k_p	Cost of preferred stock
k_{RF}	Rate of return on a risk-free security
k_s	(1) Cost of retained earnings
	(2) Required rate of return on a stock
M	Maturity value of a bond
M/B	Market/book ratio
MCC	Marginal cost of capital
n	Life of a project or financial asset
NPV	Net present value
P	(1) Price of a share of stock; P_0 = price of the stock today
	(2) Sales price per unit of product sold
P/E	Price/earnings ratio
PMT	Periodic level payment of an annuity
PV	Present value
PVA_n	Present value of an annuity for n periods
$PVIF_{k,n}$	Present value interest factor for a lump sum at k percent for n periods
$PVIFA_{k,n}$	Present value interest factor for an annuity at k percent for n periods
Q	Quantity produced or sold
Q_{BE}	Breakeven volume in units
r	Correlation coefficient
ROA	Return on assets
ROE	Return on equity
RP	Risk premium
S	Sales
S_{BE}	Breakeven volume in dollars
SML	Security Market Line
Σ	Summation sign (capital sigma)
σ	Standard deviation (lowercase sigma)
σ^2	Variance
T	Tax rate
t	Time period
TIE	Times interest earned
V	Variable cost per unit
V_B	Market value of a bond
V_P	Market value of a share of preferred stock
VC	Total variable costs
WACC	Weighted average cost of capital
YTC	Yield to call
YTM	Yield to maturity

Introduction to
Financial Management

FOURTH EDITION

Introduction to Financial Management

FOURTH EDITION

Bodil Dickerson

Oregon State University

B. J. Campsey

San Jose State University

Eugene F. Brigham

University of Florida

The Dryden Press
Harcourt Brace College Publishers

Fort Worth • Philadelphia • San Diego • New York • Orlando • Austin • San Antonio
Toronto • Montreal • London • Sydney • Tokyo

Publisher: Elizabeth Widdicombe
Acquisitions Editor: Rick Hammonds
Developmental Editors: Shana M. Lum/Barbara J. C. Rosenberg

Project Management, Text and Cover Design: Elm Street Publishing Services, Inc.
Compositor: The Clarinda Company
Text Type: 10/12 ITC Garamond Book
Cover Image: FPG International

Address for Editorial Correspondence
The Dryden Press, 301 Commerce Street, Suite 3700, Fort Worth, TX 76102

Address for Orders
The Dryden Press, 6277 Sea Harbor Drive, Orlando, FL 32887
1-800-782-4479, or 1-800-433-0001 (in Florida)

ISBN: 0-03-097602-2

Library of Congress Catalog Number: 93-46765

Printed in the United States of America
4 5 6 7 8 9 0 1 2 3 048 9 8 7 6 5 4 3 2 1

The Dryden Press
Harcourt Brace College Publishers

The Dryden Press Series in Finance

Amling and Droms
Investment Fundamentals

Berry and Young
**Managing Investments:
A Case Approach**

Bertisch
Personal Finance

Boyet
**Security Analysis for Investment
Decisions: Text and Software**

Brigham
**Fundamentals of Financial
Management**
Seventh Edition

Brigham and Gapenski
**Cases in Financial Management:
Directed, Non-Directed, and by
Request**

Brigham and Gapenski
**Cases in Financial Management:
Module A**

Brigham and Gapenski
**Cases in Financial Management:
Module B**

Brigham and Gapenski
**Cases in Financial Management:
Module C**

Brigham and Gapenski
**Financial Management:
Theory and Practice**
Seventh Edition

Brigham and Gapenski
**Intermediate Financial
Management**
Fourth Edition

Brigham, Aberwald, and Gapenski
Finance with Lotus 1-2-3
Second Edition

Chance
**An Introduction to Options and
Futures**
Third Edition

Clauretie and Webb
**The Theory and Practice of Real
Estate Finance**

Cooley
**Advances in Business Financial
Management: A Collection of
Readings**

Cooley
Business Financial Management
Third Edition

Curran
Principles of Corporate Finance

Dickerson, Campsey, and Brigham
**Introduction to Financial
Management**
Fourth Edition

Evans
**International Finance:
A Markets Approach**

Fama and Miller
The Theory of Finance

Gardner and Mills
**Managing Financial Institutions:
An Asset/Liability Approach**
Third Edition

Gitman and Joehnk
Personal Financial Planning
Sixth Edition

Greenbaum and Thakor
**Contemporary Financial
Intermediation**

Harrington and Eades
**Case Studies in Financial
Decision Making**
Third Edition

Hayes and Meerschwam
**Financial Institutions:
Contemporary Cases in the
Financial Services Industry**

Hearth and Zaima
**Contemporary Investments:
Security and Portfolio Analysis**

Johnson
**Issues and Readings in
Managerial Finance**
Fourth Edition

Kidwell, Peterson, and Blackwell
**Financial Institutions, Markets,
and Money**
Fifth Edition

Koch
Bank Management
Third Edition

Kohn
**Money, Banking, and Financial
Markets**
Second Edition

Lee and Finnerty
**Corporate Finance: Theory,
Method, and Application**

Maisel
Real Estate Finance
Second Edition

Martin, Cox, and MacMinn
The Theory of Finance:
Evidence and Applications

Mayo
Finance: An Introduction
Fifth Edition

Mayo
Investments: An Introduction
Fourth Edition

Pettijohn
PROFIT +

Reilly
Investment Analysis and
Portfolio Management
Fourth Edition

Reilly and Norton
Investments
Fourth Edition

Sears and Trennepohl
Investment Management

Seitz and Ellison
Capital Budgeting and Long-
Term Financing Decisions
Second Edition

Siegel and Siegel
Futures Markets

Smith and Spudeck
Interest Rates: Principles and
Applications

Stickney
Financial Statement Analysis:
A Strategic Perspective
Second Edition

Turnbull
Option Valuation

Weston and Brigham
Essentials of Managerial Finance
Tenth Edition

Weston and Copeland
Managerial Finance
Ninth Edition

Wood and Wood
Financial Markets

The Harcourt Brace College Outline Series

Baker
Financial Management

Preface

To the Student

Whether you envision your future as a financial manager or any other business professional, the financial environment and the strengths and weaknesses of your company will play an integral part in your career. Although you may not be directly responsible for making financial decisions that affect the whole corporation, you will contribute to its overall financial success through sales, marketing, management, accounting, research and development, and/or production. So it is important that you understand how financial decisions are made and what your part will be in those decisions. The goal of *Introduction to Financial Management,* fourth edition, is to explain all aspects of corporate financial management so that you gain the insight necessary to actively participate in your company's business future.

The study of financial management is by no means dull. As the responsibilities of the financial manager have broadened, so have the opportunities for learning about new areas of the corporate world, both internal and external. The last ten years have shown how unpredictable our business world can be with the stock market crash of 1987 (in which stock values fell by 25 percent in a single day) and the 1990–1991 recession. The uncertainty surrounding the strong economy of 1993 and concerns about inflation and interest rates, combined with the "normal" surprises of the stock market, public opinion, and government policies, illustrate how financial decision making can be both extremely difficult and incredibly exciting.

In today's rapidly changing economic environment, many in the financial world have turned to academicians for answers, and academic researchers have made a number of important contributions. Business practitioners gain insights from the use of financial theory and, in turn, provide feedback from their real-world perspective, which has led to modifications and improvements in financial theory. Although we present both theory and practice in this book, *Introduction to Financial Management* focuses primarily on the practitioner, particularly one who will own or manage a small to medium-sized business.

Furthermore, we have designed this book for the general business student, not just for the finance major. Too often, introductory texts seem to be designed primarily for finance or accounting majors. These may be excellent textbooks, but in their efforts to include the latest theories (some of which seem to contain little of practical use) or detailed financial models, the nonfinance major is often lost or turned off to the study of finance. All business students should have a thorough knowledge of finance, and it is our hope that this book provides that knowledge in a manner that is interesting and enjoyable to all students, regardless of major.

Relationship with Our Other Books

As the body of knowledge in finance expanded, it first became difficult, then impossible, to provide "everything one needs to know about financial management" in one text, especially in one undergraduate text. This recognition led us to limit the scope of this book and also to write other texts, with other coauthors, to deal with the materials that must necessarily be deleted from *Introduction to Financial Management*. Thus, Gene Brigham has coauthored with Lou Gapenski both an intermediate undergraduate text (*Intermediate Financial Management,* fourth edition) and a comprehensive book aimed primarily at MBAs (*Financial Management: Theory and Practice,* seventh edition). Brigham has also written two other introductory undergraduate texts, *Fundamentals of Financial Management,* seventh edition, and *Essentials of Managerial Finance,* tenth edition, coauthored with Fred Weston. *Essentials* and *Fundamentals* are written at the same level, but their organizational structures differ significantly. *Introduction* differs in organization and is somewhat less complex than the other undergraduate books.

Intended Market and Use

As indicated by its title, *Introduction to Financial Management,* fourth edition, is intended for use in an introductory course in financial management. The main parts of the text can be covered in a one-term course, but, when supplemented with cases and some outside readings, the text can also be used over two terms.

If the book is to be used in a one-term course, instructors will probably want to cover only selected chapters, leaving the others for students to examine on their own or to use as references in conjunction with work in other courses. In our own courses, we are seldom able to complete an entire book. The material we tend to omit is contained in Chapters 22 and 23; finance majors cover these topics in subsequent courses. Other instructors have indicated that they often save material in Chapters 15, 18, 20, and 21 for an advanced course. In institutions in which a money and banking course is required, instructors may wish to omit parts of Chapters 2, 3, and 4, and in schools that do not require such a course, instructors may wish to present the material in Chapters 13, 16, and 17 earlier in the course than the chapter sequence indicates. Many other course structures are possible, and we have written the book in "modules" to make it easy to cover chapters in a sequence different from the one in the book. The Glossary and Appendix C (which summarizes the equations contained in the text) facilitate the use of alternative course outlines.

Special Features of This Text

1. **Streamlined Quantitative Material.**   A conscious effort has been made to streamline as much of the quantitative material as possible without

lowering the quality of the text. Thus, where possible, very detailed mathematical formulas or concepts have been simplified or deleted. For example, our chapter on risk analysis assumes no previous statistical knowledge. Further, the text uses straightforward language and easy-to-follow examples to emphasize its practical orientation.

2. **Decisions in Finance.**   Each chapter begins with a real financial decision faced by a firm and ends with the resolution to the decision. These sections challenge students to consider how knowledge of the material contained in the chapter would help financial decision makers in the real world.

3. **Industry Practice.**   In most chapters we present a real-world industry practice section, which highlights or expands on a key issue. These illustrations also help to enliven the material in the chapter.

4. **Focus on Small Business.**   Roughly half of the chapters contain small business sections, written by Professor Christopher Barry of Texas Christian University and Professor Shirley Love of the University of Idaho. These sections are especially useful for giving students a view of finance from the smaller firm's standpoint.

5. **Learning Objectives.**   Each chapter begins with a set of clearly stated objectives which serve to guide students through the material of the chapter.

6. **Running Glossary.**   Brief definitions of important terms appear in the margin of the text. In addition, the key terms in each chapter are bold-faced when they are first defined.

7. **Self-Test Section.**   After each major section in the chapter, we have inserted a set of self-test questions which students can review to test their understanding of the material they just read.

8. **Bulleted Summary.**   Key terms in the chapter are highlighted and briefly explained in the end-of-chapter summary. This recapitulation corresponds to the learning objectives at the beginning of each chapter and serves as an additional review tool for students.

9. **Self-Test Problems.**   A set of fairly rigorous self-test problems, with detailed solutions, is given at the end of the more difficult quantitative chapters. These problems serve (1) to test the student's ability to set up problems for solution and (2) to explain the solution setup for those who need help.

10. ***Lotus*-Based Mini Cases.**   Five all-new case studies in Chapters 6, 7, 9, 14, and 16 teach students the value of computer spreadsheets as they build their own *Lotus 1-2-3* models.

Major Changes in the Fourth Edition

Both the theory and practice of finance are dynamic, and as important new developments occur, they must be incorporated into a textbook such as this one. In addition, we and a team of reviewers are constantly looking for ways to improve the book's relevance, clarity, and readability. As a result, we have made several important changes in this edition, including the following:

1. In the five model-building mini cases, students learn to solve problems the way professionals do. The unique classroom-tested cases, together with a basic *Lotus* tutorial contained in the *Instructor's Manual,* form a complete yet flexible package: students with prior spreadsheet experience will not need the tutorial (except possibly for review purposes), while students with few or no spreadsheet skills will need approximately two hours to work through the tutorial and will then be ready to complete any of the five *Lotus* assignments. These cases have been developed specifically to (1) reinforce chapter concepts, (2) teach students a step-by-step approach to computer modeling in finance, (3) stress the dynamic nature of a good computer model and the value of performing sensitivity analysis on critical variables, and (4) provide students with the confidence and general tools necessary to construct computer models in other settings.

2. The learning objectives at the beginning of each chapter were developed in response to reviewer comments and requests. These objectives further organize each chapter, are linked to the self-test questions at the end of each main text section, and tie directly into the end-of-chapter summary. The overall goal of this approach is to help students identify major concepts and specific competencies to be mastered in each chapter.

3. All sections of the book have been updated to reflect current business developments and 1993 tax laws.

4. Chapter 1 has been expanded to include (1) earlier introduction of the risk-return tradeoff, (2) agency relationships, and (3) discussion of the major developing trends of the 1990s.

5. Common money and capital market instruments are now more clearly defined in Chapter 2.

6. Chapter 3 has been reorganized, and major portions of the chapter have been rewritten. The Federal Reserve System is introduced first, and the chapter moves from the broad topics of monetary policy and demand deposit creation to specific instances of Federal Reserve intervention, the commercial banking system, and important recent trends.

7. In Chapter 6, the extended Du Pont equation is used to highlight the concepts of financial leverage and financial risk and prepares students for the more in-depth discussion of leverage and target capital structure in Chapter 20.

8. The discussion of additional, external financing requirements in Chapter 7 now includes nonquantitative analysis of each of the major determinants of needed financing, tied back to the formula method of forecasting.

9. Chapter 9 has been reorganized and largely rewritten to reflect recent developments in the management of cash and marketable securities.

10. Diversification of risk at the corporate level now receives a more balanced treatment in Chapters 12 and 15. Examples are given on both sides of the issue: of (1) firms that have strongly endorsed diversification strategies and (2) companies that have recently abandoned attempts at diversification and decided to emphasize their core businesses.

11. Bond valuation has been moved to the beginning of Chapter 16. This change facilitates comparison of capital budgeting techniques, as presented

in Chapters 14 and 15, with the discounted cash flow approach used to determine bond value. This also reflects a deliberate strategy of presenting the *general model* before introducing such variations as zero coupon bonds and floating-rate debt.

12. New graphs are used to clarify marginal cost of capital in Chapter 19.

13. A brief, nonquantitative discussion of Modigliani and Miller has been added in Chapter 20.

14. Chapter 22 has been largely rewritten to include the free cash flow analysis in valuing mergers, a technique that is used almost exclusively in real-world mergers and acquisitions.

15. Chapter 23 is entirely new, focusing on specific issues in the management of a multinational firm's finances.

16. The sections entitled "Decision in Finance," "Industry Practice," and "Small Business" have been updated with new examples which reflect current business practices and problems. These examples demonstrate to students that an understanding of the material in the chapter is crucial to solving real-world problems, and they also provide guides to the material in the chapter.

Ancillary Materials

The extensive package of ancillary materials that accompanies the fourth edition of *Introduction to Financial Management* provides information specifically designed to enhance the text's usefulness for both students and instructors. Materials developed for the fourth edition include the following:

1. Instructor's Manual/Transparency Masters. A complete *Instructor's Manual* is available to instructors who adopt the book. The manual contains (1) a brief *Lotus 1-2-3* tutorial to complement the book's new mini cases and the end-of-chapter problems, (2) answers to all text questions, (3) solutions to all text problems, and (4) extensive lecture notes which focus on the more difficult topics and which are keyed to special lecture transparencies.

   A set of transparency masters is included in the *Instructor's Manual*. These masters highlight key material in the text and can be used as the basis for lectures in both large and small classes.

2. Test Bank. A revised and enlarged *Test Bank* with more than 1,500 class-tested questions and problems, in objective format, is available to instructors both in text form and on IBM and Macintosh computer diskettes. The diskettes come in either the regular computerized test bank format or in WordPerfect®. The new questions are well suited for both quizzes and exams. Also, the questions are arranged, within each chapter, by type (true/false questions, multiple-choice conceptual questions, and multiple-choice numerical problems), by topic, and by degree of difficulty.

3. Supplemental Problems. A set of additional problems, organized according to topic and level of difficulty, is also available to instructors from The Dryden Press.

4. **Problem Diskette.** A diskette containing *Lotus 1-2-3* models for the computer-related end-of-chapter problems is also available to instructors. To obtain the diskette, instructors can contact their Dryden sales representative or the Dryden sales office.

A number of additional items are available for purchase by students:

1. **Study Guide.** The *Study Guide* outlines the key sections of each chapter, provides students with self-test questions, and also provides them with a set of problems and solutions similar to those in the text.

2. **Customized Casebooks.** Two new casebooks, *Cases in Financial Management, Directed Versions,* and *Cases in Financial Management, Non-Directed Versions,* by Eugene F. Brigham and Louis C. Gapenski, contain cases which illustrate applications of the concepts and methodologies developed in *Introduction to Financial Management.* The directed casebook contains 41 cases with end-of-case questions which, in essence, direct students toward a reasonable resolution to each case. The non-directed casebook contains 20 cases selected from the directed casebook, but with a guidance paragraph in place of the questions. Thus, the non-directed version requires students to develop their own solution strategy for each case. Most of the cases (both directed and non-directed) have accompanying *Lotus* models. *Lotus* is not essential for working the cases, but it does reduce number crunching and thus leaves more time for students to consider conceptual issues.

   In addition to the two casebooks, The Dryden Press has developed the *By Request* case system, which allows instructors to create their own casebooks by combining any set of cases selected from the directed and non-directed casebooks. This system gives instructors the flexibility to mix and match cases to best meet the needs of each class and section.

3. **Readings Books.** A readings book, *Issues and Readings in Managerial Finance,* fourth edition (Dryden Press, 1995), edited by Ramon E. Johnson, provides an excellent mix of theoretical and practical articles which can be used to supplement the text. Another supplemental reader is *Advances in Business Financial Management: A Collection of Readings* (Dryden Press, 1990), edited by Philip L. Cooley, which provides a broader selection of articles from which to choose.

4. **Finance with Lotus 1-2-3: Text and Models, second edition.** This text by Eugene F. Brigham, Dana A. Aberwald, and Louis C. Gapenski (Dryden Press, 1992) enables students to learn, on their own, how to use *Lotus 1-2-3,* and it explains how many commonly encountered problems in managerial finance can be analyzed with electronic spreadsheets.

5. **PROFIT+.** This software supplement by James Pettijohn contains 18 user-friendly programs that include the time value of money, forecasting, and capital budgeting. The supplement includes a user's manual, and it is available for the IBM PC.

Acknowledgments

This book reflects the efforts of a great many people over a number of years. First, we would like to acknowledge the special critical evaluation and suggestions of Dana Aberwald of the University of Florida and John McDowell of Davenport College. Professor McDowell reviewed and/or worked all end-of-chapter questions and problems and made numerous helpful comments. Dana Aberwald authored many of the new "Decision in Finance" and "Small Business" sections and helped with all phases of the revision, from designing questionnaires for reviewers to computer solutions; without her help, the revision would never have been completed.

The following reviewers merit special thanks for their help on the fourth edition:

Joseph Black
San Jose State University

Fayez A. Elayan
Southwest Missouri State
University

James Howard Finch
University of Tennessee at
Chattanooga

Martin Laurence
The William Patterson College
of New Jersey

John McDowell
Davenport College

Patricia Parker
Columbus State Community
College

James R. Scott
Southwest Missouri State
University

Jan R. Squires
Southwest Missouri State
University

Marvin T. Travis
Saint Leo College

James Wheeler
Vance Granville Community
College

Philip J. Young
Southwest Missouri State
University

In addition, we would like to thank the following people, whose reviews and comments on prior editions have contributed to this edition: Frank Aleman, Bruce Berlin, Dan Best, Mike Binder, Joseph H. Black, Sandra Cece, Harlan Cheney, Terrence Clauretie, Bill Colclough, James Collier, Maurice Corrigan, Roy Crum, Faramarz Damanpour, Zane Dennick-Ream, Gene Dunham, Philip Fanara, Jr., Timothy Gallagher, David A. Garraty, George Granger, Damon J. Johnston, Frank Jorden, Kimberly McCollough, Ambrose P. McCoy, Charles W. McKinney, Joseph Moosally, Austin Murphy, Don Nast, H. R. Pickett, Eugene Poindexter, Antonio Rodriguez, Clarence C. Rose, Dennis Schlais, George Seldat, Gary Simpson, Rodney Smith, Les Strickler, Francis Thomas, John E. Thompson, Marvin Travis, G. W. Ulseth, Paul Vanderheiden, JoAnn Vaughan, John Wachowicz, James W. Walden, Richard Whiston, Howard R. Whitney, Sally Jo Wright, Elizabeth Yelland, and Terry Zivney.

Special thanks are due to Fred Weston, who has done much to help develop the field of financial management and who provided us with instruction and inspiration; to Ann Pierce, who authored many of the "Decision in Finance" and "Industry Practice" sections; to Christopher Barry and Shirley Love, who authored the "Small Business" sections at the ends of several chapters; to Bruce

Cochran, who helped us with the chapter on financial institutions; to Michael H. Moffett, who authored the international chapter; to Susan Block, who coauthored the chapter on mergers, divestitures, holding companies, and LBOs; to J. Howard Finch, who coauthored the chapter on hybrid financing; to Art Herrmann and Larry A. Lynch, who helped us with the bankruptcy material; to Patricia A. Frishkoff, who coauthored the *Lotus 1-2-3* tutorial; to Jeffrey Smith, who provided 1993 tax information; to Rodolfo A. Camacho, who provided valuable research assistance; to Jennifer Scott-Tsiatsios, who helped us with up-to-date data on financial institutions; to Susan Ball, Mary Alice Hanebury, and Kay Mangan, who helped us develop the *Lotus 1-2-3* models; to Steve Bouchard, who helped with the ancillaries; and to Bob Karp and Carol Stanton, who provided both word processing and editorial support.

Both our colleagues and our students at the University of Florida and Oregon State University gave us many useful suggestions, and The Dryden Press and Elm Street Publishing Services staffs — especially Liz Widdicombe, Rick Hammonds, Ann Coburn, Lisé Johnson, Diana Farrell, Shana Lum, Barbara Rosenberg, Karen Hill, Sue Nodine, Barb Bahnsen, Jan Huskisson, Melissa Morgan, and Jane Perkins — helped greatly with all phases of the text development and production. We sometimes complain, but based on our many years of work on textbooks, the Dryden staff is the greatest.

Finally, to our friends and colleagues at Oregon State University, San Jose State, the University of Florida, and around the country, thanks for your suggestions and support.

Conclusion

Finance is, in a real sense, the cornerstone of the free enterprise system, so good financial management is vitally important to the economic health of businesses and hence to our nation and the world. Because of its importance, finance should be widely and thoroughly understood, but this is easier said than done. The field is relatively complex, and it is undergoing constant changes in response to economic conditions. All this makes finance stimulating and exciting, but also challenging and sometimes perplexing. We hope that the fourth edition of *Introduction to Financial Management* will meet its own challenge by contributing to a better understanding of the financial system.

Bodil Dickerson   B. J. Campsey   Eugene F. Brigham
Corvallis, Oregon   San Jose, California   Gainesville, Florida

April 1994

About the Authors

Bodil "Bodie" Dickerson has taught courses in finance at Oregon State University College of Business since 1981 and has also taught at Aarhus Handelshøjskole (Aarhus Graduate School of Management), Denmark. A textbook reviewer since 1985, she was a major contributor to the first three editions of *Introduction to Financial Management.* The coauthor of a *Lotus 1-2-3* tutorial, Dickerson has served as a member of the planning committee and the computer users' advisory group for the College of Business and has coordinated the introduction of *Lotus* computer spreadsheets and modeling into the school's finance curriculum. Dickerson is a native of Silkeborg, Denmark, who now makes her home in Albany, Oregon. She is a member of the Financial Management Association and currently serves on the board of directors of the Federal-Metals Central Credit Union, located in Albany, Oregon.

B. J. Campsey is professor of finance at San Jose State University. He has taught undergraduate and graduate courses in managerial finance and investments, and he has served as a consultant for financial and industrial firms as well as having been the Director of Candidate Programs for the Chartered Financial Analysts from 1979 to 1980. He has written articles for several professional journals and has served as a consultant for several Silicon Valley firms.

Eugene F. Brigham, graduate research professor at the University of Florida College of Business Administration, is the author of 21 books on financial management, including the first three editions of *Introduction to Financial Management.* His books have been published in 10 languages. Brigham has chaired both the Department of Finance at the University of Florida and the Department of Finance and Business Economics at UCLA. He has been director of the Public Utility Research Center at the University of Florida since 1971 and has served as a consultant to many firms and government agencies, including AT&T, Shell Oil, and the Federal Reserve Board.

Brief Contents

Part I — **The Financial Environment and the Firm** 1

Chapter 1 — Defining Financial Management 2
Chapter 2 — Taxes and the Financial Environment 36
Chapter 3 — Financial Institutions 86
Chapter 4 — Interest Rates 122

Part II — **Financial Statements and Financial Planning** 153

Chapter 5 — Examining a Firm's Financial Data 154
Chapter 6 — Interpreting Financial Statements 184
Chapter 7 — Determining Future Financial Needs 228

Part III — **Working Capital Management** 265

Chapter 8 — Working Capital Policy and Management 266
Chapter 9 — Managing Cash and Marketable Securities 300
Chapter 10 — Accounts Receivable and Inventories 340
Chapter 11 — Short-Term Financing 386
Appendix 11A Use of Security in Short-Term Financing 417

Part IV — **Capital Budgeting: Investment in Long-Term Assets** 425

Chapter 12 — Risk and Return 426
Chapter 13 — Time Value of Money 468
Appendix 13A Semiannual and Other Compounding Periods 510
Chapter 14 — The Process of Capital Budgeting 514
Appendix 14A Conflicts between NPV and IRR 555
Chapter 15 — Decisions in Capital Budgeting 562

Part V — **Long-Term Financing** 593

Chapter 16 — Bonds and Preferred Stock 594
Chapter 17 — Common Stock 644
Chapter 18 — Hybrid Financing: Leasing and Option Securities 684

Part VI — **Factors That Influence How the Firm Is Financed** 719

Chapter 19 — The Cost of Capital 720
Chapter 20 — Leverage and the Target Capital Structure 762
Appendix 20A Bankruptcy 812
Chapter 21 — Determining the Dividend Policy 820

Part VII — **Other Topics in Financial Management** 855

Chapter 22 — Mergers, Divestitures, Holding Companies, and LBOs 856
Chapter 23 — International Financial Management 890

Appendix A — Mathematical Tables A-1

Appendix B — Answers to Selected End-of-Chapter Problems B-1

Appendix C — Selected Equations C-1

Glossary G-1

Index I-1

Contents

Part I   **The Financial Environment and the Firm   1**

Chapter 1   **Defining Financial Management   2**

Decision in Finance: Changing the Guard at IBM 3,   Career Opportunities in Finance 5, Historical Perspective on the Study of Finance 6,   Financial Management in the 1990s 7,   The Financial Manager's Responsibilities 9,   The Increasing Importance of Financial Management 10,   Alternative Forms of Business Organization 11,   Finance in the Organizational Structure of the Firm 15,   Industry Practice: Do Partnerships Still Make Sense? 16,   The Goals of the Corporation 17,   Business Ethics 21,   Agency Relationships 23,   Managerial Actions to Maximize Shareholder Wealth 27,   The Risk-Return Tradeoff 28,   Organization of the Book 30,   Small Business: Resources and Goals in the Small Firm 31,   **Summary** 33,   Resolution to Decision in Finance: Changing the Guard at IBM 34

Chapter 2   **Taxes and the Financial Environment   36**

Decision in Finance: The Clinton Administration and Its Tax Proposals 37,   The Federal Income Tax System 38,   Depreciation 48,   The Role of Financial Markets 51,   The Role of Financial Intermediaries 57,   Industry Practice: Dismantling the Financial Supermarkets 63,   The Stock Market 65,   Market Efficiency 75,   Small Business: What Is Venture Capital? 76,   **Summary** 77,   Resolution to Decision in Finance: The Clinton Administration and Its Tax Proposals 79

Chapter 3   **Financial Institutions   86**

Decision in Finance: The New Banking Law Gets Tough with Banks 87,   The Federal Reserve System 88,   Overview of Financial Institutions 100,   The Commercial Banking System 101,   Industry Practice: The Thrift Crisis: What Happened, and Who Is Going to Pay? 108,   The Savings and Loan Crisis 109,   The Changing Economic Environment of Our Financial Institutions 110,   Small Business: Building a Banking Relationship 114,   **Summary** 116,   Resolution to Decision in Finance: The New Banking Law Gets Tough with Banks 118

Chapter 4   **Interest Rates   122**

Decision in Finance: Alan Greenspan Responds to Critics 123,   The Cost of Funds 124, Interest Rates 125,   The Determinants of Market Interest Rates 129,   The Term Structure of Interest Rates 135,   Specific Factors That Influence Interest Rate Levels 140,   Industry Practice: When the World Speaks . . . The Fed Listens 144, Interest Rate Levels and Stock Prices 145,   Interest Rates and Business Decisions 146,

Summary 147,   Resolution to Decision in Finance: Alan Greenspan Responds to
Critics 149

Part II   **Financial Statements and Financial Planning   153**

Chapter 5   Examining a Firm's Financial Data   154

Decision in Finance: Letters from Chairman Buffett 155,   The Annual Report 156,
The Income Statement 157,   The Balance Sheet 160,   The Statement of Retained
Earnings 164,   The Cash Flow Cycle 165,   Industry Practice: Are Accounting Methods
Too Flexible? 166,   The Statement of Cash Flows 170,   Summary 175,   Resolution to
Decision in Finance: Letters from Chairman Buffett 176

Chapter 6   Interpreting Financial Statements   184

Decision in Finance: Cooking the Books 185,   Importance of Financial Statements 186,
Ratio Analysis 187,   Industry Practice: Manipulating Financial Statements 188,   Sources
of Comparative Ratios 206,   Industry Practice: Trying to Deleverage Corporate
America 208,   Limitations of Ratio Analysis 210,   Summary 211,   Resolution to
Decision in Finance: Cooking the Books 212

Chapter 7   Determining Future Financial Needs   228

Decision in Finance: When Forecasts Are Wide of the Mark 229,   Sales Forecasts 230,
Percentage of Sales Forecasting 231,   Industry Practice: A Maverick's Forecasting
Approach 233,   The Formula Method for Forecasting AFN 238,   Forecasting Financial
Requirements When the Balance Sheet Ratios Are Subject to Change 243,
Computerized Financial Planning Models 248,   Small Business: Franchising 249,
Summary 250,   Resolution to Decision in Finance: When Forecasts Are Wide of the
Mark 251

Part III   **Working Capital Management   265**

Chapter 8   Working Capital Policy and Management   266

Decision in Finance: Florida Orange Springs Inc. — Abundance of Water, Shortage of
Working Capital 267,   Working Capital Terminology 268,   Overview of the Cash
Conversion Cycle 270,   Working Capital Investment Policies 275,   Alternative
Working Capital Financing Policies 279,   Industry Practice: The Credit Crunch, Cash
Flow Problems, and Bankruptcy 285,   Combining Current Asset and Liability
Decisions 287,   Small Business: Growth and Working Capital Needs 288,
Summary 291,   Resolution to Decision in Finance: Florida Orange Springs Inc. —
Abundance of Water, Shortage of Working Capital 292

Chapter 9   Managing Cash and Marketable Securities   300

Decision in Finance: What Do You Do with Surplus Cash? 301,   Cash Management 302,
The Cash Budget 303,   Cash Management Techniques 309,   Matching the Costs and
Benefits of Cash Management 318,   Marketable Securities 319,   Industry Practice:
Turning 'Em Around 322,   Summary 328,   Resolution to Decision in Finance: What Do
You Do with Surplus Cash? 330

Chapter 10   Accounts Receivable and Inventories   340

Decision in Finance: The Data Are Available, but Should Companies Use Them? 341,
Accounts Receivable Management 343,   Credit Policy 345,   Other Factors Influencing
Credit Policy 353,   Evaluating the Effectiveness of a Firm's Credit Policy 354,
Inventory Management 360,   Industry Practice: Keeping Inventories Lean 370,
Summary 373,   Resolution to Decision in Finance: The Data Are Available, but Should
Companies Use Them? 375

Chapter 11   Short-Term Financing   386

Decision in Finance: Will Your Banker Be There When You Need Her? 387,   Accrued
Wages and Taxes 388,   Accounts Payable (Trade Credit) 388,   Short-Term Bank
Loans 394,   Commercial Paper 403,   Use of Security in Short-Term Financing 406,
Industry Practice: Commercial Paper: An "Iffy" Source of Funds 407,   Small Business:
Financing Receivables Directly 408,   Summary 409,   Resolution to Decision in
Finance: Will Your Banker Be There When You Need Her? 411,   *Appendix 11A Use of
Security in Short-Term Financing   417*

Part IV   **Capital Budgeting: Investment in Long-Term Assets   425**

Chapter 12   Risk and Return   426

Decision in Finance: Diversifying Risk — Is It Always the Way to Go? 427,   Defining
and Measuring Risk 428,   Portfolio Risk and the Capital Asset Pricing Model 438,
The Relationship between Risk and Rates of Return 451,   Changes in the Security
Market Line and Betas 454,   Risk in a Global Context 458,   Physical Assets versus
Securities 458,   Summary 460,   Resolution to Decision in Finance: Diversifying Risk —
Is It Always the Way to Go? 461

Chapter 13   Time Value of Money   468

Decision in Finance: Can Boomers Retire? 469,   Future (or Compound) Value 471,
Present Value 475,   Future Value versus Present Value 478,   Solving for Time and
Interest Rate 480,   Future (or Compound) Value of an Annuity 482,   Present Value of
an Annuity 485,   Present Value of a Perpetuity 488,   Present Value of an Uneven
Stream of Cash Flows 489,   Solving for Time and Interest Rate of an Annuity 491,
Solving for the Payment of an Annuity 493,   Summary 494,   Review of Chapter
Concepts 497,   Resolution to Decision in Finance: Can Boomers Retire? 501,
Appendix 13A Semiannual and Other Compounding Periods   510

Chapter 14   The Process of Capital Budgeting   514

Decision in Finance: An Aged Giant Remains Nimble 515,   Importance of Capital
Budgeting 516,   Project Proposals and Classifications 518,   Steps in the Capital
Budgeting Process 520,   Estimating Cash Flows 523,   Methods Used to Evaluate
Proposed Projects 529,   Evaluation of Payback, NPV, and IRR Methods 539,   A Capital
Budgeting Case 540,   Conclusion 542,   Summary 543,   Resolution to Decision in
Finance: An Aged Giant Remains Nimble 544,   *Appendix 14A Conflicts between NPV
and IRR   555*

Chapter 15   Decisions in Capital Budgeting   562

Decision in Finance: The Collapse of a $10 Billion Empire 563,   Risk Analysis in
Capital Budgeting 564,   Other Topics in Capital Budgeting 574,   Incorporating
Inflation into Capital Budgeting Analysis 580,   Summary 582,   Resolution to Decision
in Finance: The Collapse of a $10 Billion Empire 584

Part V   **Long-Term Financing   593**

Chapter 16   Bonds and Preferred Stock   594

Decision in Finance: The Bluff-and-Threat Call Gambit 595,   Bonds 596,   Valuation of
Bonds 598,   Funded Debt 607,   Specific Bond Contract Features 607,   Types of
Bonds 611,   Recent Bond Innovations 613,   Industry Practice: To Market, to Market
. . . 615,   Bond Ratings 619,   Term Loans 624,   Pros and Cons of Long-Term Debt
626,   Preferred Stock 627,   Small Business: Contracting with Providers of Risk Capital
633,   Summary 634,   Resolution to Decision in Finance: The Bluff-and-Threat Call
Gambit 636

Chapter 17   Common Stock   644

Decision in Finance: Muscling the Underwriters 645,   Legal Rights and Privileges of
Common Stockholders 646,   Industry Practice: Shareholders Are Flexing Their
Muscle 649,   Common Stock Valuation 651,   Pros and Cons of Common Stock 661,
The Decision to Go Public 664,   The Investment Banking Process 667,   Small
Business: Going Public for Less than You're Worth 671,   Summary 672,   Resolution to
Decision in Finance: Muscling the Underwriters 674

Chapter 18   Hybrid Financing: Leasing and Option Securities   684

Decision in Finance: Looking for a New Lease on Life 685,   Leasing 686,   Options 694,
Warrants 699,   Convertibles 702,   Reporting Earnings when Warrants or Convertibles
Are Outstanding 708,   Small Business: Lease Financing for Small Businesses 708,
Summary 709,   Resolution to Decision in Finance: Looking for a New Lease on Life 710

Part VI   **Factors That Influence How the Firm Is Financed   719**

Chapter 19   The Cost of Capital   720

Decision in Finance: McDonnell Douglas's Quandary 721,   The Logic of the Weighted
Average Cost of Capital 722,   Basic Definitions 723,   Cost of Debt, $k_d(1 - T)$ 725,
Cost of Preferred Stock, k_p 726,   Cost of Retained Earnings, k_s 726,   Cost of Newly
Issued Common Stock, or External Equity, k_e 731,   Weighted Average, or Composite,
Cost of Capital, WACC 732,   Changes in the Cost of Capital Due to the Level of the
Budget 733,   Industry Practice: A Silver Lining for a Dark Economy 742,   Combining
the MCC and Investment Opportunity Schedules 743,   Some Problem Areas in Cost of
Capital 746,   Recent Trends 747,   Small Business: The Real Costs of Going Public 748,
Summary 749,   Resolution to Decision in Finance: McDonnell Douglas's Quandary 751

Chapter 20   Leverage and the Target Capital Structure   762

Decision in Finance: Ripe for the Picking 763,   Types of Risk 764,   Operating
Leverage and Breakeven Analysis 766,   Industry Practice: Leaner and Meaner 774,

Financial Leverage 775, Determining the Optimal Capital Structure 777, Capital Structure Theory: Taxes, Bankruptcy-Related Costs, and the Value of the Stock 785, Degree of Leverage 788, Practical Considerations in Determining Capital Structure 794, Variations in Capital Structures Among Firms 799, Small Business: Financing Growth Businesses in the Nineties 800, Summary 802, Resolution to Decision in Finance: Ripe for the Picking 804, *Appendix 20A Bankruptcy 812*

Chapter 21   Determining the Dividend Policy   820

Decision in Finance: To Cut or Not to Cut Dividends 821, Residual Dividend Policy 822, Factors That Influence Dividend Policy 826, Dividend Payment Policies 830, Dividend Payment Procedure 833, Dividend Reinvestment Plans (DRIPs) 834, Industry Practice: Corporate Get-Rich-Slowly Plans 835, Stock Dividends and Stock Splits 837, Stock Repurchases 841, Establishing a Dividend Policy: Some Illustrations 845, Summary 847, Resolution to Decision in Finance: To Cut or Not to Cut Dividends 849

Part VII   **Other Topics in Financial Management   855**

Chapter 22   Mergers, Divestitures, Holding Companies, and LBOs   856

Decision in Finance: An Orbiting Deal 857, Rationale for Mergers 858, Types of Mergers 861, Examples of Merger Activity 861, Procedures for Combining Firms 864, Merger Analysis 865, Valuing the Target Firm 868, The Role of Investment Bankers 871, Corporate Alliances 873, Divestitures 874, Industry Practice: A Spate of Spin-Offs 877, Holding Companies 878, Leveraged Buyouts (LBOs) 881, Small Business: Merging as a Means of Exiting a Closely Held Business 882, Summary 883, Resolution to Decision in Finance: An Orbiting Deal 885

Chapter 23   International Financial Management   890

Decision in Finance: Exchange Rates and Small-Town America 891, Exchange Rate Fundamentals 893, International Capital Budgeting 903, Industry Practice: Invading Russia 906, Capital Structure of Foreign Subsidiaries 908, International Working Capital and Cash Flow Management 909, Import/Export Trade Financing 913, Classification of Firm Exposure to Foreign Currency Movements 914, Interest Rate and Currency Swaps 922, Summary 924, Resolution to Decision in Finance: Exchange Rates and Small-Town America

Appendix A   Mathematical Tables   A-1

Appendix B   Answers to Selected End-of-Chapter Problems   B-1

Appendix C   Selected Equations   C-1

Glossary   G-1

Index   I-1

Introduction to
Financial Management

FOURTH EDITION

The Financial Environment and the Firm

The goal of financial management is to maximize stockholders' wealth. It sounds like a simple goal, but this entire book is dedicated to evaluating how alternative decisions will influence the value of the firm. By maximizing the firm's value (and thereby increasing the value of its common stock), the goal of shareholder wealth maximization can be implemented.

Chapter 1 contains an overview of financial management, including the responsibilities of a financial manager, the forms of business organization, and the role of finance in a business organization. Chapters 2, 3, and 4 describe the financial environment in which we all work. The job of financial intermediaries is to efficiently transfer funds from surplus economic units to deficit economic units. Chapter 2 briefly discusses taxes and then introduces the markets and institutions involved in successfully converting savings to productive investments. Chapter 3 describes financial institutions and the means by which the Federal Reserve System influences the economy. Both businesses and individuals are affected by interest rates, and Chapter 4 examines the factors which determine those rates.

Defining Financial Management

OBJECTIVES

After reading this chapter, you should be able to:

▸ Explain where career opportunities are found within the three interrelated areas of finance.

▸ List some of the significant changes in the study of finance since 1900, with emphasis on developments in the 1980s and early 1990s.

▸ Briefly explain the responsibilities of financial managers.

▸ Describe the advantages and disadvantages of alternative forms of business organization.

▸ State the primary goal in a publicly traded firm, and explain where social responsibility and business ethics fit in.

▸ Define an agency relationship, and give at least two examples of potential agency problems.

▸ Explain what is meant by a risk-return tradeoff and what the connection is between this concept, managerial decisions, and the value of the firm's common stock.

DECISION IN FINANCE

CHANGING THE GUARD AT IBM

More than 2,200 angry shareholders greeted Louis V. Gerstner, IBM's new chairman and chief executive officer (CEO), when he convened the troubled company's 1993 annual meeting after only 18 workdays on the job. The crowd urged the first "outsider" head of the 79-year-old corporation to kick out the board of directors in the hope that a new slate would help him restore some of Big Blue's lost luster—and profits.

Just six days before the April 26 meeting, Gerstner had announced a $285 million first-quarter loss and a 7 percent decline in revenue. This quarterly loss followed a stunning 1992 annual loss of nearly $5 billion, the elimination of 80,000 jobs since the beginning of 1991, and a $77 billion decline in market value since 1987. One shareholder at the annual meeting told Gerstner, "If I were a director, I would be embarrassed to even show up here. . . . How can you work with that group of people when their attitudes, their trusted decisions, caused this company's demise?"

There was some justification in these criticisms; IBM's board had stubbornly supported former CEO John Akers through most of his eight-year tenure, during which the company's troubles multiplied. Only after criticism grew to hailstorm proportions did directors finally withdraw their support in January 1993 and allow Akers to resign.

Most commentators blamed company woes on Akers's outdated strategy and an insider mentality that failed to acknowledge the cataclysmic changes engulfing the computer industry. Apparently mesmerized

by the 60 percent of profits and 50 percent of revenues provided by IBM's mainframe business, Akers continued to push them while the rest of the industry concentrated on increasingly popular PCs, minicomputers, and workstations.

Although he finally acknowledged that mainframe revenues were declining—and at last reduced budgets and employees in mainframe divisions—Akers shocked analysts by rehiring two retired mainframe-era executives to help him turn the company around. That was only one item in a "damning bill of particulars" that one observer said finally brought Akers down.

Akers was not the only CEO to feel shareholders' and directors' wrath in the early 1990s.

See end of chapter for resolution.
Photo source: Brad Markel/Liaison International.

"Yesterday's CEOs" are losing their grip on corporate America, announced a recent issue of *Business Week*, and *Fortune* reported a seven-day period in January 1993 as "A Week of Woe for the CEO," citing the almost simultaneous falls of James Robinson III at American Express, Paul Lego at Westinghouse, and Akers. Still other leaders had recently departed unhappily from Macy's, Sunbeam-Oster, Tenneco, Time Warner, Digital Equipment, Ames Stores, and General Motors.

What is happening? Analysts seem to agree that old-style managers, used to the power and success of American dominance in the marketplace, simply cannot move their companies fast enough to keep up in the global economy. "It's not just age, it's mindset," said a Michigan management professor. "Today's chief executives can't have an emotional commitment to the past. They can't be afraid to shake things up."

IBM was a prototype of the hierarchical, overblown bureaucracy, where promotions always came from within, and the "company man" dominated the innovator. With explicit chains of command, some managers felt more responsibility to each other than to customers.

As his defeat loomed, Akers announced "a fundamental redefinition of the company." But a former employee said, "How can a guy who has been inside IBM for 30 years change a culture and an environment when all [he knows] is the IBM way?" A research company executive said, "IBM is a ship out of control."

Akers's desperate attempts seemed, in fact, merely a response to crises rather than a demonstration of active leadership. As a University of California institute director said, "The real tragedy of corporate life is that changes occur only after it's too late."

Shareholders tried to warn the IBM board long before it woke up to the urgent need for change. Big institutional investors clamored, and small shareholders by the hundreds wrote and called company headquarters in the months be-fore Akers's departure, personifying what a corporate attorney calls "a sea change in the relationship among managements, boards, and shareholders."

Recent Securities and Exchange Commission (SEC) rules removed restrictions on joint actions by shareholders to influence management. In particular, the new SEC rules allow private discussions among shareholders, out of the public's and the company's eye. Anyone who has owned at least $1,000 of a company's stock for a year or more can now sponsor a proposal and have it voted on by all shareholders. The results are nonbinding, but corporate executives are paying attention to them. United Shareholders Association (USA), a nonprofit group of 65,000 small investors, helps stockholders apply pressure to underperforming companies. "As owners, shareholders should have a big say," says one member. Several months before Akers's departure, IBM's management accused USA and its president, Ralph Whitworth, of "badgering" the company about its poor performance.

Once they decided to withdraw support from Akers, IBM directors then faced the daunting challenge of finding a replacement. "Who Can Run IBM?" blared one publication, calling the chairmanship "the hardest job in all corporate America." One candidate for the post said, "I've never seen a situation where so many well-known CEOs have not wanted a job." After an intense three-month search, a committee of seven IBM directors chose Gerstner, head of RJR Nabisco, as the captain to steer IBM out of its sea of troubles.

As you read this chapter, consider the changing relationships among managers, directors, and investors in the modern corporation. How should Gerstner respond to these changes as he seeks to convert a lumbering, aging giant into a lean machine capable of success in the 21st century? What steps is he likely to take to restore IBM's profitability and creditability?

The purpose of this chapter is to give you an overview of managerial finance. After you finish the chapter, you should have a reasonably good idea of what finance majors might do after graduation. You should also have a better understanding of (1) some of the forces that will affect managerial finance in the future; (2) the way businesses are organized; (3) the place finance has in a firm's organization; (4) the relationships of financial managers with their counterparts in accounting, marketing, production, and personnel departments; and (5) the goals of a firm and the way financial managers can contribute to the attainment of these goals.

Career Opportunities in Finance

Finance consists of three interrelated areas: (1) *money and capital markets,* which deals with many of the topics covered in macroeconomics; (2) *investments,* which focuses on the decisions of investors, both individuals and institutions, as they choose securities for their investment portfolios; and (3) *managerial finance,* or "business finance," which involves the actual financial management of the firm. The career opportunities within each field are many and varied, but financial managers must have a knowledge of all three areas if they are to do their jobs well.

Money and Capital Markets

Many finance majors go to work for financial institutions, including banks, insurance companies, savings and loans, and credit unions. To succeed here one needs a knowledge of the factors that cause interest rates to rise and fall, the regulations to which financial institutions are subject, and the various types of financial instruments (mortgages, auto loans, certificates of deposit, and so on). One also needs a general knowledge of all aspects of business administration because the management of a financial institution involves accounting, marketing, personnel, and computer systems, as well as financial management. An ability to communicate, both orally and in writing, is important, and "people skills," or the ability to get others to do their jobs, is critical.

  The most common initial job in this area is as a bank officer trainee, where you go into bank operations and learn about the business, from the tasks performed by tellers, to cash management, to making loans. You could expect to spend a year or so being rotated among these different areas, after which you would settle into a department, often as an assistant manager in a branch. Alternatively, you might become a specialist in some area such as real estate, and be authorized to make loans going into the millions of dollars, or in the management of trusts, estates, and pension funds. Similar career paths are available with insurance companies, credit unions, and consumer loan companies.

Investments

Finance graduates who go into investments generally work for a brokerage house such as Merrill Lynch, either in sales or as a securities analyst. Others work for a bank, a mutual fund, or an insurance company in the management of their investment portfolios or for a financial consulting firm which advises individual investors or pension funds on how to invest their funds. The three main functions in the investments area are (1) sales, (2) the analysis of individual securities, and (3) determining the optimal mix of securities for a given investor.

Financial Management

Financial management is the broadest of the three areas, and the one with the greatest number of job opportunities. Financial management is important in all types of businesses, including banks and other financial institutions, as well as industrial and retail firms. Financial management is also important in governmental operations, from schools to hospitals to highway departments. The types of jobs one encounters in financial management range from those dealing with decisions on plant expansions to the job of choosing what types of securities to issue to finance expansion. Financial managers also have the responsibility for deciding the credit terms under which customers may buy, how much inventory the firm should carry, how much cash to keep on hand, whether to acquire other firms (merger analysis), and how much of the firm's earnings to plow back into the business versus pay out as dividends.

Regardless of which area you go into, you will need a knowledge of all three areas. For example, a banker lending to businesses cannot do his or her job well without a good understanding of financial management because he or she must be able to judge how well a business is operated. The same is true for one of Merrill Lynch's securities analysts, and stockbrokers must also have an understanding of general financial principles if they are to give intelligent advice to their customers. At the same time, corporate financial managers need to know what their bankers consider important and how investors are likely to judge their corporations' performances and thus determine their stock prices. So, if you decide to make finance your career, you will need to know something about all three areas.

? Self-Test

What are the three main areas of finance?

If you have definite plans to go into one area, why is it necessary that you know something about the other two areas?

Historical Perspective on the Study of Finance

When managerial finance emerged as a separate field of study in the early 1900s, the emphasis was on the legal aspects of mergers, the formation of new firms, and the various types of securities firms could issue to raise capital. During the Depression era of the 1930s, the emphasis shifted from expansion to survival, and the focus was on bankruptcy and reorganization, corporate liquidity, and regulation of securities markets. During the 1940s and early 1950s, finance continued to be taught as a descriptive, institutional subject, viewed more from the standpoint of an outsider rather than from that of management. However, a movement toward theoretical analysis began during the 1960s, and the focus of managerial finance shifted to managerial decisions regarding the choice of assets and liabilities so as to maximize the value of the firm.

The focus on valuation continued on through the 1980s, but other important issues and developments of the decade included the following:

1. *Inflation* and its implications for business decisions. In the late 1970s and early 1980s this country experienced double-digit inflation, and financial managers found that they were spending much of their time trying to deal with high wage demands from workers, high prices on raw materials and components, and high interest rates—all directly linked to the high rate of inflation.

2. Increased recognition of the *social responsibilities* of businesses in such areas as air and water pollution, worker safety, and product safety. More will be said on this topic later in the chapter.

3. *Deregulation of financial institutions,* which resulted in a trend toward large, broadly diversified financial services companies.

4. Considerable *merger activity,* sometimes in the form of friendly mergers, but frequently as hostile takeovers or so-called leveraged buyouts (LBOs).

5. An increased importance of *global markets* and global business operations.

6. A dramatic increase in the use of *computers,* both for purposes of analysis and in the electronic transfer of funds and information.

Financial Management in the 1990s

The following are likely to be among the most important trends and developments of the 1990s:

1. Four factors have made the trend toward *continued globalization* mandatory for many businesses: (a) Improvements in transportation and communications have lowered shipping costs and made international trade more feasible. (b) The political clout of consumers who desire low-cost, high-quality products has helped lower trade barriers designed to protect inefficient, high-cost domestic manufacturers. (c) As technology has become more advanced, the cost of developing new products has increased, and, as development costs rise, so must unit sales if the firm is to be competitive. (d) In a world populated with multinational firms able to shift production to wherever costs are lowest, a firm whose manufacturing operations are restricted to one country cannot compete unless costs in its home country happen to be low, a condition that does not necessarily exist for many U.S. corporations. As a result of these four factors, survival requires that most manufacturers produce and sell globally.

   Service companies, including banks, advertising agencies, and accounting firms, are also being forced to "go global" because such firms can better serve their multinational clients if they have worldwide operations. There will, of course, always be some purely domestic companies, but you should keep in mind that the most dynamic growth, and the best opportunities, are often with companies that operate worldwide.

2. The 1990s will also see *continued advances in computer and communications technology,* and this technology will revolutionize the way financial decisions are made. Companies will have networks of personal computers linked to one another, to the firm's own mainframe computers, and to their customers' and suppliers' computers. Thus, financial managers will be able to share data and programs and to have "face-to-face" meetings with distant colleagues through video teleconferencing. The ability to access and analyze data on a real-time basis will also mean that quantitative analyses will be used routinely to "test out" alternative courses of action. As a result, the next generation of financial managers will need stronger computer and quantitative skills than were required in the past.

3. *Restructuring and debt reduction* is occurring among firms and consumers alike, following the highly leveraged decade of the 1980s. This represents a major trend reversal, in part brought on by the 1990–1991 recession and renewed recognition in both sectors of the risks associated with high debt levels. Facilitating this move toward a strengthening of balance sheets and a reduction of financing costs have been the lowest long-term interest rates in at least 20 years. Corporations have rushed to market with new debt offerings to replace older issues on which they had been making significantly higher interest payments—much the way homeowners by the summer of 1993 had already been able to save millions in future interest payments by refinancing existing mortgage loans at rates not seen since the 1970s. Furthermore, a strong stock market in 1992 and 1993 made it possible for many corporations to issue stock for the first time to the general public or to "come to market" a second or even a third time to increase their equity as a percentage of total financing.

4. A number of large corporations are taking steps toward a *partial reversal of the diversification into financial services.* These are often firms which were not originally financial institutions, such as Sears, Roebuck & Co., and which are now rethinking their strategy. During a single week in late 1981, management of Sears had developed a plan that involved the purchase of Dean Witter Reynolds, the nation's fifth-largest stockbroker, Coldwell Banker, the country's largest real estate brokerage firm, and the incorporation of these into a "financial supermarket" which would also include Allstate Insurance (bought back in 1934) and Sears's newly issued Discover credit card. Yet, in September of 1992 the company's board of directors unanimously voted to break up the $56 billion firm by spinning off Dean Witter and the Discover Card, selling Coldwell Banker in its entirety, and offering for sale 20 percent of Allstate Insurance. Significantly, proceeds from sales would be used to reduce Sears's debt by $3 billion. Management further announced its intent to focus on the firm's core retailing business in the future.

5. Another developing trend of the 1990s is *changes in corporate governance and shareholder rights.* More and more, corporate giants such as Sears, General Motors, and IBM have faced strong shareholder activism, often leading to boardroom revolts, and increasingly this activism has come from large institutional investors such as pension funds. These funds have targeted companies where they have concluded that managers were not acting in the best interests of the stockholders. The result has in some

cases been the ouster of top management (GM and IBM); at other times, it has been a cooperative, negotiated change accomplished jointly by the existing management and large stockholders, as happened at Westinghouse. The $72 billion California Public Employees' Retirement System (Calpers) has been one of the pioneers in this area and certainly has the necessary financial muscle to make itself heard. Other institutional investors are following its lead, and even smaller stockholders have been able to organize their efforts more effectively, since the SEC recently gave stockholders broader rights to communicate among themselves. Boardroom reform may well do for the 1990s what LBOs did for the 1980s: Oust entrenched managements to make way for new ones who will better represent the interests of the firms' shareholders.

Self-Test

How has financial management changed from the early 1900s to the 1990s?

How might a person become better prepared for a career in financial management?

What are some of the significant developments and trends in the 1990s?

The Financial Manager's Responsibilities

financial management

The acquisition and utilization of funds to maximize the efficiency and value of an enterprise.

While the function of accounting is to provide quantitative financial information for use in economic decisions, the main functions of **financial management** are to plan for, acquire, and utilize funds in order to maximize the efficiency and value of the enterprise.[1] The specific activities involved are as follows:

1. **Forecasting and planning.** The financial manager must interact with other executives as they look ahead and lay the plans which will shape the firm's future position.

2. **Major investment and financing decisions.** A successful firm usually has rapid growth in sales, which requires investments in plant, equipment, and inventory. The financial manager must help determine the optimal sales growth rate, and he or she must help decide on the specific assets to acquire and the best way to finance those assets. For example, should the firm finance with debt or equity, and if debt is used, should it be long term or short term?

3. **Coordination and control.** The financial manager must interact with other executives to ensure that the firm is operated as efficiently as possible. All business decisions have financial implications, and all managers — financial and otherwise — need to take this into account.

4. **Dealing with the financial markets.** The financial manager must deal with the money and capital markets. As we shall see in Chapter 2, each firm affects and is affected by the general financial markets where funds are raised, where the firm's securities are traded, and where its investors are either rewarded or penalized.

---

[1] American Institute of Certified Public Accountants, *AICPA Professional Standards,* Section 100 (New York, November 1987).

In summary, financial managers make decisions regarding which assets their firms should acquire, how those assets should be financed, and how the firm should manage its existing resources. If these responsibilities are performed optimally, financial managers will help to maximize the values of their firms, and this will also maximize the long-run welfare of those who buy from or work for the company.

Self-Test

What are four specific activities with which financial managers are involved?

The Increasing Importance of Financial Management

In earlier times the marketing manager would project sales, the engineering and production staffs would determine the assets necessary to meet those demands, and the financial manager's job was simply to raise the money needed to purchase the required plant, equipment, and inventories. That situation no longer exists—decisions are now made in a much more coordinated manner, and the financial manager generally has direct responsibility for the control process.

Eastern Airlines and Delta can be used to illustrate both the importance of financial management and the effects of financial decisions. In the 1960s, Eastern's stock sold for more than $60 per share while Delta's sold for $10. By early 1991, Delta had become one of the world's strongest airlines, and its stock was selling for more than $60 per share. Eastern, on the other hand, had gone bankrupt and was no longer in existence. Although many factors combined to produce these divergent results, financial decisions exerted a major influence. Because Eastern had traditionally used a great deal of debt while Delta had not, Eastern's costs increased significantly, and its profits were lowered, when interest rates rose during the late 1970s and early 1980s. Rising rates had only a minor effect on Delta. Further, when fuel price increases made it imperative for the airlines to buy new, fuel-efficient planes, Delta was able to do so, but Eastern was not. Finally, when the airlines were deregulated, Delta was strong enough to expand into developing markets and to cut prices as necessary to attract business, but Eastern was not.

In spite of its earlier successes, Delta has recently been buffeted by forces affecting the entire airline industry as well as by the consequences of its own decisions. During the summer of 1991, Delta purchased Pan Am's European routes for $506 million, a move which tripled its capacity in the North Atlantic but also increased its operating expenses by 25 percent. This major purchase coincided with downturns in the economies on both sides of the Atlantic, and Delta began operating these routes during the traditionally slower winter season. Further aggravating the situation was a series of fare wars among U.S. carriers, causing a downdraft of reduced profitability for all. In March of 1993, Delta reported the *sixth* consecutive unprofitable quarter and was engaged in the third round of massive cost-cutting measures to again become profitable. At the end of March 1993, Delta's stock traded at $54.75, after having briefly surged above $75 per share in the spring of 1991.

The stories of Eastern and Delta illustrate the importance of financial planning and of the corporate financial staff. (The story of Delta also shows how quickly the financial fortunes of a company can be reversed when a huge acquisition is made at, what in retrospect turns out to be, an unfortunate time.)

The value of financial management is reflected in the fact that more CEOs in the top 1,000 U.S. companies started their careers in finance than in any other functional area. And, as Professor Gordon Donaldson of Harvard points out, "In harder times and with expensive money, the importance of the financial function grows."[2] It is also becoming increasingly important for people in marketing, accounting, production, personnel, and other areas to understand finance in order to do a good job in their own fields. For example, marketing decisions affect sales growth, which in turn influences investment requirements. Thus, marketing decision makers must consider how their actions affect (and are affected by) such factors as the availability of funds, inventory policies, and plant capacity utilization. Similarly, accountants must understand how accounting data are used in corporate planning and are viewed by investors. *Thus, there are financial implications in virtually all business decisions, and nonfinancial executives simply must know enough finance to work these implications into their own specialized analyses.*[3] Because of this, every student of business, regardless of major, should be concerned with finance.

? *Self-Test*

Explain why financial planning is important to today's chief executives.

Why do marketing people need to know something about managerial finance?

Alternative Forms of Business Organization

There are three main forms of business organization: (1) sole proprietorships, (2) partnerships, and (3) corporations. In terms of numbers, about 80 percent of businesses are operated as sole proprietorships, while the remainder are divided equally between partnerships and corporations. Based on dollar value of sales, however, about 80 percent of all business is conducted by corporations, about 13 percent by sole proprietorships, and about 7 percent by partnerships. A fourth form of organization represents a subset under the corporate heading; this subset is called S corporations and will be covered last. Because most business is conducted by corporations, we will concentrate on them in this book. However, it is important to understand the differences among the alternative forms of organization.

Sole Proprietorship

sole proprietorship
An unincorporated business owned by one individual.

A **sole proprietorship** is an unincorporated business owned by one individual. Going into business as a single proprietor is easy—one merely begins business operations. However, even the smallest establishments must be licensed by a governmental unit.

---

[2]"Why the Finance Man Calls the Plays," *Business Week*, April 8, 1972, 54.

[3]It is an interesting fact that the course "Managerial Finance for Nonfinancial Executives" has the highest enrollment in most executive development programs.

The proprietorship has three important advantages: (1) It is easily and inexpensively formed, (2) it is subject to few government regulations, and (3) the business pays no corporate income taxes.

The proprietorship also has three important limitations: (1) It is difficult for a proprietorship to obtain large sums of capital; (2) the proprietor has unlimited personal liability for business debts, which can result in losses exceeding the money he or she invested in the company; and (3) the life of a business organized as a proprietorship is limited to the life of the individual who created it. For these three reasons, sole proprietorships are restricted primarily to small business operations. However, businesses are frequently started as proprietorships and then converted to corporations when their growth causes the disadvantages of being a proprietorship to outweigh the advantages.

Partnership

partnership

An unincorporated business owned by two or more persons.

A **partnership** exists whenever two or more persons associate to conduct a noncorporate business. Partnerships may operate under different degrees of formality, ranging from informal, oral understandings to formal agreements filed with the secretary of the state in which the partnership does business. The major advantage of a partnership is its low cost and ease of formation. The disadvantages are similar to those associated with proprietorships: (1) unlimited liability, (2) limited life of the organization, (3) difficulty in transferring ownership, and (4) difficulty in raising large amounts of capital. The tax treatment of a partnership is similar to that of proprietorships, which is generally an advantage.

Regarding liability, the partners in a regular, or *general,* partnership can potentially lose all of their personal assets, even those assets not invested in the business, because under partnership law each partner is liable for the business's debts. Therefore, if any partner is unable to meet his or her pro rata claim in the event the partnership goes bankrupt, the remaining partners must make good on the unsatisfied claims, drawing on their personal assets if necessary. The partners of the national accounting firm Laventhol & Horwath, a huge partnership which went bankrupt recently as a result of suits filed by investors who relied on faulty audit statements, are learning all about the perils of doing business as a partnership. Thus, a Texas partner who audits a savings and loan which goes under can bring ruin to a millionaire New York partner who never went near the S&L.

The first three disadvantages of a general partnership—unlimited liability, impermanence of the organization, and difficulty in transferring ownership—combine to cause the fourth, the difficulty partnerships have in attracting substantial amounts of capital. This is no particular problem for a slow-growing business, but if a business's products really catch on, and if it needs to raise large amounts of capital to expand and thus capitalize on its opportunities, the difficulty in attracting capital becomes a real drawback. Thus, growth companies such as Hewlett-Packard and Apple Computer generally begin life as proprietorships or partnerships, but at some point they find it necessary to convert to corporations.

limited partnership

An unincorporated business owned both by general partners having unlimited liability and by limited partners whose liability is limited to their investment in the firm.

A **limited partnership** may be formed under the statutes of some states. In a limited partnership, one or more *general partners* have all the managerial rights but also have the same unlimited liabilities as in any general partnership. In addition, other partners are designated as *limited partners,* and the liability of these partners extends only to the amount of their investment in the partnership. Limited partners are often called *silent partners* because they have no active voice in management. Limited partnerships are common in such areas as oil and gas exploration ventures, equipment leasing, and commercial real estate development. In the latter area they have not worked well in recent years, mostly because of the extended real estate slump, which began in the 1980s and is lasting well into the 1990s, but also because the resale market for limited partnerships, in general, is low volume and quite fragmented—a far cry from the very liquid markets which exist for almost all other financial assets. However, real estate limited partners may soon receive some help; the SEC recently gave permission for a group of large securities firms, such as Merrill Lynch, to provide "matching services" for customers wanting to buy or sell limited partnership investments. Of course, an end to the real estate recession would help as well. Limited partnerships constitute only a relatively small fraction of all partnership businesses.

Corporation

corporation

A legal entity created by a state, separate and distinct from its owners and managers, having unlimited life, easy transferability of ownership, and limited liability.

A **corporation** is a legal entity created by the state. This form of organization, which originated in Scotland in the early 1800s, is considered an important factor in the economic advancement of the West during the nineteenth and twentieth centuries. It eliminated the need for an entrepreneur to fully finance his or her ideas into productive reality, which in turn allowed managers to become separate and distinct from the capital-providing owners of the firm.

This separation gives the corporation three major advantages: (1) It has an *unlimited life*—it can continue after its original owners and managers are deceased; (2) it permits *easy transferability of ownership interests* because ownership interests can be divided into shares of stock, which in turn can be transferred far more easily than partnership interests; and (3) it permits *limited liability.* Limited liability means that capital providers can invest in a firm with a limit on how much they can lose, but with an unlimited opportunity for profits. To illustrate, suppose you and three friends invested $25,000 each in a general partnership, which then went bankrupt owing $1 million. Because the owners are liable for the debts of a partnership, you would lose your original investment and be liable for your share of the $1 million loss, $250,000. However, if your partners could not pay their shares of the remaining $750,000 of losses, you could be held liable for the entire $1 million. Thus, an investor in a general partnership is exposed to unlimited liability. On the other hand, if you invested $25,000 in the stock of a corporation which then went bankrupt, your potential loss on the investment would be limited to your $25,000 investment.[4] These three factors—unlimited life, easy transferability of ownership interests,

---

[4] In the case of small corporations, the limited liability feature is often a fiction because bankers and credit managers frequently require personal guarantees from the stockholders of small, weak businesses.

and limited liability — make it much easier for corporations to raise money in the capital markets than for proprietorships or partnerships.

The corporate form offers significant advantages over proprietorships and partnerships, but it does have two primary disadvantages: (1) Corporate earnings are subject to double taxation — the earnings of the corporation are taxed, and then any earnings paid out as dividends are taxed again as income to the stockholders. (2) Setting up a corporation is more complex and time-consuming than starting a proprietorship or partnership.

Although a proprietorship or partnership can commence operations without much paperwork, setting up a corporation is a bit more involved. The incorporators must hire a lawyer to prepare a *charter* and a set of *bylaws*. The **charter** includes the following information: (1) name of the proposed corporation, (2) type of activities it will pursue, (3) amount of capital stock, (4) number of directors, and (5) names and addresses of directors. The charter is filed with the secretary of the state in which the firm will be incorporated, and, when it is approved, the corporation is officially in existence.[5] Then, after the corporation is in operation, quarterly and annual financial statements and tax reports must be filed with state and federal authorities.

The **bylaws** are a set of rules drawn up by the founders of the corporation to aid in governing the internal management of the company. Included are such points as (1) how directors are to be elected (all elected each year or perhaps one third each year for three-year terms); (2) whether the existing stockholders will have the first right to buy any new shares the firm issues; (3) what provisions there are for management committees (such as an executive committee or a finance committee) and their duties; and (4) what procedures there are for changing the bylaws themselves, should conditions require it.

S Corporation

Subchapter S of the Internal Revenue Code provides that some small, incorporated businesses may elect to be taxed as proprietorships or partnerships if certain technical requirements are met. For example, the firm must be a domestic corporation with no more than 35 stockholders. Such a corporation is called an **S corporation.** When the owners of a firm elect S corporation status, all of the income of the business is reported as personal income by the owners, and it is taxed at the rates that apply to individuals. The major advantages to this form of organization are the following: (1) Owners enjoy the protection of the limited liability, and (2) they obtain some tax advantages, such as avoiding double taxation. S corporation status has been the preferred alternative by owners of small corporations in which all or most of the income earned each year is distributed as dividends because the income is taxed only at the individual level.

charter

A formal legal document that describes the scope and nature of a corporation and defines the rights and duties of its stockholders and managers.

bylaws

A set of rules for governing the management of a company.

S corporation

A small corporation which, under Subchapter S of the Internal Revenue Code, elects to be taxed as a proprietorship or partnership yet retains limited liability and other benefits of the corporate form of organization.

---

[5]Note that over 60 percent of major U.S. corporations are chartered in Delaware, which has, over the years, provided a favorable legal environment for corporations. It is not necessary for a firm to be headquartered, or even to conduct operations, in its state of incorporation.

Evaluating Alternative Forms of Business Organization

The value of any business other than a very small one will probably be maximized if it is organized as a corporation. The reasons are as follows:

1. Limited liability reduces the risks borne by investors, and, other things held constant, *the lower the firm's risk, the greater its value.*

2. A firm's value depends on its *growth opportunities,* which in turn depend on the firm's ability to attract capital. Since corporations can attract capital more easily than can unincorporated businesses, they have superior growth opportunities.

3. The value of an asset also depends on its **liquidity,** which means the ease of selling the asset and converting it to cash at a fair, or reasonable, price and on short notice. Since an investment in the stock of a corporation is much more liquid than a similar investment in a proprietorship or partnership, this too means that the corporate form of organization can enhance the value of a business.

4. Regular corporations are taxed differently than proprietorships, partnerships, and S corporations, and, under certain conditions, the tax laws favor regular corporations. As we shall see in Chapter 2, the top corporate tax rate is now significantly lower than the top individual tax rate.

liquidity
The ability to sell an asset at a reasonable price on short notice.

Most firms are managed with value maximization in mind, and this, in turn, has caused most large businesses to be organized as corporations.[6]

 Self-Test

What are the key differences among a sole proprietorship, a partnership, a regular corporation, and an S corporation?

Explain why the value of any business other than a very small one will probably be maximized if it is organized as a corporation.

Finance in the Organizational Structure of the Firm

No single organizational structure will serve for all businesses. A huge, worldwide corporation needs a large, complex finance department. For example, Du Pont's finance department contains 9 divisions with a total of 29 sections, as well as separate areas of investor relations, personnel relations, accounting policy, and international finance. A small firm, of course, would not need as much specialization as a vast, multinational corporation like Du Pont. In fact, in a small firm all the necessary financial functions may be handled by only a few persons whose other duties may include such diverse areas as market planning or production management. The smaller the organization, the more the financial duties

---

[6]Note that from here on, when we refer to corporations, we mean regular corporations, not S corporations.

DO PARTNERSHIPS STILL MAKE SENSE?

The status of partnerships as one of the three main forms of business organization is precarious at best, especially in the wake of huge court damage awards against U.S. accounting and law firms resulting from the savings and loan debacle, the banking industry crisis, and the recession. It is a bit discouraging to the New York partner of a national accounting firm to be personally bankrupted by the actions of a Texas partner whom he has never even met. In the words of the former director of DePaul University's school of accountancy, "With such risks, the partnership may go the way of the dodo."

While the partnership form of organization offers the advantages of low cost and ease of formation, one of its principal disadvantages is the unlimited liability of the partners. And it is this disadvantage that might cause partnerships to become extinct. U.S. accounting and law firms, which generally operate as partnerships, had close to $1 billion of judgments against them in 1991 alone. Because of unlimited liability, the partners of these firms, many of whom were not involved in the particular client's case from which the damage award resulted, are having to foot the bill out of their own pockets.

As a result, many partners are questioning whether the partnership form of organization makes sense. And it is not only accountants and attorneys who are asking this question but also architects, investment bankers, and other professionals. But of all the partnerships, accountants are the most concerned about their increasing liability exposure. As of mid-1992, there were more than 3,000 suits filed against accounting firms alleging negligence, and plaintiffs were asking for nearly $10 billion in damages. This is twice the number of lawsuits and five times the damage amounts that were asked for five years ago. Dan Goldwasser, an attorney who advises the New York State Society of CPAs stated, "It's conceivable that one or two major accounting firms will seek bankruptcy-law protection over the next five years unless their legal status is changed." In fact, some of the partners of the

accounting firm of Laventhol & Horwath were forced to file for personal bankruptcy when their firm went under. They are trying to protect their savings and homes from the claims of creditors who are still owed $47.3 million by L&H's partners and principals.

Given this situation, can partnerships remain a viable form of business organization? Furthermore, if partnerships do remain in existence, what can they do to reduce their liability exposure? Finally, how will their actions to decrease their liability exposure affect their clients and society in general?

Professional partners are campaigning hard to reduce their personal vulnerabilities to litigation. In January 1992, the American Institute of Certified Public Accountants (AICPA) agreed to let accountants create professional corporations in which the principals would have limited liability. Previously, the AICPA, which has 300,000 members, had resisted such action because of its belief that accountants should jointly stand behind their work. But due to the recent onslaught of large negligence awards, the AICPA changed its tune, and it has been instrumental in launching a drive for laws limiting professionals' liability. As of mid-1992, 13 states, including Florida, Texas, and Virginia, had agreed to provide protection for the personal assets of partners not involved in wrongdoing committed by their firms' other members.

Accountants are not the only professionals seeking state legislative change. In New York, the accountants, joined by the bar associations and by Goldman Sachs, one of the few major investment banking houses which remain partnerships, are pushing for limits on the use of partners' personal assets to settle claims against their firms.

Currently, accountants are working with their state boards of accountancy to develop guidelines permitting them to form limited liability corporations (LLCs). For legal purposes, by operating as an LLC, these firms would limit the liability of owners so that their personal assets would not be put at risk if the firm failed. For tax purposes, though, these firms would be treated as partnerships, and the firm's income would be taxed at personal tax rates. In addition, the LLC is simpler and more flexible than another alternative form of business organization, the S corporation.

Sources: "Seeking Shelter: Partnership Structure Is Called in Question as Liability Risk Rises," *The Wall Street Journal,* June 10, 1992; and "Limited Liability Corporation Bill Mulled," *The Boston Globe,* March 28, 1993.

How do these actions affect us, as clients, and what are the repercussions for society as a whole? If laws are passed which limit partnership liability, then clients will be less able to get at partners' personal assets in malpractice judgments. Therefore, if partners' liability is lessened, some big corporate clients might demand additional safeguards such as extra negligence insurance or personal guarantees. These safeguards would add to the cost of services provided. Also, clients would lose the assurance that they have retained professionals willing to stake all they have on the work they and their partners do.

If partnerships cannot limit their liability, then it will be tougher to find accountants and lawyers who are willing to take on risky business. They might stop handling business from troubled banks, savings and loan associations, brokerage houses, and real estate operations. Even now, a survey of accountants conducted by Johnson & Higgins Financial Group indicated that more than half are either limiting services or shunning certain businesses altogether as a means of protecting themselves from lawsuits. Also, national accounting firms might limit their practice in highly litigious states like California. As you can see, the implications of potential liability damages and their effects on the way professional services are provided are important and far reaching.

will be shared among individual managers or perhaps between the accountant and the president.

A fairly typical picture of the role of finance in the organizational structure of a firm is presented in Figure 1-1. The chief financial officer — who has the title of vice-president: finance — reports to the president. The financial vice-president's key subordinates are the treasurer and the controller. In most firms the treasurer has direct responsibility for managing the firm's cash and marketable securities, for planning its capital structure, for selling stocks and bonds to raise capital, and for overseeing the corporate pension fund. The treasurer also supervises the credit manager, the inventory manager, and the director of capital budgeting (who analyzes decisions related to investments in fixed assets). The controller is responsible for the activities of the accounting and tax departments. To a large extent, we leave a discussion of the controller's function to accounting courses.

Self-Test

Identify the two subordinates who report to the firm's chief financial officer, and indicate the primary responsibilities of each.

The Goals of the Corporation

stockholder wealth maximization

The appropriate goal for management decisions in publicly traded firms; it considers the risk and timing associated with expected earnings per share in order to maximize the firm's stock price.

Business decisions are not made in a vacuum — decision makers have some objective in mind. *Throughout this book we operate on the assumption that management's primary goal is* **stockholder wealth maximization**, which, as we shall see, translates into *maximizing the price of the firm's common stock.* Firms do, of course, have other objectives — in particular, managers, who make the actual decisions, are interested in their own personal satisfaction, in their employees' welfare, and in the good of the community and of society at large. Still, for the reasons set forth in the following sections, *stock price maximization should be the primary goal of management in publicly traded firms.*

Figure 1-1   Finance in the Organizational Structure of a Typical Firm

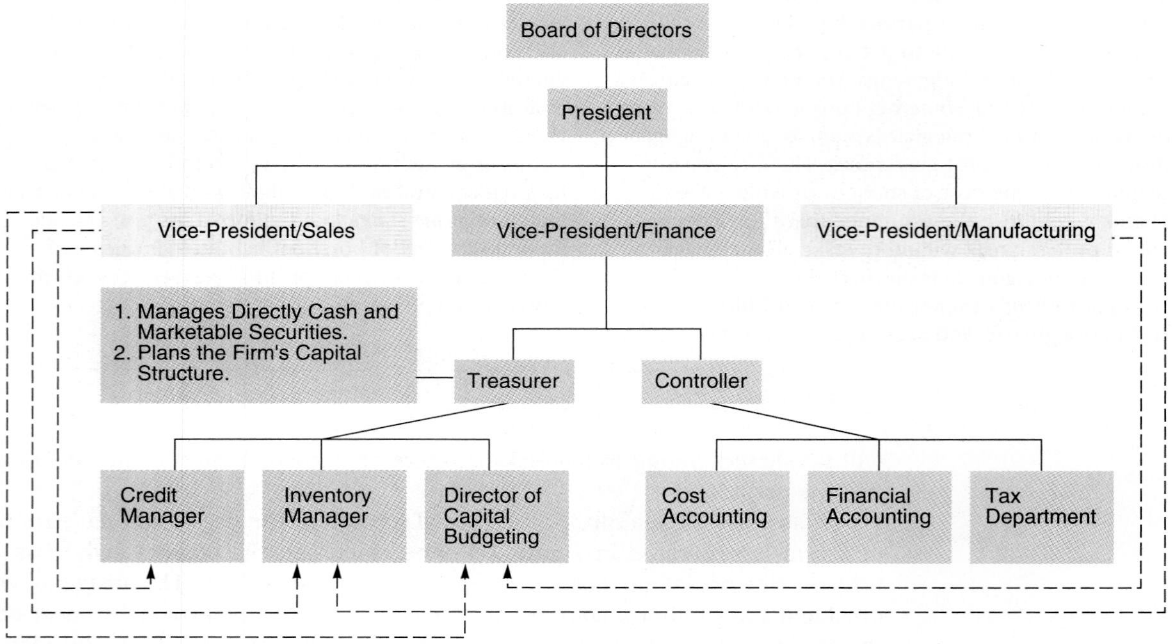

In a typical business organization such as that shown here, most general financial management functions fall to the treasurer. The treasurer is responsible for overall financial planning plus selection and management of the firm's assets. The treasurer may also be directly responsible for the management of cash, accounts receivable, and inventory. To plan and manage effectively, the treasurer needs constant input from the sales and manufacturing areas of the business. The controller oversees all accounting, auditing, and tax matters of the firm.

Managerial Incentives to Maximize Shareholder Wealth

Stockholders are the owners of the firm, and, in theory at least, control management by electing the members of the board of directors, which in turn appoints the management team. Management, therefore, is supposed to operate in the best interests of the stockholders. We know, however, that because the stock of most large firms is widely held, the managers of large corporations have a great deal of autonomy. This being the case, might not managers pursue goals other than stock price maximization? For example, some have argued that entrenched managers of a large corporation could work just hard enough to keep stockholder returns at a "fair" or "reasonable" level and then devote the remainder of their efforts and resources to public service activities, to employee benefits, to higher executive salaries, or to golf.

The argument has also been made that an established and well-compensated management might avoid risky ventures, even if the possible gains to stockholders appeared to be high enough to warrant taking the gamble. The theory behind this argument is that, since stockholders are generally well diversified in the sense that they hold portfolios of many different stocks, if a company takes a chance and loses, then its stockholders lose only a small part of their wealth. Managers, on the other hand, are not so well diversified; a manager's salary generally represents his or her largest asset. Thus, a potential setback, which might result in the manager's demotion or dismissal, is probably more devastating to the manager than it would be to a diversified stockholder. Accordingly, corporate managers may be less motivated to take on risky projects that, if successful, would benefit stockholders (and to some extent managers, if they own or have options to own the firm's stock). However, if the project is unsuccessful, it might result in the manager's rebuke, demotion, or even ouster. Therefore, some maintain that managers are not well enough compensated for their successes, and that they incur disproportionate penalties for their failures. If this is true, would a manager risk his or her job just to maximize the stockholders' wealth, or might the manager be satisfied in providing a less risky but still acceptable rate of return for the stockholder?

It is almost impossible to determine whether a particular management team is trying to maximize shareholder wealth or is merely attempting to keep stockholders satisfied while pursuing other goals. For example, how can we tell whether employee or community benefit programs are in the long-run best interests of the stockholders? Similarly, are relatively high executive salaries really necessary to attract and retain excellent managers, who, in turn, will keep the firm ahead of its competition, or are they "just another example of managers' taking advantage of stockholders"? When a risky venture is turned down, does this reflect management conservatism, or is it a correct judgment regarding the risks of the venture versus its potential rewards?

It is not possible to give definitive answers to these questions. Although several studies have suggested that managers are not completely stockholder-oriented, the evidence is cloudy. In any event, more and more firms are tying management's compensation to the company's performance, and research suggests that this motivates managers to operate in a manner consistent with stock price maximization. If they depart from this goal, they run the risk of being removed from their jobs through a hostile takeover or a proxy fight.

A *hostile takeover* is the purchase by one company of the stock of another over the opposition of its management, whereas a *proxy fight* involves an attempt to gain control by getting stockholders to vote a new management group into place. Both actions are triggered by low stock prices, so for the sake of self-preservation, management will try to keep the stock value as high as possible. Therefore, while some managers may be more interested in their own personal positions than in maximizing shareholder wealth, the threat of losing their jobs still motivates them to try to maximize stock prices.[7] We will have more to say about the conflict between managers and shareholders later in the chapter.

---

[7]Wilbur G. Lewellen, "Management and Ownership in the Large Firm," *Journal of Finance,* May 1969, 299–322. Lewellen concluded that managers seem to make decisions that are largely oriented toward stock price maximization. More recent studies indicate that Lewellen's conclusions are still valid.

Social Responsibility

social responsibility

The concept that businesses should be actively concerned about the welfare of society at large, even to the detriment of their stockholders.

normal profits/ rates of return

Those profits and rates of return that are close to the average for all firms and are just sufficient to attract capital.

Another issue that deserves consideration is **social responsibility:** Should businesses operate strictly in their stockholders' best interests, or are firms also partly responsible for the welfare of society at large? Certainly firms have an ethical responsibility to provide a safe working environment, to avoid polluting the air and water, and to produce safe products. However, socially responsible actions have costs, and it is questionable whether businesses would incur these costs voluntarily. If some firms do act in a socially responsible manner while others do not, then the socially responsible firms will be at a disadvantage in attracting capital. To illustrate, suppose the firms in a given industry have **profits** and **rates of return on investment** that are close to **normal,** that is, close to the average for all firms and just sufficient to attract capital. If one company attempts to exercise social responsibility, it will have to raise prices to cover the added costs. If the other businesses in its industry do not follow suit, their costs and prices will be lower. The socially responsible firm will not be able to compete, and it will be forced to abandon its efforts. Thus, any voluntary socially responsible acts that raise costs will be difficult, if not impossible, in industries that are subject to keen competition.

What about oligopolistic firms with profits above normal levels—cannot such firms devote resources to social projects? Undoubtedly they can, and many large, successful firms do engage in community projects, employee benefit programs, and the like to a greater degree than would appear to be called for by pure profit or wealth maximization goals.[8] Still, publicly owned firms are constrained in such actions by capital market factors. To illustrate, suppose a saver who has funds to invest is considering two alternative firms. One firm devotes a substantial part of its resources to social actions, while the other concentrates on profits and stock prices. Many investors are likely to shun the socially oriented firm, thus putting it at a disadvantage in the capital markets. After all, why should the stockholders of one corporation subsidize society to a greater extent than those of other businesses? For this reason, even highly profitable firms (unless they are privately rather than publicly owned) are generally constrained against taking unilateral cost-increasing socially responsible actions.

Does all this mean that firms should not exercise social responsibility? Not at all, but it does mean that most significant cost-increasing actions will have to be put on a *mandatory* rather than a voluntary basis, at least initially, to ensure that the burden falls uniformly on all businesses. Thus, such social benefit programs as fair hiring practices, minority training, product safety, pollution abatement, and antitrust actions are most likely to be effective if realistic rules are established initially and then enforced by government agencies. Of course, it is critical that industry and government cooperate in establishing the rules of corporate behavior, that the costs as well as the benefits of such actions be accurately estimated and taken into account, and that firms follow the spirit as well as the letter of the law in their actions. In such a setting, the rules of the game become constraints. Throughout this book, we shall assume that managers are

---

[8]Even firms like these often find it necessary to justify such projects at stockholder meetings by stating that these programs will contribute to long-run profit maximization.

stock-price maximizers who operate subject to a set of socially imposed constraints.

Stock Price Maximization and Social Welfare

If a firm attempts to maximize its stock price, is this good or bad for society? In general, it is good. Aside from such illegal actions as attempting to form monopolies, violating safety codes, and failing to meet pollution control requirements, *the same actions that maximize stock prices also benefit society*. First, note that stock price maximization requires efficient plants that produce high-quality goods and services at the lowest possible cost. Second, stock price maximization requires the development of products that consumers want and need, so the profit motive leads to new technology, to new products, and to new jobs. Finally, stock price maximization necessitates efficient and courteous service, adequate stocks of merchandise, and well-located business establishments— these factors are all necessary to make sales, and sales are necessary for profits. Therefore, actions which help a firm increase the price of its stock are also beneficial to society at large. This is why profit-motivated, free-enterprise economies have been so much more successful than communistic economic systems. Since managerial finance plays a crucial role in the operation of successful firms, and since successful firms are absolutely necessary for a healthy, productive economy, it is easy to see why finance is important from a social standpoint.[9]

Self-Test

What should be management's primary goal in a publicly traded corporation?

What actions could be taken to remove management if it departed from the goal of maximizing shareholder wealth?

Explain the difference between a hostile takeover and a proxy fight. How does a firm's stock price influence the likelihood of those actions?

What would happen if one firm were to engage in cost-increasing, socially responsible actions while its competitors did *not*?

How does the goal of stock price maximization benefit society at large?

Business Ethics

Related to the issue of social responsibility is the question of business ethics. The word *ethics* is defined in Webster's dictionary as "standards of conduct or moral behavior." Business ethics can be thought of as a company's attitude and

---

[9]People sometimes argue that firms, in their efforts to raise profits and stock prices, increase product prices and gouge the public. In a reasonably competitive economy, which we have, prices are constrained by competition and consumer resistance. If a firm raises its prices beyond reasonable levels, it will simply lose its market share. Even giant firms like General Motors lose business to the Japanese and Germans, as well as to Ford and Chrysler, if they set prices above levels necessary to cover production costs plus a "normal" profit. Of course, firms *want* to earn more, and they constantly try to cut costs, to develop new products, and so on, and thereby to earn above-normal profits. Note, though, that if they are indeed successful and do earn above-normal profits, those very profits will attract competition which will eventually drive prices down, so again the main long-term beneficiary is the consumer.

conduct toward its employees, customers, community, and stockholders. High standards of ethical behavior demand that a firm treat each party that it deals with in a fair and honest manner. A firm's commitment to business ethics can be measured by the tendency of the firm and its employees to adhere to laws and regulations relating to such factors as product safety and quality, fair employment practices, fair marketing and selling practices, and community involvement. The use of confidential information for personal gain, bribery, and illegal payments to foreign governments to obtain business are clearly unethical.

There are many instances of firms engaging in unethical behavior. For example, in recent years the employees of several prominent Wall Street investment banking houses have been sentenced to prison for illegally using insider information on proposed mergers for their own personal gain, and E. F. Hutton, a large brokerage firm, lost its independence through a forced merger after it was convicted of cheating its banks out of millions of dollars in a check kiting scheme. Drexel Burnham Lambert, one of the largest investment banking firms, went bankrupt, and its "junk bond king," Michael Milken, who had earned $550 million in just one year, was sentenced to 10 years in prison plus charged a huge fine for securities-law violations. (Mr. Milken's prison sentence has since been reduced to two years, plus three years of full-time community service while on probation; he will be barred from working in the securities industry.)

More recently, Salomon Brothers Inc. was implicated in a Treasury-auction bidding scandal which has resulted in the removal of key officers and a significant reorganization of the firm. Also, serious questions have been raised by consumers, their lawyers, and the financial press about the safety of such products as breast implants (Dow Corning) and pickup trucks with so-called "sidesaddle" gas tanks (General Motors) and about the work of the Council for Tobacco Research (established in 1954 and funded by cigarette manufacturers, tobacco growers, and others), to mention just a few examples.

In spite of all this, the results of a recent study indicate that the executives of most major firms in the United States believe that their firms should, and do, try to maintain high ethical standards in all of their business dealings.[10] Further, most executives believe that there is a positive correlation between ethics and long-run profitability. For example, Chemical Bank suggested that ethical behavior has increased its profitability because such behavior (1) avoids fines and legal expenses, (2) builds public trust, (3) attracts business from customers who appreciate and support its policies, (4) attracts and keeps employees of the highest caliber, and (5) supports the economic viability of the communities in which it operates.

Most firms today have in place strong codes of ethical behavior, and they conduct training programs designed to ensure that all employees understand the correct behavior in different business situations. However, it is imperative that top management—the chairman, president, and vice presidents—be openly committed to ethical behavior, and that they communicate this commitment through their own personal actions as well as through company policies, directives, and punishment/reward systems.

---

[10]The Business Roundtable, *Corporate Ethics: A Prime Business Asset* (New York, February 1988).

Self-Test

How would you define "business ethics"?

Is "being ethical" good for profits in the long run? In the short run?

Agency Relationships

An *agency relationship* exists when one or more people (the principals) hire another person (the agent) to perform a service and then delegate decision-making authority to that agent. Important agency relationships exist (1) between stockholders and managers and (2) between stockholders and creditors (debtholders).

Stockholders versus Managers

agency problem

A potential conflict of interest between (1) stockholders and managers or (2) stockholders and creditors.

A potential **agency problem** arises whenever the manager of a firm owns less than 100 percent of the firm's common stock. If a firm is a proprietorship managed by the owner, the owner-manager will presumably operate so as to improve his or her own welfare, with welfare measured in the form of increased personal wealth, more leisure, or perquisites.[11] However, if the owner-manager incorporates and sells some of the firm's stock to outsiders, a potential conflict of interests immediately arises. For example, the owner-manager may now decide not to work as hard to maximize shareholder wealth because less of this wealth will go to him or her, or to take a higher salary or enjoy more perquisites because part of those costs will fall on the outside stockholders. This potential conflict between two parties, the principals (outside shareholders) and the agent (manager), is an agency problem.

Another potential conflict between management and stockholders arises in a *leveraged buyout (LBO),* a term used to describe the situation in which management itself (1) arranges a line of credit; (2) makes an offer, called a *tender offer,* to buy the stock not already owned by the management group; and then (3) "takes the company private." Dozens of such buyouts of major corporations have occurred recently, mostly in the 1980s, and a potential conflict clearly exists whenever one is contemplated. For example, RJR Nabisco's President, Ross Johnson, attempted in 1988 to take the company private in an LBO. If he had been successful, Johnson and several other RJR executives would have ended up owning about 20 percent of the company, worth over a billion dollars. Management tried to pave the way for the LBO in various ways that were questionable from the stockholders' point of view. Management argued that its bid was in all stockholders' interests, but many disagreed: If management itself was buying the stock, would it not be in management's own best interest to keep the price down until the deal was completed, and thus didn't a clear conflict of interest exist?

In general, if a conflict of interest exists, what can be done to ensure that management treats the outside stockholders fairly? For one thing, the SEC,

---

[11]*Perquisites* are executive fringe benefits such as luxurious offices, use of corporate planes and yachts, personal assistants, and general use of business assets for personal purposes.

which regulates our securities markets, now requires that management disclose all material information relating to a proposed deal and that a committee of outside (i.e., nonofficer) directors be established (1) to seek other bids for the company, (2) to evaluate and compare any other bids with that of management, and (3) then to recommend the best bid to stockholders. Further, the outside directors/committee members cannot have any interest in the reorganized company; this requirement is designed to ensure their independence, and lawsuits would quickly be filed if a conflicting situation developed.

In RJR's case, the outside directors' committee received bids from several groups, including one from Kohlberg Kravis Roberts (KKR), an investment company that specializes in LBOs using pension funds as its primary source of equity capital. (KKR generally finances with about 10 percent equity and 90 percent debt, with the debt divided between short-term bank loans and longer-term junk bonds.) A bidding war ensued, and in the end KKR beat out the management group with a bid of $109 per share, up from management's original $75 offer. The final management and KKR bids were similar, but the outside directors recommended KKR in part because of the widespread feeling that management had tried to "steal" the company. This whole episode is a good example of the fact that leveraged buyouts constitute an important type of agency problem between stockholders and managers.

Several mechanisms are used to motivate managers to act in the shareholders' best interests. These include (1) the threat of firing, (2) the threat of takeover, and (3) managerial compensation.

1. **The threat of firing.** Until recently, the probability of a large firm's management being ousted by its stockholders was so remote that it posed little threat. This situation existed because ownership of most firms was so widely distributed, and management's control over the proxy (voting) mechanism was so strong, that it was almost impossible for dissident stockholders to gain enough votes to overthrow the managers. However, today 55 percent of the stock of an average large corporation is owned by a relatively few large institutions rather than by thousands of individual investors, and, as we have already discussed, the institutional money managers have the clout to influence a firm's operations. In addition to General Motors and IBM, examples of major corporations where individual managers or entire management teams have been ousted in recent years include United Airlines, Disney, Bank of America, American Express, Sunbeam-Oster, and Time Warner.

2. **The threat of takeover.** Hostile takeovers (where management does not want the firm to be taken over) are most likely to occur when a firm's stock is undervalued relative to its potential. In a hostile takeover, the managers of the acquired firm are generally fired, and any who are able to stay on lose the autonomy they had prior to the acquisition. Thus, managers have a strong incentive to take actions which maximize stock prices. In the words of one company president, "If you want to keep control, don't let your company's stock sell at a bargain price."

3. **Managerial compensation.** Firms are increasingly tying managers' compensation to the company's performance, and this motivates managers to operate in a manner consistent with stock price maximization.

**executive
stock option**

A type of incentive plan
that allows managers to
purchase stock at some
future time at a given
price.

In the 1950s and 1960s, most performance-based incentive plans involved **executive stock options,** which allowed managers to purchase stock at some future time at a given price. Since the value of the options was tied directly to the price of the stock, it was assumed that granting options would provide an incentive for managers to take actions which would maximize the stock's price. This type of managerial incentive lost favor in the 1970s, however, because the general stock market declined, and stock prices did not necessarily reflect companies' earnings growth. Incentive plans ought to be based on those factors over which managers have control, and since they cannot control the general stock market, stock option plans were not good incentive devices. Therefore, whereas 61 of the 100 largest U.S. firms used stock options as their sole incentive compensation in 1970, not even one of the largest 100 companies relied exclusively on such plans in 1992.

performance shares

A type of incentive plan in
which managers are
awarded shares of stock on
the basis of the firm's performance over given
intervals with respect to
earnings per share or other
measures.

An important incentive plan now is **performance shares,** which are shares of stock given to executives on the basis of performance as measured by earnings per share or by various profitability ratios, which we will examine in Chapter 6. For example, Honeywell uses growth in earnings per share as its primary performance measure.

All incentive compensation plans — executive stock options, performance shares, profit-based bonuses, and so forth — are designed to accomplish two things. First, these plans provide inducements to executives to act on those factors under their control in a manner that will contribute to stock price maximization. Second, the existence of such plans helps companies attract and retain top-level executives. Well-designed plans can accomplish both goals.

Stockholders versus Creditors

A second agency problem involves conflicts between stockholders and creditors (debtholders). Creditors lend funds to the firm at rates that are based on (1) the riskiness of the firm's existing assets, (2) expectations concerning the riskiness of future asset additions, (3) the firm's existing capital structure (that is, the amount of debt financing it uses), and (4) expectations concerning future capital structure changes. These are the factors that determine the riskiness of the firm's debt, so creditors base the interest rate they charge on expectations regarding these factors.

Now suppose the stockholders, acting through management, cause the firm to take on new ventures that have much greater risk than was anticipated by the creditors. This increased risk will cause the value of the outstanding debt to fall. If the risky ventures turn out to be successful, all of the benefits will go to the stockholders because the creditors get only a fixed return. However, if things go sour, the bondholders will have to share the losses. What this amounts to, from the stockholders' point of view, is a game of "heads I win, tails you lose," which is obviously not a good game for the bondholders.

Similarly, if the firm increases its use of debt in an effort to boost the return to stockholders, the value of the old debt will decrease, so we have another "heads I win, tails you lose" situation. To illustrate, consider what happened to RJR Nabisco's bondholders when RJR's CEO announced his plan to take the company private in an LBO. Stockholders saw their shares jump in value from $56 to over $90 in just a few days, but RJR's bondholders suffered losses of approximately 20 percent. Investors immediately realized that the LBO would cause the amount of RJR's debt to rise dramatically, and thus its riskiness would soar. This, in turn, led to a huge decline in the price of RJR's outstanding bonds.

The entire industrial bond market was shaken by the RJR announcement because bond investors realized that virtually any company could become an LBO target. Indeed, the state of Ohio's pension fund administrator announced that he was liquidating the fund's entire industrial bond portfolio and switching to Treasury bonds because of the danger of other corporate LBOs.

The bond market's disarray caught many experts by surprise. Even though bond investors had been stung many times in the 1980s by LBOs and restructurings, the gargantuan size of the RJR Nabisco deal made investors realize that no firm is too large to be a target. "Now, bond investors are going to have to pay much closer attention to the fine print in the credit agreements," said one analyst. He went on to say that "anybody who holds an industrial bond that is not protected against something like this is sitting on a credit toxic waste site." The RJR situation illustrates what has become known as *event risk,* the probability that some event (such as an LBO) will occur, which will increase the firm's chance of default and, therefore, reduce the value of outstanding bonds.

Can and should stockholders, through their managers/agents, try to expropriate wealth from the firm's creditors? The answer is no. First, because such attempts have been made in the past, creditors today protect themselves reasonably well against stockholder actions through restrictions in credit agreements. Second, if potential creditors perceive that a firm will try to take advantage of them in unethical ways, they will either refuse to deal with the firm or else will require a much higher than normal rate of interest to compensate for the risks of such underhanded actions. Thus, firms which try to deal unfairly with creditors either lose access to the debt markets or are saddled with higher interest rates, both of which decrease the long-run value of the stock.

In view of these constraints, it follows that the goal of maximizing shareholder wealth requires fair play with creditors: Stockholder wealth depends on continued access to capital markets, and access depends on abiding by both the letter and the spirit of credit agreements. Managers, as agents of both the creditors and the shareholders, must act in a manner which is fairly balanced between the interests of these two classes of security holders. Similarly, because of other constraints and sanctions, management actions which would expropriate wealth from any of the firm's *stakeholders* (employees, customers, suppliers, and so on) will ultimately be to the detriment of shareholders. Therefore, maximizing shareholder wealth requires the fair treatment of all stakeholders.

? Self-Test

What is an agency relationship, and what two major agency relationships affect financial management?

Give some examples of potential agency problems between stockholders and managers.

List several factors which motivate managers to act in the shareholders' interests.

Give an example of how an agency problem might arise between stockholders and creditors.

Managerial Actions to Maximize Shareholder Wealth

profit maximization

The maximization of the firm's net income.

To maximize the price of a firm's stock, what types of actions should its management take? First, consider the question of stock prices versus profits: Will **profit maximization** also result in stock price maximization? The answer is no, but in answering this question, we must initially consider the matter of total corporate profits versus *earnings per share (EPS)*.

For example, suppose Xerox had 100 million shares outstanding and earned $400 million, or $4 per share. If you owned 100 shares of the stock, your share of the total profits would be $400. Now suppose Xerox sold another 100 million shares and invested the funds received in assets which produced $100 million of income. Total income would rise to $500 million, but earnings per share would decline from $4 to $500/200 = $2.50. Now your share of the firm's earnings would be only $250, down from $400. You (and other current stockholders) would have suffered an earnings dilution, even though total corporate profits had risen. Therefore, as a first approximation, *if management is interested in the well-being of its current stockholders, it should concentrate on earnings per share rather than on total corporate profits.*

Will maximization of expected earnings per share always maximize stockholder welfare, or should other factors be considered? The answer is that the *timing of the earnings* and *risk* will matter as well. Suppose Xerox had one project that would cause earnings per share to rise by $0.20 per year for 5 years, or $1 in total, while another project would have no effect on earnings for 4 years but would increase earnings by $1.25 in the fifth year. Which project is better—in other words, is $0.20 per year for 5 years better or worse than $1.25 in Year 5? The answer depends on which project adds the most to the value of the stock, which in turn depends on the time value of money to investors. Thus, the timing of earnings is an important reason to concentrate on wealth as measured by the price of the stock rather than on earnings alone.

The other important issue is the risk of the earnings stream. Suppose one project is expected to increase earnings per share by $1, while another is expected to raise earnings by $1.20 per share. The first project is not very risky —if it is undertaken, earnings will almost certainly rise by about $1 per share. However, the other project is quite risky, so, although our best guess is that earnings will rise by $1.20 per share, we must recognize the possibility that there may be no increase whatsoever, or even a loss. Depending on how averse stockholders are to risk, the first project might be preferable to the second.

The riskiness inherent in projected EPS in part depends on *how the firm is financed.* As we shall see, many firms go bankrupt every year, and the greater the use of debt, the greater the threat of bankruptcy. *Consequently, while debt financing is usually used to increase projected EPS, debt also increases the riskiness of projected future earnings.*

Another, related, issue is the matter of paying dividends to stockholders versus retaining earnings and reinvesting them in the firm, thereby causing the earnings stream to grow over time. Stockholders like cash dividends, but they also like the growth in EPS that results from plowing earnings back into the

dividend policy decision

The decision as to how much of current earnings to pay out as dividends rather than to retain for reinvestment in the firm.

business. The financial manager must decide exactly how much of the current earnings to pay out as dividends rather than to retain and reinvest — this is called the **dividend policy decision.** The optimal dividend policy is the one that maximizes the firm's stock price.

We see, then, that the firm's stock price depends on the following three factors:

1. Projected earnings per share
2. Timing of the earnings stream
3. Riskiness of the projected earnings stream

These factors in turn depend on decisions regarding the use of debt in the firm's overall financing, its dividend policy, and numerous other policies and decisions which we will explore in the remainder of this text.

The problem with focusing on total profits or EPS is that these two measures deal *only* with profitability, but *the price of a firm's common stock incorporates a risk assessment as well, applied to the future profitability of the firm.*

Every significant corporate decision should be analyzed in terms of its effect on these factors and hence on the price of the firm's stock. For example, suppose Occidental Petroleum's coal division is considering opening a new mine. If this is done, can it be expected to increase EPS? Is there a chance that costs will exceed estimates, that prices and output will fall below projections, and that EPS will be reduced because the new mine was opened? How long will it take for the new mine to show a profit? How should the capital required to open the mine be raised? If debt is used, by how much will this increase Occidental's riskiness? Should Occidental reduce its current dividends and use the cash thus saved to finance the project, or should it maintain its dividends and finance the mine with external capital? Managerial finance is designed to help answer questions like these, plus many more.

 Self-Test

Will maximization of total profits or of earnings per share (EPS) necessarily result in stock price maximization? Why or why not?

Identify the three main factors which affect the firm's stock price?

The Risk-Return Tradeoff

risk-return tradeoff

The basic rule that higher expected return will be accompanied by higher risk and that lower risk is generally achieved in combination with lower expected return.

Financial decisions affect the value of a company's stock by influencing (1) the amount and timing of the firm's expected future profitability — its earnings stream or *return* — and (2) the riskiness of this earnings stream. Whenever financial decisions are made, there will be this link between expected profitability and risk; it is known as the **risk-return tradeoff.** If a decision is made which will reduce the firm's risk, the price that will be "paid" for the reduction in risk is lower expected profitability. On the other hand, if a very risky project is undertaken, it would be with the expectations of a very high rate of return, at least enough to compensate for the high level of risk. If that were not the case, risky projects would not be undertaken; there simply would be no incentive to do so. Therefore, risk and expected return should go up together—and they should go down together. For example, assume that the managers of a firm want to increase the amount of cash the company holds in its checking account to reduce the risk of not being able to pay bills as they are presented. Since cash is not an earning asset (most business checking accounts do not pay interest), converting other assets into cash will also reduce profitability (return).

Individual investors make risk-return decisions as well and on a regular basis. A conservative saver may opt for Treasury bills or certificates of deposit because of their very low risk, but that person then usually has to be content with a low interest rate. On the other hand, someone who is comfortable with a much higher level of risk might invest in junk bonds (we will discuss these further in Chapter 16) or highly speculative common stocks in the hope of "making a killing." It follows that you—now that you understand this basic risk-return relationship—should be highly suspicious if anyone were to approach you with an investment that "will double your money in a year and has hardly any risk!" It just does not work that way, and there is probably no other single lesson which is more important for investors to learn.

In the remainder of the text, you will come across many other examples of this basic link between risk and return, instances where corporate financial decisions will impact both and, therefore, the price of the firm's common stock. Financial managers must try to find that balance between risk and return which will maximize the price of the firm's common stock (and the value of the firm), and they must do so within such external constraints as the social concerns and legislation discussed earlier.

The Economic Environment

Although managerial actions affect the value of a firm's stock, there are additional factors that influence stock prices. Included among these are external constraints and developments, the general level of economic activity, taxes, and conditions in the stock market. Figure 1-2 summarizes these general relationships. Working within the set of external constraints shown in the box at the extreme left, management makes a set of long-run strategic policy decisions which chart a future course for the firm. These policy decisions, along with the general levels of economic activity and of corporate income taxes, influence the firm's expected profitability, the timing of its earnings, and the degree of risk inherent in the projected earnings. These, in turn, affect the price of the firm's stock, but so does the state of the stock market as a whole, because all stock prices tend to move up and down together to some extent.

Self-Test

Explain what is meant by a risk-return tradeoff.

Give an example of a situation where a decision made by management will change the risk-return characteristics of the firm.

Do individual investors ever face risk-return tradeoffs? Explain.

Identify some factors beyond the firm's control which influence its stock price.

Figure 1-2   Summary of Major Factors Affecting Stock Prices

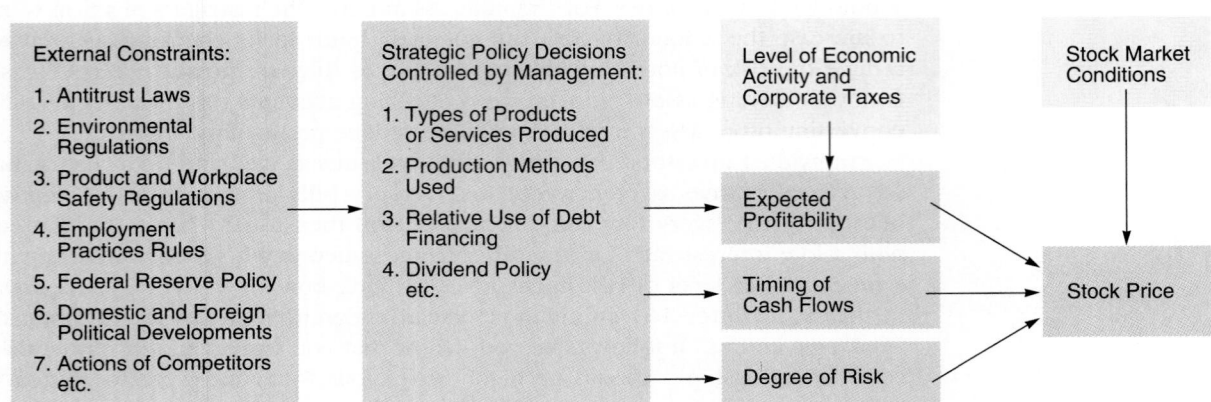

Although managers can take actions which affect the values of their firms' stocks, additional factors influence stock prices. Working within external constraints, like environmental regulations, antitrust laws, etc., management makes long-term strategic policy decisions that plot the firm's future course. These policy decisions, along with the general level of economic activity and corporate income taxes, influence the firm's expected profitability, the timing of its earnings, and the degree of risk inherent in projected earnings. Of course, stock market conditions also affect a firm's stock price because all stock prices tend to move up and down together to some extent.

Organization of the Book

This introductory chapter has described, in broad terms, the duties of the financial manager and the goals of the firm. Someone once said, "Any road will do if you don't know where you're going." We have therefore carefully charted our destination — the goal of shareholder wealth maximization — and attempted to indicate how this goal influences the duties and actions of the financial manager.

The remaining chapters in Part I will examine the economic environment in which the financial manager operates. In Chapter 2 taxes are briefly discussed, and then the general purpose of financial markets — to transfer savings to firms and individuals with attractive investment opportunities — is analyzed. Chapter 3 goes on to examine the major financial institutions in our financial markets, and in Chapter 4 we explore the role of interest rates in the economy.

Part II deals with financial statements and financial planning. Both long- and short-term plans are analyzed in terms of future financial statements, so it is important to understand how these statements are developed and then used by managers and other interested parties, such as creditors and investors. We first review how financial statements are constructed; we then show how they are used to analyze past operations, in part through the application of ratio analysis; and, finally, we discuss how financial statements can be projected into the future to forecast profits under different strategic plans and operating conditions.

In Part III we move into the execution phase of the financial management process. Here current, ongoing operations are examined. From our study of accounting we know that assets which are expected to be converted to cash within a year, such as inventories and accounts receivable, are called *current assets* and that liabilities which must be paid off within a year are called *current liabilities.* The management of current assets and current liabilities is known as *working capital management,* and Part III deals with this topic.

In Part IV we focus on long-term assets, which produce cash flows over many years. We begin, in Chapter 12, with a further discussion of the relationship between risk and return. Then, since dollars received in different years are worth different amounts, we examine *the time value of money.* Finally, we apply the risk, return, and time value concepts in our discussion of *capital budgeting,* which relates to the acquisition of long-term, usually fixed, assets. Since major capital expenditures take years to plan and execute, and since decisions in this area are generally not reversible and affect operations for many years, their effect on the value of the firm is obvious.

Part V focuses on various types of long-term financing available to a firm and describes the means by which investors evaluate the firm's debt and equity instruments. Hybrid financing methods that are not strictly debt or equity are also discussed here.

Part VI looks specifically at the cost to the firm of each type of long-term financing used, how the costs are calculated or estimated, and how much of each kind of financing the firm should employ. The effect of different levels of debt and equity on the value of the firm is addressed here, and the interrelationships among value, cost of capital, capital structure, and dividend policy serve to integrate the book and to show how the parts meld into a cohesive whole.

Finally, in Part VII, we consider some subjects that, although important, are best studied within the basic framework of the material presented earlier in the text. Included in this section are mergers and acquisitions and international financial management.

SMALL BUSINESS

RESOURCES AND GOALS IN THE SMALL FIRM

This book is about financial management, and the concepts it covers apply to small businesses as well as to large corporations. The context of financial management, however, is quite different in a small business than in a large firm, and the special characteristics of small firms must be considered. Two key characteristics of small firms are that (1) they suffer from resource poverty, and (2) their goals are often complex and even conflicting.

Resource Poverty

Consider the scenario in a large firm when a decision must be made about building a new plant. The chief executive officer (CEO) calls on a financial vice president and asks her to organize the financial analysis.

She turns to the manager in charge of financial analysis in the division considering the expansion, and he organizes a team to conduct the analysis. The team employs 20 to 30 recent graduates with masters of business administration or bachelors of business administration degrees to do the calculations, and they in turn depend on engineering and marketing staffs to provide them with the necessary input data. The treasurer will ask an investment banker (whose function is to buy securities from a firm and sell them to securities dealers or to the investing public) to recommend ways to obtain funds, such as new equity issues, new debt issues, private securities sales, a large-bank relationship, and the like. The investment banker may organize a team of experienced professionals (each earning an average of more than $250,000 annually) who will work on the plan and prepare recommendations. In general, in a large corporation, there are plenty of people to share the work, and the public securities markets are available to fund the projects.

That is not the case in a small firm. Suppose John Thompson, owner of 75 percent of Board Products Inc., wishes to expand his company's production line. He considers the proposal, obtains several bids on the project, and consults his banker, who says she's very busy now but she will get back to him. Meanwhile, Thompson is in the process of hiring three new laborers and a secretary, and he is preparing for a meeting with a potential client. He has spent the past three weeks trying to get the financial statements and paperwork for the quarterly tax payments completed. Thompson has little time and virtually no assistance in considering the financial aspects of the production line decision. Because he has no formal training in capital budgeting, he conducts a "seat-of-the-pants" analysis and decides to go ahead with the project. Later, it turns out that he overlooked many details which combine to make the project a bad idea.

Thompson's case is not unusual. Small businesses are characterized by resource poverty. In small firms, one or two key people frequently end up taking on far more responsibility than they can reasonably handle. Thompson, for example, may argue that other priorities in the business prevent him from spending much time putting together a budget or checking regularly to see how well the company is adhering to this budget. He might say, "I have a pretty good feel for how we're doing in terms of cash, and I really don't have time to go into more detail. Making budgets doesn't make money."

Management's lack of resources contributes to the failure of many small firms. An owner-manager deciding in a "seat-of-the-pants" fashion not to develop a detailed, accurate budget may realize too late that his cash flow is insufficient.

Not only is management "spread thin" in small firms, but small firms also frequently cannot acquire new funds needed for business expansion, or they can obtain funds only under very stringent conditions. Until Board Products achieves a fairly substantial size (say, $15 million in sales), the company will probably not be able to sell stock or bonds successfully in public markets. Furthermore, any public stock offering the firm did have would be very expensive compared with a similar stock offering by a larger firm. Thus,

Board Products has only limited access to public capital markets. Banks also may be reluctant to loan money to Board Products because the firm lacks a track record.

We see, then, that small firms are limited both in their access to managerial talent and in their ability to muster adequate financial resources. It is no wonder that small firms often fail, either because of poor (or overworked) management or because of undercapitalization.

Goals of the Small Firm

Small businesses' goals also may differ from those of big firms. Share price maximization is taken to be the goal of all publicly held firms. John Thompson, however, provides a good example of an owner whose life is tied up in his company. He depends on the firm for his livelihood, and he has staked his future on its success. His personal wealth portfolio is not at all diversified; he has put everything he owns into the company.

Thompson has a different attitude toward risk taking in his firm than would a typical investor in a public company. Such an investor would hold a number of other investments, all contributing to a well-diversified portfolio of holdings, and most of this investor's personal income would come from a job in an altogether separate industry.

The typical owner-manager of a small firm is, of course, keenly interested in the value of the company itself; after all, it is the most valuable asset the individual owns. In addition, the owner-manager may be considering expansion either by venture capital financing, a bond issue, "taking the firm public," or having it be the target of acquisition by a larger firm some day (hopefully at the highest share price possible!).

Nevertheless, the owner-manager has complex motives. One of them might be the desire to continue being his or her own boss, even if this means not allowing the firm to progress as rapidly or as efficiently as it otherwise could. There is a value associated with being in control, a value that is recognized in the finance literature, but that value is extremely difficult to quantify. As a result, small business owners may be observed taking actions that are in conflict with a value maximization standard but that are reasonable on the basis of other objectives.

To the extent that the goals of the small firm go beyond value maximization, some of the prescriptions in this text may not be entirely applicable. Most of the concepts will be useful for the small business, even if its objectives are different, but they may need to be modified or given different emphasis. For example,

small firms may be more interested in financial statement and cash flow analysis and in working capital management than in long-term financing and dividend policy.

Summary

This chapter has provided an overview of financial management. The key concepts covered are listed below:

▷ Finance consists of three interrelated areas: (1) **money and capital markets,** (2) **investments,** and (3) **financial management.**

▷ Financial management has undergone significant changes over the years, and in the 1980s important issues and developments have included: (1) inflation and its effects on interest rates, (2) deregulation of financial institutions, (3) a dramatic increase in the use of computers for analyzing financial decisions, and (4) the trend toward the globalization of business.

Of these four, the last two are likely to increase in importance in the 1990s. In addition, in this decade the following three trends are emerging: (1) restructuring and debt reduction, (2) a partial reversal of an earlier trend toward diversification into financial services, and (3) major changes in corporate governance and shareholder rights.

▷ **Financial managers** are responsible for **obtaining and using funds** in a way that will **maximize the value of the firm.**

▷ The three main forms of business organization are the **sole proprietorship,** the **partnership,** and the **corporation.**

Although each form of organization offers some advantages and disadvantages, **most business is conducted by corporations because this organizational form maximizes most firms' values.**

▷ The primary goal of management in a publicly traded firm should be to **maximize stockholders' wealth,** and this means **maximizing the price of the firm's stock.**

Socially responsible actions such as cleaning up air and water pollution and providing safe work places and safe products are important to society at large and are, therefore, typically mandated by law to make sure that all companies bear their proper burden in the form of cost increases.

In spite of recent examples of unethical corporate behavior, most firms today have put into place strong **codes of ethical behavior** to try to ensure that each group of constituents (employees, customers, etc.) are dealt with in a fair and honest manner.

▷ An **agency relationship** exists when one or more people (the principals) hire another person (the agent) to perform a service and then delegate decision-making authority to that agent.

An **agency problem** is a potential conflict of interest that can arise between (1) the owners of the firm and its management or (2) the stockholders and the creditors (debtholders).

▷ A **risk-return tradeoff** is a link between risk and expected profitability such that managerial decisions which increase expected profitability (return) also tend to produce higher risk for the firm and vice versa. Managers must try to find that balance, or combination, of risk and return that will maximize the price of the firm's common stock.

Resolution to
DECISION IN FINANCE

CHANGING THE GUARD AT IBM

Facing stockholders for the first time at IBM's April 1993 annual meeting, Gerstner said, "IBM has changed, but most people would say not fast enough. This . . . failure to act quickly is really the root cause of IBM's problems." He promised "bold strides," not "pussyfooting," in completing major staff reductions, in deciding what businesses IBM will pursue, in improving customer relations, and in decentralizing.

Gerstner will find no shortage of advice. A Massachusetts consultant said his first task

Sources: Pamela Sherrid, "Whose company is it, anyway?" *U.S. News and World Report,* April 22, 1991, 69–70; John W. Verity and Stephanie Anderson Forest, "Does IBM Get It Now?" *Business Week,* December 28, 1992, 32–33; Thomas A. Stewart, "The King Is Dead," *Fortune,* January 11, 1993, 34–40; Judith H. Dobrzynski, "IBM's Board Should Clean Out the Corner Office," *Business Week,* February 1, 1993, 27; Michael Schroeder, "The Ross Perot of Investor Rights," *Business Week,* February 8, 1993, 93–94; John A. Byrne, "Requiem for Yesterday's CEO," *Business Week,* February 15, 1993, 32–33; Carol J. Loomis and David Kirkpatrick, "The Hunt for Mr. X: Who Can Run IBM?" and Bill Saporito, "A Week of Woe for the CEO," *Fortune,* February 22, 1993, 68–72 and 10; Associated Press, "Former RJR Nabisco head now leads IBM," *The Gainesville* (Fla.) *Sun,* March 26, 1993; Catherine Arnst, Judith H. Dobrzynski, and Bart Ziegler, "Faith in a Stranger," *Business Week,* April 5, 1993, 18–21; Marc Levinson, "Can He Make an Elephant Dance?" *Newsweek,* April 5, 1993, 46–47; Judith H. Dobrzynski, "I'm Going to Let the Problems Come to Me," *Business Week,* April 12, 1993, 32–33; Associated Press, "IBM greets new chief with $285 million loss," *The Arizona Republic* (Phoenix), April 21, 1993, C-1; Stefan Fatsis, Associated Press, "IBM chief faces investors," *The Arizona Republic,* April 27, 1993, C-1.

should be internal—"to simultaneously stop the chaos, focus people on results, and reassure people that the company has a future." Bolstering employee morale is critical, he said, especially since some staffers were dismayed at the choice of a CEO with no computer background. Gerstner's selection also initially dismayed Wall Street—investors knocked 6 percent off IBM's market value in the days following his election.

An advisor consulted by the search committee confirmed a view held by many: "IBM's No. 1 problem is to change the internal culture. That kind of cultural change can only be achieved by an outsider."

Gerstner himself, barely seated in the CEO's chair, told an interviewer, "I have no idea how best to organize IBM. I've got to immerse myself in this company. . . . I'm also going to spend as much time with customers as I can."

Known to favor decentralization, he may let stand Akers's split of the company into 13 separate divisions, and he may take it much further. "To get effective change, you build on the values of the company, but IBM's values don't mesh with the structure of a holding company with small independent units," says one observer.

Others insist that deeper cuts in IBM's remaining 300,000 person work force will be necessary and suggest that some units must be axed. Consultant Charles Ferguson, coauthor of an analysis of IBM's problems entitled *Computer*

Wars, notes the "absurdity" of a single sales organization handling all the company's products. "These are totally different businesses, and the proper distribution system for each will be quite different." An example of the benefits of change is a company called Lexmark International that took over IBM's consumer printer, keyboard, and typewriter businesses and then consistently exceeded performance projections. Lexmark executives say their success would have been impossible without their own dedicated sales force.

Whatever he chooses to do, Gerstner will face critics who think he can never do enough. James O'Toole of the University of Southern California says, "No matter who was chosen, the odds are against him." And Ferguson concurs: "It's an impossible job." Only time will tell who is right.

Questions

1-1   What are the three principal forms of business organization? What are the advantages and disadvantages of each? What are the advantages of an S corporation?

1-2   Would the normal rate of return on investment be the same in all industries? Would normal rates of return change over time? Explain.

1-3   Would the role of the financial manager be likely to increase or decrease in importance relative to other executives if the rate of inflation increased? Explain.

1-4   Should stockholder wealth maximization be thought of as a long-term or a short-term goal; that is, if one action would probably increase the stock price from a current level of $40 to $50 in 6 months and then to $60 in 5 years, but another action would probably keep the stock price at $40 for several years but then increase it to $80 in 5 years, which action would be better? Can you think of actual examples that might have these general tendencies?

1-5   What is the difference between stock price maximization and profit maximization? Which of the two should be the primary goal in a publicly traded firm?

1-6   What are some actions stockholders could take to ensure that management's interests and those of stockholders coincided? What are some other factors that might influence management's actions?

1-7   The president of NanoSecond Semiconductor Corporation made this statement in the company's annual report: "NanoSecond's primary goal is to increase the value of the common stockholders' equity over time." Later in the report, the following announcements were made:
   a. The company contributed $1 million to the symphony orchestra in its home office city.
   b. The company spent $300 million to open a new plant in South America. No revenues will be produced by the plant for 3 years, so earnings will be depressed during this period versus what they would have been had the decision been made not to open the new plant.
   c. The company uses a great deal of electricity in its manufacturing operations, and it generates most of this power itself. The company plans to utilize nuclear fuel rather than coal to produce electricity in the future.
   d. The company has been paying out half of its earnings as dividends and retaining the other half. Henceforth, it will pay out only 20 percent as dividends.
   Discuss how each of these actions might affect NanoSecond's stock price.

1-8   Would the management of a firm in an oligopolistic or in a competitive industry be more likely to engage in what might be called "socially responsible" practices? Explain your reasoning.

Taxes and the Financial Environment

OBJECTIVES

After reading this chapter, you should be able to:

▶ Explain why financial managers must be concerned with taxation, and list some of the most important elements of the current tax law.

▶ Briefly define what is meant by MACRS depreciation and explain how it is used.

▶ List some of the many different types of financial markets, and describe three ways in which the transfer of capital takes place.

▶ Briefly define some of the most important money and capital market instruments.

▶ Specify what types of stock and bond market information are found daily in the financial press, explain how bond trading differs from the trading of stocks, and state how securities markets are regulated.

▶ Describe what is required for an efficient capital market to exist.

DECISION IN FINANCE

THE CLINTON ADMINISTRATION
AND ITS TAX PROPOSALS

When Bill Clinton replaced George Bush as president in January 1993, he promised to reduce the deficit, to increase jobs, and to get our stagnant economy going again. How does he intend to accomplish all this? Within a month of taking office, Clinton announced a comprehensive economic plan, including a massive tax increase, which would have far-reaching ramifications for both individuals and corporations.

For individuals, Clinton's tax proposal would increase the marginal tax rate from 31 to 36 percent. For single individuals, this rate would begin at $115,000 of taxable income, and for married couples filing joint returns it would begin at an income of $140,000. In addition, a 10 percent surtax would be applied to all taxable income over $250,000. As a result of the surtax, the marginal tax rate on over $250,000 of income would be 39.6 percent [calculated as 36% + 0.10(36%)], or roughly, 40 percent. At the same time, however, the proposal would hold the tax rate on capital gains at 28 percent.

In addition to raising regular tax rates, Clinton's tax proposal would add a 2.9 percent Medicare tax to all earned income (wages and self-employment income). Employees pay half (1.45 percent) of the Medicare tax, while employers pay the other half (self-employed individuals must pay the entire 2.9 percent).

See end of chapter for resolution.
Photo source: Reuters/Bettmann.

Therefore, the top income tax rate is really 39.6% + 1.45% ≈ 41% for someone not self-employed plus Social Security taxes of 6.2 percent (12.4 percent for self-employed individuals) on up to $57,600 of earned income.

Finally, Clinton proposed to increase the inheritance taxes and to establish a broad-based energy tax. Under the Clinton plan the inheritance tax rate would rise to 53 percent for estates with assets between $2.5 and $3 million and to 55 percent on assets greater than $3 million. The energy tax would be based on the heat content of fuel, and it is designed both to raise money and to control the use of relatively dirty fuels such as coal and oil.

For corporations, the president proposed to increase the top tax rate from 34 to 36 percent and to apply the 36 percent rate to taxable income over $10 million. The benefit of lower tax rates on income up to $10 million would be phased out, and as a result, large companies would be taxed at a flat rate of 36 percent. In addition, Clinton's plan would (1) disallow deductions for lobbying expenses; (2) require securities dealers to value their inventories at market prices, hence to pay taxes on unrealized income; (3) prohibit thrift institutions from taking certain write-offs if they have received funds from federal deposit insurance companies; and (4) pull in more taxes from multinational companies.

As you read this chapter, think about all the factors the Clinton administration had to consider in developing its proposals. Also, consider the impact of each of the key features of the new administration's tax proposals — if passed — on you, your family, businesses which might employ you, and society as a whole.

A financial manager's decision to invest in new assets, or to determine the ways in which assets are to be financed, is not made in a vacuum. An understanding of financial management requires a knowledge of the environment in which financial managers operate. In this chapter, we examine the tax system under which the firm operates and the markets in which capital is raised, securities are traded, and stock prices are established. We also examine the institutions through which these transactions are conducted, and we introduce the most important money and capital market instruments used.

The Federal Income Tax System

The value of any financial asset, such as a share of stock, a bond, or a mortgage, as well as the values of most real assets such as plants or even entire firms, depends on the stream of cash flows produced by the asset. Cash flows from an asset consist of *usable* income plus depreciation, and usable income means income *after taxes*. Proprietorship and partnership income must be reported by the owners, and it is taxed as their personal income. Most corporations, however, must first pay taxes on the corporation's own income, and then stockholders must pay additional taxes on all corporate after-tax income distributed as dividends. Therefore, both *personal* and *corporate* income taxes are important in the determination of the cash flows produced by financial assets.

Our tax laws can be changed by Congress, and in recent years changes have occurred almost every year. Indeed, a major change has occurred, on average, every 3 to 4 years since 1913, when our federal income tax system began. Further, certain parts of our tax system are tied to the rate of inflation, so changes automatically occur each year, depending on the rate of inflation during the previous year.

By the end of the first week of August 1993, the Clinton economic program had passed Congress, although by only the slimmest and most partisan of margins. On August 5, the House passed the $496 billion deficit-reduction package by two votes, 218 to 216. On August 6, Vice-President Al Gore broke a Senate tie, and the Senate gave its 51 to 50 approval; the following week President Clinton signed the program into law — six months after its unveiling.

The new tax law, officially known as *The Omnibus Reconciliation Act of 1993,* is a compromise of separate House and Senate versions of the Clinton

" 'Guide to the IRS Tax Code'? You'll find that in the mystery section."

Source: From *The Wall Street Journal* — Permission, Cartoon Features Syndicate.

plan. As in any compromise, specific items were modified. For example, the top corporate tax rate did not increase as much as proposed. On the other hand, certain corporate tax benefits that were originally included (notably the investment tax credit, which we will discuss later in this chapter) were deleted from the final version. This chapter will include the major changes made by the new tax law. Where an effective date is not specifically mentioned, the changes are *retroactive to December 31, 1992.*

Although this chapter will give you a good background on the basic nature of our tax system, you should consult current rate schedules and other data published by the Internal Revenue Service (and available in U.S. post offices) before you file your personal or business tax return!

Under the 1993 tax law, federal income tax rates for individuals go up to 39.6 percent, and when state and city income taxes are included, the marginal tax rate on an individual's income can easily exceed 45 percent. Business income is also taxed heavily. The income from partnerships and proprietorships, because it is reported by the individual owners as personal income, is also taxed at state-plus-federal rates going up to 45 percent or more. Corporate profits are subject to federal income tax rates of up to 39 percent, in addition to state income taxes. Because of the magnitude of the tax bite, taxes play an important role in many financial decisions.

Taxes are so complicated that university law schools offer master's degrees in taxation to practicing lawyers, many of whom are also CPAs. In a field complicated enough to warrant such detailed study, we can cover only the highlights. This is really enough, though, because business managers and investors should and do rely on tax specialists rather than trusting their own limited knowledge. Still, it is important to know the basic elements of the tax system as a starting point for discussions with tax experts.

Individual Income Taxes

Individuals pay taxes on wages and salaries, on investment income (dividends, interest, and profits from the sale of securities), and on the profits of proprietorships, partnerships, and S corporations. Our tax rates are **progressive** — that is, the higher one's income, the larger the percentage paid in taxes. Table 2-1 gives the tax rates for single individuals and married couples filing joint returns under the rate schedules in effect for 1993.

progressive tax

A tax that requires a higher percentage payment on higher incomes. The federal personal income tax in the United States, which goes from a rate of 0 percent on the lowest increments of income to 39.6 percent, is progressive.

taxable income

Gross income minus exemptions and allowable deductions as set forth in the Tax Code.

marginal tax rate

The tax applicable to the last unit of income.

average tax rate

Taxes paid divided by taxable income.

bracket creep

A situation that occurs when progressive tax rates combine with inflation to cause a greater portion of each taxpayer's real income to be paid as taxes.

1. **Taxable income** is defined as gross income less a set of exemptions and deductions which are spelled out in the instructions to the tax forms individuals must file. When filing a tax return in 1994 for the tax year 1993, each taxpayer will receive an exemption of $2,350 for each dependent, including the taxpayer, which reduces taxable income. However, this exemption is indexed to rise with inflation, and the exemption is phased out for high-income taxpayers. Also, certain expenses, such as mortgage interest paid, state and local income taxes paid, and charitable contributions, can be deducted and thus be used to reduce taxable income, but again, high-income taxpayers lose some of this benefit.

2. The **marginal tax rate** is defined as the tax on the last unit of income. Marginal rates begin at 15 percent, rise to 28, 31, 36, and then to 39.6 percent. Note, though, that when consideration is given to the phase-out of exemptions and deductions, plus Social Security taxes, the marginal tax rate actually goes up to over 47 percent (not counting state taxes).

3. One can calculate **average tax rates** from the data in Table 2-1. For example, if Jill Smith, a single individual, had taxable income of $35,000, her tax bill would be $3,315 + ($35,000 − $22,100)(0.28) = $3,315 + $3,612 = $6,927. Her *average tax rate* would be $6,927/$35,000 = 19.8%, versus a *marginal rate* of 28 percent. If Jill received a raise of $1,000, bringing her income to $36,000, she would have to pay $280 of it as taxes, so her after-tax raise would be $720. In addition, her Social Security taxes would also increase.

4. As indicated in the notes to the table, current legislation provides for tax brackets to be indexed to inflation to avoid the **bracket creep** that occurred during the 1970s and that, de facto, raised tax rates substantially.[1]

---

[1]For example, if you were single and had a taxable income of $22,100, your tax bill would be $3,315. Now suppose inflation caused prices to double and your income, being tied to a cost-of-living index, rose to $44,200. Because our tax rates are progressive, if tax brackets were not indexed, your taxes would jump to $9,503. Your after-tax income would thus increase from $18,785 to $34,697, but, because prices have doubled, your real income would *decline* from $18,785 to $17,348.50 (calculated as one-half of $34,697). You would be in a higher tax bracket, so you would be paying a higher percentage of your real income in taxes. If this happened to everyone, and if Congress failed to change tax rates sufficiently, real disposable incomes would decline because the federal government would be taking a larger share of the national product. This is called the federal government's "inflation dividend." However, since tax brackets are now indexed, if your income doubled due to inflation, your tax bill would double, but your after-tax real income would remain constant at $18,785. Bracket creep was a real problem during the 1970s and early 1980s, but indexing — if it stays in the law — will put an end to it.

Table 2-1   Federal Individual Tax Rates for 1993

Single Individuals

If Your Taxable Income Is	You Pay This Amount on the Base of the Bracket	Plus This Percentage on the Excess over the Base	Average Tax Rate at Top of Bracket
$0 to $22,100	$ 0	15.0%	15.0%
$22,100–$53,500	3,315	28.0	22.6
$53,500–$115,000	12,107	31.0	27.1
$115,000–$250,000	31,172	36.0	31.9
Over $250,000	79,772	39.6	39.6

Married Couples Filing Joint Returns

If Your Taxable Income Is	You Pay This Amount on the Base of the Bracket	Plus This Percentage on the Excess over the Base	Average Tax Rate at Top of Bracket
$0 to $36,900	$ 0	15.0%	15.0%
$36,900–$89,150	5,535	28.0	22.6
$89,150–$140,000	20,165	31.0	25.7
$140,000–$250,000	35,928	36.0	30.2
Over $250,000	75,528	39.6	39.6

Notes:

a. These are estimated tax rates for 1993 and beyond. The income ranges at which each tax rate takes effect, as well as the ranges for the additional taxes discussed below, are indexed to inflation each year, so they will change from those shown in the table.

b. In 1993, a *personal exemption* of $2,350 per person or dependent can be deducted from gross income to determine taxable income. Thus, a husband and wife, with two children, would have a 1993 exemption of 4 × $2,350 = $9,400. The amount of the exemption is scheduled to increase with inflation. However, if the gross income exceeds certain limits ($162,700 for joint returns and $108,450 for single individuals in 1993), the exemption is phased out, and this has the effect of raising the tax rate on incomes over the specified limit by about 0.5 percent per family member, or 2.0 percent for a family of four. In addition, taxpayers can claim *itemized deductions* for charitable contributions and certain other items, but these deductions are reduced if the gross income exceeds $108,450 (for single individuals and for joint returns), and this also raises the effective tax rate for high-income taxpayers. The combined effect of the loss of exemptions and reduction of itemized deductions is about 3 percent, so the marginal tax rate for high-income individuals goes up to about 42.6 percent.

In addition, there is the Social Security tax, which amounts to 6.2 percent (12.4 percent for a self-employed person) up to $57,600. Also, a 1.45 percent Medicare payroll tax (2.9 percent for self-employed individuals) will apply to *all* earned income (as opposed to income such as dividends), effective *after* 1993. Finally, high-income, older taxpayers who are eligible for Social Security payments will pay taxes on a higher percentage of their Social Security payments under the 1993 tax law than previously (a maximum of 85 percent of the Social Security payments will be taxed—*after* 1993—up from 50 percent). All of this pushes the effective tax rate up even further.

The Tax Code is extremely complex with respect to the items covered in this note, so we make no attempt to go into great detail.

Taxes on Dividend and Interest Income.   Dividend and interest income received by individuals from corporate securities is added to other income and thus is taxed at rates going up to 39.6 percent. Since corporations pay dividends out of earnings that have already been taxed, there is *double taxation* of corporate income.

It should be noted that under U.S. tax laws, interest on most state and local government bonds, called *municipals* or *"munis,"* is not subject to federal income taxes. Thus, investors get to keep all of the interest received from most municipal bonds but only a fraction of the interest received from bonds issued by corporations or by the U.S. government. This means that a lower-yielding muni can provide the same after-tax return as a higher-yielding corporate bond. For example, a taxpayer in the 36 percent marginal tax bracket who could buy a muni that yielded 6 percent would have to receive a before-tax yield of about

9.38 percent on a corporate or U.S. Treasury bond to have the same after-tax income:

$$\begin{array}{c}\text{Equivalent pretax yield} \\ \text{on taxable bond}\end{array} = \frac{\text{Yield on muni}}{1 - \text{Marginal tax rate}} = \frac{6\%}{1 - 0.36} = 9.38\%.$$

If we know the yield on the taxable bond, we can use the following equation to find the equivalent yield on a muni:

$$\begin{array}{c}\text{Equivalent yield} \\ \text{on muni}\end{array} = \begin{array}{c}\text{After-tax yield} \\ \text{on taxable bond}\end{array}$$

$$= \left(\begin{array}{c}\text{Pretax yield on} \\ \text{taxable bond}\end{array}\right)\left(1 - \begin{array}{c}\text{Marginal} \\ \text{tax rate}\end{array}\right)$$

$$= 9.38\%(1 - 0.36)$$

$$= 9.38\%(0.64) = 6.0\%.$$

The exemption from federal taxes stems from the separation of federal and state powers, and its primary effect is to help state and local governments borrow at lower rates than would otherwise be available to them.

Capital Gains versus Ordinary Income.   Assets such as stocks, bonds, and real estate are defined as *capital assets.* If you buy a capital asset and later sell it for more than your purchase price, the profit is called a **capital gain;** if you suffer a loss, it is called a **capital loss.** An asset sold within one year of the time it was purchased produces a *short-term gain or loss,* whereas one held for more than one year produces a *long-term gain or loss.* Thus, if you buy 100 shares of Disney stock for $45 per share and sell them for $55 per share, you realize a capital gain of 100 $\times$ $10, or $1,000. However, if you sell the stock for $35 per share, you will have a $1,000 capital loss. If you hold the stock for more than one year, the gain or loss is long-term; otherwise, it is short-term. If you sell the stock for exactly $45 per share, you have neither a gain nor a loss; you simply get your $4,500 back, and no tax is due.

From 1921 through 1986, long-term capital gains were taxed at substantially lower rates than ordinary income. The tax law changes which took effect in 1987 eliminated this differential, and from 1987 through 1990 all capital gains income (both long-term and short-term) was taxed as if it were ordinary income. However, beginning in 1991, the maximum tax rate on long-term capital gain was capped at 28 percent, and this was not changed by the 1993 tax law.

There has been a great deal of controversy over the proper tax rate for capital gains. It has been argued that lower tax rates on capital gains (1) stimulates the flow of **venture capital** to new, start-up businesses (which generally provide capital gains as opposed to dividend income) and (2) causes companies to retain and reinvest a high percentage of their earnings in order to provide their stockholders with capital gains as opposed to highly taxed dividend income. Thus, it was argued that elimination of the favorable rates on capital gains held back investment and economic growth. The proponents of preferential capital gains tax rates lost the argument in 1986, but they did succeed in getting the rate capped at 28 percent in 1990, and, because this rate was left unchanged

capital gain or loss

The profit (loss) from the sale of a capital asset for more (less) than its purchase price.

venture capital

An investment into new, privately held firms; it is intended to facilitate the growth of small firms not yet able to "go public."

by the 1993 tax law, the rate differential between long-term capital gains and ordinary income has once again become substantial.

The lower capital gains tax has implications for dividend policy (it favors lower payouts and hence higher earnings retention). It also favors stock investments over bond investments because part of the income from stock normally comes from capital gains. We will discuss common stock as an investment in Chapter 17.

Corporate Income Taxes

The corporate tax structure is shown in Table 2-2. To illustrate, if a firm had $75,000 of taxable income, its tax bill would be

$$\text{Taxes} = \$7,500 + 0.25(\$25,000)$$
$$= \$7,500 + \$6,250$$
$$= \$13,750,$$

and its average tax rate would be $13,750/$75,000 = 18.3%. Note that for all income over $18,333,333 one can simply calculate the federal corporate tax as 35 percent of all taxable income. Thus, the corporate tax is progressive up to $18,333,333 of income, but it is constant thereafter.[2]

Interest and Dividend Income Received by a Corporation.   Interest income received by a corporation is taxed as ordinary income at regular corporate tax rates. However, 70 percent of the dividends received by one corporation from another is excluded from taxable income, while the remaining 30 percent is taxed at the ordinary tax rate.[3] Thus, a corporation earning $20 million and paying a 35 percent marginal tax rate would pay only an effective tax

---

[2]Prior to 1987, many large, profitable corporations such as General Electric and Boeing paid no income taxes. The reasons for this were as follows: (1) expenses, especially depreciation, were (and still are) defined differently for calculating taxable income than for reporting earnings to stockholders, so some companies reported positive profits to stockholders but losses — hence no taxes — to the Internal Revenue Service; and (2) some companies which did have tax liabilities used various tax credits, including the investment tax credit (discussed later in the chapter), to offset taxes that would otherwise have been payable. This situation was effectively eliminated in 1987.

The principal method used to eliminate this situation is the Alternative Minimum Tax (AMT). Under the AMT, both corporate and individual taxpayers must figure their taxes in two ways, the "regular" way and the AMT way, and then pay the higher of the two. The AMT is calculated as follows: (1) Figure your regular taxes. (2) Take your taxable income under the regular method and then add back certain items, especially income on certain municipal bonds, depreciation in excess of straight line depreciation, certain research and drilling costs, itemized or standard deductions (for individuals), and a number of other items. (3) The income determined in (2) is defined as AMT income, and it must then be multiplied by the AMT tax rate to determine the tax due under the AMT system. An individual or corporation must then pay the higher of the regular tax or the AMT tax. Starting in 1993, there are two AMT tax rates for individuals (26 percent and 28 percent, depending on the level of AMT income and the filing status); the corporate AMT remains unchanged at 20 percent.

[3]The size of the dividend exclusion actually depends on the degree of ownership. Corporations that own less than 20 percent of the stock of the dividend-paying company can exclude 70 percent of the dividends received, firms that own over 20 percent but less than 80 percent can exclude 80 percent of the dividends, and firms that own over 80 percent can exclude the entire dividend payment. Since for investment (as opposed to control) purposes most companies own less than 20 percent of other companies, we will, in general, assume a 70 percent dividend exclusion.

Table 2-2

Federal Corporate Tax Rates

If a Corporation's Taxable Income Is	It Pays This Amount on the Base of the Bracket	Plus This Percentage on the Excess over the Base	Average Tax Rate at Top of Bracket
$0 to $50,000	$ 0	15%	15.0%
$50,000 to $75,000	7,500	25	18.3
$75,000 to $100,000	13,750	34	22.3
$100,000 to $335,000	22,250	39[a]	34.0
$335,000 to $10,000,000	113,900	34	34.0
$10,000,000–$15,000,000	3,400,000	35	34.3
$15,000,000–$18,333,333	5,150,000	38[b]	35.0
Over $18,333,333	6,416,667	35	35.0

[a]For income in the range of $100,000 to $335,000, a surtax of 5% is added to the base rate of 34%. This surtax, which eliminates the effects of the lower rates on income below $75,000, results in a marginal tax rate of 39% for income in the $100,000 to $335,000 range.

[b]For income in the range of $15,000,000 to $18,333,333, a surtax of 3% is added to eliminate the effective (average) rate of 34% on the first $10,000,000 of income.

Note: This table is based on a preliminary professional summary; more in-depth interpretations were not yet available when the text went to press. Also, when state taxes are included, corporate taxes will frequently reach or exceed 40 percent.

rate of $(0.30)(0.35) = 0.105 = 10.5\%$ on its dividend income. If this firm had $10,000 in pretax dividend income, its after-tax dividend income would be $8,950:

$$
\begin{aligned}
\text{After-tax income} &= \text{Before-tax income} - \text{Taxes} \\
&= \text{Before-tax income}(1 - \text{Effective tax rate}) \\
&= \$10,000\,[1 - (0.30)(0.35)] \\
&= \$10,000(1 - 0.105) \\
&= \$10,000(0.895) = \$8,950.
\end{aligned}
$$

If the corporation pays its own after-tax income out to its stockholders as dividends, the income is ultimately subjected to *triple taxation:* (1) The original corporation is first taxed, (2) the second corporation is then taxed on the dividends it receives, and (3) the individual stockholders who receive the dividends from the second corporation are taxed as well. This is the reason for the 70 percent exclusion on *intercorporate* dividends.

If a corporation has surplus funds that can be invested in marketable securities, the tax factor favors investment in stocks, which pay dividends, rather than in bonds, which pay interest. For example, suppose GE had $100,000 to invest, and it could buy bonds that paid interest of $8,000 per year or stock expected to pay dividends of $7,000 (the stock investment may also provide capital gains when it is sold at a later time). GE is in the 35 percent tax bracket; therefore, its tax on the interest, if it bought bonds, would be $0.35(\$8,000) = \$2,800$ and its after-tax income would be $5,200. If it bought stock, its tax would be $0.35[(0.30)(\$7,000)] = \$735$ and its after-tax income would be $6,265. Other factors might lead GE to invest in bonds, but the tax factor certainly favors stock investments when the investor is a corporation.

Table 2-3

Cash Flows to Investors
under Bond and Stock
Financing

	Use Bonds (1)	Use Stock (2)
Earnings before interest and taxes (EBIT)	$1,500,000	$1,500,000
Interest	1,500,000	0
Taxable income	$ 0	$1,500,000
Federal-plus-state taxes (40%)	0	600,000
After-tax income	$ 0	$ 900,000
Income to investors	$1,500,000	$ 900,000
Advantage to bonds	$ 600,000	

Interest and Dividends Paid by a Corporation.   A firm's operations can be financed either with debt or equity capital. If it uses debt, it must pay interest on this debt, whereas if it uses equity, it may pay dividends to the equity investors (stockholders). The interest paid by a corporation is deducted from its operating income to obtain its taxable income, but dividends paid are not deductible. Therefore, a firm needs $1 of pretax income to pay $1 of interest, but if it is in the 40 percent federal-plus-state tax bracket, it needs $1.67 of pretax income to pay $1 of dividends:

$$\frac{\text{Pretax income needed}}{\text{to pay \$1 of dividends}} = \frac{\$1}{1 - \text{Tax rate}} = \frac{\$1}{0.60} = \$1.67$$

To illustrate, Table 2-3 shows the situation for a firm with $1.5 million of earnings before interest and taxes (EBIT). As shown in Column 1, if the firm were financed entirely by bonds, and if it made interest payments of $1.5 million, its taxable income would be zero, taxes would be zero, and its investors would receive the entire $1.5 million. (The term *investors* includes both stockholders and bondholders.) As shown in Column 2, if the firm had no debt and was therefore financed only by stock, all of the $1.5 million of EBIT would be taxable income to the corporation, the tax would be $1,500,000(0.40) = $600,000, and investors would receive only $0.9 million versus $1.5 million under debt financing.

Of course, it is generally not possible to finance exclusively with debt capital, and the risk of doing so would be extremely high and would offset the benefits of the higher expected income. *Still, the fact that interest is a deductible expense has a profound effect on the way businesses are financed — our tax system favors debt financing over equity financing.* This point is discussed in more detail in Chapters 19 and 20.

Corporate Capital Gains.   Before 1987, corporate long-term capital gains were taxed at rates lower than ordinary income, as was true for individuals. Under current law, however, corporations' capital gains are taxed at the same rates as their operating income.

tax loss carry-back and carry-forward

Ordinary operating losses that can be carried backward or forward in time to offset taxable income in a given year.

Corporate Loss Carry-Back and Carry-Forward.   Ordinary corporate operating losses can be carried back (**carry-back**) to each of the preceding 3 years and forward (**carry-forward**) for the next 15 years to offset taxable income in

Table 2-4		1991	1992	1993
Apex Corporation: Calculation of Loss Carry-Back and Carry-Forward for 1991–1993 Using $12 Million 1994 Loss	Original taxable income	$2,000,000	$2,000,000	$2,000,000
	Carry-back credit	− 2,000,000	− 2,000,000	− 2,000,000
	Adjusted profit	$ 0	$ 0	$ 0
	Taxes previously paid (40%)	800,000	800,000	800,000
	Difference = Tax refund	$ 800,000	$ 800,000	$ 800,000

Total refund check received in 1995: $800,000 × 3 = $2,400,000.
Amount of loss carry-forward available for use in 1995–2009:

1994 loss	$12,000,000
Carry-back losses used	6,000,000
Carry-forward losses still available	$ 6,000,000

those years. For example, an operating loss in 1994 could be carried back and used to reduce taxable income in 1991, 1992, and 1993, and forward, if necessary, and used in 1995, 1996, and so on, up to and including the year 2009. When carrying a loss forward, the loss must first be applied to the earliest year, then to the next earliest year, and so on, until losses have been used up or the 15-year carry-forward limit has been reached.

To illustrate, suppose Apex Corporation had a $2 million *pretax* profit (taxable income) in 1991, 1992, and 1993, and then, in 1994, Apex lost $12 million as shown in Table 2-4. Also, assume that Apex's tax rate is 40 percent. The company would use the carry-back feature to recompute its taxes for 1991, using $2 million of the 1994 operating losses to reduce the 1991 pretax profit to zero. This would permit it to recover the amount of taxes paid in 1991 ($800,000). Therefore, in 1995 Apex would receive a refund of its 1991 taxes because of the loss experienced in 1994. Because $10 million of the unrecovered losses would still be available, Apex would repeat this procedure for 1992 and 1993. Thus, in 1995 the company would pay zero taxes for 1994 and also would receive a refund of $2,400,000 for taxes paid from 1991 through 1993. Apex would still have $6 million of unrecovered losses to carry forward, subject to the 15-year limit, until the entire $12 million loss had been used to offset taxable income. The purpose of permitting this treatment of ordinary operating losses is, of course, to avoid penalizing corporations whose incomes fluctuate substantially from year to year.

Improper Accumulation to Avoid Payment of Dividends.   Corporations could refrain from paying dividends to permit their stockholders to avoid personal income taxes on dividends. To prevent this, the Tax Code contains an **improper accumulation** provision which states that earnings accumulated by a corporation are subject to penalty rates *if the purpose of the accumulation is to enable stockholders to avoid personal income taxes*. A cumulative total of $250,000 (the balance sheet item "retained earnings") is by law exempted from the improper accumulation tax for most corporations. This is a benefit primarily to small corporations.

The improper accumulation penalty applies only if the retained earnings in excess of $250,000 are *shown to be unnecessary to meet the reasonable needs*

improper accumulation

Retention of earnings by a corporation for the purpose of enabling stockholders to avoid personal income taxes.

of the business. A great many companies do indeed have legitimate reasons for having retained more than $250,000 of earnings over time. For example, earnings may have been retained and used to pay off debt, to finance growth, or to provide the corporation with a cushion against possible cash drains caused by losses. How much a firm should properly accumulate for uncertain contingencies is a matter of judgment. We shall consider this matter again in Chapter 21, which deals with corporate dividend policy.

Consolidated Corporate Tax Returns.   If a corporation owns 80 percent or more of another corporation's stock, it can aggregate income and file one consolidated tax return; thus, the losses of one company can be used to offset the profits of another. (Similarly, one division's losses can be used to offset another division's profits.) No business ever wants to incur losses (you can go broke losing $1 to save 35¢ in taxes), but tax offsets do make it more feasible for large, multidivisional corporations to undertake risky new ventures or ventures that will suffer losses during a developmental period.

Taxation of Small Business: S Corporations.   As discussed in Chapter 1, to qualify for S corporation status, a corporation must meet the legal definition of a small business, must be a domestic corporation, must be owned by no more than 35 individuals, and must make a proper S corporation election.[4] Owners of S corporations are then taxed as if they were partners in a partnership. This tax treatment is especially beneficial in the early stages of a firm's development, when it is both making heavy investments in fixed assets and incurring start-up costs, which lead to operating losses. If such firms were proprietorships or partnerships, the businesses' losses would be used to offset the owners' other income. *S corporation status allows the corporation to pass on those benefits as if the firm were a partnership, with the shareholders receiving the benefits on a pro rata basis in accordance with their fractional ownership of the firm's equity.* If the firm is profitable during a year in which S corporation status is elected, the earnings are added to the individual owners' ordinary incomes. Likewise, if an S corporation has an unprofitable year, the losses reduce the owners' ordinary incomes.

Many factors other than taxes bear on the question of whether or not a firm should be organized as a corporation. However, the provision for S corporation status makes it possible for most small businesses to enjoy the benefits of a corporation yet avoid double taxation.

Self-Test

Explain what is meant by the statement, "Our tax rates are progressive."

Explain the difference between marginal tax rates and average tax rates.

What is "bracket creep," and how has it been avoided in recent years?

What are capital gains and losses?

---

[4]The full set of conditions that must be met to qualify for S corporation status is spelled out in the Tax Code. Because these provisions are subject to change by Congress, it is important to consult the current version of the Tax Code.

How does the federal income tax system tax dividends received by a corporation and those received by an individual? Why is this distinction made?

Briefly explain how tax loss carry-back and carry-forward procedures work.

Depreciation

depreciation

The accounting process whereby the cost of a productive asset is allocated against the revenues that it helps to produce.

Depreciation is the accounting process whereby the cost of a productive asset is allocated (written off) against the revenues that it helps to produce, and depreciation plays an important role in income tax calculations. Suppose a firm buys a milling machine for $100,000 and uses it for 5 years, after which it is scrapped. The cost of the goods produced by the machine must include a charge for the machine, and this charge is called depreciation. Because depreciation reduces profits as calculated by the accountants, the higher a firm's depreciation charges, the lower its reported net income. However, depreciation is not a cash charge, so higher depreciation does not reduce cash flows. Indeed, higher depreciation *increases* cash flows because the greater a firm's depreciation, the lower its tax bill.

Companies often calculate depreciation one way when figuring taxes and another way when reporting income to investors: many use the *straight line* method for stockholder reporting (or "book" purposes), but they use the fastest rate permitted by law for tax purposes. Under the straight line method *as used for stockholder reporting,* one normally takes the cost of the asset, subtracts its estimated salvage value, and divides the net amount by the asset's useful economic life. For an asset with a 5-year life, which costs $100,000 and has a $12,500 salvage value, the annual straight line depreciation charge is ($100,000 − $12,500)/5 = $17,500. (Note, however, as we discuss later in this chapter, that salvage value is *not* considered for tax depreciation purposes.)

For tax purposes, Congress changes the permissible tax depreciation methods from time to time. Prior to 1954, the straight line method was required for tax purposes, but in 1954 *accelerated* methods (double declining balance and sum-of-years'-digits) were permitted. Then, in 1981, the old accelerated methods were replaced by a simpler procedure known as the Accelerated Cost Recovery System (ACRS). The ACRS system was changed again in 1986 as a part of the Tax Reform Act, and it is now known as the **Modified Accelerated Cost Recovery System (MACRS);** the 1993 tax law has made only minimal changes in this area.

Modified Accelerated Cost Recovery System (MACRS)

A depreciation system that allows businesses to write off the cost of an asset over a period much shorter than its operating life.

Tax Depreciation Life

For tax purposes, the entire cost of an asset is expensed over its depreciable life. Historically, an asset's depreciable life was determined by its estimated useful economic life; it was intended that an asset would be fully depreciated at approximately the same time that it reached the end of its useful economic life. However, MACRS totally abandons that practice and sets simple guidelines which create several classes of assets, each with a more or less arbitrarily prescribed life called a *recovery period* or *class life.* The MACRS class life bears only a rough relationship to the expected useful economic life.

A major effect of the MACRS system has been to shorten the depreciable lives of assets, thus giving businesses larger tax deductions in the early years of

Table 2-5

Major Classes and Asset
Lives for MACRS

Class	Type of Property
3-year	Certain special manufacturing tools
5-year	Automobiles, tractor units, light-duty trucks, computers, and certain special manufacturing equipment
7-year	Most industrial equipment, office furniture, and fixtures
10-year	Certain longer-lived types of equipment
27.5-year	Residential rental real property such as apartment buildings
39-year	All nonresidential real property, including commercial and industrial buildings

Table 2-6

Recovery Allowance
Percentages for Personal
Property

Ownership Year	Class of Investment			
	3-Year	5-Year	7-Year	10-Year
1	33%	20%	14%	10%
2	45	32	25	18
3	15	19	17	14
4	7	12	13	12
5		11	9	9
6		6	9	7
7			9	7
8			4	7
9				7
10				6
11				3
	100%	100%	100%	100%

Note: Residential rental property (apartments) is depreciated over a 27.5-year life, whereas commercial and industrial structures are depreciated over 39 years. In both cases, straight line depreciation must be used. The depreciation allowance for the first year is based, pro rata, on the month the asset was placed in service, with the remainder of the first year's depreciation being taken in the 28th or 40th year.

an asset's life and thereby increasing early cash flows available for reinvestment.[5] Table 2-5 describes the types of property that fit into the different depreciation classes, and Table 2-6 gives the MACRS recovery allowance percentages for the various classes of investment property.

Consider Table 2-5 first. The first column shows the MACRS class life, while the second column describes the types of assets which fall into each category. Property in the 27.5- and 39-year categories (real estate) must be depreciated by the straight line method, but 3-, 5-, 7-, and 10-year property (personal property) can be depreciated either by the accelerated method which uses the rates shown in Table 2-6 or by an alternate straight line method.[6]

---

[5]As we shall see in Chapter 13, which deals with the time value of money, it is always valuable to receive cash flows early as opposed to late. Common sense also tells us that this is the case.

[6]As a benefit to very small companies, the Tax Code also permits companies to *expense,* which is equivalent to depreciating over one year, up to $17,500 of equipment. Thus, if a small company bought one asset worth up to $17,500, it could write the asset off in the year it was acquired. We shall disregard this provision throughout the book.

Since higher depreciation expenses result in lower taxes and hence higher cash flows, when a firm has the option of using straight line or the MACRS rates shown in Table 2-6, it would usually elect to use the MACRS rates. The yearly recovery allowance, or depreciation expense, is determined by multiplying each asset's *depreciable basis* by the applicable recovery percentage shown in Table 2-6. Calculations are discussed in the following sections.

Half-Year Convention.   Under MACRS, the assumption is generally made that property is placed in service in the middle of the first year. Thus, for 3-year class life property, the recovery period begins in the middle of the year the asset is placed in service and ends 3 years later. The effect of the **half-year convention** is to extend the recovery period out one more year, so 3-year class life property is depreciated over 4 calendar years, 5-year property is depreciated over 6 calendar years, and so on. This convention is incorporated into Table 2-6's recovery allowance percentages.[7]

Depreciable Basis.   The **depreciable basis** is a critical element of MACRS, because each year's allowance (depreciation expense) depends jointly on the asset's depreciable basis and its MACRS class life. The depreciable basis under MACRS is equal to the purchase price of the asset plus any shipping and installation costs. *The basis is not reduced for salvage value* (which is the estimated market value of the asset at the end of its useful life) regardless of whether MACRS or the straight line method is used.

Sale of a Depreciable Asset.   If a depreciable asset is sold, the sale price (actual salvage value) minus the then-existing undepreciated book value is added to operating income and taxed at the firm's marginal tax rate. For example, suppose a firm buys a 5-year class life asset for $100,000 and sells it at the end of the fourth year for $25,000. The asset's book value is equal to $100,000(0.11 + 0.06) = $100,000(0.17) = $17,000. Therefore, a profit (book gain) of $25,000 − $17,000 = $8,000 is added to the firm's operating income and is taxed. Since the asset is an operating asset, not a capital asset, the profit is operating income rather than a capital gain. It is, of course, also possible to sell an asset for less than its book value, if you sell it before it is fully depreciated. The result would be a book loss and tax savings; we will return to this topic in Chapter 15.

MACRS Illustration.   Assume that Apex Corporation buys a $150,000 computer, which falls into the MACRS 5-year class life, and places it into service on March 15, 1994. Apex must pay an additional $30,000 for delivery and installation. *Salvage value is not considered,* so the computer's depreciable basis is

half-year convention

A feature of MACRS in which assets are assumed to be put into service at midyear and thus are allowed a half-year's depreciation regardless of when they actually go into service.

depreciable basis

The dollar amount which can be depreciated for tax purposes in connection with the purchase of an asset. The depreciable basis under MACRS is equal to the cost of the asset, including shipping and installation charges.

---

[7]The half-year convention also applies if the straight line alternative is used, with half of one year's depreciation taken in the first year, a full year's depreciation taken in each of the remaining years of the asset's class life, and the remaining half-year's depreciation taken in the year following the end of the class life. You should recognize that virtually all companies have computerized depreciation systems. Each asset's depreciation pattern is programmed into the system at the time of its acquisition, and the computer aggregates the depreciation allowances for all assets when the accountants close the books and prepare the financial statements and tax returns.

$180,000 ($150,000 + $30,000). Each year's recovery allowance (tax depreciation expense) is determined by multiplying the depreciable basis by the applicable recovery allowance percentage. Thus, the depreciation expense for 1994 is 0.20($180,000) = $36,000, and for 1995 it is 0.32($180,000) = $57,600. Similarly, the depreciation expense is $34,200 for 1996, $21,600 for 1997, $19,800 for 1998, and $10,800 for 1999. The total depreciation expense over the 6-year recovery period is $180,000, which is equal to the depreciable basis of the machine.

Investment Tax Credit (ITC)

investment tax credit (ITC)

A specified percentage of the cost of new assets that businesses are *sometimes* allowed by law to deduct as a credit against their income taxes. ITCs were eliminated by the 1986 Tax Reform Act.

An **investment tax credit (ITC)** provides for a direct reduction of taxes, and its purpose is to stimulate business investment. ITCs were first introduced during the Kennedy administration in 1961, and they have subsequently been repealed and reintroduced into the tax system a number of times, depending on how Congress felt about the need to stimulate business investment versus the need for federal revenues. Immediately prior to the 1986 Tax Reform Act, ITCs applied to depreciable personal property with a life of 3 or more years and was either 6 or 10 percent, depending on the life of the asset. The credit was determined by multiplying the cost of the asset by the applicable percentage. However, ITCs were eliminated by the 1986 tax revision and were not brought back in 1993. Nevertheless, you should be aware of what ITCs are, because they may be reinstated at some future date if Congress deems that they are needed to stimulate investment.

Self-Test

What is the difference between the concept of useful economic life and the MACRS recovery period, or class life?

How do you determine the depreciable basis of an asset for tax purposes, and how does expected salvage value affect the depreciable basis?

How does one calculate an asset's MACRS depreciation expense?

How would you calculate the tax involved if a partially depreciated asset were sold for more than its book value at that time?

What is the purpose of the ITC, and is it available under current tax laws?

The Role of Financial Markets

Our economy consists of many different economic units, ranging from individuals, to businesses, to the various local and state governments, to the federal government.[8] If a unit's income exceeds its spending, then the unit is a surplus

---

[8]As discussed previously, the most important economic units within the domestic economy are business firms, individuals (often referred to as households), and governments (local, state, and national). Although our comments are directly concerned with business firms, the statements are valid for the other economic units as well.

economic unit, a *net saver;* if its spending exceeds its income, the unit is a deficit economic unit, a *net borrower.* (Technically, businesses which are deficit economic units can raise funds either by borrowing or by issuing new common stock.)

In primitive societies, where financial markets do not exist, each economic unit must be self-supporting. In modern economies such as ours, *financial markets* enable us to convert savings into productive investments. For example, suppose Houston Power and Light Company forecasts an increased demand for power in their Texas Gulf Coast service area and decides to build a new power plant. Because it will almost certainly not have the $2.5 billion necessary to pay for the plant, it will have to raise this capital in the market. Or suppose Jim Strachan, the proprietor of a Cleveland hardware store, decides to expand into appliances. Where will he get the money to buy the initial inventory of TV sets, washers, and refrigerators? Similarly, if the Martingales want to buy a home that costs $110,000, but they only have $25,000 in savings, how can they raise the additional $85,000? Also, if the City of Baltimore wants to borrow $30 million for civic improvements, and the federal government needs $300 billion to help it cover its projected 1994 deficit, they each need ways of raising capital.

On the other hand, some individuals and firms have incomes that exceed their current expenditures, so they have funds available to invest. For example, Susan Ashley has an income of $56,000, but her expenses are only $42,000, while, at the end of 1992, Ford Motor Company had accumulated over $3.5 billion of cash which it could make available for investment.

Individuals and organizations wanting to raise capital are brought together with those having surplus funds in the *financial markets.* Note that "markets" is plural — there are a great many different financial markets, each one consisting of many institutions, in a developed economy such as ours. Within these markets, capital is allocated among firms by interest rates: Firms with the most profitable investment opportunities are willing and able to pay the most for capital, so they tend to attract it from inefficient firms or from those whose products are not in demand. Thus, in the U.S. economy most capital is allocated through the price system, with *interest rates* representing the price of borrowed capital.

Figure 2-1 shows how supply and demand interact to determine interest rates in two different markets for capital, Market A, where relatively low-risk corporate bonds are traded, and Market B, where riskier firms borrow in the "junk" bond market.[9] Naturally, savers will save more if the interest rate is higher, but borrowers will borrow more at lower interest rates, so the supply curve is upward sloping, and the demand curve is downward sloping. The intersection of the supply and demand curves determines the going, or *equilibrium,* interest rates in each market. These interest rates, k_A and k_B, are market-clearing rates. Recognize that the difference between the two rates illustrates the risk-return tradeoff introduced in Chapter 1. Riskier securities simply must offer higher rates of return than lower-risk securities or there would be no market for them.

---

[9]Note that if we had chosen the market for *short-term* debt, IOUs of various economic units, for our Market A we would have seen an even greater contrast; such instruments were providing a return of only approximately 3 percent in April 1993.

Figure 2-1   Interest Rates as a Function of Supply and Demand for Funds

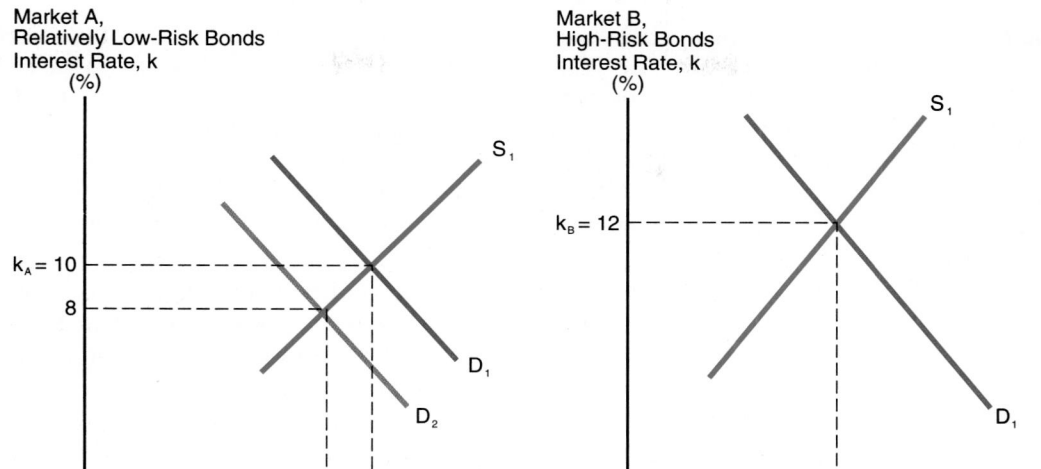

The graphs above demonstrate how capital is allocated in two financial markets, Market A, where relatively low-risk corporate bonds are traded, and Market B, where riskier securities are traded. The intersection of the supply and demand curves in each market determines the equilibrium, or market-clearing, interest rate, where a balance between supply and demand is reached. Because of its lower risk, Market A's interest rate is lower than that of Market B, an illustration of the risk-return tradeoff. Market A's graph also demonstrates that interest rates will decrease, and the supply of capital will fall, when the demand curve shifts from D_1 to D_2, as it would during a recession.

The equilibrium rates in the different markets change over time, depending on conditions. For example, if the economy slips into a recession, the demand curves tend to shift to the left and interest rates fall, while the opposite tends to be true if the economy strengthens. Similarly, if the Federal Reserve reduces the availability of credit, the supply curve shifts to the left, and interest rates rise (although the Federal Reserve's influence is felt more on short-term rates than on long-term bond rates, as we shall see in the next chapter). Note, too, that the financial markets are interrelated—savers can shift funds between markets, so if rates rise in Market A because of an increase in demand, some funds will probably be shifted from B to A, which will lower rates in Market A and raise them in Market B.

As we noted previously, each market deals with a somewhat different type of security, serves a different set of customers, or operates in a different part of the country. The following paragraphs discuss some of the major types of markets:

1. *Physical asset markets* (also called "tangible" or "real" asset markets) are those for such products as wheat, autos, real estate, computers, and machinery. *Financial asset markets* deal with stocks, bonds, notes, mortgages, and other *claims on real assets.*

2. *Spot markets* and *futures markets* are terms that refer to whether the assets are being bought or sold for "on the spot" delivery (literally, within a

few days) or for delivery at some future date, such as six months or a year later. The futures markets, which include options markets, are growing in importance. We shall discuss options in Chapter 18.

money markets

Financial markets in which funds are borrowed or loaned for short periods (less than one year).

capital markets

Financial markets for stocks and for long-term debt (one year or longer).

3. **Money markets** are the markets for debt securities with maturities of less than one year. The New York and London money markets have long been the world's largest, but Tokyo is rising rapidly. **Capital markets** are the markets for long-term debt and corporate stocks. The New York Stock Exchange, which handles the stocks of most of the largest U.S. corporations, is a prime example of a capital market. The stocks and bonds of smaller corporations are handled in other segments of the capital market.

4. *Mortgage markets* deal with loans on residential, commercial, and industrial real estate, and on farmland, while *consumer credit markets* involve loans on autos and appliances, as well as loans for education, vacations, and so on.

5. *World, national, regional,* and *local markets* also exist. Thus, depending on an organization's size and scope of operations, it may be able to borrow all around the world, or it may be confined to a strictly local, even neighborhood, market.

primary markets

Financial markets in which corporations and government units raise capital by issuing new securities.

secondary markets

Financial markets in which securities are traded among investors after the securities have been initially issued.

6. **Primary markets** are the markets in which corporations (and government units) raise new capital. If GE were to sell a new issue of common stock to raise capital, this would be a primary market transaction. The corporation selling the newly created stock receives the proceeds from the sale in a primary market transaction. **Secondary markets** are markets in which existing, already outstanding, securities are traded among investors. Thus, if Susan Ashley decided to buy 100 shares of Wal-Mart stock, the purchase would occur in the secondary market. The New York Stock Exchange is a secondary market since it deals in outstanding as opposed to newly issued stocks and bonds. Secondary markets also exist for mortgages, various other types of loans, and other financial assets. All secondary markets are extremely important because they provide liquidity for the financial assets in question. The corporation whose securities are being traded is not involved in a secondary market transaction and, thus, does not receive any funds from such a sale.

Other classifications could be made, but this breakdown is sufficient to show that there are many types of financial markets. Although savings must equal investment, financial markets allow the savings and investment processes to be separated. Thus, savers do not necessarily have to have their own productive investment opportunities. Because savings and investment are rarely equal for individual economic units, a healthy economy depends on efficient transfers of funds from savers to firms and individuals who need capital; that is, the economy depends on *efficient financial markets*. Without efficient transfers, the economy simply could not function. Houston Power and Light could not raise capital, so the citizens in the Texas gulf coast area would not have enough electricity; the Martingale family would not have adequate housing; Susan Ashley would have no place to invest her savings; and so on. Obviously, the level of employment and productivity, and hence our standard of living, would be much lower. It is therefore absolutely essential that financial markets function efficiently — not only quickly, but also at a low cost.[10]

Table 2-7 lists a number of the many important instruments traded in the various financial markets. The instruments are arranged from top to bottom in ascending order of typical length of maturity. To help clarify this table, a few brief, selected definitions are in order:

Money Market Instruments

U.S. Treasury bills

Short-term, marketable federal government debt.

1. **U.S. Treasury bills** *(T-bills)* are short-term, marketable federal government debt, that is, short-term IOUs issued by the federal government.
2. *Negotiable certificates of deposit* are large time deposits, that is, short-term IOUs issued by commercial banks.
3. *Commercial paper* are unsecured promissory notes issued by the most financially secure corporations, that is, short-term corporate IOUs.
4. *Banker's acceptances* are also short-term corporate IOUs, but these have been signed or guaranteed by a bank; banker's acceptances are used especially in import-export transactions.

All money market instruments represent *debt,* a promise to pay at some future time. On the other hand, capital market instruments may be either debt or equity.

Capital Market Instruments

U.S. Treasury notes and bonds

Long-term, marketable federal government debt.

municipal bonds

Long-term debt issued by state and local governments.

corporate bonds

Long-term debt securities issued by corporations.

preferred stock

Long-term equity securities which pay a fixed dividend.

common stock

Long-term equity claim on the issuing corporation; does not guarantee dividend payments.

1. **U.S. Treasury notes and bonds** are marketable federal government debt, long-term IOUs issued by the federal government. The difference between them is that notes have maturities of 1 to 10 years, while bonds have longer maturities.
2. *State and local government bonds,* or **municipal bonds** (munis), are long-term debt as well but issued at the state and local level, for example, to build a bridge or a sewage plant.
3. **Corporate bonds** are long-term debt issues of corporations, that is, long-term IOUs, usually in denominations of $1,000.
4. **Preferred stock** are long-term, corporate equity securities which pay a fixed dividend.
5. **Common stock** also represents an equity claim on the issuing firm but has no guarantee of any dividend.

Note that all these securities represent debt *except* preferred and common stock.

As we go through the book, we will look in much more detail at many of these instruments. In Chapter 16 we will see that there are actually many vari-

---

[10]As the Commonwealth of Independent States (the former Soviet Union) and the Eastern European nations move toward capitalism, just as much attention must be paid to the establishment of cost-efficient financial markets as to electrical power, transportation, communications, and other infrastructure systems. Economic efficiency is simply impossible without a good system for allocating capital within the economy.

Table 2-7   Summary of Major Market Instruments, Market Participants, and Security Characteristics

| Instrument (1) | Market (2) | Major Participants (3) | Security Characteristics | | Interest Rate on 4/14/93[a] (6) |
			Riskiness (4)	Maturity (5)	
U.S. Treasury bills	Money	Sold by U.S. government to institutional investors	Default-free	91 days to 1 year	3.0%
Negotiable certificates of deposit (CDs)	Money	Issued by major money-center commercial banks to large investors	Riskier than Treasury bills	Up to 1 year	3.0
Commercial paper	Money	Issued by financially secure firms to large investors	Low default risk	Up to 270 days	3.2
Banker's acceptances	Money	Firm's promise to pay, guaranteed by a bank	Low degree of risk if guaranteed by a strong bank	Up to 180 days	3.0
Money market mutual funds	Money	Invest in Treasury bills, CDs, and commercial paper; held by individuals and businesses	Low degree of risk	No specific maturity (instant liquidity)	3.0
Eurodollar market time deposits	Money	Issued by banks outside U.S.	Default risk is a function of the issuing bank	Up to 1 year	3.2
U.S. Treasury notes and bonds	Capital	Issued by U.S. government	No default risk, but price can decline if interest rates rise	1 to 30 years	6.8
Consumer credit loans	Money or Capital	Issued by banks/ credit unions/finance companies to individuals	Variable	Variable	Variable

[a]Interest rates are for longest maturity and for the strongest securities of a given type. Thus, the 7.8% interest rate shown for corporate bonds reflects the rate on 30-year, Aaa bonds. Lower-rated bonds had higher interest rates.

eties of corporate bonds, ranging from "plain vanilla" bonds, to bonds that are convertible into common stock, to bonds whose interest payments vary depending on the rate of inflation. Still, the brief definitions and the table above give an idea of the characteristics and costs of the instruments traded in the major financial markets.

Self-Test

Who are the principal suppliers and demanders of capital?

Define what is meant by the equilibrium interest rate in a given market.

Distinguish between physical asset markets and financial asset markets.

What is the difference between spot and futures markets?

Table 2-7 *continued*

Instrument (1)	Market (2)	Major Participants (3)	Security Characteristics		
			Riskiness (4)	Maturity (5)	Interest Rate on 4/14/93[a] (6)
Mortgages	Capital	Borrowings from commercial banks and S&Ls by individuals and businesses	Variable	Up to 30 years	7.5
State and local government bonds (munis)	Capital	Issued by state and local governments to individuals and institutional investors	Riskier than U.S. government securities, but exempt from most taxes	Up to 30 years	5.7
Corporate bonds	Capital	Issued by corporations to individuals and institutional investors	Riskier than U.S. government securities, but less risky than preferred and common stocks; risk depends on strength of issuer	Generally up to 30 years	7.8%
Leases	Capital	Firms contract to use assets, title to the assets held by institutional lenders	Risk similar to corporate bonds	Generally 3 to 20 years	Similar to bond yields
Preferred stocks	Capital	Issued by corporations to individuals and institutional investors	Riskier than corporate bonds, but less risky than common stock	Unlimited	4 to 6.5
Common stocks[b]	Capital	Issued by corporations to individuals and institutional investors	Risky	Unlimited	8 to 10

[b]Common stocks are expected to provide a "return" in the form of dividends and capital gains rather than interest. Of course, if you buy a stock, while you may *expect* to earn 10 percent on your money, the stock's price may decline and cause you to experience a 100 percent loss.

Distinguish between money and capital markets.

Briefly describe some of the most common money and capital market instruments.

What is the difference between primary and secondary markets?

Why are financial markets essential for a healthy economy?

financial intermediaries

Specialized financial firms that facilitate the transfer of funds from savers to demanders of capital and, in the process, create new financial products.

The Role of Financial Intermediaries

The transfer of funds from savers to those who need funds is facilitated by **financial intermediaries.** Financial intermediaries include commercial banks, savings and loan associations, credit unions, pension funds, life insurance companies, and mutual funds. These intermediaries aid the capital allocation process in several ways.

By way of explanation, let us consider an economy devoid of financial intermediaries. Further, let's assume that a businesswoman, Ms. Rossi, has discovered a cure for the common cold but requires $400,000 to obtain the proper productive assets for manufacture and distribution of the product. She must find someone with savings to invest in her project.[11]

Ms. Rossi has several problems if no financial intermediaries exist. First, she must find someone with savings. Through family and friends, she finds a saver, Mr. Davis. Ms. Rossi's problems are not over, however. In persuading Mr. Davis to invest, Ms. Rossi will encounter several obstacles. First, Mr. Davis may not have enough savings to cover the entire $400,000 investment; therefore, Ms. Rossi must search for additional investors. Second, Mr. Davis realizes that by putting all of his money into a single project, he is facing more risk than he would be if he diversified by investing in several projects.[12] With this higher risk Mr. Davis may require a greater return than Ms. Rossi wishes to pay. Third, Mr. Davis may need to withdraw his funds for retirement or to meet a financial emergency before the project is completed, causing refinancing problems for Ms. Rossi. Any or all of these problems — difficulty in locating savers, savers' need to diversify, and savers' need for liquidity — may end the investment project before it begins. We see, then, that if productive investments cannot be financed, economic growth cannot be maintained.

In a developed economy such as that of the United States, many of the problems encountered by entrepreneurs like Ms. Rossi can be alleviated by a financial intermediary. Thus, transfers of capital between savers and those who need funds can take place in three different ways, as diagrammed in Figure 2-2:

1. *Direct transfers* of money and securities, as shown in the top section, occur when a business sells its stocks or bonds directly to savers, without going through any type of intermediary or middleman. Dollars flow from savers to the business, which then delivers its securities to the savers.

investment banking house

A financial institution that underwrites and distributes new investment securities to help businesses obtain financing.

2. As the middle section illustrates, transfers may also go through an **investment banking house,** which serves as a middleman and facilitates the issuance of securities. The company sells its stocks or bonds to the investment bank, which in turn sells these same securities to the ultimate savers. The businesses' securities and the savers' money merely "pass through" the investment banking house. Even so, the investment bank is taking a risk since it is purchasing securities that it may not be able to resell to savers for as much or more than it paid; taking on this risk is called *underwriting* the securities issue. The issuing corporation, on the other hand, is assured of getting the funds it needs whether investors buy its securities from the investment banker or not. Since the corporation receives money from the sale of the securities, this is a primary market transaction. Although they serve as financial middlemen, technically, investment bankers

---

[11]For the purposes of our example, the investment may be in the form of either an equity share or a loan.

[12]We discuss diversification and how it reduces risk in Chapter 12.

Figure 2-2

Diagram of the Capital
Formation Process

1. Direct Transfers

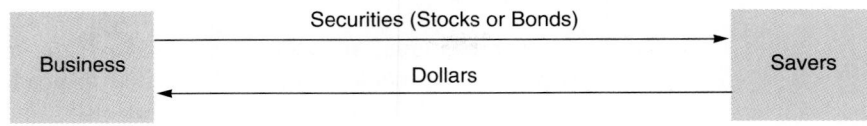

2. Indirect Transfers through an Investment Banker

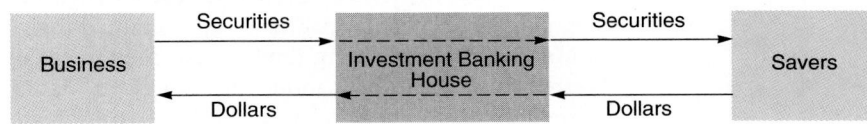

3. Indirect Transfers through a Financial Intermediary

There are three traditional ways of transferring capital between savers and those who need funds. Direct transfers without intermediaries are possible, but they are often inefficient. Investment banking houses serve as middlemen in indirect transfers, but they do not create their own financial claims. Financial intermediaries actually create new financial products such as checking and savings accounts, mutual fund shares, and insurance policies. The intermediary uses savers' funds to purchase borrowers' financial claims such as stock, bonds, and mortgages. The financial products offered by intermediaries help meet savers' needs for diversification and liquidity.

are not intermediaries because they do not create their own financial claims.

Although direct transfers between businesses and savers do occur on occasion, it is generally more efficient for a business to obtain the services of an investment banking house. Merrill Lynch and Salomon Brothers are examples of financial service corporations which offer investment banking services. In general, investment bankers (1) help corporations design securities with the features that will be most attractive to investors, (2) buy these securities from the issuing corporation, (3) resell them to savers in the primary market, and (4) bear the risk of adverse price fluctuations on these securities during the offering period. We will examine the investment banking process in greater detail in Chapter 17.

3. The bottom section of Figure 2-2 shows that transfers may occur through a *financial intermediary,* such as a bank or mutual fund, which obtains funds from savers and then *issues its own securities* in exchange. For example, a saver might deposit dollars into a bank, receiving a certificate of deposit, and then the bank might lend the money to a small business in the form of a mortgage loan. Thus, intermediaries literally create new financial products — in this case, a certificate of deposit, which is more

liquid than a mortgage. This transformation of one financial claim into another that better meets the needs of the saver increases general market efficiency.[13]

For example, Mr. Davis may not have the capital or the inclination to finance Ms. Rossi's loan for assets needed to produce her common cold cure. A direct loan of this type would be quite risky since Ms. Rossi could default and since, once the loan was made, Mr. Davis's savings could not be withdrawn and would not be repaid for many years. However, when Mr. Davis deposits his savings in a commercial bank, the bank can then make the loan to Ms. Rossi. So, Mr. Davis is indirectly lending the money to Ms. Rossi. By opening a savings account instead of loaning the money to Ms. Rossi directly, Mr. Davis enjoys several advantages: He does not have to evaluate Ms. Rossi's cure or the likelihood that she will repay the loan; the money is available on demand; and it is insured, within limits, by a government agency. *Thus, intermediaries repackage the original financial claims of borrowers into financial claims on themselves.* Financial obligations of intermediaries are also called "indirect securities" because they represent a rearrangement of the borrower's original promise to pay into one that is more compatible with the saver's needs for safety, liquidity, and maturity. These indirect claims include checking accounts, mutual fund shares, money market accounts, passbook savings, certificates of deposit and life insurance policies.

In addition, the cost of the intermediary's funds to the borrower will be lower than if a direct loan from the original saver could be negotiated. Because intermediaries are generally large institutions, they gain economies of scale in analyzing the creditworthiness of potential borrowers, in processing and collecting loans, and in pooling risks, thus helping individual savers avoid "putting all their financial eggs into one basket." These factors allow intermediaries to lend at lower rates than can individual savers. From the savers' point of view this represents a risk-return tradeoff: Safer investments do not require the high rates of return demanded on high-risk, illiquid investments. Further, intermediaries are better able to attract funds since a system of specialized intermediaries can enable savings to do more than just draw interest. Thus, people can deposit money into banks and get both interest and a convenient way of making payments (checking), buy life insurance policies and receive both interest and financial protection in the event of early death, and so on.

In the United States and other developed nations, a large set of specialized, highly efficient financial intermediaries has evolved; the major types of intermediaries are discussed next:

Commercial Banks.   These are the traditional financial department stores serving a wide variety of savers and those with needs for funds. Commercial banks are continuing to expand into an ever-widening range of services, including stock brokerage services and insurance. Historically, the commercial banks were the major financial institutions that handled checking accounts and through which the Federal Reserve System expanded or contracted the money

---

[13]For simplicity, our example assumed that the entity which needs capital is a business, although it is easy to visualize the demander of capital as an individual, a government unit, and so on.

supply. Today, however, several other institutions discussed here also provide checking accounts and significantly influence the money supply. Commercial banks are discussed in more detail in Chapter 3.

Savings and Loan Associations (S&Ls). S&Ls, also called "thrifts," have traditionally served individual savers and residential and commercial mortgage borrowers, taking the funds of many small savers, then lending the money to home buyers and other types of borrowers. The savers are provided a degree of liquidity that would be absent if they bought the mortgages or other securities directly. Also, the S&Ls should have more expertise in analyzing credit, setting up loans, and making collections than individual savers could possibly have; hence, they reduce the cost and increase the availability of real estate loans. Finally, the S&Ls hold large, diversified portfolios of loans and other assets and thus spread risks in a manner that would be impossible if small savers were making mortgage loans directly. The savings and loan industry has been going through some tough times in recent years. We merely present an overview of the industry here, and we discuss S&Ls in more detail in Chapter 3.

Mutual Savings Banks. Operating primarily in the northeastern states, these institutions accept savings mostly from individuals, and lend mainly on a long-term basis to home buyers and consumers. Mutual savings banks are very similar to S&Ls.

Credit Unions. These are cooperative associations whose members have a common bond, such as being employees of the same firm. Members' savings are loaned only to other members, generally for automobile purchases, home improvements, and the like; in recent years, credit unions have also started making mortgage loans to members. Credit union loans are often the least expensive source of funds available to an individual borrower.

Pension Funds. These are retirement plans funded by corporations or government agencies for their workers and administered primarily by the trust departments of commercial banks or by life insurance companies. Pension funds invest primarily in bonds, stocks, mortgages, and real estate.

Life Insurance Companies. These institutions take savings in the form of annual premiums, invest the funds in stocks, bonds, real estate, and mortgages, and finally make payments to the beneficiaries of the insured parties. In recent years, life insurance companies have also offered a variety of tax-deferred savings plans designed to provide benefits to the participants when they retire.

mutual fund

A financial intermediary that invests the pooled funds of savers, thus obtaining economies of scale in investing and reducing risk by diversification.

Mutual Funds. These are corporations which accept dollars from savers and then use the funds to buy stocks, bonds, or short-term debt (money market) instruments issued by businesses and government units. These organizations pool funds and thus reduce risk by diversification. They also gain economies of scale, which lower the costs of analyzing securities, managing portfolios, and buying and selling securities. Different **mutual funds** are designed to meet the objectives of different types of savers. Hence, there are bond funds for those who desire a fixed return; stock funds for savers who are willing to accept

money market fund

A mutual fund that invests in short-term, low-risk debt securities and allows investors to write checks against their accounts.

substantial risk in the hope of higher return; and still other funds that are used as interest-bearing checking accounts, the **money market funds.** There are literally hundreds of different mutual funds with dozens of different goals and purposes.

Pension funds, life insurance companies, and mutual funds — collectively known as *institutional investors* — are becoming increasingly important players in the financial markets, simply because they have such enormous amounts to invest and, therefore, have considerable clout. For example, in January 1993 individual investors were pouring $1 billion a day into mutual funds, and total mutual fund assets totaled $1.6 trillion, compared with less than $50 billion in 1977. Pension funds have also accumulated tremendous sums which they invest on behalf of their policyholders. As mentioned in Chapter 1, pension fund managers holding large stakes in major corporations have recently become quite vocal in the area of corporate governance.

Financial institutions have historically been heavily regulated, with the primary purpose of this regulation being to insure the safety of the institutions and, thus, to protect the depositors. However, these regulations — which have taken the form of prohibitions on nationwide branch banking, restrictions on the types of assets the institutions can buy, ceilings on the interest rates they can pay, and limitations on the types of services they can provide — have tended to impede the free flow of capital from surplus to deficit units and thus have hurt the efficiency of our capital markets. Recognizing this fact, Congress authorized some major changes in 1980 when it passed the *Depository Institutions Deregulation and Monetary Control Act (DIDMCA)*. This legislation resulted in fierce competition among financial institutions, a blurring of distinctions between the different types of institutions, and a trend toward huge **financial service corporations,** which own banks, S&Ls, insurance companies, pension fund operations, and mutual funds — often with branches across the country and even around the world. Until recently, Sears, Roebuck & Co. was one of the largest of these financial service corporations but has now, as mentioned earlier, changed direction and shifted its emphasis back to retailing.

financial service corporations

Institutions which offer a wide range of financial services, including pension fund operations, brokerage services, insurance, and commercial banking.

Other financial service corporations, most of which started in one area and diversified to cover the full spectrum of financial services, include (or have included) Transamerica, Merrill Lynch, American Express, Citicorp, and Prudential. However, many large companies, hurt by the 1990–1991 recession, have recently had to consider either selling off financial service units to raise cash or have gone even further in a total dismantling of the financial supermarkets they had built in the 1980s. The list of companies that have divested themselves of financial service units includes such well-known names as American Express, Westinghouse, and Xerox, in addition to Sears. (See the Industry Practice reading nearby for additional detail.)

Of course, for every seller there has to be a buyer. GE Capital, a subsidiary of General Electric, appears to be such a buyer, boasting in the fall of 1992 that it could pick and choose the best financial service assets because the financial services industry had overexpanded in the 1980s and now had to reverse course, selling off assets. The net result is an industry that is in flux in early 1993. It also appears to be headed toward further consolidation (mergers) and specialization and *away* from the 1980s' movement toward ever more financial services under one roof.

DISMANTLING THE FINANCIAL SUPERMARKETS

Diversification, a watchword of the 1980s for many companies, has become "divestification" in the 1990s as they seek to shed sidelines to strengthen their core businesses.

Xerox, Sears, American Express, and Westinghouse are all sloughing off financial services subsidiaries that seemed such a good idea when they were acquired in the last decade. Although each company acquired them in the first place because their core businesses were slumping, now they are selling them to concentrate again on their respective specialties — office equipment, retailing, charge cards, and electrical equipment.

Xerox will remove $2.6 billion in debt from its books if it manages to sell all four of its financial services, although those units have been paying the interest on the debt, so the sales will not free up any cash for the rest of the corporation.

Its Crum & Forster Inc. insurance business will be divided up and sold in pieces — an easier task than finding a buyer for the whole thing. However, the company will not just take the first offer. "The intent is to do this as soon as we can, but we're not going to fire-sale it," said Xerox Chairman Paul Allaire.

He expects that divestiture to take several years but sees a quicker turnover for the Furman Selz investment banking operation and Xerox Life. The latter attracted interest from potential buyers even when it was not on the market, Allaire said, and should move within a year. The company's mutual fund business,

Van Kampen Merritt, was sold to a New York investment "boutique" for $360 million.

For some time before the decision to divest, analysts had urged Xerox to abandon financial services as a poor investment. When the announcement finally came, Xerox stock dropped $3.62 per share and there was some fear that the company's plans to sell more stock might also weaken the value of current investors' holdings.

Xerox acquired the financial services units when its copier business faded in the shadow of Japanese competition. Ironically, copiers strengthened again under stricter management and quality control, while financial services sagged. When Allaire — one of the architects of the copier resurgence — became CEO in 1990, the financial services units had become a poorly performing liability. Under his direction, Xerox "fenced off" that segment from the rest of the company and declined to use profits from copiers and printers to prop it up. "It (quickly) became apparent that . . . the shareholders might be better served" by a complete disengagement, Allaire said.

Another financial supermarket considering dismantlement in 1993 was American Express. It bought the Shearson Lehman Brothers brokerage firm for $888 million in 1981 and sold part of it to the public six years later. In 1990, the parent company was forced to pump $1 billion into Shearson to strengthen it before buying back the remaining shares of stock. One of the AmEx moves to raise capital was the sale of a Shearson money-management unit, Boston Company, to Mellon Bank for $1.45 billion.

The latest divestiture plan would sell enough of Shearson to the public to reduce American Express ownership below 50 percent. Officials now acknowledge that the two firms have never meshed well. However, Shearson's fortunes rebounded in the early 1990s while AmEx's core charge-card business came under increasing pressure from rival card issuers. In fact, nearly a million of its 35 million cardholders jumped ship in 1992, and merchants are not happy with the higher fees AmEx charges them.

As the company changed top management following the December 1992 departure of Chairman/CEO James Robinson III, it was trying to cut $1 billion in operating expenses in its Travel Related Services card

Sources: Malcolm Berko, "Sears' corporate tower needs a good cleaning," *The Gainesville Sun Business Monday,* March 22, 1993, 11; Michael Schroeder and Stephen Baker, "The Decline and Fall of Westinghouse's Paul Lego," *Business Week,* March 8, 1993, 68–70; Laurence Hooper, "Xerox Plans to Withdraw Completely from the Financial-Services Industry," *The Wall Street Journal,* January 19, 1993, A-3; Stuart Mieher, "Westinghouse Posts 4th-Quarter Loss of $1.18 Billion After Big Write-Downs," *The Wall Street Journal,* January 21, 1993, A-2; Michael Siconolfi, "American Express to Get Plan for Shearson Sale," *The Wall Street Journal,* December 17, 1992, C-1; Steven Lipin, Peter Pae, and Fred R. Bleakley, "Robinson to Resign at American Express, Denies Receiving Pressure from Board," *The Wall Street Journal,* December 7, 1991, A-3; Gabriella Stern and Stuart Mieher, "Westinghouse Decides To Retrench, but CEO Remains Under Fire," *The Wall Street Journal,* November 24, 1992, A-1; Julia Flynn, David Greising, Kevin Kelly, and Leah Nathans Spiro, "Smaller But Wiser," *Business Week,* October 12, 1992, 28–29.

business within three years. It slashed the staff by 4,800 and consolidated several facilities in a restructuring. The gradual dismantling of its financial services takes apart most of what Mr. Robinson put together in his 15 years with the company. While considering the Shearson sale, AmEx had already sold 46 percent of its credit-card processing unit, First Data Corporation, and was looking into the sale of the Amex Life Assurance and American Express Bank subsidiaries.

Yet another firm shedding assets in the early 1990s was Westinghouse, which discontinued half a dozen units, including financial services and its credit division. The latter reported more than $5 million in write-downs in 1991 and 1992 as it struggled with bad loans. One of the company's outside directors said that Westinghouse would henceforth focus on "what we're really good at—electrical engineering."

In the fourth quarter of 1992, Westinghouse Financial Services Inc. lost $1.27 billion, or $3.66 a share. The parent company hoped to disengage the hemorrhaging unit and sell as much as possible of its $8.3 billion loan portfolio. Some executives started pushing for such a move in 1990, when a fourth-quarter write-off of $975 million was not enough to cover the losses.

Under pressure, CEO Paul Lego said, "We're going to be a dynamic, solid operation focused in high-manufacturing-type businesses. I've done a terrific job in terms of bringing the credit unit under control. How could I have anticipated what happened with real estate values and the economy?" In fact, he did try to shrink the credit corporation but charged parent-company executives with the task. Knowing little about the subsidiary business, they nevertheless discounted advice from the credit executives (who "got them into this mess" in the first place) and fumbled the ball. A later deal with General Electric to buy the credit unit fell through, and on January 27, 1993, Lego was out.

Meanwhile, a grandiose vision of management at the "Great American Company"—Sears, Roebuck—also shattered. Relying on the long-standing trust of consumers built through its retail business, Sears decided to enter the fast-growing financial services field in 1981. It bought Coldwell Banker, the nation's largest real estate broker, and Dean Witter Reynolds, the fifth largest stock broker.

In 1992, desperately needing cash, Sears could no longer afford to expand financial services. "There was a growing understanding that we needed more capital to fund our financial services businesses," said Sears Chairman Edward A. Brennan. "It's a sign of their success." The company will net about $3 billion when it spins off Dean Witter (including the successful Discover Card), dumps Coldwell Banker, and sells 20 percent of Allstate Insurance, which it acquired in 1934. Some $15 billion of debt may leave the balance sheet, giving Sears greater financial flexibility to revive its dry-goods business.

If it seemed unwise to divest the net income—almost half of Sears's total—provided by Dean Witter, Brennan was faced with a shareholders' revolt and may have felt he had no choice. Sears stock was selling in late 1992 for less than it did in 1987. Given its share price, the company could not sell stock to raise more cash, so the directors voted for a breakup. In the days after the announcement, Sears stock price rose 8 percent.

Managers do not see the breakup as a failure of their financial services strategy. "I'm just thankful we diversified," said former Chairman Edward R. Telling. "It's helped the company through some difficult times." Others, however, are more pessimistic. A retail consultant, Carol Farmer, said, "The Titanic is still there, the iceberg is still there, but the lifeboats are gone. When you really don't know what to do, you start selling assets."

Self-Test

Identify the three different ways capital is transferred between savers and borrowers.

Distinguish between investment banking houses and financial intermediaries.

List the major classes of intermediaries, and briefly describe each one's function.

Explain what has happened in terms of financial service corporations during the 1980s and early 1990s.

The Stock Market

As noted earlier, secondary markets are the markets in which outstanding, previously issued securities are traded. By far the most active secondary market, and the one most important to financial managers, is the *stock market*. It is here that the prices of firms' stocks are established. Since, in a publicly traded corporation, the primary goal of financial management should be to maximize the firm's stock price, a knowledge of the market in which this price is established is essential for anyone involved in managing such a business.

The Stock Exchanges

organized securities exchanges

Formal organizations having tangible, physical locations that conduct auction markets in designated ("listed") securities.

New York Stock Exchange (NYSE); American Stock Exchange (AMEX)

The two major U.S. securities exchanges.

There are two basic types of stock markets. First, the **organized securities exchanges,** which include the **New York Stock Exchange (NYSE),** the **American Stock Exchange (AMEX),** and several regional stock exchanges, have actual physical market locations. The second type of stock market is the less formal over-the-counter market, which consists of brokers and dealers connected by computers and telephone networks, but which has no central location. We shall consider the organized exchanges first.

Each of the larger exchanges occupies its own building, has specifically designated members, and has an elected governing body — its board of governors. Members are said to have "seats" on the exchange, although everyone stands up on the trading floor. Memberships (or seats) are sold to the highest bidder and represent the right to trade on the exchange. The price of the 1,366 seats on the NYSE, which is based on the volume and price levels of stock activity, can fluctuate dramatically. As recently as 1979, seats on the NYSE sold for as little as $40,000, but the highest price ever recorded was $1,150,000 on October 8, 1987, less than two weeks before the 1987 crash. Recent prices have been much lower than their pre-crash high. It is interesting to note that in March 1993 when the average trading volume on the NYSE was at record levels and when stock prices as measured by the Dow Jones Industrial Average were setting new highs, the most recent price of a seat on the *"Big Board"* (NYSE) was precisely half of the 1987 record price. If business is booming on Wall Street, then why has the price of a seat on the NYSE not gone up as well? Two factors help explain this seeming contradiction: (1) Securities firms have increasingly been pressured to cut the commissions they charge large customers, mostly institutional investors, and this has resulted in cost cutting throughout the industry, thus reducing the value of exchange seats. (2) Brokerage firm mergers have caused many brokerage firms to reduce their personnel on the floor of the NYSE and other organized exchanges.

Most of the larger investment banking houses operate *brokerage departments* that own seats on the exchanges, and they designate one or more of their officers as members. The exchanges are open on all normal working days, with the members meeting in a large room equipped with telephones and other electronic equipment that enable each brokerage house member to communicate with the firm's offices throughout the country.

Like other markets, securities exchanges facilitate communication between buyers and sellers. For example, Merrill Lynch (the largest brokerage firm) might receive an order in its Atlanta office from a customer who wants to buy

The trading floor of the New York Stock Exchange is the central location where registered members of the exchange meet to buy and sell shares for customers.

Source: Jon Riley/Tony Stone Images.

100 shares of General Motors stock. Simultaneously, Dean Witter's Denver office might receive an order from a customer wishing to sell 100 shares of GM. Each broker communicates by wire with the firm's representative on the NYSE. Other brokers throughout the country are also communicating with their own exchange members. The exchange members with *sell orders* offer the shares for sale, and they are bid for by the members with *buy orders*. Thus, the exchanges operate as *auction markets*.

Roughly one-fourth of all members of an exchange are known as *specialists*, so called because they specialize in "making a market" in one or more stocks. This means that they act as dealers in those stocks, hold an inventory, and stand ready to buy for as well as sell from this inventory when necessary, that is, when there is a temporary discrepancy between supply and demand. Specialists are expected to, within reason, maintain fair and orderly markets in the stocks assigned to them, and their role is important because it ensures liquidity of the market.

over-the-counter (OTC) market

A large collection of brokers and dealers, connected electronically by telephones and computers, that provides for trading in unlisted securities.

The Over-the-Counter (OTC) Market

While the NYSE turned 200 years old on May 17, 1992, the over-the-counter market is a relative newcomer and is a very different kind of market. In contrast to the organized securities exchanges, the **over-the-counter (OTC) market** is a nebulous, intangible organization. An explanation of the term "over the counter" will help clarify exactly what this market is. On the exchanges, buy and sell orders come in more or less simultaneously, and exchange members match these orders. But if a stock is traded infrequently, perhaps because it is the stock of a new or a small firm, few buy and sell orders come in, and matching them within a reasonable length of time would be difficult. To avoid this problem, some brokerage firms maintain an inventory of such stocks; they buy when individual investors want to sell and sell when investors want to buy. At one time the inventory of securities was kept in a safe, and when bought and sold, the stocks were literally passed over the counter.

Today, the OTC market is defined to include all facilities needed to conduct securities transactions *not* conducted on the organized exchanges. These facilities consist of (1) the relatively few *dealers* who hold inventories of OTC securities and who make a market in these securities, (2) the thousands of *brokers* who act as agents in bringing these dealers together with investors, and (3) the computers, terminals, and electronic networks that provide a communications link between dealers and brokers. The dealers who make a market in a particular stock continuously quote a price at which they are willing to buy the stock (the **bid price**) and a price at which they will sell shares (the **asked price**). Each dealer's prices, which are adjusted as supply and demand conditions change, can be read off computer screens all across the country. The bid price is always the lower of the two prices, and the spread between bid and asked prices represents the dealer's markup, or profit.

Brokers and dealers who make up the OTC market are members of a self-regulating body known as the **National Association of Securities Dealers (NASD),** which licenses both brokers and dealers and oversees trading practices. The computerized trading network used by NASD is known as the NASD Automated Quotation System (NASDAQ), and *The Wall Street Journal* and other newspapers contain information on NASDAQ transactions.

In terms of the number of issues, the majority of stocks are traded over the counter. However, because the stocks of larger companies are listed on the exchanges, about two-thirds of the dollar volume of stock trading takes place on the organized securities exchanges.

Some Trends in Securities Trading

From the NYSE's inception until the 1970s, the vast majority of all stock trading occurred on the exchanges and was conducted by member firms. The NYSE established a set of minimum brokerage commission rates, and no member firm could charge a commission lower than the set rate. However, the Securities and Exchange Commission (SEC), with strong prodding from the Antitrust Division of the Justice Department, forced the NYSE to abandon its fixed commissions effective May 1, 1975. Commission rates declined dramatically, falling in some cases as much as 90 percent from former levels.

This change was a boon to the investing public but not to the brokerage industry. A number of *full-service* brokerage houses went bankrupt, and others were forced to merge with stronger firms. The number of brokerage houses has declined from literally thousands in the 1960s to a much smaller number of large, strong, nationwide companies, many of which are units of diversified financial service corporations. Deregulation has also produced a number of *dis-*

bid price
The price a dealer in securities will pay for a stock.

asked price
The price at which a dealer in securities will sell shares of stock out of inventory.

National Association of Securities Dealers (NASD)
An organization of securities dealers that works with the SEC to regulate operations in the over-the-counter market.

count brokers, some of which are affiliated with commercial banks, and several of these are growing quite rapidly.[14]

Another trend in recent years has been increasing competition between the organized exchanges and the OTC market, a contest which the over-the-counter market appears to be winning. Today, more and more large companies choose to stay in the OTC market, although they could easily qualify for a listing on one of the major exchanges. Institutional investors have also increasingly been drawn to the OTC market, and the result is that the dollar volume traded here is now greater than that of the AMEX and is challenging the volume traded on the NYSE.

Stock Market Reporting

Information on transactions both on the organized exchanges and in the over-the-counter market is contained in local newspapers, and in specialized business publications such as *Investor's Daily* and *The Wall Street Journal.* Although the details of financial reporting are covered in investment analysis, it is useful to understand now what information is available on the financial pages and how it is presented.

Table 2-8 is a section of the stock market page for stocks listed on the New York Stock Exchange taken from *The Wall Street Journal* published on Friday, April 9, 1993. For each listed stock the *Journal* provides specific data on the trading that took place the prior day (Thursday, April 8, in this case), as well as other more general information. Similar information is available on stocks listed on the other organized exchanges as well as those traded over the counter.

Stocks listed on the NYSE are arranged in alphabetical order from AAR Industries to the Zweig Fund; the data in Table 2-8 were taken from the top of the listing. We will examine the data for Abbott Laboratories (AbbotLab), shown about halfway down the table. The two columns on the left show the highest and lowest prices at which the stock sold during the past year. Abbott traded in the range of 34 to 22⅝ (that is, from a high of $34.00 to a low of $22.625) during the preceding 52 weeks. The letters just to the right of the company's abbreviated name are its *ticker symbol* (ABT) and the following number is the dividend; Abbott had a current indicated annual dividend of $0.68 per share and a *dividend yield* of 2.9 percent.[15] Next comes the ratio of the stock's price to its annual earnings (the P/E ratio), which is 16 for Abbott. Although controversy

---

[14]Full-service brokers give investors information on different stocks and make recommendations as to which stocks to buy. Discount brokers do not give advice — they merely execute orders. Some brokerage houses (institutional houses) cater primarily to institutional investors such as pension funds and insurance companies, while others cater to individual investors and are called "retail houses." Large firms such as Merrill Lynch generally have both retail and institutional brokerage operations.

[15]To avoid confusion later, it is important to note that there is often more than one definition for certain financial terms. The term "dividend yield" is an excellent example. In the remainder of this text, we will use the terms "dividend yield" and "expected dividend yield" interchangeably; that is, we define the dividend yield to mean next year's expected dividend divided by the current market price of the common stock, D_1/P_0. In contrast, *The Wall Street Journal* defines the term "dividend yield" as the current, or indicated, dividend yield, which is calculated as the most recent dividend divided by the current market price of the common stock, D_0/P_0. Also, note that we and most others take the latest closing price as the "current" price when we calculate the dividend yield.

Table 2-8   Stock Market Transactions, April 8, 1993

| 52 weeks | | | | | | | | | | | |
Hi	Lo	Stock	Sym	Div	Yld. (%)	PE	Vol 100s	Hi	Lo	Close	Net Chg
				—A—A—A—							
14⅜	10¾	AAR	AIR	.48	4.0	...	279	12½	12⅛	12⅛	...
11⅜	10⅛	ACM Gvt Fd	ACG	.96e	8.6	...	453	11¼	11⅛	11⅛	...
10	9	ACM OppFd	AOF	.80	8.5	...	153	9⅜	9¼	9⅜	+ ⅛
11⅞	9⅞	ACM SecFd	GSF	.96	8.7	...	806	11⅛	11	11	...
9¾	8½	ACM SpctmFd	SI	.80	8.5	...	303	9⅜	9⅛	9⅜	+ ¼
11	8¾	ACM MgdIncFd	AMF	1.08	10.2	...	635	10¾	10½	10⅝	− ⅛
11¾	8⅝	ACM MgdMultFd	MMF	.91e	10.0	...	96	9¼	9⅛	9⅛	...
9⅞	6⅜	ADT	ADT	...	...	...	406	9	8⅞	9	...
n 2½	⅞	ADT wt		...	...	...	45	1½	1⅜	1½	+ ⅛
36⅞	24	AFLAC	AFL	.44	1.3	16	1164	35½	34⅝	34¾	− ⅝
28½	18	AL Labs A	BMD	.18	.7	29	598	24½	23¾	24½	+ ¾
2	³⁄₁₆	AM Int	AM		...	dd	265	¼	¹⁵⁄₆₄	¼	+ ¹⁄₆₄
65⅞	52⅝	AMP	AMP	1.60f	2.6	22	1202	60⅞	60⅜	60¾	+ ¼
72½	54⅜	AMR	AMR		...	dd	13270	69½	67¾	68	− 1
47¼	39¼	ARCO Chm	RCM	2.50	5.8	21	162	43⅜	42⅞	43⅛	− ⅜
2¼	1⅜	ARX	ARX		...	12	100	1⅞	1⅞	1⅞	+ ⅛
46⅛	29¾	ASA	ASA	2.00	5.0	...	528	41⅛	40⅜	40⅜	− ⅞
sx 34	22⅝	AbbotLab	ABT	.68f	2.9	16	20449	24	23¼	23¾	− ⅝
n 9⅞	3⅝	Abex	ABE	...	...		394	4⅛	4⅛	4⅛	...
s 15	6	AcceptIns	AIF	...	...	dd	158	12⅜	12⅛	12⅜	...
n 4⅛	2¼	AcceptIns wt		...	...		10	3⅝	3⅝	3⅝	...
n 29⅝	28	ACE Ltd	ACL	...	...		5185	29¼	28⅞	28⅞	− ¼
9½	4¾	AcmeCleve	AMT	.40	4.9	17	148	8⅛	7⅞	8⅛	+ ¼
9¼	3¾	AcmeElec	ACE	...		cc	19	7¼	7¼	7¼	− ⅛
n 24¾	15⅛	Acordia	ACO	.18e	.8	...	40	21¾	21½	21⅝	− ¼
23¾	12⅛	Acuson	ACN	...		12	607	13⅝	13⅜	13⅜	− ⅛
22¼	18⅛	AdamsExp	ADX	1.62e	7.7	...	103	21⅜	21⅛	21⅛	− ⅛
▲ 25⅛	7⅜	AdvMicro	AMD		...	11	12077	25½	24¾	24⅞	− ¼
55	29½	AdvMicro pf		3.00	5.6	...	604	54¾	53¾	54	− ¼
7¾	4⅞	Advest	ADV		...	dd	30	6⅞	6⅞	6⅞	...

Source: *The Wall Street Journal*, April 9, 1993, C3.

exists among analysts as to the intrinsic value of the P/E ratio as an analytical tool, its existence on the financial page allows for the computation of the firm's current earnings per share. Since the P/E is 16, we can use Abbott's closing price, shown in the next to last column, to determine Abbott's indicated earnings per share which is approximately $1.48: $23.75/E = 16, so E = $23.75/16 = $1.48.

The P/E ratio is followed by the volume of trading for the day; 2,044,900 shares of Abbott's common stock were traded on Thursday, April 8, 1993. After the trading volume is information on the highest, lowest, and closing (last) prices paid for Abbott's stock on that trading day. Thus, on April 8, 1993, Abbott's common stock sold for as high as $24.00 and as low as $23.25, and its closing price was $23.75. The last column indicates the net change in price from the closing price on the previous trading day. Because Abbott was down by ⅝ ($0.625), the previous close must have been $24.375 ($24.375 − $0.625 = $23.75).

The stock market page also provides other information about equity instruments. For example, the far-left column contains various informational notes. The upward-pointing arrow (▲) indicates that Advanced Micro Devices's common stock hit a 52-week high. Similarly, a downward-pointing arrow (none shown) would indicate that a stock hit a 52-week low. In the same far-left column, the *n* notation means a stock is newly listed (within the last 52 weeks) *s* indicates a stock split or dividend, and *x* shows that Abbott has gone "ex-dividend" (is now selling without its dividend). Notice also that an *e* in the dividend column, shown for Acordia and others, indicates that a dividend has been declared or paid in the preceding 12 months but that there is no regular annual dividend rate; the *f* after Abbott's dividend indicates that this is the annual dividend rate and represents an increase on the latest declaration. The *pf* following the second entry for Advanced Micro Devices tells us that this is a preferred stock issue rather than the firm's common stock, and, in this same column, *wt* marks a warrant (a type of option, covered in Chapter 18). In the PE column you will see *dd* for AMR, which indicates that the firm experienced a loss for the most recent four quarters; a *cc* in this column, as for Acme Electric, tells us that the P/E ratio is 100 or more. Additional explanatory notes appear at the bottom of the first page of the transactions listing.

Bond Markets

The majority of bond transactions occur in the OTC market. Bond holdings are concentrated in the hands of large financial institutions, such as life insurance companies, mutual funds, and pension funds. Therefore, it is relatively easy for OTC bond dealers to arrange the trade of large blocks of bonds among the comparatively few bondholders for one of their infrequent trades. It would be much more difficult to arrange similar trades in the stock market among the literally millions of large and small stockholders. Thus, most equity shares are traded on one of the organized exchanges.

Information on bond trades in the OTC market is not published. However, a representative number of bonds are listed and traded on the bond division of the NYSE. Information on NYSE bond trades is published daily in *The Wall Street Journal* under the heading New York Exchange Bonds.[16] While information on the entire spectrum of bond trading is not available, the published data on NYSE bond transactions reflects reasonably well the conditions in the larger OTC market. Table 2-9 is a section of the bond market page in the Friday, April 9, 1993, issue of *The Wall Street Journal,* reporting the bond trades of the previous trading day. A total of $41.84 million in bonds, representing 466 issues, were traded on that date, but we show only those of American Telephone & Telegraph (ATT). Bonds can have any denomination, but most have a *par* (or maturity) value of $1,000; this is how much the company borrowed and how

[16]A limited number of bonds are also traded on the American Stock Exchange. The results of these trades are also published in *The Wall Street Journal.*

Table 2-9

NYSE Bond Market
Transactions, April 8, 1993

**CORPORATION BONDS
Volume, $41,840,000**

Bonds	Cur Yld	Vol	Close	Net Chg
ATT 4¾98	4.9	20	96⅜	+ ⅜
ATT 5½97	5.5	12	100¼	+ ¼
ATT 4⅜99	4.7	26	92⅜	− ⅜
ATT 6s00	6.1	394	99⅛	+ ¼
ATT 5⅛01	5.5	106	93	+ ¾
ATT 7cld	...	1	100¾	...
ATT 7⅛cld	...	9	101⁹⁄₁₆	...
ATT 8⅝cld	...	165	105¹³⁄₁₆	...
ATT 8⅝31	7.8	82	111	− 1
ATT 7⅛02	6.8	20	104⅜	− ⅛
ATT 8⅛22	7.6	190	107	+ 1¼
ATT 8⅛24	7.7	10	106⅛	+ ⅝
ATT 4½96	4.5	55	99¾	...

Note: *The Wall Street Journal* only lists those American Telephone & Telegraph bonds that were actually traded on the NYSE on April 8, 1993. The company has many more outstanding bond issues but only 13 issues traded on April 8th.

Source: *The Wall Street Journal*, April 9, 1993, C14.

much it must repay when the bond matures. Because other denominations are possible, however, for trading and reporting purposes bond prices are quoted as percentages of par. Looking at the last bond listed, we see that the number 4½ appears after the company's name; this indicates that the bond pays 4½ percent interest; thus it pays 0.045($1,000) = $45 in interest per year.[17] The 4½ percent is defined as the bond's **coupon rate.** The 96, shown after the coupon rate, indicates that the bond must be repaid in the year 1996. It is not shown in the table, but this debt instrument was issued on April 7, 1993, and so, technically speaking, it is a *note* (as opposed to a long-term bond) because of its short maturity; however, notes and bonds are shown in the same section of *The Wall Street Journal.* Other AT&T debt securities clearly have much longer maturities, coming due in 2022, 2024, and even 2031. Also, three of the AT&T issues shown have been *called,* indicated by the letters *cld,* which means that they have been repaid early. We will discuss callable bonds in Chapter 16.

coupon rate

The stated, or nominal, rate of interest on a bond.

The 4.5 in the second column is the bond's **current yield,** which is the annual interest payment divided by the bond's closing price: Current yield = $45/$997.50 = 4.511%, which is rounded to 4.5%. The column labeled "Vol" indicates that 55 of this particular issue were traded on April 8, 1993. Because bond prices are quoted as percentages of par, the closing value of 99¾ indicates that the bond sold for $997.50 (99.75% of the bond's $1,000 par value). As with common stock, the net change column refers to the change in the bond's price from the closing on the prior trading day.

current yield

The annual interest payment on a bond divided by its current market price.

---

[17]AT&T's bonds, like most in the United States, pay interest semiannually; therefore, the company would send a check for $22.50 every six months to the holder of one of the 4½s of 1996.

Companies generally set their coupon rates at levels which reflect the "going rate of interest" on the day a bond is issued. If the rates were set lower, investors simply would not buy the bonds at the $1,000 par value, so the company could not borrow the money it needed. Thus, bonds generally sell at their par values when they are issued, but their prices fluctuate thereafter as a result of changes in either the general level of interest rates or the financial strength of the firm.

As you can see from Table 2-9, AT&T's $4\frac{1}{2}$ percent notes maturing in 1996 were selling for approximately their par value due to the fact that they were issued so recently, while its $4\frac{3}{8}$ percent bonds which mature in 1999 were selling for $923.75. These bonds are said to sell at a *discount,* or an amount less than their par value. This is because their coupon rate, at time of issuance, was set at a level that is low relative to today's going rate on similar bonds. On the other hand, bonds will sell at a *premium,* an amount greater than their par value, when they were originally sold with a higher coupon rate than the rate now required on new bonds of similar quality.

We will see in later chapters that bonds with longer maturities generally require higher coupon rates than short-term securities of the same issuer. For example, notice that the coupon rate on AT&T's bonds maturing in 2031 is $8\frac{5}{8}$ or $8.625 and is the highest coupon rate of any of the still-outstanding AT&T issues traded on April 8, 1993. (AT&T is one of the relatively few issuers that sell bonds with maturities longer than 30 years.) We will discuss the relationship between interest rate and maturity further in Chapter 4, and we will explain how investors determine the price of these debt instruments in Chapter 16.

Regulation of Securities Markets

Securities and Exchange Commission (SEC)
The U.S. government agency which regulates the issuance and trading of stocks and bonds.

Sales of new securities, as well as operations in the secondary markets, are regulated by the **Securities and Exchange Commission (SEC)** and, to a lesser extent, by each of the 50 states. Certain rules apply to the issuance of new securities, while other rules apply to the trading of existing securities in the secondary markets.

1. **Elements in the Regulation of New Issues:**
   a. The SEC has jurisdiction over all interstate offerings to the public in amounts of $1,500,000 or more.

registration statement
A statement of facts filed with the SEC about a company planning to issue securities.

   b. Securities must be registered with the SEC at least 20 days before they are publicly offered. The **registration statement** provides financial, legal, and technical information about the company. A **prospectus** summarizes this information for use in selling the securities. SEC lawyers and accountants analyze both the registration statement and the prospectus. If the information is inadequate or misleading, the SEC will delay or stop the public offering.

prospectus
A document describing a new securities issue and the issuing company.

   c. After the registration has become effective, the securities may be offered, but any sales solicitation must be accompanied by the prospectus. Preliminary or "red herring" prospectuses may be distributed to potential buyers during the 20-day waiting period, but no sales can be finalized during this time. The red herring prospectus contains all the key information that will appear in the final prospectus except the price.

d. If the registration statement or prospectus contains misrepresentations or omissions of material facts, any purchaser who suffers a loss may sue for damages. Severe penalties may be imposed on the issuer, its officers, directors, accountants, engineers, appraisers, underwriters, and all others who participated in the preparation of the registration statement or prospectus.

2. **Elements in the Regulation of Outstanding Securities:**

   a. The SEC also regulates all national securities exchanges. Companies whose securities are listed on an exchange must file annual reports similar to the registration statement with both the SEC and the stock exchange, and must provide periodic reports as well.

   b. The SEC has control over corporate **insiders.** Officers, directors, and major shareholders of a corporation must file monthly reports of changes in their holdings in the corporation's stock. Any short-term profits from such transactions are payable to the corporation. The prohibition against trading on information not available to the public goes beyond those directly connected to the firm; anyone who obtains information not available to the public from a corporate insider is prohibited from acting on this information to gain profits. The recent insider trading scandals prove that the SEC is very thorough in finding those who attempt to make profits by trading on inside information.

   c. The SEC has the power to prohibit manipulation by such devices as pools (aggregations of funds used to affect prices artificially) or wash sales (sales between members of the same group to record artificial transaction prices).

   d. The SEC has control over the form of the proxy and the way the company uses it to solicit votes.

   e. Control over the flow of credit into securities transactions is exercised by the Board of Governors of the Federal Reserve System. The Fed exercises this control through **margin requirements,** which stipulate the percentage of the securities' purchase price that must be supplied by the purchaser. Thus, if the margin requirement is 60 percent, the purchaser must initially supply 60 percent of the securities' financing, and the remaining 40 percent ($1 -$ the margin requirement) may be borrowed. The margin requirement has been 50 percent since 1974. A decline in a stock's price can result in inadequate coverage, forcing the stockbroker to issue a *margin call,* which in turn requires investors either to put up more money or to have their margined stock sold to pay off their loans. Without a margin requirement to limit borrowing to purchase securities, such forced sales could further depress stock prices, setting off a disastrous downward spiral. Before the Great Crash of 1929, no margin was required to purchase stock, so many investors used close to 100 percent debt to obtain their securities. When prices fell, these investors were unable to cover their debts, forcing the sale of their securities at successively lower and lower

insiders

Officers, directors, major stockholders, or others who may have access to information not available to the public about a company's operations.

margin requirement

The minimum percentage of his or her own money that a purchaser must put up when buying securities.

values. Thus, without the stabilizing influence of a margin requirement, the spiral of lower prices and margin calls was an important contributor to the 1929 stock market crash.

3. State Regulations:

   a. States have some control over the issuance of new securities within their boundaries. This control is usually exercised by a "corporation commissioner" or someone with a similar title.

blue sky laws

State laws that prevent the sale of securities having little or no asset backing.

   b. State laws relating to securities sales are called **blue sky laws** because they were put into effect to keep unscrupulous promoters from selling securities that offered the "blue sky" but which actually had little or no asset backing.

The securities industry itself realizes the importance of stable markets, sound brokerage firms, and the absence of stock manipulation. Therefore, the various organized exchanges work closely with the SEC to police transactions on the exchanges and to maintain the integrity and credibility of the system. Similarly, the National Association of Securities Dealers (NASD) cooperates with the SEC to police trading in the OTC markets. These industry groups also cooperate with regulatory authorities to set net worth and other standards for securities firms, to develop insurance programs to protect customers of brokerage houses, and the like.

In general, government regulation of securities trading, as well as industry self-regulation, is designed to ensure that investors receive information that is as accurate as possible, that no one artificially manipulates (that is, drives up or down) the market price of a given stock, and that corporate insiders do not take advantage of their position to profit in their companies' stocks at the expense of other stockholders. Neither the SEC, the state regulators, nor the industry itself can prevent investors from making foolish decisions or from having bad luck, but the regulators can and do help investors obtain the best data possible for making sound investment decisions.

❓ *Self-Test*

What are the two basic types of stock markets, and how do they differ?

What are the role and functions of specialists on the organized exchanges?

Go to Table 2-8, find ARCO Chemical (ARCO Chm), and identify (1) ARCO's April 8, 1993 closing price, (2) its P/E ratio, (3) its current dividend yield, and (4) its price range over the last 52 weeks.

Briefly explain why the majority of corporate bonds are traded on the OTC market, while most common stocks are traded on one of the organized exchanges.

Go to Table 2-9, find AT&T's 5⅛ bond, and identify (1) its coupon rate, (2) the year in which the bond matures, (3) its current yield, and (4) the bond's closing prices on both April 8 and 9, 1993.

Differentiate among a registration statement, a prospectus, and a red herring prospectus.

Who are generally considered corporate insiders?

Market Efficiency

During the last two decades, a great deal of financial research has focused on the question of capital market efficiency. Efficiency in this context refers to the ability of stock prices to (1) react quickly to new information and (2) reflect, at any point in time, all available information about the securities. Thus, in an efficient market, prices are "fair."

efficient capital market

Market in which securities are fairly priced in the sense that the price reflects all publicly available information on each security.

Requirements for an **efficient capital market** are relatively few, and realistic, in today's investment world. First and perhaps foremost, there must be a reasonably large number of profit-seeking individuals engaged in securities analysis who operate independently of one another. Second, many (but not all) investors should have quick and full access to any news about present and potential investments. Announcements of new information will be disseminated as soon as the news breaks; thus, new information will come to the market in a random fashion. Finally, the efficient markets hypothesis assumes that investors are rational in that they will act (buy or sell) quickly to adjust securities prices in light of new information.

One of the critical requirements for an efficient market is the free flow of reliable information to analysts and investors. The SEC and other government agencies have labored to ensure that accurate information is quickly disseminated and that no special interest group is able to profit from special access to nonpublic information. The majority of academic studies, found in summary form in most textbooks on securities analysis, agree that financial markets, although not perfect, are very efficient. An efficient market is therefore one in which securities prices adjust rapidly to new information, reflecting all information available on a particular security.

As we stressed in Chapter 1, all financial decisions involve a tradeoff between risk and expected return. In an efficient market, securities will be priced to reflect the risks involved, with higher-risk issues expected to provide higher returns, as illustrated by Figure 2-3. If an investor is unwilling to accept risk, he or she should invest in low-return but risk-free U.S. Treasury bills. If the investor desires higher returns, however, then he or she must be willing to accept higher levels of risk. Thus, as investors move from risk-free U.S. Treasury bills to riskier securities, they do so in the expectation of receiving higher returns.

Studies of the realized returns on securities in the capital markets have supported the concept of a tradeoff between risk and return. In one such study by Ibbotson Associates, which covered the investment period from 1926 to 1989, the securities with the least risk (U.S. Treasury bills) were found to have provided the lowest rate of return, whereas the securities with the most risk (common stock) provided the highest rate of return.[18] Therefore, because of the efforts of the SEC, which ensures that financial information is quickly and accurately provided, and because of the competition among many analysts, financial markets appear to be efficient in pricing securities relative to their risk.

---

[18]A word of caution is probably necessary at this point. Remember that the Ibbotson study was based on past data for many securities over long periods of time. A selected high-risk security may not provide superior returns over any given time period. After all, if high-risk securities *always* provided the highest returns, there would be no risk.

Figure 2-3

Risk and Expected Returns on Different Classes of Securities

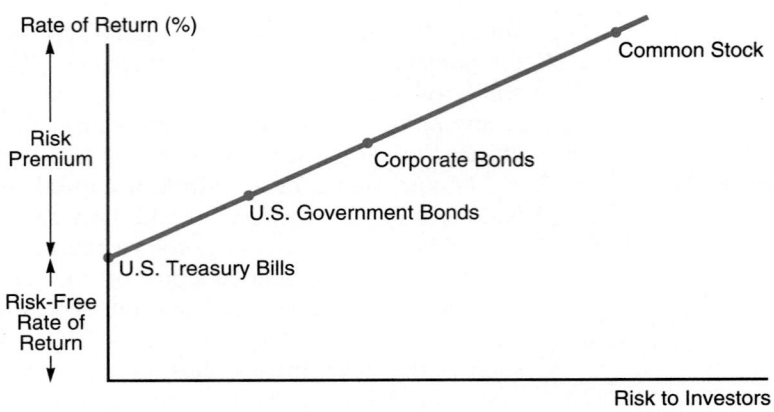

The risk-return tradeoff in the financial markets is illustrated in this figure. An investor willing to invest in the most risky type of security, common stock, has the *potential* to earn the highest rate of return. Investing in the least risky security, U.S. Treasury bills, will provide the lowest return. This risk-return tradeoff hypothesis has been empirically demonstrated in a study by Ibbotson Associates covering more than 60 years.

 *Self-Test*

Identify the requirements for an efficient capital market.

Briefly explain the following statement: "The tradeoff between risk and return should prevail in a rational economic environment."

SMALL BUSINESS

WHAT IS VENTURE CAPITAL?

Venture capital is the name given to organized private financing that can provide substantial amounts of capital, mostly through equity purchases but occasionally through debt offerings to help growth-oriented companies develop and succeed. Venture capital investors include many types of organizations—separate companies owned by wealthy individuals such as the

Rockefeller family and J. H. Whitney; subsidiaries of large financial and industrial corporations; separate public corporations, and most common, professional partnerships and corporations that raise money from large institutional investors such as pension funds, insurance companies, foundations, and foreign investors.

Several reasons are given for seeking venture capital. Perhaps the best is that professional venture investors often provide technical and managerial assistance that would be very expensive otherwise. Also, venture capitalists usually commit to additional rounds of financing as the company achieves its growth targets.

Sources: Deloitte and Touche, *Financing Business Growth: An Entrepreneur's Guidebook,* 1990, 58; "How to Finance Anything," *INC.,* February 1993, 58; "How to Finance Anything," *INC.,* February 1993, 56; and "When the Venture Capital Dries Up," *The Boston Globe,* May 16, 1993, 76–77.

In exchange for such financing, venture capitalists will assume membership on the board of directors and will choose to invest in a controlling position of equity ownership, usually through preferred stock that gives them priority of payment in the event of bankruptcy. Even if they hold a majority interest, however, control is in the hands of management — unless management is in danger of failing to meet its objectives and more direct leadership is required. Finally, prospective venture capital investors seek a minimum 25 to 30 percent (and upwards of 50 percent) return compounded annually. Common return on investment objectives range from ten times their investment in five years for start-up companies to as low as five times their investment in five years for more mature (less risky) companies. The venture capitalist's investment horizon is typically three to five years, at which time they will look to liquidate their interest in the company through a public offering of the company's stock or through acquisition.

At present, venture capital funding is approximately half of what it was in 1987. Most venture capital money has gone into older, more developed companies, where opportunities for strong returns appear brighter. Examples of such companies are mostly later stage expansions of technology companies and, to some extent, the retail and health-care industries. Yet, as a result of the sheer abundance of venture capital funding available (more than $4 billion in 1987 alone) the overall returns fell substantially short of what investors expected. "It was the classic case of too much money chasing too few deals," claims one venture capital manager. By 1991 new funding going into venture capital partnerships was off more than 70 percent, compared with the 1987 peak. Realistically, only those companies with extraordinary growth prospects (that is, companies that have a good shot at being $40 million businesses in four or five years) and with managers capable of leading them in that direction can expect to attract the attention of venture capital firms.

As a result, an attractive alternative investment vehicle has emerged in the midst of the prolonged credit crunch. Syndicated retail *private placements,* similar to venture capital funding, provide money from more than one source, usually arranged by an investment banker whose brokers line up the money from wealthy clients. The clients buy blocks of stock in the company but are, in contrast to venture capital investors, generally more passive investors. Although costly to the company, there is no loss of control or equity. Nationally, money flowing into these private offerings has continued to climb since 1989 and has doubled to $6 billion in 1992 over the previous years. The money is coming from investors anxious to leave an overheated initial public offering market and a highly competitive mutual fund market as well as from the venture capital base. In return, investors expect to earn a return of three to five times their investment within three to five years.

Summary

In this chapter we discussed (1) taxes, (2) the nature of financial markets — where capital is raised, securities are traded, and stock prices are established — (3) the types of instruments offered in these markets, (4) the types of institutions that operate in these markets, (5) the regulation of securities markets, and (6) the concept of market efficiency. The key points covered are listed below:

▷ The value of any asset depends on the stream of **after-tax cash flows** it produces. Tax rates and other aspects of our tax system are changed frequently by Congress.

In the United States, income tax rates are **progressive** — the higher one's income, the larger the percentage paid in taxes, up to a point.

Assets such as stocks, bonds, and real estate are defined as **capital assets.** If a capital asset is sold for more than the purchase price, the profit is called a **capital gain.** If the capital asset is sold at a loss, it is called a **capital loss.**

Operating income paid out as dividends is subject to **double taxation:** the income is first taxed at the corporate level, and then shareholders must pay personal taxes on their dividends.

Interest income received by a corporation is taxed as ordinary income; however, 70 percent of the **dividends** received by one corporation from another are excluded from taxable income. The reason for this exclusion is that this income is ultimately subjected to **triple taxation.**

Because interest paid by a corporation is a **deductible** expense, while dividends are not, our tax system favors debt financing over equity financing.

Ordinary corporate operating losses can be carried back **(carry-back)** to each of the preceding 3 years and forward **(carry-forward)** for the next 15 years to offset taxable income in those years.

Fixed assets are depreciated over time to reflect the decline in value of the assets. **Depreciation** is a **tax-deductible,** but noncash, expense. The higher the firm's depreciation in a given year, the lower its taxes and the higher its cash flows in that year, other things held constant.

▷ Current tax laws permit fixed assets to be depreciated using the **Modified Accelerated Cost Recovery System (MACRS).** Tax depreciation rules have a major impact on the profitability of long-term assets such as plant and equipment.

Under MACRS, depreciation expense is calculated as the yearly **recovery allowance percentage** multiplied by the asset's depreciable basis. The asset's **depreciable basis** is equal to the purchase price of the asset plus any shipping and installation costs.

If a depreciable asset is sold, the sale price minus the then-existing **undepreciated book value** is added to operating income and taxed at the firm's marginal tax rate.

▷ There are many different types of **financial markets.** Each market serves a different set of customers or deals with different types of securities.

Transfers of capital between borrowers and savers take place (1) by **direct transfers** of money and securities; (2) by transfers through **investment banking houses,** which act as middlemen; and (3) by transfers through **financial intermediaries,** which create new securities.

The **stock market** is an especially important market because this is where stock prices are established.

There are two basic, and very different, types of stock markets — the **organized exchanges** and the **over-the-counter (OTC) market.**

▷ Some of the most important **money market instruments** are (1) U.S. Treasury bills, (2) negotiable certificates of deposit, (3) commercial paper, and (4) banker's acceptances. All money market instruments represent debt, but the issuer may be the federal government, a bank, or a corporation.

Among the most important **capital market instruments** you will find (1) U.S. Treasury notes and bonds, (2) municipal bonds, and (3) corporate bonds, all of which are long-term debt securities. Preferred stock and common stock are also long-term securities, but these represent an equity claim on the issuing corporation.

▶ *The Wall Street Journal* publishes the following **information on stock market transactions:** (1) the high and low price for the previous 52 weeks; (2) the current, or indicated, annual dividend; (3) the current dividend yield; (4) the P/E ratio; (5) trading volume; (6) the high, low, and closing prices for the trading day; and (7) the net change in price from the previous day's closing price.

The majority of **corporate bonds** are traded in the OTC market. Bonds are (1) traded with less frequency than stocks and (2) concentrated in the hands of large financial institutions, which makes it relatively easy for OTC bond dealers to arrange bond trades.

The Wall Street Journal publishes the following **information on NYSE bond trades:** (1) coupon rate, (2) maturity, (3) current yield, (4) volume, (5) closing price (expressed as a percentage), and (6) net change from the previous day's closing price.

Securities markets are primarily regulated by the **Securities and Exchange Commission (SEC).**

▶ The requirements for an **efficient capital market** are (1) a large number of profit-seeking individuals engaged in securities analysis who operate independently from one another, (2) quick and full access by most investors to any news about present and potential developments, and (3) quick action by investors to adjust securities prices in light of new information.

Resolution to
DECISION IN FINANCE

THE CLINTON ADMINISTRATION
AND ITS TAX PROPOSALS

In announcing his package, President Clinton stated, "The test of our program cannot simply be, 'What's in it for me?' The question must be, 'What's in it for us?'" He went on to say, "Unless we reduce the deficit, increase investment, raise productivity, and generate jobs, we will condemn our children and our children's children to a lesser life and a diminished

Sources: "Proposed Tax Increases Hit the Rich Hardest," "Winners and Losers in Clinton's Economic Plan," and "A Plan for Change: Clinton Stresses Taxes Over Spending Cuts in Attack on Deficit," *The Wall Street Journal,* February 18, 1993; "Plan to Lift Top Tax Rate Will Resurrect Tax Shelters," *The Wall Street Journal,* February 19, 1993; and "With Signature, President Will Erase Reagan's Legacy," *The Wall Street Journal,* August 9, 1993.

destiny." His proposal offered a shared sacrifice, where taxes would increase (he called the increases a "contribution"), but government spending would be reduced. The package was specifically designed to lower interest rates and inflation by reducing the deficit and laying a firmer foundation for future prosperity.

The outcome for President Clinton's economic program was in doubt until the very end. Senator Robert Kerrey (Democrat)—a rival of Mr. Clinton's during the presidential race — announced only 1½ hours before the August 6 Senate vote that he would, reluctantly, vote for the program. Said Senator Kerrey (from the Senate floor), "President Clinton, if you are watching now, as I suspect you are, I could not and would not cast a vote that would bring down your presidency."

Much of Mr. Clinton's original blueprint survived, with some notable exceptions. For example, the president did not get his broad-based energy tax but, instead, a 4.3 cent-a-gallon tax on gasoline and other transportation fuels (effective October 1, 1993). The fuel tax is expected to cause only about a 1 percent increase, on average, in the taxes paid by the middle class. There will, of course, be both winners and losers under the new tax law. Workers earning less than $30,000 are likely to benefit from a tax cut (mainly due to an expansion in the so-called earned-income tax credit). By contrast, people earning $200,000 annually will pay an average of 17.4 percent more in taxes, and estimates are that 98.5 percent of all individual taxpayers will see no increase in their income taxes.

The changes in the inheritance taxes went through as proposed, as did the Medicare payroll tax change. By removing the ceiling on earnings subject to the Medicare tax (which had been $135,000), successful small businesses, sole proprietorships, and professionals will be especially hard hit. However, with the top capital gains rate remaining at 28 percent, close to 12 percentage points less than the highest marginal tax rate, taxpayers with capital gains from the sale of securities or real estate will not fare so badly. Because the differential between the rate on ordinary income and that on capital gains will widen, there will be an incentive for high-income investors to shift investments which provided taxable interest and dividend income into tax-exempt state and local government securities (munis) and into investments which will provide capital gains.

Treasury officials stated that the increase in the corporate tax rate would affect only 2,700 of the country's 2.2 million corporations. Of course, these 2,700 corporations are the largest ones, with millions of stockholders and employees, and higher taxes for corporations mean higher costs of goods and services for consumers.

Of the four specific proposals listed at the beginning of this chapter, only the first one was modified — lobbying expenses will be "limited" but not disallowed. The other three survived essentially intact. Because of the proposal to mark to market their trading portfolios, securities dealers will pay higher taxes, reflecting the appreciation in their portfolios. Clinton's proposal to obtain more taxes from multinational corporations was designed to prevent those companies from improperly avoiding their U.S. tax liability by transferring costs between home and abroad. To accomplish this goal, the Treasury says that the number of Internal Revenue Service agents will be doubled to police transfer pricing actions. By doing this, the federal government will try to make sure that everyone, corporations and individuals alike, pays his or her fair share.

Other significant provisions of the new tax law include (1) cutting Medicare, Medicaid, and defense, but expanding the food stamp program and childhood immunizations; (2) allowing small businesses to write off as much as $17,500 for equipment purchased during the year — up from $10,000; (3) reducing by half the capital gains tax rate for certain investments in start-up firms, where the investment is held for at least five years; and (4) reforming the student-loan program mainly by phasing in direct government lending.

According to congressional analysts, and based on available data as of August 1993, the Clinton tax plan is projected to increase taxes by a net $241 billion and cut spending by $255 billion for a total reduction in the federal budget deficit of $496 billion over five years. Keep in mind, however, that certain assumptions had to be made to obtain these projections — assumptions about world politics and the ability to reduce defense, about the level of economic activity both in the United States and abroad (and the resulting tax receipts), and about the actions of investors and taxpayers in general in response to the new tax realities, to mention just a few.

Questions

2-1   Suppose you owned 100 shares of Exxon stock, and the company earned $4 per share during the last reporting period. Suppose further that Exxon could either pay all its earnings out as dividends (in which case you would receive $400) or retain the earnings in the business, buy more assets, and cause the price of the stock to go up by $4 per share (in which case the value of your stock would rise by $400).

    a. How would the tax laws influence what you, as a typical stockholder, would want the company to do?

    b. Would your choice be influenced by how much other income you had? Why might the preference of a 45-year-old physician differ with respect to corporate dividend policy from those of a pension fund manager or a retiree living on a small income?

    c. How might the corporation's decision about dividend policy influence the price of its stock?

2-2   What does *double taxation of corporate income* mean?

2-3   If you were starting a business, what tax considerations might cause you to prefer to set it up as a proprietorship or a partnership rather than as a corporation?

2-4   Explain how the federal income tax structure affects the choice of financing (use of debt versus equity) of U.S. business firms.

2-5   How can the federal government influence the level of business by adjusting the ITC?

2-6   For someone planning to start a new business, is the average or the marginal tax rate more relevant?

2-7   What would happen to the standard of living in the United States if people lost faith in the safety of our financial institutions? Explain.

2-8   How does a cost-efficient capital market hold down the prices of goods and services?

2-9   In what way does the secondary market contribute to the efficient functioning of the primary market?

2-10   What is the financial intermediary's primary role in the economy?

2-11   What are the most important services provided by financial intermediaries?

2-12   What would happen to required rates of return if no financial intermediaries existed?

Self-Test Problems

ST-1   Austin Sound Company had 1993 income of $200,000 from operations after all operating costs but before (1) interest charges of $5,000, (2) dividends paid of $10,000, and (3) income taxes. What is the firm's income tax liability?

ST-2   Margaret Considine earned a salary of $32,000 this year, and, in addition, she received $5,000 in dividends from some stock she owns. If Considine is a single individual and takes her $2,350 personal exemption, what is her taxable income and her tax liability for this year?

ST-3   Sections of *The Wall Street Journal* are provided for the student to use in answering the questions concerning Commonwealth Edison's (ComwEd) common stock quotation and its (CmwE) 9⅛08 bond quotation that follow.

New York Stock Exchange Composite Transactions

52 Weeks Hi	52 Weeks Lo	Stock	Sym	Div	Yld %	PE	Vol 100s	Hi	Lo	Close	Net Chg
34¼	21¾	ComwEd	CWE	1.60	5.8	13	5131	27⅞	27⅜	27⅝	+ ⅛
25½	22	ComwEd pfC		1.90	7.8	...	20	24½	24⅛	24⅜	+ ¼
26	23⅛	ComwEd pfD		2.00	7.8	...	7	25⅝	25½	25½	− ⅜
95¼	85	ComwEd pfE		7.24	7.6	...	z10	95	95	95	+ ½
102	94⅝	ComwEd pfF		8.40	8.4	...	50	100	100	100	+ ⅜
33½	28½	ComwEd pfG		2.88	8.6	...	5	33⅝	33½	33½	+ ¼

Source: *The Wall Street Journal,* Friday, April 9, 1993.

New York Exchange Bonds

Quotations as of 4 p.m. Eastern Time Thursday, April 8, 1993.

Bonds	Cur Yld	Vol	Close	Net Chg
CmwE 8s03	7.8	5	102½	+ ⅜
CmwE 8¾05	8.4	6	104	+ ⅛
CmwE 9⅜04	9.0	18	103⅞	− ⅛
CmwE 8¼07	8.1	21	102¼	− ⅝
CmwE 9⅛08	8.7	47	104⅞	+ ¼

Source: *The Wall Street Journal,* Friday, April 9, 1993.

I. Common Stock

a. What is the stock's dividend per share and its dividend yield?

b. What is the stock's price/earnings ratio, based on the closing price, and the firm's most recent 12 months' earnings per share?

c. How many shares were sold on the trading day you investigated?

d. How much did the stock's price rise or fall from the close of the previous day's trading?

e. Is the stock's closing price closer to the stock's high or low for the year?

II. 9⅛08 Bond

a. In what year will the bond mature?

b. How much interest will the investor receive during the year?

c. If an investor purchased the bond at the end of the trading day, what price would be paid for this bond?

d. What was the bond's price at the close of the previous day's trading?

e. Was the bond selling above, below, or at par?

Problems

Note: At the time when you read this book, Congress may again have changed tax rates and other provisions. Work all problems under the assumption that the information in the chapter is still current.

2-1

Corporate tax liability

In 1993 Beckwith Industries had $150,000 in taxable income.

a. What federal income tax will the firm pay?

b. What is the firm's average tax rate?

c. What is the firm's marginal tax rate?

2-2

Corporate tax liability

Vanagas Corporation had $110,000 of taxable income from operations in 1993.

a. What is the company's federal income tax bill for the year?

b. Assume Vanagas receives an additional $30,000 of interest income from some bonds it owns. What is the tax on this interest income?

c. Now assume that the firm does *not* receive the interest income but does receive an additional $30,000 as dividends on some stock it owns. What is the tax on this dividend income?

2-3

Corporate taxable income

Given the following information for Northwest Tools Inc., calculate the firm's taxable income for the year:

Net operating income	$400,000
Interest income	20,000
Interest expense	90,000
Dividends received from small holdings of several stocks	30,000
Dividends paid to firm's stockholders	40,600

2-4

Corporate interest and dividend income

Management of Up-N-Coming Enterprises wants to invest $100,000 into either bonds that pay 8 percent annually or common stock of the Bodine Corporation on which it would expect to receive annual dividends of $6,500. (Assume that Up-N-Coming's ownership of Bodine stock represents less than 20 percent of Bodine's total common stock.) If Up-N-Coming expects to pay state-plus-federal taxes of 40 percent this year, what is the *difference* in expected after-tax returns on the two investments?

2-5

MACRS depreciation

A new machine was purchased for $80,000. Another $10,000 was spent on installing the machine. The machine has a 5-year MACRS class life. What is the tax depreciation expense in Year 2?

2-6

Individual tax liability

Maxine Chomsky earned a salary of $50,000 this year, and, in addition, she received $2,500 in dividends from stock she owns. Chomsky is a single individual and takes $2,350 in personal exemption.

a. What is her taxable income this year?

b. What federal income tax will she pay?

c. What is her average tax rate?

d. What is her marginal tax rate?

2-7

Loss carry-back, carry-forward

Calais Computers Inc. has made $200,000 before taxes during each of the previous 15 years, and it expects to make $200,000 a year before taxes in the future. However, last year (1993) Calais incurred a loss of $1,200,000. Calais will claim a tax credit at the time it files its 1993 income tax returns and will receive a check from the U.S. Treasury. Show how it calculates this credit, and then indicate Calais's tax liability for each of the next 5 years. To ease calculations, assume a 30 percent tax rate on *all* income.

2-8

Individual taxes

Lisa Werksman has the following situation for the year 1993: salary of $80,000; dividend income of $10,000; interest on GMAC bonds of $4,000; interest on state of Oregon municipal bonds of $10,000; and proceeds of $13,600 from the sale of 200 shares of Exxon stock purchased in 1990 at a cost of $10,000. Lisa gets one exemption ($2,350), and she has allowable itemized deductions of $5,000; these amounts will be deducted from her gross income to determine her taxable income.

a. If she files an individual return, what is Lisa's tax liability for 1993?

b. What are her marginal and average tax rates?

c. If she had some money to invest and was offered a choice of either Oregon municipal bonds with a yield of 6 percent or additional GMAC bonds with a yield of 8 percent, which should she choose and why?

d. At what marginal tax rate would Lisa be indifferent to the choice between Oregon and GMAC bonds?

2-9

MACRS depreciation

Dawson & Reins Inc. purchased two new assets in 1993. The first is a 3-year class asset and the other is classified as a 5-year asset for MACRS depreciation (cost recovery) purposes. The assets each cost $100,000. What depreciation expense will the company report for tax purposes over the next 6 years?

2-10

MACRS depreciation

Tillicum Industries (TI) will commence operations on January 2, 1994. It expects to have sales of $200,000 in 1994, $250,000 in 1995, and $400,000 in 1996. TI also forecasts that operating expenses excluding depreciation will total 60 percent of sales in each year during this period and that it will have interest expenses of $12,000 in 1994, $15,000 in 1995, and $20,000 in 1996. TI will make an investment in fixed assets of $100,000 on January 2, 1994. These assets will be depreciated over their 3-year class life. Use the corporate tax rates from Table 2-2.

a. What is the depreciation expense in each year (1994 through 1996) on the 3-year class life equipment? (Note that the assets will not have been fully depreciated by the end of 1996.)

b. What is TI's tax liability in each year from 1994 to 1996?

2-11

Stock quotations

Look up General Electric's common stock in *The Wall Street Journal* or another appropriate financial publication.

a. On what exchange is the stock listed?

b. What is the dividend per share?

c. What is the stock's dividend yield?

d. What is the price/earnings ratio, based on the closing price, and the most recent 12 months' earnings per share?

e. How many shares were sold on the trading day you investigated?

f. How much did the stock's price rise or fall from the close of the previous day's trading?

g. Is the stock's closing price closer to the stock's high or low for the year?

2-12

Bond quotations

Look up General Motors Acceptance Corporation's bonds in *The Wall Street Journal* or another appropriate financial publication. The firm's bonds are identified by "GMA" in *The Wall Street Journal's* bond listings. Specifically, answer the following questions based on GMA's 8¼16 bond. (*Note:* If this bond is not listed in *The Wall Street Journal* when you are working on this problem, choose another GMA bond with a similar coupon and maturity.)

a. On what exchange is the bond listed?

b. In what year will the bond mature?

c. How much interest will the investor receive during the year?

d. If an investor purchased the bond at the end of the trading day, what price would be paid?

e. What was the bond's price at the close of the previous day's trading?

f. Was the bond selling above, below, or at par?

g. If General Motors Acceptance Corporation were to sell a new issue of bonds, approximately what coupon rate would be required for the issue to sell at par?

Solutions to Self-Test Problems

ST-1

Operating income	$200,000
Less: interest deduction	5,000
Taxable income	$195,000

Note that dividends paid are not tax deductible; therefore, they are not deducted from operating income to obtain taxable income.

From Table 2-2 we obtain the corporate tax rates as follows:

$$\text{Tax} = \$22,250 + 0.39(\$195,000 - \$100,000)$$
$$= \$22,250 + \$37,050$$
$$= \$59,300.$$

ST-2 Taxable income:

Salary earned	$32,000
Dividends received	5,000
Personal exemption	(2,350)
	$34,650

Tax liability:

Since Margaret Considine is a single individual, we use the tax rates for single individuals shown at the top of Table 2-1.

$$\text{Taxes} = \$3,315 + 0.28(\$34,650 - \$22,100)$$
$$= \$3,315 + \$3,514$$
$$= \$6,829.$$

ST-3 **I. Common Stock**

a. You should notice that there are 6 stock issues listed for Commonwealth Edison, only 1 of which is common stock — the first Commonwealth issue shown. (The other 5 issues are preferred stock, denoted by "pf".) Looking at the 5th column, you should see that Commonwealth's dividend per share is $1.60. The next column to the right indicates the dividend yield of 5.8 percent.

b. Looking at the 7th column, you should see that the P/E ratio is 13 times. Since the P/E ratio is 13 times and the closing price (shown in the next-to-last column) is $27.625, the earnings per share is calculated as follows:
P/E = 13; E = $27.625/13; E = $2.125.

c. Looking at the 8th column, you should see that 513,100 shares were sold. Notice that this column indicates volume in hundreds.

d. The last column shows the change in price from the previous trading day. For Commonwealth, the price rose by $0.125 from the previous day's close.

e. The first 2 columns give the 52-week high and low price. For the 52-week period, Commonwealth's price ranged from $34.25 to $21.75. Since Commonwealth's closing stock price is shown as $27.625, its stock was trading closer to its low than to its high price, but it is trading roughly in the middle of its trading range.

II. 9⅛08 Bond

a. This particular bond is the last issue shown for Commonwealth. The maturity date is indicated in the first column by the two digits 08, indicating that the bond matures in the Year 2008.

b. Again, the interest rate for this particular bond is shown in the first column after the company's ticker symbol (CmwE) by the digits 9⅛. Since a bond's par value is typically $1,000, and the interest rate is 9⅛ percent, the annual interest is calculated as 0.09125 × $1,000 = $91.25.

c. The next-to-last column shows the percentage of par value at which the bond closed — 104⅞. Therefore, the price paid for the bond at the end of the day is calculated as 1.04875 × $1,000 = $1,048.75.

d. The last column shows the change in price (calculated as a percentage of par) from the previous day's close — +¼. Thus, the change in price was 0.0025 × $1,000 = $2.50, so the previous day's close was $1,048.75 − $2.50 = $1,046.25.

e. Because the next-to-last column shows a number greater than 100, the bond is selling above par.

Financial Institutions

OBJECTIVES

After reading this chapter, you should be able to:

▶ Explain how the Federal Reserve influences the money supply through the commercial banking system, and give the Fed's three main monetary tools.

▶ Define deposit expansion, explain how it works, and give some reasons that the full expansion potential may not always be reached.

▶ Trace the events that occurred in 1981 and 1991 in terms of monetary policy, and explain why a "credit crunch" occurred in both cases.

▶ Compare and contrast major financial institutions, noting their assets and liabilities.

▶ List the sources and uses of commercial bank funds, and explain the importance of a bank's capital account.

▶ Give an overview of major banking legislation during the 1980s and early 1990s.

▶ List the major trends in banking that are likely to continue during this decade.

DECISION IN FINANCE

THE NEW BANKING LAW GETS TOUGH WITH BANKS

In late 1991, Congress passed a new banking law which created a much tougher regulatory system for banks. The Bush administration had proposed to modernize the banking system by allowing well-capitalized banks to establish nationwide branch systems and to become financial supermarkets which could sell insurance, broker stocks, underwrite securities issues, and provide other financial services. The Bush package was designed to strengthen the U.S. banking system, making it more like banking systems in other developed nations, by expanding banking's horizons. However, the legislation passed by Congress rejected most of Bush's proposals and even imposed new restrictions on banks.

Congress had recently been forced to authorized the expenditure of over $200 billion to bail out the savings and loan (S&L) industry, and banking regulators were seeking another $70 billion to keep the Bank Insurance Fund solvent. Congress reasoned that the bank and S&L problems had been caused by granting these institutions too much leeway and by regulation that was too loose, so it was reluctant to let banks go into new business areas. Now, though, many bankers and industry analysts fear that Congress went too far with its legislation — they

think the new banking law will undermine banks further by keeping them out of profitable businesses and that rules designed to prevent banks from failing will mainly keep them from prospering.

The new legislation (1) will mandate that regulators move more quickly to correct problems and close banks before they become insolvent rather than working with them to correct developing problems, (2) will limit the Federal Reserve Board's ability to keep ailing banks open with long-term loans from its discount window, and (3) will end the Federal Deposit Insurance Corporation's authority to pay off uninsured deposits (those over $100,000) when banks fail. The Bush administration was forced to accept the tougher regulation in a political compromise to get the $70 billion needed to support the Bank Insurance Fund, which had been depleted

See end of chapter for resolution.
Photo source: Andrew Sacks/Tony Stone Images.

This chapter was co-authored by Bruce Cochran of San Jose State University.

88   Part I   The Financial Environment and the Firm

by the failure of more than 1,100 banks since 1984.

As you read this chapter, consider how the new restrictions will impact banks' lending policies and how that will affect consumers and the economy. Will the newer restrictions lead to more bank failures, and if so, what impact will that have on the remaining banks and on the economy? Also, consider possible changes that the Clinton administration may make in banking regulations.

In Chapter 2, we provided a general overview of financial markets and the main function of financial intermediaries, namely, to channel funds from surplus economic units to deficit economic units (from savers to borrowers). In that chapter, we also discussed how financial intermediaries provide a complete change in the financial product, in the process better meeting the savers' needs for liquidity and diversification and, therefore, lowering the cost of funds to borrowers.

In this chapter, we will continue our coverage of the financial environment by focusing on the largest of the financial intermediaries, the commercial banking system. However, to understand the crucial role that commercial banks play in our economic system, it is essential that we first examine the functions of our central bank, the *Federal Reserve System.* We will discuss how the Fed conducts its *monetary policy,* primarily through the commercial banking system, in order to influence the nation's money supply and the level of interest rates throughout the economy. We will look at the specific monetary tools available to the Fed and the likely effectiveness of each.

Next we will examine the process by which commercial banks (and other depository institutions) "create money" through deposit expansion, look at bank balance sheets and banking regulation, and provide a brief summary of the assets and liabilities of other financial intermediaries. We will conclude the chapter with a look at the continuing bailout of the savings and loan industry, and we will stress some recent trends and developments within the commercial banking system, including the impact of globalization.

The Federal Reserve System

Federal Deposit Insurance Corporation (FDIC)

An agency created by Congress in 1933 to protect depositors in insured banks from the effects of a bank failure.

Federal Reserve (Fed)

The central banking system in the United States; the chief regulator of the banking system.

Commercial banks are at the center of our nation's financial system, and a number of regulatory agencies have been developed to control the banking system and its ability to create credit. The primary bank regulators are the Office of the Comptroller of the Currency (OCC), the Federal Reserve, and the **Federal Deposit Insurance Corporation (FDIC),** created by Congress in 1933 to protect depositors in insured banks from the effects of a bank failure. As we will discuss later in this chapter, banks in this country may be chartered at either the national or state level, and the OCC charters, examines, and, if necessary, closes nationally chartered banks, while the FDIC insures deposits and examines some state-chartered banks. However, the most important of the bank regulators is the **Federal Reserve (the Fed),** which is the central banking system in the United States. The Fed is involved in examinations, regulates bank holding company activities, and acts as a last-resort lender to banks, but its chief responsibility is regulating the nation's money supply. The Fed attempts to influence the ability of banks to create credit (and hence to influence the money supply), primarily by increasing or reducing the reserves available to the banking system. Later in the chapter, we will review the three major tools that the Fed uses to exercise control over reserves. We will also explain *how* banks use new reserves into the banking system to expand the money supply.

Organization and Structure

The Federal Reserve System is a decentralized central bank. The Federal Reserve Act of 1913 divided the country into 12 Federal Reserve districts. The districts' operations are conducted through a Federal Reserve Bank located in each district. These banks are located in Boston, New York, Philadelphia, Cleveland, Richmond, Atlanta, Chicago, St. Louis, Minneapolis, Kansas City, Dallas, and San Francisco. Branches of the district banks are located in 24 additional cities.

Board of Governors of the Federal Reserve System

Seven-member decision-making authority of the Fed.

The real decision-making authority is given to the seven-member **Board of Governors of the Federal Reserve System,** in Washington, D.C. The seven members of the Board are appointed by the president and confirmed by the Senate. The current chairman of the Board of Governors is Alan Greenspan, a highly respected economist and inflation fighter who took office in the fall of 1987. He was quickly put to the test when, on October 19 of that year, the stock market plummeted a record 508 points in a single nearly catastrophic day of trading — dubbed "Black Monday." Mr. Greenspan earned high marks for his handling of the crisis. He and other Fed officials responded quickly to the stock market collapse and used the full powers of the Fed to keep the market crash from spiraling out of control.

The framers of the Federal Reserve Act wished to keep the Board as free from political influence as possible, so Board members are appointed for terms of 14 years, and their terms are arranged so that one expires every two years. Thus, it would, theoretically, take a president almost a full two terms to appoint a majority of the Board members. However, circumstances such as resignations or deaths can create a faster turnover on the Board. For example, President Carter appointed five members to the Board in just over three years. Thus, although the Fed has legal independence from the executive and legislative branches of government, great influence is still exerted on the Fed's policies by the political sector of the government.[1]

All national banks are legally required to be members of the system. In addition, approximately 10 percent of all state banks are voluntary members of the Federal Reserve System. One reason that more state banks did not join the system is that the Fed's reserve requirements generally were higher than the

[1]Even though the Fed's designers attempted to shield it from political influence, it is unlikely that the members of the Board are immune to political pressures. It raised a few eyebrows, for example, when Alan Greenspan was prominently seated next to Hillary Rodham Clinton at President Clinton's first State of the Union Address on February 17, 1993. There were charges that he had compromised the Federal Reserve's independence. However, by the summer of 1993, there were signs that the Fed chairman was about to demonstrate the Fed's independence and that Bill Clinton — like every other president in the last 30 years — might be headed toward a confrontation with the Fed over rising interest rates.

Depository Institutions Deregulation and Monetary Control Act (DIDMCA)

An act that eliminated many of the distinctions between commercial banks and other depository institutions.

Federal Open Market Committee (FOMC)

Committee of the Federal Reserve System that makes decisions relating to open-market operations.

open-market operations

The purchase and sale of U.S. government securities by the Federal Reserve.

state-imposed reserve requirements. The **Depository Institutions Deregulation and Monetary Control Act (DIDMCA)** of 1980 eliminated many of the differences between national- and state-chartered and between Fed member and nonmember banks. Also, DIDMCA made the Fed's services available to all depository institutions for a fee, which has allowed development of private competition for many of these services.

An important element of the Federal Reserve System is the **Federal Open Market Committee (FOMC),** which has responsibility for decisions relating to **open-market operations.** Open-market operations are the purchase and sale of U.S. government securities conducted through the Federal Reserve Bank of New York. As we shall see, open-market operations are the most effective monetary tool available to the Fed, so the FOMC is at the heart of the Fed's power. It consists of 12 members — the seven members of the Board of Governors and representatives from five of the 12 Federal Reserve District Banks. One of these five District Bank representatives is always the president of the Federal Reserve Bank of New York because this bank is responsible for the transaction of the open-market operations. The other four District Bank memberships rotate among the presidents of the remaining 11 Federal Reserve Districts.

Tools of Monetary Policy

The Board of Governors of the Federal Reserve System, by affecting reserves in the system, influences the money supply and hence interest rates.[2] The three principal tools of control are (1) changes in the reserve requirements, (2) changes in the discount rate, and (3) open-market operations. Reserve requirements refer to the percentage of each type of deposit that depository institutions must hold as reserves, that is, may not lend out. Discount policy refers to the terms under which depository institutions may borrow from the Fed. Open-market operations, as mentioned previously, involve the purchase or sale of U.S. government securities.

Reserve Requirements

required reserves

The minimum reserves that a depository institution must hold as vault cash or reserve deposits with the Federal Reserve.

excess reserves

Reserves held by a commercial bank (or other depository institution) with a Federal Reserve bank in excess of the bank's required reserves.

The Federal Reserve System requires all depository institutions to hold reserves against their deposits. For checking account deposits, the amount of **required reserves** is based on the two-week average level ending on the second Monday of the period, and banks must settle their reserve requirements the following Wednesday.

Reserve requirements work in the following way: If there is a reserve requirement of, say, 10 percent, then banks have to hold $1 in every $10 deposited in idle balances (vault cash or a reserve deposit with the Fed), but the other $9 may be lent out or invested in marketable securities. The $9 is called free or **excess reserves.**

---

[2]The interrelationship of reserves, money supply, and interest rates is not a simple one and is open to much debate and controversy. We will provide some simplified illustrations later in this chapter, but the interested reader should refer to any of the many excellent money and banking or economics texts for further details.

A relatively small change in reserve requirements has a very large potential effect on the amount of deposits outstanding. Any new deposits into the banking system (from the Fed) can be expanded by the *reciprocal* of the reserve requirement, at least in theory. Therefore, if we continue with our assumption of a reserve requirement of 10 percent, the money supply would increase by $1/0.10 = 10$ times the amount of the initial deposit. The banking system does this, as we shall see, by lending excess reserves (the $9 out of every $10 in our example) which become new demand deposits, checking accounts, somewhere within the banking system, not necessarily in the same bank. The bank which receives the new demand deposits can also lend $9/10$, and the expansion process continues.

The authority to make changes in reserve requirements is the Fed's most powerful tool, and for this reason it is reluctant to use it. In fact, reserve requirements are seldom changed. From 1963 until the time the Monetary Control Act was implemented in 1980, reserve requirements on demand deposits were changed only five times, and those on savings deposits were changed only twice. After 1980, some reserve requirements were changed in 1983, some in December 1990, and others in February 1992, but these changes are still relatively infrequent and not appropriate when "fine tuning" the economy. Consider the effect of an increase in reserve requirements in a tight money period. Even a 1 percent increase in the reserve requirements would increase required reserves by hundreds of millions of dollars. This would then cause a decrease in excess reserves which would reduce demand deposits by a multiple much larger than the original 1 percent change in the reserve requirement and would force banks to call in outstanding loans. Such a radical decline in money and credit could be damaging to the economic system. Thus, the potential impact of even a modest change in reserve requirements makes it a tool that is used cautiously by the Federal Reserve System.[3]

The Discount Rate

discount rate

The interest rate charged by the Fed for loans of reserves to depository institutions.

The **discount rate** is the rate of interest the Fed charges depository institutions when they borrow reserves. Institutions may find themselves temporarily short of reserves when there has been a large or unexpected shift in reserves, perhaps due to a large withdrawal, and institutions may also need to borrow from the Fed during times of tight money to relieve temporary reserve imbalances.

It is important to note that the Federal Reserve System views these loans as a *temporary* mechanism for the adjustment of the specific institution's reserve position, and it discourages the use of these funds for profit making. Moreover, loans from the Fed are viewed as a privilege, not as a right. Thus, the Fed can and does exert pressure on institutions to limit their borrowing. Although the borrowing privilege offers a safety valve to relieve temporary strains on reserves, there are strong incentives to repay loans quickly. For example, if a particular bank shows a borrowing pattern that is characterized by frequent or continuing indebtedness over an extended period, the Fed may press for repay-

---

[3]We will look at the actual process whereby the deposit expansion (or contraction) takes place later in this chapter.

Federal funds market

The market in which banks lend reserve funds among themselves for short periods of time.

Federal funds rate

The interest rate, set by market forces, at which banks borrow in the Federal funds market.

prime rate

A published rate of interest charged by commercial banks on short-term loans to very large, strong corporations.

ment, even if it means that the bank must call in some loans or liquidate some investments. Therefore, banks are reluctant to use the Fed for other than temporary needs. In fact, some banks, particularly large banks, avoid the Fed altogether even as a source of temporary credit by borrowing instead in the **Federal funds market.** Federal funds are interbank loans of excess reserves, a market where banks borrow from other banks for short periods of time. A bank with excess reserves (available funds) lends funds, typically overnight, to a bank that has a temporary need for reserves. The **Federal funds rate** is the prevailing interest rate in this market and is an extremely sensitive short-term interest rate. The Fed funds rate, despite its name, is set by market forces, not by the Fed.[4]

When the Federal Reserve System was established in 1913, it was thought that the discount rate would be the principal instrument of monetary control. Such has not been the case, however, at least not historically. As Figure 3-1 shows, the discount rate has frequently lagged behind other short-term rates, such as the Treasury bill rate. This has also typically been the case with the **prime rate,** which is the interest rate commercial banks charge on short-term loans to very large, strong corporations. For example, the prime rate rose to 10.5 percent in November 1988 and increased to 11.5 percent by February 1989 before the discount rate was increased from 6.5 to 7 percent. The prime rate started falling in June 1989; however, the discount rate remained at 7 percent. Obviously, an effective instrument of monetary policy would consistently lead, not follow, market rates.

Even though the discount rate is not the active tool of monetary policy that the Fed's founders envisioned, announcements of changes in the discount rate have an important psychological effect in the financial community. For example, increases in the discount rate generally signal a movement toward tighter monetary policy. If such an announcement causes financial institutions to become more stringent in loan policies or causes businesses to reconsider expansion plans, then the discount rate, in a roundabout fashion, has done its job.

In December 1991, we saw an example of the psychological impact that cuts in the discount rate can have on financial markets. A stagnant economy, not yet officially out of recession, convinced the Fed to abandon its previous, cautious approach of ¼ and ½ percentage point reductions to cut the discount rate by a full percentage point from a 4.5 to 3.5 percent, its lowest level in 27 years. Financial markets took notice, and in the two weeks that followed, stock prices soared. Banks also reduced the prime rate from 7.5 to 6.5 percent, an indication that the discount rate is, perhaps, becoming more effective as the direct monetary tool it was intended to be.

Open-Market Operations

Although the ability to change reserve requirements and the discount rate are both important elements of Federal Reserve monetary policy, the infrequency of change in the reserve requirements and the generally lagged nature of the

---

[4]The Fed explicitly sets the discount rate; however, the Fed may *influence* the Federal funds rate through its open-market operations, discussed later in the chapter.

Figure 3-1 The Discount Rate and the Treasury Bill Rate, 1978–1993

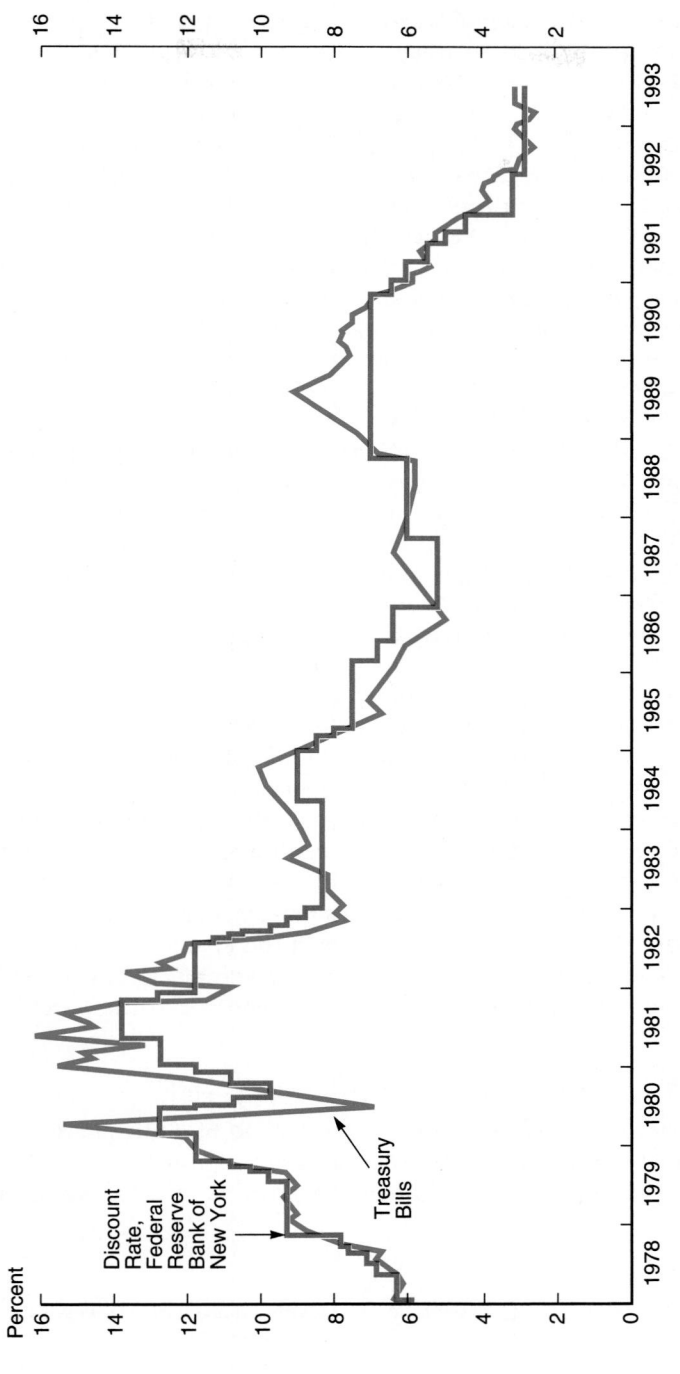

The Federal Reserve System makes loans to banks to correct temporary imbalances in their required reserves, charging a rate of interest known as the discount rate. First envisioned as a major instrument of monetary control, the Fed's discount rate has instead frequently lagged behind other short-term rates. This figure, for example, shows how the Treasury bill rate often led the discount rate from 1978 to 1993.

Sources: Economic Indicators, December 1992; *Monetary Trends*, The Federal Reserve Bank of St. Louis, January 1993; *The Wall Street Journal*, March–July 1993; and *Federal Reserve Bulletin*, March 1993.

discount rate indicate that they are not the Fed's most important tools. *Open-market operations are the most useful instrument of monetary policy available to the Federal Reserve.* Unlike changes in the reserve requirements, which would be likely to trigger massive changes in bank reserves, securities may be bought and sold in any quantity to effect slight changes in the economy.

Assume that the Federal Open Market Committee has determined that an expansion in the money supply and a lowering of interest rates is desirable to stimulate a depressed economy. The FOMC will direct the Federal Reserve Bank of New York to *buy* government securities through government securities dealers.[5] The Federal Reserve Bank pays for its purchases with a check drawn on its own account. The securities dealer deposits the check in a bank, which now has an increase in excess reserves. It is important to note that this increase in reserves does not take away from the reserves of any other bank; rather, it comes from new funds that the Fed has created by drawing a check on its own account. This action obtains the desired results in two ways. First, as the Fed purchases securities, demand will exceed supply and the price of securities will rise. The increase in price has the effect of reducing the securities' yield.[6] This interest rate effect will spread to other sectors of the financial markets, reducing yields on other interest-bearing securities, including the rates charged for loans. Second, the bank will usually wish to lend the excess reserves, which were generated by the government securities dealer's deposit of the Fed's check. To stimulate borrowing, the bank will further lower the interest rate it charges on loans. Thus, the purchase of government securities by the Fed has increased the money supply and put in motion events which will serve to lower interest rates. These lower interest rates and easier credit will encourage additional borrowing and spending, providing benefits to the depressed economy.[7]

On the other hand, during a period of excessive expansion, or inflation, the FOMC will *sell* securities to reduce bank reserves. Then, as the supply of securities increases relative to demand, the securities' prices will fall, resulting in an increase in interest rates. Through a series of steps exactly opposite to those traced before, the Fed's sale of government securities will ultimately translate into a shrinking of the nation's money supply and higher interest rates throughout the economy. A little later in the chapter, we will look at the sequence of events that followed the Fed's intervention in two specific instances, but first we need to examine exactly how deposit expansion occurs.

demand deposits

Transaction deposits at commercial banks that are available on demand, usually through a check.

Demand Deposit Creation

Demand deposits are deposits made by individuals, businesses, and government units that are available on demand, usually through a check. Banks are the most important element in our financial system, not so much because of the

---

[5]The Fed does not buy securities directly from individuals or banks. A designated set of government securities dealers buys the securities from, or sells them to, the general public and the banks.

[6]The inverse relationship between securities prices and rates of return will be discussed in Chapters 4 and 16.

[7]The Federal Reserve must take care not to overstimulate the economy through excessive creation of credit, which would lead to expectations of greater inflation.

services they provide, but because of two other important factors. First, commercial banks are important to the economy because demand deposits are money, and the bank can create demand deposits through the extension of credit in the form of loans. Second, banks are important because the Federal Reserve Board utilizes the banking system to affect the money supply and, therefore, interest rates. Thus, in the United States, demand deposits, not currency, are the most important form of money, and commercial banks are at the heart of the nation's financial system because of their ability to create money.[8]

As mentioned earlier in the chapter, the Fed requires a bank to maintain stated percentages of its demand, time, and savings deposits on reserve at the Fed or in vault cash, but the bank can lend the remainder of the deposited funds to others. For example, if the overall reserve requirement were 25 percent, a $1,000 deposit would require a reserve of $250, and the remaining $750 would be considered excess or free reserves, which could be loaned or invested by the bank. It is primarily through its loans, and, secondarily, through its investments, that the bank makes a profit.

The economy has a certain amount of productive capacity. Given our labor force, natural resources, and capital equipment, we can turn out only so many autos, hamburgers, houses, and so forth. If the economy is operating close to capacity, any increase in the money supply will simply lead to price increases, or inflation. The Federal Reserve has a primary goal of controlling inflation, and it seeks to exercise this control through the money supply. The money supply consists of two elements, currency and the far larger and more important element, bank deposits. For every $100 of deposits shown among total claims on the balance sheet, banks can have loans and investments of something less than $100, with the difference being a reserve held by a Federal Reserve bank.

If the economy slows down, as it would during a recession, and the Fed wants to expand the money supply in an effort to stimulate production, then the Fed will make additional reserves available to the banking system. The banks will then typically make credit available to borrowers. The way this will work is as follows: The bank will grant a loan, creating a deposit in the name of the borrower, who can then spend the money by writing checks. Those checks will, in turn, be deposited in the same or a different bank, and the money supply (bank deposits) will increase. (Of course, the Fed can reverse the process — it can reduce the supply of reserves, which will force the banking system to contract the amount of deposits, hence reduce the money supply.)

We see, then, that the banking system's ability to expand the money supply depends on the existence of excess reserves. By lending excess reserves, banks create money; furthermore, the action is perfectly legal. To illustrate the process, assume that there are currently no excess reserves in the banking system and that the Fed's reserve requirement is 15 percent.[9] The Fed can increase reserves, hence the money supply, by buying short-term Treasury securities.

---

[8]Recently other financial intermediaries have gained the right to expand money and credit, but these efforts are *quite* limited when compared with those of the banking system. However, in the discussion of demand deposit creation, when we refer to "banks," other depository institutions are considered included.

[9]Actually, reserve requirements depend on the size and type of deposits at a commercial bank.

Table 3-1

Deposit Expansion —
Commercial Banking
System

	New Loans	Reserves Required	Reserves Excess	Total Demand Deposits
Initial demand deposit of $1,000		$ 150	$850	$1,000
Expansion stage				
1	$ 850	128	722	1,850
2	722	108	614	2,572
3	614	92	522	3,186
4	522	78	444	3,708
5	444	67	377	4,152
6	377	57	320	4,529
7	320	48	272	4,849
8	272	41	231	5,121
.	.	.	.	.
.	.	.	.	.
.	.	.	.	.
Cumulative effect	$5,667	$1,000	$ 0	$6,667

Assume that the Fed buys $1,000 of Treasury bills from a government securities dealer. The dealer deposits the $1,000 into a checking account, and that deposit becomes an addition to the reserves in the commercial banking system.

Think of this initial $1,000 reserve infusion into the banking system as funds which had previously been out of circulation, inaccessible to the banking system, which now flow into the banking system. With a reserve requirement of 15 percent, the bank which receives the $1,000 dealer deposit must now hold $150 as required reserves, but the other $850 may be lent out.

Total reserves gained from the Fed's purchase of T-bills	$1,000
Required reserves based on initial $1,000 deposit	$ 150
Excess reserves after initial $1,000 deposit	$ 850

The $1,000 becomes the first increment of a potentially much larger increase in the money supply, and this deposit expansion is shown in Table 3-1.

Assume that a creditworthy customer applies for a loan of $850 to purchase some major appliances. If the bank which received the $1,000 initially decides to make this loan, the $850 is credited to the customer's account, and when the appliances have been bought and paid for, the $850 ends up in the appliance dealer's account. Possibly, this account is in a different bank but this will not end the expansion process. Whichever bank receives the deposit also acquires an equal amount of reserves, of which all but 15 percent will be excess and may become a new loan. Thus, at each stage of the process, total loans and total deposits increase by an amount equal to the excess reserves before the last loan was made. In other words, each succeeding loan can equal, at most, 85 percent of the previous one. In theory, this process can continue through several stages until there are no excess reserves remaining.

In our example, we see that it is theoretically possible for the commercial banking system to expand the original $1,000 initial deposit into $5,667 in new loans since banks need to maintain only 15 percent of each deposited dollar in reserves. We can also determine the maximum possible expansion in deposits by using the following formula:

$$\text{Maximum deposit expansion} = \frac{\text{Initial reserve infusion}}{\text{Reserve requirement}}. \qquad (3\text{-}1)$$

In our example,

$$\text{Maximum deposit expansion} = \frac{\$1,000}{0.15} = \$6,667,$$

which includes the $5,667 in new loans and the initial $1,000 deposit.

Realistically, however, three factors may lessen the *actual* deposit expansion. (1) If customers decide to keep some of their newly created demand deposits as cash rather than in the bank, there will be less excess reserves available to lend. (2) Banks may decide, as a matter of policy, to keep some excess reserves in case of unexpected losses therefore lending out less than 85 percent in each case. (3) There may be a scarcity of qualified borrowers, again resulting in less than the entire excess reserves being lent out at each stage of the process. These factors could create "leakages" that would reduce the deposit-expansion potential within the commercial banking system. Of course, the Fed can also *decrease* the money supply by *selling* Treasury securities and thus reversing the process; we will look at such a case in the next section.

Two Illustrations of Federal Reserve Open-Market Operations

In the fall of 1981, after two years of record-high inflation, the Fed used its open-market operations to slow down the overheated economy and reduce inflation. The following sequence of events took place:

1. The FOMC sold government securities to government securities dealers.

2. Dealers paid for these securities by check.

3. The supply of government securities in the market increased relative to demand.

4. Prices of government securities dropped due to the greater supply, and prices of debt securities, in general, declined as well. This happened because markets are interrelated and changes in one market will, therefore, cause changes in other segments of the financial markets — a ripple effect.

5. There is an inverse relationship between the market price of a debt security and its yield, or interest rate.[10] Therefore, interest rates rose on all debt securities.

---

[10]You are not expected to understand at this point *why* this inverse relationship exists. We will prove mathematically in Chapter 16 that this is always the case, as long as we are dealing with fixed-rate debt securities. For now, simply take on faith that this is a fact; we will refer to this relationship again in Chapter 4.

6. As government securities dealers' checks for the purchased securities cleared, banks lost reserves. The effect of reserve deficiencies for individual banks quickly spread throughout the banking system, as banks attempted to replenish their reserves through the interbank Federal funds market.

7. The rate of interest on Federal funds was bid up due to the greater demand.

8. Banks were also forced to sell securities and reduce their loan portfolios to generate needed reserves.

9. The sale of securities by banks, along with those sold by the Fed, further depressed the securities' prices and increased their yields (interest rates).

10. Because banks had fewer excess reserves, the availability of credit declined, further increasing interest rates.

In summary, the sale of securities by the Fed reduced the ability of banks to lend and resulted in higher interest rates throughout the economy, which acted as a deterrent to borrowing. The resulting reduction in debt-financed spending had the effect of curbing inflation.

The sequence of events described generally takes anywhere from 6 to 12 months to work its way through the economy. This means that, in practice, it is very easy for the Fed to overshoot the mark since the effects of any steps it takes at a particular point in time will not be seen for at least 6 months, and during that time, other factors will also influence the economy.

In retrospect, we can see that the Fed's action in 1981 was highly successful in terms of curbing inflation. The annual rate of inflation fell from a high of around 12 percent to today's level of about 3 percent. But the process was painful; short-term interest rates shot up above 16 percent, long-term rates were nearly as high for a brief period, and a severe recession followed. Finally, you should understand that the Fed is constantly conducting open-market operations, sometimes easing and at other times tightening, in its attempt to fine tune the economy. The action it took in the fall of 1981 was chosen as an illustration because it was a very extreme move by the Fed and its consequences, therefore, were easier to observe.

credit crunch

A period in which capital is scarce and interest rates, typically, are high.

The series of events described above ended in what is commonly called a **credit crunch,** a period of scarce capital and, usually, high interest rates. That was precisely the point of the Fed's intervention in 1981 since this was a necessary step in "squeezing out" inflation. Now let us turn to a very different situation, namely, the one facing the Fed in early 1991. While the United States was engaged in war against Saddam Hussein in Iraq, the country was battling a recession at home. In response to rising unemployment, the Fed had already cut the discount rate twice in less than two months (and would go on to cut it many more times), had completely eliminated the reserve requirement on certain corporate certificates of deposit in late 1990 (the first time the reserve requirements had been changed since 1983), and was considering *encouraging* banks to borrow at the "discount window," a most unusual step since the Fed typically frowns on repeated borrowing by banks. Why such drastic measures? By way of answering, let us trace the initial Fed action and the subsequent results in the financial markets.

The Fed wanted to boost the recessionary economy, and it, therefore, initiated the opposite chain of events from that discussed earlier:

1. The Fed bought government securities from dealers.
2. Dealers deposited their receipts into the banking system.
3. The supply of government securities decreased relative to demand.
4. Prices of government and corporate debt securities increased due to the lower overall supply.
5. Interest rates (yields) fell.
6. Banks gained reserves, as dealers deposited their checks.
7. The Federal funds rate dropped, as banks had less need to borrow in the interbank Federal funds market.
8. Banks had excess reserves and could expand their holdings of securities, if they chose to do so.
9. Prices of securities increased further, and their yields (interest rates) declined.
10. Because banks had more reserves, they had the option of making more loans, and *credit should have been readily available.*

This series of steps depicts the way the economy, interest rates, and bankers *normally* react when the Fed introduces easier monetary policy. Yet, in spite of the Fed's (and the Bush administration's) strong wish to end the recession by bringing down interest rates and making credit widely available, only half of the desired outcome resulted. Short-term interest rates did come down as planned, but banks were reluctant to lend to all but the very strongest firms, and a very different kind of credit crunch developed: Low interest rates *and scarce capital for expansion.* This is not the way monetary policy is supposed to work! In fact, bankers and analysts alike agreed in February 1991 that low interest rates and plentiful reserves alone would *not* induce bankers to lend. What was going on?

The short answer is that regulation of banks had become much more severe in the late 1980s and early 1990s, and so, rather than run afoul of bank regulators, bankers chose to curtail their lending to most small and medium-sized firms and instead invested excess reserves into U.S. Treasury securities, an action which did nothing for deposit expansion and the money supply. (Refer back to the earlier discussion of leakages, which have the effect of reducing deposit expansion.) This phenomenon, where banks are not willing to lend, for whatever reason, has been likened to the Fed "pushing on a string"; unless you have a mighty stiff string, nothing happens at the other end.

At this point, you should begin to understand that being a central banker and trying to keep inflation under control while keeping the economy on an even keel — or getting it back on track when it is already in a recession — is far from an easy task. This particular case of Fed intervention was used to illustrate that the Fed indeed cannot control all the variables needed to fine tune the economy.

To more fully understand our commercial banking system, we next need to compare commercial banks with other large financial institutions in terms of the composition of their assets and liabilities, as well as their overall size. We must also look at the differences between our system and those of other large, industrialized countries, examine a typical U.S. bank balance sheet at different points in time to highlight trends, and discuss briefly the regulations that govern our banks. The reference made previously to recent tighter banking regulation can then be put in its proper perspective.

? Self-Test

Name the primary bank regulators identified in this section. What is the purpose of the Federal Deposit Insurance Corporation (FDIC)?

What is the Federal Reserve System?

What are the three principal tools used by the Fed to conduct monetary policy? Briefly explain how each of these tools works.

Banks enjoy their status in our financial system, not so much because of the services they provide, but because of two other very important factors. What are these two factors?

If the Fed's reserve requirement were increased from 15 percent to 20 percent in the example given in this section, what would the maximum deposit expansion be on the $1,000 initial deposit?

Briefly describe the nature of the Fed's monetary policy in 1981 and 1991. Were the results of the Fed intervention, in terms of interest rates and credit availability, as intended in both instances? Explain.

Overview of Financial Institutions

In Table 3-2 we present a brief summary of the major financial institutions in the U.S. economy. As you can see from the table, commercial banks are one of the largest of the U.S financial institutions in terms of asset size, further demonstrating the importance of banks in our economy.

As we learned in Chapter 2, the financial institutions listed in Table 3-2 are intermediaries — they take funds deposited by individuals and businesses, and they then lend those funds to various borrowers. Column 2 of Table 3-2, labeled "Principal Assets," shows the type of assets held by each institution, and Column 3 shows the principal types of liabilities each institution issues. Financial intermediaries increase the efficiency of our economy by bringing together economic units with surplus funds and those in need of funds.

An important trend has emerged in terms of pension funds and mutual funds over the last few years: These two types of financial intermediaries have shown enormous growth. While total assets of all commercial banks grew by only a little over 12 percent from mid-1990 to December 1992 (in large part due to regulatory restraints), pension fund assets increased by about 54 percent, and mutual fund assets by an astounding 188 percent over the same time period. Mutual funds have become hugely popular because, although these institutions do not offer insurance protection, as do banks and other depository institutions, they have attracted individual savers who have increasingly become dissatisfied with the low interest rates offered by banks, S&Ls, and others in the early 1990s.

Table 3-2   Financial Institutions Summary: December 1992

Type of Institution (1)	Principal Assets (2)	Principal Liabilities (3)	Total Assets (Millions) (4)	Principal Regulators (5)
Commercial banks	Business and consumer loans, mortgages, and government securities	Checking, savings, and time deposits	$3,651,345	Federal Reserve Board, Comptroller of the Currency, and FDIC
Savings and loan associations (thrifts)	Mortgages	Savings and time deposits	849,823	Office of Thrift Supervision and FDIC/SAIF
Credit unions	Consumer loans	Savings deposits	299,135	National Credit Union Administration
Life insurance companies	Corporate bonds, mortgages, and real estate	Life insurance policies	1,643,699	State insurance commissioners
Pension funds	Government securities, corporate stocks and bonds	Pension fund reserves	3,800,000	Federal government, Employee Retirement Income Security Act of 1974 (ERISA)
Mutual funds	Government securities, municipal bonds, corporate stocks, bonds, and short-term debt instruments	Mutual fund shares	1,600,000	Securities and Exchange Commission

Sources: *Federal Reserve Bulletin,* March 1993, Tables A19 and A71; "The Power of Mutual Funds," *Business Week,* January 18, 1993; "Pension-Fund Executives Spin Scenarios That Might Bring Next Market Crash," *The Wall Street Journal,* October 16, 1992; and Sheshunoff Information Services, Inc.

Bond and common stock mutual funds do offer higher expected returns, but on these types of investments, there will always be the potential for loss as well. There is some concern among financial advisors and market analysts in 1993 that many individuals do not fully understand this risk-return tradeoff as they reach for higher yields. Although each institution listed in Table 3-2 is important, our major focus in this chapter is on the commercial banking industry.

Self-Test

For each intermediary listed in Table 3-2, list the principal assets and liabilities.

Which two types of financial institutions have shown particularly rapid growth during the last few years?

The Commercial Banking System

The commercial banking system, as shown in Table 3-2, held well above $3.6 trillion in deposits at the end of 1992. Banks convert most of these deposits into loans and securities, making them the primary source of short- to intermediate-term credit for state and local governments, businesses, and consumers.

The U.S. banking system is quite different from that in other industrialized countries, as we shall see later in the chapter in our discussion of globalization. Canada, Great Britain, Germany, and Japan all have a few large banks with nationwide operations. In the United States, however, there are approximately 11,500 separately chartered commercial banks (down from more than 14,000 in 1990). We have so many banks because of our history of restricting the activities of banks to a single state and, in some states, to just one office (no branches). The early designers of our banking system were concerned over the apparent concentration of economic power in European banks. Consequently, they allowed each state to design its own banking system, and, until the 1980s, all states prohibited interstate banking. Many states, including Texas, Illinois, and Florida, would not allow any bank to operate more than one office. Such restrictive banking regulations encouraged the development of small, local institutions.

As mentioned earlier, another unique feature of U.S. banking is the dual (state and federal government) chartering system. Prior to 1863, all banks were chartered by their home states. Then, the federal government began chartering banks after the passage of the National Bank Act of 1863. This Act set up the Office of the Comptroller of the Currency (OCC) to charter, examine, and if necessary close national banks. National banks, however, do not operate nationwide; they are subject to the same interstate banking restrictions as state-chartered banks. Recently, however, many of the restrictions on branch and interstate banking have been eased. These changes will be discussed in greater detail later in the chapter. Many states have made regional banking pacts which allow interstate banking within the region. Such pacts exist in New England, the Southeast, and the Midwest. Moreover, California and other states either have opened or will be opening their borders to banks from all states. The breakdown of geographic barriers is leading to a system with larger banks and more competition, as well as to innovation in the banking markets.

Banking Regulation of the 1980s

The banking system has changed dramatically during the past 10 to 15 years. During the 1980s, many banks became virtual financial supermarkets, offering savings certificates, retirement plans, trust and leasing departments, discount brokerage services, and insurance products. Many of these products and services are actually offered by subsidiaries of the banks' holding companies. A **bank holding company (BHC)** is an organizational structure, which owns banks and nonbank subsidiaries. BHCs were originally designed to circumvent bank regulations, but their activities are now restricted by the Bank Holding Company Acts of 1956 and 1970, under which the Federal Reserve determines the products and services a BHC may offer. Much of the deregulation of the 1980s has resulted from Fed decrees increasing the number of permissible activities under the Bank Holding Company Acts.

During the 1980s, a number of Congressional Acts were also passed which affected banking. One of these was DIDMCA, commonly known as the Monetary Control Act of 1980, which eliminated deposit rate and loan rate ceilings and removed differences between Fed member and nonmember banks. For example, after an initial phase-in period, the reserve requirements became the same for all depository institutions, regardless of whether they are members of the Fed-

bank holding company (BHC)

A corporation which owns banks and nonbank subsidiaries, originally designed to circumvent bank regulation.

In general, competition is fierce, both within banking and from nonbank financial services firms encroaching on banks' traditional turf. Whatever this competition may mean for banks, it is clear that customers already have a wide range of options when seeking financial services.

Source: Andrew Powell, Illustrator.

eral Reserve System or not. At the present time, reserve requirements range from 0 percent on certain corporate time deposits to 10 percent on demand deposits in very large banks. This legislation also increased deposit insurance limits for all depository institutions from $40,000 to $100,000 per account. More than any other piece of legislation, the Monetary Control Act of 1980 has lead to increased competition among financial institutions, as each seeks to invade the areas of financial services previously the domains of others. This heightened competition continues today.

Garn–St. Germain Act

A thrift bailout act which allowed banks to buy failing thrifts.

The **Garn–St. Germain Act** of 1982, primarily a thrift bailout act, allowed banks to buy failing thrifts; the crisis surrounding the savings and loan industry will be discussed in detail later in the chapter. In 1987, Congress passed the

Competitive Equality in Banking Act (CEBA)

An act passed in 1987 to stem the growth of bank-like corporations.

Financial Institutions Reform, Recovery, and Enforcement Act (FIRREA)

An act passed in 1989 that restructured the thrift industry.

Competitive Equality in Banking Act (CEBA) to stem the growth of bank-like subsidiaries of companies such as Sears, Roebuck and Merrill Lynch, and in 1989 Congress voted for a major restructuring of the thrift industry in the **Financial Institutions Reform, Recovery, and Enforcement Act (FIRREA).**

We will take up the discussion of banking regulation again toward the end of this chapter, with emphasis on developments of the 1990s, but first we need to look at bank balance sheets to understand the implications of more recent legislation.

Sources and Uses of Bank Funds

A review of a typical commercial bank's balance sheet provides information about the sources of bank funds and the uses to which those funds are put.[11] Look at Table 3-3 as you read this section.

Bank Liabilities and Equity. Deposits are a bank's primary source of funds and a major component of the economy's money supply, so Congress has been careful to protect these accounts. While the stated deposit insurance limit is $100,000, virtually all deposits have, until quite recently, been covered. The FDIC maintains that, from its creation through the 1980s, 98 percent of all deposits in failing banks have been recovered.[12] Because deposit insurance allows banks and thrifts to issue risk-free debt, but then to invest funds received in highly speculative ventures, this insurance has been somewhat controversial. Deposit insurance has played a crucial role in the savings and loan crisis, which is discussed later in this chapter.

There are three types of deposits—demand, savings (passbook), and time deposits. Demand deposits, at one time the primary source of bank funds, are the major source of liquidity for all economic units. Banks attract deposits by offering transactions services and by paying interest. A bank's ability to pay interest was in the past limited in order to hold down banks' costs and thus make them safer. From 1933 through 1980, banks were prohibited from paying interest on demand deposits by **Regulation Q.** During this period, banks attracted deposits by offering such features as free checks, free services, and an occasional toaster or blender. Late in the 1970s, however, it became clear that toasters were not enough. Depositors, faced with inflation rates of 7 to 12 percent, were taking their money out of banks and placing it in money market mutual funds. Through the lobbying efforts of banks, regulators, and consumers, Congress passed the Monetary Control Act of 1980, which has already been discussed. However, the relevant aspect in this connection is that it created a new type of transaction account—one which pays interest. That account, a form of savings

Regulation Q

A rule which, from 1933 through 1980, prohibited banks from paying interest on demand deposits.

---

[11]Although this presentation of a bank's balance sheet is not technical, some readers may wish to refer to Chapter 5, "Examining a Firm's Financial Data," where balance sheets are discussed in greater detail, before continuing with this chapter.

[12]Similar programs such as the Federal Savings and Loan Insurance Corporation (FSLIC) and the National Credit Union Insurance Fund (NCUIF) were set up to protect deposits for the savings and loan and credit union industries. The FSLIC has since been eliminated due to large losses in the thrift industry, and thrift industry deposits are now insured by the Savings Association Insurance Fund (SAIF), which is administered by the FDIC.

Table 3-3

Banking Industry
Percentage Balance Sheet

Percentage of Total Assets	1980	1987	1989	1992
Cash	17.90%	11.54%	8.01%	6.47%
Federal funds and repos	3.80	2.55	2.33	5.38
Securities	18.00	14.65	17.72	21.87
Loans	54.30	62.05	62.23	58.16
Miscellaneous assets	6.00	9.21	9.71	8.12
Total assets	100.00%	100.00%	100.00%	100.00%
Demand deposits	23.30%	14.96%	19.86%	21.89%
Time and savings deposits	40.70	55.81	50.08	47.72
Federal funds and repos	7.20	8.61	8.24	8.53
Other short-term debt	23.00	5.51	6.06	5.14
Long-term debt	0.00	9.36	9.47	9.39
Capital (equity)	5.80	5.75	6.29	7.33
Total claims	100.00%	100.00%	100.00%	100.00%

NOW (negotiable order of withdrawal) account

A form of savings account that allows withdrawal by check.

certificate of deposit (CD)

A time deposit evidenced by a negotiable or non-negotiable receipt issued for funds deposited for a specified period of time.

repurchase agreement (repo)

A collateralized loan by one financial institution to another.

account that allows withdrawal by check and which is offered by banks, savings and loans, and credit unions, is referred to as a **NOW (negotiable order of withdrawal) account.** NOW accounts, however, are not available to a bank's corporate customers.

Today, as you can see from Table 3-3, the most important sources of bank funds are time and savings deposits. Savings accounts generally pay close to the market interest rates and offer limited transactions services. Time deposits offer higher rates but do not allow transactions. The most common type of time deposit is a **CD,** or **certificate of deposit.** A CD is a receipt for funds deposited in an institution for a specified time which pays a specific interest rate. Generally, the interest rate on CDs increases with the term to maturity. Certificates of deposit were known but not widely used until 1961, when Citibank of New York announced that it would issue CDs in negotiable form, meaning that the funds could be obtained before maturity by selling the CD in a secondary market to another investor. Because these CDs are negotiable, they attract business funds and other deposits in large denominations, beginning at $100,000. Other certificates in much smaller denominations are available to individuals and other small savers, but, unlike the larger $100,000 CDs, the smaller savings certificates are not negotiable.[13]

In addition to deposits, banks may choose to finance a part of their assets with borrowed funds. The primary source of borrowed funds is the Federal funds market which was discussed in connection with the Fed's monetary policy earlier in the chapter. Another source of short-term borrowings for a bank is the repo market. A **repurchase agreement,** or **repo,** is a collateralized loan (one for which security is held) by one financial institution to another financial institution. Treasury securities are generally used as collateral for these short-term loans. A small portion of a bank's short-term borrowings may be obtained

---

[13]CD rates are set by the institution; however, if a saver must redeem a certificate before its maturity date, the interest rate paid is the passbook rate minus an early withdrawal penalty, generally three months' interest.

from the Federal Reserve System itself; however, banks are restricted in what they can do with funds obtained as loans from the Fed, and, consequently, they prefer not to borrow from the Fed unless absolutely necessary. Finally, banks can obtain funds by selling long-term bonds.

capital account

The account that represents a bank's total assets minus its liabilities.

A bank's **capital account** is similar to a business firm's net worth or common stock equity account. This account reveals the owners' contributions to the bank's financing, both through the purchase of common stock and through undistributed profits which are retained by the bank. The total assets of the bank minus liabilities equal the bank's capital. Note also that regulatory capital rules allow banks to count some portion of their long-term debt as capital.

Bank capital is important both to the bank and to its regulators. Before deposits were insured, bank capital protected depositors from losses, and, today, a bank's capital protects the deposit insurance fund, taxpayers, and the bank's unsecured creditors from losses. Bank losses generally occur as a result of loans that cannot be repaid or poor investments, and these losses are charged against the bank's capital. The typical commercial bank has only 7 to 10 percent of its assets financed by capital. Thus, the traditional banker's conservative attitude is well founded because loans or investments can decline by only 7 to 10 percent before the bank becomes insolvent.

Although we have not yet looked at balance sheets of other types of corporations, you should know that manufacturing firms, in general, are usually not considered financially sound, unless at least 50 percent of their total financing has been provided by equity. In other words, banks have much slimmer margins for error, and that by itself, is probably a good reason why banks should be subject to relatively strict regulations, especially since taxpayers bear the ultimate risk when banks fail. Finally, note that capital as a percentage of total assets, for the banking industry as a whole, has increased and is higher for 1992 than for any of the other years shown. This is not by accident. As we will discuss later in the chapter, this is the result of much tighter banking regulation taking effect in 1991 and 1992.

Bank Assets.   Banks do more than simply act as safekeepers for depositors' funds. In fact, they keep very little of a depositor's cash on hand. According to Table 3-3, cash today accounts for less than 7 percent of a bank's total assets. This percentage is down substantially from earlier periods, signifying that bankers have become more efficient cash managers. The cash account includes more than just vault cash. Part of the **cash account** includes "items in process of collection," which is the value of checks drawn on other banks but not yet collected. The cash account also includes funds that are required to be kept on deposit at the district Federal Reserve Bank.

cash account

The account that represents a bank's vault cash, checks in process of collection, and funds required to be kept on deposit with the Federal Reserve.

Of the three components of the cash account — vault cash, checks in process, and funds on deposit at the District Bank — actual cash kept at the bank for daily transactions, or vault cash, would be the smallest amount for most banks. First, banks are able to maintain relatively small amounts of vault cash because normal transactions generally result in approximately the same amount of cash deposits as cash withdrawals. Second, like other businesses, banks prefer to keep their funds invested in productive, income-producing assets. Excess cash is therefore channeled into more productive loans and investments.

Another use of funds is the purchase of investment securities. These securities are legally required to be of the highest investment quality — highly liquid and having low risk — so that they may be converted into cash quickly, and with little chance of loss. Typically, most of these securities are issued by the state and other political subdivisions in the bank's geographic area. U.S. Treasury securities also account for a large portion of the bank's investment portfolio. Investments provide a return for a bank, and they can also be sold quickly to raise additional cash if it is needed.

A bank will usually consider one of its main purposes to be lending money in support of economic growth in its area, and loans also have a higher expected rate of return than investments. However, if there is not enough demand for loans, banks must turn to investment in securities as a source of revenue. Also keep in mind that banks are corporations and have stockholders, so, like other publicly traded firms (which most banks are), their primary goal should be to maximize stockholder wealth.

Banks are the major source of short-term credit for the business sector. Historically, they have preferred to make "self-liquidating loans." For example, in our agrarian past, a farmer would borrow money to buy seed and, upon harvest, would repay the loan with the proceeds of the crop's sale. A modern example of a self-liquidating loan would be a merchant's borrowing to increase inventory before Christmas. After Christmas, the merchant would repay the loan from the proceeds of the holiday sales. These short-term loans were the historical rule for banks because their primary source of funds was short-term demand deposits. However, since the greater proportion of funds now comes from time and savings deposits, banks are today generally more willing to provide intermediate-term loans (three- to seven-year maturities). Some loans, such as real estate loans, have even longer maturities.

As Table 3-3 illustrates, in 1992 approximately 58 percent of bank assets were the loans banks had extended. Note also that 1992 loans represent a decline from 1989 of approximately 4 percentage points, while securities held by banks increased by about 4 percentage points over the same time period. Although loan demand normally drops off during a recession, this is not the entire reason. As we will explain later in the chapter, this shift in bank assets — away from loans and toward investment in securities — is due primarily to changes in the regulatory environment of banks and has contributed to the credit crunch of the early 1990s.

? Self-Test

In terms of number of banks, how does the U.S. banking system differ from those of other industrialized nations?

How did the U.S. banking system change during the 1980s?

Briefly explain the difference between demand deposits and certificates of deposit (CDs).

What is meant by a bank's capital account, and why is it important to regulators?

What are the three components of a bank's cash account?

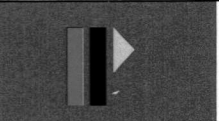

INDUSTRY PRACTICE

THE THRIFT CRISIS: WHAT HAPPENED, AND WHO IS GOING TO PAY?

What has happened to the savings and loan industry? How could an industry created with such a noble goal — promoting home ownership — turn into such a nightmare? The cost of the S&L fiasco to taxpayers will be hundreds of billions of dollars, and, when interest on the debt incurred to fund the bailout is considered, the cost rises to trillions of dollars. How did the losses occur? How are we going to pay to clean up the mess? And, finally, what is the current status of the bailout?

To understand how the crisis arose, we must examine the S&L industry's history. Congress, in an effort to encourage thrift and to promote home ownership, passed legislation in the early 1930s which created a regulatory structure similar to that for banks but specifically designed to make capital available to homeowners. The Federal Home Loan Bank (FHLB) system was set up to mimic the functions of the Federal Reserve, while the Federal Savings and Loan Insurance Corporation (FSLIC) insured deposits for the thrift industry. S&Ls were also given favorable tax and regulatory treatment, including permission to offer a higher rate to savers than banks, if they invested 80 to 85 percent of their assets in mortgage-related investments. For the next 40 years, S&Ls thrived in their specially created market niche.

Unfortunately, the typical S&L portfolio mix represented a "ticking time bomb." To keep their regulatory and tax advantages, S&Ls invested in 20- and 30-year fixed-rate mortgages, but they got their investible funds as relatively short-term, interest-rate-sensitive deposits. This strategy was profitable as long as short-term interest rates were below long-term rates, but it proved disastrous when the opposite happened in the late 1970s and early 1980s. The S&Ls' assets consisted of mortgages acquired back when interest rates were low, but liabilities required interest payments based on the high current level of interest rates. If they did not offer a competitive rate to depositors, funds would be withdrawn, and people making withdrawals wanted cash, not old mortgages which paid low rates

Sources: "Time to Speed Up the S&L Cleanup," *Fortune,* November 16, 1992; and "Package to Complete S&L Bailout Gets Approval of House Banking Committee," *The Wall Street Journal,"* May 7, 1993.

and whose current market values were below their stated values. As a result, by 1980 the S&Ls profits had vanished, most of their equity was wiped out, and the industry was collapsing.

Congress reacted to the growing crisis by partially deregulating the industry. In 1980, the S&Ls were allowed to offer checking accounts, and the deposit insurance limit was expanded. However, these new powers did little to improve S&L profitability, so in 1982 Congress changed the very nature of the industry by greatly expanding the investment powers of S&Ls. They were suddenly allowed to offer a wide variety of consumer loans, to make some commercial loans, to invest in junk bonds, and, most importantly, to make direct investments in real estate. Previously, S&Ls simply made loans, but now they were allowed to develop condominium projects, office buildings, housing subdivisions, and shopping centers.

These new powers brought in a new breed of S&L owner. Real estate developers saw ownership of an S&L as a gold mine — they could raise money through federally insured deposits and then use those funds to finance risky real estate projects or invest in junk bonds.

These problems pointed out a fatal flaw in the nation's deposit insurance system, a flaw particularly exploited by the owners of Vernon, Empire, American, and Lincoln Savings — just to name a few of the S&Ls involved. Under the deposit insurance system, accounts up to $100,000 are guaranteed, but those above $100,000 are not. However, in most failures, larger depositors recovered most if not all of their funds. Depositors, consequently, paid little attention to the management or financial condition of their institutions. They simply evaluated thrifts on the basis of their interest rates, convenience, and services offered, not on their financial strength. Therefore, an S&L could grow rapidly by simply offering the highest interest rates. Money brokers would then send millions into high-rate CD accounts. Hundreds of banks and S&Ls grew 20 to 40 percent a year by using brokered deposits. Without depositor discipline, S&L managers and owners could play a game of "heads we win, tails you lose." If high-risk real estate and junk bond investments paid off, the thrift managers and owners would reap the benefits. If not, the thrift would fail and deposit insurance (backed by U.S. taxpayers) would cover the loss. Unfortunately, the latter situation occurred for hundreds of S&Ls. To make matters worse, many losses also resulted from fraudulent activities that were not detected by inexperienced accountants and examiners.

In 1989, Congress ordered a complete reorganization of the thrift industry. The Federal Home Loan Bank Board was replaced by the Office of Thrift Supervision (OTS), a new division of the Treasury. The OTS is responsible for taking over failing S&Ls and then handing them over to the Resolution Trust Corporation (RTC), which was created to sell foreclosed property. Congress also created the Resolution Financing Corporation (RFC) to raise the billions of dollars needed to pay off the depositors in failed thrifts. Deposit insurance was taken over by an arm of the FDIC, and premiums charged to thrifts were increased, but the bulk of the bailout cost will be borne by taxpayers.

So, we go back to our original questions:

1. What happened? Savings and loans have lost hundreds of billions of dollars; no one knows exactly how much. Hundreds of S&Ls have been closed, and several hundred additional thrift failures are anticipated.

2. How did this happen? Savings and loans were designed in the 1930s, in a calmer economic climate. The industry had a fatal structural defect that made it unable to survive the volatile economic conditions of the past two decades — it financed long-term assets with short-term deposits. Also, deregulation occurred at the wrong time, without a corresponding change in the deposit insurance system and without adequate controls and audits. The new thrift owners and managers were able to gamble on risky real estate deals, and many lost.

3. How did the losses occur? What happened to the money? It did not just disappear, but it has been filtered into the economy. The media focuses on fraud, and it is true that several billions were lost to fraud. However, most of the hundreds of billions that were lost did not just evaporate. Some of the money went to finance unnecessary construction projects and, consequently, was paid to contractors and employees. Much of the money went to mortgage customers, who received cheap credit, and to depositors, who received high interest rates. So, we really had a shifting of funds from taxpayers to other parties.

4. How are we going to pay for this crisis? The money the thrift industry lost was distributed widely throughout the economy. Many of us benefited indirectly from the losses, and we are all being asked to pay for them, either directly or indirectly. Taxes will be higher than they otherwise would be. Mortgage loans will be tougher to get, will require larger down payments, and will be more expensive than they otherwise might be. Rates on deposits have fallen, partly due to thrifts passing along the increase in deposit insurance premiums. Real estate prices have dropped as foreclosed properties have been sold into already saturated markets. Finally, the money used to pay for the cleanup could have been used for better social purposes or by private companies to support economic growth.

5. What is the current status, in 1993, of the bailout? For over a year, the S&L cleanup had been stalled because Congress has refused to vote for additional RTC funding. According to the Treasury Department, each day of congressional inaction adds $6 million to the cost of the cleanup. Now, in May 1993, it looks as though progress is being made in Congress, but we have heard this before, and disputes between the House and the Senate must still be resolved. In the meantime, the meter keeps ticking.

The Savings and Loan Crisis

The "Industry Practice" boxed feature in this chapter discusses in detail what led up to the nation's crisis in the S&L (or thrift) industry. So, what is the latest on the bailout that began more than four years ago? And how are the remaining savings and loan associations doing? One of the most important developments in the financial environment impacting S&Ls has been low short-term interest rates which have boosted the profitability of surviving S&Ls by widening their interest-rate spreads. The interest-rate spread, or net interest margin, is the difference between the interest rate an S&L earns on loans and/or securities and the rate it pays, on average, to depositors. It was *because* the interest-rate spread became *negative* in the late 1970s that the S&L industry began the long slide that would ultimately lead to the bankruptcies of hundreds of institutions. Therefore, the high *positive* interest-rate spreads experienced lately (courtesy of the Fed) have been a real lifesaver. As of March 31, 1992, the industry was able to report the first quarterly gain since 1987, and the favorable interest rate environment is lasting into 1993. In fact, the nation's remaining 1,855 private thrifts ended 1992 with record profits of $5.14 billion, almost three times the 1991 profits of $1.83 billion, and more than 30 percent above the previous record set in 1978.

Certainly, there are still "problem" thrifts. Estimates of necessary closures range from 30 to 50 for the rest of 1993. Therefore, estimates of funds required to finish the massive bailout also vary widely. In March 1993, the White House budget office tentatively concluded that it would take $34 billion to complete the job, while — less than a week later — Treasury Secretary Lloyd Bentsen expressed hope that $45 billion would be enough. Some members of Congress, however, find it difficult to vote for sizeable amounts of S&L bailout funds at a time when the overwhelming efforts of the Clinton administration are aimed at deficit reduction. A Vermont Independent, Representative Bernard Sanders, asked during a March hearing where the bailout money would come from but received no answer. He was referring to the $45 billion estimate which, he said, "to some of us, is a lot of money."

? Self-Test

What is the significance of a positive interest-rate spread for savings and loan associations? Is the interest-rate spread positive or negative in the early 1990s?

What was the status of the S&L industry at the end of 1992?

The Changing Economic Environment of Our Financial Institutions

In recent years questions have surfaced about the long-term strength of the U.S. financial system. The October 1987 stock market crash led to the demise of a number of old, established investment banking concerns such as E.F. Hutton and to the loss of thousands of jobs on Wall Street and throughout the nation. Commercial banks have had to take large losses on loans to developing countries, on energy-related projects, and on real estate developments. The S&Ls — and U.S. taxpayers — have incurred horrible losses. And, since 1990, when the real estate market began a three-year slump, life insurance companies have also seen the quality of their assets deteriorate, and many have not yet owned up to their losses by writing off the decline in value of their holdings. In short, crises have occurred in many segments of our financial markets.

Reasons for the Changing Environment

It is difficult to pinpoint the reasons for all the crises in our financial system. Some analysts blame bankers for being overly ambitious in lending money to real estate developers and to expansion-minded corporations. Some blame the soft lending controls that were characteristic of the banking industry during the 1980s. Others blame the Congress and our huge budget and trade deficits for the problems, while still others blame regulators for letting things get out of control. All of these factors probably contributed to the turmoil.

The banking industry has experienced increased competition from other financial institutions worldwide, higher deposit insurance premiums, tougher regulation and supervision, and more stringent capital adequacy requirements. Because of these conditions, hundreds of banks have been merged or closed and huge cutbacks in staffing have occurred. There is a growing consensus that the system no longer needs more than 11,000 banks, and commercial banks are restructuring themselves before they become victims of unwanted takeovers.

Commercial Banks in the 1990s

The opening vignette to this chapter discussed the tough new banking law which, in spite of the Bush administration's efforts, was passed by Congress in 1991 and which effectively reversed the deregulatory banking climate of much of the 1980s. Having recently been forced to authorize over $200 billion to bail out the savings and loan industry, Congress was in no mood to see the banking industry go the way of the S&Ls.

Federal Deposit Insurance Corporation Improvement Act of 1991 (FDICIA)

Legislation designed to reduce the number and cost of bank failures.

The Federal Deposit Insurance Corporation Improvement Act of 1991 (FDICIA) was designed to reduce the number and cost of bank failures. However, many bankers, acutely aware of the new regulatory climate with its much stricter rules, simply became less inclined to lend. In other words, while the Fed was easing credit in 1991, legislation was being passed which virtually required banks to *tighten* credit. No wonder we had the unusual credit crunch described earlier, which lasted throughout all of 1992 and into 1993.

A final piece of the regulatory puzzle has been the transition to new capital (equity) requirements. In mid-1989, Congress ratified new international capital rules for banks, the so-called *Basle Accord of 1988.* December 1992 marked the completion of the final phase-in period for the *risk-based capital standards* established by the Basle Accord. Under these standards, bank assets are assigned a risk weight of 0, 20, 50, or 100 percent, based on the perceived degree of credit risk. Assets such as cash and U.S. Treasury securities receive a zero-percent risk weight; banks are not required to hold capital against these assets. In contrast, most business loans receive a risk weight of 100 percent. FDICIA placed additional emphasis on bank capital by linking many supervisory actions to a bank's capital ratio. The result has been that banks have shifted the composition of their assets from higher risk weights to lower risk weights. In plain English, this means that banks had a powerful incentive to make fewer business loans and to invest more in U.S. Treasury securities in order to meet the new capital requirements by year-end 1992. In addition, banks have limited their overall asset growth and have raised new capital both by retaining earnings and selling new capital instruments. Financial analyst Kelly Klemme of the Federal

Reserve Bank of Dallas reported in *Financial Industry Issues* (first quarter, 1993) that "the health of the U.S. banking industry continues to improve" and that "the risk-based capital framework will continue to influence the composition of bank asset portfolios."

In March 1993, the nation's commercial banks announced sharp increases in earnings for 1992, although lending showed a decline. Acting FDIC Chairman Andrew Hove made the statement on March 9, 1993, that "the banking cleanup isn't turning out to be the tragedy that some people had expected." (Still, banks continue to fail; the official estimate for 1993 is 120.) The wave of bank failures that started with defaults in oil, farming, and real estate loans in the 1980s may finally be tapering off. Banks have been able to improve their profitability for two reasons: (1) fewer bad loans and (2) higher net interest margins.[14] Rebounding from a dismal 1991, in 1992 banks could borrow at record low rates, paying their depositors 3 percent or less, and could lend at relatively high rates, typically above the prime rate, which is currently at 6 percent. This generous spread between banks' borrowing costs and lending rates is not expected to continue, but in 1992, for the first time since 1988, large U.S. banks emerged as the most profitable in the world.

The Impact of Globalization on U.S. Banks

universal (global) banks
Banks that offer both commercial and investment banking services to their customers.

specialist banks
Banks that act only as investment banks, concentrating on the origination, distribution, and trading of securities.

Capital markets are becoming integrated into a global capital market. As a result, we are seeing *universal (global) banks* competing directly with *specialist banks*. **Universal (global) banks** offer both commercial and investment banking services to their customers, while **specialist banks** act only as investment banks, concentrating on the origination, distribution, and trading of securities. An important question in the development of a global capital market is how successful universal banks will be relative to specialized investment banks and whether they will dominate the capital markets. True universal banks exist only in Germany and Switzerland, while an example of a specialist bank would be the U.S. investment banking houses.

The success of the universal banks will depend on their advantages and disadvantages when compared with specialist banks. The universal banks' advantages include these: (1) They can cross-sell a wider range of products, which will reduce initial marketing costs and the costs of developing and maintaining customer relationships. (2) They can cross-subsidize. This means that they can offer products in highly competitive fields at a lower cost than specialist banks and can subsidize them through higher profit margins on products in less competitive fields. Conceivably, they could use cross subsidies to eliminate competition, then raise prices. (3) They can offer the customer the full range of products he or she may require, thus encouraging customer loyalty. (4) They have greater opportunities for smoothing income fluctuations in different areas of their business.

Their disadvantages include the following: (1) They face various conflicts of interest in different areas of their business. (2) The quality of service they

---

[14]This is the same healthy interest-rate spread that allowed many remaining S&Ls to become profitable, as discussed earlier.

offer may sometimes be lower than that offered by specialist banks. (3) Coordination becomes more difficult, and reaction time longer, the larger and more complex the organization.

The advantages appear to outweigh the disadvantages, because there is a clear trend towards universal banking throughout the world. This trend has been fueled by the commercial banks rather than by the investment banks. In the United States, development of universal banks is still constrained by the Glass Steagall Act of 1933, the Bank Holding Company Act of 1956, and the International Banking Act of 1978, which still enforce the strict separation of commercial and investment banking. None of this legislation has been repealed, but commercial banks have recently been empowered to underwrite and distribute commercial paper, municipal bonds, and mortgage-backed securities. Such activities represent a trend toward a universal banking system in the United States.

Conclusion

In order to survive, the U.S. commercial banking system is changing. After a period of transition, the following types of banks are emerging: *niche banks* — specialists in a single product or market segment; *regional banks* — dominating the middle market in their part of the country; *super-regionals* — involved in the consumer and middle markets in several states and offering some services on a national scale; and *global banks* — offering full-service banking to virtually everyone, everywhere.

The trends influencing our commercial banking system during the next several years are likely to be the following:

1. **Constraints on asset growth** for many banks, as they move to comply with the new risk-based capital requirements. These requirements will also likely continue to impact the loan-investment mix of banks and, in general, will make banks less inclined to take risk.

2. **Continued fierce competition** both within the banking industry and from nonbank financial service firms.

3. **An increase in nationwide branching.**

4. **A continued high level of banking mergers.** Although some have questioned that fewer banks are better, it is expected that bank consolidation will continue. Many bankers believe that mergers will make the industry stronger, more efficient, and better able to fight competitors, both at home and abroad.

Self-Test

Identify some of the factors that have contributed to the changing environment of our financial institutions.

What are some of the major regulatory changes affecting commercial banks in the 1990s?

Differentiate between universal banks and specialist banks.

Explain which trends are likely to dominate the commercial banking system for much of the 1990s.

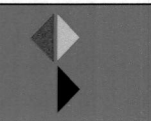

BUILDING A BANKING RELATIONSHIP

Building a good banking relationship is important for a small business for two reasons. The most obvious is that the banker may lend the business money for working capital expansion, equipment, and so on, which will allow the firm to grow. A less obvious reason is that the banker may be a valuable source of financial advice for an inexperienced small business owner. Once the bank has loaned the business money, it is in both the bank's and the business's best interest for the company to survive. Thus, a good banker will take a genuine interest in the firm and will care about how it is doing.

Even though the bank is interested in the firm's survival, it is likely to be more risk averse than the business because the bank shares in the firm's risk but not in its positive potential. If the firm fails, the entrepreneur and the bank both lose their investment. If things go well, on the other hand, the bank gets back only the loaned money plus the interest, but the entrepreneur has the potential for huge profits. The entrepreneur, therefore, may be willing to take greater risks in the hope of earning great rewards, whereas the banker will want to avoid risks.

There is a possibility, then, of a conflict of interest between the banker and the entrepreneur. Because of that potential conflict, the bank will often impose restrictions on how the firm can use its revenues or profits, on how much the firm can pay the entrepreneur in salary, and on other such matters. The bank probably will require some or all of the business's assets as collateral to safeguard the loan. The banker will be concerned about and be watchful for the one thing the entrepreneur most wants to avoid — the failure of the business. To that end, the banker will follow the firm's financial progress very closely, and that watchful eye can be of great benefit to the entrepreneur.

The banking environment in the 1990s has changed markedly. With industry regulators monitoring banks so strictly, the Federal Reserve reports that

bank commercial and industrial lending to U.S. businesses has decreased to the lowest level in a decade. The loans banks do make are almost always heavily collateralized by homes and other personal assets. Loans to good customers (businesses that are meeting their forecasts, making money, and meeting their debt payments) are now only about 75 percent (down from 80 to 90 percent) of receivables and even less for inventory. Businesses report that if there is any slight alteration in earnings or if a brief sales decline is experienced, they are often pushed to find new lenders. The reports are similar from coast to coast as well, with no region escaping the credit crunch. Still, as a result of innovations in financial services and of competition, a growing business today can expect to find a wider array of options available from banks than in the past.

Finding the Right Bank

Often the small business owner may be unsure about how to find the right bank. Looking for funds, the entrepreneur might go to the nearest bank and ask for money to fund an idea or proposal. Not all banks are willing to lend to start-ups or to ongoing small businesses; instead they may target large, well-established corporations that have much larger funding needs (wholesale banks), or they may specialize in consumer lending (retail banks). Size is important because large banks can make bigger loans than small banks. Bank management will typically target the specific type and size (in terms of assets) of customer on whom they will concentrate.

Another fact that a small business owner must be aware of is that banks themselves are facing such enormous competitive pressure that there is a great deal of mobility among bank managers. Consequently, when the small business owner finds a bank that will meet his or her business needs, it would be wise to build the relationship with the lending department manager as well, in case the banker with whom he or she is working is transferred to another bank and the entrepreneur is forced to start all over again. The right banker and department should satisfy at least three conditions:

1. The banker should understand the entrepreneur's business.

Sources: "How to Finance Anything," *INC.*, February 1993, 64; "How to Finance Anything," *INC.*, February 1993, 62; and "Financing Your Franchise," *Nation's Business,* September 1992, 57.

2. The banker should be interested in the business and commit to follow it closely.

3. The banker should be experienced and understand the pitfalls that tend to wipe out small firms.

The banker and the entrepreneur should have a rapport. If they cannot communicate candidly and easily with each other, things may go wrong that might have been avoided. In addition, the bank itself should be adequately capitalized to offer funds at the level the business needs, and it should also provide other services (such as cash management).

The Approach

The first meeting between the banker and the entrepreneur should not involve a detailed discussion of the firm's financial statements. Rather, it should be a "get acquainted" session in which the banker learns about the business and the entrepreneur learns about the bank and the banker. At that first meeting, the entrepreneur should leave the business's historical financial statements with the banker for review. It is suggested that the entrepreneur establish a relationship at a time when financing is not urgently needed.

By not immediately delving into problems and projections, the two parties will have an opportunity to become acquainted without pressure. Also, at such a meeting, the entrepreneur has the chance to convey the impression that he or she is in control of the business, rather than appearing excessively anxious to resolve some financial crisis.

The second meeting (if there is one) should begin with a discussion of the historical financial statements, which should then be followed by a presentation of projections, and if possible an on-site visit by the banker so he or she can become fully acquainted with the operations of the business. Together, the banker and the entrepreneur should discuss the business's financing needs. If the banker is effective, he or she will have some suggestions for improving the projections or will perhaps anticipate some potential problems.

What the Banker Evaluates

In the past, bankers have traditionally evaluated a customer's creditworthiness based on the following "*five Cs of credit*":

▶ Character

▶ Capacity

▶ Capital

▶ Collateral

▶ Conditions

Today, it takes more than that to qualify for a loan. In addition to these 5 factors, 3 other considerations "combine to cement relationships between the banker, the business, and the community." They are:

▶ Commitment

▶ Customers

▶ Community

The small business owner seeking a loan should be prepared to show his or her strengths in all of these areas.

The *character* factor considers whether the entrepreneur and his or her team are people who take obligations seriously, are honest, and are straightforward. The second management factor, *capacity,* questions whether management can handle the business. The banker will want to know about the depth of leadership and experience of the key people in the business. Finally, the business owner should demonstrate how past credit payments have been handled.

The *capital* issue involves how the firm will generate the cash flow to repay this loan, or if it is a revolving line of credit, how it will generate the cash flow to service the debt and keep it current. The banker may ask if the money that the business generates is put back into the business or if it is taken out by the owners. The entrepreneur should also indicate the sources of capital.

Many loans are made to finance specific assets, such as equipment or receivables, and those are matched against *collateral.* Today, because bankers have so recently been burned by collateral that has lost considerable value (real estate, for instance) the entrepreneur should emphasize the business's ability to repay the loan and should offer collateral merely as a secondary protection for the bank. The banker will carefully evaluate if the bank is protected by the value and the ongoing quality of the collateral.

Another factor considered is current economic *conditions* that prevail within an industry. For example, oil-based lending at one time was highly profitable, whereas now, bankers are very reluctant because oil revenues are unpredictable.

Commitment refers to the loyalty and dedication to the business of the entrepreneur and the employees. This commitment may be in the form of the amount of capital or time that the two parties contribute to the business.

Today more than ever before, when collateral was plentiful, the banker will want to know how well the business "knows" its *customer base*. The entrepreneur should be able to answer questions regarding the competition in his or her market, the business's image and its distinctiveness in the market, and its plan for maintaining market share. Finally, regarding the *community,* bankers will want to know how this business relates to the community in areas such as the environment and job creation.

Tips from a Credit Department Manager

The credit department manager of a large commercial bank was interviewed to obtain his point of view about establishing a banking relationship with a small business. He summarized the points he teaches new officers to consider when reviewing a proposal to grant credit.

First, he tells officers to simply ask, "Why do you need the money?" He wants to know not only how the funds will be used but also why the company cannot generate the funds itself. By carefully considering the answers, the banker is able to ascertain that the entrepreneur thoroughly understands the business.

Next, the manager tells loan officers to carefully investigate how the loan will be repaid. If the funds will come from operating cash flows, how realistic are the projections in comparison with cash flows of similar businesses within the industry? If it is a seasonal working capital loan, what is the company's track record for managing receivables and inventory? If the business is not seasonal, is the firm sufficiently profitable to meet payments on the debt from operating profits?

The manager realizes that some working capital in a growing business is essentially permanent. The next concern is whether management is truly in control of the business and whether the financing can be supported by assets.

The final question the credit manager asks, which is the most important of all, is "What are your biggest problems?" The loan officer should explain that he or she is not looking for firms that have no problems because every firm has its problems. What the banker is really trying to find out is whether the entrepreneur is (1) perceptive of present problems, (2) aware of potential problems before they occur, (3) in control of the business, and (4) frank and candid; that is, if he or she is willing to talk honestly about the business's problems.

The ability to earnestly communicate with and to learn from another, in this case the lender, whose outside expertise can make the difference before the business is overcome with problems, is what the credit manager is looking for in the entrepreneur. Frankness is the key to success. The business owner's willingness to share concerns is viewed by the manager as the bank's greatest protection against "surprises."

Conclusion

For a small business, a good banking relationship can mean the difference between success and failure. Establishing that relationship is important. Both sides are better off if it is an open relationship, where the banker and the business owner understand each other and communicate honestly when dealing with the various problems of the small, but growing, firm.

Summary

This chapter contained a discussion of the Federal Reserve System and the tools available to the Fed as it conducts monetary policy, reasons that monetary policy tools do not always work as intended, the commercial banking system and other important financial institutions, and the changing economic environment of our financial institutions. The key concepts covered are listed below.

▷ The **Federal Reserve System** works through the banking system to affect the level of economic activity via the money supply and interest rates.

The **Federal Reserve** has examination responsibilities, it regulates bank holding company activities, and it acts as a lender of last resort to banks, but its chief responsibility is regulating the nation's money supply.

The Fed's principal tools in conducting monetary policy are (1) **reserve requirements,** (2) the **discount rate,** and (3) **open-market operations.**

Other bank regulators include the **Office of the Comptroller of the Currency (OCC)** and the **Federal Deposit Insurance Corporation (FDIC),** which protects most depositors in insured banks from the effects of a bank failure.

▶ **Demand deposit creation** occurs primarily through the commercial banking system through the extension of credit. The full expansion may not always be reached due to "leakages" from the system. For example, banks may decide to keep some excess reserves and, therefore, lend less.

▶ **When the Fed wants to slow down an inflationary economy,** as it did in 1981, it drains reserves from the banking system by selling government securities, thereby raising the level of interest rates and making credit hard to obtain. This situation is commonly called a **credit crunch.**

When the Fed wants to boost a slow, recessionary economy, as it did in 1991, it buys government securities, and funds flow into the banking system, which expands the money supply. However, major new banking regulation prevented the Fed from reaching its goal of easier credit in the early 1990s, and as a result, the nation again experienced a credit crunch, but of a very different nature than the one a decade earlier.

▶ Besides commercial banks, major financial institutions include: (1) **savings and loan associations,** (2) **credit unions,** (3) **life insurance companies,** (4) **pension funds,** and (5) **mutual funds.** Of these, the last two have shown particularly dramatic growth in assets in recent years.

▶ The **U.S. banking system** is quite different from that of other industrialized countries in (1) the number of banks and (2) the dual chartering system (state and federal).

The banking system has changed dramatically during the past 10 to 15 years. During the 1980s many banks became virtual **financial supermarkets,** offering savings certificates, retirement plans, trusts, leasing departments, discount brokerage services, and insurance products.

The primary source of funds for a bank is its deposits. Deposits are either demand, savings, or time deposits. **Demand deposits** are deposits made by individuals, businesses, and government units that are available on demand, usually through checks. **Savings** (passbook) **accounts** generally pay near-market interest rates and offer limited transactions services. **Time deposits (CDs)** offer higher rates but do not allow transactions.

Another source of funds for banks is the **Federal funds market.** In this market, banks borrow for short periods of time from other banks at the **Federal funds rate.**

Before deposit insurance was implemented, **bank capital,** which is total assets minus liabilities, protected depositors from losses. Today, a bank's capital cushions the deposit insurance fund, taxpayers, and unsecured creditors from losses.

Bank assets include **cash,** federal funds (loans to other banks), **securities, loans** to nonbank entities, and miscellaneous assets. Of these the largest components are loans and securities, but in recent years there has been a shift toward fewer loans and more securities held, for example, U.S. Treasury securities.

▶ The overall trend in banking legislation in the 1980s was toward greater deregulation. The **Depository Institutions Deregulation and Monetary Control Act of 1980 (DIDMCA)** (1) eliminated interest rate ceilings, (2) removed differences between Fed member and nonmember banks, and (3) allowed for much greater competition among financial institutions.

In the early 1990s the tide turned, to a large extent, as tough new banking laws have been passed to avoid a banking crisis. Important lessons learned from the **savings and loan crisis** and taxpayer bailout, have resulted in the **Federal Deposit Insurance Corporation Improvement Act of 1991 (FDICIA),** which was designed to reduce the number and cost of bank failures.

▶ Among the trends likely to affect banking for the rest of this decade are (1) renewed regulation, as mentioned above; (2) the impact of more **globalized, integrated capital markets;** (3) **risk-based capital requirements,** resulting in **constraints on asset growth** for many banks; (4) **increased nationwide branching;** (5) continuing **fierce competition** between banks and nonbank financial firms; and (6) a high level of **banking mergers.**

Resolution to
DECISION IN FINANCE

THE NEW BANKING LAW GETS TOUGH WITH BANKS

Many bankers believe that the new legislation has made it more difficult for them to lend money at a time when the Clinton administration is urging them to stimulate the economy with easier credit. They also worry that, if many more banks fail, the premiums the surviving banks must pay for deposit insurance will rise sharply. Then, the banks' customers will have to pay for the premium increases through increases in loan charges and reductions in rates paid on deposit accounts.

This situation could hurt both the banks and the economy.

Robert Litan of the Brookings Institution argued that in the long run the legislation will strengthen banks but that in the short run it may well exacerbate the credit squeeze and further slow the economy. Thus, while the Fed is easing credit, the new legislation requires bank regulators to tighten it. Still, Mr. Litan believes that this is "modest good news" for taxpayers because the new regulations will lead to sounder banking.

The new regulations are related to banks' capital—when a bank's capital declines, its regulators will be required to take prompt action to make the bank slow its growth rate, reduce or suspend dividends and/or sell stock to raise capi-

Sources: "The New Banking Law Toughens Regulation, Some Say Too Much," *The Wall Street Journal,* November 29, 1991; and "Banking Industry Is in Long-Term Fall Despite Current Health, Greenspan Says," *The Wall Street Journal,* May 7, 1993.

tal, and, in extreme cases, to replace the management team. Regulators can even force banks to close when their ratio of capital to assets falls below 2 percent; this provision alone might lead to the closure of at least 100 small and medium-sized banks.

Thus, the new law will require many banks to boost their capital at a time of low stock prices, which is not a time when the sale of stock will provide the bank with the maximum benefit, nor will it necessarily be easy to sell. De facto, the new capital requirements will force many weaker banks to merge with stronger banks.

Both bank shareholders and borrowers could be hurt by the new legislation. Due to higher capital requirements, and the fact that some banks will have to sell more stock to raise capital, current stockholders could see their positions diluted. Also, if a bank's capital falls to the 2 percent threshold level and if regulators then close the bank even though it is not insolvent, stockholders will be wiped out before the bank has a chance to get back on a sound footing. All this will make weak banks reluctant to lend to all but their strongest customers, which will compound the difficulty smaller firms, and those in financial difficulty, are having in rolling over existing loans and getting new credit. Finally, banks will think a little harder about whether they want to fund high-risk ventures, which the nation may need if we are to grow and prosper.

The new legislation also ends the "too big to fail" doctrine. Under this doctrine, large banks, whose failure might have brought down the banking system, either were granted sufficient loans by the Fed to keep them afloat or were merged with healthy banks under terms whereby the government reimbursed the acquiring bank for any losses it incurred.

Recently, in a speech at a Chicago Federal Reserve Bank Conference, Fed Chairman Alan Greenspan noted that banks' commercial and industrial lending as a percentage of total borrowing by nonfinancial business has been declining for several decades. In 1960, the banking industry accounted for 40 percent of the country's total financial assets, while today the banking industry accounts for only 25 percent. Greenspan further noted that this decline raises questions about the future role of U.S. banks in the overall provision of financial services, not just loans. He also commented that the banking industry is less competitive and less efficient than it should be, and he blamed unnecessary laws and regulations for the decline.

To date, the Clinton administration has not taken a position on the politically charged issue of banking reform. However, Eugene Ludwig, the newly appointed comptroller of the currency, has emphasized the need to address the banking industry's decreasing economic role, and he stated that he does not agree with congressional arguments that giving banks broader powers to sell insurance or to underwrite securities would increase the risks of the banking system. Even though the new administration does not plan to propose legislation to overhaul the banking system in 1993, it has promised to push for regulatory changes to spur lending. One can only wait and see.

Questions

3-1 What are the three principal tools that the Federal Reserve System uses in affecting the nation's money supply?

3-2 When the Fed buys government securities, is it attempting to increase or decrease the money supply?

3-3 Why is the Fed reluctant to use the reserve requirement as an active tool in monetary policy?

3-4   From the standpoint of a commercial bank's balance sheet, evaluate the following statement: "One financial unit's asset is another's liability."

3-5   If the primary goal of the financial manager is to maximize shareholder wealth, what is the bank manager's primary goal?

3-6   Why do banks usually attempt to minimize their investments in excess reserves?

3-7   What are the characteristics of securities that banks would obtain for their investment portfolios?

3-8   Why have banks, among financial institutions, historically been the major suppliers of short-term funds to borrowers?

3-9   What is the importance of the Depository Institutions Deregulation and Monetary Control Act of 1980?

3-10 What are the trends that are likely to influence banking during the 1990s? Why has tougher banking legislation been passed?

Self-Test Problem

ST-1   What is the potential increase (decrease) in demand deposits if
a. The Fed buys $12 million in government securities and the reserve requirement is 10 percent?
b. The Fed sells $18 million in government securities and the reserve requirement is 3 percent?

Problems

3-1
Open-market operations
The Fed buys $24 million in government securities.
a. Will the money supply expand or contract?
b. If the reserve requirement is 3 percent, what is the potential increase (decrease) in demand deposits?

3-2
Open-market operations
The Fed sells $5 million in government securities.
a. Will the money supply expand or contract?
b. If the reserve requirement is 10 percent, what is the potential increase (decrease) in demand deposits?

3-3
Comparative financial statements
Obtain the financial statement of a local bank. Compare the bank's balance sheet with that of a manufacturer (or see Carter Chemical Company's balance sheet in Chapter 5). What major differences are apparent?

Solution to Self-Test Problem

ST-1   **a.** Demand deposits would potentially increase by $12,000,000/0.1 = $120,000,000.
b. Demand deposits would potentially decrease by $18,000,000/0.03 = $600,000,000.

Interest Rates

After reading this chapter, you should be able to:

▶ Explain how capital is allocated in a supply/demand framework, and list the fundamental factors which affect the cost of money.

▶ Write out two equations for the nominal, or quoted, interest rate, and briefly discuss each component or premium.

▶ Define what is meant by the term structure of interest rates, and graph a yield curve for a given set of data.

▶ Account for how each of the three theories explain the slope of the yield curve.

▶ List four additional, specific factors that influence the level of interest rates and the slope of the yield curve.

▶ Briefly explain how interest rate levels affect stock prices and corporate financial policy.

DECISION IN FINANCE

ALAN GREENSPAN RESPONDS TO CRITICS

In December 1991, after 17 months of recession, Chairman Alan Greenspan of the Federal Reserve Board took two drastic actions in an attempt to halt the recession: He announced that the Fed (1) was cutting the discount rate that it charges on loans to banks from 4.5 percent to 3.5 percent, its lowest level in almost three decades and (2) was lowering the Federal funds rate (the interest rate charged on overnight loans between banks) from 4.5 percent to 4 percent. The announcement came as a surprise—this was the biggest interest rate cut in a decade. Previous Fed actions had been restricted to small, cautious quarter-point reductions which had been announced with minimum fanfare to keep the financial markets convinced of the Fed's commitment to fight inflation.

Mr. Greenspan's announcement came in response to growing criticism from the White House, Congress, and private economists, who accused the Fed of worrying too much about bond-market psychology and too little about the rapidly deteriorating confidence of both consumers and business executives. In addition, new forecasts by the Fed's economists (who had

See end of chapter for resolution.
Photo source: © 1992, Chris Usher

earlier been confident that the economy was recovering) showed an economy "dead in the water." Finally, a survey of manufacturers revealed that manufacturing activity had fallen to its lowest level of the year.

As you read this chapter, consider the Federal Reserve's importance to the U.S. banking system as well as its role in international finance. Think about the kinds of decisions that Alan Greenspan and the Fed's Board of Governors routinely must make. Also, think about all the factors the Fed must consider before deciding to cut rates to stimulate the economy and the effects lower short-term interest rates might have on inflation, on the financial markets, and on the economy as a whole. Finally, think about how the Fed's policies will need to work with the newly elected Clinton administration's economic and deficit-reduction policies.

interest rate

The price paid by borrowers to lenders for the use of funds.

Capital in a free economy is allocated through the price system. In the case of debt, the **interest rate** is the price paid to borrow capital from investors, whereas in the case of equity capital, investors' returns come in the form of dividends and capital gains. The factors which affect the supply of and demand for investment capital, and hence the cost of funds, are discussed in this chapter.

The Cost of Funds

production opportunities

The returns available within an economy from investment into productive assets.

time preferences for consumption

The preferences of consumers for current consumption as opposed to saving for future consumption.

risk

In a financial market context, the chance that a loan will not be repaid as promised.

inflation

The tendency of prices to increase over time.

The four most fundamental factors affecting the cost of funds are (1) **production opportunities,** (2) **time preferences for consumption,** (3) **risk,** and (4) **inflation.** To see how these factors operate, visualize an isolated island community where the people live on fish. They have a stock of fishing gear that permits them to survive reasonably well, but they would like to have more fish. Now suppose Mr. Crusoe had a bright idea for a new type of fishnet that would enable him to double his daily catch. However, it would take him a year to perfect his design, to build his net, and to learn how to use it efficiently, and Mr. Crusoe would probably starve before he could put his new net into operation. Therefore, he might suggest to Ms. Robinson, Mr. Friday, and several others that if they would give him one fish each day for a year, he would return two fish a day during all of the next year. If someone accepted the offer, then the fish which Ms. Robinson or one of the others gave to Mr. Crusoe would constitute *savings;* these savings would be *invested* in the fishnet; and the extra fish the net produced would constitute a *return on the investment.*

Obviously, the more productive Mr. Crusoe thought the new fishnet would be, the higher his expected return on the investment would be, and the more he could offer to pay Ms. Robinson, Mr. Friday, or other potential investors for their savings. In this example we assume that Mr. Crusoe thought he would be able to pay, and thus he offered, a 100 percent rate of return — he offered to give back two fish for every one he received. He might have tried to attract savings for less; for example, he might have decided to offer only 1.5 fish next year for every one he received this year, which would represent a 50 percent rate of return to Ms. Robinson and the other potential savers.

How attractive Mr. Crusoe's offer would appear to potential savers would depend in large part on their time preferences for consumption. For example, Ms. Robinson might be thinking of retirement, and she might be willing to trade fish today for fish in the future on a one-for-one basis. On the other hand, Mr. Friday might have a wife and several young children and need his current fish, so he might be unwilling to "lend" a fish today for anything less than three fish next year. Mr. Friday would be said to have a high time preference for current consumption and Ms. Robinson a low time preference for current consumption. Note also that if the entire population were living right at the subsistence level, time preferences for current consumption would necessarily be high, aggregate savings would be low, interest rates would be high, and capital formation would be difficult.

The risk inherent in the fishnet project, and thus in Mr. Crusoe's ability to repay the loan, would also affect the return investors would require: The higher the perceived risk, the higher the required rate of return. As we will discuss in this chapter, there are actually several different types of risk that must be considered. Also, in a more complex society there are many businesses like Mr. Crusoe's, many goods other than fish, and many savers like Ms. Robinson and Mr. Friday. Further, people use money as a medium of exchange rather than barter with fish. When money is used, rather than fish, its value in the future, which is affected by inflation, comes into play: Other things equal, the higher the expected rate of inflation, the larger the required return.

Thus, we see that the interest rate paid to savers depends in a basic way (1) on the rate of return producers expect to earn on invested capital, (2) on consumers'/savers' time preferences for current versus future consumption, (3) on the riskiness of the loan, and (4) on the expected rate of inflation. Producers' expected returns on their business investments set an upper limit on how much they can pay for savings, while consumers' time preferences for consumption establish how much consumption they are willing to defer and hence how much they will save at different rates of interest offered by producers.[1] Higher risk and higher inflation also lead to higher interest rates.

Self-Test

What do we call the price paid to borrow capital?

What four fundamental factors affect the cost of funds?

Interest Rates

A firm's cost of capital is determined by the rate of return required by its debt and equity investors. That return is dependent, in part, on factors specific to the firm itself: its financing, product innovation, competition, and management skills, to name a few. However, the firm's cost of capital is not determined just by factors that apply exclusively to the firm; cost considerations also include the general level of interest rates in the economy. The level of interest rates, in turn, is shaped by the Fed's monetary policy, as we saw in Chapter 3, but also by broader market forces — the supply of and demand for funds, risk factors, inflation, and overall investor expectations about the future. The way in which various economic forces combine to determine market interest rates is analyzed in the following sections.

Figure 4-1 is a graph of the production/consumption situation in a supply/demand framework, similar to Figure 2-1 discussed in Chapter 2. What it shows is that savers will save more if producers offer higher interest rates on savings, and producers will borrow more if savers accept a lower return on their savings. There is an **equilibrium rate (k)** which produces a balance between the aggregate supply of and demand for a particular type of capital. The equilibrium rate is that rate which is required to induce savers to invest and, simultaneously,

equilibrium rate (k)

A market-clearing interest rate which obtains a balance between the supply of and the demand for a particular type of capital.

----

[1]The term *producers* is really too narrow. As we discussed earlier in Chapter 2, a better word might be *"borrowers,"* which would include corporations, home purchasers, people borrowing to go to college, or even people borrowing to buy autos or to pay for vacations. However, our emphasis in this text will indeed be on those business units that borrow in order to invest into productive, cash-generating assets, hence the term *producers.*

Figure 4-1

Supply of and Demand for
Savings

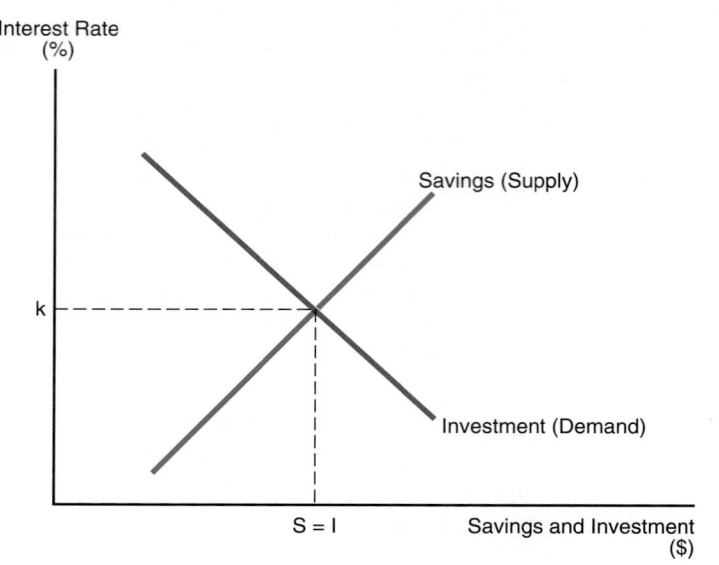

This figure shows how the supply/demand system works to determine the equilibrium
rate of interest (k) on savings. The investment (demand) curve indicates that borrowers
(producers) will try to attract more savings from savers as interest rates decrease. Conversely, the savings (supply) curve shows that savers will tend to save more as interest
rates increase. These conflicting desires of savers and borrowers come together at some
equilibrium rate, k, creating a balance between supply of and demand for savings. At that
point, savings will equal investment (S = I).

---

it is the rate which borrowers are willing to pay. This rate is not static; it
changes over time, depending on conditions. For example, if a major technological breakthrough occurs and raises the rate of return on producers' investments, the investment (demand) curve in Figure 4-1 will shift to the right, causing both k and S = I to increase. Similarly, if consumers' attitudes change and
they become more thrifty, the savings curve will shift to the right, causing k to
decline but S = I to increase. Clearly, aggregate savings must equal aggregate
investment, since a dollar cannot be invested unless someone, somewhere, has
saved that dollar.

As you learned from our discussion in Chapter 2, there are many capital
markets in the United States. U.S. firms also invest and raise capital throughout
the world, and foreigners both borrow and lend capital in the United States.
There are markets in the United States for home loans; farm loans; business
loans; federal, state, and local government loans; and consumer loans. Within
each category, there are regional markets as well as different types of submar-
kets. For example, in real estate, there are separate markets for first and second
mortgages and for loans on owner-occupied homes, apartments, office buildings,
shopping centers, undeveloped land, and so on. Within the business sector,
there are dozens of types of debt and also several sharply differentiated markets
for common stocks. There is a price for each type of capital. However, even
with all the differentiation in the capital markets, rates in the various capital

Figure 4-2   Long- and Short-Term Interest Rates, 1956–1993

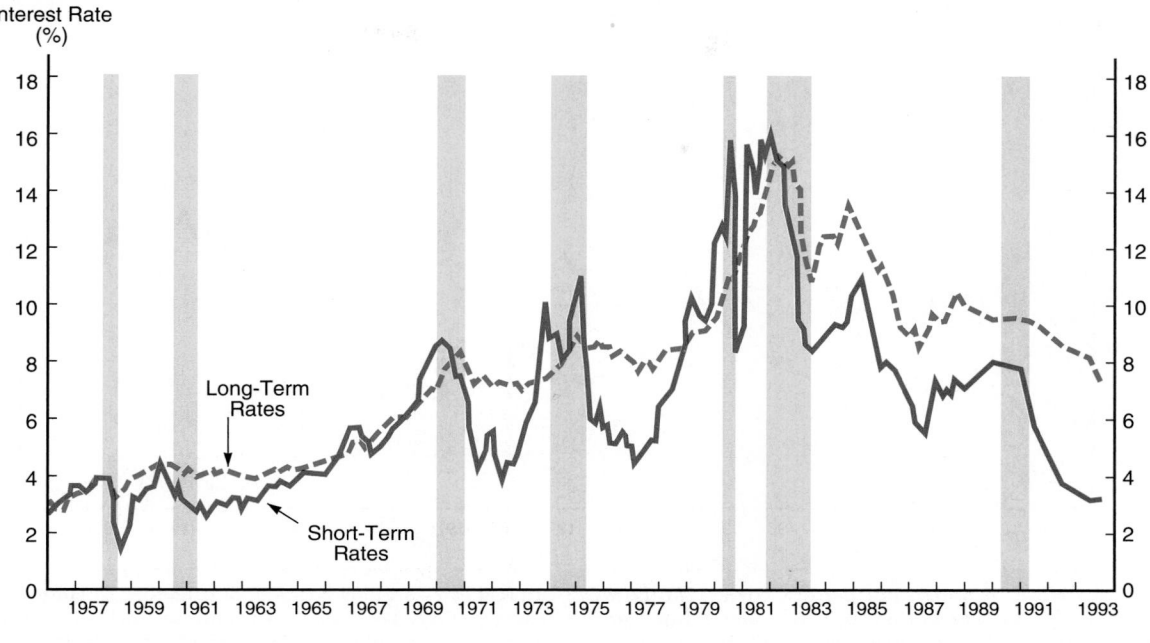

This figure depicts the fluctuation of long- and short-term interest rates over the past 38 years, and it shows how these rates have responded to business recessions. Recessions have caused sharp drops in short-term rates because of Federal Reserve intervention and falling demand for money. Long-term rates are much less affected by recessions since these rates are based on long-range expectations that are not significantly changed by relatively temporary recessions or by Fed intervention.

Note: The shaded areas designate business recessions. Short-term rates are measured by four- to six-month loans to very large, strong corporations, and long-term rates are measured by Aaa corporate bonds.

Source: *Federal Reserve Bulletin,* various issues.

markets are interrelated. Thus, when demand rises and causes the interest rate on business loans to increase, the interest rate on home mortgages will also increase.

The price of each type of capital changes over time as shifts occur in supply and demand conditions and in other underlying determinants. Figure 4-2 shows how long- and short-term interest rates to business borrowers have varied since the mid-1950s. Notice that short-term interest rates are more volatile than long-term rates. This is because short-term rates are responsive to current economic conditions and the Fed's monetary policy moves, while long-term rates primarily reflect long-run expectations for the economy, especially inflation. Thus, short-term rates are especially prone to rise during booms and then to fall during recessions (indicated by the shaded areas in Figure 4-2). As a result, short-term rates are sometimes above and sometimes below long-term rates. The relationship between long- and short-term rates, which is called the *term structure of interest rates,* is discussed later in this chapter.

When the economy is expanding, firms need capital, and this demand for funds pushes interest rates up. Also, because inflationary pressures are strongest

Figure 4-3   Relationship between Annual Inflation Rates and Long-Term Interest Rates

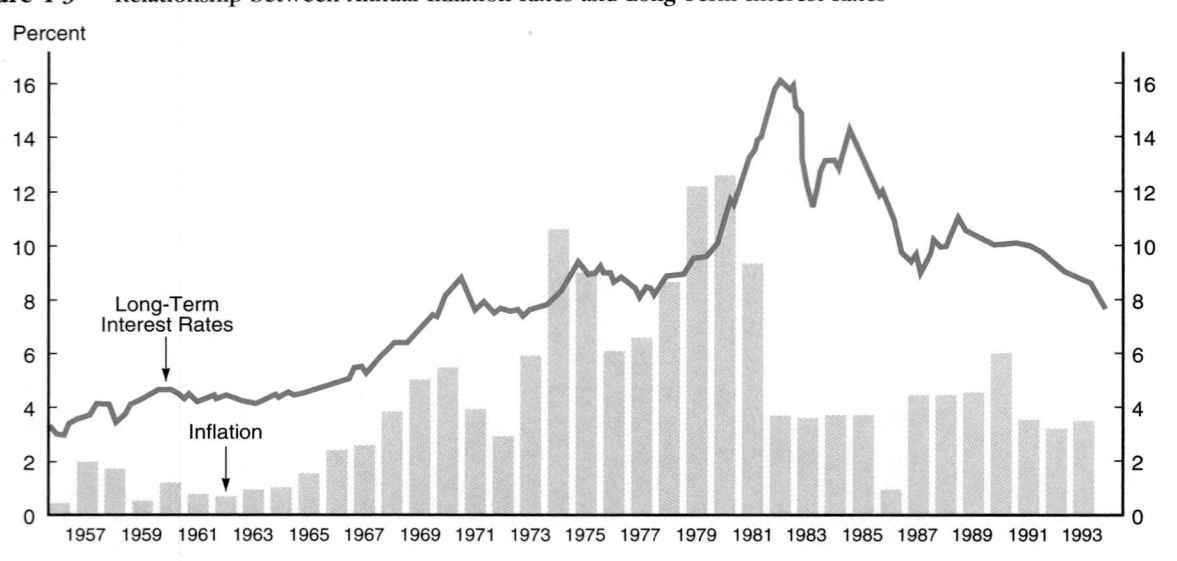

There is a close, although not perfect, correlation between interest rates and actual rates of inflation, as shown in this figure. Over a 38-year period, the two rates tended to fluctuate together. The inflation premium built into long-term interest rates is based on expectations of future inflation, with these expectations arising largely from actual past and present inflation rates.

Notes:

1. Interest rates are those on Aaa long-term corporate bonds.
2. Inflation is measured as the annual rate of change in the consumer price index (CPI).
3. 1993 inflation is estimated.

during business booms, the Federal Reserve tends to tighten the money supply at such times, which also exerts upward pressure on rates. Conditions are reversed during recessions: slack business reduces the demand for credit, the Fed increases the money supply, and the result is a drop in interest rates. In addition, inflationary pressures are normally weakest during recessions, and this too helps to keep interest rates down.

These tendencies do not hold exactly, and the period after 1984 is a case in point. The price of oil decreased dramatically in 1985 and 1986, reducing inflationary pressures on other prices and easing fears of serious, long-term inflation. Earlier, these fears had pushed interest rates to record levels. The economy was fairly strong from 1984 to 1987, but the declining fears about inflation more than offset the normal tendency of interest rates to rise during good economic times, and the net result was lower interest rates.

The relationship between inflation and long-term interest rates is highlighted in Figure 4-3, which plots actual (experienced) rates of inflation along with long-term interest rates. Prior to 1965, when the average rate of inflation was about 1 percent, interest rates on Aaa-rated bonds generally ranged from 4 to 5 percent. As the war in Vietnam accelerated in the mid-1960s, the rate of inflation increased, and interest rates began to rise. The inflation rate dropped after 1970, and so did long-term interest rates. However, the 1973 Arab oil embargo was followed by a quadrupling of oil prices in 1974, which caused a spurt in the price level, which in turn drove interest rates to new record highs in 1974 and 1975. Inflationary pressures eased in late 1975 and 1976 but then rose again after 1976. In 1980, inflation rates hit the highest level on record, and fears of continued double-digit inflation pushed interest rates up to historic highs. From 1981 through 1986, the inflation rate dropped steadily, and in 1986 inflation was only 1.1 percent, the lowest level in 25 years; yet, investors' fears of a renewal of double-digit inflation kept long-term interest rates at relatively high levels. As confidence built that inflation was under control, interest rates declined. Currently (1993), inflation is in the 3 to 3.5 percent range, and the long-term interest rate on Aaa corporate bonds is about 7.25 percent.

Self-Test

Identify some company-specific factors which influence a firm's cost of capital.

What is meant by the term "equilibrium rate"? Is this rate static? Explain.

Briefly explain why interest rates change during booms and recessions.

The Determinants of Market Interest Rates

In general, the nominal, or quoted, interest rate on a debt security, k, is composed of a real risk-free rate of interest, k*, plus several premiums that reflect inflation, the riskiness of the security, and the security's liquidity. This relationship can be expressed as follows:

$$\text{Nominal interest rate} = k = k^* + IP + DRP + LP + MRP. \quad (4\text{-}1)$$

Here:

  k = the *nominal,* or quoted, rate of interest on a given security. The nominal rate of interest is the stated rate which includes a premium for expected inflation. In contrast, a *real* rate of interest is one which is adjusted to remove the effects of inflation.[2] There are many different securities, hence many different nominal interest rates.

  k* = the real risk-free rate of interest; k* is pronounced "k-star," and it is the rate that would exist on a risk-free security if zero inflation were expected.

  k_{RF} = the nominal risk-free rate of interest. This is the stated interest rate on a security such as a U.S. Treasury bill, which is very liquid and free from most risks. Notice that k_{RF} does include a premium for expected inflation, so $k_{RF} = k^* + IP$.

  IP = inflation premium. IP is equal to the average expected inflation rate over the life of the security.

---

[2]If you had bought a 10-year Treasury bond in April 1993, the quoted or nominal rate was about 6 percent, but if inflation averaged 3.5 percent over the next 10 years the real rate you would earn would be about 6% − 3.5% = 2.5%. In Chapter 13 we will use the term *nominal* in yet another way: to distinguish between stated rates and effective annual rates when compounding occurs more frequently than once a year.

DRP = default risk premium. This premium reflects the possibility that the issuer will not pay interest or principal on a security at the stated time and in the stated amount. DRP is zero for U.S. Treasury securities, but it rises as the riskiness of an issuer increases.

LP = liquidity premium. This is a premium charged by lenders to reflect the fact that some securities cannot be converted to cash on short notice at a fair market price. LP is essentially zero for Treasury securities, but quite high on securities issued by very small companies.

MRP = maturity risk premium. As we will explain later, longer-term bonds are exposed to a significant risk of price declines, and a maturity premium is charged by lenders to reflect this risk.

If we combine $k^* + IP$ and obtain k_{RF}, then we have this equation:

$$k = k_{RF} + DRP + LP + MRP. \qquad (4\text{-}2)$$

We will discuss the components of the quoted, or nominal, interest rate on a given security in the following sections.

The Real Risk-Free Rate of Interest, k^*

real risk-free rate of interest, k^*

The rate of interest that would exist on short-term default-free U.S. Treasury securities if no inflation were expected.

The **real risk-free rate of interest, k^***, is defined as the interest rate that would exist on a riskless security if no inflation were expected, and it may be thought of as the rate of interest on short-term U.S. Treasury securities (T-bills) in an inflation-free world. As with the equilibrium rate, discussed at the beginning of this chapter, the real risk-free rate also changes over time depending on economic conditions. It is difficult to measure k^* precisely, but most experts think that in the United States it has fluctuated in the range of 1 to 4 percent in recent years.

The Nominal, or Quoted, Risk-Free Rate of Interest, k_{RF}

nominal (quoted) risk-free rate, k_{RF}

The rate of interest on a security that is free of all risk; k_{RF} is proxied by the T-bill rate or the T-bond rate. k_{RF} includes an inflation premium.

The **nominal, or quoted, risk-free rate, k_{RF}**, is the real risk-free rate plus a premium for expected inflation: $k_{RF} = k^* + IP$. To be strictly correct, the risk-free rate should be the interest rate on a *totally* risk-free security—one that has no risk of default, no maturity risk, no liquidity risk, and no risk of loss if inflation increases. (We will discuss each of these risks in detail in this chapter.) There is no such security, and hence there is no observable truly risk-free rate. However, there is one security that is free of most risks—a U.S. Treasury bill (T-bill), which is a short-term security issued by the U.S. government. Treasury bonds (T-bonds), which are longer-term government securities, are free of default and liquidity risks, but T-bonds are exposed to some risk due to changes in the general level of interest rates.[3]

If the term "risk-free rate" is used without either the modifier "real" or "nominal," people generally mean the nominal rate, and we will follow that convention in this book. Therefore, when we use the term risk-free rate, we mean k_{RF}, which includes an inflation premium equal to the average expected inflation rate over the life of the security. In general, we use the T-bill rate to

---

[3]Treasury bills and Treasury bonds were both defined and briefly discussed in Chapter 2.

approximate the short-term risk-free rate, and the T-bond rate to approximate the long-term risk-free rate.[4]

Inflation Premium (IP)

Inflation has a major impact on interest rates because it erodes the purchasing power of the dollar and lowers the real rate of return on investments. To illustrate, suppose you save $1,000 and invest it in a Treasury bill that matures in 1 year and pays 4 percent interest. At the end of the year, you will receive $1,040 — your original $1,000 plus $40 of interest. Now suppose the rate of inflation during the year is 6 percent, and it affects all items equally. If beer had cost $1 per bottle at the beginning of the year, it would cost $1.06 at the end of the year. Therefore, your $1,000 would have bought $1,000/$1 = 1,000 bottles at the beginning of the year but only $1,040/$1.06 = 981 bottles at the end. Thus, in *real terms,* you would be worse off; you would receive $40 of interest, but it would not be sufficient to offset inflation. You would thus be better off buying 1,000 bottles of beer (or some other storable asset such as land, timber, apartment buildings, wheat, or gold) than buying the Treasury bill.

inflation premium (IP)

A premium for expected inflation that investors add to the real risk-free rate of interest.

Investors are well aware of all of this, so when they lend money, they build in an **inflation premium (IP)** equal to the expected inflation rate over the life of the security. As discussed previously, for a short-term default-free U.S. Treasury bill, the actual interest rate charged, $k_{T\text{-bill}}$, would be the real risk-free rate of interest, k^*, plus the inflation premium (IP):

$$k_{T\text{-bill}} = k_{RF} = k^* + IP. \qquad (4\text{-}3)$$

Therefore, if the real risk-free rate of interest were $k^* = 3\%$, and if inflation were expected to be 4 percent (and hence IP = 4%) during the next year, then the quoted rate of interest on 1-year T-bills would be 7 percent. In January of 1990, the expected 1-year inflation rate was about 5 percent, and the yield on 1-year T-bills was about 7.9 percent, which implies that the real risk-free rate of interest at that time was about 2.9 percent.[5]

It is important to note that the rate of inflation built into interest rates is the *rate of inflation expected in the future,* not the rate experienced in the past. Thus, the latest reported figures might show an annual inflation rate of 3 percent, but that is for the *past* period. If people on the average expect a 5 percent inflation rate for the future, then 5 percent would be built into the current rate of interest. Note also that the inflation rate reflected in the interest rate on any security is the *average rate of inflation expected over the security's life.* Thus, the inflation rate built into a 1-year Treasury bill is the expected inflation rate for the next year, but the inflation rate built into a 30-year Treas-

---

[4]For example, we will use the Treasury bond rate in later chapters when we want to compare rates on *long-term* securities, such as stocks, with a "risk-free rate"; the T-bond rate is the closest thing we have to a risk-free, long-term rate.

[5]Although the real risk-free rate is assumed to be in the range of one to four percentage points, on rare occasions it may be lower. In April 1993, for example, the T-bill rate was roughly 3 percent. If expected inflation was also about 3 percent, which is a reasonable assumption, this would make k^* close to zero or even slightly negative. Since investors typically do require to be compensated for expected inflation *and* to realize some positive return besides, even on a risk-free security, such a situation would not be likely to exist for long.

ury bond is the average rate of inflation expected over the next 30 years. The same would be true for corporate securities.

If you turn once again to Figure 4-3, you will note the high correlation between actual inflation and interest rates over the years. The relationship is not perfect, however, because it is built on expectations. Studies have shown that inflation expectations for the future are closely related to recent inflation rates. In 1974–1975 and again in the late 1970s to 1980, when high inflation rates were unusual for the United States, investors' forecasts of inflation were too low, and inflation was greater than interest rates. Therefore, investors' purchasing power eroded as price increases exceeded the rate of return they earned on their investments. Because of these experiences with high inflation, the rates in the early to mid-1980s remained high relative to current inflation as investors' fears of renewed high inflation kept the inflation premium (at least with hindsight) artificially high.

Because expectations for future inflation are closely related to recent inflation experience, if the inflation reported for the past few months were to show an increase, people would tend to raise their expectations for future inflation, and this change in expectations would cause an increase in interest rates.

Default Risk Premium (DRP)

bond ratings

Ratings assigned to bonds based on the probability of their default. Those bonds with the smallest default probability are rated Aaa and carry the lowest interest rates.

The risk that a borrower will *default* on a loan, which means not pay the interest or the principal, also affects the market interest rate on a security; the greater the default risk, the higher the interest rate lenders charge. Treasury securities have no default risk, hence they carry the lowest interest rates of taxable securities in the United States. For corporate bonds, the higher the bond's rating, the lower its default risk, and, consequently, the lower its interest rate.[6] **Bond ratings** range from Aaa, which is the rating for the financially strongest firms, down to D, which is the rating applied to companies already in bankruptcy. The following are some representative interest rates on long-term bonds during December 1992.[7]

Security	Rate	Default Risk Premium
U.S. Treasury bond	7.36%	—
Aaa corporate bond	7.93	0.57
Aa corporate bond	8.18	0.82
A corporate bond	8.32	0.96
Baa corporate bond	8.75	1.39

default risk premium (DRP)

The difference between the interest rate on a U.S. Treasury bond and a corporate bond of equal maturity and liquidity.

The difference between the quoted interest rate on a Treasury bond and that on a corporate bond *with similar maturity, liquidity, and other features* is defined as the **default risk premium (DRP).** Therefore, if the previously listed bonds are otherwise similar, the default risk premium is relatively low for Aaa

---

[6]Bond ratings, and bonds' riskiness in general, will be discussed in detail in Chapter 16. For now, merely note that bonds rated AAA are judged to have less default risk than bonds rated AA, which are less risky than bonds rated A, and so on. Ratings are expressed as AAA or Aaa, AA or Aa, etc., depending on the rating agency. In this book the designations are used interchangeably.

[7]*Federal Reserve Bulletin,* March 1993, p. A25.

corporate bonds (DRP = 7.93% − 7.36% = 0.57%), but the default risk premium is higher for the higher-risk Baa corporate bonds (DRP = 8.75% − 7.36% = 1.39%). Default risk premiums vary somewhat over time, but the December 1992 figures are representative of levels in recent years.

Liquidity Premium (LP)

liquidity premium (LP)

A premium included in the nominal interest rate on a security if that security cannot be converted to cash on short notice and at a fair market price.

Liquidity generally is defined as the ability to convert an asset to cash quickly at a fair market value. Assets have varying degrees of liquidity, depending on the characteristics of the market in which they are traded. For instance, there exist very active and easily accessible secondary markets for financial assets such as government notes and bonds, the stocks and bonds of large corporations, and most short-term debt instruments, but the markets for real estate are limited because they are geographically constrained. Therefore, most financial assets are considered more liquid than real assets. However, less actively traded securities, for example, those of small corporations, are said to have a "thin market" and are not very liquid.[8] Because liquidity is important, investors evaluate liquidity and include a **liquidity premium (LP)** in the nominal rates of all illiquid securities. Although it is very difficult to accurately measure liquidity premiums, a differential of at least two and probably four or five percentage points exists between the least liquid and the most liquid financial assets of similar default risk and maturity.

Maturity Risk Premium (MRP)

U.S. Treasury securities are free of default risk in the sense that one can be virtually certain that the federal government will pay interest on its bonds and will also pay them off when they mature. Therefore, the *default* risk premium on Treasury securities is essentially zero. Further, active markets exist for Treasury securities, so the *liquidity* premium may also be assumed to be zero. Thus, as a first approximation, the rate of interest on a Treasury bond should be the risk-free rate, k_{RF}, which is equal to the real risk-free rate, k^*, plus an inflation premium, IP.

However, an adjustment is needed for long-term Treasury bonds, and for *all* fixed-rate debt instruments, for that matter, especially those with a long maturity. Remember from Chapter 3 that you were asked to take on faith that there is an inverse relationship between the price, or market value, of an existing, fixed-rate debt instrument and the general level of interest rates. (This was discussed in connection with the Fed's open market operations.) Although the proof of the statement will be presented in Chapter 16, we can, at this point, explain the inverse relationship between interest rate and market value in a common-sense fashion:

Suppose that you inherited a bond some years ago and that it pays a coupon rate of 14 percent for an interest payment of $140 annually. Now you need to

---

[8]Another example of lack of liquidity would be the junk bond market in 1989–1990, after the principal market maker, Drexell Burnham Lambert, had declared bankruptcy (junk bonds will be discussed further in Chapter 16). A third example of a less-than-liquid market is the secondary market for limited partnership interests which was covered in Chapter 1.

sell it. Assume that new bonds with exactly the same characteristics currently sell with a coupon of only 8 percent, or an annual interest of $80 per bond. Ask yourself which of these two bonds, yours or the new one, is most valuable to a potential bond buyer. The answer is, of course, yours. Because it pays so much more in annual interest and is no different in any other respect, it will have risen in value and will now sell for more than its original issue price of $1,000. The annual coupon rate is fixed and cannot adjust; therefore, the market value must adjust to reflect the changed interest rate environment.

This illustration is an example of what is called *interest rate risk,* but it is that portion of the total risk that you could live with! You would have had a significant capital gain on the bond simply because interest rates, in general, had declined over time. The problem is that the opposite is also true: If interest rates rise (as they very well might from the record low levels of 1993), you would experience a capital loss on a fixed-rate debt instrument. For example, if someone had bought a 30-year Treasury bond for $1,000 in 1972, when the interest rate (coupon) on such bonds was 7 percent, and held it until 1981, when T-bond rates were about 14.5 percent, the value of the bond would have declined to about $514. This would represent a loss of almost half the money invested, and it demonstrates that even U.S. Treasury bonds are not riskless.[9]

In summary, interest rate risk is the risk of incurring capital losses on a fixed-rate debt instrument due to changing interest rates over time. (Check Figure 4-2 again to remind yourself just how extreme interest rate fluctuations have been.) Note two important points: (1) Interest rate risk affects *all* fixed-rate debt securities, therefore, also Treasury securities, because it has nothing to do with the creditworthiness of the issuer or the liquidity of the asset; (2) it is when you want to trade a bond *prior* to its maturity that you are likely to have a capital gain or loss on the investment. If you could hold it until maturity, the assumption is that you would get back the $1,000 initially invested.

Finally, and most importantly in this context, *the longer the period until a bond's maturity, the more it is subject to interest rate risk.* If interest rates were to increase by 1 percentage point, an investor would suffer a much greater capital loss on a T-bond with 30 years until maturity than on a 2-year Treasury note. Therefore, a **maturity risk premium (MRP),** which is higher the longer the period of years to maturity, must be included in the nominal interest rate.

The effect of maturity risk premiums is to raise interest rates on long-term bonds relative to those on short-term securities. This premium, like the others, is extremely difficult to measure, but (1) it seems to vary over time, rising when interest rates are more volatile and uncertain and falling when they are more stable, and (2) in recent years, the maturity risk premium on 30-year T-bonds appears to have been in the range of one to two percentage points.[10]

We should mention that although long-term bonds are heavily exposed to interest rate risk, short-term securities are heavily exposed to **reinvestment rate risk.** When short-term securities mature and the funds are reinvested, or

maturity risk premium (MRP)

A premium which compensates investors for interest rate risk.

reinvestment rate risk

The risk that a decline in interest rates will lead to lower income when securities mature and funds are reinvested.

---

[9]On the other hand, had the investor purchased short-term T-bills in 1972 and subsequently reinvested the principal each time the bills matured, he or she would still have had the $1,000 principal intact—plus whatever interest had been earned.

[10]The MRP has averaged 1.3 percentage points over the last 65 years. See *Stocks, Bonds, Bills, and Inflation: 1992 Yearbook* (Chicago: Ibbotson Associates, 1992).

"rolled over," a decline in interest rates would result in reinvestment at a lower rate, and hence would lead to a decline in interest income. To illustrate, suppose you had $100,000 invested in 1-year T-bills, and you lived on the income. In 1981, short-term rates were about 15 percent, so your income would have been about $15,000. However, your income would have declined to about $9,000 by 1983, and to only about $3,000 by 1993. Had you invested your money in long-term T-bonds, your income (but not the value of your principal) would have been stable.[11] Thus, although "investing short" preserves one's principal, the interest income provided by short-term T-bills (and other short-term money market instruments) varies from year to year, depending on reinvestment rates.

Self-Test

Write out the two equations for the nominal interest rate on any debt security.

Distinguish between the *real* risk-free rate of interest, k*, and the *nominal*, or quoted, risk-free rate of interest, k_{RF}.

How are inflation expectations incorporated into interest rates by investors?

Does the interest rate on a T-bond include a default risk premium? Explain.

Explain what is meant by liquidity, and identify some assets that are liquid and some that are illiquid.

Briefly explain the following statement: "Although long-term bonds are heavily exposed to interest rate risk, an investment into short-term instruments is heavily exposed to reinvestment rate risk."

The Term Structure of Interest Rates

term structure of interest rates

The relationship between interest rates (yields) and maturities of debt securities.

From Figure 4-2, we can see that at certain times, such as in 1993, short-term interest rates are lower than long-term rates, while at other times, such as in 1980 and 1981, short-term rates were higher than long-term rates. The **term structure of interest rates** is the relationship between long- and short-term interest rates on debt securities. It is important to both corporate treasurers and investors to understand (1) how long- and short-term rates are related to each other and (2) what causes shifts in their relative positions.

In sources such as *The Wall Street Journal* and the *Federal Reserve Bulletin,* we can find interest rates on debt securities of different maturities. When we look up these rates, it is important (1) that they are all obtained at the same point in time (on the same date) and (2) that all the securities are issued by

---

[11]Long-term bonds also have some reinvestment rate risk. To actually earn the quoted rate on a long-term bond, the interest payments must be reinvested at the quoted rate. However, if interest rates fall, the interest payments must be reinvested at a lower rate; thus, the realized return would be less than the quoted rate. Note, though, that the reinvestment rate risk is lower on a long-term bond than on a short-term security because on the long-term bond only the interest payments (not the principal) are exposed to reinvestment rate risk. Only zero coupon bonds, discussed in Chapter 16, are completely free of reinvestment rate risk.

Figure 4-4

Yield Curves for U.S.
Treasury Securities on
Different Dates

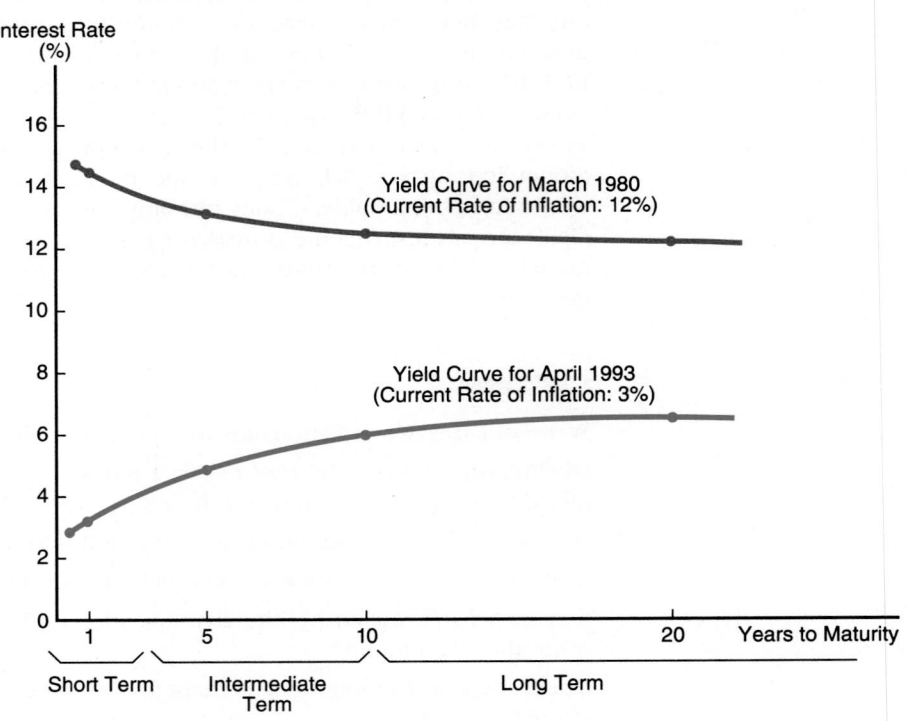

This figure shows the actual yield curves for U.S. Treasury securities of different maturities in two recent years. In 1993 investors expected inflation to rise from the then-current 3 percent; this produced an upward-sloping yield curve, meaning that long-term bonds offered a higher interest rate than did short-term securities. In 1980, however, inflation was expected to decline, creating a downward-sloping yield curve.

Term to Maturity	Interest Rate	
	March 1980	**April 1993**
6 months	15.0%	3.0%
1 year	14.0	3.1
5 years	13.5	5.2
10 years	12.8	6.0
20 years	12.5	6.5

yield curve

A graph showing the relationship between yields and maturities of debt securities.

the same entity, for example, one corporation or the federal government. In the table at the bottom of Figure 4-4, interest rates are given for Treasury securities with a variety of maturities, first in March 1980 and then in April 1993. Each of the two sets of data, when plotted on a graph as in Figure 4-4, is called the **yield curve** for that date. The yield curve changes both in position and in slope over time. In March 1980, all rates were relatively high, and short-term rates were higher than long-term rates, so the yield curve on that date was *downward sloping*. However, by April 1993, all rates had fallen, and short-term rates were lower than long-term rates, so the yield curve at that time was *upward sloping*. If the yield curve had been drawn in January 1982, it would have been essentially horizontal, or flat, since long-term and short-term securities at that time had about the same rate of interest. (See Figure 4-2.)

The yield curves shown in Figure 4-4 are for U.S. Treasury securities, but yield curves could have been constructed for corporate securities; for example, we could have developed yield curves for IBM, Chrysler, or any other company that borrows money over a range of maturities. If the corporate yield curves had been plotted on Figure 4-4, these curves would have been above those for Treasury securities on the same dates because the corporate yields would include default risk premiums, but they would have had the same general shape as the Treasury curves. Also, the riskier the corporation, the higher its yield curve.

In a stable economy such as the United States had in the 1950s and early 1960s, in which (1) inflation fluctuated in the 1 to 3 percent range, (2) the expected future rate of inflation was about equal to the current rate, and (3) the Federal Reserve did not actively intervene in the markets, all interest rates were relatively low, and the yield curve generally had a slight upward slope to reflect maturity effects. People often define such an upward-sloping yield curve as a **normal yield curve,** and a yield curve which slopes downward as an **inverted, or abnormal, yield curve.** Thus, in Figure 4-4 the yield curve for March 1980 was inverted, but the one for April 1993 was normal. Note also that we have not had an inverted, or downward-sloping, yield curve since the early 1980s.

normal yield curve

An upward-sloping yield curve.

inverted (abnormal) yield curve

A downward-sloping yield curve.

Term Structure Theories

Several theories have been proposed to explain the shape of the yield curve. The three major ones are (1) the *market segmentation theory,* (2) the *liquidity preference theory,* and (3) the *expectations theory.*

market segmentation theory

The theory that each borrower and lender has a preferred maturity and that the slope of the yield curve depends on the supply of and demand for funds in the long-term market relative to the short-term market.

Market Segmentation Theory. The **market segmentation theory** states that each lender and borrower has a preferred maturity. For example, a person borrowing to buy a long-term asset, such as a house, would want a long-term loan, while a retailer borrowing in September for Christmas inventory would prefer a short-term loan. Similar differences exist among savers — for example, a person saving to take a vacation next summer would want to lend in the short-term market, but someone saving for retirement 20 years hence would probably buy long-term securities.

The essence of the market segmentation theory is that the slope of the yield curve depends on supply/demand conditions in the long-term and short-term markets. According to the theory, the yield curve could at any given time be flat, upward sloping, or downward sloping. An upward-sloping yield curve would occur when there was a large supply of short-term funds relative to demand but a shortage of long-term funds. Similarly, a downward-sloping curve would indicate relatively strong demand in the short-term market compared with that in the long-term market. A flat curve would indicate a balance between the relative supply and demand in the two markets.

**liquidity
preference theory**
The theory that lenders prefer to make short-term loans rather than long-term loans; hence, they will lend short-term funds at lower rates than long-term funds.

Liquidity Preference Theory.   The **liquidity preference theory** states that long-term bonds normally yield more than short-term securities for two reasons: (1) Investors generally prefer to hold short-term securities and will accept lower yields on these because such securities are more liquid in the sense that they can be converted to cash with little danger of loss of principal.[12] (2) Borrowers, on the other hand, generally prefer long-term debt because short-term debt exposes them to the risk of having to repay the debt under adverse conditions. Accordingly, borrowers are willing to pay a higher rate, other things held constant, for long-term funds than for short-term funds. Taken together, these preferences — and hence the liquidity preference theory — imply that under normal conditions, a positive maturity risk premium (MRP) exists, and the MRP increases with years to maturity, causing the yield curve to be upward sloping. Notice that the liquidity preference theory offers no explanation for an inverted, or downward-sloping, yield curve.

expectations theory
The theory that the shape of the yield curve depends primarily on investors' expectations about future inflation rates.

Expectations Theory.   The **expectations theory** states that the yield curve depends on investor expectations about future inflation rates. Specifically, k_t, the nominal interest rate on a U.S. Treasury security that matures in t years, is found as follows:

$$k_t = k^* + IP_t + MRP.$$

Here k^* is the real, risk-free interest rate, IP_t is an inflation premium equal to the average expected rate of inflation over the t years before the security matures, and MRP is the maturity risk premium. Remember from the discussion earlier in this chapter that the default risk premium (DRP) and liquidity premium (LP) are zero for U.S. Treasury securities. *Under the pure expectations theory, the maturity risk premium (MRP) is also assumed to be zero,* so the equation reduces to

$$k_t = k^* + IP_t.$$

Note that (1) the Treasury can borrow on a short-term basis, on a long-term basis, or anywhere in between, and (2) the inflation premium built into any security's interest rate is the *average expected inflation rate* over the security's life, or its *term to maturity.* Therefore, it is appropriate to add a subscript, t, to the inflation premium, depending on years to maturity. Thus IP_3 is the inflation premium for a 3-year security (note), and it is equal to the average expected inflation rate over the next 3 years.

To illustrate, suppose that in late December 1993 the real risk-free rate of interest was $k^* = 2\%$, and expected inflation rates for the next 3 years were as follows:

---

[12]Recognize that, in spite of the name of this theory, the risk of concern to investors is really *interest rate risk* since this is the risk that is linked to the maturity of the instrument.

	Expected Annual (1-Year) Inflation Rate	Expected Average Inflation Rate from 1993 to Indicated Year
1994	4%	4%/1 = 4.0%
1995	6%	(4% + 6%)/2 = 5.0%
1996	8%	(4% + 6% + 8%)/3 = 6.0%

Given these expectations, the following pattern of interest rates should exist on 1-, 2-, and 3-year Treasury securities:

	Real Risk-free Rate (k^*)		Inflation Premium, Which Is Equal to the Average Expected Inflation Rate (IP_t)		Nominal Interest Rate for Each Maturity (k_t)
1 year	2%	+	4.0%	=	6.0%
2 years	2%	+	5.0%	=	7.0%
3 years	2%	+	6.0%	=	8.0%

Had the pattern of expected inflation rates been reversed, with inflation expected to fall from 8 percent to 6 percent and then to 4 percent, the following situation would have existed for Treasury securities:

	Real Risk-free Rate (k^*)		Average Expected Inflation Rate (IP_t)		Nominal Interest Rate for Each Maturity (k_t)
1 year	2%	+	8.0%	=	10.0%
2 years	2%	+	7.0%	=	9.0%
3 years	2%	+	6.0%	=	8.0%

These hypothetical data are plotted in Figure 4-5. According to the expectations theory, whenever the annual rate of inflation is expected to increase, the yield curve must be upward sloping, as shown in Yield Curve a, whereas it must be downward sloping if inflation is expected to decline, as shown in Yield Curve b.

Various tests of these theories have been conducted and indicate that all three theories have some validity. Thus, the shape of the yield curve at any given time is affected by (1) supply/demand conditions in the long- and short-term markets, (2) liquidity preferences, and (3) expectations about future inflation. One factor may dominate at one time, another at another time, but all three affect the structure of interest rates.

Self-Test

What is a yield curve, and what information would you need to draw such a curve?

Figure 4-5

Expectations Theory: Hypothetical Example of the Term Structure of Interest Rates

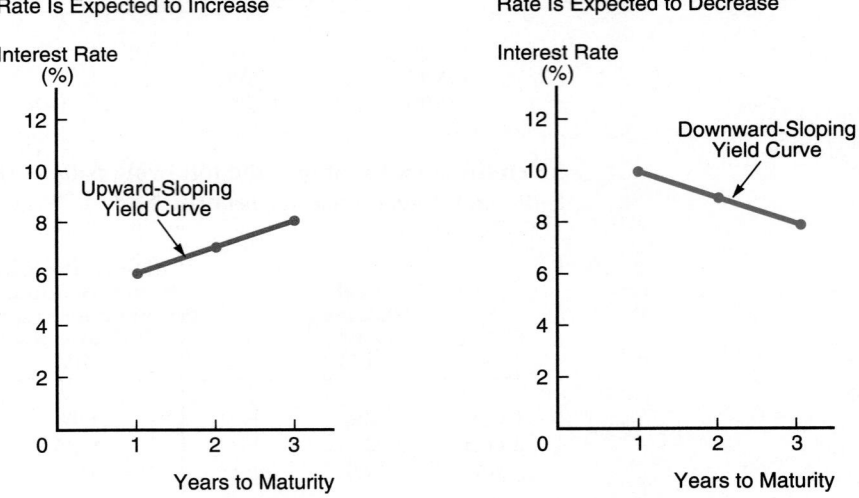

The inflation premium built into the interest rate for any security is the average expected inflation rate over the life, or term to maturity, of the security. The term structure of interest rates is depicted by the hypothetical yield curves shown in this figure. If inflation is expected to increase, short-term securities will yield less than long-term securities, as shown in Yield Curve a. Conversely, if inflation is expected to decline, as shown in Yield Curve b, short-term securities will yield more than long-term securities.

Distinguish among the following theories: (1) market segmentation theory, (2) liquidity preference theory, and (3) expectations theory.

Distinguish between the shapes of a normal yield curve and an inverted yield curve, and explain why each might exist.

Specific Factors That Influence Interest Rate Levels

In addition to inflationary expectations, liquidity preferences, and normal supply/demand fluctuations, a number of specific factors also influence the general level of interest rates and the shape of the yield curve. The four most important ones are (1) Federal Reserve policy, (2) the level of the federal budget deficit, (3) the foreign trade balance, and (4) the level of business activity.

Federal Reserve Policy

As you learned in Chapter 3 and in your studies of economics, (1) the money supply has a major effect on both the level of economic activity and the rate of inflation, and (2) in the United States the Federal Reserve System controls (or *attempts* to control) the money supply. When the Fed wants to stimulate the economy, as it did in the early 1990s, it takes steps to increase growth in the money supply. The initial effect of such an action is to cause interest rates to decline, but the action also may lead to an increase in the expected rate of inflation, which in turn could push interest rates up. The reverse holds if the Fed tightens monetary policy and reduces the money supply.

As we have already seen, in 1981 inflation was quite high, so the Fed tightened monetary policy. The Fed deals primarily in the short-term end of the market, so this tightening had the direct effect of pushing short-term interest rates up sharply. At the same time, the very fact that the Fed was taking strong action to reduce inflation led to a decline in expectations for long-run inflation, which led to a drop in long-term bond yields. The net effect was a downward-sloping, or inverted, yield curve. After the Fed's intervention ended, short-term rates declined, and the yield curve resumed its normal upward slope.

In 1991 and 1992, the situation was just the reverse. To combat the recession, the Fed took steps to reduce interest rates. Short-term rates fell dramatically (see Figure 4-2), and later long-term rates also dropped, but not as sharply. These lower rates have provided a huge benefit to heavily indebted businesses and individual borrowers. Savers have, of course, lost out, but the net effect has been a boost to the economy.

We see, then, that during periods when the Fed is actively intervening in the markets, the yield curve will be distorted. Short-term rates will be temporarily "too high" if the Fed is tightening credit and "too low" if it is easing credit. Long-term rates are not affected as much by Fed intervention, except to the extent that such intervention affects expectations for long-term inflation.

Federal Deficits

If the federal government spends more than it takes in from tax revenues, it runs a deficit, and that deficit must be covered either by borrowing or by printing money. If the government borrows, this added demand for funds pushes up interest rates. If it prints money, this increases expectations for future inflation, which also drives up interest rates. Thus, the larger the federal deficit, other things held constant, the higher the level of interest rates. Whether long- or short-term rates are affected more depends on how the deficit is financed, so we cannot state, in general, how deficits will affect the slope of the yield curve.

Events in early 1993 provide a powerful example of the link between the federal deficit and interest rates. In spite of the Fed's easier monetary policy, long-term interest rates remained stubbornly high going into 1993. Then, in mid-February, President Clinton presented his economic plan to the nation. The package included sharp tax increases to bring about a significant reduction in the federal budget deficit. In response to the Clinton tax plan, bond prices surged, and the yield on 30-year Treasury bonds dropped below 7 percent, the lowest level since the Treasury began issuing 30-year bonds in 1977. (It should be mentioned that an alternative interpretation of the bond market rally was that higher taxes would send the economy back into recession. This would dampen inflation fears, which, in turn, would also lead to lower interest rates.)

Another way in which the federal government's actions can influence the shape of the yield curve has to do with the mix of short-term versus long-term Treasury securities used to finance the federal deficit. In May 1993, after considering the matter for several months, the Treasury announced that it would sharply reduce its sale of 30-year bonds (a reduction of about 45 percent is expected) and instead sell more Treasury securities with maturities of three years or less. This would be done, said the Clinton administration, in an attempt to cut borrowing costs and save taxpayer money.

By shifting a significant portion of its total borrowing to much shorter maturities, there would be less overall demand for long-term funds, and long-term rates should fall; however, the more the Treasury borrows short term, the more short-term rates would be pushed up, other things equal. The effect of such a financial shift would be a flatter yield curve. Would such a policy change by the Treasury save taxpayers money? The answer is by no means certain and depends on the time horizon used. The Treasury's total financing cost would decline *in the short run,* but as just discussed, the Treasury's action would, by itself, contribute to *rising* short-term interest rates. In addition, if short-term rates were to rise further for other reasons (for example, higher inflation or greater demand from nongovernment borrowers), the Treasury's plan could backfire and cost the taxpayers dearly. We know that short-term rates will fluctuate more than long-term rates (see Figure 4-2). Therefore, as we will discuss toward the end of this chapter, overreliance on short-term financing subjects the borrower to considerable uncertainty. Many Wall Street economists, bond dealers, and at least one former Treasury secretary have been strongly recommending that the Treasury *not* make this potentially risky bet on the direction of interest rates. (It is worth noting that while the Treasury is moving to shorten its debt, many corporations are doing just the opposite—they are rushing to take advantage of the lowest long-term interest rates in about two decades by selling long-term bonds and reducing their reliance on shorter-term debt.)

Foreign Trade Balance

Businesses and individuals in the United States buy from and sell to people and firms in other countries. If we import more than we export, we are said to be running a *foreign trade deficit.* When trade deficits occur, they must be financed, and the main source of financing is debt. In other words, if we import $200 billion of goods but export only $100 billion, we run a trade deficit of $100 billion and must borrow the $100 billion.[13] Therefore, the larger our trade deficit, the more we must borrow, and as we increase our borrowing, this drives up interest rates. Also, foreigners are willing to hold U.S. debt if and only if the interest rate on this debt is competitive with interest rates in other countries. Therefore, if the Federal Reserve attempts to lower interest rates in the United States, causing our rates to fall below rates abroad, then foreigners will sell U.S. bonds, those sales will depress bond prices, and the result will be higher U.S. rates. Thus, the existence of a deficit trade balance limits the Fed's ability to combat a recession through lower interest rates.

The United States has been running annual trade deficits since the mid-1970s, and the cumulative result of these deficits is that the United States is by far the largest debtor nation of all time. As a result, our interest rates are very

---

[13]The deficit could also be financed by selling assets, including gold, corporate stocks, entire companies, and real estate. The United States has financed its massive trade deficits by all of these means in recent years, but the primary method has been by borrowing.

much influenced by interest rate trends in other countries around the world (higher rates abroad tend to lead to higher U.S. rates). Because of this, U.S. corporate treasurers must keep up with developments in the world economy.

Business Activity

Figure 4-2, presented earlier, can be examined to see how business conditions influence interest rates. Here are the key points revealed by the graph:

1. Because inflation has generally been increasing since 1956, the tendency has been toward higher interest rates. However, since the 1981 peak, the trend has been reversed.

2. Until 1966, short-term rates were almost always below long-term rates. Thus, in those years the yield curve was almost always normal, or upward sloping.

3. The shaded areas in the graph represent recessions, during which both the demand for money and the rate of inflation tend to fall, and, at the same time, the Federal Reserve tends to increase the money supply in an effort to stimulate the economy. As a result, interest rates generally decline during recessions—this is seen especially clearly in the early 1980s.

4. During recessions, short-term rates experience sharper declines than long-term rates. This occurs because (1) the Fed operates mainly in the short-term sector, and hence, its intervention has the major effect here, and (2) long-term rates reflect the average expected inflation rate over the next 20 to 30 years, and this expectation generally does not change much, even when the current rate of inflation is low because of a recession.

In summary, note that (1) the four specific factors just discussed are interrelated and also tie in with the underlying determinants identified earlier by the three theories and (2) our government's foreign policy is very much linked to these important variables.

For example, the level of business activity and the level of the federal budget deficit both contribute to general supply and demand conditions, and large federal budget deficits make it difficult for the government to provide a fiscal stimulus to a sagging economy, which means that more of the burden falls on the shoulders of the Fed. The Fed may then respond by dramatically lowering short-term interest rates, as in the early 1990s. Meanwhile, our government may put pressure on other governments, such as Germany's, to lower their interest rates to avoid having capital flow from the United States to Germany in search of higher yields. We have also seen several recent attempts by the U.S. government to convince the Japanese government to lower trade barriers and allow more U.S. products into Japan. The goal is, of course, to lower our trade deficit with Japan.

Self-Test

Other than inflationary expectations, liquidity preferences, and normal supply/demand fluctuations, name four specific factors which influence interest rates, and explain their effects.

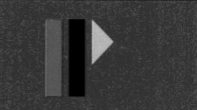

WHEN THE WORLD SPEAKS . . . THE FED LISTENS

A fail-safe way to boost the U.S. economy in case of a slump has always been to lower interest rates. But the traditional remedy is no longer automatically available, and this is quite a change from the past. In earlier times, when the Fed spoke, the world listened. Today, the Fed must listen to the world—especially to Germany and Japan.

Because of our foreign trade deficits, the United States has become the world's largest debtor nation—foreign nationals hold a tremendous amount of U.S. bonds and other securities. If our interest rates decline, international investors will pull money out or, at the very least, stop putting more in. If the supply of foreign funds to U.S. borrowers is cut back, U.S. interest rates can go only one way—up.

Today there's a fear that big bond investors hold unprecedented power—maybe even a veto—over U.S. economic policy. If inflation accelerates, or if big spending programs are enacted, the reaction could be swift and painful. Anticipation by global bondholders of just such possibilities under President Clinton pushed down the price of U.S. Treasury bonds and increased long-term interest rates from 7.3 to 7.7 percent during one month in the fall of 1992. However, if Clinton fulfills his promises to reinvigorate the U.S. economy and create jobs without increasing either the budget deficit or the inflation rate, bondholders will probably bestow their blessings and allow long-term rates to ease.

In the past, presidents paid little attention to Wall Street except to note if stock prices were rising (signifying satisfaction with economic policy) or falling (signifying dissatisfaction). But the government does not sell stock to pay for its operations; instead it borrows money by using Treasury bills (with a maturity of several months), notes (2 to 10 years), and bonds (up to 30 years).

Foreign investors hold some $400 billion of our government's debt. Global trading in U.S. government bonds averages around $150 billion a day. With computer linkups, millions of dollars of bonds can be sold in a matter of seconds, 24 hours a day. Since long-term interest rates move inversely to bond prices, rates would shoot up if thousands of investors worldwide decided to dump their U.S. bonds. In the worst case, a mass withdrawal could plunge the nation back into recession.

There is anxiety among U.S. traders and investors every time the Treasury seeks new funds through a bond auction. In early 1990, interest rates in Germany rose above U.S. rates, and Japanese rates reached a six-year high about the same time. When the U.S. Treasury offered rare 40-year bonds at a $5 billion auction, it expected demand to be strong. Instead, both domestic and foreign investors turned a cold shoulder. After that, fears were widespread that foreign investors would not participate in later, much larger, auctions of Treasury bonds, and that this would push U.S. rates dramatically higher. One financial analyst said, "If the Japanese suddenly cut back and buy only 10 percent instead of 40 percent [of an issue], somebody else has to buy that 30 percent, and that buyer, more than likely, will only come in if the rate is set at a higher level."

The first months of the Clinton administration inspired some hesitancy worldwide, according to Sandy Batten, senior economist at Citibank, since no one knew what changes in economic policy might emerge. "It's just not clear that foreign investors will want to put funds into the U.S. with the uncertainty about the possibility of a fiscal drag on the economy," he said.

Many money managers still remember the soaring inflation and wildly fluctuating interest rates we experienced during the tenure of the last Democratic president, Jimmy Carter. Says Richard Hoey, chief economist of Dreyfus Corporation, "Conditions are different now, but the memory is still in the minds of all who lived through that period."

Robert Hormats, a former State Department official who is now vice-chairman of Goldman Sachs International, warns, "Bond buyers have a very conservative bias . . . they'll be looking very hard at whatever Clinton does."

Sources: Douglas R. Sease and Constance Mitchell, "World's Bond Buyers Gain Huge Influence Over U.S. Fiscal Plans," *The Wall Street Journal,* November 6, 1992, page A-1; David Wessel and Constance Mitchell, "Fed has Lost Much of Its Power to Sway U.S. Interest Rates," *The Wall Street Journal,* March 12, 1990, p. A-1; J. M. Laderman, "Boxed in at the Fed," *Business Week,* February 5, 1990, pp. 22–23.

In fact, if the actions of worried investors caused a rise of just one percentage point in long-term interest rates, the deficit would increase another $20 billion.

Interest rates are tied to inflation, and worries about inflation may force the Federal Reserve to keep money tight and short-term interest rates up. But even when the Fed wants to lower rates, the situation in Frankfurt and Tokyo can make it difficult, if not impossible. When the 6 Federal Reserve Board governors and the 12 regional Fed bank presidents met at the end of 1989 to consider the direction interest rates should take, they were worried about a possible recession and decided to lower short-term rates with the goal of calming the financial markets and leading to a lowering of long-term rates.

Long rates did fall slightly, supporting the traditional dictum that long-term rates follow changes in short-term rates. However, the theory did not hold up very long. Within three months, the rate on 30-year Treasury bonds was three-fourths of a percentage point *higher* than it had been when the Fed acted. Part of the rise was accounted for by optimism that the United States would avoid a recession, but the major influence apparently came from across both oceans. Accelerating inflation caused rates to rise in Japan, while in Europe there were also fears of inflation plus a new demand for capital to modernize liberated eastern European nations.

Lyle Gramley, who was chief economic forecaster for the Fed during the 1970s, emphasized how things have changed: "I considered the international division more of a nuisance. The direct link from interest rates abroad to interest rates in the U.S. to the outlook for the U.S. economy—I never had to deal with that intellectually before. Who ever thought that developments in . . . Germany were going to be a very important influence on interest rates in the U.S.?"

Government economists and bond traders are not the only ones affected by the global marketplace. Prospective homeowners also feel the effect because lenders may set their mortgage rates according to the latest news from Tokyo or Frankfurt rather than Washington or New York.

Wall Street economists are not immune either. David Jones, chief economist at Aubrey G. Lanston, says, "I spend 80 percent of my time worrying about the foreign side, or at least how the foreign side affects the domestic side."

Edward Yardeni, chief economist of C.J. Lawrence Inc., coined the term "bond vigilantes" a decade ago when he recognized the growing power of global investors in U.S. government bonds. He says, "The federal deficit is a Frankenstein's monster. By having such a large deficit, we have created a situation that puts a lot of power in the hands of money managers around the world. We created the monster, and now it's coming back to tell us what we can and can't do. "I think the bond vigilantes are forcing Clinton to recognize that they will be voting every day the market is open, and they have the ability to act as a governor on the steam engine."

Interest Rate Levels and Stock Prices

Interest rates have two effects on corporate profits and influence stock prices in yet another way: (1) First, because interest is a cost, the higher the rate of interest, the lower a firm's profits, other things held constant. (2) Second, interest rates affect the level of economic activity, and economic activity affects corporate profits. Thus, interest rates obviously affect stock prices because of their effects on profits, but, perhaps even more important, they have an effect due to competition in the marketplace between stocks and bonds. (3) If interest rates rise sharply, investors can get higher returns in the bond market, which induces them to sell stocks and to transfer funds from the stock market to the bond market. Stock sales in response to rising interest rates will depress stock prices. Of course, the reverse occurs if interest rates decline. Indeed, the bull market of December 1991, when the Dow Jones Industrial Index rose 10 percent in less than a month, was caused almost entirely by the sharp drop in long-term interest rates.

The experience of Commonwealth Edison, the electric utility serving the Chicago area, can be used to illustrate the effects of interest rates on stock prices. In 1984 Edison's stock sold for $21 per share, and, since the company paid a $3 dividend, the dividend yield was $3/$21 = 14.3%. Edison's bonds at the time also yielded about 14.3 percent. Thus, if someone had saved $100,000 and invested it in either the stock or the bonds, his or her annual income would have been about $14,300. (The investor might also have expected the stock price to grow over time, providing some capital gains, but that point is not relevant for the example.)

By 1992, all interest rates were lower, and Edison's bonds were yielding only 8.5 percent. If the stock still yielded 14.3 percent, investors could switch $100,000 out of Edison's bonds and into its stock and, in the process, increase their annual income from $8,500 to $14,300. Many people did exactly that—as interest rates dropped, orders poured in for the stock, and its price was bid up. In January 1992, Edison's stock sold for $37, up about 76 percent over the 1984 level, and the dividend yield (8.1%) was close to the bond yield (8.5%).

? Self-Test

In what three ways do changes in interest rates affect stock prices?

Interest Rates and Business Decisions

The yield curve for April 1993, shown earlier in Figure 4-4, indicates how much the U.S. government had to pay at that time to borrow money for 1 year, 5 years, 10 years, and so on. A business borrower would have had to pay somewhat more, but assume for the moment that we are back in April 1993 and that the yield curve also applies to your company. Now suppose your company has decided (1) to build a new plant with a 20-year life which will cost $1 million and (2) to raise the $1 million by selling an issue of debt (or borrowing) rather than by selling stock. If you borrowed in April 1993 on a short-term basis—say, for one year—your interest cost for that year would be only 3.1 percent, or $31,000, whereas if you used long-term (20-year) financing, your cost would be 6.5 percent, or $65,000. Therefore, at first glance, it would seem that you should use short-term debt.

However, this could prove to be a horrible mistake. If you use short-term debt, you will have to renew your loan every year, and the rate charged on each new loan will reflect the then-current short-term rate. Interest rates could return to their March 1980 levels, so in a few years you might be paying 14 percent, or $140,000, per year. These high interest payments would cut into and perhaps eliminate your profits. Your reduced profitability could easily increase your firm's risk to the point where your bond rating would be lowered, causing lenders to increase the default risk premium built into the interest rate they charge, which in turn would force you to pay even higher rates. These very high interest rates would further reduce your profitability, worrying lenders even more, and making them reluctant to renew your loan. If your lenders refused to renew the loan and demanded payment, as they have every right to do, you might have trouble raising the cash. If you had to make price cuts to convert physical assets to cash, you might incur heavy operating losses, or even bankruptcy.

On the other hand, if you used long-term financing in 1993, your interest costs would remain constant at $65,000 per year, so an increase in interest rates would not hurt you. You might even be able to buy up some of your bankrupted competitors at bargain prices — bankruptcies increase dramatically when interest rates rise, primarily because many firms do use short-term debt.

Does all this suggest that firms should always avoid short-term debt? Not necessarily. If inflation remains low in the next few years, so will interest rates. If you had borrowed on a long-term basis at 6.5 percent in April 1993, your company would be at a major disadvantage if its debt were locked in at 6.5 percent while its competitors had a borrowing cost of close to 3 percent. On the other hand, if larger than expected federal deficits or other factors were to drive inflation and interest rates up to new record levels, you would wish you had borrowed on a long-term basis in 1993.

Financing decisions would be easy if we could develop accurate forecasts of future interest rates. Unfortunately, predicting future interest rates with consistent accuracy is somewhere between difficult and impossible — people who make a living by selling interest rate forecasts say it is difficult, but many others say it is impossible.

Even if it is difficult to predict future interest rate *levels,* it is easy to predict that interest rates will *fluctuate* — they always have, and they always will. This being the case, sound financial policy calls for using a mix of long- and short-term debt, as well as equity, in such a manner that the firm can survive in most interest rate environments. Further, the optimal financial policy depends in an important way on the nature of the firm's assets; the easier it is to sell off assets and thus to pay off debts, the more appropriate it is to use large amounts of short-term debt. This makes it more feasible to finance current assets than fixed assets with short-term debt. We will return to this issue later in the book, when we discuss working capital management.

Self-Test

If short-term interest rates are lower than long-term rates, why might a firm still choose to finance with long-term debt?

Explain the following statement: "The optimal financial policy depends in an important way on the nature of the firm's assets."

Summary

In this chapter we primarily discussed how interest rates are determined, but we also explained some of the ways in which interest rates affect business decisions. The key concepts covered are listed next.

▶   Capital is allocated through the price system — a price is charged to "rent" money. Lenders charge **interest** on funds they lend, while equity investors expect to receive dividends and/or capital gains in return for letting the firm use their money.

Four fundamental factors affect the cost of money: (1) **production opportunities**, (2) **time preferences for consumption**, (3) **risk**, and (4) **inflation.**

▶ The **nominal, or quoted, interest rate** on a debt security, **k,** is composed of the real risk-free rate (k^*) plus premiums that reflect inflation (IP), default risk (DRP), liquidity (LP), and maturity, or interest rate, risk (MRP): $k = k^* + IP + DRP + LP + MRP$.

The **nominal, or quoted, risk-free rate of interest (k_{RF})** is defined as the real risk-free rate (k^*) plus an inflation premium (IP): $k_{RF} = k^* + IP$.

The **inflation premium (IP)** represents the average rate of inflation expected over the life of the security and is intended to protect the purchasing power of the lender. A **default risk premium (DRP)** is incorporated into the nominal interest rate on all securities other than those issued by the federal government. Bond ratings reflect default risk, and the higher the rating the lower the chance that the issuer will default on the obligation.

If there is the possibility that a security cannot be converted into cash quickly and at a fair market price, then its nominal interest rate must include a **liquidity premium (LP).** A **maturity risk premium (MRP)** exists to compensate investors for interest rate risk. This is the risk of capital loss on existing fixed-rate debt instruments due to rising interest rates, and there is more of this risk the longer an instrument's term to maturity.

▶ The relationship between the yields on debt securities and their maturities is known as the **term structure of interest rates,** and the **yield curve** is a graph of this relationship.

The yield curve is normally **upward sloping** — this is called a **normal yield curve** — but the curve can slope downward (an **inverted yield curve**) if the demand for short-term funds is relatively strong, if the rate of inflation is expected to decline, or if the Fed is actively intervening.

▶ Three major theories used to explain the shape of the yield curve are (1) the **market segmentation theory,** (2) the **liquidity preference theory,** and (3) the **expectations theory.**

▶ Four specific factors that also influence interest rate levels are (1) **Federal Reserve Policy,** (2) **federal deficits,** (3) the **foreign trade balance,** and (4) the general level of **business activity.**

▶ **Interest rate levels have a profound effect on stock prices.** Higher interest rates (1) increase interest expenses and thus lower corporate profits, (2) depress the economy, and (3) cause investors to sell stocks and transfer funds to the bond market. Each of these factors tends to depress stock prices.

Interest rate levels have a significant influence on corporate financial policy. Because interest rate levels are difficult if not impossible to predict, **sound financial policy** calls for using a mix of short- and long-term debt, with the goal being to position the firm to survive in any future interest rate environment.

Resolution to
DECISION IN FINANCE

ALAN GREENSPAN RESPONDS
TO CRITICS

The Federal Reserve system is the government's most important instrument for regulating the U.S. banking system. Although the Fed's mandate is to create an environment for sustained economic growth by regulating the commercial banks' ability to create credit, the effects of its policies and actions are felt well beyond the confines of the banking system. The Fed is one of the cornerstones of the U.S. economy and an important factor in international finance.

In December 1991, the financial system responded immediately to Mr. Greenspan's announcement. Morgan Guaranty Trust cut its prime lending rate from 7.5 percent to 6.5 percent, and other large banks followed Morgan's actions. Long-term rates in the bond market decreased to levels not seen in years.

What did these actions mean for the economy? On the one hand, lower rates cut the interest payments of heavily indebted businesses and homeowners. Home mortgage refinancings put billions of dollars into consumers' pockets and did it more quickly than would have been accomplished by a tax cut. Lower rates should also encourage businesses to borrow for investment, provide new life for the housing market, and help exporters by decreasing the value of the dollar relative to other currencies, which will make U.S. goods less expensive overseas.

On the other hand, lower interest rates take income away from elderly Americans who live on the income they receive from their bonds

Sources: "Changing Its Course, The Fed Boldly Tries to Bolster Economy," *The Wall Street Journal,* December 31, 1991; "Will the Fed Put America Back to Work?," *Business Week,* September 21, 1992; "Greenspan and Clinton Could Play Some Snazzy Duets," *Business Week,* February 8, 1993; and "Gonzalez Urges Clinton to Push Fed Toward Looser Monetary Policy," *United Press International,* February 8, 1993.

and savings accounts. (Overall, U.S. households receive significantly more in interest income than they pay out in interest expense.) Although the reduction of income to elderly Americans will limit the favorable effect of lower interest rates to some extent, it is not likely to offset the rate cut because (1) the excess of interest income over interest expense represents less than 2 percent of all personal income and (2) many individuals with substantial interest income are wealthy, and their day-to-day spending is not affected very much by changes in their interest income.

What were the responses of the critics immediately after the Fed's actions? Martin Feldstein, a Harvard economist and former presidential adviser, made this statement: "Although they've come down a number of times, interest rates are still very high in real [inflation-adjusted] terms, relative to where they've been in previous business cycles." Economist Robert Brusca of Nikko Securities International, who had been criticizing the Fed for months for not doing more, said, "People think monetary policy has been used and it's not effective. Monetary policy works. It's just not been used aggressively enough to fight this recession."

At the time of the 1991 announcement, most economists believed that if Greenspan's move did not work, the Fed still had room to cut rates further. Therefore, when the economy did not recover as quickly as anticipated, the Fed continued to decrease the discount and Federal funds rates, but by much smaller cuts than it made in 1991. Presently (1993), the discount rate is 3 percent, the Federal funds rate is 3 percent (its lowest level since 1963), and the prime rate is 6 percent. Despite these lower rates, the economy's recovery is still slow. With lower interest rates, consumers have reduced the liability side of their balance sheets, but with no new jobs and high unemployment, income growth has suffered, and this keeps consumers from spending.

Along with the election of a Democratic president, Republican-appointed Chairman Greenspan is coming under attack for the Fed's monetary policy from the chairman of the House Banking Committee, Representative Henry Gonzalez. Gonzalez questions whether Greenspan supports the new administration's economic goals in light of what he considers to be tight monetary policies, which have delayed the country's economic growth. In a letter to President Clinton regard-

ing Greenspan, Gonzalez wrote, "While he praises your budgetary proposals, his approach to monetary policy risks economic stagnation and recession." Gonzalez urged the President to watch the Fed carefully and to do all he could do to dissuade it from adopting policies that would choke off any chances for a recovery.

Although statements made by the Fed's chairman indicate that he supports the new administration's policies, it remains to be seen whether the Fed's actions will work harmoniously with the Clinton administration's budgetary and economic proposals.

Questions

4-1   Suppose interest rates on residential mortgages of equal risk were 8 percent in California and 10 percent in New York. Could this differential persist? What forces might tend to equalize rates? Would differentials in borrowing costs for businesses of equal risk located in California and New York be more or less likely to exist than residential mortgage rate differentials? Would differentials in the cost of money for New York and California firms be more likely to exist if the firms being compared were very large or if they were very small? What are the implications of all this for the pressure now being put on Congress to permit banks to engage in nationwide branching?

4-2   Which fluctuate more, long-term or short-term interest rates? Why?

4-3   Suppose you believe that the economy is just entering a recession. Your firm must raise capital immediately, and debt will be used. Should you borrow on a long-term or a short-term basis? Explain.

4-4   Suppose the population of Area Y is relatively young, whereas that of Area O is relatively old, but everything else about the two areas is equal.
   a. Would interest rates be the same or different in the two areas? Explain.
   b. Would trends toward nationwide branching by banks and S&Ls, and the development of diversified nationwide financial corporations, affect your answer to Part a?

4-5   Suppose a new and much more liberal Congress and administration were elected, and their first order of business was to take away the independence of the Federal Reserve System and force the Fed to greatly expand the money supply. What effect would this have
   a. on the level and slope of the yield curve immediately after the announcement?
   b. on the level and slope of the yield curve that would probably exist two or three years in the future?

4-6   The federal government (1) encouraged the development of the S&L industry; (2) virtually forced the industry to make long-term, fixed interest rate mortgages; and (3) restricted the S&Ls' liabilities largely to deposits that were withdrawable on demand or very short notice.
   a. Would S&Ls be better off in a world with a normal or an inverted yield curve? Explain.
   b. If federal actions such as deficit spending and expansion of the money supply produced a sharp increase in inflation, why would this have contributed to the need for a federal bailout of the S&L industry?

c. Under the conditions described in Part b, would the savings and loan industry be better off if the individual institutions sold mortgages to federal agencies and collected servicing fees or if the institutions held the mortgages that they originated?

4-7 Assume that the yield curve is horizontal (flat). You and other investors now receive information that suggests the economy is headed into a recession. You and most other investors think that the Fed will soon relax credit and that this will lead to a decline in short-term interest rates. Over the long run (the next 5, 10, or 15 years) people expect a fairly high rate of inflation, and they expect that this will keep long-term rates fairly high. Explain what all of this will probably do to the yield curve. Use a graph to illustrate your answer.

4-8 Suppose interest rates on Treasury bonds rose from 7 percent to 10 percent. Other things held constant, what do you think would happen to the price of an average company's common stock?

4-9 Why are T-bills popular short-term investments for corporations and commercial banks?

4-10 Other things held constant, how would each of the following factors affect the slope and the general position of the yield curve? Indicate by a (+) if it would lead to a steeper slope or an upward shift in the curve, a (−) if it would cause the slope of the yield curve to become less steep or the curve to shift downward, or a (0) if it would have no effect or an indeterminate effect on the slope or position of the curve.

	Effect on the Yield Curve	
	Slope	Position
a. Investors perceive the risk of default to increase on securities with longer maturities; that is, they become increasingly uncertain about the more distant future.	_____	_____
b. Future interest rates are expected to fall.	_____	_____
c. The Federal Reserve pumps a large amount of money into the banking system.	_____	_____
d. An inexpensive method of harnessing solar power is developed. This development leads to a decline in the expected rate of inflation.	_____	_____

Self-Test Problem

ST-1 Assume that it is now January 1, 1994. The rate of inflation is expected to average 3 percent throughout 1994. However, increased government deficits and renewed vigor in the economy are then expected to push inflation rates higher. Investors expect the inflation rate to be 4 percent in 1995, 5 percent in 1996, and 6 percent in 1997. Assume that the real risk-free rate of interest, k^*, is currently 2 percent and that no maturity risk or liquidity premiums are required on securities with 5 years or less to maturity. Finally, assume the current interest rate on 5-year Treasury notes is 7 percent.
a. What is the average expected inflation rate over the period from 1994 through 1997?
b. What should be the prevailing interest rate on 4-year T-notes?
c. What is the implied expected inflation rate in 1998, or Year 5, given that notes which mature in that year yield 7 percent?

Problems

4-1
Yield curves
Suppose you and most other investors expect the rate of inflation to be 8 percent next year, to fall to 4 percent during a recession in the following year, and then to run at a rate of 7 percent thereafter. Assume that the real risk-free rate, k^*, is 2 percent and that maturity risk premiums on Treasury securities rise from zero on very short-term bills

(those that mature in a few days) by 0.20 percentage points for each year to maturity, up to a limit of 1.0 percentage point on 5-year or longer Treasury securities.

a. Calculate the interest rates on 1-, 2-, 3-, 4-, 5-, 10-, and 20-year Treasury securities, and plot the yield curve.

b. Now suppose AT&T, an Aaa-rated company, has securities with the same maturities as the Treasury securities. As an approximation, plot an AT&T yield curve on the same graph with the Treasury yield curve. (Hint: Think about the default risk premium on AT&T's long-term versus its short-term securities.)

4-2
Yield curves

Look in *The Wall Street Journal* or some other newspaper which publishes interest rates on U.S. Treasury securities. Identify some Treasury securities which mature at various dates in the future, record the years to maturity and the interest rate for each, and then plot a yield curve. (Note: Some of the bonds — for example, the 3 percent issue which matures in February 1995 — will show very low yields. Disregard them — these are "flower bonds," which can be turned in and used at par value to pay estate taxes, so they always sell at close to par and have a yield which is close to the coupon yield, irrespective of the going rate of interest. Also, the yields quoted in the *Journal* are not for the same point in time for all bonds, so random variations will appear. An interest rate series that is purged of flower bonds and random variations, and hence one that provides a better picture of the true yield curve, can be obtained from the *Federal Reserve Bulletin.*)

4-3
Risk premiums

Look in *The Wall Street Journal.* Examine the interest rates for comparable maturity dates of U.S. Treasury securities and government agency securities.

a. Which group of securities carries the slightly higher interest rate?

b. Why do you think this relationship exists?

4-4
Expected interest rates

Assume that the real risk-free rate is 3 percent and that the liquidity and maturity risk premiums are zero. If the nominal rate of interest on 1-year Treasury securities is 9 percent and that on 2-year Treasury securities is 11 percent, what rate of inflation is expected during Year 2? What is the 1-year interest rate that is expected for Year 2? Comment on why the average interest rate during the 2-year period differs from the 1-year interest rate expected for Year 2.

4-5
Expected rate of interest

Suppose the annual yield on a 2-year Treasury security is 4.75 percent, while that on a 1-year Treasury security is 4 percent. k^* is 1%, and the liquidity and maturity risk premiums are zero.

a. Using the expectations theory, forecast the interest rate on a 1-year security during the second year. (Hint: Under the expectations theory, the yield on a 2-year security is equal to the average yield on 1-year securities in Years 1 and 2.)

b. What is the expected inflation rate in Years 1 and 2?

Solution to Self-Test Problem

ST-1
a. Average $= IP_4 = (3\% + 4\% + 5\% + 6\%)/4 = 18\%/4 = 4.50\%$.

b. $k_{T\text{-note}} = k^* + IP_4 = 2\% + 4.5\% = 6.5\%$.

c. If the 5-year T-note rate is 7 percent, the inflation rate is expected to average approximately $7\% - 2\% = 5\%$ over the next 5 years. Thus, the Year 5 implied inflation rate (I_5) is 7 percent:

$$5\% = (3\% + 4\% + 5\% + 6\% + I_5)/5$$

$$25\% = 18\% + I_5$$

$$I_5 = 7\%.$$

Financial Statements and
Financial Planning

A company's financial statements tell an important story about its operations, and a financial manager or financial analyst should be able to interpret these statements and understand them thoroughly. In Chapter 5 we discuss the four basic financial statements — the *income statement,* the *balance sheet,* the *statement of retained earnings,* and the *statement of cash flows.* Financial analysis, explored in Chapter 6, allows the analyst to  evaluate the firm's financial strengths and weaknesses and to utilize this knowledge to develop a plan for the future. Determining future financial needs is an important requisite to effective financial management. Chapter 7 provides useful tools for making projections of future financial statements. Managers use these financial projections to evaluate future operating alternatives.

Examining a Firm's Financial Data

OBJECTIVES

After reading this chapter, you should be able to:

▶ List the types of information found in a corporation's annual report.

▶ Construct an income statement.

▶ Arrange assets and claims on assets on a balance sheet and identify who bears the risk of asset-value fluctuations.

▶ Specify the changes reported in a firm's statement of retained earnings.

▶ Describe what is meant by a firm's cash flow cycle.

▶ Construct a statement of cash flows and indicate its purposes.

DECISION IN FINANCE

LETTERS FROM CHAIRMAN BUFFETT

Savvy readers of corporate annual reports usually check three elements: the auditor's opinion, the financial results, and the footnotes. Few give more than a glance to the chairman's letter, which they assume will be pure puffery.

But even the most jaded analysts settle back in their chairs and prepare for a good read when the Berkshire Hathaway report arrives. It invariably contains two things to which they look forward: good news about the company's financial performance and a long, insightful, and entertaining letter from Chairman Warren Buffett. In fact, the letters are so popular that Berkshire Hathaway often receives requests for reprints and, to meet demand, has assembled an anthology of the last five letters.

Most chairmen's letters try to paint a rosy corporate picture, regardless of the reality of the situation. But Buffett believes that stockholders are too smart to buy such an approach. Describing his attitude toward his readers, he says, "I assume I've got a very intelligent partner who has been away for a year and needs to be filled in on all that's happened." Consequently, in his letters he often admits mistakes and emphasizes the negative. In 1979, for example, he wrote, "We continue to look for ways to expand our insurance operation, but your reaction to this intent should not be unrestrained joy. Some of

our expansion efforts—largely initiated by your chairman—have been lackluster, others have been expensive failures."

Buffett also uses his letters to educate his shareholders and to help them interpret the data presented in the rest of the report. In one letter he lamented the complexities of accounting and observed, "The Yãnomamö Indians employ only three numbers: one, two, and more than two. Maybe their time will come."

As you read this chapter, think about the kinds of information that corporations provide their stockholders. Do the four basic financial statements provide adequate data for investment decisions? What other information might be helpful?

Also consider the pros and cons of Chairman Buffett's decision to include long, frank, and frequently self-critical letters in his company's annual reports. Would you suggest that other companies follow suit? Why or why not?

See end of chapter for resolution.

Photo source: Dan Budnik/Woodfin Camp & Associates

Any analysis of a firm, whether by management or investors, must include an examination of the company's financial data. The most obvious and readily available source of these financial data is the company's *annual report*. In this chapter we examine the *basic financial data* included in the firm's annual report. In following chapters we discuss the *techniques of financial analysis* used to evaluate financial data in an effort to determine the firm's relative riskiness, its profit potential, and its general managerial competence.

The Annual Report

annual report

A report issued annually by a corporation to its stockholders. It contains the basic financial statements, along with management's opinion of the past year's operations and of the firm's future prospects.

Of the various reports corporations issue to their stockholders, the **annual report** is by far the most important. Two types of information are given in this report. First, there is a verbal section, often presented as a letter from the president, that describes the firm's operating results during the past year and discusses new developments that will affect future operations. Second, the annual report presents four basic financial statements — the *income statement,* the *balance sheet,* the *statement of retained earnings,* and the *statement of cash flows.* Taken together, these statements give an accounting picture of the firm's operations and financial position. Detailed data are provided for the two most recent years, along with historical summaries of key operating statistics for the past five to ten years.

The quantitative and verbal information are equally important. The financial statements report *what has actually happened* to earnings and dividends over the past few years, whereas the verbal statements attempt to explain *why things turned out the way they did.* For example, suppose earnings dropped sharply last year. Management may report that the drop resulted from a strike at a key facility at the height of the busy season but then will go on to state that the strike has now been settled and that future profits are expected to bounce back. Of course, this return to profitability may not occur, and investors and analysts should compare management's past statements with subsequent results. In any event, *the information contained in an annual report is used by investors to form expectations about future earnings and dividends, and about the riskiness of these expected cash flows.* Therefore, the annual report is obviously of great interest to investors.

For illustrative purposes, we shall use data taken from Carter Chemical Company, a major producer of industrial and consumer chemical products. The company was originally formed in 1950, it has prospered throughout the years, and it is now recognized as an industry leader. However, in recent years, the firm's earnings have started declining. Because of the competitive nature of the industry, Carter's president, Bruce Berlin, has asked the chief financial officer to conduct a careful appraisal of the firm's position and, on the basis of this analysis, to draw up a plan for future operations.

Self-Test

Identify the two types of information given in the annual report. Which one is more important? Explain.

AMERITECH *Annual Report 1991*

Beyond tomorrow...

Building the future through communication

The theme for Ameritech's 1991 Annual Report was "Beyond tomorrow . . . Building the future through communication." Ameritech, one of the world's leading information companies, is the parent of five Bell companies serving the Great Lakes region and other information businesses. In its annual report, Ameritech stresses that broad access to electronic information is opening new windows of opportunity for consumers, for American businesses, and for Ameritech. The company continues to make investments to enhance network intelligence and to make possible a wide range of services such as electronic transactions, work at home, remote monitoring, and distance learning . . . services that are transforming how consumers work and live.

Source: Courtesy of Ameritech Corporation

The Income Statement

income statement

A statement summarizing the firm's revenues and expenses over an accounting period.

An **income statement** summarizes a firm's revenues and expenses over an accounting period — generally a quarter or a year. Table 5-1 presents an income statement as it might appear in an annual report. This financial statement records the 1992 and 1993 profits and disbursements of Carter Chemical Company.

Table 5-1		1993	1992
Carter Chemical Company: Income Statement for Year Ending December 31 (Millions of Dollars, except per-Share Data)	Net sales	$3,000	$2,850
	Less: Cost of goods sold	2,544	2,413
	Gross profit	$ 456	$ 437
	Less: Other operating expenses:		
	Depreciation	100	90
	Selling	22	20
	General and administrative	40	35
	Lease payments on buildings	28	28
	Earnings before interest and taxes (EBIT)	$ 266	$ 264
	Less: Interest expense:		
	Interest on notes payable	$ 8	$ 2
	Interest on first mortgage bonds	40	42
	Interest on debentures	18	3
	Earnings before taxes (EBT)	$ 200	$ 217
	Less: Federal and state taxes (40%)	80	87
	Net income available to common stockholders[a]	$ 120	$ 130
	Disposition of net income:		
	Dividends to common stockholders	$ 100	$ 90
	Addition to retained earnings	$ 20	$ 40
	Per share of common stock:		
	Earnings per share (EPS)[b]	$ 2.40	$ 2.60
	Dividends per share (DPS)[b]	$ 2.00	$ 1.80

[a]Carter Chemical Company does not currently use preferred stock in its financing; therefore, no preferred dividends have to be paid, and all the firm's after-tax earnings for the year are available to common stockholders.

[b]Fifty million shares are outstanding: see Table 5-2. Calculations of EPS and DPS for 1993 are as follows:

$$EPS = \frac{\text{Net income available to common stockholders}}{\text{Shares outstanding}} = \frac{\$120,000,000}{50,000,000} = \$2.40.$$

$$DPS = \frac{\text{Dividends paid to common stockholders}}{\text{Shares outstanding}} = \frac{\$100,000,000}{50,000,000} = \$2.00.$$

Reported at the top of the statement are net sales (net of returns and discounts). As for the format of a firm's income statement from this point on, several equally valid variations exist. In Table 5-1, cost of goods sold is deducted from net sales to arrive at *gross profit*. Gross profit is then reduced by all other operating expenses to obtain *earnings before interest and taxes (EBIT)*, also called **net operating income** or *operating profit*. Various costs, such as interest expense and taxes, are then subtracted from EBIT to obtain net income available to common stockholders.

net operating income
Earnings before interest and taxes (EBIT); is also called operating profit.

Operating Costs and Expenses

In a typical manufacturing firm, the operating costs and expense accounts include all costs required to obtain raw materials and convert them into finished products, plus the costs of selling, plus the costs associated with overseeing operations. *Cost of goods sold* represents costs associated with raw materials acquisition and direct production costs. Expenses for salaries, travel, commissions, promotion, and advertising generally are the most important items in *selling expenses.* Staff and executive salaries and office expenses are the major items in *general and administrative expenses.* Of course, expenses attributable to assets employed in the business must be accounted for through *depreciation* or, if the firm leases assets, through *lease payments.*

Even though the computation of these expenses appears to be unambiguous, great discretion is allowed managers in calculating depreciation and in valuing inventory for the cost of goods sold calculation.[1]

Remaining Disbursements

The *earnings before interest and taxes,* or *operating profit,* is further reduced by interest payments on debt, which must be paid whether the company is profitable or not. Repayments of principal are not indicated on the income statement but are reported, as we shall see, on the balance sheet.

All firms have a partner, some might say an "uninvited" partner, who demands a predetermined percentage of profits. This partner is, of course, the U.S. government, which requires that a portion of the firm's profits be paid in the form of income taxes. State and local governments require tax payments as well. However, certain accounting conventions allow the firm to postpone these tax payments for a while.

If Carter Chemical Company had used preferred stock as part of its long-term financing mix, preferred dividends would be paid *after* taxes, further reducing net income available to common stockholders.

The Bottom Line

Financial managers often refer to net income as "the bottom line," and of all the items on the income statement, net income draws the greatest attention. A manager once noted, "Net income is so important that we underline it twice!"[2]

The firm's net income is either paid to the shareholders in the form of dividends or retained by the firm to support its growth. Net income and dividends paid are reported both in total dollars and on a per-share basis as **earnings per share (EPS)** and **dividends per share (DPS),** respectively. These are calculated as follows:

earnings per share (EPS)
Net income available to common stockholders divided by the number of shares of common stock outstanding.

dividends per share (DPS)
Total dividends paid to common stockholders divided by the number of shares of common stock outstanding.

$$\text{EPS} = \frac{\text{Net income available to common stockholders}}{\text{Shares outstanding}} \quad (5\text{-}1)$$

$$\text{DPS} = \frac{\text{Dividends paid to common stockholders}}{\text{Shares outstanding}} \quad (5\text{-}2)$$

Carter earned $2.40 per share in 1993, down from $2.60 in 1992, but it raised the dividend per share from $1.80 to $2.00.

---

[1]These are not the only areas of managerial discretion in financial reporting. Such items as the determination of pension fund liabilities and the decision between expensing or capitalizing certain costs also have an important effect on reported profits.

[2]In the remainder of this text we will use the term "net income" to mean "net income available to common stockholders."

Self-Test

What does an income statement summarize?

Outline the general format for an income statement.

Differentiate among cost of goods sold, selling expenses, and general and administrative expenses.

What must be subtracted from operating profit to arrive at net income?

The Balance Sheet

balance sheet
A statement of the firm's financial position at a specific point in time.

equity
Financing supplied by the firm's owners.

liabilities
All the legal claims held against the firm by nonowners.

The income statement as discussed above reports on operations *over a period of time* — for example, during the calendar year 1993. The **balance sheet,** on the other hand, may be thought of as a snapshot of the firm's financial position *at a point in time* — for example, on December 31, 1993.

The left-hand side of Carter's balance sheet, which is shown in Table 5-2, shows the firm's assets, and the right-hand side of the statement shows claims on assets. These claims are divided into two types — claims that arise from the investment of funds by the owners of the firm, which constitutes the firm's **equity,** and claims associated with debt the firm owes the nonowners of the firm. These debts must be repaid, and they constitute the firm's **liabilities.**

Assets

assets
All items which the firm owns.

The **assets** are listed in the order of their liquidity, or the length of time it typically takes to convert them to cash. The current assets, or working capital, consist of assets that are normally converted into cash within one year. *Cash* and *marketable securities* are temporary stores of liquidity. Examples of securities included here were listed briefly in Chapter 2 and will be discussed again in Chapter 9. *Inventories* include raw materials used in the production process, work in process, and finished goods awaiting sale. *Accounts receivable* result when the firm sells a product on credit, and when the customer pays, the account receivable is converted to cash.

Assets with a useful life of more than one year are referred to as *fixed assets.* These assets typically include the plant, equipment, office furniture, and other assets which are used in the production process. With extended usage, these assets will eventually wear out. *Depreciation* was at one time supposed to reflect the decline in an asset's useful productive value, but today the actual relationship between an asset's productive value and its book value is low. In fact, with the introduction of the Accelerated Cost Recovery System (ACRS) method of depreciation in 1981, and again under MACRS, in effect after 1986, the tax life of an asset is no longer tied to its productive life; an asset's tax life is generally shorter than its economic or productive life.

Liabilities

A liability is a claim against the assets of the firm. On the balance sheet, liabilities are listed in the order in which they mature and must be repaid. Current liabilities are those debts that mature within one year.

Table 5-2   Carter Chemical Company: Balance Sheet as of December 31 (Millions of Dollars)

Assets	1993	1992	Liabilities and Equity	1993	1992
Cash	$ 50	$ 55	Accounts payable	$ 60	$ 30
Marketable securities	0	25	Notes payable	100	60
Accounts receivable	350	315	Accrued wages	10	10
Inventories	300	215	Accrued income taxes	130	120
Total current assets	$ 700	$ 610	Total current liabilities	$ 300	$ 220
Gross fixed assets	$1,800	$1,470	First mortgage bonds	$ 500	$ 520
Less: Accumulated			Debentures	300	60
depreciation	500	400	Total long-term debt	$ 800	$ 580
Net fixed assets	$1,300	$1,070	Stockholders' equity:		
			Common stock (50,000,000 shares, $1 par)	$ 50	$ 50
			Paid-in capital	100	100
			Retained earnings	750	730
			Total stockholders' equity (common net worth)[a]	$ 900	$ 880
Total assets	$2,000	$1,680	Total liabilities and equity	$2,000	$1,680

[a]Note the residual nature of Total stockholders' equity (common net worth): Total assets − Total liabilities = Total stockholders' equity.

Accounts payable represent the amount the company owes to other businesses for purchases of goods on "open account." Each purchase is recorded on the seller's balance sheet as an account receivable. *Notes payable* represent short-term debt owed to banks or other lenders. *Accruals* are current expenses which have not yet been paid as of the date of the balance sheet. *Accrued wages* and *accrued income taxes* are payable on a periodic basis — weekly or monthly for wages and quarterly for income taxes. These accounts build up as the wage and tax liabilities increase during the period. Once paid, the accounts are reduced by the amounts paid, and then they begin to build again as the process continues.

Long-term debt represents liabilities with more than one year remaining until maturity. The funds may have been borrowed from any source, such as from financial intermediaries or from the public through the sale of bonds. Table 5-2 indicates that Carter Chemical Company has two types of bonds outstanding, a *first mortgage bond* issue and a *debenture* issue.[3]

The bond's principal may have to be repaid either at maturity in a lump sum or in periodic repayments. One device which helps ensure the orderly repayment of a bond issue is a *sinking fund.* Carter's bonds contain a sinking fund provision which requires it to pay off $20 million each year. Accordingly, its outstanding mortgage bonds declined by $20 million from December 31, 1992, to December 31, 1993. The current portion of the long-term debt is included in notes payable here, although in a more detailed balance sheet it would be shown as a separate item.

---

[3]We discuss different types of bonds in Chapter 16.

Stockholders' Equity

**stockholders' equity
(net worth)**

The capital supplied by
stockholders — capital
stock, paid-in capital,
and retained earnings.
Common equity is that
part of total claims be-
longing to the common
stockholders.

The **stockholders' equity,** or **net worth,** account represents the owners'
claim against the assets of the firm. *Common equity* is another term used to
designate the owner's claim on the firm's assets; these three terms are used
interchangeably, and are also equal to *total stockholders' equity,* when a firm
has no preferred stock, as is the case with Carter. When the word "equity" is
used in finance, we generally mean common equity, or net worth.[4] This equity
claim differs significantly from the claims of creditors (or debtholders). For one
thing, the equity claim does not mature and thus never needs to be paid off.
Second, the equity is not fixed at a set amount; rather, it is a residual which can
rise or fall. That is,

$$\text{Assets} \quad - \quad \text{Liabilities} \quad = \text{Stockholders' equity} \qquad (5\text{-}3)$$

$$\$2,000,000,000 \ - \ \$1,100,000,000 \ = \ \$900,000,000.$$

Suppose assets decline in value; for example, suppose some of the firm's inventory becomes obsolete and must be written off. Because liabilities remain constant, the value of the net worth declines. Therefore, the risk of asset-value
fluctuations is borne entirely by the stockholders. Note, however, that if asset
values rise, these benefits accrue exclusively to the stockholders. Note, too, that
if the firm retains some of its earnings, this also causes equity to increase.

The equity section of the balance sheet is divided into three accounts —
common stock, paid-in capital, and *retained earnings.* The first two accounts
arise when the firm issues new common stock to raise capital. A **par value** is
generally assigned to common stock — Carter's stock has a par value of $1.[5]
Now suppose Carter were to sell 1 million additional shares at a price of $30
per share. The company would raise $30 million, and the cash account would
go up by this amount. On the right-hand side of the balance sheet, the transaction would be reflected by an increase of $1 per share, or a total increase of
$1 million in the common stock account. The remaining $29 per share would
be added to the **paid-in capital** account. This account is occasionally referred
to by its more descriptive title, *capital in excess of par.* The results of a sale of
new common stock are as follows:

par value

The nominal or face value
of a stock or bond.

paid-in capital

Funds received in excess
of par value when a firm
sells stock.

	Before Sale of Stock
Common stock (50,000,000 shares, $1 par)	$ 50,000,000
Paid-in capital	100,000,000
Retained earnings	750,000,000
Total stockholders' equity	$900,000,000

---

[4]When preferred stock is used it appears on the balance sheet after long-term debt but before
common equity. Preferred stock is considered equity but not *common* equity; these investors receive preferential treatment both in the payment of dividends and in the event of bankruptcy and
liquidation of the firm. Many firms do not use preferred stock, and those that do generally do not
use very much of it. We will defer detailed discussion of this security to Chapter 16.

[5]The par value assigned to common stock does not really mean much to the average stockholder;
there is no direct relationship between a stock's par value and its market value.

	After Sale of Stock
Common stock (51,000,000 shares, $1 par)	$ 51,000,000
Paid-in capital	129,000,000
Retained earnings	750,000,000
Total stockholders' equity	$930,000,000

Thus, after the sale, the common stock account would show $51 million, paid-in capital would show $129 million, and there would be 51 million shares of common stock. The retained earnings account is not affected by the sale of new common stock.

The common stock and paid-in capital accounts provide information about external sources of equity funds. Self-generated, or internal, equity comes from the undistributed profits of the firm. The retained earnings account is built up over time by the firm's "saving" a part of its net income rather than paying all of its earnings out as dividends.[6] Thus, since its inception Carter has retained, or plowed back, a total of $750 million, and $20 million was added during the last year.

The breakdown of the equity accounts is important for some purposes but not for others. For example, a potential stockholder would want to know whether the company had actually earned the funds reported in its equity accounts or whether the funds had come mainly from selling stock. A potential creditor, on the other hand, would be more interested in the total amount of money the owners had put up than in the form in which they put it up.

Note that most real-world corporate reports have a much more complex equity section than the one shown here for Carter Chemical Company. For example, you might see a *negative* equity account called *treasury stock*. This would indicate that the firm in question had repurchased, or "retired," some of its common equity. This topic will be dealt with in Chapter 21. Another entry in the equity section might refer to *foreign currency translation adjustments*, which will be covered in Chapter 23. At this point, however, we want to focus on the basics.[7]

 Self-Test

How does the balance sheet differ from the income statement?

Identify the two types of claims on assets shown on the right-hand side of the balance sheet.

In what order are assets and liabilities listed on the balance sheet?

Differentiate between current assets and fixed assets and between accounts payable and accounts receivable.

---

[6]A word of caution is in order here. The retained earnings account does *not* represent a pool of cash from which funds may be withdrawn. The retained earnings account simply indicates the source from which some of the firm's assets were originally procured.

[7]Also, equity is sometimes referred to simply as "capital," as in "the firm is undercapitalized," which means that its balance sheet shows too little equity (and other long-term financing). Students frequently ask why so many terms are used to refer to the same thing; unfortunately, all we can say is that this is the way it is done! Common equity provides a good example, but you will find other cases as you continue your study of finance.

How do the stockholders' claims differ from the claims of nonowners?

Into what three accounts is the equity section of the balance sheet divided? Briefly explain what information each account provides.

The Statement of Retained Earnings

statement of retained earnings

A statement reporting how much of the firm's earnings were not paid out in dividends. The figure for retained earnings that appears here is the sum of the annual retained earnings for each year of the firm's history.

Changes in the retained earnings account of the equity section between balance sheet dates are reported in the **statement of retained earnings;** Carter's statement is shown in Table 5-3. The company earned $120 million during 1993, paid out $100 million in dividends, and plowed $20 million back into the business. Thus the balance sheet item "retained earnings" increased from $730 million at the end of 1992 to $750 million at the end of 1993.

Note that the balance sheet account "retained earnings" represents a *claim on assets,* not assets per se. Furthermore, firms typically retain earnings to expand the business; this means investing in plant and equipment, inventories, and so on, *not* in a bank account. Thus, retained earnings as reported on the balance sheet do not represent cash, and they are not available for the payment of dividends or anything else.[8] A positive number in the retained earnings account indicates only that, in the past and according to generally accepted accounting principles, the firm has earned an income, and its total dividends have been less than its reported income over the same period.

A desire to expand assets and sales may not be the only reason that firms retain earnings. Incremental retained earnings may be used in a given year to pay down debt. This action might not change total assets or total claims from the year before; in other words, the size of the firm might not change, but it would increase the percentage of assets financed by equity and lower the percentage financed through debt. As mentioned in Chapter 1, the amount of debt used has a direct impact on the firm's risk and on the value of its stock. In the early 1990s, many corporations are retaining earnings for this reason, following unsustainably high levels of debt in the 1980s. Many of these firms are banks, required by law to boost their capital (equity).

Earnings and Dividends

Although dividends and dividend policy are discussed in detail in Chapter 21, two points should be made here:

dividend payout ratio

The percentage of earnings paid out in dividends.

1. In any given year dividends per share (DPS) may exceed earnings per share (EPS), but in the long run dividends are paid from earnings, so DPS is normally smaller than EPS.[9] The percentage of earnings paid out in dividends, or the ratio of DPS to EPS, is called the **dividend payout ratio.**

---

[8]However, *incremental* (this year's) retained earnings do represent a source of financing and may be applied to new uses.

[9]Maintaining a given dividend in spite of *temporarily* declining earnings is a logical move since a cut in dividends normally causes a decline in the stock price. A firm could pay out a DPS greater than its current EPS by (1) borrowing, (2) liquidating marketable securities or other assets, or (3) selling new common stock.

Table 5-3	Balance of retained earnings, December 31, 1992	$730
Carter Chemical Company:	Add: Net income, 1993	120
Statement of Retained	Less: Dividends to stockholders	(100)
Earnings for Year Ending	Balance of retained earnings, December 31, 1993	$750
December 31, 1993		
(Millions of Dollars)		

This ratio may also be calculated using total dividends to net income. From Table 5-3 we see that Carter Chemical's dividend payout ratio is: $100,000,000/$120,000,000 = 83.3\%$. Carter is therefore retaining $1 - 0.833 = 0.167 = 16.7\%$.

2. Dividends per share represent the basic cash flows passed from the firm to its stockholders. It follows that dividends are a key element in the stock valuation models which we will develop in Chapter 17.

? *Self-Test*

Explain the following statement: "Retained earnings as reported on the balance sheet do not represent cash, and they are not 'available' for the payment of dividends or anything else."

Why would DPS normally be less than EPS?

The Cash Flow Cycle

As a company like Carter Chemical goes about its business, it makes sales, which lead (1) to a reduction of inventories, (2) to an increase in cash, and, (3) if the sales price exceeds the cost of the item sold, to a profit. If the item is sold on credit rather than for cash, the transaction is slightly more complicated. The inventory account is reduced and accounts receivable are increased; then, when the customer pays, accounts receivable are reduced, and the cash account is increased. These transactions cause the balance sheet to change, and they are also reflected in the income statement.

It is important that you understand (1) that businesses deal with *physical* units like autos, computers, and chemicals; (2) that physical transactions are translated into dollar terms through the accounting system; and (3) that the purpose of financial analysis is to examine the accounting numbers in order to determine how efficient the firm is at making and selling physical goods and services. In other words, financial analysis helps determine how good the company is at taking resources in the form of labor and materials and converting them into some product or service that people want and are willing to pay for.

Several factors make financial analysis difficult. One of them is variations in accounting methods among firms. For example, different methods of inventory valuation and depreciation can lead to differences in reported profits for otherwise identical firms, and a good financial analyst must be able to adjust for these differences if he or she is to make valid comparisons among companies. Another factor involves timing. An action is taken at one point in time, but even though

ARE ACCOUNTING METHODS TOO FLEXIBLE?

Financial institutions in the United States have experienced serious problems recently. Many savings and loan associations (S&Ls) have either failed or been bailed out by a government agency, at an estimated cost to taxpayers of $150 billion. The banks have not been in as much trouble, but many have failed or have had to be bailed out by the government, and taxpayers can expect a substantial hit here, too. There is also fear that a number of corporate pension plans will not be able to make good on their promises to make payments to retirees, and if that happens, the burden will be shared by retirees and taxpayers. Finally, a number of insurance companies have gone under, dragging down unsuspecting policyholders and disrupting lives. Insurance companies are generally not government backed; hence, their failure affects primarily policyholders, not taxpayers.

These problems surfaced in the 1970s, they accelerated in the 1980s, and the bills started coming due in the 1990s. Uninsured investors have lost millions so far, and U.S. taxpayers can look forward to payments of nearly $500 per year per taxpayer well into the 21st century.

What happened? What went wrong? Who was responsible? There is actually plenty of blame, and it is shared by a number of groups. First, Congress and several presidents changed the laws under which financial institutions are regulated. In general, regulations were relaxed, permitting the institutions to make investments outside their traditional areas of expertise. With hindsight, we now know that the new types of investments were extremely risky. Second, the federal and state agencies which regulate the institutions were not as vigilant as they should have been in enforcing various regulations. Third, some "bad apples"

Sources: "For Charlie Keating, the Best Defense Is a Lawsuit," *Business Week*, May 1, 1989; "Regulators: Accounting failed in S&L collapse," *San Jose Mercury News*, December 28, 1989; "SEC Pushes for Market Value Accounting," *Financial Regulation Report*, December 16, 1991; "Banks Face A Nervous New Year," *Fortune*, December 14, 1992; "Tough Legal Battles Shaped Business World," *The National Law Journal*, December 28, 1992/January 4, 1993; "Keating S&L Case Goes to Jury," *USA Today*, December 29, 1992; "Securities Accounting: Half a Loaf," *U.S. Banker*, January 1993; "Accountants' Bottom Line: Home Free," *Newsday*, January 19, 1993; "It's Time to Free the FASB Seven," *Business Week*, May 3, 1993; and several other materials.

assumed control of some of the institutions, and they literally stole the assets they were supposed to be managing. Finally, the accounting profession let institutions present grossly misleading financial statements that concealed the depth of the problem.

At least some of those responsible have suffered. For example, Jim Wright, Speaker of the U.S. House of Representatives, and once one of the most powerful men in Washington, was disgraced and forced to resign from Congress when his involvement with failed S&Ls came out, and Charles Keating, chairman of Lincoln S&L, whose bankruptcy cost U.S. taxpayers $2.5 billion, is currently serving a 10-year prison sentence. Several accounting firms have been sued by the federal government for the use of accounting methods which deceived federal regulators about institutions' net worth. Among them are Arthur Andersen (for $400 million), Deloitte & Touche (for $150 million), and KPMG Peat Marwick (for more than $100 million).

Accounting firms are also being sued by investors who held uninsured deposits in the institutions. In the Lincoln S&L case, investors collected $63 million from Ernst & Young, $30 million from Arthur Andersen, and $7.5 million from Deloitte & Touche.

The accountants overlooked obvious warning signs and did not conduct audits with proper care and diligence. Experts agree that three factors caused these lapses:

1. Deregulation of the financial institutions, which brought about the need for greater auditing vigilance.

2. Auditing procedures which did not keep up with changes in the financial industries.

3. Fierce competition for big auditing accounts, which resulted in a "give the client what he wants" attitude.

According to John Burton, former chief accountant of the Securities and Exchange Commission, "We should not be surprised that this happened. Whenever you have substantial changes in an industry, you will find auditing problems. Accounting rules may no longer apply, and auditors are asked to look into things with which they are unfamiliar. Also, there is evidence that competitiveness among accounting firms increases the risk of auditing failure."

One accounting procedure which contributed to the problem was the rule which permitted financial institutions to report loans and investments at original cost rather than at current market values. Thus, if a bank paid $10 million for a long-term bond that paid a 6 percent interest rate and if rising interest rates caused the value of the bond to decline to $5 million, the bank was nevertheless permitted to carry the bond on its books at $10 million. So, under generally accepted accounting principles (GAAPs), a financial institution could conceal massive losses—until it went bankrupt.

If a bank's assets are earning 6 percent but it is paying 12 percent on the deposits it uses to finance the assets, the bank will eventually go bankrupt, even if its balance sheet indicates that its liabilities are well covered by assets. However, if assets were reported at their market values rather than at original cost, the balance sheet would reveal a problem—the value of the assets would be less than the liabilities, and the institution would be seen to be insolvent.

The original cost valuation rule led to another deceptive practice, "cherry picking," whereby the financial institution sells off loans and investments that have gone up in value and reports the gains as profits but holds on to losing investments and does not report the losses because they are unrealized. Using this tactic, some banks, S&Ls, and insurance companies were able to show marvelous profits—up to the time they failed.

It would seem that an obvious solution to the problem would be to require banks and other financial institutions to report financial assets at market values rather than at historical costs. However, that is easier said than done, and it could cause other problems. First, since many of the assets held by banks and other institutions are not traded in the marketplace, the "market" values of such assets would, at best, be approximations. Second, if banks' assets are to be "marked to market," would it not also be reasonable to treat their liabilities similarly? Third, market values tend to fluctuate over time, and there is a danger that depositors would panic if they saw a deterioration in their bank's financial position. They might start withdrawing money, force the bank to sell assets at

distressed prices, and in the process literally drive the bank to ruin. Fourth, and as a result of the first three items, banks would (1) concentrate on short-term as opposed to long-term loans and investments because short-term financial assets are less prone to decline in value when interest rates rise and (2) make loans only to the safest of investors. All of this would inhibit long-term investments in new, entrepreneurial businesses, which a vibrant economy needs. Given these problems, the banking industry has resisted calls to mark assets to market.

The bankers have lost the argument. The SEC and other governmental agencies have been pressuring the accounting profession to change generally accepted accounting principles to require market value reporting, and the huge judgments against accounting firms have weakened the profession's resistance to change. As a result, the Financial Accounting Standards Board, in 1993, issued Statement of Financial Accounting Standards (SFAS) 107, which goes a long way toward forcing financial institutions to report a large fraction of their assets at market values. When SFAS 107 takes effect in 1997, stocks which have a readily determined market value, as well as all debt securities, must be classified into three categories and accounted for as follows: (1) "Trading securities," which are held for resale at any time, must be reported at fair market value, and even unrealized gains and losses must be reflected in net income. (2) "Securities available for sale but held for future liquidity management" also must be reported at fair market value; here unrealized gains and losses are to be excluded from the income statement but reported as a separate component of equity. (3) "Securities planned to be held to maturity" are to be accounted for at amortized book value.

SFAS 107 will surely help make financial statements more meaningful, but problems remain. There will be controversy over the category in which given assets should be placed, and there will be arguments over the fair market value of assets for which reliable market quotations are not readily available. In addition, banks and other institutions will declare that they plan to hold certain assets to maturity but later decide to sell them, which will call the true effectiveness of SFAS 107 into question. Still, SFAS 107 is a step in the right direction.

cash flow

The actual net cash, as opposed to accounting net income, that flows into or out of the firm during a specified period; equal to net income plus depreciation and other noncash expenses.

its full effects are not felt until some later period, the effects of the action need to be evaluated before its final results are known.

To understand how timing influences the financial statements and hence financial analysis, one must understand the **cash flow** cycle within a firm, as set forth in Figure 5-1. Here rectangles represent balance sheet accounts (assets and claims on assets), and circles represent actions taken by the firm. Each rectangle may be thought of as a reservoir, and the wavy lines designate the amount in the reservoir (account) on a balance sheet date. Various transactions cause changes in the accounts, just as adding or subtracting water changes the level in a reservoir. For example, the purchase of raw materials inventory increases accounts payable and eventually reduces cash, while the collection of accounts receivable increases cash. The diagram is by no means a complete representation of the cash flow cycle — to avoid undue complexity, it shows only the major flows (for example, we assume that all sales and purchases are on credit).

The cash account is the focal point of the figure.[10] Certain events, such as collecting accounts receivable or borrowing money will cause the cash account to increase, while the payment of dividends, taxes, interest, accruals, and accounts payable will cause it to decline. Similar comments could be made about all the balance sheet accounts — their balances rise, fall, or remain constant depending on events that occur during the period under study, which for Carter is January 1, 1993, through December 31, 1993.

Projected sales increases may require the firm to raise cash by borrowing or selling new stock. For example, if Carter anticipates an increase in sales, it will (1) expend cash to buy or build fixed assets through the capital budgeting process; (2) step up purchases of raw materials, thereby increasing both raw materials inventories and accounts payable; (3) increase production, which will cause an increase in both accrued wages and work-in-process inventories; and (4) eventually build up its finished goods inventory. The firm will have obligated itself to pay off its accounts payable and its accrued wages within a few weeks and frequently *before* any new cash has been generated from sales. Even when the expected sales do occur, there will still be a lag in the generation of cash until receivables are collected. For example, if Carter grants credit for 30 days, it will have to wait 30 days after a sale is made before cash comes in. Depending on how much cash the firm had at the beginning of the buildup, on the length of its production-sales-collection cycle, and on how long it can delay payment of its own payables and accrued wages, the company may have to obtain substantial amounts of additional cash by selling stock or bonds or by borrowing from a bank or other financial institution.

If the firm is profitable, its sales revenues will exceed its costs, and its cash inflows will eventually exceed its cash outlays. However, even a profitable business can experience a cash shortage if it is growing rapidly. It typically has to pay for plant, materials, and labor before cash from the expanded sales starts flowing in. For this reason, rapidly growing firms generally require either large bank loans or capital from other sources, or both.

---

[10]If a firm holds marketable securities, these are normally included here as well since such securities are highly liquid.

Figure 5-1   Cash and Materials Flows within the Firm

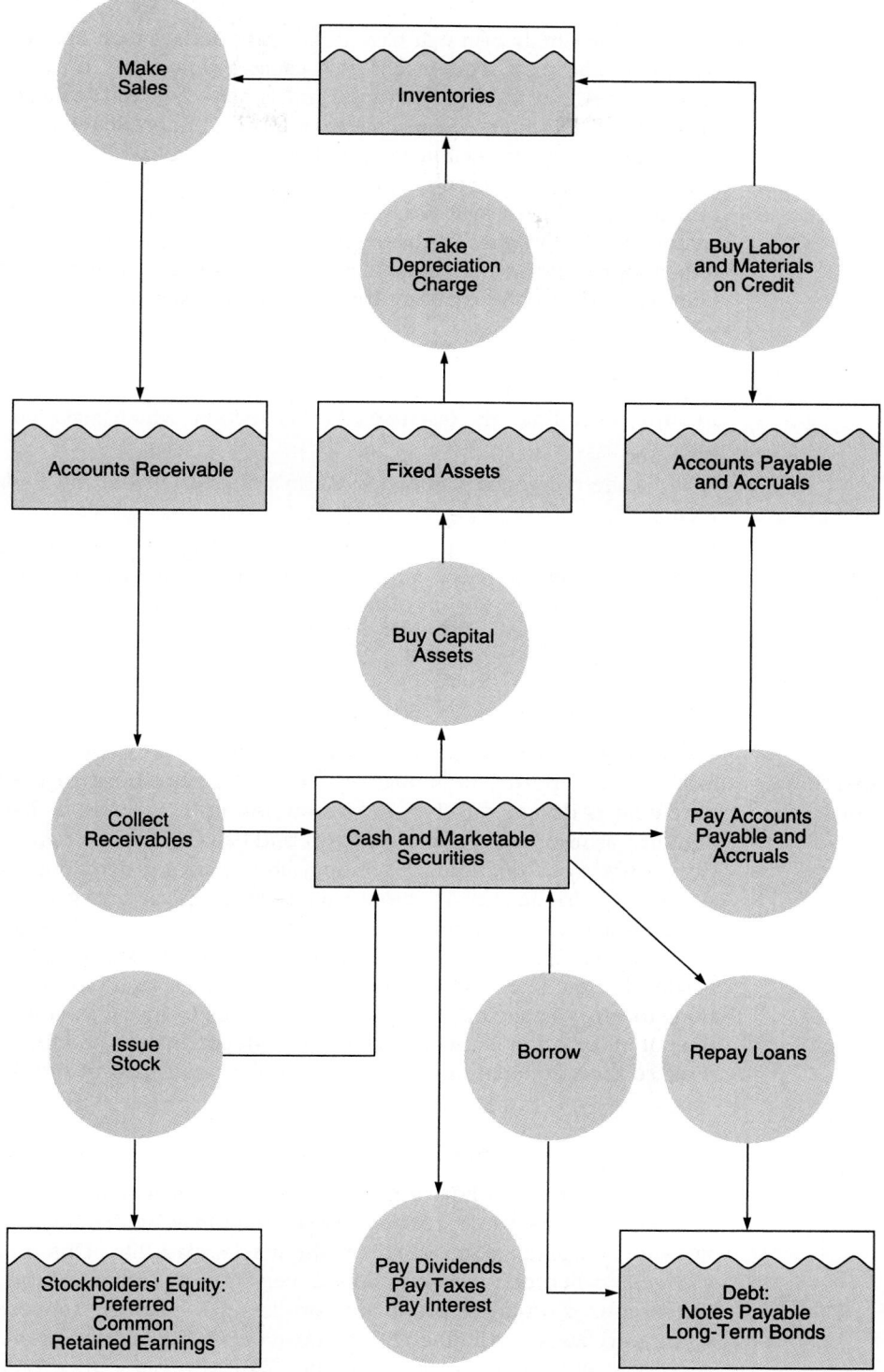

The focal point of a firm's cash flow cycle is its cash account, which is influenced by the firm's other accounts (rectangles) and activities (circles). The lower part of this diagram shows how the cash account is increased through stock issues and borrowing. The cash is then used to purchase raw materials inventory and to acquire fixed assets, both of which feed into the production of goods and replenish the cash account through sales. Note that cash flows continuously through this cycle, so an action in any portion will, after a lag, influence other portions and ultimately affect the cash account.

An unprofitable firm will have larger cash outlays than inflows. This, in turn, will lower the cash account and also cause a slowdown in the payment of accrued wages and accounts payable, and it may also lead to heavy borrowings. Accordingly, liabilities rise to excessive levels in unprofitable firms. Similarly, an overly ambitious expansion plan will result in excessive inventories and fixed assets, while a poor credit and collection policy will result in bad debts and reduced profits that will first show up as high accounts receivable. Financial analysts are well aware of these relationships, and they use the analytical techniques discussed in the remainder of this chapter and in the next chapter to help discover problems before they become too serious.

Self-Test

Identify several factors, discussed in this section, which make financial analysis difficult.

What is the relationship between a firm's physical assets and its financial statements?

In terms of the cash flow cycle, as shown in Figure 5-1, what happens to unprofitable firms that have larger cash outlays than inflows and to firms with overly ambitious expansion plans?

The Statement of Cash Flows

statement of cash flows
A statement reporting the impact of a firm's operating, investing, and financing activities on cash flows over an accounting period.

The graphic cash flow analysis shown in Figure 5-1 is converted to numerical form and is reported in annual reports as the **statement of cash flows.** This statement is designed (1) to show how the firm's operations have affected its liquidity, as measured by its cash flows, and (2) to show the relationships among cash flows from operating, investing, and financing activities. The cash flow statement helps answer questions such as these: Is the firm generating internally the cash it needs to buy additional fixed assets for growth? Is growth so rapid that external financing is required both for maintaining operations and for investing in new fixed assets? Does the firm have enough cash flows from operations to repay financing from earlier periods or to invest in new products? This type of information is useful both for investment analysis and for corporate planning, so the statement of cash flows is an important part of the annual report.

The Role of Depreciation

In Chapter 2 we saw how firms, under the current tax laws, calculate that percentage of an asset's depreciable basis which may be deducted from operating income in a given year, based on the asset's class life. This *annual noncash charge* is called depreciation and is a very rough estimate of the dollar cost of the asset used up in the production process. For example, suppose that in 1993 a firm purchases a machine with a MACRS class life of 5 years for $50,000. This $50,000 cost is not expensed in the purchase year but, rather, is charged against production over the machine's 6-year depreciable life. If the depreciation expense were not taken, profits would be overstated, and taxes would be too high. The annual depreciation allowance is deducted from sales revenues, along with

Table 5-4

Carter Chemical Company:
Cash Flows versus
Reported Income for 1993
(Millions of Dollars)

	Income Statement (1)	Cash Flows (2)
Sales	$3,000	$3,000
Operating costs and expenses:		
All operating costs except depreciation	2,634	2,634
Depreciation (DEP)	100	—[a]
Earnings before interest and taxes (EBIT)	$ 266	—[a]
Interest expense	66	66
Earnings before taxes (EBT)	$ 200	—[a]
Taxes	80	80
Net income (NI)	$ 120	—[a]
Cash flow: CF = NI + DEP = $120 + $100 =	$ 220	$ 220

[a]Depreciation is not deducted because it is a noncash charge. Also, the terms EBIT, EBT, and NI are not meaningful in the calculation of cash flows.

such other costs as labor and raw materials, to determine taxable income. However, depreciation is not a cash outlay; funds were expended back in 1993, so the depreciation charged against the income in years 1993 through 1998 is not a cash outlay, as are labor or raw materials charges.

The primary importance of depreciation is its effect on cash flows. In the income statement, depreciation shields income from taxation; therefore, the larger the depreciation charge in a particular year, the lower the taxable income, and the lower the taxes paid. The value of depreciation is this tax shelter it provides: reducing taxes increases after-tax, spendable cash flows. When a firm has depreciation charges (or other noncash charges), its cash flows will exceed net income by the amount of these charges:

$$\text{Cash flow} = \text{Net income} + \text{Depreciation (and other noncash expenses)}. \quad (5\text{-}4)$$

This point is illustrated with data for Carter Chemical Company in Table 5-4. Here Column 1 shows an abbreviated version of Carter's income statement, whereas Column 2 shows the statement on a cash flow basis. Assume for the moment that (1) all sales are for cash, (2) all costs except depreciation were paid during 1993, and (3) no buildups or depletions occurred in inventories or other assets. How much cash would have been generated from operations? From Column 2 we see that the answer is $220 million. The sales are all for cash, so Carter took in $3 billion in cash. Its costs, other than depreciation, were $2,634 million, and these were paid in cash, leaving $366 million. Again, depreciation is *not* a cash charge — the firm does not pay out the $100 million of depreciation expenses — so $366 million of cash is still left after depreciation. Taxes and interest, however, are paid in cash, so $66 million for interest and $80 million for federal and state income taxes must be deducted from the $366 million EBIT cash flow, leaving a net cash flow from operations of $220 million. As shown in Column 1, this $220 million is, of course, exactly equal to net income plus depreciation: $120 million plus $100 million equals $220 million. Therefore, because depreciation is a noncash charge, it is added back to net income to approximate cash flows from operations, and it is included as a source of funds in the statement of cash flows, as discussed in the next section.

Before leaving the subject of depreciation, we should sound a word of caution. Depreciation does not *really* provide funds; it is simply a noncash charge. Hence, it is added back to net income to obtain an estimate of the cash flow from operations. If the firm made no sales, however, depreciation certainly would not provide cash flows. To see this point more clearly, consider the situation of Communications Satellite Corporation (Comsat), which derives its income principally from two satellites, one positioned over the Atlantic and one over the Pacific. Comsat's cash flows are approximately equal to its net income plus its depreciation charges. Yet, if its two satellites stopped working, sales would vanish, and although accountants might still calculate depreciation, this depreciation would provide no cash flows (except possibly some tax refunds).

Preparing the Statement of Cash Flows

The statement of cash flows is designed to answer at a glance these three questions: (1) What were the firm's sources of funds during the year? (2) How did the firm use its available funds? (3) Did operations during the year tend to increase or decrease the firm's liquidity as measured by its cash and marketable securities balances?[11] Note that in the following discussion of the statement of cash flows we abandon the somewhat unrealistic assumptions of the previous example, Table 5-4. (One of these assumptions was that no buildups or depletions occurred in the asset accounts.) We will now broaden our analysis and look specifically at the changes in Carter's balance sheet accounts during the year.

The first step in preparing a statement of cash flows is to identify which balance sheet items provided cash and which used cash during the year. This is done on a "sources and uses of funds" worksheet. The change in each balance sheet account is determined, and this change is recorded as either a source or a use of funds according to the following rules:

Sources:

1. **Increase in a claim on assets** (that is, an increase in a liability or equity account). Borrowing from the bank is an example of a source of funds.
2. **Decrease in an asset account.**   For example, selling some fixed assets or reducing inventories are also sources of funds. Depreciation is called a "contra-asset" account. It has the effect of reducing net fixed assets (a decrease in an asset account); an increase in depreciation must, therefore, be considered a source of funds. We saw this also in Table 5-4.

Uses:

1. **Decrease in a claim on assets.**   Paying off a loan is an example of a use of funds.
2. **Increase in an asset account.**   Buying fixed assets or building up inventories are examples of uses of funds.

---

[11]There are several different formats for presenting the statement of cash flows, which was formerly called the statement of changes in financial position. The older format focused on net working capital (current assets minus current liabilities). The cash flow approach is now used since it provides information in the most useful way to financial analysts.

Table 5-5

Carter Chemical Company:
Changes in Balance Sheet
Accounts during 1993
(Millions of Dollars)

	Dec. 31, 1993	Dec. 31, 1992	Change	
			Source	Use
Cash	$ 50	$ 55	$ 5	$
Marketable securities	0	25	25	
Accounts receivable	350	315		35
Inventories	300	215		85
Gross fixed assets	1,800	1,470		330
Accumulated depreciation[a]	500	400	100	
Accounts payable	60	30	30	
Notes payable	100	60	40	
Accrued wages	10	10		
Accrued taxes	130	120	10	
Mortgage bonds	500	520		20
Debentures	300	60	240	
Common stock	50	50		
Paid-in capital	100	100		
Retained earnings	750	730	20	
Totals			$470	$470

[a]Depreciation is a "contra-asset," not an asset. Hence an increase in depreciation is a source of funds.

Thus, sources of funds include increases in short- and long-term loans, accounts payable, accruals, and retained earnings, as well as money generated by selling assets, by collecting receivables, and even by drawing down the cash account. Uses include acquiring fixed assets, building up receivables or inventories, and paying off debts.

Table 5-5 shows the changes in Carter's balance sheet accounts during the calendar year 1993, with each change designated as a source or a use. A caution is in order before we proceed. Although it may at first appear backward and confusing, it is the generally accepted accounting practice today to show the *most recent year's data first.* In this case, Carter's balance sheet accounts are shown for 1993, then for 1992. (You should always check since the older format showing the earliest year first is still used occasionally.)[12]

Carter's sources and uses each total $470 million; in fact, these two columns must always show the same total for a given year, since a dollar cannot be used unless it has been raised somewhere. Note that the table does not contain any summary accounts, such as total current assets or net fixed assets. If we included summary accounts in Table 5-5 and then used these accounts to prepare the statement of cash flows, we would be "double counting."

The data contained in Table 5-5 are next used to prepare the formal statement of cash flows. The one contained in Carter's annual report is shown in Table 5-6. Each balance sheet change in Table 5-6 is classified as resulting from (1) operations, (2) long-term investments, or (3) financing activities. Operating cash flows are those associated with the production and sale of goods and ser-

---

[12]The worksheet in Table 5-5 is flexible enough to allow for *negative* net income, which would *reduce* retained earnings, and for a *decrease* in depreciation, as when depreciable assets not yet fully depreciated have been sold during the year and have not been offset by the purchase of new depreciable assets.

Table 5-6

Carter Chemical Company: 1993 Statement of Cash Flows (Millions of Dollars)

Cash Flows from Operations:		
Net income	$120	
Additions (sources of cash):		
Increase in depreciation[a]	100	
Increase in accounts payable	30	
Increase in accrued taxes	10	
Subtractions (uses of cash):		
Increase in accounts receivable[b]	(35)	
Increase in inventories	(85)	
Net cash flow from operations		$140
Cash Flows Associated with Long-Term Investments:		
Acquisition of fixed assets		(330)
Cash Flows Associated with Financing Activities:		
Increase in notes payable	$ 40	
Increase in debentures	240	
Repayment of mortgage bonds	(20)	
Common dividends paid	(100)	
Net cash flow from financing		160
Net reduction in cash and marketable securities		($ 30)

[a]Depreciation is a noncash expense that was deducted when calculating net income. It must be added back to show the correct cash flow from operations.
[b]Recall that parentheses denote negative numbers here and throughout the book.

vices. Net income is usually a firm's primary operating cash flow, but changes in depreciation, accounts payable, accounts receivable, inventories, and accruals are also classified as operating cash flows. Investment cash flows arise from the purchase or sale of plant, property, and equipment. Financing cash inflows result from issuing debt or common stock, while financing outflows occur when the firm pays dividends, repays debt, or repurchases its own common stock. The cash inflows and outflows from these three sections are totaled to determine their impact on the firm's liquidity position, which is measured by the change in the cash and marketable securities accounts.

Note that every item in the "change" columns of Table 5-5 is carried over to Table 5-6 except retained earnings. The statement of cash flows reports net income as the first line item in the "operations" section, while dividends paid are shown as a negative cash flow in the "financing activities" section, rather than netting these items out and simply reporting the increase in retained earnings. Cash and marketable securities are combined by most large companies in this statement because marketable securities are regarded as cash equivalents.

Table 5-6 shows the sources as positive numbers and the uses as negative numbers with regard to their effects on Carter's cash and marketable securities. In the first section we see that Carter's operations provided net cash flows of $140 million. The major sources of operating cash flows were net income and depreciation, while the primary operating use was to increase inventories. The second section shows that Carter purchased fixed assets totaling $330 million; this was its only long-term investment activity during 1993. Carter's financing activities, shown in the third section of the table included borrowing from banks (notes payable), selling debentures, paying off part of its mortgage bonds, and paying dividends on its common stock. Carter raised $280 million from the capital markets, but it paid $20 million on its mortgage loan and $100 million in dividends, so its net inflow of funds from financing activities during 1993 was $160 million.

When all of these sources and uses of cash are totaled, we see that Carter had a $30 million shortfall during 1993. It met that shortfall by selling its marketable securities for a total of $25 million and by reducing its cash balance by $5 million, as can be seen in Table 5-5. Carter Chemical Company is a strong, well-managed company, and its statement of cash flows shows nothing unusual or alarming. It does show a cash drain which resulted primarily from the purchase of fixed assets, but it also shows positive cash flows from operations, so if the company were to cut back on its fixed asset expansion, it would generate positive cash flows. Thus, the cash outflow does not appear likely to continue, so it will not bleed the company to death.

Finally, the argument could be made that the statement of cash flows treats all sources of financing as equal and that, in fact, there is a dramatic difference between obtaining a short-term bank loan which has to be paid back in, say, one year and obtaining equity funds through the sale of new common stock or by being profitable and paying out less than 100 percent in dividends. The argument is valid. Equity additions are lasting, permanent sources of funds, while short-term borrowing is not. We will return to specific sources of financing in later chapters.

Self-Test

What is depreciation, and how does it relate to cash flows from operations?

Does an increase in depreciation use or provide funds? Explain.

What three questions does the statement of cash flows answer?

List the rules that determine whether a change in a balance sheet item is recorded as a source or a use of funds.

Outline the general format of the statement of cash flows.

Summary

The primary purpose of this chapter was to describe the basic financial statements. The key concepts covered are listed below:

▶   The four basic statements contained in the annual report are the **income statement,** the **balance sheet,** the **statement of retained earnings,** and the **statement of cash flows.**

The **annual report** contains both **quantitative** and **verbal** information. The financial statements report **what has actually happened** to earnings and dividends over the past few years, while the verbal statements attempt to explain **why things turned out the way they did.**

Investors use the information contained in these statements to form **expectations about the future levels of earnings and dividends,** and about the **riskiness of these expected values.**

▷   The **income statement** summarizes a firm's revenues and expenses over an accounting period — generally one year.

▷   The **balance sheet** may be thought of as a snapshot of the firm's financial position **at a point in time.** The balance sheet shows the firm's **assets and claims** on the assets.

The claims on assets are divided into two types — those claims that arise from the investment of funds by the owners of the firm, which constitute the firm's **equity,** and those claims that arise from the debt the firm owes, which constitute the firm's **liabilities.** The risk of asset-value fluctuations is borne, primarily, by the firm's common stockholders; if assets are written off, equity will shrink by the same amount.

▷   The **statement of retained earnings** reports changes in retained earnings between balance sheet dates.

▷   To understand how the timing of cash flows influences the financial statements and hence financial analysis, one must understand the **cash flow cycle** within a firm.

▷   The **statement of cash flows** converts the graphical cash flow analysis into numerical form. This statement is designed (1) to show how the firm's operations have affected its liquidity, as measured by its cash flows, and (2) to show the relationship among cash flows from operating, investing, and financing activities.

Resolution to
DECISION IN FINANCE

LETTERS FROM CHAIRMAN BUFFETT

Of all the documents that large companies publish, none receives so much attention within the firm as the annual report to shareholders. At some companies top executives begin work on the report as much as six months before its publication, and most hire professional designers and writers to ensure that the final product looks sharp and reads well.

Obviously, so much fuss would hardly be necessary if the only goal of an annual report

Sources: "Letters from Chairman Buffett," *Fortune,* August 22, 1983, 137–141; "Annual Reports Get an Editor in Washington," *Fortune,* May 7, 1979, 210–222; "Annual Reports: The Rites of Spring," *The Wall Street Journal,* March 12, 1984, 26.

were to inform shareholders about financial results. But, in fact, most big companies have turned their annual reports into flashy management showcases. In slick magazine format, using four-color photos, feature stories, and elaborate graphics, each firm tells the story its chairman would like to see told. To get the desired results, most annual reports are now produced by the director of public relations instead of the chief financial officer.

Because of their puffery, annual reports have lost credibility with serious seekers of financial information. Instead, Wall Street analysts and other sophisticated investors prefer more straightforward financial disclosure documents, such as 10-Ks, proxies, 8-Ks, and 13-Ds, all of which contain more detailed and unadorned information and must by law be filed with the Securities and Exchange Commission.

Of course, a company's philosophy and personality do count, and few other documents can offer better insight into these intangibles than an annual report. Most financial experts believe, however, that companies owe it to their investors to distinguish between the fanfare and the facts. They want to see more annual reports that realistically examine management's conduct of business affairs and factually discuss projects that will improve corporate welfare in the future. They'd like to see annual reports become the equivalent of management report cards, detailing strengths and weaknesses and plans for improvement. Given such information, they claim, shareholders would be better equipped to make intelligent investment decisions.

Chairman Warren Buffett's letters, although probably a bit too subjective for financial reporting purists, represent a giant step in the desired direction. In fact, Berkshire Hathaway's annual reports contain no photographs, colored ink, bar charts, or graphs, freeing readers to focus on the company's financial statements and Buffett's interpretation of them. Some CEOs might contend that such a bare-bones approach is too dull for the average stockholder and, further, that some readers may actually be intimidated by the information overload. But Buffett would no doubt counter that, whatever its shortcomings, his approach shows much greater respect for shareholders' intelligence and capacity to understand than does the average annual report.

A. A. Sommer, Jr., who chaired an SEC panel which studied disclosure practices, says that his group agreed that letters like Buffett's were important. But, he says, "Warren's letters are unique. Few CEOs are as smart in as many ways as Warren. It would be awfully hard to require that kind of discussion from all CEOs." In other words, it takes a chairman with interesting ideas to write an interesting chairman's letter.

Questions

5-1   What four statements are contained in most annual reports?

5-2   Is it true that if a "typical" firm reports $20 million of retained earnings on its balance sheet, its directors could declare a $20 million cash dividend without any qualms whatsoever?

5-3   What is the relationship between each rectangle in Figure 5-1 and each individual source and use in a statement of cash flows?

Self-Test Problems

ST-1   Webster Investment Services has the following net worth section reported on its balance sheet:

Common stock ($2 par)	$ 10,000,000
Paid-in capital	60,000,000
Retained earnings	50,000,000
Total shareholders' equity	$120,000,000

The company is planning to sell 1,000,000 new shares at $15.00 per share. After the sale, what will be the value of the common stock, paid-in capital, and retained earnings accounts?

ST-2   The consolidated balance sheets for the Clouse Lumber Company at the beginning and end of 1993 follow. The company bought $50 million worth of fixed assets. The charge for depreciation in 1993 was $10 million. Net income was $33 million, and the company paid out $5 million in dividends.

a. Fill in the amount of source or use in the appropriate column.
b. Prepare a statement of cash flows.
c. Briefly summarize your findings.

Clouse Lumber Company:
Balance Sheets at Beginning and End of 1993
(Millions of Dollars)

	12/31/1993	1/1/1993	Change Source	Use
Cash	$ 15	$ 7		
Marketable securities	11	0		
Accounts receivable	22	30		
Inventories	75	53		
Total current assets	$123	$ 90		
Gross fixed assets	125	75		
Less accumulated depreciation	35	25		
Net fixed assets	$ 90	$ 50		
Total assets	$213	$140		
Accounts payable	$ 15	$ 18		
Notes payable	15	3		
Other current liabilities	7	15		
Total current liabilities	$ 37	$ 36		
Long-term debt	24	8		
Common stock	57	29		
Retained earnings	95	67		
Total liabilities and equity	$213	$140		

Note: Total sources must equal total uses.

Problems

5-1
Income statement construction

Arrange these income statement items in their proper order:

Labor and material expense
Depreciation
Earnings before interest and taxes
Selling and administrative expense
Earnings before taxes

Net income
Lease payments on buildings
Sales
Taxes
Interest payments

(Hint: Labor and material expense equals cost of goods sold.)

5-2
Income computation

Engeman's Card Shop Inc. sold 50,000 cards at $1.25 each this month. The cards cost 95 cents wholesale. Engeman's newspaper and radio advertising expenses are $1,400 monthly. Mr. and Mrs. Engeman work in the shop and pay themselves a combined monthly salary of $4,000. The monthly rent payment for the shop is $2,900, and the depreciation on the store fixtures is $1,000 per month. The effective tax rate is 30 percent. What is the store's profit or loss for the month?

5-3
Income computation

Hickory Inc. had total revenue of $300,000 last year. For the period, labor costs were $112,000, material costs were $48,000, depreciation expense was $20,000, administrative expenses were $56,000, interest on its loan was $8,000, and the principal repayment on the loan was $4,000. The firm's effective tax rate is 20 percent.
a. What is the firm's reported net income?
b. Where does the principal repayment appear on the income statement?

5-4

Income computation

Wiemeyer International's retained earnings account on its 1992 balance sheet was $1,500,000, and the account equaled $1,800,000 at the end of 1993.

a. If the firm paid no dividends (zero dividend payout) in 1993, what was Wiemeyer's reported net income after dividends for 1993?

b. If, unlike Part a, Wiemeyer paid 20 percent of net income to its shareholders in the form of common stock dividends, what was the firm's reported net income for the 1993 period?

c. If, unlike Parts a or b, Wiemeyer retained 60 percent of earnings (net income), what was the firm's reported net income for the period?

5-5

Net income and cash flow calculations

The records of Horwitz & Sons were damaged recently in a fire. You have been given the task of reconstructing last year's income statement from the following data:

Sales	$4,290,000
All operating costs except depreciation	3,950,320
Depreciation	159,000
Earnings before interest and taxes (EBIT)	_____
Interest expense	60,550
Earnings before taxes (EBT)	_____
Taxes (40%)	_____

a. What was last year's net income for Horwitz & Sons?

b. If Horwitz & Sons have 30,000 shares of common stock outstanding and if the dividend payout ratio for last year was 40 percent, what were EPS and DPS?

c. What is your estimate of last year's cash flows if you also know that (1) all sales were for cash, (2) all costs except depreciation were paid last year, and (3) no buildups or depletions occurred in inventories or other assets?

5-6

Categorizing balance sheet accounts

Balance sheet items may be categorized as follows:

Current assets (CA)   Long-term debt (LTD)
Fixed assets (FA)   Common stock equity (CSE)
Current liabilities (CL)

Categorize each of the following accounts:

_____ Debt maturing in less than one year   _____ Cash
_____ Accounts receivable   _____ Common stock
_____ Debt maturing in more than one year   _____ Short-term notes payable
_____ Paid-in capital   _____ Retained earnings
_____ Mortgage bond   _____ Accruals
_____ Inventory   _____ Plant and equipment
_____ Accounts payable   _____ Short-term marketable securities

5-7

Net worth and per share calculations

D'Alelio Corporation has the following net worth section reported on its 1993 balance sheet:

Common stock ($2 par)	$10,000
Paid-in capital	12,000
Retained earnings	28,000
Total shareholders' equity	$50,000

In addition, reported net income for 1993 was $9,000, and the company announced it would pay dividends totaling $5,000. D'Alelio sold no new common stock during the year.

a. What is D'Alelio's earnings per share for 1993?

b. What is D'Alelio's dividends per share for 1993?

c. What is the addition to retained earnings for 1993?

5-8   Swingle & Company has the following net worth section reported on its balance sheet:

Net worth accounts

Common stock ($2 par)	$ 8,000,000
Paid-in capital	9,600,000
Retained earnings	42,400,000
Total shareholders' equity	$60,000,000

The company is planning to sell an issue of $6,800,000 in equity at $6.80 per share. Fill in the following net worth section to reflect the sale of the new equity:

Common stock ($2 par)	$_____
Paid-in capital	_____
Retained earnings	_____
Total shareholders' equity	$_____

5-9   Shortly after the sale of the stock, Swingle & Company (from Problem 5-8) reported that net income for the year was $28,950,000. The company announced that it would pay dividends totaling $16,750,000.

Net worth accounts

a. What was the firm's earnings per share?
b. What was the firm's dividends per share?
c. Complete the following net worth section to reflect the stock sale and the effect of the firm's earnings and dividend payment:

Common stock ($2 par)	$_____
Paid-in capital	_____
Retained earnings	_____
Total shareholders' equity	$_____

5-10   Munza Mills had $7,875,000 in retained earnings on December 31, 1992. The firm paid $630,000 in dividends during 1993 and reported retained earnings on December 31, 1993, to be $8,426,250. What was Munza Mills's reported net income for 1993?

Income computation

5-11   Peabody Corporation reported $994,000 in cumulative retained earnings at the end of last year. Assume that by the end of this year the retained earnings balance sheet account has grown to $1,154,500. If Peabody's net income for this year is $268,000 and the firm has 50,000 shares of common stock outstanding, what dividends per share was paid for this year?

Dividends per share calculation

5-12   What effect would each of the following events have on a firm's balance sheet? (Discuss changes in individual accounts, then resulting changes in total assets and total claims.)

Balance sheet effects

a. Purchase of a new asset for $2 million cash.
b. Purchase of a new asset for $2 million financed with 35 percent debt and 65 percent cash.
c. Sale of $100,000 in merchandise for cash.
d. Sale of $100,000 in merchandise on credit.
e. Inventory write-off of $200,000 due to obsolescence.
f. Payment of $50,000 to trade creditors.

5-13   Refer to Tables 5-1 and 5-2 to answer the following questions:

Balance sheet effects

a. What would Carter Chemical Company's balance sheet item "retained earnings" for 1993 have been if the firm paid $60 million in dividends for the year?
b. What would Carter's 1993 EPS have been had net income for that year been $150 million rather than $120 million?
c. Suppose that you knew that Carter's EPS was $2.40 and that net income was $120 million. Could you use this information to determine the number of shares outstanding?
d. If Carter sold inventories carried at $150 million for only $37.5 million, what effects would this have on the firm's balance sheet? (Disregard tax effects and assume cash sales.)

e. Carter's accountants find that MACRS depreciation shortens the tax life of assets. This would increase the firm's depreciation expense in the early years. How will this action affect the company's cash flows? No calculations are necessary.

5-14 Determine last year's increase or decrease in cash for Radke Manufacturing Inc., given
Sources and uses the following information, in millions. (Assume no other changes have occurred over the past year.)

Decrease in marketable securities	=	$ 50
Increase in accounts receivable	=	100
Increase in notes payable	=	60
Decrease in accounts payable	=	40
Increase in accrued wages and taxes	=	30
Increase in inventories	=	70
Increase in depreciation	=	10

5-15 On its December 31, 1993, balance sheet, Attas Graphics Inc. reported gross fixed as-
Sources and uses sets of $4,150,000 and net fixed assets of $2,500,000. Depreciation for the year was $750,000. Net fixed assets on December 31, 1992, had been $2,350,000. What figure for "cash flows associated with long-term investments—fixed assets" should Attas Graphics report on its statement of cash flows for 1993?

5-16 Determine the total sources and uses of funds for T. J. Luepke Inc., given the following
Sources and uses information (in thousands):

	12/31/93	12/31/92
Cash	$ 10	$ 30
Marketable securities	50	0
Accounts receivable	150	90
Inventories	200	200
Gross fixed assets	2,500	2,000
Depreciation	1,000	800
Accounts payable	130	100
Notes payable	0	30
Common stock	650	500
Paid-in capital	920	730
Retained earnings	210	160

5-17 The consolidated balance sheets for Manion Associates at the beginning and end of
Statement of cash flows 1993 follow. The company bought $75 million worth of fixed assets. The charge for depreciation in 1993 was $15 million. Net income was $38 million, and the company paid out $10 million in dividends.
a. Fill in the amount of source or use in the appropriate column.
b. Prepare a statement of cash flows.
c. Briefly summarize your findings.

Manion Associates:
Balance Sheet, Beginning and End of 1993
(Millions of Dollars)

	12/31/93	1/1/93	Change Source	Use
Cash	$ 7	$ 15	_____	_____
Marketable securities	0	11	_____	_____
Accounts receivable	30	22	_____	_____
Inventories	75	53	_____	_____
Total current assets	$112	$101	_____	_____

continued

Manion Associates:
Balance Sheet, Beginning and End of 1993
(Millions of Dollars) *(continued)*

| | | | Change | |
| | | | Source | Use |
	12/31/93	1/1/93		
Gross fixed assets	224	149	_____	_____
Less: Depreciation	(41)	(26)	_____	_____
Net fixed assets	$183	$123	_____	_____
Total assets	$295	$224	_____	_____
Accounts payable	$ 28	$ 25	_____	_____
Notes payable	3	15	_____	_____
Accrued wages and taxes	15	7	_____	_____
Total current liabilities	$ 46	$ 47	_____	_____
Long-term debt	90	72	_____	_____
Common stock	64	38	_____	_____
Retained earnings	95	67	_____	_____
Total liabilities and equity	$295	$224	_____	_____

Solutions to Self-Test Problems

ST-1   The common stock sale results in 1,000,000 × $15 = $15,000,000 new equity. The breakdown of this money to the equity accounts is as follows:

	Before Sale	Transaction	After Sale
Common stock	$10,000,000	1,000,000 × $2 = $2,000,000	$12,000,000
Paid-in capital	60,000,000	$15,000,000 - $2,000,000 = $13,000,000	73,000,000
Retained earnings	50,000,000	0	50,000,000
Total shareholders' equity	$120,000,000	$15,000,000	$135,000,000

ST-2   **a.** Sources and uses of funds analysis:

Clouse Lumber Company:
Balance Sheets (Millions of Dollars)

	12/31/1993	1/1/1993	Source	Use
Cash	$ 15	$ 7		$ 8
Marketable securities	11	0		11
Accounts receivable	22	30	$ 8	
Inventories	75	53		22
Total current assets	$123	$ 90		
Gross fixed assets	125	75		50
Less: accumulated depreciation	35	25	10	
Net fixed assets	$ 90	$ 50		
Total assets	$213	$140		
Accounts payable	$ 15	$ 18		3
Notes payable	15	3	12	
Other current liabilities	$ 7	$ 15		8
Total current liabilities	$ 37	$ 36		
Long-term debt	24	8	16	
Common stock	57	29	28	
Retained earnings	95	67	28	
Total liabilities and equity	$213	$140	$102	$102

b.   **Clouse Lumber Company:**
     Statement of Cash Flows, 1993
     (Millions of Dollars)

Cash Flows from Operations:		
Net income	$ 33	
Additions (sources of cash):		
Increase in depreciation	10	
Decrease in accounts receivable	8	
Subtractions (uses of cash):		
Increase in inventories	(22)	
Decrease in accounts payable	(3)	
Decrease in other current liabilities	(8)	
Net cash flows from operations		$ 18
Long-Term Investments:		
Acquisition of fixed assets		(50)
Financing Activities:		
Increase in notes payable	$ 12	
Sale of long-term debt	16	
Sale of common stock	28	
Dividends paid	(5)	
Net cash flows from financing		51
Net increase in cash and marketable securities		$ 19

c.   Investments were made in plant and inventories, and funds were utilized to reduce
     accounts payable and other current liabilities. The cash and marketable securities
     accounts were also increased. Most funds were obtained by increasing long-term
     debt, selling common stock, and retaining earnings. The remainder was obtained
     from an increase in depreciation, increasing notes payable, and reducing receivables.

Interpreting Financial Statements

After reading this chapter, you should be able to:

▶ Explain why ratio analysis is usually the first step in the analysis of a company's financial statements.

▶ List the five groups of ratios and specify which ratios belong in each group.

▶ State why trend analysis is important.

▶ Describe how the Du Pont system is used and how it may be modified to include the effect of financial leverage.

▶ List several limitations of ratio analysis.

DECISION IN FINANCE

COOKING THE BOOKS

Phantom sneakers, invisible copper rods, and a barrel full of floor sweepings—what do they all have in common? Each was used by a different corporation to inflate its financial reports through inventory fraud—one of the latest and fastest-growing methods of cooking the books.

Accounting irregularities are not new in the business world, and not all such instances are fraud—many are the result of honest mistakes or of different interpretations of financial information. Manipulating inventory figures, however, appears on its face to be intentional, and it is not always caught even by the most careful auditors. Overstating inventory is a quick way to pad profits.

"When companies are desperate to stay afloat, inventory fraud is the easiest way to produce instant profits and dress up the balance sheet," says Felix Pomerantz of Florida International University's Center for Accounting, Auditing, and Tax Studies. The "profits" appear because current inventory figures are subtracted from those of the previous year to show the cost of supplies used to produce items for sale. This, plus the cost of labor, is then deducted from the sale price to calculate profits.

Among the many companies where such manipulation has been discovered are L.A. Gear, which listed nonexistent sneakers in its inventory, Digital Equipment, which failed to set aside reserves for obsolete inventory, and Phar-Mor, alleged to have overstated its inventory by more than $50 million.

Comptronix Corporation, embroiled in a financial scandal, disclosed that inventory manipulations played a "significant role." Then there was the company that reported a value of several thousand dollars for the contents of a barrel which, when examined, proved to be full of floor sweepings.

It was copper rods, however, that played the central role in the downfall of Laribee Wire Manufacturing Company in New York. The heavily debt-ridden firm needed a big loan to meet its obligations, and it borrowed $130 million from six banks. Collateral for the loans included inventories of the copper rods used to make the wire at the six Laribee factories.

Laribee's management misstated the amount and value of their supplies in various ways. For instance, when shipments of stocks were made

See end of chapter for resolution.
Photo source: Barbara Filet/Tony Stone Images

from one plant to another, they were recorded as existing at both plants; sometimes they were never shipped at all, and transfer documents were simply made up. Some stocks were inventoried at a higher price than their actual value. And $5 million worth of copper rods, about 4.5 million pounds, were reported as stored in two warehouses. In fact, it would have taken six warehouses of that size to hold such a large amount of stock.

As you read this chapter, consider how falsified inventory reports would affect the analysis of a company's financial statements. Who gets hurt by this type of fraud? How does such deception go undiscovered, and what is the result likely to be if it is found out?

In Chapter 5 we examined the major sources of financial information — the income statement and the balance sheet. We also discussed other statements, such as the statement of retained earnings and the statement of cash flows, which aid in the interpretation of the available financial data. In this chapter we continue our discussion of the techniques of financial analysis, especially ratio analysis, by which firms' relative riskiness, creditworthiness, profit potential, and general managerial competence can be appraised.

Importance of Financial Statements

In addition to the ratios discussed in this chapter, financial analysts also employ a tool known as *common-size* balance sheets and income statements. To form a common-size balance sheet, one simply divides each asset, liability, and equity item by total assets and then expresses the result as a percentage. To form a common-size income statement, one divides each income statement item by sales. The percentage statements that this produces can be compared with common-size statements of larger or smaller firms or with those of the same firm over time.[1]

Financial statements report both on a firm's position at a point in time and on its operations over some past period. However, their real usefulness lies in the fact that they can be used to help predict the firm's future earnings and dividends as well as the riskiness of these cash flows. From an equity investor's viewpoint, *predicting the future* is what financial statement analysis is all about. Of course, current debtholders and others who are considering lending to the firm are also concerned with the firm's future. As we shall see, the firm's debt and equity investors are usually concerned with different aspects of the firm's prospects. From management's viewpoint, *financial statement analysis is useful both as a way to anticipate future conditions and, more important, as a starting point for planning actions that will influence the future course of events for the firm.*

---

[1]For a more complete discussion of common-size statements, see Eugene F. Brigham and Louis C. Gapenski, *Intermediate Financial Management,* Fourth Edition, 1993, Chapter 18.

Self-Test

How are common-size statements created?

What is the real usefulness of financial statements?

Ratio Analysis

ratio analysis

Analysis of the relationships among financial statement accounts.

Financial ratios are designed to show relationships among financial statement accounts. Ratios put numbers into perspective. For example, Firm A may have $5,248,760 of debt and annual interest charges of $419,900, while Firm B's debt may total $52,647,980 versus interest charges of $3,948,600. The true burden of these debts, and the companies' ability to repay them, can be ascertained only by comparing each firm's debt to its assets, and its interest charges to the income available for payment of interest. Such comparisons are made by **ratio analysis.**

A single ratio is relatively useless in making relevant evaluations of a firm's health. To be effectively interpreted, a ratio must be systematically applied in one of the following ways:

1. Compared with several ratios in a network such as the Du Pont system of analysis, discussed later in this chapter, or other logical grouping.

2. Compared with the trends of the firm's own ratios.

3. Compared with management's goals for key ratios.

4. Compared with selected ratios of other firms in the same industry (or with a published industry average).

When comparing a firm's ratios with those of other companies, care must be taken to select similar firms of corresponding size and industry type to ensure the appropriate comparison of financial data. For example, small firms must often rely on trade credit and other short-term liabilities to finance the firms' assets, whereas larger firms have access to the capital markets for financing. This fact may lead to significant differences in liquidity and debt ratios if these firms are compared. Similarly, cross-industry comparisons often lead to incorrect conclusions. Thus, an acceptable inventory turnover ratio for a retail jeweler would lead to disaster if adopted by a meat packer.

Analysts who use financial ratios extensively may be characterized as belonging to three main groups: (1) *managers,* who use ratios to help analyze, control, and thus improve the firm's operations; (2) *credit analysts,* such as bank loan officers or credit managers for industrial companies, who analyze ratios to help ascertain a company's ability to pay its debts; and (3) *securities analysts,* including both stock analysts, who are interested in a company's efficiency and growth prospects, and bond analysts, who are concerned with a company's ability to pay interest on its bonds and with the assets that would be available to bondholders if the company were to go bankrupt.

Thus, each group of analysts has specific areas of interest which it wishes to investigate. A bank loan officer would concentrate on the short-term health of the firm, while a stock analyst would be more concerned with the firm's long-term prospects. Analysts, then, calculate specific groups of ratios rather than all

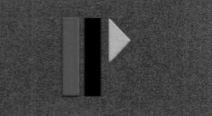

MANIPULATING FINANCIAL STATEMENTS

Call it by any other name—and many do—a company's annual report is usually still the first source investors turn to when deciding whether to buy or sell a stock. The annual report should describe a company's recent performance and current health accurately. If profits shown in the report are healthy, then presumably the company is too.

But wait! Finger pointing abounds every year in the business press, suggesting that all is not what is should be in corporate reportland. "Annual obfuscation," "camouflage caper," and "hornblowing festival" are some of the descriptive terms for the spring flood of annual reports that deluges shareholders and others with the good news of a company's previous year— or bad news made to look as good as possible.

A report from General Motors, when its business was terrible, indicated that the company was merely undergoing "a transitional period of lower volume." And Carter Hawley Hale Stores chairman Philip Hawley said in his firm's 1990 report that "we are fully committed to accomplishing a major improvement in . . . profitability . . . in the current difficult retail environment." In fact, the environment, or something, was so difficult that Carter Hawley Hale filed for bankruptcy protection two months later, and General Motors' top managers have all been replaced.

Two business writers studying annual reports noted that the more verbiage an executive's letter to stockholders contained, the worse off the company usually was. Applying their "fog factor" to several years of annual reports from big firms that later failed, they found that the chairman's letter grew 64 percent longer over three years at Continental Information Systems, and at Southmark the letter length doubled.

Sources: Grace M. Kang, "It's Corporate America's Spring Hornblowing Festival," *Business Week,* April 12, 1993, 31; Michael W. Miller and Lee Berton, "As IBM's Woes Grew, Its Accounting Tactics Got Less Conservative," *The Wall Street Journal,* April 7, 1993, A1ff; Mary Beth Grover, "Generally Vague Accounting Principles," *Forbes,* September 14, 1992, 462–463; "Autos" Section, *Fortune,* November 16, 1992, 74; Craig Torres, "Lone Star Steakhouse's Sizzle Is Cooking Up Doubts," *The Wall Street Journal,* November 3, 1992, C1, C3; Jason Zweig and John Chamberlain, "Windbag Theory," *Forbes,* August 3, 1992, 43–44; Andrea Rothman and Lisa Driscoll, "Won't You Pleeeease Read Our Annual Report?" *Business Week,* May 13, 1991, 50; "Discounting for Creativity," *The Economist,* January 19, 1991, 70; and Gary Hector and Terence P. Pare, "Cute Tricks on the Bottom Line," *Fortune,* April 24, 1989, 193.

The average letter in all the reports studied fattened an average 26 percent.

Possibly report readers can cope with descriptive gibberish and gobbledegook, but what about misleading numbers? The only really solid number in any financial report is the one specifying cash. Everything else is calculated according to certain assumptions. Managers and accountants can be scrupulously honest yet still produce annual reports that confuse and mislead rather than enlighten. They can also intentionally adjust or skirt reality, using aggressive, though still legal, accounting. Among the most common abuses are the following:

1. **Hiding inventory.** Sales to consumers may be slow and retailers may be overstocked, but manufacturers can still record a sale every time they ship a product and can keep their profit picture bright in the short run. IBM, racked by almost $5 billion in losses in 1992 that led to the layoff of tens of thousands, a much-publicized change at the top, and a 60 percent stock price decline, is reported to have delayed its fall by applying this method, among others. An outside auditor criticized IBM's practice of recording as revenue products shipped to dealers without waiting for sales at the other end and even without being sure the dealer would not return the product. Sometimes IBM even booked revenue for shipments to its own warehouses. Some other companies also record sales upon shipment of a product, but better companies are more conservative.

2. **Creating income.** When companies enter into long-term contracts for the development of products, they often do not receive any payment until the project is completed. Even so, accounting rules allow them to report income based on the percentage of completion they calculate has been achieved. One biotech company annually reported $4.5 million in revenue from two long-term contracts relating to a developing product, even though it had not received nearly that much. It spent millions of its own money on development but offset those costs with *expected* income, which obviously props up profits.

3. **Storing up profits.** A big gain in profits in a particular quarter may look great—until the next quarter, when profits slump badly after the one-time bonanza. What to do to avoid investor shock? Some companies create special reserve funds into which portions of unusual one-time profits can be shunted and use those reserves to mask losses in later years.

4. **Consolidating the bad news.** "Taking a bath" by writing off a number of different projects all at once relieves a company of future expenses and allows it to look good the following year. Federal Express found a way to get it over with even more quickly. The courier service wrote off $254 million in early 1992 connected with a planned overseas expansion that soured, resulting in a loss of $3.58 per share. However, its books showed a profit of $36 million the very next quarter. How was it done? If a write-off estimate turns out to be higher than was actually needed, accounting rules allow companies to put the excess into operating income. "The problem for investors," says an accounting professor, "is that you can get an accounting turnaround when you don't necessarily get a business turnaround."

5. **Deferring costs.** Lone Star Steakhouse figured out an accounting treatment that is worth about 3 cents a share annually. When they have managers in training at their restaurants, the trainees' salaries are accrued for the first eight weeks and then listed as a capital expense that is amortized over a year. After the eight-week period, the sal-

ary is treated as expense to the outlet where the trainee is assigned. An analyst who follows Lone Star says, "They are not doing anything differently with their accounting than most other restaurant companies." Another firm, CUC International, admitted that its profits had been inflated by aggressive accounting, including deferring for several years the costs of attracting new customers. When it decided to write off all the deferred costs at once, three years of profits were totally erased.

6. **Changing depreciation.** A British firm, Cable & Wireless, had been depreciating its fixed assets at 8.9 percent for several years but then changed the depreciation to 7.0 percent in 1990. Longer asset lives mean less depreciation per year, and that translates into higher reported profits. Although the company's technical reasons may have been sound, most people usually assume that the life of mechanical assets is less today than it used to be, so analysts questioned the move.

All these methods, and others, can be used by creative accountants without stepping outside the law, but they may also screen or distort the truth. Investors and others trying to decipher what annual reports really say would be well advised to read the fine print in the footnotes, where more detailed information can modify that available in the financial statements. In the final analysis, true costs may be hidden and true profits inflated, but the real world of cash flow is not altered at all.

possible ratios, as their purpose dictates. Therefore, ratios may be categorized into specific task groupings. We have categorized ratios into five groups: (1) liquidity ratios, (2) asset management ratios, (3) debt management ratios, (4) profitability ratios, and (5) market value ratios. Some of the most valuable ratios in each category are discussed and illustrated next, using Carter Chemical Company's financial data as they were presented back in Tables 5-1 and 5-2.

Liquidity Ratios

One of the first concerns of most financial analysts is liquidity: Will the firm be able to meet its maturing obligations? Carter Chemical Company has debts totaling $300 million that must be paid off within the coming year. Can these obligations be satisfied? A full liquidity analysis requires the use of cash budgets (described in Chapter 9); but, by relating the amount of cash and other current assets to the current obligations, ratio analysis provides a quick and

liquidity ratios

Ratios that show the relationship of a firm's cash and other current assets to its current liabilities.

current ratio

This ratio is computed by dividing current assets by current liabilities. It indicates the extent to which the claims of short-term creditors are covered by assets expected to be converted to cash in the near future.

easy-to-use measure of liquidity. Two commonly used **liquidity ratios** are presented in this section.[2]

Current Ratio.   The **current ratio** is computed by dividing current assets by current liabilities. Current assets normally include cash, marketable securities, accounts receivable, and inventories. Current liabilities consist of accounts payable, short-term notes payable, current maturities of long-term debt, accrued income taxes, and other accrued expenses (principally wages).

If a company is getting into financial difficulty, it begins paying its bills (accounts payable) more slowly, building up bank loans, and so on. If these current liabilities are rising faster than current assets, the current ratio will fall, and this could spell trouble. Accordingly, the current ratio is the most commonly used measure of short-term solvency because it provides an indicator of the extent to which the claims of short-term creditors are covered by assets that are expected to be converted to cash in a period roughly corresponding to the maturity of the claims.

The calculation of the current ratio for Carter at year-end 1993 follows. (All dollar amounts in this section are in millions.)

$$\text{Current ratio} = \frac{\text{Current assets}}{\text{Current liabilities}} = \frac{\$700}{\$300} = 2.3 \text{ times.}$$

$$\text{Industry average} = 2.5 \text{ times.}$$

Carter's current ratio is slightly below the average for the industry, 2.5, but it is not low enough to cause concern. It appears that Carter is about in line with most other chemical firms. Since current assets are scheduled to be converted to cash in the near future, it is highly probable that they could be liquidated at close to their stated value. With a current ratio of 2.3, Carter could liquidate current assets at only 43 percent of book value and still pay off current creditors in full.[3]

Although industry average figures are discussed later in some detail, it should be stated at this point that an industry average is not a magic number that all firms should strive to maintain. In fact, some well-managed firms will be above the average, while other good firms will be below it. However, if a firm's ratios are far removed from the average for its industry, an analyst should be concerned about why this variance occurs. Thus, a deviation from the industry average should signal the analyst (or management) to check further.

If we were also to calculate Carter's current ratio for 1992, we would find that it had declined to 2.3 in 1993 from 2.8 in 1992. Thus the *trend* is poor, and this could indicate potential future difficulties. More will be said about *trend analysis* later in the chapter.

---

[2]Liquidity ratios are generally considered better if higher, but only within reason. Very high values for these ratios tend to have a negative impact on profitability because this reflects a relatively high level of short-term assets, and such current assets usually earn a lower return than long-term assets, plant and equipment. We will return to this risk-return tradeoff in Chapter 8.

[3]$(1/2.3) = 0.43$, or 43 percent. Note that $(0.43)(\$700) \approx \$300$, the amount of current liabilities.

quick, or acid test, ratio

This ratio is computed by deducting inventories from current assets and dividing the remainder by current liabilities.

Quick, or Acid Test, Ratio. The **quick, or acid test, ratio** is calculated by deducting inventories from current assets and then dividing the remainder by current liabilities. Inventories are typically the least liquid of a firm's current assets, hence they are the assets on which losses are most likely to occur in the event of liquidation. Therefore, a measure of the firm's ability to pay off short-term obligations without relying on the sale of inventories is important.

$$\text{Quick, or acid test, ratio} = \frac{\text{Current assets} - \text{Inventory}}{\text{Current liabilities}} = \frac{\$400}{\$300}$$

$$= 1.3 \text{ times.}$$

$$\text{Industry average} = 1.0 \text{ time.}$$

The industry average quick ratio is 1.0, so Carter's 1.3 quick ratio compares favorably with the quick ratios of other firms in the industry. If the accounts receivable can be collected, the company can pay off its current liabilities even without selling any inventory. Again, the trend is downward — 1.3 in 1993 versus 1.8 in 1992.

Asset Management Ratios

asset management ratios

A set of ratios which measures how effectively a firm is managing its assets; also called *activity ratios*.

The second group of ratios, the **asset management ratios,** measures how effectively the firm is managing its assets. These ratios are sometimes called *activity ratios* and are designed to answer this question: Does the total amount of each type of asset as reported on the balance sheet seem reasonable, too high, or too low in view of current and projected operating levels? Carter Chemical Company and other companies must borrow or obtain capital from other sources to acquire assets. If they have too many assets, their interest expenses will be too high, and hence their profits will be depressed. On the other hand, if assets are too low, profitable sales may be lost. So, having the proper level of each type of asset is important.

inventory turnover ratio

The ratio computed by dividing sales by inventories; also called the *inventory utilization ratio.*

Inventory Turnover. The **inventory turnover ratio**, also called the *inventory utilization ratio,* is defined as sales divided by inventories[4]:

$$\text{Inventory turnover, or utilization, ratio} = \frac{\text{Sales}}{\text{Inventory}} = \frac{\$3,000}{\$300} = 10 \text{ times.}$$

$$\text{Industry average} = 9 \text{ times.}$$

As a rough approximation, each item of Carter's inventory is sold out and restocked, or "turned over," 10 times per year. Its gross profit is therefore 10 times the difference between its selling prices and the cost of its inventory. Carter's ratio of 10 times compares favorably with an industry average of 9 times. This suggests that the company does not hold excessive stocks of inventory; excess stocks are, of course, unproductive and represent an investment with a low or zero rate of return. Carter's high inventory turnover ratio also

---

[4]Any reference to "Sales" in this and subsequent ratios is "Net sales" from Table 5-1.

reinforces our faith in the current ratio. If the turnover were low — say, 3 or 4 times — we might wonder whether the firm was holding damaged or obsolete goods not actually worth their stated value.

Two problems arise in calculating and analyzing the inventory turnover ratio. First, sales are stated at market prices, so if inventories are carried at cost, as they generally are, it would be more appropriate to use cost of goods sold in place of sales in the numerator of the formula. However, established compilers of financial ratio statistics, such as Dun & Bradstreet, use the ratio of sales to inventories carried at cost. To develop a figure that can be compared with those published by Dun & Bradstreet and similar organizations, it is necessary to measure inventory turnover with sales in the numerator, as we do here.

The second problem lies in the fact that sales occur over the entire year, while the inventory figure is for one point in time. This makes it better to use an average inventory measure.[5] If the firm's business is highly seasonal, or if there has been a strong upward or downward sales trend during the year, it is essential to make some such adjustment. To maintain comparability with industry averages, however, we did not use the average inventory figure.

days sales outstanding (DSO)

The ratio computed by dividing average *credit* sales per day into accounts receivable; indicates the average length of time the firm must wait after making a credit sale before receiving payment.

Days Sales Outstanding. **Days sales outstanding (DSO)**, also called the *average collection period (ACP),* is used to appraise the accounts receivable, and it is computed by dividing average daily sales into accounts receivable to find the number of days' sales tied up in receivables.[6] Thus, the DSO represents the average length of time that the firm must wait after making a sale before receiving cash. The calculations for Carter show that 42 days' sales are outstanding, slightly above the 36-day industry average:

$$\text{DSO} = \frac{\text{Days sales}}{\text{outstanding}} = \frac{\text{Receivables}}{\text{Average sales per day}} = \frac{\text{Receivables}}{\text{Annual sales}/360}$$

$$= \frac{\$350}{\$3,000/360} = \frac{\$350}{\$8.333} = 42 \text{ days.}$$

$$\text{Industry average} = 36 \text{ days.}$$

Note that in this and several later calculations where we need to make an assumption regarding the number of days in the year, we will always use 360 days, not 365. This may not be logical, but it is how published ratios are calculated, and for our ratios to be comparable, we must use a 360-day year also.

The DSO can be evaluated by comparison with the terms on which the firm sells its goods. For example, Carter's sales terms call for payment within 30 days, so the fact that 42 days' sales, not 30 days, are outstanding indicates that customers, on the average, are not paying their bills on time. If the trend in DSO

---

[5]Preferably, the average inventory value should be calculated by summing the monthly figures during the year and dividing by 12. If monthly data are not available, one can add the beginning and ending figures and divide by 2; this will adjust for growth but not for seasonal effects.

[6]Because information on the proportion of credit sales to total sales is generally unavailable, total sales may be used as a substitute in the DSO calculation. However, since all firms do not have the same percentage of credit sales, there is a good chance that the DSO will be understated if total sales are used rather than credit sales. The smaller the percentage of credit sales, the greater this understatement.

over the past few years has been rising but the credit policy has not been changed, this would be even stronger evidence that steps should be taken to expedite the collection of accounts receivable.[7]

fixed assets turnover ratio

The ratio of sales to net fixed assets; also called the *fixed assets utilization ratio.*

Fixed Assets Turnover.   The **fixed assets turnover ratio,** also called the *fixed assets utilization ratio,* measures how effectively the firm uses its plant and equipment. It is the ratio of sales to net fixed assets:

$$\text{Fixed assets turnover, or utilization, ratio} = \frac{\text{Sales}}{\text{Net fixed assets}} = \frac{\$3,000}{\$1,300} = 2.3 \text{ times.}$$

Industry average = 3.0 times.

Carter's ratio of 2.3 times compares poorly with the industry average of 3.0 times, indicating that the firm is not using its fixed assets to as high a percentage of capacity as are the other firms in the industry. The financial manager should bear this fact in mind when production people request funds for new capital investments.

A major potential problem exists when the fixed assets turnover ratio is used to compare different firms. All assets except cash and accounts receivable reflect the historical cost of the assets, and inflation has caused the value of many assets that were purchased in the past to be seriously understated. Therefore, if we were comparing an old firm which had acquired many of its fixed assets years ago at low prices with a new company which had acquired its fixed assets only recently, we probably would find that the old firm reported a higher turnover ratio. However, this would be more reflective of the inability of accountants to deal with inflation than of any inefficiency on the part of the new firm. The accounting profession is trying to devise ways of making financial statements reflect current values rather than historical values. If balance sheets were stated on a current value basis, this would eliminate the problem of comparisons, but at the moment the problem still exists. Because financial analysts typically do not have the data necessary to make adjustments, they must simply recognize that a problem may exist and deal with it judgmentally. In Carter's case, the issue is not a serious one because all firms in the industry have been expanding at about the same rate; thus, the balance sheets of the comparison firms are indeed comparable.

total assets turnover ratio

The ratio computed by dividing sales by total assets; also called the *total assets utilization ratio.*

Total Assets Turnover.   The **total assets turnover ratio** measures the turnover, or utilization, of all the firm's assets; it is calculated by dividing sales by total assets:

$$\text{Total assets turnover, or utilization, ratio} = \frac{\text{Sales}}{\text{Total assets}} = \frac{\$3,000}{\$2,000} = 1.5 \text{ times.}$$

Industry average = 1.8 times.

[7]A similar ratio, which is often used to measure the effectiveness of a firm's accounts receivable management, is the *accounts receivable turnover ratio,* found by dividing receivables into sales *or* by dividing DSO into 360 days. For Carter Chemical Company, the accounts receivable turnover ratio is \$3,000/\$350 = 8.6 times. (Alternatively: 360/42 = 8.6 times.)

Carter's ratio is somewhat below the industry average, meaning that the company is not generating a sufficient volume of business for the size of its total asset investment. Sales should be increased, some assets should be disposed of, or a combination of these steps should be taken.

Debt Management Ratios

financial leverage

The extent to which a firm uses debt (or preferred stock) financing.

The extent to which a firm uses debt financing, or **financial leverage,** has three important implications. (1) By raising funds through debt, the owners can maintain control of the firm with a limited investment. (2) Creditors look to the equity, or owner-supplied funds, to provide a margin of safety; if the owners have provided only a small proportion of the total financing, the risks of the enterprise are borne mainly by its creditors. (3) If the firm earns more on investments financed with borrowed funds than it pays in interest, the return on the owners' capital is magnified, resulting in "favorable leverage." Preferred stock also provides financial leverage, but we will defer our discussion of preferred stock to Chapter 16.

To understand better how the use of debt, or financial leverage, affects risk and return, consider Table 6-1. Here we are analyzing two companies that are identical except for the way they are financed. Firm U (for "unleveraged") has no debt, whereas Firm L (for "leveraged") is financed half with equity and half with debt which has an interest rate of 15 percent. Both companies have $100 million of assets and $120 million in sales. Their ratio of EBIT to total assets, called the *basic earning power ratio,* is $30 million/$100 million = 0.30 = 30%. Even though both companies' assets have the same earning power, *under expected conditions,* Firm L provides its stockholders with a *return on equity* of 27 percent versus only 18 percent for Firm U. This difference is caused by Firm L's use of debt.[8]

Financial leverage has the potential to raise the rate of return to stockholders for two reasons: (1) Because interest is deductible, the use of debt financing lowers the tax bill and leaves more of the firm's operating income available to its investors. (2) If the firm's basic earning power ratio exceeds the interest rate on debt, as it generally does, then a company can use debt to finance assets, pay the interest on the debt, and have something left over as a "bonus" for its stockholders. For our hypothetical firms, these two effects have combined to push Firm L's rate of return on equity up to a level 50 percent higher than that of Firm U. Thus, debt can be used to "leverage up," or magnify, a firm's rate of return on equity.[9]

However, financial leverage makes a firm riskier. As shown in Column 2 of the income statements, if sales are lower and costs are higher than expected,

---

[8]The basic earning power ratio and the return on equity ratio both belong in the fourth category, profitability ratios, which will be discussed shortly. While it would be ideal *not* to use these two ratios until profitability ratios have been fully explained, what we have here is a type of chicken-and-egg situation. Profitability ratios are normally presented *after* both asset and debt management ratios because they reflect the impact on profits of decisions relating to asset and debt levels. At the same time, these two profitability ratios provide convenient tools for analyzing the use of debt.

[9]As mentioned, preferred stock also provides financial leverage, but in this chapter the underlying assumption will be that the firms in question do not use preferred stock in their capital structures.

Table 6-1

Effect of Financial Leverage on Stockholders' Returns (Millions of Dollars)

Firm U (Unleveraged)

Current assets	$ 50	Debt	$ 0
Fixed assets	50	Common equity	100
Total assets	$100	Total liabilities and equity	$100

	Expected Conditions (1)	Bad Conditions (2)
Sales	$100.00	$82.50
Operating costs	70.00	80.00
Operating income (EBIT)	$ 30.00	$ 2.50
Interest	0.00	0.00
Earnings before taxes (EBT)	$ 30.00	$ 2.50
Taxes (40%)	12.00	1.00
Net income (NI)	$ 18.00	$ 1.50
ROE_U = NI/Common equity = NI/$100 =	18.00%	1.50%

Firm L (Leveraged)

Current assets	$ 50	Debt (interest = 15%)	$ 50
Fixed assets	50	Common equity	50
Total assets	$100	Total liabilities and equity	$100

	Expected Conditions (1)	Bad Conditions (2)
Sales	$100.00	$82.50
Operating costs	70.00	80.00
Operating income (EBIT)	$ 30.00	$ 2.50
Interest	7.50	7.50
Earnings before taxes (EBT)	$ 22.50	($ 5.00)
Taxes (40%)	9.00	(2.00)
Net income (NI)	$ 13.50	($ 3.00)
ROE_L = NI/Common equity = NI/$50 =	27.00%	(6.00%)

the basic earning power ratio will be lower than expected for both firms: EBIT/Total assets = $2.5 million/$100 million = 0.025 = 2.5%. But notice that, under these conditions, the leveraged firm's return on equity falls especially sharply. Under the "bad conditions" in Table 6-1, the unleveraged firm still shows a profit, but the firm which uses debt shows a loss and a negative return on equity. Firm U, because of its strong balance sheet, could ride out the decline in sales and be around when sales recover. Firm L, on the other hand, would be under great pressure. Because of its losses, its cash might be depleted, requiring it to raise funds. However, because it is running a loss, Firm L would have a hard time selling stock to raise capital, and because the firm now looks riskier to lenders, they would raise the interest rate they charge, increasing Firm L's problems still further. In short, Firm L is vulnerable to declines in the business cycle and might not be around to enjoy the next boom.

This illustration provides another clear example of the risk-return tradeoff introduced in Chapter 1. We see that firms with relatively high debt usage are able to magnify returns when the economy is normal or booming, but they are exposed to greater risk of loss when the economy is in a recession. Firms which use little or no debt financing are less risky, but they forgo the opportunity to "leverage up," or magnify, their returns on equity. The possibility of high returns is desirable, but investors are averse to risk. Therefore, decisions about the use of debt require that managers balance higher expected returns against increased risk and attempt to find the particular level of debt that will maximize the value of the firm's common stock. This is no small task. Although sales are clearly influenced by many other factors, the business cycle of expansion and recession is one of the major determinants for most firms. If you look back to Figure 4-2, you will see that no two business cycles are the same. Recessions in the past have varied considerably in duration and in the number of years of expansion between them. What you cannot see from Figure 4-2 is that recessions also differ significantly in severity, that is, the extent to which an average firm's sales will be hurt by the downturn. Given the difficulties associated with forecasting, it is no wonder that firms with above average use of debt are concerned about declining sales (or increasing operating costs) and the resulting impact on their returns on equity (ROEs).

Determining the optimal amount of debt for a given firm is a complicated process, and we defer a discussion of this topic until Chapter 20. For now we will simply look at two procedures analysts use to examine the firm's debt in a financial statement analysis: (1) They check balance sheet ratios to determine the extent to which borrowed funds have been used to finance assets, and (2) they review income statement ratios to determine the number of times interest and total fixed charges are covered by operating profits. These two sets of ratios are complementary, and most analysts use both types.

debt ratio

The ratio of total debt to total assets.

Total Debt to Total Assets.   The ratio of total debt to total assets, generally called the **debt ratio**, measures the percentage of total funds provided by creditors. Debt includes both current liabilities and long-term debt. Creditors prefer low debt ratios because the lower the ratio, the greater the cushion against creditors' losses in the event of liquidation. The owners, on the other hand, may seek higher leverage, either to magnify earnings or because selling new stock would mean giving up some degree of control.

$$\text{Debt ratio} = \frac{\text{Total debt}}{\text{Total assets}} = \frac{\$1,100}{\$2,000} = 55.0\%.$$

Industry average = 40.0%.

Carter's debt ratio is 55 percent; this means that its creditors have supplied more than half the firm's total financing. Since the average debt ratio for this industry is 40 percent, Carter would find it difficult to borrow additional funds without first raising more equity capital. Creditors would be reluctant to lend the firm more money, and management would probably be subjecting the firm to the risk of bankruptcy if it sought to increase the debt ratio still more by borrowing additional funds. At the current relatively high level of debt, Carter is also more vulnerable to a downturn in sales than is the average chemical company.

**times-interest-earned
(TIE) ratio**

The ratio of earnings be-
fore interest and taxes
(EBIT) to interest charges;
measures the ability of the
firm to meet its annual
interest payments.

Times Interest Earned.   The **times-interest-earned (TIE) ratio** is determined by dividing earnings before interest and taxes (EBIT) by the interest
charges. The TIE ratio measures the extent to which operating income can decline before the firm is unable to meet its annual interest costs. Failure to meet
this obligation can bring legal action by the firm's creditors, possibly resulting
in bankruptcy. Note that the earnings before interest and taxes, rather than net
income, is used in the numerator. Because income taxes are computed after
interest expense is deducted, the ability to pay current interest is not affected
by income taxes.

$$\text{TIE} = \frac{\text{EBIT}}{\text{Interest charges}} = \frac{\$266}{\$66} = 4.0 \text{ times.}$$

Industry average = 6.0 times.

Compared with its industry, Carter is covering its interest charges by a relatively low margin of safety, and it deserves only a fair rating. The TIE ratio
reinforces our conclusions based on the debt ratio — namely, that the company
would face some difficulties if it attempted to borrow additional funds and that
a decline in sales, or an increase in operating costs, would jeopardize its ability
to pay interest as scheduled.

**fixed charge
coverage ratio**

This ratio expands upon
the TIE ratio to include
the firm's annual long-
term lease and sinking
fund obligations.

Fixed Charge Coverage.   The **fixed charge coverage ratio** is similar to the
times-interest-earned ratio, but it is more inclusive because it recognizes that
many firms lease assets and incur long-term obligations both under certain lease
contracts, which cannot be canceled, and for sinking funds. Leasing has become
widespread in certain industries in recent years, making this ratio preferable to
the times-interest-earned ratio for many purposes. Note that a sinking fund payment goes toward the retirement of a bond. As discussed earlier in Chapter 5,
Carter is required to pay off $20 million each year. Because sinking fund pay-
ments are *not* tax deductible and because interest and lease payments are deductible, the sinking fund payment is divided by (1 − Tax rate) to find the
before-tax income required to pay taxes and have enough left to make the sinking fund payment.

Fixed charges include interest, annual long-term lease obligations, and sinking fund payments, and the fixed charge coverage ratio is defined as follows:

$$\frac{\text{Fixed charge}}{\text{coverage ratio}} = \frac{\text{EBIT + Lease payments}}{\text{Interest charges + Lease payments} + \dfrac{\text{Sinking fund payments}}{(1 - \text{Tax rate})}}$$

$$= \frac{\$266 + \$28}{\$66 + \$28 + \dfrac{\$20}{(1 - 0.4)}}$$

$$= \$294/\$127 \qquad = 2.3 \text{ times.}$$

Industry average = 2.5 times.

Lease payments must be added back to EBIT in the numerator because they
were previously deducted to arrive at EBIT. Carter's fixed charges are covered
2.3 times, as opposed to an industry average of 2.5 times. Again, this indicates
that the firm is somewhat weaker than creditors would prefer it to be, and it

points out the difficulties that Carter would probably encounter if it attempted to increase its debt.

Profitability Ratios

profitability ratios

A group of ratios showing the combined effects of liquidity, asset management, and debt management on operating income and net income.

Profitability is the net result of a large number of policies and decisions. Although the ratios examined thus far provide some information about the way the firm is operating, the **profitability ratios** show the combined effects of liquidity, asset management, and debt management on operating income and net income.

Profit Margin on Sales.   The **profit margin on sales,** computed by dividing net income by sales, gives the profit per dollar of sales:

profit margin on sales

This ratio measures income per dollar of sales; it is computed by dividing net income by sales.

$$\text{Profit margin} = \frac{\text{Net income}}{\text{Sales}} = \frac{\$120}{\$3,000} = 4.0\%.$$

$$\text{Industry average} = 5.0\%.$$

Carter's profit margin is somewhat below the industry average of 5 percent, indicating that its sales prices are relatively low, that its costs are relatively high, or both.[10]

basic earning power (BEP) ratio

This ratio indicates the ability of the firm's assets to generate operating income; computed by dividing EBIT by total assets.

Basic Earning Power.   The **basic earning power (BEP) ratio,** which was discussed earlier in connection with financial leverage, is calculated by dividing earnings before interest and taxes (EBIT) by total assets:

$$\text{Basic earning power (BEP) ratio} = \frac{\text{EBIT}}{\text{Total assets}} = \frac{\$266}{\$2,000} = 13.3\%.$$

$$\text{Industry average} = 17.2\%.$$

This ratio shows the raw earning power of the firm's assets, before the influence of taxes and leverage, and it is useful for comparing firms with different tax situations and different degrees of financial leverage. Carter is not getting as high a return on its assets as is the average chemical company because of its low total assets turnover ratio and low operating income.

return on total assets (ROA)

The ratio of net income to total assets.

Return on Total Assets.   The ratio of net income to total assets, also known as the *return on investment (ROI)* ratio, measures the **return on total assets (ROA)** after interest and taxes:

$$\text{Return on total assets (ROA)} = \frac{\text{Net income}}{\text{Total assets}} = \frac{\$120}{\$2,000} = 6.0\%.$$

$$\text{Industry average} = 9.0\%.$$

Carter's 6 percent return is well below the 9 percent average for the industry. This low rate results from three primary factors: (1) the low utilization of total

---

[10]Carter's *gross profit margin* may also be calculated and contrasted with the above *net* profit margin to yield important insights into the specific nature of cost control problems. The gross profit margin is found by dividing gross profit by sales; for Carter this ratio is $456/$3,000 = 15.2%.

assets, (2) Carter's above average use of debt, which causes its interest payments to be high and which, in turn, contributes to (3) the low profit margin on sales.

Return on Common Equity. The ratio of net income to common equity (consisting of three accounts: common stock, paid-in capital, and retained earnings) measures the **return on common equity (ROE),** or the *rate of return on the stockholders' investment:*

return on common equity (ROE)

The ratio of net income to common equity; measures the rate of return on common stockholders' investment.

$$\text{Return on common equity (ROE)} = \frac{\text{Net income}}{\text{Common equity}} = \frac{\$120}{\$900} = 13.3\%.$$

$$\text{Industry average} = 15.0\%.$$

Carter's 13.3 percent ROE is below the 15 percent industry average, but it is not as far below as the return on total assets. This results from the company's greater use of debt, a point that is analyzed in detail later in the chapter.[11]

Market Value Ratios

market value ratios

A set of ratios that relates the firm's stock price to its earnings and book value per share.

Market value ratios relate the firm's stock price to its earnings and book value per share. These ratios give management an indication of what investors think of the company's past performance and future prospects. If the firm's liquidity, asset management, debt management, and profitability ratios are all good, then its market value ratios will be high, and its stock price will probably be as high as can be expected.

price/earnings (P/E) ratio

The ratio of price per share to earnings per share; shows how many times earnings investors will pay for the stock.

Price/Earnings Ratio. The **price/earnings (P/E) ratio** shows how many times earnings investors are willing to pay for the stock. Carter's stock sells for $28.50, so with an EPS of $2.40, its P/E ratio is 11.9:

$$\text{Price/earnings ratio} = \frac{\text{Market price per share}}{\text{Earnings per share}} = \frac{\$28.50}{\$2.40} = 11.9 \text{ times.}$$

$$\text{Industry average} = 12.5 \text{ times.}$$

Stated another way, Carter's P/E ratio shows that investors are paying $11.90 for every $1 of Carter's earnings per share. Generally, P/E ratios are higher for firms with high growth prospects, but P/Es are lower for riskier firms. Carter's P/E ratio is slightly below those of other large chemical producers, which suggests that the company is regarded as being somewhat riskier than most, as having poorer growth prospects, or both.

Market/Book Ratio. The ratio of a stock's market price per share to its book value per share gives another indication of how investors regard the company. Companies with relatively high rates of return on assets generally sell at higher multiples of book value than those with low returns. Carter's book value per

---

[11]The fact that Carter's basic earning power and ROE are both 13.3 percent is a coincidence; normally, they differ. Actually, if more decimal places had been shown, the two ratios would have been different from each other.

share is the sum of the three equity accounts (common stock, paid-in capital, and retained earnings) divided by the number of shares outstanding:

$$\text{Book value per share} = \frac{\text{Total stockholders' equity}}{\text{Shares outstanding}} = \frac{\$900}{50} = \$18.00.$$

market/book (M/B) ratio

The ratio of a stock's market price to its book value.

Dividing the market price per share by the book value per share gives a **market/book (M/B) ratio** of 1.6 times:

$$\text{Market/book ratio} = \frac{\text{Market price per share}}{\text{Book value per share}} = \frac{\$28.50}{\$18.00} = 1.6 \text{ times.}$$

$$\text{Industry average} = 1.8 \text{ times.}$$

Investors are willing to pay slightly less for Carter's book value than for that of an average chemical company.

The typical railroad, which has a very low rate of return on assets, has a market/book ratio of less than 0.5. On the other hand, very successful firms such as Hewlett-Packard achieve healthy rates of return on their assets and have market values well in excess of their book values. In January 1992, Hewlett-Packard's book value per share was $29.90 versus a market value of $74, so the firm's market/book ratio was $74/$29.90 = 2.5.

Summary of Ratios

The individual types of ratios, which are summarized in Table 6-2, give Carter's president, Bruce Berlin, a fairly good idea of Carter's main strengths and weaknesses. First, the company's liquidity position is reasonably good; its current and quick ratios appear to be satisfactory by comparison with the industry averages. Second, the inventory turnover ratio indicates that the company's inventories are in reasonable balance, but the low fixed assets turnover suggests that there has been too heavy an investment in fixed assets. This low turnover means, in effect, that the company probably could have operated with a smaller investment in fixed assets. Also, the high DSO figure suggests that the credit policy should be examined.

The debt management ratios suggest that the company is relatively indebted. With a debt ratio substantially higher than the industry average, and with coverage ratios well below the industry averages, it is doubtful that Carter could do much additional debt financing except on relatively unfavorable terms. Even if the company could borrow more, to do so would be to subject the company to the danger of default and bankruptcy in the event of a business downturn. The company could have avoided some of its debt financing, thus, lowering its interest payments, if excessive fixed asset investments had not been made. This, in turn, would have led to improved leverage and coverage ratios.

The profit margin on sales is low, indicating that costs are too high, or prices are too low, or both. When Berlin checked, he found that sales prices were in line with those of other firms, so he concluded that high costs are, in fact, the cause of the low profit margin. Further, he traced the high costs to high depreciation charges and high interest expenses, both of which are attributable to the excessive investment in fixed assets.

Table 6-2   Summary of Carter Chemical Company's Ratios (Millions of Dollars)

Ratio	Formula for Calculation	Calculation	Ratio	Industry Average	Comment
Liquidity					
Current	$\dfrac{\text{Current assets}}{\text{Current liabilities}}$	$\dfrac{\$\ 700}{\$\ 300} =$	2.3 times	2.5 times	Slightly low
Quick, or acid, test	$\dfrac{\text{Current assets} - \text{Inventory}}{\text{Current liabilities}}$	$\dfrac{\$\ 400}{\$\ 300} =$	1.3 times	1 time	OK
Asset Management					
Inventory turnover	$\dfrac{\text{Sales}}{\text{Inventory}}$	$\dfrac{\$3,000}{\$\ 300} =$	10 times	9 times	OK
Days sales outstanding (DSO)	$\dfrac{\text{Receivables}}{\text{Sales}/360}$	$\dfrac{\$\ 350}{\$8.333} =$	42 days	36 days	High
Fixed assets turnover	$\dfrac{\text{Sales}}{\text{Net fixed assets}}$	$\dfrac{\$3,000}{\$1,300} =$	2.3 times	3 times	Low
Total assets turnover	$\dfrac{\text{Sales}}{\text{Total assets}}$	$\dfrac{\$3,000}{\$2,000} =$	1.5 times	1.8 times	Low
Debt Management					
Debt to total assets	$\dfrac{\text{Total debt}}{\text{Total assets}}$	$\dfrac{\$1,100}{\$2,000} =$	55 percent	40 percent	High
Times interest earned (TIE)	$\dfrac{\text{EBIT}}{\text{Interest charges}}$	$\dfrac{\$\ 266}{\$\ 66} =$	4 times	6 times	Low
Fixed charge coverage	$\dfrac{\text{EBIT} + \text{Lease payments}}{\text{Interest charges} + \text{Lease payments} + \dfrac{\text{Sinking fund payments}}{1 - \text{Tax rate}}}$	$\dfrac{\$\ 294}{\$\ 127} =$	2.3 times	2.5 times	Low
Profitability					
Profit margin on sales	$\dfrac{\text{Net income}}{\text{Sales}}$	$\dfrac{\$\ 120}{\$3,000} =$	4 percent	5 percent	Low
Basic earning power (BEP)	$\dfrac{\text{EBIT}}{\text{Total assets}}$	$\dfrac{\$\ 266}{\$2,000} =$	13.3 percent	17.2 percent	Low
Return on total assets (ROA)	$\dfrac{\text{Net income}}{\text{Total assets}}$	$\dfrac{\$\ 120}{\$2,000} =$	6 percent	9 percent	Very low
Return on common equity (ROE)	$\dfrac{\text{Net income}}{\text{Common equity}}$	$\dfrac{\$\ 120}{\$\ 900} =$	13.3 percent	15 percent	Low
Market Value					
Price/earnings (P/E)	$\dfrac{\text{Market price per share}}{\text{Earnings per share}}$	$\dfrac{\$28.50}{\$\ 2.40} =$	11.9 times	12.5 times	Slightly low
Market/book (M/B)	$\dfrac{\text{Market price per share}}{\text{Book value per share}}$	$\dfrac{\$28.50}{\$18.00} =$	1.6 times	1.8 times	Slightly low

Figure 6-1

Trend Analysis: Carter
Chemical Company, Rate
of Return on Common
Equity, 1989–1993

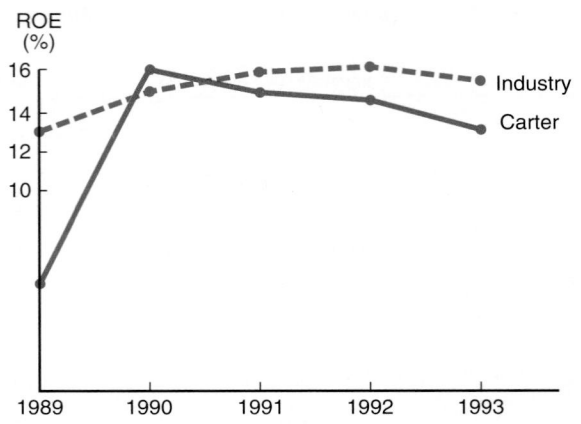

In addition to comparing ratios to industry averages, it is important to analyze what trends
the various ratios are taking. By simply plotting Carter's rate of return on common equity
for each year, one can determine improvement and deterioration over the period. A potential investor can quickly see that Carter's ROE first increased from 1989 to 1990, but has
declined since 1990, and has been below the industry average for the last three years.

The basic earning power ratio and the returns on total assets and equity are
also below the industry averages. These relatively poor results are directly attributable to the firm's low profitability, which lowers the numerators of the ratios,
and to the excessive investment in fixed assets. Finally, Carter's market value
relationships are also unfavorable — investors don't like firms with subnormal
profits, and that fact is reflected in a low stock price and in low P/E and
M/B ratios.

Trend Analysis

trend analysis

An analysis of a firm's
financial ratios over
time; used to determine
the improvement or
deterioration of its
financial situation.

It is important to analyze trends in ratios as well as their absolute levels, for
trends give clues as to whether the financial situation is improving or deteriorating. To do a **trend analysis,** one simply graphs a ratio against years, as shown
in Figure 6-1. This graph shows that Carter's rate of return on common equity
has been declining since 1990, while the industry average has been relatively
stable. Other ratios could be analyzed similarly.

Summary of Ratio Analysis: The Du Pont System

modified Du Pont chart

A chart designed to show
the relationships among return on total assets, total
assets turnover, profit margin, and financial leverage.

While Table 6-2 summarizes Carter Chemical Company's ratios, Figure 6-2,
which is called a **modified Du Pont chart** because that company's managers
developed the general approach, shows the relationships among ROA, total assets turnover, the profit margin, and financial leverage. The left-hand side of the
chart develops the *profit margin on sales.* The various expense items are listed
and then summed to obtain Carter's total costs. Subtracting costs from sales
yields the company's net income. When we divide net income by sales, we find

Figure 6-2   Modified Du Pont Chart Applied to Carter Chemical Company (Millions of Dollars)

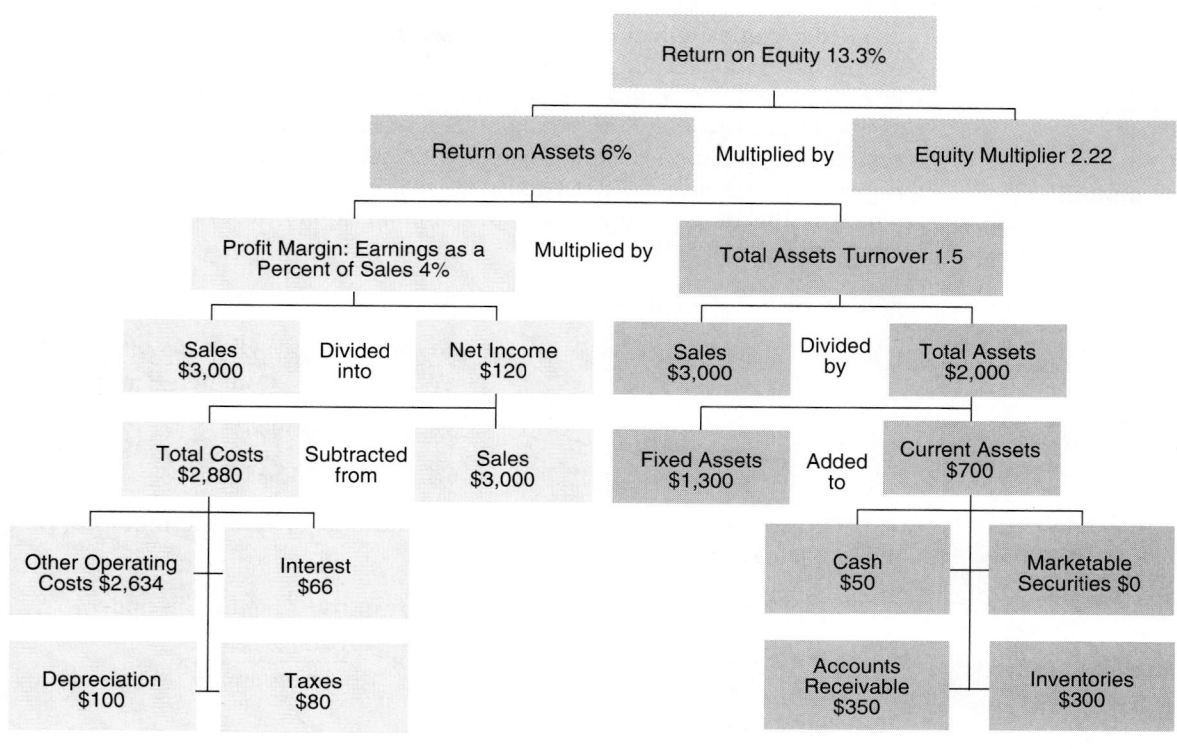

The Du Pont chart was created to illustrate the relationships among key financial ratios. The left side of the chart develops a firm's profit margin; the right side develops its total assets turnover ratio. The profit margin is then multiplied by the total assets turnover ratio to arrive at the return on total assets (ROA). The use of debt is brought into the chart by multiplying the ROA by the equity multiplier to arrive at the return on common equity (ROE). The ROE could be calculated more simply, but the modified Du Pont chart is useful for illustrating how debt, assets turnover, and profitability ratios interact to determine the ROE.

that 4 percent of each sales dollar is left over for stockholders. If the profit margin is low or trending down, one can examine the individual expense items to identify and then try to correct the problem.

The right-hand side of Figure 6-2 lists the various categories of assets, totals them, and then divides sales by total assets to find the number of times Carter "turns its assets over" each year. The company's *total assets turnover ratio* is 1.5 times.

Du Pont equation

A formula that finds the rate of return on assets by multiplying the profit margin by the total assets turnover.

The profit margin times the total assets turnover is called the **Du Pont equation,** which gives the return on total assets (ROA):

$$ROA = \text{Return on total assets} = \text{Profit margin} \times \text{Total assets turnover}$$

$$= \frac{\text{Net income}}{\text{Sales}} \times \frac{\text{Sales}}{\text{Total assets}} \qquad \textbf{(6-1)}$$

$$= 4\% \times 1.5 = 6\%.$$

Carter made 4 percent, or 4 cents, on each dollar of sales. Assets were "turned over" 1.5 times during the year, so Carter earned a return of 6 percent on its assets.

If the company had used only equity, the 6 percent return on total assets would have equaled the rate of return on equity. However, 55 percent of the firm's capital was supplied by creditors. Because the 6 percent return on total assets all goes to common stockholders, who put up only 45 percent of the capital, the return on common equity is higher than 6 percent. Specifically, the return on total assets (ROA) must be multiplied by the **equity multiplier,** which is the ratio of total assets to common equity, to obtain the return on common equity (ROE):

equity multiplier
The ratio of total assets to total common equity.

$$ROE = \text{Return on common equity} = ROA \times \text{Equity multiplier}$$

$$= \frac{\text{Net income}}{\text{Total assets}} \times \frac{\text{Total assets}}{\text{Common equity}} \quad (6\text{-}2)$$

$$= 6\% \times (\$2{,}000/\$900)$$

$$= 6\% \times 2.22 = 13.3\%.$$

We can also combine Equations 6-1 and 6-2 to form the modified, or extended, Du Pont equation:

$$ROE = (\text{Profit margin})(\text{Total assets turnover})(\text{Equity multiplier}) \quad (6\text{-}3)$$

$$= \frac{\text{Net income}}{\text{Sales}} \times \frac{\text{Sales}}{\text{Total assets}} \times \frac{\text{Total assets}}{\text{Common equity}}.$$

Thus, for Carter, we have

$$ROE = (4\%)(1.5)(2.22)$$

$$= 13.3\%.$$

This 13.3 percent ROE could, of course, be calculated directly: Net income/Common equity = \$120/\$900 = 13.3 percent. However, the Du Pont equation shows how the profit margin, the total assets turnover ratio, and the use of debt interact to determine the return on equity.

Management can use the modified Du Pont chart to analyze ways of improving the firm's performance. On the left, or profit margin, side of Figure 6-2, Carter's marketing people can study the effects of raising sales prices (or lowering them to increase volume), of moving into new products or markets with higher margins, and so on. The company's cost accountants can study various expense items and, working with engineers, purchasing agents, and other operating personnel, seek ways of holding down costs. On the assets turnover side, Carter's financial analysts, working with both production and marketing people, can investigate ways of reducing investments in various types of assets. At the same time, the treasurer's staff can analyze the effects of alternative financing strategies, seeking to hold down interest expenses and the risks of debt while

As a result of this analysis, Bruce Berlin recently announced a series of moves designed to cut operating costs by more than 20 percent per year. Berlin also announced that the company intended to concentrate its capital in markets where profit margins are reasonably high and that if competition increased in certain of its product markets, Carter would withdraw from those markets. Carter is seeking a high return on equity, and since the firm's debt ratio is already too high, it cannot boost its ROE by taking on additional debt — in fact, it is doubtful that lenders would allow it to borrow more. Berlin recognizes that if competition drives profit margins too low in a particular market, it then becomes impossible to earn high returns on the capital invested to serve that market. Therefore, if it is to achieve a higher ROE, Carter may have to develop new products and shift capital into new areas. The company's future depends on this type of analysis, and if it succeeds in the future, then the Du Pont system will have helped it achieve that success.

An alternative method sometimes used in calculating the equity multiplier will help emphasize that the link between Carter's ROA of 6 percent and its ROE of 13.3 percent is *financial leverage.* Remember that in our discussion earlier in this chapter of Firm U and Firm L (Table 6-1), we saw that as long as a firm's basic earning power ratio exceeds the interest rate paid on debt, debt can be used to boost or "leverage up" the firm's ROE. We now find that the following equation will also give us Carter's ROE of 13.3 percent:

$$\text{ROE} = \text{ROA} \times \frac{1}{1 - \text{Debt ratio}} \qquad (6\text{-}4)$$

$$= 6\% \times \frac{1}{1 - 0.55}$$

$$= 6\% \times 2.22$$

$$= 13.3\%.$$

Equation 6-4 is not so very different from Equation 6-2. Both show that the greater the use of financial leverage, the lower equity will be relative to total assets and the higher the magnification that will occur in ROE from a given ROA. If a firm uses no debt in its financing, its equity multiplier will be 1. In Equation 6-2, total assets will equal common equity, and the fraction becomes 1; in Equation 6-4, the last term in the equation becomes $1/(1 - 0.00) = 1$. If, on the other hand, a firm uses any debt at all, its equity multiplier must be greater than 1, and the higher the debt ratio, the greater the equity multiplier.

We can use Equation 6-4 to find the equity multiplier of the average chemical firm with a debt ratio of 40 percent and at the same time check to see if we get the previously stated industry average ROE of 15 percent:

$$\text{ROE}_{\text{Industry}} = \text{ROA}_{\text{Industry}} \times \frac{1}{1 - \text{Debt ratio}_{\text{Industry}}}$$

$$= 9\% \times \frac{1}{1 - 0.40}$$

$$= 9\% \times 1.67$$

$$= 15\%.$$

Finally, remember from the previous discussion that financial leverage will also magnify a *negative* ROA, and the amount of the magnification is again seen in the equity multiplier. For example, if Carter were to experience a year with a return on assets of *minus* 6 percent, a 55 percent debt ratio would translate this into a return on equity of *minus* 13.3 percent.

⟨?⟩ *Self-Test*

What is ratio analysis?

A single ratio is relatively useless in making relevant evaluations of a firm's "health." How are ratios effectively interpreted?

What three main groups use ratio analysis? What types of ratios does each group emphasize?

List the five categories of financial ratios.

Identify those ratios that would be used for analyzing a firm's liquidity, and write out those equations.

Identify those ratios that would be used to measure how effectively a firm is managing its assets, and write out those equations.

Identify the debt management ratios, and write out those equations.

Identify those ratios that show the combined effects of liquidity, asset management, and debt management on operating income and net income, and write out those equations.

Identify those ratios that relate a firm's stock price to its earnings and book value per share, and write out those equations.

Explain how the modified Du Pont system combines ratios to reveal the basic determinants of ROE.

Explain how the use of debt financing may, at times, increase the return to the firm's common stockholders. When will the use of debt not work to the advantage of the stockholders?

Sources of Comparative Ratios

comparative ratio analysis

An analysis based on a comparison of a firm's ratios with those of other firms in the same industry.

The preceding analysis of Carter Chemical Company is an example of **comparative ratio analysis.** Comparative ratios are available from a number of sources. One useful set of comparative data is compiled by Dun & Bradstreet Inc. (D&B), which provides 14 ratios calculated for a large number of industries; nine of these are shown for a small sample of industries in Table 6-3. Useful ratios can also be found in the *Annual Statement Studies* published by Robert Morris Associates, the national association of bank loan officers. The U.S. Commerce Department's *Quarterly Financial Report,* which is found in most libraries, gives a set of ratios for manufacturing firms by industry group and size of firm. Trade associations and individual firms' credit departments also compile industry average financial ratios. Finally, financial statement data are available on magnetic tapes and diskettes for thousands of publicly owned corporations, and because most of the larger brokerage houses, banks, and other financial institutions have access to these data, security analysts can and do generate comparative ratios tailored to their specific needs.

Table 6-3 Dun & Bradstreet Ratios for Selected Industries: Upper Quartile, Median, and Lower Quartile[a]

SIC Codes, Line of Business, and Number of Concerns Reporting	Quick Ratio (x)	Current Ratio (x)	Total Liabilities to Net Worth (%)	Days Sales Outstanding (Days)	Net Sales to Inventory (x)	Total Assets to Net Sales (%)	Return on Net Sales (%)	Return on Total Assets (%)	Return on Net Worth (%)
2879 Agricultural chemicals (52)	2.0	3.6	46.7	22.1	20.8	31.8	5.8	13.3	24.9
	1.1	2.4	77.1	41.3	11.5	46.7	1.8	3.1	6.2
	0.7	1.5	158.8	59.1	5.7	78.9	(1.6)	(0.5)	(0.3)
3724 Aircraft parts, including engines (105)	1.7	4.0	27.7	40.7	12.2	50.4	8.6	10.6	18.2
	0.9	2.3	90.7	50.9	5.4	64.0	3.3	3.0	10.7
	0.7	1.3	227.0	63.6	3.5	92.4	0.8	1.1	1.9
2051 Bakery products (177)	2.3	3.0	35.7	12.8	68.5	21.6	6.3	16.7	37.8
	1.0	1.6	80.8	23.6	38.7	33.0	2.7	7.8	18.9
	0.6	0.9	165.2	32.2	19.8	51.6	1.1	2.7	6.4
2086 Beverages (119)	2.5	4.2	22.3	17.2	30.6	28.6	5.0	11.0	18.5
	1.1	2.1	61.5	24.8	17.4	38.6	2.2	3.8	10.1
	0.6	1.1	194.9	46.0	12.1	72.0	0.5	0.5	2.3
3312 Blast furnaces and steel mills (284)	2.0	3.2	51.8	30.7	27.9	31.7	8.9	13.7	35.5
	1.1	1.8	126.9	42.8	9.6	48.6	3.7	5.8	15.2
	0.6	1.2	296.4	58.8	6.0	78.0	0.9	0.9	2.6
2731 Book publishing (360)	2.5	5.3	24.2	30.2	9.5	42.5	13.7	13.4	27.8
	1.2	2.6	65.9	50.7	5.2	63.0	5.4	5.6	13.2
	0.6	1.5	143.3	72.5	2.7	94.2	0.9	0.6	1.9

Source: Industry Norms and Key Business Ratios, 1991–92 Edition, Dun & Bradstreet Credit Services.

[a]The median and quartile ratios can be illustrated by an example. The median quick ratio for agricultural chemical manufacturers, as shown in this table, is 1.1. To obtain this figure, the ratios of current assets less inventories to current debt for each of the 52 concerns were arranged in a graduated series, with the largest ratio at the top and the smallest at the bottom. The median ratio of 1.1 is the ratio halfway between the top and the bottom. The ratio of 2.0, representing the upper quartile, is one-quarter of the way down from the top (or halfway between the top and the median). The ratio 0.7, representing the lower quartile, is one-quarter of the way up from the bottom (or halfway between the median and the bottom). SIC codes are Standard Industrial Classification codes used by the U.S. government to classify companies.

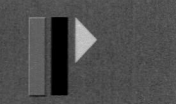

TRYING TO DELEVERAGE CORPORATE AMERICA

When investment bankers Kohlberg Kravis Roberts (KKR) acquired RJR Nabisco in a $25.1 billion leveraged buyout in 1988, the transaction was christened "the sale of the century," and it climaxed a decade of high-flying, debt-financed deals. Nabisco's interest payments came to $2.5 billion annually on the $22.8 billion of borrowed funds used to finance the buyout.

Such massive debt was thought to spur better performance, and observers of the buyout frenzy of the 1980s felt the new manager-owners of LBO companies would watch costs and monitor resources more closely, thus increasing profits. At Nabisco, the new owners quickly sold assets worth $3.5 billion and trimmed deadwood by laying off more than 2,500 workers and managers. They also grounded most of the fleet of jet aircraft, including the former chairman's jet which had been used, among other things, to ferry his dog (as the sole passenger) around the country.

Many LBOs were financed with more than 90 percent debt. However, the "net advantages" of debt are being questioned in the 1990s. The staggering loads assumed by hundreds of corporations have destroyed some of those corporations, and many companies that survived now have a severe case of debt fright. As a result, in 1991, for the first time in eight years, corporate debt/equity ratios actually declined.

"Equity and balance-sheet quality are in fashion," said the treasurer of Colgate-Palmolive, which has lowered its debt/equity ratio from 50/50 to 30/70. Goodyear Tire and Rubber raised $423 million in a 1992 stock offering to ease its hefty debt burden, and RJR Nabisco, which had a debt/equity ratio of 25/1 at the time of its buyout, is now considered a "classic case" of a company trying to deleverage. When Louis V. Gerstner, Jr., signed on as CEO in 1989, Nabisco's debt load totaled almost $30 billion. In four years (before he moved on in 1993 to take over troubled IBM), Gerstner managed to cut RJR Nabisco's debt in half.

Even so, RJR Nabisco planned to float another stock issue in 1993 to raise approximately $1.7 billion to retire more of its still-mountainous debt. In addition, it has been counting on its "cash cow"—its tobacco business—to help pay down debt, and it is worried that the federal health-care initiative might cut the flow with still bigger taxes on cigarettes.

RJR Nabisco is only one among hundreds of LBO companies seeking to get out from under a mountain of debt. "Debt is now a four-letter word," said a managing director of First Boston Corporation. At York International, an air conditioning and refrigeration equipment manufacturer, a common stock offering in 1991 raised $270 million to help reduce the debt from a 1988 buyout and to save the firm more than $1 million a week in interest. Said the president, "We were running ahead of a freight train, and God help us if we stubbed our toe."

Without so much debt, companies can afford to go after new markets by lowering prices, and they can invest in new technology to improve their productivity. However, not all will be able to raise equity through sale of stock to the public. For example, the steel, publishing, and chemical businesses are out of favor in the stock market, and many other companies with a heavy debt load are unattractive to investors.

Multi-Local Media Corporation discovered its wallflower status when, despite three years of healthy growth, a stock offering designed to reduce debt failed to garner anywhere near the asking price, and the publisher of regional yellow-pages directories was forced to withdraw it. Similarly, when Stone Container Corporation announced refinancing plans, investors backed off even before its equity offer materialized. Proceeds expected to total $500 million were to be used to pay Stone's bank loans. "It is important to understand that the proposal to deleverage our balance sheet was initiated by us, and not imposed upon us by the banks," said Roger Stone, chairman and CEO. Even so, investors apparently thought the company was in financial distress, and when they started selling Stone stock they already owned, the price declined by 42 percent. "At this share price level," said Stone chief financial officer (CFO) Arnold Brookstone, "it doesn't make sense to sell the equity."

Sources: "Financing the 90s," *Business Week*, November 4, 1991, 113–115, 118–120; Terence P. Pare, "Why Banks Are Still Stingy," *Fortune*, January 25, 1993, 73–75; Laura Zinn, "The RJR Nabisco He's Leaving Behind," *Business Week*, April 5, 1993, 24; James P. Miller, "Stone Container Opts to Suspend Equity Offering," *The Wall Street Journal*, April 9, 1993, A8.

Aside from corporations' new aversion to high debt loads, bank regulators are also restraining the formerly lavish lenders who might now provide fresh cash. As RJR Nabisco CFO Karl von der Heyden said, the firm had to restructure to reduce debt because of "restrictive bank credit agreements that gave us virtually no flexibility in diverting cash, say, for small acquisitions that would help our growth."

Financial services companies such as banks, brokerages, and insurance companies, decimated by the results of excesses during the 1980s, are shrinking. They are closing offices right and left and are laying off thousands of workers. For companies seeking fresh cash, banks are the most prominent skinflints, and regulators have pressured them to avoid making loans to highly leveraged borrowers. Insurance companies and foreign investors are also pulling back, so credit-starved, highly leveraged smaller companies have had to look elsewhere to finance their growth and pay down their high-priced debt. The lending activity of commercial finance companies has been growing 30 percent per year, even though their loans are of shorter duration than banks' and they also charge more. Business loans at banks dropped from $642 billion to $603 billion from mid-1990 to the fall of 1992, while finance company loans grew from 45 percent of the bank share to more than 50 percent.

When President Clinton asked bankers at an economic conference early in his term if they could let some cash go, they said they would be glad to if regulations were eased. Many banks have put most of their funds into ultraconservative U.S. Treasury securities because they are not allowed to do much with them. The vice-chairman of the Federal Reserve, David W. Mullins, Jr., said overregulation of the banking system may be causing economic damage. "Launch a search-and-destroy mission to eliminate these regulatory impediments," he urged. The president of a Midwest bank said lenders worry that "examiners are going to come in with both barrels blasting and shoot everyone in sight" if banks lend money to firms with even slightly below par credit ratings.

Still, many major players in the debt-reduction game are successfully deleveraging, and as the economy improves, some of those who have not made it yet will probably find a way. There is no doubt, says business experts, that the rip-roaring 1980s' Era of Excess has given way to the sober 1990s' Era of Atonement.

Each of the data-supplying organizations uses a somewhat different set of ratios, designed for its own purposes. For example, D&B deals mainly with small firms, many of which are proprietorships, and it is concerned largely with the creditors' viewpoint. Accordingly, its ratios do not emphasize market value ratios. Therefore, when you select a comparative data source, you should either be sure that your emphasis is similar to that of the agency whose ratios you use or recognize the limitations of its ratios for your purposes. In addition, there are often definitional differences in the ratios presented by different sources, so before using a source, be sure to verify the exact definitions of the ratios to ensure consistency.

Finally, recognize that there are many more possible ratios than the ones we have discussed. Any meaningful relationship between two or more pieces of financial data may be expressed as a ratio, and you would need some very different ratios if you were analyzing the annual statements of a bank or other financial institution than if you were looking at a typical manufacturing firm.

Self-Test

Differentiate between trend analysis and comparative ratio analysis.

List several sources of comparative ratios.

Limitations of Ratio Analysis

Ratio analysis can provide useful information about a company's operations and financial condition. However, it does have some inherent problems and limitations that necessitate care and judgment. Some potential problems are listed here:

1. Many large firms operate a number of different divisions in quite different industries, making it difficult to develop a meaningful set of industry averages for comparative purposes. This tends to make ratio analysis more useful for small than for large firms.

2. Most firms want to be better than average (although half will be above and half below the median), so merely attaining average performance is not necessarily good. As a target for high-level performance, it is best to look at the industry leaders' ratios.

3. Inflation has badly distorted firms' balance sheets. Further, because inflation affects both depreciation charges and inventory costs, profits are also affected. Thus, a ratio analysis for one firm over time, or a comparative analysis of firms of different ages, must be interpreted with considerable judgment.

4. The ratios can be distorted by seasonal factors. For example, the inventory turnover ratio for a food processor will be radically different if the balance sheet figure used for inventory is the one just before versus the one just after the end of the canning season. This problem can be minimized by using monthly averages for inventory (and receivables) when calculating some ratios.

"window dressing"
Techniques employed by a firm to make its financial statements look better than they really are.

5. Firms can employ **"window dressing"** techniques to make their financial statements look better to credit analysts. To illustrate, a manufacturer borrowed on a two-year basis on December 29, 1993, held the proceeds of the loan as cash for a few days, and then paid off the loan ahead of time on January 4, 1994. This improved the firm's current and quick ratios and made the year-end 1993 balance sheet look good. However, the improvement was strictly temporary, and a week later the balance sheet was back at the old level.

6. Different accounting and operating practices can also distort comparisons. As noted earlier, inventory valuation and depreciation methods will affect the financial statements and thus distort comparisons among firms. And, if one firm leases a substantial amount of its productive equipment, then its assets may appear low relative to sales because leased assets often do not appear on the balance sheet. At the same time, the lease liability may not be shown as a debt. Therefore, leasing can artificially improve both the debt and turnover ratios. The accounting profession has recently taken steps that reduce this problem, and we will discuss them in Chapter 18.

7. It is difficult to generalize about whether a particular ratio is "good" or "bad." For example, a high current ratio may indicate a strong liquidity position, which is good, or excessive cash, which is bad (because excess cash in the bank is a nonearning asset). Similarly, a high fixed assets turnover ratio may denote either a firm that uses assets efficiently or one that is undercapitalized and simply cannot afford to buy enough assets.

8. A firm may have some ratios which look "good" and others which look "bad," making it difficult to tell whether the company is, on balance, in a strong or a weak position. However, statistical procedures can be used to analyze the *net effects* of a set of ratios. Many banks and other lending organizations use statistical procedures to analyze firms' financial ratios and, on the basis of their analyses, classify companies according to their probability of getting into financial distress.[12]

Ratio analysis provides a good starting point in evaluating a firm, but analysts should be aware of these limitations and make adjustments as necessary. Ratio analysis conducted in a mechanical, unthinking manner is dangerous; however, used intelligently and with good judgment, ratios can provide useful insights into a firm's operations. Your judgment in interpreting a set of ratios is probably weak at this point, but it will improve with practice.

Self-Test

List several potential problems with ratio analysis.

Summary

The primary purpose of this chapter was to discuss techniques used by investors and managers when they analyze the basic financial statements. The key concepts we covered are listed below:

▶ **Financial statement analysis** generally begins with the calculation of a set of **financial ratios** designed to reveal the relative strengths and weaknesses of a company as compared with other companies in the same industry.

▶ Managers, credit analysts, and securities analysts are often interested in specific areas of the firm's operations and look at different ratios. Therefore, it is useful to categorize ratios into five groups:

Liquidity ratios show the relationship of a firm's current assets to its current obligations, and, thus, liquidity ratios indicate the firm's ability to meet its maturing short-term debts.

Asset management ratios measure how effectively a firm is managing its assets.

Debt management ratios measure (1) the extent to which the firm is financed with debt and (2) the firm's ability to meet its interest and other fixed obligations.

Profitability ratios show the combined effects of liquidity, asset management, and debt management on operating results.

Market value ratios show what investors think of the firm by relating the stock price to earnings and book value per share.

---

[12]The technique used is discriminant analysis. For a discussion, see Edward I. Altman, "Financial Ratios, Discriminant Analysis, and the Prediction of Corporate Bankruptcy," *Journal of Finance,* September 1968, 589–602, or Eugene F. Brigham and Louis C. Gapenski, *Intermediate Financial Management,* Fourth Edition, Chapter 26. We will return to this topic in Chapter 10.

> ▶ **Trend analysis** is important because it reveals whether the firm's financial position is improving or deteriorating over time.

> ▶ The modified **Du Pont system** shows how the profit margin on sales, the total assets turnover ratio, and the use of debt interact to determine the rate of return on equity.

> ▶ **Ratio analysis** has **limitations,** but used with care and judgment, it can be most helpful.

Resolution to
DECISION IN FINANCE

COOKING THE BOOKS

The Laribee Company's debt amounted to almost seven times its equity, and despite the large loan it negotiated in 1990, by 1991 it had to seek bankruptcy protection. The court investigated and found the fraud; the court-appointed trustee, John Turbidy, said, "It was one of the biggest inventory overstatements I've ever seen."

Without the manipulation, the court found, Laribee would have reported a $6.5 million loss for fiscal year 1989 instead of the $3 million of net income claimed in the company's audited financial statements used to convince the banks to okay the big loan.

Since Laribee was under bankruptcy-court protection, creditors in four states sued Deloitte & Touche, the accounting firm which had given it a clean bill of health, charging them with malpractice and gross negligence. One creditor also sued the Deloitte partner who had been in charge of the Laribee audit. Trustee Turbidy commented, "The auditor was either taken in or missed the obvious. Giving the auditors the benefit of the doubt, I assume that it was inexperience on their part. . . . Otherwise, how could they have overlooked such blatant inventory manipulations?"

Deloitte is not the only firm that has faced such lawsuits. The six biggest accounting firms spent almost $500 million in 1991 to defend themselves against fraud and malpractice charges. Accounting Professor Douglas Carmichael of the City University of New York noted, "The recent rise in inventory fraud is one of the biggest single reasons for the proliferation of accounting scandals."

Why there is so much fraud is open to speculation. Professor Carmichael feels that some accounting firms may not have enough employees to do a proper inventory sampling for an audit because they have reduced their staffs to cut costs: "With their jobs in peril, the remaining auditors are less likely to make waves for fear of losing a client and possibly their jobs."

Other critics point out that current auditing standards do not specify the size of the inventory sample auditors should check but simply require auditors to watch closely how employees count inventory and then to count a "representative sample" themselves.

Some auditing firms apparently believe everything management tells them; others seem to overlook obvious signals of potential fraud. In one case, auditors told a retailer in advance the stores where they planned to conduct "surprise" audits. In another case, a manager reported that new shipments of the material an auditor had counted the previous day had just been received. Without checking, the auditor simply

Source: Lee Berton, "Inventory Chicanery Tempts More Firms, Fools More Auditors," *The Wall Street Journal,* December 14, 1992, A1.

accepted the new figures the manager reported for the inventory.

When profits of a company are overstated because of inventory fraud and are not detected by auditors, the results can be far reaching. Creditors, shareholders, stock analysts, and the general public may draw false conclusions and make wrong decisions based on the erroneous information. When the fraud is finally uncovered, the reputations of both the company and the original auditors are tarnished, and the price of the company's stock generally plunges. Overcoming such betrayal of the public trust can take a very long time.

Questions

6-1 How does inflation distort ratio analysis comparisons, both for one company over time (trend analysis) and when different companies are compared? Are only balance sheet items, or both balance sheet and income statement items, affected?

6-2 If a firm's ROE is low (but positive) and management wants to improve it, explain how using more debt might help.

6-3 Suppose a firm used debt to leverage up its ROE, and in the process its EPS was also boosted. Would this necessarily lead to an increase in the price of the firm's stock?

6-4 How might (a) seasonal factors and (b) different growth rates distort a comparative ratio analysis? Give some examples. How might these problems be alleviated?

6-5 Seasonal factors and inflation are two problems that distort ratio analysis comparisons. What are some of the other factors that limit the effectiveness of ratio analysis?

6-6 Why would the inventory turnover ratio be more important to a grocery chain than to an insurance company?

6-7 Ratios vary from one industry to another. What differences would you expect to find between a grocery chain like Safeway and a steel company? Think particularly about the turnover ratios and the profit margin, and think about the Du Pont equation.

6-8 Indicate the effects of the transactions listed in the following table on total current assets, current ratio, and net income. Use (+) to indicate an increase, (−) to indicate a decrease, and (0) to indicate either no effect or an indeterminate effect. Be prepared to state any necessary assumptions, and assume an initial current ratio of more than 1.0. (Note: As an introductory finance student, you are not expected to be familiar with all of the transactions listed. The purpose of this question is to stimulate thought about the effects of these transactions.)

	Total Current Assets	Current Ratio	Net Income
1. Cash is acquired through issuance of additional common stock.	_____	_____	_____
2. Merchandise is sold for cash.	_____	_____	_____
3. Federal income tax due for the previous year is paid.	_____	_____	_____
4. A fixed asset is sold for less than book value.	_____	_____	_____
5. A fixed asset is sold for more than book value.	_____	_____	_____
6. Merchandise is sold on credit.	_____	_____	_____
7. Payment is made to trade creditors for previous purchases.	_____	_____	_____

	Total Current Assets	Current Ratio	Net Income
8. A cash dividend is declared and paid.	___	___	___
9. Cash is obtained through short-term bank loans.	___	___	___
10. Short-term notes receivable are sold at a discount.	___	___	___
11. Short-term marketable securities are sold below cost.	___	___	___
12. Advances are made to employees.	___	___	___
13. Short-term promissory notes are issued to trade creditors for prior purchases.	___	___	___
14. Ten-year notes are issued to pay off accounts payable.	___	___	___
15. A fully depreciated asset is retired.	___	___	___
16. Accounts receivable are collected.	___	___	___
17. Equipment is purchased with short-term notes.	___	___	___
18. Merchandise is purchased on credit.	___	___	___
19. The estimated taxes payable are increased.	___	___	___

Self-Test Problems

ST-1   H. B. Jones & Co. had earnings per share of $3 last year, and it paid a $1.50 dividend. Book value per share at year-end was $30, while total retained earnings increased by $9 million during the year. Jones has no preferred stock, and no new common stock was issued during the year. If Jones's year-end debt (which equals its total liabilities) was $90 million, what was the company's year-end total debt/total assets ratio?

ST-2   The following data apply to Cavendish & Company (dollar amounts in millions):

Cash and marketable securities	$100.00
Fixed assets	$283.50
Sales	$1,000.00
Net income	$50.00
Quick ratio	2.0×
Current ratio	3.0×
Days sales outstanding (DSO)	40 days
ROE	0.12 or 12%

Cavendish has no preferred stock — only common equity, current liabilities, and long-term debt. Find Cavendish's (a) accounts receivable, (b) current liabilities, (c) current assets, (d) total assets, (e) ROA, (f) common equity, and (g) long-term debt.

ST-3   In the preceding problem you should have found that Cavendish's accounts receivable = $111.1 million. If Cavendish could reduce its DSO from 40 days to 30 days while holding other things constant, how much cash would it generate? If this cash were used to buy back common stock (at book value) and thus reduced the amount of common equity, how would this affect (a) the ROE, (b) the ROA, and (c) the total debt/total assets ratio?

Problems

6-1
Du Pont analysis

Yelland Corporation's profit margin on sales is 5 percent, its total assets turnover ratio is 1.6 times, and its equity multiplier (assets/equity ratio) is 1.4 times. What is its rate of return on equity?

6-2
Return on equity

Kielech Equipment is 100 percent equity financed. Given the following information, calculate the firm's return on equity:

$$
\begin{aligned}
\text{Earnings before taxes (EBT)} &= \text{\$6 million} \\
\text{Sales} &= \text{\$30 million} \\
\text{Dividend payout ratio} = \frac{\text{DPS}}{\text{EPS}} &= 45 \text{ percent} \\
\text{Total assets turnover} &= 1.2 \text{ times} \\
\text{Combined federal and state tax rate} &= 40 \text{ percent}
\end{aligned}
$$

6-3
Debt ratio

Travel Air, an emerging regional airline, earns 6 percent on total assets but has a return on equity of 24 percent. What percentage of the airline's assets are financed with debt?

6-4
Du Pont analysis

Barbara Beal, president of Beal & Co., has been reviewing her firm's financial statements. She knows that the firm's return on equity is 13 percent, total debt/total assets is 20 percent, and total assets turnover is 2.6 times. She is sure the firm's accountant told her the profit margin before he went home, but she can't remember. Would you determine the firm's profit margin for her?

6-5
Days sales outstanding

LaBant Manufacturing had sales of $9,000,000 this year. Of those sales, 25 percent were for cash. If the firm maintains an accounts receivable balance of $712,500, what is the firm's days sales outstanding (DSO)?

6-6
Inventory turnover

Gjerde Inc. had sales of $1,800,000 last year. If the firm maintains $600,000 in inventory, what is its inventory turnover? What is its inventory turnover period? (Found: 360 days/inventory turnover.)

6-7
Days sales outstanding

Burton Paper Products has sales of $5,760,000. Its accounts receivable balance is $784,000.
a. If all sales are on credit, what is the company's days sales outstanding?
b. What is the firm's days sales outstanding if 10 percent of the firm's sales are for cash?

6-8
Liquidity ratios

Finmark Textile Inc. has $2,500,000 in current assets and $1,000,000 in current liabilities. Its initial inventory level is $700,000, and it will raise funds as additional notes payable and use them to increase inventory. How much can its short-term debt (notes payable) increase without falling below a current ratio of 2 times? What will be the firm's quick ratio after the company has raised the maximum amount of short-term funds and purchased inventory with these funds?

6-9
Ratio calculations

Swift Software Inc. finds itself with more debt than it would like to have. Currently, the firm has $18 million in sales, days sales outstanding (DSO) equal to 40 days, and an inventory turnover of 6 times. Benson Fong, the firm's financial manager, is certain he can lower the DSO to 30 days and increase inventory turnover to 8 times without lowering sales. How much would be available to reduce debt if Fong succeeds in his proposed reduction of current assets?

6-10
Liquidity ratios

MacGill Corporation had sales last year of $4 million and total assets of $2.2 million. Current liabilities were $750,000 on December 31. The firm's current ratio was 2.5 and its quick ratio was 1.8. What was MacGill's investment in inventory?

6-11
Market value ratios

Chen, Sorini, & Cook Inc. has 500,000 shares of common stock outstanding. The firm uses only debt and common equity in its financing (no preferred stock). Selected financial information follows:

Total assets	$7,000,000
Total liabilities	$2,450,000
Net income	$685,000
Market price per share	$19

Calculate the firm's P/E and M/B ratios.

6-12

Return on equity

T&R Broadcasting has the following long-term financing, according to its end-of-year balance sheet:

Long-term debt	$20,000,000
Common stock	$8,000,000
Paid-in capital	$12,500,000
Retained earnings	$28,590,910

If sales for the year were $180 million and the profit margin was 4.8 percent, what was T&R Broadcasting's return on equity (ROE)?

6-13

Du Pont analysis

Assume you are given the following relationships for the Kielsheimer Corporation:

Sales/Total assets	1.8×
Return on assets (ROA)	7.5%
Return on equity (ROE)	12.5%

a. Calculate Kielsheimer's profit margin and debt ratio.

b. Suppose you are considering investing in either Kielsheimer or another firm in the same industry. The two firms are virtually identical except that the other firm has a debt ratio of only 20 percent and therefore a lower ROE this year than the 12.5 percent achieved by Kielsheimer. Which of the two firms would have the better ROE (least negative) next year if they both experience an ROA of −15 percent? Explain your answer with or without calculations.

6-14

Ratio calculations

Cotchett Company has a quick ratio of 1.2 times, a current ratio of 3.6 times, an inventory turnover of 7.2 times, and current assets of $600,000. What are the firm's annual sales and, if cash and marketable securities are negligible, what is its DSO ratio?

6-15

Balance sheet construction

Complete the balance sheet below by using the following financial information:

$$\text{Total assets turnover} = 2.0\times$$
$$\text{Current ratio} = 2.5\times$$
$$\text{Days sales outstanding} = 37.5 \text{ days}$$
$$\text{Inventory turnover} = 4.8\times$$
$$\text{Debt/Total assets} = 45\%$$
$$\text{Fixed assets turnover} = 6\times$$
$$\text{Sales} = \$2,400,000$$

Cash	$ 50,000	Current liabilities	$
Accounts receivable		Long-term debt	
Inventory	_____	Total debt	
Current assets		Common stock	100,000
Net fixed assets	_____	Retained earnings	_____
Total assets	$_____	Total liabilities and equity	$_____

6-16

Ratio analysis

Data for Zanjini Computer Concepts and its industry averages follow.

a. Calculate the indicated ratios for Zanjini. (All sales are on credit.)

b. Construct the extended Du Pont equation for both Zanjini and the industry.

c. Outline Zanjini's strengths and weaknesses as revealed by your analysis.

Zanjini Computer Concepts:
Balance Sheet as of December 31, 1993

Cash	$ 155,000	Accounts payable	$ 258,000
Receivables	672,000	Notes payable	168,000
Inventory	483,000	Other current liabilities	234,000
Total current assets	$1,310,000	Total current liabilities	$ 660,000
Net fixed assets	585,000	Long-term debt	513,000
		Common equity	722,000
Total assets	$1,895,000	Total liabilities and equity	$1,895,000

Zanjini Computer Concepts:
Income Statement for Year Ended December 31, 1993

Sales		$3,215,000
Cost of goods sold:		
Materials	$1,434,000	
Labor	906,000	
Heat, light, and power	136,000	
Indirect labor	226,000	
Depreciation	83,000	2,785,000
Gross profit		430,000
Selling expenses		230,000
General and administrative expenses		60,000
Earnings before interest and taxes		$ 140,000
Interest expense		49,000
Earnings before taxes		91,000
Federal and state income taxes (40%)		36,400
Net income		$ 54,600

Ratio	Zanjini	Industry Average
Current assets/Current liabilities	_____	2.0 ×
Days sales outstanding	_____	35 days
Sales/Inventory	_____	6.7 ×
Sales/Total assets	_____	2.9 ×
Net income/Sales	_____	1.2%
Net income/Total assets	_____	3.4%
Net income/Equity	_____	8.7%
Total debt/Total assets	_____	60.0%

d. Suppose that Zanjini's sales as well as its inventories, accounts receivable, and common equity had doubled during 1993. How would the information about this rapid growth affect the validity of your ratio analysis? (*Hint:* Think about averages and the effects of rapid growth on ratios if averages are not used. No calculations are needed.)

6-17

Du Pont analysis

Owen Furniture Company (OFC), a manufacturer and wholesaler of high-quality home furnishings, has been experiencing low profitability in recent years. As a result, the board of directors has replaced the president of the firm with a new president, Richard Whiston, who has asked you to make an analysis of the firm's financial position using the Du Pont system. The most recent industry average ratios and OFC's financial statements follow.

a. Calculate ratios to compare OFC with the industry averages.

b. Construct an extended Du Pont equation for the firm, and comment on how OFC compares with the industry with regard to each ratio used in this equation.

c. Do the balance sheet accounts or the income statement figures seem to be primarily responsible for OFC's low return on equity?

Industry Average Ratios

Current assets/Current liabilities	2×	Sales/Net fixed assets	6×
Total debt/Total assets	30%	Sales/Total assets	3×
Times interest earned (TIE)	7×	Net income/Sales	3%
Sales/Inventory	10×	Return on total assets (ROA)	9%
Days sales outstanding (DSO)	24 days	Return on common equity (ROE)	12.8%

Owen Furniture Company:
Balance Sheet as of December 31, 1993 (Millions of Dollars)

Cash	$ 99	Accounts payable	$ 126
Marketable securities	78	Notes payable	90
Accounts receivable	120	Other current liabilities	54
Inventories	375	Total current liabilities	$ 270
Total current assets	$ 672	Long-term debt	66
Gross fixed assets	555	Total liabilities	$ 336
Less: Depreciation	183	Common stock	228
Net fixed assets	$ 372	Retained earnings	480
		Total stockholders' equity	$ 708
Total assets	$1,044	Total liabilities and equity	$1,044

Owen Furniture Company:
Income Statement for Year Ended December 31, 1993
(Millions of Dollars)

Net sales	$1,680
Cost of goods sold	1,395
Gross profit	$ 285
Depreciation	39
Selling expenses	100
General and administrative expenses	53
EBIT	$93
Interest expense	15
EBT	$ 78
Taxes (40%)	31
Net income	$ 47

d. Which specific accounts seem to be most out of line in relation to other firms in the industry?

e. If OFC had a pronounced seasonal sales pattern, or if it had grown rapidly during the year, how might this affect the validity of your ratio analysis? How might you correct for such potential problems?

6-18

Ratio analysis

The following data pertain to Gomez & Ivy Inc. (GII):

1. GII has outstanding debt in the form of accounts payable, notes payable, and long-term bonds. The notes carry a 14 percent interest rate, and the bonds carry a 12 percent rate. Both the notes and bonds were outstanding for the entire year.
2. Retained earnings at the beginning of the year are $7,000 million.
3. The dividend payout ratio (Dividends/Earnings) is 33.3 percent.
4. The debt ratio is 60 percent.
5. The profit margin is 6 percent.
6. The return on equity (ROE) is 5 percent.
7. The inventory turnover ratio is 5 times.
8. The days sales outstanding (DSO) is 122.4 days.

a. Given this information, complete GII's balance sheet and income statement that follow.

b. The industry average inventory turnover ratio is 6.25 times, and the industry average DSO is 72 days. Assume that at the beginning of 1993, GII had been able to adjust its inventory turnover and DSO to the industry averages and that this (1) freed up capital and (2) reduced storage costs and bad debt losses. Assume that the reduction of storage costs and bad debts raised the profit margin to 10 percent. Assume further that the freed-up capital was used at the start of the year to pay an extra, one-time dividend which reduced the beginning retained earnings figure. What would have been the effect on GII's ROE for 1993? (*Hint:* Construct a new balance sheet which will show lower inventories and accounts receivable and a different value for December 31, 1993, retained earnings. Keep common stock, long-term debt, and notes payable at the values obtained in Part a. The balance sheet will not balance; force it into balance by reducing accounts payable. Then calculate the new ROE. You can get the new net income figures directly.)

Gomez & Ivy Inc.:
Balance Sheet as of December 31, 1993
(Millions of Dollars)

Cash	$ 3,750	Accounts payable	$
Accounts receivable		Notes payable	5,000
Inventories	————	Total current liabilities	
Total current assets		Long-term debt	15,000
Net fixed assets	27,000	Total debt	
		Common stock	
		Retained earnings	————
		Total common equity	————
Total assets	════	Total liabilities and equity	════

Gomez & Ivy Inc.:
Income Statement for Year Ended December 31, 1993
(Millions of Dollars)

Sales	$12,500
Cost of goods sold	————
Gross profit	
Selling expenses	1,350
General and administrative expenses	950
EBIT	
Interest expense	————
Earnings before taxes (EBT)	
Taxes	600
Net income	════

6-19

The Englewood Corporation's balance sheets for 1993 and 1992 are as follows (millions of dollars):

	1993	1992
Cash	$ 21	$ 45
Marketable securities	0	33
Receivables	90	66
Inventories	225	159
Total current assets	$336	$303
Gross fixed assets	450	225
Less: Accumulated depreciation	123	78
Net fixed assets	$327	$147
Total assets	$663	$450

continues

	1993	1992
Accounts payable	$ 54	$ 45
Notes payable	9	45
Accruals	45	21
Total current liabilities	$108	$111
Long-term debt	78	24
Common stock	192	114
Retained earnings	285	201
Total equity	$477	$315
Total liabilities and equity	$663	$450

Additionally, Englewood's 1993 income statement is as follows (millions of dollars):

Sales	$1,365
Cost of goods sold	888
General expenses	282
EBIT	$ 195
Interest	10
EBT	$ 185
State and federal taxes (46%)	85
Net income	$ 100

a. What was Englewood's dividend payout ratio in 1993?

b. The following extended Du Pont equation is the industry average for 1993:

$$\frac{\text{Profit margin} \times \text{Total assets turnover} \times \text{Equity multiplier} = \text{ROE}}{6.52\% \quad\quad\quad 1.82 \quad\quad\quad\quad 1.77 \quad\quad = 21.00\%}.$$

Construct Englewood's 1993 extended Du Pont equation. What does the Du Pont analysis indicate about Englewood's expense control, assets utilization, and debt utilization? What is the industry's debt to assets ratio?

c. Construct Englewood's 1993 statement of cash flows. What does it suggest about the company's operations?

6-20

Ratio sensitivity analysis

Tel-Tech Corporation's forecasted 1994 financial statements follow, along with some industry average ratios.

a. Calculate Tel-Tech's 1994 forecasted ratios, compare them with the industry average data, and comment briefly on Tel-Tech's projected strengths and weaknesses.

Tel-Tech Corporation:
Forecasted Balance Sheet as of December 31, 1994

Cash	$ 60,000
Accounts receivable	530,400
Inventory	1,050,000
Total current assets	$1,640,400
Land and buildings	285,600
Machinery	158,400
Other fixed assets	84,000
Total assets	$2,168,400
Accounts and notes payable	$ 537,600
Accruals	199,000
Total current liabilities	$ 736,600
Long-term debt	486,000
Common stock	690,000
Retained earnings	255,800
Total liabilities and equity	$2,168,400

Tel-Tech Corporation:
Forecasted Income Statement for 1994

Sales	$5,184,000
Cost of goods sold	4,380,000
Gross profit	$ 804,000
General, administrative, and selling expenses	270,330
Depreciation	200,500
Miscellaneous	130,200
Earnings before interest and taxes	$ 202,970
Interest	60,000
Earnings before taxes	$ 142,970
Taxes (40%)	57,188
Net income	$ 85,782

Additional Data:

Number of shares outstanding	50,000
EPS	$1.72
P/E ratio	9×
Market price (average)	$15.44

Industry Financial Ratios (1994)[a]

Quick ratio	1.0×
Current ratio	2.7×
Inventory turnover[b]	7×
Days sales outstanding (DSO)	32 days
Fixed assets turnover[b]	13.0×
Total assets turnover[b]	2.6×
Return on total assets (ROA)	9.1%
Return on equity (ROE)	18.2%
Debt ratio	50%
Profit margin on sales	3.5%
P/E ratio	12×
M/B ratio	1.6×

[a]Industry average ratios have been constant for the past four years.
[b]Based on year-end balance sheet figures.

(Do Part b only if you are using the computerized problem diskette.)

b. Suppose Tel-Tech is considering installing a new computer system, which would provide tighter control of inventory, accounts receivable, and accounts payable. If the new system is installed, the following data are projected rather than the data now given in certain balance sheet and income statement categories:

Cash	$ 96,000
Accounts receivable	474,000
Inventory	894,000
Other fixed assets	102,000
Accounts and notes payable	354,000
Accruals	156,000
Long-term debt	504,000
Retained earnings	306,000
Cost of goods sold	4,260,000
General, administrative, and selling expenses	270,000
Depreciation	203,020
Interest	55,850
P/E ratio	10×

1. How does this affect the projected ratios and the comparison to the industry averages?

2. If the new computer system is either more efficient or less efficient and causes the cost of goods sold to decrease or increase by $100,000 from the new projections, what effect does that have on the company's position?

Solutions to Self-Test Problems

ST-1   Jones paid $1.50 in dividends and retained $1.50 per share. Since total retained earnings (RE) increased by $9 million, there must be 6 million shares outstanding.

$$\Delta RE = (EPS \times \text{Number of shares}) - (DPS \times \text{Number of shares})$$

$$\Delta RE = \text{Number of shares}\,(EPS - DPS)$$

$$\$9,000,000 = \text{Number of shares}\,(\$3.00 - \$1.50)$$

$$\frac{\$9,000,000}{\$1.50} = \text{Number of shares}$$

$$\text{Number of shares} = 6,000,000.$$

With a book value of $30 per share, total common stock equity must be $30(6 million) = $180 million. Thus the debt ratio must be 33.3 percent:

$$\frac{\text{Total debt}}{\text{Total assets}} = \frac{\text{Debt}}{\text{Debt} + \text{Equity}} = \frac{\$90 \text{ million}}{\$90 \text{ million} + \$180 \text{ million}} = 33.3\%.$$

ST-2   **a.**
$$DSO = \frac{\text{Accounts receivable}}{\text{Sales}/360}$$

$$40 = \frac{A/R}{\$1,000/360}$$

$$A/R = 40(\$2.778) = \$111.1 \text{ million.}$$

b.
$$\text{Quick ratio} = \frac{\text{Current assets} - \text{Inventories}}{\text{Current liabilities}} = 2.0$$

$$= \frac{\text{Cash and marketable securities} + A/R}{\text{Current liabilities}} = 2.0.$$

$$\text{Current liabilities} = (\$100 + \$111.1)/2 = \$105.6 \text{ million.}$$

c.
$$\text{Current ratio} = \frac{\text{Current assets}}{\text{Current liabilities}} = 3.0.$$

$$\text{Current assets} = 3.0(\$105.6) = \$316.8 \text{ million.}$$

d.
$$\text{Total assets} = \text{Current assets} + \text{Fixed assets}$$

$$= \$316.8 + \$283.5 = \$600.3 \text{ million.}$$

e.
$$ROA = \text{Profit margin} \times \text{Total assets turnover}$$

$$= \frac{\text{Net income}}{\text{Sales}} \times \frac{\text{Sales}}{\text{Total assets}}$$

$$= \frac{\$50}{\$1,000} \times \frac{\$1,000}{\$600.3}$$

$$= 0.05 \times 1.666 = 0.0833 = 8.33\%.$$

f.
$$ROE = ROA \times \frac{\text{Total assets}}{\text{Common equity}}$$

$$12.0\% = 8.33\% \times \frac{\$600.3}{\text{Common equity}}$$

$$\text{Common equity} = \frac{(8.33\%)(\$600.3)}{12.0\%}$$

$$= \$416.7 \text{ million.}$$

g.

$$\text{Total assets} = \text{Total claims} = \$600.3$$

$$\text{Current liabilities} + \text{Long-term debt} + \text{Common equity} = \$600.3$$

$$\$105.6 + \text{Long-term debt} + \$416.7 = \$600.3$$

$$\text{Long-term debt} = \$600.3 - \$105.6 - \$416.7 = \$78 \text{ million.}$$

Note: We could have found ROA and common equity as follows:

$$\text{ROA} = \frac{\text{Net income}}{\text{Total assets}}$$

$$= \frac{\$50}{\$600.3}$$

$$= 0.0833 = 8.33\%.$$

$$\text{ROE} = \frac{\text{Net income}}{\text{Common equity}}$$

$$0.12 = \frac{\$50}{\text{Common equity}}$$

$$\text{Common equity} = \$50/0.12$$

$$= \$416.7 \text{ million.}$$

Then we could have gone on to find long-term debt.

ST-3   Cavendish would have reduced its accounts receivable (A/R) by 10 average days of sales, from a DSO of 40 days to a DSO of 30 days. This reduction in A/R would generate cash equal to 10 days of sales:

$$\text{New cash generated} = \frac{\text{Sales}}{360} \times 10$$

$$= \frac{\$1,000}{360} \times 10$$

$$= \$27.8 \text{ million.}$$

a.

$$\text{New common equity} = \text{Old common equity} - \text{Stock repurchased}$$

$$= \$416.7 - \$27.8$$

$$= \$388.9.$$

Thus

$$\text{New ROE} = \frac{\text{Net income}}{\text{New common equity}}$$

$$= \frac{\$50}{\$388.9}$$

$$= 12.86\% \text{ (versus old ROE of } 12.00\% \text{).}$$

b.

$$\text{Old total assets} = \$600.3 \text{ million.}$$

$$\text{New total assets} = \text{Old total assets} - \text{Reduction in A/R}$$

$$= \$600.3 - \$27.8$$

$$= \$572.5 \text{ million.}$$

$$\text{New ROA} = \frac{\text{Net income}}{\text{New total assets}}$$

$$= \frac{\$50}{\$572.5}$$

$$= 8.73\% \text{ (versus old ROA of 8.33\%).}$$

c. The old debt is the same as the new debt:

$$\text{New debt} = \text{Total claims} - \text{Equity}$$

$$= \$600.3 - \$416.7 = \$183.6 \text{ million.}$$

Therefore

$$\frac{\text{Old debt}}{\text{Old total assets}} = \frac{\$183.6}{\$600.3} = 30.6\%,$$

whereas

$$\frac{\text{New debt}}{\text{New total assets}} = \frac{\$183.6}{\$572.5} = 32.1\%.$$

MINI CASE

COMPUTER MODELING: PROJECTED FINANCIAL STATEMENTS AND RATIO ANALYSIS

Wyatt Industries is a manufacturer of specialized equipment used by airlines. Management of Wyatt is in the process of constructing projected financial statements for 1994. You have been asked to complete the following statements and provide a brief analysis of the proposed financing alternative.

Wyatt Industries: Projected 1994 Interest Expense and Retained Earnings

Interest on notes payable	$ _____
Interest on mortgage bonds	$ _____
Interest on other long-term debt	$ _____
Total interest	$ _____
1993 Retained earnings	$ 559,340
1994 Net income	$ _____
1994 Dividends	$ 0
1994 Retained earnings	$ _____

Wyatt Industries: Projected Income Statement for Year Ending December 31, 1994

Sales	$ 5,250,000
Cost of goods sold	$ 3,900,000
Gross profit	$ _____
Selling and administrative expenses	$ 620,000
Depreciation expense	$ 80,000
Net operating income (EBIT)	$ _____
Interest expense	$ _____
Earnings before tax (EBT)	$ _____
Taxes (34%)	$ _____
Net income	$ _____
Shares outstanding	_____
Earnings per share	$ _____

Wyatt Industries: Projected Balance Sheet, December 31, 1994

Assets		Liabilities and Equity		
Cash	$ 40,000	Accounts payable		$ 375,000
Marketable securities	$ 22,870	Notes payable	(7%)	$ 50,000
Accounts receivable	$ 500,000	Accrued wages and taxes		$ 15,000
Inventories	$ 480,000	Total current liabilities		$
Total current assets	$	Mortgage bonds	(9%)	$ 900,000
Gross fixed assets	$2,950,000	Other long-term debt	(10%)	$ 450,000
Less: depreciation	$ 800,000	Total long-term debt		$
Net fixed assets	$	Common stock	(par $1.00)	$ 200,000
		Paid-in capital		$ 300,000
		Retained earnings		$ 490,000
		Total net worth		$
Total assets	$	Total liabilities and equity		$

Using *Lotus 1-2-3,* do the following:

a. Enter into the spreadsheet all of the above information as shown. Calculate all items not shown to complete the projected statements for Wyatt Industries. Be sure to use the @SUM function where appropriate and, except for 1993 retained earnings, never enter an amount as a constant if it can be calculated using information entered elsewhere. Refer to these other cell addresses. (*Hint:* Placing percentages such as the interest rate on debt in a separate column, as opposed to each one being part of a label, makes for better modeling.)

b. Calculate the following ratios and save Parts a and b as W-AB. Print out everything.

Liquidity:	*Profitability:*
Current	Profit margin on sales
Quick	Basic earning power (BEP)
	Return on total assets (ROA)
Asset Management:	Return on common equity (ROE)
Inventory turnover	
Days sales outstanding (DSO)	*Market Value:*
Fixed assets turnover	Price/earnings (P/E)[a]
Total assets turnover	Market/Book (M/B)[a]
Debt Management:	
Debt to total assets	
Times interest earned (TIE)	

[a]Assume that Wyatt's common stock will sell for $13.25 per share on December 31, 1994.

c. Management has been discussing the possibility of issuing an additional 100,000 shares of common stock in 1994. The firm expects to net $12.50 per share after paying its investment banker for services rendered. The proceeds from the new stock issue would be utilized as follows:

▷ Accounts payable would be reduced by half.

▷ The cash account would be increased to $90,000.

▷ Inventories would be increased by 20 percent.

▷ New equipment would be purchased at a cost of $600,000 on which additional depreciation of $84,000 would be taken during 1994.

▷ Any remaining funds would be invested in short-term marketable securities to meet future seasonal or cyclical expansion needs.

Hint: Check to make sure that the balance sheet account "Retained earnings" reflects the change in projected 1994 net income (no dividends paid).

Assume that balance sheet accounts not specifically mentioned — and expense items other than depreciation — remain unchanged. The tax percentage is also assumed unchanged.

If your model is constructed correctly, the account "Marketable securities" should always take up the slack; that is, it should recalculate *automatically* and cause the balance sheet to balance.

When you change the financial statements to reflect the above information, this should cause ratios to change, without any additional effort on your part.

d. Assume that Wyatt goes ahead with the changes discussed in Part c. At the bottom of the spreadsheet, type in your answers to the following questions:

(1) Will these actions place the firm in a more or less risky position? Explain your answer.

(2) Why has ROE increased (decreased)? Print out everything and save as W-CD.

Determining Future Financial Needs

OBJECTIVES

After reading this chapter, you should be able to:

▶ Explain why managers must construct pro forma, or projected, financial statements.

▶ State the assumptions implicit in the percentage of sales method of forecasting needed external financing.

▶ Calculate additional funds needed (AFN), using both the balance sheet approach and the formula method.

▶ List the five important determinants of AFN, and indicate how changes in each would influence additional funds needed.

▶ Explain the conditions under which the percentage of sales method should not be used unless modified.

▶ Give two or three reasons why forecasting of future financial needs is crucial.

DECISION IN FINANCE

WHEN FORECASTS ARE WIDE OF THE MARK

Before Bristol-Myers merged with Squibb in 1989 to become the nation's second largest drug company, investors could count on steady earnings increases of around 15 percent year after year for each company. After the merger, however, analysts expected Bristol-Myers-Squibb's earnings to grow as much as 20 percent and the firm to challenge Merck as the top drug company.

Earnings increased by 17.6 percent in 1991, but they slumped in the first quarter of 1992, falling well short of company forecasts. Still, shareholders were soothed by CFO Michael Autera's statement that "everything was on track" for the second quarter. Two months later, CEO Richard Gelb had to release the news that earnings had come up short again; they would not reach double-digit levels because sales projections had been in error. Indeed, when the final figures came in, second-quarter results showed a mere 5 percent growth in sales and flat earnings.

The problem, claimed management, was that the firm's wholesalers had piled up inventory at the end of 1991 and then sharply reduced it at the beginning of the new year. Wholesalers insisted that their buying patterns did not fluctuate any more than usual. "I think they're looking for a scapegoat," said an executive at one of the largest, Bergen Brunswig Corporation.

See end of chapter for resolution.
Photo sources: (top) Charles West/The Stock Market; (bottom) Brownie Harris/The Stock Market

Competition from lower priced generic drugs might be one reason for the decline in earnings. During a recent three-year period, Bristol had helped push up earnings by raising prices of its best-selling drugs an average 12.5 percent while rival Merck's prices went up only half that amount. Bristol even raised prices twice in the same year on some products. Those price increases stimulated sales of generic products, and in the face of that new competition, Bristol can no longer count on price hikes to boost its earnings.

In fact, some of its newer drugs are priced lower than rival products, and the company is also giving large discounts to some government agencies to boost market share.

Bristol is hardly the only company where rosy forecasts have turned gray in the unforgiving light of the real world. Another is Sequoia Systems, which seemed to be riding high with its "fault-tolerant" computers that are designed to keep running even if a component fails.

Beginning an embarrassing series of miscalculations, the company forecast sales of $85 million for its fiscal year ending June 30, 1992. In August it reduced the estimate to $71 million, then again to $65.7 million, and in late 1992 it lowered the figure once more.

How did Sequoia get so far off track? The problem came to light when a Virginia firm complained to the Securities and Exchange Commission that it had been billed by Sequoia for merchandise never delivered on an order it had canceled. An investigation found that Sequoia was recording sales before they were completed, and the errant forecasts had been based on faulty accounting. Some sales were counted as revenues when computers were delivered to customers who were unable to pay for them. As a result, Sequoia's accounts receivable were almost half as large as their annual revenues.

A big sale to a steel mill in Siberia was stalled by difficulties getting hard currency to pay for it, yet Sequoia booked the sale just as if it had received cash money. Payment for another foreign sale, this time in Poland, was delayed by a turnover in government and turmoil in the currency, yet Sequoia again booked the sale as if no problems had been encountered.

Sequoia's former chief financial officer, who quit two months after the first sales forecast revision, said, "There was enormous pressure in this company to make sales. The culture and [the] environment encourged people to sometimes take risks, and those risks accumulated." The former CEO said, "Mistakes were made, but they were honest mistakes. No one deliberately misled anyone or deliberately mispresented revenue."

As you read this chapter, consider the possible consequences to Bristol-Myers and Sequoia of their erroneous and misleading forecasts. What would be the reaction of shareholders to such errors and subsequent embarrasing correction announcements? Consider what each of these companies might be able to do next to find its way back to financial respect.

---

pro forma financial statement

A projected financial statement which shows how an actual statement will look if certain specified assumptions are realized.

As noted in Chapter 6, both managers and investors are deeply concerned with *future* financial statements. Therefore, managers regularly construct **pro forma,** or projected, **financial statements,** and they consider alternative courses of action in terms of how the actions will affect these projections. In this chapter we discuss how pro forma statements are constructed and then used to help estimate the need for capital.

Sales Forecasts

sales (demand) forecast

A forecast of a firm's unit and dollar sales for some future period, generally sales based on recent trends plus forecasts of the economic prospects for the nation, region, industry, and so forth.

The most important element in financial planning is a **sales (demand) forecast.** Because such forecasts are critical for production scheduling, for plant design, for financial planning, and so on, the entire management team participates in their preparation. In fact, most larger firms have a *planning group* or *planning committee,* with its own staff of economists, which coordinates the corporation's sales forecast. A great deal of work lies behind all good sales forecasts. Companies must project the state of the national economy, economic conditions within their own geographic areas, and conditions in the product markets they serve. Further, they must consider their own pricing strategies, credit policies, advertising programs, capacity limitations, and the like. Companies also must consider the strategies and policies of their competitors, including the introduction of new products and changes in competitive pricing of key products.

If the sales forecast is off, the consequences can be serious. First, if the market expands *more* than the firm has expected and geared up for, the company will not be able to meet its customers' needs. Orders will back up, delivery times will lengthen, repairs and installations will be harder to schedule, and customer dissatisfaction will increase. Customers will end up going elsewhere, and the firm will lose market share and will have missed a major opportunity. On the other hand, if its projections are overly optimistic, the firm could end up with too much plant, equipment, and inventory. This would mean low turnover ratios, high costs for depreciation and storage, and, possibly, write-offs of obsolete inventory and equipment. All of this would result in a low rate of return on equity, which in turn would depress the company's stock price. If the company had financed the expansion with debt, its problems would, of course, be compounded.

We see, then, that an accurate sales forecast is critical to the well-being of the firm. Because sales forecasting is a rather specialized subject, we do not consider the mechanics of the forecasting process in this text. Rather, we simply take the sales forecast as given and use it to illustrate various types of financial decisions.

Once a forecast of sales has been made, several methods may be used to develop pro forma, or projected, financial statements. In this chapter we will focus on the *percentage of sales method,* and we will explain how this method may be modified as needed. We will conclude the chapter by discussing briefly the growing use of computerized financial planning models.

? *Self-Test*

List some items which should be considered when developing the sales forecast.

Briefly explain why an accurate sales forecast is critical to the well-being of the firm.

Percentage of Sales Forecasting

percentage of sales method

A method of forecasting financial requirements by expressing various balance sheet items as percentages of sales and then multiplying these percentages by expected future sales to construct pro forma balance sheets.

Financial forecasting involves projecting financial statements on the basis of a set of assumed operating conditions; the **percentage of sales method** is a simple but often practical method of forecasting financial statement variables. In its simplest form, the procedure is based on two assumptions: (1) that most balance sheet accounts are tied directly to sales and (2) that the current levels of all assets are optimal for the current sales level.

In using and analyzing the percentage of sales method of forecasting financial requirements we will do the following:

▸ **Project a complete balance sheet** and statement of cash flows based on the two stated assumptions and on the data for a specific company. The end result of this three-step process will be a projection of additional funds needed (AFN).

▸ **Discuss how needed funds may be raised,** subject to typical contractual constraints.

Table 7-1

Addison Products
Company: 1993 Financial
Statements

I. Balance Sheet, December 31, 1993 (Thousands of Dollars)

Cash	$ 10	Accounts payable	$ 40
Accounts receivable	90	Notes payable	10
Inventories	200	Accrued wages and taxes	50
Total current assets	$300	Total current liabilities	$100
Net fixed assets	300	Mortgage bonds	150
		Common stock	50
		Retained earnings	300
Total assets	$600	Total liabilities and equity	$600

II. Summary Income Statement, 1993 (Thousands of Dollars)

Sales	$400
Net income	40
Dividends paid	24

▶ **Project additional funds needed (AFN) based on the formula method** which is, in essence, a shortcut method and which will, therefore, give the same estimate of AFN as the balance sheet method.

▶ **Consider situations in which balance sheet ratios are not constant,** but are subject to change. This typically leads to modification of the forecast, based on the firm's actual situation.

We illustrate the process by examining the Addison Products Company, a highly capital-intensive manufacturing company, whose December 31, 1993, balance sheet and summary income statement are given in Table 7-1. Addison operated its fixed assets at full capacity in 1993 to support its $400,000 of sales, and it had no unnecessary current assets. Its profit margin on sales was 10 percent, and it paid out 60 percent of its net income to stockholders as dividends. If Addison's sales increase to $600,000 in 1994, what will be its pro forma December 31, 1994, balance sheet, and how much additional financing will the company require during 1994?

The Projected Balance Sheet Method

spontaneous assets

Assets which vary proportionately with sales and, therefore, remain constant percentages of sales; investment in these assets must increase by the same percentage as projected sales.

The first task is to identify those balance sheet items that vary directly and proportionately with sales; these are called **spontaneous assets.** Because Addison has been operating at full capacity (it has no excess manufacturing capacity), each asset item, including plant and equipment, must increase if the higher level of sales is to be attained. More cash will be needed for transactions; receivables will be higher, as sales increase by 50 percent and credit policy is assumed unchanged; additional inventory must be stocked; and new fixed assets must be added.[1]

---

[1] Some assets, such as marketable securities, are not tied directly to operations and hence do not vary directly with sales. If anything, there will generally be an *inverse* relationship between marketable securities and growth in sales. Also, as we shall see later in this chapter, if some assets (such as fixed assets) are not being fully utilized, sales can increase without increasing those assets. For now, we are deliberately keeping the analysis simple by assuming that Addison holds *no* marketable securities and that *all* the firm's assets must increase proportionately with sales.

A MAVERICK'S FORECASTING APPROACH

A public company, whose shareholders are interested primarily in quarterly profits, might not adapt well to his system, but Larry Stifler, admittedly a maverick in the art of forecasting, wonders why most other firms don't analyze their current status and future needs the way he does. Stifler is the founder and head of Health Management Resources Inc. (HMR), a weight-loss company, and he projects and plans for impressive growth without relying on standard techniques. "It takes my accountants months to find out that I've got a problem," he says. "My system tells me immediately, and it tells me how bad things really are."

Although his system is totally quantitative, most of the numbers on which he relies are not straight dollar amounts. Instead, they are ratios, expressing relationships between one thing and another. In his two dozen locations, budgets are not drafted, and costs are not projected. But, in six years, the Stifler concept has worked well enough so that sales tripled every year, and revenues totaled $50 million in 1989. Cost controls are quite stringent, even though employees claim they don't know how much money their particular divisions spent in the past or how much they will spend in the future.

Merely knowing how much something costs and how much revenue it brings in is not enough, Stifler insists. He prefers to capture relationships within the business by building mathematical models, one of which was the catalyst for the birth of his company. Health Management Resources sprang from the founder's differences with management of the Institute for Health Maintenance (IHM), which hired him from an academic position as a behavioral psychologist to help people in the IHM program lose weight. Stifler developed a behavior modification support program which, combined with a medically supervised, very-low-calorie diet, distinguished IHM from other weight-loss firms.

Stifler agreed that IHM's program was outstanding, but he disagreed with their ideas on the future of the business and how it should be run. He worked out a mathematical model to show IHM that the company could not survive by operating free-standing, independent clinics. He tried to demonstrate that patient fees

would not be enough to cover both operating costs and the big initial investment required to open a clinic. Instead, he argued, the company should cooperate with, and run its clinics in, existing hospitals, as part of physician group practices, or in other medical establishments. When IHM management couldn't be persuaded, Stifler left to found his own company, based on his own guidelines. IHM should have taken his advice, because, with its free-standing clinics, it suffered 18 months of losses before shutting them down. Meanwhile, Stifler's HMR continues to grow, relying on more of his mathematical models to keep current operations and future plans on track.

Stifler's method depends on the number of patients enrolled in his program. In a different company, the key might be the number of autos sold or clients serviced. He began building his model by estimating that a reasonable patient/staff ratio is 50 to 1. Knowing how much each employee receives in salary and benefits, he then established a direct relationship between clients and payroll. Since each staff member needs a telephone, a desk, and a chair, he also related patient enrollment directly to furniture and telephone expenses. Thus, his model shows that, for every 50 patients, he will have to spend a certain amount for payroll, telephones, and furniture. Clinic managers merely need to keep track of patient enrollment and to hire a new employee for every 50 new patients. They know the money will be available to pay for the additions because each new enrollee brings in a known amount of revenue. Says a health educator at one HMR clinic, "I never write a budget or proposals. I just work with patients, and in a year of working here, there's nothing we've wanted that we couldn't get. The model tells us."

Stifler can build a model to test almost any plan by showing exactly how each facet of his business works. For instance, even though HMR offers a consumer-oriented service, the company does no consumer advertising. The model says it doesn't have to.

Patients enrolled in the weight-loss plan agree to a medically supervised fasting period followed by an 18-month maintenance program. Throughout the industry, about half of diet customers drop out after three months. From company records, Stifler learned that each patient who made it through the fast and entered maintenance brought in 2.2 new referrals to the pro-

Source: "The Language of Business," *Inc.,* February 1990.

gram. If only 46 percent of the enrollees stayed on into maintenance, the program would sustain itself (since 46% × 2.2 = 100%). Management could easily project growth based on retainment of over 46 percent. Says Stifler, "Set up the business for quality care and it'll grow by itself."

In other words, the numbers say that every dollar spent providing good patient care comes back 2.2 times. Thus, a plan that would "save" $1 by changing the patient/staff ratio or otherwise reducing the costs of patient care might actually cost the company $2.20 in revenue. This proved to be a powerful argument to use with hospital administrators, who had been accustomed to increasing profits by cutting costs.

Stifler does monitor costs, but again, by using ratios instead of dollar amounts. He keeps a running check on productivity by dividing each month's net revenue by the number of employees (figured as full-time equivalents) to get the ratio of revenues per employee. "If productivity is the same or better each month," he says, "then we're O.K." Unlike the data that accounts would provide, the number gives him

an instant view of the "forest," instead of a belated "head count of the trees." If productivity does falter, he then goes a step further to try to locate the problem. Using net revenue as the constant denominator, he divides it into approximately 18 cost categories to see whether each relationship corresponds to the model. If not, he then digs further to determine the cause of the problem.

The company even uses numbers to monitor the quality of its services—not usually an easy thing to do—and to foresee problems before they cause a patient to leave. For instance, each enrollee keeps careful records and reports on such things as calories consumed and the amount worked off through exercise. Combined with other clinic records, such as the amount of weight lost, HMR not only can monitor patients' progress, but also can monitor the clinic's performance. "You can look at those numbers," says one employee, "and without even talking to patients know whether they're in trouble." Says another, "The quality-control data lets us see we have a problem before it shows up in attrition."

spontaneously generated funds

Funds that are obtained automatically from routine business transactions; also called *spontaneous liabilities,* this financing is assumed to increase by the same percentage as projected sales.

If Addison's assets are to increase, its liabilities and/or equity must likewise rise: the balance sheet must balance, and any increases in assets must be financed in some manner. Some of the required funds will come spontaneously from routine business transactions, whereas other funds must be raised from outside sources. **Spontaneously generated funds** will come from such sources as accounts payable and accruals, which are assumed to increase spontaneously and proportionately with sales. As sales increase, so will Addison's own purchases, and larger purchases will automatically result in higher levels of accounts payable. Thus, if sales double, accounts payable will also double. Similarly, because a higher level of operations will require more labor, accrued wages will increase, and, assuming profit margins are maintained, an increase in profits will pull up accrued taxes. Retained earnings will also increase, but not in direct proportion to the increase in sales. Other sources of financing require formal action by the firm's financial manager. For example, neither notes payable, mortgage bonds, nor common stock will increase spontaneously with sales, so management must obtain funds from these sources by taking some specific, planned action.

Let us summarize our assumptions about the relationship of Addison's asset accounts and certain liability accounts to sales:

Spontaneous Assets	Spontaneous Liabilities
Cash	Accounts payable
Accounts receivable	Accrued wages and taxes
Inventories	
Net fixed assets	

No other balance sheet accounts are spontaneous, but all entries in the income statement are assumed (for simplicity) to vary directly and proportionately with sales.

We will begin our analysis by constructing first-approximation projected financial statements for December 1994, proceeding as follows:

Step 1. Project Spontaneous Balance Sheet and Income Statement Items.   In Table 7-2, Column 2, we multiply those balance sheet items that vary directly with sales by $(1 + \text{Sales growth rate}) = (1 + g) = 1.50$. For example, since sales will grow by 50 percent, inventories must also grow by 50 percent, to $300,000. An item such as notes payable that does not vary directly with sales is simply carried forward from Column 1 to Column 2 to develop the first-approximation balance sheet. We also carry forward figures for mortgage bonds and for common stock from 1993 to 1994. One or more of the three accounts will have to be changed later in the analysis, when we make our second-approximation forecast.

In the lower part of Table 7-2, we multiply the income statement items by $(1 + \text{Sales growth rate}) = (1 + g) = 1.50.$[2] Thus, we are assuming that each income statement item increases at the same rate as sales, which means that we are assuming constant returns to scale.

Step 2. Project Cumulative Retained Earnings.   We next combine the addition to retained earnings estimated for 1994 and the December 31, 1993, balance sheet figure to obtain the December 31, 1994, projected retained earnings. Addison will have a net income of $60,000 in 1994. If the firm continues to pay out 60 percent of its income as dividends, the dividend payment will be $36,000, leaving $60,000 − $36,000 = $24,000 of new retained earnings. Thus, the 1994 balance sheet account retained earnings is projected to be $300,000 + $24,000 = $324,000.

Step 3. Calculate Additional Funds Needed (AFN).   Next, we sum the balance sheet asset accounts, obtaining a projected total assets figure of $900,000, and we also sum the projected liability and equity items to obtain $669,000. At this point, the 1994 balance sheet does not balance: assets total $900,000, but only $669,000 of liabilities and equity are projected. Thus, we have a shortfall, or **additional funds needed (AFN)** of $231,000, which will presumably be raised by bank borrowings and/or by selling securities. (For simplicity, we disregard depreciation by assuming that cash flows generated from depreciation will be used to replace worn-out fixed assets.)

additional funds needed (AFN)

Funds that a firm must acquire through borrowing or by selling new stock.

---

[2]We have simplified the process for projecting the income statement items. For example, interest expense does not vary directly with sales but will vary depending on the financing obtained to support asset growth. This refinement is dealt with in advanced finance textbooks. See Brigham and Gapenski, *Intermediate Financial Management,* Fourth Edition, Chapter 19.

In addition, recognize that since all firms have both fixed and variable costs, the fixed costs (such as executive salaries) will not increase with sales over some reasonable range of sales and that, for this reason, our assumption of a constant profit margin as sales increase is also a simplification. We will come back to this topic in Chapter 20.

Table 7-2   Addison Products Company: Financial Projections (Thousands of Dollars)

	As of 12/31/93 (1)	1994 Projections	
		First Approximation: Column 1 × 1.5 (2)	Second Approximation: Includes Financings (3)
Balance Sheet			
Cash	$ 10	$ 15	$ 15
Accounts receivable	90	135	135
Inventories	200	300	300
Total current assets	$300	$450	$450
Net fixed assets	300	450	450
Total assets	$600	$900	$900
Accounts payable	$ 40	$ 60	$ 60
Notes payable	10	10[a]	15[d]
Accrued wages and taxes	50	75	75
Total current liabilities	$100	$145	$150
Mortgage bonds	150	150[a]	300[e]
Common stock	50	50[a]	126[f]
Retained earnings	300	324[b]	324
Total liabilities and equity	$600	$669	$900
Additional funds needed (AFN)		$231[c]	

	For the Year Ended 12/31/93	Forecasted for 1994
Income Statement		
Sales	$400	$600
Total costs	333	500
Taxable income	$ 67	$100
Taxes (40%)	27	40
Net income	$ 40	$ 60
Dividends	24	36
Addition to retained earnings	$ 16	$ 24

[a]This account does not increase spontaneously with sales, so for the first-approximation projection, the 1993 balance is carried forward. Later decisions could change the figure shown.
[b]1993 retained earnings plus 1994 addition = $300,000 + $24,000 = $324,000.
[c]AFN is a balancing item found by subtracting projected total liabilities and equity from projected total assets.
[d]$5,000 of new notes payable has been added to the first-approximation balance. This is the maximum addition based on limitations on total current liabilities.
[e]$150,000 of new bonds has been added to the first-approximation balance. This is the maximum additional debt due to total liability limitations.
[f]The addition to common equity is determined as a residual; it is that amount of AFN that still remains after the additon to notes payable and mortgage bonds.

Raising the Additional Funds Needed

Addison could use short-term bank loans (notes payable), mortgage bonds, common stock, or a combination of these securities to make up the shortfall.[3] Ordinarily, it would make this choice on the basis of the relative costs of these

---

[3]Assume that Addison has not used preferred stock in the past and does not plan to do so in the immediate future.

different types of securities, subject to certain constraints. For example, Addison has a contractual agreement with its bondholders to keep total debt at or below 50 percent of total assets and also to keep the current ratio at a level of 3.0 or greater. These provisions restrict the financing choices as follows:

a. **Restriction on additional debt**

Maximum debt permitted = 0.5 × Total assets

= 0.5 × $900,000 = $450,000

Less: Debt already projected for December 31, 1994:

Current liabilities $145,000

Mortgage bonds   150,000 =   295,000

Maximum additional debt $155,000

b. **Restriction on additional current liabilities**

Maximum current liabilities = Current assets ÷ 3.0

= $450,000 ÷ 3 = $150,000

Current liabilities already projected   145,000

Maximum additional current liabilities $ 5,000

c. **Common equity requirements**

Total additional funds needed (from Table 7-2) $231,000

Maximum additional debt permitted   155,000

Common equity funds required $ 76,000

From Table 7-2, we saw that Addison needs a total of $231,000 from external sources. Its existing debt contract limits new debt to $155,000, and of that amount, only $5,000 can be short-term debt. Thus, assuming that Addison wants to make maximum use of debt financing, it must plan to sell common stock in the amount of $76,000, in addition to its debt financing, to cover its financial requirements. Here is a summary of its projected nonspontaneous external financings:

Short-term debt (notes payable) $ 5,000

Long-term debt   150,000

New common stock   76,000

Total $231,000

Addison's financial manager can use the pro forma financial statements developed in Table 7-2, Column 3, to analyze the ratios implied by these statements and to construct a projected statement of cash flows. Table 7-3 shows Addison's projected statement of cash flows, and below it we show the projected key 1994 ratios.

These statements can be used by the financial manager to show the other executives the implications of the planned sales increase. For example, the projected rate of return on equity is 13.3 percent. Is this a reasonable target, or can it be improved? Also, the preliminary forecast calls for the sale of some common stock, but does top management really want to sell any new stock? Suppose Addison Products Company is owned entirely by Maddie Addison, who does not want to sell any stock and thereby lose her exclusive control of the company. How then can the needed funds be raised, or what adjustments could be made? In the remainder of the chapter, we consider approaches to answering questions such as these.

Table 7-3

Addison Products Company: Projected Statement of Cash Flows for 1994 (Thousands of Dollars)

Cash Flows from Operations		
Net income	$60	
Additions (sources of cash):		
Increase in accounts payable	20	
Increase in accruals	25	
Subtractions (uses of cash):		
Increase in accounts receivable	(45)	
Increase in inventories	(100)	
Total cash flows from operations[a]		($40)
Cash Flows Associated with Long-Term Investments		
Increase in net fixed assets		(150)
Cash Flows from Financing Activities		
Increase in notes payable	5	
Proceeds from sale of bonds	150	
Proceeds from sale of common stock	76	
Dividends paid	(36)	
Net cash flows from financing activities		195
Net increase in cash		$ 5

Key Ratios Projected for December 31, 1994:

1. Current ratio — $3.0\times$[b]
2. Total debt/Total assets — 50%[b]
3. Rate of return on equity — 13.3%
4. Sales/Inventory — $2\times$
5. DSO — 81 days

[a]*Cash flows from operations* normally includes depreciation. Here we have assumed that depreciation is reinvested in fixed assets; that is, depreciation is netted out against fixed asset additions.

[b]Many firms would find it prudent to stay *well below* the stipulated maximum debt ratio and *well above* the required current ratio. In other words, if Addison wants to maintain a margin of safety, it must raise *more* than $76,000 through sale of common stock.

? Self-Test

What are the key assumptions on which the percentage of sales method is based?

Briefly explain the process you would go through to develop a forecast of additional funds needed (AFN), using the projected balance sheet method.

What type of factors determine how additional funds needed (AFN) will actually be raised?

The Formula Method for Forecasting AFN

The forecast of capital requirements is normally made by constructing pro forma financial statements, as described previously. However, a simple forecasting formula provides a shortcut to projecting additional funds needed (AFN) and can be used to clarify the relationship between sales growth and financial requirements, as well as the influence of other relevant variables on AFN.

$$\begin{bmatrix} \text{Additional} \\ \text{funds} \\ \text{needed} \end{bmatrix} = \begin{bmatrix} \text{Required} \\ \text{increase} \\ \text{in assets} \end{bmatrix} - \begin{bmatrix} \text{Spontaneous} \\ \text{increase in} \\ \text{liabilities} \end{bmatrix} - \begin{bmatrix} \text{Increase in} \\ \text{retained} \\ \text{earnings} \end{bmatrix} \quad (7\text{-}1)$$

$$\text{AFN} = \text{A*/S } (\Delta S) - \text{L*/S } (\Delta S) - MS_1(1 - d).$$

Here,

AFN = additional, or external, funds needed.

A*/S = assets that increase spontaneously with sales as a percentage of sales, or required dollar increase in assets per $1 increase in sales. A*/S = $600,000/$400,000 = 150%, or 1.5, for Addison. Thus, for every $1 increase in sales, assets must increase by $1.50. Note that A designates total assets and A* those assets that must increase if sales are to increase. When the firm is operating at full capacity, as is the case here, A* = A.

L*/S = liabilities that increase spontaneously with sales as a percentage of sales, or spontaneously generated financing per $1 increase in sales. L*/S = $90,000/$400,000 = 22.5% for Addison. Thus, every $1 increase in sales generates $0.225 of spontaneous financing. L* is normally less than L, total liabilities.

S_1 = total sales projected for next year. Note that S_0 = $400,000 = last year's sales. S_1 = $600,000 for Addison.

ΔS = change in sales = $S_1 - S_0$ = $600,000 - $400,000 = $200,000 for Addison. ΔS is also equal to $S_0(g)$, where g equals the rate of growth: $400,000(0.50) = $200,000.

M = profit margin, or rate of profit per $1 of sales. M = 10%, or 0.10, for Addison.

d = percentage of earnings paid out in dividends, or the dividend payout ratio; d = 60%. Notice that 1 − d = 1.0 − 0.6 = 0.4, or 40%. This is the percentage of earnings that Addison retains, and it is called the **retention rate** or *retention ratio*.

retention rate

The percentage of its earnings retained by the firm after payment of dividends, which is equal to 1 minus the dividend payout ratio.

excess capacity

Capacity that exists when an asset is not being fully utilized.

Because no **excess capacity** exists and ratios are assumed constant, we can insert these values for Addison into Equation 7-1 to find the additional funds needed as follows:

$$\text{AFN} = 1.5 \, (\Delta S) - 0.225(\Delta S) - 0.1(S_1) \, (1 - 0.6)$$

$$= 1.5(\$200,000) - 0.225(\$200,000) - 0.1(\$600,000)(0.4)$$

$$= \$300,000 - \$45,000 - \$24,000$$

$$= \$231,000.$$

To increase sales by $200,000, Addison must increase assets by $300,000. The $300,000 of new assets must be financed in some manner. Of the total,

$45,000 will come from a spontaneous increase in liabilities, while another $24,000 represents the 1994 addition to retained earnings. The additional funds needed (AFN) to finance this projected growth amount to $231,000, which must be raised over and above the internally and spontaneously generated funds. This value must, of course, agree with the number developed in Table 7-2.

Determinants of Financial Requirements

It should be clear by now that each of the terms A*/S, L*/S, g, M, and d have a bearing on the amount of additional, or external, funds needed by a firm, in this case Addison. Let us look at each one, starting with the growth rate, g.

Rate of Growth.   The faster the rate of growth in sales (g), the greater ΔS, and the greater the firm's need for additional, external financing. Equation 7-1 quantifies this relationship and is plotted for Addison in Figure 7-1. The lower section of the figure shows the firm's additional funds needed from external sources at various growth rates.

Of particular interest is the growth rate at which Addison can support the level of sales entirely from spontaneous liabilities and internally generated equity (retained earnings). We can solve for this rate of growth where AFN = $0. First we rewrite ΔS and S_1 as follows:

$$\Delta S = S_0(g)$$

and

$$S_1 = S_0(1 + g).$$

Using Equation 7-1, we then substitute into the equation the known values for A*/S, L*/S, M, d, and S_0 as they apply to Addison, set the equation equal to $0, and solve for g:

$$
\begin{aligned}
\$0 &= 1.5(\$400,000)(g) - 0.225(\$400,000)(g) - 0.1[\$400,000(1 + g)](1 - 0.6) \\
&= \$600,000g - \$90,000g - 0.04(\$400,000 - \$400,000g) \\
&= \$600,000g - \$90,000g - \$16,000 - \$16,000g \\
\$494,000g &= \$16,000 \\
g &= \$16,000/\$494,000 = 0.03239 = 3.239\%.
\end{aligned}
$$

At very low growth rates, Addison needs no additional, external financing, and it even generates surplus cash. However, if the company grows faster than approximately 3.239 percent in 1994, it must raise capital from outside sources. If management foresees difficulties in raising the required capital—perhaps because Addison's owner does not want to sell additional stock—the company should reconsider the feasibility of its expansion plans. Alternatively, management could look closely at the remaining determinants of external financing to see if any of these can be adjusted to lower the firm's overall need for additional financing during the coming year.

Dividend Policy.   Dividend policy as reflected in the payout ratio, also affects external capital requirements—the higher the payout ratio, the smaller the addition to retained earnings, and hence the greater the requirements for external capital. Therefore, if Addison foresees difficulties in raising capital, it might want

Figure 7-1

Addison Products Company: Relationship between Growth in Sales and Financial Requirements, $S_0 = \$400,000$

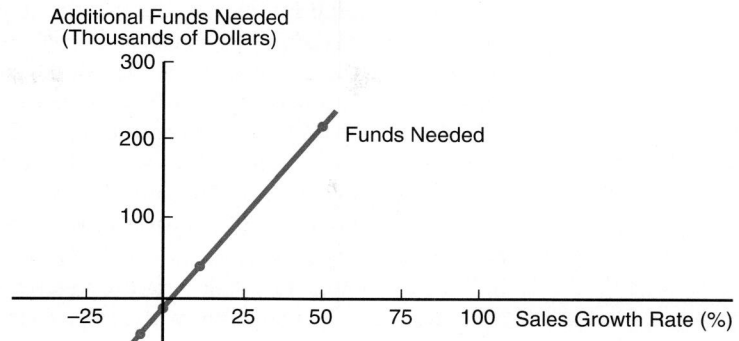

Growth Rate in Sales, g (1)	Increase (Decrease) in Sales, ΔS (2)	Forecasted Sales, S_1 (3)	Additional Funds Needed[a] (4)
50%	$200	$600	$231.0
10	40	440	33.4
3.239	12.956	412.956	0.0
0	0	400	(16.0)
(10)	(40)	360	(65.4)

Explanation of Columns:
Column 1: Growth rate in sales, g.
Column 2: Increase (decrease) in sales, $\Delta S = (S_0)g$.
Column 3: Forecasted sales, $S_1 = S_0 + (S_0)g = S_0(1 + g)$.
Column 4: Additional funds needed $= 1.5(\Delta S) - 0.225(\Delta S) - 0.1(S_1)(1 - 0.6)$.
[a]Negative additional funds required $=$ Surplus funds available.

External financing and a firm's sales growth rate are related. The higher a firm's growth rate in sales, the greater its need for external financing. If Addison's sales growth rate is greater than about 3.239 percent, the company will need to raise capital from outside sources as shown by this graph. At growth rates of less than 3.239 percent, the company will actually have surplus funds.

to consider a reduction in the dividend payout ratio. This would lower, or shift to the right, the line in Figure 7-1, indicating lower external capital requirements at all growth rates. Before changing its dividend policy, however, management should consider the effects of such a decision on stock prices. These effects are described in Chapter 21.

Notice that the line in Figure 7-1 does *not* pass through the origin. Thus, if Addison's rate of growth is below 3.239 percent, surplus funds (negative additional funds needed) will be produced because new retained earnings plus spontaneously generated funds will exceed the required asset increases. Only if the dividend payout ratio is 100 percent, meaning that the firm does not retain any of its earnings, would the "funds needed" line pass through the origin.

capital intensity ratio

The amount of assets required per dollar of sales (A*/S).

Capital Intensity.   The amount of assets required per dollar of sales, A*/S in Equation 7-1, is often called the **capital intensity ratio.** This factor has a major effect on capital requirements per unit of sales growth. If the capital intensity ratio is low, sales can grow rapidly without much outside capital. However, if the firm is capital intensive, which is the case with Addison, even a small growth in output will require a great deal of outside capital. Note that the capital intensity ratio is the reciprocal of the total assets turnover ratio only if *all* assets must grow proportionally with sales, as they do here.

If Addison finds that it cannot raise $231,000 in external financing, as previously calculated, one option would be to try to reduce the firm's capital intensity ratio. If *less* than $1.50 could be invested into new current and fixed assets for every $1 increase in Addison's sales, the total external funds needed would be lower as well. This could possibly be accomplished by (1) managing the firm's cash better, (2) reducing the investment into accounts receivables and/or inventory, or (3) managing with fewer fixed assets than originally projected. For example, if the plant currently has two shifts of workers operating at full capacity, maybe it is possible to add a third shift, instead of adding new fixed assets, to reach the higher level of sales. Or, if the firm is currently manufacturing many parts and components used in the final products, it may be advantageous to purchase some of these items instead. Both of these steps would reduce additional funds needed.

Spontaneous Liabilities.   When it comes to spontaneous liabilities, L*/S, exactly the opposite is true: Addison's management would want to *increase* this percentage because accounts payable and accruals both provide financing. There is usually not much a firm can do to raise the portion of L*/S that is due to accrued wages and taxes. However, suppliers can sometimes be persuaded to give customers longer to pay, when that customer is financially sound and is in need of financing to support a significant growth in sales (after all, suppliers will also benefit by being able to sell more to that customer). In fact, longer credit terms can, at times, be almost a subsidy by the supplier.[4]

Profit Margin.   The profit margin, M, is also an important determinant of the funds required; the higher the margin, the lower the funds requirements, other things held constant. Addison's profit margin is 10 percent. This is already a fairly healthy profit margin, but if Addison could reduce costs and raise M to, say, 12 percent, the effect would be to reduce the additional funds needed at all growth rates. In terms of the graph, an increase in the profit margin would cause the line to shift down, and its slope would also become less steep. Because of the relationship between profit margins and external capital requirements, some very rapidly growing firms do not need much external capital. For example, in the 1960s Xerox grew very rapidly with very little borrowing or stock sales. However, as the company lost patent protection and as competition intensified in the copier industry, Xerox's profit margin declined, its needs for external capital rose, and it began to borrow heavily from banks and other sources. IBM has had a similar experience.

---

[4]We will return to the management of current assets and liabilities in Chapters 8, 9, 10, and 11. Our intent, at this point, is merely to show how these variables fit into the forecasting of future financial needs.

In summary, if Addison can increase spontaneous liabilities, L*/S, or the profit margin, M, the firm's need for additional, external financing would decrease, other things constant. A reduction in AFN could also be accomplished if either the capital intensity ratio, A*/S, or the dividend payout ratio, d, were reduced. If all else fails, it may become necessary for Addison to curtail its growth in sales. The firm would simply have no choice if it cannot raise the entire $231,000; the balance sheet must balance. If funds are not available to finance asset growth, then sales growth can only occur at a modest rate.

The options available to a firm such as Addison are of more than academic interest. Starting in 1990 and lasting throughout all of 1992, many small and medium-sized firms have experienced what is commonly called a "credit crunch." This topic was discussed in connection with commercial banks in Chapter 3. At still other times, the bond and equity markets are simply not receptive to a particular firm's new issues of bonds or equity. Therefore, managements of companies such as Addison should never assume that projected funds needed can be raised. Managers must be ready to deal with a situation where less than 100 percent of the needed financing can be obtained.

Self-Test

Write out Equation 7-1, and briefly explain it.

How do each of the following affect external capital requirements?
a. Rate of growth
b. Dividend policy
c. Capital intensity
d. Spontaneous liabilities
e. Profit margin

Explain why it has been especially important in recent years that managers understand what their options are, if the projected external funds cannot be obtained.

Forecasting Financial Requirements When the Balance Sheet Ratios Are Subject to Change

To this point we have been assuming that the balance sheet ratios of assets and liabilities to sales (A*/S and L*/S) remain constant over time. For this to happen, each spontaneous asset and liability item must increase at the same rate as sales. In graph form, this assumes the type of relationship indicated in Panel a of Figure 7-2, a relationship that is linear and passes through the origin. Under these conditions, if the company's sales expand from $200 million to $400 million, accounts receivable will increase proportionately, from $100 million to $200 million.

The assumption of constant ratios is appropriate at times, but there are times when it is incorrect. Three such conditions are described in the following sections.

Figure 7-2   Three Possible Ratio Relationships (Millions of Dollars)

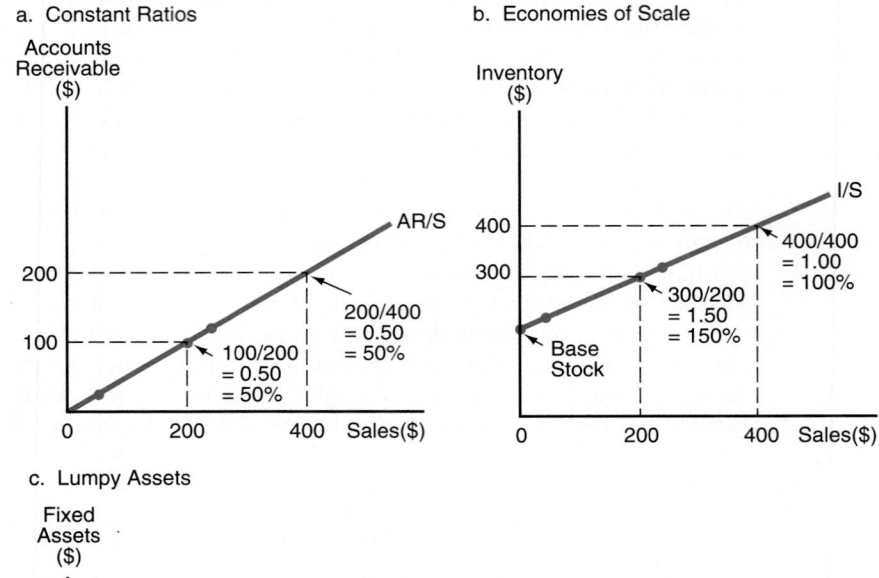

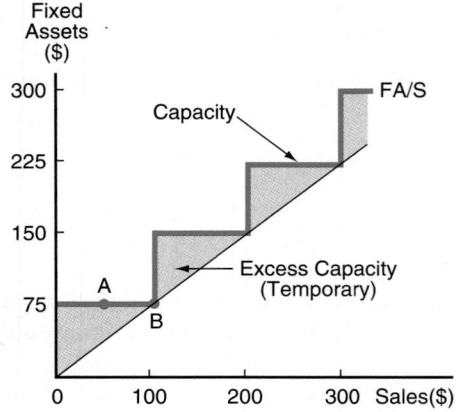

a. Constant Ratios

b. Economies of Scale

c. Lumpy Assets

| | Panel a | | | Panel b | | Panel c | |
	Sales	AR	AR/S	I	I/S	FA	FA/S
Year 1	$ 50	$ 25	0.5	$225	4.500	$ 75	1.50
Year 2	200	100	0.5	300	1.500	150	0.75
Year 3	250	125	0.5	343.75	1.375	225	0.90

Three of the possible assets to sales relationships that may exist: Constant ratios, economies of scale, and lumpy assets. If the balance sheet ratios of assets (and liabilities) to sales remain constant over time (i.e, they increase at the same rate as sales), a linear relationship exists, and that line passes through the origin. Panel a shows this relationship. With economies of scale, ratios are likely to decline over time as the size of the firm increases. A base stock of assets is needed for even low sales levels, but the asset level grows less rapidly than the sales level. This situation is depicted in Panel b. Many industries must add fixed assets in large, discrete, or "lumpy," units; this situation is illustrated in Panel c.

Economies of Scale

There are economies of scale in the use of many kinds of assets, and where economies occur, the ratios are likely to change over time as the size of the firm increases. For example, firms often need to maintain base stocks of different inventory items, even if current sales levels are quite low. Then, as sales expand, inventories grow less rapidly than sales, so the ratio of inventory to sales (I/S) declines. This situation is depicted in Panel b of Figure 7-2. Here we see that the inventory/sales ratio is 1.5, or 150 percent, when sales are $200 million, but it declines to 1.0 when sales climb to $400 million. When economies of scale exist, firms may use simple linear regression to arrive at a relationship between an asset account and sales, such as that shown in Panel b.[5]

Although the relationship shown here for economies of scale is linear, this is not necessarily the case. Indeed, as we shall see in Chapter 10, if the firm uses the most popular model for establishing inventory levels, the EOQ model, inventories will rise with the square root of sales. In this case, the graph in Panel b of Figure 7-2 would show a curved line the slope of which decreases at higher sales levels.

Lumpy Assets

lumpy assets

Assets that cannot be acquired in small increments but must be obtained in large, discrete amounts.

In many industries, technological considerations dictate that if a firm is to be competitive, it must add fixed assets in large, discrete units; such assets are often referred to as **lumpy assets.** In the paper industry, for example, there are strong economies of scale in basic paper mill equipment, so when paper companies expand capacity, they must do so in large, or lumpy, increments. This type of situation is depicted in Panel c of Figure 7-2. Here we assume that the smallest efficient plant has a cost of $75 million, and that such a plant can produce enough output to attain a sales level of $100 million. If the firm is to be competitive, it simply must have at least $75 million of fixed assets.

This situation has a major effect on the fixed assets/sales (FA/S) ratio at different sales levels, and, consequently, on financial requirements. At Point A in Figure 7-2, Panel c, which represents a sales level of $50 million, the fixed assets are $75 million, so the ratio FA/S = $75/$50 = 1.5. However, sales can expand by $50 million, out to $100 million, with no additions to fixed assets. At that point, represented by Point B, the ratio FA/S = $75/$100 = 0.75. However, if the firm is operating at capacity (sales of $100 million), even a small increase in sales would require a doubling of plant capacity, so a small projected sales increase would bring with it very large financial requirements.[6]

In reality, most fixed assets are lumpy to some extent, so, when we include fixed assets among a firm's spontaneous assets (for a firm operating at full capacity), we should recognize that this is a simplification. For example, assume that

---

[5]For a more complete discussion of simple linear regression in financial forecasting, see J. Fred Weston and Eugene F. Brigham, *Essentials of Managerial Finance,* Tenth Edition, 1993, Chapter 7.

[6]Firms often make arrangements to share excess capacity with other firms in their industry. For example, consider the situation in the electric utility industry, which is very much like that depicted in Panel c. Electric companies often build jointly owned plants, or they "take turns" building plants and buy power from or sell power to other utilities to avoid building new plants that may be underutilized.

a firm is operating at full capacity with one plant and five pieces of machinery, model number KL-102. If this firm's sales are projected to increase by 20 percent next year, and if no additional shifts of workers can be added, it is possible to add one more machine, model KL-102, for a 20 percent increase in equipment, but it is *not* possible to add one-fifth of a new plant (incomplete plants tend to be both drafty and not very efficient). Still, in the end-of-chapter problems, you should assume that fixed assets are spontaneous when they are clearly included in A*/S and when you are not told otherwise.

An alternative approach to dealing with lumpy assets would be to do the following: (1) determine whether the firm is at full capacity; (2) include in the spontaneous assets, A*/S, only those assets that realistically increase in proportion to sales, mainly current assets; and (3) add into Equation 7-1 a new term, FA, representing those lumpy, fixed assets that must be purchased and/or built, and therefore financed, to reach the projected level of sales. We would then have the following equation:

$$AFN = A^*/S(\Delta S) + FA - L^*/S(\Delta S) - MS_1(1 - d) \qquad (7\text{-}2)$$

The only change is that fixed assets, FA, is now stated not as a percentage but simply as the estimated dollar amount of lumpy, fixed assets needed for the year in question.

Cyclical/Seasonal Changes

Panels a, b, and c of Figure 7-2 all focus on target, or projected, relationships between sales and assets. Actual sales, however, are often different from projected sales, and the actual asset/sales ratio for a given period may thus be quite different from the planned ratio. To illustrate, the firm depicted in Panel b of Figure 7-2 might, when its sales are at $200 million and its inventories at $300 million, project a sales expansion to $400 million and then increase its inventories to $400 million in anticipation of the projected growth. Yet suppose an unforeseen economic downturn held sales down to only $300 million. In this case, actual inventories would be $400 million, but inventories of only $350 million would be needed to support the actual sales of $300 million. If the firm were making its forecast for the following year, it would have to recognize that sales could expand by $100 million with no increase in inventories but that any sales expansion beyond $100 million would require additional financing to build inventories.

Modifying the Forecast of Additional Funds Needed

Someone once said "Forecasting is always difficult, especially when you are forecasting the future!" At this point, you should have gained some sympathy for individuals who make their living at this difficult task. We have seen in the Addison example that a firm's forecast of needed financing, *which must be lined up in advance,* is sensitive not only to the level of sales but also to many other variables. In addition, we have to start out with some set of assumptions, as we did in the percentage of sales method, which may not be a perfect representation of actual conditions for that firm.

Although the percentage of sales method provides, admittedly, only a rough estimate of projected asset needs and AFN, it is quite possible to refine, or modify, the forecast through seasoned judgment. In other words, a manager may *override* any one of the forecasted balance sheet or income statement items, *given a valid reason.* For example, if any of the asset/sales ratios that can be calculated from data in Table 7-2 are subject to any of the conditions noted earlier, then it will be necessary (1) to make separate forecasts of the requirements for each type of asset, (2) to forecast spontaneously generated funds, and (3) to subtract the spontaneously generated funds and the addition to retained earnings from the forecasted asset requirements to determine the external funds needed.

To illustrate, consider again the Addison example set forth in Tables 7-1, 7-2, and 7-3. Now suppose that a ratio analysis along the lines described in Chapter 6 suggests that the cash, receivables, and inventory ratios indicated by the data in Table 7-2 are appropriate, as are the liability ratios and the retained earnings calculations, but that excess capacity exists in fixed assets. Specifically, assume that in 1993 fixed assets were being utilized at only 80 percent of capacity. Also, assume that fixed assets are *not* considered lumpy. To use the existing fixed assets at full capacity, 1993 sales could have been as high as $500,000:

$$\text{Full capacity sales} = \frac{\text{Current sales}}{\% \text{ fixed assets operated}} = \frac{\$400,000}{0.80} = \$500,000.$$

This suggests that Addison's target fixed assets/sales ratio should be

$$\text{Target FA/Sales ratio} = \frac{\text{Current level of fixed assets}}{\text{Full capacity sales}} = \frac{\$300,000}{\$500,000} = 0.6,$$

not the 0.75 that actually exists. Therefore, at the projected sales level of $600,000, Addison would need fixed assets of only $0.6(\$600,000) = \$360,000$, up only $60,000 from the $300,000 currently on hand, rather than the increase of $150,000 which was forecasted by the percentage of sales method.

We estimated earlier, in Table 7-2, that Addison would need an additional $231,000 of capital and that at least $76,000 of this amount would have to be raised by selling common stock. However, those estimates were based on the assumption that $450,000 − $300,000 = $150,000 of additional fixed assets would be required. If Addison could attain a sales level of $600,000 with only $360,000 of fixed assets, then external funds needed would decline by $90,000, to $141,000, and no new stock would have to be issued.

Self-Test

Identify and describe three conditions under which the assumption that each spontaneous asset item increases at the same rate as sales is not correct.

Explain how one might adjust the AFN formula when fixed assets are mostly lumpy and a firm is at or close to full capacity.

Explain how one might adjust the AFN formula to calculate full capacity sales and the target FA/S ratio when excess capacity exists in fixed assets and fixed assets are treated as spontaneous.

Computerized Financial Planning Models

Although the type of financial forecasting described in this chapter can be done by hand, most well-managed firms with sales greater than a few million dollars employ some type of computerized financial planning model. Such models can be programmed to show the effects of different sales levels, different ratios of operating assets to sales, and different assumptions about sales prices and input costs (labor, materials, and so forth). Plans are then made regarding how financial requirements are to be met — through bank loans, thus increasing short-term notes payable; by selling long-term bonds; or by selling new common stock. Pro forma balance sheets and income statements are generated under the different financing plans, and earnings per share are projected, along with such risk measures as the current ratio, the total debt/total assets ratio, and the times-interest-earned ratio.

Depending on how these projections look, management may modify its initial plans. For example, the firm may conclude that its projected sales must be cut because the requirements for external capital exceed the firm's ability to obtain financing. Or management may decide to reduce dividends and thus generate more funds internally. Alternatively, the company may decide to investigate production processes that require fewer fixed assets, or it may consider the possibility of buying rather than manufacturing certain components, thus eliminating raw materials and work-in-process inventories, as well as certain manufacturing facilities. We have already discussed these options in connection with the Addison example.

In subsequent chapters we examine in detail ways of analyzing various types of policy change. In all such considerations, the basic issue is the effect that a specific action will have on future earnings, on the riskiness of earnings, and hence on the price of the firm's stock. Because computerized planning models help management assess these effects, they are playing an ever-growing role in corporate management.[7]

 Self-Test

Why are computerized planning models playing an increasingly important role in corporate management?

---

[7]It is becoming increasingly easy for companies to develop planning models as a result of the dramatic improvements that have been made in computer hardware and software in recent years. *Lotus 1-2-3* is one system that can be used, and a more elaborate system is the *Interactive Financial Planning System (IFPS)*. Both systems are used by literally thousands of companies, including 3M Corporation, Shell Oil, and Florida Power & Light. Increasingly, a knowledge of these or similar planning systems is becoming a requirement for getting even an entry-level job in the finance department of many corporations.

Note that in this chapter we have concentrated on long-run, or strategic, financial planning. Within the framework of the long-run strategic plan, firms also develop short-run financial plans. For example, in Table 7-2 we saw that Addison expects to need $231,000 by the end of 1994, and that it plans to raise this capital by using short-term debt, long-term debt, and common stock. However, we do not know *when* during the year the need for funds will occur, or when Addison will obtain each of its different types of capital. To address these issues, the firm must develop a short-run financial plan, the centerpiece of which is the *cash budget,* which is a projection of cash inflows and outflows on a daily, weekly, or monthly basis during the coming year (or other budget period). Although considering the cash budget here would complete our examination of the basic types of analysis done in connection with financial planning, we shall defer this discussion to Chapter 9 because cash budgets can best be understood after we have discussed the firm's target cash balance.

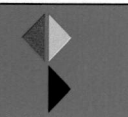

SMALL BUSINESS

FRANCHISING

As was mentioned in Chapter 1, small businesses often have both limited access to capital markets and limited human resourcs. What can a small business owner with limited resources do to fully capitalize on a great idea? There is an attractive avenue to follow, particularly if developing the idea requires both substantial capital and human resources that the owner can't provide; this avenue is called franchising.

Franchising involves other people's money, energy, and desire to own their own business to promote a concept originally developed by the franchiser. In an ideal franchise setting, the franchiser benefits by being able to expand the business with less capital outlay than traditional strategies. Regardless of the type of franchise selected (sale of product trade name or sale of a business format or conversion of an independent firm to an existing franchised company), the franchiser benefits as franchises are sold by having access to capital at lower risk by sharing the cost, rapid market penetration at a relatively lower cost, economies of scale, and a motivated work force. The franchisee has the opportunity to enter a business at less cost with a proven service or brand name.

Typically, the franchiser will have already paid the costs of product or service development and will have built one or more prototypes of the business which the franchiser can test for any "bugs" in the system. Thus, the franchisee is spared the expense of unanticipated problems with the business. Once the prototypes are successful, the franchiser is ready to begin marketing the franchises. The franchiser is paid a franchise fee and royalties on sales. When the franchise is purchased, the franchisee benefits by receiving specific benefits such as:

▶ An idea.
▶ A recognized trade name.
▶ A volume buying service.
▶ Advertising and market research.

▶ Training in operations.
▶ Plans and designs for facilities.
▶ Profit planning.

Everyone is familiar with McDonald's, Taco Bell, and other large, fast-food franchise operations. According to the International Franchise Association, consumers spent one-third of every retail dollar in 1992 at a franchise. Franchising typically has offered innovative product or service businesses that are niche driven and customer oriented; for example, video rentals, personnel services, exercise studios, repair services, and even medical care.

Successful Franchising
Over the last ten years, the franchising industry's size has more than doubled, and sales are approaching $800 billion. An attractive avenue of franchise growth in the 1990s, for example, is in the home-based sector. The ease of organizing from start-up, minimal capital requirements, low overhead, and the flexibility that it affords franchisees has made it popular domestically. A list of franchise investments requiring less that $30,000 include Chem-Dry, Jazzercise Inc., and Kinderdance International Inc., each suitable for home-based operations. A Choice Nanny, Coffee Beanery Ltd., Computertots, Cost Cutters, Shipping Connection Inc., Sox Appeal Franchising Inc., and Travelplex International Inc. are others of similar affordability to name a few.

Meanwhile, overseas franchising is expanding at a rapid pace. The International Franchise Association reported that more than 500 U.S. franchisers were operating in foreign countries since 1990. With the unification of the European market in 1992, Europe has become a key target for franchisers. On the other hand, franchisers expanding overseas must be prepared to deal with cultural and language differences, differences in consumer preferences, difficulties in obtaining supplies, and foreign exchange risk exposure.

Problems in Franchising
The foundation of any successful franchise system is a strong partnership between the franchiser and the franchisees. Franchisers have reported problems in the field that stem from inconsistencies in meeting the

Sources: "Franchising: Selecting a Strategy for Rapid Growth," *Long-Range Planning,* August 1991, 74–85; "An Upbeat Forecast for Franchising," *Nation's Business,* January 1993, 49–55; "Hot Franchises You Can Afford," *Working Woman,* April 1992, 50–52, 102; "The Best Franchises for Women," *Working Woman,* November 1992, 73–75, 97–101; and "Franchisees to Feel Financial Crunch of 1992," *Hotel and Motel Management,* January 13, 1992, 21–22, 24.

goals of the partnership, a lack of high-quality people interested in becoming franchisees, and maintaining quality control while growing rapidly. For example, early in the life of the franchise operation, the franchiser attempts to establish wide distribution and recognition. The franchiser may not initially be concerned about such matters as maintenance and remodeling of franchise locations since all of them are new. Later this can change. Such chains as Kentucky Fried Chicken (KFC), Howard Johnson, and Holiday Inn have hundreds of franchises, some dating back to the 1950s. Modernization of facilities is essential. But therein lies potential conflict. The franchiser desires a degree of control in the modernization, and the franchisee enjoys relative autonomy. Therefore, financing schemes providing remodeling incentives and matched funding have been offered by Howard Johnson and Holiday Inn, for example, to help franchisees with upgrades. When setting up the original franchise

agreement, it is difficult for a new franchiser to be far-sighted enough to anticipate all future problems. A sound agreement should, however, carefully delineate exactly who is required to do what.

Today's franchisees need to focus even more on the future than did their predecessors. Continued franchise success depends on high-quality franchisees who constantly evaluate the market in which they operate and who are consistently providing customers with value and convenience.

Conclusion

Small businesses suffer from resource poverty. Franchising can offer an alternative to help the business overcome some of its capital and human resource constraints. In a well-conceived franchise operation, both the franchiser and the franchisees benefit by their agreement to work together.

Summary

This chapter described in broad outline how firms project their financial statements and determine their capital requirements. The key concepts covered are listed below.

▶ **Pro forma,** or **projected, financial statements** are developed to help estimate the firm's future financial requirements.

▶ The **percentage of sales method** for forecasting financial statements is based on the assumptions (1) that certain balance sheet accounts vary directly with sales and (2) that the firm's existing level of assets is optimal for its sales volume.

▶ A firm can determine the amount of **additional funds needed (AFN)** by estimating the amount of new assets necessary to support the forecasted level of sales and then subtracting from that amount both the spontaneous funds that will be generated from operations and the addition to retained earnings.

The **balance sheet approach** sets up a complete **projected balance sheet,** as well as a brief forecasted income statement and a statement of cash flows. The **formula method** for forecasting AFN is a shortcut that gives us a quick estimate of the total amount of external funds needed. Neither method indicates, by itself, how much will be raised through short-term debt, long-term debt, and equity.

Among the **factors that help determine the actual mix** of short- and long-term financing and debt and equity financing will be the firm's desired (or required) risk ratios, the costs of different types of financing, and other constraints.

The firm will then enter into talks with financial institutions in order to raise the required AFN through bank borrowing, by issuing securities, or both.

▶ Five major variables that determine the firm's need for additional, external funds are (1) the **rate of growth,** (2) the **dividend policy,** (3) **capital intensity,** (4) **spontaneous liabilities,** and (5) the **profit margin.** The higher the rate of growth in sales, the higher the dividend payout ratio, and the more capital intensive the firm, the greater will be the firm's need for additional, external funds (AFN). On the other hand, the higher the spontaneous liabilities and the higher the profit margin the lower the firm's AFN.

▶ The percentage of sales method cannot be used if **economies of scale** exist in the use of assets, if **excess capacity** exists, or if some assets must be added in **lumpy increments.** If these conditions exist, we must modify our projection.

▶ The type of forecasting described in this chapter is important for several reasons: (1) If the projected operating results are unsatisfactory, management can "go back to the drawing board," reformulate its plans, and develop more reasonable targets for the coming year. (2) It is possible that the funds required to meet the sales forecast simply cannot be obtained; if so, it is obviously better to know this in advance and to scale back the projected level of operations than to suddenly run out of cash and have operations grind to a halt. (3) Even if the required funds can be raised, it is desirable to plan for their acquisition well in advance. As we shall see in later chapters, raising capital takes time, and both time and money can be saved by careful planning.

Resolution to
DECISION IN FINANCE

WHEN FORECASTS ARE WIDE OF THE MARK

Both Bristol-Myers and Sequoia are being sued by shareholders. The unpleasant surprise of sales projection goofs that resulted in lower earnings sent Bristol stock down 11 percent within a week of the June

1992 announcement. Angry stock purchasers claimed in their suit that Bristol deliberately misled investors. If wholesalers' actions did indeed cause the miscalculation by piling up inventory at the end of 1991, as Bristol claimed, the shareholders said it was Bristol's fault because it announced a price hike which would take place at the end of the year. The company should have known, the suit said, that wholesalers would then stock up on products before the

Sources: Laurel Touby, "That Queasy Feeling at Bristol-Myers," *Business Week,* August 10, 1992, 44–45; and John R. Wilke, "Sequoia Systems Remains Haunted by Phantom Sales," *The Wall Street Journal,* October 30, 1992.

new prices took effect, thus increasing 1991's numbers at the expense of 1992's.

Bristol had used price hikes in recent years to boost earnings, but increased competition makes that path an unlikely one for the future. Indeed, President Clinton's medical cost containment program may well lead to price reductions. Chief rival Merck is fighting the cheaper generics by developing and marketing its own, and Merck appears better able to come to grips with federally mandated cost controls.

Despite all its problems, however, Bristol insists it is well positioned for the future, with five new drugs approved and a consolidation plan that calls for closing or shrinking 15 plants by 1994. It announced plans to sell one of its consumer divisions, Drackett Company, maker of Drano and Windex. However, it is hanging on to other low-profitability units, and it has already gone astray on sales forecasts for one of its new drugs, which got off to a slower-than-expected start.

As for Sequoia, in addition to facing stockholder suits and an investigation by the SEC, it is trying to recover from the 80 percent plunge its stock took in the fall of 1992 from the previous year's price. A Salomon Brothers analyst said,

"They've almost completely wiped out their credibility." Attrition among top management included the CEO, who stepped aside; the CFO, who resigned; and a senior vice-president, who was fired. The latter was responsible for international sales and, despite the stalled Siberian and Polish deals, he said, "The business is there. . . . It is a solid opportunity." He also insisted that booking the incomplete sales as revenues "was supported by the revenue recognition policy that we had in place."

Richard Goldman, the new CFO and acting co-chief executive at Sequoia, says the company's problems were caused by a judgment error complicated by unforeseen events.

No one knows how long it will take Sequoia to overcome its crisis or whether there are more surprises in store. However, its products are sound, and it still has strong support from major computer companies. An executive at Hewlett-Packard, which owns 8 percent of Sequoia, says, "They have the best fault-tolerant technology and extremely well designed products." And an industry analyst, noting that sales of that technology are growing dramatically, says, "Sequoia is in a good position to benefit from that — if they get their act together."

Questions

7-1 Put a check ($\checkmark$) by those balance sheet accounts that typically increase spontaneously, and proportionately, with increases in sales.

Marketable securities	_____
Accounts receivable	_____
Accounts payable	_____
Notes payable to banks	_____
Accrued wages	_____
Accrued taxes	_____
Mortgage bonds	_____
Common stock	_____
Retained earnings	_____

7-2 The following equation can, under certain assumptions, be used to forecast financial requirements:

$$\text{Additional funds needed} = A^*/S(\Delta S) - L^*/S(\Delta S) - MS_1(1 - d).$$

Under what conditions does the equation give satisfactory predictions, and when should it not be used?

7-3 Assume that an average firm in the office supply business has a 6 percent after-tax profit margin, a 40 percent total debt/total assets ratio, a total assets turnover of 2 times, and a dividend payout ratio of 40 percent. Is it true that if such a firm is to have *any* sales growth ($g > 0\%$), it will be forced to sell either bonds or common stock (that is, will it need some nonspontaneous external capital, even if g is very small)?

7-4 Is it true that computerized corporate planning models were a fad during the 1970s, but, because of a need for flexibility in corporate planning, they have been dropped by most firms?

7-5 Suppose a firm makes the following policy changes. If the change means that external, nonspontaneous financial requirements for any rate of sales growth will increase, indicate this by a ($+$); indicate a decrease by a ($-$); and indicate indeterminate or no effect by a (0). Think in terms of the immediate, short-run effect on financial requirements.

  a. The dividend payout ratio is increased. _____
  b. The firm contracts to buy rather than make certain components used in its products. _____
  c. The firm decides to pay all suppliers on delivery, rather than after a 30-day delay, to take advantage of discounts for rapid payment. _____
  d. The firm begins to sell on credit; previously all sales had been on a cash basis. _____
  e. The firm's profit margin is eroded by increased competition; sales are steady. _____
  f. Advertising expenditures are stepped up. _____
  g. A decision is made to substitute long-term mortgage bonds for short-term bank loans. _____
  h. The firm begins to pay employees on a weekly basis; previously it paid them at the end of each month. _____

Self-Test Problems

ST-1 J. Sarwark Productions Inc., has the following ratios: $A^*/S = 1.6$; $L^*/S = 0.4$; profit margin = 0.10; and dividend payout ratio = 0.45. Sales last year were $100 million. Assuming that all these ratios will remain constant, what is the maximum growth rate Sarwark can achieve without having to obtain additional, external funds?

ST-2 Suppose Sarwark's financial consultants report (1) that the inventory turnover ratio is 3 times versus an industry average of 4 times and (2) that Sarwark could raise its turnover ratio to 4 times without affecting sales, the profit margin, or the other asset turnover ratios. Under these conditions, what amount of external funds would Sarwark require during each of the next 2 years if sales grew at a rate of 20 percent per year?

Problems

7-1

Pro forma balance sheet

A group of investors is planning to set up a new company, Kim-Sacks Inc. To help plan the new operation's financial requirements, you have been asked to construct a pro forma balance sheet for December 31, 1994, the end of the first year of operations. Sales for 1994 are projected at $30 million, and the following are industry average ratios for similar companies:

Sales to common equity	$5\times$
Current debt to equity	50%
Total debt to equity	80%
Current ratio	$2.2\times$
Net sales to inventory	$8\times$
Accounts receivable to sales	9%
Fixed assets to equity	70%
Profit margin	4%
Dividend payout ratio	20%

Kim-Sacks Inc.:
Pro Forma Balance Sheet, December 31, 1994 (Millions of Dollars)

Cash	$_____		Current debt	$_____
Accounts receivable	_____		Long-term debt	_____
Inventories	_____		Total debt	$_____
Total current assets	$_____		Common equity	_____
Net fixed assets	_____			
Total assets	$_____		Total liabilities and equity	$_____

a. Complete the preceding pro forma balance sheet, assuming that 1994 sales are $30 million.

b. If the group supplies all of the new firm's equity, how much external capital will it be required to put up by December 31, 1994?

7-2

Debt financing needed

At year-end 1993, Ramirez Company's total assets were $3.4 million. Sales, which were $5 million, will increase by 20 percent in 1994. The 1993 ratio of total assets to sales will be maintained in 1994. Common stock amounted to $850,000 in 1993, and retained earnings were $590,000. Spontaneous liabilities will continue to be 22 percent of sales in 1994, and the company plans to sell new common stock in the amount of $100,000. Net income is expected to be 5 percent of sales, and 60 percent of earnings will be paid out as dividends.

a. What was Ramirez Company's total debt in 1993?

b. How much new debt financing will be needed in 1994? (*Hint:* AFN − New stock = New debt.)

7-3

Ratios and short-term financing needed

QRM Health Systems has been growing at a rapid rate lately. As a result Mr. Quigley, one of the firm's founders, has been unable to devote proper attention to the management of the firm's assets. Expected sales for next year are $2.7 million with a net profit margin of 3 percent. The expected beginning-of-the-year retained earnings are $390,000, and current liabilities are $200,000. Long-term debt and common stock have remained constant for some time. Quigley computed the following financial ratios:

$$\text{Days sales outstanding} = 40 \text{ days,}$$

$$\text{Inventory turnover} = 6 \text{ times,}$$

$$\text{Fixed assets turnover} = 4 \text{ times.}$$

Quigley anticipates no dividend payout next year. Complete the following pro forma balance sheet. Short-term debt is the appropriate balancing item. According to your projections:

a. Including the expected increase in cumulative retained earnings, how much will QRM have to raise to support the expected level of sales?

b. How much of the total will be generated internally (equity) and externally (debt)?

c. What is QRM's debt ratio?

d. What is QRM's current ratio?

e. What is the firm's return on assets?

QRM Health Systems: Pro Forma Balance Sheet

Cash	$ 60,000		Short-term debt	$_____
Accounts receivable	_____		Long-term debt	375,000
Inventory	_____		Total debt	$_____
Total current assets	$_____		Common stock	150,000
Net fixed assets	_____		Retained earnings	_____
Total assets	$_____		Total liabilities and equity	$_____

7-4

After making the projections in Problem 7-3, Mr. Quigley is determined to streamline his company's balance sheet. He is certain that the days sales outstanding can be reduced to 32 days and that the inventory turnover can be increased to 7.5 times. He believes that cash and fixed assets will remain at their current levels, however. Make another projection regarding QRM's financial needs. Specifically:

a. How much will QRM have to raise to support sales under these new conditions?

b. How much of the total will be generated internally (equity) and externally (debt)?

c. What is QRM's debt ratio?

d. What is QRM's current ratio?

e. What is the firm's return on assets?

7-5

Greensburg Distributors Inc. has these ratios:

$$A^*/S = 1.3,$$

$$L^*/S = 0.5,$$

$$\text{Profit margin, } M = 8\%,$$

$$\text{Dividend payout ratio, } d = 40\%.$$

Sales last year were $150 million. Assuming that these ratios remain constant, what is the maximum growth rate the firm can achieve without having to obtain nonspontaneous external funds?

7-6

The 1993 balance sheet for Horan and Associates is shown below (in millions of dollars):

Cash	$12	Accounts payable and accruals	$20
Accounts receivable	12	Notes payable	10
Inventory	20	Long-term debt	18
Total current assets	$44	Total debt	$48
Net fixed assets	52	Common equity	48
Total assets	$96	Total liabilities and equity	$96

a. Management believes that sales will increase in the next year by 15 percent over the current level of $300 million. The profit margin is expected to be 5 percent, and the dividend payout will remain at 40 percent. If the firm has no excess capacity, what additional funding is required for 1994?

b. Horan and Associates would like to raise the additional funds needed calculated in Part a by issuing additional long-term debt. Would doing so violate an agreement with bondholders that total debt should not exceed 50 percent of total assets?

7-7

Refer to Problem 7-6. Assume that all relationships hold *except* for the capacity constraint. *Now* assume that the firm has excess capacity and that no increase in fixed assets will be required to support the sales increase. Under this new condition, how much additional funding will be required for 1994?

7-8

A firm has the following balance sheet and other data (in thousands of dollars):

Cash	$ 20	Accounts payable	$ 20
Accounts receivable	20	Notes payable	40
Inventories	20	Long-term debt	80
Net fixed assets	180	Common stock	80
		Retained earnings	20
Total assets	$240	Total liabilities and equity	$240

Fixed assets are being used at 80 percent of capacity, sales for the year just ended were $400,000, sales will increase $20,000 per year for the next 4 years, the profit margin is 5 percent, and the dividend payout ratio is 60 percent. What are the total outside financing requirements for the entire 4 years? (Assume that fixed assets cannot be sold.)

7-9

AFN equation

Ogawa Inc. expects its 1994 sales to be 30 percent above the 1993 sales of $145 million. In 1993, assets which varied directly with sales equaled $113.1 milion, and spontaneous liabilities were $37.7 million. These relationships are likely to hold in 1994. Ogawa's profit margin is expected to be 6.2 percent in 1994, and management wants to continue a dividend payout rate of 40 percent. Using the percentage of sales method, calculate the amount of additional, external financing the firm will need in 1994.

7-10

AFN equation

Calculate the total assets for BentCo given the following information: Sales this year = $1,500,000; increase in sales projected for next year = 20 percent; net income this year = $105,000; dividend payout ratio = 40 percent; projected external funds needed next year = $59,400; accounts payable = $300,000; notes payable = $50,000; accrued wages and taxes = $225,000. (*Note:* The company is operating at full capacity, and all its assets are considered to be spontaneous.)

7-11

Additional funds needed

Riverside Garden Center has estimated that the following balance sheet accounts from this year should equal the same percentages of next year's sales:

Cash	$ 90,000	(5%)	Payables	$342,000	(19%)
Receivables	396,000	(22%)	Accruals	180,000	(10%)
Inventory	666,000	(37%)			

The forecasted sales level for next year represents a $450,000 increase over this year's sales. In keeping with past dividend policy, management plans to pay out $56,925 in dividends next year and retain $46,575. The firm has excess capacity and therefore does not need new fixed assets.

a. How much additional, external financing does Riverside need next year?

b. If Riverside has to maintain a current ratio of at least 2, how much of the projected external financing can be short-term bank loans? (Assume that the firm has no short-term debt at this time other than payables and accruals.)

c. What is the expected profit margin and dividend payout ratio for next year?

d. Now assume that one of Riverside's competitors has just gone out of business. This creates an opportunity for Riverside to increase its sales dramatically next year to $3.5 million by purchasing the other firm's building and land for $500,000. There will still be some excess capacity at the original garden center, but that cannot be helped. Treat this as a lumpy fixed asset, and use Equation 7-2 to calculate Riverside's AFN for next year if it goes ahead with the purchase and realizes $3.5 million in combined sales. (Profit margin and dividend payout ratio are assumed to be unchanged, as are A^*/S and L^*/S.)

7-12

Additional funds needed — excess capacity

Ameritronic's December 31, 1993, balance sheet is given below (in millions of dollars):

Cash	$ 20	Accounts payable	$ 40
Accounts receivable	50	Notes payable	40
Inventory	80	Accrued wages and taxes	20
Net fixed assets	150	Long-term debt	60
		Common equity	140
Total assets	$300	Total liabilities and equity	$300

Sales during 1993 were $200 million, and they were expected to rise by 50 percent to $300 million during 1994. Also, during 1993, fixed assets were being utilized to only 80 percent of capacity; that is, Ameritronic could have supported $200 million of sales with fixed assets that were only 80 percent of the actual 1993 fixed assets. Assuming that Ameritronic's profit margin will remain constant at 5 percent and that the company will continue to pay out 60 percent of its earnings as dividends, what amount of non-spontaneous external funds will be needed during 1994?

7-13

Pro forma statements
and ratios

Knapp Computers makes bulk purchases of small computers, stocks them in conveniently located warehouses, and then ships them to its chain of retail stores. Knapp's balance sheet as of December 31, 1993, is shown here (in millions of dollars):

Cash	$ 3.0	Accounts payable	$ 7.0
Accounts receivable	22.5	Notes payable	15.0
Inventories	49.5	Accruals	8.0
Total current assets	$ 75.0	Total current liabilities	$ 30.0
Net fixed assets	30.3	Mortgage bonds	5.1
		Common stock	12.6
		Retained earnings	57.6
Total assets	$105.3	Total liabilities and equity	$105.3

Sales for 1993 were $300 million, while net income for the year was $9 million. Knapp paid dividends of $3.6 million to common stockholders. The firm is operating at full capacity.

a. If sales are projected to increase by $75 million, or by 25 percent, during 1994, what are Knapp's projected external capital requirements?

b. Construct Knapp's pro forma balance sheet for December 31, 1994. Assume that all external capital requirements are met by bank loans and are reflected in notes payable.

c. Now calculate the following ratios, based on your projected December 31, 1994, balance sheet. Knapp's 1993 ratios and industry average ratios are shown here for comparison.

	Knapp Computers Dec. 31, 1994	Knapp Computers Dec. 31, 1993	Industry Average Dec. 31, 1993
Current ratio	_____	2.5×	3×
Total debt/total assets	_____	33.3%	30%
Return on equity	_____	12.8%	12%

If Knapp's restrictions on the use of additional debt are that (1) the current ratio may not decline below 2 and (2) the debt ratio may not exceed 45 percent, can the firm raise all the funds needed through short-term bank loans?

d. Now assume that Knapp grows by the same $75 million but that the growth is spread over 5 years; that is, sales grow by $15 million each year.

1. Calculate total external financial requirements over the 5-year period.

2. Construct a pro forma balance sheet as of December 31, 1998, using notes payable as the balancing item.

3. Calculate the current ratio, debt ratio, and return on equity as of December 31, 1998. [*Hint:* Be sure to use *total sales,* which amount to $1,725 million, to calculate retained earnings, but use 1998 profits to calculate the return on equity — that is, (1998 profits)/(December 31, 1998, equity).]

e. Set up a modified Du Pont equation for Knapp (1) using data from Parts a through c and (2) using data from Part d, where the 25 percent growth is spread over five years instead of one. Use this equation to explain why the ROE ratio is lower when Knapp grows more slowly. Next, look at the current ratio, and comment on the firm's risk and expected return under each scenario.

7-14

Additional funds needed

Embry International's 1993 sales were $36 million. Each of the following balance sheet items varies directly with sales and each account can be calculated as a percentage of sales as follows:

Cash	3%
Accounts receivable	20
Inventories	25
Net fixed assets	40
Accounts payable	15
Accruals	10
Profit margin on sales	5

The dividend payout ratio is 40 percent; the December 31, 1992, balance sheet account for retained earnings was $12.3 million; and both common stock and mortgage bonds are constant and equal to the amounts shown on the following balance sheet.
a. Complete the following balance sheet.

Embry International:
Balance Sheet, December 31, 1993
(Thousands of Dollars)

Cash	$_____	Accounts payable	$_____	
Accounts receivable	_____	Notes payable	3,300	
Inventories	_____	Accruals	_____	
Total current assets	$_____	Total current liabilities	$_____	
Net fixed assets	_____	Mortgage bonds	3,000	
		Common stock	3,000	
		Retained earnings	_____	
Total assets	$_____	Total liabilities and equity	$_____	

b. Now suppose that 1994 sales increase by 10 percent over 1993 sales. How much additional, external capital will be required? The company was operating at full capacity in 1993. Use both the balance sheet methodology and Equation 7-1 to answer this question.

c. Develop a finalized pro forma balance sheet for December 31, 1994, showing any required financing as notes payable.

d. What would happen to external funds requirements under each of the following conditions? Answer in words, without calculations.
  1. The profit margin went (i) from 5 to 7 percent, (ii) from 5 to 3 percent.
  2. The dividend payout ratio (i) was raised from 40 to 90 percent, (ii) was lowered from 40 to 20 percent.
  3. Credit terms on sales were relaxed substantially, giving customers longer to pay.
  4. The company had excess manufacturing capacity on December 31, 1993.

7-15

Excess capacity

Adamson & Wien's 1993 sales were $100 million. Each of the following balance sheet items except notes payable, mortgage bonds, and common stock varies directly with sales and each account can be calculated as a percentage of sales as follows:

Cash	4%
Accounts receivable	25
Inventory	30
Net fixed assets	50
Accounts payable	15
Accruals	5
Profit margin on sales	5

The dividend payout ratio is 60 percent; the December 31, 1992, balance sheet account for retained earnings was $58 million; and both common stock and mortgage bonds are constant and equal to the amounts shown on the following balance sheet.
a. Complete the following balance sheet.

Adamson & Wien:
Balance Sheet, December 31, 1993
(Millions of Dollars)

Cash	$_____	Accounts payable	$_____
Accounts receivable	_____	Notes payable	9.5
Inventory	_____	Accruals	_____
Total current assets	$_____	Total current liabilities	$_____
Net fixed assets	_____	Mortgage bonds	13.5
		Common stock	6.0
		Retained earnings	_____
Total assets	$_____	Total liabilities and equity	$_____

b. Assume that the company was operating at full capacity in 1993 with regard to all items *except* fixed assets; had the fixed assets been used to full capacity, the fixed assets/sales ratio would have been 40 percent in 1993. By what percentage could 1994 sales increase over 1993 sales without the need for an increase in fixed assets?

c. Now suppose that 1994 sales increase by 20 percent over 1993 sales. How much additional, external capital will be required? Assume the same condition as in Part b with respect to fixed assets and that Adamson & Wien cannot sell any fixed assets. Assume that any required financing is borrowed as notes payable.

d. Suppose the industry averages for receivables and inventories are 20 percent and 25 percent, respectively, and that the firm matches these figures in 1994 and then uses the funds released to reduce equity. (It could pay a special dividend out of retained earnings.) What would this do to the return on year-end 1994 equity?

7-16
Additional funds needed

The 1993 sales of Marsh's Department Store were $3 million. Common stock and notes payable are constant. The dividend payout ratio is 50 percent. Retained earnings as shown on the December 31, 1992, balance sheet were $105,000. Each of the following balance sheet items varies directly with sales, and each account can be calculated as a percentage of sales as follows:

Cash	4%
Accounts receivables	10
Inventory	20
Net fixed assets	35
Accounts payable	12
Accruals	6
Profit margin on sales	3

a. Complete the balance sheet that follows.

Marsh's Department Store:
Balance Sheet, December 31, 1993

Cash	$	Accounts payable	$
Accounts receivables	_____	Notes payable	130,000
Inventory	_____	Accruals	_____
Total current assets	$	Total current liabilities	$
Net fixed assets	_____	Common stock	1,250,000
		Retained earnings	_____
Total assets	$_____	Total liabilities and equity	$_____

b. Suppose that in 1994 sales will increase by 10 percent over 1993 sales levels. How much additional capital will be required? Assume that the firm operated at full capacity in 1993.

    c. Construct the year-end 1994 balance sheet. Assume that 50 percent of the additional capital required will be financed by selling common stock and the remainder by borrowing as notes payable.

    d. If the profit margin remains at 3 percent and the dividend payout rate remains at 50 percent, at what growth rate in sales will the additional financing requirements be exactly zero?

Solutions to Self-Test Problems

ST-1   To solve this problem, we will use the three following equations:

$$\Delta S = S_0(g).$$

$$S_1 = S_0(1 + g).$$

$$AFN = A^*/S(\Delta S) - L^*/S(\Delta S) - MS_1(1 - d).$$

Set $AFN = \$0$, substitute in known values for A^*/S, L^*/S, M, d, and S_0, and then solve for g:

$$\$0 = 1.6(\$100g) - 0.4(\$100g) - 0.1[\$100(1 + g)](0.55)$$

$$= \$160g - \$40g - 0.055(\$100 + \$100g)$$

$$= \$160g - \$40g - \$5.5 - \$5.5g$$

$$\$114.5g = \$5.5$$

$$g = \$5.5/\$114.5 = 0.048 = 4.8\% = \quad \begin{array}{l}\text{Maximum growth rate} \\ \text{without external financing.}\end{array}$$

ST-2   Note that assets consist of cash, marketable securities, receivables, inventories, and fixed assets. Therefore, we can break the A^*/S ratio into its components — cash/sales, inventories/sales, and so forth. Then

$$A^*/S = \frac{A^* - \text{Inventories}}{S} + \frac{\text{Inventories}}{S} = 1.6.$$

We know that the inventory turnover ratio is sales/inventories = 3 times, so inventories/sales = $\frac{1}{3}$ = 0.3333. Furthermore, if the inventory turnover ratio could be increased to 4 times, then the inventories/sales ratio would fall to $\frac{1}{4}$ = 0.25, a difference of 0.3333 − 0.2500 = 0.0833. This, in turn, would cause the A^*/S ratio to fall from A^*/S = 1.6 to A^*/S = 1.6 − 0.0833 = 1.5167.

    This change would have two effects: (1) it would change the AFN equation, and (2) it would mean that Sarwark currently has excessive inventories, so there could be some sales growth without any additional inventories. Therefore, we could set up the revised AFN equation, estimate the funds needed next year, and then subtract out the excess inventories currently on hand:

Present conditions:

$$\frac{\text{Sales}}{\text{Inventories}} = \frac{\$100}{\text{Inventories}} = 3,$$

so

$$\text{Current level of inventories} = \$100/3 = \$33.3 \text{ million.}$$

New conditions:

$$\frac{\text{Sales}}{\text{Inventories}} = \frac{\$100}{\text{Inventories}} = 4,$$

so

$$\text{New level of inventories} = \$100/4 = \$25 \text{ million.}$$

Therefore,

$$\text{Excess inventories} = \$33.3 - \$25 = \$8.3 \text{ million.}$$

Forecast of funds needed, first year:

$$\Delta S \text{ in first year} = 0.2(\$100 \text{ million}) = \$20 \text{ million.}$$

$$AFN = 1.5167(\$20) - 0.4(\$20) - 0.1(\$120)(0.55) - \$8.3$$

$$= \$30.3 - \$8 - \$6.6 - \$8.3$$

$$= \$7.4 \text{ million.}$$

Forecast of funds needed, second year:

$$\Delta S \text{ in second year} = 0.2(\$120 \text{ million}) = \$24 \text{ million.}$$

$$AFN = 1.5167(\$24) - 0.4(\$24) - 0.1(\$144)(0.55)$$

$$= \$36.4 - \$9.6 - \$7.9$$

$$= \$18.9 \text{ million.}$$

MINI CASE	COMPUTER MODELING: EXTERNAL FINANCING REQUIREMENTS AND RATIOS

Corcoran, Case & Wolfe (CCW) has emerged as one of the true growth companies of the 1980s and early 1990s. The firm designs and builds trash-to-energy plants throughout the eastern United States and has become a leader in the field of waste management. However, the rapid growth in sales has caused an almost constant need for additional, external funds, and CCW, therefore, pays out only a token dividend equal to 10 percent of each year's earnings. The firm's profit margin was 9 percent in 1993, and this percentage is expected to apply to 1994 as well. Assume that the following balance sheet accounts have historically been fairly stable percentages of sales as shown below:

Cash	5%	Account payable	22%
Accounts receivable	34	Accruals	14
Inventories	40		
Net fixed assets	55		

Further assume that at year-end 1993 the following was true:

▷ Cumulative retained earnings = $25,500,000.

▷ Notes payable = $2,000,000.

▷ Common stock (no par) = $26,600,000.

▷ Marketable securities = $0.

▷ Long-term debt = $14,500,000.

▷ CCW is operating at full capacity.

▷ Fixed assets are not considered to be lumpy.

CCW's 1994 sales are expected to increase by 25 percent over 1993's sales of $70 million, and management wants to use the percentage of sales method to forecast its 1994 need for additional, external funds.

Using *Lotus 1-2-3,* do the following:

a.   State the basic assumptions of the problem. This means that you need to read through the entire problem, and isolate those variables that change as well as any other quantitative information needed for your calculations (for example, 1993 cumulative retained earnings, the given spontaneous percentages, the rate of growth in sales, etc.). Display this information in the upper left-hand corner of the spreadsheet. This is called an "assumption block."

b.   Construct CCW's statement of retained earnings for 1994, based on the above information, and complete the following pro forma balance sheet. Note that notes payable, long-term debt, and common stock are assumed to be unchanged from 1993 and that AFN appears as a separate (temporary) account among long-term claims. In the event that this account is negative, it would indicate funds available.

While you could certainly use Equation 7-1 to calculate AFN, this is rather cumbersome in Lotus 1-2-3 and other spreadsheets. Recognize, however, that AFN is simply the dollar amount that, in each case, forces total liabilities and equity to equal total assets. This should suggest to you a much simpler equation. You may then *confirm* the dollar amount calculated for AFN in this manner through a pencil-and-paper calculation of AFN using Equation 7-1. The two AFNs should agree (giving you a check figure!), the balance sheet should balance, and when you have accomplished this, you should have some confidence in your model.

Corcoran, Case & Wolfe:
Balance Sheet as of December 31, 1994

Assets		Claims on assets	
Cash	$ _____	Accounts payable	$ _____
Accounts receivable	$ _____	Notes payable	$ 2,000,000
Inventory	$ _____	Accruals	$ _____
Total current assets	$ _____	Total current liabilities	$ _____
Net fixed assets	$ _____	Long-term debt	$14,500,000
		AFN	$ _____
		Common stock	$26,600,000
		Retained earnings	$ _____
Total assets	$ _____	Total liabilities and equity	$ _____

The real power of electronic spreadsheets is the ability to perform sensitivity analysis (answer "what if" questions). It is, therefore, crucial that you set up your model, in this case a balance sheet, such that the stated assumptions in Part a are the underlying determinants of the dollar amounts shown in the balance sheet. A change in any one of the assumptions in Part a will then automatically change the dollar amount of additional, external funds needed, AFN. In other words, be sure to use formulas, and refer back up to earlier cell addresses wherever appropriate.

Assuming that the additional funds needed, AFN, will be raised as additional long-term debt, calculate CCW's: (1) debt ratio, (2) current ratio, and (3) return on equity. Save assumption block, pro forma balance sheet, and ratios as CCW-B. Print all of this. If you have set up your model correctly, the sensitivity analysis in Parts c through f should take very little time to complete.

c. After some discussion of recent cost-cutting measures, management comes to the conclusion that 1994's profit margin is more likely to be 11 percent, on the same level of sales as previously projected for 1994. This will *not* affect 1993's profit margin or other financial data for 1993. What will be the new AFN? Other assumptions as in Part b. Answer the question by printing assumption block, balance sheet, and ratios. Save as CCW-C.

d. Continue with all assumptions from Part c, except for sales. If 1994 sales were to increase by 40 percent over 1993 sales, what difference would this make? Answer by providing yet another complete printout. Save as CCW-D.

e. CCW is constrained by its existing long-term debt contract, which states that new debt may only be issued if the debt ratio stays below 50 percent. Given all other assumptions as in Part d, what is the maximum rate of growth that the firm can achieve and not exceed a 50 percent debt ratio? Find through trial and error. (*Note:* It is useful to *duplicate* the debt ratio somewhere close to the cell containing the rate of growth in sales so that you can keep an eye on it while you experiment.) Print out everything and save as CCW-E.

f. Find the approximate rate of growth at which CCW can support the level of sales entirely from spontaneous liabilities and retained earnings. In other words, find the rate of growth in sales where AFN is approximately $0, again through trial and error. (Now, duplicate *AFN* near the assumption block, and watch it change as you gradually change the rate of growth.)

g. Note that ROE should be different in each part of the analysis. Finally, answer two questions: (1) Would any of the cases violate a restriction that the current ratio must not drop below 2? (2) Would it make any difference if CCW wanted to raise a portion of AFN through short-term borrowing? Simply type in your answers on the spreadsheet. Print out everything and save as CCW-FG.

Working Capital Management

Most financial managers would tell you that the greater part of their work day is taken up with managing and financing the firm's short-term assets. Thus, this section devotes four chapters to the important topic of working capital policy and management.

Chapter 8 deals primarily with policy decisions and demonstrates that the level of current assets and how those assets are financed contribute significantly to the firm's profitability and risk exposure. Then, in the next two chapters we turn to the management of four current asset accounts: Chapter 9 considers cash and marketable securities, while Chapter 10 analyzes accounts receivable and inventories. Finally, in Chapter 11, we discuss the various types of short-term credit that can be used to finance current assets.

Working Capital Policy and Management

OBJECTIVES

After reading this chapter, you should be able to:

▶ List the two main areas in which managers make working capital decisions.

▶ Define basic working capital terminology.

▶ Calculate the cash conversion cycle for a given firm and explain each of the four terms used in this model.

▶ Distinguish between a conservative and an aggressive working capital **investment** policy, and explain the effect of each on risk and expected return.

▶ Explain what is meant by permanent current assets, temporary current assets, and maturity matching.

▶ Distinguish between a conservative and an aggressive working capital **financing** policy, and explain the effect of each on risk and expected return.

▶ Discuss the pros and cons of short-term credit.

DECISION IN FINANCE

FLORIDA ORANGE SPRINGS INC. — ABUNDANCE OF WATER, SHORTAGE OF WORKING CAPITAL

Orange Springs, near Ocala, has perhaps the best water in Florida, and it is also one of the largest privately owned springs in the state. Recognizing the spring's potential as a source of bottled water, Roger Wood, a real estate developer, purchased the property in 1986, founded Florida Orange Springs Inc. (FOS) in 1989, and entered the rapidly growing bottled water business.

FOS targeted three market segments: (1) bulk sales to large, established bottlers for bottling under those bottlers' own labels; (2) retail sales in five-gallon containers to offices and homes in the north central Florida area; and (3) wholesale sales to supermarkets and convenience stores. Bulk sales were neither very profitable nor very dependable, but they did provide badly needed cash flow, and they could be made without much capital investment. Retail sales, on the other hand were both profitable and stable, and FOS's business plan called for "locking up" that segment of the market in the Jacksonville-Gainesville-Ocala area before the "majors" could move in and preempt it. And for additional growth, FOS was counting on the wholesale market, which is where most industry growth is occurring.

Wood purchased the spring and 85 surrounding acres with his own funds (and a mortgage from the people who sold him the property), and he obtained additional capital from ten private investors. That money was sufficient to construct a bottling plant and to get the company started. However, FOS experienced an unexpected capital shortage that delayed full implementation of its business plan and even threatened the company's future.

The marketing program was successful — FOS was signing up doctors, lawyers, and homeowners for its retail business, and it was close to closing deals with such major supermarkets as Publix, the largest grocery chain in Florida. The deal with Publix called for FOS to bottle water for Publix under Publix's own label, and the company was seeking other private label business as well as promoting its own brand name. But instead of

See end of chapter for resolution.

Photo source: Telegraph Colour Library/FPG International Corp.

solving the cash flow problem, new business was making the financial problem worse!

As you read this chapter, consider how firms plan for, manage, and finance their working capital needs. How important is short-term planning?

How does short-term planning contribute to the success of a company? Think about the reasons for FOS's cash flow shortage in spite of its increasing sales.

In Part II we saw that a firm's investment in assets is closely related to its present and projected sales. We shall see in later chapters how a firm's risk, profitability, and stock price are influenced by its investment into fixed assets and its long-term financing. However, in the next four chapters we will focus on what is commonly called *working capital management,* and we will deal with two very important questions:

1. How much should be invested into each category of current assets?
2. How should the current asset investment be financed?

Chapter 8 will provide an overview of both of these topics.

About 60 percent of a financial manager's time is devoted to working capital management, and many finance students' first assignments on the job will be in this area. These are two reasons working capital management is important. A third reason is that, in this respect as in many others in financial management, decisions made will have an impact on both the risk and the expected return of the firm, and, since a typical firm has about 40 percent of its capital invested in current assets, that impact is significant.

Working Capital Terminology

The term *working capital* originated in the days when the old Yankee peddler would load up his wagon with goods and then go off on his route to sell his wares. The merchandise was defined as his "working capital" because it was actually sold or "turned over" to produce profits; the wagon and horse were his fixed assets. If he bought $4,000 of goods and sold them for $5,000, he would make $1,000 per trip. If he made five trips per year, he would turn over his working capital five times and make a profit of $5 \times \$1,000 = \$5,000$ for the year.

The days of the Yankee peddler have long since passed, but the importance of working capital remains. Financial managers spend more of their daily time and energy on working capital matters than on any other single function discussed in this text. In contrast, the choice of business projects and the associated fixed asset commitment occurs, for most firms, perhaps once or twice a year. It is useful to begin our discussion of working capital by defining (in some cases reviewing) several basic terms and concepts:

working capital

A firm's investment in short-term assets — cash, marketable securities, inventory, and accounts receivable.

1. **Working capital,** sometimes called *gross working capital,* simply refers to the firm's total current assets (often called *short-term assets*) — cash, marketable securities, accounts receivable, and inventory.

net working capital

Current assets minus current liabilities; also equal to the current assets financed by long-term funds.

2. **Net working capital** is defined as current assets minus current liabilities. As we discuss later in this chapter, net working capital is, therefore, the current assets financed by long-term funds.

3. One key working capital ratio is the *current ratio,* which was defined in Chapter 6 as current assets divided by current liabilities. This ratio is intended to measure a firm's liquidity, or its ability to meet obligations that will come due within a year. However, a high current ratio does not ensure that a firm will have the cash required to meet its needs. If inventories cannot be sold and receivables cannot be collected in a timely manner, then the apparent safety reflected in a high current ratio would be an illusion.

4. The *quick,* or *acid test,* ratio was discussed in Chapter 6 as well and was defined as current assets minus inventories, divided by current liabilities. This ratio, which also measures liquidity, removes inventories (the least liquid current asset) from total current assets, and it thus provides an "acid test" of a company's ability to meet its current obligations.

5. In Chapter 5, the importance of a firm's *cash flows* from operations was stressed—the actual cash, as opposed to accounting income, that flows into or out of the firm during a specified period, such as a year. For example, in Carter Chemical Company's statement of cash flows we saw that the increase in accumulated depreciation from one year to the next provided a source of funds. This was not reflected in the firm's current and quick ratios, and, for this reason as well as others, the two ratios cannot be said to provide a complete picture of the firm's liquidity. As we concluded in Chapter 6, ratios should provide only a starting point in analyzing a firm's financial position. In the next section, we will look at the concept of the *cash conversion cycle,* yet another tool used by managers in trying to estimate the firm's liquidity and its need for financing.

6. The best and most comprehensive picture of a firm's liquidity position is obtained by examining its *cash budget.* This statement, which forecasts cash inflows and outflows, focuses on what really counts, the firm's ability to generate sufficient cash inflows to meet its required cash outflows within a given time period such as a month or even a week. We will discuss cash budgeting in detail in Chapter 9.

working capital policy

Basic policy decisions regarding target levels for each category of current assets and how current assets will be financed.

7. **Working capital policy** refers to the firm's basic policies regarding the target levels for each category of current assets as well as policies concerning how current assets will be financed.

working capital management

The administration, within policy guidelines, of current assets and current liabilities.

8. **Working capital management** involves the administration, within policy guidelines, of current assets and current liabilities. Important elements of working capital management include cash management, credit and collections, inventory management, and short-term borrowings.

While long-term financial analysis primarily concerns strategic planning, working capital management deals with day-to-day operations—making sure that production lines do not stop because the firm runs out of raw materials, that inventories do not build up because production continues unchanged when sales dip, that customers pay on time, and that enough cash is on hand to make payments when they are due. Obviously, without good working capital management, no firm can be efficient and profitable.

Self-Test

Which two important questions are dealt with in working capital management?

Where did the term "working capital" originate?

What is meant by the term "liquidity"?

Overview of the Cash Conversion Cycle

Let us return to the Yankee peddler. He generally owned the horse and wagon, so these were financed with equity, but he borrowed the funds to buy inventory, his working capital. The borrowed funds were, therefore, called working capital loans, and they had to be repaid after each trip to show the banker that the credit was sound. If the peddler was able to repay the loan, the bank would then extend a new loan, and the peddler would set out again to turn over his merchandise and, in the process, realize a profit for himself. This cycle would be repeated. The bank would earn interest on the short-term loans and would be following sound banking practices by making sure that each previous loan could be repaid before a new loan was extended.

The general concept of the *working capital cash flow cycle* just described is still valid today and may be applied to much more complex businesses. The essence of the concept is that (1) the longer the cycle and (2) the greater the investment into working capital per cycle, the greater the need for external financing, such as short-term bank loans. This cycle is frequently called the *cash conversion cycle* because it is the process of converting cash into inventory which is sold—often on credit, in which case receivables result—and ultimately cash is again available and may be reinvested into current assets. Profits generated through this cycle will, in turn, increase equity. Figure 8-1 shows the short-term financial operations of the firm and their effects on its current asset and current liability accounts.

For illustrative purposes, we will consider Addison Products, for which we have already presented pro forma financial statements in Chapter 7. On December 31, 1994, Addison expects to have $15,000 in cash. Addison has received information from its forecasting department about an increase in the demand for its product. Addison must accommodate this demand increase, or it will lose market share to its competitors. Thus, Addison places orders for additional materials to produce more inventory. The $15,000 is not enough to pay for the entire materials order, so Addison must purchase on credit from its suppliers, creating an account payable on Addison's balance sheet. Addison will sell its inventory for more than cost, creating a profit for the firm. Addison makes both cash and credit sales; however, when credit sales are made an account receivable is created at the time of sale, and the money is received from the customer at a later date. Then, Addison will use the cash to pay off the account payable, and the cycle repeats itself in a continuous, ongoing manner. Of course, the amount of cash the firm has on hand at the end of each cycle will be higher than at the beginning of each cycle because of the profit made on sales.

However, Addison's accounts payable may have to be paid before the firm's receivables have been collected, and this will require some type of financing, typically short-term bank loans. The proceeds from this financing will be used

Figure 8-1   Short-Term Financial Operations: Working Capital Management

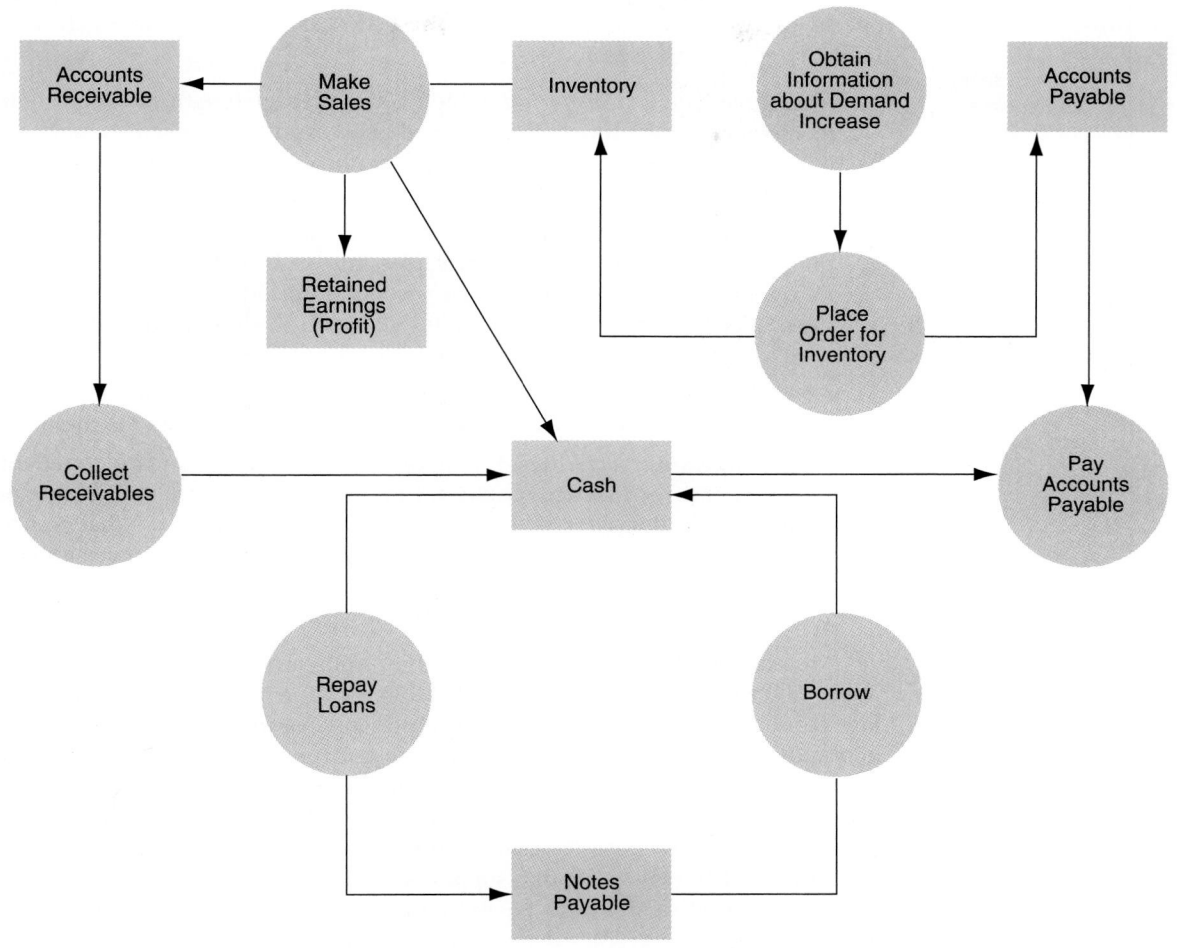

Short-term financial operations affect the firm's current assets and current liabilities. The firm starts with some cash on hand and receives information on the demand for its product. On the basis of this forecast the firm orders materials to produce inventories of finished goods (a current asset), which it then sells to customers. When the firm orders materials, it creates an account payable (a current liability). When the firm sells inventory, it either receives cash directly from the sale or receives a promise to pay from the customer — an account receivable. When the firm collects the account receivable, it receives cash. This cycle repeats itself many times during the course of the year, and the firm typically needs external financing, such as short-term bank loans, to complete each working capital cycle. (In this figure, squares represent accounts, and circles represent actions.)

to pay suppliers, so when cash is collected from receivables, it will be used to pay off the loans that were obtained to finance production. If we look again at the projected balance sheet for Addison Products, we see that short-term debt (notes payable) has been estimated at $15,000 for December 31, 1994.

This concept of the cash conversion cycle is important in working capital management. In Figure 8-1 we generalize the cycle without adding numbers to

cash conversion cycle

The length of time from the payment for raw materials and labor to the collection of accounts receivable generated by the sale of the final product.

the picture; however, numbers could be added to this analysis. In fact, Verlyn Richards and Eugene Laughlin developed a useful approach for analyzing the cash conversion cycle.[1] Their approach centers on the conversion of operating events to cash flows, and thus it is called the **cash conversion cycle** model. Here are the terms used in the model:

1. *Inventory conversion period,* which is the average length of time required to convert raw materials into finished goods and then to sell these goods. Note that the inventory conversion period can be calculated as 360 days divided by the inventory turnover ratio (Sales/Inventory).

2. *Receivables conversion period,* which is the average length of time required to convert the firm's receivables into cash — that is, to collect cash following a sale. The receivables conversion period is also called the days sales outstanding (DSO), and it was calculated in Chapter 6 as Receivables/Average sales per day = Receivables/(Sales/360).

3. *Payables deferral period,* which is the average length of time between the purchase of raw materials and labor and the cash payments for them.

4. *Cash conversion cycle,* which nets out the three periods just defined and which equals the average length of time from the firm's actual cash expenditures on productive resources (raw materials and labor) — that is, from the day labor and suppliers are paid — to the day receivables are collected. Thus, the cash conversion cycle measures the length of time, on average, that the firm has funds tied up in current assets.

We can use these definitions to analyze Addison's cash conversion cycle. In Table 8-1 we give the December 31, 1994, pro forma financial statements and key ratios for Addison that were developed in Chapter 7. We will use these to generate some of the numbers for the cash conversion cycle analysis. Addison's inventory turnover is 2 times. Thus, Addison's inventory conversion period is 360/2 = 180 days. Addison's days sales outstanding (DSO) equals 81 days, so this is Addison's receivables conversion period. Because of the highly specialized nature of the materials that suppliers provide to Addison, their credit terms are more liberal than would be the case for other types of manufacturers. In Addison's case, its payables deferral period (including materials and labor) is 90 days. Now, we are ready to calculate Addison's cash conversion cycle.

The cash conversion cycle is diagrammed in Figure 8-2. Notice that we have put the corresponding data for Addison on the diagram. Each component is given a number, and the cash conversion cycle can be expressed by this equation:

$$
\begin{matrix}
\underset{(1)}{\begin{array}{c}\text{Inventory}\\ \text{conversion}\\ \text{period}\end{array}} + \underset{(2)}{\begin{array}{c}\text{Receivables}\\ \text{conversion}\\ \text{period}\end{array}} - \underset{(3)}{\begin{array}{c}\text{Payables}\\ \text{deferral}\\ \text{period}\end{array}} = \underset{(4)}{\begin{array}{c}\text{Cash}\\ \text{conversion}\\ \text{cycle}\end{array}}
\end{matrix}
\qquad \textbf{(8-1)}
$$

---

[1]See Verlyn D. Richards and Eugene J. Laughlin, "A Cash Conversion Cycle Approach to Liquidity Analysis," *Financial Management,* Spring 1980, 32–38.

Table 8-1

Addison Products Company: Pro Forma Financial Statements and Key Ratios December 31, 1994 (Thousands of Dollars)

I. Balance Sheet

Cash	$ 15	Accounts payable	$ 60
Accounts receivable	135	Notes payable	15
Inventories	300	Accrued wages and taxes	75
Total current assets	$450	Total current liabilities	$150
Net fixed assets	450	Mortgage bonds	300
		Common stock	126
		Retained earnings	324
Total assets	$900	Total liabilities and equity	$900

II. Income Statement

Sales	$600
Total costs	500
Taxable income	$100
Taxes (40%)	40
Net income	$ 60
Dividends	36
Addition to retained earnings	24

III. Key Ratios

1. Current ratio	3.0×
2. Total debt/Total assets	50%
3. Rate of return on equity	13.3%
4. Sales/Inventory	2×
5. DSO	81 days

Figure 8-2

Addison Products Company: The Cash Conversion Cycle

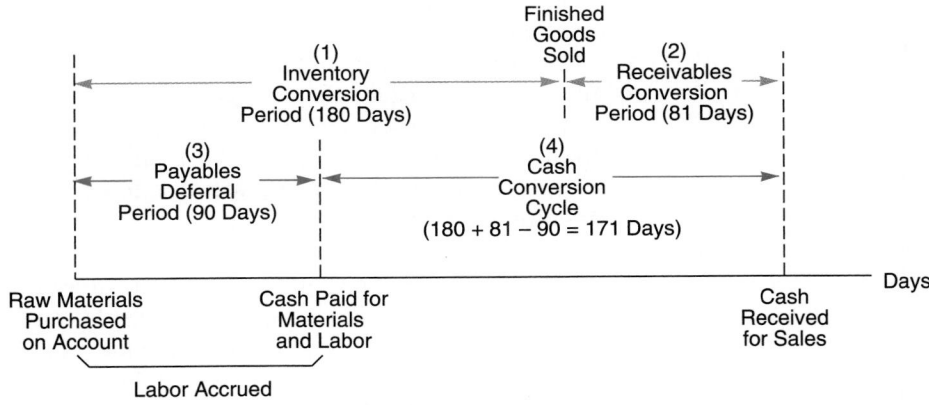

The cash conversion cycle measures the length of time it takes for cash invested in the firm's current assets to be returned. Cash invested in inventory is recaptured only when the firm collects its accounts receivable. Generally, the shorter the cash conversion cycle, the more profitable the firm will be.

Substituting Addison's numbers for each of these components, we obtain the following results:

$$180 \text{ days} + 81 \text{ days} - 90 \text{ days} = 171 \text{ days}.$$

Given these data, Addison knows, when it decides to accept and fill an order, that it will have to finance the processing of that order for a 171-day period, including the 81 days it takes the firm to collect on an average credit sale. The firm's goal should be to shorten the cash conversion cycle as much as possible without hurting operations or sales. This would improve profits because the *longer* the cash conversion cycle, the *greater* the need for external financing— and such financing has a cost.[2]

The cash conversion cycle can be shortened (1) by reducing the inventory conversion period, that is, by processing and selling goods more quickly; (2) by reducing the receivables conversion period (or DSO) by speeding up collections; or (3) by lengthening the payables deferral period by slowing down the firm's own payments. To the extent that these actions can be taken *without increasing costs or depressing sales,* they should be carried out. You should keep the cash conversion cycle in mind as we go through the remainder of this chapter and the other chapters on working capital management.

Reducing the Cash Conversion Cycle

As noted above, the firm's goal should be to keep the cash conversion cycle as short as possible, thus freeing up cash for other uses. Some actions which Addison could take to shorten its cash conversion cycle of 171 days are discussed below.

Inventories.   Looking again at Table 8-1, we see that Addison's inventories total $300,000. If the company were to reduce its inventories by a third, or to $200,000, its inventory conversion period would decline from 180 days to 120 days. Its new inventory conversion period would be calculated as 360/(Sales/Inventory) = 360/($600,000/$200,000) = 120 days. Of course, we assume that Addison could reduce its inventory without any adverse effects on sales or operating costs. As we shall see in Chapter 10, a firm needs to keep sufficient inventory to prevent stock-outs. Stock-outs create customer ill will and decrease sales. Also, in Chapter 10 we will develop a formula to calculate the optimal inventory amount to order.

Receivables.   In Table 8-1 we see that Addison's receivables total $135,000. If Addison were to reduce its receivables by $35,000, or to $100,000, its receivables conversion period would decline from 81 days to 60 days. Its new receivables conversion period would be calculated as (A/R)/(Sales/360) = $100,000/($600,000/360) = 60 days. Again, we assume that Addison could reduce its receivables without affecting sales adversely. As we shall see in Chapter 10, changing the receivables balance involves the firm's credit policy. In Chap-

---

[2]We will discuss the cost of short-term financing in Chapter 11.

ter 10, we will develop a methodology which will enable you to analyze the effect of a change in credit policy on the firm's income statement.

Payables.   We assumed that Addison's suppliers' credit policy called for payment of bills within 90 days. What if Addison extended its payment period by 10 days, to 100 days? This action might incur the wrath of its suppliers, and such an action would be easier to pursue during times of supplier excess capacity rather than when the suppliers have no such excess capacity. In Chapter 11, we will evaluate different credit terms and their resulting costs.

For the purposes of this illustration, we will assume that Addison was able to make changes to each of the cash conversion cycle components as mentioned here. Addison's new cash conversion cycle would then equal 80 days:

$$120 \text{ days} + 60 \text{ days} - 100 \text{ days} = 80 \text{ days}.$$

The combined effect of each of the actions discussed would cut the cash conversion cycle by more than 50 percent, and this would have a dramatic effect on the firm. Again, we assumed that none of the actions taken would adversely affect operating costs or sales. This is probably not a realistic assumption, as you will see in the remaining working capital management chapters.

Before we leave this topic, note that the concept just introduced ties back nicely to Equation 7-1 which was used to forecast AFN, additional, external funds needed. In Chapter 7 we were concerned with the entire balance sheet and not just current assets and current liabilities. However, at one point several options were discussed, just in case Addison could not raise the projected financing needed to balance its balance sheet. Two of these options were (1) to try to reduce the firm's capital intensity ratio, A*/S (which includes accounts receivable and inventory) and (2) to try to increase spontaneous liabilities, L*/S (which includes accounts payable). What we have done here is look at possible changes in these current asset and liability accounts on a time line, rather than as part of the terms A*/S and L*/S, respectively; the idea is the same.

Self-Test

Briefly explain the following terms:
a. Inventory conversion period.
b. Receivables conversion period.
c. Payables deferral period.

Briefly explain the importance of the cash conversion cycle.

How can the cash conversion cycle be shortened?

Working Capital Investment Policies

Because it is inherently difficult to quickly change the level of fixed assets, the current asset accounts, the firm's working capital, are used to make initial adjustments in operations as economic conditions change. If demand begins to rise or fall, the immediate response is in the current asset accounts, and the appropriateness of this response can spell success or failure for the firm.

Remember from the beginning of this chapter that working capital policy involves two basic questions: (1) What is the appropriate level of current assets, both in total and by specific accounts? (2) How should this level of current assets be financed? We now turn to the first of these two questions: An examination of alternative policies regarding the level of investment in current assets.

Effect of Current Asset Levels on Risk and Return

Under conditions of certainty — when sales, costs, order lead times, collection periods, and so on are known with certainty — all firms within an industry would hold the same level of current assets relative to sales. Any larger amount would increase the need for external funds without a corresponding increase in profits, whereas any smaller amount would cause late payments to suppliers, lost sales, and production inefficiencies because of inventory shortages. The picture changes when uncertainty is introduced. Here the firm requires some minimum amount of cash and inventories based on expected payments, sales, order lead times, and so on, plus additional amounts, or *safety stocks,* to help it cope if events vary from their expected values. Similarly, accounts receivable levels are affected by credit terms, and the easier those terms, the higher the receivables for any given level of sales.

A brief review of risk and return is appropriate at this point, exactly because the real world is one of uncertainty and because different individuals, and that includes managers, do not have the same risk-return preferences. Some individuals have a very low tolerance for risk and, therefore, trade off a certain amount of return for safety (and the ability to sleep well at night). Such individuals are often called financially *conservative.* When we check the dictionary we find that one definition of conservative is "cautious, safe." A very conservative investor is likely to choose, say, U.S. Treasury bills or certificates of deposit where there is virtually no chance that the principal invested will be lost, but where the return is also low. On the other hand, an *aggressive* investor might buy highly speculative common stocks or junk bonds.[3] An aggressive investor takes on much greater risk motivated by the expectation of higher returns. A second illustration can be found when we look at the amount of financial leverage that different firms choose to employ. Remember from Chapter 6 that financial leverage makes the firm riskier. But debt financing has the *potential* to boost the firm's return on equity, ROE. A firm that is conservatively financed would use relatively little total debt; an aggressively financed firm would attempt to leverage up its ROE by using more debt, accepting, at the same time, higher risk.

Now the topic is working capital policy, specifically the *level* of current assets, and we see that the risk-return tradeoff applies here as well. To be "conservative" again means to take the low-risk road, be cautious, play it safe; to be "aggressive" is the opposite, being willing to accept more risk in the hope of realizing higher returns.

Table 8-2 depicts three alternative policies that a firm like Addison might have regarding the level of current assets that it carries. Under each policy, a

---

[3]Junk bonds are debt instruments of low quality; these will be discussed in greater detail in Chapter 16.

	Conservative	Moderate	Aggressive
Expected sales	$40	$40	$40
Expected EBIT	3	3	3
Current assets	$15	$10	$ 5
Fixed assets	10	10	10
Total assets	$25	$20	$15
Expected basic earning power (EBIT/TA)	12%	15%	20%

Table 8-2

Effect of Working Capital Investment Policies on Basic Earning Power (Millions of Dollars)

conservative working capital investment policy

A policy under which relatively large amounts of cash, marketable securities, and inventories are carried and under which sales are stimulated by a generous credit policy, resulting in a high level of receivables.

aggressive working capital investment policy

A policy under which holdings of cash, securities, inventories, and receivables are minimized.

moderate working capital investment policy

A policy that is between the conservative and the aggressive working capital policies.

different amount of working capital is carried to support each level of sales. A **conservative working capital investment policy** means that the firm invests in larger amounts of cash or marketable securities, accounts receivable, and inventory than its level of sales seems to require. Conversely, with an **aggressive working capital investment policy,** the levels of cash or marketable securities, inventories, and receivables are reduced to the minimum possible amount at a given level of operations. A **moderate working capital investment policy** is between these two extremes.

In general, the greater the proportion of current assets to fixed assets at any given level of output, the less risky the firm's working capital investment policy.[4] How does the conservative policy reduce risk? In essence, all risk of shortages is removed. With high levels of current assets there will be ample inventory so that no stock outages will ever occur, as well as sufficient cash or near-cash marketable securities to prevent any conceivable liquidity problem. Of course, there is a price to pay for all this safety. That price, as we illustrate in Table 8-2, comes in the form of a relatively low expected basic earning power ratio.

The lower return associated with the conservative working capital investment policy stems from the fact that the firm has acquired more current assets than the minimum required to support the current level of sales. Obviously, any level of sales requires the supporting assets of inventory, accounts receivable, and cash balances for business transactions. An overabundance of these assets, however, directs resources away from more productive investments. Therefore, assuming that EBIT is constant, the basic earning power will be lower as the level of current assets increases.[5] We can conclude, therefore, that an overly conservative working capital policy misallocates resources, which lowers the overall earning power of the firm.

---

[4]It is important to distinguish between planned and unplanned increases in current assets. Unplanned increases in inventory that cannot be sold or accounts receivable that cannot be collected are *not* examples of a conservative risk-reducing working capital investment policy. Of course, such a buildup in current assets is risky and even life-threatening to the firm. The planned conservative policy that we are considering here concentrates on keeping more cash and inventory on hand to ensure that no shortages occur.

[5]The same principle holds true for fixed assets. Idle excess capacity bloats the asset side of the balance sheet, requiring financing to support it. Because idle assets are not producing revenues but are increasing the firm's financing charges, the profitability of the firm declines.

From this discussion, an unwary reader might conclude that the best working capital investment policy would be one which slashes current assets to the bare minimum. As seen in Table 8-2, the expected basic earning power rises from 12 percent under the conservative policy to 20 percent under the aggressive policy. However, just as lower returns were the price for the safety of a conservative working capital policy, there is a price associated with the higher *potential*[6] returns in the aggressive policy — higher risk.

The probability that a given level of sales cannot be maintained is one of the risks associated with an aggressive working capital policy. For example, the expected high rate of return resulting from the aggressive policy in Table 8-2 explicitly assumes no change in sales as levels of current assets are manipulated. How could an aggressive working capital policy affect sales? First, with lower levels of inventory, sales could decline as a result of stock outages. Second, sales revenues might also be lost because of a stringent credit policy that is designed to reduce accounts receivable. Of course, a decline in sales could result in lower returns.

Reduced sales are not the only risk associated with an aggressive policy. Since current assets provide liquidity, their reduction may lead to difficulties in paying bills or other obligations as they come due. Slow payment could lead to poor credit ratings or even to a reduction in suppliers' willingness to extend trade credit.

Therefore, an overly aggressive working capital policy can lead to exactly the opposite result of that intended. As is often the case in finance, the preferred policy lies somewhere between the extreme levels of aggressive and conservative policies. Even though it is difficult to prescribe an optimal level of current assets for each firm, a general guideline for working capital investment policy does exist. *The level of current assets should be reduced as long as the expected marginal return from such an action is greater than or equal to the expected marginal cost.* Thus, inventory should be reduced to a point where there is only an acceptably low probability of lost sales due to stock outages. Similarly, the savings resulting from lower levels of accounts receivable must be compared with the potential losses from the more stringent credit policy. Finally, the return from minimizing cash holdings, in either demand deposits or marketable securities, must be compared with the potential losses if cash were in short supply.

Self-Test

In general, what is meant by the terms financially "conservative" and financially "aggressive"?

Differentiate among the three alternative working capital investment policies.

What "price" is associated with a conservative working capital investment policy?

How could an overly aggressive working capital investment policy affect sales?

Identify the general guideline for working capital investment decisions.

---

[6]If returns were *always* higher under the aggressive working capital policy, there wouldn't be any risk, would there?

Alternative Working Capital Financing Policies

The second important topic in connection with working capital policy and management has to do with how the firm's current asset investment is financed.

At the time of the Yankee peddler, when the term *working capital* was first used, most industries were closely related to agriculture. Just like the peddler, who would repay the bank after every trip, other working capital loans were, in essence, self-liquidating. Farmers would borrow to buy seed in the spring and, when the crops were harvested in the fall, repay the loan with the proceeds of the crop's sale. Similarly, processors would buy crops in the fall, process them, sell the finished product, and end up just before the next harvest with relatively low inventories. Bank loans with maximum maturities of one year were used to finance both the purchase and the processing costs, and these loans were retired with the proceeds from the sale of the finished products.

This situation is depicted in Figure 8-3, from the processor's point of view. Fixed assets are shown to be growing steadily over time, while the processor's current assets jump at harvest season, decline during the year, and end at zero just before the next crop is harvested. Short-term credit is used to finance current assets, and long-term funds are used to finance fixed assets. The upward trend in fixed assets in this and the following examples indicates that we are assuming *growth in sales over time,* accompanied by an increased need for assets, even before considering seasonal and cyclical factors.

The figure represents an idealized situation — actually, the processor's current assets build up gradually as crops are purchased and processed; inventories are drawn down less regularly; and ending inventory balances do not decline to zero. Nevertheless, the example does illustrate the general nature of the production and financing process, and working capital management consists of decisions relating to the top section of the graph — managing current assets and arranging short-term credit.

Although our modern economy has become less oriented toward agriculture, seasonal and cyclical fluctuations of current assets and current liabilities still exist. For example, construction firms have peaks in the spring and summer, whereas retail sales often peak around Christmas. Consequently, manufacturers who supply either construction companies or retailers follow patterns much like those of their customers, but with a lead time of several months. Similarly, virtually all businesses must build up current assets when the economy is strong, but their inventories and receivables decline when the economy slacks off. Even when a business is at its seasonal or cyclical low, however, its current assets do not drop to zero, and this realization has led to the development of the concept of **permanent current assets.** Even when a firm is experiencing the lowest point in its own seasonal cycle, or in the overall business cycle, its sales are not zero. Therefore, its current assets cannot be zero either; it must have some cash on hand, it will have some receivables outstanding, and it will, likewise, hold some inventories. *There will be, for a given firm, some level of current assets which is needed — and must be financed — at all times.* This permanent level of current assets includes safety stocks of cash and inventories.

In addition, the firm must invest in **temporary current assets** when its sales increase for seasonal or cyclical reasons. There is a close and direct link between a firm's sales and its need to hold current assets, as we saw in

permanent current assets

Current assets that are still on hand when business activity is at seasonal or cyclical lows.

temporary current assets

Current assets that fluctuate with seasonal or cyclical sales variations.

Figure 8-3

Fixed and Current Assets and Their Financing

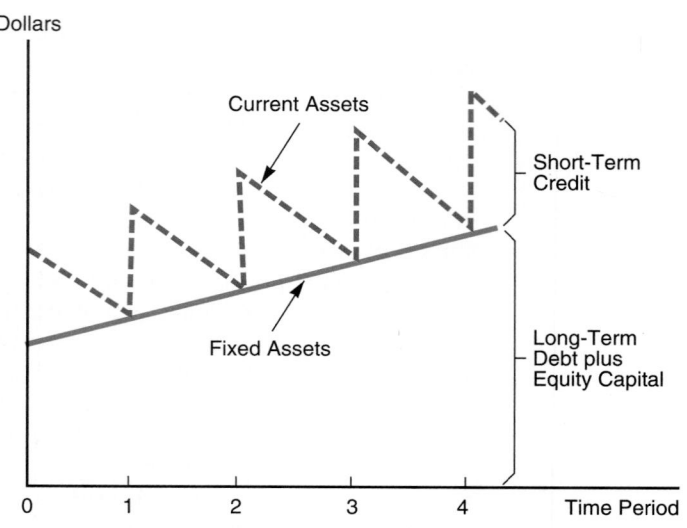

This figure shows an idealized model of the financing of current and fixed assets. Each season, current assets rise sharply, then gradually fall to zero. Short-term loans, used to finance these current assets, are repaid and renewed each season. Fixed assets, on the other hand, are financed with long-term debt and owners' equity. (The underlying assumption in this and following illustrations is one of growth over time in the firm's sales and total assets.)

Chapter 7. The manner in which the permanent and temporary current assets are financed constitutes the firm's **working capital financing policy.**

working capital financing policy

The manner in which the firm's permanent and temporary current assets are financed.

Maturity Matching, or Self-Liquidating, Approach.   One commonly used financing policy is to match asset and liability maturities, as shown in Figure 8-4. Here both fixed assets and permanent current assets are financed with long-term capital — equity plus long-term debt — while temporary current assets are financed with current liabilities. This strategy reduces the risk that the firm will be unable to pay off its maturing obligations. To illustrate, suppose a firm borrowed on a one-year basis and used the funds to build and equip a plant. Because cash flows from the plant (net income plus depreciation) would not be sufficient to pay off the loan after only one year, the loan would have to be renewed annually. Thus, the company's ability to continue operating would depend on its ability to renew the loan each year. If for some reason the lender refused to renew the loan, the firm would have serious problems. Had the plant been financed with a 20-year loan, however, the required loan payments (interest plus a small part of the principal) would have been better matched with cash flows from net income and depreciation, and the problem of renewal would arise, if at all, only once every 20 years.[7]

---

[7]Examples of maturity matching can also be found in our personal financial lives. Few of us would even think of financing a home with only a one-year note or financing a car for 30 years. In the first case, almost no one could pay for a home in one year. In the second case, the car would have turned to rust before our payments ended. Therefore, we typically finance an asset over a period that, in some manner, reflects its expected useful life.

Figure 8-4

Temporary versus
Permanent Assets: Exactly
Matching Maturities

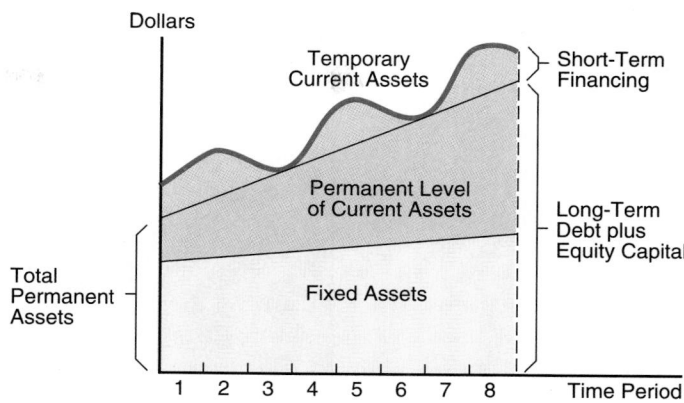

Because in the modern business world current assets rarely drop to zero, the idea of permanent current assets was developed. This figure shows these assets being financed, along with fixed assets, by long-term debt and equity capital. Those current assets that are still seasonal or cyclical continue to be financed by short-term credit. Figures 8-3 and 8-4 illustrate the traditional approach of matching asset and liability maturities.

At the extreme, a firm could attempt to exactly match the maturity structure of its assets and liabilities. Inventory expected to be sold in 30 days would be financed with a 30-day bank loan; receivables expected to be collected in 45 days would be financed for 45 days; a machine expected to last for 5 years would be financed with a 5-year loan; a 20-year building would be financed with a 20-year mortgage; and so on. Of course, uncertainty about the lives of assets prevents this exact maturity matching. For example, a firm may finance inventories with a 30-day loan, expecting to sell the inventories and to use the cash generated to retire the loan. However, if sales are slower than expected, the cash will not be forthcoming, and the use of short-term credit may cause a problem. Still, if a firm makes an attempt to match asset and liability maturities, we would define this as a moderate working capital financing policy.

There are inherent problems with highly simplified graphs, such as the ones used in this chapter to illustrate working capital financing. First, while trying to keep things simple, figures such as Figure 8-4 show an even, steady growth in fixed assets and permanent current assets over time. That is, of course, seldom the case. Fixed assets are particularly likely to grow unevenly; in Chapter 7 we saw that they may be what we called "lumpy." A second problem is more closely tied to the topic of this chapter. The rise and fall in temporary current assets *appears* to be nice and smooth, with each cycle looking very much like the one before it and the one following it. That is certainly not the case in reality. No two seasonal cycles are the same for a given firm, and no two overall business cycles are alike. (Look back to Figure 4-2 to remind yourself of the differences in the durations of booms and recessions in the United States over the last four decades.)

Given so much uncertainty in forecasting sales and required assets, managers can move away from an attempt to precisely match maturities of assets and liabilities. They can finance in a more conservative (safer) manner, or they can take a more aggressive course in financing working capital needs.

Figure 8-5

Temporary versus
Permanent Assets:
Aggressive Approach

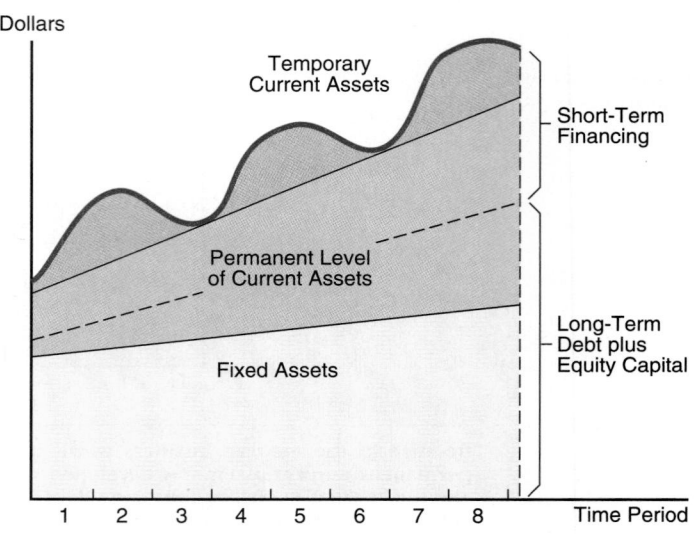

To take advantage of flexible, and usually cheaper, short-term credit, a firm may finance a portion of its permanent current assets with short-term credit. The remainder of its permanent current assets, along with fixed assets and temporary current assets, are financed in the traditional way as shown in the prior two figures. A firm taking this approach sacrifices a measure of safety to lower its financing costs in hopes of increasing profits.

Aggressive Approach.   Figure 8-5 illustrates an aggressive working capital financing policy. Here a firm continues to finance all of its fixed assets with long-term capital, but part of its permanent current assets plus all of its temporary current assets are financed with short-term credit. Why would a firm wish to increase the amount of assets it finances with short-term credit? Basically, short-term credit is desirable because it is flexible and usually cheaper than long-term credit. Consider the sources of short-term debt. First, some sources of short-term financing are spontaneous; that is, they increase as the level of the firm's operations increases. Accounts payable and accruals are examples of spontaneous financing. As we saw in Chapter 7 and will examine in more detail in Chapter 11, when sales increase, a company obtains more raw materials from suppliers, and the increased trade credit offered by the suppliers finances the buildup in assets. Similarly, as operations increase, there is a resulting increase in accrued wages and taxes, which helps to finance the buildup in operations. Used within limits, these sources constitute "free" capital. Second, the yield curve is usually upward sloping, or normal, which means that firms can obtain funds in the short-term market at a lower cost than by selling long-term bonds or issuing equity. Most such nonspontaneous, short-term borrowing is in the form of bank loans. For these two reasons, virtually all firms — even the most conservative ones — will show some current liabilities on their books. Thus, working capital financing policy is a matter of degree; the more aggressive the firm, the more it will rely on short-term financing.

Short-term credit could be used to finance all current assets (both temporary and permanent), and even to finance a portion of the fixed assets. This

Figure 8-6

Temporary versus
Permanent Assets:
Conservative Approach

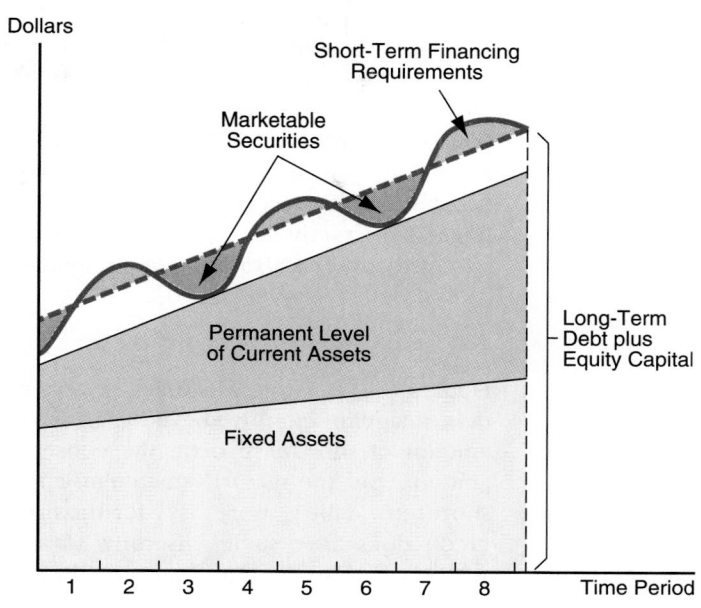

A very conservative approach to financing current assets is illustrated in this figure. Part
of the short-term financing requirement is met by using long-term capital to "store up"
liquidity in the form of marketable securities during the off season. During peak seasons
these securities are sold to provide needed liquidity, and they are augmented by a small
amount of short-term borrowing.

would be represented in Figure 8-5 by drawing the dashed line *below* the line
designating fixed assets. This very aggressive financing policy would be extremely risky because it would subject the firm even more to the fluctuations
of volatile short-term interest rates, and loan renewal problems would have a
greater impact on the firm, possibly leading to the sale of assets to avoid bankruptcy. Even so, since short-term debt is often cheaper than long-term debt,
some firms are willing to sacrifice safety for possibly higher profits.

Conservative Approach.   Alternatively, the firm could finance not only its
fixed and permanent current assets with long-term debt and equity capital, but
a portion of its temporary current assets as well. This is shown in Figure 8-6 by
drawing the dashed line *above* the line designating the firm's investment into
permanent current assets. In this case, permanent capital is being used to finance all permanent assets as well as some or all of the seasonal and cyclical
demands. The humps above the dashed line in Figure 8-6 represent short-term
financing; the troughs below it represent short-term securities holdings. Our
illustrative firm uses a small amount of short-term credit to meet its peak requirements, but it also meets a part of its seasonal needs by "storing liquidity"
in the form of marketable securities during the off season. This represents a very
safe, conservative working capital financing policy, but one that results in lower
expected profits.

Remember from Chapter 7 that we did not include marketable securities among the firm's spontaneous assets. It now becomes clear why not; marketable securities tend to run *counter* to the changes in such asset accounts as receivables and inventory. The firm needs more inventory when higher sales are projected, and immediately after the sale the investment in receivables will have increased. However, if the firm held marketable securities during times of seasonally and cyclically low sales, these will now be liquidated and invested into other current assets, in effect postponing the need for external short-term financing. Exactly the opposite will occur when sales decline and the need for inventory and receivables is no longer as great.

Advantages and Disadvantages of Short-Term Credit

Figures 8-4, 8-5, and 8-6 differ in terms of the relative amounts of short-term debt financing employed. The aggressive financing policy calls for the greatest amount of short-term debt, the conservative financing policy uses the lowest amount, and the maturity matching approach falls in between. Although using short-term debt is more risky for the firm than using long-term debt, short-term credit does have some offsetting advantages. The pros and cons of financing with short-term debt are considered in this section.

Speed.   A short-term loan can be obtained much more quickly than a long-term loan. Lenders will insist on a more thorough financial examination before granting long-term credit, and the loan agreement will have to be spelled out in considerably more detail because a great deal can happen during the life of a 10- to 20-year loan. Therefore, if funds are needed in a hurry, the firm should look to the short-term markets.

Flexibility.   If its needs for funds are seasonal or cyclical, or just hard to predict for whatever reason, a firm may not want to commit itself to long-term debt. First, loan initiation costs are generally higher for long-term debt. Second, although long-term debt can be repaid early, provided the loan agreement contains a prepayment provision, prepayment penalties can be expensive. Accordingly, if a firm thinks its need for funds will diminish in the near future, it should choose short-term debt for the repayment flexibility it provides. Finally, long-term loan agreements always contain provisions, or *covenants,* which constrain the firm's future actions, but short-term credit agreements are generally less restrictive.

Cost of Long-Term versus Short-Term Debt.   As noted earlier, the yield curve is typically upward sloping, indicating that interest rates are lower on short-term than on long-term debt. Thus, under normal conditions, interest expense will generally be lower if the firm borrows on a short-term rather than a long-term basis.

Risk of Long-Term versus Short-Term Debt.   Even though short-term debt is generally less expensive than long-term debt, financing with short-term debt subjects the firm to more risk for three reasons: (1) If a firm borrows on a long-term basis, its interest costs will be fixed (or if the interest rate is floating, the

THE CREDIT CRUNCH, CASH FLOW PROBLEMS, AND BANKRUPTCY

During the early 1990s, a combination of cash flow shortfalls and cautious lenders resulted in an increase in bankruptcies, especially among small and medium-sized firms. According to the Administrative Office of the U.S. Courts, 24,000 companies entered into Chapter 11 reorganization proceedings during the 12 months ending June 30, 1992, an increase of 38 percent from three years earlier. Most of the bankrupt companies are small businesses, says Administrative Office bankruptcy analyst Ed Flynn. Small-business owners are at a disadvantage — they have few assets to redeploy or sell, and they have a tougher time persuading lenders or investors to supply more capital.

Industries that have been hard hit by bankruptcies include clothing, retailing, real estate, and construction. Although small firms are hardest hit, large companies are not immune — at least 40 firms with liabilities of $1 billion or more filed for bankruptcy from 1988 to 1992. Some of these larger bankruptcies included Macy's, Olympia & York, TWA, Memorex Telex N.V., Zale Corporation, El Paso Electric, and Wang Laboratories. "It's a result of the generally weak economy," said Harvey R. Miller, co-managing partner of a New York law firm with many bankruptcy clients.

Other specialists cited other causes. Savings and loans, in deep trouble themselves as exhibited by massive thrift failures and subsequent bailouts, can no longer help troubled companies. The market for junk bonds, which in the 1980s financed so many young or struggling firms, virtually disappeared in the wake of Wall Street scandals and indictments. This situation made it difficult for firms to "roll over" loans when they matured, and the rollover problem has contributed to bankruptcies. Also, the debt burden from

earlier leveraged buyouts sent companies such as Macy's into bankruptcy court.

With commercial banks as the primary source of funds, many troubled firms are finding themselves shut out. Melvin Jaffe, president and CEO of a California-based chain of building-supply stores, said, "We ran out of cash. Our lender wouldn't give us any more. I think they were scared by what they saw happening to other retailers." Jaffe's company continues to operate under the protection of Chapter 11 of the Bankruptcy Code (which prevents its creditors from seizing its assets and closing it down) as it seeks to work out an agreement with its creditors.

Troubled companies are not the only firms finding themselves shut out — healthy firms are having trouble arranging credit, too. Anthony Lombardi, president of Kemvolt of Connecticut Inc., a circuit board maker with a 25-person staff, is turning away business because he cannot get bank loans to finance inventory. The banks do not want to see purchase orders; they want to see profits. As one prospective borrower put it, "The only companies the banks want to lend to are those who don't need the money."

Even a healthy after-interest cash flow is not sufficient, as Walter Grant, chief executive of Camellia Food Stores, discovered. The weak economy had reduced average store sales in his 50-unit chain, so Mr. Grant decided to add new stores. But his bank would not extend additional credit to him, and other banks have not been interested in helping with his expansion either.

Even when firms are granted credit, the amounts have been reduced. A few years ago, firms were given loans against plant and equipment for 75 percent of appraised value. Now, the amounts lent are typically 40 to 50 percent. Banks have also become more cautious about lending against accounts receivable. Omega World Travel's president, Gloria Bohan, says her firm's banks are lending only 75 percent against receivables, compared with 90 percent a few years ago. Also, lenders have toughened up on the age of receivables against which they will lend. A few years ago, 90-day receivables might have been acceptable, but today 60-days receivables are the cut-off point.

Sources: "Bankruptcy-Law Filings by Firms Spurt," *The Wall Street Journal*, April 6, 1990; Associated Press, May 10, 1990; "U.S. Officials Urge Bankers to Avoid Tightening Credit," *The New York Times*, May 11, 1990; "Victims of the Credit Crunch," *Fortune*, January 27, 1992; "For Many Small Businesses, Chapter 11 Closes the Book," *The Wall Street Journal*, November 4, 1992; "Continuing Crunch," *The Wall Street Journal*, November 16, 1992; "Largest U.S. Bankruptcies," E. Altman, NYU Salomon Center, Stern School of Business; "Why Banks Are Still Stingy," *Fortune*, January 25, 1993; "Regulators Adopt Policies to Ease Credit Crunch," *The Reuter Business Report*, March 30, 1993; "OCC, Senate Confirms Clinton's Choice for Comptroller of the Currency," *Daily Report for Executives*, April 6, 1993.

Tight credit "has become a self-fulfilling prophecy," in the opinion of New York economic consultant A. Gary Shilling. "As lenders get more worried, they stop lending to the people who most need to borrow, causing what the lenders most fear, bankruptcy."

What lies behind this credit crunch? There are two schools of thought. One is that the excesses of the 1980s are entirely responsible — companies are just too leveraged, and banks and other lenders are too weak to take a chance on doing anything other than operating in a highly conservative manner. Proponents of this view argue that the situation is like a child who has eaten too much candy and now has to pay the price and take the bitter medicine.

The other school of thought is that the main culprit of the credit crunch is the Federal Deposit Insurance Corporation Improvement Act (FDICIA) of 1991. Enacted at year-end 1991 to protect the bank insurance fund from further fiascos like that of the 1980s, this law requires federal regulators to enforce a large number of new and costly rules. Regulators are now charged with seeing that institutions meet the law's tough new standards for asset quality, loan documentation, credit underwriting, and even minimum earnings. Regulators are emphasizing soundness to the point that bankers feel the best way to avoid trouble with loans is to avoid all risky loans. Few financial institutions are willing to take risks for which they may have to reserve additional capital, and many are cutting expenses by laying off staff.

The regulations require as much paperwork and loan documentation for a small loan as for a large one. As a result, many small loans are either unprofitable to the bank or uneconomical to the borrower, depending on whether the bank passes on the higher fixed costs in the interest rate.

Due to the new guidelines, bankers are worried that regulators will question what were formerly routine lending decisions, so they are refusing all but the soundest borrowers. The principal victims of the bankers' fears are small businesses. Large companies can raise capital by issuing bonds and commercial paper, but small companies depend on banks for most of their financing.

The situation, whatever its cause, is dealing a major blow to our economy because small companies grow faster and create more jobs than larger firms. Small companies, typically defined as those with fewer than 500 employees, account for approximately 57 percent of the jobs in the private sector and for virtually all of the net new jobs. If President Clinton is going to jump-start the economy, he will have to attack the credit crunch currently confronting small businesses.

President Clinton has begun the attack on the credit crunch with his appointment for Comptroller of the Currency. As for the guidelines, U.S. banking regulators have been instructed to adopt new policies which will make it easier for banks to lend to smaller companies. The goal is to eliminate unnecessary paperwork that healthy, well-run institutions are required to go through for loans of less than $1 million to small and medium-sized firms. Further, bankers are being encouraged to look at a loan applicant's reputation and character, not just at his or her financial status. The new policies are expected to free up as much as $46 billion in additional credit to small and medium-sized firms.

cost will still be relatively stable over time), but if it borrows on a short-term basis, its interest expense will fluctuate widely, at times going quite high. For example, from 1977 to 1980 the short-term rate for large corporations (the prime rate) more than *tripled,* going from 6.25 percent to 21 percent. (2) If a firm borrows on a short-term basis, there will be less time in the borrowing period to generate cash to pay the debt's principal and interest as they come due. If the firm finds itself in a weak financial position on the loan's maturity date, it is possible that the lender will not extend the loan, thereby forcing the firm into bankruptcy. (3) The lender may choose not to renew the loan, for reasons that have little to do with the potential borrower's financial position. For example, in the 1990–1992 credit crunch, many smaller firms found themselves unable to renew short-term loans, which they could have renewed easily only a few years before. Bankers had become more cautious for a number of market-related reasons (the S&L crisis, declining real estate values, and the recession), and stricter banking regulation contributed to their suddenly very conservative lending practices. The result was that many smaller firms were left "out in the cold," having to scale back operations for lack of short-term, non-spontaneous financing, or, worse yet, facing bankruptcy, as is discussed in the "Industry Practice" boxed feature in this chapter.

Self-Test

What is meant by the term "working capital financing policy"?

How do the three alternative working capital financing policies compare with respect to their use of short-term debt?

What are the main advantages and disadvantages of short-term credit?

Combining Current Asset and Liability Decisions

From the preceding discussion, it is obvious that a potentially profitable, yet risky, strategy would be to minimize the firm's investment in current assets and to finance a large proportion of total assets with short-term debt. Alternatively, risk could be minimized, at the expense of potential profits, by increasing current assets and financing a large proportion of total assets with long-term debt and equity.

In Table 8-3 we illustrate the effects of different working capital investment and financing policies. For these strategies, the current ratio and the net working capital are our measures of risk, and return on equity measures the profitability of each plan.

The conservative policy of building current assets and financing with more expensive long-term debt will reduce the firm's expected return. The firm's level of risk is quite low, however — its high current ratio indicates that the firm has sufficient liquidity to meet almost any emergency. In contrast, the aggressive policy of minimizing current asset investment and utilizing more low-cost short-term debt has led to a much higher expected return. There are dangers associated with this higher return, however. First, at this low level of current assets, it is quite possible that the firm will be unable to maintain the proposed level of sales. Second, a potentially critical problem is indicated by the firm's low level of liquidity, as measured by the current ratio and the negative net working capital.[8] With this low current ratio, the firm may find future financing more difficult to obtain, and certainly it will be more expensive (due to the higher liquidity risk) if it can be obtained at all. The low current ratio also indicates that the firm may have substantial problems paying bills and making interest and principal payments as they come due. Thus, although an aggressive policy may lead to higher profits for the firm, it also increases the potential for bankruptcy. A more moderate approach, which represents a balancing of risk and return, may be preferred by many financial managers.

---

[8]Note that net working capital mirrors the liquidity risk identified by the current ratio.

Table 8-3		Conservative	Moderate	Aggressive
Combined Effects of Current Asset Levels and Debt Maturity Mix on Risk and Expected Return (Thousands of Dollars)	Current assets	$15,000	$10,000	$ 5,000
	Fixed assets	10,000	10,000	10,000
	Total assets	$25,000	$20,000	$15,000
	Short-term debt (cost = 10%)	$ 3,750	$ 5,000	$ 6,000
	Long-term debt (cost = 14%)	8,750	5,000	1,500
	Common equity	12,500	10,000	7,500
	Total liabilities and equity	$25,000	$20,000	$15,000
	Sales	$40,000	$40,000	$40,000
	EBIT	3,000	3,000	3,000
	Less: Interest	1,600	1,200	810
	EBT	$ 1,400	$ 1,800	$ 2,190
	Less: Taxes (40%)	560	720	876
	Net income	$ 840	$ 1,080	$ 1,314
	Current ratio (current assets/current liabilities)	4×	2×	0.83×
	Net working capital (current assets − current liabilities)	$11,250	$5,000	($1,000)
	Expected return on equity (net income/common equity)	6.7%	10.8%	17.5%

Procedures for evaluating the investment in each of the current asset and liability accounts are considered in the remaining chapters on working capital management.

 Self-Test

Briefly explain why a potentially profitable, yet risky, strategy would be to minimize investment in current assets while financing a large portion of total assets with short-term debt.

SMALL BUSINESS

GROWTH AND WORKING CAPITAL NEEDS

Working capital is the requirement that entrepreneurs most often underestimate when seeking funds to finance a new business. The entrepreneur generally provides for the plant and equipment required for production, as well as the research and new product development, but often overlooks the impact of the magnitude of the working capital investment required by daily operations early on. A common misconception among entrepreneurs is the expectation that the product will immediately sell and will provide high profit margins. They expect that selling at a premium price will provide the source of future financing of the firm's additional cash needs. A high profit margin is the ideal, of course, but it is not often the rule.

Sources: "Smart Ways to Manage Cash," *Nation's Business,* August 1992, 43; "Small Business Financial Management Practices in North America: A Literature Review," *Journal of Small Business Management,* April 1991, 19–29.

Even in the ideal setting, if the entrepreneur is able to sell all that has been produced, very often the sale is made on credit and may not be paid for another month or two. Payment periods are determined by industry practices. The entrepreneur must learn to operate within the industry's terms. In the meantime, as the bills mount within the firm for salaries, research and development expenses, utilities, and advertising, to name a few, the entrepreneur faces his or her own payment responsibilities. Therein lies the crunch. To make timely payments to ensure his or her own "creditability," the entrepreneur is forced to dip into his or her own personal savings. If this process begins to recur, without some additional sources of liquidity, the business will soon fail. Thus, the need for sound working capital practices becomes essential at the outset of the business's life.

Consider for example a small firm that finances its activities solely through the funds it generates. Recall the financial analysis presented earlier in this chapter. Suppose the firm has an average of 120 days of sales in inventory and an average of 60 days of sales in receivables. If the firm pays cash for all its materials and labor, it has a cash conversion cycle of 180 days; that is, between the payment for goods at the beginning of the cycle and the receipt of cash at the end, 180 days pass. Thus, the company "turns over" its cash only twice per year.

If the company earns, say, 3 percent on its sales dollar (as measured by the net profit margin), it has about 3 percent more money available after a cycle than before it. With two cycles per year, about 6 percent more is available for investment at the end of the year than at the beginning. Thus, annual growth of approximately 6 percent can be supported.

If, for example, the company is growing at a rate of 20 percent per year but can generate only 6 percent internally, it must either obtain funds externally or face enormous problems. Rapid growth consumes cash; it does not generate cash. Rapid growth may generate profits, but profits do not pay the bills—cash does. Close attention to a statement of cash flows indicates the demands from operating, investment, and financing needs that quickly deplete the liquidity available internally.

As the tight credit conditions continue to prevail, a small firm is forced to rely on its own internally generated funds. How can the small firm improve its ability to fund its operations internally? First, a firm can support more rapid growth either by raising the profit margin, if the market will bear it, or by shortening the cash conversion cycle (increasing the number

of cycles). To increase the profit margin, the company must raise prices, cut costs, or do both. Unfortunately, many small businesses make the mistake of attempting to solve their cash flow problems solely by boosting sales. Second, shortening the cash conversion cycle requires collecting receivables more efficiently, reducing inventory, or paying supplies more slowly if possible. Improving the cash conversion cycle by increasing the rate at which the firm can support growth internally reduces the firm's needs for outside funds to a more manageable level. In fact, analysis of rapidly growing firms consistently reveals the borrower's inability to make principal payments during the growth period.

To avoid future problems with receivables, small companies should establish a strict policy on how and when to extend credit. When setting policy for credit on new accounts, the small business owner should thoroughly investigate the creditworthiness of its potential customers. A good source of credit information is other credit managers who may have had direct experience with the customer. Surprisingly different from what one might expect, a credit manager will be very candid with another credit manager—even if they are competitors. They know that if they withhold something important, they will not be able to get information when *they* need it.

Another cash drain is excessive inventory. More efficient inventory management can be facilitated by tracking inventory with computer software. Integrating inventory management with customer service and delivery programs can cut costs by a considerable amount. Many small business owners are not aware of the true cost of carrying inventory. For example, a typical manufacturing company pays 25 to 30 percent of the value of inventory for the cost of the borrowed money, warehouse space, materials handling, staff, lift-truck expenses, and fixed costs.

Cash flow can be improved markedly simply by monitoring expenses throughout an organization. Improved expense control is a potential cash source in the following areas of operation.

Supplies

Careful and regular review of expenses regarding business supplies and services, even those provided by long-term vendors, is highly recommended. Itemized petty cash expenses may uncover unnecessary expense. Employees who are aware of the costs of supplies will be more likely to conserve on their use. Having one person responsible and accountable for expenses in each department will tighten up on any waste.

Travel and Advertising

Scrutinize expenses for travel and entertainment. Investigate whether ads are reaching the business's intended market and monitor the results of current advertising.

Insurance

Determine ways to reduce accidents and premiums as per the suggestions made by companies that provide workers' compensation and other coverage. Consider the tradeoffs of increasing deductibles for employee health insurance.

Recordkeeping

Since 90 percent of the businesses that fail do not know why, establishing, maintaining, and monitoring a good recordkeeping system will alert the entrepreneur when expenses begin to head off in directions that are inconsistent with goals. Also, small business owners mistakenly assume that the accounting firms that prepare statements will necessarily alert them to financial trouble. The compilation of financial records is solely for reporting purposes. Unless an accounting firm is retained to do so, it will not analyze the company for problems.

Compensation

Justify salaries and pay schedules by evaluating the volume of work and the way it is accomplished. Reconcile the work load with employee responsibilities by having everyone log his or her daily, weekly, and monthly activities to locate duplication and to gauge productivity.

Purchasing

Consolidate purchasing and overnight mail services with one employee who maintains responsibility.

Cash Management

A firm can also improve its working capital management by focusing on the firm's cash position. By ensuring that the sales, purchases, and finance departments communicate regularly, frequently reviewing the collection and payments cycles, checking to see whether the most cost-effective cash transmission methods are in use, and by critically reviewing exist-ing bank relations to simplify daily cash management, the firm can more effectively manage its own internal cash resources. Further, limiting the number of people who can authorize expenditures and handle cash and requiring invoices and purchase orders before issuing checks enables the owner to make adjustments where necessary.

In addition, by prompt investment of idle funds (funds not required within the next month), management can earn additional revenues; however small they may seem in the short-term, the no-longer-idle excess cash has the potential of accumulating handsomely.

Credit Management

A final untapped source of internal funds is the use of accounts payables, as cited by a recent survey. The survey determined that only about half the small business owners view accounts payable as a source of financing for their businesses. (Others apparently pay the bill as it arrives "to get it out of the way," as many have said.)

Borrowing

Forecasting the cash budget, additional financing needs, and cash flow schedules providing for the repayment of a loan allow the entrepreneur to set goals. By planning ahead and regularly monitoring operations in hopes of uncovering *early on* any unexpected departures in revenues or expenses, the entrepreneur can seek the lowest cost of funds that may be available. In practice, owners of small businesses admit they rarely evaluate forecasted financial statements and compare these with the firm's actual performance, and that this is a direct result of time constraints.

For the small business owner with serious constraints on obtaining outside funds, these discretionary policies can help bring the firm's rate of growth into balance with its ability to finance that growth. Maintaining control is a matter of constantly scrutinizing every aspect of the business—which means looking well beyond the bottom line. Furthermore, such control on the part of management may impress bankers and others who have funds and, thus, may help the firm obtain the outside financing it would have preferred to have had all along.

Summary

This chapter examined working capital policy and management, which includes working capital investment policies and alternative ways of financing current assets. The key concepts covered are listed below.

▷ The two main areas in which managers must make working capital decisions are (1) the **level** of the current assets investment and (2) the **financing** of those current assets.

▷ **Working capital** refers to total current assets, and **net working capital** is defined as current assets minus current liabilities.

Working capital management involves the administration, within policy guidelines, of current assets, including the financing of those assets.

▷ The **cash conversion cycle** is the length of time from paying for raw materials and labor to receiving cash from the sale of products. The cash conversion cycle can be calculated as follows:

$$
\begin{array}{c}
\text{Inventory} \\
\text{conversion} \\
\text{period}
\end{array}
+
\begin{array}{c}
\text{Receivables} \\
\text{conversion} \\
\text{period}
\end{array}
-
\begin{array}{c}
\text{Payables} \\
\text{deferral} \\
\text{period}
\end{array}
=
\begin{array}{c}
\text{Cash} \\
\text{conversion.} \\
\text{cycle}
\end{array}
$$

The **inventory conversion period** is the length of time required to convert raw materials into finished goods and then to sell them.

The **receivables conversion period** is the additional length of time required to convert the firm's receivables into cash, and it is equal to the days sales outstanding (DSO).

The **payables deferral period** is the length of time between the purchase of raw materials and labor and the payment for them.

Under a **conservative working capital investment policy,** a firm holds relatively large amounts of each type of current asset and reduces risk and expected return. An **aggressive working capital investment policy** entails holding minimal amounts of these items and, therefore, entails higher risk and higher expected return. A **moderate working capital investment policy** falls between these two policies.

▷ **Permanent current assets** are those current assets that the firm holds even during slack times, whereas **temporary current assets** are the additional current assets that are needed during seasonal or cyclical peaks. The methods used to finance permanent and temporary current assets define the firm's **working capital financing policy.**

▷ A **maturity matching** approach to current asset financing involves matching the maturities of assets and liabilities in such a way that temporary current assets are financed with short-term debt and permanent current assets and fixed assets are financed with long-term debt or equity. Under an **aggressive** approach, some permanent current assets and perhaps even some fixed assets are financed with short-term debt. A **conservative** approach would be to use long-term capital to finance all fixed and permanent current assets plus some of the temporary current assets. In general, the more aggressively a firm finances its working capital, the higher the expected return, but the higher also the risk.

▷   The advantages of short-term credit are (1) the **speed** with which short-term loans can be arranged, (2) increased **flexibility,** and (3) the fact that **short-term interest rates** are generally **lower** than long-term rates. The principal disadvantage of short-term credit is the **extra risk** that the borrower must bear because (1) the lender can demand payment on short notice, (2) the cost of the loan will increase if short-term interest rates rise, and (3) at times, lenders may refuse to make loans for market-related reasons.

Resolution to
DECISION IN FINANCE

FLORIDA ORANGE SPRINGS INC. — ABUNDANCE OF WATER, SHORTAGE OF WORKING CAPITAL

Every time a new retail customer signed on, FOS had to buy and install a water cooler in the customer's office, and also provide a supply of full five-gallon bottles, at an out-of-pocket cost of about $300 per new customer. This money would be returned, plus a profit, over time as the customer paid monthly bills, but in the meantime, the sale caused FOS to experience a cash shortfall. Sales to Publix and other potentially large customers created a similar problem. Such customers deal only with suppliers who can provide large quantities of product on short notice. This meant that FOS would have to carry a large inventory of bottled water, and that required an investment in labor and materials (bottles and cases) long before sales were made and even longer before receivables created by sales were collected.

So, whereas FOS thought it was adequately financed, in fact it was not because it had not recognized fully the investment in working capital needed to support growing sales. FOS was able to obtain the capital it needed, but its financing difficulties delayed implementation of the business plan by a full year. Many other businesses are less fortunate and are literally pulled under by the combination of working capital requirements and inadequate capital.

Source: Original material from Florida Orange Springs's business plan.

Questions

8-1   What are the differences between permanent and temporary current assets?

8-2   What is the tradeoff between risk and return in the management of the firm's current assets?

8-3   Why do excess current assets reduce profits?

8-4   How would a period of rapidly increasing inflation affect the firm's level of current assets?

8-5   During a tight-money period, would you expect a business firm to hold higher or lower cash balances (demand deposits) than during an easy-money period? Assume the firm's volume of business remains constant over both economic periods.

8-6   How would management's ability to predict sales trends and patterns affect working capital policy?

8-7   From the standpoint of the borrower, is long-term or short-term credit riskier? Explain. Would it ever make sense to borrow on a short-term basis if short-term rates were above long-term rates?

8-8   If long-term credit exposes a borrower to less risk, why would people or firms ever borrow on a short-term basis?

8-9   Considering the fact that an increase in the inventory turnover and total assets turnover ratios correspond with a decrease in the cash conversion cycle, with what group of ratios would you classify the cash conversion cycle?

Self-Test Problems

ST-1   Vanderheiden Press Inc., and the Herrenhouse Publishing Company had the following balance sheets as of December 31, 1993 (thousands of dollars):

	Vanderheiden Press	**Herrenhouse Publishing**
Current assets	$100,000	$ 80,000
Net fixed assets	100,000	120,000
Total assets	$200,000	$200,000
Current liabilities	$ 20,000	$ 80,000
Long-term debt	80,000	20,000
Common stock	50,000	50,000
Retained earnings	50,000	50,000
Total liabilities and equity	$200,000	$200,000

Earnings before interest and taxes (EBIT) for both firms are $30 million, and the effective federal-plus-state tax rate is 40 percent.

a. What is the return on equity for each firm if the interest rate on current liabilities is 10 percent and the rate on long-term debt is 13 percent?

b. Assume that the short-term rate rises to 20 percent. While the rate on new long-term debt rises to 16 percent, the rate on existing long-term debt remains unchanged. What would be the return on equity for Vanderheiden Press and Herrenhouse Publishing under these conditions?

c. Which company is in a riskier position? Why?

ST-2   The Calgary Company is attempting to establish a working capital investment policy. Net fixed assets are $300,000, and the firm plans to maintain a 50 percent debt-to-assets ratio. The interest rate is 10 percent on all debt. Three alternative current asset levels are under consideration: 40, 50, and 60 percent of projected sales. The company expects to earn 15 percent before interest and taxes on sales of $1.5 million. Calgary's effective federal-plus-state tax rate is 40 percent. What is the expected return on equity under each alternative?

Problems

8-1
Working capital policy

Consider the following balance sheet:

**National Business Machines (NBM):
Balance Sheet, December 31, 1993**

Assets	
Cash	$ 100,000
Marketable securities	40,000
Accounts receivable	660,000
Inventory	1,000,000
Net plant and equipment	1,800,000
Total assets	$3,600,000

Liabilities and Shareholders' Equity	
Accounts payable	$ 160,000
Notes payable	240,000
Accrued wages	40,000
Accrued taxes	140,000
Mortgage bonds	800,000
Other long-term debt	420,000
Common stock	200,000
Paid-in capital	400,000
Retained earnings	1,200,000
Total liabilities and shareholders' equity	$3,600,000

a. Determine NBM's investment in gross working capital.

b. Determine NBM's net working capital investment.

c. Does the firm's financing mix (long-term versus short-term) appear to be conservative or aggressive?

8-2
Cash conversion cycle

The Shay Container Company has an inventory conversion period of 72 days, a receivables conversion period of 52 days, and a payables deferral period of 38 days.

a. What is the length of the firm's cash conversion cycle?

b. If Shay's sales are $3,240,000 and all sales are on credit, what is the firm's investment in accounts receivable?

c. How many times per year does Shay turn over its inventory?

8-3
Cash conversion cycle

T. J. Peroni & Company has $2.4 million in sales for the year (all credit sales), inventory of $280,000, and net fixed assets of $1 million. The firm has $100,000 in cash and marketable securities combined, and its total assets turnover ratio is 1.5 times.

a. What is T. J. Peroni's investment into accounts receivable?

b. If the payables deferral period is 30 days, what is T. J. Peroni's cash conversion cycle?

c. What is the firm's inventory turnover ratio?

8-4
Return on equity

Hunter & Tharp Inc. has sales of $12 million, earnings before interest and taxes of $1.4 million, and total assets of $5 million. Assets have been financed with $2,250,000 of 9 percent debt, the balance by common equity. The firm's average federal-plus-state tax rate is 40 percent.

a. What is Hunter & Tharp's return on equity?

b. If half of the firm's debt were short-term bank borrowing and short-term rates raise to 14 percent because of an inverted yield curve, what would be Hunter & Tharp's new ROE? (Assume long-term funds still cost 9 percent.)

8-5

Net working capital

A company has a quick ratio of 1.3× and a current ratio of 2.5×. Total current assets are $1.9 million. What is the firm's net working capital?

8-6

Current asset investment

Kazuya Motors Inc. (KMI) is a leading manufacturer of small electric motors. KMI turns out 1,000 motors a day at a cost of $9 per motor for materials and labor. It takes the firm 30 days to convert the raw materials into a motor. The motors are shipped to dealers immediately upon completion of the manufacturing process. KMI allows its customers 45 days in which to pay for the motors, and the firm generally pays its suppliers in 30 days.

a. What is the length of KMI's cash conversion cycle?

b. In a steady state in which KMI produces 1,000 motors a day, what amount of current assets must it finance?

c. By what amount could KMI reduce its current asset financing needs if it were able to stretch its payables deferral period to 35 days?

d. KMI's management is trying to analyze the effect of a proposed new manufacturing process on the firm's current asset investment. The new production process would allow KMI to decrease its inventory conversion period to 27 days and to increase its daily production to 1,200 motors. However, the new process would increase the cost of materials and labor to $10 per unit. Assuming the change does not affect the receivables conversion period (45 days) or the payables deferral period (30 days), what will be the length of the cash conversion cycle and the current asset financing requirement if the new production process is implemented? Assume finished goods inventory remains near zero.

8-7

Working capital financing policies

Martin Bassman has been evaluating his firm's financing mix of short-term and long-term debt. He has projected the two following condensed balance sheets:

	Plan 1	Plan 2
Current assets	$2,500,000	$2,500,000
Net fixed assets	2,500,000	2,500,000
Total assets	$5,000,000	$5,000,000
Current liabilities	$ 500,000	$2,000,000
Long-term debt	2,000,000	500,000
Common stock equity	2,500,000	2,500,000
Total liabilities and equity	$5,000,000	$5,000,000

Earnings before interest and taxes (EBIT) are $750,000, and the tax rate is 40 percent under either plan.

a. If current liabilities have a 7 percent interest rate and long-term debt has an 11 percent interest rate, what is the rate of return on equity under each plan?

b. Assume that the yield curve is inverted and that the short-term rate is 15 percent while the long-term rate is still 11 percent. What is the rate of return on equity for the two plans?

c. Which plan is riskier? Explain.

8-8

Working capital policy

Jack Galanis, financial manager for Nassau Tool Works has a problem. The firm's board of directors has complained about the firm's low liquidity. Jack has been ordered to raise the current ratio to at least 2.0 within a reasonable time period. One of his plans is to sell $5,000,000 in equity and invest the proceeds in Treasury bills, which yield 5 percent before taxes. The firm has a 40 percent tax rate, and, if no Treasury bills are purchased, net income is expected to be $2,000,000. Assume 100 percent dividend payout.

Nassau Tools Works:
Balance Sheet, December 31, 1993

Current assets	$10,000,000	Current liabilities	$ 6,250,000
Net fixed assets	15,000,000	Long-term debt	3,750,000
		Common stock equity	15,000,000
Total assets	$25,000,000	Total liabilities and equity	$25,000,000

a. Using the financial information in the accompanying balance sheet (which does not include the proposed purchase of Treasury bills), calculate the firm's current ratio, net working capital, and return on equity.
b. If Jack follows his plan and sells $5,000,000 in equity in order to purchase the 5 percent Treasury bills, what are the firm's resulting current ratio, net working capital, and return on equity?
c. What result would the plan have on the firm's liquidity?
d. Would you suggest acceptance of this plan?

8-9

Alternative working capital financing policies

Management of Li Fibre Inc. is concerned about the way in which its new firm will be financed. The three alternative plans that have been proposed are as follows:

	Plan 1	Plan 2	Plan 3
Current assets	$4,500,000	$4,500,000	$4,500,000
Fixed assets	8,000,000	8,000,000	8,000,000
Current liabilities (8.5%)	4,500,000	1,500,000	3,000,000
Long-term debt (12%)	1,500,000	4,500,000	0
Common stock equity	6,500,000	6,500,000	9,500,000

Whichever plan is chosen, sales are expected to be $20 million and operating profits (EBIT) will be $2 million. The marginal tax rate is 40 percent.
a. For each plan, calculate the following: (1) current ratio, (2) net working capital, (3) total debt/total assets ratio, and (4) return on equity.
b. Compare the risk and return associated with each plan. Which plan would you accept?

8-10

Cash conversion cycle

The balance sheet of Caspersen Enterprises follows:

Cash	$ 200,000	Debt	$ 816,000
Accounts receivable	620,000		
Inventory	540,000	Equity	1,344,000
Net fixed assets	800,000		
Total assets	$2,160,000	Total liabilities and equity	$2,160,000

The company's sales are $3,600,000 annually, the payables deferral period is 35 days, and the net profit margin is 6 percent. Compute the firm's (a) inventory turnover (S/Inv), (b) inventory conversion period, (c) days sales outstanding (DSO), (d) cash conversion cycle, and (e) return on assets (ROA).

8-11

Cash conversion cycle

Refer to the data in Problem 8-10. The company's owner, Marianne Caspersen, is too busy to oversee all the financial aspects of the business. She decides to hire Mel Brannigan to reduce current assets. After some study, Brannigan concludes he can reduce the firm's inventory conversion period by 14 days and the days sales outstanding (DSO) by 20 days without reducing its sales or profit margin. Under these new conditions:
a. What is the new level of inventory?
b. What is the new level of accounts receivable?
c. What is the length of the firm's cash conversion cycle after these changes are implemented?

d. If all of the savings (from the reduction in inventory and accounts receivable) are used to reduce debt, what is the firm's return on assets? (Assume the profit margin remains constant.)

8-12

Cash conversion cycle

Plank & Capaldi Inc. (P&C) is trying to determine the effects of its inventory turnover ratio and days sales outstanding (DSO) on its cash conversion cycle. P&C's 1993 sales (all on credit) were $150,000, and it earned a net profit of 6 percent, or $9,000. It turned over its inventory 6 times during the year, and its DSO was 36 days. The firm had fixed assets totaling $40,000. P&C's payables deferral period is 40 days.

a. Calculate P&C's cash conversion cycle.
b. Assuming P&C holds negligible amounts of cash and marketable securities, calculate its total assets turnover and ROA.
c. P&C's managers believe that the inventory turnover can be raised to 8 times. What would P&C's cash conversion cycle, total assets turnover, and ROA have been if the inventory turnover had been 8 for 1993?

8-13

Working capital policy

Three companies—Aggressive, Between, and Conservative—have different working capital management policies as implied by their names. For example, Aggressive employs only minimal current assets, and it finances almost entirely with current liabilities plus equity. This "tight-ship" approach has a dual effect. It keeps total assets low, which tends to increase return on assets, but because of stock-outs and credit rejections, total sales are reduced, and since inventory is ordered more frequently and in smaller quantitites, variable costs are increased. Condensed balance sheets for the three companies are presented below.

	Aggressive	Between	Conservative
Current assets	$150,000	$200,000	$300,000
Net fixed assets	200,000	200,000	200,000
Total assets	$350,000	$400,000	$500,000
Current liabilities (cost = 8%)	$200,000	$100,000	$ 50,000
Long-term debt (cost = 10%)	0	100,000	200,000
Total debt	$200,000	$200,000	$250,000
Common equity	150,000	200,000	250,000
Total liabilities and equity	$350,000	$400,000	$500,000
Current ratio	0.75	2	6

Cost of goods sold = Fixed costs + Variable costs.
Aggressive: Cost of goods sold = $200,000 + 0.70(Sales).
Between: Cost of goods sold = $270,000 + 0.65(Sales).
Conservative: Cost of goods sold = $385,000 + 0.60(Sales).

The cost of goods sold functions for the three firms are as follows:

Because of the working capital differences, sales for the three firms under different economic conditions are expected to vary as indicated next:

	Aggressive	Between	Conservative
Strong economy	$1,200,000	$1,250,000	$1,300,000
Average economy	900,000	1,000,000	1,150,000
Weak economy	700,000	800,000	1,050,000

a. Construct income statements for each company for strong, average, and weak economies using the following format:

Sales
Less: cost of goods sold
Earnings before interest and taxes (EBIT)
Less: interest expense
Earnings before taxes (EBT)
Less: taxes (at 40%)
Net income

b. Compare the basic earning power (EBIT/Total assets) and return on equity (Net income/Common equity) for the companies. Which company is best in a strong economy? In an average economy? In a weak economy?
(Do Parts c, d, and e only if you are using the computerized diskette.)
c. Suppose, with sales at the average economy level, short-term interest rates rose to 20 percent. How would that affect the three firms?
d. Suppose that because of production slowdowns caused by inventory shortages, the aggressive company's variable cost ratio rises to 80 percent. What would happen to its ROE, assuming an average economy and a short-term rate of 8 percent?
e. What considerations for management of working capital are indicated by this problem?

Solutions to Self-Test Problems

ST-1   a. and b.

Income Statements for Year Ended December 31, 1993 (Thousands of Dollars)

	Vanderheiden Press		Herrenhouse Publishing	
	a	b	a	b
EBIT	$ 30,000	$ 30,000	$ 30,000	$ 30,000
Interest	12,400	14,400	10,600	18,600
Earnings before taxes	$ 17,600	$ 15,600	$ 19,400	$ 11,400
Taxes (40%)	7,040	6,240	7,760	4,560
Net income	$ 10,560	$ 9,360	$ 11,640	$ 6,840
Equity	$100,000	$100,000	$100,000	$100,000
Return on equity	10.56%	9.36%	11.64%	6.84%

The Vanderheiden Press has a higher ROE when short-term interest rates are high, whereas Herrenhouse Publishing does better when rates are lower.
c. Herrenhouse's position is riskier. First, its profits and return on equity are much more volatile than Vanderheiden's. Second, Herrenhouse must renew its large short-term loan every year, and if the renewal comes up at a time when money is very tight, when its business is depressed, or both, then Herrenhouse could be denied credit, which could put it out of business.

ST-2   **The Calgary Company:
Alternative Balance Sheets**

	Aggressive (40%)	Moderate (50%)	Conservative (60%)
Current assets	$ 600,000	$ 750,000	$ 900,000
Net fixed assets	300,000	300,000	300,000
Total assets	$ 900,000	$1,050,000	$1,200,000
Debt	$ 450,000	$ 525,000	$ 600,000
Equity	450,000	525,000	600,000
Total liabilities and equity	$ 900,000	$1,050,000	$1,200,000

**The Calgary Company:
Alternative Income Statements**

	Aggressive (40%)	Moderate (50%)	Conservative (60%)
Sales	$1,500,000	$1,500,000	$1,500,000
EBIT	225,000	225,000	225,000
Interest (10%)	45,000	52,500	60,000
Earnings before taxes	$ 180,000	$ 172,500	$ 165,000
Taxes (40%)	72,000	69,000	66,000
Net income	$ 108,000	$ 103,500	$ 99,000
ROE	24.0%	19.7%	16.5%

Managing Cash and Marketable Securities

OBJECTIVES

After reading this chapter, you should be able to:

▷ State the primary goal of cash management and the types of cash balances that should be considered.

▷ Construct a cash budget, and explain its purpose.

▷ Explain how synchronized cash flows can improve cash management and how a lockbox plan can speed up a firm's collections.

▷ Define the terms "disbursement float," "collections float," and "net float."

▷ List several techniques used by firms to slow down and control their own disbursements.

▷ Explain what is meant by "matching the costs and benefits of cash management."

▷ Explain why firms are likely to hold marketable securities, what types of risk should be considered, and which securities are appropriate as near-cash reserves.

WHAT DO YOU DO WITH SURPLUS CASH?

Businesses cannot survive without enough cash to pay bills and to finance growth. On the other hand, having too much cash is inefficient because cash earns considerably less than a firm's cost of capital. Therefore, it is essential that firms put their money to work to maximize value, and when they invest excess cash, they must strike a balance between risk and expected returns.

Several large entertainment companies, who went through the 1980s buying, selling, merging, and purging, are sitting on huge cash stockpiles. Currently, Paramount, Disney, Capital Cities/ABC, and CBS each have over $1 billion in cash, and they expect their stockpiles to increase during 1993. For most of these companies, cash holdings are only temporary, while they seek out strategic acquisitions. But, as a Merrill Lynch media analyst states: "There's a liquidity trap. Companies sit on cash looking around for opportunities but don't find them because of the maturity of the business. There isn't enough to buy at the right price at the current time." Another analyst put it more bluntly: During these times, when interest rates are so low, "cash is trash."

Companies receive pressure from Wall Street and shareholders to use their excess cash. But

See end of chapter for resolution.
Photo source: © COMSTOCK, INC.

how much cash is too much? And if a firm really does have excess cash—defined as cash that cannot be invested in the firm's core business except at a rate of return below its cost of capital—should this cash be used to acquire another company, to repurchase its own stock, or to increase dividends? All these alternatives are possible uses for excess cash. As you read this chapter, consider the reasons for holding  cash and marketable securities, the strategies involved in investing cash, and the factors influencing the choice of securities held in the firm's investment portfolio. Think about the alternatives each treasurer must consider in reaching his or her decision regarding what to do with excess cash.

Any business firm requires cash to pay for labor and materials, to buy fixed assets, to pay taxes, and so on. As we discussed in Chapter 8, the financial manager must consider the risk and return implications of working capital decisions. Because currency (and most commercial checking accounts) earns no interest, cash is generally considered a "nonearning" asset. Overinvestment in cash may reduce the firm's earning power, but underinvestment may cause the firm to be unable to meet some of its operating obligations. Thus, the goal of the cash manager is to reduce the amount of cash held to the minimum necessary to conduct business. Like cash, marketable securities provide lower yields than the firm's operating assets; however, many corporations report sizable securities balances on their financial statements. As we will learn later in this chapter, corporations do have good reasons for holding marketable securities.

Cash Management

Approximately 1.5 percent of the average industrial firm's assets are held in the form of **cash,** which is defined as demand deposits plus currency. In addition, sizable holdings of near-cash, short-term marketable securities such as U.S. Treasury bills (T-bills) or bank certificates of deposit (CDs) are often reported on corporate financial statements. However, cash balances vary widely both across industries and among the firms within a given industry, depending on the individual firms' specific conditions and on their owners' and managers' aversion to risk. We begin our analysis with a discussion of the reasons why firms hold cash. These same factors, incidentally, apply to the cash holdings of individuals and nonprofit organizations, including government agencies.

Reasons for Holding Cash (or Marketable Securities)

Firms hold cash for four primary reasons, but although the first two of these are generally satisfied by holding actual cash (a checking account balance), the last two requirements may be met instead by holding highly liquid marketable securities. These can be turned into cash very quickly and, thus, serve as "near cash," or as a substitute for cash. The advantage to this approach is that marketable securities will provide a return — even at today's low interest rate level — while most business checking accounts do not earn interest. The reasons that firms hold cash are as follows:

1. **Transactions.**   Cash balances are necessary in business operations. Payments must be made in cash, and receipts are deposited in the cash account. Those cash balances associated with routine payments and collections are known as **transactions balances.**

2. **Compensation to banks for providing loans and services.**   A bank makes money by lending out funds that have been deposited with it, so the larger its deposits, the better the bank's profit position. If a bank is providing services to a customer, it generally requires the customer to leave a minimum balance on deposit to help offset the costs of providing the services. This type of balance, defined as a **compensating balance,** is discussed in detail later in this chapter.

---

cash

The total of bank demand deposits plus currency.

transactions balances

Cash balances associated with payments and collections; those balances necessary to conduct day-to-day operations.

compensating balance

A checking account balance that a firm must maintain with a commercial bank to compensate the bank for services rendered.

3. **Precaution.** Cash inflows and outflows are somewhat unpredictable, with the degree of predictability varying among firms and industries. Therefore, firms need to hold some cash (or, more often, marketable securities) in reserve for random, unforeseen fluctuations in inflows and outflows. These "safety stocks" are called **precautionary balances,** and the less predictable the firm's cash flows, the larger the necessary cash balances. However, if the firm has easy access to borrowed funds—that is, if it can borrow on short notice—its need to hold cash or marketable securities for precautionary purposes is reduced.

4. **Speculation.** Cash balances may also be held to enable the firm to take advantage of any bargain purchases that might arise; these funds are defined as **speculative balances.** As with precautionary balances, firms today are more likely to rely on reserve borrowing capacity and on marketable securities portfolios than on cash per se for speculative purposes.

Although the cash accounts of most firms can be thought of as consisting of transactions, compensating, precautionary, and speculative balances, we cannot calculate the amount needed for each purpose, add them together, and produce a total desired cash balance because the same money often serves more than one purpose. For instance, precautionary and speculative balances can also be used to satisfy compensating balance requirements. Firms do, however, consider these four factors when establishing their target cash positions.

While there are good reasons for holding *adequate* cash balances, there is an important reason for not holding *excessive* balances. Since cash is a nonearning asset, excessive cash balances simply lower the total assets turnover, thereby reducing both the firm's rate of return on equity and the value of its stock. Therefore, firms are interested in establishing procedures for increasing the efficiency of their cash management, and the higher the level of short-term interest rates, the greater the **opportunity cost** associated with holding excess cash. Opportunity cost is the return that could be earned on the best alternative investment available *of equal risk*—in this case, the return that could be earned on, say, U.S. Treasury bills. If firms can make their cash work harder, they can reduce cash balances. We now turn to a discussion of the procedures business firms use to increase cash management efficiency.

precautionary balances
Cash balances *or marketable securities* held in reserve for random, unforeseen fluctuations in cash inflows and outflows.

speculative balances
Cash balances *or marketable securities* that are held to enable the firm to take advantage of any bargain purchases that might arise.

opportunity cost
The return on the best alternative investment available of equal risk.

Self-Test

Why is cash management important?

Which of the four primary reasons for holding cash typically require that firms hold *actual cash* (a checking account balance)?

Which types of balances may be satisfied by holding marketable securities instead of actual cash?

The Cash Budget

A firm normally estimates its need for cash as a part of its general budgeting, or forecasting, process. First, it forecasts sales. Next, it forecasts the fixed assets and inventories that will be required to meet the forecasted sales levels. Asset

cash budget

A schedule showing cash flows (receipts, disbursements, and cash balances) for a firm over a specified period.

purchases and the actual payments for them are then put on a time line, along with the actual and forecasted sales and the expected timing of collections on sales. For example, the typical firm makes a 5-year sales forecast, which is then used to help plan fixed asset acquisitions (capital budgeting). Then, the firm develops an annual forecast, in which sales and inventory purchases are projected on a monthly basis, along with the times when payments for both fixed assets and inventory purchases must be made. These forecasts are combined with the expected timing of collected accounts receivable, the schedule for payment of taxes, the dates when dividend and interest payments will be made, and so on. Finally, all of this information is summarized in the **cash budget,** which shows the firm's projected cash inflows and outflows over some specified period of time.

Cash budgets provide much more detailed information about a firm's expected future cash flows than that provided by forecasted financial statements, and the cash budget can be constructed on a monthly, weekly, or even daily basis. Generally, firms use a monthly cash budget over the next 6 to 12 months, plus a more detailed daily or weekly cash budget for the coming month. The longer-term budget is used for general planning purposes, and the shorter-term one for actual cash control.

Constructing the Cash Budget

We shall illustrate the process with a monthly cash budget covering the last six months of 1994 for the Dayton Card Company, a leading producer of greeting cards. Dayton's birthday and get-well cards are sold year-round, but the bulk of the company's sales occur during September, when retailers are stocking up for Christmas. At the present time, Dayton offers no cash discount for early payment but it does offer a generous 45-day credit period to its customers. Small accounts, which compose 20 percent of its total sales, are on a "cash only" basis and pay within the month of sale. However, credit customers take full advantage of Dayton's sales terms. Thus, for 70 percent of its sales, payment is made during the month after sales. A small percentage of Dayton's customers (10 percent) pay during the second month after sales. Dayton has had virtually no problem with bad debts, so all bills are paid within 90 days of the original date of sale.

Rather than produce at a uniform rate throughout the year, Dayton prints cards immediately before they are required for delivery. Paper, ink, and other materials amount to 70 percent of sales and are bought the month before the company expects to sell the finished product. Its own purchase terms permit Dayton to delay payment on its purchases for one month. Accordingly, if July sales are forecasted at $10 million, purchases during June will amount to $7 million, and this amount will actually be paid in July.

target cash balance

The cash balance that a firm plans to maintain in order to conduct business.

Other cash expenditures such as wages and rent are also built into the cash budget in Table 9-1. Dayton Card Company must make tax payments of $2 million on September 15 and December 15, as well as a progress payment in October for a new plant that is under construction. Assuming that it needs to keep a **target cash balance** of $2.5 million at all times and that it will have $3 million on July 1, what are Dayton's financial requirements for the period from July through December?

The monthly cash requirements are worked out in Table 9-1. Section I of the table provides a worksheet for calculating collections on sales and payments on purchases. Line 1 gives the sales forecast for the period May through December; May and June sales are necessary to determine collections for July and August. Next, on Lines 2 through 5, cash collections are projected. Line 2 shows that 20 percent of the sales during any given month are expected to be collected during that month. These sales are on a "cash only" basis, and these customers, of course, pay during the month of sale. Line 3 shows the expected collections on the previous month's sales, or 70 percent of sales in the preceding month; for example, in July, 70 percent of the $5 million June sales, or $3.5 million, will be collected. Line 4 gives expected collections from sales two months earlier, or 10 percent of sales in that month; for example, the July collections for May sales are $(0.10)($5 million$) = $0.5 million. The collections during each month are summed and shown on Line 5; thus, the July collections represent 20 percent of July sales plus 70 percent of June sales plus 10 percent of May sales, or $6 million in total. We assume in this example that the firm will, in fact, be able to collect on all its credit sales. As we shall see in Chapter 10, credit losses are sometimes incurred.

Next, payments for purchases of raw materials are shown. July sales are forecasted at $10 million, so Dayton will purchase $7 million of materials in June (Line 6) and pay for these purchases in July (Line 7). Similarly, Dayton will purchase $10.5 million of materials in July to print cards to meet August's forecasted sales of $15 million.

With Section I completed, Section II can be constructed. Cash from collections is shown on Line 8. Lines 9 through 14 list payments made during each month, and these payments are summed on Line 15. The difference between cash receipts and cash payments (Line 8 minus Line 15) is the net cash gain or loss during the month; for July there is a net cash loss of $2.1 million, as shown on Line 16.

In Section III, we first determine Dayton's cumulative cash balance at the end of each month, assuming no borrowing is done. Then, we determine the company's forecasted cash surplus or the loan balance, if any, that is needed to force Dayton's cash balance to equal the target cash balance. The cash on hand at the beginning of the month is shown on Line 17. We assume that Dayton will have $3 million on hand on July 1, but thereafter the beginning cash balance is the cumulative cash balance (Line 18) from the previous month. The beginning cash balance (Line 17) is added to the net cash gain or loss during the month (Line 16) to obtain the cumulative cash that would be on hand *if no financing were done* (Line 18); at the end of July, Dayton forecasts a cumulative cash balance of $0.9 million in the absence of borrowing.

The target cash balance, $2.5 million, is then subtracted from the cumulative cash balance to determine the firm's borrowing requirements or surplus cash. Because Dayton expects to have cumulative cash, as shown on Line 18, of $0.9 million in July, it will have to borrow $1.6 million to bring the cash account up to the target balance of $2.5 million. Assuming that this amount is indeed borrowed, loans outstanding will total $1.6 million at the end of July. (We assume that Dayton did not have any loans outstanding on July 1, because its beginning cash balance exceeded the target balance.) The cash surplus or

Table 9-1 Dayton Card Company: Cash Budget (Thousands of Dollars)

	May	June	July	Aug.	Sept.	Oct.	Nov.	Dec.
I. Collections and Purchases Worksheet								
(1) Sales[a]	$5,000	$5,000	$10,000	$15,000	$20,000	$10,000	$10,000	$5,000
Collections During:								
(2) Month of sales (20%)	1,000	1,000	2,000	3,000	4,000	2,000	2,000	1,000
(3) First month after sale month (70%)		3,500	3,500	7,000	10,500	14,000	7,000	7,000
(4) Second month after sale month (10%)			500	500	1,000	1,500	2,000	1,000
(5) Total collections	$1,000	$4,500	$6,000	$10,500	$15,500	$17,500	$11,000	$9,000
(6) Purchases (70% of next month's sales)	$3,500	$7,000	$10,500	$14,000	$7,000	$7,000	$3,500	
(7) Payments (1-month lag)		$3,500	$7,000	$10,500	$14,000	$7,000	$7,000	$3,500
II. Cash Gain or Loss for Month								
(8) Collections (from Line 5)			$6,000	$10,500	$15,500	$17,500	$11,000	$9,000
Payments (Outflows):								
(9) Payments for purchases (from Line 7)			$7,000	$10,500	$14,000	$7,000	$7,000	$3,500
(10) Wages and salaries			750	1,000	1,250	750	750	500
(11) Rent			250	250	250	250	250	250
(12) Other expenses			100	150	200	100	100	50
(13) Taxes					2,000			2,000
(14) Payment for plant construction						5,000		
(15) Total payments			$8,100	$11,900	$17,700	$13,100	$8,100	$6,300
(16) Net cash gain (loss) during month (Line 8 – Line 15)			($2,100)	($1,400)	($2,200)	$4,400	$2,900	$2,700
III. Cash Surplus or Loan Requirements								
(17) Cash at start of month if no borrowing is done[b]			$3,000	$900	($500)	($2,700)	$1,700	$4,600
(18) Cumulative cash prior to financing (cash at start + gain or – loss = Line 16 + Line 17)			$900	($500)	($2,700)	$1,700	$4,600	$7,300
(19) Target cash balance			2,500	2,500	2,500	2,500	2,500	2,500
(20) Surplus cash or total loans outstanding required to maintain $2,500 target cash balance (Line 18 – Line 19)[c]			($1,600)	($3,000)	($5,200)	($800)	$2,100	$4,800

[a] Although the budget period is July through December, sales and purchases data for May and June are needed to determine collections and payments during July and August.

[b] The amount shown on Line 17 for the first budget period month, the $3,000 balance on July 1, is assumed to be on hand initially. The values shown for each of the following months on Line 17 are equal to the cumulative cash as shown on Line 18 for the preceding month; for example, the $900 shown on Line 17 for August is taken from Line 18 in the July column.

[c] When the target cash balance of $2,500 (Line 19) is deducted from the cumulative cash balance (Line 18), a resulting negative figure on Line 20 represents a required loan, whereas a positive figure represents surplus cash. Loans are required from July through October, and surpluses are expected during November and December. Note also that firms can borrow or pay off loans on a daily basis, as needed, and during October the $5,200 loan that existed at the beginning of the month would be reduced daily to the $800 ending balance, which in turn would be completely paid off during November.

required loan balance is given on Line 20; a positive value indicates a cash surplus, whereas a negative value indicates a loan requirement. Note that the surplus cash or loan requirement shown on Line 20 is a *cumulative amount.* Thus, Dayton must borrow $1.6 million in July; it has a cash shortfall during August of $1.4 million as reported on Line 16; and, therefore, its total loan requirement at the end of August is $1.6 million + $1.4 million = $3 million, as reported on Line 20. Dayton's arrangement with the bank permits it to increase its outstanding loans on a daily basis, up to a prearranged maximum, just as you could increase the amount you owe on a credit card. Dayton will use any surplus funds it generates to pay off its loans, and because the loan can be paid down at any time, Dayton will never have both a cash surplus and an outstanding loan balance.

This same procedure is used in the following months. Sales will peak in September, accompanied by increased payments for purchases, wages, and other items. Receipts from sales will also go up, but the firm will still be left with a $2.2 million net cash outflow during the month. The total loan requirement at the end of September will be $5.2 million, the cumulative cash plus the target cash balance. This amount is also equal to the $3 million needed at the end of August plus the $2.2 million cash deficit for September. Thus, loans outstanding will hit a high of $5.2 million at the end of September.

Sales, purchases, and payments for past purchases will fall sharply in October, and collections will be the highest of any month because they will reflect the high September sales. As a result, Dayton will enjoy a healthy $4.4 million net cash gain during October. This net gain will be used to pay off borrowings, so loans outstanding will decline by $4.4 million, to $0.8 million.

Dayton will have another cash surplus in November, which will permit it to pay off all of its loans. In fact, the company is expected to have $2.1 million in surplus cash by the month's end, and another cash surplus in December will swell the extra cash to $4.8 million. With such a large amount of unneeded funds, Dayton's treasurer will certainly want to invest in interest-bearing securities or to put the funds to use in some other way. Various types of investments into which Dayton might put its excess funds are discussed later in this chapter.

Before concluding our discussion of the cash budget, we should make some additional points:

1. Our cash budget example does not reflect interest on loans required to maintain the target level cash balance or income from the investment of surplus cash. These refinements could easily be added.

2. If cash inflows and outflows are not uniform during the month, Dayton could be seriously understating the firm's peak financing requirements. The data in Table 9-1 show the situation expected on the last day of each month, but on any given day during the month it could be quite different. For example, if all payments must be made on the fifth of the month, but collections come in uniformly throughout the month, Dayton would need to borrow much larger amounts than those shown in Table 9-1. In this case, the company would need to prepare a cash budget on a daily basis.[1]

---

[1] Note that the cash budget framework presented in Table 9-1 is as valid for Monday/Tuesday/Wednesday, etc., as it is for July/August/September, etc.

3. Because depreciation is a noncash expense, it does not appear in the cash budget.

4. Because the cash budget represents a forecast, all the values in the table are *expected* values. If actual sales, collections, and so on, are different from the forecasted levels, then the projected cash deficits and surpluses will also be incorrect. Therefore, the financial manager will wish to constantly monitor the cash budget during the period and modify it to conform to actual changes in the amount and timing of cash inflows or disbursements.

5. Computerized spreadsheet programs such as *Lotus 1-2-3* are particularly well suited for constructing and analyzing cash budgets, especially with respect to the sensitivity of cash flows to changes in sales levels, collection periods, and the like. With computerized models, one can instantly answer questions such as, "If collections slow down, what will the firm's cash needs be?"

6. Methods have been developed for setting and controlling a firm's cash balance, based on such variables as the fixed costs of obtaining a loan or of liquidating marketable securities and the opportunity cost of holding cash. One such method is the Baumol model, which is based on the observation that cash balances are, in many respects, similar to inventories. Therefore, the EOQ model (covered in Chapter 10) can be used to establish a firm's target cash balance. The essence of this model is minimization of the total costs associated with holding and obtaining cash, in light of the firm's typical cash needs.[2]

7. Finally, we should note that the target cash balance probably will be adjusted over time, rising and falling with seasonal patterns and with long-term changes in the scale of the firm's operations. Factors that influence the target cash balance are discussed in the following section.

Factors Influencing the Target Cash Balance

Any firm's target cash balance is normally set as the larger of (1) its transactions balances plus precautionary (safety stock) balances or (2) its required compensating balances as determined by its agreements with banks. The transactions and the precautionary balances depend on the firm's volume of business, on the degree of uncertainty inherent in its forecast of cash inflows and outflows, and on its ability to borrow on short notice to cover cash shortfalls. Recalling our cash budget for Dayton Card Company, the target cash balance could have been reduced if the firm had been able to predict its inflows and outflows with greater precision. Dayton, like most firms, does not know exactly when bills will come in or when payments will be received. Therefore, balances must be sufficient to allow for a random increase in required payments at a time when receipts lag behind expectations. Most firms keep higher cash balances than ab-

[2]See William J. Baumol, "The Transactions Demand for Cash: An Inventory Theoretical Approach," *Quarterly Journal of Economics,* November 1952, 545–556. See also Brigham and Gapenski, *Intermediate Financial Management,* Fourth Edition, Chapter 21.

solutely necessary for transactions purposes to lower the probability that reduced inflows or unexpected outflows will cause them to run out of cash. Although we do not consider them in this book, statistical procedures are available to help improve cash flow forecasts, and the better the cash flow forecast, the lower the minimum cash balance.

Self-Test

What is the purpose of the cash budget?

What is done in each of the three sections of the cash budget?

Why is depreciation not included in the cash budget?

What would happen to the monthly cash budget if cash inflows and outflows were not uniform during the month? How might the cash budget be modified when this situation occurs?

Cash Management Techniques

Cash management has changed significantly over the last 20 years as a result of two factors. First, from the early 1970s to the early 1980s, there was a clear upward trend in interest rates which increased the opportunity cost of holding cash and, therefore, encouraged financial managers to search for more efficient ways of managing the firm's cash. This trend in interest rates was reversed in the second decade from about 1982 until today, a period of largely declining rates, but the newly developed focus on cash management remained. Second, new techniques, particularly computerized electronic funds transfer mechanisms, have made improved cash management possible.

Although a carefully prepared cash budget is a necessary starting point for managing the firm's cash, there are other elements of a good cash management program. The primary cash management activities are performed jointly by the firm and its main bank, but the financial manager is responsible for the effectiveness of the cash management program. The most commonly used cash management techniques will be discussed in the following sections.

Cash Flow Synchronization

If you, as an individual, were to receive income once a year, you would probably put it in the bank, draw down your account periodically, and have an average balance during the year equal to about half your annual income. If you received income monthly instead of once a year, you would operate similarly, but now your average balance would be much smaller. If you could arrange to receive income daily and to pay rent, tuition, and other charges on a daily basis, and if you were quite confident of your forecasted inflows and outflows, then you could hold a very small average cash balance.

Exactly the same situation holds for business firms; by improving their forecasts and by arranging things so that cash receipts coincide with the timing of cash outflows, firms can reduce their transactions balances to a minimum. Recognizing this point, utility companies, oil companies, department stores, and

synchronized cash flows

A situation in which inflows coincide with outflows, thereby permitting a firm to reduce transactions balances to a minimum.

other firms arrange to bill customers and to pay their own bills on regular "billing cycles" throughout the month. In our cash budgeting example, if Dayton Card Company could arrange more **synchronized cash flows** and could increase the certainty of its forecasts, it would be able to reduce its cash balances, decrease its required bank loans, lower interest expenses, and boost profits.

The Check-Clearing Process

When a customer writes and mails a check, this does *not* mean that the funds are immediately available to the receiving firm. Most of us have been told by someone that "the check is in the mail," and we have also deposited a check in our account and then been told that we cannot write our own checks against this deposit until the **check-clearing** process has been completed. Our bank must first make sure that the check we deposited is good and then receive funds itself from the customer's bank before giving us cash.

check clearing

The process of converting a check that has been written and mailed into cash in the payee's account.

As shown on the left side of Figure 9-1, quite a bit of time may be required for a firm to process incoming checks and obtain the use of the money. A check must first be delivered through the mail and then be cleared through the banking system before the money can be put to use. Checks received from customers in distant cities are especially subject to delays because of mail time and also because more parties are involved. For example, assume that we receive a check and deposit it in our bank. Our bank must send the check to the bank on which it was drawn. Only when this latter bank transfers funds to our bank are the funds available for us to use. Checks are generally cleared through the Federal Reserve System or through a clearinghouse set up by the banks in a particular city. Of course, if the check is deposited in the same bank on which it was drawn, that bank merely transfers funds by bookkeeping entries from one of its depositors to another. The length of time required for checks to clear is thus a function of the distance between the payer's and the payee's banks. In the case of private clearinghouses, it can range from one to three days. The maximum time required for checks to clear through the Federal Reserve System is two days, but mail delays can slow down things on each end of the Fed's involvement in the process.

Speeding Collections

An important aspect of cash management deals with processing the checks a company writes and receives. It is obviously inefficient to put checks received in a drawer and deposit them every week or so; no well-run business would follow such a practice. Similarly, cash balances are drawn down unnecessarily if bills are paid earlier than required. In fact, efficient firms go to great lengths to speed up the processing of incoming checks, thus putting the funds to work faster, and they try to stretch out their own payments as long as possible. At this point we will focus on a firm's efforts to collect faster from its customers; disbursement techniques will be covered in a later section.

Financial managers have searched for ways to collect receivables faster since credit transactions began. Although cash collection is the financial manager's responsibility, the speed with which checks are cleared is dependent on the banking system. Several techniques are now used both to speed collections

Figure 9-1   Diagram of the Check-Clearing Process

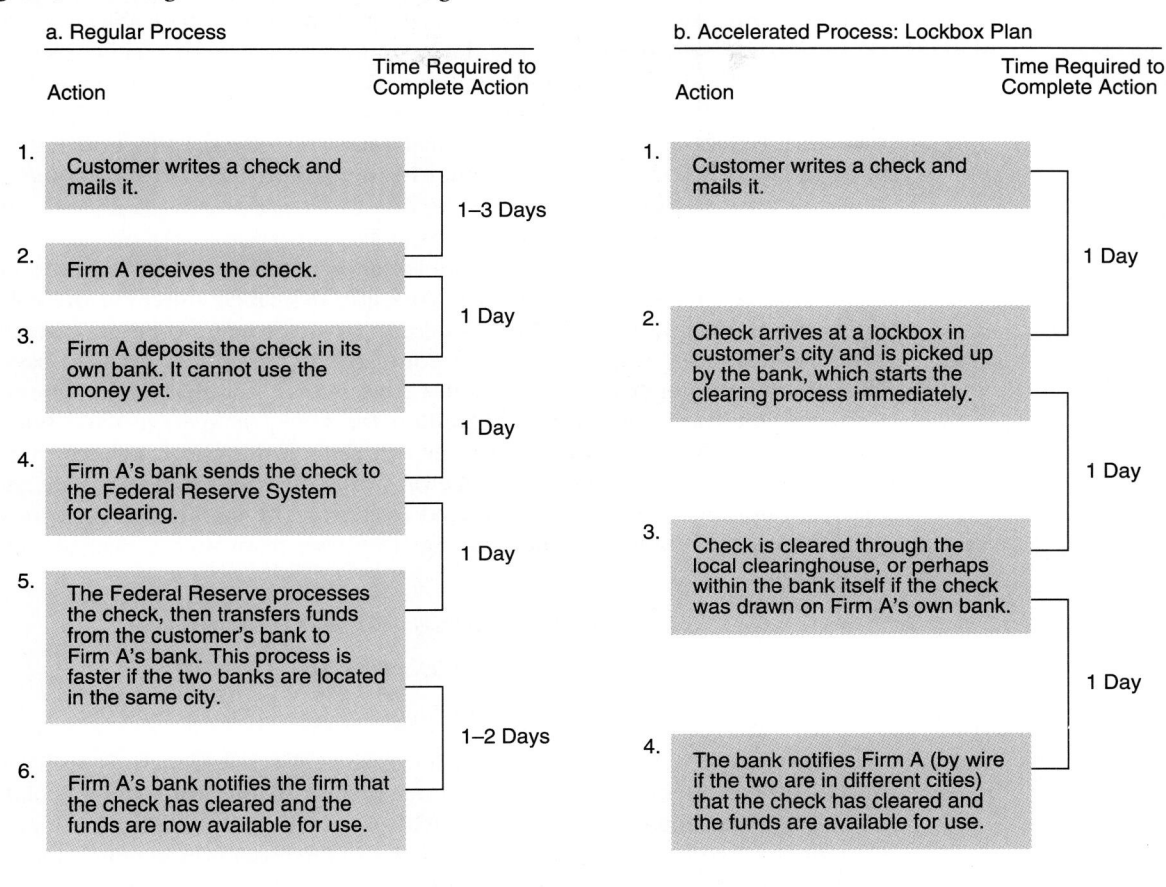

a. Regular Process

Action	Time Required to Complete Action
1. Customer writes a check and mails it.	1–3 Days
2. Firm A receives the check.	1 Day
3. Firm A deposits the check in its own bank. It cannot use the money yet.	1 Day
4. Firm A's bank sends the check to the Federal Reserve System for clearing.	1 Day
5. The Federal Reserve processes the check, then transfers funds from the customer's bank to Firm A's bank. This process is faster if the two banks are located in the same city.	1–2 Days
6. Firm A's bank notifies the firm that the check has cleared and the funds are now available for use.	

5–8 Working Days

b. Accelerated Process: Lockbox Plan

Action	Time Required to Complete Action
1. Customer writes a check and mails it.	1 Day
2. Check arrives at a lockbox in customer's city and is picked up by the bank, which starts the clearing process immediately.	1 Day
3. Check is cleared through the local clearinghouse, or perhaps within the bank itself if the check was drawn on Firm A's own bank.	1 Day
4. The bank notifies Firm A (by wire if the two are in different cities) that the check has cleared and the funds are available for use.	

3 Working Days

This figure illustrates how a lockbox plan can accelerate a company's collection of receivables by two to five working days. With the regular check-clearing process, a company must wait five to eight working days for a customer's payment to pass through the mail and clear through the banks and the Federal Reserve System. When a company uses a mailing address and bank in a customer's hometown, however, the check-clearing process is expedited and the company gains quicker access to its funds. It is possible for a company to free up several million dollars in cash by using lockboxes.

and to get funds where they are needed. Included are (1) lockbox plans, (2) pre-authorized debits, and (3) concentration banking.

lockbox plan

A procedure used to speed up collections through the use of post office boxes in payers' local areas.

Lockboxes.   A **lockbox plan** is one of the oldest cash management tools. In a lockbox system, incoming checks are sent to post office boxes rather than to corporate headquarters. For example, a firm headquartered in New York City might have its West Coast customers send their payments to a box in San Francisco, its customers in the Southwest send their checks to Dallas, and so on, rather than having all checks sent to New York City. Several times a day a local bank will collect the contents of the lockbox and deposit the checks into the company's local account. The bank would then provide the firm with a daily record of the receipts collected, usually via an electronic data transmission system in a format that permits on-line updating of the firm's receivables accounts.

A lockbox system reduces the time required for a firm to receive incoming checks, to deposit them, and to get them cleared through the banking system so that the funds are available for use. As shown on the right side of Figure 9-1, this time reduction occurs because mail time and check collection time are both reduced if the lockbox is located in the geographic area where the customer is located. Lockbox services can often increase the availability of funds by two to five days over the "regular" system.

Partly offsetting the advantages of a lockbox system is the fact that the local banks will, of course, charge the New York firm described above for the collections and funds-transfer services rendered. To determine whether a lockbox system is advantageous, the firm must compare the banks' fees with the savings from freeing up funds. For example, in Chapter 5 we saw that Carter Chemical Company had net sales of $3,000 million for 1993, or average daily sales of approximately $8.333 million. If Carter can reduce the check collection time on its customers' checks by an average of 3 days through a lockbox plan, and if the freed-up funds will then be invested in short-term, marketable securities to yield 4 percent, the gross annual savings to Carter from such a plan would be $1 million:

$$\text{Annual savings} = (\text{Average daily sales})\,(3)\,(0.04)$$

$$= (\$3,000 \text{ million}/360)\,(3)\,(0.04)$$

$$= \$1 \text{ million}$$

Therefore, if Carter can set up a lockbox plan for less than $1 million, it should do so, since it would result in net savings to the firm. The calculation also shows that higher annual savings will be realized by firms from a lockbox plan when (1) their volume of sales is high, (2) the reduction in collection time is significant, and (3) the opportunity cost is high, that is, what can be earned on freed-up funds by investing in marketable securities or paying down short-term debt. Other things equal, if short-term interest rates were to double to 8 percent, the gross savings to Carter (before the costs of the lockbox plan) would double also, to $2 million. Small wonder that in the early 1980s, when the prime rate was close to—and briefly above—20 percent, cash management techniques such as lockbox plans became extremely important.

pre-authorized debits

A method used to speed up collections through automatic transfers from customers' accounts on specified dates.

Pre-authorized Debits.   Another method of speeding collections is the use of **pre-authorized debits.** A pre-authorized debit allows funds to be automatically transferred from a customer's account to the firm's account on specified dates. These transactions are also called "checkless" or "paperless" transactions since they are accomplished without using traditional paper checks. However, a record of payment does appear on both parties' bank statements. Pre-authorized debiting accelerates the transfer of funds because mail and check-clearing times are totally eliminated, and they are used frequently for the payment of mortgages, taxes, utility bills, and payrolls. Although pre-authorized debits are efficient and appear to be the trend of the future, the pace of acceptance by payers has been much slower than was originally predicted, partly because peo-

disbursement float

The amount of a payer's checks that have been written but are still being processed and that have not been deducted from the account balance by the bank.

collections float

The amount of checks received but not yet credited to the payee's account.

concentration bank

Larger bank to which the firm channels funds from the local depository banks which operate its lockboxes.

depository transfer check (DTC)

A check that is restricted to use in making deposits to a particular account at a particular bank.

net float

The difference between a firm's checkbook balance and the balance shown on the bank's books, i.e., the difference between disbursement float and collections float.

ple like to be able to use cancelled checks as receipts and partly because a payer who agrees to a pre-authorized debit system is disadvantaged by the elimination of the inherent delay in the paper-based system. We say that the payer loses the use of **disbursement float.** Disbursement float is the amount of a payer's checks that have not been deducted from that payer's account balance by the bank because the checks have not yet cleared. With pre-authorized debits the disbursement float is zero. Compare this with the two check-clearing processes in Figure 9-1. Here the payer would have 5 to 8 working days of disbursement float under the regular process and 3 working days of disbursement float if the payee sets up a lockbox system and expedites the check-clearing process.

On the other hand, we saw that the firm which is collecting from its customers will benefit when float (funds in transit) is reduced to the absolute minimum, assuming that annual savings exceed annual costs of making the change. It would, therefore, prefer pre-authorized debits, which would reduce its **collections float** to zero. In other words, disbursement float is simply one side of the coin; collections float is the other: the amount of checks *received* but not yet *credited* to the payee's account. We will come back to this topic in a moment.

Concentration Banking.   Lockbox plans and pre-authorized debits, although efficient in speeding up collections, result in the firm's cash being spread around among many banks. The primary purpose of *concentration banking* is to mobilize funds from decentralized receiving locations into one or more central cash pools. The cash manager then uses these pools for short-term investing or reallocation among the firm's banks.

In a typical concentration system, the firm's collection banks record deposits received each day. Then, based on disbursement needs, the corporate cash manager transfers the funds from these collection points to a **concentration bank.** Concentration banking allows firms to take maximum advantage of economies of scale in cash management and investment, and funds transfers are typically either electronic, via a telecommunications network, or by **depository transfer check (DTC),** a check that is restricted to use in making deposits to a particular account at a particular bank, here the concentration bank.

Using Float

Float was briefly defined earlier as funds in transit. A more complete definition would be to say that float is the difference between the balance shown in a firm's (or individual's) checkbook and the balance on the bank's records. Suppose a firm writes, on the average, checks in the amount of $5,000 each day, and it takes six days for these checks to clear and be deducted from the firm's bank account. In other words, the firm has six days of disbursement float. Now suppose the same firm also receives checks in the amount of $5,000 daily but loses only four days while these checks are being deposited and cleared; the firm's collections float is four days. The firm's **net float**—the difference between the $30,000 ($5,000 × 6) positive disbursement float and the $20,000 ($5,000 × 4) negative collections float—is $10,000.

Net float = Disbursement float − Collections float

If the firm's own collection and clearing process is more efficient than that of the recipients of its checks—which is generally true of larger, more efficient firms—then the firm could actually show a *negative* balance on its own books but have a *positive* balance on the records of its bank. Some firms indicate that they *never* have positive book cash balances. One large manufacturer of construction equipment stated that while its account, according to its bank's records, shows an average cash balance of about $20 million, its *book* cash balance is *minus* $20 million—it has $40 million of net float. Obviously the firm must be able to forecast its disbursements and collections accurately in order to make such heavy use of float.

E. F. Hutton provides an example of pushing cash management too far. Hutton, a prominent, independent brokerage firm at the time, did business with banks all across the country, and it had to keep compensating balances in these banks. The sizes of the required compensating balances were known, and any excess funds in these banks were sent electronically, on a daily basis, to concentration banks, where they were immediately invested in interest-bearing securities. However, rather than waiting to see what the end-of-day balances actually were, Hutton began estimating inflows and outflows, and it transferred out for investment the *estimated* end-of-day excess. But then Hutton got greedy and began *kiting* checks. Hutton deliberately overestimated its deposits and underestimated clearings of its own checks, thereby deliberately overstating the estimated end-of-day balances. As a result, Hutton was chronically overdrawn at its local banks, and it was in effect earning interest on funds which really belonged to those local banks. It is entirely proper to forecast what your bank will have recorded as your balance and then to make decisions based on the estimate, even if that balance is different from the balance your own books show. However, it is illegal to forecast an overdrawn situation but then to tell the bank that you forecast a positive balance.[3]

Basically, the size of a firm's net float is a function of its ability to speed up collections on checks received and to slow down collections on checks written. As we have seen, efficient firms go to great lengths to speed up the processing of incoming checks, thus putting the funds to work faster. At the same time, they try to slow down their own payments as much as possible.

Slowing and Controlling Disbursements

One way for a firm to keep its cash on hand longer would simply be to delay payments, but this would lead to such obvious difficulties as being labeled a "deadbeat." Firms have, in the past, devised rather ingenious methods for

---

[3]A question raised during the Hutton investigation was this: "Why didn't the banks recognize that Hutton was systematically overdrawing its account and call the company to task?" The answer is that some banks, with tight controls, did exactly that—they refused to let Hutton get away with the practice. Other banks were lax. Still other banks apparently let Hutton get away with being chronically overdrawn out of fear of losing its business: Hutton used its economic muscle to force the banks to let it get away with an illegal act. In many people's opinion, the banks were as much at fault as Hutton. Still, in business dealings, honesty is presumed, and Hutton was dishonest in its dealings with the banks. This dishonesty severely damaged Hutton's reputation, cost the company profits totaling hundreds of millions of dollars, cost its top managers their jobs, and contributed to the ultimate demise of the company.

lengthening the collection periods for their own checks. Some of these disbursement techniques will be discussed in this section.

draft

A check-like instrument used in delaying payments; must be sent to the payer before funds can be collected.

Drafts.   **Drafts** are a widely used procedure for delaying payments. While a check is payable when presented to the bank on which it was drawn, a draft must be transmitted to the issuer, who approves it and then deposits funds to cover it, after which it can be collected. Insurance companies often use drafts in handling claims. For instance, Aetna can pay a claim by draft on Friday. The recipient deposits the draft at a local bank, which must then send it to Aetna's Hartford bank. It may be Wednesday or Thursday before the draft arrives. The bank then sends it to the company's accounting department, which has until 3 P.M. that day to inspect and approve it. Not until then does Aetna have to deposit funds in the bank to pay the draft.

payables centralization

The centralized processing of payables, which allows more efficient monitoring of payables and float balances.

Payables Centralization.   No single action controls cash outflows more effectively than **payables centralization.** This permits the financial manager to evaluate the payments coming due for the entire firm and to schedule cash transfers to meet these needs on a company-wide basis. Centralizing disbursements also permits more efficient monitoring of payables and float balances. Of course, there are also disadvantages to a centralized disbursement system—regional offices may not be able to make prompt payment for services rendered, which can create ill will and raise the company's operating costs. More than one firm has saved a few pennies by using a cheaper check-disbursing system but lost far more as a result of higher operating costs caused by ill will.

overdraft system

A system whereby firms may write checks in excess of their balances, with the banks automatically extending loans to cover the shortages.

Overdraft Systems.   When a firm is actively trying to use float, it will often arrange with its bank to have the use of an **overdraft system.** In such a system, a firm writes checks in excess of its actual balance, and its bank automatically extends loans to cover the shortage. The maximum amount of such loans must, of course, be established beforehand. Although statistics are not available on the usage of overdrafts in the United States, a number of firms have worked out informal, and in some cases formal, overdraft arrangements. Also, both banks and credit card companies regularly establish cash reserve systems for individuals. In general, the use of overdrafts has been increasing in recent years, and, if this trend continues, it will lead to a reduction of cash balances.

zero-balance account (ZBA)

A checking account in which a zero balance is maintained; as checks are presented against the account, funds are transferred from a master account.

Zero-Balance Accounts.   **Zero-balance accounts (ZBAs)** are special disbursement accounts having a zero-dollar balance on which checks are written. Typically, a firm establishes several ZBAs in the concentration bank and funds them from a master account. As checks are presented to a ZBA for payment, funds are automatically transferred from the master account. Zero-balance accounts simplify the control of disbursements and cash balances, hence reduce the amount of idle (non-interest-bearing) cash.

Larger corporations often set up accounts for special purposes, such as paying dividends. Suppose IBM planned to pay dividends of $1.25 per share on 600 million shares, or $750 million in total, on September 10, 1994. It could deposit $750 million in an account and then write checks to its stockholders, but because some stockholders would surely delay cashing their dividend checks, a great deal of money would be sitting idle in the account. One alternative would be for IBM to write the checks, forecast how rapidly they would be cashed and presented for payment, and then make a series of daily deposits based on those forecasts. Another procedure would be to set up a zero-balance account, in which case (1) it would write the dividend checks, (2) each day the bank would notify IBM by 11 A.M. of the total dollar amount of checks that had been received for payment that day, and (3) IBM would have until 4 P.M. to deposit the funds to cover those checks. (Because of the nature of the clearinghouse process, all checks will have been presented by 11 A.M. for payment.) IBM could obtain the funds by transferring them to the account from its master account, by selling marketable securities, or by borrowing in the commercial paper market. IBM could even arrange to borrow the necessary funds from the bank itself. In any event, the account would be zeroed out at the end of each day. This type of account is being used with increasing frequency.

controlled disbursement account

An account which is not funded until the day's checks are presented against it; originally called remote disbursement.

Controlled Disbursement Accounts. Whereas zero-balance accounts are typically established at concentration banks, **controlled disbursement accounts** can be set up at any bank. In fact, controlled disbursement accounts were initially used only in relatively remote banks, hence this technique was originally called *remote disbursement.* The basic technique is simple: Controlled disbursement accounts are not funded until the day's checks are presented against the account. The key to controlled disbursement is the ability of the bank having the account to report the total daily amount of checks received for clearance by 11 A.M., New York time. This early notification gives financial managers sufficient time (1) to wire funds to the controlled disbursement account to cover the checks presented for payment and (2) to invest excess cash at midday, when money market trading is at a peak.

Cash Management in the Multidivisional Firm

Most business is conducted by large firms, many of which operate regionally, nationally, or even worldwide. They collect cash from many sources and make payments from a number of different cities. The concepts, techniques, and procedures described thus far in the chapter must be extended when applied to large, multidivisional or multinational firms which deal with banks in all of their operating territories. For example, companies like IBM, General Motors, and Hewlett-Packard have manufacturing plants all around the world, even more sales offices, and bank accounts in virtually every city where they do business. Thus, a major corporation might have hundreds or even thousands of bank accounts. These companies must maintain compensating balances in each of their banks, and they must be sure that no bank account becomes overdrawn. (After E. F. Hutton's problems, this has become especially important.) Cash inflows and outflows are subject to random fluctuations, and there is no reason to think that inflows and outflows will balance in each account. A system must, therefore, be in place to transfer funds from where they are to where they are needed, to arrange loans to cover net corporate shortfalls, and to invest net corporate surpluses without delay.

General Motors provides an example of a firm which has extended the electronic transfer system for use in paying its suppliers. The electronic system utilizes eight banks across the nation, and it not only speeds up the payment process but also decreases uncertainty about the timing of the payment. This system benefits both GM and its suppliers, as it reduces the required level of each firm's transactions and precautionary cash balances. GM's suppliers especially like the electronic system because overdue bills from GM have been reduced considerably, and suppliers take this into account when they bid for GM's business.

A sound cash management program for a multidivisional firm necessarily includes provisions for keeping strict control over the level of funds in each account and for shifting funds among accounts to minimize the total corporate cash balance. Mathematical models and electronic connections between a central computer and each branch location have been developed to help with such situations; however, an in-depth discussion of these topics would go beyond the scope of this book.

Compensating Balance Requirements

At the beginning of this chapter we defined a compensating balance as a checking account balance that a firm must maintain with a commercial bank to compensate the bank for services rendered, and we identified compensating balances as one of two main reasons that firms hold cash (the other was transactions). In addition to extending loans, banks provide many types of services to firms — indeed most of the collections and disbursement techniques just discussed would be impossible without the cooperation of banks. They clear checks, operate lockbox plans, supply credit information, and the like. Because these services cost the banks money, they must be compensated.

Banks earn most of their income by lending money at interest, and most of the funds they lend are obtained in the form of deposits. If a firm maintains a deposit account with an average balance of $100,000, and if the bank can lend these funds at a net return of $8,000, then the account is, in a sense, worth $8,000 to the bank. Thus, it is to the bank's advantage to provide services worth up to $8,000 to attract and hold the account.

Banks first determine the costs of the services rendered to their larger customers, and then they estimate the average account balances necessary to provide enough income to compensate for these costs. Firms can make direct fee payments for these services, but they often find it more convenient to maintain compensating balances to avoid paying cash service charges to the bank.[4]

Compensating balances are also required by some bank loan agreements. During periods when the supply of credit is restricted and interest rates are high, banks frequently require that borrowers maintain accounts which average

---

[4]Compensating balance arrangements apply to individuals as well as to business firms. Thus, you might get "free" checking services if you maintain a minimum balance of $500, but you might be charged 10 cents per check if your balance falls below $500 during the month.

a specified percentage of the loan amount as a condition for granting a loan; 15 percent is a typical figure. If the required balance is larger than the firm would otherwise maintain, the effective cost of the loan is increased. The excess balance presumably compensates the bank for making a loan at a rate below what it could earn on the funds if they were invested elsewhere.[5]

Compensating balances can be established as either (1) an *absolute minimum* (say, $100,000) below which the actual balance must never fall or (2) a *minimum average balance* (perhaps $100,000) during some period, generally a month. The absolute minimum is a much more restrictive requirement because the total amount of cash held during the month must be above $100,000 by the amount of the firm's transactions balances. The $100,000 in this case is "dead money" from the firm's standpoint. With a minimum average balance, however, the account could fall to zero on one day provided it was $200,000 some other day, with the average working out to $100,000. Thus, the $100,000 in this case would be available for transactions.

Statistics on compensating balance requirements are not available, but average balances are typical and absolute minimums rare for business accounts. Discussions with bankers, however, indicate that absolute minimums are less rare during times of extremely tight money.

Self-Test

How can a firm speed up its collections?

How does a lockbox plan contribute to faster collections on customer accounts, and when would a firm benefit from using such a system?

Why would payers be likely to resist pre-authorized debits?

Is it better for a firm to have positive or negative net float? Explain.

List several techniques used by firms to slow and/or control their disbursements.

What are overdraft systems, and how do they work?

Why would a firm use a zero-balance account, and how does one work?

Why do firms maintain compensating balances?

Matching the Costs and Benefits of Cash Management

Although a number of procedures may be used to hold down cash balances, implementing these procedures is not a costless operation. How far should a firm go in making its cash operations more efficient? As a general rule, the firm should incur these expenses as long as marginal returns exceed or equal marginal expenses.

For example, we saw earlier that Carter Chemical Company, with its $3,000 million in annual sales for 1993, would have gross annual savings of $2 million if it instituted a lockbox plan, assumed to reduce the firm's collections float by 3 days, and *assuming that Carter can invest freed-up funds to yield 8 percent.*

---

[5]The interest rate effect of compensating balances is discussed further in Chapter 11.

If the cost of such a plan is less than $2 million per year, the move is a good one. If the cost is equal to $2 million, we have a breakeven situation; there would be neither a positive nor a negative impact on the firm's financial situation if it were to set up the lockbox plan. If the cost is above $2 million, the reduction in collections float is not worth the cost. It is clear that larger firms, with larger cash balances, can better afford to hire the personnel necessary to maintain tight control over their cash positions. Cash management is one element of business operations in which economies of scale are present.

In summary, the value of careful cash management depends greatly on the costs of funds invested in cash, which in turn depend on the current rate of interest. Although interest rates have receded from their historic highs of the early 1980s, business firms continue to devote considerable care to cash management.

Self-Test

How far should a firm go in making its cash operations more efficient?

Is cash management more important when interest rates are high or low? Explain.

Marketable Securities

marketable securities

Securities that can be sold on short notice for close to their quoted market prices.

As noted at the beginning of the chapter, sizable holdings of such short-term **marketable securities** as U.S. Treasury bills or bank certificates of deposit are often reported on corporations' financial statements. The reasons for such holdings, as well as the factors that influence the choice of securities held, are discussed in this section.

Reasons for Holding Marketable Securities

Many companies show sizable amounts of marketable securities among their current assets. For example, at the end of June 1992, Microsoft held $1,144 million of short-term investments (marketable securities), up from $641 million a year earlier. Since such securities usually yield much less than operating assets, why would a company like Microsoft have such large holdings of low-yielding assets? There are two basic reasons for these holdings: (1) they serve as a substitute for cash balances, and (2) they are used as a temporary investment. These points are considered next.

Marketable Securities as a Substitute for Cash.   Some firms hold portfolios of marketable securities in lieu of larger cash balances, then sell some securities from the portfolios whenever they need to replenish the cash account. In such situations the marketable securities could be a substitute for transactions balances, precautionary balances, speculative balances, or all three. In most cases the securities are held primarily for precautionary purposes. Most firms prefer to rely on bank credit—when readily available—to meet temporary transactions or speculative needs, but they may hold some liquid assets to guard against a possible shortage of bank credit.

Several years ago IBM had approximately $6 billion in marketable securities. This large liquid balance had been built up primarily as a reserve to cover possible damage payments resulting from pending antitrust suits. When it became clear that IBM would win most of the suits, the liquidity need declined, and the company spent some of the funds on other assets, including repurchases of its own stock. This is a prime example of a firm's building up its precautionary balances to handle possible emergencies.

Marketable Securities Held as a Temporary Investment.   Whenever a firm has more than 1 or 2 percent of its total assets invested in marketable securities, chances are good that these funds represent a strictly temporary investment. Such temporary investments generally occur in one of the three following situations:

1. **When the firm must finance seasonal or cyclical operations.**   Firms engaged in seasonal operations frequently have surplus cash flows during one part of the year and deficit cash flows during another. For example, retailers such as Sears often purchase marketable securities during their surplus periods and then liquidate them when cash deficits occur. Other firms, however, choose to use short-term bank financing to cover such shortages.

2. **When the firm must meet some known financial requirements.**   If a major plant construction program is planned for the near future, or if a bond issue is about to mature, a firm may build up its marketable securities portfolio to provide the required funds. Furthermore, marketable securities holdings are frequently built up immediately before quarterly corporate tax payment dates.

3. **When the firm has just sold long-term securities.**   Expanding firms generally have to sell long-term securities (stocks or bonds) periodically. The funds from such sales are often invested in marketable securities, which are then sold off to provide cash as it is needed to pay for permanent investments in operating assets.

Strategies Regarding Marketable Securities Holdings

Actually, each of the needs mentioned previously can be met either by obtaining short-term loans or by holding marketable securities. Consider a firm like Dayton Card Company, which we discussed earlier in this chapter, whose sales are growing over time but also fluctuate on a seasonal basis. As we saw from Dayton's cash budget (Table 9-1), the firm plans to borrow to meet seasonal needs. As an alternative financial strategy, Dayton could hold a portfolio of marketable securities and then liquidate these securities to meet its peak cash needs.

A firm's marketable securities policy is an integral part of its overall working capital policy. If a firm like Dayton uses maturity matching in its working capital financing policy, as shown in Figure 9-2, Plan A, it will never hold marketable securities and will borrow heavily in the short-term market to meet peak needs. Under the extremely conservative Plan B, the firm would stockpile marketable securities during slack periods and then sell these securities to raise funds for peak seasonal and cyclical needs. Plan C is still fairly conservative but is a com-

Figure 9-2   Alternative Strategies for Meeting Seasonal or Cyclical Cash Needs

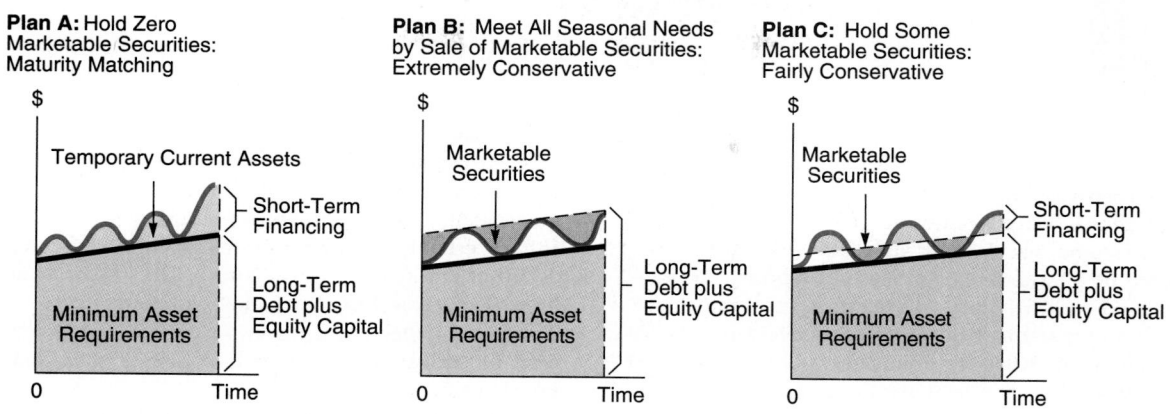

This figure shows the effects of three different approaches to the use of marketable securities in financing temporary current assets. Under Plan A, a company holds no marketable securities and relies entirely on bank loans for its short-term cash. Although it may create problems in borrowing funds or repaying loans, Plan A should provide a higher return on total assets and equity because no funds are locked into low-yielding marketable securities. Under Plan B, a company accumulates a large amount of marketable securities that it then sells off to raise cash for seasonal and cyclical asset needs. This plan avoids short-term borrowing but lowers the company's return on total assets and equity. The disadvantages of Plans A and B are moderated under Plan C, which uses a combination of marketable securities and short-term loans to finance temporary current assets.

promise between the other two plans; under this alternative, the company would hold some securities but not enough to meet all of its peak needs. Dayton actually follows Plan C. (Note that in this example we do not show the working capital financing policy which in Chapter 8 was labeled "aggressive" — see Figure 8-5 — but we show two variations of the conservative option since it is the *amount* of marketable securities that is relevant here.)

There are advantages and disadvantages to each of these strategies. Plan A is clearly the most risky of the three shown; the firm's current ratio is always lower than under the other plans, indicating that it might encounter difficulties either in borrowing the funds needed or in repaying the loan. On the other hand, Plan A requires no holdings of low-yielding marketable securities, and this will probably lead to a relatively high rate of return on both total assets and equity.

Factors Influencing the Choice of Securities

A wide variety of securities, differing in terms of default risk, interest rate risk, liquidity risk, and expected rate of return, are available to firms that choose to hold marketable securities. In this section we first consider the different types of risk, we then look at the extent to which each type of risk is found in different securities, and, finally, we look at specific instruments which are suitable investments for temporary excess cash. These same considerations are, incidentally, as important for individuals' investment decisions as for businesses' decisions.

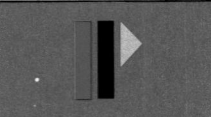

TURNING 'EM AROUND

In the chapter introduction, some successful companies were considering management strategies for use of excess cash. But, what strategies are available to companies that are performing poorly? Many companies assume that the best alternative for a firm battered by a business downturn or the pressures of increased competition is to seek protection under the bankruptcy statutes, but that is not necessarily the case.

Enter the turnaround specialist — a corporate hired gun whose job it is to shake things up, to cut the deadwood, to reorganize the business to snatch it from the jaws of bankruptcy, and, generally, to breathe new life into the corporate corpse. The turnaround executive is a special breed. He or she must have the crisis skills of an intensive care doctor and the strategic genius of a military commander.

According to one expert, turnarounds are a lot like wars. By the time a turnaround specialist is called in, the situation is critical. The corporation is drowning in a sea of its own red ink. There is no time for introspection. Action is everything. The turnaround specialist must be strong, decisive, even dictatorial.

Anyone considering taking on a turnaround assignment should be sure of the banks' support before plunging ahead. The worst news a turnaround executive can hear on arriving at a company is that its banks are going to call in its loans. This may just be a bluff, and a face-to-face meeting, possibly with a bankruptcy lawyer in tow, can convince the bankers that they will not get as much as they think by calling in the loans. Still, if the bankers do pull the plug, the situation may be terminal.

Once there is a commitment of bank support, the turnaround executive must get control of cash. No purchases over a certain amount should be made without the new leader's approval. In small companies that may mean the executive has to approve all purchase orders, at least for the first month or so, just to find out what is really going on. All capital expendi-

tures should also be canceled until they can be reassessed by the turnaround executive.

With cash flow under control, the next task is to start making cash projections, even if they are fraught with uncertainty. Cash projections give the executive his or her first glimpse of the future. They show what the projected level of sales is, how much money is going to be collected, whether business is getting softer or weaker, and whether the company's customers are paying their bills.

In developing the cash projection, the new leader should be willing to sidestep established lines of communication to get a realistic view of the situation. The new boss should speak directly to employees on the floor, directly to key customers, and directly to vendors. He or she should also speak at length with the bankers who, if the business is in really bad shape, may be the ones who actually control the company's future.

Another critical task facing the turnaround specialist is finding internal sources of cash, which usually means collecting accounts receivable faster and reducing inventory. Past due accounts must be pursued, and care must be taken to collect promptly on new sales. Getting cash from inventory is a longer and more delicate process. It is important not to run out of key inventory items, for if that happens, rumors of corporate demise will run rampant and turn into a self-fulfilling prophecy. However, companies should refrain from carrying as many secondary inventory items as they would under normal circumstances.

While turnaround executives must first concentrate on correcting control, cash, financial, and management information problems, a good leader will also think about marketing. Going into new markets is generally too expensive and risky, but by concentrating on serving existing markets better, corporate performance can often be improved.

Given the economic climate of the 1990s, numerous firms are employing turnaround specialists in an attempt to get themselves back on their feet again. These firms include American Express, Eastman Kodak, IBM, L.A. Gear, and Allied Signal.

Eastman Kodak recruited Christopher J. Steffen from Honeywell to serve as chief financial officer and to direct its turnaround. During his earlier stint as

Sources: *Venture,* December 1986; "Getting the Picture," *Business Week,* February 1, 1993; "Eastman Kodak: Higher Rewards in Lowered Goals," *Fortune,* March 8, 1993; "New Boss Vows to Boost Shareholder Value," *Computer Reseller News,* March 29, 1993; and *The Wall Street Journal,* May 4, 1993, "IBM Appoints Chrysler's York as Finance Chief," and "Kodak's Outside Directors Voice Support for Chairman, but Press for Results."

treasurer of Chrysler (which was bailed out by the government in 1980 with a guaranteed loan package), Steffen squeezed out hidden costs, and, during his time at Honeywell, he put every manager through a financial training course, forcing them to think about the cash implications of their actions. As a result, Honeywell pared down its working capital from $2.2 to $1.6 billion. At Kodak, Steffen began by identifying which assets needed to be disposed of, such as Kodak's copier division, which was a money loser. Analysts believe that this division alone could be sold for $1 to $1.5 billion. Steffen needed to build cost consciousness into Kodak's culture and to reduce both the company's debt and its number of employees. Because of his efforts, analysts expected Kodak to trim $100 million from its $1.6 billion research and development budget. Also, Steffen wanted to decrease Kodak's debt ratio from 59 percent to somewhere in the range of 30 to 40 percent. He stated that he believed Kodak would be easier to turn around than Chrysler because of the strength of its products, its distribution system, and its reputation for quality.

However, Steffen ran into a problem. As CFO, he reported to Chairman and CEO Kay R. Whitmore, who wanted to take a "go slower" approach. As a result, Steffen resigned in April 1993. Kodak's directors have indicated that they support Whitmore for now, but he must either "get results or get out."

In early 1993, IBM selected Louis Gerstner, former chief executive of RJR Nabisco Inc., as its new chairman and chief executive, and one of Gerstner's first acts was to replace IBM's chief financial officer with Jerome York, another architect of Chrysler's recovery. Both Gerstner and York are regarded as tough turnaround specialists known for aggressive cost cutting. At RJR, Gerstner sold assets and cut costs, reducing the company's $29 billion debt by more than half. York helped slash Chrysler's costs, and he sold off billions of dollars of assets to help pare the company's debt. By bringing in York, Gerstner gave a strong signal that he plans to subject IBM to a truly drastic restructuring. Industry analysts predict that in Gerstner's and York's first year on the job, they will eliminate at least 50,000 jobs, will begin to sell off smaller parts of IBM, and will break the remainder into independent business units which will be more directly responsible for their own fates. When he took the job, Gerstner stated that he has an immense task ahead and that he does not underestimate the challenge before him.

The best turnaround specialists share many of the same characteristics as successful entrepreneurs. Both face limited resources and a sense of urgency, as well as confusion. Senior managers in both startups and turnarounds have to be adaptable and flexible. They must be able to see promising opportunities and be able to shift resources to profit from an advantage. Turnaround specialists, like entrepreneurs, are not resource driven—they are opportunity driven.

Recall that in Chapter 4 we developed Equation 4-1 for determining the nominal interest rate:

$$k = k^* + IP + DRP + LP + MRP.$$

Here k^* is the real risk-free rate which is a component of *all* nominal interest rates, IP is a premium for expected inflation, DRP is the default risk premium, LP is the liquidity premium, and MRP is the maturity (or interest rate) risk premium. Also, remember from Chapter 4 that the risk-free rate, k_{RF}, is equal to $k^* + IP$ and that a U.S. Treasury bill comes closest to having a nominal interest rate equal to the risk-free rate.

inflation risk

The risk that inflation will reduce the purchasing power of a given sum of money.

Inflation Risk.   One type of risk is **inflation risk,** or the risk that inflation will reduce the purchasing power of a given sum of money. Inflation risk, which is important both to firms and to individual investors during times of rising prices, is lower on assets whose returns tend to rise with inflation than on assets whose returns are fixed. Thus, real estate and common stocks are generally better hedges against inflation than are bonds and other fixed-income securities. As you should recall from our discussion in Chapter 4, a security's interest rate reflects the average rate of inflation expected over the security's life in the form of an inflation premium (IP). Therefore, a 3-month Treasury bill would include the average rate of inflation expected over the 3-month period, while a 30-year Treasury bond would include the average rate of inflation expected over a 30-year period. Thus, if a high rate of inflation is expected in the future, that expectation is built into interest rates. Accordingly, the real risk of inflation to holders of fixed-rate debt securities is that actual inflation will exceed the expected level.

It is usually somewhat easier to assess what inflation will be over the next 3 months to a year than to estimate inflation over 30 years. It is, therefore, more likely that the inflation premium built into the nominal interest rate of short-term securities such as U.S. Treasury bills, CDs, and commercial paper is "correct," that is, close to actual inflation, than when the inflation premium is based on the average expected inflation over 30 years and incorporated into the nominal rate of a 30-year bond.

default risk

The risk that a borrower will not pay the interest or principal on a loan.

Default Risk.   As you may remember from Chapter 4, the risk that a borrower will be unable to make interest payments, or to repay the principal amount on schedule, is known as **default risk.** If the issuer is the U.S. Treasury, the default risk is negligible, so Treasury securities are regarded as being default-free. However, corporate securities, as well as securities issued by state and local governments, are subject to some degree of default risk, so these securities' returns include a default risk premium (DRP). Several organizations (for example, Moody's Investment Service and Standard & Poor's Corporation) rate bonds and also short-term corporate debt issues. They classify them on a scale that ranges from very high quality to highly speculative with a definite chance of going into default. Ratings change from time to time. Finally, recognize that it is usually somewhat easier to correctly estimate the default risk on a short-term than on a long-term instrument.

liquidity risk

The risk that securities cannot be sold at close to the quoted price on short notice.

Liquidity Risk.   An asset that can be sold on short notice for close to its quoted market price is considered to be highly liquid. If a company such as Dayton purchased $1 million of infrequently traded bonds of a relatively obscure company like Bigham Pork Products, it would probably have to accept a price reduction in order to sell the bonds on short notice; the nominal interest rate on Bigham's bonds would, therefore, include a liquidity premium (LP). On the other hand, if Dayton invested in U.S. Treasury bonds, in bonds issued by AT&T, General Motors, or Exxon, or in short-term securities, it would be able to dispose of them almost instantaneously at close to the quoted market price. These latter issues are therefore said to have very little **liquidity risk.**

Liquidity is sometimes set equal to *marketability.* Strictly speaking, this is not correct. Marketability means only that something can be sold quickly; liquidity, on the other hand, indicates that an asset can be sold not only quickly but also *at its fair market value.* In other words, being able to sell something for 10 cents on the dollar (when its fair market value is actually $1) is marketability; it is not liquidity.

Interest Rate Risk.   We learned in Chapter 4 that fixed-rate bond prices vary inversely with changes in interest rates. Also, the prices of long-term bonds are

interest rate risk

The risk to which investors are exposed due to rising interest rates.

much more sensitive to changes in interest rates than are the prices of short-term securities—long-term bonds have more **interest rate risk.** Thus, if Dayton's treasurer purchased at par $1 million of 25-year U.S. government bonds paying 9 percent interest, and if interest rates then rose to 14.5 percent, the market value of the bonds would fall from $1 million to just below $635,000 —a loss of almost 40 percent.[6] (This actually happened from 1980 to 1982.) If 3-month Treasury bills had been held during a period of rising interest rates, however, the loss would have been negligible. In Equation 4-1, the Treasury bill would have a zero maturity risk premium (MRP), but the long-term Treasury bond would have a positive maturity risk premium included in its nominal interest rate.

Rate of Return (Yield).   As we know from earlier chapters, the higher a security's risk, the higher the required rate of return on the security. Thus corporate treasurers, like other investors, must make a tradeoff between risk and return when choosing investments for their marketable securities portfolios. Because this portfolio is generally held either for a specific known need or for use in emergencies, the firm might be financially embarrassed should the portfolio decline in value. Also, most nonfinancial corporations do not have investment departments specializing in appraising securities and determining the probability of their going into default. Accordingly, the marketable securities portfolio is generally composed of highly liquid short-term securities issued either by the U.S. government or by the very strongest corporations. These are the money market instruments defined briefly in Chapter 2. Given the purpose of the securities portfolio, treasurers are generally unwilling to sacrifice safety for higher rates of return. There are many types of safe, highly liquid, short-term securities in which a company can invest temporary excess cash. These instruments will be discussed next.

Types of Marketable Securities

Although any investor wishes to minimize needless risks, a manager investing temporary excess cash must be especially aware of default risk, liquidity risk, and interest rate risk. The manager has a wide variety of available securities to hold as near cash. These alternatives, both government and nongovernment securities, are discussed in this section, with special emphasis given to these three types of risk. Table 9-2 provides a listing of various investment alternatives, an indication of their suitability as short-term investments, and an indication of their returns at different points in time.

Government Securities.   The U.S. Treasury and other federal agencies issue a wide variety of securities with different maturities. Treasury bills are a popular outlet for temporary excess funds because they have a large and active secondary market to ensure liquidity and because they are free of default risk. Treasury bills, as well as all other short-term securities, have relatively little interest rate risk because of their short maturities.

---

[6]These computations are explained in detail in Chapter 16.

Table 9-2 Securities Available for Investment of Surplus Cash

Security	Typical Maturity at Time of Issue	Approximate Yields			Appropriate as a Near-Cash Reserve?
		2/10/82	3/8/90	1/28/93	
Suitable to Hold as Near-Cash Reserve					
U.S. Treasury bills	91 days to 1 year	15.1%	7.9%	3.0%	Yes
Banker's acceptances	Up to 180 days	15.0	8.0	3.1	Yes
Commercial paper	Up to 270 days	15.3	8.2	3.2	Yes
Negotiable certificates of deposit (CDs) of U.S. banks	Up to 1 year	15.5	7.8	3.2	Yes
Money market mutual funds	Instant liquidity	14.0	7.6	2.8	Yes
Eurodollar bank time deposits	Up to 1 year	16.2	8.4	3.3	Questionable
Not Suitable to Hold as Near-Cash Reserve					
U.S. Treasury notes	2 to 10 years	14.8	8.6	6.0	Questionable
U.S. Treasury bonds	Up to 30 years	14.6	8.6	7.2	No
Corporate bonds (AAA)	Up to 50 years	16.0	9.4	7.8	No
State and local government bonds[a]	Up to 30 years	12.8	7.4	6.2	No
Common stocks of other corporations	None	Variable	Variable	Variable	No
Common stock of the firm in question	None	Variable	Variable	Variable	No

[a]Rates are usually lower on state/municipal government bonds because the interest they pay is exempt from federal income taxes.

Treasury bills are sold at regular auctions and have either 13-week (91-day), 26-week (182-day), or 1-year original maturities. Alternatively, they can be bought or sold in the secondary market with as little as one day remaining to maturity. Thus, the investor has a wide choice of available maturities.

Other government securities with longer maturities are available. Treasury notes are government obligations with maturities of 2 to 10 years. Treasury bonds are issued with maturities of up to 30 years. However, because of their long maturities and potentially unstable near-term prices, these longer-term securities may be poor choices as investments for **near-cash reserves,** reserves that might have to be quickly converted to cash—unless, of course, they are bought when they have a year or less remaining until maturity. Again, the longer the maturity of a fixed-rate debt security, the greater its interest rate risk. This works against the use of bonds, in general, as a short-term investment since temporary excess cash should be invested such that the principal is safe.

U.S. federal agencies, such as the Federal Home Loan Bank and the Federal National Mortgage Association (FNMA), also issue notes and bonds. These securities are riskier than Treasury issues because they are not directly backed by the U.S. Treasury. Therefore, they yield a slightly higher return than Treasury issues. For example, on January 29, 1993, FNMA bonds with 5 years until maturity yielded 5.9 percent versus 5.6 percent for 5-year Treasury notes.

near-cash reserves

Reserves that can be quickly and easily converted to cash.

Nongovernment Securities. In the discussion that follows, we identify four different nongovernment investments that are appropriate as near-cash reserves because of their short maturities, low default risk, and liquidity. The fifth security, Eurodollars, is questionable as a near-cash reserve.

banker's acceptance

A promissory note which has been endorsed, or guaranteed, by a bank.

commercial paper

Short-term, unsecured promissory notes of large, financially strong firms, usually issued in denominations of $100,000 or more and having an interest rate somewhat below the prime rate.

negotiable certificate of deposit

A marketable receipt for a large bank time deposit, usually issued in denominations of $100,000 or more.

Banker's Acceptances.   A **banker's acceptance** is the promissory note of a business debtor resulting from a business transaction. A bank, by endorsing the note, assumes the obligation of payment at the due date. The instrument is widely used, especially in foreign trade. It has a low degree of risk if guaranteed by a strong bank, and there is a ready market for it, making it easy for the holder to sell the acceptance to raise immediate cash. Banker's acceptances are sold at a discount below face value and then paid off at face value when they mature, so the discount amounts to interest on the acceptance. The effective yield on a strong banker's acceptance is generally a little above the Treasury bill rate.

Commercial Paper.   Short-term, unsecured promissory notes issued by the largest, most financially secure corporations are called **commercial paper.** Dealers in commercial paper prefer to handle the paper of firms whose net worth is $100 million or more and whose annual borrowing exceeds $10 million. Regular issuers include General Motors Acceptance Corporation, Ford Motor Credit Corporation, and C.I.T. Financial Corporation. Commercial paper is sold primarily to other business firms, to insurance companies, to pension funds, to money market mutual funds, and to banks. It has a secondary market, but this market is not quite as well developed as is the secondary market for, say, Treasury bills. The amount of commercial paper has grown rapidly in recent years; at the end of March 1993, there was more than $536 billion of commercial paper outstanding, compared with about $594 billion of bank loans to businesses.

Maturities of commercial paper generally vary from one to nine months, with an average of about five months.[7] The rates on commercial paper fluctuate with supply and demand conditions; they are determined in the marketplace, varying daily as conditions change. However, the rates on commercial paper are low relative to other securities. The low rates reflect, among other things, the fact that default risk is low since only the most creditworthy corporations can sell commercial paper. Recently, commercial paper rates have ranged from one to three percentage points below the stated prime rate but slightly above the T-bill rate. For example, in March 1993, the average rate on 3-month commercial paper was 3.2 percent, whereas the stated prime rate was 6 percent, and the T-bill rate was 3.0 percent.

Negotiable Certificates of Deposit.   Major money-center commercial banks will issue certificates of deposit (CDs) as marketable receipts for large time deposits. A **negotiable certificate of deposit** is in denominations of at least $100,000 and matures within 1 year. The interest paid is negotiated and is paid at maturity.

A secondary market for CDs exists, but it is also not as well developed as that for Treasury bills. This is one reason that the yield on CDs is generally above that on Treasury bills.

These securities should not be mistaken for the type of CDs purchased by individual small investors. The small CDs are different from the marketable se-

[7]The maximum maturity without SEC registration is 270 days. Commercial paper can be sold only to "sophisticated" investors; otherwise, SEC registration would be required even for maturities of 270 days or less.

curities in that their interest is established by the financial institution rather than negotiated, and smaller CDs are not marketable.

Money Market Mutual Funds.   Money market mutual funds are a popular source of liquidity for both businesses and individuals. These mutual funds hold only short-term securities such as Treasury bills, CDs, banker's acceptances, and commercial paper. Shares in these funds are easily obtained — often without commissions (the so-called "no-load" funds). Because the required initial investment is small and the liquidity is comparable to lower-yielding checking and savings accounts, money market mutual funds are a popular temporary investment alternative, especially for smaller firms.

Eurodollar Bank Time Deposits.   Eurodollars are interest-bearing time deposits, denominated in U.S. dollars and placed in banks outside the United States. The term **Eurodollars** may be misleading because banks in Canada, Japan, and the Caribbean are important players in this market.

Eurodollars

Interest-bearing time deposits, denominated in U.S. dollars, placed in banks outside the United States.

In many respects the Eurodollar is an international counterpart to the negotiable certificate of deposit. Interest and maturities are negotiated; however, Eurodollars are outside the direct control of the U.S. monetary authorities, so U.S. banking regulations, such as fractional reserves and FDIC insurance premiums, do not apply. The absence of these costs means that the interest paid on Eurodollar deposits tends to be higher than the domestic U.S. rates on equivalent instruments. As with CDs, there is a secondary market for Eurodollars, but it is still in the developmental stage, and it is not a source of certain liquidity. Default risk is a function of the issuing bank's strength.

? *Self-Test*

What are the major reasons for a firm to hold marketable securities?

List three situations in which a firm would hold marketable securities as a temporary investment.

What are the three alternative strategies for meeting seasonal cash needs as identified in Figure 9-2? What makes one strategy more conservative than the other two?

What risks do financial managers consider when developing their marketable securities portfolios?

What government securities are suitable as near-cash reserves? What nongovernment securities are suitable as near-cash reserves?

Summary

This chapter dealt with cash and marketable securities management. In it we examined the motives for holding cash, the construction of the cash budget, several ways in which firms can minimize their cash holdings, cash management in the multidivisional firm, and the different types of marketable securities that can be used as substitutes for cash. The key concepts covered in the chapter are listed below:

▶   The primary **goal of cash management** is to reduce the amount of cash held to the minimum necessary to conduct business.

The **transactions balance** is the cash necessary to conduct day-to-day business, whereas the **precautionary balance** is the cash reserve held to meet random, unforeseen needs. A **compensating balance** is a minimum, or average, checking account balance that a bank requires as compensation either for services provided or as part of a loan agreement. Firms also hold **speculative balances,** which allow them to take advantage of bargain purchases. Note, though, that borrowing capacity and marketable securities reduce the need for both precautionary and speculative cash balances.

➤ A **cash budget** is a statement which shows projected cash inflows and outflows over a specified period. The cash budget is used to determine when the firm will have cash surpluses and shortfalls, and thus to help management plan to invest surpluses or to cover projected shortfalls.

➤ A firm can lower its cash balances if it can **synchronize** its cash outflows and inflows. Also, the use of **lockboxes** can speed collections by expediting the check-clearing process and thus reduce a firm's required cash holdings.

➤ **Disbursement float** is the amount of funds associated with checks written by the firm that are still in the process of clearing and hence have not yet been deducted by the bank from the firm's account.

Collections float is the amount of funds associated with checks written to the firm that have not been cleared and hence are not yet available for use.

Net float is the difference between disbursement float and collections float, and it also is equal to the difference between the balance in a firm's checkbook and the balance on the bank's records. The larger the net float, the smaller the cash balances the firm must maintain.

➤ Techniques used by firms for slowing down and controlling their own disbursements include **drafts, payables centralization, overdraft systems, and zero-balance accounts.** These and other tools of cash management make it possible for firms to keep their cash balances to a minimum.

➤ Steps should be taken and expenses incurred in cash management so long as the expected **marginal returns** are greater than or equal to the expected **marginal costs.**

➤ Firms can reduce their cash balances by holding **marketable securities,** which can be sold on short notice at close to their quoted market values. Marketable securities serve both as a substitute for cash and as a temporary investment for funds that will be needed in the near future. Safety is the primary consideration when treasurers select marketable securities.

In choosing a marketable securities portfolio, a financial manager must consider **inflation risk, default risk, liquidity risk,** and **interest rate risk.**

Securities that are appropriate as **near-cash reserves** are U.S. Treasury bills, banker's acceptances, commercial paper, negotiable CDs, and money market mutual funds. Eurodollars and U.S. Treasury notes are questionable as near-cash reserves.

Resolution to
DECISION IN FINANCE

WHAT DO YOU DO WITH
SURPLUS CASH?

Paramount's cash stockpile was a direct result of the 1989 sale of its consumer finance division for $3.35 billion. Since that time, Paramount has been actively seeking acquisition targets. Rumors of Paramount's interest in additional publishing or cable companies abound, but Paramount has been reluctant to buy because of high prices and possible recession problems. Says Marti Rohm, an analyst for First Boston, "Companies are cautious about redeploying capital when they're not sure of the values of acquired assets." Thus, rather than use its cash to purchase companies, Paramount has opted (1) to buy back 3 million shares of its stock over the last three-year period, (2) to repay high-interest debt, and (3) to increase its quarterly dividend from 70 to 80 cents. Further, Paramount has taken a conservative investment approach with its remaining cash ($1.27 billion), choosing to invest in short-term money market instruments. It could have earned more if it had invested in long-term bonds, but it would then be exposed to a decline in the value of its portfolio if interest rates rose.

Disney considers its excess cash a potential profit center. The company has $2 billion of cash on hand and manages it with a handful of in-house professionals. According to its chief financial officer, Richard Naunula, "We attempt to earn an attractive return for our shareholders." Management estimates that its cash stockpile will earn about $150 million in interest during 1992, representing a total return of approximately 7.5 percent.

While Disney considers its excess cash a profit center, Capital Cities does not. The firm's

chief financial officer, Ron Doerfler, has taken an investment philosophy of better safe than sorry. Consequently, virtually all of Capital Cities's $1.5 billion of excess cash is invested in short-term government securities, such as Treasury bills. Through the first three quarters of 1992, the firm's portfolio has earned a return of 3.6 percent, roughly the same as the interest rate on short-term U.S. Treasury bills. Top management does not want to tie up its cash with financial instruments having maturities greater than 90 days because the firm's goal is to purchase another company. Its current cash position would allow it to leverage the firm into a $5 to $8 billion acquisition.

In addition to making short-term investments, Capital Cities has retired $1.1 billion of high interest debt, repurchased $100 million of its common stock, and made $100 million in small acquisitions. Its cash stockpile earned $40.6 million of interest during 1992. Doerfler's approach is not to aggressively manage cash by taking risks to earn an extra 10 cents a share. He believes that the interest earned on his cash stockpile has a "minimal amount of influence on [the firm's] stock price."

For CBS, 50 percent of its third-quarter 1992 earnings resulted from the interest and capital gains earned on its investment portfolio. CBS's cash stockpile was the result of its selling common stock during the late 1980s. Its current cash and marketable securities portfolio totals $1 billion, and it earned net interest of $83.9 million during the first three quarters of 1992, representing approximately an 11 percent annual return. CBS's strategy stems in part from the fact that its chairman and major stockholder, Larry Tisch, is primarily an investor as opposed to a corporate manager, and companies'

Sources: "Surplus Cash Works while Companies Wait," *Daily Variety,* December 15, 1992; and "Knowing How Cash Flows Is Key to Running Business," *The Plain Dealer,* March 9, 1993.

"styles" often reflect the backgrounds of their top managers.

How have investors reacted to each company's investment strategy? Overall, the stock market has reacted positively to the way these firms have put their excess cash to work. According to Debra Cohen, a consultant with Stern Stewart & Co., "Instead of throwing cash at frivolous opportunities, which certainly exist in the volatile entertainment environment today, these companies are waiting until true value-creating opportunities arise, and the market is rewarding their patience with significant market price premiums."

Questions

9-1 How can better methods of communication reduce the necessity for firms to hold large cash balances?

9-2 What are the four principal reasons for holding cash or marketable securities? Can a firm estimate its target cash balance by summing the cash held to satisfy each of these reasons?

9-3 Explain how each of the following factors would probably affect a firm's target cash balance if all other factors were held constant. (In each case assume that transactions balances are the primary determinant of the firm's target cash balances, not bank compensating balances.)

  a. The firm institutes a new billing procedure which better synchronizes its cash inflows and outflows.

  b. The firm develops a new sales forecasting technique which improves its forecasts.

  c. The firm reduces its portfolio of U.S. Treasury bills.

  d. The firm arranges to use an overdraft system for its checking account.

  e. The firm borrows a large amount of money from its bank and also begins to pay suppliers twice as frequently as in the past; thus it must write far more checks than it did in the past even though the dollar volume of business has not changed.

  f. Interest rates on Treasury bills rise from 3 percent to 8 percent.

9-4 In the cash budget shown in Table 9-1, is the projected loan requirement of $5,200,000 in September known with certainty, or should it be regarded as the expected value of a probability distribution? Consider how this peak requirement probably would be affected by each of the following:

  a. A lengthening of the days sales outstanding (DSO).

  b. An unanticipated decline in sales that occurred when sales were supposed to peak.

  c. A sharp drop in sales prices required to meet competition.

  d. A sharp increase in interest rates for a firm with a large amount of short-term debt outstanding.

9-5 Would a lockbox plan make more sense for a firm that makes sales all over the United States or for a firm with the same volume of business, but whose business is concentrated in its home city?

9-6 Would a corporate treasurer be more tempted to invest the firm's liquidity portfolio in long-term as opposed to short-term securities when the yield curve was upward sloping or downward sloping?

9-7 What does the term *liquidity* mean? Which would be more important to a firm that held a portfolio of marketable securities as precautionary balances against the possibility of losing a major lawsuit — liquidity or rate of return? Explain.

9-8 Firm A's management is very conservative, whereas Firm B's managers are more aggressive. Is it true that, other things being equal, Firm B would probably have larger holdings of short-term marketable securities? Explain.

9-9   Is it true that *interest rate risk* refers to the risk that a firm will be unable to pay the interest on its bonds? Explain.

9-10   Corporate treasurers, when selecting securities for portfolio investments, must make a tradeoff between risk and return. Is it true that most treasurers are willing to assume a fairly high exposure to risk to gain higher expected returns?

Self-Test Problems

ST-1   David Banner, Limited, has grown from a small Houston firm, with customers concentrated in the Texas Gulf Coast area, to a large national firm serving customers throughout the United States. Despite its broad customer base, Banner has maintained its headquarters in the Houston area and keeps its central billing system there. Banner's management is considering an alternative collection procedure to reduce its collections float. On average, it takes 6 days from the time customers mail payments until the company receives, processes, and deposits them. Banner would like to set up a lockbox collection system, which it estimates would reduce the time lag from customer mailing to deposit by 4 days, bringing it down to 2 days. Banner receives an average of $1,000,000 in payments per day.

    a. How many days of collections float now exist (Banner's customers' disbursement float), and what would it be under the lockbox system? By what amount would Banner be able to reduce the firm's financing if the lockbox system is used?

    b. If Banner has an opportunity cost of 10 percent, how much is the lockbox system worth on an annual basis?

    c. What should be Banner's maximum monthly cost for this lockbox system?

ST-2   The Weston Company is setting up a new checking account with Howe National Bank. Weston plans to issue checks in the amount of $1 million each day and to deduct them from its own records at the close of business on the day they are written. On average, the bank will receive and clear the checks at 5 P.M. the third day after they are written; for example, a check written on Monday will be cleared on Thursday afternoon. The firm's agreement with the bank requires it to maintain a $500,000 average compensating balance. It makes a $500,000 deposit at the time it opens the account.

    a. Assuming that the firm makes deposits at 4 P.M. each day (and the bank includes them in that day's transactions), how much must it deposit daily in order to maintain a sufficient balance once it reaches a steady state? Indicate the required deposit on Day 1, Day 2, Day 3, if any, and each day thereafter, assuming that the company will write checks for $1 million on Day 1 and each day thereafter.

    b. How many days of disbursement float does Weston have?

    c. What ending daily balance should the firm try to maintain (1) on the bank's records and (2) on its own records?

Problems

9-1
Net float

The Sohn Company is setting up a new bank account with the First National Bank. Sohn plans to issue checks in the amount of $2 million each day and to deduct them from its own records at the close of business on the day they are written. On average, the bank will receive and clear (that is, deduct from the firm's bank balance) the checks at 5 P.M. the fourth day after they are written. For example, a check written on Monday will be cleared on Friday afternoon. The firm's agreement with the bank requires it to maintain a $1.5 million average compensating balance. This is $500,000 greater than the cash balance the firm would otherwise have on deposit; that is, without the compensating balance, it would carry an average deposit of $1 million. It makes a $1.5 million deposit at the time it opens the account.

a. Assuming that the firm makes deposits at 4 P.M. each day (and the bank includes the deposit in that day's transactions), how much must the firm deposit each day to maintain a sufficient balance on the day it opens the account, during the first 4 days after it opens the account, and once it reaches a "steady state"? (Ignore weekends.)

b. What ending daily balance should the firm try to maintain (1) on the bank's records and (2) on its own records?

c. Explain how net float can help increase the value of the firm's common stock.

9-2
Lockbox system

Valley Medical Inc. (VMI) started 5 years ago as a small medical products firm serving customers in the Seattle area. Its reputation and market area grew quickly, however, so that today VMI has customers throughout the United States. Despite its broad customer base, VMI has maintained its headquarters in the Seattle area and keeps its central billing system there. VMI's management is considering an alternative collection procedure to reduce its collections float. On average, it takes 5 days from the time customers mail payments until the company receives, processes, and deposits them. VMI would like to set up a lockbox collection system, which it estimates would reduce the time lag from customer mailing to deposit by 2 days, bringing it down to 3 days. VMI receives an average of $900,000 in payments per day.

a. How many days of collections float now exist (VMI's customers' disbursement float), and what would it be under the lockbox system? What reduction in receivables would VMI achieve by initiating the lockbox system?

b. If VMI has an opportunity cost of 8 percent, how much is the lockbox system worth on an annual basis?

c. What is the maximum monthly charge VMI should pay for this lockbox system?

9-3
Cash receipts

E. W. Jorling & Company had actual sales of $50,000 during November and $75,000 during December. The company expects to have sales of $60,000 in January, $66,000 in February, and $76,000 in March. During any given month, 10 percent of the sales are for cash, 50 percent are credit sales paid in the month following the sale, and 40 percent are credit sales paid 2 months after the sale. Prepare the firm's schedule of cash receipts for January through March.

9-4
Cash receipts

Ramirez Farm Supply had sales of $30,000 in May, and it has forecasted sales for its peak season as follows:

Actual:	April	$22,500
	May	30,000
Forecast:	June	48,750
	July	67,500
	August	56,250

From experience, management estimates that 25 percent of sales are for cash, 65 percent of sales are paid after 30 days, 8 percent of sales are paid after 60 days, and 2 percent of sales are uncollectable. Prepare a schedule of cash receipts for the firm's peak season (June through August).

9-5
Cash disbursements

Interactive Communications Unlimited (ICU) is scheduling the production of video-phones to be sold next summer. Orders for the next 5 months are as follows: April, 80,000 units; May, 100,000 units; June, 130,000 units; July, 80,000 units; and August, 40,000 units. Manufacturing costs for materials are $1,300 per unit, paid 1 month before manufacture. Direct labor costs equal $600 per unit, paid in the month of production. Shipping costs are $240 per unit, paid the month after manufacture. Depreciation expense is allocated on a units-of-production basis of $100 per unit in the month of production. Advertising expense is zero for April and May but will be $400,000 in June and $1,000,000 in July. Fixed overhead is $600,000 monthly. Taxes of $16 million will be paid at the end of June. Prepare a schedule of cash disbursements for May through July.

9-6

Cash budgeting

Ben and Clara Dwyer recently leased space in the Lone Pine Mall and opened a new business, B & C Sporting Goods. Business has been good, but the Dwyers have frequently run out of cash. This has necessitated late payment on certain orders, which, in turn, is beginning to cause a problem with suppliers. The Dwyers plan to borrow from the bank to have cash ready as needed, but first they need to determine how much they must borrow. Accordingly, they have asked you to prepare a cash budget for a critical period around Christmas, when needs will be especially high.

Sales are made on a *cash basis only*. The Dwyers' purchases must be paid for in the month following the purchase. The Dwyers pay themselves a salary of $4,800 per month, and the rent is $2,000 per month. In addition, the Dwyers must make a tax payment of $12,000 in December. The current cash on hand (on December 1) is $400, but the Dwyers have agreed to maintain an average bank balance of $6,000; this is their target cash balance. (Disregard till cash, which is insignificant because the Dwyers keep only a small amount on hand to lessen the chances of robbery.)

The estimated sales and purchases for December, January, and February are shown in the following table. Purchases during November amounted to $140,000.

	Sales	Purchases
December	$160,000	$40,000
January	40,000	40,000
February	60,000	40,000

a. Prepare a cash budget for December, January, and February.
b. Now suppose that the Dwyers were to start selling on a credit basis on December 1, giving customers 30 days to pay. All customers accept these terms, and all other facts in the problem are unchanged. What would the firm's loan requirements be at the end of December in this case? (*Hint:* The calculations required to answer this question are minimal.)

9-7

Cash budgeting

South Beach Home Decor is trying to improve its cash management. You have been assigned to help in this task and are given the following data to use in your analysis:

Sales Forecast for the Month of	Sales
December	$20,000
January	27,000
February	27,000
March	10,000
April	10,000

Collection estimates were obtained from the credit and collection department as follows: 10 percent collected within one month of sale, 80 percent collected in the month following sale, and 10 percent collected in the second month following sale. Payments for labor and raw materials are typically made during the month following the one in which these costs are incurred.

Labor and Raw Materials for the Month of	Cost
January	$15,000
February	15,000
March	7,500
April	8,500

General and administrative salaries will amount to approximately $4,080 a month; lease payments under long-term lease contracts will be $1,380 a month; depreciation charges are $5,400 a month; miscellaneous expenses will be $420 a month. Cash on hand February 1 will amount to $500, and a minimum cash balance of $7,500 should be maintained throughout the cash budget period. (Assume that the minimum cash balance policy has only just started.) Prepare a cash budget for South Beach for February through April.

9-8

Cash budgeting

The McGirr Corporation is planning to request a line of credit from its bank. The following sales forecasts have been made for 1994 and 1995:

May 1994	$ 75,000
June	75,000
July	150,000
August	225,000
September	300,000
October	150,000
November	150,000
December	37,500
January 1995	75,000

Collection estimates obtained from the credit and collection department are as follows: collections within the month of sale, 20 percent; collections the month following the sale, 65 percent; collections the second month following the sale, 15 percent. Payments for labor and raw materials are typically made during the month following the one in which these costs have been incurred. Total labor and raw materials costs are estimated for each month as follows:

May 1994	$ 37,500
June	37,500
July	52,500
August	367,500
September	127,500
October	97,500
November	67,500
December	37,500

General and administrative salaries will amount to approximately $13,250 a month; lease payments under long-term lease contracts will be $4,500 a month; depreciation charges will be $15,000 a month; miscellaneous expenses will be $1,125 a month; income tax payments of $26,250 will be due in both September and December; and a progress payment of $75,000 on new construction must be paid in October. Cash on hand on July 1 will amount to $35,000, and a minimum cash balance of $30,000 will be maintained throughout the cash budget period.

a. Prepare a monthly cash budget for the last six months of 1994.

b. Prepare an estimate of the required financing (or excess funds) — that is, the amount of money that McGirr will need to borrow (or will have available to invest) — for each month during that period.

c. Assume that receipts from sales come in uniformly during the month (that is, cash receipts come in at the rate of 1/30 each day) but that all outflows are paid on the fifth of the month. Will this have an effect on the cash budget? In other words, would the cash budget you have prepared be valid under these assumptions? If not, what can be done to make a valid estimate of peak financing requirements? No calculations are required, although calculations can be used to illustrate the effects.

d. McGirr produces on a seasonal basis, just ahead of sales. Without making any calculations, discuss how the company's current ratio and debt ratio would vary during the year assuming all financial requirements were met by short-term bank loans. Could changes in these ratios affect the firm's ability to obtain bank credit?

Solutions to Self-Test Problems

ST-1 **a.** The collection float period is now 6 days and can be reduced by 4 days under the proposed collection system. Since Banner receives $1,000,000 daily, the 4 day reduction in float would either increase the firm's marketable securities or reduce needed financing by $4,000,000.

b. $4,000,000 × 0.10 = $400,000.

c. $400,000/12 = $33,333.

ST-2 **a.** First determine the balance on the firm's checkbook and the bank's records as follows:

	Firm's Checkbook	Bank's Records
Day 1: Deposit $500,000; write checks for $1,000,000	($ 500,000)	$500,000
Day 2: Write checks for $1,000,000	($1,500,000)	$500,000
Day 3: Write checks for $1,000,000	($2,500,000)	$500,000
Day 4: Write checks for $1,000,000; deposit $1,000,000	($2,500,000)	$500,000

After Weston has reached a steady state, it must deposit $1,000,000 each day to cover the checks written 3 days earlier.

b. The firm has 3 days of disbursement float; not until Day 4 does the firm have to make any additional deposits.

c. As shown above, Weston should try to maintain a balance on the bank's records of $500,000. On its own books it will have a balance of *minus* $2,500,000.

MINI CASE

COMPUTER MODELING: CASH BUDGETING

Follow-the-Sun RV Services (FTS) is a medium-sized Idaho-based corporation, specializing in the manufacture and repair of customized appliances for a wide range of recreational vehicles. The firm also repairs exterior surfaces, upholstery, and cabinets of such vehicles and has had a booming business in recent years due to its quality craftsmanship and excellent reputation for on-time delivery.

FTS typically experiences peak demands for its products and services in March and April, as RV manufacturers gear up for the summer season and families with school age children start planning their vacations — and again in late summer, when retired couples either buy a recreational vehicle for the first time or make repairs to their vehicles in order to head south for the winter.

The firm is getting ready to construct a cash budget for the period March through August 1995, and Anna Petrovic, FTS's vice president of finance, has asked you to build a spreadsheet model which (1) can be used to test the sensitivity of future cash flows to various assumptions and (2) can be updated for each subsequent 6-month period. FTS has not previously used computers in cash budgeting, but management understands that this is one of the areas where computerized planning and forecasting models have gained the greatest popularity. In addition, management is always concerned about running low on cash and has had problems with this in the past. The following actual and forecasted information is available (all dollar amounts in millions):

		Jan.	Feb.	March	April	May	June	July	Aug.	Sept.
(1)	Sales	$10	$30	$50	$40	$30	$25	$20	$40	$50
	Collections:									
(2)	Month of sale (10%)									
(3)	Month after sale (60%)									
(4)	Second month after sale (27%)									

Additional data:

▷ FTS does not offer any cash discounts at this time.

▷ In the past, the firm has been able to collect on only 97 percent of its sales; in other words, 3 percent of total sales represent bad debt losses.

▷ Purchases for materials are equal to 70 percent of the following month's projected sales, and FTS pays its suppliers after 1 month. FTS has tried to negotiate longer trade credit from its suppliers but has not been successful. Therefore, you may treat the 1-month lag in payment for purchases as a constant.

▷ Wages and salaries are paid in the month incurred and are projected as follows (in millions):

March	April	May	June	July	August
$5.0	$4.0	$3.0	$2.5	$2.0	$4.0

▷ Rent is $250,000 per month.

▷ Other expenses are $100,000 per month.

▷ Tax payments of $7.8 million each are due on March 15 and June 15.

▷ FTS's cash balance on March 1 is estimated to be $300,000, but the firm has agreed to keep a cash balance of $500,000 with First Street Bank at all times to compensate the bank for services rendered. The $500,000 becomes the firm's target cash balance.

▷ FTS does not have any bank loans outstanding at this time.

Using *Lotus 1-2-3,* do the following:

a. State the basic assumptions of the problem in an "assumption block." This means that you should display in the upper left-hand corner of the spreadsheet all the information given above, with quantitative data in separate columns and not part of labels (for example, "Sales" is a label and so is "Month of sale," but the three collection percentages are quantitative data and should be accessible). It is this set of assumptions that should "drive" your model, and changes should only be made in the assumption block.

b. Construct a cash budget for the period March through August 1995 for Follow-the-Sun RV Services. Use Table 9-1 for general format. The bottom line should show cumulative surplus cash (or cumulative loans required, if negative) for each of the six months.

Note: The real power of an electronic spreadsheet is its ability to perform a sensitivity analysis (answer "what if" questions). It is therefore crucial that the stated assumptions in Part a are the underlying determinants of the model in Part b, your cash budget. Therefore, your cash budget must not use constants (the only exception is the 1-month lag in payments for purchases) but formulas, and these formulas must refer back up to earlier cell addresses. You may want to review how to make reference to a cell *absolute,* as opposed to relative. Any time a change is made in one or more assumptions in Part a, surplus funds (required loans) in the cash budget should *automatically* recalculate. If that happens, you have succeeded in building a dynamic model. And if your model is constructed correctly, the remaining questions should require very little time to answer. Save your work in Parts a and b as FTS-B. Print out all of this.

c. Marketing manager, Jack Tan, feels that the sales forecast for March and April is actually on the conservative side. What would FTS's cash budget look like if sales were higher by $5 million in each of these two months? Assume that this would cause wages and salaries to rise by $0.5 million above the previously projected levels in March and April but that all other assumptions would remain unchanged. Answer by printing out both assumption block and cash budget, and save the file as FTS-C.

d. Collection of accounts receivable has been a problem for Follow-the-Sun for some time. Management realizes that the firm has an awful lot of money tied up in receivables. Slim Gittner, the credit manager, wants to know what the effect would be on the cash budget if collections were 20 percent in the month of sale, 70 percent in the month after sale, and 7 percent in the second month after sale. Assume that this could be done without hurting the level of sales and that bad debt losses would still be 3 percent.

If all other data remain as in Part c, would Follow-the-Sun RV Services have surplus funds of $10 million in May to purchase a badly needed piece of equipment? In other words, can the firm buy the equipment without relying on additional borrowing? If not in May, then when? Simply type in a brief answer. Provide a new printout and save your work as FTS-D.

Accounts Receivable and Inventories

After reading this chapter, you should be able to:

▶ Explain how management of accounts receivable and inventory influences a firm's overall profitability.

▶ List the four elements of a firm's credit policy.

▶ Specify how the "five Cs of credit," management by exception, credit-scoring systems, and an aging schedule help managers determine, apply, or evaluate credit policy.

▶ Analyze proposed changes in credit policy.

▶ State the goal of inventory management and explain the specific decisions and the categories of inventory involved.

▶ Find the economic ordering quantity (EOQ) for a given firm, with or without safety stocks.

▶ Explain the use of several inventory control systems and define just-in-time and out-sourcing.

DECISION IN FINANCE

THE DATA ARE AVAILABLE, BUT SHOULD COMPANIES USE THEM?

At least once a month, the nation's banks and retailers, among others, give credit bureaus computer tapes or electronic files detailing the purchases and payments of nearly every U.S. consumer. Twenty years ago, credit bureaus guarded this information so closely that even individual consumers could not see their own files. The files are still closely guarded, and they are virtually impossible to steal. However, until recently it has been easy to obtain data from the files. "For very little cost," says the editor of *Privacy Journal,* a newsletter, "anybody can learn anything about anybody."

Credit file information covers the entire life of an individual, literally from birth until death. Anyone who applies for credit to buy a car, a house, or any other item must submit detailed information about his or her financial status—including checking account balances, telephone bill information, payment records, family size and ages, Social Security numbers, medical records, racial or ethnic background, employment history, annual income, insurance records, available credit balance on credit cards, and, of course, addresses and telephone numbers. Until very recently, all of this information was available to almost anyone who was willing to pay for it.

The "big three" credit bureaus—TRW, Trans Union, and Equifax—each have about a

one-third share of the U.S. credit-reporting market, estimated at a total of about $1 billion. To give you an idea of how lucrative the sale of information from their databases is, for example, Trans Union advertises a list of 104 million credit card holders for 6.5 cents a name. And, for an extra fee, the company will divide the list into a number of different categories, including "Premium Bankcard" holders and "Upscale Retail Card" holders. The stored information is becoming so detailed that marketers can distinguish the spending habits of one family from their next-door neighbors of the same age and with the same number of children.

With 971,517 bankruptcy petitions filed nationwide in 1992, with personal bankruptcies accounting for 92 percent of that total, and with the credit card delinquency rate at 3.29 percent nationally, businesses are eager to find out about and screen potential customers. To help in this regard, credit bureaus, in the past, have provided forecasts on the financial soundness of individuals.

See end of chapter for resolution.
Photo source: Copyright © 1992, Comstock, Inc.

Companies also spend about $2 billion a year with information providers to identify good prospects for their products, in addition to obtaining credit information. They can obtain such specific characteristics as names of Hispanics earning $500,000 a year and having $10,000 available on their credit cards or people with $1 million in the bank who live within a 50-mile radius of Dallas. According to a lawyer specializing in consumer financial services, "Consumers don't understand that for each ad stuffing their mailbox, a company without their knowledge or permission has asked a credit bureau to review their file and provide information to the advertiser."

Legislators and consumer advocates have long been concerned about these increasing invasions of personal privacy. Ten privacy laws already exist, but they have had only limited effects on credit bureau operations. One law aimed primarily at the private sector is the Fair Credit Reporting Act of 1971. It requires that consumers be allowed to see their own credit records and that they be told of investigations for insurance or employment purposes. It also bars credit agencies from giving information to anyone but "authorized customers." However, that definition is so broad that it includes anyone who claims to have "a legitimate business need." The real problem is that the law was written long before the rise of electronic databases. Although this legislation limits the "permissible" purposes of credit data, it did not anticipate the mailing-list boom; therefore, it does not address this market.

The Video Privacy Protection Act of 1988 forbids disclosure or sale of retailers' video rental records—kinky habits are protected. Several other acts restrict the government's use of certain types of personal information.

Nevertheless, the computer age has made it increasingly difficult to control the flow of data. "Computers have outstripped the ability of our legal system to safeguard privacy," says a professor who chaired the 1977 U.S. Privacy Protection Commission. A researcher says few people have any idea of the kinds of information available about them, and they have no way of finding out who may be using such information. However, public opinion polls show that 90 percent of the population is worried about the invasion of privacy via electronic data collection, and this concern is likely to be translated into laws. For example, in late 1989, California passed a law limiting commercial use of personal records, and it allows its residents to use a post office box or business address instead of a home address on driver's license applications and in transactions with state agencies. Thus, even though people continue to fill out credit applications and to divulge information about their private lives, they seem to be increasingly concerned that it not be passed along for uses other than the one for which they furnished it.

As you read this chapter, consider the many uses to which a business might put personal information about individuals. Then consider how those individuals might react when they learn about such uses. Finally, do you think businesses should assume a more responsible position about private information before government steps in and does it for them?

In the previous chapter, we examined the firm's investment in cash and marketable securities. To complete the analysis of current assets management, we now turn to accounts receivable and inventories. These accounts are essential for a firm's profitability and even for its existence. Inventories are needed for sales to occur, and, although firms would rather sell for cash than on credit, competition forces most companies to offer credit.

Since firms often have as much as 25 percent of their assets in receivables and another 25 percent in inventories, effective management of these two accounts is clearly important for the firm's profitability. Remember from Chapter 6 that the Du Pont equation finds return on total assets (ROA) as the product of profit margin and total assets turnover:

$$\text{ROA} = \text{Profit margin} \times \text{Total assets turnover} \qquad (6\text{-}1)$$

$$= \frac{\text{Net income}}{\text{Sales}} \times \frac{\text{Sales}}{\text{Total assets}}.$$

If receivables and inventories are allowed to build up to excessive levels, Du Pont analysis shows that this will result in a lower total assets turnover and a lower return on total assets (ROA) than would otherwise have been the case. Extending too much credit and carrying too much inventory will also lead to lower net income, other things equal, since some portion of these current assets is typically financed through debt, on which interest must be paid. This lowers the profit margin and results in a still lower return on total assets. On the other hand, carrying too little inventory and denying credit to potential customers are likely to result in lost sales and profits. The goal becomes—in credit management as in so many other areas of financial management—to find just the right balance.

In Chapter 8 we saw the effect of the firm's inventory and receivables management on its cash conversion cycle. Two components of the cash conversion cycle are the inventory conversion period, which is the average length of time required to convert raw materials and labor into finished goods and then to sell these goods, and the receivables conversion period, which is the length of time required to convert the firm's receivables into cash. Naturally, the larger the amount of inventories and receivables held, the longer the inventory and receivables conversion periods will be, hence, the longer the cash conversion cycle and the greater the firm's need for nonspontaneous financing will be. Again, there are costs associated with such a working capital policy. In this chapter we discuss procedures that will help the firm optimize its investment in accounts receivable and inventories.

Accounts Receivable Management

account receivable

A balance due from a customer.

As mentioned earlier, most firms sell on credit. When goods are shipped, inventories are reduced, and an **account receivable** is created.[1] Eventually, the customer will pay the account, at which time receivables will decline and the cash account will increase. Carrying receivables is costly, but the costs involved can be offset by the fact that granting credit helps the firm by increasing its sales. The financial manager tries to balance the costs and benefits of granting credit when determining the firm's credit policy. A good receivables control system is important, for without an adequate system, receivables will build up to exces-

---

[1]Whenever goods are sold on credit, two accounts are actually created; an asset item called an *account receivable* appears on the books of the selling firm, and a liability item called an *account payable* appears on the books of the purchaser. At this point we are analyzing the transaction from the seller's viewpoint, so we are concentrating on the variables under its control — in this case, the receivables. The transaction will be examined from the purchaser's viewpoint in Chapter 11, where we discuss accounts payable as a source of funds and consider their cost relative to the cost of funds obtained from other sources.

sive levels, cash flows will decline, and bad debts will rise to unacceptable levels. *The optimal credit policy is the one at which the marginal benefits of increased sales are exactly offset by the marginal costs of granting credit;* this is the credit policy that maximizes the value of the firm.

The optimal credit policy, and hence the optimal level of accounts receivable, depends on the firm's own unique operating conditions. Thus, a firm with excess capacity and low variable production costs should extend credit more liberally, and therefore should carry a higher level of accounts receivable, than if it were operating at full capacity or had a slim gross profit margin. Although optimal credit policies vary among firms, or even for a single firm over time, it is still useful to analyze the effectiveness of the firm's credit policy in an overall, aggregate sense.

Determinants of Accounts Receivable

The total amount of a firm's accounts receivable outstanding at any given time is determined by two factors: (1) the volume of credit sales and (2) the average length of time between sales and collections. For example, suppose that Cascade Lumber Company, a distributor of wood products, opens a lumber yard on January 1 and, starting the first day, makes sales of $1,000 each day. For simplicity, we assume that all sales are on credit. Customers are given 10 days in which to pay. At the end of the first day, accounts receivable will be $1,000; they will rise to $2,000 by the end of the second day; and by January 10, they will have risen to $10,000. On January 11, another $1,000 will be added to receivables, but payments for sales made on January 1 will reduce receivables by $1,000 so that total accounts receivable will remain constant at $10,000. In general, assuming that all customers pay on time, once Cascade's operations have stabilized, this situaion will exist:

$$\frac{\text{Accounts}}{\text{receivable}} = \frac{\text{Credit sales}}{\text{per day}} \times \frac{\text{Length of collection}}{\text{period (DSO)}}$$

$$= \$1,000 \times 10 \text{ days} = \$10,000.$$

If either the volume of credit sales or the length of the collection period changes, this will be reflected in the level of accounts receivable, which, in turn, would require a change in the level of financing.

Recognize also that both the volume of credit sales and DSO are functions of (1) economic conditions that are not controllable by management and (2) credit policy variables which, subject to such considerations as industry practice, *are* factors that management can change, if such change appears to offer benefits that at least match the costs involved. These policy variables will be discussed next.

Self-Test

In general terms, what credit policy maximizes the value of the firm?

Explain what is meant by the following statement: "The optimal credit policy, hence the optimal level of accounts receivable, depends on the firm's own unique operating conditions."

Which two factors determine a firm's total level of accounts receivable?

Credit Policy

The success or failure of a business depends primarily on the demand for its products; as a rule, the higher the demand, the greater its sales and profits, and the higher the value of its stock. The major controllable variables that affect sales are product price and quality, advertising, and the firm's credit policy. **Credit policy,** in turn, consists of these four elements:

1. The *credit period,* which is the length of time buyers are given to pay for their purchases.
2. *Cash discounts* given to encourage early payment.
3. *Credit standards,* which refer to the minimum financial strength of acceptable credit customers and the amount of credit available to different customers.
4. The firm's *collection policy,* which reflects the firm's toughness or leniency in following up on slow-paying accounts.

The credit period and the discount allowed (if any), when combined, are called the **credit terms.** Thus, if a company allows its customers 30 days in which to pay, but then gives a 2 percent discount if payment is made within 10 days, it is said to offer credit terms of 2/10, net 30. The credit manager has the responsibility for enforcing the credit terms and administering the firm's credit policy. However, because of the pervasive importance of credit, the credit policy itself — both setting the credit terms and specifying the credit standards and collection policy — is established by the executive committee, which usually consists of the president and the vice presidents in charge of finance, marketing, and production.

Credit Period

The **credit period,** as mentioned above, is the length of time a company gives its customers to pay; for example, credit might be extended for 30, 60, or 90 days. Several factors influence the length of time over which the firm offers credit. In part, this credit period is influenced by the terms offered by competitors. Further, there is generally a relationship between the normal inventory holding period of the firm's customers and the credit period it will extend to these customers. For example, fresh fruits and vegetables normally are sold on very short credit terms, whereas jewelry may involve a 90-day or even a 6-month credit period.

Within these parameters there is still plenty of leeway for setting more or less generous credit terms. Lengthening the credit period may stimulate sales, but there is a cost to tying up funds in receivables. For example, if a firm changes its terms from net 30 to net 60, the average receivables for the year might rise from $100,000 to $300,000, with the increase in accounts receivable of $200,000 being caused in part by higher sales and in part by the longer credit period. Assuming that the firm's required rate of return on investment is 12 percent, the marginal return required on lengthening the credit period is $200,000 $\times$ 12% = $24,000. If the incremental profit (sales price minus all direct production and selling costs, as well as any credit

---

credit policy

A set of decisions that include a firm's credit period, discounts offered, credit standards, and collection policy.

credit terms

A statement of the credit period and any discounts offered—for example, 2/10, net 30.

credit period

The length of time for which credit is granted.

losses associated with the additional sales) exceeds or equals $24,000, the change in credit policy should be made. Thus determining the optimal credit period involves many factors, but the bottom line in establishing a credit period is determining the point at which marginal profits on increased sales just offset the marginal costs, such as the costs of carrying the higher amount of accounts receivable.

Cash Discounts

cash discount

A reduction in the price of goods, given to encourage early payment.

The second element in the credit policy decision, the use of **cash discounts** to encourage early payment, is analyzed by balancing the costs and benefits of different discount terms. For example, a firm might decide to change its credit terms from "net 30," which means that customers must pay within 30 days, to "2/10, net 30," which means that it will allow a 2 percent discount if payment is received within 10 days, whereas the full invoice price must otherwise be paid within 30 days. This change should produce two benefits: (1) it should attract new customers who consider discounts a type of price reduction, and (2) it should cause a reduction in the days sales outstanding (DSO) because some old customers will begin to pay within 10 days to take advantage of the discount. Offsetting these benefits is the dollar cost of the discounts taken. The optimal discount is the one at which the marginal costs and benefits are exactly offsetting. The methodology for analyzing changes in the discount is developed later in this chapter.

Offering cash discounts for prompt payment may lead to increased profits for the selling firm if its customers follow the terms of credit, but discounts can be quite costly if buyers pay late and still take the discount. One such case involved Carter Hawley Hale Stores Inc. Arizona Wholesale Supply Company, a distributor of household products such as television sets, sold merchandise to Carter Hawley Hale on terms which allowed a 2 percent discount on invoices paid within 20 days. Arizona Wholesale filed a lawsuit charging that Carter Hawley Hale had illegally deducted $53,000 in discounts on invoices which were not paid within the stated 20-day credit period. Arizona Wholesale also charged that federal antitrust laws were being violated because firms which allow some customers to take discounts on late payments are discriminating against other customers who are not allowed to take such discounts. Thus, Arizona Wholesale would have been guilty of antitrust violations if it had permitted Carter Hawley Hale to take discounts after the 20-day credit period but had not allowed other customers to also take such discounts. This example illustrates the fact that firms have two incentives to enforce their credit policies: profitability and the avoidance of antitrust violations.

seasonal dating

Terms to induce customers to buy early by not requiring payment until the customers' selling season, regardless of when the merchandise is shipped.

If sales are seasonal, a firm may use **seasonal dating** on discounts. For example, Jenson Inc., a swimsuit manufacturer, sells on terms of 2/10, net 30, May 1 dating. This means that the effective invoice date is May 1, even if the sale was made back in January. The discount may be taken up to May 10; otherwise, the full amount must be paid on May 30. If Jenson produces throughout the year, but retail sales of bathing suits are concentrated in the spring and early summer, offering seasonal dating may induce some customers to stock up early, saving Jenson storage costs and also "nailing down" sales.

Credit Standards

If a firm makes credit sales only to its strongest customers, it will never have bad debt losses nor will it incur much in the way of expenses for its credit department. On the other hand, it will probably lose sales, and the profit forgone on these lost sales could be far larger than the costs it has avoided. Determining the optimal credit standards involves equating the marginal costs of credit to the marginal profits on the increased sales.

credit standards

Standards that stipulate the minimum financial strength that an applicant must demonstrate in order to be granted credit.

Credit standards refer to the strength and creditworthiness a customer must exhibit in order to qualify for credit. If a customer does not qualify for the regular credit terms, he or she can still purchase from the firm, but under more restrictive terms. For example, a firm's "regular" credit terms might call for payment after 30 days, and these terms might be extended to all qualifed customers. The firm's credit standards would be applied to determine which customers qualified for the regular credit terms and how much credit each customer should receive. The major factors considered when setting credit standards relate to the likelihood that a given customer will pay slowly, or perhaps even end up as a bad debt loss.

Setting credit standards implicitly requires a measurement of *credit quality*, which is defined in terms of the probability of a customer's default. The probability estimate for a given customer is, for the most part, a subjective judgment. Nevertheless, credit evaluation is a well-established practice, and a good credit manager can make reasonably accurate judgments of the probability of default by the different classes of customers. In this section we discuss some of the methods used by firms (and by bank loan officers) to measure credit quality.

The Five Cs System. The traditional method of measuring credit quality, where no computerized system is to be used, is to investigate potential credit customers with respect to five factors called the **five Cs of credit:**

five Cs of credit

The factors used to evaluate credit risk: character, capacity, capital, collateral, and conditions.

1. *Character* refers to the probability that a customer will *try* to honor his or her obligations. This factor is of considerable importance because every credit transaction implies a *promise* to pay. Will debtors make an honest effort to pay their debts, or are they likely to try to get away with something? Experienced credit managers frequently insist that the moral factor is the most important issue in a credit evaluation. Thus, credit reports provide background information on people's and firms' past performances. Often credit analysts will seek this type of information from a firm's bankers, its other suppliers, its customers, and even its competitors.

2. *Capacity* is a subjective judgment of a customer's ability to pay. It is gauged in part by the customer's past records and business methods, and it may be supplemented by physical observation of the plant or store. Again, credit analysts and bank loan officers will obtain information of this type from a variety of sources.

3. *Capital* is measured by the cash flows and the general financial condition of a customer firm as indicated by an analysis of its financial statements, with special emphasis on the risk ratios — the debt ratio, the current ratio, and the times-interest-earned ratio.

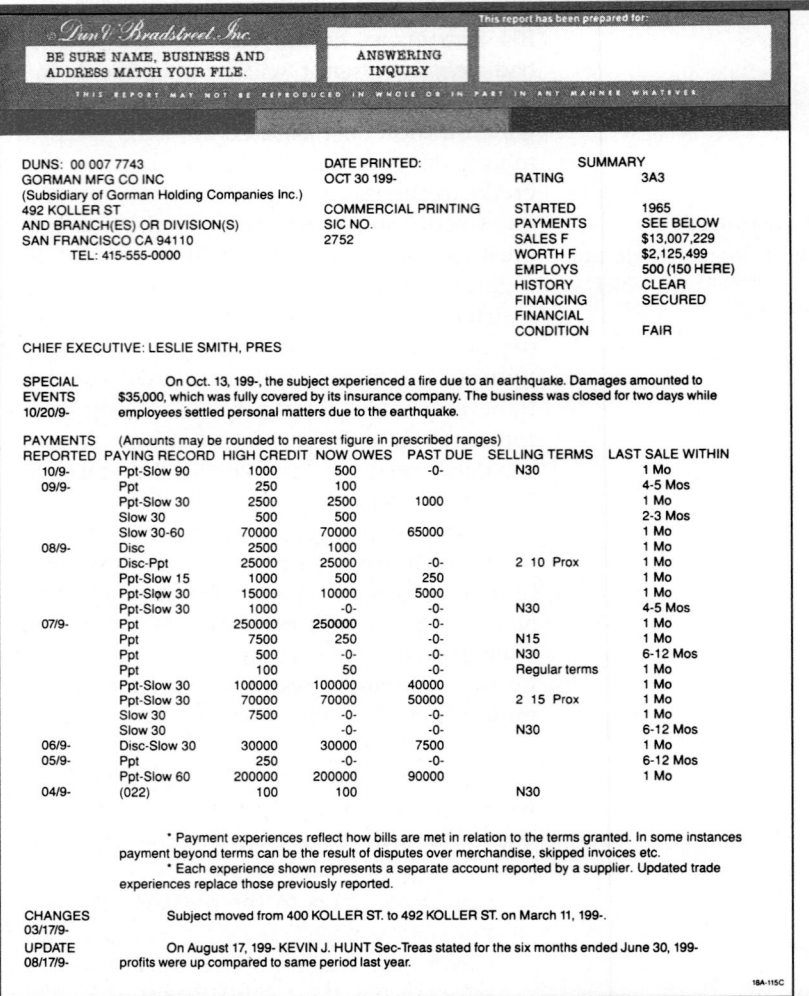

Credit reporting agencies (such as Dun & Bradstreet) compile and sell reports on specific companies; in this example, the information is on Gorman Manufacturing Co. Inc. These reports provide a credit rating (in top right corner) as well as factual information about

4. *Collateral* refers to any assets that the customer may offer as security in order to obtain credit.

5. *Conditions* refers both to general economic trends and to special developments in certain geographic regions or sectors of the economy that may affect customers' ability to meet their obligations.

Information on these five factors comes from the firm's previous experience with its customers, and it is supplemented by a well-developed system of exter-

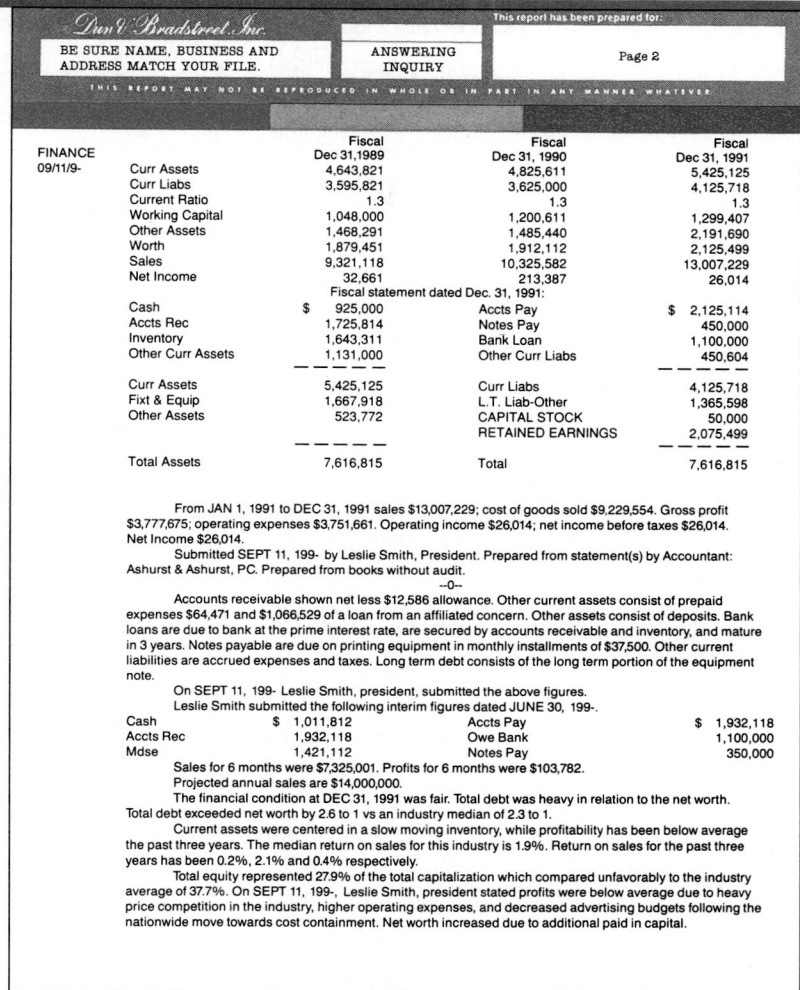

Dun & Bradstreet, Inc.

BE SURE NAME, BUSINESS AND
ADDRESS MATCH YOUR FILE.

ANSWERING
INQUIRY

Page 2

THIS REPORT MAY NOT BE REPRODUCED IN WHOLE OR IN PART IN ANY MANNER WHATEVER

FINANCE		Fiscal Dec 31,1989	Fiscal Dec 31, 1990	Fiscal Dec 31, 1991
09/11/9-	Curr Assets	4,643,821	4,825,611	5,425,125
	Curr Liabs	3,595,821	3,625,000	4,125,718
	Current Ratio	1.3	1.3	1.3
	Working Capital	1,048,000	1,200,611	1,299,407
	Other Assets	1,468,291	1,485,440	2,191,690
	Worth	1,879,451	1,912,112	2,125,499
	Sales	9,321,118	10,325,582	13,007,229
	Net Income	32,661	213,387	26,014

Fiscal statement dated Dec. 31, 1991:

Cash	$ 925,000	Accts Pay	$ 2,125,114
Accts Rec	1,725,814	Notes Pay	450,000
Inventory	1,643,311	Bank Loan	1,100,000
Other Curr Assets	1,131,000	Other Curr Liabs	450,604
Curr Assets	5,425,125	Curr Liabs	4,125,718
Fixt & Equip	1,667,918	L.T. Liab-Other	1,365,598
Other Assets	523,772	CAPITAL STOCK	50,000
		RETAINED EARNINGS	2,075,499
Total Assets	7,616,815	Total	7,616,815

From JAN 1, 1991 to DEC 31, 1991 sales $13,007,229; cost of goods sold $9,229,554. Gross profit $3,777,675; operating expenses $3,751,661. Operating income $26,014; net income before taxes $26,014. Net Income $26,014.

Submitted SEPT 11, 199- by Leslie Smith, President. Prepared from statement(s) by Accountant: Ashurst & Ashurst, PC. Prepared from books without audit.

--0--

Accounts receivable shown net less $12,586 allowance. Other current assets consist of prepaid expenses $64,471 and $1,066,529 of a loan from an affiliated concern. Other assets consist of deposits. Bank loans are due to bank at the prime interest rate, are secured by accounts receivable and inventory, and mature in 3 years. Notes payable are due on printing equipment in monthly installments of $37,500. Other current liabilities are accrued expenses and taxes. Long term debt consists of the long term portion of the equipment note.

On SEPT 11, 199- Leslie Smith, president, submitted the above figures.
Leslie Smith submitted the following interim figures dated JUNE 30, 199-.

Cash	$ 1,011,812	Accts Pay	$ 1,932,118
Accts Rec	1,932,118	Owe Bank	1,100,000
Mdse	1,421,112	Notes Pay	350,000

Sales for 6 months were $7,325,001. Profits for 6 months were $103,782. Projected annual sales are $14,000,000.

The financial condition at DEC 31, 1991 was fair. Total debt was heavy in relation to the net worth. Total debt exceeded net worth by 2.6 to 1 vs an industry median of 2.3 to 1.

Current assets were centered in a slow moving inventory, while profitability has been below average the past three years. The median return on sales for this industry is 1.9%. Return on sales for the past three years has been 0.2%, 2.1% and 0.4% respectively.

Total equity represented 27.9% of the total capitalization which compared unfavorably to the industry average of 37.7%. On SEPT 11, 199-, Leslie Smith, president stated profits were below average due to heavy price competition in the industry, higher operating expenses, and decreased advertising budgets following the nationwide move towards cost containment. Net worth increased due to additional paid in capital.

the company's current financial status, public record of legal activities, banking, company history, and a brief description of the business.

nal information gatherers. Of course, once the information on the five Cs is developed, the credit manager must still make the final decision on the potential customer's overall credit quality. Because this decision is normally judgmental in nature, credit managers must rely on their background knowledge and instincts.

Sources of Credit Information.   Two major sources of external information are available. First there are the *credit associations,* which are local groups that meet frequently and correspond with one another to exchange information on credit customers. These local groups have also banded together to create Credit Interchange, a system developed by the National Association of Credit Management for assembling and distributing information about customers' past performances. The interchange reports show the paying records of different credit customers, the industries from which they are buying, and the geographic areas in which purchases are being made.

The second source of external information is the *credit-reporting agencies,* which collect credit information and sell it for a fee. The best known of these agencies are Dun & Bradstreet (D&B), Equifax, and TRW. These and other agencies provide factual data that can be used in credit analysis; they also provide ratings similar to those available on corporate bonds.[2]

Managing a credit department requires fast, accurate, up-to-date information, and to help make such information available, the National Association of Credit Management (a group with 43,000 member firms) persuaded TRW to develop a computer-based telecommunications network for the collection, storage, retrieval, and distribution of credit information. The TRW system contains credit data on over 120 million individuals, and it electronically transmits credit reports which are available within seconds to its thousands of subscribers. Dun & Bradstreet has a similar electronic system, plus another service which provides more detailed reports through the U.S. mail.

A typical credit report would include the following pieces of information:

1. A summary balance sheet and income statement.
2. A number of key ratios, including trends.
3. Information obtained from the firm's banks and suppliers about whether it generally pays promptly or slowly and whether it has recently failed to make any payments.
4. A verbal description of the physical condition of the firm's operations.
5. A verbal description of the backgrounds of the firm's owners, including any previous bankruptcies, lawsuits, fraud, and the like.
6. A summary rating, ranging from A for the best credit risks down to F for those judged likely to default.

Although a great deal of credit information is available, it must still be processed in a judgmental manner. Computerized information systems can assist managers in making better credit decisions, but in the final analysis credit determinations are really exercises in informed judgment.

As discussed in the opening vignette to this chapter, serious questions are being raised today about the credit bureaus' practice of selling the credit information they have collected. Also, consumers often encounter enormous difficulties in trying to correct erroneous credit records. The *Federal Trade Commission* reports that problems involving credit-reporting agencies remain the number 1 consumer complaint — however crucial the role of these agencies may be when seen from the point of view of the selling firm. In March 1993,

---

[2]For additional information, see *Credit Management,* a publication of the National Association of Credit Management; and also see Peter Nulty, "An Upstart Takes on Dun & Bradstreet," *Fortune,* April 9, 1979, 98–100.

two bills were introduced in the U.S. House of Representatives to overhaul the 23-year old laws which regulate the credit-reporting industry. One of these bills proposes that consumers should be provided with free annual reports, and it would prohibit credit bureaus from selling prescreened lists to marketers. The second bill would do neither but would require that credit disputes be resolved within 30 days. The length of time needed to clear up credit mixups, which currently may be as long as two years, is one of the major frustrations expressed by consumers.

credit-scoring system

Statistical method similar to multiple regression analysis; it is used to assess a customer's credit risk.

Credit-Scoring Systems.   Although most credit decisions are subjective, many firms now use a sophisticated statistical **credit-scoring system** method called *multiple discriminant analysis (MDA)* to assess credit quality. MDA is similar to multiple regression analysis. The dependent variable is, in essence, the probability of default, and the independent variables are factors associated with financial strength and the ability to pay off the debt if credit is granted. For example, if a firm such as Sears is evaluating consumers' credit quality, then the independent variables in the credit scoring system would be such factors as these: (1) Does the credit applicant own his or her own home? (2) How long has the applicant worked on his or her current job? (3) What is the applicant's outstanding debt in relation to his or her annual income? (4) Does the potential customer have a history of paying his or her debts on time?

One major advantage of an MDA credit-scoring system is that a customer's credit quality is expressed in a single numerical value rather than as a subjective assessment of various factors. This is a tremendous advantage for a large firm that must evaluate many customers in many different locations using many different credit employees, for without an automated procedure, the firm would have a hard time applying equal standards to all credit applicants. Therefore, most credit card companies, department stores, oil companies, and the like use credit-scoring systems to determine who gets how much credit, as do the larger building supply chains and manufacturers of electrical products, machinery, and so on.

To illustrate the use of MDA, suppose Hanover Company, a North Carolina furniture manufacturer, has historical information on 500 of its customers, all of whom are retail businesses. Of these 500, assume that 400 have always paid on time, but the other 100 either paid late or, in some cases, went bankrupt and did not pay at all. Further, the firm has historical data on each customer's quick ratio, times-interest-earned ratio, debt ratio, years in existence, and so on. Multiple discriminant analysis relates the experienced record (or historical probability) of late payment or nonpayment with various measures of a firm's financial condition and then assigns weights to each of the critical factors. In effect, MDA produces an equation that looks much like a regression equation, and when data on a customer are plugged into the equation, then a credit score for that customer is produced.

For example, suppose Hanover's multiple discriminant analysis indicates that the critical factors affecting prompt payment are the customer's times-interest-earned ratio (TIE), quick ratio, debt ratio, and number of years in business. Here is the equation produced, the so-called discriminant function:

Score = 3.5(TIE) + 10.0(Quick ratio) − 25.0(Debt ratio) + 1.3(Years in business).

Further, assume that a score of less than 40 indicates a poor credit risk, 40 to 50 indicates an average credit risk, and a score above 50 signifies a good credit risk. Now suppose a firm with the following conditions applies for credit:

$$TIE = 4.2$$
$$Quick\ ratio = 3.1$$
$$Debt\ ratio = 0.30$$
$$Years\ in\ business = 10$$

This firm's credit score would be $3.5(4.2) + 10.0(3.1) - 25.0(0.30) + 1.3(10) = 51.2$. Therefore, it would be considered a good credit risk, and consequently it would be offered favorable credit terms.

Management by Exception.   Modern credit managers often practice *management by exception*. Under such a system, statistical procedures are used to classify customers into five or six categories according to degree of risk, and the credit manager then concentrates time and attention on the customers judged most likely to cause problems. For example, the following classes might be established:

Risk Class	Percentage of Uncollectible Credit Sales	Percentage of Customers in This Class
1	0–½%	60%
2	½–2	20
3	2–5	10
4	5–10	5
5	Over 10	5

Firms in Class 1 might be extended credit automatically, and their credit status might be reviewed only once a year. Those in Class 2 might also receive credit (up to specified limits) automatically, but a ratio analysis of their financial condition would be conducted more frequently (perhaps quarterly), and they would be moved down to Class 3 if their position deteriorated. Specific approvals might be required for credit sales to Classes 3 and 4, whereas sales to Class 5 might be on a COD (cash on delivery) basis only.

Collection Policy

collection policy

The procedures used to collect accounts receivable.

Collection policy refers to the procedures used to collect accounts receivable. For example, a letter might be sent to any account when the bill is 10 days past due; a more severe letter, followed by a telephone call, might be used if payment is not received within 30 days; and the account might be turned over to a collection agency after 90 days. The collection process can be expensive in terms of both out-of-pocket expenditures and lost goodwill, but some firmness is needed both to prevent an undue lengthening of the collection period and to minimize outright losses. A balance must be struck between the costs and benefits of different collection policies.

Changes in collection policy influence the level of sales, the collection period, the bad debt loss percentage, and the percentage of customers who take discounts. The effects of a change in collection policy, along with changes in the other credit policy variables, will be analyzed later in the chapter.

Self-Test

Identify and briefly explain the four elements of credit policy.

What is the purpose of a cash discount?

Identify and briefly explain the five Cs of credit.

What are some sources of credit information?

What is meant by a credit-scoring system, and what type of data does such a system typically require?

How do credit managers practice management by exception?

Other Factors Influencing Credit Policy

In addition to the four basic policy variables discussed in the previous sections, three other considerations should be mentioned regarding credit policy.

Profit Potential in Carrying Accounts Receivable

Thus far we have emphasized the costs of granting credit. *However, if it is possible to sell on credit and to assess a carrying charge on the receivables that are outstanding, then credit sales can actually be more profitable than cash sales.* This is especially true for consumer durables (automobiles, appliances, clothing, and so on), but it is also true for certain types of industrial equipment. Thus, General Motors Acceptance Corporation (GMAC), which finances automobiles, is highly profitable, as is Sears, Roebuck's credit subsidiary.[3] Some encyclopedia companies even lose money on cash sales but more than make up for these losses from the carrying charges on their credit sales; obviously, such companies would rather sell on credit than for cash!

The carrying charges on outstanding credit generally run about 18 percent on an annual interest rate basis ($1\frac{1}{2}\%$ per month, so $1.5\% \times 12 = 18\%$). Except for the early 1980s, when short-term interest rates rose to unprecedented levels, having receivables outstanding that earn 18 percent is highly profitable.

Use of Receivables in Obtaining Short-Term Credit

As we shall see in Chapter 11, having receivables often means that a firm has access to short-term financing it otherwise might not have obtained. This financing takes two forms: (1) *pledging of receivables* as collateral for short-term borrowing and (2) *factoring of receivables,* where a third party such as a bank or a finance company purchases the receivables outright. In both cases, the cost of the financing tends to be relatively high, but the methods are often used by small firms unable to borrow without collateral and where raising working capital and reducing the cash conversion cycle are high priorities.

---

[3]Companies that do a large volume of sales financing typically set up subsidiary companies called *captive finance companies* to do the actual financing. Thus, General Motors, Chrysler, and Ford all have captive finance companies, as do Sears, Roebuck, Montgomery Ward, and General Electric.

Legal Considerations

It is illegal, under the Robinson-Patman Act, for a firm to charge prices that discriminate between customers unless these differential prices are cost justified. The same holds true for credit—it is illegal to offer more favorable credit terms to one customer or class of customers than to another, unless the differences are cost justified.

Self-Test

Identify other factors that influence credit policy and explain the effect of each.

Evaluating the Effectiveness of a Firm's Credit Policy

Earlier in this chapter we discussed the impact of a firm's management of receivables—and inventories—on the return on total assets (ROA). Recall from Chapter 6 that, because of the equity multiplier (Total assets/Common equity), whenever a firm uses some debt financing, any increase or decrease in the ROA will be accompanied by a greater than proportional increase or decrease in the return on equity (ROE). And, the return on equity is one of the ratios that present and potential equity investors watch closely. Therefore, a change in this measure will usually translate into a change in the price of the firm's common stock, other things equal.

The effectiveness of a firm's credit policy may also be evaluated by way of its days sales outstanding (DSO). For example, in Chapter 6 we saw that Carter Chemical Company's days sales outstanding was 42 days, compared with an industry average of 36 days. If Carter lowered its days sales outstanding by 6 days to 36 days, this would mean a reduction of $8,333,333 \times 6 = $49,999,998, or approximately $50 million, in the amount of capital tied up in receivables. Assuming that the cost of funds to finance receivables is 10 percent, this would mean a savings of $5 million per year, other things held constant.

The DSO can also be compared with Carter's credit terms. Carter typically sells on terms of 1/10, net 30, so its customers, on average, are not paying their bills on time; the 42-day DSO is greater than the 30-day credit period. Note, however, that some of the customers are probably paying within 10 days to take advantage of the cash discount, so others must be taking much longer than 42 days to pay. One way to get a better view of the situation is to construct an **aging schedule,** which breaks down accounts receivable according to how long they have been outstanding. Carter's aging schedule is as follows:

aging schedule

A report showing how long accounts receivable have been outstanding; it gives the percentage of receivables currently past due and the percentages past due by specified periods.

Age of Accounts (Days)	Percentage of Total Value of Accounts Receivable
0–10	52%
11–30	20
31–45	13
46–60	4
Over 60	11
Total	100%

Although most of the accounts pay on schedule or after only a slight delay, a significant number are more than 1 month past due. This indicates that even though the majority of the firm's receivables are collected within the 30-day credit period, Carter has quite a bit of capital tied up in slow-paying accounts, some of which may eventually result in bad debt losses.

Management should constantly monitor the firm's days sales outstanding and aging schedule to detect trends, to see how the firm's collection experience compares with its credit terms, and to see how effectively the credit department is operating in comparison with other firms in the industry. If the DSO begins to lengthen, or if the aging schedule begins to show an increasing percentage of past-due accounts, then the firm's credit policy may need to be tightened.

Although a change in the DSO or the aging schedule should be a signal to the firm to investigate its credit policy, a deterioration in either of these measures does not *necessarily* indicate that the firm's credit policy has weakened. In fact, if a firm experiences sharp seasonal variations, or if its sales have been growing or declining rapidly, then both the aging schedule and the DSO will be distorted.[4]

Investors and bank loan officers should pay close attention to accounts receivable management; otherwise, they could be misled by the firm's financial statements and later suffer serious losses on their investments. When a sale is made, the following events occur: (1) Inventories are reduced by the cost of the goods sold, (2) accounts receivable are increased by the sales price, and (3) the difference is recorded as a profit. If the sale is for cash, the profit is definitely earned, but if the sale is on credit, the profit is not actually earned unless and until the account is collected. Firms have been known to use credit policy to encourage "sales" to very weak customers in order to inflate reported profits. This can boost the stock price but only until credit losses show up and begin to lower earnings, at which time the stock price will fall. An analysis along the lines suggested above will detect any such questionable practices, as well as any undetected deterioration in the quality of accounts receivable. Such early detection could help both investors and bankers avoid losses.

Analyzing Proposed Changes in Credit Policy

If a firm's credit policy is eased by such actions as lengthening the credit period, relaxing credit standards, following a less tough collection policy, or offering cash discounts, sales should increase. *Easing the credit policy normally stimulates sales.* However, if credit policy is eased and sales *do* rise, costs will also rise because (1) more labor, materials, and so on, will be required to produce the additional goods; (2) receivables outstanding will increase, which will increase financing costs; and (3) bad debt or discount expenses may also increase. Thus, the key question when deciding on a credit policy change is this: Will

[4]While an overall corporate aging schedule may not be useful for a firm with fluctuating sales, individual aging schedules, that is, for individual customers, do provide useful information as to whether the customer is paying on time. See Eugene F. Brigham and Louis C. Gapenski, *Intermediate Financial Management,* 4th ed., Chapter 23, for a more complete discussion of the problems with the DSO and aging schedules and how to correct for these problems.

Table 10-1   Roark Restaurant Supply Company: Analysis of Proposed
Changes in Credit Policy (Millions of Dollars)

	Projected 1994 Income Statement under Current Credit Policy (1)	Effect of Credit Policy Change (2)	Projected 1994 Income Statement under New Credit Policy (3)
Gross sales	$400.0	+ $130.0	$530.0
Less: Discounts	2.0	+ 4.0	6.0
Net sales	$398.0	+ $126.0	$524.0
Production costs, including overhead (70%)	280.0	+ 91.0	371.0
Profit before credit costs and taxes	$118.0	+ $ 35.0	$153.0
Credit-related costs:			
Cost of carrying receivables	2.5	+ 1.2	3.7
Credit analysis and collection expenses	5.0	− 3.0	2.0
Bad debt losses	10.0	+ 22.0	32.0
Profit before taxes	$100.5	+ $ 14.8	$115.3
Taxes (40%)	40.2	+ 5.9	46.1
Net income	$ 60.3	+ $ 8.9	$ 69.2

sales revenues rise more than costs, causing net income to increase, or will the increase in sales revenues be more than offset by higher costs?

Table 10-1 illustrates the general idea behind credit policy analysis. Column 1 shows the projected 1994 income statement for Roark Restaurant Supply Company under the assumption that the firm's current credit policy is maintained throughout the year. In this particular case, excess capacity exists, so sales could be increased without adding either new plant or general overhead expense. Column 2 shows the expected effects of easing the credit policy by extending the credit period, offering larger discounts, relaxing credit standards, and easing collection efforts. (Note, however, that firms often do not change all four variables at one time because this makes it hard to determine what caused the observed changes; we do it here for illustrative purposes.) Specifically, Roark is analyzing the effects of changing its credit terms from 1/10, net 30, to 2/10, net 40, relaxing its credit standards, and putting less pressure on slow-paying customers. Column 3 shows the projected 1994 income statement incorporating the expected effects of an easing in credit policy. The generally easier policy is expected to increase sales and lower credit analysis and collection costs, but discounts and several other types of cost would rise. The overall, bottom-line effect is an $8.9 million increase in projected profits. In the following paragraphs, we explain how the numbers in the table were calculated.

Roark's annual sales are currently projected at $400 million. Under its current credit policy, 50 percent of those customers who pay do so on Day 10 and take the discount, 40 percent pay on Day 30, and 10 percent pay late, on Day 40. Thus, Roark's days sales outstanding is 21 days:

$$(0.50)(10) + (0.40)(30) + (0.10)(40) = 21 \text{ days.}$$

Even though Roark spends $5 million annually to analyze accounts and to collect bad debts, 2.5 percent of sales will never be collected. Therefore, bad debt losses amount to $(0.025)($400,000,000) = 10 million. In addition, Roark's cash collections will be reduced by the amount of discounts taken. Fifty percent of the customers who pay (and 97.5 percent of all customers pay) take the 1 percent discount, so discounts equal $($400,000,000)(0.975)(0.01)(0.50) = $1,950,000 \approx 2 million. Notice that total sales are multiplied by $(1 -$ Bad debt ratio), 97.5 percent, to obtain collected sales, and collected sales are then multiplied by the discount percentage and by the percentage of paying customers who take the discount.

The annual cost of carrying receivables is equal to the average amount of receivables times the variable cost percentage, which gives the dollars of capital invested in receivables, times the cost of money used to carry receivables:

$$\begin{pmatrix} \text{Average} \\ \text{amount of} \\ \text{receivables} \end{pmatrix} \begin{pmatrix} \text{Variable} \\ \text{cost} \\ \text{ratio} \end{pmatrix} \begin{pmatrix} \text{Cost} \\ \text{of} \\ \text{funds} \end{pmatrix} = \begin{matrix} \text{Cost of} \\ \text{carrying} \\ \text{receivables} \end{matrix}.$$

The average receivables balance, in turn, is equal to the days sales outstanding times sales per day. Roark's DSO is 21 days, as previously calculated, its variable cost ratio is 70 percent, and its cost of funds invested in receivables is 15 percent. Therefore, its annual cost of carrying receivables is approximately $2.5 million:

$$(\text{DSO}) \begin{pmatrix} \text{Sales} \\ \text{per} \\ \text{day} \end{pmatrix} \begin{pmatrix} \text{Variable} \\ \text{cost} \\ \text{ratio} \end{pmatrix} \begin{pmatrix} \text{Cost} \\ \text{of} \\ \text{funds} \end{pmatrix} = \begin{matrix} \text{Cost of} \\ \text{carrying} \\ \text{receivables} \end{matrix}. \qquad (10\text{-}1)$$

$$(21)\left(\frac{$400,000,000}{360}\right)(0.70)(0.15) = $2,450,000 \approx $2.5 \text{ million}.$$

Only variable costs enter into this calculation because this is the only cost element that must be financed as a result of a change in the credit policy. In other words, if a new customer buys goods worth $100, Roark will have to invest only $70 (in labor and materials); therefore, it will have to finance only $70, even though accounts receivable rise by $100. Variable costs thus represent the company's investment in the goods sold.

Roark's new credit policy calls for a larger discount, a longer payment period, a relaxed collection effort, and lower credit standards. The company believes that these changes will increase sales by $130 million, to $530 million per year. Under the new credit terms, management believes that 60 percent of the customers who pay will take the 2 percent discount and that bad debt losses will total 6 percent of sales. Therefore, discounts will increase to $($530,000,000)(0.94)(0.02)(0.60) = 5,978,400 \approx 6 million. Half of the remaining paying customers (20 percent of the paying customers) will pay on Day 40, and the remainder on Day 50. Therefore, the new DSO is estimated to be 24 days:

$$(0.6)(10) + (0.2)(40) + (0.2)(50) = 24 \text{ days}.$$

As a result, the cost of carrying receivables will increase to $3.7 million:

$$(24)\left(\frac{\$530,000,000}{360}\right)(0.70)(0.15) = \$3,710,000 \approx \$3.7 \text{ million.}^5$$

Because it will relax credit standards, hence credit checking expenses, and also ease up on collections, the company expects to reduce its annual credit analysis and collection expenditures from $5 million to $2 million. However, these changes are also expected to raise bad debt losses from 2.5 percent to 6 percent of sales, or to $(0.06)(\$530,000,000) = \$32.0$ million, an increase of $22 million, with a portion of the increase due to the higher level of sales.

The combined effect of the changes in Roark's credit policy is a projected $8.9 million increase in net income. There would, of course, be corresponding changes on the projected balance sheet. The higher sales would necessitate somewhat larger cash balances, inventories, and perhaps more fixed assets. As we have already seen, accounts receivable would also increase. Since these asset increases would have to be financed, certain liability accounts and/or equity would also have to be increased.

The $8.9 million expected increase in net income is, of course, an estimate, and the actual effects of the change could be quite different. Most important, there is likely to be considerable uncertainty about the projected $130 million increase in sales. Conceivably, if Roark's competitors match its credit policy changes, sales may not rise at all. Similar uncertainties must be attached to the number of customers who would take discounts, to production costs at higher sales levels, to the costs of carrying additional receivables, and to the bad debt losses.

The preceding analysis provides Roark's managers with a quantitative method of evaluating a proposed change in credit policy and its likely impact on the firm's income statement and balance sheet. However, a great deal of judgment must also be applied because consumer response to credit policy changes is typically quite difficult to estimate, not to mention the response of competitors. Still, this type of numerical analysis can provide a good starting point for credit policy decisions.

Use of Computers in Receivables Management

Except possibly in the inventory and payroll areas, nowhere in the typical firm have computers had more of an impact than in accounts receivable management. A well-run business will use a computer system to record sales, to send

---

[5]Since the credit policy change will result in a longer DSO, Roark will have to wait longer to receive its profit on the goods it sells. Therefore, the firm will incur an opportunity cost as a result of not having the cash from these profits available for investment. The dollar amount of this opportunity cost is equal to the old sales per day times the change in DSO times the contribution margin $(1-v)$ times the cost of carrying the receivables:

$$\text{Opportunity cost} = (\text{Old sales}/360)(\Delta\text{DSO})(1 - v)(k)$$
$$= (\$400 \text{ million}/360)(3)(0.3)(0.15) = \$0.15 \text{ million.}$$

Here v = variable cost ratio and k = cost of funds. For simplicity, and because it is not large, we ignored opportunity costs in our analysis. For a more complete discussion of the analysis of changes in credit policy, see Eugene F. Brigham and Louis C. Gapenski, *Intermediate Financial Management,* 4th ed., Chapter 23.

out bills, to keep track of when payments are made, to alert the credit manager when an account becomes past due, and to ensure that actions are taken to collect past due accounts (for example, to prepare form letters requesting payment). Additionally, the payment history of each customer can be summarized and used to help establish credit limits for customers and classes of customers, and the data on each account can be aggregated and used for the firm's accounts receivable monitoring system. Historical data can be stored in the firm's database and used to develop inputs for analyses of changes in credit policy variables, such as those illustrated by Roark Restaurant Supply Company. Finally, computerizing the analysis process itself by setting up a relatively simple spreadsheet along the lines of Table 10-1, gives management the ability to perform sensitivity analyses, answer "what if" questions, and be able to see quickly and in advance how different values of crucial input variables would impact the bottom line, incremental net income.

Conclusion

We will end our discussion of accounts receivable management with two examples in which well-known companies developed their own unique credit policy strategies.

1. During a recent recession, the sales and earnings of Xerox had been forecasted by securities analysts to decline, but instead earnings rose by 10 percent on a 23 percent increase in sales. The explanation was that Xerox had instituted a major change in its credit policy. It had built up a pool of cash which it then loaned to its customers at bargain rates to increase sales of its products. Profits on the added sales more than offset the cost to Xerox of the low-rate loans, boosting the company's net income at a time when its competitor's profits were falling.

2. While Xerox liberalized its credit policy and profited from the change, other companies, faced with different conditions, have increased their profits by tightening or even eliminating credit. For example, Atlantic Richfield Company (Arco) eliminated the use of credit cards at all of its service stations, based on the following beliefs held by its management: (1) that customers were very sensitive to gasoline prices; (2) that the cost of extending credit to customers amounted to about 4 cents per gallon; (3) that if it eliminated credit sales it could cut gas prices at the pump by 3 cents a gallon, which would boost profit per gallon by 1 cent and at the same time double its number of customers; and (4) that consequently it would enjoy a substantial increase in net income. The plan worked beautifully and contributed to Arco's overall success.

? Self-Test

Briefly explain what the DSO and the aging schedule are, and tell how they are used to help evaluate a firm's credit policy.

Describe the procedure used to evaluate a change in credit policy.

Should credit policy decisions be made more on the basis of numerical analysis or judgmental factors?

List several ways in which computers have had great impact in the management of accounts receivable.

Inventory Management

As discussed at the beginning of this chapter, the typical firm has a large percentage of its total assets invested in inventory, as well as in receivables, and the Du Pont equation illustrates that poor inventory control and excessive build-up of inventories will lead to low profitability. Still, inventories are necessary for sales, and sales are necessary for profits, so the goal becomes finding the right level of inventory investment for a given firm, a proper balance between the costs associated with having too much inventory and those incurred when the firm has too little.

Actual inventory control is generally not within the domain of the financial manager. Rather, in manufacturing firms, production people typically have control over inventories, and in retail concerns this control is exercised by merchandising personnel. However, the financial manager is still vitally concerned with inventory levels because he or she has the responsibility both for tracking factors which affect the overall profitability of the firm and for raising the capital needed to finance inventory. In this portion of the chapter we will discuss the basics of inventory management.

Inventories, which include (1) *raw materials*, (2) *work-in-process*, and (3) *finished goods* (or *merchandise* for a retailer), are an essential part of virtually all business operations. Like accounts receivable, inventory levels depend heavily on sales. However, while receivables build up *after* sales have been made, inventories must be acquired *before* sales are made. This is a critical difference, and the necessity of forecasting sales before establishing target inventory levels makes **inventory management** a difficult task. Also, because errors in establishing inventory levels can lead either to lost sales and profits or to excessive carrying costs, inventory management is as important as it is difficult.

The manner in which its inventory is managed can have a direct effect on the value of a firm. Any procedure that allows a firm to achieve a given sales volume with a lower investment in inventories will increase the rate of return and, hence, increase the firm's value. However, actions to reduce inventory investment can also lead to lost sales because of stock-outs or costly production slowdowns. Managers must maintain inventories at levels which balance the benefits of reducing the level of investment against the costs associated with lowering inventories.

Inventory management focuses on three basic questions: (1) How many units of each inventory item should the firm hold in stock? (2) How many units should be ordered (or produced) at a given time? (3) At what point should inventory be ordered (or produced)? The remainder of this chapter is devoted to answering these questions.

Determining the Inventory Investment

In part, inventory policy is determined by the economics of the firm's industry; thus retailers have large stocks of finished goods but little, if any, raw materials or work-in-process. Moreover, the inventory policies of firms in a given industry

inventory management

The balancing of a set of costs that increase with larger inventory holdings with a set of costs that decrease with larger order size.

can vary widely—no one inventory policy is suitable for all firms, although the policies of successful firms are often emulated by others.

No single executive establishes inventory policy. Rather, the firm's inventory policy is set by its executive committee, and production, marketing, and financial people all have somewhat different perspectives on inventory management. The production manager is concerned with the raw materials inventory to ensure continuous production; he or she has direct control over the length of the production process (which influences work-in-process inventories) and is vitally concerned with whether the firm produces on a smooth, continuous basis throughout the year, stockpiling finished goods inventories for seasonal sales, or whether it produces irregularly in response to orders. The marketing manager wants the firm to hold large stocks of inventories to ensure rapid deliveries; this will make it easier to close sales. The financial manager is concerned with the level of inventories because of the effects excessive inventories have on profitability: (1) they reduce the total assets turnover ratio; (2) there are substantial costs of carrying inventories, so excessive inventories erode the profit margin; and (3) other things equal, when these two ratios are low, the firm's return on total assets (ROA) and return on equity (ROE) will also suffer.

Through the accounting staff, the financial manager also maintains the records relating to inventories, and in this capacity he or she is responsible for establishing information systems to monitor inventory usage and to replenish stocks as necessary. This information system is not complex in a single-product, single-plant firm, but in most modern corporations the inventory control process is as complex as it is important. Visualize an automobile or an appliance manufacturer, with thousands of dealers stocking hundreds of styles and colors of various automobiles, stoves, or refrigerators, as well as thousands of spare parts, all across the country. Production must reflect both stocks on hand and the current sales levels, and any mistake can result either in excessive stocks (which will lose value when the new models appear) or in lost sales. Grocery stores, department stores, plumbing manufacturers, textbook publishers, and most other firms are faced with similar problems. It is not surprising that computerized inventory control systems have become tremendously popular in recent years. We will discuss these later in the chapter.

Inventory Costs

The goal of inventory management is to provide the inventories required to sustain operations at the minimum cost. The first step is to identify all the costs involved in purchasing and maintaining inventory. Table 10-2 lists the typical costs associated with inventory, broken down into three categories: costs associated with carrying inventory, costs associated with ordering and receiving inventory, and costs associated with running short of inventory, which are called *stock-out costs*.

Although they may well be the most important element, we shall at this point disregard the third category of costs—stock-out costs—these are dealt with by adding safety stocks, which we will discuss later. The costs that remain for consideration at this stage, then, are carrying costs and ordering, shipping, and receiving costs.

Table 10-2

Costs Associated with Inventory

	Approximate Annual Cost as a Percentage of Inventory Value
Carrying Costs	
Cost of capital tied up	12.0%
Storage and handling costs	0.5
Insurance	0.5
Property taxes	1.0
Depreciation and obsolescence	12.0
Total	26.0%
Ordering, Shipping, and Receiving Costs	
Cost of placing orders, including production and set-up costs	Varies
Shipping and handling costs	2.5%
Costs of Running Short (Stock-out Costs)	
Loss of sales	Varies
Loss of customer goodwill	Varies
Disruption of production schedules	Varies

Note: These costs vary from firm to firm, from item to item, and over time. The figures shown are U.S. Department of Commerce estimates for an average manufacturing firm. When costs vary so widely that no meaningful numbers can be assigned, this is indicated by the term "Varies."

The Economic Ordering Quantity (EOQ) Model

Inventories are obviously necessary, but it is equally obvious that a firm will suffer if it has too much or too little inventory. How can management determine the *optimal* inventory level? One commonly used approach is the *economic ordering quantity (EOQ) model,* which is described in this section, and which attempts to minimize total inventory costs.

Figure 10-1 illustrates the basic premise on which inventory theory is built, namely, that some costs rise with larger inventories while other costs decline, and that there is an optimal order size which minimizes the total costs associated with inventories. The average investment in inventories depends on how frequently orders are placed; if a small order is placed every day, average inventories will be much smaller than if one large order is placed annually. Further, as Figure 10-1 shows, inventory **carrying costs** rise with larger orders; because larger orders mean larger average inventories, warehousing costs, interest on financing needed to carry inventory, insurance costs, and obsolescence costs all will increase. At the same time, total **ordering costs** decline with large orders because the total costs of placing orders, setting up production runs, and handling shipments will all decline if the firm orders infrequently. Ordering costs are assumed to be a fixed amount per order.

When the carrying and ordering cost curves in Figure 10-1 are summed, the sum represents the total cost of ordering and carrying inventories, the total inventory cost. The point where the total inventory cost curve is minimized represents the **economic ordering quantity (EOQ),** and this, in turn, determines the optimal average inventory level. A graph like Figure 10-1 is useful in helping the firm determine its approximate optimal ordering quantity, but to

carrying costs

The costs associated with carrying inventories, including storage, capital, and depreciation costs. Carrying costs generally increase in proportion to the average amount of inventory held.

ordering costs

The costs of placing and receiving an order; these costs are fixed regardless of the average size of inventories.

economic ordering quantity (EOQ)

The optimal, or least-cost, quantity of inventory that should be ordered.

Figure 10-1

Determination of the
Economic Ordering
Quantity (EOQ)

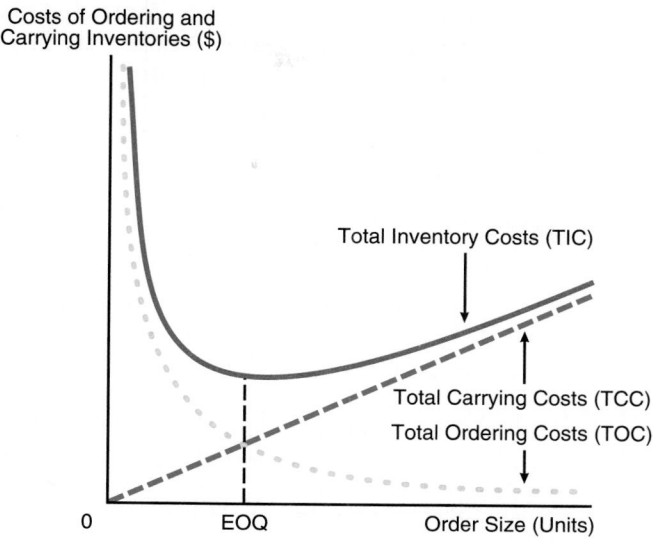

To avoid the problems that may arise from carrying too much or too little inventory, a
business must determine the optimal quantity of a product to purchase each time an order
is placed. As this figure shows, total carrying costs rise steadily as order size increases;
total ordering costs, on the other hand, decline with larger order sizes. The sum of these
two curves is the total inventory costs curve, and the lowest point on that curve is the
optimal order size, or economic ordering quantity (EOQ).

EOQ model

Formula for determining
the ordering quantity that
will minimize total
inventory costs.

find the exact value it would be necessary to plot every possible ordering quantity or, better yet, use the economic ordering quantity, or **EOQ, model.** It can be shown that under certain reasonable assumptions, the ordering quantity that minimizes the total cost curve in Figure 10-1 can be found by using the following formula:

$$EOQ = \sqrt{\frac{2(F)(S)}{(C)(P)}}. \tag{10-2}$$

Here

EOQ = the economic ordering quantity, or the optimal
        quantity to be ordered each time an order is placed.
    F = fixed costs of placing and receiving an order.
    S = annual sales in units.
    C = carrying cost expressed as a percentage of average inventory value.
    P = purchase price the firm must pay per unit of inventory.[6]

---

[6]The EOQ model may also be written as

$$EOQ = \sqrt{\frac{2(F)(S)}{C^*}}$$

where C^* is the annual carrying cost per unit expressed in *dollars.*

The assumptions of the economic ordering quantity (EOQ) model include the following: (1) sales can be forecasted perfectly; (2) sales are evenly distributed throughout the year; (3) orders are received with no delays; and (4) F, C, and P are all fixed and independent of the ordering procedures.

To illustrate the EOQ model, consider the following data, supplied by Romantic Books Inc., publisher of the classic novel *Madame Boudoir*:

S = sales = 26,000 copies per year.
C = carrying cost = 20 percent of inventory value.
P = purchase price per book to Romantic Books from a printing company = $6.1538 per copy. (Each book sells for $9, but this is irrelevant for our purposes.)
F = fixed cost per order = $1,000. The bulk of this cost is the labor cost for setting the page plates on the presses, as well as for setting up the binding equipment for the production run. The printer bills this cost separately from the $6.1538 cost per copy.

Substituting these data into Equation 10-2, we obtain an EOQ of 6,500 copies:

$$EOQ = \sqrt{\frac{2(F)(S)}{(C)(P)}}$$

$$= \sqrt{\frac{2(\$1,000)(26,000)}{(0.2)(\$6.1538)}}$$

$$= \sqrt{42,250,317}$$

$$\approx 6,500 \text{ copies.}$$

With an EOQ of 6,500 copies and annual sales of 26,000 copies, Romantic Books will place 26,000/6,500 = 4 orders per year. Note that average inventory depends directly on the EOQ; this relationship is illustrated graphically in Figure 10-2, where we see that average inventory = EOQ/2. Immediately after an order is received, 6,500 copies are in stock. The usage rate, or sales rate, is 500 copies per week (26,000/52 weeks), so inventories are drawn down by this amount each week, and this determines the slope of the line. Thus, if the sales rate increases, the line will become steeper.

The actual number of units held in inventory will vary from 6,500 books just after an order is received to zero just before the next order arrives. On average, the number of units held will be 6,500/2 = 3,250 books. At a cost of $6.1538 per book, the average investment in inventory will be 3,250 × $6.1538 = $19,999.85 ≈ $20,000. If inventory is financed by a bank loan, the loan will vary from a high of $40,000 to a low of $0, but the average amount outstanding over the course of a year will be $20,000.

The EOQ, hence average inventory holdings, rises with the square root of sales. Therefore, a given increase in sales will result in a less than proportionate increase in inventory so the inventory/sales ratio will decline as sales grow. For example, Romantic Books's EOQ is 6,500 copies at an annual sales level of 26,000, and the average inventory is 3,250 copies, worth $20,000. However, if sales increase by 100 percent, to 52,000 copies per year, the EOQ will rise to

Figure 10-2   Inventory Position without Safety Stock

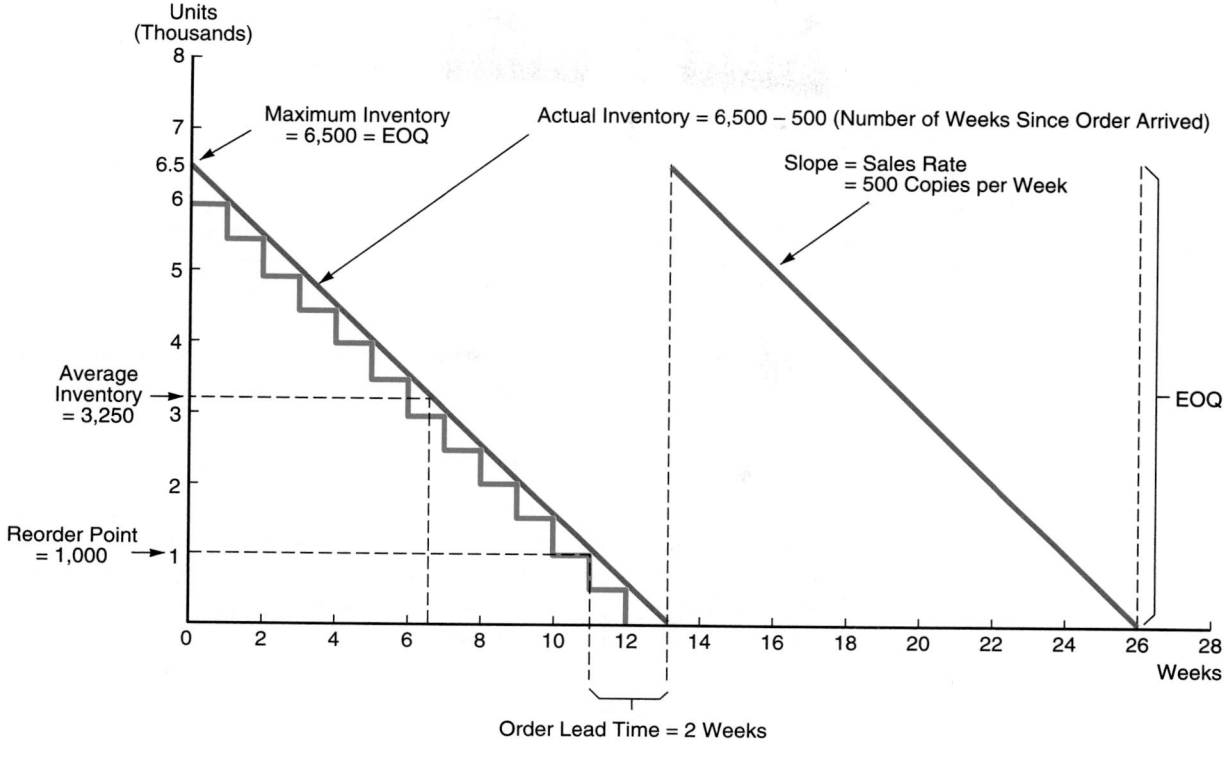

This figure shows Romantic Books's average inventory position between orders. The EOQ of 6,500 copies represents the maximum inventory and determines the average inventory (6,500/2 = 3,250). The expected sales rate of 500 copies per week determines the order frequency (every 13 weeks since 52 weeks/4 orders per year = 13 weeks). Because a 2-week lead time is required on orders, the reorder point is reached when inventories reach 1,000 copies. This model assumes that both the sales rate and the required lead time on orders are constant and, therefore, predictable.

only 9,192 copies, or by roughly 41 percent, and the average inventory will rise by this same percentage. There are economies of scale in holding inventory.[7]

Setting the Reorder Point

reorder point

The inventory level at which an order should be placed.

If a 2-week lead time is required for production and shipping, what is Romantic Books's **reorder point,** or the inventory level at which an order should be placed? Romantic Books sells 26,000/52 = 500 books per week. Thus, if a 2-week lag occurs between placing the order and taking delivery, Romantic Books must place the order when there are 1,000 books on hand.

---

[7]Note, however, that these economies of scale relate to each particular item, not to the entire firm. Thus, a large company with $500 million in sales might have a higher inventory/sales ratio than a much smaller company, if the small company has only a few items with high sales volume, while the large firm sells a great many low-volume items.

$$\text{Reorder point} = \text{Lead time} \times \text{Usage rate}$$

$$= 2 \times 500 = 1,000.$$

At the end of the 2-week production and shipping period, the new inventory balance will be down to zero, but just at that time a new supply of books will arrive.

Goods in Transit

goods in transit
Goods which have been ordered but have not yet been received.

If a new order must be placed before the previous order is received, a **goods-in-transit** inventory will build up. Goods in transit are items which have been ordered but have not yet been received. A goods-in-transit inventory will exist if the normal delivery lead time is longer than the time between orders. This complicates matters somewhat, but the simplest solution to the problem is to deduct goods in transit when calculating the reorder point. The reorder point would then be calculated as follows:

$$\text{Reorder point} = (\text{Lead time} \times \text{Usage rate}) - \text{Goods in transit}.$$

Goods in transit is not an issue for Romantic Books because the firm orders $26,000/6,500 = 4$ times a year, or once every 13 weeks, and the delivery lead time is 2 weeks. However, suppose that Romantic Books ordered 1,000 copies of *Madame Boudoir* every 2 weeks and the delivery lead time was 3 weeks. In that case, whenever an order was placed, another order of 1,000 books would be in transit. Therefore, Romantic Books's reorder point would be:

$$\text{Reorder point} = (3 \times 500) - 1,000$$

$$= 1,500 - 1,000$$

$$= 500.$$

Safety Stocks

If Romantic Books knew for certain that both the sales rate and the order lead time would never vary, it could operate exactly as shown in Figure 10-2. However, sales rates do change, and because production and shipping delays are frequently encountered, the company must carry additional inventories, or **safety stocks.**

safety stocks
Additional inventory carried to guard against increases in sales rates or production/shipping delays.

The concept of a safety stock is illustrated in Figure 10-3. First, note that the slope of the sales line again measures the expected rate of sales. The company still *expects* to sell 500 copies each week, but let us assume a maximum likely sales rate of twice this amount, or 1,000 copies each week. Romantic Books sets the safety stock at 1,000 copies, so it initially orders 7,500 copies, the EOQ plus 1,000 copies. Subsequently, it reorders the EOQ, 6,500 copies, whenever the inventory level falls to 2,000 copies (the safety stock of 1,000 copies plus the 1,000 copies expected to be used while awaiting delivery of the order). Notice that the company could, during the 2-week delivery period, sell 1,000 copies a week, doubling its normal expected sales. This maximum rate of sales is shown by the steeper dashed line in Figure 10-3. The condition that makes this higher sales rate possible is the introduction of a safety stock of

Figure 10-3   Inventory Position with Safety Stock Included

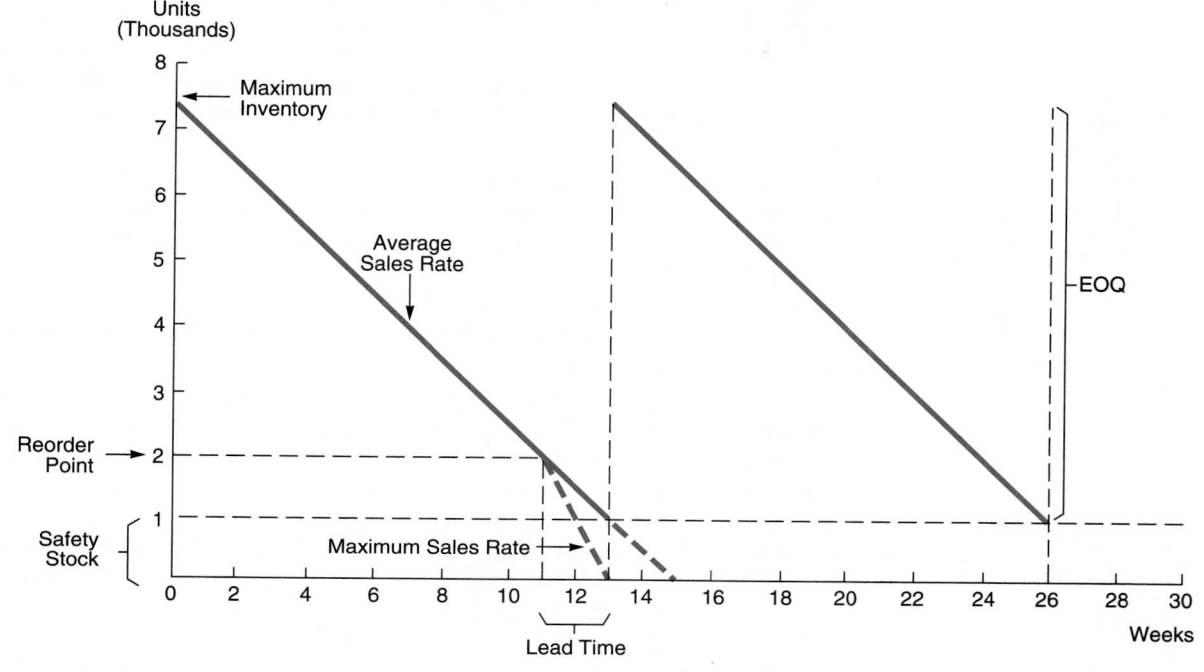

Because sales rates and required lead times do vary, a business must carry safety stocks. In this example 1,000 copies of safety stock are initially ordered, in addition to the EOQ of 6,500 copies. The reorder point now becomes 2,000 copies. This safety stock allows the firm to handle a sales increase to 1,000 copies per week during the 2-week reorder lead time, should that occur, or if delays are encountered in receiving orders, the company could continue at its average sales rate for 2 weeks beyond the usual 2-week delivery time.

1,000 copies; without it, the firm would run out of stock after 1 week if the sales rate rose from 500 to 1,000 copies per week.

The safety stock is also useful in guarding against delays in receiving orders. The expected delivery time is 2 weeks; however, with a 1,000-copy safety stock, the company could maintain sales at the expected rate of 500 copies per week for an additional 2 weeks if production or shipping delays held up an order.

Safety stocks are obviously useful under conditions of uncertainty, but they do have a cost. For Romantic Books, the average inventory is now EOQ/2 plus a safety stock of 1,000 units, or $6,500/2 + 1,000 = 3,250 + 1,000 = 4,250$ copies, and the average inventory value is $(4,250)(\$6.1538) \approx \$26,154$. The increase in average inventory resulting from the safety stock causes an increase in inventory carrying costs equal to $(\text{Safety stock})(P)(C) = 1,000(\$6.1538)(0.20) = \$1,230.76 \approx 1,231$.

The optimal safety stock varies from situation to situation, but in general it *increases* with (1) the uncertainty of sales forecasts, (2) the costs (in terms of lost sales and lost goodwill) that would result from inventory shortages, and (3) the probability of delays in receiving shipments. The optimal safety stock *decreases* as the cost of carrying the extra inventory increases.

Inventory Control Systems

The EOQ model, and the concept of safety stocks, can be used to establish the proper inventory level, but inventory management also involves the establishment of an *inventory control system*. There are various types of control systems that can be used—some simple and others extremely complex. One simple control procedure is the **red-line method**. Here inventory items are stocked in a bin, a red line is drawn around the inside of the bin at the level of the reorder point, and the inventory clerk places an order when the red line shows. For the **two-bin method**, inventory items are stocked in two bins, and when the working bin is empty, an order is placed and inventory is drawn from the second bin. These procedures work well for items such as bolts in a manufacturing process and for many items in retail businesses.

Larger companies employ **computerized inventory control systems.** The computer starts with an inventory count in memory. As withdrawals are made, they are recorded by the computer, and the inventory balance is revised. When the reorder point is reached, the computer automatically places an order, and when the order is received, the recorded balance is increased. Retailers such as Wal-Mart have carried this system quite far—each item has a bar code, and, as an item is checked out, the code is read, a signal is sent to the computer, and the inventory balance is adjusted at the same time the price is fed into the cash register tape. When the balance drops to the reorder point, an order is placed, in Wal-Mart's case directly from its computers to those of its suppliers.

Other large companies which in recent years have developed highly sophisticated computerized inventory systems, both to gather data and to control inventory, include Walt Disney Company (in its retailing of video cassettes to stores), Hallmark Cards, Kmart Stores, and Dayton Hudson. Even Revco D.S., emerging from Chapter 11 bankruptcy proceedings in June 1992, managed to find the funds to install companywide computer systems for inventory control and customer prescriptions throughout the drugstore chain.

A good inventory control system is dynamic, not static. A company such as IBM or General Motors (GM) stocks hundreds of thousands of different items. The sales (or use) of these various items can rise or fall quite separately from rising or falling overall corporate sales. As the usage rate for an individual item begins to rise or fall, the inventory manager must adjust its balance to avoid running short or ending up with obsolete items. If the change in the usage rate appears to be permanent, then the EOQ should be recomputed, the safety stock level should be reconsidered, and the computer model used in the control process should be reprogrammed.

Usage rates do tend to change over time, and both purchase prices and ordering costs may depend on the buyer's arrangements with the seller, such as Wal-Mart's with its suppliers. Therefore, a good inventory management system must respond promptly to any changes in these conditions. One system that is used to monitor inventory usage rates and then to modify EOQs and inventory item levels is the **ABC system.** Under this system, the firm analyzes each inventory item on the basis of its cost, frequency of usage, seriousness of a stock-out, order lead time, and other criteria related to the item's importance. Items that are expensive, are frequently used, have serious consequences if a stock-out occurs, and have long order lead times are put in the A category; somewhat less

red-line method
An inventory control procedure in which a red line is drawn around the inside of an inventory-stocked bin to indicate the reorder point level.

two-bin method
An inventory control procedure in which the reorder point is reached when one of two inventory-stocked bins is empty.

computerized inventory control system
A system of inventory control in which a computer is used to determine reorder points and to adjust inventory balances.

ABC system
A system used to categorize inventory items to ensure that the most important ones are reviewed most often.

important items are put in the B category; and the least important items are designated C items. Management reviews the A items' recent usage rates, stock positions, and delivery time situations quite frequently, say monthly, and adjusts the EOQ and reorder points as necessary. Category B items are reviewed and adjusted less frequently, say, every quarter, and C items are reviewed perhaps annually. Thus, inventory management resources are concentrated where they will do the most good.

Major inventory changes should also be evaluated using the firm's forecasting model and cash budget. For example, increases in inventory, if not accompanied by increases in sales, would tend to decrease profitability and increase the need for additional funding. Further, cash outlays for the additional inventory would increase cash outflows as reported on the firm's cash budget. Efficient inventory management will result in relatively low levels of inventories, in low write-offs of obsolete or deteriorated inventories, and in few work stoppages or lost sales due to inventory shortages. All this, in turn, will contribute to a high total assets turnover, a high profit margin, a high return on equity, and a high stock price.

Other Inventory Issues

just-in-time (JIT) system
A system of inventory control in which a manufacturer coordinates production with suppliers so that raw materials and components arrive just as they are needed in the production process.

Two other inventory-related issues should be mentioned. The first is the **just-in-time (JIT) system,** in which a manufacturer coordinates production with suppliers so that raw materials or components arrive from suppliers just as they are needed in the production process. Japanese firms developed just-in-time, and the system has since gained popularity throughout the world. To some extent, the just-in-time system reduces the need for the purchaser to carry inventories by passing the problem back to its suppliers; however, with a coordinated production schedule, the supplier may also benefit (1) by being able to schedule production runs better and (2) by having to carry lower finished goods inventory safety stock. In any event, coordination between suppliers and users lessens total inventory requirements and also reduces total production costs.

Toyota provides a good example of the just-in-time system. Eight of Toyota's ten factories, along with most of Toyota's suppliers, dot the countryside around Toyota City. Delivery of components is tied to the speed of the assembly line, and parts are generally delivered no more than a few hours before they are used. Not surprisingly, U.S. automobile manufacturers were among the first domestic firms to move toward just-in-time systems. Ford has been restructuring its production system with a goal of increasing its inventory turnover from 20 times a year to 30 or 40 times. As already indicated, just-in-time systems place considerable pressure on suppliers. GM formerly kept a ten-day supply of seats and other parts made by Lear Siegler; now GM sends in orders at four- to eight-hour intervals and expects immediate shipment. A Lear Siegler spokesman stated, "We can't afford to keep things sitting around either," so Lear Siegler has had to be tougher on its own suppliers.

As pointed out in the "Industry Practice" boxed feature in this chapter, just-in-time systems are also being adopted by many smaller firms, and, in fact, it *should* be easier to redefine job functions and to educate people in small firms. However, when Allen-Edmonds Shoe Corportion, a small firm, introduced just-in-time inventory methods, the result was a painful and expensive flop. In

KEEPING INVENTORIES LEAN

What do just-in-time (JIT) inventory methods and supercomputers have in common? The answer is, both are being used, in a coordinated manner, to keep U.S. business inventories remarkably lean. Recent statistics show that retail, wholesale, and factory inventories—taken together and adjusted for inflation—amount to just 1.4 times monthly sales, the lowest reading in the 40 years that records have been kept. And leaner inventories mean lower inventory carrying costs for businesses, hence greater profits.

JIT became the watchword for many U.S. manufacturers in the mid-1980s, as they began to adopt this Japanese method of inventory delivery. JIT involves redesigning production so that parts and raw materials flow into the factory just as they are needed, thus allowing manufacturers to save the cost of carrying inventories. Large firms, including General Motors, Campbell Soup, Motorola, Hewlett-Packard, and Intel, as well as dozens of small firms, such as Omark Industries, an Oregon manufacturer of power saw chains, have converted to JIT. A recent survey of 385 manufacturing plants in the United States, conducted for the National Association of Manufacturers, found that more than 16 percent were "extremely skilled" in JIT procedures, and another 44 percent had plans under way to "excel" in JIT operations. Importantly, the inventory turnover ratios of plants using JIT procedures were twice as high as those for the survey group as a whole.

Large corporations started the just-in-time trend in the United States, but Robert W. Hall of Indiana University, who has written several books on the subject, says smaller companies are actually better positioned to adopt the method. Hall points out that small firms usually have only one plant to convert, and they usually have simpler accounting and planning systems. Also, their management groups are smaller and can make faster decisions than can larger firms. Another advantage for many small firms is that smaller, non-

unionized labor forces make it easier to redesign job functions.

Worker attitudes toward these changes have generally been the greatest stumbling block for companies—large or small—that convert to JIT methods. One company president says employee acceptance depends on management. "It's just a matter of managers getting their mind-sets correct." This can be difficult, though, since managers must give up the security of large inventories and trust their suppliers more than they ever have before. It is essential for managers to work closely with suppliers to ensure that parts or materials get to the plant at the right time and in the right sequence for the assembly line.

Allen Hagstrand, director of purchasing for the Stamford, Connecticut, unit of Cadbury Schweppes PLC, the London food and beverage producer, stated that his company's inventory levels are at a fraction of what they were in the mid-1980s as a result of "closer cooperation with a smaller but better informed assortment of suppliers." The Schweppes unit gets 80 percent of its glass containers from a single supplier, as compared with 30 percent seven years ago. Mr. Hagstrand stated, "We used to play one off against the other and keep them guessing, but now we work very closely together, providing sales forecasts and other data we once kept to ourselves." By working in this way, Mr. Hagstrand's unit has been able to reduce its inventory carrying costs, including financing and warehousing costs, dramatically.

When a company adopts the JIT method, it is essential that managers be concerned not only with their own problems but also with those faced by their suppliers. Xerox, for instance, went into the new system with the idea that "this was an inventory reduction program for our benefit," according to Fred McClintock, materials manager for the copier division, "and we treated it that way, asking suppliers to hold inventories without compensation." Suppliers protested, and good relationships built over many years began to deteriorate. To improve the situation, Xerox reorganized its production and ordering schedules so suppliers could plan better. It also formed classes about JIT for the suppliers. One supplier, Rockford Dynatorq, reduced the time needed to make one

Sources: "Small Manufacturers Shifting To 'Just-in-Time' Techniques," *The Wall Street Journal,* December 21, 1987; "Having a Hard Time," *Fortune,* June 9, 1986; "General Motors' Little Engine That Could," *Business Week,* August 3, 1987; "Firms' Inventories Are Remarkably Lean," *The Wall Street Journal,* November 3, 1992; and "Supercomputers Manage Holiday Stock," *The Wall Street Journal,* December 23, 1992.

brake part from three and a half weeks to just one day with the help of Xerox. Rockford's inventory dropped by 10 percent in just six months.

Improvement in quality control is a common by-product of JIT. Before its conversion, Lifeline Systems assembled its emergency patient monitoring devices in lots of several hundred and tested them only when an entire lot was produced. Now each device is assembled and tested individually. "If you make them one at a time, you can't go any further if one is bad," says a manufacturing consultant with Coopers & Lybrand. "You have to say, 'Whoops, halt!' "

Many wasteful procedures are also uncovered when manufacturers reevaluate their production processes for JIT conversion. Costs that add nothing to a product's value are incurred every time an item is moved, inspected, or stored in inventory, and JIT helps trim these costs. One compamy, U.S. Repeating Arms of New Haven, Connecticut, used JIT techniques to lower its minimum lot size for the manufacture of wooden gun stocks from 500 to 100 and to reduce production time from five weeks to two.

Retailers, such as Kmart Corporation, Wal-Mart Stores Inc., and Dayton Hudson Corporation, are using a sophisticated approach to maintaining lean inventories and reducing carrying costs. These firms are using supercomputers, extraordinarily powerful parallel computers, to help managers decide what to buy, where to stock it, and when to cut prices. Wayne Hood, a retail analyst with Prudential Securities Inc., states that "Technology like this is absolutely critical . . . It's going to separate the winners from the losers in retailing in the 1990s. Companies that don't invest in technology—even in the hard times—won't make it."

The parallel design of these supercomputers, where thousands of small processors work as one, instead of having two to four large precessors as in mainframe computers, permits the retailing managers to quickly access data. For example, managers can obtain data through on-line searches instantly from every register, in every store, during the last year: What was sold, when, and what were the colors, styles, sizes, and prices? These managers can then act on this informa-

tion. Mainframe computers would choke on this tera-byte of data (a trillion characters of information). In addition to having the capability of accessing such information, the supercomputers are less costly than the mainframes.

Kmart's managers get feedback from its supercomputers daily. For example, one manager got a note from the computer system telling him that a certain inventory item was selling slower than in other Kmart stores. It asked him to make sure that the item was well displayed and to determine whether its price was being undercut by a competitor. In addition, the computer let him know the item's cost to Kmart. As a result of the query, the manager cut the price of the item and displayed the item so that it was the first thing shoppers saw as they came into the store.

Supercomputers have been especially effective in managing seasonal inventory items. Seasonal merchandise, such as Christmas and Valentine's Day items, have high profit margins, so it is bad to have them go out of stock, but they also have a "death date"—a time at which they need to be completely sold out. Therefore, such items need to be tightly managed. By using the supercomputers, Kmart was able to determine that it sold 50 percent of its Valentine inventory in a particular store in the last two days, hence that there was no need to panic and mark down prices to move the stock. Thus, the store managers were able to avoid unnecessary price cuts, and this increased the stores' profits.

It is apparent from firm's statements and from reported statistics that the trend to lower inventory levels represents a long-term, serious commitment. According to Geoffrey Moore, a Columbia University economist, the trend toward leaner inventories will reduce the volatility of U.S. business cycles because with smaller stockpiles of inventories, inventory draw-downs during recessions cannot last as long; hence, production must pick up sooner than would be the case if initial inventories were larger. Thus, it appears that JIT procedures and supercomputers will both lower companies' costs and help stabilize the economy, but they will also make life increasingly difficult for smaller, less efficient firms.

analyzing the experience, President John Stollenwerk pointed to several likely reasons. First, the firm did not have the clout to get all its suppliers to go along with the strategy of matching delivery to need. For example, European tanneries, which were supplying calfskin hides, refused to cooperate and continued to send huge batches of hides. Also, just-in-time inherently encourages a production focus on quality and teamwork, but the workers at Allen-Edmonds were used to a piecework pay system, and when the switch was made to teamwork and hourly wages, although inventory gains were realized, *productivity de-clined.* Finally, small companies with short production runs of a variety of products (41,000 styles of shoes in the case of Allen-Edmonds) must continually switch product lines, which reduces efficiency. In 1991, after losing $1 million on the project, Allen-Edmonds abandoned its attempt at just-in-time production. John Stollenwerk complains that efficiency experts still need to develop a just-in-time solution for small manufacturers with much more limited production runs than their larger rivals. And, of course, no single production method or concept will work for every company since each is constrained by its own unique set of circumstances.

out-sourcing

The practice of purchasing components rather than making them in-house.

Another important development related to inventories is **out-sourcing,** which is the practice of purchasing components rather than making them in-house. Thus, if General Motors arranges to buy radiators, axles, and other parts from suppliers rather than making them itself, it has increased its use of out-sourcing. Out-sourcing is often combined with just-in-time systems to reduce inventory levels. However, one important reason for out-sourcing has nothing to do with inventory policy—because of wage-rate differentials, a heavily unionized company like GM can often buy parts from a nonunionized supplier at a lower cost than it could make them.

A final point relating to inventory levels is the *relationship between production scheduling and inventory levels.* A firm like Dayton Card Company, whose cash budget was discussed in Chapter 9, has sales which are highly seasonal. Dayton could produce on a steady, year-round basis, or it could let production rise and fall with sales. If it established a level production schedule, its inventories would rise sharply during periods when sales were low and then would decline during peak sales periods, but the average inventory held would be substantially higher than if production were geared to rise and fall with sales.

Our discussion of just-in-time systems, out-sourcing, and production scheduling all point out the necessity of coordinating inventory policy with manufacturing/procurement policies. Companies try to minimize *total production and distribution costs,* and inventory costs are just one part of total costs. Still, they are an important cost, and financial managers should be aware of the determinants of inventory costs and how they can be minimized.

? *Self-Test*

Into what three classifications can inventories be grouped?

Identify the three basic questions on which inventory management focuses.

What is the goal of inventory management?

What are some specific inventory carrying costs?

What is meant by ordering costs?

What is the basic premise on which inventory theory is built?

Give the equation for the EOQ model.

How do you calculate the reorder point (1) when there are no goods in transit and (2) when there are goods in transit?

Identify some conditions that would normally cause the safety stock to increase and one that would cause the safety stock to decrease.

Identify and briefly explain some inventory control systems described in the text.

Explain what is meant by just-in-time and out-sourcing.

Summary

In this chapter we discussed accounts receivable and inventory management. Also, we presented an inventory model for helping the firm minimize its inventory investment. The key concepts covered are listed below.

▶   When a firm sells goods to a customer on credit, an **account receivable** is created, and since a firm's accounts receivable are a large part of its total assets, the level of investment into this current asset account has implications for the firm's total assets turnover, return on total assets, and return on equity. Excessive investment in receivables will lead to a reduction in profitability, but tightening receivables management may result in lost sales; a balance must be found.

▶   A firm's **credit policy** consists of four elements: (1) **credit period,** (2) **discounts** given for early payment, (3) **credit standards,** and (4) **collection policy.** The first two, when combined, are called the **credit terms.**

▶   The traditional method of measuring credit quality, where no computerized system is to be used, is to investigate potential credit customers with respect to five factors called the **five Cs of credit.** These factors are: **character, capacity, capital, collateral,** and **conditions.**

Modern credit managers often practice **management by exception.** Under this system, statistical procedures are used to classify customers into five or six categories according to degree of risk, and the credit manager then concentrates time and attention on customers judged most likely to cause problems.

Credit-scoring systems are statistical methods similar to multiple regression analysis which make it possible to express the estimate of a customer's credit quality as a single numerical value.

A firm can use an **aging schedule** and the **days sales outstanding (DSO)** to monitor and evaluate the firm's accounts receivable policy.

▶   Proposed changes in credit policy are analyzed within a quantitative framework and judgment must also be used. The **optimal credit policy** is the one at which the marginal benefits of a change in credit policy are exactly equal to the marginal costs of the change, but higher profits may be due to either an easing or a tightening of credit, depending on the firm's own unique set of circumstances.

Computers are increasingly used in managing accounts receivable and are valuable in conducting a sensitivity analysis of proposed changes in credit policy.

▷ **The goal of inventory management** is to provide the inventory required to sustain operations at the minimum cost. Inventory management involves determining how much inventory to hold, when to place orders, and how many units to order at a time. Because the cost of holding inventory is high, inventory management is important and has a direct impact on a firm's profitability, as well as on its level of sales.

Inventory can be grouped into three categories: (1) raw materials, (2) work-in-process, and (3) finished goods.

▷ The **economic ordering quantity (EOQ) model** is a formula for determining the ordering quantity that will minimize total inventory costs:

$$EOQ = \sqrt{\frac{2(F)(S)}{(C)(P)}}.$$

Here F is the fixed cost per order, S is annual sales in units, C is the percentage cost of carrying inventory, and P is the purchase price per unit.

Carrying costs include the costs of financing inventory, of storage and handling, insurance, property taxes, and depreciation; these costs tend to increase in proportion to the amount of inventory held.

Ordering costs are the costs of placing an order, including production and set-up costs, plus the costs of shipping and handling.

The costs of running short of inventory include lost sales and lost customer goodwill. These costs can be avoided by carrying **safety stocks.** Safety stocks help avoid shortages if (1) demand becomes greater than expected and/or (2) shipping delays are encountered.

▷ Firms use inventory control systems, such as the **red-line method,** the **two-bin method,** and the **ABC method,** as well as **computerized inventory control systems,** to help them keep track of actual inventory levels and to ensure that inventory levels are adjusted as sales change.

Just-in-time (JIT) systems are also used to hold down inventory costs and, simultaneously, to improve the production process.

Out-sourcing, the practice of purchasing components rather than making them in-house, is often combined with JIT systems to reduce inventory levels.

Resolution to
DECISION IN FINANCE

THE DATA ARE AVAILABLE, BUT SHOULD COMPANIES USE THEM?

A consumer advocate said, "When people find out what's going on, they are appalled." One such customer received a call urging her to switch to ITT for long-distance service. Responding that she didn't make many out-of-town calls, she was told, "I'm surprised to hear you say that. I see from your phone records that you frequently call Newark, Delaware, and Stamford, Connecticut." The customer later reported, "I was shocked, scared, and paranoid. If people are able to find out who I call, what else could they find out about me?" In that case, ITT's only response was that they have very little control over the telemarketing companies who sell their services.

American Express took a different approach and salvaged an account in the process. A new customer paid his previous two months of charges in full and on time. Then, he was notified that his credit privileges were suspended because American Express had looked at his bank records and found that there was not enough money in his checking account to pay his bill for the current month. "I felt violated," said the customer. "When I gave them my bank account number, I never thought they would use it routinely to look over my shoulder." American Express later apologized, and a spokesman said the company was wrong and should have asked permission before looking into the

customer's bank balance. The customer paid his bill from his savings account, and his credit was restored.

In 1991, Equifax succumbed to increasing public pressure and got out of the target-marketing business altogether, but TRW and Trans Union remained in it. However, in 1993, the FTC made a move to stop TRW and Trans Union from using confidential financial data to create lists for junk mailers. Because of the FTC's pressure, TRW agreed to stop using credit data in its mailing-list business. Under the agreement, TRW's mailing-list business can still use demographic information (name, address, phone number, age, Social Security number, and mother's maiden name) from its credit files. Meanwhile, Trans Union has insisted that its mailing-list business is perfectly legal and has said that it will fight the FTC in court.

Despite the FTC's crackdown on credit-reporting companies, one loophole remains in the mailing-list business—they may still sell credit information for use when soliciting individuals for credit cards. Under the FTC's interpretation of the law, this usage is legal because the credit-reporting companies are using credit data to make an offer of credit.

Consumer advocates are pleased with the FTC's recent crackdown. They have been pushing for new laws to bring the 1971 act up to date. In fact, revisions to the act made some progress in Congress last year but died because of the lobbying efforts made by banks, stores, and credit-reporting companies. Still, consumer advocates call the FTC's recent actions important moves against violations of privacy of which many people are not even aware.

Sources: "Is Nothing Private?" *Business Week,* September 4, 1989; "The Rising Tide of Privacy Laws," *American Demographics,* March 1990; "NY Loan Delinquencies Up," *Newsday,* February, 29, 1992; "FTC Takes Aim at Trans Union, TRW Mail Lists," *The Wall Street Journal,* January 13, 1993; and "Bankruptcies Hit a Record," *The New York Times,* March 18, 1993.

Questions

10-1 Is it true that when one firm sells to another on credit, the seller records the transaction as an account receivable while the buyer records it as an account payable and that, disregarding discounts, the receivable typically exceeds the payable by the amount of profit on the sale?

10-2 What are the four elements in a firm's credit policy? To what extent can firms set their own credit policies as opposed to having to accept credit policies that are dictated by "the competition"?

10-3 Suppose that a firm makes a purchase and receives the shipment on February 1. The credit terms as stated on the invoice read, "2/10, net 40, May 1 dating." What is the latest date on which payment can be made and the discount still be taken? What is the date on which payment must be made if the discount is not taken?

10-4 **a.** What is the days sales outstanding (DSO) for a firm whose sales are $2,880,000 per year and whose accounts receivable are $312,000? (Use 360 days per year.)
  b. Is it true that if this firm sells on terms of 3/10, net 40, its customers probably all pay on time?

10-5 Is it true that if a firm calculates its days sales outstanding (DSO), it has no need for an aging schedule?

10-6 Firm A had no credit losses last year, but 1 percent of Firm B's accounts receivable proved to be uncollectible and resulted in losses. Should Firm B fire its credit manager and hire A's?

10-7 Indicate by a (+), (−), or (0) whether each of the following events would probably cause accounts receivable (A/R), sales, and profits to increase, decrease, or be affected in an indeterminate manner:

	A/R	Sales	Profits
a. The firm tightens its credit standards.	____	____	____
b. The credit terms are changed from 2/10, net 30, to 3/10, net 30.	____	____	____
c. The credit terms are changed from 2/10, net 30, to 3/10, net 40.	____	____	____
d. The firm's major competitor changes its credit policy from 2/10, net 30 to 2/10, net 60.	____	____	____
e. The credit manager gets tough with past-due accounts.	____	____	____

10-8 Indicate by a (+), (−), or (0) whether each of the following events would probably cause average annual inventories (the sum of the inventories held at the end of each month of the year divided by 12) to rise, fall, or be affected in an indeterminate manner:
  a. The firm's suppliers switch from delivering by train to air freight.   ____
  b. The firm changes from producing just in time to meet seasonal sales to steady year-round production. (Sales peak at Christmas.)   ____
  c. Competition in the markets in which the firm sells increases.   ____
  d. The fixed ordering cost increases.   ____
  e. Interest rates rise; other things are constant.   ____

10-9 A firm can reduce its investment in inventory by having its suppliers hold raw materials inventories and its customers hold finished goods inventories. Explain actions a firm can take which would result in larger inventories for its suppliers and customers and smaller inventories for itself. What are the limitations of such actions?

10-10 The toy business is subject to large seasonal demand fluctuations. What effect would such fluctuations have on inventory decisions of toy manufacturers and toy retailers?

Self-Test Problems

ST-1   The Carson Company expects to have sales of $10 million this year under its current operating policies. Its variable costs are 80 percent of sales, and its cost of capital is 16 percent. Currently Carson's credit policy is net 25 (no discount for early payment). However, its DSO is 30 days, and its bad debt loss percentage is 2 percent. Carson spends $50,000 per year to collect bad debts, and its effective federal-plus-state tax rate is 40 percent.

The credit manager is considering two alternative proposals (given next) for changing Carson's credit policy. Find the expected change in net income, taking into consideration anticipated changes in carrying costs for accounts receivable, the probable bad debt losses, and the discounts likely to be taken, for each proposal. Should a change in credit policy be made?

Proposal 1: Lengthen the credit period by going from net 25 to net 30. The bad debt collection expenditures will remain constant. Under this proposal, sales are expected to increase by $1 million annually, and the bad debt loss percentage on *new* sales is expected to rise to 4 percent (the loss percentage on old sales should not change). In addition, the DSO is expected to increase from 30 to 45 days on all sales.

Proposal 2: Shorten the credit period by going from net 25 to net 20. Again, collection expenses will remain constant. The anticipated effects of this change are (1) a decrease in sales of $1 million per year, (2) a decline in the DSO from 30 to 22 days, and (3) a decline in the bad debt loss percentage to 1 percent on all sales.

ST-2   The Mrs. Morris Bread Company buys and then sells (as bread) 2.6 million bushels of wheat annually. The wheat must be purchased in multiples of 2,000 bushels. Ordering costs, which include grain elevator removal charges of $3,500, are $5,000 per order. Annual carrying costs are 2 percent of the purchase price of $5 per bushel. The company maintains a safety stock of 200,000 bushels. The delivery time is 6 weeks.

a. What is the EOQ?

b. At what inventory level should an order be placed to prevent having to draw on the safety stock?

c. What are the total inventory costs?

d. The wheat processor agrees to pay the elevator removal charges if Mrs. Morris Bread Company will purchase wheat in quantities of 650,000 bushels. Would it be to Mrs. Morris Bread Company's advantage to order under this alternative?

Problems

10-1
Receivables investment
Sam MacEwen, the new credit manager for Athletic Shoe Inc., is studying the firm's credit accounts. The company sells all its products on credit terms of 2/10, net 30. MacEwen's predecessor told him that the company's DSO is 40 days and that 60 percent of the customers take the discount. What is the DSO for the firm's customers who elect not to take the discount?

10-2
Receivables investment
Kimpel & Losh Inc. (KLI) sells on terms of 2/15, net 45. Total sales for the year are $720,000. Forty percent of KLI's customers pay on the fifteenth day and take the discount; the other 60 percent pay, on average, 55 days after their purchases.

a. What is the days sales outstanding (DSO)?

b. What is the average amount of receivables?

c. What would happen to the average receivables if KLI toughened up on its collection policy with the result that all nondiscount customers paid on Day 45?

10-3
Tightening credit terms
The Bilby Corporation with annual sales of $14.4 million, sells on terms of 2/10, net 30. Currently 45 percent of its customers pay on the tenth day and take discounts; the other 55 percent pay, on average, 40 days after their purchases. Bilby plans to tighten

its credit policy so that all nondiscount customers will pay on Day 30.
a. What is the days sales outstanding both before and after the change?
b. What is the average investment in receivables both before and after the change?

10-4

Credit scoring

Jack Perret, credit manager of National Appliance Distributors, uses multiple discriminant analysis in assessing its customers' credit risk. The firm has an extensive database
of historical information on its customers, and Perret has developed the following discriminant function:

$$\text{Score} = 4(\text{TIE}) + 8.5(\text{Quick ratio}) - 31.5(\text{Debt ratio}) + 2.3(\text{Years in business}).$$

National Appliance considers a score above 50 indicative of a good credit risk. One of
the firm's customers, A-Z Appliance Inc. asks for credit, and Perret must decide whether
to grant the request. A-Z Appliance has the following ratios:

$$\text{TIE} = 3.5$$
$$\text{Quick ratio} = 1.8$$
$$\text{Debt ratio} = 0.40$$
$$\text{Years in business} = 17$$

What is A-Z Appliance's credit score, and should Perret grant the customer credit?

10-5

Credit scoring

Four retail customers have applied for credit from Hausman Inc., which uses a scoring
system to determine whether credit should be extended. Hausman has used the following discriminant function for a number of years and feels that it provides a good
measure of customer credit risk:

$$\text{Score} = 3(\text{TIE}) + 9.2(\text{Quick ratio}) - 27.8(\text{Debt ratio}) + 1.8(\text{Years in business}).$$

Data as it applies to the four customer firms are as follows:

Customer	TIE	Quick Ratio	Debt Ratio	Years in Business
1	2.5	1.7	0.30	13
2	6.2	2.5	0.35	11
3	1.7	1.0	0.40	17
4	4.8	3.9	0.20	8

Hausman will extend credit to a customer if that firm's score is greater than or equal to
45. Which of the above firms will receive credit?

10-6

Easing credit terms

Varveres Inc. is considering changing its credit terms from 2/15, net 30, to 3/10, net 30,
to speed collections. At present, 50 percent of Varveres's customers who pay take the 2
percent discount. Under the new terms, discount customers are expected to rise to 60
percent. Regardless of the credit terms, half of the customers who do not take the discount are expected to pay on time, while the remainder will pay 10 days late. The
change does not involve a relaxation of credit standards; therefore, bad debt losses are
not expected to rise above their present 2 percent level. However, the more generous
cash discount terms are expected to increase sales from $2 million to $2.6 million per
year. Varveres's variable cost ratio is 70 percent, its cost of capital invested in accounts
receivable is 10 percent, and its average tax rate is 40 percent.
a. What is the days sales outstanding before and after the change?
b. Calculate the discount costs before and after the change.
c. Calculate the dollar cost of carrying receivables before and after the change.
d. Calculate the bad debt losses before and after the change.
e. What is the incremental profit from the change in credit terms? Should Varveres
change its credit terms?

10-7
Credit analysis

The Steenberg Corporation makes all sales on a credit basis, selling on terms of 2/10, net 30. Once a year it evaluates the creditworthiness of all its customers. The evaluation procedure ranks customers from 1 to 5, with 1 indicating the "best" customers. Results of the ranking are as follows:

Customer Category	Percentage of Bad Debts	DSO	Credit Decision	Annual Sales Lost Due to Credit Restrictions
1	None	10	Unlimited credit	None
2	1.0	12	Unlimited credit	None
3	3.0	20	Limited credit	$365,000
4	9.0	60	Limited credit	$182,500
5	16.0	90	Limited credit	$230,000

The firm's variable cost ratio is 75 percent, and its average tax rate is 40 percent. The cost of capital invested in receivables is 15 percent. What would be the effect on profitability of extending unlimited credit to each of the Categories 3, 4, and 5? (*Hint:* Determine separately the effect on the income statement of changing each policy. In other words, find the change in sales, change in production costs, change in receivables and the cost of carrying receivables, change in bad debt costs, and so forth, down to the change in net income. What should be calculated in each case is what corresponds to the *middle* column in Table 10-1. Assume that none of the customers in these three categories will take the discount.)

10-8
Tightening credit terms

Karen Edens, the new credit manager of Donaho Industries, was alarmed to find that Donaho sells on credit terms of net 60 days even though industry-wide credit terms have recently been lowered to net 30 days. On annual credit sales of $2.5 million, Donaho currently averages 70 days' sales in accounts receivable. Edens estimates that tightening the credit terms to 30 days would reduce annual sales to $2.2 million, but accounts receivable would drop to 35 days of sales, and the savings on investment in receivables should more than overcome any loss in profit. Donaho's variable cost ratio is 85 percent, and its average tax rate is 40 percent. If Donaho's cost of funds invested in receivables is 14 percent, should the change in credit terms be made? (Assume that Donaho has no bad debt losses.)

10-9
Relaxing collection efforts

The Fujita Corporation has annual credit sales of $6.5 million. Current expenses for the collection department are $200,000, bad debt losses are 3 percent of sales, and the days sales outstanding is 32 days. Fujita is considering easing its collection efforts so that collection expenses will be reduced to $175,000 per year. The change is expected to increase bad debt losses to 5 percent as well as to increase the days sales outstanding to 48 days. However, sales should increase to $7.2 million per year.

Fujita's opportunity cost of funds is 10 percent, its variable cost ratio is 75 percent, and its average tax rate is 40 percent. (Assume that no discounts are offered for early payment under the current or the proposed credit policy.)
a. Should Fujita relax its collection efforts?
(Do Parts b and c only if you are using the computerized problem diskette.)
b. Would the change in collection efforts be profitable if sales rose only to $7.1 million?
c. What would be the change in Fujita's net income if sales in fact rose only to $7.1 million as a result of the relaxed collection efforts but the firm's credit manager was able to limit bad debt losses to 4.5 percent?

10-10
Economic ordering quantity

Newport Hardware expects to sell 7,000 pounds of nails this year. Ordering costs are $35 per order, and carrying costs are $1 per pound.
a. What is the economic ordering quantity (EOQ)?
b. How many orders will be placed this year?
c. What is the average inventory under this plan, expressed in pounds?

10-11
Inventory cost

Computer-World Inc. must order diskettes from its supplier in lots of one dozen boxes. Given the following information, complete the table below and determine the economic ordering quantity for diskettes for Computer-World.

Annual demand: 2,800 dozen
Cost per order placed: $5.25
Carrying cost: 20%
Price per dozen: $30

Order size (dozens)	35	56	70	140	200	2,800
Number of orders	___	___	___	___	___	___
Average inventory	___	___	___	___	___	___
Carrying cost	___	___	___	___	___	___
Ordering cost	___	___	___	___	___	___
Total cost	___	___	___	___	___	___

[*Hint*: Calculate carrying cost as (Average inventory)(C)(P) and calculate ordering cost as (Number of orders)(F).]

10-12
Economic ordering quantity

Twin Rivers Garden Centers Inc. sells 240,000 bags of lawn fertilizer annually. The optimal safety stock (which is on hand initially) is 1,200 bags. Each bag costs Twin Rivers $4, inventory carrying costs are 20 percent, and the cost of placing an order with its supplier is $25.
a. What is the economic ordering quantity (EOQ)?
b. What is the maximum inventory of fertilizer in both quantity and dollar value?
c. What will the garden center's average inventory be in both quantity and dollar value?
d. How often must the company order?

10-13
Ordering discounts

Suppose that Double Delights Inc. purchases 100,000 boxes of ice cream cones every year. Order costs are $200 per order, and carrying costs are $0.40 per box. Moreover, management has determined that the EOQ is 10,000 boxes. The vendor now offers a quantity discount of $0.02 per box if the company buys cones in order sizes of 20,000 boxes. Determine the before-tax benefit or loss of accepting the quantity discount for Double Delights. (Assume the carrying cost remains at $0.40 per box whether or not the discount is taken.)

10-14
Ordering discounts

Stockton Recreational Center (SRC) purchases 25,000 gallons of distilled water each year. Ordering costs are $20 per order, and the carrying cost, as a percentage of inventory value, is 80 percent. The purchase price to SRC is $0.20 per gallon. Management currently orders the EOQ each time an order is placed. No safety stock is carried. The supplier is now offering a quantity discount of $0.01 per gallon if SRC orders 8,000 gallons at a time. Should SRC take the discount? (Assume the carrying cost percentage is not influenced by whether the discount is taken.)

10-15
EOQ and ordering discounts

Thermenos Electric Inc. purchases 11,875 reels of copper wiring annually. Inventory carrying costs are $4.75 per reel, and the cost of placing an order is $50.
a. What is the economic ordering quantity (EOQ)?
b. What is the average inventory if Thermenos holds a safety stock of 800 reels?
c. The supplier offers a discount of $0.08 per reel if Thermenos will buy 1,000 reels at a time. Assuming that carrying costs and safety stock remain unchanged, should Thermenos order in batches of 1,000 reels and take the discounts? [*Hint:* Calculate carrying cost as (Average inventory)(C*), ordering costs as (Number of orders per year)(F), and total inventory costs as the sum of carrying costs and ordering costs for each of the alternatives.]

10-16
EOQ and ordering discounts

Wonder Toys, a large manufacturer of toys and dolls, uses large quantities of flesh-colored cloth in its doll production process. Throughout the year, the firm uses 1,080,000 square yards of this cloth. The fixed costs of placing and receiving an order are $1,500, including a $1,125 set-up charge at the mill. The price of the cloth is $2 per square yard, and the annual cost of carrying this inventory item is 20 percent of the price. Wonder Toys maintains 10,000 square yards of safety stock. The cloth supplier requires a 2-week lead time from order to delivery.

a. What is the EOQ for this cloth?

b. What is the average inventory dollar value, including the safety stock?

c. What is the total cost of ordering and carrying the inventory, including the safety stock? (Assume that the safety stock is on hand at the beginning of the year.)

d. Using a 52-week year, at what inventory unit level should an order be placed? (Again, assume the 10,000 unit safety stock is already on hand.)

e. Suppose the cloth supplier offers to lower the fixed ordering cost to $1,000 if Wonder Toys will increase its order size from 90,000 to 150,000 square yards. Would it be to Wonder Toys's advantage to order under this alternative?

f. Now, suppose the cloth supplier offers to lower the fixed ordering cost to $1,200 if Wonder Toys will order 125,000 yards at a time. Should the firm accept this alternative?

10-17

Changes in the EOQ

The following relationships for inventory costs have been established for the Jessup Corporation:

1. Annual sales are 735,000 units.

2. The purchase price per unit is $1.

3. The carrying cost is 15 percent of the purchase price of goods.

4. The cost per order placed is $45.

5. Desired safety stock is 7,000 units (on hand initially).

6. One week is required for delivery.

a. What is the EOQ? What is the total cost of ordering and carrying inventories at the EOQ?

b. What is the optimal number of orders to be placed per year?

c. At what inventory level should Jessup order?

d. If annual unit sales double, what is the percentage increase in the EOQ? What is the elasticity of EOQ with respect to sales (Percentage change in EOQ/Percentage change in sales)?

e. If the cost per order doubles, what is the elasticity of EOQ with respect to cost per order?

f. If the carrying cost declines by 50 percent, what is the elasticity of EOQ with respect to that change?

g. If the purchase price declines by 50 percent, what is the elasticity of EOQ with respect to that change?

Solutions to Self-Test Problems

ST-1

Under the current credit policy, the Carson Company has no discounts, has collection expenses of $50,000, has bad debt losses of $(0.02)($10,000,000) = $200,000, and has average accounts receivable of (DSO)(Average sales per day) = (30)($10,000,000/360) = $833,333. The firm's cost of carrying these receivables is (A/R)(Variable cost ratio)(Cost of capital) = ($833,333)(0.80)(0.16) = $106,667. It is necessary to multiply by the variable cost ratio because the actual *investment* in receivables is less than the dollar amount of the receivables.

Proposal 1: Lengthen the credit period to net 30 so that:

1. Sales increase by $1 million.

2. Discounts = $0.

3. Bad debt losses $= (0.02)(\$10,000,000) + (0.04)(\$1,000,000)$

$$= \$200,000 + \$40,000$$

$$= \$240,000.$$

4. DSO $= 45$ days on all sales.

5. New average receivables $= (45)(\$11,000,000/360) = \$1,375,000.$

6. Cost of carrying receivables $= (A/R)(\text{Variable cost ratio})(\text{Cost of capital})$

$$= (\$1,375,000)(0.80)(0.16)$$

$$= \$176,000.$$

7. Collection expenses $= \$50,000.$

Analysis of proposed change:

	Income Statement under Current Policy	Effect of Change	Income Statement under New Policy
Gross sales	$10,000,000	+ $1,000,000	$11,000,000
Less: Discounts	0	0	0
Net sales	$10,000,000	+ $1,000,000	$11,000,000
Production costs (80%)	8,000,000	+ 800,000	8,800,000
Profits before credit costs and taxes	$ 2,000,000	+ $ 200,000	$ 2,200,000
Credit-related costs:			
Cost of carrying receivables	106,667	+ 69,333	176,000
Collection expenses	50,000	0	50,000
Bad debt losses	200,000	+ 40,000	240,000
Profit before taxes	$ 1,643,333	+ $ 90,667	$ 1,734,000
Taxes (40%)	657,333	+ 36,267	693,600
Net income	$ 986,000	+ $ 54,400	$ 1,040,400

The proposed change appears to be a good one, if the assumptions are correct.

Proposal 2: Shorten the credit period to net 20 so that:

1. Sales decrease by $1 million.

2. Discount $= \$0.$

3. Bad debt losses $= (0.01)(\$9,000,000) = \$90,000.$

4. DSO $= 22$ days.

5. New average receivables $= (22)(\$9,000,000/360) = \$550,000.$

6. Cost of carrying receivables $= (A/R)(\text{Variable cost ratio})(\text{Cost of capital})$

$$= (\$550,000)(0.80)(0.16)$$

$$= \$70,400.$$

7. Collection expenses $= \$50,000.$

Analysis of proposed change:

	Income Statement under Current Policy	Effect of Change	Income Statement under New Policy
Gross sales	$10,000,000	− $1,000,000	$9,000,000
Less: Discounts	0	0	0
Net sales	$10,000,000	− $1,000,000	$9,000,000
Production costs (80%)	8,000,000	− 800,000	7,200,000
Profits before credit costs and taxes	$ 2,000,000	− $ 200,000	$1,800,000
Credit-related costs:			
Cost of carrying receivables	106,667	− 36,267	70,400
Collection expenses	50,000	0	50,000
Bad debt losses	200,000	− 110,000	90,000
Profit before taxes	$ 1,643,333	− $ 53,733	$1,589,600
Taxes (40%)	657,333	− 21,493	635,840
Net income	$ 986,000	− $ 32,240	$ 953,760

This change reduces net income, so it should be rejected. Carson will increase profits by accepting Proposal 1 to lengthen the credit period from 25 days to 30 days, *if all assumptions are correct.* This may or may not be the *optimal,* or profit-maximizing, credit policy, but it does appear to be a movement in the right direction.

ST-2   a.

$$\text{EOQ} = \sqrt{\frac{2(F)(S)}{(C)(P)}}$$

$$= \sqrt{\frac{(2)(\$5,000)(2,600,000)}{(0.02)(\$5)}}$$

$$= 509,902 \text{ bushels.}$$

Since the firm must order in multiples of 2,000 bushels, it should order in quantities of 510,000 bushels.

b.

$$\text{Average weekly sales} = 2,600,000/52$$

$$= 50,000 \text{ bushels.}$$

$$\text{Reorder point} = 6 \text{ weeks' sales} + \text{Safety stock}$$

$$= 6(50,000) + 200,000$$

$$= 300,000 + 200,000$$

$$= 500,000 \text{ bushels.}$$

c. Total inventory costs = Ordering costs + Carrying costs.

(*Note:* Ordering costs do not apply to safety stock.)

$$\frac{\text{Ordering}}{\text{costs}} = \left(\begin{array}{c}\text{Number of}\\\text{orders}\end{array}\right)\left(\begin{array}{c}\text{Fixed order}\\\text{cost}\end{array}\right)$$

$$= \left(\frac{2,600,000}{510,000}\right)(\$5,000)$$

$$= \$25,490.20.$$

Carrying costs apply to EOQ + Safety stock.

$$\frac{\text{Carrying}}{\text{costs}} = (\text{Average inventory})(C)(P)$$

$$= \left(\frac{510,000}{2} + 200,000\right)(0.02)(\$5)$$

$$= \$45,500.00.$$

$$\frac{\text{Total inventory}}{\text{costs}} = \$25,490.20 + \$45,500.00$$

$$= \$70,990.20.$$

d. Ordering costs would be reduced to $1,500. By ordering 650,000 bushels at a time, Mrs. Morris Bread Company can lower its total inventory costs.

$$\frac{\text{Ordering}}{\text{costs}} = \left(\begin{array}{c}\text{Number of}\\\text{orders}\end{array}\right)\left(\begin{array}{c}\text{Fixed order}\\\text{cost}\end{array}\right)$$

$$= \left(\frac{2{,}600{,}000}{650{,}000} \right) \left(\$1{,}500 \right)$$

$$= \$6{,}000.$$

$$\frac{\text{Carrying}}{\text{costs}} = \left(\frac{650{,}000}{2} + 200{,}000 \right)(0.02)(\$5)$$

$$= \$52{,}500.$$

$$\frac{\text{Total inventory}}{\text{costs}} = \$6{,}000 + \$52{,}500 = \$58{,}500.$$

Since the firm can reduce its total inventory costs by ordering 650,000 bushels at a time, it should accept the offer and place larger orders. (Incidentally, this same type of analysis is used to consider any quantity discount offer.)

Short-Term Financing

O B J E C T I V E S

After reading this chapter, you should be able to:

▷ Define short-term credit and list the four major sources of short-term credit.

▷ Distinguish between free and costly trade credit and calculate the approximate annual percentage cost of not taking a discount, given specific credit terms.

▷ Describe the importance of bank loans as a source of short-term financing and discuss some of the characteristics of bank lending.

▷ Calculate the effective annual rate for (1) simple interest, (2) discount interest, and (3) add-on interest, using equations provided in the chapter.

▷ Discuss the impact of a compensating balance requirement when a firm would not normally hold cash balances with the bank in question.

▷ Explain why large, financially strong corporations issue commercial paper and why this source of short-term credit is typically less reliable than bank loans if the firm gets into financial difficulties.

DECISION IN FINANCE

WILL YOUR BANKER BE THERE
WHEN YOU NEED HER?

One of the most important "assets" on a firm's balance sheet is never actually reported there. The reason is simple: This "asset," which is a lasting and supportive banking relationship, is not quantifiable, hence the accountants cannot show it on the financial statements. Although it may seem that developing a good banking relationship would be easy, it is actually extremely difficult for both small and early-stage companies to accomplish, especially given the recent condition of both the economy and the banking industry. Therefore, it is extremely hard for many firms to get bank support, that is, credit, when needed, and the smaller and newer the firm, the more difficult the task of getting credit.

As you read this chapter, think about how to choose a bank, how to apply for a bank loan, and what variety of features are available on short-term bank loans. Also, consider the cost of bank loans and how that cost varies depending on the different terms quoted. Would you be able to

make an intelligent choice among banks? What things would be important to you in making your decision? Would you be able to "comparison shop" among banks for a loan, even though the loan terms among different banks are not stated on the same basis? Are there things you can do to make sure your banker stays with you, even during the rough times? Further, how would you decide on the proper amount of trade credit to employ, given the availability and cost of bank credit as a substitute for trade credit?

See end of chapter for resolution.
Photo source: Jay Brousseau/The Image Bank.

As we noted in Chapter 8, working capital management involves decisions relating to current assets, including decisions about how these assets are to be financed. Any statement about the flexibility, cost, and riskiness of short-term versus long-term credit depends to a large extent on the nature of the short-term credit that is actually used. The choice of the short-term credit instrument will affect both the firm's riskiness and its expected rate of return, and, hence, the market value of its stock. This chapter examines the sources and characteristics of the major types of short-term credit available to the firm.

Short-term credit is defined as any liability originally scheduled for payment within one year. The four major sources of short-term credit are (1) accruals such as accrued wages and taxes, (2) accounts payable (trade credit), (3) loans from commercial banks and finance companies (notes payable), and (4) commercial paper.

Accrued Wages and Taxes

Because firms generally pay employees on a weekly, biweekly, or monthly basis, the balance sheet typically will show some accrued wages. Similarly, because the firm's own estimated income taxes, sales taxes collected, and payroll taxes are usually paid on a weekly, monthly, or quarterly basis, the balance sheet will show some accrued taxes along with accrued wages.

accruals

Continually recurring short-term liabilities, especially accrued wages and accrued taxes.

As we saw in Chapter 7, **accruals** increase automatically as a firm's operations expand, and this type of credit is "free" in the sense that no explicit interest is paid on funds raised through accruals. However, a firm cannot ordinarily control its accruals: the timing of wage payments is set by economic forces and industry custom, while tax payment dates are established by law. Thus, firms use all the accruals they can, but they have little control over the level of these accounts.

 Self-Test

Define short-term credit.

What are the four major sources of short-term credit?

Why are accruals considered "free" credit?

How much control do financial managers have over the dollar amount of accruals?

Accounts Payable (Trade Credit)

trade credit

Inter-firm debt arising from credit sales; recorded as an account receivable by the seller and as an account payable by the buyer.

Firms generally make purchases from other firms on credit, recording the debt as an *account payable*. Accounts payable, or **trade credit,** as it is commonly called, is the largest single category of short-term debt, representing about 40 percent of the current liabilities of the average nonfinancial corporation. The percentage is somewhat larger for smaller firms; because small companies often do not qualify for financing from other sources, they rely rather heavily on trade credit.[1]

Trade credit, like accruals, is a spontaneous source of financing in the sense that it arises from ordinary business transactions. For example, suppose a firm makes average purchases of $2,000 a day on terms of net 30, meaning that it must pay for goods 30 days after the invoice date. On average, it will owe 30 times $2,000, or $60,000, to its suppliers. If its sales, and consequently its purchases, doubled, its accounts payable would also double, to $120,000. Simply by growing, the firm would have *spontaneously* generated an additional $60,000 of financing. Similarly, if the terms of credit were extended from 30 to 40 days, its accounts payable would expand from $60,000 to $80,000. Therefore, lengthening the credit period, as well as expanding sales and purchases, generates additional financing.

The Cost of Trade Credit

As we saw in Chapter 10 in connection with accounts receivable management, firms that sell on credit have a *credit policy* that includes certain *credit terms.* For example, McCue Electronics sells on terms of 2/10, net 30, meaning that a 2 percent discount is given if payment is made within 10 days of the invoice date, with the full invoice amount being due and payable within 30 days if the discount is not taken.

Note that the true price of McCue's products is the net price, or 98 percent of the list price, because any customer can purchase an item at a 2 percent "discount" as long as the customer pays within 10 days. Consider Personal Computer Company (PCC), which buys its memory chips from McCue. One commonly used memory chip is listed at $100, so the true cost to PCC is $98. Now if PCC wants an additional 20 days of credit beyond the 10-day discount period, it must incur a finance charge of $2 per chip for that credit. Thus, the $100 list price can be thought of as follows:

$$\text{List price} = \$98 \text{ true price} + \$2 \text{ finance charge.}$$

The question that PCC must ask before it takes the additional 20 days of credit from McCue is whether the firm could obtain similar credit under better terms from some other lender, say a bank. In other words, could 20 days of credit be obtained for less than 2 percent?

PCC buys an average of $11,760,000 of memory chips from McCue each year at the net or true price, which amounts to $11,760,000/360 = $32,666.67 per day. For simplicity, assume that McCue is PCC's only supplier. If PCC de-

---

[1]In a credit sale, the seller records the transaction as an account receivable, and the buyer records it as an account payable. We examined accounts receivable as an asset investment in Chapter 10. Our focus in this chapter is on accounts payable, a liability item. Note that if a firm's accounts payable exceed its accounts receivable, it is said to be *receiving net trade credit,* whereas if its accounts receivable exceed its accounts payable, it is *extending net trade credit.* Smaller firms frequently receive net credit; larger firms extend it.

clines the additional trade credit offered by McCue—that is, if it pays on the 10th day and takes the discount—its payables will average 10(\$32,666.67) ≈ \$326,667. Thus, PCC will be receiving \$326,667 of credit from its only supplier, McCue Electronics.

Now suppose PCC decides to take the additional 20 days of credit and thus must pay the finance charge. Since PCC will now pay on the 30th day, its accounts payable will increase to 30(\$32,666.67) = \$980,000.[2] McCue will now be supplying PCC with an additional \$653,333 of credit, which it could use to build up its cash account, to pay off debt, to expand inventories, or even to extend more credit to its own customers and hence to increase its own accounts receivable.

The additional credit offered by McCue has a cost—PCC must pay the finance charge by forgoing the 2 percent discount on its purchases from McCue. Since PCC buys \$11,760,000 of chips at the true price of 98 percent of the list price, the added finance charge increases the total cost to PCC to \$11,760,000/ 0.98 = \$12 million, so the annual financing cost is \$12,000,000 − \$11,760,000 = \$240,000. Dividing the \$240,000 financing cost by the \$653,333 in average annual additional credit, we find the implicit cost of the additional trade credit to be 36.7 percent:

$$\text{Approximate percentage cost} = \frac{\$240,000}{\$653,333} = 36.7\%.$$

Assuming that PCC can borrow from its bank (or from other sources) at an interest rate of less than 36.7 percent, it should *not* obtain credit in the form of accounts payable by forgoing discounts; it should borrow from the bank, pay on the 10th day, and take the discounts offered.

The following equation can be used to calculate the approximate percentage cost, on an annual basis, of not taking discounts:

$$\begin{matrix} \text{Approximate} \\ \text{percentage} \\ \text{cost} \end{matrix} = \frac{\text{Discount percent}}{100 - \begin{matrix} \text{Discount} \\ \text{percent} \end{matrix}} \times \frac{360}{\begin{matrix} \text{Days credit is} \\ \text{outstanding} \end{matrix} - \begin{matrix} \text{Discount} \\ \text{period} \end{matrix}}. \quad (11\text{-}1)$$

The numerator of the first term, Discount percent, is the cost per dollar of credit, while the denominator in this term, 100 − Discount percent, represents the funds made available by not taking the discount. Thus, the first term is the periodic cost of the trade credit. The denominator of the second term is the number of days of extra credit obtained by not taking the discount, so the entire second term shows how many times each year the cost is incurred. To illustrate

---

[2]A question arises here: Should accounts payable reflect gross purchases or purchases net of discounts? Although generally accepted accounting principles permit either treatment on the grounds that the difference is not material, most accountants prefer to record payables net of discounts, or at "true" prices, and then to report the higher payments that result from not taking discounts as an additional expense, called "discounts lost." *Thus, we show accounts payable net of discounts even if the company does not expect to take the discount.*

the equation, the approximate cost of not taking a discount when the terms are 2/10, net 30, is calculated as follows:[3]

$$\text{Approximate percentage cost} = \frac{2}{98} \times \frac{360}{20} = 2.04\% \times 18 = 36.7\%.$$

Notice, however, that the cost of trade credit is lower if the firm pays late. Thus, if PCC could get away with paying in 60 days rather than in the specified 30, then the effective credit period would become $60 - 10 = 50$ days, the number of times per year that the periodic cost of the additional trade credit is incurred would fall to $360/50 = 7.2$, and the approximate annual percentage cost would drop from 36.7 percent to 14.7 percent:

$$\text{Approximate percentage cost} = \frac{2}{98} \times \frac{360}{50} = 2.04\% \times 7.2 = 14.7\%.$$

stretching accounts payable

The practice of deliberately paying accounts payable late.

If their suppliers have excess capacity, firms may be able to get away with late payments, but this is an *unethical practice,* and it will lead to a variety of problems associated with **stretching accounts payable** and being labeled a "slow payer" account. These problems are discussed later in the chapter.

The cost of the additional trade credit obtained by not taking discounts can be worked out for other purchase terms. Some illustrative costs are as follows:

Credit Terms	Cost of Additional Credit if Cash Discount Is Not Taken
1/10, net 20	36%
1/10, net 30	18
2/10, net 20	73
3/15, net 45	37

As these figures show, the cost of not taking discounts can be substantial, and the differential between the cost of trade credit and bank borrowing is especially great in the low-interest-rate environment of 1993, even though smaller firms must be prepared to pay several percentage points above the 6 percent prime rate on commercial bank loans. Incidentally, throughout the chapter we assume that payments are made either on the *last day* for taking discounts or on the *last day* of the credit period. It would be foolish to pay (and take discounts), say, on the fifth day or to pay the full amount on the twentieth day if the credit terms were 2/10, net 30.

---

[3]Equation 11-1 may be roughly approximated as follows:

1. Divide the number of days in the year (360) by the difference in days between the end of the discount period and the date of payment.
2. Multiply this quotient by the forgone discount percentage.

Using the preceding illustration, there are $360/(30 - 10) = 18$ 20-day periods in a year. Therefore, $(18)(0.02) = 36$ percent is the approximate cost of forgoing the discount.

Of course, both of these methods used to determine the cost of not taking advantage of the discount are approximations of the "true" or compound interest rate to be discussed in Chapter 13. As such, Equation 11-1 and its approximation, detailed in this note, may understate the cost of trade credit in a compound interest sense.

Effects of Trade Credit on the Financial Statements

A firm's policy with regard to taking or not taking discounts can have a significant effect on its financial statements. To illustrate, let us assume that PCC is just beginning its operations. On the first day, it makes net purchases of $32,666.67. This amount is recorded on its balance sheet under accounts payable.[4] The second day it buys another $32,666.67. The first day's purchases are not yet paid for, so at the end of the second day, accounts payable total $65,333.34. Accounts payable increase by another $32,666.67 on the third day, for a total of $98,000, and after 10 days, accounts payable are up to $326,667.

If PCC takes discounts, then on the 11th day it will have to pay for the $32,666.67 of purchases made on the first day, which will reduce accounts payable. However, it will buy another $32,666.67, which will increase payables. Thus, after the 10th day of operations, PCC's balance sheet will level off, showing a balance of $326,667 in accounts payable, assuming that the company pays on the 10th day in order to take discounts.

Now suppose PCC decides not to take discounts. In this case, on the 11th day it will add another $32,666.67 to payables, but it will not pay for the purchases made on the 1st day. Thus, the balance sheet figure for accounts payable will rise to 11($32,666.67) = $359,333.37. This buildup will continue through the 30th day, at which point payables will total 30($32,666.67) = $980,000. On the 31st day, PCC will buy another $32,666.67 of goods, which will increase accounts payable, but it will also pay for the purchases made the 1st day, which will reduce payables. Thus, the balance sheet item accounts payable will stabilize at $980,000 after 30 days, assuming PCC does not take discounts but pays on day 30.

The upper section of Table 11-1 shows PCC's balance sheet, after it reaches a steady state, under the two trade credit policies. Total assets are unchanged by this policy decision, and we also assume that the accruals and common equity accounts are unchanged. The differences show up in accounts payable and notes payable; when PCC elects to take discounts and thus gives up some of the trade credit it otherwise could have obtained, it will have to raise $653,333 from some other source. It could have sold more common stock, or it could have used long-term bonds, but it chose to use bank credit, which we will assume has a 10 percent cost and is reflected in the notes payable account.

The lower section of Table 11-1 shows PCC's income statement under the two policies. If the company does not take discounts, then its interest expense will be zero, but it will have a $240,000 expense for discounts lost. On the other hand, if it does take discounts, it will incur an interest expense of $65,333, but it will avoid the cost of discounts lost. Since discounts lost exceed the interest expense, the take-discounts policy results in a higher net income and, thus, in a higher stock price.

---

[4]Inventories also increase by $32,666.67, but we are not concerned with inventories at this point. Again note that both inventories and receivables are recorded net of discounts regardless of whether discounts are taken.

	Take Discounts; Borrow from Bank (1)	Do Not Take Discounts; Use Maximum Trade Credit (2)	Difference (1) − (2)
Table 11-1			
PCC's Financial Statements with Different Trade Credit Policies			
I. Balance Sheets			
Cash	$ 500,000	$ 500,000	$ 0
Receivables	1,000,000	1,000,000	0
Inventories	2,000,000	2,000,000	0
Fixed assets	2,980,000	2,980,000	0
Total assets	$ 6,480,000	$ 6,480,000	$ 0
Accounts payable	$ 326,667	$ 980,000	$ −653,333
Notes payable (10%)	653,333	0	+653,333
Accruals	500,000	500,000	0
Common equity	5,000,000	5,000,000	0
Total liabilities and equity	$ 6,480,000	$ 6,480,000	$ 0
II. Income Statements			
Sales	$15,000,000	$15,000,000	$ 0
Less: Purchases	11,760,000	11,760,000	0
Labor	2,000,000	2,000,000	0
Interest	65,333	0	+65,333
Discounts lost	0	240,000	−240,000
Earnings before taxes (EBT)	$ 1,174,667	$ 1,000,000	$ +174,667
Taxes (40%)	469,867	400,000	+69,867
Net income	$ 704,800	$ 600,000	$ +104,800

Components of Trade Credit: Free versus Costly

Based on the preceding discussion, trade credit can be divided into two components:

free trade credit

Credit received during the discount period.

1. **Free trade credit,** which involves credit received during the discount period. For PCC, this amounts to ten days of net purchases, or $326,667.[5]

costly trade credit

Credit taken in excess of free trade credit; the cost is equal to the discounts lost.

2. **Costly trade credit,** which involves credit in excess of the free credit. This credit has an implicit cost equal to the forgone discounts. PCC could obtain $653,333, or 20 days' net purchases, of nonfree trade credit at a cost of approximately 37 percent.

Financial managers should always use the free component, but they should use the costly component only after analyzing the cost of this capital and determining that it is less than the costs of funds obtained from other sources.

---

[5]Accounts payable where no discount is offered, for example, where the purchase terms are net 30, are also regarded as "free." Actually, there is some question as to whether any credit is really "free" because the supplier will have a cost of carrying receivables, which must be passed on to the customer in the form of higher prices. Still, where suppliers sell on standard terms such as 2/10, net 30, and where the base price cannot be negotiated downward for early payment, for all intents and purposes the 10 days of trade credit is indeed free.

Under the terms of trade found in most industries, the costly component involves a relatively high percentage cost, so stronger firms with access to bank credit should generally use only the free component of trade credit.

We noted earlier that firms sometimes can and do deviate from the stated credit terms, thus altering the percentage cost figures cited earlier. For example, a California manufacturing firm that buys on terms of 2/10, net 30, makes a practice of paying in 15 days (rather than 10), but it still takes discounts. Its treasurer simply waits until 15 days after the invoice date to pay and then writes a check for the invoiced amount less the 2 percent discount. The company's suppliers want its business, so they tolerate this practice. Similarly, a Wisconsin firm that also buys on terms of 2/10, net 30, does not take discounts, but it pays in 60 rather than in 30 days, thus "stretching" its trade credit. As we saw earlier, this will reduce the cost of trade credit. Neither of these firms is "loved" by its suppliers, and neither could continue these practices in times when suppliers were operating at full capacity and had order backlogs. Indeed, both firms have bad reputations in their industries, and both will have a hard time getting deliveries when their suppliers are operating at full capacity. However, these practices do reduce the nominal costs of trade credit during times when suppliers have excess capacity.

? Self-Test

Give the equation used to calculate the approximate percentage cost, on an annual basis, of not taking discounts.

What is the difference between free and costly trade credit?

How does the cost of costly trade credit generally compare with the cost of short-term bank loans?

Short-Term Bank Loans

Commercial banks, whose loans generally appear on firms' balance sheets as notes payable, are second in importance to trade credit as a source of short-term financing.[6] However, banks' influence is actually greater than it appears from the dollar amounts they lend, because banks provide *nonspontaneous* funds. As a firm's financing needs increase, it requests additional funds from its bank. If the request is denied, often the firm is forced to abandon attractive growth opportunities. In this section we discuss factors that influence the choice of a bank, how to approach a bank for a business loan, some features of bank loans, and the cost of bank loans.

---

[6]Although commercial banks remain the primary source of short-term loans, other sources are available. For example, GE Capital Corporation (GECC) has recently had several billion dollars in commercial loans outstanding. Firms such as GECC, which was initially established to finance consumers' purchases of GE's durable goods, often find business loans to be more profitable than consumer loans.

Choosing a Bank

Individuals whose only contact with their bank is through the use of its checking services generally choose a bank for the convenience of its location and the competitive cost of its services. Businesses that borrow from banks must look at other criteria, however, and potential borrowers seeking banking relationships should recognize that important differences exist among banks. Some of these differences include the following:

1. Banks have different basic *policies toward risk*. Some banks follow relatively conservative lending practices, while others engage in what are properly termed "creative banking practices." These policies reflect both the personalities of the banks' officers and the characteristics of the banks' deposit liabilities. Thus, a bank with fluctuating deposit liabilities in a static community will tend to be a conservative lender, while a bank whose deposits are growing with little interruption can more safely follow liberal credit policies. Similarly, a large bank with broad diversification over geographic regions or among industries served can obtain the benefit of combining and averaging risks. Thus, marginal credit risks that might be unacceptable to a small or specialized bank can be pooled by a large branch banking system to reduce the overall risk of a group of marginal accounts.

2. Some bank loan officers are active in providing *advice and counsel* and in making developmental loans to firms in their early and formative years. Certain banks have specialized departments which make loans to firms that are expected to grow and thus become more important customers. The personnel of these departments can provide valuable counseling to customers. The bankers' experience with other firms in growth situations may enable them to spot, and then warn their customers about, developing problems.

3. Banks differ in the extent to which they will support the activities of borrowers in bad times. This characteristic is referred to as the banks' degree of *loyalty*. Some banks may put great pressure on a business to liquidate its loans when the firm's outlook becomes unfavorable, while others will stand by the firm and work diligently to help it get back on its feet. An especially dramatic illustration of this point was Bank of America's bailout of Memorex Corporation some years ago. The bank could have forced Memorex into bankruptcy, but instead it loaned the company additional capital and helped it survive a bad period. Memorex's stock price subsequently rose on the New York Stock Exchange from $1.50 to $68, so Bank of America's help was indeed substantial. (Memorex has again encountered financial adversity in recent years. In the spring of 1992 it emerged from Chapter 11 bankruptcy reorganization; by May 1993 it was trading at only about $0.28 per share. However, recent events by no means diminish the importance of the bank's loyalty to the firm in the earlier crisis.) We will discuss the topic of bank loyalty again later in this chapter.

4. Banks differ greatly in their degree of *loan specialization*. Larger banks have separate departments specializing in different kinds of loans — for example, real estate loans, farm loans, and commercial loans. Within these

broad categories there may be a specialization by line of business, such as steel, machinery, cattle, or textiles. The banks' strengths are also likely to reflect the nature of the business and economic environments in which they operate. For example, Seattle banks have become specialists in lending to timber and fisheries companies, some California banks have specialized in lending to electronics companies, and many Midwestern banks are agricultural specialists. A sound firm can obtain more creative cooperation and more active support by going to the bank that has the greatest experience and familiarity with its particular type of business. The financial manager should choose a bank with care. Therefore, a bank that is excellent for one firm may be unsatisfactory for another.

5. The size of a bank can be an important factor. Since the *maximum loan amount* a bank can make to any one customer is limited to 15 percent of the bank's capital accounts (capital stock plus retained earnings), it is generally not appropriate for large firms to develop borrowing relationships with small banks.

6. Businesses need to consider the extent to which a bank is able to provide a full range of commercial and *merchant banking services.* The term "merchant bank" was originally applied to banks which not only loaned depositors' money but also provided customers with equity capital and financial advice. Prior to 1933, U.S. commercial banks performed all types of merchant banking functions. However, about one-third of the U.S. banks failed during the Great Depression, in part because of these activities, so in 1933 the Glass-Steagall Act was passed in an effort to reduce banks' exposure to risk. In recent years, commercial banks have been attempting to get back into merchant banking, in part because their foreign competitors offer such services, and U.S. banks need to be able to compete with their foreign counterparts for multinational corporations' business. Currently, the larger banks, often through holding companies, are being permitted to get back into merchant banking, at least to a limited extent. This trend will probably continue.

7. Banks may also supply *other services,* such as providing lockbox systems, assisting with electronic funds transfers, helping firms obtain foreign currency, and the like. Such supplementary services should be taken into account when selecting a bank. Finally, if the firm is a small business whose manager owns most of its stock, the bank's ability to provide trust and estate services should be considered.

Applying for a Bank Loan

Both large and small firms often find a temporary need for short-term funds above current resources. At such times, most business firms seek interim financing from a commercial bank.

Requests for loans take many forms. A request from a major corporation may be supported by professionally prepared and audited financial statements, complete credit analysis reports from agencies such as Dun & Bradstreet, and documentation from the company's legal counsel. On the other hand, a small firm may have only an unaudited financial statement to support the loan request.

Whatever the degree of sophistication of the data presented to support the loan request, bankers use the financial statements, both historical and pro forma, to answer questions about the term and adequacy of the loan, sources of repayment, and the certainty of those sources. The borrower therefore should anticipate the banker's questions and attempt to answer them in the loan application package. A successful application package generally would contain (1) a cover letter; (2) historical financial data; (3) projected, or pro forma, financial statements; and (4) a brief history of the firm and the resumés of its major officers.

The cover letter should indicate only the most relevant factors about the loan: the purpose of the loan, the amount requested, and the loan period. Balance sheets, income statements, and perhaps even tax records for the past three years of operation constitute an integral part of the loan application package. These data will be used by bankers to learn more about the business, and they are especially helpful in determining management's business and financial acumen. Another important factor in a banker's evaluation is the firm's capitalization. Many small businesses are undercapitalized; that is, their long-term or permanent financing is insufficient to support a larger volume of business. A bank is not the proper source of permanent capital. Additionally, bankers demand that the owner's equity investment in the business be sufficient to give the owner a considerable stake in the success or failure of the firm.

Of course, the pro forma financial statements will receive a great deal of attention from the bank's loan officer. First, the officer will consider whether the requested loan amount is sufficient for its intended purpose. Bankers note that one of the most prevalent mistakes that novice borrowers make is to underestimate the loan amount needed. Second, the banker will review the projected financial statements and even the firm's order book (a listing of its customers' orders) for an indication of the sources of repayment from operations and the relative certainty of the payments. If the loan is to cover only seasonal working capital requirements, a monthly or even weekly cash budget, such as the one developed in Chapter 9, is an excellent addition to the loan documentation package. Finally, if the bank's credit officers are unfamiliar with the applicants or their business, a summary of the educational and managerial backgrounds of the firm's principals and a brief history of the firm, including a review of recent company and industry trends and future prospects, should be provided. Recall that the *five Cs of credit,* discussed in Chapter 10, is a traditional method used by credit managers to evaluate a customer's credit quality. These are the same five factors that would normally be of interest to a banker who receives a request for a short-term bank loan.

collateral

Assets that are pledged to secure a loan.

Banks and bankers are in business to lend money, but the loan documentation package must provide the banker with enough data to support a positive response to the loan request. In addition, the loan request should indicate any security or **collateral** that is available to support the loan. Unpleasant as the prospect may be, collateral is important since it indicates a source of funds available to the bank if unforeseen events cause default. Because collateral reduces the lending risk to the bank, it may reduce the cost of the loan or even be the determining factor in the decision to accept or reject the loan request. The use of collateral is discussed in more detail later in this chapter.

There are times, however, when even offering collateral does not assure the firm a loan. Such a time has been the credit crunch of the early 1990s, which was first discussed in Chapter 3. For example, in November 1992 many small and mid-sized companies found that bankers were less willing to lend against accounts receivable and that even real estate was no longer the ideal collateral because lenders did not want to end up with this collateral in the middle of a real estate slump. As a result, many small and medium-sized firms were denied the working capital loans they needed just when business was picking up and they had opportunities for expansion.

Some Features of Bank Loans

Maturity. Although banks do make longer-term loans, *the bulk of their lending is on a short-term basis;* about two-thirds of all bank loans mature in a year or less. Bank loans to businesses frequently are written as 90-day notes, so the loan must be repaid or renewed at the end of 90 days. Of course, if a borrower's financial position has deteriorated, or if the bank has other internal or regulatory reasons for cutting back on lending in general, it may refuse to renew the loan. This can mean serious trouble for the borrower.

promissory note

A document specifying the terms and conditions of a loan, including the amount, interest rate, and repayment schedule.

Promissory Note. When a bank loan is approved, the agreement is executed by signing a **promissory note.** The note specifies (1) the amount borrowed; (2) the percentage interest rate; (3) the repayment schedule, which can involve either a lump sum or a series of installments; (4) any collateral that might be put up as security for the loan; and (5) any other terms and conditions to which the bank and the borrower have agreed. When the note is signed, the bank credits the borrower's checking account with the amount of the loan, so on the borrower's balance sheet, both cash and notes payable increase.

compensating balance (CB)

A minimum checking account balance that a firm must maintain with a commercial bank, generally equal to 10 to 20 percent of the amount of loans outstanding.

Compensating Balances. In Chapter 9 compensating balances were discussed in connection with a firm's cash account as a way to compensate banks for services rendered. Banks will also typically require a regular borrower to maintain an average checking account balance of 10 to 20 percent of the face amount of the loan. This is called a **compensating balance (CB),** and, as we shall see later in this chapter, such a balance generally raises the effective interest rate on the loan.[7] Note that these *loan* compensating balances are in addition to any compensating balances that the bank may require for *services performed,* such as clearing checks.

line of credit

An arrangement in which a bank agrees to lend up to a specified maximum amount of funds during a designated period.

Line of Credit. A **line of credit** is an agreement between the bank and the borrower indicating the maximum amount of credit the bank will extend to the borrower. For example, on December 31, a bank loan officer may indicate to a corporate treasurer that the bank considers the firm to be "good" for up to $80,000 during the forthcoming year. On January 10 the treasurer signs a promissory note for $15,000 for 90 days; this is called "taking down" $15,000 of the total line of credit. This amount is credited to the firm's checking account at the bank, and before repayment of the $15,000, the firm may borrow additional amounts up to a total of $80,000 outstanding at any one time. When the firm

---

[7]The compensating balance may be set as a minimum monthly *average* or as an absolute minimum; if, however, the firm would maintain this amount anyway, the compensating balance requirement will not raise the effective interest rate.

has surplus cash, it can pay down the loan, which will both reduce its interest expense and increase its available remaining credit.

revolving credit agreement

A formal line of credit extended to a firm by a bank or other financial institution.

Revolving Credit Agreement.   A **revolving credit agreement** is a more formal line-of-credit arrangement often used by large firms. To illustrate, Carter Chemical Company negotiated a revolving credit agreement for $100 million with a group of banks. The banks were formally committed for 4 years to lend Carter up to $100 million if the funds were needed. Carter, in turn, paid an annual commitment fee of one quarter of 1 percent on the unused balance of the committed funds to compensate the banks for making the funds available. Thus, if Carter did not take down any of the $100 million commitment during a given year, it would still be required to pay a $250,000 fee. If it borrowed $50 million on the first day of the agreement, the unused portion of the line of credit would fall to $50 million, and the annual fee would fall to $125,000. Of course, interest also must be paid on the amount of money Carter actually borrowed. As a general rule, the interest rate on "revolvers" is pegged to the prime rate, so the cost of the loan varies over time as interest rates change.[8] Carter's rate was set at prime plus 0.5 percentage point, to be adjusted on the first of every month.

Note that a revolving credit agreement is very similar to a regular line of credit. However, there is an important distinguishing feature: the bank has a legal obligation to honor a revolving credit agreement, and it charges a fee for this commitment. No legal obligation exists under the regular line of credit.

The Cost of Bank Loans

The cost of bank loans varies for different types of borrowers at a given point in time, and for all borrowers over time. Interest rates are higher for riskier borrowers. Rates also are higher on smaller loans because of the fixed costs of making and servicing loans. If a firm can qualify as a "prime risk" because of its size and financial strength, it can borrow at the prime rate, which has traditionally been the lowest rate banks charge. Rates on other loans are generally scaled up from the prime rate, which currently (May 1993) is 6 percent.

---

[8]Each bank sets its own prime rate, but, because of competitive forces, most banks' prime rates are identical. Further, most banks follow the rate set by the large New York City banks, and they, in turn, generally follow the rate set by Citibank, the largest bank in the United States. Citibank formerly set the prime rate each week at $1\frac{1}{4}$ to $1\frac{1}{2}$ percentage points above the average rate on certificates of deposit (CDs) during the three weeks immediately preceding.

However, recently banks' net interest margins (discussed in Chapter 3) have widened considerably. In May 1993 the prime rate remained at 6 percent, while rates on CDs ranged from 3.12 percent on three-month maturities to only slightly higher yields on longer-term CDs. This wide interest-rate spread has been the major reason for the recovery of many commercial banks in 1992 and 1993. Not surprisingly, depositors have reacted to the miserly CD rates by shifting savings out of low-yielding CDs and into such investments as bond and stock mutual funds.

In recent years the prime rate has been held relatively constant even during periods when open market rates fluctuated. For example, during the period from January 1992 to May 1993, the prime rate was cut only once (from 6.5 percent to 6 percent). Also, in recent years many banks have been lending to the very strongest companies at rates below the prime rate. As we discuss later in this chapter, larger firms have ready access to the commercial paper market, and if banks want to do business with these larger companies, they must match or at least come close to the commercial paper rate. As competition in financial markets increases, "administered" rates such as the prime rate are giving way to flexible, negotiated rates based on market conditions.

Bank lending rates vary widely over time depending on economic conditions and Federal Reserve policy. When the economy is weak, loan demand is usually slack, inflation is low, and the Fed also makes plenty of money available to the system. As a result, interest rates on all types of loans decline. Conversely, when the economy is booming, loan demand is typically strong, and the Fed restricts the money supply. This results in an increase in interest rates, especially short-term rates. An example will illustrate how quickly changes can occur: In just five months (from August to December 1980), the prime rate rose from 11 percent to 21 percent. Then it fell steadily until the winter of 1987, when the rate was only 7.5 percent, the lowest since 1978. From 1987 to mid-1989, the prime rate first rose until it reached 11.5 percent then began falling to its current rate of 6 percent. Interest rates on other bank loans also vary, generally moving with the prime rate.

Interest rates on bank loans are calculated in three ways: (1) *simple* interest, (2) *discount* interest, and (3) *add-on* interest. These three methods are explained in the following sections.

simple interest

Interest that is charged on the basis of the amount borrowed; it is paid when the loan matures rather than when it is taken out.

Regular, or Simple, Interest.   When a loan is based on **simple interest,** the borrower receives the face value of the loan and repays both principal and interest at maturity. For example, in a simple interest loan of $10,000 at 10 percent for 1 year, the borrower receives the $10,000 upon approval of the loan and pays back the $10,000 principal plus $10,000(0.10) = $1,000 of interest at maturity (after 1 year). In the case of a simple interest loan, the stated, or nominal, rate is also the effective annual rate, which is 10 percent in this example:

$$\text{Effective annual rate}_{\text{Simple}} = \frac{\text{Interest}}{\text{Amount received}} \qquad (11\text{-}2)$$

$$= \frac{\$1,000}{\$10,000} = 10\%.$$

discount interest

Interest that is calculated on the face amount of a loan but is paid in advance.

Discount Interest.   In a **discount interest** loan, the bank deducts the interest in advance (*discounts* the loan). Because the borrower receives less than the face value of the loan, the effective rate of interest on the loan is increased. Thus, on a $10,000 loan with a nominal interest rate of 10 percent, the interest is $1,000 but the borrower has the use of only $9,000 and the effective rate of interest is 11.1 percent versus 10 percent on a 1-year simple interest loan[9]:

---

[9]Note that the firm receives less than the face amount of the loan:

$$\text{Funds received} = \text{Face amount of loan} (1.0 - \text{Nominal interest rate}),$$

and we can solve for the face amount as follows:

$$\text{Face amount of loan} = \frac{\text{Amount received}}{1.0 - \text{Nominal rate (decimal)}}.$$

Therefore, if the borrowing firm actually *requires* $10,000 of cash, it must borrow $11,111.11:

$$\text{Face amount of loan} = \frac{\$10,000}{1.0 - 0.1} = \frac{\$10,000}{0.9} = \$11,111.11.$$

$1,111.11 of this amount is interest, so the borrower will receive only $10,000. Increasing the face value of the loan does not change the effective annual rate of 11.1 percent on the $10,000 of usable funds (see Equation 11-3).

$$\text{Effective annual rate}_{\text{Discount}} = \frac{\text{Interest}}{\text{Amount received}} = \frac{\text{Interest}}{\text{Face value} - \text{Interest}} \quad (11\text{-}3)$$

$$= \frac{\$1,000}{\$9,000} = 11.1\%.$$

add-on interest

Interest that is calculated and added to funds received to determine the face amount of an installment loan.

Installment Loans: Add-On Interest. Banks (and other lenders) typically charge **add-on interest** on automobile, appliance, and other types of small installment loans. The term *add-on* means that interest is calculated and added to the amount received to determine the loan's face value. To illustrate, suppose the $10,000 is borrowed on an add-on basis and is to be repaid in 12 monthly installments. At a 10 percent add-on rate, the borrower pays a total interest charge of $1,000. Thus, the signed note is for $11,000. However, because the loan is paid off in installments, the borrower has the full $10,000 only during the first month, and the outstanding balance declines until, during the last month, only $\frac{1}{12}$ of the original loan will still be outstanding. Thus, the borrower is paying $1,000 for the use of only about half the amount initially received, as the *average* outstanding balance of the loan is only about $5,000. Therefore, the effective annual rate on the loan is *approximately* 20 percent, calculated as follows:

$$\begin{array}{c}\text{Approximate} \\ \text{effective annual rate}_{\text{Add-on}}\end{array} = \frac{\text{Interest}}{(\text{Amount received})/2} \quad (11\text{-}4)$$

$$= \frac{\$1,000}{\$5,000} = 20\%.$$

The main point to note here is that interest is paid on the *original* amount of the loan, not on the outstanding balance, which causes the effective interest rate to be approximately double the stated rate.[10]

Simple Interest with Compensating Balances. A compensating balance tends to raise the effective interest rate on a loan. To illustrate, suppose a firm needs $10,000 to pay for some equipment that it recently purchased. A bank offers to lend the company money for 1 year at a 10 percent simple interest rate, but the company must maintain a *compensating balance (CB)* equal to 20 percent of the loan amount. Assume that if the firm did not take the loan, it would keep no deposits with the bank. What is the effective annual interest rate on the loan?

First, note that although the firm needs only $10,000, it must borrow $12,500, calculated as follows:

$$\text{Face amount of loan}_{\text{Simple/CB}} = \frac{\text{Funds needed}}{1.0 - \text{CB (decimal)}}. \quad (11\text{-}5)$$

$$= \frac{\$10,000}{1.0 - 0.2} = \frac{\$10,000}{0.8} = \$12,500.$$

---

[10]Equation 11-4 is an approximation of the true interest rate, which is determined by utilizing the compound interest techniques described in Chapter 13.

Even though the interest paid will be $(0.10)(\$12,500) = \$1,250$, the firm will get to use only $10,000. Therefore the effective annual interest rate is

$$\text{Effective annual rate}_{\text{Simple/CB}} = \frac{\text{Interest}}{\text{Amount received}} \qquad (11\text{-}6)$$

$$= \frac{\$1,250}{\$10,000} = 0.125 = 12.5\%.$$

In general, we can use this formula to find the effective annual interest rate when compensating balances apply:

$$\text{Effective annual rate}_{\text{Simple/CB}} = \frac{\text{Nominal interest rate (\%)}}{1.0 - \text{CB (decimal)}}. \qquad (11\text{-}6a)$$

In this example,

$$\text{Effective annual rate}_{\text{Simple/CB}} = \frac{10\%}{1 - 0.2} = \frac{10\%}{0.8} = 12.5\%.$$

Note that if a firm normally carries cash balances with the bank, then those balances can be used to meet all or part of the compensating balance requirement, and this will reduce the effective cost of the loan. In this case, the calculations required to determine the effective annual rate are a bit more complicated.[11]

Discount Interest with Compensating Balances.   The analysis can be extended to the case where compensating balances are required and the loan is on a discount basis. For example, assume that a firm needs $10,000 and is offered a loan with a nominal interest rate of 10 percent, discount interest, and with a 20 percent compensating balance. The amount that the firm would need to borrow would be

---

[11]To illustrate, if our firm normally carries a cash balance of $1,000, then the effective annual cost of a $10,000 loan requiring a 20 percent compensating balance would be found as follows:

Step 1. $\dfrac{\text{Additional funds to meet}}{\text{compensating balance}} = 0.2(\text{Loan} - \$1,000).$

Step 2. $\text{Loan} = \$10,000 + 0.2(\text{Loan}) - \$1,000$
$0.8(\text{Loan}) = \$9,000$
$\text{Loan} = \$11,250.$

Step 3. $\text{Effective annual interest rate} = \dfrac{(\text{Nominal interest rate})(\text{Loan})}{\text{Amount received}}$

$$= \frac{(0.10)(\$11,250)}{\$10,000} = 11.25\%.$$

Thus, the firm will borrow $11,250, use $10,000 of this amount to meet its obligations, leave $1,250 on deposit as part of the compensating balance requirement, meet the remainder of the compensating balance requirement with the currently available $1,000, and pay an effective annual interest rate of 11.25 percent for the $10,000 net usable funds it received.

In our experience, most firms that require significant bank loans do not have much in the way of cash balances available for compensating balances. Therefore, in most situations Equation 11-6a can be used to find the cost of a bank loan with compensating balance requirements.

$$\text{Face amount of loan}_{\text{Discount/CB}} = \frac{\text{Funds needed}}{1.0 - \text{Nominal rate (decimal)} - \text{CB (decimal)}} \quad (11\text{-}7)$$

$$= \frac{\$10,000}{1.0 - 0.1 - 0.2} = \frac{\$10,000}{0.7} = \$14,285.71.$$

It would use this $14,285.71 as follows:

To make required payment	$10,000.00
Prepaid interest (10% of $14,285.71)	1,428.57
Compensating balance (20% of $14,285.71)	2,857.14
Total	$14,285.71

The effective annual interest rate would be

$$\text{Effective annual rate}_{\text{Discount/CB}} = \frac{\text{Nominal interest rate (\%)}}{1.0 - \text{Nominal rate (decimal)} - \text{CB (decimal)}}. \quad (11\text{-}8)$$

$$= \frac{10\%}{1.0 - 0.1 - 0.2} = \frac{10\%}{0.7} = 14.3\%.$$

In this example, compensating balances and discount interest combine to push the effective annual rate of interest up from 10 percent to 14.3 percent. Note, however, that our analysis assumes that the compensating balance requirement forces the firm to increase its bank deposits. If the company normally carries cash balances that could be used to supply all or part of the compensating balance, the effective interest rate would be less than 14.3 percent. Also, if the firm earns interest on its bank deposits, including the compensating balance, the effective annual interest rate would decrease further.

Self-Test

What are some factors that should be considered when choosing a bank?

What would a successful loan application package include?

Explain how a firm that expects to need funds during the coming year might make sure that the needed funds would be available. Would there be a cost for that assurance?

Explain the difference between a regular, or simple, interest loan and a discount interest loan.

Explain how you would calculate the approximate effective annual rate on an add-on interest installment loan.

What is a compensating balance? What impact will a compensating balance requirement typically have on the effective annual rate?

Commercial Paper

Commercial paper was briefly defined in Chapter 2, and later, in Chapter 9, we discussed this money market instrument and identified it as one of several short-term, relatively safe securities that are appropriate investments when a firm has temporary excess cash. However, the present chapter would be incomplete if we did not include a discussion of commercial paper as a *source* of short-term financing. Commercial paper consists of unsecured promissory notes of large, strong firms, in denominations of $100,000 or more, and it is sold primarily to other business firms, insurance companies, pension funds, money market funds, and banks. Although the amount of commercial paper outstanding is smaller than bank loans outstanding, this form of financing has grown rapidly in recent years. At the end of December 1992, there was more than $545 billion of commercial paper outstanding versus about $599 billion of bank loans to businesses.

Maturity and Cost

Maturities of commercial paper generally vary from 1 to 9 months from the original date of issue. The rates on commercial paper fluctuate with supply and demand conditions; they are determined in the marketplace and vary daily as conditions change. Recently, commercial paper rates have ranged from two to almost three percentage points below the stated prime rate and only slightly above the T-bill rate. For example, in May 1993 the average rate on 3-month commercial paper was 3.10 percent, while the stated prime rate was 6 percent. The T-bill rate at the time was 3.06 percent. Also, because compensating balances are not required for commercial paper, the *effective* cost differential versus the prime rate is still wider.

Use of Commercial Paper

The use of commercial paper is restricted to a comparatively small number of large firms that are exceptionally good credit risks. As we discussed in Chapter 9, purchasers of commercial paper hold it in their temporary marketable securities portfolios as liquidity reserves, and, therefore, safety is a paramount concern.

One potential problem with commercial paper is that a debtor who is in temporary financial difficulty may receive little help because commercial paper dealings are generally less personal than bank relationships. Thus, banks are generally more able and willing to help a good customer weather a temporary storm; that is, they are more likely to show loyalty to the firm, than are the commercial paper dealers. On the other hand, using commercial paper permits a corporation to tap a wide range of credit sources, including financial institutions outside its own area and industrial corporations across the country, and this can reduce interest costs. Like bonds, commercial paper is rated, and the quality of the commercial paper is reflected in the rating.

An illustration of the lack of loyalty in the commercial paper market is provided by the case of Olympia & York Developments Ltd. of Toronto, Canada. In March 1992 the real estate giant announced its intention to cancel two of its three commercial paper programs, totaling $780 million Canadian. Less than two weeks later the company had to retire the remainder of its commercial paper worth C$400 million. These were the first indications that O&Y, previously considered one of the soundest real estate companies in the world, was in serious financial trouble. Rumors had circulated in the Toronto market that O&Y was facing imminent collapse, and, although the company categorically

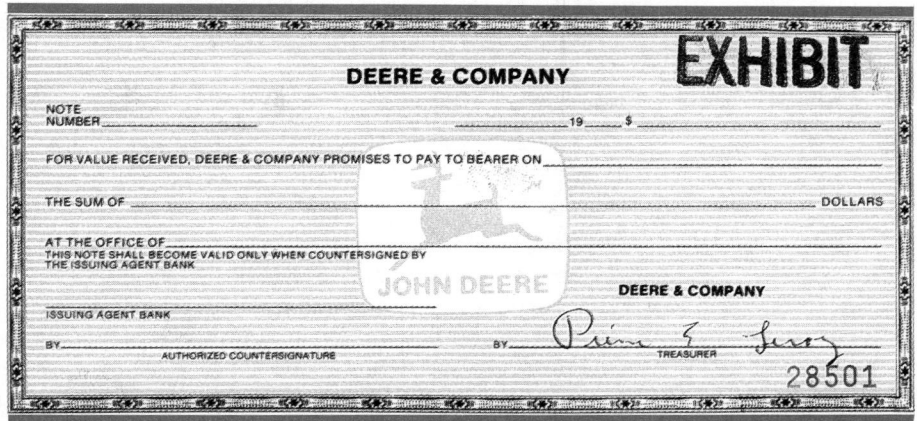

An increasingly popular form of short-term financing among large, secure firms, *commercial paper* looks very much like a bank check, except that it is issued by a large corporation. Commercial paper is really just a promise to pay the bearer. It is used only by firms that are excellent credit risks.

Source: Courtesy of Deere & Company.

denied these rumors, it simply could not roll over (renew) its outstanding commercial paper amid investor nervousness about its financial health.

Contributing factors to investor skittishness and reluctance to hold O&Y's short-term debt were the general slump in real estate worldwide as well as the fact that a Canadian rating agency had just announced a possible downgrading of O&Y's commercial paper. Olympia & York's inability to use this low-cost source of funds and its urgent need to replace the lost financing with other funds sparked a liquidity crisis for the firm. What followed was a scramble to sell assets and to line up additional bank financing to avoid a complete financial "meltdown." More than two dozen banks had loans outstanding to O&Y totaling nearly $20 billion; these lenders were now being asked to extend additional credit to the struggling firm.

By late March, 11 lenders had offered $89 million in interim financing (so-called bridge loans); however, other banks balked at allowing O&Y to delay debt repayments. Ultimately, O&Y's attempts to restructure its debt ran into a major stumbling block: in mid-April 1992 the firm's long-time ally, Canadian Imperial Bank of Commerce (CIBC) staged a full-scale rebellion. In spite of a 36-year relationship between O&Y and CIBC, the bank said no to extending $84 million in short-term financing, illustrating that even the loyalty of a bank is not something a firm can take for granted. Several other long-term "friendly" institutions also rebelled, among them J. P. Morgan, despite the fact that this U.S. bank served as adviser to the troubled real estate conglomerate. By mid-May 1992 O&Y had announced its decision to file for bankruptcy protection in Canada and the United States.[12]

---

[12]Although Olympia & York (U.S.A.) did not file for bankruptcy-court protection in the United States, several holding companies of Olympia & York Developments, through which it holds the U.S. subsidiary, are in Chapter 11.

Self-Test

What types of firms use commercial paper?

Give an advantage and a disadvantage to a firm's using commercial paper.

Use of Security In Short-Term Financing

secured loan
A loan backed by collateral, often inventories or receivables.

Thus far we have not addressed the question of whether loans should be secured. Commercial paper is never secured, but all other types of loans can be secured if this is deemed necessary or desirable. Given a choice, it is ordinarily better to borrow on an unsecured basis since the bookkeeping costs of **secured loans** are often high. However, small or weak firms may find that they can borrow only if they put up some type of security to protect the lender or that by offering security they can borrow at a much lower rate.

Several different kinds of collateral can be employed, including stocks or bonds, land or buildings, equipment, inventory, and accounts receivable. Marketable securities make excellent collateral, but few firms that need loans hold portfolios of stocks and bonds. Similarly, real property (land and buildings) and equipment are good forms of collateral, but they are generally used as security for long-term loans rather than for working capital loans. Therefore, most secured short-term business borrowing involves the use of accounts receivable and inventories as collateral.

To understand the use of security, consider the case of a San Jose hardware dealer who wants to modernize and expand his store. He requests a $200,000 bank loan. After examining his business's financial statements, the bank indicates that it will lend him a maximum of $100,000 and that the interest rate will be 12 percent discount, or an effective rate of 13.6 percent. The owner has a substantial personal portfolio of stocks, and he offers to put up $300,000 of high-quality stocks to support the $200,000 loan. The bank then grants the full $200,000 loan, and at a rate of only 10 percent, simple interest. The store owner also might have used his inventories or receivables as security for the loan, but processing costs would have been high.[13]

Uniform Commercial Code
A system of standards that simplifies and standardizes procedures for establishing loan security.

In the past, state laws varied greatly with regard to the use of security in financing. Today, however, all states except Louisiana operate under the **Uniform Commercial Code,** which standardized and simplified the procedures for establishing loan security. The heart of the Uniform Commercial Code is the *Security Agreement,* a standardized document or form on which the specific pledged assets are listed. The assets can be items of equipment, accounts receivable, or inventories. Procedures for using accounts receivable and inventories as security for short-term credit under the Uniform Commercial Code are described in Appendix 11A.

---

[13]The term "asset-based financing" is often used as a synonym for "secured financing." In recent years accounts receivable have also been used as security for long-term bonds, and this permits corporations to borrow from lenders such as pension funds rather than being restricted to banks and other traditional short-term lenders.

COMMERCIAL PAPER: AN "IFFY" SOURCE OF FUNDS

You have learned from this chapter that commercial paper is an important source of short-term financing but that it is available only to large, financially secure companies. Historically, commercial paper rates have been below the prime rate and only slightly above the T-bill rate, so strong companies have found commercial paper to be a very low cost source of short-term financing. Purchasers of commercial paper, typically insurance companies, pension funds, money market funds, and banks, hold the paper in their marketable securities portfolios as liquidity reserves; therefore, safety is extremely important to them, and that is why they are willing to sacrifice return for safety.

Although the cost to a commercial paper borrower is low, if a firm issues commercial paper and then finds itself in financial difficulty, it will receive little help in rolling over the short-term debt because commercial paper dealings are less personal than banking relationships. Corporations that have recently found out how difficult it is to roll over commercial paper include Olympia & York, Hees-Edper Enterprises, and Old Stone Corporation.

When O&Y experienced a run on its commercial paper, its problems were compounded by the fact that its commercial paper was not backed up by a bank line of credit, which would have assured holders that the paper could be redeemed. Instead, the paper was secured by buildings, the value of which is not very stable in a crumbling real estate market! The end result for O&Y was, as previously stated, bankruptcy and, for some holders of its commercial paper, large losses.

Historically, commercial paper has been a cheaper source of funding than certain other forms of short-term financing, such as banker's acceptances; however, because of O&Y's problems, this cost advantage has virtually disappeared. Further, companies that would have qualified for the market in the past are now find-

ing themselves frozen out. This is most unfortunate for somewhat marginal companies that depend heavily on the commercial paper market. Hees-Edper Enterprises, a diversified conglomerate, illustrates this point. One of the firm's executives stated, "A tremendous degree of unease has developed in the market . . . The historical cost advantage of using commercial paper is evaporating." Hees-Edper's costs have risen, and it has experienced difficulty in issuing commercial paper. The firm has reduced its average outstanding commercial paper by about $150 million.

During the last decade, Old Stone Corporation in Rhode Island, which had operated successfully for over 100 years, has gone from an international financial conglomerate with hundreds of offices to a company with a single local bank with a portfolio of bad loans. In the 1980s, Old Stone bought and revived troubled savings and loans, and it tripled in size and earned record profits. It had a reputation of cleaning up other bank's problems, and it maintained that reputation until the fall of 1991. At that time, however, federal regulators told Old Stone to concentrate on its own problems rather than rescuing other banks from theirs. It had overexpanded, concentrated too much on real estate, and been poorly managed. In addition, Old Stone had another problem—it depended too heavily on commercial paper.

In 1980, Old Stone began selling low-cost commercial paper to raise money, which it loaned to its finance company subsidiary, which, in turn, extended credit at much higher rates to consumers. This worked well for 10 years. The firm's commercial paper was bought by the Rhode Island pension fund, as well as area municipalities and colleges, and it offered a yield that was one-half to one percentage point higher than alternative short-term investments such as CDs. So, what was the problem? Old Stone was not doing anything that other corporations were not doing, or was it? Other companies sold *rated* paper to investors around the country (independent agencies such as Moody's and Standard & Poor's grade the quality, giving investors an idea about the risk of the investment). By contrast, Old Stone's commercial paper was sold locally—there was no demand for it

Sources: "Hees-Edper Cuts Its Commercial Paper," *The Financial Post,* June 9, 1992; "Heady Days' Hangover Threatens Survival," *The Providence Journal-Bulletin,* July 26, 1992; "Troubles Mounting at Olympia & York," *Chicago Tribune,* November 25, 1992; and "Another Creditor Group Backs O&Y Restructuring Plan," *The Financial Post,* January 14, 1993.

outside New England—because it was *not rated.* However, the paper's short maturity and its relatively high rate of return caused unsophisticated government officials to use public money to buy the firm's commercial paper.

In 1990, as the financial markets became increasingly unsettled, cities, towns, and state governments wanted investments that were more secure. Also, federal regulators became concerned about the effect of low-quality commercial paper on the pension funds' balance sheets. Regulators correctly saw commercial paper as a volatile source of funding—if it cannot be rolled over when it matures, then the firm has a difficult time trying to raise the funds from other sources.

In late 1991, Old Stone was unable to pay off more than $150 million of its commercial paper, of which $57 million was owed to Rhode Island's Investment Commission, which oversees the state's pension fund. A deal was finally struck, and the state bought Old Stone's bank and a portion of its finance company. This permitted Old Stone to pay off the remainder of its commercial paper.

Many Rhode Island constituents say that the state and municipal investments in Old Stone's commercial paper were a bad idea, one that bordered on being irresponsible. One candidate for state treasurer added, "You just don't purchase unrated paper. Not when you have a fiduciary duty to current and future retirees."

 Self-Test

Why is it ordinarily better to borrow on an unsecured basis rather than on a secured basis?

Why do firms borrow on a secured basis?

What types of collateral can be used for working capital loans? Is one type of collateral preferred over another?

What is the Security Agreement?

SMALL BUSINESS

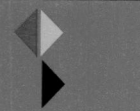

FINANCING RECEIVABLES DIRECTLY

The growing small firm that offers its customers credit will often find that its accounts receivable grow rapidly. As discussed in Chapter 10, growth usually entails a growing need to finance the firm's current assets, and accounts receivable are a major portion of current assets. Even though growth in accounts receivable places a strain on the firm's financing ability, it may also offer the firm special opportunities to obtain financing.

Accounts receivable constitute important asset accounts within the firm, assets that may be particularly liquid and thus attractive to a lender as collateral. Two common strategies for financing receivables that make use of these desirable features are (1) pledging

of receivables as collateral for debt and (2) factoring of receivables.

In the case of pledged receivables, the firm needing capital merely borrows funds and offers its receivables as collateral for the loan. For example, suppose Main Street Builders' Supply sells materials wholesale to builders. To increase its sales, Main Street offers trade credit terms of 2/10, net 60. Most of its customers elect to delay payment. As Main Street grows, it realizes that its cash reserves are being badly strained, making it difficult to finance inventory requirements. The firm arranges to pledge its receivables to the First West National Bank. The bank, in turn, agrees to review Main Street's major receivable accounts and to select the acceptable accounts to serve as collateral. The bank lends Main Street about 70 percent of the face value of the acceptable accounts, reducing some of the financial pressure the firm had experienced.

Pledging receivables makes sense when the customers of the small firm have better credit histories than the firm itself. However, the small business still bears the credit risk if its customers do not pay, and it receives only a fraction of the funds due from its accounts. Factoring receivables may be a better alternative.

Factoring involves the sale of receivables to a third party, called a factor, usually without recourse. The factor performs all of the credit services the firm might otherwise have to provide itself. It bears credit risk, it checks the creditworthiness of the customers, and it collects the receivable accounts themselves. Of course, it charges a price for these services.

The small firm employing a factor gets more than just credit. If Main Street Builders' Supply financed through a factor, the factor would take over Main Street's collection function almost entirely. It would be up to the factor to decide which of Main Street's customers merited credit. Also, if one of Main Street's customers, such as Reliable Homes, became unable to pay its debts, the factor rather than Main Street would absorb the loss. Of course, if Main Street wanted to sell to a customer that the factor found unacceptable, Main Street could still do so, but it would have to bear the credit risk itself.

Main Street must decide if it is worthwhile to use a comparatively high-cost factor or to maintain its own credit and collection services. The cost of funds through the factor must be compared with the direct cost of replacing all of the factor's services internally.

There is a good reason why many small firms find that using a factor's services is indeed an economical alternative; the small firm has its own special expertise (in Main Street's case, buying and selling building materials), whereas the factor has its own profession (credit services). Because managerial talent is often especially limited in small firms, it may turn out that

the factors' services are a bargain in comparison with the cost of the firm's maintaining its own credit services and exposing itself to credit risks.

The fees charged by the factor normally include an interest charge for lending the funds in advance of payment, a credit fee for evaluating customers' credit, and sometimes a charge that reflects the credit risk of the customers. Also, the factor usually does not advance all of the net proceeds, making an allowance for possible returns because of disputes between the buyer and seller.

To illustrate, suppose Main Street agrees to deliver $25,000 in building supplies to Reliable Homes on terms of net 30. Main Street approaches Factor Inc., a wholly owned subsidiary of the major local bank holding company, and Factor accepts the account. Factor charges Main Street interest at the rate of 12 percent, resulting in an interest charge of $1/12 \times 12\% \times \$25,000 = \$250$ on the $25,000 invoice amount. Factor charges an additional 2 percent as a credit fee, for another $500. Finally, Factor advances only $21,750 rather than $24,250, holding a 10 percent (or $2,500) allowance in case Reliable disputes the order or finds some problem with the merchandise.

At the end of the month, Reliable pays $24,000 directly to Factor after deducting $1,000 for defective sinks it had to return to Main Street. At that point Factor pays Main Street the remaining $1,500 due the firm on its net $24,000 sale of materials to Reliable Homes.

Considering the $750 total fee paid by Main Street to Factor for 30 days' use of $21,750, the factor seems to be an expensive source of financing. Main Street must consider, however, the cost of duplicating the additional services provided by the factor.

The firm's comparative advantage is delivering a product; the factor's advantage is in providing financial and credit services. In small firms with limited managerial resources and perhaps limited experience in monitoring and collecting credit accounts, factors may be economical sources of financing and credit services.

Summary

This chapter examined (1) different types of short-term credit available to firms, (2) decisions the financial manager must make in selecting among the types of short-term credit, and (3) the use of security to obtain credit. The key concepts covered are listed below:

▷ **Short-term credit** is any liability originally scheduled for payment within one year. The four major sources of short-term credit are (1) accruals, (2) accounts payable, (3) loans from commercial banks and finance companies, and (4) commercial paper.

Accruals, which are continually recurring short-term liabilities, represent free, spontaneous credit.

▷ **Accounts payable,** or **trade credit,** is the largest category of short-term debt. This credit arises spontaneously as a result of purchases on credit. Firms should use all the **free trade credit** they can obtain, but they should use **costly trade credit** only if it is less expensive than other forms of short-term debt. Suppliers often offer discounts to customers who pay within a stated discount period. The following equation may be used to calculate the approximate percentage cost, on an annual basis, of not taking discounts:

$$\begin{array}{l} \text{Approximate} \\ \text{percentage} \\ \text{cost} \end{array} = \frac{\text{Discount percent}}{100 - \begin{array}{c} \text{Discount} \\ \text{percent} \end{array}} \times \frac{360}{\begin{array}{c} \text{Days credit} \\ \text{is outstanding} \end{array} - \begin{array}{c} \text{Discount} \\ \text{period} \end{array}}.$$

▷ **Bank loans** are an important source of short-term credit, especially because banks provide nonspontaneous funds. Interest on bank loans may be quoted as **simple interest, discount interest,** or **add-on interest.** The effective annual rate on a discount or add-on loan always exceeds the stated nominal rate.

When a bank loan is approved, a **promissory note** is signed. It specifies: (1) the amount borrowed, (2) the percentage interest rate, (3) the repayment schedule, (4) the collateral, and (5) any other conditions to which the parties have agreed.

Lines of credit are agreements between the bank and the borrower indicating the maximum amount of credit the bank will extend to the borrower.

A **revolving credit agreement** is a formal line of credit often used by large firms. Because the bank in this case has a legal obligation to honor its commitment, it charges the firm a **commitment fee.**

The **prime rate** is a published interest rate charged by banks to very large, strong corporations.

▷ **Simple interest** is interest charged on the basis of the amount borrowed; the borrower receives the entire amount of loan and repays principal and interest at maturity. On a simple interest loan (without a compensating balance) the stated, or nominal, rate is also the effective annual rate.

Discount interest is interest calculated on the face amount of a loan but deducted in advance; the effective annual rate on a discount interest loan is greater than the stated, or nominal, rate because the borrower receives less than the face value of the loan.

Add-on interest is interest calculated and added to funds received to determine the face amount of an installment loan; the effective annual rate on an add-on interest loan is approximately double the stated, or nominal, rate because, on average, only half the face amount is available to the borrower.

▶ Banks often require borrowers to maintain **compensating balances,** which are required deposits set at between 10 and 20 percent of the loan amount. Compensating balances usually raise the effective annual rate of interest on bank loans.

▶ **Commercial paper** is unsecured short-term debt issued by large, financially strong corporations. Although the cost of commercial paper is lower than the cost of bank loans, commercial paper's maturity is limited to 270 days, and it can be used only by large firms with exceptionally strong credit ratings.

The major disadvantage to the commercial paper market as a source of short-term financing is that it is completely impersonal and lacks loyalty to any given issuer. A corporation that encounters temporary difficulties would not be able to roll over (renew) its commercial paper and might, therefore, face a liquidity crisis.

Resolution to
DECISION IN FINANCE

WILL YOUR BANKER BE THERE
WHEN YOU NEED HER?

By doing homework on the choice of the "right" bank for a firm, you are ensuring that the banker will be there when the company needs him or her the most—when the firm needs to borrow money. But, the "right" bank for one company is not necessarily the right bank for another company. When choosing a bank, ask individuals familiar with the business and industry (distributors, suppliers, trade groups, competitors, and the like) which banks understand the industry and are actively lending to similar companies. Reference checks should be done on the banker and his or her boss, as they will certainly do reference checks on the company before taking it on as a loan customer. It is important for the firm to ask for the bank's financial statements, to make sure that the bank has "staying power" during hard times. In partic-

ular, it is important to do business with a profitable bank since a bank that is making money is more likely to take risks than an unprofitable one, especially given the banking industry's current regulatory climate.

Competition among banks cannot hurt either, so a representative of the firm should visit several banks and ask what additional kinds of services the bank offers besides making loans. Often, a good banking relationship is based on "chemistry," so it is important that you feel comfortable with your banker. It is important to get to know him or her. In addition, there is nothing wrong with doing business with two banks at the same time, and letting them know that you are doing it. One bank can be the firm's primary bank; the other can be its secondary bank. Competition never hurts!

The firm should provide the prospective bank with a copy of its most recent, and also its projected, income statement, balance sheet, and

Source: "How to Make Sure a Banker Is There When Needed," *The San Francisco Chronicle,* May 4, 1992.

statement of cash flows. It might also be useful to provide a scenario analysis for the financial statements, showing what they would look like under best-case, worst-case, and most-likely-case conditions. But if projections are provided, be prepared for some tough questions regarding the assumptions you used. A cynical—but good—banker once told the authors that he had never seen a poor projection, even by companies that went bankrupt shortly after the projections were made. Still, carefully prepared and defendable projections will show the bank that you have done your homework.

After a firm has chosen a bank, it should not make itself scarce until the time comes when it needs a loan. The banker should be kept informed of the firm's progress and should be visited often. Remember, you want to build a trusting relationship, and regular reports and visits will go a long way in creating that relationship. Because you are trying to build a good relationship, it is important to never mislead your

banker, either intentionally or unintentionally. Bankers (and almost everyone else in business) hate surprises!

The firm should establish a line of credit, even if it is not needed, and the line should be used —it should be drawn down occasionally and then paid back on time. This will establish a good payment history, which is important to a loan committee. Finally, if for some reason you are unable to make a scheduled loan payment, the bank should be notified immediately and presented with a report outlining the problem, how the company got in the position it now finds itself in, and what remedial action is being taken. Pro forma financial statements will definitely be needed here.

The important point to remember about banks is that they operate in a competitive environment, just like any other company. Banks have to compete to sell their products, to get deposits, and to sell their services. So, comparison shopping is a must!

Questions

11-1   "Firms can control their accruals within fairly wide limits; depending on the cost of accruals, financing from this source will be increased or decreased." Discuss.

11-2   Is it true that both trade credit and accruals represent a spontaneous source of capital for financing growth? Explain.

11-3   Is it true that most firms are able to obtain some free trade credit and that additional trade credit is often available, but at a cost? Explain.

11-4   What is meant by the term *stretching accounts payable?*

11-5   The chapter indicated that required compensating balances usually increase the cost of a bank loan. In what situation would a compensating balance not increase the cost of a bank loan?

11-6   The availability of bank credit is often more important to a small firm than to a large one. Why?

11-7   From the standpoint of the borrower, is long-term or short-term credit riskier? Explain.

11-8   If long-term credit exposes a borrower to less risk, why would people or firms borrow on a short-term basis?

11-9   What kinds of firms use commercial paper? Could Mamma and Pappa Gus's Corner Grocery borrow using this form of credit?

11-10   Suppose a firm can obtain funds by borrowing at the prime rate or by selling commercial paper. If the prime rate is 7 percent, what is a reasonable estimate for the cost of commercial paper?

11-11   Given that commercial paper interest rates are generally lower than bank loan rates to a given borrower, why might firms which are capable of selling commercial paper also use bank credit?

Self-Test Problem

ST-1   Kitty Burton, owner of MovieTime Rentals, is negotiating with Mechanics and Merchants Bank for a $30,000, 1-year loan. The bank has offered Burton the following alternatives. Rank the alternatives from the one with the lowest effective annual interest rate to the one with the highest rate. The firm will hold no balances in the bank if it does not obtain a loan from the bank.
   1.   A 13 percent annual rate on a simple interest loan, with no compensating balance required, interest and principal due at the end of the year.
   2.   An 8 percent annual rate on a simple interest loan, with a 15 percent compensating balance required and interest due at the end of the year.
   3.   A 7 percent annual rate on a discounted loan with a 15 percent compensating balance.
   4.   Interest is figured as 8 percent add-on interest, with the $30,000 principal to be paid off in monthly installments during the year.

Problems

11-1   Calculate the implicit cost of nonfree trade credit under each of the following terms.
Cost of trade credit   Assume that the discount is not taken and that payment is made on the due date.
   a. 1/10, net 30.
   b. 1/15, net 30.
   c. 2/10, net 30.
   d. 2/15, net 40.
   e. 1/10, net 60.
   f. 3/10, net 60.
   g. 3/10, net 20.
   h. What conclusion may be drawn from the above calculations?

11-2   Oaksdale Manufacturing buys on terms of 3/15, net 60, but actually pays on the 20th
Cost of credit   day and *still* takes the discount.
   a. What is the cost of its nonfree trade credit?
   b. Does it receive more or less trade credit than it would if it paid within 15 days?
   c. When terms are 3/15, net 60 as stated above, is the practice of paying on Day 20 and *taking* the discount ethical?

11-3   Suppose Sullivan Auto Parts makes purchases of $2.5 million per year on terms of
Cash discounts   2/15, net 30. It takes discounts.
   a. What is the average amount of its accounts payable, net of discounts? (Assume the $2.5 million purchases are net of discounts; that is, gross purchases are $2,551,020, discounts are $51,020, and net purchases are $2.5 million. Also, use 360 days in a year.)
   b. Is there a cost to the trade credit the firm uses?
   c. If it did not take discounts, what would Sullivan's average payables be, and what would be the cost of this nonfree trade credit if the firm pays on the 30th day?

11-4   Nugroho Appliances Inc. has two primary sources of short-term debt: trade credit and
Short-term financing   bank loans. One supplier, which supplies Nugroho with $50,000 of materials a year, offers the firm terms of 2/10, net 50.
   a. What are Nugroho's net daily purchases from this supplier?

b. What is the average level of Nugroho's accounts payable to this supplier if the discount is taken? What is the average level if the discount is not taken? What are the amounts of free credit and costly credit under both discount policies?

c. What is the approximate cost of the costly trade credit?

11-5
Cost of bank loan

You plan to borrow $100,000 from the bank. The bank offers to lend you the money at an 11 percent interest rate on a 1-year loan. What is the true, or effective, annual rate of interest for **(a)** simple interest, **(b)** discount interest, and **(c)** add-on interest, if the loan is a 12-month installment loan?

11-6
Cost of bank loans

Kim Haswell of Haswell Office Equipment is negotiating a $500,000, 1-year working capital loan with four area banks. The banks have provided the loan opportunities listed below. What is the effective annual interest rate being offered by each bank? Unless otherwise required by the terms of the loan arrangement, Haswell prefers to keep cash balances as close to zero as possible.

a. First National Bank offered a 14 percent loan with principal and interest due at the end of 1 year. No compensating balance is required.

b. Second National Bank would lend at 11 percent stated interest if Ms. Haswell kept a 20 percent compensating balance. Ms. Haswell had not planned to keep any borrowed funds in the bank.

c. Third National Bank suggested it would approve a loan at 11 percent if Ms. Haswell kept a 10 percent compensating balance and discounted the loan.

d. Fourth National Bank would lend to the company at 9 percent if the principal and interest were paid in 12 equal monthly installments (add-on interest).

11-7
Cost of bank loan

Angvick & Andersen (A&A) needs to purchase $816,000 in inventory. The local bank agrees to the loan with a stated interest rate of 9 percent and a compensating balance of 15 percent. The loan will mature in 1 year.

a. What is the loan's effective annual interest rate if A&A had not planned to keep any of the borrowed funds in the bank?

b. How much interest will A&A pay if it agrees to the loan as stated? (*Hint:* Remember that A&A needs the loan proceeds to be $816,000.)

11-8
Cost of bank loan

Cox Electric wishes to borrow $100,000 for one year. Its bank agrees to loan Cox the money at 13.5 percent, on the condition that the firm keep a 10 percent compensating balance in a 4 percent savings account for the duration of the loan. If Cox usually keeps a zero account balance, what is the effective annual cost of this loan? (*Hint:* Cox only needs $90,000.)

11-9
Trade credit versus bank credit

Jim Schultz of The Lamp Gallery is worried. Cash flow problems have prevented him from taking a 2/15, net 40, discount from his trade creditors. In fact, he has stretched payment to 55 days after purchase, and his suppliers are threatening a cutoff of credit. First Western National Bank has agreed to lend enough money to alleviate the firm's cash flow problems and to allow Jim to take all discounts offered. The loan provides a 13 percent stated interest rate and requires a 20 percent compensating balance.

a. What is the firm's effective annual cost of not taking discounts?

b. What is the effective annual cost of the bank loan offered?

c. What should Jim do? Be sure to include a brief discussion of the hard-to-quantify cost of the firm's current, unethical practice of stretching accounts payable.

11-10
Cost of bank loan

Phil Danilov of Danilov Manufacturing is borrowing $200,000 from his local bank. Terms of the loan require a 15 percent compensating balance to qualify for an 11 percent stated interest rate. If Mr. Danilov always keeps his bank cash balance as close to zero as possible, what is the effective annual cost of the loan? Interest and principal are due at the end of the year.

11-11
Cost of bank loan

Refer to Problem 11-10. Assume that rather than a zero balance, Mr. Danilov, as a matter of company policy, always keeps $6,000 in the company's checking account as a cushion against unexpected needs. These precautionary balances may be used as part of the compensating balance. What is the effective annual cost of the loan under these conditions?

11-12

Trade credit versus bank credit

Jack Rivers Inc. has a cash flow problem that is preventing the firm from taking the trade discounts it is offered. The terms of sale are 3/10, net 30, but Jack Rivers has been unable to pay before 70 days after purchases are made. Understandably, its suppliers are threatening to hold the company to its credit terms or withhold future credit. Jack Rivers has discussed the matter with its bank, and the bank will offer it a 16.5 percent discounted loan that requires a 15 percent compensating balance.

a. What is the effective annual cost of (1) paying payables on the 30th day; (2) continuing to pay on the 70th day; and (3) taking the bank loan?

b. What should Jack Rivers do?

11-13

Cost of revolving credit agreement

The Metroplex Corporation has entered into a revolving credit agreement with Atlantic National Bank. Terms of the agreement allow the firm to borrow up to $30 million as the funds are needed. The firm will pay ¼ percent for the unused balance and prime plus 2 percent for the funds that are actually borrowed. The prime rate is expected to remain at 6 percent during the period covered by the loan. Determine the effective annual percentage cost under the revolving credit agreement if **(a)** no funds are used; **(b)** $9 million is borrowed; **(c)** $15 million is borrowed; **(d)** $24 million is borrowed; **(e)** the entire $30 million is borrowed.

11-14

Trade credit versus bank credit

Acevedo Brothers Inc. projects an increase in sales from $2.5 million to $3 million, but the company needs an additional $500,000 of assets to support this expansion. The money can be obtained from the bank at an interest rate of 10 percent discount interest. Alternatively, Acevedo Brothers can finance the expansion by no longer taking discounts, thus increasing accounts payable. Acevedo Brothers purchases under terms of 2/10, net 30, but it can delay payment for an additional 30 days, paying in 60 days and thus becoming 30 days past due, without penalty at this time.

a. Based strictly on an interest rate comparison, how should Acevedo Brothers finance its expansion? Show your work.

b. What additional qualitative factors should Acevedo Brothers consider in reaching a decision?

11-15

Bank financing

Hogan Construction had sales of $2 million last year and earned a 3 percent return, after taxes, on sales. Although its terms of purchase are net 30 days, its accounts payable represent 60 days' purchases. The president of the company is seeking to increase the company's bank borrowings to become current in meeting its trade obligations (that is, have 30 days' payables outstanding). The company's balance sheet follows.

a. How much bank financing is needed to eliminate past-due accounts payable?

b. Would you as a bank loan officer make the loan? Explain your answer. (*Hint:* You have the data needed to calculate a few relevant ratios.)

Hogan Construction: Balance Sheet

Cash	$ 25,000	Accounts payable	$ 300,000
Accounts receivable	225,000	Bank loans	250,000
Inventory	550,000	Accruals	125,000
Current assets	$ 800,000	Current liabilities	$ 675,000
Land and buildings	250,000	Mortgage bond	250,000
Equipment	250,000	Common stock	125,000
		Retained earnings	250,000
Total assets	$1,300,000	Total liabilities and equity	$1,300,000

11-16

Cost of trade credit

Elaine's Fashions Inc. sells on terms of 2/10, net 40. Annual sales last year were $3.6 million. Half of Elaine's customers pay on the tenth day and take discounts.

a. If accounts receivable averaged $350,000, what is Elaine's days sales outstanding *on nondiscount sales?*

b. What rate of return is Elaine's Fashions earning on its nondiscount receivables, where this rate of return is defined as being equal to the cost of this trade credit to the nondiscount customers?

11-17

Short-term financing analysis

The Bayless-Curry Corporation (BCC) has the following balance sheet:

Bayless-Curry Corporation: Balance Sheet

Cash	$ 50,000	Accounts payable[a]	$ 500,000
Accounts receivable	450,000	Notes payable	50,000
Inventories	750,000	Accruals	50,000
Total current assets	$1,250,000	Total current liabilities	$ 600,000
		Long-term debt	150,000
Net fixed assets	750,000	Common equity	1,250,000
Total assets	$2,000,000	Total liabilities and equity	$2,000,000

[a]Stated net of discounts, even though discounts may not be taken.

BCC buys on terms of 1/10, net 30, but it has not been taking discounts and has actually been paying in 70 days rather than 30 days. Now BCC's suppliers are threatening to stop shipments unless the company begins making prompt payments (that is, pays in 30 days or less). BCC can borrow on a 1-year note (call this a current liability) from its bank at a rate of 9 percent, discount interest, with a 20 percent compensating balance required. (All of the cash now on hand is needed for transactions; it cannot be used as part of the compensating balance.)

a. Determine what action BCC should take by (1) calculating the cost of nonfree trade credit and (2) calculating the effective, annual cost of the bank loan.

b. Based on your decision in Part a, construct a pro forma balance sheet. (*Hint:* You will need to include an account called "prepaid interest" under current assets. Also, ignore discounts lost, if any, in your calculations.)

11-18

Alternative financing arrangements

CampingLand Inc. estimates that because of the seasonal nature of its business, it will require an additional $1 million of cash for the month of June. CampingLand has the following four options available for raising the needed funds:

(1) Establish a 1-year line of credit for $1 million with a commercial bank. The commitment fee will be 0.5 percent per year on the unused portion, and the interest charge on the used funds will be 8 percent per annum. Assume that the funds are needed only in June, and that there are 30 days in June and 360 days in the year.

(2) Forgo the trade discount of 2/10, net 60, on $1 million of purchases during June.

(3) Issue $1 million of 30-day commercial paper at a 4.5 percent per annum interest rate. The total transactions fee, including the cost of a backup credit line, on using commercial paper is 0.5 percent of the amount of the issue.

(4) Issue $1 million of 60-day commercial paper at a 4 percent per annum interest rate, plus a transactions fee of 0.5 percent. Since the funds are required for only 30 days, the excess funds ($1 million) can be invested in 4.3 percent per annum marketable securities for the month of July. The total transactions cost of purchasing and selling the marketable securities is 0.4 percent of the amount of the issue.

a. What is the cost of each financing arrangement?

b. Is the source with the lowest expected cost necessarily the one to select? Why or why not?

Solution to Self-Test Problem

ST-1 Effective annual rates:

1. $\dfrac{0.13(\$30,000)}{\$30,000} = \dfrac{\$3,900}{\$30,000} = 0.13 = 13\%.$

2. $\dfrac{0.08(\$30,000)}{\$30,000 - \$4,500} = \dfrac{\$2,400}{\$25,500} = 0.0941 = 9.41\%.$

Alternative solution:

$\dfrac{8\%}{1.0 - 0.15} = 9.41\%.$

3. $\dfrac{0.07(\$30,000)}{\$30,000 - \$2,100 - \$4,500} = \dfrac{\$2,100}{\$23,400} = 0.0897 = 8.97\%.$

Alternative solution:

$\dfrac{7\%}{1.0 - 0.07 - 0.15} = 8.97\%.$

4. $\dfrac{0.08(\$30,000)}{\$30,000/2} = \dfrac{\$2,400}{\$15,000} = 0.16 = 16\%.$

Use of Security in Short-Term Financing

APPENDIX 11A

Procedures under the Uniform Commercial Code for using accounts receivable and inventories as security for short-term credit are described in this appendix. As noted in the chapter, secured short-term loans involve quite a bit of paperwork and other administrative costs; hence they are relatively expensive. However, weak firms often find that they can borrow only if they put up some type of collateral to protect the lender, or they find that by using security they can borrow at a lower rate than would otherwise be possible.

pledging of accounts receivable

Putting accounts receivable up as security for a loan.

recourse

A situation in which the lender can require payment from the selling firm if an account receivable is uncollectible.

Accounts Receivable Financing

Accounts receivable financing involves either the pledging of receivables or the selling of receivables (called factoring). The **pledging of accounts receivable** is characterized by the fact that the lender not only has a claim against the receivables but also has **recourse** to the borrower: if the person or firm that bought the goods does not pay, the selling firm must take the loss. Therefore, the risk of default on the pledged accounts receivable remains with the borrower. The buyer of the goods is not ordinarily notified about the pledging of the receivables. The financial institution that lends on the security of accounts receivable is generally either a commercial bank or a large industrial finance company.

factoring

Outright sale of accounts receivable.

Factoring, or *selling accounts receivable,* involves the purchase of accounts receivable by the lender, generally without recourse to the borrower, which means that if the buyer of the goods does not pay for them, the lender rather than the seller of the goods takes the loss. Under a factoring arrangement, the buyer of the goods is typically notified of the transfer and is asked to make payments directly to the financial institution. Because the factoring firm assumes the risk of default on bad accounts, it must make the credit check. Accordingly, factors provide not only money but also a credit department. Incidentally, the same financial institutions that make loans against pledged receivables also serve as factors. Thus, depending on the circumstances and the wishes of the firm, a financial institution will provide either form of receivables financing.

Procedure for Pledging Accounts Receivable

The financing of accounts receivable is initiated by a legally binding agreement between the seller of the goods and the financing institution. The agreement sets forth in detail the procedures to be followed and the legal obligations of both parties. Once the working relationship has been established, the seller periodically takes a batch of invoices to the financing institution. The lender reviews the invoices and makes credit appraisals of the buyers. Invoices of companies that do not meet the lender's credit standards are not accepted for pledging.

The financial institution seeks to protect itself at every phase of the operation. First, it attempts to select only sound invoices. Second, if the buyer of the goods does not pay the invoice, the lender still has recourse against the seller of the goods. Third, additional protection is afforded the lender because the loan generally will be made for less than 100 percent of the pledged receivables; for example, the lender may advance the selling firm only 75 percent of the amount of the pledged invoices.

Procedure for Factoring Accounts Receivable

The procedures used in factoring are somewhat different from those used for pledging. Again, an agreement between the seller and the factor specifies legal obligations and procedural arrangements. When the seller receives an order from a buyer, a credit approval slip is written and immediately sent to the factoring company for a credit check. If the factor approves the credit, shipment is made and the invoice is stamped to notify the buyer to make payment directly to the factoring company. If the factor does not approve the sale, the seller generally refuses to fill the order; if the sale is made anyway, the factor will not buy the account.

The factor normally performs three functions: (1) credit checking, (2) lending, and (3) risk bearing. However, the seller can select various combinations of these functions by changing provisions in the factoring agreement. For example, a small or medium-sized firm may have the factor perform the credit-checking and risk-bearing functions and thus avoid having to establish a credit department. The factor's charge for this service may well be less costly than maintaining a credit department that would have excess capacity for the firm's small credit volume. At the same time, if the selling firm uses someone who is not really qualified for the job of credit checking, then that person's lack of education, training, and experience could result in excessive losses.

Thus, the seller may have the factor perform the credit-checking and risk-taking functions but *not* the lending function. The following procedure illustrates the handling of a $10,000 order under this arrangement. The factor checks and approves the invoices. The goods are shipped on terms of net 30. Payment is made to the factor, who remits to the seller. If the buyer defaults, however, the $10,000 must still be remitted to the seller, and if the $10,000 is never paid, the factor will sustain a $10,000 loss. Note that in this situation the factor does not remit funds to the seller until either they are received from the buyer of the goods or the credit period has expired. Thus, the factor does not supply any credit.

Now consider the more typical situation in which the factor performs the lending, risk-bearing, and credit-checking functions. The goods are shipped, and even though payment is not due for 30 days, the factor immediately makes funds available to the seller. Suppose $10,000 of goods are shipped. Further, assume that the factoring commission (sometimes called a credit fee) for credit checking and risk bearing is 2.5 percent of the invoice price, or $250, and that the interest expense is computed at a 9 percent annual rate on the invoice balance, or $75.[1] The seller's accounting entry is as follows:

Cash	$ 9,175	
Interest expense	75	
Factoring commission	250	
Reserve due from factor on collection of account	500	
Accounts receivable		$10,000

The $500 due from the factor upon collection of the account is a reserve established by the factor to cover disputes between the seller and buyers over damaged goods, goods returned by the buyers to the seller, and the failure to make an outright sale of goods. The reserve is paid to the selling firm when the factor collects on the account.

Factoring is normally a continuous process instead of the single cycle just described. The selling firm receives an order; it transmits this order to the factor for approval; upon approval, the firm ships the goods; the factor advances to the seller the invoice amount minus withholdings; the buyer pays the factor when payment is due; and the factor periodically remits any excess in the reserve to the seller of the goods. Once a routine has been established, a continuous circular flow of goods and funds takes place between the seller, the buyers of the goods, and the factor. Thus, once the factoring agreement is in force, funds from this source are *spontaneous,* in the sense that an increase in sales will automatically generate additional credit.

Cost of Receivables Financing

Both accounts receivable pledging and factoring are convenient and advantageous, but they can be costly — especially factoring. The credit-checking and risk-bearing fee is 1 to 3 percent of the dollar amount of invoices accepted by the factor, and it may be even more if the buyers are poor credit risks. The cost of money is reflected in the interest rate (usually two to three percentage points over the prime rate) charged on the unpaid balance of the funds advanced by the factor or charged by the lender on a loan secured by pledged receivables.

Evaluation of Receivables Financing

It cannot be said categorically that accounts receivable financing is always either a good or a bad way to raise funds. Among the advantages is, first, the flexibility of this source of financing. As the firm's sales expand, and more financing is needed, a larger volume of invoices is generated automatically. Because the dollar amounts of invoices vary directly

[1]Because the interest is for only 1 month, we multiply 1/12 of the stated rate, 9 percent, by the $10,000 invoice price:

$$(1/12)(0.09)($10,000) = $75.$$

Note that the effective rate of interest is really above 9 percent because (1) the term is for less than one year and (2) since a discounting procedure is used, the borrower does not get the full $10,000. In many instances, however, the factoring contract calls for interest to be computed on the invoice price less the factoring commission and the reserve account.

with sales, the amount of readily available financing increases at the same time. Second, receivables provide security for a loan that might otherwise not be granted. Third, factoring can provide the services of a credit department that might otherwise be available to the firm only at a higher cost.

Accounts receivable financing also has disadvantages. First, when invoices are numerous and each dollar amount is relatively small, the administrative costs involved may be excessive. Second, some of a firm's trade creditors may refuse to sell to it on credit if it factors or pledges its receivables. This refusal is due in part to the fact that for a long time accounts receivable financing was frowned upon by most trade creditors as a sign of a firm's unsound financial position. It is no longer regarded in this light by most firms because many financially sound firms engage in receivables factoring or pledging. Another reason for refusal is that since accounts receivables represent a firm's most liquid noncash assets (after marketable securities), factoring removes these liquid assets and accordingly weakens the position of other creditors.

Future Use of Receivables Financing

We will make a prediction at this point: in the future, accounts receivable financing will increase in relative importance. Computer technology is rapidly advancing toward the point where credit records of individuals and firms can be kept on disks and magnetic tapes. For example, one device used by retailers consists of a box which, when an individual's magnetic credit card is inserted, gives a signal that the credit is "good" and that a bank is willing to "buy" the receivable created as soon as the store completes the sale. The cost of handling invoices will be greatly reduced over present-day costs because the new systems will be so highly automated. This will make it possible to use accounts receivable financing for very small sales, and it will reduce the cost of all receivables financing. The net result will be a marked expansion of accounts receivable financing. In fact, when consumers use credit cards such as MasterCard or Visa, the seller is in effect factoring receivables. The seller normally receives the amount of the purchase, minus a percentage fee, the next working day. The buyer receives about 30 days' free credit, at which time she or he remits payment to the credit card company or sponsoring bank.

Inventory Financing

A substantial amount of credit is secured by business inventories. If a firm is a relatively good credit risk, the mere existence of the inventory may be a sufficient basis for receiving an unsecured loan. However, if the firm is a relatively poor risk, the lending institution may insist on security, which often takes the form of a *blanket lien* against the inventory. Alternatively, *trust receipts* or *warehouse receipts* can be used to secure the loan. These methods of using inventories as security are discussed in the following sections.

inventory blanket lien

A lending institution's claim on all of the borrower's inventories as security for a loan.

Inventory Blanket Liens.   The **inventory blanket lien** gives the lending institution a lien against all the borrower's inventories. However, the borrower is free to sell inventories; thus the value of the collateral can be reduced below the level that existed when the loan was granted.

trust receipt

An instrument acknowledging that the borrower holds certain goods in trust for the lender.

Trust Receipts.   Because of the inherent weakness of the blanket lien for inventory financing, another procedure for inventory financing has been developed — the **trust receipt.** A trust receipt is an instrument acknowledging that the borrower holds the goods in trust for the lender. With this method, the borrowing firm, as a condition for receiving funds from the lender, signs and delivers a trust receipt for the goods. The goods can be stored in a public warehouse or held on the borrower's premises. The trust receipt states that the goods are held in trust for the lender, or are segregated on the borrower's premises on behalf of the lender, and that any proceeds from the sale of the goods must be transmitted to the lender at the end of each day. Automobile dealer financing is one of the best examples of trust receipt financing.

One defect of trust receipt financing is the requirement that a trust receipt must be issued for specific goods. For example, if the security is autos in a dealer's inventory, the trust receipts must indicate the cars by registration number. To validate its trust receipts, the lending institution must send someone to the borrower's premises periodically to see that the auto numbers are correctly listed. Such care is necessary because auto dealers who are in financial difficulty have been known to sell the cars backing trust receipts and then use the funds obtained for other operations rather than to repay the bank. Problems are compounded if the borrower has a number of different locations, especially if they are separated geographically from the lender. To offset these inconveniences, *warehousing* has come into wide use as a method of securing loans with inventory.

warehouse receipt financing

An arrangement under which the lending institution employs a third party to exercise control over the borrower's inventory and to act as the lender's agent.

Warehouse Receipts.   Like trust receipts, **warehouse receipt financing** uses inventory as security. A *public warehouse* is an independent third-party operation engaged in the business of storing goods. Under a warehouse receipt financing arrangement, the lending institution employs the warehousing company to exercise control over the inventory and to act as its agent. Items that must age, such as tobacco and liquor, are often financed and stored in public warehouses. The value of the inventory increases as it ages, so the lender's position improves with the passage of time. However, at times a public warehouse is not practical because of the bulkiness of goods, the expense of transporting them to and from the borrower's premises, or the need for the borrower to process them on a continuous basis. In such cases, a *field warehouse* may be established on the borrower's grounds. The field warehouse arrangement is overseen by an independent third party, the field warehouse company, just as a public warehouse is run by a warehousing firm.

Field warehousing can be illustrated by a simple example. Suppose a firm which has iron stacked in an open yard on its premises needs a loan. A field warehousing concern can place a temporary fence around the iron, erecting a sign stating: "This is a field warehouse supervised by the Smith Field Warehousing Corporation," and then assigning an employee to supervise and control the inventory.

The example illustrates the three essential elements for the establishment of a field warehouse: (1) public notification, (2) physical control of the inventory, and (3) supervision by a custodian of the field warehousing concern. When the field warehousing operation is relatively small, the third condition is sometimes violated by hiring one of the borrower's employees to supervise the inventory. This practice is viewed as undesirable by most lending institutions because there is no control over the collateral by a person independent of the borrowing firm.[2]

The procedure involved in a field warehouse financing operation is best described by an actual case. A Florida vegetable cannery was interested in financing its operations by bank borrowing. The cannery had sufficient funds to finance 15 to 20 percent of its operations during the canning season. These funds were adequate to purchase and process only an initial batch of vegetables. As the cans were put into boxes and rolled into the storerooms, the cannery needed additional funds for both raw materials and labor.

---

[2]This absence of independent control was the main cause of a breakdown that resulted in more than $200 million in losses on loans to the Allied Crude Vegetable Oil Company by Bank of America and other banks. American Express Field Warehousing Company was handling the operation, but it hired men from Allied's own staff as custodians. Their dishonesty was not discovered because of another breakdown — the fact that the American Express touring inspector did not actually take a physical inventory of the warehouses. As a consequence, the swindle was not discovered until losses running into the hundreds of millions of dollars had been suffered. See N. C. Miller, *The Great Salad Oil Swindle* (Baltimore, Md.: Penguin Books, 1965), 72–77.

Because of the cannery's poor credit rating, the bank decided that a field warehousing operation would be necessary to secure its loans.

The field warehouse was established, and the custodian notified the bank of the description, by number, of the boxes of canned vegetables in storage and under warehouse control. With this inventory as collateral, the bank established a line of credit for the cannery on which it could draw. From this point on, the bank financed the operations. The cannery needed only enough cash to initiate the cycle. Farmers brought in more vegetables; the cannery processed them; the cans were boxed, and the boxes were put into the field warehouse; field warehouse receipts were drawn up and sent to the bank; the bank increased the credit line for the cannery on the basis of additional collateral; and the cannery could draw on the credit line to continue the cycle.

Of course, the cannery's ultimate objective was to sell the canned vegetables. As it received purchase orders, it transmitted them to the bank, and the bank directed the custodian to release the inventories. It was agreed that, as remittances were received by the cannery, they would be turned over to the bank. These remittances by the cannery thus paid off the loans.

Typically, a seasonal pattern exists in this type of financing. In the above example, at the beginning of the harvesting and canning season, the cannery's cash needs and loan requirements began to rise, and they reached a maximum level at the end of the canning season. It was expected that well before the new canning season began, the cannery would have sold a sufficient volume to have paid off the loan completely. If for some reason the cannery had a bad year, the bank might carry part of the loan over for another year to enable the company to work off its inventory.

Acceptable Products.   In addition to canned goods, which account for about 17 percent of all field warehousing loans, many other types of products provide a basis for field warehouse financing. Some of these are miscellaneous groceries, which represent about 13 percent; lumber products, about 10 percent; and coal and coke, about 6 percent. These products are relatively nonperishable and are sold in well-developed, organized markets. Nonperishability protects the lender if it should have to take over the security. For this reason, a bank would not make a field warehousing loan on perishables such as fresh fish; however, frozen fish, which can be stored for a long time, can be field warehoused. An organized market aids the lender in disposing of an inventory that it takes over. Banks are not interested in going into the canning or the fish business. They want to be able to dispose of an inventory with a minimum expenditure of time.

Cost of Financing.   The fixed costs of a field warehousing arrangement are relatively high; such financing is, therefore, not suitable for a very small firm. If a field warehousing company sets up the field warehouse itself, it will typically set a minimum charge of about $25,000 a year, plus about 1 to 2 percent of the amount of credit extended to the borrower. Furthermore, the financing institution will charge an interest rate of two to three percentage points over the prime rate. An efficient field warehousing operation requires a minimum inventory of about $1 million.

Evaluation of Inventory Financing.   The use of inventory financing, especially field warehouse financing, as a source of funds for business firms has many advantages. First, the amount of funds available is flexible because the financing is tied to the growth of inventories, which in turn is related directly to financing needs. Second, the field warehousing arrangement increases the acceptability of inventories as loan collateral. Some inventories simply would not be accepted by a bank as security without a field warehousing arrangement. Third, the necessity for inventory control and safekeeping, as well as the use of specialists in warehousing, often results in improved warehousing practices, which in turn save handling costs, insurance charges, theft losses, and so on. Thus, field warehousing companies often have saved money for firms in spite of the financing charges. The major disadvantages of a field warehousing operation include the paperwork, physical separation requirements, and, for small firms, the fixed-cost element.

Problems

11A-1
Factoring receivables

Fleckman Industries is considering two methods of raising working capital: (1) a commercial bank loan secured by accounts receivable and (2) factoring accounts receivable. Fleckman's bank has agreed to lend the firm 75 percent of its average monthly accounts receivable balance of $250,000 at an annual interest rate of 9 percent. The loan would be discounted, and a 20 percent compensating balance would also be required.

A factor has agreed to purchase Fleckman's accounts receivable and to advance 85 percent of the balance to the firm. The factor would charge a 3.5 percent factoring commission and annual interest of 9 percent on the invoice price, minus both the factoring commission and the reserve account. The monthly interest payment would be deducted from the advance. If Fleckman chooses the factoring arrangement, it can eliminate its credit department and reduce operating expenses by $4,000 per month. In addition, bad debt losses of 2 percent of the monthly receivables will be avoided.
a. What is the annual cost associated with each financial arrangement?
b. Discuss some considerations other than cost that might influence management's decision between factoring and a commercial bank loan.

11A-2
Inventory financing

Because of crop failures last year, Sunset Valley Produce Inc. has no funds available to finance its canning operations during the next 6 months. It estimates that it will require $1,800,000 for inventory financing during the period. One alternative is to establish a 6-month, $2,250,000 line of credit with terms of 9 percent annual interest on the used portion, a 1 percent commitment fee on the unused portion, and a $450,000 compensating balance at all times.

Expected inventory levels to be financed are as follows:

Month	Amount
July 1994	$ 375,000
August	1,500,000
September	1,800,000
October	1,425,000
November	900,000
December	0

Calculate the cost of funds from this source, including interest charges and commitment fees. (*Hint:* Each month's borrowings will be $450,000 greater than the inventory level to be financed because of the compensating balance requirement.)

11A-3
Field warehouse financing

Because canned vegetables have a relatively long shelf life, field warehouse financing would also be appropriate for Sunset Valley Produce Inc. in Problem 11A-2. The costs of the field warehousing alternative in this case would be a flat fee of $2,000, plus 8 percent annual interest on all outstanding credit, plus 1 percent of the maximum amount of credit extended.
a. Calculate the total cost of the field warehousing operation.
b. Compare the cost of the field warehousing arrangement to the line of credit cost in Problem 11A-2.

Which alternative should Sunset Valley choose?

11A-4
Factoring receivables

The Sievers Corporation needs an additional $500,000, which it plans to obtain through a factoring arrangement. The factor would purchase Sievers's accounts receivable and advance the invoice amount, minus a 1 percent commission, on the invoices purchased each month. Sievers sells on terms of net 30 days. In addition, the factor charges a 13 percent annual interest rate on the total invoice amount, to be deducted in advance.
a. What amount of accounts receivable must be factored to net $500,000?
b. If Sievers can reduce credit expenses by $1,000 per month and avoid bad debt losses of 2 percent on the factored amount, what is the total dollar cost of the factoring arrangement?

(Do Parts c and d only if you are using the computerized problem diskette.)

c. Would it be to Sievers's advantage to offer to pay the factor a commission of 1.25 percent if it would lower the interest rate to 12 percent annually?

d. Assume a commission of 1 percent and an interest rate of 13 percent. What would be the total cost of the factoring arrangement if the amount of funds Sievers needed rose to $1,000,000? Would the factoring arrangement be profitable under these circumstances?

e. Retain the assumptions of a 1 percent commission and an interest rate of 13 percent. Would the factoring arrangement be profitable if the firm's need for funds from this source rose to $1,200,000?

f. Through trial and error, find the level of funds needed where the factoring arrangement would be a "breakeven proposition," in other words, where the net savings realized by Sievers would be $0. (Assume that commission and interest rate charged by the factor are as in Part e.)

Capital Budgeting: Investment in Long-Term Assets

Part III dealt with working capital management, that is, investment decisions regarding current assets and short-term financing. In the following four chapters we present techniques for evaluating investment opportunities in long-term assets.

Chapter 12 formally introduces risk — in it we discuss ways of defining and measuring the risk of investments, both on a stand-alone basis and in a portfolio context. Because fi-

nancial management often deals with situations in which we make expenditures today in exchange for future cash flows, techniques that correctly evaluate cash flows from different time periods must be developed. This important concept, the time value of money, is presented in Chapter 13, and then applied in Chapter 14, where the basic methods of capital budgeting analysis are introduced. Chapter 15 extends and refines our treatment of capital budgeting analysis, with an emphasis on how risk is handled.

Risk and Return

OBJECTIVES

After reading this chapter, you should be able to:

▷ Define risk and calculate the expected rate of return, standard deviation, and coefficient of variation for a probability distribution.

▷ Specify how risk aversion influences required rates of return.

▷ State the basic proposition of the Capital Asset Pricing Model and explain how and why a portfolio's risk may be reduced.

▷ Graph company-specific risk and market risk; explain which of these is relevant to a well-diversified investor.

▷ Explain the significance of a stock's beta coefficient, and use the Security Market Line to calculate a stock's required rate of return.

▷ List changes in the market or within a firm which would cause the required rate of return on the firm's stock to change.

▷ Explain why it is typically easier to diversify with a portfolio of securities than with a portfolio of physical assets.

DECISION IN FINANCE

DIVERSIFYING RISK — IS IT ALWAYS THE WAY TO GO?

Well-heeled bankers and stock-brokers used to spend several thousand dollars per visit for a couple of suits at Brian George's exclusive menswear store, which opened in New Jersey in 1983. A former corporate executive himself, George apparently knew what his colleagues wanted and originally sold clothing from his office before setting up shop as Northshore Inc. and going into the retail business full time.

The heady days of big spending were short lived, however, and George's profits declined with the economy. He laid off some of his staff, and he began trying out different ideas to keep Northshore's sales figures healthy and thus minimize his risk of going out of business.

Since customers had stopped buying suits, George emphasized shirts and ties — customers could give their old suits a sharp new look, and the new emphasis was designed to draw buyers who would not otherwise come into the store. To lure women shoppers, who often buy clothes for their husbands, he reintroduced a small line of women's wear. He even advertised some mens' items as suitable for women — an Austrian smoking jacket, for instance, became a feminine "outer coat." All these steps diversified his product line and reduced his exposure to risk.

In addition, George expanded his services to make shopping more convenient by launching Northshore One on One, which permitted cus-

tomers to make private in-store appointments on weekends. Finally, with a partner to share the added risk, George opened a second store in 1988 in Manhattan — Northshore on the Hudson.

Despite his innovations, however, George was bucking a downward trend. The number of men's clothing stores in the United States has declined during the last 20 years from 21,000 to about 15,000. Del Beukelman, president of the Menswear Retailers of America, says, "A residential community that 25 years ago sustained five men's specialty stores now probably has just one."

Two primary reasons for the decline are shopping malls and discount stores. However, the owner of a successful San Francisco menswear store and catalog company believes many customers still want quality and are willing to pay for it. "People know you can buy from us today and not see the same suit on sale next week," says Sidney Goodwill of Bullock & Jones.

See end of chapter for resolution.
Photo source: Jan Doty Huskisson.

Nevertheless, Brian George continued to struggle. The going got even tougher when his Manhattan store failed in 1990, and, despite the shared liability with his partner, it took the entire next year to pay off his debts. "I had trouble putting food on the table," George said, "and I had to ask for favors from suppliers."

As you read this chapter, think about the concept of risk in general, of portfolio risk, and of how diversification can be used to reduce risk. If you had been in Brian George's position, what further actions might you have taken to reduce your risk? Also, think about the question posed in the title of this reading.

Recall that the risk-return tradeoff was briefly introduced in Chapter 1. Remember also that in Chapter 4 we looked at nominal, or quoted, interest rates on debt securities and saw that these are influenced by several distinct types of risk for which lenders require compensation. In this chapter, we will discuss risk and return concepts in greater depth, define more precisely what the term *risk* means, and discuss how it may be measured.

Risk and return are relevant considerations not only for lenders but for investors in general, whether they are individuals investing in stocks or corporations investing in physical assets and other long-term projects. All types of investments involve expected future returns. The riskiness of these returns can be considered on a *stand-alone basis* (each asset by itself) or in a *portfolio context,* where the investment is combined with other assets and where risk may be reduced through *diversification.* These are the topics of this chapter. We will focus on how the risk-return relationship enters into the decision process; then, in Chapter 15, we will apply these same concepts specifically to the capital budgeting process.

Defining and Measuring Risk

risk

The chance that some unfavorable event will occur.

Risk is defined in *Webster's* as "a hazard; a peril; exposure to loss or injury." Thus, risk refers to the chance that some unfavorable event will occur. If you engage in skydiving, you take a chance with your life — skydiving is risky. If you bet on the horses, you risk losing your money. If you invest in speculative stocks (or, really, in *any* stock), you are taking a risk in the hope of making an appreciable return.

To illustrate the riskiness of financial assets, suppose an investor buys $100,000 of U.S. Treasury bills with an interest rate of 4 percent. In this case the rate of return on the investment, 4 percent, can be estimated quite precisely, and the investment is said to be risk-free. However, if the $100,000 were invested in the stock of a company just being organized to prospect for oil in the mid-Atlantic, then the investment's return could not be estimated precisely. One might analyze the situation and conclude that the *expected* rate of return is 20 percent. However, the *actual* rate of return could range from an extremely large positive return, say +1,000 percent, to a total loss of invested capital, −100 percent. Because there is a significant danger of actually earning a return considerably less than the expected return, the investment would be described as being relatively risky.

The relationship between risk and return is such that *no investment will be made unless the expected rate of return is high enough to compensate the investor for the perceived risk of the investment.* In this example, it is clear that few, if any, investors would be willing to buy the oil company stock if its expected return were the same as that of the T-bill. Naturally, the risky investment might not actually produce the higher rate of return; if the highest-risk projects always provided the highest returns, there would be no risk.

Investment risk, then, is related to the probability of actually earning significantly less than the expected return — the greater the chances of low or negative returns, the riskier the investment. We can define risk more precisely, however, and in the following sections we will do so.

Probability Distributions

An event's *probability* is defined as the chance that the event will occur. For example, a weather forecaster may state, "There is a 40 percent chance of rain today and a 60 percent chance that it will not rain." If all possible events, or outcomes, are listed, and if a probability is assigned to each event, the listing is called a **probability distribution.** For our weather forecast, we could set up the following probability distribution:

Outcome (1)	Probability (2)
Rain	0.4 = 40%
No rain	0.6 = 60%
	1.0 = 100%

probability distribution

A listing of all possible outcomes, or events, with a probability (chance of occurrence) assigned to each outcome.

The possible outcomes are listed in Column 1, and the probabilities of these outcomes, expressed both as decimals and as percentages, are given in Column 2. Notice that the probabilities must sum to 1.0, or 100 percent. Given that probabilities can be attached to specific events, or outcomes, we can then calculate some statistics to help us summarize a situation of risk or uncertainty. An example will illustrate the procedure.

Eastern Communications Inc., a manufacturer and retailer of business and consumer telephones, is considering the projected rates of return on two telephones, its Standard Phone line and its new Designer Phone. Most of the firm's marketing managers believe that the Designer line should have a higher return than the Standard line in "boom" and "normal" economic periods, but in recessionary periods, when consumers typically have less to spend on luxury items, the Designer line is not expected to be profitable. Before money is invested to manufacture the phones, Eastern Communications wishes to determine the risk and return of these two products in a more precise manner.

The states of the economy and the resulting rates of return on each phone are presented in Table 12-1. Here we see that there is a 30 percent chance of a boom, in which case both products will enjoy high rates of return; a 40 percent chance of a normal economy and moderate returns; and a 30 percent probability of a recession, which will mean a low return for the Standard phone and a negative return for the Designer phone. Of course, the profits of the luxury Designer phone are more sensitive to the economic environment than the profits of the Standard phone. In fact, in recessionary periods the return on the

Table 12-1

Eastern Communications
Inc.: Projected Rates of
Return on Each Phone,
Based on the State of the
Economy

	Designer Phone	
State of the Economy	**Probability of This State Occurring**	**Rate of Return under This State**
Boom	0.3	100%
Normal	0.4	15
Recession	0.3	−70
	1.0	

	Standard Phone	
State of the Economy	**Probability of This State Occurring**	**Rate of Return under This State**
Boom	0.3	20%
Normal	0.4	15
Recession	0.3	10
	1.0	

Designer phone will drop significantly, resulting in a loss of 70 percent, while the Standard phone has no loss. (Consumers will still need phones in a recession, but they will tend to buy the less expensive model.)

Expected Rate of Return ($\hat{k}$)

If we multiply each possible outcome by its probability of occurrence and then sum these products, we have a *weighted average* of outcomes. This weighted average of outcomes, *the mean of the distribution,* can be expressed in equation form as the **expected rate of return, $\hat{k}$,** of a probability distribution:

expected rate of return, $\hat{k}$

The rate of return expected to be realized from an investment; the mean value of the probability distribution of possible outcomes.

$$\text{Expected rate of return} = \hat{k} = \sum_{i=1}^{n} P_i k_i. \quad (12\text{-}1)$$

Here k_i is the *i*th possible outcome, P_i is the probability of the *i*th outcome, and n is the number of possible outcomes. Thus, $\hat{k}$ is a weighted average of the possible outcomes (the k_i values), with each outcome's weight being its probability of occurrence.[1] Using the data for the Designer line, we obtain its expected rate of return as follows:

$$\hat{k} = P_1(k_1) + P_2(k_2) + P_3(k_3)$$
$$= 0.3(100\%) + 0.4(15\%) + 0.3(-70\%)$$
$$= 15\%.$$

---

[1] In this equation, sigma (Σ) means "sum up," or add the values of n factors. If i = 1, then $P_i k_i = P_1 k_1$; if i = 2, then $P_i k_i = P_2 k_2$; and so on until i = n, the last possible outcome. The symbol $\sum_{i=1}^{n}$ simply says, "Go through the following process: First, let i = 1 and find the first product; then let i = 2 and find the second product; then continue until each individual product up to i = n has been found, and then add these individual products to find the weighted average, the expected rate of return.

Figure 12-1   Eastern Communications Inc.:
Probability Distributions of the Rates of Return for the Designer and Standard Telephone Projects

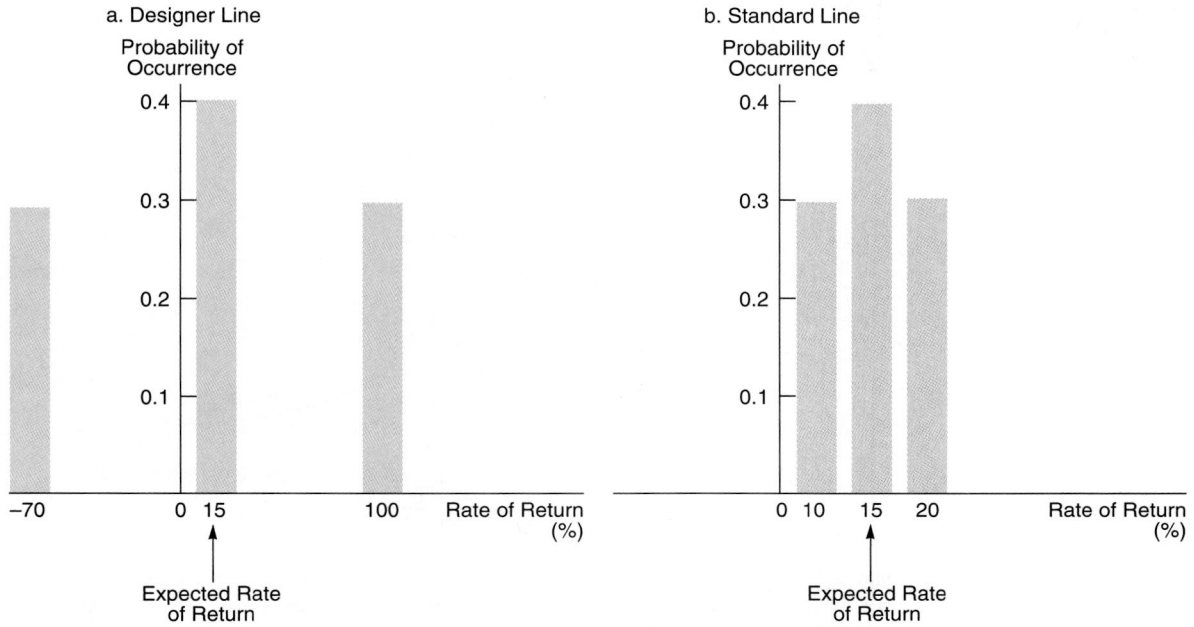

The expected rate of return on a project is equal to the average of all possible outcomes, with each outcome weighted by the probability of its occurrence. These bar charts show the variability of possible outcomes for each of the two projects. A weighted average (or expected) return of 15 percent is projected for both, but the Designer line has a much wider range of possible returns than that of the Standard line. Thus, the Designer line is the riskier project.

Similarly, we can use Equation 12-1 to determine the expected rate of return for the Standard line:

$$\hat{k} = 0.3(20\%) + 0.4(15\%) + 0.3(10\%)$$

$$= 15\%.$$

We can graph the rates of return to obtain a picture of the variability of the possible outcomes; this is shown in the bar charts of Figure 12-1. The height of each bar signifies the probability that a given outcome will occur. The range of possible returns for the Designer line is from 100 percent to −70 percent, with a weighted average, or expected, return of 15 percent. The expected return for the Standard line is also 15 percent, but with a much narrower range of possible returns. Note that instead of finding an expected rate of return (a percentage measure), we could have calculated the expected *cash flows* (a dollar measure) for each of the two telephone projects. The procedure would have been the same; the only change would have been that we would have estimated cash flows for each state of the economy and would then have substituted CF_i for k_i in Equation 12-1:

$$\text{Expected cash flows} = \hat{CF} = \sum_{i=1}^{n} P_i CF_i. \qquad \textbf{(12-1a)}$$

Figure 12-2

Eastern Communications
Inc.: Continuous
Probability Distributions of
the Designer and Standard
Lines' Rates of Return

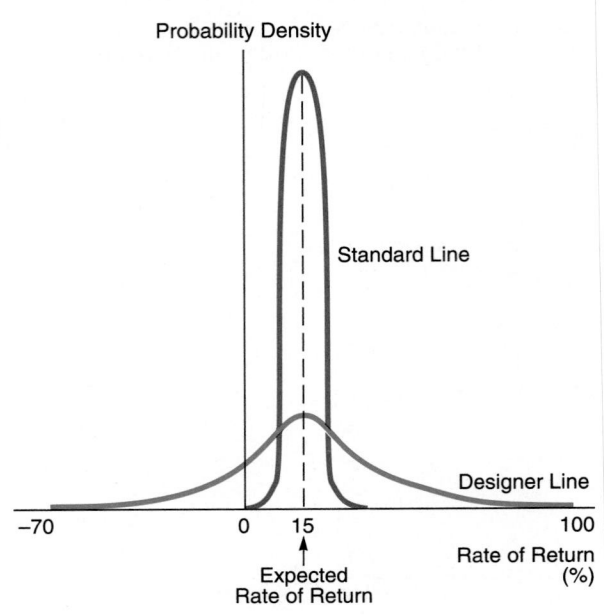

Figure 12-1 graphed the probabilities of three possible outcomes for each telephone project. In reality, both projects could have numerous rates of return, which could be illustrated best by the continuous probability curves shown here. These curves indicate that
the most likely rate of return for both products is 15 percent. In addition, the relative
flatness of the curves indicates the extent to which returns are likely to vary from 15
percent. The height of the curve for the Standard line indicates a tight probability distribution and reflects the fact that there is essentially a zero probability that the rate of
return will be below 0 percent or above 30 percent. The curve for the Designer line is
much flatter, meaning that this project has a higher probability of returning either more
or less than 15 percent, so it has the higher risk.

Note: The assumptions about the probabilities of various outcomes have been changed from those in Figure
12-1. There the probability of obtaining exactly 15 percent was 40 percent; here it is *much smaller* because
there are many possible outcomes instead of just three.

Continuous Probability Distributions

Thus far, we have assumed that only three states of the economy can exist:
recession, normal, and boom. Actually, of course, the state of the economy
could range from a deep depression to a fantastic boom, and there is an unlimited number of possibilities in between. Suppose we had the time and patience
to assign a probability to each possible state of the economy (with the sum of
the probabilities still equaling 1.0) and to estimate a rate of return on each
project for each state of the economy. We would again be using Equation 12-1
except that our weighted average would now have many more entries. The
probabilities and outcomes could be approximated by the continuous curves
presented in Figure 12-2. Here we have changed the assumptions so that there
is essentially a zero probability that the Designer line's rate of return will be
less than −70 percent or more than 100 percent, or that the Standard line's
rate of return will be less than 0 percent or more than 30 percent, but virtually
any return within these limits is possible.

The tighter, or more peaked, the probability distribution, the more likely it is that the actual outcome will be close to the expected value, and, consequently, the less likely it is that the actual return will end up far below the expected return. Thus, the tighter the probability distribution, the lower the risk of a project. Since the Standard line has a relatively tight probability distribution, its *actual return* is likely to be closer to the 15 percent *expected return* than is the actual return of the Designer line.

Measuring Risk: The Standard Deviation (σ)

standard deviation, σ

A statistical measure of the variability of a set of observations.

Risk is a difficult concept to grasp, and a great deal of controversy has surrounded attempts to define and measure it. To be most useful, any measure of risk should have a definite value; we need a measure of the tightness of the probability distribution. One such measure is the **standard deviation,** the symbol for which is **σ,** pronounced "sigma." The smaller the standard deviation, the tighter the probability distribution and, accordingly, the lower the riskiness of the project. The calculation of the standard deviation follows these steps:

1. Calculate the expected rate of return, as shown previously:

$$\text{Expected rate of return} = \hat{k} = \sum_{i=1}^{n} P_i k_i. \tag{12-1}$$

2. Subtract the expected rate of return from each possible outcome to obtain a set of deviations about the expected rate of return, $\hat{k}$:

$$\text{Deviation}_i = k_i - \hat{k}.$$

3. Square each deviation, multiply the squared deviation by the probability of occurrence for its related outcome, and sum these products to obtain the **variance, σ²**, of the probability distribution:

variance, σ²

The square of the standard deviation.

$$\text{Variance} = \sigma^2 = \sum_{i=1}^{n} (k_i - \hat{k})^2 P_i. \tag{12-2}$$

4. Find the standard deviation by taking the square root of the variance:

$$\text{Standard deviation} = \sigma = \sqrt{\sum_{i=1}^{n} (k_i - \hat{k})^2 P_i}. \tag{12-3}$$

We can illustrate these procedures by calculating the standard deviation for both the Designer and Standard lines:

a. **Designer line:**

(1) The expected rate of return, $\hat{k}$, was already found, using Equation 12-1, to be 15 percent. Following the steps just outlined, we set up a table to calculate the standard deviation, using Equation 12-3.

(2) In Column 1, we subtract the expected return from each possible outcome to obtain Column 2, a set of deviations about $\hat{k}$.

(3) In Column 3, we square each of these deviations. In Column 4, these squared deviations are multiplied by the probability of their occurrence. In Column 5, these products are summed to obtain the variance of the probability distribution, 4,335.

(4) Below the table, we take the square root of the variance to obtain the probability distribution's standard deviation, 65.84%.

1		2	3	4	5
$k_i - \hat{k}$	$=$	$(k_i - \hat{k})$	$(k_i - \hat{k})^2$	$(k_i - \hat{k})^2 P_i$	
$100 - 15$		85	$7{,}225$	$(7{,}225)(0.3) = 2{,}167.5$	
$15 - 15$		0	0	$(0)(0.4) = \phantom{2{,}16}0.0$	
$-70 - 15$		-85	$7{,}225$	$(7{,}225)(0.3) = \underline{2{,}167.5}$	
				Variance $= \sigma_k^2 = \overline{\underline{4{,}335.0}}$	

Standard deviation $= \sigma_k = \sqrt{\sigma_k^2} = \sqrt{4{,}335.0} = 65.84\%$.

b.   Standard line: The expected rate of return, $\hat{k}$, is 15 percent. As before, we compute the project's risk measure, the standard deviation, by following the previously outlined steps and solving Equation 12-3:

1		2	3	4	5
$k_i - \hat{k}$	$=$	$(k_i - \hat{k})$	$(k_i - \hat{k})^2$	$(k_i - \hat{k})^2 P_i$	
$20 - 15$		5	25	$(25)(0.3) = 7.5$	
$15 - 15$		0	0	$(0)(0.4) = 0.0$	
$10 - 15$		-5	25	$(25)(0.3) = \underline{7.5}$	
				Variance $= \sigma_k^2 = \underline{\underline{15.0}}$	

Standard deviation $= \sigma_k = \sqrt{\sigma_k^2} = \sqrt{15} = 3.87\%$.

We can summarize as follows: The standard deviation gives an idea of how far above or below the expected value (the mean) actual outcomes are likely to fall; it is a measure of dispersion around the mean. From the calculations above, we can conclude that the Designer line, with its standard deviation of 65.84 percent, has much more risk than the Standard line where σ is much lower at 3.87 percent.[2]

---

[2]In the example we described the procedure for finding the mean and standard deviation when the data are in the form of a known probability distribution. If only sample returns data over some past period are available, the standard deviation of returns can be estimated using this formula:

$$\text{Estimated } \sigma = S = \sqrt{\frac{\sum\limits_{t=1}^{n} (\bar{k}_t - \bar{k}_{Avg})^2}{n - 1}} \tag{12-3a}$$

Here $\bar{k}_t$ ("k bar t") denotes the past realized rate of return in Period t, and $\bar{k}_{Avg}$ is the average annual return earned during the last n years. Here is an example:

Year	$\bar{k}_t$
1991	15%
1992	-5
1993	20

$$\bar{k}_{Avg} = \frac{(15 - 5 + 20)}{3} = 10.0\%.$$

$$\text{Estimated } \sigma \text{ (or S)} = \sqrt{\frac{(15 - 10)^2 + (-5 - 10)^2 + (20 - 10)^2}{3 - 1}}$$

$$= \sqrt{\frac{350}{2}} = 13.2\%.$$

The historical σ is often used as an estimate of the future σ. Much less often, and generally incorrectly, $\bar{k}_{Avg}$ for some past period is used as an estimate of $\hat{k}$, the expected future return. Because past variability is likely to be repeated, σ may be a good estimate of future risk, but it is much less reasonable to expect that the past *level* of return (which could have been as high as $+100\%$ or as low as -50%) is the best expectation of what investors think will happen in the future.

Figure 12-3

Probability Ranges for a
Normal Distribution

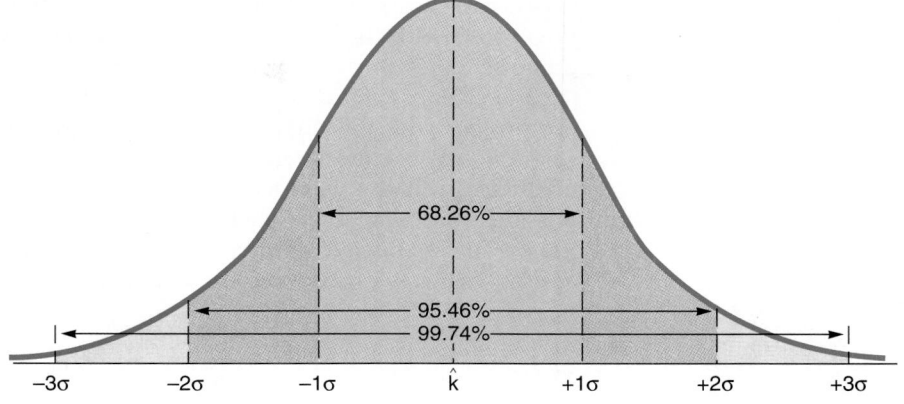

This figure illustrates a normal probability curve. In a normal distribution the actual value
will fall within ±1 standard deviation of the expected value (the mean) about 68 percent
of the time. Thus, *if we assume normal distributions* in the Eastern Communications Inc.
example, about 68 percent of the time the Standard line's actual return will be in the range
of 15 percent ± 3.87 percent. Similarly, there is roughly a 68 percent chance that the
Designer line's return will fall in the range of 15 percent ± 65.84 percent. The normal
curve again highlights the greater risk associated with the Designer line.

Notes:
1. The area under the normal curve equals 1.0, or 100%. *Thus, the areas under any pair of normal curves
drawn on the same scale, whether they are peaked or flat, must be equal.*
2. Half of the area under a normal curve is to the left of the mean, indicating that there is a 50% probability
that the actual outcome will be less than the mean, and a 50% probability that it will be greater than the mean,
or to the right of it.
3. Of the area under the curve, 68.26% is within ±1σ of the mean, indicating that the probability is 68.26%
that the actual outcome will be within the range $\hat{k} - 1\sigma$ to $\hat{k} + 1\sigma$.
4. Procedures are available for finding the probability of other earnings ranges. These procedures are covered in
statistics courses.
5. For a normal distribution, the larger the value of σ, the greater the probability that the actual outcome will
vary widely from, hence perhaps be far below, the expected, or most likely, outcome. Because the probability of
having the actual result turn out to be far below the expected result is one definition of risk, and because σ
measures this probability, we can use σ as a measure of risk. This definition may not be a good one, however, if
we are dealing with an asset held in a diversified portfolio. This point is covered later in the chapter.

Furthermore, *if we have a continuous probability distribution which is
also a normal, bell-shaped distribution,* the actual return will lie within ±1
standard deviation of the *expected* return about 68 percent (68.26 percent, to
be exact) of the time. Figure 12-3 illustrates this point and also shows the situation for ±2σ and ±3σ.

Assume for now that the two telephone projects in fact have *continuous,
normal distributions,* and that we have found the expected value, $\hat{k}$, to be 15
percent for both and the standard deviations to be 65.84 percent for the Designer line but only 3.87 percent for the Standard line. Thus, for the Designer
line there is a 68.26 percent probability that the actual return will be in the
range of 15 percent ± 65.84 percent, or from −50.84 percent to 80.84 percent. In a similar fashion, for the Standard line there is a 68.26 percent
probability that the actual return will be in the range of 15 percent ± 3.87
percent, or from 11.13 to 18.87 percent. With such a small standard deviation
for the Standard line, we can conclude that there will be little chance of significant loss from investing in that product line, so the project is not very risky.

If a choice has to be made between two projects which have the same expected returns but different standard deviations, most people would choose the project with the lower standard deviation and, therefore, lower risk. On the other hand, given a choice between two investments with the *same* risk (standard deviations) but different expected returns, investors would tend to prefer the project with the higher expected return. To most people this is common sense; return is considered "good," risk is considered "bad," and, consequently, investors generally want as much of the former, and as little of the latter, as possible. But, how do we decide when we have to pick one of two projects and *neither* the expected returns nor the standard deviations are the same? The answer is that we need yet another measure of risk, which will be discussed next.

Measuring Risk: The Coefficient of Variation (CV)

coefficient of variation (CV)

A standardized measure of the risk per unit of return; calculated as the standard deviation divided by the expected return.

The **coefficient of variation (CV)** shows the risk per unit of return, whether that unit is a percentage, as in our example, or in dollars. It is calculated by dividing the standard deviation by the expected return (or expected cash flows) of the investment:

$$\text{Coefficient of variation} = CV = \frac{\sigma}{\hat{k}}. \qquad (12\text{-}4)$$

The coefficient of variation provides a more meaningful comparison when the expected returns *and* the standard deviations on two alternatives are not the same. Since the Designer line and the Standard line have the same expected return, the calculation of the coefficient of variation is not really necessary in this case because the result is obvious; the project with the larger standard deviation, the Designer line, will have the larger coefficient of variation. In fact, the Designer line is almost 17 times as risky as the Standard line based on this measure of risk:

$$\text{Coefficient of variation}_{\text{Designer line}} = \frac{65.84\%}{15\%} = 4.39,$$

while

$$\text{Coefficient of variation}_{\text{Standard line}} = \frac{3.87\%}{15\%} = 0.26.$$

Now consider two other projects, A and B, which have different expected rates of return as well as different standard deviations. Project A has a 45 percent expected rate of return and a standard deviation of 15 percent, while Project B has an expected rate of return of 20 percent and a standard deviation of 10 percent. Is Project A riskier because it has the larger standard deviation? If we calculate the coefficients of variation for these two projects, we find that Project A has a coefficient of variation of 0.33:

$$CV_A = \frac{\sigma_A}{\hat{k}_A} = \frac{15\%}{45\%} = 0.33,$$

and for Project B the coefficient of variation is 0.50:

$$CV_B = \frac{\sigma_B}{\hat{k}_B} = \frac{10\%}{20\%} = 0.50.$$

Thus, we see that Project B actually has more risk per unit of return than Project A, even though Project A's standard deviation is larger. When such differences occur, the coefficient of variation is generally a better measure of risk than the standard deviation alone.

Risk Aversion and Required Returns

In our previous examples, we have been looking at projects as investments. Now, let us turn to financial assets. Suppose you have worked hard and saved $100,000, which you plan to invest. You can buy a 6 percent U.S. Treasury note, and at the end of 1 year you will have $106,000, which is your original investment plus $6,000 in interest. The risk on this investment is quite low, and it is risk-free from the standpoint of default risk. Alternatively, you can buy stock in GeneTech Innovations Inc. (GII). If GII's medical research programs are successful, you think the stock will increase in value to $212,000; however, if the research is a failure, the value of your stock will be zero, and you will lose all of your savings. You regard GII's chances of success or failure as being 50/50, so the expected value of the stock investment is 0.5($0) + 0.5($212,000) = $106,000. Subtracting the $100,000 cost of the stock leaves an expected profit of $6,000, or an expected (but risky) 6 percent rate of return:

$$\text{Expected rate of return} = (\text{Expected ending investment value} - \text{Cost})/\text{Cost}$$

$$= (\$106,000 - \$100,000)/\$100,000$$

$$= \$6,000/\$100,000$$

$$= 6 \text{ percent.}$$

Thus, you have a choice between a sure $6,000 profit (representing a 6 percent rate of return) on the Treasury note or a risky expected $6,000 profit (also representing a 6 percent expected rate of return) on the GeneTech Innovations stock. Which one would you choose? *If you choose the less risky investment, you are risk averse. Most investors are indeed risk averse, and certainly the average investor is risk averse, at least with regard to his or her "serious money." Because this is a well-documented fact, we shall assume* **risk aversion** *throughout the remainder of this book.* However, the concept of risk aversion does *not* mean that investors are afraid of taking chances; rather, risk aversion indicates that individuals or businesses will take on risk only if a stock's or project's expected rate of return is sufficiently high to justify taking the risk.

What are the implications of risk aversion for securities prices and rates of return? The answer is that, other things held constant, the higher a security's risk, (1) the lower its price and (2) the higher its required rate of return. To see how this works, assume that two stocks are available for investment. Suppose, initially, that each stock has the same expected rate of return and the same stock price, but they have very different risk profiles. The first firm, TotWear Products, a respected manufacturer of children's clothing, has little risk, and its expected rate of return is 15 percent. TotWear's common stock sells for $75. The second firm, SilTek, is involved in new technology for superconductors. SilTek's rate of return is also expected to be 15 percent, but its returns have always been highly variable and thus risky, and they will remain so in the future

risk aversion
A dislike for risk. Risk averse investors require higher rates of return on higher-risk investments.

due to the nature of the firm's products. Investors are risk averse, and if SilTek's stock were to sell for $75 also, there would be a general preference for the less risky TotWear's stock. Therefore, people with money to invest would purchase TotWear's rather than SilTek's stock, and SilTek's stockholders would start selling shares and using the money to buy TotWear's stock. Buying pressure would drive up the price of TotWear's stock, and selling pressure would simultaneously cause SilTek's stock price to decline.

These price changes would, in turn, cause changes in the expected rates of return on the two securities. Suppose, for example, that the price of TotWear's stock was bid up from $75 to $112.50, while the price of SilTek's stock declined from $75 to $56.25. Further, suppose this caused TotWear's expected rate of return to fall to 10 percent, while SilTek's expected rate of return rose to 20 percent. The difference in rates of return, $20\% - 10\% = 10\%$, is a **risk premium, RP,** which represents the compensation investors require for assuming the additional risk of SilTek's stock.[3]

risk premium, RP
The difference between the required (and expected) rate of return on a given risky asset and that on a less risky asset.

This example demonstrates a very important principle: *In a market dominated by risk averse investors, riskier securities must have higher expected returns as estimated by the average investor than less risky securities, for if this situation does not hold, market participants will act, and stock prices will change to force it to come about.* We will discuss how the market prices financial assets such as bonds and common stock in subsequent chapters. Later in this chapter, we will consider the question of *how much higher* the returns on risky securities must be, after we see how diversification affects the way risk should be measured.

? *Self-Test*

Briefly explain the differences between the assumptions used in Figures 12-1 and 12-2.

Which of the two projects graphed in Figure 12-2 is less risky? Explain your answer.

Which is a better measure of risk: (1) standard deviation or (2) coefficient of variation? Explain.

What is meant by the following statement: "Most investors are risk averse"?

How does risk aversion affect relative rates of return?

Portfolio Risk and the Capital Asset Pricing Model

In the preceding section we considered the description and measurement of risk for investments held in isolation, or on a stand-alone basis. Now we will analyze the effect of diversifying by combining two or more investments into a

---

[3]The relationship between a stock's price and its expected rate of return will be explored in greater detail in Chapters 17 and 19.

portfolio

A collection of investments.

Capital Asset Pricing Model (CAPM)

A model based on the proposition that any stock's required rate of return is equal to the risk-free rate of return plus a risk premium, where risk reflects the effects of diversification.

portfolio.[4] As we shall see, an investment held as part of a portfolio is less risky than the same investment held in isolation. This fact has been incorporated into a procedure used to analyze the relationship between risk and rates of return, the **Capital Asset Pricing Model,** or **CAPM.** The CAPM is an extremely important analytical tool in both investment analysis and managerial finance. Indeed, the 1990 Nobel Prize was awarded to the developers of the CAPM, Professors Harry Markowitz and William F. Sharpe. In the following sections we discuss the elements of the CAPM.[5]

The basic concepts of the Capital Asset Pricing Model were developed specifically for common stocks, and we will, therefore, first examine the theory in this context. However, it has become common practice to extend the concepts to capital budgeting and to speak of firms having "portfolios of tangible assets and projects." We will come back to these assets and projects later in this chapter and again in Chapter 15, where we will discuss the implications of CAPM in capital budgeting and in the diversification of the firm.

Portfolio Risk and Return

Most financial assets are not held in isolation; rather, they are held as parts of portfolios. Banks, pension funds, insurance companies, mutual funds, and other financial institutions are required by law to hold diversified portfolios. Individual investors — at least those whose securities holdings constitute a significant part of their total wealth — will also generally hold stock portfolios, not just the stock of one firm. Even individuals with relatively small amounts of money to invest can obtain diversification quite easily by investing in mutual funds. Since investors can and do hold portfolios, the fact that a particular stock goes up or down is not very important; *what is important is the rate of return on the portfolio and the portfolio's risk. Logically, then, the risk and return of an individual security should be analyzed in terms of how that security affects the risk and return of the portfolio in which it is held.*

To illustrate, Payco American is a collection agency company which operates nationwide through 37 offices. The company is not well known, its stock is not very liquid, its earnings have fluctuated quite a bit in the past, and it doesn't even pay a dividend. All this suggests that Payco is risky and that its required rate of return should be relatively high. However, Payco's required rate of return has in fact been quite low in relation to those of most other companies. This indicates that investors regard Payco as being a low-risk company in spite of its uncertain profits and its nonexistent dividend stream. The reason for this somewhat counterintuitive fact has to do with diversification and its effect on risk. Payco's stock price rises during recessions, whereas other stocks tend to decline when the economy slumps. Therefore, holding Payco in a portfolio of "normal" stocks tends to stabilize returns on the entire portfolio.

---

[4]If you owned some General Motors stock, some Exxon stock, and some IBM stock, you would be holding a three-stock portfolio. For the reasons given in this section, the majority of all stocks are held as parts of portfolios.

[5]The CAPM is a relatively complex subject, and we present only its basic elements in this text. For a more detailed discussion, see any standard investments textbook.

expected return on a portfolio, $\hat{k}_p$

The weighted average of expected returns on the stocks held in the portfolio.

Portfolio Returns. The **expected return on a portfolio, $\hat{k}_p$,** is simply the weighted average of the expected returns on the individual stocks in the portfolio, with the weights being the fraction of the total portfolio invested in each stock:

$$\hat{k}_p = \sum_{i=1}^{n} w_i \hat{k}_i. \qquad (12\text{-}5)$$

Here the $\hat{k}_i$'s are the expected returns on the individual stocks, the w_i's are the weights, and there are n stocks in the portfolio. Note (1) that w_i is the proportion of the portfolio's dollar value invested in Stock i (that is, the value of the investment in Stock i divided by the total value of the portfolio) and (2) that the w_i's must sum to 1.0.

Assume that in January 1993, a securities analyst had estimated the following returns on four large companies:

	Expected Return, $\hat{k}$
Lotus Development	11%
General Electric	20%
Exxon	13%
McDonald's	18%

If we formed a $100,000 portfolio, investing $25,000 in each stock, the expected portfolio return would be 15.50%:

$$\hat{k}_p = w_1\hat{k}_1 + w_2\hat{k}_2 + w_3\hat{k}_3 + w_4\hat{k}_4$$
$$= 0.25(11\%) + 0.25(20\%) + 0.25(13\%) + 0.25(18\%)$$
$$= 15.50\%.$$

realized rate of return, $\bar{k}$

The return that is actually earned. The actual return ($\bar{k}$) is usually different from the expected return ($\hat{k}$).

Of course, after the fact and a year later, the actual **realized rates of return, $\bar{k}$,** on the individual stocks—the $\bar{k}_i$, or "k-bar," values—will almost certainly be different from their expected values, so $\bar{k}_p$ will be somewhat different from $\hat{k}_p = 15.50\%$. For example, Lotus stock might double in price and provide a return of +100%, whereas Exxon stock might have a terrible year, fall sharply, and have a return of −75%. Note, though, that those two events would be somewhat offsetting, so the portfolio's return might still be close to its expected return, even though the individual stocks' actual returns were far from their expected returns.

Portfolio Risk. As we just saw, the expected return on a portfolio is simply a weighted average of the expected returns on the individual stocks in the portfolio. However, unlike returns, the riskiness of a portfolio, σ_p, is generally *not* a weighted average of the standard deviations of the individual securities in the portfolio; the portfolio's risk will be *smaller* than the weighted average of the stocks' σs. In fact, it may even be theoretically possible to combine two stocks which are individually quite risky as measured by their standard deviations and to form a portfolio which is completely riskless, with $\sigma_p = 0\%$.

To illustrate the effect of combining securities, consider the situation in Figure 12-4. The bottom section gives data on rates of return for Stocks W and M individually, and also for a portfolio invested 50 percent in each stock. The

Figure 12-4 Rate of Return Distributions for Two Perfectly Negatively
Correlated Stocks (r = −1.0) and for Portfolio WM

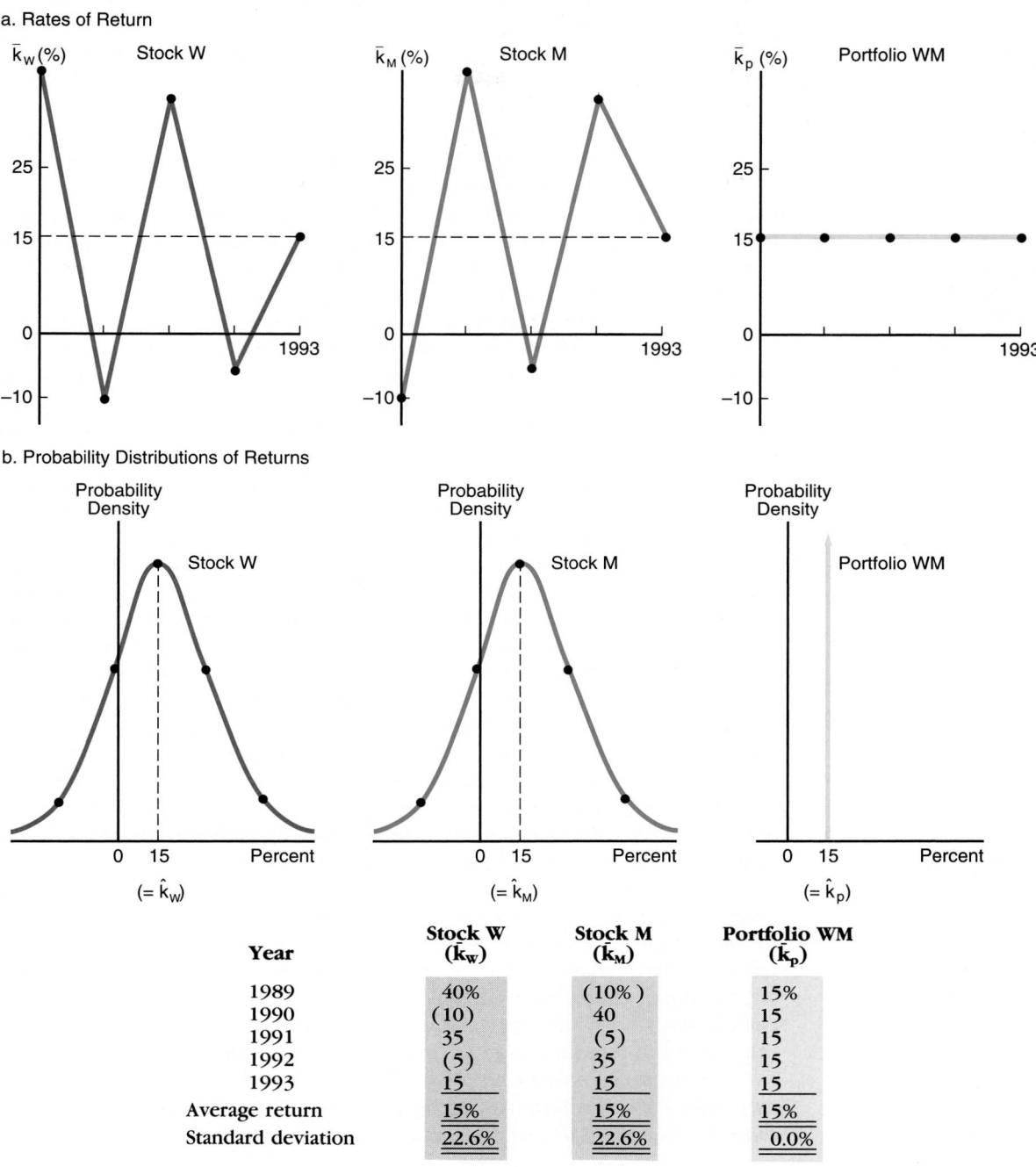

a. Rates of Return

b. Probability Distributions of Returns

Year	Stock W ($\bar{k}_W$)	Stock M ($\bar{k}_M$)	Portfolio WM ($\bar{k}_p$)
1989	40%	(10%)	15%
1990	(10)	40	15
1991	35	(5)	15
1992	(5)	35	15
1993	15	15	15
Average return	15%	15%	15%
Standard deviation	22.6%	22.6%	0.0%

If it were possible to find two stocks where the returns were perfectly negatively correlated (r = −1.0), such as Stocks W and M, then a completely riskless portfolio could be constructed. Although each of the two stocks has considerable risk if held in isolation, a diversified portfolio made up of 50 percent of each stock would provide the investor with the same average rate of return as on each individual stock, and yet zero risk. This result occurs because the returns on Stock W and Stock M move countercyclically to each other. It is *theoretically possible*, but highly unlikely, that two such stocks can be found.

correlation coefficient, r

A measure of the degree of relationship between two variables.

three top graphs show plots of the data in a time series format, and the lower graphs show the probability distributions of returns, assuming that the future is expected to be like the past. The two stocks would be quite risky if they were held in isolation, but when they are combined to form Portfolio WM, they are not risky at all. (Note: These stocks are called W and M because their returns graphs in Figure 12-4 resemble a W and an M.)

The reason Stocks W and M can be combined to form a riskless portfolio is that their returns move countercyclically to each other—when W's returns fall, those of M rise, and vice versa. The tendency of two variables to move together is called *correlation,* and the **correlation coefficient, r,** measures this tendency.[6] In statistical terms, we say that the returns on Stocks W and M are *perfectly negatively correlated,* with r = −1.0.

The opposite of perfect negative correlation, with r = −1.0, is *perfect positive correlation,* with r = +1.0. Returns on two perfectly positively correlated stocks would move up and down together, and a portfolio consisting of two such stocks would be exactly as risky as the individual stocks. This point is illustrated in Figure 12-5, where we see that the portfolio's standard deviation is equal to that of the individual stocks. Thus, diversification does nothing to reduce risk if the portfolio consists of perfectly positively correlated stocks.

Figures 12-4 and 12-5 demonstrate that when stocks are perfectly negatively correlated (r = −1.0), all risk can be diversified away, but when stocks are perfectly positively correlated (r = +1.0), diversification does no good whatsoever. In reality, most stocks are positively correlated, but not perfectly so. On average, the correlation coefficient for the returns on two randomly selected stocks would be about +0.6, and for most pairs of stocks, r would lie in the range of +0.5 to +0.7. *Under such conditions, combining stocks into portfolios reduces risk but does not eliminate it completely.* Figure 12-6 illustrates this point with two stocks whose correlation coefficient is r = +0.67. The portfolio's average return is 15.0 percent, which is exactly the same as the average return for each of the two stocks, but its standard deviation is 20.6 percent, which is less than the standard deviation of either stock. Thus, the portfolio's risk is *not* an average of the risks of its individual stocks—diversification has reduced, but not eliminated, risk.

What would happen if we included more than two stocks in the portfolio? *As a rule, the riskiness of a portfolio will be reduced as the number of stocks in the portfolio increases.* If we added enough partially correlated stocks, could we completely eliminate risk? In general, the answer is no, but the extent to which adding stocks to a portfolio reduces its risk depends on the *degree of correlation* among the stocks: The smaller the positive correlation coefficient, the lower the risk in a large portfolio. If we could find a set of stocks whose correlations were zero or negative, all risk could be eliminated. *In the typical case, where the correlations among the individual stocks are positive but less than +1.0, some, but not all, risk can be eliminated.*

---

[6]The *correlation coefficient, r,* can range from +1.0, denoting that the two variables move up and down in perfect synchronization, to −1.0, denoting that the variables always move in exactly opposite directions. A correlation coefficient of zero suggests that the two variables are not related to each other—that is, changes in one variable are *independent* of changes in the other.

If a choice has to be made between two projects which have the same expected returns but different standard deviations, most people would choose the project with the lower standard deviation and, therefore, lower risk. On the other hand, given a choice between two investments with the *same* risk (standard deviations) but different expected returns, investors would tend to prefer the project with the higher expected return. To most people this is common sense; return is considered "good," risk is considered "bad," and, consequently, investors generally want as much of the former, and as little of the latter, as possible. But, how do we decide when we have to pick one of two projects and *neither* the expected returns nor the standard deviations are the same? The answer is that we need yet another measure of risk, which will be discussed next.

Measuring Risk: The Coefficient of Variation (CV)

coefficient of variation (CV)

A standardized measure of the risk per unit of return; calculated as the standard deviation divided by the expected return.

The **coefficient of variation (CV)** shows the risk per unit of return, whether that unit is a percentage, as in our example, or in dollars. It is calculated by dividing the standard deviation by the expected return (or expected cash flows) of the investment:

$$\text{Coefficient of variation} = \text{CV} = \frac{\sigma}{\hat{k}}. \tag{12-4}$$

The coefficient of variation provides a more meaningful comparison when the expected returns *and* the standard deviations on two alternatives are not the same. Since the Designer line and the Standard line have the same expected return, the calculation of the coefficient of variation is not really necessary in this case because the result is obvious; the project with the larger standard deviation, the Designer line, will have the larger coefficient of variation. In fact, the Designer line is almost 17 times as risky as the Standard line based on this measure of risk:

$$\text{Coefficient of variation}_{\text{Designer line}} = \frac{65.84\%}{15\%} = 4.39,$$

while

$$\text{Coefficient of variation}_{\text{Standard line}} = \frac{3.87\%}{15\%} = 0.26.$$

Now consider two other projects, A and B, which have different expected rates of return as well as different standard deviations. Project A has a 45 percent expected rate of return and a standard deviation of 15 percent, while Project B has an expected rate of return of 20 percent and a standard deviation of 10 percent. Is Project A riskier because it has the larger standard deviation? If we calculate the coefficients of variation for these two projects, we find that Project A has a coefficient of variation of 0.33:

$$CV_A = \frac{\sigma_A}{\hat{k}_A} = \frac{15\%}{45\%} = 0.33,$$

and for Project B the coefficient of variation is 0.50:

$$CV_B = \frac{\sigma_B}{\hat{k}_B} = \frac{10\%}{20\%} = 0.50.$$

Figure 12-3

Probability Ranges for a
Normal Distribution

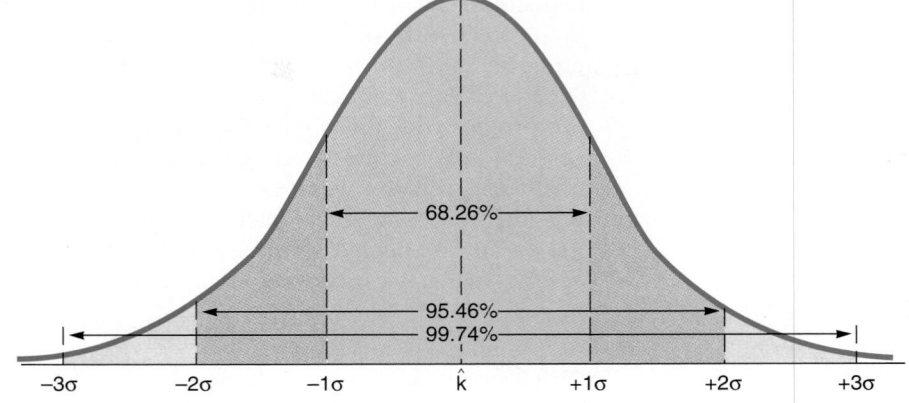

This figure illustrates a normal probability curve. In a normal distribution the actual value will fall within ±1 standard deviation of the expected value (the mean) about 68 percent of the time. Thus, *if we assume normal distributions* in the Eastern Communications Inc. example, about 68 percent of the time the Standard line's actual return will be in the range of 15 percent ± 3.87 percent. Similarly, there is roughly a 68 percent chance that the Designer line's return will fall in the range of 15 percent ± 65.84 percent. The normal curve again highlights the greater risk associated with the Designer line.

Notes:
1. The area under the normal curve equals 1.0, or 100%. *Thus, the areas under any pair of normal curves drawn on the same scale, whether they are peaked or flat, must be equal.*
2. Half of the area under a normal curve is to the left of the mean, indicating that there is a 50% probability that the actual outcome will be less than the mean, and a 50% probability that it will be greater than the mean, or to the right of it.
3. Of the area under the curve, 68.26% is within ±1σ of the mean, indicating that the probability is 68.26% that the actual outcome will be within the range $\hat{k} - 1\sigma$ to $\hat{k} + 1\sigma$.
4. Procedures are available for finding the probability of other earnings ranges. These procedures are covered in statistics courses.
5. For a normal distribution, the larger the value of σ, the greater the probability that the actual outcome will vary widely from, hence perhaps be far below, the expected, or most likely, outcome. Because the probability of having the actual result turn out to be far below the expected result is one definition of risk, and because σ measures this probability, we can use σ as a measure of risk. This definition may not be a good one, however, if we are dealing with an asset held in a diversified portfolio. This point is covered later in the chapter.

Furthermore, *if we have a continuous probability distribution which is also a normal, bell-shaped distribution,* the actual return will lie within ±1 standard deviation of the *expected* return about 68 percent (68.26 percent, to be exact) of the time. Figure 12-3 illustrates this point and also shows the situation for ±2σ and ±3σ.

Assume for now that the two telephone projects in fact have *continuous, normal distributions,* and that we have found the expected value, $\hat{k}$, to be 15 percent for both and the standard deviations to be 65.84 percent for the Designer line but only 3.87 percent for the Standard line. Thus, for the Designer line there is a 68.26 percent probability that the actual return will be in the range of 15 percent ± 65.84 percent, or from −50.84 percent to 80.84 percent. In a similar fashion, for the Standard line there is a 68.26 percent probability that the actual return will be in the range of 15 percent ± 3.87 percent, or from 11.13 to 18.87 percent. With such a small standard deviation for the Standard line, we can conclude that there will be little chance of significant loss from investing in that product line, so the project is not very risky.

Figure 12-5   Rate of Return Distributions for Two Perfectly Positively
Correlated Stocks (r = +1.0) and for Portfolio MM′

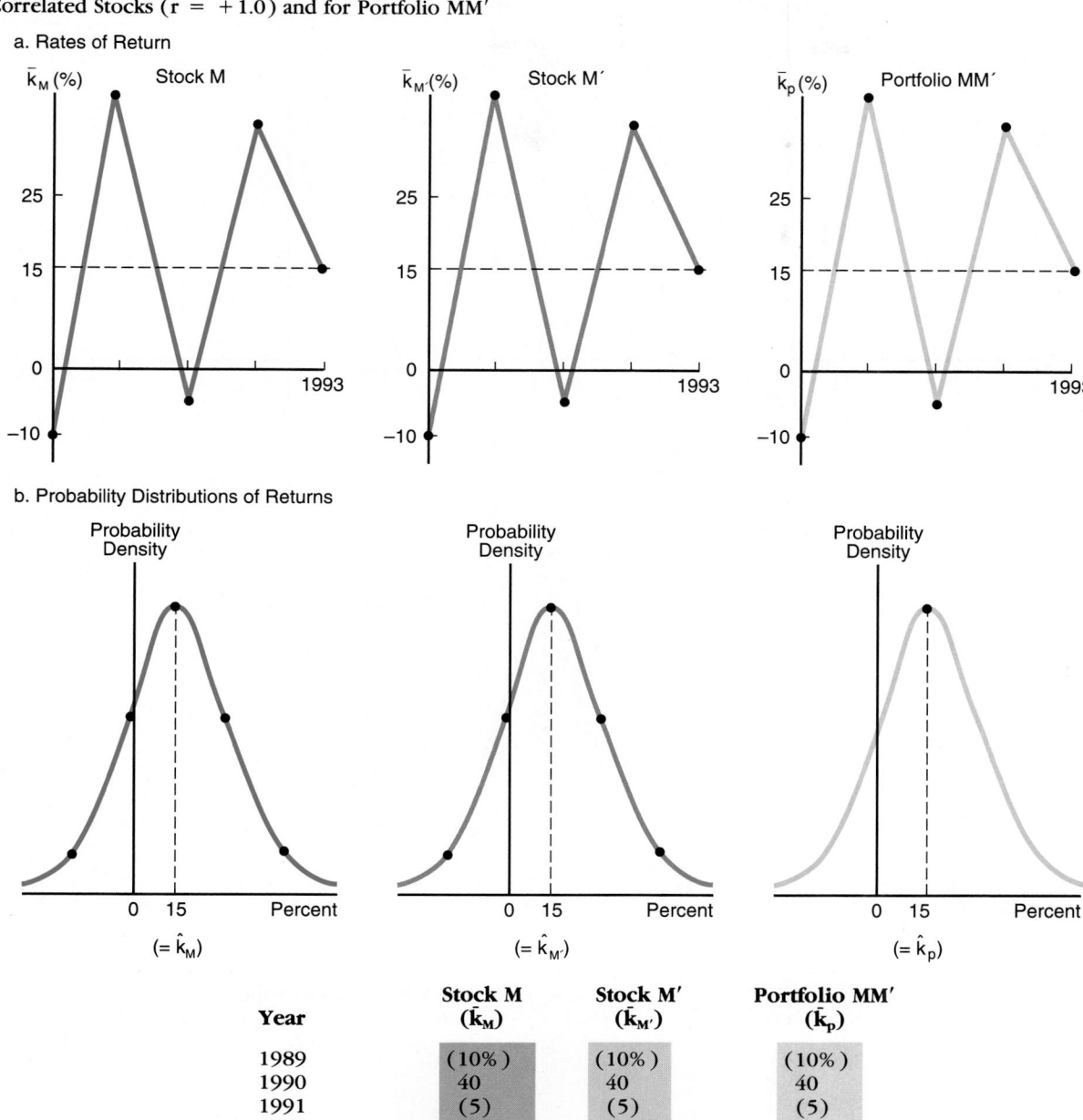

a. Rates of Return

b. Probability Distributions of Returns

Year	Stock M $(\bar{k}_M)$	Stock M′ $(\bar{k}_{M'})$	Portfolio MM′ $(\bar{k}_p)$
1989	(10%)	(10%)	(10%)
1990	40	40	40
1991	(5)	(5)	(5)
1992	35	35	35
1993	15	15	15
Average return	15%	15%	15%
Standard deviation	22.6%	22.6%	22.6%

A portfolio consisting of two stocks where the returns are perfectly positively correlated (r = +1.0), such as Stocks M and M′ shown here, would obtain no benefit from diversification whatsoever. Combining these two stocks, on which returns move up and down in perfect synchronization, merely produces a portfolio with the same average rate of return *and the same standard deviation* as would be obtained on each of the two stocks if held separately. Therefore, risk is not reduced. Fortunately, most stocks are less than perfectly positively correlated.

Figure 12-6   Rate of Return Distributions for Two Partially Correlated Stocks (r = +0.67) and for Portfolio WY

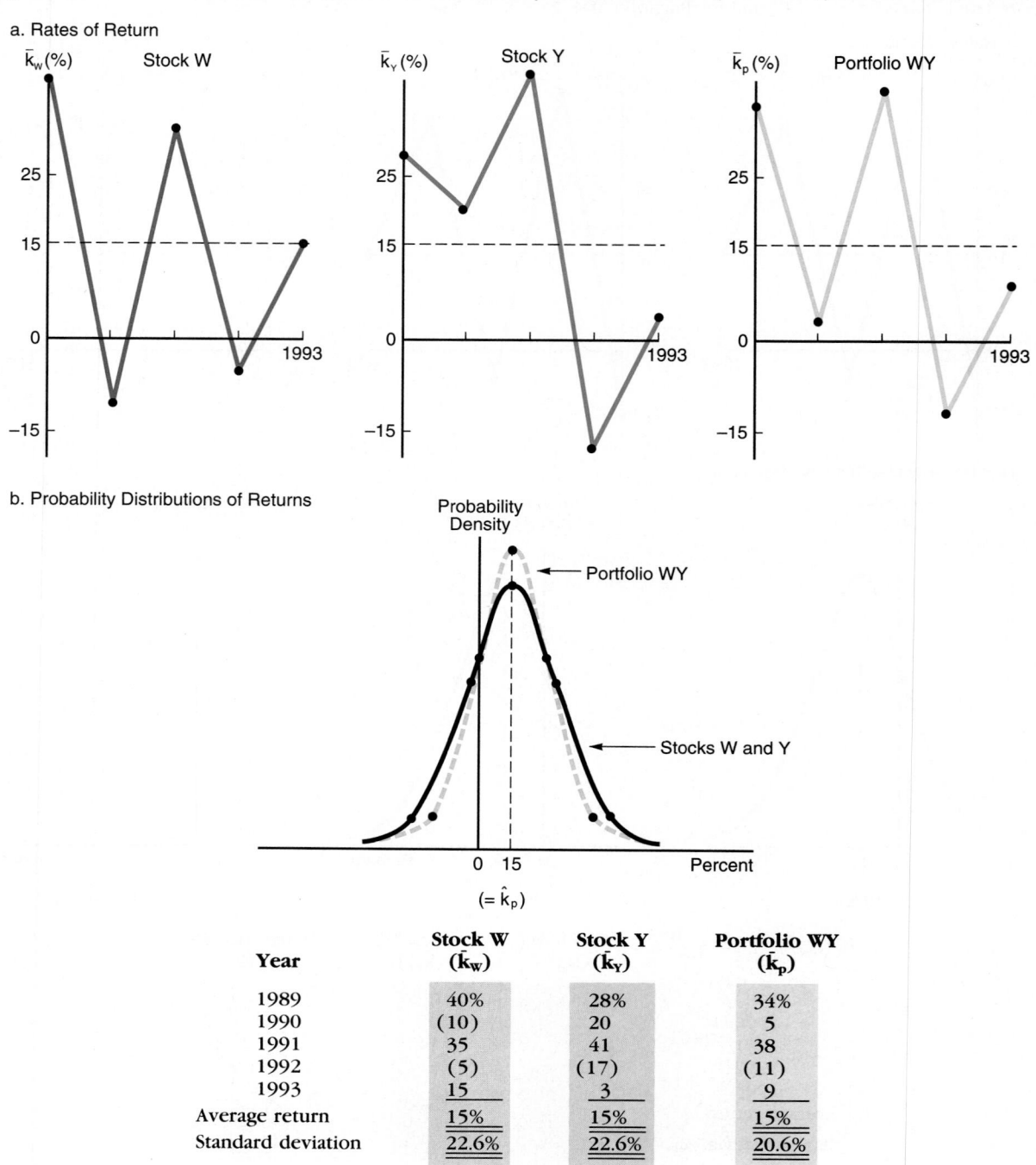

a. Rates of Return

b. Probability Distributions of Returns

Year	Stock W ($\bar{k}_W$)	Stock Y ($\bar{k}_Y$)	Portfolio WY ($\bar{k}_p$)
1989	40%	28%	34%
1990	(10)	20	5
1991	35	41	38
1992	(5)	(17)	(11)
1993	15	3	9
Average return	15%	15%	15%
Standard deviation	22.6%	22.6%	20.6%

When the returns on two stocks are less than perfectly positively correlated, as is the case with Stocks W and Y, diversification will reduce risk. If an investor holds both of these two stocks, the return on the two-stock portfolio is the same as on each individual stock, but the standard deviation is smaller than on the returns of either Stock W or Stock Y held alone. The reason is that factors and events that influence the returns on each stock will, *to some extent,* cancel each other out.

To test your understanding, would you expect to find higher correlations between the returns on two companies in the same or in different industries? For example, would the correlation of returns on Ford's and General Motors's stocks be higher, or would the correlation coefficient be higher between either Ford or GM and IBM, and how would those correlations affect the risk of portfolios containing them?

Answer: Ford's and GM's returns have a correlation coefficient of about 0.9 with one another because both are affected by auto sales, but only about 0.6 with those of IBM.

Implications: A two-stock portfolio consisting of Ford and GM would be riskier than a two-stock portfolio consisting of either Ford or GM, plus IBM. Thus, to minimize risk, portfolios should be diversified across industries.

Company-Specific Risk versus Market Risk. As noted earlier, it is very difficult, if not impossible, to find stocks whose expected returns are not positively correlated—most stocks tend to do well when the national economy is strong and badly when it is weak.[7] Thus, even very large portfolios end up with a substantial amount of risk, but not as much risk as if all the money were invested in only one stock.

To see more precisely how portfolio size affects portfolio risk, consider Figure 12-7, which shows the effect on portfolio risk of forming larger and larger portfolios from randomly selected NYSE stocks. Standard deviations are plotted for an average one-stock portfolio, a two-stock portfolio, and so on, up to a portfolio consisting of all 1,500-plus common stocks that were listed on the NYSE at the time the data were graphed. The graph illustrates that, in general, the riskiness of a portfolio consisting of average NYSE stocks tends to decline and to approach some limit as the size of the portfolio increases. According to data accumulated in recent years, σ_1, the standard deviation of a one-stock portfolio (or an average stock), is approximately 28 percent. A portfolio consisting of all stocks, which is called the *market portfolio,* would have a standard deviation, σ_M, of about 15.1 percent, which is shown as the horizontal dashed line in Figure 12-7.

Thus, almost half of the riskiness inherent in an average individual stock can be eliminated if the stock is held in a reasonably well-diversified portfolio, which is one containing 40 or more stocks. Some risk always remains, however, due to the fact that it is virtually impossible to diversify away the effects of broad stock market movements that affect almost all stocks.

That part of the risk of a stock which can be eliminated is called *diversifiable,* or *company-specific,* or *unsystematic, risk;* that part which cannot be eliminated is called *nondiversifiable,* or *market,* or *systematic, risk.* The name is not especially important, but the fact that a large part of the riskiness of any individual stock can be eliminated is vitally important.

Company-specific risk is caused by such things as lawsuits, strikes, successful and unsuccessful marketing programs, the winning and losing of major

company-specific risk
That part of a security's risk associated with random events; it *can* be eliminated by proper diversification.

---

[7]It is not too hard to find a few stocks that happened to rise because of a particular set of circumstances in the past while most other stocks were declining; it is much harder to find stocks that could logically be *expected* to go up in the future when other stocks are falling. Payco American, the collection agency discussed earlier, is one of those rare exceptions.

Figure 12-7

Reduction of Portfolio Risk through Diversification

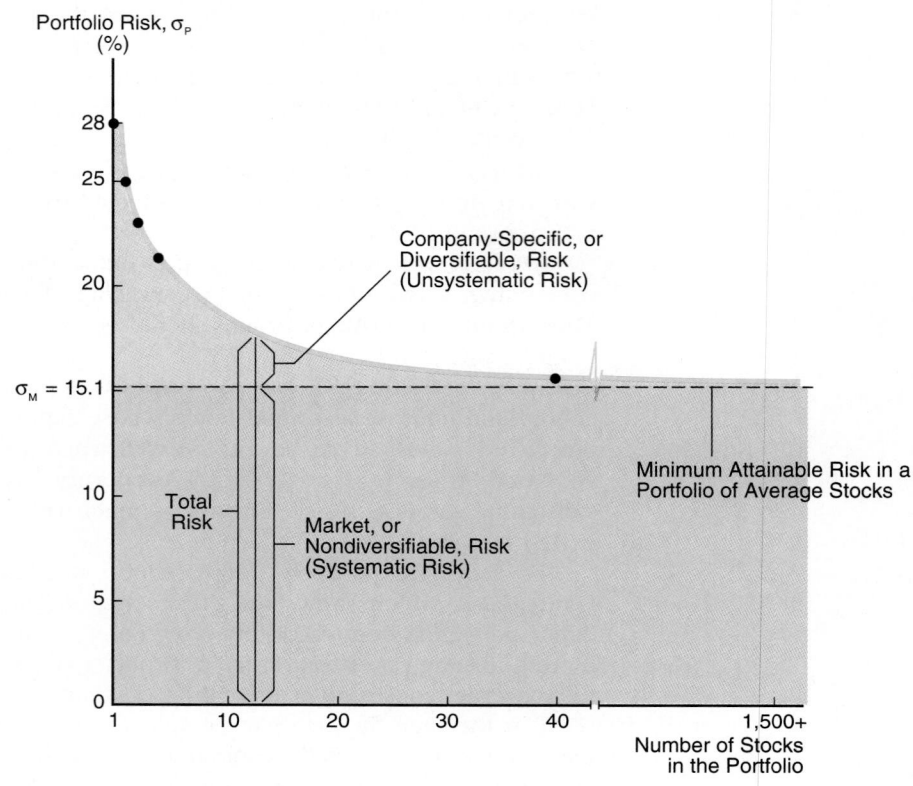

Increasing diversification decreases the risk of an investor's portfolio. When an investor owns only one stock, the risk equals the standard deviation of the returns on that stock, or, in this case, approximately 28 percent. Portfolio risk declines as more stocks are added, until the level of market risk (here, about 15.1 percent) is reached. Market risk is related to broad swings in the stock market as a whole and cannot be eliminated through diversification. Therefore, even very large stock portfolios still contain quite a bit of risk.

market risk

That part of a security's risk that *cannot* be eliminated by diversification.

contracts, and other events that are unique to a particular firm. Since these events are essentially random, their effects on a portfolio can be eliminated by diversification—bad events in one firm will be offset by good events in another. **Market risk,** on the other hand, stems from factors which systematically affect most firms, such as war, inflation, recessions, and high interest rates. Since most stocks will tend to be negatively affected by these factors, systematic risk cannot be eliminated by diversification.

We know that investors demand a premium for bearing risk; that is, the higher the riskiness of a security, the higher the expected return required to induce investors to buy (or to hold) it. However, if investors are primarily concerned with *portfolio risk* rather than the risk of the individual securities in the portfolio, how should the riskiness of an individual stock be measured? The answer, as provided by the Capital Asset Pricing Model (CAPM), is this: *The relevant riskiness of an individual stock is its contribution to the riskiness of a well-diversified portfolio.* In other words, the riskiness of General Electric's stock to a doctor who has a portfolio of 40 stocks, to a trust officer managing a 150-stock portfolio, or to an individual who has invested via a broadly diversified mutual fund is the contribution that the GE stock makes to a portfolio's riskiness. The stock might be quite risky if held by itself, but if most of its risk can be eliminated by diversification, then its **relevant risk,** which is its *contribution to a portfolio's risk,* may be small.

relevant risk

The risk of a security that cannot be diversified away, or its *market risk*. This reflects a security's contribution to the risk of a portfolio.

A simple example will help make this point clear. Suppose you are offered the chance to flip a coin once; if a head comes up, you win $20,000, but if it comes up tails, you lose $16,000. This is a good bet—the expected return is $0.5(\$20,000) + 0.5(-\$16,000) = \$2,000$. However, it is a highly risky proposition because you have a 50 percent chance of losing $16,000. Thus, you might well refuse to make the bet. Alternatively, suppose you were offered the chance to flip a coin 100 times, and you would win $200 for each head but lose $160 for each tail. It is possible that you would flip all heads and win $20,000, and it is also possible that you would flip all tails and lose $16,000, but the chances are very high that you would actually flip about 50 heads and about 50 tails, winning a net of about $2,000. Although each individual flip is a risky bet, collectively you have a low-risk proposition because most of the risk has been diversified away. This is the idea behind holding portfolios of stocks rather than just one stock, except that with stocks all of the risk cannot be eliminated by diversification—those risks related to broad, systematic changes in the stock market will remain.

Are all stocks equally risky in the sense that adding them to a well-diversified portfolio would have the same effect on the portfolio's riskiness? The answer is no. Different stocks will affect the portfolio differently, so different securities have different degrees of relevant risk. How can the relevant risk of an individual stock be measured? As we have seen, all risk except that related to broad market movements can, and presumably will, be diversified away. After all, why accept risk that can easily be eliminated? *The risk that remains after diversifying is market risk, or risk that is inherent in the market, and it can be measured by the degree to which a given stock's returns tend to move up and down with returns on the market.* In the next section, we introduce a measure of a stock's market risk, and then, in a later section, we explain an equation for determining the required rate of return on a stock, given its market risk.

The Concept of Beta

beta coefficient, b

A measure of the extent to which the returns on a given stock move with the stock market.

The tendency of a stock's returns to move with the market is reflected in its **beta coefficient, b,** which is a measure of the stock's *volatility* relative to that of an average stock. Beta is a key element of the CAPM.

An *average-risk stock* is defined as one whose returns tend to move up and down in step with the general market as measured by some index, such as the Dow Jones Industrials, the S&P 500, or the New York Stock Exchange Index. Such a stock will, *by definition,* have a beta, b, of 1.0, which indicates that, in general, if market returns move up by 10 percent, returns on the stock will also move up by 10 percent, while if market returns fall by 10 percent, the stock's returns will likewise fall by 10 percent. A portfolio of such b = 1.0 stocks will

Table 12-2

Illustrative List of
Beta Coefficients

Stock	Beta
Biogen	1.80
Harley-Davidson	1.60
Black & Decker	1.50
Lotus Development	1.45
Deere & Company	1.30
Walt Disney	1.20
Albertson's Inc.	1.20
Apple Computer	1.15
Delta Airlines	1.10
General Motors	1.10
Anheuser Busch	1.05
Campbell Soup Company	1.05
Kellogg	1.00
Gibson Greetings	1.00
Upjohn Company	1.00
Heinz	0.95
Smucker	0.90
BellSouth Corporation	0.85
Exxon	0.75
Potomac Electric Power	0.65

Source: *Value Line,* February 5, 1993.

move up and down with the broad market averages, and it will be just as risky as the averages. If b = 0.5, the stock is only half as volatile as the market—its returns will rise and fall only half as much—and a portfolio of such stocks will be half as risky as a portfolio of b = 1.0 stocks. On the other hand, if b = 2.0, the stock's returns are twice as volatile as the returns on an average stock, so a portfolio of such stocks will be twice as risky as an average portfolio. The value of such a portfolio could double—or be reduced to half—in a short time, and if you held such a portfolio, you could quickly become a millionaire—or take a significant loss.

Betas are regression coefficients, and betas for literally thousands of companies are calculated and published by Merrill Lynch, Value Line, and numerous other organizations. The beta coefficients of some well-known companies are shown in Table 12-2. Most stocks have betas in the range of 0.50 to 1.50; the average for all stocks is 1.0, by definition.[8]

The beta of a stock reflects that company's industry characteristics and management policies. It would, therefore, be reasonable if we were to detect certain patterns where betas are concerned. For example, even without knowning specific management policies of each of the firms listed in Table 12-2, it should intuitively make sense to you that firms such as Harley-Davidson and Deere &

---

[8]Betas can, in theory, be negative—if a stock's returns tend to rise when those of other stocks decline, and vice versa, then the stock's beta will be negative. Note though, that *Value Line* follows 1,700 stocks, and none have negative betas. Payco American, the collection agency company, might have a negative beta, but it is too small to be followed by *Value Line* and most other services which calculate and report betas.

Company, which sell expensive, big-ticket items, should have more market risk and higher betas than, say, Kellogg and Heinz. Sales of the first two companies are likely to suffer more from higher interest rates and/or recessions than are the sales of Kellogg and Heinz. Consumers could be expected to postpone purchases of Harleys and farm equipment during tough economic times (while waiting for financing costs to come down or the recession to end)—they would be much less likely to postpone purchases of corn flakes and ketchup. As a result, the returns on the stocks of Harley-Davidson and Deere *ought* to be more volatile than the returns on an average stock. Following the same line of reasoning, it should not surprise us to find utilities more often than not with below-average betas. The major factors which contribute to market risk (war, inflation, high interest rates, recessions, etc.) simply do not affect consumers' purchases as much when it comes to these basic services.

If a relatively high-beta stock (one whose beta is greater than 1.0) is added to an average-risk (b = 1.0) portfolio, both the portfolio's beta and the riskiness of the portfolio will increase. Conversely, if a relatively low-beta stock (one whose beta is less than 1.0) is added to an average-risk portfolio, the portfolio's beta and risk will decline. *Thus, because a stock's beta measures its contribution to the riskiness of any portfolio, beta is the appropriate measure of the stock's riskiness. Therefore, a stock's market risk is measured by its beta coefficient, and we use the terms "market risk" and "beta risk" interchangeably.*

The preceding analysis of risk in a portfolio setting is part of the Capital Asset Pricing Model (CAPM), and we can summarize our discussion to this point as follows:

1. A stock's risk consists of two components, market, or beta, risk and company-specific risk.

2. Company-specific risk can be eliminated by diversification, and most investors do indeed diversify, either by holding large portfolios or by purchasing shares in a mutual fund. We are left, then, with market risk, which is caused by general movements in the stock market and which reflects the fact that most stocks are systematically affected by certain overall economic events like war, recessions, and inflation. Market risk is the only relevant risk to a rational, diversified investor, because he or she should have already eliminated company-specific risk.

3. Investors must be compensated for bearing risk—the greater the riskiness of a stock, the higher its required return. However, compensation is required only for risk which cannot be eliminated by diversification. If risk premiums existed on stock with high diversifiable risk, well-diversified investors would start buying these securities and bidding up their prices, and their final (equilibrium) expected returns would reflect only nondiversifiable market risk.

   If this point is not clear, an example may help clarify it. Suppose half of Stock A's risk is market risk (it occurs because Stock A moves up and down with the market). The other half of A's risk is diversifiable. You plan to buy only Stock A, so you would be exposed to all of its risk. As compensation for bearing so much risk, you want a risk premium of 8 percent over the 7 percent T-bond rate. Thus, your required return is $k_A = 7\% + 8\% = 15\%$. But suppose other investors, including your professor, are well diversified; they also hold Stock A, but they have eliminated its diversifiable risk and thus are exposed to only half as much risk as you. Therefore, their risk premium will be only half as large as yours, and their required rate of return will be $k_A = 7\% + 4\% = 11\%$.

If the stock were yielding more than 11 percent in the market, others, including your professor, would buy it. If it were yielding 15 percent, you would be willing to buy it, but well-diversified investors would bid its price up and its yield down, and keep you from getting it. In the end, you would have to accept an 11 percent return if you still wanted the stock. Thus, risk premiums in a market populated with rational investors will reflect only market risk.

4. The market risk of a stock is measured by its beta coefficient, which is an index of the stock's relative volatility. Some benchmark betas follow:

$b = 0.5$: Stock's returns are only half as volatile, or risky, as returns of the average stock.

$b = 1.0$: Stock is of average risk.

$b = 2.0$: Stock's returns are twice as risky as returns of the average stock.

5. *Since a stock's beta coefficient determines how the stock affects the riskiness of a diversified portfolio, beta is the most relevant measure of a stock's risk.*

Portfolio Beta

Earlier in the chapter, we found the expected return on a portfolio, $\hat{k}_p$, to be the weighted average of the expected returns on the individual stocks in the portfolio, with the weights equal to the fraction invested in each. Similarly, the beta of a portfolio, b_p, is the weighted average of the betas of the specific securities in that portfolio:

$$b_p = \sum_{i=1}^{n} w_i b_i. \tag{12-6}$$

Here b_p is the beta of the portfolio, and it reflects how volatile the portfolio is in relation to the market; w_i is the fraction of the portfolio invested in the ith stock; and b_i is the beta coefficient of the ith stock. For example, if an investor holds a \$100,000 portfolio consisting of \$33,333.33 invested in each of 3 stocks, and each of the stocks has a beta of 0.7, then the portfolio's beta will be $b_p = 0.7$:

$$b_p = 0.3333(0.7) + 0.3333(0.7) + 0.3333(0.7) = 0.7.$$

Such a portfolio will be less risky than the market; it should experience relatively narrow price swings and have relatively small rate-of-return fluctuations.

Now suppose one of the existing stocks is sold and replaced by a stock with $b_i = 2.0$. This action will increase the riskiness of the portfolio from $b_{p1} = 0.7$ to $b_{p2} = 1.13$:

$$b_{p2} = 0.3333(0.7) + 0.3333(0.7) + 0.3333(2.0) = 1.13.$$

Had a stock with $b_i = 0.2$ been added instead, the portfolio beta would have declined from 0.7 to 0.53. Adding a low-beta stock, therefore, would reduce the riskiness of the portfolio.

? Self-Test

Explain the following statement: "A stock held as part of a portfolio is generally less risky than the same stock held in isolation."

What is meant by perfect positive correlation, by perfect negative correlation, and by zero correlation?

In general, can the riskiness of a portfolio be reduced to zero by increasing the number of stocks in the portfolio? Explain.

What is an average-risk stock in a market-risk sense?

Why is beta the theoretically correct measure of a stock's riskiness?

The Relationship between Risk and Rates of Return

In the preceding section we saw that under the CAPM theory, beta is the appropriate measure of a stock's relevant risk. Now we must specify the relationship between risk and return: for a given level of beta, what rate of return will investors require on a stock in order to compensate them for assuming the risk? The **Security Market Line (SML)** quantifies the risk-return relationship and is given by the following equation:

Security Market Line (SML)

The line that shows the relationship between risk as measured by beta and the required rate of return for individual securities. SML = Equation 12-7.

$$k_i = k_{RF} + (k_M - k_{RF})b_i, \qquad (12\text{-}7)$$

where:

k_i = required rate of return on the ith stock. Note that $\hat{k}_i$ is the *expected* rate of return on the ith stock. If $\hat{k}_i$ is less than k_i, you would not purchase this stock, or you would sell it if you owned it. If $\hat{k}_i$ were greater than k_i, you would want to buy the stock, and you would be indifferent if $\hat{k}_i = k_i$.

k_{RF} = risk-free rate of return. In this context, k_{RF} is generally measured by the return on long-term U.S. Treasury bonds.[9]

b_i = beta coefficient of the ith stock. The beta of an average stock, by definition, is $b_A = 1.0$.

[9]It should be noted that k_{RF} in a CAPM analysis can be proxied by either a long-term rate (the T-bond rate) or a short-term rate (the T-bill rate). Traditionally, the T-bill rate was used, but in recent years there has been a movement toward use of the T-bond rate because there is a closer relationship between T-bond yields and stocks than between T-bill yields and stocks. See Ibbotson and Sinquefield, *Stocks, Bonds, Bills, and Inflation; 1992, Yearbook* (Chicago: Ibbotson & Associates, 1992), for a discussion. Because the T-bond rate is used, k_{RF} is not literally a risk-free rate since Treasury bonds, as you will remember from Chapter 4, do have interest rate risk. However, *the T-bond rate is the closest thing we have to a risk-free long-term interest rate.*

k_M = required rate of return on a portfolio consisting of all stocks, which is the market portfolio. k_M is also the required rate of return on an average ($b_A = 1.0$) stock.

$RP_M = (k_M - k_{RF})$ = market risk premium. This is the additional return over the risk-free rate required to compensate an average investor for assuming an average amount of risk. Average risk means $b_A = 1.0$.

$RP_i = (k_M - k_{RF})b_i$ = risk premium on the ith stock. The stock's risk premium is less than, equal to, or greater than the premium on an average stock, depending on whether its beta is less than, equal to, or greater than 1.0. If $b_i = b_A = 1.0$, then $RP_i = RP_M$.

market risk premium, RP_M

The additional return over the risk-free rate needed to compensate investors for assuming an average amount of risk.

The **market risk premium, RP_M,** depends on the degree of aversion that investors, on average, have to risk.[10] Let us assume that at the current time, Treasury bonds yield $k_{RF} = 9\%$ and an average share of stock has a required rate of return of $k_M = 13\%$. Therefore, the market risk premium is 4 percent:

$$RP_M = k_M - k_{RF} = 13\% - 9\% = 4\%.$$

It follows that if one stock were twice as risky as another, its risk premium would be twice as high, and, conversely, if its risk were only half as much, its risk premium would be half as large. Further, we can measure a stock's relative riskiness by its beta coefficient. Therefore, if we know the market risk premium, RP_M, and the stock's risk as measured by its beta coefficient, b_i, we can find its risk premium as the product $(RP_M)b_i$. For example, if $b_i = 0.5$ and $RP_M = 4\%$, then RP_i is 2 percent:

$$\text{Risk premium for Stock i} = RP_i = (RP_M)b_i$$

$$= (4\%)(0.5) = 2\%.$$

The required return for any investment can be expressed in general terms as

$$\text{Required return} = \text{Risk-free return} + \text{Premium for risk}.$$

Using the SML equation presented above (Equation 12-7), the required rate of return for Stock i can be found to equal 11%:

$$\text{Required rate of return for Stock i} = k_i = k_{RF} + (k_M - k_{RF})b_i$$

$$= 9\% + (13\% - 9\%)(0.5)$$

$$= 9\% + 4\%(0.5)$$

$$= 9\% + 2\%$$

$$= 11\%.$$

---

[10]This concept, as well as other aspects of CAPM, is discussed in more detail in Chapter 3 of Brigham and Gapenski, *Intermediate Financial Management*. It should be noted that the risk premium of an average stock, $k_M - k_{RF}$, cannot be measured with great precision because it is impossible to obtain precise values for the expected future return on the market, k_M. However, empirical studies suggest that where long-term U.S. Treasury bonds are used to measure k_{RF} and where k_M is an estimate of the expected return on the S&P 400 Industrial Stocks, the market risk premium varies somewhat from year to year, and it has generally ranged from 4 to 8 percent during the last 20 years.

Figure 12-8   The Security Market Line (SML)

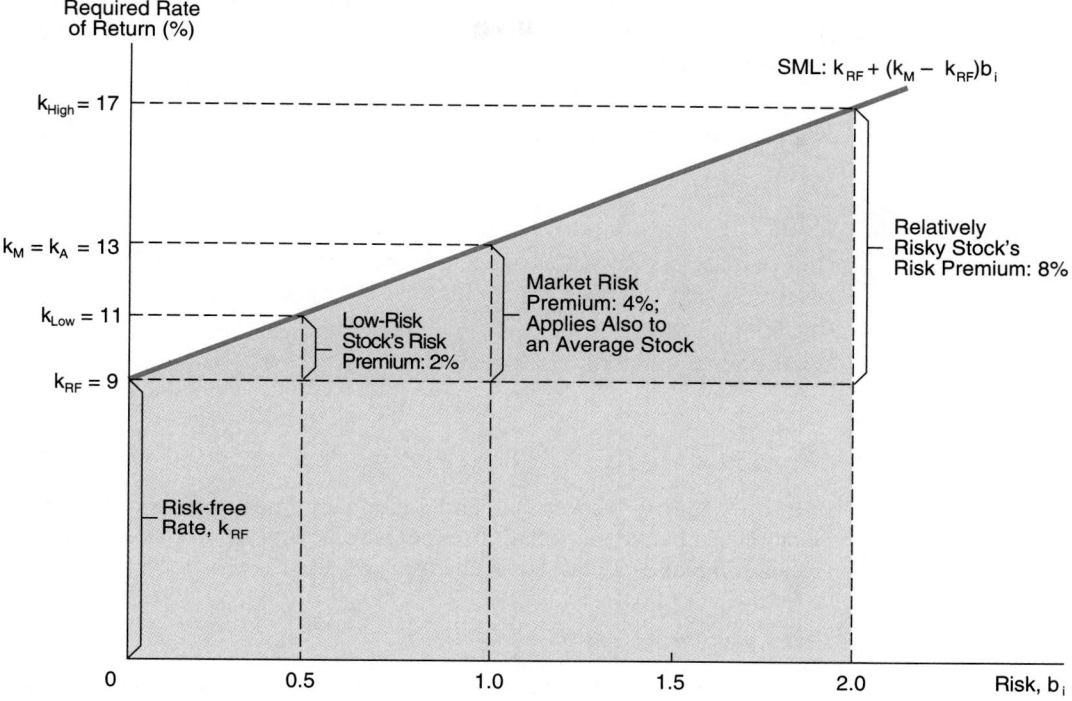

The Security Market Line reflects the relationship between a stock's riskiness and its rate of return. According to the SML equation, a stock's required rate of return equals the rate for risk-free securities (U.S. Treasury bonds) plus a risk premium. This premium is set according to whether a stock is considered to be of average risk (beta = 1.0), less than average risk (beta < 1.0), or greater than average risk (beta > 1.0). When the slope of the SML ($k_M - k_{RF}$) is 4 percent, a stock with a beta of 0.5 will have a 2 percent risk premium, a stock with a beta of 1.0 will have a 4 percent risk premium, and a stock with a beta of 2.0 will have an 8 percent risk premium.

Stock i is a relatively low-risk stock and, therefore, has a lower-than-average required rate of return; its risk premium has been scaled down. On the other hand, if another stock, j, were four times riskier than Stock i and had $b_j = 2.0$, then its required rate of return would be 17 percent:

$$k_j = 9\% + (4\%)2.0 = 17\%.$$

An average stock, with b = 1.0, would naturally have a required rate of return of 13 percent, the same as the market return, k_M:

$$k_A = 9\% + (4\%)1.0 = 13\% = k_M.$$

The Security Market Line (SML) equation is often expressed in graph form, as in Figure 12-8, which shows the SML when $k_{RF} = 9\%$ and $k_M = 13\%$. Note the following points:

1. Required rates of return are shown on the vertical axis, while risk as measured by beta is shown on the horizontal axis.

2. Riskless securities have $b_i = 0$; therefore, k_{RF} appears as the vertical axis intercept in Figure 12-8.

3. The slope of the SML reflects the degree of risk aversion in the economy; the greater the average investor's aversion to risk, (1) the steeper the slope of the line, (2) the greater the risk premium for any stock, and (3) the higher the required rate of return on stocks.[11] These points are discussed further in a later section.

4. The values we worked out for stocks with $b_i = 0.5$, $b_i = 1.0$, and $b_i = 2.0$ agree with the values shown on the graph for k_{Low}, k_A, and k_{High}.

Self-Test

Differentiate between the expected rate of return ($\hat{k}_i$) and the required rate of return (k_i) on the ith stock. Which would have to be larger to get you to buy the stock?

What does the market risk premium, RP_M, measure?

Changes in the Security Market Line and Betas

Both the Security Market Line and a company's position on it change over time because of changes in inflation expectations, investors' risk aversion, and individual companies' betas. Such changes are discussed in the following sections.

Changes in Expected Inflation

As we discussed in Chapter 4, interest amounts to "rent" on borrowed money, or the price of money; thus k_{RF} is the price of money to a riskless borrower. The risk-free rate as measured by the rate on U.S. Treasury securities is called the *nominal rate,* and it consists of two elements: (1) a *real, inflation-free rate of return, k*,* and (2) an *inflation premium, IP,* equal to the anticipated rate of inflation. Thus, $k_{RF} = k^* + IP$.[12] The real rate on long-term Treasury bonds has historically ranged from 2 to 4 percent, with a mean of about 3 percent. Therefore, if no inflation were expected, long-term Treasury bonds would yield about 3 percent. However, as the expected rate of inflation increases, a premium must be added to the real risk-free rate to compensate investors for the loss of purchasing power that results from inflation. Therefore, the 9 percent k_{RF} shown in Figure 12-8 might be thought of as consisting of a 3 percent real risk-free rate of return plus a 6 percent inflation premium: $k_{RF} = k^* + IP = 3\% + 6\% = 9\%$.

If the expected rate of inflation rose by 2 percent to 8 percent, this would cause k_{RF} to rise to 11 percent. Such a change is shown in Figure 12-9. Notice

---

[11]Students sometimes confuse beta with the slope of the SML. This is a mistake. The slope of any line is equal to the "rise" divided by the "run," or $(y_1 - y_0)/(x_1 - x_0)$. Consider Figure 12-8. If we let $y = k$ and $x = $ beta, and we go from the origin to $b = 1.0$, we see that the slope is $(k_M - k_{RF})/(beta_M - beta_{RF}) = (13 - 9)/(1 - 0) = 4$. Thus, the slope of the SML is equal to $(k_M - k_{RF})$, the market risk premium. To put it another way, the slope coefficient of the SML is the numerical value of the market risk premium, in this case, 4.

[12]Long-term Treasury bonds also contain a maturity risk premium, MRP. Here we include the MRP in k* to simplify the discussion.

Figure 12-9

Shift in the SML Caused by an Increase in Expected Inflation

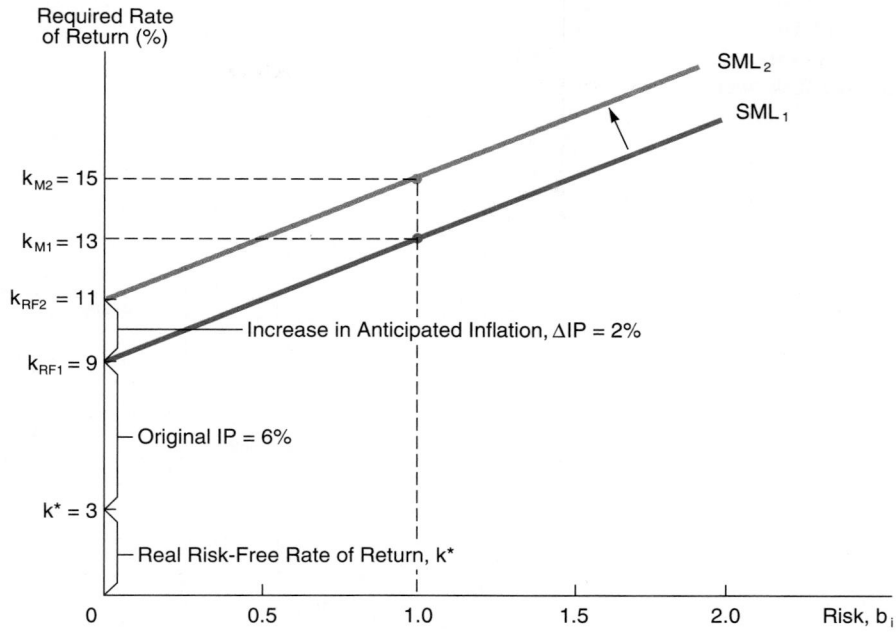

If market participants expect a 2 percent increase in inflation, the return on Treasury bonds would rise from its original 9 percent to 11 percent to compensate purchasers for the expected inflation. This rise in k_{RF} would cause an equal rise in the rate of return for all risky assets because the inflation premium is part of the required rate of return for all assets. The change in inflationary expectations would therefore cause a parallel shift in the SML from SML_1 to SML_2, indicating a 2 percent greater required rate of return for each investment risk level.

that under the CAPM, the increase in k_{RF} causes an *equal* increase in the rate of return on all risky assets because the inflation premium is built into the required rate of return of both risk-free and risky assets.[13] For example, in the figure the rate of return on an average stock, k_M, increases from 13 to 15 percent. Other risky securities' returns also rise by two percentage points; the new Security Market Line, SML_2, is parallel to SML_1, but is 2 percent higher. On the other hand, if inflation expectations decline, and if other things are equal, SML_2 will be at a new lower level, again parallel to the original Security Market Line, SML_1.

Changes in Risk Aversion

As we noted earlier, the slope of the Security Market Line reflects the extent to which investors are averse to risk; the greater the average investor's risk aversion, the steeper the slope of the SML. If investors were indifferent to risk, and

---

[13]Recall that the inflation premium for any asset is equal to the average expected rate of inflation over the life of the asset. Thus, in this analysis we must assume either that all securities plotted on the SML graph have the same life or else that the expected rate of future inflation is constant.

Figure 12-10

Shift in the SML Caused by
Increased Risk Aversion

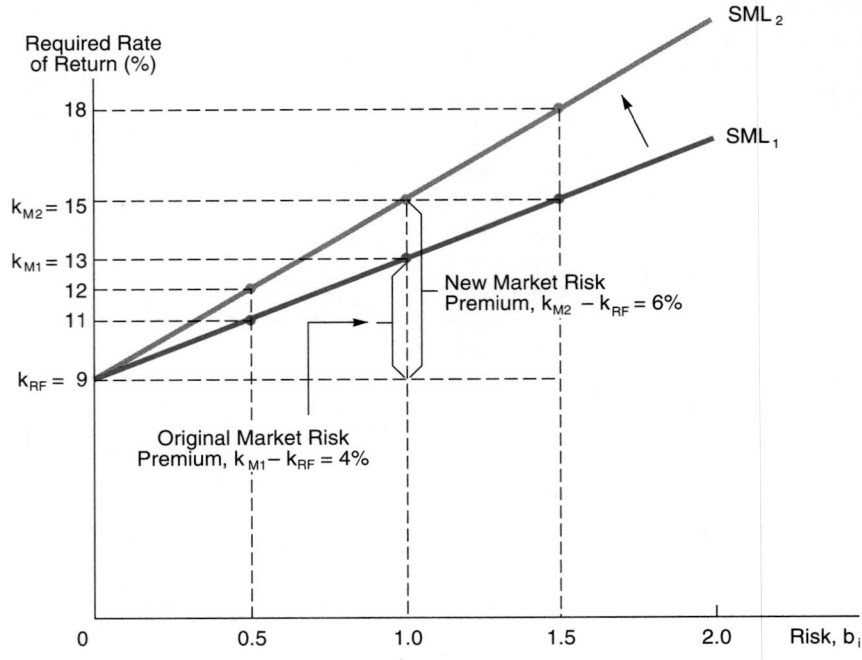

If market participants grow more risk averse, they will require a higher rate of return on
risky investments. Therefore, the difference between the required rate of return on an
average-risk investment and the risk-free rate, known as the market risk premium ($k_M -
k_{RF}$), will grow. In this case, the new SML (SML_2) will have a greater slope than the old one
(SML_1). Note that the shift in risk aversion has no effect on either the risk-free rate or an
individual stock's beta.

if k_{RF} was 9 percent, then risky assets would also sell to provide an expected
return of 9 percent. If there were no risk aversion, there would be no risk
premium, so the SML would be horizontal. As risk aversion increases, so does
the risk premium, and, thus, the slope of the SML.

Figure 12-10 illustrates an increase in risk aversion. The market risk premium rises from 4 to 6 percent, and k_M rises from 13 to 15 percent. The returns
on other risky assets also rise, and the effect of this shift in risk aversion is
greater for riskier securities. For example, the required return on a stock with
$b_i = 0.5$ increases by only one percentage point, from 11 to 12 percent, but
that on a stock with $b_i = 1.5$ increases by three percentage points, from 15 to
18 percent. Instead of the parallel upward shift seen in Figure 12-9, due to
increased inflation expectations, here we see an upward pivoting of the SML
with the risk-free rate acting as an "anchor"; the risk-free rate, by definition, will
not be influenced by changes in investor risk aversion, but the required rate on
all stocks will. Of course, the opposite could also occur: a downward pivoting
of the SML, if investors became less reluctant to take on risk.

Changes in a Stock's Beta Coefficient

As mentioned earlier, the beta of a stock reflects the firm's industry characteristics and its own management policies. For example, a firm can affect its beta risk through changes in the composition of its assets as well as through its use of debt financing, as we shall see in later chapters. A company's beta can also change as a result of external factors such as increased competition in its industry, the expiration of basic patents, major changes in technology, and the like. When such changes occur, the required rate of return also changes, and, as we shall see in Chapter 17, this will affect the price of the firm's stock. For example, consider Allied Food Products, with a beta equal to 1.0. Now suppose some action occurred that caused Allied's beta to increase from 1.0 to 1.5. If the conditions depicted in Figure 12-8 held, Allied's required rate of return would increase from

$$k_1 = k_{RF} + (k_M - k_{RF})b_i$$

$$= 9\% + (13\% - 9\%)1.0 = 13\%$$

to

$$k_2 = 9\% + (13\% - 9\%)1.5 = 15\%.$$

Any change which affects the required rate of return on a security, such as a change in its beta coefficient, in expected inflation, or in investors' risk aversion, will have an impact on the price of the security. We will examine in detail the relationship between a security's required rate of return and its stock price in Chapter 17.

A Word of Caution

A word of caution about betas and the Capital Asset Pricing Model (CAPM) is in order. Although these concepts are logical, the entire theory is based on *ex ante,* or *expected,* conditions, yet we have available only *ex post,* or *past,* data. The betas we calculate show how volatile a stock has been in the past, but conditions may change, and the stock's *future volatility,* which is the item of real concern to investors, may be quite different from its past volatility. Thus, problems may arise when one attempts to forecast *future* events on the basis of *past* data. Indeed, the CAPM does have some potentially serious deficiencies when applied in practice, so estimates of k_i found through the SML may be subject to considerable error. In spite of the potential problems in the application of the CAPM in practice, the CAPM does represent an important step forward in understanding how markets adjust for risk.

Self-Test

What happens to the SML graph (1) when expected inflation increases or (2) when it decreases?

What happens to the SML graph (1) when risk aversion increases or (2) when it decreases? What would the SML look like if investors were indifferent to risk, i.e., had zero risk aversion?

How can a firm influence its market, or beta, risk?

Does the fact that the CAPM theory is based on ex ante, or expected, conditions, while we generally have only ex post, or historical, data, affect the application of CAPM in practice? Explain your answer.

Risk in a Global Context

It seems reasonable to think that investments outside the United States are, for a U.S. citizen or company, riskier than investments in U.S. assets. However, this is not necessarily true—because returns on foreign investments may not be perfectly positively correlated with returns on U.S. assets, it has been argued that multinational corporations may be less risky than companies which operate strictly within the boundaries of any one country. Similarly, portfolio managers have argued that to minimize risk investors should diversify not only across stocks but also across countries. We will address these issues in more depth in Chapter 23, but you should understand the logic behind the case for global diversification.

? *Self Test*

Why are investments made abroad by a U.S. citizen or company not always riskier than those made in U.S. assets?

Physical Assets Versus Securities

In a book on managerial finance for business firms, why do we spend so much time on the riskiness of stocks? Why not begin by looking at the riskiness of such business assets as plant and equipment? *The reason is that, for a management whose goal is stock price maximization, the overriding consideration is the riskiness of the firm's stock, and the relevant risk of any physical asset must be measured in terms of its effect on the stock's risk.* For example, suppose Goodyear Tire Company is considering a major investment in a new product, recapped tires. Sales of recaps and hence earnings on the new operation are highly uncertain, so it would appear that the new venture is quite risky. However, suppose returns on the recap business are negatively correlated with Goodyear's regular operations—when times are good and people have plenty of money, they buy new tires, but when times are bad, they tend to buy more recaps. Therefore, returns would be high on regular operations and low on the recap division during good times, but the opposite situation would occur during recessions. The result might be a pattern somewhat similar to that shown in Figure 12-4 earlier in the chapter for Stocks W and M. Thus, what appears to be a risky investment when viewed on a stand-alone basis might not be very risky when viewed within the context of the company as a whole.

This analysis can be extended to the corporation's owners, the stockholders. Because the stock of Goodyear is owned by diversified stockholders, the primary issue each time the company makes a major asset investment is this: How does this investment affect the risk of our stockholders? Again, the stand-alone risk of an individual project may look quite high, but viewed in the context of the project's effect on stockholders' risk, it may not be very large. We will address this subject again in Chapter 15, where we will examine the effects of capital budgeting projects on companies' beta coefficients and thus on their risk to stockholders.

Finally, the "Decision in Finance" vignette at the beginning and end of this chapter raises an important question: Is diversification always the way to go? Unfortunately, there is no single answer. If you are an *individual* investing in securities, the answer is generally yes. Financial advisers typically recommend reducing your risk by investing in a broadly diversified portfolio, either directly or indirectly through mutual funds. Assets may also be allocated among different *types* of securities, such as U.S. stocks, bonds, money market instruments, and foreign securities, with the mix determined primarily by the investor's risk tolerance and investment time horizon. Note that when diversifying via mutual funds, the individual investor does *not* need to be an expert on every security these funds hold, as long as the funds themselves are well managed and the investor understands each fund's investment objective and has chosen the fund on this basis.

However, if the question is whether *business firms* should always try to diversify their divisions, physical assets, and projects, the answer is less clear. There are many instances in which firms have found diversification to be part of the answer — *and there are cases in which too much diversification has been part of the problem.* For example, in 1992 and 1993, firms as diverse as Rockwell International Corporation and Chemical Banking Corporation are strongly endorsing diversification strategies. Rockwell has had little choice. As defense spending has been reduced in the post–Cold War era, the maker of military aircraft, space shuttles, and guidance systems for nuclear missiles has diversified into more down-to-earth product lines such as factory automation gear and printing presses. Chemical, for its part, has deliberately chosen to become an old-fashioned, widely diversified bank doing business with almost every kind of customer from retail to corporate banking — at the very time that other major banks are moving in the opposite direction toward a narrower focus and a niche in specialized areas of banking.

The danger of a diversification strategy at the *corporate* level is that a firm may find itself trying to do too many things at once. When this happens, the firm's resources may be spread too thin, and it may lose its focus and stray too far from its core business. Examples of such firms include Ball Corporation, whose president notes that "every company is resource-limited" (Ball was planning the spinoff of seven noncore operations during the spring of 1993), and JWP Inc. JWP acts as subcontractor and superintendent to companies; it designs, installs, and services a variety of electrical and mechanical systems for everything from hotels to power plants. JWP's strategy of diversifying into computer services and gobbling up smaller mechanical and electrical companies backfired, according to one analyst, because it left JWP facing "an inability to control a far-flung empire at the same time the economy went in the wrong direction." As of September 1992, JWP was also paring noncore businesses.

A company that has had both successes and failures in terms of diversification is Johnson & Johnson. Against a background of great success in developing new products and markets, J&J's "single most expensive mistake ever" came when it branched off into diagnostic imaging equipment. J&J, a maker of mostly disposable, consumable, small-ticket products such as health-care items, simply did not have the expertise to develop and market highly technical equipment priced as high as $1 million. "We didn't understand that this wasn't a health-care business, it was an electronics business," says chairman and CEO Ralph Larson. You should keep these illustrations in mind when we return to the topic of diversification *within* the firm, which we will do in Chapter 15.

? Self-Test

Explain the following statement: "The stand-alone risk of an individual project may look quite high, but viewed in the context of a project's effect on stockholders' risk, the project's risk may not be very large."

How would the correlation between returns on the project and other assets' returns affect the preceding statement?

Is it possible for a business firm to be too diversified? Explain.

Summary

The primary goals of this chapter were (1) to show how risk is measured in financial analysis and (2) to explain how risk affects required rates of return. The key concepts covered are listed below:

▷ **Risk** can be defined as the chance that some unfavorable event will occur.

The **expected rate of return** on an investment is the mean value of the probability distribution of its possible outcomes.

The **higher the probability** that the actual return will be far below the expected return, the **greater the risk** associated with owning an asset.

The **standard deviation** measures the dispersion around the mean or the risk of an asset on a stand-alone basis.

The **coefficient of variation** is a standardized measure of risk used when comparing assets which have neither the same expected rate of return nor the same standard deviation.

▷ The average investor is **risk averse,** which means that he or she must be compensated for holding risky securities. Therefore, riskier securities must have higher expected returns than less risky securities.

▷ The **Capital Asset Pricing Model (CAPM)** is based on the proposition that any stock's required rate of return is equal to the risk-free rate plus a risk premium.

Most rational investors hold **portfolios of stocks,** and they are more concerned with the risk of their portfolios than with the risks of individual stocks.

Diversification will reduce **portfolio risk**—but not eliminate it—so long as the stocks combined are less than perfectly positively correlated. The reduction in portfolio risk occurs because factors which influence the returns on each stock will, to some extent, cancel each other out.

▶ A stock's risk consists of (1) **company-specific risk,** which can be eliminated by diversification, plus (2) **market risk,** which cannot be eliminated by diversification.

The **relevant risk** of an individual security is its contribution to the riskiness of a well-diversified portfolio, which is the security's **market risk.** Since market risk cannot be eliminated by diversification, investors must be compensated for it.

▶ A stock's **beta coefficient, b,** is a measure of the stock's market (beta) risk. Beta measures the extent to which the stock's returns move with the market, or the stock's **relative volatility.**

A **high-beta stock** is more volatile than an average stock, while a **low-beta stock** is less volatile than average. An **average stock** has b = 1.0 by definition.

The **Security Market Line (SML)** equation shows the relationship between securities' risks and rates of return. The return required for any security i is equal to the **risk-free rate** plus the **market risk premium** times the **security's beta: $k_i = k_{RF} + (k_M - k_{RF})b_i$.**

▶ A number of things can happen to cause the required rate of return on a firm's stock to change, for example (1) **changes in expected inflation,** (2) **changes in investors' aversion to risk,** and (3) **changes in the stock's beta.**

▶ A **diversified portfolio of securities** may be obtained quite easily by investing in one or more mutual funds. In theory, **diversification of physical assets,** occurring within a business firm, should provide benefits as well but, if carried too far, may cause the firm to lose its focus.

Resolution to
DECISION IN FINANCE

DIVERSIFYING RISK—IS IT ALWAYS THE WAY TO GO?

Today, George is eating better and enjoying dreams of expansion rather than nightmares of failure. The answer to his problems was further diversification plus his new role as a traveling salesman.

In addition to his former lines, he now also sells rugby jerseys and other sportswear featur-

Sources: Brenton R. Schlender, "The Perils of Losing Focus," *Fortune,* May 17, 1993, 100; Brent Bowers, "A Clothier Discovers a Sideline Can Dress Up Results," *The Wall Street Journal,* December 7, 1992, B2; and Ann de Rouffignac, "Entergy Pursues Tricky Path of Utility Diversification," *The Wall Street Journal,* December 1, 1992, B4.

ing college letters. He travels around the Northeast and the Midwest to interest campus stores in his Varsity Raggs Inc. So far, Princeton, Dartmouth, Cornell, Notre Dame, and Georgetown are among the campus stores selling his college sportswear. The Georgetown store resisted his sales pitch until a newspaper photo appeared showing President Clinton on the golf course wearing a jersey with the G monogram for his alma mater. He had received it as a gift from Brian George, who also sent shirts with the appropriate initial to former President Bush, Ross Perot, a senator, and other politicians.

The business, says George, "has developed into this national thing. The potential isn't just national. It's global. We sell pure Americana."

By late 1992 the sideline had brought in a modest $75,000 in sales (compared with $450,000 a year for the Northshore store), but it was providing nearly all the company's growth in sales and profits. George has now expanded even further, adding "a whole line of nostalgic items" such as varsity jackets, sweaters, blankets, towels, and caps. He is considering publishing his own national Varsity Raggs catalog. "I don't like to be stagnant," he says. "This gives me an opportunity to get out of the store and sell a concept." As a small business owner, George found diversification into a related product line his key to success.

An exponentially larger business—the Entergy Corporation, a giant utility holding company—is hoping for the same result as it, too, diversifies. An energy research firm reports that electricity sales are growing only about 2 percent a year, and many investor-owned utilities hope to branch out. If they, like Entergy, stay in related areas, they may be all right. "Utilities should stick to their knitting," says Daniel Scotto, a utility bond analyst.

Fears about utility diversification date back to some disastrous decisions of the early 1980s, when some investor-owned utilities went into hotels, insurance, cable television, and other totally unrelated fields. El Paso Electric and Tucson Electric both went bankrupt largely as a result of ill-conceived diversification, and the share price of the Phoenix utility plummeted from $32 to $5 after it moved into the savings and loan business.

Entergy's sidelines, like George's, will be closely related to its primary product. Plans include the energy-efficient audit business, energy management and conservation, foreign power projects, and independent power generation in areas of the United States not regulated by state utility commissions. "They could be real successful since the investments are focused," says analyst Scotto.

If a company strays too far from its original area of expertise, it may find that diversification is not the best way to go. Sears, Xerox, and other major U.S. firms have been shedding their financial services subsidiaries, which were acquired originally because their core businesses were slumping. As noted in the Chapter 2 "Industry Practice" boxed feature, these companies are now selling their financial sidelines and concentrating again on their specialties. American Express is divesting too, acknowledging that its core business never meshed well with the brokerage firm it acquired in 1981.

Seisuke Ueshima, president of Yamaha Corporation, discovered the perils of branching out too far when he expanded outside his firm's world-leading line of musical instruments. Skis, tennis rackets, and furniture require the same wood-shaping techniques as piano cases, but they were not what consumers associated with Yamaha. Similarly, Ueshima's expansion of his electronic organ business into the highly competitive TV, VCR, and audio market proved ill advised.

A Tokyo securities analyst said, "Instead of just worrying about whether they are building things right, they should be asking, 'Why are we building this product?'" Indeed, Yamaha is moving more methodically toward growth these days. Ueshima said, "We are studying new markets very carefully now before introducing new products."

Questions

12-1 The probability distribution of a less risky expected return is more peaked than that of a riskier return. What shape would the probability distribution have for (a) completely certain returns and (b) completely uncertain returns?

12-2 Security A has an expected return of 6 percent, a standard deviation of expected returns of 30 percent, a correlation coefficient with the market of −0.25, and a beta coefficient of -0.5. Security B has an expected return of 11 percent, a standard deviation of returns of 10 percent, a correlation with the market of 0.75, and a beta coefficient of 1.0. Which security is riskier? Why?

12-3   Suppose you owned a portfolio consisting of $500,000 worth of long-term U.S. government bonds.

    a. Would your portfolio be riskless?

    b. Now suppose you hold a portfolio consisting of $500,000 worth of 30-day Treasury bills. Every 30 days your bills mature, and you reinvest the principal ($500,000) in a new batch of bills. Assume that you live on the investment income from your portfolio and that you want to maintain a constant standard of living. Is your portfolio truly riskless?

    c. You should have concluded that both long-term and short-term portfolios of government securities have some element of risk. Can you think of any asset that would be completely riskless?

12-4   A life insurance policy is a financial asset. The premiums paid represent the investment's cost.

    a. How would you calculate the expected return on a life insurance policy?

    b. Suppose the owner of the life insurance policy has no other financial assets — the person's only other asset is "human capital," or lifetime earnings capacity. What is the correlation coefficient between returns on the insurance policy and returns on the policyholder's human capital?

    c. Life insurance companies have to pay administrative costs and sales representatives' commissions; hence, the expected rate of return on insurance premiums is generally low or even negative. Use the portfolio concept to explain why people buy life insurance in spite of negative expected returns.

12-5   If investors' aversion to risk increased, would the risk premium on a high-beta stock increase more or less than that on a low-beta stock? Explain.

Self-Test Problem

ST-1   Stocks A and B have the following historical returns:

Year	Stock A's Returns, k_A	Stock B's Returns, k_B
1989	(10.00%)	(3.00%)
1990	18.50	21.29
1991	38.67	44.25
1992	14.33	3.67
1993	33.00	28.30

    a. Calculate the average rate of return for each stock during the period 1989 through 1993. Assume that someone held a portfolio consisting of 50 percent of Stock A and 50 percent of Stock B. What would have been the realized rate of return on the portfolio in each year from 1989 through 1993? What would have been the average return on the portfolio during this period?

    b. Now calculate the standard deviation of returns for each stock and for the portfolio.

    c. Looking at the annual returns data on the two stocks, would you guess that the correlation coefficient between returns on the two stocks is closer to 0.9 or to -0.9?

    d. If you added more randomly selected stocks to the portfolio, which of the following is the most accurate statement of what would happen to σ_p?

        1. σ_p would remain constant.

        2. σ_p would decline to somewhere in the vicinity of 15 percent.

        3. σ_p would decline to zero if enough stocks were included.

Problems

12-1
Expected return and risk

Analysts have determined the following probability distribution of returns for Jarvi & Ness Inc. (JNI):

Probability	Returns
0.1	(5.0%)
0.2	2.5
0.4	7.5
0.2	12.5
0.1	20.0

a. Calculate the expected rate of return for JNI.
b. Calculate the standard deviation of these returns for JNI.

12-2
Expected returns and risk

The market and Stock J have the following probability distributions:

Probability	k_M	k_J
0.3	15%	20%
0.4	9	5
0.3	18	12

a. Calculate the expected rates of return for the market and Stock J.
b. Calculate the standard deviations for the market and Stock J.
c. Calculate the coefficients of variation for the market and Stock J.

12-3
Expected returns and risk

Projects X and Y have the following probability distributions of future rates of return:

Probability	X	Y
0.1	(40%)	(25%)
0.2	0	5
0.4	20	15
0.2	40	30
0.1	70	45

a. Calculate the expected rate of return for Project Y. The expected rate of return for Project X is 19%.
b. Calculate the standard deviation of expected returns for Project X. The standard deviation of expected returns for Project Y is 17.75%.
c. Calculate the coefficients of variation for Projects X and Y.
d. Is it possible that the firm's management might regard Project X as being *less* risky than Project Y? Explain.

12-4
Required rate of return

Solomon & Sons is evaluating three investment opportunities. Its financial manager has forecasted the risk-free rate and the expected market rate of return as being k_{RF} = 7% and k_M = 11%, respectively. What is the appropriate required rate of return for each stock if
a. Stock A has a beta of 0.5?
b. Stock B has a beta of 1.0?
c. Stock C has a beta of 2.0?

12-5
Required rate of return

Suppose k_{RF} = 8%, k_M = 11%, and k_A = 12.5%.
a. Calculate Stock A's beta.
b. Assume that changes within the firm cause stock A's beta to change to 1.3. What would be A's new required rate of return?

12-6
Required rate of return

Suppose that k_{RF} = 8%, k_M = 12%, and the beta for Computer Concepts Inc. (CCI) is 1.6.
a. What is the required rate of return for CCI's stock?

b. Now suppose that k_{RF} (1) increases to 10 percent or (2) decreases to 6 percent. The slope of the Security Market Line (SML) remains constant (that is, $[k_M - k_{RF}]$ remains at 4 percent). How would each of these changes affect k_M and the required rate of return on CCI's stock?

c. Now assume that the risk-free rate remains at 8 percent but that k_M (1) increases to 14 percent or (2) falls to 10 percent. The slope of the SML does not remain constant. How would each of these changes affect investors' required rate of return on CCI's stock?

12-7

Expected returns

Suppose you were offered (1) $10,000 or (2) a gamble in which you would get $20,000 if a head was flipped but zero if a tail came up.

a. What is the expected value of the gamble?

b. Would you take the sure $10,000 or the gamble?

c. If you choose the sure $10,000, are you a risk averter or a risk seeker?

d. Suppose that you actually take the sure $10,000. You can invest it in either a U.S. Treasury bond that will return $10,700 at the end of a year or a common stock that has a 50/50 chance of being either worthless or worth $23,600 at the end of the year.

1. What is the expected dollar profit on the stock investment? (The expected profit on the T-bond investment is $700.)

2. What is the expected rate of return on the stock investment? (The expected rate of return on the T-bond investment is 7 percent.)

3. Would you invest in the bond or the stock?

4. Just how large would the expected profit (or the expected rate of return) have to be on the stock investment to make *you* invest in the stock?

5. How might your decision be affected if, rather than buying one stock for $10,000, you could construct a portfolio consisting of 100 stocks with $100 in each? Each of these stocks has the same return characteristics as the one stock; that is, a 50/50 chance of being worth either zero or $236 at year-end. Would the correlation between returns on these stocks matter?

12-8

Security Market Line

The Vance Value Fund has a total investment of $500 million in five stocks:

Stock	Investment	Stock's Beta Coefficient
A	$150 million	0.40
B	125 million	1.20
C	75 million	1.60
D	100 million	0.80
E	50 million	1.40

The beta coefficient for a fund like Vance Value can be found as a weighted average of the fund's investments. The current risk-free rate is 9 percent. Market returns have the following estimated probability distribution for the next period:

Probability	Market Return
0.1	10%
0.2	12
0.4	14
0.2	16
0.1	18

a. What is the estimated equation for the Security Market Line (SML)? (*Hint:* Determine the expected market return.)

b. Compute the fund's required rate of return for the next period.

c. Suppose Vance Value Fund's management receives a proposal for a new stock. The investment needed to take a position in the stock is $50 million, it will have an expected return of 17 percent, and its estimated beta coefficient is 2.0. Should the new stock be purchased? At what expected rate of return should management be indifferent to purchasing the stock?

12-9
Portfolio beta

Suppose you hold a diversified portfolio consisting of a $7,500 investment in each of 20 different common stocks. The portfolio beta is equal to 1.12. Now, suppose you have decided to sell one of the stocks in your portfolio with a beta equal to 1.0 for $7,500 and to use these proceeds to buy another stock for your portfolio. Assume the new stock's beta is equal to 1.6. Calculate your portfolio's new beta.

12-10
Required rates of return

Stock R has a beta of 1.5, Stock S has a beta of 0.75, the expected rate of return on an average stock is 15 percent, and the risk-free rate of return is 9 percent. By how much does the required return on the riskier stock exceed the required return on the less risky stock?

12-11
Risky cash flows

Kulkarni Inc. is faced with two investment projects. Annual net cash flows from each project and their probability distributions are shown below:

	Project A		Project B	
Probability	Cash Flow		Probability	Cash Flow
0.2	$4,000		0.2	$ 0
0.6	4,500		0.6	4,500
0.2	5,000		0.2	12,000

a. What is the expected value of the annual net cash flows from each project? What is each project's coefficient of variation (CV)? (*Hint:* Use Equation 12-3 to calculate the standard deviation of Project A. $\sigma_B = \$3,865.23$.)

b. If it were known that Project B was negatively correlated with other cash flows of the firm whereas Project A was positively correlated, how should this knowledge affect the decision? If Project B's cash flows were negatively correlated with gross domestic product (GDP), would that influence your assessment of its risk?

12-12
Realized rates of return

Stocks Y and Z have the following historical returns:

Year	Stock Y's Returns, k_Y	Stock Z's Returns, k_Z
1989	(18.00%)	(14.50%)
1990	33.00	21.80
1991	15.00	30.50
1992	(0.50)	(7.60)
1993	27.00	26.30

a. Calculate the average rate of return for each stock during the period 1989 through 1993.

b. Assume that someone held a portfolio consisting of 50 percent of Stock Y and 50 percent of Stock Z. What would have been the realized rate of return on the portfolio in each year from 1989 through 1993? What would have been the average return on the portfolio during this period?

c. Calculate the standard deviation of returns for each stock and for the portfolio.

d. Calculate the coefficient of variation for each stock and for the portfolio.

e. If you are a risk averse investor, would you prefer to hold Stock Y, Stock Z, or the portfolio? Why?

Solution to Self-Test Problem

ST-1   **a.** The average rate of return for each stock is calculated by simply averaging the returns over the five-year period. The average return for each stock is 18.90 percent, calculated for Stock A as follows:

$$k_{Avg} = (-10.00\% + 18.50\% + 38.67\% + 14.33\% + 33.00\%)/5$$

$$= 18.90\%.$$

The realized rate of return on a portfolio made up of Stock A and Stock B would be calculated by finding the average return in each year as (% of Stock A) k_A + (% of Stock B) k_B and then averaging these yearly returns:

Year	Portfolio AB's Return, k_{AB}
1989	(6.50%)
1990	19.89
1991	41.46
1992	9.00
1993	30.65
	k_{Avg} = 18.90%

b. If only sample returns data over some past period are available, the standard deviation of returns is estimated, using Equation 12-3a, as follows:

$$\text{Estimated } \sigma = S = \sqrt{\frac{\sum_{t=1}^{n} (\bar{k}_t - \bar{k}_{Avg})^2}{n-1}}. \qquad \textbf{(12-3a)}$$

For Stock A, the estimated σ is 19.0 percent:

$$\sigma_A = \sqrt{\frac{(-10.00 - 18.90)^2 + (18.50 - 18.90)^2 + \ldots + (33.00 - 18.90)^2}{5-1}}$$

$$= \sqrt{\frac{1,445.92}{4}} = 19.0\%.$$

The standard deviation of returns for Stock B and for the portfolio are similarly determined, and they are as follows:

	Stock A	Stock B	Portfolio AB
Standard deviation	19.0%	19.0%	18.6%

c. Since the risk reduction from diversification is small (σ_{AB} falls only from 19.0 to 18.6 percent), the most likely value of the correlation coefficient is 0.9. If the correlation coefficient were -0.9, the risk reduction would be much larger. In fact, the correlation coefficient between Stocks A and B is 0.93.

d. If more randomly selected stocks were added to the portfolio, σ_p would decline to somewhere in the vicinity of 15 percent, as we discussed earlier in connection with Figure 12-7. σ_p would remain constant only if the correlation coefficients were $+1.0$, which is most unlikely. σ_p would decline to zero only if the correlation coefficients were less than or equal to zero, but greater than -1.0 and a large number of stocks were added to the portfolio, or if the proper proportions were held in a two-stock portfolio with $r = -1.0$.

Time Value of Money

OBJECTIVES

After reading this chapter, you should be able to:

▶ Explain the relationship between compounding and discounting; between future and present value.

▶ Compute the future value of some beginning amount, and find the present value of a single payment to be received in the future.

▶ Find the future value of a series of equal, periodic payments (an annuity) as well as the present value of such an annuity.

▶ Demonstrate how to find the present value of an uneven series of cash flows, and explain the options available if a portion of this series is an annuity.

▶ Show how you would use the four basic equations to solve for (1) the interest rate, (2) the number of periods, or (3) the periodic payment, if an annuity.

▶ Construct a loan amortization schedule.

DECISION IN FINANCE

CAN BOOMERS RETIRE?

I t's a lot easier to be poor when you're young than when you're in your seventies," says a pension expert who saves 15 percent of her income for her retirement. She acts on information that many young workers are aware of, but ignore — that a comfortable retirement in the 21st century will require years of planning and saving, beginning in this century. The more workers make, the more they need to save to secure the 70 percent of preretirement income that is required to maintain an accustomed standard of living when working days are over. However, most people under the age of 50 give little thought to their retirement needs. If they give it any thought at all, they apparently either plan to keep working after age 65 or else believe that their pensions and Social Security will somehow be sufficient. Blind optimism, rather than logic, seems to rule. As Donald Kanter, coauthor of the book *The Cynical Americans: Living and Working in an Age of Discontent and Disillusion,* says, "These people have seen inflation, layoffs, and a stock market crash. Ordinarily, looking out for 'Number One' would lead to planning for retirement. But if it seems society is going to hell, the whole effort isn't worth it."

In 1991, the average monthly Social Security check was $569. Job holders making $30,000 at retirement today might, nevertheless, have

enough with Social Security and a typical company pension to maintain their lifestyles. As workers' incomes climb, however, the percentage of income that will be replaced by Social Security after retirement shrinks. Those currently earning $125,000 at retirement typically need to replace 21 percent of  their income with savings to maintain their standard of living.

And what about retirement in the future? A 45-year-old currently earning $83,000 (*Fortune*'s median subscriber) would need $1.2 million in total financial assets to be able to retire in the year 2013, at age 65, with no lowering of living standards. This figure does not even take inflation into account. Assuming an average inflation rate over the next 20 years of 4.5 percent, the amount needed would be $2.8 million; to achieve it, the worker would have to save 17 percent of his or her pre-tax income every year. To retire at age 62 instead, almost 30 percent of income should be saved. "If they don't start actively planning for it," says an employee benefits

See end of chapter for resolution.

Photo source: © 1992, Comstock, Inc.

expert, "the future of retirement for the baby boomers is work."

Actually, "saving" is more a generic than a descriptive term since the income set aside should be managed more aggressively if maximum future benefits are to result. Employees who can participate in tax-deferred savings plans at work are advised by the experts to treat them not as savings accounts but as investment vehicles. Tax-deferred opportunities such as 401(k) and profit-sharing plans usually offer employees a choice of investment types—several stock mutual funds, their own company's stock, and several fixed-income investments. Most employees opt for the latter, but they find their earnings seriously eroded by inflation over time. If inflation averaged a modest 4 percent a year, $70,000 would buy only $47,000 worth of goods and services after ten years. Says one financial advisor, "Shifting from fixed-income to

growth stocks could double one's account over 20 to 30 years." (Still, remember that the key word here is "could." In Chapter 12, we learned that the higher the risk of an investment, the higher its required rate of return. People invest in savings accounts, money market mutual funds, and U.S. Treasury securities because the principal is relatively protected and the probability distribution of returns is tighter; thus, the risk of receiving less than the expected return is lower.

Assume that you are planning to participate in your employer's tax-deferred savings plan. As you read this chapter, consider the options that, under differing circumstances, would give you the best expected return over time. Also, suppose your father plans to retire in 20 years, and he plans to invest $5,000 per year for the next 20 years at an average expected annual rate of 10 percent. What would this retirement nest egg be at the end of 20 years?

In Chapter 1 we stated that the firm's goal is to maximize the shareholders' wealth by maximizing the market value of its common stock. One of the determinants of a stock's value is the *timing* of the cash flows investors expect to receive if they invest in that stock. In this chapter we learn why earlier cash flows are better than later ones. This concept is then used in later chapters.

Because the time value of money principles, as developed in this chapter, have many applications, ranging from determining the value of stocks and bonds to making decisions about the acquisition of new equipment, we must emphasize that *of all the techniques used in finance, none is more important than the time value of money, or discounted cash flow (DCF) analysis.* A thorough understanding of the material in this chapter is vital because this concept will be used throughout the remainder of the text to evaluate a wide array of financial topics.[1]

---

[1]This chapter (indeed the entire book) is written assuming that some students do not have financial calculators. The cost of these calculators is falling rapidly, however, so most students do have them. As a result, procedures for obtaining financial calculator solutions are set forth in each of the major sections, along with procedures for obtaining solutions by using regular calculators or tables. It is highly desirable for each student to obtain a financial calculator and to learn how to use it, for calculators — and not clumsy, rounded, and incomplete tables — are used exclusively in well-run, efficient businesses.

However, financial calculators do pose a danger: People sometimes learn to use them in a "cookbook" fashion without understanding the logical processes that underlie the calculations, and then when confronted with a new type of problem, they cannot figure out how to set it up. Therefore, we urge you not only to get a good calculator and to learn how to use it but also to work through the illustrative problems "the long way" to ensure that you understand the concepts involved.

Future (or Compound) Value

The first law of finance, simply stated, is: *A dollar today is worth more than a dollar tomorrow.* Why? Because today's dollar can be invested today so that tomorrow the dollar will have earned interest, and you would end up with an amount greater than the original one dollar.[2] The process of going from present values to future values is called **compounding.** Before we begin, let us define terms that will be used throughout this chapter:

compounding

The arithmetic process of determining the final value of a payment or series of payments when compound interest is applied.

rate of return (k)

The rate of interest expected, or required, on an investment.

future value (FV$_n$)

The amount to which a payment or series of payments will grow over a given future time period when compounded at a given interest rate; also called compound value.

PV = the *present value,* principal, or beginning amount, at Time 0.

  k = the **rate of return** expected, or required, on an investment opportunity.

  I = dollars of interest earned during the year = PV(k).

FV$_n$ = the **future value,** or ending amount, of an investment some number of periods, n, from now; sometimes referred to as *compound value* or *terminal value.* FV$_n$ is the value n years into the future, after compound interest has been earned.

  n = the *number of years* (or, more generally, periods) covered by an investment.

To illustrate, suppose you have $100 that you wish to invest for 1 year at a rate of 8 percent compounded annually. How much would you have at the end of 1 year? In this example, n = 1, so FV$_n$ = FV$_1$ and, using our general terminology, we have

$$FV_1 = PV + I$$
$$= PV + PV(k)$$
$$= PV(1 + k). \tag{13-1}$$

This means that the future value, FV$_n$, at the end of 1 period is the present value times 1 plus the interest rate.

We can now use Equation 13-1 to find how much your $100 will be worth at the end of 1 year at an 8 percent interest rate:

$$FV_1 = \$100(1 + 0.08) = \$100(1.08) = \$108.$$

Your investment will earn $8 of interest (I = $8) so you will have $108 at the end of the year.

Another way to view this problem is through a tool called a *time line.* At Time 0, you have $100. The following time line shows $100 at Year 0. You would like to know how much you will have at the end of the year, Year 1 on the time line, if the investment earns an interest rate of 8 percent. Year 1 on the time line shows a question mark and an arrow that starts at Year 0 and ends

---

[2]What about inflation? Doesn't that lower the value of tomorrow's dollar? The answer is that the rate of return must compensate the investor for all the risks faced in the investment. This includes the risk of lost purchasing power. The investor must believe an investment will provide a rate of return that will be larger than the inflation rate; otherwise, the investor would not make the investment. This need to be compensated for lost purchasing power is reflected in an inflation premium which is incorporated into nominal required interest rates, as we saw in Chapter 4.

at Year 1. The interest rate of 8 percent is shown below the arrow to indicate how much your deposit will increase. From Equation 13-1 we know that the investment will increase to $108 at the end of the year, so you could replace the first question mark with $108.

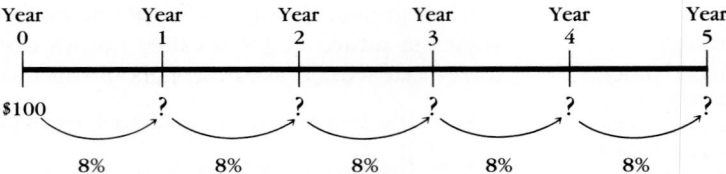

Now suppose you invest your money for 5 years; how much will you have at the end of the fifth year? The answer is $146.93; this value is worked out in Table 13-1. Notice the following points: (1) You start with $100, earn $8 of interest during the first year, and end the year with $108. (2) You start the second year with $108, earn $8.64 on this now larger amount, and end the second year with $116.64. Your second-year earnings, $8.64, were higher because you earned interest on the first year's interest as well as on the initial $100. (3) This process continues, and because in each year the beginning balance is higher, your annual interest income increases — it is "compounding." (4) The total interest earned, $46.93, is reflected in the ending balance, $146.93, so you could replace the last question mark in the time line with $146.93.

Notice that the Table 13-1 value for FV_2, the value of the account at the end of Year 2, is equal to

$$FV_2 = FV_1(1 + k)$$
$$= PV(1 + k)(1 + k)$$
$$= PV(1 + k)^2$$
$$= \$100(1.08)^2$$
$$= \$116.64.$$

Continuing, we see that FV_3, the balance at the end of Year 3, is

$$FV_3 = FV_2(1 + k)$$
$$= PV(1 + k)^3$$
$$= \$100(1.08)^3$$
$$= \$125.97.$$

In general, FV_n, the future value at the end of n years, is found as follows:

$$FV_n = PV(1 + k)^n. \qquad (13\text{-}2)$$

Applying Equation 13-2 to our 5-year, 8 percent example, we obtain

$$FV_5 = \$100(1.08)^5$$
$$= \$100(1.4693)$$
$$= \$146.93,$$

which is the same as the value worked out in Table 13-1.

Table 13-1

Compound Interest
Calculations

Year	Beginning Amount, PV	× (1 + k)	=	Ending Amount, FV_n	Interest Earned, PV(k)
1	$100.00	1.08		$108.00	$ 8.00
2	108.00	1.08		116.64	8.64
3	116.64	1.08		125.97	9.33
4	125.97	1.08		136.05	10.08
5	136.05	1.08		146.93	10.88
					$46.93

In general, we can solve time value of money problems, such as the one just shown, in three ways: (1) with a regular calculator, (2) using interest tables, or (3) with a financial calculator.

1.   **Regular calculator.**   One can simply use a regular calculator, either by multiplying (1 + k) by itself n − 1 times or by using the exponential function to raise (1 + k) to the nth power. In our example, you would enter 1 + k = 1.08 and multiply it by itself four times, or else enter 1.08, press 5, and then press the y^x (or exponential) function key. In either case, the result would be 1.4693 (if you set your calculator to display four decimal places), which you would then multiply by $100 to get the final answer, $146.93.

future value interest factor ($FVIF_{k,n}$)

The future value of $1 left in an account for n periods paying k percent per period, which is equal to $(1 + k)^n$.

2.   **Interest tables.**   The term **future value interest factor for k,n ($FVIF_{k,n}$)** is defined as $(1 + k)^n$, and tables have been constructed for the term $(1 + k)^n$ using a number of k and n values. Table 13-2 is illustrative, and a more complete table, with a wider range of k and n values, is given in Table A-3 in Appendix A at the end of the book.[3]

Equation 13-2 can be written as $FV_n = PV(FVIF_{k,n})$. It is necessary only to go to an appropriate interest table (13-2 or A-3) to find the proper interest factor. For example, the correct interest factor for our 5-year, 8 percent illustration can be found in Table 13-2. We look down the period column to 5 and then across this row to the 8 percent column to find the interest factor, 1.4693. Then, using this interest factor, we find the value of $100 after 5 years to be $FV_5 = PV(FVIF_{8\%,5 \text{ years}}) = $100(1.4693) = $146.93, which is identical to the value obtained by the long method in Table 13-1.

3.   **Financial calculator.**   Financial calculators have been programmed to solve most time value of money problems. In this example, the calculators first generate the $FVIF_{k,n}$ for the specified pair of k and n values, and then multiply the computed factor by the PV to produce the FV_n. You would simply enter PV = 100, k = i = 8, and n = 5, then press the FV key, and the answer $146.93, rounded to two decimal places, will appear. (The FV

---

[3]Notice that we have used the word *period* rather than *year* in Table 13-2. Although annual compounding will be assumed in most of the text material, compounding can occur over periods of time other than years. Appendix 13A demonstrates how the time value of money is affected by "other than annual compounding" (semiannual, quarterly, monthly, and the like).

Table 13-2   Future Value of $1 at the End of n Periods: $FVIF_{k,n} = (1 + k)^n$

Period (n)	1%	2%	3%	4%	5%	6%	7%	8%	9%	10%
1	1.0100	1.0200	1.0300	1.0400	1.0500	1.0600	1.0700	1.0800	1.0900	1.1000
2	1.0201	1.0404	1.0609	1.0816	1.1025	1.1236	1.1449	1.1664	1.1881	1.2100
3	1.0303	1.0612	1.0927	1.1249	1.1576	1.1910	1.2250	1.2597	1.2950	1.3310
4	1.0406	1.0824	1.1255	1.1699	1.2155	1.2625	1.3108	1.3605	1.4116	1.4641
5	1.0510	1.1041	1.1593	1.2167	1.2763	1.3382	1.4026	1.4693	1.5386	1.6105
6	1.0615	1.1262	1.1941	1.2653	1.3401	1.4185	1.5007	1.5869	1.6771	1.7716
7	1.0721	1.1487	1.2299	1.3159	1.4071	1.5036	1.6058	1.7138	1.8280	1.9487
8	1.0829	1.1717	1.2668	1.3686	1.4775	1.5938	1.7182	1.8509	1.9926	2.1436
9	1.0937	1.1951	1.3048	1.4233	1.5513	1.6895	1.8385	1.9990	2.1719	2.3579
10	1.1046	1.2190	1.3439	1.4802	1.6289	1.7908	1.9672	2.1589	2.3674	2.5937
11	1.1157	1.2434	1.3842	1.5395	1.7103	1.8983	2.1049	2.3316	2.5804	2.8531
12	1.1268	1.2682	1.4258	1.6010	1.7959	2.0122	2.2522	2.5182	2.8127	3.1384
13	1.1381	1.2936	1.4685	1.6651	1.8856	2.1329	2.4098	2.7196	3.0658	3.4523
14	1.1495	1.3195	1.5126	1.7317	1.9799	2.2609	2.5785	2.9372	3.3417	3.7975
15	1.1610	1.3459	1.5580	1.8009	2.0789	2.3966	2.7590	3.1722	3.6425	4.1772

will appear with a minus sign on some calculators. The logic behind the negative output is that you deposit the initial amount [the PV] and withdraw the ending amount [the FV], so one is an inflow and the other is an outflow. The negative sign reminds you of that. At this point, though, you can ignore the minus sign. Also, on some calculators you may need to press the Compute key before pressing the FV button.)

Financial calculators allow you to specify the number of decimal places to be displayed. Twelve significant digits are actually *used* in the calculations (which makes financial calculators more accurate than interest tables), but we generally round to two places for answers denominated in dollars and to four places when working with other decimals. The nature of the problem tends to dictate how many decimal places should be displayed.

The most efficient way to solve most problems is to use a financial calculator. Therefore, you should get one and learn how to use it. However, you ought to understand how the tables are developed and used, and you should also understand the logic and the math that underlie all types of financial analysis. Otherwise, you simply will not understand stock and bond valuation, lease analysis, capital budgeting, and other critically important topics.

Graphic View of the Compounding Process: Growth

Figure 13-1 shows how $1 (or any other sum) grows over time at various rates of interest. The 5 and 10 percent curves are based on values given in Table 13-2 for these two interest rates. Notice that the higher the rate of interest, the faster the rate of growth. The interest rate is, in fact, a growth rate. If a sum is invested at a rate of 5 percent and if interest earned is left in the account, then the investment will grow at a rate of 5 percent per period. The compounding

Figure 13-1

Relationships among
Future Value Interest
Factors, Interest Rates, and
Time

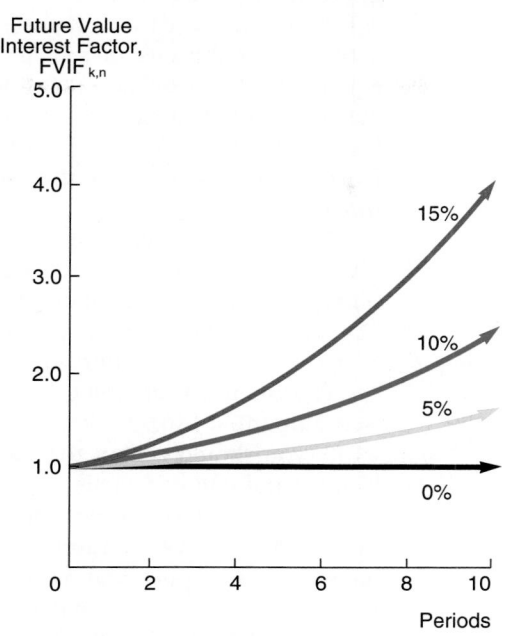

This figure shows the future value interest factors for several interest rates over various periods of time. Because of compounding, the higher the interest rate, the faster the growth in future value. $1.00 invested at 10 percent will grow *more than* twice as fast as $1.00 invested at 5 percent. Refer back to Table 13-2 and note, for example, that for a 10-year period, the future value of $1.00 at 5 percent is only $1.63, but its future value at 10 percent is $2.59. The dollar interest earned, when the interest rate is 5 percent, equals $1.63 − $1.00 = $0.63; the interest earned at 10 percent, however, is $2.59 − $1.00 = $1.59. The point is that although the interest rate was merely doubled, the dollar interest *more than doubled* ($1.59 is greater than 2 × $0.63).

process can be applied to anything that is growing — sales, population, earnings per share, inflation, and so on.

Self-Test

Explain why the following statement is true: "A dollar today is worth more than a dollar to be received next year."

What is compounding? What is "interest on interest"?

Explain the following equation: $FV_1 = PV + I$. (No calculations are necessary.)

Set up a time line showing the following situation: (1) Your initial deposit is $100. (2) The account pays 5% interest annually. (3) You want to know what the balance (FV_3) will be at the end of 3 years.

Present Value

Suppose you are offered the alternatives of receiving $146.93 at the end of 5 years or some currently unspecified amount today. Assume that there is no question that the $146.93 will be paid in full (perhaps the payer is the U.S.

government). Further, assume that you have no current need for the money and will therefore invest it at 8 percent. (Eight percent is defined as your *opportunity cost,* or the rate of return on the best alternative investment available of equal risk.) What dollar amount would it take to make you indifferent to receiving that amount today or the $146.93 at the end of 5 years? Or, wording it a little differently, what is the future promise of $146.93 at the end of 5 years worth to you *today,* when the appropriate interest rate (also called the *discount rate*) is 8 percent?

present value (PV)

The value today of a future payment or series of payments discounted at the appropriate interest rate.

Table 13-1 showed that an initial investment of $100 growing at 8 percent a year yields $146.93 at the end of 5 years. Therefore, in a strictly financial sense, you should be indifferent to $100 today or $146.93 at the end of 5 years. The $100 is defined as the **present value,** or **PV,** of the future $146.93, due in 5 years, when the opportunity cost is 8 percent. Therefore, if the unknown present amount is anything less than $100, you should prefer the future promised amount, $146.93. Conversely, if the amount offered now is greater than $100, you should accept that amount because, when invested at 8 percent, its value at the end of 5 years would be greater than $146.93.

The concept of present value can also be illustrated using a time line which, in this case, shows the future value amount of $146.93 at the end of Year 5. A question mark appears at Year 0; this is the value in which we are interested. Arrows begin at Year 0 and end at Year 5, and the interest rate of 8 percent appears below the arrows, indicating your opportunity cost.

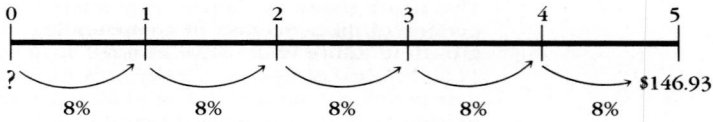

The present value of any future sum is the amount that must be invested today in order to provide that future amount. Because $100 would grow to $146.93 in 5 years at an 8 percent interest rate, the $100 amount is the *present value* of $146.93 due at the end of 5 years when the appropriate interest rate is 8 percent.

discounting

The process of finding the present value of a future payment or a series of future payments; the reverse of compounding.

Finding present values is called **discounting** and is simply the reverse of compounding. We can use Equation 13-2 to illustrate this point.

$$FV_n = PV(1 + k)^n. \qquad (13\text{-}2)$$

To solve for the present value, PV, divide both sides of the equation by the interest factor, $(1 + k)^n$

$$PV = \frac{FV_n}{(1 + k)^n}. \qquad (13\text{-}3)$$

Since dividing by a number and multiplying by its reciprocal give equivalent results,[4] we can rewrite Equation 13-3 as follows:

$$PV = FV_n \left[\frac{1}{(1 + k)^n}\right]. \qquad (13\text{-}3a)$$

---

[4]For example, dividing by 2 is the same as multiplying by ½, or dividing by 4 is equivalent to multiplying by ¼.

Table 13-3   Present Value of $1 Due at the End of n Periods: $PVIF_{k,n} = 1/(1 + k)^n$

Period (n)	1%	2%	3%	4%	5%	6%	7%	8%	9%	10%	12%	14%	15%
1	.9901	.9804	.9709	.9615	.9524	.9434	.9346	.9259	.9174	.9091	.8929	.8772	.8696
2	.9803	.9612	.9426	.9246	.9070	.8900	.8734	.8573	.8417	.8264	.7972	.7695	.7561
3	.9706	.9423	.9151	.8890	.8638	.8396	.8163	.7938	.7722	.7513	.7118	.6750	.6575
4	.9610	.9238	.8885	.8548	.8227	.7921	.7629	.7350	.7084	.6830	.6355	.5921	.5718
5	.9515	.9057	.8626	.8219	.7835	.7473	.7130	.6806	.6499	.6209	.5674	.5194	.4972
6	.9420	.8880	.8375	.7903	.7462	.7050	.6663	.6302	.5963	.5645	.5066	.4556	.4323
7	.9327	.8706	.8131	.7599	.7107	.6651	.6227	.5835	.5470	.5132	.4523	.3996	.3759
8	.9235	.8535	.7894	.7307	.6768	.6274	.5820	.5403	.5019	.4665	.4039	.3506	.3269
9	.9143	.8368	.7664	.7026	.6446	.5919	.5439	.5002	.4604	.4241	.3606	.3075	.2843
10	.9053	.8203	.7441	.6756	.6139	.5584	.5083	.4632	.4224	.3855	.3220	.2697	.2472

present value interest factor ($PVIF_{k,n}$)

The present value of $1 due n periods in the future discounted at k percent per period.

Tables have been constructed for the term inside the brackets for various values of k and n; Table 13-3 is an example. (For a more complete table, see Table A-1 in Appendix A at the end of the book.) For our illustrative case, look down the 8 percent column in Table 13-3 to the fifth row. The number shown there, 0.6806, is the **present value interest factor ($PVIF_{k,n}$)** used to determine the present value of $146.93 payable in 5 years, discounted at 8 percent:

$$PV = FV_5(PVIF_{8\%,5 \text{ years}})$$
$$= \$146.93(0.6806)$$
$$= \$100.00.$$

Again, you could use a financial calculator to find the PV of the $146.93. Just enter n = 5, k = i = 8, and FV = 146.93, and then press the PV button to find PV = $100. (Again, on some calculators, the PV will be given as $-\$100$, and on some calculators you need to press the Compute key before pressing the PV button.)

Graphic View of the Discounting Process

Note in Table 13-3 that the higher the discount rate, k, and the higher the value of n, the lower the $PVIF_{k,n}$. The lowest interest factor shown is $PVIF_{15\%,10} = 0.2472$ in the bottom right-hand corner of the table. This relationship between discount rate, number of periods, and present value is shown graphically in Figure 13-2. These curves, plotted with data from Table 13-3, show that the present value of a sum to be received at some future time decreases both as the payment date is extended further into the future and as the discount rate increases. To illustrate, the present value of $1 due in 10 years is about 61 cents if the discount rate is 5 percent, but the PV is only approximately 25 cents in 10 years if the discount rate is 15 percent. If you are investing in a project with a higher rate of return, a smaller initial payment is required to earn $1 in the future. The length of time until money is paid or received is also important. For example, $1 due in 5 years at 10 percent is worth 62 cents today, but at the same discount rate $1 due in 10 years is worth only about 39 cents today. (In each case, confirm the amount by referring back to Table 13-3.)

Figure 13-2

Relationships among
Present Value Interest
Factors, Interest Rates, and
Time

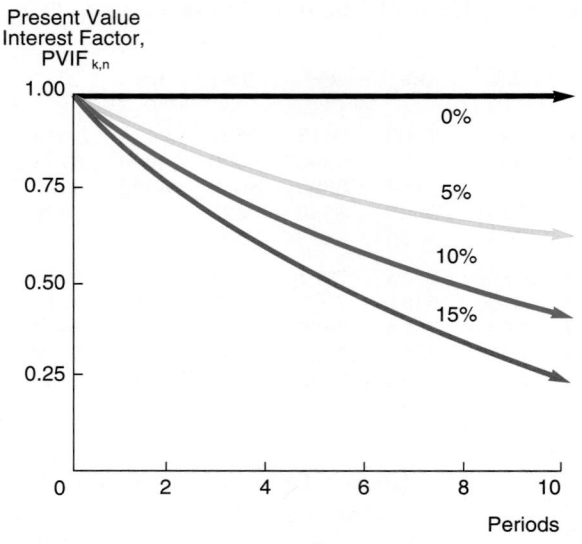

This graph shows the discounting process at various interest rates. The *longer* the time until payment or the *higher* the interest rate, the *less* future payments will be worth in today's dollars. For example, if the interest rate is 10 percent, the present value of $1.00 due in 5 years is $0.62, but the value drops to about $0.39 if due in 10 years. If we vary the interest rate, we see that $1.00 received in 10 years has a present value of about $0.61 when the opportunity cost is 5 percent, but if the interest rate is 15 percent, its present value is only about $0.25.

Thus, if relatively high discount rates apply, funds due in the future are worth comparatively little today. Even at relatively low discount rates, the present values of funds due in the distant future are quite small. Notice also that if the interest rate is zero, or if no time will lapse before the future funds will be received ($n = 0$), then the present and future values of a dollar are the same.

Self-Test

What is meant by the term "opportunity cost"?

What is discounting? How does it relate to compounding?

Briefly discuss how the present value of an amount to be received in the future changes as the time is extended and as the interest rate increases.

Future Value versus Present Value

By now you have noticed that Equations 13-2 and 13-3 are really two ways of looking at the same process. People must decide in everyday life, just as financial managers do, how much to invest in order to receive future returns. Also, it should be apparent that present and future amounts cannot be directly compared: We must either compound present amounts into the future, or discount future dollars back to the present, before making comparisons.

To illustrate this point, let's use the following example. Conrad Dunn is a college student who plans to sell his car for $5,000 and to invest the money in a project that promises a 12 percent return. An uncle suggests that he would like to have the car, but he cannot pay cash for it. He does, however, have several zero coupon government bonds that mature in 15 years.[5] Although their current value is below $5,000, they will mature in 15 years at $20,000, which is four times the car's value, Conrad's uncle notes. Should Conrad give his uncle the car in anticipation of the future $20,000 or sell it for $5,000 cash today?

Even though the value of the future sum is four times the value of the car, we cannot compare the amounts directly because one is a future value and the other is a present value. To make the values comparable, we must either discount the future payment back to the present or compound the present amount into the future. The two procedures will lead to the same decision (to accept or reject the uncle's offer), but we will use both methods.

If we wish to discount the future amount back to the present, we can use Equation 13-3a, employing a present value interest factor from Table A-1 in Appendix A for 12 percent, 15 years:

$$PV = FV_n \left[\frac{1}{(1 + k)^n} \right] = FV_{15}(PVIF_{12\%,15})$$

$$= \$20,000(0.1827)$$

$$= \$3,654.00.$$

Obviously, the offer made by Conrad's uncle is not financially attractive to Conrad because the present value of $20,000 discounted at 12 percent for 15 years is less than the $5,000 Conrad would receive if he sold the car today.

We come to the same conclusion if the present value of the car, $5,000, is compounded 15 years into the future. We use the future value interest factor from Table A-3 in Appendix A for 12 percent, 15 years, in Equation 13-2:

$$FV_n = PV(1 + k)^n = PV(FVIF_{12\%,15})$$

$$= \$5,000(5.4736)$$

$$= \$27,368.00.$$

As we expected, the value of $5,000 invested at a 12 percent rate of interest for 15 years exceeds the $20,000 future value of Conrad's uncle's bonds.

Figure 13-3 illustrates the point that present and future values cannot be directly compared. A present amount can be compounded into the future and then compared with a promised future amount. Conversely, a future sum can be discounted back to the present and then compared with the present value of the uncle's offer. Thus, we can compare $5,000 with $3,654, or $27,368 with $20,000, but we cannot compare $5,000 with $20,000. Conrad may still wish

---

[5]Zero coupon bonds will be discussed in Chapter 16. For now, what matters is that they are purchased for a lump sum, pay no interest, but pay back a much greater lump sum at some future date.

Figure 13-3

Discounting and
Compounding Compared

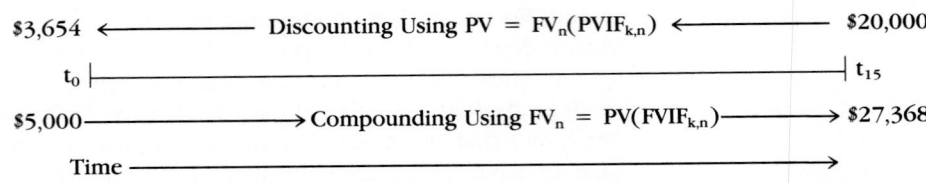

$3,654 ⟵——————— Discounting Using PV = $FV_n(PVIF_{k,n})$ ⟵——————— $20,000

t_0 ├————————————————————————————————┤ t_{15}

$5,000 ——————————→ Compounding Using FV_n = $PV(FVIF_{k,n})$ ——————→ $27,368

Time ————————————————————————————→

To compare a present value to a future value, we must either compound the present sum into the future or discount the future amount back to the present. Whichever method is used, the result gives a proper basis on which to compare the two values. In this figure, the future values are shown on the right ($27,368 was obtained by compounding $5,000 at 12 percent over 15 periods), and the present values are shown on the left ($3,654 was reached by discounting $20,000 at 12 percent over 15 periods).

---

to give his uncle the car for the promise of $20,000 in the future, but not for financial reasons.[6]

 Self-Test

Briefly explain the following statement: "Present and future values cannot be directly compared."

If you know a future amount, the interest rate, and the number of periods, how do you convert the future amount to a present value?

If you know a present amount, the interest rate, and the number of periods, how do you convert the present amount to a future value?

Solving for Time and Interest Rate

You should recognize that we have been dealing with one equation, Equation 13-2, and its transformed version, Equation 13-3:

$$FV_n = PV(1 + k)^n = PV(FVIF_{k,n}). \tag{13-2}$$

$$PV = \frac{FV_n}{(1 + k)^n} = FV_n(PVIF_{k,n}). \tag{13-3}$$

Notice that there are four variables in the equations:

PV = present value.

FV_n = future value.

k = interest (or discount) rate.

n = number of periods.

---

[6]Note that *present value does not have to be today,* and *future value does not have to occur in the future.* Present value is simply the value at the earliest point in time, while future value is at some later time. For example, suppose Conrad had inherited $5,000 from his grandfather when he was six years old and that the money had been earning 12 percent ever since. If today is 15 years later, then the account should have a value of $27,368. The only difference in this illustration is that the present value, $5,000, was 15 years ago, and the future value, $27,368, is today. Both have shifted on the time line by 15 years. Whenever you are in doubt, put the information on a time line, as shown in Figure 13-3.

If you know the values of three of the variables, you can solve for the fourth. Thus far we have always given you the interest rate (k) and the number of periods (n), as well as either the PV or the FV_n. In many situations, though, you will need to solve for either k or n. Solution procedures for these values are discussed next.

Solving for Time, n

Suppose you were given the following information: The present value is $100, the future value is $146.93, and the interest rate is 8 percent. Could you determine the length of time, n, involved? The answer is yes. To do this, you could set up the problem as follows:

$$FV_n = PV(FVIF_{k,n})$$

$$\$146.93 = \$100(FVIF_{8\%,n})$$

$$FVIF_{8\%,n} = \$146.93/\$100$$

$$= 1.4693.$$

Because you were given the interest rate of 8 percent and you were solving for the future value interest factor, all you need to do is to refer to Table A-3 in Appendix A. In Table A-3, look down the 8% column until you reach the future value interest factor of 1.4693. This interest factor is in Row 5; thus, n, the number of time periods it takes for $100 to grow to $146.93, is equal to 5.

You could also work the problem using Equation 13-3 and solve for n:

$$PV = FV_n(PVIF_{k,n})$$

$$\$100 = \$146.93(PVIF_{8\%,n})$$

$$PVIF_{8\%,n} = \$100/\$146.93$$

$$= 0.6806.$$

Because you were given the interest rate of 8 percent and you are solving for the present value interest factor, all you need to do is to refer to Table A-1 in Appendix A. In Table A-1, look down the 8% column until you reach the present value interest factor of 0.6806. This interest factor is in Row 5; thus, n, the number of time periods it takes for $100 to grow to $146.93, is equal to 5.[7]

Finally, you could solve the problem using a financial calculator. Just enter k = i = 8, PV = 100, FV = 146.93 (or −146.93), and then press the n button to find n = 5 periods.

---

[7]Note that whenever you are solving a problem that has only *one* beginning amount and *one* future value and you are trying to find k or n, you always have a choice. You can solve for $FVIF_{k,n}$ or for $PVIF_{k,n}$ and then for either k or n. The example above illustrates that the two approaches will always give the same answer. Remember also that in the example with Conrad and his uncle, we could solve the problem two ways. This is only true for so-called *lump sum* calculations. As we shall see in a moment, when we deal with *annuities* (a series of equal payments) there is generally one preferred method.

Solving for Interest Rate (Growth Rate), k

Suppose we were given the following facts: The present value equals $100, the future value in n years is $146.93, and n, the time period, equals 5. We need to determine the interest rate at which $100 would grow to $146.93 over 5 periods. We could set up the equation as follows:

$$FV_5 = PV(FVIF_{k,5})$$

$$\$146.93 = \$100(FVIF_{k,5})$$

$$FVIF_{k,5} = 1.4693.$$

Because we are given the number of time periods, 5, and we have solved for the future value interest factor, all we need to do is to refer to Table A-3 in Appendix A. We look across the Period 5 row until we reach the future value interest factor of 1.4693. We find this interest factor in the 8% column; thus, the interest rate, k, at which $100 grows to $146.93 over 5 years is equal to 8 percent.

Alternatively, we could set up this equation as follows:

$$PV = FV_5(PVIF_{k,5})$$

$$\$100 = \$146.93(PVIF_{k,5})$$

$$PVIF_{k,5} = 0.6806.$$

Because we are given the number of time periods, 5, and we have solved for the present value interest factor, all we need to do is to refer to Table A-1 in Appendix A. We look across the Period 5 row until we find the present value interest factor of 0.6806. This interest factor is in the 8% column, so the interest rate, k, at which $100 grows to $146.93 over 5 years is equal to 8 percent.

We could also solve the problem with a financial calculator. Simply enter PV = 100, FV = 146.93 (or −146.93), and n = 5, and then press the k = i button to find k = i = 8%.

Self-Test

Write out the two equations that can be used to determine the time period, assuming that you are given PV, FV_n, and the interest rate, k.

Write out the two equations that can be used to determine the interest rate, assuming that you are given PV, FV_n, and the time period, n.

Future (or Compound) Value of an Annuity

So far we have been dealing with cases involving a single payment or receipt in the present and a single amount in the future, that is, lump sums. We now turn to a discussion of situations where there is a series of equal annual payments or receipts, called *annuities*. An **annuity** is defined as *a series of payments of an equal, or constant, amount of money at fixed intervals for a specified number of periods*. Payments are given the symbol PMT, and if the payments are made

annuity
A series of payments of an equal, or constant, amount for a specified number of periods.

Figure 13-4

Time Line for an Ordinary (Deferred) Annuity: Future Value with k = 7%

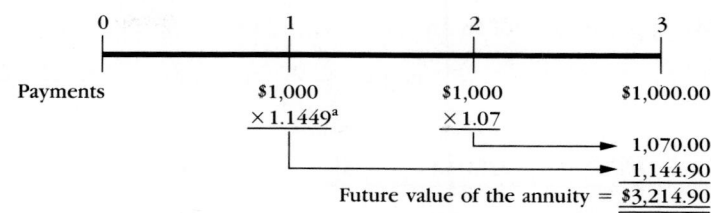

This figure shows how the future value of an annuity is calculated. In this case there is a promise to pay $1,000 per year for 3 years, and the $1,000 payment is received at the *end* of each of the three periods. Upon receipt, each payment is invested at 7 percent interest. The first payment is compounded for 2 years, the second for 1 year, and the third is not compounded at all. The sum of the three future values is the total value of the annuity.

$^a(1.07)^2 = 1.1449$

or received at the beginning of each period, it is called an *annuity due*. However, because *ordinary (deferred) annuities* where payments occur at the end of each period are far more common in finance, when the word annuity is used in this book, you may assume that payments are received at the end of each period, unless otherwise indicated.

Ordinary (Deferred) Annuity

A promise to pay $1,000 annually for 3 years is a 3-year annuity, and if each payment is made at the end of the year, it is an **ordinary (deferred) annuity.** If you were to receive such an annuity and if you deposited each annual payment in an account paying 7 percent interest, how much would you have at the end of 3 years? The answer is shown graphically on a time line in Figure 13-4. The first payment is made at the end of Year 1, the second at the end of Year 2, and the third at the end of Year 3. The last payment is not compounded at all, the second year's payment is compounded for 1 year, and the first is compounded for 2 years. When the future values of each of the $1,000 payments are added, their total is the future value of the annuity, also called the *sum of the annuity*, FVA_n, which in this case is equal to $3,214.90.

Of course, you could calculate the interest factors yourself,[8] but the future value interest factors for an annuity, $FVIFA_{k,n}$, have already been calculated for various combinations of interest rates, k, and time periods, n, in Table A-4 in Appendix A. An illustrative set of these annuity factors is given in Table 13-4.

ordinary (deferred) annuity

An annuity in which the payments occur at the end of each period.

FVA_n

The future value of an annuity over n periods; also called the sum of an annuity.

$FVIFA_{k,n}$

The future value interest factor for an annuity of n periodic payments compounded at k percent.

---

[8]Expressed algebraically, the future value of an annuity, FVA_n, can be computed by multiplying the annuity amount, PMT, by each FVIF, year by year, and then summing *or* by the future value interest factor for an annuity, $FVIFA_{k,n}$:

$$FVA_n = PMT(1 + k)^{n-1} + PMT(1 + k)^{n-2} + \cdots + PMT(1 + k)^1 + PMT(1 + k)^0$$

$$= PMT[(1 + k)^{n-1} + (1 + k)^{n-2} + \cdots + (1 + k)^1 + (1 + k)^0]$$

$$= PMT \sum_{t=1}^{n}(1 + k)^{n-t}$$

$$= PMT(FVIFA_{k,n}).$$

Table 13-4   Future Value of an Annuity of $1 per Period for n Periods:

$$FVIFA_{k,n} = \sum_{t=1}^{n} (1 + k)^{n-t} = \frac{(1 + k)^n - 1}{k}.$$

Period (n)	1%	2%	3%	4%	5%	6%	7%	8%
1	1.0000	1.0000	1.0000	1.0000	1.0000	1.0000	1.0000	1.0000
2	2.0100	2.0200	2.0300	2.0400	2.0500	2.0600	2.0700	2.0800
3	3.0301	3.0604	3.0909	3.1216	3.1525	3.1836	3.2149	3.2464
4	4.0604	4.1216	4.1836	4.2465	4.3101	4.3746	4.4399	4.5061
5	5.1010	5.2040	5.3091	5.4163	5.5256	5.6371	5.7507	5.8666
6	6.1520	6.3081	6.4684	6.6330	6.8019	6.9753	7.1533	7.3359
7	7.2135	7.4343	7.6625	7.8983	8.1420	8.3938	8.6540	8.9228
8	8.2857	8.5830	8.8923	9.2142	9.5491	9.8975	10.2598	10.6366
9	9.3685	9.7546	10.1591	10.5828	11.0266	11.4913	11.9780	12.4876
10	10.4622	10.9497	11.4639	12.0061	12.5779	13.1808	13.8164	14.4866

To answer the preceding question, you would utilize Equation 13-4:

$$FVA_n = PMT(FVIFA_{k,n}), \tag{13-4}$$

where

FVA_n = the future (compound) value of an annuity.

PMT = the annuity payment or receipt.

$FVIFA_{k,n}$ = the future value interest factor for an annuity at k percent for n periods.

To find the future value of the 3-year, $1,000 annuity problem posed earlier, first find the future value interest factor for an annuity, $FVIFA_{k,n}$, by simply referring to Table 13-4. Look down the 7 percent column to the Period 3 row, and then multiply the factor 3.2149 by the $1,000:

$$FVA_3 = PMT(FVIFA_{7\%,3})$$

$$= \$1,000(3.2149)$$

$$= \$3,214.90.$$

Thus, the future value of a 3-year, $1,000 annuity, received at the end of each year and invested at 7 percent annually, is $3,214.90. Notice also that Equation 13-4 is simply the summation of n values of Equation 13-2, i.e., the FV of an annuity is the sum of n individual FVs and, in an ordinary (deferred) annuity, the longest any payment can compound is *one period less* than the life of the annuity.

We can also solve annuity problems with a financial calculator. To solve our illustrative problem, merely key in n = 3, k = i = 7, and PMT = 1000, and then press the FV button to get the answer, $3,214.90. The calculator actually calculates the future values of the three $1,000 payments and sums them to produce the answer, just as we show in Figure 13-4.

Annuity Due

annuity due

An annuity in which the payments occur at the beginning of each period.

Had the annuity in the previous example been an **annuity due**, each of the three payments would have occurred at the beginning rather than the end of the period, or at $t = 0$, $t = 1$, and $t = 2$. In terms of Figure 13-4, each payment would have been shifted to the left, so there would have been $1,000 under Period 0 and a zero under Period 3, meaning that each payment would be compounded for one more period.

We can modify Equation 13-4 to handle annuities due as follows:

$$FVA_n(\text{Annuity due}) = PMT(FVIFA_{k,n})(1 + k). \qquad (13\text{-}4a)$$

Because each payment is compounded for one extra year, multiplying the term $PMT(FVIFA_{k,n})$ by $(1 + k)$ takes care of this extra compounding. Applying Equation 13-4a to the previous example, we obtain

$$FVA_n(\text{Annuity due}) = \$1,000(3.2149)(1.07) = \$3,439.94$$

versus the $3,214.90 for the ordinary annuity.[9] Since payments on an annuity due come earlier, it will always have a higher future value than an ordinary (deferred) annuity.

Annuity due problems can also be solved with financial calculators, most of which have a switch or key marked "Due" or "Beginning" that permits you to convert from ordinary annuities to annuities due. *Since most time value of money problems specify end-of-year payments, you should always switch your calculator back to the "End" mode after you have worked an annuity due problem.*

? Self-Test

What is the difference between an ordinary (deferred) annuity and an annuity due?

How do you modify the equation used to determine the value of an ordinary annuity in order to determine the value of an annuity due?

Which annuity has the greater future value: an ordinary annuity or an annuity due?

Present Value of an Annuity

The preceding section presented techniques that allow you to determine the *future value* of a stream of equal annual payments. You may also wish to determine the *present value* of an annuity. Suppose you were offered the alternatives

---

[9]Another technique can also be used to solve for the future value of an annuity due. First look up the $FVIFA_{k,n}$ for $n + 1$ years in the table. Then subtract 1.0 from that amount to get the $FVIFA_{k,n}$ for the annuity due. Using the previous example, the fourth period interest factor is 4.4399. This factor assumes 4 payments and 3 compounding periods, so by subtracting one payment, we will have the desired 3 payments and 3 compounding periods. Thus:

$$FVIFA_{k,n}(\text{Annuity due}) = \$1,000(4.4399 - 1.0) = \$3,439.90.$$

Notice a rounding difference of $0.04.

Figure 13-5

Time Line for an Ordinary (Deferred) Annuity: Present Value with k = 9%

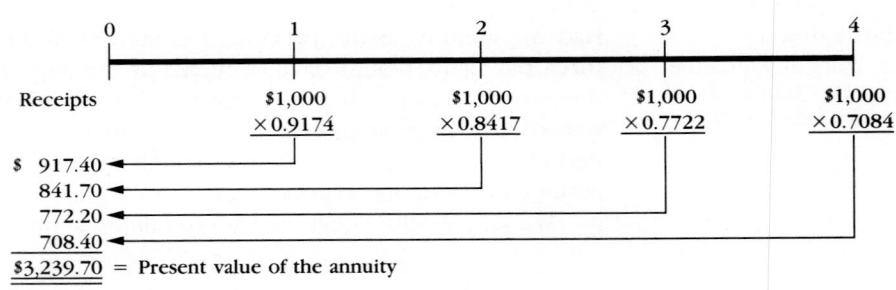

This figure shows how to calculate the present value of a 4-year annuity of $1,000 per year at an interest rate of 9 percent. The present value is calculated by multiplying each year's receipt by the appropriate present value interest factor from Table 13-3 and summing the resulting amounts. Note that *all* the payments must be discounted because they are received at the *end* of each year.

of a 4-year annuity of $1,000 at the *end* of each year (an ordinary, or deferred, annuity) or a single payment today. Let's assume that you have no immediate need for the money during the next 4 years, so if you accept the annuity, you would simply deposit the annual payments in an investment that pays 9 percent interest. The single payment today, if you choose it, would also be deposited in an investment which pays 9 percent interest, compounded annually. How large must the single payment be to make it equivalent to the annuity?

The time line in Figure 13-5 will help you visualize the problem. Note also that, rather than multiplying each year's receipt by factors from Table 13-3 and summing the results, as suggested by Figure 13-5, a table has been constructed to facilitate the computation of the present value of an annuity, PVA_n. Table 13-5 is illustrative of the more complete set of present value interest factors for an annuity, $PVIFA_{k,n}$,[10] that is presented in Table A-2 in Appendix A. Utilizing Equation 13-5 and the appropriate $PVIFA_{k,n}$ contained in Table 13-5, we can solve the problem in a direct fashion:

PVA_n

The present value of an ordinary (deferred) annuity of n periods.

$PVIFA_{k,n}$

The present value interest factor for an annuity of n periodic payments discounted at k percent.

$$PVA_n = PMT(PVIFA_{k,n}) \qquad (13\text{-}5)$$

$$= \$1,000(3.2397)$$

$$= \$3,239.70.$$

---

[10]The present value interest factor for an annuity, $PVIFA_{k,n}$, is computed by summing the present value interest factors for each period. The present value interest factor for the first period is $[1/(1 + k)]^1$, the second is $[1/(1 + k)]^2$, and so on. Thus:

$$PVA_n = PMT \left(\frac{1}{1 + k}\right)^1 + PMT \left(\frac{1}{1 + k}\right)^2 + \cdots + PMT\left(\frac{1}{1 + k}\right)^n$$

$$= PMT \left[\frac{1}{(1 + k)^1} + \frac{1}{(1 + k)^2} + \cdots + \frac{1}{(1 + k)^n}\right]$$

$$= PMT \sum_{t=1}^{n} \frac{1}{(1 + k)^t}$$

$$= PMT(PVIFA_{k,n}). \qquad (13\text{-}5)$$

Table 13-5   Present Value of an Annuity of $1 per Period for n Periods:

$$PVIFA_{k,n} = \sum_{t=1}^{n} \frac{1}{(1 + k)^t} = \frac{1 - [1/(1 + k)^n]}{k}$$

Period (n)	1%	2%	3%	4%	5%	6%	7%	8%	9%	10%
1	0.9901	0.9804	0.9709	0.9615	0.9524	0.9434	0.9346	0.9259	0.9174	0.9091
2	1.9704	1.9416	1.9135	1.8861	1.8594	1.8334	1.8080	1.7833	1.7591	1.7355
3	2.9410	2.8839	2.8286	2.7751	2.7232	2.6730	2.6243	2.5771	2.5313	2.4869
4	3.9020	3.8077	3.7171	3.6299	3.5460	3.4651	3.3872	3.3121	3.2397	3.1699
5	4.8534	4.7135	4.5797	4.4518	4.3295	4.2124	4.1002	3.9927	3.8897	3.7908
6	5.7955	5.6014	5.4172	5.2421	5.0757	4.9173	4.7665	4.6229	4.4859	4.3553
7	6.7282	6.4720	6.2303	6.0021	5.7864	5.5824	5.3893	5.2064	5.0330	4.8684
8	7.6517	7.3255	7.0197	6.7327	6.4632	6.2098	5.9713	5.7466	5.5348	5.3349
9	8.5660	8.1622	7.7861	7.4353	7.1078	6.8017	6.5152	6.2469	5.9952	5.7590
10	9.4713	8.9826	8.5302	8.1109	7.7217	7.3601	7.0236	6.7101	6.4177	6.1446

Thus, the present value of an annuity, PVA_n, equals the annuity payment multiplied by the present value interest factor for an annuity, $PVIFA_{k,n}$, given a value of k and n. In the present problem, the $PVIFA_{k,n}$ for a 4-year, 9 percent annuity is found from Table 13-5 to be 3.2397. Multiplying this factor by the $1,000 annual receipt gives $3,239.70, the present value of the annuity. This amount is, of course, identical to that found by the long method suggested by Figure 13-5.

Notice that the entry for each period n in Table 13-5 is equal to the sum of the entries in Table 13-3 up to and including Period n. For example, the $PVIFA_{k,n}$ for 9 percent, 4 periods in Table 13-5 could have been calculated by summing the PVIFs for Periods 1 through 4 from Table 13-3:

$$0.9174 + 0.8417 + 0.7722 + 0.7084 = 3.2397.$$

Also, as you might expect, the easiest way to solve for the present value of an annuity is with a financial calculator. For our illustrative problem, simply enter n = 4, k = i = 9, and PMT = 1000, and then press the PV button to find the answer, PV = $3,239.72. Note the 2 cent rounding difference.[11]

Present Value of an Annuity Due

Had the payments in the preceding example occurred at the beginning of each year, the annuity would have been an *annuity due.* In terms of Figure 13-5 each payment would have been shifted to the left so that $1,000 would have appeared under Periods 0, 1, 2, and 3 but a zero under Period 4. Each payment occurs one period earlier, so the annuity has a higher present value. To account

---

[11]As mentioned earlier, calculators are more accurate than tables, but even if only tables are used, it is not uncommon to see rounding differences depending on the actual method used.

for these shifts, we multiply Equation 13-5 by $(1 + k)$ to find the present value of an annuity due:

$$PVA_n(\text{Annuity due}) = PMT(PVIFA_{k,n})(1 + k). \qquad (13\text{-}5a)$$

Our illustrative 9 percent, 4-year annuity, with payments made at the beginning of each year thus has a present value of $3,531.27 versus a value of $3,239.70 on an ordinary (deferred) annuity basis:

$$PVA_3 = \$1,000(3.2397)(1.09)$$
$$= \$3,239.70(1.09)$$
$$= \$3,531.27.$$

Since each payment comes earlier, an annuity due is worth more than an ordinary (deferred) annuity.

Again, you can use a financial calculator to solve the problem. Simply set the switch to "Due" or "Begin" instead of "End" and proceed as before. When you finish, remember to switch back to "End."

? Self-Test

Which annuity has the greater present value: an ordinary (deferred) annuity or an annuity due? Why?

Present Value of a Perpetuity

perpetuity
A stream of equal payments expected to continue forever.

Most annuities call for payments to be made over a finite time period, for example, $1,000 per year for 4 years. However, some annuities go on indefinitely; here the payments constitute an *infinite series,* and this is called a **perpetuity.** The present value of a perpetuity is found by applying Equation 13-6:

$$PV(\text{Perpetuity}) = \frac{\text{Payment}}{\text{Interest rate}} = \frac{PMT}{k}. \qquad (13\text{-}6)$$

consol
A perpetual bond originally issued by the British government to consolidate past debts; in general, any perpetual bond.

Perpetuities can be illustrated by some British securities issued after the Napoleonic Wars. In 1815, the British government sold a huge bond issue and used the proceeds to pay off many smaller issues that had been floated in prior years to finance the wars. Because the purpose of the new bonds was to *consolidate* past debts, the bonds were called **consols.** Suppose each consol promised to pay $90 interest per year in perpetuity. (Actually, the interest was stated in pounds.) What would each bond be worth if the going rate of interest, or discount rate, was 8 percent? The answer is $1,125:

$$\text{Value} = \$90/0.08 = \$1,125.00.$$

Perpetuities are discussed further in Chapter 16, where procedures for finding the values of various types of securities are analyzed.

Figure 13-6   Time Line for an Uneven Cash Flow Stream: Present Value with k = 6%

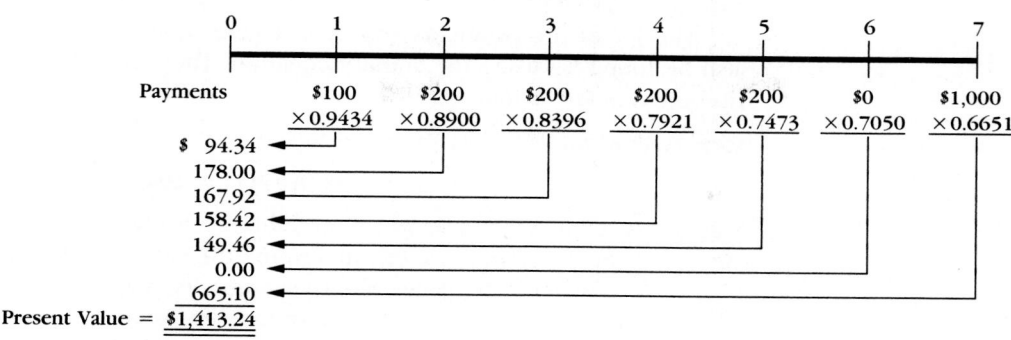

The method used to calculate the present value of an uneven stream of future payments is illustrated in this figure. Each payment is multiplied by the appropriate present value interest factor from Table 13-3 to arrive at its individual present value. The resulting amounts are then totaled to arrive at the present value of the stream of payments. Note that all payments are assumed to occur at year end.

 Self-Test

In what sense is a perpetuity also an annuity?

How is the present value of a perpetuity calculated?

Would it make sense to try to calculate the future value of a perpetuity? Explain.

Present Value of an Uneven Stream of Cash Flows

The definition of an annuity includes the words *equal, or constant, amount;* in other words, annuities involve situations in which payments are *identical* in every period. Although many financial decisions do involve such constant cash flows, some important decisions concern *uneven* flows of cash.[12] In particular, common stock investments ordinarily involve uneven, hopefully increasing, dividend payments over time, and *capital budgeting* projects usually provide uneven cash flows.[13] Consequently, it is necessary to expand our analysis to deal with **uneven cash flow streams.**

uneven cash flow stream

A series of payments in which the amount varies from one period to the next.

The present value of an uneven stream of future payments is equal to the sum of the PVs of the individual components of the stream. For example, suppose we are trying to find the PV of the stream of payments shown in Figure 13-6,

---

[12]We use the terms "payments" and "cash flows" synonymously at this point. Recognize, however, that "cash flows" is a more general term in that it covers both inflows (payments received) and outflows (payments made). In later chapters we will primarily use the term "cash flows."

[13]Capital budgeting is the process of analyzing investments into long-term projects and assets; we will deal with this topic in Chapters 14 and 15.

discounted at 6 percent. As shown in this figure, we multiply each payment by the appropriate $PVIF_{6\%,n}$, then sum these products to obtain the PV of the entire stream, $1,413.24.

The PV of the payments shown in Figure 13-6 for Years 2 through 5 can also be found by using the annuity equation. The steps in this alternative solution process are as follows:

Step 1. Find the PV of $100 due in Year 1:

$$\$100(0.9434) = \$94.34.$$

Step 2. Recognize that a $200 annuity will be received during Years 2 through 5. Thus, we can determine the value of a 5-year annuity, subtract from it the value of a 1-year annuity, and have remaining the value of a 4-year annuity where the first payment occurs in 2 years. This result is achieved by subtracting the PVIFA for a 1-year, 6 percent annuity from the PVIFA for a 5-year, 6 percent annuity and then multiplying the difference by $200:

$$\text{PV of the annuity} = \$200[(PVIFA_{6\%,5}) - (PVIFA_{6\%,1})]$$

$$= \$200(4.2124 - 0.9434)$$

$$= \$200(3.2690) = \$653.80.$$

Thus, the present value of the annuity component of the uneven stream is $653.80.

Step 3. Find the PV of the $1,000 due in Year 7:

$$\$1,000(0.6651) = \$665.10.$$

Step 4. Sum the components:

$$\$94.34 + \$653.80 + \$665.10 = \$1,413.24.$$

Either of the methods can be used to solve problems of this type; note that minor rounding differences may occur. However, the alternative (annuity) solution is easier if the annuity component runs for many years. For example, the alternative solution would be clearly superior for finding the PV of a stream of cash flows consisting of $100 in Year 1, $200 in Years 2 through 29, and $1,000 in Year 30.

The present value of a stream of future cash flows can always be found by summing the present values of each individual cash flow. However, cash flow regularities within the stream may allow the use of shortcuts, such as finding the present value of several cash flows that compose an annuity. Also, in some instances we may want to find the value of a stream of payments at some point other than the present (Year 0). In this situation, we proceed as before but compound and discount to some other point in time, say Year 2 rather than Year 0.

Problems involving uneven cash flows can be solved relatively easily with most financial calculators. First, you enter the individual cash flows, in chronological order, into the cash flow register. Cash flows are usually designated CF_0, CF_1, CF_2, CF_3, and so on. Next, you enter the interest rate, k = i. Finally, you press the NPV key to find the present value of the cash flow stream. (NPV stands for *net* present value, that is, *net* of the cost associated with the stream of future payments. Since no cost is given here, the calculator assumes a zero cost at Time 0. We will expand on this topic in the next chapter.) The calculator has been programmed to find the present value of each cash flow and then to sum these values to find the present value of the entire cash flow stream. For the above problem, enter 0 (because $CF_0 = 0$), 100, 200, 200, 200, 200, 0, 1000, in that order, into the cash flow register. Then enter $k = i = 6$, and press NPV to obtain the answer, $1,413.19, which differs slightly from the long-form solution due to rounding.

Our example has no negative cash flows, but if such cash flows occur, we will simply enter them with negative signs; in other words, this is a general all-purpose method. Second, notice that many calculators allow the annuity portion of the cash flow stream to be entered into the cash flow register more efficiently by using the N_j key. (On some calculators you will be prompted to enter the number of times the cash flow occurs.) In our example, after you have entered the first 200, you could then key in $N_j = 4$, which tells the calculator that 200 occurs four times, then proceed as before.

Also, note that amounts entered into the cash flow register remain in the register until they are cleared. Thus, if you had previously worked a problem with eight cash flows and then moved to a problem with only four cash flows, the calculator would assume that the cash flows from the first problem belonged to the second problem. Therefore, be sure to clear the cash flow register before starting a new problem.

We are generally more interested in the present value of a stream of payments from an asset than in the future (or compound) value because the PV is the value today, and hence the market value of the asset.

Self-Test

What are two types of financial decisions that typically involve uneven cash flows?

Solving for Time and Interest Rate of an Annuity

Earlier in the chapter, we solved for n, the number of periods, and for k, the interest (or growth) rate, when the equation involved only one present value, PV, and one future value, FV_n. Now we see that a similar approach is followed when dealing with annuities and we want to find either n or k.

Solving for Time, n

Suppose you are given the following information: the present value of an ordinary annuity is $75,000, the annual payment is $7,635.48, and the interest rate is 9 percent. What is n? For example, how many years would it take you to pay off a $75,000 home mortgage loan received today, if you make payments of $7,635.48 at the end of each year? To solve this problem, you would go through the following steps:

$$PVA_n = PMT(PVIFA_{k,n}) \qquad (13\text{-}5)$$

$$\$75{,}000 = \$7{,}635.48 \,(PVIFA_{9\%,n})$$

$$PVIFA_{9\%,n} = \$75{,}000/\$7{,}635.48$$

$$= 9.8226.$$

Next you turn to Table A-2 in Appendix A and look at the 9% column. Follow this column down until you find the PVIFA of 9.8226. This interest factor is in Row 25; therefore, it would take 25 years to pay off the loan. To solve this problem with a financial calculator, enter PV = 75000, PMT = 7635.48 (or −7635.48), and k = i = 9; then press n, and obtain the solution, 25 years.

Solving for Interest Rate (Growth Rate), k

On the other hand, if you had been given the present value of a 25-year ordinary annuity as $75,000 (the beginning balance of the mortgage loan), and the constant annual payment of $7,635.48, it should be possible to solve for k, the interest rate that the bank is charging you. If you guess 9 percent, you would be right. The steps are as follows:

$$PVA_n = PMT(PVIFA_{k,n}) \qquad (13\text{-}5)$$

$$\$75{,}000 = \$7{,}635.48 \,(PVIFA_{k,25})$$

$$PVIFA_{k,25} = 9.8226.$$

Because we know the number of periods, we only have to look across the Period 25 row in Table A-2 of Appendix A to find the interest factor 9.8226 in the 9% column. Therefore, the bank is receiving 9 percent interest on the mortgage loan. Using a financial calculator, you would enter PV = 75000, PMT = 7635.48 (or −7635.48), and n = 25. By pressing k = i you would find the interest rate to be 9 percent.

In dealing with the *future* value of an annuity, we could similarly solve for k, given FVA_n, PMT, and n, *or* we could solve for n, given FVA_n, PMT, and k.

Note that these problems would be more difficult to solve if you were using Table A-2 in Appendix A and the interest rate was not an even number. The approximate interest rate could be found by "linear interpolation," which is discussed in algebra texts, but exact solutions can be found easily with calculators.

Although the tables can be used to find the interest rate implicit in single payments and annuities, it is also more difficult to find the interest rate implicit in an uneven series of payments. One can use a trial-and-error procedure, a financial calculator with an IRR feature (IRRs are discussed in Chapter 14), or a graphic procedure (which is also discussed in Chapter 14). We defer further discussion of this problem for now, but we will take it up later, in the capital budgeting chapters and again in our discussion of bonds in Chapter 16.

Self-Test

How would you solve for n, the number of periods, in an annuity?

How would you solve for k, the implicit interest rate, in an annuity?

Solving for the Payment of an Annuity

Suppose that a corporation has to pay off a bond issue of $1 million in 20 years and that the agreement with bondholders requires it to set aside a constant annual amount at the end of each of the 20 years to be able to do so. This is a type of sinking fund, and the $1 million is the future value of a 20-year annuity. If the payments into the sinking fund are expected to earn 6 percent interest, compounded annually, we can solve for the required annual payment as follows:

$$FVA_n = PMT(FVIFA_{k,n}) \qquad\qquad (13\text{-}4)$$

$$\$1{,}000{,}000 = PMT(FVIFA_{6\%,20})$$

$$\$1{,}000{,}000 = PMT(36.786)$$

$$PMT = \$27{,}184.25.$$

If you want to use a financial calculator to solve this problem, you would enter FV = 1000000 (or − 1000000), n = 20, and k = i = 6. Then press PMT, and obtain $27,184.56 (minor difference due to rounding).

Amortized Loans

One of the most important applications of compound interest involves loans that are to be paid off in installments, where the installments include both principal and interest. Examples include automobile loans, home mortgage loans, and most business debt other than very short-term debt. If a loan is to be repaid in equal periodic amounts (monthly, quarterly, or annually), it is said to be an **amortized loan.**

amortized loan

A loan that is repaid in equal payments over its life.

To illustrate, suppose a firm borrows $1,000 to be repaid in 3 equal payments at the end of each of the next 3 years. The lender is to receive 6 percent interest on the loan balance that is outstanding at the beginning of each year. The first task is to determine the amount the firm must repay each year, or the annual payment. To find this amount, recognize that the $1,000 represents the present value of an ordinary annuity of PMT dollars per year for 3 years, discounted at 6 percent, and that we would solve as follows:

$$PVA_n = PMT(PVIFA_{k,n}) \qquad\qquad (13\text{-}5)$$

$$\$1{,}000 = PMT(PVIFA_{6\%,3})$$

$$\$1{,}000 = PMT(2.6730)$$

$$PMT = \$374.11.$$

amortization schedule

A schedule showing precisely how a loan will be repaid. It gives the required payment on each specified date and a breakdown of the payment showing how much constitutes interest and how much constitutes repayment of principal.

Therefore, if the firm pays the lender $374.11 at the end of each of the next 3 years, the percentage cost to the borrower, and the rate of return to the lender, will be 6 percent.

To solve the problem with a financial calculator, simply enter n = 3, k = i = 6, and PV = 1000, and then press PMT. The solution, PMT = 374.11 (or − 374.11) will appear.

Each payment consists partly of interest and partly of a repayment of principal. This breakdown is given in the **amortization schedule** shown in Table 13-6. The interest component is largest in the first year, and it declines as

	Beginning Amount	Payment	Interest[a]	Repayment of Principal[b]	Remaining Balance
Year	(1)	(2)	(3)	(4)	(5)
1	$1,000.00	$ 374.11	$ 60.00	$ 314.11	$685.89
2	685.89	374.11	41.15	332.96	352.93
3	352.93	374.11	21.18	352.93	0
		$1,122.33	$122.33	$1,000.00	

Table 13-6

Loan Amortization Schedule

[a]Interest is calculated by multiplying the loan balance at the beginning of the year by the interest rate. Therefore, interest in Year 1 is $1,000(0.06) = $60; in Year 2 interest is $685.89(0.06) = $41.15; and in Year 3 interest is $352.93(0.06) = $21.18.
[b]Repayment of principal is equal to the payment of $374.11 minus the interest charge for each year.

the outstanding balance of the loan decreases. For tax purposes, the borrower reports the interest payments in Column 3 as a deductible cost each year, while the lender reports these same amounts as taxable income.

Self-Test

How would you find the constant annual payments required to accumulate a given future sum?

In an amortization schedule, in general terms, how do you determine the amount of the periodic payments? How do you determine the portion of the payment that goes to interest and to principal?

Summary

Financial decisions often involve situations where someone pays money at one point in time and receives money at some later time. Dollars that are paid or received at two different points in time are different, and this difference is recognized and accounted for in *time value of money, or discounted cash flow (DCF), analysis.* We summarize below the types of DCF analysis and the key concepts covered in this chapter, using the data shown in Figure 13-7 to illustrate the various points. Refer to the figure constantly, and find in it an example of each point covered as you go through this section.

▷ **Compounding** is the process of determining the **future value (FV)** of a payment or a series of payments. The future (or compound) value, is equal to the beginning amount plus the interest earned.

Future value: $FV_n = PV(1 + k)^n = PV(FVIF_{k,n})$.   (13-2)
(single, lump-sum payment)

Example: $961.50 compounded for 1 year at 4%.

$$FV_1 = \$961.50(1.04)^1 = \$1,000.$$

Figure 13-7

Illustration for Chapter
Summary (k = 4%)

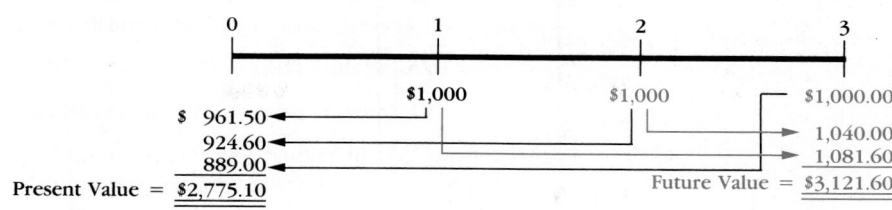

> **Discounting** is the process of finding the **present value (PV)** of a future payment or a series of payments; discounting is the reverse of compounding.

Present value:
(single, lump-sum payment)

$$PV = FV_n \left[\frac{1}{(1 + k)^n} \right] = FV_n(PVIF_{k,n}).$$ **(13-3)**

Example: $1,000 discounted back for 2 years at 4%.

$$PV = \$1,000 \frac{1}{(1.04)^2} = \$1,000(0.9246) = \$924.60.$$

> An **annuity** is defined as a series of equal, periodic payments (PMT) for a specified number of periods.

Future value:
(annuity)

$$FVA_n = PMT(FVIFA_{k,n}).$$ **(13-4)**

Example: FVA of 3 payments of $1,000 each when k = 4%.

$$FVA_3 = 3.1216(\$1,000) = \$3,121.60.$$

Present value:
(annuity)

$$PVA_n = PMT(PVIFA_{k,n}).$$ **(13-5)**

Example: PVA of 3 payments of $1,000 when k = 4%.

$$PVA_3 = 2.7751(\$1,000) = \$2,775.10.$$

An annuity that has payments occurring at the *end* of each period is called an **ordinary (deferred) annuity.** The formulas above are for ordinary (deferred) annuities.

If each payment occurs at the beginning of the period rather than at the end, then we have an **annuity due.** In Figure 13-7, the payments would be shown at Years 0, 1, and 2 rather than at 1, 2, and 3. The PV of each payment would be larger because each payment would be discounted back one year less, and hence the present value of the annuity would also be larger. Similarly, the future value of the annuity due would be larger because each payment would be compounded for an extra year. These formulas can be used to convert the present value and the future value of an ordinary (deferred) annuity to an annuity due:

$$PVA_n(\text{annuity due}) = PVA_n \text{ of an ordinary annuity} \times (1 + k).$$

$$FVA_n(\text{annuity due}) = FVA_n \text{ of an ordinary annuity} \times (1 + k).$$

If the time line in Figure 13-7 were extended out forever, so that the $1,000 payments went on forever, we would have a **perpetuity,** and the perpetuity's present value could be found as follows:

$$\text{PV of perpetuity} = \frac{PMT}{k} = \frac{\$1,000}{0.04} = \$25,000. \qquad \textbf{(13-6)}$$

▷   If the payments in Figure 13-7 were **unequal,** we could not use the annuity formulas. To find the present value or the future value of the series, find the present value or the future value of each individual payment, and then sum them. However, if some of the payments constitute an annuity, then the annuity formula could be used to calculate the present value or future value of that part of the payment stream.

Financial calculators have built-in programs which perform all of the operations discussed in this chapter. It is very helpful to get such a calculator and to learn how to use it. However, it is essential that you also understand the logical processes involved.

▷   Recognize that, given all other relevant information, it is possible to solve for (1) **interest (or growth) rate,** (2) **number of periods,** or (3) **equal, periodic payment.** For the interest rate and number of periods, this is true whether the calculation involves one present value, PV, and one future value, FV_n, or whether you are dealing with annuities.

Example: $961.50 is compounded for 1 year and results in a $FV_1 = \$1,000$.

$FVIF_{k,n} = \$1,000/\$961.50 = 1.0400$;

the interest rate, k, is found in Table A-3 to be 4 percent.

In annuity calculations you can find the equal, periodic payment, when given the interest factor and either the present value or the future value of the annuity. We can use Figure 13-7 to illustrate:

Example: $PVA_3 = PMT\ (PVIFA_{4\%,3})$

$PMT = \$2,775.10/2.7751 = \$1,000$.

▷   An **amortized loan** is one that is paid off in equal payments over a specified period, and the first step is to calculate the PMT which will accomplish this. An **amortization schedule** shows how much of each payment constitutes interest, how much is used to reduce the principal, and the remaining balance at the end of each period.

Note that in all calculations, except the one solving for the present value of a perpetuity, we relied on the four basic equations shown in Table 13-7. These equations, used either alone or in combination, can answer a variety of time value of money questions.

Table 13-7

Time Value of Money Equations

Equation	Equation Number	Chapter Table	Appendix A Table
$FV_n = PV(FVIF_{k,n})$	13-2	13-2	A-3
$PV = FV_n(PVIF_{k,n})$	13-3	13-3	A-1
$FVA_n = PMT(FVIFA_{k,n})$	13-4	13-4	A-4
$PVA_n = PMT(PVIFA_{k,n})$	13-5	13-5	A-2

When solving such problems, you should begin by asking yourself "What do I *know?*" in order to isolate the one variable you do not know and for which you must solve. But, equally important is the question you should ask after you have completed your calculations, namely, *"Is my answer reasonable?"* For example, suppose you are trying to determine what amount must be deposited at the end of the next 5 years, if the interest rate is 5 percent, in order to have $20,000 5 years hence. Recognize that if you receive *no interest* on the funds deposited, you would have to set aside $20,000/5 = $4,000 each year. Therefore, when you *do* receive interest, the annual deposit must be *less* than $4,000 (the answer is $3,619.52). In other words, a little common sense at this point will usually catch your mistake if you have used the wrong table.

The concepts covered in this chapter will be used throughout the remainder of the book. In the next two chapters, the same basic concepts are applied to corporate decisions involving expenditures on capital assets. In later chapters we apply present value concepts to the process of valuing stocks and bonds; there we will see that the market prices of securities are established by determining the present values of the cash flows they are expected to provide.

Review of Chapter Concepts

In light of the importance of this chapter, a review of the equations is warranted. If you have a financial calculator, you should work the problems with it as well as with the equations shown in Table 13-7.

Sample Problems

Problem: Compounding a Single Payment, or Lump Sum, to a Future Period. Your aunt has given you a $3,000 tax-free gift. If you invest it in a 5-year, 8 percent certificate of deposit which compounds interest annually, how much will you have when the certificate matures?

Discussion. The variables in this problem are a present amount, PV, of $3,000; a length of time for the investment, n, of 5 years; and an interest rate, k, of 8 percent. A future amount, FV_n — the value of $3,000 compounded at 8 percent for 5 years — is to be found. Because a single, lump sum is being compounded, we use the $FVIF_{k,n}$ found in either Table 13-2 or Table A-3 in Appendix A.

Solution.

$$FV_5 = PV(FVIF_{8\%,5}) \tag{13-2}$$

$$= \$3,000(1.4693)$$

$$= \$4,407.90.$$

Problem: Present Value of a Future Lump Sum. Your friend Howard has suggested that you invest, along with him, in a real estate deal. He predicts that your portion of the property in question will be worth $40,000 in 8 years. If, as an alternative, you can make an investment with equal risk likely to yield 10 percent, what is the maximum that you should pay for your share of the venture?

Discussion. Here we are concerned with finding the present value, PV, of a future amount, FV_n, of $40,000 to be received in 8 years, n, with a discount rate, k, of 10 percent. With a lump-sum amount to be discounted back to the present, we use a present value interest factor, $PVIF_{k,n}$, found in Table 13-3 or in Table A-1 in Appendix A.

Solution.

$$PV = FV_8(PVIF_{10\%,8}) \tag{13-3}$$

$$= \$40,000(0.4665)$$

$$= \$18,660.00.$$

Problem: Future Value of an Ordinary (Deferred) Annuity. You are planning a great vacation to Europe in 15 years. You plan to save $500 annually, beginning next year, after you graduate. How much will you have in your vacation fund in 15 years if you invest at 9 percent?

Discussion. In this situation you need to determine the future value, FVA_n, of an annuity of $500, PMT, deposited annually for 15 years, n, at 9 percent, k. To do so you would use the interest factor for an annuity, $FVIFA_{k,n}$ where n = 15 and k = 9%, from Table A-4 in Appendix A.

Solution.

$$FVA_{15} = PMT(FVIFA_{9\%,15}) \tag{13-4}$$

$$= \$500(29.361)$$

$$= \$14,680.50.$$

Alternative Problem. Let's keep the scenario that you are saving for your vacation to Europe but change some of the elements of the problem. Now let's assume that you still want to save $500 each year for 15 years, but this time assume that you know the trip will cost $14,680.50. What is the rate of return you must earn to reach your goal?

Discussion. In this situation you again use Equation 13-4, but this time you solve for the future value interest factor for an annuity, $FVIFA_{k,n}$. Once you have the $FVIFA_{k,n}$, you can determine the rate of return required to meet the goal.

Solution.

$$FVA_{15} = PMT(FVIFA_{k,15}) \qquad (13\text{-}4)$$

$$\$14,680.50 = \$500(FVIFA_{k,15})$$

$$FVIFA_{k,15} = \$14,680.50/\$500$$

$$= 29.361.$$

Now go to Table A-4 in Appendix A and find the 15-year row. Moving to the right along the 15-year row, find the future value interest factor 29.361 in the 9 percent column. Thus 9 percent is the rate at which you must invest the annuity of $500 annually for 15 years to have a future value of $14,680.50.

Problem: Future Value of an Annuity Due.   Again, let's keep the scenario that you are saving for your vacation to Europe but change the problem a bit. Now assume that you still want to save $500 each year for 15 years, but that you begin saving today by placing $500 into an investment earning 8 percent, not 9 percent as before. If the trip will cost $14,680, will you have enough money?

Discussion.   In this example we will want to find the future value of an annuity due utilizing Equation 13-4a. You will be saving $500 annually, PMT, for 15 years, n, which will be invested at 8 percent, k. The future value interest factor for an annuity is found in Table A-4 in Appendix A. Recall that in this example the annuity is an annuity due, so the $FVIFA_{k,n}$ must be multiplied by $(1+k)$ to account for this fact.

Solution.

$$FVA_{15}(\text{Annuity due}) = PMT(FVIFA_{8\%,15})(1+0.08) \qquad (13\text{-}4a)$$

$$= \$500(27.152)(1.08)$$

$$= \$14,662.08.$$

Thus, you will fall short of your goal of $14,680 by $17.92.

Problem: Present Value of an Ordinary (Deferred) Annuity.   Lefty Holland, star center for Central State College, has been approached by the Buffalo Bouncers of the Professional Basketball League. The Bouncers have offered Lefty a generous contract that gives him a choice in the payment of his bonus. He may choose between receiving a payment of $25,000 annually (at the end of each year) for 15 years or receiving an equivalent amount today. If Lefty can invest at 8 percent, what would be the equivalent amount if the bonus were paid today? (Ignore tax consequences.)

Discussion.   Under the conditions outlined, we want to find the present value of an annuity, PVA_n, of $25,000 annually, PMT, for 15 years, n, which could be invested at 8 percent, k. The present value interest factor for an annuity, $PVIFA_{k,n}$, is found in Table A-2 of Appendix A.

Solution.

$$PVA_{15} = PMT(PVIFA_{8\%,15}) \qquad (13\text{-}5)$$

$$= \$25,000(8.5595)$$

$$= \$213,987.50.$$

Alternative Problem. To demonstrate again how a single formula (Equation 13-5) can be used to determine unknowns other than PVA_n, let's change the basketball scenario. Now assume that Lefty is given the choice of taking an immediate bonus of \$213,987.50 or taking an annuity for 15 years that he could invest at 8 percent. What is the annual receipt from the annuity?

Discussion. Utilizing Equation 13-5, we now solve for the annuity amount, PMT. The present value interest factor for the annuity, 8.5595, is again found in Table A-2.

Solution.

$$PVA_{15} = PMT(PVIFA_{8\%,15}) \qquad (13\text{-}5)$$

$$\$213,987.50 = PMT(8.5595)$$

$$PMT = \$213,987.50/8.5595$$

$$= \$25,000.00.$$

Problem: Present Value of an Annuity Due. Suppose Lefty's contract allows him to choose between receiving a payment of \$25,000 annually, at the *beginning* of each year, for 15 years or receiving an equivalent amount today. If Lefty can invest at 8 percent, what would be the equivalent amount if the bonus were paid today? (Again, ignore tax consequences.)

Discussion. Under the conditions outlined, we want to find the present value of an annuity due of \$25,000 annually, PMT, for 15 years, n, which could be invested at 8 percent, k. The formula for solving this problem is given in Equation 13-5a.

Solution.

$$PVA_{15} \text{ (Annuity due)} = PMT(PVIFA_{8\%,15})(1+0.08) \qquad (13\text{-}5a)$$

$$= \$25,000(8.5595)(1.08)$$

$$= \$231,106.50.$$

Problem: Present Value of a Perpetuity. Suppose you invest in a security which promises to pay you \$100 per year forever. Assume that the going rate of interest is 10 percent. What is the value of this security?

Discussion. Here we are concerned with finding the PV of a perpetuity (because the payments go on indefinitely) with payments, PMT, of \$100 at an interest rate, k, of 10 percent. The formula for solving this problem is given in Equation 13-6.

Solution.

$$PV(\text{Perpetuity}) = \frac{PMT}{k} \qquad (13\text{-}6)$$

$$= \$100/0.10$$

$$= \$1,000.00.$$

Conclusion

With a bit of practice, perhaps gained by working the end-of-chapter problems, you will find that time value of money questions are not as difficult as they may at first appear. Especially in the beginning, it is often useful to place the dollar amounts on a time line, as shown throughout the chapter, to help you visualize when the various cash flows occur. When you have become comfortable with the concepts just covered, you will continue to discover new applications in many areas. Let's conclude with a recent real-world example: In early February 1993, in an environment of record-breaking low interest rates, General Motors Corporation announced that it had changed its assumption about the rate of interest that its pension fund assets would earn from 11 percent to 10 percent. As a result of this downward revision in the interest rate assumed to apply — part of an overall change toward more conservative accounting practices — *GM's continuing pension expenses would increase by about $428 million per year,* said a company spokesman. In other words, when pension fund assets earn less, more has to be deposited each year to meet future pension obligations. What a difference one percentage point can make!

Resolution to
DECISION IN FINANCE

CAN BOOMERS RETIRE?

Regardless of a person's age or financial circumstances, experts advise a mix of growth and income securities in a retirement portfolio. The nature of this mix, however, varies with the individual. Workers in their twenties or thirties should put 70 percent or more of their retirement money into stocks,

Sources: "Will You Be Able to RETIRE?" *Fortune,* July 31, 1989; "What's Wall Street's First Rule? Diversify," *The Wall Street Journal,* January 25, 1990; "Taking Full Control of Retirement Funds," *The Wall Street Journal,* April 27, 1990; and "Consider IRAs as Tax Deadline Draws Near," *Investor's Business Daily,* April 2, 1993.

with the rest in bonds or liquid assets such as Treasury bills or money market mutual funds. Employees should not overload the stock portion of their portfolios with their own company's stock (as IBM employees recently discovered) because diversification is necessary within that portfolio.

As workers grow older, they are advised to change the mix of their retirement assets. Laurence B. Siegel, managing director of Ibbotson Associates, an investment research firm, says stocks alone are fine "if you're interested only in making the most money possible, and your time horizon is very long. . . ." But for people with less time to realize results, he suggests "a diversified mix of U.S. and international stocks, bonds, and other assets—certainly including real estate."

Although bonds have traditionally been less volatile than stocks, events during the past decade have shown that an all-bond portfolio can be almost as risky as one containing all stocks. Annual returns on U.S. government and corporate bonds during the period from 1982 through 1992 ranged from −2.7 to +43.8 percent.

Several strategies for long-term investing have been proposed. One suggests 60 percent stocks, 35 percent bonds, and 5 percent cash. Such a mix would have produced an average annual return of 9.4 percent over the last 25 years. (Of course, past returns do not necessarily indicate what future returns will be.) A more controversial formula calls for investing equally in five types of no-load mutual funds: funds which specialize in U.S. stocks, in bonds, in real estate, in liquid assets, and in foreign stocks. At the end of each year, investors should realign their holdings and rebalance them among the five groups. This generally involves selling some of the assets that have been performing well and using the proceeds to add to the badly performing groups. However, critics claim this "fixed mix" is a "lazy" and even dangerous strategy since many investors would be putting some of their money into areas they know little or nothing about, such as foreign stocks.

When individual employees decide about retirement fund strategies, they should select the type of plan offered by their employers which best complements their other investments. For instance, some employer plans may be invested only in guaranteed investment contracts (GICs) that pay fixed interest rates close to those paid on certificates of deposit. If so, employees in those companies should probably keep their personal IRAs (individual retirement accounts) in something without a fixed return. (An IRA is allowed to earn tax-deferred interest, and for some individuals the $2,000 contribution is fully or partially tax-deferred as well.) Where compa-

nies offer a choice between a stock fund and a GIC, employees can select the one that is most different from their personal investment accounts.

One good idea is to invest, usually up to 6 percent of one's pre-tax pay, in 401(k) plans. Such an investment reduces current taxable income and also provides for the future. Also, even if after-tax dollars must be contributed, people should always seek plans in which the employer matches employee contributions. Most employers with 401(k) plans provide from 50 cents to $1 for every dollar the employee contributes. As a pension consultant points out, "Getting 50 cents on the dollar is like getting an instant 50 percent return on your money."

Let's now consider the question posed at the beginning of the chapter concerning your father's nest egg. From your reading in this chapter, you should realize that we must solve for the future value of an annuity. We know that PMT = $5,000, n = 20 years, and k = 10 percent, so we are solving for FVA_{20}. The formula is

$$FVA_{20} = PMT\,(FVIFA_{10\%,20})$$
$$= \$5,000\,(57.275)$$
$$= \$286,375.$$

Thus, your father would have $286,375 at the end of 20 years. If your father's investment had earned 12 percent rather than 10 percent, his nest egg would have been $360,260 rather than $286,375.

Suppose your father's nest egg was $286,375 when he retired, and it was earning 10 percent. How much could he withdraw each year for the next 20 years? From your reading of this chapter, you should realize that we must use the present value of an annuity formula. We know that PVA_n = $286,375, k = 10 percent, and n = 20 years, so we are looking for PMT. The formula is

$$PVA_{20} = PMT\,(PVIFA_{10\%,20})$$
$$\$286,375 = PMT\,(8.5136)$$
$$PMT = \$33,637.36.$$

Thus, your father, after he retires, could withdraw $33,637.36 for each of the next 20 years if the account continues to earn 10 percent. If his nest egg had been $360,260 and continued to earn 12 percent rather than 10 percent, he could have withdrawn $48,231.45 for 20 years.

From these two examples, you can see how the return on your investment determines both the total amount accumulated and how much can be withdrawn on an annual basis from this account. However, another important concept to remember is the risk-return relationship that we learned about in Chapter 12—the higher an investment's expected return, the higher its exposure to risk.

Questions

13-1 Is it true that for all positive interest rates the following conditions hold: $FVIF_{k,n} > 1.0$; $PVIF_{k,n} < 1.0$; $FVIFA_{k,n} >$ number of periods the annuity lasts; $PVIFA_{k,n} <$ number of periods the annuity lasts?

13-2 An *annuity* is defined as a series of payments of a fixed amount for a specific number of periods. Thus, $100 a year for 10 years is an annuity, but $100 in Year 1, $200 in Year 2, and $400 a year in Years 3 through 10 does *not* constitute an annuity. However, the second series *contains* an annuity. Is this last statement true or false? Explain.

13-3 If a firm's earnings per share grew from $1 to $2 over a 10-year period, the *total growth* would be 100 percent, but the *annual growth rate* would be *less than* 10 percent. Why is this so?

13-4 To find the present value of an uneven series of payments, you must use the $PVIF_{k,n}$ table; the $PVIFA_{k,n}$ table can never be of use, even if some of the payments constitute an annuity (for example, $100 each year for Years 3, 4, 5, and 6), because the entire series is not an annuity. Is this statement true or false? Explain.

Self-Test Problems

ST-1 Assume it is now January 2, 1993. If you put $1,000 into a savings account on January 2, 1994, at an 8 percent interest rate, compounded annually:
    a. How much would you have in your account on January 2, 1997?
    b. Suppose that you deposited the $1,000 in 4 payments of $250 each on January 2 of 1994, 1995, 1996, and 1997. How much would you have in your account on January 2, 1997, based on 8 percent annual compounding?
    c. Suppose that you made 4 equal payments into your account as suggested in Part b. How large would each of your payments have to be for you to obtain the same ending balance you calculated in Part a?

ST-2 Assume that it is now January 2, 1993, and you will need $1,000 on January 2, 1997. Your bank compounds interest at an 8 percent rate annually.
    a. If only one deposit is made, how much must you place in your account today to have a balance of $1,000 on January 2, 1997?
    b. If you want to make equal payments on each January 2 from 1994 through 1997 to accumulate the $1,000 you need, how large must each of the 4 payments be?
    c. If your father offered either to make the payments calculated in Part b ($221.92) or to give you a lump sum of $750 on January 2, 1994, which would you choose?
    d. If you have only $750 on January 2, 1994, what interest rate, compounded annually, would you have to earn to have the necessary $1,000 on January 2, 1997?

e. Suppose that you can deposit only $186.29 each January 2 from 1994 through 1997 but you still need $1,000 on January 2, 1997. What interest rate, with annual compounding, must you seek out to achieve your goal?

ST-3 Due to unfortunate circumstances, your sister must borrow $5,000 from you. She wants to repay the loan in 3 equal annual installments that include 9 percent interest. How much should she pay for each of the next 3 years? (Note: The first payment is due one year from today.)

ST-4 Your Uncle Henry promises that if you invest $7,500 today in his latest "get rich quick" scheme, he will pay you $2,651.50 at the end of each year for the next 3 years. What rate of return is his project offering?

Problems

13-1

Present and future values for different periods

Find the following values *without* using the tables, then work the problems *with* the tables to check your answers. Disregard rounding errors.

a. An initial $1,000 compounded for 1 year at 6 percent.
b. An initial $1,000 compounded for 2 years at 6 percent.
c. The present value of $1,000 due in 1 year at a discount rate of 6 percent.
d. The present value of $1,000 due in 2 years at a discount rate of 6 percent.

13-2

Present and future values for different interest rates

Use the tables to find the following values:

a. An initial $1,000 compounded for 10 years at 5 percent.
b. An initial $1,000 compounded for 10 years at 10 percent.
c. The present value of $1,000 due in 10 years at a 5 percent discount rate.
d. The present value of $2,594 due in 10 years at a 10 percent discount rate.

13-3

Time for a lump sum to double

To the closest year, how long will it take any given amount to double if it is deposited and earns the following interest rates?

a. 5 percent.
b. 10 percent.
c. 15 percent.
d. 100 percent.

13-4

Future value of an ordinary annuity

Find the *future value* of the following annuities if the first payment in each annuity is made at the end of the year; that is, it is an ordinary (deferred) annuity.

a. $1,000 per year for 10 years at 6 percent.
b. $2,000 per year for 5 years at 12 percent.
c. $1,000 per year for 5 years at zero percent.

13-5

Future value of an annuity due

Find the *future value* of the following annuities if the first payment is made today; that is, each one is an annuity due.

a. $1,000 per year for 10 years at 6 percent.
b. $2,000 per year for 5 years at 12 percent.
c. $1,000 per year for 5 years at zero percent.

13-6

Present value of an ordinary annuity

Find the *present value* of the following ordinary (deferred) annuities:

a. $1,000 per year for 10 years at 6 percent.
b. $2,000 per year for 5 years at 12 percent.
c. $1,000 per year for 5 years at zero percent.

13-7

Present value of an annuity due

Find the *present value* of the following annuities if the first payment is made today; that is, each one is an annuity due.

a. $1,000 per year for 10 years at 6 percent.
b. $2,000 per year for 5 years at 12 percent.
c. $1,000 per year for 5 years at zero percent.

13-8
Uneven cash flows

a. Find the present value of the following cash flow streams when the discount rate is 10 percent. (Assume end-of-year payments.)

Year	Cash Flow Stream A	Cash Flow Stream B
1	$1,000	$5,000
2	3,000	3,000
3	3,000	3,000
4	3,000	3,000
5	5,000	1,000

b. What is the value of each cash flow stream at a zero percent discount rate?
c. What are the implications of your findings?

13-9
Uneven cash flows

Find the present value of the following cash flow stream, discounted at 12 percent: Year 1, $10,000; Year 2, $5,000; Years 3 to 20, $1,000. (Assume end-of-year cash flows.)

13-10
Future value of an ordinary annuity

Joe Cargill has decided to set up an individual retirement account (IRA) and to contribute $2,000 to the account at the end of each of the next 15 years, at which time he plans to retire. Joe's broker has recommended a mutual stock fund which has yielded an average annual rate of return of 10 percent for a number of years and is expected to continue to yield 10 percent indefinitely. Find the expected total value of Joe's IRA when he retires.

13-11
Growth rates

Last year The Keane Company's sales were $6 million. Sales were $3 million 5 years earlier.
a. To the nearest percentage point, at what rate have sales been growing?
b. Suppose someone calculated the sales growth in Part a as follows: "Sales doubled in 5 years. This represents a growth of 100 percent in 5 years; so dividing 100 percent by 5, we find the growth rate to be 20 percent per year." Explain what is wrong with this calculation.

13-12
Growth rate

The stock of Northern Gas & Electric sold recently for $6 per share. The stock's price 15 years ago was $2.50. What has been the approximate annual growth rate in the value of this stock?

13-13
Ordinary annuity versus annuity due

a. You have decided to turn over a new leaf and begin to save money for a change. If you save $2,000 annually for the next 5 years in an investment expected to yield 6 percent, what will be the total at the end of the period? Assume that your investment will occur at the end of each year.
b. Since the savings look so good in Part a, you want to get your savings started today. What is the future value of the $2,000 annual investment if your first payment is made today and you continue as before with 5 annual payments at an assumed rate of 6 percent?

13-14
Effective rate of interest

Find the interest rates, or rates of return, on each of the following:
a. You borrow $2,000 and promise to pay back $2,200 at the end of 1 year.
b. You lend $2,000 and receive a promise of $2,200 at the end of 1 year.
c. You borrow $20,000 and promise to pay back $62,112 at the end of 10 years.
d. You borrow $20,000 and promise to make payments of $5,141.78 per year for 5 years. (Assume end-of-year payments.)

13-15
Expected rate of return

Routzahn Tool Works buys equipment for $1,340,300 and expects a return of $247,260 per year for the next 12 years. What is the expected rate of return on the equipment?

13-16
Expected rate of return

Pacific Corp. invests $1.2 million to clear a tract of land and plant some young pine trees. The trees will mature in 30 years, at which time the firm plans to sell the lumber at an expected price of $61.14 million. What is Pacific Corp.'s expected rate of return?

13-17
Expected rate of return

Your cousin who works at Wilsonville Realty has approached you with an offer. For an investment of $25,000 today, she will practically guarantee you a property that will sell for $61,900 in 8 years. If your cousin's estimate is correct, what would your annual yield be on this investment?

13-18
Effective rate of interest

Your broker offers to sell you a note for $4,100 that will pay $1,000 per year for 5 years. If you buy the note, what approximate rate of interest will you be earning?

13-19
Effective rate of interest

Amano Finance Corporation offers to lend you $75,000; the loan calls for annual payments of $9,860.51 for 15 years. What interest rate is the company charging you?

13-20
Interest rate and sinking fund payments

Dombrowski Inc. must provide a sinking fund to retire a $2 million bond issue in 20 years.
a. If an amount of $39,093 is deposited into marketable securities at the end of each year, what annual rate of interest must be earned on these securities to reach the goal of $2 million in 20 years?
b. If funds deposited can only be expected to earn 6 percent interest, what amount must then be deposited at the end of each year in order to have the $2 million in 20 years?

13-21
Required lump-sum payment

To enable you to complete your last year in college and then go through law school, you need $15,000 per year for the next 4 years, starting next year (that is, you need the first payment of $15,000 one year from today). Your rich aunt has offered to provide you with a sum of money sufficient to put you through school. She plans to deposit this sum today in an investment that is expected to yield 7 percent interest.
a. How large must the deposit be?
b. How much will be in the account immediately after you make the first withdrawal? After the last withdrawal?

13-22
Required lump-sum investment

Midland Mortgage Company is offering a note that matures in 5 years at $10,000. If you wish a 12 percent return on your investment, how much would you be willing to pay for this note? (Assume that no other cash flows accrue from the note other than the single lump-sum maturity payment.)

13-23
Annual payment

If a loan of $50,000 is to be paid off on an amortized basis over 5 years and if the interest rate is 10 percent, what approximate annual payment will be required?

13-24
Present value of an ordinary annuity

You have just been notified that you hold a winning ticket in the lottery. Your prize will be $50,000 per year for the next 20 years, with each payment occurring at the end of the year.
a. What is the value of your winnings in today's dollar if the appropriate discount rate is 9 percent?
b. If someone were to offer you $500,000 for your winning ticket, should you accept? Explain.

13-25
Present value of an ordinary annuity

Susan Tatera took out a personal loan of $8,000 three years ago which she is paying back in equal annual payments of $2,330.26. The interest rate on the loan is 14 percent, and it still has two years (and two payments) remaining. Susan has just received an inheritance and would like to pay off the loan. What would it cost her to do so? (Assume no prepayment penalties.)

13-26
Ordinary annuity versus annuity due

Coleon Developers has just purchased equipment costing $500,000. The firm can finance the equipment at 12 percent for 15 years.
a. If the annual payment is computed as an *ordinary annuity,* what is the annual payment?
b. If, however, the annual payment is computed as an *annuity due* (that is, the first payment is due today), what is the amount of the payment?

13-27
Compound growth

Houston Chemicals plans to increase sales at an annual rate of 10 percent for the next 5 years from its current $5,000,000 level.

a. What is the expected level of sales each year?

b. Graph each year's sales.

13-28
Present value of a perpetuity

What is the present value of a perpetuity of $1,500 per year if the appropriate discount rate is 3 percent? If interest rates in general doubled and the appropriate discount rate rose to 6 percent, what would happen to the present value of the perpetuity?

13-29
Term loan

Management of Oscar's Restaurant has arranged with Friendly Finance Inc. to receive a $10,000 loan to be repaid in equal installments at the end of each of the next 3 years. The interest rate is 9 percent.

a. What annual payment will be required?

b. Set up a loan amortization schedule.

c. Explain the significance of the interest column both to Oscar's and to Friendly Finance.

13-30
Number of periods

A rare stamp would fit beautifully into your collection, and you are seriously considering buying it. The dealer wants $21 for it and tells you that he bought it when he was just 10 for $2. He also claims that the asking price would only yield him a 4 percent annual return on his original investment. If that is true, how old is the dealer now?

13-31
Number of periods

Suppose that you have just graduated from college and have found a good job. You have decided to start saving up for the down payment on a home by setting aside $2,940 at the end of each year. You calculate that you need $20,000 for the down payment, and you find an investment where your savings should earn 5 percent annually. Approximately how many years must you save to have the $20,000?

13-32
Finding missing cash flow

The present value ($t = 0$) of the following cash flow stream is $8,972.15 when discounted at 10 percent annually. What is the value of the missing ($t = 2$) cash flow?

0	1	2	3	4
$0	$1,500	?	$3,000	$3,000

13-33
Effect of inflation

At an inflation rate of 9 percent, the purchasing power of $1 would be cut in half in approximately 8 years. How long to the nearest year would it take the purchasing power of $1 to be cut in half if the inflation rate were only 4 percent?

13-34
Present value of perpetuities

You are currently at Time Period 0. At Time Period 1 you will begin to receive an annual payment of $50 in perpetuity. At Time Period 6 you will begin to receive an additional $100 in perpetuity, and at Time Period 10 you will begin to receive an additional $150 in perpetuity. If you require a 10 percent rate of return, then what is the combined present value of these 3 perpetuities?

13-35
Present and future value of a lump sum; annual payment

Your grandfather deposited a lump sum 22 years ago intended for your college education. When you started college *two years ago* this account was worth $13,743, and the broker who manages the account told you at that time that the account had yielded an average annual return of 14 percent over the 20-year period.

a. What amount did your grandfather initially deposit?

b. Assume that you have not touched the money your grandfather intended for your education because you received help from your parents the first two years and have also received a small scholarship. If nothing more has been added to the account and the money has earned 12 percent compounded annually during the two years, what is the balance today?

c. Now suppose that you have won in the lottery and you deposit the money into the account your grandfather set up for you, bringing the total up to $32,000. Your dad has just been laid off, and your parents can no longer help you financially. If you plan to withdraw the funds from your account over the next four years (to complete college and get started on a career — maybe relocate), what approximate dollar amount can you withdraw at the end of each of the next four years? (Assume the interest rate earned is 12 percent.)

Solutions to Self-Test Problems

ST-1   a.

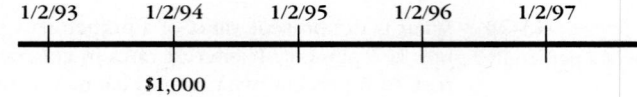

$1,000 is being compounded for 3 years, so your balance on January 2, 1997, is $1,259.70:

$$FV_3 = PV(FVIF_{8\%,3})$$

$$= \$1,000(1.2597)$$

$$= \$1,259.70.$$

b.

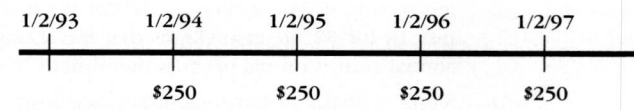

Future value of an annuity:

$$FVA_4 = PMT(FVIFA_{8\%,4})$$

$$= \$250(4.5061)$$

$$= \$1,126.53.$$

c.

$$FVA_4 = PMT(FVIFA_{8\%,4})$$

$$\$1,259.70 = PMT(4.5061)$$

$$PMT = \$1,259.70/4.5061$$

$$= \$279.55.$$

Therefore, you would have to make 4 payments of $279.55 at the end of each year to accumulate a balance of $1,259.70 on January 2, 1997.

ST-2   a. Set up a time line like those in Self-Test Problem 1 and note that your deposit will grow for 4 years at 8 percent. The deposit on January 2, 1993, is the present value, and $1,000 is the future value. The solution is as follows:

$$PV = FV_4(PVIF_{8\%,4})$$

$$= \$1,000(0.7350)$$

$$= \$735.00.$$

The initial deposit necessary to accumulate $1,000 is $735.00.

b. Here we are dealing with a 4-year annuity where the first payment occurs one year from today, on January 2, 1994, and where the future value must equal $1,000. The solution is as follows:

$$FVA_4 = PMT(FVIFA_{8\%,4})$$

$$\$1,000 = PMT(4.5061)$$

$$PMT = 1,000/4.5061$$

$$= \$221.92.$$

c. This problem can be approached in several ways. Perhaps the simplest is to ask the question, "If I received $750 on January 2, 1994, and deposited it to earn 8 percent, would I have the required $1,000 on January 2, 1997?" The answer is no:

$$FV_3 = PV(FVIF_{8\%,3})$$

$$= \$750(1.2597)$$

$$= \$944.78.$$

This indicates that you should let your father make the payments rather than accept the lump sum of $750 in one year.

You could also compare the $750 with the PV of the payments:

$$PVA_4 = PMT(PVIFA_{8\%,4})$$

$$= \$221.92(3.3121)$$

$$= \$735.02.$$

Because this is less than the $750 lump-sum offer, your initial reaction might be to accept the lump sum of $750. However, this would be a mistake. Note that if you deposited the $750 on January 2, 1994, at an 8 percent interest rate to be withdrawn on January 2, 1997, interest would be compounded for only 3 years, and the future value would be only $944.78 as shown above.

The problem is that when you found the $735.02 present value of the annuity, you were finding the value of the annuity *today,* on January 2, 1993. You were comparing $735.02 today with the lump sum of $750 *one year from now.* Such a comparison is, of course, invalid. What you should have done was take the $735.02, recognize that this is the present value of an annuity as of January 2, 1993, multiply $735.02 by 1.08 to get $793.82, and compare $793.82 with the lump sum of $750. You would then take your father's offer to pay off the loan rather than the lump sum on January 2, 1994.

d.

$$FV_3 = PV(FVIF_{k,3})$$

$$\$1,000 = \$750(FVIF_{k,3})$$

$$(FVIF_{k,3}) = \$1,000/\$750$$

$$= 1.3333.$$

Use Table A-3 in Appendix A, and look across the Period 3 row for a FVIF of 1.3333. The closest value is 1.3310 in the 10 percent column. Therefore, you would require an interest rate of approximately 10 percent to achieve your $1,000 goal. The exact rate required, found with a financial calculator, is 10.0642 percent.

e.

$$FVA_4 = PMT(FVIFA_{k,4})$$

$$1,000 = \$186.29(FVIFA_{k,4})$$

$$FVIFA_{k,4} = \$1,000/\$186.29$$

$$= 5.3680.$$

Use Table A-4 in Appendix A, and look across the Period 4 row until you find the interest factor of 5.3680. This FVIFA corresponds to a 20 percent interest rate. You might be able to find a borrower willing to offer you a 20 percent interest rate, but there would be some risk involved, and he or she might not actually pay you your $1,000!

ST-3

$$PVA_3 = PMT(PVIFA_{9\%,3})$$
$$\$5,000 = PMT(2.5313)$$
$$PMT = \$5,000/2.5313$$
$$= \$1,975.27.$$

The equal annual installment required to repay the loan in 3 years with a 9 percent return to the lender is $1,975.27.

ST-4

$$PVA_3 = PMT(PVIFA_{k,3})$$
$$\$7,500 = \$2,651.50(PVIFA_{k,3})$$
$$PVIFA_{k,3} = \$7,500/\$2,651.50$$
$$= 2.8286.$$

Use Table A-2 of Appendix A, go down to the third row, and follow the row across until you find the interest factor, $PVIFA = 2.8286$. This factor corresponds to only a 3 percent rate of return. Apparently this is not a very profitable investment opportunity.

Semiannual and Other Compounding Periods

APPENDIX 13A

In all of the examples in the chapter, we assumed that returns are received once a year, or annually. Suppose, however, that you put $1,000 in a bank which advertises that it pays 6 percent compounded *semiannually*. How much will you have at the end of 1 year? Semiannual compounding means that interest is actually paid every 6 months. The procedures for semiannual compounding are illustrated in the calculations in Table 13A-1. Here the annual interest rate is divided by 2, but twice as many compounding periods are used because interest is paid twice a year. Comparing the amount on hand at the end of the second 6-month period, $1,060.90, with what would have been on hand under annual compounding, $1,060, you see that semiannual compounding is better from your standpoint as a saver. This result occurs because you can earn *interest on interest* more frequently.

Throughout the economy, different types of investments use different compounding periods. For example, bank accounts generally pay interest monthly or daily; most bonds pay interest semiannually; stocks pay dividends quarterly; and many loans pay interest annually. Thus, if securities with different compounding periods are to be compared, one needs to put them on a common basis. This means that we must distinguish between the *nominal*, or *stated, interest rate* and the *effective annual rate (EAR)*.

The **nominal**, or **stated**, **interest rate** is the quoted rate; thus, in the previous example, the nominal rate is 6 percent. The nominal interest rate is often called the *annual percentage rate (APR)* when it is reported by banks and other lending institutions. The **effective annual rate (EAR)** is the interest rate that would have produced the final compound value, $1,060.90, under annual rather than semiannual compounding.

nominal (stated) interest rate
The contracted, or quoted, interest rate.

effective annual rate (EAR)
The annual rate of interest actually being earned as opposed to the nominal or stated rate.

Table 13A-1

Future Value Calculations
with Semiannual
Compounding

Period	Beginning Amount, PV	×	(1 + k/2)	=	Ending Amount, FV
1	$1,000.00		(1.03)		$1,030.00
2	1,030.00		(1.03)		1,060.90

In this case, the effective annual rate is 6.09 percent, found by solving for k in the following equation:

$$\$1,000(1 + k) = \$1,060.90$$

$$k = \frac{\$1,060.90}{\$1,000} - 1 = 0.0609 = 6.09\%.$$

Thus, if one bank offered 6 percent with semiannual compounding while another offered 6.09 percent with annual compounding, they would both be paying the same effective annual rate of interest.

In general, the effective annual rate can be determined, given the nominal rate, by solving Equation 13A-1:

$$\text{Effective annual rate (EAR)} = \left(1 + \frac{k_{Nom}}{m}\right)^m - 1.0. \qquad (13A-1)$$

Here k_{Nom} is the nominal, or stated, interest rate, and m is the number of compounding periods per year. For example, to find the effective annual rate if the nominal rate is 6 percent, compounded semiannually, the following calculation is made:

$$\text{Effective annual rate} = \left(1 + \frac{0.06}{2}\right)^2 - 1.0$$

$$= (1.03)^2 - 1.0$$

$$= 1.0609 - 1.0$$

$$= 0.0609 = 6.09\%.$$

Semiannual compounding can be handled easily with a financial calculator. Simply enter k = i = 3, n = 2, and PV = 1000, and then press the FV button to get the solution, FV = $1,060.90.

The points made about semiannual compounding can be generalized as follows. When compounding periods are more frequent than once a year, we use a modified version of Equation 13A-2 to find the future value of a lump sum:

$$\text{Annual compounding: } FV_n = PV(1 + k)^n. \qquad (13A-2)$$

$$\text{More frequent compounding: } FV_n = PV\left(1 + \frac{k_{Nom}}{m}\right)^{mn}. \qquad (13A-2a)$$

Here m is the number of times per year compounding occurs, and n is the number of years. Therefore, if $1,000 is invested for 3 years at a nominal rate of 6 percent, compounded semiannually, the ending value can be computed using Equation 13A-2a:

$$FV_3 = \$1,000[1 + (0.06/2)]^{2\times3}$$

$$= \$1,000(1.1941)$$

$$= \$1,194.10.$$

The interest tables often can be used when compounding occurs more than once a year. Simply divide the nominal, or stated, interest rate (k_{Nom}) by the number of times compounding occurs during the year (m), then multiply the years (n) by the number of compounding periods per year (m), as shown in Equation 13A-2a. For example, to find the amount to which $1,000 will grow after 5 years if semiannual compounding is applied to a stated 8 percent interest rate, divide 8 percent by 2, the number of compounding periods in the year when semiannual compounding is used, and multiply the 5-year period by 2, also because of semiannual compounding. Then look in Table A-3 of Appendix A under the 4 percent column and the row for Period 10. You will find an interest factor of 1.4802. Multiplying this by the initial $1,000 gives a value of $1,480.20, the amount to which $1,000 will grow in 5 years at 8 percent, compounded semiannually. This compares with $1,469.30 for annual compounding.

The same procedure is applied in all the cases covered — compounding, discounting, single payments, and annuities. To illustrate semiannual discounting when finding the present value of an annuity, consider the case of an annuity of $1,000 a year for 3 years, discounted at 12 percent. With annual discounting, the present value interest factor is 2.4018, and the present value of the annual annuity is $2,401.80. For semiannual discounting, look under the 6 percent column and in the Period 6 row of Table A-2 in Appendix A to find the PVIFA of 4.9173. This present value interest factor for an annuity is now multiplied by half of the $1,000, or $500 received each six months, and the present value of the semiannual annuity is found to be $2,458.65. Because the payments come a little more rapidly (the first $500 is paid after only six months), the annuity is a little more valuable if payments are received semiannually rather than annually.

Problems

13A-1

Future value for various compounding periods

Find the amount to which $500 will grow under each of the following conditions:
a. 12 percent compounded annually for 4 years.
b. 12 percent compounded semiannually for 4 years.
c. 12 percent compounded quarterly for 4 years.
d. 12 percent compounded monthly for 1 year.

13A-2

Present value for various compounding periods

Find the present value of $500 due in the future under each of the following conditions:
a. 12 percent nominal rate, semiannual compounding, discounted back 4 years.
b. 12 percent nominal rate, quarterly compounding, discounted back 4 years.
c. 12 percent nominal rate, monthly compounding, discounted back 1 year.

13A-3

Annuity values for various compounding periods

Find the value of the following ordinary (deferred) annuities:
a. FV of $200 each 6 months for 4 years at a nominal rate of 12 percent, compounded semiannually.
b. PV of $200 each 3 months for 4 years at a nominal rate of 12 percent, compounded quarterly.

13A-4

Effective versus nominal interest rates

The First National Bank pays 11 percent interest, compounded annually, on time deposits. The Second National Bank pays 10 percent interest, compounded quarterly.
a. In which bank would you prefer to deposit your money?
b. Is your choice of banks influenced by the fact that you might want to withdraw your funds during the year rather than at the end of the year? In answering the question, assume that funds must be left on deposit during the entire compounding period for you to receive any interest.

The Process of Capital Budgeting

OBJECTIVES

After reading this chapter, you should be able to:

▶ Define capital budgeting, explain why it is
important, and state how project proposals
are generally classified.

▶ List the steps that the capital budgeting
process should follow.

▶ Discuss difficulties and relevant
considerations in estimating net cash flows.

▶ Calculate payback period, NPV, and IRR for a
given project and evaluate each method.

▶ Find the NPV for an expansion project
where initial net working capital investment
is required and where the asset's salvage
value exceeds its future book value.

DECISION IN FINANCE

AN AGED GIANT
REMAINS NIMBLE

Motorola Inc., a leading manufacturer of electronic equipment and components, provides an example to companies, both large and small, of manufacturing supremacy and market-share dominance. Motorola is the global market leader in the production of cellular phones, pagers, two-way radios, and microchips used to control devices other than computers. Motorola obtained promises from Japan of access to previously closed Japanese markets under a 1989 trade agreement and the opportunity to compete with giant Japanese companies manufacturing consumer electronics.

Motorola started 1993 with $277 million in operating cash flow and has been investing heavily to keep up with soaring demand. For example, the company is both increasing plant capacity in the United States and is constructing a new $120 million facility in China. Motorola plans to boost capital outlays by $2 billion for 1993, up 45 percent from 1992. Why has Motorola been so successful? One illustration is presented below.

Recently, a small Oregon company, In Focus Systems Inc., demonstrated a revolutionary type of video screen that Motorola badly wanted to produce. But Motorola had to act quickly because some Japanese executives had seen the same demonstration, and Motorola was afraid it

might lose the project to the Japanese. Within 22 days, Motorola's CEO met with the officers of the Oregon firm, and three months later, the two companies announced a joint venture to manufacture the video screens in the United States. One month later, the two companies launched the project, which involves a $70

million plant plus working capital and marketing expenses.

The speed with which Motorola moved to undertake this project surprised In Focus officers. The firm's chief technologist stated, "I was amazed that a company that large could make decisions of this magnitude in such a short period." Motorola illustrates that there is nothing inherently wrong with being either a big corporation or an old established one. However, Motorola's success is in stark contrast to the well-publicized problems of other large, established corporations such as GM, IBM, and Westinghouse.

As you read this chapter, consider (1) the importance of capital budgeting to the firm, (2)

See end of chapter for resolution.
Photo source: Photo courtesy of Motorola Inc.

the capital budgeting process, (3) estimation and evaluation of relevant cash flows, and (4) the post-audit process. Now, consider Motorola and the speed with which it was able to act on the video screen project. How was such a large company able to act so quickly? Think about the steps the company's financial managers had to follow before the project could be undertaken. What is the company's secret to its manufacturing success in such a competitive environment?

In Part III we analyzed decisions relating to the investment of funds in current assets. Now that we have covered the important topics of risk and return, followed by the time value of money, we are ready to consider decisions involving long-term investments, the process of *capital budgeting*. The term *capital* refers to fixed assets used in production, and a *budget* is a plan detailing projected inflows and outflows during some future period. Thus, the *capital budget* sets forth planned expenditures on fixed assets and other long-term projects and **capital budgeting** is the entire process of analyzing projects and deciding whether they should be included in the capital budget.

capital budgeting
The process of planning expenditures on assets and projects whose returns extend beyond one year.

Our treatment of capital budgeting is divided into two parts. First, this chapter gives an overview of the process and explains the basic techniques used in capital budgeting analysis. Then, in Chapter 15, we go on to consider special capital budgeting situations, plus risk analysis in capital budgeting.

Importance of Capital Budgeting

Capital budgeting decisions are among the most important ones that financial managers must make; indeed, a good decision can boost earnings sharply and increase the price of the firm's stock, but a bad decision can lead to bankruptcy. Major factors that contribute to the importance of capital budgeting are discussed next.

1. **Capital expenditures limit the firm's future flexibility.**   Because the consequences of capital budgeting decisions are in effect over an extended period, the forecasts for revenues and costs associated with a given project or asset become crucial. In fact, behind every capital budget is an implicit sales forecast, and if projected cash flows fall far short of estimates, a firm is often in a situation where it can cancel a project only at a great loss. Therefore, by their very nature, such investment decisions *determine* the firm's future. There are many cases where, with perfect 20/20 hindsight, it is apparent that firms' capital expenditures were based on wildly optimistic forecasts and where projects clearly should not have been undertaken. For example, when Washington Public Power Supply System (WPPSS, also commonly known as Whoops) ended up "moth balling" two half-completed nuclear power plants in 1983—and defaulted on $2.25 billion of municipal bonds it had issued to finance these plants—it was due to overestimated demand for electricity as well as vast cost overruns. More recently, when, in 1988, Coca-Cola launched its minature soda fountain intended for U.S. offices too small for standard vending machines, it had high hopes of this becoming a new method of distribution. This project, which

Coca-Cola saw as a winning weapon in the "cola wars" and which it hoped would lead to a similar machine installed in homes, turned into Coca-Cola's largest development project ever. By June 1993, the project had cost $30 million, and the company had yet to see a profit.

2. **Capital expenditures frequently require large sums.** The two preceding examples illustrate this point as well. And, before a firm can spend a substantial sum, it must raise the funds; large amounts of money are not available automatically. A firm contemplating a major capital expenditure program may need to arrange its financing several years in advance to be sure the needed funds can be obtained. The sums are mind boggling at times: In March 1993, Ford revealed that it had spent $6 *billion* in developing the new Mondeo, a small sedan to be introduced in Europe that same spring and in North America in mid-1994. *The Wall Street Journal* called this project Ford's "$6 billion roll of the dice"—which should remind you of the risk-return concepts in Chapter 12.

3. **The impact of capital expenditures is significant.** Not only is the firm's future flexibility influenced by the projects and assets in which it decides to invest, but the results of these decisions can also be seen directly in the standard ratios. Erroneous forecasts of asset requirements can have serious consequences. If the firm has invested too much in assets, it will incur unnecessarily heavy expenses, which will lower both the profit margin and the total assets turnover, therefore also lowering return on assets (ROA) and return on equity (ROE), other things being equal. On the other hand, if the firm has not spent enough on fixed assets, two problems arise. First, the firm's equipment may not be sufficiently modern to enable it to produce competitively. Second, if it has inadequate capacity, it may lose market share to rival firms, and regaining lost customers typically requires heavy selling expenses, price reductions, and/or product improvements, all of which are costly.

4. **Timing is an important consideration in capital budgeting.** Capital assets must be ready to come "on line" when they are needed. Edward Ford, executive vice-president of Western Design, a decorative tile company, gave the authors an illustration of the importance of capital budgeting. His firm tried to operate near capacity most of the time. During a four-year period, Western experienced intermittent spurts in the demand for its products, which forced it to turn away orders. After these sharp increases in demand, Western would add capacity by renting an additional building, then purchasing and installing the appropriate equipment. It would take six to eight months to get the additional capacity ready, but frequently by that time demand had dried up—other firms had already expanded their operations and had taken an increased share of the market. If Western had properly forecasted demand and planned its capacity requirements a year or so in advance, it would have been able to maintain or perhaps even increase its market share.

Effective capital budgeting can improve not only the timing of asset acquisitions but also the *quality* of assets purchased. A firm which forecasts its needs for capital assets in advance will have an opportunity to purchase and install the assets before they are needed. Unfortunately, many firms do not order capital goods until they approach full capacity or are forced to replace worn-out equipment. If sales increase because of an increase in general market demand, all firms in the industry will tend to order capital goods at about the same time. This results in backlogs, long waiting times for machinery, a deterioration in the quality of the capital goods, and an increase in their prices. If a firm foresees its needs and purchases capital assets early, it can avoid these problems. Note, though, that if a firm forecasts an increase in demand and then expands to meet the anticipated demand, but sales then do not increase, it will be saddled with excess capacity and high costs. This can lead to losses or even bankruptcy. Thus, an accurate sales forecast is critical.

? *Self-Test*

Why are capital budgeting decisions so important to the success of a firm?

Why is the sales forecast a key element in a capital budgeting decision?

Project Proposals and Classification

Capital budgeting proposals are created by the firm. For example, a sales representative may report that customers are asking for a particular product that the company does not now produce. The sales manager then discusses the idea with the marketing research group to determine the size of the market for the proposed product. If it appears likely that a significant market does exist, cost accountants and engineers will be asked to estimate production costs. If it appears that the product can be produced and sold to yield a sufficient profit, the project will be undertaken.

A firm's growth, development, and even its ability to remain competitive and to survive depend on a constant flow of ideas for new products and for ways to make existing products better, or to produce them at a lower cost. Accordingly, a well-managed firm will go to great lengths to develop good capital budgeting proposals. For example, a senior executive of a major corporation indicated that his company takes the following steps to generate proposals:

strategic business plan

A long-run plan which outlines in broad terms the firm's basic strategy for the next 5 to 10 years.

Our R&D department is constantly searching for new products and also for ways to improve existing products. In addition, our executive committee, which consists of the president plus senior executives in marketing, production, and finance, identifies the products and markets in which our company will compete, and the committee sets long-run targets for each division. These targets, which are spelled out in the corporation's **strategic business plan,** *provide a general guide to the operating executives who must meet them. These executives then seek new products, set expansion plans for existing products, and look for ways to reduce production and distribution costs. Since bonuses and promotions are based in large part on each unit's ability to meet or exceed its targets, these economic incentives encourage our operating executives to seek out profitable investment opportunities.*

While senior executives are judged and rewarded on the basis of how well their units perform, people further down the line are given bonuses for specific suggestions, including ideas that lead to profitable investments. Additionally, a percentage of our corporate profit is set aside for distribution to nonexecutive employees, and we have an Employees' Stock Ownership Plan (ESOP) to provide further incentives. Our objective is to encourage lower-level workers to keep on the lookout for good ideas, including those that lead to capital investments.

It is clear that not all capital project ideas come from the research and development department. If the firm has capable and imaginative executives and employees, and if its incentive system is working properly, many ideas for capital investment will be advanced. Because some ideas will be good ones while others will not, procedures must be established for evaluating the likely benefits to the firm of each proposal.

The process of carefully screening and analyzing capital expenditure proposals does, however, have a cost. For certain types of projects, a relatively refined analysis may be warranted; for others, cost/benefit studies may suggest that simpler procedures should be used. Therefore, firms generally classify projects into the following categories and then analyze projects in each category somewhat differently:

1. **Replacement: maintenance of business.** One category consists of expenditures to replace worn-out or damaged equipment used in the production of profitable products or services. Such replacement is necessary if the operation is to continue, so the only issues here are (a) should we, in fact, continue to produce these products or services, and (b) should we continue to use our existing production processes? The answers are usually yes, so maintenance decisions are normally made without going through an elaborate decision process. Also, cost and benefit estimates tend to be fairly accurate.

2. **Replacement: cost reduction.** This category includes expenditures to replace serviceable but obsolete equipment. The purpose here is to lower the costs of labor, materials, or other inputs such as electricity. These decisions are discretionary, and a more detailed analysis is generally required to support them.[1]

3. **Expansion of existing products or markets.** Expenditures to increase output of existing products, or to expand outlets or distribution facilities in markets now being served, are included here. These decisions are more complex because they require an explicit forecast of growth in demand. Mistakes in estimating cash flows are more likely, so a still more detailed analysis is required, and the final decision is made at a higher level within the firm.

---

[1]In recent years, this category of projects has gained in importance as many U.S. companies have been striving to cut costs and become "lean and mean." We shall return to this topic later in the chapter.

4. **Expansion into new products or markets.** These are expenditures necessary to produce a new product or to expand into a geographic area not currently being served. These projects involve strategic decisions that could change the fundamental nature of the business, and they normally require the expenditure of large sums of money over long periods. Invariably, a very detailed analysis is required, and the final decision is generally made at the very top — by the board of directors as a part of the firm's strategic plan. Statistical data are generally lacking for new product decisions, so here judgment is a key element in the decision process.

5. **Safety and/or environmental projects.** Expenditures necessary to comply with government orders, labor agreements, or insurance policy terms fall into this category. These expenditures are often called *mandatory investments,* or *nonrevenue-producing projects.* How they are handled depends on their size, with small ones being treated much like the Category 1 projects described above.

6. **Other.** This catch-all category includes office buildings, parking lots, executive aircraft, and so on. How they are handled varies among companies. And, to illustrate that capital budgeting includes more than tangible fixed asset expenditures, if a company were to consider a major image-building advertising campaign, the project would fall into this category as well.

In general, within each category, projects are broken down by their dollar costs: the larger the required investment, the more detailed the analysis, and the higher the level of the officer who must authorize the expenditure. A plant manager may be authorized to approve maintenance expenditures up to $25,000 on the basis of a relatively unsophisticated analysis, but the full board of directors may have to approve decisions that involve amounts over $1 million.

? Self-Test

How does a firm get ideas for capital projects?

Identify and briefly explain how projects are generally classified.

Steps in the Capital Budgeting Process

Although the financial manager does not usually initiate capital budgeting proposals, he or she evaluates and coordinates these requests and, therefore, plays a crucial role in the sequence of events outlined next. The capital budgeting process should generally follow these steps:

1. **Review of goals and objectives.**   Company goals and objectives are reviewed to make sure that the projects considered are consistent with the firm's intended direction and strategic business plan.

2. **Search for capital budgeting proposals.**   A search is undertaken for capital budgeting proposals which qualify according to Step 1. This is where creativity comes into the picture and where ideas are gathered from the R&D department, executives, employees in general, and sources outside the firm.

This small segment of a 220-foot-long robotic production line at Lamb Electric's Graham, North Carolina, manufacturing plant tests and balances armatures for AMETEK's exclusive 2.43-inch vacuum cleaner motors. These U-shaped lines are fed metal shafts, laminations, and windings at one end and produce finished armatures at the other end — an example of a capital project in which equipment replaces human labor.

Source: Ed Wheeler photography

3. **Estimation of project cash flows.** Project cash flows are estimated to provide input for the analysis phase which follows. *In the entire capital budgeting process, nothing is of greater importance than reliable estimates of the revenue increases and/or cost savings associated with a given project.* Projecting cash flows is also typically the most difficult step — the previous examples of WPPSS and Coca-Cola gave us a feel for just how far off the mark forecasts may be. Because this topic is absolutely crucial to a project's success, we will consider cash flows in much greater detail later in the chapter.

4. **Ranking of proposals.** Capital budgeting proposals are ranked in terms of their attractiveness to the firm. This step represents the analysis phase of the process and is the domain of the financial manager. We will look at several ranking techniques later in the chapter. At this point, some assumption also has to be made about the riskiness of projected cash flows from each proposal.

5. **Selection of projects.** Projects are selected, based on the above analysis. Firms may also consider qualitative factors, as well as quantitative information, in the selection — decisions are seldom based entirely on dollars and cents.

6. **Implementation.** Decisions are implemented: construction is begun, orders for equipment are placed, and so forth.

7. **Post-audit.**   A post-audit should be conducted to compare actual results with expected outcomes at later points in time. The post-audit is the feedback and control mechanism of the process and should attempt to explain why any discrepancies occurred. The post-audit is discussed in greater detail in the next section.

The Post-Audit

post-audit

A comparison of the actual and expected results for a given capital project.

The **post-audit** is the last, but by no means least important, step in the capital budgeting process. It is accomplished in many firms by requiring that operating divisions send a monthly report for the first six months after a project goes into operation, and a quarterly report thereafter, until the project's results are up to expectations. From then on, reports on the project are handled like those of other operations.

The post-audit has two main purposes:

1. **Improve forecasts.**   When decision makers are forced to compare their projections with actual outcomes, there is a tendency for estimates to improve. Conscious or unconscious biases are observed and eliminated; new forecasting methods are sought as the need for them becomes apparent; and people simply tend to do everything better, including forecasting, if they know that their actions are being monitored.

2. **Improve operations.**   Businesses are run by people, and people can perform at higher or lower levels of efficiency. When a divisional team has made a forecast about an investment, its members are, in a sense, putting their reputations on the line. If costs are above predicted levels, sales below expectations, and so on, executives in production, marketing, and other areas will strive to improve operations and to bring results into line with forecasts. In a discussion related to this point, an IBM executive made this statement: "You academicians worry only about making good decisions. In business, we also worry about making decisions good."

The post-audit is not a simple process—a number of factors can cause complications. First, we must recognize that each element of the cash flow forecast is subject to uncertainty, so a percentage of all projects undertaken by any reasonably venturesome firm will necessarily go awry. This fact must be considered when appraising the performances of the operating executives who submit capital expenditure requests. Second, projects sometimes fail to meet expectations for reasons beyond the control of the operating executives and for reasons that no one could realistically be expected to anticipate. For example, the 1990–1991 recession adversely affected many projects. Third, it is often difficult to separate the operating results of one investment from those of a larger system. Although some projects stand alone and permit ready identification of costs and revenues, the actual cost savings that result from a new computer system, for example, may be very hard to measure. Fourth, it is often hard to hand out blame or praise because the executives who were actually responsible for a given decision may have moved on by the time the results of a long-term investment are known.

Because of these difficulties, some firms tend to play down the importance of the post-audit. However, observations of both businesses and governmental units suggest that the best-run and most successful organizations are the ones that put the greatest emphasis on post-audits. Accordingly, we regard the post-audit as being one of the most important elements in a good capital budgeting system.

? Self-Test

List the general sequence of steps that the capital budgeting process should follow.

Which step in this process is typically the most important as well as the most difficult?

What is a post-audit, and what are its two main purposes?

What are some factors which can cause complications in the post-audit?

Estimating Cash Flows

Cash flows associated with the project include the initial investment outlays required and the annual net cash flows that the project will produce after it goes into operation. Note that we defined cash flow back in Chapter 5, when we discussed Carter Chemical Company, as the actual net cash (as opposed to accounting net income) that flows into, or out of, the firm during a specified period. Many variables are involved in the cash flow forecast, and many individuals and departments participate in the process. For example, the market research group projects sales by means of industry analysis and test marketing of proposed products; the marketing department determines pricing policy and anticipates competitors' actions; the production and engineering departments work together to determine the necessary capital outlays and to establish production and labor requirements; and the industrial relations department determines appropriate wage and benefit packages. In addition, the accounting department estimates overhead costs for the new project.

The better the firm's cash flow forecast, the more likely it is that poor projects will be rejected and good ones accepted. However, obtaining accurate estimates of the costs and revenues associated with a large, complex project can be exceedingly difficult, and forecast errors can, therefore, be quite large, as we have seen already. A few more examples should further emphasize this point: When several oil companies decided to build the Alaska Pipeline, the original cost estimates were in the neighborhood of $700 million, but the final cost was closer to $7 billion. Similar (or even worse) miscalculations are common in product design cost estimates for items like new personal computers. Furthermore, as difficult as plant and equipment costs are to estimate, sales revenues and operating costs over the life of a project are even more uncertain. For example, several years ago Federal Express developed an electronic delivery system (ZapMail). It used the correct capital budgeting technique, but it incorrectly estimated the project's cash flows: Projected revenues were too high, and projected costs were too low, and virtually no one was willing to pay the price required to cover the project's costs. As a result, cash flows failed to meet the forecasted levels, and Federal Express ended up losing about $200 million on the venture. This example demonstrates a basic truth — if cash flow estimates are not reasonably accurate, any analytical technique, no matter how sophisticated, can lead to poor decisions and hence to operating losses and lower stock prices.[2] Because of its financial strength, Federal Express was able to absorb losses on the project with no problem, but the ZapMail venture could have forced a weaker firm into bankruptcy.

The financial staff's role in the forecasting process includes (1) coordinating the efforts of the other departments, such as engineering and marketing; (2) ensuring that everyone involved with the forecast uses a consistent set of economic assumptions; and (3) making sure that no biases are inherent in the forecasts. This last point is extremely important because division managers often become emotionally involved with pet projects or develop empire-building complexes, which leads to cash flow forecasting biases that make bad projects look good — on paper. The ZapMail project is a good example of this problem.

It is not sufficient that the financial staff has unbiased point estimates of the key variables; data on probability distributions or other indications of the probable ranges of error are also essential. It is useful as well to know the relationship between each input variable and some basic economic variable, such as gross domestic product. If all production and sales variables can be related to such a basic variable, the financial manager can forecast how the project will do under different economic conditions.

It is almost impossible to overstate the importance of cash flow estimates — or of the difficulties that are encountered in making these forecasts. However, observing the principles discussed in the next several sections will help to minimize forecasting errors.

Identifying Relevant Cash Flows

relevant cash flows
The specific set of cash flows that should be considered in a capital budgeting decision.

An important element in cash flow estimation is the identification of **relevant cash flows,** defined as that set of cash flows which should be considered for the decision at hand. Errors are often made in this area, but two cardinal rules can help financial analysts avoid mistakes: (1) Capital budgeting decisions must be based on *cash flows,* not on accounting income; and (2) only *incremental cash flows* are relevant to the accept/reject decision. These two rules are discussed in detail in the following sections.

Cash Flow versus Accounting Net Income

Cash flows and accounting net income can be very different, and this point was first made in connection with Carter Chemical Company. In fact, Table 14-1, which shows how the firm's accounting profits and cash flows are related to one another, is a replication of Table 5-4. As discussed in Chapter 5, Carter's 1993 cash flow may be found either by subtracting all *cash* expenses from sales (Column 2) or by adding depreciation charges back to the accounting net income (Column 1). Remember: *Depreciation is a noncash charge,* merely an accounting write-off, and therefore, does not represent a cash outflow. (If this does not

---

[2]At the annual convention of the Financial Management Association (FMA) in San Francisco in October 1992, practicing financial managers met with academicians in a round-table discussion of capital budgeting. Here, financial managers reconfirmed that coming up with the correct inputs for revenue and cost projections is by far the most difficult aspect of the capital budgeting process.

Table 14-1

Carter Chemical Company:
Cash Flows versus
Reported Income for 1993
(Millions of Dollars)

	Income Statement (1)	Cash Flows (2)
Sales	$3,000	$3,000
Costs and expenses:		
All costs except depreciation	2,634	2,634
Depreciation (DEP)	100	—[a]
Earnings before interest and taxes (EBIT)	$ 266	—[a]
Interest expense	66	66
Earnings before taxes (EBT)	$ 200	—[a]
Taxes (40%)	80	80
Net income (NI)	$ 120	—[a]
Cash flow: CF = NI + DEP = $120 + $100 =	$ 220	$ 220

[a]Depreciation is not deducted because it is a noncash charge. Also, the terms EBIT, EBT, and NI are not meaningful in the calculation of cash flows.

Table 14-2

Carter Chemical Company:
Project X

	Effect of Project X on Income Statement
Sales	$90,000
Costs and expenses:	
All costs except depreciation	55,000
Depreciation (DEP)	20,000
Earnings before interest and taxes (EBIT)	$15,000
Interest expense	0
Earnings before taxes (EBT)	$15,000
Taxes (40%)	6,000
Net income	$ 9,000
Cash flow: CF = NI + DEP = $9,000 + $20,000 =	$29,000

sound familiar, you may want to review the discussion of depreciation and cash flows in Chapter 5.)

Exactly the same principle applies when we are looking at an individual capital budgeting proposal instead of the entire firm. Again, we are interested in net cash flow, not in accounting net income, because net income typically understates the actual cash that a project is expected to generate. If we assume that Carter is considering a project, Project X, which is expected to result in sales of $90,000 in a given year and has cash expenses and depreciation as shown in Table 14-2, then the expected cash flow for the project during the year in question would, similarly, be net income plus depreciation: CF = NI + DEP.[3] For Project X, the expected cash flow would be $29,000.

---

[3]Actually, net cash flow should be adjusted to reflect all noncash charges, not just depreciation. However, for most projects, depreciation is by far the largest noncash charge.

Accounting profits are important for some purposes, but *in capital budgeting, we are interested only in cash flows.* An equivalent method of determining the cash flow is presented in Equation 14-1:

$$\text{Net cash flow} = (\$REV - \$EXP)(1 - T) + (DEP)(T), \qquad \textbf{(14-1)}$$

where

REV = cash revenues generated by the project.

EXP = cash expenses associated with the project.

T = marginal tax rate.

DEP = depreciation for the year on the project's fixed assets.

Using this formula and the data for Carter's Project X in Table 14-2, we obtain

$$
\begin{aligned}
\text{Net cash flow}_X &= (\$REV - \$EXP)(1 - T) + (DEP)(T) \\
&= (\$90,000 - \$55,000)(1 - 0.4) + (\$20,000)(0.4) \\
&= (\$35,000)(0.6) + (\$20,000)(0.4) \\
&= \$21,000 + \$8,000 \\
&= \$29,000.
\end{aligned}
$$

We see that Equation 14-1 produces exactly the same result as found in Table 14-2, namely, that the annual net cash flow for Project X is $29,000.

Note that, for capital budgeting purposes, interest expense is not deducted in calculating cash flow. (Interest expense is given as $0 in Table 14-2.) As you will learn in a subsequent chapter, the minimum acceptable rate of return for an average-risk project is the firm's **cost of capital,** which is the weighted average of the required returns, or costs, of all sources of financing. The net cash flow for each year is *discounted,* or converted to a present value, to account for these financing costs. If interest charges were also *deducted* when determining the project's cash flow and the net cash flows then were discounted by the cost of capital, double counting of this financing cost would occur. Therefore, interest charges should *not* be dealt with explicitly in capital budgeting. In effect, we compute the project's cash flow *as if* it were financed entirely with common stock equity, but then we discount by the cost of capital, which does incorporate all financing costs. In essence, this approach allows the analyst to concentrate on selecting the best projects available. Note also that the financing cost associated with common stock does not present a problem. Since common stock dividends are paid *after* net income has been calculated, there is no danger of double counting this financing cost.[4] Finally, if you look back to the earlier section detailing steps in the capital budgeting process, you will see that choosing specific project financing was *not* one of these steps. The decision regarding the financing of the entire firm is deliberately kept sep-

cost of capital

The discount rate that should be used in the capital budgeting process.

---

[4]If a firm uses preferred stock, we would also have to be careful *not* to deduct the financing expense of preferred dividends. Again, *in capital budgeting, we assume that the firm is financed solely by common equity.* This may all be a bit difficult to grasp at this point but should become clearer in Chapter 19, which deals with the cost of capital.

arate from capital budgeting decisions; we will come back to this topic in Chapter 20.

Incremental Cash Flows

incremental cash flows

The net cash flows attributable to an investment project.

sunk cost

A cash outlay that has already been incurred and which cannot be recovered regardless of whether the project is accepted or rejected.

In evaluating a capital project, we are concerned only with those cash flows that would result directly from a decision to accept the project. These cash flows, called **incremental cash flows,** represent the changes in the firm's total cash flows that are attributable to the project in question. Four special problems in determining incremental cash flows are discussed next.

Sunk Costs.   Sunk costs are not incremental costs, and they should not be included in the analysis. A **sunk cost** is an outlay that has already been committed or that has already occurred and, hence, is not affected by the accept/reject decision under consideration. To illustrate, in 1993 Northeast BankCorp was considering the establishment of a branch office in a newly developed section of Boston. To help with its evaluation, Northeast had, back in 1992, hired a consulting firm to perform a site analysis; the cost was $100,000, and this amount was paid and then expensed for tax purposes in 1992. Is this 1992 expenditure a relevant cost with respect to the 1993 capital budgeting decision? The answer is no — the $100,000 is a sunk cost, and Northeast cannot recover it regardless of whether or not the new branch is built.

Opportunity Costs.   The second potential problem relates to opportunity costs, which we defined in Chapter 9 as the percentage return on the best alternative investment available of equal risk. Here, we will use the term to mean the *dollar* cash flows that can be generated from assets the firm already owns provided they are not used for the project in question. To illustrate, Northeast BankCorp already owns a piece of land that is suitable for the branch location. When evaluating the prospective branch, should the cost of the land be disregarded because no additional cash outlay would be required? The answer is no because there is an opportunity cost inherent in the use of the property. In this case, the land could be sold for $150,000 after taxes. Use of the site for the branch would require forgoing this inflow, so the $150,000 must be charged as an opportunity cost against the project. Note that the amount in this example is the $150,000 market-determined value, irrespective of whether Northeast originally paid $50,000 or $500,000 for the property. (What Northeast paid would, of course, have an effect on taxes and hence on the after-tax opportunity cost, but we made the assumption above that the $150,000 was already on an after-tax basis.)

externalities

Effects of a project on cash flows in other parts of the firm.

Effects on Other Parts of the Firm: Externalities.   The third potential problem involves the effects of a project on other parts of the firm; economists call these effects **externalities.** For example, some of Northeast's customers who would use the new branch are already banking with Northeast's downtown office. The loans and deposits, and hence profits, attributable to these customers would not be new to the bank; rather, they would represent a transfer from the main office to the branch. Thus, the net revenues produced by these customers should not be treated as incremental income in the capital budgeting decision.

On the other hand, having a suburban branch would help the bank attract new business to its downtown office because some people like to be able to bank both close to home and close to work. In this case, the additional revenues that would actually flow to the downtown office should be attributed to the branch. Although often difficult to quantify, externalities such as these should be considered.

Shipping and Installation Costs.   When a firm acquires fixed assets, it often must incur substantial costs for shipping and installing the equipment. These charges are added to the invoice price of the equipment when the cost of the project is being determined. Also, as was mentioned briefly in Chapter 2, shipping and installation costs increase the asset's depreciable basis. Thus, if Northeast BankCorp bought a computer with an invoice price of $100,000 and paid another $10,000 for shipping and installation, the full cost of the computer, and its depreciable basis, would be $110,000.

Changes in Net Working Capital

change in net working capital

The increased current assets required for a new project, minus the simultaneous increase in accounts payable and accruals.

Normally, additional inventories are required to support a new operation, and expanded sales also produce additional accounts receivable; both of these increases in assets must be financed. At the same time, however, accounts payable and accruals will increase spontaneously as a result of the expansion, and this will reduce the net cash needed to finance inventories and receivables. The difference between the required increase in current assets and the spontaneous increase in current liabilities is a required **change in net working capital.** If this change is positive, as it generally is for expansion projects, then the firm must raise this much additional capital, over and above the cost of the fixed assets, to undertake the project.[5] The additional net working capital is part of the required initial cost of the project, and it is just as necessary as the investment in the project's fixed assets.

As the end of the project's life approaches, inventories will be sold off and not replaced, and receivables will be collected. As these changes occur, the firm receives a positive end-of-project cash inflow equal to the net working capital investment that occurred when the project began. Thus, additional net working capital must be financed when the project is begun, but those dollars are recovered at the end of the project's life, and the recovery is not taxable since it represents a conversion of assets without economic gain.[6]

---

[5]Recall Equation 7-1 from Chapter 7:

$$\text{AFN} = \text{A*/S}(\Delta S) - \text{L*/S}(\Delta S) - \text{MS}_1(1 - d).$$

Now recognize that a change in net working capital is basically equal to $\text{A*/S}(\Delta S) - \text{L*/S}(\Delta S)$ in cases where only current assets are considered spontaneous. It follows that an *increase* in net working capital is most likely to be required when a capital budgeting proposal involves an *increase* in sales (as opposed to one undertaken to reduce costs).

[6]It is possible for a change in net working capital to be *negative* at the beginning of the project, that is, an *inflow.* This is most likely to happen when there is no expected increase in sales but, instead, a reduction in operating costs. An example would be an investment into a computerized inventory management system, which is expected to reduce inventory and, possibly, labor costs. In such a situation, the *inflow* when the asset is purchased is matched by an *outflow* of the same amount at the end of the project's life.

? Self-Test

Describe a couple of cases where estimating cash flows turned out to be extremely difficult.

What is the financial staff's role in the capital budgeting forecasting process?

Briefly explain the difference between accounting net income and net cash flow. Which should be used in capital budgeting? Why?

Explain what these terms mean, and assess their relevance in capital budgeting: incremental cash flows, sunk cost, opportunity cost, externalities, and shipping plus installation costs.

How is an initial increase in net working capital dealt with in the capital budgeting analysis?

Does the company get back the dollars it invests in working capital? Explain.

Methods Used to Evaluate Proposed Projects

ranking methods

Techniques used to evaluate capital expenditure proposals in terms of their attractiveness to the firm.

A number of different methods are used to rank projects and to decide whether or not they should be accepted for inclusion in the capital budget. The three most commonly used **ranking methods** are payback, net present value (NPV), and internal rate of return (IRR).[7]

1. **Payback period.**   This is the expected number of years required to recover the original investment.

2. **Net present value (NPV).**   This is the present value of future cash flows, discounted at the appropriate cost of capital, minus the cost of the investment. The NPV method is a *discounted cash flow (DCF)* method.

3. **Internal rate of return (IRR).**   This is the discount rate that equates the present value of future cash flows to the initial cost of the project. The IRR is also a discounted cash flow (DCF) method.

investment outlay

Funds expended for an asset or a project (including delivery and installation) plus additional net working capital if required.

Future cash flows are, in all cases, defined as the incremental net cash flows from the investments. The nature and characteristics of the three methods are illustrated and explained in the following sections, using the cash flow data shown in Table 14-3 for two projects that we call Project E and Project L. Note that the returns from Project E are much greater early in its life compared with those of Project L, whose returns are larger late in its life. We assume that the two projects are equally risky. Note that the cash flows, CF_t, are expected values and that they have been adjusted to reflect taxes, depreciation, and salvage values. Further, since many projects require an investment in both fixed assets and working capital, the **investment outlay** includes any necessary changes in net working capital. Finally, when using the NPV and IRR methods, we assume that all cash flows occur at the end of the designated year.

---

[7]You should be aware that there are three other ranking methods that are sometimes used: (1) the accounting rate of return, (2) the profitability index, and (3) the discounted payback period. Each of these methods can lead to incorrect rankings for projects and are thus potentially misleading. Also, a modified version of the IRR is seeing increased usage today. For a discussion of these methods, see Brigham and Gapenski, *Intermediate Financial Management,* 4th ed., Chapter 7.

Table 14-3

Cash Flows for Projects E and L (Investment Outlay for Each Project Is $25,000)

	Net Cash Flow (Net Income Plus Depreciation)	
Year	Project E	Project L
1	$12,000	$ 5,400
2	10,000	8,000
3	8,000	10,000
4	5,400	12,000
Total inflows	$35,400	$35,400

Payback Period

payback period

The number of years required to recover the firm's original investment.

The **payback period** is defined as the expected number of years required for a firm to recover its original investment from a project's net cash flows. The process is a simple one—sum the future cash flows for each year until the initial cost of the capital project is at least covered. The total amount of time, including the fraction of a year if appropriate, that it takes to recapture the original amount invested is the payback period. The payback method provides a measure of project *liquidity*, or the speed with which cash invested in the project will be returned. In Table 14-3 each project costs $25,000. If the cash flows come in evenly during the year, it will take 2.375 years for cash flows from Project E to equal the $25,000 cost. Therefore, the payback period for Project E is 2.375 years: $12,000 + $10,000 + ($3,000/$8,000) = the cash flows for the first two years plus 0.375 of the third year's cash flow. The general method for calculating payback is as follows:

$$\text{Payback} = \text{Year before full recovery} + \frac{\text{Unrecovered cost at start of year}}{\text{Cash flow during year}}.$$

Applying the same procedure to Project L, we find its payback to be 3.133 years:

$$\text{Payback}_L = 3 + \frac{\$1,600}{\$12,000} = 3.133 \text{ years.}$$

Because Project E's largest cash flows occur early in its life, it is not surprising that it has the faster recovery of the initial investment. On the basis of payback, Project E is superior to Project L.

The payback method's principal strength is that it is easy and inexpensive to calculate and apply. This was an important consideration in the precomputer days, and prior to the 1960s, payback was the most commonly used method for screening capital budgeting proposals. However, the payback method has conceptual problems that make total reliance on this technique undesirable. Two of the major conceptual weaknesses of payback are the following:

1. **It ignores returns beyond the payback period.** One glaring weakness of the payback method is that it ignores any cash flow that occurs beyond the payback period. For example, if Project L had an additional return of $20,000 in Year 5, this fact would not influence the payback ranking of Projects E and L. Ignoring returns in the distant future means that the pay-

back method is biased against long-term projects and tends to sacrifice future growth for current liquidity.

2. **It ignores the time value of money.**   The timing of cash flows is obviously important (as the last chapter emphasized), yet the payback method ignores the time value of money. By this method, a dollar in Year 3 is given the same weight as a dollar in Year 1.

In spite of the conceptual drawbacks to the payback technique, this project-screening device has shown remarkable vitality over the years. Managers still use payback because it tells them something they want to know. Firms that are short of cash necessarily place a higher value on projects with a higher degree of liquidity, and a project that returns its investment quickly will allow these funds to be reinvested quickly in other projects. Such a project would be especially valuable to a small or growing firm that is unable to raise capital quickly or in large amounts. Also, the payback period is often used as an indicator of projects' relative risk. Because firms can usually forecast near-term events better than more distant ones, projects whose returns come in relatively rapidly are, other things held constant, generally less risky than longer-term projects. We see, then, that by focusing on the speed of cash inflows, the payback period provides important information to the financial manager. However, in light of payback's weaknesses, the technique should be used in conjunction with other, more technically correct, project-screening methods such as net present value (NPV) and internal rate of return (IRR), which are discussed next.

Net Present Value (NPV)

discounted cash flow (DCF) techniques

Methods of evaluating investment proposals that employ time value of money concepts; two of these are the *net present value* and *internal rate of return* methods.

net present value (NPV) method

A method of evaluating investment proposals by finding the present value of future net cash flows, discounted at an appropriate interest rate, minus the cost of the investment.

As the flaws in the payback method were recognized, people began to search for ways of evaluating projects which would recognize that a dollar received immediately is preferable to a dollar received at some future date. This led to the development of **discounted cash flow (DCF) techniques** to take into account the time value of money. One such DCF technique is called the *net present value (NPV) method.* To implement this approach, find the present value of the expected net cash flows of an investment, discounted at an appropriate interest rate, and subtract from it the initial cost outlay of the project. If its net present value is zero or positive, the project should be accepted; if negative, it should be rejected.

The equation for the **net present value (NPV) method** is as follows:

$$\text{NPV} = \sum_{t=1}^{n} \frac{CF_t}{(1+k)^t} - C \tag{14-2}$$

$$= \left[\frac{CF_1}{(1+k)^1} + \frac{CF_2}{(1+k)^2} + \cdots + \frac{CF_n}{(1+k)^n} \right] - C$$

$$= CF_1(PVIF_{k,1}) + CF_2(PVIF_{k,2}) + \cdots + CF_n(PVIF_{k,n}) - C.$$

Here CF_t is the expected net cash flow from the project at Period t, n is the project's expected life, and k, incorporated into the present value interest factor, PVIF, is the appropriate discount rate, or the cost of capital. The cost of capital, k, depends on the riskiness of the project, on the level of interest rates in the economy, and on several other factors. In this chapter we take k as a given, but it is discussed in detail in Chapter 19.

	Project E			Project L		
Year	**Cash Flow**	**PVIF (12%)**	**PV of Cash Flow**	**Cash Flow**	**PVIF (12%)**	**PV of Cash Flow**
1	$12,000	0.8929	$ 10,715	$ 5,400	0.8929	$ 4,822
2	10,000	0.7972	7,972	8,000	0.7972	6,378
3	8,000	0.7118	5,694	10,000	0.7118	7,118
4	5,400	0.6355	3,432	12,000	0.6355	7,626
		PV of inflows	$ 27,813		PV of inflows	$ 25,944
		Less: Cost	−25,000		Less: Cost	−25,000
		NPV	$ 2,813		NPV	$ 944

Table 14-4 Calculating the Net Present Values (NPVs) of Projects E and L

The initial cost of the investment, C, such as the cost of buying equipment or building factories, is a *negative* cash flow and is given a minus sign. In evaluating Projects E and L, only the initial outlay (CF_0) is negative, but for many large projects, such as General Motors's Saturn project, an electric power plant, or IBM's lap-top computer, outflows occur for several years before operations begin and positive cash flows are generated.

Under the assumption that the two projects are equally risky, the net present values of Projects E and L are calculated in Table 14-4, based on the discounting procedures developed in Chapter 13 and used in Equation 14-2. Assuming an appropriate discount rate (a required rate of return) of 12 percent for both projects, Project E has an NPV of $2,813, and Project L has an NPV of $944.[8] On the basis of the calculations shown in Table 14-4, both projects should be accepted if possible; however, if only one can be chosen, Project E is the better choice because it has the higher NPV.

The rationale for the NPV method is straightforward. The value of a firm is the sum of the values of its parts; that is, the values of its various projects and investments. If the firm takes on a zero-NPV project, the position of the original stockholders is unchanged — the firm becomes larger, but its value does not change. Thus, when the NPV is zero, the project has covered all required operating and financial costs, but it has no excess returns. However, when a firm adopts a project with a positive NPV, the project's returns exceed required financial and operating costs. Therefore, the value of the firm increases by the amount of the NPV, thereby improving the position of the original stockholders. In this example, the value of the firm, and hence the original stockholders' wealth, increases by $2,813 if the firm chooses Project E but by only $944 if it chooses Project L. Of course, the firm's value will increase by $3,757 if it is possible to accept both projects. *The increase in the value of the firm from its*

---

[8]It is often helpful to place cash flows on a time line, as was done in Chapter 13. Also, although calculating NPV with a regular calculator and interest rate tables (the method shown in Table 14-4) is not difficult, the most efficient way to find NPV is with a financial calculator. Review the section in Chapter 13 on the use of financial calculators in solving for uneven cash flows. This approach provides the general method for the time value of money calculations needed here. For example, for Project E, enter into the cash flow register: $CF_0 = -25000$, $CF_1 = 12000$, $CF_2 = 10000$, $CF_3 = 8000$, and $CF_4 = 5400$. Next enter the interest rate, $k = i = 12$, and press the NPV key. The calculator will provide the answer: $2,812.26 (remember, slight rounding errors are common).

capital budget for the year is the sum of the NPVs of all accepted projects.[9] Thus, if Projects E and L are mutually exclusive, it is easy to see why Project E is preferable to Project L, but if they are independent, both are acceptable since each has a positive NPV. **Mutually exclusive projects** are alternative investments that serve the same purpose; if one project is taken on, the other must be rejected. The installation of a conveyor belt system in a warehouse and the purchase of a fleet of forklift trucks to do the same job for the same warehouse would be an example of mutually exclusive projects—accepting one implies rejection of the other. **Independent projects** are those whose costs and revenues are independent of one another. For example, the purchase of the company president's automobile and the purchase of a major piece of machinery would represent independent projects.

mutually exclusive projects

A situation where if one project is accepted, the other must be rejected.

independent projects

Two or more projects where all can be accepted; the opposite of mutually exclusive.

The Internal Rate of Return (IRR)

In the previous section on NPV we said that if a project's NPV is zero or positive, the project is acceptable, and if the NPV is negative, the project is unacceptable. The **internal rate of return (IRR) method** finds the specific discount rate that equates the present value of the expected future cash flows to the initial cost of the project. (The future cash flows are normally *inflows* but, as we shall see in Appendix 14A, may occasionally be outflows.) The equation for calculating this rate is as follows:

internal rate of return (IRR) method

A method of evaluating investment proposals by calculating the discount rate that sets equal the present value of future cash flows to the investment's cost.

$$NPV = \sum_{t=1}^{n} \frac{CF_t}{(1 + IRR)^t} - C = \$0 \qquad (14\text{-}3)$$

$$\frac{CF_1}{(1 + IRR)^1} + \frac{CF_2}{(1 + IRR)^2} + \cdots + \frac{CF_n}{(1 + IRR)^n} - C = \$0$$

$$CF_1(PVIF_{IRR,1}) + CF_2(PVIF_{IRR,2}) + \cdots + CF_n(PVIF_{IRR,n}) - C = \$0.$$

Here we know the value of the investment outlay, $C = CF_0$, and the cash flows, $CF_1, CF_2, \cdots CF_n$ as well, but we do not know the value of the discount rate, **IRR,** that equates the future cash flows and the present value of the investment outlay. *There is a value of IRR which will cause the sum of the discounted cash flows to equal the initial cost of the project, making the NPV equal to zero: this value is defined as the internal rate of return.*

IRR

The discount rate which forces the PV of a project's cash flows to equal the PV of its costs and, thus, forces the project's NPV to equal zero.

   A simple example may make this concept easier to understand. If we invest $10,000 for 6 years at 14 percent, then, by using Equation 13-2 from Chapter 13, we can determine the future (compound) value of the investment:

$$FV_6 = PV(FVIF_{14\%,6})$$

$$= \$10,000(2.1950)$$

$$= \$21,950.$$

Now assume that we know that if we invest $10,000 today, the investment will return $21,950 in 6 years. What is the rate of return on this investment? We need to find the discount rate, or IRR, that equates the value of the investment today, $10,000, with the future value of $21,950 to be received 6 years hence. This is the same as finding the discount rate that causes the NPV of the investment to equal zero. Therefore, we solve for the present value interest factor as a step in determining the IRR:

$$PV = FV_6(PVIF_{k,6})$$

$$PVIF_{k,6} = PV/FV_6$$

$$= \$10,000/\$21,950$$

$$= 0.455581 = 0.4556.$$

Now we can find the PVIF of 0.4556 in Table A-1 of Appendix A by looking across the sixth-year row to the 14 percent column. A 14 percent discount rate equates the investment's cost and the PV of the future cash flows, so 14 percent is the internal rate of return.

Because the IRR equation (14-3) is simply the NPV equation (14-2), solved for the particular discount rate that forces the NPV to equal zero, the same basic equation is used for both methods. In the NPV method the discount rate, k, is specified, and the NPV is found, while in the IRR method the NPV is specified to equal zero, and the discount rate that forces the NPV to equal zero is found.

The internal rate of return may be found in a number of ways, and we have just given a simple lump-sum example, using tables. Several other methods are discussed in the following sections.

Procedure 1: IRR with Constant Cash Inflows. If the cash flows from a project are constant, or equal in each year, the project's internal rate of return can be found by a relatively simple process. In essence, such a project is an annuity: the firm makes an outlay, C, and receives a stream of cash flow benefits, PMT, for a given number of years. The IRR for the project is found by applying Equation 13-5, discussed in Chapter 13.

To illustrate, suppose a project has a cost of $10,000 and is expected to produce cash flows of $1,627.45 each year for 10 years. The cost of the project, $10,000, is the present value of an annuity of $1,627.45 a year for 10 years. Applying Equation 13-5, we obtain

$$PVA_{10} = PMT(PVIFA_{k,10})$$

$$Cost = CF(PVIFA_{k,10})$$

$$PVIFA_{k,10} = Cost/CF = \$10,000/\$1,627.45$$

$$= 6.1446.$$

Looking up the PVIFA in Table A-2 of Appendix A, across the row for Year 10, we find it located under the 10 percent column. Accordingly, 10 percent is the project's IRR. In other words, 10 percent is the discount rate that would force Equation 14-3 to equal zero when the cash flows are constant at $1,627.45 for 10 years and C is $10,000. This procedure works only if the project has con-

Table 14-5

Finding the Internal Rate
of Return of Project L

Year	Cash Flow	12%		14%	
		PVIF	PV	PVIF	PV
1	$ 5,400	0.8929	$ 4,822	0.8772	$ 4,737
2	8,000	0.7972	6,378	0.7695	6,156
3	10,000	0.7118	7,118	0.6750	6,750
4	12,000	0.6355	7,626	0.5921	7,105
		PV of inflows	$ 25,944		$ 24,748
		Less: Cost	− 25,000		− 25,000
		NPV$_L$	$ 944		$ (252)

stant annual cash flows; if it does not, the IRR must be found by one of the other methods discussed below.

Procedure 2: Trial and Error. In the trial-and-error method, the present value of an investment's future cash flows is first computed using a somewhat arbitrarily selected discount rate. Generally, the firm's cost of capital, in this case 12 percent, is a good starting point for most problems. Then the present value of these cash flows, based on a 12 percent discount rate, is compared with the investment's cost. If the present value of the future cash flows is *larger* than the project's cost, the NPV is positive. Therefore, we must *lower* the NPV, and to do this we must *raise* the discount rate and go through the process again. Conversely, if the present value of the future cash flows is lower than the cost (NPV is negative), we must lower the discount rate and repeat the process. This process is continued until the present value of the future cash flows from the investment is approximately equal to its cost. The discount rate that brings about this equality—and forces NPV to equal zero—is the internal rate of return.

This calculation process is illustrated next for Projects E and L which were analyzed earlier. In Table 14-5 the steps required to find the IRR for Project L are reviewed. Earlier, in Table 14-4, we found the NPV of Project L to be $944, when future cash flows are discounted at a 12 percent cost of capital. This calculation is shown again in the center columns of Table 14-5. Because the NPV of Project L is positive at a discount rate of 12 percent, we know that the internal rate of return of this investment opportunity is *greater* than 12 percent. However, the NPV is rather small, indicating that the IRR is close to 12 percent. Thus we increase the discount rate slightly, to 14 percent. At 14 percent the NPV of Project L is a negative $252. Because the internal rate of return (IRR) causes the NPV to equal zero, we know that the internal rate of return for Project L is between 12 and 14 percent.

If we wish the IRR to be more accurate, we can interpolate between these results. To do so, we bracket the discount rate that causes the project's NPV to equal zero:

$$NPV = \$944 \text{ at } 12.0\% \left.\right\} \$944$$
$$NPV = \$0 \text{ at IRR} \left.\right\} \$1,196$$
$$NPV = (\$252) \text{ at } \underline{14.0\%} \left.\right\} (\$252)$$
$$\underline{2.0\%}$$

Table 14-6 Finding the Internal Rate of Return of Project E

Year	Cash Flow	12% PVIF	12% PV	16% PVIF	16% PV	18% PVIF	18% PV
1	$12,000	0.8929	$ 10,715	0.8621	$ 10,345	0.8475	$ 10,170
2	10,000	0.7972	7,972	0.7432	7,432	0.7182	7,182
3	8,000	0.7118	5,694	0.6407	5,126	0.6086	4,869
4	5,400	0.6355	3,432	0.5523	2,982	0.5158	2,785
		PV of inflows	$ 27,813		$ 25,885		$ 25,006
		Less: Cost	− 25,000		− 25,000		− 25,000
		NPV_E	$ 2,813		$ 885		$ 6

Thus,

$$IRR = 12.00\% + (\$944/\$1,196)(2.0\%)$$

$$= 12.00\% + 0.789(2.0\%)$$

$$\approx 13.6\%.$$

The IRR lies 944/1,196 of the way between 12 and 14 percent. Since there is a 2-percentage-point difference between 12 and 14 percent, we multiply the fraction by 2 percent and then add this product to 12 percent to obtain the IRR of approximately 13.6 percent. For all practical purposes, an IRR that is accurate to within one-half of a percentage point is usually sufficient, especially when the uncertainty of the underlying cash flows is considered.

Just as we found the IRR of Project L, we now trace the steps in determining the IRR for Project E (see Table 14-6). Again, the 12 percent discount rate is used as a starting point in our search for the project's internal rate of return. At 12 percent the NPV is positive, so we know the project's IRR is greater than 12 percent. Because the NPV is significantly larger than zero at 12 percent, we know the IRR is much greater than 12 percent. At a discount rate of 16 percent we find that the NPV is still positive. At 18 percent the NPV is barely larger than zero; thus, for all practical purposes the IRR of Project E is 18 percent because at that rate the project's NPV is essentially zero.

Procedure 3: Graphic Solution. The graphic method for finding IRRs involves plotting a curve that shows the relationship between a project's NPV and the discount rate used to calculate the NPV. Such a curve is defined as the project's **net present value profile.** NPV profiles for Projects E and L are shown in Figure 14-1. To construct such NPV profiles, first note that at a zero percent discount rate, the NPV is simply the total of the undiscounted cash flows of the project less the project's cost; thus, at a zero percent discount rate, the NPV of both projects is $10,400. This value is plotted as the vertical axis intercept in Figure 14-1. Next, we calculate the projects' NPVs at three discount rates, say, 5, 10, and 15 percent, and plot these values. The data points plotted on the graph are shown at the bottom of the figure. When we connect these points, we have the net present value profiles.

net present value profile

A curve showing the relationship between a project's NPV and the discount rate used.

Figure 14-1

Net Present Value Profiles: NPVs of Projects E and L at Different Discount Rates

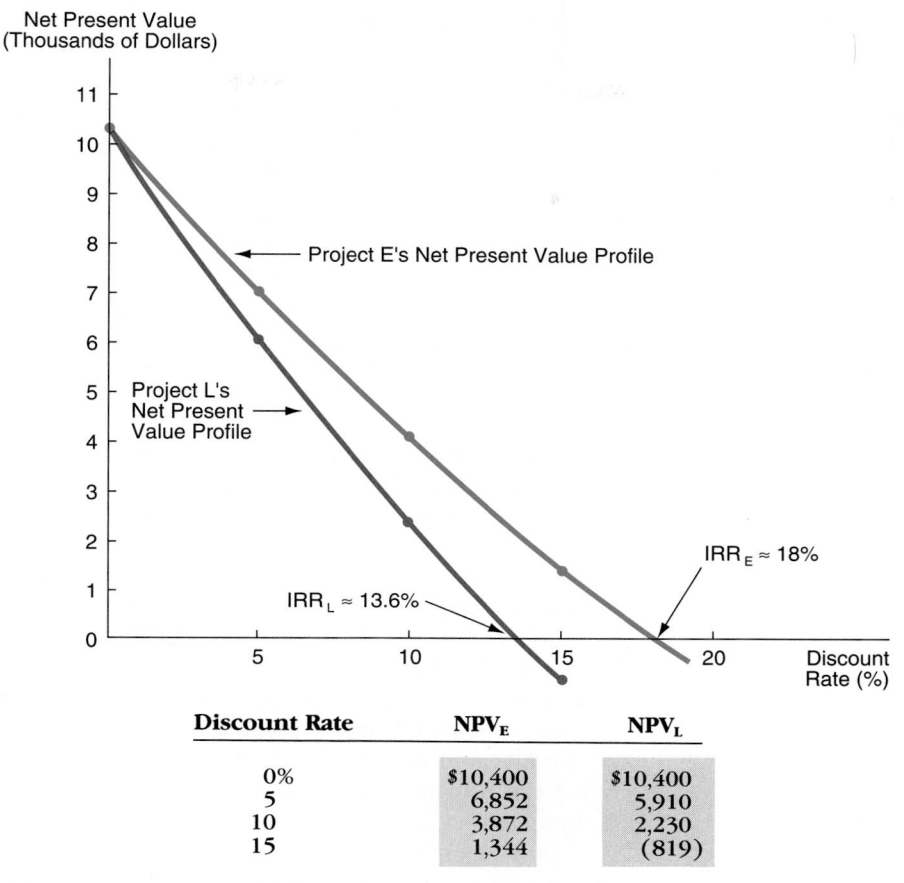

Discount Rate	NPV_E	NPV_L
0%	$10,400	$10,400
5	6,852	5,910
10	3,872	2,230
15	1,344	(819)

A net present value profile shows a project's NPV at different discount rates. In the graph above, NPV profiles are shown for Projects E and L. The Y intercept for each curve gives the project's NPV at a zero percent discount rate, while the X intercept is the project's internal rate of return.

Since the IRR is defined as the discount rate at which a project's NPV equals zero, *the point at which a project's net present value profile crosses the horizontal axis indicates the project's internal rate of return.* In Figure 14-1 we see that IRR_E is about 18 percent, while IRR_L is approximately 13.6 percent. Using graph paper and a sharp pencil, we can make reasonably accurate estimates of IRRs, at least sufficiently accurate for most purposes.

Procedure 4: Financial Calculator and Computer Solutions. Internal rates of return can be calculated easily by financial calculators and by computers. Most larger firms have computerized their capital budgeting processes and automatically generate IRRs, NPVs, and paybacks for all projects. On a financial calculator, once the cash flows have been entered into the cash flow register, as shown in Footnote 8, instead of keying in k = i and solving for NPV, simply

Table 14-7   Analysis of Project E's IRR as a Loan Rate

Year (1)	Loan Amount at Beginning of Year (2)	Cash Flow (3)	Interest on the Loan at 18% $0.18 \times (2) = (4)$	Repayment of Principal $(3) - (4) = (5)$	Ending Loan Balance $(2) - (5) = (6)$
1	$25,000	$12,000	$4,500	$7,500	$17,500
2	17,500	10,000	3,150	6,850	10,650
3	10,650	8,000	1,917	6,083	4,567
4	4,567	5,400	822	4,578	(11)[a]

[a]The exact value of IRR_E is 18.01324 percent. Had that value been used, the ending balance would have been zero. Note that the difference between this residual and that in Table 14-6 is simply the result of rounding differences.

press the IRR key, and the calculator will, through trial and error, solve for the internal rate of return. (If you plan to continue your study of finance, a financial calculator is a good investment.)

Rationale and Use of the IRR Method.   What is so special about the particular discount rate that equates a project's cost with the present value of its future cash flows? To answer this question, first assume that our illustrative firm obtains the $25,000 needed to take on Project E by borrowing from a bank at an interest rate of 18 percent. Since the internal rate of return on this project was calculated to be 18 percent, the same as the cost of the bank loan, the firm can invest in the project, use the cash flows generated by the investment to pay off the principal and interest on the loan, and come out exactly even on the transaction. This point is demonstrated in Table 14-7, which shows that Project E provides cash flows that are just sufficient to pay 18 percent interest on the unpaid balance of the bank loan, retire the loan over the life of the project, and end up with a balance that differs from zero only by a rounding error of ($11).

If the internal rate of return exceeds the cost of the funds used to finance a project, a surplus remains after paying for the capital. This surplus will accrue to the firm's stockholders, so taking on a project on which the IRR exceeds the firm's cost of capital increases the value of the firm's stock. If the internal rate of return is less than the cost of capital, taking on the project will impose a cost on existing stockholders, so accepting the project results in a reduction of value. It is this "breakeven" characteristic that makes us interested in the internal rate of return.[10]

Continuing with the example of Projects E and L, if both projects have a cost of capital of 12 percent, the internal rate of return rule indicates that if the projects are independent, both should be accepted — they both do better than break even. If they are mutually exclusive, E ranks higher and should be accepted, whereas L should be rejected. If the cost of capital is above 18 percent, both projects should be rejected.

---

[10]This example illustrates the logic of the IRR method, but for technical correctness, the capital used to finance the project should be assumed to be a mix of debt and equity, not debt alone. We will discuss this in greater detail in Chapter 19. For right now, we will continue with our earlier assumption of 100% equity financing.

? Self-Test

Identify the three methods presented for evaluating proposed capital budgeting projects.

How is the payback period of a project calculated, and what information does it provide to the firm?

Briefly explain the net present value (NPV) method.

What is the rationale behind the NPV method?

How would you calculate the IRR of a project?

Describe how NPV profiles are constructed.

What is the rationale behind the IRR method?

Evaluation of Payback, NPV, and IRR Methods

We have presented three possible capital budgeting methods, all of which are used to a greater or lesser extent in practice. However, because these methods can lead to quite different accept/reject decisions, we need to answer this question: Which one is best? Obviously, the best approach is the one that selects from all available projects that particular set of projects which maximizes the firm's value and hence its shareholders' wealth. If more than one method does this, then the best method would be the one that is easiest to use in practice.

There are three properties that must be exhibited by a capital budgeting method if it is to lead to consistently correct decisions:

1. The method must consider all cash flows over the entire life of a project.

2. The method must consider the time value of money — that is, it must reflect the fact that dollars which come in sooner are more valuable than dollars which are received in the distant future.

3. When the method is used to select from a set of mutually exclusive projects, it must pick the project which maximizes the firm's stock price.

How do the three methods compare with regard to the required properties? The payback method violates Properties 1 and 2: it does not consider all cash flows, and it ignores the time value of money. Both the NPV and IRR methods satisfy Properties 1 and 2, and both lead to identical (and correct) accept/reject decisions for *independent* projects. However, only the NPV method satisfies Property 3 in all cases. As we demonstrate in Appendix 14A, there are certain conditions under which the IRR method fails to correctly identify that project, within a set of *mutually exclusive* projects, which maximizes the firm's stock price.

? Self-Test

What are the three properties that a capital budgeting method must have in order to consistently lead to correct decisions?

Do payback period, NPV, and IRR satisfy the three properties equally well? Explain.

A Capital Budgeting Case

expansion project
A project that is intended to increase sales.

An **expansion project** is one that calls for the firm to invest in new facilities in order to increase sales. For example, suppose Houston Trucking Company buys a new delivery van at a cost of $10,000. The van has a 5-year MACRS class life (see Chapter 2 for a review of MACRS depreciation), additional sales attributable to the new van will amount to $28,000 per year for 6 years, and Houston expects to be able to sell the van for $500 at the end of its 6-year service life. (Remember that a 5-year MACRS class life means that the asset is depreciated over 6 years because only one-half year of depreciation is taken in the year that the asset is acquired.) Operating costs (fuel, labor, and so forth) will amount to $20,000 per year. Houston's marginal federal-plus-state income tax rate is 40 percent, its cost of capital is 12 percent, and the firm must increase its net working capital by $3,000 if it purchases the van.

First, we need to determine the company's initial investment, or CF_0. Houston must write a check for $10,000 to pay for the van. Also, Houston will have to increase its net working capital by $3,000 to support the higher level of sales attributable to the van, but this net working capital will be recovered when the van is sold. Thus, the net investment in the van at (approximately) time zero is as follows:

Purchase price of van	$10,000
Plus investment in net working capital	3,000
Net investment at t = 0	$13,000

Next, we find the annual net cash flows attributable to the investment in the van, equal to net income plus depreciation. These cash flows are developed in Table 14-8.

Note that depreciation under MACRS for a 5-year class life project such as the van is calculated as follows:

1. The *depreciable basis* is equal to the total cost of the van, which is $10,000. Note that any delivery, installation, and similar charges are included in the depreciable basis.

2. Annual depreciation:

Year	MACRS Allowance	×	Basis	=	Annual Depreciation
1	0.20		$10,000		$ 2,000
2	0.32		10,000		3,200
3	0.19		10,000		1,900
4	0.12		10,000		1,200
5	0.11		10,000		1,100
6	0.06		10,000		600
	1.00				$10,000

When the van is disposed of at the end of 6 years, Houston expects to sell it for $500. Since the van will be fully depreciated (book value = $0), yet will have a market value of $500, in economic terms it has been "overdepreciated." Under the tax laws, the government gets to "recapture" this depreciation by treating any salvage value in excess of the book value at that time as ordinary income. Therefore, the $500 will be taxed as ordinary income at a rate of 40

Table 14-8 Houston Trucking Company: Analysis of an Expansion Project

	Year 1	Year 2	Year 3	Year 4	Year 5	Year 6
Sales attributable to the project	$28,000	$28,000	$28,000	$28,000	$28,000	$28,000
Operating costs	20,000	20,000	20,000	20,000	20,000	20,000
Depreciation (DEP)	2,000	3,200	1,900	1,200	1,100	600
Earnings before taxes (EBT)	$ 6,000	$ 4,800	$ 6,100	$ 6,800	$ 6,900	$ 7,400
Taxes (40%)	2,400	1,920	2,440	2,720	2,760	2,960
Net income (NI)	$ 3,600	$ 2,880	$ 3,660	$ 4,080	$ 4,140	$ 4,440
Net cash flow (CF = NI + DEP)	$ 5,600	$ 6,080	$ 5,560	$ 5,280	$ 5,240	$ 5,040

percent. The after-tax proceeds from the sale, recovered at the end of Year 6, will be as follows:

$$\text{Salvage (market) value after tax} = \text{Amount before tax} - \text{Tax}$$
$$= \text{Amount before tax}(1 - T)$$
$$= \$500(0.6)$$
$$= \$300.$$

Also in Year 6, Houston will recover the $3,000 initially invested in additional current assets (net working capital).

Now we have all the information necessary for calculating the project's NPV at the 12 percent cost of capital:

Year	Cash Flow	$PVIF_{12\%,t}$	PV of Cash Flow
1	$5,600	0.8929	$ 5,000
2	6,080	0.7972	4,847
3	5,560	0.7118	3,958
4	5,280	0.6355	3,355
5	5,240	0.5674	2,973
6	8,340[a]	0.5066	4,225
		Total	$24,358
		Less: Net investment at t = 0	13,000
		NPV	$11,358

[a]$5,040 from operations + $3,000 recovery of net working capital + $300 after-tax salvage value.

Alternatively, we could set up the problem as follows:

$$NPV = \sum_{t=1}^{n} \frac{CF_t}{(1 + k)^t} - \text{Net investment at t = 0}$$

$$= \frac{\$5,600}{(1.12)^1} + \frac{\$6,080}{(1.12)^2} + \frac{\$5,560}{(1.12)^3} + \frac{\$5,280}{(1.12)^4} + \frac{\$5,240}{(1.12)^5} + \frac{\$8,340}{(1.12)^6} - \$13,000$$

$$= \$11,358.$$

We could enter the cash flow data and the cost of capital into a financial calculator (the net investment at t = 0 is C_0 and is entered first as −13000), press the NPV button, and obtain $11,359. (Note the $1 rounding difference.) If the project had a fairly long life, the calculator solution would be much more efficient.

We could also solve for IRR in the following equation to find the van's IRR:

$$\text{NPV} = \frac{\$5,600}{(1 + \text{IRR})^1} + \frac{\$6,080}{(1 + \text{IRR})^2} + \frac{\$5,560}{(1 + \text{IRR})^3}$$

$$+ \frac{\$5,280}{(1 + \text{IRR})^4} + \frac{\$5,240}{(1 + \text{IRR})^5} + \frac{\$8,340}{(1 + \text{IRR})^6} - \$13,000 = \$0.$$

The solution value is IRR = 38.30%, found with a financial calculator.

The question still remains: Should Houston invest in the delivery van? Assuming the forecasts of revenues and costs are reasonably correct, the answer is yes; the NPV is positive, and the IRR is greater than Houston's cost of capital.

Self-Test

Explain the steps required in setting up an expansion project analysis, such as that described for Houston Trucking Company.

How is a required initial increase in net working capital handled in calculating a project's net investment at time zero? Will such an initial investment in net working capital have any impact on cash flows in the project's last year? Explain.

What difference will it make if the salvage value of the new asset is expected to exceed the book value in the last year?

Conclusion

This chapter has primarily been about the "nuts and bolts" of capital budgeting, the "how to" of the process, but it is important not to lose sight of the long-range consequences of capital spending on a national level. Capital spending ebbs and flows with business cycles and interest rate levels, with utilization of existing capacity, with lenders' willingness to make funds available, and with tax incentives such as the investment tax credit, which has tended to be of the "now you see it, now you don't" variety.

However, as mentioned early in the chapter, in recent years there has been a wave of cost-cutting capital spending in the United States, and a considerable amount of this has been technology related. Companies as diverse as Pitney Bowes, Bausch & Lomb, and Greyhound have invested millions of dollars in computerized systems and other information technology. So have DuPont, General Electric, Aetna Life & Casualty, Wal-Mart Stores, Levi Strauss, and countless other companies less well known. Says Frank Stotz of Bausch & Lomb, "Like everyone else, we're investing in computer systems to do things more efficiently." *BusinessWeek* reported in June 1993, that businesses had spent $1 *trillion* on information technology during the last decade.

As recently as a few years ago, economists and business people alike had not seen positive results from the huge investment, but the payoff may now have begun: In 1992, U.S. businesses boosted their productivity by 2.7 percent — the largest increase in 20 years. According to *BusinessWeek*, this wave of new technology, coupled with a sweeping reorganization of work itself, may ultimately lead to a "new industrial revolution" and an era of economic growth in the United States.

Self-Test

What types of variables tend to have an impact on capital spending overall?

Which area of capital spending has been predominant during the most recent decade? Are we seeing any results of this spending? Explain.

Summary

This chapter discussed the capital budgeting process, and the key concepts covered are listed below:

▷ **Capital budgeting** is the process of analyzing potential expenditures on fixed assets and other long-term projects and deciding whether the firm should undertake those investments.

Capital budgeting is important for a number of reasons, for example, capital expenditures **limit the firm's future flexibility.** Also, **large sums** are typically involved, and the firm needs time to line up financing.

Capital budgeting proposals are often grouped by categories such as **replacement** or **expansion.**

▷ **The capital budgeting process** should follow these steps: (1) a review of company goals and objectives, (2) a search for proposals, (3) estimates of cash flows, (4) ranking of proposals, (5) selection of projects, (6) implementation, and (7) a post-audit.

The most important, but also the most difficult, step in analyzing a capital budgeting project is **estimating the project's net cash flows.**

The **post-audit** is a key element in the capital budgeting process. By comparing actual results with predicted results and then determining why differences occurred, decision makers can improve both their operations and their forecasts of projects' outcomes.

▷ **Net cash flows** consist of net income plus depreciation and, therefore, do not equal accounting profits.

Net cash flows are difficult to estimate because **revenue and cost projections are subject to error,** and these projections are the required inputs into the analysis.

Considerations in estimating net cash flows include (1) **identifying relevant cash flows** and (2) **counting only incremental cash flows.**

Capital projects often require an additional investment in **net working capital.** An increase in net working capital must be included in the initial cash outlay at time zero and then shown as a cash inflow in the final year of the project.

▷ The **payback period** is defined as the expected number of years required to recover the original investment. The payback method ignores cash flows beyond the payback period, and it does not consider the time value of money. The payback does, however, provide an indication of a project's risk and liquidity, because it shows how long the original capital will be "at risk."

The **net present value (NPV)** is the present value of all future net cash flows, discounted at the project's **cost of capital,** minus the cost of the project. The project is acceptable if the NPV is positive or zero; the project should be rejected if the NPV is negative.

The **internal rate of return (IRR)** is defined as the discount rate which forces the present value of the future cash flows of a project to equal the cost of the project (NPV = $0). The project is accepted if the IRR is greater than or equal to the project's cost of capital.

The NPV and IRR methods lead to the same accept/reject decisions for **independent projects,** but if projects are **mutually exclusive,** then ranking conflicts can arise. These two methods are both better than payback because they discount cash flows; however, only the NPV method will maximize the firm's stock price under all conditions.

▶   An **expansion problem,** such as the Houston Trucking Company example, includes a number of steps: (1) calculate the net investment at t = 0, including possible changes in net working capital; (2) calculate annual net cash flows attributable to the investment (NI + DEP); (3) consider any additional cash flows in the asset's last year, such as **recovery of net working capital** and, possibly, **after-tax benefits from salvage,** whenever the asset is expected to sell for more than its book value at the time; and (4) discount all future cash flows and determine NPV.

Although this chapter has presented the basic elements of the capital budgeting process, there are many other aspects of this crucial topic. Some of the more important ones are discussed in the following chapter.

Resolution to
DECISION IN FINANCE

AN AGED GIANT
REMAINS NIMBLE

Throughout the company's history, Motorola has been forced to anticipate change, something that many large, bureaucratized companies are not very good at doing. In fact, some of the problems encountered by firms such as IBM and Westinghouse stem, in part, from their managements' failure to anticipate and embrace change, to foster a participative culture, and to organize large groups of workers into smaller, more productive work teams.

In general, Motorola has done an excellent job foreseeing changes in technology and mar-

Sources: "Staying Power: How an Aged Giant Can Remain Vibrant," *The Wall Street Journal,* December 9, 1992; "Nationwide Quality Improvement Network Urged," *Chicago Tribune,* April 1, 1993; "Quality Goes to School; Consortium to Train Suppliers at Community Colleges," *The Dallas Morning News,* May 20, 1993; "Money Talks and Cash-Rich Companies Have Begun to Invest," *Business Week,* November 1, 1993; "U.S. Says Japan Violated Trade Agreement," *Albany Democrat-Herald,* February 15, 1994; and "U.S. Set to Press Japan in Trade Fight; Tactics Include 'Super 301' Provision," *The Wall Street Journal,* February 15, 1994.

kets, but this did not happen by accident. Anticipation is a religion at Motorola, embedded in its culture in a number of ways and designed to keep important information flowing to the top.

One way that Motorola has been able to stay on top of leading technology is through its intelligence department, which reports on the latest technological developments obtained from conferences, journals, and the like. From this information, staff members assess where breakthroughs are likely to happen, when these developments can be incorporated into new products, how much money new product development will cost, and where the competition stands.

Only about ten other American companies spend more on research and development (R&D) than Motorola, which in 1992 alone spent an estimated $1.3 billion on R&D and another $1.4 billion on plant and equipment. But spending money on R&D does not necessarily mean success, as evidenced by the problems GM, IBM, and Digital Equipment Corporation (DEC) are experiencing. What really distinguishes Motorola is its skill in spending money on canny technology bets and manufacturing improvements. Those skills stem from a corporate culture that inspires rather than stifles conflict and dissent, locates promising but neglected projects, and generates a constant flow of information and innovation from thousands of small teams that are held to rigorous, statistically evaluated goals.

In 1979, one of the company's department heads remarked that some of the company's competitors offered better quality. In response, Motorola's chairman began a series of discussions on the increasing superiority of Japanese electronics conglomerates. From those discussions, Motorola concluded that it had to make its products better and cheaper than its Japanese rivals if it wanted to survive. In the early 1980s the company instituted a massive quality improvement program, and Motorola's phones and pagers were made with fewer parts and a high degree of automation. In 1987, Motorola's chairman announced two additional productivity goals: He wanted Motorola to reduce manufac-

turing defects by 90 percent every two years and to reduce cycle time (that is, the time required to complete tasks such as filling a customer's order or developing a new product) by 90 percent every five years. If these two goals were achieved, then by 1992, Motorola would drive its defect rate to 3.4 per million parts from 6,000, a level of near perfection referred to in engineering terminology as "six-sigma quality." To try to reach that low defect rate, Motorola had to spend heavily on redesign and automation, and the work force had to be reorganized into small teams. "Total customer satisfaction" teams are given authority to make production changes or changes in other work procedures, are paid bonuses that are tied into improved defect rates and cycle times, and compete against one another in companywide performance tests.

In 1988, Motorola was one of the first winners of the Malcolm Baldrige National Quality Award. This prestigious award is given to companies or other organizations that have excelled in total quality management (TQM)—a concept based on the principles of J. Edward Demming and first put into practice in the Japanese auto industry. However, Motorola has continued in its drive for near perfection; in 1991 alone, the company spent $70 million training employees on techniques for identifying and fixing problems.

Although Motorola's sales have doubled in the last five years, its work force has grown only slightly. A continuing audit of expenses for such things as factory downtime and warranty repairs indicates that Motorola's costs in 1992 are $900 million lower than they would have been without its investments and reorganization. Also, Motorola calculates that its project teams produce an average of four new or improved products each day.

The former editor of the *Harvard Business Review* and author of a study of giant corporations entitled "When Giants Learn to Dance" states that "Motorola is one of the few genuine role models of industry transformation." But change is not without its costs. Managers at Motorola burn out, and jobs are eliminated by its investment in automation. Competition from

Japan's NEC and from AT&T is relentless. The prices of Motorola's pagers drop an average of 8 to 12 percent a year, and its cellular phone prices drop an average of 25 percent a year. This keen competition, and the amount of investment

Some question whether other companies can imitate Motorola. The company has a totally nonunion work force and a macho work culture that suits its highly professional trained engineers. In addition, it has tremendous cash flows to support its R&D, capital investment, and training. Even so, it is hazardous to assume that such a successful giant will continue to be successful, as one look at DEC and IBM indicates.

Motorola itself has fallen short of its 1992 six-sigma quality goal of 3.4 defects per million parts, currently achieving 30 defects. Still, in the last five years, Motorola has reduced its defect rate in manufacturing 99.5 percent, which has

generated cost savings of $900 million in 1992 alone and $3.1 billion overall. To grow, Motorola must continue to make breakthroughs and expand overseas. In addition, its management will not be satisfied when it does achieve six-sigma quality, and it will then start designing for a defect rate that is measured in parts per billion.

Incidentally, in early 1994 the Clinton administration accused Japan of failing to live up to the terms of the 1989 trade agreement in which it had promised to open up its lucrative cellular phone market to American firms. It appears that Motorola had not, in fact, received the promised access to Japanese markets. Motorola officials said that the company's percentage of cellular phone business in the Tokyo area had been kept under 5 percent, in spite of the at least one-third promised under the agreement.

Questions

14-1   How is project classification (for example, replacement, expansion into new markets, etc.) used in the capital budgeting process?

14-2   Explain how net working capital is recovered at the end of a project's life and why it is included in a capital budgeting analysis.

14-3   Why are spontaneous liabilities such as accounts payable and accruals deducted from working capital in the analysis of capital budgeting costs?

14-4   If a firm used straight line rather than an accelerated depreciation method, how would this affect **(a)** the total amount of depreciation, net income, and net cash flows over the project's expected life; **(b)** the timing of depreciation, net income, and net cash flows; and **(c)** the project's payback, NPV, and IRR?

14-5   Net cash flows rather than accounting profits are emphasized throughout the chapter. What is the basis for this emphasis on cash flows as opposed to net income?

14-6   Explain why the NPV of a long-term project, defined as one with a high percentage of its cash flows expected in the distant future, is more sensitive to changes in the cost of capital than the NPV of a short-term project.

14-7   Are there conditions under which a firm might be better off if it were to choose a project with a rapid payback rather than one with a larger NPV?

14-8   A firm has $100 million available for capital expenditures. It is considering investment in one of two projects, each costing $100 million. Project A has an IRR of 20 percent and an NPV of $9 million. It will be terminated at the end of one year at a profit of $20 million, resulting in an immediate increase in earnings per share (EPS). Project B, which cannot be postponed for one year in order to take on Project A, has an NPV of $50 million and an IRR of 30 percent. However, the firm's short-run EPS will be reduced if it accepts Project B because no revenues will be generated by the project for several years.
a. Should the short-run effects on EPS influence the choice between the two projects?

b. How might situations like the one described here influence a firm's decision to use payback as a part of the capital budgeting process?

Self-Test Problems

ST-1 Paschal Products is considering the purchase of a new machine that will dramatically increase the firm's manufacturing capacity. The machine, if purchased today, would cost $40,550,000 and provide annual net cash flows (net income plus depreciation) of $13,425,000 for 6 years.

a. Determine the project's payback period.

b. Determine the project's NPV if the required return is 15 percent.

c. Determine the project's IRR.

ST-2 Bio-Technical Engineering (BTE) is considering an investment in a gene splicing project. The investment involves acquiring land, developing a new plant, operating the plant during the project, and then disposing of the salvageable assets from the project. The following is a summary of the project's characteristics (dollars in millions):

1. A total of $50 has been spent thus far to investigate the feasibility of the process used in the project.

2. BTE will purchase the land immediately at a cost of $300.

3. A BTE operations building will be put up at a cost of $400. This expenditure will occur at t = 1, that is, at the end of Year 1.

4. Equipment will be installed at a cost of $200. This outlay will occur at t = 2, the end of Year 2.

5. BTE will need additional net working capital of $100. This outlay will occur at the end of Year 3, t = 3, and the net working capital will be recovered at the end of the project's life, t = 8, the end of Year 8.

6. The plant will commence operations at the beginning of Year 4. The operations will continue for 5 years, until the end of Year 8. Net cash flows from the project (net income plus depreciation) will equal $425 annually for the 5-year operating period.

7. Even though the operating assets will be fully depreciated, management believes the building and equipment will have a combined salvage value of $150 at the end of Year 8.

8. BTE's effective tax rate is 40 percent.

9. Assume that there is no investment tax credit available at this time.

If the required rate of return for a high-risk project, such as the gene splicing project at BTE, is 20 percent, should the firm invest in this project?

Problems

14-1 Shaw Publications is evaluating a project with a cost of $754,290 and expected annual
Payback, NPV, and   net cash flows of $150,000 per year for 11 years.
IRR calculations

a. What is the project's payback period?

b. The firm's cost of capital is 12 percent. What is the project's NPV?

c. What is the project's IRR? (*Hint:* Recognize that the project's cash flows are an annuity.)

14-2 Videcon Corporation's proposed project has a cost of $3,244,320, and its expected net
Payback, NPV, and   cash flows are $900,000 per year for 5 years.
IRR calculations

a. What is the payback period for this project?

b. The cost of capital is 10 percent. What is the project's NPV?

c. What is the project's IRR? (*Hint:* Recognize that the project's net cash flows are an annuity.)

14-3 RaeTel Inc. is investigating a project that costs $1,312,150 and is expected to produce
Payback, NPV, and   net cash flows of $500,000 annually for 3 years.
IRR calculations

a. What is the project's payback period?

b. If the cost of capital is 9 percent, what is the project's NPV?

c. What is the project's IRR? (*Hint:* Recognize that the project's net cash flows are an annuity.)

14-4
Payback, NPV, and IRR calculations

The management of B&N Towing is evaluating the following investment opportunity, which costs $47,678.50 today but promises to return the following net cash flows:

Year	Net Cash Flow
1	$20,000
2	15,000
3	10,000
4	20,000

a. What is this project's payback period?
b. What is the project's NPV if B&N's cost of capital is 14 percent?
c. What is the project's IRR?

14-5
Payback, NPV, and IRR calculations

Portland Surgical Corporation is evaluating an investment opportunity that costs $100,000 today but promises to return the following net cash flows (net income plus depreciation) over the next 4 years:

Year	Net Cash Flow
1	$20,000
2	40,000
3	36,000
4	24,000

a. What is the investment's payback period?
b. What is the NPV of the project if the required return is 7 percent?
c. Is the IRR of the investment greater or less than the required return?
d. Without relying on a financial calculator, what would be a reasonable estimate of IRR? (*Hint:* IRR may be found by interpolation.)

14-6
NPV and IRR calculations

Obstbaum & Lee is considering an investment in a new machine that will provide dramatic cost savings over the next 5 years. The cost of the machine is $72,107.10. Annual net cash flows (net income plus depreciation) are projected as follows:

Year	Net Cash Flow
1	$18,000
2	25,000
3	22,000
4	20,000
5	20,000

a. If the firm's required return for a project of this type is 12 percent, what is the investment's NPV?
b. What is the project's IRR?

14-7
Net cash flows and NPV

Westworld Inc. has the opportunity to invest in a new type of robot. The initial outlay is $250,000, and the before-tax cash revenues generated by the robot are expected to be $55,000 per year for the next 20 years, after which it will be scrapped as potentially unreliable. There will be no additional annual cash expenses associated with the investment. Westworld uses straight line depreciation (no salvage), the firm's tax rate is 40 percent, and the required rate of return on this asset is 16 percent.
a. What are the estimated annual net cash flows?
b. Should the robot be purchased? Explain.

14-8
NPV calculation

Management of Accurex Associates is evaluating a computerized inventory system which would cost the firm $70,000. It is estimated that the system will provide net cash flows of $15,000 per year for 11 years (including cost reductions and depreciation), and at the end of Year 11, when the system has been fully depreciated, its salvage value is expected to be $2,000. If the firm's tax bracket is 40 percent and the appropriate discount rate is 15 percent, what is the NPV of the inventory system?

14-9
NPV calculation

Capital Services has estimated the following net cash flows in connection with Project A:

Year	Net Cash Flow
1	$10,000
2	8,500
3	7,000
4	6,000
5	4,000

The firm's cost of capital is 12 percent, and the payback period is exactly 4 years. What is the NPV of Project A? Should Capital Services accept the project?

14-10
NPVs and IRRs for mutually exclusive projects

Florida Industries is considering including one of two pieces of equipment, a truck or an overhead pulley system, in this year's capital budget. These projects are mutually exclusive. The cash outlay for the truck is $19,889 and that for the pulley system is $31,754. The firm's cost of capital is 15 percent. Net cash flows, including depreciation, are as follows:

Years	Truck	Pulley
1–5	$6,360	$9,700

Calculate the IRR and the NPV for each project, and indicate the correct accept/reject decision for each.

14-11
NPVs and IRRs for mutually exclusive projects

TMI Manufacturing must choose between a gas-powered and an electric-powered forklift for moving materials in its factory. Because both forklifts perform the same function, the firm will choose only one. (They are mutually exclusive investments.) The electric-powered forklift will cost more, but it will be less expensive to operate; it will cost $27,500, whereas the gas-powered one will cost $22,000. The cost of capital that applies to both investments is 16 percent. The life for both equipment types is estimated to be 6 years, during which time the net cash flows for the electric-powered forklift will be $8,250 annually and for the gas-powered forklift will be $6,625 per year. Annual net cash flows include depreciation expenses. Calculate the NPV and IRR for each type of forklift, and decide which to recommend for purchase.

14-12
NPVs and IRRs for independent projects

The net cash flows for Projects X and Y follow. Each project has a cost of $40,000.

Year	Project X	Project Y
1	$26,000	$14,000
2	12,000	14,000
3	12,000	14,000
4	4,000	14,000

a. Calculate each project's payback period.
b. Calculate each project's NPV at a 10 percent cost of capital.
c. Calculate each project's IRR. (*Hints:* Use the graphic approach for Project X, and notice that Project Y is an annuity.)
d. Should Project X, Project Y, or both projects be accepted if they are independent projects?
e. Which of the two projects should be accepted if they are mutually exclusive?

14-13
Expected NPV and IRR

D. Harrington and Company has provided the following net cash flow estimates (net income plus depreciation) for a proposed investment project:

Annual Net Cash Flows

Probability	Amount
0.3	$30,000
0.4	45,000
0.2	56,250
0.1	67,500

This project has a life of 10 years and is expected to have a zero salvage value. An investment of $188,662.50 is required to make the project operational.

a. If the firm requires a 16 percent return, what is the project's NPV?

b. What is the project's IRR?

c. Should D. Harrington and Company accept or reject the proposed project?

14-14
Expected NPVs

Southwest Energy Inc. has a cost of capital of 12 percent. The company is choosing between two mutually exclusive projects. Alpha Project is of average risk, so its cost of capital is 12 percent, and it costs $1 million. Its expected cash flows are $220,000 annually for 8 years. The Omega Project is of above-average risk, and management estimates that its cost of capital should be 15 percent. Omega also costs $1 million, and it promises to provide net cash flows of $240,000 annually for 8 years. Each project is expected to have a zero salvage value at the end of its life. Calculate the NPV for each project, and indicate which project should be accepted and which should be rejected by Southwest Energy. What is the basis for your conclusion?

14-15
Project evaluation

The Skyline Corporation is considering a new production line for its rapidly expanding camping equipment division. The line will have a cost of $288,000 and will be depreciated toward a zero salvage value over the next 3 years, using straight line depreciation. Other important factors are: (1) The new camping products will be responsible for new sales of $300,000 next year, $330,000 the following year, and $360,000 in the last year. (2) Cost of goods sold (excluding depreciation) is 40 percent of sales. (3) The increase in selling and administrative expenses caused by the new line is predicted to be $24,000 annually. (4) The company's cost of capital is 16 percent, and its tax rate is 40 percent.

a. What are the project's annual net cash flows?

b. What is the project's NPV?

14-16
Project evaluation

Preedy Industries is evaluating a capital asset for its Salem division. The asset's cost is $420,000, and incremental sales, if it is purchased, are expected to be as follows: Year 1, $250,000; Year 2, $350,000; Year 3, $450,000; Year 4, $550,000. The asset will be depreciated using MACRS over 4 years (3-year class life) and is expected to have a zero salvage value at the end of Year 4. MACRS percentages are 33, 45, 15, and 7 percent. Further assume that cost of goods sold (not counting depreciation) is 55 percent of sales and that selling and administrative expenses attributable to the new asset are expected to be constant at $20,000 per year. The company's tax rate is 40 percent, and its cost of capital is 10 percent.

a. What are the project's annual net cash flows for Years 1 through 4? (*Hint:* If earnings before taxes are negative in any year, this should result in a *negative tax,* representing a tax credit or a refund of taxes paid in earlier years. You may assume that the tax refund occurs in the year of the negative EBT.)

b. What is the asset's NPV?

c. Management of Preedy Industries would like to know how much of a difference MACRS depreciation makes. What would be the project's NPV if straight line depreciation were used? (Other assumptions unchanged.)

d. If, instead of a zero salvage value, the asset is assumed to have a market value of $50,000 at the end of Year 4, how much would this add to the asset's NPV?

14-17
Project evaluation

The director of capital budgeting for Diaz Enterprises is analyzing a proposal to build a new plant in Arizona. The following data have been developed thus far:

Land acquisition, cost incurred at start of Year 1 ($t = 0$)	$ 300,000
Plant construction, cost incurred at start of Year 2 ($t = 1$)	700,000
Equipment purchase, cost incurred at start of Year 3 ($t = 2$)	1,000,000
Net working capital, investment made at start of Year 4 ($t = 3$)	400,000

Operations will begin in Year 4 and will continue for 10 years, through Year 13. Sales revenues and operating costs are assumed to come at the end of each year; since the plant will be in operation for 10 years, operating costs and revenues occur at the end of Years 4 through 13 ($t = 4$ to 13). The following additional assumptions are made: (1) The plant and equipment will be depreciated over a 10-year life, starting in Year 4. The buildings and equipment will be worthless after 10 years' use, but Diaz expects to sell the land for $300,000 when the plant is closed down. The firm's management also expects that its investment in net working capital for the plant will be fully recoverable when the plant is closed. Diaz uses straight line depreciation. (2) Diaz uses a cost of capital of 14 percent to evaluate projects like this one. (3) Annual sales = 10,000 units at $140 per unit; annual sales revenue = $1,400,000. (4) Annual fixed operating costs *excluding* depreciation are $213,333. (5) Annual variable operating costs are $300,000, *assuming the plant operates at full capacity.* (6) Diaz's marginal tax rate is 40 percent. (7) The project is not eligible for an investment tax credit.
a. Calculate the project's NPV. Should Diaz accept this project?
b. Assuming constant sales prices and constant variable costs per unit, what will happen to the NPV if unit sales fall 10 percent below the forecasted level?

14-18

Cash flow estimation

Lanway-Linch & Company is considering the installation of a new production line for its rapidly expanding skate division. The line will have a cost of $150,000. The asset will be 5-year-class property for the purpose of MACRS depreciation. No salvage value is expected for the asset when the project ends in 6 years. Sales are expected to be $150,000 annually. Operating costs other than depreciation will be $105,000 annually. The company's required rate of return is 12 percent, and its tax rate is 40 percent.

Determine the project's net cash flows, and then calculate the project's net present value. (The following MACRS recovery allowances are in effect: Year 1, 20%; Year 2, 32%; Year 3, 19%; Year 4, 12%; Year 5, 11%; and Year 6, 6%.)

Solutions to Self-Test Problems

ST-1   **a.** The payback period is defined as the length of time it takes to recover the investment in a project. Since this project's cash flows are constant at $13,425,000 per year, we can find the payback: $40,550,000/$13,425,000 = 3.02 years, which is approximately 3 years and 1 week.
b. The NPV is calculated thus:

$$NPV = CF(PVIFA_{15\%,6}) - Cost$$

$$= \$13,425,000(3.7845) - \$40,550,000$$

$$= \$50,806,913 - \$40,550,000$$

$$= \$10,256,913.$$

Using a financial calculator, the solution is found through the following steps:

$$CF_0 = -40550000$$

$$CF_1 - CF_6 = 13425000$$

$$k = i = 15$$

$$NPV = ?$$

Calculator solution: NPV = $10,256,680. (Note: The difference between the two answers is due to rounding of the PVIFA.)

c. Since the cash flows of this project take the form of an annuity, we can solve the following equation to determine the present value interest factor for an annuity:

$$PVA_6 = PMT(PVIFA_{k,6})$$

$$\$40,550,000 = \$13,425,000(PVIFA_{k,6})$$

$$PVIFA_{k,6} = \$40,550,000/\$13,425,000$$

$$= 3.0205.$$

For a 6-year annuity, the PVIFA of 3.0205 corresponds to a 24 percent rate of return. Using a financial calculator, the solution is found through the following steps:

$$CF_0 = -40550000$$

$$CF_1 - CF_6 = 13425000$$

$$IRR = ?$$

Calculator solution: IRR = 24.00%.

(Note that we do not need to enter cash flows *twice* into the financial calculator in order to find NPV *and* IRR. Simply find NPV as shown in Part b, $10,256,680, then press IRR, and obtain 24.00%.)

ST-2   The costs associated with the gene splicing project (in millions of dollars) are as follows:

Time	Cost	Purpose
t = 0	$300	Land
t = 1	$400	Building
t = 2	$200	Equipment
t = 3	$100	Net working capital

$$\text{Present value of costs} = -\$300 - \$400(0.8333)$$
$$- \$200(0.6944) - \$100(0.5787)$$
$$= -\$830.07.$$

Notice that we did not include in the cost of the project the $50 million spent on the feasibility study. This is a sunk cost and, as such, is not a relevant cash flow.

The net cash inflows associated with the project (in millions of dollars) are as follows:

Time	Net Cash Inflow	Source
t = 4 − 8	$425	Cash flow from operations
t = 8	$100	Recovery of net working capital
t = 8	$150	Sale of salvageable assets (taxed as ordinary income)

$$\text{Present value of net cash flows} = \$425(1.7307)^* + \$100(0.2326)$$
$$+ \$150(1 - 0.4)(0.2326)$$
$$= \$779.7415.$$

---

*$PVIFA_{20\%,8} - PVIFA_{20\%,3} = 3.8372 - 2.1065 = 1.7307.$

$$\text{Net present value} = \text{Discounted cash inflows} - \text{Discounted costs}$$
$$= \$779.7415 - \$830.07$$
$$= (\$50.3285).$$

Since all dollar amounts above are in millions, the project's NPV = ($50,328,500). Because the project's NPV is negative, BTE should abandon the project. Of course, the same decision would have been reached if we had found the project's IRR. A negative NPV indicates that the IRR of the project is less than the required rate of return for the project. Whichever method is used, BTE should not invest in the gene splicing project.

We could also find the solution to this problem by using a financial calculator. To do this, we would begin by identifying the relevant cash flows on a time line as follows:

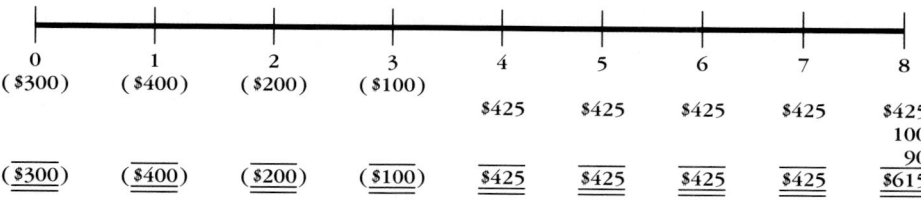

	0	1	2	3	4	5	6	7	8
Cash outflows	($300)	($400)	($200)	($100)					
Operating cash inflows					$425	$425	$425	$425	$425
Net working capital recovery									100
After-tax salvage value									90
Net cash flow	($300)	($400)	($200)	($100)	$425	$425	$425	$425	$615

Then, we would enter each cash flow in our financial calculator, enter k = i = 20, and press NPV to arrive at the solution of −$50.3664 million, or ($50,366,400). (Note: The difference in values obtained is due to rounding.) Of course, the same decision would be reached, that is, BTE should not invest in the gene splicing project.

After having solved for NPV, press IRR. The calculator will ignore the k = i = 20 given earlier and will calculate an IRR of 18.46%.

MINI CASE

COMPUTER MODELING: CAPITAL BUDGETING, EXPANSION

In 1982, Dr. James W. Conklin mortgaged his home, sold his practice in internal medicine, and used his pension fund for collateral to start Value-Care Inc., a so-called utilization-review firm. Such companies, which review hospital costs for employers and point out unnecessary treatments, have exploded in number over the past several years, spurred by soaring health-care costs. Today, approximately 200 such firms exist nationwide. In 1983, James's younger brother, Scott—also a physician—decided to join the firm.

Utilization-review firms—often started by physicians—are firms that, for instance, will look at a $5,000 three-day hospital stay for lower back treatment and suggest to a client that the patient could be treated for $500 at home with medication and therapy just as effectively. If a patient needs surgery, one of the firm's 600 staff members, which include nurses and physicians, will call doctors for relevant information on the patient's treatment plan. Information is reviewed, fed into a computer, and compared with national norms on the procedure. The staff then confers with doctors on whether the patient should be admitted and on what treatment is appropriate. "We save our corporate clients $4 to $8 for every dollar they spend with us," says James Conklin.

The client list of Value-Care Inc. has grown dramatically and today includes some of the largest corporate employers in the country. Over the last few years the firm's revenue has doubled, but competition is now intensifying within the industry. "The ones doing the best nowadays are those who spent every dime they had on new technology," states Scott Conklin.

At this point the Conklin brothers are considering expanding the services offered into psychiatric and substance-abuse treatment and want to install a new and highly sophisticated computer system, which would cost $75 million. Delivery and installation would add another $600,000 to the initial cost. The new computer system has a 5-year class life under MACRS. Because of the half-year convention, it will take six years for Value-Care to fully depreciate the cost of the system (MACRS percentages: 20, 32, 19, 12, 11, and 6 percent), and at the end of Year 6 the salvage value of the system is estimated to be $3 million.

Additional data:

▷ If the new system is purchased, revenue is expected to increase over the present level by $94.5 million in each of the first three years, by $90 million in Year 4, and by $85 million in Years 5 and 6.

▷ The increase in operating costs is projected at $69 million for each of the six years.

▷ Value-Care's federal-plus-state income tax rate is 40 percent.

▷ The project's cost of capital is 9.5 percent.

▷ It is expected that installation of the new system would cause the following changes in working capital accounts: (1) an increase in receivables of $24.2 million because of expanded services, (2) an increase in inventories of $2.1 million, and (3) an increase in accounts payable and accruals combined equal to $9 million.

Using *Lotus 1-2-3*, do the following:

a. State the basic assumptions of the problem in an "assumption block." This means that you should display in the upper left-hand corner of the spreadsheets all the *relevant* quantitative information given above, whether it actually changes in the problem or not. Include an entry for the discount rate, k, so that you can later *calculate* the present value interest factors by referring to this cell. (To raise something to a power in *Lotus 1-2-3* use the caret, ^.)

b. (1) Calculate the net cash outflow at time zero (t = 0) if Value-Care goes ahead with this expansion project.

(2) Construct a table along the following lines to calculate net operating cash flows for Years 1 through 6 (in thousands) and the present value of each year's cash flows. Note that negative taxes may occur in some scenarios, indicating tax credits.

Year	1	2	3	4	5	6
Revenue						
Operating costs						
Depreciation (DEP)						
Income before tax						
Taxes						
Net income (NI)						
Net cash flow (NI + DEP)						
PVIF						
PV of operating cash flows						

(3) Calculate the present value of any additional cash flows for Year 6. *Be sure to label these.*

(4) Calculate the NPV of this expansion project (NPV = PV of all cash flows − Cash outflow at t = 0).

The real power of electronic spreadsheets is their ability to perform sensitivity analyses (answer "what-if" questions). It is therefore crucial that you set up your model such that the stated assumptions in Part a are the underlying determinants of the capital budgeting calculations performed in Part b. A change in any one of the assumptions in Part a will then automatically cause a recalculation of the project's NPV. In other words, be sure to use formulas and refer back up to earlier cell addresses whenever appropriate. If your model is constructed correctly, the remaining questions should require very little time to answer.

Save all of your work in Parts a and b as VC-B. Print out all of this.

c.   Because computer hardware and software prices are notoriously difficult to estimate beyond a couple of years—let alone resale values—the salvage value of the new system is somewhat "iffy." However, Scott guesses that it will not drop below $1 million. Using this worst-case scenario as far as salvage is concerned, what is the new NPV? Other assumptions are as in Part b. Answer by printing out the assumption block and NPV analysis again. Save as VC-C.

d.   While analyzing the project, the brothers suddenly realize that the current tax law actually allows them to depreciate the computer system over four years instead of six. Assume percentages of 33, 45, 15, and 7 percent, and assume that the system will, in fact, be used for six years as originally planned. All other assumptions are as in Part c. Calculate a new NPV, print out everything, and save as VC-D.

e.   Scott and James would also like to know just how sensitive the NPV of the project is to operating costs. To the nearest $1,000, what is the highest annual operating cost increase associated with the project that would result in a positive NPV? Find through trial and error. All other assumptions are as in Part d (salvage = $1 million). Print out everything, showing the new NPV, and save as VC-E.

f.   *Change annual operating costs back to $69 million.* Find the IRR of the project through trial and error; all other assumptions are as in Part e. You should get the NPV to within $100 on either side of a NPV = $0. (Recognize, however, that in the "real world" an IRR rounded to the nearest half of a percentage point is usually considered accurate enough.) Save as VC-F and provide a final printout of your IRR solution.

Conflicts between NPV and IRR

Appendix 14A

In Chapter 14 we indicated that the two appropriate procedures for evaluating capital budgeting projects are the NPV and the IRR methods. For single projects and for two (or more) *independent projects,* the NPV and IRR methods *always* lead to the same accept/reject decisions. As noted in Table 14A-1, if the project's internal rate of return, IRR, is greater than the company's or project's required rate of return, k, the NPV will be positive, and the project will thus be deemed acceptable. Under normal circumstances (that is, when a project is not mandated by law), any project that provides a return less than the required return will be rejected. In this situation the project's NPV will always be negative. Of course, where NPV = $0, the project's required and internal rates of return are equal, operating and financing costs are only just covered, and the firm will be indifferent with respect to accepting this project.

However, when we consider *ranking* several investment projects, as in the following example, these decision rules may not agree, and this matters if two or more projects

Table 14A-1

Comparison of NPV and IRR
Project Evaluation Rules for
Independent Projects

Method	Accept	Reject	Indifferent
NPV	Positive	Negative	Zero
IRR	Greater than k	Less than k	k = IRR

Table 14A-2   Calculating the NPVs of Projects A and B where k = 5%

	Project A			Project B		
Year	Cash Flow	$PVIF_{5\%,t}$	Discounted Cash Flow	Cash Flow	$PVIF_{5\%,t}$	Discounted Cash Flow
1	$500,000	0.9524	$ 476,200	$100,000	0.9524	$ 95,240
2	400,000	0.9070	362,800	300,000	0.9070	272,100
3	300,000	0.8638	259,140	400,000	0.8638	345,520
4	100,000	0.8227	82,270	600,000	0.8227	493,620
		PV of inflows	$1,180,410			$1,206,480
		Less: Cost	1,000,000			1,000,000
		NPV	$ 180,410			$ 206,480

are *mutually exclusive.* Assume that MBI Corporation has two competing, mutually exclusive projects, Projects A and B. Recall that with such projects, we can choose either Project A or Project B, or we can reject both, but we cannot accept both projects. In this example, each project requires an initial investment outlay of $1,000,000. Notice in Figure 14A-1 that if the firm's cost of capital (the discount rate used) is above 7.2 percent, both the NPV and IRR methods indicate that Project A should be selected. However, if the firm's cost of capital is below 7.2 percent, a conflict between the two methods arises.[1] If the firm's cost of capital is 5 percent, for example, the NPV of Project A is $180,410, whereas the NPV of Project B is $206,480, as seen in Table 14A-2. We approximate the IRRs of both projects graphically in Figure 14A-1. The IRR of Project A is 14.5 percent, but the IRR of Project B, 11.8 percent, is lower. Therefore, the IRR method indicates that Project A should be selected, while, *at any discount rate below the crossover point, the NPV method indicates that Project B is preferable.* The critical question is, which method should we use in making capital budgeting decisions when the methods are in conflict with respect to the *ranking* of projects?

Comparison of the NPV and IRR Methods

As we noted in Chapter 14, the NPV method exhibits all the desired decision rule properties and, in all cases, provides the best approach to evaluating projects. Because the NPV method is theoretically superior to the IRR, it is tempting to explain only the NPV, state that it should be used for all capital budgeting decisions, and move on to the next topic. However, the IRR method is familiar to many corporate executives, and it is widely entrenched in industry practices. We will also use IRRs in Chapter 19 in determining a firm's optimal capital budget. Therefore, it is important that finance students thoroughly understand the IRR method and be prepared to explain why at times a project with a lower IRR may be preferable to one with a higher IRR.

---

[1]The crossover rate for these two projects is *approximately* 7.2 percent. You can satisfy yourself that this is correct if you have a financial calculator. Simply enter CF_0-CF_4 for Project A, enter k = i = 7.2, and obtain NPV_A = $133,734. Then enter CF_0-CF_4 for Project B, enter k = i = 7.2, and obtain NPV_B = $133,364.

Figure 14A-1

Net Present Value Profiles of Projects A and B at Different Discount Rates (Thousands of Dollars)

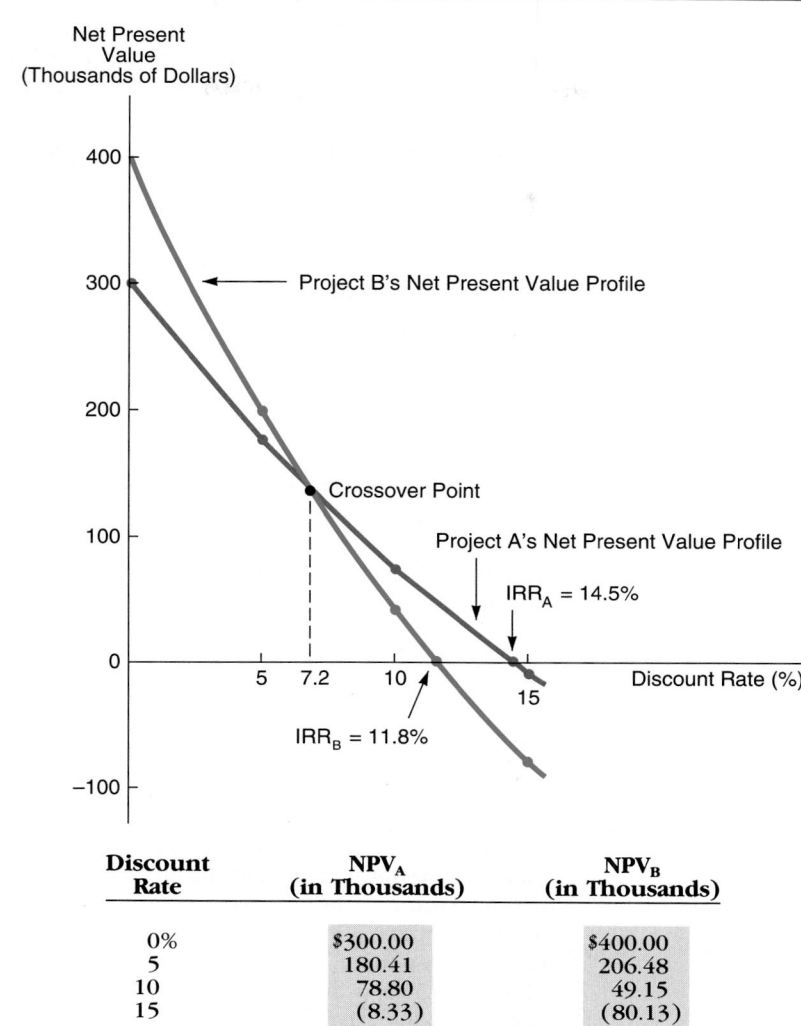

Discount Rate	NPV$_A$ (in Thousands)	NPV$_B$ (in Thousands)
0%	$300.00	$400.00
5	180.41	206.48
10	78.80	49.15
15	(8.33)	(80.13)

Conflicting results may arise when both net present value (NPV) and internal rate of return (IRR) are used to *rank mutually exclusive* capital projects. In this example, Project A has an IRR of 14.5 percent, and Project B's IRR is 11.8 percent. However, if the discount rate is 5 percent, Project A has an NPV of $180.41, whereas Project B has an NPV of $206.48. Based on NPV, Project B would be preferred, but based on IRR, Project A would seem more attractive. In such cases, the project with the higher NPV should be chosen.

Note: Notice that the net present value profiles are curved — they are *not* straight lines. We should also mention that under certain conditions, the NPV profiles can cross the horizontal axis several times or never cross it.

Causes of Conflicting Rankings

There are two basic conditions that cause NPV profiles to cross, as in Figure 14A-1, and thus lead to potential conflicts between the NPV and IRR methods.

1. **Project size (or scale) differences.**   If the cost of one project is significantly larger than that of the other, the larger project will generally have a higher NPV than the smaller one at low discount rates. If the larger project has the higher NPV at a zero discount rate, and the smaller project has the higher IRR, the NPV profiles

will cross each other. For example, Project S calls for an investment of $1.00 and yields $1.50 at the end of one year. Its IRR is 50 percent and at a 10 percent cost of capital, its NPV is 36 cents. Project L costs $1 million and yields $1.25 million at the end of the year. Its IRR is only 25 percent, but its NPV at 10 percent is $136,375.

2. **Timing differences.**   If most of the cash flows from one project come in the early years whereas most of those from the other project come in the later years, as occurred with Projects A and B, the project with the larger cash flows occurring late may have a higher vertical axis intercept, in which case the NPV profiles are likely to cross each other. This situation is caused by the fact that high discount rates do not significantly lower the NPVs of projects having early cash flows but impose a greater penalty on projects having cash flows that are slow to accrue.

Resolving the NPV versus IRR Conflict

When either size or timing differences occur, the rankings provided by the NPV and IRR methods may be in conflict. When this happens, the project with the highest NPV should be chosen. The choice of the NPV method avoids two problems associated with the IRR method plus a scenario where the IRR criterion can also provide an incorrect capital budgeting decision: (1) absolute value versus relative returns, (2) the reinvestment rate assumption, and (3) multiple IRRs.[2]

Absolute Value versus Relative Returns

Recall the example used a moment ago, when we identified project size (or scale) differences as one of the two causes of conflicting rankings. We had a choice between Project S with an IRR of 50 percent, but a NPV of only 36 cents, and Project L with an IRR of only 25 percent, but a NPV of $136,375. The NPV method provides an *absolute* measure; it tells us the expected absolute dollars that a project will add to the firm's value. On the other hand, the IRR method is a *relative* measure; it calculates the expected return on a project *relative to its initial outlay.* (In the case of Project S, the initial cost was so small that it could have been paid out of petty cash.) This is not a hard choice to make. Common sense should tell us that it is better to increase the firm's value by $136,375 than by 36 cents. Thus, we would opt for Project L which has the higher NPV, the higher absolute value.

Reinvestment Assumption

reinvestment rate assumption

The assumption that cash flows from a project can be reinvested (1) at the cost of capital, if using the NPV method, or (2) at the internal rate of return of the project, if using the IRR method.

When either timing or size differences occur, the firm will have different amounts of funds to invest in the intervening years of the project's life, depending on which of the mutually exclusive projects it chooses. For example, if one project costs more than the other, the firm will have more money at t = 0 to invest elsewhere if it selects the less costly project. Similarly, for projects of equal cost, the one with the larger early net cash flows will provide more funds for reinvestment in the early years. Thus the rate of return at which differential cash flows can be invested is an important consideration.

Although we do not prove it in this book, the fundamental reason behind the NPV/IRR conflict has to do with the **reinvestment rate assumptions** underlying the two

---

[2]For a much more detailed and complete discussion of these factors, see Brigham and Gapenski, *Intermediate Financial Management,* 4th ed., Chapter 7.

methods.[3] The NPV method assumes that the firm can reinvest net cash flows at the cost of capital, whereas *the IRR method assumes that net cash flows can be reinvested at the IRR of the project.* The NPV method makes a much more conservative reinvestment assumption than the IRR method. Thus, if a project has a calculated, expected IRR of 40 percent, but the best alternative for reinvesting the net cash flows from the project is 8 percent, the realized rate of return from the project will definitely be less than 40 percent. (Put another way, just because you have one project available on which the expected IRR is 40 percent, what are the chances that the net cash flows from that project can be invested into *another* project that will also yield a generous 40 percent? The chances are usually slim.) This does not mean that the project may not be acceptable, only that its *actual* return will be less than its calculated IRR.

Naturally, the closer the project's IRR is to the firm's cost of capital, the less the reinvestment assumption matters. Yet, there will *never* be a problem using the NPV rule in ranking competing, or mutually exclusive, investment opportunities.

Multiple IRRs

A third reason that the NPV method provides a better criterion for ranking capital budgeting projects is that, in certain situations, there can be more than one IRR. In Figure 14A-1, Projects A and B each have only one IRR, which is found where the NPV profile crosses the X axis — that is, where the NPV = $0. These are both normal projects in that their cash outflow is followed by future cash inflows. However, capital budgeting projects can have outflows followed by inflows, then by more outflows, and so on. Strip mining for coal provides an example of nonnormal cash flows. First, the land is purchased, then the coal is mined for several years, and finally the land must be returned to its natural state at the expense of the mine's owners. Oil-well drilling provides a similar example of nonnormal cash flows, as the rig must be periodically shut down and refurbished before the well can produce more cash flows.

An example of a project with nonnormal cash flows, Project N, is as follows (in millions of dollars):

Expected Net Cash Flow		
Year 0	Year 1	Year 2
($1.6)	$10	($10)

As shown in Figure 14A-2, if one were ranking projects based on the IRR method, this nonnormal project would create a problem because the project's IRR is 25 percent *and* 400 percent. Both IRRs cause the NPV to equal zero, so both are correct. This situation creates confusion for firms that rely on the IRR method to select projects.[4]

The example just presented illustrates one problem, multiple IRRs, that can arise when the IRR criterion is used with a project that has nonnormal cash flows. Use of the

---

[3]Both the NPV and the IRR methods are discounted cash flow techniques. Because both techniques utilize the time value of money, we should consider again how the present value tables are constructed. Recall that the present value of any future sum is defined as the beginning amount that, when compounded at a specified and constant rate, will grow to equal the future amount over the stated time period. From Table 13-1 we can see that the present value of $146.93 due in 5 years, when discounted at 8 percent, is $100, because $100, when reinvested and compounded at 8 percent for 5 years, will grow to $146.93. Thus, compounding and discounting are reciprocal relationships, and *the very construction of the discounting and compounding tables implies a reinvestment process.*

[4]Financial calculators may also be "confused" by multiple IRRs and, if so, will give you an error message. However, if you enter an estimate of one of the two IRRs in the example just given, say, 20 percent, it will go on to solve for IRR_1 = 25 percent. Next you may choose to enter k = i = 350, and the calculator will solve for IRR_2 = 400 percent.

Figure 14A-2

NPV Profile for Project N

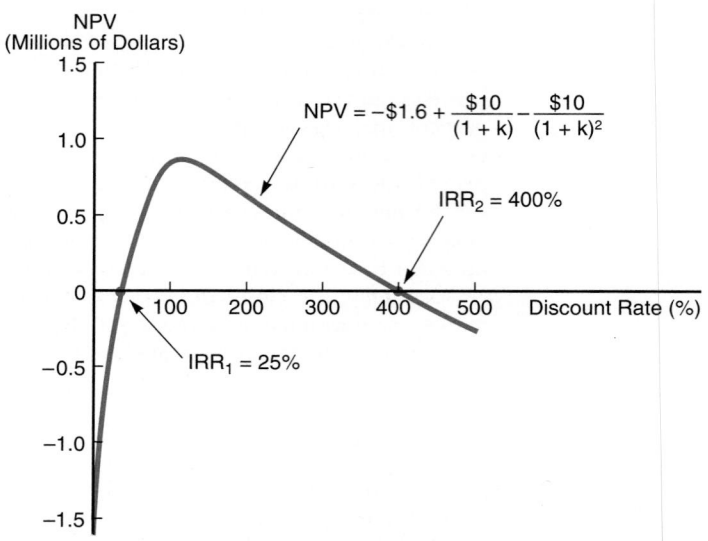

NPV
(Millions of Dollars)

$$NPV = -\$1.6 + \frac{\$10}{(1 + k)} - \frac{\$10}{(1 + k)^2}$$

$IRR_2 = 400\%$

$IRR_1 = 25\%$

When a capital budgeting project has initial outflows, followed by inflows, then by more outflows, we call the cash flows *nonnormal*. In such cases, illustrated by Project N, multiple IRRs are likely to occur. Project N's IRR is both 25 percent and 400 percent. Using *either* of these two discount rates will give an NPV of zero, so both are correct. Since this is confusing, managers should rely on the NPV method when ranking capital budgeting projects with nonnormal cash flows.

IRR method on nonnormal cash flow projects could produce other problems such as no IRR or, as we have seen for normal cash flows, an IRR which leads to an incorrect accept/reject decision. In all such cases, the NPV criterion could be easily applied, and the NPV leads to conceptually correct capital budgeting decisions.[5]

Problems

14A-1

NPV and IRR analysis, scale differences

The Chaplinsky Publishing Company is considering two mutually exclusive expansion plans. Plan A calls for the expenditure of $40 million on a large-scale, integrated plant which will provide an expected net cash flow stream of $6.4 million per year for 20 years. Plan B calls for the expenditure of $12 million to build a somewhat less efficient, more labor-intensive plant which has an expected net cash flow stream of $2.72 million per year for 20 years. Chaplinsky's cost of capital is 10 percent.

a. Calculate each project's NPV and IRR.

b. Graph the NPV profiles for Plan A and Plan B. From the NPV profiles constructed, approximate the crossover rate.

c. Give a logical explanation, based on reinvestment rates and opportunity costs, of why the NPV method is better than the IRR method when the firm's cost of capital is constant at some value such as 10 percent.

---

[5]For an in-depth discussion of multiple IRRs see James R. Sisson and James F. Nielsen, "Multiple Internal Rates of Return: A Revisitation," *Review of Financial Economics,* Spring 1993 (Volume 2, Number 2), 85–97.

14A-2

NPV and IRR analysis,
timing differences

Two projects each involve an investment of $36,000. Net cash flows (net income plus depreciation) are $24,000 a year for 2 years for Project S and $9,600 annually for 6 years for Project L.

a. Compute the NPV for each project if the firm's cost of capital is zero percent and if it is 6 percent. NPVs for Project S at 10 and 20 percent, respectively, are $5,652.00 and $667.20, whereas NPVs for Project L at 10 and 20 percent are $5,810.88 and ($4,075.20).

b. Graph the net present value profiles of the two projects, putting NPV on the Y axis and the discount rate on the X axis, and use the graph to estimate each project's IRR.

c. Estimate the IRR for each project, using tables or a financial calculator.

d. If these projects were mutually exclusive, which one would you select, assuming a cost of capital of (1) 8 percent, (2) 10.2 percent, or (3) 12 percent? Explain. For this problem, assume that the operation will terminate at the end of the project's life.

14A-3

NPV and IRR analysis,
timing differences

Each of two mutually exclusive projects involves an investment of $180,000. Net cash flows (net income plus depreciation) for the two projects have different time patterns. Project X will provide the highest net cash flows in the early years; however, Project Y will provide much lower net cash flows in the early years and higher net cash flows in the later years. The net cash flows from the two investments are as follows:

Year	Project X	Project Y
1	$105,000	$ 15,000
2	60,000	30,000
3	45,000	45,000
4	15,000	75,000
5	15,000	120,000

a. Calculate each project's payback period.

b. Compute the NPV of each project when the firm's cost of capital is 0 percent, 6 percent, and 20 percent. At 10 percent, the NPV for X is $18,410 and the NPV for Y is $17,975.

c. Graph the net present value profiles of the two projects. Use the graph to estimate each project's IRR. If you have a financial calculator, use it to check your graphic estimate.

d. Which project would you select, assuming a cost of capital of 8 percent? Of 10 percent? Of 12 percent? Explain.

e. How might a change in the cost of capital produce a conflict between NPV and IRR results? At what values of k would this conflict exist?

f. The company's capital budgeting manual states that no project with a payback period greater than 4 should be accepted. Discuss this rule and its effects, both in general and in this specific case.

14A-4

NPV and IRR analysis,
multiple IRRs

The Upton Uranium Company is deciding whether or not it should open a strip mine, the net cost of which is $2 million. Net cash inflows are expected to be $13 million, all coming at the end of Year 1. The land must be returned to its natural state at a cost of $12 million, payable at the end of Year 2.

a. Plot the project's NPV profile. (*Hint:* Calculate NPV at k = 0, 10, 80, and 450 percent, and possibly at other k values.)

b. Should the project be accepted if k = 10 percent? If k = 20 percent? Explain your reasoning.

c. Can you think of any other capital budgeting situation in which negative cash flows during or at the end of the project's life might lead to multiple IRRs?

Decisions in Capital Budgeting

OBJECTIVES

After reading this chapter, you should be able to:

▷ Identify the three types of project risk.

▷ Explain why stand-alone risk is often used as a proxy for the other two types of risk.

▷ Show how the Capital Asset Pricing Model is used to evaluate projects, and describe how the Security Market Line concept is used in capital budgeting.

▷ Explain the advantages and disadvantages of diversification at the corporate level.

▷ Explain how the financial manager incorporates his or her assessment of project risk to adjust a project's cost of capital.

▷ Evaluate a replacement decision.

▷ Compare projects with unequal lives using the replacement chain method, and specify some potential weaknesses of this approach.

▷ Explain how to incorporate inflation into the capital budgeting analysis.

DECISION IN FINANCE

THE COLLAPSE OF A
$10 BILLION EMPIRE

Taking big risks with no assurance of a return for many years was a hallmark of Canada's Reichmann brothers, former floor tile importers who went on to develop a real estate empire which spanned the globe. Their giant firm, Olympia & York (discussed also in Chapter 11 in connection with commercial paper), was the richest and most powerful real estate development company in the world, and their family fortune rivaled that of Great Britain's Queen Elizabeth.

Today, it is all gone. A court-appointed trustee is overseeing the orderly liquidation of Olympia & York, and Paul Reichmann, the brother in charge through the company's 30-year history, is accepting the blame. It appears that he risked too much and ignored the warnings of outsiders and even his own bankers, who argued that his sophisticated and complex financial dealings were getting out of hand. His strategy was to buy or build office towers and then borrow against those buildings when prices were rising to finance the next one. He also diverted several billion dollars from his property holdings to invest in natural resource companies.

Among the properties O&Y developed were Manhattan's World Financial Center; London's Canary Wharf project, which was Europe's largest real estate development; First Canadian Place

See end of chapter for resolution.

Photo source: John Lamb/Tony Stone Images.

in Toronto, the company's home base; and more than 50 other office buildings in the United States and Canada.

As it grew into the colossus of its industry, O&Y was known as an innovator. It helped finance public projects that complemented its private developments and created, with local governments, whole new urban centers. The World Financial Center was built on cheap land provided by New York City. The Reichmanns spent $300 million of their company's money on the center before seeking outside financing. The project helped subsidize neighboring housing and also created public spaces, changing the face of lower Manhattan.

Although that project was hugely successful, attaining a 90 percent office occupancy rate for the center with such prestigious firms as American Express, Merrill Lynch, and Dow Jones as key tenants, the much larger Canary Wharf project fell far short of expectations. Expected to cost $7 billion and to house 50,000 workers in

20 office buildings, the project gobbled up $3 billion in its beginning stages—including $2 billion of Olympia & York's own money. Reichmann was hoping to repeat his New York success by attracting a few large clients who would, in turn, draw smaller companies. However, by early 1990 clients had signed up for only 20 percent of Canary Wharf's office space.

Reichmann justified the massive risk undertaken by his firm on the Canary Wharf project on the grounds that office space in most European cities is woefully inadequate compared with that in North America. Believing that the service revolution was just beginning in Europe, he argued that the growing banking, insurance, and trade industries would need modern offices. "Europe is still at a relatively early stage of renewal. London will be the business capital of Europe."

Reichmann's reputation for seemingly infallible business acumen had been tarnished earlier, in the late 1980s, when he tried to bail out fellow Canadian Robert Campeau's real estate and retailing company. Some critics had raised questions about Olympia & York then, but Reichmann

dismissed them as "children who don't know what they're talking about." He also ignored his bankers' advice to overhaul his company's finances when real estate values started collapsing, assuring them that everything was all right.

Today, Canary Wharf stands less than half finished. Negotiations with Barclays Bank to lease a huge block of space dragged on, and Olympia & York's cash squeeze sent it down the drain before the deal could be completed.

As you read this chapter, note that Canary Wharf provides a prime example of what we shall call "corporate, or within-firm, risk," which is the potential of a project to destabilize the entire firm. Consider the other two types of project risk with respect to Canary Wharf and the signs that should have indicated the coming collapse. Consider also what part the personality and leadership style of Paul Reichmann played, what the role of his bankers and other financial advisors might have been, and recall from earlier chapters the importance of dealing openly and honestly with your bankers. (See the Small Business feature in Chapter 3, "Building a Banking Relationship.")

In Chapter 12 we explained, in general terms, how risk is defined, the procedures managers and securities analysts use to measure risk, and the relationship between risk and return. In Chapter 13 we discussed time value of money concepts, which enabled us to cover the basic principles of capital budgeting in Chapter 14. In this chapter, we combine the topics of risk and capital budgeting to explain how managers incorporate risk measures into capital budgeting decisions. In addition, we cover several special topics in capital budgeting, including replacement analysis, evaluation of projects with unequal lives, and effects of inflation on capital budgeting decisions.

Risk Analysis in Capital Budgeting

stand-alone risk
The risk an asset would have if it were a firm's only asset and if the firm's stockholders held only that one stock; it is measured by the variability of the asset's expected returns.

corporate (within-firm) risk
Risk not considering the effects of stockholders' diversification; it is measured by a project's effect on the firm's earnings variability.

Risk analysis is important in all financial decisions, especially those relating to capital budgeting. Three separate and distinct types of project risk can be identified: (1) the project's own **stand-alone risk,** or its risk disregarding the facts that it is but one asset within the firm's portfolio of assets and that the firm in question is but one stock in most investors' stock portfolios; (2) **corporate,** or **within-firm, risk,** which is the effect a project has on the company's risk without consideration for the effects of the stockholders' own personal diversifica-

beta (market) risk

That part of a project's risk that cannot be eliminated by diversification; it is measured by the project's beta coefficient.

tion; and (3) **beta** (or **market**) **risk** which is project risk assessed from the standpoint of an equity investor who holds a highly diversified portfolio. As we shall see, a particular project may have high stand-alone risk, yet taking it on may not have much effect on either the firm's risk or that of its owners because of portfolio effects.

A project's stand-alone risk is measured by the variability of the project's expected returns, its corporate risk is measured by the project's impact on the firm's earnings variability, and its beta risk is measured by the project's effect on the firm's beta coefficient. Taking on a project with a high degree of either stand-alone or corporate risk will not necessarily affect the firm's beta to any great extent, and hence the project might not appear very risky to a well-diversified stockholder. To better illustrate this point, let us recall that the beta coefficient reflects only that part of an investor's risk which cannot be eliminated by forming a large portfolio of stocks. If an investor holds a portfolio consisting of 100 companies' stocks, and if each company is considering 20 equal-sized projects, then the project in question is only one of 2,000 projects from the investor's point of view. Therefore, even if the project produces a return of negative 100 percent, this would not make much difference within the overall portfolio, and the law of large numbers suggests that the loss would be offset by gains in some of the other 1,999 remaining projects.

In theory, a project's stand-alone risk should be of little or no concern. However, it is actually of great practical importance, for the following reasons:

1.   It is much easier to estimate a project's stand-alone risk than its corporate risk or its beta risk.

2.   In the majority of cases, all three types of risk are highly correlated — if the general economy does well, so will the firm, and if the firm does well, so will most of its projects. Thus, stand-alone risk is generally a good indicator of hard-to-measure beta risk.

3.   Because of Points 1 and 2, if management wants a reasonably accurate assessment of a project's riskiness, it ought to spend considerable effort on ascertaining the riskiness of the project's own cash flows — that is, its stand-alone risk. The starting point for analyzing a project's stand-alone risk involves determining the uncertainty inherent in the project's cash flows, which can be done through informal judgments or through complex economic and statistical analyses involving large-scale computer models.

Now let's consider corporate and beta risk. To illustrate the difference between corporate and beta risk, suppose 100 start-up firms in the oil business each drill one wildcat well. Each company has $1 million of capital that it will invest in its well. (Note that since each firm has only one well, *in this case,* the stand-alone risk of the well equals the corporate risk of the firm.) If a firm strikes oil, it will get a return of $2.4 million and earn a profit of $1.4 million, whereas if it hits a dry hole, it will lose its $1 million investment and go bankrupt. The probability of striking oil is 50 percent. Each firm's expected rate of return is 20 percent, calculated as follows:

$$\text{Expected rate of return} = \frac{\text{Expected profit}}{\text{Investment}} = \frac{0.5(-\$1\text{ million}) + 0.5(+\$1.4\text{ million})}{\$1\text{ million}}$$

$$= \frac{-\$500,000 + \$700,000}{\$1,000,000} = 20\%.$$

Note, however, that even though the expected return is 20 percent, there is a 50 percent probability of each firm's being wiped out. From the standpoint of the individual firms, this is a very risky business.

Although the risk to each individual firm is high, if a stockholder constructs a portfolio consisting of a few shares of each of the 100 companies, the riskiness of this portfolio will not be high at all. Some of the firms will strike oil and do well, others will miss and go out of business, but the portfolio's return will be very close to the expected 20 percent. Therefore, because investors can diversify away some of the risks inherent in each of the individual companies, these risks are *not market-related;* that is, they do not affect the companies' beta coefficients. The firms remain quite risky from the standpoint of their managers and employees, however, who bear risks similar to those borne by undiversified stockholders.

With this background, *we may define the corporate risk of a capital budgeting project as the probability that the project will incur losses which will, at a minimum, destabilize the corporation's earnings and, at the extreme, cause it to go bankrupt.* Furthermore, the larger a project is relative to the size of the firm, in dollar terms, the greater its potential to destabilize the firm will be. A project with a high degree of either stand-alone or corporate risk will not necessarily affect the firm's beta to any great extent, as our hypothetical example demonstrated. On the other hand, if a project has highly uncertain returns, if the project is large, and if its returns are highly correlated with returns on the firm's other assets and also with most other assets in the economy, the project will have a high degree of all types of risk.

For example, suppose General Motors decides to undertake a major expansion to build solar-powered automobiles. GM is not sure how its technology will work on a mass production basis, so there are great risks in the venture — its stand-alone risk is high. Management also estimates that the project will have a higher probability of success if the economy is strong, for then people will have more money to spend on the new automobiles. This means that the project will tend to do well if GM's other divisions also do well and to do badly if other divisions do badly. This being the case, the project will also have high corporate risk. Finally, since GM's profits are highly correlated with those of most other firms, the project's beta coefficient will also be high. Thus, this project will be risky under all three definitions of risk.

Beta risk is important because of its direct effect on a firm's stock price: Beta affects k, and k affects the stock price. (As we shall see in Chapter 17, the higher the required rate on a firm's common stock, other things equal, the lower the stock's price.) At the same time, corporate risk is also important for three primary reasons:

1. Undiversified stockholders, including the owners of small businesses, are more concerned about corporate risk than about beta risk.

2. Empirical studies of the determinants of required rates of return (k) generally find that both beta and corporate risk affect stock prices. This suggests that investors, even those who are well diversified, consider factors other than beta risk when they establish required returns.

3. The firm's stability is important to its managers, workers, customers, suppliers, and creditors, as well as to the community in which it operates. Firms that are in serious danger of bankruptcy, or even of suffering low

profits and reduced output, have difficulty attracting and retaining good managers and workers. Also, both suppliers and customers are reluctant to depend on weak firms, and such firms have difficulty borrowing money at reasonable interest rates. These factors tend to reduce risky firms' profitability and hence the price of their stocks, and, thus, they also make corporate risk significant.[1]

For these three reasons, corporate risk is important even if a firm's stockholders are well diversified.

Beta (or Market) Risk

The types of risk analysis discussed thus far in the chapter provide insights into a project's risk and thus help managers make better accept/reject decisions. However, these risk measures do not take into account the reduction of risk that is possible when projects are combined and evaluated as part of a portfolio of projects. In this section, we show how the Capital Asset Pricing Model (CAPM) can be used to evaluate projects as portfolios and thereby overcome the shortcomings of these risk measures. Of course, the CAPM has shortcomings of its own, but it nevertheless offers useful insights into risk analysis in capital budgeting.

The CAPM provides a framework for analyzing the relationship between risk and return, and we used it in Chapter 12 to analyze the relationship between risk and return in portfolios of financial assets. The fundamental premise of this analysis is that the higher the beta risk associated with an investment, the higher the expected rate of return must be to compensate investors for assuming risk. This same principle holds for managers evaluating capital budgeting investment opportunities for a firm. The CAPM holds that there is a minimum required rate of return, even if there are no risks, plus a premium for all nondiversifiable risks associated with the investment. Thus

$$\text{Required rate of return} = \text{Risk-free rate} + \text{Risk premium},$$

which translates into the Security Market Line (SML) equation to express this risk/return relationship:

$$k_i = k_{RF} + (k_M - k_{RF})b_i. \qquad (12\text{-}7)$$

Here the required return on an investment, k_i, is equal to the risk-free rate, k_{RF}, plus a risk premium that is equal to the market risk premium $(k_M - k_{RF})$ times the stock's beta coefficient, b_i.[2] The greater the nondiversifiable risk associated with a stock or project, the larger the beta, and hence, the larger the risk premium.

For example, consider the case of Chicago Steel Company, an integrated steel producer operating in the Great Lakes region. Chicago Steel's beta is 1.1; $k_{RF} = 8\%$; and $k_M = 12\%$. Thus, Chicago's required rate of return is 12.4 percent:

---

[1] In Chapter 12, we noted that one measure of risk was the standard deviation. Other techniques for measuring corporate risk such as sensitivity analysis, scenario analysis, and simulation techniques are discussed in Brigham and Gapenski, *Intermediate Financial Management,* 4th ed., Chapter 9.

[2] Note that both the risk-free rate, k_{RF}, and the return on a diversified portfolio of securities, k_M, are market determined and thus outside the control of the firm.

$$k = 8\% + (12\% - 8\%)1.1$$
$$= 8\% + (4\%)1.1$$
$$= 12.4\%.$$

This suggests that investors would be willing to give Chicago Steel money to invest in average-risk projects if the company expects to earn 12.4 percent or more on this money. Here again, by average-risk projects we mean projects having risk similar to the firm's existing assets. *Therefore, as a first approximation, Chicago Steel should invest in capital projects if and only if these projects have an expected return of 12.4 percent or more.*[3] In other words, Chicago Steel should use 12.4 percent as its discount rate to determine the NPVs of any average-risk project which it is considering, or as the **hurdle rate** if the IRR method is used.

hurdle rate

The minimum acceptable IRR; the rate which determines whether a project should be accepted or rejected.

Suppose, however, that taking on a particular project would cause a change in Chicago's beta coefficient and, hence, change the company's cost of equity capital. For example, suppose Chicago Steel is considering the construction of a fleet of barges to haul iron ore, and barge operations have betas of 1.5 rather than 1.1. Since the firm itself may be regarded as a "portfolio of assets" and since the beta of any portfolio is a weighted average of the betas of its individual assets, taking on the barge project would cause the overall corporate beta to rise to somewhere between the original beta of 1.1 and the barge project's beta of 1.5. The exact value of the company's new beta would depend on the relative size of the investment in barge operations versus Chicago's other assets. If 80 percent of Chicago's total funds ended up in basic steel operations with a beta of 1.1 and 20 percent in barge operations with a beta of 1.5, the new corporate beta would be 1.18:

$$\text{New beta} = 0.8(1.1) + 0.2(1.5)$$
$$= 1.18.$$

This increase in Chicago's beta coefficient would cause its stock price to decline *unless the increased beta were offset by a higher expected rate of return.* Note that taking on the new project would cause the overall corporate cost of capital to rise from the original 12.4 percent to 12.72 percent:

$$k_{(new)} = 8\% + (4\%)1.18$$
$$= 12.72\%.$$

Therefore, to keep the barge investment from lowering the value of the firm, Chicago's overall expected rate of return must also rise from 12.4 percent to 12.72 percent.

If investments in basic steel must earn 12.4 percent, how much must the barge investment earn in order for the new overall rate of return to equal 12.72 percent? We know that if Chicago Steel undertakes the barge investment, it will have 80 percent of its assets invested in basic steel projects earning 12.4 percent and 20 percent in barge operations earning "X" percent, and that the average required rate of return will be 12.72 percent. Therefore,

---

[3]To simplify things somewhat, we assume at this point that the firm uses only equity capital. If debt is used, the cost of capital used must be a weighted average of the cost of debt and equity. This point is discussed at length in Chapters 19 and 20.

$$0.8(12.4\%) + 0.2(X) = 12.72\%$$

$$0.2(X) = 2.8\%$$

$$X = 14.0\%.$$

Because $X = 14\%$, we see that the barge project must have an expected return of 14 percent if the corporation is to earn its new cost of capital.

In summary, if Chicago Steel takes on the barge project, its corporate beta will rise from 1.1 to 1.18, its overall required rate of return will rise from 12.4 percent to 12.72 percent, and the barge investment will have to earn 14 percent if the company is to earn its new overall cost of capital. If the barge investment has an expected return of more than 14 percent, taking it on will increase the value of Chicago's stock. If the expected return is less than 14 percent, taking it on will decrease the stock's value. If its expected return is exactly 14 percent, the barge project will be a breakeven proposition in terms of its effect on the firm's stock price.

This line of reasoning leads to the conclusion that, *if the beta coefficient for each project could be determined, then an individual project's cost of capital could be found as follows:*

$$k_{Project} = k_{RF} + (k_M - k_{RF})b_{Project}. \tag{15-1}$$

Thus, for basic steel projects with $b = 1.1$, Chicago should use 12.4 percent as the discount rate. The barge project, with $b = 1.5$, should be evaluated at a 14 percent discount rate:

$$k_{Barge} = 8\% + (4\%)1.5$$

$$= 8\% + 6\%$$

$$= 14\%.$$

On the other hand, a low-risk project such as a new steel distribution center with a beta of only 0.5 would have a cost of capital of 10 percent:

$$k_{Center} = 8\% + (4\%)0.5$$

$$= 10\%.$$

Figure 15-1 gives a graphic summary of these concepts as applied to Chicago Steel. Note the following points:

1.   The SML is a Security Market Line like the one we developed in Chapter 12. It shows how investors are willing to make tradeoffs between risk, as measured by beta, and expected returns. The higher the beta risk, the higher the rate of return needed to compensate investors for bearing this risk. The SML specifies the nature of this relationship.

2.   Chicago Steel initially had a beta of 1.1, so its required rate of return on average-risk investments was 12.4 percent.

3.   High-risk investments such as the barge project require higher rates of return, whereas low-risk investments such as the distribution center require lower rates of return. It is not shown in Figure 15-1, but if Chicago concentrates its new investments in either high- or low-risk projects, as opposed to those with average risks, its corporate beta, and therefore its required rate of return on common stock (k), will change from its current value of 12.4 percent.

Figure 15-1

Chicago Steel Company:
Using the Security Market
Line Concept in Capital
Budgeting

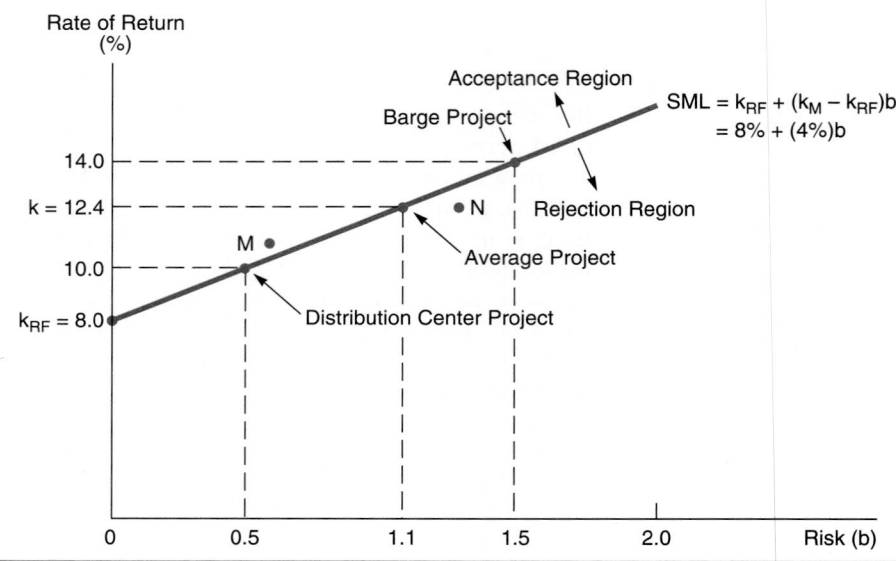

The Security Market Line (SML) can be used in the accept/reject decision for potential projects in capital budgeting decisions. A project whose expected rate of return lies on or above the SML should be accepted. A project whose return falls below the SML should be rejected because its return will not be high enough to compensate for its higher risk. In this case Project M would be accepted, while Project N would be rejected.

4. If the expected rate of return on a given capital project lies *above* the SML, the expected rate of return on the project is more than enough to compensate for its risk, and the project should be accepted. Conversely, if the project's rate of return lies *below* the SML, it should be rejected. Thus, Project M in Figure 15-1 is acceptable, while Project N should be rejected. Even though Project N has a higher expected rate of return than Project M, its return differential is not enough to offset its much higher risk. Projects that lie *on* the SML should be accepted, as their returns exactly compensate for their risk.

Diversification to Reduce Risk

As we learned in Chapter 12, a security may be risky if held in isolation but not very risky if held as part of a well-diversified portfolio. The same is true of capital budgeting; returns on an individual project may be highly uncertain, but if the project is small relative to the total firm and if its returns are not highly correlated with the firm's other assets, the project may not be very risky in either the corporate or the beta sense.

Many firms do make serious efforts to diversify; often this is a specific objective of the long-run strategic plan. For example, KeyCorp, a bank holding company with offices in New England, has weathered that region's economic storms because it also owns banks in the Pacific Northwest that have been profitable. Similarly, NCNB, a North Carolina–based banking concern that acquired Atlanta-based C&S/Sovran to become NationsBank, the third largest U.S. bank, stated, "We like having textiles and tobacco in North Carolina, citrus growing and tourism in Florida, cattle ranching and oil in Texas." One objective of moves such as those of KeyCorp and NCNB is to stabilize earnings, reduce corporate risk, and raise the value of the firm's stock.

The wisdom of corporate diversification designed to reduce risk has been questioned — why should a firm diversify when stockholders can easily diversify on their own? In other words, although it may be true that if the returns on NCNB's and C&S/Sovran's stocks are not perfectly positively correlated then merging the companies will reduce their risks somewhat, would it not be as easy for investors to diversify directly, without the trouble and expense of a merger?

The answer is not so simple. Although stockholders could directly obtain some of the risk-reducing benefits through personal diversification, other benefits can be gained only by diversification at the corporate level. For example, a more stable bank might be able to attract a better work force and also obtain funds cheaper than could two less stable banks. Also, there may be spillover effects from mergers. For example, NCNB became expert at cleaning up bad real estate loans after it acquired banks in Texas, and that expertise will help it clean up bad loans at C&S/Sovran. Finally, combining the administrative offices of the two banks, and closing some branches, will result in economies of scale, lower costs, and, thus, higher profits.

In the previous paragraph we pointed out some benefits obtained from diversification at the corporate level. We should also mention some complications that corporations have experienced in recent years in their rush to diversify. Such negative results might include (1) a corporate culture clash which hurts both firms, (2) a management which is spread "too thin" or loses its corporate focus, and (3) a situation in which top management of the acquiring firm has insufficient expertise in the business of the acquired firm to direct its operations. In fact, in recent years we have seen numerous thrift institutions and banks diversify themselves right into bankruptcy. Their regulators gave them the power to venture into new areas, but no one gave them the expertise to manage the acquired businesses properly. (At this point, you should also recall our discussion of diversification at the corporate level in Chapter 12.)

Conclusions on Project Risk

We have discussed the three types of risk normally considered in capital budgeting analyses — stand-alone risk, corporate (or within-firm) risk, and beta (or market) risk — and we have discussed ways of assessing each. However, two important questions remain: (1) To what extent should a firm be concerned with stand-alone and corporate risk in its capital budgeting decisions, and (2) what do we do when the stand-alone or corporate risk assessments and the beta risk assessment lead to different conclusions?

These questions do not have easy answers. From a theoretical standpoint, well-diversified investors should be concerned only with beta risk, managers should be concerned only with stock price maximization, and these two factors should lead to the conclusion that beta risk ought to be given virtually all the weight in capital budgeting decisions. However, if investors are not well diversified, if market imperfections prevent the CAPM from operating exactly as theory says it should, if measurement problems keep managers from having confidence in the CAPM approach in capital budgeting, or if project betas are simply not available, it may be appropriate to give stand-alone and corporate risk more weight than financial theorists suggest. Note also that the CAPM ignores bankruptcy costs and other costs associated with financial weakness, even though such costs can be substantial, and that the probability of bankruptcy depends on a firm's corporate risk, not on its beta risk. Therefore, one can easily conclude that even well-diversified investors should want a firm's management to give at least some consideration to a project's corporate risk instead of concentrating entirely on beta risk.

Although it would be desirable to reconcile these problems and to measure project risk on some absolute scale, the best anyone can do in practice is to determine project risk in a somewhat nebulous, relative sense. For example: (1) The financial manager can generally say with a fair degree of confidence that a particular project has more or less stand-alone risk than the firm's average project. (2) Assuming that stand-alone and corporate risk are highly correlated (which is typical), the project's stand-alone risk will be a good measure of its corporate risk. (3) Finally, assuming that beta risk and corporate risk are highly correlated (as is true for most companies), a project with more corporate risk than average will also have more beta risk, and vice versa for projects with low corporate risk.

What does all this mean to the financial manager? He or she should make as good an assessment as possible of each project's relative stand-alone risk, corporate risk, and beta risk. If these three types of risk are estimated to be higher than average for a given project, that project's cost of capital should be increased relative to the firm's overall cost of capital. If these three types of risk are below average, the adjustment should be reversed. Unfortunately, it is impossible to specify exactly how large the adjustments should be. However, one rule-of-thumb some companies follow is to rank projects into three groups, low risk, average risk, and high risk. Then, the corporate cost of capital is used to evaluate average-risk projects, that rate is reduced by one to two percentage points for low-risk projects, and it is increased by one to two percentage points for high-risk projects. This process is arbitrary, but it does force management to address the issue of risk, and it appears to be a step in the right direction.

Divisional Cost of Capital

As we have just discussed, it is generally agreed that riskier projects should be evaluated with a higher cost of capital than the overall corporate cost, whereas for lower-risk projects a lower cost of capital should be used. Unfortunately, there is no good way of specifying exactly how much higher or lower these cost rates should be; given the present state of the art, risk adjustments are necessarily judgmental, and somewhat arbitrary.

The problem is, primarily, that it is almost impossible to determine the beta (market) risk of individual projects. Likewise, there are no published betas for divisions within a company. Therefore, if a firm's divisions are recognized as having different levels of beta risk, some risk adjustment should be made in the divisional costs of capital, followed by risk adjustments for projects' perceived risk within each division.

One approach that has been used for estimating the betas of divisions is the *pure play method*. With this approach, the company tries to find one or more nonintegrated, single-product companies in the same line of business as the division in question. If these "pure plays" (single-product companies) are also publicly traded, their betas will be published, and an average beta for such companies can be obtained. With some adjustments (for example, for differential tax brackets and uses of financial leverage), it is then possible to arrive at an estimate of a divisional beta and cost of capital. The pure play method is often difficult to implement because it is difficult to find pure play proxy firms. However, there are times when the method is feasible. For example, when IBM was considering going into personal computers, it was able to get data on Apple Computer and several other essentially pure play personal computer companies. Similarly, Pillsbury has been able to employ this technique when making capital budgeting decisions in its Burger King, Godfather's Pizza, Steak and Ale, and Bennigan's divisions.

risk-adjusted discount rate

The discount rate that applies to a particular risky stream of cash flows; the firm's or division's cost of capital plus a risk premium appropriate to the level of risk attached to a particular project's income stream.

When no pure play can be found, many companies develop **risk-adjusted discount rates** for use in capital budgeting in a two-step process: (1) a divisional cost of capital is established for each of the major operating divisions on the basis of the division's estimated risk, and (2) within each division, all projects are classified into three categories—high risk, average risk, and low risk. Each division then uses its basic divisional cost of capital as the discount rate for average-risk projects, reduces the discount rate by one to two percentage points when evaluating low-risk projects, and raises the rate by one to two percentage points for high-risk projects.

For example, if a division's basic cost of capital is estimated to be 10 percent, a 12 percent discount rate might be used for high-risk projects and a 9 percent rate for low-risk ones. Average-risk projects would be evaluated at the 10 percent divisional cost of capital. This procedure is not very elegant, but at least it recognizes that different divisions have different characteristics and hence different costs of capital, and it acknowledges differential project riskiness within divisions.

Self-Test

What are the three types of project risk?

How is a project's stand-alone risk measured?

How is corporate risk measured?

How is beta risk measured?

List three reasons why corporate risk is important.

List three reasons why, in practice, a project's stand-alone risk is important.

What is meant by the term "average-risk project?" How would one find the cost of capital for such a project, for a "low-risk project," and for a "high-risk project?"

Complete the following sentence: An increase in a company's beta coefficient would cause its stock price to decline unless . . .

Explain why a firm should accept a given capital project if its expected rate of return lies above the SML. What if the expected rate of return lies on the SML? Below the SML?

Does a merger which lowers a company's risk by stabilizing earnings necessarily benefit stockholders?

Are there any good reasons why a firm might want to engage in mergers even though its stockholders could diversify on their own?

In recent years, what types of complications have corporations experienced in their rush to diversify?

In theory, is it correct for a firm to be concerned with stand-alone and corporate risk in its capital budgeting decisions? Should the firm be concerned with these risks in practice?

If a project's stand-alone, corporate, and beta risk are highly correlated, would this make the task of measuring risk easier or harder? Explain.

Briefly explain the two-step process used by many multidivisional companies to develop risk-adjusted discount rates.

Other Topics in Capital Budgeting

In Chapter 14 we identified the techniques financial managers use to evaluate capital budgeting projects. Several important topics were omitted from that discussion, however. In the remainder of this chapter we will consider some of these special topics, including (1) replacement analysis, (2) evaluation of projects with unequal lives, and (3) effects of inflation on the evaluation of real assets.

Replacement Analysis

The example of Houston Trucking Company's decision to purchase a new van was used in Chapter 14 to illustrate how expansion projects are analyzed. Not all project analysis is for new projects, however — some investment opportunities are evaluated as part of replacement decisions, and the analysis of replacements is somewhat different from that of expansion projects because the cash flows from the old asset must be considered. **Replacement analysis** is illustrated here with an example for Gourmet Coffee International (GCI), a maker of fine coffees.

replacement analysis

An analysis involving the decision of whether or not to replace an existing asset that is still productive with a new one. Replacement projects are by definition mutually exclusive.

GCI of New Orleans roasts, blends, and packages coffee from imported beans for specialty shop owners in the Gulf Coast area. The company's management is evaluating the purchase of a new coffee bean roaster that is quicker and more efficient than GCI's old roasting machine. This old, relatively inefficient roaster was purchased 9 years ago at a cost of $300,000. The machine had an original expected life of 15 years and a zero estimated salvage value at the end of its expected life. It is being depreciated on a straight line basis; therefore, its annual depreciation charge is $20,000, and its present book value is $120,000.

The production manager reports that a new, faster machine can be purchased for $325,000 (including freight and installation). Over its 6-year life, the new machine is expected to expand sales from $200,000 to $230,000 a year and, furthermore, to reduce labor usage sufficiently to cut annual operating costs from $140,000 to $100,000. The new machine falls into the 5-year MACRS class; therefore, it is depreciated over 6 years. The new machine has an estimated salvage value of $40,000 at the end of its 6-year life. The old machine's current market value is $20,000; the firm's marginal tax rate is 40 percent; and its cost of capital is 10 percent. Should GCI buy the new coffee roasting machine?

Table 15-1   Gourmet Coffee International: Replacement Decision Worksheet

I. *Investment Outlay at t = 0*

1. Cost of new machine	($325,000)
2. Market value of old machine	20,000
3. Tax savings on sale of old machine	40,000
4. Total net investment at t = 0	($265,000)

II. *Operating Inflows over the Project's Life*

Year:	0	1	2	3	4	5	6
5. After-tax increase in sales and decrease in costs		$42,000	$ 42,000	$42,000	$42,000	$42,000	$42,000
6. Depreciation on new machine		$65,000	$104,000	$61,750	$39,000	$35,750	$19,500
7. Depreciation on old machine		20,000	20,000	20,000	20,000	20,000	20,000
8. Change in depreciation (6 − 7)		$45,000	$ 84,000	$41,750	$19,000	$15,750	($ 500)
9. Tax savings from change in depreciation (8 × 0.4)		18,000	33,600	16,700	7,600	6,300	(200)
10. Net operating cash flows (5 + 9)		$60,000	$ 75,600	$58,700	$49,600	$48,300	$41,800

III. *Terminal Year Cash Flows*

11. Estimated salvage value of new machine							$40,000
12. Tax on salvage value							16,000
13. Total terminal year cash flows							$24,000

IV. *Net Cash Flows*

	0	1	2	3	4	5	6
14. Total net cash flows	($265,000)	$60,000	$ 75,600	$58,700	$49,600	$48,300	$65,800

V. *Results*

Payback period: 4.4 years
IRR: 9.6% versus 10% cost of capital
NPV: ($2,862.68)

Table 15-1 shows the worksheet format the company uses to analyze replacement projects.[4] Each line is numbered, and a line-by-line description of the table follows.

---

[4]We have chosen to illustrate this replacement analysis using a worksheet approach rather than using Equation 14-1, which is discussed at the beginning of Chapter 14. However, Equation 14-1 could have been used to develop any of the operating cash inflows shown in Table 15-1. For example, GCI's Year 1 operating cash inflow could have been calculated as

$$CF_1 = [\$30,000 - (-\$40,000)](1 - 0.4) + (\$65,000 - \$20,000)(0.4)$$
$$= \$42,000 + \$18,000 = \$60,000.$$

The systematic worksheet approach makes it less likely that some relevant cash flow or tax effect may be missed. Also, most firms conduct analyses like this one by using personal computers and spreadsheet programs such as *Lotus 1-2-3*, and the worksheet format we use fits perfectly into a *Lotus 1-2-3* format.

Line 1.   Part I of the table, Lines 1 through 4, shows the cash flows which occur at (approximately) t = 0, the time the investment is made. Line 1 shows the purchase price of the new machine, including installation and freight charges. Since it is an outflow, it is negative.

Line 2.   Here we show the price received from the sale of the old machine.

Line 3.   Because the old machine would be sold at less than its $120,000 book value, the sale would create a $100,000 loss, which would reduce the firm's taxable income and hence its next quarterly income tax payment. The tax savings is equal to (Loss)(T) = ($100,000)(0.40) = $40,000, where T is the marginal corporate tax rate. The Tax Code defines this loss as an operating loss because it reflects the fact that inadequate depreciation was taken on the old asset. If there had been a profit on the sale (that is, if the sale price had exceeded book value), Line 3 would have shown taxes *paid,* a cash outflow. In the actual case, the machine would be sold at a loss so no taxes would be paid, and the company would realize a tax savings of $40,000.

Line 4.   Here we show the total net cash outflow at the time the replacement is made. The company writes a check for $325,000 to pay for the machine; however, this outlay is partially offset by proceeds from the sale of the old machine and by reduced taxes. *Note that if additional net working capital were required as a result of the capital budgeting decision, this factor would have to be taken into account.* The amount of net working capital (additional current assets required as a result of an expansion in sales minus any spontaneously generated funds) would be estimated and added to the initial cash outlay; see the Houston Trucking Company example in Chapter 14. We assume that GCI will not need any additional working capital, so that factor is not relevant in this example.

Line 5.   Part II of the table shows the *incremental operating cash flows,* or benefits, that are expected if the replacement is made. The first of these benefits is the increase in sales and the reduction in operating costs shown on Line 5. Cash flows increase because sales are increased (by $30,000) and cash operating costs are reduced (by $40,000), for a total of $70,000, but increased sales and reduced costs also mean higher taxable income, hence higher income taxes. This is really the first part of Equation 14-1:

$$\text{Net cash flow} = (\$REV - \$EXP)(1 - T) + (DEP)(T) \qquad \textbf{(14-1)}$$

$$= [\$30,000 - (-\$40,000)](1 - 0.4) + (DEP)(T)$$

$$= \$70,000\,(1 - 0.4) + (DEP)(T)$$

$$= \$42,000 + (DEP)(T).$$

GCI will pay $70,000 × 0.40 = $28,000 in taxes on the $70,000 sales increase and cost savings which are assumed to occur in each of the 6 years. (Note that in other cases there might be an increase in sales accompanied by an *increase* in cash expenses associated with a project, or there could be *no change* in sales but only a reduction in cash operating costs. Both Equation 14-1 and the worksheet approach in Table 15-1 are flexible enough to allow for these possibilities.) If the term ($REV − $EXP) had been expected to change over time, this fact could be built into our analysis.

Again comparing our worksheet with the equation, the next four lines will calculate (DEP)(T) for each year—the only difference is that we now have to focus on *incremental* depreciation, that is, the increase (or decrease) in depreciation expense for each year.

Line 6. The depreciable basis of the new machine, $325,000, is multiplied by the appropriate MACRS recovery allowances for 5-year class property (20, 32, 19, 12, 11, and 6 percent, respectively) to obtain the depreciation figures shown on Line 6. Note that if you summed across Line 6, the total would be $325,000, the machine's depreciable basis.

Line 7. Line 7 shows the $20,000 straight line depreciation taken annually on the old machine. This is found by dividing the old machine's original life of 15 years into its purchase price of $300,000. Nine years' worth of depreciation has been taken, while 6 years' has not.

Line 8. The depreciation expense on the old machine as shown on Line 7 can no longer be taken if the replacement is made, but the new machine's depreciation will be available instead. Therefore, the $20,000 depreciation on the old machine is subtracted from that on the new machine to show the net change in annual depreciation. The change is positive in Years 1 through 5 but negative in Year 6. The Year 6 negative net change in annual depreciation signifies that the purchase of the replacement machine results in a *decrease* in depreciation expense during that year.

Line 9. The net change in depreciation results in a tax reduction (increase in Year 6) which is equal to the change in depreciation multiplied by the tax rate: Depreciation tax savings for Year 1 = $45,000(0.40) = $18,000. Note again that the relevant cash flow is the tax savings on the *net change* in depreciation, not just the depreciation on the new equipment. Capital budgeting decisions are based on *incremental* cash flows, and since GCI will lose $20,000 of depreciation if it replaces the old machine, that fact must be taken into account.

Line 10. Here we show the net operating cash flows over the project's 6-year life. These flows are found by adding the after-tax sales increase and cost decrease to the depreciation tax savings, or Line 5 plus Line 9.

Line 11. Part III shows the cash flows associated with the termination of the project. To begin, Line 11 shows the estimated **salvage value** of the new machine at the end of its 6-year life, $40,000.

salvage value
The market price of a capital asset at the end of a specified period. In a capital budgeting decision, it is also the current market price of an asset being considered for replacement.

Line 12. Since the book value of the new machine at the end of Year 6 will be zero, the company will have to pay taxes of $40,000(0.4) = $16,000.

Line 13. Here we show the total cash flows resulting from terminating the project. *Note that if additional working capital had been required and included in the initial cash outlay, that amount would have been added to the final year's cash flows because the working capital would be recovered when the project was completed.*

Line 14. Part IV shows, on Line 14, the total net cash flows in a form suitable for capital budgeting evaluation. In effect, Line 14 is a time line.

These cash flows can now be used to determine the project's NPV based on GCI's 10 percent cost of capital:

$$\text{NPV} = \sum_{t=1}^{6} \frac{CF_t}{(1 + k)^t} - \text{Cost}$$

$$= \left(\frac{\$60,000}{(1.1)^1} + \frac{\$75,600}{(1.1)^2} + \frac{\$58,700}{(1.1)^3} + \frac{\$49,600}{(1.1)^4} + \frac{\$48,300}{(1.1)^5} + \frac{\$65,800}{(1.1)^6} \right) - \$265,000$$

$$= [\,\$60,000(0.9091) + \$75,600(0.8264) + \$58,700(0.7513)$$

$$+ \$49,600(0.6830) + \$48,300(0.6209) + \$65,800(0.5645)\,] - \$265,000$$

$$= \$262,133.52 - \$265,000$$

$$= (\$2,866.48).$$

Part V of the table, "Results," shows the replacement project's payback period, IRR, and NPV. Because the NPV is negative, GCI should not replace the old coffee bean roaster with the newer, more efficient machine. If the NPV had been positive, the decision would have been to replace the old machine. Alternatively, had we set NPV equal to zero and solved for the IRR, we would have found that the IRR $\approx$ 9.6%. Since the required rate of return = 10%, and the IRR < 10%, this second method reaffirms the decision not to replace the old machine. (Note that in Part V a financial calculator was used to find IRR and NPV; therefore, the NPV differs slightly from the NPV found using PVIFs from the table.)

Comparing Projects with Unequal Lives

Note that a replacement decision involves comparing two mutually exclusive projects: retaining the old asset versus buying a new one. To simplify matters, in our replacement example we assumed that the new coffee roasting machine had a life equal to the remaining life of the old machine. Suppose, however, that we must choose between two mutually exclusive replacement alternatives that have *different* lives. For example, Machine S has an expected life of 10 years, whereas Machine L has a 15-year life. An adjustment would need to be made to the analysis.[5]

The most typical procedure for solving problems of this type is to set up a series of *replacement chains* extending out to the "common denominator" year—that is, the year in which both alternatives require replacement. For Machines S and L this would be Year 30, so it would be necessary to compare a 3-chain cycle for S, the 10-year machine, with a 2-chain cycle for L, the 15-year one.

---

[5]We discuss only one of the approaches available to compare projects with unequal lives. For a discussion of the second approach, the equivalent annual annuity method, refer to Brigham and Gapenski, *Intermediate Financial Management*, 4th ed., Chapter 8.

replacement chain (common life) method

A method of comparing projects of unequal lives which assumes that each project can be replicated as many times as necessary to reach a common life span; the NPVs over this life span are then compared, and the project with the higher common life NPV is chosen.

To illustrate the **replacement chain (common life) method,** suppose a firm is considering the replacement of a fully depreciated printing press with a new one. The plant in which the press is used is profitable and is expected to continue in operation for many years. The old press could continue to be used indefinitely, but it is not as efficient as new presses. Two replacement machines are available. Press A has a cost of $36,100, will last for 5 years, and will produce after-tax incremental cash flows of $9,700 per year for 5 years. Press B has a cost of $57,500, will last for 10 years, and will produce net cash flows of $9,500 per year. Both the costs and cash flows of Presses A and B have been constant in recent years and are expected to remain constant in the future. The company's cost of capital is 10 percent.

Should the old press be replaced and, if so, with Press A or with Press B? To answer these questions, we first calculate Press A's NPV as follows:

$$NPV_A = \$9,700(3.7908) - \$36,100 = \$36,771 - \$36,100 = \$671.$$

Press B's NPV is calculated as follows:

$$NPV_B = \$9,500(6.1446) - \$57,500 = \$58,374 - \$57,500 = \$874.$$

These calculations suggest that the old press should indeed be replaced and that Press B should be selected. However, the analysis is incomplete, and the decision to choose Press B is *incorrect.* If the company chooses Press A, it will have an opportunity to repeat the investment after 5 years, and this second investment will *also* be profitable. However, if it chooses Press B, it will not have this second investment opportunity. Therefore, to make a proper comparison of Presses A and B, we must find the present value of Press A over a 10-year period and compare it with Press B over the same 10 years.

The NPV for Press B as calculated previously is correct as it stands. For Press A, however, we must take three additional steps: (1) determine the NPV of the second Press A five years hence, (2) bring this NPV back to the present, and (3) sum these two component NPVs:

1.   If we assume that the cost and annual cash flows of Press A will not change if the project is repeated in 5 years and that the firm's cost of capital will remain at 10 percent, then Press A's NPV will remain the same as its first-stage NPV, $671. However, the second NPV will not accrue for five years, and hence it represents a present value at t = 5.

2.   The present value (at t = 0) of the purchase of a second printing Press A is determined by discounting the second NPV (at t = 5) back five years as a lump sum at 10 percent to determine its present value at t = 0: $671(PVIF_{10\%,5}) = \$671(0.6209) = \$417.$

3.   The true (or common life) NPV of Press A is $671 + $417 = $1,088. This is the value that should be compared with the NPV of Press B, $874.

The value of the firm will increase more if the old press is replaced by Press A *twice* than if the firm goes with Press B; therefore, Press A should be selected.

When should we worry about unequal life analysis? As a general rule, the unequal life issue (1) does not arise for independent projects but (2) can arise if mutually exclusive projects with significantly different lives are being evaluated. However, even for mutually exclusive projects, it is not always appropriate to extend the analysis to a common life. This should only be done if there is a high probability that the projects will actually be replicated beyond their initial lives.

We should note several potentially serious weaknesses inherent in this type of unequal life analysis: (1) If inflation is expected, then replacement equipment will have a higher price, and both sales prices and operating costs will probably change. Thus, the static conditions built into the analysis would be invalid. (2) Replacements that occur down the road would probably employ new technology, which in turn might change the cash flows. This factor is not built into the replacement chain analysis. (3) It is difficult enough to estimate the lives of most projects, so estimating the lives of a series of projects is often just a speculation. (4) If reasonably strong competition is present, the profitability of projects will be eroded over time and that would reduce the need to extend the analysis beyond the projects' initial lives.

In view of these problems, no experienced financial analyst would be too concerned about comparing mutually exclusive projects with lives of, say, 8 years and 10 years. Given all the uncertainties in the estimation process, such projects would, for all practical purposes, be assumed to have the same life. Still, it is important to recognize that a problem does exist if mutually exclusive projects have substantially different lives. When we encounter such problems in practice, we build expected inflation and/or possible efficiency gains directly into the cash flow estimates, and then use the replacement chain approach. The cash flow estimation is more complicated, but the concepts involved are exactly the same as in our example.

? *Self-Test*

Briefly explain the steps involved in the capital budgeting analysis required for replacement projects.

What are the primary differences between a replacement analysis and an expansion analysis?

Briefly describe the replacement chain (common life) approach.

Why is it not always necessary to adjust project cash flow analyses for unequal lives?

Incorporating Inflation into Capital Budgeting Analysis

Inflation is a fact of life in the United States and most other nations, and thus, it must be considered in any sound capital budgeting analysis. Several procedures are available for dealing with inflation. The most valid approach is to (1) make no explicit adjustment in the discount rate, which already contains an inflation premium when inflation is expected, and (2) adjust the cash flows upward to reflect expected inflation. This method will be discussed next. Note that the logic of the approach will be developed in three steps: First, we will deal with capital budgeting in the *absence of inflation*. Next, we examine how the situation changes if the *same rate of inflation* is expected to influence cost of capital, sales prices, and all the firm's input costs. Finally, we will suggest the appropriate procedure where a firm's sales prices, input costs, and cost of capital are expected to be influenced by *different rates of inflation*.

To see how inflation enters the picture, suppose an investor lends $100 for 1 year at a rate of 5 percent. At the end of the year the investor will have $100(1.05) = $105. However, if prices rise by 6 percent during the year, the ending $105 will have a purchasing power, in terms of beginning-of-year values, of only $105/1.06 = $99. Thus the investor will have lost $1, or 1 percent of the original purchasing power, in spite of having earned 5 percent interest: $105 at the end of the year will buy only as much in goods as $99 would have bought at the beginning of the year.

Investors recognize this problem, and, as we learned in earlier chapters, they incorporate expectations about inflation into the required rate of return. For example, suppose investors seek a *real rate of return (k_r)* of 8 percent on an investment with a given degree of risk. Suppose further that they anticipate an *annual rate of inflation (i)* of 4 percent. Then, to end up with the 8 percent real rate of return, the *nominal rate of return (k_n)* must be a value such that

$$k_n = k_r + i$$
$$= 8\% + 4\% = 12\%.$$

Here the expected inflation rate, i, is equivalent to the inflation premium, IP, that we discussed in Chapter 4. (Note also that, except for U.S. Treasury securities, k_r includes a default risk premium and, possibly, a liquidity premium; for *all* medium- and long-term securities, a maturity risk premium would also be included in k_r.)

1. We can use these concepts to analyze capital budgeting under inflation. First, note that a project's NPV in the absence of inflation, where $k_r = k_n$, RCF_t = the *real* net cash flow in Year t (based on t = 0 dollars), and C = cost, is calculated as follows:

$$NPV = \sum_{t=1}^{n} \frac{RCF_t}{(1 + k_r)^t} - C.$$

2. Next, suppose the situation changes. We now expect inflation to occur, and we expect both sales prices and input costs to rise at the rate i, the same inflation rate that is built into the estimated cost of capital. Under these conditions, the *nominal* cash flow (CF_t) will increase annually at the rate of i percent, producing this situation:

$$CF_t = \text{Actual (nominal) cash flow}_t = RCF_t(1 + i)^t.$$

For example, if a net cash flow of $100 is expected in Year 5 in the absence of inflation, then with a 4 percent rate of inflation, $CF_5 = $100(1.04)^5 = $121.67.

Now if net cash flows increase at the rate of i percent per year and if this same inflation factor is built into the cost of capital by investors seeking to protect their purchasing power, then

$$\text{Inflation-adjusted NPV} = \sum_{t=1}^{n} \frac{RCF_t(1 + i)^t}{(1 + k_n)^t} - C. \tag{15-2}$$

Remember that $k_n = k_r + i$, so the denominator in the equation has been adjusted for inflation by market forces.

This procedure is the recommended approach, but it may not be followed. People sometimes discount cash flows that have *not* been adjusted upward for inflation by the *nominal* cost of capital, which *does* include an inflation premium. This is wrong! Therefore, when the cost of capital, which includes an inflation risk premium, is used to discount constant dollar cash flows (not adjusted upward for expected inflation), *the resulting NPV will be downward biased.* The denominator will reflect inflation, but the numerator will not, which produces the bias. If sales prices and all costs are expected to rise at approximately the same rate, the bias can be corrected by having current cash flows increase at the inflation rate, or by using the real rate as the cost of capital.

3. Although it is often appropriate to assume that *variable costs* will rise at the same rate as sales prices, fixed costs generally increase at a lower rate, and depreciation will not increase at all. *In any situation where revenues and different types of costs are not all expected to rise at exactly the same inflation rate as is built into the cost of capital, the best procedure is to build inflation into the basic cash flow component projections for each year.* If high rates of inflation are projected, and if expected inflation rates for sales prices and input costs differ materially, this method must be followed. While such adjustments may sound daunting, the process becomes manageable if a spreadsheet such as *Lotus 1-2-3* is used.

Self-Test

What is the most valid approach in adjusting the capital budgeting analysis for inflation?

What happens to the NPV when cash flows have *not* been adjusted for inflation, but a nominal discount rate (which includes an inflation premium) has been used?

Summary

In this chapter, we discussed four issues in capital budgeting: risk analysis in capital budgeting, replacement decisions, replacement chains for mutually exclusive assets with unequal lives, and the effects of inflation on capital budgeting analysis.

▷   **Risk analysis** is important in all financial decisions, especially those relating to capital budgeting. Three distinct types of project risk can be identified: (1) *stand-alone risk,* (2) *corporate, or within-firm, risk,* and (3) *beta, or market, risk.*

A project's **stand-alone risk** is the risk the project would have if it were the firm's only asset and if the firm's stockholders held only that one stock. Stand-alone risk is measured by the variability of the asset's expected returns.

Corporate (within-firm) risk reflects the effects of a project on the firm's risk, and it is measured by the project's effect on the firm's earnings variability. Stockholder diversification is not taken into account. Corporate risk is important because it influences the firm's ability to use low-cost debt, to maintain smooth operations over time, and to avoid crises that might consume management's energy and disrupt employees, customers, suppliers, and the community.

Beta (market) risk is that part of a project's risk which cannot be eliminated by diversification. It is measured by the project's beta coefficient. In theory, beta risk should be the most relevant type of risk.

▷ Stand-alone risk is often used as a **proxy for both corporate and beta risk** because (1) corporate and beta risk are difficult to measure and (2) the three types of risk are usually highly correlated.

▷ The **Capital Asset Pricing Model (CAPM),** which provides a framework for analyzing the relationship between risk and return, can be used to evaluate projects as portfolios. The fundamental premise of this analysis is that the higher the risk associated with an investment, the higher the expected rate of return must be to compensate investors for assuming risk.

The **Security Market Line (SML) equation** expresses the risk-return relationship as follows:

$$k_i = k_{RF} + (k_M - k_{RF})b_i.$$

If the expected rate of return on a project lies *above* the SML, the project's expected rate of return is more than enough to compensate for its risk, so the project should be accepted. If the project's rate of return lies *below* the SML, it should be rejected. Finally, if the project's return lies *on* the SML, the project should be accepted as its return exactly compensates for the risk.

▷ **Corporate diversification** has both potential advantages and disadvantages. Although stockholders could directly obtain some of the risk-reducing benefits through personal diversification, other benefits can be gained only by corporate diversification, such as spillover effects from mergers.

Complications from diversification have arisen as well. Such negative results include (1) *corporate culture clash,* (2) *management* that has been *spread "too thin"* or has lost its focus, and (3) situations in which the top management of the acquiring firm has *insufficient expertise* in the business of the acquired firm to direct operations.

▷ Both the **measurement of risk** and its incorporation into capital budgeting involve judgment. It is possible to use quantitative techniques as an aid to judgment, but in the final analysis the assessment of risk in capital budgeting is a subjective process.

Projects which are **riskier** than the firm's (or division's) average project require **higher rates of return,** while **low-risk projects** require **lower rates of return.** In this manner, **risk-adjusted discount rates** are estimated and applied to a particular risky stream of cash flows, and these risk-adjusted discount rates represent a scaling up or down from the firm's (or division's) cost of capital.

▶   A **replacement analysis** involves the decision of whether or not to replace an existing asset that is still productive with a new one. Replacement projects are by definition **mutually exclusive.**

A replacement analysis is more complicated than an expansion analysis because it is more difficult to calculate **incremental cash flows.** Cash flows are produced by the new asset, but cash flows are lost from the old asset, and it is the difference between these two sets of cash flows which must be determined and evaluated.

▶   The **replacement chain (common life) method** is used to evaluate *mutually exclusive projects of unequal lives.* This method assumes that each project can be replicated as many times as necessary to reach a common life span; the NPVs over this life span are then compared, and the project with the higher common life NPV is chosen.

There are several potentially serious weaknesses in this type of unequal life analysis. (1) If **inflation** is expected, then static conditions built into the analysis would be invalid. (2) **Technological advancements** might change cash flows. (3) **Estimating the lives of a series of projects** is often just speculation. (4) If **strong competition** is present, the profitability of projects will be eroded over time and that would reduce the need to extend the analysis beyond the project's initial lives.

▶   **Expected inflation** should be accounted for in capital budgeting analysis. The most efficient way to deal with inflation is to build it into each cash flow element.

Resolution to
DECISION IN FINANCE

THE COLLAPSE OF A
$10 BILLION EMPIRE

Olympia & York's destruction began with the severe downturn in global commercial real estate in 1990 that its bankers had warned it about. Paul Reichmann said, "It is

Sources: Richard D. Hylton and Tricia Welsh, "The Man Who Blew $10 Billion," *Fortune,* May 17, 1993, 92–95; Larry M. Greenberg, "Dismantling of Olympia & York Set to Begin Following Restructuring Vote," *The Wall Street Journal,* January 11, 1993, A4.

my fault. I did not concentrate on risk management, and I did not realize the change in the marketplace that came about with the Gulf War. Psychologically, a lot of things I should have done I didn't, because I knew that when this big tenant — Barclays Bank — moved in, Canary Wharf would have been acclaimed as the greatest success of the century. In the end, the blame is all mine."

The Canadian banks that had financed his projects for 30 years felt betrayed because Reichmann told them until the end that there was no problem. One banker said, "We trusted him and gave him great license to do things. For a long time we thought he was different from the other developers. He seemed wise. But yes, he was also a gambler."

Part of the problem was the Reichmanns' secretiveness. Only they knew the facts about their company's debt structure and cash flows, keeping their bankers and even their own executives virtually in the dark. When Salomon Brothers underwrote a $1 billion mortgage bond offering, the brothers refused to provide financial statements and only allowed Salomon a brief examination—note taking was not allowed, and they had to memorize what they could.

Finally, the Reichmanns should have been warned by their previous experience with Campeau. Although they lost only $250 million, their reputation was damaged. And after the Campeau crash, Paul Reichmann admitted that his company stepped outside familiar territory and lost its way. "The main focus for us is real estate and real estate investments internationally. The only way to succeed in the global marketplace is if you strive to be the best in one area, perhaps two."

He should have rememberd his own words when he decided to finance Abitibi-Price, a huge paper products manufacturer, and Gulf Canada Resources, an oil and gas company. After Olympia & York filed for bankruptcy in April 1992 and was subject to liquidation by the bankruptcy court. Reichmann said, "The mistakes were not in real estate but in our financings of other things . . . that we did during an inflationary period. We should never have invested in things we were not experts in."

Perhaps he will not make the same mistakes again. In any case, Olympia & York will no longer be on his family's shoulders. The restructuring plan for some $7 billion in debt related to the company's Canadian operations will free the Reichmanns from any further liability for the Olympia & York debt and will allow them to get on with new ventures.

At age 62, Reichmann is not discouraged. "I fully expect to work on two or three more projects as big as Canary Wharf in my life," he says.

Questions

15-1   Think about the example of GCI's coffee roasting machine purchase in Table 15-1, and answer these questions:

    a. Why is the salvage value of the new machine on Line 11 reduced for taxes on Line 12?

    b. Why is depreciation on the old machine deducted on Line 7 to get Line 8?

    c. How would the analysis be affected if the new machine permitted a *reduction* in net working capital?

    d. Why were the sales increase and cost savings figures shown on Line 5 reduced by multiplying the before-tax figure by $(1 - T)$, while the change in the depreciation figure on Line 8 was multiplied by T?

15-2   Distinguish among stand-alone risk, corporate (or within-firm) risk, and beta (or market) risk for a project being considered for inclusion in the capital budget. Which type of risk do you believe should be given the greatest weight in capital budgeting decisions? Explain.

15-3   Suppose Gonzo Technologies, which has a high beta as well as a great deal of corporate risk, merged with E-Z Patterns Inc. E-Z Patterns's sales rise during recessions, when people are more likely to make their own clothing; consequently, its beta is negative, but its corporate risk is relatively high. What would the merger do to the costs of capital in the consolidated company's technology division and in its patterns division?

15-4   Suppose a firm estimates its cost of capital for the coming year to be 10 percent. What are reasonable costs of capital for evaluating average-risk projects, high-risk projects, and low-risk projects?

15-5   Why is it true, in general, that a failure to adjust expected cash flows for expected inflation biases the calculated NPV downward?

15-6   Suppose a firm is considering two mutually exclusive projects. One has a life of 6 years and the other a life of 10 years. Would the failure to employ some type of replacement chain analysis bias an NPV analysis against one of the projects? Explain.

Self-Test Problem

ST-1   Wofford Novelty Plastics (WNP) currently uses an injection molding machine that was purchased 2 years ago. This machine is being depreciated on a straight line basis, it has 6 years of remaining life, and its current book value is $2,100. Thus, the annual depreciation expense is $2,100/6 = $350 per year. The machine currently can be sold for $2,500.

WNP has been offered a replacement machine that has a cost of $8,000, an estimated useful life of 6 years, and an estimated salvage value of $800. This machine falls into the MACRS 5-year class. The replacement machine would permit an output expansion, so sales would rise by $1,000 per year; even so, its much greater efficiency would still cause operating expenses to decline by $1,500 per year. The new machine would require inventories to be increased by $2,000, but accounts payable would simultaneously increase by $500.

WNP's effective tax rate is 40 percent, and its cost of capital is 15 percent. Should it replace the old machine?

Problems

15-1
Replacement decision

McDowell Equipment Company is considering the purchase of a new machine to replace an obsolete one. The machine being used in current operations has both a book value and a market value of zero; it is in good working order, however, and will operate at an acceptable level for an additional 5 years. McDowell's engineers estimate that the proposed machine will perform operations so much more efficiently that if it is installed, labor, materials, and other direct costs of the operation will decline by $42,000 annually. The proposed machine costs $112,500 delivered and installed. The new machine falls into the MACRS 5-year class and will be sold for its book value at the end of 5 years. The MACRS depreciation percentages are as follows: 0.20, 0.32, 0.19, 0.12, 0.11, and 0.06. The company's cost of capital is 14 percent and its tax rate is 40 percent.

a. What is the replacement project's annual cash flow?
b. What is the project's NPV?
c. Should the old machine be replaced?

15-2
Replacement decision

Continental Construction Company is considering replacing an old machine with a new one that will increase cash earnings before taxes by $45,000 annually. The new machine will cost $90,000 and will have an estimated life of 8 years. The new machine falls into the MACRS 5-year class and will be sold for $10,000 at the end of 8 years. The MACRS depreciation percentages are as follows: 0.20, 0.32, 0.19, 0.12, 0.11, and 0.06. The applicable corporate tax rate is 40 percent, and the firm's cost of capital is 16 percent. The old machine has been fully depreciated and has no salvage value. Calculate the net present value for the replacement project. Should the old machine be replaced by the new one?

15-3
Replacement decision

Garraty Manufacturing currently uses an injection molding machine that was purchased several years ago. This old machine is being depreciated on a straight line basis. It has 5 years of remaining life with zero expected salvage value. Its current book value is $4,000, and it can be sold for $4,800 at this time.

Garraty has been offered a replacement machine that has a cost of $12,800, it falls under the 5-year MACRS class life, and it has an estimated salvage value of $1,600 in Year 5. The MACRS depreciation percentages are as follows: Year 1 = 20%; Year 2 = 32%; Year 3 = 19%; Year 4 = 12%; and Year 5 = 11%. At the end of the fifth year the new machine will be sold for its salvage value. The replacement machine will permit an output expansion, so sales will rise by $1,600 annually; yet the new machine's much greater efficiency will cause operating expenses to decline by $2,400 per year. The new machine will cause inventories to increase by $3,200 and accounts payable to increase by $800.

Garraty's effective tax rate is 40 percent, and its cost of capital is 15 percent. Should it replace the old machine? (*Hint:* Remember to calculate the tax on the difference between the salvage value and the book value of the replacement machine.)

15-4
Risk adjustment

The risk-free rate of return is 7 percent, and the market risk premium ($k_M - k_{RF}$) is 4 percent. The beta of the project under analysis is 1.25, and the expected after-tax net cash flow is estimated at $1,942 annually for 5 years. The required investment outlay for the project is $7,000.
a. What is the required risk-adjusted return on the project?
b. What is the project's NPV?
c. What is the project's IRR?
d. Should this project be accepted?

15-5
Required rate of return

Jordan-McCoy Technology (JMT) is considering investing in a 5-year project that has expected annual cash flows of $56,000. The project's cost is $175,000. JMT bases its required rate of return on the Security Market Line (SML). The risk-free rate is expected to be 7 percent, and the return on an average security in the market is forecasted to be 11 percent. The firm's beta is 2.0, and the project is assumed to have the same level of beta risk as the firm's existing assets.
a. What is the firm's required rate of return?
b. What is the project's NPV?
c. What is the project's IRR?
d. Should the firm invest in this project?

15-6
Risk adjustment

The Vaughan Corporation has two independent projects under consideration. Vaughan's beta is 1.2. The average-risk security in the market has a return of 13 percent, and the risk-free rate is 8 percent. Project E has the same risk as Vaughan's current projects, whereas Project F has a beta of 1.6. Project E has a cost of $200,000 and expected after-tax cash flows of $51,400 annually for the next 5 years. Project F also has a cost of $200,000 and expected after-tax cash flows of $58,000 annually for 5 years.
a. What is the required rate of return for each project?
b. What is the NPV for each project?
c. Which project(s) should Vaughan accept?

15-7
Risk-adjusted NPV

Pickett International is considering investing in a new capital project. The project, which has an expected productive life of 10 years, would require a $300,000 investment and promises to provide a cash flow (net income plus depreciation) of $60,000 annually. Pickett's cost of capital is 12 percent. However, management has determined that the project is much riskier than the firm's average projects. Pickett requires an 18 percent return on high-risk projects.
a. Which rate of return, 12% or 18%, should management use in evaluating this project?
b. What is the project's NPV?
c. Should Pickett invest in this project?

15-8
Risk-adjusted NPVs

Arlington Mills has an average cost of capital equaling 10 percent. The company is choosing between two mutually exclusive projects. Project B is of average risk, has a cost of $50,000, and has expected cash flows of $14,701.80 per year for 5 years. Project A is of above-average risk, and management estimates that its cost of capital would be 12 percent. Project A also costs $50,000, and it is expected to provide cash flows of $14,980.03 per year for 5 years. Calculate risk-adjusted NPVs for the two projects, and use these NPVs to choose between them.

15-9
Replacement project

McKinney-Best Publishing Company is contemplating the replacement of one of its bookbinding machines with a newer and more efficient one. The old machine has a book value of $300,000 and a remaining useful life of 6 years. The firm does not expect to realize any return from scrapping the old machine in 6 years, but it can sell it now to another firm in the industry for $150,000. The old machine is being depreciated toward a zero salvage value, or by $50,000 per year, using the straight line method (assume that at the time the machine was purchased this was permissible).

The new machine has a purchase price of $1 million, a MACRS class life of 5 years, and an estimated salvage value of $75,000. It is expected to economize on electric power usage, labor, and repair costs, as well as to reduce the number of defective bindings. In total, an annual savings of $250,000 will be realized if it is installed. The company is in the 40 percent marginal tax bracket, and it has a 12 percent cost of capital.

a. What is the initial cash outlay required for the new machine?

b. Calculate the annual depreciation allowances for both machines, and compute the change in the annual depreciation expense if the replacement is made. (The appropriate MACRS depreciation percentages for a 5-year class life are these: Year 1 = 20%; Year 2 = 32%; Year 3 = 19%; Year 4 = 12%; Year 5 = 11%; and Year 6 = 6%.)

c. What are the after-tax operating cash flows in Years 1 to 6?

d. What is the after-tax cash flow from the salvage value of the new machine in Year 6?

e. Should McKinney-Best purchase the new machine? Support your answer.

f. In general, how would each of the following factors affect the investment decision, and how should each be treated? (Give verbal answers.)

   1. The expected life of the existing machine decreases.

   2. The cost of capital is not constant but is increasing.

(Do Parts g, h, and i only if you are using the computerized problem diskette.)

g. McKinney-Best Publishing may be able to purchase an alternative new bookbinding machine from another supplier. Its purchase price would be $850,000, but its salvage value would only be $25,000. This machine would lower annual operating costs by only $185,000. Should McKinney-Best purchase this machine?

h. If the salvage value on the alternative new machine were $60,000 rather than $25,000, how would this affect the decision?

i. With everything as in Part h, assume that the cost of capital increased from 12 percent to 12.5 percent. How would this affect the decision?

15-10
Unequal lives

Corrigan Technology has two mutually exclusive projects code-named Gold and White. The firm must determine which of the two projects to select. The following table provides the necessary information to evaluate the projects.

	Gold	White
Cost	$30,000	$30,000
Annual after-tax cash flow	$11,000	$ 7,000
Life	4 years	8 years

If the firm's cost of capital for the projects is 14 percent, which of the two projects should be selected for investment?

15-11

Cash flow estimate and replacement analysis

Wonder Bakers, whose motto is, "If it's good, it's a Wonder," is considering the replacement of its oven. The old oven, with a book value of $100,000, has a remaining useful life of 4 years and is being depreciated using the straight line method to a salvage value of zero (assume that this is permissible). If the old oven is sold today, its market value will be only $33,000. The new oven has a total cost, delivered and installed, of $120,000 and an expected salvage value of $20,000 at the end of its 4-year life. The new oven would have no effect on operating income. The firm uses the MACRS depreciation methodology and has a tax rate of 40 percent. (The MACRS depreciation percentages for a 3-year class life are these: Year 1 = 33%; Year 2 = 45%; Year 3 = 15%; and Year 4 = 7%.)

a. What is the initial cash outlay required for the new oven?

b. What are the after-tax operating cash flows that would result from the replacement of the old oven?

c. What is the after-tax cash flow from the salvage value of the new oven in Year 4?

d. If the firm's cost of capital is 10 percent, should Wonder replace the old oven?

15-12

Cash flow estimate and replacement analysis

Barak Industries is considering replacing an old crane with a new one that will increase cash earnings before taxes by $120,000 per year. The new crane, which costs $240,000, will have an estimated useful life of 8 years and a salvage value of $32,000 at the end of that time. The new machine will be depreciated using a 5-year MACRS class life. (The appropriate MACRS depreciation percentages for a 5-year class life are these: Year 1 = 20%; Year 2 = 32%; Year 3 = 19%; Year 4 = 12%; Year 5 = 11%; and Year 6 = 6%.) The old crane currently has a book value of $80,000 and a remaining life of 8 years. It is being depreciated by $10,000 per year toward a zero salvage value using the straight line method. The marginal tax rate is 40 percent for Barak Industries. If replaced, the old crane can be sold now for $60,000.

a. What is the initial cash outlay required for the new crane?

b. What are the after-tax operating cash flows that occur each year as a result of the replacement decision?

c. What is the after-tax cash flow from the salvage value of the new crane in Year 6?

d. If the firm's cost of capital is 18 percent, should the replacement be made?

15-13

CAPM approach to risk adjustments

Toledo Rubber Company has two divisions: (1) the Tire Division, which manufactures tires for new automobiles, and (2) the Recap Division, which manufactures recapping materials that are sold to independent tire recapping shops throughout the United States. Since auto manufacturing moves up and down with the general economy, the Tire Division's earnings contribution to Toledo's stock price is highly correlated with returns on most other stocks. If the Tire Division were operated as a separate company, its beta coefficient would be about 1.60. The sales and profits of the Recap Division, on the other hand, tend to be countercyclical, as recap sales boom when people cannot afford to buy new tires. The Recap Division's beta is estimated to be 0.40. Approximately 75 percent of Toledo's corporate assets are invested in the Tire Division and 25 percent in the Recap Division.

Currently, the rate of interest on Treasury securities is 7 percent, and the expected rate of return on an average share of stock is 12 percent. Toledo uses only common equity capital, and it has no debt outstanding.

a. What is the required rate of return on Toledo's stock?

b. What discount rate should be used to evaluate capital budgeting projects in each division? Explain your answer fully, and in the process illustrate your answer with a project that costs $104,322, has a 10-year life, and provides after-tax cash flows of $20,000 per year.

15-14

Capital budgeting considering inflation

The Stanton-Karp Company is considering an average-risk investment in a mineral water spring project that has a cost of $125,000. The project will produce 1,000 cases of mineral water per year indefinitely. The current sales price is $125 per case, and the cost per case is $100. (Assume that all costs are *variable*; that is, all costs will vary directly with sales. Assume also that the price per case and cost per case are in constant dollars; that is, t = 0 dollars.) The firm is taxed at a rate of 40 percent. Inflation is assumed to be 5 percent per year, indefinitely, affecting all sales and costs equally, including the company's cost of capital. The firm's nominal cost of capital is 15 percent (a real rate of return plus an inflation premium). Assume that cash flows consist only of after-tax profits because the spring has an indefinite life and will not be depreciated.

a. What is the company's cost of capital in real terms?

b. Should the firm accept the project? (*Hint:* The project is a perpetuity, so you must use the formula for a perpetuity to find the NPV.)

15-15

Capital budgeting
considering inflation

The Adams-Clarke Company is evaluating an average-risk capital project that has a 4-year economic life and a 3-year MACRS class life. The initial net investment outlay (at t = 0) is $18,800. The expected end-of-year cash flows, expressed in t = 0 dollars (in other words, in constant dollars) are listed below:

	Year 1	Year 2	Year 3	Year 4
Revenues	$28,000	$28,000	$28,000	$28,000
Operating costs (excluding depreciation)	21,500	21,500	21,500	21,500
Depreciation	6,204	8,460	2,820	1,316

The firm has a marginal tax rate of 40 percent. Adams-Clarke's current cost of capital is 12 percent, which includes an inflation premium of 6 percent. Should the firm accept this project? (*Hints:* After-tax depreciation must be added to the firm's after-tax cash earnings to arrive at the firm's net cash flow. Also, since you are given *real* cash flows above, recognize that you can use the equation in Step 1 of the chapter discussion and find $k_r = k_n - i$.)

Solution to Self-Test Problem

ST-1 First determine the net cash outflow at t = 0:

Purchase price	($8,000)
Sale of old machine	2,500
Tax on sale of old machine	(160)[a]
Net working capital	(1,500)[b]
Total investment	($7,160)

[a]The market value is $2,500 − $2,100 = $400 above the book value. Thus, there is a $400 recapture of depreciation, and WNP would have to pay 0.40($400) = $160 in taxes.
[b]The change in net working capital is a $2,000 increase in current assets minus a $500 increase in current liabilities, or $1,500.

Now examine the annual operating cash inflows:

Sales increase	$1,000
Cost decrease	1,500
Pretax operating revenue increase	$2,500

$$\text{After-tax operating revenue increase} = \$2,500(1 - T)$$
$$= \$2,500(0.60)$$
$$= \$1,500.$$

Depreciation:

	1	2	3	4	5	6
New[a]	$1,600	$2,560	$1,520	$ 960	$ 880	$ 480
Old	350	350	350	350	350	350
Change	$1,250	$2,210	$1,170	$ 610	$ 530	$ 130
Depreciation tax savings[b]	$ 500	$ 884	$ 468	$ 244	$ 212	$ 52

[a]Depreciation expense each year equals depreciable basis times the MACRS factors of 0.20 for Year 1, 0.32 for Year 2, 0.19 for Year 3, 0.12 for Year 4, 0.11 for Year 5, and 0.06 for Year 6.
[b]Depreciation tax savings = Δ Depreciation(T).

Now recognize that, at the end of Year 6, WNP will recover its net working capital investment of $1,500, and it will also receive $800 from the sale of the replacement machine. However, the firm will have to pay 0.40($800) = $320 in taxes on the sale of the machine since it had been depreciated to a zero book value.

Finally, place all the cash flows on a time line:

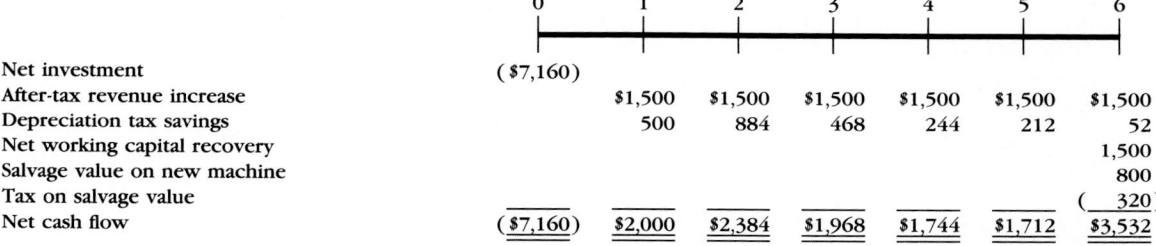

	0	1	2	3	4	5	6
Net investment	($7,160)						
After-tax revenue increase		$1,500	$1,500	$1,500	$1,500	$1,500	$1,500
Depreciation tax savings		500	884	468	244	212	52
Net working capital recovery							1,500
Salvage value on new machine							800
Tax on salvage value							(320)
Net cash flow	($7,160)	$2,000	$2,384	$1,968	$1,744	$1,712	$3,532

The net present value of this incremental cash flow stream, when discounted at 15 percent, is $1,051. Thus the replacement should be made.

Long-Term Financing

In Part IV we discussed means by which a firm can identify and evaluate long-term investment opportunities. Now we will identify the primary types of long-term capital used to finance those investments. In Chapters 16, 17, and 18 we examine the characteristics of long-term debt, preferred stock, common stock, and hybrid financing. The hybrid financing chapter includes discussions of leasing, warrants, convertibles, and options. Portions of Chapters 16 and 17 explain the determination of bond and stock values.

Bonds and Preferred Stock

O B J E C T I V E S

After reading this chapter, you should be able to:

▶ Calculate the value of a bond with annual or semiannual interest payments.

▶ Explain why the market value of an outstanding fixed-rate bond will fall when interest rates rise on new bonds of equal risk.

▶ Calculate the yield to maturity on a bond.

▶ Define common bond terms, specify bond contract features, and list major types of bonds, including recent innovations.

▶ Explain the importance of bond ratings and the differences between bond yields over time.

▶ List the major characteristics of term loans.

▶ Define preferred stock, specify how it differs from bonds, and describe its typical provisions.

DECISION IN FINANCE

THE BLUFF-AND-THREAT CALL GAMBIT

How can a borrower, who in the 1980s issued high-interest-rate non-refundable debt, get bondholders to relinquish their high-yielding investments in exchange for lower yielding debt? Some corporate borrowers, along with a number of Wall Street investment banking firms, have been using a strategy that is very common to the game of poker — bluffing — but they have elevated it to an even higher level.

In the 1980s, investors, including many pension fund managers and insurance companies, bought high-interest-rate debt believing that it could not be called easily. Since that time, however, interest rates have fallen sharply, leaving corporate borrowers frantic to rid themselves of this high-cost debt. Obviously, the bondholders would not willingly give up their investments; they enjoy earning 10 percent or more in an 8 percent market.

Corporate borrowers have turned to Wall Street for help, and some have been successful at prying high-yielding investments away from bondholders through a strong-arm maneuver called STAC (simultaneous tender [offer] and call). This has pension fund managers in an uproar.

Normally, the nonrefundable debt to which we refer cannot be called (or redeemed) from investors by using proceeds from additional debt

issues — the bonds can only be called through a "cash call," where money is raised from stock offerings, internally generated funds, or selling firm assets. Bond investors use the jargon "clean, or segregated money" to refer to a cash call.

However, a STAC works differently. In a STAC, the corporate borrower says, "Turn over your bonds to us voluntarily, and you'll get a little extra money. Fight us, and we've got enough money to cash-call them anyway." The bondholder must then determine whether the borrower is bluffing — and the stakes are quite high. A Federal Reserve economist estimated that U.S. corporations have issued $50 billion in nonrefundable bonds that are now cash-callable. According to Morgan Stanley, at least $12 billion of those bonds are prime STAC candidates with coupons of at least 10 percent.

The Retirement System of Alabama was one outraged bondholder who was approached, in the summer of 1992, with a STAC for May Department Stores' 10¾ percent bonds, maturing in 2018. The Alabama fund owned about half of the issue, worth approximately $140 million. The fund's CEO, Dr. David G. Bronner, was repeatedly approached by Morgan Stanley representatives stating that May was going to cash-call the bonds but that May would offer an extra $2.50 for each $1,000 of the fund's bonds "as a good-faith gesture" if it voluntarily turned over the bonds.

As you read this chapter, consider the definitions associated with a bond and its accompanying indenture. What are the bondholders' rights? What are the corporate borrowers' rights? What would you do if you were in the same situation as this pension fund's CEO? Is the company bluffing, or does it have enough money to cash-call the issue?

Most firms find it both necessary and desirable to use long-term debt financing, and some also use preferred stock. These both provide a fixed income to investors. There are many types of fixed-income securities: marketable and nonmarketable, secured and unsecured, convertible and nonconvertible, and so on. Different groups of investors prefer different types of securities, and their preferences change over time. An astute financial manager knows how to package securities at a given point in time to make them appealing to the greatest possible number of potential investors, thereby keeping the firm's cost of capital to a minimum. In this chapter we analyze the three most important types of *fixed-income securities* — bonds, term loans, and preferred stocks — and we discuss how the values of bonds and preferred stock are determined in the marketplace. Later chapters deal with other types of long-term capital.

Bonds

bond

A long-term debt instrument.

A **bond** is a long-term promissory note issued by a business or governmental unit; it is a contract under which a borrower agrees to make payments of interest and principal, on specific dates, to the holder of the bond. A bond issue is generally advertised, offered to the general public, and typically sold to many different investors. Indeed, thousands of individual and institutional investors may purchase bonds when a firm sells a bond issue, whereas there is usually only one lender in the case of a term loan, as we shall see later in this chapter. There are a number of different types of bonds, the more important of which are discussed in this chapter. We will start by looking at a standard, fixed-rate bond (often called a "plain vanilla" bond), and we will explain how the value of such bonds is determined. To illustrate, assume that on January 2, 1994, Carter Chemical Company borrowed $50 million by selling 50,000 individual bonds for $1,000 each. Carter received the $50 million, and it promised to pay the bondholders annual interest and to repay the $50 million on a specified date. The lenders (investors) were willing to pay $50 million for the bonds, so the value of the bond issue was $50 million. To see just how bond value is established — both initially and later in the secondary market — we need to define some terms:

coupon payment

The specified dollar interest paid each period, generally each six months, on a bond.

coupon interest rate

The stated annual rate of interest on a bond.

maturity date

A specified date on which the par value of a bond must be repaid.

original maturity

The number of years to maturity at the time a bond is issued.

call provision

A provision in a bond contract that gives the issuer the right to pay off the bonds under specified terms prior to the stated maturity date.

1. **Par value.**   The *par value* is the stated face value of the bond; it is usually set at $1,000, although multiples of $1,000 (for example, $5,000) are often used. The par value generally represents the amount of money the firm borrows and promises to repay at some future date.

2. **Coupon interest rate.**   The bond requires the issuer to pay a specified number of dollars of interest each year (or, more typically, each six months). When this **coupon payment,** as it is called, is divided by the par value, the result is the **coupon interest rate.** For example, Carter's bonds have a $1,000 par value, and they pay a $90 coupon payment each year. The bond's coupon interest rate is, therefore, $90/$1,000 = 9 percent. The $90 is the yearly "rent" on the $1,000 loan. This payment, which is fixed at the time the bond is issued, remains in force, by contract, during the life of the bond. Incidentally, some time ago, most bonds literally had a number of small (½- by 2-inch) dated coupons attached to them, and on the interest payment date, the owner would clip off the coupon for that date and either cash it at his or her bank or mail it to the company's paying agent, who then mailed back a check for the interest. A 30-year, semiannual bond would start with 60 coupons, whereas a 5-year annual payment bond would start with only 5 coupons. Today most bonds are *registered*—no physical coupons are involved, and interest checks are mailed automatically to the registered owners of the bonds. Even so, people continue to use the terms *coupon* and *coupon interest rate* when discussing registered bonds.

3. **Maturity date.**   Bonds generally have a specified **maturity date** on which the par value must be repaid. Carter's bonds, which were issued on January 2, 1994, will mature on January 1, 2009; thus, they had a 15-year maturity at the time they were issued. Most bonds have **original maturities** (the maturity at the time the bond is issued) of from 10 to 40 years, but any maturity is legally permissible.[1] Of course, the effective maturity of a bond declines each year after it has been issued. Thus, Carter's bonds had a 15-year original maturity, but in 1995 they will have a 14-year maturity, and so on.

4. **Call provision.**   Many bonds have a provision whereby the issuer may pay them off prior to maturity. This feature is known as a **call provision,** and it is discussed in detail later in this chapter. If a bond is callable, and if interest rates in the economy decline, then the company can sell a new issue of low-interest-rate bonds and use the proceeds to retire the old, high-interest-rate issue, just as a homeowner can refinance a home mortgage.

---

[1]When Tennessee Valley Authority (TVA), a federally owned utility, sold $1 billion of *50-year* bonds in April 1992, it became the first U.S. issuer in decades to sell bonds with such a long original maturity. Since then, other large issuers have followed TVA's example. Among these are Boeing, Conrail, Texaco, and Ford. In July 1993, Walt Disney Company and Coca-Cola surprised investors by offering *100-year* bonds, the first debt with such a long maturity since the late 1800s. In each case the attraction, for the issuer, has been locking in low long-term rates. (It is interesting to note that the U.S. government has been doing exactly the opposite. As mentioned in Chapter 4, in early 1993 the U.S. Treasury announced a plan to *reduce* the government's reliance on 30-year bonds and issue more U.S. Treasury securities with original maturities of less than three years.)

5. **New issues versus outstanding bonds.**   As we shall see, a bond's market price is determined primarily by its coupon interest payments—the higher the coupon, other things held constant, the higher the market price of the bond. At the time a bond is issued, the coupon is generally set at a level that will cause the market price of the bond to equal its par value. If a lower coupon were set, investors simply would not be willing to pay $1,000 for the bond, while if a higher coupon were set, it would be so attractive, that investors would bid its price up over $1,000. Investment bankers can, generally, judge quite precisely the coupon rate that will cause a bond to sell at its $1,000 par value.

A bond that has just been issued is known as a *new issue.* (*The Wall Street Journal* classifies a bond as a new issue for about one month after it has first been issued.) Once the bond has been on the market for a while, it is classified as an *outstanding bond,* also called a *seasoned issue.* Although newly issued bonds generally sell very close to par, the prices of outstanding bonds may vary widely from par. Coupon interest payments are constant, so when economic conditions change, a bond with a $90 coupon that sold at par originally will sell for more or less than $1,000 thereafter.

Self-Test

Explain the following terms: (1) par value, (2) coupon payment, (3) coupon interest rate, (4) maturity date, (5) call provision.

Why is the coupon on a newly issued bond generally set at a level that will cause the market price of the bond to equal its par value?

Valuation of Bonds

In Chapters 14 and 15 we saw that the value of a capital budgeting project is the sum of its discounted net cash flows. What is true for the valuation of real assets is also true for financial asset valuation. In other words, the value of a financial asset—a bond, a share of preferred stock, or a share of common stock—is equal to the cash flows provided by the security discounted back to the present.

Since a bond calls for the payment of a specified amount of interest for a stated number of years, and for the repayment of the par value on the bond's maturity date, the bond's cash flows are represented by an annuity plus a lump sum, and its value is found as the present value of this cash flow stream. The following equation is used to find a bond's value:

$$\text{Value} = V_B = \sum_{t=1}^{n} I \frac{1}{(1 + k_d)^t} + M \frac{1}{(1 + k_d)^n} \qquad (16\text{-}1)$$

$$= I(\text{PVIFA}_{k_d,n}) + M(\text{PVIF}_{k_d,n}).$$

Here:

I = dollars of interest paid each year = Coupon interest rate × Par value.[2]

M = the par value, or maturity value, which typically is $1,000.

k_d = the appropriate rate of interest on the bond, or the "going rate" on new bonds with this degree of risk.[3]

n = the number of years until the bond matures; n declines each year after the bond is issued.

We can use Equation 16-1 to find the value of Carter Chemical Company's bonds, which we have already described. Each holder of a $1,000 bond would be entitled to annual interest of $90. The bonds are due to mature in 15 years, at which time the maturity value of $1,000 will be paid to each bondholder. Simply substitute $90 for I, $1,000 for M, and the values for PVIFA and PVIF at 9 percent, Period 15 into the equation:

$$V_B = I(PVIFA_{9\%,15}) + M(PVIF_{9\%,15})$$

$$= \$90(8.0607) + \$1,000(0.2745)$$

$$= \$725.46 + \$274.50$$

$$= \$999.96 \approx \$1,000.$$

Figure 16-1 gives a graphic view of the bond valuation process.[4]

If k_d remained constant at 9 percent, what would the value of the bond be 1 year after it was issued? We can find this value using the same equation, but now the term to maturity is only 14 years; that is, n = 14:

$$V_B = I(PVIFA_{9\%,14}) + M(PVIF_{9\%,14})$$

$$= \$90(7.7862) + \$1,000(0.2992)$$

$$= \$999.96 \approx \$1,000.$$

This same result will hold for every year as long as the appropriate interest rate (the going rate) for the bond remains constant at 9 percent.

---

[2]Since most bonds actually pay interest semiannually rather than annually, we will modify this equation slightly in the next section. However, for simplicity of calculations, we will assume annual interest payments initially.

[3]The appropriate interest rate was discussed in Chapter 4. The bond's riskiness, liquidity, and years to maturity, as well as supply and demand conditions in the capital markets and expected inflation, all influence the nominal, or quoted, interest rate on a new bond.

[4]To solve for bond value with a financial calculator, enter n = 15, k = i = 9, PMT = 90, FV = 1000, then press the PV key to obtain the bond's value, $1,000. (Some calculators will show this as a negative number because this is what you have to *pay* to purchase the bond.) You can quickly calculate new values for the same bond (as we shall be doing shortly, using tables). For example, enter k = i = 12 (to override k = i = 9) and n = 14 (to override n = 15), then press PV again, and you have the value of the bond if the going rate increases to 12 percent over the next year. Slight rounding differences are likely, but the calculator is more accurate than the tables.

Figure 16-1   Time Line for Carter Chemical Company Bonds

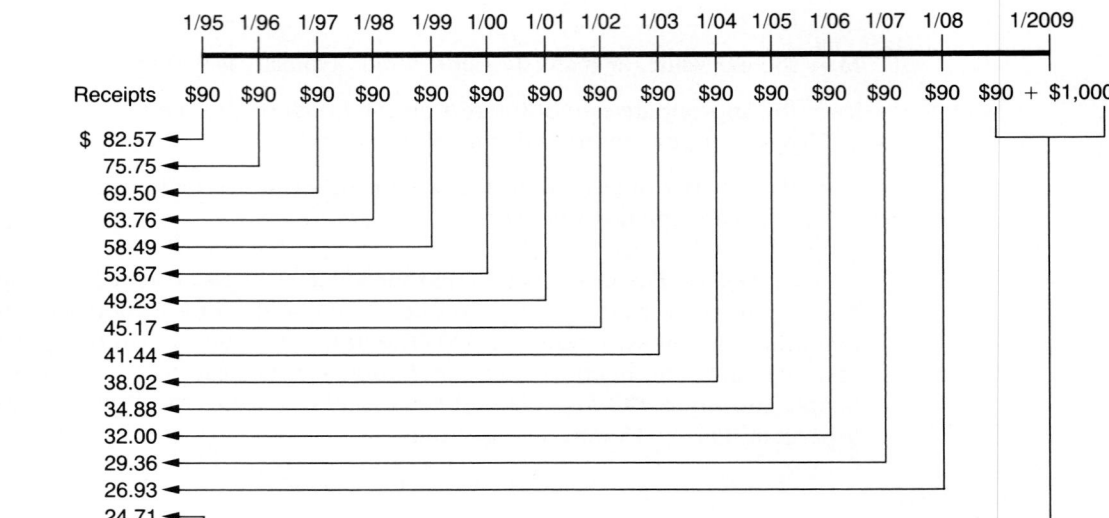

A bond's value is equal to the sum of its future interest payments and its $1,000 maturity value discounted at an appropriate rate of interest, given the bond's risk. For example, the discounted cash flows from a 15-year, 9 percent Carter Chemical Company bond purchased in January 1994 totaled approximately $1,000; the first interest payment of $90 was discounted for one year to a present value of $82.57, the second interest payment of $90 was discounted for two years to a present value of $75.75, and so on.

Now suppose instead that interest rates in the economy rose during the year after the sale of Carter's 9 percent bonds, and as a result k_d increased from 9 to 12 percent.[5] Of course, the interest and principal payments on the bonds are fixed, but now a new PVIFA and PVIF would be used in Equation 16-1, and these should reflect a k_d of 12 percent and n equal to 14. Thus, the bond's value would be $801.14 if investors require a 12 percent return:

$$V_B = \$90(PVIFA_{12\%,14}) + \$1,000(PVIF_{12\%,14})$$
$$= \$90(6.6282) + \$1,000(0.2046)$$
$$= \$596.54 + \$204.60$$
$$= \$801.14.$$

The bond would sell at a discount—that is, at a price below its par value.

The arithmetic of the bond's price decrease should be clear, but what is the logic behind it? The reason for the decrease is simple. Carter's bondholders

[5]Long-term interest rates do not normally change by three full percentage points during a single year; this is merely an illustration. In fact, had Carter's bonds been issued with a 9 percent coupon *any number of years earlier*—now having 14 years until maturity—the market value would be the same as that calculated here, assuming a going rate of 12 percent.

notice that other companies are issuing new bonds with the same risk characteristics as Carter's outstanding bonds but with higher rates of return. Carter's bondholders, eager to receive the higher yield, sell Carter's 9 percent bonds in order to purchase the new 12 percent bonds. The increased supply of Carter's bonds on the market means that the price of the bonds will fall. As investors continue selling Carter's bonds, the price will be further depressed until, at the price of $801.14, Carter's bonds will yield the same rate of return to an investor as the new 12 percent bonds which are selling at par.

If interest rates were to remain constant at 12 percent for the next 14 years (which is not very likely), what would happen to the price of this Carter bond? It would rise gradually from $801.14 to $1,000 at maturity, when Carter must redeem each bond for $1,000. This point can be illustrated by calculating the value of the bond 2 years after issue, when it has 13 years to maturity:

$$V_B = \$90(PVIFA_{12\%,13}) + \$1,000(PVIF_{12\%,13})$$

$$= \$90(6.4235) + \$1,000(0.2292)$$

$$= \$578.12 + \$229.20$$

$$= \$807.32$$

The value of the bond will have risen from $801.14 to $807.32, or by $6.18. If you were to calculate the value of the bond at other future dates, while holding k_d constant at 12 percent, you would see that the price would continue to rise as the maturity date approached.

Current yield was defined in Chapter 2 as the annual interest payment on a bond divided by its current (beginning) market price. But notice that if you had purchased Carter's bond at a price of $801.14 and sold it a year later (with k_d still at 12 percent), you would also have had a capital gain of $6.18. We can calculate a *capital gains yield* by dividing the dollar gain by the bond's beginning price. The total rate of return, or yield, is calculated as follows:

$$\text{Current yield} = \$90.00/\$801.14 = 0.1123 = 11.23\%$$

$$\text{Capital gains yield} = \$6.18/\$801.14 = 0.0077 = \underline{0.77\%}$$

$$\text{Total rate of return, or yield} = \$96.18/\$801.14 = 0.1201 \approx \underline{12.00\%}$$

Now let us look at a very different scenario. If interest rates had *fallen* from 9 to 6 percent when Carter Chemical Company's bonds had 14 years to maturity, the value of each of Carter's bonds would have risen to $1,278.85:

$$V_B = \$90(PVIFA_{6\%,14}) + \$1,000(PVIF_{6\%,14})$$

$$= \$90(9.2950) + \$1,000(0.4423)$$

$$= \$836.55 + \$442.30$$

$$= \$1,278.85.$$

In this case, *the bond would sell at a premium* above its par value. If interest rates remain at 6 percent for the next 14 years, the value of the bond would fall gradually from $1,278.85 to $1,000 at maturity. Two years after Carter's bond was issued (n = 13), if the going rate remains at 6 percent, Carter's bond would have a market value of $1,265.54:

$$V_B = \$90(PVIFA_{6\%,13}) + \$1,000(PVIF_{6\%,13})$$

$$= \$90(8.8527) + \$1,000(0.4688)$$

$$= \$796.74 + \$468.80$$

$$= \$1,265.54.$$

This represents a *capital loss* of $13.31, which partially offsets the relatively high coupon of 9 percent. Total rate of return, or yield, is calculated as follows:

$$\text{Current yield} = \$90/\$1,278.85 = 0.0704 = 7.04\%$$

$$\text{Capital gains yield} = -\$13.31/\$1,278.85 = -0.0104 = \underline{-1.04\%}$$

$$\text{Total rate of return, or yield} = \$76.69/\$1,278.85 = 0.0600 = \underline{6.00\%}$$

Figure 16-2 graphs the value of the bond over time, assuming that the going rate either remains constant at 9 percent, rises to 12 percent, or falls to 6 percent one year after the issue date and, in the case of the 12 and 6 percent rates, also stays constant after the initial change. Of course, if interest rates do *not* remain constant, and they rarely do, the price of the bond will fluctuate. Regardless of interest rate changes, however, the bond's price will approach $1,000 as the maturity date comes nearer (barring bankruptcy, in which case the bond's value might drop to zero).

Figure 16-2 illustrates the following key points:

1. Whenever the going rate of interest, k_d, is equal to the coupon rate, a bond will sell at its par value.

2. Interest rates do change over time, but the coupon rate remains fixed after the bond has been issued. Whenever the going rate of interest is *greater than* the coupon rate, a bond's price will fall *below* its par value. Such a bond is called a **discount bond.**

3. Whenever the going rate of interest is *less than* the coupon rate, a bond's price will rise *above* its par value. Such a bond is called a **premium bond.**

4. Thus, an *increase* in interest rates will cause the price of an outstanding bond to *fall*, whereas a *decrease* in rates will cause it to *rise.*

5. The market value of a bond will always approach its par value as its maturity date approaches, provided the firm does not go bankrupt.

6. In general, *the longer the period until a bond's maturity date, the more sensitive its market value will be to changes in the going rate of interest.* This follows from Point 5.

discount bond

A bond that sells below its par value; occurs whenever the going rate of interest *rises above* the coupon rate.

premium bond

A bond that sells above its par value; occurs whenever the going rate of interest *falls below* the coupon rate.

These points are very important, for they show that bondholders may suffer capital losses or realize capital gains, depending on whether interest rates rise or fall after the bond was purchased.

It is this risk which, in Chapters 4 and 9, was labeled *interest rate risk.* Note that investors holding U.S. Treasury bonds are subject to this risk as well. Remember also from Chapter 4 that investors will incorporate into the nominal, or quoted, interest rate (which we now call k_d) a maturity risk premium (MRP) in order to be compensated for this risk of a capital loss. In general, the pre-

Figure 16-2

Time Path of the Value of a 9% Coupon, $1,000 Par Value Bond when Interest Rates Are 6%, 9%, and 12%

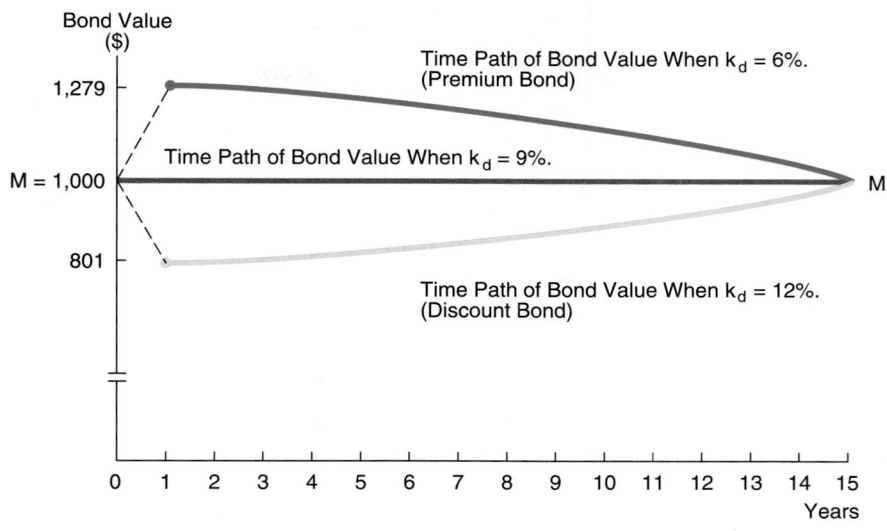

The value of a bond fluctuates in response to changes in the market interest rate on bonds with the same level of risk. When a bond's coupon rate is equal to the market rate of interest (the going rate) the bond sells at par. When the going rate falls below a bond's coupon rate, the bond sells above par. And when the going rate rises above a bond's coupon rate, the bond sells below par. This graph shows how the selling price of a 15-year, 9 percent bond with a par value of $1,000 will change if the going rate rises to 12 percent or falls to 6 percent the year after issue, *and remains at that level until maturity.* Note that as the bond's maturity date approaches, its value fluctuates less and less until it finally reaches par.

Note: The curves for 6% and 12% appear to be straight, but they actually have a slight bow.

mium has to be larger as the number of years until the bond's maturity becomes greater because long-term bonds have more interest rate risk.

What the preceding calculations have demonstrated is something that you were asked to take on faith in earlier chapters: *There is an inverse relationship between the market value of existing, fixed-rate bonds and interest rates;* you have just seen the mathematical proof of this statement.

Semiannual Interest

Although some bonds do pay interest annually, most actually pay interest semiannually. The same methodology discussed in Appendix 13A for other than annual compounding periods applies to the valuation of bonds when interest is paid twice each year. To evaluate bonds paying semiannual interest, we must modify the bond valuation model (Equation 16-1) as follows:

1.   Divide the annual coupon interest payment by 2 to determine the amount of interest paid every 6 months.

2.   Multiply the years to maturity, n, by 2 to determine the number of semiannual periods.

3.   Divide the annual interest rate, k_d, by 2 to determine the semiannual interest rate.

By making these changes, we arrive at the following equation for finding the value of a bond that pays semiannual interest:

$$V_B = \sum_{t=1}^{2n} \frac{I}{2} \frac{1}{(1 + k_d/2)^t} + M \frac{1}{(1 + k_d/2)^{2n}} \qquad (16\text{-}1a)$$

$$= I/2(\text{PVIFA}_{k_d/2,2n}) + M(\text{PVIF}_{k_d/2,2n}).$$

To illustrate, assume now that Carter's bond actually paid interest semiannually. Carter will pay \$45 interest per bond every 6 months rather than \$90 at the end of each year. Thus, each interest payment is only half as large, but there are twice as many of them. When the going rate of interest is 6 percent, and if we assume 13 years until maturity ($n = 13$), the value of this 13-year bond is found as follows:

$$V_B = \$45(\text{PVIFA}_{3\%,26}) + \$1,000(\text{PVIF}_{3\%,26})$$

$$= \$45(17.8768) + \$1,000(0.4637)$$

$$= \$804.46 + \$463.70$$

$$= \$1,268.16.$$

We had previously calculated the value of Carter's bond, with *annual* interest payments to be \$1,265.54, when $k_d = 6$ percent and when there are 13 years until maturity. The \$1,268.16 value with semiannual interest payments is slightly larger than \$1,265.54, the bond's value when interest is paid annually. The higher value occurs because interest payments are received somewhat faster.

When bonds pay interest semiannually, as in the above example, students sometimes want to discount the maturity value ($M = \$1,000$) at 6 percent over 13 periods, rather than at the correct 3 percent over 26 six-month periods. This is *incorrect*; logically, all cash flows in a given contract must be discounted on the same basis — semiannually in this instance. For consistency, bond traders *must* apply semiannual discounting to the maturity value, and they do.

Finding the Interest Rate on a Bond: Yield to Maturity (YTM)

yield to maturity (YTM)

The rate of return earned on a bond if it is bought at a given market price and held to maturity.

Suppose you were offered a 14-year, 9 percent, annual coupon, \$1,000 par value bond at a price of \$1,082.48. What rate of interest would you earn if you bought the bond and held it to maturity? This rate is defined as the bond's **yield to maturity (YTM),** and it is the interest rate discussed by bond traders when they talk about rates of return. To find the yield to maturity, you could solve Equation 16-1 for k_d:

$$V_B = \$1,082.48 = \frac{\$90}{(1 + k_d)^1} + \frac{\$90}{(1 + k_d)^2} + \cdots + \frac{\$90}{(1 + k_d)^{14}} + \frac{\$1,000}{(1 + k_d)^{14}}$$

$$= \$90(\text{PVIFA}_{k_d,14}) + \$1,000(\text{PVIF}_{k_d,14}).$$

Just as we did in finding the IRR for a project in Chapter 14, we can substitute values of PVIFA and PVIF into the equation until we find a rate that *just equates* the present market price of the bond with the present value of its future cash flows of interest and principal. (The YTM is, in fact, an internal rate of return.)

What would be a good interest rate to use as a starting point? First, from earlier discussions, we know that since the bond is selling at a premium over its par value ($1,082.48 versus $1,000), the bond's yield is *below* the 9 percent annual coupon rate. Therefore, we might try a rate of 7 percent. Substituting present value interest factors for 7 percent, we obtain

$$\$90(8.7455) + \$1,000(0.3878) = \$1,174.90 \neq \$1,082.48.$$

Our calculated bond value, $1,174.90, is *above* the actual market price, so the yield to maturity is *not* 7 percent. To lower the calculated value, we must *raise* the interest rate used in the process. Inserting present value interest factors for 8 percent, we obtain

$$V_B = \$90(8.2442) + \$1,000(0.3405)$$

$$= \$741.98 + \$340.50$$

$$= \$1,082.48.$$

This calculated value is exactly equal to the market price of the bond; thus 8 percent is the bond's yield to maturity.[6] Of course, the easiest way to find the yield to maturity of a bond is with a financial calculator.[7]

The yield to maturity is the total rate of return discussed earlier, and this rate of return is equal to the bond's coupon rate, if the bond is selling at par. If a bond is purchased at a price *other* than its par value, the YTM consists of the current yield plus either a positive capital gains yield (if the bond was purchased at a discount) or a negative capital gains yield (if the bond was purchased at a premium). Note also that a bond's yield to maturity changes whenever interest rates in the economy change, and this is almost daily. An investor who purchases a bond and holds it until maturity will receive the YTM that existed on the purchase date, but the bond's calculated YTM will change frequently between the purchase date and the maturity date.

Yield to Call (YTC)

If you purchased a bond that was callable and the company called it, you would not have the option of holding it until it matured, so the yield to maturity would not be earned. For example, if Carter's 9 percent coupon bonds were callable,

---

[6]A formula developed by R. J. Rodrigues can be used to find the approximate yield to maturity on a bond:

$$k_d = YTM = \frac{I + (M - V)/n}{(M + 2V)/3}.$$

In the situation where I = $90, M = $1,000, V = $1,082.48, and n = 14,

$$k_d = \frac{\$90 + (\$1,000 - \$1,082.48)/14}{(\$1,000 + \$2,164.96)/3} = 0.07972 = 7.972\%.$$

This is close to the exact value, 8 percent. This formula can also be used to obtain a starting point for the trial-and-error method.

[7]In the example given, enter PV = 1082.48 (or −1082.48), FV = 1000, PMT = 90, and n = 14. Then press k = i, and obtain 7.9996 ≈ 8 percent. If the bond pays semiannual interest, enter PMT = 45 and n = 28 (these values will override PMT = 90 and n = 14, if already entered); the calculator solves for k = i = 4.0047 percent ≈ 4 percent. Notice that semiannual interest gives a slightly higher YTM since 4.0047 percent is more than half of the 7.9996 percent calculated above.

and if interest rates fell from 9 percent to 6 percent, then the company could call in the bonds, replace them with 6 percent bonds, and save $90 - $60 = $30 interest per bond per year. This would be beneficial to the company, but not to its bondholders.

yield to call (YTC)

The rate of return earned on a bond if it is called before its maturity date.

If current interest rates are well below an outstanding bond's coupon rate, then a callable bond is likely to be called, and investors should estimate the expected rate of return on the bond as the **yield to call (YTC)** rather than as the yield to maturity. To calculate the YTC, you would need to solve this equation for k_d:

$$V_B = \sum_{t=1}^{n} I \frac{1}{(1 + k_d)^t} + \text{Call price} \frac{1}{(1 + k_d)^n} \qquad (16\text{-}2)$$

Here n is the number of years until the company can call the bond, call price is the price the company must pay in order to call the bond (it is often set equal to the par value plus one year's interest), and k_d is the YTC.

To illustrate the yield-to-call calculation, suppose Carter's bonds had a provision that the company could call the bonds, at the earliest, 5 years after the issue date at a price of $1,090. Suppose further that interest rates had fallen, such that one year after issuance k_d was 6 percent and the price of the bonds was $1,278.85. Here, by far the easiest way of finding the bond's YTC is with a financial calculator.[8] (You will *not* be asked to solve for YTC on a coupon bond with a regular calculator, merely to understand the concept. In the balance of this chapter, we assume that bonds are not callable, unless otherwise noted.) The YTC on Carter's bond, under the circumstances and terms described, would be 3.54 percent—this is the return you would earn if you bought the bond at a price of $1,278.85 and it was called 4 years later. Clearly, the 3.54 percent YTC is more relevant than the 6 percent YTM since it is likely that Carter will call the bond at the earliest possible date, barring any significant increase in market rates over the next 4 years.

? Self-Test

Explain the following equation:

$$V_B = I(\text{PVIFA}_{k_d,n}) + M(\text{PVIF}_{k_d,n}).$$

Explain what happens to the price of a bond if (1) interest rates rise above the bond's coupon rate or (2) interest rates fall below the bond's coupon rate.

How is the bond valuation equation changed to deal with bonds that have semiannual interest payments rather than annual interest payments?

Explain the following statement: "An investor who purchases a bond and holds it until maturity will receive the YTM that existed on the purchase date, but the bond's calculated YTM will change frequently between the date the bond is purchased and the time it matures."

---

[8]Enter into the financial calculator PV = 1278.85 (or -1278.85), FV = 1090, PMT = 90, n = 4. Then press k = i, and obtain a YTC of approximately 3.54 percent.

Would a bond be most likely to be called when the going rate of interest is above or below the bond's coupon? Explain.

Explain the general method used to calculate yield to call (YTC).

Funded Debt

funded debt

Long-term debt; "funding" means replacing short-term debt with securities of longer maturity.

Long-term debt is often called **funded debt,** and when a firm "funds" its debt, this means that it replaces short-term debt with securities of longer maturity. Funding does not imply that the firm places money with a trustee or other repository; it is simply part of the jargon of finance, and it means that the firm replaces short-term debt with long-term capital. Pacific Gas & Electric Company (PG&E) provides a good example of funding. PG&E has a continuous construction program, and it typically uses short-term debt to finance construction expenditures. Once short-term debt has built up to about $100 million, however, the company sells a stock or a bond issue, uses the proceeds to pay off (or fund) its bank loans, and starts the cycle again. There is a high fixed cost involved in selling stocks or long-term bonds, which makes it quite expensive to issue small amounts of these securities, and this makes the procedure followed by PG&E and other companies very logical.

 Self-Test

What is meant when it is said that a firm is funding its debt?

Specific Bond Contract Features

A firm's managers are concerned with both the effective cost of debt and any restrictions in debt contracts which might limit the firm's future flexibility. In this section, we will look at a number of such features.

In Chapter 1 we discussed *agency problems,* which relate to conflicts of interest among corporate stakeholders—stockholders, bondholders, and managers. Bondholders have a legitimate fear that once they lend money to a company and are "locked in" for up to 50 years, the company will take some action that is designed to benefit stockholders but that harms bondholders. For example, RJR Nabisco, when it was highly rated, sold 30-year bonds with a low coupon rate, and investors bought those bonds in spite of the low yield because of their low risk. Then, after the bonds had been sold, the company announced plans to issue a great deal more debt, increasing the expected rate of return to stockholders but also increasing the riskiness of the outstanding bonds. RJR's bonds fell 20 percent the week the announcement was made. Safeway Stores and a number of other companies have done the same thing, and their bondholders also lost heavily as the required yield on the bonds rose and drove the prices of the bonds down.

Bondholders attempt to reduce agency problems by use of legal restrictions designed to ensure, insofar as possible, that the company does nothing to cause the quality of its bonds to deteriorate after they have been issued. These legal restrictions are listed in the bond indenture.

Bond Indenture and Trustee

indenture

A formal agreement between the issuer of a bond and the bondholders.

trustee

An official who ensures that the bondholders' interests are protected and that the terms of the indenture are carried out.

restrictive covenant

A provision in a debt contract that constrains the actions of the borrower.

An **indenture** is a legal document that spells out the rights of both the bondholders and the issuing corporation. A **trustee** is an official (usually of a bank) who represents the bondholders and makes sure the terms of the indenture are carried out. The indenture may be several hundred pages in length, and it includes **restrictive covenants,** or specific constraints on the firm, which we will discuss in the next section. The trustee monitors the situation and, in the event that the issuer violates any provision in the indenture, takes appropriate action on behalf of the bondholders. Exactly what constitutes "appropriate action" varies with the circumstances. It might be that to insist on immediate compliance would result in bankruptcy, which in turn might lead to large losses for the bondholders. In such a case, the trustee may decide that the bondholders would be better served by giving the company a chance to work out its problems rather than by forcing it into bankruptcy.

The SEC approves indentures and makes sure that all indenture provisions are met before allowing a company to sell new securities to the public. The indentures of most larger corporations were actually written back in the 1930s or 1940s, and many issues of new bonds, all covered by this same indenture, have been sold through the years. The interest rates on the bonds, and perhaps their maturities, will change from issue to issue, but bondholders' protection as spelled out in the indenture will be the same for all bonds of a given type. Some of the more important provisions contained in most indentures are discussed in the following sections.

Restrictive Covenants

Restrictive covenants require the issuer of the bond to meet certain stated conditions. These provisions typically include (1) that debt not exceed a specific percentage of total capital; (2) that the current ratio be maintained above a specific level; (3) that the times-interest-earned ratio be kept above a given level, if the issuer is to sell additional bonds; and (4) that dividends not be paid on common stock unless earnings are maintained at a given level. Overall, these covenants are designed to protect bondholders by safeguarding the quality of their bonds. As with other provisions in the indenture, the trustee is responsible for making sure that the restrictive covenants are not violated or that violations are quickly corrected in the best interests of the bondholders.

Bond Repayment Provisions

sinking fund

A required annual payment designed to amortize a bond or preferred stock issue.

Sinking Fund.   A **sinking fund** is a provision that facilitates the orderly retirement of a bond issue (or, in some cases, an issue of preferred stock). Typically, the sinking fund provision requires the firm to retire a portion of the bond issue each year, but on rare occasions the firm may be required to deposit money with a trustee, who invests the funds and then uses the accumulated sum to retire the bonds when they mature. Sometimes the stipulated sinking fund payment is tied to sales or earnings of the current year, but usually it is a mandatory fixed amount. If it is mandatory, a failure to meet the sinking fund requirement causes the bond issue to be thrown into default, which may force the company into bankruptcy. Obviously, then, a sinking fund can constitute a dangerous cash drain on the firm.

In most cases, the firm is given the right to handle the sinking fund in either of two ways:

1. The company can call in for redemption, *at par value,* a certain percentage of the bonds each year. The bonds are numbered serially, and those called for redemption are determined by a lottery administered by the trustee.

2. The company may buy the required amount of bonds on the open market.

The firm will choose the least-cost method. If interest rates have risen, causing bond prices to fall, it will buy the bonds at a discount in the open market; if interest rates have fallen, it will call the bonds.

Although sinking funds are designed to protect bondholders by ensuring that an issue is retired in an orderly fashion, sinking funds will, at times, work to the detriment of bondholders. If, for example, the bond carries a 14 percent interest rate and if similar bonds are yielding 10 percent, the bond will sell above par. A sinking fund call at par would greatly disadvantage the bondholders whose securities were called for retirement purposes, as this would require an investor to give up $140 of interest per year and then to reinvest in a bond that pays only $100.

On balance, however, bonds that provide for a sinking fund are regarded as being safer than those without such a provision, so they are offered initially on a lower-yield basis than otherwise similar bonds without sinking funds.

Call Provision.   Earlier in this chapter we defined a call provision, which gives the issuer the right to pay off the bonds under specified terms prior to the stated maturity date. If it is used, the call provision generally states that the company must pay the bondholder an amount greater than the par value for the bond, with this additional sum being termed the **call premium.** The call premium is typically set equal to one year's interest if the bond is called during the first year, with the premium declining at a constant rate each year thereafter. For example, the call premium on a $1,000 par value, 10-year, 9 percent coupon bond would generally be $90 if it were called during the first year, $81 if it were called during the second year (calculated by reducing the $90 call premium by one-tenth annually), and so on. However, bonds are often not callable for several years (generally 5 to 10) after they are issued; this is known as a *deferred call.*

Suppose a company sold bonds when interest rates were relatively high, such as in the early 1980s. Provided the issue is callable, the company could sell a new issue of low-yielding securities if interest rates drop. It could then use the proceeds to retire the high-yield issue and thus reduce its interest expenses. This procedure is called a *refunding operation.*

The call privilege is valuable to the firm but potentially detrimental to the investor, especially if the bond is issued in a period when interest rates are

call premium

The amount in excess of par value that a company must pay when it calls a security.

cyclically high. Accordingly, the interest rate on a new issue of callable bonds will exceed that on a new issue of noncallable bonds, typically by 0.25 to 0.375 percent. (Note that the call for refunding purposes is quite different from the call for sinking fund purposes. The call for sinking fund purposes generally has no call premium, but only a small percentage of the issue is callable each year.)

From mid-1992 to mid-1993, U.S. corporations have rushed to load up on long-term debt, as interest rates have headed down across the board. With each new decline in the 30-year U.S. Treasury bond rate, to which corporate long-term yields are linked, another wave of corporate notes and bonds has flooded the market. Much of this debt is intended to replace older, higher-yielding debt. A study by Fitch Investors Services and Andrew Kalotay Associates in early May 1993 reported a record $19 billion in bond calls for the first quarter of 1993 and an expected $97 billion in calls for the remainder of the year.[9] This would represent an increase in corporate bond calls of 73 percent over 1992—also a year of declining interest rates and an avalanche of bond calls.

Although the rules are more complex in the municipal bond market and refinancings, therefore, are more difficult, hundreds of cities, including Boston, Buffalo, and San Francisco, have been able to plug budget deficits and reduce the need for tax increases by issuing new debt and paying off high-yielding bonds originally sold in the mid-1980s. In March 1992, Towson State University, the largest liberal arts school in the Baltimore area, paid off $44 million of tax-exempt bonds with interest rates as high as 14 percent after having sold new bonds with coupons of only 6.5 percent. The windfall of nearly $800,000 a year may be used to cut each student's annual dormitory bill by at least $100. Also in 1992, St. Alexius Hospital of Bismarck, North Dakota, cut its annual interest expense by $325,000 by slashing its borrowing cost from 10 percent to just under 7 percent.

From an investor's point of view, having a bond called—especially if the investor had reason to think the bond could not be called—can be financially devastating. Every dollar saved on lower interest costs by a corporation or municipality is a dollar lost by some individual bondholder, pension fund, or insurance company. (Incidentally, most Treasury bonds cannot be called.) Bondholders sometimes fight for their right to hang on to high-yielding bonds—one such example is given in the "Decision in Finance" boxed feature in this chapter.

? *Self-Test*

What are some of the typical restrictive covenants found in a bond indenture?

What are the two ways a sinking fund can be handled? Which method will be chosen by the firm if interest rates have risen? If interest rates have fallen?

Are securities that provide for a sinking fund regarded as being riskier than those without this type of provision? Explain.

Why is a call provision advantageous to the issuer of a bond?

---

[9]The study only looked at so-called *investment grade* bonds, which means those of the highest quality, BBB or better. Bond ratings will be covered in greater detail later in this chapter.

Types of Bonds

Mortgage Bonds

mortgage bond

A bond backed by fixed assets. *First mortgage bonds* are senior in priority to claims of *second mortgage bonds.*

Under a **mortgage bond** the corporation pledges certain real assets as security for the bond. To illustrate, suppose that in 1993 the Collier Corporation needed $15 million to purchase land and to build a major research and development center. Bonds in the amount of $7 million, secured by a mortgage on the property, were issued. (The remaining $8 million was financed with equity funds.) If Collier defaults on the bonds, the bondholders can foreclose on the property and sell it to satisfy their claims.

If Collier chooses to, it can issue *second mortgage bonds* secured by the same $15 million plant. In the event of liquidation, the holders of these second mortgage bonds would have a claim against the property only after the first mortgage bondholders had been paid off in full. Thus second mortgages are sometimes called *junior mortgages* because they are junior in priority to the claims of senior mortgages, or *first mortgage bonds.*

The first mortgage bond indentures of most major corporations were written 20, 30, 40, or more years ago. These indentures are generally "open ended," meaning that new bonds may be issued from time to time under the existing indenture. However, the amount of new bonds that can be issued is almost always limited by clauses in the indenture to a specified percentage of the firm's total "bondable property," which generally includes all plant and equipment. For example, Savannah Electric can issue first mortgage bonds totaling up to 60 percent of its fixed assets. If its fixed assets total $1 billion and if it had $500 million of first mortgage bonds outstanding, it could, by the property test, issue another $100 million of first mortgage bonds (60 percent of $1 billion = $600 million).

At times, Savannah Electric has been unable to issue any new first mortgage bonds because of another indenture provision — its times-interest-earned (TIE) ratio was below 2.5, the minimum coverage that it must maintain to sell new bonds. Savannah Electric passed the property test but failed the coverage test, so it could not issue first mortgage bonds, and it had to finance with junior securities. Since first mortgage bonds carry lower rates of interest than junior long-term debt, this restriction was a costly one.

Savannah Electric's neighbor, Georgia Power Company, has more flexibility under its indenture; its interest coverage requirement is only 2.0. In hearings before the Georgia Public Service Commission, it was suggested that Savannah Electric should change its indenture coverage to 2.0 so that it could issue more first mortgage bonds. However, this was simply not possible; the holders of the outstanding bonds would have to approve the change, and it is inconceivable that they would vote for a change that would seriously weaken their position.

Debentures

debenture

A bond that is not secured by a mortgage on specific property.

A **debenture** is an unsecured bond, and as such it provides no lien against specific property as security for the obligation. Debenture holders are, therefore, general creditors whose claims are protected by property not otherwise pledged. In practice, the use of debentures depends on the nature of the firm's assets and on its general credit strength. An extremely strong company, such as AT&T, will tend to use debentures — it simply does not need to put up property as security for its debt. Debentures are also issued by companies in industries in which it would not be practical to provide security through a mortgage on fixed assets. Examples of such industries are the large mail-order houses and commercial banks, which characteristically hold most of their assets in the form of inventory or loans, neither of which is satisfactory security for a mortgage bond.[10]

Subordinated Debentures

subordinated debenture

A bond which, in the event of bankruptcy and liquidation, has a claim on assets only after the senior debt has been paid off.

The term *subordinate* means "below," or "inferior to," and, in the event of bankruptcy, subordinated debt has claims on assets only after senior debt, such as mortgage bonds, has been paid off. Debentures may be subordinated either to designated notes payable (usually bank loans) or to all other debt. In the event of liquidation or reorganization, holders of **subordinated debentures** cannot be paid until all senior debt, as named in the debentures' indenture, has been paid. Precisely how subordination works, and how it strengthens the position of senior debtholders, is explained in Appendix 20A.

Other Types of Bonds

convertible bond

A bond that is exchangeable, at the option of the holder, for common stock of the issuing firm.

Several other types of bonds are used sufficiently often to warrant mention. First, **convertible bonds** are securities that are convertible into shares of common stock, at a fixed price, at the option of the bondholder. Basically, convertibles provide investors with a chance to receive capital gains from a rising stock price in exchange for a lower coupon rate, while the issuing firm gets the advantage of that lower rate. Bonds issued with warrants are similar to convertibles. *Warrants* are options that permit the holder to buy stock for a stated price, thereby providing a capital gain if the price of the stock rises. Like convertibles, bonds that are issued with warrants carry lower coupon rates than do straight bonds. Warrants and convertibles are discussed in detail in Chapter 18.

income bond

A bond that pays interest only if the interest is earned.

Income bonds pay interest only when the interest is earned. This provides the issuer some flexibility in that these securities cannot bankrupt a company. However, from an investor's perspective they are clearly riskier than regular bonds and must, therefore, offer a higher yield. Firms that issue income bonds are generally quite weak and are often in reorganization.

indexed (purchasing power) bond

A bond that has interest payments based on an inflation index so as to protect the holder from inflation.

Another type of bond that has been discussed in the United States but not yet used here to any extent is the **indexed,** or **purchasing power, bond,** which is popular in Brazil, Israel, and a few other countries plagued by high rates of inflation. The interest rate paid on these bonds is based on an inflation index such as the consumer price index (CPI), so the interest paid rises automatically when the inflation rate rises, thus protecting the bondholders against

---

[10]In the late 1980s and early 1990s, as banks were getting into financial difficulty which required them to raise more nondeposit capital, they began packaging up some of their best loans, especially credit card loans, and using those loans as collateral for bonds. These asset-backed securities are, conceptually, exactly like mortgage bonds. Industrial companies are also increasingly issuing bonds backed by accounts receivable and other non-real-estate assets.

inflation. The British government has issued an indexed bond on which the interest rate is set equal to the British inflation rate plus 3 percent. Thus, these bonds provide a real rate of return of 3 percent. Also, Mexico has used bonds on which the interest rate is pegged to the price of oil to finance the development of its huge petroleum reserves; since oil prices and inflation are correlated, these bonds offer some protection to investors against inflation.

? Self-Test

Differentiate between mortgage bonds and debentures.

Define convertible bonds, bonds with warrants, income bonds, and indexed bonds.

Why do bonds with warrants and convertible bonds have lower coupons than bonds without these features?

Recent Bond Innovations

Zero Coupon Bonds

Some bonds pay no interest but are offered at a substantial discount below their par values and hence provide capital appreciation rather than interest income. These securities are called **zero coupon bonds (zeros).**

zero coupon bonds (zeros)

Bonds that pay no annual interest but are sold at a discount below par, thus providing compensation to investors in the form of capital appreciation.

Zeros were first used in a major way in 1981. Since then, IBM, Alcoa, J.C. Penney, ITT, Cities Service, GMAC, Martin-Marietta, and many other companies have used them to raise billions of dollars. Moreover, investment bankers have in effect created zero coupon Treasury bonds. Treasury zeros are, of course, safer than corporate zeros, which has made them very popular with pension fund managers and risk-averse individual investors wishing to lock in a particular rate of return.

An example will help illustrate the calculations required for zero coupon bonds: In 1982 BankAmerica Corporation issued $500 million of zero coupon securities. Its preliminary prospectus stated that for $250 investors could purchase one of these securities, which would mature at $1,000 in late 1992. It is relatively easy to calculate the yield to maturity an investor would have received from this investment. The present value is the $250 sale price in 1982, the future value is the $1,000 maturity value, n = 10, and we solve for k_d, using Equation 13-3:

$$PV = \frac{FV_n}{(1 + k)^n} \tag{13-3}$$

$$PV = FV_{10}(PVIF_{k,10})$$

$$\$250 = \$1,000(PVIF_{k,10})$$

$$PVIF_{k,10} = \$250/\$1,000$$

$$= 0.2500.$$

Using the table, we find $k = k_d$ to be approximately 15 percent. (The calculator solution is 14.87 percent.)

It is equally straightforward to calculate the market value of a zero, given the number of years until maturity, an appropriate discount rate, *and* a bond that is not callable (as we shall see in a moment, some are). If a zero will mature and pay $1,000 in 10 years and if the going rate is 12 percent, then its current market price should be the present value of the future $1,000, or $322.00:

$$V_B = PV = FV_{10}\,(PVIF_{12\%,10})$$

$$= \$1,000(0.3220)$$

$$= \$322.00.$$

When zero coupon bonds were first introduced in 1981, most were not callable. This has since changed. Corporations quickly recognized that committing themselves to an effective yield of 15 or even 12 percent over 10 or more years was not to their advantage in an environment of declining interest rates. (Remember, no one *knew* back in 1981 or 1982 which way interest rates would go, but it was feared that they would head higher.) Today many corporate (and municipal) zeros are callable, just like many coupon bonds, usually after some stated call protection period.[11]

For example, in June 1993 Time Warner offered $2.1 billion in 20-year zero coupon bonds (due 2013). These are senior securities with a relatively high credit rating, and each bond was priced at $372.43 for a YTM of about 5 percent (gross proceeds to the firm: approximately $782 million). However, the zeros will be callable any time after the fifth year.[12] Time Warner issued the zeros to redeem 8¾ percent convertible subordinate debentures and, thus, reduce its annual cash interest expense by over $68 million ($782 million × 0.0875 = $68.425 million).

Advantages to zeros from the viewpoint of the issuer include the following: (1) no cash outlays until the bonds are redeemed; (2) zeros may sell with relatively low yields to maturity; especially if noncallable, and (3) the issuer receives an annual tax deduction equal to the yearly amortization of the discount, which means that the bonds actually provide a positive cash flow in the form of tax savings over their life. The major disadvantage to the issuer is that the firm will have a very large nondeductible cash outlay coming up in the year the bonds mature.

The main advantage to the purchasers of zero coupon bonds is that they are guaranteed a "true" yield, irrespective of what happens to interest rates. Thus, the holders of these bonds do not have to worry about having to reinvest coupons received at low rates if interest rates should fall (although, if the bonds are callable, holders do have to face the possibility of them being called). This feature is extremely important to pension funds, life insurance companies, and other institutions that make actuarial contracts based on assumed reinvestment

---

[11]Such zero coupon bonds are usually callable at their accrued value calculated as the issue price compounded at the implied interest rate for the number of years since issue. For example, the accrued value of our illustrative bond after five years would be $322 $(1.12)^5$ = $567.47. A call premium of, say, 2 percent might also be added, making the call price $567.47(1.02) = $587.82.

[12]These zeros are also so-called *putable bonds,* which means that the bonds can be redeemed at the *bondholder's* option. In the Time Warner case, investors may exercise this option on the fifth, tenth, and fifteenth anniversaries of the issue.

INDUSTRY PRACTICE

TO MARKET, TO MARKET . . .

When interest rates plunged in early 1993, corporations rushed to take advantage of the decline by flooding the markets with $4.7 billion of new notes and bonds in just one day. January 6 was the second highest single-day bond total ever, after the record $5.2 billion of corporate bonds issued a year earlier on January 8, 1992, and ahead of the $4.6 billion recorded one day in May 1989.

Barbara Kenworthy of Dreyfus Corporation termed investors' demand for corporate bonds a "feeding frenzy," spurred especially by those seeking maturities of 20 years or more. "One of my salesmen was telling me that people practically started fighting on our trading floor to get their allocations" of some new corporate bonds, she said.

Because of the strong demand, one company more than doubled its offering of 10-year notes and 30-year bonds, to $1.05 billion. Mark Siegel of investment banking house Morgan Stanley said other corporations would be pushing out bonds while demand was strong and that the month's total might top $30 billion. That would make it the biggest month since the previous January, when $35.3 billion in new corporate bonds were sold.

One factor pushing up the demand for corporate debt was the very low level of rates prevailing in short-term issues—the lowest in almost two decades. Investors whose CDs were maturing were moving into the higher yielding corporate bond market in an effort to maintain their income levels. That, combined with the general decline in interest rates, provided an "incredibly friendly environment" for corporations who wanted to borrow, said Thomas Pura, a managing director at Goldman Sachs.

To compete with a $9.51 billion seven-year Treasury issue at 6.4 percent, General Motors Acceptance Corporation and the Tennessee Valley Authority (TVA) offered slightly higher yields, and each was able to sell $500 million of new seven-year notes that day, stealing some of the thunder from the Treasury's auction. (Even though the TVA is a federal agency, its notes are traded in the corporate bond market.)

Other big issuers were Ford, Shell Oil, International Paper, and Michigan Bell. And, just 48 hours earlier, AT&T had issued $1 billion worth of 10-year notes and 30-year bonds.

A few months after its seven-year issue, TVA went to market again with a 50-year bond, surprising analysts who did not expect a maturity of such extreme length to attract investors. However, the $1 billion offering proved popular despite a yield of only 9 percent—considered low for such a long-term issue. One investment manager who bought some of the bonds said he expects inflation to maintain a moderate rate for the next 10 years or so, in which case the issue will provide a most attractive real return. After a slow start, said an officer at one of the investment banking firms, "the deal started to warm up, and we got orders for ten times as many bonds as we could sell."

Institutional investors bought most of the TVA issue, according to Jon Winkelreid of Goldman Sachs, who noted that managers of pension funds, state retirement funds, and insurance companies often need to match the maturities of bonds in their portfolios to dates when they expect to be paying out claims. An example would be a company with many young workers in their twenties who would be expected to collect their pensions 50 years hence, at about age 70.

Some of the TVA bonds also ended up in individual retirement accounts. Half of the issue consisted of zero coupon bonds, which are bought at big discounts from face value and are often held in tax-deferred programs such as IRAs or 401(k) plans. Offering the zeros, said the TVA's chief financial officer, "probably saved the authority about a million dollars a year in interest expense by enhancing the issue's marketability, and thus driving down its yield."

Long maturities are currently popular because investors are not as worried as they had been about the budget deficit and the Clinton administration's proposed spending increases. For example, Dillard Department Stores offered $100 million of 30-year bonds yielding close to 8 percent, or just 0.67 percentage point above the yield on the Treasury's 30-year issue in early 1993. An official with the lead underwriter (investment banker) said that "the deal went very well" in large part because investors wanted the longer maturities. "Investors are basically becoming more comfortable, more bullish," and are "looking for ways to enhance their returns."

Sources: Thomas T. Vogel, Jr., "Corporate Bond Sales Near Record," *The Wall Street Journal,* January 7, 1993, page C-1; Constance Mitchell, "TVA's Huge 50-Year Bond Sale Is a Hit," *The Wall Street Journal,* April 10, 1992, page C-1; Constance Mitchell and Anita Raghavan, "Companies Issue Flood Of Debt, Heaviest in Years," *The Wall Street Journal,* January 9, 1992, page C-1.

rates; for such investors the risk of *declining* interest rates, hence an inability to reinvest cash inflows at the assumed rates, is greater than the risk of an increase in rates and the accompanying fall in bond values.

Because of tax considerations (the difference between the purchase price and the maturity value for individuals is treated as amortized annual interest income and not as a capital gain), these bonds are best suited for tax-exempt organizations, especially pension funds, and for tax-deferred individual savings, such as individual retirement accounts (IRAs). However, since pension funds are by far the largest purchasers of corporate bonds, the potential market for zero coupon bonds is by no means small.

Floating-Rate Debt

Recall from the earlier discussion of bond valuation that an increase in the level of interest rates (the going rate) will cause a decline in the market value of outstanding, fixed-rate bonds. In the early 1980s, when inflation pushed interest rates up to unprecedented levels, even some supposedly "risk-free" long-term, U.S. Treasury bonds lost fully half their value, and a similar situation occurred with corporate bonds, mortgages, and other fixed-rate, long-term securities. The lenders who held the fixed-rate debt were, of course, hurt very badly. Bankruptcies (or forced mergers to avoid bankruptcy) were commonplace in the banking and especially the savings and loan industry. Insurance company reserves also plummeted. As a result, many lenders became reluctant to lend money at fixed rates on a long-term basis, and they would do so only at extraordinarily high rates.

The maturity risk premium which is incorporated into nominal interest rates is designed to offset the risk of declining bond prices if interest rates rise. Prior to the 1970s, the maturity risk premium on 30-year bonds was about one percentage point, meaning that under normal conditions, a firm might expect to pay about 1 percent more to borrow on a long-term than on a short-term basis. In the early 1980s, however, the maturity risk premium is estimated to have jumped to about three percentage points, which made long-term debt very expensive. If you look back to Figure 4-3, you will see that although long-term interest rates did start to decline in 1982, they were slow to come down, relative to the rate of inflation. *Actual* inflation dropped much faster than inflation *expectations* throughout the first half of the 1980s, and *real* long-term rates (after subtracting out inflation) were very high. Lenders were basically "once burned, twice shy." After having experienced negative real rates of return on many fixed-rate debt instruments in the late 1970s, they were guarding against still higher inflation and interest rates by demanding high long-term yields. They were able and willing to lend on a short-term basis, but corporations were correctly reluctant to borrow on a short-term basis to finance long-term assets — such action is, as we saw in Chapter 8, extremely dangerous. Therefore, there was a situation in which lenders did not want to lend on a long-term basis, but corporations needed long-term money. The problem was solved by the introduction of *long-term, floating-rate debt.*

floating-rate bond
A bond whose interest rate fluctuates with shifts in the general level of interest rates.

A typical **floating-rate bond** works as follows. The coupon rate is set for, say, the initial six-month period, after which it is adjusted every six months based on some market rate. Some corporate issues have been tied to the Treasury bond rate, while other issues have been tied to short-term rates. Many additional provisions can be included in floating-rate issues; for example, some are convertible to fixed-rate debt, whereas others have a minimum coupon rate as well as a cap on how high the rate can go.

Floating-rate debt is advantageous to lenders because the interest rate moves up if market rates rise. This, in turn, causes the market value of the bond to remain very close to the $1,000 par value at all times. It provides lenders such as banks with income which is better matched to their own obligations. (Banks' deposit costs rise with interest rates, so the income on floating-rate bonds rises just when banks' deposit costs are rising.) Moreover, floating-rate debt is advantageous to borrowers because by using it, firms can issue debt with a long maturity without committing themselves to paying an historically high rate of interest for the entire life of the loan. Of course, if interest rates increase after a floating-rate bond has been sold, the borrower would have been better off issuing conventional, fixed-rate debt.

Junk Bonds

junk bond

A high-risk, high-yield bond used originally to finance mergers, leveraged buyouts, and troubled companies.

Prior to the 1980s, fixed-income investors such as pension funds and insurance companies were generally unwilling to buy risky bonds, so it was almost impossible for risky companies to raise capital in the public bond markets. These companies, if they could raise debt capital at all, had to do so in the term loan market, where the loan could be tailored to satisfy the lender. Then, in the late 1970s, Michael Milken of the investment banking firm Drexel Burnham Lambert, relying on historical studies which showed that risky bonds yielded more than enough to compensate for their risk, began to convince certain institutional investors of the merits of purchasing risky debt. Thus was born the **junk bond,** a high-risk, high-yield bond issued originally to finance a leveraged buyout, a merger, or a troubled company. For example, when Ted Turner attempted to buy CBS, he planned to finance the acquisition by issuing junk bonds to CBS's stockholders in exchange for their shares. Similarly, Public Service of New Hampshire financed construction of its troubled Seabrook nuclear plant with junk bonds, and junk bonds were used in the RJR Nabisco LBO. In junk bond deals, the debt ratio is generally extremely high, so the bondholders must bear as much risk as stockholders normally would. The bonds' yields reflect this fact —a coupon rate of 25 percent per annum was required to sell the Public Service of New Hampshire bonds.

The emergence of junk bonds as an important type of debt is another example of how the investment banking industry adjusts to and facilitates new developments in capital markets. In the 1980s, mergers and takeovers increased dramatically. People like T. Boone Pickens and Ted Turner thought that certain old-line, established companies were run inefficiently and were financed too conservatively, and they wanted to take these companies over and restructure them. Michael Milken and his staff at Drexel Burnham Lambert began an active campaign to persuade certain institutions (often S&Ls) to purchase high-yield bonds. Milken developed expertise in putting together deals that were attractive to the institutions yet apparently feasible in the sense that projected cash flows were sufficient to meet the required interest payments. The fact that interest on the bonds was tax deductible, combined with the much higher debt ratios of the restructured firms, also increased after-tax cash flows and helped make the deals appear feasible.

The development of junk bond financing has done as much as any single factor to reshape the U.S. financial scene. The existence of these securities led directly to the loss of independence of Gulf Oil and hundreds of other companies, and it led to major shake-ups in such companies as CBS, Union Carbide, and USX (formerly U.S. Steel). It also caused Drexel Burnham Lambert to leap from essentially nowhere in the 1970s to become the most profitable investment banking firm during the 1980s.

The phenomenal growth of the junk bond market was impressive, but controversial. In early 1989, Drexel Burnham Lambert was forced into bankruptcy, and in 1990 "junk bond king" Michael Milken pleaded guilty to six securities-related felonies and was sentenced to ten years in prison. (In August 1992, Mr. Milken won an early release after having served two years.) These events badly tarnished the junk bond market, which also came under severe criticism for fueling takeover fires and adding to the cost of the S&L bailout.

Do junk bonds have a future role in corporate finance aside from takeovers and LBOs? The answer is, undoubtedly, yes. In spite of all the publicity surrounding the use of junk bonds in mergers and acquisitions, statistics show that well over half of the junk bond issues in recent years have been used for normal expansion purposes. And, although it appeared at the beginning of this decade that junk bonds would play a much smaller role in corporate financings than had been the case in the 1980s, they have staged a remarkable comeback. By the end of 1991, junk bond issuance had rebounded to levels not seen since 1988. Declining interest rates were the driving force, sending investors scrambling for higher yields than those available on other alternatives, and corporations, again, benefited from this trend. For example, Safeway was able to refinance older junk bonds carrying rates as high as $14\frac{1}{2}$ percent with new junk bonds yielding less than 10 percent.

Another wave of junk bond offerings hit the market during the spring of 1992, including numerous issues of zero coupon junk bonds. These are among the most speculative types of junk bonds and had been stopped entirely when the junk bond market went into its deep slide in 1989. The sizzling pace of new junk bond issuance continued throughout 1992; the largest junk bond offerings to come to market included Comcast Cellular ($1,000 million), Tele-Communications ($600 million), and Chrysler ($300 million), in addition to Safeway ($300 million).

In a number of ways the junk bond market is now a very different market than the one dominated by Drexel Burnham Lambert in the 1980s. Today, there are more securities firms underwriting junk bonds, competition is keeping some of the most ill-conceived deals from making it to market, and mutual funds are now the leading buyers of junk bonds, not S&Ls and insurance companies. Although the junk bond market has its ups and downs, as of June 1993 the offerings were still coming at a furious pace. Issuers including Bell & Howell, American Standard, Gaylord Container, and Revlon—several of these companies back again after successful offerings in 1992. During the first six months of 1993, more than $25.8 billion of junk bonds had been sold, up from $19.3 billion for the first half of 1992. To be sure, the $25.8 billion was only about 5.5 percent of total taxable debt sold during the six-month period, but this sector of the market is expected to continue its growth.

?   *Self-Test*

Explain how the yield on a noncallable zero coupon bond is determined.

Would it be easier or harder to calculate the yield on a *callable* zero coupon bond? Explain.

Identify the principal advantages of zero coupon bonds to the issuer.

In what sense do holders of zero coupon bonds not have to be concerned about reinvestment risk?

What problem was solved by the introduction of long-term floating-rate debt, and how is the rate on such bonds actually set?

For what purposes were junk bonds typically used in the 1980s?

Bond Ratings

Since the early 1900s, bonds have been assigned quality ratings that reflect their probability of going into default. The two major rating agencies are Moody's Investors Service (Moody's) and Standard & Poor's Corporation (S&P). These agencies' rating designations are shown in Table 16-1.[13]

investment-grade bonds

Bonds rated A or triple-B; many banks and other institutional investors are permitted by law to hold only investment-grade or better bonds.

The triple- and double-A bonds are extremely safe. The single-A and triple-B rated bonds are strong enough to be termed **investment-grade bonds,** and they are the lowest-rated bonds that many banks and other institutional investors are permitted by law to hold. Double-B and lower-rated bonds are considered speculative grade securities, or junk bonds, with increasingly higher probabilities of default as ratings decline.

Bonds ratings are based on both qualitative and quantitative factors, some of which are listed below:

▷   **Ratio analysis.** The firm's liquidity, debt level, and debt coverage are among the first factors considered by the bond-rating agencies. Recall from Chapter 6 that the two most important coverage ratios are the times-interest-earned and the fixed charge coverage ratios.

▷   **Security provisions.** Whether the bond is backed by real assets (mortgage bond) or not (debenture), or by another firm (guaranteed bond), or whether the bonds are subordinated, are important factors in the rating scheme.

▷   **Sinking fund.** If the issue has a sinking fund to ensure systematic repayment, this is a positive factor to the rating agencies.

▷   **Maturity.** Other things equal, a bond with a shorter maturity will be judged less risky than a longer-term bond, and this will be reflected in the rating.

▷   **Stability.** As a general rule, the more stable the firm's sales and earnings, the higher the rating.

▷   **Legal actions.** Any major legal controversies such as antitrust or product liability suits could erode the ratings.

---

[13]In the discussion to follow, reference to the S&P code is intended to imply the Moody code as well. Thus, for example, *triple-B bonds* means both BBB and Baa bonds, *double-B bonds* both BB and Ba bonds, and so on.

Table 16-1

Comparison of Bond
Ratings

| | High Quality | | Investment Grade | | "Junk" | | |
					Substandard		Speculative
Moody's	Aaa	Aa	A	Baa	Ba	B	Caa to D
S&P	AAA	AA	A	BBB	BB	B	CCC to D

Note: Both Moody's and S&P use "modifiers" for bonds rated below triple-A. S&P uses a plus and minus system; thus, A+ designates the strongest A-rated bonds and A− the weakest. Moody's uses a 1, 2, or 3 designation, with 1 denoting the strongest and 3 the weakest. Thus, within the double-A category, Aa1 is the best, Aa2 is average, and Aa3 is the weakest.

▶ **Pension liabilities.** If the firm has unfunded pension liabilities that could cause a problem, this fact is reflected in its bond ratings.

▶ **Other.** Many other factors enter into the bond-rating scheme used by agencies. Examples of other factors include accounting policies, potential for labor problems, political unrest in host countries for multinational firms, and the regulatory climate for public utilities and other regulated industries.[14]

Analysts at the rating agencies have consistently stated that no precise formula is used to set a firm's rating; all the factors listed, plus others, are taken into account, but not in a mathematically precise manner. Statistical studies have borne out this contention; researchers who have tried to predict bond ratings on the basis of quantitative data have had only limited success, indicating that the agencies do indeed use a good deal of subjective judgment when establishing a firm's rating.[15]

Importance of Bond Ratings

Bond ratings are important both to firms and to investors. First, because a bond's rating is an indicator of its default risk, the rating has a direct, measurable influence on the bond's interest rate and the firm's cost of debt capital. Second, most bonds are purchased by institutional investors rather than individuals, and many institutions are restricted to investment-grade securities. Thus, if a firm's bonds fall below BBB, it will have a difficult time selling new bonds since many potential purchasers will not be allowed to buy them. Also, because there is always a possibility that a given security may be downgraded, many institutions restrict their bond portfolios to at least A, or even AA, bonds. Thus, the lower a firm's bond rating, the smaller the group of available purchasers for its new issues.

As a result of their higher risk and more restricted market, lower-grade bonds have much higher required rates of return than do high-grade bonds. Figure 16-3 illustrates this point. In each of the years shown on the graph, U.S.

[14]Municipal bonds are also rated, and in October 1992, *The Wall Street Journal* reported that Moody's and S&P had begun basing credit ratings for municipal debt on cities' *quality of life* as well as previously used criteria. S&P, for example, is looking at health programs, "harmony" and other socioeconomic conditions, and the quality of a city's schools. Said the director of Moody's public finance department, Daniel Heimowitz, "We have to question [a city's] long-term viability."

[15]See Ahmed Belkaoui, *Industrial Bonds and the Rating Process* (London: Quorum Books, 1983).

Figure 16-3   Yields on U.S. Treasury Bonds, AAA Corporates, and BBB Corporates, 1956–1993

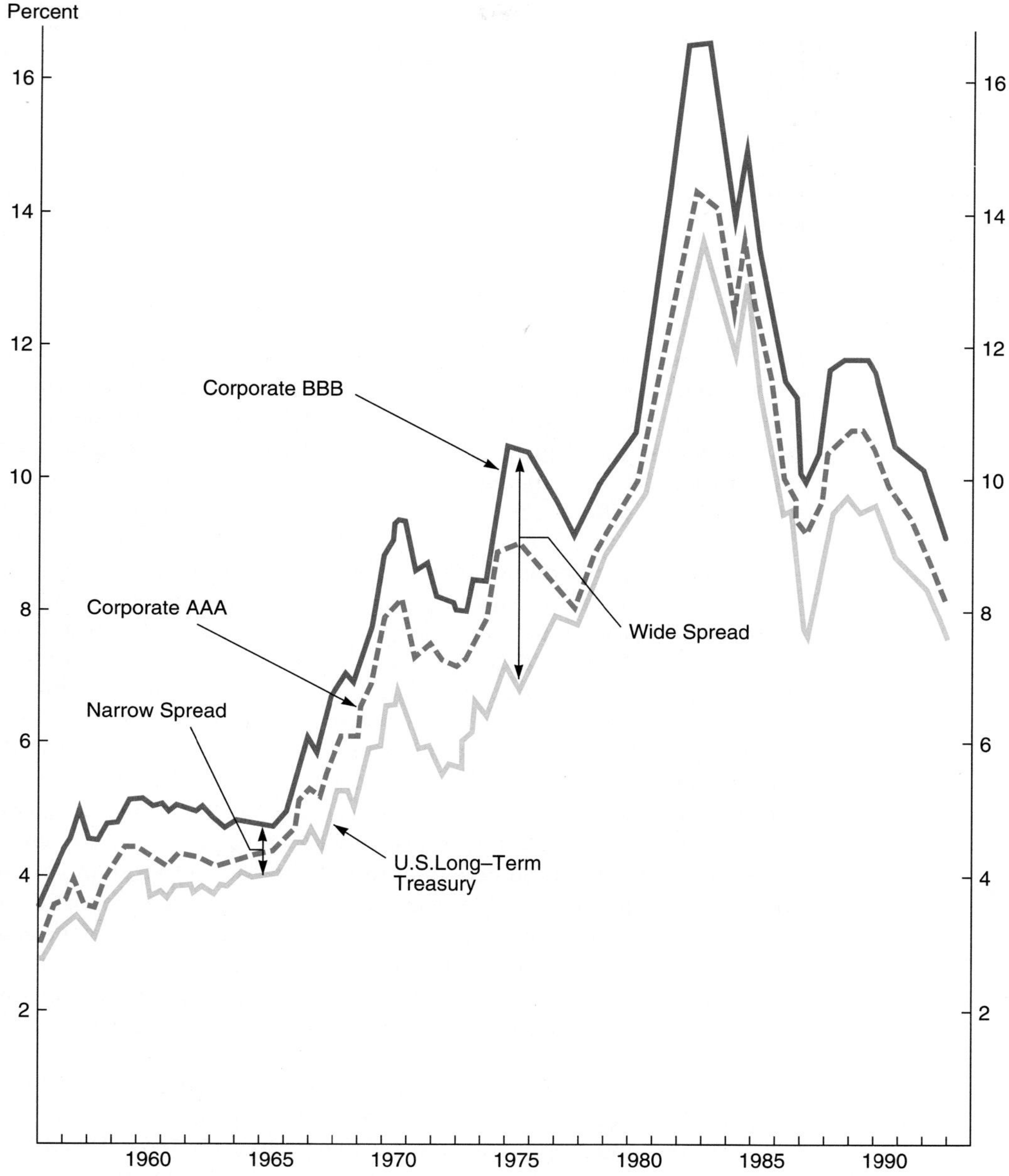

A bond's rating is an indicator of its default risk. Because a lower-grade bond entails greater default risk, it must pay a higher interest rate to attract investors. During the 38 years shown here, long-term, U.S. Treasury bonds, which are default-free, paid the lowest interest rates. Corporate AAA bonds paid somewhat higher interest rates, while corporate BBB bonds paid the highest rates of the three shown. The spreads between the curves indicate the risk premiums that corporate bond issuers had to pay to raise capital.

Sources: *Federal Reserve Board Historical Chart Book,* 1983, and *Federal Reserve Bulletin,* various issues.

Table 16-2   Risk Premiums in Selected Economic Periods

	Long-Term U.S. Treasury Bonds (Default-Free) (1)	AAA Corporate Bonds (2)	BBB Corporate Bonds (3)	Risk Premiums AAA (4) = (2) − (1)	BBB (5) = (3) − (1)
June 1963	4.00%	4.23%	4.84%	0.23%	0.84%
June 1975	6.86	8.77	10.40	1.91	3.54
April 1989	9.17	9.88	10.69	0.71	1.52
March 1993	6.82	7.58	8.15	0.76	1.33

Source: *Federal Reserve Bulletin,* various issues; *Federal Reserve Statistical Release,* June 4, 1990.

Treasury bonds have had the lowest yields, AAA bonds have been next, and the BBB bonds have had the highest yields of the three shown. The figure also shows that the spreads between the yields on the three types of bonds vary over time; in other words, the cost differentials, or risk premiums, fluctuate from year to year. This changing yield spread reflects the degree of risk aversion in the market at different points in time. U.S. Treasury bonds have no default risk, AAA corporate bonds have some, and BBB corporate bonds have more. (If we were to chart junk bond yields in Figure 16-3 as well, they would, of course, all be above the three shown.) Investors require a higher return on AAA and BBB corporate securities than on Treasury bonds at all times because default premiums are built into the required rates of return on the two corporate securities, but the *size* of the default premium is linked to investor inclination to take on risk. For example, in Figure 16-3 we see that from 1963 to 1965, very little additional yield was needed to convince investors to hold AAA and BBB corporate bonds, as opposed to Treasury bonds. On the other hand, the yield spread widened considerably in 1975. That year, the United States was emerging from a severe recession caused by a quadrupling of oil prices in 1973 and 1974, and investors were afraid the economy would slip back into a slump. At such times, people seek safe investments, Treasury bonds are in great demand, and the premiums on all corporate bonds increase, even those of investment grade. Such a shift toward the safe end of the spectrum is often called a "flight to quality."

This point is highlighted in Table 16-2, which gives the yields on the three types of bonds, plus the risk premiums for AAA and BBB bonds on selected dates.

These relationships for the same years (1963, 1975, 1989, and 1993) are graphically depicted in Figure 16-4. Note that the U.S. Treasury bond yield (the vertical axis intercept) rose during the period 1963 to 1989 because of increases in realized and expected inflation, but declined between 1989 and 1993 because of expectations of lower inflation. (Incidentally, by mid-October 1993, 30-year Treasury bond yields had dropped by more than a full percentage point to 5.79 percent.) Next compare the slope of the lines for 1975 and 1993. Although the Treasury bond rate is almost identical for the two years (6.86 versus 6.82 percent), the level of risk aversion in the market is again seen to be much higher in 1975 than in 1993. In fact, the 1975 risk premium on BBB corporate bonds is more than 2.6 times the risk premium on such bonds in 1993. This confirms what we were able to observe in Figure 16-3.

Figure 16-4   Relationship between Bond Ratings and Bond Yields, 1963, 1975, 1989, and 1993

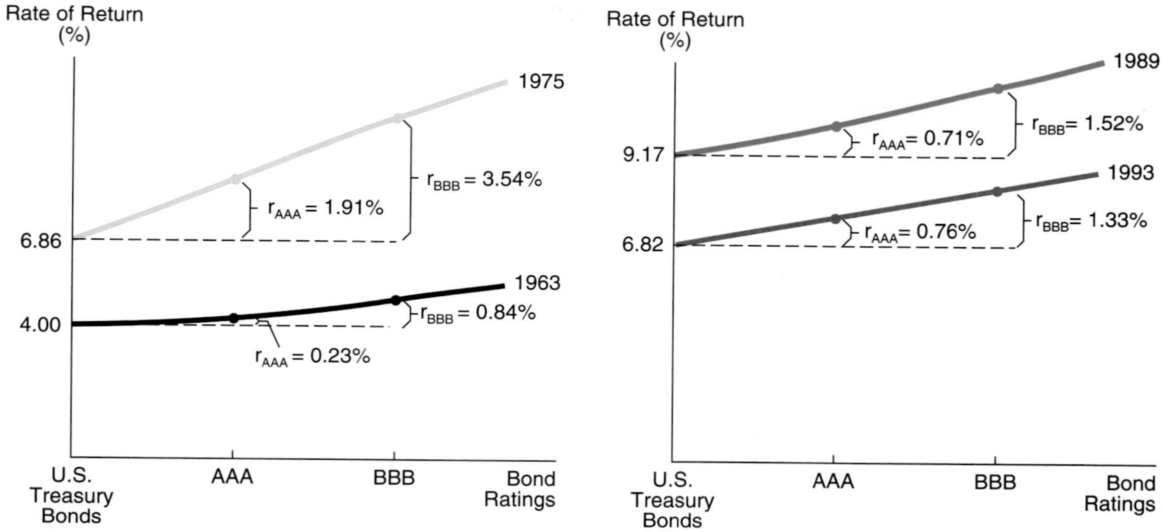

In this figure we take a closer look at the relationship between bond ratings and bond yields. Between 1963 and 1989, the default-free rate of interest rose from 4.00 percent to 9.17 percent to reflect both realized and anticipated inflation. Corporate borrowers, of course, had to pay a default risk premium in addition. In 1963, corporate AAA bonds paid a default risk premium of 0.23 percent, and corporate BBB bonds paid a default risk premium of 0.84 percent. In 1975, this risk premium rose to 1.91 percent for AAA bonds and to 3.54 percent for BBB bonds. In 1989, this risk premium dropped to 0.71 percent for AAA bonds and to 1.52 percent for BBB bonds, and in 1993 the two premiums were 0.76 and 1.33 percent, respectively. The default risk premiums fluctuate to reflect changes in investors' attitudes toward assuming risk. (Note that this graph assumes that maturity is held constant for the three types of securities shown.)

Source: Table 16-2.

r_{AAA} = risk premium on AAA bonds.
r_{BBB} = risk premium on BBB bonds.

Changes in Ratings

Rating agencies review outstanding bonds on a periodic basis, occasionally upgrading or downgrading a bond as a result of its issuer's changed circumstances. For example, as IBM struggled with a drop in sales of its mainframe computers, it was placed on S&P's *CreditWatch* list in December 1992, "with negative implications." The rating service cited concerns about the computer giant's near-term progress and reports that IBM would "take another round of write-offs" before year end. Moody's had already downgraded IBM by two notches from its previous triple-A rating to double-A2. In January 1993, IBM reported a record $4.97 billion loss for 1992 — the largest single-year loss in U.S. corporate history — and S&P downgraded its debt by three grades, to double-A minus from triple-A (leaving only 13 industrial companies with a triple-A rating from S&P). As a result, IBM's cost of borrowing rose, and the market value of its bonds declined. In April, Moody's again lowered its ratings, this time to single-A1, on about $18 billion of IBM debt.

Meanwhile in the automotive industry, S&P in February 1993 downgraded General Motors's senior debt, citing GM's pension and medical benefits liabilities, now materially larger than previously assumed. But at the same time, the rating agency raised the ratings on rival Chrysler, following the company's successful issue of new common stock. S&P also cited Chrysler's success with new product launches.

Self-Test

What are the two major rating agencies, and what are some factors that affect bond ratings?

Why are bond ratings important both to firms and to investors?

What is measured by the changing spreads in Figure 16-3 which compares Treasury bond yields to the yields on AAA and BBB corporate bonds?

Term Loans

term loan

A loan, generally obtained from a bank or insurance company, with a maturity greater than one year.

So far in this chapter, we have been dealing entirely with bonds, long-term debt instruments which may be sold to many investors through a public offering. In contrast to bonds, **term loans** are long-term debt where the borrower negotiates directly with a financial institution, for example, a bank, an insurance company, or a pension fund. This type of financing is, therefore, called *direct financing.*[16] A term loan is a contract under which a borrower agrees to make payments of interest and principal, on specific dates, to the lender. Although the maturities of term loans vary, most are for periods in the 3- to 15-year range.

Advantages of Term Loans

Term loans have three major advantages over publicly issued securities — *speed, flexibility,* and *low issuance costs.* Because they are negotiated directly between the lender and the borrower, formal documentation is minimized. The key provisions of a term loan can be worked out much more quickly than can those for a public issue, and it is not necessary for a term loan to go through the SEC registration process. A further advantage of term loans over publicly held debt securities has to do with future flexibility: if a bond issue is held by many different bondholders, it is virtually impossible to obtain permission to alter the terms of the agreement, even though new economic conditions may make such changes desirable. With a term loan, the borrower can generally sit down with the lender and work out mutually agreeable modifications to the contract.

Amortization

Most term loans are *amortized,* or paid off, in equal installments over the life of the loan. (At this point you should review the discussion of amortization in Chapter 13.) The purpose of amortization is to have the loan repaid gradually

---

[16]Another type of direct financing is a *private placement.* The only major difference between a term loan and this form of financing is that the private placement tends to have a longer maturity. Corporations may use private placements for preferred stock as well as for debt.

over its life rather than fall due all at once. Amortization forces the borrower to retire the loan slowly; this protects both the lender and the borrower against the possibility that the borrower will not make adequate provisions for its retirement during the life of the loan. Amortization is especially important whenever the loan is used to purchase a specific item of equipment; here the repayment schedule should be matched to the productive life of the equipment, with the payments being made from cash flows resulting from its use.

Interest Rate

The interest rate on a term loan can either be fixed for the life of the loan or be variable. If it is fixed, the rate used will be close to the rate on bonds with an equivalent maturity and risk. If the rate is variable, it will usually be set at a certain number of percentage points over the prime rate, the commercial paper rate, the T-bond rate, or some other market-determined rate. Thus, when these rates go up or down, so does the rate on the outstanding balance of the term loan.

Recent Developments

Earlier in this chapter we discussed junk bonds and the resurgence of this market in recent years. Remember also from Chapter 3 that banks are facing increasingly stiff competition from other financial institutions encroaching on their turf. One trend that has emerged in 1993 is that many firms which, in the past, would have taken out bank term loans are now selling junk bonds instead, causing banks to lose a large slice of their traditional business. In the first quarter of 1993, 75 percent of all junk bond offerings were of so-called "senior" junk bonds with claims on the firm's earnings and assets often equal to those of bank loans, no longer subordinated to senior bank debt, as was usually the case in the 1980s. This has made the junk bonds easier to sell; only a few years ago, such senior junk bonds barely existed. Other reasons that this shift in financing is occurring are that borrowers want to avoid (1) the current highly restrictive banking practices and constant scrutiny and (2) the amortization payments which can be a serious cash drain on the firm. Issuing junk bonds instead gives the borrower longer to pay back.

Quantum Chemical Company provides an example of this growing trend. In April 1993, Quantum sold $300 million of 10-year first mortgage notes (short-term bonds) in the junk bond market and paid off its bank term loans. Even though the notes would cost the firm nearly 4 percentage points *more* than the bank debt, Quantum—which expects its revenue and earnings to suffer until the economy picks up—bought itself some much needed breathing room until year 2003.

Self-Test

What are the three major advantages that term loans have over publicly issued securities?

What is the purpose of amortizing loans?

Why have a number of firms, which in the past would have obtained bank term loans, turned to the junk bond market in recent years?

Pros and Cons of Long-Term Debt

The advantages and disadvantages to the use of long-term debt instruments are discussed briefly in the following sections.

Issuer's Viewpoint

There are several advantages to the corporation from the use of long-term debt such as bonds or term loans, as opposed to equity financing. First, the cost of debt is limited. Since bondholders are not owners but creditors, they have no claim on extra earnings in a good year; they simply get the interest they have been promised. This fixed, limited financing cost provides financial leverage, and, as we discussed in Chapter 6 (and will come back to again in Chapter 20), *financial leverage has the potential to boost the return to common stockholders.* (Preferred stock is the other source of financial leverage.) Second, because creditors, including bondholders, have prior claims on the firm's earnings and assets, this lowers the risk to these lenders. Therefore, the cost to the firm is lower on debt than on preferred and common stock, and the fact that interest expense is tax deductible makes the after-tax cost of debt lower yet. (We shall return to this topic in Chapters 19 and 20.) Another advantage to the use of debt is that owners of the firm do not have to give up any of their control of the firm since bondholders typically do not vote. Finally, it is possibly for the firm to build some flexibility into the bond indenture by including a call provision.

The disadvantages associated with the use of long-term debt include the fact that *debt must be serviced.* The fixed interest charge must be paid, whether the firm is having a good or a bad year. Fluctuating earnings means that the firm may find itself unable to cover fixed charges; it would then have defaulted on the obligation. Also, as we have seen, most debt has a fixed maturity date so the firm must have a plan to repay lenders or refinance the debt. And, while the bond is outstanding, the indenture provisions are likely to be much more severe than any restrictions that apply to short-term loans. Last, but by no means least important, *there are limits to the amount of funds that can be raised through debt.* We will expand on this in much greater detail in Chapter 20, but the essence is that there comes a point for every firm where the higher risk associated with higher financial leverage will *reduce* the value of the firm's common stock.

Investor's Viewpoint

Bondholders and other long-term lenders, such as banks making term loans, are likely to focus on three aspects of debt: risk, return, and control. Compared with the preferred and common stockholders of a given firm, investors holding the firm's debt have less risk. This is primarily because of their prior claims on earnings and assets but also because of the protective covenants of the indenture. With lower risk, the expected return to the lenders should also be lower than what common stockholders hope to realize. Unfortunately, bondholders tend to suffer during inflationary periods when a sufficiently large inflation premium has not been built into the nominal interest rate. Finally, in the area of control, bondholders and other creditors do not have any under normal circumstances since they typically do not have the right to vote. This is precisely why their interests must be protected via restrictive provisions in the bond indenture (or the term loan contract). However, if the bonds go into default, the bondholders in effect take control of the firm.

? *Self-Test*

What are some of the advantages and disadvantages to long-term debt, seen from both the issuer's and the investor's viewpoints?

Preferred Stock

Preferred stock was defined in Chapter 2 as long-term equity which pays a fixed dividend. It is a *hybrid* — it is similar to bonds in some respects and to common stock in others. The hybrid nature of preferred stock becomes apparent when we try to classify it in relation to bonds and common stock. Like bonds, preferred stock has a par value.[17] Preferred dividends are also similar to interest payments on bonds in that they are fixed in amount and generally must be paid before common stock dividends can be paid. However, if the preferred dividend is not earned, the directors can omit (or "pass") it without throwing the company into bankruptcy. So, even though preferred stock has a fixed payment like bonds, a failure to make this payment will not lead to bankruptcy.

Accountants classify preferred stock as equity and report it in the equity portion of the balance sheet under "preferred stock" or "preferred equity." However, financial analysts sometimes treat preferred stock as debt and sometimes as equity, depending on the type of analysis being made. If the analysis is done by a common stockholder, the key consideration is that the fixed preferred dividends must be paid ahead of common stock dividends, so the preferred stock will be viewed much like debt. Suppose, however, that the analysis is being made by a bondholder studying the firm's vulnerability to failure in the event of a future decline in sales and income. If the firm's income declines, the debtholders have a prior claim to the available income ahead of preferred stockholders, and if the firm fails, debtholders have a prior claim to assets when the firm is liquidated. Thus, to a bondholder, preferred stock is similar to common equity.

From management's perspective, preferred stock lies between debt and common equity. Since failure to pay dividends on preferred stock will not force the firm into bankruptcy, preferred stock is safer to use than debt. At the same time, if the firm is highly successful, the common stockholders will not have to share that success with the preferred stockholders because preferred dividends are fixed. Preferred stock is used in situations where conditions are such that neither debt nor common stock is entirely appropriate.

---

[17]Common stock may also have a par value, but while the par value is meaningful for bonds and preferred stock (because it represents what these investors should be paid in case the company is liquidated), it is *not* meaningful for common stock. It bears no relationship to the common stock's actual market price for a going concern, and if the company is liquidated, the common stockholders are not likely to receive anything.

Major Provisions of Preferred Stock Issues

Preferred stock has a number of features, the most important of which are covered in the following sections.

Priority with Regard to Earnings and Assets.   Preferred stockholders have priority over common stockholders with regard to earnings and assets. Thus, dividends must be paid on preferred stock before they can be paid on common stock, and, in the event of bankruptcy, the claims of the preferred shareholders must be satisfied before the common stockholders receive anything. To reinforce these features, most preferred stock contracts have coverage requirements, similar to those on bonds. These restrictions limit the amount of preferred stock a company can use, and they also require a minimum level of retained earnings before common dividends can be paid.

Par Value.   Unlike common stock, preferred stock always has a par value (or its equivalent under some other name), and this value is important. First, the par value establishes the amount due the preferred stockholders in the event of liquidation. Second, the preferred dividend is frequently stated as a percentage of the par value. For example, Duke Power has preferred stock with a par value of $100 and a stated dividend of 7.8 percent of par. It would, of course, be just as appropriate for Duke's preferred stock to simply call for an annual dividend of $7.80.

cumulative dividends

A protective feature on preferred stock that requires preferred dividends in arrears to be paid before any common dividends can be paid.

arrearage

An omitted dividend on preferred stock.

Cumulative Dividends.   Most preferred stock provides for **cumulative dividends;** that is, all preferred dividend **arrearages** must be paid before common dividends can be paid. The cumulative feature is a protective device, for if the preferred stock dividends were not cumulative, a firm could avoid paying preferred and common stock dividends for, say, 10 years and thus "save" a large amount of earnings, and then pay a large common stock dividend but pay only the stipulated annual amount to the preferred stockholders. Obviously, such an action could be used to effectively void the preferred position that the preferred stockholders are supposed to have. The cumulative feature prevents such abuses.[18] Clearly, it is not to a firm's advantage to fall in arrears on its preferred dividends since this is likely to lower the value of its common stock.

Convertibility.   Approximately 40 percent of the preferred stock that has been issued in recent years is convertible into common stock. For example, each share of Enron's $10.50 Class J preferred stock can be converted into 3.413 shares of its common stock at the option of the preferred shareholders. (Convertibility is discussed in more detail in Chapter 18.)

---

[18]Note, however, that compounding is absent in most cumulative plans — in other words, the arrearages themselves earn no return. Also, many preferred issues have a limited cumulative feature; for example, arrearages might accumulate for only three years.

Other Provisions.   Some other provisions one occasionally encounters in preferred stocks include the following:

1. **Voting rights.**   Preferred stockholders are generally given the right to vote for directors if the company has not paid the preferred dividend for a specified period, such as ten quarters. This feature motivates management to make every effort to pay preferred dividends.

2. **Participating.**   A rare type of preferred stock is one that participates with the common stock in sharing the firm's earnings. Participating preferred stocks generally work as follows: (a) the stated preferred dividend is paid — for example, $5 a share; (b) the common stock is then entitled to a dividend in an amount up to the preferred dividend; (c) if the common dividend is raised, say, to $5.50, the preferred dividend must likewise be raised to $5.50.

3. **Sinking fund.**   In the past (before the mid-1970s), few preferred issues had sinking funds. Today, however, most newly issued preferred stocks have sinking funds which call for the purchase and retirement of a given percentage of the preferred stock each year. If the amount is 2 percent, which is used frequently, the preferred issue will have an average life of 25 years and a maximum life of 50 years.

4. **Call provision.**   A call provision gives the issuing corporation the right to call in the preferred stock for redemption. As in the case of bonds, call provisions generally state that the company must pay a call premium. For example, Trivoli Corporation's 12 percent, $100 par value preferred stock, issued in 1988, is noncallable for 10 years, but it may be called at a price of $112 after 1998.

5. **Maturity.**   Before the mid-1970s, most preferred stock was perpetual — it had no maturity and never needed to be paid off. However, today most new preferred stock has a sinking fund and thus an effective maturity date.

Valuation of Preferred Stock

Despite the fact that preferred stock dividends can be omitted without throwing the firm into bankruptcy, most financial managers attempt to pay these dividends without omission. Thus, the dividends may reasonably be expected to be paid on time, and, because few preferred stocks are participating, these dividends should not change in value from period to period.

Just as bondholders value debt instruments as the present value of the bond's future cash flows, discounted at a required rate of return, k_d, preferred stockholders also discount future cash flows, in this case a perpetuity of fixed dividends, to arrive at a current market price for preferred stock:[19]

---

[19]Note that we previously mentioned that today many newly issued preferred stocks have sinking funds, which call for the purchase and retirement of a given percentage of the issue in each year. In that case, the valuation of the preferred stock would also involve discounting future cash flows, but the cash flows would have a *finite* life. Thus, the valuation would be similar to that for a bond.

$$V_p = \frac{D_p}{k_p}.$$ (16-3)

Here:

V_p = the market price of preferred stock today.
D_p = the fixed dividend payment.
k_p = the required rate of return on preferred stock with this degree of risk.

Thus, if a company has a $100 par value preferred stock issue outstanding which pays a dividend of $12 per year and which has no sinking fund provision, the stock's price will be determined by the investors' required return, k_p. If investors are satisfied with a 12 percent rate of return, they will pay a price equal to the stock's par value:

$$V_p = \$12/0.12$$

$$= \$100.$$

If, however, investors require a 14 percent rate of return, they will pay less than the preferred stock's par value: $V_p = \$12/0.14 = \$85.71$. Similarly, if rates on competing investment opportunities of equal risk fall to 8 percent, the price of the preferred stock will rise to $150: $V_p = \$12/0.08 = \$150$.

We can transpose the V_p and the k_p in Equation 16-3 and solve for k_p. We look up the price of the stock and the preferred dividend in the financial section of the newspaper, and we can then calculate our expected rate of return if we buy the stock at the current market price:

$$k_p = \frac{D_p}{V_p}.$$ (16-4)

Thus, if we buy the preferred stock, which pays a constant dividend of $12, for $150, the stock's rate of return will be: $k_p = \$12/\$150 = 0.08 = 8\%$. However, if investors are paying only $85.71 for a preferred stock that pays a constant $12 dividend, their required rate of return is: $k_p = \$12/\$85.71 = 0.14 = 14\%$.

Pros and Cons of Preferred Stock

There are both advantages and disadvantages to financing with preferred stock. These are discussed in the following sections.

Issuer's Viewpoint.   As is the case with bonds, by using preferred stock, a firm can fix its financial costs and thus keep more of the potential future profits for its existing set of common stockholders. Yet, unlike with bonds, by issuing preferred stock the firm can avoid the danger of being in default if earnings are too low to meet these fixed charges. Also, by selling preferred rather than common stock, the firm avoids sharing control with new investors.

However, preferred stock does have a major disadvantage from the issuer's standpoint: It has a higher after-tax cost of capital than debt. The major reason for this higher cost is taxes: Preferred dividends are not deductible as a tax expense, while interest expense is deductible, which makes the effective after-tax cost of preferred stock much greater than that of bonds. The after-tax cost of debt is approximately two-thirds of the stated coupon rate for profitable firms, whereas the cost of preferred stock is the full percentage amount of the preferred dividend. Of course, the deductibility differential is most important for issuers that are in relatively high tax brackets. If a company pays little or no taxes because it is unprofitable or because it has a great deal of accelerated depreciation, the deductibility of interest does not make much difference. Thus, the lower a company's tax bracket, the more likely it is to use preferred stock financing.

Investor's Viewpoint. In designing securities, the financial manager must also consider the investor's point of view. It is sometimes said that preferred stock has so many disadvantages to both the issuer and the investor that it should never be issued. Nevertheless, preferred stock is issued in substantial amounts. It provides investors with reasonably steady and assured income plus a preference over common stockholders in the event of liquidation. In addition (as with common stock dividends), 70 percent of the preferred dividends received by corporations are not taxable. For this reason, most outstanding preferred stock is owned by corporations.

The principal disadvantage of preferred stock from an investor's standpoint is that although preferred stockholders bear some ownership risk, their returns are limited. Other disadvantages are that (1) preferred stockholders have no legally enforceable right to dividends, even if a company earns a profit, and (2) companies often manage to avoid paying off all accumulated dividends when they emerge from a troubled, low-income period. Such companies frequently go through reorganization under the Bankruptcy Act, and preferred stockholders often do not fare well in these proceedings.

Recent Trends

Because preferred dividends are not tax deductible, many companies have retired their preferred stocks and replaced them with debentures or subordinated debentures. However, as the following examples illustrate, preferred is still used to raise long-term capital when conditions are such that neither common stock nor long-term debt can be issued on reasonable terms.

1. Chrysler's issue of preferred stock with warrants several years ago proved a successful means of raising capital in the face of adverse circumstances. Because of its losses, Chrysler's common stock was depressed and very much out of favor. Investors were so worried about the company's ability to survive that they were unwilling to make additional commitments without receiving some sort of senior position. Therefore, common stock was ruled out. Chrysler had already borrowed to the hilt, and it could not obtain any more debt without first building its equity base (and preferred is equity from the bondholders' viewpoint). Various incentives were offered to the brokers who handled the preferred issue, and a relatively high yield was set. As a result, the issue was so successful that its size was raised from $150 to $200 million while the underwriting was under way. Chrysler got the money it needed, and that money helped the company survive.

2. Utility companies often use preferred stock to bolster the equity portion of their balance sheets. These companies are capital intensive, and they make

heavy use of debt financing, but lenders and rating agencies require minimum equity ratios as a condition for maintaining bond ratings. Also, the utilities have made very heavy investments in fixed assets and thus have high depreciation charges, which has held down their effective tax rates and thus has lowered the tax disadvantage of preferred stock in relation to debt.

3. As previously mentioned, in recent years there has been a pronounced movement toward convertible preferred, which is often used in connection with mergers. For example, when Belco Petroleum was negotiating its acquisition by Enron, it was pointed out that if the buyout were for cash, Belco's stockholders (one of whom owned 40 percent of the stock and thus could block the merger) would be required to immediately pay huge capital gains taxes. However, under U.S. tax laws, if preferred stock is exchanged for the acquired company's common stock, this constitutes a tax-free exchange of securities. Thus, Belco's stockholders could obtain a fixed-income security yet postpone the payment of taxes on their capital gains.

    Enron actually offered a choice of straight or convertible preferred to Belco's stockholders. Those stockholders who were interested primarily in income could take the straight preferred, whereas those interested in capital gains could take the convertible preferred. After the exchange, both preferred issues traded on the NYSE; the straight preferred had a yield of 11 percent, and the convertible preferred yielded 7.5 percent. However, the convertibles had a chance of gains — indeed, by October 1990 the Enron convertible preferred had risen from its initial price of $100 to $203 per share because of an increase in the price of the common into which it could be converted. Meanwhile, the price of the nonconvertible preferred remained close to its $100 par value.

floating-rate preferred stock

Preferred stock on which the dividend rate fluctuates with changes in the general level of interest rates.

4. In 1984, Alabama Power introduced a new type of security, **floating-rate preferred stock.** Since this stock has a floating rate, its market price stays relatively constant, as with floating-rate bonds, making it suitable for liquid asset portfolios (marketable securities held by corporations to provide funds either for planned expenditures or to meet emergencies). The combination of a floating rate, and hence a stable price, and the 70 percent tax exemption for corporations makes this preferred quite attractive, and it enabled Alabama Power to obtain capital at a low cost.

5. Starting in 1991, preferred stock has become one of the hottest financial products around. Yield-hungry investors apparently decided that, as the rates on money market funds and other short-term alternatives declined, the much higher preferred dividends looked tempting, even when accompanied by higher risk. Scores of companies, eager to raise their equity and bolster their credit ratings, have offered preferred stocks yielding up to 9 percent. Issuers have included such well-known names as RJR Nabisco, Kmart, General Motors (twice), and Ford, which first tripled the size of a planned offering in 1991 to $2.3 billion, then surprised analysts in late 1992 by announcing its intent to sell another $1 billion of preferred. Banks have been especially anxious to strengthen their balance sheets; among the large banks which have offered preferred stock in recent years are Chase Manhattan, Citicorp, and Wells Fargo.

Self-Test

Explain the following statement: "Preferred stock is a hybrid."

Identify and briefly explain some of the key features of preferred stock.

What are the advantages and disadvantages of preferred stock from an issuer's viewpoint?

What are the advantages and disadvantages of preferred stock from an investor's viewpoint?

SMALL BUSINESS

CONTRACTING WITH PROVIDERS OF RISK CAPITAL

Venture capitalists and others providing risk capital to support firms with high growth prospects often lose much or all of their investments. In fact, a recent study showed that more than a third of all venture capital (VC) investments lost money. In a sixth of the cases, the VC firm lost its entire investment. That fact and other aspects of the behavior of small business investments mean that the structure of the financial contract between an entrepreneur and a venture capitalist may have a decided effect on the decision to provide capital to the business. Bill Sahlman of Harvard University argues that ". . . an effective financial design may well be the difference between a flourishing and a failed (if not a still-born) enterprise." The points discussed below are largely based on his article.

The financial contract between a VC firm and an entrepreneur must contain a number of key points relating to the ultimate success or failure of the venture. Among the points that need to be considered are these:

▶ What can go wrong?

▶ What can go right?

▶ Who gets what in the case of the two above points?

▶ What expected return is required?

▶ What are the risks, and who bears them?

▶ What are the incentives for each of the two sides?

A deal in which the venture capitalist receives a large share and the entrepreneur receives very little will fail because the entrepreneur will have little or no incentive to make it work. So, the deal itself can destroy incentives. A good contract will ensure that both sides do well if things go right.

The entrepreneur is probably optimistic about his or her project. Anyone who would devote all of his or her time and resources to a project would have to be optimistic. As a result of this optimism, the entrepreneur's viewpoint may not be realistic. The contract should delineate some conditions under which the entrepreneur is not meeting projections, and, under those conditions, the VC firm might have a greater share of the venture — perhaps also including the right to actually remove the entrepreneur from the project. To protect the VC firm, the contract must provide for the possibility that things will not work out as expected. Often, this is achieved by the VC firm's investing in the venture in the form of preferred stock (with a preference on liquidation) or convertible debt. Such an investment gives the venture capitalist's claim top priority in the event of the firm's failure and provides some "downside" protection. If holding a convertible security, the VC firm can convert to straight equity if the deal goes well. Convertible debt is a sort of a "have my cake and eat it too" option.

By allocating much of the risk to the entrepreneur, the venture capitalist is forcing the entrepreneur to take *actions* to confirm his or her forecasts. Any entrepreneur can produce a set of lofty forecasts, but, by

Sources: See Linda A. Vincent, "Setting Realistic Expectations for Potential Returns — Part II," *Investing in Venture Capital* (Washington, D. C.: The Institute of Chartered Financial Analysts, 1989); and William A. Sahlman, "Aspects of Financial Contracting in Venture Capital," *Journal of Applied Corporate Finance, V1,* No. 2 (Summer 1988), 23–36.

agreeing to a contract under which the entrepreneur gets nothing if the venture does not meet those forecasts, the entrepreneur says, in no uncertain terms, "I believe in this deal."

Another feature of VC investment is that it does not necessarily provide all the capital a firm needs in the beginning. For example, suppose you have developed an idea for a new product, and you estimate you will need $10 million to develop a prototype, set up the manufacturing process, and begin to market the product. You will not get the $10 million in advance, and, indeed, it may be in the best interest of both the entrepreneur and the venture capitalist that you not get all of the money in advance. It makes sense to get the investment from the venture capitalist in stages, rather than all at once. The product is, at this stage, only an idea; there is at least some risk that the product will not be successful. Typically, only a small fraction of the total capital requirement is needed to develop and test a product. Once it is developed, both the entrepreneur and the investors may agree that they should not proceed with it, perhaps because by that time there is already a superior competitor on the market.

If the entrepreneur insists on the full $10 million in advance, he or she will probably get *nothing*. This is the stage at which the project faces its greatest risks, and few people would be foolish enough to invest at this stage. Accordingly, the entrepreneur would have to give up virtually all ownership rights to get the money in advance. So, he or she should accept only the money that is needed for that stage, and thus retain what he or she can of the ownership claim.

As the entrepreneur moves toward developing production facilities, he or she will want to obtain some market data to measure the need for the product, and to help determine prices. This is another source of risk, and, again, the entrepreneur is better off not insisting on capital infusions at this point since he or she is still more willing than others to bear the risk of failure. At each stage of the project, risk is reduced, and in the later stages the entrepreneur should be able to obtain larger amounts of funding while giving up smaller fractions of ownership. Accepting money in stages, under a set of prearranged conditions, is known as "staged capital commitment."

A final suggestion for the entrepreneur designing the terms under which funds are accepted is to remain flexible. Sahlman tells of a case in which the initial investors insisted on receiving an option that permitted them to maintain 51 percent ownership of a venture, regardless of how much additional capital was raised from others after the initial deal. The effect of this provision was to ruin the company's chances of raising any additional capital. Potential investors felt that their investment would be diluted by the "rolling option" of the initial investors.

In a similar case, a new software firm raised funds by selling stock to investors at $5.00 per share. The CEO decided he would not let any new investors buy stock at a better price than that of the original investors. Later, when the company had problems and was in worse shape than in the beginning, it couldn't raise additional funds because the price was too steep. Thus, a provision intended to *protect* the early shareholders turned out to prevent the firm from raising capital, and, ultimately, it reduced the chances that investors would see returns on their capital. Beware of conditions that limit your options with respect to future financial needs. Even conditions created with good intentions may do more harm than good.

In summary, a good financing contract must encompass many issues. It must provide incentives for both sides in the agreement. It must lead to an appropriate sharing of both risks and returns. It must allow for raising additional funds in the future. Finally, it must be clear, as well as fair, to both sides. A deal is not good unless it is fair for all parties involved.

Summary

This chapter contained a discussion of the characteristics, advantages, and disadvantages of the major types of long-term debt securities and preferred stock. The valuation of both debt and preferred stock was also discussed. The key concepts covered are listed below.

▷ The **value of a bond** is found as the present value of an **annuity** (the interest payments) plus the present value of a lump sum (the **principal**).

An adjustment to the formula must be made if the bond pays interest **semi-annually.** The semiannual dollar interest is half of the annual amount, but there are twice as many periods.

▶ Whenever the market interest rate, **the going rate,** rises on bonds of equal risk, the market value of an outstanding fixed-rate bond will fall. If the going rate declines, the existing fixed-rate bond's value will increase. This **inverse relationship** exists because the bond's coupon payment is fixed for the life of the bond, yet it has to compete in the secondary market with newly issued bonds. Thus, an outstanding bond may sell at a **discount** or at a **premium** to its par value.

▶ The return earned on a bond purchased at a given market price and held to maturity is defined as the bond's **yield to maturity (YTM).** However, if a bond is callable and if interest rates are falling, **yield to call (YTC)** is typically more relevant to investors.

▶ There are many different types of bonds. They include **mortgage bonds, debentures, convertibles, bonds with warrants, income bonds,** and **indexed (purchasing power) bonds.** The return required on each type of bond is determined by the bond's riskiness.

A bond's **indenture** is a legal document that spells out the rights of the bondholders and of the issuing corporation. A **trustee** is assigned to make sure that the terms of the indenture are carried out.

A **call provision** gives the issuing corporation the right to redeem the bonds prior to maturity under specified terms, usually at a price greater than the maturity value (the difference is a **call premium**). A firm will typically call a bond and refund it if interest rates fall substantially.

A **sinking fund** is a provision which requires the corporation to pay off a portion of the bond issue each year. The purpose of the sinking fund is to provide for the orderly retirement of the issue. No call premium is paid to the holders of bonds called for sinking fund purposes.

Some recent innovations in long-term financing include **zero coupon bonds,** which pay no annual interest but which are issued at a discount; **floating-rate debt,** on which interest payments fluctuate with changes in the general level of interest rates; and **junk bonds,** which are high-risk, high-yield instruments.

▶ Bonds are assigned **ratings** which reflect the probability of their going into default. The higher a bond's rating, the lower its interest rate.

When a wide yield spread exists between, for example, U.S. Treasury bonds and BBB corporate bonds, this indicates a relatively high degree of **risk aversion** in the market.

▶ **Term loans** are long-term debt contracts under which a borrower agrees to make a series of interest and principal payments on specific dates to the lender; the term loan is **amortized.** A term loan is generally obtained from one (or a few) lenders, while a bond is typically offered to the public and sold to many different investors.

▶ **Preferred stock** is a hybrid security having some characteristics of debt and some of equity. Common stockholders view preferred stock as being similar to debt because it provides a claim on the firm's earnings ahead of their claim. Bondholders, however, view preferred as equity because debtholders have a prior claim on the firm's income, and, in the event of bankruptcy, on the firm's assets.

Although preferred dividends are fixed, failure to pay preferred dividends does not represent default on an obligation. Preferred stock, therefore, gives the issuing corporation some **flexibility.** From the investors' point of view this feature adds an element of risk since investors have no assurance of receiving dividends every year.

Resolution to
DECISION IN FINANCE

THE BLUFF-AND-THREAT
CALL GAMBIT

D r. Bronner wondered why May Department Stores would offer a premium to tender the bonds if the company really had enough money to cash-call the issue. He asked a Morgan Stanley representative about the offer, and he received the following reply, "It's coercion; it's a threat — it is standard operating procedure." At about this same time, May Department Stores was in the capital market issuing $200 million of 8⅜ percent, 30-year bonds. Dr. Bronner was disturbed about this. He believed that the company was trying to refinance the pension fund's bonds with this lower-yielding debt — in direct conflict with what a cash-call is supposed to be.

Dr. Bronner called the company's bluff and refused to tender his securities. And, so far, May has not announced either a tender offer or a cash-call on the 10¾ percent bond issue. But, Dr. Bronner believes, "They've taken a very legal method of retiring very-high-coupon bonds and thrown it into the gutter . . . It's really questionable how they're doing it." Morgan Stanley claims that it never told Dr. Bronner that May

was definitely going to cash-call the issue and that it was merely measuring investor sentiment toward a cash-call.

However, May did announce a STAC for a different issue (10⅞ percent coupon), in which Dr. Bronner's pension fund had $1 million invested. At that time, Dr. Bronner organized an ad hoc committee (consisting of holders of the 10⅞ issue) which wrote complaints to the SEC. One of the members of the committee stated, "This is one case where it's worth looking into their legal right to do what they did and worth considering whether it should be contested." In addition to organizing the committee, Dr. Bronner tried to determine May's funding sources for the cash-call, but he was unsuccessful. The committee also wrote to May demanding that the company stop its efforts to redeem both bond issues. The company replied that the tender offer and redemption of the 10⅞ percent issue were proper and that the company had complied with the appropriate rules and regulations. The company never mentioned the 10¾ percent issue.

Did the ad hoc committee do any good? The deadline for tendering the 10⅞ percent bonds has passed, and only half of the bonds were tendered. Most of the committee members did not tender their bonds; however, most other bondholders did. In contrast, in three other STAC

Sources: "Corporate Issuers Use Bluff-and-Threat Call Gambit," *The Wall Street Journal,* November 2, 1992.

deals, over 90 percent of the bonds were tendered.

What was Morgan Stanley's reply? Morgan Stanley notes that pension funds are sophisticated investors, that they are aware of the extra risk that a nonrefundable bond carries, and that they have been compensated accordingly for that risk. In addition, Morgan Stanley officials pointed out that it was in Dr. Bronner's best interest to see fewer bondholders tender the 10⅞ percent issue, forcing May to use up its "clean"

money to redeem that issue, consequently protecting his pension fund's 10¾ percent issue from a STAC.

Is the STAC a wave of the future? Morgan Stanley, Goldman Sachs, and Merrill Lynch have all managed STAC deals since the spring of 1992. Some of the corporate borrowers involved in these deals included Mercantile Stores, Houston Industries, and James River Corporation. And, underwriters expect many more bond issues to be called using this approach.

Questions

16-1 What effect would each of the following items have on the interest rate a firm must pay on a new issue of long-term debt? Indicate by a plus (+), minus (−), or zero (0) whether the factor will tend to raise, lower, or have an indeterminate effect on the firm's interest rate, and then explain *why*.

Effect on Interest Rate

a. The firm uses bonds rather than a term loan. _____

b. The firm uses nonsubordinated debentures rather than first mortgage bonds. _____

c. The firm makes its bonds convertible into common stock. _____

d. The firm makes its debentures subordinated to its bank debt. What will the effect be:
 (1) On the debentures? _____
 (2) On the bank debt? _____
 (3) On the average total debt? _____

e. The firm sells income bonds rather than debentures. _____

f. The firm must raise $100 million, all of which will be used to construct a new plant, and is debating the sale of first mortgage bonds or debentures. If it decides to issue $50 million of each type, as opposed to $75 million of mortgage bonds and $25 million of debentures, how will this affect:
 (1) The debentures? _____
 (2) The mortgage bonds? _____
 (3) The average cost of the $100 million? _____

g. The firm is planning to raise $25 million of long-term capital. Its outstanding bonds yield 9 percent. If it sells preferred stock, how will this affect the yield on the outstanding debt? _____

h. The firm puts a call provision on its new issue of bonds. _____

i. The firm includes a sinking fund on its new issue of bonds. _____

j. The firm's bonds are downgraded from A to BBB. _____

k. The firm uses zero coupon bonds rather than coupon bonds. _____

16-2 Rank the following securities from lowest (1) to highest (10) in terms of their riskiness for an investor. All securities (except the government bond) are for a given firm. If you think two or more securities are equally risky, indicate so.

	Rank (10 = Highest Risk)
a. Income bond	_____
b. Subordinated debentures — noncallable	_____
c. First mortgage bond — no sinking fund	_____
d. Preferred stock	_____
e. Common stock	_____
f. U.S. Treasury bond	_____
g. First mortgage bond — with sinking fund	_____
h. Subordinated debentures — callable	_____
i. Amortized term loan	_____
j. Nonamortized term loan	_____

16-3 A bond that pays interest forever and has no maturity date is a perpetual bond. In what respect is a perpetual bond similar to a share of preferred stock?

16-4 "The values of outstanding fixed-rate bonds change whenever the going rate of interest changes. In general, short-term interest rates are more volatile than long-term interest rates. Therefore, short-term bond prices are more sensitive to interest rate changes than are long-term bond prices." Is this statement true or false? Explain.

16-5 A sinking fund can be set up in one of two ways:
(1) The corporation makes annual payments to the trustee, who invests the proceeds in securities (frequently government bonds) and uses the accumulated total to retire the bond issue at maturity.
(2) The trustee uses the annual payments to retire a portion of the issue each year, either calling a given percentage of the issue by a lottery and paying a specified price per bond or buying bonds on the open market, whichever is cheaper.
Discuss the advantages and disadvantages of each procedure from the viewpoints of both the firm and the bondholders.

Self-Test Problem

ST-1 A firm issued a new series of bonds on January 2, 1973. The bonds were sold at par ($1,000), have an 8 percent annual coupon, and mature 30 years after the date of issue. Interest is paid on December 31.
a. What was the yield to maturity (YTM) of the bonds on January 2, 1973?
b. What was the price of the bond on January 2, 1978, five years later, assuming that the level of interest rates had risen to 10 percent?
c. If, for this type of bond, interest rates had been 6 percent on January 2, 1978, what would investors have paid for the bond?
d. Find the current yield and capital gains yield on the bond if interest rates as of January 2, 1978, were 6 percent, as in Part c.
e. On January 2, 1983, the bonds sold for $525.70. What was the YTM on that date?
f. What was the current yield and capital gains yield for the bond under the conditions described in Part e?
g. It is now January 2, 1994. The going rate of interest is 12 percent. How large a check must you write to buy the bond?

Problems

16-1
Preferred stock valuation

Ashley Resources has a $100 par, $9 dividend perpetual preferred stock outstanding. Investors require a 7 percent return on investments of this type.
a. What is the current market price of Ashley's preferred stock?
b. If the investment community's required return rose for Ashley's preferred stock, what would happen to the price?

16-2
Yield computations

Hopewell & James Inc. sold a 20-year, 14 percent annual coupon, $1,000 par value bond issue 10 years ago. Today, the bond issue is selling for $1,113.03. What is the bond's:
a. Current yield?
b. Yield to maturity?

16-3
Bond valuation

United Circuits sold a 25-year, 15 percent annual coupon bond issue at a par value of $1,000 in September 1980. In September 1993 the bond issue's yield to maturity was 12 percent. What was the price of the bond?

16-4
Bond valuation, semiannual interest

Assume the same facts as for Problem 16-3, except that, rather than issuing annual coupon bonds, United Circuits had issued semiannual coupon bonds. What was the price in September 1993 of these semiannual coupon bonds?

16-5
Zero coupon bond valuation

J. Lizotte and Company wants to sell 15-year zero coupon bonds. The bonds will mature at $1,000 and will be sold to yield 10 percent. At what price will these bonds be offered?

16-6
Zero coupon bond, YTM, and YTC

Maria Romero is considering the purchase of zero coupon bonds being issued by Wilder Publications. The bonds have a 10-year maturity, will mature at $1,000, and are selling for $508.30.
a. What are the bonds' yield to maturity, YTM?
b. If Wilder's bonds are callable in 5 years at $746.84 per bond, what is the yield to call, YTC? (*Hint:* You do not need a financial calculator to answer this question.)
c. Suppose that interest rates, in general, and Wilder's cost of debt as well, rise slowly but steadily over the next decade. Is it more likely that Maria will receive the YTM or the YTC on this investment? Explain.

16-7
Bond valuation, semiannual interest

a. Hytec Electronics's bonds pay $50 semiannual interest, mature in 5 years, and pay $1,000 on maturity. What will be the value of these bonds when the going annual rate of interest is: (1) 8 percent, (2) 10 percent, and (3) 12 percent?
b. Now suppose that Hytec has issued some other bonds that pay $50 semiannual interest, $1,000 at maturity, and mature in 1 year. What is the price of these bonds if the going annual rate of interest is: (1) 8 percent, (2) 10 percent, and (3) 12 percent?
c. Why do the longer-term bond prices fluctuate more when interest rates change than do the shorter-term bond prices?

16-8
Yield to maturity

The Scheffler Company's bonds have 5 years remaining to maturity. Interest is paid annually, the bonds have a $1,000 par value, and the annual coupon interest rate is 9 percent.
a. What is the yield to maturity at a current market price of: (1) $892 and (2) $1,126? You may wish to use the approximation formula found in Footnote 6.
b. Would you pay $892 for the bond described in Part a if you thought that the appropriate rate of interest for these bonds was 10 percent? Explain your answer.

16-9
Bond valuation

Suppose Wibisono Industries sold an issue of bonds with a 10-year maturity, a $1,000 par value, and a 10 percent coupon rate paid annually.
a. Suppose that 4 years after the issue, the going rate of interest had risen to 14 percent. At what price would the bonds sell?

b. Suppose that the conditions in Part a continued (that is, interest rates remained at 14 percent throughout the bond's life). What would happen to the price of Wibisono's bonds over time?

16-10

Loan amortization

Suppose that a firm is setting up an amortized term loan. What are the annual payments for a $2 million loan under the following terms:
a. 9 percent, 3 years?
b. 9 percent, 7 years?
c. 12 percent, 3 years?
d. 12 percent, 7 years?
e. Suppose you know that the more exact calculator solution to Part d is $438,235.47. Using this payment for a 12 percent, 7-year loan, what would be the remaining balance immediately after the third annual payment has been made? (*Hint:* You may answer this question by setting up a partial amortization schedule or by recognizing that the remaining balance represents the present value of a 4-year annuity. Some rounding difference may occur depending on the method used.)

16-11

Amortization schedule

Set up an amortization schedule for a $1 million, 3-year, 8 percent term loan.

16-12

Amortization payments

A company borrows $1 million on a 3-year, 8 percent, partially amortized term loan. The annual payments are to be set so as to amortize $700,000 over the loan's 3-year life and also to pay interest on the $300,000 nonamortized portion of the loan.
a. How large must each annual payment be? (*Hint:* Think of the loan as consisting of two loans, one fully amortized for $700,000 and one on which interest only is paid each year until the end of the third year.)
b. Suppose the firm requests a $1 million, 8 percent, 3-year loan with payments of $250,000 per year (interest plus some principal repayment) for the first 2 years and the remainder to be paid off at the end of the third year. How large must the final payment be?

16-13

Bond interest payments

Blessing Inc. has two bond issues outstanding, and both sell for $668.84. The first issue has an annual coupon rate of 9 percent and 20 years to maturity. The second has a yield to maturity identical to the first but only 5 years until maturity. Both issues pay interest annually. What is the annual interest payment on the second issue?

16-14

Bond valuation

Suppose that the time is June 1993. You have $10,000 which you want to invest in long-term bonds, and your broker is suggesting (1) investing the $10,000 in 30-year Treasury bonds, (2) buying ten 30-year bonds issued by Ford Motor Company, or (3) buying ten 50-year bonds also issued by Ford. The Treasuries yield 6.89 percent, the 30-year Ford bond sells at par with a 7.7 percent coupon, and the 50-year Ford bond, also selling at par, has a coupon of 7.85 percent.
a. In which of these bonds would you have the lowest default risk?
b. In which of these bonds would you have the greatest interest rate risk.
c. Calculate the value of each of the three investments in 20 years, June 2013, if rising inflation and changes in investor risk aversion has resulted in the following situation for new issues selling at par: (1) 10-year Treasury securities yield 12 percent, (2) 10-year securities issued by Ford yield 14 percent, and (3) 30-year bonds issued by Ford yield 15 percent.
d. Can you think of any reason that you might choose to buy the 50-year Ford bond in June 1993? Why might institutional investors like insurance companies and pension funds choose the 50-year Ford bonds?
e. If the interest rate changes described in Part c occurred instead over the following *five* years, as opposed to 20 years, would the market values of the three types of bonds be greater or smaller in June 1998 than the values calculated earlier for June 2013? Explain your answer. (No calculations are needed.)

16-15

(Do this problem only if you are using the computerized problem diskette or a financial calculator.) It is now January 1, 1994, and you are considering the purchase of an outstanding Figone Corporation bond that was issued on January 1, 1992. Figone's bond has an 11.5 percent annual coupon and a 30-year original maturity (it matures in 2022). There was originally a 5-year call protection (until December 31, 1996), after which time the bond can be called at 120 (that is, at 120 percent of par, or $1,200). Interest rates have declined since the bond was issued, and the bond is now selling at 128.625 percent of par, or $1,286.25. You want to determine both the yield to maturity and the yield to call for this bond. (*Note:* The yield to call includes the impact of a call provision on the bond's probable yield. In the calculation, we assume that the bond will be called on December 31, 1996. Thus, the investor will have received interest payments for the call-protected period and then will receive the call price — in this case, $1,200 — on the call date.)

a. What is the yield to maturity in 1994 for Figone's bond? What is its yield to call?

b. If you bought this bond, which return do you think you would actually earn? Explain your reasoning.

c. Suppose that the bond had sold at a discount. Would the yield to maturity or the yield to call have been more relevant?

d. Suppose that the bond's price suddenly jumps to $1,350. What is the yield to maturity now, and what is the yield to call?

e. Suppose that the price suddenly falls to $900; now what would the YTM and the YTC be?

Solution to Self-Test Problem

ST-1

a. The bonds were sold at par. Therefore, the YTM equals the coupon interest rate, which is 8 percent.

b. We must find the PV of the 25 remaining interest payments of $80 each and the $1,000 lump sum payment of principal to be paid when the bond matures in 25 years. Therefore:

$$\text{Bond value} = V_B = \$80(\text{PVIFA}_{10\%,25}) + \$1,000(\text{PVIF}_{10\%,25})$$

$$= \$80(9.0770) + \$1,000(0.0923)$$

$$= \$726.16 + \$92.30$$

$$= \$818.46.$$

c. Using the 6 percent present value interest factors, we find

$$\text{Bond value} = V_B = \$80(12.7834) + \$1,000(0.2330)$$

$$= \$1,022.67 + \$233.00$$

$$= \$1,255.67.$$

d. If interest rates were 6 percent on January 1, 1978, the bond's price was $1,255.67, as found in Part c. Thus,

$$\text{Current yield} = \frac{\text{Annual interest payment}}{\text{Current market price}}$$

$$= \frac{\$80}{\$1,255.67} = 0.0637 = 6.37\%.$$

$$\text{Capital gains yield} = \text{Total yield} - \text{Current yield}$$

$$= 6\% - 6.37\% = -0.37\%.$$

e. Use the approximation formula from Footnote 6 to get a starting point:

$$\text{Approximate YTM} = \frac{I + (M - V)/n}{(M + 2V)/3}$$

$$= \frac{\$80 + [(\$1,000 - \$525.70)/20]}{(\$1,000 + \$1,051.40)/3}$$

$$= \frac{\$103.715}{\$683.80} = 15.17\%.$$

Suppose we try a k_d of 15 percent:

$$V_B = I(\text{PVIFA}_{15\%,20}) + \$1,000(\text{PVIF}_{15\%,20})$$

$$= \$80(6.2593) + \$1,000(0.0611)$$

$$= \$500.74 + \$61.10 = \$561.84.$$

Because this present value is greater than the $525.70 bond price given we will try a higher discount rate of $k_d = 16$ percent:

$$V_B = I(\text{PVIFA}_{16\%,20}) + M(\text{PVIF}_{16\%,20})$$

$$= \$80(5.9288) + \$1,000(0.0514)$$

$$= \$474.30 + \$51.40 = \$525.70.$$

Therefore, the YTM at the beginning of January 1983 was 16 percent.

f.
$$\text{Current yield} = \$80/\$525.70$$

$$= 15.22\%.$$

$$\text{Capital gains yield} = 16\% - 15.22\%$$

$$= 0.78\%.$$

g. The bond has 9 years until it matures; at 12 percent the price would be

$$V_B = \$80(5.3282) + \$1,000(0.3606)$$

$$= \$426.26 + \$360.60 = \$786.86.$$

MINI CASE   COMPUTER MODELING: AMORTIZED TERM LOAN

Susan Hawkins, M.D., and Frank Lane, M.D., met originally when both were interning at a large Baltimore hospital in the 1970s. Following the completion of their internships, they each chose general practice, but in different parts of the country. Frank returned to his native state, Vermont, and Susan set up practice in Billings, Montana.

Then in 1993 they met again at a convention for radiologists in St. Louis and discovered, much to their surprise, that they had chosen this same specialty and had each obtained the needed additional training in the intervening years. By the time the convention ended, Susan and Frank had made the decision to go into practice together in Olympia, Washington.

They have now moved west, have leased an appropriate space in a large, new professional plaza, and have bought the standard office equipment needed. The next step is obtaining a term loan for the purchase of general X-ray equipment. Susan and Frank have approached a large insurance company known for its willingness to lend to the medical profession and are now negotiating the terms of the contract.

The cost of state-of-the-art, general-purpose X-ray equipment is $320,000, and this is the amount that the two radiologists are asking to borrow. They are quoted a 9¼ percent fixed interest rate, compounded annually, with the term loan maturing in 15 years.

Using *Lotus 1-2-3,* do the following:

a.   State the basic assumptions of the problem. The "assumption block" can be extremely simple but should include values of n and k, the discount factor for the annuity, PVIFA, and a cell to show the annual payment needed to pay off the term loan. These last two should be *calculated* in the assumption block. In other words, don't pull a PVIFA from the table (since only certain whole percentages are found there) but arrive at a PVIFA using the following equation:

$$PVIFA = \frac{1 - [1/(1 + k)^n]}{k}.$$

Hints: You may find that an additional parenthesis is needed to get this to work, and the symbol needed to raise someting to a power is ^ in *Lotus 1-2-3.*

b.   Set up a complete amortization schedule for the term loan, given the assumptions/ terms listed in Part a. The copy command is very useful in a case like this. *Note:* The real power of electronic spreadsheets is the ability to perform sensitivity analysis (answer "what if" questions). It is therefore crucial that you use formulas and refer back up to earlier cell addresses wherever appropriate. You may want to review how to make reference to a cell *absolute,* as opposed to relative. Also show a total for each of the three columns headed "PAYMENT," "INTEREST," and "REPAYMENT OF PRINCIPAL." Use the @SUM function to arrive at the three totals. Print out everything and save as HL-B. If you have set up your model correctly, Parts c, d, and e should take much less time to complete.

c.   Frank has recently inherited a portfolio of stocks from his grandfather, and since he does not want to sell the stocks, he offers the portfolio as collateral for the term loan. In response, the insurance company agrees to lower the interest rate on the loan to 7¾ percent. What difference will this make in the annual payment? In the total amount of interest paid? Answer by printing out the new solution, including the assumption block, and save as HL-C. All other assumptions are as in Part b.

d.   Susan points out that the highly sophisticated X-ray equipment they are considering is likely to be technologically obsolete in about 10 years—well before the term loan has been paid back.

Since it is desirable to match the cash flows from the asset to the payments on the loan, they agree that a 10-year term loan would probably be better. If net income plus depreciation on the equipment is expected to total $95,000 per year and if the loan is for 10 years instead of 15, will the annual cash flows be sufficient to meet the annual payment? (Disregard the tax effect of interest payments.) Answer by printing out everything and save as HL-D. (*Hint:* Be sure to "clean up" or delete years 11 through 15 of the amortization schedule to avoid having these rows contain "nonsense.") All other assumptions are as in Part c.

e.   What if the payments were to be made on a *quarterly* basis, rather than annually? Recognize that the quarterly interest rate will be one-fourth of the annual interest rate and that there will be four times as many periods and payments. All other assumptions are as in Part d. What is the increase (decrease) in total interest paid over the life of the loan if payments are made quarterly? After changing your spreadsheet, simply type in a brief answer. Print out everything and save as HL-E.

Common Stock

OBJECTIVES

After reading this chapter, you should be able to:

▶ Define the terms "proxy" and "preemptive right" and explain the use of each.

▶ Determine the value of a share of common stock where dividends are expected to grow at some constant rate.

▶ Calculate the expected rate of return on a constant growth stock.

▶ State and demonstrate the steps required to find the value of a supernormal, or nonconstant, growth stock.

▶ Discuss the pros and cons of common stock financing from the issuer's viewpoint as well as from the viewpoint of the investor.

▶ List some advantages and disadvantages to a corporation of going public.

▶ Identify the primary functions of investment bankers and define some of the terms commonly used in the investment banking process.

DECISION IN FINANCE

MUSCLING THE UNDERWRITERS

When we think of Wall Street investment banking firms, we do not generally think of firms that permit themselves to be pushed around by their clients. Rather, we think of powerful firms that have control of their situations. However, recent events with a Time Warner note and bond offering indicate just the opposite. Time Warner wanted to raise cash and then retire some high-cost preferred stock (which carried a coupon rate of 11 percent), and it blitzed the securities market during the last two weeks of 1992 and the first four weeks of January 1993 with a series of note and bond offerings that totaled $3.43 billion. The problem for the company's investment bankers came when Time Warner, eager to take advantage of declining interest rates, dumped another $1 billion in 30-year bonds on the market at the end of January 1993. (The company's two most recent issues were rated BBB minus by Standard & Poor's, the lowest investment grade rating, and Ba2, a junk bond rating, by Moody's Investors Service.)

What was the investment bankers' problem? The Wall Street firms that had underwritten Time Warner's most recent note offering (which had taken place only a week earlier) were still trying to find buyers for the five- and seven-year notes. (It was estimated that 50 to 80 percent of the five- and seven-year notes bought by the un-

derwriters from the prior offering remained unsold when Time Warner announced its 30-year offering.) As a result, Salomon Inc., the lead underwriter, and Lazard Freres & Company, who comanaged the prior offering with Merrill Lynch, were left with several millions of dollars in paper losses because they still held $500 million of Time Warner notes in the now overloaded market.

As you read this chapter, consider the investment banking process. Think about the decisions that are made by both the issuing company and its investment bankers, the selling procedures involved, shelf registration procedures, and the importance of maintaining a strong secondary market. How and why did the Time Warner fiasco happen? Was it avoidable? Could the investment bankers have protected themselves, and might Time Warner's actions hurt the company when it tries to sell new securities in the future?

See end of chapter for resolution.
Photo source: Roger Tully/Tony Stone Images.

Common stock—or, for unincorporated businesses, the proprietor's or partner's capital—represents the ownership of a firm. In earlier chapters we discussed the accounting aspects of common stock and the markets in which it is traded. Now we consider some of the rights and privileges of equity holders, the process by which investors establish the value of equity shares in the marketplace, and the procedures involved when firms raise new capital by issuing additional shares of stock.

Legal Rights and Privileges of Common Stockholders

The common stockholders are the *owners* of a corporation, and as such they have certain rights and privileges. The most important of these rights are discussed in this section.

Control of the Firm

The stockholders have the right to elect the firm's directors, who in turn elect the officers who manage the business. In a small firm, the major stockholder typically assumes the positions of president and chairperson of the board of directors. In a large, publicly owned firm, the managers typically have some stock, but their personal holdings are likely to be insufficient to exercise voting control. Thus, the managements of most publicly owned firms can be removed by the stockholders if they decide that a management team is not effective.

Various state and federal laws stipulate how stockholder control is to be exercised. First, corporations must hold an election of directors periodically, usually once a year, with the vote taken at the annual meeting. Each share of stock has one vote; thus, the owner of 1,000 shares has 1,000 votes. Stockholders can appear at the annual meeting and vote in person, but typically they transfer their right to vote to a second party by means of an instrument known as a **proxy.** Management always solicits stockholders' proxies and often gets them. However, if earnings are poor and stockholders are dissatisfied, an outside (or inside) group may solicit the proxies in an effort to overthrow management and take control of the business. This is known as a **proxy fight.**

The question of control has become a central issue in finance in recent years. When a person, group, or company succeeds in ousting a firm's management by *purchasing* a majority of the outstanding stock the action is called a *takeover.* Takeovers are *hostile,* as opposed to friendly mergers in which terms are approved by the managements of the two companies. Both are discussed in detail in Chapter 22. Some well-known examples of recent takeover battles include KKR's acquisition of RJR Nabisco, Chevron's acquisition of Gulf Oil, and AT&T's takeover of NCR. As this book went to press in late 1993, a takeover battle was raging around Paramount Communications. Viacom had made a friendly bid, which Paramount favored; however, the company was forced by the courts to consider the higher bid from unwelcome suitor QVC.

Managers who do not have majority control of their firms' stocks (over 50 percent) are naturally concerned about proxy fights and hostile takeovers, and many have attempted to introduce changes in their corporate charters that

proxy

A document giving one person the authority to act for another, typically the power to vote shares of common stock.

proxy fight

An attempt by a person, group, or company to gain control of a firm by convincing stockholders to vote a new management team into office.

would make takeovers more difficult. For example, a number of companies have in the past gotten their stockholders to agree (1) to elect only one-third (rather than all) of the directors each year, (2) to require 75 percent of the stockholders (rather than 50 percent) to approve a merger, and (3) to vote in a "poison pill" provision which would allow the stockholders of a firm that is taken over by another firm to buy shares in the second firm at a reduced price. The third provision makes the acquisition unattractive and, thus, wards off hostile takeover attempts.

However, by mid-1993 important developments were occurring in this area. You may recall from Chapter 1 our discussion of a major new trend toward increased shareholder activism. This is especially true for large institutional investors such as state employee pension funds, for example, Calpers.[1] (The "Industry Practice" boxed feature later in this chapter will give additional details.) With top managements ousted during 1992 in such giant companies as General Motors, IBM, and American Express—not through hostile takeovers but through "revolt" by their large shareholders—the message has been very clear: Managements that do not have majority control *must* listen to their shareholders, at any rate to the big ones with clout. *The Economist* summed up the situation nicely with its April 24, 1993, headline: "American corporate governance; Shareholders call the plays."

As a result, the 1993 season of annual meetings for many U.S. corporations (March through June) was relatively uneventful, almost anticlimactic. Under relaxed SEC rules, shareholders can now openly communicate with each other and, sometimes, manage to do so also with corporate boards. Through negotiated settlements with management or by implied threats of proxy resolutions and resulting proxy fights, changes had already taken place. In the words of one observer, "Shareholder activism has become a year-round activity."

Major changes in a number of corporations have included (1) getting rid of poison pill provisions instituted in the 1980s, (2) electing entire corporate boards every year, (3) electing a majority of *independent* directors to boards, and (4) splitting the jobs of chairman and CEO, positions which traditionally have been held by the same individual more often than not.

Hostile takeovers have not totally disappeared from the corporate landscape. Although there were no such actual takeovers in 1992, a number of unsolicited takeover offers occurred from late 1992 through early 1993. It is likely that takeover activity will again pick up with interest rates low and bank lending on the rise.[2]

---

[1]Some mutual funds and union pension funds have taken activist shareholder roles as well. And, in July 1993 Campbell Soup Company announced its plan to become one of the first *corporate* pension funds to put pressure on companies that do not follow basic corporate governance principles, that is, manage in the best interests of their stockholders. Harvard Professor John Pound expressed the view that other corporate pension funds would likely follow Campbell's lead. If correct, this would mark an important development; corporate pension funds control $1.1 trillion in stocks (as of July 1993), compared with $464 billion in stock investments by state and local pension funds.

[2]There have been plenty of acquisitions and *friendly mergers* (also sometimes called takeovers) since roughly mid-1992. These have been due to such factors as (1) increased optimism among corporate executives over the U.S. economy, (2) general consolidation in the banking and health-care industries, and (3) industrial firms trying to reverse earlier diversification strategies by divesting units no longer seen to fit with their core businesses. Mergers and acquisitions are covered in Chapter 22.

The Right to Purchase New Stock: The Preemptive Right

preemptive right
A provision in the corporate charter or bylaws that gives common stockholders the right to purchase on a pro rata basis new issues of common stock (or securities convertible into common stock).

Common stockholders often have the right, called the **preemptive right,** to purchase, on a pro rata basis, any additional shares sold by the firm. In some states the preemptive right is automatically included in every corporate charter; in others it is necessary to specifically insert it into the charter.

The purpose of the preemptive right is twofold. First, it protects the power of control of present stockholders. If it were not for this safeguard, the management of a corporation under criticism from stockholders could prevent stockholders from removing it from office by issuing a large number of additional shares and purchasing these shares itself. Management could thereby secure control of the corporation and frustrate the will of the current stockholders.

The second, and by far the more important, reason for the preemptive right is that it protects stockholders against a dilution of value. For example, suppose 1,000 shares of common stock, each with a price of $100, were outstanding, making the total market value of the firm $100,000. If an additional 1,000 shares were sold at $50 a share, or for $50,000, this would raise the total market value of the firm to $150,000. When the total market value is divided by the new total shares outstanding, a value of $75 a share is obtained. The original stockholders thus lose $25 per share, and the new stockholders would have an instant profit of $25 per share. Therefore, selling common stock at below-market values dilutes its price and would transfer wealth from the present stockholders to those who were allowed to purchase the new shares. The preemptive right prevents this.[3]

Types of Common Stock

classified stock
Common stock that is given special designations, such as Class A, Class B, and so forth, to meet the special needs of the company.

founders' shares
Stock owned by the firm's founders that has sole voting rights but pays no dividends until retained earnings reach some specified level.

Although most firms have only one type of common stock, in some instances **classified stock** is created to meet the special needs of the company. Generally, when different types of stock are used, one type is designated *Class A,* the second *Class B,* and so on. Small, new companies seeking to acquire funds from outside sources frequently use different types of common stock. Such a company might sell Class A stock to the public, and this stock is typically *nonvoting* for a number of years, for example, five. Class B stock would be retained by the organizers of the firm and would have sole voting rights initially, during the firm's formative years. In such a situation, the Class B stock is often called **founders' shares.** On the other hand, the public investors holding Class A stock would receive dividends, but the Class B stock would typically receive no dividends until the firm's retained earnings have reached some designated level. By holding this type of classified stock, the public can take a position in a conservatively financed growth firm without sacrificing income and is protected against excessive withdrawals of funds by the original owners. Note that "Class A," "Class B," and so on, have no standard meanings. Most firms have no classified shares, but a firm that does could designate its Class A shares as founders' shares and its Class B shares as those sold to the public, while another firm could reverse these designations or use them for entirely different purposes.

---

[3]The procedure for issuing stock to existing stockholders, called a *rights offering,* is discussed in detail in Eugene F. Brigham and Louis C. Gapenski, *Intermediate Financial Management,* 4th ed., Chapter 14.

INDUSTRY PRACTICE

SHAREHOLDERS ARE FLEXING THEIR MUSCLE

Eastman Kodak Chairman Kay R. Whitmore announced in mid-1993 that he would unveil a turnaround plan for his troubled company in September. Denying that angry shareholders drove him to it, he repeatedly told reporters that he was personally motivated to make changes.

Nevertheless, analysts who upgraded their expectations for Kodak stock in light of the forthcoming plan credited investor complaints about the company's problems for the move toward change. "The dynamics have gone beyond the company, to shareholder activism and the outside board," said Jack Kelly of Goldman Sachs. And Brenda Lee Landry of Morgan Stanley said of Chairman Whitmore, "He may be bowing to shareowner pressure." If so, Kodak has joined a growing trend among America's largest corporations.

Events at General Motors in late 1992 are widely seen as the bellwether of similar corporate upheavals in response to growing shareholder activism. GM separated the roles of chairman and CEO and then named an outsider as chairman and charged him to serve as the representative of shareholders in overseeing management.

John Nash, president of the National Association of Corporate Directors, predicted that 40 or 50 percent of Fortune 500 companies will separate the two posts within five years: "The train has left the station," he said. "There's no stopping it."

Big institutional investors have been pushing for the change, contending that a split in the chairman/CEO positions strengthens the directors' ability to monitor a corporate chief while curbing his or her control over a board's agenda and makeup. A survey of large corporations' directors found that 35 percent

favored separation of the two positions, and 49 percent added that retired CEO's should not continue to serve on companies' boards.

At Kodak, Chairman Whitmore acknowledged that his job was on the line, and he promised that he and his management team had the best chance of turning the company around "more completely . . . and with better long-term outcome than anyone else."

Hopes had soared for improvement in Kodak's listless performance when Christopher J. Steffen, a man noted for his ability to ram through cost cuts, was appointed chief financial officer. However, just a few weeks later the widely respected executive quit after a clash with Whitmore, and confidence in Kodak took a dive. Just weeks after that, though, the stock moved two-thirds of the way to its previous high because Whitmore appeared to have taken the hint that shareholders were demanding strong actions. Whitmore promised that his plan would slash costs, increase cash flows, and put more money in shareholders' pockets with solid earnings in 1993 and record earnings in 1994.

Whitmore also said his plan would make Kodak "less large and less complex." He formed a finance committee composed of four outside directors and a new corporate directions committee which would meet regularly with investors. Additionally, retired Kodak chairmen will no longer serve on the company's board.

A leader in the push for greater board independence for all companies is the nation's largest public pension fund, the California Public Employees Retirement System (Calpers) and its head, Dale Hanson. "The people at Calpers have consistently been not just the first to identify issues but also the ones with the courage to follow up on them," said Sara Teslik, head of the Council of Institutional Investors.

Calpers targets 12 poorly performing companies each year and requests meetings with their CEOs or outside directors. Suggested changes have come about in more than half the selected firms, including GM, Sears, and Westinghouse. At Westinghouse, cooperation between shareholders and management was the key to tackling the firm's problems, not a boardroom coup or hostile takeover that would have been the likely action in the past. The company's stock price had dropped more than half in less than a year during

Sources: Joan E. Rigdon, "Kodak Bounces Back on Hopes for True Turnaround," *The Wall Street Journal,* May 18, 1993, C1; Joan E. Rigdon, "Kodak Holders Send a Warning to Directors," *The Wall Street Journal,* May 13, 1993, A3; George Anders, "While Head of Calpers Lectures Other Firms, His Own Board Frets," *The Wall Street Journal,* January 29, 1993, A1; John Pound, "Westinghouse Lights Boardroom Path," *The Wall Street Journal,* December 11, 1992, A12; Joann S. Lublin, "Recent Wave of Activism in Boardroom Will Gain Momentum, Survey Suggests," *The Wall Street Journal,* December 9, 1992; Joann S. Lublin, "Other Concerns Are Likely to Follow GM in Splitting Posts of Chairman and CEO," *The Wall Street Journal,* November 4, 1992, B1; and Paul Ingrassia, "Board Reform Replaces the LBO," *The Wall Street Journal,* October 30, 1992, A14.

1992, primarily because of loan problems in its credit and finance unit.

Several different groups, including Calpers, the Council of Institutional Investors, and the United Shareholders Association, focused on Westinghouse and requested meetings to discuss its performance and structure. There was an implied threat of shareholder proposals, including separating the CEO and chairman positions, hiring an outside consultant to explore financial restructuring, and rearranging the board.

Because of those threats, CEO Paul Lego opened the door to the various groups, meeting with them and explaining Westinghouse's problems and attempts at solutions. The sessions led to reforms that set new rules for oversight, gave investors more input, and ensured a more responsive and energized board. For instance, Westinghouse established a board committee made up only of outside directors to oversee director nominations; it set up an independent compensation committee which hired its own consultants; it mandated annual election of the entire board rather than staggered elections of one-third at a time; it ensured full confidentiality in shareholder voting; and it ruled that independent, outside directors would make up the majority of its board.

John Pound, finance professor at Harvard's John F. Kennedy School, says the overall result of the changes at Westinghouse "will not be a sudden earnings increase, but enhanced long-term competitiveness."

As changes come to company after company, one analyst's comments about Kodak seem applicable to all. What has changed, said Michael Ellmann of Wertheim Schroder, is "not management but the environment." Now that shareholders are angry, "investors' tolerance . . . is much lower."

General Motors provides an example of another type of classification. When General Motors acquired Electronic Data Systems (EDS), it established a separate class of stock, GME, so that EDS's management would have a substantial equity stake in the business as an incentive for high-level performance. The GME shareholders have limited voting rights, but they receive dividends based on EDS's earnings rather than on those of GM. GM later acquired Hughes Aircraft and paid in part with a new Class H common, GMH, which also has limited voting rights and on which dividends are tied to Hughes's performance as a GM subsidiary.

Companies that have more recently created separate classes of stock include USX Corporation, Ralston Purina, Hovnanian Enterprises, and Mitchell Energy & Development Corporation. As with GM, in several of these cases the separate classes of stock were for very dissimilar types of businesses within a corporation. This was true for USX (steel versus energy) and Ralston Purina (pet foods versus bakery products). In June 1993, RJR Nabisco was likewise planning a new class of stock for its food unit, separate from its badly slumping tobacco business. Yet, hours after obtaining stockholders approval for the new class of stock, RJR abandoned the plan and blamed poor market conditions. Market analysts were guessing that investors would have balked at buying the new class of stock because of the company's tobacco business and the "risk of tobacco liability [lawsuits]."

Self-Test

Identify some approaches that corporate managements have used in the past to make hostile takeovers more difficult.

What are the two primary reasons for the existence of the preemptive right?

What are some reasons that a company might use classified stock?

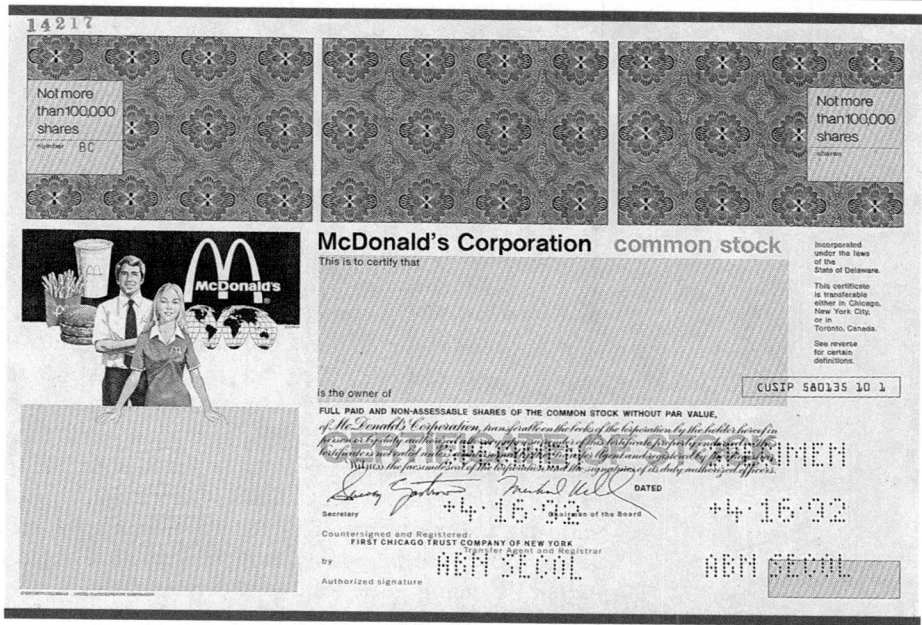

Stock certificates, such as this sample from McDonald's Corporation, are issued to common stockholders as proof of ownership in the corporation. McDonald's stock has no par value; however, when a stock has a par value it would be stated on the certificate. The stock certificate would also show the number of shares purchased (found in the boxed area in the upper right corner). The intricate design is intended to make counterfeiting difficult, as with U.S. dollar bills.

Source: Reprinted with the permission of McDonald's Corporation.

Common Stock Valuation

Common stock represents an ownership interest in a corporation, but to the typical investor, a share of common stock is simply a piece of paper characterized by two features:

1. It entitles its owner to dividends, but only if the company has earnings out of which dividends can be paid and only if management chooses to pay dividends rather than to retain and reinvest all the earnings. Whereas a bond contains a *promise* to pay interest, common stock provides no such promise to pay dividends—if you own a stock, you may *expect* a dividend, but your expectations may not in fact be met. To illustrate, Long Island Lighting Company (LILCO) had paid dividends on its common stock for more than 50 years, and people expected these dividends to continue. However, when the company encountered severe problems a few years ago, it stopped paying dividends. Note, though, that LILCO continued to pay interest on its bonds; if it had not, then it would have been declared bankrupt, and the bondholders could have taken over the company.

2. Stock can be sold at some future date, hopefully at a price greater than the purchase price. If the stock is actually sold at a price above its purchase price, the investor will receive a *capital gain*. Generally, at the time

people buy common stocks, they do expect to receive capital gains; otherwise, they would not buy the stocks. However, after the fact, one can end up with capital losses rather than capital gains. LILCO's stock price dropped from $17.50 to $3.75 in one year, so the *expected* capital gains on that stock turned out to be *actual* capital losses.

Definitions of Terms Used in the Stock Valuation Models

As we saw in capital budgeting, as well as in the evaluation of bonds and preferred stock, an asset's value is determined by the discounted benefits that the asset provides a purchaser. These benefits are the expected future cash flows, and a stock's value is, therefore, the present value of (1) the dividends expected in each year plus (2) the price investors expect to receive when they sell the stock, which includes the return of the original investment.

We saw in Chapter 1 that managers seek to maximize the values of their firms' stocks. A manager's actions affect both the stream of income to investors and the riskiness of that stream. Therefore, the manager needs to know how alternative actions are likely to affect stock prices, so at this point we develop some models to help show how the value of a share of stock is determined. We begin by defining the following terms:

D_t = dividend the stockholder *expects* to receive at the end of Year t. D_0 is the most recent dividend, which has already been paid; D_1 is the first dividend expected, and it will be paid at the end of this year; D_2 is the dividend expected at the end of 2 years; and so on. D_1 represents the first cash flow a new purchaser of the stock will receive. Note that D_0, the dividend which has just been paid, is known with certainty. However, all future dividends are expected values, so the estimate of D_t may differ among investors.[4]

market price, P_0

The price at which a stock sells in the market.

intrinsic value, $\hat{P}_0$

The value of an asset that, in the mind of a particular investor, is justified by the facts; $\hat{P}_0$ may be different from the asset's actual market price.

P_0 = actual **market price** of the stock today.

$\hat{P}_t$ = expected price of the stock at the end of each Year t (pronounced "P hat t"). $\hat{P}_0$ is the **intrinsic**, or *theoretical*, **value** of the stock today as seen by the particular investor doing the analysis; $\hat{P}_1$ is the price expected at the end of 1 year; and so on. Note that whereas P_0 is fixed and is identical for all investors, $\hat{P}_0$ could differ among investors depending on their estimates of the stock's cash flows and of the risk associated with these future cash flows. The caret, or "hat," is used to indicate that $\hat{P}_t$ is an estimated value. $\hat{P}_0$, the individual investor's estimate of the intrinsic value today, could be above or below P_0, the actual current stock price, but an investor would buy the stock only if his or her estimate of $\hat{P}_0$ were equal to or greater than P_0.

Since there are many investors in the market, there can be many values for $\hat{P}_0$. However, we can think of a group of "average," or "marginal," investors whose actions actually

---

[4]Stocks generally pay dividends quarterly, so theoretically we should evaluate them on a quarterly basis. However, in stock valuation, most analysts work on an annual basis because the data generally are not precise enough to warrant refinement to a quarterly model.

determine the market price. For these marginal investors, P_0 must equal $\hat{P}_0$; otherwise, a disequilibrium would exist, and buying and selling in the market would occur until P_0 and $\hat{P}_0$ are equal; at that point we say that the stock is in *equilibrium.*

g = expected **growth rate** in dividends as predicted by a marginal investor. (If we assume that dividends are expected to grow at a constant rate, g is also equal to the expected rate of growth in the stock's price.)

k_s = minimum acceptable, or **required, rate of return** on the stock, considering both its riskiness and the returns available on other investments. Again, this term generally relates to marginal investors. We found this rate in Chapter 12 using the SML equation; the only difference is that we have now added the subscript "s."

$\hat{k}_s$ = **expected rate of return** which an investor who buys the stock actually anticipates receiving. $\hat{k}_s$ (pronounced "k hat s") could be above or below k_s, but one would buy the stock only if $\hat{k}_s$ were equal to or greater than k_s. When $\hat{k}_s = k_s$, $\hat{P}_0 = P_0$, and the stock is in **equilibrium.**

$\bar{k}_s$ = **actual,** or **realized,** *after the fact* **rate of return** (pronounced "k bar s"). You may *expect* to obtain a return of $\hat{k}_s = 15$ percent if you buy a given stock today, but if the market goes down, you may end up next year with an actual realized return that is much lower, perhaps even negative.

D_1/P_0 = expected **dividend yield** on the stock during the coming year. If the stock is expected to pay a dividend of $1 during the next 12 months, and if its current price is $10, then the expected dividend yield is $1/$10 = 0.10 = 10\%$.

$\dfrac{\hat{P}_1 - P_0}{P_0}$ = expected **capital gains yield** on the stock during the coming year. If the stock sells for $10 today, and if it is expected to rise to $10.50 at the end of 1 year, then the expected capital gain is $\hat{P}_1 - P_0 = \$10.50 - \$10.00 = \$0.50$, and the expected capital gains yield is $0.50/$10 = 0.05 = 5\%$.

Expected total return = $\hat{k}_s$ = expected dividend yield (D_1/P_0) plus expected capital gains yield $[(\hat{P}_1 - P_0)/P_0]$. In our example, the **expected total return** = $\hat{k}_s = 10\% + 5\% = 15\%$.

growth rate
The expected rate of growth in dividends per share.

required rate of return, k_s
The minimum rate of return on a common stock that a stockholder considers acceptable.

expected rate of return, $\hat{k}_s$
The rate of return on a common stock that a stockholder expects to receive.

equilibrium
The condition under which the expected rate of return, $\hat{k}_s$, equals the required rate of return, k_s, and the price of the stock is stable.

actual (realized) rate of return, $\bar{k}_s$
The rate of return on a common stock actually received by stockholders. $\bar{k}_s$ may be greater or less than k_s and/or k_s.

dividend yield
The expected dividend divided by the current price of a share of stock.

capital gains yield
The capital gain during a given year divided by the beginning price.

expected total return
The sum of the expected dividend yield and the expected capital gains yield on a share of stock.

Expected Dividends as the Basis for Stock Values

In our discussion of bonds, we found the value of a bond as the present value of interest payments over the life of the bond plus the present value of the bond's maturity (or par) value. Stock prices are likewise determined as the present value of a stream of cash flows. What are the cash flows that corporations provide to their stockholders? First, think of yourself as an investor who buys a stock with the intention of holding it (in your family) forever. In this case, all that you and your heirs will receive is a stream of dividends, and the value of the stock today is calculated as the present value of *an infinite stream of dividends* since common stock has no maturity date:

$$\text{Value of stock} = \hat{P}_0 = \text{PV of expected future dividends}$$

$$= \frac{D_1}{(1 + k_s)^1} + \frac{D_2}{(1 + k_s)^2} + \cdots + \frac{D_\infty}{(1 + k_s)^\infty} \quad (17\text{-}1)$$

$$= \sum_{t=1}^{\infty} \frac{D_t}{(1 + k_s)^t}.$$

What about the more typical case, where you expect to hold the stock for a finite period and then sell it — what will be the value of $\hat{P}_0$ in this case? Unless the company is likely to be liquidated and thus to disappear, *the value of the stock is again determined by Equation 17-1*. To see this, recognize that for any individual investor, the expected cash flows consist of expected dividends plus the expected sale price of the stock. However, the sale price the current investor receives will depend on the dividends some future investor expects. Therefore, for all present and future investors, *in total*, expected cash flows are the expected future dividends. To put it another way, unless a firm is liquidated or sold to another concern, the cash flows it provides to its stockholders will consist only of a stream of dividends; therefore, the value of a share of its stock must be established as the present value of that expected dividend stream.

The general validity of Equation 17-1 can also be confirmed by asking the following question: Suppose you buy a stock and expect to hold it for 1 year. You will receive dividends during the year plus the value $\hat{P}_1$ when you sell at the end of the year. But what will determine the value of $\hat{P}_1$? The answer is that it will be determined as the present value of the dividends during Year 2 plus the stock price at the end of that year, which in turn will be determined as the present value of another set of future dividends and an even more distant stock price. This process can be continued ad infinitum, and the ultimate result is Equation 17-1.[5]

Equation 17-1 is a generalized stock valuation model in the sense that the pattern of dividend payments can be anything; D_t can be rising, falling, constant, or fluctuating randomly, and Equation 17-1 will still hold. Often, however, the projected stream of dividends can reasonably be assumed to follow some pattern, in which case we can simplify our model. In the next section we will show a much less complex version of Equation 17-1, which makes only two simplifying assumptions: (1) that the growth in earnings and dividends for the firm will progress at a constant rate into the future, and (2) that k_s is greater than g.

Normal, or Constant, Growth

As firms reach the maturity phase of their life cycles, the growth of their earnings and dividends tends to stabilize. This period of stability is not one of stagnation but rather one of moderate growth, and, in general, this growth is expected to continue into the foreseeable future at about the same rate as that of

---

[5]We should note that investors periodically lose sight of the long-run nature of stocks as investments and forget that in order to sell a stock at a profit, one must find a buyer who will pay the higher price. If you analyze a stock's value in accordance with Equation 17-1, conclude that the stock's market price exceeds a reasonable value, and then buy the stock anyway, you are following the "bigger fool" theory of investment — you think that you may be a fool to buy the stock at its excessive price, but you also think that when you get ready to sell it, you can find someone who is an even bigger fool.

the nominal gross domestic product (real GDP plus inflation). On this basis, one may expect the dividend of an average, or "normal," company to grow at a rate of 6 to 8 percent a year.

normal (constant) growth

Growth which is expected to continue into the fore-seeable future at about the same rate as that of the economy as a whole; g = a constant.

If we wish to determine next year's dividend, D_1, for a **normal (constant) growth** firm we need only to multiply last year's dividend, D_0, by one plus the expected growth rate. Thus, if Carter Chemical Company has just paid a dividend of $2.00 and if investors expect a 7 percent growth rate for the company throughout the foreseeable future, then the estimated dividend one year hence would be $D_1 = \$2.00(1.07) = \$2.14$, D_2 would be approximately $2.29, and the estimated dividend five years hence would be

$$D_t = D_0 (1 + g)^t = \$2.00 (1.07)^5 \approx \$2.81.$$

If g is constant, Equation 17-1 may be rewritten as follows.[6]

$$\hat{P}_0 = \frac{D_0(1 + g)}{k_s - g} = \frac{D_1}{k_s - g}. \tag{17-2}$$

If investors require a 12 percent rate of return, k_s, from an investment in Carter's common stock, the value of the firm's common stock is found to be $42.80:

$$\hat{P}_0 = \frac{\$2.00(1.07)}{0.12 - 0.07} = \frac{\$2.14}{0.05} = \$42.80.$$

constant growth model

Also called the Gordon Model; used to find the value of a constant growth stock.

The **constant growth model** Equation 17-2 is often called the Gordon Model, after Myron J. Gordon, who did much to develop and popularize it. Recall that we could reach the same conclusion—that the price of Carter's common stock is $42.80—by utilizing the more cumbersome Equation 17-1.

The concept underlying the valuation process is graphed in Figure 17-1. The upper step function curve represents the dollar value of Carter's dividends growing at a 7 percent rate. The lower step function plots the present value of those dividends.

Carter's dividends are growing at the rate $g = 7\%$, but because $k_s > g$, the present value of each future dividend is declining. We have already found the expected dividend in Year 1 to be $2.14. However, the present value of this dividend, discounted at 12 percent, is PV $D_1 = \$2.14/(1.12)^1 = \$1.9107$ or $\approx$ $1.91. The dividend expected in Year 2 grows to $\$2.14(1.07) \approx \$2.29$, but the present value of this dividend falls to $\$2.29/(1.12)^2 \approx \$1.825$, and so on. Thus, the expected dividends are growing, but the present value of each successive dividend is declining because the dividend growth rate (7%) is less than the rate used for discounting the dividends to the present (12%).

If we summed the present values of each future dividend, this summation would be the value of the stock, $\hat{P}_0$. Therefore, if we extended the lower step function curve in Figure 17-1 on out to infinity and added up the present values of each future dividend, the sum would equal $42.80. When g is constant, this is also the value obtained using Equation 17-2.

Note that Equation 17-2 is sufficiently general to encompass a case where growth is zero or even negative. *If Carter's expected rate of growth had been*

[6]We spare the reader the mathematical proof of our assertion. For those who are interested, the derivation of Equation 17-2 is provided in Eugene F. Brigham and Louis C. Gapenski, *Intermediate Financial Management,* 4th ed., Appendix 4A.

Figure 17-1

Carter Chemical Company: Constant Growth Dividend Stream and Present Value of the Stream, Assuming $D_0 = \$2.00$, $g = 7\%$, $k_s = 12\%$

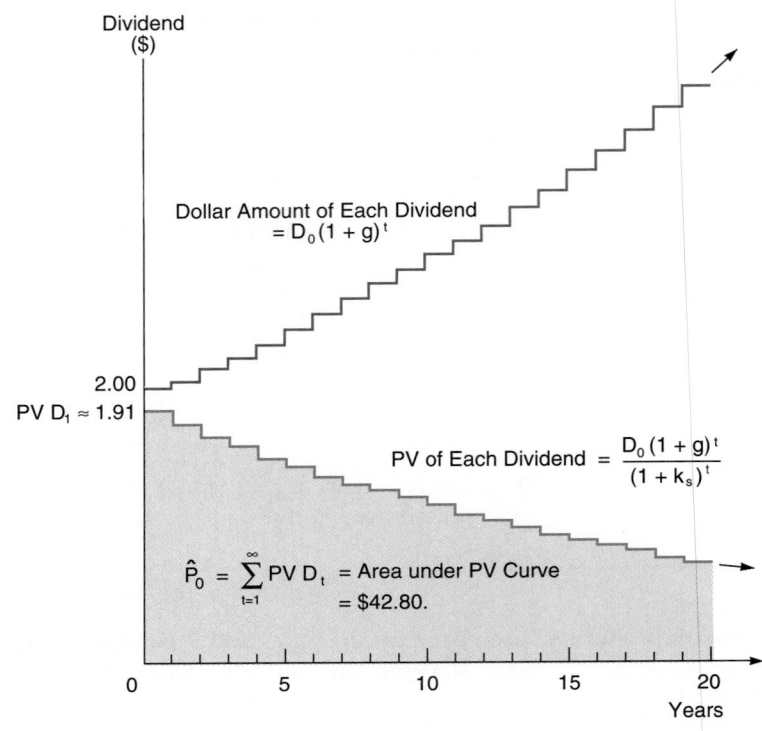

This figure illustrates constant growth stock valuation. The value of a share of common stock equals the present value of all future dividends. This example assumes that these dividends will grow at a constant rate, g, of 7 percent and that Carter has a required rate of return, k_s, of 12 percent. We can plot the growing dividend stream both in actual dollar amounts and in present values into infinity. The sum of the discounted future dividends is equal to the intrinsic value of the firm's stock, P_0.

zero, $D_0 = D_1 = D_t = \$2.00$, and the intrinsic value of Carter's stock would have been $16.67.

$$\hat{P}_0 = \frac{D}{k_s} = \frac{\$2.00}{0.12} \approx \$16.67.$$

In effect, the value is found as we would calculate the value of any perpetuity.[7] Note also that a necessary condition for using the simplified Equation 17-2 is that k_s be greater than g. If the equation is used in situations where k_s is not

---

[7]As we will see in Chapter 21, if there are no growth opportunities for a given firm, it would pay out all earnings as dividends, so $E_1 = D_1 = E_2$, etc. Therefore, an alternative measure of the stock price of a *no-growth* firm is $\hat{P} = E/k_s$.

As for the case of *negative growth*, a mining company whose profits are falling because of a declining ore body is an example. Someone buying such a company would expect its earnings, and consequently its dividends and stock price, to decline each year, and this would lead to capital losses rather than capital gains. Obviously, a declining company's stock price will be relatively low, and its dividend yield must be high enough to offset the expected capital loss and still produce a competitive total return. Students sometimes argue that they would not be willing to buy a stock whose price was expected to decline. However, if the annual dividends are large enough to *more than offset* the falling stock price, the stock still could provide a good return.

greater than g, the results will be meaningless. For example, if Carter's k_s = 12%, D_1 = \$2.14, but g = 15%, then

$$\hat{P}_0 = \frac{\$2.14}{0.12 - 0.15} = \frac{\$2.14}{-0.03} \approx -\$71.33.$$

This result indicates that a present owner of Carter's equity would be willing to give you a share of the stock *and* \$71.33 to get you to take it. A highly unlikely scenario!

It should be emphasized that the constant growth valuation model is intended to price the equity shares of a company that has normal or constantly growing earnings and dividends. However, for a firm that is exhibiting unusually high growth in the early stages of its life cycle or that is in a highly variable economic environment, Equation 17-2 would not provide an effective means of equity valuation. For example, Equation 17-2 would be a poor choice to use in evaluating the share price of a new high-technology firm, but it would probably provide an excellent approximation of the economic value of a mature company. Therefore, the more variable the growth rate in earnings and hence dividends, the less satisfactory a job the model represented by Equation 17-2 will do in valuing a firm's common stock. We will discuss procedures for dealing with nonconstant growth in a later section.

Finally, notice that an investor's expected holding period is *not* a factor in Equation 17-2. The implication is that *if* investors agree on the next dividend on a given stock, D_1, on a constant rate of growth, g, and on the riskiness of the future dividend stream, as reflected in k_s, they should then arrive at the same intrinsic value, $\hat{P}_0$, for the stock.

Expected Rate of Return on a Constant Growth Stock

We can solve Equation 17-2 for the required rate of return, k_s. And, if the stock market is in equilibrium, k_s will equal $\hat{k}_s$, the expected rate of return. We obtain the following equation:

$$\begin{array}{ccc} \text{Expected} & \text{Expected} & \text{Expected growth rate,} \\ \text{rate of return} = & \text{dividend yield} + & \text{or capital gains yield} \end{array}$$

$$\hat{k}_s = \frac{D_1}{P_0} + g. \qquad (17\text{-}3)$$

Thus, if you buy a stock for a price P_0 = \$42.80, and if you expect the stock to pay a dividend D_1 = \$2.14 one year from now and to grow at a constant rate g = 7% in the future, your expected rate of return is 12 percent:

$$\hat{k}_s = \frac{\$2.14}{\$42.80} + 7\% = 5\% + 7\% = 12\%$$

In this form, we see that $\hat{k}_s$ is the *expected total return* and that it consists of an *expected dividend yield*, D_1/P_0 = 5%, plus an *expected growth rate* or *capital gains yield*, g = 7%.

Suppose the previously described analysis had been conducted on December 31, 1993, so P_0 = \$42.80 is the stock price at that time and D_1 = \$2.14 is the dividend expected at the end of 1994. What should the *stock price* be at the end of 1994? We would again apply Equation 17-2, but this time we would use the 1995 dividend, $D_2 = D_1(1 + g) = \$2.14(1.07) = \$2.29$:

$$\hat{P}_{12/31/1994} = \frac{D_{1995}}{k_s - g} = \frac{\$2.29}{0.12 - 0.07} = \$45.80.$$

Now notice that $\hat{P}_1$, \$45.80, is 7 percent greater than P_0, the \$42.80 price on December 31, 1993:

$$P_0(1 + g) = \hat{P}_1$$

$$\$42.80(1.07) = \$45.80.$$

Thus, you would expect to make a capital gain of $\$45.80 - \$42.80 = \$3.00$ during 1994 and to have a capital gains yield of 7 percent:

$$\text{Capital gains yield}_{1994} = \frac{\text{Capital gain}}{\text{Beginning price}} = \frac{\hat{P}_1 - P_0}{P_0} = \frac{\$3.00}{\$42.80} = 0.07 = 7\%.$$

We could extend the analysis on out, and in each future year the expected capital gains yield would always equal g, the expected dividend growth rate.

The dividend yield for 1995 can be estimated as follows:

$$\text{Dividend yield}_{1995} = \frac{D_{1995}}{\hat{P}_{1994}} = \frac{\$2.29}{\$45.80} = 0.05 = 5\%.$$

The dividend yield for 1996 could also be calculated, and again it would be 5 percent. Thus, *for a constant growth stock,* these conditions must hold:

1. The dividend is expected to grow forever at a constant rate, g. This also requires that earnings grow at the rate g.
2. The stock price is expected to grow at this same rate.
3. The expected dividend yield is a constant.
4. The expected capital gains yield is also a constant, and it is equal to g.
5. The expected total rate of return, $\hat{k}_s$, is equal to the expected dividend yield plus the expected growth rate.

Supernormal, or Nonconstant, Growth

Firms typically go through *life cycles.* During the early part of their lives, their growth is much faster than that of the economy as a whole; then they match the economy's growth; and, if management cannot prevent it, they enter a final period when their growth is slower than that of the economy. Automobile manufacturers in the 1920s and computer software firms such as Microsoft in the 1990s are examples of firms in the early part of the cycle, and these firms are called **supernormal,** or **nonconstant, growth** firms. Figure 17-2 illustrates such nonconstant growth and compares it with normal growth, zero growth, and negative growth.

In the figure, the dividends of the supernormal growth firm are expected to grow at a 30 percent rate for 3 years, after which the growth rate is expected to fall to 8 percent, the assumed average for the economy. The value of this firm, like any other, is the present value of its expected future dividends as determined by Equation 17-1. In the case in which D_t is growing at a constant rate, we obtained Equation 17-2: $\hat{P}_0 = D_1/(k_s - g)$. In the supernormal growth case, however, the expected growth rate is not a constant, but it drops to a lower, normal, rate of growth at the end of the supernormal growth period. To

supernormal (nonconstant) growth

The part of the life cycle of a firm in which its growth is much faster than that of the economy as a whole.

Figure 17-2

Illustrative Dividend
Growth Rates

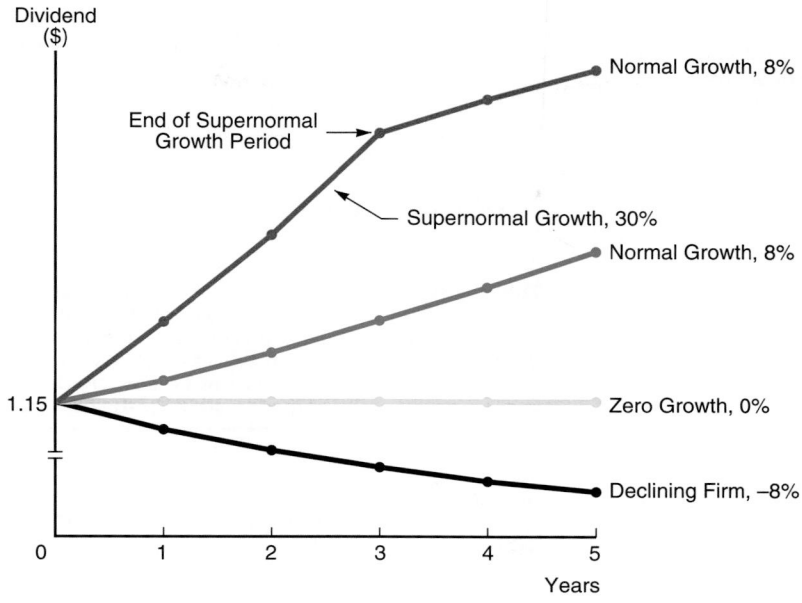

This figure compares dividend growth patterns for a supernormal growth firm, a normal growth firm, a zero growth firm, and a firm with declining growth. Notice that the supernormal firm's dividend growth is 30 percent per year for 3 years, and it then follows a normal growth pattern of 8 percent per year. The normal firm's dividend growth is a steady 8 percent per year, while the zero growth firm's dividend remains at $1.15 per year. (The zero growth pattern is the same as a preferred stock dividend pattern.) Finally, the last case illustrated is that of declining dividend growth.

find the value of such a stock, or of any nonconstant growth stock when the growth rate will eventually stabilize, we proceed in three steps:

1.   Find the dividends expected at the end of each year during the period of supernormal growth.

2.   Find the expected price of the stock at the end of the supernormal growth period, at which point it has become a normal, constant growth stock.

3.   Discount all the expected cash flows through the end of the supernormal growth period, and sum to find the intrinsic value of the stock, $\hat{P}_0$.

To illustrate the process for valuing nonconstant growth stocks, suppose the following facts exist:

k_s = stockholders' required rate of return = 13.4%.
N = expected years of supernormal growth = 3.
g_s = expected rate of growth in both earnings and dividends during the supernormal growth period = 30%. (Note: The growth rate during the supernormal growth period could, in some cases, vary from year to year. Also, there could be several different supernormal growth periods, e.g., 30% for 3 years, then 20% for 3 years, and then a constant 8%.)
g_n = expected rate of constant growth after the supernormal period = 8%.
D_0 = last dividend the company paid = $1.15.

Figure 17-3

Process for Finding the
Value of a Supernormal
Growth Stock

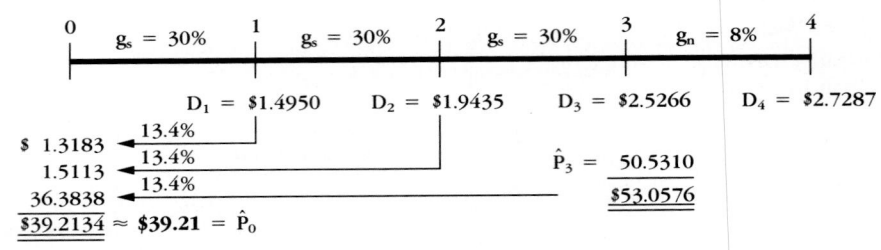

This figure illustrates the steps for evaluating a nonconstant, or supernormal, growth stock. The first step is to find the expected dividends during each of the supernormal growth years. The next step is to find the price of the stock at the end of the supernormal growth period based on, in this case, D_4. The stock now becomes a constant growth stock, therefore, the Gordon Model can be used. Each year's cash flow is then discounted back to the present and summed to arrive at the expected current stock price.

The valuation process is graphed in Figure 17-3 and explained in the steps that follow.

Step 1. Calculate the dividends expected at the end of each year during the supernormal growth period. Calculate the first dividend, $D_1 = D_0(1 + g_s) = \$1.15(1.30) = \$1.4950$. Show the $1.4950 on the time line as the cash flow for Year 1.

Now calculate $D_2 = D_1(1 + g_s) = \$1.4950(1.30) = \$1.9435$, and then $D_3 = D_2(1 + g_s) = \$1.9435(1.30) = \$2.5266$. Show these values on the time line as cash flows for Years 2 and 3.

Step 2. The price of the stock is the PV of dividends from Year 1 to infinity, so in theory we could project each future dividend, with growth at the normal growth rate of 8% from this point on. However, we know that after D_3 has been paid, which is at the end of Year 3, the stock becomes a constant growth stock, so we can use the constant growth equation to find $\hat{P}_3$, which is the PV of the dividends from Year 4 to infinity as evaluated at the end of Year 3.

First, we determine $D_4 = \$2.5266(1.08) = \$2.7287$ for use in the equation, and then we calculate $\hat{P}_3$ as follows:

$$\hat{P}_3 = \frac{D_4}{k_s - g_n} = \frac{\$2.7287}{0.134 - 0.08} = \$50.5310.$$

Note that the only reason we have to calculate D_4 is to use it in calculating $\hat{P}_3$. The price of a constant growth stock is always based on the *next* dividend.

Now we show $\hat{P}_3 = \$50.5310$ on the time line as a *second* cash flow in Year 3. The $50.5310 is a Year 3 cash flow in the sense that the owner of the stock could sell it for $50.5310 at the end of Year 3 because this price represents the present value of all future dividends, from Year 4 to infinity. Note that the *total cash flow* at Year 3 consists of the sum of D_3 and $\hat{P}_3 = \$2.5266 + \$50.5310 = \$53.0576$.

Step 3. Now that the cash flows have been placed on the time line, we can discount each cash flow at the required rate of return, $k_s = 13.4\%$. Since 13.4% is not shown in the tables, it is necessary to discount each flow by dividing by $(1.134)^t$, where $t = 1$ for Year 1, $t = 2$ for Year 2, and $t = 3$ for Year 3. If you do this, you should get the PVs shown in the column to the left below the time line. The sum of the PVs is the value of the supernormal growth stock, $39.21. (Recognize that it makes no difference if you discount D_3 and $\hat{P}_3$ separately.)[8]

Self-Test

Explain the following statement: "Whereas a bond contains a promise to pay interest, common stock provides an expectation but no promise of dividends."

What are the two elements of a stock's expected returns?

How are the capital budgeting project valuation model, the general bond valuation model, and the general stock valuation model (Equation 17–1) similar to one another?

Write out and explain the Gordon Model for a constant growth stock.

What conditions must hold if we are to be able to use the Gordon Model (Equation 17-2)?

How does one calculate the capital gains yield and the dividend yield of a stock?

Explain how one would find the value of a supernormal growth stock?

Pros and Cons of Common Stock

Thus far the chapter has covered some of the legal rights of common stockholders and the main characteristics of common stock, and we have seen how its price is determined. Now we will evaluate the advantages and disadvantages of stock financing from the point of view of the issuing corporation, investors, and society in general.

Issuer's Viewpoint

Advantages. Common stock financing offers several advantages to the corporation:

1. Common stock does not obligate the firm to make payments to stockholders: Only if the company generates earnings and has no pressing internal needs for them will it pay dividends. Had it used debt, it would have incurred a legal obligation to pay interest, regardless of its operating condition and cash flows.

2. Common stock carries no fixed maturity date — it never has to be "repaid" as would a debt issue. And yet, the issuer usually has the option of buying

---

[8]If you have a financial calculator, you can find the PV of the cash flows as shown on the time line by using the cash flow register of your calculator. Here you would enter 0 for CF_0 because you get no cash flow at Time 0, $CF_1 = 1.495$, $CF_2 = 1.9435$, and $CF_3 = 2.5266 + 50.531 = 53.0576$. Then enter $k = i = 13.4$, and press the NPV key to find the value of the stock, $39.21.

back some portion of its common stock in the open market. (We will discuss stock repurchase in Chapter 21.)

3. Since common stock cushions creditors against losses, the sale of common stock increases the creditworthiness of the firm. This, in turn, raises its bond rating, lowers its cost of debt, and increases its future ability to use debt.

4. If a company's prospects look bright, then common stock can often be sold on better terms than debt.

5. When a company is having operating problems, it often needs new funds to overcome its problems. However, investors are reluctant to supply capital to a troubled company, and if they do they generally require some type of security. From a practical standpoint, this often means that a firm which is experiencing problems can only obtain new capital by issuing debt, which is safer from the investor's standpoint. Because corporate treasurers are well aware of this, they often opt to finance with common stock during good times in order to maintain a **reserve borrowing capacity.** Indeed, surveys have indicated that maintenance of an adequate reserve of borrowing capacity is a primary consideration in many financing decisions.

reserve borrowing capacity

Unused debt capacity that permits borrowing if a firm needs capital in troubled times.

Disadvantages.   Disadvantages associated with issuing common stock include the following:

1. The sale of common stock gives some voting rights, and perhaps even control, to new stockholders. For this reason, additional equity financing is often avoided by managers who are concerned about maintaining control. The use of classified stock can mitigate this problem.

2. Common stock gives new owners the right to share in the income of the firm; if profits soar, then new stockholders will share in this bonanza, whereas if debt had been used, new investors would have received only a fixed return, no matter how profitable the company had been.

3. As we shall see, the costs of underwriting and distributing common stock are usually higher than those for preferred stock or debt. Issuance costs for common stock are characteristically higher because (1) the costs of investigating an equity security investment are higher than those for a comparable debt security and (2) stocks are riskier than debt, meaning that investors must diversify their equity holdings, so a given dollar amount of new stock must be sold to a larger number of purchasers than the same amount of debt.

4. As we will learn in Chapter 19, the cost of equity capital is greater than the cost of debt, even *before* factoring in issuance costs (also called *flotation costs*). Therefore, if the firm has more equity than is called for in its optimal capital structure (the appropriate mix of debt and equity), the average cost of capital will be higher than necessary.

5. Under current tax laws, common stock dividends are not deductible as an expense for tax purposes, but bond interest is deductible. As we will also see in Chapter 19, taxes raise the relative cost of equity as compared with debt.

Investor's Viewpoint

Advantages.   Common stock appeals to certain groups of investors for a number of reasons, some of which are the following:

1. Common stock typically carries a higher expected total return (dividends plus capital gains) than does preferred stock or debt.

2. Common stockholders have unlimited ownership rights to remaining profits after other security holders have received their limited contractual payments. This means that there is considerable growth potential associated with a common stock investment.

3. Because common stock represents ownership of the firm, and, therefore, ownership of real assets, it tends to provide investors with a better hedge against unanticipated inflation than would fixed-income securities such as bonds and preferred stock. However, this tendency to keep investors ahead of inflation only holds over relatively long periods of time.

4. Common stock cannot be called away from the investors under normal circumstances.

5. Since common stockholders control the corporation through their right to vote, corporate policies are usually developed to further their interests and maximize the price of the common stock.

Disadvantages.   Disadvantages associated with common stock ownership include the following:

1. A common stock investment in a given firm is riskier than holding debt or preferred stock in that same firm (which means—as mentioned earlier—that the investor has a greater need to diversify). This is the basic risk-return tradeoff again, the price that must be paid for the higher expected return. The higher risk is due to the next four factors.

2. Common stockholders have no legal rights to dividends. Even when they do consistently receive dividends, there is no promise that these will be stable or growing, although one or the other may be the goal of management. Since common dividends are paid *after* all fixed financing charges (interest on debt and dividends on preferred stock), the residual amount available for common stock dividends will fluctuate more than total corporate earnings. This is the effect of financial leverage, which will be discussed further in Chapter 20.

3. Not only do common stockholders have a residual claim on earnings, but, in case of corporate bankruptcy and liquidation, their claim on corporate assets is also residual (last). In practice, this usually means that common stockholders' investment is wiped out if the firm is liquidated.

4. There is no promise from the issuing corporation to ever buy back, or redeem, the shares sold.

5. Common stock prices are quite volatile. Market price fluctuations are often so extreme that the timing of purchases and sales of even high-quality common stocks presents a major investment problem.

Social Viewpoint

From a social viewpoint, common stock is a desirable form of financing because it makes business firms less vulnerable to the consequences of declines in sales and earnings. Common stock financing involves no fixed financing payments which might force a faltering firm into bankruptcy. From the standpoint of the economy as a whole, if too many firms used too much debt, business fluctuations would be amplified, and minor recessions could turn into major ones. In the 1980s, when many leveraged mergers and buyouts were occurring and were raising the aggregate debt ratio (the average debt ratio of all firms), the Federal Reserve and other authorities voiced concern over the situation, and Congressional leaders debated the wisdom of social controls over corporations' use of debt.

Self-Test

What are the major advantages and disadvantages of common stock financing to the issuing corporation?

Seen from an investor's viewpoint, what are the major advantages and disadvantages associated with common stock ownership?

From a social viewpoint, why may common stock be considered a desirable form of financing?

The Decision to Go Public

closely held corporation

A corporation that is owned by a few individuals who are typically associated with the firm's management.

going public

The act of selling stock to the public at large by a closely held corporation or its principal stockholders.

initial public offering (IPO) market

The market consisting of stocks of companies that have just gone public.

As we noted in Chapter 1, most businesses begin their lives as proprietorships or partnerships, and the more successful ones, as they grow, eventually find it desirable to convert into a corporation. The ownership of these young corporations is often kept in the hands of the founders, a few key employees, and perhaps a limited number of investors who are not actively involved in management. As the firm grows, it will probably outgrow its ability to finance its equity needs through internal sources or the increased investment of the owners. Whenever a **closely held corporation** offers stock to the public for the first time, it is said to be **going public.** The market for stock that has recently gone public is often called the **initial public offering (IPO) market.** The advantages and disadvantages of becoming a *publicly owned* corporation are discussed next.

Advantages of Going Public

Facilitates Stockholder Diversification.   As a company grows and becomes more valuable, its founders often have most of their wealth tied up in the company. By selling some of their stock in a public offering, the founders can diversify their holdings and thereby reduce somewhat the riskiness of their personal portfolios.

Increases Liquidity.   The stock of a closely held firm is illiquid — it cannot be easily sold because no ready market exists for it. If an owner wishes to sell

publicly owned corporation

A corporation that is owned by a relatively large number of individuals of which many are not actively involved in its management.

some shares to raise cash, it is hard to find potential buyers, and even if a buyer is located, there is no established price at which to complete the transaction. These problems do not exist with **publicly owned corporations.**

Facilitates Raising New Corporate Cash.   If a privately held company wants to raise cash through a sale of new stock, it must either go to its existing owners, who may not have the wherewithal or may not want to put any more eggs into this particular basket, or it must shop around for wealthy investors who are willing to make an investment in the company. However, it is usually difficult to get outsiders to put money into a closely held company because if the managers have voting control (over 50 percent of the stock), they can run roughshod over outsiders. The insiders can pay or not pay dividends, pay themselves exorbitant salaries, have private deals with the company, and so on. Insiders can even keep outsiders from knowing the company's actual earnings or its real worth. There are not many positions more vulnerable than that of an outside stockholder in a closely held company, and for this reason it is hard for closely held companies to raise new equity capital. Going public, which brings with it disclosure requirements and regulation by the Securities and Exchange Commission (SEC), greatly reduces these problems and thus makes people more willing to invest in the company.

Establishes a Value for the Firm.   For a number of reasons, it is often useful to establish a firm's value in the marketplace. For one thing, when the owner of a privately held business dies, state and federal inheritance tax appraisers must set a value on the company for estate tax purposes. Often, these appraisers set too high a value, which creates all sorts of problems. However, a company that is publicly owned has its value established, with little room for argument. Similarly, if a company wants to give incentive stock options to key employees, it is useful to know the exact value of these options. In addition, employees much prefer to own stock, or options on stock, that is publicly traded because of the previously mentioned increased liquidity.

Disadvantages of Going Public

Cost of Reporting.   A publicly owned company must file quarterly and annual reports with the SEC, with various state officials, or with both. These reports can be costly, especially for small firms.

Disclosure.   Management may not like the idea of reporting operating data because such data will then be available to competitors. Similarly, the owners of the company may not want people to know their net worth. Since publicly owned companies must disclose the number of shares owned by officers, directors, and major stockholders, it is easy enough for anyone to multiply number of shares held by price per share to estimate the net worth of an insider.

Self-dealings.   The owners/managers of closely held companies have many opportunities for various types of questionable but legal self-dealings, including the payment of high salaries, nepotism, personal transactions with the business (such as leasing arrangements), excellent retirement programs, and not-truly necessary fringe benefits. Such self-dealings are much harder to arrange if a company is publicly owned; they must be disclosed, and the managers are also subject to stockholder lawsuits.

Inactive Market/Low Price.   If a firm is very small and if its shares are not traded with much frequency, then its stock will not truly be liquid, and the market price may not be representative of the stock's real value. Securities analysts and stockbrokers simply will not follow or recommend the stock because there will not be sufficient trading activity to generate enough sales commissions to cover the analysts' or brokers' costs of keeping up with it.

Control.   As mentioned earlier in this chapter, managers of publicly owned firms who do not have at least 50 percent of the stock must be concerned about maintaining control. Further, there is pressure on such managers to produce annual earnings gains, even when it would be in the shareholders' best long-term interest to adopt a strategy that might penalize short-run earnings but lead to higher earnings in future years. These factors have led a number of public companies to "go private" in leveraged buyout (LBO) deals in which the managers and some related investors borrow the money to buy out the public stockholders. The RJR Nabisco deal, the largest LBO on record at about $25 billion, is an example.

Conclusions on Going Public

It should be obvious from this discussion that there are no hard-and-fast rules about whether or when a company should go public. In each case, the decision should be made on the basis of the company's and its stockholders' unique circumstances.

If a company does decide to go public, either by the sale of newly issued stock to raise new capital for the corporation or by the sale of stock by the current owners, one key issue is that of setting the price at which shares will be offered to the public. The company and its current owners want to set the price as high as possible — the higher the offering price, the smaller the fraction of the company the current owners will have to give up to obtain any specified amount of money. On the other hand, potential buyers will want the price set as low as possible. The valuation models presented earlier in this chapter aid investment bankers in determining the initial selling price.

It should be mentioned that the 1993 pace of initial public offerings (IPOs) has been sizzling. A record 275 IPOs came to market in the first six months, and as of early July 1993, there were 727 additional new stock issues ready to be sold within a few months. A managing director at investment banker Shearson Lehman Brothers commented that, as companies abandon their 1980s penchant for borrowing, "they are . . . issuing equity" more often. Another investment banker from Shearson pointed out that — as with corporate debt markets — the decline in interest rates has been "the fuel that fired the U.S. equity market." As we know from the common stock valuation models in this chapter, the lower the interest rate (k_s), the higher the intrinsic value of a firm's common stock, and the more attractive a stock issue would be from the corporate point of view, other things equal. In the biggest stock deal *ever,* investment banking firm

Goldman Sachs brought Sears's IPO of Allstate Insurance to market in June 1993, in a $2.4 billion offering. By mid-December, new issues of stocks and bonds were about to hit an annual record of $1 trillion—called a historic breakthrough on Wall Street—and another 35 new stock issues were scheduled to come to market before year's end.

Self-Test

Differentiate between a closely held and a publicly owned corporation.

What are the major advantages and disadvantages of going public?

What has been the driving force behind the rush of corporations to issue equity in the early 1990s?

The Investment Banking Process

The role of investment bankers was discussed in general terms in Chapter 2. There we learned (1) that the major investment banking houses are often divisions of large financial service corporations engaged in a wide range of activities and (2) that investment bankers help firms issue new securities in the primary markets and also operate as brokers in the secondary markets. Merrill Lynch, the nation's largest brokerage concern, operates thousands of offices, and its investment banking department is the top underwriter of U.S. debt and equity. In this section we describe how securities are issued, and we explain the role of investment bankers in this process.

Raising Capital: Stage I Decisions

The firm's management makes some initial, preliminary decisions on its own, including the following:

1. **Dollars to be raised.**   How much new capital is needed?
2. **Type of securities used.**   Should stock, bonds, or a combination be used? Further, if stock is to be issued, should it be offered to existing stockholders or sold directly to the general public? (Of course, if the preemptive right is included in the corporate charter, the latter question need not be asked; existing stockholders must then have first option to purchase the new issue of stock.)
3. **Competitive bid versus negotiated deal.**   Should the company simply offer a block of its securities for sale to the highest bidder, or should it sit down with an investment banker and negotiate a deal? These two procedures are called *competitive bids* and *negotiated deals.* Only about 100 of the largest firms on the NYSE, whose securities are already well known to the investment banking community, are in a position to use the competitive bid process. The investment banks would have to do a large amount of investigative work in order to bid on an issue unless they were already quite familiar with the firm, and the costs involved would be too high to make it worthwhile unless the investment bank was sure of getting the deal. Therefore, the vast majority of offerings of stock or bonds are made on a negotiated basis.

4. **Selection of an investment banker.**   Assuming the issue is to be negotiated, which investment banker should the firm use? Older firms that have "been to market" before will have already established a relationship with an investment banker, although it is easy enough to change bankers if the firm is dissatisfied. However, a firm that is just going public will have to choose an investment banker, and different investment banking houses are better suited for different companies. Some investment banking houses specialize in new issues of firms going public for the first time, whereas others are not well suited to handle such IPOs because their brokerage clients are relatively conservative.

Raising Capital: Stage II Decisions

After the firm has decided to issue new securities, there are still decisions to be made jointly by the firm and its selected investment banker, including the following:

1. **Reevaluating the company's initial decisions.**   The firm and its investment banker will reevaluate the firm's initial decisions about the size of the issue and the type of securities to use. For example, the firm may have initially decided to raise $50 million by selling common stock, but the investment banker may convince management that it would be better off, in view of existing market conditions, to limit the stock issue to $25 million and to raise the other $25 million as debt.

2. **Best efforts or underwritten issues.**   The firm and its investment banker must decide whether the banker will work on a best efforts basis or will underwrite the issue. In a **best efforts arrangement,** the banker does not guarantee that the securities will be sold or that the company will get the cash it needs. In an **underwritten arrangement,** the company does get a guarantee, so the banker bears significant risks in such an offering. For example, the very day that IBM signed an underwritten agreement to sell $1 billion of bonds in 1979, interest rates rose sharply and bond prices fell. IBM's investment bankers lost somewhere between $10 million and $20 million. Had the offering been on a best efforts basis, IBM would have been the loser.

3. **Issuance costs.**   The investment banker's fee must be negotiated, and the firm must also estimate the other expenses it will incur in connection with the issue—lawyers' fees, accountants' costs, printing and engraving, and so on. Usually, the investment banker will buy the issue from the company at a discount below the price at which the securities are to be offered to the public, and this **spread** covers the investment banker's costs and provides a profit.

Table 17-1 gives an indication of the **flotation costs** associated with public issues of bonds, preferred stock, and common stock. As the table shows, costs as a percentage of the proceeds are higher for stocks than for bonds, and percentage costs are also higher for small issues than for large issues. The relationship between size of issue and flotation costs is primarily due to the existence of fixed costs. Certain costs must be incurred regardless of the size of the issue, so the percentage flotation cost is quite high for small issues.

best efforts arrangement
Agreement for the sale of securities in which the investment bank handling the transaction gives no guarantee that the securities will be sold.

underwritten arrangement
Agreement for the sale of securities in which the investment bank guarantees the sale of the securities, thus agreeing to bear any risks involved in the transaction.

spread
The difference between the price a securities dealer offers to pay for securities (the "bid" price) and the price at which the dealer offers to sell the securities (the "asked" price).

flotation costs
The cost of issuing new common stock, preferred stock, or bonds.

Table 17-1 Costs of Flotation for Underwritten, Nonrights Offerings (Expressed as a Percentage of Gross Proceeds)

Size of Issue (Millions of Dollars)	Bonds			Preferred Stock			Common Stock		
	Underwriting Commission	Other Expenses	Total Costs	Underwriting Commission	Other Expenses	Total Costs	Underwriting Commission	Other Expenses	Total Costs
Under 1.0	10.0%	4.0%	14.0%	—	—	—	13.0%	9.0%	22.0%
1.0–1.9	8.0	3.0	11.0	—	—	—	11.0	5.9	16.9
2.0–4.9	4.0	2.2	6.2	—	—	—	8.6	3.8	12.4
5.0–9.9	2.4	0.8	3.2	1.9%	0.7%	2.6%	6.3	1.9	8.2
10.0–19.9	1.2	0.7	1.9	1.4	0.4	1.8	5.1	0.9	6.0
20.0–49.9	1.0	0.4	1.4	1.4	0.3	1.7	4.1	0.5	4.6
50.0 and over	0.9	0.2	1.1	1.4	0.2	1.6	3.3	0.2	3.5

Notes:
1. Small issues of preferred are rare, so no data on preferred issues below $5 million are given.
2. Flotation costs tend to rise somewhat when interest rates are cyclically high because when money is in relatively tight supply, the investment bankers will have greater difficulty placing issues with permanent investors. Thus, the figures shown here represent averages, and actual flotation costs vary somewhat over time.

Sources: Securities and Exchange Commission, *Cost of Flotation of Registered Equity Issues* (Washington, D.C.: U.S. Government Printing Office, December 1974); Richard H. Pettway, "A Note on the Flotation Costs of New Equity Capital Issues of Electric Companies," *Public Utilities Fortnightly,* March 18, 1982; Robert Hansen, "Evaluating the Costs of a New Equity Issue," *Midland Corporate Finance Journal,* Spring 1986; and informal surveys of common stock, preferred stock, and bond issuers conducted by the authors.

When relatively small companies go public to raise new capital, the investment bankers frequently take part of their compensation in the form of options to buy stock in the firm. For example, if a company were to go public with a $10 million issue in 1994 by selling 1 million shares at a price of $10 per share, its investment bankers might buy the stock from the company at a price of $9.75 per share, so the direct underwriting fee would be only $1,000,000($10.00 − $9.75) = $250,000 or 2.5 percent. However, the investment bankers might also receive a 5-year option to buy 200,000 shares at a price of $10, so if the stock goes up to $15, which the investment bankers expect it to do, they will make a $1 million profit on top of the $250,000 underwriting fee.

4. **Setting the offering price.** If the company is already publicly owned, the **offering price** will be based on the existing market price of the stock or the yield on the bonds. For common stock, the most typical arrangement calls for the investment banker to buy the securities at a prescribed number of points below the closing price on the last day of registration.

offering price

The price at which common stock is sold to the public.

If the company is going public for the first time, there will be no established price, so the investment bankers will have to estimate the *equilibrium price,* the price that will be low enough to induce investors to buy the stock, but not so low that it will rise sharply immediately after the stock is issued. Recall that earlier in this chapter we defined a stock as being in equilibrium when $\hat{k}_s = k_s$ and $\hat{P}_0 = P_0$. Note that if the offering price is set below the true equilibrium price, the stock will rise sharply after issue and the company and its original stockholders will have given away too much stock to raise the required capital. If the offering price is set above the true equilibrium price, either the issue will fail or, if the bankers succeed in selling the stock, their investment clients will be unhappy when the stock subsequently falls to its equilibrium level. Therefore, it is important that the equilibrium price be approximated as closely as possible.

Selling Procedures

Once the company and its investment bankers have decided how much money to raise, the type of securities to issue, and the basis for pricing the issue, they will prepare and file a registration statement and a prospectus with the SEC. It generally takes about 20 days for the issue to be approved by the SEC. The final price of the stock (or the yield on a bond issue) is set at the close of business the day the issue clears the SEC, and the securities are offered to the public the following day.

Investors are not required to pay for the stock until ten days after they place their buy orders, but the investment bankers must pay the issuing firm within four days of the time the offering officially begins. Typically, the investment bankers sell the stock within a day or two after the offering begins, but on occasion they miscalculate, set the offering price too high, and are unable to move the issue. Similarly, the market might decline during the offering period, forcing the bankers to reduce the price of the stock. In either instance, on an underwritten offering the firm receives the price that was agreed upon, and the investment bankers must absorb any losses that are incurred.

Because they are exposed to potentially large losses, investment bankers typically do not handle the purchase and distribution of an issue singlehandedly unless it is a very small one. If the amount of money involved is large, and the risk of price fluctuations substantial, investment bankers form **underwriting syndicates** in an effort to minimize the amount of risk each one carries. The investment banking house that sets up the deal is called the **lead, or managing, underwriter.**

In addition to the underwriting syndicate, on larger offerings still more investment bankers are included in a **selling group,** which handles the distribution of securities to individual investors. The selling group includes all members of the underwriting syndicate plus additional dealers who take relatively small participations (or shares of the total issue) from the syndicate members. Thus the underwriters act as *wholesalers,* whereas members of the selling group act as *retailers.* The number of participants in a selling group depends partly on the size of the issue; for example, the one set up when Communications Satellite Corporation (Comsat) went public consisted of 385 members.

Shelf Registrations

The selling procedures described previously, including the 20-day minimum waiting period between registration with the SEC and sale of the issue, apply to most securities sales. However, large, well-known public companies which issue securities frequently may file a *master registration statement* with the SEC and then update it with a *short-form statement* just prior to each individual offering. In such a case, a company could decide at 10 A.M. to sell registered securities and have the sale completed before noon. This procedure is known as **shelf registration** because in effect the company puts its new securities "on the shelf" and then sells them to investors when it thinks the market is right. The Time Warner example in the opening vignette of this chapter illustrates the use of shelf registration; of course, the procedure itself does not inherently lead to losses for investment bankers as it did in the Time Warner case.

underwriting syndicate

A syndicate of investment banking firms formed to spread the risk associated with the purchase and distribution of a new issue of securities.

lead, or managing, underwriter

The member of an underwriting syndicate that actually manages the new securities issue.

selling group

A group of brokerage firms formed for the purpose of distributing a new issue of securities.

shelf registration

A procedure under which a large, well-established firm can sell new securities on very short notice.

Maintenance of the Secondary Market

In the case of a large, established firm like Carter Chemical Company, the investment banking firm's job is finished once it has disposed of the stock and turned the net proceeds over to the issuing company. However, in the case of a company going public for the first time, the investment banker is under an obligation to maintain a market for the shares after the issue has been completed. Such stocks are typically traded in the over-the-counter market, and the lead underwriter generally agrees to "make a market" in the stock so as to keep it reasonably liquid. The company wants a good market to exist for its stock, as do the stockholders. Therefore, if the banking house wants to do business with the company in the future, keep its own brokerage customers happy, and have future referral business, it will hold an inventory of the shares and help to maintain an active secondary market in the stock.

? Self-Test

What is the sequence of events when a firm decides to issue new securities?

What is an underwriting syndicate, and why is it important in the investment banking process?

What type of firm would use a shelf registration? Explain.

SMALL BUSINESS

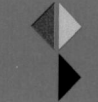

GOING PUBLIC FOR LESS THAN YOU'RE WORTH

For many entrepreneurs, making an initial public offering (IPO) of their company's equity is a dream come true. After their years of sacrifice and hard work, the company is finally a success. The value of that offering is realized by going public. Many observers are amazed that the successful entrepreneur appears willing to sell equity in his or her firm for too little money—IPOs are "underpriced" on average.

Stocks are underpriced if they begin trading in the public markets at a price that is higher than the price in the IPO. An example would be a stock that was sold in an IPO for $12.00 which begins trading immediately after the IPO for $13.50 to $15.00 per share. Some stocks have traded for as much as twice their IPO prices in the public market.

This underpricing is a puzzle. The company going public, and any current shareholders of the privately owned firm who are selling as part of the public offering, receive, on average, the IPO price minus a commission or "discount" of roughly 8 percent. Thus, shareholders selling for $12.00 per share in an IPO

would typically receive about $11.00 per share. If the share price increases to $15.00 after the IPO, then the former shareholders (and the company) have received $4.00 per share less than their shares were worth. Even if the shareholders don't sell any of their own shares in the IPO, but instead sell only the company's shares, they are still hurt by underpricing, because their ownership in the firm is diluted more than it would have been had the shares been fully priced.

Underpricing is especially severe during periods known as "hot issue periods" in the market. During such periods, the *average* issue sold in an IPO has increased in price by 25 to 50 percent after issuance. In general, the definition of a hot issue period is one in which issue values increase after the IPO in the public market.

The large returns of IPOs in the public market are not caused by the company's performance after the IPO. They do not mean that the firm showed high earnings growth after the IPO—the higher returns generally occur on the *first trading day.* This simply means that the IPO securities were sold at a price below their value.

Why would issuers in IPOs (i.e., selling companies) willingly sell their stocks for less than their true value? There are a number of theories to explain underpricing, which are being tested by scholars, but there is no widespread consensus on the reasons for underpricing. Some possible explanations are described next.

One theory holds that issues are underpriced because the issuing companies' owners do not know everything that their underwriters know. The assumption is that there is an "information asymmetry" between issuers and underwriters, and that without this asymmetry, issues would be fully priced. This theory may explain some occurrences of underpricing, such as isolated instances in which an unethical underwriter (who presumably would not last long in the business) knowingly misinforms the issuer. However, some underwriters themselves have gone public, acting as their own underwriters, and they have also had substantial first-day returns.

A popular theory among academicians is that underpricing occurs to keep uninformed investors in the market. According to this theory, there are some well-informed investors who regularly watch the IPO market. They see new issues, and they can tell which ones are mispriced. They, therefore, buy only the underpriced issues and avoid all others. However, such informed investors do not have enough capital to buy all of the shares of any offering.

An uninformed investor may place an offer to buy some shares in every offering. This uninformed investor will get to buy a lot of stock in the overpriced or correctly priced offerings, but will obtain only a small portion of the offerings in which the informed investors are active. Unless the set of all offerings is underpriced on average, the uninformed investors would consistently lose money, they would leave the market, and the market would break down. Thus, this theory argues, the IPO market must experience general un-

derpricing to function. Early empirical evidence is consistent with this theory. In particular, it shows that offerings about which there is great uncertainty will tend to be more underpriced, and that is observed in practice.

The most popular theory with underwriters and venture capitalists is what might be called the "good taste in the mouth" theory. According to this theory, if the company underprices its issue in an IPO, investors will be more receptive to future "seasoned" issues from the same firm. Note, too, that most IPOs involve only 10 to 20 percent of the stock, so the original owners still have 80 to 90 percent of the shares.

All of these theories have a similar implicaton: An IPO with less uncertainty concerning its value will tend to be more fully priced. This suggests some ways that firms can prepare themselves for public offerings at higher prices. For example, offerings through more prestigious underwriters are, on average, less underpriced than offerings through less reputable underwriters. Issuers that use reputable, well-known accountants for their audits also experience less underpricing than those with less reputable accountants, and firms that received venture capital investment from more reputable capitalists are less underpriced. In fact, even the successful application for a bank loan that is revealed in the offering prospectus is associated with less underpricing. Firms with a longer financial history and which have achieved a higher level of sales also appear to be able to obtain a better price for their shares.

The phenomenon of underpricing IPO shares remains a puzzle to finance academicians. We think we have some of the answers, but the questions are not yet settled. Meanwhile, an issuer should be aware that most IPOs are underpriced by a meaningful amount, and that this underpricing is almost certainly related to the risk and uncertainty of the business. This is important information to consider when deciding when and if the firm should make its initial public offering.

Summary

This chapter describes the valuation of common stock, the characteristics of common stock financing, and the investment banking process. The key concepts covered are listed below:

▶   A **proxy** is a document which gives one person the power to act for another person, typically the power to vote shares of common stock. A proxy fight occurs when an outside, or inside, group solicits stockholders' proxies in order to vote a new management team into office.

Stockholders often have the right to purchase any additional shares sold by the firm. This right, called the **preemptive right,** protects the control of the present stockholders and prevents dilution of the value of their stock.

▶   The **value of a share of stock** is calculated as the **present value of the stream of dividends** to be received in the future.

The equation used to find the **value of a constant,** or **normal, growth stock** is

$$\hat{P}_0 = \frac{D_1}{k_s - g}.$$

▶   The **expected rate of return** from a stock consists of an **expected dividend yield** plus an **expected capital gains yield.** For a constant growth firm, both the expected dividend yield and the expected capital gains yield are constant.

The equation for $\hat{k}_s$, **the expected rate of return on a constant growth stock,** can be expressed as follows:

$$\hat{k}_s = \frac{D_1}{P_0} + g.$$

▶   A **supernormal growth stock** is one for which earnings and dividends are expected to grow much faster than the economy as a whole over some specified time period.

To find the **value of a supernormal (nonconstant) growth stock,** (1) estimate the dividends during the supernormal growth period, (2) find the expected price of the stock at the end of the supernormal growth period, and (3) discount all the expected cash flows through the end of the supernormal growth period and sum.

▶   The major **advantages to the issuer of common stock financing** are as follows: (1) there is no obligation to make fixed payments, (2) common stock never matures, (3) the use of common stock increases the creditworthiness of the firm, (4) stock can often be sold on better terms than debt, and (5) using stock helps the firm maintain its reserve borrowing capacity.

The major **disadvantages to the issuer of common stock financing** are that (1) it extends voting privileges to new stockholders, (2) new stockholders share in the firm's profits, (3) the issuance costs of stock financings are high, (4) using stock can raise the firm's cost of capital, and (5) dividends paid on common stock are not tax deductible.

From the **investor's viewpoint,** common stock has the **advantages** of (1) higher expected total return, (2) unlimited ownership rights to remaining profits after payment of contractual obligations, (3) providing a relatively good hedge against inflation, (4) no danger of a call, and (5) the right to vote.

Disadvantages to the investor include that (1) common stock is riskier than bonds or preferred stock; (2) common stockholders have no legal right to dividends; (3) in case of bankruptcy, common stockholders' claims on assets come last; (4) the issuing corporation has made no promise to buy back the stock; and (5) common stock prices are quite volatile.

▶ A **closely held corporation** is one that is owned by a few individuals who are typically associated with the firm's management.

A **publicly owned corporation** is one that is owned by a relatively large number of individuals, of which many are not actively involved in its management.

Going public facilitates stockholder diversification, increases liquidity of the firm's stock, makes it easier for the firm to raise capital, and establishes a value for the firm. However, reporting costs are high, operating data must be disclosed, management self-dealings are harder to arrange, the price may sink to a low level if the stock is not actively traded, and public ownership may make it harder for management to maintain control of the firm.

▶ An **investment banker** assists in the issuing of securities by helping the firm determine the size of the issue and the type of securities to be used, by establishing the selling price, by selling the issue, and, in some cases, by maintaining an aftermarket for the stock.

A securities issue may be on a **best efforts** basis, where the investment banker gives no guarantee that the issue will be sold, or it may be an **underwritten** issue, where the firm does receive such a guarantee and where the investment banker, therefore, bears the risk of loss. On underwritten issues, an **underwriting syndicate** will typically be formed to spread the risk over a number of investment banks.

In recent years **shelf registrations** have made it possible for large, well-known firms to sell new issues much more quickly than was previously the case.

Flotation costs are the costs associated with public issues of bonds, preferred stock, and common stock. These issuance costs are lowest for large issues of bonds and highest for small issues of common stock, when calculated as a percentage of proceeds.

Resolution to
DECISION IN FINANCE

MUSCLING THE UNDERWRITERS

Some 15 years ago, before the advent of shelf registration procedures, it took considerable time and planning to arrange the sale of a large securities offering, and corporations planned their entire financing program with a small group of underwriters. Now, due to

shelf registrations, companies can register a large amount of securities long before the funds are actually needed and then "fire off" bond sales at a moment's notice to take advantage of market conditions. This is why Time Warner was able to issue its securities so quickly.

Salomon, as the lead underwriter, had the legal right to delay the bond sale by three days through a so-called blackout agreement with

Source: "Time Warner Muscles Its Underwriters," *The Wall Street Journal,* January 28, 1993.

Time Warner. This is a standard provision in underwriting agreements which gives underwriters time to sell the securities without being overwhelmed by an unexpected new offering. However, Salomon bowed to the demands of the entertainment giant, which made it clear that if Salomon did not acquiesce and waive the blackout period, Salomon's entire relationship with the company would be in jeopardy. Of course, this action would mean that Salomon would forfeit its chance for large fees on future Time Warner asset and securities sales. For example, the fees for Time Warner's seven-year notes were 0.75 percent, equivalent to $3,750,000 for the $500 million issue, and the fee on the $1 billion of 30-year bonds was 1 percent, or $10 million. Consequently, Salomon agreed to the waiver.

According to bond traders, the 30-year bond offering pummeled the price of the Time Warner notes held by Salomon, Lazard, and their customers. During the eight-day period at the end of January 1993, when the offerings occurred, the price of $10 million of seven-year U.S. Treasury notes rose by $50,000, while the same amount of Time Warner seven-year notes fell by

$25,000. For bond portfolio managers, who live and die by small differentials, this 0.75 percent decline in principal in just eight days really hurt.

While the investment bankers caved in to the company, they were not at all happy about it. Investment bankers have a reputation to protect, and many of the investment banking firms' customers who had bought the Time Warner notes were angry with Salomon for waiving the blackout period, with Time Warner for flooding the market with securities, and with Merrill Lynch for leading the latest sale. As one portfolio manager at Dreyfus Corporation stated, "It creates a bad taste in everybody's mouth to have a billion, and another billion, and then another billion [in securities sales]." The managing director of Pacific Investment Management stated that for Time Warner "to be able to bring $2 billion of debt with that kind of rating shows a lot of moxie or muscle or a combination of both, so for the company, it was a coup." Bond market watchers say this episode shows the ability of corporate giants, such as Time Warner, to play big Wall Street investment banking firms against one another.

Questions

17-1 Two investors are evaluating the common stock of Multiple Basic Industries (MBI) for possible purchase. MBI is in the mature stage of its life cycle, and its earnings and dividends are growing at a constant rate. The investors agree on the expected value of D_1 and also on the expected future dividend growth rate. Furthermore, they agree on the riskiness of the stock. However, one investor normally holds stock for 2 years, while the other normally holds stock for 10 years. Based on the analysis presented in this chapter, they should both be willing to pay the same price for MBI's stock. True or false? Explain.

17-2 The firm's expected dividend yield is defined as the next expected dividend, D_1, divided by the current price of the stock, P_0. What is the relationship between the dividend yield, the total yield, and the remaining years of supernormal (nonconstant) growth for a supernormal (nonconstant) growth firm?

17-3 Is it true that the following expression can be used to determine the value of a constant growth stock:

$$\hat{P}_0 = \frac{D_0}{k_s + g} \quad ?$$

Explain your answer.

17-4 Draw a Security Market Line graph. Put dots on the graph to show (approximately) where you think a particular company's (1) common stock and (2) bonds would lie. Now where would you add a dot to represent the common stock of a riskier company?

17-5 The SEC attempts to protect investors who are purchasing newly issued securities by making sure that the information put out by a company and its investment bankers is correct and is not misleading. However, the SEC *does not* provide any information about the real value of the securities; hence, an investor might pay too much for some new stock and consequently lose heavily. Do you think the SEC should, as part of every new stock or bond offering, render an opinion to investors as to the proper value of the securities being offered? Explain.

17-6 Before entering a formal agreement, investment bankers carefully investigate the companies whose securities they underwrite; this is especially true of the issues of firms going public for the first time. Since the investment bankers do not themselves plan to hold the securities but intend to sell them to others as soon as possible, why are they so concerned about making careful investigations?

Self-Test Problems

ST-1 You are considering buying the stock of two very similar companies. Both companies are expected to earn $4.50 per share this year. However, Alliance Manufacturing (AM) is expected to pay all of its earnings out as dividends, whereas Bascombe Industries (BI) is expected to pay out only one-third of its earnings, or $1.50. AM's stock price is $30. Which of the following is most likely to be true?
   a. BI will have a faster growth rate than AM. Therefore, BI's stock price should be greater than $30.
   b. Although BI's growth rate should exceed AM's, AM's current dividend exceeds that of BI, and this should cause AM's price to exceed BI's.
   c. An investor in AM will get his or her money back faster because AM pays out more of its earnings as dividends. Thus, in a sense, AM's stock is like a short-term bond, and BI's is like a long-term bond. Therefore, if economic shifts cause k_d and k_s to increase and if the expected streams of dividends from AM and BI remain constant, AM's and BI's stock prices will both decline, but AM's price should decline further.
   d. AM's expected and required rate of return is $\hat{k}_s = k_s = 15$ percent. BI's expected return will be higher because of its higher expected growth rate.
   e. Based on the available information, the best estimate of BI's growth rate is 10 percent.

ST-2 You can buy a share of the Crown Company's stock today for 33⅛. Crown's last dividend was $2.50. Crown's required rate of return is 14 percent. If dividends are expected to grow at a constant rate, g, in the future, and if k_s is expected to remain at 14 percent, what is Crown Company's expected stock price 5 years from now?

ST-3 TGI Group Inc. is experiencing a period of rapid growth. Earnings and dividends are expected to grow at a rate of 18 percent during the next 2 years and 15 percent in the third year, then at a constant rate of 6 percent thereafter. TGI's last dividend was $1.15, and the required rate of return on the stock is 12 percent.
   a. Calculate the price of the stock today, $\hat{P}_0$.
   b. Calculate $\hat{P}_1$ and $\hat{P}_2$.
   c. Calculate the dividend yield and capital gains yield for Years 1, 2, and 3.

Problems

Constant growth stock valuation

17-1 Compuware Inc. has enjoyed many years of growth through franchising. Financial analysts now believe that the firm is moving into a mature, constant growth phase of its life cycle. Next year's dividend is expected to be $2.90, and dividends and earnings are expected to grow at a constant 5 percent rate in the future. What price should investors pay for a share of Compuware common stock if they require a 13 percent rate of return on their investment?

17-2
Constant growth stock valuation

Detroit Steel's last dividend was $3.00 ($D_0 = \$3.00$). The company's growth is expected to remain at a constant 6 percent. If investors demand a 12 percent rate of return, what is Detroit Steel's current market price?

17-3
Constant growth stock valuation

What would you expect Detroit Steel's (Problem 17-2) stock price to be in 4 years? That is, solve for $\hat{P}_4$. Assume that growth projections and investor-required returns will remain constant.

17-4
Zero growth stock valuation

The Sponberg Corporation has been paying a $5.39 dividend for several years. Growth prospects for higher earnings are dim, but the company's treasurer is confident that the firm can continue to provide the current dividend into the foreseeable future. If investors require a 14 percent return, what is the current market price of the stock?

17-5
Return on common stock

Bay Harbor Industries' earnings and dividends have grown at a constant 7 percent rate over the past few years. This growth rate is expected to continue into the future. The firm's current dividend, D_0, is $3.00, and the current market price of the firm's stock is $32.10.

a. What is the firm's dividend yield?

b. What rate of return are the firm's investors expecting?

17-6
Calculating the growth rate

You can buy a share of Chung Engineering today for $60. Last year's dividend was $5.09. The required rate of return for stocks in Chung Engineering's risk class is 15 percent. Earnings and dividends are expected to grow at a constant rate, g, in the future, and k_s is also expected to remain at 15 percent.

a. What rate of growth in earnings and dividends is the firm expecting?

b. What is Chung Engineering's expected stock price 4 years from now?

17-7
Calculating the growth rate

The Paschke Company has just paid a $2.45 dividend. Three years ago its dividend was $2.00. This growth in dividends is expected to remain constant in the future. If investors expect a 16 percent return, what is Paschke's common stock price today?

17-8
Constant growth stock valuation

R. A. Camacho and Company paid a dividend of $2.00 last year. The dividend is expected to grow at a constant rate of 5 percent into the future. You plan to buy the stock today, hold it for 3 years, and then sell it — if indeed you do decide to purchase it.

a. What is the expected dividend for each of the next 3 years? That is, calculate D_1, D_2, and D_3. Note that $D_0 = \$2.00$.

b. If the appropriate discount rate is 12 percent, and the first of these dividend payments will occur one year from today, what is the present value of the dividend stream? That is, calculate the PV of D_1, D_2, and D_3, and sum these PVs.

c. You expect the price of the stock to be $34.73 in 3 years; that is, you expect P_3 to equal $34.73. Discounted at a 12 percent rate, what is the present value of this future stock price? In other words, calculate the PV of $34.73.

d. If you plan to buy the stock, hold it for 3 years, and then sell it for $34.73, what is the most you should pay for it if your minimum required return is 12 percent?

e. Use Equation 17-2 to calculate the present value of this stock. Assume that the rate of growth is a constant 5 percent.

f. Is the value of this stock to you dependent on how long you plan to hold it? In other words, if your planned holding period were 2 years or 5 years rather than 3 years, would this affect the value of the stock today, $\hat{P}_0$?

17-9
Return on common stock

Kaufman & Koenig's current market price is $54. Your stockbroker has determined that the firm's dividends will be $5.40 next year, $5.832 in 2 years, and $6.298 in 3 years. Although your broker expects that the dividends will continue to grow at the same growth rate in the future, she recommends that you sell the stock for $68 at the end of 3 years.

a. Calculate the growth rate in dividends.

b. Calculate the stock's dividend yield.

c. If the growth rate continues as expected, what is this stock's expected rate of return? Confirm your answer using Equation 17-2.

17-10

Constant growth stock
valuation

a. Investors require a 12 percent rate of return on Nortex Corporation's stock (k_s = 12%). At what price will the stock sell if the previous dividend was D_0 = $3 and investors expect dividends to grow at a constant compound rate of (1) minus 5 percent, (2) 0 percent, (3) 5 percent, (4) 9 percent, and (5) 11 percent? [*Hint:* Use $D_1 = D_0 (1 + g)$, not D_0, in the formula.]

b. What is the price of Nortex Corporation's stock (using Equation 17-2) if the required rate of return is 12 percent and the expected growth rate is (1) 12 percent or (2) 15 percent? Are these results reasonable? Explain.

17-11

Constant growth stock
valuation

Tom Jackson is an analyst with Widicus Investments and is currently evaluating the common stock of Vineyard Mountain Inc. Vineyard Mountain's earnings and dividends have been growing at an annual rate of 8 percent in the past, and this rate of growth is expected to continue. Vineyard Mountain's earnings per share were $3.20 last year, and the company follows a policy of paying out 40 percent in dividends. If the required rate of return on Vineyard Mountain is 13 percent, what is the stock worth today?

17-12

Constant growth stock
valuation

Scott-Tsiatsios Inc. paid dividends of $2.40 recently. The risk-free rate of return is 8 percent, and the required rate of return on the market is 12.5 percent. Scott-Tsiatsios has a beta of 0.8 and is expected to have constant annual growth of 6.5 percent. What is a fair price for the company's common stock?

17-13

Declining growth stock
valuation

The Barely Able Coal Mining Company has had difficulty complying with government regulations concerning strip mining. As a result, the company's earnings and dividends are declining at a constant rate of 9 percent per year. If the last dividend per share was $2.20 and the required rate of return on the firm's common equity is 14 percent, what is the most an investor should be willing to pay for the firm's common stock?

17-14

Declining growth stock
valuation

TRX Energy's oil and gas reserves are being depleted, and the costs of recovering a declining amount of crude petroleum products are rising each year. As a result, the company's earnings and dividends are declining at the rate of 5 percent per year. If D_0 = $3.00 and k_s = 12.5%, what is the value of TRX Energy's stock?

17-15

Supernormal growth stock
valuation

Acorn Industries has been growing at a rate of 20 percent per year in recent years. This same growth rate is expected to last another 3 years. After that time Acorn's financial manager expects the firm's growth to slow to a constant 7 percent.

a. Assuming that D_0 = $1.50 and that the firm's required rate of return, k_s, is 16 percent, what is Acorn's stock worth today?

b. Calculate the dividend yield and capital gains yield for Years 1, 2, and 3.

c. Now assume that the period of supernormal (20 percent) growth for Acorn Industries will last for 6 years rather than 3 years. Describe how this longer supernormal growth period will affect the stock's price, dividend yield, and capital gains yield. (No calculations are necessary.)

17-16

Supernormal growth stock
valuation

The earnings per share of Waluja Imports Inc. are currently $2.00 ($E_0$ = $2.00). These earnings are expected to grow at a rate of 25 percent for the next 2 years and at 12 percent for the following 3 years, then to slow to a sustainable growth rate of 6 percent thereafter. The firm has previously had a policy of paying zero dividends because of its rapid growth. However, since its growth will be slower in the future, the payout policy will change. Payout for the next 2 years will remain at zero but will increase to 25 percent for the following 3 years. The payout will be 75 percent after Year 5. Waluja's shareholders require a 12 percent rate of return. What is the current market price for Waluja Imports Inc.?

17-17
Nonconstant growth stock valuation

A firm expects to pay dividends over each of the next 4 years of $3.50, $2.00, $3.00, and $4.50. If growth is then expected to level off at 5 percent and if you require a 14 percent rate of return, how much should you be willing to pay for this stock?

17-18
Supernormal growth stock valuation

Silverton International has been growing at a rate of 30 percent per year in recent years. This same growth rate is expected to last for another 2 years.
a. If $D_0 = \$2.75$, $k_s = 16\%$, and $g_n = 7\%$, what is Silverton's stock worth today? What are its current dividend yield and capital gains yield?
b. Now assume that Silverton's period of supernormal growth is 5 years rather than 2 years. How does this affect its price, dividend yield, and capital gains yield? Answer in words only.
c. What will be Silverton's dividend yield and capital gains yield the year after its period of supernormal growth ends? (*Hint:* These values will be the same regardless of whether you examine the case of 2 or 5 years of supernormal growth; the calculations are trivial.)
d. Of what interest to investors is the changing relationship between dividend yield and capital gains yield over time?
e. Return to the assumption that the supernormal growth will only last for the next 2 years and that $g_n = 7\%$ from that point on. What would be the effect on Silverton's stock price if, because of declining interest rates throughout the economy, its required rate of return, k_s, dropped to 14 percent? (*Hint:* Remember that this change will influence $\hat{P}_2$.)

17-19
Nonconstant growth stock valuation

Due to unfavorable economic conditions, Ezzell Electronic's earnings and dividends are expected to remain unchanged for the next 3 years. After 3 years, dividends are expected to grow at a 10 percent annual rate into the foreseeable future. The last dividend (and also the next dividend) was $1.00, and the required rate of return is 18 percent. What should be the current market value of Ezzell's stock?

17-20
Equilibrium stock price

The risk-free rate of return, k_{RF}, is 9 percent; the required rate of return on the market, k_M, is 13 percent; and Griffin-Gunawan-Holbo's (GGH's) stock has a beta coefficient of 1.5.
a. If the dividend expected during the coming year, D_1, is $3.50, and if g = a constant 5%, at what price should GGH's stock sell?
b. Now suppose that the Federal Reserve Board increases the money supply, causing the risk-free rate to drop to 8 percent. If k_M also declines by 1 percent, what would this do to the price of the stock?
c. In addition to the change in Part b, suppose that investors' risk aversion declines; this fact, combined with the decline in k_{RF}, causes k_M to fall to 11 percent. At what price would GGH's stock sell?
d. Assume the changes in Part c, and suppose that GGH has a change in management. The new group institutes policies that increase the expected constant growth rate to 6 percent. Also, the new management stabilizes sales and profits and thus causes the beta coefficient to decline from 1.5 to 1.2. After all these changes, what is GGH's new equilibrium price? (*Note:* D_1 goes to $3.53.)

17-21
Stock valuation

Assume that the stock of Olympic Enterprises has just paid an annual dividend of $2.50 and that this dividend is expected to grow for the next 2 years at an annual rate of 20 percent, then to grow indefinitely at an annual rate of 10 percent. If the risk-free rate is 7 percent, the expected return on the market is 11.8 percent, and the firm's beta is 1.25, then how much should you be willing to pay for this stock?

17-22
Beta coefficients

Suppose Pfaff Company's management conducts a study and concludes that if Pfaff expanded its consumer products division (which is less risky than its primary business, industrial chemicals), the firm's beta would decline from 1.4 to 1.1. However, consumer products have a somewhat lower profit margin, and this would cause Pfaff's constant growth rate in earnings and dividends to fall from 8 to 6 percent.

 a. Should management make the change? Assume the following: $k_M = 12\%$; $k_{RF} = 9\%$; $D_0 = \$1.75$.

 b. Assume all the facts as given previously except the change in the beta coefficient. What would the beta have to equal to cause the expansion to be a good one? (*Hint:* Set $\hat{P}_0$ under the new policy equal to $\hat{P}_0$ under the old one, and find the new beta that will produce this equality.)

17-23

Stock pricing

B. R. Roth and Company is a small jewelry manufacturer. The company has been successful and has grown. Now Roth is planning to sell an issue of common stock to the public for the first time, and it faces the problem of setting an appropriate price on its common stock. The company and its investment bankers believe that the proper procedure is to select firms similar to it with publicly traded common stock and to make relevant comparisons.

 Several jewelry manufacturers are reasonably similar to Roth with respect to product mix, size, asset composition, and debt/equity proportions. Of these, Gemex and Diamond Gallery are most similar. Data are given in the following table. When analyzing these data, assume that 1988 and 1993 were reasonably normal years for all 3 companies; that is, these years were neither especially good nor bad in terms of sales, earnings, and dividends. At the time of the analysis, k_{RF} was 10 percent and k_M was 15 percent. Gemex is listed on the American Exchange and Diamond Gallery on the NYSE, whereas B. R. Roth will be traded in the OTC market.

	Gemex (Per Share)	Diamond Gallery (Per Share)	B. R. Roth (Totals)
Earnings			
1993	$2.25	$3.75	$600,000
1988	1.50	2.75	408,000
Price			
1993	$18.00	$32.50	———
Dividends			
1993	$1.125	$1.875	$300,000
1988	0.750	1.375	210,000
Book value			
1993	$15.00	$27.50	$4,500,000
Market/book ratio			
1993	120%	118%	———
Total assets, 1993	$14 million	$41 million	$10 million
Total debt, 1993	$6 million	$15 million	$5.5 million
Sales, 1993	$20.5 million	$70 million	$18.5 million

 a. Assume that B. R. Roth has 100 shares of stock outstanding. Use this information to calculate earnings per share (EPS), dividends per share (DPS), and book value per share for Roth. (*Note:* Since there are only 100 shares outstanding, your results may seem a bit large.)

 b. Based on your answer to Part a, do you think Roth's stock would sell at a price in the same "ballpark" as Gemex's and Diamond Gallery's—that is, sell in the range of $25 to $100 per share?

 c. Assuming that Roth's management can split the stock so that the 100 shares could be changed to 1,000 shares, 100,000 shares, or any other number, would such an action make sense in this case? Why?

 d. Now assume that Roth did split its stock and has 400,000 shares. Calculate new values for EPS, DPS, and book value per share.

 e. What can you say about the relative growth rates of the 3 companies?

f. What can you say about their dividend payout policies?

g. Return on equity (ROE) can be measured as EPS/book value per share, or as total earnings/total equity. Calculate 1993 ROEs for the 3 companies.

h. Calculate total debt/total assets ratios for the 3 companies.

i. Calculate P/E ratios for Gemex and Diamond Gallery. Are these P/Es consistent with the growth and ROE data? If not, what other factors could explain the relative P/E ratios?

j. Now determine a range of values for Roth's stock, with 400,000 shares outstanding, by applying Gemex's and Diamond Gallery's P/E ratios, price/dividend ratios, and price/book value ratios to your data for Roth. For example, one possible price for Roth's stock is (P/E Gemex)(EPS Roth) = (8)($1.5) = $12 per share. Similar calculations would produce a range of prices based on both Gemex and Diamond Gallery data.

k. Using the equation $k_s = D_1/P_0 + g$, find approximate k_s values for Gemex and Diamond Gallery. Then use these values in the constant growth stock price model to find a price for Roth's stock.

l. At what price do you think Roth's shares should be offered to the public? You will want to find the *equilibrium price* (i.e., a price that will be low enough to induce investors to buy the stock but not so low that it will rise sharply immediately after it is issued). Think about relative growth rates, ROEs, dividend yields, and total returns ($k_s = D_1/P_0 + g$). Also, as you think about the appropriate price, recognize that when Howard Hughes let the Hughes Tool Company go public, different investment bankers proposed prices that ranged from $20 to $30 per share. Hughes naturally accepted the $30 price, and the stock jumped to $40 almost immediately. Nobody's perfect!

Solutions to Self-Test Problems

ST-1 **a.** This is not necessarily true. Since BI plows back two-thirds of its earnings, its growth rate should exceed that of AM, but AM pays higher dividends ($4.50 versus $1.50). We cannot say which stock should have the higher price.

b. Again, we just do not know which price would be higher.

c. This is false. The changes in k_d and k_s would have a greater effect on BI's stock—its price would decline more.

d. Once again, we just do not know which expected return would be higher. The total expected return for AM is $k_{AM} = D_1/P_0 + g = 15\% + 0\% = 15\%$. The total expected return for BI will have D_1/P_0 less than 15 percent and g greater than 0 percent, but k_{BI} could be either greater or less than AM's total expected return, 15 percent.

e. We have eliminated a, b, c, and d, so e must be correct. Based on the available information, AM's and BI's stocks should sell at about the same price, $30. Thus $k_s = \$4.50/\$30 = 15\%$ for both AM and BI. BI's current dividend yield is $1.50/$30 = 5\%$. Therefore g = 15\% - 5\% = 10\%$.

ST-2 The first step is to solve for g, the unknown variable, in the constant growth equation. Since D_1 is unknown, substitute $D_0(1 + g)$ as follows:

$$\hat{P}_0 = \frac{D_0(1 + g)}{k_s - g}$$

$$\$33.125 = \frac{\$2.50(1 + g)}{0.14 - g}.$$

Solving for g, we find the growth rate to be 6 percent. The next step is to use the growth rate to project the stock price 5 years hence:

$$\hat{P}_5 = \frac{D_0(1 + g)^6}{k_s - g}$$

$$= \frac{\$2.50(1.06)^6}{0.14 - 0.06}$$

$$= \$44.33.$$

[Alternatively, $\hat{P}_5 = \$33.125(1.06)^5 = \$44.33$.]

Therefore, Crown Company's expected stock price 5 years from now, $\hat{P}_5$, is $44.33.

ST-3   **a.** *Step 1:* Calculate the dividends paid during the supernormal growth period:

$$D_1 = \$1.1500(1.18) = \$1.3570.$$

$$D_2 = \$1.3570(1.18) = \$1.6013.$$

$$D_3 = \$1.6013(1.15) = \$1.8415.$$

Step 2: Find the stock's price at the end of Year 3:

$$\hat{P}_3 = \frac{D_4}{k_s - g} = \frac{D_3(1 + g_n)}{k_s - g_n}$$

$$= \frac{\$1.8415(1.06)}{0.12 - 0.06}$$

$$= \$32.53.$$

Step 3: Discount cash flows and sum to find the price of the stock today, $\hat{P}_0$:

$$\hat{P}_0 = \$1.3570(0.8929) + \$1.6013(0.7972) + (\$1.8415 + \$32.53)(0.7118)$$

$$= \$1.2117 + \$1.2766 + \$24.4656$$

$$= \$26.9539 \approx \$26.95.$$

b. $$\hat{P}_1 = \$1.6013(0.8929) + (\$1.8415 + \$32.53)(0.7972)$$

$$= \$1.4298 + \$27.4010$$

$$= \$28.8308 \approx \$28.83.$$

$$\hat{P}_2 = (\$1.8415 + \$32.53)(0.8929)$$

$$= \$30.6903 \approx \$30.69.$$

c.

Year	Dividend Yield	Capital Gains Yield	Total Return
1	$\dfrac{\$1.3570}{\$26.95} = 5.04\%$	$\dfrac{\$28.83 - \$26.95}{\$26.95} = 6.98\%$	$\approx 12\%$
2	$\dfrac{\$1.6013}{\$28.83} = 5.55\%$	$\dfrac{\$30.69 - \$28.83}{\$28.83} = 6.45\%$	12%
3	$\dfrac{\$1.8415}{\$30.69} = 6.00\%$	$\dfrac{\$32.53 - \$30.69}{\$30.69} = 6.00\%$	12%

Hybrid Financing: Leasing and Option Securities

OBJECTIVES

After reading this chapter, you should be able to:

▶ Characterize the various types of leases and perform the analysis necessary to make lease-versus-borrow-and-purchase decisions.

▶ Determine how options are valued, including both the formula value and the premium which comprise the market value of an option.

▶ Discuss warrants and the way in which corporations utilize warrants together with bonds as alternative means of raising investment capital.

▶ Explain how convertible securities work, how they are valued, and how they affect the issuing firm's capital structure.

DECISION IN FINANCE

LOOKING FOR A NEW
LEASE ON LIFE

Airlines all over the world fly planes belonging to GPA Group PLC, a Shannon, Ireland, company with a fleet of 443 aircraft. In Mexico, the Philippines, and Malaysia the airliners leased from GPA by local carriers handle nearly a third of the domestic traffic. Companies lease planes for the same reasons they lease cars or equipment—either they cannot afford to purchase aircraft, which may cost up to $100 million for a large jet, or they prefer the economics of renting.

GPA's growth has been phenomenal since its founding two decades ago by a former Aer Lingus executive, Tom Ryan. Its 100 salespeople—twice as many as its nearest rival, International Lease Finance Company (ILFC)—cover 60 countries.

Ryan has pushed the company aggressively. He started as a middleman for third-world carriers, tapping millions and then billions of dollars in credit from 100 of the world's largest banks and buying hundreds of aircraft to lease. In early 1989 he took arguably his boldest step—ordering $16.8 billion of new aircraft on speculation to add 600 jets and 100 turboprops to his existing fleet, which then numbered only 172. He joked then about the potential risk, noting that the worst thing that could happen to GPA would be the invention of a beaming device (as in *Star Trek*) to transport people around.

_____
See end of chapter for resolution.
Photo source: Mark Wagner/Tony Stone Images.

By the end of 1991, it became apparent that science-fiction technology was not the only thing Ryan should have worried about. His aggressive strategy of the 1980s was not working in the troubled 1990s. GPA's cost of capital soared as it ordered more and more planes. Then an initial stock offering failed when GPA

admitted that it did not have customers for future orders and that it could not get new financing because its banks were refusing to make additional loans.

Meanwhile, GPA's chief rival, ILFC, was ordering aircraft much more conservatively and had also received a $200 million equity infusion from its parent insurance company. ILFC's total assets at the end of 1992 were valued higher than GPA's, and its pretax profits had risen 50 percent from January through September.

Should GPA go down the drain, its own stockholders and employees will not be the only ones to suffer—the shock waves will be felt throughout the industry. Airlines, big banks, and

_____
This chapter was co-authored by Dr. J. Howard Finch of the University of Tennessee at Chattanooga.

aircraft manufacturers worldwide will be seriously affected. Jet makers already face many order delays and cancellations from troubled airlines, so a GPA failure would be sour icing on a falling cake. Northwest Airlines, for instance, canceled orders from a European manufacturer for 74 aircraft and delayed the delivery of 44 more from Boeing. United Airlines cut back its orders twice in just 10 months.

If Ryan's company goes under, its fleet would be dumped on an already saturated market, further depressing aircraft prices. Ultimately, a GPA downfall could even lead to a smaller global airline industry because a key source of inexpensive aircraft would be grounded. The airlines most at risk would be those with short-term leases from GPA due for renewal in the near future. Some will also miss the financing GPA offered them in the past—something it can no longer afford to do.

But Ryan believes GPA can pull through. "We started this company in a recession in 1974 to 1975," he said. "We went through the recession in the early 1980s. I still believe the fundamentals of the business are as strong today as they were 20 years ago."

As you read this chapter, consider the steps Ryan and his staff might take to restore GPA to health. They have created a plan dubbed "Project Rebound" and insist they can avoid a court-protected financial restructuring. They also point out that they have not yet missed any note payments.

In the two preceding chapters, we examined the use of common stock and various types of debt. In this chapter, we examine two other types of long-term capital which financial managers can use to lower their firms' costs of capital: *leasing,* which is used by financial managers as an alternative to borrowing to finance fixed assets, and option securities, particularly *warrants* and *convertibles*, which are attractive to investors because they allow debtholders to acquire common stock at bargain prices and thus to share in the capital gains if a company is especially successful.[1]

Leasing

Firms generally own fixed assets and report them on their balance sheets, but it is the *use* of buildings and equipment that is important, not their ownership per se. One way of obtaining the use of assets is to buy them, but an alternative is to lease them. Prior to the 1950s, leasing was generally associated with real estate—land and buildings. Today, however, it is possible to lease virtually any kind of fixed asset, and in 1992 about 25 percent of all new capital equipment acquired by businesses was leased.

Types of Leases

Leasing takes three different forms: (1) *sale-and-leaseback* arrangements, (2) *operating leases,* and (3) straight *financial,* or *capital, leases.*

---

[1]Even though both of the topics covered in this chapter are important, time pressures may preclude detailed coverage of them. Accordingly, the chapter is written in a modular form so as to permit instructors to cover one or both of these topics.

sale and leaseback

An operation whereby a firm sells land, buildings, or equipment and simultaneously leases the property back for a specified period under specific terms.

lessee

The party that uses, rather than the one who owns, the leased property.

lessor

The owner of the leased property.

Sale and Leaseback.   Under a **sale and leaseback,** a firm that owns land, buildings, or equipment sells the property and simultaneously executes an agreement to lease the property back for a specified period under specific terms. The purchaser of the property desires a long-term investment with a stable rate of return. The purchaser could be an insurance company, a commercial bank, a specialized leasing company, or even an individual investor. The sale-and-lease-back plan is an alternative to taking out a mortgage loan.

The firm which is selling the property, or the **lessee,** immediately receives the purchase price put up by the buyer, or the **lessor.**[2] At the same time, the seller-lessee firm retains the use of the property just as if it had borrowed and mortgaged the property to secure the loan. Note that under a mortgage loan arrangement, the financial institution would normally receive a series of equal payments just sufficient to amortize the loan while providing a specified rate of return to the lender on the outstanding balance. Under a sale-and-leaseback arrangement, the lease payments are set up in exactly the same way; the payments are set so as to return the purchase price to the investor-lessor while providing a specified rate of return on the lessor's outstanding investment.

operating lease

A lease under which the lessor maintains and finances the property; also called a *service lease.*

Operating Leases.   **Operating leases,** sometimes called *service leases,* provide for both *financing* and *maintenance.* IBM is one of the pioneers of the operating lease contract, and computers and office copying machines, together with automobiles and trucks, are the primary types of equipment involved. Ordinarily, these leases call for the lessor to maintain and service the leased equipment, and the cost of providing maintenance is built into the lease payments.

Another important characteristic of operating leases is the fact that they are frequently *not fully amortized;* in other words, the payments required under the lease contract are not sufficient to recover the full cost of the equipment. However, the lease contract is written for a period considerably shorter than the expected economic life of the leased equipment, and the lessor expects to recover all investment costs through subsequent renewal payments, through subsequent leases to other lessees, or by selling the leased equipment.

A final feature of operating leases is that they frequently contain a *cancellation clause,* which gives the lessee the right to cancel the lease before the expiration of the basic agreement. This is an important consideration for the lessee, for it means that the equipment can be returned if it is rendered obsolete by technological developments or if it is no longer needed because of a decline in the lessee's business.

financial lease

A lease that does not provide for maintenance services, is not cancelable, and is fully amortized over its life; also called a *capital lease.*

Financial, or Capital, Leases.   **Financial leases,** sometimes called *capital leases,* are differentiated from operating leases in three respects: (1) they do *not* provide for maintenance services, (2) they are *not* cancelable, and (3) they *are* fully amortized (that is, the lessor receives rental payments which are equal to the full price of the leased equipment plus a return on the investment). In a typical financial lease arrangement, the firm that will use the equipment (the lessee) selects the specific items it requires and negotiates the price and delivery terms with the manufacturer. The user firm then negotiates terms with a

---

[2]The term *lessee* is pronounced "less-ee," not "lease-ee," and *lessor* is pronounced "less-or."

Table 18-1   Balance Sheet Effects of Leasing

Before Asset Increase				After Asset Increase						
				Firm B, Which Borrows and Purchases				**Firm L, Which Leases**		
Firms B and L										
Current assets	$ 50	Debt	$ 50	Current assets	$ 50	Debt	$150	Current assets	$ 50	Debt	$ 50
Fixed assets	50	Equity	50	Fixed assets	150	Equity	50	Fixed assets	50	Equity	50
Total	$100		$100	Total	$200		$200	Total	$100		$100
	Debt ratio: 50%				Debt ratio: 75%				Debt ratio: 50%	

leasing company and, once the lease terms are set, arranges to have the lessor buy the equipment from the manufacturer or the distributor. When the equipment is purchased, the user firm simultaneously executes the lease agreement.

Financial leases are similar to sale-and-leaseback arrangements, the major difference being that the leased equipment is new and the lessor buys it from a manufacturer or a distributor instead of from the user-lessee. A sale and leaseback may thus be thought of as a special type of financial lease, and both sale and leasebacks and financial leases are analyzed in the same manner.[3]

Financial Statement Effects

Lease payments are shown as operating expenses on a firm's income statement, but under certain conditions, neither the leased assets nor the liabilities under the lease contract appear on the firm's balance sheet. For this reason, leasing is often called **off balance sheet financing.** This point is illustrated in Table 18-1 by the balance sheets of two hypothetical firms, B (for Buy) and L (for Lease). Initially, the balance sheets of both firms are identical, and both have debt ratios of 50 percent. Each firm then decides to acquire fixed assets which cost $100. Firm B borrows $100 to make the purchase, so both an asset and a liability are recorded on its balance sheet, and its debt ratio is increased to 75 percent. Firm L leases the equipment, so its balance sheet is unchanged. The lease may call for fixed charges as high as or even higher than those on the loan, and the obligations assumed under the lease may be equally or more dangerous from the standpoint of financial safety, but the firm's debt ratio remains at 50 percent.

To correct this problem, the Financial Accounting Standards Board issued **FASB #13,** which requires that for an unqualified audit report, firms that enter into financial (or capital) leases must restate their balance sheets to report leased assets as fixed assets and the present value of future lease payments as a

off balance sheet financing

Financing in which the assets and liabilities involved do not appear on the firm's balance sheet.

FASB #13

The statement of the Financial Accounting Standards Board that details the conditions and procedures for capitalizing leases.

---

[3]For a lease transaction to qualify as a lease for *tax purposes,* and thus for the lessee to be able to deduct the lease payments, the life of the lease must not exceed 80 percent of the expected life of the asset, and the lessee cannot be permitted to buy the asset at a nominal value. These conditions are IRS requirements, and they should not be confused with the FASB requirements discussed later in the chapter concerning the capitalization of leases. It is important to consult lawyers and accountants to ascertain whether or not a prospective lease meets current IRS regulations.

debt. This process is called *capitalizing the lease,* and its net effect is to cause Firms B and L to have similar balance sheets, both of which will resemble the one shown for Firm B after the asset increase.[4]

The purpose of FASB #13 is to avoid investor deception. Because a lease is a long-term fixed liability, off balance sheet financing may cause unwary investors to understate the firm's use of leverage. Lease disclosure allows investors to analyze the "true" capital structure of the firm and adjust their required returns accordingly.[5]

A lease will be classified as a capital lease, and hence be capitalized and shown directly on the balance sheet, if any one of the following conditions exists:

1. Under the terms of the lease, ownership of the property is effectively transferred from the lessor to the lessee.

2. The lessee can purchase the property or renew the lease at less than a fair market price when the lease expires.

3. The lease runs for a period equal to or greater than 75 percent of the asset's life. Thus, if an asset has a 10-year life and if the lease is written for more than 7.5 years, the lease must be capitalized.

4. The present value of the lease payments is equal to or greater than 90 percent of the initial value of the asset.[6]

These rules, together with strong footnote disclosures for operating leases, are sufficient to ensure that no one will be fooled by lease financing. Thus, leases are recognized to be essentially the same as debt, and they have the same effects as debt on the firm's required rate of return. Therefore, leasing will not generally permit a firm to use more financial leverage than could be obtained with conventional debt.

Evaluation by the Lessee

Any prospective lease must be evaluated by both the lessee and the lessor. The lessee must determine whether leasing an asset will be less costly than buying it, and the lessor must decide whether or not the lease will provide a reasonable

---

[4]FASB #13, "Accounting for Leases," November 1976, spells out in detail the conditions under which leases must be capitalized, and the procedures for doing so.

[5]There are, however, certain legal differences between loans and leases. In a bankruptcy liquidation, the lessor is entitled to take possession of the leased asset, and, if the value of the asset is less than the required payments under the lease, the lessor can enter a claim (as a general creditor) for one year's lease payments. In a bankruptcy reorganization, the lessor receives the asset plus three years' lease payments if needed to bring the value of the asset up to the remaining investment in the lease. Under a secured loan arrangement, on the other hand, the lender has a security interest in the asset, meaning that if it is sold, the lender will be given the proceeds, and the full unsatisfied portion of the lender's claim will be treated as a general creditor obligation (see Appendix 20A). It is not possible to state as a general rule whether a supplier of capital is in a stronger position as a secured creditor or as a lessor. Since one position is usually regarded as being about as good as the other at the time the financial arrangements are being made, a lease is about as risky as a secured term loan from both the lessor-lender's and the lessee-borrower's viewpoints.

[6]The discount rate used to calculate the present value of the lease payments must be the lower of (1) the rate used by the lessor to establish the lease payments or (2) the rate of interest which the lessee would have paid for new debt with a maturity equal to that of the lease.

rate of return. Since our focus in this book is primarily on managerial finance as opposed to investments, we restrict our analysis to that conducted by the lessee.[7]

In a typical case, the events leading to a lease arrangement follow this sequence, which has produced the correct lease-versus-purchase decision in every case we have ever encountered:

1. The firm decides to acquire a particular building or piece of equipment. This decision is based on regular capital budgeting procedures, and it is not an issue in the typical lease analysis. In a lease analysis, we are concerned simply with whether to finance the machine by a lease or by a loan. However, if the effective cost of the lease is substantially lower than that of debt—and this could occur for several reasons, including the situation in which the lessor is able to utilize the depreciation tax shelters but the lessee is not—then the capital budgeting decision would have to be reevaluated, and projects formerly deemed unacceptable might become acceptable.

2. Once the firm has decided to acquire the asset, the next question is how to finance it. Well-run businesses do not have excess cash lying around, so new assets must be financed in some manner.

3. Funds to purchase the asset could be obtained by borrowing, by retaining earnings, or by issuing new stock. Alternatively, the asset could be leased. Because of the FASB #13 capitalization/disclosure provision for leases, we assume that a lease would have the same capital structure effect as a loan.

As indicated earlier, a lease is comparable to a loan in the sense that the firm is required to make a specified series of payments, and a failure to make these payments can result in bankruptcy. Thus, it is most appropriate to compare the cost of lease financing with that of debt financing.[8] The lease-versus-borrow-and-purchase analysis is illustrated with data on the Mitchell Electronics Company. The following conditions are assumed:

1. Mitchell plans to acquire equipment with a 5-year life which has a cost of $10,000,000, delivered and installed.

2. Mitchell can borrow the required $10 million, using a 10 percent loan to be amortized over 5 years. Therefore, the loan will call for payments of $2,637,965.60 per year, calculated as follows:

---

[7]The lessee is typically offered a set of lease terms by the lessor, which is generally a bank, a finance company such as General Electric Capital (the largest U.S. lessor), or some other institutional lender. The lessee can accept or reject the lease or shop around for a better deal. In this chapter, we take the lease terms as given for purposes of our analysis. See Chapter 17 of Eugene F. Brigham and Louis C. Gapenski, *Intermediate Financial Management,* 4th ed., for a discussion of lease analysis from the lessor's standpoint, including a discussion of how a potential lessee can use such an analysis in bargaining for better terms.

[8]The analysis should compare the cost of leasing to the cost of debt financing *regardless* of how the asset is actually financed. The asset may actually be purchased with available cash if it is not leased, but because leasing is a substitute for debt financing, a comparison between the two is still appropriate.

$$\text{Payment} = \frac{\$10,000,000}{\text{PVIFA}_{10\%,5}}$$

$$= \frac{\$10,000,000}{3.7908} = \$2,637,965.60.$$

With a financial calculator, input $n = 5$, $k = i = 10$, $PV = -10000000$, and $FV = 0$, and then press PMT to find the payment, $2,637,974.81. Note the rounding difference; the calculator solution is more accurate.

3. Alternatively, Mitchell can lease the equipment for 5 years at a rental charge of $2,800,000 per year, payable at the end of the year, but the lessor will own it upon the expiration of the lease.[9] (The lease payment schedule is established by the potential lessor, and Mitchell can accept it, reject it, or negotiate.)

4. The equipment will definitely be used for 5 years, at which time its estimated net salvage value will be $715,000. Mitchell plans to continue using the equipment, so (1) if it purchases the equipment, the company will keep it, and (2) if it leases the equipment, the company will exercise an option to buy it at its estimated salvage value, $715,000.

5. The lease contract stipulates that the lessor will maintain the equipment. However, if Mitchell borrows and buys, it will have to bear the cost of maintenance, which will be performed by the equipment manufacturer at a fixed contract rate of $500,000 per year, payable at year-end.

6. The equipment falls in the MACRS 5-year class life, and for this analysis we assume that Mitchell's effective federal-plus-state tax rate is 40 percent. Also, the depreciable basis is the original cost of $10,000,000.

NPV Analysis.   Table 18-2 shows the cash flows that would be incurred each year under the two financing plans. The table is set up to produce a time line of cash flows:

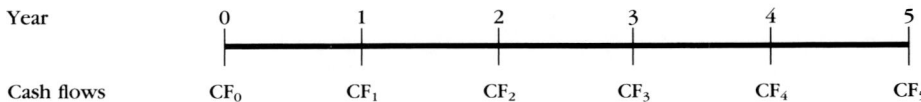

All cash flows occur at the end of the year, and the CF_t values are shown on Lines 5 and 10 of Table 18-2 for buying and leasing, respectively.

The top section of the table (Lines 1–6) is devoted to the cost of owning (borrowing and buying). Lines 1–4 show the individual cash flow items. Line 5 summarizes the annual net cash flows that Mitchell will incur if it finances the equipment with a loan. The present values of these cash flows are summed to find the *present value of the cost of owning,* which is shown on Line 6 in the Year 0 column. (Note that with a financial calculator, we would enter the cash

---

[9]Lease payments can occur at the beginning of the year or at the end of the year. In this example, we assume end-of-year payments, but we demonstrate beginning-of-year payments in Self-Test Problem ST-1.

Table 18-2   Mitchell Electronics Company: NPV Lease Analysis (Thousands of Dollars)

	0	1	2	3	4	5
I. Cost of Owning						
1. Net purchase price	($10,000)					
2. Maintenance cost		($ 500)	($ 500)	($ 500)	($ 500)	($ 500)
3. Maintenance tax savings		200	200	200	200	200
4. Depreciation tax savings		800	1,280	760	480	440
5. Net cash flow	($10,000)	$ 500	$ 980	$ 460	$ 180	$ 140
6. PV cost of owning	($ 8,023)					
II. Cost of Leasing						
7. Lease payment		($2,800)	($2,800)	($2,800)	($2,800)	($2,800)
8. Lease payment tax savings		1,120	1,120	1,120	1,120	1,120
9. Purchase option price						(715)
10. Net cash flow	$ 0	($1,680)	($1,680)	($1,680)	($1,680)	($2,395)
11. PV cost of leasing	($ 7,611)					

III. Cost Comparison

12. Net advantage to leasing = NAL
    = PV cost of owning − PV cost of leasing
    = $8,023 − $7,611 = $412.

Explanation of Lines

1. If Mitchell buys the equipment, it will have to spend $10,000,000 on the purchase. Alternatively, we could show all of the financing flows associated with a $10,000,000 loan, net of taxes, but the end result would be the same because the PV of those flows would be exactly $10 million.

2. If the equipment is owned, Mitchell must pay $500,000 at the end of each year for maintenance.

3. The $500,000 maintenance expense is tax deductible, so it will produce a (Tax rate)(Maintenance expense) = 0.4($500,000) = $200,000 tax savings in each year.

4. If Mitchell buys the equipment, it can depreciate the equipment for tax purposes, and thus lower taxable income and taxes. The tax savings in each year is equal to (Tax rate)(Depreciation expense) = 0.4(Depreciation expense). As shown in Chapters 2 and 14, the MACRS rates for 5-year property are 0.20, 0.32, 0.19, 0.12, and 0.11 in Years 1–5, respectively. To illustrate the calculation of the depreciation tax savings, consider Year 2. The depreciation expense is 0.32($10,000,000) = $3,200,000, and the tax savings is 0.4($3,200,000) = $1,280,000.

5. The net cash flows associated with owning are found by summing Lines 1–4.

6. The PV (in thousands) of the Line 5 cash flows, when discounted at the after-tax cost of debt of 6 percent, is − $8,023.

7. The annual end-of-year lease payment is $2,800,000.

8. Since the lease payment is tax deductible, a tax savings of (Tax rate)(Lease payment) = 0.4($2,800,000) = $1,120,000 results.

9. Because Mitchell plans to continue to use the equipment after the lease expires, it must purchase the equipment for $715,000 at the end of Year 5 if it leases.

10. The net cash flows associated with leasing are found by summing Lines 7–9.

11. The PV (in thousands) of the Line 10 cash flows, when discounted at the after-tax cost of debt of 6 percent, is − $7,611.

12. The net advantage to leasing is merely the difference between the PV cost of owning (in thousands) and the PV cost of leasing (in thousands) = $8,023 − $7,611 = $412. Since the NAL is positive, leasing is favored over borrowing and buying.

flows as shown on Line 5 into the cash flow register, enter the interest rate, i = 6, and then press the NPV key to obtain the PV of owning the equipment.)

Section II of the table calculates the present value cost of leasing. The lease payments are $2,800,000 per year; this rate, which in this example but not in all cases includes maintenance, was established by the prospective lessor and offered to Mitchell Electronics. If Mitchell accepts the lease, the full $2,800,000 will be a deductible expense, so the tax savings is (Tax rate)(Lease payment) = (0.4)($2,800,000) = $1,120,000. These amounts are shown on Lines 7 and 8.

Line 9 in the lease section shows the $715,000 which Mitchell expects to pay in Year 5 to purchase the equipment. We include this amount as a cost of leasing because Mitchell will almost certainly want to continue the operation and thus will be forced to purchase the equipment from the lessor. If we had assumed that the operation would not be continued, then no entry would have appeared on this line. However, in that case, we would have included the $715,000, minus applicable taxes, as a Year 5 inflow in the cost of owning analysis because if the asset were purchased originally, it would be sold after 5 years. Line 10 shows the net cash flows associated with leasing for each year, and Line 11 shows the PV cost of leasing. (As indicated earlier in the cost of owning analysis, using a financial calculator we would enter the cash flows as shown on Line 10 into the cash flow register, enter the interest rate, i = 6, and then press the NPV key to obtain the PV cost of leasing the equipment.)

The rate used to discount the cash flows is a critical issue. In Chapter 12, we saw that the riskier a security, the higher its required return will be. This same principle was observed in our discussion of capital budgeting, and it also applies in lease analysis. Just how risky are the cash flows under consideration here? Most of them are relatively certain, at least when compared with the types of cash flow estimates that were developed in capital budgeting. For example, the loan payment schedule is set by contract, as is the lease payment schedule. The depreciation expenses are also established by law and are not subject to change, and the $500,000 annual maintenance cost is fixed by contract as well. The tax savings are somewhat uncertain because tax rates may change. The residual value is the least certain of the cash flows, but even here Mitchell's management is fairly confident that it will want to acquire the property and also that the cost of doing so will be close to $715,000.

Since the cash flows under both the lease and the borrow-and-purchase alternatives are all reasonably certain, they should be discounted at a relatively low rate. Most analysts recommend that the company's cost of debt be used, and this rate seems reasonable in our example. Further, since all the cash flows are on an after-tax basis, *the after-tax cost of debt should be used.* Mitchell's after-tax cost of debt is $k_d(1 - T) = 10\% (1 - 0.4) = 6\%$. Accordingly, in Table 18-2 we used a 6 percent discount rate to obtain the present values of the costs of owning and leasing. The financing method that produces the smaller present value of costs is the one that should be selected. The example shown in Table 18-2 indicates that leasing has a net advantage over buying: the present value of the cost of leasing is $412,000 less than that of buying. Therefore, it is to Mitchell's advantage to lease.

Factors That Affect Leasing Decisions

The basic method of analysis set forth in Table 18-2 is sufficient to handle most situations. However, certain factors warrant additional comments.

residual value

The value of leased property at the end of the lease term.

Estimated Residual Value.   It is important to note that the lessor will own the property upon the expiration of the lease. The estimated end-of-lease value of the property is called the **residual value.** Superficially, it would appear that if residual values are expected to be large, owning would have an advantage over leasing. However, if expected residual values are large—as they may be under inflation for certain types of equipment as well as if real property is involved—then competition among leasing companies will force leasing rates down to the point where potential residual values will be fully recognized in the lease contract rates. Thus, the existence of large residual values on equipment is not likely to bias the decision against leasing.

Increased Credit Availability. As noted earlier, leasing is sometimes said to have an advantage for firms that are seeking the maximum degree of financial leverage. First, it is sometimes argued that a firm can obtain more money, and for a longer period, under a lease arrangement than under a loan secured by the asset. Second, because some leases do not appear on the balance sheet, lease financing has been said to give the firm a stronger appearance in a *superficial* credit analysis, thus permitting it to use more leverage than it could if it did not lease. There may be some truth to these claims for smaller firms. However, now that larger firms are required to capitalize major leases and to report them on their balance sheets, this point is of questionable validity.

 Self-Test

Define each of these terms: (1) sale-and-leaseback arrangements, (2) operating leases, and (3) financial, or capital, leases.

What is off balance sheet financing, what is FASB #13, and how are the two related?

List the sequence of events, for the lessee, leading to a lease arrangement.

What is the appropriate discount rate to use in lease-versus-purchase analysis? Why is it appropriate to compare the cost of lease financing with that of debt financing?

Options

option

A contract that gives the option holder the right, but not the obligation, to buy or sell an asset at some predetermined price within a specified period of time.

An **option** is a contract that gives its holder the right, but not the obligation, to buy (or sell) an asset at some predetermined price within a specified period of time. "Pure options" are instruments that are created by outsiders (generally investment banking firms) rather than by the firm itself; they are bought and sold primarily by investors (or speculators). However, financial managers should understand the nature of options because this will help them structure warrant and convertible financings.

Option Types and Markets

There are many types of options and option markets.[10] To understand how options work, suppose you owned 100 shares of IBM stock, which on October 7, 1993, sold for $44.125 per share. You could sell to someone else the right to

---

[10]For more information on options, see any standard investments textbook.

striking (exercise) price

The price that must be paid (buying or selling) for a share of common stock when an option is exercised.

call option

An option to buy, or "call," a share of stock at a certain price within a specified period.

buy your 100 shares at any time during the next 3 months at a price of, say, $50 per share. The $50 is the **striking, or exercise, price.** Such options exist, and they are traded on a number of stock exchanges, with the Chicago Board of Options Exchange (CBOE) being the oldest and largest. This type of option is known as a **call option,** as the purchaser has a "call" on 100 shares of the stock. The seller of a call option is known as an *option writer.* An investor who writes a call option against stock held in his or her portfolio is said to be selling *covered options;* options sold without the stock to back them up are called *naked options.*

On October 7, 1993, IBM's 3-month, $50 call options sold on the CBOE for $1.00 each. Option contracts are normally written on 100 share lots. Thus, for ($1.00)(100) = $100.00, an investor could buy an option contract that would give him or her the right to purchase your 100 shares of IBM at a price of $50 per share at any time before expiration. If the stock price stayed below $50 during the period, the option would not be exercised since there would be no reason for the purchaser of the call option to pay more for the stock than its market price. As the option writer (seller), you would pocket the $100.00 price paid to you for selling the call option. However, if the stock's price rose to $60, the option buyer's $100.00 investment would be worth ($60 − $50)(100) = $1,000. That translates into a very healthy return on a $100.00 investment. Incidentally, if the stock price did go up, the option buyer would probably not actually exercise the option and buy your stock; rather, he or she would sell the same call options, which would then each have a price of at least $10 per share versus the $1.00 originally paid. By having both buy (long) and sell (short) positions on the same call contract, the option buyer would cancel out his or her position with the exchange, and the profit would be the difference in the buying price paid and the selling price received on the IBM call option contract.

put option

An option to sell a share of stock at a certain price, within a specified period.

Options are also traded which give the buyer the right to *sell* a stock at a specified price at some time in the future—this is called a **put option.** For example, suppose you expect IBM's stock to decline from its current level some time during the next 3 months. For $675.00 you could buy a 3-month put option giving you the right to sell 100 shares (which you would not necessarily own) at a price of $50 per share ($50 is the put option striking price). If you bought a 100-share put contract for $675.00 and IBM's stock price actually fell to $40, you would profit since your put contract gives you the right to sell the stock for $50 per share. You would make ($50 − $40)(100) = $1,000 minus the $675.00 you paid for the put option, for a net profit (before taxes and commissions) of $325.00

Options trading is one of the hottest financial activities in the United States today. The leverage involved makes it possible for speculators with just a few dollars to make a fortune almost overnight. Also, investors with sizable portfolios can sell options against their stocks and earn the value of the options (minus brokerage commissions) even if the stocks' prices remain constant. Still, those who have profited most from the development of options trading are securities firms, which earn very healthy commissions on such trades.

The corporations on whose stocks options are written, such as IBM, have nothing to do with the options market. They neither raise money in that market nor have any direct transactions in it, and option holders neither receive dividends nor vote for corporate directors (unless they exercise their options to purchase the stock, which few actually do). There have been studies by the SEC and others as to whether options trading stabilizes or destabilizes the stock market and whether it helps or hinders corporations seeking to raise new capital. The studies have not been conclusive, but options trading is here to stay, and many regard it as the most exciting game in town.

Formula Value versus Option Price

How is the actual price of an option determined in the market? In this section, we consider some of the basic relationships that can help investors determine the market price of a *call* option. Because a *call* option is the option to *purchase* shares of stock and a *put* option is the option to *sell* shares of stock, the relationships discussed will differ somewhat for puts. To begin, we define an option's **formula value** as follows:

formula value

The value of an option security, calculated as the stock price minus the striking, or exercise, price.

$$\text{Formula value} = \text{Current price of the stock} - \text{Striking price.} \quad (18\text{-}1)$$

For example, if a stock sells for $50 and its options have a striking price of $20, then the formula value of the option is $30. As we shall see, options generally sell at a price greater than their formula value.

Now consider Figure 18-1, which presents some data on Space Technology Inc. (STI), a company which recently went public and whose stock has fluctuated widely during its short history. Column 1 in the lower section shows the trading range of the stock; Column 2 shows the striking price of the option; Column 3 shows the formula values for STI's option when the stock sells at different prices; Column 4 gives the actual market prices of the option; and Column 5 shows the premium, or excess of the actual option price over its formula value. These data are plotted in the graph.

In this example, for any stock price below $20, the formula value is negative; above $20, each $1 increase in the price of the stock brings with it a $1 increase in the option's formula value. Note, however, that the actual market price of the option lies above the formula value at all prices of the common stock, but that the premium declines as the price of the stock increases. For example, when the common stock sold for $20 and the option had a zero formula value, its actual price, and the premium, was $9. Then, as the price of the stock rose, the formula value matched the stock increase dollar for dollar, but the market price of the option climbed less rapidly, causing the premium to decline. Thus, the premium was $9 when the stock sold for $20 a share, but it had declined to $1 by the time the stock price reached $73 a share, and beyond that point the premium virtually disappeared.

Why does this pattern exist? Why should the option ever sell for more than its formula value, and why does the premium decline as the price of the stock increases? The answer lies in the speculative appeal of options; they provide an investor with a high degree of leverage when buying securities. To illustrate, suppose STI's stock was selling for $21, and its options sold for exactly their formula value, $1. Now suppose you were thinking of investing in the company. If you bought a share of stock and the price rose to $42, you would make a 100 percent capital gain. However, if you bought the option at its $1 formula value, your capital gain would be $21 on a $1 investment, a 2,100 percent gain! At

Figure 18-1

Space Technology Inc.:
Option Price and Formula
Value

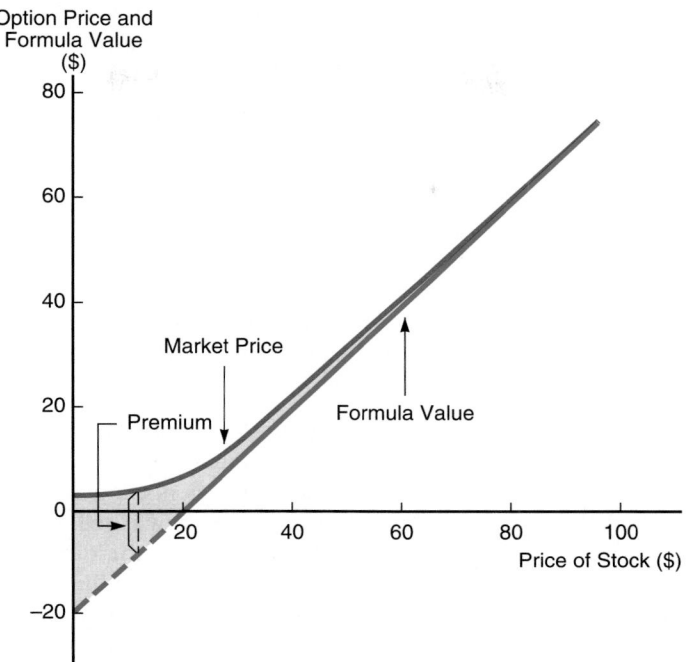

Price of Stock (1)	Striking Price (2)	Formula Value of Option (1) − (2) = (3)	Market Price of Option (4)	Premium (4) − (3) = (5)
$12.00	$20.00	($ 8.00)	$ 5.00	$13.00
20.00	20.00	0.00	9.00	9.00
21.00	20.00	1.00	9.75	8.75
22.00	20.00	2.00	10.50	8.50
35.00	20.00	15.00	21.00	6.00
42.00	20.00	22.00	26.00	4.00
50.00	20.00	30.00	32.00	2.00
73.00	20.00	53.00	54.00	1.00
98.00	20.00	78.00	78.50	0.50

Options have both a formula value and a market value, as illustrated here. The difference between the market price of the option and its formula value is the premium, the amount investors will pay for the potential gains available prior to the option's maturity. While increases in the stock price are reflected dollar for dollar in the formula value, the amount of the premium declines at higher stock prices. This highlights the fact that at low stock prices, an investor has large gain and small loss potential, but as the stock price increases, the leverage effect diminishes. The decreasing premium reflects this change in profit and loss potential.

the same time, your total loss potential with the option would be only $1, whereas the potential loss if you purchased the stock would be $21. The huge capital gains potential, combined with the loss limitation, is clearly worth something; the exact amount it is worth to investors is the amount of the premium.

Why does the premium decline as the price of the stock rises? Part of the answer is that both the leverage effect and the loss protection feature decline at high stock prices. For example, if you were thinking of buying the stock when its price was $73 a share, the formula value of the option would be $53. If the stock price doubled to $146, the formula value of STI's option would go from $53 to $126, an increase of 138 percent versus the 2,100 percent gain when the stock price doubled from $21. Notice also that the potential loss on the option is much greater when the option is selling at a high price. These two factors—the declining leverage effect and the increasing danger of losses—help explain why the premium diminishes as the price of the common stock rises.

In addition to the stock price and the striking price, the value of an option also depends on (1) the option's time to maturity and (2) the variability of the underlying stock's price, as explained below:

time effect

A principle of option valuation that states that the longer the time remaining to maturity, the greater the market price of an option.

volatility effect

A principle of option valuation that states that the greater the volatility of the stock price, the greater the market price of an option written on the stock.

1. **Time effect.**   The **time effect** states that the longer an option has to run, the greater its value, and the larger its premium. If an option expires at 4 P.M. today, there is not much chance that the stock price will go way up. Therefore, the option will sell at close to its formula value, and its premium will be small. On the other hand, if it has a year to go, the stock price could rise sharply, pulling the option's value up with it.

2. **Volatility effect.**   The **volatility effect** states that an option on an extremely volatile stock will be worth more than one on a very stable stock. We know that an option on a stock whose price rarely moves will not offer much chance for a large gain. On the other hand, an option on a stock that is highly volatile could provide a large gain, so such an option will be valuable. Note also that because losses on options are limited, large declines in a stock's price do not have a corresponding bad effect on option holders. Therefore, stock price volatility can only enhance the value of an option.[11]

If everything else were held constant, then in a graph like Figure 18-1, the longer an option's life, the higher its market price line would be above the

---

[11]To illustrate this point, suppose that for $2 you could buy an option on a stock now selling for $20. The striking price is also $20. Now suppose the stock is highly volatile, and you think it has a 50 percent probability of selling for either $10 or $30 when the option expires in one month. What is the expected value of the option? If the stock sells for $30, the option will be worth $30 − $20 = $10. If the stock sells for $10, the option to buy at $20 will be worthless ($0). Since there is a 50-50 chance that the stock will be worth $10 or $30, the expected value of the option is $5:

$$\text{Expected value of option} = 0.5(\$0) + 0.5(\$10) = \$5.$$

To be exactly correct, we would have to discount the $5 back for one month.

Now suppose the stock was more volatile, with a 50-50 chance of being worth zero or $40. Here the option would be worth

$$\text{Expected value of option} = 0.5(\$0) + 0.5(\$20) = \$10.$$

This demonstrates that the greater the volatility of the stock, the greater the value of the option. The reason this result occurs is that the large loss on the stock ($20) had no more of an adverse effect on the option holder than the small loss ($10). Thus, option holders benefit greatly if a stock goes way up, but they do not lose too badly if it drops all the way to zero. These concepts have been used to develop formulas for pricing options, with the most widely used formula being the Black-Scholes model, which is discussed in most investments texts.

formula value line. Also, the more volatile the price of the underlying stock, the higher the option's market price line would be.

Self-Test

Differentiate between a call option and a put option.

Do the corporations on whose stocks options are written raise money in the options market? Explain.

How does one calculate the formula value of an option? How is the premium on the option calculated?

Why does the premium on the option decline as the price of the stock increases?

Explain how these factors affect the premium on an option: (1) the time remaining before the option expires and (2) the volatility of the underlying stock.

Warrants

warrant

A long-term option to buy a stated number of shares of common stock at a specified price.

A **warrant** is an option issued by a company which gives the holder the right to buy a stated number of shares of the company's stock at a specified price. Generally, warrants are distributed along with debt, and they are used to induce investors to buy a firm's long-term debt at a lower interest rate than would otherwise be required. For example, when Pan-Pacific Airlines (PPA) wanted to sell $50 million of 20-year bonds in 1992, the company's investment bankers informed the financial vice president that straight bonds would be difficult to sell and that an interest rate of 14 percent would be required. However, the bankers suggested as an alternative that investors would be willing to buy bonds with an annual coupon rate as low as 10⅜ percent if the company would offer 30 warrants with each $1,000 bond, each warrant entitling the holder to buy one share of common stock at a price of $22 per share. The stock was selling for $20 per share at the time, and the warrants would expire in 1998 if they had not been exercised previously.

Why would investors be willing to buy Pan-Pacific's bonds at a yield of only 10⅜ percent in a 14 percent market just because warrants were offered as part of the package? The answer is that warrants are long-term *options,* and they have a value for the reasons set forth in the previous section. In the PPA case, this value offset the low interest rate on the bonds and made the entire package of low interest bonds plus warrants attractive to investors.

Initial Market Price of Bond with Warrants

If the PPA bonds had been issued as straight debt, they would have carried a 14 percent interest rate. With warrants attached, however, the bonds were sold to yield 10⅜ percent. Someone buying one of the bonds at its $1,000 initial offering price would thus have been receiving a package consisting of a 10⅜ percent, 20-year bond plus 30 warrants. Since the going interest rate on bonds as risky as those of PPA was 14 percent, we can find the pure-debt value of the bonds, assuming an annual coupon, as follows:

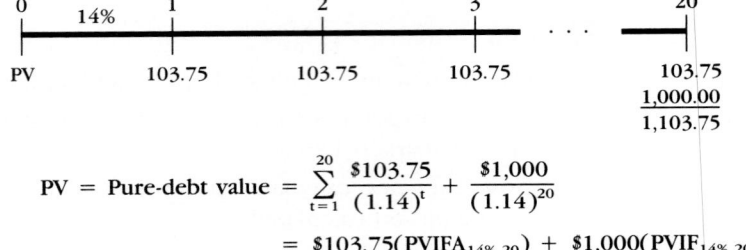

$$PV = \text{Pure-debt value} = \sum_{t=1}^{20} \frac{\$103.75}{(1.14)^t} + \frac{\$1,000}{(1.14)^{20}}$$

$$= \$103.75(\text{PVIFA}_{14\%,20}) + \$1,000(\text{PVIF}_{14\%,20})$$

$$= \$687.15 + \$72.80$$

$$= \$759.95 \approx \$760.$$

Alternatively, using a financial calculator we would enter the following data: n = 20, k = i = 14, PMT = 103.75, and FV = 1000. Then, we would press the PV key to obtain the answer of $759.91, or approximately $760. Thus, a person buying the bonds in the initial underwriting would pay $1,000 and receive in exchange a pure bond worth about $760 plus warrants presumably worth about $1,000 − $760 = $240:

$$\begin{array}{ccccc} \text{Price paid for} & = & \text{Pure-debt} & + & \text{Value of} \\ \text{bond with warrants} & & \text{value of bond} & & \text{warrants} \end{array} \qquad \text{(18-2)}$$

$$\$1,000 \quad = \quad \$760 \quad + \quad \$240.$$

Because investors receive 30 warrants with each bond, each warrant has an implied value of $240/30 = $8.

The key issue in setting the terms of a bond-with-warrants offering is finding the value of the warrants. The pure-debt value of the bond can be estimated quite accurately. However, it is much more difficult to estimate the value of the warrants. If their value is overestimated relative to their true market value, it will be difficult to sell the issue at its par value. Conversely, if the warrants' value is underestimated, investors in the issue will receive a windfall profit because they can sell the warrants in the market for more than they implicitly paid for them, and this windfall profit would come out of the pockets of PPA's current stockholders.

Use of Warrants in Financing

Warrants are generally used by small, rapidly growing firms as "sweeteners" to help sell either debt or preferred stock. Such firms are frequently regarded as being highly risky, and their bonds can be sold only if the firms are willing to pay extremely high rates of interest and to accept very restrictive indenture provisions. To avoid this, firms such as Pan-Pacific often offer warrants along with their bonds. However, some strong firms also have used warrants. In one of the largest financings of any type ever undertaken by a business firm, AT&T raised $1.57 billion by selling bonds with warrants. This marked the first use ever of warrants by a large, strong corporation.

Getting warrants along with bonds enables investors to share in a company's growth if that firm does in fact grow and prosper; therefore, investors are willing to accept a lower bond interest rate and less restrictive indenture provisions. A bond with warrants has some characteristics of debt and some of equity. It is a hybrid security that provides the financial manager with an opportunity to expand the firm's mix of securities and to appeal to a broader group of investors, thus lowering the firm's cost of capital.

detachable warrant

A warrant that can be detached from a bond and traded independently of it.

Virtually all warrants today are **detachable warrants,** meaning that after a bond with attached warrants has been sold, the warrants can be detached and traded separately from the bond. Further, when these warrants are exercised, the bonds themselves (with their low coupon rate) will remain outstanding. Thus, the warrants will bring in additional equity while leaving low interest rate debt on the books.

The warrants' exercise price is generally set at from 10 to 30 percent above the market price of the stock on the date the bond is issued. For example, if the stock sells for $10, the exercise price will probably be set in the $11 to $13 range. If the firm does grow and prosper and if its stock price rises above the exercise price at which shares may be purchased, warrant holders will turn in their warrants, along with cash equal to the stated exercise price, in exchange for stock. Without some incentive, however, many warrants would never be exercised until just before expiration. Their value in the market would be greater than their formula, or exercise, value, and hence holders would sell warrants rather than exercise them.

Recognize that the issuing firm benefits from financing by issuing bonds with warrants in two ways. First, the before-tax cost of debt is reduced, from 14 percent to $10\frac{3}{8}$ percent for PPA. Second, the exercising of warrants results in the issuance of new common shares, representing new equity capital for the firm. Thus, firms wishing to raise additional equity capital would prefer for their warrants to be exercised rather than held or sold for speculative purposes. There are three conditions which encourage holders to exercise their warrants: (1) Warrant holders will *surely* exercise warrants and buy stock if the warrants are about to expire with the market price of the stock above the exercise price. This means that if a firm wants its warrants exercised soon in order to raise capital, it should set a relatively short expiration date. (2) Warrant holders will tend to exercise *voluntarily* and buy stock if the company raises the dividend on the common stock by a sufficient amount. Since no dividend is paid on the warrant, it provides no current income. However, if the common stock pays a high dividend, it provides an attractive dividend yield. Therefore, the higher the stock's dividend, the greater the opportunity cost of holding the warrant rather than exercising it. Thus, if a firm wants its warrants exercised, it can raise the common stock's dividend. (3) Warrants sometimes have **stepped-up exercise prices,** which prod owners into exercising them. For example, the Shome Scientific Company has warrants outstanding with an exercise price of $25 until December 31, 1994, at which time the exercise price will rise to $30. If the price of the common stock is over $25 just before December 31, 1994, many warrant holders will exercise their options before the stepped-up price takes effect.

stepped-up exercise price

An exercise price that is specified to be higher if a warrant is exercised after a designated date.

Another useful feature of warrants is that they generally bring in funds only if such funds are needed. If the company grows, it will probably need new equity capital. At the same time, this growth will cause the price of the stock to rise and the warrants to be exercised, thereby allowing the firm to obtain additional cash. If the company is not successful and cannot profitably employ additional money, the price of its stock will probably not rise sufficiently to induce exercise of the options.

? Self-Test

Explain (showing two formulas, but without doing any calculations) how you would determine the value of warrants attached to bonds.

What three conditions would encourage holders to exercise their warrants?

Do warrants bring in additional funds to the firm when exercised? Explain.

Explain how a firm can use warrants to issue debt with a lower cost than similar debt without warrants.

Convertibles

convertible security

A security, usually a bond or preferred stock, that is exchangeable at the option of the holder for the common stock of the issuing firm.

Convertible securities are bonds or preferred stocks that can be exchanged for common stock at the option of the holder. Unlike the exercise of warrants, which provides the firm with additional funds, conversion does not bring in additional capital—debt (or preferred stock) is simply replaced by common stock. Of course, this reduction of debt or preferred stock will strengthen the firm's balance sheet and make it easier to raise additional capital, but this is a separate action.

Conversion Ratio and Conversion Price

conversion ratio (CR)

The number of shares of common stock that may be obtained by converting a convertible bond or share of convertible preferred stock.

conversion price (P_c)

The effective price paid for common stock obtained by converting a convertible security.

One of the most important provisions of a convertible security is the **conversion ratio (CR),** defined as the number of shares of stock the convertible holder receives upon conversion. Related to the conversion ratio is the **conversion price (P$_c$),** which is the effective price paid for the common stock obtained by converting a convertible security. The relationship between the conversion ratio and the conversion price can be illustrated by the Jackson Company's convertible debentures, issued at their $1,000 par value in 1993. At any time prior to maturity on July 1, 2013, a debenture holder can exchange a bond for 20 shares of common stock; therefore, CR = 20. The bond has a par value of $1,000, so the holder would be relinquishing this amount upon conversion. Dividing the $1,000 par value by the 20 shares received gives a conversion price of P$_c$ = $50 a share:

$$\text{Conversion price} = P_c = \frac{\text{Par value of bond}}{\text{CR}} \qquad (18\text{-}3)$$

$$= \frac{\$1,000}{20} = \$50.$$

Similarly, if we know the conversion price, we can find CR:

$$\text{Conversion ratio} = \text{CR} = \frac{\text{Par value of bond}}{P_c} \qquad (18\text{-}4)$$

$$= \frac{\$1,000}{\$50} = 20 \text{ shares.}$$

Once CR is set, the value of P_c is established, and vice versa.

Like a warrant's exercise price, the conversion price is characteristically set at from 10 to 30 percent above the prevailing market price of the common stock at the time the convertible issue is sold. Generally, the conversion price and ratio are fixed for the life of the bond, although sometimes a stepped-up conversion price is used. Arden Industries's convertible debentures, for example, are convertible into 12.5 shares until 1995; into 11.76 shares from 1995 until 2000; and into 11.11 shares from 2000 until maturity in 2005. The conversion price thus started at $80, will rise to $85 in 1995, and then will go to $90 in 2000. Arden's convertibles, like most, are callable at the option of the company after a 3-year call protection period.

Another factor that may cause a change in the conversion price and ratio is a standard feature of almost all convertibles—the clause protecting the convertible against dilution from stock splits, stock dividends, and the sale of common stock at prices below the conversion price.[12] The typical provision states that if common stock is sold at a price below the conversion price, the conversion price must be lowered (and the conversion ratio raised) to the price at which the new stock was issued. Also, if the stock is split (or if a stock dividend is declared), the conversion price must be lowered by the percentage of the stock split (or stock dividend). For example, if the Jackson Company were to have a two-for-one stock split, the conversion ratio would automatically be adjusted from 20 to 40, and the conversion price lowered from $50 to $25. If this protection were not contained in the contract, a company could completely thwart conversion by the use of stock splits. Warrants are similarly protected against such dilution.

The standard protection against dilution from selling new stock at prices below the conversion price can, however, get a company into trouble. For example, Arden Industries's stock was selling for only $64 in 1992 versus the conversion price of $80. Thus, Arden would have had to give its bondholders a tremendous break if it wanted to sell new common stock. Problems like this must be kept in mind by firms considering the use of convertibles or bonds with warrants.[13]

Convertible Bond Analysis

In 1993 the Jackson Company was thinking of issuing 20-year convertible bonds at a price of $1,000 each. Each bond would pay a 10 percent annual coupon interest rate, or $100 per year, and each would be convertible into 20 shares of

---

[12]Stock splits and stock dividends will be discussed in Chapter 21.

[13]For a more complete discussion of how the terms are set on a convertible offering, see M. Wayne Marr and G. Rodney Thompson, "The Pricing of New Convertible Bond Issues," *Financial Management,* Summer 1984, 31–37.

stock. Thus, the conversion price would be $1,000/20 = $50. If the bonds did not have the conversion feature, investors would require a yield of 12 percent, because k_d = 12%. Knowing k_d, the coupon rate, and the maturity, we can find the pure-debt (or pure-bond) value of the convertibles at the time of issue, B_0, using the bond valuation model developed back in Chapter 16. The bonds would initially sell at a price of $851:

$$\text{Pure-debt value at time of issue} = B_0 = \sum_{t=1}^{n} I \frac{1}{(1 + k_d)^t} + M \frac{1}{(1 + k_d)^n} \quad (18\text{-}5)$$

$$= \sum_{t=1}^{20} \frac{\$100}{(1.12)^t} + \frac{\$1,000}{(1.12)^{20}} = \$851.$$

B_0 is the initial pure-debt value of the bond, and B_t is the value each year after issue, as the bond's maturity changes from 20 to 19, then 18, and so forth. As maturity approaches, the pure-debt value approaches $1,000.

Jackson's stock is expected to pay a dividend of $2.80 in the coming year; it currently sells at $35 per share, and this price is expected to grow at a constant rate of 8 percent per year. Thus, the stock price expected in each future Year t is $\hat{P}_t = P_0(1 + g)^t = \$35(1.08)^t$. Further, since Jackson's convertibles would allow their holders to convert them into 20 shares of stock, the value a bondholder would expect to receive if he or she converted, defined as C_t, would be

$$\text{Conversion value} = C_t = \text{Initial stock price } (1 + g)^t(CR) \quad (18\text{-}6)$$

$$= \$35(1.08)^t(20).$$

The convertible bonds would not be callable for 10 years, after which they could be called at a price of $1,000. If after 10 years the conversion value exceeded the call price by at least 20 percent, management has indicated that it would call the bonds.

Figure 18-2 shows the expectations of both an average investor and the company:

1. The horizontal line $MM'' = \$1,000$ represents the par (and maturity) value. Also, $1,000 is the price at which the bond would initially be offered to the public.

2. The pure-debt (or pure-bond) value of the convertible would initially be $851, but it would rise to $1,000 over the 20-year life of the bond. The bond's pure-debt value is shown by the line B_t in Figure 18-2.

conversion value, C_t
The value of common stock obtained by converting a convertible security.

3. The bond's initial **conversion value, C_t,** or the value of the stock the investor would receive if the bond were converted at t = 0, is $700: Conversion value = $P_0(CR)$ = $35(20 shares) = $700. As indicated previously, the stock's price is expected to grow at an 8 percent annual rate, so $\hat{P}_t = \$35(1.08)^t$. If the price of the stock rises over time, so will the conversion value of the bond. For example, in Year 3 the conversion value should be $C_3 = P_3(CR) = \$35(1.08)^3(20) = \$882$. The expected conversion value over time is given by the line C_t in Figure 18-2.

4. The actual market price of the bond must always be equal to or greater than the *higher* of its pure-debt value or its conversion value. Therefore,

Figure 18-2

Jackson Company:
Model of a Convertible
Bond

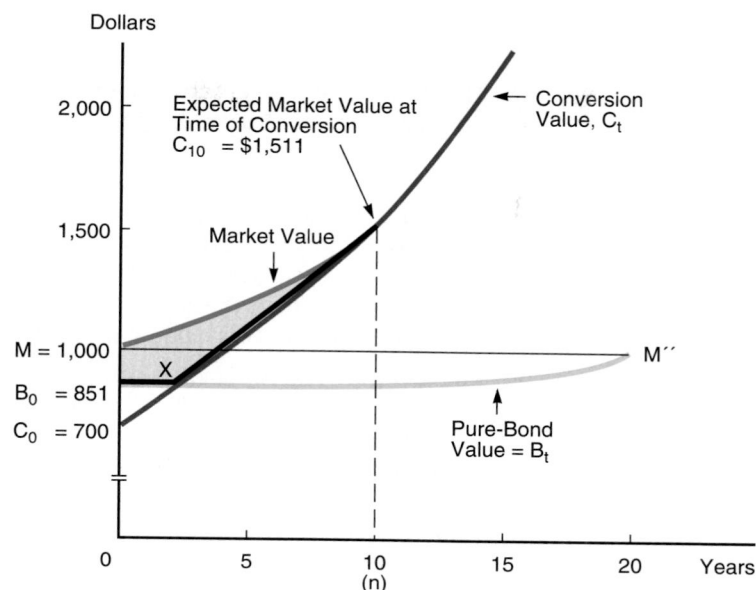

Year	Pure-Bond Value, B_t	Conversion Value, C_t	Maturity Value, M	Market Value	Floor Value	Premium
0	$ 851	$ 700	$1,000	$1,000	$ 851	$149
1	853	756	1,000	1,042	853	189
2	855	816	1,000	1,086	855	231
3	858	882	1,000	1,132	882	250
4	861	952	1,000	1,180	952	228
5	864	1,029	1,000	1,229	1,029	200
6	867	1,111	1,000	1,281	1,111	170
7	872	1,200	1,000	1,335	1,200	135
8	876	1,296	1,000	1,391	1,296	95
9	881	1,399	1,000	1,450	1,399	51
10	887	1,511	1,000	1,511	1,511	0
11	893	1,632	1,000	1,632	1,632	0
.	.	.	.	.	.	.
.	.	.	.	.	.	.
.	.	.	.	.	.	.
20	1,000	3,263	1,000	3,263	3,263	0

This graph compares the pure-bond value, the "floor" value, the conversion value, and the market value lines for the Jackson Company's 20-year convertible bond. As this graph illustrates, the market value of a convertible will exceed the floor price because investors are willing to pay a premium over the pure-bond value for the possiblity of earning large capital gains if the stock price shoots up. The gap between the market price of the convertible and the floor, or the premium investors are willing to pay, declines over time, and it is zero in Year 10.

the higher of the bond value or the conversion value curves in Figure 18-2 represents a "floor price" for the bond; this is represented by the heavy line B_0XC_t.

5.   The market value of a convertible generally will exceed the floor price for the same reasons that an option's or a warrant's price will exceed its formula value. Investors are willing to pay a premium over the pure-debt value (which establishes the initial floor) because of the possibility of earning large capital gains if the stock price shoots up. After Year 3, when the conversion value exceeds the pure-bond value and thus establishes the floor, the market price will still exceed the floor. This is because the convertible is safer than the stock, for even if profits decline and the stock price drops, the bond's value will never fall below its pure-debt value.[14]

6.   The gap between the market price of the convertible and the floor, or the premium investors are willing to pay, declines over time and is zero in Year 10. This decline occurs for two reasons. First, the dividends received on the stock presumably are growing at 8 percent a year, whereas the interest on the bond is fixed at $100 annually. After 8 years, the dividends which would be received from 20 shares of stock, $2.80(1.08)^8(20) = \$103.65$, would exceed the $100 of interest paid by the bond; beyond that point the opportunity cost of holding the bond rather than converting it would become increasingly heavy. Second, after 10 years the bond would become callable at a price of $1,000. If Jackson called the issue, the bondholder could either convert the bond to common stock worth $C_{10} = \$1,511$ or receive $1,000 in cash. The holder would, of course, choose the $1,511 of stock. Note, however, that if the convertible were selling at a price greater than $C_{10} = \$1,511$ when the call occurred, the holder would suffer an immediate loss equal to the difference between the bond's price and $1,511. Therefore, because of the call provision, the market value of the bond cannot logically exceed the higher of the call price or the conversion price after the bond becomes callable.

7.   If investors purchased Jackson's stock, they would expect a return of $k_s = D_1/P_0 + g = \$2.80/\$35 + 8\% = 16\%$. If they bought a pure bond, they would earn 12 percent. The convertible has some guaranteed interest plus the expectation of some capital gains, so its risk and therefore its expected rate of return should lie between $k_d = 12\%$ and $k_s = 16\%$. We can find the expected return on the convertible by solving for k_c in the following equation:

$$\text{Initial price} = \sum_{t=1}^{n} I\frac{1}{(1 + k_c)^t} + C_t\frac{1}{(1 + k_c)^n} \qquad (18\text{-}7)$$

$$\$1,000 = \sum_{t=1}^{10} \frac{\$100}{(1 + k_c)^t} + \frac{\$1,511}{(1 + k_c)^{10}}.$$

Using a financial calculator, if we enter n = 10, PV = –1000, PMT = 100, and FV = 1511, then we could find $k_c = i = 12.8\%$. Therefore, un-

---

[14]Note, however, that the bond value line B_0M'' would fall if interest rates rose in the economy or if the company's credit risk deteriorated, both of which would cause k_d to rise.

der the assumptions of this example, an investor who purchased the convertible at its initial $1,000 offering price could expect to earn a rate of return of 12.8 percent.

Use of Convertibles in Financing

Convertibles offer three important advantages from the issuer's standpoint. First, convertibles, like bonds with warrants, permit a company to sell debt with a lower interest rate and with less restrictive covenants than straight bonds. Second, convertibles are generally subordinated to mortgage bonds, bank loans, and other senior debt, so financing with convertibles leaves the company's access to "regular" debt unimpaired. Third, convertibles provide a way of selling common stock at prices higher than those currently prevailing. Many companies actually want to sell common stock and not debt, but they believe that the price of their stock is temporarily depressed. The financial manager may know, for example, that earnings are depressed because of start-up costs associated with a new project, but he or she may expect earnings to rise sharply during the next year or so, pulling the price of the stock along. In this case, if the company sold stock now it would be giving up too many shares to raise a given amount of money. However, if it sets the conversion price at 20 to 30 percent above the present market price of the stock, then 20 to 30 percent fewer shares will have to be given up when the bonds are converted. Notice, however, that management is counting on the stock price's rising sufficiently above the conversion price to make the bonds attractive in conversion. If earnings do not rise and pull the stock price up, and hence if conversion does not occur, the company could be saddled with debt in the face of low earnings, which could be disastrous.

How can the company be sure that conversion will occur if the price of the stock rises above the conversion price? Typically, convertibles contain a call provision that enables the issuing firm to force bondholders to convert. Suppose the conversion price is $50, the conversion ratio is 20, the market price of the common stock has risen to $60, and the call price on the convertible bond is $1,050. If the company calls the bond, bondholders could either convert into common stock with a market value of $1,200 or allow the company to redeem the bond for $1,050. Naturally, bondholders prefer $1,200 to $1,050, so conversion will occur. The call provision therefore gives the company a means of forcing conversion, but only if the market price of the stock is greater than the conversion price.

Convertibles are useful, but they do have three important disadvantages. (1) The use of a convertible security may in effect give the issuer the opportunity to sell common stock at a price higher than it could sell stock otherwise. However, if the common stock increases greatly in price, the company would probably have been better off if it had used straight debt in spite of its higher interest rate and then later sold common stock to refund the debt. (2) If the company truly wants to raise equity capital and if the price of the stock does not rise sufficiently after the bond is issued, then the firm will be stuck with debt. (3) Convertibles typically have a low coupon interest rate, an advantage that will be lost when conversion occurs. Warrant financings, on the other hand, permit the company to continue to use the low-coupon debt for a longer period.

Self-Test

Does the exchange of convertible securities for common stock bring in additional funds to the firm? Explain.

How do you calculate (1) the conversion price, P_c, and (2) the conversion ratio, CR?

How is a convertible bond's initial conversion value, C_0, calculated? How does the conversion value change over time?

Why does the premium (the excess of the market value of a convertible over either the conversion value or the straight bond value) decline over time and eventually go to zero?

What are the key advantages and disadvantages of convertibles?

Reporting Earnings when Warrants or Convertibles Are Outstanding

If warrants or convertibles are outstanding, a firm can theoretically report earnings per share in one of three ways:

1. **Simple EPS.** The earnings available to common stockholders are divided by the average number of shares actually outstanding during the period.

2. **Primary EPS.** The earnings available are divided by the average number of shares that would have been outstanding if warrants and convertibles likely to be converted in the near future had actually been exercised or converted.

3. **Fully diluted EPS.** This is similar to primary EPS except that *all* warrants and convertibles are assumed to be exercised or converted, regardless of the likelihood of either occurring.

Simple EPS is virtually never reported by firms which have warrants or convertibles likely to be exercised or converted; the SEC prohibits use of this figure, and it requires that primary and fully diluted earnings be shown on the income statement.

 Self-Test

Differentiate between simple EPS, primary EPS, and fully diluted EPS.

SMALL BUSINESS

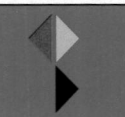

LEASE FINANCING FOR SMALL BUSINESSES

Earlier in this chapter we saw that, under certain conditions, leasing an asset can be less costly than borrowing to purchase the asset. For the small firm, leasing often offers three additional advantages: it (1) conserves cash, (2) makes better use of managers' time, and (3) provides financing quickly.

Conserving Cash

Small firms often have limited cash resources. Because many leasing companies do not require the lessee to make even a small down payment and because leases are often for longer terms and thus require lower payments than bank loans, leasing can help the small firm conserve its cash. Leasing companies also may be willing to work with a company to design a flexible leasing package that will help the lessee preserve its cash during critical times. For example, when Surgicare of Central Jersey opened its first surgical center, the firm did not have sufficient cash to pay for the necessary equipment. Surgicare's options were to borrow at a high interest rate, to sell stock to the public (which is difficult for a start-up firm), or to lease the equipment. Surgicare's financial vice president, John Rutzel, decided to lease the needed equipment from Copelco Financial Services, a leasing company which specializes in health care equipment. Copelco allowed Surgicare to make very low payments for the first 6 months, slightly higher payments during the second 6 months, and level payments thereafter. These unique lease terms "got Surgicare through the start-up phase, when cash flow was the critical consideration."

Freeing Managers for Other Tasks

Most small business owners find that they never have enough time to get everything done—being in charge of sales, operations, budgeting, and everything else, they are simply spread too thin. If an asset is owned, the firm must maintain it in good working condition and also keep records on its use for tax depreciation purposes. However, leasing assets frees the business's owner of these duties. First, paperwork is reduced because maintenance records, depreciation schedules, and other records do not have to be maintained on leased assets. Second, less time may have to be spent "shopping around" for the right equipment because leasing companies, which generally specialize in a particular industry, can often provide the manager with the information necessary to select the needed assets. Third, since the assets can be traded in if they become obsolete, the initial choice of equipment is less critical. And fourth, the burden of servicing and repairing the equipment can be passed on to the lessor.

Obtaining Assets Quickly and Inexpensively

Many new, small firms find that banks are unwilling to lend them money at a reasonable cost. However, because leasing companies retain the ownership of the equipment, they may be more willing to take chances with start-up firms. When Ed Lavin started Offset Printing Company, his bank would not lend him the money to purchase the necessary printing presses—the bank wanted to lend only to firms with proven track records. Lavin arranged to lease the needed presses from Eaton Financial, which also advised him on the best type of equipment to meet his needs. Recently, Lavin's firm achieved sales of $250,000, and as his company grew, he expanded by leasing additional equipment. Thus, (1) leasing allowed Lavin to go into business when his bank was unwilling to help, (2) his leasing company provided him with help in selecting equipment, and (3) the leasing company also provided additional capital to meet his expansion needs.

Summary

This chapter discussed two hybrid forms of long-term financing: (1) leasing and (2) option securities, including warrants and convertibles.

▶ **Leasing** is a means of obtaining the use of an asset without purchasing that asset.

The three most important forms of leasing are **sale-and-leaseback** arrangements, under which a firm sells an asset to another party and leases the asset back for a specified period under specific terms; **operating leases,** under which the lessor both maintains and finances the asset; and **financial leases,** under which the asset is fully amortized over the life of the lease, the lessor does not normally provide maintenance, and the lease is not cancelable.

The **decision whether to lease or to buy an asset** is made by comparing the financing costs of the two alternatives and choosing the financing method with the lower cost. All cash flows should be discounted at the

after-tax cost of debt because lease analysis cash flows are relatively certain and are on an after-tax basis.

▶ An **option** is a contract that gives its holder the right, but not the obligation, to buy (or sell) an asset at some predetermined price within a specified period of time. Option features are used by firms to "sweeten" debt offerings.

An option's **formula value** is equal to the stock price less the striking, or exercise, price.

Premium value can be calculated by subtracting the formula value from the actual option price. This difference exists due to the speculative appeal of options.

▶ A **warrant** is an option issued by a firm which gives the holder the right to purchase a stated number of shares of stock at a specified price within a given period.

A warrant will be exercised if it is about to expire and if the stock price is above the exercise price.

Companies offer warrants in conjunction with bonds to entice investors to buy long-term debt at lower interest rates.

▶ A **convertible security** is a bond or preferred stock which can be exchanged for common stock. When conversion occurs, debt or preferred stock is replaced with common stock, but no money changes hands.

The actual market price of a convertible bond is always equal to or greater than the *higher* of its pure-debt value or its **conversion value,** that is, the value of the common stock obtained on conversion.

The **conversion of bonds** by their holders **does not provide additional funds** to the company, but it does result in a lower debt ratio. The **exercise of warrants does provide additional funds,** which strengthens the firm's equity position, but it still leaves the debt on the balance sheet. Thus, low interest rate debt remains outstanding when warrants are exercised, but the firm loses this advantage when convertibles are converted.

Resolution to
DECISION IN FINANCE

LOOKING FOR A NEW
LEASE ON LIFE

Negotiation is the key to GPA's future—negotiation with aircraft manufacturers, with its lenders, and with its shareholders.

Source: "Troubles of a Lessor of Jet Airliners Touch Many Parts of Industry," *The Wall Street Journal,* December 17, 1992, A1.

Boeing reluctantly agreed to delay delivery on 65 planes. A Boeing official said, "We're disappointed," but he also said he expects GPA to pull through "one way or another." Some workers at Boeing's Everett, Washington, wide-body assembly plant north of Seattle are looking into other job possibilities in case things do not work out. "Everybody is concerned about this, and hoping we don't lose those orders because it would mean layoffs," said one.

Other delays, and 20 cancellations, were sought from Airbus Industrie in Europe, and GPA is dickering with McDonnell Douglas to reschedule orders for 18 big jets, valued at about $2 billion, plus 9 smaller planes.

GPA has put some of its fleet up for sale, a move that in better times would bring the company plenty of cash. In the present state of the economy, however, even "fire sale" pricing is not much help. In eight months in 1992, the company sold only 25 planes for about $700 million.

In negotiating with its lenders, GPA Deputy Chairman Maurice Foley said, "We've been quite encouraged. The lead banks all support the broad principles we've put forward." The primary banks include National Westminster Bank PLC, Swiss Bank Corporation, Citicorp, and Mitsubishi Trust and Banking Corporation. However, at least one of them insisted that all 100 lenders would need to agree on any restructuring plan.

Stockholders may be even harder to persuade to hang in there with GPA. The company approached big investors with a plan to offer convertible stock to raise some $200 million. Those who did not participate would see their holdings diluted. However, many would undoubtedly rather sell their stock than buy more.

Deputy Chairman Foley said, "We recognize that some of our major shareholders would like to reduce their stakes, but we have to put it to them that they have to put more money into the company instead of taking it out. The company needs more primary equity."

Questions

18-1 Distinguish between operating leases and financial leases. Would a firm be more likely to finance a fleet of trucks or a manufacturing plant with an operating lease?

18-2 One alleged advantage of leasing voiced in the past was that it kept liabilities off the balance sheet, thus making it possible for a firm to obtain more leverage than it otherwise could have. This raised the question of whether or not both the lease obligation and the asset involved should be capitalized and shown on the balance sheet. Discuss the pros and cons of capitalizing leases and related assets.

18-3 Suppose there were no IRS restrictions on what constitutes a valid lease. Explain in a manner that a legislator might understand why some restrictions should be imposed.

18-4 Suppose Congress changed the tax laws in a way that (1) permitted equipment to be depreciated over a shorter period, (2) lowered corporate tax rates, and (3) reinstated the investment tax credit. Discuss how each of these changes would affect the relative use of leasing versus conventional debt in the U.S. economy.

18-5 Why do options typically sell at prices higher than their formula values?

18-6 What effect does the expected growth rate of a firm's stock price (subsequent to issue) have on its ability to raise additional funds through (a) convertibles and (b) warrants?

18-7 **a.** How would a firm's decision to pay out a higher percentage of its earnings as dividends affect each of the following?
   (1) The value of its long-term warrants.
   (2) The likelihood that its convertible bonds will be converted.
   (3) The likelihood that its warrants will be exercised.
b. If you owned the warrants or convertibles of a company, would you be pleased or displeased if it raised its payout rate from 20 percent to 80 percent? Why?

18-8 Evaluate the following statement: "Issuing convertible securities represents a means by which a firm can sell common stock at a price above the existing market price."

18-9   Suppose a company simultaneously issues $50 million of convertible bonds with a coupon rate of 9 percent and $50 million of pure bonds with a coupon rate of 12 percent. Both bonds have the same maturity. Does the fact that the convertible issue has the lower coupon rate suggest that it is less risky than the pure bond? Would you regard the company's cost of capital as being lower on the convertible than on the pure bond? Explain. (*Hint:* Although it might appear at first glance that the convertible's cost of capital is lower, this is not necessarily the case because the interest rate on the convertible understates its cost. Think about this.)

Self-Test Problem

ST-1   The Olsen Company has decided to acquire a new truck. One alternative is to lease the truck on a 4-year contract for a lease payment of $10,000 per year, with payments to be made at the *beginning* of each year. The lease would include maintenance. Alternatively, Olsen could purchase the truck outright for $40,000, financing with a bank loan for the net purchase price, amortized over a 4-year period at an interest rate of 10 percent per year, payments to be made at the *end* of each year. Under the borrow-to-purchase arrangement, Olsen would have to maintain the truck at a cost of $1,000 per year, payable at year-end. The truck falls into the MACRS 3-year class. It has a salvage value of $10,000, which is the expected market value after 4 years, at which time Olsen plans to replace the truck irrespective of whether it leases or buys. Olsen has a federal-plus-state tax rate of 40 percent.

   a. What is Olsen's PV cost of leasing?

   b. What is Olsen's PV cost of owning? Should the truck be leased or purchased?

   c. The appropriate discount rate for use in Olsen's analysis is the firm's after-tax cost of debt. Why?

   d. The salvage value is the least certain cash flow in the analysis. How might Olsen incorporate the higher riskiness of this cash flow into the analysis?

Problems

18-1

Establishing lease payments

Sav-U-Lease specializes in leasing trucks and equipment to construction firms in the metropolitan Atlanta area. Nelson-Long Construction wishes to lease $3 million in equipment from Sav-U-Lease for a 5-year period. What is the annual lease payment Nelson-Long would pay if the lease is based on a 14 percent lease rate? The lease payments are to be made at the end of each year. (Note that the 14 percent rate is simply the rate used to establish the lease payments; it is not Sav-U-Lease's rate of return.)

18-2

Establishing lease payments

Refer to Problem 18-1. What would the annual lease payments be if Sav-U-Lease required lease payments to be made at the beginning of the year rather than at the end of the year? Note that 5 payments will be made, with the first due immediately.

18-3

Balance sheet effects of leasing

Two textile companies, Meyer Manufacturing and Haugen Mills, began operations with identical balance sheets. A year later, both required additional manufacturing capacity at a cost of $200,000. Meyer obtained a 5-year, $200,000 loan at an 8 percent interest rate from its bank. Haugen, on the other hand, decided to lease the required $200,000 capacity from American Leasing for 5 years; an 8 percent return was built into the lease. The balance sheet for each company, before the asset increases, is as follows:

		Debt	$200,000
		Equity	200,000
Total assets	$400,000	Total liabilities and equity	$400,000

a. Show the balance sheet of each firm after the asset increase, and calculate each firm's new debt ratio. (Assume Haugen's lease is kept off the balance sheet.)

b. Show how Haugen's balance sheet would have looked immediately after the financing if it had capitalized the lease.

c. Would the rate of return (1) on assets and (2) on equity be affected by the choice of financing? How?

18-4
Lease analysis

As part of its overall plant modernization and cost reduction program, the management of Teweles Textile Mills has decided to install a new automated weaving loom. In the capital budgeting analysis of this equipment, the IRR of the project was found to be 20 percent versus a project required return of 12 percent.

The loom has an invoice price of $250,000, including delivery and installation charges. The funds needed could be borrowed from the bank through a 4-year amortized loan at a 10 percent interest rate, with payments to be made at the end of each year. In the event that the loom is purchased, the manufacturer will contract to maintain and service it for a fee of $20,000 per year paid at the end of each year. The loom falls in the MACRS 5-year class, and Teweles's marginal federal-plus-state tax rate is 40 percent.

Apilado Automation Inc., maker of the loom, has offered to lease the loom to Teweles for $70,000 upon delivery and installation (at t = 0) plus 4 additional annual lease payments of $70,000 to be made at the end of Years 1 through 4. (Note that there are 5 lease payments in total.) The lease agreement includes maintenance and servicing. Actually, the loom has an expected life of 8 years, at which time its expected salvage value is zero; however, after 4 years, its market value is expected to equal its book value of $42,500. Teweles plans to build an entirely new plant in 4 years, so it has no interest in either leasing or owning the proposed loom for more than that period.

a. Should the loom be leased or purchased?

b. The salvage value is clearly the most uncertain cash flow in the analysis. Assume that the appropriate salvage value pretax discount rate is 15 percent. What would be the effect of a salvage value risk adjustment on the decision?

c. The original analysis assumed that Teweles would not need the loom after 4 years. Now assume that the firm will continue to use it after the lease expires. Thus, if it leased, Teweles would have to buy the asset after 4 years at the then existing market value, which is assumed to equal the book value. What effect would this requirement have on the basic analysis? (No numerical analysis is required; just verbalize.)

18-5
Convertibles

The Swift Company was planning to finance an expansion in the summer of 1994. The principal executives of the company agreed that an industrial company like theirs should finance growth by means of common stock rather than by debt. However, they believed that the price of the company's common stock did not reflect its true worth, so they decided to sell a convertible security. They considered a convertible debenture but feared the burden of fixed interest charges if the common stock did not rise enough to make conversion attractive. They decided on an issue of convertible preferred stock, which would pay a dividend of $1.05 per share.

The common stock was selling for $21 a share at the time. Management projected earnings for 1994 at $1.50 a share and expected a future growth rate of 10 percent a year in 1995 and beyond. It was agreed by the investment bankers and management that the common stock would continue to sell at 14 times earnings, the current price/earnings ratio.

a. What conversion price should be set by the issuer? The conversion rate will be 1.0; that is, each share of convertible preferred can be converted into one share of common. Therefore, the convertible's par value (as well as the issue price) will be equal to the conversion price, which in turn will be determined as a percentage over the current market price of the common. Your answer will be a guess, but make it a reasonable one.

b. Should the preferred stock include a call provision? Why or why not?

18-6
Financing alternatives

The Cox Computer Company has grown rapidly during the past 5 years. Recently its commercial bank urged the company to consider increasing its permanent financing. Its bank loan under a line of credit has risen to $150,000, carrying a 10 percent interest rate, and Cox has been 30 to 60 days late in paying trade creditors.

Discussions with an investment banker have resulted in the decision to raise $250,000 at this time. Investment bankers have assured Cox that the following alternatives are feasible (flotation costs will be ignored):

▶ *Alternative 1:* Sell common stock at $10 per share.

▶ *Alternative 2:* Sell convertible bonds at a 10 percent coupon, convertible into 80 shares of common stock for each $1,000 bond (that is, the conversion price is $12.50 per share).

▶ *Alternative 3:* Sell debentures with a 10 percent coupon; each $1,000 bond will have 80 warrants to buy one share of common stock at $12.50.

Charles Cox, the president, owns 80 percent of Cox's common stock and wishes to maintain control of the company; 50,000 shares are outstanding. The following are summaries of Cox's latest financial statements:

Balance Sheet

		Current liabilities	$200,000
		Common stock, $1 par	50,000
		Retained earnings	25,000
Total assets	$275,000	Total liabilities and equity	$275,000

Income Statement

Sales	$550,000
All costs except interest	495,000
EBIT	$ 55,000
Interest	15,000
EBT	$ 40,000
Taxes at 40%	16,000
Net income	$ 24,000
Shares outstanding	50,000
Earnings per share	$0.48
Price/earnings ratio	18×
Market price of stock	$8.64

a. Show the new balance sheet under each alternative. For Alternatives 2 and 3, show the balance sheet after conversion of the debentures or exercise of the warrants. Assume that $150,000 of the funds raised will be used to pay off the bank loan and the rest to increase total assets.

b. Show Charles Cox's control position under each alternative, assuming that he does not purchase additional shares.

c. What is the effect on earnings per share of each alternative if it is assumed that earnings before interest and taxes will be 20 percent of total assets?

d. What will be the debt ratio under each alternative?

e. Which of the three alternatives would you recommend to Charles Cox, and why?

18-7

Convertibles

Rentz Computers Inc. needs to raise $35 million to begin producing a new microcomputer. Rentz's straight, nonconvertible debentures currently yield 12 percent. Its stock sells for $38 per share, the last dividend was $2.46, and the expected growth rate is a constant 8 percent. Investment bankers have tentatively proposed that Rentz raise the $35 million by issuing convertible debentures. These convertibles would have a $1,000 par value, carry a coupon rate of 10 percent, have a 20-year maturity, and be convertible into 20 shares of stock. The bonds would be noncallable for 5 years, after which they would be callable at a price of $1,075; this call price would decline by $5 per year in Year 6 and each year thereafter. Management has called convertibles in the past (and presumably will call them again in the future), once they were eligible for call, as soon as their conversion value was about 20 percent above their par value (not their call price).

a. Draw an accurate graph similar to Figure 18-2 representing the expectations set forth in the problem.

b. Suppose the previously outlined projects work out on schedule for 2 years, but then Rentz begins to experience extremely strong competition from Japanese firms. As a result, Rentz's expected growth rate drops from 8 percent to zero. Assume that the dividend at the time of the drop is $2.87. The company's credit strength is not impaired, and its value of k_s is also unchanged. What would happen (1) to the stock price and (2) to the convertible bond's price? Be as precise as you can.

18-8

Lease versus buy

Malitz Mining Company must install $1.5 million of new machinery in its Nevada mine. It can obtain a bank loan for 100 percent of the required amount. Alternatively, a Nevada investment banking firm which represents a group of investors believes that it can arrange for a lease financing plan. Assume that the following facts apply:

(1) The equipment falls in the MACRS 3-year class.

(2) Estimated maintenance expenses are $75,000 per year.

(3) Malitz's federal-plus-state tax rate is 40 percent.

(4) If the money is borrowed, the bank loan will be at a rate of 15 percent, amortized in 4 equal installments to be paid at the end of each year.

(5) The tentative lease terms call for end-of-year payments of $400,000 per year for 4 years.

(6) Under the proposed lease terms, the lessee must pay for insurance, property taxes, and maintenance.

(7) Malitz must use the equipment if it is to continue in business, so it will almost certainly want to acquire the property at the end of the lease. If it does, then under the lease terms it can purchase the machinery at its fair market value at that time. The best estimate of this market value is the $250,000 salvage value, but it could be much higher or lower under certain circumstances.

To assist management in making the proper lease-versus-buy decision, you are asked to answer the following questions.

a. Assuming that the lease can be arranged, should Malitz lease, or should it borrow and buy the equipment? Explain.

b. Consider the $250,000 estimated salvage value. Is it appropriate to discount it at the same rate as the other cash flows? What about the other cash flows—are they all equally risky? (*Hint:* Riskier cash flows are normally discounted at higher rates, but when the cash flows are *costs* rather than *inflows,* the normal procedure must be reversed.)

(Do parts c and d only if you are using the computerized problem diskette.)

c. Determine the lease payment at which Malitz would be indifferent to buying or leasing; that is, find the lease payment which equates the NPV of leasing to that of buying. (*Hint:* Use trial-and-error.)

d. Using the $400,000 lease payment, what would be the effect if Malitz's tax rate fell to 20 percent? What would be the effect if the tax rate fell to zero percent? What do these results suggest?

18-9   Hawke Industries Inc. has warrants outstanding that permit its holders to purchase one
Warrants   share of stock per warrant at a price of $21.

a. Calculate the formula value of Hawke's warrants if the common stock sells at each of the following prices: $18, $21, $25, and $70.

b. At what approximate price do you think the warrants would actually sell under each condition indicated in Part a? What premium is implied in your price? Your answer will be a guess, but your prices and premiums should bear reasonable relationships to each other.

c. How would each of the following factors affect your estimates of the warrants' prices and premiums in Part b?

(1) The life of the warrant is lengthened.

(2) The expected variability (σ_p) in the stock's price decreases.

(3) The expected growth rate in the stock's EPS increases.

(4) The company announces the following change in dividend policy: whereas it formerly paid no dividends, henceforth it will pay out *all* earnings as dividends.

d. Assume Hawke's stock now sells for $18 per share. The company wants to sell some 20-year, annual interest, $1,000 par value bonds. Each bond will have 50 warrants, each exercisable into one share of stock at an exercise price of $21. Hawke's pure bonds yield 10 percent. Regardless of your answer to Part b, assume that the warrants will have a market value of $1.50 when the stock sells at $18. What coupon interest rate and dollar coupon must the company set on the bonds with warrants if they are to clear the market? Round to the nearest dollar or percentage point.

Solution to Self-Test Problem

ST-1   a. *Cost of leasing:*

	Beginning of Year			
	0	1	2	3
Lease payment (AT)[a]	$ 6,000	$6,000	$6,000	$6,000
PVIFs (6%)[b]	1.000	0.9434	0.8900	0.8396
PV of leasing	$ 6,000	$5,660	$5,340	$5,038
Total PV cost of leasing =	$22,038			

[a]After-tax payment = $10,000(1 − T) = $10,000(0.60) = $6,000.

[b]This is the after-tax cost of debt: 10%(1 − T) = 10%(0.60) = 6.0%.

b. *Cost of owning:*

$$\text{Purchase price} = \$40,000.$$

$$\text{Loan payment} = \$40,000/(\text{PVIFA}_{10\%,4})$$

$$= \$40,000/(3.1699)$$

$$= \$12,619.$$

$$\text{Depreciable basis} = \$40,000.$$

Here are the cash flows under the borrow-and-buy alternative:

	End of Year			
	1	2	3	4
1. Amortization schedule				
(a) Loan payment	$12,619	$12,619	$12,619	$12,619
(b) Interest	4,000	3,138	2,190	1,147
(c) Principal payment	8,619	9,481	10,429	11,472
(d) Remaining balance	31,381	21,900	11,472	0
2. Depreciation schedule				
(e) Depreciable basis	$40,000	$40,000	$40,000	$40,000
(f) MACRS percentage	0.33	0.45	0.15	0.07
(g) Depreciation	13,200	18,000	6,000	2,800
3. Cash outflows				
(h) Loan payment	$12,619	$12,619	$12,619	$12,619
(i) Interest tax savings	(1,600)^a	(1,255)	(876)	(459)
(j) Depreciation tax savings	(5,280)^b	(7,200)	(2,400)	(1,120)
(k) Maintenance (AT)	600	600	600	600
(l) Salvage value (AT)				(6,000)
(m) Total cash outflows	$ 6,339	$ 4,764	$ 9,943	$ 5,640
PVIFs	0.9434	0.8900	0.8396	0.7921
PV of owning	$ 5,980	$ 4,240	$ 8,348	$ 4,467
Total PV cost of owning =	$23,035			

^{a}Interest(T) = $4,000(0.40) = $1,600.
^{b}Depreciation(T) = $13,200(0.40) = $5,280.

   Because the present value of the cost of leasing is less than that of owning, the truck should be leased: $23,035 − $22,038 = $997, net advantage to leasing.

c. The discount rate is based on the cost of debt because most cash flows are fixed by contract and, consequently, are relatively certain. Thus, the lease cash flows have about the same risk as the firm's debt. Also, leasing is considered to be a substitute for debt. We use an after-tax cost rate because the cash flows are stated net of taxes.

d. Olsen could increase the discount rate on the salvage value cash flow. This would increase the PV cost of owning and make leasing even more advantageous.

Factors That Influence How the Firm is Financed

In the previous section, we examined the characteristics and valuation of long-term debt, preferred stock, and common stock. We also looked at hybrid forms of financing, such as leasing, warrants, and convertibles. The values of stocks and bonds are determined, in part, by the rates of return required by investors. In Chapter 19, we see how the investors' required returns are combined to determine the firm's weighted average cost of capital. In Chapter 20 we explain how the concepts of business and financial risk are used to determine the optimal capital structure, defined as that mix of debt, preferred stock, and common equity which maximizes the value of the firm. Finally, in Chapter 21 we explain how the interaction of financing and investment decisions determines the firm's dividend policy.

The Cost of Capital

After reading this chapter, you should be able to:

▶ Explain what is meant by a firm's weighted average cost of capital.

▶ Define and calculate the component costs of debt and preferred stock.

▶ Explain why retained earnings are not free and use three approaches to estimate the component cost of retained earnings.

▶ Calculate the component cost of new common equity and explain why it is higher than that of retained earnings.

▶ Define optimal capital structure; point out its importance in cost of capital calculations.

▶ Construct a firm's marginal cost of capital (MCC) schedule and explain what causes the break points in this schedule.

▶ Graph and explain the importance of the intersection between the MCC schedule and the investment opportunity schedule (IOS).

▶ List several problem areas in estimating cost of capital.

DECISION IN FINANCE

DECISION IN FINANCE

MCDONNELL DOUGLAS'S QUANDARY

McDonnell Douglas Corporation, a manufacturer of military and commercial aircraft, recently received some startling news from Moody's Investors Service, a major credit rating agency—Moody's had downgraded McDonnell's long-term senior debt from investment grade (Baa3) to junk status (Ba2) and its short-term commercial paper from Prime-3 to Not Prime. McDonnell's officials, who had been upbeat about 1993 financial prospects, were surprised by the rating agency's action.

Why was McDonnell's management caught by surprise? First, the company was given no advance word by Moody's. Second, S&P, the other major credit rating agency, had recently reaffirmed McDonnell's BBB investment-grade rating. S&P based its decision on expectations of a meaningful improvement in the firm's 1993 operating performance and, as a result, the strengthening of its balance sheet. McDonnell's executive vice-president and chief financial officer expressed management's opinion of the downgrading: "I was totally shocked . . . Our balance sheet is getting stronger, not weaker. The facts simply do not point to a Ba2 rating in our long-term debt."

What was Moody's reasoning for the downgrading? Moody's cited the expectation that the company's defense business would decline because of shrinking defense budgets worldwide.

See end of chapter for resolution.

Photo source: © 1991, Comstock, Inc.

In addition, Moody's was concerned that financial uncertainties relating to the C-17 military aircraft program and the termination of the A-12 aircraft development program would persist. Also, Moody's thought that orders for McDonnell's commercial aircraft would decline at a rate greater than that of other producers because of the firm's relatively limited product line and its reduced financial flexibility. They reasoned that those two pressures alone would put McDonnell at a disadvantage in offering aircraft financing, a growing industry trend. Finally, the rating agency believed that even if McDonnell's operating cash flows improve moderately, the increase would not be sufficient to materially improve the balance sheet. So, as a result of all these factors, the company's debt ratings were lowered.

As you read this chapter, consider each component cost in the weighted average cost of capital, the way each component is calculated, and the logic behind the weighted average cost of capital. Think about why changes in the marginal cost of capital schedule occur, and think about how the firm's cost of capital is determined for use in the capital budgeting process. Consider the importance of the cost of capital to the firm. Then, put yourself in the position of McDonnell Douglas's financial managers. Why are they so upset about Moody's downgrading their debt? What are the implications for the firm's cost of debt, its cost of equity, and its ability to raise additional capital? Are holders of McDonnell's existing securities affected by the downgrade, or does it affect only new capital suppliers?

The cost of capital is critically important in finance for several reasons. First, capital budgeting decisions have a major impact on a firm, and correct capital budgeting decisions require an estimate of the cost of capital. Second, many other types of decisions, including those related to leasing and to bond refunding, require estimates of the cost of capital. Finally, maximizing the value of a firm requires that the costs of all inputs, including capital, be minimized, and to minimize the cost of capital managers must be able to measure it.[1]

In Chapter 14, in order to focus on the basic steps of the net present value (NPV) method, the firm's cost of capital was always *given* and was simply defined as the weighted average of the required rates of return, or costs, associated with all sources of financing. In Chapter 15 we saw that, for a given company, the discount rate must then be increased for projects with higher-than-average risk and decreased for projects with lower-than-average risk, but again, for average-risk projects, the firm's cost of capital was either given or could be found fairly easily.

We begin this chapter with an explanation of the logic of the weighted average cost of capital. Next, we consider the costs of the major types of capital. Third, the costs of the individual components of the capital structure are brought together to form a weighted average cost of capital. Fourth, we look at how a firm's weighted average cost of capital changes as it expands the level of its budget (the total amount of new capital raised and invested). Finally, we use the concepts developed to determine a firm's optimal capital budget, that is, the projects it should accept in a given year.

The Logic of the Weighted Average Cost of Capital

When we calculated cash flows for capital budgeting purposes in Chapter 14, we assumed that equity was the only source of financing used by the firm. We made this assumption so we could concentrate on the investment decision with-

---

[1]The cost of capital is also vitally important in regulated industries, including electric, gas, telephone, and water companies. In essence, regulatory commissions first seek to measure a utility's cost of capital and then set prices so that the company will earn just this rate of return. If the cost of capital estimate is too low, the company will not be able to attract sufficient capital to meet long-term demands for service, and the public will suffer. If the estimate of capital costs is too high, customers will pay too much for service.

out being concerned about how the project was to be financed. Of course, few firms are financed entirely with equity—most firms finance a substantial portion of their new assets with debt, and some use preferred stock as well. For these firms, the cost of capital must reflect the average cost of the various sources of long-term funds used, not just the cost of equity.

To illustrate this point, assume that Precision Associates (PA), a subcontractor of engineering systems to many of the nation's largest aerospace firms, has an effective (after-tax) cost of debt of 5.4 percent and a cost of equity of 13.2 percent. Suppose the firm decides to finance all of next year's projects with debt. The argument is sometimes made that the cost of capital for a project financed exclusively with debt is equal to the cost of debt. However, this position is *incorrect*. To finance a particular set of projects exclusively with debt implies that the firm will be using up some of its potential for obtaining new low-cost debt in the future. As the firm continues to expand in subsequent years, PA will at some point find it necessary to use additional equity financing to prevent the debt ratio from becoming too large.

Suppose PA borrows heavily at the effective rate of 5.4 percent during 1994 to finance projects yielding 7 percent, using up its debt capacity in the process. Now assume that in 1995 it has new projects available that yield 9.3 percent, well above the return on the 1994 projects, but PA cannot accept these because they would have to be financed with 13.2 percent equity money.[2]

To avoid this problem, every firm should be viewed as an ongoing concern, and the cost of capital used in capital budgeting should be calculated as a weighted average, or composite, of the various types of funds it generally uses, regardless of the specific financing used to fund a particular project.

Self-Test

Why should the cost of capital used in capital budgeting be calculated as a weighted average of the various types of funds the firm generally uses, regardless of the specific financing used to fund a particular project?

Basic Definitions

capital component

One of the types of capital used by firms to raise money.

Capital components are the long-term items on the right-hand side of a firm's balance sheet: various types of debt, preferred stock, and common equity. Any increase in total assets is generally financed by an increase in one or more of these capital components. *Capital* is a necessary factor of production, and, like any other factor, it has a cost. The cost of each component is defined as the *component cost* of that particular type of capital. Throughout this chapter we concentrate on debt, preferred stock, retained earnings, and new issues of com-

[2]As we saw in Chapter 18, firms have both a before-tax and an after-tax cost of debt. PA's *before-tax* component cost of debt is 9 percent, but, as we shall show in a moment, the relevant cost of debt is the *after-tax* cost, here 5.4 percent. In the remainder of the chapter we will see that PA can also choose to use preferred stock with a cost of 9.5 percent as part of its financing; however, in 1995 this option would not have helped the firm since raising funds at a cost of 9.5 percent to invest in projects yielding 9.3 percent does not make sense.

mon stock. These are the major capital structure components; their component costs are identified by the following symbols:

k_d = interest rate on the firm's new debt = before-tax component cost of debt. For Precision Associates (PA), $k_d = 9\%$.

$k_d(1 - T)$ = after-tax component cost of debt, where T is the firm's marginal tax rate. The term $k_d(1 - T)$ is the debt cost used to calculate the weighted average cost of capital. For PA, $T = 40\%$, so $k_d(1 - T) = 9\%(1 - 0.4) = 9\%(0.6) = 5.4\%$.[3]

k_p = component cost of preferred stock. For PA, $k_p \approx 9.5\%$.

k_s = component cost of retained earnings (or internal equity). This k_s is identical to the k_i and k_s developed in Chapters 12 and 17 and defined there as the required (or expected) rate of return on common stock. It is quite difficult to estimate k_s, but, as we shall see shortly, for PA, $k_s \approx 13.2\%$.

k_e = component cost of external equity obtained by issuing new common stock as opposed to retained earnings. As we shall see, it is necessary to distinguish between equity raised by retained earnings and that raised by selling new stock. This is why we distinguish between internal and external equity, k_s and k_e. Further, k_e is always greater than k_s because of flotation costs. For PA, $k_e \approx 14.2\%$.

k_a = WACC = the weighted average cost of capital. If PA raises new capital to finance asset expansion and if it is to keep its capital structure in balance (that is, if it is to keep the same percentage of debt, preferred stock, and common equity funds), then it must raise part of its new funds as debt, part as preferred stock, and part as common equity (with equity coming either from retained earnings or from the issuance of new common stock).[4] The terms k_a and WACC are used interchangeably. We will calculate WACC for Precision Associates shortly.

These definitions and concepts are explained in detail in the remainder of the chapter, where we develop a marginal cost of capital (MCC) schedule that can be used in capital budgeting. Then, in Chapter 20, we extend the analysis to determine the capital structure (the weights used in the WACC) that will minimize a firm's cost of capital and thereby maximize its value.

Self-Test

Identify the firm's four major capital components, and give their respective component cost symbols.

---

[3]Note that only the component cost of *debt* needs to be put on an after-tax basis because interest expense is the only financing charge that is tax deductible.

[4]Firms try to keep their debt, preferred stock, and common equity in optimal proportions; we will see how they establish these proportions (weights) in Chapter 20. However, firms do not try to maintain any proportional relationship between the common stock and retained earnings accounts as shown on the balance sheet — common equity is common equity, whether it is represented by common stock or by retained earnings.

Cost of Debt, $k_d(1 - T)$

The component cost of debt used to calculate the weighted average cost of capital is the interest rate on new debt, k_d, less the tax savings that result because interest is deductible. This is the same as k_d multiplied by $(1 - T)$, where T is the firm's marginal tax rate:[5]

$$\text{After-tax component cost of debt} = \text{Interest rate} - \text{Tax savings}$$
$$= k_d - k_dT$$
$$= k_d(1 - T). \qquad (19\text{-}1)$$

after-tax cost of debt, $k_d(1 - T)$

The relevant cost of new debt financing, taking into account the tax deductibility of interest; used to calculate the WACC.

In effect, the government pays part of the cost of debt because interest is tax deductible. Therefore, if Precision Associates can borrow at a rate of 9 percent and if it has a marginal federal-plus-state tax rate of 40 percent, then its **after-tax cost of debt** is

$$k_d(1 - T) = 9\%(0.6) = 5.4\%.$$

The reason for using the after-tax cost of debt is as follows. The value of the firm's stock, which we want to maximize, depends on *after-tax* cash flows. Because interest is a deductible expense, it produces tax savings which reduce the net cost of debt, so the after-tax cost of debt is less than the before-tax cost. Since cash flows and rates of return should be on a comparable basis, we adjust the interest rate downward to account for the preferential tax treatment of debt.[6]

Our primary concern with the cost of capital is to use it in a decision-making process — to determine the minimum acceptable return on new capital budgeting projects. Thus, the appropriate cost of debt is the cost for *new* borrowing, not the historical interest rates on old, previously outstanding debt. In other words, we are interested in the cost of the next dollar borrowed, or the *marginal* cost of debt. The rate at which the firm has borrowed in the past is a *sunk cost*, and it is irrelevant for cost of capital purposes.

Self-Test

Why is the after-tax rather than the before-tax cost of debt used to calculate the weighted average cost of capital?

Is the relevant cost of debt the interest rate on already *outstanding* debt or that on *new* debt? Explain your answer.

---

[5]In our discussion of the required return on equity, flotation costs (or the cost of selling equity through an investment banker) will be an integral part of the *cost of common equity* and of the *cost of preferred stock*. However, when we evaluate the *cost of debt,* flotation costs will be ignored. This is common practice since the flotation cost for a debt issue, sold through investment bankers in the capital markets, is usually quite low as a percentage of the issue. In fact, over 99 percent of all debt is privately placed with banks, insurance companies, pension funds, and the like, and therefore has virtually no flotation cost.

[6]The tax rate is *zero* for a firm with losses. Therefore, for a company that does not pay taxes, the cost of debt is not reduced; that is, in Equation 19-1 the tax rate equals zero, so the after-tax cost of debt is equal to the interest rate.

Cost of Preferred Stock, k_p

cost of preferred stock, k_p

The rate of return investors require on the firm's preferred stock, adjusted for flotation costs. k_p is calculated as the preferred dividend, D_p, divided by the net issuing price, P_n.

The component **cost of preferred stock, k_p**, used to calculate the weighted average cost of capital is the preferred dividend, D_p, divided by the net issuing price, P_n, or the price the firm receives after deducting flotation costs:

$$\text{Component cost of preferred stock} = k_p = D_p/P_n. \qquad \text{(19-2)}$$

In Equation 19-2, we assume that the dividend from the preferred stock remains constant — that is, that the dividend will always be paid — that the preferred stock is not a participating preferred issue, and that it does not have a sinking fund.

Precision Associates's preferred stock pays a $9.25 dividend per share and sells for $100 per share in the market. If PA issues new shares of preferred, it will incur an underwriting (or flotation) cost of 2.5 percent, or $2.50 per share, so it will net $97.50 per share. Therefore, PA's cost of preferred stock is approximately 9.5 percent:

$$k_p = \$9.25/\$97.50 \approx 9.5\%.$$

Equation 19-2 can also be used to determine the cost of preferred stock if an issue is already outstanding. Suppose the price of PA's preferred stock falls to $84.50 per share in the secondary market. This is a signal to the firm that investors will no longer accept a return of 9.25 percent; now they will require a return of approximately 10.95 percent: $9.25/$84.50 ≈ 10.95%. Furthermore, if PA chooses to issue new preferred stock at *that* time the cost to the firm will, again, be higher than the rate of return required by investors because of flotation costs. Assuming that PA sells preferred stock at par ($100) with a $10.95 dividend and flotation costs of $2.50, the cost to PA would be

$$k_p = \$10.95/\$97.50 \approx 11.23\%.$$

No tax adjustments are made when calculating k_p because, unlike interest on debt, dividends are not tax deductible; hence there are no tax savings associated with the use of preferred stock.

? *Self-Test*

Does the component cost of preferred stock include or exclude flotation costs? Explain.

Is a tax adjustment made to the cost of preferred stock? Why or why not?

cost of retained earnings, k_s

The rate of return required by stockholders on a firm's common stock.

Cost of Retained Earnings, k_s

The costs of debt and preferred stock are based on the returns investors require on these securities. Similarly, the **cost of retained earnings, k_s**, is the rate of return stockholders require on equity capital the firm obtains by retaining earnings.[7]

---

[7]The term *retained earnings* can be interpreted to mean either the balance sheet item "retained earnings," consisting of all the earnings retained in the business throughout its history, or the income statement item "additions to retained earnings." The latter definition is used in this chapter. For our purpose, *retained earnings* refers to the company's *change in retained earnings*, in other words, to that part of the year's earnings not paid out in dividends and hence available for reinvestment in the business during the year.

At one time many managers believed that retained earnings were a costless source of funds. Now, however, managers realize that retained earnings are not free. The reason that a cost of capital must be assigned to retained earnings involves the *opportunity cost principle.* Recall from earlier chapters that opportunity cost is the rate of return available on the best alternative investment of equal risk. The firm's after-tax earnings literally belong to its stockholders. Bondholders are compensated by interest payments and preferred stockholders by preferred dividends, but the earnings remaining after interest and preferred dividends have been paid belong to the common stockholders, and these earnings serve to compensate the stockholders for the use of their capital. Management may either pay out earnings in the form of dividends or retain earnings and reinvest them in the business. If management decides to retain earnings, there is an opportunity cost involved — stockholders could have received the earnings as dividends and then invested this money in other stocks, in bonds, in real estate, or in anything else. The opportunity cost principle implies that the firm should earn on its retained earnings at least as much as its stockholders could earn on alternative investments *of equivalent risk.*

What rate of return can stockholders expect to earn on equivalent-risk investments? Answer: the rate of return that they expect to earn in PA's stock, k_s. Recall from Chapter 17 that stocks are normally in equilibrium, with the expected and required rates of return being equal: $\hat{k}_s = k_s$ (and with the price of the stock stable). Therefore, we can assume that PA's stockholders require and expect to earn k_s on their investment. If PA were to invest retained earnings and earn *less* than this rate of return on the retained earnings, the price of the stock would fall. *Therefore, if the firm cannot invest retained earnings and earn at least k_s, it should pay these funds to its stockholders and let them invest directly in other assets that do provide this return.*

The majority of U.S. business firms have debt-to-total-assets ratios that are less than 50 percent. Thus, common stock equity provides the largest proportion of financing in the average firm's capital structure. Unfortunately, the cost of equity is the most difficult of the cost of capital components to determine. Other sources of capital have periodic fixed payment schedules, such as debt's interest and principal payments, which are contractual obligations, and preferred stock's dividends, which are not contractually guaranteed but are generally treated as fixed obligations by financial managers. The amount and timing of cash flows from these securities can be forecasted with a high degree of certainty, making investors' required returns (and hence the costs of capital from these sources) easy to determine. Unlike debt and preferred stock, however, the cash flows resulting from the purchase of common stock are difficult to forecast. Still, although it is not easy to measure k_s, we can employ the principles developed in Chapters 12 and 17 to produce reasonably good *estimates* of the cost of equity.

To begin, we know that for stocks in equilibrium (which is the typical situation), the *required* rate of return, k_s, is also equal to the *expected* rate of return, $\hat{k}_s$. Further, the required return is equal to a risk-free rate, k_{RF}, plus a premium for all risks, RP, and the expected return on a constant growth stock is equal to a dividend yield, D_1/P_0, plus an expected growth rate, g:

$$\text{Required rate of return} = \text{Expected rate of return}$$

$$k_s = k_{RF} + RP = D_1/P_0 + g = \hat{k}_s.$$

Therefore, k_s can be estimated either directly as $k_s = k_{RF} + RP$ or indirectly as $k_s = \hat{k}_s = D_1/P_0 + g$. Actually, three methods are commonly used for finding the cost of retained earnings: (1) the CAPM approach, which was introduced in Chapter 12, (2) the discounted cash flow (DCF) approach, which was introduced in Chapter 17, and (3) the bond-yield-plus-risk-premium approach, which we will present shortly. These three approaches are discussed in the following sections.

CAPM Approach

The Capital Asset Pricing Model (CAPM) as developed in Chapter 12 can be used to help estimate k_s as follows:

Step 1. Estimate the risk-free rate, k_{RF}, generally taken to be either the U.S. Treasury bond rate or the 30-day Treasury bill rate.

Step 2. Estimate the stock's beta coefficient, b_i, and use this as an index of the stock's market risk. The i signifies the *i*'th company's beta.

Step 3. Estimate the required rate of return on the market or on an "average" stock, k_M.

Step 4. Substitute the preceding values into the CAPM equation to estimate the required rate of return on the stock in question:

$$k_s = k_{RF} + (k_M - k_{RF})b_i.$$

This equation shows that the CAPM estimate of k_s begins with the risk-free rate, k_{RF}, to which is added a risk premium set equal to the premium on an average stock $(k_M - k_{RF})$, scaled up or down to reflect the particular stock's relative risk as measured by its beta coefficient. This is the Security Market Line (SML) equation which we discussed in Chapter 12.

To illustrate the CAPM approach, assume that $k_{RF} = 6.5\%$, $k_M = 11.5\%$, and $b_i = 1.25$ for PA's stock. PA's k_s is calculated as follows:

$$k_s = 6.5\% + (11.5\% - 6.5\%)1.25 = 6.5\% + 6.25\% = 12.75\%.$$

Had b_i been 0.7, indicating that the stock was less risky than average, its k_s would have been

$$k_s = 6.5\% + (5\%)0.7 = 6.5\% + 3.5\% = 10\%.$$

For an average stock,

$$k_s = k_M = 6.5\% + (5\%)1.0 = 6.5\% + 5\% = 11.5\%.$$

It should be noted that although the CAPM approach appears to yield accurate, precise estimates of k_s, there are actually several problems with this approach. First, as we saw in Chapter 12, if a firm's stockholders are not well diversified, they may be concerned with *total risk* rather than beta, or market, risk only; in that case the firm's true investment risk will not be measured by its beta, and the CAPM procedure will understate the correct value of k_s. Further, even if the CAPM method is valid, it is hard to obtain correct estimates of the inputs required to make it operational because (1) there is uncertainty about whether to use the rate on long-term or short-term Treasury securities for k_{RF}, (2) it is hard to estimate the beta that investors expect the company to have in the future, and (3) it is difficult to estimate the market risk premium.

Dividend-Yield-plus-Growth-Rate or Discounted Cash Flow (DCF) Approach

In Chapter 17 we saw that for a constant growth stock

$$\hat{k}_s = \frac{D_1}{P_0} + g. \tag{17-3}$$

Thus, investors expect to receive a dividend yield, D_1/P_0, plus a capital gains yield (a measure of the expected growth in the firm's value), g, for a total expected return of $\hat{k}_s$.[8]

To illustrate, suppose Precision Associates begins to retain some earnings rather than paying them all out as dividends. The stock is in equilibrium, it sells for $30.00, the next expected dividend is $2.16, and the expected growth rate is 6 percent. Therefore, the firm's expected and required rate of return, and hence its cost of retained earnings, is

$$\hat{k}_s = k_s = \frac{\$2.16}{\$30.00} + 6\% = 7.2\% + 6\% = 13.2\%.$$

Thus, according to this method, 13.2 percent is the minimum rate of return that PA's management must expect to earn on the equity-financed projects to justify retaining earnings and plowing them back into the business rather than paying them out to stockholders as dividends. Throughout this chapter, we assume that equilibrium exists, so k_s and $\hat{k}_s$ are equal. Therefore, we use the terms k_s and $\hat{k}_s$ interchangeably.

It is relatively easy to determine the dividend yield, but it is difficult to establish the proper growth rate. If past growth rates in earnings and dividends have been relatively stable and if investors appear to be projecting a continuation of past trends, then g may be based on the firm's historical growth rate. *However, if the company's past growth rate has been abnormally high or low, either because of its own unique situation or because of general economic conditions, investors will not blindly project the past growth rate into the future.*

Securities analysts regularly make forecasts of the growth in both dividends and earnings, looking at such factors as projected sales, profit margins, and competitive factors. For example, *Value Line,* which is available in most libraries, provides growth rate forecasts for 1,700 companies, and Merrill Lynch, Salomon Brothers, and other organizations make similar forecasts. Therefore, someone making a cost of capital estimate can obtain several analysts' forecasts, average them, use the average as a proxy for the growth expectations of investors in general, and then combine the forecasted growth with the current dividend yield to estimate the cost of equity capital, as follows:

$$\hat{k}_s = D_1/P_0 + \text{growth rate, g, as projected by securities analysts.}$$

[8]Note, however, that if a firm's growth rate is not expected to remain constant, Equation 17-3 cannot be used.

Again, note that this estimate of k_s is based on the assumption that g is expected to remain constant in the future.[9]

Bond-Yield-plus-Risk-Premium Approach

Although it is essentially an ad hoc, subjective procedure, analysts often estimate a firm's cost of common equity by adding a risk premium of three to five percentage points to the interest rate on the firm's own long-term debt. It is logical to think that firms with risky, low-rated, and consequently high-interest-rate debt will also have risky, high-cost equity, and the procedure of basing the cost of equity on a readily observable debt cost utilizes this precept. For example, if PA's bonds, which are rated A, yield 9 percent, its cost of equity might be estimated as follows:

$$k_s = \text{Bond rate} + \text{Risk premium}$$

$$= 9\% + 4.5\% = 13.5\%.$$

Because this 4.5 percent risk premium is a judgmental estimate, the estimated value of k_s is also judgmental.[10] A judgmental estimate is not likely to result in a precise measure of the cost of equity capital — about all that it can do is "get us into the right ballpark." Low premiums occur when interest rates are quite high and people are reluctant to invest in long-term bonds for fear of runaway inflation, further increases in interest rates, and losses on bond investments. High premiums occur when interest rates are relatively low as in the early 1990s.

Conclusions on the Cost of Equity Capital

Which of the methods used to determine the cost of equity is most correct? The answer depends on the data that are available — for which method, in a specific instance, do we have the most reasonable data? Many business firms use all of these methods or more to approximate the cost of equity. In fact, the Du Pont Corporation uses five different methods to evaluate and approximate its cost of equity capital. Therefore, we suggest that in practice it is best to use all three of the methods discussed here and then apply judgment when the meth-

---

[9]Analysts' growth rate forecasts are usually for 5 years into the future, and the rates provided represent the average growth rate over that 5-year horizon. Studies have shown that analysts' forecasts represent the best source of growth data for DCF cost of capital estimates. See Robert Harris, "Using Analysts' Growth Rate Forecasts to Estimate Shareholder Required Rates of Return," *Financial Management,* Spring 1986, 58–67.

Another method for estimating g involves first forecasting the firm's average future dividend payout ratio and its complement, the *retention rate,* and then multiplying the retention rate by the company's average projected rate of return on equity (ROE):

$$g = (\text{Retention rate})(\text{ROE}) = (1.0 - \text{Payout rate})(\text{ROE}).$$

Securities analysts often use this procedure when they estimate growth rates.

[10]Analysts who use this procedure often cite studies of historical returns on stocks and bonds and use the difference between the average yield (dividends plus capital gains) on stocks and the average yield on bonds as the risk premium of stocks over bonds. The most frequently cited study is R. G. Ibbotson and R. A. Sinquefield, "Stocks, Bonds, Bills, and Inflation: Year-By-Year Historical Returns (1926–1974)," *Journal of Business,* January 1976, 11–47.

ods produce differing results. Managers experienced in estimating equity capital costs recognize that both careful analysis and some good judgment are required. *It would be nice to pretend that judgment is unnecessary and to specify an easy, precise way of determining the exact cost of equity capital. Unfortunately, this is not possible. Finance is in large part a matter of judgment, and we simply must face this fact.*

Precision Associates's financial managers used the three methods discussed above and obtained a range for PA's common equity from 12.75% to 13.5%. After much discussion, they decided to use 13.2 percent as the firm's cost of common equity. Finally, just because the CAPM approach and the discounted cash flow approach did not produce the same value for PA's cost of equity does not mean that the stock is not in equilibrium. The difference simply reflects the fact that all the data used are subject to uncertainty and that management only has estimates and assumptions on which to base its calculations.

 Self-Test

Why must a cost be assigned to retained earnings?

What are the three approaches for estimating the cost of retained earnings?

Identify some problems with the CAPM approach.

Which of the components of the constant growth DCF formula — dividend yield or growth rate — is more difficult to estimate? Explain your answer.

What is the reasoning behind the bond-yield-plus-risk-premium approach?

Cost of Newly Issued Common Stock, or External Equity, k_e

cost of new common equity, k_e
The cost of external equity; based on the cost of retained earnings but increased for flotation costs.

The cost of new common equity, k_e, or external equity capital, is higher than the cost of retained earnings, k_s, because of flotation costs involved in selling new common stock. What rate of return must be earned on funds raised by selling stock in order to make issuing new stock worthwhile? To put it another way, what is the cost of new common stock?

For a firm with a constant growth rate, the answer is found by applying the following formula:

$$k_e = \frac{D_1}{P_0(1 - F)} + g. \qquad (19\text{-}3)$$

flotation cost, F
The percentage cost of issuing new common stock.

Here **F** is the percentage **flotation cost** incurred in selling the new stock issue, so $P_0(1 - F)$ is the net price per share, P_n, received by the company when it sells new shares. Equation 19-3 may, therefore, also be expressed as

$$k_e = \frac{D_1}{P_n} + g. \qquad (19\text{-}3a)$$

Recall that Precision Associates has a required return of 13.2 percent on its common equity from retained earnings. If the firm wishes to issue new stock, however, there will be a flotation cost charged by the investment banker, and that will affect the cost of equity. If the flotation charge for PA's new issue is 12 percent, the cost of new outside equity is computed as follows:

$$k_e = \frac{\$2.16}{\$30(1 - 0.12)} + 6\%$$

$$= \frac{\$2.16}{\$26.40} + 6\%$$

$$= 8.18\% + 6\%$$

$$\approx 14.2\%.$$

Investors require a return on equity capital that consists of a current dividend yield, D_1/P_0, and a growth or capital gains component, g. For PA this required return, k_s, was 13.2 percent. However, because of flotation costs, the company *must earn more* than 13.2 percent on funds obtained by selling new common stock if it is to provide a return of 13.2 percent to its stockholders. What causes this seeming contradiction? New investors will expect to receive the same stream of dividends as that expected by the present stockholders, but the funds available to be invested by the firm from the proceeds of the sale are less than P_0 per share because of flotation costs. Specifically, the firm will have to provide the $2.16 in dividends next year and maintain a 6 percent growth based on only $26.40 of assets, even though stockholders put up $30. The firm must meet these investor expectations with only 88 percent of the share price because 12 percent goes to the investment banker for services rendered in selling the stock. Therefore, if PA earns less than 14.2 percent on the new equity, the investment will be unable to provide the required dividend of $2.16 and the anticipated 6 percent growth. Such a decline in either dividends, growth, or both would cause the value of the stock to decline below the $30 price investors paid. Conversely, if the equity raised and invested into the new project earns more than 14.2 percent, the firm's dividend and/or growth will be larger than required, and the price of PA's stock will rise.

 ### Self-Test

Why is the cost of external equity capital higher than the cost of retained earnings?

How can the DCF model be modified to incorporate flotation costs?

Weighted Average, or Composite, Cost of Capital, WACC

target (optimal) capital structure

The percentages of debt, preferred stock, and common equity that will minimize the firm's weighted average cost of capital (WACC) and, therefore, maximize the price of the firm's stock.

As we shall see in Chapter 20, each firm has a **target (optimal) capital structure,** which is that mix of debt, preferred stock, and common equity that minimizes the firm's weighted average cost of capital (WACC) and, therefore, causes the firm's stock price to be maximized. A rational, value-maximizing firm will establish its optimal capital structure and then raise new capital in a manner that will keep the actual capital structure on target over time. *In this chapter we assume that the firm has already identified its optimal capital structure* (that is, *the weights are given*), that it uses this optimum as the target, and that it finances so as to remain constantly on target. How the target is established will be examined in Chapter 20.

The target proportions of debt, preferred stock, and common equity, along with the component costs of capital, are used to calculate the firm's **weighted average cost of capital, WACC = k$_a$.** To illustrate, suppose Precision Associates has a target capital structure calling for 30 percent debt, 10 percent preferred stock, and 60 percent common equity (retained earnings initially, then new common stock). Its before-tax cost of debt, k$_d$, is 9 percent; its after-tax cost of debt = k$_d$(1 − T) = 9%(0.6) = 5.4% (based on a marginal tax rate of 40 percent); its cost of preferred stock, k$_p$, is 9.5 percent; and its cost of common equity from retained earnings, k$_s$, is 13.2 percent. These are the component costs that we have been calculating in the preceding sections. Now we can calculate PA's weighted average cost of capital, WACC, as follows:

$$\text{WACC} = k_a = w_d k_d (1 - T) + w_p k_p + w_s k_s \qquad (19\text{-}4)$$
$$= 0.3(9\%)(0.6) + 0.1(9.5\%) + 0.6(13.2\%) = 10.49\%.$$

Here w$_d$, w$_p$, and w$_s$ are the weights used for debt, preferred, and common equity, respectively.

Every dollar of new capital that Precision Associates obtains consists of 30 cents of debt with an after-tax cost of 5.4 percent, 10 cents of preferred stock with a cost of 9.5 percent, and 60 cents of common equity (all initially from additions to retained earnings) with a cost of 13.2 percent. The average cost of each whole dollar, WACC, is 10.49 percent.

The weights could be based either on the accounting values shown on the firm's balance sheet (book values) or on the market values of the different securities. Theoretically, the weights should be based on market values, but if a firm's book value weights are reasonably close to its market value weights, book value weights can be used as a proxy for market value weights. This point is discussed further in Chapter 20, but in the remainder of this chapter we shall assume that the firm's market values are approximately equal to its book values, and we will use book value capital structure weights.

 Self-Test

How does one calculate the weighted average cost of capital?

Changes in the Cost of Capital, Due to the Level of the Budget

The *marginal cost* of any item is the cost of another unit of that item; for example, the marginal cost of labor is the cost of adding one additional worker. The marginal hourly cost of labor may be $20 per person for a particular job if 10 workers are added but $22 per person if the firm tries to hire 100 new workers because it may be harder to find 100 people willing and able to do the work. The same concept applies to capital. As the firm tries to attract more new dollars, the cost of each dollar will at some point rise. *Thus, the* **marginal cost of capital (MCC)** *is defined as the weighted average cost of the last dollar of*

weighted average cost of capital, WACC

A weighted average of the component costs of debt, preferred stock, and common equity.

marginal cost of capital (MCC)

The cost of obtaining another dollar of new capital; the weighted average cost of the last dollar of new capital raised.

new capital that the firm raises, and the marginal cost increases as more and more capital is raised during a given period.

The cost of capital changes as the *proportions* of debt, preferred, and common equity in the capital structure change. As a general rule, a different marginal cost of capital (MCC) will exist for every possible capital structure; *the optimal capital structure is the one that produces the lowest WACC,* given a certain budget level. In this chapter, a firm such as Precision Associates has already determined its mix of long-term capital; in other words, *in this chapter, a firm's target (optimal) capital structure is given and constant for every dollar raised (the weights are constant).* On the other hand, in Chapter 20 the primary topic will be how a firm decides on a particular target capital structure.

Can PA raise an unlimited amount of new capital at the 10.49 percent cost as long as its capital structure is maintained at 30 percent debt, 10 percent preferred, and 60 percent common equity? The answer is no. As companies raise larger and larger sums during a given time period, the costs of the debt, preferred, and common equity components begin to rise, and as this occurs, the MCC, the weighted average cost of each new dollar, also rises.

This increase in the weighted average cost of capital occurs any time one or more component costs increase, and that may, in turn, happen for several reasons. (1) Even if PA does not deviate from its 30 percent debt ratio, it may have to go to new lenders as it tries to expand the level of its budget further and further. (2) As the amount of preferred and common stock sold increases, the flotation costs on one or both may increase as investment bankers have to attract new buyers. (3) Generating larger amounts of common equity means that the firm will exhaust its internal equity (retained earnings) and will have to turn to more expensive new common equity.

We can use Precision Associates to illustrate the marginal cost of capital concept. The company's current capital structure is assumed to be optimal and, therefore, represents the target capital structure. Other data follow:

Long-term debt	$ 507,000,000	30%
Preferred stock	169,000,000	10
Common equity	1,014,000,000	60
Total capital	$1,690,000,000	100%

$$k_d = 9\%.$$
$$T = 40\%.$$
$$k_d(1 - T) = 5.4\%.$$
$$k_p = 9.5\%.$$
$$P_0 = \$30.$$
$$g = 6\%, \text{ and growth is expected to remain constant.}$$
$$D_1 = \text{the } next \text{ dividend} = \$2.16$$
$$k_s = D_1/P_0 + g = (\$2.16/\$30) + 0.06 = 0.072 + 0.06 = 13.2\%.$$
$$F = 0.12 = 12\%.$$
$$k_e = D_1/P_0(1 - F) + g = \$2.16/[\$30(1 - 0.12)] + 0.06$$
$$= 0.082 + 0.06 = 14.2\%.$$

On the basis of these data, the weighted average cost of capital (WACC) is *initially* 10.49 percent, as previously calculated using Equation 19-4.

Figure 19-1

Precision Associates:
Marginal Cost of Capital
(MCC) Schedule

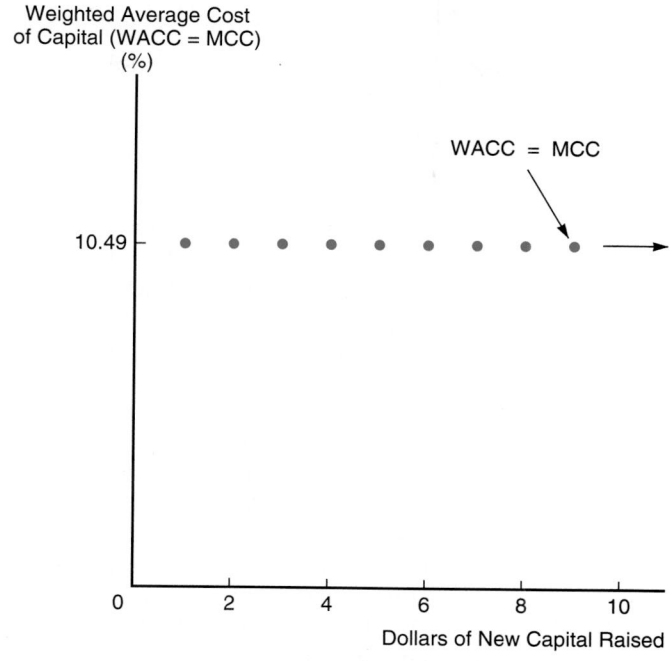

The marginal cost of capital, MCC, is shown here for Precision Associates, as it applies to *the first few dollars* of new capital raised. Each dollar is raised in accordance with PA's current capital structure, which is also its target capital structure. Therefore, the weights are 30 percent debt, 10 percent preferred stock, and 60 percent common equity. Initially, PA has retained earnings available to satisfy the equity requirement, and the weighted average cost of capital (WACC) is 10.49 percent for each dollar raised.

Note that only long-term debt is included in the capital structure. PA uses its cost of capital in the capital budgeting process, which involves long-term assets, and it finances those assets with long-term capital. Thus, current liabilities do not enter the calculation at this point. (However, recall that in Chapters 14 and 15, certain current liabilities—*spontaneous liabilities*—*did* become part of the capital budgeting process in that any changes in these accounts contributed to potential changes in *net working capital*.)

As long as PA keeps its capital structure on target and as long as its debt has an after-tax cost of 5.4 percent, its preferred stock a cost of 9.5 percent, and its common equity a cost of 13.2 percent, then its weighted average cost of capital will be WACC = MCC = 10.49%. Each dollar the firm raises will consist of some long-term debt, some preferred stock, and some common equity, and the cost of the whole dollar will be 10.49 percent.

marginal cost of capital (MCC) schedule

A graph that relates the firm's weighted average cost of each dollar of capital to the total amount of new capital raised.

A graph which shows how the WACC changes as more and more new capital is raised during a given year is called the **marginal cost of capital schedule.** The graph shown in Figure 19-1 is PA's MCC schedule. Here the dots represent dollars raised, and because each dollar of new capital has a cost of 10.49

percent, the marginal cost of capital (MCC) for PA is *initially* constant at 10.49 percent.[11]

Breaks in the MCC Schedule

We have already stated that PA *cannot* raise an unlimited amount of new capital at the 10.49 percent cost and we have given some reasons why component costs, and the weighted average, are likely to increase as a firm raises larger and larger sums during a given time period. Where will breaks in the MCC schedule occur for PA? As a first step in determining the point at which the MCC begins to rise, recognize that although the company's balance sheet shows total long-term capital of $1,690,000,000, all of this capital was raised in the past, and it has been invested in assets which are being used in operations. New (or marginal) capital will also be raised so as to maintain the 30/10/60 debt/preferred/common relationship. Therefore, if PA wants to raise $1,000,000 in new capital, it should obtain $300,000 of debt, $100,000 of preferred stock, and $600,000 of common equity. The new common equity could come from two sources: (1) retained earnings, defined as that part of this year's profits which management decides to retain in the business rather than use for dividends (but not earnings retained in the past, for these have already been invested in plant, equipment, inventories, and so on), or (2) proceeds from the sale of new common stock.

The debt will have an interest rate of 9 percent, or an after-tax cost of 5.4 percent, and the preferred stock will have a cost of 9.5 percent. *The cost of common equity will be $k_s = 13.2\%$ as long as the equity is obtained from retained earnings, but it will jump to $k_e = 14.2\%$ once the company uses up all of its retained earnings and is thus forced to sell new common stock.*

We saw in an earlier section that PA nets only $26.40 per share when it sells new stock, and it must earn 14.2 percent on this $26.40 in order to provide investors with a 13.2 percent return on the $30 they actually put up.

PA's weighted average cost of capital, when it uses new retained earnings and also when it uses new common stock, is shown in Table 19-1. We see that the weighted average cost of each dollar is 10.49 percent as long as retained earnings are used, but the MCC jumps to 11.09 percent as soon as the firm exhausts its retained earnings and must sell new common stock.

How much total new capital can Precision Associates raise before it exhausts its retained earnings and is forced to sell new common stock; that is, where will an increase in the MCC schedule occur? We find this point as follows:

1. Assume that the company expects to have total earnings of $156 million in 1994, and it has a target payout ratio of 45 percent, so it plans to pay out 45 percent of its earnings as dividends. Thus, the retained earnings for the year are projected to be $156 million(1.0 − 0.45) = $85.8 million.

2. If PA is to remain at its optimal capital structure, it must raise each dollar as 30 cents of debt, 10 cents of preferred stock, and 60 cents of common equity. Therefore, each 60 cents of retained earnings will support $1 of

---

[11]PA's MCC schedule in Figure 19-1 would be different (higher) if the company used any capital structure other than 30 percent debt, 10 percent preferred, and 60 percent equity.

Table 19-1

Precision Associates: MCC Using New Retained Earnings and New Common Stock

I. MCC when Equity Is from New Retained Earnings

	Weight ×	Component Cost =	Product
Debt	0.30	5.4%	1.62%
Preferred stock	0.10	9.5	0.95
Common equity (Retained earnings)	0.60	13.2	7.92
	1.00	$MCC_1 =$	10.49

II. MCC when Equity Is from Sale of New Common Stock

	Weight ×	Component Cost =	Product
Debt	0.30	5.4%	1.62%
Preferred stock	0.10	9.5	0.95
Common equity (New common stock)	0.60	14.2	8.52
	1.00	$MCC_2 =$	11.09%

break point (BP)

The dollar value of total new capital that can be raised before an increase in the firm's marginal cost of capital occurs.

capital, and the $85.8 million of retained earnings will not be exhausted, hence the MCC will not rise, until $85.8 million of retained earnings, plus some additional amount of debt and preferred stock, have been used up.

3. We now want to know how much *total new capital*—debt, preferred stock, and retained earnings—can be raised before the $85.8 million of retained earnings is exhausted. In effect, we are seeking some amount of capital, X, which is called a **break point (BP)** and which represents the total financing that can be raised before PA must sell new common stock.

4. We know that 60 percent, or 0.60, of X, the total new capital raised, will be retained earnings, whereas 40 percent will be debt plus preferred stock. We also know that retained earnings will amount to $85.8 million. Therefore,

$$\text{Retained earnings} = 0.60X = \$85,800,000.$$

5. Solving for X, which is the *retained earnings break point*, we obtain $BP_{RE} = \$143$ million:

$$X = BP_{RE} = \frac{\text{Retained earnings}}{\text{Equity fraction (weight)}} = \frac{\$85,800,000}{0.60} = 143 \text{ million}.$$

6. Thus, PA can raise a total of $143 million, consisting of 0.60($143 million) = $85.8 million of retained earnings plus 0.10($143 million) = $14.3 million of preferred stock and 0.30($143 million) = $42.9 million of new debt supported by these new retained earnings, without altering its capital structure (dollars in millions):

New debt supported by retained earnings	$42.9	30%
Preferred stock supported by retained earnings	14.3	10
Retained earnings	85.8	60
Total capital, or break point for retained earnings	$143.0	100%

Figure 19-2   Precision Associates: Marginal Cost of Capital Schedule Using
                    Both Retained Earnings and New Common Stock

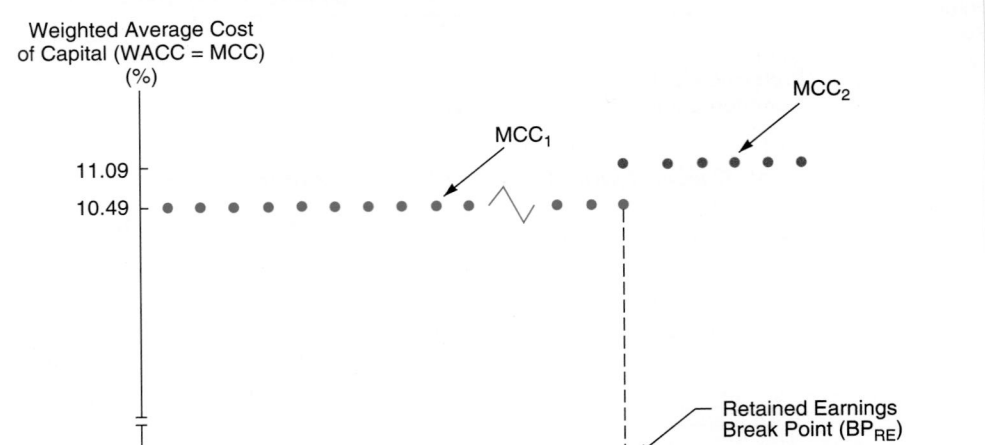

As PA raises larger and larger sums during a given time period, it is likely that one or several component costs will increase. Each time there is an increase in a component cost of capital due to the level of capital raised, the MCC schedule will break, or jump. In this figure we see that PA can raise a total of $143 million at a constant weighted average cost of capital of 10.49 percent. At that level of the budget, however, PA has used up its retained earnings available for the year. To raise *one more dollar* (with 60 cents still coming from equity) the firm must issue new common stock which has a higher component cost, and the marginal cost of capital increases to 11.09 percent.

break, or jump, in the MCC schedule

An increase in the weighted average cost of capital that occurs when there is an increase in a component cost of capital.

7. The value of X, or BP_{RE} = $143 million, is defined as the *retained earnings break point,* and it is the amount of total capital at which a break, or jump, occurs in the MCC schedule.

8. In general, there will be a **break, or jump, in the MCC schedule** any time there is an increase in a component cost of capital.

Figure 19-2 graphs PA's marginal cost of capital schedule with the retained earnings break point. Each dollar has a weighted average cost of 10.49 percent until the company has raised a total of $143 million. This $143 million will consist of $42.9 million of new debt with an after-tax cost of 5.4 percent, $14.3 million of preferred stock with a cost of 9.5 percent, and $85.8 million of retained earnings with a cost of 13.2 percent. However, if PA raises one dollar over $143 million, the new dollar will contain 60 cents of equity *obtained by selling new common equity at a cost of 14.2 percent;* therefore, the MCC jumps from 10.49 percent to 11.09 percent, as calculated in Table 19-1.

Note that we don't *really* think the MCC jumps by precisely 0.6 percent when we raise $1 over $143 million. Thus, Figure 19-2 should be regarded as an approximation rather than as a precise representation of reality. We will return to this point later in the chapter.

Other Breaks in the MCC Schedule

Most likely there will be additional breaks in PA's MCC schedule. For example, suppose PA could obtain only $60 million of debt at a 9 percent interest rate, with additional debt costing 10 percent. This would result in a second break point in the MCC schedule, at the point where the lower cost debt is exhausted. At what amount of *total financing* would the 9 percent debt be used up? We know that this total financing will amount to $60 million of debt plus some amount of preferred stock and common equity. If we let BP_{Debt} represent the *total financing* at this second break point, then we know that 30 percent, or 0.30, of BP_{Debt} will be debt, so

$$0.30(BP_{Debt}) = \$60,000,000,$$

and, solving for BP_{Debt}, we obtain

$$BP_{Debt} = \frac{\text{Amount of 9\% debt}}{\text{Debt fraction (weight)}} = \frac{\$60,000,000}{0.30} = \$200,000,000.$$

Thus, there will be another break in the MCC schedule after PA has raised a total of $200 million, and this second break results from an increase in the cost of debt.

As we have seen, from $0 to $143 million of new capital the MCC is 10.49 percent, whereas just beyond $143 million the MCC rises to 11.09 percent. Then, at $200 million of new capital, the MCC rises again, to 11.27 percent, as a result of the increase in k_d from 9 percent to 10 percent:

MCC above $200 Million when Cost of Debt has Increased

Component	Weight		Component Cost		Product
Debt ($k_d = 10\%$)	0.30	×	6.0%[a]	=	1.80%
Preferred stock	0.10	×	9.5	=	0.95
Common equity	0.60	×	14.2	=	8.52
	1.00			MCC_3 =	11.27%

[a]$10\%(1 - T) = 10\%(0.6) = 6\%$, up from $9\%(0.6) = 5.4\%$.

In other words, the next dollar beyond $200 million will consist of 30 cents of 10 percent debt (6 percent after taxes), 10 cents of 9.5 percent preferred stock, and 60 cents of new common stock at a cost of 14.2 percent (retained earnings were used up much earlier), and this marginal dollar will have a cost of $MCC_3 = 11.27\%$.

The effect of this second increase in PA's weighted average cost of capital is shown in Figure 19-3. Now there are two break points, one caused by using up all the retained earnings and the other by using up all the 9 percent debt. With the two breaks, there are three different MCCs: $MCC_1 = 10.49\%$ for the first $143 million of new capital; $MCC_2 = 11.09\%$ in the interval between $143 million and $200 million; and $MCC_3 = 11.27\%$ for all new capital beyond $200 million.

Figure 19-3

Precision Associates: Marginal Cost of Capital Schedule Showing the Effects of a Switch from Retained Earnings to New Common Stock, and from Lower Cost to Higher Cost Debt

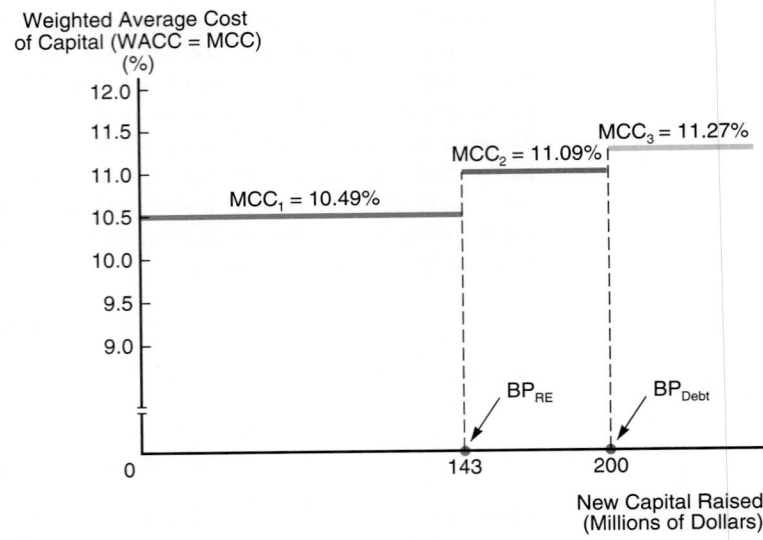

PA can expect to encounter a second break in its marginal cost of capital (MCC) schedule if it tries to raise more than $200 million in total financing for the period. The second break occurs because, when the firm has used $60 million of 9 percent debt, the component cost of debt will increase to 10 percent. This, in turn, will pull up the WACC to 11.27 percent, as the debt financing continues to represent 30 percent of every dollar raised.

There could, of course, be still more break points; they would occur if the interest rate continued to rise, if the cost of preferred stock rose, or if the cost of common stock rose.[12] *In general, a break point will occur whenever the cost of one of the capital components rises, and the break point can be determined by the following equation:*

$$\frac{\text{Break}}{\text{point}} = \frac{\text{Total dollar amount of lower cost capital of a given type}}{\text{Fraction of this type of capital in the capital structure (weight)}}. \quad (19\text{-}5)$$

We see, then, that numerous break points can occur. At the limit, we can even think of an MCC schedule with so many break points that it rises almost continuously beyond some given level of new financing. Such an MCC schedule is shown in Figure 19-4.

---

[12]The first break point is not necessarily the point at which retained earnings are used up; it is possible for low-cost debt to be exhausted *before* retained earnings have been used up. For example, if PA had available only $25 million of 9 percent debt, BP_{Debt} would occur at approximately $83.3 million:

$$BP_{Debt} = \frac{\$25,000,000}{0.30} = \$83,333,333 \approx \$83.3 \text{ million.}$$

This is well before the break point for retained earnings, which occurs at $143 million.

a. Show the balance sheet of each firm after the asset increase, and calculate each firm's new debt ratio. (Assume Haugen's lease is kept off the balance sheet.)

b. Show how Haugen's balance sheet would have looked immediately after the financing if it had capitalized the lease.

c. Would the rate of return (1) on assets and (2) on equity be affected by the choice of financing? How?

18-4
Lease analysis

As part of its overall plant modernization and cost reduction program, the management of Teweles Textile Mills has decided to install a new automated weaving loom. In the capital budgeting analysis of this equipment, the IRR of the project was found to be 20 percent versus a project required return of 12 percent.

The loom has an invoice price of $250,000, including delivery and installation charges. The funds needed could be borrowed from the bank through a 4-year amortized loan at a 10 percent interest rate, with payments to be made at the end of each year. In the event that the loom is purchased, the manufacturer will contract to maintain and service it for a fee of $20,000 per year paid at the end of each year. The loom falls in the MACRS 5-year class, and Teweles's marginal federal-plus-state tax rate is 40 percent.

Apilado Automation Inc., maker of the loom, has offered to lease the loom to Teweles for $70,000 upon delivery and installation (at t = 0) plus 4 additional annual lease payments of $70,000 to be made at the end of Years 1 through 4. (Note that there are 5 lease payments in total.) The lease agreement includes maintenance and servicing. Actually, the loom has an expected life of 8 years, at which time its expected salvage value is zero; however, after 4 years, its market value is expected to equal its book value of $42,500. Teweles plans to build an entirely new plant in 4 years, so it has no interest in either leasing or owning the proposed loom for more than that period.

a. Should the loom be leased or purchased?

b. The salvage value is clearly the most uncertain cash flow in the analysis. Assume that the appropriate salvage value pretax discount rate is 15 percent. What would be the effect of a salvage value risk adjustment on the decision?

c. The original analysis assumed that Teweles would not need the loom after 4 years. Now assume that the firm will continue to use it after the lease expires. Thus, if it leased, Teweles would have to buy the asset after 4 years at the then existing market value, which is assumed to equal the book value. What effect would this requirement have on the basic analysis? (No numerical analysis is required; just verbalize.)

18-5
Convertibles

The Swift Company was planning to finance an expansion in the summer of 1994. The principal executives of the company agreed that an industrial company like theirs should finance growth by means of common stock rather than by debt. However, they believed that the price of the company's common stock did not reflect its true worth, so they decided to sell a convertible security. They considered a convertible debenture but feared the burden of fixed interest charges if the common stock did not rise enough to make conversion attractive. They decided on an issue of convertible preferred stock, which would pay a dividend of $1.05 per share.

The common stock was selling for $21 a share at the time. Management projected earnings for 1994 at $1.50 a share and expected a future growth rate of 10 percent a year in 1995 and beyond. It was agreed by the investment bankers and management that the common stock would continue to sell at 14 times earnings, the current price/ earnings ratio.

a. What conversion price should be set by the issuer? The conversion rate will be 1.0; that is, each share of convertible preferred can be converted into one share of common. Therefore, the convertible's par value (as well as the issue price) will be equal to the conversion price, which in turn will be determined as a percentage over the current market price of the common. Your answer will be a guess, but make it a reasonable one.

b. Should the preferred stock include a call provision? Why or why not?

18-6   The Cox Computer Company has grown rapidly during the past 5 years. Recently its

Financing alternatives   commercial bank urged the company to consider increasing its permanent financing. Its bank loan under a line of credit has risen to $150,000, carrying a 10 percent interest rate, and Cox has been 30 to 60 days late in paying trade creditors.

Discussions with an investment banker have resulted in the decision to raise $250,000 at this time. Investment bankers have assured Cox that the following alternatives are feasible (flotation costs will be ignored):

▷   *Alternative 1:* Sell common stock at $10 per share.

▷   *Alternative 2:* Sell convertible bonds at a 10 percent coupon, convertible into 80 shares of common stock for each $1,000 bond (that is, the conversion price is $12.50 per share).

▷   *Alternative 3:* Sell debentures with a 10 percent coupon; each $1,000 bond will have 80 warrants to buy one share of common stock at $12.50.

Charles Cox, the president, owns 80 percent of Cox's common stock and wishes to maintain control of the company; 50,000 shares are outstanding. The following are summaries of Cox's latest financial statements:

Balance Sheet

		Current liabilities	$200,000
		Common stock, $1 par	50,000
		Retained earnings	25,000
Total assets	$275,000	Total liabilities and equity	$275,000

Income Statement

Sales	$550,000
All costs except interest	495,000
EBIT	$ 55,000
Interest	15,000
EBT	$ 40,000
Taxes at 40%	16,000
Net income	$ 24,000
Shares outstanding	50,000
Earnings per share	$0.48
Price/earnings ratio	18×
Market price of stock	$8.64

a. Show the new balance sheet under each alternative. For Alternatives 2 and 3, show the balance sheet after conversion of the debentures or exercise of the warrants. Assume that $150,000 of the funds raised will be used to pay off the bank loan and the rest to increase total assets.

b. Show Charles Cox's control position under each alternative, assuming that he does not purchase additional shares.

c. What is the effect on earnings per share of each alternative if it is assumed that earnings before interest and taxes will be 20 percent of total assets?

Figure 19-4

Smooth, or Continuous, Marginal Cost of Capital Schedule

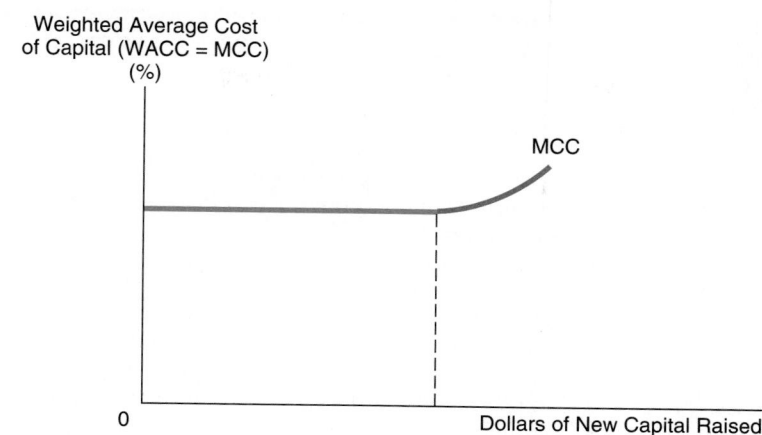

Numerous break points can occur as a firm attempts to increase the total dollar amount of new capital raised and invested within a given budget period. At the limit, the MCC schedule may be shown with so many break points that it becomes smooth or continuously rising beyond a given level of new financing.

The easiest sequence for calculating MCC schedules is as follows:

1. Use Equation 19-5 to determine each point at which a break occurs. (It is possible that two capital components could increase at the same point with both contributing to one break point and causing MCC to jump sharply.) After determining the break points, make a list of them.

2. Determine the cost of capital for each component in the intervals between breaks.

3. Calculate the weighted averages of these component costs to obtain the MCCs in each interval, as we did in Table 19-1. The MCC is constant within each interval, but it rises at each break point.

Notice that if there are n separate breaks, there will be n + 1 different MCCs. For example, in Figure 19-3 we see two breaks and three different MCCs.

Before closing this section, we should note again that a different MCC schedule would result if a different capital structure were used. As we will show in Chapter 20, the optimal capital structure produces the lowest MCC schedule.

? *Self-Test*

What are break points, and why do they occur in MCC schedules?

Write out and explain the equation for determining break points.

How does one calculate a firm's MCC schedule?

If there are n breaks in the MCC schedule, how many different MCCs are there? Why?

A SILVER LINING FOR A DARK ECONOMY

Just as homeowners in the early 1990s took advantage of falling interest rates to refinance their mortgages, some American corporate treasurers did the same thing with their companies' high-cost debt.

Throughout the 1980s, U.S. firms were at a disadvantage in the international market, compared with Japan and Germany, because interest rates overseas were much lower than those at home. An international strategist at Shearson Lehman Brothers calculated that the cost of capital in the second half of the 1980s averaged 7.5 percent in the United States, 5.4 percent in Japan, and 4.3 percent in Germany. By 1991 a reversal was under way, with U.S. rates at 5.9 percent, Japan's at 6.1 percent, and Germany's at 4.8 percent. "Much of the cost-of-capital advantage of Japan and Germany has gone away," said Hewlett-Packard CEO John A. Young.

Between 1990 and 1992, short-term rates in the United States dropped five percentage points, and long-term rates declined about half that much. As a result, estimated David Wyss, research director at DRI/McGraw Hill, American companies were saving about $30 billion a year. "That's equal to about a 10 percent increase in pretax corporate earnings each year," he said.

Other executives were excited about the choices made available to them by lower rates. Michael Murphy, CFO of Sara Lee Corporation, said, "We'll be able to spend more money advertising our brands" because of the drop in rates on $400 million of its short-term debt. The Tennessee Valley Authority (TVA) was able to avoid a rate increase for its customers because the utility issued new bonds to pay off higher interest securities.

Dozens of companies—including Merck, Kmart, Polaroid, and Deere—saved interest on their old debt or else raised cheap new money. In the first three weeks of 1992, new bond offerings totaled $23 billion —more than twice as much as in any other recent January. The senior vice-president–finance of United Airlines, which issued $200 million in bonds several months earlier than planned, said, "It was totally opportunistic on our part."

Corporate treasurers do face a dilemma in the refinancing/new money binge: whether to opt for short-term or long-term debt. Rates for issues of a year or less are much lower than those for longer maturity debt, but in early 1992 long-term rates were still as low as they had been in the past 20 years. This prompted Motorola to issue 15-year bonds to pay off its short-term commercial paper. Garth Milne, Motorola's treasurer, said, "We thought maybe rates might get a little better, but by midyear we expect them to be higher." An insurance holding company, W. R. Berkley Corporation, issued 30-year bonds for the first time in its history to lock in the historically low rates.

"In past recessions, corporations tended to take advantage of commercial paper as long as they could," said Roger Vasey, an executive vice-president with Merrill Lynch. This time, though, they are locking in long-term rates.

Investors have been eager to buy up the issues. TVA's CFO, William Malec, was surprised that the power supplier was able to raise $2 billion so fast, and Ford Motor Company decided to raise more money than originally planned when demand for its first-ever 30-year bonds turned out to be extremely strong.

Nevertheless, some companies are gambling that interest rates will stay low for a while, and they have decided go to the short-term route. For instance, Allied-Signal Corporation retired long-term debt by issuing commercial paper, bringing those obligations to $1 billion with an average maturity of less than 45 days. Roger Matthews, assistant treasurer of the firm, said, "By using commercial paper, we get the benefit of paying 4.25 percent instead of 8 percent." He expected no "major increase in rates for 12 months."

Since companies were finding it easy to raise money, the low-rate climate also enabled them to avoid layoffs, to hold larger inventories, and to look farther ahead. "It is giving corporations a higher degree of confidence that they will have the capital to support expansion over the years," said Vasey of Merrill Lynch. And a Sara Lee executive enthused, "This is a great time for companies like ourselves to be looking at acquisitions."

Sources: Fred R. Bleakley, "Decline in Rates Offers Chief Financial Officers Some Happy Choices," *The Wall Street Journal,* January 23, 1992, A1; Christopher Farrell and Ted Holden, "The U.S. Has a New Weapon: Low-Cost Capital," *Business Week,* July 29, 1991, 72–73.

Investment decisions for long-term projects are strongly affected by interest rates. Japan's much-praised willingness in the past to invest for the long haul might have been due to its favorable costs of capital rather than to a cultural predilection. When Japan's interest rates were almost four points lower than those in the United States, the difference in the cost of financing a five-year project in each country was only a 19 percent advantage for Japan. With a long-term project of 15 years, the difference was a whopping 69 percent. That might explain why, in the last three years of the 1980s, business investment in Japan rose 51 percent and in the United States, only 15 percent. But when rates in Japan moved higher, a Tokyo-based Salomon Brothers Asia executive said capital investment there was expected to grow only 3.1 percent in eight months.

There are still some drawbacks for the United States in the Japan/Germany/America rivalry. Foreign businesses have a more stable source of capital than U.S. ones because of more cross-ownership overseas of companies and banks—banks in Germany and Japan can make equity investments in corporations, whereas U.S. banks are restricted to making loans. As a result, foreign investors are usually willing to wait longer for a payback than their U.S. counterparts, and they are also more willing to help ailing companies recover rather than to force them to declare bankruptcy.

Nevertheless, the lower interest rates have made the future look much brighter for American business. "The cost of capital affects the rate of investment, especially in research and development," said the CEO of a Massachusetts technology company. These are things, he added, "that could lead the U.S. to be competitive in the future." An economist with Goldman, Sachs agreed. "A low cost of capital can encourage more risk-taking and more innovation, and maybe more productivity growth."

Combining the MCC and Investment Opportunity Schedules

Now that we have calculated the MCC schedule, we can use it to develop a discount rate for use in the capital budgeting process; *that is, we can use the MCC schedule to find the cost of capital for determining projects' net present values (NPVs) as discussed in Chapters 14 and 15.*

To understand how the MCC schedule is used in capital budgeting, assume that Precision Associates has three financial executives: a financial vice-president (VP), a treasurer, and a director of capital budgeting (DCB). The financial VP asks the treasurer to develop the firm's MCC schedule, and the treasurer produces the schedule shown earlier in Figure 19-3. At the same time, the financial VP asks the DCB to draw up a list of all projects that are potentially acceptable. The list shows each project's cost, projected annual net cash inflows, life, and IRR. These data are presented at the bottom of Figure 19-5. For example, Project A has a cost of $80 million, it is expected to produce inflows of $15.10 million per year for 8 years, and, therefore, it has an IRR of 10.2 percent. Similarly, Project B has a cost of $50 million, it is expected to produce inflows of $11.31 million per year for 7 years, and it has an IRR of 13 percent. Projects C, D, and E likewise have costs, inflows, project lives, and IRRs as shown. For simplicity, we assume that all projects are independent as opposed to mutually exclusive, that they are equally risky, and that their risk is equal to that of the firm's existing assets.

The director of capital budgeting then plots the IRR data shown at the bottom of Figure 19-5 as the **investment opportunity schedule (IOS)** shown in

investment opportunity schedule (IOS)
A graph of the firm's investment opportunities ranked in order of the projects' internal rates of return.

Figure 19-5

Precision Associates:
Combining the MCC and
IOS Schedules to
Determine the Optimal
Capital Budget

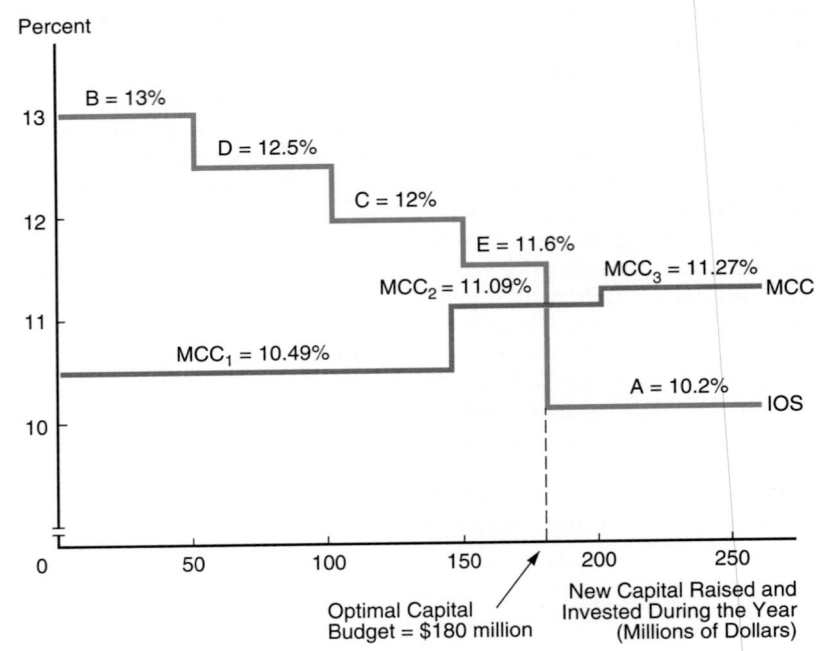

Project	Cost (in Millions)	Annual Inflows (in Millions)	Project Life (Years)	IRR, or Discount Rate, at which NPV = $0
A	$80	$15.10	8	10.2%
B	50	11.31	7	13.0
C	50	13.87	5	12.0
D	50	9.03	10	12.5
E	30	12.40	3	11.6

This figure shows how the MCC and the investment opportunity schedules are used in
capital budgeting. The IOS indicates how much PA can invest at different rates of return.
The two schedules intersect at an MCC of 11.09 percent, which is the cost of capital that
should be used in evaluating projects in capital budgeting. Projects B, D, C, and E, which
have returns in excess of the cost of capital, would thus be acceptable, making the optimal
capital budget $180 million. Because Project A would have to be financed with 11.27 per-
cent money—and is expected to provide an IRR of only 10.2 percent—it should be rejected.

the graph. The IOS schedule shows, in rank order, how much money PA could
invest at different rates of return. Figure 19-5 also shows PA's MCC schedule as
it was developed by the treasurer and plotted in Figure 19-3. Now consider
Project B: its IRR is 13 percent, and it can be financed with capital that costs
only 10.49 percent; consequently, it should be accepted. Recall from Chapter
14 that if a project's IRR exceeds its cost of capital, its NPV will also be positive;
therefore, Project B must also be acceptable by the NPV criterion. Projects D,
C, and E can be analyzed similarly; they are all acceptable because IRR > MCC

and, hence, NPV > $0. Project A, on the other hand, should be rejected because its IRR < MCC and therefore its NPV < $0.

Notice that if the cost of capital had started at a point above 13 percent, none of the available projects would have had positive NPVs; hence, none of them would be accepted. In that case, Precision Associates simply would not expand. However, in the actual situation, where the MCC starts at 10.49 percent and then rises, PA would accept the four projects (B, D, C, and E) which have rates of return in excess of the cost of the capital that would be used to finance them, ending up with a capital budget of $180 million.[13]

The preceding analysis as summarized in Figure 19-5 reveals a very important point: *The cost of capital used in the capital budgeting process as discussed in Chapters 14 and 15 is actually determined at the intersection of the IOS and MCC schedules. If the cost of capital at the intersection (MCC_2 = 11.09% in Figure 19-5) is used, then the firm will make correct accept/reject decisions, and its level of financing and investment will be optimal. If it uses any other rate, its capital budget will not be optimal.*

If PA had fewer good investment opportunities, its IOS would be shifted to the left, causing the intersection to occur at a lower level on the MCC curve. Conversely, if the firm had more and better investment opportunities, the IOS would be shifted to the right, and the intersection would occur at a higher MCC. In either event, the MCC at the intersection could change. *Thus, we see that the cost of capital used in capital budgeting is influenced both by the shape of the MCC curve and by the set of available projects.*

We have, of course, abstracted from differential project riskiness in this chapter; for simplicity, we have assumed that all projects are equally risky. As we learned in Chapter 15, the cost of capital used to evaluate riskier projects should be adjusted upward, whereas a lower rate should be used for projects with below-average risk. The intersection MCC as determined in Figure 19-5 should be used to find the NPVs of new projects that are about as risky as the firm's existing assets, but this corporate cost of capital should be adjusted up or down to find NPVs for projects with higher or lower risk than the average project. This point was discussed in Chapter 15.

Self-Test

Differentiate between the MCC and IOS schedules.

How are the MCC and IOS schedules used to determine a firm's cost of capital?

As a general rule, should a firm's cost of capital as determined in this chapter be used to evaluate all of its capital budgeting projects? Explain.

---

[13]A question that sometimes arises is this: "What would happen if the MCC cut through one of the projects? Should we then accept that project?" The answer is that if the project could be accepted *in part,* we would take on only part of it. Otherwise, the answer would be determined by (1) finding the average cost of the funds needed to finance the project in question and (2) comparing the average cost of this money with the IRR of the project. We should accept the project if its IRR exceeds the average cost of the funds needed to finance it.

Some Problem Areas in Cost of Capital

A number of difficult issues relating to the cost of capital either have not been mentioned or were glossed over in this chapter. These topics are covered in advanced finance courses, but they deserve some mention now to alert you to potential dangers as well as to provide you with a preview of some of the matters dealt with in advanced courses.

1. **Depreciation-generated funds.** The largest single source of capital for many firms is depreciation, yet we have not discussed the cost of funds from this source. In brief, depreciation cash flows can either be reinvested or returned to investors (stockholders *and* creditors). The cost of depreciation-generated funds is approximately equal to the weighted average cost of capital in the interval in which capital comes from retained earnings and low-cost debt.[14]

2. **Privately owned firms.** Our discussion of the cost of equity was related to publicly owned corporations, and we have concentrated on the rate of return required by public stockholders. However, there is a serious question about how one should measure the cost of equity for a firm whose stock is not traded.

3. **Measurement problems.** One cannot overemphasize the practical difficulties encountered when one actually attempts to estimate the cost of equity. It is very difficult to obtain good input data for the CAPM, for g in the formula $k_s = D_1/P_0 + g$, and for the risk premium in the formula $k_s = $ Bond yield + Risk premium. As a result, we can never be sure just how accurate our estimated cost of capital is.

4. **Costs of capital for projects of differing riskiness.** As we saw in Chapter 15, it is difficult to assign proper risk-adjusted discount rates to capital budgeting projects of differing degrees of riskiness.

5. **Capital structure weights.** In this chapter we have simply taken as given the target capital structure and used it to obtain the weights for calculating the WACC (MCC). As we shall see in Chapter 20, establishing the target capital structure is a major task in itself.

6. **Dynamic considerations.** Capital budgeting and cost of capital estimates are a part of the *planning process*—they deal with ex ante, or estimated, data rather than ex post, or historical, data. Hence, we can be wrong about the location of the IOS and the MCC. For example, we can underestimate the MCC and then accept projects which, with 20/20 hindsight, we should have rejected. In a dynamic, changing world this is a real problem. For example, interest rates and money costs could be low at the time plans are being made and contracts to build plants are signed, but six or eight months later, when we actually raise the money, capital costs could have risen substantially. Thus, a project that formerly looked good

---

[14]See Eugene F. Brigham and Louis C. Gapenski, *Intermediate Financial Management,* 4th ed., Chapter 6.

could turn out to be a bad one because we improperly forecasted the MCC schedule.

Although this listing of problems may appear formidable, the state of the art in cost of capital estimation is really not in bad shape. The procedures outlined in this chapter can be used to obtain cost of capital estimates that are sufficiently accurate for practical purposes, and the problems listed here merely indicate the desirability of refinements. The refinements are not unimportant, but the problems we have identified do not invalidate the usefulness of the procedures outlined in the chapter.

?   *Self-Test*

Identify some problem areas in cost of capital analysis. Do these problems invalidate the cost of capital procedures discussed in the chapter? Explain.

Recent Trends

This chapter has focused on the methodology of cost of capital calculations. However, it is important to relate all this to recent economic and financial developments. The "Industry Practice" boxed feature in this chapter emphasized the decline of corporate costs of capital in a general environment of falling interest rates. By August 1993 this trend had vastly accelerated, following passage of the Clinton administration's deficit-reduction plan. The 30-year Treasury bond yield set new record lows, and, since all interest rates in the debt markets are interrelated, corporate costs of capital declined dramatically as well. Corporate borrowers continued their rush to issue new long-term debt (also discussed in Chapter 16), frequently calling older high-coupon debt in the process. The fact that many of these new issues were *non*callable, coupled with the tendency of some issuers to sell bonds with much longer maturities (up to 100 years in a few cases), indicates that many borrowers felt long-term interest rates were not likely to go much lower and that 1993 represented a "window of opportunity."

At the same time, the Dow Jones Industrial Average and other stock market indices repeatedly set record highs. Since high stock prices, other things equal, mean lower costs of equity to firms ($k_s = D_1/P_0 + g$), it is no surprise that new stock offerings flooded the market. Finally, since all interest rates tend to be linked, the cost of preferred stock has declined as well. In short, by August 1993, as savers and investors desperately tried to obtain higher yields by going into longer term instruments, corporations and other long-term borrowers enjoyed the lowest cost of capital in decades.

?   *Self-Test*

What happened in the early 1990s with respect to long-term interest rates and the corporate cost of capital? What is the implication for corporate capital budgets, if we assume that investment opportunity schedules have not changed?

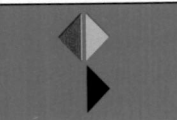

THE REAL COSTS OF GOING PUBLIC

In Chapter 17, we discussed some of the costs of going public, including the underwriter's discount (or commission) and the other cash expenses in public offerings. As we explained in Chapter 17's Small Business section, initial public offerings (IPOs) of common stock are generally underpriced, and that underpricing is an additional cost of going public. Furthermore, some underwriters ask for and obtain warrants allowing them to buy, at a future date, some of the issuer's shares at a lower price than the stock's initial market price. Such warrants represent another cost. Finally, some hard-to-quantify costs are involved in going public. In this section, we will describe these additional costs of the public offering.

IPOs are typically underpriced, and Professor Jay Ritter has argued that such underpricing is itself a cost of going public. Consider this example: Suppose your firm sold shares to the public at a price of $10 and those shares rose to $15 in the immediate aftermarket. You have sold shares worth $15 for only $10, so, in essence, you have discounted your shares by one-third. If you only counted the underwriter's commission and other cash expenses, you would be severely understating the cost of your public offering. Ritter's analysis takes this into account.

Ritter examines underpricing, underwriters' commissions, and other cash expenses, and he calculates the total cost of going public, including these three sources of cost. However, rather than looking at these costs as a fraction of gross proceeds (as in Chapters 17 and 19), he looks at costs as a fraction of the realized market values of the equities. To explain, consider again the example of the $10 IPO stock that rose to a market value of $15. If the underwriter's commission was 10% (of the $10 offered price) and cash expenses were 6% (again, of this $10), then the total costs were: $5.00 Underpricing + $1.00 Commission + $0.60 Cash expenses = $6.60. Since the

stock had a market value of $15, then the total costs of going public were $6.60/$15 = 44% of the market value. Ignoring underpricing and computing cost only on the basis of the offered price, the cost would have been calculated as just 16% instead of the more realistic 44%.

By computing the costs of going public in his own way, Ritter found that the average total cost of going public was 21.22% for firm commitment offers and 31.87% for best-efforts offers. It was not surprising that the costs of the best-efforts offers were higher (on a percentage basis) because they involved smaller offers by riskier, less-established firms. As indicated in Chapter 17, the costs were much higher for smaller offerings than for larger offerings.

The breakdown into best-efforts versus firm commitment offerings was useful in Ritter's analysis in another way as well. He argued that an additional factor to consider is the possibility that an offer might fail entirely. Underwritten offers are in essence guaranteed against failure. In a best-efforts offering, however, the offering is "called off" if the offering does not achieve a minimum number of sales as stated in the prospectus. Ritter found that nearly half (47%) of the best-efforts offerings in a sample failed entirely. An additional cost to consider, therefore, is that the firm may not receive any funds, in spite of having invested considerable effort in preparing for an offering. If the funds to be raised in the offering are necessary for the business's survival, then using a best-efforts offering presents a serious risk to the firm.

Barry, Muscarella, and Vetsuypens (BMV) examined public offerings in which the underwriter was paid, in part, through the receipt of warrants to buy the issuer's stock. Such warrants, called underwriter warrants (UWs), enable the underwriter to buy a fixed number of shares of the issuer's stock at a fixed price over a number of years, usually five. (Chapter 18 provided some details about warrants.) BMV found that these warrants themselves have values almost as high as the explicit commissions paid to the underwriters. These warrants also present a problem for the issuer. If the underwriter underprices the issue by a large amount, then the warrants the underwriter holds will be more valuable. There is, therefore, an incentive for the un-

Sources: Jay R. Ritter, "The Costs of Going Public," *Journal of Financial Economics,* 19(2) (December 1987), 269–283; and Christopher B. Barry, Chris J. Muscarella, and Michael R. Vetsuypens, "Underwriter Warrants, Underwriter Compensation and the Costs of Going Public," Working paper, Texas Christian University and Southern Methodist University, 1990.

derwriter to price the issue too low. Evidence from the sample examined by BMV, for example, shows that among offerings through the lowest tier of underwriters, issues with UWs had average underpricing (measured by initial returns) of nearly 65%, while offerings through the lowest tier of underwriters without UWs had an average underpricing (measured by initial returns) of only 5%. Thus, the issuer should be careful about the decision to use UWs in a public offering.

Some additional costs of going public also exist. One obvious cost involves the issuer's requirement to do a "road show" before the offering. In this road show, the CEO and/or some other key representatives of the issuing company spend six weeks or more traveling and talking with investor groups and telling the company's story. This road show, therefore, represents a real loss of productive time for the company.

Also, the public company has a serious reporting responsibility since it must file quarterly and annual reports with the Securities and Exchange Commission and provide material information to investors. Any failure to report, or reporting incorrect information, exposes the officers, directors, and the corporation to possible securities litigation. In fact, some authors contend that a motivation for underpricing an IPO is to make sure that the stock price does not fall in the aftermarket and trigger investor lawsuits against the firm. Such drops in stock price often trigger investor or lawyer searches to try to ascertain whether the company failed to report or reported inaccurately. Such information could then serve as the basis for a lawsuit. Directors' and officers' insurance against such lawsuits is, consequently, becoming very expensive.

In summary, the cost of going public includes many elements, and it is much greater than it would appear from an evaluation of only the commissions paid to underwriters and the other cash expenses of the offering. For many firms, the costs of going public at an early stage in their existence, when there are still many risks, are simply too high in relation to other alternative sources of financing.

Summary

This chapter showed how the MCC schedule is developed for use in the capital budgeting process. The key concepts covered are listed below.

▷ The cost of capital to be used in capital budgeting decisions is the **weighted average** of the various types of capital the firm uses, typically debt, preferred stock, and common equity.

▷ The **component cost of debt** is the **after-tax** cost of new debt. It is found by multiplying the cost of new debt by $(1 - T)$, where T is the firm's marginal tax rate: $k_d(1 - T)$.

The **component cost of preferred stock** is calculated as the preferred dividend divided by the net issuing price, where the net issuing price is the price the firm receives after deducting flotation costs: $k_p = D_p/P_n$.

▷ The **cost of common equity** is the cost of retained earnings as long as the firm has retained earnings, but the cost of equity becomes the cost of new common stock once the firm has exhausted its retained earnings.

The **cost of retained earnings** is the rate of return required by stockholders on the firm's common stock; if less than this rate is earned on retained earnings, the price of the stock will fall. It can be estimated using one of three methods: (1) the **CAPM approach**, (2) the **dividend-yield-plus-growth-rate**, or **DCF**, **approach**, and (3) the **bond-yield-plus-risk-premium approach**.

To use the **CAPM approach,** one (1) estimates the firm's beta, (2) multiplies this beta by the market risk premium to determine the firm's risk premium, and (3) adds the firm's risk premium to the risk-free rate to obtain the firm's cost of retained earnings: $k_s = k_{RF} + (k_M - k_{RF})b_i$.

To use the **dividend-yield-plus-growth-rate approach,** which is also called the **DCF approach,** one adds the firm's expected growth rate to its expected dividend yield: $k_s = D_1/P_0 + g$.

The **bond-yield-plus-risk-premium approach** calls for adding a risk premium of from 3 to 5 percentage points to the firm's interest rate on long-term debt: $k_s = $ Bond yield $+$ RP.

▷ The **cost of new common equity** is higher than the cost of retained earnings because the firm must incur **flotation expenses** to sell stock. To find the cost of new common equity, the stock price is first reduced by the flotation expense, then the dividend yield is calculated on the basis of the price the firm will actually receive, and finally the expected growth rate is added: $k_e = D_1/[P_0(1 - F)] + g$.

▷ Each firm has an **optimal capital structure,** defined as that mix of debt, preferred stock, and common equity which minimizes its **weighted average cost of capital (WACC):**

$$\text{WACC} = w_d k_d (1 - T) + w_p k_p + w_s (k_s \text{ or } k_e).$$

The firm's optimal (target) capital structure is important because it provides the weights (w_d, w_p, and w_s) in the WACC equation.

▷ The **marginal cost of capital (MCC)** is defined as the cost of the last dollar of new capital that the firm raises. The MCC increases as the firm raises more and more capital during a given period. A graph of the MCC plotted against dollars raised is the **MCC schedule.**

A **break point** will occur in the MCC schedule each time the cost of one of the capital components increases.

▷ The **investment opportunity schedule (IOS)** is a graph of the firm's investment opportunities, ranked in order of their internal rates of return.

The MCC schedule is combined with the IOS schedule, and the intersection defines the **corporate cost of capital,** which is used to evaluate average-risk capital budgeting projects.

▷ Some of the **problem areas in cost of capital estimation** are (1) finding a cost for depreciation-generated funds; (2) finding a cost of equity for privately owned firms; (3) measurement problems, in general, in trying to obtain inputs for cost of equity calculations; (4) projects of differing riskiness; (5) establishing capital structure weights; and (6) dynamic considerations.

The concepts developed in this chapter are extended in Chapter 20, where we consider the effect of the capital structure on the cost of capital.

Resolution to
DECISION IN FINANCE

MCDONNELL DOUGLAS'S QUANDARY

McDonnell Douglas is expected to generate $1 billion in cash in 1993 as the result of the sale of noncore assets, increased cash flow from the MD-11 commercial air transport program, and anticipated profits on the C-17 military air transport. This financial assessment is shared by a number of securities analysts, including S&P. Assuming that the expectations are met, nearly all the cash flow is earmarked to pay off debt, thus strengthening the firm's balance sheet. However, Moody's downgrading action will sting. When a company's debt is downgraded, the company's cost of borrowing increases. McDonnell's CFO stated that this was not a concern because he does not foresee the need to borrow during 1993. However, he also made the following statement: "It [the downgrading] creates the perception that McDonnell Douglas's financial risks have increased, which is blatantly false . . . It also unduly punishes debtholders, who are not at greater risk."

As a result of Moody's downgrading, whether the company's CFO likes it or not, the company's overall cost of capital will increase—the cost of both debt and equity will rise. Investors perceive the company as being riskier, so they will require a higher return to compensate them for taking on the additional risk. In the long run, this means that it will cost the firm more money to raise capital than it would have without the downgrade. Thus, capital investments that once would have been acceptable may not be acceptable now.

The cost of capital is not the only concern—an even greater concern is whether the firm will be able to raise capital at all. Moody's Ba2 rating puts McDonnell's senior debt below investment grade, the level that many banks and institutional investors, such as pension funds, are required by law to hold. Thus, it is critical for the company to maintain an investment grade rating from at least one of the rating agencies, or a very large and important source of capital will dry up.

The increased cost of capital affects both new and old investors. Current bondholders that thought they were holding triple-B (investment grade) debt now find themselves holding junk bonds, at least according to one of the rating agencies. However, these old investors are not being compensated for the additional risk because the interest payments on the debt were fixed at the time of issuance, when the debt was rated higher.

McDonnell's CFO suggests that "Moody's has 'misconceptions' about McDonnell Douglas that need to be worked out." However, both Moody's and S&P were briefed on the company's operating strategy only a month before Moody's downgrade announcement. States an S&P analyst, "We agree that there are a number of uncertainties affecting McDonnell Douglas's outlook, but S&P is looking at them in a different light . . . In our opinion, the C-17 and MD-11 have turned the corner, and the company is in a better position to make significant improvements in its operating performance in 1993." Obviously, McDonnell Douglas hopes that its 1993 expectations will be met because if they are not, S&P will surely reevaluate its assessment and also downgrade the debt.

Source: "McDonnell Douglas in Quandary over Contradictory Debt Ratings," *Aviation Week and Space Technology,* February 8, 1993.

Questions

19-1   In what sense does the marginal cost of capital (MCC) schedule represent a series of average costs?

19-2   How would each of the following affect a firm's cost of debt, $k_d(1 - T)$; its cost of equity, k_s; and its weighted average cost of capital, WACC? (Note: The financing mix is held constant, as it was throughout the chapter, and the firm in question uses only debt and common equity, no preferred stock.) Indicate by a plus (+), a minus (−), or a zero (0) if the factor would raise, lower, or have an indeterminate effect on the items in question. Assume other things are held constant. Be prepared to justify your answer, but recognize that several of the parts probably have no single correct answer; these questions are designed to stimulate thought and discussion.

	Effect on		
	$k_d(1 - T)$	k_s	WACC
a. The corporate tax rate is lowered.	———	———	———
b. The Federal Reserve tightens credit.	———	———	———
c. The dividend payout ratio is increased.	———	———	———
d. The firm doubles the amount of capital it raises during the year.	———	———	———
e. The firm expands into a risky new area.	———	———	———
f. The firm merges with another firm whose earnings are countercyclical both to those of the first firm and to the stock market.	———	———	———
g. The stock market falls drastically, and the firm's stock falls along with the rest.	———	———	———
h. Investors become more risk averse.	———	———	———
i. The firm is an electric utility with a large investment in nuclear plants. Several states propose a ban on nuclear power generation.	———	———	———

19-3   Suppose a firm estimates its MCC and IOS schedules for the coming year and finds that they intersect at the point 10%, $10 million. What cost of capital should be used to evaluate average-risk projects, high-risk projects, and low-risk projects?

Self-Test Problem

ST-1   L. H. Clore Inc. has the following capital structure, which it considers to be optimal:

Debt	25%
Preferred stock	15
Common equity	60
	100%

Clore's expected net income this year is $150,000, its established dividend payout ratio is 20 percent, its federal-plus-state tax rate is 40 percent, and investors expect earnings and dividends to grow at a constant rate of 7 percent in the future. Clore paid a dividend of $3.30 per share last year. Its stock currently sells at a price of $60 per share.

Clore can obtain new capital in the following ways:

● *Common:* New common stock would have a flotation cost of 10 percent for up to $60,000 of new stock and of 20 percent for all common over $60,000.

● *Preferred:* New preferred can be sold to the public at its par value of $100 per share, with a dividend of $8.10. However, flotation costs of $5 per share will be incurred

for up to $37,500 of preferred, rising to $10, or 10 percent, on all preferred over
$37,500.

- *Debt:* Up to $25,000 of debt can be sold at an interest rate of 8 percent; debt in the
range of $25,001 to $50,000 must carry an interest rate of 9 percent; and all debt
over $50,000 will have an interest rate of 10.2 percent.

Clore has the following investment opportunities:

Project	Cost at t = 0	Annual Net Cash Flow	Project Life (Years)	IRR
A	$ 50,000	$ 9,934	7	
B	50,000	14,704	5	14.4%
C	50,000	9,785	8	11.2
D	100,000	16,767	10	10.7
E	100,000	25,015	6	13.0

a. Find the break points in the MCC schedule.
b. Determine the cost of each capital structure component.
c. Calculate the weighted average cost of capital in the interval between each break in
the MCC schedule.
d. Calculate the IRR for Project A.
e. Construct a graph showing the MCC and IOS schedules.
f. Which projects should L. H. Clore accept?

Problems

19-1
After-tax cost of debt
Calculate the after-tax cost of debt under each of the following conditions:
a. Interest rate = 7 percent; tax rate = 0 percent.
b. Interest rate = 7 percent; tax rate = 34 percent.
c. Interest rate = 7 percent; tax rate = 40 percent.
d. Interest rate = 7 percent; tax rate = 60 percent.

19-2
After-tax cost of debt
Barbara Brewer Enterprises can sell a bond with a 9.5 percent coupon. Analysts believe
the company can sell the bond at a price that will provide a yield to maturity of 9.5
percent. If the tax rate is 40 percent, what is the firm's after-tax cost of debt?

19-3
Cost of debt
Sierra International has a 10 percent, $1,000 par bond issue outstanding with 15 years
left to maturity.
a. If investors require a 9 percent return (yield to maturity), what is the current market price of the bond?
b. If the company wishes to sell a new issue of equal-risk bonds at par, what coupon
rate will the investors require?

19-4
Cost of preferred stock
Juarez Publications plans to issue some $50 par value preferred stock with a 13 percent
dividend. To issue the stock, the company must pay flotation costs of 8 percent to the
investment bankers. What is the cost of capital for this preferred stock?

19-5
Cost of preferred stock
Ash Grove Apparel Inc. plans to issue some $100 par preferred stock with an 11 per-
cent dividend. The stock is selling on the market for $97.00, and Ash Grove must pay
flotation costs equal to 10 percent of the market price.
a. What is the cost of preferred stock to Ash Grove?
b. If the firm's tax rate is 40 percent, what is the after-tax component cost of preferred
stock to Ash Grove?

19-6
Cost of debt
Wachowicz Corporation has a bond issue outstanding with the following financial characteristics: 14 percent coupon; 5 years to maturity; $1,000 par value; and $1,200
current market price.

a. Using the formula found in Footnote 6 of Chapter 16, calculate the bond's approximate yield to maturity.

b. With the information obtained in Part a, determine the bond's exact yield to maturity.

c. What is the relationship between the yield to maturity on outstanding bonds and the cost of debt for new debt securities the firm wishes to issue?

19-7
Cost of retained earnings

Talbot Department Stores paid a dividend of $5.00 per share recently; that is, $D_0 = $5.00. The company's stock sells for $71.42 per share. The expected growth rate is 6 percent. Calculate Talbot's cost of retained earnings.

19-8
Cost of retained earnings

NewAge Home Decor's EPS 5 years ago was $3.90; its EPS today is $6.00. The company pays out 45 percent of its earnings as dividends, and the firm's stock sells for $49.05.

a. Calculate the firm's growth rate. (Assume that the growth rate and payout rate have been constant over the 5-year period.)

b. Calculate the expected dividend, D_1. (Note: $D_0 = 0.45($6.00) = 2.70.) Assume that the payout rate and past growth rate will continue into the foreseeable future.

c. What is the cost of retained earnings for the firm?

19-9
Cost of retained earnings

The risk-free rate is 7 percent and the required rate of return on an average-risk security in the market is 12 percent. Calculate a firm's cost of retained earnings for each of the following betas:

a. Beta = 1.5.

b. Beta = 0.6.

c. Beta = 1.0.

19-10
Cost of retained earnings

The earnings, dividends, and stock price of Mangano Inc. are expected to grow at a rate of 5 percent into the foreseeable future. Mangano's common stock sells for $28.00 per share, and its last dividend, D_0, was $2.40.

a. Using the discounted cash flow (DCF) approach, what is the firm's cost of retained earnings?

b. The firm's beta is 1.4, the risk-free rate is 8 percent, and the required rate of return on the market is 12 percent. What is the firm's cost of retained earnings as computed by the CAPM approach?

c. If Mangano's bonds yield 10.5 percent, what is k_s, according to the bond-yield-plus-risk-premium approach?

d. Based on the results in Parts a through c, what would you estimate Mangano's cost of retained earnings to be?

19-11
Cost of equity

Tucker & Tolle's (T&T's) last dividend was $2.00, its growth rate is 6 percent (which is expected to continue at a constant rate), and the stock now sells for $23.56. New stock can be sold to net the firm $21.91 after flotation costs.

a. What is T&T's cost of retained earnings?

b. What is T&T's percentage flotation cost, F?

c. What is T&T's cost of new common stock, k_e?

19-12
Return on common stock

DuVall Hardware's common stock is currently selling for $15.75 per share. The firm is expected to earn $5.40 and to pay a year-end dividend of $1.89. The firm's return on assets is 6 percent, but 45 percent of its assets are financed with debt.

a. What is the firm's return on equity (ROE)?

b. What is the firm's expected growth rate? (*Hint:* g = b(ROE), where b = the fraction of earnings that are retained. See Footnote 9.)

c. What is the firm's cost of equity capital?

19-13
Cost of equity

You have been hired as the treasurer of Jernigan Resources. The firm's president has asked you to compute the firm's cost of capital. You have gathered all pertinent financial data to make the calculations. Jernigan's EPS this year will be $5.00, whereas 7 years ago EPS was $1.40. The firm's expected dividend, D_1, will be $2.75, and Jernigan's market price is $30.50. The risk-free rate is 7 percent, and the return on an average security is 13 percent. Jernigan's beta is 1.5. Its bond issue is currently selling to yield investors 11 percent to maturity.

a. Using all three approaches, calculate the firm's cost of equity capital.

b. What conclusions can be drawn from your calculations? What is your best estimate of Jernigan Resources's cost of equity capital? Explain your findings to the firm's president, Bob Jernigan.

19-14

Break point calculations

Sandoval Imports Inc. expects earnings of $10 million next year. Its dividend payout ratio is 30 percent, and its debt/assets ratio is 40 percent. The firm uses no preferred stock.

a. How much will the firm pay in dividends next year?

b. What amount of additional retained earnings does the firm expect next year?

c. At what amount of total financing will there be a break point in the MCC schedule because of an increase in the component cost of equity?

d. The firm can borrow $7.5 million at an interest rate of 8 percent, but additional borrowing up to $12.5 million will require a rate of 9.75 percent, and above $12.5 million, additional debt will cost 11.50 percent. At what points will rising debt costs cause breaks in the MCC schedule?

19-15

Required cash flow

Hoffberger and Company is making final calculations on the purchase of a new production assembler. The equipment is valued at $1,000,000. It will be in service for 5 years and will be depreciated at $200,000 annually. (Assume straight-line depreciation is allowed.) There is no salvage value. Additional annual costs include the following:

Labor	$125,000
Materials	166,667
Building lease	100,000
Overhead	41,667

If all costs are constant during the 5-year period, what is the minimum level of sales that will allow Hoffberger to earn at least its 14 percent cost of capital? Hoffberger's marginal tax rate is 40 percent.

19-16

Weighted average cost of capital

The Perry Company has the following capital structure, which is considered optimal:

Long-term debt	$1,200,000
Preferred stock	200,000
Common stock equity	2,600,000
Total long-term debt and equity	$4,000,000

The cost of debt is 10 percent before tax, the cost of preferred stock is 12.5 percent, and the cost of equity is 15.4 percent. The firm's marginal tax rate is 40 percent. What is Perry's cost of capital?

19-17

Marginal cost of capital

Underhill Manufacturing's earnings and dividends per share have been growing at a steady 5 percent during the last 10 years. The firm's stock, 500,000 shares outstanding, is now selling for $80 a share, and the expected dividend for next year, D_1, is $6.00. The firm pays out 48 percent of its earnings in dividends. The current interest rate on new debt is 8.5 percent. The firm's marginal tax rate is 40 percent. The firm's capital structure, considered to be optimal, is as follows:

Long-term debt	$ 5,000,000
Common equity	5,000,000
Total long-term debt and equity	$10,000,000

a. Calculate the after-tax cost of new debt and the cost of common equity, assuming that new equity comes only from retained earnings. Because the historical growth rate is expected to continue, we may calculate the cost of equity as $\hat{k}_s = D_1/P_0 + g$.

b. Find the marginal cost of capital, again assuming that no new common stock is to be sold.

c. If this year's addition to retained earnings is $3.9 million, how much can be spent for capital investments before external equity must be sold? (*Hint:* Calculate the retained earnings break point.)

d. What is the marginal cost of capital (cost of funds raised in excess of the amount calculated in Part c) if new common stock can be sold to the public at $80 a share to net the firm $72 a share after flotation costs? The cost of debt is constant.

19-18

Optimal capital budget

Ramsing Inc. has a debt ratio of 25 percent. Management has concluded that this capital structure is optimal. Ramsing has analyzed its investment opportunities for the coming year and has identified 4 possible additions to assets which generate IRRs greater than zero.

Investment	Size	IRR
A	$ 6 million	16.2%
B	12 million	15.3
C	12 million	14.1
D	6 million	13.0

Ramsing is forecasting net income for the coming year of $15 million and expects to pay out 40 percent in dividends to the 1 million outstanding shares of common stock. Earnings have been growing at a constant rate of 8 percent over the past few years, and this rate is expected to continue indefinitely. If Ramsing has to sell new common stock, it will be faced with flotation costs of 15 percent (current market price = $75 per share). Ramsing uses no preferred stock in its capital structure, and any debt that is raised, up to $7.5 million, will require a coupon rate of 8 percent. However, if the total debt required is greater than $7.5 million, the coupon rate will have to be 10 percent. The marginal tax rate is 40 percent. How large will the capital budget be if all investments with IRR > MCC are accepted? (Note: Your answer should include a graph showing the MCC and investment opportunity schedules for Ramsing Inc.)

19-19

Optimal capital budget

CNI Semiconductors has the following (independent) investment opportunities:

	Cost	Annual Cash Inflows	Life (Years)
Project A	$ 5,000,000	$1,216,130	6
Project B	13,000,000	2,348,770	8
Project C	10,000,000	1,746,870	14

The optimal capital structure calls for financing all projects with 60 percent common equity and 40 percent debt. The following information applies to the financial position of CNI. The last dividend (D_0) was $3.50. The constant growth rate of earnings and dividends is 6 percent. The current price per share of common stock is $46. If CNI issues new common stock, a flotation cost of 12 percent will be incurred. The company can issue debt at a before-tax cost of 12 percent. The firm's dividend payout ratio is 30 percent, and it is in the 40 percent tax bracket. CNI expects net income to equal $15,000,000 for the current year. In which projects (if any) should CNI invest, and what is the firm's optimal capital budget? Provide an MCC-IOS graph to support your answer.

19-20

Optimal capital budget

The Loden Corporation expects to earn $50,000 before taxes this year. Its tax rate is 25 percent, and the dividend payout ratio is 40 percent. The company can raise debt at a 12 percent (before-tax) cost up to $15,000. However, a 13 percent rate will apply to all debt above $15,000. The cost of retained earnings has been calculated to be 17 percent, and the cost of new common stock is 18.2 percent. Loden has the opportunity to invest in the following projects:

Project	Cost	Annual Cash Inflows	Life (Years)
A	$10,000	$2,983	5
B	14,000	3,265	7
C	45,000	9,311	10

The company will finance all capital expenditures with 30 percent debt and 70 percent common equity. In which projects should Loden invest? What is Loden's capital budget? (Your answer should include a graph.)

19-21
Optimal capital budget

On January 1 the total assets of Audiomax Corporation were $35 million. During the year the company plans to raise and invest $15 million. The firm's present capital structure, shown below, is considered to be optimal. Assume that there is no short-term debt.

Debt	$14,000,000
Common equity	21,000,000
Total liabilities and equity	$35,000,000

New bonds will have an 11 percent coupon rate and will be sold at par. Common stock, currently selling at $50 a share, can be sold to net the company $42.50 a share. The stockholders' required rate of return is estimated to be 15 percent, consisting of a dividend yield of 6 percent and an expected growth rate of 9 percent. (The next expected dividend is $3, so $3/$50 = 6%.) Net income for the year is estimated to be $5,475,000, and dividends of $1.65 per share will be paid on 1,500,000 shares of common equity. The marginal corporate tax rate is 40 percent.

a. Assuming that all asset expansion (gross expenditures for fixed assets plus related working capital) is included in the capital budget, what is the dollar amount of the capital budget?

b. To maintain the present capital structure, how much of the capital budget must be financed by common equity?

c. How much of the needed new common equity funds will be generated internally? Externally?

d. What is the cost of each of the common equity components?

e. At what level of capital expenditures will there be a break in the MCC schedule?

f. Calculate the MCC **(1)** below and **(2)** above the break in the schedule.

g. Plot the MCC schedule. Also, draw in an investment opportunity schedule that is consistent with both the MCC schedule and the projected capital budget. *Any* IOS that is consistent will do.

19-22
Optimal capital budget

Birmingham Industries has the following capital structure, which it considers to be optimal under present and forecasted conditions:

Debt (long-term only)	40%
Common equity	60
Total liabilities and equity	100%

For the coming year, management expects net income of $2.4 million. Birmingham's past dividend policy of paying out 60 percent of net income will continue. Present commitments from its banker will allow Birmingham to borrow according to the following schedule:

Loan Amount	Interest Rate
$0 to $750,000	9% on this increment of debt
$750,001 to $1,350,000	11% on this increment of debt
$1,350,001 and above	13% on this increment of debt

The company's average tax rate is 40 percent, the current market price of its stock is $48 per share, its *last* dividend was $4.57 per share, and the expected growth rate is 5 percent. External equity (new common) can be sold at a flotation cost of 10 percent.

Birmingham has the following investment opportunities for the next year:

Project	Cost	Annual Cash Flows	Project Life (Years)	IRR
1	$ 900,000	$186,210	10	
2	1,200,000	316,904	6	15.0%
3	500,000	303,644	2	
4	750,000	246,926	4	12.0
5	1,000,000	194,322	8	11.0

Management asks you to help determine which projects (if any) should be undertaken. You proceed with this analysis by answering the following questions as posed in a logical sequence:

a. How many breaks are there in the MCC schedule?

b. At what dollar amounts do the breaks occur, and what causes them?

c. What is the weighted average cost of capital, WACC, in each of the intervals between the breaks?

d. What are the IRR values for Projects 1 and 3?

e. Graph the IOS and MCC schedules.

f. Which projects should Birmingham's management accept?

g. What assumptions about project risk are implicit in this problem? If you learned that Projects 1, 2, and 3 were of above-average risk, yet Birmingham chose the projects that you indicated in Part f, how would this affect the situation?

h. The problem stated that Birmingham pays out 60 percent of its net income as dividends. In words, how would the analysis change if the payout ratio were changed to zero, to 100 percent, or somewhere in between? If you are using the computerized problem diskette, reanalyze the firm's capital budgeting decision using dividend payout ratios of zero, 100 percent, and 40 percent.

(Do Parts i through l only if you are using the computerized problem diskette.)

i. Suppose Birmingham's tax rate fell to zero, with other variables remaining constant. How would that affect the MCC schedule and the capital budget?

j. Return the tax rate to 40 percent. Now assume that the debt ratio is increased to 65 percent, causing all interest rates to rise by 1 percentage point, to 10 percent, 12 percent, and 14 percent, and causing g to increase from 5 percent to 6 percent. What happens to the MCC schedule and the capital budget?

k. New information becomes available. Change the Part j scenario to assume net income of only $1,000,000 but a growth rate of 9 percent. How does that affect the capital budget?

l. Would it be reasonable to use the model to analyze the effects of a change in the payout ratio without changing other variables?

Solution to Self-Test Problem

ST-1   a. A break point will occur each time a low-cost type of capital is used up. We establish the break points as follows, after first noting that Clore has $120,000 of retained earnings:

$$\text{Retained earnings} = (\text{Total earnings})(1.0 - \text{Payout})$$

$$= \$150,000(0.8)$$

$$= \$120,000.$$

$$\text{Break point} = \frac{\text{Total dollar amount of lower cost capital of a given type}}{\text{Fraction of this type of capital in the capital structure (weight)}}.$$

Capital Used Up	Break Point Calculation		Break Number
Retained earnings	$BP_{RE} = \dfrac{\$120,000}{0.60}$	$= \$200,000$	2
10% flotation common	$BP_{10\%E} = \dfrac{\$120,000 + \$60,000}{0.60}$	$= \$300,000$	4
5% flotation preferred	$BP_{5\%P} = \dfrac{\$37,500}{0.15}$	$= \$250,000$	3
8% debt	$BP_{8\%D} = \dfrac{\$25,000}{0.25}$	$= \$100,000$	1
9% debt	$BP_{9\%D} = \dfrac{\$50,000}{0.25}$	$= \$200,000$	2

A summary of the break points follows:

1. There are three common equity costs, and hence two changes, and, therefore, two equity breaks in the MCC. There are two preferred costs and hence one preferred break. There are three debt costs and hence two debt breaks.

2. The numbers in the third column of the table above designate the sequential order of the breaks, determined after all the break points were calculated. Note that the second debt break and the break for retained earnings both occur at $200,000.

3. The first break point occurs at $100,000, when the 8 percent debt is used up. The second break point, $200,000, results from using up both retained earnings and the 9 percent debt. The MCC curve also rises at $250,000 and $300,000 as preferred stock with a 5 percent flotation cost and common stock with a 10 percent flotation cost, respectively, are used up.

b. Component costs within indicated total capital intervals are as follows:
Retained earnings (used in interval $0 to $200,000):

$$\hat{k}_s = \frac{D_1}{P_0} + g = \frac{D_0(1 + g)}{P_0} + g$$

$$= \frac{\$3.30(1.07)}{\$60} + 7\%$$

$$= 5.89\% + 7\% = 12.89\%.$$

Common with F = 10% ($200,001 to $300,000):

$$k_c = \frac{D_1}{P_0(1.0 - F)} + g = \frac{\$3.531}{\$60(0.9)} + 7\% = 13.54\%.$$

Common with F = 20% (over $300,000):

$$k_c = \frac{\$3.531}{\$60(0.8)} + 7\% = 14.36\%.$$

Preferred with F = 5% ($0 to $250,000):

$$k_p = \frac{D_p}{P_n} = \frac{\$8.10}{\$100(0.95)} = 8.53\%.$$

Preferred with F = 10% (over $250,000):

$$k_p = \frac{\$8.10}{\$100(0.90)} = 9.00\%.$$

Debt at $k_d = 8\%$ ($0 to $100,000):

$$k_d(1 - T) = 8\%(0.6) = 4.80\%.$$

Debt at $k_d = 9\%$ ($100,001 to $200,000):

$$k_d(1 - T) = 9\%(0.6) = 5.40\%.$$

Debt at $k_d = 10.2\%$ (over $200,000):

$$k_d(1 - T) = 10.2\%(0.6) = 6.12\%.$$

c. WACC calculations within indicated total capital intervals:

1. $0 to $100,000 (debt $= 4.8\%$, preferred $= 8.53\%$, and RE $= 12.89\%$):

$$MCC_1 = w_d k_d(1 - T) + w_p k_p + w_s k_s$$

$$= 0.25(4.8\%) + 0.15(8.53\%) + 0.60(12.89\%) = 10.21\%.$$

2. $100,001 to $200,000 (debt $= 5.4\%$, preferred $= 8.53\%$, and RE $= 12.89\%$):

$$MCC_2 = 0.25(5.4\%) + 0.15(8.53\%) + 0.60(12.89\%) = 10.36\%.$$

3. $200,001 to $250,000 (debt $= 6.12\%$, preferred $= 8.53\%$, and equity $= 13.54\%$):

$$MCC_3 = 0.25(6.12\%) + 0.15(8.53\%) + 0.60(13.54\%) = 10.93\%.$$

4. $250,001 to $300,000 (debt $= 6.12\%$, preferred $= 9.00\%$, and equity $= 13.54\%$):

$$MCC_4 = 0.25(6.12\%) + 0.15(9.00\%) + 0.60(13.54\%) = 11.00\%.$$

5. Over $300,000 (debt $= 6.12\%$, preferred $= 9.00\%$, and equity $= 14.36\%$):

$$MCC_5 = 0.25(6.12\%) + 0.15(9.00\%) + 0.60(14.36\%) = 11.50\%.$$

d. IRR calculation for Project A:

$$PVIFA_{k,7} = \frac{\$50,000}{\$9,934} = 5.0332.$$

This is the approximate factor for 9 percent, so $IRR_A = 9\%$.

e. See the following graph of the MCC and IOS schedules for Clore.

f. Clore clearly should accept Projects B, E, and C. It should reject Projects A and D, because their IRRs do not exceed the marginal costs of funds needed to finance them. The firm's optimal capital budget would total $200,000.

MCC and IOS Schedules
for L. H. Clore Inc.

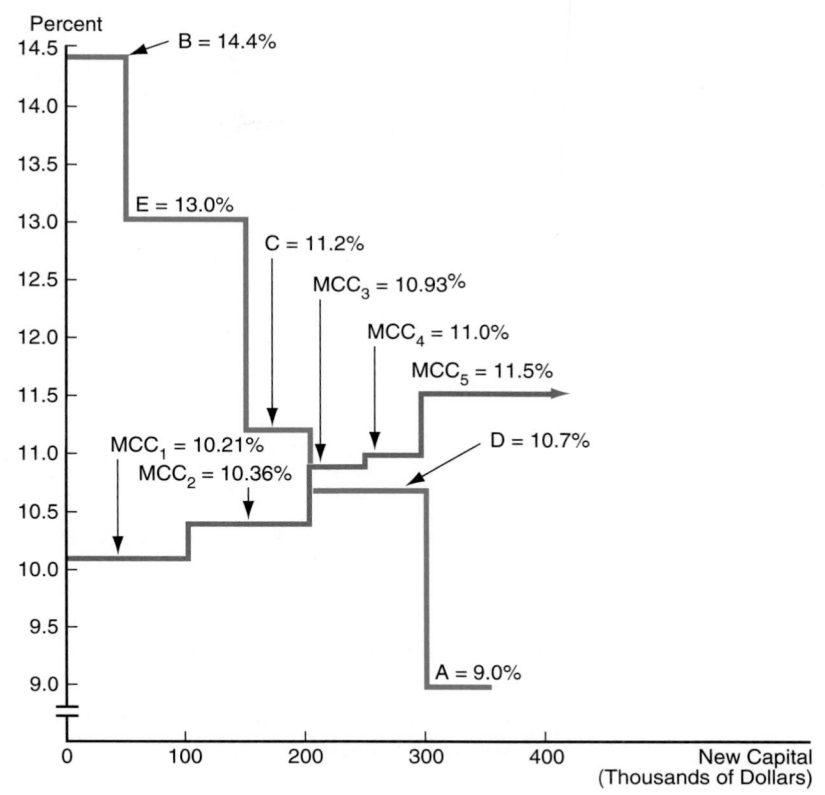

C H A P T E R

20

Leverage and the Target Capital Structure

O B J E C T I V E S

After reading this chapter, you should be able to:

▶ Distinguish between a firm's business risk and its financial risk.

▶ Explain how operating leverage contributes to a firm's business risk and conduct a linear breakeven analysis, complete with breakeven chart.

▶ Define financial leverage and explain the risk-return tradeoff associated with capital structure policy.

▶ State what is meant by a firm's optimal capital structure.

▶ Demonstrate how the degree of operating leverage, DOL, and the degree of financial leverage, DFL, interact to determine a firm's degree of total leverage, DTL.

▶ List several practical considerations which influence the determination of a firm's target capital structure.

DECISION IN FINANCE

RIPE FOR THE PICKING

I f an offer came in that was just too good to refuse, then it would be accepted, according to Rohr Inc.'s interim chairman, James J. Kerley. Otherwise, the troubled aircraft parts manufacturer says it is not seeking a buyout and has not received any proposals.

Rohr provides 43 percent of the world demand for jet engine housings, or nacelles, and also makes pylons that connect engines to planes. It has valuable contracts with Airbus Industrie of Europe and with Boeing, which uses Rohr thrust reversers and fan cowls for its 757s.

Nevertheless, Rohr has problems. Its expansion during the 1980s led to debt of $700 million, compared with its total equity of only $450 million. "We took on a large amount of production risk that required a great deal more investment," said Kerley, a former outside director who had been tapped to replace Chairman Robert H. Goldsmith, who retired. "We didn't analyze the capital structure requirements as carefully as we might have."

A problem that developed in early 1992 led to an investigation into possible defective testing at a Riverside, California, plant. Management expected that the investigation would lead to an indictment by a grand jury, but a year later, the U.S. attorney's office in Los Angeles said the inquiry was continuing, and Rohr officials said they thought a settlement could be worked out.

See end of chapter for resolution.

Source: © Telegraph Colour Library, FPG International Corp.

"There was no purposeful mischief," commented former chairman Goldsmith, "and nobody was harmed."

The company also faces a wrongful termination suit that could lead to as much as $5.9 million in damages, and in November 1992 it lost a lucrative contract for Pratt & Whit-

ney engine nacelles to Martin Marietta. Another apparent problem was the early retirement of Goldsmith after just two years in an expected five-year term of office and the resignation of Rohr's chief financial officer after he had been on the job for just six months. Finally, and most importantly, there was a general slump in the airline industry—reduced orders caused Rohr's sales to drop an expected 10 percent for fiscal 1993. As a result of all this, Rohr had 1,770 fewer employees at the end of 1992 than in August 1991, and it was talking of 2,000 more layoffs over the next few years.

Despite its problems, Rohr's management rejected an offer in December 1992 to provide

$150 million in exchange for convertible preferred stock, which would have given the bidder a one-third interest in the firm. The proposal, by an investment company called the Carlyle Group and some unnamed U.S. and European partners, also included the replacement of $150 million of Rohr's short-term debt with a longer term, lower-interest-rate issue. The Carlyle Group also wanted a seat on the 11-member Rohr board of directors.

As you read this chapter, consider the risks under which Rohr continues to operate and the possible solutions to its problems. Does its debt position make it unusually vulnerable to a takeover? Should its stockholders, as opposed to its management, fear a takeover?

In Chapter 19, when we calculated the weighted average cost of capital for use in capital budgeting, we took the capital structure weights, or the mix of securities the firm uses to finance its assets, as a given. However, if the weights are changed, the calculated cost of capital, and thus the set of acceptable projects, will also change. Further, changing the capital structure will affect the riskiness inherent in the firm's common stock, and this will affect k_s and P_0. Therefore, the choice of a capital structure is an important decision.

In this chapter we will do the following: (1) We will break down a firm's total risk in yet another way, namely, into *business risk* versus *financial risk*. (2) Next we will examine *operating leverage*, one of several contributing factors to a firm's business risk, and, in the process, we will look at linear *break-even analysis*. (3) A discussion of *financial leverage* will follow, and this is where we will return to consider capital structure weights, as we attempt to determine a firm's *optimal capital structure*. (4) The discussion of *degree of leverage* will serve to show the interrelationship between operating leverage and financial leverage. Neither can be discussed in isolation since both contribute to a firm's total risk. (5) Finally, we will discuss *practical determinants of capital structure*, including a checklist of considerations where some will apply to a given firm while others may not.

Types of Risk

Throughout this text we have emphasized many different facets of risk. In Chapter 1, we introduced the concept of the risk-return tradeoff, and we indicated that corporate financial decisions will affect both risk and return and, therefore, the value of the firm. We have seen several illustrations of the risk-return tradeoff, for example, in the chapters on working capital management. Then, in Chapter 12, we examined risk from the viewpoint of the individual investor, and we distinguished between *market risk*, which cannot be diversified away and is measured by the beta coefficient, and *company-specific risk* which *can* be eliminated by diversification. In Chapter 15 we again viewed risk from the firm's viewpoint, considering how capital budgeting decisions affect the riskiness of the firm. There we distinguished between *beta (or market) risk* (the effect of a project on the firm's market risk) and *corporate (or within-firm) risk* (the effect of the project on the firm's total risk).

Now we introduce two new dimensions of risk:

1. *Business risk,* which is the riskiness of the firm's operations if it uses only common equity financing.

2. *Financial risk,* which is the additional risk placed on the common stockholders as a result of the firm's decision to use debt or preferred stock in its financing.

Conceptually, the firm has a certain amount of risk inherent in its operations; this is its business risk. When it uses fixed-rate financing (debt or preferred stock), there is the additional risk to common stockholders that the fixed payments (interest and preferred dividends) must be paid *prior* to any common stock dividends. We will come back to financial risk later in this chapter, but for now we will focus on the first of the two risk elements, business risk.

Business Risk

business risk

The risk associated with future operating income; the risk that would exist even if the firm's operations were all equity financed.

The uncertainty associated with forecasting and realizing future operating income—earnings before interest and taxes (EBIT)—is called **business risk.** The element of uncertainty associated with business risk includes both the chance of not reaching a positive level of operating profits and the problems associated with fluctuating returns. Year-to-year fluctuations can be caused by many events—booms or recessions in the national economy, successful new products introduced either by the firm or by its competitors, labor strikes, price controls, changes in the prices of raw materials, or disasters such as fires, floods, hurricanes, and the like.

Business risk derives from a number of sources, the more important of which are the following:

1. **Demand (unit sales) variability.**   The less stable the unit sales of a firm's products, other things held constant, the higher its business risk.

2. **Sales price variability.**   Firms whose products are sold in highly volatile markets are exposed to more business risk than similar firms whose sales prices are relatively stable.

3. **Input price variability.**   Firms whose input prices are highly uncertain are exposed to greater business risk.

4. **Inability to adjust output prices for changes in input prices.**   Some firms have considerable difficulty in raising their own sales prices when input costs rise, and such firms experience a great deal of business risk. This factor is especially important during periods of high inflation.

5. **Changing technology.**   If a company operates in an industry where technology is changing rapidly and where new products are constantly being introduced, it will be exposed to a high level of business risk.

6. **The extent to which operating costs are fixed: operating leverage.** If a high percentage of a firm's operating costs are fixed, and hence do not decline when demand falls off, this increases the company's business risk. This factor is called *operating leverage,* and it is discussed at length in the next section.

Each of these factors is determined in part by the firm's industry characteristics, but most of them are also controllable to some extent by management. For example, most firms can, through their marketing policies, take actions to stabilize both unit sales and sales prices. However, this stabilization may require either large expenditures on advertising or price concessions to induce customers to commit to purchasing fixed quantities at fixed prices in the future. Similarly, firms can reduce the volatility of future input costs by negotiating long-term labor and materials supply contracts, but they may have to agree to pay prices above the current market prices to obtain these contracts.

As should be clear from the points listed, business risk varies not only from industry to industry but also among firms within a given industry. Furthermore, business risk can change over time. For example, electric utilities, regarded for years as having little business risk, were affected by a combination of events in the 1970s and 1980s that drastically altered their situation, producing sharp declines in operating income for some companies, and greatly increasing the industry's business risk. Two other examples of "safe" industries that turned out to be risky are the railroads just before automobiles, airplanes, and trucks took away most of their business, and the telegraph business just before telephones came on the scene. Today food processors and grocery retailers are frequently given as examples of industries with low business risk, whereas cyclical manufacturing industries, such as steel, are regarded as having especially high business risk.

Again, business risk is the risk associated with forecasting and realizing future operating income; that is, it has to do with the variability of EBIT. *Note that if a firm uses no financial leverage (debt and preferred stock), the variability of its ROE (return on equity) will be exactly equal to the variability of its EBIT.* In that case, the firm's total risk is equal to its business risk; it has no financial risk. On the other hand, any time a firm uses financial leverage, any given change in its EBIT will be accompanied by a greater than proportional change in its ROE.[1] We will come back to this topic later in the chapter.

Self-Test

What is the difference between business risk and financial risk?

Identify and briefly explain some of the more important sources of business risk.

Why does business risk vary from one industry to another?

Give two or three examples of industries where the level of business risk has changed over time.

Operating Leverage and Breakeven Analysis

operating leverage
The extent to which fixed costs are used in a firm's operation.

If a high percentage of a firm's total costs are fixed, the firm is said to have high **operating leverage.** In physics, leverage implies the use of a lever to raise a heavy object with a small amount of force. In politics, people who have lever-

---

[1]The same can be said for earnings per share (EPS), if we assume no change in the number of shares outstanding.

Table 20-1	**Fixed Operating Costs**[a]	**Variable Operating Costs**
Fixed and Variable Operating Costs	Depreciation on plant and equipment Rent and lease payments Salaries of research staff Salaries of executive staff General office expenses	Factory labor Materials Sales commissions

[a]Some of these costs—for example, salaries and office expenses—can be variable to some degree; hence, they are often called *semivariable* costs. However, firms are reluctant to reduce these expenditures in response to temporary fluctuations in sales, and they are often constrained from doing so by labor agreements and other contractual arrangements. Hence, de facto, fixed costs are generally greater than one might think.

age can accomplish a great deal with their smallest word or action. *In business terminology, high operating leverage means that, other things held constant, a relatively small change in sales will result in a large change in operating income (and ROE).* The common element in all of these examples is that a small initiating change is followed by a proportionally greater effect.

fixed operating costs

Operating costs that do not vary directly with sales; that is, costs that would exist even if no sales were made. Examples include depreciation and lease payments.

variable operating costs

Operating costs that vary directly with sales. For example, factory labor, materials, and sales commissions.

breakeven analysis

An analytical technique for studying the relationship between fixed costs, variable costs, sales volume, and operating profits.

Fixed operating costs are operating costs that do not vary directly with sales but would be incurred even if a firm made no sales. **Variable operating costs,** on the other hand, vary directly with sales. Examples of both types of costs are listed in Table 20-1. Note that interest charges are not included in the table. Interest charges is a *financial* cost as opposed to an *operating* cost; it will, therefore, influence financial leverage but not operating leverage.

Breakeven Analysis

The relationship between fixed and variable operating costs, sales volume, and operating profits is explored in breakeven analysis. **Breakeven analysis** is a method of determining the point at which sales revenue will just cover operating costs—that is, the point at which the firm will break even—but it also shows the magnitude of the firm's operating profits or losses if sales exceed or fall below that point. Breakeven analysis is important in the planning process because the cost-volume-profit relationship can be greatly influenced by the firm's investment in assets which have fixed operating costs, such as depreciation, and changes in the ratio of fixed to variable costs are a result of the firm's ongoing capital budgeting decisions. A sufficient volume of sales must be achieved such that fixed and variable costs will be covered, or else the firm will incur operating losses.

Breakeven analysis, as developed here, shows the breakeven point *before* interest charges. The reason for this emphasis is that, at this point, we are concerned with the firm's *operating plan* rather than its *financing plan*. We will expand the analysis to include financial charges later in this chapter, when we take up the issue of debt versus equity financing.

Breakeven Chart.   The essentials of breakeven analysis are depicted in Figure 20-1, the basic linear breakeven chart. Here units produced and sold are shown on the horizontal axis, and revenues and costs are measured on the vertical axis. We assume that the number of units sold is equal to the number of units

Figure 20-1
Breakeven Chart

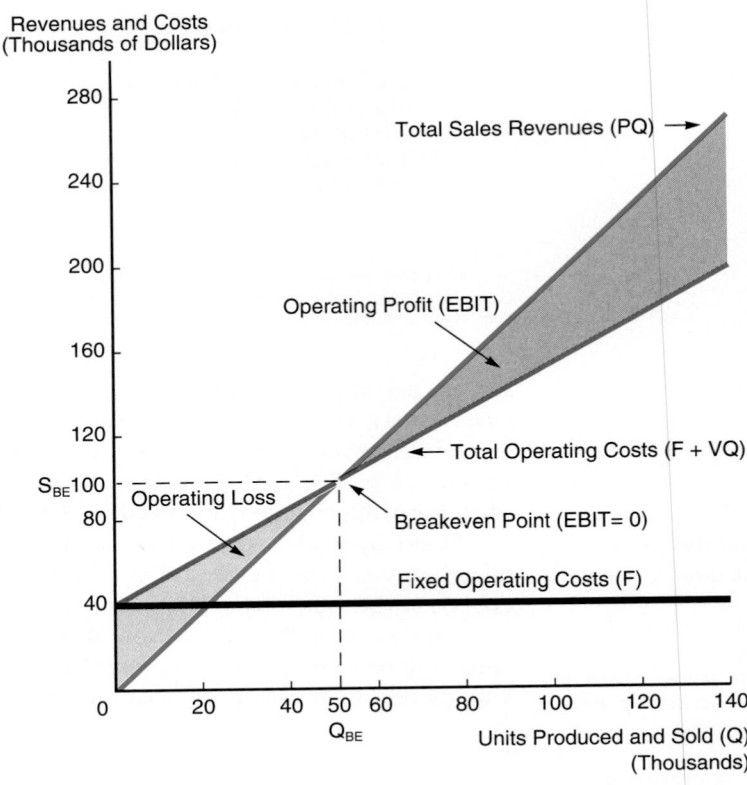

Revenues and Costs
(Thousands of Dollars)

Total Sales Revenues (PQ)

Operating Profit (EBIT)

Total Operating Costs (F + VQ)

S_{BE} 100   Operating Loss

Breakeven Point (EBIT= 0)

Fixed Operating Costs (F)

Q_{BE}

Units Produced and Sold (Q)
(Thousands)

Notes:
S = sales in dollars; S_{BE} = breakeven sales in dollars.
Q = sales in units; Q_{BE} = breakeven sales in units.
F = fixed operating costs = $40,000.
V = variable costs per unit = $1.20.
P = price per unit = $2.00.

A breakeven chart shows both the breakeven sales in dollars (here $100,000) and the breakeven sales in units (here 50,000) needed to cover all operating costs, both fixed and variable. At the breakeven point, operating income (EBIT) is $0, below the breakeven point the firm will experience an operating loss, while above the breakeven point sales revenue will exceed total operating costs and the result will be an operating profit.

---

produced. Fixed operating costs of $40,000 are represented by a horizontal line; they are the same (fixed) regardless of the number of units produced. Variable costs are assumed to be $1.20 a unit, so (1) total variable costs are found by multiplying $1.20 by the number of units sold, and (2) the total cost line rises at a rate of $1.20 for each unit produced and sold. Therefore, the total operating costs function, which is equal to fixed costs plus total variable costs, is shown on the graph as a straight line with a Y intercept of $40,000 and a slope of $1.20.

Each unit produced is assumed to be sold at a price of $2. Therefore, a second straight line, with a Y intercept of zero and a slope of $2, is used to depict total sales revenues. The slope of the total revenues line is steeper than that of the total operating costs line because the firm is gaining $2 of revenue for every $1.20 it pays out for labor and materials as each new unit is produced and sold. At the point where the total revenues line cuts the total operating costs line, the firm's total revenues are just equal to its total operating costs, and at that volume the firm breaks even. Before the breakeven volume is reached, the firm suffers operating losses, but after that point, it earns larger and larger operating profits as sales increase.

Breakeven Sales Volume.   Figure 20-1 shows that the breakeven sales volume is 50,000 units; at that volume, sales revenues and total operating costs are both $100,000. We could calculate the breakeven point algebraically, rather than graphically. From the data given, the firm's total sales revenues are

$$S = PQ \tag{20-1}$$
$$= \$2Q,$$

where S is total sales in dollars, P is the sales price per unit, and Q is the volume in units. The total operating cost equation is

$$TC = F + VQ \tag{20-2}$$
$$= \$40{,}000 + \$1.20Q,$$

where F is total fixed operating costs and V is the variable operating cost per unit.

breakeven point (Q_{BE})
The volume of sales at which total operating costs equal total revenues and operating income (EBIT) equals zero.

At the **breakeven point, Q_{BE},** total sales revenues and total operating costs are equal. Therefore, the sales and cost functions are equal to one another, and, solving, we find the breakeven volume to be 50,000 units:

$$\$2Q_{BE} = \$40{,}000 + \$1.20Q_{BE}$$
$$Q_{BE} = 50{,}000 \text{ units.}$$

In general, we can use this formula to find the breakeven volume in units, Q_{BE}:

$$Q_{BE} = \frac{F}{P - V}. \tag{20-3}$$

Thus, in our example,

$$Q_{BE} = \frac{\$40{,}000}{\$2.00 - \$1.20} = \frac{\$40{,}000}{\$0.80} = 50{,}000 \text{ units.}$$

If we know both the breakeven volume in units and the sales price, then we can find the breakeven volume in dollars, S_{BE}:

$$S_{BE} = PQ_{BE}. \tag{20-3a}$$

Thus,

$$S_{BE} = \$2(50{,}000) = \$100{,}000.$$

Thus, the breakeven point in either units or in dollar sales can be calculated by use of Equation 20-3 or 20-3a.

The breakeven point based on dollar sales may also be calculated directly:

$$S_{BE} = \frac{F}{1 - \dfrac{V}{P}}. \qquad (20\text{-}4)$$

In our example,

$$S_{BE} = \frac{\$40,000}{1 - \dfrac{\$1.20}{\$2.00}} = \frac{\$40,000}{1 - 0.60} = \$100,000.$$

Breakeven analysis can shed light on three important types of business decisions: (1) When one is making new product decisions, breakeven analysis can help determine how large the sales of a new product must be for the firm to achieve profitability. (2) Breakeven analysis can be used to study the effects of a general expansion in the level of the firm's operations; an expansion would cause the levels of both fixed and variable costs to rise, but it would also increase expected sales. (3) When the firm is considering modernization and automation projects, where the fixed investment in equipment is increased in order to lower variable costs, particularly the cost of labor, breakeven analysis can help management analyze the consequences of these projects. In addition, breakeven analysis ties in closely with the concepts of business risk and operating leverage.

Operating Leverage

As noted previously, business risk would exist even if the firm had no fixed operating costs and, thus, used no operating leverage. However, when the firm has some fixed operating expenses, as the majority of firms do, by definition, it is using operating leverage and a change in its sales will result in a greater than proportional change in operating profits and ROE. Business risk is intensified to the extent that a firm builds fixed costs into its operations. If fixed costs are high, the breakeven point is high, and even a small decline in sales can lead to a large decline in EBIT and ROE. Thus, other things held constant, the higher a firm's fixed operating costs, the greater its operating leverage and business risk. Higher fixed operating costs are generally associated with more highly automated, capital intensive firms and industries. Also, businesses that employ highly skilled workers who must be retained and paid even during business recessions have relatively high fixed operating costs.

Figure 20-2 provides an illustration by comparing the results that All-Technology Manufacturing (ATM) can expect if it uses different amounts of operating leverage. Option 1 calls for a relatively small amount of fixed operating costs, which will be accomplished by using less automated equipment. Depreciation, maintenance, property taxes, and so on, will be lower than in the case of the other operating option. Note, however, that under Option 1 the total cost line in Figure 20-2 has a relatively steep slope, indicating that variable operating costs are higher per unit than if the firm were to use more operating leverage. Option 2 calls for a higher level of fixed operating costs in order to reduce variable costs per unit. Here the firm uses more automated equipment, thereby

Figure 20-2 All-Technology Manufacturing: Effect of Operating Leverage

Option 1

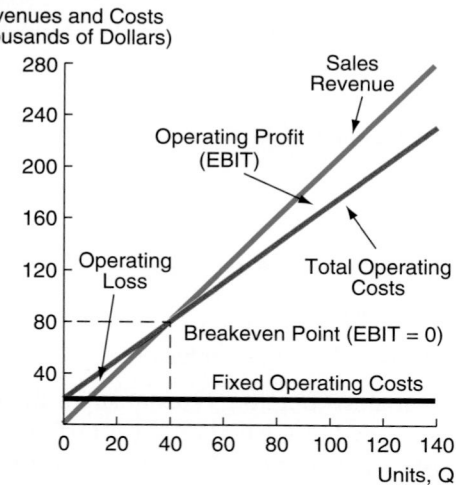

Price per unit = $2.00
Fixed operating costs = $20,000
Variable costs per unit = $1.50

Option 2

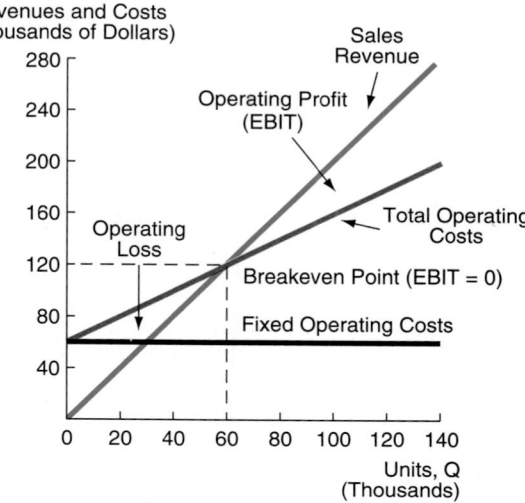

Price per unit = $2.00
Fixed operating costs = $60,000
Variable costs per unit = $1.00

Units Sold, Q	Sales Revenue	Option 1 Total Operating Costs	Option 1 Operating Profit (EBIT)	NI	ROE	Option 2 Total Operating Costs	Option 2 Operating Profit (EBIT)	NI	ROE
0	$ 0	$ 20,000	($20,000)	($12,000)	(6.0%)	$ 60,000	($60,000)	($36,000)	(18.0%)
40,000	80,000	80,000	0	0	0.0	100,000	(20,000)	(12,000)	(6.0)
60,000	120,000	110,000	10,000	6,000	3.0	120,000	0	0	0.0
80,000	160,000	140,000	20,000	12,000	6.0	140,000	20,000	12,000	6.0
100,000	200,000	170,000	30,000	18,000	9.0	160,000	40,000	24,000	12.0
110,000	220,000	185,000	35,000	21,000	10.5	170,000	50,000	30,000	15.0
160,000	320,000	260,000	60,000	36,000	18.0	220,000	100,000	60,000	30.0
180,000	360,000	290,000	70,000	42,000	21.0	240,000	120,000	72,000	36.0
200,000	400,000	320,000	80,000	48,000	24.0	260,000	140,000	84,000	42.0
Expected value			$30,000	$18,000	9.0%		$40,000	$24,000	12.0%

Notes:
a. ATM has a 40 percent federal-plus-state tax rate.
b. The firm has no debt, so Assets = Equity = $200,000.
c. ATM's expected sales are 100,000 units ($2.00) = $200,000.

This figure demonstrates that higher operating leverage (i.e., higher fixed operating costs) will create higher business risk and greater potential variability in EBIT and ROE. *Assume that ATM's expected sales are 100,000 units at $2.00 each.* Option 1 has one-third the fixed operating costs of Option 2, and as a result, Option 2 has a higher breakeven point. As both the graphs and tables show, the further sales move away from the breakeven point, the more profits or losses under Option 2 exceed those under Option 1.

requiring fewer workers to make its product. Automation allows an operator to turn out few or many products at the same labor cost. Therefore, to reduce variable cost per unit, Option 2 employs more fixed operating costs. The differences in the way fixed and variable operating costs are apportioned between Option 1 and Option 2 result in a breakeven point that is higher under Option 2:

For Option 1,

$$Q_{BE} = \$20,000/(\$2.00 - \$1.50)$$

$$= 40,000 \text{ units.}$$

For Option 2,

$$Q_{BE} = \$60,000/(\$2.00 - \$1.00)$$

$$= 60,000 \text{ units.}$$

Based on Figure 20-2, we can reach the following conclusions:

1. Changing the mix of fixed and variable operating costs changes the breakeven point. The breakeven point is higher for Option 2 (at 60,000 units) because the fixed operating costs are higher for this option than for Option 1.

2. By definition, Option 2 uses higher operating leverage than Option 1, and Option 2 would—other things equal—result in higher business risk for ATM.

3. Assuming an underlying probability distribution such that expected sales equal 100,000 units ($200,000), we see an expected EBIT of $40,000 under Option 2 versus only $30,000 under Option 1.

4. The higher business risk for Option 2 is seen in the greater *variability* of its EBIT, which ranges from −$60,000 to $140,000, while the range of EBIT if Option 1 is used is only from −$20,000 to $80,000. If we had a complete probability distribution, we could calculate a standard deviation for EBIT under both options, and it would be greater for Option 2.

5. The greater variability of EBIT under Option 2 is the *direct cause* of the greater variability in NI and ROE (compare the ranges of these to the ranges of NI and ROE under Option 1); this is because of our assumption, *at this point,* that ATM is 100 percent equity financed. We will change this assumption in the next section when we bring financial leverage into our analysis.

6. The ATM illustration provides us with another example of the risk-return tradeoff: Higher expected EBIT, NI, and ROE are available at a price; that price is higher business risk.

Holding other things constant, the higher a firm's operating leverage, the greater its business risk as measured by the variability of EBIT, net income, and ROE.

To what extent can firms control their operating leverage? For the most part, operating leverage is determined by technology. Electric utilities, telephone companies, airlines, steel mills, and chemical companies simply *must* have heavy investments in fixed assets; this results in high fixed operating costs and high operating leverage. Grocery stores, on the other hand, generally have substantially lower fixed operating costs and, hence, lower operating leverage. Still, although industry factors do exert a major influence, all firms have some control over their operating leverage. For example, an electric utility can expand its generating capacity by building either a nuclear reactor or a coal-fired plant. The nuclear plant would require a larger investment in fixed assets, which would involve higher fixed operating costs, but its variable operating costs would be relatively low. The coal plant, on the other hand, would require a smaller investment in fixed assets and would have lower fixed operating costs, but the variable operating costs (for coal) would be high. Thus, by its capital budgeting decisions a utility (or any other company) can influence its operating leverage and, hence, its basic business risk.

The concept of operating leverage was, in fact, originally developed for use in capital budgeting. Alternative methods for producing a given product often have different amounts of operating leverage and, therefore, different breakeven points and different levels of business risk. Companies regularly undertake some type of breakeven analysis as part of their evaluation of proposed new projects. Still, once established, the firm's operating leverage, and hence the extent to which operating leverage will cause future operating profits to fluctuate, is an important factor in determining the firm's capital structure, as we demonstrate in the next section.[2]

? Self-Test

Is interest paid considered in a breakeven analysis? Why or why not?

Give the equations used to calculate the breakeven point in units and in dollar sales.

Give some examples of business decisions for which breakeven analysis might be useful.

What is the association between the concepts of breakeven and operating leverage?

What happens to a firm's business risk, other things equal, if it increases its operating leverage?

In which dollar and percentage measures would we see greater variability if a firm increases its operating leverage?

To what extent can firms control their operating leverage?

---

[2]It is interesting to note that ATM chose neither Option 1 nor Option 2 for its operating leverage. Rather, as is often the case, the firm chose a compromise between the two options. Recall that Option 1 had the higher variable-cost ratio (75 percent of sales) but a lower level of fixed costs, $20,000, and Option 2 had lower variable costs (50 percent of sales) but higher fixed costs, $60,000. The compromise option selected a mid-level for both costs, with variable operating costs at 60 percent of sales and fixed operating costs of $40,000, as we shall see in the next section. ATM's breakeven chart would, therefore, be like the one shown in Figure 20-1.

LEANER AND MEANER

Changes in top management and in the way corporations operate mark many U.S. firms' drive to cut costs. This often means slashing bureaucratic lard, closing plants, selling off sidelines, and even adopting more conservative accounting practices. Among major companies that recently named outsiders with reputations for tough cost cutting to top positions are General Motors, Kodak, Westinghouse, and IBM.

Paul H. O'Neill, chairman of Alcoa, was tapped for the GM board of directors to help it cope with the company's struggling domestic auto operations. Its activist board undertook a major review of GM's past financial management and its financial plan for the future "to confirm that our financial and operating plans are on target," the company announced.

Known for his cost-reduction campaign at Alcoa, where he closed factories and cut headquarters staff, O'Neill apparently thinks like GM's top bosses. Both Chairman John G. Smale and President/CEO John F. Smith, Jr., have emphasized the importance of shrinking bureaucracy and tightening operations.

Meanwhile, the cost-cutting efforts at a GM rival, Chrysler, lowered its breakeven point on vehicle sales from 1.9 million in 1991 to 1.7 million in 1992. Standard & Poor's upgraded Chrysler's bonds, announcing that "Chrysler's competitive position is improving significantly as a result of successful new products and its extensive, ongoing cost-cutting initiatives."

At Kodak, Christopher J. Steffen was hired from Honeywell to become chief financial officer and senior vice-president — the first outsider in 20 years to be tapped for a top position. Steffen led a successful turnaround of Honeywell, where he was known as an aggressive cost-cutter. When his predecessor came to Kodak, it had one of the strongest financial positions in corporate America. By the time he retired, 10 years later, the company was burdened with debt. Steffen said Kodak needs a "definitive change." Meanwhile,

rumors abounded that as many as 4,000 employees would soon be laid off.

Just months after the major changes took place at Kodak and GM, an outsider was also chosen by Westinghouse as chairman and chief executive officer. For that company, it was the first time in 64 years that the top post was not filled from within. The new man, Michael H. Jordan, formerly headed international operations at PepsiCo.

When he took over in July 1993, Jordan said he would accelerate Westinghouse's efforts to "cut out the losers and adjust the cost structure." He is also expected to cut out some layers of management. A major shareholder said, "There's an awfully big need for somebody to come in, draw a line in the sand, and say 'We're going to do this and do this' and then do it." Another commented that "patience is running thin" with the company's troubles. "We want [Jordan] to act quickly."

Meanwhile, not just personnel changes but new ways of operating are being undertaken by an entire industry in an effort to cut costs. Airlines in the United States lost about $8 billion in the first three years of the 1990s. In an effort to boost profits, some lines have reduced their meal service and started charging higher fees for replacing lost tickets. But both individuals and businesses will feel the effects of a much more drastic change that major players in the industry are initiating — cutting service to unprofitable areas by eliminating some hubs and spokes from the route systems. Among smaller hubs cut in 1992 were those at Milwaukee, Dayton, and Washington, D.C.'s National Airport. An air industry consultant said as many as 10 more of the nation's remaining 32 hubs may be shut down within a few more years.

Airlines are in "a death march for market share," said John Garel of Northwest Airlines. The economic boom of the 1980s fueled a high demand for the growing number of flights generated by the innovative hub and spoke system. When recession hit, passenger volume fell, and the high costs of maintaining hubs could not be covered by the reduced loads. The airlines' routes spread over the country like spiderwebs, and the carriers found themselves with too many hubs too close together, competing for the same passengers.

Sources: Joseph B. White, "GM Taps Alcoa's Chairman O'Neill, Known for Cost-Cutting Drive, for Board," *The Wall Street Journal,* January 12, 1993, A3; Joan E. Rigdon, "Kodak Selects C. J. Steffen for Senior Post," *The Wall Street Journal,* January 12, 1993, A3; James S. Hirsch, "Big Airlines Scale Back Hub-Airport System to Curb Rising Costs," *The Wall Street Journal,* January 12, 1993, A1; Erle Norton, "Westinghouse Names Jordan to Top Posts," *The Wall Street Journal,* July 1, 1993, A3.

USAir reduced flights to its former Dayton hub by 66 percent and eliminated its nonstop service to many cities throughout the country. A local business has found its product shipment time tripled as a result.

United Airlines said it would cut its service to Washington's Dulles Airport by 38 percent, among other reductions, and Delta also announced cutbacks in routes. The hubs most likely to close are those in smaller cities that do not generate much traffic as well as those operated by airlines under Chapter 11 bankruptcy proceedings. The latter group includes Continental's hubs in Houston, Cleveland, and Newark; TWA's in St. Louis; and America West's in Phoenix and Las Vegas.

All these changes have inconvenienced many passengers. The president of a farm equipment company in Sioux City, Iowa, complained, "Now, a one-day trip to the West Coast takes three days of travel." The same customer, when he goes east from his small city, must also suffer the inconvenience of slower and smaller planes. "When I stand up," said the 6-foot 7-inch executive, "my shoulders are on the ceiling."

Many airlines have replaced some jet flights with less expensive commuter planes. American eliminated 10 jets and substituted 7 turboprops at its San Jose, California, hub. USAir did much the same thing in Baltimore. Passengers who do not like to fly in small planes may have to travel farther on the ground to complete their trips in jets. A travel agent in Iowa said some of his customers drive an hour and a half to a larger airport in Nebraska rather than take a small connecting carrier from their hometown.

The moves by the airlines do result in lower costs —but not to passengers. As routes are eliminated and as more small planes are flown, ticket prices go up because there are fewer excess seats to sell.

"Airlines are becoming less concerned with the price-sensitive passenger," said Michael Boyd, a Denver aviation consultant. "Eventually, the airlines have to figure out a way to produce more revenue, and that likely means higher prices one way or the other."

Financial Leverage

Financial leverage was defined in Chapter 6 as the extent to which a firm uses debt (or preferred stock) financing. Financial leverage is thus the extent to which *fixed-rate* securities are used in a firm's capital structure. You should see a parallel between operating leverage and financial leverage: in operating leverage we were talking about fixed *operating* costs; now we are dealing with fixed *financing* costs and the implications of these for the firm and its stockholders. That being said, recognize that many firms do not use preferred stock. For this reason, and in order to simplify matters somewhat, we will assume that ATM uses only debt and common equity, and we will use the debt ratio as our measure of financial leverage in the remainder of this chapter.

Not only did we define and discuss financial leverage in Chapter 6 when we introduced the debt ratio, but later in the chapter, financial leverage was shown to be an important link in the extended, or modified, Du Pont equation, Equation 6-3 (you may want to review these sections at this point). Recall also from Chapter 6 the "Industry Practice" boxed feature, "Trying to Deleverage Corporate America." The essence of this feature was that hundreds of companies in the 1990s are attempting to get out from under the burden of debt that they took on during the 1980s (sometimes called "the decade of debt"). Many of these companies have succeeded in cleaning up their balance sheets; that is, they have substituted equity for much of their debt.[3] So, does that mean that

---

[3]Others, as we discussed in Chapter 16, have been able to call large amounts of high-coupon debt and issue lower cost bonds instead, as long-term interest rates have continued their downward trend. This group of firms may or may not have changed their debt ratios, but they have dramatically reduced the fixed costs associated with their outstanding bonds: the interest charges.

debt is bad? As you might suspect, the answer is not so simple. Financial leverage has the *potential* to boost, or increase, the returns to the common stockholders (typically measured either by ROE or EPS); however, financial leverage places additional risk on the common stockholders—over and above the business risk of the firm. Capital structure policy involves a risk-return tradeoff: Higher expected returns to stockholders should raise the stock's price, but the greater risk resulting from the use of debt tends to lower it. *Therefore, the optimal capital structure is the one that strikes a balance between risk and return to maximize the price of the stock.*

Note that in Chapter 19, capital structure was held constant (the weights were not changed) as we increased the level of the budget in order to observe the effect on the WACC. In this chapter, we will do precisely the opposite: *We will assume a constant budget level,* and we will change the mix of long-term financing in an attempt to find the optimal capital structure weights.

Financial Risk

financial risk

The portion of stockholders' risk, over and above basic business risk, resulting from the use of financial leverage.

Conceptually, the firm has a certain amount of risk inherent in its operations; this is its business risk. **Financial risk** is the additional risk placed on the common stockholders as a result of using financial leverage. By using financial leverage, the firm concentrates its business risk on the common stockholders. To illustrate, suppose 10 people decide to form a corporation to manufacture running shoes. There is a certain amount of business risk in the operation. If the firm is financed only with common equity and if each person buys 10 percent of the stock, then each investor will bear an equal share of the business risk. However, suppose the firm is financed with 50 percent debt and 50 percent equity, with 5 of the investors putting up their capital as debt and the other 5 putting up their money as equity. In this case, the investors who put up the equity will have to bear essentially all of the business risk, so their common stock will be twice as risky as it would have been had the firm been financed only with equity. *Thus, the use of debt concentrates the firm's business risk on its stockholders.*

In the next section, we will explain how financial leverage affects a firm's expected earnings per share, the riskiness of those earnings, and, consequently, the price of the firm's stock. As you will see, the value of a firm that has no debt first rises as it substitutes debt for equity, then hits a peak, and finally declines as the use of debt becomes excessive. The objective of our analysis is to determine the capital structure at which value is maximized; this point is then used as the *target capital structure.*[4]

---

[4]We will examine capital structures on a *book value* (or *balance sheet) basis.* An alternative approach is to calculate the market values of debt, preferred stock, and common equity and then to reconstruct the balance sheet on a *market value basis.* Although the market value approach is more consistent with financial theory, bond rating agencies and most financial executives focus their attention on book values. Moreover, the conversion from book to market values is a complicated process, and since market value capital structures change with stock market fluctuations, they are thought by many to be too unstable to serve as operationally useful targets. Finally, exactly the same insights are gained from the book value and market value analyses. For all these reasons, a market value analysis of capital structure is better suited for advanced finance courses.

Self-Test

Is there any similarity, with respect to costs, between operating leverage and financial leverage? Explain.

State the risk-return tradeoff associated with the use of financial leverage.

What is meant by an optimal capital structure?

Determining the Optimal Capital Structure

We can analyze the effects of financial leverage using the data shown in Table 20-2 for our illustrative company, All-Technology Manufacturing (ATM). As shown in the top section of the table, the company currently has no debt. Should ATM continue the policy of using no debt, or should it start using financial leverage? If it does decide to substitute debt for equity, how high should its debt ratio be? As in all such decisions, *the correct answer is that it should choose the capital structure that will maximize the price of its stock.*

Because the price of a share of stock is the present value of the stock's expected future dividends, if the use of financial leverage is to affect the stock's price, it must do so by changing either the expected dividend stream or the required rate of return on equity, k_s, or both. We first consider the effect of capital structure on earnings (and dividends); then we examine its effect on k_s.

Table 20-2

Data on All-Technology Manufacturing

I. Balance Sheet on 12/31/93

Current assets	$100,000	Debt	$ 0
Net fixed assets	100,000	Common equity (10,000 shares outstanding)	200,000
Total assets	$200,000	Total liabilities and equity	$200,000

II. Income Statement for 1993

Sales		$200,000
Fixed operating costs	$ 40,000	
Variable operating costs	120,000	160,000
Earnings before interest and taxes (EBIT)		$ 40,000
Interest		0
Taxable income		$ 40,000
Taxes (40%)		16,000
Net income		$ 24,000

III. Other Data

1. Earnings per share = EPS = $24,000/10,000 shares = $2.40.
2. Dividends per share = DPS = $24,000/10,000 shares = $2.40. (Thus, ATM pays all of its earnings out as dividends. Alternatively stated, ATM has a 100 percent payout ratio.)
3. Book value per share = $200,000/10,000 shares = $20.
4. Market price per share = P_0 = $20. Thus the stock sells at its book value.
5. Price/earnings ratio = P/E = $20/$2.40 = 8.33 times.
6. Variable operating costs equal 60 percent of sales.

Table 20-3

Interest Rates for ATM with Different Debt/Assets Ratios

Amount Borrowed[a]	Debt/Assets Ratio	Interest Rate, k_d, on All Debt
$ 20,000	10%	8.0%
40,000	20	8.3
60,000	30	9.0
80,000	40	10.0
100,000	50	12.0
120,000	60	15.0

[a]We assume that the firm must borrow in increments of $20,000. We also assume that ATM is unable to borrow more than $120,000, or 60 percent of assets, because of restrictions in its corporate charter.

The Effect of Financial Leverage on Expected EPS and Risk

Changes in the use of debt will cause changes in earnings per share (EPS) and consequently in the stock price. To understand the relationship between financial leverage and EPS, consider first Table 20-3, which shows how ATM's cost of debt would vary if it used different percentages of debt in its capital structure. Naturally, the higher the percentage of debt, the riskier the debt, and hence the higher the interest rate lenders will charge.

Table 20-4 goes on to show how expected EPS varies with changes in financial leverage. Section I of the table begins with a probability distribution of sales; we assume for simplicity that sales can take on only three values: $100,000, $200,000, or $300,000. Note that we also assume that EBIT is independent of financial leverage. Therefore, the three EBIT figures ($0, $40,000, and $80,000) will remain the same, no matter which of the six levels of debt ATM chooses.[5]

Section II of Table 20-4 goes on to show the situation if ATM continues to use no debt. Net income is divided by the 10,000 shares outstanding to calculate EPS. If sales are as low as $100,000, EPS will be zero, but at sales of $300,000, EPS will rise to $4.80.

The EPS at each sales level is next multiplied by the probability of that sales level and summed to calculate the expected EPS, which is $2.40 if ATM uses no debt. We also calculate the standard deviation of EPS and the coefficient of varia-

---

[5]*In the real world, capital structure does at times affect EBIT, especially if debt levels are excessive.* A firm with excessive debt will probably not be able to finance at all if its earnings are low at a time when interest rates are high. This could lead to stop-start construction and R&D programs, as well as to the necessity of passing up good investment opportunities. Second, a weak financial condition (i.e., too much debt) could cause a firm to lose sales. For example, prior to the time that its huge debt forced Eastern Airlines into bankruptcy, many people refused to buy Eastern tickets because they were afraid the company would go bankrupt and leave them holding unusable tickets. Third, financially strong companies are able to bargain hard with unions as well as with their suppliers, whereas weaker ones may have to give in simply because they do not have the financial resources to carry on the fight. Finally, a company with so much debt that bankruptcy is a serious threat will have difficulty attracting and retaining managers and employees, or it will have to pay premium salaries. People value job security, and financially weak companies simply cannot provide such protection. For all these reasons, it is not totally correct to say that a firm's financial policy has no effect on its operating income, however, the effect is usually difficult to quantify.

Table 20-4

ATM: EPS with Different Amounts of Financial Leverage (Thousands of Dollars except Per-Share Figures)

I. Calculation of EBIT

Probability of indicated sales	0.2	0.6	0.2
Sales	$100.0	$200.0	$300.0
Fixed operating costs	40.0	40.0	40.0
Variable operating costs (60% of sales)	60.0	120.0	180.0
Total operating costs	$100.0	$160.0	$220.0
Earnings before interest and taxes (EBIT)	$ 0.0	$ 40.0	$ 80.0

II. Situation if Debt/Assets (D/A) = 0%

EBIT (from Section I)	$ 0.0	$ 40.0	$ 80.0
Less: Interest	0.0	0.0	0.0
Earnings before taxes (EBT)	$ 0.0	$ 40.0	$ 80.0
Taxes (40%)	0.0	16.0	32.0
Net income	$ 0.0	$ 24.0	$ 48.0
Earnings per share on 10,000 shares (EPS)	$ 0.0	$ 2.40	$ 4.80
Expected EPS		$ 2.40	
Standard deviation of EPS (σ_{EPS})		$ 1.52	
Coefficient of variation (CV_{EPS})		0.63	

III. Situation if Debt/Assets (D/A) = 50%

EBIT (from Section I)	$ 0.0	$ 40.0	$ 80.0
Less: Interest (0.12 × $100,000)	12.0	12.0	12.0
Earnings before taxes (EBT)	($ 12.0)	$ 28.0	$ 68.0
Taxes (40%)	(4.8)[a]	11.2	27.2
Net income	($ 7.2)	$ 16.8	$ 40.8
Earnings per share on 5,000 shares (EPS)	($ 1.44)	$ 3.36	$ 8.16
Expected EPS		$ 3.36	
Standard deviation of EPS (σ_{EPS})		$ 3.04	
Coefficient of variation (CV_{EPS})		0.90	

[a]Assumes tax credit on losses.

tion as indicators of the firm's risk at a zero debt ratio: σ_{EPS} = $1.52, and CV_{EPS} = 0.63.[6]

Section III of the table shows the financial results that would occur if the company financed with a debt/assets ratio of 50 percent. In this situation, $100,000 of the $200,000 total capital would be debt. The interest rate on the debt, 12 percent, is taken from Table 20-3. With $100,000 of 12 percent debt outstanding, the company's interest expense is shown in Table 20-4 to be $12,000 per year. This is a fixed financing cost — it is the same regardless of the level of sales — and it is deducted from EBIT as calculated in the top section. Next, taxes are taken out, to derive net income, and EPS is calculated as net income divided by shares outstanding. With debt = $0, there are 10,000 shares outstanding. However, if half the equity were replaced by debt (debt = $100,000), there would be only 5,000 shares outstanding; we use this number

---

[6]See Chapter 12 for a review of procedures for calculating standard deviations and coefficients of variation. Recall that the advantage of the coefficient of variation is that it permits better comparisons when both the expected values and the standard deviations of EPS vary, as they do here.

Figure 20-3

ATM: Probability
Distribution of EPS with
Different Amounts of
Financial Leverage

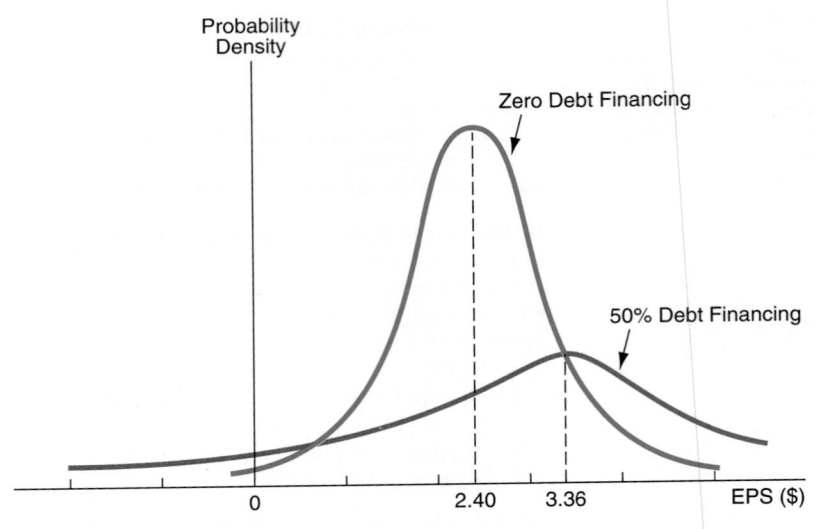

Financial leverage (debt or other fixed-rate securities) affects a firm's expected earnings per share and thus the price of its stock. With zero financial leverage, expected EPS is lower than expected EPS with 50 percent debt ($2.40 versus $3.36). However, with greater financial leverage, the probability of lower or even negative earnings is increased. Clearly, increased financial leverage carries with it both higher expected earnings and greater risk.

to determine the EPS figures that would result at each sales level in Section III.[7] With a debt/assets ratio of 50 percent, EPS would be a negative $1.44 if sales were as low as $100,000; it would rise to $3.36 if sales were $200,000; and it would soar to $8.16 if sales were as high as $300,000. Note that with a debt ratio of 50 percent, expected EPS is higher at $3.36, but our two risk measures have increased as well to $\sigma_{EPS} = \$3.04$ and $CV_{EPS} = 0.90$.

The EPS distributions under the two financial structures are graphed in Figure 20-3, where we use continuous distributions to approximate the discrete distributions contained in Table 20-4. Although expected EPS would be much higher if financial leverage were employed, the graph makes it clear that the risk of low or even negative EPS would also be higher if debt were used.

The relationships among financial leverage, expected EPS, and risk are extended in Table 20-5, and the Table 20-5 data are then plotted in Figure 20-4. Here we see that ATM's expected EPS rises until the firm is financed with 50 percent debt. Interest charges rise, but this is more than offset by the declining number of shares outstanding as debt is substituted for equity. ATM's expected EPS will peak at $3.36 when the firm's debt ratio is 50 percent. Beyond this

---

[7]We assume in this example that the firm could change its capital structure by repurchasing common stock at its book value of $100,000/5,000 shares = $20 per share. However, the firm may actually have to pay a higher price to repurchase its stock on the open market. If the firm had to pay $22 per share, then it could repurchase only $100,000/$22 = 4,545 shares, and in this case, expected EPS would be only $16,800/(10,000 − 4,545) = $16,800/5,455 = $3.08 rather than $3.36.

Table 20-5

ATM: Expected EPS, Standard Deviation, and Coefficient of Variation with Different Amounts of Financial Leverage

Debt/Assets Ratio	Expected EPS	Standard Deviation of EPS	Coefficient of Variation
0%	$2.40[a]	$1.52[a]	0.63[a]
10	2.56	1.69	0.66
20	2.75	1.90	0.69
30	2.97	2.17	0.73
40	3.20	2.53	0.79
50	3.36[a]	3.04[a]	0.90[a]
60	3.30	3.79	1.15

[a]Values for D/A = 0 and 50 percent were taken from Table 20-4. Values for other D/A ratios were calculated similarly.

Figure 20-4   ATM: Relationships among Financial Leverage, Expected EPS, and Risk

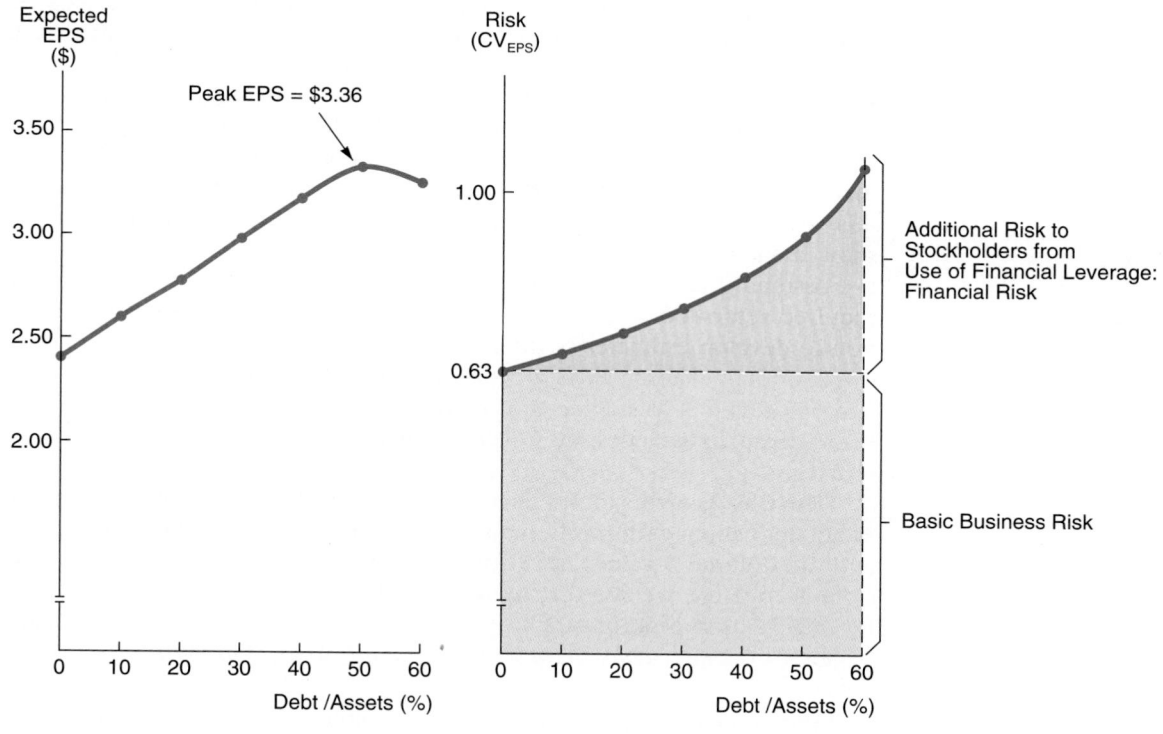

As shown in the right panel of this figure, financial risk rises at an increasing rate with each addition of financial leverage. Earnings per share, on the other hand, rises only to a certain point, as shown on the left. Beyond this peak, interest rates become prohibitively high, and EPS begins to fall.

ratio, interest rates rise so rapidly that EPS is depressed in spite of the decreasing number of shares outstanding. The right panel of Figure 20-4 shows that risk, as measured by the coefficient of variation of EPS, rises continuously and at an increasing rate as debt is substituted for equity.

We see, then, that using financial leverage has both good and bad effects: higher leverage increases expected earnings per share (at least for a while—in this example, until the D/A ratio equals 50 percent), but greater leverage also increases the firm's risk. We are *seeing* the risk-return tradeoff which earlier was simply stated. Clearly, the debt ratio for ATM should not exceed 50 percent, but where, in the range of 0 to 50 percent, should it be set? Exactly how this tradeoff should be resolved is discussed in the next section.

The Effect of Capital Structure on Stock Price and the Cost of Capital

As we saw in Figure 20-4, ATM's EPS is maximized at a debt/assets ratio of 50 percent. Does this mean that ATM's optimal capital structure is 50 percent debt, 50 percent equity? The answer is a resounding no—*the optimal capital structure is the one that maximizes the price of the firm's stock, and this always calls for a debt ratio which is lower than the one that maximizes expected EPS.*

This statement is demonstrated in Table 20-6, where we develop ATM's estimated stock price and weighted average cost of capital at different debt/assets ratios. The values for k_d and EPS were taken from Tables 20-3 and 20-5. The beta coefficients shown in Column 4 were estimated. Recall from Chapter 12 that a stock's beta measures its relative volatility as compared with that of an average stock. It has been demonstrated both theoretically and empirically that a firm's beta increases with its use of financial leverage. The exact nature of this relationship is difficult to estimate, but the values given in Column 4 do show the approximate nature of the relationship for ATM.

Assuming that the risk-free rate of return, k_{RF}, is 6 percent and that the required return on an average stock, k_M, is 10 percent, we use the CAPM equation to develop estimates of the required rate of return, k_s, for ATM at different levels of debt. These values are shown in Column 5. Here we see that k_s is 12 percent if no financial leverage is used, but k_s rises to an estimated 16.8 percent if the company finances with 60 percent debt, the maximum permitted by its charter.

The zero growth stock valuation model developed in Chapter 17 is used in Table 20-6 along with the Column 3 values of dividends and earnings per share and the Column 5 values of k_s, to develop the estimated stock prices shown in Column 6. Here we see that the expected stock price first rises with financial leverage, hits a peak of $22.86 at a debt/assets ratio of 40 percent, and then begins to decline. *Thus, ATM's optimal capital structure calls for 40 percent debt.*

The price/earnings ratios shown in Column 7 were calculated by dividing the estimated price in Column 6 by the expected earnings given in Column 3. We use the pattern of P/E ratios as a check on the "reasonableness" of the other data. As a rule, P/E ratios should decline as the riskiness of a firm increases. Also, at the time ATM's data were being analyzed, the P/Es

Table 20-6   ATM: Stock Price Estimates with Different Debt/Assets Ratios

Debt/ Assets (1)	k_d (2)	Expected EPS (and DPS)[a] (3)	Estimated Beta (4)	k_s[b] (5)	Estimated Price[c] (6)	Resulting P/E Ratio (7)	Weighted Average Cost of Capital (8)[d]
0%	—	$2.40	1.50	12.0%	$20.00	8.33	12.00%
10	8.0%	2.56	1.55	12.2	20.98	8.20	11.46
20	8.3	2.75	1.65	12.6	21.83	7.94	11.08
30	9.0	2.97	1.80	13.2	22.50	7.58	10.86
40	**10.0**	**3.20**	**2.00**	**14.0**	**22.86**	**7.14**	**10.80**
50	12.0	3.36	2.30	15.2	22.11	6.58	11.20
60	15.0	3.30	2.70	16.8	19.64	5.95	12.12

[a]ATM pays all of its earnings out as dividends, so EPS = DPS.

[b]We assume that k_{RF} = 6% and k_M = 10%. Therefore, at D/A = 0%, k_s = 6% + (10% − 6%)1.5 = 6% + 6% = 12%. Other values of k_s were calculated similarly.

[c]Since all earnings are paid out as dividends, no retained earnings will be plowed back into the business, and growth in EPS and DPS will be zero. Hence, the zero growth stock price model developed in Chapter 17 can be used to estimate the price of ATM's stock. For example, at D/A = 0%,

$$P_0 = \frac{DPS}{k_s} = \frac{\$2.40}{0.12} = \$20.$$

Other prices were calculated similarly.

[d]Column 8 was found by use of the weighted average cost of capital (WACC) equation developed in Chapter 19:

$$WACC = w_d k_d (1 - T) + w_s k_s$$

$$= (D/A)(k_d)(1 - T) + (1 - D/A)k_s.$$

For example, at D/A = 40%,

$$WACC = 0.4(10\%)(0.6) + 0.6(14.0\%) = 10.80\%.$$

shown here were generally consistent with those of zero growth companies with varying amounts of financial leverage. Thus, the data in Column 7 reinforce our confidence in the estimated prices shown in Column 6.[8]

Finally, Column 8 shows ATM's weighted average cost of capital, WACC, calculated as described in Chapter 19, at the different capital structures. If the firm uses zero debt, its assets are all equity financed, and in that case ATM's WACC = k_s = 12%. As the firm begins to employ lower-cost debt, its weighted average cost of capital declines. However, as the debt ratio increases the costs of both debt and equity rise, and the increasing costs of the two components begin to offset the fact that a larger proportion of the lower-cost debt component is being used. At 40 percent debt, WACC reaches a minimum, and it rises after that as the debt ratio is increased.

---

[8]As mentioned earlier, we are assuming that ATM can change its capital structure by repurchasing any number of shares of its common stock at $20 per share. However, if the repurchase were done in an incremental fashion, as opposed to all at one time (say, from one large stockholder), the company most likely would have to pay more than $20 for the most recently purchased shares. This would cause the expected EPS and the estimated price on remaining shares to be somewhat lower than the values shown for each level of debt in Table 20-6. To avoid this complication, think of the debt ratios in Table 20-6 as *options* available to ATM in establishing its target capital structure, as opposed to incremental changes.

Figure 20-5

ATM: Relationships among
Debt/Assets Ratio,
Expected EPS, Cost of
Capital, and Estimated
Stock Price

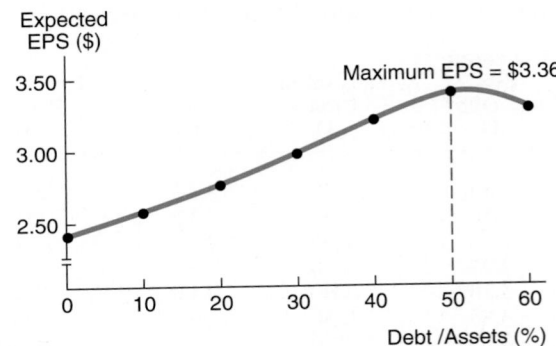

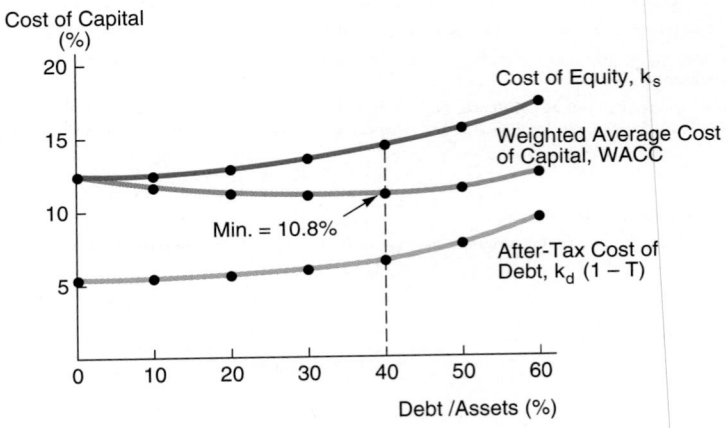

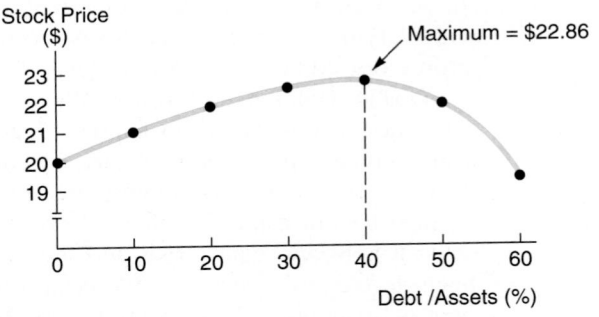

The amount of financial leverage that maximizes a firm's estimated stock price is always
lower than the amount that will maximize its expected EPS. In this example, with the
graphed data obtained from Table 20-6, the stock price is maximized and the cost of capital
is minimized at a debt/assets ratio of 40 percent, even though expected EPS would be
higher at 50 percent debt. ATM should, therefore, target its capital structure at 40 percent
debt, 60 percent equity.

The debt/assets ratio, EPS, cost of capital, and stock price data in Table 20-6 are plotted in Figure 20-5. As the graph shows, the debt/assets ratio that maximizes ATM's expected EPS is 50 percent. However, the expected stock price is maximized, and the cost of capital is minimized, at a 40 percent debt ratio. *Thus, the optimal capital structure calls for 40 percent debt and 60 percent equity.* Management should set its target capital structure at these ratios, and if the present ratios are off target, it should move toward the target when new securities offerings are made.

In wrapping up this section, three points need to be stressed:

1. The reason that the maximum expected stock price occurs at a *lower* debt ratio (40 percent) than the maximum EPS (50 percent) is simple. EPS is a measure of expected return only, while *the stock price incorporates both risk and return.* That makes the stock price the better measure.

2. It is no accident that the level of debt that minimizes the WACC is the same debt ratio that maximizes the estimated stock price; this will always be the case.

3. Note that the WACC curve in Figure 20-5 is fairly flat. What this means, in practice, is that although a 40 percent debt ratio is ATM's optimal capital structure, its actual debt ratio may be either a little above or a little below 40 percent without the firm being "penalized" much in the form of a higher WACC. This is extremely important because it provides ATM's financial managers with some flexibility.

? Self-Test

Explain the following statement: "Using financial leverage has both good and bad effects."

Is the optimal capital structure the one that maximizes expected EPS? Explain.

Explain the following statement: "At the optimal capital structure, a firm has minimized its cost of capital." Do stockholders want the firm to minimize its cost of capital?

Capital Structure Theory: Taxes, Bankruptcy-Related Costs, and the Value of the Stock

Why does the expected stock price first rise as the firm begins to use financial leverage, then hit a peak, and finally decline when leverage becomes excessive? This pattern occurs primarily as a result of *corporate income taxes* and *bankruptcy-related costs.* To understand this answer better we first need to look at the capital structure theory and research which has evolved since the late 1950s. Later in the chapter we will add a number of practical determinants of capital structure to round out the picture.

Capital Structure Theory

Modern capital structure theory began in 1958, when Professors Franco Modigliani and Merton Miller (hereafter MM) published what has been called the most influential finance article ever written.[9] MM proved, under a very restrictive set of assumptions, that because of the tax deductibility of interest on debt, a firm's value rises continuously as it uses more debt, and hence its value will be maximized by financing almost entirely with debt. MM's assumptions included the following:

1. There are no brokerage costs.

2. There are no personal taxes.

3. Investors can borrow at the same rate as corporations.

4. Investors have the same information as management about the firm's future investment opportunities.[10]

5. All the firm's debt is riskless, regardless of how much debt it uses.

6. EBIT is not affected by the use of debt.

Since several of these assumptions were obviously unrealistic, MM's position was only the beginning of capital structure research.

Subsequent researchers, and MM themselves, extended the basic theory by relaxing the assumptions. Other researchers attempted to test the various theoretical models with empirical data to see exactly how stock prices and capital costs are affected by capital structure. Both the theoretical and the empirical results have added to our understanding of capital structure, but none of these studies has produced results that can be used to precisely identify a firm's optimal capital structure. A summary of the theoretical and empirical research to date is expressed graphically in Figure 20-6, as applied to our illustrative firm, ATM. Here are the key points in the figure:

1. The fact that interest is a deductible expense makes debt less expensive than common or preferred stock. In effect, the government pays part of the cost of debt capital, or, to put it another way, debt provides *tax shelter benefits*. As a result, using debt causes more of the firm's operating income (EBIT) to flow through to investors, so the more debt a company uses, the higher its value, and the higher the price of its stock. Under the assumptions of the original Modigliani-Miller paper, their analysis led to the conclusion that the firm's stock price will be maximized if it uses virtually 100 percent debt, and the line labeled "Pure MM Result" in Figure 20-6 expressed their relationship between stock prices and debt.

2. *The MM assumptions do not hold in the real world.* First, interest rates rise as the debt ratio rises. Second, EBIT declines at extreme levels of le-

---

[9]Franco Modigliani and Merton H. Miller, "The Cost of Capital, Corporation Finance, and the Theory of Investment," *American Economic Review,* June 1958. Modigliani and Miller both won Nobel Prizes for their work.

[10]A second line of capital structure theory which does not make this assumption is *signaling theory.* For a discussion of signaling theory, see J. Fred Weston and Eugene F. Brigham, *Essentials of Managerial Finance,* 10th ed., Chapter 17.

Figure 20-6   ATM: Effect of Financial Leverage on Stock Value

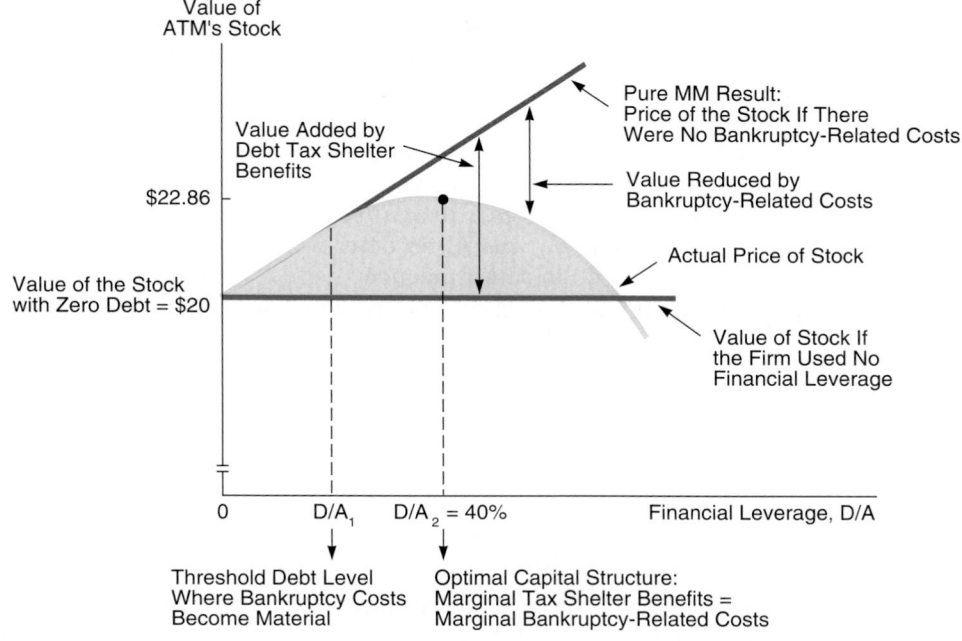

When a firm uses financial leverage, its expected stock price first rises and then falls. The initial rise occurs because the interest payments on corporate debt are tax deductible. Thus, as a firm's debt load increases, more of its operating income escapes taxation and flows through to investors. As levels of debt increase, however, so does the risk of bankruptcy. Consequently, at Point D/A_1, when investors begin to worry about the effects of debt, the potential risk of bankruptcy begins to offset the benefits of the tax-deductible interest. At Point D/A_2 the balance between the marginal benefits of financial leverage and the marginal bankruptcy-related costs is reached and the firm's capital structure is optimized. Beyond Point D/A_2 the potential costs of bankruptcy exceed the marginal benefits of financial leverage and the stock's price falls.

verage. Third, expected tax rates fall at high debt levels, and this also reduces the expected value of the debt tax shelter. And, fourth, the probability of bankruptcy, which brings with it lawyers' fees and other costs, increases as the debt ratio rises.[11]

3. There is some threshold level of debt, labeled D/A_1 in Figure 20-6, below which the effects noted in Point 2 are immaterial. Beyond D/A_1, however, the bankruptcy-related costs become increasingly important, and they reduce the tax benefits of debt at an increasing rate. In the range from D/A_1 to D/A_2, bankruptcy-related costs reduce but do not completely offset the tax benefits of debt, so the firm's stock price rises (but at a decreasing

---

[11]Bankruptcy-related costs also include the following hard-to-quantify costs which are likely to occur with a firm's increasing proximity to actual bankruptcy: (1) key employees may leave the firm, (2) suppliers may deny credit for fear of not getting paid, (3) customers may loose confidence in the firm and shop elsewhere, and (4) management may have to start selling off fixed assets to raise needed working capital.

rate) as the debt ratio increases. However, beyond D/A$_2$, marginal bankruptcy-related costs exceed the marginal tax benefits, so from this point on increasing the debt ratio lowers the value of the stock. Therefore, D/A$_2$ is the optimal capital structure; for ATM this point was assumed to be 40 percent debt, where the price of the firm's common stock peaked at $22.86.[12]

4. Both theory and empirical evidence support the preceding discussion. However, statistical problems prevent researchers from identifying Points D/A$_1$ and D/A$_2$. *The only way we could calculate an optimal capital structure for ATM was to assume we knew the values of crucial inputs, such as beta, k$_M$, and k$_d$.* In other words, this type of analysis is extremely difficult to do in actual practice.

5. While theoretical and empirical work supports the general shape of the curves in Figures 20-5 and 20-6, these graphs must be taken as approximations, not as precisely defined functions. Several of the numbers in Figure 20-5 are shown out to two decimal places, but that is merely for illustrative purposes—the numbers are not nearly that accurate in view of the fact that the data on which the graph is based are judgmental estimates. In fact, management rarely, if ever, has sufficient confidence in the type of analysis set forth in Table 20-6 to use it as the sole determinant of the target capital structure.

Let us close our discussion of capital structure theory by again emphasizing the interaction of tax shelter benefits (obtained by using debt) with potential bankruptcy-related costs in determining the stock's value. The fact that the theory does not allow us to specify, for a given firm, the precise debt ratio which represents that firm's optimal capital structure in no way invalidates the theory. It only means that, *in practice,* we need additional guidelines. We will return to discuss a number of such guidelines, or considerations, later in this chapter, and bankruptcy is discussed in greater detail in Appendix 20A. At this point, however, we will turn to a very specific measure of a firm's operating and financial leverage called *degree of leverage.*

Self-Test

Why does the expected stock price first rise as the firm begins to use financial leverage, then hit a peak, and finally decline when leverage becomes excessive?

Why is capital structure theory difficult to apply in practice? What is the solution to this problem?

Degree of Leverage

In our discussion of operating leverage in an earlier section of this chapter we made only a brief mention of financial leverage, and when we discussed financial leverage, operating leverage was assumed to be given. Actually, the two types of leverage are interrelated. For example, if ATM *reduced* its operating leverage,

---

[12]This entire concept—including (1) the reasons the tax shelter benefits cause a linear increase in value and (2) the effects of personal income taxes on capital structure decisions—is discussed in Eugene F. Brigham and Louis Gapenski, *Intermediate Financial Management,* 4th ed., Chapter 11.

it could probably *increase* its use of financial leverage. On the other hand, if it decided to *increase* its operating leverage, its optimal capital structure would probably call for *less* debt.

The theory of finance has not been developed to the point where we can actually specify simultaneously the optimal levels of operating and financial leverage. However, we can see how operating and financial leverage interact through an analysis of the *degree of leverage* concept.

degree of leverage

The percentage change in one variable, given a percentage change in another variable; a form of elasticity.

Degree of leverage is a form of *elasticity,* similar to other elasticity measures studied in microeconomics. It measures the percentage change in one variable, given a percentage change in another variable. Degree of leverage is a *point concept.* That means that it applies, in our case, to percentage changes up or down in the quantity produced and sold by ATM from a specific starting level. You should, therefore, keep in mind throughout this section that whenever we calculate a degree of leverage, it applies only to one particular level of output, Q. Degree of leverage is a more precise way of calculating the effects of operating and financial leverage on stockholder returns.

Degree of Operating Leverage (DOL)

degree of operating leverage (DOL)

The percentage change in EBIT resulting from a given percentage change in sales.

The **degree of operating leverage (DOL)** is defined as the percentage change in operating income (or EBIT) associated with a given percentage change in sales:

$$DOL = \frac{\text{Percentage change in EBIT}}{\text{Percentage change in sales}} = \frac{\dfrac{\Delta EBIT}{EBIT}}{\dfrac{\Delta S}{S}}. \tag{20-5}$$

DOL is an index number which measures the effect of a change in sales on operating income, or EBIT. DOL can also be calculated by using Equation 20-6, which is derived from Equation 20-5.

$$DOL_Q = \text{Degree of operating leverage at Point Q}$$

$$= \frac{Q(P - V)}{Q(P - V) - F}, \tag{20-6}$$

or, based on dollar sales rather than units,

$$DOL_S = \frac{S - VC}{S - VC - F}. \tag{20-6a}$$

Here Q is the initial units of output, P is the sales price per unit, V is the variable cost per unit, F is fixed operating costs, S is initial total sales in dollars, and VC is total variable costs.

Look back to Table 20-2 for the basic data on All-Technology Manufacturing (ATM). Now apply Equation 20-6a to this data, at a sales level of $200,000 and we find ATM's degree of operating leverage to be 2.0:

$$DOL_{\$200,000} = \frac{\$200,000 - \$120,000}{\$200,000 - \$120,000 - \$40,000}$$

$$= \frac{\$80,000}{\$40,000} = 2.0.$$

Thus, an X percent increase in sales will produce a 2X percent increase in EBIT. For example, a 50 percent increase in sales, *starting from sales of $200,000,* will result in a 50%(2.0) = 100% increase in EBIT. This situation is confirmed by examining Section I of Table 20-4, where we see that a 50 percent increase in sales, from $200,000 to $300,000, causes EBIT to double from $40,000 to $80,000. Note, however, that *if sales decrease by 50 percent, then EBIT will decrease by 100 percent;* according to Table 20-4, EBIT decreases to $0 if sales decrease to $100,000.[13]

Because the DOL is specific to the initial sales level, if we evaluated a change from a sales base of $300,000, there would be a different DOL:

$$DOL_{\$300,000} = \frac{\$300,000 - \$180,000}{\$300,000 - \$180,000 - \$40,000}$$

$$= \frac{\$120,000}{\$80,000} = 1.5.$$

In general, if a firm is operating close to its breakeven level, the degree of operating leverage will be high, but DOL declines the higher the base level of sales is above breakeven sales. Looking back at the top section of Table 20-4, we see that the company's operating breakeven point (EBIT = $0) is at sales of $100,000. At that level, DOL is infinite:

$$DOL_{\$100,000} = \frac{\$100,000 - \$60,000}{\$100,000 - \$60,000 - \$40,000}$$

$$= \frac{\$40,000}{\$0} = \text{undefined but} \approx \text{infinity.}$$

When evaluated at higher and higher sales levels, DOL progressively declines.

---

[13]To use *Equation 20-5* to solve for DOL, first note that the method for calculating a percentage change in a given variable is as follows:

$$\text{Percentage change} = \frac{\text{New value} - \text{Old value}}{\text{Old value}}.$$

For example, if ATM's sales were to increase from $200,000 to $240,000, what effect would this have on EBIT? Using symbols already defined, we can set up the following:

Q	P	S = PQ	V	VC = VQ	F	EBIT = S − VC − F
100,000	$2	$200,000	$1.20	$120,000	$40,000	$40,000
120,000	2	240,000	1.20	144,000	40,000	56,000

$$\text{Percentage change in sales} = \frac{\$240,000 - \$200,000}{\$200,000} = 20\%,$$

$$\text{Percentage change in EBIT} = \frac{\$56,000 - \$40,000}{\$40,000} = 40\%,$$

$$DOL = \frac{\% \Delta \text{ EBIT}}{\% \Delta \text{ Sales}} = \frac{40\%}{20\%} = 2.0.$$

Since we obtained the same DOL (2.0) when we increased sales by 20 percent as when we increased sales by 100 percent (just using two different methods), we can conclude that *any change in ATM's sales from an initial level of $200,000 will be accompanied by a change in ATM's EBIT that is twice as large.*

Degree of Financial Leverage (DFL)

Operating leverage affects earnings before interest and taxes (EBIT), whereas financial leverage affects earnings after interest and taxes, or the earnings available to common stockholders. In terms of Table 20-4, operating leverage affects the top section, whereas financial leverage affects the lower sections. Thus, if ATM decided to use more operating leverage, its fixed operating costs would be higher than $40,000, its variable cost ratio would be lower than 60 percent of sales, and its EBIT would be more sensitive to changes in sales. *Financial leverage takes over where operating leverage leaves off, further magnifying the effects on earnings per share of changes in the level of sales.* For this reason, operating leverage is sometimes referred to as *first-stage leverage* and financial leverage as *second-stage leverage.*

The **degree of financial leverage (DFL)** is defined as the percentage change in earnings per share (EPS) that results from a given percentage change in earnings before interest and taxes (EBIT), and it is calculated as follows:

degree of financial leverage (DFL)

The percentage change in earnings per share associated with a given percentage change in earnings before interest and taxes.

$$DFL = \frac{\text{Percentage change in EPS}}{\text{Percentage change in EBIT}} = \frac{\frac{\Delta EPS}{EPS}}{\frac{\Delta EBIT}{EBIT}}. \tag{20-7}$$

DFL is an index number which measures the effect of a change in EBIT on earnings per share. DFL can also be calculated by using Equation 20-8, which is derived from Equation 20-7:

$$DFL_Q = \text{Degree of financial leverage at Point Q}$$

$$= \frac{Q(P - V) - F}{Q(P - V) - F - I} = \frac{EBIT}{EBIT - I}. \tag{20-8}$$

Here I is the total fixed financing charges.

For ATM at sales of $200,000 and an EBIT of $40,000, the degree of financial leverage with a 50 percent debt ratio is

$$DFL_{\$200,000,\ 50\%} = \frac{\$40,000}{\$40,000 - \$12,000}$$

$$= 1.43.$$

Therefore, a 100 percent increase in EBIT would result in a 100%(1.43) = 143% increase in earnings per share. This may be confirmed by referring to the lower section of Table 20-4, where we see that a 100 percent increase in EBIT, from $40,000 to $80,000, produces a 143 percent increase in EPS:

$$\%\Delta EPS = \frac{\Delta EPS}{EPS} = \frac{\$8.16 - \$3.36}{\$3.36} = \frac{\$4.80}{\$3.36} = 1.43 = 143\%.$$

If ATM's EBIT were to increase by 20 percent, its EPS would increase by 20%(1.43) = 28.6%. However, if ATM's EBIT *declines* by 20 percent the decline in EPS would also be greater by a factor of 1.43 (EPS decline = 28.6%).

If no debt were used, the degree of financial leverage would by definition be 1.0, so a 100 percent increase in EBIT would produce exactly a

100 percent increase in EPS.[14] This can be confirmed from the data in Section II of Table 20-4, where we see ATM's EPS double from $2.40 to $4.80, as EBIT doubles from $40,000 to $80,000 (D/A = 0%).

Degree of Total Leverage (DTL): Combining Operating and Financial Leverage

We have seen (1) that the greater the degree of operating leverage (or fixed operating costs), the more sensitive EBIT will be to changes in sales, and (2) that the greater the degree of financial leverage (fixed financing costs), the more sensitive EPS will be to changes in EBIT. Therefore, if a firm uses a considerable amount of both operating and financial leverage, then even small changes in sales will lead to wide fluctuations in EPS.

degree of total leverage (DTL)

The percentage change in EPS brought about by a given percentage change in sales; DTL shows the effects of both operating leverage and financial leverage.

The **degree of total leverage (DTL)** is defined as the percentage change in earnings per share that results from a given percentage change in sales, and it is calculated as follows:

$$DTL = \frac{\text{Percentage change in EPS}}{\text{Percentage change in sales}} = \frac{\frac{\Delta EPS}{EPS}}{\frac{\Delta S}{S}}. \qquad (20\text{-}9)$$

Alternatively, we may use the fact that degree of total leverage is the *product* of the firm's DOL and DFL at a given level of sales to obtain three equivalent equations for DTL at Point Q:

$$DTL_Q = (DOL_Q)(DFL_Q). \qquad (20\text{-}10)$$

$$DTL_Q = \frac{Q(P - V)}{Q(P - V) - F - I}. \qquad (20\text{-}10a)$$

$$DTL_Q = \frac{S - VC}{S - VC - F - I}. \qquad (20\text{-}10b)$$

For ATM at sales of $200,000 (Q = 100,000 units), we can substitute data from Table 20-4 into Equation 20-10b to find the degree of total leverage if the debt ratio is 50 percent:

$$DTL_{\$200,000,\ 50\%} = \frac{\$200,000 - \$120,000}{\$200,000 - \$120,000 - \$40,000 - \$12,000}$$

$$= \frac{\$80,000}{\$28,000} = 2.86.$$

Using Equation 20-10, we get the same result:

$$DTL_{\$200,000,\ 50\%} = (2.00)(1.43) = 2.86.$$

---

[14]You might remember from Chapter 6 that when a firm uses no debt financing, the equity multiplier in the extended Du Pont equation is also 1.0. This should not be a surprise since both of these (DFL and equity multiplier) measure the use of financial leverage.

Table 20-7   Operating, Financial, and Total Leverage Effects for ATM with a 50 Percent Increase in Sales from a Sales Level of $200,000

Income Statement		Original Status	Percentage Increase	Resulting Status
	PQ = Sales	$200,000	50%	$300,000
DOL (2.0)	VQ = Variable operating costs (60% of sales)	120,000	50	180,000
	F = Fixed operating costs	40,000	0	40,000
	EBIT = Operating profits	$ 40,000	100	$ 80,000
DFL (1.43)	I = Fixed financing charges[a]	12,000	0	12,000
	EBT = Earnings before taxes	$ 28,000	143[b]	$ 68,000
	T = Taxes (40%)	11,200	143[b]	27,200
	NI = Net income	$ 16,800	143[b]	$ 40,800
	Common stock equity shares outstanding	5,000	0	5,000
	Earnings per share	$3.36	143[c]	$8.16

DTL (2.86) brackets DOL and DFL.

[a]In this case all fixed financing costs result from interest charges.

[b]Note that EBT also increases by the same 143 percent. Since taxes are a variable cost in this example, they do not affect the degree of leverage.

[c]Note that because of operating leverage (DOL = 2.0), a 50 percent increase in sales will result in twice as large a change in operating profits. Similarly, the effects of the combination of operating and financial leverage cause a change in sales to be magnified by 2.86×. DOL = 2.0 and DFL = 1.43; therefore DTL = 2.0 × 1.43 = 2.86, and if sales increase by 50 percent then the result would be a 143 percent increase in EBT, NI, EPS, and ROE. Unfortunately, a 50 percent decrease in sales will likewise be magnified into a 143 percent decline in EBT, NI, EPS, and ROE!

We can also use the degree of total leverage (DTL) to find the new earnings per share (EPS_1) for any given percentage increase in sales (%Δ Sales), where EPS_0 represents the initial level of earnings per share. We proceed as follows:

$$EPS_1 = EPS_0 + EPS_0[(DTL)(\%\Delta Sales)]$$

$$= EPS_0[1.0 + (DTL)(\%\Delta Sales)]. \qquad (20\text{-}11)$$

For example, a 50 percent (or 0.5) increase in sales, from $200,000 to $300,000, would cause EPS_0 ($3.36 as shown in Section III of Table 20-4) to increase to $8.16:

$$EPS_1 = \$3.36[1.0 + (2.86)(0.5)]$$

$$= \$3.36(2.43)$$

$$= \$8.16.$$

This figure agrees with the EPS at sales of $300,000 shown in Table 20-4.

Table 20-7 provides a summary of the combined effects of DOL and DFL on ATM, when its sales increase from $200,000 to $300,000. Note specifically that while we have been referring to changes in *EPS* in our DFL and DTL calculations, *the magnitude of changes in EBT, NI, and ROE would exactly equal the change in EPS;* that is, these would also increase by 143 percent when sales increase by 50 percent. (Implicit assumptions in these calculations include that the number of shares does not change and that the tax rate stays constant at 40 percent.)

The degree of leverage concept is useful primarily for the insights it provides regarding the joint effects of operating and financial leverage on earnings per share. The concept can be used to show the management of a business, for example, that a decision to automate a plant and to finance the new equipment with debt would result in a situation wherein a 10 percent decline in sales would produce a 50 percent decline in EPS, whereas with a different combination of operating and financial leverage, a 10 percent sales decline would cause EPS to decline by only 20 percent. Having the alternatives stated in this manner gives decision makers a better idea of the ramifications of alternative actions.

? *Self-Test*

Give a formula for calculating the degree of operating leverage (DOL), and explain what DOL is.

Why is the DOL different at various sales levels?

Give a formula for calculating the degree of financial leverage (DFL), and explain what this calculation means.

Give a formula for calculating the degree of total leverage (DTL), and explain what DTL is.

Why is the degree of leverage concept useful?

Practical Considerations in Determining Capital Structure

Our discussion of degree of leverage in the previous section was intended to highlight the interaction between the use of operating leverage and financial leverage, between the concepts of business risk (to which operating leverage contributes) and financial risk. However, it did not bring us much closer to finding the precise optimal structure for a given firm, such as ATM. Recall that when we ended our discussion of capital structure theory in an earlier section we did so by concluding that *financial theory at the present time does not allow us to specify a firm's optimal capital structure* and that additional guidelines are needed. Therefore, we now turn to a number of factors which, in practice, have proven to be important considerations when actual capital structures are determined.

The TIE Ratio as an Indicator of Financial Strength

Managers are concerned about the effects of financial leverage on the risk of bankruptcy, and an analysis of this factor is an important input in all capital structure decisions. Accordingly, managements give considerable weight to financial strength indicators such as the *times-interest-earned (TIE) ratio*. The lower this coverage ratio, the higher the probability that a firm will default on its debt and be forced into bankruptcy.

Table 20-8 shows how ATM's expected TIE ratio declines as the debt/assets ratio increases. When the debt/assets ratio is only 10 percent, the expected TIE is a high 25 times, but the interest coverage ratio declines rapidly as debt rises.

Table 20-8

ATM: Expected Times-Interest-Earned Ratio at Different Debt/Assets Ratios

Debt/Assets	TIE[a]
0%	Undefined
10	25.0
20	12.0
30	7.4
40	5.0
50	3.3
60	2.2

[a]TIE = EBIT/Interest. For example, if debt/assets = 50%, then TIE = $40,000/$12,000 = 3.3. Data are from Tables 20-3 and 20-4.

Figure 20-7

ATM: Probability Distributions of Times-Interest-Earned Ratios with Different Capital Structures

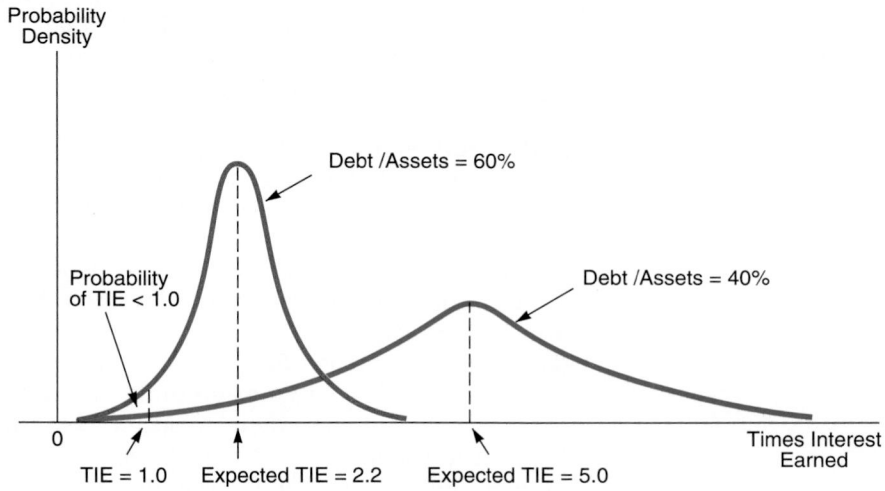

The times-interest-earned ratio is an important indicator of bankruptcy risk. The lower the expected TIE, the greater the potential for bankruptcy. Management will be especially concerned about keeping the actual TIE above 1.0, the point below which a firm's earnings will not cover its required interest payments. This figure shows that a 60 percent debt/assets ratio not only creates lower expected TIE than a 40 percent debt/assets ratio but also results in a much higher probability of TIE falling below 1.0.

Note, however, that these TIE ratios are the expected values; the actual TIE will be higher if sales exceed the expected $200,000 level but lower if sales fall below $200,000. The variability of the TIE ratios is highlighted in Figure 20-7, which shows the probability distributions of these ratios at debt/assets ratios of 40 percent and 60 percent. The expected TIE is much higher if only 40 percent debt is used. Even more important, with less debt there is a much lower probability of a TIE of less than 1.0, the level at which the firm is not earning enough to meet its required interest payments and is seriously exposed to the threat of bankruptcy.[15]

Capital Structure and Mergers

One of the most dramatic developments in the financial world during the 1980s was the high level of merger activity, especially hostile takeovers, and leveraged buyouts. The target firm's stock was considered to be undervalued by the acquiring firm, so the acquirer was willing to pay a premium of 50 to 100 percent to gain control. For example, General Electric offered $66.50 per share for RCA (which owned the NBC television network, among other things) versus RCA's preannouncement price of $45 per share, and Kohlberg Kravis Roberts paid $106 for RJR Nabisco's stock versus RJR's preannouncement price of $55. Mergers and acquisitions are discussed at length in Chapter 22, but it is useful to mention several points now: (1) very often the acquiring firm issues debt and uses it to buy the target firm's stock, (2) the new debt effectively changes the enterprise's capital structure, and (3) the value enhancement resulting from the use of debt is sufficient to cover the premium offered for the stock and still leave a profit for the acquiring company.

An understanding of the type of analysis described in this chapter has led to the creation of companies whose major function is to acquire other companies through debt-financed takeovers. The managers of these acquiring companies have made huge personal fortunes, and shrewd individual investors, including a few finance professors, have selected stock portfolios heavily weighted with prime acquisition targets and have done well in the market.

Of course, the managements of firms with low leverage ratios who do not want to be taken over can be expected to react by attempting to find their optimal debt levels and then issuing debt and repurchasing stock, thus bringing their firms' actual debt ratios up to the levels that maximize the prices of their stocks, which will make these companies less attractive acquisition targets. This is called *restructuring,* and a great deal of it has been going on lately. CBS, for example, did this when it was fighting off an acquisition attempt by Ted Turner, and Phillips Petroleum did likewise to fend off T. Boone Pickens.

Checklist for Capital Structure Decisions

The factors listed and briefly discussed in this section all have an important, though hard to measure, bearing on a firm's choice of a target capital structure. You will recognize that we have touched on a few of these factors already in this chapter, while others we have not.

1. **Sales stability.**   A firm whose sales are relatively stable can safely take on more debt and incur higher fixed charges than a company with unstable

---

[15]Note that cash flows, which include depreciation, can be sufficient to cover required interest payments even though the TIE is less than 1.0. Thus, at least for a while, a firm may be able to avoid bankruptcy even though its operating income is less than its interest charges. However, most debt contracts stipulate that firms must maintain the TIE ratio above some minimum level, say, 2.0 or 2.5, or else they cannot borrow any additional funds. This can severely constrain operations, and potential constraints, as much as the threat of actual bankruptcy, limit the use of debt.

sales. Utility companies, because of their stable demand, have historically been able to use more financial leverage than industrial firms.

2. **Asset structure.** Firms whose assets are suitable as security for loans tend to use debt rather heavily. General purpose assets which can be used by many businesses make good collateral, whereas special-purpose assets do not. Thus, real estate companies are usually highly leveraged, whereas companies involved in technological research using specialized equipment employ less debt.

3. **Operating leverage.** Other things equal, a firm with less operating leverage is better able to employ financial leverage because, as we saw, the interaction of operating and financial leverage determines the overall effect of a decline in sales on net income and earnings per share.

4. **Growth rate.** Other things equal, faster growing firms must rely more heavily on external capital (see Chapter 7). Further, the flotation costs involved in selling common stock exceed those incurred when selling debt. Thus, rapidly growing firms tend to use somewhat more debt than slower growing companies.

5. **Profitability.** One often observes that firms with very high rates of return on investment use relatively little debt. Although there is no theoretical justification for this fact, one practical explanation is that very profitable firms such as Intel, Microsoft, and Coca-Cola simply do not need to do much debt financing. Their high rates of return enable them to do most of their financing with retained earnings.

6. **Taxes.** Interest is a deductible expense, and deductions are most valuable to firms with high tax rates. Hence, the higher a firm's corporate tax rate, the greater the advantage of debt.

7. **Control.** The effect that issuing debt versus stock might have on a management's control position may influence the firm's capital structure. If management currently has voting control (over 50 percent of the stock) but is not in a position to buy any more stock, it may choose debt for new financings. On the other hand, the management group may decide to use equity rather than debt if the firm's financial situation is so weak that the use of debt might subject the firm to serious risk of default because, if the firm goes into default, the managers will almost surely lose their jobs. However, if too little debt is used, management runs the risk of a takeover. Thus, control considerations could lead to the use of *either* debt or equity because the type of capital that best protects management will vary from situation to situation. In any event, if management is at all insecure, it will definitely take into account the effects of capital structure on control.

8. **Management attitude toward risk.** Since no one can prove that one capital structure will lead to higher stock prices than another, management can exercise its own judgment about the proper capital structure. Some managements use more debt than the average firm in their industry in a quest for higher profits, while other managements tend to be more conservative and, thus, use less debt. However, if management is far off target on the low side, then the probability is high that some other firm or management group will take over the company, increase its leverage, and thereby raise its value. This point was discussed in some detail earlier.

9. **Lender and rating agency attitudes.** Regardless of managers' own analyses of the proper leverage factors for their firms, there is no question that lenders' and rating agencies' attitudes frequently influence capital structure decisions (see Chapter 16; recall also the "Decision in Finance" opening vignette in Chapter 19 on McDonnell Douglas). In the majority of cases, the corporation discusses its capital structure with lenders and rating agencies and gives much weight to their advice. For example, one large utility was recently told by Moody and Standard & Poor that its bonds would be downgraded if it issued more bonds. This influenced its decision to finance its expansion with common equity.

10. **Market conditions.** Conditions in the stock and bond markets undergo both long- and short-run changes that can have an important bearing on a firm's optimal capital structure. For example, during the credit crunch in the winter of 1991, the junk bond market dried up, and there was simply no market at any "reasonable" interest rate for new long-term bonds rated below BBB. Therefore, low-rated companies in need of capital were forced to go to the stock market or to the short-term debt market, regardless of their target capital structures. By contrast, in September 1993 conditions in *both* the stock and bond markets were extremely favorable — long-term interest rates were the lowest in over two decades, and many companies were able to sell stock at P/E multiples that were quite high by historical standards.

11. **The firm's internal condition.** A firm's own internal condition can also have a bearing on its target capital structure. For example, suppose a firm has just successfully completed an R&D program, and it projects higher earnings in the immediate future. However, the new earnings are not yet anticipated by investors and hence are not reflected in the price of the stock. This company would not want to issue stock — it would prefer to finance with debt until the higher earnings materialize and are reflected in the stock price. Then it could sell an issue of common stock, retire the debt, and return to its target capital structure.

12. **Financial flexibility.** An astute corporate treasurer made this statement to the authors:

> Our company can earn a lot more money from good capital budgeting and operating decisions than from good financing decisions. Indeed, we are not sure exactly how financing decisions affect our stock price, but we know for sure that having to turn down a promising venture because funds are not available will reduce our long-run profitability. For this reason, my primary goal as treasurer is to always be in a position to raise the capital needed to support operations.
>
> We also know that when times are good, we can raise capital with either stocks or bonds, but when times are bad, suppliers of capital are much more willing to make funds available if we give them a secured position, and this means bonds. Further, when we sell a new issue of stock, this sends a negative "signal" to investors, so stock sales by a mature company such as ours are not generally desirable.

Combining these thoughts leads to the goal of *maintaining financial flexibility,* which, from an operational viewpoint, means *maintaining adequate reserve borrowing capacity.* Determining an "adequate" reserve borrowing capacity is judgmental, but it clearly depends on the factors mentioned previously in the chapter, including the firm's forecasted need for funds, predicted capital market conditions, management's confidence in its forecasts, and the consequences of a capital shortage.

Self-Test

Why do managers give considerable weight to the TIE ratio when they make capital structure decisions?

Why does capital structure sometimes cause one firm to take over another?

How does sales stability affect capital structure?

How does asset structure affect capital structure?

How does growth rate affect capital structure?

How do taxes affect capital structure?

How do lender and rating agency attitudes affect capital structure?

How might the firm's internal condition affect capital structure?

What is "financial flexibility," and is it increased or decreased by having a high debt ratio?

Variations in Capital Structures Among Firms

As might be expected, wide variations in the use of financial leverage occur both across industries and among the individual firms in each industry. Table 20-9 illustrates this point for selected industries, ranked in descending order of common equity ratios, as shown in Column 1.[16]

The drug companies do not use much debt (their common equity ratios are high); the uncertainties inherent in any industry that is either cyclical, oriented toward research, or subject to huge product liability suits render the heavy use. Retailers and utility companies both use more long-term debt then the other two industries shown. Retailers use long-term debt secured by mortgages on their stores; the utility companies have traditionally used large amounts of debt, particularly long-term debt because their fixed assets make good security for mortgage bonds, and their relatively stable sales make it safe for them to carry more debt than would be true for firms with more business risk.

Particular attention should be given to the times-interest-earned (TIE) ratio because it gives a measure of how safe the debt is and how vulnerable the company is to financial disasters. The TIE ratio depends on three factors: (1) the amount of debt, here expressed as a percentage of total financing; (2) the interest rate on the debt; and (3) the company's operating profits (EBIT). Generally, the least leveraged industries, such as the drug industry, have the highest coverage ratios, whereas the utility industry, which finances heavily with debt, has a low average coverage ratio.

---

[16]Information on capital structures and financial strength is available from a multitude of sources. We used the *Compustat* data tapes to develop Table 20-9, but published sources include *The Value Line Investment Survey, Robert Morris Association Annual Studies,* and *Dun & Bradstreet Key Business Ratios.*

Table 20-9   Capital Structure Percentages, 1992: Four Industries Ranked by Common Equity Ratios

Industry	Common Equity (1)	Preferred Stock (2)	Total Debt (3)	Long-Term Debt (4)	Short-Term Debt (5)	Times-Interest-Earned Ratio (6)	Return on Equity (7)
Drugs	76.2%	0.0%	23.8%	14.7%	9.1%	24.0 ×	33.4%
Electronics	65.8	0.4	33.8	18.2	15.6	5.2	14.6
Retailing	62.0	2.6	35.4	33.8	1.6	5.0	14.7
Utilities	39.0	6.2	54.8	51.5	3.3	2.6	10.4
Composite (average of all industries, not just those listed above)	45.2%	1.8%	53.0%	34.6%	18.4%	2.2 ×	9.6%

Note: These ratios are based on accounting (or book) values. Stated on a market-value basis, the equity percentages would rise because most stocks sell at prices that are much higher than their book values.

Source: *Compustat* Industrial Data Tape, 1993.

Wide variations in capital structures also exist among firms within given industries—for example, although the average common equity ratio in 1992 for the drug industry was 76.2 percent, Upjohn's equity ratio was approximately 73 percent, while the equity ratio of Mylan Laboratories was nearly 100 percent. Thus, factors unique to individual firms, including managerial attitudes, do play an important role in setting target capital structures.

 Self-Test

Why do wide variations in the use of financial leverage occur both across industries and among the individual firms in each industry?

SMALL BUSINESS

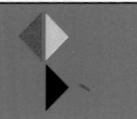

FINANCING GROWTH BUSINESSES IN THE NINETIES

Growth requires cash. The financing needs of small but rapidly growing firms are often greater than the firms can meet from internal sources. The "most com-

mon form of torture known to small-business owners is undercapitalization. It is a problem that derails countless small businesses every year, even when their products sell briskly and everything else seems to go well." So, small businesses that hope to become more substantial have to look to financial markets for capital. Where should they look?

Sources of start-up financing are proliferating. From networks of wealthy individuals to state-sponsored funds with mandates to promote economic development, the funds may not be greater than a decade ago, but the wider variety of financing sources, with differ-

Sources: Brent Bowers, "This Store Is a Hit but Somehow Cash Flow Is Missing," *The Wall Street Journal,* March 14, 1993, B2; Meg Whittemore, "Financing Your Franchise," *Nation's Business,* September 1992, 51–56; Michael Siconolfi, "Merrill Lynch, Pushing into Many New Lines, Expands Bank Services," *The Wall Street Journal,* July 7, 1993, A1, A8; Steve Bingaman and James Howard, *D&B Reports,* March/April, 1993, 34–36; Maria Shao, "The Johnny Appleseed of State Street," *The Boston Globe,* June 20, 1993, 78; "Courting Private Backers," *INC.,* July 1992, 125; and Udayan Gupta, "Beyond the Banks," *The Wall Street Journal,* October 15, 1993, R7.

ent missions and outlooks, make it more likely that a venture will find money somewhere.

In the early to mid-1980s, firms were looking increasingly at the use of venture capital. As a result of the many successful high-tech start-ups in the late 1970s and early 1980s, money poured into venture capital funds. New venture capital firms continued to be formed, often by people who were less experienced than those associated with venture capital in the past. By 1988, new businesses received about 42 percent of the total invested by the funds. Then, because so much money was available for investment and so many entrepreneurs were trying to get financing, rates of return went way down in the venture capital industry during the mid-to-late 1980s. The "euphoria" over venture capital investment disappeared —some venture capitalists left the business because of losses, and others became more discriminating when choosing projects in which to invest. Thus, venture capital has become somewhat less available than in the past.

To compound matters, in the early nineties commercial banks made only about 26 percent of all loans in the United States. The remaining 74 percent of loans came from nonbank lending institutions, such as Capital Credit Corporation, GMAC, and American Express. Merrill Lynch is among these nonbank heavy hitters. They have been described as having all the resources of a bank but not having those resources tied up in bureaucratic regulatory matters, so they can respond very quickly. Merrill Lynch claims that it is "not looking just to have loan accounts, but instead [is] interested in lending as a way to capture the money of wealthy clients and to have access to their working capital and to the securities-related services they need." The Merrill Lynch Interfunding unit lent roughly $2 billion to about 80 small companies between 1982 and 1991. Despite earning substantial profits on the best deals, they are still "holding the bag" on loans to about 50 of the companies that are facing some financial difficulty.

Other alternatives to financing small-business growth include private placements which can be completed quickly due to a minimum of regulatory requirements. Often customized as they are arranged, private placements can take the form of debt that must be paid back with interest, a private stock sale which has the advantage of not requiring a payback, or a combination of these methods. A typical private placement may have several different components. The safer parts of a privately placed loan will probably

be at rates competitive with those of the commercial banks, and in some cases, even lower.

Insurance companies are the largest players in the nonbank corporate lending market. But in the last decade, private commerical investors have begun to participate in the middle-market financing game, and they provide a substantial amount of capital for the private-placement market. By most estimates, private placements now account for about $170 billion per year in working capital loans and investments for U.S. industry. Heller Financial is one of the most aggressive commercial lenders in the private-placement market. However, the largest by far is GE Capital.

Private individual investors or "angels" have become more active with the advent of enterprise forums in which start-up entrepreneurs make presentations before gatherings of angels. Angel investments are quicker than usual venture-capital deals, and, more important, start-ups receive valuable mentoring from investors who have traveled the same path earlier.

Private placements can also be arranged through state-owned venture capital funds and limited partners. Federal and state governments have allocated far greater resources for new businesses; examples of each are concentrated in Boston and San Francisco, although other cities boast similar ventures. The Massachusetts Technology Development Corporation (MTDC) is one of the few organizations to provide equity to early-stage technology ventures. Its principal mission is economic development—the creation of new companies, new jobs, and the improved health of the economy. Since its inception, MTDC has invested $21 million in 64 companies in software, telecommunications, medical devices, and other leading-edge industries. The venture firm says that its investments have helped create more than 3,500 new jobs in the state. Although it does not officially take board seats on its portfolio companies, MTDC says much of its work is in coaching and in counseling the entrepreneurs it backs. By sticking to the niche of seed funding (early-stage financing), MTDC has made respectable returns, notwithstanding losses incurred on its investment on 12 of the original 64 firms.

The other alternative, limited partners, was the approach taken by a veteran restaurateur when he was seeking to launch a new seafood establishment. When no bank (after approaching 15) was willing to provide more than a token amount of money, he was able to attract a group of limited partners, with terrific incentives. Repayment terms included paying nearly all his pretax income (97.5 percent) after expenses until they recouped their entire investment. After that, he proposed (and they accepted) paying out 75 percent of the restaurant's income until they doubled their money. Assuming the business hit that milestone, they would get 25 percent of the income for the remainder of the eatery's 10-year lease. The business has since repaid the original limited partners and has raised more than $900,000 in similar deals for subsequent restaurants. The limited partners doubled their money in less than six years. In spite of the expense that the owner considers as "having to pay his dues," it was a way to work for himself.

Corporations are also increasingly providing start-up financing as they downsize and shed operations that are not part of their core businesses. They are looking to small ventures to perform some necessary tasks. Especially in pharmaceuticals and health care, big companies are turning to smaller businesses to develop technology faster and more cheaply than they often can. Big companies such as SmithKline Beecham PLC and Genentech are among those that have established development units to find and to finance ventures developing new technologies.

Thus, through creative means, entrepreneurial companies with high-growth prospects will continue to need and to find financing to support their growth in the future. The sources of that financing will increasingly include new funds from nonbank lending institutions, state and local governments, private groups of friends, relatives, and weathly individuals, as well as larger corporations, foreign investors, and other, yet-uncreated sources.

Summary

In this chapter we have examined the concepts of operating and financial leverage as well as a number of other factors which have a bearing on a firm's target capital structure. Management should seek to find a firm's *optimal* capital structure, which is that mix of debt and equity that will maximize the price of the firm's common stock. At any point in time, the firm's management has a specific **target capital structure** in mind, although this target is likely to change over time. Throughout the chapter, risk was an important consideration; the key concepts covered are listed below.

▶ **Business risk** is the uncertainty associated with a firm's future operating income (EBIT). A firm will tend to have *low business risk* if (1) the demand for its products is stable, (2) the prices of its inputs *and* products remain relatively constant, (3) it can adjust its prices freely as its costs increase, (4) it operates in an industry where technology does not change rapidly, and (5) it has relatively low fixed operating costs. Other things equal, the lower a firm's business risk, the higher its optimal debt ratio.

Financial risk is the added risk to stockholders which results from financial leverage—the use of debt or preferred stock as part of a firm's financing.

▶ **Operating leverage** is the extent to which fixed costs are used in operations. High fixed operating costs contribute to business risk because these costs are incurred at all times; hence, there is a greater chance that the firm's operating income (EBIT) will not be sufficient to cover fixed operating costs, resulting in an operating loss.

Breakeven analysis examines the use of fixed and variable costs in operations to find the **breakeven point**, the volume of sales where total revenue equals total costs and where EBIT equals zero.

▷ **Financial leverage** is the extent to which fixed costs are used in financing; that is, it is the extent to which the firm uses fixed-rate securities (debt and preferred stock) in its capital structure.

The **risk-return tradeoff** associated with capital structure refers to the fact that using debt has the potential to boost the return to common stockholders, but using debt makes the stock (and the firm) riskier.

Financial leverage increases expected EPS, at least to a point. **The variability of EPS also increases** and at an increasing rate.

▷ **The optimal capital structure** strikes a balance between risk and return such that the price of the stock is maximized, and, simultaneously, the firm's weighted average cost of capital, WACC, is minimized.

The optimal capital structure is determined jointly by the **tax benefits of using debt** and **bankruptcy-related costs.**

▷ The **degree of operating leverage (DOL)** shows how changes in sales affect operating income, whereas the **degree of financial leverage (DFL)** shows how changes in operating income affect earnings per share. The **degree of total leverage (DTL)** shows the percentage change in EPS resulting from a given percentage change in sales: $DTL = DOL \times DFL$. Degree of leverage is a point concept; that is, it applies to changes in output from a specific starting level.

▷ **Practical considerations** in setting a target capital structure include such factors as (1) the **TIE ratio** and (2) the link between **capital structures and mergers.**

A checklist of factors provides guidelines for financial managers in choosing a firm's target capital structure. These include such considerations as (1) the **growth rate** of the firm, (2) **control**, (3) **management attitude toward risk**, (4) **market conditions**, and (5) the firm's need for **financial flexibility.**

Although it is theoretically possible to determine a firm's optimal capital structure, as a practical matter we cannot estimate this structure with precision. Accordingly, financial executives generally treat the optimal capital structure as a range—for example, 40 to 50 percent debt—rather than as a precise point, such as 45 percent. The concepts discussed in this chapter help managers understand the factors they should consider when they set the target capital structure ranges for their firms.

Resolution to
DECISION IN FINANCE

RIPE FOR THE PICKING

The aerospace industry is consolidating in the face of reduced national defense spending, and Rohr appears to be a likely candidate for takeover by a larger company despite management's apparent determination to go it alone.

Securities analysts believe the company is fundamentally strong. One commented, "Rohr has considerable potential looking ahead for the next 20 years. The engines and programs they're on will generate a strong and long-term revenue base."

Northrop Corporation is believed to have been the American partner with Carlyle in the rejected equity deal, and it has indicated interest in expanding its commercial jet work as its defense business shrinks. Martin Marietta would also be a likely candidate to take over Rohr, except that it already has a buy offer under way for GE Aerospace.

Source: Sarah Lurman, "Bidders Look at Rohr as Aerospace Industry Shrinks," *The Wall Street Journal,* January 14, 1993, B4.

Nevertheless, some observers are certain a takeover will occur. Both insiders and outsiders see Chairman Goldsmith's retirement as an open invitation. A middle manager at Rohr commented bitterly, reflecting employees' low morale, "Last year, [Goldsmith] made a speech saying in the next year some of you won't be here. He should have said some of us." And a Washington consultant, David Smith, said a takeover "is just a matter of time. You have a low stock price, a management shakeup, an outside director in control, irate shareholders—one and one usually makes two. With a consolidating industry, the strong survivors are going to eat these guys."

From management's viewpoint, a takeover would mean loss of authority and possibly their jobs, but from the stockholders' standpoint, a takeover would not necessarily be bad news. Stock prices generally gain when other companies start bidding for a company like Rohr, so Rohr's stockholders probably should regard the merger rumors as good news.

Questions

20-1   "One type of leverage affects both EBIT and EPS. The other type affects only EPS." Explain what this statement means.

20-2   What is the relationship between beta (or market) risk and leverage?

20-3   Explain why the following statement is true: "Other things the same, firms with relatively stable sales are able to carry relatively high debt ratios."

20-4   Why do public utility companies usually pursue a different financial policy than retail firms?

20-5   Some economists believe that swings in business cycles will not be as wide in the future as they have been in the past. Assuming that they are correct in their analysis, what effect might this added stability have on the types of financing used by firms in the United States? Would your answer be true for all firms?

20-6   Why is EBIT generally considered to be independent of financial leverage? Why might EBIT actually be influenced by financial leverage at high debt levels?

20-7   How might increasingly volatile inflation rates, interest rates, and bond prices affect the optimal capital structure for corporations?

20-8   If a firm went from zero debt to successively higher levels of debt, why would you expect its stock price to first rise, then hit a peak, and then begin to decline?

20-9   Why is the debt level that maximizes a firm's expected EPS always higher than the debt level that maximizes its stock price?

20-10   In public utility rate cases, a utility's riskiness is a key issue, as utilities are supposed to be allowed to earn the same rate of return on common equity as unregulated firms of comparable risk. The difficulty is in specifying in quantitative terms the riskiness of utilities and nonutilities. Describe how the degree of leverage concepts (DOL, DFL, and DTL) might be used as indicators of risk in a rate case.

20-11   When the Bell System was broken up, the old AT&T was split into a new AT&T plus 7 regional telephone companies. The specific reason for forcing the breakup was to increase the degree of competition in the telephone industry. AT&T had had a monopoly on local service, long distance, and the manufacture of all the equipment used by telephone companies, and the breakup was expected to open most of these markets to competition. In the court order that set the terms of the breakup, the capital structures of the surviving companies were specified, and much attention was given to the increased competition telephone companies could expect in the future. Do you think the optimal capital structure after the breakup was the same as the prebreakup optimal capital structure? Do you think competition could force companies to use more debt in order to reduce taxes? Explain your position.

20-12   Assume that you are advising the management of a firm that is about to double its assets to serve its rapidly growing market. It must choose between a highly automated production process and a less automated one, and it must also choose a capital structure for financing the expansion. Should the asset investment and financing decisions be jointly determined, or should each decision be made separately? How would these decisions affect one another? How could the degree of leverage concept be used to help management analyze the situation?

Self-Test Problems

ST-1   Visical Inc. produces medical test equipment for ophthalmologists, which sells for $500 per unit. Visical's fixed operating costs are $1 million; 5,000 units are produced and sold each year; operating profits total $250,000; and the firm's assets (all equity financed) are $2,500,000. Visical estimates that it can change its production process, thereby adding $2 million to investment and $250,000 to fixed operating costs. This change will reduce variable operating costs per unit by $50 and increase output by 2,000 units, but the sales price on all units will have to be lowered to $475 to permit sales of the additional output. Visical has tax loss carry-forwards that cause its tax rate to be zero. It uses no debt, and its cost of capital (cost of equity) is 10 percent.
   a. Should Visical make the change?
   b. Would Visical's operating leverage as measured by DOL increase or decrease if it made the change? Would Visical's business risk increase or decrease, other things equal? What about its breakeven point?

ST-2   Brosky Production's situation is as follows: (1) EBIT = $2.86 million; (2) tax rate = T = 40%; (3) debt outstanding = D = $4 million; (4) k_d = 9%; (5) k_s = 12%; and (6) shares of stock outstanding = 500,000. Since Brosky's product market is stable and the company expects no growth, all earnings are paid out as dividends. The debt consists of perpetual bonds.
   a. What are Brosky's earnings per share (EPS) and its price per share (P_0)?
   b. What is Brosky's weighted average cost of capital (WACC)? Assume that Brosky's stock is selling at its book value (M/B = 1.0).
   c. Brosky can increase its debt by $4 million, to a total of $8 million, using the new

debt to buy back and retire some of its shares at the current price. Its interest rate on debt will be 12 percent (it will have to call and refund the old debt), and its cost of equity will rise from 12 percent to 15 percent. EBIT will remain constant. Should Brosky change its capital structure?

d. What is Brosky's TIE ratio under the original situation and under the conditions in Part c?

Problems

20-1
Combined leverage effects

Waters Inc. has a DOL of 1.5 and a DFL of 2.4 at a given level of sales. If sales increase by 5 percent, what will happen to net income?

20-2
Operating leverage effects

Sattem & Dane (S&D) has a single product, which sells for $45 and has a variable cost of $30 per unit. Fixed operating costs are $750,000.
a. What is the firm's breakeven point in units?
b. What is the firm's breakeven point in sales dollars?
c. What is the firm's DOL if sales are 15,000 units above the breakeven point?
d. What is the firm's EBIT for the period if S&D's sales are 7,500 units below the breakeven point?

20-3
Operating leverage effects

Now assume that Sattem & Dane (Problem 20-2) has begun an impressive modernization program. To reduce its variable costs to $15 per unit, the company's fixed operating costs have been allowed to rise to $2.1 million annually. Under these new conditions:
a. What is the firm's breakeven point in units?
b. What is the firm's breakeven point in sales dollars?
c. What is the firm's DOL if sales are 15,000 units above the breakeven point?
d. What is the firm's EBIT for the period if S&D's sales are 7,500 units below the breakeven point?
e. What are the financial implications of the new level of operating leverage as compared with S&D's operating leverage before the modernization?

20-4
Operating leverage

Abrassart Manufacturing is selling 300,000 units of its only product at $100 per unit. Variable costs are $40 per unit, whereas annual fixed operating costs are $15 million.
a. What is the firm's operating income (EBIT) at this level of sales?
b. What is the firm's DOL at this level of sales?
c. If sales increase by 5 percent, what is the resulting operating income? Use the DOL to answer this question.
d. Confirm your answer in Part c by preparing an income statement showing the dollar level of sales, fixed and variable operating costs, and operating income after the 5 percent growth in sales.
e. What would happen to operating income if sales decline by 5 percent? Confirm your answer with a pro forma income statement.

20-5
Operating leverage

Emory Supplies had sales of only $150,000 last year. However, management expects this year's sales to reach $187,500 and further estimates that this will cause operating income (EBIT) to increase by 67.5 percent. What was Emory's DOL at a sales level of $150,000?

20-6
Operating leverage

Refer back to Figure 20-2.
a. Calculate the degree of operating leverage for Options 1 and 2 at sales of $40,000, $120,000, and $360,000. The degree of operating leverage for other levels of sales are as follows:

Sales	DOL_1	DOL_2
$ 80,000	Undefined (or ∞)	(2.0)
160,000	2.0	4.0
200,000	1.67	2.5

b. Is it true that the DOL is approximately equal to infinity just above the breakeven point, implying that a very small increase in sales will produce a huge percentage increase in EBIT, but that the DOL declines when calculated at higher levels of sales?

c. Is it true for both options for all sales levels where DOL > 0 that $DOL_2 < DOL_1$? Explain.

20-7
Breakeven analysis

Educators Inc. will produce 200,000 units this year of "The Magic Speller," a learning device for children. Variable costs are $40 per unit, and fixed operating costs are $3,400,000. What selling price is required for the firm to obtain operating profits of $1,800,000 if all 200,000 units are sold?

20-8
Breakeven point

Adventure Books sells paperback books for $6.25 each. The variable cost per book is $4.50. At current annual sales of 150,000 books, the publisher is just breaking even. It is estimated that if the author's royalties are reduced, the variable cost per book will drop by $0.75. Assume the author's royalties are reduced and sales remain constant; how much more money can the publisher put into advertising (a fixed operating cost) and still break even?

20-9
Breakeven analysis

The Coate Corporation, which manufactures ski goggles, has decided to also manufacture ski poles. The ski poles will sell for $44 per set. Fixed operating costs are $480,000 annually. The company expects to sell 30,000 sets of ski poles during its first year of operations. What is the maximum allowable variable cost per set if the company is to just break even in its first year of operations?

20-10
Combined leverage effects

Munk International has sales of $9.6 million, and variable cost is 65 percent of sales. Fixed operating costs are $1.8 million. The firm just received an $8.4 million loan with an interest rate of 11 percent. Assume that this loan is the firm's only debt.
a. What is the firm's DOL at this level of sales?
b. What is the firm's DFL at this level of sales?
c. What is the firm's DTL at this level of sales?

20-11
Combined leverage effects

Condor Air Service expects sales of $15 million this year. Variable costs are 70 percent of sales, and fixed operating costs are $4 million. The firm has debt of $10 million on which it pays 8 percent interest.
a. What is the firm's DOL at this level of sales?
b. What is the firm's DFL at this level of sales?
c. What is the firm's DTL at this level of sales?
d. If Condor's sales were to increase by 3 percent, what would happen to operating income (EBIT)?

20-12
Financial leverage

Kostecki Inc. has annual sales of $7.4 million, variable costs are 40 percent of sales, and fixed operating costs are $4 million. The firm's DFL = 4.0. How much interest does the firm pay annually?

20-13
Degree of financial leverage

A company currently sells 150,000 units annually. At this sales level, its EBIT is $8 million, and its degree of total leverage is 2.0. The firm's debt consists of $20 million in bonds with a 12 percent coupon. The company is considering a new production method which will entail an increase in fixed operating costs, resulting in a degree of operating leverage of 1.8. Being concerned about the total risk of the firm, the president wants to keep the degree of total leverage at 2.0. If EBIT remains at $8 million, what amount of bonds must be retired to accomplish this?

20-14
Combined leverage effects

Management of Ironhill Inc. has calculated that if sales increase from $6,200,000 to $7,130,000, EBIT will increase by 30 percent and net income will increase from $372,000 to $520,800. What is Ironhill's degree of total leverage (DTL) at a sales level of $6,200,000?

20-15

Combined leverage effects

Berggren & Company has the following financial characteristics:

$$\text{Sales in units} = 50,000.$$
$$\text{Unit sales price} = \$140.$$
$$\text{Variable cost per unit} = \$77.$$
$$\text{Fixed operating costs} = \$2.1 \text{ million.}$$
$$\text{Annual interest charges} = \$350,000.$$
$$\text{Tax rate} = 40\%.$$
$$\text{Shares outstanding} = 200,000.$$

a. Determine the firm's EPS if sales increase by 20 percent next year. Use the DTL equation as the basis for your computations.

b. Confirm your answer in Part a by preparing a projected income statement.

20-16

Combined leverage effects

Chan Software Inc. has a single product, which it sells for $50. Variable costs per unit are $35, and total fixed costs are $600,000, which include interest payments of $120,000. The firm plans to produce and sell 48,000 units this year.

a. What is the firm's DOL?

b. What is the firm's DFL?

c. What is the firm's DTL?

d. If sales were to increase from 48,000 units to 53,760 units this year, what would be the impact on (1) EBIT and (2) net income?

e. Confirm your answers in Part d by setting up two income statements, one before and one after the change in sales.

f. If, instead of an increase, the firm's sales were to drop to 44,640 units from the current level of 48,000 units, what would be the resulting percentage change in net income?

20-17

Combined leverage effects

Trinity Valley Corporation is a new firm that will manufacture and sell replacement parts for equipment to construction firms. The firm must determine the operating and financial leverage under which it will operate. Trinity Valley can use a low operating leverage (LOL) plan under which variable costs are $15 per unit (75 percent of sales) and fixed operating costs are $200,000. Alternatively, Trinity Valley can use high operating leverage (called the HOL plan) under which the variable costs are $10 per unit (50 percent of sales) and fixed operating costs are $600,000. Whichever production plan is implemented, the firm's product will sell for $20 per unit.

a. Calculate the degree of operating leverage (DOL) for the LOL and HOL production plans at sales of $1.2 million and $1.6 million.

b. Assume that the LOL and HOL plans can be financed in either of the following ways: (1) no debt or (2) $900,000 of debt at 10 percent interest. Calculate the degree of financial leverage (DFL) for the LOL plan at sales levels of both $1.2 and $1.6 million. The DFLs for the HOL plan at $900,000 of debt and these same sales levels are 0 and 1.82, respectively.

c. Calculate the degree of total leverage (DTL) under the LOL plan with $900,000 of debt at sales of $1.2 and $1.6 million. The DTLs for the HOL plan at these same sales levels are -6.67 and 7.27, respectively.

d. At the sales level of $1.2 million, the DTL for the HOL plan was negative ($DTL_{HOL} = -6.67$). Does a negative degree of operating leverage imply that an increase in sales will *lower* profits?

20-18

Financing alternatives

Zuccaro Enterprises plans to raise a net amount of $360 million to finance new equipment and working capital in 1994. Two alternatives are being considered: Common stock may be sold to net $40 per share, or debentures yielding 10 percent may be issued. Zuccaro's balance sheet and income statement prior to financing are as follows:

Zuccaro Enterprises:
Balance Sheet as of December 31, 1993
(Millions of Dollars)

Current assets	$1,200	Accounts payable	$ 230
Net fixed assets	600	Notes payable to bank	370
		Other current liabilities	300
		Total current liabilities	$ 900
		Long-term debt	370
		Common stock, $2 par	80
		Retained earnings	450
Total assets	$1,800	Total liabilities and equity	$1,800

Zuccaro Enterprises:
Income Statement for Year Ended December 31, 1993
(Millions of Dollars)

Sales	$3,300
Operating costs	2,970
Earnings before interest and taxes (10%)	$ 330
Interest on debt	60
Earnings before taxes	$ 270
Federal-plus-state taxes (40%)	108
Net income	$ 162

The probability distribution for 1994 sales is as follows:

Probability	Annual Sales (Millions of Dollars)
0.30	$3,000
0.40	3,600
0.30	4,200

a. Assuming that EBIT is equal to 10 percent of sales, calculate earnings per share under both the debt financing and the stock financing alternatives at each possible level of sales. Then calculate expected earnings per share and σ_{EPS} under both debt and stock financing. Also calculate the debt ratio and the times-interest-earned (TIE) ratio at the expected sales level under each alternative. The old debt will remain outstanding. Which financing method would you recommend?

(Do Part b only if you are using the computerized problem diskette.)

b. Suppose each of the following happens, with other values held at Part a levels:
  (1) The interest rate on new debt falls to 5 percent.
  (2) The interest rate on new debt rises to 20 percent.
  (3) The stock price falls to $20 (return k_d to 0.10 = 10%).
  (4) The stock price rises to $70.
  (5) With P_0 = $40 and k_d = 0.10 = 10%, now change the sales probability distribution to the following:

	Sales	Probability		Sales	Probability
(a)	$3,000	0	(b) $	0	0.3
	3,600	1.0		3,600	0.4
	4,200	0		10,000	0.3

What are the implications of these changes?

Solutions to Self-Test Problems

ST-1   a. 1. Determine the variable cost per unit at present, using the following definitions and equations:

P = average sales price per unit of output = $500.

F = fixed operating costs = $1 million.

Q = units of output (sales) = 5,000.

V = variable costs per unit, found as follows:

$$EBIT = PQ - VQ - F$$

$$\$250,000 = \$500(5,000) - 5,000V - \$1,000,000$$

$$5,000V = \$1,250,000$$

$$V = \$250.$$

2. Determine the new operating profit level if the change is made:

$$\text{New operating profit (EBIT)} = P_2Q_2 - V_2Q_2 - F_2$$

$$= \$475(7,000) - \$200(7,000) - \$1,250,000$$

$$= \$675,000.$$

3. Determine the incremental operating profit (ΔEBIT):

$$\Delta EBIT = \$675,000 - \$250,000 = \$425,000.$$

4. Estimate the approximate rate of return on the new investment:

$$ROI = \frac{\Delta EBIT}{\Delta Investment} = \frac{\$425,000}{\$2,000,000} = 21.25\%.$$

Since the ROI exceeds Visical's cost of capital, this analysis suggests that Visical should go ahead and make the investment.

b. 1.

$$DOL = \frac{Q(P - V)}{Q(P - V) - F}$$

$$\textit{Old}: DOL_{Q=5,000} = \frac{5,000(\$500 - \$250)}{5,000(\$500 - \$250) - \$1,000,000} = 5.00.$$

2. Note that we cannot compare DOL_{Old} at 5,000 units of output with DOL_{New} at 7,000 units of output. This would not be a valid comparison because DOL declines as the sales level increases above the breakeven point. The only valid way to compare Visical's operating leverage before and after the change is by calculating DOL at the *same* level of output for both plans, for example, 5,000 units (even though the company expects to sell 7,000 units under the new plan):

$$\textit{New}: DOL_{Q=5,000} = \frac{5,000(\$475 - \$200)}{5,000(\$475 - \$200) - \$1,250,000} = 11.00.$$

This indicates that, *at any given level of sales, Visical's operating income will be more sensitive to changes in sales* if the production process is modified to include greater use of operating leverage. The proposal would, therefore, increase the firm's business risk. This is also reflected in the higher breakeven point under the new plan:

$$Old: Q_{BE} = \frac{F}{P - V} = \frac{\$1,000,000}{\$500 - \$250} = 4,000 \text{ units.}$$

$$New: Q_{BE} = \frac{F_2}{P_2 - V_2} = \frac{\$1,250,000}{\$475 - \$200} = 4,545 \text{ units.}$$

This does not mean that Visical should not make the change (clearly, with a lower sales price, it might be easier to achieve the new higher breakeven volume). It simply means that the firm's management should be aware of the added risk.

ST-2 **a.**

EBIT	$2,860,000
Interest ($4,000,000 × 0.09)	360,000
Earnings before taxes (EBT)	2,500,000
Taxes (40%)	1,000,000
Net income	$1,500,000

$$EPS = \$1,500,000/500,000 = \$3.00.$$

$$P_0 = \$3.00/0.12 = \$25.00.$$

b.
$$Equity = 500,000 \times \$25 = \$12,500,000.$$

$$Debt = \$4,000,000.$$

$$Total \ capital = \$16,500,000.$$

$$WACC = w_d k_d (1 - T) + w_s k_s$$

$$= (\$4,000,000/\$16,500,000)(9\%)(1 - 0.4) + (\$12,500,000/\$16,500,000)(12\%)$$

$$= 1.31\% + 9.09\%$$

$$= 10.40\%.$$

c.

EBIT	$2,860,000
Interest ($8,000,000 × 0.12)	960,000
Earnings before taxes (EBT)	$1,900,000
Taxes (40%)	760,000
Net income	$1,140,000

Shares bought and retired = ΔDebt/P_0 = $4,000,000/$25 = 160,000.

New outstanding shares = 500,000 − 160,000 = 340,000.

New EPS = $1,140,000/340,000 = $3.35.

New price per share P_0 = $3.35/0.15 = $22.33 versus $25.00.

Therefore, Brosky should not change its capital structure.

Alternative solution:

$$New \ total \ equity = \$12,500,000 - \$4,000,000 = \$8,500,000.$$

$$New \ total \ debt = \$4,000,000 + \$4,000,000 = \$8,000,000.$$

$$Total \ capital = \$16,500,000.$$

$$k_d = 12\%.$$

$$k_s = 15\%.$$

$$\text{WACC} = w_d k_d (1 - T) + w_s k_s$$

$$= (\$8,000,000/\$16,500,000)(12\%)(0.6) + (\$8,500,000/\$16,500,000)(15\%)$$

$$= 3.49\% + 7.73\%$$

$$= 11.22\%.$$

This represents an increase in the WACC, and again, we conclude that Brosky should keep its present capital structure.

d.
$$\text{TIE} = \frac{\text{EBIT}}{\text{I}}.$$

$$\text{Original TIE} = \frac{\$2,860,000}{\$360,000} = 7.94.$$

$$\text{New TIE} = \frac{\$2,860,000}{\$960,000} = 2.98.$$

Bankruptcy

Appendix 20A[1]

In the event of bankruptcy, debtholders have a prior claim to a firm's income and assets over common and preferred stockholders. Because different classes of debtholders are accorded different treatments in bankruptcy settlements, it is important for one to know who gets what if the firm fails. These topics are discussed in this appendix.[2]

Federal Bankruptcy Laws

Bankruptcy actually begins when a debtor is unable to meet scheduled payments to creditors or when the firm's cash flow projections indicate that it will soon be unable to meet payments. As the bankruptcy proceedings go forward, the following central issues arise:

1. Is the inability to meet scheduled debt payments a temporary cash flow problem, or does it represent a permanent problem caused by asset values' having fallen below debt obligations?

2. If the problem is a temporary one, an extension that gives the firm time to recover and to satisfy creditors will be worked out. If basic long-run asset values have truly declined, economic losses have occurred. In this event, who should bear the losses?

3. Is the company "worth more dead than alive"? In other words, would the business be more valuable if it were maintained and continued in operation or if it were liquidated and sold off in pieces?

---

[1]This appendix was co-authored by Arthur L. Hermann of the University of Hartford and Larry A. Lynch of Roanoke College.

[2]Much of the current work in this area is based on writings of Edward I. Altman. For a summary of his work and that of others, see Edward I. Altman, "Bankruptcy and Reorganization," in *Financial Handbook,* ed. Edward I. Altman (New York: Wiley, 1986), Chapter 19.

4. Who should control the firm while it is being liquidated or rehabilitated? Should the existing management be left in control, or should a *trustee* be placed in charge of operations?

These primary issues are addressed in the federal bankruptcy statutes.

The U.S. bankruptcy laws were first enacted in 1898, modified substantially in 1938, changed again in 1978, and further fine-tuned in 1984. The 1978 act, which provides the basic laws that govern bankruptcy today, was a major revision designed to streamline and expedite proceedings, and it consists of eight odd-numbered chapters, the even-numbered chapters of the earlier act having been incorporated into the remaining chapters. Chapters 1, 3, and 5 of the 1978 act contain general provisions applicable to the other chapters; Chapter 7 details the procedures to be followed when liquidating a firm; Chapter 9 provides for financially distressed municipalities; Chapter 11 is the business reorganization chapter; Chapter 13 covers the adjustment of debts for "individuals with regular income"; and Chapter 15 sets up a system of trustees who help administer proceedings under the act.

Chapter 11

A chapter of the Bankruptcy Reform Act that governs reorganizations, or restructurings, due to bankruptcy.

Chapter 7

A chapter of the Bankruptcy Reform Act that governs liquidations, or selling of the firm's assets, due to bankruptcy.

Chapters 11 and 7 are the most important ones for financial management purposes. When you read in the paper that Eastern Airlines or some other company has "filed for **Chapter 11,**" this means that the company is bankrupt and is trying to reorganize under Chapter 11 of the act. If a reorganization plan cannot be worked out, then the company will be liquidated as prescribed in **Chapter 7** of the act.

The 1978 act is quite flexible, and it provides a great deal of scope for informal negotiations between a company and its creditors. Under this act, a case is opened by filing a petition with a federal district bankruptcy court. The petition may be either voluntary or involuntary; that is, it may be filed either by the firm's management or by its creditors. A committee of unsecured creditors is then appointed by the court to negotiate with management for a *reorganization,* which may include the restructuring of debt and other claims against the firm. (A restructuring could involve lengthening the maturity of debt, lowering the interest rate on it, reducing the principal amount owed, exchanging common or preferred stock for debt, or some combination of these actions.) A trustee may be appointed by the court if it is in the best interests of the creditors and stockholders; otherwise, the existing management will retain control. Under Chapter 11, if no fair and feasible reorganization can be worked out, the firm will be liquidated under the procedures spelled out in Chapter 7.

Financial Decisions in Bankruptcy

liquidation

The dissolution of a firm by selling off its assets.

reorganization

The restructuring of debt and other claims against the firm.

When a business becomes insolvent, a decision must be made whether to dissolve the firm through **liquidation** or to keep it alive through **reorganization.** Fundamentally, this decision depends on a determination of the value of the firm if it is rehabilitated as compared with the value of the assets if they are sold off individually. The procedure that promises higher returns to the creditors and owners will be adopted. Often the greater indicated value of the firm in reorganization versus its value in liquidation is used to force a compromise agreement among the claimants in a reorganization, even when each group believes that its relative position has not been treated fairly in the reorganization plan. Both the SEC and the courts are called upon to determine the *fairness* and the *feasibility* of proposed plans of reorganization.

Standard of Fairness.   The basic doctrine of *fairness* states that claims must be recognized in the order of their legal and contractual priority. Carrying out this concept of fairness in a reorganization (as opposed to a liquidation) involves the following steps:

1. Future sales must be estimated.
2. Operating conditions must be analyzed so that the future earnings and cash flows can be predicted.

3.   The capitalization (or discount) rate to be applied to these future cash flows must be determined.

4.   This capitalization rate must be applied to the estimated cash flows to obtain a present value figure, which is the indicated value for the reorganized company.

5.   Provisions for the distribution of the restructured firm's securities to its claimants must be made.

Standard of Feasibility.   The primary test of *feasibility* in a reorganization is whether the fixed charges after reorganization can be adequately covered by cash flows. Adequate coverage generally requires an improvement in operating earnings, a reduction of fixed charges, or both. Among the actions that must generally be taken are the following:

1.   Debt maturities are usually lengthened, interest rates may be scaled back, and some debt may be converted into equity.

2.   When the quality of management has been substandard, a new team must be given control of the company.

3.   If inventories have become obsolete or depleted, they must be replaced.

4.   Sometimes the plant and the equipment must be modernized before the firm can operate on a competitive basis.

A firm may undergo internal reorganization with existing management retaining control or being replaced, should they be considered incompetent. The internal restructuring must be deemed fair and feasible by the court. A firm may undergo external reorganization in the form of a merger with or acquisition by an outside entity. Again, claimants may be asked to make concessions to guarantee fairness and feasibility.

Liquidation Procedures

If a company is too far gone to be reorganized, it must be liquidated. Liquidation should occur if the business is worth more dead than alive, or if the possibility of restoring it to financial health is so remote that the creditors would face a high risk of even greater losses if operations were continued.

Chapter 7 of the Bankruptcy Reform Act is designed to do three things: (1) provide safeguards against the withdrawal of assets by the owners of the bankrupt firm; (2) provide for an equitable distribution of the assets among the creditors; and (3) allow insolvent debtors to discharge all their obligations and to start new businesses unhampered by a burden of prior debt. Liquidation is time-consuming, it can be costly, and it results in the loss of the business.

The distribution of assets in a liquidation under Chapter 7 of the Bankruptcy Act is governed by the following priority of claims:

1.   *Secured creditors, who are entitled to the proceeds of the sale of specific property pledged for a lien or a mortgage.* If the proceeds from the sale of property do not fully satisfy the secured creditors' claims, the remaining balance owed them is treated as a general creditor claim. See Item 9.

2.   *Trustee's costs to administer and operate the bankrupt firm.*

3.   *Expenses incurred after an involuntary case has begun but before a trustee is appointed.*

4.   *Wages due workers if earned within three months prior to the filing of the petition of bankruptcy.* The amount of wages is limited to $2,000 per person.

5. *Claims for unpaid contributions to employee benefit plans that were to have been paid within six months prior to filing.* However, these claims, plus wages in Item 4, are not to exceed the $2,000-per-employee limit.

6. *Unsecured claims for customer deposits, not to exceed a maximum of $900 per individual.*

7. *Taxes due a federal, state, county, or any other government agency.*

8. *Unfunded pension plan liabilities.* These have a claim above that of general creditors for an amount up to 30 percent of the common and preferred equity; any remaining unfunded pension claims rank with general creditors.

9. *General, or unsecured, creditors.* Holders of trade credit, unsecured loans, the unsatisfied portion of secured loans, and debenture bonds are classified as *general creditors.* Holders of subordinated debt also fall into this category, but they must turn over required amounts to the holders of senior debt.

10. *Preferred stockholders,* who can receive an amount up to the par value of the issue.

11. *Common stockholders,* who receive any remaining funds.

To illustrate how this priority of claims works out, consider the balance sheet of Panhandle Drilling Inc., shown in Table 20A-1. Assets total $90 million. The claims are indicated on the right-hand side of the balance sheet. Note that the debentures are subordinated to the notes payable to banks. Panhandle has filed for reorganization under Chapter 11, but since no fair and feasible reorganization could be arranged, the trustee is liquidating the firm under Chapter 7.

Now assume that the assets are sold. The assets as reported in the balance sheet in Table 20A-1 are greatly overstated — they are, in fact, worth less than half of the $90 million at which they are carried. The following amounts are realized on liquidation:

Proceeds from sale of current assets	$28,000,000
Proceeds from sale of fixed assets	5,000,000
Total receipts	$33,000,000

The order of priority for payment of claims is shown in Table 20A-2. The first mortgage is paid from the net proceeds of $5 million from the sale of fixed property, leaving

---

Table 20A-1

Panhandle Drilling Inc.: Balance Sheet

Current assets	$80,000,000	Accounts payable	$20,000,000
Net fixed assets	10,000,000	Notes payable (due bank)	10,000,000
		Accrued wages, 1,400 at $500	700,000
		U.S. taxes	1,000,000
		State and local taxes	300,000
		Total current liabilities	$32,000,000
		First mortgage	6,000,000
		Second mortgage	1,000,000
		Subordinated debentures[a]	8,000,000
		Long-term debt	$15,000,000
		Preferred stock	2,000,000
		Common stock	26,000,000
		Paid-in capital	4,000,000
		Retained earnings	11,000,000
		Total equity	$43,000,000
Total assets	$90,000,000	Total liabilities and equity	$90,000,000

[a]Subordinated to $10 million of notes payable to the First National Bank.

Table 20A-2

Panhandle Drilling Inc.:
Order of Priority of Claims

Distribution of Proceeds on Liquidation

1. Proceeds from sale of assets	$33,000,000
2. First mortgage, paid from sale of fixed assets	5,000,000
3. Fees and expenses of administration of bankruptcy	6,000,000
4. Wages due workers earned within 3 months prior to filing of bankruptcy petition	700,000
5. Taxes	1,300,000
6. Available to general creditors	$20,000,000

Claims of General Creditors	Claim[a] (1)	Application of 50 Percent[b] (2)	After Subordination Adjustment[c] (3)	Percentage of Original Claims Received[d] (4)
Unsatisfied portion of first mortgage	$ 1,000,000	$ 500,000	$ 500,000	92
Unsatisfied portion of second mortgage	1,000,000	500,000	500,000	50
Notes payable	10,000,000	5,000,000	9,000,000	90
Accounts payable	20,000,000	10,000,000	10,000,000	50
Subordinated debentures	8,000,000	4,000,000	0	0
	$40,000,000	$20,000,000	$20,000,000	

[a]Column 1 is the claim of each class of general creditor. Total claims equal $40 million.
[b]From Line 6 in the upper section of the table, we see that $20 million is available for general creditors. This sum, divided by the $40 million of claims, indicates that general creditors will initially receive 50 percent of their claims. This is shown in Column 2.
[c]The debentures are subordinated to the notes payable, so $4 million is reallocated from debentures to notes payable in Column 3.
[d]Column 4 shows the results of dividing the amount in Column 3 by the original claim amount given in Column 1, except for the first mortgage, for which $5 million received from the sale of fixed assets is included.

$28 million available to other creditors. Next come the fees and expenses of the trustee's administration, which are typically about 20 percent of gross proceeds; in this example they are assumed to be $6 million. Next in priority are wages due workers, which total $700,000. The total amount of taxes to be paid is $1.3 million. Thus far, the total of claims paid from the $33 million is $13 million, leaving $20 million for the general creditors.

The claims of the general creditors total $40 million. Since $20 million is available, claimants would each receive 50 percent of their claims before the subordination adjustment. This adjustment requires that the holders of subordinated debentures turn over to the holders of notes payable all amounts received until the notes are satisfied. In this situation the claim of the holders of the notes payable is $10 million, but only $5 million is available; the deficiency is therefore $5 million. After transfer of $4 million from the subordinated debentures, there remains a deficiency of $1 million on the notes. This amount will remain unsatisfied.

Note that 90 percent of the bank claim is satisfied, whereas a maximum of 50 percent of other unsecured claims will be satisfied. These figures illustrate the usefulness of the subordination provision to the security to which the subordination is made. Because no other funds remain, the claims of the holders of preferred and common stock are completely wiped out. Studies of bankruptcy liquidations indicate that unsecured creditors receive, on the average, about 15 cents on the dollar, whereas common stockholders generally receive nothing.

It is clear to see why representatives of the stockholders strive for reorganization over liquidation. Current bankruptcy and tax laws may actually favor reorganization over liquidation, allowing for the potential breakdown of the absolute priority rules just described. Junior creditors and residual claimants have the ability to delay resolution of a filing and raise the costs of settling the claims. Senior claimants may cooperate with equity holders in the hope of faring better by preserving tax loss carry-forwards.

Social Issues in Bankruptcy Proceedings

An interesting social issue arose in connection with bankruptcy during the 1980s—the role of bankruptcy in settling labor disputes and product liability suits. Normally, bankruptcy proceedings originate after a company has become so financially weak that it cannot meet its current obligations. However, provisions in the Bankruptcy Act permit a company to file for protection under Chapter 11 if *financial forecasts* indicate that a continuation of business under current conditions will lead to insolvency. These provisions were applied by Frank Lorenzo, the principal stockholder of Continental Airlines, who demonstrated that if Continental continued to operate under its then-current union contract, it would become insolvent in a matter of months. The company then filed a plan of reorganization which included major changes in its union contract. The court found for Continental and allowed the company to abrogate its contract. The airline then reorganized as a nonunion carrier, and that reorganization turned the company from a money loser into a money maker. However, under pressure from labor, Congress changed the bankruptcy laws after the Continental affair to make it more difficult to use the laws to break union contracts.

The bankruptcy laws have also been used to bring about settlements in major product liability suits, the Manville asbestos case being the first, followed by the Dalkon Shield case. In both instances, the companies were being bombarded by literally thousands of lawsuits, and the very existence of such huge contingent liabilities made continued operations virtually impossible. Further, in both cases, it was relatively easy to prove (1) that if the plaintiffs won, the companies would be unable to pay off the full amounts claimed, (2) that a larger amount of funds would be available if the companies continued to operate than if they were liquidated, (3) that continued operations were possible only if the suits were brought to a conclusion, and (4) that a timely resolution of all the suits was impossible because of the number of suits and the different positions taken by different parties. At any rate, the bankruptcy statutes were used to consolidate all the suits and to reach a settlement under which all the plaintiffs obtained more money than they otherwise would have gotten, and the companies were able to stay in business. The stockholders did not do very well because most of the companies' future cash flows were assigned to the plaintiffs, but, even so, the stockholders probably came out better than they would have if the individual suits had been carried through the jury system to a conclusion, because of the high costs of extended litigation.

While we have no opinion about the use of bankruptcy laws to settle social issues such as labor disputes and product liability suits, bankruptcy filing has become an acceptable strategic choice for some firms. The examples illustrate how financial projections can be used to demonstrate the effects of different legal decisions. Financial analysis is being used to an increasing extent in various types of legal work, from antitrust cases to suits against stockbrokers by disgruntled customers, and this trend is likely to continue.

Problems

20A-1
Liquidation effects

At the time it defaulted, Tapley Technologies had net current assets valued on the books at $30 million and net fixed assets valued at $37.5 million. At the time of final settlement its debts were as follows:

Current liabilities	$18.0 million
First mortgage bonds	15.0 million
Second mortgage bonds	7.5 million
Debentures	6.0 million

None of the current liabilities have preferences in liquidation as provided for in the bankruptcy laws, and none have been secured by the pledge of assets.

Assume that the amount shown for each of the four classes of liabilities includes all unpaid interest to the date of settlement. The fixed assets were pledged as security for the first mortgage bonds and repledged for the second mortgage bonds. Determine the appropriate distribution of the proceeds of liquidation under the following conditions:

a. Liquidation of current assets realizes $27 million, and $10.5 million is obtained from fixed assets.

b. Liquidation of current assets realizes $13.5 million, and $6 million is obtained from fixed assets.

20A-2

Bankruptcy distributions

The Mathys Marble Company has the following balance sheet:

Current assets	$5,040	Accounts payable	$1,080
Fixed assets	2,700	Notes payable (to bank)	540
		Accrued taxes	180
		Accrued wages	180
		Total current liabilities	$1,980
		First mortgage bonds	900
		Second mortgage bonds	900
		Total mortgage bonds	$1,800
		Subordinated debentures	1,080
		Total debt	$4,860
		Preferred stock	360
		Common stock	2,520
Total assets	$7,740	Total liabilities and equity	$7,740

The debentures are subordinated only to the notes payable. Suppose Mathys Marble goes bankrupt and is liquidated, with $1,800 being received from the sale of the fixed assets, which were pledged as security for the first and second mortgage bonds, and $2,880 received from the sale of current assets. The trustee's costs total $480.

a. How much will each class of investors receive?

(Do Part b only if you are using the computerized problem diskette.)

b. How much would each class of investors receive if (1) $960 were received from the sale of fixed assets and $2,040 from the sale of current assets and (2) if $1,680 were received from the sale of fixed assets and $3,720 from the sale of current assets?

Determining the Dividend Policy

O B J E C T I V E S

After reading this chapter, you should be able to:

▶ Define optimal dividend policy.

▶ Explain the logic of the residual dividend policy, and state why firms are more likely to use this policy in setting a long-run target than as a strict determinant of dividends in a given year.

▶ List a number of factors that influence dividend policy in practice, and explain the meaning of "signaling" and "clientele effect."

▶ State the three major dividend policies in use and specify which of these is most common.

▶ Explain the use of dividend reinvestment plans and why they are popular with certain investors.

▶ Specify why a firm might split its stock or pay a stock dividend.

▶ Discuss stock repurchases, including the effects on EPS, the price of the stock, and the firm's capital structure.

DECISION IN FINANCE

TO CUT OR NOT TO CUT DIVIDENDS

Delta Air Lines, one of the three largest U.S. carriers and awash in red ink during 1992, is looking for ways to slash costs to stop its hemorrhaging. Delta lost a record $564.8 million in 1992, which was more than double the $239.5 million it lost in calendar 1991, and, to make matters worse, its losses have been much greater than those of its rivals. Due to the most severe and prolonged loss period in its history, the company is considering a number of steps, including cutting its common dividend (which is currently the largest in the industry), deferring aircraft deliveries, reducing planned capital expenditures for facilities and ground equipment, and paring salaries. The board of directors scheduled a meeting for January 28, 1993, to discuss its plan of action. Of particular importance to the board is the avoidance of a possible debt downgrading by Standard & Poor's and Moody's.

Regarding a dividend cut, one Delta spokesman stated, "Mulling it over is something any responsible company should do." Delta had considered a dividend cut previously and rejected the idea. Says the company spokesman, "Our small stockholders depend on this dividend." The 30-cent quarterly common dividend is one of the hottest financial issues facing the company, since a dividend cut goes emphatically against the company's tradition. Prior to the

board's announcement of the January meeting, Delta officials discussed the dividend question with industry financial analysts. Delta officials believed that common shareholders already had suffered sufficiently — through dilution caused by issuing additional stock and by poor stock price performance. They believed that the shareholders had contributed enough and that they should not be asked to give any more.

How did Delta get into this position? Actually, the entire airline industry is in a quandary. Says one industry analyst, "If the airline industry were a savings and loan institution, the government would have seized and liquidated it." In 1990, the airline industry's "Waterloo" was Iraq's invasion of Kuwait, resulting in a near-doubling of fuel prices, which is a huge cost for the airlines. Then, in 1991 the industry was faced with the recession and the Gulf War, and in 1992 weak domestic traffic produced fare cutting and eliminating all hopes of

See end of chapter for resolution.
Photo source: Bruce Ayres/Tony Stone Images

profits. Everyone hoped that 1993 would be the transition year to a profitable 1994 for the industry, but only time will tell, and in the meantime, management must act if the company is to make it to 1994.

As you read this chapter, consider the factors that influence dividend policy, alternative dividend payment policies, and how a dividend policy is actually established. Think about the situation facing the airline industry in general and Delta in particular. Consider the board's dilemma. What options other than cutting the common dividend might they consider? What effect is a dividend cut likely to have on the company's financial situation, on its reputation, on its future ability to raise capital, and on the likelihood of a stockholder revolt which leads to a change in management?

Dividend policy involves the decision to pay out earnings or to retain them for reinvestment in the firm. The basic stock price model, $\hat{P}_0 = D_1/(k_s - g)$, shows that if the firm adopts a policy of paying out more cash dividends, D_1 will rise, which will tend to increase the price of the stock. However, if cash dividends are increased, then less money will be available for reinvestment, the expected future growth rate will be lowered, and this will depress the price of the stock. Thus, changing the dividend has two opposing effects. *The **optimal dividend policy** for a firm strikes that balance between current dividends and future growth which maximizes the price of the firm's stock.*

optimal dividend policy

The dividend policy which strikes a balance between current dividends and future growth and maximizes the firm's stock price.

A number of factors influence dividend policy, among them the investment opportunities available to the firm, alternative sources of capital, and stockholders' preferences for current versus future income. The primary goal of this chapter is to show how these and other factors interact to determine a firm's optimal dividend policy.

Residual Dividend Policy

residual dividend policy

A policy in which dividends paid equal total earnings minus the amount of retained earnings necessary to finance the firm's optimal capital budget.

In the preceding chapters on capital budgeting and the cost of capital, we indicated that the marginal cost of capital and investment opportunity schedules must be combined before the cost of capital can be established. In other words, the optimal capital budget, the marginal cost of capital, and the marginal rate of return on investment are determined *simultaneously*. In this section we use this framework to develop what is called the **residual dividend policy**, which states that a firm should follow these steps when deciding on its payout ratio: (1) determine the optimal capital budget; (2) determine the amount of equity capital needed to finance that budget, given a target capital structure; (3) use retained earnings to supply the equity component to the greatest extent possible; and (4) pay dividends only if more earnings are available than are needed to support the optimal capital budget. The word *residual* means "left over," and the residual policy implies that dividends should be paid only out of leftover earnings.

The basis for the residual policy is the premise that *investors prefer to have the firm retain and reinvest earnings rather than pay them out in dividends if the rate of return the firm can earn on reinvested earnings exceeds the rate investors, on average, can themselves obtain on other investments of compa-*

Figure 21-1 Georgia Paper Products: Marginal Cost of Capital

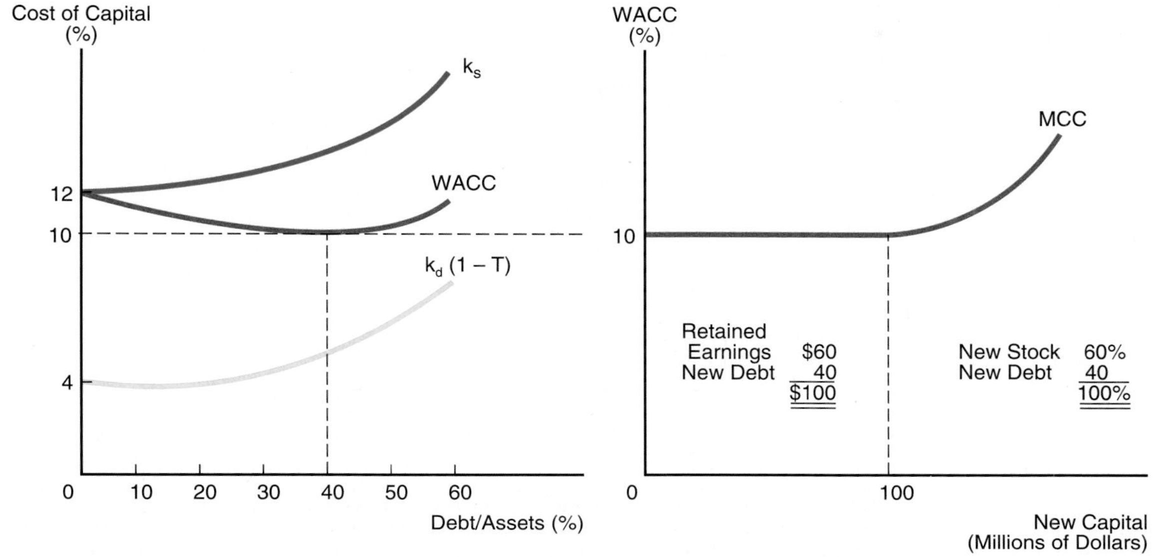

The marginal cost of capital is the weighted average of the costs of equity (k_s) and debt [$k_d(1 - T)$], as shown on the left. With a target debt ratio of 40 percent, the MCC will be 10 percent as long as GPP finances the equity portion through retained earnings. The right side of this figure shows that retaining earnings of $60 million will allow the firm to finance $100 million at an MCC of 10 percent. Beyond $100 million, new stock must be issued, which means an increase in the cost of equity and, therefore, a rise in the MCC.

rable risk. For example, if the corporation can reinvest retained earnings at a 14 percent rate of return, whereas the best rate the average stockholder can obtain if the earnings are passed on in the form of dividends is 12 percent, then stockholders will prefer to have the firm retain the profits.

We saw in Chapter 19 that the cost of retained earnings is an *opportunity cost* that reflects rates of return available to equity investors on investments of similar quality. If a firm's stockholders can buy other stocks of equal risk and obtain a 12 percent dividend-plus-capital-gains yield, then 12 percent is the firm's cost of retained earnings. The cost of new outside equity raised by selling common stock will be higher than 12 percent because of the costs of floating the issue.

Because most firms have a target capital structure that calls for at least some debt, new financing is done partly with debt and partly with equity. As long as the firm finances with the optimal mix of debt and equity and as long as it uses only internally generated equity (retained earnings), its marginal cost of capital will be minimized. Internally generated equity is available for financing a certain amount of new investment; beyond this amount the firm must turn to more expensive new common stock. At the point where new stock must be sold, the cost of equity, and consequently the marginal cost of capital, rises.

These concepts, which were developed in Chapter 19, are illustrated in Figure 21-1 with data from Georgia Paper Products (GPP). The firm has a mar-

Figure 21-2

Georgia Paper Products:
Investment Opportunity
Schedules

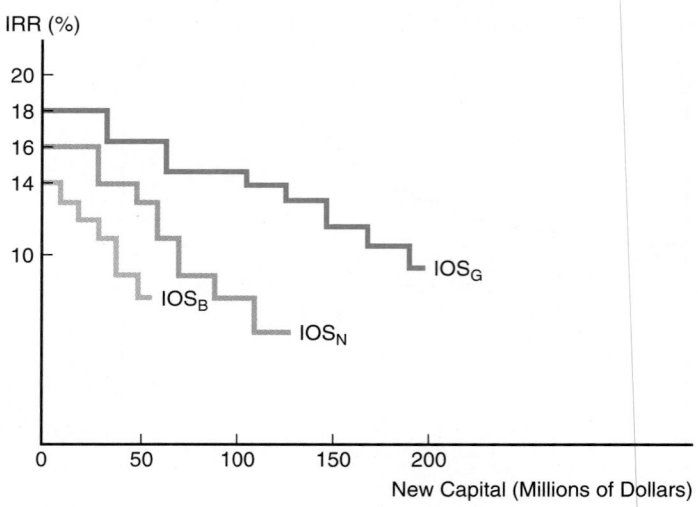

Investment opportunity schedules show the new investments available to a firm at various internal rates of return. In this figure, IOS_G represents a good economy, IOS_N a normal economy, and IOS_B a bad economy. When investment opportunities are good, internal rates of return are higher and GPP can invest large amounts. On the other hand, when opportunities are poor, as in IOS_B, the firm will cut back on its investment.

ginal cost of capital of 10 percent as long as retained earnings are available, but the MCC begins to rise at the point where new stock must be sold. GPP has $60 million of net income and a 40 percent optimal debt ratio. Provided it does not pay cash dividends, GPP can make net investments (investments in addition to asset replacements financed from depreciation) of $100 million, consisting of $60 million from retained earnings plus $40 million of new debt supported by the retained earnings, at a 10 percent marginal cost of capital. Therefore, its MCC is constant at 10 percent up to $100 million of capital, beyond which it rises as the firm begins to use more expensive new common stock. Of course, if GPP does not retain all of its earnings, its MCC will begin to rise before $100 million. For example, if GPP retained only $30 million, its MCC would begin to rise at $30 million retained earnings + $20 million debt = $50 million.

Now suppose GPP's director of capital budgeting constructs investment opportunity schedules under three economic scenarios and plots them on a graph. The investment opportunity schedules for three different states of the economy—good (IOS_G), normal (IOS_N), and bad (IOS_B)—are shown in Figure 21-2. GPP can invest the most money, and earn the highest rates of return, when the investment opportunities are as given by IOS_G.

In Figure 21-3, we combine these investment opportunity schedules with the MCC schedule that would exist if the company retained all of its earnings. The point where the relevant IOS curve cuts the MCC curve defines the proper level of new investment. If investment opportunities are relatively bad (IOS_B), the optimal level of investment is $40 million; if opportunities are normal

Figure 21-3

Georgia Paper Products:
Cost of Capital, Investment
Opportunities, and New
Investment

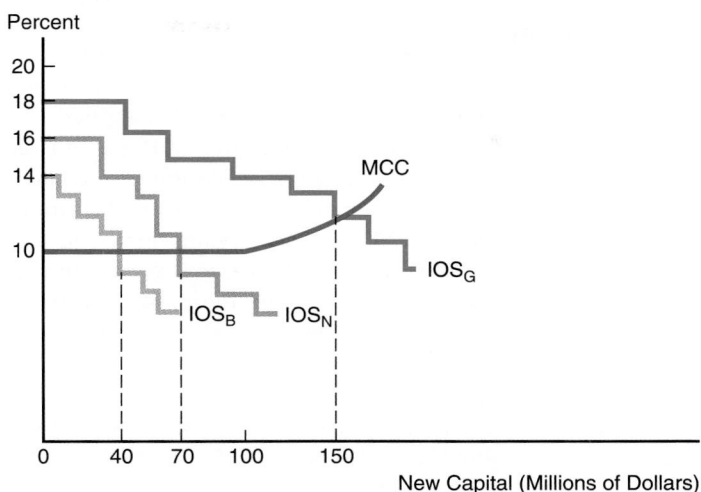

A firm's optimal level of new investment can be determined by combining the MCC and IOS schedules. For example, the IOS_N curve is crossed by the MCC curve at an investment level of $70 million. In a normal year, any investment beyond $70 million would generate returns lower than the 10 percent marginal cost of capital and thus should not be undertaken.

(IOS_N), $70 million should be invested; and if opportunities are relatively good (IOS_G), GPP should make new investments in the amount of $150 million.[1]

Consider the situation in which IOS_G is the appropriate schedule. GPP should invest $150 million. It has $60 million in earnings and a 40 percent target debt ratio. Thus, if it retained all of its earnings, it could finance $100 million, consisting of $60 million of retained earnings plus $40 million of new debt, at a cost of 10 percent. The remaining $50 million would include external equity and thus would have a higher cost. If GPP paid out part of its earnings in dividends, it would have to begin using more costly new common stock earlier, so its MCC curve would rise sooner than it otherwise would. This suggests that under the conditions of IOS_G, GPP should retain all of its earnings. According to the residual policy, GPP's payout ratio should in this case be zero. Note that even so, new common stock would have to be issued as well.

Under the conditions of IOS_N, however, GPP should invest only $70 million. How should this investment be financed? First, notice that if GPP retained all of its earnings, $60 million, it would need to sell only $10 million of new debt. However, if GPP retained $60 million and sold only $10 million of new debt, it would move away from its target capital structure. To stay on target, GPP must finance 60 percent of the required $70 million with equity (retained earnings)

[1]Figure 21-3 shows one MCC schedule and three IOS schedules for three possible sets of investment opportunities. Actually, both the MCC and the IOS schedules would normally change from year to year as interest rates and stock prices change. Figure 21-3 is designed to illustrate a point, not to duplicate reality. In reality, there would be one MCC and one IOS schedule for each year, but those schedules would change from year to year.

and 40 percent with debt. This means that it would retain only $42 million and sell $28 million of new debt. Since GPP would retain only $42 million of its $60 million total earnings, it would have to distribute the residual, $18 million, to its stockholders. Thus, its optimal payout ratio would be $18 million/$60 million = 30 percent, if IOS_N applied.

Under the conditions of IOS_B, GPP should invest only $40 million. Because it has $60 million in earnings, it could finance the entire $40 million out of retained earnings and still have $20 million available for dividends. Should this be done? Under our assumptions, this would not be a good decision because it would cause GPP to move away from its optimal capital structure. To stay at the 40 percent target debt/assets ratio, GPP must retain $24 million of earnings and sell $16 million of debt. When the $24 million of retained earnings is subtracted from the $60 million in total earnings, GPP would be left with a residual of $36 million, the amount that should be paid out in dividends. Thus, under IOS_B, the payout ratio as prescribed by the residual policy would be $36 million/$60 million = 60 percent. In summary, under the residual dividend policy as investment opportunities become more scarce, the IOS shifts to the left, and the dividend payout ratio increases.

Since both the IOS and the earnings level vary from year to year, strict adherence to the residual dividend policy would result in considerable dividend variability—one year the firm might declare zero dividends because investment opportunities were good, but the next year it might pay a large dividend because investment opportunities were poor. Similarly, fluctuating earnings would also lead to variable dividends even if investment opportunities were stable over time. Thus, following the residual dividend policy would be optimal only if investors were not bothered by fluctuating dividends. However, if investors prefer stable, dependable dividends, k_s would be higher, and the stock price lower, if the firm followed the residual policy in a strict sense. *Therefore, firms use the residual policy to help set their long-run target payout ratios, not as a strict determinant of the payout in any one year.*

As we shall see later in the chapter, many companies do, in fact, prefer paying a stable, predictable dividend. We will examine ways in which a stable dividend may be accomplished, even with both earnings and investment opportunities fluctuating from year to year.

? Self-Test

Explain the logic of the residual dividend policy.

List and describe the steps a firm would take to implement the residual policy.

If you owned stock in a company, would you want it to follow the residual policy? Would it matter if you relied on dividends to meet your living costs instead of simply saving any dividends received?

Factors That Influence Dividend Policy

The residual dividend policy is only a starting point in establishing the final dividend policy. Specific considerations that influence dividend policy may be grouped into four broad categories: (1) constraints on dividend payments or on earnings retention, (2) investment opportunities, (3) availability and costs of alternative sources of capital, and (4) effects of dividend policy on the required rate of return, k_s. Each of these categories and related factors are discussed in the following sections.

Constraints

1. **Bond indentures.** Debt contracts often restrict dividend payments to earnings generated after the loan was granted. Also, debt contracts often stipulate that no dividends can be paid unless the current ratio, the times-interest-earned ratio, and other safety ratios exceed stated minimums.

2. **Impairment of capital rule.** Dividend payments cannot exceed the balance sheet item "retained earnings." This legal restriction, known as *the impairment of capital rule,* is designed to protect creditors. Without this rule, a company in trouble might distribute most of its assets to stockholders and leave its debtholders "out in the cold." (*Liquidating dividends* can be paid out of capital, but they must be indicated as such, and they must not reduce capital below the limits stated in the debt contracts.)

3. **Availability of cash.** Cash dividends can be paid only with cash. Thus, a shortage of cash can restrict dividend payments; however, the ability to borrow can offset this factor.

4. **Penalty tax on improperly accumulated earnings.** To prevent wealthy individuals from using corporations to avoid personal taxes, the Tax Code provides for a special surtax on improperly accumulated income. Thus, if the IRS can demonstrate that a firm's dividend payout ratio is being deliberately held down to help its stockholders avoid personal taxes, the firm is subject to heavy penalties. This factor is generally relevant only to privately owned firms.

Investment Opportunities

1. **Location of the investment opportunity schedule.** If a firm's "typical" IOS, as shown in Figure 21-3, is far to the right, this will tend to produce a low target payout ratio, while if the IOS is far to the left, a higher dividend payout ratio is likely to result. For example, companies in new industries with rapid growth, such as many technology firms today, pay no dividends, and their investors want it that way. On the other hand, companies in mature industries with limited growth opportunities, such as tobacco and textiles, are more likely to pay high dividends.

   When companies adopt a dividend policy *other* than what this basic rule would seem to indicate, they stand out. For example, when Intel surprised the investment community in September 1992 by announcing that it would pay its first cash dividend ever, the company—known for its dominance of the computer microprocessor market—became a rarity in Silicon Valley. Most electronics makers have no choice but to plow back earnings into R&D and factories just to keep up with technological changes. Intel, however, was sitting on $2.9 billion in cash, and Chairman Gordon Moore stressed that the company could afford both to pay dividends ($0.10 per share initially) and to fund $2 billion in capital spending and R&D each year. In other words, Intel will remain a growth company with numerous investment opportunities, but the very profitable firm will still have residual earnings and will, therefore, pay dividends. The price of Intel's stock rose following the announcement, and an analyst commented, "It positions Intel a cut above others who are forced to invest earnings back into the company. It says they've arrived."

2. **Possibility of accelerating or delaying projects.** The ability to accelerate or postpone projects will permit a firm to adhere more closely to its target dividend policy.

Alternative Sources of Capital

1. **Cost of selling new stock.** If a firm needs to finance a given level of investment, it can obtain equity by retaining earnings or by selling new common stock. If flotation costs are high, k_e will be well above k_s, and this would favor a low payout ratio. On the other hand, if flotation costs are low, a high dividend payout ratio will be more feasible. Flotation costs differ among firms — for example, the flotation percentage is generally higher for small firms, so they tend to set low payout ratios.

2. **Control.** If management is concerned about maintaining control, it may be reluctant to sell new stock, hence, the company may retain more earnings than it otherwise would. However, if stockholders want higher dividends and a proxy fight looms, then the dividend will be increased.

3. **Capital structure flexibility.** A firm can finance a given level of investment with either debt or equity. If the firm can adjust its debt ratio without raising costs sharply, it can maintain a constant dollar dividend, even if earnings fluctuate, by using a variable debt ratio. The shape of the WACC curve (left panel in Figure 21-1) determines the practical extent to which the firm can deviate from its optimal debt ratio. If the WACC curve is relatively flat over a wide range (which is normally the case), then a higher payout ratio will be more feasible than it would be if the curve had a V shape because the firm is better able to substitute debt for equity on a temporary basis.[2]

Effects of Dividend Policy on k_s

1. **Stockholders' desire for current versus future income.** Some stockholders desire current income; retired individuals and university endowment funds are examples. Other stockholders have no need for current investment income, so they simply reinvest any dividends received, after first paying income taxes on the dividend income. If dividends are paid, then these stockholders will also incur brokerage costs to reinvest their dividends. On the other hand, if the firm retains and reinvests income rather than paying dividends, those stockholders who need current income will

---

[2]You may recall that this point was stressed in Chapter 20 in our discussion of ATM's optimal capital structure and WACC (see Figure 20-5, middle panel).

be disadvantaged. Although they will presumably receive capital gains, they will be forced to sell off some of their shares to obtain cash. This will also involve brokerage costs, which are relatively high unless large sums are involved. Furthermore, some institutional investors (or trustees for individuals) may be precluded from selling stock and then "spending capital."

clientele effect

The tendency of a firm to attract the type of investor who likes its dividend policy.

The argument has been made that a firm tends to attract a "clientele" of investors who like its particular dividend policy. This is called the **clientele effect.** Investors can, of course, switch companies if they own stock in a firm whose dividend policy differs from the policy they desire. However, there are costs associated with selling and buying other stock (brokerage costs and, potentially, capital gains taxes), and there may be a shortage of investors to replace those seeking to switch, in which case the stock price would fall.

2. **Riskiness of dividends versus riskiness of capital gains.**   It has been argued that investors regard returns coming in the form of dividends as being less risky than capital gains returns. Others disagree, arguing that if an investor receives dividends, then turns around and reinvests them in the same firm or one of similar risk, there is little difference in risk between this action and that of the company retaining and reinvesting the earnings in the first place. This question has been subjected to statistical studies, but without conclusive results.

3. **Information content of dividends: signaling.**   It has been observed that an increase in the dividend (for example, the annual dividend per share is raised from $2 to $2.50) is often accompanied by an increase in the price of the stock, whereas an unexpected dividend cut generally leads to a stock price decline. This suggests to some observers that investors like dividends more than capital gains. However, others argue differently. They state that corporations are always reluctant to cut dividends, so firms do not raise dividends unless they anticipate higher, or at least stable, earnings in the future. Thus, a dividend increase is a signal to investors that the firm's management forecasts good future earnings. Conversely, a dividend reduction signals that management is forecasting poor earnings in the future. Therefore, the price changes following a change in dividend policy may not reflect investors' preferences for either dividends or earnings growth, but may simply be a reflection of the important information regarding future earnings that is contained in the dividend announcement.[3]

---

[3]As you may suspect, real-life situations are often more complex. When troubled computer giant IBM announced in July 1993 that it had posted an $8.04 billion net loss for the second quarter and would slash its quarterly common stock dividend from $0.54 to $0.25 per share, IBM's stock *rose* by $3.25 (or 7.7 percent). What was going on? Part of the answer was that investors had feared even worse news from IBM, whose stock had plunged to 18-year lows just the week before. Also, there appeared to be relief that Chairman Louis Gerstner was taking aggressive steps to try to bring IBM's costs into line with the rest of the computer industry. "We have got to get behind us this Chinese water torture we've been going through quarter after quarter," said Gerstner, referring to IBM's seven years of reductions in work force and overhead. The dividend cut will save IBM $700 million a year, according to the company's new financial officer, Jerome York. The two major rating agencies, however, did not applaud IBM's actions. Standard & Poor's lowered its ratings on the company's senior debt, and Moody's placed its debt under review for a possible downgrade.

information content (signaling) of dividends

The theory that stock price changes following dividend announcements simply reflect the fact that investors regard dividend changes as signals of management's earnings forecasts.

As with many other controversies about dividend policy, empirical studies of the importance of the **information content (signaling) of dividends** have been inconclusive. There is clearly some information content in dividend announcements, but it may or may not completely explain the stock price changes that follow increases or decreases in dividends.

These points are considered by financial executives when they are establishing their firms' dividend policies, but the only real generalizations we can make are these:

1.   The optimal dividend policy for a firm is influenced by many factors. Some factors suggest a higher payout than would be called for by the residual policy, whereas others suggest a lower optimal payout.

2.   Much research has been done on dividend policy, but many points are still unresolved. Researchers are far from being able to specify a precise model for establishing corporate dividend policy.

Although no one has been able to construct a usable model for finding an optimal dividend policy, the residual policy does at least provide a good starting point, and we do have a good checklist of factors to consider before finalizing the dividend policy. Later in the chapter we return to the process of establishing a dividend policy, but first we must take up several other components of dividend policy.

Self-Test

Identify four broad categories of considerations that influence dividend policy.

What constraints affect dividend policy?

How do investment opportunities affect dividend policy?

How does the availability and costs of alternative capital sources affect dividend policy?

List the three factors that should be considered when assessing the effects of dividend policy on the cost of equity, k_s.

Dividend Payment Policies

In practice, corporations tend to use one of three major dividend payment policies: (1) *constant, or steadily increasing, dollar dividends,* (2) *constant payout ratio,* or (3) *low regular dividends plus extras.* These alternatives are discussed in this section.

Constant, or Steadily Increasing, Dollar Dividends

In the past, many firms set a specific annual cash dividend per share and then maintained it, increasing the annual dividend only if it seemed clear that future earnings would be sufficient to allow the new dividend to be maintained. A corollary of the policy is this rule: *Never reduce the annual dividend.*[4]

---

[4]The case of IBM only goes to prove that it is not always possible to abide by this rule.

Figure 21-4   Shoal Creek Engineering: Dividends and Earnings over Time

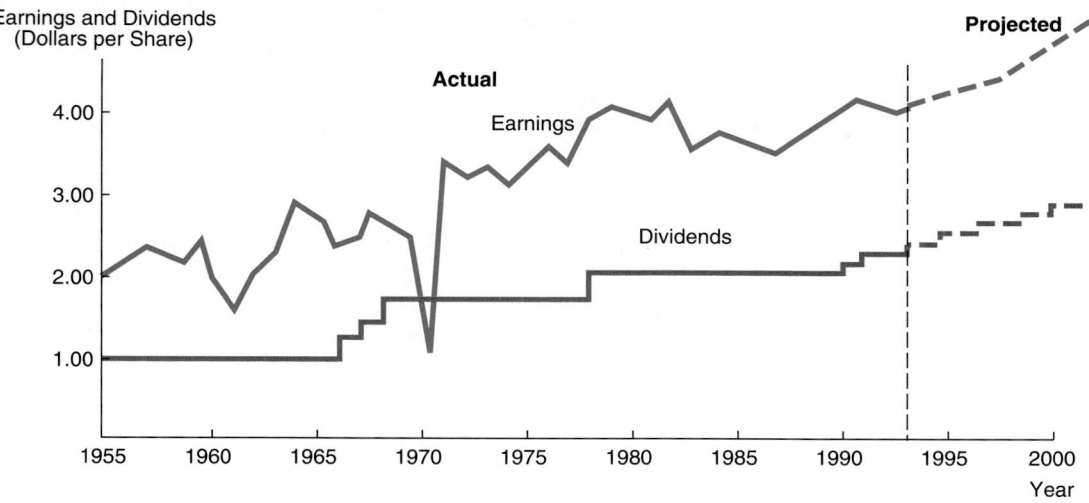

Many firms use a stable dividend payment policy, maintaining a specific dollar dividend and raising it only if earnings increase on an apparently permanent basis. As shown in this figure, Shoal Creek Engineering paid a dividend of $1.00 beginning in 1955 and maintained it for 10 years. Note that a temporary drop in earnings below the dividend level in 1970 did not affect the amount of dividend paid. In the 1990s, though, Shoal Creek expects earnings to grow steadily, and it plans to increase its dividend each year at a stable rate.

More recently, inflation plus reinvested earnings have tended to push earnings up, so many firms that would otherwise have followed the stable dividend payment policy have switched over to what is called the "stable growth rate" policy. Here the firm sets a target growth rate for dividends (for example, 5 percent per year, which is a little above the long-run average inflation rate) and strives to increase dividends by this amount each year. Obviously, earnings must be growing at a reasonably steady rate for this policy to be feasible, but where it can be followed, such a policy provides investors with a stable real income.

Figure 21-4, which illustrates a fairly typical dividend policy, presents data for Shoal Creek Engineering from 1955 to 1993 with earnings and dividends projected to 2000. Initially, earnings were $2 and dividends were $1 a share, so the payout ratio was 50 percent. Earnings rose for 4 years, while dividends remained constant; thus the payout ratio fell during this period. During 1960 and 1961 earnings fell substantially; however, the dividend was maintained, and the payout percentage rose. During the period between 1961 and 1965 earnings experienced a sustained rise. Dividends were held constant while management sought to determine whether the earnings increase would be permanent. By 1966, when it was apparent that the earnings gain would be maintained, dividends were raised in 3 steps to reestablish the long-run target payout level. During 1970 a strike caused earnings to fall below the regular dividend. Expecting the earnings decline to be temporary, management maintained the dividend. Earnings fluctuated on a fairly high plateau from 1972 through 1977, during which time dollar dividends remained constant. A new increase in earnings permitted management to raise the dividend in 1978 to reestablish the target payout level. In 1990, Shoal Creek adopted a stable growth rate dividend policy, as illustrated in Figure 21-4, and plans to continue this policy throughout the 1990s, if earnings grow as projected.

There are two good reasons for paying a stable, predictable dividend rather than exactly following the residual dividend policy. First, given the existence of the information content, or signaling, theory, a fluctuating payment policy would lead to greater uncertainty, hence to a higher k_s and a lower stock price, than would exist under a stable dividend policy. Second, because stockholders who use dividends for current consumption want to be able to count on receiving dividends regularly, irregular dividends would cause anxiety for these stockholders plus brokerage costs, if they have to sell a portion of their shares. This, in turn might lower demand for the stock, causing a decline in its price.

It is often possible for firms to avoid these problems. Even though the optimal dividend as prescribed by the residual policy might vary somewhat from year to year, actions such as delaying some investment projects, departing from the target capital structure during a particular year, or even issuing new common stock may make it possible for a company to stabilize its dividends.

Constant Payout Ratio

Very few firms follow a policy of paying out a constant percentage of earnings every year. Because earnings surely will fluctuate, following this policy would necessarily mean that the dollar amount of dividends would vary from year to year. For reasons discussed in the preceding section, this policy is not likely to maximize a firm's stock price. However, before its bankruptcy, Penn Central Railroad did follow the policy of paying out one half its earnings: "A dollar for the stockholders and a dollar for the company," as one director put it. Logic like this could drive any company to bankruptcy!

Most companies will conduct an analysis similar to the residual analysis described earlier in the chapter and will then establish a target payout based on the most likely set of conditions. The target will not be reached in every year, but over time the average payout will probably be close to the target level. Of course, the target would change if fundamental changes in the company's position were to occur.

Low Regular Dividend plus Extras

extra dividend

A supplementary dividend paid in years when excess funds are available.

A policy of paying a low regular dividend plus a year-end extra in good years is a compromise between a stable dividend (or stable growth rate) and a constant payout rate. Such a policy gives the firm flexibility, yet investors can count on receiving at least a minimum dividend. Therefore, if a firm's earnings and cash flows are quite volatile, this policy may well be its best choice. The directors can set a relatively low regular dividend—low enough so that it can be maintained even in low-profit years or in years when a considerable amount of retained earnings is needed—and then supplement it with an **extra dividend** in years when excess funds are available. Ford, General Motors, and other auto companies, whose earnings fluctuate widely from year to year, formerly followed such a policy, but in recent years they have joined the crowd and now follow a stable dollar dividend policy.

❔ *Self-Test*

Describe the constant, or steadily increasing, dollar dividend policy, and give two reasons why a firm might follow such a policy of stable dividends.

Explain what a low-regular-dividend-plus-extras policy is, and tell why a firm might follow such a policy.

Dividend Payment Procedure

Dividends are normally paid quarterly, and, if conditions permit, the dividend is increased once each year. For example, in September 1993, Quaker Oats Company increased its quarterly common stock dividend from $0.48 to $0.53 a share. In common financial language, we say that Quaker's *regular quarterly dividend* is now $0.53, and that its *indicated annual dividend* is $2.12. The actual dividend payment procedure is as follows:

declaration date

Date on which a firm's directors issue a statement declaring a regular dividend.

1. **Declaration date.**   On the **declaration date,** the directors of Quaker meet and declare the regular dividend. When they met on September 8, 1993, they issued a statement similar to the following: "On September 8, 1993, the directors of Quaker Oats Company met and declared a 10.4 percent increase in the quarterly dividend to $0.53 per share, payable to stockholders of record on September 17, 1993, payment to be made on October 15, 1993." For accounting purposes, the declared dividend becomes an actual liability on the declaration date, and if a balance sheet were constructed, the amount ($0.53) × (Number of shares outstanding) would appear as a current liability, and retained earnings would be reduced by a like amount.

holder-of-record date

If the company lists the stockholder as an owner on this date, then the stockholder receives the dividend.

2. **Holder-of-record date.**   At the close of business on the **holder-of-record date,** September 17 (a Friday), the company closes its stock transfer books and makes up a list of the shareholders as of that date. If Quaker is notified of the sale and transfer of some stock before 5 P.M. on September 17, then the new owner receives the dividend. However, if notification is received after September 17, the previous owner of the stock gets the dividend check.

3. **Ex-dividend date.**   Suppose Jean Buyer purchases 100 shares of Quaker stock from John Seller on September 15. Will the company be notified of the transfer in time to list Buyer as the new owner and thus pay the dividend to her? To avoid conflict, the securities industry has set up a convention of declaring that the right to the dividend remains with the stock until four business days prior to the holder-of-record date; on the fourth business day before the holder-of-record date, the right to the dividend no longer goes with the shares. The date when the right to the

ex-dividend date

The date on which the right to the current dividend no longer accompanies a stock; it is four working days prior to the holder-of-record date.

dividend leaves the stock is called the **ex-dividend date.** In this case, the ex-dividend date is September 13:

	......	September 10
Weekend:	......	September 11 & 12
Ex-dividend date	......	September 13
	......	September 14
	......	September 15
	......	September 16
Holder-of-record date:	......	September 17

Therefore, if Buyer wishes to receive the dividend, she must buy the stock on or before Friday, September 10. If she buys it on Monday, September 13 or later, Seller will receive the dividend. Note that if Quaker had paid its dividend to holders of record the *previous* Friday, September 10, the Labor Day holiday on Monday of that week would have placed the ex-dividend date on Thursday, September 2 (again, counting back four business days).

The dividend is $0.53 per share, so the ex-dividend date is important. Barring fluctuations in the stock market, we would normally expect the price of a stock to drop by approximately the amount of the dividend on the ex-dividend date. Thus, if Quaker closed at $68¾ on Friday, September 10, it would probably open at about $68¼ on Monday, September 13.

payment date

The date on which a firm actually mails dividend checks.

4. **Payment date.**   The company actually mailed the checks to the holders of record on October 15, 1993, the **payment date.**

  Self-Test

Briefly explain the steps in the dividend payment procedure.

Dividend Reinvestment Plans (DRIPs)

dividend reinvestment plan (DRIP)

A plan that enables a stockholder to automatically reinvest dividends received in the stock of the paying firm.

During the 1970s most of the larger companies instituted **dividend reinvestment plans (DRIPs),** whereby stockholders can automatically reinvest dividends received in the stock of the paying corporation.[5] There are two types of DRIPs: (1) plans which involve only "old" stock that is already outstanding, and (2) plans which involve newly issued stock. In either case, the stockholder must pay income taxes on the amount of the dividends, even though stock rather than cash is received.

Under the "old-stock" type of plan, the stockholder chooses between receiving dividend checks or having the company use the dividends to buy more stock in the corporation. If the stockholder elects reinvestment, a bank, acting as trustee, takes the total funds available for reinvestment (minus a nominal fee to cover costs), purchases the corporation's stock on the open market, and allocates the shares purchased to the participating stockholders' accounts on a

---

[5]See R. H. Pettway and R. P. Malone, "Automatic Dividend Reinvestment Plans," *Financial Management,* Winter 1973, 11–18, for an excellent discussion of the topic.

CORPORATE GET-RICH-SLOWLY PLANS

For investors who do not need immediate cash income, more than 900 public companies offer a plan that is an almost guaranteed money-maker. It is a dividend reinvestment plan (DRIP), which allows stockholders to use their dividends to buy more stock. Instead of receiving checks, they automatically get additional shares of the firm's stock.

Banks and electric utilities are well represented in the DRIP listings, and a few foreign companies with American Depository Receipts (ADRs), representing shares of foreign companies traded in the United States, also offer DRIPs. The list includes SmithKline Beecham and British Petroleum.

Participants in DRIPs benefit whether the market moves up or down because a DRIP is a form of dollar-cost averaging—a proven way to lower the cost of investments. If dividends are reinvested regularly (and the payment period for most companies is every quarter), the same dividend buys more shares when the price is low and fewer when it is high. Over time, the result for a reasonably stable company is an average cost per share that is lower than the stock's average market price.

The shareholder gets another important advantage—most DRIPs involve no brokerage fees, so the entire dividend check goes toward more shares of stock. Although investors must own at least one share in a company to be eligible for its reinvestment plan, they pay a stockbroker only for that first purchase, and they do not need to work with the broker again. Regular purchases through a broker can cost from $35 to $100 or more for each transaction, so the savings in a reinvestment plan can be substantial.

However, if you agree to have dividends reinvested, a handful of companies, such as Bank of New York, Minnesota Power & Light, Texaco, Citibank, and W. R. Grace, will sell you your first shares directly, up to a set dollar amount. "From the corporate point of view, it's a goodwill gesture," says the editor of a reinvestment-plan directory. "Most of those are consumer-oriented companies trying to attract long-term shareholders." Note, though, that Procter & Gamble recently terminated its direct purchase program, citing that huge investor demand drove up their costs, making the program too expensive.

The advantages of keeping shares for a long time are demonstrated by the profits enjoyed by a retired Texas engineer. In 25 years, his 700 shares of a utility stock, purchased for just under $10,000, grew to 5,000 shares, worth about $102,500, through dividend reinvestment alone—a 925 percent gain with no work involved. Still more can be amassed if a stockholder adds cash to the dividend reinvestments. Many companies allow this practice, with $3,000 being the typical maximum per quarter, but in some cases, the maximum can be in the hundreds of thousands.

Corporations also benefit from DRIPs because the plans strengthen shareholders' commitment to the company. Also, the plans can be used to raise capital when firms keep the cash and issue new shares. For example, NYNEX, which owns New York Telephone and New England Telephone, recently announced that it would issue new shares under its DRIP, and it expected to raise approximately $250 million of equity per year to help fund its investment program.

As an additional lure to stockholders, some companies offer stock at a discount of from 3 to 5 percent below the market price. However, Chemical Bank and Chase Manhatttan Bank both had to change their discount policies when arbitragers figured out that they could sell shares short (the practice of selling borrowed shares) and then cover their positions by buying the stock at a 5 percent discount. This short selling caused the banks' stock prices to fluctuate. As a result, Chemical lowered its discount for cash purchases from 5 percent to 2.5 percent, and then eliminated it altogether. Similarly, Chase Manhattan

Sources: Daniel M. Kehrer, "Make Your Dividends Pay Again and Again," *Changing Times,* November 1988; "Buying Stocks—Without a Stockbroker," *Business Week,* November 7, 1988; Robert Guenther, "Chase Drops Parts of Dividend Plan Due to Stock Fall," *The Wall Street Journal,* February 16, 1990; "Chemical Banking Cuts Reinvestment Plan Following Stock Drop," *The Wall Street Journal,* February 23, 1990; "Chemical Banking Ends Discount on Stock Buys," *The Wall Street Journal,* March 29, 1990; "DRIPs Can Help Your Dividends Multiply," *Money,* May 1990; "Smart Money—Replanting Dividends: It's Easy and Cheap," *Business Week,* February 24, 1992; "Bookshelf: Investing Wisely," *The Wall Street Journal,* January 15, 1993; and "Dividend Reinvestment Plans Take on New Look," *The Wall Street Journal,* March 3, 1993.

amended its cash option plan to 3 percent from 5 percent, and it reduced the maximum amount of stock a shareholder could buy from $250,000 a quarter to $40,000 a month. Arbitragers had not only been selling Chase shares short and covering this action with discount purchases, but they also avoided the $250,000 limit by buying the discounted shares under multiple names. Even so, neither Chase nor Chemical Bank is thinking of eliminating their DRIPs. Both banks need new equity, and Chase's plan raised $257 million in new equity in just two months, while Chemical's raised $106 million during a four-month period.

Although investors continue to respond well to DRIPs, there are some drawbacks to them. For example, all reinvested dividends are taxable in the year they were paid, even though no cash goes directly to the shareholder. Obviously, the plans are inappropriate for those who need cash income for living expenses or for tax payments.

The latest trend appears to be the revamping of companies' plans from "limited" DRIPs to plans that offer shareholder services that are similar to those provided by mutual funds. Exxon offers these expanded investment services, permitting people to buy the stock directly, to open individual retirement accounts, and even to set up automatic transfers from their bank accounts to buy Exxon stock. The response to its new services has been tremendous. Exxon has signed up 187,000 direct investment accounts (out of about 1 million shareholders) since it started the program a little over a year ago.

The number of companies offering these enhanced services could increase if stock transfer agents are able to get their proposal of an "investor registration option" approved. The main feature of this proposal is a bookkeeping system that would eliminate paper stock certificates unless specifically requested. In addition, the system would make it easy for the issuer to offer a host of services to individual investors. Each company would come up with its own package, but the critical element to the package would be the ability to buy and sell stock directly from the company without a broker. Even if this package were offered to a limited population—for example, company employees—the investor registration option might require a company to file with the SEC to change the way it handles stock.

Obviously, the brokerage community does not like the idea. It says that shareholders would be deprived of their basic rights—the right to a stock certificate without additional paperwork and the right to the best market price. However, proponents of the idea are optimistic. James Volpe, a vice-president at First Chicago Trust, says that a handful of these programs will be in place by year-end 1993. He also stated, "I see 80 percent of issuers offering a version of this plan in the next four years." And many corporations are clearly interested in the plan. For example, Dan Bulla, director of financial relations for Houston Industries, stated, "We don't have one yet, but we are investigating it for the same reasons as everyone from IBM on down . . . It may offer some attractive benefits for the investors."

These direct investment plans are not aimed at the active trader who wants to buy and sell quickly. Rather, they are aimed at the small investor who has only a limited amount to invest. While none of the pieces for this type of plan are new, putting all the pieces together in a package would be quite revolutionary. Dividend reinvestment plans are an easy, low-risk way for shareholders to compound growth in a stock. A DRIP will not make anyone rich overnight, but as a long-term investment, it is hard to beat.

---

pro rata basis. The transactions costs of buying shares (brokerage costs) are low because of volume purchases, so these plans benefit small stockholders who do not need cash dividends for current consumption.

The "new-stock" type of DRIP provides for dividends to be invested in newly issued stock; hence, these plans raise new capital for the firm. AT&T, Florida Power & Light, Union Carbide, and many other companies have had such plans in effect in recent years, using them to raise substantial amounts of new equity capital. No fees are charged to stockholders, and many companies offer stock at a discount of 3 to 5 percent below the actual market price. The companies absorb these costs as a tradeoff against the flotation costs that would have been incurred had they sold stock through investment bankers rather than through the dividend reinvestment plans.[6]

As mentioned in the "Industry Practice" boxed feature in this chapter, DRIPs have in recent years begun to take on a new look, as some companies, including Exxon, have expanded the services they offer their shareholders through these plans.

? *Self-Test*

Describe the two different types of dividend reinvestment plans.

Stock Dividends and Stock Splits

Stock dividends and stock splits are related to the firm's cash dividend policy. The rationale for stock dividends and splits can best be explained through an example; we will use Allied Food Products to illustrate.

Allied is a processor and distributor of a wide variety of foods. Formed in 1977 when several regional firms merged, Allied's markets have been expanding, and the company has enjoyed growth in sales and earnings. Some of its earnings have been paid out in dividends, but some are also retained each year to allow the firm to grow. After some years of growth, Allied's shares had a very high EPS and DPS. When a "normal" P/E ratio was applied, the derived market price was so high that few people could afford to buy a "round lot" of 100 shares. This limited the demand for the stock and thus kept the total market value of the firm below what it would have been if more shares, at a lower price, had been outstanding. To correct this situation, Allied "split its stock," as described in the next section.

Stock Splits

stock split

An action taken by a firm to increase the number of shares outstanding, such as doubling the number of shares outstanding by giving each stockholder two new shares for each one formerly held.

Although there is little empirical evidence to support the contention, there is nevertheless a widespread belief in financial circles that an *optimal price range* exists for stocks. "Optimal" means that if the price is within this range, the price/earnings ratio, hence the value of the firm, will be maximized. Many observers, including Allied's management, believe that the best range for most stocks is from $20 to $80 per share. Accordingly, if the price of Allied's stock rose to $80, management would probably declare a two-for-one **stock split,** thus doubling the number of shares outstanding, halving the earnings and divi-

---

[6]One interesting aspect of DRIPs is that they are forcing corporations to reexamine their basic dividend policies. A high participation rate in a DRIP suggests that stockholders might be better off if the firm simply reduced cash dividends, as this would save stockholders some personal income taxes. Quite a few firms are surveying their stockholders to learn more about their preferences and to find out how they would react to a change in dividend policy. A more rational approach to basic dividend policy decisions may emerge from this research.

Also, it should be noted that companies either use or stop using new-stock DRIPs depending on their need for equity capital. Florida Power & Light recently stopped offering a new-stock DRIP with a 5 percent discount because its need for equity capital declined once it had completed a nuclear-powered generating plant.

dends per share, and thereby lowering the price of the stock. Each stockholder would have twice as many shares, but each share would be worth less. If the post-split price were $40, Allied's stockholders would be exactly as well off as they were before the split. However, if the price of the stock were to stabilize above $40, stockholders would be better off. Stock splits can be of any size — for example, the stock could be split two-for-one, three-for-one, one-and-a-half-for-one, or in any other way.[7]

Stock Dividends

stock dividend

A dividend paid in the form of additional shares of stock rather than in cash.

Stock dividends are similar to stock splits in that they "divide the pie into smaller slices" without affecting the fundamental position of the current stockholders. With a 5 percent stock dividend, the holder of 100 shares would receive an additional 5 shares (without cost); with a 20 percent stock dividend, the same holder would receive 20 new shares; and so on. Again, the total number of shares is increased, so earnings, dividends, and price per share all decline. If a firm wants to reduce the price of its stock, should it use a stock split or a stock dividend? Stock splits are generally used after a sharp price run-up to produce a large price reduction. Stock dividends are typically used on a regular annual basis to keep the stock price more or less constrained. For example, if a firm's earnings and dividends were growing at about 10 percent per year, its stock price would tend to go up at about that same rate, and it would soon be outside the desired trading range. A 10 percent annual stock dividend would maintain the stock price within the optimal trading range.

Balance Sheet Effects

Although the economic effects of stock splits and stock dividends are virtually identical, accountants treat them somewhat differently. In a two-for-one split, the shares authorized and outstanding are doubled, and the stock's par and book values are halved. This treatment is shown in the middle section of Table 21-1 for Allied Food Products, using a pro forma 1994 balance sheet.

The bottom section of Table 21-1 shows the effect of a 20 percent stock dividend. With a stock dividend, the par value is not reduced, but an accounting entry is made transferring capital from the retained earnings account to the common stock and paid-in capital accounts. The transfer from retained earnings is calculated as follows:

$$\begin{matrix} \text{Dollars} \\ \text{transferred from} \\ \text{retained earnings} \end{matrix} = \begin{pmatrix} \text{Number} \\ \text{of shares} \\ \text{outstanding} \end{pmatrix} \begin{pmatrix} \text{Percentage} \\ \text{of the} \\ \text{stock dividend} \end{pmatrix} \begin{pmatrix} \text{Market} \\ \text{price of} \\ \text{the stock} \end{pmatrix}. \quad \textbf{(21-1)}$$

Allied has 5 million shares outstanding, and they sell for $80 each, so a 20 percent stock dividend would require the transfer of $80 million:

$$\text{Dollars transferred} = (5,000,000)(0.2)(\$80) = \$80,000,000.$$

---

[7]*Reverse splits,* which reduce the shares outstanding, can even be used. For example, a company whose stock sells for $5 might employ a 1-for-5 reverse split, exchanging 1 new share for 5 old ones and raising the value of the shares to about $25, which is within the optimal range. LTV Corporation did this after several years of losses had driven its stock price down below the optimal range.

Table 21-1

Allied Food Products:
Stockholders' Equity
Accounts, Pro Forma,
December 31, 1994

Before a Stock Split or Stock Dividend

Common stock (6 million shares authorized, 5 million outstanding, $1 par)	$ 5,000,000
Paid-in capital	10,000,000
Retained earnings	155,000,000
Total common stockholders' equity	$170,000,000
Book value per share	$34.00

After a Two-for-One Stock Split

Common stock (12 million shares authorized, 10 million outstanding, $0.50 par)	$ 5,000,000
Paid-in capital	10,000,000
Retained earnings	155,000,000
Total common stockholders' equity	$170,000,000
Book value per share	$17.00

After a 20 Percent Stock Dividend

Common stock (6 million shares authorized, 6 million outstanding, $1 par)[a]	$ 6,000,000
Paid-in capital[b]	89,000,000
Retained earnings[b]	75,000,000
Total common stockholders' equity	$170,000,000
Book value per share	$28.33

[a]Shares outstanding are increased by 20 percent, from 5 million to 6 million.

[b]A transfer equal to the market value of the new shares is made from the retained earnings account to the common stock and paid-in capital accounts:

$$\text{Transfer} = (5{,}000{,}000 \text{ shares})(0.2)(\$80) = \$80{,}000{,}000.$$

Of this $80 million, ($1 par)(1,000,000 shares) = $1,000,000 goes to common stock and $79 million to paid-in capital.

As shown in the table, $1 million of this $80 million is added to the common stock account and $79 million to the paid-in capital account. The retained earnings account is reduced from $155 million to $75 million.[8]

Price Effects

Several empirical studies have examined the effects of stock splits and stock dividends on stock prices.[9] The findings of the Barker study, which are typical of those reported in the financial literature, are presented in Table 21-2. When

---

[8]Note that Allied could not pay a stock dividend that exceeded 38.75 percent; a stock dividend of that percentage would exhaust the retained earnings. Thus, a firm's ability to declare stock dividends is constrained by the amount of its retained earnings. Of course, if Allied had wanted to pay a 50 percent stock dividend, it could have switched to a 1.5-for-one stock split and accomplished the same thing.

[9]See C. A. Barker, "Evaluation of Stock Dividends," *Harvard Business Review,* July–August 1958, 99–144. Barker's study has been replicated several times in recent years, and his results are still valid; they have withstood the test of time. Another excellent study, using an entirely different methodology yet reaching similar conclusions, is that of E. Fama, L. Fisher, M. C. Jensen, and R. Roll, "The Adjustment of Stock Prices to New Information," *International Economic Review,* February 1969, 1–21.

Table 21-2

Price Effects of Stock Dividends

	Price at Selected Dates (in Percentages)		
	Six Months before Ex-Dividend Date	At Ex-Dividend Date	Six Months after Ex-Dividend Date
Cash dividend increase after stock dividend	$100	$109	$108
No cash dividend increase after stock dividend	100	99	88

a stock dividend was associated with a cash dividend increase, the value of the company's stock six months after the ex-dividend date had risen by 8 percent. On the other hand, when a stock dividend was not accompanied by a cash dividend increase, the stock value had fallen by 12 percent, which approximated the size of the average stock dividend, within six months.

These data suggest that investors see stock dividends for what they are — simply additional pieces of paper which do not represent true income. When they are accompanied by higher earnings and cash dividends, investors bid up the price of the stock. However, when stock dividends are not accompanied by increases in earnings and cash dividends, the dilution of earnings and dividends per share causes the price of the stock to drop by about the same percentage as the stock dividend. *Thus, the fundamental determinants of stock prices are the underlying earnings and dividends per share.*

Well-known companies that have split their stock in 1992 or 1993 include Coca-Cola, Walt Disney, Wal-Mart, Goodyear, May Department Stores, and Microsoft. Yet, one prominent and respected CEO does not believe in stock splits, at least not for his own company. Remember Warren Buffett of Berkshire Hathaway ("Decision in Finance," Chapter 5)? Chairman Buffett has steadfastly refused to split his company's stock, which closed on September 9, 1993, at *$17,025 per share!* Back in 1983 Berkshire's stock was selling for a mere $1,300 per share. (You should be able to calculate the annual rate of growth in the value of Berkshire's stock, and you would find it impressive.) When asked, Chairman Buffett explains his policy on stock splits as a deliberate strategy not to attract unsophisticated investors, which Buffett, in his company's 1983 annual report, defined as those "preferring paper to value [who] feel wealthier with nine $10 bills than with one $100 bill." Instead, Berkshire has cultivated a loyal group of owners (a clientele) which is unlikely to sell in a stampede.[10]

---

[10]And, at the other end of the spectrum when it comes to stock splits, there is Oregon Steel Mills Inc., owned by its workers, which in 1991 split its shares *112-for-1!* For details, see "Newly Rich —Here Is One LBO Deal Where the Workers Became Millionaires," *The Wall Street Journal,* October 27, 1992.

? *Self-Test*

What is the rationale for a stock split? What economic conditions might suggest that a series of stock dividends be used rather than a stock split?

Differentiate between the accounting treatments for stock splits and stock dividends.

What have been the results of studies concerning the effect of stock dividends on stock prices? What difference does it make if a cash dividend does or does not accompany the stock dividend?

Can an argument be made for not splitting a stock, even though its price appears to be well above the so-called optimal trading range? Explain.

Stock Repurchases

stock repurchase

A transaction in which a firm buys back shares of its own stock, thereby decreasing shares outstanding, increasing EPS, and, often, increasing the price of the stock.

Many companies have been repurchasing shares of their own stock in recent years, and some of these actions have been on a considerable scale. Until the 1980s, most repurchases amounted to a few million dollars, but in 1985 Phillips Petroleum announced plans for the largest repurchase on record: 81 million of its shares with a market value of $4.1 billion. Since then, hundreds of companies have taken similar steps, usually to a lesser extent, and often for very diverse reasons. This section explains what a **stock repurchase** is, how it is carried out, and how the financial manager should analyze a possible repurchase program. We will conclude our discussion of the topic by looking at specific cases of stock repurchases from the 1990s. We shall see that unique developments, especially in 1992 and 1993, have made this an attractive financial alternative in a number of very different industries.

There are two principal types of repurchases: (1) situations in which the firm has cash available for distribution to its stockholders, and it distributes this cash by repurchasing shares rather than by paying cash dividends; and (2) situations in which the firm concludes that its capital structure is too heavily weighted with equity, and it then obtains debt financing and uses the proceeds to buy back some of its stock.

treasury stock

Common stock that has been repurchased by the issuing corporation.

Stock that has been repurchased by a firm is called **treasury stock.** If some of the outstanding stock is repurchased, fewer shares will remain outstanding. Assuming that the repurchase does not adversely affect the firm's future earnings, the earnings per share on the remaining shares will increase, and this should result in a higher market price per share. Consequently, capital gains will have been substituted for dividends.

The Effects of Stock Repurchases

The effects of a repurchase can be illustrated with data on American Development Corporation (ADC). The company expects to earn $4.4 million in 1994, and 50 percent of this amount, or $2.2 million, has been allocated for distribution to common shareholders. There are 1.1 million shares outstanding, and the market price is $20 a share. ADC believes that it can either use the $2.2 million to repurchase 100,000 of its shares through a tender offer for $22 a share or else pay a cash dividend of $2 a share.[11]

The effect of the repurchase on the EPS and market price per share of the remaining stock can be analyzed in the following way:

1. Current EPS $= \dfrac{\text{Total earnings}}{\text{Number of shares}} = \dfrac{\$4.4 \text{ million}}{1.1 \text{ million}} = \$4$ per share.

2. P/E ratio $= \dfrac{\$20}{\$4} = 5\times$.

3. EPS after repurchase of 100,000 shares $= \dfrac{\$4.4 \text{ million}}{1 \text{ million}} = \$4.40$ per share.

4. Expected market price after repurchase $= (\text{P/E})(\text{EPS}) = (5)(\$4.40)$
$= \$22$ per share.

It should be noted that, in this example, investors would receive before-tax benefits of $2 per share in any case, either in the form of a $2 cash dividend or a $2 increase in the stock price. This result would occur because we assumed, (1) that shares could be repurchased at exactly $22 a share and (2) that the P/E ratio would remain constant. If shares could be bought for less than $22, the repurchase would be even better for *remaining* stockholders, but the reverse would hold if ADC had to pay more than $22 a share. Furthermore, the P/E ratio might change as a result of the repurchase operation, rising if investors viewed it favorably and falling if they viewed it unfavorably. Some factors that might affect P/E ratios are considered next.

Pros and Cons of Stock Repurchases

Advantages.   The advantages of repurchases are as follows:

1. Repurchase announcements are viewed as positive signals by investors because the repurchase is often motivated by management's belief that the firm's shares are undervalued.

2. Aside from the vote of confidence in the firm's future which is expressed by management when it launches a buy-back program, the per-share price

---

[11]Stock repurchases are generally made in one of three ways: (1) A publicly owned firm can simply buy its own stock through a broker on the open market. (2) It can make a *tender offer*, under which it permits stockholders to send in (that is, "tender") their shares to the firm in exchange for a specified price per share. When a firm makes a tender offer, it generally indicates that it will buy up to a specified number of shares within a particular time period (usually about two weeks); if more shares are tendered than the company wishes to purchase, purchases are made on a pro rata basis. (3) The firm can purchase a block of shares from one large holder on a negotiated basis. If a negotiated purchase is employed, care must be taken to ensure that this one stockholder does not receive preferential treatment over other stockholders or that any preference given can be justified by "sound business reasons." For example, when Texaco repurchased about $600 million of stock from the Bass Brothers at a substantial premium over the market price, Texaco's management was sued by unhappy stockholders who were *not* able to sell back their shares and receive a similar premium. The suit charged that Texaco's management, afraid the Bass Brothers would attempt a takeover, used the buyback to get them off its back. Such payments have been dubbed "greenmail."

of the stock after the buy-back should be higher than before, other things equal. As we saw in the ADC example, fewer outstanding shares will boost EPS and stock price since treasury stock is not included when calculating EPS and DPS.

3. The stockholders have a choice when the firm repurchases stock—to sell or not to sell. However, if the firm were to opt for paying a special dividend instead, stockholders must accept the dividend payment and pay the tax. With a repurchase of stock, those stockholders who need cash can sell back some of their shares, while those who do not want additional cash can simply retain their stock. From a tax standpoint, in a repurchase both types of stockholders get what they want.

    In addition, the new tax law has widened the gap between the maximum capital gains tax rate (still at 28 percent) and the top rate on individuals' ordinary income including dividends (now at 39.6 percent). This, by itself, would make stock repurchases more attractive to investors in high tax brackets; the ability to defer capital gains taxes adds to this advantage, and it is likely, therefore, that the new tax law will quicken the pace of buy-backs.

4. Dividends are "sticky" in the short run because managements are reluctant to raise the dividend if the increase cannot be maintained in the future—as discussed earlier, managements dislike cutting cash dividends. Hence, if the excess cash flow is thought to be only temporary, management may prefer to make the distribution in the form of a share repurchase rather than to declare an increased cash dividend that cannot be maintained.

5. Repurchases can be used to produce large-scale changes in capital structures. For example, Consolidated Edison recently decided to repurchase $400 million of its common stock in order to increase its debt ratio. The repurchase was necessary because even if the company financed its capital budget only with debt, it would still have taken years to get the debt ratio up to the target level. Con Ed used repurchases to produce an instant change in its capital structure.

Disadvantages. The disadvantages of repurchases include the following:

1. Stockholders may not be indifferent between dividends and capital gains, and the price of the stock might benefit more from cash dividends than from repurchases. Cash dividends are generally dependable, but repurchases are not.

2. The *selling* stockholders may not be fully aware of all the implications of a repurchase, or they may not have all pertinent information about the corporation's present and future activities. However, firms generally announce repurchase programs before embarking on them to avoid potential stockholder suits.

3. The corporation may pay too high a price for the repurchased stock, to the disadvantage of remaining stockholders. If its shares are inactively traded and if the firm seeks to acquire a relatively large amount of the stock, then the price may be bid above its equilibrium level and then fall after the firm ceases its repurchase operations.

4. There is an "announcement effect" when a company repurchases its own shares. Management is basically making it known that the company does not have enough investment opportunities available yielding rates greater than its cost of equity capital. If it did, that is where the funds would be invested.

5. A stock buy-back program is, in essence, the company reducing its size. In the past, companies have sometimes turned down this alternative because they were in no mood to shrink themselves; on the other hand, in the 1990s many firms have found that smaller can be better. The fact that debt increases and equity shrinks in a repurchase (each as a percentage of total) can, however, pose problems. The firm, of course, ends up with higher financial leverage and greater financial risk. For example, General Electric suspended its stock buy-back program in 1992, partly to reassure credit rating agencies and maintain its triple-A rating.

On balance, companies probably ought to be doing more repurchasing and distributing less cash as dividends than they are. However, increases in the size and frequency of repurchases in recent years suggest that companies are rapidly reaching this same conclusion.

Recent Developments

In the 1980s, buying back a company's own shares was often a defensive move. A firm with excess cash, especially one that also had a debt ratio well below the optimal level, was a beautiful target for a takeover. Getting rid of the excess cash and raising the debt ratio in one fell swoop proved to be one of the most successful defensive measures a firm could take. In addition, after the stock market crashed in 1987, hundreds of companies stepped in and repurchased their own stock to prop up share prices and boost investor confidence. Even after the stock market rebounded, the introduction of new buy-back programs continued.

By the early 1990s, the takeover threat had largely disappeared, and high levels of debt were no longer "in." Yet, a new wave of buy-back activity began in the spring of 1992, and by mid-August 1993 a *Business Week* article reported on "The Great Buyback Boom of '93."[12] This time around, some of the companies, and their reasons for repurchasing shares, have been the following:

▶ Phillip Morris, which initiated its buy-back program in 1992 while a tobacco-liability case was before the Supreme Court, has seen its share price beaten down further recently because of a public and government backlash against smoking and the possibility of a new tax on cigarettes.

▶ Merck, Bristol-Meyers Squibb, and other pharmaceutical companies have seen their stock prices plunge because of fears that health-care reform will hurt their profits.

▶ General Dynamics, the defense contractor, sold off several divisions in 1992, increased its cash dividends, and returned 30 percent of its cash stockpile to shareholders in the form of stock repurchases, as the entire defense industry contracted.

---

[12]*Business Week,* August 23, 1993.

- ▶ Mattel, with sufficient plant capacity for sales to grow at an annual rate of 10 to 12 percent, plans to earmark half of its $200 million annual build-up in cash for buy-backs and dividends.

- ▶ Sun Microsystems, with $1.1 billion in cash as of July 1993, has decided to use $280 million of this hoard to buy back shares.

- ▶ Quaker Oats, like many consumer-products companies, has little choice but to repurchase its own shares. "We spend on new products, we make acquisitions, and we raise the dividend, and we still can't soak up all the cash," says Janet K. Cooper, Quaker's treasurer.

Other companies that have launched repurchase programs recently include Nike, Heinz, Pepsico, and Reebok. The economic environment of much of 1993 has been one of modest growth or actual retrenchment in some sectors. This, combined with the tax benefits previously discussed and with low interest rates on fixed-rate investments that firms might consider as alternatives for excess cash, has caused hundreds of management teams to authorize stock repurchase programs (359 by mid-August). As *Business Week* put it, "In this era of lame interest rates, what better investment than your own stock?"

Self-Test

Explain how repurchases can (1) help stockholders hold down taxes and (2) help firms change their capital structures.

What is treasury stock?

What are the three ways a firm can make repurchases?

What are the key advantages and disadvantages of stock repurchases?

State some of the reasons that stock repurchase programs have increased in the early 1990s.

Establishing a Dividend Policy: Some Illustrations

Many factors interact to determine a firm's optimal dividend policy. Because these interactions are too complex to permit the development of a rigorous model for use as a guide to dividend policy, firms are forced to consider their dividend policies in a relatively subjective manner. Some illustrations of how dividend policies are actually set follow.

Shoal Creek Engineering

Shoal Creek Engineering analyzed its situation in terms of the residual policy, as shown earlier, and the residual policy suggested a dividend of $2.40 per share during 1994. Shoal Creek's stock is widely held, and a number of tax-exempt institutions are important stockholders. A questionnaire to its stockholders revealed no strong preferences for dividends versus capital gains. Shoal Creek's long-range planning group projected a cost of capital and a set of investment opportunities during the next 3 to 5 years similar to those shown for this year.

On the basis of this information, Shoal Creek's treasurer recommended to the board of directors that it establish a dividend of $2.40 for 1994, payable 60 cents quarterly. The 1993 dividend was $2.28, so the $2.40 represented an increase of about 5 percent. The treasurer also reported to the board that, in the event of an unforeseen earnings downturn, the company could obtain additional debt to meet its capital expenditure requirements. The board accepted the treasurer's recommendation, and in December 1993 it declared a dividend of 60 cents per share, payable January 15, 1994. The board also announced its intention of maintaining this dividend for the balance of 1994.

Hytec Electronics

Hytec Electronics has a residual policy position that resembles IOS_G in Figure 21-3. This suggests that no dividend should be paid. Hytec has, in fact, paid no dividend since its inception in 1978, even though it has been continuously profitable and its earnings have recently been growing at a 25 percent rate. Informal conversations with the firm's major stockholders, all of whom are in high tax brackets, suggest that they neither expect nor want dividends; they would prefer to have the firm retain earnings, have good earnings growth, and provide capital gains, which are taxed at a maximum rate of 28 percent and not until the shares are sold. The stock now sells for $126 per share. Hytec's treasurer recommended a three-for-one split, no cash dividend, and a future policy of declaring an annual stock dividend geared to earnings for the year. The board of directors concurred.

Northwest Electric Company

Northwest Electric Company has an acute need for new equity capital. The company has a major expansion program under way and absolutely must come up with the money to meet construction payments. The debt ratio is high, and if the times-interest-earned ratio falls any lower, (1) the company's bonds will be downgraded, and (2) it will be barred by bond indenture provisions from further debt issues. These facts suggest a cut in dividends from the $3.75 per share paid last year. However, the treasurer knows that many of the stockholders rely on dividends for current living expenses, so if dividends are cut, these stockholders may be forced to sell, thus driving down the price of the stock. This would be especially bad in view of the treasurer's forecast that there will be a need to sell new common stock during the coming year. (New outside equity would be needed even if the company totally eliminated the dividend.) The treasurer is aware that many other utilities face similar problems. Some have cut their dividends, and their stock prices invariably have fallen by amounts ranging from 30 to 70 percent.

Northwest's earnings were forecasted to increase from $5.00 to $5.26. The treasurer recommended that the dividend be raised by 4 percent, from $3.75 to $3.90, with the dividend increase being announced a few weeks before the company floated a new stock issue. The hope was that this action would cause the price of the stock to increase, after which the company could sell a new issue of common stock at a better price.

Pacific Brands

Pacific Brands Inc. has experienced solid cash flows in recent years and this is expected to continue for at least the next three years. The company's treasurer is hard put to find good temporary investments for the rising level of cash in the corporate coffer, given today's environment of low interest rates. Pacific has developed several new products since 1990, but management does not feel that the stock's price, at this point, fully reflects the value of these new product lines. Expansion of plant capacity a few years back has left Pacific with considerable excess capacity. Management now expects only modest growth in sales for several years, and the director of capital budgeting recommends that capital expenditures be held at a low and relatively constant level.

Pacific's 1993 dividend was $2.76 per share, up from $2.60 in 1992. Both figures represent about 60 percent of earnings, and this payout was consistent with a residual dividend policy analysis. Earnings for 1994 are expected to be such that Pacific could raise its annual dividend to $3.58 per share, on a residual basis; however, a recent survey of stockholders has revealed that many are in high tax brackets and are concerned about the much higher taxes on dividend income than on capital gains under the new tax law. Pacific's financial vice-president points out that if the firm's cash flows were to dry up — or if new investment opportunities were to arise unexpectedly — it would be difficult to cut dividends. On the other hand, there are some compelling arguments in favor of a stock repurchase program: (1) the stock price could be expected to improve; (2) stockholders would receive capital gains income instead of extra dividends, if they chose not to sell their shares now; and (3) a repurchase program could be halted more easily than a dividend could be cut, should the cash be needed elsewhere. The board voted to approve an increase in the dividend to $2.93 and to make an announcement that Pacific intended to repurchase 15 percent of its common stock over two years.

Summary

Dividend policy involves the decision to pay out earnings versus retaining them for reinvestment in the firm, and dividend policy decisions can have either favorable or unfavorable effects on the price of a firm's stock. The key concepts covered are listed below.

- ▶ The **optimal dividend policy** is that policy which strikes the balance between current dividends and future growth that maximizes the price of the firm's stock.

- ▶ The **residual dividend policy** assumes that investors would prefer having the firm retain and reinvest earnings on their behalf any time the firm can obtain a higher rate of return than they themselves can receive elsewhere on investments of comparable risk.

  Since both investment opportunities and earnings vary from year to year for the typical firm, strict adherence to the residual policy would be likely to result in unstable dividends.

Because **research on dividend policy has been inconclusive,** academi- cians simply cannot tell corporate managers how a change in dividend policy will affect stock prices and capital costs. Thus, actually determining the optimal dividend policy is a matter of judgment.

▶ Practical determinants of dividend policy include factors that fall into four broad categories: (1) **constraints** on either dividend payments or earnings retention, (2) **investment opportunities,** (3) **availability and costs of alternative sources of capital,** and (4) **effects of dividend pol- icy on k_s.**

Dividend policy should reflect the existence of the **information content of dividends (signaling)** and the **clientele effect.** The information con- tent, or signaling, theory states that investors regard dividend changes as a signal of management's forecast of future earnings. The clientele effect sug- gests that a firm will attract investors who like the firm's dividend policy.

▶ The three major dividend policies used are: (1) **constant, or steadily in- creasing, dollar dividends,** (2) **constant payout ratio,** and (3) **low regular dividend plus extras.**

In practice, most firms try to follow a policy of paying constant, or steadily increasing, dollar dividends. This policy provides investors with a stable, dependable income, and it also gives investors information about manage- ment's expectations for earnings growth.

▶ A **dividend reinvestment plan (DRIP)** allows stockholders to have the company automatically use their dividends to purchase additional shares of the firm's stock. DRIPs are popular with investors who do not need cur- rent income because the plans allow stockholders to acquire additional shares without incurring normal brokerage fees.

▶ A **stock split** is an action taken by a firm to increase the number of shares outstanding. Normally, splits reduce the price per share in proportion to the increase in shares because splits merely "divide the pie into smaller slices." A **stock dividend** is a dividend paid in additional shares of stock rather than in cash. Both stock dividends and splits are used to keep stock prices within an "optimal" range.

▶ Under a **stock repurchase plan,** a firm buys back some of its outstanding stock, thereby decreasing the number of shares, which in turn increases both EPS and the stock price. Repurchases are useful for making major changes in a firm's capital structure.

Stock repurchases give shareholders a choice. If they choose not to sell back their shares, they have presumably substituted capital gains for divi- dends. Not only are capital gains taxed at a maximum rate of 28 percent, but this also allows stockholders to defer taxes until some future time when the stock is sold.

Resolution to
DECISION IN FINANCE

TO CUT OR NOT TO CUT DIVIDENDS

Delta implemented cost cuts which included laying off 5,000 temporary and part-time employees. In addition, it cut $5 billion from its capital budget for the period through 2001 and returned nine Airbus Industrie airplanes to lessors as replacements were delivered. Delta also announced plans to cut wages of its nonunion personnel by 5 percent, effective February 1, 1993. The carrier is now negotiating for wage and benefits concessions from its unionized pilots, and the company has reduced its interest costs by refunding its high-interest-rate debt with proceeds from a preferred stock issue. Overall, it plans to reduce costs by $375 million during fiscal 1993, which ends in June.

On December 22, 1992, three days before Christmas, S&P downgraded Delta's senior debt from BBB to BBB minus and its commercial paper from A-2 to A-3. S&P cited as its reasons for the downgrading the impact of a slowing European economy on Delta's efforts to decrease losses on its transatlantic routes, which it acquired from the now-defunct Pan Am, and the increased expense and reduced equity resulting from the implementation of new accounting rules for reporting retirees' health benefits. In addition, S&P noted that Delta had experienced larger losses than any other U.S. airline over the past 12 months, in spite of the fact that its competitive exposure to U.S. carriers operating in bankruptcy and to low-cost Southwest Airlines was more limited than that of its two chief rivals.

The downgradings reflect the increasing business and financial risk that the company is experiencing. As a result of this increased risk, the cost of the company's capital — both debt and equity — has been increasing. Thus, until the situation improves, investors are going to require a higher return to compensate for the company's increased risk exposure.

On January 29, 1993, Delta's board of directors voted to cut the quarterly common dividend from 30 cents to 5 cents, an 83 percent decrease. While the dividend cut was a drastic move, Delta is virtually the last big airline still paying any common dividends. AMR Corporation, American Airlines's parent company, eliminated its dividend in 1978; UAL Corporation eliminated its dividend in 1987; USAir Group Inc. suspended its 3 cent quarterly dividend in September 1990; and Alaska Air Group Inc. suspended its dividend in December 1992. Besides Delta, only Southwest Airlines, the one money-maker in the entire airline industry, pays a common dividend. And even at the drastically reduced rate, Delta's dividend still tops Southwest's dividend of 1.4 cents. Investors anticipated Delta's dividend cut, and on the day the reduction was announced, the common shares dropped a minuscule 12.5 cents, to $51.

Sources: "Delta Seeks Ways to Slash Costs Further," *The Wall Street Journal*, December 11, 1992; "Delta Cuts Dividend, Salaries," *The Buffalo News*, December 18, 1992; "Delta Debt Rating Downgraded by S&P," *Financial Times*, December 23, 1992; "U.S. Airlines Exit Dismal 1992 Seeking Profits," *Reuters*, December 28, 1992; "Delta Loses $126 Million in Last 3 Months of '92," *The Atlanta Journal and Constitution*, January 28, 1993; and "Delta, UAL, and Continental Report Losses," *The Wall Street Journal*, January 29, 1993.

Questions

21-1   As an investor, would you rather invest in a firm that has a policy of maintaining **(a)** a constant payout ratio, **(b)** a constant or steadily increasing dollar dividend per share, or **(c)** a constant regular quarterly dividend plus a year-end extra when earnings are sufficiently high or corporate investment needs sufficiently low? Explain your answer, stating how these policies would affect your k_s. Discuss also how your answer might change if you were a 21-year-old student, a 48-year-old professional with peak earnings, or a retiree.

21-2   How would each of the following changes probably affect aggregate (that is, the average for all corporations) payout ratios, other things held constant? Explain your answers.
   a. An increase in the personal income tax rate.
   b. A liberalization of depreciation for federal income tax purposes; that is, faster tax write-offs.
   c. A rise in interest rates.
   d. An increase in corporate profits.
   e. A decline in investment opportunities.
   f. Permission for corporations to deduct dividends for tax purposes as they now do interest charges.
   g. A change in the Tax Code so that both realized and unrealized capital gains in any year would be taxed at the same rate as dividends.

21-3   Discuss the pros and cons of having the directors formally announce what a firm's dividend policy will be in the future.

21-4   Most firms would like to have their stock selling at a high P/E ratio, and they would also like to have extensive public ownership (many different shareholders). Explain how stock dividends or stock splits may help achieve these goals.

21-5   What is the difference between a stock dividend and a stock split? As a stockholder, would you prefer to see your company declare a 100 percent stock dividend or a 2-for-1 split? Assume that either action is feasible.

21-6   "The cost of retained earnings is less than the cost of new outside equity capital. Consequently, it is totally irrational for a firm to sell a new issue of stock and to pay dividends during the same year." Discuss this statement.

21-7   Would it ever be rational for a firm to borrow money in order to pay dividends? Explain.

21-8   Explain the rationale that a financial vice-president might give his or her board of directors to support a stock split/dividend recommendation.

21-9   One position expressed in the financial literature is that firms set their dividends as a residual after using income to support new investment.
   a. Explain what a residual dividend policy implies, illustrating your answer with a graph showing how different conditions could lead to different dividend payout ratios.
   b. Could the residual dividend policy be consistent with (1) a constant growth-rate policy, (2) a constant payout policy, and/or (3) a low-regular-dividend-plus-extras policy? Answer in terms of both short-term, year-to-year consistency and longer term consistency.
   c. Think back to Chapter 20, in which we considered the relationship between capital structure and the cost of capital. If the WACC curve were shaped like a sharp V,

would this have a different implication for the importance of setting dividends according to the residual policy than when the plot is shaped like a shallow bowl (or a flattened U)?

d. Assume that Companies A and B both have IOS schedules that intersect their MCC schedules at a point which, under the residual policy, calls for a 30 percent payout. In both cases, a 30 percent payout would require a cut in the annual dividend from $3 to $1.50. One company cuts its dividend, whereas the other does not. One company has a relatively steep IOS curve, whereas the other has a relatively flat one. Explain which company probably has the steeper curve.

Self-Test Problem

ST-1   Campos Aircraft Corporation (CAC) has an all-equity capital structure that includes no preferred stock. It has 500,000 shares of $2 par value common stock outstanding.

When CAC's founder and chief engineer, Jennifer Campos, retired suddenly in late 1993, CAC was left suddenly and permanently with materially lower growth expectations and relatively few attractive new investment opportunities. Unfortunately, there was no way to replace the founder's contributions to the firm. Previously, CAC had found it necessary to plow back most of its earnings to finance growth, which had averaged 12 percent per year. Future growth of 5 percent appears to be realistic, but that would call for an increase in the dividend payout. Further, it now appears that new investment projects with at least the 14 percent rate of return required by CAC's shareholders ($k_s = 14\%$) would amount to only $2,800,000 for 1994, in comparison to a projected $7 million of net income. If the existing 25 percent dividend payout were continued, incremental retained earnings would be $5.25 million in 1994, but, as noted, investments that yield the 14 percent cost of capital amount to only $2.8 million.

The one encouraging thing is that the high earnings from existing assets are expected to continue, and net income of $7 million is still expected for 1994. Given the dramatically changed circumstances, CAC's management is reviewing the firm's dividend policy.

a. Assuming that the acceptable 1994 investment projects would be financed entirely by retained earnings during the year, calculate DPS in 1994, if CAC uses the residual dividend policy.

b. What payout ratio does this imply for 1994?

Problems

21-1

Dividend payout

Magnusson-Hess had net income for 1993 of $12 million.

a. What was the firm's payout ratio if it paid $7.5 million in dividends?

b. If the firm's payout was 25 percent, what was the dividend payment?

c. If the payout ratio was 40 percent, what was the retention rate?

d. In 1992 the firm's payout ratio was 60 percent, and $6.3 million was paid in dividends. What was Magnusson-Hess's net income in 1992?

21-2

Payout ratio

Fucetti Enterprises expects net income of $880,000 for the next year. Its target, and current, capital structure is 45 percent debt and 55 percent common equity. The director of capital budgeting has determined that the optimal capital budget for next year is $1,200,000. If Fucetti uses the residual dividend policy to determine next year's dividend payout, what is the expected payout ratio?

21-3
Payout ratio

C. J. Hansen & Company is expecting net income for next year to be $1,762,000. The company's target capital structure is 30 percent debt and 70 percent equity. The optimal capital budget for the next year has been determined to be $1,400,000. If the firm uses the residual dividend policy to determine next year's payout, what is the payout ratio?

21-4
External equity financing

Wei Manufacturing is expanding its productive capacity with a $9.6 million investment. The board of directors approved the expansion under the following conditions:
1. The firm would not exceed its current 40 percent debt/assets ratio.
2. The dividend payout ratio would remain at 30 percent.
If net income is expected to be $6 million this year, how much external equity must Wei seek during the year?

21-5
Stock dividend

Bueso Sporting Goods Inc. has the following common stock equity accounts on its balance sheet:

Common stock ($0.50 par)	$ 400,000
Paid-in capital	3,000,000
Retained earnings	8,000,000
Total equity	$11,400,000

The market price of the firm's stock is $20. Restate the equity accounts of Bueso to reflect a 20 percent stock dividend.

21-6
Stock split

O'Connor Industries has just announced a 3-for-1 stock split. Prior to the split, dividends were $3.75 per share. The firm plans to pay a dividend of $1.35 per share after the split. What is the percentage increase in the cash dividend that occurs after the split?

21-7
Stock split

After a 5-for-1 split, Stendardi Resources paid a dividend of $2.50 per new share, which represents a 10 percent increase over last year's pre-split dividend. What was last year's dividend per share?

21-8
Cash and stock dividends

Zaic Metals Corporation declared a 15 percent stock dividend and a cash dividend of $0.75 per share. The cash dividend is paid on both the old shares and the shares received in the stock dividend. Construct a pro forma balance sheet showing the effect of these actions; use one new balance sheet that incorporates both actions. The stock sells for $60 per share. A condensed version of Zaic's end-of-year balance sheet (before dividends) is given below (in millions of dollars):

Cash	$ 75		Debt	$1,500
Other assets	2,925		Common stock (30 million shares	
			authorized, 25 million outstand-	
			ing, $3 par)	75
			Paid-in capital	300
			Retained earnings	1,125
Total assets	$3,000		Total liabilities and equity	$3,000

21-9
Alternate dividend policies

In 1992 Suntime Boats, Limited (SBL) paid dividends of $3,125,000. The firm's net income for 1992 was $12.5 million. For the past 5 years SBL's earnings and dividends have grown at a constant 8 percent rate. However, 1993 was an especially profitable year, with net income totaling $25 million. For 1994 SBL has $20 million of profitable investment opportunities planned. Even so, the surge in earnings enjoyed in 1993 cannot last, and the firm's profits are expected to return to the previous 8 percent stable growth rate. Calculate the 1993 dividends for SBL under each of the following dividend policies:
a. A constantly growing dividend payment.

b. Stable payout based on the 1992 payout ratio.

c. Residual dividend policy if the firm uses no debt to finance investment opportunities.

d. Residual dividend policy if the firm maintains a 40 percent debt/assets ratio.

21-10

Dividend policy and
capital structure

North Carolina Tobacco Inc. has for many years enjoyed a moderate but stable growth in sales and earnings. However, cigarette consumption and consequently North Carolina's sales have been falling recently, primarily because of an increasing awareness of the dangers of smoking to health. Anticipating further declines in tobacco sales in the future, North Carolina's management hopes eventually to move almost entirely out of the tobacco business and into a newly developed, diversified product line in growth-oriented industries. The company is especially interested in the prospects for pollution-control devices because its research department has already done much work on the problems of filtering smoke. Right now the company estimates that an investment of $15 million is necessary to purchase new facilities and to begin operations on these products, but the investment could be earning a return of about 18 percent within a short time. The only other available investment opportunity totals $6 million, is expected to return about 10.8 percent, and is indivisible; that is, it must be accepted in its entirety or else be rejected.

The company is expected to pay a $1.50 dividend on its 6 million outstanding shares, the same as its dividend last year. The directors may change the dividend, however, if there are good reasons for doing so. Total earnings for the year are expected to be $14.25 million; the common stock is currently selling for $28⅛; the firm's target debt ratio (debt/assets ratio) is 45 percent; and its tax rate is 40 percent. The costs of various forms of financing are as follows:

New bonds, $k_d = 11\%$. This is a before-tax rate.

New common stock sold at $28⅛ per share will net $25⅝.

Required rate of return on retained earnings, $k_s = 15\%$.

a. Calculate North Carolina's expected payout ratio, the break point where the MCC rises, and its marginal cost of capital above and below the point of exhaustion of retained earnings at the current payout. (*Hint:* k_s is given, and D_1/P_0 can be found. Then, knowing k_s and D_1/P_0, g can be determined.)

b. How large should North Carolina's capital budget be for the year?

c. What is an appropriate dividend policy for North Carolina? How should the capital budget be financed?

d. How might risk factors influence North Carolina's cost of capital, capital structure, and dividend policy?

e. What assumptions, if any, do your answers to the preceding questions make about investors' preferences for dividends versus capital gains — that is, their preferences regarding the D_1/P_0 and g components of k_s?

(Do Part f only if you are using the computerized problem diskette.)

f. Assume that North Carolina's management is considering changing the company's capital structure to include more debt, and thus, it would like to analyze the effects of an increase in the debt ratio to 60 percent. However, the treasurer believes that such a move would cause lenders to increase the required rate of return on new bonds to 12 percent before tax and that k_s would rise to 15.5 percent. How would this change affect the optimal capital budget? If k_s rose to 17 percent, would the low-return project be acceptable?

Solution to Self-Test Problem

ST-1　**a.**　Projected net income　　　　　　　　　$7,000,000
　　　　　　Less: Projected capital investments　　　2,800,000
　　　　　　Available residual　　　　　　　　　$4,200,000

　　　　　　Shares outstanding　　　500,000

$$DPS = \$4,200,000/500,000 \text{ shares} = \$8.40.$$

b.

$$EPS = \$7,000,000/500,000 \text{ shares} = \$14.$$

$$Payout\ ratio = DPS/EPS = \$8.40/\$14 = 60\%$$

$$or:\ Total\ dividends/NI = \$4,200,000/\$7,000,000 = 60\%.$$

Other Topics in Financial Management

Throughout this text we have been developing the basic framework for making financial decisions. At this point we still have two important topics to discuss: Chapter 22 deals with mergers, divestitures, holding companies, and LBOs, and Chapter 23 covers international finance. We deferred these final topics so that they could be analyzed on an integrated basis using analytical tools developed in earlier chapters.

Mergers, Divestitures, Holding Companies, and LBOs

OBJECTIVES

After reading this chapter, you should be able to:

▸ Define "merger" and understand the main objectives for mergers.

▸ Characterize the different types of mergers.

▸ Determine the value of a target firm using the free cash flow (FCF) method.

▸ Discuss the roles investment bankers play in merger transactions.

▸ Recognize other restructuring techniques such as corporate alliances, divestitures, and leveraged buyouts.

▸ Discuss the nature of holding companies and list their advantages and disadvantages.

AN ORBITING DEAL

The deal that created America's newest defense giant began at a resort — the Homestead in Hot Springs, Virginia — during a meeting of the Business Council, a business group composed of senior executives of the nation's top companies. At the meeting, General Electric Chairman Jack Welch approached his old friend, Martin Marietta Chairman Norman Augustine, with a stunning proposal: Why not buy GE's aerospace division?

Intrigued by the offer, Martin's Augustine and GE's Welsh met to thrash out the details. On November 22, 1992, they announced the deal that stunned the industry. The merger marked the biggest defense consolidation to date, making Martin Marietta the world's largest maker of defense electronics.

As you read this chapter, consider the economic implications of mergers and the different types of mergers. Think about the procedures for combining firms and the financial analysis that must be made by both the acquiring and target firms when a merger is proposed. The acquisition of GE Aerospace by Martin Marietta poses many interesting questions. Why did GE's chairman propose the deal? What did Martin Marietta gain from the deal? What type of merger was this? How do you think the merger will fare in terms of corporate culture clash? How are deals valued? What is the best way to structure a deal? And, are mergers such as this one good or bad for the nation?

See end of chapter for resolution.

Photo source: Telegraph Colour Library, FPG International Corp.

_____

This chapter was co-authored by Susan Block of the University of California at Santa Barbara.

merger

The combination of two firms to form a single firm.

Mergers, acquisitions, and divestitures are a natural process in the life cycle of a business or an industry. What varies over time, however, is the pace at which these transactions take place. The frenzied pace of the 1980s slowed considerably as the adverse financial repercussions of hastily made and strategically inappropriate transactions became apparent. Up to this point we have discussed the financing, capital budgeting, and operating decisions financial managers face. However, the most dramatic changes in a firm's size, operations, value, and stock price are often a result of restructuring programs, in which major new businesses are acquired, large segments of the firm are sold off, or the capital structure is changed radically. Such events can occur either separately or in combination, and they can be decided by management or be forced on management by outsiders. We discuss such restructurings in this chapter, examining mergers, divestitures, holding companies, strategic alliances, and leveraged buyouts (LBOs). There are many important legal and tax implications to consider when structuring a merger transaction.[1] However, the scope of this chapter will focus primarily on the financial and business aspects of merger-related business transactions.

Rationale for Mergers

Although the driving force behind most mergers is the desire to increase, or at times protect, shareholders' wealth, the manner in which this is accomplished depends on the specific situation the firm faces. The following section discusses several sources of additional value which may serve as to motivate a merger transaction.

Synergy

synergy

The condition wherein the whole is greater than the sum of its parts; in a synergistic merger, the postmerger value exceeds the sum of the separate companies' premerger values.

Synergistic effects account for the additional value driving many mergers. If Companies A and B merge to form Company C, and if C's value exceeds that of A and B taken separately, then **synergy** is said to exist.[2] Synergistic effects can arise from four sources: (1) *operating economies* resulting from economies of scale in management, production, purchasing, or distribution; (2) *financial economies,* which could include a higher price/earnings ratio, a lower cost of debt, or a greater debt capacity; (3) *differential management efficiency,* which implies that the management of one firm is relatively inefficient, so the profitability of the acquired assets can be improved by merger; and (4) *increased market power* resulting from reduced competition. Operating and financial

---

[1]As we use the term, *merger* means any combination that forms one firm from two or more existing firms. For legal purposes, there are distinctions among the various ways these combinations can occur, but our emphasis is on the fundamental business and financial aspects of mergers.

[2]If synergy exists, the whole is greater than the sum of the parts. Synergy is also called the "2 plus 2 equals 5 effect." The distribution of the synergistic gain between A's and B's stockholders is determined by negotiation, a point discussed later in the chapter.

economies are socially desirable, as are mergers that increase managerial efficiency, but mergers that reduce competition are both undesirable and illegal.[3]

Tax Considerations

Tax considerations have stimulated a number of mergers. For example, a firm which is highly profitable and in the highest corporate tax bracket could acquire a company with large accumulated tax losses, then use those losses to shelter its own income.[4] Similarly, a company with large losses could acquire a profitable firm. Also, tax considerations could cause mergers to be a desirable use for excess cash. For example, if a firm has a shortage of internal investment opportunities compared with its cash flows, it will have excess cash, and its options for disposing of this excess cash are (1) paying an extra dividend, (2) investing in marketable securities, (3) repurchasing its own stock, or (4) purchasing another firm. If the firm pays an extra dividend, its stockholders will have to pay taxes on the distribution. Marketable securities such as Treasury bonds provide a good temporary parking place for money, but the rate of return on such securities is less than that required by stockholders. A stock repurchase might result in a capital gain for the remaining stockholders, but it could be disadvantageous if the company had to pay a high price to acquire the stock, and, if the repurchase was designed solely to avoid paying dividends, it might be challenged by the IRS. However, using surplus cash to acquire another firm has no immediate tax consequences for either the acquiring firm or its stockholders, and this fact has motivated a number of mergers.

Purchase of Assets below Their Replacement Cost

Sometimes a firm will become an acquisition candidate because the replacement value of its assets is considerably higher than its market value. For example, in the 1980s oil companies could acquire reserves more cheaply by buying out other oil companies than by exploratory drilling. This factor was a motive in Chevron's acquisition of Gulf Oil.

The acquisition of Republic Steel (the sixth largest steel company) by LTV (the fourth largest) provides another example of a firm's being purchased because its purchase price was less than the replacement value of its assets. LTV found that it was less costly to purchase Republic Steel for $700 million than it

---

[3]In the 1880s and 1890s, many mergers occurred in the United States, and some of them were clearly directed toward gaining market power rather than increasing operating efficiency. As a result, Congress passed a series of acts designed to ensure that mergers are not used as a method of reducing competition. The principal acts include the Sherman Act (1890), the Clayton Act (1914), and the Celler Act (1950). These acts make it illegal for firms to combine in any manner if the combination will lessen competition. They are administered by the antitrust division of the Justice Department and by the Federal Trade Commission.

[4]Mergers undertaken only to use accumulated tax losses would probably be challenged by the IRS. However, because many factors are present in any given merger, it is hard to prove that a merger was motivated only, or even primarily, by tax considerations.

would have been to construct a new steel mill. At the time, Republic's stock was selling for less than one-third of its book value.

Diversification

Managers often claim that diversification helps to stabilize the firm's earnings and thus reduce corporate risk. Therefore, diversification is often given as a reason for mergers. Stabilization of earnings is certainly beneficial to a firm's employees, suppliers, and customers, but its value to stockholders and debtholders is less clear. If an investor is worried about earnings variability, he or she could probably diversify through stock purchases more easily than the firm could through acquisitions. Therefore, why should Firms A and B merge to stabilize earnings when a stockholder in Firm A could sell half of his or her stock in A and use the proceeds to purchase stock in Firm B, especially since the stockholder could take this action at a much lower cost than would be involved if the firms merged?

Of course, if you were the owner-manager of a closely held firm, it might be virtually impossible for you to sell part of your stock to diversify because this would dilute your ownership and also generate a large tax liability. For such a firm, a merger might well be the best way to achieve personal diversification. However, for publicly held firms, diversification to reduce stockholder risk is generally not a valid motive for a merger.

Maintaining Control

defensive merger

A merger designed to make a company less vulnerable to a takeover.

As we discuss in a later section, in recent years many hostile mergers and take-overs have occurred. The managers of the acquired companies generally lose their jobs, or at least their autonomy. Therefore, managers who own less than 51 percent of the stock in their firms look to devices that will lessen the chances of their firms' being taken over. Mergers can serve as such a device. For example, when Enron was under attack, it arranged to buy Houston Natural Gas Company, paying for Houston primarily with debt. That merger made Enron much larger and hence harder for any potential acquirer to "digest." Also, the much higher debt level resulting from the merger made it hard for any acquiring company to use debt to buy Enron. Such **defensive mergers** are difficult to defend on economic grounds. The managers involved invariably argue that synergy, not a desire to protect their own jobs, motivated the acquisition, but there can be no question that many mergers have been designed more for the benefit of managers than for stockholders.

Self-Test

What is the primary motive behind most mergers?

From what sources might synergistic effects arise?

How have tax considerations stimulated mergers?

Is diversification to reduce stockholder risk a valid motive for mergers? Explain.

List and discuss sources of additional value which may drive a merger transaction.

Types of Mergers

horizontal merger

A combination of two firms that produce the same type of good or service.

vertical merger

A merger between a firm and one of its suppliers or customers.

congeneric merger

A merger of firms in the same general industry but for which no customer or supplier relationship exists.

conglomerate merger

A merger of companies in totally different industries.

Economists classify mergers into four groups: (1) horizontal, (2) vertical, (3) congeneric, and (4) conglomerate. A **horizontal merger** occurs when one firm combines with another in its same line of business—for example, the merger of Shearson Lehman and E. F. Hutton was a horizontal merger because both firms were brokerage houses. An example of a **vertical merger** is a steel producer's acquisition of one of its own suppliers, such as an iron or coal mining firm, or an oil producer's acquisition of a company which uses its products, such as a petrochemical firm. *Congeneric* means "allied in nature or action"; hence, a **congeneric merger** involves related enterprises but not producers of the same product (horizontal) or firms in a producer-supplier relationship (vertical). Examples of congeneric mergers include Unilever's takeover of Chesebrough-Ponds, a toiletry maker, and Philip Morris's acquisitions of General Foods and Kraft. A **conglomerate merger** occurs when unrelated enterprises combine, as illustrated by Mobil Oil's acquisition of Montgomery Ward.

Operating economies (and also anticompetitive effects) are dependent on the type of merger involved. Vertical and horizontal mergers generally provide the greatest synergistic operating benefits, but they are also the ones most likely to be attacked by the U.S. Department of Justice. In any event, it is useful to think of these economic classifications when analyzing the feasibility of a prospective merger.

 Self-Test

Explain briefly the four economic classifications of mergers.

Examples of Merger Activity

Four major "merger waves" have occurred in the United States. The first was in the late 1800s, when consolidations occurred in the oil, steel, tobacco, and other basic industries. The second was in the 1920s, when the stock market boom helped financial promoters consolidate firms in a number of industries, including utilities, communications, and autos. The third was in the 1960s, when conglomerate mergers were the rage, while the fourth occurred in the 1980s.

The "merger mania" of the 1980s was sparked by seven factors: (1) the depressed level of the dollar relative to Japanese and European currencies, which made U.S. companies look cheap to foreign buyers; (2) the unprecedented level of inflation that existed during the 1970s and early 1980s, which increased the replacement value of firms' assets even while a weak stock market reduced their market values; (3) the Reagan and Bush administrations' stated view that "bigness is not necessarily badness," which resulted in a more tolerant attitude toward large mergers; (4) the general belief among the major natural resource companies that it was cheaper to "buy reserves on Wall Street" through mergers than to explore and find them in the field; (5) attempts to ward off raiders by use of defensive mergers; (6) the development of the junk bond market, which made it possible to use far more debt in acquisitions than had been possible

Table 22-1

Illustrative Large
Acquisitions (Billions of
Dollars)

Companies	Year	Value	Percent of Book Value	Type of Transaction
Time-Warner	1989	$14.0	350%	Acquisition for cash, stock, and debt
Chevron-Gulf	1984	13.3	136	Acquisition for cash
Philip Morris-Kraft	1988	12.9	609	Acquisition for stock
Bristol Myers-Squibb	1989	11.5	250	Acquisition for stock
Texaco-Getty	1984	10.1	191	Acquisition for cash and notes

Note: KKR's acquisition of RJR Nabisco exceeded $25 billion, but that transaction was an LBO, not a merger.

earlier; and (7) the increased globalization of business, which has led to increased economies of scale and to the formation of worldwide corporations. Financial historians have not yet compiled the statistics and done the analysis necessary to compare the latest merger wave with the earlier ones, but it is virtually certain that this wave will rank as the largest. Table 22-1 lists the top five mergers of all time, and they all occurred in the 1980s.

We present the highlights of several large mergers to give you a flavor of how actual mergers occur.

1. Getty Oil, the fourteenth largest U.S. oil company, was acquired by Texaco, the fourth largest, at a cost of $10.1 billion. Prior to the merger activity, Getty's shares were selling at around $65, and the descendants of J. Paul Getty, the founder and richest man in the world, were complaining of inefficient management. Then the controlling trustees of the Sarah C. Getty Trust, together with Pennzoil, announced plans to take the firm private by buying the shares which they did not already control at a price of $112.50 per share. Texaco then jumped in with an offer of $125 per share.

   The merger doubled Texaco's domestic oil and gas reserves and, with Getty's retail outlets, gave Texaco a larger share of the gasoline market. Some analysts claimed that Texaco, with its sprawling network of refineries and rapidly dwindling reserves, made the correct decision by acquiring Getty, with its large reserves and minimal refining operations. Other analysts contended that Texaco paid too much for Getty. Acquiring Getty's reserves may have been cheaper for Texaco than finding new oil, but the value of these reserves will depend on the price of oil.

   Two side issues arose during the Getty merger. The first concerned the Bass Brothers of Texas, an immensely wealthy family that had acquired over $1 billion of Texaco stock during all the action. Texaco's management was afraid the Basses would try to take over Texaco, so they bought out the Bass interests at a premium of about 20 percent over the market value. Some of Texaco's stockholders argued that the payment amounted to "greenmail," or a payoff made with stockholders' money just to ensure that Texaco's managers could keep their jobs. This situation, along with several similar ones, has led to the introduction of bills in Congress to limit the actions that a management group can take in its efforts to avoid being taken over. However, Congress has not actually passed such a law to date. The second side issue was a suit by Pennzoil, which charged that Texaco caused Getty to breach its contract with Pennzoil. Pennzoil won a $12 billion judgment, but Texaco appealed, and Pennzoil eventually settled for $3 billion, of which Pennzoil's lawyers will get $400 million.

2. Conoco, which had assets with a book value of $11 billion and which was, based on sales, the thirteenth largest company in the United States, was the target of three other giants: Mobil (the second largest U.S. corporation), Du Pont (the fifteenth largest U.S. corporation), and Seagram (a large Canadian company). This merger alone almost equaled in dollar amount the previous record for all mergers in any one year. Conoco's stock sold for about $50 just before the bidding started, but the bid price got up to over $100 per share before it was over because Conoco's oil and coal reserves, plus its plant and equipment, were worth far more than the company's initial stock market value.

   If Mobil had won, this would have been a horizontal merger. If Seagram had won, it would have been a conglomerate merger. Yet Du Pont won, and it was classified as a vertical merger because Du Pont uses petroleum in its production processes. The Justice Department would have fought a merger with Mobil, but it indicated that it would not do so in the case of Seagram or Du Pont. For this reason, even though Mobil made the highest bid of $115 per share, Du Pont ended up the winner with a bid of $98. Stockholders chose the Du Pont bid over that of Mobil because they were afraid a Mobil merger would be blocked, causing Conoco's stock to fall below the level of the Du Pont bid.

   This was a *hostile merger*—Conoco's management would rather have had the company remain an independent entity. Obviously, though, that was not to be, and Conoco's top managers found themselves working for someone else (or out of a job). This is a good illustration of a point made in Chapter 1, namely, that managers have a strong motivation to operate in a manner that will maximize the value of their firms' stock, for otherwise they can find themselves in the same boat as Conoco's managers.

3. Marathon Oil, a company only slightly smaller than Conoco, was the object of an attempted acquisition by Mobil after that company lost its bid for Conoco. Marathon's management resisted strongly, and again other bidders entered the picture. In the end, U.S. Steel picked up Marathon for about $6 billion, making this the fourth largest merger up to that time. U.S. Steel's bid for Marathon was unusual in that the firm offered to pay cash for only 51 percent of the stock and to exchange bonds for the remainder, with cash going to those stockholders who agreed to the merger at the earliest date. This is called a **two-tier offer,** and it prompted many stockholders to tender their stock to U.S. Steel out of fear of having to accept bonds if they waited to see if the bid might go higher.

two-tier offer

A merger offer which provides different (better) terms to those who tender their stock earliest.

4. Schlitz, once the largest U.S. brewer, had been losing both money and market share. By the 1980s it had become only the fourth largest brewer, with a market share of 8.5 percent, and it seemed to be on a collision course with bankruptcy. Schlitz's troubles arose from its poor marketing strategy, a problem that it was unable to conquer. G. Heileman, the sixth largest brewer, with a market share of 7.5 percent, was better managed, and its

sales were growing rapidly. (Heileman's ROE was 27.3 percent; Schlitz's was negative.) Because of its successful marketing programs, Heileman needed more brewing capacity, whereas because of its poor sales performance, Schlitz had 50 percent excess capacity. Heileman offered to buy Schlitz's common stock for $494 million. If the takeover attempt had been successful, Heileman would have acquired capacity at an effective cost of $19 per barrel versus a construction cost of about $50 per barrel. The merger would also have made Heileman the third largest brewer in the nation. However, the Justice Department opposed this merger because, in its judgment, the resulting concentration would substantially reduce competition in the brewing industry. Therefore, Heileman abandoned the merger effort. However, Schlitz was still in trouble, and it was later acquired by Stroh Brewery, another good marketer, which was smaller than G. Heileman.

5. At the start of the 1990s, the hottest area for mergers was in the banking and S&L industries. In both cases, the primary motive was a quest for synergies. Both banks and S&Ls were plagued with problem loans, and both industries suffered from excess capacity. Therefore, mergers, which can cut costs and thus boost profits, were desperately needed. In December 1991, NCNB, a North Carolina–based bank which, through a merger, had recently become the largest bank in Texas, acquired C&S/Sovran, a bank holding company which operated through the Southeast and which had serious problems with bad real estate loans. The acquisition was for $4.6 billion in stock. Also, in December 1991, Chemical Banking acquired Manufacturers Hanover for $1.8 billion in stock. The Chemical–Manny Hanny combination beat out the NationsBank merger as the second largest U.S. bank (second to Citibank of New York). Both of these mergers have the potential to greatly reduce costs and thus raise profits, but many jobs have been lost. For example, when Chemical's managers announced their merger, they also announced that some 6,000 to 8,000 jobs would be eliminated in the New York City area.

Self-Test

What are the seven factors that sparked the "merger mania" of the 1980s?

Procedures for Combining Firms

In the vast majority of mergers, one firm (generally the larger of the two) simply decides to buy another company, negotiates a price, and then acquires the target company. Occasionally, the acquired firm will initiate the action, but it is much more common for a firm to seek acquisitions than to seek to be acquired.[5]

---

[5]However, if a firm is in financial difficulty, if its managers are elderly and do not think that suitable replacements are on hand, or if it needs the support (often the capital) of a larger company, then it may seek to be acquired. Thus, when a number of Texas banks were in trouble in the late 1980s, they lobbied to get the state legislature to pass a law that made it easier for them to be acquired. Out-of-state banks then moved in to help salvage the situation and minimize depositor losses.

acquiring company

A company that seeks to acquire another.

target company

A firm that another company seeks to acquire.

friendly merger

A merger whose terms are approved by the managements of both companies.

hostile merger (takeover)

A merger in which the target firm's management resists acquisition.

tender offer

The offer of one firm to buy the stock of another by going directly to the stockholders, frequently (but not always) over the opposition of the target company's management.

Following convention, we shall call a company that seeks to acquire another the **acquiring company** and the one it seeks to acquire the **target company.**

Once an acquiring company has identified a possible target, it must establish the price that it is willing to pay. With this in mind, it will then approach the target company's managers. If the acquiring firm has reason to believe that the target's management will approve the merger, it will propose the merger and try to work out suitable terms. If an agreement can be reached, the two management groups will issue statements to their stockholders recommending that they approve the merger. Assuming the stockholders do approve, the acquiring firm will then buy the target company's shares from its stockholders, paying for them either with its own shares (in which case the target company's stockholders become stockholders of the acquiring company), with cash, or with bonds. Such a transaction is defined as a **friendly merger.** Examples of friendly mergers include Time's merger with Warner Communications, General Electric's acquisition of RCA, and Federal Express's acquisition of Tiger International.

Under other circumstances, the target company's management may resist the merger. Perhaps the managers believe that the price offered for the stock is too low, or perhaps they simply want to keep their jobs. In either case, the target firm's management is said to be *hostile* rather than friendly, and in a **hostile merger (a takeover),** the acquiring firm must make a direct appeal to the target firm's stockholders. In a hostile merger, the acquiring company generally makes a **tender offer,** in which it asks the stockholders of the firm it is seeking to control to submit, or "tender," their shares in exchange for a specified price. The price is generally stated as so many dollars per share of the stock to be acquired, although it can be stated in terms of shares of stock of the acquiring firm. Because the tender offer is a direct appeal to stockholders, it need not be approved by the target firm's management. Tender offers are not new, but their frequency has increased greatly in recent years.[6]

 Self-Test

Differentiate between an acquiring company and a target company.

Merger Analysis

The acquisition decision involves consideration of both "strategic fit," or how well the proposed merger will fulfill or meet the corporate objectives, and financial value. From a pure financial theory perspective, the merger analysis is quite simple. The financial value is evaluated using the same discounted cash flow methods used in prior chapters with other capital budgeting decisions; if the net present value exceeds the price the acquiring firm must pay, the transaction appears favorable. Conversely, the target company's board of directors should accept an offer if the price offered exceeds the present value of the cash flows they would receive if they continued to operate the firm.

---

[6]Tender offers can be friendly, with the target firm's management recommending that stockholders go ahead and tender their stock.

However, the process of estimating future cash flows is quite complex with an acquisition because one must take into account the effect of potential synergy and the new ownership. In fact, overestimating financial projections up front, and thus, overstating the purchase price, is one of the major reasons that merger transactions fail. Consequently, pro forma financial statements, cash flow projections, and valuations are often developed with the assistance of investment banking firms — serving as a professional, unbiased third party.

Beyond estimating future cash flows, several other merger issues must be resolved, such as (1) what effect, if any, the purchase will have on the acquiring firm's required rate of return on equity; (2) what consideration will be used for the purchase — cash, stock, or some combination of both; and (3) how to best negotiate all the terms of the transaction to benefit the shareholders of both the target and the acquiring firm.

Operating Mergers versus Financial Mergers

From the standpoint of financial analysis, there are two basic types of mergers: *operating mergers* and *financial mergers*.

operating merger

A merger in which operations of the firms involved are integrated in hope of achieving synergistic benefits.

1. An **operating merger** is one in which the operations of two companies are integrated with the expectation of obtaining synergistic effects. The Chemical–Manufacturers Hanover and the NCNB-C&S/Sovran deals are good examples of operating mergers.

financial merger

A merger in which the firms involved will not be operated as a single unit and from which no operating economies are expected.

2. A **financial merger** is one in which the merged companies will not be operated as a single unit and from which no significant operating economies are expected. Coca-Cola's acquisition of Columbia Pictures is an example of a financial merger.

Of course, mergers may actually combine these two features. Thus, if Mobil had acquired Marathon Oil, the merger would have been primarily an operating one. However, with U.S. Steel emerging as the victor, the merger was more financial than operating in nature.

Estimating Future Operating Income

In a financial merger, the postmerger cash flows are simply the sum of the expected cash flows of the two companies if they continued to operate independently. However, if the two firms' operations are to be integrated, or if the acquiring firm plans to change the target firm's management to get better results, then accurate estimates of future cash flows, which are difficult to obtain but absolutely essential to sound merger decisions, will be required.

The basic rationale for any operating merger is synergy. Del Monte Corporation provides a good example of a series of well-thought-out, favorable operating mergers. Del Monte successfully merged and integrated numerous small canning companies into a highly efficient, profitable organization. It used standardized production techniques to increase the efficiency of all of its plants, a national brand name and national advertising to develop customer brand loyalty, a consolidated distribution system, and a centralized purchasing office to obtain substantial discounts due to volume purchases. Because of these economies, Del

Monte became the most efficient and profitable U.S. canning company, and its merger activities helped make possible the size that produced these economies. Consumers also benefited, because Del Monte's efficiency enabled the company to sell high-quality products at relatively low prices.

An example of a poor pro forma analysis that resulted in a disastrous merger was the consolidation of the Pennsylvania and New York Central railroads. The premerger analysis suggested that large cost savings would result, but the analysis was grossly misleading because it failed to recognize that certain key elements in the two rail systems were incompatible and hence could not be meshed together. Thus, rather than gaining synergistic benefits, the combined system actually incurred additional overhead costs which led to bankruptcy. *In planning operating mergers, the development of accurate pro forma cash flows is the single most important aspect of the analysis.*[7]

Merger Terms

The terms of a merger include answers to two important questions: (1) Who will control the combined enterprise? (2) How much will the acquiring firm pay for the acquired company?

Postmerger Control.   The employment/control situation is often of vital interest. First, consider the situation in which a small, owner-managed firm sells out to a larger concern. The owner-manager may be anxious to retain a high-status position, and he or she may also have developed a camaraderie with the employees and thus be concerned about keeping operating control of the organization after the merger. If so, these points are likely to be stressed during the merger negotiations.[8] When a publicly owned firm not controlled by its managers is merged into another company, the acquired firm's management also is worried about its postmerger position. If the acquiring firm agrees to retain the old management, then management may be willing to support the merger

---

[7]Firms heavily engaged in mergers have "acquisition departments" whose functions include (1) seeking suitable merger candidates and (2) taking over and integrating acquired firms into the parent corporation. The first step involves the estimation of future cash flows and a plan for making the projections materialize. The second step involves streamlining the operations of the acquired firm and instituting a system of controls that will permit the parent to effectively manage the new division and to coordinate its operations with those of other units.

[8]The acquiring firm may also be concerned about this point, especially if the acquired firm's management is quite good. A condition of the merger may be that the management team agree to stay on for a period, such as five years, after the merger. Also, the price paid may be contingent on the acquired firm's performance subsequent to the merger. For example, when International Holdings acquired Walker Products, the price paid was 200,000 shares of International Holdings stock (which sold for $63 per share) at the time the deal was closed plus an additional 30,000 shares each year for the next three years, provided Walker Products earned at least $2 million during each of these years. Since Walker's managers owned the stock and would receive the bonus, they had a strong incentive to stay on and help the firm meet its targets.

If the managers of the target company are highly competent but do not wish to remain on after the merger, the acquiring firm may build into the merger contract a noncompetitive agreement with the old management. Thus, Walker Products's principal officers had to agree not to affiliate with a new business which is competitive with the one they sold for a period of five years. Such agreements are especially important with service-oriented businesses.

and to recommend its acceptance to the stockholders. If the old management is to be removed, it will probably resist the merger.[9]

Purchase Price.   The second key element in a merger is the price to be paid for the target company — the cash or securities to be given to the target firm's stockholders. The analysis is similar to a regular discounted cash flow analysis: The *free cash flows* are estimated; a discount rate is applied to find the present value of those cash flows; and, if the present value of the future cash flows exceeds the price to be paid for the target firm, the merger is approved. Thus, only if the target firm is worth more to the acquiring firm than its market value as a separate entity will the merger be feasible. Obviously, the acquiring firm tries to buy at as low a price as possible, whereas the target firm tries to sell out at the highest possible price. The final price is determined by negotiations, with the party that negotiates best capturing most of the incremental value. *The larger the synergistic benefits, the more room there is for bargaining, and the higher the probability that the merger actually will be consummated.*[10]

Self-Test

What is the essential difference between an operating merger and a pure financial merger?

In analyzing a proposed operating merger, what is the single most important factor?

When negotiating a friendly merger, what are the two most important considerations?

Valuing the Target Firm

Virtually all acquisition valuation methods utilize a discounted cash flow (DCF) methodology, under which two key items are needed: (1) a set of pro forma financial statements which develop the expected cash flows and (2) a discount rate, or cost of capital, to use in finding the present value of the projected cash flows. However, the various valuation approaches differ as to the relevant cash flows and appropriate discount rates used. Perhaps the most widely used valuation method involves using yearly free cash flow (FCF) estimates as the relevant cash flows in determining the valuation of the target firm. We will illustrate the determination of free cash flows in a moment.

---

[9]Managements of firms that are thought to be attractive merger candidates occasionally arrange "golden parachutes" for themselves. Golden parachutes are extremely lucrative retirement plans which take effect if a merger is consummated. Thus, when Bendix was acquired by Allied, Bill Agee, Bendix's chairman, "pulled the ripcord of his golden parachute" and walked away with $4 million. Congress is currently considering controls on golden parachutes as a part of its takeover legislative proposals.

[10]It has been estimated that of all merger negotiations seriously begun, fewer than one-third actually result in mergers. Also, in contested merger situations, the company that offers the most will usually make the acquisition, and the company that stands to gain the greatest synergistic benefits can generally bid the most.

Table 22-2		1994	1995	1996	1997	1998
CompuEd Corporation: Projected Postmerger Income Statements as of December 31 (Millions of Dollars)	Net sales	$105.0	$126.0	$151.0	$174.0	$191.0
	Cost of goods sold	80.0	94.0	111.0	127.0	137.0
	Selling and administrative expenses	10.0	12.0	13.0	15.0	16.0
	Depreciation	8.0	8.0	9.0	9.0	10.0
	EBIT	$ 7.0	$ 12.0	$ 18.0	$ 23.0	$ 28.0
	Interest[a]	3.0	4.0	5.0	6.0	6.0
	EBT	$ 4.0	$ 8.0	$ 13.0	$ 17.0	$ 22.0
	Taxes (40.0%)[b]	1.6	3.2	5.2	6.8	8.8
	Net income	$ 2.4	$ 4.8	$ 7.8	$ 10.2	$ 13.2
	Investments for growth[c]	4.0	4.0	7.0	9.0	12.0

[a]Interest payment estimates are based on CompuEd's existing debt plus additional debt to increase the debt ratio to 50 percent, plus additional debt after the merger to finance asset expansion but subject to the 50 percent target capital structure.

[b]American will file a consolidated tax return after the merger. Thus, the taxes shown here are the full corporate taxes attributable to CompuEd's operations; there will be no additional taxes on the cash flowing from CompuEd to American.

[c]Some of the net income generated by CompuEd after the merger will be retained to finance its own asset growth, and some will be transferred to American to pay dividends on its stock or for redeployment within the corporation.

Pro Forma Income Statements

Table 22-2 contains the projected income statements for CompuEd Corporation, which is being considered for acquisition by American Technologies, a large high-tech company. The projected data are postmerger, so all synergistic effects are included. CompuEd currently uses 30 percent debt, but if it were acquired, American would increase CompuEd's debt ratio to 50 percent. Both American and CompuEd have a 40 percent marginal federal-plus-state tax rate.

In a complete merger valuation, just as in a complete capital budgeting analysis, the component cash flow probability distributions would be specified, and sensitivity, scenario, and simulation analyses would be conducted. Indeed, in a friendly merger, the acquiring firm would send a team to the target firm's headquarters to carefully go over its books and verify all assets, holdings, and liabilities.

Estimating the Discount Rate

The discount rate used in valuing a target firm is a weighted average cost of capital, determined using the average cost of equity and average cost of debt for firms comparable to the target firm—with the weights determined as the expected relative proportions of debt and equity in the target firm after the acquisition. In our example, the capital structure of the target firm is expected to be 50 percent debt and 50 percent equity. The average cost of equity for firms similar to the target firm is 18.5 percent, and the average after-tax cost of debt for similar firms is 16.9 percent. We then use Equation 19-4 to find the weighted average cost of capital:

$$\text{WACC} = w_d k_d (1 - T) + w_p k_p + w_s k_s \qquad (19\text{-}4)$$

Table 22-3		1994	1995	1996	1997	1998
CompuEd Corporation: FCF Projections (Millions of Dollars)	Net income	$2.40	$ 4.80	$ 7.80	$10.20	$13.20
	+ Depreciation	8.00	8.00	9.00	9.00	10.00
	+ After-tax interest [interest $\times$ (1 $-$ T)]	1.80	1.92	3.12	4.08	5.28
	$-$ Investment	4.00	4.00	7.00	9.00	12.00
	= Free cash flow (FCF)	$8.20	$10.72	$12.92	$14.28	$16.48

because there is no preferred stock the second term is zero and we have

$$\text{WACC} = 0.5(16.9\%) + 0.5(18.5\%) = 17.70\%.$$

Determining Free Cash Flow

free cash flow

The sum of a target firm's net income, depreciation, and after-tax interest, minus any annual investment required.

Free cash flow estimates are calculated as Net income + Depreciation + After-tax interest $-$ Investment required (such as increases in working capital or additional plant and equipment). An after-tax interest is used to reflect the true cost of interest to the firm, net of the tax shelter effect of interest expense. After-tax interest is calculated as: Interest $\times$ (1 $-$ Tax rate).

Terminal Value

Obviously, the firm does not cease to have value or generate cash beyond the five-year projected FCFs. However, the inaccuracy of projections beyond a five-year time frame precludes extending this out any further, and instead, a residual value is determined and added to the fifth year's FCF. The residual value is calculated using what is basically a constant growth valuation model and using the fifth year's FCF estimate, an estimated annual growth in free cash flow (g) of 5 percent into perpetuity, and the weighted average cost of capital (WACC) calculated earlier of 17.70 percent:

$$\text{Terminal value} = \frac{[\text{FCF year 5 } (1 + g)]}{\text{WACC} - g}$$

$$= \frac{\$16.48(1.05)}{.1770 - 0.05}$$

$$= \$136.25.$$

Valuing the Cash Flows

The value of CompuEd is the present value of the expected free cash flows and of the terminal value, discounted at 17.70 percent:

$$\text{Total value} = \frac{\$8.20}{(1.1770)^1} + \frac{\$10.72}{(1.1770)^2} + \frac{\$12.92}{(1.1770)^3} + \frac{\$14.28}{(1.1770)^4} + \frac{\$16.48 + \$136.25}{(1.1770)^5}$$

$$= \$97.68 \text{ million.}$$

(Using a financial calculator, you would enter the cash flows for each year in the cash flow register, enter $k = i = 17.70$, and press the NPV key to arrive at the value of $97.68 million.) Consequently, if the purchase price for CompuEd is $97.68 million or below, the transaction appears favorable from a financial perspective.

? Self-Test

How are the free cash flows in a merger analysis determined?

How is the discount rate that is used to evaluate the postmerger cash flows of the target firm obtained?

The Role of Investment Bankers

Investment bankers serve several critical functions in merger transactions: (1) structuring and negotiating the merger, (2) valuing the target firm, and (3) developing and implementing tactics. Merger-related activities can be quite profitable for investment banking firms. Paramount Communications incurred fees and related costs of about $50 million in its failed attempt to acquire Time, and Time's costs to fend off Paramount and to acquire Warner were over $100 million. No wonder investment banking houses are able to make top offers to finance graduates!

Arranging Mergers

Major investment banking firms have merger and acquisition groups which operate within their corporate finance departments. (Corporate finance departments offer advice, as opposed to underwriting or brokerage services, to business firms.) Members of these groups strive to identify firms with excess cash that might want to buy other firms, companies that might be willing to be bought, and firms that might, for a number of reasons, be attractive to others. If an oil company, for instance, decided to expand into coal mining, it might enlist the aid of an investment banker to help it locate, value, and then negotiate with a target coal company.

Developing Defense Tactics

white knight

A company that is more acceptable to the management of a firm under attack in a hostile takeover attempt.

Target firms that do not want to be acquired generally enlist the help of an investment banking firm, along with a law firm that specializes in helping to block mergers. Defenses include such tactics as (1) changing the bylaws so that only one-third of the directors are elected each year and/or so that a 75 percent approval (a "supermajority") versus a simple majority is required to approve a merger, (2) trying to convince stockholders that the price offered by the potential acquirer is too low, (3) raising antitrust issues in the hope that the Justice Department will intervene, (4) issuing debt and using the proceeds to repurchase stock in the open market in an effort to push the price above that being offered by the potential acquirer, (5) persuading a **white knight** more

poison pill

An action which will seriously hurt a company if it is acquired by another.

golden parachutes

Large payments made to the managers of a firm if it is acquired.

acceptable to the target firm's management that it should compete with the potential acquirer, and (6) taking a "poison pill," as described below.

Some examples of **poison pills** — some of which really do amount to virtually committing suicide to avoid a takeover — are such tactics as borrowing on terms that require immediate repayment of all loans if the firm is acquired, selling off at bargain prices the assets that originally made the firm a desirable target, granting such lucrative **golden parachutes** to the firm's executives that the cash drain from these payments would render the merger infeasible, and planning defensive mergers which would leave the firm with new assets of questionable value plus a huge amount of debt to service. Companies are even giving their stockholders the right to buy at half price the stock of an acquiring firm should the firm be acquired. The blatant use of poison pills is constrained by directors' awareness that such use could trigger personal suits by stockholders against directors who voted for them, and, perhaps in the near future, bylaws that would limit management's use of these tactics. Still, investment bankers are busy thinking up new poison pill formulas, and others are just as actively trying to come up with antidotes.

Establishing a Fair Value

If a friendly merger is being worked out between two firms' managements, it is important to be able to document that the agreed-upon price is a fair one; otherwise, the stockholders of either company could sue to block the merger. Therefore, in most large mergers, each side will hire an investment banking firm to evaluate the target company and render a fair value opinion. For example, General Electric employed Morgan Stanley to determine a fair price for Utah International, as did Royal Dutch to help establish the price it paid for Shell Oil. Even if the merger is not friendly, investment bankers may still be asked to help establish a price. If a surprise tender offer is to be made, the acquiring firm will want to know the lowest price at which it might be able to acquire the stock, whereas the target firm may seek help in proving that the price being offered is too low.[11]

? Self-Test

What roles do investment bankers play in merger transactions?

List some defense tactics that can be used by target firms to block mergers.

List some examples of poison pills.

---

[11]Such investigations must obviously be done in secret, for if someone knew that Company A was thinking of offering, say, $50 per share for Company T, which was currently selling at $35 per share, huge profits could be made. The biggest scandal to hit Wall Street in the 1980s was the disclosure that Ivan Boesky, a well-known investor, was buying from Dennis Levine, a senior member of the investment banking house of Drexel Burnham Lambert, information about prospective takeovers of companies that Drexel Burnham was analyzing for others. Boesky's purchases, of course, raised the prices of the stocks and thus forced Drexel's clients to pay more than they otherwise would have had to pay. Incidentally, Boesky and Levine both went to jail for improper use of inside information, as did others involved in the scheme.

Corporate Alliances

corporate alliance

A cooperative agreement between two firms that can range from a simple marketing agreement to the joint ownership of a third corporation.

Mergers are not the only way in which the resources of two firms can be combined. In fact, many companies are striking cooperative deals which fall far short of merging. Such cooperative deals are called **corporate alliances.** Corporate alliances and partnering have become a dynamic element in the development of firms and markets. It is now often imperative for companies to partner to remain competitive in today's environment — namely, an increasingly global market characterized by rapid technological change. Especially prevalent are joint venture and partnership agreements between large corporations and small entrepreneurial firms. Small firms often need capital and access to distribution channels, and large companies lack the innovation and flexibility to create new product developments. By partnering, large and small firms can use their complementary strengths to take a new product or service from concept to the marketplace. The process by which a new idea gets to the end user is called the *value chain,* composed of the following sequential stages: research, development, design, production, marketing, sales, and distribution. All the stages in the value chain must be in place before a product can make it from an idea to the end consumer. Few companies are competitive at every stage of the value chain. Traditionally, large firms are best at the later stages, such as production, marketing, sales, and distribution, while small companies excel at innovation, research, development, and design. A simple solution is corporate partnering — joint ventures and corporate agreements between large corporations and small firms.

joint venture

A corporate alliance in which two independent companies combine their resources to achieve a specific, limited objective.

Corporate alliances are broadly defined as cooperative agreements between two firms and can take many forms — from marketing or production agreements to joint venture ownership of a third corporation. A **joint venture** is the strongest form of corporate alliance and entails two firms combining resources to accomplish a specific, limited objective such as developing, and subsequently marketing, a high-technology product or new drug. Often a third corporation, which is jointly owned, is formed to accomplish the joint venture objective. The exact structure of the joint venture is a function of the needs of the contributing firms and the objective to be accomplished. Joint ventures are quite common in the pharmaceutical industry where the large established pharmaceutical firms contribute the up-front capital, and later the marketing and distribution channels, while a small biotech firm provides the research and development skills to develop a drug for a specific disease state.

Joint ventures have also been used often by U.S., Japanese, and European firms to share technology and marketing expertise. For example, Whirlpool recently announced a joint venture with the Dutch electronics giant Philips that will produce appliances under the Philips brand names in five European countries. By joining with their foreign counterparts, U.S. firms are trying to establish a strong foothold in Europe before the European community becomes one unified market.

Self-Test

What is the difference between a merger and a joint venture?

Divestitures

As a part of corporate restructuring, firms will often decide to sell a portion of their business. The decision to sell an operating unit may be driven by either (1) strictly financial motives, such as a negative cash flow or the need to raise capital to pay outstanding debt obligations, or (2) strategic business motives, such as discontinuing an unrelated product line and concentrating on what the firm does best. In this section we briefly discuss the major types of divestitures, and then we present some recent examples of and rationales for divestitures.

Types of Divestitures

divestiture

The sale of some of a company's operating assets.

There are four types of **divestitures:** (1) sale of an operating unit to another firm, (2) sale to the managers of the unit being divested, (3) setting up the business to be divested as a separate corporation and then giving (or "spinning off") its stock on a pro rata basis to the divesting firm's stockholders, and (4) outright liquidation of assets.

Sale to another firm generally involves the sale of an entire division or unit, usually for cash but sometimes for stock of the acquiring firm. In a *managerial buyout,* the managers of the division purchase the division themselves, usually for cash plus notes. Then, as owners-managers, they reorganize it as a closely held firm. In a **spin-off,** the firm's existing stockholders are given new stock representing separate ownership rights in the company that was divested. The new company establishes its own board of directors and officers, and it operates as a separate company. The stockholders end up owning shares of two firms instead of one, but no cash has been transferred. Finally, in a *liquidation,* the assets of a division are sold off piecemeal rather than as a single entity. We present some recent examples of the different types of divestitures in the next section.

spin-off

A divestiture in which the stock of a subsidiary is given to the parent company's stockholders.

Divestiture Illustrations

1. Esmark Inc., a holding company which owned such consumer products companies as Swift Meats and Playtex, sold off several of its nonconsumer-oriented divisions, including petroleum properties for which Mobil and some other oil companies paid $1.1 billion. Investors had generally thought of Esmark as a meat packing and consumer products company, and its stock price had reflected this image rather than that of a company with huge holdings of valuable oil reserves carried at low balance sheet values. Thus, Esmark's stock was undervalued, according to its managers, and the company was in danger of a takeover bid. Selling the oil properties helped Esmark raise its stock price from $19 to $45.

2. IU International, a multimillion-dollar conglomerate listed on the NYSE, spun off three major subsidiaries—Gotaas-Larson, an ocean shipping company which owned Carnival Cruise Lines; Canadian Utilities, an electric utility; and Echo Bay Mines, a gold mining company. IU also owned (and retained) some major trucking companies (Ryder and PIE), several manu-

facturing businesses, and some large agribusiness operations. IU's management originally had acquired and combined highly cyclical businesses such as ocean shipping and gold mining with stable ones such as utilities in order to gain overall corporate stability through diversification. The strategy worked reasonably well from an operating standpoint, but it failed in the financial markets. According to its management, IU's very diversity kept it from being assigned to any particular industrial classification, so securities analysts tended not to follow the company and therefore did not understand it or recommend it to investors. (Analysts tend to concentrate on an industry, and they do not like to recommend—and investors do not like to invest in—a company they do not understand.) As a result, IU had a low P/E ratio and a low market price. After the spin-offs, IU's stock price plus those of the spun-off companies rose from $10 to over $75.

leveraged buyout (LBO)

A situation in which a buyer borrows heavily against the target firm's assets and purchases the company primarily using debt.

3. The managers of Beatrice Companies and some private investors borrowed $6.9 billion from a group of banks and used this money to buy all of the firm's stock. This type of debt-financed transaction is called a **leveraged buyout (LBO),** and Beatrice was said to have "gone private" because the public stockholders were bought out, and all of the stock went into the hands of the management group. We will look at LBOs in more detail in a later section. The new Beatrice has been busily selling off divisions to raise money to reduce its bank loans; its loan agreements required it to sell off at least $1.45 billion in assets within a year, but Beatrice beat that schedule. The company sold Avis for $250 million just 12 days after it went private, and it later sold off its Coca-Cola bottling operations for about $1 billion. Beatrice also sold its refrigerated warehouse network, its Max Factor cosmetic line, its dairy products line, and other operations, raising another $2.4 billion in total.

4. In 1984 AT&T was broken up to settle a Justice Department antitrust suit filed in the 1970s. For almost 100 years AT&T had operated as a holding company which owned Western Electric (its manufacturing subsidiary), Bell Labs (its research arm), a huge long-distance network system, and 22 Bell operating companies, such as Pacific Telephone, New York Telephone, Southern Bell, and Southwestern Bell. In preparation for the breakup, AT&T was divided into eight separate companies: a slimmed-down AT&T, which kept Western Electric, Bell Labs, and all interstate long-distance operations, and seven new regional telephone holding companies that were created from the 22 old operating telephone companies. The stock of the seven new telephone companies was then spun off to the old AT&T's stockholders. Thus, a person who held 100 shares of old AT&T stock owned, after the divestiture, 100 shares of the "new" AT&T plus 10 shares of each of the seven new operating companies. These 170 shares were backed by the same assets that had previously backed 100 shares of AT&T common.

   The AT&T divestiture occurred as a result of a suit by the Justice Department, which wanted to break up the Bell System into a regulated monopoly segment (the seven regional telephone companies) and a manufacturing/long-distance segment which would be subjected to competition.

The breakup was designed to strengthen competition in those parts of the telecommunications industry which are not natural monopolies.[12]

5. Woolworth recently liquidated every one of its 336 Woolco discount stores. This made the company, which had had sales of $7.2 billion before the liquidation, 30 percent smaller. Woolco had posted operating losses of $19 million in the year before the liquidation, and its losses in the six months preceding it had climbed to an alarming $21 million. Woolworth's CEO, Edward F. Gibbons, was quoted as saying: "How many losses can you take?" Woolco's demise necessitated an after-tax write-off of $325 million, but management believed that it was better to go ahead and "bite the bullet" than to let the losing stores bleed the company to death.

6. As a result of some imprudent loans to oil companies and to developing nations, Continental Illinois, one of the largest U.S. bank holding companies, was recently threatened with bankruptcy. Continental then sold off several profitable divisions, such as its leasing and credit card operations, to raise funds to cover bad-loan losses and deposit withdrawals. In effect, Continental sold assets in order to stay alive. Ultimately, Continental was bailed out by the Federal Deposit Insurance Corporation and the Federal Reserve, which (1) arranged a $7.5 billion rescue package and (2) provided a blanket guarantee for all of Continental's $40 billion of deposits, which kept deposits larger than $100,000 from fleeing the bank because of their uninsured status.

The preceding examples illustrate the varied reasons for divestitures. Sometimes the market does not appear to properly recognize the value of a firm's assets when they are held as part of a conglomerate; the Esmark oil properties case was an example. Similarly, IU International had become so complex and diverse that analysts and investors did not understand it and consequently ignored it. Other companies need cash either to finance expansion in their primary business lines or to reduce a large debt burden, and divestitures can be used to raise this cash. Running a business is a dynamic process—conditions change, corporate strategies change in response, and, as a result, firms alter their asset portfolios by acquisitions, divestitures, or both. Some divestitures, such as Woolworth's liquidation of its Woolco stores, occur in order to unload losing assets that would otherwise drag the company down, while the AT&T example is one of the many instances in which a divestiture is the result of an antitrust settlement. Finally, Continental's actions represented a desperate effort to get the cash needed to stay alive.

Self-Test

What are the four types of divestitures?

What are some reasons for divestitures?

---

[12]Another forced divestiture involved Du Pont and General Motors. In 1921, GM was in serious financial trouble, and Du Pont supplied capital plus managerial talent in exchange for 23 percent of GM's stock. Many years later, the Justice Department won an antitrust suit which required Du Pont to spin off (to Du Pont stockholders) its GM stock.

A SPATE OF SPIN-OFFS

For years, Tandy Corporation has been spinning off parts of itself. The owner of Radio Shack removed from its corporate umbrella such firms as Bombay Company, a specialty furniture retailer; Pier 1 Imports; Color Tile; and the home improvement company Tandycrafts. The latest move involved the spin-off of its technology and manufacturing operations into a separate company called TE Electronics. "Tandy has had a history of reinventing itself over the years," said Chairman John Roach. "This allows the company to focus with a passion."

Focus was also on the mind of Shearson Lehman Brothers, a unit of American Express, when it separated into three operating divisions in 1993. A major reorganization created new executive titles and switched around some top personnel. T. Christopher Pettit was put in charge of the Lehman Brothers investment banking and trading division, and Joseph Plumeri was named to head the flagship brokerage. John R. Laird, formerly CEO of the entire Shearson brokerage and money-management unit, heads a new division that will stand on its own as SLB Asset Management. Shearson Chairman/CEO, Howard L. Clark, Jr., said the breakout "will focus more attention" on the asset management business.

Weak earnings had been a problem at both Shearson and Tandy; the spin-offs and other changes were seen as positive moves by Wall Street. At Tandy, the spin-off also was symbolic of a return to the company's root business—retailing. The 7,000 Radio Shack stores have been transformed into what Roach calls "the ultimate electronics convenience store." The company will also focus on megastores to compete with Circuit City, opening as many as 32 "Computer City" and several "Incredible Universe" electronic and appliance superstores by 1995. Applauding Tandy's moves, a New York technology analyst said, "It's been hard for them to get the right following. They are finally going to be treated as a true retailer."

However, not everyone is optimistic. Tandy's spun-off manufacturing arm sold two-thirds of its products to customers other than Tandy, and thus, it provided a hedge against slow times in the company's retail outlets. After the spin-off, that hedge is gone. Also, the company created by the spin-off will compete directly with Tandy by opening some retail operations of its own, including computers-by-mail.

Then there is the performance of Tandy's new megastores. Although "Superstores are clearly winning the day . . . [with] hyper selection, hyper convenience, and, hopefully, hyper low prices" according to one industry watcher, the Incredible Universe stores may not be achieving the success that others are. Sales have been slow, and suppliers have complained about weak orders. An analyst said, "I can't possibly fathom in my mind that they could be making a profit. I am very skeptical about its success."

Regardless of the possibility of failure, however, spin-offs are in vogue. An executive at First Boston Corporation said, "We have seen an increase in this activity, and we expect a continuous, steady flow." An analyst at the monthly publication *Spinoff Report* said in 1992 that "this is the busiest year for spin-offs in 30 years."

Some companies get rid of their slow-growth businesses when they can not find cash buyers for them, but investors often foresee profits in the spin-offs. When Ecolab announced it would shed its Chemlawn unit, its stock price went up more than seven points. The Pet food company's valuation on the market went up when it was spun off by Whitman Industries. A managing director at J. P. Morgan & Company said spin-offs not only allow companies to focus on their core business, they also make it easier for investors to focus their own choices as well.

When a company splits itself, stockholders then hold shares in two firms instead of one, and they can decide to sell or keep either or both. For instance, when Ralston-Purina spun off Continental Baking (maker of Wonder Bread and Hostess Twinkies), investors who liked the dog food business but not bakeries could stay with Ralston and shed Continental.

Many prefer to stay with a discarded company, however. An academic study at Pennsylvania State University found that spin-off stocks often outperform

Sources: Kyle Pope, "Tandy's Roach Decides to Try His Hand at Megastores," *The Wall Street Journal,* January 13, 1993, B4; Michael Siconolfi, "Shearson Names Fuld, Hill to New Office of Chairman in Wide Reorganization," *The Wall Street Journal,* January 12, 1993, B6; Randall Smith, "Spate of Spinoffs Turns Investors' Heads," *The Wall Street Journal,* May 12, 1992, C1.

the market and other companies in their industry. The authors' conclusions were based on a sample of 146 spin-offs between 1965 and 1988.

To the parent corporation, the advantages of spin-offs include tax savings and easing of the distractions to management of a slow-growth division. If a company decided to sell a business, it might incur a large capital gains tax bill. A spin-off, however, is tax free. Another advantage some see is that top executives who would balk at joining a huge bureaucracy might be recruited to run stand-alone companies. Finally, when businesses are broken up, the managers of the separate companies can see the results of their individual efforts more clearly, and results can be better reflected in incentive compensation packages. In the words of one manager of a spun-off operation, "The effects of our executives' efforts are now clearly reflected in earnings per share and in the stock price. When we were just a small part of a huge operation, we just couldn't move the stock price, so giving us stock options didn't provide much incentive."

Nevertheless, there is always the danger of failure, and few top managers are willing to spin off the corporation's "crown jewels." An analyst at a Baltimore investment counseling firm says of spin-offs, "In the vast majority of cases you're dealing with mundane, low-growth businesses."

Holding Companies

holding company

A corporation that owns sufficient common stock of another firm to achieve working control of it.

parent company

A holding company; a firm which controls another firm by owning a large block of its stock.

operating company

A subsidiary of a holding company; a separate legal entity.

Strictly defined, any company that owns stock in another firm could be called a holding company. However, as the term is generally used, a **holding company** is a firm whose primary function is to hold the stock of other corporations, but that has no operating units of its own. The holding company is often called the **parent company,** it owns sufficient common stock of one or more firms to achieve working control of each firm, and the controlled companies are known as *subsidiaries* or **operating companies.** The parent can own 100 percent of the subsidiaries' stock, but control can generally be exercised with far fewer shares.

Many of the advantages and disadvantages of holding companies are identical to those of large-scale operations already discussed in connection with mergers and consolidations. However, as we show next, the holding company form of large-scale operations has some distinct advantages (as well as a few disadvantages) over those of completely integrated, divisionalized operations.

Advantages of Holding Companies

Holding companies have three potential advantages: (1) control with fractional ownership, (2) isolation of risks, and (3) legal and accounting separation when regulations make such separation desirable.

1. **Control with fractional ownership.**   Through a holding company operation, a firm may buy 5, 10, 50, or any other percentage of another corporation's stock. Such fractional ownership may be sufficient to give the acquiring company effective working control over the operations of the firm in which it has acquired stock ownership. Working control is often considered to require more than 25 percent of the common stock, but it can be as low as 10 percent if the stock is widely distributed. One financier recently made this statement: "The attitude of management is more important than the number of shares you own. If they think you can control the company, then you do."

2. **Isolation of risks.**   Because the various operating companies in a holding company system are separate legal entities, the obligations of any one unit are separate from those of the others. Therefore, catastrophic losses incurred by one unit might not be transmitted as claims on the assets of the other units. However, although this is a customary generalization, it is not always valid. First, the parent company may feel obligated to make good on the subsidiary's debts, even though it may not be legally bound to do so, to keep its good name and thus retain customers. Examples of this would include American Express's payment of more than $100 million in connection with a swindle that was the responsibility of one of its subsidiaries, and United California Bank's coverage of a multimillion-dollar fraud loss incurred by its Swiss affiliate. Second, a parent company may feel obligated to supply capital to an affiliate to protect its initial investment; General Public Utilities' continued support of its subsidiaries' Three Mile Island nuclear plant is an example. Third, when lending to one of the units of a holding company system, an astute loan officer may require a guarantee by the parent holding company. Finally, an accident such as the one at Union Carbide's Bhopal, India, plant may be deemed the responsibility of the parent company, voiding the limited liability rules that would otherwise apply. Still, holding companies can at times be used to prevent losses in one unit from bringing down other units in the system.

3. **Legal separation.**   Certain regulated companies such as utilities and financial institutions find it easier to operate as holding companies than as divisional corporations. For example, an electric utility such as The Southern Company, which operates in and is regulated by several states, found it most practical to set up a holding company (Southern) which in turn owns a set of subsidiaries (Georgia Power, Alabama Power, Mississippi Power, Gulf Power, and Savannah Electric). All of the Bell telephone companies are parts of holding company systems, and even utilities which operate only within a single state often find it beneficial to operate within a holding company format in order to separate those assets under the control of regulators from those not subject to utility commission regulation. Thus, Florida Power & Light reorganized as a holding company called FPL Group, which owns a utility (Florida Power & Light) plus subsidiaries engaged in insurance, real estate development, orange groves, and the like.

    Banks, insurance companies, and other financial service corporations have also found it convenient to be organized as holding companies. Thus, Citicorp is a holding company which owns Citibank of New York, a leasing company, a mortgage service company, and so on. Transamerica is a holding company which owns insurance companies, small loan companies, title companies, auto rental companies, and an airline.

Disadvantages of Holding Companies

Holding companies have three disadvantages: (1) partial multiple taxation, (2) ease of enforced dissolution, and (3) a "management by financial statements" approach.

1. **Partial multiple taxation.**   Provided the holding company owns at least 80 percent of a subsidiary's voting stock, the Tax Code permits the filing

of consolidated returns, in which case dividends received by the parent are not taxed. However, if less than 80 percent of the stock is owned, returns cannot be consolidated, and taxes must be paid on 30 percent of the dividends received by the holding company. With a tax rate of 34 percent, this means that the effective tax rate on intercorporate dividends is $0.30 \times 34\% = 10.2\%$. This partial double taxation somewhat offsets the benefits of holding company control with limited ownership, but whether or not the penalty of 10.2 percent of dividends received is sufficient to offset other possible advantages is a matter that must be decided in individual situations.

2. **Ease of enforced dissolution.**   It is relatively easy for the Justice Department to require dissolution by disposal of stock ownership of a holding company operation that it finds unacceptable. Thus, Du Pont was required to dispose of its 23 percent stock interest in General Motors Corporation, an interest that had been acquired back in the early 1920s. Because there had been no fusion between the two corporations, there were no difficulties, from an operating standpoint, in requiring their separation. If complete amalgamation had taken place, however, it would have been much more difficult to break up the company after so many years, and the likelihood of forced divestiture would have been reduced. Still, the forced breakup of AT&T shows that even fully integrated companies can be broken up.

3. **"Management by financial statements" approach.**   High-level management decisions concerning the operating units are often made based on financial information with no insight or strategies regarding the firm's products, industry, or competition. These shortsighted decisions often prove disastrous to the firm over time.

Holding Companies as a Leveraging Device

The holding company vehicle has been used to obtain huge amounts of financial leverage. In the 1920s, several tiers of holding companies were established in the electric utility and other industries. In those days, an operating company at the bottom of the pyramid might have had $100 million of assets, financed by $50 million of debt and $50 million of equity. A first-tier holding company might have owned the stock of the operating firm as its only asset and then been financed with $25 million of debt and $25 million of equity. A second-tier holding company, which owned the $25 million of stock of the first-tier company as its only asset, might have been financed with $12.5 million of debt and $12.5 million of equity. Such systems were extended to four or more levels, but even with only two holding companies, we see that $100 million of operating assets could be controlled at the top by only $12.5 million of second-tier equity, and the $100 million of operating assets would have had to provide enough cash flow to support $87.5 million of debt. Such a holding company system is highly leveraged, even though the individual components each report 50 percent debt/assets ratios. Because of this *consolidated leverage,* even a small decline in profits at the operating company level could bring the whole system down like a house of cards.

? *Self-Test*

Differentiate between holding companies and operating companies.

What are the major advantages and disadvantages of holding companies?

Explain how holding companies can be used to obtain huge amounts of financial leverage.

Leveraged Buyouts (LBOs)

Leveraged buyouts, or LBOs, differ from ordinary acquisitions in several ways: (1) the way in which they are financed, (2) motivation for the transaction, and (3) future plans for the firm. The buyer in an LBO situation is often a group of investors, which may or may not include members of the existing management of the firm. Leveraged buyouts generally take place for purely financial reasons, with the equity group expecting to "cash out" and reap their profits by either selling the firm or taking it public within five years.

What makes an acquisition a leveraged buyout is the fact that it is purchased almost entirely with debt, a large portion of which was borrowed using the firm's assets as collateral. It is not uncommon for an LBO purchase to be financed with 80 percent or more debt. The debt is then repaid with the cash flow generated from the firm's operations. Once the debt level is paid down and reduced to a manageable level, the firm is sold or taken public with an enormous return on investment to the buying group.

The 1980s witnessed a huge increase in the number and size of LBOs. This development occurred for the same reasons that mergers and divestitures occurred — the existence of potential bargains, situations in which companies were using insufficient financial leverage, and the development of the junk bond market, which facilitated the use of leverage in takeovers.

LBOs can be initiated in one of two ways: (1) The firm's own managers can set up a new company whose equity comes from the managers themselves, plus some equity from pension funds and other institutions. This new company then arranges to borrow a large amount of money from banks, large asset-based lenders, and institutional investors (such as insurance companies). With the financing arranged, the management group then makes an offer to purchase all the publicly owned shares through a tender offer. (2) A specialized LBO firm, with Kohlberg, Kravis, & Roberts (KKR) being the largest and best known, will identify a potential target company, structure an LBO transaction, and make an offer to the firm's board of directors. KKR and other LBO firms have billions of dollars of equity, most put up by pension funds and other large investors, available for the equity portion of the deals, and they arrange debt financing just as would a management-led group. Again, the newly formed company will generally have at least 80 percent debt, and sometimes the debt ratio is as high as 98 percent. Thus, the term "leveraged" is most appropriate.

A major risk facing LBO transactions, and the main reason that LBO transactions run into severe posttransaction financial difficulties, is that the massive debt load is incurred assuming that the firm will maintain or increase their pretransaction level of cash flow to service the debt. Consequently, recessionary periods or changes in the competitive environment which adversely affect the firm's operations will render the firm unable to meet the interest payments on its debt. Moreover, many LBO structuring plans also assume the sale of various divisions in order to meet debt payment obligations. If the sale price for these divisions is less than anticipated, the firm once again cannot meet its debt obligations. A perhaps more insidious, but nonetheless dangerous, side effect of the high debt obligation is the fact that LBO firms are often forced to cut advertising, marketing, and R&D spending in order to pay the debtholders. These functions are critical to the long-term viability of the firm, and the firm begins to falter and lose its competitive position without adequate funding in these areas.

To illustrate an LBO, consider the $25 billion leveraged buyout of RJR Nabisco by KKR. RJR, a leading producer of tobacco and food products with brands such as Winston, Camel, Planters, Ritz, and Oreo, was trading at about $55 a share. Then F. Ross Johnson, the company's president and CEO, announced a $75 per share, or $17.6 billion, offer to take the firm private. The day after the announcement, RJR's stock soared to $77.25, which indicated that investors thought that the final price would be even higher than Johnson's opening bid. A few days later, KKR offered $90 per share, or $20.6 billion, for the firm. The battle between the two bidders continued until late November 1988, when RJR's board accepted a revised KKR bid of cash and securities worth about $106 per share, for a total value of about $25.1 billion.

 Self-Test

What characteristics make an acquisition a leveraged buyout?

Identify and briefly explain the two ways in which an LBO may be initiated.

SMALL BUSINESS

MERGING AS A MEANS OF EXITING A CLOSELY HELD BUSINESS

Imagine a small family-run business that has achieved some success. The entire family fortune may be tied up in the firm, as might be the case if a successful entrepreneur — say, Grandpa — started a business, brought his sons and daughters in as they reached adulthood, and continued to run the enterprise as it grew.

In such a situation, particularly if the firm is valued in the millions, the family's entire financial well-being may depend on the success of this business. As long as Grandpa is healthy and continues to run things, everything is fine. Grandpa may, in fact, be reluctant to sell the business; it gives him something to pass on to his family, and it provides a place for his children and grandchildren to work.

Closely held family businesses are fairly common in the United States. Yet, for several reasons, maintaining the business in its closely held form may not be in the family's best interests. First, there is the problem of succession. Because at some point Grandpa will retire or die, the issue of who will succeed him is important. Sometimes there is a clear choice for the successor, and everyone agrees with the choice. More often, however, even in families that are very close, the problem of succession can be an issue that splits the family apart. This problem is especially acute if Grandpa dies unexpectedly. At a highly emotional time, a key business decision needs to be made, and the choice is not a simple one. It is, therefore, essential that Grandpa and the other principals set up a plan of succession. If the issue is not resolvable, plans should be made for the outright sale of the business in the event of Grandpa's death.

A second problem is that the business represents the family's primary asset, but family members have no easy way to realize that value when they need cash: the business has no liquidity. Sometimes a plan will be made for someone to buy a family member's stock at a predetermined rate, such as at its book value per share. This enables the family member to obtain cash, but the price paid probably bears little relation to the market value of the shares. Thus, a family member gives up a valuable asset for the sake of liquidity, taking a potential loss in the process. An alternative, as discussed in Chapter 17, is to register the shares and take the company public so that family members can use their equity as they choose. A disadvantage to this approach is the potential loss of control as the number of shares held by the public increases.

A third problem is that as the firm grows, the family may be unable to provide the financial resources necessary to support that growth. If external funding is needed, it will generally be more difficult to obtain in a private, closely held business.

A perhaps even more serious problem is that, since the family's entire wealth is tied up in a single business, the family holds an *undiversified portfolio*. As was explained in earlier chapters, diversification through investment in a variety of securities reduces a portfolio's risk. Thus, the goals of maintaining control and reducing risk through diversification are in conflict. Again, a public offering would allow family members to sell some of their stock and to diversify their own personal portfolios.

Both the diversification motive and family members' liquidity needs indicate that the business's ownership structure should be changed. There is,

however, another alternative besides going public — that of selling the business outright to another company or of merging it into a larger firm. This alternative is often overlooked by owners of closely held businesses, because it frequently means an immediate and complete loss of control. It deserves special consideration, however, because it can often be accomplished with far greater realization of value than can be achieved in a public offering.

With the sale of the business, the family gives up control, yet that control is what makes the firm more valuable in a merger than in a public offering. Merger premiums for public companies often range from 50 to 70 percent over the market price. Therefore, a company worth $10 million in the public market might be acquired for a price of $15 to $17 million in a merger. A merger provides several advantages to both the selling firm and to the acquiring firm. The selling firm liquidates its investment, thereby affording it other investment opportunities and, therefore, diversification. The acquiring firm, as the new owner, is provided a new avenue of business — perhaps a new product or service line — or even a new geographic location without incurring the costs of a start-up. Many times the acquiring firm inherits rich customer and/or supplier relationships as well as an established distribution network.

What are the disadvantages to a merger? An obvious disadvantage is the loss of control. Also, family members risk losing employment in the firm. In such a case, however, they will have additional wealth to sustain them while they seek other opportunities.

Owners of the closely held family business must consider the cost/benefit tradeoffs of continuing to be closely held versus going public or being acquired in a merger. Of the three alternatives, the acquisition alternative is likely to provide the most immediate wealth and security to the family members.

Summary

This chapter discussed mergers, divestitures, holding companies, and LBOs. The key concepts covered are listed below.

▷ A **merger** occurs when two firms combine to form a single company. The primary motives for mergers are (1) synergy, (2) tax considerations, (3) purchase of assets below their replacement costs, (4) diversification, and (5) gaining control over a larger enterprise.

Mergers can provide economic benefits through **economies of scale** or through the **concentration of assets** in the hands of more efficient managers — these mergers reduce operating costs. However, mergers also have the potential for reducing competition, and for this reason they are carefully regulated by governmental agencies.

In most mergers, one company **(the acquiring firm)** initiates action to take over another **(the target firm).**

▶   The nature of the companies involved and the method by which the **merger** is completed classifies the merger.

A **horizontal merger** occurs when two firms in the same line of business combine.

A **vertical merger** is the combination of a firm with one of its customers or suppliers.

A **congeneric merger** involves firms in related industries, but for which no customer-supplier relationship exists.

A **conglomerate merger** occurs when firms in totally different industries combine.

In a **friendly merger,** the managements of both firms approve the merger, while in a **hostile merger (a takeover)** the target firm's management opposes the merger.

An **operating merger** is one in which the operations of the two firms are combined. A **financial merger** is one in which the firms continue to operate separately, and hence no operating economies are expected.

▶   In a **merger analysis,** (1) the price to be paid for the target firm and (2) the employment/control situation are the key issues to be resolved.

To determine the **value of the target firm,** the acquiring firm must (1) forecast the cash flows that will result after the merger and (2) develop a discount rate to apply to the projected cash flows.

The most widely used method for merger valuation is the **free cash flow (FCF) method** which uses yearly free cash flow estimates over a five-year period as the relevant cash flows.

▶   **Investment bankers** assist the acquiring or target firm in merger transactions by structuring and negotiating the merger, determining the value of the target firm, and developing tactics for the successful execution of or defense against the merger.

Poison pills are actions a firm can take that will make it less valuable if it is acquired in a hostile takeover. **Golden parachutes** are a form of poison pill in which large payments are to be made to a firm's managers if it is acquired.

▶   A **joint venture** is a **corporate alliance** in which two companies combine some of their resources to achieve a specific, limited objective.

A **divestiture** is the sale of some of a company's operating assets. A divestiture may involve (1) selling an operating unit to another firm, (2) selling a unit to that unit's managers, (3) **spinning off** a unit as a separate company, or (4) the outright **liquidation** of a unit's assets.

The **reasons for divestitures** include antitrust actions, the clarification of what a company actually does, and the raising of capital needed to strengthen the corporation's core business.

A **leveraged buyout** is a transaction where a firm is purchased almost entirely with debt, a large portion of which is secured by the firm's assets, and the debt is then repaid using cash flows from the firm's operations.

▶ A **holding company** is a corporation whose primary function is to hold the stock of other corporations, but that has no operating units of its own. The holding company is also known as the **parent company,** and the companies which it controls are called subsidiaries, or **operating companies.**

Advantages to holding company operations include the following: (1) control can often be obtained for a smaller cash outlay, (2) risks may be segregated, and (3) regulated companies can separate regulated from unregulated assets.

Disadvantages to holding company operations include (1) partial multiple taxation; (2) the ease of enforced dissolution; and (3) a narrow "financial statement only" management perspective.

Resolution to
DECISION IN FINANCE

AN ORBITING DEAL

Why would GE's chairman suggest such a deal? GE prefers businesses in which it can be one of the market leaders, especially in global markets. Although GE Aerospace was a world leader in technology, it was not in a position to dominate the defense electronics market, especially on a global scale. For GE, the aerospace division was never more than a peripheral business. Furthermore, cutbacks in defense spending, especially in the United States, meant that business would be sagging and that an industry consolidation was inevitable. Put simply, it was a graceful way out of a slumping business that generated less than 10 percent of GE's annual revenues. Furthermore, selling the subsidiary would provide immediate cash to GE, which would leave it in a good position to acquire nondefense assets that troubled companies are eager to dump.

For Martin Marietta, the acquisition cemented its position as one of the top players in the industry. With the deal, Martin nearly doubled in size, with annual revenues of $11 billion. Until this point in time, Martin had principally supplied weapons subsystems, but as a result of the merger, Martin has been propelled into the top tier of military contractors. Also, electronics, which will be Martin's primary focus, appears to be the safest place for defense contractors—as the armed services shrink and buy fewer ships, tanks, and planes, it will be increasingly important for them to have "smart" weapons systems along with the latest surveillance, command-and-control, and computer systems.

GE Aerospace was a perfect complement for Martin Marietta. GE Aerospace was a major supplier to the Navy, while Martin dealt mainly with the Army. GE Aerospace built satellites, while Martin made rockets. Now the combined company can make the entire system. Similarly, GE supplies the radar that guides Martin Marietta's missiles for the Aegis fleet air-defense system. "There's very little overlap between the two companies," said a defense analyst. "It's almost like two pieces of a jigsaw puzzle."

Source: "This Deal Could Send Martin Marietta into Orbit," *Business Week,* December 7, 1992.

This merger clearly illustrates that classifying mergers is not always crystal clear. The merger could be placed into any one of the following categories: (1) a congeneric merger, for it involved a merger of firms in the same general industry; (2) a horizontal merger, for it represented the combination of two firms that produce the same general type of good or service; or (3) a vertical merger, which combines firms where one sells materials to the other.

Often mergers fail because the two corporate cultures cannot be blended into one well-functioning team. Analysts expect no problem in this regard, as both companies are run by engineers and both have strong reputations for financial discipline.

Martin agreed to pay approximately $3 billion for GE Aerospace, including $1.25 billion in cash, $1 billion in convertible preferred stock (which would give GE up to 23.5 percent ownership of Martin), and $750 million of GE Aerospace debt assumptions. The market loved the deal, and both companies' stocks jumped when the sale was announced.

Martin now faces some big challenges. Its debt ratio was increased from 27 to 46 percent by the deal, and successfully merging large enterprises is always a difficult task, even when the cultures are similar. Still, even with defense budgets shrinking, the Pentagon will spend $100 billion a year on research and procurement. "Weaker companies will shrink and sink," concedes Martin Marietta Chairman Augustine, but, he adds, "There is room for strong survivors." He is betting $3 billion that Martin Marietta will be one of the survivors.

Questions

22-1 Four economic classifications of mergers are *horizontal, vertical, conglomerate,* and *congeneric.* Explain the significance of these terms in merger analysis with regard to (**a**) the likelihood of governmental intervention and (**b**) possibilities for operating synergy.

22-2 Firm A wants to acquire Firm B. Firm B's management agrees that the merger is a good idea. Might a tender offer be used?

22-3 Distinguish between operating mergers and financial mergers.

Self-Test Problem

ST-1 Perrin-Stewart, a large conglomerate that has grown in the past through mergers, is analyzing its latest takeover target, Cleburne Pharmaceuticals (CP). Perrin-Stewart's financial analysts have made a projection of CP's cash flows for the next 5 years. Their 5-year projection of CP's postmerger year-end cash flows (in millions) is reproduced in the following table:

	1995	1996	1997	1998	1999
Sales	$147	$176	$211	$244	$267
Cost of goods sold	112	132	155	178	192
Sales and administrative expenses	14	17	18	21	22
Depreciation	8	8	9	9	10
EBIT	$ 13	$ 19	$ 29	$ 36	$ 43
Interest	4	5	5	6	6
EBT	$ 9	$ 14	$ 24	$ 30	$ 37
Taxes (34%)	3	5	8	10	13
Net income	$ 6	$ 9	$ 16	$ 20	$ 24
Retained earnings	2	4	7	10	14
Terminal growth rate (5%)					

Cleburne currently has a capital structure of 17 percent debt, but if Perrin-Stewart's merger plans are successful, CP's debt ratio will rise to 50 percent of assets. CP's mar-

ginal tax rate will remain at 34 percent after the merger. The average cost of equity for firms similar to the target firm is 17.4 percent, and the average after-tax cost of debt is 16.9 percent.
a. What is the appropriate discount rate for valuing the proposed acquisition?
b. What is Cleburne's value to Perrin-Stewart?
c. CP has 9 million shares outstanding, and its common stock currently sells for $18.55. What is the maximum price per share that Perrin-Stewart should offer for Cleburne's stock?

Problems

22-1
Capital budgeting analysis

Gentry Gifts & Stationery Shoppe wishes to acquire Celec's Card Gallery for $400,000. Gentry expects the merger to provide incremental earnings of about $64,000 a year for 10 years. Jim Gentry has calculated the marginal cost of capital for this investment to be 10 percent. Conduct a capital budgeting analysis for Gentry to determine whether he should purchase Celec's Card Gallery.

22-2
Merger analysis

TransWorld Products Inc., a large conglomerate, is evaluating the possible acquisition of Georgia Siding Company (GSC), a small aluminium-siding manufacturer. TransWorld's analysts project the following postmerger data for GSC (in thousands):

	1995	1996	1997	1998	1999
Net sales	$450	$518	$555	$600	$638
Selling and administrative expenses	45	53	60	68	74
Depreciation	8	8	9	9	10
Interest	18	21	24	27	30

Tax rate after merger (35%)
Cost of goods sold as a percentage of sales (65%)
Terminal growth rate of cash flow available to TransWorld (7%)

If the acquisition is made, it will occur on January 1, 1995. All cash flows shown in the income statements are assumed to occur at the end of the year. GSC currently has a capital structure of 40 percent debt, but TransWorld would increase that to 50 percent if the acquisition were made. GSC, if independent, would pay taxes at 20 percent, but this percentage would rise to 35 percent if it were consolidated. The average cost of equity for companies like GSC is 18.5 percent, and the average after-tax cost of debt is 14 percent. TransWorld typically retains one quarter of its earnings for future investments.
a. What is the appropriate discount rate for valuing the acquisition?
b. What is the terminal value? What is the value of GSC to TransWorld?

22-3
Merger analysis

Mehran Electric Corporation is considering a merger with the Rodriguez Lamp Company. Due to rough economic times, Rodriguez has been barely profitable and has only paid 20 percent in taxes over the last several years. Additionally, Rodriguez has used little debt, only 25 percent.

If the acquisition were made, Mehran plans to operate Rodriguez as a separate, wholly owned subsidiary. Mehran would pay taxes on a consolidated basis; thus, the federal-plus-state tax rate would increase to 40 percent. Mehran would also increase the debt ratio of the Rodriguez subsidiary to 40 percent of assets. Mehran's analysts project the following postmerger data for Rodriguez (in thousands):

	1995	1996	1997	1998	1999
Net sales	$300	$345	$375	$405	$460
Selling and administrative expenses	30	40	45	50	60
Interest	15	18	20	21	21
Depreciation	8	8	9	9	10

Cost of goods sold as a percentage of sales (65%)
Terminal growth rate (8%)
Retained earnings (25% of earnings)

This information includes all acquisition effects. Mehran's cost of equity is 16 percent and its after-tax cost of debt is 12 percent.

a. What discount rate should be used to value the acquisition?

b. What is the dollar value of Rodriguez to Mehran?

c. Rodriguez has 1.2 million common shares outstanding, at $6.53 per share. What is the maximum price per share that Mehran should offer for Rodriguez?

22-4

Merger analysis

O'Brien Enterprises, a large conglomerate, is evaluating the possible acquisition of McCue Manufacturing Corporation (MMC). O'Brien's analysts project the following postmerger data for MMC (in thousands):

	1995	1996	1997	1998	1999
Net sales	$250.00	$287.50	$312.50	$337.50	$362.50
Selling and administrative expenses	25.00	31.25	37.50	40.00	43.75
Depreciation	8	8	9	9	10
Interest	12.50	15.00	16.25	17.50	19.00

Tax rate after merger (39%)
Cost of goods sold as a percentage of sales (70%)
Terminal growth rate of cash flow available to O'Brien (8%)
Retained earnings (20%)

If the acquisition is made, it will occur on January 1, 1995. All cash flows shown in the income statements are assumed to occur at the end of the year. MMC currently has a market value capital structure of 40 percent debt, but O'Brien would increase that to 50 percent if the acquisition were made. O'Brien's after-tax cost of debt is 14 percent, and its cost of equity is 18.4 percent. This information takes into account all acquisition effects.

a. What is the appropriate discount rate for valuing the acquisition?

b. What is the terminal value? What is MMC's value to O'Brien?

Solution to Self-Test Problem

ST-1   **a.** The appropriate discount rate, WACC, is determined as follows:

$$WACC = w_d k_d (1 - T) + w_s k_s$$

$$= 0.5\,(16.9\%) \ + \ 0.5(17.4\%)$$

$$= 8.45\% \qquad + \ 8.7\%$$

$$= 17.15\%$$

b. Cleburne Pharmaceutical's value to Perrin-Stewart is determined by first finding the free cash flows (in millions):

	1995	1996	1997	1998	1999
Net income	$ 6.00	$ 9.00	$16.00	$20.00	$24.00
+Depreciation	8.00	8.00	9.00	9.00	10.00
+After-tax-interest	2.64	3.30	3.30	3.96	3.96
−Investment (RE)	2.00	4.00	7.00	10.00	14.00
=Free cash flow	$14.64	$16.30	$21.30	$22.96	$23.96

Then, we find the terminal value as follows:

$$Terminal\ value = \frac{[Free\ cash\ flow\ Year\ 5\ (1\ +\ g)]}{WACC\ -\ g}$$

$$= \frac{\$23.96\,(1\ +\ 0.05)}{0.1715 - 0.05}$$

$$= \frac{\$23.96\,(1.05)}{0.1215} = \$207.06$$

The value is the present value of the expected free cash flows and of the terminal value, discounted at 17.15%:

$$\frac{\$14.64}{(1.1715)^1} + \frac{\$16.3}{(1.1715)^2} + \frac{\$21.3}{(1.1715)^3} + \frac{\$22.96}{(1.1715)^4} + \frac{\$23.96 + \$207.06}{(1.1715)^5}$$

$$= \$12.496 + \$13.914 + \$18.182 + \$19.599 + \$197.20$$

$$= \$261.40 \text{ million}$$

c. The maximum price that Perrin-Stewart should offer for Cleburne's stock on a per-share basis is:

$$\$261.40 \text{ million}/9 \text{ million shares} = \$29.00$$

Therefore, Perrin-Stewart should make its initial offer above the current market price of \$18.55 but below its maximum offering price of \$29.00.

International Financial Management

OBJECTIVES

After reading this chapter you should be able to:

▷ Understand the special issues involved in international financial management.

▷ Calculate exchange rates between any two or three countries.

▷ Discuss purchasing power parity as a means for determining exchange rates.

▷ Identify the various risks related to international investing.

▷ Explain several different cash flow management techniques that a multinational firm can utilize.

▷ Define the three types of foreign currency exposure and detail the options for managing each one.

DECISION IN FINANCE

EXCHANGE RATES AND
SMALL-TOWN AMERICA

People in and out of business in the United States often feel that international issues such as exchange rates do not directly affect them. The people of small-town America—Troy, Ohio, population 19,000, for example—are finding out differently. The rise of the Japanese yen in 1993 is a prime example of how international finance affects every dimension of their lives.

As the value of the Japanese yen rose over 15 percent against the U.S. dollar in 1993, the prices of products produced in Japan and sold in America also rose. Importers of Japanese products must buy Japanese currency first, then purchase the goods. As the yen rises, so does the price of Japanese goods to outsiders like U.S. consumers.

At the Harris jewelry store in Troy, the price of an 18-inch strand of cultured pearls rose from a sizeable $899 a few years ago to an unaffordable $3,000 at the end of the year. Japanese cameras and camera lenses were no exception. Nikon cameras that were sold at B-K Photo in Troy posted price increases twice in the first ten months of 1993. Sharp copiers sold at Trojan Business Machines not only went up in price but experienced three price increases in one week.

Jim Witmer, a professional photographer in Troy, now buys used cameras lenses rather than

pay the $1,000 for a new Nikon 300-millimeter lens, which has gone up $250 since the start of the year. For others, the purchase price of a Japanese automobile is also higher. Most models actually produced in Japan now cost more than $2,000 over their sticker prices of the previous model year. These are costs and

burdens which most of the residents of Troy never suspected would affect their lives, here in the heart of the American Midwest. In fact, many of the residents of Troy are not sure what a yen is.

But the members of the business community know all too well the value of a yen. Hobart Brothers Company of Troy employs over 2,000 workers in the manufacturing of arc-welding equipment. Hobart has been a member of a joint-venture agreement with Yaskawa Electric America Inc. of Japan (known locally as Motoman Inc.) in the adaptation of Japanese-produced robotics equipment for U.S. companies. Because Hobart buys the robots from Japan,

See end of chapter for resolution.

Photo source: Michele Burgess/The Stock Market

This chapter was co-authored by Dr. Michael H. Moffett of Oregon State University.

the price of their inputs have risen with the yen. If Hobart has to pay more for the basic robots, it must pass along the higher costs to its customers. Hobart's customers are not always accommodating, however; many are switching to other companies which have production and costs based more in America or Europe, rather than Japan. If Hobart continues to lose customers, some of the workers at its factory in downtown Troy will have to be laid off.

Theoretically, the rise in the yen versus the dollar would not only slow the import of Japanese products but also increase the export of U.S. goods to Japan. The problem is that this process takes some time. PMI Food Equipment of Troy exports over $8 million of commercial dishwashers and food mixers to buyers in Japan. If PMI's products were priced in yen with no other added costs, its prices would actually drop in Japanese markets. However, PMI — like many American manufacturers — uses a Japanese company for its distribution and sales in Japan, and the Japanese firm has not passed along the lower prices to consumers, choosing instead to enjoy a wider profit margin on existing sales. PMI is frustrated.

A second way in which U.S. exports are slowed is the toll the high yen takes on the Japanese economy itself. Falling export sales of Japanese firms has dampened the Japanese economy, reducing the spending of Japanese consumers and manufacturers. Firms such as B.F. Goodrich in Troy are dependent on the health of many related Japanese companies for their sales. For example, if the business of major Japanese airlines continues to decline, then B.F. Goodrich will also feel the pinch.

As you read this chapter, consider the problems of a rising foreign currency and the impact on the financial management activities of an American firm. Consider also the alternatives available to businesses located in the United States or other countries when trading and working with Japanese firms in a world of a rapidly rising Japanese yen.

International financial management is not a separate set of issues from domestic or traditional financial management, but it does involve a number of risks and complexities not confronted domestically. These complexities (different laws, different methods, different markets, different interest rates, and, most of all, different currencies) require specific knowledge of how these foreign financial markets work and how the modern firm must adapt its financial management practices. There is also an important distinction between a firm which only imports and exports, an **international firm,** and a firm which not only conducts direct import/export business but also possesses foreign affiliate and subsidiary operations, a **multinational firm.**

International financial management means that all the standard financial activities and decisions within a firm (capital budgeting, capital structure, raising long-term capital, working capital and cash flow management, and so forth) will be complicated by the differences in markets, languages, cultures, governments, laws, and especially currencies of conducting business internationally. This management requires many activities different from the domestic financial management practices described up to now. All firms, no matter how domestic they may seem in structure, are influenced by exchange rate changes. The financial management of a firm which has any dimension of international activity must pay special attention to these issues if the firm is to succeed in its international endeavors.

international firm

A firm which conducts international business through imports and exports.

multinational firm

A firm which not only actively imports and exports but also possesses affiliate operations in other countries.

Exchange Rate Fundamentals

The price of one country's currency in terms of another country's currency is called a foreign currency **exchange rate.** For example, the exchange rate between the U.S. dollar (US$) and the German mark (Deutschemark, or DM) may be 1.5 marks per dollar, or simply abbreviated DM 1.5000/US$. This is the same exchange rate as when it is stated US$ 1.00 = DM 1.50. Since most international business activities require at least one of the two parties to first purchase the country's currency before purchasing any good, service, or asset, a proper understanding of exchange rates and exchange rate markets is very important to the conduct of international business.

Exchange Rate Quotations and Terminology

The order in which the foreign exchange (FX) rate is stated is sometimes confusing to the uninitiated. For example, when the rate between the U.S. dollar and the German mark was stated earlier, a direct quotation on the German mark was used. This is simultaneously an indirect quotation on the U.S. dollar. The *direct quote* on any currency is the form when that currency is stated *first;* an *indirect quotation* refers to when the subject currency is stated *second.* Figure 23-1 illustrates both forms, direct and indirect quotations, for major world currencies on Monday, March 1, 1993.

The majority of the quotations listed in Figure 23-1 are **spot rates.** A spot transaction is the exchange of currencies for immediate delivery. Although it is defined as immediate, in practice, settlement actually occurs two business days following the agreed-upon exchange. The other time-related quotations listed in Figure 23-1 are the **forward rates.** Forward exchange rates are contracts which provide for two parties to exchange currencies on a future date at an agreed-upon exchange rate. Forwards are typically traded for the major-volume currencies for maturities of 30, 90, 120, 180, and 360 days (from the present date). The forward rate, like the basic spot exchange rate, can be for any amount of currency the two parties wish. Forward contracts serve a variety of purposes, but their primary purpose is to allow a firm to lock in a future rate of exchange. This is a valuable tool in a world in which exchange rates are continually changing.

The quotations listed may also differentiate between rates applicable to business trade (commercial rates) or for financial asset purchases or sales (financial rates). Those countries which have government regulations regarding the exchange of their currency may post official rates, while the markets operating outside those countries' jurisdiction will list a floating rate. In this case, any exchange of currency which is not under the control of that government is interpreted to be a better indication of the currency's true market value.

Direct and Indirect Quotations

The Wall Street Journal quotations list the rates of exchange between major national currencies, both in direct and indirect forms. The exchange rate for the German mark versus the U.S. dollar, in the third column of Figure 23-1, is DM 1.6555/US$. This is a **direct quote** on the German mark or an **indirect quote** on the U.S. dollar. The inverse of this spot rate is listed in the first column, the indirect quote on the German mark or direct quote on the U.S. dollar, US$

Figure 23-1

Exchange Rate Quotations

Monday, March 1, 1993

The New York foreign exchange selling rates below apply to trading among banks in amounts of $1 million and more, as quoted at 3 p.m. Eastern time by Bankers Trust Co., Telerate and other sources. Retail transactions provide fewer units of foreign currency per dollar.

The foreign exchange rates for Friday, Feb. 26, 1993 are unavailable from Bankers Trust Co. because of the explosion at the World Trade Center. The comparison rates provided are for Thursday, Feb. 25.

Country	U.S. $ equiv. Mon.	U.S. $ equiv. Thurs.	Currency per U.S. $ Mon.	Currency per U.S. $ Thurs.
Argentina (Peso)	1.01	1.01	.99	.99
Australia (Dollar)	.7045	.6957	1.4194	1.4374
Austria (Schilling)	.08584	.08684	11.65	11.52
Bahrain (Dinar)	2.6522	2.6522	.3771	.3771
Belgium (Franc)	.02935	.02966	34.08	33.71
Brazil (Cruzeiro)	.0000519	.0000539	19259.00	18543.24
Britain (Pound)	1.4380	1.4305	.6954	.6991
30-Day Forward	1.4341	1.4266	.6973	.7010
90-Day Forward	1.4279	1.4199	.7003	.7043
180-Day Forward	1.4207	1.4121	.7039	.7082
Canada (Dollar)	.8009	.7980	1.2486	1.2532
30-Day Forward	.7992	.7960	1.2512	1.2563
90-Day Forward	.7958	.7924	1.2566	1.2620
180-Day Forward	.7903	.7865	1.2653	1.2715
Czechoslovakia (Koruna)				
Commercial rate	.0353232	.0352485	28.3100	28.3700
Chile (Peso)	.002638	.002645	379.11	378.11
China (Renminbi)	.171233	.171233	5.8400	5.8400
Colombia (Peso)	.001558	.001564	641.75	639.20
Denmark (Krone)	.1576	.1593	6.3464	6.2765
Ecuador (Sucre)				
Floating rate	.000556	.000556	1798.01	1799.01
Finland (Markka)	.16645	.16816	6.0078	5.9469
France (Franc)	.17811	.17994	5.6145	5.5575
30-Day Forward	.17673	.17853	5.6583	5.6013
90-Day Forward	.17435	.17595	5.7355	5.6835
180-Day Forward	.17172	.17310	5.8235	5.7770
Germany (Mark)	.6040	.6112	1.6555	1.6360
30-Day Forward	.6011	.6083	1.6636	1.6438
90-Day Forward	.5966	.6034	1.6761	1.6572
180-Day Forward	.5908	.5973	1.6925	1.6741
Greece (Drachma)	.004464	.004511	224.00	221.70
Hong Kong (Dollar)	.12931	.12930	7.7333	7.7337
Hungary (Forint)	.0117481	.0118245	85.1200	84.5700
India (Rupee)	.03048	.03338	32.81	29.96
Indonesia (Rupiah)	.0004852	.0004859	2061.01	2058.04
Ireland (Punt)	1.4686	1.4841	.6809	.6738
Israel (Shekel)	.3662	.3671	2.7309	2.7240
Italy (Lira)	.0006358	.0006282	1572.75	1591.85
Japan (Yen)	.008421	.008524	118.75	117.32
30-Day Forward	.008421	.008524	118.75	117.32
90-Day Forward	.008420	.008522	118.76	117.34
180-Day Forward	.008424	.008527	118.71	117.28
Jordan (Dinar)	1.4767	1.4832	.6772	.6742
Kuwait (Dinar)	3.2497	3.2573	.3077	.3070
Lebanon (Pound)	.000574	.000573	1742.00	1745.00
Malaysia (Ringgit)	.3798	.3801	2.6330	2.6310
Malta (Lira)	2.6281	2.6295	.3805	.3803
Mexico (Peso)				
Floating rate	.3237294	.3233107	3.09	3.09
Netherland (Guilder) ..	.5372	.5434	1.8616	1.8403
New Zealand (Dollar) .	.5270	.5230	1.8975	1.9120
Norway (Krone)	.1421	.1433	7.0359	6.9800
Pakistan (Rupee)	.0383	.0383	26.12	26.10
Peru (New Sol)	.5762	.5844	1.74	1.71
Philippines (Peso)	.04032	.04032	24.80	24.80
Poland (Zloty)	.00006349	.00006410	15750.00	15600.02
Portugal (Escudo)	.006589	.006637	151.78	150.68
Saudi Arabia (Riyal) ...	.26702	.26665	3.7450	3.7502
Singapore (Dollar)	.6078	.6086	1.6453	1.6430
South Africa (Rand)				
Commercial rate	.3171	.3191	3.1538	3.1343
Financial rate	.2202	.2208	4.5420	4.5300
South Korea (Won)	.0012580	.0012574	794.90	795.30
Spain (Peseta)	.008427	.008495	118.67	117.71
Sweden (Krona)	.1281	.1277	7.8082	7.8332
Switzerland (Franc) ...	.6502	.6590	1.5380	1.5175
30-Day Forward	.6488	.6576	1.5412	1.5207
90-Day Forward	.6466	.6551	1.5465	1.5266
180-Day Forward	.6443	.6524	1.5521	1.5327
Taiwan (Dollar)	.038745	.039063	25.81	25.60
Thailand (Baht)	.03928	.03936	25.46	25.41
Turkey (Lira)	.0001105	.0001108	9046.01	9027.01
United Arab (Dirham) .	.2723	.2723	3.6725	3.6725
Uruguay (New Peso)				
Financial	.000273	.000268	3657.00	3729.01
Venezuela (Bolivar)				
Floating rate	.01227	.01230	81.51	81.33
	---	---		
SDR	1.37405	1.38145	.72778	.72388
ECU	1.17380	1.18120	....	....

Special Drawing Rights (SDR) are based on exchange rates for the U.S., German, British, French and Japanese currencies. Source: International Monetary Fund.

European Currency Unit (ECU) is based on a basket of community currencies.

Forward Rates — [arrow to 90-Day Forward under Britain]

Floating Rate — [arrow to Floating rate under Ecuador]

DM 1.6555/US$ [pointing to Germany (Mark)]

Commerical and Financial Rates — [arrow to Commercial rate / Financial rate under South Africa]

Exchange rates quoted daily in periodicals like *The Wall Street Journal* include both spot exchange rates and forward exchange rates. Rate quotations are listed in both direct and indirect forms (for example, US$/DM and DM/US$).

Source: *The Wall Street Journal*, Tuesday, March 2, 1993

0.6040/DM. The two forms of the exchange rate are of course equal, one being the inverse of the other[1]:

$$\frac{1}{DM\ 1.6555/US\$} = US\$\ 0.6040/DM.$$

Luckily, the world foreign currency markets do follow some conventions so that confusion is minimized. With only a few exceptions, most currencies are quoted in direct form quotes versus the U.S. dollar (DM/US\$, ¥/US\$, FFr/US\$). The major exceptions are those currencies that at one time or another have been associated with the British Commonwealth, including the Australian dollar and of course the British pound sterling. These currencies are customarily quoted as US\$ per pound sterling or US\$ per Australian dollar. Once again, it makes no real difference whether one quotes US\$/¥, or ¥/US\$, as long as one knows which is being used for the transaction.

Cross-Exchange Rates

cross rate

Any exchange rate which does not include the U.S. dollar.

Although it is common among exchange traders worldwide to quote currency values against the U.S. dollar, it is not necessary. Any currency's value can be stated in terms of any other currency. When the exchange rate for a currency is stated without using the U.S. dollar as a reference it is referred to as a **cross rate.** For example, the German mark and Japanese yen are both quoted on Monday, March 1, 1993, versus the U.S. dollar: DM 1.6555/US\$, and ¥ 118.75/US\$. But if the ¥/DM cross rate is needed, it is simply a matter of division:

$$\frac{¥\ 118.75/US\$}{DM\ 1.6555/US\$} = ¥\ 71.731/DM.$$

triangular arbitrage

The process of trading three different currencies within a few moments in time in order to obtain a tiny margin of profit from rates which are not perfectly aligned.

The ¥/DM cross rate of 71.731 can be thought of as the third leg of a triangle. If the first two exchange rates are known, the third can be found also. If one of the exchange rates changes due to market forces, the others will have to adjust in order for the three cross rates to be once again aligned. If they are out of alignment, it would be possible to make a profit simply by exchanging one currency for a second, the second for a third, and the third back to the first. This is known as **triangular arbitrage.** Besides the potential profitability of arbitrage which may occasionally occur, cross rates have become increasingly common in a world of rapidly expanding trade and investment.

Percentage Change Calculations

The quotation form is important when calculating the percentage change in an exchange rate. For example, if the spot rate between the Japanese yen and the U.S. dollar changed from ¥ 125/US\$ to ¥ 150/US\$, the percentage change in the value of the Japanese yen is

$$\frac{¥\ 125/US\$ - ¥\ 150/US\$}{¥\ 150/US\$} \times 100 = -16.67\%.$$

---

[1]Rounding errors are solved quite simply with exchange rates. With a few notable exceptions, all active trading takes place using direct quotations on foreign currencies versus the U.S. dollar (for example, DM 1.5390/US\$, ¥ 123.21/US\$) and for a conventional number of decimal places. These are the base rates which are then used for the calculation of the inverse indirect quotes on the foreign currencies if needed.

The Japanese yen has declined in value versus the U.S. dollar by 16.67 percent. This is consistent with the intuition that it now requires more yen (150) to buy a dollar than it used to (125).

The same percentage change result can be achieved by using the inverted forms of the same spot rates (indirect quotes on the Japanese yen) if care is taken to also "invert" the basic percentage change calculation. Using the inverse of ¥ 125/US$ (US$ 0.0080/¥) and the inverse of ¥ 150/US$ (US$ 0.0067/¥), the percentage change is still −16.67 percent:

$$\frac{US\$ \ 0.0067/¥ \ - \ US\$ \ 0.0080/¥}{US\$ \ 0.0080/¥} \times 100 = -16.67\%.$$

If the percentage changes calculated are not identical, it is normally the result of rounding errors introduced when inverting the spot rates. Both methods are identical, however, when calculated properly.

Foreign Currency Market Structure

The market for foreign currencies is a worldwide market which is informal in structure. This means that it has no central place, pit, or floor like the floor of the New York Stock Exchange in which the trading takes place. The market for currencies is composed of the thousands of telecommunications links between financial institutions around the globe and is, therefore, open 24 hours a day. Someone, somewhere, is nearly always open for business.

The structure of the foreign currency market leads to some interesting problems. For example, since there is no one exchange, no one floor, no world central bank, is there a single exchange rate? The answer is no, there is no single agreed-upon rate of exchange between all financial institutions. Since all the banks and financial institutions which are trading the currencies are calling and communicating with dozens or hundreds of different banks all over the world. The speed with which this market moves, and the multitude of players playing on a field which is open 24 hours long and the circumference of the earth wide, results in many different "single prices." A good example of this lack of one price is to look back at Figure 23-1. The explanation of the exchange rate quotes states:

The New York foreign exchange selling rates below apply to trading among banks in amounts of $1 million and more, as quoted at 3 P.M. Eastern time by Bankers Trust Company, Telerate, and other sources. Retail transactions provide fewer units of foreign currency per dollar.

Those are pretty specific prices![2] The rates quoted are the foreign exchange rates as seen by only one or a few members of the world of participants and at a specific point in time (3 P.M. Eastern time). The rates are obviously "wholesale

---

[2]Note that the exchange rate quotations are particulary unusual on this date due to the closing of the World Trade Center on Friday, February 26, 1993, after a bomb blast in the basement of the east tower.

rates," applicable to large-scale trading, and will, therefore, be better than one might trade at in an airport when exchanging currencies on international trips.

One way to put this ever-changing market in perspective is to think of the foreign exchange market as a never-ending horse race. The winner is whoever is ahead at one point on the track, at one point in time, from the viewpoint of where in the stands the audience is sitting. The markets continue, as would the theoretical horses, forever. The rates quoted by Bankers Trust or Telerate are, therefore, only daily Polaroid snapshots of the race, the daily photo-finish from the individual bank's seat in the stands.

International Money Markets

A money market is traditionally defined as a market for deposits, accounts, or securities which have maturities of one year or less. The international money markets, often termed the *Eurocurrency markets,* constitute an enormous financial market which is in many ways outside the jurisdiction and supervision of world financial and governmental authorities.

Eurocurrency

A bank loan or deposit denominated in a foreign currency; for example, a U.S. dollar deposit in a London bank is a Eurodollar deposit.

A **Eurocurrency** is any foreign currency–denominated deposit or account at a financial institution outside the country of the currency's issuance. For example, U.S. dollars which are held on account in a bank in London are termed *Eurodollars.* Similarly, Japanese yen held on account in a Parisian financial institution would be classified as *Euroyen.* The *Euro* prefix does not mean these currencies or accounts are only European, as German marks on account in Singapore would also be classified as a Eurocurrency, a *Euromark* account.

Eurocurrency Interest Rates

What is the significance of these foreign currency denominated accounts? Simply put, it is the purity of value which comes from no governmental interference or restrictions on their use. Because Eurocurrency accounts are not controlled or managed by governments (for example, the Bank of England has no control over Eurodollar accounts), the financial institutions pay no deposit insurance, hold no reserve requirements, and are normally not subject to any interest-rate-setting restriction with respect to these accounts. Eurocurrencies are one of the purest indicators of what these currencies should yield in terms of interest.

LIBOR

The London InterBank Offer Rate, which is the rate of interest charged by the most creditworthy banks to other large banks for short-term loans; the interest rate used as the base rate in many international loan agreements.

There are literally hundreds of different major interest rates around the globe, but the international financial markets focus on a very few, the interbank interest rates. Interbank rates charged by banks to banks in the major international financial centers such as London, Frankfurt, Paris, New York, Tokyo, Singapore, and Hong Kong are generally regarded as *the interest rate* in the respective market. The interest rate which is used most often in international loan agreements is the Eurocurrency interest rate on U.S. dollars (Eurodollars) in London between banks: **LIBOR,** the London InterBank Offer Rate. Because it is a Eurocurrency rate, it floats freely without regard to any governmental restrictions on reserves or deposit insurance or any other regulation or restriction which would add expense to transactions using this capital. The interbank rates for other currencies in other markets are often named similarly: PIBOR (Paris-interbank offer rate), MIBOR (Madrid interbank offer rate), HIBOR (either Hong Kong or Helsinki interbank offer rate), and so forth. While LIBOR is the offer rate, the cost of funds offered to those acquiring a loan, the equivalent deposit rate in the Euromarkets is *LIBID,* the London InterBank Bid Rate, which is the rate of interest other banks can earn on Eurocurrency deposits.

How do these international Eurocurrency and interbank interest rates differ from domestic rates? The answer is, not by much. They generally move up and down in unison, by currency, but often differ by the percent by which the restrictions alter the rates of interest in the domestic markets. For example, because the Euromarkets have no restrictions, the spread between the offer rate and the bid rate (the loan rate and the deposit rate) is substantially smaller than in domestic markets. This means the loan rates in international markets are a bit lower than domestic market loan rates, and deposit rates are a bit higher in the international markets than in domestic markets. This is, however, only a big-player market. Only well-known international firms, financial or nonfinancial, have access to the quantities of capital necessary to operate in the Euromarkets. But as described in later sections on international debt and equity markets, more and more firms are gaining access to the Euromarkets.

Forward Exchange Rates

The Eurocurrency interest rates just described also play a large role in the foreign exchange markets themselves. They are, in fact, the interest rates used in the calculation of the forward rates we noted earlier (for examples of forward rate quotes refer back to Figure 23-1). Recall that a forward rate is a contract for a specific amount of currency to be exchanged for a second currency at a future date, usually 30, 60, 90, 180, or even 360 days in the future. Forward rates are calculated from the spot rate in effect on the day the contract is written along with the respective Eurocurrency interest rates for the two currencies.

For example, to determine the 90-day forward rate on February 19, 1993, the spot rate on that date is multiplied by the ratio of the two Eurocurrency interest rates. Table 23-1 provides spot rates and Eurocurrency interest rates (deposit rates) for February 19, 1993. Note that to correctly calculate the forward rate it is important to adjust the interest rates for the actual period of time needed — 90 days (3 months) of a 360-day financial year.

90-day forward rate (Currency A/Currency B)

$$= \text{Spot rate} \times \left[\frac{1 + i_{90}^{A}\left(\dfrac{90}{360}\right)}{1 + i_{90}^{B}\left(\dfrac{90}{360}\right)} \right]. \quad (23\text{-}1)$$

Now, plugging in the spot exchange rate of DM 1.6360/US\$ and the two 90-day (3-month) Eurocurrency interest rates from Table 23-1 (3.0625% for the dollar and 8.2500% for the mark), the 90-day forward exchange rate is

Table 23-1

Eurocurrency Interest
Rates (percent per annum)

		United States Dollar	German Mark	Japanese Yen
Exchange rate (bid rate)	Spot rate	---	DM 1.6360	¥ 119.00
Eurocurrency deposit rate	1 month	3.0000	8.5625	3.1875
London rates	3 months	3.0625	8.2500	3.2500
(bid rates)	6 months	3.1875	7.8125	3.2188
	12 months	3.5000	7.2500	3.2188

Source: *Harris Bank Foreign Exchange Weekly Review,* Harris Trust and Savings Bank, Chicago, February 19, 1993.

$$
\text{DM } 1.6360/\text{US\$} \times \left[\frac{1 + 0.082500\left(\dfrac{90}{360}\right)}{1 + 0.030625\left(\dfrac{90}{360}\right)} \right]
$$

$$
= \text{DM } 1.6360/\text{US\$} \times \left(\frac{1.020625}{1.007656}\right) = \text{DM } 1.6571/\text{US\$}.
$$

The forward rate of DM 1.6571/US$ is a "weaker rate" for the German mark than the spot rate of DM 1.6360/US$. This is because US$ 1 is worth 1.6360 marks spot, but the forward rate states that US$ 1 will be exchanged for 1.6571 marks in 90 days according to the provisions of the contract. The German mark is *selling forward at a discount,* meaning that the forward contract possesses a rate for purchasing marks which is cheaper than the present spot rate.

But why is this the case? The reason is that interest rates on German marks are higher than U.S. interest rates. If the preceding forward rate was calculated with U.S. Eurocurrency interest rates, which are higher than German Eurocurrency interest rates, the result would be the opposite. The German mark would be *selling forward at a premium,* meaning more expensive versus the dollar than the present spot rate. The forward rates quoted in the foreign exchange markets simply reflect the interest differentials between the two currencies. Forward exchange rate contracts are frequently used by businesses around the world to manage their exposure to currency risk.

What Should a Currency Be Worth?

At what rate should one currency be exchanged for another currency? For example, what should the exchange rate be between the U.S. dollar and the Japanese yen? The simplest answer is that the exchange rate should equalize purchasing power. For example, if the price of a movie ticket in the United States is $6, the *correct* exchange rate would be one which exchanges $6 for the amount of Japanese yen it would take to purchase a movie ticket in Japan. If ticket prices are ¥ 750 in Japan, then the exchange rate which would equalize purchasing power would be

$$\frac{¥\ 750}{US\ \$6} = ¥\ 125/US\$.$$

Therefore, if the exchange rate between the two currencies was ¥ 125/US $, regardless of which country the moviegoer was in, he or she could purchase a ticket. This is the theory of **purchasing power parity,** generally considered the definition of what exchange rates should ideally be. The purchasing power parity (PPP) exchange rate is simply that rate which equalizes the price of the identical product or service in two different currencies:

Price in Country A = Exchange rate × Price in Country B.   (23-2)

For example, if the price of the same product in each currency is $P^{¥}$ and $P^{\$}$ and if the spot exchange rate between the Japanese yen and the U.S. dollar is $S^{¥/\$}$, the price in yen is simply the price in dollars multiplied by the spot exchange rate:

$$P^{¥} = S^{¥/\$} \times P^{\$}.$$

If this is rearranged (dividing both sides by $P^{\$}$), the spot exchange rate between the Japanese yen and U.S. dollar is the ratio of the two product prices:

$$S^{¥/\$} = \frac{P^{¥}}{P^{\$}}.$$

These prices could be the price of just one good or service like the movie ticket mentioned previously, or they could be price indexes for each country which cover many different goods and services. Either form is an attempt to find comparable products in different countries (and currencies) in order to determine a purchasing power parity–based exchange rate. The problem has been that currency values have differed significantly in recent history from their PPP values.

Finally, what should a currency be worth *tomorrow?* It should simply be the ratio of prices adjusted for general price level changes—inflation—between now and tomorrow. The future spot exchange rate, $S_{t+1}^{¥/\$}$, is simply the present spot rate, $S_{t}^{¥/\$}$, multiplied by the ratio of the two expected rates of inflation:

$$S_{t+1}^{¥/\$} = S_{t}^{¥/\$} \times \left[\frac{1\ +\ ¥\ \text{inflation}}{1\ +\ US\$\ \text{inflation}} \right].$$

If Japanese inflation is expected to be 2 percent annually while U.S. inflation is expected to be 3 percent, the future spot exchange rate is calculated as

$$S_{t+1}^{¥/\$} = ¥\ 125/US\$ \times \left[\frac{1\ +\ 0.02}{1\ +\ 0.03} \right] = ¥\ 123.79/US\$.$$

The result is one of the fundamental principles of inflation and exchange rates. The currency with the higher rate of inflation generally loses value relative to the lower inflation currency; that is, it depreciates.

purchasing power parity (PPP)

The theory that the price of internationally traded goods should be the same in every country, and therefore, the exchange rate between the two currencies should simply be the ratio of prices in the two countries.

Brief History of Exchange Rates

The international monetary system has seen many changes since the beginning of the twentieth century. The major Western countries—Great Britain, Germany, France, the United States, and others—exchanged currencies on a gold standard until the outbreak of World War I in 1913. Under the gold standard each currency was convertible into a specific weight of gold, thereby "fixing" the rates at which one currency exchanged for another currency. The U.S. dollar was fixed at a rate of $20.67/oz of gold, while the British pound was fixed at £4.2474/oz. Each country stood ready to buy or sell their own currency in exchange for gold to assure that these rates remained in effect. Governments were the main players in this international monetary system.

After World War I, although several countries like Great Britain and the United States attempted to return to the gold standard, world trade and economic conditions deteriorated significantly. Whenever international investors feared that a country's currency would lose value in the near future, these investors would demand gold in exchange for paper. This convertibility caused rapid depletions in the gold stocks held by the respective governments. Eventually, each country ended convertibility of their currency into gold.

As each country left the gold standard, it would officially declare its currency to be worth less of other currencies; it was officially devalued. Large devaluations made products produced and exported from these countries cheaper on world markets, and thus, exports grew. These competitive devaluations, as they were called, contributed to much of the international political and economic tensions of the 1930s. With the onset of World War II, world trade came to a standstill.

In the summer of 1944, representatives of the Allied Powers met in Bretton Woods, New Hampshire, to plan the structure of the postwar international monetary system. The resulting system of fixed exchange rates, known as the Bretton Woods Agreement, established stable exchange rates which allowed the reopening of world markets. The system was constructed about the U.S. dollar. All currencies would be fixed in value versus the U.S. dollar (they could generally vary ± 1 percent, and the U.S. dollar itself would be convertible into gold.[3]

The reindustrialization of Europe and Asia after the ravages of World War II was aided greatly by this stability. But, like all systems, it was designed for a specific world. The Bretton Woods Agreement was premised on the dominance of the U.S. economy and the U.S. dollar. As the economies of Europe and Asia once more flourished, the demands of the world economy forced continuing outflows of gold from the United States as other countries exchanged U.S. paper money for gold. In 1971, President Richard Nixon of the United States ended convertibility of the U.S. dollar into gold, and the world was effectively shifted to a floating exchange rate system in which governments no longer dictated currency values.

The current floating exchange rate system, now over 20 years old, is one which confronts modern businesses and governments with a complex market for currencies. In today's markets, the price of one currency in terms of another

---

[3]Actually the convertibility was limited to foreign governments. Private individuals could not exchange paper money for gold, only the central banking institutions of other countries.

Figure 23-2   The U.S. Dollar under Floating Exchange Rates (Morgan Index, foreign currency per U.S. dollar)

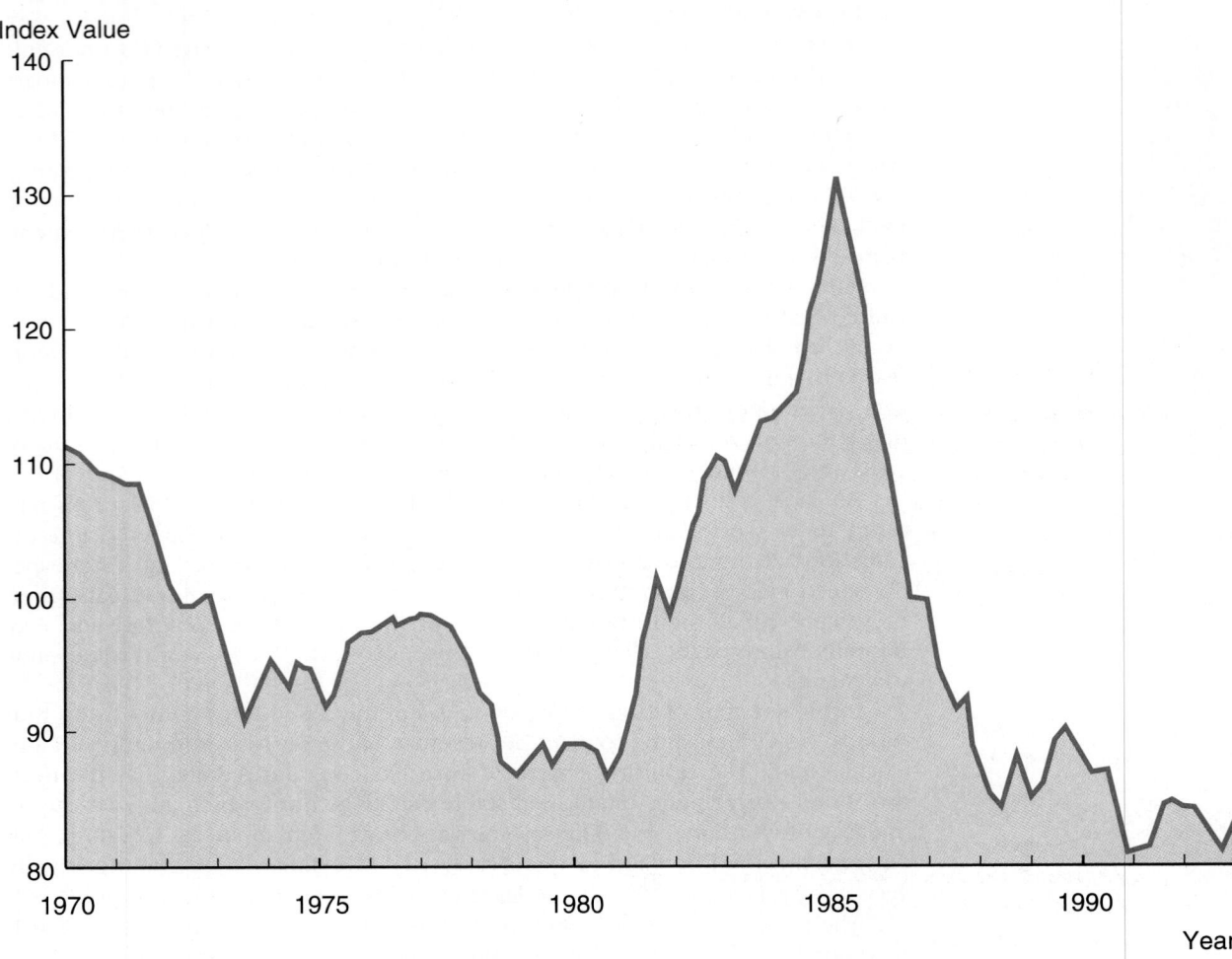

The value of the U.S. dollar has moved as if on a roller coaster in the past two decades. After the dollar fell in value from 1970 to 1981, it rose astronomically against other major world currencies until peaking in early 1985. Since 1985, the dollar has declined and stabilized at a relatively weak level versus other major currencies.

Source: Derived from *World Financial Markets,* Morgan Guaranty, New York, various issues. The Morgan 15 country nominal index is calculated using trade weights of the United States's 15 largest bilateral trading partners. 1980–1982 average = 100.

changes by the day, the hour, and even the minute for some of the world's largest currencies. Although the current system is generally categorized as a *floating rate system,* it must be noted that this is representative of the exchange of the largest currencies: the U.S. dollar, the Japanese yen, and the German mark. Many of the currencies of small countries even today are fixed in value to other currencies like the German mark, the French franc, or the U.S. dollar. It is, therefore, always important to be specific about which currencies are being discussed.

Figure 23-2 illustrates the changing value of the U.S. dollar over the past two decades against a weighted average of the United States' major trading partners. The volatility of the dollar's value has complicated trade and finance significantly. As the following sections will explain, financial management internationally must now deal effectively with this exchange rate risk if the firm of tomorrow is to remain competitive in the world's marketplace.

Self-Test

What problems exist as a result of an unstructured foreign currency market?

What is a cross rate?

How is LIBOR essential to international interest rates?

Briefly explain the concept of purchasing power parity.

International Capital Budgeting

Any investment, whether it be the acquisition of real estate or the construction of a manufacturing facility in another country, is financially justified if the present value of expected cash inflows is greater than the present value of expected cash outflows — in other words, if it has a positive net present value (NPV). The construction of a capital budget is the process of projecting the net operating cash flows of the potential investment in order to determine if it is indeed a good investment.

Capital Budget Components

All capital budgets, either domestic or international, are only as good as the accuracy of the cost and revenue assumptions. Adequately anticipating all of the incremental expenses that the individual project imposes on the firm is critical to a proper analysis. If the undertaking of a new project in a foreign country requires the establishment of a new office in the parent firm for handling shipments of people and materials, this needs to be added into the incremental cash flows of the project. As you may recall from Chapter 14, a capital budget is composed of three primary cash flow components: (1) initial expenses and capital outlays, (2) operating cash flows, and (3) terminal cash flows. All three components are altered in an international capital budget.

The decision criterion for an individual investment is whether the net present value of the project is positive or negative, as explained in the previous chapters.[4] Traditional capital budgeting exercises, when conducted domestically, discount expected future net cash flows by the weighted average cost of capital for the firm if the project is of the same risk as the firm. International capital budgeting, however, must also address the issue of whether the added

---

[4]There are of course other traditional decison criteria used in capital budgeting, such as the internal rate of return (IRR), modified internal rate of return (MIRR), and payback period. For the sake of simplicity, NPV is used throughout the analysis in this chapter.

risk introduced by cross-border investments — including the risk components of currency values, potential government restrictions on the movements of capital, or even the potential lack of political stability of the country in which the investment is to take place — should be captured in the analysis by adding a risk premium to the discount rate used. Although there are those who believe that the added risk should result in a higher discount rate, there are also those who believe that the additional risk of international projects should be captured in the estimation of the net cash flows themselves and through added sensitivity analysis in the conduct of the capital budgeting exercise.

A Proposed Project Evaluation

The capital budget for a manufacturing plant in Singapore serves as a basic example. ACME, a U.S. manufacturer of household consumer products is considering the construction of a plant in Singapore in 1994. It will cost $1,660,000 in Singapore dollars to build and would be ready for operation on January 1, 1995. ACME will operate the plant for three years, at the end of which it will sell the plant to the Singapore government.

To analyze the proposed investment, ACME must estimate what the sales revenues would be per year, the costs of production, the overhead expenses of operating the plant per year, the depreciation allowances for the new plant and equipment, and the Singapore tax rate on corporate income. The estimation of all net operating cash flows is very important to the analysis of the project. Often the entire acceptability of a foreign investment may depend on the sales forecast for the foreign project.

But ACME needs U.S. dollars, not Singapore dollars. The only way the stockholders of ACME would be willing to undertake this investment is if it would be profitable in terms of their own currency, the U.S. dollar. This is the primary theoretical distinction between a domestic capital budget and a multinational capital budget. The evaluation of the project in the viewpoint of the parent will focus on whatever cash flows, either operational or financial, will find their way back to the parent firm in U.S. dollars.

ACME must, therefore, forecast the movement of the Singapore dollar (S$) over the four-year period as well. The spot rate on January 1, 1994, is S$ 1.6600/US$. ACME concludes that the rate of inflation will be roughly 5 percent higher per year in Singapore than in the United States. If the theory of purchasing power parity (PPP) holds, it should take roughly 5 percent more Singapore dollars to buy a U.S. dollar per year. Using this assumption, ACME forecasts the exchange rate from 1994 through 1997.

After considerable study and analysis, ACME estimates that the net cash flows of the Singapore project, in Singapore dollars, would be those on Line 1 in Table 23-2. Line 2 lists the expected exchange rate between Singapore dollars and U.S dollars over the four-year period, assuming it takes 5 percent more Singapore dollars per U.S. dollar each year (the Singapore dollar is, therefore, expected to depreciate versus the U.S. dollar). Combining the net cash flow forecast in Singapore dollars with the expected exchange rates, ACME can now calculate the net cash flow per year in U.S. dollars. ACME notes that although the initial expense is sizeable, S$ 1,660,000 or US$ 1,000,000, the project produces net positive cash flows in its first year of operations, US$ 229,489.

Table 23-2

Preliminary Capital Budget:
Singapore Manufacturing
Facility

	1994	1995	1996	1997
1 Net cash flow in S$	(1,660,000)	400,000	700,000	1,600,000
2 Exchange rate, S$/US$	1.6600	1.7430	1.8302	1.9217
3 Net cash flow in US$	(1,000,000)	229,489	382,472	832,596
4 Present value interest factor	1.000	0.8475	0.7182	0.6086
5 Present value in US$	(1,000,000)	194,492	274,691	506,718
6 NPV from parent viewpoint	**US$ (24,098)**			
7 Present value in S$	(1,660,000)	339,000	502,740	973,760
8 NPV from project viewpoint	**S$ 155,500**			

ᵃThe spot exchange rate of S$ 1.6600/US$ is assumed to change by 5% per year, 1.6600 × 1.05 = 1.7430.

ᵇThe present value interest factor assumes a weighted average cost of capital, the discount rate, of 18%. The present value factor is then found using the standard formula of $1/(1 + 0.18)^t$, where t is the number of years in the future (1, 2, or 3).

ACME estimates that its cost of capital, both debt and equity combined (the WACC), is about 18 percent per year. Using this as the rate of discount, the discount factor (PVIF) for each of the future years is found. Finally, the net cash flow in U.S. dollars multiplied by the present value interest factor yields the present values of each net cash flow. The net present value of the Singapore project to the U.S. parent firm is negative, − $24,098, and ACME may now decide to not proceed with the investment.

Risks in International Investments

How is this capital budget different from a similar project constructed in Phoenix, Arizona? It is riskier, at least from the standpoint of cross-border risk. The higher risk of an international investment arises from the different countries; their laws, regulations, and potential for interference with the normal operations of the investment project; and, obviously, currencies—all of which are unique to international investment.

The risk of international investment is considered greater because the proposed investment will lie within the jurisdiction of a different government. Governments have the ability to pass new laws, including the potential nationalization of the entire project. The typical problems which may arise from operating in a different country are changes in foreign tax laws, restrictions placed on when or how much in profits may be repatriated (sent back) to the parent company, and other types of restrictions which hinder the free movement of merchandise and capital between the proposed project, the parent, and any other country relevant to its material inputs or sales.

The other major distinction between a domestic investment and a foreign investment is that the viewpoint or perspective of the parent and the project are no longer the same. The two perspectives differ because the parent only values cash flows it derives from the project. So, for example, in Table 23-2, the project generates sufficient net cash flows in Singapore dollars that it is acceptable from the project's viewpoint, a positive NPV of S$ 155,500. However, as noted earlier, from the parent's viewpoint the net present value of the

INVADING RUSSIA

Business is more complicated in the former Soviet Union than it used to be. A foreign company looking for opportunities there in the past could simply go through a one-man office and visit the centralized state trade organization several times a year. Today, 15 independent governments exist where there was only one, and small regions and individual enterprises often make deals on their own, without help from the state.

Nevertheless, some foreign companies are entering the market. Marc Rich & Company, a multibillion dollar firm whose namesake and founder moved the firm to Switzerland to escape U.S. racketeering and tax evasion charges, is making big deals with the Soviets, and taking big risks. Danny Posen, who works at the new Marc Rich office in central Moscow, said "The breakup of the Soviet Union has created huge opportunities, but that doesn't mean things are easy. It's a madhouse. At this point, we're all kind of in the dark."

Founder Rich, however, says, "I am amazed at how timid the West has been in investing in the former Soviet Union. We've approached this market very aggressively."

Despite local suspicions that the illegal behavior that got the company in trouble in the United States is continuing in Russia, Rich is building a vast trading empire there that accounts for 10 percent of its global business. Its staff in the area grew from 10 to 150 in slightly over a year, and it has engineered a number of multimillion dollar deals across political and ethnic borders.

Five newly independent countries in the former Soviet Union were involved in a 1992 arrangement that one employee called "a very Soviet deal. When you don't have money, you pay with what you do have." This particular deal involved sugar, copper, and oil, and it eventually resulted in hard-currency profits for Rich.

The complicated bartering arrangement began when Rich purchased 70,000 tons of raw sugar from

Brazil and shipped it to Ukraine for refining. After paying the refinery with part of the sugar, Rich sent 30,000 tons of it to several Siberian oil refineries that needed to provide sugar for their employees. The refineries paid for the sugar with low-grade gasoline, which Rich then shipped to Mongolia in exchange for 35,000 tons of copper ore concentrate. The ore went to Kazakhstan to be refined into metal, which was then shipped to a Baltic port and out to the world market, where its sale finally brought hard currency back to Rich.

Ari Zalkinder, one of Rich's financial officers, says, "Basically, we play the role of financier in the region. Nobody else is going to do it."

Sometimes, however, the deals do not work out. Last year Marc Rich contracted to ship 40,000 tons of grain to Kazakhstan in exchange for metals. Trains were waiting to take on the cargo as grain ships arrived at a port 3,000 miles from the final destination, but Kazakhstan suddenly canceled the agreement. Posen said, "There are times here when a signed contract doesn't mean a whole lot. You just try to be as agile as possible." Agility in this case meant turning the other cheek so as not to lose a trading partner, then negotiating a sale of the grain elsewhere, but at a loss.

Different standards of business conduct have required agility of other firms as well. When Microsoft Corporation opened its first office in Russia in late 1992, it found that its MS-DOS computer operating system had already captured the lion's share of the market. The only problem was, the tens of thousands of users obtained the software by following entrenched local custom and pirating it. "The former Soviet Union is a piracy superpower," said Robert Clough, managing director of the Microsoft Russian subsidiary. One reason is that foreign computer firms refused to accept rubles for their wares until last year, so legal purchases could be made only by governments or by the few individuals with access to hard currency. Everybody else turned to pirating since Russia had no copyright laws. The government even financed bootlegging operations and provided service centers where citizens could come and copy the software they wanted.

Sources: Laurie Hays, "Microsoft Urges Russian Software Bootleggers: Join Us," *The Wall Street Journal*, May 18, 1993, B4; Adi Ignatius, "Marc Rich & Co. Does Big Deals at Big Risk in Former U.S.S.R.," and Joseph B. White, "GM Starts to Ship Control Systems to Volga Auto Works," *The Wall Street Journal*, May 13, 1993, A1, B4.

Microsoft tackled the problem first by joining with other Western companies and 40 local ones to lobby Russia's parliament to pass copyright legislation which made it illegal to duplicate and sell software without a license. Then Microsoft set out to turn the pirates into licensed distributors by pointing out the new law and its penalties. "If they come to work for us, they don't get punished," said Nikolai Lubovny, manager of large accounts for Microsoft in Russia. Added the subsidiary's marketing manager, "Francis Drake was a pirate, but became an admiral in the fleet after he signed a contract with the Queen."

By mid-1993, Microsoft had signed on 13 distributors and 250 dealers throughout the former Soviet Union, although some pirates turned down the company because they can make more money the illegal way. "We're trying to make it attractive to be a dealer," said Lubovny. One way is to build a partnership relationship and provide special services such as repairs and information sharing through the dealers.

The campaign also means finding a way to change long-standing cultural differences. The idea of personal ownership is still an alien concept to many Russians, according to Lubovny. "We want an environment where people are interested in protecting their own property. The idea is that if you steal somebody's program, they can steal yours, too."

Another concept Russians are not used to is the advantage of buying an official product from the company that makes it—getting an operating manual and a guarantee as part of the package. Although pirating groups try to copy the manuals too, they often leave out critical commands, and consumers can not make the software do what they want it to.

Trying to change the Russian mindset and standard operating procedures is also a challenge for General Motors, which inaugurated a five-year deal in May 1993 to provide engine and emission control systems to the Volga Auto Works so that the Russian company could sell its low-priced Lada car in Western markets. GM executives sent to Volga's plant 600 miles southeast of Moscow found that cost accounting was a mystery to the Russians, that phone calls took days to go through, and that logistics were a nightmare. Rick Merrill, sales manager for Russia, said, "After 20 years with GM, I thought I was used to . . . decision processes that dragged on forever. The Russians wrote the book."

Nevertheless, GM's automotive components group sees the Russian deal as a big step toward entering the world market as a major supplier of sophisticated technological systems. Being paid in dollars generated when Volga sells its cars overseas, GM expects to earn $140 million a year from the agreement.

U.S. dollar cash flows to be generated and returned to the U.S. firm are negative and, therefore, unacceptable.

But what if the spot exchange rate were not to deteriorate? What if the rate were to remain the same over the four-year period or if the Singapore dollar were to even appreciate versus the U.S. dollar? Or what if the Singapore government were to restrict the payment of dividends back to the U.S. parent firm or somehow prohibit the Singapore subsidiary from exchanging Singapore dollars for U.S. dollars (capital controls)? Without cash flows in U.S. dollars, the parent would have no way of justifying the investment. All of this occurs while the project itself is sufficiently profitable when measured in its own local currency. This split between project and parent viewpoint is a critical difference in international investment analysis. Any individual investment can be judged only on the basis of the future cash flows it generates in the investor's own currency.

 Self-Test

What special considerations are necessary when evaluating an international capital budgeting proposal?

Explain the unique risks involved in international investments.

Table 23-3   Financing Alternatives for Foreign Affiliates

Foreign affiliate can raise equity capital:	*Foreign affiliate can raise debt capital:*
1. From the parent	1. From the parent
2. From a joint-venture partner in the parent's country, a joint-venture partner in the host country, or a share issue in the host country	2. From the parent firm's home market through a bank loan or bond issue or from a bank loan or bond issue in the host-country market
3. From a third-country market such as a share issue in the Euro-equity market	3. From a third-country bank loan, bond issue, Euro-syndicated credit, or Eurobond issue

Capital Structure of Foreign Subsidiaries

The choice of what proportions of debt and equity to use in international investments is usually dictated by either the debt-equity structure of the parent firm or by the debt-equity structure of the competitive firms in the foreign country—host country to the investment.[5] The parent firm sees equity investment as capital at risk; it therefore would normally prefer to provide less equity capital of its own than more. Because international investments are subject to higher risks from political sources or financial sources, the parent firm would ideally prefer to risk little of its own capital and instead fund the foreign subsidiary with large quantities of debt. Although this would still be putting the parent's capital at risk, debt service provides a strict schedule for cash flow repatriation to the lender—regular principal and interest payments according to the debt agreement. Equity capital's return, dividends from profits if realized, are returned to the parent through managerial discretion. It is this discretion, the proportion of profits which are to be returned to the parent versus profits which are to be retained and reinvested in the project or firm, which often leads to conflict between host-country authorities and the multinational firm's parent.

The sources of debt for a foreign subsidiary are, theoretically, quite large but, in reality, often quite limited. The alternatives listed in Table 23-3 are often reduced radically in practice because many countries possess relatively small capital markets of their own. These countries often either officially restrict the borrowing by foreign-owned firms in their countries or simply do not have affordable capital available for the foreign firm's use. The parent firm is then often forced to provide not only the equity but a large proportion of the debt to its own foreign subsidiaries. If the project or subsidiary is a new project, it has no existing line of business or credit standing. The parent must then represent the subsidiary's credit worth and provide the debt capital at least until the project is operating and showing (hopefully) positive net cash flows.

Internationally, the larger firms will often have their own financial subsidiaries, companies purely for the purpose of acquiring the capital needed for the entire company's continuing growth needs. These financial subsidiaries will often be the actual unit extending the debt or equity capital to the foreign project or subsidiary. Hopefully, with time and success, the foreign investment will

---

[5]Chapters 19 and 20 previously covered the theory of capital structure.

grow sufficiently to establish its own credit standing and acquire more and more of its capital needs from the local markets in which it operates, or even from the international markets which become aware of its growth.

Self-Test

What options do multinational firms have for financing international investments?

International Working Capital and Cash Flow Management

Working capital management is the financing of short-term or current assets but is used here to generally describe all short-term financing and financial management of the firm. Even a relatively small multinational firm will have a number of different cash flows moving throughout its system at one time. The maintenance of proper liquidity, the monitoring of payments, and the acquisition of additional capital when needed require a great degree of organization and planning in international operations today.

Operating and Financial Cash Flows

operating cash flows
The cash flows associated with the everyday business activities of the firm; for example, the purchasing of inputs from a foreign supplier.

Firms possess both operating cash flows and financial cash flows. **Operating cash flows** are those which arise from the everyday business activities of the firm such as paying for materials or resources (accounts payable) or receiving payments for items sold (accounts receivable). In addition to the direct cost and revenue cash flows from operations, there are a number of indirect cash flows. These indirect cash flows are primarily license fees paid to the owners of particular technological processes and royalties paid to the holders of patents or copyrights. Many multinational firms also spread their overhead and management expenses incurred at the parent over their foreign affiliates and subsidiaries who are utilizing the parent's administrative services.

financial cash flows
The cash flows associated with the principal and periodic payments on the financial structure of the firm; for example, the principal and interest payments on debt.

The second category of cash flows, **financial cash flows,** arise from the funding activities of the firm. The servicing of existing funding sources, interest on existing debt, and dividend payments to existing shareholders constitute potentially large and frequent cash flow sources. Periodic additions to debt or equity through new bank loans, new bond issuances, or supplemental stock sales may constitute additional financial cash flows in the international firm.

A Sample Cash Flow Mapping

Figure 23-3 provides an overview of how these cash flows may appear for a U.S.-based multinational firm. In addition to having some export sales in Canada, it may import some materials from Mexico. The firm accesses several different European markets by first selling its product to its German subsidiary, which then provides the final touches necessary for sales in Germany, France, and Switzerland. Sales and purchases by the parent with Canada and Mexico give

Figure 23-3   Operational and Financial Cash Flows of a U.S. Multinational Firm with a German Subsidiary

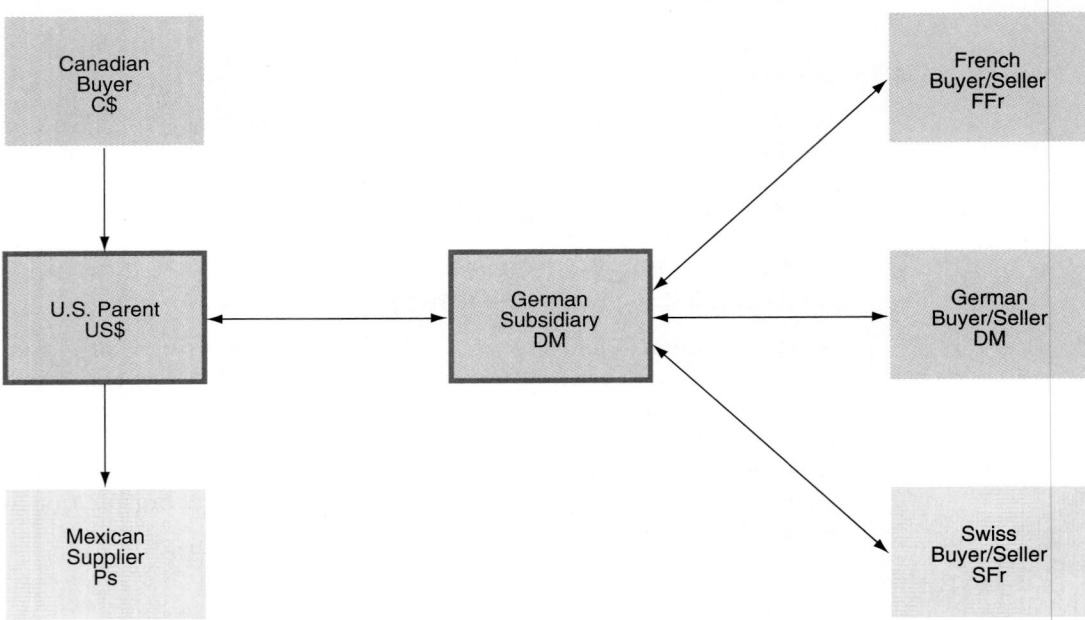

A U.S.-based multinational firm possesses operating cash flows with third parties such as Canadian buyers and Mexican suppliers, as well as with its own German subsidiary, which also purchases product from the parent. The U.S. parent also possesses financial cash flows with its German subsidiary, as it provides the majority of the capital for the German subsidiary's financial structure.

rise to a continuing series of accounts receivable and accounts payable, many of which may be denominated in Canadian dollars, Mexican pesos, or its own currency, the U.S. dollar.

Cash flows between the U.S. parent and the German subsidiary will be both operational and financial in nature. The sale of the major product line to the German subsidiary creates intrafirm receivables and payables. These payments may be denominated in either U.S. dollars or German marks. And these intrafirm sales may in fact be two-way if the German subsidiary is actually producing a form of the product not made in the United States but needed there. The German subsidiary may also be utilizing techniques, machinery, or processes that are owned or patented by the parent firm, so royalties and license fees must also be paid to the parent. These cash flows are usually calculated as a percentage of the sales price in Germany.

There are also a number of financial cash flows between the U.S. parent and the German subsidiary. If the subsidiary is partially financed by loans extended by the parent, principal and interest payments will need to be made on a regular basis by the subsidiary to the parent. If the German subsidiary is successful in its operations and generates a profit, that portion of the profits not reinvested in the subsidiary will need to be sent back to the parent as dividends.[6] If, at some point in the operations of the German subsidiary, it needs additional capital over and above what it can retain from its own profits, it may need additional debt or equity capital (from any of the potential sources listed in Table 23-3). These would obviously add to the potential financial cash flow volume.

The subsidiary, in turn, is dependent on its sales in Germany (German mark revenues), France (French franc revenues), and Switzerland (Swiss franc revenues) to generate the needed cash flows for paying everyone else! This "map" of operating and financial cash flows does not even attempt to describe the frequency of these various foreign currency cash flows or specify who will be responsible for managing the currency risks. The management of cash flows in a larger multinational firm, one with possibly 10 or 20 subsidiaries, is obviously complex. The proper management of these cash flows is, however, critical to the success or failure of the international business.

Cash Flow Management

The structure of the firm dictates in what ways cash flows and financial resources can be managed. The trend in the past decade has been for the increasing centralization of most financial and treasury operations. The centralized treasury is often responsible for both funding operations and cash flow management. The centralized treasury may often enjoy significant economies of scale, offering more services and expertise to the various units of the firm worldwide than the individual units themselves could support. However, regardless of whether the firm follows a centralized or decentralized approach, there are a number of operating structures which aid the multinational firm in managing its cash flows.

Cash Pooling.   A large firm with a number of units operating both within an individual country and across countries may be able to economize on the amount of firm assets needed in cash if operated through one central pool. With one pool of capital and up-to-date information on the cash flows in and out of the various units, the firm spends much less in terms of forgone interest on precautionary cash balances which are held against unforeseen cash flow shortfalls. A single large pool may also be able to negotiate better financial service rates with banking institutions for clearing purposes.

Netting.   As illustrated in Figure 23-3, many of the cash flows between units of a multinational firm are two-way and may result in unneeded transfer costs and transaction expenses. Coordination between units simply requires some planning and budgeting of intrafirm cash flows in order that two-way flows are "netted" against one another, with only one smaller cash flow having to be

---

[6]One of the most difficult pricing decisions many multinational firms must make is the price at which they sell their own products to their own subsidiaries and affiliates. These prices, called transfer prices, are theoretically equivalent to what the same product would cost if purchased on the open market. However, it is often impossible to find such a product on the open market; it is unique to this firm and this firm's product line. The result is a price set internally which may result in the subsidiary being more or less profitable. This, in turn, affects taxes paid in host countries.

undertaken as opposed to two. This is particularly helpful if the two-way flow is in two different currencies, as each would be suffering currency exchange charges for intrafirm transfers.

Leads and Lags.   The timing of payments between units of a multinational firm is somewhat flexible. This flexibility in deciding which currencies are paid to which units allows the firm to not only position cash flows where they are needed most, but it may actually aid in currency risk management. A foreign subsidiary unit that must obtain U.S. dollars to pay the parent for intrafirm shipments, who is expecting its own local currency of business to fall in value relative to the U.S. dollar, may wish to try to speed up or "lead" its payments to the parent. Similarly, if the local currency was expected to rise versus the dollar, it may wish to wait or "lag" payments until exchange rates are more favorable.

Reinvoicing.   Multinational firms with a variety of manufacturing and distribution subsidiaries scattered over a number of countries within a region may often find it more economical to have one office or subsidiary taking ownership of all invoices and payments between units. This subsidiary literally buys from one unit and sells to a second unit, therefore taking ownership of the goods and reinvoicing the sale to the next unit. Once ownership is taken, the sale/purchase can be redenominated in a different currency, netted against other payments, hedged against specific currency exposures, or repriced in accordance with potential tax benefits of the reinvoicing center's host country. The additional flexibility achievable in cash flow management, product pricing, and profit placement may be substantial.

Internal Banks.   Some multinational firms have found that their financial resources and needs are becoming either too large or too sophisticated for the financial services which are available in many of their local subsidiary markets. One solution to this has been the establishment of an internal bank within the firm. This bank actually buys and sells payables and receivables from the various units. This frees the units of the firm from struggling for continual working capital financing and allows them to focus on their primary business activities.

These structures and procedures are often combined in different ways to fit the needs of the individual multinational firm. Some techniques are encouraged or prohibited by laws and regulations depending on the host country's government and stage of capital market liberalization. In fact, it is not uncommon to find one type of system at work in one hemisphere of firm operations and a very different system in use in the other hemisphere. Multinational cash flow management requires a good deal of flexibility in thinking on the part of managers.

Self-Test

Characterize the different cash flows that can occur within a multinational firm. What methods help manage international cash flows?

Import/Export Trade Financing

Unlike most domestic business, international business often occurs between two parties who do not know each other very well. Yet, in order to conduct business, a large degree of financial trust must exist. This financial trust is basically the belief that the buyer of a product will actually pay for it on or after delivery. For example, if a furniture manufacturer in South Carolina receives an order from a Midwestern distributor located in Cleveland, Ohio, the furniture maker will ordinarily fill the order, ship the furniture, and await payment. Payment terms are usually 30 to 60 days. This is trade on an *open-account basis*. The furniture manufacturer has placed a considerable amount of financial trust in the buyer but is normally paid with little problem.

letter of credit

A written statement by an importing firm's bank testifying to the firm's ability to make payment, often guaranteeing payment to the exporter or the exporter's bank.

Internationally, however, this financial trust is pushed to its limit. An order from a foreign buyer may constitute a degree of credit risk (the risk of not being repaid) which the producer—the exporter—cannot afford to take. The exporter needs some guarantee that the importer will indeed pay for the goods. Other factors which tend to intensify this problem include the increased lag times necessary for international shipments and the potential risks of payments in different currencies. For this reason, arrangements which provide guarantees to exports are important to countries and companies wishing to expand international sales. This is accomplished through a sequence of documents surrounding the **letter of credit.**

An Example of Trade Financing Mechanics

A lumber manufacturer in the Pacific Northwest of the United States, Vanport, receives a large order from a Japanese construction company, Endaka, for a shipment of old-growth pine lumber. Vanport has not worked with Endaka before and, therefore, wishes some assurance that payment for the lumber will actually be made. Vanport ordinarily does not require any assurance of the buyer's ability to pay (sometimes a small down payment or deposit is made as a sign of good faith), but an international sale of this size is too large to risk. If Endaka could not or would not pay, the cost of returning the lumber products to the United States would be prohibitive. Vanport needs some assurance of payment. The following sequence of events will complete the transaction.

1. Endaka Construction requests a *letter of credit* to be issued by its own bank, Yokohama Bank.

2. Yokohama Bank will determine whether Endaka is financially sound and capable of making the payments as required. This is actually a very important step because Yokohama Bank simply wishes to guarantee the payment, not make the payment.

3. Yokohama Bank, once satisfied with Endaka's application, issues the letter of credit to a representative in the United States or to the exporter's bank, Pacific First Bank. The letter of credit guarantees payment for the merchandise if the goods are shipped as stipulated in accompanying documents. Customary documents include the commercial invoice, customs clearance and invoice, the packing list, certification of insurance, and a bill of lading.

4. The exporter's bank, Pacific First, assures Vanport that payment will be made after evaluating the letter of credit. At this point the credit standing of Yokohama bank has been substituted for the credit standing of the importer itself, Endaka Construction.

5. When the pine lumber order is ready, it is loaded on board the *shipper* (called a *common carrier*). When the exporter signs a contract with a shipper, the signed contract serves as the receipt that the common carrier has received the goods and is termed the *bill of lading*.

6. Vanport draws a *draft* against Yokohama Bank for payment. The draft is the document used in international trade to effect payment and explicitly requests payment for the merchandise which is now shown to be shipped and insured consistent with all requirements of the previously issued letter of credit. (If the draft is issued to the bank issuing the letter of credit, Yokohama Bank, it is termed a *bank draft*. If the draft is issued against the importer, Endaka Construction, it is a *trade draft*.) The draft, letter of credit, and other appropriate documents are presented to Pacific First Bank for payment.

7. If Pacific First Bank had confirmed the letter of credit from Yokohama Bank, it would immediately pay Vanport for the lumber and then collect from the issuing bank, Yokohama. If Pacific First Bank had not confirmed the letter of credit, it only passes the documents to Yokohama Bank for payment (to Vanport). The *confirmed* letter of credit obviously speeds up payment to the exporter as opposed to an *unconfirmed letter of credit*.

Regardless, with the letter of credit as the financial assurance, the exporter or the exporter's bank is collecting payment from the importer's bank, not the importer itself. Specific arrangements between the importer (Endaka) and the importer's bank (Yokohama) will determine the final settlement on that end of the purchase.

If this trade relationship continues over time, both parties will gain faith and confidence in the other. With this strengthening of financial trust, a loosening of the trade financing relationship will come. Sustained cross-border buyer-seller relations eventually end up operating on an open-account basis similar to domestic commerce.

? *Self-Test*

Why is a letter of credit important to international trade?

Classification of Firm Exposure to Foreign Currency Movements

Companies today know the risks of international operations. They are aware of the substantial risks to balance sheet values and annual earnings that interest rates and exchange rates may inflict upon any firm at any time. And, as is the case with most potential risks or problems to the firm, senior management expects junior management to do something about it. Financial managers, international treasurers, and financial officers of all kinds are expected to "protect the firm" from these risks. But before you can manage a risk, you must be able to measure it. There are three types of foreign currency exposures which firms possess to varying degrees:

transaction exposure

The risk to a firm of making or receiving a foreign currency–denominated cash flow at a future date.

1. **Transaction exposure.**   The risk associated with a contractual payment of foreign currency is known as **transaction exposure.** For example, a U.S. firm who exports products to France will receive a guaranteed (by contract) payment in French francs in the future. Firms who buy or sell internationally, either inputs or outputs, will possess transaction exposures if any of the cash flows of these transactions are denominated in foreign currency.

economic exposure

The risk to a firm's value of unexpected exchange rate changes and their impacts on the value of future cash flows over the long run.

2. **Economic exposure.**   The risk to the firm of its long-term cash flows being affected, positively or negatively, by unexpected future exchange rate changes is known as **economic exposure.** Many firms who consider themselves to be purely domestic may not realize that all firms are in some way or another exposed to economic exchange rate risk.

translation exposure

The risk to a firm's consolidated balance sheet and income statement from the valuation of foreign affiliates and subsidiaries; also called accounting exposure.

3. **Translation exposure.**   The risk that arises from the legal requirement that all firms annually consolidate their financial statements (balance sheets and income statements) for their worldwide operations is called **translation exposure.** Therefore, any firm with operations outside its home country — operations which will be either earning foreign currency or valued in foreign currency — will represent potential risks to the firm.

Transaction exposure and economic exposure are true exposures in the financial sense. This means they both present potential threats to the value of a firm's cash flows over time. The third exposure, translation, is a problem which arises from accounting. Under the present accounting principles in practice across most of the world's industrialized countries, translation exposure is not the problem it once was. For the most part, little in the way of real resource use should therefore be devoted to the management of a purely accounting-based event.

Transaction Exposure

Transaction exposure is the most commonly observed type of exchange rate risk. Only two conditions are necessary for a transaction exposure to exist: (1) a cash flow which is denominated in a foreign currency and (2) the cash flow will occur at a future date. Any contract, agreement, purchase, or sale that is denominated in a foreign currency and will be settled in the future constitutes a transaction exposure.[7]

The risk associated with a transaction exposure is that the exchange rate between the present date and the settlement date will change. The change may be for the better or for the worse. For example, an American firm signs a con-

---

[7]Many firms only acknowledge the existence of a transaction exposure when they ship the order to the customer and issue the account receivable, In fact, whether they realize it or not, when they accepted the order at a fixed price in terms of foreign currency, they gave birth to a transaction exposure.

tract to purchase heavy rolled-steel pipe from a South Korean steel producer for 21,000,000 Korean won. The payment is due in 30 days upon delivery. This 30-day account payable, so typical of international trade and commerce, is a transaction exposure of the U.S. firm. If the spot exchange rate on the date the contract is signed is Won 700/US$, the U.S. firm would expect to pay

$$\frac{\text{Won } 21,000,000}{\text{Won } 700/\text{US\$}} = \text{US\$ } 30,000.$$

But the firm is not assured of what the actual exchange rate will be in 30 days. If the spot rate at the end of 30 days is Won 720/US$, the U.S. firm would actually find itself paying *less.* The payment would now be US$ 29,167. If, however, the exchange rate changed in the opposite direction—for example to Won 650/US$, the payment could just as easily increase to US$ 32,308. This type of price risk, transaction exposure, is a major problem for international commerce.

Transaction Exposure Management.   Management of transaction exposures is usually accomplished by either *natural hedging* or *contractual hedging.* **Natural hedging** is the term used to describe how a firm might arrange to have foreign currency cash flows coming in and going out at roughly the same times and same amounts. This is referred to as *natural hedging* because the management or hedging of the exposure is accomplished by matching offsetting foreign currency cash flows and, therefore, does not require the firm to undertake specific financial contracts or activities to manage the exposure. For example, a Canadian firm which generates a significant portion of its total sales in U.S. dollars may acquire U.S. dollar debt. The U.S. dollar earnings from sales could then be used to "service" the dollar debt as needed. In this way, regardless of whether the C$/US$ exchange rate goes up or down, the firm would be naturally hedged against the movement. If the U.S. dollar went up in value against the Canadian dollar, the U.S. dollar needed for debt service would be generated automatically by the export sales to the United States. U.S. dollar cash inflows would match U.S. dollar cash outflows.

Contractual hedging is when the firm uses financial contracts to hedge the transaction exposure. The most common foreign currency contractual hedge is the *forward contract,* although other financial instruments and derivatives such as *currency futures* and *options* are also used. The forward contract described previously in this chapter would ensure the firm a fixed rate of exchange between the desired two currencies at the precise future date. The forward contract would also be for the exact amount of the exposure.

Before proceeding further into financial and currency risk management, it is important to be precise regarding the definition of hedging. A *hedge* is an asset or a position whose value moves in the equal but opposite direction of the exposure. This means that if an exposure experienced a loss in value of US$ 50, the hedge asset would offset the loss with a gain in value of US$ 50. The total value of the position would not change. This would be termed a *perfect hedge*.

But perfect hedges are hard to find. And many people would not use them if they were readily available. Why? Because, while the presence of a perfect hedge eliminates all downside risk, it also eliminates all upside potential. And

---

natural hedging

The hedging of a currency risk through an offsetting currency position resulting from operational or financial cash flows; for example, the hedging of German mark (DM) cash inflows by a U.S.-based firm by borrowing DM and then servicing the DM debt with the DM earnings from operations.

contractual hedging

The hedging of a currency risk through the acquisition of a financial contract such as a forward contract.

many businesses accept this two-sided risk as part of the risk of doing business. However, it is generally best to accept risk in the line of business, not in the cash payment process of settling the business. By hedging the value of the currency, the total value of the position will now be protected against either good or bad exchange rate changes.

Currency Risk Sharing.   Firms which import and export on a continuing basis have constant transaction exposures. If a firm is interested in maintaining a good business relationship with one of its suppliers, it must work with that supplier to assure it that it will not force all currency risk or exposure off on the other party on a continual basis. Exchange rate movements are inherently random; therefore, some type of mutual risk-sharing arrangement may prove useful.

If Ford (United States) imports automotive parts from Mazda (Japan) every month, year after year, major swings in exchange rates can benefit one party at the expense of the other. One solution would be for Ford and Mazda to agree that all purchases by Ford will be made in Japanese yen, as long as the actual spot rate on the date payment is due is between ¥ 120/US$ and ¥ 130/US$. If the exchange rate is between these values on the payment dates, Ford agrees to accept whatever transaction exposure exists (because it is paying in a foreign currency). If, however, the exchange rate falls outside of this range on the payment date, Ford and Mazda will "share" the difference. If the spot rate on the settlement date was ¥ 110/US$, the Japanese yen would have appreciated versus the dollar causing Ford's costs of purchasing automotive parts to rise. Since this rate falls outside the contractual range, Mazda would agree to accept a total payment in Japanese yen which would result from a "shared" difference of ¥ 10. Thus, Ford's total payment in Japanese yen would be calculated using an exchange rate of ¥ 115/US$.

Risk-sharing agreements like these have been in use for nearly 50 years on world markets. They became something of a rarity during the 1950s and 1960s, when exchange rates were relatively stable (under the Bretton Woods Agreement). With the return to floating exchange rates in the 1970s, firms with long-term customer-supplier relationships across borders have returned to some old ways of keeping old friends. And sometimes old ways work very well.

Economic Exposure

Economic exposure is the change in the value of a firm arising from unexpected changes in exchange rates. Economic exposure emphasizes that there is a limit to the individual firm's ability to predict either cash flows or exchange rate changes over the long term. All firms, either directly or indirectly, possess economic exposure.

It is customary to think of only firms which actively trade internationally as having any type of currency exposure. Actually, all firms which operate in economies which are impacted by international financial events are affected. A barber in Ottumwa, Iowa, seemingly isolated from international exchange rate chaos is still affected when the dollar rises as it did in the early 1980s. When U.S. products become increasingly expensive to foreign buyers, American manufacturers like John Deere & Company in Iowa are forced to cut back

Figure 23-4

How Exchange Rate
Changes May Alter the
Value of Eastman Kodak

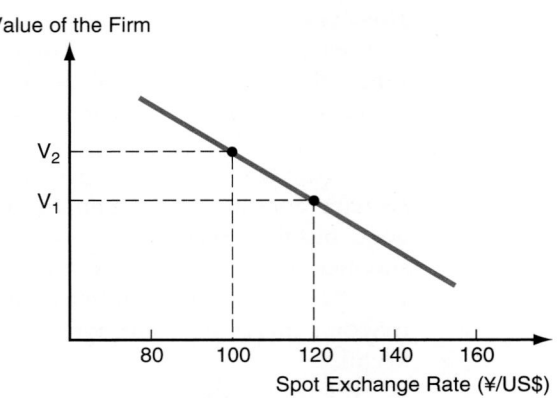

Eastman Kodak's value as a firm increases as the value of the U.S. dollar falls versus the Japanese yen.

---

production and lay off workers. Businesses of all types decline, even the business of barbers. The impacts are real, and they affect all firms, domestic or international, alike.

But how exposed is an individual firm in terms of economic exposure? It is impossible to say. Measuring economic exposure is subjective and, for the most part, depends on the degree of internationalization in the firm's present cost and revenue structure, as well as on potential changes over the long run. But simply because it is difficult to measure does not mean that management cannot take some steps to prepare the firm for the unexpected.

For example, a U.S. exporter like Eastman Kodak pays specific attention to the value of the U.S. dollar. One of Kodak's major competitors is Fuji of Japan. If the value of the Japanese yen rises on world markets versus the U.S. dollar, Fuji's products which are exported to the United States would increase in price, eventually causing a fall in its market share in the United States. Kodak, however, would benefit from the rising value of the yen both in its increased sales in the United States (what Fuji loses Kodak gains) but also in its export sales to Japan. Kodak's exports to Japan would now be cheaper in the eyes of Japanese consumers and its market share in Japan should eventually increase.

Figure 23-4 illustrates this negative relationship between the exchange rate and the value of Kodak as a firm. The value of any firm such as Kodak is simply the present value of all future cash flows. If the spot exchange rate moves from ¥ 120/US$ to ¥ 100/US$, the net cash flows which will flow to Kodak in the future should increase. Therefore, as the value of the U.S. dollar "falls," the value of Kodak as a firm increases.

Effect of Economic Exposure.   The effects of economic exposure are as diverse as firms are in their international structure. Take the case of a U.S. corporation with a successful British subsidiary. The British subsidiary manufactures and then distributes the firm's products in Great Britain, Germany, and France.

The profits of the British subsidiary are paid out annually to the American parent corporation. What would be the impact on the profitability of the British subsidiary and the entire U.S. firm if the British pound suddenly fell in value against all other major currencies (as it did in September and October 1992)?

If the British firm had been facing competition in Germany and France and in its own home market from firms based in those other two continental countries, it would now be more competitive. If the British pound is cheaper, so are the products sold internationally by British-based firms. The British subsidiary of the American firm would, in all likelihood, see rising profits from increased sales.

But what of the value of the British subsidiary to the U.S. parent corporation? The same fall in the British pound which allowed the British subsidiary to gain profits would also result in substantially fewer U.S. dollars when the British pound earnings are converted to U.S. dollars at the end of the year! It seems that it is nearly impossible to win in this situation. Actually, from the perspective of economic exposure management, the fact that the firm's total value—subsidiary and parent together—is roughly a wash as a result of the exchange rate change is desirable. Sound financial management assumes that a firm will profit and bear risk in its line of business, not in the process of settling payments on business already completed.

Economic Exposure Management. Management of economic exposure is being prepared for the unexpected. A firm such as Eastman Kodak which is highly dependent on its ability to remain cost competitive in markets both at home and abroad, may choose to take actions now which would allow it to passively withstand any sudden unexpected rise of the dollar. This could be accomplished through diversification: diversification of operations and diversification of financing.

Diversification of operations would allow the firm to be desensitized to the impacts of any one pair of exchange rate changes. For example, many multinational firms such as Hewlett Packard produce the same products in manufacturing facilities in Singapore, the United States, Puerto Rico, and Europe. If a sudden and prolonged rise in the dollar made production in the United States prohibitively expensive and uncompetitive, they are already *positioned* to shift production to a relatively cheaper currency environment. Although firms rarely diversify production location for the sole purpose of currency diversification, it is a substantial additional benefit from such global expansion.

Diversification of financing serves in hedging economic exposure much in the same way it did with transaction exposures. A firm with debt which is denominated in many different currencies is sensitive to many different interest rates. If one country or currency experiences rapidly rising inflation rates and interest rates, the firm, if diversified, will not be subject to the full impact of such movements. Purely domestic firms, however, are actually somewhat captive to these local conditions and are unable to ride out such interest rate storms as easily.

It should be noted that, in both cases, diversification is a passive solution to the exposure problem. This means that—without knowing when or where or what the problem may be—the firm simply spreads its operations and financial structure out over a variety of countries and currencies to be prepared.

Translation Exposure

Translation exposure results from the conversion or *translation* of foreign currency–denominated financial statements of foreign subsidiaries and affiliates into the home currency of the parent. This is necessary in order to prepare consolidated financial statements for all firms as country law requires. The purpose is to have all operations worldwide stated in the same currency terms for comparison purposes. Management often uses these translated statements to judge the performance of foreign affiliates and their personnel on the same currency terms as the parent itself.

The problem, however, arises from the translation of balance sheets in foreign currencies into the domestic currency. Which assets and liabilities are to be translated at current exchange rates (at the current balance sheet date) versus historical rates (those in effect on the date of the initial investment)? Or should all assets and liabilities be translated at the same rate? The answer is somewhere in between, and the process of translation is dictated by financial accounting standards.

The Current Rate Method. At present in the United States, the proper method for translating foreign financial statements is given in Financial Accounting Standards Board statement No. 52 (FASB #52). According to FASB #52, if a foreign subsidiary is operating in a foreign currency functional environment,[8] most assets, liabilities, and income statement items of foreign affiliates are translated using current exchange rates (the exchange rate in effect on the balance sheet date). For this reason, it is often referred to as the current rate method. Table 23-4 provides an example of how this translation process might work.

A U.S. firm, Walport, established a Canadian subsidiary three years ago. The subsidiary, Walport-Canada, is wholly owned and operated by Walport. The balance sheet of Walport-Canada on December 31, 1992, is shown in Canadian dollars in Column (1) of Table 23-4. In order for Walport to construct a consolidated financial statement, all Walport-Canada's assets and liabilities must be translated into U.S. dollars at the end-of-year exchange rate. This rate is C$ 1.20/US$. All assets and liabilities are translated at the current rate except for equity capital, which is translated at the exchange rate in effect at the time of the Canadian subsidiary's establishment, C$ 1.10/US$. The exchange rates used to translate each individual asset and liability of the Canadian subsidiary are in Column (2).

The U.S. dollar value of all translated assets and liabilities are shown in Column (3). Because all assets and liabilities — except equity capital — were translated at the current rate, an imbalance results. A new account must be created in order for the translated balance sheet to balance. This new account, the cumulative translation adjustment (CTA), takes on a gain or loss value necessary

---

[8]The determination of the "functional currency" of a foreign subsidiary or affiliate operation depends on a number of factors, including the currency which dominates expenses and revenues. If the foreign subsidiary's dominant currency is the local currency, the current rate method of translation is used. If, however, the functional currency of the foreign subsidiary is identified as the currency of the parent, for example, the U.S. dollar, the temporal method of translation is used. The temporal method is that translation procedure which was used in the United States from 1975 to 1981 under FASB #8.

Table 23-4

Translation of a Foreign
Affiliate's Balance Sheet:
Canadian Subsidiary of a
U.S. Firm

	(1) Canadian Dollars (Thousands)	(2) Current Rate C$/US$	(3) U.S. Dollars (Thousands)
Assets			
Cash	120	1.20	100
Accounts payable	240	1.20	200
Inventory	120	1.20	100
Net plant and equipment	480	1.20	400
Total	C$ 960		US$ 800
Liabilities and Net Worth			
Accounts payable	120	1.20	100
Short-term debt	120	1.20	100
Long-term debt	240	1.20	200
Equity capital	480	1.10	436
Cumulative translation adjustment	—	—	(36)
Total	C$ 960		US$ 800

to maintain a balanced translation. Walport-Canada, because the equity capital
was invested when the Canadian dollar was stronger, now represents a CTA
translation loss of US$ 36,000 to the parent company.

But what does this translation loss mean to the company? The CTA account
is an accounting construction. It is created in order to produce a consolidated
balance sheet. Neither the Canadian subsidiary nor the U.S. parent experiences
any cash flow effect as a result of the translation gain or loss. It is quite possible
that consolidation in the following year or years could result in CTA translation
gains which could reduce or even cancel this year's loss.

The translation of the income statement of Walport-Canada offers no such
problems under FASB #52 so that consolidated reporting results in no other
surprises or problems. The CTA account remains a "paper fiction" until the time
the Canadian subsidiary is either sold or liquidated. On the sale or liquidation
of the Canadian subsidiary, the CTA gains or losses attributed to Walport-Canada
must be realized by the parent company. The result is that these gains or losses
are included with other current income of the parent for that period.[9]

Translation Exposure Management. Translation exposure under FASB52
results in no cash flow effects under normal circumstances. Although consolidated accounting does result in CTA translation losses/gains on the parent's consolidated balance sheet, these accounting entries are not ordinarily realized.

---

[9]Prior to the passage of FASB #52, FASB #8 had been the primary directive on translation in the
United States. FASB #8, often termed the monetary/nonmonetary method, differed from FASB #52
in two very important ways: (1) It applied historical exchange rates to several of the long-term asset
categories, normally resulting in a lower net exposed asset position. (2) All translation gains and
losses were passed through the parent's consolidated income for the current period. This resulted
in volatile swings in the critical earnings per share (EPS) reported by multinational firms. Although
this was still only an accounting convention, the volatility introduced to EPS caused much concern
among firms.

Unless liquidation or sale of the subsidiary is anticipated, neither the subsidiary nor the parent firm should expend real resources on the management of an accounting convention.

In the event that the realization of the CTA translation gain or loss is imminent, traditional currency hedging instruments can be used. If Walport planned on liquidating Walport-Canada this year, Walport could use a *forward contract hedge* to protect the firm's income for the period. The value of the forward contract would make up for part of the expected loss if the firm believed the Canadian dollar would be lower than C$ 1.10/US$ by the end of the year. Firms that are more concerned with their CTA position will structure their foreign subsidiaries to reduce the degree of net translation exposure. The primary method for this is the holding of some assets which are not denominated in the functional currency. For example, in the previous Walport-Canada balance sheet shown in Table 23-4, if some portion of cash or accounts payable had been denominated in U.S. dollars rather than Canadian dollars, Walport-Canada's net exposure — its translation loss in this case — would have been less. This restructuring of the foreign subsidiary's balance sheet is termed a *balance sheet hedge*. Although this will protect the parent against translation losses or gains, it is often difficult or costly to achieve in practice.

Self-Test

What risks, particular to foreign currency, must financial managers consider?

Explain the difference between natural and contractual hedging. In what situations would each be used?

Why are all firms affected by economic exposure?

What role does the cumulative translation adjustment play in the consolidation of a multinational firm's financial statements?

Interest Rate and Currency Swaps

One of the most significant developments in international finance in the 1980s was the development of the *interest rate and currency swap market*. Although markets of all kinds — goods, services, labor, and capital — have continued to open up across the world in the past two decades, there are still invisible barriers between many capital markets. Firms operating in their home markets are both helped and hindered; they are well known in their own capital markets but still may not be recognized in other potentially larger capital markets. The interest rate and currency swap markets which developed in the 1980s have allowed firms to arbitrage the differences between markets, using their comparative advantage of borrowing in their home market and swapping for interest rates or currencies which are not as readily accessible.

Interest Rate Swaps

Firms which are considered to be better borrowers in financial markets borrow at lower rates. These lower rates may be lower fixed rates or at lower spreads over floating-rate bases. In fact, lower quality borrowers often are limited in

interest rate swap

The exchange of a fixed interest rate debt-servicing cash flow stream for a floating interest rate debt-servicing cash flow stream (or vice versa), both calculated on the same principal amount.

their choices to floating rates in many markets. The **interest rate swap,** often called the "plain vanilla swap," allows one firm to use its good credit standing to borrow capital at low fixed rates and exchange its interest payments with a slightly lower credit-rated borrower who has debt-service payments at floating rates. Each borrower ends up making net interest payments at rates below those they could have achieved on their own.

If Firm Alpha is considered an extremely sound borrower, it can borrow capital at lower interest rates, probably fixed rates, than a second firm, Zeta. Zeta, although profitable and sound, is simply not as much of a high-quality borrower in the eyes of the financial markets. Zeta must borrow at higher interest rates if borrowing at fixed rates, although it may only be able to currently borrow at floating rates. If each firm were to borrow where it is "well received," using their respective comparative advantages, they may then *swap* or exchange their debt-service payments. Alpha, who has taken on fixed-rate debt-service payments will exchange these payments for Zeta's floating-rate payments. Both companies end up paying less interest in the form which they desired by negotiating rates between themselves which are better than what the markets had offered directly.

Currency Swaps

currency swap

The exchange of debt-service payments denominated in one currency for debt-service payments in a different currency, both calculated on the same principal value based on the spot rate in effect on the initial swap date.

The **currency swap** is the equivalent of the interest rate swap except that the currency of denomination of the debt is different. Many international and multinational firms need capital denominated in different currencies for international investments or even for the purpose of risk management (for natural hedging, as described previously). Foreign firms often find themselves at a disadvantage, however, when trying to enter new markets for the first time. The interest rates available to them in the currencies which they desire may simply not be affordable.

Figure 23-5 illustrates how a currency swap arrangement would work for a Swedish firm desiring U.S. dollar debt and a U.S. firm desiring Swedish krona debt. The mechanics of the swap are actually quite simple. The Swedish firm, Nobel, borrows capital in its home market where it is well known and can obtain capital at attractive interest rates. The U.S. firm, Sioux, also acquires local debt in its own advantaged access market. Then, working through a swap dealer, each firm exchanges the debt-service payment schedule on its own debt for the debt-service payment schedule of the other firm's debt. The principal amounts borrowed must be equal at current exchange rates in order for the swap to be made. The U.S. firm, Sioux, now agrees to make interest payments in Swedish kronor, and the Swedish firm, Nobel, agrees to make U.S. dollar interest payments. The two firms have swapped payment streams.

But what of the risk of nonpayment? If one of the swap parties does not make its agreed-upon payments, who is responsible for meeting the obligations of the original debt agreement? The answer is that the initial borrower is responsible for covering any shortfall or nonpayment by the swap party. This risk, termed **counterparty risk,** is an increasing concern in the interest rate and currency swap markets as more and more firms utilize these markets to manage their debt structures.

counterparty risk

The risk that the other participant or party of a swap agreement will not fulfill their obligations under the swap agreement.

The currency swap market allows any firm to exchange its own comparative advantage in acquiring capital for the advantaged access of another firm in the

Figure 23-5

Sample Currency Swap: Arbitrage between the U.S. Dollar and Swedish Krona Debt Markets

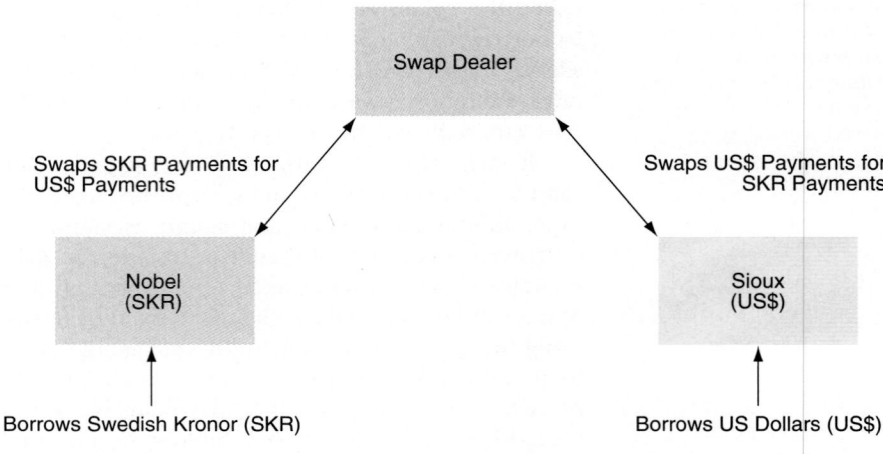

Each firm first acquires debt in its home market, Nobel borrowing Swedish kronor and Sioux borrowing U.S. dollars, and then they "swap" the debt-service payments. Sioux would then make interest payments in Swedish kronor and Nobel would make interest payments in U.S. dollars.

foreign currency market. Both parties benefit from the free exchange of their comparative advantages. Although the currency (or interest rate) swap market is not a source of capital, it is a very important way to change the characteristics of capital.

The swap markets have grown rapidly over the past decade as more and more firms in small and large countries have sought to diversify their operations and their financing. In the early days of the market (the early 1980s), most swaps were literally matched pairs of firms and debt issues as described earlier. The market has since grown and matured to the stage where most firms can now simply contact the swap desk of a major international bank and arrange a swap directly with the bank. The bank is able to find the counterparty for the transaction on its own, without involving the other firm. As more and more firms attempt to expand internationally, the swap market is expected to grow in significance as a means of managing the international financial risks and exposures of the firm.

 Self-Test

What is the interest rate swap?

Why are currency swaps useful in managing international risks?

Summary

This chapter discusses the special issues that a multinational firm must consider as it performs international financial management. The key concepts covered are listed below.

▷ All traditional functional areas of financial management are affected by the internationalization of the firm. Aside from different cultures, languages, governments, and laws, the **existence of different currencies** has the greatest effect on international financial management.

▷ The **exchange rate** is the price of one country's currency in terms of another's.

A **spot rate** is an exchange rate that is established for an immediate transaction. In contrast, a **forward rate** is a contract to exchange currencies at a future date at a specified exchange rate.

The number of units of the "home" country's currency required to purchase one unit of foreign currency is called a **direct quotation,** while the number of units of foreign currency that can be purchased for one unit of the home currency is an **indirect quotation.**

When two currencies are valued against one another without the use of the U.S. dollar, this rate is known as a **cross rate.**

Eurocurrency is a foreign-currency deposit at an institution in a different country from that which issued the currency. These accounts are generally free from any government's restrictions.

LIBOR, the London InterBank Offer Rate, is the most widely used interest rate for international loans.

▷ **Purchasing power parity** is the currency exchange rate theory which professes that the exchange rate between two countries should equalize the price of identical products in those countries.

▷ **International investment** evaluations must consider the effects of currency exchange, government restrictions, and political stability. These factors, combined with capital budgeting issues encountered in regular domestic project analyses, make international investment opportunities more risky.

▷ A multinational firm's **working capital management** involves the careful orchestration of many different cash flows crossing different currencies. Cash flow difficulties can be reduced by cash pooling, netting cash flows, adjusting payment timing, reinvoicing, and establishing an internal bank.

▷ There are three types of **foreign currency exposures,** or effects of currency exchanges, that firms experience in international business.

The most immediate risk to all international firms is **transaction exposure,** which occurs because of the fluctuation of the exchange rate between the issue and fulfillment date of a transaction. This risk can be mitigated by hedging.

Economic exposure, which really affects all businesses, is the change in a firm's value resulting from unexpected changes in exchange rates.

In order to report earnings, a firm must convert all foreign currency–denominated operations into its own currency, causing **translation exposure.** In this translation process, the **current rate method** is used to determine foreign assets and liabilities.

Resolution to
DECISION IN FINANCE

EXCHANGE RATES AND
SMALL-TOWN AMERICA

Changes in the value of foreign currencies alter international trade flows and the international competitiveness of firms. Many of the solutions to the rising value of the Japanese yen for the Troy, Ohio, firms can be observed in the day-to-day business of those benefiting from the yen's appreciation.

For example, Matsushita Electronics Corporation, a subsidiary of Matsushita of Japan, employs thousands of workers along Interstate 75 outside Troy. The same economic and financial forces which have led to declining exports from Matsushita of Japan have led it and similar firms to shift production to other countries such as the United States. Matsushita (U.S.) expects to increase its work force soon, as does Honda Motor Company's parts-distribution plant on I-75. Gokoh Corporation, a parts manufacturer for automobile engines and a supplier to Honda Motor Company, is a regional supplier which also expects to benefit from the shift of production from Japan to the United States.

Many of Troy's workers are quickly learning of the local implications of international events.

Source: "Currency Waves—Global Money Trends Rattle Shop Windows in Heartland America," by Valerie Reitman, *The Wall Street Journal*, Friday, November 26, 1993, A1, A5.

Tommy Moorehead earns $11.24 an hour as a quality inspector for PMI in Troy, and he realizes that if PMI did not earn over 25 percent of its revenues through exports, there would be a lot less to go around, including jobs. Others, however, see the rising value of the yen as a reflection of the unwillingness of many Americans to "buy American," arguing that if people would buy domestically produced goods, there would be a lower level of demand for Japanese goods and the yen would not rise so much. Many of these workers will nevertheless ultimately benefit from the relocation of much of the world's industries and jobs to America itself.

Troy resident Joe Newman knows better than to be sidetracked by the "buy American" debate. Joe has held a wider world view since his days spent recuperating in a Yokosuka, Japan, air force base during the Korean War. Today, Joe is a purchasing agent for Wright Patterson Air Force base. His job requires him to keep track of the yen's movements against the dollar, since he regularly purchases Japanese electronics equipment for the Air Force. "I think it's a good thing to be aware of. Sometimes we fail to look around us and just live in our own little cocoon," he says.

Questions

23-1 When can cross rates result in a profitable currency exchange?

23-2 What is a Eurodollar? If a French citizen deposits $10,000 in Chase Manhattan Bank in New York, have Eurodollars been created? What if the deposit is made in Barclay's Bank in London? Chase Manhattan's Paris branch?

23-3 Exchange rates fluctuate under both the fixed exchange rate and floating exchange rate systems. What, then, is the difference between the two systems?

23-4 Most firms require higher rates of return on foreign projects than on identical projects located at home. Why?

23-5 Why do the domestic parent company and its foreign subsidiaries have different perspectives of the value of a foreign investment?

23-6 Explain the process by which a Danish furniture manufacturer can establish an export relationship with a Chicago-based retail outlet.

Self-Test Problem

ST-1 Merck, the U.S.-based pharmaceutical giant, has a Swiss subsidiary which has had a very profitable year. The subsidiary, Merck-Switzerland, has declared a dividend of 15 million Swiss francs (SFr). The dividend will not, however, be paid to the U.S. parent for 90 days because of Swiss legal restrictions on capital flows. Using the exchange rate quotations on the Swiss franc from Figure 23-1 (Monday's quotes), answer the following questions.

    a. If Merck (U.S.) actually received the Swiss franc dividend payment today, what would its value be in U.S. dollars?

    b. If Merck (U.S.) decided that the risk of leaving the dividend payment uncovered was too large, what would be the U.S. dollar value of the dividend if it was covered with a 90-day forward contract?

    c. What is the percentage gain or loss on the U.S. dollar value of the dividend payment if a 90-day forward contract was used?

    d. Explain why the 90-day forward rate is different from the existing spot rate.

Problems

23-1
Exchange rate
If British pounds sell for $1.68 (U.S.) per pound, what should dollars sell for in pounds per dollar?

23-2
Exchange rates
Table 23-1 lists foreign exchange rates for March 1, 1993. On that day how many dollars would be required to purchase 1,000 units of each of the following: Indian rupees, Italian lira, Japanese yen, Mexican pesos, and Saudi Arabian riyals?

23-3
Exchange rates
Look up the five currencies in Problem 23-2 in the foreign exchange section of a current issue of *The Wall Street Journal*.

    a. What is the current exchange rate for changing dollars into 1,000 units of rupees, lira, yen, pesos, and riyals?

    b. What is the percentage gain or loss between the March 1, 1993, exchange rate and the current exchange rate for each of the currencies in Part a?

23-4
Cross exchange rates
Recently the exchange rate between the U.S. dollar and the French franc was FFr 5.50 = $1, and the exchange rate between the dollar and the British pound was US$ 1.68/STG. What was the exchange rate between francs and pounds?

23-5
Cross exchange rates
Look up the three currencies in Problem 23-4 in the foreign exchange section of a current issue of *The Wall Street Journal*. What is the current exchange rate between francs and pounds?

23-6
Results of exchange rate changes
Early in September 1983, it took 245 Japanese yen to equal $1. Almost ten years later, in June 1993, that exchange rate had fallen to 106 yen to $1. Assume the price of a Japanese-manufactured automobile was $8,000 in September 1983 and that its price changes were in direct relation to exchange rates.

    a. Has the price of the automobile, in dollars, increased or decreased during the ten-year period because of changes in the exchange rate?

    b. What would the dollar price of the automobile be in June 1993, again assuming that the car's price changes only with exchange rates?

23-7
Forward exchange rates
Use Table 23-1 to determine the six-month forward exchange rate of the yen against the U.S. dollar. Is this forward rate more favorable than the spot rate?

Solution to Self-Test Problem

ST-1   **a.** The value of the SFr 15,000,000 dividend payment at the current spot rate of SFr 1.5380/US$ is

$$\frac{\text{SFr } 15,000,000}{\text{SFr } 1.5380/\text{US\$}} = \text{US\$ } 9,752,925.88.$$

b. The value of the SFr 15,000,000 dividend payment at the 90-day forward rate of SFr 1.5465/US$ is

$$\frac{\text{SFr } 15,000,000}{\text{SFr } 1.5465/\text{US\$}} = \text{US\$ } 9,699,321.05.$$

c. The forward contract would assure Merck of receiving $9,699,321.05, which is .55% less than what might be "expected" if the dividend were paid today.

$$\frac{\text{US\$ } 9,699,321.05 - \text{US\$ } 9,752,925.88}{\text{US\$ } 9,752,925.88} \times 100 = -.55\%.$$

d. The 90-day forward rate is calculated from the present spot rate and the Eurocurrency interest rates on U.S. dollars and Swiss francs for the 90-day maturity. Since the forward rate on Swiss francs, SFr 1.5465/US$, indicates a "weaker" rate than the spot rate of SFr 1.5380/US$ (it takes more Swiss francs to buy a dollar at the forward rate), the 90-day Euro-Swiss franc interest rate must be larger than the Eurodollar rate. For example, the 90-day forward rate may be the result of the following two interest rates with the current spot rate:

$$\text{Forward} = \text{SFr } 1.5380/\text{US\$} \left[\frac{1 + 0.06233 \left(\frac{90}{360}\right)}{1 + 0.0400 \left(\frac{90}{360}\right)} \right] = \text{SFr } 1.5465/\text{US\$}.$$

Mathematical Tables

Table A-1   Present Value of $1 Due at the End of n Periods: $PVIF_{k,n} = 1/(1 + k)^n$

Period	1%	2%	3%	4%	5%	6%	7%	8%	9%	10%
1	.9901	.9804	.9709	.9615	.9524	.9434	.9346	.9259	.9174	.9091
2	.9803	.9612	.9426	.9246	.9070	.8900	.8734	.8573	.8417	.8264
3	.9706	.9423	.9151	.8890	.8638	.8396	.8163	.7938	.7722	.7513
4	.9610	.9238	.8885	.8548	.8227	.7921	.7629	.7350	.7084	.6830
5	.9515	.9057	.8626	.8219	.7835	.7473	.7130	.6806	.6499	.6209
6	.9420	.8880	.8375	.7903	.7462	.7050	.6663	.6302	.5963	.5645
7	.9327	.8706	.8131	.7599	.7107	.6651	.6227	.5835	.5470	.5132
8	.9235	.8535	.7894	.7307	.6768	.6274	.5820	.5403	.5019	.4665
9	.9143	.8368	.7664	.7026	.6446	.5919	.5439	.5002	.4604	.4241
10	.9053	.8203	.7441	.6756	.6139	.5584	.5083	.4632	.4224	.3855
11	.8963	.8043	.7224	.6496	.5847	.5268	.4751	.4289	.3875	.3505
12	.8874	.7885	.7014	.6246	.5568	.4970	.4440	.3971	.3555	.3186
13	.8787	.7730	.6810	.6006	.5303	.4688	.4150	.3677	.3262	.2897
14	.8700	.7579	.6611	.5775	.5051	.4423	.3878	.3405	.2992	.2633
15	.8613	.7430	.6419	.5553	.4810	.4173	.3624	.3152	.2745	.2394
16	.8528	.7284	.6232	.5339	.4581	.3936	.3387	.2919	.2519	.2176
17	.8444	.7142	.6050	.5134	.4363	.3714	.3166	.2703	.2311	.1978
18	.8360	.7002	.5874	.4936	.4155	.3503	.2959	.2502	.2120	.1799
19	.8277	.6864	.5703	.4746	.3957	.3305	.2765	.2317	.1945	.1635
20	.8195	.6730	.5537	.4564	.3769	.3118	.2584	.2145	.1784	.1486
21	.8114	.6598	.5375	.4388	.3589	.2942	.2415	.1987	.1637	.1351
22	.8034	.6468	.5219	.4220	.3418	.2775	.2257	.1839	.1502	.1228
23	.7954	.6342	.5067	.4057	.3256	.2618	.2109	.1703	.1378	.1117
24	.7876	.6217	.4919	.3901	.3101	.2470	.1971	.1577	.1264	.1015
25	.7798	.6095	.4776	.3751	.2953	.2330	.1842	.1460	.1160	.0923
26	.7720	.5976	.4637	.3607	.2812	.2198	.1722	.1352	.1064	.0839
27	.7644	.5859	.4502	.3468	.2678	.2074	.1609	.1252	.0976	.0763
28	.7568	.5744	.4371	.3335	.2551	.1956	.1504	.1159	.0895	.0693
29	.7493	.5631	.4243	.3207	.2429	.1846	.1406	.1073	.0822	.0630
30	.7419	.5521	.4120	.3083	.2314	.1741	.1314	.0994	.0754	.0573
35	.7059	.5000	.3554	.2534	.1813	.1301	.0937	.0676	.0490	.0356
40	.6717	.4529	.3066	.2083	.1420	.0972	.0668	.0460	.0318	.0221
45	.6391	.4102	.2644	.1712	.1113	.0727	.0476	.0313	.0207	.0137
50	.6080	.3715	.2281	.1407	.0872	.0543	.0339	.0213	.0134	.0085
55	.5785	.3365	.1968	.1157	.0683	.0406	.0242	.0145	.0087	.0053

Period	12%	14%	15%	16%	18%	20%	24%	28%	32%	36%
1	.8929	.8772	.8696	.8621	.8475	.8333	.8065	.7813	.7576	.7353
2	.7972	.7695	.7561	.7432	.7182	.6944	.6504	.6104	.5739	.5407
3	.7118	.6750	.6575	.6407	.6086	.5787	.5245	.4768	.4348	.3975
4	.6355	.5921	.5718	.5523	.5158	.4823	.4230	.3725	.3294	.2923
5	.5674	.5194	.4972	.4761	.4371	.4019	.3411	.2910	.2495	.2149
6	.5066	.4556	.4323	.4104	.3704	.3349	.2751	.2274	.1890	.1580
7	.4523	.3996	.3759	.3538	.3139	.2791	.2218	.1776	.1432	.1162
8	.4039	.3506	.3269	.3050	.2660	.2326	.1789	.1388	.1085	.0854
9	.3606	.3075	.2843	.2630	.2255	.1938	.1443	.1084	.0822	.0628
10	.3220	.2697	.2472	.2267	.1911	.1615	.1164	.0847	.0623	.0462
11	.2875	.2366	.2149	.1954	.1619	.1346	.0938	.0662	.0472	.0340
12	.2567	.2076	.1869	.1685	.1372	.1122	.0757	.0517	.0357	.0250
13	.2292	.1821	.1625	.1452	.1163	.0935	.0610	.0404	.0271	.0184
14	.2046	.1597	.1413	.1252	.0985	.0779	.0492	.0316	.0205	.0135
15	.1827	.1401	.1229	.1079	.0835	.0649	.0397	.0247	.0155	.0099
16	.1631	.1229	.1069	.0930	.0708	.0541	.0320	.0193	.0118	.0073
17	.1456	.1078	.0929	.0802	.0600	.0451	.0258	.0150	.0089	.0054
18	.1300	.0946	.0808	.0691	.0508	.0376	.0208	.0118	.0068	.0039
19	.1161	.0829	.0703	.0596	.0431	.0313	.0168	.0092	.0051	.0029
20	.1037	.0728	.0611	.0514	.0365	.0261	.0135	.0072	.0039	.0021
21	.0926	.0638	.0531	.0443	.0309	.0217	.0109	.0056	.0029	.0016
22	.0826	.0560	.0462	.0382	.0262	.0181	.0088	.0044	.0022	.0012
23	.0738	.0491	.0402	.0329	.0222	.0151	.0071	.0034	.0017	.0008
24	.0659	.0431	.0349	.0284	.0188	.0126	.0057	.0027	.0013	.0006
25	.0588	.0378	.0304	.0245	.0160	.0105	.0046	.0021	.0010	.0005
26	.0525	.0331	.0264	.0211	.0135	.0087	.0037	.0016	.0007	.0003
27	.0469	.0291	.0230	.0182	.0115	.0073	.0030	.0013	.0006	.0002
28	.0419	.0255	.0200	.0157	.0097	.0061	.0024	.0010	.0004	.0002
29	.0374	.0224	.0174	.0135	.0082	.0051	.0020	.0008	.0003	.0001
30	.0334	.0196	.0151	.0116	.0070	.0042	.0016	.0006	.0002	.0001
35	.0189	.0102	.0075	.0055	.0030	.0017	.0005	.0002	.0001	*
40	.0107	.0053	.0037	.0026	.0013	.0007	.0002	.0001	*	*
45	.0061	.0027	.0019	.0013	.0006	.0003	.0001	*	*	*
50	.0035	.0014	.0009	.0006	.0003	.0001	*	*	*	*
55	.0020	.0007	.0005	.0003	.0001	*	*	*	*	*

*The factor is zero to four decimal places.

Table A-2   Present Value of an Annuity of $1 per Period for n Periods:

$$\text{PVIFA}_{k,n} = \sum_{t=1}^{n} \frac{1}{(1+k)^t} = \frac{1 - \dfrac{1}{(1+k)^n}}{k}$$

Number of Periods	1%	2%	3%	4%	5%	6%	7%	8%	9%
1	0.9901	0.9804	0.9709	0.9615	0.9524	0.9434	0.9346	0.9259	0.9174
2	1.9704	1.9416	1.9135	1.8861	1.8594	1.8334	1.8080	1.7833	1.7591
3	2.9410	2.8839	2.8286	2.7751	2.7232	2.6730	2.6243	2.5771	2.5313
4	3.9020	3.8077	3.7171	3.6299	3.5460	3.4651	3.3872	3.3121	3.2397
5	4.8534	4.7135	4.5797	4.4518	4.3295	4.2124	4.1002	3.9927	3.8897
6	5.7955	5.6014	5.4172	5.2421	5.0757	4.9173	4.7665	4.6229	4.4859
7	6.7282	6.4720	6.2303	6.0021	5.7864	5.5824	5.3893	5.2064	5.0330
8	7.6517	7.3255	7.0197	6.7327	6.4632	6.2098	5.9713	5.7466	5.5348
9	8.5660	8.1622	7.7861	7.4353	7.1078	6.8017	6.5152	6.2469	5.9952
10	9.4713	8.9826	8.5302	8.1109	7.7217	7.3601	7.0236	6.7101	6.4177
11	10.3676	9.7868	9.2526	8.7605	8.3064	7.8869	7.4987	7.1390	6.8052
12	11.2551	10.5753	9.9540	9.3851	8.8633	8.3838	7.9427	7.5361	7.1607
13	12.1337	11.3484	10.6350	9.9856	9.3936	8.8527	8.3577	7.9038	7.4869
14	13.0037	12.1062	11.2961	10.5631	9.8986	9.2950	8.7455	8.2442	7.7862
15	13.8651	12.8493	11.9379	11.1184	10.3797	9.7122	9.1079	8.5595	8.0607
16	14.7179	13.5777	12.5611	11.6523	10.8378	10.1059	9.4466	8.8514	8.3126
17	15.5623	14.2919	13.1661	12.1657	11.2741	10.4773	9.7632	9.1216	8.5436
18	16.3983	14.9920	13.7535	12.6593	11.6896	10.8276	10.0591	9.3719	8.7556
19	17.2260	15.6785	14.3238	13.1339	12.0853	11.1581	10.3356	9.6036	8.9501
20	18.0456	16.3514	14.8775	13.5903	12.4622	11.4699	10.5940	9.8181	9.1285
21	18.8570	17.0112	15.4150	14.0292	12.8212	11.7641	10.8355	10.0168	9.2922
22	19.6604	17.6580	15.9369	14.4511	13.1630	12.0416	11.0612	10.2007	9.4424
23	20.4558	18.2922	16.4436	14.8568	13.4886	12.3034	11.2722	10.3711	9.5802
24	21.2434	18.9139	16.9355	15.2470	13.7986	12.5504	11.4693	10.5288	9.7066
25	22.0232	19.5235	17.4131	15.6221	14.0939	12.7834	11.6536	10.6748	9.8226
26	22.7952	20.1210	17.8768	15.9828	14.3752	13.0032	11.8258	10.8100	9.9290
27	23.5596	20.7069	18.3270	16.3296	14.6430	13.2105	11.9867	10.9352	10.0266
28	24.3164	21.2813	18.7641	16.6631	14.8981	13.4062	12.1371	11.0511	10.1161
29	25.0658	21.8444	19.1885	16.9837	15.1411	13.5907	12.2777	11.1584	10.1983
30	25.8077	22.3965	19.6004	17.2920	15.3725	13.7648	12.4090	11.2578	10.2737
35	29.4086	24.9986	21.4872	18.6646	16.3742	14.4982	12.9477	11.6546	10.5668
40	32.8347	27.3555	23.1148	19.7928	17.1591	15.0463	13.3317	11.9246	10.7574
45	36.0945	29.4902	24.5187	20.7200	17.7741	15.4558	13.6055	12.1084	10.8812
50	39.1961	31.4236	25.7298	21.4822	18.2559	15.7619	13.8007	12.2335	10.9617
55	42.1472	33.1748	26.7744	22.1086	18.6335	15.9905	13.9399	12.3186	11.0140

Number of Periods	10%	12%	14%	15%	16%	18%	20%	24%	28%	32%
1	0.9091	0.8929	0.8772	0.8696	0.8621	0.8475	0.8333	0.8065	0.7813	0.7576
2	1.7355	1.6901	1.6467	1.6257	1.6052	1.5656	1.5278	1.4568	1.3916	1.3315
3	2.4869	2.4018	2.3216	2.2832	2.2459	2.1743	2.1065	1.9813	1.8684	1.7663
4	3.1699	3.0373	2.9137	2.8550	2.7982	2.6901	2.5887	2.4043	2.2410	2.0957
5	3.7908	3.6048	3.4331	3.3522	3.2743	3.1272	2.9906	2.7454	2.5320	2.3452
6	4.3553	4.1114	3.8887	3.7845	3.6847	3.4976	3.3255	3.0205	2.7594	2.5342
7	4.8684	4.5638	4.2883	4.1604	4.0386	3.8115	3.6046	3.2423	2.9370	2.6775
8	5.3349	4.9676	4.6389	4.4873	4.3436	4.0776	3.8372	3.4212	3.0758	2.7860
9	5.7590	5.3282	4.9464	4.7716	4.6065	4.3030	4.0310	3.5655	3.1842	2.8681
10	6.1446	5.6502	5.2161	5.0188	4.8332	4.4941	4.1925	3.6819	3.2689	2.9304
11	6.4951	5.9377	5.4527	5.2337	5.0286	4.6560	4.3271	3.7757	3.3351	2.9776
12	6.8137	6.1944	5.6603	5.4206	5.1971	4.7932	4.4392	3.8514	3.3868	3.0133
13	7.1034	6.4235	5.8424	5.5831	5.3423	4.9095	4.5327	3.9124	3.4272	3.0404
14	7.3667	6.6282	6.0021	5.7245	5.4675	5.0081	4.6106	3.9616	3.4587	3.0609
15	7.6061	6.8109	6.1422	5.8474	5.5755	5.0916	4.6755	4.0013	3.4834	3.0764
16	7.8237	6.9740	6.2651	5.9542	5.6685	5.1624	4.7296	4.0333	3.5026	3.0882
17	8.0216	7.1196	6.3729	6.0472	5.7487	5.2223	4.7746	4.0591	3.5177	3.0971
18	8.2014	7.2497	6.4674	6.1280	5.8178	5.2732	4.8122	4.0799	3.5294	3.1039
19	8.3649	7.3658	6.5504	6.1982	5.8775	5.3162	4.8435	4.0967	3.5386	3.1090
20	8.5136	7.4694	6.6231	6.2593	5.9288	5.3527	4.8696	4.1103	3.5458	3.1129
21	8.6487	7.5620	6.6870	6.3125	5.9731	5.3837	4.8913	4.1212	3.5514	3.1158
22	8.7715	7.6446	6.7429	6.3587	6.0113	5.4099	4.9094	4.1300	3.5558	3.1180
23	8.8832	7.7184	6.7921	6.3988	6.0442	5.4321	4.9245	4.1371	3.5592	3.1197
24	8.9847	7.7843	6.8351	6.4338	6.0726	5.4509	4.9371	4.1428	3.5619	3.1210
25	9.0770	7.8431	6.8729	6.4641	6.0971	5.4669	4.9476	4.1474	3.5640	3.1220
26	9.1609	7.8957	6.9061	6.4906	6.1182	5.4804	4.9563	4.1511	3.5656	3.1227
27	9.2372	7.9426	6.9352	6.5135	6.1364	5.4919	4.9636	4.1542	3.5669	3.1233
28	9.3066	7.9844	6.9607	6.5335	6.1520	5.5016	4.9697	4.1566	3.5679	3.1237
29	9.3696	8.0218	6.9830	6.5509	6.1656	5.5098	4.9747	4.1585	3.5687	3.1240
30	9.4269	8.0552	7.0027	6.5660	6.1772	5.5168	4.9789	4.1601	3.5693	3.1242
35	9.6442	8.1755	7.0700	6.6166	6.2153	5.5386	4.9915	4.1644	3.5708	3.1248
40	9.7791	8.2438	7.1050	6.6418	6.2335	5.5482	4.9966	4.1659	3.5712	3.1250
45	9.8628	8.2825	7.1232	6.6543	6.2421	5.5523	4.9986	4.1664	3.5714	3.1250
50	9.9148	8.3045	7.1327	6.6605	6.2463	5.5541	4.9995	4.1666	3.5714	3.1250
55	9.9471	8.3170	7.1376	6.6636	6.2482	5.5549	4.9998	4.1666	3.5714	3.1250

Table A-3   Future Value of $1 at the End of n Periods: $FVIF_{k,n} = (1 + k)^n$

Period	1%	2%	3%	4%	5%	6%	7%	8%	9%	10%
1	1.0100	1.0200	1.0300	1.0400	1.0500	1.0600	1.0700	1.0800	1.0900	1.1000
2	1.0201	1.0404	1.0609	1.0816	1.1025	1.1236	1.1449	1.1664	1.1881	1.2100
3	1.0303	1.0612	1.0927	1.1249	1.1576	1.1910	1.2250	1.2597	1.2950	1.3310
4	1.0406	1.0824	1.1255	1.1699	1.2155	1.2625	1.3108	1.3605	1.4116	1.4641
5	1.0510	1.1041	1.1593	1.2167	1.2763	1.3382	1.4026	1.4693	1.5386	1.6105
6	1.0615	1.1262	1.1941	1.2653	1.3401	1.4185	1.5007	1.5869	1.6771	1.7716
7	1.0721	1.1487	1.2299	1.3159	1.4071	1.5036	1.6058	1.7138	1.8280	1.9487
8	1.0829	1.1717	1.2668	1.3686	1.4775	1.5938	1.7182	1.8509	1.9926	2.1436
9	1.0937	1.1951	1.3048	1.4233	1.5513	1.6895	1.8385	1.9990	2.1719	2.3579
10	1.1046	1.2190	1.3439	1.4802	1.6289	1.7908	1.9672	2.1589	2.3674	2.5937
11	1.1157	1.2434	1.3842	1.5395	1.7103	1.8983	2.1049	2.3316	2.5804	2.8531
12	1.1268	1.2682	1.4258	1.6010	1.7959	2.0122	2.2522	2.5182	2.8127	3.1384
13	1.1381	1.2936	1.4685	1.6651	1.8856	2.1329	2.4098	2.7196	3.0658	3.4523
14	1.1495	1.3195	1.5126	1.7317	1.9799	2.2609	2.5785	2.9372	3.3417	3.7975
15	1.1610	1.3459	1.5580	1.8009	2.0789	2.3966	2.7590	3.1722	3.6425	4.1772
16	1.1726	1.3728	1.6047	1.8730	2.1829	2.5404	2.9522	3.4259	3.9703	4.5950
17	1.1843	1.4002	1.6528	1.9479	2.2920	2.6928	3.1588	3.7000	4.3276	5.0545
18	1.1961	1.4282	1.7024	2.0258	2.4066	2.8543	3.3799	3.9960	4.7171	5.5599
19	1.2081	1.4568	1.7535	2.1068	2.5270	3.0256	3.6165	4.3157	5.1417	6.1159
20	1.2202	1.4859	1.8061	2.1911	2.6533	3.2071	3.8697	4.6610	5.6044	6.7275
21	1.2324	1.5157	1.8603	2.2788	2.7860	3.3996	4.1406	5.0338	6.1088	7.4002
22	1.2447	1.5460	1.9161	2.3699	2.9253	3.6035	4.4304	5.4365	6.6586	8.1403
23	1.2572	1.5769	1.9736	2.4647	3.0715	3.8197	4.7405	5.8715	7.2579	8.9543
24	1.2697	1.6084	2.0328	2.5633	3.2251	4.0489	5.0724	6.3412	7.9111	9.8497
25	1.2824	1.6406	2.0938	2.6658	3.3864	4.2919	5.4274	6.8485	8.6231	10.835
26	1.2953	1.6734	2.1566	2.7725	3.5557	4.5494	5.8074	7.3964	9.3992	11.918
27	1.3082	1.7069	2.2213	2.8834	3.7335	4.8223	6.2139	7.9881	10.245	13.110
28	1.3213	1.7410	2.2879	2.9987	3.9201	5.1117	6.6488	8.6271	11.167	14.421
29	1.3345	1.7758	2.3566	3.1187	4.1161	5.4184	7.1143	9.3173	12.172	15.863
30	1.3478	1.8114	2.4273	3.2434	4.3219	5.7435	7.6123	10.063	13.268	17.449
40	1.4889	2.2080	3.2620	4.8010	7.0400	10.286	14.974	21.725	31.409	45.259
50	1.6446	2.6916	4.3839	7.1067	11.467	18.420	29.457	46.902	74.358	117.39
60	1.8167	3.2810	5.8916	10.520	18.679	32.988	57.946	101.26	176.03	304.48

Period	12%	14%	15%	16%	18%	20%	24%	28%	32%	36%
1	1.1200	1.1400	1.1500	1.1600	1.1800	1.2000	1.2400	1.2800	1.3200	1.3600
2	1.2544	1.2996	1.3225	1.3456	1.3924	1.4400	1.5376	1.6384	1.7424	1.8496
3	1.4049	1.4815	1.5209	1.5609	1.6430	1.7280	1.9066	2.0972	2.3000	2.5155
4	1.5735	1.6890	1.7490	1.8106	1.9388	2.0736	2.3642	2.6844	3.0360	3.4210
5	1.7623	1.9254	2.0114	2.1003	2.2878	2.4883	2.9316	3.4360	4.0075	4.6526
6	1.9738	2.1950	2.3131	2.4364	2.6996	2.9860	3.6352	4.3980	5.2899	6.3275
7	2.2107	2.5023	2.6600	2.8262	3.1855	3.5832	4.5077	5.6295	6.9826	8.6054
8	2.4760	2.8526	3.0590	3.2784	3.7589	4.2998	5.5895	7.2058	9.2170	11.703
9	2.7731	3.2519	3.5179	3.8030	4.4355	5.1598	6.9310	9.2234	12.166	15.917
10	3.1058	3.7072	4.0456	4.4114	5.2338	6.1917	8.5944	11.806	16.060	21.647
11	3.4785	4.2262	4.6524	5.1173	6.1759	7.4301	10.657	15.112	21.199	29.439
12	3.8960	4.8179	5.3503	5.9360	7.2876	8.9161	13.215	19.343	27.983	40.037
13	4.3635	5.4924	6.1528	6.8858	8.5994	10.699	16.386	24.759	36.937	54.451
14	4.8871	6.2613	7.0757	7.9875	10.147	12.839	20.319	31.691	48.757	74.053
15	5.4736	7.1379	8.1371	9.2655	11.974	15.407	25.196	40.565	64.359	100.71
16	6.1304	8.1372	9.3576	10.748	14.129	18.488	31.243	51.923	84.954	136.97
17	6.8660	9.2765	10.761	12.468	16.672	22.186	38.741	66.461	112.14	186.28
18	7.6900	10.575	12.375	14.463	19.673	26.623	48.039	85.071	148.02	253.34
19	8.6128	12.056	14.232	16.777	23.214	31.948	59.568	108.89	195.39	344.54
20	9.6463	13.743	16.367	19.461	27.393	38.338	73.864	139.38	257.92	468.57
21	10.804	15.668	18.822	22.574	32.324	46.005	91.592	178.41	340.45	637.26
22	12.100	17.861	21.645	26.186	38.142	55.206	113.57	228.36	449.39	866.67
23	13.552	20.362	24.891	30.376	45.008	66.247	140.83	292.30	593.20	1178.7
24	15.179	23.212	28.625	35.236	53.109	79.497	174.63	374.14	783.02	1603.0
25	17.000	26.462	32.919	40.874	62.669	95.396	216.54	478.90	1033.6	2180.1
26	19.040	30.167	37.857	47.414	73.949	114.48	268.51	613.00	1364.3	2964.9
27	21.325	34.390	43.535	55.000	87.260	137.37	332.95	784.64	1800.9	4032.3
28	23.884	39.204	50.066	63.800	102.97	164.84	412.86	1004.3	2377.2	5483.9
29	26.750	44.693	57.575	74.009	121.50	197.81	511.95	1285.6	3137.9	7458.1
30	29.960	50.950	66.212	85.850	143.37	237.38	634.82	1645.5	4142.1	10143.
40	93.051	188.88	267.86	378.72	750.38	1469.8	5455.9	19427.	66521.	*
50	289.00	700.23	1083.7	1670.7	3927.4	9100.4	46890.	*	*	*
60	897.60	2595.9	4384.0	7370.2	20555.	56348.	*	*	*	*

*$FVIF_{k,n} > 99{,}999$.

Table A-4   Future Value of an Annuity of $1 per Period for n Periods:

$$\text{FVIFA}_{k,n} = \sum_{t=1}^{n} (1 + k)^{n-t} = \frac{(1 + k)^n - 1}{k}$$

Number of Periods	1%	2%	3%	4%	5%	6%	7%	8%	9%	10%
1	1.0000	1.0000	1.0000	1.0000	1.0000	1.0000	1.0000	1.0000	1.0000	1.0000
2	2.0100	2.0200	2.0300	2.0400	2.0500	2.0600	2.0700	2.0800	2.0900	2.1000
3	3.0301	3.0604	3.0909	3.1216	3.1525	3.1836	3.2149	3.2464	3.2781	3.3100
4	4.0604	4.1216	4.1836	4.2465	4.3101	4.3746	4.4399	4.5061	4.5731	4.6410
5	5.1010	5.2040	5.3091	5.4163	5.5256	5.6371	5.7507	5.8666	5.9847	6.1051
6	6.1520	6.3081	6.4684	6.6330	6.8019	6.9753	7.1533	7.3359	7.5233	7.7156
7	7.2135	7.4343	7.6625	7.8983	8.1420	8.3938	8.6540	8.9228	9.2004	9.4872
8	8.2857	8.5830	8.8923	9.2142	9.5491	9.8975	10.260	10.637	11.028	11.436
9	9.3685	9.7546	10.159	10.583	11.027	11.491	11.978	12.488	13.021	13.579
10	10.462	10.950	11.464	12.006	12.578	13.181	13.816	14.487	15.193	15.937
11	11.567	12.169	12.808	13.486	14.207	14.972	15.784	16.645	17.560	18.531
12	12.683	13.412	14.192	15.026	15.917	16.870	17.888	18.977	20.141	21.384
13	13.809	14.680	15.618	16.627	17.713	18.882	20.141	21.495	22.953	24.523
14	14.947	15.974	17.086	18.292	19.599	21.015	22.550	24.215	26.019	27.975
15	16.097	17.293	18.599	20.024	21.579	23.276	25.129	27.152	29.361	31.772
16	17.258	18.639	20.157	21.825	23.657	25.673	27.888	30.324	33.003	35.950
17	18.430	20.012	21.762	23.698	25.840	28.213	30.840	33.750	36.974	40.545
18	19.615	21.412	23.414	25.645	28.132	30.906	33.999	37.450	41.301	45.599
19	20.811	22.841	25.117	27.671	30.539	33.760	37.379	41.446	46.018	51.159
20	22.019	24.297	26.870	29.778	33.066	36.786	40.995	45.762	51.160	57.275
21	23.239	25.783	28.676	31.969	35.719	39.993	44.865	50.423	56.765	64.002
22	24.472	27.299	30.537	34.248	38.505	43.392	49.006	55.457	62.873	71.403
23	25.716	28.845	32.453	36.618	41.430	46.996	53.436	60.893	69.532	79.543
24	26.973	30.422	34.426	39.083	44.502	50.816	58.177	66.765	76.790	88.497
25	28.243	32.030	36.459	41.646	47.727	54.865	63.249	73.106	84.701	98.347
26	29.526	33.671	38.553	44.312	51.113	59.156	68.676	79.954	93.324	109.18
27	30.821	35.344	40.710	47.084	54.669	63.706	74.484	87.351	102.72	121.10
28	32.129	37.051	42.931	49.968	58.403	68.528	80.698	95.339	112.97	134.21
29	33.450	38.792	45.219	52.966	62.323	73.640	87.347	103.97	124.14	148.63
30	34.785	40.568	47.575	56.085	66.439	79.058	94.461	113.28	136.31	164.49
40	48.886	60.402	75.401	95.026	120.80	154.76	199.64	259.06	337.88	442.59
50	64.463	84.579	112.80	152.67	209.35	290.34	406.53	573.77	815.08	1163.9
60	81.670	114.05	163.05	237.99	353.58	533.13	813.52	1253.2	1944.8	3034.8

Number of Periods	12%	14%	15%	16%	18%	20%	24%	28%	32%	36%
1	1.0000	1.0000	1.0000	1.0000	1.0000	1.0000	1.0000	1.0000	1.0000	1.0000
2	2.1200	2.1400	2.1500	2.1600	2.1800	2.2000	2.2400	2.2800	2.3200	2.3600
3	3.3744	3.4396	3.4725	3.5056	3.5724	3.6400	3.7776	3.9184	4.0624	4.2096
4	4.7793	4.9211	4.9934	5.0665	5.2154	5.3680	5.6842	6.0156	6.3624	6.7251
5	6.3528	6.6101	6.7424	6.8771	7.1542	7.4416	8.0484	8.6999	9.3983	10.146
6	8.1152	8.5355	8.7537	8.9775	9.4420	9.9299	10.980	12.136	13.406	14.799
7	10.089	10.730	11.067	11.414	12.142	12.916	14.615	16.534	18.696	21.126
8	12.300	13.233	13.727	14.240	15.327	16.499	19.123	22.163	25.678	29.732
9	14.776	16.085	16.786	17.519	19.086	20.799	24.712	29.369	34.895	41.435
10	17.549	19.337	20.304	21.321	23.521	25.959	31.643	38.593	47.062	57.352
11	20.655	23.045	24.349	25.733	28.755	32.150	40.238	50.398	63.122	78.998
12	24.133	27.271	29.002	30.850	34.931	39.581	50.895	65.510	84.320	108.44
13	28.029	32.089	34.352	36.786	42.219	48.497	64.110	84.853	112.30	148.47
14	32.393	37.581	40.505	43.672	50.818	59.196	80.496	109.61	149.24	202.93
15	37.280	43.842	47.580	51.660	60.965	72.035	100.82	141.30	198.00	276.98
16	42.753	50.980	55.717	60.925	72.939	87.442	126.01	181.87	262.36	377.69
17	48.884	59.118	65.075	71.673	87.068	105.93	157.25	233.79	347.31	514.66
18	55.750	68.394	75.836	84.141	103.74	128.12	195.99	300.25	459.45	700.94
19	63.440	78.969	88.212	98.603	123.41	154.74	244.03	385.32	607.47	954.28
20	72.052	91.025	102.44	115.38	146.63	186.69	303.60	494.21	802.86	1298.8
21	81.699	104.77	118.81	134.84	174.02	225.03	377.46	633.59	1060.8	1767.4
22	92.503	120.44	137.63	157.41	206.34	271.03	469.06	812.00	1401.2	2404.7
23	104.60	138.30	159.28	183.60	244.49	326.24	582.63	1040.4	1850.6	3271.3
24	118.16	158.66	184.17	213.98	289.49	392.48	723.46	1332.7	2443.8	4450.0
25	133.33	181.87	212.79	249.21	342.60	471.98	898.09	1706.8	3226.8	6053.0
26	150.33	208.33	245.71	290.09	405.27	567.38	1114.6	2185.7	4260.4	8233.1
27	169.37	238.50	283.57	337.50	479.22	681.85	1383.1	2798.7	5624.8	11198.0
28	190.70	272.89	327.10	392.50	566.48	819.22	1716.1	3583.3	7425.7	15230.3
29	214.58	312.09	377.17	456.30	669.45	984.07	2129.0	4587.7	9802.9	20714.2
30	241.33	356.79	434.75	530.31	790.95	1181.9	2640.9	5873.2	12941.	28172.3
40	767.09	1342.0	1779.1	2360.8	4163.2	7343.9	22729.	69377.	*	*
50	2400.0	4994.5	7217.7	10436.	21813.	45497.	*	*	*	*
60	7471.6	18535.	29220.	46058.	*	*	*	*	*	*

*$FVIFA_{k,n} > 99,999$.

Answers to Selected
End-of-Chapter Problems

In this appendix we present some intermediate steps and final answers to selected end-of-chapter problems. Please note that your answer may differ slightly from ours due to rounding errors. Also, although we hope not, some of the problems may have more than one correct solution, depending on the assumptions made in working the problem. Finally, many of the problems involve some verbal discussion as well as numerical calculations; that verbal material is not presented here.

2-1   **a.** $41,750
      b. 27.83%
      c. 39%

2-2   **a.** $26,150
      b. $11,700
      c. $3,510

2-3 $339,000

2-4 $920

2-6   **a.** $50,150
      b. $11,169
      c. 22.27%
      d. 28%

2-7   1993 refund = $180,000

2-8   **a.** $23,392
      b. Marginal rate = 31%;
         Average rate = 25.92%
      d. 25%

2-9 $53,000; $77,000; $34,000;
      $19,000; $11,000; $6,000

2-10   **a.** $33,000; $45,000; $15,000
      b. $5,250; $6,000; $32,000

3-1   **b.** $800,000,000

3-2   **b.** $50,000,000

4-1   **a.** $k_1 = 10.2\%$; $k_5 = 9.6\%$;
         $k_{20} = 9.9\%$

4-4 $IP_2 = 10\%$; k_1 in Year 2 = 13%

4-5   **a.** k_1 in Year 2 = 5.5%
      b. $IP_1 = 3\%$; $IP_2 = 4.5\%$

5-2 $3,990

5-3   **a.** $44,800

5-4   **a.** $300,000
      b. $375,000
      c. $500,000

5-5   **a.** $72,078
      c. $231,078

5-7   **a.** $1.80
      b. $1.00
      c. $4,000

5-8   CS = $10,000,000; Paid-in capital = $14,400,000; Total equity = $66,800,000

5-9   **a.** $5.79
      b. $3.35
      c. RE = $54,600,000

5-10 $1,181,250

5-12 **a.** $0
         b. + $700,000
         c. + Profit
         d. + Profit
         e. − $200,000
         f. − $50,000

5-13 **a.** $790,000,000
         b. $3.00

5-14 − $60

5-15 − $900,000

5-16 Total sources: $640

5-17 Total sources = $117 million

6-1   11.2%

6-2   14.4%

6-3   75%

6-4   4%

6-5   38 days

6-6   3×; 120 days

6-7   **a.** 49 days
         b. 54.44 days

6-8 $500,000; quick ratio = 1.2×

6-9 $1,250,000

6-10 $525,000

6-11 13.9×; 2.1×

6-12 17.6%

6-13 4.17%; 40%

6-14 $2,880,000; DSO = 25 days

6-15 Net fixed assets = $400,000;
         Total assets = $1,200,000;
         CL = $320,000;
         A/R = $250,000;
         Total debt = $540,000;
         RE = $560,000

6-16 **a.** Current ratio 1.98; DSO = 75 days; Total assets turnover = 1.7; Debt ratio = 61.9%

6-17 **a.** TIE = 6.2×; S/TA = 1.6×; ROA = 4.5%

6-18 **a.** Inv. = $2,500; RE = $7,500; Interest expense = $2,500

6-19 **a.** 16%
         b. ROE = 20.99%

6-20 **a.** Quick ratio = 0.8; DSO = 37 days; ROE = 9.1%; Debt ratio = 56.4%

7-1   **a.** TA = $10.8 million
         b. $5.04 million

7-2   **a.** Total debt = $1,960,000
         b. $240,000

7-3   **a.** $370,000
         b. $81,000; $289,000
         c. 58.18%
         d. Current ratio = 1.66
         e. ROA = 5.45%

7-4   **a.** $220,000
         b. $81,000; $139,000
         c. 53.48%
         d. Current ratio = 1.95
         e. 6.07%

7-5   6.38%

7-6   **a.** $1,050,000

7-7 $6,750,000 excess funds

7-8 $28,000 excess funds

7-10 $1,200,000

7-11 **a.** $110,925
         c. 4.6%; 55%

7-12 $69,000,000

7-13 **a.** $15,825,000
         c. Current ratio = 1.89; ROE = 14.62%
         d. (1) $8,475,000 excess funds
               (3) Current ratio = 3.71; ROE = 11.11%

7-14 **b.** $1,080,000

7-15 **b.** 25% sales increase
c. $5,400,000
d. 10.64%

7-16 **b.** $103,500
d. 3.03%

8-1 **a.** $1,800,000
b. $1,220,000

8-2 **a.** 86 days
b. $468,000
c. 5 times

8-3 **a.** $220,000
c. $8.6 \times$

8-4 **a.** 26.13%

8-6 **a.** 45 days
b. $405,000
c. $45,000
d. 42 days; $504,000

8-7 **a.** 11.88%; 13.32%
b. 10.92%; 9.48%

8-8 **a.** Current ratio = 1.6;
NWC = $3,750,000;
ROE = 13.33%
b. Current ratio = 2.4;
NWC = $8,750,000;
ROE = 10.75%

8-9 **a.** Plan 1: Current ratio =
1.0; NWC = $0;
D/TA = 0.48; ROE =
13.27%
Plan 2: Current ratio =
3.0; NWC = $3,000,000;
D/TA = 0.48; ROE =
12.30%

8-10 **a.** Inventory turnover =
$6.67 \times$
b. Inventory turnover period
= 54 days
c. DSO = 62 days
d. Cash cycle = 81 days
e. ROA = 10%

8-11 **a.** $400,000
b. $420,000
c. 47 days
d. ROA = 11.87%

8-12 **a.** 56 days
b. $1.875 \times$; 11.25%
c. 41 days; $2.03 \times$; 12.2%

9-1 **b.** (1) $1,500,000
(2) $-$ $6,500,000

9-2 **a.** $1,800,000
b. $144,000
c. $12,000

9-3 Jan. $63,500; Feb. $66,600;
Mar. $64,600

9-4 June $33,487.50; July
$50,962.50; August
$61,837.50

9-5 May $248,800,000; June
$223,000,000; July
$132,800,000

9-6 **a.** Dec. $-$ $4,400; Jan.
$-$ $11,200; Feb. $+$ $2,000
b. $164,400

9-7 Feb. $-$ $1,580; Mar. $+$ $2,840;
Apr. $+$ $1,160

9-8 **a.** July surplus cash =
$38,625; October loans =
$25,500

10-1 DSO = 85 days

10-2 **a.** DSO = 39 days
b. A/R = $78,000
c. DSO = 33 days; A/R =
$66,000

10-3 **a.** DSO before = 26.5 days;
after = 21 days
b. Before $1,060,000; after
$840,000

10-4 55.8; Yes

10-5 Customer 1: 38.20; Customer
4: 59.12

10-6 **a.** DSO before = 25 days;
             after = 20 days
         b. Discount costs are $19,600
             before; $45,864 after
             change
         c. $9,722.22 before;
             $10,111.11 after change
         d. Bad debt loss is $40,000
             before; $52,000 after
             change
         e. $84,808

10-7 $NI_3 = \$46,811$; $NI_4 = \$15,467$; $NI_5 = \$8,539$

10-8 No, $\Delta NI = -\$7,564$

10-9 **a.** $NI_O = \$712,000$; $NI_N = \$715,800$

10-10 **a.** 700 pounds
          b. 10 orders
          c. 350 pounds

10-11 EOQ = 70 dozen boxes

10-12 **a.** 3,873 bags
          b. 5,073 bags; $20,292
          c. 3,137 bags; $12,548
          d. 5.81 days

10-13 BT net benefit = $1,000

10-15 **a.** 500 reels
          b. 1,050 reels

10-16 **a.** 90,000 square yards
          b. $110,000
          c. $40,000
          d. 51,538 square yards

10-17 **a.** 21,000 units
          b. 35 orders
          c. 21,135 units

11-1 **a.** 18.18%
          b. 24.24%
          c. 36.73%
          d. 29.39%
          e. 7.27%
          f. 22.27%
          g. 111.34%

11-2 **a.** 27.84%

11-3 **a.** $104,167
          c. $208,333; 48.98%

11-4 **a.** $136.11
          b. Avg. A/P w/discount =
              $1,361.11; w/o discount =
              $6,805.56;
              Free credit = $1,361.11;
              Costly credit = $5,444.45
          c. 18.37%

11-5 **a.** 11%
          b. 12.36%
          c. ≈ 22%

11-6 **a.** 14%
          b. 13.75%
          c. 13.92%
          d. 18%

11-7 **a.** 10.59%
          b. $86,400

11-8 14.56%

11-9 **a.** 18.37%
          b. 16.25%

11-10 12.94%

11-11 12.50%

11-12 **a.** (1) 55.67% (2) 18.56%
              (3) 24.09%

11-13 **b.** 8.58%
          c. 8.25%
          d. 8.06%
          e. 8.00%

11-14 **a.** Bank 11.11%; trade credit
              14.69%

11-15 **a.** $150,000

11-16 **a.** 60 days
          b. 14.69%

11-17 **a.** (1) Trade credit 18.18%
              (2) Bank 12.68%

11-18 **a.** (1) $11,250;
              (2) $12,244.90;
              (3) $8,750;
              (4) $12,083.34

11A-1 **a.** $Cost_L = \$124,875$;
              $Cost_F = \$123,338$

11A-2 $69,250

11A-3   **a.** $60,000

11A-4   **a.** $510,638
 b. Mos. cost = $10,638;
  Mos. savings = $11,213;
  Mos. net savings = $574

12-1   **a.** 7.5%
 b. 6.42%

12-2   **a.** $\hat{k}_M = 13.5\%$; $\hat{k}_j = 11.6\%$
 b. $\sigma_M = 3.85\%$; $\sigma_j = 6.22\%$

12-3   **a.** 15%
 b. 27.73%
 c. $CV_x = 1.46$; $CV_y = 1.18$

12-4   **a.** 9%
 b. 11%
 c. 15%

12-5   **a.** 1.5
 b. 11.9%

12-6   **a.** 14.4%

k_M	k_i

 b. (1) 14%   16.4%
    (2) 10%   12.4%
 c. (1) $k_s = 17.6\%$
    (2) $k_s = 11.2\%$

12-7   **a.** $10,000
 d. (1) $1,800
    (2) 18%

12-8   **a.** $\hat{k}_M = 14\%$
 b. 13.8%
 c. 19%

12-9   1.15

12-10   4.5%

12-11   **a.** Project A $4,500; Project B
  $5,100

12-12   **a.** $k_y = 11.30\%$; $k_z =$
  11.30%
 b. $k_p = 11.30\%$
 c. $\sigma_y = 20.79\%$; $\sigma_z =$
  20.78%; $\sigma_p = 20.13\%$
 d. $CV_y = 1.84$; $CV_z = 1.84$;
  $CV_p = 1.78$

13-1   **a.** $1,060.00
 b. $1,123.60
 c. $943.40
 d. $890.00

13-2   **a.** $1,628.90
 b. $2,593.70
 c. $613.90
 d. $1,000.00

13-3   **a.** 14 years
 b. 7 years
 c. 5 years
 d. 1 year

13-4   **a.** $13,181.00
 b. $12,705.60
 c. $5,000.00

13-5   **a.** $13,971.86
 b. $14,230.27
 c. $5,000.00

13-6   **a.** $7,360.10
 b. $7,209.60
 c. $5,000.00

13-7   **a.** $7,801.71
 b. $8,074.75
 c. $5,000.00

13-8   **a.** $PV_A = \$10,795.70$;
   $PV_B = \$11,948.50$
 b. $15,000

13-9 $18,694.30

13-10 $63,544

13-11   **a.** 15%

13-13   **a.** $11,274.20
 b. $11,950.65

13-14   **a.** 10%
 b. 10%
 c. 12%
 d. 9%

13-15   15%

13-16   14%

13-17   12%

13-19   10%

13-20   **a.** 9%

13-21   a. $50,808.00
           b. $39,364.56; $0.00

13-22 $5,674

13-23 $13,190

13-24   a. $456,425

13-26   a. $73,411.74
           b. $65,546.26

13-27   a. Year 1 $5,500,000; Year 5
              $8,052,500

13-28 $50,000; $25,000

13-29   a. $3,950.54

13-30   70 years

13-32 $4,000

13-33   18 years

13-34 $1,757.05

13-35   b. $17,239.22

13A-1   a. $786.75
           b. $786.90
           c. $802.35
           d. $563.40

13A-2   a. $313.70
           b. $311.60
           c. $443.70

13A-3   a. $1,979.50
           b. $2,512.22

13A-4   a. Effective interest rates:
              11% and 10.38%

14-1   a. 5 years
           b. $136,365
           c. 16%

14-2   a. 3.6 years
           b. $167,400
           c. 12%

14-3   a. 2.6 years
           b. − $46,500
           c. 7%

14-4   a. 3.13 years
           b. $0
           c. 14%

14-5   a. 3.17 years
           b. $1,324.40

14-6   a. $3,612.70
           b. 14%

14-7   a. $38,000
           b. − $24,705.60

14-8 $8,763.38

14-9   − $4,729.60

14-10

	NPV	IRR
Truck	$1,430.99	18%
Pulley	762.34	16%

14-11

	NPV	IRR
Elec.	$2,898.78	≈ 20%
Gas	2,411.14	≈ 20%

14-12

	X	Y
a.	2.17 years	2.86 years
b.	$5,301.00	$4,378.60
c.	18%	15%

14-13   a. $28,831.50
           b. 20%

14-14 NPV_A = $92,872; NPV_O =
           $76,952

14-15

	Year 1	Year 2	Year 3
a.	$132,000	$142,800	$153,600
b.	$30,337.68		

14-16

	Year 1	Year 2	Year 3	Year 4
a.	$110,940	$158,100	$134,700	$148,260
b.	$13,971.08			
c.	$7,261.50			
d.	$20,490			

14-17   a. $286,410

		Year 1	Year 2	Year 3	Year 4	Year 5	Year 6
14-18	Cash flow	$39,000	$46,200	$38,400	$34,200	$33,600	$30,600

NPV = $5,287.56

	A	B
14A-1 a.	$14,486,808	$11,156,893
	15.03%	22.26%

14A-2 a. 0%: NPV_s = $12,000.00;
NPV_L = $21,600.00
6%: NPV_s = $8,001.60;
NPV_L = $11,206.08
c. IRR_s = 21.53%; IRR_L = 15.34%

14A-3 a. $Payback_X$ = $2\frac{1}{3}$ yrs;
$Payback_Y$ = $4\frac{1}{8}$ yrs
b. 0%: NPV_X = $60,000;
NPV_Y = $105,000
6%: NPV_X = $33,331;
NPV_Y = $47,717
20%: NPV_X = − $11,533;
NPV_Y = − $36,225

14A-4 a. 0%: NPV = − $1,000,000
10%: NPV = − $99,174
80%: NPV = $1,518,519

15-1 a. $25,200
b. $8,034

15-2 $53,415

15-3 NPV = $1,475.53

15-4 a. 12%
b. ≈ $0
c. 12%

15-5 a. 15%
b. $12,723.20
c. ≈18%

15-6 a. k_E = 14%; k_F = 16%
c. NPV_E @ 14% = − $23,538.66;
NPV_F @ 16% = − $10,090.60

15-7 a. 18%
b. − $30,354

15-8 NPV_A = $4,000.01;
NPV_B = $5,731.58

15-9 a. − $790,000
b. ΔDep_1 = $150,000; ΔDep_6 = $10,000
c. Cash flow: Year 1 = $210,000; Year 6 = $154,000
d. $45,000

15-10 NPV_G = $3,264.92;
NPV_W = $2,472.30

15-11 a. − $60,200
b. CF_1 = $5,840;
CF_3 = − $2,800
c. $12,000
d. NPV = − $43,747.38

15-12 a. − $172,000
b. CF_1 = $87,200; CF_8 = $68,000
c. $19,200
d. NPV = $172,504.46

15-13 a. 13.5%
b. Recap NPV = $24,032;
Tire NPV = − $3,946

15-14 a. k_r = 10%
b. $15,000

15-15 a. k_r = 6%
b. NPV = $1,430.88

16-1 a. $128.57

16-2 a. 12.58%
b. 12%

16-3 $1,185.86

16-4 $1,188.28

16-5 $239.40

16-6 a. 7%
b. 8%

16-7 **a.** (1) $1,081.15;
(2) $1,000.00;
(3) $926.41
b. (1) $1,018.91;
(2) $1,000.00;
(3) $981.67

16-8 **a.** (1) 12.0%; (2) 6.0%

16-9 **a.** $844.47

16-10 **a.** $790,107.85
b. $397,377.31
c. $832,708.80
d. $438,231.30
e. $1,331,074.23

16-11 PMT = $388,033.06

	Year 1	Year 2	Year 3
16-12 a.	$295,623.14	$295,623.14	$595,623.14
b.	$698,112		

16-13 $43.53

16-14 **c.** (1) $7,112.99;
(2) $6,713.40;
(3) $5,305.31

16-15 **a.** YTM = 8.73%; YTC = 6.85%

17-1 $36.25

17-2 $53.00

17-3 $66.91

17-4 $38.50

17-5 **a.** 10%
b. 17%

17-6 **a.** 6%
b. $75.75

17-7 $29.13

17-8 **a.** D_1 = $2.10; D_2 = $2.205;
D_3 = $2.3153
b. $5.29
c. $24.72
d. $30.01
e. $30.00

17-9 **a.** 8%
b. 10%
c. 18%

17-10 **a.** (1) $16.76; (2) $25.00;
(3) $45.00; (4) $109.00;
(5) $333.00
b. (1) Undefined;
(2) − $115.00

17-11 $27.65

17-12 $50.12

17-13 $8.70

17-14 $16.29

17-15 **a.** $24.54

17-16 $34.88

17-17 $40.38

17-18 **a.** $47.60; 7.51%; 8.49%

17-19 $10.54

17-20 **a.** $35.00
b. $38.89
c. $46.67
d. $63.04

17-21 $108.85

17-22 **a.** No, new price = $29.44
b. Beta = 0.70

17-23 a.	1988	1993
EPS	$4,080	$ 6,000
DPS	$2,100	$ 3,000
Book value per share		$45,000

d.

	1988	1993
EPS	$1.02	$ 1.50
DPS	$0.525	$ 0.75
Book value per share		$11.25

g.

	ROE
Gemex	15.00%
Diamond Gallery	13.64%
Roth	13.33%

h.

	Debt Ratio
Gemex	42.86%
Diamond Gallery	36.59%
Roth	55.00%

i.

	P/E
Gemex	$8.00 \times$
Diamond Gallery	$8.67 \times$

k.

	k_s
Gemex	15.18%
Diamond Gallery	12.54%

18-1 $873,846

18-2 $766,538

18-4 $PV_O = -\$185,112$; $PV_L = -\$187,534$; Purchase

18-5 $25.20

18-6
b. Original = 80%; Plan 1 = 53%; Plan 2 = 57%; Plan 3 = 57%
c. $EPS_0 = \$0.48$; $EPS_1 = \$0.60$; $EPS_2 = \$0.64$; $EPS_3 = \$0.86$
d. $D/A_1 = 13\%$; $D/A_2 = 13\%$; $D/A_3 = 48\%$

18-8 **a.** $PV_L = -\$954,639$; lease

18-9 **a.** FV = $0; FV = $4; FV = $49
d. 9%; $90

19-1 **a.** 7%
b. 4.62%
c. 4.2%
d. 2.8%

19-2 5.7%

19-3 **a.** $1,080.57
b. 9%

19-4 14.13%

19-5 **a.** 12.6%
b. 12.6%

19-6 **a.** 8.82%
b. 9%

19-7 13.42%

19-8 **a.** 9%
b. $2.943
c. 15%

19-9 **a.** 14.5%
b. 10%
c. 12%

19-10 **a.** 14%
b. 13.6%
c. 13.5% − 15.5%; Avg = 14.5%
d. 13.6% − 14.5%; ≈ 14%

19-11 **a.** 15%
          b. 7%
          c. 15.68%

19-12 **a.** 10.91%
          b. 7.09%
          c. 19.09%

19-13 **a.** DCF = 29%; CAPM = 16%; BY = 14–16%

19-14 **a.** $3,000,000
          b. $7,000,000
          c. $11,666,666.67
          d. $18,750,000; $31,250,000

19-15 $785,471

19-16 12.435%

19-17 **a.** k_d = 5.1%; k_s = 12.5%
          b. 8.8%
          c. $7,800,000
          d. 9.2%

19-18 $18,000,000

19-19 Projects A and C; $15,000,000

19-20 Project C; $45,000

19-21 **a.** $15,000,000
          b. $9,000,000
          c. $3,000,000; $6,000,000
          d. k_s = 15%; k_e = 16.06%
          e. $5,000,000
          f. (1) 11.64%; (2) 12.28%

19-22 **a.** 3
          c. 11.16%; 11.83%; 12.31%; 12.79%
          d. 16%; 14%

20-1 18% increase

20-2 **a.** 50,000 units
          b. $2,250,000
          c. 4.33
          d. − $112,500

20-3 **a.** 70,000 units
          b. $3,150,000
          c. 5.67
          d. − $225,000

20-4 **a.** $3,000,000
          b. 6
          c. $3,900,000
          e. $2,100,000

20-5 2.7

20-6 **a.**

Sales	Option 1	Option 2
$ 40,000	− 1.00	− 0.50
$120,000	3.00	∞
$360,000	1.29	1.50

20-8 $112,500

20-9 $28

20-10 **a.** DOL = 2.15
           b. DFL = 2.45
           c. DTL = 5.28

20-11 **a.** DOL = 9
           b. DFL = − 1.67
           c. DTL = − 15

20-12 $330,000

20-13 $13,333,333

20-14 2.67

20-15 **a.** $3.99

20-16 **a.** DOL = 3
           b. DFL = 2
           c. DTL = 6

20-17 **a.**

	DOL	
Sales	LOL	HOL
$1.2 million	3	∞
$1.6 million	2	4

b.

		DFL		
		LOL		HOL
Sales	**No Debt**	**$900,000 Debt**	**No Debt**	**$900,000 Debt**
$1.2 million	1.00	10.00	1.00	0.00
$1.6 million	1.00	1.82	1.00	1.82

c.

	DTL	
Sales	**LOL**	**HOL**
$1.2 million	30.00	−6.67
$1.6 million	3.64	7.27

20A-1 a. Distribution: CL = $13,500,000; FA = $13,875,000
b. Distribution: 2nd Mtg. = $2,500,000; Deb. = $2,000,000

21-1 a. 62.5%
b. $3,000,000
c. 60%
d. $10,500,000

21-2 25%

21-3 44.4%

21-4 $1,560,000

21-5 Total equity = $11,400,000; Paid-in capital = $6,120,000

21-6 8%

21-7 ≈$11.36

21-8 Paid-in capital = $513.75; Total assets = $2,978.4375

21-9 a. $3,375,000
b. $6,250,000
c. $5,000,000
d. $13,000,000

22-1 − $6,746

22-2 a. 16.25%
b. $1,226.43

22-3 a. WACC = 14.4%
b. $1,340,020
c. $11.17/share

22-4 a. WACC = 16.2%
b. $570,490

23-1 0.5952 pounds per dollar

23-2

Dollars per 1,000 Units of				
Rupees	**Lira**	**Yen**	**Pesos**	**Riyals**
$30.48	$6.36	$8.42	$323.73	$267.02

23-4 9.24 francs per pound

23-6 b. $18,491

23-7 118.71

Selected Equations

Chapter 3

$$\text{Maximum deposit expansion} = \frac{\text{Initial reserve infusion}}{\text{Reserve requirement}}.$$

Chapter 4

$$\text{Nominal interest rate} = k = k^* + IP + DRP + LP + MRP.$$

$$k = k_{RF} + DRP + LP + MRP.$$

$$k_{\text{T-bill}} = k_{RF} = k^* + IP.$$

Chapter 5

$$EPS = \frac{\text{Net income available to common stockholders}}{\text{Shares outstanding}}.$$

$$DPS = \frac{\text{Dividends paid to common stockholders}}{\text{Shares outstanding}}.$$

$$\text{Assets} - \text{Liabilities} = \text{Stockholders' equity}.$$

$$\text{Cash flows} = \text{Net income} + \text{Depreciation (and other noncash expenses)}.$$

Chapter 6

$$\frac{\text{Current}}{\text{ratio}} = \frac{\text{Current assets}}{\text{Current liabilities}}.$$

$$\frac{\text{Quick, or}}{\text{acid test,}}_{\text{ratio}} = \frac{\text{Current assets} - \text{Inventory}}{\text{Current liabilities}}.$$

$$\frac{\text{Inventory}}{\text{turnover}} = \frac{\text{Sales}}{\text{Inventory}}.$$

$$\frac{\text{Days sales}}{\text{outstanding}}_{(DSO)} = \frac{\text{Receivables}}{\text{Average sales per day}} = \frac{\text{Receivables}}{\text{Annual sales}/360}.$$

$$\frac{\text{Fixed assets}}{\text{turnover}} = \frac{\text{Sales}}{\text{Net fixed assets}}.$$

$$\frac{\text{Total assets}}{\text{turnover}} = \frac{\text{Sales}}{\text{Total assets}}.$$

$$\frac{\text{Debt}}{\text{ratio}} = \frac{\text{Total debt}}{\text{Total assets}}.$$

$$TIE = \frac{\text{EBIT}}{\text{Interest charges}}.$$

$$\text{Fixed charge coverage} = \frac{\text{EBIT} + \text{Lease payments}}{\text{Interest charges} + \text{Lease payments} + \left(\dfrac{\text{Sinking fund payments}}{1 - \text{Tax rate}}\right)}.$$

$$\text{Basic earning power (BEP) ratio} = \frac{\text{EBIT}}{\text{Total assets}}.$$

$$\text{Return on common equity (ROE)} = \frac{\text{Net income}}{\text{Common equity}}.$$

$$\text{Book value per share} = \frac{\text{Stockholders' equity}}{\text{Shares outstanding}}.$$

$$\text{ROA} = \frac{\text{Profit margin}} \times \frac{\text{Total assets turnover}}.$$

$$\text{Profit margin on sales} = \frac{\text{Net income}}{\text{Sales}}.$$

$$\text{Return on total assets (ROA)} = \frac{\text{Net income}}{\text{Total assets}}.$$

$$\text{Price/earnings (P/E) ratio} = \frac{\text{Market price per share}}{\text{Earnings per share}}.$$

$$\text{Market/book (M/B) ratio} = \frac{\text{Market price per share}}{\text{Book value per share}}.$$

$$\text{ROE} = \text{ROA} \times \frac{\text{Total assets}}{\text{Common equity}}.$$

$$\text{ROE} = \text{ROA} \times \frac{1}{1 - \text{Debt ratio}}.$$

Chapter 7

$$\text{AFN} = A^*/S(\Delta S) - L^*/S(\Delta S) - MS_1(1 - d).$$

$$\text{AFN} = A^*/S(\Delta S) + FA - L^*/S(\Delta S) - MS_1(1 - d).$$

$$\text{Full capacity sales} = \frac{\text{Current sales}}{\%\ \text{fixed assets operated}}.$$

Chapter 8

$$\text{Inventory conversion period} + \text{Receivables conversion period} - \text{Payables deferral period} = \text{Cash conversion cycle}.$$

Chapter 9

$$\text{Net float} = \text{Disbursement float} - \text{Collections float}.$$

Chapter 10

$$(\text{DSO})\left(\frac{\text{Sales per day}}\right)\left(\frac{\text{Variable cost ratio}}\right)\left(\frac{\text{Cost of funds}}\right) = \text{Cost of carrying receivables}.$$

$$\text{EOQ} = \sqrt{\frac{(F)(S)}{(C)(P)}}.$$

$$\text{Reorder point} = (\text{Lead time} \times \text{Usage rate}) - \text{Goods in transit}.$$

Chapter 11

$$\text{Approximate percentage cost} = \frac{\text{Discount percent}}{100 - \text{Discount percent}} \times \frac{360}{\text{Days credit is outstanding} - \text{Discount period}}.$$

$$\text{Effective annual rate}_{\text{Simple}} = \frac{\text{Interest}}{\text{Amount received}}.$$

$$\text{Effective annual rate}_{\text{Discount}} = \frac{\text{Interest}}{\text{Face value} - \text{Interest}}.$$

$$\text{Approximate effective annual rate}_{\text{Add-on}} = \frac{\text{Interest}}{(\text{Amount received})/2}.$$

$$\text{Face amount of loan}_{\text{Simple/CB}} = \frac{\text{Funds needed}}{1.0 - \text{CB(decimal)}}.$$

$$\text{Effective annual rate}_{\text{Simple/CB}} = \frac{\text{Nominal interest rate}(\%)}{1.0 - \text{CB(decimal)}}.$$

$$\text{Face amount of loan}_{\text{Discount/CB}} = \frac{\text{Funds needed}}{1.0 - \text{Nominal rate (decimal)} - \text{CB(decimal)}}.$$

$$\text{Effective annual rate}_{\text{Discount/CB}} = \frac{\text{Nominal interest rate}(\%)}{1.0 - \text{Nominal rate (decimal)} - \text{CB(decimal)}}.$$

Chapter 12

$$\text{Expected rate of return} = \hat{k} = \sum_{i=1}^{n} P_i k_i.$$

$$\text{Variance} = \sigma^2 = \sum_{i=1}^{n} (k_i - \hat{k})^2 P_i.$$

$$\text{Standard deviation} = \sigma = \sqrt{\sum_{i=1}^{n} (k_i - \hat{k})^2 P_i}.$$

$$\text{Coefficient of variation (CV)} = \frac{\sigma}{\hat{k}}.$$

$$\hat{k}_p = \sum_{i=1}^{n} w_i \hat{k}_i.$$

$$b_p = \sum_{i=1}^{n} w_i b_i.$$

$$k_i = k_{RF} + (k_M - k_{RF}) b_i.$$

Chapter 13

$$FV_n = PV(FVIF_{k,n}). \qquad FVIF_{k,n} = (1 + k)^n.$$

$$PV = FV_n(PVIF_{k,n}). \qquad PVIF_{k,n} = [1/(1 + k)^n] = (1/FVIF_{k,n}).$$

$$FVA_n = PMT(FVIFA_{k,n}). \qquad FVIFA_{k,n} = \frac{(1 + k)^n - 1}{k}.$$

$$FVA_n(\text{Annuity due}) = PMT(FVIFA_{k,n})(1 + k).$$

$$PVA_n = PMT(PVIFA_{k,n}). \qquad PVIFA_{k,n} = \frac{1 - \dfrac{1}{(1 + k)^n}}{k}.$$

$$PVA_n(\text{Annuity due}) = PMT(PVIFA_{k,n})(1 + k). \qquad PV(\text{perpetuity}) = \frac{PMT}{k}.$$

Appendix 13A

$$\text{Effective annual rate (EAR)} = \left(1 + \frac{k_{Nom}}{m}\right)^m - 1.0.$$

$$FV_n = PV\left(1 + \frac{k_{Nom}}{m}\right)^{mn}.$$

Chapter 14

$$\text{Net cash flow} = (\$REV - \$EXP)(1 - T) + (DEP)(T).$$

$$\text{Payback} = \text{Year before full recovery} + \frac{\text{Unrecovered cost at start of year}}{\text{Cash flow during year}}.$$

$$NPV = \sum_{t=1}^{n} \frac{CF_t}{(1 + k)^t} - C. \qquad NPV = \sum_{t=1}^{n} \frac{CF_t}{(1 + IRR)^t} - C = \$0.$$

Chapter 15

$$k_{Project} = k_{RF} + (k_M - k_{RF})b_{Project}.$$

$$k_n = k_r + i.$$

$$NPV = \sum_{t=1}^{n} \frac{RCF_t}{(1 + k_r)^t} - C.$$

$$\text{Inflation-adjusted NPV} = \sum_{t=1}^{n} \frac{RCF_t(1 + i)^t}{(1 + k_n)^t} - C.$$

Chapter 16

$$\text{Value} = V_B = \sum_{t=1}^{n} I \frac{1}{(1 + k_d)^t} + M \frac{1}{(1 + k_d)^n}$$

$$= I(PVIFA_{k_d,n}) + M(PVIF_{k_d,n}).$$

$$V_B = \sum_{t=1}^{2n} \frac{I}{2} \frac{1}{(1 + k_d/2)^t} + M \frac{1}{(1 + k_d/2)^{2n}}$$

$$= I/2 \, (PVIFA_{k_d/2,2n}) + M(PVIF_{k_d/2,2n}).$$

$$k_d = YTM = \frac{I + (M - V)/n}{(M + 2V)/3}.$$

$$V_B = \sum_{t=1}^{n} I \frac{1}{(1 + k_d)^t} + \text{Call price} \frac{1}{(1 + k_d)^n}.$$

$$V_P = \frac{D_p}{k_p}.$$

Chapter 17

$$\hat{P}_0 = \frac{D_1}{(1 + k_s)^1} + \frac{D_2}{(1 + k_s)^2} + \cdots + \frac{D_\infty}{(1 + k_s)^\infty}$$

$$= \sum_{t=1}^{\infty} \frac{D_t}{(1 + k_s)^t}.$$

$$\hat{P}_0 = \frac{D_0(1 + g)}{k_s - g} = \frac{D_1}{k_s - g}.$$

$$\hat{k}_s = \frac{D_1}{P_0} + g.$$

Chapter 18

$$\text{Formula value} = \text{Current price of the stock} - \text{Striking price}.$$

$$\begin{array}{c}\text{Price paid for bond} \\ \text{with warrants}\end{array} = \begin{array}{c}\text{Pure-debt} \\ \text{value of bond}\end{array} + \begin{array}{c}\text{Value of} \\ \text{warrants}.\end{array}$$

$$\text{Conversion price} = P_c = \frac{\text{Par value of bond}}{CR}.$$

$$\text{Conversion ratio} = CR = \frac{\text{Par value of bond}}{P_c}.$$

$$\begin{array}{c}\text{Pure-debt value} \\ \text{at time of issue}\end{array} = B_0 = \sum_{t=1}^{n} I \frac{1}{(1 + k_d)^t} + M \frac{1}{(1 + k_d)^n}.$$

$$\text{Conversion value} = C_t = \text{Initial stock price } (1 + g)^t(CR).$$

$$\begin{array}{c}\text{Convertible's} \\ \text{initial price}\end{array} = \sum_{t=1}^{n} I \frac{1}{(1 + k_c)^t} + C_t \frac{1}{(1 + k_c)^n}.$$

Chapter 19

$$\text{After-tax } k_d = k_d(1 - T). \qquad k_e = \frac{D_1}{P_0(1 - F)} + g.$$

$$k_p = D_p/P_n. \qquad \text{WACC} = k_a = w_d k_d(1 - T) + w_p(k_p) + w_s(k_s).$$

$$\text{Break point} = \frac{\text{Total dollar amount of lower cost capital of a given type}}{\text{Fraction of this type of capital in the capital structure (weight)}}.$$

Chapter 20

$$S = PQ. \qquad TC = F + VQ.$$

$$Q_{BE} = \frac{F}{P - V}. \qquad S_{BE} = \frac{F}{1 - V/P}.$$

$$\text{DOL} = \frac{\text{Percentage change in EBIT}}{\text{Percentage change in sales}} = \frac{\dfrac{\Delta\text{EBIT}}{\text{EBIT}}}{\dfrac{\Delta S}{S}}.$$

$$\text{DOL}_Q = \frac{Q(P - V)}{Q(P - V) - F}. \qquad \text{DOL}_S = \frac{S - VC}{S - VC - F}.$$

$$\text{DFL} = \frac{\text{Percentage change in EPS}}{\text{Percentage change in EBIT}} = \frac{\dfrac{\Delta\text{EPS}}{\text{EPS}}}{\dfrac{\Delta\text{EBIT}}{\text{EBIT}}}.$$

$$\text{DFL}_Q = \frac{Q(P - V) - F}{Q(P - V) - F - I} = \frac{\text{EBIT}}{\text{EBIT} - I}.$$

$$\text{DTL} = \frac{\text{Percentage change in EPS}}{\text{Percentage change in sales}} = \frac{\dfrac{\Delta\text{EPS}}{\text{EPS}}}{\dfrac{\Delta S}{S}}.$$

$$\text{DTL}_Q = \frac{Q(P - V)}{Q(P - V) - F - I}. \qquad \text{DTL}_Q = (\text{DOL}_Q)(\text{DFL}_Q).$$

$$\text{EPS}_1 = \text{EPS}_0\,[1.0 + (\text{DTL})(\%\,\Delta\text{Sales})].$$

Chapter 21

$$\begin{array}{c}\text{Dollars}\\\text{transferred from}\\\text{retained earnings}\end{array} = \left(\begin{array}{c}\text{Number}\\\text{of shares}\\\text{outstanding}\end{array}\right)\left(\begin{array}{c}\text{Percentage}\\\text{of the}\\\text{stock dividend}\end{array}\right)\left(\begin{array}{c}\text{Market}\\\text{price of}\\\text{the stock}\end{array}\right).$$

Chapter 23

$$\begin{matrix} \text{90-day forward rate} \\ \text{(Currency A/Currency B)} \end{matrix} = \text{Spot rate} \times \left[\frac{1 + i_{90}^{A}\left(\dfrac{90}{360}\right)}{1 + i_{90}^{B}\left(\dfrac{90}{360}\right)} \right].$$

Price in Country A = Exchange rate × Price in Country B.

Glossary

ABC System A system used to categorize inventory items to ensure that the most important ones are reviewed most often.

Account Receivable A balance due from a customer. *See also trade credit.*

Accruals Continually recurring short-term liabilities, especially accrued wages and accrued taxes.

Acquiring Company A company that seeks to acquire another.

Actual (Realized) Rate of Return, $\bar{k}_s$ The rate of return on a common stock actually received by stockholders; $\bar{k}_s$ may be greater or less than $\hat{k}_s$ and/or k_s.

Additional Funds Needed (AFN) Funds that a firm must acquire through borrowing or by selling new stock.

Add-On Interest Interest that is calculated and added to funds received to determine the face amount of an installment loan.

After-Tax Cost of Debt, $k_d(1 - T)$ The relevant cost of new debt financing, taking into account the tax deductibility of interest; used to calculate the WACC.

Agency Problem A potential conflict of interest between (1) stockholders and managers or (2) stockholders and creditors (debt holders).

Aggressive Working Capital Investment Policy A policy under which holdings of cash, securities, inventories, and receivables are minimized.

Aging Schedule A report showing how long accounts receivable have been outstanding; it gives the percentage of receivables currently past due and the percentages past due by specified periods.

Amortization Schedule A schedule showing precisely how a loan will be repaid. It gives the required payment on each specified date and a breakdown of the payment showing how much constitutes interest and how much constitutes repayment of principal.

Amortized Loan A loan that is repaid in equal payments over its life.

Annual Report A report issued annually by a corporation to its stockholders. It contains the basic financial statements, along with management's opinion of the past year's operations and of the firm's future prospects.

Annuity A series of payments of an equal, or constant, amount for a specified number of periods.

Annuity Due An annuity in which the payments occur at the beginning of each period.

Arrearage An omitted dividend on preferred stock.

Asked Price The price at which a dealer in securities will sell shares of stock out of inventory.

Asset Management Ratios A set of ratios which measures how effectively a firm is managing its assets; also called *activity ratios.*

Assets All items which the firm owns.

Average Tax Rate Taxes paid divided by taxable income.

Balance Sheet A statement of the firm's financial position at a specific point in time.

Bank Holding Company (BHC) A corporation which owns bank and nonbank subsidiaries, originally designed to circumvent bank regulation.

Banker's Acceptance A promissory note which has been endorsed, or guaranteed, by a bank.

Basic Earning Power (BEP) Ratio   This ratio indicates the ability of the firm's assets to generate operating income; computed by dividing EBIT by total assets.

Best Efforts Arrangement   Agreement for the sale of securities in which the investment bank handling the transaction gives no guarantee that the securities will be sold.

Beta Coefficient, b   A measure of the extent to which the returns on a given stock move with the stock market.

Beta (Market) Risk   *See market risk.*

Bid Price   The price a dealer in securities will pay for a stock.

Blue Sky Laws   State laws that prevent the sale of securities having little or no asset backing.

Board of Governors of the Federal Reserve System   Seven-member decision-making authority of the Fed.

Bond   A long-term debt instrument.

Bond Ratings   Ratings assigned to bonds based on the probability of their default. Those bonds with the smallest default probability are rated Aaa and carry the lowest interest rates.

Bracket Creep   A situation that occurs when progressive tax rates combine with inflation to cause a greater portion of each taxpayer's real income to be paid as taxes.

Break, or Jump, in the MCC Schedule   An increase in the weighted average cost of capital that occurs when there is an increase in a component cost of capital.

Break Point (BP)   The dollar value of total new capital that can be raised before an increase in the firm's marginal cost of capital occurs.

Breakeven Analysis   An analytical technique for studying the relationship between fixed costs, variable costs, sales volume, and operating profits.

Breakeven Point (Q_{BE})   The volume of sales at which total operating costs equal total revenues and operating income (EBIT) equals zero.

Business Risk   The risk associated with future operating income; the risk that would exist even if the firm's operations were all equity financed.

Bylaws   A set of rules for governing the management of a company.

Call Option   An option to buy, or "call," a share of stock at a certain price within a specified period.

Call Premium   The amount in excess of par value that a company must pay when it calls a security.

Call Provision   A provision in a bond contract that gives the issuer the right to pay off the bonds under specified terms prior to the stated maturity date.

Capital Account   The account that represents a bank's total assets minus its liabilities.

Capital Asset Pricing Model (CAPM)   A model based on the proposition that any stock's required rate of return is equal to the risk-free rate of return plus a risk premium, where risk reflects the effects of diversification.

Capital Budgeting   The process of planning expenditures on assets and projects whose returns extend beyond one year.

Capital Component   One of the types of capital used by firms to raise money.

Capital Gain or Loss   The profit (loss) from the sale of a capital asset for more (less) than its purchase price.

Capital Gains Yield   The capital gain during a given year divided by the beginning price.

Capital Intensity Ratio   The amount of assets required per dollar of sales (A*/S).

Capital Markets   Financial markets for stocks and for long-term debt (one year or longer).

Carrying Costs   The costs associated with carrying inventories, including storage, capital, and depreciation costs. Carrying costs generally increase in proportion to the average amount of inventory held.

Cash   The total of bank demand deposits plus currency.

Cash Account   The account that represents a bank's vault cash, checks in process of collection, and funds required to be kept on deposit with the Federal Reserve.

Cash Budget   A schedule showing cash flows (receipts, disbursements, and cash balances) for a firm over a specified period.

Cash Conversion Cycle   The length of time from the payment for raw materials and labor to the collection of accounts receivable generated by the sale of the final product.

Cash Discount A reduction in the price of goods, given to encourage early payment.

Cash Flow The actual net cash, as opposed to accounting net income, that flows into or out of the firm during a specified period; equal to net income plus depreciation and other noncash expenses.

Certificate of Deposit (CD) A time deposit evidenced by a negotiable or nonnegotiable receipt issued for funds deposited for a specified period of time.

Change in Net Working Capital The increased current assets required for a new project, minus the simultaneous increase in accounts payable and accruals.

Chapter 7 A chapter of the Bankruptcy Reform Act that governs liquidations, or selling of the firm's assets, due to bankruptcy.

Chapter 11 A chapter of the Bankruptcy Reform Act that governs reorganizations, or restructurings, due to bankruptcy.

Charter A formal legal document that describes the scope and nature of a corporation and defines the rights and duties of its stockholders and managers.

Check Clearing The process of converting a check that has been written and mailed into cash in the payee's account.

Classified Stock Common stock that is given special designations, such as Class A, Class B, and so forth, to meet the special needs of the company.

Clientele Effect The tendency of a firm to attract the type of investor who likes its dividend policy.

Closely Held Corporation A corporation that is owned by a few individuals who are typically associated with the firm's management.

Coefficient of Variation (CV) A standardized measure of the risk per unit of return; calculated as the standard deviation divided by the expected return.

Collateral Assets that are pledged to secure a loan.

Collections Float The amount of checks received but not yet credited to the payee's account.

Collection Policy The procedures used to collect accounts receivable.

Commercial Paper Short-term, unsecured promissory notes of large, financially strong firms, usually issued in denominations of $100,000 or more and having an interest rate somewhat below the prime rate.

Common Stock Long-term equity claim on the issuing corporation; does not guarantee dividend payments.

Company-Specific Risk That part of a security's risk associated with random events; it *can* be eliminated by proper diversification.

Comparative Ratio Analysis An analysis based on a comparison of a firm's ratios with those of other firms in the same industry.

Compensating Balance (CB) A minimum checking account balance that a firm must maintain with a commercial bank, generally equal to 10 to 20 percent of the amount of loans outstanding. Also, a checking account balance that a firm must maintain with a commercial bank to compensate the bank for services rendered.

Competitive Equality in Banking Act (CEBA) An act passed in 1987 to stem the growth of bank-like corporations.

Compounding The arithmetic process of determining the final value of a payment or series of payments when compound interest is applied.

Computerized Inventory Control System A system of inventory control in which a computer is used to determine reorder points and to adjust inventory balances.

Concentration Bank Larger bank to which the firm channels funds from the local depository banks which operate its lockboxes.

Congeneric Merger A merger of firms in the same general industry but for which no customer or supplier relationship exists.

Conglomerate Merger A merger of companies in totally different industries.

Conservative Working Capital Investment policy A policy under which relatively large amounts of cash, marketable securities, and inventories are carried and under which sales are stimulated by a generous credit policy, resulting in a high level of receivables.

Consol   A perpetual bond originally issued by the British government to consolidate past debts; in general, any perpetual bond.

Constant Growth Model   Also called the Gordon Model; used to find the value of a constant growth stock.

Contractual Hedging   The hedging of a currency risk through the acquisition of a financial contract such as a forward contract.

Controlled Disbursement Account   An account which is not funded until the day's checks are presented against it; originally called remote disbursement.

Conversion Price (P_c)   The effective price paid for common stock obtained by converting a convertible security.

Conversion Ratio (CR)   The number of shares of common stock that may be obtained by converting a convertible bond or share of convertible preferred stock.

Conversion Value (C_t)   The value of common stock obtained by converting a convertible security.

Convertible Bond   A bond that is exchangeable, at the option of the holder, for common stock of the issuing firm.

Convertible Security   A security, usually a bond or preferred stock, that is exchangeable at the option of the holder for the common stock of the issuing firm.

Corporate Alliance   A cooperative agreement between two firms that can range from a simple marketing agreement to the joint ownership of a third corporation.

Corporate Bonds   Long-term debt securities issued by corporations.

Corporate (Within-Firm) Risk   Risk not considering the effects of stockholders' diversification; it is measured by a project's effect on the firm's earnings variability.

Corporation   A legal entity created by a state, separate and distinct from its owners and managers, having unlimited life, easy transferability of ownership, and limited liability.

Correlation Coefficient, r   A measure of the degree of relationship between two variables.

Cost of Capital   The discount rate that should be used in the capital budgeting process.

Cost of New Common Equity, k_e   The cost of external equity; based on the cost of retained earnings but increased for flotation costs.

Cost of Preferred Stock, k_p   The rate of return investors require on the firm's preferred stock, adjusted for flotation costs. k_p is calculated as the preferred dividend, D_p, divided by the net issuing price, P_n.

Cost of Retained Earnings, k_s   The rate of return required by stockholders on a firm's common stock.

Costly Trade Credit   Credit taken in excess of free trade credit; the cost is equal to the discounts lost.

Counterparty Risk   The risk that the other participant or party of a swap agreement will not fulfill their obligations under the swap agreement.

Coupon Interest Rate   The stated annual rate of interest on a bond.

Coupon Payment   The specified dollar interest paid each period, generally each six months, on a bond.

Coupon Rate   The stated, or nominal, rate of interest on a bond.

Credit Crunch   A period in which capital is scarce and interest rates, typically, are high.

Credit Period   The length of time for which credit is granted.

Credit Policy   A set of decisions that includes a firm's credit period, discounts offered, credit standards, and collection policy.

Credit-Scoring System   Statistical method similar to multiple regression analysis; it is used to assess a customer's credit risk.

Credit Standards   Standards that stipulate the minimum financial strength that an applicant must demonstrate in order to be granted credit.

Credit Terms   A statement of the credit period and any discounts offered — for example, 2/10, net 30.

Cross Rate   Any exchange rate which does not include the U.S. dollar.

Cumulative Dividends   A protective feature on preferred stock that requires preferred dividends in arrears to be paid before any common dividends can be paid.

Currency Swap   The exchange of debt-service payments denominated in one currency for debt-service payments in a different currency, both calculated on the same principal value based on the spot rate in effect on the initial swap date.

Current Ratio   This ratio is computed by dividing current assets by current liabilities. It indicates the extent to which the claims of short-term creditors are covered by assets expected to be converted to cash in the near future.

Current Yield   The annual interest payment on a bond divided by its current market price.

Days Sales Outstanding (DSO)   The ratio computed by dividing average *credit* sales per day into accounts receivable; indicates the average length of time the firm must wait after making a credit sale before receiving payment.

Debenture   A bond that is not secured by a mortgage on specific property.

Debt Ratio   The ratio of total debt to total assets.

Declaration Date   Date on which a firm's directors issue a statement declaring a regular dividend.

Default Risk   The risk that a borrower will not pay the interest or principal on a loan.

Default Risk Premium (DRP)   The difference between the interest rate on a U.S. Treasury bond and a corporate bond of equal maturity and liquidity.

Defensive Merger   A merger designed to make a company less vulnerable to a takeover.

Degree of Financial Leverage (DFL) The percentage change in earnings available to common shareholders associated with a given percentage change in earnings before interest and taxes.

Degree of Leverage   The percentage change in one variable, given a percentage change in another variable; a form of elasticity.

Degree of Operating Leverage (DOL) The percentage change in EBIT resulting from a given percentage change in sales.

Degree of Total Leverage (DTL)   The percentage change in EPS brought about by a given percentage change in sales; DTL shows the effects of both operating leverage and financial leverage.

Demand Deposits   Transaction deposits at commercial banks that are available on demand, usually through a check.

Depository Institutions Deregulation and Monetary Control Act (DIDMCA) An act that eliminated many of the distinctions between commercial banks and other depository institutions.

Depository Transfer Check (DTC)   A check that is restricted to use in making deposits to a particular account at a particular bank.

Depreciable Basis   The dollar amount which can be depreciated for tax purposes in connection with the purchase of an asset. The depreciable basis under MACRS is equal to the cost of the asset, including shipping and installation charges.

Depreciation   The accounting process whereby the cost of a productive asset is allocated against the revenues that it helps to produce.

Detachable Warrant   A warrant that can be detached from a bond and traded independently of it.

Direct Quote   The form of an exchange rate in which the home currency is stated first; for example, a direct quote on the U.S. dollar versus the Japanese yen is US$ 0.00800/¥.

Disbursement Float   The amount of a payer's checks that have been written but are still being processed and that have not been deducted from the account balance by the bank.

Discount Bond   A bond that sells below its par value; occurs whenever the going rate of interest *rises above* the coupon rate.

Discount Interest   Interest that is calculated on the face amount of a loan but is paid in advance.

Discount Rate   The interest rate charged by the Fed for loans of reserves to depository institutions.

Discounted Cash Flow (DCF) Techniques   Methods of evaluating investment proposals that employ time value of money concepts; two of these are the *net present value* and *internal rate of return* methods.

Discounting   The process of finding the present value of a future payment or a series of future payments; the reverse of compounding.

Divestiture   The sale of some of a company's operating assets.

Dividend Payout Ratio   The percentage of earnings paid out in dividends.

Dividend Policy Decision   The decision as to how much of current earnings to pay out as dividends rather than to retain for reinvestment in the firm.

Dividend Reinvestment Plan (DRIP)   A plan that enables a stockholder to automatically reinvest dividends received in the stock of the paying firm.

Dividend Yield   The expected dividend divided by the current price of a share of stock.

Dividends per Share (DPS)   Total dividends paid to common stockholders divided by the number of shares of common stock outstanding.

Draft   A check-like instrument used in delaying payments; must be sent to the payer before funds can be collected.

Du Pont Equation   A formula that finds the rate of return on assets by multiplying the profit margin by the total assets turnover.

Earnings per Share (EPS)   Net income available to common stockholders divided by the number of shares of common stock outstanding.

Economic Exposure   The risk to a firm's value of unexpected exchange rate changes and their impacts on the value of future cash flows over the long run.

Economic Ordering Quantity (EOQ)   The optimal, or least-cost, quantity of inventory that should be ordered.

Effective Annual Rate (EAR)   The annual rate of interest actually being earned as opposed to the nominal or stated rate.

Efficient Capital Market   Market in which securities are fairly priced in the sense that the price reflects all publicly available information on each security.

EOQ Model   Formula for determining the ordering quantity that will minimize total inventory costs.

Equilibrium   The condition under which the expected rate of return, $\hat{k}_s$,

equals the required rate of return, k_s, and the price of the stock is stable.

Equilibrium Rate (k)   A market-clearing interest rate which obtains a balance between the supply of and the demand for a particular type of capital.

Equity   Financing supplied by the firm's owners.

Equity Multiplier   The ratio of total assets to total common equity.

Eurocurrency   A bank loan or deposit denominated in a foreign currency; for example, a U.S. dollar deposit in a London bank is a Eurodollar deposit.

Eurodollars   Interest-bearing time deposits, denominated in U.S. dollars, placed in banks outside the United States.

Ex-Dividend Date   The date on which the right to the current dividend no longer accompanies a stock; it is four working days prior to the holder-of-record date.

Excess Capacity   Capacity that exists when an asset is not being fully utilized.

Excess Reserves   Reserves held by a commercial bank (or other depository institution) with a Federal Reserve bank in excess of the bank's required reserves.

Exchange Rate   The rate at which one country's currency or money is exchanged for another country's currency.

Executive Stock Option   A type of incentive plan that allows managers to purchase stock at some future time at a given price.

Expansion Project   A project that is intended to increase sales.

Expectations Theory   The theory that the shape of the yield curve depends primarily on investors' expectations about future inflation rates.

Expected Rate of Return, $\hat{k}$ The rate of return expected to be realized from an investment; the mean value of the probability distribution of possible outcomes.

Expected Rate of Return, $\hat{k}_s$ The rate of return on a common stock that a stockholder expects to receive.

Expected Return on a Portfolio, $\hat{k}_p$ The weighted average of expected returns on the stocks held in the portfolio.

Expected Total Return   The sum of the expected dividend yield and the expected capital gains yield on a share of stock.

Externalities Effects of a project on cash flows in other parts of the firm.

Extra Dividend A supplementary dividend paid in years when excess funds are available.

Factoring Outright sale of accounts receivable.

FASB #13 The statement of the Financial Accounting Standards Board that details the conditions and procedures for capitalizing leases.

Federal Deposit Insurance Corporation (FDIC) An agency created by Congress in 1933 to protect depositors in insured banks from the effects of a bank failure.

Federal Deposit Insurance Corporation Improvement Act of 1991 (FDICIA) Legislation designed to reduce the number and cost of bank failures.

Federal Funds Market The market in which banks lend reserve funds among themselves for short periods of time.

Federal Funds Rate The interest rate, set by market forces, at which banks borrow in the Federal funds market.

Federal Open Market Committee (FOMC) Committee of the Federal Reserve System that makes decisions relating to open-market operations.

Federal Reserve (Fed) The central banking system in the United States; the chief regulator of the banking system.

Financial Institutions Reform, Recovery, and Enforcement Act (FIRREA) An act passed in 1989 that restructured the thrift industry.

Financial Intermediaries Specialized financial firms that facilitate the transfer of funds from savers to demanders of capital and, in the process, create new financial products.

Financial Lease A lease that does not provide for maintenance services, is not cancelable, and is fully amortized over its life; also called a *capital lease.*

Financial Leverage The extent to which a firm uses debt (or preferred stock) financing.

Financial Management The acquisition and utilization of funds to maximize the efficiency and value of an enterprise.

Financial Merger A merger in which the firms involved will not be operated as a single unit and from which no operating economies are expected.

Financial Risk The portion of stockholders' risk, over and above basic business risk, resulting from the use of financial leverage.

Financial Service Corporations Institutions which offer a wide range of financial services, including pension fund operations, brokerage services, insurance, and commercial banking.

Financing Cash Flows The cash flows associated with the principal and periodic payments on the financial structure of the firm; for example, the principal and interest payments on debt.

Five Cs of Credit The factors used to evaluate credit risk: character, capacity, capital, collateral, and conditions.

Fixed Assets Turnover Ratio The ratio of sales to net fixed assets; also called the *fixed assets utilization ratio.*

Fixed Charge Coverage Ratio This ratio expands upon the TIE ratio to include the firm's annual long-term lease and sinking fund obligations.

Fixed Operating Costs Operating costs that do not vary directly with sales; that is, costs that would exist even if no sales were made. Examples include depreciation and lease payments.

Floating-Rate Bond A bond whose interest rate fluctuates with shifts in the general level of interest rates.

Floating-Rate Preferred Stock Preferred stock on which the dividend rate fluctuates with changes in the general level of interest rates.

Flotation Cost, F The percentage cost of issuing new common stock.

Flotation Costs The costs of issuing new common stock, preferred stock, or bonds.

Formula Value The value of an option security, calculated as the stock price minus the striking, or exercise, price.

Forward Rates Exchange rates used in contracts which guarantee the contract participants a specific future spot rate of exchange for a specific amount of currency.

Founders' Shares Stock owned by the firm's founders that has sole voting rights but pays no dividends until retained earnings reach some specified level.

Free Cash Flow   The sum of a target firm's net income, depreciation, and after-tax interest, minus any annual investment required.

Free Trade Credit   Credit received during the discount period.

Friendly Merger   A merger whose terms are approved by the managements of both companies.

Funded Debt   Long-term debt; "funding" means replacing short-term debt with securities of longer maturity.

Future Value (FV_n)   The amount to which a payment or series of payments will grow over a given future time period when compounded at a given interest rate; also called compound value.

Future Value Interest Factor ($FVIF_{k,n}$)   The future value of $1 left in an account for n periods paying k percent per period, which is equal to $(1 + k)^n$.

FVA_n   The future value of an annuity over n periods; also called the sum of an annuity.

$FVIFA_{k,n}$ The future value interest factor for an annuity of n periodic payments compounded at k percent.

Garn–St. Germain Act   A thrift bailout act which allowed banks to buy failing thrifts.

Going Public   The act of selling stock to the public at large by a closely held corporation or its principal stockholders.

Golden Parachutes   Large payments made to the managers of a firm if it is acquired.

Goods in Transit   Goods which have been ordered but have not yet been received.

Growth Rate, g   The expected rate of growth in dividends per share.

Half-Year Convention   A feature of MACRS in which assets are assumed to be put into service at midyear and thus are allowed a half-year's depreciation regardless of when they actually go into service.

Holder-of-Record Date   If the company lists the stockholder as an owner on this date, then the stockholder receives the dividend.

Holding Company   A corporation that owns sufficient common stock of another firm to achieve working control of it.

Horizontal Merger   A combination of two firms that produce the same type of good or service.

Hostile Merger (Takeover)   A merger in which the target firm's management resists acquisition.

Hurdle Rate   The minimum acceptable IRR; the rate which determines whether a project should be accepted or rejected.

Improper Accumulation   Retention of earnings by a corporation for the purpose of enabling stockholders to avoid personal income taxes.

Income Bond   A bond that pays interest only if the interest is earned.

Income Statement   A statement summarizing the firm's revenues and expenses over an accounting period.

Incremental Cash Flows   The net cash flows attributable to an investment project.

Indenture   A formal agreement between the issuer of a bond and the bondholders.

Independent Projects   Two or more projects where all can be accepted; the opposite of mutually exclusive projects.

Indexed (Purchasing Power) Bond   A bond that has interest payments based on an inflation index so as to protect the holder from inflation.

Indirect Quote   The form of an exhange rate in which the home currency is stated last; for example, an indirect quote on the U.S. dollar versus the Japanese yen is ¥ 125/US$.

Inflation   The tendency of prices to increase over time.

Inflation Premium (IP)   A premium for expected inflation that investors add to the real risk-free rate of interest.

Inflation Risk   The risk that inflation will reduce the purchasing power of a given sum of money.

Information Content (Signaling) of Dividends   The theory that stock price changes following dividend announcements simply reflect the fact that investors regard dividend changes as signals of management's earnings forecasts.

Initial Public Offering (IPO) Market
The market consisting of stocks of companies that have just gone public.

Insiders   Officers, directors, major stockholders, or others who may have access to information not available to the public about a company's operations.

Interest Rate   The price paid by borrowers to lenders for the use of funds.

Interest Rate Risk   The risk to which investors are exposed due to rising interest rates.

Interest Rate Swap   The exchange of a fixed interest rate debt-servicing cash flow stream for a floating interest rate debt-servicing cash flow stream (or vice versa), both calculated on the same principal amount.

Internal Rate of Return (IRR) Method   A method of evaluating investment proposals by calculating the discount rate that sets equal the present value of future cash flows to the investment's cost.

International Firm   A firm which conducts international business through imports and exports.

Intrinsic Value, $\hat{P}_0$ The value of an asset that, in the mind of a particular investor, is justified by the facts; $\hat{P}_0$ may be different from the asset's actual market price.

Inventory Blanket Lien   A lending institution's claim on all of the borrower's inventories as security for a loan.

Inventory Management   The balancing of a set of costs that increase with larger inventory holdings with a set of costs that decrease with larger order size.

Inventory Turnover Ratio   The ratio computed by dividing sales by inventories; also called the *inventory utilization ratio*.

Inverted (Abnormal) Yield Curve   A downward-sloping yield curve.

Investment Banking House   A financial institution that underwrites and distributes new investment securities to help businesses obtain financing.

Investment-Grade Bonds   Bonds rated A or triple-B; many banks and other institutional investors are permitted by law to hold only investment-grade or better bonds.

Investment Opportunity Schedule (IOS)   A graph of the firm's investment opportunities ranked in order of the projects' internal rates of return.

Investment Outlay   Funds expended for an asset or a project (including delivery and installation) plus additional net working capital, if required.

Investment Tax Credit (ITC)   A specified percentage of the cost of new assets that businesses are *sometimes* allowed by law to deduct as a credit against their income taxes. ITCs were eliminated by the 1986 Tax Reform Act.

IRR   The discount rate which forces the PV of a project's cash flows to equal the PV of its costs and, thus, forces the projects NPV to equal zero.

Joint Venture   A corporate alliance in which two independent companies combine their resources to achieve a specific, limited objective.

Junk Bond   A high-risk, high-yield bond used originally to finance mergers, leveraged buyouts, and troubled companies.

Just-in-Time (JIT) System   A system of inventory control in which a manufacturer coordinates production with suppliers so that raw materials and components arrive just as they are needed in the production process.

Lead, or **Managing, Underwriter**   The member of an underwriting syndicate that actually manages the new securities issue.

Lessee   The party that uses, rather than the one who owns, the leased property.

Lessor   The owner of the leased property.

Letter of Credit   A written statement by an importing firm's bank testifying to the firm's ability to make payment, often guaranteeing payment to the exporter or the exporter's bank.

Leveraged Buyout (LBO)   A situation in which a group (often the firm's management) borrows heavily against the target firm's assets and purchases the company primarily using debt.

Liabilities   All the legal claims held against the firm by nonowners.

LIBOR   The London InterBank Offer Rate, which is the rate of interest charged by the most creditworthy banks to other large banks for short-term loans; the interest rate used as the base rate in many international loan agreements.

Limited Partnership   An unincorporated business owned both by general partners having unlimited liability and by limited partners whose liability is limited to their investment in the firm.

Line of Credit   An arrangement in which a bank agrees to lend up to a specified maximum amount of funds during a designated period.

Liquidation   The dissolution of a firm by selling off its assets.

Liquidity   The ability to sell an asset at a reasonable price on short notice.

Liquidity Preference Theory   The theory that lenders prefer to make short-term loans rather than long-term loans; hence, they will lend short-term funds at lower rates than long-term funds.

Liquidity Premium (LP)   A premium included in the nominal interest rate on a security if that security cannot be converted to cash on short notice and at a fair market price.

Liquidity Ratios   Ratios that show the relationship of a firm's cash and other current assets to its current liabilities.

Liquidity Risk   The risk that securities cannot be sold at close to the quoted price on short notice.

Lockbox Plan   A procedure used to speed up collections through the use of post office boxes in payers' local areas.

Lumpy Assets   Assets that cannot be acquired in small increments but must be obtained in large, discrete amounts.

Margin Requirement   The minimum percentage of his or her own money that a purchaser must put up when buying securities.

Marginal Cost of Capital (MCC)   The cost of obtaining another dollar of new capital; the weighted average cost of the last dollar of new capital raised.

Marginal Cost of Capital (MCC) Schedule   A graph that relates the firm's weighted average cost of each dollar of capital to the total amount of new capital raised.

Marginal Tax Rate   The tax applicable to the last unit of income.

Market/Book (M/B) Ratio   The ratio of a stock's market price to its book value.

Market Price, P_0   The price at which a stock sells in the market.

Market Risk   That part of a security's risk that *cannot* be eliminated by diversification. Also, that part of a *project's* risk that cannot be eliminated by diversification; it is measured by a project's beta coefficient.

Market Risk Premium, RP_M   The additional return over the risk-free rate needed to compensate investors for assuming an average amount of risk.

Market Segmentation Theory   The theory that each borrower and lender has a preferred maturity and that the slope of the yield curve depends on the supply of and demand for funds in the long-term market relative to the short-term market.

Market Value Ratios   A set of ratios that relates the firm's stock price to its earnings and book value per share.

Marketable Securities   Securities that can be sold on short notice for close to their quoted market prices.

Maturity Date   A specified date on which the par value of a bond must be repaid.

Maturity Risk Premium (MRP)   A premium which compensates investors for interest rate risk.

Merger   The combination of two firms to form a single firm.

Moderate Working Capital Investment Policy   A policy that is between the conservative and the aggressive working capital policies.

Modified Accelerated Cost Recovery System (MACRS)   A depreciation system that allows businesses to write off the cost of an asset over a period much shorter than its operating life.

Modified Du Pont Chart   A chart designed to show the relationships among return on total assets, total assets turnover, profit margin, and financial leverage.

Money Markets   Financial markets in which funds are borrowed or loaned for short periods (less than one year).

Money Market Fund   A mutual fund that invests in short-term, low-risk debt securities and allows investors to write checks against their accounts.

Mortgage Bond   A bond backed by fixed assets. *First mortgage bonds* are senior in priority to claims of *second mortgage bonds*.

Multinational Firm   A firm which not only actively imports and exports but also possesses affiliate operations in other countries.

Municipal Bonds   Long-term debt issued by state and local governments.

Mutual Fund   A financial intermediary that invests the pooled funds of savers, thus obtaining economies of scale in investing and reducing risk by diversification.

Mutually Exclusive Projects   A situation where if one project is accepted, the other must be rejected.

National Association of Securities Dealers (NASD)   An organization of securities dealers that works with the SEC to regulate operations in the over-the-counter market.

Natural Hedging   The hedging of a currency risk through an offsetting currency position resulting from operational or financial cash flows; for example, the hedging of German mark (DM) cash inflows by a U.S.-based firm by borrowing DM and then servicing the DM debt with the DM earnings from operations.

Near-Cash Reserves   Reserves that can be quickly and easily converted to cash.

Negotiable Certificate of Deposit   A marketable receipt for a large bank time deposit, usually issued in denominations of $100,000 or more.

Net Float   The difference between a firm's checkbook balance and the balance shown on the bank's books, i.e., the difference between disbursement float and collections float.

Net Operating Income   Earnings before interest and taxes (EBIT); is also called operating profit.

Net Present Value (NPV) Method   A method of evaluating investment proposals by finding the present value of future net cash flows, discounted at an appropriate interest rate, minus the cost of the investment.

Net Present Value Profile   A curve showing the relationship between a project's NPV and the discount rate used.

Net Working Capital   Current assets minus current liabilities; also equal to the current assets financed by long-term funds.

New York Stock Exchange (NYSE); American Stock Exchange (AMEX)   The two major U.S. securities exchanges.

Nominal (Stated) Interest Rate   The contracted, or quoted, interest rate.

Nominal (Quoted) Risk-Free Rate, k_{RF}   The rate of interest on a security that is free of all risk; k_{RF} is proxied by the T-bill rate or the T-bond rate. k_{RF} includes an inflation premium.

Normal (Constant) Growth   Growth which is expected to continue into the foreseeable future at about the same rate as that of the economy as a whole; g = a constant.

Normal Profits/Rates of Return   Those profits and rates of return that are close to the average for all firms and are just sufficient to attract capital.

Normal Yield Curve   An upward-sloping yield curve.

NOW (Negotiable Order of Withdrawal) Account   A form of savings account that allows withdrawal by check.

Off Balance Sheet Financing   Financing in which the assets and liabilities involved do not appear on the firm's balance sheet.

Offering Price   The price at which common stock is sold to the public.

Open-Market Operations   The purchase and sale of U.S. government securities by the Federal Reserve.

Operating Cash Flows   The cash flows associated with the everyday business activities of the firm; for example, the purchasing of inputs from a foreign supplier.

Operating Company   A subsidiary of a holding company; a separate legal entity.

Operating Lease   A lease under which the lessor maintains and finances the property; also called a *service lease*.

Operating Leverage   The extent to which fixed costs are used in a firm's operations.

Operating Merger   A merger in which operations of the firms involved are integrated in hope of achieving synergistic benefits.

Opportunity Cost   The return on the best alternative investment available of equal risk.

Optimal Dividend Policy   The dividend policy which strikes a balance between current dividends and future growth and maximizes the firm's stock price.

Option   A contract that gives the option holder the right, but not the obligation, to buy or sell an asset at some predetermined price within a specified period of time.

Ordering Costs   The costs of placing and receiving an order; these costs are fixed regardless of the average size of inventories.

Ordinary (Deferred) Annuity   An annuity in which the payments occur at the end of each period.

Organized Securities Exchanges   Formal organizations having tangible, physical locations that conduct auction markets in designated ("listed") securities.

Original Maturity   The number of years to maturity at the time a bond is issued.

Out-Sourcing   The practice of purchasing components rather than making them in-house.

Overdraft System   A system whereby firms may write checks in excess of their balances, with the banks automatically extending loans to cover the shortages.

Over-the-Counter Market   A large collection of brokers and dealers, connected electronically by telephones and computers, that provides for trading in unlisted securities.

Paid-in Capital   Funds received in excess of par value when a firm sells stock.

Par Value   The nominal or face value of a stock or bond.

Parent Company   A holding company; a firm which controls another firm by owning a large block of its stock.

Partnership   An unincorporated business owned by two or more persons.

Payables Centralization   The centralized processing of payables, which allows

more efficient monitoring of payables and float balances.

Payback Period   The number of years required to recover the firm's original investment.

Payment Date   The date on which a firm actually mails dividend checks.

Percentage of Sales Method   A method of forecasting financial requirements by expressing various balance sheet items as a percentage of sales and then multiplying these percentages by expected future sales to construct pro forma balance sheets.

Performance Shares   A type of incentive plan in which managers are awarded shares of stock on the basis of the firm's performance over given intervals with respect to earnings per share or other measures.

Permanent Current Assets   Current assets that are still on hand when business activity is at seasonal or cyclical lows.

Perpetuity   A stream of equal payments expected to continue forever.

Pledging of Accounts Receivable   Putting accounts receivable up as security for a loan.

Poison Pill   An action which will seriously hurt a company if it is acquired by another.

Portfolio   A collection of investments.

Post-Audit   A comparison of the actual and expected results for a given capital project.

Pre-Authorized Debits   A method used to speed up collections through automatic transfers from customers' accounts on specified dates.

Precautionary Balances   Cash balances or *marketable securities* held in reserve for random, unforeseen fluctuations in cash inflows and outflows.

Preemptive Right   A provision in the corporate charter or bylaws that gives common stockholders the right to purchase on a pro rata basis new issues of common stock (or securities convertible into common stock).

Preferred Stock   Long-term equity securities which pay a fixed dividend.

Premium Bond   A bond that sells above its par value; occurs whenever the going rate of interest falls below the coupon rate.

Present Value (PV)   The value today of a future payment or series of payments discounted at the appropriate interest rate.

Present Value Interest Factor (PVIF$_{k,n}$) The present value of $1 due n periods in the future discounted at k percent per period.

Price/Earnings (P/E) Ratio   The ratio of price per share to earnings per share; shows how many times earnings investors will pay for the stock.

Primary Markets   Financial markets in which corporations and government units raise capital by issuing new securities.

Prime Rate   A published rate of interest charged by commercial banks on short-term loans to very large, strong corporations.

Pro Forma Financial Statement   A projected financial statement which shows how an actual statement will look if certain specified assumptions are realized.

Probability Distribution   A listing of all possible outcomes, or events, with a probability (chance of occurrence) assigned to each outcome.

Production Opportunities   The returns available within an economy from investment into productive assets.

Profit Margin on Sales   This ratio measures income per dollar of sales; it is computed by dividing net income by sales.

Profit Maximization   The maximization of the firm's net income.

Profitability Ratios   A group of ratios showing the combined effects of liquidity, asset management, and debt management on operating income and net income.

Progressive Tax   A tax that requires a higher percentage payment on higher incomes. The federal personal income tax in the United States, which goes from a rate of 0 percent on the lowest increments of income to 39.6 percent, is progressive.

Promissory Note   A document specifying the terms and conditions of a loan, including the amount, interest rate, and repayment schedule.

Prospectus   A document describing a new securities issue and the issuing company.

Proxy   A document giving one person the authority to act for another, typically the power to vote shares of common stock.

Proxy Fight   An attempt by a person, group, or company to gain control of a firm by convincing stockholders to vote a new management team into office.

Publicly Owned Corporation   A corporation that is owned by a relatively large number of individuals of which many are not actively involved in its management.

Purchasing Power Parity (PPP)   The theory that the price of internationally traded goods should be the same in every country, and therefore the exchange rate between the two currencies should simply be the ratio of prices in the two countries.

Put Option   An option to sell a share of stock at a certain price, within a specified period.

PVA$_n$ The present value of an ordinary (deferred) annuity of n periods.

PVIFA$_{k,n}$ The present value interest factor for an annuity of n periodic payments discounted at k percent.

Quick, Acid Test, Ratio   This ratio is computed by deducting inventories from current assets and dividing the remainder by current liabilities.

Ranking Methods   Techniques used to evaluate capital expenditure proposals in terms of their attractiveness to the firm.

Rate of Return (k)   The rate of interest expected, or required, on an investment.

Ratio Analysis   Analysis of the relationships among financial statement accounts.

Realized Rate of Return, $\bar{k}$ The return that is actually earned. The actual return ($\bar{k}$) is usually different from the expected return ($\hat{k}$).

Real Risk-Free Rate of Interest, k*   The rate of interest that would exist on short-term default-free U.S. Treasury securities if no inflation were expected.

Recourse   A situation in which the lender can require payment from the selling firm if an account receivable is uncollectible.

Red-Line Method An inventory control procedure in which a red line is drawn around the inside of an inventory-stocked bin to indicate the reorder point level.

Registration Statement A statement of facts filed with the SEC about a company planning to issue securities.

Regulation Q A rule which, from 1933 through 1980, prohibited banks from paying interest on demand deposits.

Reinvestment Rate Assumption The assumption that cash flows from a project can be reinvested (1) at the cost of capital, if using the NPV method, or (2) at the internal rate of return of the project, if using the IRR method.

Reinvestment Rate Risk The risk that a decline in interest rates will lead to lower income when securities mature and funds are reinvested.

Relevant Cash Flows The specific set of cash flows that should be considered in a capital budgeting decision.

Relevant Risk The risk of a security that cannot be diversified away, or its *market risk*. This reflects a security's contribution to the risk of a portfolio.

Reorder Point The inventory level at which an order should be placed.

Reorganization The restructuring of debt and other claims against the firm.

Replacement Analysis An analysis involving the decision of whether or not to replace an existing asset that is still productive with a new one. Replacement projects are by definition mutually exclusive.

Replacement Chain (Common Life) Method A method of comparing projects of unequal lives which assumes that each project can be replicated as many times as necessary to reach a common life span; the NPVs over this life span are then compared, and the project with the higher common life NPV is chosen.

Repurchase Agreement (Repo) A collateralized loan by one financial institution to another.

Required Rate of Return, k_s The minimum rate of return on a common stock that a stockholder considers acceptable.

Required Reserves The minimum reserves that a depository institution must hold as vault cash or reserve deposits with the Federal Reserve.

Reserve Borrowing Capacity Unused debt capacity that permits borrowing if a firm needs capital in troubled times.

Residual Dividend Policy A policy in which dividends paid equal total earnings minus the amount of retained earnings necessary to finance the firm's optimal capital budget.

Residual Value The value of leased property at the end of the lease term.

Restrictive Covenant A provision in a debt contract that constrains the actions of the borrower.

Retention Rate The percentage of its earnings retained by the firm after payment of dividends, which is equal to 1 minus the dividend payout ratio.

Return on Common Equity (ROE) The ratio of net income to common equity; measures the rate of return on common stockholders' investment.

Return on Total Assets (ROA) The ratio of net income to total assets.

Revolving Credit Agreement A formal line of credit extended to a firm by a bank or other financial institution.

Risk The chance that some unfavorable event will occur. Also, in a financial market context, the chance that a loan will not be repaid as promised.

Risk-Adjusted Discount Rate The discount rate that applies to a particular risky stream of cash flows; the firm's or division's cost of capital plus a risk premium appropriate to the level of risk attached to a particular project's income stream.

Risk Aversion A dislike for risk. Risk averse investors require higher rates of return on higher-risk investments.

Risk Premium, RP The difference between the required (and expected) rate of return on a given risky asset and that on a less risky asset.

Risk-Return Tradeoff The basic rule that higher expected return will be accompanied by higher risk and that lower risk is generally achieved in combination with lower expected return.

S Corporation A small corporation which, under Subchapter S of the Internal Revenue Code, elects to be taxed as a proprietorship or partnership yet retains limited liability and other benefits of the corporate form of organization.

Safety Stocks Additional inventory carried to guard against increases in sales rates or production/shipping delays.

Sale and Leaseback An operation whereby a firm sells land, buildings, or equipment and simultaneously leases the property back for a specified period under specific terms.

Sales (Demand) Forecast A forecast of a firm's unit and dollar sales for some future period, generally sales based on recent trends plus forecasts of the economic prospects for the nation, region, industry, and so forth.

Salvage Value The market price of a capital asset at the end of a specified period. In a capital budgeting decision, it is also the current market price of an asset being considered for replacement.

Seasonal Dating Terms to induce customers to buy early by not requiring payment until the customers' selling season, regardless of when the merchandise is shipped.

Secondary Markets Financial markets in which securities are traded among investors after the securities have been initially issued.

Secured Loan A loan backed by collateral, often inventories or receivables.

Securities and Exchange Commission (SEC) The U.S. government agency which regulates the issuance and trading of stocks and bonds.

Security Market Line (SML) The line that shows the relationship between risk as measured by beta and the required rate of return for individual securities. SML = Equation 12-7.

Selling Group A group of brokerage firms formed for the purpose of distributing a new issue of securities.

Shelf Registration A procedure under which a large, well-established firm can sell new securities on very short notice.

Simple Interest Interest that is charged on the basis of the amount borrowed; it is paid when the loan matures rather than when it is taken out.

Sinking Fund A required annual payment designed to amortize a bond or preferred stock issue.

Social Responsibility The concept that businesses should be actively concerned about the welfare of society at large, even to the detriment of their stockholders.

Sole Proprietorship An unincorporated business owned by one individual.

Specialist Banks Banks that act only as investment banks, concentrating on the origination, distribution, and trading of securities.

Speculative Balances Cash balances or *marketable securities* that are held to enable the firm to take advantage of any bargain purchases that might arise.

Spin-Off A divestiture in which the stock of a subsidiary is given to the parent company's stockholders.

Spontaneous Assets Assets which vary proportionately with sales and, therefore, remain constant percentages of sales; investment in these assets must increase by the same percentage as projected sales.

Spontaneously Generated Funds Funds that are obtained automatically from routine business transactions; this financing is assumed to increase by the same percentage as projected sales.

Spot Rates Exchange rates established for immediate delivery or settlement (actually settled within two business days).

Spread The difference between the price a securities dealer offers to pay for securities (the "bid" price) and the price at which the dealer offers to sell the securities (the "asked" price).

Stand-Alone Risk The risk an asset would have if it were a firm's only asset and the firm's stockholders held only that one stock; it is measured by the variability of the asset's expected returns.

Standard Deviation, σ A statistical measure of the variability of a set of observations.

Statement of Cash Flows A statement reporting the impact of a firm's operating, investing, and financing activities on cash flows over an accounting period.

Statement of Retained Earnings A statement reporting how much of the firm's earnings were not paid out in dividends. The figure for retained earnings that appears here is the sum of the annual retained earnings for each year of the firm's history.

Stepped-Up Exercise Price An exercise price that is specified to be higher if a warrant is exercised after a designated date.

Stock Dividend A dividend paid in the form of additional shares of stock rather than in cash.

Stock Repurchase A transaction in which a firm buys back shares of its own stock, thereby decreasing shares outstanding, increasing EPS, and, often, increasing the price of the stock.

Stock Split An action taken by a firm to increase the number of shares outstanding, such as doubling the number of shares outstanding by giving each stockholder two new shares for each one formerly held.

Stockholder Wealth Maximization
The appropriate goal for management decisions in publicly traded firms; it considers the risk and timing associated with expected earnings per share in order to maximize the firm's stock price.

Stockholders' Equity (Net Worth) The capital supplied by stockholders — capital stock, paid-in capital, and retained earnings. *Common equity* is that part of total claims belonging to the common stockholders.

Strategic Business Plan A long-run plan which outlines in broad terms the firm's basic strategy for the next 5 to 10 years.

Stretching Accounts Payable The practice of deliberately paying accounts payable late.

Striking (Exercise) Price The price that must be paid (buying or selling) for a share of common stock when an option is exercised.

Subordinated Debenture A bond which, in the event of bankruptcy and liquidation, has a claim on assets only after the senior debt has been paid off.

Sunk Cost A cash outlay that has already been incurred and which cannot be recovered regardless of whether the project is accepted or rejected.

Supernormal (Nonconstant) Growth
The part of the life cycle of a firm in which its growth is much faster than that of the economy as a whole.

Synchronized Cash Flows A situation in which inflows coincide with outflows, thereby permitting a firm to reduce transactions balances to a minimum.

Synergy The condition wherein the whole is greater than the sum of its parts; in a synergistic merger, the postmerger value exceeds the sum of the separate companies' premerger values.

Target (Optimal) Capital Structure
The percentages of debt, preferred stock, and common equity that will minimize the firm's weighted average cost of capital (WACC) and, therefore, maximize the price of the firm's stock.

Target Cash Balance The cash balance that a firm plans to maintain in order to conduct business.

Target Company A firm that another company seeks to acquire.

Taxable Income Gross income minus exemptions and allowable deductions as set forth in the Tax Code.

Tax Loss Carry-Back and Carry-Forward Ordinary operating losses that can be carried backward or forward in time to offset taxable income in a given year.

Temporary Current Assets Current assets that fluctuate with seasonal or cyclical sales variations.

Tender Offer The offer of one firm to buy the stock of another by going directly to the stockholders, frequently (but not always) over the opposition of the target company's management.

Term Loan A loan, generally obtained from a bank or insurance company, with a maturity greater than one year.

Term Structure of Interest Rates The relationship between interest rates (yields) and maturities of debt securities.

Time Effect A principle of option valuation that states that the longer the time remaining to maturity, the greater the market price of an option.

Time Preferences for Consumption
The preferences of consumers for current consumption as opposed to saving for future consumption.

Times-Interest-Earned (TIE) Ratio
The ratio of earnings before interest and taxes (EBIT) to interest charges; measures the ability of the firm to meet its annual interest payments.

Total Assets Turnover Ratio The ratio computed by dividing sales by total assets;

also called the *total assets utilization ratio*.

Trade Credit Inter-firm debt arising from credit sales; recorded as an account receivable by the seller and as an account payable by the buyer.

Transaction Exposure The risk to a firm of making or receiving a foreign currency-denominated cash flow at a future date.

Transactions Balances Cash balances associated with payments and collections; those balances necessary to conduct day-to-day operations.

Translation Exposure The risk to a firm's consolidated balance sheet and income statement from the valuation of foreign affiliates and subsidiaries; also called accounting exposure.

Treasury Stock Common stock that has been repurchased by the issuing corporation.

Trend Analysis An analysis of a firm's financial ratios over time; used to determine the improvement or deterioration of its financial situation.

Triangular Arbitrage The process of trading three different currencies within a few moments in time in order to obtain a tiny margin of profit from rates which are not perfectly aligned.

Trust Receipt An instrument acknowledging that the borrower holds certain goods in trust for the lender.

Trustee An official who ensures that the bondholders' interests are protected and that the terms of the indenture are carried out.

Two-Bin Method An inventory control procedure in which the reorder point is reached when one of two inventory-stocked bins is empty.

Two-Tier Offer A merger offer which provides different (better) terms to those who tender their stock earliest.

Underwriting Syndicate A syndicate of investment banking firms formed to spread the risk associated with the purchase and distribution of a new issue of securities.

Underwritten Arrangement Agreement for the sale of securities in which the investment bank guarantees the sale of the securities, thus agreeing to bear any risks involved in the transaction.

Uneven Cash Flow Stream A series of payments in which the amount varies from one period to the next.

Uniform Commercial Code A system of standards that simplifies and standardizes procedures for establishing loan security.

Universal (Global) Banks Banks that offer both commercial and investment banking services to their customers.

U.S. Treasury Bills Short-term, marketable federal government debt.

U.S. Treasury Notes and Bonds Long-term, marketable federal government debt.

Variable Operating Costs Operating costs that vary directly with sales. For example, factory labor, materials, and sales commissions.

Variance, σ^2 The square of the standard deviation.

Venture Capital An investment into new, privately held firms; it is intended to facilitate the growth of small firms not yet able to "go public."

Vertical Merger A merger between a firm and one of its suppliers or customers.

Volatility Effect A principle of option valuation that states that the greater the volatility of the stock price, the greater the market price of an option written on the stock.

Warehouse Receipt Financing An arrangement under which the lending institution employs a third party to exercise control over the borrower's inventory and to act as the lender's agent.

Warrant A long-term option to buy a stated number of shares of common stock at a specified price.

Weighted Average Cost of Capital, WACC A weighted average of the component costs of debt, preferred stock, and common equity.

White Knight A company that is more acceptable to the management of a firm under attack in a hostile takeover attempt.

"Window Dressing" Techniques employed by a firm to make its financial statements look better than they really are.

Working Capital A firm's investment in short-term assets — cash, marketable securities, inventory, and accounts receivable.

Working Capital Financing Policy The manner in which the firm's permanent and temporary current assets are financed.

Working Capital Management The administration, within policy guidelines, of current assets and current liabilities.

Working Capital Policy Basic policy decisions regarding target levels for each category of current assets and how current assets will be financed.

Yield Curve A graph showing the relationship between yields and maturities of debt securities.

Yield to Call (YTC) The rate of return earned on a bond if it is called before its maturity date.

Yield to Maturity (YTM) The rate of return earned on a bond if it is bought at a given market price and held to maturity.

Zero-Balance Account (ZBA) A checking account in which a zero balance is maintained; as checks are presented against the account, funds are transferred from a master account.

Zero Coupon Bonds (Zeros) Bonds that pay no annual interest but are sold at a discount below par, thus providing compensation to investors in the form of capital appreciation.

Index

ABC system of inventory control, 368–369
Abnormal yield curve, 137
Absolute value, vs. relative returns, 558
Accelerated Cost Recovery System (ACRS), 48, 160
Accelerated depreciation methods, 48–51, 160
Accounting methods, flexibility of, 166–167(IP)
Accounting net income, vs. cash flow, 524–527
Accounts payable, 161. *See also* Trade credit
  centralization of, 315
  deferral period for, 272
  extending payment period for, 275
  as source of short-term credit, 388–394, 408–409(SB)
  stretching, 391, 394
Accounts receivable, 160, 161, 343–359
  collection policy for, 352
  computers and, 358–359
  cost of financing, 419
  credit policy and, 345–359
  determinants of, 344
  direct financing of, 408–409(SB)
  evaluation of financing of, 419–420
  factoring of, 353, 418–419
  future use of financing of, 420
  pledging of, 353, 417, 418
  profit potential in carrying, 353
  receivables conversion period, 272
  reducing, 274–275
  short-term credit and, 353
  speeding collection of, 310–313
Accounts receivable turnover ratio, 193n
Accruals, 161, 388
Acid test ratio, 191, 201, 269
ACME, 904–905
ACP (average collection period), 192–193
Acquiring company, 865
Acquisition departments, 867n
ACRS (Accelerated Cost Recovery System), 48, 160
Activity ratios, 191. *See also* Asset management ratios
Actual rate of return, 653
Addison Products Company, 232–243, 270–277
Additional funds needed (AFN), 232, 235–243
  formula method for forecasting, 238–243
  modifying forecast of, 246–247
Add-on interest, 401
AFN. *See* Additional funds needed
After-tax cost of debt, $k_d(1 - T)$, 725
Agency problem, 23–26
Aggressive working capital financing policy, 282–283
Aggressive working capital investment policy, 276, 277
Aging schedule, 354–355
Akers, John, 3–4(DIF)
Alabama Power, 632
Allaire, Paul, 63(IP)
Allen-Edmonds Shoe Corporation, 369, 371–372
Allied Crude Vegetable Oil Company, 421n

Allied Food Products, 838–839
All-Technology Manufacturing (ATM), 770–773, 777–785, 787, 788, 789–795
Alternative Minimum Tax (AMT), 43n
American Development Corporation (ADC), 841–842
American Express, 63–64(IP), 375(DIF)
American Express Field Warehousing Company, 421n
American Institute of Certified Public Accountants (AICPA), 16(IP)
American Stock Exchange (AMEX), 65
Amortization schedule, 493–494
Amortized loan, 493–494, 624–625, 642–643
AMT (Alternative Minimum Tax), 43n
Annual report, 156, 157
  abuses in, 188–189(IP)
  chairman's letter in, 155(DIF), 176–177(DIF)
Annuity, 482
  deferred, 483–484, 486
  future value of, 482–485
  ordinary, 483–484, 486
  present value of, 485–488
  solving for interest rate of, 492
  solving for payment of, 493–494
  solving for time of, 491–492
  sum of, 483
Annuity due, 483, 485, 487–488
Arbitrage, triangular, 895
Arrearage, 628
Asked price, 67
Asset(s), 160
  on balance sheet, 160
  of banks, 106–107
  capital, 42
  claim on, 164
  combining current asset and liability decisions, 287–288
  depreciable, 50
  fixed, 160, 193
  lumpy, 245–246
  permanent current, 279–280
  physical, 53, 458–460
  rate of return and, 276–278
  risk and, 276–278
  spontaneous, 232
  temporary current, 279–280
Asset-based financing, 406n. *See also* Secured loans
Asset management ratios, 191–194, 201
AT&T, 875–876
Auction markets, 66
Augustine, Norman, 857(DIF), 886(DIF)
Autera, Michael, 229(DIF)
Average collection period (ACP), 192–193
Average tax rate, 40

Balance sheet, 160–163
  changing ratios of assets and liabilities, 243–248
  common-size, 186

  effects of stock dividends and stock splits, 838–839
  leasing and, 688–689
  projected, 232–236
  trade credit and, 392, 393
Balance sheet basis, 776n
Ball Corporation, 459
Bank(s)
  accounting methods of, 166–167(IP)
  assets of, 106–107
  capital account of, 106
  cash account of, 106
  choosing, 395–396
  commercial, 60–61, 101–107, 111–113
  concentration, 313
  demand deposits and, 94–97, 104, 105
  discount rate and, 91–92, 93
  dual chartering system for, 102
  internal, in international financial management, 912
  investment, 58–59, 645(DIF), 667–674, 674–675(DIF), 871–872
  liabilities and equity of, 104–106
  mutual savings, 61
  regulation of, 87(DIF), 102–104, 118–119(DIF)
  relationship with customer, 387(DIF), 411–412(DIF)
  reserve requirements and, 90–91, 95
  savings deposits in, 104, 105
  sources and uses of funds of, 104–107
  specialist, 112–113
  time deposits in, 104, 105
  universal (global), 112–113
  See also Federal Reserve
Banker's acceptances, 55, 56, 327
Bank holding company (BHC), 102
Bank Holding Company Acts of 1956 and 1970, 102
Banking relationships, building, 114–116(SB)
Bank loans. *See* Loans
Bank of America, 421n, 613
Bankruptcy, 285–286(IP), 812–817
  Chapter 7, 813, 814–815
  Chapter 11, 813
  federal laws concerning, 812–813, 817
  financial decisions in, 813–814
  liquidation procedures in, 813, 814–817
  social issues in, 817
Basic earning power (BEP) ratio, 194, 198, 201
Basle Accord of 1988, 111
Beatrice Companies, 875
Belco Petroleum, 632
BEP (basic earning power) ratio, 194, 198, 201
Best efforts arrangement, 668
Beta coefficient, 447–451, 457
Beta risk, 565, 566, 567–570
Beukelman, Del, 427(DIF)
BHC (bank holding company), 102
Bid, competitive, 667
Bid price, 67
Blackout agreement, 674–675(DIF)

Note: Boldface terms in the index refer to key terms in the text, and the boldface number refers to the page on which the key term is defined. (DIF) refers to "Decision in Finance" and "Resolution to Decision in Finance," (SB) to "Small Business," and (IP) to "Industry Practice" sections, and an "n" beside a page number indicates information is found in a footnote on that page.

Blanket lien, inventory, 420
Blue sky laws, 74
Board of Governors of Federal Reserve System, 89
Bohan, Gloria, 285(IP)
Bond(s), 596–624
 advantages and disadvantages of, 626–627
 calling, 595–596(DIF), 597, 609–610, 636–637(DIF)
 convertible, 612, 702–707
 corporate, 55, 57
 debentures, 161, 611–612
 demand for, 615(IP)
 discount, 72, 600–601, 602
 features of contracts for, 607–610
 floating-rate, 616–617
 income, 612
 indexed (purchasing power), 612–613
 interest rate on, 604–605
 investment-grade, 619
 junk, 617–618
 maturity of, 597, 619
 mortgage, 161, 611
 municipal ("munis"), 41, 55, 57
 new issues, 598
 outstanding, 598
 premium, 72, 601, 602
 putable, 614n
 reinvestment rate risk of, 135n
 repayment provisions of, 608–610
 Treasury, 55, 56, 136–137, 326, 621, 622
 types of, 611–613
 valuation of, 598–606
 with warrants, 699–702
 yield to call on, 605–606
 yield to maturity on, 604–605
 zero coupon, 135n, 479n, 613–616
Bond indenture, 608, 827
Bond markets, 70–72
Bond ratings, 132, 619–624
Bond-yield-plus-risk-premium approach, 730
Book value basis, 776n
Borrowers, 52, 60, 125n
Borrowing. See Credit; Loans
"Bottom line," 159
Boyd, Michael, 775(IP)
Bracket creep, 40
Break in MCC schedule, 738–741
Breakeven analysis, 767–770
Breakeven chart, 767–769
Breakeven point, 769–770
Break point (BP), 737
Brennan, Edward A., 64(IP)
Bristol-Myers-Squibb, 229(DIF), 251–252(DIF), 844
Brokerage departments, 66
Brokerage houses, 67–68
Bronner, David G., 596(DIF), 636–637(DIF)
Brookstone, Arnold, 208(IP)
Brusca, Robert, 149(DIF)
Budget, cash. See Cash budget
Buffett, Warren, 155(DIF), 177(DIF), 840
Burton, John, 166–167(IP)
Business activity, and interest rates, 143
Business decisions
 in bankruptcy, 813–814
 in capital budgeting, 562–585
 on capital structure, 794–799
 combining current asset and liability decisions, 287–288
 interest rates and, 146–147
 in raising capital, 667–669
 reevaluating, 668
Business organization, 11–17
 corporation, 13–14
 evaluating alternative forms of, 15
 finance and, 15–17, 18
 partnership, 12–13, 16–17(IP)
 reorganization, 813
 S corporation, 14
 sole proprietorship, 11–12
Business risk, 765–766
Buyout
 leveraged, 23–24, 26, 208–209(IP), 617–618, 666, 875, 881–882
 managerial, 874
Bylaws, 14

Cadbury Schweppes PLC, 370(IP)
Calculators, financial, 473–474, 537–538
Call option, 695
Call premium, 609
Call provision, 597
 of bonds, 595–596(DIF), 609–610, 636–637(DIF)
 of preferred stock, 629
Calpers (California Public Employees Retirement System), 647, 649–650(IP)
Campbell Soup Company, 647n
Canadian Imperial Bank of Commerce (CIBC), 405
Cancellation clause, 687
Capital
 alternative sources of, 828
 cost of. See Cost of capital; Interest rate(s)
 credit and, 347
 decisions in raising, 667–669
 impairment of capital rule, 827
 paid-in, 162
 venture, 42, 76–77(SB), 633–634(SB), 800–802(SB)
 See also Working capital
Capital account, 106
Capital asset, 42
Capital Asset Pricing Model (CAPM), 439, 446–450, 567, 571, 728–729
Capital budgeting, 516–544
 anticipating change and, 515–516(DIF), 544–546(DIF)
 case study in, 540–542
 classifying projects for, 518–520
 comparing projects with unequal lives in, 578–580
 computer modeling for, 553–555
 cost in, 519–520
 decisions in, 562–585
 estimating cash flows in, 523–528
 evaluating proposed projects in, 529–539, 555–560
 importance of, 516–518
 inflation and, 580–582
 international, 903–909
 replacement analysis in, 574–578
 replacement chain method in, 579–580
 risk analysis in, 564–573
 steps in, 520–523
 timing in, 517
Capital Cities, 330(DIF)
Capital components, 723–724
Capital gain or loss, 42–43
 common stock and, 651–652
 corporate, 45
Capital gains yield, 601, 653
Capital intensity ratio, 241–242
Capitalizing the lease, 689
Capital lease, 687–688, 689
Capital markets, 5, 54
 career opportunities in, 5
 efficient, 75–76
 instruments of, 55, 56, 57
Capital spending, 542
Capital structure
 cost of capital and, 782–785
 determining, 794–799
 dividend policy and, 828
 earnings before interest and taxes and, 778n
 of foreign subsidiaries, 908–909
 mergers and, 796
 stock price and, 782–785
 target (optimal), 732–733, 777–785
 theory of, 785–788
 times-interest-earned ratio and, 794–796, 799
 variations in, 799–800
CAPM. See Capital Asset Pricing Model
Captive finance companies, 353n
Career opportunities, 5–6
Carlyle Group, 764(DIF), 804(DIF)
Carmichael, Douglas, 212(DIF)
Carry-back and carry-forward of operating losses, 45–46
Carrying costs, 362
Carter Chemical Company, 157–175, 189–206, 399, 524–525, 596–606, 655–657
Carter Hawley Hale Stores, 188(IP)
Cash, 302–329
 on balance sheet, 160, 161
 dividend policy and, 827
 marketable securities as substitute for, 319–320

reasons for holding, 302–303
 slowing and controlling disbursements of, 314–316
 speed collection of, 310–313
 surplus, 301(DIF), 330–331(DIF)
Cash account, 106
Cash balances
 compensating, 302, 317–318
 precautionary, 303
 speculative, 303
 target, 304, 308–309
 transactions, 302
Cash budget, 248n, 303, **304**–309
 computer modeling for, 336–338
 constructing, 304–308
 working capital and, 269
Cash call, 595–596(DIF)
Cash conversion cycle, 269, 270–271, **272,** 273–275
Cash discount, 346
Cash flow, 168
 accounting net income vs., 524–527
 cycle of, 165, 168–170
 estimating for capital budgeting, 523–528
 financial, 909, 910
 forecasting, 523–528
 free, 868, 870
 incremental, 524, 527–528
 in international financial management, 909–912
 operating, 909, 910
 relevant, 524
 statement of, 170–175, 238
 synchronized, 309–310
 uneven stream of, 489–491
 valuing, for mergers, 870–871
 working capital and, 269
Cash management, 302–319
 matching costs and benefits of, 318–319
 in multidivisional firm, 316–317
 techniques for, 309–316
Cash pooling, 911
CBS, 330(DIF)
CDs. See Certificates of deposit
CEBA (Competitive Equality in Banking Act of 1987), 104
Certificates of deposit (CDs), 105
 interest rates for, 399n
 negotiable, 55, 56, 327–328
Change in net working capital, 528
Chapter 7, 813, 814–815
Chapter 11, 813
Charter, 14
Chase Manhattan Bank, 835–836(IP)
Check clearing, 310, 311
Chemical Bank, 459, 835–836(IP), 864
"Cherry picking," 167(IP)
Chicago Board of Options Exchange (CBOE), 695
Chicago Steel Company, 567–570
Chief financial officer, 17
Chrysler Corporation, 624, 631, 774(IP)
C.I.T. Financial Corporation, 327
Clark, Howard L., Jr., 877(IP)
Classified stock, 648
Class life, 48
Clientele effect, 829
Clinton, Bill, 37–38(DIF), 79–80(DIF)
Closely held corporation, 664
Clough, Robert, 906(IP)
Coca-Cola, 516–517
Coefficient of variation (CV), 436–437
Colgate-Palmolive, 208(IP)
Collateral, 348, **397**–398
Collection policy, 352
Collection process, speeding up, 310–313
Collections float, 313
Commercial banks, 60–61, 101–107, 111–113
Commercial paper, 55, 56, **327**
 cost of, 404
 maturity of, 404
 in short-term financing, 403–405, 407–408(IP)
 use of, 404–405
Common equity, 162–163
 cost of new, 731–732
 return on, 199, 201, 354
Common life (replacement chain) method, 579–580

Common-size balance sheets and income statements, 186
Common stock, 55, 57, 162, 644–675
    advantages and disadvantages of, 661–664
    control of firm and, 646–648, 649–650(IP), 666
    cost of newly issued, 731–732
    decision to go public with, 664–667
    going public and, 664–667, 671–672(SB)
    investment banking and, 645(DIF), 667–674, 674–675(DIF)
    issuance costs of, 668–669
    legal rights and privileges of stockholders, 646–650
    selling procedures for, 670
    types of, 648, 650
    valuation of, 651–661
Commonwealth Edison, 146
Company-specific risk, 445–446
Comparative ratio analysis, 206–209
Compensating balance, 302, 398
    cash, 317–318
    discount interest with, 402–403
    short-term bank loans and, 398
    simple interest with, 401–402
Compensation, managerial, 24–25
Competitive bid, 667
Competitive Equality in Banking Act of 1987 (CEBA), 104
Composite cost of capital, 732–733
Compounding, 471–475. See also Future value
Compounding periods, 510–512
Comptronix Corporation, 185(DIF)
CompuEd Corporation, 869–870
Computer(s)
    accounts receivable and, 358–359
    consumer credit information and, 342(DIF)
    in finance, 7, 8
    in inventory control, 368, 371(IP)
Computerized inventory control system, 368
Computer modeling
    amortized term loan, 642–643
    capital budgeting, 553–555
    cash budgeting, 336–338
    external financing requirements and ratios, 261–263
    in financial planning, 248
    projected financial statements and ratio analysis, 224–226
Concentration bank, 313
Congeneric merger, 861
Conglomerate merger, 861
Conklin, James W., 553–555
Conklin, Scott, 553–555
Conoco, 863
Conservative working capital financing policy, 283–284
Conservative working capital investment policy, 276, 277
Consol, 488
Consolidated corporate tax returns, 47
Consolidated Edison, 843
Consolidated leverage, 880
Constant growth, 655–658
Constant growth model, 655
Consumer credit information, 341–342(DIF), 349–351
Consumer credit loans, 56
Continental Airlines, 817
Continental Illinois, 876
Continental Information Systems, 188(IP)
Continuous probability distributions, 432–433, 435
Contractual hedging, 916–917
Control
    capital structure decisions and, 797
    common stock and, 646–648, 649–650(IP), 666
    dividend policy and, 828
    as financial manager's responsibility, 9
    holding companies and, 878
    mergers and, 860, 867–868
Controlled disbursement account, 316
Controller, 17
Conversion price (P_c), 702–703
Conversion ratio (CR), 702–703
Conversion value (C_t), 704
Convertible bonds, 612, 702–707
Convertible securities, 686, 702–707
    analysis of, 703–707
    conversion ratio and conversion price of, 702–703
    use in financing, 707

Cooper, Janet K., 845
Coordination, as financial manager's responsibility, 9
Corcoran, Case & Wolfe (CCW), 261–263
Corporate alliance, 873
Corporate bonds, 55, 57
Corporate risk, 564, 565, 566–567
Corporation, 13–14
    advantages of, 13–14
    closely held, 664
    disadvantages of, 14
    goals of, 17–21
    income taxes on, 43–47, 80(DIF)
    interest and dividend income received by, 43–44
    interest and dividends paid by, 45
    limited liability, 16–17
    publicly owned, 665–667
    S, 4, 47
Correlation coefficient, 442
Cost(s)
    in capital budgeting, 519–520
    carrying, 362
    of cash management, 318–319
    of commercial paper, 404
    cutting, 774–775(IP)
    deferring, 189(IP)
    flotation, 668, 731–732
    of funds, 124–125
    of going public, 748–749(SB)
    of installation, 528
    of inventory, 361–362, 422
    of issuing stock, 668–669
    of long-term vs. short-term debt, 284
    operating, 158–159, 767
    opportunity, 303, 527, 727, 823
    ordering, 362
    replacement, 519
    of shipping, 528
    of short-term bank loans, 399–403
    stock-out, 361, 362
    sunk, 527
    of trade credit, 389–391
Costly trade credit, 393–394
Cost of capital, 526, 572–573, 720–751
    capital structure and, 782–785
    changes due to level of budget, 733–741
    composite, 732–733
    credit rating and, 721–722(DIF), 751(DIF)
    divisional, 572–573
    importance of, 722
    marginal, 733–741
    problem areas in, 746
    trends in, 747
    weighted average, 722–723, 724, 732–733
    See also Interest rate(s)
Cost of debt, k_d(1 − T), 725
Cost of goods sold, 158
Cost of new common equity (k_e), 731–732
Cost of preferred stock (k_p), 726
Cost of retained earnings (k_s), 726–731
Counterparty risk, 923
Coupon interest rate, 597
Coupon payment, 597
Coupon rate, 71, 72
Coverage ratios, 187–206, 619–624
Covered options, 695
Credit
    capital structure decisions and, 798
    five Cs of, 347–349
    information available on, 341–342(DIF)
    law on, 354
    leasing and, 694
    letter of, 913–914
    line of, 398–399
    profit potential in granting, 353
    quality of, 347
    revolving, 399
    short-term, 279–287, 353
    trade, 388–394
Credit analysts, 187
Credit associations, 349–351
Credit bureaus, 341(DIF), 349–351
Credit crunch, 98, 285–286(IP)
Credit information
    privacy and, 341–342(DIF)
    sources of, 348, 349–351

Creditors, vs. shareholders, 25–26
Credit period, 345–346
Credit policy, 345–359
    analyzing proposed changes in, 355–358
    elements of, 345–353
    evaluating effectiveness of, 354–359
    other factors influencing, 353
Credit-reporting agencies, 341, 348–349, 350
Credit-scoring system, 351–352
Credit standards, 347–352
Credit terms, 345
Credit unions, 61, 101, 104n
Cross rate, 895
CTA (cumulative translation adjustment), 920–922
Cumulative dividends, 628
Cumulative translation adjustment (CTA), 920–922
Currency, foreign. See Exchange rates; Foreign currency
Currency swap, 923–924
Current assets, permanent vs. temporary, 279–280
Current ratio, 190, 201, 269
Current yield, 71, 601
Cyclical changes, 246

Days sales outstanding (DSO), 192–193, 201, 354
Dayton Card Company, 304–307, 320, 372
Dayton Hudson Corporation, 371(IP)
DCF (discounted cash flow) techniques, 529, 531, 729–730
Debentures, 161, 611–612
Debits, pre-authorized, 312–313
Debt
    cost of, 725
    floating-rate, 616–617
    funded, 607
    long-term, 284–287, 626–627
    reduction of, 8
    short-term vs. long-term, 284–287
Debt management ratios, 194–198, 201
Debt ratio, 196
Decisions. See Business decisions
Declaration date, 833
Default risk, 324
Default risk premium (DRP), 130, 132–133
Defensive merger, 860
Deferred annuity, 483–484, 486
Deferred call, 609
Deficit, federal, and interest rates, 141–142
Degree of financial leverage (DFL), 791–792
Degree of leverage, 788, 789–794
Degree of operating leverage (DOL), 789–790
Degree of total leverage (DTL), 792–794
Del Monte Corporation, 866–867
Deloitte & Touche, 212(DIF)
Delta Air Lines, 10, 821–822(DIF), 849(DIF)
Demand deposits, 94–97, 104, 105
Demand forecast, 230–231
Depository Institutions Deregulation and Monetary Control Act of 1980 (DIDMCA), 62, 90, 102–103
Depository transfer check (DTC), 313
Depreciable asset, sale of, 50
Depreciable basis, 50
Depreciation, 48–51
    accelerated methods of, 48–51, 160
    on balance sheet, 160, 161
    cash flow and, 170–172
    changing, in financial reports, 189(IP)
    as operating expense, 159
    straight line method of, 48
    tax depreciation life, 48–51
Deregulation of financial institutions, 7
Detachable warrant, 701
DFL (degree of financial leverage), 791–792
DIDMCA (Depository Institutions Deregulation and Monetary Control Act of 1980), 62, 90, 102–103
Digital Equipment Corporation, 185(DIF)
Dillard Department Stores, 615(IP)
Direct financing, 408–409(SB), 624
Direct quote, 893–895
Direct transfers of money and securities, 58–59
Disbursement(s), slowing and controlling, 314–316
Disbursement float, 313
Discount bonds, 72, 600–601, **602**
Discount brokers, 67–68
Discounted cash flow (DCF) techniques, 529, 531, 729–730

Discounting, 476–478
Discount interest, 400–401, 402–403
Discount rate, 91–92, 93
  estimating, for mergers, 869–870
  risk-adjusted, 573
Discounts lost, 390n
Discriminant analysis, 211n, 351
Disney Corporation, 330(DIF)
Diversifiable risk. *See* Company-specific risk
Diversification, 8, 63–64(IP)
  global, 458
  mergers and, 860, 883(SB)
  of risk, 427–428(DIF), 458, 461–462(DIF), 570–571
Divestitures, 874–876
  illustrations of, 874–876
  spin-offs, 874, 877–878(IP)
  types of, 874
Dividend(s)
  as basis for stock values, 653–654
  constant or steadily increasing, 830–832
  constant payout ratio, 832
  corporate, 45
  cumulative, 628
  cutting, 821–822(DIF), 849(DIF)
  extra, 832–833
  improper accumulation to avoid payment of, 46–47
  information content of (signaling), 829–830
  intercorporate, 44
  payment policies for, 830–833
  payment procedure for, 833–834
  riskiness of, 829
  stock, 838–840
  taxes and, 41–42, 43–44
Dividend payout ratio, 164–165
Dividend policy, 820–849
  factors influencing, 826–830
  financial requirements and, 240–241
  illustrations of, 845–848
  optimal, 822
  residual, 822–826
Dividend policy decision, 28
Dividend reinvestment plans (DRIPs), 834–837
Dividends per share (DPS), 159, 164–165
Dividend yield, 68n, 653
Dividend-yield-plus-growth-rate approach, 729–730
Doerfler, Ron, 330(DIF)
DOL (degree of operating leverage), 789–790
DPS (dividends per share), 159, 164–165
Draft, 315
Drexel Burnham Lambert, 22, 133n, 617, 618
DRIPs (dividend reinvestment plans), 834–837
DRP (default risk premium), 130, 132–133
DSO (days sales outstanding), 192–193, 201, 354
DTC (depository transfer check), 313
DTL (degree of total leverage), 792–794
Dun & Bradstreet, 192, 207, 348–349, 350
Du Pont chart, modified, 202–206
Du Pont Corporation, 863
Du Pont equation, 203–204

EAR (effective annual rate), 510–511
Earnings before interest and taxes (EBIT), 45, 159
Earnings per share (EPS), 27, 159, 164, 778–782
Eastern Airlines, 10
Eastern Communications Inc., 429–436
Eastman Kodak, 322–323(IP), 649(IP), 774(IP), 918
EBIT (earnings before interest and taxes), 45, 159
Economic environment, 29, 30, 110–113
Economic exposure, 915, 917–919
Economic ordering quantity (EOQ), 362–365
Economies of scale, 245
Effective annual rate (EAR), 510–511
Efficient capital market, 75–76
Electronic Data Systems (EDS), 650
Electronic spreadsheets, 554–555
Ellmann, Michael, 650(IP)
Employees' Stock Ownership Plan (ESOP), 519
Entergy Corporation, 462(DIF)
Environment, economic, 29, 30, 110–113
EOQ (economic order quantity), 362–365
EOQ model, 363–364
EPS (earnings per share), 27, 159, 164, 778–782
Equifax, 341, 350, 375(DIF)
Equilibrium, 653
Equilibrium price, 669
Equilibrium rate, 52–53, **125**–126

Equity, 160
  of banks, 104–106
  stockholders', 162–163
Equity capital, cost of. *See* Cost of capital
Equity multiplier, 204
Esmark Inc., 874, 876
ESOP (Employees' Stock Ownership Plan), 519
Ethics, 21–22
Eurocurrency, 897–898, 899
Eurodollar, 328, 897
Eurodollar bank time deposits, 328
Eurodollar market time deposits, 56
Excess capacity, 239
Excess reserves, 90, 91
Exchange rates, 893–903
  cross-exchange rates, 895
  floating, 902
  foreign currency market structure and, 896–897
  forward, 893, 898–899
  history of, 901–903
  quotations for, 893–895
  small-town America and, 891–892(DIF), 926(DIF)
Ex-dividend date, 833-834
Executive stock options, 25
Exercise price, 695, 701
Expansion project, 540–542, 553–555
Expectations theory, 138–139, 140
Expected rate of return, 430–432, 440, **653,** 657–658
Expected return on a portfolio, 440
Expected total return, 653
Expense, operating, 158–159
Exposure, to foreign currency movements, 914–922
  economic, 915, 917–919
  transaction, 915–917
  translation, 915, 920–922
Externalities, 527–528
Extra dividend, 832–833
Exxon, 836(IP)

Factoring, 353, 418–419
Fair Credit Reporting Act of 1971, 342(DIF)
Fairness, standard of, 813–814
Farmer, Carol, 64(IP)
FASB #13, 688–689
FDIC (Federal Deposit Insurance Corporation), 88
FDICIA (Federal Deposit Insurance Corporation
    Improvement Act of 1991), 111, 286(IP)
Feasibility, standard of, 814
Federal Deposit Insurance Corporation (FDIC), 88
**Federal Deposit Insurance Corporation
    Improvement Act of 1991 (FDICIA), 111,** 286(IP)
Federal Express, 523–524
Federal funds market, 92
Federal funds rate, 92
Federal Home Loan Bank (FHLB), 108(IP), 109(IP),
    326
Federal National Mortgage Association (FNMA), 326
Federal Open Market Committee (FOMC), 90, 94
Federal Reserve (Fed), 88–100
  Board of Governors of, 89
  discount rate and, 91–92, 93
  interest rates and, 123(DIF), 140–141, 149–150(DIF)
  open-market operations of, 90, 92–94, 97–100
  organization and structure of, 89–90
  reserve requirements of, 90–91, 95
Federal Savings and Loan Insurance Corporation
    (FSLIC), 104n, 108(IP)
Federal Trade Commission (FTC), 375(DIF)
Feldstein, Martin, 149(DIF)
Ferguson, Charles, 34–35(DIF)
FHLB (Federal Home Loan Bank), 108(IP), 109(IP),
    326
Field warehouse, 421–422
Finance
  career opportunities in, 5–6
  historical perspective on, 6–7
  organizational structure and, 15–17, 18
Finance companies, 327, 353
Financial Accounting Standards Board, 167(IP), 688–
    689
Financial cash flows, 909, 910
Financial flexibility, 798–799
Financial institutions
  accounting methods of, 166–167(IP)
  commercial banks, 60–61, 101–107, 111–113
  demand deposits in, 94–97, 104, 105

  deregulation of, 7
  discount rate and, 91–92, 93
  economic environment of, 110–113
  Federal Reserve System and, 88–100
  open-market operations of the Fed, 90, 92–94, 97–
    100
  reserve requirements and, 90–91, 95
  types of, 101
**Financial Institutions Reform, Recovery, and
    Enforcement Act of 1989 (FIRREA), 104**
Financial intermediaries, 57–62
Financial lease, 687–688, 689
Financial leverage, 194, 195, 205, 775–776
  degree of, 791–792
  effect on expected EPS and risk, 778–782
  stock value and, 786–788
Financial management, 9
  career opportunities in, 6
  importance of, 10–11
  international. *See* International financial management
    in 1990s, 7–9
Financial manager, responsibilities of, 9–10
Financial markets
  capital markets, 5, 54, 55–56, 57, 75–77
  capital structure decisions and, 798
  efficiency of, 75–77
  as financial manager's responsibility, 9
  money markets, 54, 55, 56
  mortgage markets, 54, 57
  for options, 694–696
  physical asset markets, 53
  primary, 54
  role of, 51–57
  secondary, 54, 671
  spot (futures) markets, 53–54
Financial merger, 866
Financial requirements
  computer modeling of, 261–263
  determinants of, 240–243
  forecasting, 243–247
Financial risk, 765, 776
Financial service corporations, 62
Financial services, diversification of, 8
Financial statements
  annual report, 155(DIF), 156, 157, 176–177(DIF),
    188–189(IP)
  balance sheet, 160–163
  importance of, 186
  income statement, 157–159
  interpreting, 184–213
  inventory fraud in, 185–186(DIF), 212–213(DIF)
  leasing and, 688–689
  manipulating, 188–189(IP), 210
  pro forma, 230, 869
  projected, 224–226, 232–236, 238
  ratio analysis of, 187–211
  statement of cash flows, 170–175, 238
  statement of retained earnings, 164–165
  trade credit and, 392, 393
  See also names of specific statements
Financial vice-president, 17
Financing. *See* Hybrid financing; Long-term financing;
    Short-term financing
**FIRREA (Financial Institutions Reform, Recovery,
    and Enforcement Act of 1989), 104**
First mortgage bond, 161, 611
Five Cs of credit, 347–349
Fixed assets, 160, 193
Fixed assets turnover ratio, 193, 201
Fixed charge coverage ratio, 197–198, 201
Fixed-income securities. *See* Bond(s); Preferred stock;
    Term loans
Fixed operating costs, 767
Float
  collections, 313
  disbursement, 313
  net, 313–314
Floating-rate bonds, 616–617
Floating-rate preferred stock, 632
Floating rate system, 902
Florida Orange Springs Inc., 267–268(DIF), 292(DIF)
Florida Power & Light, 836, 837n
Flotation cost, 668, 731–732
Flynn, Ed, 285(IP)
FNMA (Federal National Mortgage Association), 326
Foley, Maurice, 711(DIF)

Follow-the-Sun RV Services (FTS), 336–338
FOMC (Federal Open Market Committee), 90, 94
Ford Motor Company, 369, 517, 632
Ford Motor Credit Corporation, 327
Forecasting, 229–252
  cash flow, 523–528
  changing balance sheet ratios and, 243–248
  computerized models for, 248
  as financial manager's responsibility, 9
  formula method for, 238–243
  mathematical models and, 233–234(IP)
  percentage of sales, 231–238
  problems in, 229–230(DIF), 251–252(DIF)
  sales, 230–231
Foreign currency
  Eurocurrency, 897–898, 899
  firm exposure to, 914–922
  market structure for, 896–897
  risk sharing with, 917
  value of, 899–900
  See also Exchange rates
Foreign subsidiaries, capital structure of, 908–909
Foreign trade. *See* Trade
Formula value, 696–699
Forward contract hedge, 922
Forward rates, 893, 898–899
Founders' shares, 648
Franchising, 249–250(SB)
Fraud, inventory, 185–186(DIF), 212–213(DIF)
Free cash flow, 868, 870
Free trade credit, 393–394
Friendly merger, 865
FSLIC (Federal Savings and Loan Insurance Corporation), 104n, 108(IP)
Full-service brokerage houses, 67, 68n
Fund(s)
  cost of, 124–125
  spontaneously generated, 234
Funded debt, 607
Futures markets, 53–54
Future value, 471–475
  of annuity, 482–485
  interest rates and, 474–475
  present value vs., 478–480
Future value interest factor, 473
FVA_n, **483–**484
$FVIFA_{k,n}$, **483–**484

Garel, John, 774(IP)
Garn–St. Germain Act of 1982, 103
GE Capital Corporation (GECC), 394n
Gelb, Richard, 229(DIF)
General and administrative expenses, 159
General Dynamics, 844
General Electric, 796, 857(DIF), 885–886(DIF)
Generally accepted accounting principles (GAAPs), 167(IP)
General Motors Acceptance Corporation (GMAC), 327, 353, 615(IP)
General Motors Corporation, 188(IP), 317, 369, 501, 623–624, 632, 649(IP), 650, 774(IP)
General partners, 12–13
George, Brian, 427–428(DIF), 461–462(DIF)
Georgia Paper Products (GPP), 823–826
Georgia Power Company, 611
Germany, and interest rates, 144–145(IP), 742–743(IP)
Gerstner, Louis V., 3(DIF), 4(DIF), 34(DIF), 35(DIF), 208(IP), 323(IP), 829n
Getty Oil, 862–863
Gibbons, Edward F., 876
GICs (guaranteed investment contracts), 502(DIF)
Global banks, 112–113
Global diversification, 458
Global markets, 7, 144–145(IP)
Going public, 664
  common stock and, 664–667, 671–672(SB)
  with small businesses, 748–749(SB)
Golden parachutes, 872
Goldman, Richard, 252(DIF)
Goldsmith, Robert H., 763(DIF), 804(DIF)
Goldwasser, Dan, 16(IP)
Gonzalez, Henry, 150(IP)
Goods-in-transit inventory, 366
Goodwill, Sidney, 427–428(DIF)
Goodyear Tire and Rubber, 208(IP), 458
Gordon, Myron J., 655
Gordon Model, 655

Gourmet Coffee International (GCI), 574–578
Government securities, 325–326. *See also specific securities*
GPA Group PLC, 685–686(DIF), 710–711(DIF)
Gramley, Lyle, 145(IP)
Grant, Walter, 285(IP)
Greenmail, 842n
Greenspan, Alan, 89, 119(DIF), 123(DIF), 149–150(DIF)
Gross profit margin, 198n
Gross working capital. *See* Working capital
Growth
  financial requirements and, 240, 241
  interest rates and, 474–475
  negative, 656n
  normal (constant), 655–658
  opportunities for, 15
  supernormal (nonconstant), 658–661
  working capital and, 288–290(SB)
Growth rate, 653, 797
Guaranteed investment contracts (GICs), 502(DIF)

Hagstrand, Allen, 370(IP)
Half-year convention, 50
Hall, Robert W., 370(IP)
Hanover Company, 351
Hanson, Dale, 649(IP)
Hawkins, Susan, 642–643
Hawley, Philip, 188(IP)
Health Management Resources Inc. (HMR), 233–234(IP)
Hedging, 916–917, 922
Hees-Edper Enterprises, 407(IP)
Heileman, G., 863–864
Heller Financial, 801(SB)
HIBOR (Hong Kong or Helsinki Interbank Offer Rate), 898
Hobart Brothers Company, 891–892(DIF)
Hoey, Richard, 144(IP)
Holder-of-record date, 833
Holding companies, 878–880
Hood, Wayne, 371(IP)
Horizontal merger, 861
Hormats, Robert, 144(IP)
Hostile merger (takeover), 7, **19,** 863, **865**
  common stockholders and, 646–647
  junk bonds and, 617–618
  threat of, 24
Houston Trucking Company, 540–542
Hove, Andrew, 112
Hughes Aircraft, 650
Hurdle rate, 568
Hutton, E. F., 314
Hybrid financing, 685–710
  convertibles, 702–708
  leases, 686–694
  options, 694–699
  warrants, 699–702
Hytec Electronics, 846

IBM (International Business Machines), 3–4(DIF), 34–35(DIF), 320, 323(IP), 623, 694–695, 829n
IFPS (Interactive Financial Planning System), 248n
Impairment of capital rule, 827
Import/export trade financing, 913–914
Improper accumulation, 46–47
Incentives, managerial, 18–19, 24–25
Income
  accounting net, 524–527
  capital gains vs., 42–43
  creating, 188(IP)
  from dividends and interest, 41–42, 43–44
  net operating, 158
  operating, estimating, 866–867
  taxable, 40
Income bonds, 612
Income statement, 157–159
  common-size, 186
  projected, 235, 236
  trade credit and, 392, 393
Income taxes, 38–47
  accrued, 161, 388
  corporate, 43–47, 80(DIF)
  individual, 40–43
Incremental cash flows, 524, 527–528
Indenture, 608, 827
Independent projects, 533, 539
Indexed bonds, 612–613

Indirect quote, 893–895
Individual income taxes, 40–43
Individual retirement accounts (IRAs), 502(DIF)
Inflation, 124
  capital budgeting and, 580–582
  expected, changes in, 454–455
  high rate of, 7
  interest rates and, 128–129, 145(IP)
Inflation premium (IP), 129, **130–**132
Inflation risk, 323–324
Inflow, 528n, 533
Information content of dividends, 829-830
Inheritance taxes, 80(DIF)
Initial public offering (IPO) market, 664–667, 671–672(SB)
Insiders, 73
Installation costs, 528
Installment loans, 401
Institutional investors, 62
Intel, 827–828
Interactive Financial Planning System (IFPS), 248n
Intercorporate dividends, 44
Interest
  add-on, 401
  discount, 400–401, 402–403
  paid by corporation, 45
  semiannual, 603–604
  simple, 400, 401–402
  taxes on, 41–42, 43–44
Interest rate(s), 52, 122–150
  on bonds, 604–605
  business activity and, 143
  business decisions and, 146–147
  for CDs, 399n
  coupon, 597
  determinants of, 129–135
  discount, 91–92, 93
  effective annual, 510–511
  equilibrium, 52–53, 125–126
  Eurocurrency, 897–898, 899
  federal deficits and, 141–142
  Federal funds, 92
  Federal Reserve and, 123(DIF), 140–141, 149–150(DIF)
  foreign trade balance and, 142–143
  future value and, 474–475
  global business climate and, 144–145(IP)
  inflation and, 128–129, 145(IP)
  long-term, 126–128
  nominal, 510, 511
  nominal risk-free, 129, 130–131
  present value and, 478
  prime, 92
  real risk-free, 129, 130
  and refinancing of business debt, 742–743(IP)
  short-term, 126–128, 399–400
  solving equations for, 482, 492
  stock prices and, 145–146
  on term loans, 625
  term structure of, 127, 135–140
Interest rate risk, 134, 324-**325**
Interest rate swap, 922-923
Internal rate of return (IRR) method, 529, 533–539
  evaluation of, 530
  net present value method vs., 555–560
  rationale and use of, 538
International financial management, 890–926
  capital budgeting in, 903–907
  capital structure of foreign subsidiaries and, 908–909
  cash flow management in, 909–912
  classification of firm exposure to foreign currency movements in, 914–922
  currency swaps and, 923–924
  exchange rates and, 891–892(DIF), 893–903, 926(DIF)
  import/export trade financing in, 913–914
  interest rate swaps and, 922–923
International firm, 892
International Holdings, 867n
International markets, 7, 144–145(IP)
Intrinsic value, 652
Inventory
  on balance sheet, 160, 161
  costs of, 361–362, 422
  determining investment in, 360–361
  goods-in-transit, 366
  hiding, 188(IP)

Inventory *continued*
  reducing, 274
Inventory blanket lien, 420
Inventory control systems, 368–369
Inventory conversion period, 272
Inventory financing, 420–423
  cost of, 422
  evaluation of, 422–423
  methods of, 420–422
Inventory fraud, 185–186(DIF), 212–213(DIF)
Inventory management, 360–372
  computers in, 368, 371(IP)
  determining inventory investment, 360–361
  economic ordering quantity model in, 362–365
  goods-in-transit and, 366
  inventory control systems and, 368–369
  inventory costs and, 361–362, 422
  just-in-time system in, 369–372
  out-sourcing in, 372
  production scheduling vs. inventory levels in, 372
  reorder point in, 365–366
  safety stocks and, 366–367
Inventory turnover (utilization) ratio, 191–192, 201
Inverted yield curve, 137
Investment(s)
  career opportunities in, 5–6
  as financial manager's responsibility, 9
  in inventory, 360–361
  in marketable securities, 320
  return on. *See* Rate of return
  of working capital, 275–278
Investment banking house, 58–59
  common stocks and, 645(DIF), 667–674, 674–675(DIF)
  mergers and, 871–872
Investment-grade bonds, 619
Investment opportunity schedule (IOS), 743–745, 825–826, 827–828
Investment outlay, 529, 530
Investment tax credit (ITC), 51
Investor, 45, 62
Investor's Daily, 68
IOS (investment opportunity schedule), 743–745, 825–826, 827–828
IPO (initial public offering) market, 664–667, 671–672(SB)
IRAs (individual retirement accounts), 502(DIF)
IRR. *See* Internal rate of return method
ITC (investment tax credit), 51
ITT, 375(DIF)
IU International, 874–875, 876

Jackson Company, 703–706
Jaffe, Melvin, 285(IP)
Japan, and interest rates, 144–145(IP), 742–743(IP)
JIT (just-in-time) system, 369, 370–371(IP), 372
Johnson, Ross, 23
Johnson & Johnson, 459–460
Joint venture, 873
Jordan, Michael H., 774(IP)
Jump in MCC schedule, 738–741
Junior mortgages, 611
Junk bonds, 617–618
Just-in-time (JIT) system, 369, 370–371(IP), 372
JWP Inc., 459

Kanter, Donald, 469(DIF)
Kelly, Jack, 649(IP)
Kenworthy, Barbara, 615(IP)
Kerley, James J., 763(DIF)
Kerrey, Robert, 79–80(DIF)
KeyCorp, 570–571
Klemme, Kelly, 111–112
Kmart Corporation, 371(IP)
Kohlberg Kravis Roberts (KKR), 24, 208(IP), 796, 881, 882

L.A. Gear, 185(DIF)
Lags, 912
Laird, John R., 877(IP)
Landry, Brenda Lee, 649(IP)
Lane, Frank, 642–643
Lanston, Aubrey G., 145(IP)
Laribee Wire Manufacturing Company, 185–186(DIF), 212(DIF)
Lavin, Ed, 709(SB)
Laws. *See* Regulation; *specific laws*

LBO. *See* Leveraged buyout
Leads, 912
Lead underwriter, 670
Lear Siegler, 369
Lease(s), 57
  capitalizing, 689
  evaluation of, 689–693
  financial (capital), 687–688, 689
  loans vs., 689n
  operating (service), 687
  sale and leaseback, 687
Lease payments, 159
Leasing, 686–694
  of aircraft, 685–686(DIF), 710–711(DIF)
  balance sheet effects of, 688–689
  credit availability and, 694
  residual value and, 693–694
  for small businesses, 708–709(SB)
  taxes and, 688n
Lego, Paul, 64(IP), 650(IP)
Lessee, 687, 689–693
Lessor, 687
Letter of credit, 913–914
Leverage
  consolidated, 880
  degree of, 788–794
  operating, 766–773, 789–790
  See also Financial leverage
Leveraged buyout (LBO), 23–24, 26, 208–209(IP), 617–618, 666, **875,** 881–882
Liabilities, 160
  on balance sheet, 160–161, 243–248
  of banks, 104–106
  combining current asset and liability decisions, 287–288
  spontaneous, 242
Liability
  in corporation, 13
  limited, 13, 15, 16–17
  in partnership, 12
  in sole proprietorship, 12
LIBID (London InterBank Bid Rate), 898
Lien, inventory blanket, 420
LIBOR (London InterBank Offer Rate), 897
Life insurance companies, 61, 62, 101
Lifeline Systems, 371(IP)
Limited liability, 13, 15, 16–17
Limited liability corporations (LLCs), 16–17
Limited partnership, 12–13
Line of credit, 398–399
Liquidation, 813, 814–817, 874
Liquidity, 15
Liquidity preference theory, 138
Liquidity premium, 130, 133
Liquidity ratios, 189, 190–191, 201
Liquidity risk, 324
Litan, Robert, 118(DIF)
LLCs (limited liability corporations), 16–17
Loans
  amortized, 493–494, 624–625, 642–643
  applying for, 396–398
  cost of, 399–403
  features of, 398–399
  installment, 401
  leases vs., 689n
  secured, 406, 417–423
  short-term, 394–403
  term, 624–627, 642–643
Lockbox plan, 311–312
Lombardi, Anthony, 285(IP)
Lone Star Steakhouse, 189(IP)
Long Island Lighting Company (LILCO), 651
Long-term debt, 284–287, 626–627
Long-term financing
  bonds, 596–624
  common stock, 644–675
  convertibles, 702–708
  leasing, 686–694
  options, 694–699
  preferred stock, 627–632
  warrants, 699–702
Long-term interest rates, 126–128
Lorenzo, Frank, 817
Lotus 1-2-3, 248n, 308, 554–555, 643
Lubovny, Nikolai, 907(IP)
Ludwig, Eugene, 119(DIF)
Lumpy assets, 245–246

MACRS (Modified Accelerated Cost Recovery System), 48–51, 160
Main Street Builders' Supply, 408–409(SB)
Malec, William, 742(IP)
Management
  attitude toward risk, 797
  compensation for, 24–25
  incentives for, 18–19, 24–25
  profit maximization by, 27–28
  shareholders vs., 23–25
  threat of firing, 24
Management by exception, 352
Managerial buyout, 874
Managing underwriter, 670
Manufacturers Hanover, 864
Marathon Oil, 863
Marginal cost of capital (MCC), 733–741
Marginal cost of capital (MCC) schedule, 735–745
Marginal tax rate, 40
Margin call, 73–74
Margin requirements, 73–74
Market(s)
  futures, 53–54
  international, 7, 144–145(IP)
  money, 54, 55, 56, 897
  stock, 65–74
  See also Capital markets; Financial markets
Marketable securities, 319–328
  on balance sheet, 160, 161
  as cash substitute, 319–320
  factors influencing choice of, 321–325
  reasons for holding, 302–303, 319–320
  strategies for, 320–321
  as temporary investment, 320
  types of, 325–328. *See also specific securities*
Market/book (M/B) ratio, 199–**200,** 201
Market portfolio, 445
Market price, 652
Market risk, 446–447, **565,** 566, 567–570
Market risk premium, 452
Market segmentation theory, 137–138
Market value basis, 776n
Market value ratios, 199–200, 201
Markowitz, Harry, 439
Martin Marietta, 804(DIF), 857(DIF), 885–886(DIF)
Massachusetts Technology Development Corporation (MTDC), 801(SB)
Mattel, 845
Matthews, Roger, 742(IP)
Maturity
  of bonds, 597, 619
  of commercial paper, 404
  of loans, 398
  original, 597
  of preferred stock, 629
  yield to, 604–605
Maturity date, 597
Maturity matching, 280–281
Maturity risk premium (MRP), 130, 133-**134,** 135, 454n
May Department Stores, 595–596(DIF), 636–637(DIF)
M/B (market/book) ratio, 199-**200,** 201
MCC (marginal cost of capital), 733–741
MCC (marginal cost of capital) schedule, 735–745
McClintock, Fred, 370(IP)
McCue Electronics, 389–390
McDonnell Douglas Corporation, 721–722(DIF), 751(DIF)
MDA (multiple discriminant analysis), 351
Merck, 844
Mergers, 7, 646, 647n, **858**–872
  analysis of, 865–868
  capital structure and, 796
  congeneric, 861
  conglomerate, 861
  defensive, 860
  diversification and, 860, 883(SB)
  examples of, 857(DIF), 861–864, 885–886(DIF)
  financial, 866
  friendly, 865
  horizontal, 861
  hostile. *See* Hostile merger (takeover)
  investment bankers and, 871–872
  operating, 866
  postmerger control in, 860, 867–868
  procedures for, 864–865
  purchase price in, 868

Mergers continued
    rationale for, 858–860
    regulation of, 859n
    in small businesses, 882–883(SB)
    valuing target firm in, 868–871
    vertical, 861
Merrill, Rick, 907(IP)
Merrill Lynch, 801(SB)
MIBOR (Madrid Interbank Offer Rate), 898
Microsoft, 906–907(IP)
Milken, Michael, 22, 617, 618
Miller, Merton, 786
Milne, Garth, 742(IP)
Mitchell Electronics Company, 690–693
Modeling. See Computer modeling
Moderate working capital investment policy, 277,
    278
Modified Accelerated Cost Recovery System
    (MACRS), 48–51, 160
Modified Du Pont chart, 202–206
Modigliani, Franco, 786
Monetary Control Act of 1980, 102–103. See also
    Depository Institutions Deregulation and Monetary
    Control Act of 1980
Monetary policy, tools of, 90–94
Money
    capital markets and, 5
    direct transfers of, 58–59
    time value of, 468–503
    See also Foreign currency
Money market(s), 54
    instruments of, 55, 56
    international, 897
Money market fund, 62
Moore, Geoffrey, 371(IP)
Moore, Gordon, 827
Morgan Stanley, 596(DIF), 636–637(DIF)
Mortgage bond, 161, 611
Mortgage markets, 54, 57
Motorola Inc., 515(DIF), 544–546(DIF)
MRP (maturity risk premium), 130, 133-**134,** 135,
    454n
Mullins, David W., Jr., 209(IP)
Multidivisional firms, cash management in, 316–317
Multi-Local Media Corporation, 208(IP)
Multinational firm, 892. See also International
    financial management
Multiple discriminant analysis (MDA), 351
Municipal bonds ("munis"), 41, 55, 57
Murphy, Michael, 742(IP)
Mutual funds, 61–62, 101
    as investors, 62
    money market, 328
Mutually exclusive projects, 533, 539, 557
Mutual savings banks, 61

Naked options, 695
NASD (National Association of Securities Dealers),
    67, 74
NASDAQ (NASD Automated Quotation System), 67
Nash, John, 649(IP)
National Association of Credit Management, 350
National Association of Securities Dealers (NASD),
    67, 74
National Bank Act of 1863, 102
National Credit Union Insurance Fund (NCUIF), 104n
Natural hedging, 916
Naunula, Richard, 330(DIF)
NCNB, 570–571
NCUIF (National Credit Union Insurance Fund), 104n
Near-cash reserves, 326
Negative growth, 656n
Negotiable certificates of deposit, 55, 56, 327–328
Negotiable order of withdrawal (NOW) account, 105
Negotiated deals, vs. competitive bids, 667
Net float, 313–314
Net income, 524–527
Net operating income, 158
Net present value (NPV) method, 529, 531–533
    evaluation of, 539
    internal rate of return method vs., 555–560
    in leasing, 691–693
Net present value profile, 536–537
Netting, 911–912
Net working capital, 269, 528
Net worth, 162–163
New issue, 598

New York Stock Exchange (NYSE), 65
Nominal interest rate, 510, 511
Nominal risk-free rate of interest, 129, **130**–131
Nonconstant growth, 658–661
Nongovernment securities, 326–328. See also specific
    securities
Nonvoting stock, 648
Normal growth, 655–658
Normal profits, 20
Normal yield curve, 137
Northeast BankCorp, 527–528
Northrop Corporation, 804(DIF)
Northwest Airlines, 774(IP)
Northwest Electric Company, 846
Notes
    promissory, 398
    Treasury, 55, 56, 136–137, 326
Notes payable, 161
NOW (negotiable order of withdrawal) account, 105
NPV. See Net present value method
NYSE (New York Stock Exchange), 65

Off balance sheet financing, 688
Offering price, 669
Office of the Comptroller of the Currency (OCC), 102
Office of Thrift Supervision (OTS), 109(IP)
Offset Printing Company, 709(SB)
Old Stone Corporation, 407–408(IP)
Olympia & York Developments Ltd., 404–405, 407(IP),
    563–564(DIF), 584–585(DIF)
Omnibus Reconciliation Act of 1993, 38–39
O'Neill, Paul H., 774(IP)
Open-market operations, 90, 92–94, 97–100
Operating cash flows, 909, 910
Operating company, 878
Operating costs, 158–159, 767
Operating expenses, 158–159
Operating income, estimating, 866–867
Operating lease, 687
Operating leverage, 766–773
    breakeven analysis and, 767–770
    capital structure decisions and, 797
    degree of, 789–790
Operating merger, 866
Operating profit, 159
Opportunity cost, 303, 527, 727, 823
Opportunity cost principle, 727
Optimal (target) capital structure, 732–733, 777–785
Optimal dividend policy, 822
Options, 686, 694–699
    call, 695
    covered, 695
    formula value vs. option price, 696–699
    naked, 695
    put, 695
    types of and markets for, 694–696
Option writer, 695
Ordering costs, 362
Ordinary annuity, 483–484, 486
Organized securities exchanges, 65
Original maturity, 597
OTC (over-the-counter) market, 66–67
Out-sourcing, 372
Outstanding bonds, 598
Overdraft system, 315
Over-the-counter (OTC) market, 66–67

Pacific Brands, 847
Paid-in capital, 162
Panhandle Drilling Inc., 815–816
Pan-Pacific Airlines (PPA), 699–700
Paramount Communications, 330(DIF), 646
Parent company, 878
Partnership, 12–13, 16–17(IP)
Par value, 162
    of bonds, 597
    of preferred stock, 627, 628
Payables. See Accounts payable
Payables centralization, 315
Payables deferral period, 272
Payback period, 529, 531–533
    evaluation of, 539
    weaknesses of, 530–531
Payco American, 439, 445n
Payment date, 834
Pension funds, 8–9, 61, 62, 101
P/E (price/earnings) ratio, 68–69, **199,** 201

Percentage of sales method, 231–238
Perfect hedge, 916–917
Performance shares, 25
Permanent current assets, 279–280
Perpetuity, 488
Perquisites, 23n
Personal Computer Company (PCC), 389–393
Pettit, T. Christopher, 877(IP)
Phar-Mor, 185(DIF)
Phillip Morris, 844
Physical assets
    markets for, 53
    securities vs., 458–460
PIBOR (Paris Interbank Offer Rate), 897–898
Pickens, T. Boone, 617
Planning, as financial manager's responsibility, 9
Planning committees, 230
Pledging of accounts receivable, 353, 417, 418
Plumeri, Joseph, 877(IP)
Poison pill, 872
Pomerantz, Felix, 185(DIF)
Portfolio, 439
    beta of, 450–451, 457
    market, 445
    size of, vs. risk, 446
Portfolio return, 439, 440–447
Portfolio risk, 438–451
Posen, Danny, 906(IP)
Post-audit, 522–523
Pound, John, 650(IP)
PPP (purchasing power parity), 900
Pre-authorized debits, 312–313
Precautionary balances, 303
Precision Associates, 729, 731–732, 734–740, 743–
    745
Preemptive right, 648
Preferred stock, 55, 57, 162n, 627–632
    advantages and disadvantages of, 630–631
    convertibility of, 628
    cost of, 726
    floating-rate, 632
    major provisions of, 628–629
    with sinking funds, 629
    trends in, 631–632
    valuation of, 629–630
Premium bonds, 72, 601, **602**
Present value, 476–478
    of annuity, 485–488
    future value vs., 478–480
    interest rates and, 478
    of perpetuity, 488
    of uneven stream of cash flows, 489–491
Present value interest factor, 477
Price(s)
    asked, 67
    bid, 67
    conversion, 702–703
    equilibrium, 669
    exercise, 695, 701
    market, 652
    offering, 669
    striking, 695
    See also Stock prices
Price/earnings (P/E) ratio, 68–69, **199,** 201
Primary markets, 54
Prime rate, 92
Privacy, of consumer credit information, 341–
    342(DIF)
Privacy Protection Commission, 342(DIF)
Private placements, 77(SB), 624n
Probability distributions, 429–430, 432–433, 435
Producers, 125n
Production opportunities, 124
Production scheduling, 372
Profit(s)
    normal, 20
    operating, 159
    storing up, 189(IP)
Profitability ratios, 198–199, 201, 797
Profit margin, 198n, 242
Profit margin on sales, 198, 201
Profit maximization, 27–28
Pro forma financial statements, 230, 869
Progressive tax, 40
Projects
    evaluating, 529–539, 555–560
    expansion, 540–542, 553–555
    independent, 533, 539

Projects *continued*
 mutually exclusive, 533, 539, 557
 size of, 557–558
 with unequal lives, comparing, 578–580
Promissory note, 398
Proprietorship, 11–12
Prospectus, 72
Proxy, 646
Proxy fight, 19, 646
Publicly owned corporations, 665–667
Public warehouse, 421
Pura, Thomas, 615(IP)
Purchasing power bonds, 612–613
Purchasing power parity (PPP), 900
Pure play method, 572–573
Putable bonds, 614n
Put option, 695
PVA$_n$, 486–487
PVIFA$_{k,n}$, 486–487

Quaker Oats, 845
Quantum Chemical Company, 625
Quick ratio, 191, 201, 269
Quoted risk-free rate of interest, 129, 130–131
QVC, 646

Ranking methods, 529–539, 555–560
 conflicts between, 555–560
 evaluation of, 539
 internal rate of return (IRR), 529, 533–539, 555–560
 net present value (NPV), 529, 531–533, 539, 555–560, 691–693
 payback period, 529, 530–531, 539
Rate of return, 20, 471
 actual, 653
 assets and, 276–278
 cost of funds and, 124–125
 expected, 430–432, 440, 653, 657–658
 internal, 529, 533–539, 555–560
 portfolio, 439, 440–447
 realized, 440, 653
 required, 653
 risk vs., 28–29, 276–278, 325, 428, 439–447, 451–454
Ratio analysis, 187–211
 asset management ratios, 191–194, 201
 bond ratings and, 619
 case study of, 224–226
 comparative, 206–209
 debt management ratios, 194–198, 201
 Du Pont system and, 202–206
 limitations of, 210–211
 liquidity ratios, 189–191, 201
 market value ratios, 199–200, 201
 profitability ratios, 198–199, 201
 trend analysis and, 202
Realized rate of return, 440, 653
Real risk-free rate of interest, 129, 130
Receivables. *See* Accounts receivable
Receivables conversion period, 272
Recourse, 417
Recovery period, 50
Red-line method of inventory control, 368
Refunding operation, 609
Registration statement, 72
Regulation
 of banking, 87(DIF), 102–104, 118–119(DIF)
 of bankruptcy, 812–813, 817
 of mergers, 859n
 of securities markets, 72–74
Regulation Q, 104
Reichman, Paul, 563–564(DIF), 584–585(DIF)
Reinvestment rate assumption, 558-559
Reinvestment rate risk, 134–135
Reinvoicing, 912
Relevant cash flows, 524
Relevant risk, 447
Reorder point, 365–366
Reorganization, 813
Replacement analysis, 574–578
Replacement chain method, 579–580
Replacement costs, 519
Republic Steel, 859–860
Repurchase agreement (repo), 105
Required rate of return, 653
Required reserves, 90–91, 95
Reserve borrowing capacity, 662
Reserve requirements, 90–91, 95

Residual dividend policy, 822–826
Residual value, 693–694
Resolution Trust Corporation (RTC), 109(IP)
Resources, of small businesses, 31–32(SB)
Restrictive covenant, 608
Restructuring, 8, 796
Retained earnings
 on balance sheet, 162, 163
 cost of, 726–731
 incremental, 164n
 projected, 235
 statement of, 164–165
Retention rate, 239
Retirement, saving for, 469–470(DIF), 501–502(DIF)
Return on common equity (ROE), 199, 201, 354
Return on investment. *See* Rate of return
Return on total assets (ROA), 198–199, 201, 354
Reverse splits, 838n
Revolving credit agreement, 399
Rich, Marc, 906(IP)
Rights offering, 648n
Risk, 124, 428–461
 assets and, 276–278
 bank policy toward, 395
 beta (market), 565, 566, 567–570
 business, 765–766
 company-specific, 445–446
 corporate (within-firm), 564, 565, 566–567
 counterparty, 923
 default, 324
 diversifying, 427–428(DIF), 458, 461–462(DIF), 570–571
 financial, 765, 776
 financial leverage and, 778–782
 in global context, 458
 holding companies and, 879
 inflation, 323–324
 interest rate, 134, 324–325
 in international investments, 905, 907
 liquidity, 324
 of long-term vs. short-term debt, 284–287
 management attitude toward, 797
 market, 446–447
 measuring, 428–437
 portfolio, 438–451
 relevant, 447
 and return, 439–447
 sharing, with foreign currency, 917
 stand-alone, 564, 565
Risk-adjusted discount rate, 573
Risk analysis, 564–573
Risk aversion, 437–438, 455–456
Risk premium (RP), 438
Risk-return tradeoff, 28–29, 276–278, 325, 428, 439–447, 451–454
Ritter, Jay, 748(SB)
RJR Nabisco, 23, 24, 25–26, 208(IP), 209(IP), 323(IP), 607, 617, 650, 796, 882
ROA (return on total assets), 198–199, 201, 354
Roach, John, 877(IP)
Roark Restaurant Supply Company, 356–358
Robinson, James, III, 63–64(IP)
Robinson-Patman Act, 354
Rockford Dynatorq, 370–371(IP)
Rockwell International Corporation, 459
Rodrigues, R. J., 605n
ROE (return on common equity), 199, 201, 354
Rohm, Marti, 330(DIF)
Rohr Inc., 763–764(DIF), 804(DIF)
RTC (Resolution Trust Corporation), 109(IP)
Russia, foreign businesses in, 906–907(IP)
Rutzel, John, 709(SB)
Ryan, Tim, 685–686(IP)

Safety stocks, 276, 366–367
Sahlman, William A., 634(SB)
Sale and leaseback, 687
Sales, stability of, 796–797
Sales forecast, 230–231
Sales volume, breakeven, 769–770
Salomon Brothers Inc., 22, 645(DIF), 674–675(DIF)
Salvage value, 50, 577
Sanders, Bernard, 110
Savannah Electric, 611
Savers, 52, 58–59
Savings
 retirement, 469–470(DIF), 501–502(DIF)
 supply of and demand for, 126

Savings and loan associations (S&Ls), 61, 101
 crisis of, 108–109(IP), 109–110
 protection of deposits in, 104n
Savings deposits, 104, 105
Scale, economies of, 245
Schlitz, 863–864
S corporation, 14, 47
Sears, 64(IP)
Seasonal changes, 246
Seasonal dating, 346
Seasoned issue, 598
Secondary markets, 54, 671
Second mortgage bonds, 611
Secured loans, 406, 417–423
Securities
 convertible, 686, 702–707
 government, 325–326
 nongovernment, 326–328
 physical assets vs., 458–460
 See also Marketable securities; *specific securities*
Securities analysts, 187
Securities and Exchange Commission (SEC), 72
 accounting methods and, 167(IP)
 fixed commissions and, 67
 regulation of securities markets by, 72–74
 restrictions on joint actions by shareholders, 4(DIF)
Securities exchanges, 65–66
Securities trading, trends in, 67–68
Security agreement, 406
Security Market Line (SML), 451–457, 567, 569–570
Self-liquidating approach to working capital financing, 280–281
Selling expenses, 158–159
Selling group, 670
Semiannual compounding, 510–512
Semiannual interest on bonds, 603–604
Sensitivity analysis, 555
Sequoia Systems, 229–230(DIF), 252(DIF)
Service lease, 687
Shareholders
 of common stock, 646–648, 649–650(IP)
 creditors vs., 25–26
 dividend policy and, 828–829
 managers vs., 23–25
 rights of, 8–9
 SEC restrictions on joint actions of, 4(DIF)
Sharpe, William F., 439
Shearson Lehman Brothers, 877(IP)
Shelf registration, 670–671
Shilling, A. Gary, 286(IP)
Shipping costs, 528
Shoal Creek Engineering, 831–832, 845–846
Short-term bank loans, 394–403
Short-term credit, 279–287
Short-term financing, 386–412
 accounts payable in, 388–394, 408–409(SB)
 accrued wages and taxes in, 388
 bank loans, 394–403
 commercial paper in, 403–405, 407–408(IP)
 use of security in, 406, 417–423
Short-term interest rates, 126–128, 399–400
Siegel, Mark, 615(IP)
Signaling, 829-830
Silent partners, 13
SilTek, 437–438
Simple interest, 400, 401–402
Simultaneous tender and call (STAC), 595–596(DIF), 636–637(DIF)
Sinking fund, 608
 on balance sheet, 161
 bonds with, 608–609, 619
 preferred stock with, 629
Smale, John G., 774(IP)
Small businesses
 banking relationships of, 114–116(SB)
 direct financing of receivables in, 408–409(SB)
 franchising of, 249–250(SB)
 goals of, 32–33(SB)
 going public with, 671–672(SB), 748–749(SB)
 growth and working capital needs of, 288–290(SB)
 lease financing for, 708–709(SB)
 mergers in, 882–883(SB)
 resources of, 31–32(SB)
 taxation of, 47
 venture capital for, 76–77(SB), 633–634(SB), 800–802(SB)
Smith, David, 804(DIF)
Smith, John F., Jr., 774(IP)

SML (Security Market Line), 451–457, 567, 569–570
Social issues, in bankruptcy proceedings, 817
Social responsibility, 7, 20–21
Social welfare, 21
Sole proprietorship, 11–12
Sommer, A. A., Jr., 177(DIF)
Southmark, 188(IP)
Space Technology Inc. (STI), 696–698
Specialist, 66
Specialist banks, 112–113
Speculative balances, 303
Spin-off, 874, 877–878(IP)
Spontaneous assets, 232
Spontaneous liabilities, 242
Spontaneously generated funds, 234
Spot (futures) markets, 53–54
Spot rates, 893
Spread, 668
Spreadsheets, electronic, 554–555
STAC (simultaneous tender and call), 595–596(DIF),
    636–637(DIF)
Stakeholders, 26
Stand-alone risk, 564, 565
Standard deviation, 433–436
Standard of fairness, 813–814
Standard of feasibility, 814
Start-up (venture) capital, 42, 76–77(SB), 633–
    634(SB), 800–802(SB)
Stated interest rate, 510, 511
Statement of cash flows, 170–175, 238
Statement of retained earnings, 164–165
Steffen, Christopher J., 322–323(IP), 649(IP), 774(IP)
Stepped-up exercise price, 701
Stifler, Larry, 233–234(IP)
Stock
    classified, 648
    constant growth, 655–658
    cost of selling, 828
    issuance costs of, 668–669
    nonconstant growth, 658–661
    nonvoting, 648
    options on, 694–699
    treasury, 163, 841
    See also Common stock; Preferred stock
Stock buy-back programs, 844–845
Stock dividend, 838–840. See also Dividend(s)
Stock exchanges, 65–66
Stockholders. See Shareholders
Stockholders' equity, 162–163
Stockholder wealth maximization, 17–19
Stock market, 65–74
    bond markets, 70–72
    over-the-counter market, 66–67
    regulation of, 72–74
    reporting on, 68–70
    stock exchanges, 65–66
    trading trends in, 67–68
Stock options, executive, 25
Stock-out costs, 361, 362
Stock prices
    capital structure and, 782–785
    factors affecting, 29, 30
    financial leverage and, 786–788
    interest rates and, 145–146
    maximization of, 21
Stock repurchase, 841–845
    advantages of, 842–843
    disadvantages of, 843–844
    effects of, 841–842
    recent developments with, 844–845
Stock split, 837–838
    balance sheet effects of, 838–839
    price effects of, 839–840
Stollenwerk, John, 371, 372
Stone, Roger, 208(IP)
Stone Container Corporation, 208(IP)
Straight line depreciation methods, 48
Strategic business plan, 518
Stretching accounts payable, 391, 394
Striking price, 695
Subordinated debenture, 612
Sunk cost, 527
Sun Microsystems, 845
Supercomputers, 371(IP)
Supernormal growth, 658–661
Surgicare, 709(SB)
Synchronized cash flows, 309-310
Synergy, 858–859

Takeovers. See Hostile merger (takeover)
Tandy Corporation, 877(IP)
Target capital structure, 732–733, 777–785
Target cash balance, 304, 308–309
Target company, 865, 868–871
Tax(es)
    capital structure decisions and, 797
    Clinton administration and, 37–38(DIF), 79–80(DIF)
    dividends and, 41–42, 43–44, 827
    holding companies and, 879–880
    income, 38–47, 80(DIF), 161, 388
    inheritance, 80(DIF)
    leasing and, 688n
    mergers and, 859
    progressive, 40
Taxable income, 40
Tax-deferred savings plans, 470(DIF)
Tax loss carry-back and carry-forward, 45–46
Tax returns, consolidated, 47
Telling, Edward R., 64(IP)
Temporary current assets, 279–280
Tender offer, 23, 842n, **865**
Tennessee Valley Authority (TVA), 597n, 615(IP)
Terminal value, 870
Term loans, 624–627, 642–643
Term structure of interest rates, 127, 135–140
Teslik, Sara, 649(IP)
Texaco, 862–863
Thrifts. See Savings and loan associations
Ticker symbol, 68
TIE (times-interest-earned) ratio, 197, 201, 794–796,
    799
Time, solving equations for, 481, 491–492
Time deposits, 104, 105
Time effect, 698
Time preferences for consumption, 124
Times-interest-earned (TIE) ratio, 197, 201, 794–796,
    799
Time value of money, 468–503
Time value of money equations, 483–484, 486–487
Time Warner, 614, 645(DIF), 674–675(DIF)
Tisch, Larry, 330(DIF)
Total assets turnover ratio, 193–194, 201
Total quality management (TQM), 545
TotWear Products, 437–438
Toyota, 369
Trade
    interest rates and, 142–143
    international, financing of, 913–914
Trade credit, 388–394
    cost of, 389–391
    extending net, 389n
    financial statements and, 392, 393
    free vs. costly, 393–394
    receiving net, 389n
Transaction exposure, 915–917
Transactions balances, 302
Translation exposure, 915, 920–922
Trans Union, 341, 375(DIF)
Treasurer, 17
Treasury bills, 55, 56, 93, 136–137, 325–326
Treasury notes and bonds, 55, 56, 136–137, 326,
    621, 622
Treasury stock, 163, 841
Trend analysis, 202
Triangular arbitrage, 895
Trustee, 608
Trust receipt, 420–421
TRW, 341, 350, 375(DIF)
Turbidy, John, 212(DIF)
Turnaround specialists, 322–323(IP)
Turner, Ted, 617
Two-bin method of inventory control, 368
Two-tier offer, 863

Ueshima, Seisuke, 462(DIF)
Underwriting agreements, 645(DIF), 674–675(DIF)
Underwriting syndicate, 670
Underwritten arrangement, 668
Uneven cash flow stream, 489–491
Uniform Commercial Code, 406
United Airlines, 775(IP)
Universal (global) banks, 112–113
U.S. Repeating Arms, 371(IP)
U.S. Steel, 863
U.S. Treasury bills, 55, 56, 93, 136–137, 325–326
U.S. Treasury notes and bonds, 55, 56, 136–137,
    326, 621, 622

USAir, 775(IP)
Utilization-review firms, 553–555

Valuation
    of bonds, 598–606
    of cash flow in merger, 870–871
    of common stock, 651–661
    of preferred stock, 629–630
    of target firm in merger, 868–871
Value-Care Inc., 553–555
Value chain, 873
Variable operating costs, 767
Variance, 433
Vasey, Roger, 742(IP)
Venture capital, 42, 76–77(SB), 633–634(SB), 800–
    802(SB)
Vertical merger, 861
Viacom, 646
Video Privacy Protection Act of 1988, 342(DIF)
Volatility effect, 698
Volpe, James, 836(IP)
von der Heyden, Karl, 209(IP)

Wages, accrued, 161, 388
Walker Products, 867n
Wall Street Journal, 68
Wal-Mart Stores Inc., 371(IP)
Walport-Canada, 920–921, 922
Warehouse receipt financing, 421–422
Warrants, 612, 686, **699**–702
    detachable, 701
    initial market price of bond with, 699–700
    use in financing, 700–702
Washington Public Power Supply System, 516
Weighted average cost of capital (WACC), 722–723,
    724, 732–**733**
Welch, Jack, 857(DIF)
Westinghouse, 64(IP), 650(IP), 774(IP)
"What-if" analysis, 555
White knight, 871–872
Whitmore, Kay R., 323(IP), 649(IP)
"Window dressing" techniques, 210
Winkelreid, Jon, 615(IP)
Within-firm risk, 564, 565, 566–567
Woolworth, 876
Working capital, 268
    cash conversion cycle and, 269, 270–275
    in international financial management, 909–912
    net, 269, 528
    risk vs. return and, 276–278
    shortage of, 267–268(DIF), 292(DIF)
    small business need for, 288–290(SB)
Working capital financing policies, 279–287
    aggressive approach in, 282–283
    conservative approach in, 283–284
    maturity matching, or self-liquidating approach in,
        280–281
Working capital investment policies, 275–278
    aggressive, 276, 277
    conservative, 276, 277
    moderate, 277, 278
Working capital management, 269
Working capital policy, 269
Wyatt Industries, 224–226
Wyss, David, 742(IP)

Xerox, 63(IP)

Yamaha Corporation, 462(DIF)
Yardeni, Edward, 145(IP)
Yield
    capital gains, 601, 653
    current, 71, 601
    dividend, 68n, 653
    See also Rate of return
Yield curve, 136–137
Yield to call (YTC), 605-606
Yield to maturity (YTM), 604–605
York, Jerome, 323(IP)
York International, 208(IP)
Young, John A., 742(IP)
YTC (yield to call), 605-606
YTM (yield to maturity), 604–605

Zalkinder, Ari, 906(IP)
Zero-balance accounts (ZBAs), 315–316
Zero coupon bonds (zeros), 135n, 479n, 613–616

2004
NOVEL &
SHORT STORY
WRITER'S
2,000+ PLACES TO GET
YOUR FICTION INTO PRINT
MARKET

EDITOR
ANNE BOWLING

ASSISTANT EDITORS
MICHAEL SCHWEER
& VANESSA LYMAN

D1529586

WRITER'S DIGEST BOOKS
CINCINNATI, OH

Complaint Procedure

If you feel you have not been treated fairly by a listing in *Novel & Short Story Writer's Market*, we advise you to take the following steps:

- First try to contact the listing. Sometimes one phone call or a letter can quickly clear up the matter.
- Document all your correspondence with the listing. When you write to us with a complaint, provide the details of your submission, the date of your first contact with the listing and the nature of your subsequent correspondence.
- We will enter your letter into our files and attempt to contact the listing.
- The number and severity of complaints will be considered in our decision whether or not to delete the listing from the next edition.

If you are a publisher of fiction and would like to be considered for a listing in the next edition of *Novel & Short Story Writer's Market*, send a SASE (or SAE and IRC) with your request for a questionnaire to *Novel & Short Story Writer's Market*—QR, 4700 East Galbraith Road, Cincinnati OH 45236.

Editorial Director, Writer's Digest Books: Barbara Kuroff
Supervisory Editor, Writer's Digest Books: Alice Pope
Technical Coordinator: Robert Lee Brewer

Writer's Digest Books website: www.writersdigest.com.
Writer's Market website: www.writersmarket.com.

International Standard Serial Number 0897-9812
International Standard Book Number 1-58297-193-5

Cover photo by Tristan Paviot, Getty Images.

Attention Booksellers: This is an annual directory of F&W Publications.
Return deadline for this edition is January 15, 2005.

contents at a glance

Writing Fiction:

Personal Views   6

Craft & Technique   31

Getting Published   44

For Mystery Writers   68

For Romance Writers   80

For Science Fiction/Fantasy & Horror Writers   90

The Markets:

Literary Agents   107

Literary Magazines   166

Small Circulation Magazines   275

Online Markets   306

Consumer Magazines   332

Book Publishers   361

Contests & Awards   472

Resources:

Conferences & Workshops   519

Writing Programs   568

Literary Agents Category Index   596

Contest Index by Deadline   611

Conference Index by Date   614

Category Index   618

General Index   660

Contents

1 **From the Editor**

2 **The "Quick-Start" Guide to Publishing Your Fiction**

PERSONAL VIEWS

6 **Walter Mosley: Connecting with the Rest of the World Through Words,** by W.E. Reinka

11 **Richard Russo: Master of the Tragicomedy,** by Jane Friedman

13 **Janet Evanovich: 'Out of Nowhere' to the Bestseller List,** by Anne Bowling

15 **Alice Sebold: 'The Entire Book is a Leap of Faith,'** by Jane Friedman

17 **Beyond BAM! and POW!: Four Publishing Insiders Talk About Breaking into Graphic Novels,** by Lauren Mosko

23 **Brian Michael Bendis: Riding the Rise of the Graphic Novel,** by Michelle Taute

27 **Doing Double Duty: *Missouri Review* Editor Speer Morgan Dishes on Writing and Editing,** by Elizabeth Boneau

CRAFT & TECHNIQUE

31 **Beyond Inspiration: How to 'Stay in the Chair,'** by Jack Heffron

35 **Boning Up: How to Strengthen Your Manuscript by Fixing Injured Sentences,** by I.J. Schecter

40 **Finding the Perfect Writing Community,** by Joe Feiertag, Mary Carmen Cupito, and the editors of Writer's Market

GETTING PUBLISHED

44 **For Steve Almond, Self-Promotion Takes a Backseat to Writing,** by Will Allison

47 **From Prom Night to Alien Pets: Writing for Theme Anthologies,** by Tim Wagonner

50 **The Scams are Out There!,** by Nancy Breen

54 ***Writer's Digest* Top 30 Short Story Markets,** by Maria Witte

59 **The Business of Fiction Writing**

FOR MYSTERY WRITERS

68 **Ayelet Waldman: Writing Carpool to Carpool,** by W.E. Reinka

71 *Hitchcock & Queen:* **Detecting Strong Fiction for Half a Century,** by I.J. Schecter

76 **David Schanker: 'Scratch a Lawyer, Find a Writer,'** by Will Allison

79 **Resources for Mystery Writers**

FOR ROMANCE WRITERS

80 **Katherine Sutcliffe: Moving to the Dark Side of Romance,** by Deborah Bouziden

83 **The Romance Market: Ever-Evolving, Welcoming New Writers,** by Robin Gee

89 **Resources for Romance Writers**

FOR SCIENCE FICTION/FANTASY & HORROR WRITERS

90 **Poppy Z. Brite on Writing Her 'Exquisite' Horror,** by Candi Lace

94 **Someone Else's Sandbox: Writing Media Tie-Ins,** by Roger MacBride Allen

99 **Jacqueline Cary: At Ease in an Alternate Reality,** by Vanessa Lyman

104 **Resources for Science Fiction/Fantasy & Horror Writers**

THE MARKETS

107 **Literary Agents**

166 **Literary Magazines**

    insider report
      222 *Many Mountains Moving:* Much-needed space for writers, by Denise Meyers

275 **Small Circulation Magazines**

306 **Online Markets**

332 **Consumer Magazines**

    insider report
      337 *C. Michael Curtis:* Happy to find beginners, by Katie Brogan

361 **Book Publishers**

    insider reports
      399 *Lynn Pruett:* Have faith in your craft, by Brad Vice

417 *Mark Wisniewski: Writing fiction 'rooted in real life,'* by Jack Smith

472 **Contests & Awards**

RESOURCES

519 **Conferences**

568 **Writing Programs**

585 **Publishers and Their Imprints**

589 **Canadian Writers Take Note**

590 **Printing and Production Terms Defined**

592 **Glossary**

596 **Literary Agents Category Index**

611 **Contest Index by Deadline**

614 **Conference Index by Date**

618 **Category Index**

660 **General Index**

From the Editor

Welcome to your 2004 edition of *Novel & Short Story Writer's Market*. Each year when we put together a new edition of the book, we try to balance our editorial content to offer a little something for everyone in our family of readers—novelists, short story writers, genre and literary writers, traditionalists and experimentalists. This year is no exception.

In this edition, we've broadened our content to include information for graphic novelists. If you're unfamiliar with this emerging form, our roundtable interview with four graphic novel editors may serve as an introduction to what *Publishers Weekly* has called "the wayward child of the publishing world." Our interview with graphic novelist **Brian Michael Bendis** helps shed light on how to write in this image-driven form. Also, look for market listings for the major players in graphic novel publishing in the Book Publishers section.

No matter what kind of fiction you're writing, we've got the publishing outlets you're looking for. You'll find more than 600 listings for magazines alone—literary journals, online magazines, small circulation publications and zines, and consumer magazines. In our Book Publishers section, look for more than 500 listings, including most imprints of New York's "big houses," and smaller, specialty fiction publishers. And don't forget to check our expanded Literary Agents section, which we've increased from last year's 50 listings to more than 200.

In our Personal Views section, you'll find advice and inspiration from a range of bestselling authors and top-notch editors—**Janet Evanovich, Richard Russo, Speer Morgan, Alice Sebold,** and **Walter Mosley.**

In a recent interview in *Pages* magazine, Easy Rawlins author Mosley said of fiction writing: "I love writing, I really love it . . . I love how the stories blend with experiences I've had. I love how you can change stories. I love language. I love how you can change a sentence to work better . . . that's wonderful." Despite our diversity, it's this love of writing that unites us. Best wishes for a great year, and good luck!

Anne Patterson Bowling

Anne Patterson Bowling
Editor, *Novel & Short Story Writer's Market*
anne.bowling@fwpubs.com

With many, many thanks to everyone whose hard work makes this book work hard for you: assistant editors Michael Schweer *and* Vanessa Lyman; *also* Roger MacBride Allen, Will Allison, Elizabeth Boneau, Deborah Bouziden, Nancy Breen, Robert Lee Brewer, Katie Brogan, Mary Carmen Cupito, Joe Feiertag, Jane Friedman, Robin Gee, Jack Heffron, Kim Kane, Candi Lace, Belinda McCann, Denise Meyers, Lauren Mosko, I.J. Schecter, Jack Smith, W.E. Reinka, Michelle Taute, Brad Vice, Tim Wagonner *and* Maria Witte. *Also, read more about the world of fiction writing and publishing in* Pages *magazine. Ask for* Pages *at your local bookstore, or visit online at www.ireadpages.com.*

The "Quick-Start" Guide to Publishing Your Fiction

To make the most of *Novel & Short Story Writer's Market* you need to know how to use it. And with more than 600 pages of fiction publishing markets and resources, a writer could easily get lost amid the information. This "quick-start" guide will help you wind your way through the pages of *Novel & Short Story Writer's Market*, as well as the fiction publishing process, and emerge with your dream accomplished—to see your fiction in print.

1. Read, read, read.

Read numerous magazines, fiction collections and novels to determine if your fiction compares favorably with work currently being published. If your fiction is at least the same caliber as that you're reading, then move on to step two. If not, postpone submitting your work and spend your time polishing your fiction. Writing and reading the work of others are the best ways to improve craft.

For help with craft and critique of your work:

- You'll find advice and inspiration from bestselling authors and top fiction editors in the Personal Views section, beginning on page 6.
- You'll find articles on the craft and business aspects of writing fiction in the Craft & Technique section, beginning on page 31 and in the Getting Published section, beginning on page 44.
- If you're a genre writer, you will find information in For Mystery Writers, beginning on page 68, For Romance Writers, beginning on page 80 and For Science Fiction/Fantasy & Horror Writers, beginning on page 90.
- You'll find Conference & Workshop listings beginning on page 519.
- Look for undergraduate and graduate writing program listings beginning on page 568.

2. Analyze your fiction.

Determine the type of fiction you write to best target your submissions to markets most suitable to your work. Do you write literary, genre, mainstream or one of many other categories of fiction? There are magazines and presses seeking specialized work in each of these areas as well as numerous others.

For editors and publishers with specialized interests, see the Category Index beginning on page 618.

3. Learn about the market.

Read *Writer's Digest* magazine (F&W Publications, Inc.), *Publishers Weekly*, the trade magazine of the publishing industry, and *Independent Publisher* containing information about small- to medium-sized independent presses. And don't forget the Internet. The number of sites for writers seems to grow daily, and among them you'll find www.writersmarket.com and www.writers digest.com.

4. Find markets for your work.

There are a variety of ways to locate markets for fiction. The periodicals sections of bookstores and libraries are great places to discover new journals and magazines that might be open to your type of short stories. Read writing-related magazines and newsletters for information about new markets and publications seeking fiction submissions. Also, frequently browse bookstore shelves to see what novels and short story collections are being published and by whom. Check acknowledgment pages for names of editors and agents, too. Online journals often have links to the websites of other journals that may publish fiction. And last but certainly not least, read the listings found here in *Novel & Short Story Writer's Market.*

Also, don't forget to utilize the Category Indexes at the back of this book to help you target your fiction to the right market.

5. Send for guidelines.

In the listings in this book, we try to include as much submission information as we can get from editors and publishers. Over the course of the year, however, editors' expectations and needs may change. Therefore, it is best to request submission guidelines by sending a self-addressed stamped envelope (SASE). You can also check the websites of magazines and presses which usually contain a page with guideline information. You can find updated guidelines of many of the markets listed here at www.writersdigest.com. And for an even more comprehensive and continually updated online markets list, you can obtain a subscription to www.writersmarket. com by calling 1-800-448-0915.

6. Begin your publishing efforts with journals and contests open to beginners.

If this is your first attempt at publishing your work, your best bet is to begin with local publications or those you know are open to beginning writers. Then, after you have built a publication history, you can try the more prestigious and nationally distributed magazines. For markets most open to beginners, look for the ⬭ symbol preceding listing titles. Also, look for the ◨ symbol that identifies markets open to exceptional work from beginners as well as work from experienced, previously published writers.

7. Submit your fiction in a professional manner.

Take the time to show editors that you care about your work and are serious about publishing. By following a publication's or book publisher's submission guidelines and practicing standard submission etiquette, you can better ensure your chances that an editor will want to take the time to read your work and consider it for publication. Remember, first impressions last, and a carelessly assembled submission packet can jeopardize your chances before your story or novel manuscript has had a chance to speak for itself. For help with preparing submissions read The Business of Fiction Writing, beginning on page 59.

8. Keep track of your submissions.

Know when and where you have sent fiction and how long you need to wait before expecting a reply. If an editor does not respond by the time indicated in his market listing or guidelines, wait a few more weeks and then follow up with a letter (and SASE) asking when the editor anticipates making a decision. If you still do not receive a reply from the editor within a reasonable amount of time, send a letter withdrawing your work from consideration and move on to the next market on your list.

9. Learn from rejection.

Rejection is the hardest part of the publication process. Unfortunately, rejection happens to every writer, and every writer needs to learn to deal with the negativity involved. On the other hand, rejection can be valuable when used as a teaching tool rather than a reason to doubt yourself and your work. If an editor offers suggestions with his or her rejection slip, take those comments into consideration. You don't have to automatically agree with an editor's opinion of your work. It may be that the editor has a different perspective on the piece than you do. Or, you may find that the editor's suggestions give you new insight into your work and help you improve your craft.

10. Don't give up.

The best advice for you as you try to get published is be persistent, and always believe in yourself and your work. By continually reading other writers' work, constantly working on the craft of fiction writing and relentlessly submitting your work, you will eventually find that magazine or book publisher that's the perfect match for your fiction. And, *Novel & Short Story Writer's Market* will be here to help you every step of the way.

GUIDE TO LISTING FEATURES

Below you will find an example of the market listings contained in *Novel & Short Story Writer's Market*. Also included are call-outs identifying the various format features of the listings. (For an explanation of the symbols used, see the inside front and back covers of this book.)

ICONS FOR EASY REFERENCE

WHAT KIND OF FICTION THEY BUY

COMMENTS FROM THE NSSWM EDITOR

PUBLICATION PROFILE

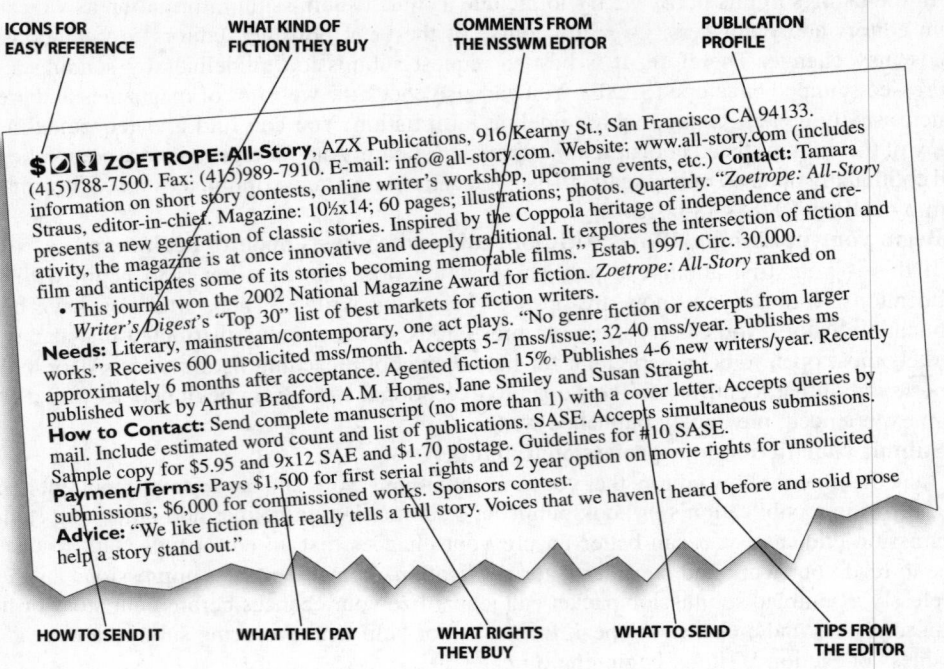

$ 🖊 📷 ZOETROPE: All-Story, AZX Publications, 916 Kearny St., San Francisco CA 94133. (415)788-7500. Fax: (415)989-7910. E-mail: info@all-story.com. Website: www.all-story.com (includes information on short story contests, online writer's workshop, upcoming events, etc.) **Contact:** Tamara Straus, editor-in-chief. Magazine: 10½x14; 60 pages; illustrations; photos. Quarterly. "*Zoetrope: All-Story* presents a new generation of classic stories. Inspired by the Coppola heritage of independence and creativity, the magazine is at once innovative and deeply traditional. It explores the intersection of fiction and film and anticipates some of its stories becoming memorable films." Estab. 1997. Circ. 30,000.

• This journal won the 2002 National Magazine Award for fiction. *Zoetrope: All-Story* ranked on *Writer's Digest*'s "Top 30" list of best markets for fiction writers.

Needs: Literary, mainstream/contemporary, one act plays. "No genre fiction or excerpts from larger works." Receives 600 unsolicited mss/month. Accepts 5-7 mss/issue; 32-40 mss/year. Publishes ms approximately 6 months after acceptance. Agented fiction 15%. Publishes 4-6 new writers/year. Recently published work by Arthur Bradford, A.M. Homes, Jane Smiley and Susan Straight.

How to Contact: Send complete manuscript (no more than 1) with a cover letter. Accepts queries by mail. Include estimated word count and list of publications. SASE. Accepts simultaneous submissions. Sample copy for $5.95 and 9x12 SAE and $1.70 postage. Guidelines for #10 SASE.

Payment/Terms: Pays $1,500 for first serial rights and 2 year option on movie rights for unsolicited submissions; $6,000 for commissioned works. Sponsors contest.

Advice: "We like fiction that really tells a full story. Voices that we haven't heard before and solid prose help a story stand out."

HOW TO SEND IT

WHAT THEY PAY

WHAT RIGHTS THEY BUY

WHAT TO SEND

TIPS FROM THE EDITOR

Writing Fiction

Personal Views... 6

Craft & Technique 31

Getting Published 44

For Mystery Writers...................................... 68

For Romance Writers.................................... 80

For Science Fiction/Fantasy & Horror Writers... 90

Walter Mosley

Walter Mosley: Connecting with the Rest of the World Through Words

BY W.E. REINKA

Walter Mosley remembers the first sentence he ever wrote: "On hot sticky days in Southern Louisiana, the fire ants swarmed." Not bad, he thought. He never used the sentence in a novel or story, but something in its texture encouraged him to continue writing fiction.

"Why was I writing that sentence about fire ants instead of doing my job? Who knows?," Mosley speculates. "I guess I was looking for some mode of expression that I hadn't found yet. I've always sketched and drawn. For a long time, I've done pottering. Those things are very satisfying. I still do them. But writing really seems to click for me. It connects me to the rest of the world. I think that's what art is supposed to do."

Recalling his days as a computer programmer for Mobil Oil, he says, "I won't say I did the minimum of work, but I wasn't pressed to seek some higher forms of excellence, to learn more, to do more, to get deeper into understanding. Without doing that, there was a feeling of dissatisfaction in life. Whereas when I write, I'm critical of every sentence and I worry, 'This is not good enough, this is not good enough.' Even though that's hard to go through, at the end when you've written the best sentence you can—not to say it's perfect by any means, but the best that you can—then there's a sense of satisfaction."

Now in his early fifties, Mosley recalls with a chuckle that he was "old—34 or 35" when those fire ants swarmed. Depending on one's age, "34 or 35" may or may not seem "old." Regardless, Mosley proves that writers who do not start devoting themselves to fiction in their teens can still succeed.

And succeed he has. His career started with publication of *Devil in a Blue Dress* (Norton, 1990). That mystery earned him an Edgar nomination. Later, Columbia TriStar turned the book into a movie starring Denzel Washington. Mosley's career also got a boost when then-President Bill Clinton cited him as one of his favorite mystery writers. Mosley continues to make up for his late start as a writer—since that first title he has published 15 books and written several big screen and TV movies.

Mosley remains best known for his Easy Rawlins series. When complete, the series will trace the life of the eponymous African-American lead character from the late 1930s, into the social changes when, as a World War II combat veteran, he joined the black migration to California, and finally up to the year 2000, when Easy will be about 80. In the latest installments, Easy has reached his mid-40s in the turbulent 1960s.

In terms of publishing pigeonholes, the Easy Rawlins titles are mysteries. Other titles in the series include *A Red Death*(1991), *White Butterfly* (1992), *Black Betty* (1994), *A Little Yellow Dog* (1996), *Bad Boy Brawly Brown* (Little, Brown, 2002), the non-color coded *Gone Fishin'* (Black Classic Press, 1997) and seven stories, six with colors in the titles, collected under the title *Six Easy Pieces* (Atria Books, 2003). The original six stories in that collection had been previously published as bonus stories, one each in various Easy Rawlins paperback editions.

W.E. REINKA *who writes frequently about books and authors, contributes to magazines and newspapers nationwide.*

("Why should readers buy the new hard cover if they have the back list?" Mosley says. "So I wrote a seventh—throwing in an extra like a baker's dozen.")

Though the Easy Rawlins series fits the mystery pigeonhole, Mosley can no longer be characterized as solely a mystery writer. A lifelong science fiction fan, his list of novels also includes *Blue Light* (Little, Brown, 1998) and *Futureland* (Warner, 2001). In *Blue Light*, a sort of cosmic ray infuses select characters with higher planes of understanding. But that doesn't mean they still don't have to battle bad guys. *Futureland* is a collection of nine linked stories that depict a bleak future landscape where capitalism triumphs over government to rule people's lives.

Linking stories is one of Mosley's favorite (and effective) storytelling techniques. He uses it in *Always Outnumbered, Always Outgunned* which introduces lead character Socrates Fortlow. After surviving 27 years in prison for murder, the marginalized Fortlow struggles to live peacefully (outwardly and inwardly) in Watts. He returns in *Walkin' the Dog*, where he tries to balance a quest for redemption with justifiable anger. No wonder Socrates is one of Mosley's favorite characters—he is one of the most complicated. Though Socrates takes an at-risk youth under his wing and adopts a crippled dog, there is never any question that he has killed people and that anger still bubbles easily within him.

In 2001, Mosley returned to crime fiction with *Fearless Jones*. Last summer, he reprised its narrator, Paris Minton, a bookstore owner who would love to be left alone, and Fearless Jones who is, well, fearless, in *Fear Itself*. The two novels cut across black society in Los Angeles, from rich to poor.

Despite his wide range of successes, chances are you'll find Mosley's books lumped into the mystery shelves of your local bookstore. Publishing loves pigeonholes, but Mosley adamantly resists pigeonholing. Take his Easy Rawlins mysteries, for instance. Like most good storytellers, Mosley deepens the characters and layers the plots so they're not merely whodunits. Certainly the book reveals who killed the victim, but the thrust of the writing is aimed toward how characters are in tune with, or victimized by, or perhaps simply accommodate socioeconomic and political forces.

Mosley's desire to round out his characters' milieu-South Central Los Angeles in the 1950s and 1960s, for instance—leads to another pigeonhole: "black writer." Seeing how he grew up in Los Angeles during that same period, he might well wonder why some would put him in a separate category from classic white writers who attempt to bring their worlds to life with historical accuracy. Mosley often cites the "PTM"—or pre-Terry McMillan—period when times were tougher for black writers. He no longer sees today's writers of color segregated in a separate room, as they once were. "A lot of black books are being sold and being bought by black people and not black people. Things are going pretty good for black writers."

But writers are not publishing's decision makers. "Editors make decisions, marketing people make decisions, salespeople make them. Writers just write books and wonder why they are or aren't selling," Mosley says. "Publishing remains 99-point-whatever percent white. And publishing doesn't really have to hire other people because they never really get money from the government. They don't get tax subsidies so you can never force them to say they're not really being diverse. The racial make-up is starting to change somewhat but only because people are making a lot of noise about it."

Mosley is one of those people making noise. He helped launch City College of New York's publishing certificate program. Under its aegis, insiders from the publishing industry come to teach young urbanites about all aspects of publishing from editing to marketing, publicity to sales. Students are offered real-world internships and early statistics show that a significant portion of students, many of them persons of color, wind up working in publishing.

It's not the only time Mosley has made a conscious effort to use his power as a respected and visible writer to promote minorities in publishing. Back in 1997, he forewent his usual large advance and published *Gone Fishin'*, a prequel to the Easy Rawlins series, with Black Classic Press in Baltimore. Mosley knew the experience might not go as smoothly as with a mainstream

New York publisher. He once likened it to a street hot dog stand suddenly assuming the concessions at a Big League park. Ultimately, Black Classic Press produced a beautifully designed book and the publicity generated by Mosley's decision sent ripples throughout the publishing world.

Mosley is also active in other venues. Past president of the Mystery Writers of America, Mosley serves on the board of directors of the National Book Awards and The Poetry Society of America. In 1996, he was named the first Artist-in-Residence at New York University's Africana Studies Institute and continues to contribute to its "Black Genius" lecture series which brings speakers from a variety of specialties to discuss contemporary issues in a public classroom format.

With all of his other activities and accomplishments, it's a wonder Mosley has time to write anything, let alone average over one book per year. He learned what it took to succeed back when he was writing about fire ants and still had a day job as a computer programmer at Mobil Oil. "I woke up at five in the morning and spent my best hours of the day writing, from five to eight. At eight o'clock I would get ready and I'd go off for work and I gave my second best hours to work."

"I'm a writer who writes many different types of things. If I don't have a publisher who can accommodate all the different ways that I write, then they're not really my publisher. I don't have a home. It's like living in a hotel. So I had to change publishers, not because there's anything wrong with the other publisher—they're very good and quite respectable—but they weren't able to accommodate the range of writing that I wanted to do."

Today, he starts a "Writers on Writing" essay in *The New York Times* with the following advice: "If you want to be a writer, you have to write every day. The consistency, the monotony, the certainty, all vagaries and passions are covered by this daily reoccurrence." Later he adds "writing a novel is gathering smoke. It's an excursion into the ether of ideas. There's no time to waste. You must work with that idea as well as you can, jotting down notes and dialogue."

Perhaps because Mosley sees writing as "gathering smoke," he doesn't take success for granted. Or maybe it's because he hasn't forgotten those days at Mobil Oil and the encouragement the fire ants lent him when he was just one of millions of unfulfilled hopefuls. Regardless, he treasures his continued success, though he sees that it, too, may dissipate like a cloud of smoke.

"Everybody always says that most writers have an arc of about 10 years and then they sink into obscurity. The fact that I've been published now for about 14 years is really amazing." As for his own obscurity, "I'm not worried about it. I'm sure it's going to happen. It's like being worried about death. Are you worried that you're going to die one day? Well, no."

For as long as his career lasts, Mosley seems determined to enjoy it, in part by writing what he wants. He has had to fight at times to control his own career. Take *Blue Light*, the first science fiction novel he penned after enjoying success as a mystery writer. His then-publisher, W.W. Norton, refused to publish it, Mosley says. "It's always hard with your first publisher because you come in like a kid. You're inexperienced. They know everything. They had an idea of my career and, because they started it, they felt a little paternal toward it, which is fine."

According to Mosley, Norton informed him that he wouldn't be happy if they published *Blue Light*, to which he replied, "Well, I'm not going to be happy if you don't publish it." Finally, Mosley accepted that. "Obviously, they were saying something to me. I was angry. But there's an issue—I'm a writer who writes many different types of things. If I don't have a publisher who can accommodate all the different ways that I write, then they're not really my publisher. I don't have a home. It's like living in a hotel. So I had to change publishers, not because there's anything wrong with Norton—they're a very good publisher and quite respectable—but they weren't able to accommodate the range of writing that I wanted to do."

Mosley now associates with a variety of publishers, though it seems that Little, Brown has become his primary, though not exclusive, outlet. In 2002, Little, Brown published *The Man in My Basement*. In it, two disparate characters—one black, one white—enter what amounts to a long political dialogue which leads to changes and revelations to them both, and leaves readers happy that Mosley didn't limit himself to mysteries and insisted on exerting professional freedom.

"I'm unusual in as much that I attempt various types of writing. There are some people who have a kind of writing that they do and they're really not interested in other types of writing. You have a mystery writer or a western writer or science fiction writer—that's what they do. On the whole, most writers don't try other types of writing because in America everything is done on the business model. You'll be most successful if, at least in the short run, you continue to write the same kind of thing again and again."

Though Mosley refused "to write the same kind of thing again and again," he has become an extremely successful writer, by any measure, including his own. Asked if he's satisfied with his progress and ability as a writer since he first wrote about fire ants, he puts a smile in his voice.

Richard Russo: Master of the Tragicomedy

BY JANE FRIEDMAN

Validation: that's how Richard Russo describes the impact of winning the 2002 Pulitzer Prize for his fifth and most recent novel, *Empire Falls* (Knopf, 2001). It gave me permission to continue," he says. "It said, 'keep doing what you're doing'."

Russo's epic story of a declining New England small town has been hailed by critics as the last great American novel of the 20th century. It was the inaugural selection of the *USA Today* book club and named 2001's best novel by *Time* magazine.

Empire Falls tells the life story of an unpretentious nice guy. Miles Roby, who's spent all his life managing the town's greasy spoon, Empire Grill. The first chapter opens with Miles waiting at the restaurant for his teenage daughter, Tick, to return from school. She eventually appears hefting a load of books.

"The overarching metaphor is at the book's opening—Tick and her books," Russo says. "The larger theme is how kids are carrying too much weight, and what will the weight be in the end? It turns out it's cruelty."

Richard Russo

Photo © Christine Polomsky

Russo modeled Tick on his own two daughters, who were high-school age when he wrote *Empire Falls*. In some ways, Russo says, the story is a father-daughter love story, but one that ends with a father's worst nightmare—cruelty against his own child.

"I was hoping (the school shooting) wouldn't be the climax. I knew where it was headed, and I didn't want to go there," Russo says. "I used a fair amount of my daughters in the character of Tick—I had grown to love this child. And to turn around and put this fictional child in that kind of mortal jeopardy! But it's a multigenerational book. Everyone's hurt or abused in some way."

As grim as the subject sounds, *Empire Falls* overflows with humorous scenes and characters, for which Russo's earlier novels are well known. *Straight Man* is an academic satire, and *Nobody's Fool* (both Random House) is another small-town life novel with tragicomic elements. The latter was made into a motion picture starring Paul Newman; Russo wrote the screenplay.

Whether he's detailing the lives of intellectuals or blue-collars, Russo always builds a vivid setting. Sense of place is crucial in all of Russo's work, particularly so in *Empire Falls*. The dying

JANE FRIEDMAN *is acquisitions editor for* Writer's Digest Books, *and former managing editor of* Writer's Digest *magazine. Before joining* Writer's Digest, *Jane spent three years at North Light Books as an acquisitions and content editor. She earned a BFA in creative writing at the University of Evansville and an MA in English at Xavier University. Her creative work has appeared in* Salon, The Formalist, The Evansville Review, *and* UE Magazine.

town envelopes Miles' activities, taunting him for never escaping. In *The Complete Handbook of Novel Writing* (Writer's Digest Books), Russo says, "place and its people are intertwined, place is character."

Typically, Russo works on a novel for several years, and during that time often returns to the story's beginning to add passages or reshuffle scenes. "In art, effects often precede the cause. I try to make the novel appear like that's what I was doing all along," he says.

Empire Falls features lengthy flashbacks, including a 14-page prologue relating the town's history. But Russo says chapter one, set during the present day, was his true start. As he progressed, he saw the need for backstory, so he started writing about Miles' childhood and the town's history. He later decided to place the flashbacks in italics, as separate sections, to deliver the information.

"I realized how much the past impinged on the present," Russo says. "I have this analogy: If you're building a house and you start digging, and you run into this rock, you have two options. You can either try to dig the rock out, not knowing how big it is or how deep it goes, or you can build around the rock and make it an architectural part of the house, as if it really belongs there. And that's kind of what these flashbacks are like."

Once Russo finishes a novel—which he revises and revises until he can't make it any better—he shows it to his wife. "She's the first reader, a good reader and a generous reader. She tells me when the book loses her attention," he says.

After his wife's read, Russo sends the work to his agents, Nat Sobel and Judith Weber. "Every single one of my books they've made better, but we don't always agree on what needs to be done. The secret to the relationship is that they're never insistent," he says.

Russo's latest release has taken a different direction. *The Whore's Child* is a collection of seven short stories—some new, some old.

Although Russo finds that short stories pose a lesser risk ("if short stories fail, it's a month out of your life—damage control"), they are much more difficult for him to write. "They are all about control, which I have never had a lot of. I'm a creature of digression. You can't allow yourself to be distracted."

Yet distraction is exactly what Russo goes after in his writing environment. He prefers to write in diners or busy places, where his mind can wander and make connections. "You can end up where you didn't mean to go, but it's probably more interesting than where you meant to go in the first place."

Russo's advice to novelists in particular is this: "Whatever you're working on, take small bites. A few pages at a time. Whatever you're working on should be the most exciting thing. The task will not be overwhelming if you can reduce it to its smallest component."

Also: "Don't keep a journal because you'll think what you remembered to write down was important, when actually it's not."

———————————

"Whatever you're working on, take small bites. Whatever you're working on should be the most exciting thing. The task will not be overwhelming if you can reduce it to its smallest component."

———————————

Janet Evanovich: 'Out of Nowhere' to the Bestseller List

BY ANNE BOWLING

Janet Evanovich will say that as a writer, she "came out of nowhere." History supports her statement, but only up to a point. A former art school student from South River, New Jersey, she was not formally trained as a writer. She knew no one who wrote, and knew no one in the industry. But Evanovich did do her time in the trenches working at craft, experimenting with content and developing her own sense of a writer's relationship with her readers.

The result? A series crime writer for whom the adjective "hot" won't do it. A signing last year in her Trenton, New Jersey home base drew 3,000 fans. Each of her last three books—*Hot Six*, *Seven Up* and *Hard Eight*—debuted at No. 1 on the New York Times bestseller list, and publisher St. Mar-

Janet Evanovich

Photo © Herman Estevez

tin's Press was pleased when the 2003 installment, *To the Nines*, was equally successful. Not too shabby for a writer who came out of nowhere.

"I got serious about getting published after about 10 years of writing," Evanovich says. "I had written three big, bizarre books that had been sent to and rejected by a seemingly endless round of publishing houses and agents. So I told myself I could try two category romances because they're short and quick. If that didn't work I was gonna quit and get a real job."

Her persistence paid off. The first romance was rejected, but the next was picked up by the Second Chance Press (an irony not lost on Evanovich), and she was on her way. Of her 10-year wait for publication, perseverance was important, "but it also helped that I always believed, when I got those rejections, that it was because I hadn't learned enough yet," Evanovich says. "Ultimately, that's what you've got to do—you've got to write it good enough."

"Good enough" for Evanovich came in the form of her Stephanie Plum crime series. Launched in 1994 with *One for the Money* (Scribner), the series quickly hit the pace of a book a year. Part romance, part crime story and part comedy, the series revolves around Stephanie, a Trenton, New Jersey-based bond enforcement agent. Attitudinal and working class, Stephanie leads a cast of offbeat characters through antic efforts to nab the bad guys, in what *The New York Times* has called "pure, classic farce—Jersey Girl style." An accessible Everywoman, Steph goes to mom's macaroni and cheese for comfort, and to cop Joe Morelli for romance.

"That's the hardest element of the Plum series," says Evanovich of sustaining Stephanie's ongoing love interest with Morelli, and handling her periodic trysts with a mysterious bond

---

ANNE BOWLING *is editor of* Novel & Short Story Writer's Market. *This interview originally appeared in* Writer's Digest *magazine, and appears here with permission.*

agent called Ranger. "It's hard keeping the tension going between Stephanie and Joe, and yet keeping it realistic enough in terms of what people really do. I love the sexual tension of romance writing, the 'keeping the characters apart.' The TV show 'Moonlighting' was much the same—it had the elements of a detective story, but ultimately it was a romantic comedy."

Evanovich had published 12 romance titles before she began the Plum series, "but by book five I suspected I was in the wrong place," she says. "I found out I liked writing action, and that I needed that something extra to move the book forward." But romance was a good place to cut her teeth, Evanovich says. Writing in that genre gave her the opportunity to work with a lot of different editors, to develop her voice in a non-threatening environment ("romance readers are loyal," she says), and to learn craft through workshops and conferences sponsored by the Romance Writers of America (RWA). Secure in that foundation, Evanovich was able to pull elements of her craft into her new genre.

"For years I'd hear people at writer's conferences say, 'I wrote the book that was in me—I wrote the book that I had to write.' And I'd think, that's fine, but what about the reader?"

Despite its slightly madcap spin, the Plum series was developed with a great deal of deliberation. "It's important for writers to be analytic, and when I decided to move out of romance, I wanted to make sure I had my formula for making a popular series." She critically read mainstream novels and listed the elements she liked. "As a producer of a product, I thought, 'what do I need to do for the consumer?'," she says. "Find a hole in the marketplace, and offer the consumer something they like but that hasn't already be done."

When Evanovich talks about writing, the reader is an integral part of the subject. "Art for art's sake" doesn't fly for the pragmatist in Jersey Janet. That attentiveness to her readers—demonstrated by book tours, her family-maintained website, and the consideration she gives them when crafting her novels—has generated a fan base so loyal they've named themselves the Plum Crazies.

"When I was in art school, the idea was art is something you create for yourself, and if someone comes along and sees something in it that's meaningful to them, great. If not, that's okay too," she says. "And for years I'd hear people at writer's conferences say, 'I wrote the book that was in me—I wrote the book that I had to write.' And I'd think, that's fine, but what about the reader?"

All the elements of Evanovich's books are crafted to keep the reader entertained and moving—dialog, narrative, and plot points. "Transitions are critically important," she says. "I want the reader to turn the page without thinking she's turning the page. It must flow seamlessly."

There's a great deal of Evanovich in Stephanie Plum, which may help explain the popularity of both the character and the author. To keep her lead character consistent, Evanovich tests her own reactions to the circumstances she faces Stephanie with. And to bridge the decades-wide age gap, Evanovich turns to her twenty-something daughter Alex (who also runs the website). "There's a danger in writing a character who's a generation removed from you," she says. Alex keeps Stephanie's slang and speech current and her wardrobe up-to-date, tight jeans, leather boots and all.

"When you give a reader a book, you give them an emotional experience. And you pick that emotional experience in the details you provide," Evanovich says. Through the reading "you smell the coffee, and the chocolate chip cookies baking in the oven, and you want to stay in that woman's kitchen."

For more on Janet Evanovich and her work, visit www.evanovich.com.

Alice Sebold: 'The Entire Book is a Leap of Faith'

BY JANE FRIEDMAN

When Alice Sebold finished *The Lovely Bones* (Little, Brown), she was 38. She had never before published a novel, just a modestly selling memoir, *Lucky* (Scribner), a book that wasn't even expected to go into paperback.

By the end of August 2002, *Lovely Bones* had become a blockbuster hit. It sold more than 1 million copies in two months without being a major book club pick, and ranked No. 1 on the major bestseller lists, including *The New York Times*.

The novel opens with the rape and murder of a 14-year-old girl, Susie, who acts as the first-person narrator from heaven. For nearly 10 years, Susie watches her family and friends on Earth, seeing how they cope, develop and experience life without her.

Alice Sebold

Sebold says persistence can be a writer's best virtue—particularly after repeated failure. "If you want to give up, give up. There's no reason to stay doing this unless part of you really is insane," she says. "Nothing else mattered to me as much as great books and wanting to try to write. One thing about failing repeatedly: If you're still doing it after you've failed that much, you really mean it."

Soon after graduating from Syracuse University in 1984—where she studied under Tess Gallagher and Tobias Wolff—Sebold moved to New York City and taught creative writing at Hunter College. Despite having an agent, she couldn't find a publisher for her two novel manuscripts, one of which was nominated for a Pushcart Editor's Award. Looking back, she says that it was probably a good thing.

"I'm thrilled to buttons that they weren't published. To those people who think I'm quite old for a first novelist, I end up saying, 'that's how long my apprenticeship took.' But what I feel a lot is that maybe there are a lot of people who maybe shouldn't publish those early novels," Sebold says.

The idea for *Lovely Bones* came to Sebold after she left New York for California in the mid-1990s, and enrolled in the MFA program at the University of California at Irvine.

In what she has described as one "mind-blowing" sitting, Sebold wrote almost word for

---

JANE FRIEDMAN *is acquisitions editor for Writer's Digest Books, and former managing editor of* Writer's Digest *magazine. Before joining* Writer's Digest, *Jane spent three years at North Light Books as an acquisitions and content editor. She earned a BFA in creative writing at the University of Evansville and an MA in English at Xavier University. Her creative work has appeared in* Salon, The Formalist, The Evansville Review, *and* UE Magazine.

word what is now the novel's first chapter. But instead of continuing Susie's story, Sebold put the chapter aside and started work on her memoir, *Lucky* (published in 1999), which details her rape and its aftermath during her undergraduate years. Sebold says it was necessary to complete the memoir first, so her experiences wouldn't become part of Susie's story.

"Writing *Lucky* was a much more rigorous, almost athletic experience . . .there were things that were essential to the story for the audience, but not necessarily pieces that were enjoyable to draft and redraft."

While composing *Lovely Bones*, however, Sebold found the writing process wonderful. "I liked keeping company with Susie, and the imagined idea of, you know, murdered girls in heaven."

The wild burst of inspiration that sparked *Lovely Bones* isn't typical of Sebold's day-to-day writing process. She doesn't have a set way of doing things. "I'm a big supporter of what I call 'disciplined mess.' I keep my hours, and I keep my goals, but beyond that I don't have any sense of 'I've got to write the scene where A meets B today'."

Sebold says she writes by drafting—she doesn't create outlines or spend time worrying that the story might not be going in the right direction. She just plows ahead. "In *Lovely Bones* there were plenty of scenes I drafted that just didn't work. You have to be ready, willing and able to cut things as soon as you sense they're going in a bad direction. You have an inner critic who knows when something's going off."

"There's a joke among my friends that no matter how much I wrote, I only ever had 100 pages," Sebold says. "That's because I would write, cut, write, cut. I'd write something and decide I wanted to use that, but something else had to be cut. It's constantly shaping and reshaping the material."

Unlike those writers who analyze their writing process, or talk about the "Aha!" moment during composition, Sebold says she's not sure how she successfully builds a scene or character. Rather she concentrates on listening to her characters' voices and desires.

"I think (understandings) come after you've finished working on some scenes and you go and you read them. Your characters provide you with what the story is and with what direction it's going. I don't believe in the idea of the writer as intellectual dominator of a text," she says.

Although many reviews of *Lovely Bones* praise Sebold's deft handling of the book's topic—admiring how she never lets it slip into sweet sentimentality—the book has its share of critics. Some say the book stumbles in a scene near the end that often reminds people of the movie *Ghost*. Sebold dismisses such criticism.

"You write the book that you're driven to write, and you really can't do more than that. It's a leap of faith, the entire book is a leap of faith, and not everybody is going to take it with me."

One person who took the leap with her from the novel's beginning was her husband, Glen David Gold, author of *Carter Beats the Devil*, whom she met at UCI. When Sebold finished writing her novel's first chapter—before they were married—she called him and read it over the phone to get his opinion. He gave it the green flag. "We're each others' first readers. We're vital to each others' processes. We believe that writing is the most important thing in the world," she says.

In their household, during heavy work times, Sebold will get up anywhere from 3 to 5 a.m. and start writing (she says her husband considers the habit "insane"). By the time she's done with her writing hours, he's up and getting his coffee.

Above her desk, while she wrote *Lovely Bones*, Sebold taped a note saying, "For those five people," indicating how many people she thought would ever read the novel. As it turns out, it may be for those 5 million people. As of Spring 2003, *Lovely Bones* still ranked in the top five on the *The New York Times* bestseller list. And the memoir, *Lucky*, was reissued in paperback by Little, Brown.

Sebold's final advice to writers who may doubt their abilities? "Just stay in the game. Throughout my 20s and early 30s, I would apply for things or send things out, and I got enough messages back to let me know I wasn't insane." Sebold is already more than 100 pages into her second novel, the topic of which she's keeping to herself. "I worked my whole life to be able to do nothing but write books, and now I have that opportunity, so I'm going to grab it."

Beyond BAM! and POW!: Four Publishing Insiders Talk about Breaking into Graphic Novels

BY LAUREN MOSKO

If you've been keeping tabs on the publishing industry, you already know comic books—and their format spin-off graphic novels—have recently attracted more attention from publishers, librarians, booksellers, and readers alike. With comics tie-ins (like Spider-Man, The Hulk, and X-Men) and graphic-novel-based movies (like *Ghost World*, *From Hell*, and *The Road to Perdition*) enjoying much success at the box office, both comics aficionados and those who stare blankly when you mention Stan Lee or Will Eisner are rediscovering the art—and not just the illustration. It's prime time for graphic novelists, but before you go running for your pen, you need a basic understanding of the format and how its segment of the industry is different from the rest of the comics-publishing world.

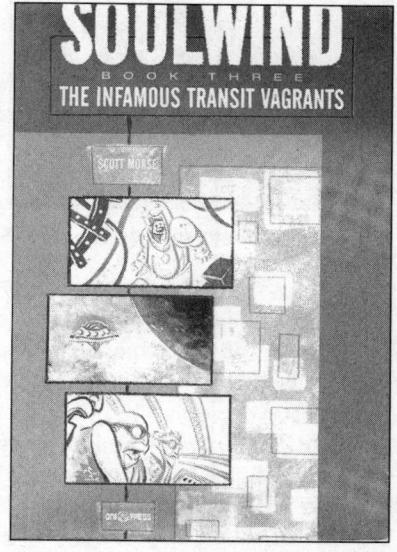

Oni Press, Soulwind series, Book Three

Although many, even within the trade, use the terms interchangeably, there are a few key differences between a comic book and a graphic novel. First, graphic novels are book-sized volumes of material not previously published in traditional "comic book" periodical form. Also, a distinction can be made regarding plot accessibility. In other words, comics periodicals are generally part of a lengthy, on-going series, so someone new to a title might have to read six or eight back issues just to understand the story. On the other hand, graphic novels are usually self-contained. Of course, there are always exceptions, such as Neil Gaiman's 10-part *Sandman* series (DC Comics), but even those installments are easily digestible on their own.

The next nomenclatural hitch is the use of the term "novel" when, in the true sense, graphic novels do not have to be works of fiction at all. It's important to understand that "graphic novel" is a format (i.e. telling a story using sequential art), *not* a genre, that encompasses works of nonfiction, as well. Joe Sacco's *The Fixer* (Drawn & Quarterly) addresses issues of western journalism while reporting from Bosnia; Chester Brown presents a comic-strip biography of the Canadian politician *Louis Riel* (Drawn & Quarterly); Pulitzer Prize winner Art Spiegelman's *MAUS* (Pantheon) is his father's Holocaust memoir.

So don't think that just because your protagonist isn't a superhero, warlock, or robot that

LAUREN MOSKO *is a Cincinnati-based journalist specializing in music, writing and design. She has contributed to both* Novel & Short Story Writer's Market *and* Children's Writer's & Illustrator's Market. *When not bent over her desk writing and editing, she's teaching journalism at the University of Cincinnati.*

DC Comics, Sandman series, volume X

you've ruled out a career in comics. It doesn't matter whether you write history, philosophy, literature, romance, mystery, fantasy, action, comedy or sci-fi; there's a place in the world of graphic novels for your work, as long as you have a story to tell.

You're bound to have some questions before delving into the oft-misunderstood realm of the graphic novel. To help you get started, we've assembled four industry insiders—Jamie S. Rich, editor-in-chief of Oni Press; Jeff Mason, publisher of Alternative Comics and *Indy Magazine*; Jennifer de Guzman, editor-in-chief of SLG (Slave Labor Graphics) Publishing; and Lee Dawson, publicist for Dark Horse Comics, Inc.-to give you some insight on breaking into the panels and navigating the gutters.

What's the best way for someone with a manuscript for a graphic novel to approach a publisher?

Jamie Rich: Whatever way they can. The big conventions are often the best starting point, something face to face. Printed preview books and online displays are also good showcases.

Jeff Mason: First, find out whether or not that publisher has submission guidelines. Check that publisher's website. Read those guidelines, and follow them exactly. Don't submit your rough draft, your first draft, or your second draft.

Jennifer de Guzman: The best thing to do is to find out what each publisher prefers. Here at SLG Publishing, for example, we don't look at art or writing on its own—we only consider projects that have both an artist and a writer attached to it. Other publishers might not take unsolicited submissions or they might have specific procedures for making proposals. As with any other writing market, you should know the submission guidelines before you send something in or approach a publisher.

Lee Dawson: Well, it is tough to break in, especially for writers. Many comic companies don't accept writing submissions—not only because of the amount of time it takes to wade through them but also because of potential legal problems (e.g. someone sends in a writing submission, and then claims at a later date that the company stole their idea). I would suggest checking the company's website for submission information. At Dark Horse, that's where we keep ours. Ideally, the best bet for both writers and illustrators is to try and self-publish and get noticed that way. We have discovered numerous writers and artists through their self-published work.

What's the biggest mistake you see new or potential writer/illustrators making?

Rich: They spend too much time worrying about what a publisher may want or too much time trying to recapture comics from their youth. We need more passion in our potential creators; we need people who have a burning desire to tell stories. You don't see novelists rehashing characters that are over half-a-century old because it gives them the tingly feeling of being a little kid. We need less people that think to themselves, "Gee, wouldn't it be cool to be in comics," and more that have an inner flame that says, "I must relate this story to the world."

Mason: The biggest mistake I see is writers and illustrators not attempting to familiarize themselves with my company, my policies, and my attitudes before attempting to submit work to me. It is essential that you know who you are trying to interact with!

de Guzman: Not knowing the submission guidelines is a big mistake. Submitting projects that don't fit the publisher is another. Writers often make the mistake of e-mailing me with ideas and asking if we'd be interested in a project like they describe, but we can't tell just based on an idea. The *execution* of the idea is more important.

Dawson: Lack of originality is probably the number one writing taboo. Illustrators need to be sure they can draw hands and faces conveying emotion, as opposed to just a static battle scene. Most importantly, writers need to be able to tell a story in sequence.

Would you encourage writers who are interested in the format to attend comic conventions? If so, what can they hope to take away from the experience?

Rich: Yeah, I would encourage them to. I think they need to network with artists and editors and generally get known, schmooze their way into maybe getting people to look at their work. It's a tough road for writers, though. It's not like they have the instant quality recognition artists have. Their work needs to be digested, to have someone spend time with it. That said, I once had a teenage kid come up during portfolio review and plunk down a couple of pages of script and say, "I know this is for artists, but just read a couple of panels, look at construction and dialogue, and tell me what you think." He was a smart, smart kid. I don't think I ever heard from him again, though, which is a shame.

Mason: I would say that this is almost essential. Go to comic book conventions to meet people, to learn about the career you are hoping to pursue, and learn to be more at ease with yourself and the notion of being a professional.

de Guzman: Writers who want to get into the business could learn a good deal from attending comic conventions. Comic-Con International in San Diego is *the* convention to attend. It might be overwhelming to someone who is not familiar with the industry, however. The convention hall is always packed, and the sheer number of booths makes it impossible to know what to do without a game plan. Check the programs and see when publishers are holding submissions workshops; as far as I know, writers and artists must attend these workshops to even have their work considered by DC. Independent publishers often hold panels on what kind of books they're looking for and how to approach submissions, as well. The other thing to do is to look at the books. Check out what is out there, what kind of books each publisher puts out, and become familiar with the market.

Dawson: Yes definitely! Comic conventions are the best way to network with other creators and a chance to talk with publishers. As a writer, you may not be able to show your work and get feedback, but a lot can be gleaned from a conversation with the right folks.

In your experience, does the industry regard creative-team jobs (i.e. when the writing and illustrating are not done by the same person) with any less respect? And what advice would you give a writer who's looking for an illustrator for a graphic-novel project?

Rich: I think there is a certain snobbery that exists amongst certain members of the indie community. I personally think it's bunk. It's like saying an actor has to also write and direct. This is classically a collaborative medium, and so there is no shame in being realistic and choosing to write the books, but realizing you can't draw and vice versa.

I would tell any writer looking for an artist to be very selective, though. Your artist is going to be the first thing a potential publisher sees about your package. That's your first foot forward, and if the artist is terrible, you may never recover. Ask yourself if you'd pay money to buy a book this guy drew. Ask yourself, "Is he as good as half the people working in comics today?" and if the answer isn't, "No, he's better," move on. Same goes for artists looking for writers, though I think it's much easier for an artist to show off, since you can look good without having the words read.

Mason: No, the industry does not give less respect to writers and illustrators than to individuals that both write and illustrate. In addition, creative teams can create comics quicker than a single cartoonist. My best advice would be for individuals to attend comic book conventions, talk to people, and use the Internet to try to connect with a creative partner.

de Guzman: Creative teams are the standard in the big two—Marvel and DC—so there's nothing disrespectable about them in the industry. They're less common in independent publishing, but in my experience, they're not looked down upon. Writers who are looking for illustrators should try to get involved in online comics communities. There are often illustrators looking for writers and writers looking for illustrators there. Comic book writers and illustrators are very active in the online world. The comic book industry still is very insular, and anyone interested in becoming part of it probably would do well to make some contacts and get his or her name out there.

Dawson: Creative teams are held in the same regard as the single writer/artist. The bulk of the industry is made up of creative teams, and some of the most esteemed and popular titles in the medium's history were co-created. It sounds obvious, but I would suggest the writer look for an illustrator who will truly compliment the tone of the work—even more than choosing the "best" artist. If the illustrator is able to capture the emotion of the writing, it will really enhance the story beyond simply being technically proficient.

What is your opinion on graphic-novel-writing contests? Do you find that they're being used as serious tools to find new talent, or are they more of a sales/publicity gimmick?

Rich: I honestly can't say. I know I am personally very cynical about such things, but I can't speak for the intentions of others.

Mason: I think they are useful to both the publishers and the new talents. They are both serious tools to find new talent as well as a sales/publicity gimmick. The best of both worlds.

Say What?

Graphic Novel: Book-length story told using sequential art, usually self-contained and previously unpublished in pamphlet form

Manga: Literally meaning "entertaining visual"; licensed editions of Japanese (or Japanese-inspired) comics re-released in English or in split-language, often read right-to-left

Pamphlet: Saddle-stitched publications with paper covers; what you think of when you hear the term "comic book"

Trade Paperback: A reprint collection of a comic series bound together as one volume

Will Eisner: Often credited with the invention of the graphic novel after publishing *A Contract with God* in 1978 (Titan Books)

de Guzman: I haven't heard much buzz about graphic-novel-writing contests. I know that Dark Horse had a contest to get new comics published on their website, but I haven't heard anything about writing contests specifically.

Dawson: Actually we are running a sort of graphic novel contest right now. It's actually a talent search but for finished projects. We are indeed using it to find talent, as opposed to getting more sales or publicity. These types of things are too much work to be used only as promotional tools!

Are graphic-novel anthologies more of a stepping stone for those seeking independent publication, or are they considered an end in themselves?

Rich: I am not sure exactly what purpose they serve. I think the short story in comics is a terribly misunderstood form. I think most people in comics don't get the short story and end up giving us not very much of a story at all. They often rely on a bad twist ending, or go nowhere, or just seem to exist, as you say, as an end unto themselves. I personally rarely read them, and honestly, have lost any taste for editing them. So, at risk of sounding like a an old grump—which I very much am—I will settle on them serving their own purpose for the most part, with the occasional gem shining through. Which, in the end, has me going from caustic to wishy-washy. Ha-ha!

Mason: Certainly both, with most anthologies leaning toward one end of the balance or the other, depending on the anthology.

de Guzman: It's certainly an accomplishment to be published in an anthology. Sometimes, as with the *Bizarro Comics* anthology that DC recently published, it's a sign that an artist or writer has "arrived" in the industry. However, it seems that the goal is usually to get a title all to oneself, whether it be writing a superhero comic for one of the big two or having one's own work published by an indie publisher.

Dawson: I think they can be an end in themselves, as getting published in any format is a great goal. It really depends on the individual and if he or she wants to take the story beyond the anthology.

What's the inside story on strictly web-based graphic novels? Do you see all print titles eventually heading in that direction?

Rich: I don't know about heading in that direction. I think in general, right now, most people aren't as well-trained to read on screen, and the interface still has issues. Perhaps a new generation will be more equipped for it, and we'll see more of it. I don't see web comics as less viable, at all, though. Whatever gets your work out there is good, and as long as you aren't using the digital element for trickery to hide problems with the work (which you can also do in print), then I think it's fine.

Mason: I don't think many print titles are soon to head to the Internet. Once truly easy-to-use, cheap, beautiful handheld electronic books are ubiquitous, I don't think that we'll see that much of a migration to the web.

de Guzman: I know that Artbomb.net and Dark Horse have done some interesting things with online comics, and there are some interesting independently-produced web comics out there, but I don't see comics moving in that direction any time soon. For them to do so would mean that the comic book industry would have to move much farther away from the collector mentality. The collector attitude is—happily, in my opinion—on the wane, especially when it comes to independent comics, but there are still collectors out there, and online comics don't lend themselves well to being collected. But, more generally, I think there is still an aesthetic aversion to reading things that aren't on paper, as well as logistical problems with transforming the publishing industry in that way. Some people were sure that the e-book would take the traditional book industry by storm, but that hasn't really happened. People have been reading books on paper for centuries, and it's going to take some time to alter people's preferences. It's a gradual process.

Dawson: Well, for a while there it was the talk of the industry that web comics might take over, but it really hasn't turned out that way. There are some great online comics, but it seems that the people have spoken, and they still love the printed versions over web-based stuff. I think this is true in the book world, as well. There's just no substitute for having that comic in your hand.

As a publisher of graphic novels, how do you feel you are regarded by the traditional publishing world?

Rich: I honestly don't know. I don't know anyone in the traditional publishing world! No one has offered me a job, so maybe that's your answer right there. Heh!

Mason: I believe I'm still pretty much under their radar. Those familiar with Alternative Comics seem to hold us in pretty high regard, and I hope to continue to earn that regard!

de Guzman: We attended BookExpo America this summer, and I got the feeling that the traditional publishing world is increasingly seeing graphic novels as a legitimate, and even important, part of the industry. BEA set up a "Graphic Novel Pavilion," and we got a lot of interest from bookstores and libraries that wanted to start up or expand a graphic novel section. There is still a declining perception that comics—or graphic novels—are a medium for kids, but we've been trying to educate people in that regard, showing them that graphic novels are a medium, not a genre. SLG, for example, publishes a large variety of graphic novels, from works that are appropriate for small children, like *Patty Cake and Friends* by Scott Roberts, to works that are aimed at mature audience, like *Johnny the Homicidal Maniac* by Jhonen Vasquez.

Works that get a lot of mainstream media attention, like Joe Sacco's *Palestine* (Fantagraphics Books) and *Persepolis* (Pantheon) by Marjane Satrapi, are doing a lot to increase people's awareness. It's an exciting time for the graphic novel industry. I wouldn't say we're entering a new Golden Age, but I definitely see this as a time of transition. Right now, I'm just hoping that graphic novels will become part of what people think of when they see the word "books."

Dawson: The last few years, we have seen an explosion of graphic novels in the book market and libraries. Book buyers and librarians tell us that once they assign a specific graphic novel section, they see a tenfold increase in traffic and demand. (In the past, many stores would stick graphic novels in the humor section next to Garfield.) As a result, I think the publishing world has gained a new respect for the quality, diversity, and sales potential of the format.

For more information about writing in this industry, see the article Writing Media Tie-Ins *on page 94.*

Conventions

Comic-Con International, WonderCon, and Alternative Press Expo (APE): www.comic-con.org.
MoCCA (Museum of Comic and Cartoon Art) Art Festival: www.moccany.org.
BookExpo America (BEA): www.bookexpoamerica.com.

Brian Michael Bendis: Riding the Rise of the Graphic Novel

BY MICHELLE TAUTE

It's a good time to be a graphic novelist. Especially one with three Eisner awards (the Oscars of the comic book world) under your belt, an ongoing deal with Marvel to chronicle iconic characters like Daredevil and Spider-Man, and your own original projects to boot. Ask anyone with a passing interest in graphic novels and comics and they'll tell you Brian Michael Bendis is hot right now. Make that unstoppable.

The writer first turned the heads of the national media with his graphic crime novel *Goldfish*, a gritty revenge tale. He followed it up with three other crime books, *Jinx*, *Torso* and *Fire* (all Image Comics, 2001). In the midst of producing these breakthrough hits, Bendis' work caught the eye of comic-book giant Marvel. The company eventually gave him the opportunity to write two major media tie-in franchises—Daredevil and Spider-Man. Today he's known for innovative graphic novels like *Fortune and Glory* (Oni Press, 2000), his Hollywood parody, and for using his savvy storytelling to make *Ultimate Spider-Man* one of the top 10 comic books in the country.

For those who've yet to be bitten by the

graphic novel bug, Bendis' writing serves up a surprising level of intelligence and complexity. His characters resonate with the same force of those in traditional literary novels—except he does it with less text than you ever thought possible. And as in any good crime tale, you're never quite sure what to expect next when Bendis is pulling the strings. Here's what he told us about the secret to his success, letting the artwork speak for itself, and where graphic novels really belong in the bookstore.

How did you get your start in graphic novels and comics?

I kind of made my own way. It's a business that has a lot of self-publishers and small publishers. I sent my senior project from college out to a few publishers, and seven months later I heard

---

MICHELLE TAUTE, *a recent graphic novel convert, writes and edits in Cincinnati, Ohio. She contributes to a wide variety of national magazines.*

from two. The best publisher for me at the time was called Caliber. They were really willing to let me get my feet wet and fall on my ass a couple of times, which is definitely what I needed. Particularly with comics, since it's such a visual medium, seeing the book in print is quite an eye-opener. You think you know what it is, and you see it in print and it's a totally different thing. I was able to do a handful of projects there and met a lot of other creators that I've become very close with. After a couple of graphic novels, I moved over to Image Comics, one of the larger publishers. They were allowing me to do my thing, and then Marvel read one of them. They liked it a lot and called me and said, "Hey you wanna do *Spider-Man*?" And then *Daredevil* and *X-men*, and it built from there. But it was definitely me making my own way for quite a few years as a graphic novelist.

What are the main differences between writing a graphic novel and a traditional one?

With a comic book or graphic novel, you're expressing yourself visually. You're expressing yourself with a sequence of panels that build a mood or build a momentum or build a theme. People think it's similar to movie-making storytelling, but it's not. It's a totally different thing because you can control the pacing, but you can't control what people see in between the panels. It's a very kind of intimate thing with the reader.

In your graphic novels and comic books, you communicate a lot of emotion and action with very little text. Do you ever wish you had more space? Are you ever tempted to crowd the artwork with a little more text?

I'd actually like to go the other way—I'd actually like to do less. I'll write a full script and then they draw. Then I go back in and re-dialogue based on their art so it really matches up. And a lot of times I'll see the art, and I'll go "Everything that needs said is said on these faces." You do not need dialogue. I'm a big fan of "show don't tell." If I can shut up, I will. I'm very much into the visuals of it.

Is it challenging to say everything you need to say in dialogue? Are you tempted to add narration?

That's actually my choice. It's fully part of the comic-book mentality to write little narration boxes filled with prose and text. You can do that all day. There's nothing wrong with it. Here's the thing with comics: There are no rules. Anything with words and pictures makes a comic. The words could be poetry. They could be prose. And the art could be line art, photography, collage, computer art. Anything that makes a sequence of pictures that tells a narrative story is a comic book. We're going way back to cave man walls. There really are no rules.

I could add narration, but I'm a huge fan of playwriting. And a lot of my motivation for writing comes from really good playwriting, which is all dialogue-motivated. And you mix that in with the visuals of the comic book, and that's kind of what you're getting from me. But that's what I like to read. That's what makes me happy. So I tend to write what I like to read. But when you're doing prose with comic book stuff, you'd better damn well have a reason for it. Not just writing prose to be lofty. You've got to be saying something that isn't in the art. The art can say a lot.

What's your working process like? Do you write for a set amount of time everyday? Do you revise a lot?

I do revise a lot. I'm writing all the time because I'm almost always concocting in my head. Sometimes the writing can go on for hours, and sometimes I can write for five great minutes and I've written the best thing I'll write all year. I'm working on stuff all night long, but how much writing gets done just depends. I got up not too long ago [mid-afternoon], and after this I will go on a very lengthy bike ride, which is an important part of the process. I know it is because the minute I started riding a bike, people started liking my work. It was weird. I get on the bike, put on some music and think about all the things I'm working on. All of a sudden, tons of stuff comes to me. By the time I get home I have so much stuff to write in my head that I'm actually bursting, and I'm working all night.

With the crime books *Jinx* and *Goldfish*, you really got a lot of mainstream media recognition. How did that change your writing life?

It only changed my writing life in the sense that someone's reading it. When I was working on *Goldfish* and it did its initial run, nobody was reading it. So it's very nice that even years later, it's selling. As far as my writing life, the only real difference is that I kind of know that more people are going to be reading it. With *Ultimate Spider-Man*, I don't mean to be bragging, but it does very well. It's the number two [comic] book in the country. So you know when it comes out people are going to be reading.

Did you feel like you'd found your true niche with crime?

I found some themes that are very important to me, styles of writing that are very important to me. It's still such an ongoing quest. To think I've found it—it never feels that way. It always feels like there's something else to do.

What are some of the challenges of writing an existing character like Daredevil as opposed to one you created yourself?

It's a big challenge in that everybody has an opinion about the character. Some of these characters have a 40-year history already. You're bound to upset somebody. With *Ultimate Spider-Man*, we are taking the Spider-Man idea and starting it from the ground up. It's really like taking a Shakespeare play and screwing around with it. You can do that, but you've got to be immensely respectful of the source material and immensely passionate about the characters.

People often comment about how great the plot twists and subplots are in your work. Is that one of your primary focuses?

Character is, but I love a good cliffhanger. And I want to see things I haven't seen before. Sometimes I'll fall on my ass, but at least I went out and fell on my ass trying too hard. We try to come up with new things. And from that I think we've created enough shockers that people don't really know what we're going to do. Sometimes you let it happen organically. And also, I have a couple quotes that I live by like a religion. And one of them is, "The best thing you can do for your characters is to put them in the worst possible situations."

What's the collaborative process like between you and the artist when you're not doing your own illustration? Is it different with every artist?

It is very different for every artist. And it's also a very addictive thing to the point where I'm not even drawing a lot anymore. Because now I get to write and have someone much better than me draw it. And we both look awesome. Basically, I write full script. It looks a lot like a movie script. You can direct in a comic strip. I lay out what the panel angles are and what would be of maximum effect, and I have all the dialog in the script. The artist can get a real sense of tone and meaning. And I can even write subtext—here's what he's thinking and here's what he's saying, which might be two different things. It can create an excellent and subtle look on the character's face. And from there, we'll talk about some of the key themes and sometimes the artist comes back with, "You know what would be a better way to do that. If it were me, I would do this." And I always say, "Do it."

What advice do you have for up-and-coming writers who'd like to get into graphic novels or comics?

It's as hard to get into as anything else. People always think it's really hard, but I think it's hard to get any job you really want. A lot of the guys you see working on the top 10 books are friends of mine, and we all came up together, and we all made our own comics. That's how we all got our break. We didn't wait for Marvel or DC to find us. We all went and made our own way. And we all needed the practice. We all needed to figure ourselves out before we were ready. So I think if you really have something to say that isn't just "Boy I'd really like to write Spider-Man versus the Green Goblin," go make your own comic. Even if you have to go to Kinko's and make your own mini-comics. Some of the best comics I've read this year are handmade mini-comics. And just get them out to anyone who can help you. Go to shows and meet people. Just like anything else. Almost everyone who reads comic books wants to make them, so you've got to show that you're really something special.

You seem to have a lot of contact with your fans through your message board and website (www.jinxworld.com). How does that interaction affect your work?

I'm sure it does affect my work, and I believe it affects my work in an immensely positive way. When you get numbers for your books or orders, it feels surreal. I don't know what 100,000 people looks like. Not to be bragging. So when I'm online and fans are there, I consider them friends of mine. They've spent bucks on something of mine. That's a pretty cool thing for someone to do. So they're hanging on the boards and they're talking. It's a big, open reminder that there are actual human beings who might not have a ton of money spending whatever free money they might have on your stuff. It makes me roll up my sleeves and get to work. It makes me want to really give them something good because they're friends of mine. I wanna knock their socks off. I find it to be a very good experience. And also you get good feedback. Even when somebody's coming by yelling crazy stuff about *Daredevil* continuity, they've got a point of view you should hear. They are the audience.

You tried to get your graphic novels *Jinx* and *Goldfish* shelved in the crime section at bookstores. Why?

It's a pet peeve of mine. It's getting much better as the bookstores have embraced graphic novels in a big way over the last year. But it drives me insane that all the graphic novels, no matter what genre they're in, get shoved into the graphic novel section next to the gaming section. I'm not just talking about mine—I'm talking about all the graphic novel stuff. There's a lot of really intense graphic novel work. Even the Anne Rice graphic novels, they're shoved in the graphic novel section, and they're not in the Anne Rice section. It's crazy. I think they should break up the graphic novel section and make a superhero section, and all the other ones should go where they're inclined to go. At the Borders near my house, I got them to put Jinx in the crime section, and low and behold, they all sold. That audience would try it.

There was a fair amount of hype last year about the rise of the graphic novel. Do you think the genre is becoming more mainstream?

It absolutely is. It's a mixture of the immense success of Marvel movies with whatever is going on with these little black-and-white Manga books (Japanese comics) that seem to be huge. That's opening a lot of bookstore doors. So between the two what you're getting is people trying new kinds of comics and people who are just running and looking for Marvel tie-in stuff. Both are awesome reasons to be reading. My worry is that people aren't reading anything. Most people don't read anything. They don't read newspapers. They don't read online. They just don't read. So anything that gets people in the bookstores is a good thing.

Doing Double Duty: *The Missouri Review* Editor Speer Morgan Dishes on Writing and Editing

BY ELIZABETH BONEAU

The credo of *The Missouri Review* could read something like the Emma Lazarus poem that graces the Statue of Liberty, "Give me your tired, your poor, your huddled masses yearning to breathe free," for the way in which it actively seeks and celebrates unknown authors, bringing them into that promised land of publication.

Begun as a fledgling offshoot of the University of Missouri English Department in 1978, *The Missouri Review* now stands on its own two feet as one of the foremost literary magazines in the country. This development is due largely in part to the devotion of editor Speer Morgan, who oversaw the magazine's conception and continues to steer it 25 years later.

Speer Morgan

Stanford-educated and personally lauded for his own fiction, Morgan is ever mindful of *The Missouri Review*'s humble beginnings, and his attitude toward submissions reflects an openness to unknown authors, as opposed to a preference for big-name authors. The focus for Morgan and his staff is on the piece itself. Morgan says that if asked to choose any book from a burning library, it would be James Joyce's *Dubliners*, not because of the Joyce byline and "not because I am supposed to like it, but because every time I've read the stories in that collection, I've grown to appreciate them more, how un-dramatically dramatic they are, how coldly compassionate." Spoken like a true editor.

As an author as well as editor, Morgan has a unique perspective on the world of literary publishing, playing both sides of the "us" versus "them" battle. He has published a collection of his early short stories, *Frog Gig and Other Stories* (University of Missouri Press, 1976), as well as five novels: *Belle Starr: A Novel* (Little, Brown, 1979); *Brother Enemy* (Little, Brown, 1981); *The Assemblers* (Dutton, 1986); *The Whipping Boy* (Houghton Mifflin, 1994); and *The Freshour Cylinders* (MacMurray & Beck, 1998), winner of the National Book Award. However, as a writer, he struggles with many of the same roadblocks that plague the ordinary struggling

ELIZABETH BONEAU *hails from Lexington, Kentucky and just graduated from the Honors Program at Xavier University with majors in both English and Classics. She interned at F&W Publications last semester, continues to write in what free time she has and will put her Bachelor's Degree to good use when she begins teaching Latin at Alter High School in Dayton this fall.*

author. Only a hardworking author could have the same kind of respect for authors that Morgan does as editor, and this is demonstrated by *The Missouri Review*'s hefty contest prizes, openness to simultaneous submissions and prompt response time. Morgan has been teaching fiction writing at The University of Missouri in Columbia for as long as he has been editor of *The Missouri Review*. When not discovering new authors, he spends his time uncovering "found" unpublished texts from well-known authors, such as Mark Twain, Charlotte Bronte, Jack Kerouac, and Zane Grey. Here, Morgan offers insight into publishing from both a writer's and editor's viewpoint as his literary magazine celebrates its 25th anniversary.

How did you continue to build up the publication until it finally became a separate entity from the university's English department in 1990?

In my opinion, few if any really good literary magazines can thrive long as an operating arm of an academic department. But really the short answer to your question is that we've built *The Missouri Review* by coming to work and caring about it. Literary magazines need to be focused on their own success, not sidetracked by departmental politics. We've stayed in business by knowing and remaining focused on our purpose, which is to discover and present the best new writing in English without prejudice—for or against—how well-known a writer is. A flashy literary magazine can be bought with enough money, but it will die without a clear and viable mission.

Our numbers float between about 4,500 and 6,800 subscribers, depending on the time of year. We actively promote the magazine through such mailings, bookstore sales and the Internet. I believe that a magazine is obligated to its contributors to be well-circulated.

Practically speaking, we've been blessed at *The Missouri Review* with a relatively stable and highly motivated staff. There's always change, though, and I try to deal with it by taking a deep breath and trying to understand how we can make something good of it. That goes for everything. Sometimes, what seems like a disastrous problem turns out to be something that can be made positive—on occasion unexpectedly so.

Do you feel your own writing influences your choice of submissions?

Three of my five novels have been historical, and the one I'm writing now is historical, and yes, *The Missouri Review* probably has published more material with an eye toward history, particularly if you include our "found text" and "history as literature" features. However, it's very hard to write good historical short fiction. It doesn't come together very often. But given the choice between a decent historical story and a superb one of some other sort, I'll choose the better story any day.

What are the top two qualities you look for in submissions? What makes that piece, out of 3,000, stand out?

Good writing, and what I call understory—which is what I call a story's larger resonance. I want to go away from a read feeling as if the author has not just told a good particular tale but one with wide resonance. My ideal response is that occasional feeling of the artistic hackles on my neck being raised by a piece.

What was the deciding factor in the last manuscript it pained you to reject?

The last one was a very solid little coming-out story. It had a good particular setting—in this case, the Midwest—and good characters. But it just didn't have anything to quite distinguish it from the large numbers of coming-out stories we receive and have published. It is natural for story writers to focus on classical transition points-death, coming of age-but they should be aware that editors are swamped with such stories.

Are good writers made or born? How can they grow?

I refuse to answer that question on the grounds that DNA research may soon prove me wrong. But if you make me answer, I'd guess that one might be born with an inborn capacity for whatever it takes to be a writer, but unless those capacities are "switched on" as the person develops she may not become one.

Sometimes I think that the primary constituents of becoming a good writer are less the warm fuzzy positive things that parents can provide than a certain amount of disappointment in life and introversion, alongside dogged ambition to leave some beautiful expression of what it means to be human.

What are the most common errors young writers make and how do you help correct them?

The most common error in story writing is sinking into vague descriptions of thoughts and feelings. My friend Brett Lott says that his model for writing is "And then, and then." That's good advice.

Do you see yourself as a champion of young, unknown writers?

If we are anything, we are that. But we are "champions" not in favoring unknowns but in giving them an equal chance. Everyone we publish, known or unknown, we consider to be our writers. We actively promote them. This year we had a piece in all three of the prize anthologies, which we jokingly call winning the "Trifecta." That happens like everything else—by actually reading all of our many thousand submissions, finding the best, editing them well, and then working hard to get the word out on our authors.

What is the best thing a writer can do if he wants to be published—persevere?

You said it. That's the word. Write it on your wall and make yourself look at it every day.

The Missouri Review accepts simultaneous submissions. Are there any other ways *The Missouri Review* is different from other literary reviews? Is it more author-friendly? Why do you think this is?

We try to be realistic about submissions. Authors can't afford the response time of most literary magazines. We try to make our response time fast and we don't hold prejudice against multiple submissions. We pay as much as we can afford, which is $40 a page. We work with authors to present their work in the best form possible—i.e. we edit rigorously. Our contest is among the high paying ones—$2,000 for the winner. We accept international submissions on our website. Finally, we try to be as friendly and helpful as possible, and to promote our authors.

Do you ever second-guess your submission decisions?

Staff members sometimes taunt each other about having rejected this or that story that was later in *The New Yorker*. But I usually feel the same about the piece no matter where they later appear.

Is there a trend toward more traditional storytelling in most literary journals? Is there still room for more postmodern writers?

The simple answer is that there isn't much good postmodern writing. I take that term to refer to writing that is self- and text-conscious, quirky in style, and that deals with some overtly contemporary theme such as confusion between media and reality and so on—the shiftiness of fact, themes that have been so worked over by movies and television that they've become something of a yawn. What some might imagine to be a highly original "postmodern" theme has been dealt with repeatedly in Arnold Schwarzenegger movies.

I'm a big fan of the natural postmodern writers such as Pynchon and William Gaddis. In fact we're working on a Gaddis found-text feature at the moment—publishing two of his previously unpublished stories. But these two novelists were writing in their own very distinct styles before anybody was called "Postmodern." While terms like this are useful as shorthand, they really break down under scrutiny. Was Nabokov a modernist or postmodernist? What about Joseph Heller?

For young writers, I'd suggest writing in your own voice, whatever sounds natural spoken aloud. If it begins to sound fake or unreal when you say it aloud, it probably is.

Do you ever have a hard time writing? How do you fight it? Is writing a spontaneous or structured activity for you?

For a lot of writers, work is torture. But at times they secretly cry with joy about what comes through their fingers. I simultaneously love and hate writing novels—which I mostly do. It's a wonderfully uncontrollable form. Every one I write I feel is going to kill me. But at least I'm not waiting for the clock to say five.

One day there will probably come a time when you are no longer in charge of *The Missouri Review*—what then? What drove you, inspired you, to take the position in the first place?

I wasn't inspired at first. *The Missouri Review* was a love that I learned by doing it. It took me ten or more years to really become a true editor. I was primarily a writer "filling in." It slowly dawned on me that I was not just being burdened by an additional responsibility but really in a position to do something for other writers. That's a blessing, not a burden.

Beyond Inspiration: How to "Stay in the Chair"

BY JACK HEFFRON

There are many parallels between writing and falling in love. The process has a similar arc and similar obstacles. They have the same kind of highs and lows and require similar resources from those who are successful.

Falling in love, for example, is the easy part. Finding someone to fall in love with can be tough, but when you find that someone, things usually launch onto a natural course. Life takes on a glow. There's a new zap of energy in the air and in everything around us. Ah, love's first tender bud. It's truly a remarkable thing.

I compare the initial "idea" stage of a project to the feeling of first falling in love. We may have to sort through some ideas, and we may find that one or two don't quite work or whose brief glimmer fades quickly. But when a good one hits, it feels great. And just like the first spark of romance, getting ideas is the easy part. It's also the most thrilling, in some ways even the most fun. There's the high of inspiration, the glorious sense that the cares and strictures of the world have fallen away or at least been pushed into their proper perspective. We feel invulnerable. We feel perfectly connected to the natural order of life. We are who we are destined to be.

Then things get a little rocky.

In love, we suddenly realize that our partner is not perfect in every way: Must she be right about everything? Is he planning on coming over every night? You may even have a spat or two. And what the heck is this relationship anyway? What are we doing? Are we in love? Are we moving toward a deep commitment? Do we both want the same things?

In writing, after the first glow of idea-hood, even as we're humming along into chapter two or scene three, we begin to suspect that this story or essay or script isn't as perfect as we'd hoped. Looked at in a certain light, it's actually kind of stupid. Or pretentious. Or dull and obvious. Or maybe it's okay but certainly not the stroke of genius it seemed to be last week.

Many apprentice writers give up on the piece when they hit this first turn. It goes bang into the file cabinet, or worse, the trash basket. Alas, another failed idea. When oh when will the Right Idea come along? The answer is that, in fact, it might already have arrived. What's required is a renewed sense of involvement, an energy that we must create ourselves, because the first glow of inspiration has passed. Now things will get more complicated, will demand insight and compromise, will demand a certain level of blind faith.

Ron Carlson, well-known fiction writer and teacher, offers some advice about this stage of the process. He says that when we reach a point where the next step appears difficult, we get restless. We squirm in our chairs. Some writers will go get a fresh cup of coffee. Some will dive into household chores or catch up on e-mails or cut the grass. Others will stay in the chair and push forward. His advice is simple: "Be the writer who stays in the chair." I have that quote taped to an imaginary wall in my mind. When I find myself fidgeting because the first rush is over or some new scene or moment challenges me, maybe I don't know what comes next or I

JACK HEFFRON *is the author of* The Writer's Idea Book *and* The Writer's Idea Workbook (*both Writer's Digest Books*). This article was excerpted from The Writer's Idea Workbook, *and is reprinted here with permission.*

am having trouble making a sentence work, I repeat Carlson's advice aloud: *Be the writer who stays in the chair.*

Whether you're struggling on one particular day, or you're entering a new and difficult phase of a project that's been soaring along for weeks, you need to stay in the chair, sometimes literally, sometimes figuratively. As we move through the stages of a project we'll find many occasions for throwing up our hands and surrendering. But these stages truly are part of the process, just as working through differences is part of the process of building a relationship. They grow naturally out of your engagement with the material. In fact, they're *signs* of your engagement with the material.

That's not writer's block, that's writing

If you bail out of the chair, you'll never know what might have happened had you faced the moment of consternation. Be the writer who stays in the chair. When you struggle to find the answers to the tricky questions posed by your story, when you push through the feeling that the piece is no longer as inspired or wonderful as it seemed at first blush, you push your project to its next level. And you push yourself forward as a writer. These are the victories that give us confidence, that make us brave enough to face the next set of difficulties.

I had the good fortune to hear a keynote speech by Billie Letts at a writers' conference. Her novel *Where the Heart Is* had been chosen the week before by the Oprah Book Club, guaranteeing huge sales. The movie version of the novel would be released in a few weeks. So she was living the dream we all hold in our hearts. Making the moment even more special, she spoke about the fact that a few years earlier, she sat in the audience at the same conference, a no-name conferee. Her very presence in the room made the dream seem that much more attainable, and the atmosphere was electrified. She could have recited bawdy limericks, and we'd have gone away inspired.

She didn't. Nor did she talk much about how it felt to be enjoying such a windfall of success. Instead, she told us about the process of writing the book and the struggle she went through when she was well into the book. She said she gave herself a daily goal of three pages. She couldn't begin her day until she met that goal. She couldn't even take a shower. Sometimes she went a few days without a shower. But she stayed in the chair, and she told us the book was made better by the effort.

Sue Grafton is another writer who stays in the chair. As you probably know, Grafton writes an enormously successful mystery series in which every title uses a letter of the alphabet. At this writing, she is up to *Q Is for Quarry*. She told me in an interview for a magazine article that she reaches a point where she thinks she won't make it to the end of the novel.

"I'm always convinced it's over," she said. "I worry that I'm out of juice, that I have nothing left to say." And yet she has managed to finish 17 novels in the series, and I have faith she'll make it all the way to *Z Is for Zero*.

These stories of perseverance rewarded give us hope that our dark moments are shared by even the most successful writers, of course, but more to the point, these stories show us that the struggle is part of the process.

Withholding judgment

A common way to block yourself from completing a draft of a piece is to sit back and judge it before you have it on paper. It's a natural instinct. We make judgments every day. We're trained readers and writers, and we know what works. If a piece isn't working, we know it.

Another way we block ourselves and limit the potential for our work is by judging how a piece should be realized—what it's about and where it should go. The first great wave of inspiration is exhilarating but it can be scary too. We want to grab control. We want to know the nature of this thing we're creating. And so we decide it's a story about our father, or we rush headlong through the plot and decide how it will end and what that will mean even as we're still scribbling the opening lines.

If you're still in the early stages of a first draft, it's not your job to make any conclusions about the piece. You don't yet know if it "sucks," because you don't yet know what it's about. The first strong wind of inspiration has passed. It may be time to break out the oars and row for a while. You also don't yet know what the piece is about—its themes, its range of dramatic possibilities. You will limit those possibilities by deciding too soon.

It's not our role at this time to say if something's good or bad, worth pursuing or destined for the wastebasket. We need to focus on the piece itself, listen to it, play with it, experiment with it. Keep putting words on paper. Keep adding ideas to the generative idea. Look for complications and possibilities. When you have a draft of something, or at least a good chunk of writing, you can allow yourself to assess its merits. For now, suspend your disbelief. Resist labeling it. Resist deciding too soon the direction the piece should take. Trust your imagination and the way your subconscious creates the piece.

Getting Past the Block

- If you've got a piece underway but are beginning to feel it lag a bit, find a place in what you've written already that excites your interest. Perhaps it's a character or an image, a setting, even a subplot that appeals to you, even if the piece itself seems to have slowed down. Focus your energy there. You could expand its role in the story. Or you could freewrite about it. If you're smitten by a character, explore her background, even if you feel that what you write won't be included in the final piece. (Remember, we're avoiding those kinds of judgments at this point.) If you like an earlier scene, revisit it. Expand it, or perhaps jump ahead in your narrative to a place where the characters in that scene return. By focusing your energy and interest in this way, you can catch a renewed sense of engagement in the piece, and before you know it you're moving again.

- Give yourself a time limit for getting through a rough spot in your piece of writing, You might say, I'll work on this section or this piece for the next five sessions. If it still seems blocked or flat, I'll let it go for a while. Make sure you give yourself enough time to get past the block—at least five sessions. If you have to put it away for a while, give yourself a time limit on when you'll revisit it.

- If you're stuck, consider changing the time of day you usually use for writing. If you've been putting in an hour on your story before heading to work in the morning, write during your lunch break, or as soon as you get home in the evening. Also consider changing where you write. If at a computer, take a notepad to a park or a library. New times and locations and routines for writing can spark new interest.

- Consider how you start and end your writing sessions. Do you write until you're exhausted? If so, consider stopping while you're still feeling energetic about the project. Ernest Hemingway made famous his method of stopping each session in the middle of a sentence, so he'd know just how to start the new session. This approach might work for you.

- Spend at least three sessions practicing the "stay in the chair" method. Set a timer for your session, and write whatever you want, perhaps responding to a prompt in this book. Do not for any reason get up from the chair. Turn off the phone, shut down your email, tell family members that for the next half hour or whatever time you choose you are not to be disturbed unless someone is facing a life-or-death situation. If the idea you're exploring stalls before you finish, begin a new one or simply write about writing or describe the room in which you're working. Our goal is to practice staying in the chair.

The grass is greener

As we've discussed, making your way through the middle of a project requires a certain amount of blind faith. It also requires withholding judgment. It also requires our focused attention. Another way we can get in our own way is by jumping from one project to the next at the first sign of difficulty. We begin to develop an idea into a draft of writing only to realize that several other ideas are much better. They're more interesting and exciting and we have a much firmer grasp of them. Well . . . maybe. Or we could be suffering from the-grass-is-greener syndrome.

When we're in the midst of writing a novel, the short story can have a powerful allure. The short story is so, well, short. It seems far less daunting than the novel we've undertaken. Or perhaps you're distracted from your novel by a memoir, with its simple demands of just telling what happened rather than having to make up everything. Of course, when we jump to the short story, we might feel constrained by the need for making every word count, for making every little action resonate within the whole of the story. When we jump to the memoir, we face research and flipping through old journals and trying to find ways to stick to the facts. Ah, so much easier to be able to create a fictional reality.

Sound familiar? We've all been there. As soon as we undertake project number two, project number one will look good again, or we'll think of a project number three. Some writers keep several projects going simultaneously until one rises to the fore. If you can balance projects in this way, feel free to do it. But if one rises to the fore, try to focus on that one. Simultaneous projects, as in romantic relationships, can be a way of avoiding a commitment.

Consider giving yourself a time limit for working on one project before moving to a new one. Also, be open to the possibility that project number two is asking to be folded into project number one. They might be related somehow in your subconscious. If the subjects and forms are radically different—such as an essay about life as a teacher and a short poem about your mother—inding the connection might not be easy, but be open to the possibility. Perhaps there's a thematic connection rather than a more obvious one directly involving the subject matter.

I wish I had a magic piece of advice to give you for how to keep moving on a project. We've looked at ways of getting started and developing a draft from a craft perspective, but often what stalls us has nothing to do with craft. More often it's a matter of our mental state. Completing a project requires persistence and tenacity. It also requires, at times, leaps of faith. Even if a piece seems aimless and pointless, trust that you're simply not at a place yet where the writing is ready to reveal its mysteries. And so we push on.

Boning Up: How to Strengthen Your Manuscript by Fixing Injured Sentences

BY I.J. SCHECTER

There are 206 bones in an adult human body, and every one of them needs to work properly for the overall machine to do its job. In your manuscript, every sentence is a bone—and unless you're an experimental writer, there will be many more than 206. If all the bones are strong, healthy and working together, they will create an impression of vibrancy and ease. Too many weak or injured ones, on the other hand, will leave your story hobbled.

As a writer, you're the doctor examining sets of X-rays. You need to be able to recognize, and fix, problems when you see them. Here are some potential injuries you may encounter and solutions you can employ to help make the bones of your story as strong as possible.

BRUISES

A bruised sentence is like a bruised bone: though healthy underneath, it's been temporarily distorted. You need to look closely at the sentence and decide how it should be restored.

There are several causes of sentence bruises—awkward construction, passive language, not-quite-right words—but one of the most common is sentence reversal, in which the right words have been put down in an order opposite to their ideal.

Consider the opening of Harper Lee's classic, *To Kill a Mockingbird*:

> When he was nearly thirteen, my brother Jem got his arm badly broken at the elbow.

Now imagine if the sentence were flipped:

> My brother Jem got his arm badly broken at the elbow when he was nearly thirteen.

Not only is the inflection flatter and less rhythmic in the made-up example, but it also places stress on the wrong element—Jem's age, rather than the badly broken elbow we want to know more about.

Let's do the same exercise for *Tortilla Flat*, by John Steinbeck:

> When Danny came home from the army he learned that he was an heir and an owner of property.

Or *Trust Me*, by John Updike:

> When Harold was three or four, his father and mother took him to a swimming pool.

Both these examples, reversed, suddenly work against the story—they end up leveling the ca-

---

I.J. SCHECTER *is a freelance writer of fiction and essays. His latest book, a collection of short stories, is titled* The Bottom of the Mug. *His nonfiction frequently appears in* Novel & Short Story Writer's Market.

dence and, moreover, failing to propel us toward the next piece of information the way they do in their correct form. The fictitious sentences aren't wounded terribly, just bruised enough to warrant treatment.

When you get to one of these sentences, it will be like noticing a slight discoloration on your skin. You know it doesn't require undue time or attention, but spending a few minutes on it is certainly worth your while.

FRACTURES

Some of your sentences, having sustained minor injuries like hairline fractures, may need to be fused or re-set. Typically these types of injuries result from a lack of grammar, the manuscript's calcium. To be able to recognize and solve grammatical issues, you'd better make sure you know your way around nouns, verbs, subjects and predicates, dangling participles, and so on.

Common culprits of fractured sentences, for example, are comma splices. (If you're not familiar with this term, it's time to hit the nearest grammar guide.) Should the following sentence appear in your manuscript . . .

> It was late in the evening, the sun was just beginning its descent.

. . . it's critical that you know how to spot the fracture and the different ways it can be fixed: in this case, a period, semi-colon or coordinating conjunction.

Some writers feel grammatical rules are constraining and that strict adherence to them serves to deaden the tone of a manuscript. But there's a reason grammar rules were set down in a particular way, and when used well they lend a piece energy, tempo and continuity.

There are exceptions, of course, like the use of sentence fragments in plenty of commercial fiction ("Her father was strict. Very.") This doesn't mean, however, that you should look for places to violate sound grammar practice just to shake things up. Your story line should be able to carry a reader's attention on its own, and any unconventional grammar you use should occur naturally and suit the overall feel of the manuscript.

EXCESS MATERIAL

Often a bone causes you pain simply because too much other stuff, like fluid or scar tissue, has accreted around it. That bone needs to be cleaned.

Writers love words—it's one of the greatest of our occupational hazards. Consequently, when a first draft comes rushing out of us, it invariably contains too many of them. It's your job to go through the manuscript and identify the bones that require scoping.

To do this, monitor your own response to the rhythms of your sentences and paragraphs. You'll know when a sentence is too lengthy if, by the end of it, you feel as you would listening to someone share an anecdote that drags on too long.

Here is the beginning of *Gone With the Wind*, by Margaret Mitchell:

> Scarlett O'Hara was not beautiful, but men seldom realized it when caught by her charm as the Tarleton twins were.

Mitchell tells us the most important thing we need to know about Scarlett and wastes no words in doing so. Assume she had instead written the following:

> Scarlett O'Hara, petite, dark-haired, and too small-mouthed for the rest of her face, was not beautiful in any conventional way, but men seldom realized it when they were caught unexpectedly by her stunning charm, as the Tarleton twins now suddenly found themselves.

You must be able to flag this kind of verbosity and, when you come across it, immediately strip the bone clean. (Adjectives and adverbs, of course, are the most common sources of excess material, as the example above demonstrates.) Even lyrical books, or stories whose themes lend themselves to a more expansive tone, must be trimmed sentence by sentence to their essence and not a word more.

It's important not to confuse mere length with wordiness. Because a sentence is long does not automatically mean it needs scoping. Look at the beginning of *Goodbye, Mr. Chips*, by James Hilton:

> When you are getting on in years (but not ill, of course), you get very sleepy at times, and the hours seem to pass like lazy cattle moving across a landscape.

Hilton employs a few techniques here to ensure the sentence *feels* languorous—adding parentheses to slow the reader down, for example, and making the first few clauses the same length and inflection—but read the sentence two or three times and you'll realize how tight it is, making the point it needs to and then getting out of the way. The lesson here is that Hilton's use of words is more important than the number of words he uses.

Let's look at one more example—from *Billy Phelan's Greatest Game*, by William Kennedy—whose tone contrasts that of Hilton but which accomplishes the same:

> Martin Daugherty, age fifty and now the scorekeeper, observed it all as Billy Phelan, working on a perfect game, walked with the arrogance of a young, untried eagle toward the ball return, scooped up his black, two-finger ball, tossed it like a juggler from right to left hand, then held it in his left palm, weightlessly.

It's a gorgeous, vivid sentence, skimming along with ease and ending on a breathless note that fills us with anticipation. (I don't know about you, but I wouldn't want to step in against Billy Phelan.) Why does this sentence work? Because it's conscious of what it wants to say and does so without getting tripped up.

To digress a moment from my own doctor metaphor, imagine yourself an archer. Your target as you review each sentence is the point you want that sentence to make, and your aim is to hit that target without veering off course even a little. Whether the target is ten feet away or a hundred, your arrow mustn't waver. Extra words in your sentences are like a breeze making the arrow flutter. So don't attack your manuscript with the idea that no sentence can exceed a certain number of words. Focus instead on the notion of each sentence flying straight toward that bulls eye.

CLEAN BREAKS

Like a person who knows his thumb is broken but decides to use it anyway, a strong story with broken sentences will be able to get by on some level, but it won't be as good as it could be were the sentences properly mended.

Rehabilitating a weak or broken bone requires patience and effort, since you don't always know just how much rehab a bone needs. For clean breaks, sometimes a small amount of physiotherapy will do. Consider the first line of Ed McBain's *Eight Black Horses*:

> The lady was extraordinarily naked.

Suppose in draft one the author had started with, "The lady was naked." Still an interesting start, but nowhere near as powerful as the actual version—all because of one word.

Here's another example (which doubles as an example of the sentence fragments I referred to earlier), from *An American Tragedy*, by Theodore Dreiser:

> Dusk—of a summer night.

Without the dash, this sentence is ordinary and thin. But that small addition acts like a brace, strengthening the bone so it can stand on its own.

MULTIPLE BREAKS

When a sentence is broken badly, or in multiple spots, you need to take serious action—saw into the bone, insert pins or screws, or even perform cosmetic surgery. The new bone will end up looking quite different than the way it looked at first. In a sense, only the idea of the original bone will be left. But your manuscript will be the better for it.

Multiple-break sentences are frequently left intact through several drafts, since you know the general thrust of the sentence is right but you haven't gotten around to fixing it. Let's assume you've had the following sentence since draft one:

> Ned tore through his neighbor's garbage not even really knowing what he was looking for, but tearing through it just the same, tossing aside candy wrappers, phone bills, orange peels, and—whoa, here was something.

Finally, in draft four or five, you decide that, in the context of your manuscript, it doesn't sound right—it's too long, the voice is inconsistent, it ends sloppily, and you refer to Ned by his nickname instead of his real name almost everywhere else in the manuscript. But you want to preserve the point the broken sentence is trying to make.

Two things can be done with a truly mangled sentence. Either you can go step-by-step through it, twisting it around and changing the language and adjusting the tone, or you can rewrite it from scratch, since you know what you want to say anyway. For the sentence in question you might perform the operation and end up instead with:

> Flipping aside an apple core, Natty had decided that twenty minutes of rifling through his neighbor's garbage was just about enough, when he found the thing he didn't even know he had been searching for.

The bone looks rather different, but its original substance remains. Operation successful.

GANGRENE

In the spring of 2003 a young man named Aaron Ralston was hiking in Utah when his arm became trapped under a boulder. He was in too remote an area to expect that someone would find him. So, after weighing every option he could think of, Aaron realized he was left with one choice only: to amputate his own arm.

Removing a sentence you've created is considerably less wrenching than Aaron Ralston's experience, but it's still hard. How do you know when a sentence needs to be amputated? Simple (infuriatingly simple, as I always remember after the fact): you've tried everything else, and it still doesn't work.

I can't count the number of times I've agonized over a particular sentence, searching endlessly for the right way to fix it, analyzing over and over whether it needed to be fused, flipped, scoped, or rehabbed, only to finally realize that the answer was so obvious I'd missed it all along. The sentence was a lost cause to begin with, and the manuscript is stronger without it.

If you're reading this, I'm willing to bet you've had this experience more than a few times yourself. And I'm sure you agree that the time spent realizing the sentence didn't belong is outweighed by the gratification you feel once it's been cut away.

Ernest Hemingway opens his famous story, "The Snows of Kilimanjaro," with the following:

> "The marvelous thing is that it's painless," he said.

Consider how this would have sounded if Hemingway had stuck in an introductory sentence like, "I watched, rapt, as he opened his mouth to speak." Booooring. The way he's got it, we're thrust directly into the action.

The same goes for the first line of *Vengeance is Mine!* by Mickey Spillane:

> The guy was dead as hell.

Imagine a draft that included a preceding line such as, "I looked down and saw a pool of blood beside his head." Such a line would function only as deadweight, weakening the bone.

It's often said that almost any story would be better if it started with sentence two. Try this test on your own manuscript, and remove the bones that don't belong. You'll feel better after you've let them go.

Sentences are the bones on which your story is built, so you owe it to yourself to hold them to high standards. Pretend you're a field archaeologist slowly dusting away the layers of debris that hide the precious thing you're after: the bone, intact, pristine, and looking just the way it should.

Now take out whatever manuscript you're working on and try to identify any weak or injured bones. See if you can determine whether they're bruised, fractured, weakened by extraneous material, broken cleanly, or crushed. And if all else fails, consign them to that great literary wasteland in the sky.

Even if this fate befalls them, remember that they weren't wasted words—they were the ones that helped you get to the next sentence. And that might be the one that lives forever.

Know When to Leave it Alone

Spotting a deficient bone is one thing, but how do you know when a sentence is just fine the way it is? I can suggest two clues. The first is intangible: sometimes you capture a sentence on the first try, and you just know it's right, whether it's a lively snippet of dialogue or an atmospheric, sinuous description of your setting. No matter how many times you read it, you know it shouldn't be touched. This feeling is usually right, so trust your instincts, and celebrate the fact that you nailed it the first time around.

The second clue is that you're reversing edits back over themselves. In other words, in draft three, you changed "Bob raced out the door" to "Bob darted out the door," and now, editing draft four, you feel you ought to change it back again. I usually find that when I start making these "double-back" edits, the sentence is just fine either way, changing it has no positive or negative consequence, and I've more than likely entered the dreaded overediting stage.

Finding the Perfect Writing Community

BY JOE FEIERTAG, MARY CARMEN CUPITO,
and the editors of WRITER'S MARKET

Even if it's only once in a blue moon, writers need to break out of their creative and physical confines to find a new sense of community among other writers. Writers' conferences and colonies, university programs and correspondence schools, provide a wealth of options and opportunities. Which, if any, of these you choose depends on where you are in your career and your needs at the time.

If your goal is to pick up skills from top professionals or expand your contacts in the business, conferences can be an excellent investment of time and money. A writer's colony is a great place to finish a project, start a new one, or reassess a stalled piece of work. University programs and correspondence schools require a long-term commitment, but are especially useful for those just getting started in the business of writing.

WRITERS' COLONIES AND RETREATS

Writers colonies offer a wonderful change of pace—providing an opportunity to get the most out of your creative powers in a short time.

Some allow you to work virtually uninterrupted. Others provide space for quiet work but also encourage participants to interact and learn from each other during breaks or through critiques, readings and workshops. Some even bring together creative people from different disciplines—painters, writers, musicians—believing you can learn more about your own art by talking with others about theirs. At some retreats, the interaction takes place randomly throughout the day.

Few if any colonies enforce a regimented schedule or keep tabs on your progress. Writers respond to this freedom differently. Some overwork and burn out in a short period of time. More commonly, writers need several days to adjust to their newfound freedom before they can develop routines.

Some colonies select writers with substantial professional credentials. Others cater to emerging talent. Still others try to foster a mix of better-known and lesser-known talent. Some colonies are highly competitive—receiving dozens of applications for every position they have open.

The typical stay at a writers' colony lasts from a couple of weeks to three months. The cost of most colonies is relatively inexpensive. Most programs charge a small application fee, then $75 to $200 per week. The majority of colonies stress that payment is voluntary and no qualified applicant will be turned away simply because he is unable to pay. Many require that writers bring along whatever equipment they plan to use.

Before you select a writers' colony, consider the following:
• Most colonies schedule visits six months in advance, so make sure you assemble your writing samples and apply at least eight months before you plan to attend.
• Look for a colony that fits your lifestyle. Some writers thrive in a rural atmosphere; others find the peace and quiet uninspiring. Some writers like to cook their own meals at their conve-

nience. Others prefer to have their meals prepared for them on a regular schedule. Compare all aspects of the colonies you're interested in before applying.

• Some colonies offer weekend programs, but the majority want you to stay two weeks to two months. Since most writers work more quickly at a colony, plan your work ahead of time, even if the colony doesn't require it. If possible, talk to other writers who've been to the colonies to find out how they used the experience.

WRITERS' CONFERENCES

Whether you are just starting out in the business or are already a professional writer, attending writers' conferences can be very beneficial. Beginners can learn a lot about the creative and business side of writing. Established writers can gain added insights into all aspects of the trade. Writers—whether beginners or seasoned—have many different goals when they attend a conference. Some want to explore a new writing area or learn from a particular instructor. Others are interested in making contacts with writers, editors and agents. Still others like the inspiration of spending time with fellow writers.

If you are thinking of attending a writers' conference, consider the following:

• Your chances of individual meetings or instruction are greater at a small conference, but smaller conferences are less likely to draw prominent speakers. Instead of focusing on the total number attending, ask about the number in each session. If the number is 30 or less, you'll have more opportunities to ask questions and discuss your work with an instructor.

• Money is a key consideration for almost any writer. But don't choose a conference solely on the basis of cost. Attending a conference is an investment in your future success. The least expensive option may not be the best for you. A one- or two-day workshop can cost up to $200. Conferences that last up to a week can cost $800 or more, which usually includes the cost of lodging and some meals. One way to work a conference into your budget is to combine it with a vacation.

• The caliber of the conference is usually the most important criterion when evaluating a conference. Look for writers who have credentials in the particular areas they will be teaching.

• Some conferences offer individual consultations with instructors, editors or agents for an additional fee. Such personal feedback generally must be arranged ahead of time. If you are

---

Elizabeth Graver on the power of writing communities

She describes herself as "a writer who needs readers," and to satisfy that need Elizabeth Graver carved a place for herself in the writing community throughout her apprenticeship. Author of the acclaimed 1999 title *The Honey Thief*, and earlier *Unravelling* (both Hyperion), Graver availed herself of the collegiality, direction and financial support of a network of writers, and says she's grateful for the opportunity.

A fellowship to Washington University kept her among a writing community as she earned her M.F.A., and retreats to the Breadloaf Writer's Conference and MacDowell Colony gave her extended periods among other writers to work at her craft.

"I've always created through an institution, or created some kind of writing community, and I've always been in a writing group," she says. "So I'm someone who needs readers. I'm not sure it's necessary to get that through the structure of an MFA program, although for me one of the main benefits of it was a grant. Before that, I'd been a secretary and a teacher, and just worked like crazy to pay the rent. Being in that kind of space, where writing should be your first priority, was very valuable."

—Anne Bowling

paying for an appointment, you have every right to know what to expect from the meeting. Don't go in expecting to find an editor who will want to publish your work or an agent who will want to represent you. Such overnight success stories are few and far between.

• Most conferences attract writers of a variety of skill levels and are geared accordingly. Check the program for clues as to whether sessions are geared toward beginners or professionals. You should avoid sessions that seem too far below or above your expertise.

• A conference's format can make a big difference. The best conferences are set up to provide interaction between the attendees and the instructors/speakers, rather than just lectures. Also, look for panel discussions where writers, editors and agents offer their opinions on subjects of interest to you.

UNIVERSITY DEGREE PROGRAMS

For some people, a university environment is a great way to develop their skills and immerse themselves in the writers' world. Yet attending a college or university writing program is expensive and requires a large commitment of time. So if you're already earning a decent living as a writer, or if you have a full-time job and can find the time to pursue a writing career, a degree may not be a wise investment of time or money. Agents have been known to scout the well-known programs for talent, but there are other ways to attract attention that cost far less than a degree.

There may be other reasons to enroll in classes, including the opportunity to study with a writer whom you admire or to develop specific skills. Universities also support more experimental writing and have literary magazines that will publish students' work.

Consider the following guidelines in making your decision:

• Programs are almost as varied as the number of schools. Some schools offer small programs where students receive individual attention. Others offer larger programs with prestigious faculties. Some are conducted in a straight classroom set-up. Others take a workshop approach in which you bring work to be critiqued by the teacher and fellow students. You can tell a lot about a program by the type of degree it offers. A master's degree usually requires more reading while a master of fine arts requires more writing. Each program has its own focus and requirements; talk to past graduates to decide which approach is best for you.

• Besides investigating the program itself, inquire about the caliber of the visiting writers, the faculty, and the literary publications affiliated with the program. The community surrounding a program can be just as important to your creative development as the program itself.

• Reading the program's literary publications and the works of its faculty is a great way to evaluate a program. It can also help you select the best submissions from your own writing. (A fiction sample usually includes three stories.)

• If cost is a major consideration—and when isn't it?—check out financial aid options and the availability of assistantships. In addition to the cost of instruction, be sure to compare the cost of living in various areas. And since you're going to be there awhile, choose a place where you feel comfortable.

• Weigh the benefits of several programs and be flexible in your choice of institutions. It's not unusual for more renowned programs to receive hundreds of applications for only a few dozen openings.

CORRESPONDENCE SCHOOLS

A correspondence course is a good choice if you lack easy access to a college or if your schedule prevents you from attending classes. Most home study courses can be finished in less than a year, and most offer one-on-one instruction with the same teacher for the length of the course. But choose your course wisely. You cannot always adapt the course to your needs if you require specialized instruction.

Correspondence courses let you work at your own pace, but only up to a point. If you have difficulty meeting deadlines, a correspondence course is not for you. Most courses have dead-lines, and getting an extension usually costs extra.

Evaluate correspondence courses with the following points in mind:

• Some courses offer a range of topics covering everything from news writing to fiction. Others focus on a single subject, such as poetry or short stories. Pick a course that suits your specific goals.

• The cost of a correspondence course can vary from a few hundred dollars to a few thousand dollars. Compare the different courses. The most costly do not always offer what is best for you. Look for a course that allows you to return the materials for a refund if you are not initially satisfied.

• Any reputable school will share information about the caliber of its instructors. Look for instructors who not only know the subject but have recent sales in their chosen genres. Of course feedback from the instructor can make or break your learning experience, so it's important to get a good match. Look for a school that is willing to assign you another instructor if things don't work out.

• Inquire about the level of feedback you can expect from your instructor. Ideally you want frequent, detailed critiques of your work—not just overall evaluations.

For program descriptions and contact information on fiction writing conferences and educational programs across the country, see our markets section Conferences, on page 519, and Writing Programs, on page 568. For information on the Writer's Digest School, visit www.writers digest.com.

For Steve Almond, Self-Promotion Takes a Backseat to Writing

BY WILL ALLISON

Shortly before Steve Almond hit the road for a reading tour in support of his first book, the story collection *My Life in Heavy Metal* (Grove/Atlantic, 2002), he e-mailed the schedule to his friends with a plea.

"In a couple of weeks," he wrote, "I'm gonna be heading out on this big ole reading tour. Here's what I want from you: 1) Print out schedule. 2) Make 50,000 copies. 3) Laminate. 4) Hire out crop duster. 5) Drop onto major metropolitan area closest to your home. If you're too 'busy' to do this, you can: 1) Come to a reading. 2) Drag a bunch of friends to a reading. 3) Forward this message to friends/relatives/people you once slept with in cities where I'll be reading and guilt-trip them into attending a reading. 4) Alert any media types (print or radio) in cities where I'll be reading and guilt-trip them into reviewing the book, interviewing me, and/or feeding me drinks."

Steve Almond

Photo © Miriam Berkley

And so began a coast-to-coast tour that saw Almond give readings in 35 cities in 54 days. Since then, he's done another 35 readings, including a cross-country spring 2003 tour for the paperback release of his collection.

Anyone who's followed Almond's on-the-road exploits (either in person or via his website, www.stevenalmond.com, which includes periodic updates from the road) might conclude that he's a master of self-promotion. A natural born bookseller. A liquor- and testosterone-fueled publicity machine. But talk to Almond about the business of promoting his work, and you get a different picture.

"My job is to move people, not product," he says. "The reason I read is to connect with people through my art. I'm pimping what I love. If a reading gets someone to pick up my book—or any book, for that matter—I'm happy. But the commercial aspect of art makes me sick. What matters is the work. Always and forever."

In the eight years since Almond gave up journalism and started writing fiction, he's estab-

WILL ALLISON *is former editor-at-large for* Zoetrope: All-Story, *former executive editor of* Story, *and former editor of* Novel & Short Story Writer's Market. *He is also a staff member at the Squaw Valley Community of Writers and the recipient of a 2000 Ohio Arts Council Grant for fiction.*

lished himself as one of the country's most talented and prolific writers of literary short stories, publishing 80 of them in magazines ranging from *Playboy* and *Ploughshares* to *Zoetrope: All-Story* and *Georgia Review*. His stories have been anthologized in *The Pushcart Prize*, *New Stories from the South*, and *The Best of Zoetrope*. His first nonfiction book, *Candyfreak: A Journey Through the Chocolate Underbelly of America* (Algonquin Books) will be published in spring 2004, and his second collection, *The Evil B.B. Chow and Other Stories* (Algonquin Books) is due out the following spring.

When he's not coming to a city near you, Almond lives in Somerville, Massachusetts, where he teaches creative writing at Boston College and publishes his ultra-hip/geeky music e-zine, *The Tip*, which can be found on his website.

Here, Almond discusses the ins and outs of self-promotion, the etiquette of readings, and the difficulty of living in a culture with so few readers.

You've given close to 70 readings in the past couple years. Why so many? Is that what it takes to sell a story collection these days?

I do readings because I love them. Period. The act of telling a story to real live humans—seeing if you can compel them to enter into the world you've created—just rocks my socks. But it's no guarantee that a book will sell. Just ask my publisher. All a story writer can do, in this era of frantic inattention, is to write like hell, try to get the word out, and pray for good fortune.

Tell us about your spring 2002 tour. Who planned it? Who paid for it?

Total punk-rock style tour. No hotels. No per diems. Stayed with old friends and whoever would put me up. I was like Blanche Dubois out there—relying on the kindness of strangers. That's the way to travel, anyway, a little desperate and by the seat of your pants. Grove planned most of the readings and kicked in about half the jack for transportation. I paid for the rest. It was incredibly unglamorous—bordering on pathetic—but I had a ball.

Are you planning a tour for your next book?

The next book is called *Candyfreak: A Journey Through the Chocolate Underbelly of America*. It's all about the history of candy bars in this country, and especially these crazy little niche candy bars that you can only find in certain cities. The Twin Bing. The Idaho Spud. So I'm going to do a series of readings/candy tastings. After I've read about these candy bars, the audience *will get to taste them*. I love doing readings that include music or food, that totally blow up the traditional model, all those uptight gatherings where people are afraid to even breathe too loud. I don't mean dressing up literature with gimmicks, but reminding the audience that art is relevant to their lives and—God forbid—fun.

How do you balance your writing time with the time you spend promoting your work?

I'm constantly ravaged by guilt because I'm not writing. Any serious writer is. I'm also well aware of my desire to escape the lonely, dogged work by flinging myself out into the world. But the self-promotion crapola only goes so far before it dissolves into narcissism. My friends who are writers know that the real success happens at home, alone, in front of the keyboard.

What makes a good Steve Almond reading, and how do you lay the groundwork for such success?

It's mostly the audience, how ready they are to imagine their way into a story. All I can do is try to get them to relax, and not mess up the sentences. I do better with bigger crowds, because the audience members feel less embarrassed, particularly if I'm reading a female orgasmic scene, as I'm wont to do from time to time.

I assume a book tour helps get your book reviewed in cities where it otherwise might be overlooked. How important are the local reviews in the cities where you read?

Yeah, part of the reason to tour is to get reviews in particular cities. But I don't think many people buy books based on reviews. Unless you get a rave in *The New York Times* or a plug from a TV show (the literary equivalent of hitting the Lotto) most sales come from word of mouth. Individual booksellers or enthusiastic readers. Unless I know someone at a particular publication, I let the publicist supplicate them.

"They" say that all publicity is good publicity. Is this true even with less-than-favorable local reviews?

No idea. But I can't imagine that the stupider reviews I got helped much. They were just these bitter little screeds that didn't have much to do with my book.

During your spring 2002 tour, only one person showed up for your reading in Memphis. What do you do in a situation like that?

Oh, hey, thanks for bringing that up. I'd almost managed to forget that episode. Actually, in that case, we decided to do a mercy killing and cancelled the reading. I did stick around in a state of polite humiliation for half an hour or so. And the bookshop owner gave me Skittles, which I totally appreciated.

What has been the most difficult aspect of promoting your book?

Simply facing how few people read in this culture. I know that sounds pretty obvious, but it really hits you in the face when you're out there screaming like hell. People these days are so desperately lonely. They need the succor of art, the emotional company. But they spend their lives running as fast as they can away from their deepest feelings. They'd rather watch TV, or the crap Hollywood puts out, than go to an exhibit or a reading.

It's easy for writers to bitch about their publisher, or bookstore owners, or the media. (I've certainly done my share.) But the bottom line is that late-model capitalism is predicated on replacing people's internal lives with frantic buy messages. The agents of commerce don't want people thinking about their fears and desires, their capacities for mercy, because this interferes with the notion that the right aftershave will cure them.

To me, this just means that writers (and artists of any kind) have to work that much harder to *wake people up.*

Last advice: What's the most important thing a writer can do to promote his or her work?

I'm reluctant to put so much emphasis on the promotion aspect of things. Because the most important thing a writer can do, in the end, is to love his or her characters and to write beautiful sentences that commemorate that love. If you've done that, then by all means, get out there, scream from the rooftops on your own behalf, take out an ad in Variety, whatever. But make sure you do so out of a genuine desire to move people, not just to be famous. History always sniffs out the phonies.

From Prom Night to Alien Pets: Writing for Theme Anthologies

BY TIM WAGONNER

Tim Wagonner

Many writers believe that the short story, while as vital as ever an art form, is past its publishing prime. The days when large circulation glossy magazines routinely ran short fiction are long gone, and while there are still plenty of literary journals around, many have a print run of only a few thousand copies, if that. Sure, it seems like there's a new web zine popping up every nanosecond or two, but the quality of such publications varies widely, and usually they don't pay.

But there is a market for short fiction that not only pays and has a decent circulation, it also has a longer shelf life than most magazines and journals. I'm talking about theme anthologies.

Theme anthologies are book-length collections of short fiction (although poetry sometimes is included) centered on a particular theme. Among the anthologies in which I've had stories published are such diverse titles—and themes—as *Vengeance Fantastic*, *Villains Victorious*, *Guardian Angels*, *Prom Night*, *Civil War Fantastic*, *Monsters From Memphis*, and (perhaps the weirdest of all) *Alien Pets*. Among the more literary theme-based anthologies are *Thema* and *Mota*.

The idea is that the theme will be an effective marketing hook for selling the collection and, for this reason, many writers are cynical about these anthologies, believing that themes constrain creativity and don't lead to a writer's best work. But in a very real sense, the plethora of "Year's Best" anthologies center on a theme as well: the best work (stories, essays, poems, etc.) published in a given year. And let's be honest; who's going to plunk down anywhere from $6 to $25 for an anthology called *Really Good Stories by Really Good Writers About Whatever They Felt Like Writing*?

Writing to a theme can be a lot of fun. It can provide structure and spark ideas in the same way that a poet might be challenged by attempting to write a sonnet or sestina. Whenever I start a story for a new anthology, I ask myself the same question: How in the world am I going to write a story about that? (Remember *Alien Pets*?) I find the challenge invigorating and sometimes frustrating, but always fun.

Let's say you want to try your hand at writing a story for a theme anthology. How do you find markets?

It's not always easy. Some anthologies are invitation-only, meaning the editor contacts specific writers and asks them to submit stories. But there are anthologies that are open to any writers, and you can frequently find their submission information in market directories like *Novel &*

TIM WAGONNER *is the author of two novels,* Dying For It *and* The Harmony Society, *as well as the short story collection* All Too Surreal. *He's published more than 70 fantasy and horror short stories. He teaches creative writing at Sinclair Community College in Dayton, Ohio. His home page is www.sff.net/people/Tim.Waggoner. This article originally appeared in* Writer's Digest *and appears here with permission.*

Short Story Writer's Market and *Writer's Market. Gila Queen's Guide to Markets* (www.gilaquee n.com) is another wonderful print and Web resource. Various writers' organizations supply market information to their members and you often can subscribe to their newsletters or market publications even if you don't yet have the credentials to join. For example, the Science Fiction and Fantasy Writers of America's quarterly bulletin contains all sorts of articles and market information of interest to professional writers and is available on newsstands as well as by subscription.

Even if an anthology is by invitation only, you still might be able to submit to it. Read and research published anthologies and compile a list of editors' names. If you find yourself at the same conference as one of these editors, introduce yourself and ask if the editor has any anthology projects to which you could submit. If you can't attend such conferences, you might be able to track down editors' e-mail addresses—especially if you are a member of a writers' organization with access to other members' contact information. Send a short, polite e-mail inquiring if the editor has any projects to which you could submit. You'll be surprised how often an editor is willing to look at a story for a supposedly "closed" anthology.

Finding the right idea

After diligent research and perhaps a little networking, you've discovered an anthology to which you'd like to submit. How do you come up with a story idea?

First, remember that your story has to center on the anthology's theme. Sometimes these themes can be broad—love, friendship or revenge, for example—and sometimes they can be very specific. I've done stories for anthologies based on TV shows like *Xena: Warrior Princess* and role-playing games like "Dark Tyrants," where the guidelines are very clear on what writers can and can't do with the characters and concepts. Whatever the theme, your story needs to add to the anthology's exploration of it while avoiding covering the same ground as all the other stories. And if the anthology is also genre-specific—horror, science fiction, mystery, romance— you have a whole host of other concerns to attend to as well.

I always begin by mulling over the personal experience I've had with the theme. For example, the cross-genre anthology *A Dangerous Magic* was built on the theme of fantasy stories dealing with romance. After thinking back on my own romantic experiences, I came up with the idea of how our view of romance evolves (or doesn't) as we mature, from putting the object of our affections on a pedestal to, hopefully, achieving a more balanced and realistic view of our loved ones. Thus my story "The Man of Her Dreams" was born, a tale about a woman whose literal (and absolutely perfect) dream lover comes to life. At first, she's thrilled but she soon realizes that it's possible to have too much perfection.

I had a harder time coming up with an idea for the anthology *Vengeance Fantastic*. I guess I'm not a very vindictive person, because I couldn't think of any time that I wished to get revenge on someone. Then I turned the question around: was there a time someone might have wished to get revenge on me? Years ago, when I worked as a reporter for a small weekly newspaper, I did some theater reviews, and I always felt uncomfortable criticizing actors' performances. What if one of those actors had wished to get back at me for a negative review? "Exits and Entrances" became a story about a theater critic with a poison pen (or more accurately, a poison keyboard) and the ghost of an actress he'd devastated. To keep this story from being a cliché, I had my critic believe the ghost has come back solely for revenge when in reality, like Marley's ghost, she's returned to help save his soul.

Avoid the obvious

That brings me to one of the most important considerations when writing a story for a theme anthology: avoiding the obvious and the cliché. Since an anthology might contain stories by a dozen or so writers, you want to avoid writing the same kind of story as everyone else. To do this, try to find an aspect of the theme that isn't apparent at first glance. For *A Dangerous Magic*, the story about the woman and her dream lover, rather than coming up with a fantasy story with romantic elements, I wrote about a central issue regarding the concept of romance itself: the difference between the ideal and the real. For *Vengeance Fantastic*, I wrote a story that at first certainly seemed to be about revenge, but turned out to be about redemption (though my character certainly does get what's coming to him in the end).

Don't go with your first, second or even third idea. Keep pushing yourself to explore the theme until you come up with an idea that's more original and perhaps more off-beat than any of the others the editor is going to see. That way, your story will stand a greater chance of being accepted for publication.

While getting a story published (and receiving a check to cash) is nice, writing for theme anthologies has meant I've written stories I never would have otherwise (need I mention *Alien Pets* again?), and they've often turned out to be some of the best work I've done. The themes have not only sparked ideas, they've taken me in directions I never would have explored otherwise and helped me grow as a writer.

And they can do the same for you.

Breaking In: Advice from the Pros

"[If] the author follows the editor's guidelines for the theme anthology, most of the time stories are turned down because there is nothing in them that makes them 'special.' Hackneyed phrases, mundane plots, and so on, are certain to get the story rejected. You need to ask yourself 'What makes this story special?' I mean, just because it has a dragon in it that doesn't make it special. Heck, all the stories in this dragon anthology have dragons in them. What is it that makes my story better? What makes it stand out?"

—Dennis L. McKiernan, author of Once Upon a Winter's Night and Dragondoom.

"Read enough anthologies to see what you like about them and what you don't. Submit to the editors whose instincts you trust. Also, if your work is to be published where editors can read it, and if an editor likes it, she will approach you to submit to an anthology."

—Ellen Datlow, fiction editor of Scifi.com, and co-editor of the Year's Best Fantasy and Horror series.

The Scams Are Out There!

BY NANCY BREEN

Are you one of those writers who worries about being ripped off? While most industry professionals are upstanding and trustworthy, there are individuals and operations that prosper at the expense of naïve writers eager to see their work in print. Such disreputable activities result in criminal investigations, class action lawsuits—and millions of dollars bilked from those unsuspecting writers who don't know how to spot an unscrupulous publisher, literary agent, or book doctor.

How do these things happen? Could they happen to *you*? With basic knowledge of how scams operate and the obvious warning signs (not to mention a well-developed sense of skepticism), you'll be better equipped to detect a scam *before* you get taken.

HOW SCAMS WORK

Publishers: They're called subsidy, or "vanity" publishers. They recruit authors through display ads in writer's magazines, spam sent to online newsgroups or even through unsolicited letters and brochures sent by regular mail. "ATTENTION: WRITERS WANTED" they trumpet. When you respond with a query or manuscript, you receive a letter awash with praise for your writing and chock full of promises of success and exaggerated claims for all the wonderful things the publisher will do for your manuscript, from printing to promotion. Then when the contract comes, you notice the clause that states how much YOU are expected to contribute, usually a significant sum of money. For this you will receive X number of books out of X number printed, your book will be widely distributed and promoted and you will all live happily ever after.

Don't bet on it. These kinds of publishers make profits from the fees they charge writers, not from sales of the books they produce. The finished books are often of dubious quality, there's actually little or no promotional effort expended by the publisher at all and you'll be hard pressed to find your book in major bookstores (or even small ones). The publisher may not even print as many total books as promised. Without sales there are no royalties, and the hoodwinked writer ends up with little to show for a considerable investment except stacks of unsold books.

Literary agents and book doctors: Shady agents recruit writers much as subsidy publishers do—through ads, online spam and direct mail. When you submit a manuscript, the agent responds that the work isn't quite up to standard and could use some editing. And, see, publishers no longer take the time and trouble to edit manuscripts but expect polished, ready-to-print work. But don't despair! The agent gives you the name of an excellent book doctor who understands just what that agent, and today's publisher, are looking for.

For an inflated fee, the book doctor works his "magic" on your manuscript. You resubmit the work to the agent, but wouldn't you know it? In the meantime, the market for your book has changed, or the agent represents an entirely different genre of writing, or . . . Well, the end of the story is you wind up with an unpublished manuscript that wasn't even particularly well "doctored," you have no representation in the marketplace and you're out of a big chunk of change.

Anthologies: You see an ad calling for poets or announcing a competition that offers thou-

NANCY BREEN *is editor of* Poet's Market *as well as a published poet and hopeful fiction writer.*

sands of dollars in cash prizes. You submit a poem and, lo and behold, you receive a heartening letter: Your poem didn't win, but it's so good it's been chosen for inclusion in a special anthology of only the *best* poems submitted. What a feather in your cap! Now, you don't *have* to purchase the anthology if you don't want to; but should you wish to see your poem among this treasure trove of literary gems, it will cost you only $45 (or whatever—could be more). Deluxe hardbound edition, mind you. Won't you be proud to show it to your family and friends? Why, they'll probably want to buy copies for themselves.

When you receive this grand volume, you may be disappointed in the quality of the other poems "chosen" to appear in this exclusive publication. Actually, everyone who entered was invited to be published, and you basically paid cash to see your poem appear in a book of no literary merit whatsoever.

These are the most common scams out there, although enterprising con artists are devising new ones all the time (modern technology, from "display" sites on the Internet to print-on-demand schemes, have opened up lots of fresh possibilities for emptying your wallet).

THE WARNING SIGNS

How do you protect yourself? It's important to learn the warning signs common to most publishing scams. Spotting even one of these danger signals should be enough to make you pause and ask some appropriate questions.

Here's what to watch out for:

A request for money. Here's how the legitimate system works: An agent sells your work to a publisher and takes a percentage of the sale amount as commission. A publisher agrees to publish your work and makes money off the sales of your book. *At no point in the process should you be paying anyone for anything.* That goes for "reading fees," "marketing fees," "contract fees," and so on.

What about contest fees? True, many literary magazines, small presses and literary organizations (such as state poetry societies) conduct contests that require entry fees (also sometimes called "reading fees"), and most of these are legitimate. The fees they charge go toward the expenses of conducting the contest, paying judges and putting up prize money, not lining someone's pocket. Also, entrants often receive a subscription to the magazine or a copy of the prize issue in exchange for the entry fee (or a copy of the winning book or chapbook in the case of small presses).

When in doubt, consider the reputation of the press, magazine or organization, how long it's been in existence and/or sponsoring the competition, how dependably winners and entrants are rewarded and the quality of the winning entries. If a competition asks for money but does not pay in cash, contributor's copies or some other tangible prize, enter your work elsewhere.

One more note about money: Do expect to pay for professional services, such as personal editing of your manuscript. However, be sure what you're being charged for (simple copyediting vs. deep revision, for example). If there's a contract, read it carefully and take pains to make sure all points are understood by both parties. And never pay the full cost of the service up front!

Referral to a specific agent, publisher or book doctor. Unscrupulous agents, publishers and book doctors could be in cahoots. For instance, an agent or publisher might suggest they'll look at your manuscript *if* it's worked on by a certain book doctor. An agent might suggest that a certain subsidy publisher is your best bet to see your work in print. And so on. If you're referred to just one individual or company, beware!

Phrases like "joint venture agreement," "author's contribution" and "co-partnership." It's that money thing again. Beware of any wording that even remotely suggests your financial participation. Your "contribution" will be bigger than you ever imagined and bring you far less than you ever wanted to believe.

Extravagant praise or unrealistic promises. Does the publisher or agent just rave about your work? Does he/she go on and on about the incredible success and financial rewards you can expect upon publication? Are you fed glorious visions of promotional campaigns and massive distribution? Don't be a chump. They're setting you up for the kill. Legitimate publishers and agents aren't going to gush all over you; and those spiels about promotional campaigns and widespread distribution are blue-sky come-ons that never materialize into anything. Great stuff for feeding your ego in the beginning, but later you'll wonder how you ever could have been so gullible.

Vagueness about details. If a publisher, agent or book doctor seems reluctant to provide basic information about his/her business activities or suggests sharing such "confidential" information could compromise the business's operation, be on guard. It's not crossing the line to ask about sales figures, how royalties are calculated and how often they're paid, a client list (i.e., references), a complete breakdown of costs to you and whatever else you'll need to help you make a sensible, well-informed decision.

Broad, inaccurate statements about the publishing industry. This is especially true of negative statements that make it seem as if you have no hope of ever selling your manuscript; at least, not without that party's assistance. If an agent, publisher or book doctor makes claims such as "publishers don't edit manuscripts any more," kick your skepticism into high gear. While it's true many editors are less involved in the nuts-and-bolts editing than they used to be, do some research on your own to find out what's really going on in the publishing world. Knowledge is power, and you'll be better able to detect the distortions in a scammer's spiel.

Display ads for agents, publishers, contests and anthologies. You're better off resisting these ads entirely. Legitimate, successful agents and publishers don't need to advertise; they're deluged with more writers than they can take on. What's more, these ads are misleading. Study them carefully and you probably won't find any mention of a fee, but you can be sure that requests for money will be introduced once you respond to the ad.

As for contests and anthologies, these ads are tempting with their promises of big cash awards. Even if the awards are actually paid to the winners, what you're more likely to receive is an

---

If You're the Victim of a Scam . . .

. . . or if you're trying to prevent one, the following resources should be of help:

Contact **The Federal Trade Commission, Bureau of Consumer Protection** at 1-877-FTC-HELP(382-4357) or log on to www.ftc.gov. While they won't resolve individual consumer problems, the FTC depends on your complaints to help them investigate fraud. Your speaking up may even lead to law enforcement action. Contact them by phone or enter your complaint through their online submission form.

Volunteer Lawyers for the Arts (1 E. 53rd St., New York NY 10022) is a group of volunteers from the legal profession who assist with questions of law pertaining to the arts, all fields. You can phone their hotline at (212)319-ARTS(2787), ext. 1 and have your questions answered for the price of the phone call. For further information you can also visit their website at www.vlany.org.

Better Business Bureau (check local listings or visit www.bbb.org)—the folks to contact if you have a complaint or if you want to investigate a publisher, literary agent or other business related to writing and writers.

In addition, you should contact your state's attorney general with information about scamming activity. Don't know your attorney general's name? Go to www. attorneygeneral.gov/ags for a wealth of contact information, including a complete list of links for each state's attorney general.

invitation to buy an anthology. Understand that writer's publications do run display ads for entirely legitimate contests, but these are usually sponsored by literary magazines and small presses. Those ads with the grandiose titles that appear in both writer and non-writer publications are what you really have to watch out for ("The Best Damn Poetry in the Cosmos Competition" or "Universal Library of Literary Giants Competition" or . . . well, you get the idea.)

These are just a few of the basic tip-offs to scams that prey on writers. When searching for an agent, publisher or book doctor, apply the same common sense that you would to finding a good mechanic, caterer or carpenter. Request a resume and references. Check with the Better Business Bureau. Talk to clients past and present. Search the Internet. You can even generate a professional background check (fees for this vary, so be careful here, too).

DON'T RUSH TO PUBLISH

Writers serious about their craft should never be so impatient for publication that they rush into dubious business arrangements. Devious publishers, agents and book doctors understand the vulnerability of unpublished authors who feel anxious—desperate, even—about ever seeing their work in print.

If you're good enough to be published, you're good enough to be the payee rather than the payer. On the other hand, if you really are not ready for publication, paying someone to rush things along isn't going to earn you the reputation and success you desire. So put away your checkbook and credit cards and dig out your manuscript. Concentrate your energies into making your writing the best it can be. If your work deserves an audience, it will find one without the process draining your bank account.

The scams are out there—but you do *not* have to be a victim!

For More Information

There are plenty of books that can help you identify reputable publishers, literary agents, and book doctors, including *Writer's Market* (Writer's Digest Books) and its online counterpart at www.writersmarket.com (subscription-based); and *Literary Marketplace* (R.R. Bowker), plus many individual titles focused on specific areas of the publishing world (finding an agent, for example).

The Internet is also a rich source of information. Simply type "publishing scams" into your favorite search engine. Here are some of our favorite sites (not only for scam information, but for good writing advice as well):

National Writers Union (www.nwu.org) for their "Writer Alert!" page (accessible to non-members).

The Science Fiction & Fantasy Writers of America (www.sfwa.org/beware) for their "Writer Beware" section.

Preditors & Editors (http://anotherealm.com/prededitors) for their "Warnings" page.

Todd Jones Pierce's Guide to Literary Agents (www.literaryagents.org) for a bounty of tips and advice (plus free e-newsletter subscription).

The Writer's Center (www.writer.org/scamkit.htm) for their online "Scam Kit."

Writer's Digest's Top 30 Short Story Markets

BY MARIA WITTE

Are you on a quest to find the best place to submit your short fiction? Look no further! Use this list to find the door that leads to short story publication.

Not surprisingly, almost every editor makes some mention of checking guidelines and reading past issues of their publication before submitting. Jill Adams, editor of *The Barcelona Review*, says, "First of all, read the submission guidelines carefully, which is, unfortunately, so rarely done." This may seem like common sense, but many writers ignore this advice, submit on their own terms, and end up with a pile of rejections—or worse, no response at all.

Other editors offer even more specific advice. "The most important advice any editor can offer is to read the previously published work prior to submission," says Sean Meriwether, editor of *Outsider Ink*. "Each venue has its own particular obsessions. By reading work the editor has already selected, you can develop an idea of what that market is looking for." And don't be put off if you're a beginner. "We especially seek out and enjoy publishing first-time writers and artists. Don't let a lack of publishing credits prevent you from submitting!" *Mindprints* Editor Paul Fahey says.

Once you've brushed up on the basics, it's time to enhance the quality of your work. Do your characters shine? Are their conflicts plausible? Does your plot move at a steady pace? "We look for a strong sense of voice, flashes of humor, concrete and condensed description in fiction that unites the heart and mind by avoiding the sentimental," says Vivian Shipley, editor of *Connecticut Review*. Humor, also, seems to be a prevalent need in many of these markets. Fahey says he looks for "a short but complete story with a change in character, great imagery and an unusual voice or point of view. We are dying for some humorous pieces. We love it when we read a short story or memoir or poem that makes us laugh."

Also, many editors are inclined to accept shorter works. "Short shorts are popular—stories under 1,000 words, and flash fiction, which generally is a story under 500 words," the editors of *Prose Ax* say. "Though it might seem easier to write one of these stories in comparison to writing a regular-length story, I think they are actually more difficult to write, because you don't have a lot of space to get your story across." Fahey says, "We love reading complete stories of 55 and 100 words. For us, the shorter, the better. That way we can publish a variety of styles and voices."

Once you're familiar with a publication's guidelines and style preferences, it's time to send your creation out into the publishing world. Always read and reread your manuscript to be sure it's clean—no grammar, punctuation and spelling errors. And make sure the story idea is appropriate for the publication to which you're submitting.

Is all of this planning worth it? Definitely. "A writer's career can be furthered by the broad national exposure we provide to an audience who reads quality fiction. After every issue, I have several agents contact me about representing authors we publish," Shipley says.

MARIA WITTE *is managing editor of* Writer's Digest *magazine. For* Writer's Digest *subscription information, visit their website at www.writersdigest.com, or call toll free at 800-448-0915.*

So, get rid of those creative inhibitions and submit, submit, submit. You never know who could be waiting on the other side of that door!

About the Listings

Every year, *Writer's Digest* rounds up the top short fiction markets for writers. In keeping with last year's ranking method, we've whittled down a list of hundreds of fiction publications to 30, which we then classified into six categories. Based on information from *Novel & Short Story Writer's Market*, WritersMarket.com and the individual magazine guidelines, we are thrilled to showcase the top 30 short story markets!

Criteria considered included circulation, payment, rights, submission response time, and the number of manuscripts a magazine receives per year vs. the number of manuscripts it's able to publish. In our **Best Bets for Beginners** category, we've found five high-caliber publications that encourage new writers to submit. Under **Internet Envy**, we've listed the top five online publications. **Genre Gems** tips its hat to notable genre markets. **Fame Without Fortune** showcases top-notch nonpaying magazines that won't add weight to your wallet but may get your writing noticed. **You're in the Money** features paying markets that remain attainable for skilled writers. And finally, we've replaced last year's long-shot category-which included distinguished publications such as **The Atlantic Monthly, Harper's** and **The New Yorker**, markets that reserve their space for the most accomplished writers—with **Around the World**, the most writer-friendly, non-U.S. publications.

—*Maria Witte*

For expanded listings on the top 30 markets, check the page number references in these market listings and see that page in this edition of Novel & Short Story Writer's Market.

Best bets for beginners

Beginnings Publishing: A Magazine for Novice Writers (scbeginnings.com), Jenine Boisits, fiction editor, P.O. Box 92, Shirley NY 11967-1525. Tel: (631) 205-5542. E-mail: Jenineb@opto nline.net. **See page 175**. Semiannual magazine; does not read in January or April. Pays one contributor copy for first rights.

Mindprints: A Literary Journal (www.hancock.cc.ca.us/studentservices/learning_assistance/ mindprints), Paul Fahey, editor, Learning Assistance Program, Allan Hancock College, 800 S. College Dr., Santa Maria CA 93454-6399. Tel: (805) 992-6966, ext. 3274. E-mail: pafahey@han cock.cc.ca.us. E-submissions accepted only from non-U.S. residents. U.S. residents query by mail. **See page 225**. Annual magazine; reads September through May. Pays one contributor copy for one-time rights. Note: "Many famous writers have started their careers by publishing work in small literary magazines," Fahey says. "In our area of California, many well-known authors such as Catherine Ryan Hyde, author of *Pay It Forward*, have graciously contributed to our magazine. What a high for a first-time writer to be published alongside such pros!"

Outsider Ink (www.outsiderink.com), Sean Meriwether, editor, Outsider Media, 201 W. 11th St., New York NY 10014. Tel: (212) 691-4345. E-mail: editor@outsidermedia.com. Submit via e-mail. **See page 322**. Quarterly e-zine. No payment; acquires e-rights. Note: "Publishing short fiction is incredibly important to the development of a new writer," Meriwether says. "You can test the markets, develop your own voice, gain experience in the submission process, and build name recognition."

Prose Ax: doses of prose, poetry, visual and audio art (www.proseax.com), J. Calma Salazar, editor, P.O. Box 22643, Honolulu HI 96823-2643. E-mail: prose_ax@att.net. Submit via e-mail. **See page 298**. Quarterly zine. Pays two contributor copies for one-time and e-rights.

The Unknown Writer (www.webpan.net/~amunno/temphome.html), Rick Maffei, fiction editor, P.O. Box 698, Ramsey NJ 07446. E-mail: unknown_writer_2000@yahoo.com. **See page 268**. Quarterly magazine. Pays two contributor copies for first rights.

Internet envy

Big Country Peacock Chronicle (www.peacockchronicle.com), Audrey Yoeckel, owner/publisher, RR1 Box 89K-112, Aspermont TX 79502. Tel: (806) 254-2322. E-mail: ayoeckel@yahoo.com. **See page 309**. Monthly e-zine. No payment; acquires e-rights. Note: "If you are unsure of your writing skills and have a good story, we can work with you," Yoeckel says. "We have help and resources for marketing and skills development available for writers, poets, journalists and storytellers."

The Blue Moon Review (www.thebluemoon.com), Theron Montgomery, fiction editor, 14313 Winter Ridge Lane, Midlothian VA 23112. E-mail: fiction@thebluemoon.com. Submit via e-mail only. **See page 310**. Quarterly e-zine. No payment; acquires first North American serial and one-time anthology rights.

The Café Irreal: International Imagination (www.cafeirreal.com), Alice Whittenburg and G.S. Evans, editors. E-mail: editors@cafeirreal.com. Submit via e-mail only. **See page 310**. Semiannual e-zine. Pays 1¢/word, $2 minimum, for first and one-time rights. Note: "Because the Internet is so readily accessible in so many parts of the world, an Internet publication such as *The Café Irreal* can help a writer reach a much wider audience than would have been possible in such a specialty publication 10 or more years ago," Evans and Whittenburg say, via an e-mail response.

PIF (www.pifmagazine.com), Rachel Sage, editor, 1426 Harvard Ave., #451, Seattle WA 98122-3813. Tel: (360) 493-0596. E-mail: editor@pifmagazine.com. Submit via e-mail only. **See page 323**. Monthly e-zine. Pays $20/printed page for first North American serial rights. Note: You must be a registered member to submit. Membership is free.

Alternate Realities Webzine (www.sff.net/estand/ezine/altreal.htm), Joan M. McCarty, editor, 26 N.E. 57th Ave., Portland OR 97218.

• As of press time, this website was no longer active.

Genre gems

Analog: Science Fiction and Fact (www.analogsf.com), Stanley Schmidt, editor, Dell Magazines, 475 Park Ave. S., New York, NY 10016. Tel: (212) 686-7188. E-mail: analog@dellmagazines.com. **See page 334**. Magazine published 11 times/year. Pays 5-8¢/word and two contributor copies for first North American serial and nonexclusive foreign serial rights.

Asimov's Science Fiction (www.asimovs.com), Gardner Dozois, editor, 475 Park Ave. S., New York NY 10016-6901. Tel: (212) 686-7188. E-mail: asimovs@dellmagazines.com. **See page 335**. Magazine published 11 times/year. Pays 5-8¢/word for first world English serial and specified foreign rights, as explained in contract.

Magazine of Fantasy & Science Fiction (www.sfsite.com/fsf), Gordon Van Gelder, editor. P.O. Box 3447, Hoboken NJ 07030. Tel: (201) 876-2551. E-mail: sandsf@aol.com. **See page 351**. Monthly magazine. Pays 5-8¢/word for first North American and foreign serial rights, and an option on anthology if requested.

Millennium Science Fiction & Fantasy (www.jopoppub.com), Diana R. Moreland, fiction editor, P.O. Box 8118, Roswell NM 88202-8118. E-mail: jopoppub@jopoppub.com. Submit online or via e-mail only. **See page 321**. Monthly e-zine; reads January through October. Pays $5-20 for one-time rights. Note: Type "Story Submission" in subject line.

Scifi.com (www.scifi.com/scifiction), Ellen Datlow, editor, PMB 391, 511 Avenue of the Americas, New York NY 10011-8436. Tel: (212) 989-3742. E-mail: datlow@www.scifi.com. Submit via standard mail only. **See page 325**. Weekly e-zine. Pays 20¢/word up to $3,500 for first (with a six-month exclusivity clause), anthology and e-rights. Note: "Publishing short fiction (if you're good at it) is a way to get your name out quickly and with less hassle than writing and publishing a novel," Datlow says. "This is only true of writers who have a talent for short fiction—if it takes you as long to write a short story as it does to write a novel, this won't help."

Fame without fortune

Connecticut Review (www.ctstateu.edu/univrel/ctreview/index.htm), Dr. Vivian Shipley, editor, Connecticut State University System, SCSU 501 Crescent St., New Haven CT 06515. Tel: (203) 392-6737. E-mail: ctreview@southernct.edu. Submit via standard mail only. **See page 189.** Semiannual magazine; reads September through May. Pays two contributor copies for first rights. Note: "I forward the agents' inquiries to the writers. Several of our stories have been reprinted by other magazines, and *Weston Magazine* is doing a feature article on a fiction writer as a result of a story published in Spring 2002."

The Literary Review: An International Journal of Contemporary Writing (www.theliteraryreview.org), René Steinke, editor in chief, Fairleigh Dickinson University, 285 Madison Ave., Madison NJ 07940. Tel: (973) 443-8564. E-mail: trl@fdu.edu. Submit via standard mail. **See page 217.** Quarterly magazine; reads September through May. Pays two contributor copies for first rights. Note: "We feel that publishing in fiction magazines helps writers to get their work out into the mainstream and add to their publishing credits," editors say.

Snake Nation Review (www.snakenationpress.org), Jean Arambula, editor, 110 W. Force St., Valdosta GA 31601. E-mail: jeana@snakenationpress.org. **See page 255.** Quarterly magazine. Pays two contributor copies for one-time rights.

Story Quarterly (www.storyquarterly.com), fiction editors, 431 Sheridan Rd., Kenilworth IL 60043-1220. Tel: (847) 256-6998. E-mail: storyquarterly@yahoo.com. Submit online only. **See page 261.** Annual magazine. Pays 10 contributor copies and a lifetime subscription ($200 value) for first North American serial rights. Note: You must be a registered member to submit. Membership is free.

Transition: An International Review, (www.transitionmagazine.com), Michael Vazquez, executive editor, Duke University Press, 69 Dunster St., Cambridge MA 02138. Tel: (617) 496-2845. E-mail: transition@fas.harvard.edu. **See page 267.** Quarterly magazine. Pays three contributor copies; right negotiable.

You're in the money

The Georgia Review (www.uga.edu/~garev), T.R. Hummer, editor, The University of Georgia, Athens GA 30602-9009. Tel: (706) 542-3481. E-mail: garev@arches.uga.edu. **See page 200.** Quarterly journal; reads Aug. 16 through May 14. Pays $40/printed page, one contributor copy and a one-year subscription for first North American serial rights.

Glimmer Train Stories (www.glimmertrain.com), Susan Burmeister-Brown and Linda Swanson-Davies, editors, Glimmer Train Press, 710 S.W. Madison St., Suite 504, Portland OR 97205. Tel: (503) 221-0836. E-mail: info@glimmertrain.com. Submit online. **See page 202.** Quarterly magazine; reads in January, April, July, October. Pays $500 and 10 contributor copies for first rights.

Ploughshares (www.pshares.org), fiction editor, Emerson College, 120 Boylston St., Boston, MA 02116. Tel: (617) 824-8753. E-mail: pshares@emerson.edu. **See page 243.** Triquarterly magazine; reads mss postmarked between Aug. 1 and March 31. Pays $25/page ($50 min., $250 max.), contributor copies and one-year subscription for first North American serial rights.

The Southern Review (www.lsu.edu/thesouthernreview), John Easterly, associate editor, Louisiana State University, 43 Allen Hall, Baton Rouge LA 70803-5005. Tel: (225) 578-5108. E-mail: jeaster@lsu.edu. **See page 258.** Quarterly magazine; reads September through May. Pays $12/printed page and two contributor copies for first North American serial rights.

Tin House (www.tinhouse.com), Rob Spillman and Elissa Schappell, fiction editors, P.O. Box 10500, Portland OR 97296-0500. Tel: (503) 274-4393. E-mail: tinhouse@aol.com. **See page**

267. Quarterly magazine. Pays $100-800 for first North American serial and anthology rights.

Around the world

The Barcelona Review (www.barcelonareview.com), Jill Adams, editor, Correu Vell 12-2, 08002 Barcelona, Spain. Tel: (00) 34 93 319 15 96. E-mail: editor@barcelonareview.com. Submit via e-mail only. **See page 308**. Bimonthly e-zine. Sometimes pays in professional Spanish translation of story for e-rights. Note: "We always help with editing if a piece is accepted, but the majority of submissions we receive are just plain sloppy: misspellings, redundancies, awkward sentence structures," Adams says.

Event (http://event.douglas.bc.ca), Christine Dewar, fiction editor, Douglas College, Box 2503, New Westminster, British Columbia V3L 5B2 Canada. E-mail: event@douglas.bc.ca. **See page 194**. Triannual magazine. Pays $22/page and two contributor copies for first North American serial rights.

Grain Magazine (www.grainmagazine.ca), Marlis Wesseler, fiction editor, Saskatchewan Writers' Guild, P.O. Box 67, Saskatoon, Saskatchewan S7K 3K1, Canada. Tel: (306) 244-2828. E-mail: grainmag@sasktel.net. **See page 202**. Quarterly magazine. Pays $40/page up to $175 and two contributor copies for first Canadian serial rights.

Prism International (prism.arts.ubc.ca), Billeh Nickerson, editor, Buch E462-1866 Main Mall, University of British Columbia, Vancouver, British Columbia V6T 1Z1, Canada. Tel: (604) 822-2514. E-mail: prism@interchange.ubc.ca. **See page 246**. Quarterly magazine; does not read in August. Pays $20 (Canadian)/printed page and one-year subscription for first North American serial rights.

Storie, all write (www.storie.it), Gianluca Bassi, editor, Leconte, Via Suor Celestina Donati 13/E, Rome, Italy 00167. Tel: (39) 06 614 8777. E-mail: storie@tiscali.it. **See page 261**. Bimonthly magazine. Pays $30-600 and two contributor copies for first English and Italian rights.

The Business of Fiction Writing

It's true there are no substitutes for talent and hard work. A writer's first concern must always be attention to craft. No matter how well presented, a poorly written story or novel has little chance of being published. On the other hand, a well-written piece may be equally hard to sell in today's competitive publishing market. Talent alone is just not enough.

To be successful, writers need to study the field and pay careful attention to finding the right market. While the hours spent perfecting your writing are usually hours spent alone, you're not alone when it comes to developing your marketing plan. *Novel & Short Story Writer's Market* provides you with detailed listings containing the essential information you'll need to locate and contact the markets most suitable for your work.

Once you've determined where to send your work, you must turn your attention to presentation. We can help here, too. We've included the basics of manuscript preparation, along with a compilation of information on submission procedures and approaching markets. In addition we provide information on setting up and giving readings. We also include tips on promoting your work. No matter where you're from or what level of experience you have, you'll find useful information here on everything from presentation to mailing to selling rights to promoting your work—the "business" of fiction.

APPROACHING MAGAZINE MARKETS

While it is essential for nonfiction markets, a query letter by itself is usually not needed by most magazine fiction editors. If you are approaching a magazine to find out if fiction is accepted, a query is fine, but editors looking for short fiction want to see *how* you write. A cover letter can be useful as a letter of introduction, but it must be accompanied by the actual piece. Include basic information in your cover letter—name, address, a brief list of previous publications—if you have any—and two or three sentences about the piece (why you are sending it to *this* magazine or how your experience influenced your story). Keep it to one page and remember to include a self-addressed, stamped envelope (SASE) for reply. See the Sample Short Story Cover Letter on page 61.

Agents: Agents are not usually needed for short fiction and most do not handle it unless they already have a working relationship with you. For novels, you may want to consider working with an agent, especially if marketing to publishers who do not look at unsolicited submissions. For more on approaching agents and listings of agents willing to work with beginning and established writers, see our Literary Agents section beginning on page 107.

APPROACHING BOOK PUBLISHERS

Some book publishers do ask for queries first, but most want a query plus sample chapters or an outline or, occasionally, the complete manuscript. Again, make your letter brief. Include the essentials about yourself—name, address, phone number and publishing experience. Include only the personal information related to your story. Show that you have researched the market with a few sentences about why you chose this publisher. See the Sample Book Query Cover Letter on page 62.

THE SAMPLE COVER LETTER

A successful cover letter is no more than one page (20 lb. bond paper), single spaced with a double space between paragraphs, proofread carefully, and neatly typed in a standard typeface (not script or italic). The writer's name, address and phone number appear at the top, and it is addressed, ideally, to a specific editor. (If the editor's name is unavailable, address to "Fiction Editor.")

The body of a successful cover letter contains the name and word count of the story, the reason you are submitting to this particular publication, and some brief biographical information, especially when relevant to your story. Mention that you have enclosed a self-addressed, stamped envelope or postcard for reply. Also let the editor know if you are sending a disposable manuscript that doesn't need to be returned. (More and more editors prefer disposable manuscripts that save them time and save you postage.) When sending a computer disk, identify the program you are using. Remember, however, that even editors who appreciate receiving your story on a disk usually also want a printed copy. Finally, don't forget to thank the editor for considering your story.

BOOK PROPOSALS

A book proposal is a package sent to a publisher that includes a cover letter and one or more of the following: sample chapters, outline, synopsis, author bio, publications list. When asked to send sample chapters, send up to three *consecutive* chapters. An **outline** covers the highlights of your book chapter by chapter. Be sure to include details on main characters, the plot and subplots. Outlines can run up to 30 pages, depending on the length of your novel. The object is to tell what happens in a concise, but clear, manner. A **synopsis** is a very brief description of what happens in the story. Keep it to two or three pages. The terms synopsis and outline are sometimes used interchangeably, so be sure to find out exactly what each publisher wants.

MANUSCRIPT MECHANICS

A professionally presented manuscript will not guarantee publication. But a sloppy, hard-to-read manuscript will not be read—publishers simply do not have the time. Here's a list of suggested submission techniques for polished manuscript presentation:

• **Use white, 8½×11 bond paper,** preferably 16 or 20 lb. weight. The paper should be heavy enough so it will not show pages underneath it and strong enough to take handling by several people.

• **Type your manuscript** on a computer using a laser or ink jet printer, or on a typewriter using a new ribbon.

• **Proofread carefully.** An occasional white-out is okay, but don't send a marked-up manuscript with many typos. Keep a dictionary, thesaurus and stylebook handy and use the spellcheck function of your computer.

• **Always double space and leave a 1¼ inch margin** on all sides of the page.

• **For a short story manuscript,** your first page should include your name, address and phone number (single-spaced) in the upper left corner. In the upper right, indicate an approximate word count. Center the name of your story about one-third of the way down, skip two or three lines and center your byline (byline is optional). Skip three lines and begin your story. On subsequent pages, put last name and page number in the upper right hand corner.

• **For book manuscripts,** use a separate cover sheet. Put your name, address and phone number in the upper left corner and word count in the upper right. Some writers list their agent's name and address in the upper right (word count is then placed at the bottom of the page). Center your title and byline about halfway down the page. Start your first chapter on the next page. Center the chapter number and title (if there is one) one-third of the way down the page. Include your last name and page number in the upper right of this page and each page to follow. Start each chapter with a new page.

• **Include a word count.** If you work on a computer, chances are your word processing program can give you a word count. If you are using a typewriter, there are a number of ways to count the number of words in your piece. One way is to count the words in five lines and divide that

SAMPLE SHORT STORY COVER LETTER

Jennifer Williamson
8822 Rose Petal Ct.
Norwood OH 45212

June 22, 2004

Rebecca Rossdale
Young Woman Magazine
4234 Market St.
Chicago IL 60606

Dear Ms. Rossdale,

As a teacher and former assistant camp director I have witnessed many a summer romance between teens working at camp. One romance in particular touched me because the young people involved helped each other through a very difficult summer. It inspired me to write the enclosed 8,000-word short story, "Summer Love," a love story about two teens, both from troubled families, who find love and support while working at a camp in upstate New York.

I think the story will fit nicely into your Summer Reading issue. My publishing credits include stories in *Youth Today* and *Sparkle* magazines as well as publications for adults. I am also working on a historical romance.

I look forward to hearing from you.

Sincerely,

Jennifer Williamson
(513)555-5555

Encl.: Manuscript
SASE

SAMPLE BOOK QUERY COVER LETTER

Bonnie Booth
1453 Nuance Blvd.
Norwood OH 45212

December 18, 2004

Ms. Thelma Collins
Bradford House Publishing
187 72nd St., Fifth Floor
New York NY 10101

Dear Ms. Collins,

I am a published mystery writer whose short stories have appeared in *Modern Mystery* and *Doyle's Mystery Magazine*. I am also a law student and professional hair designer and have brought these interests together in *Only Skin Deep*, my 60,000-word novel set in the glamorous world of beauty care, featuring hair designer to the stars and amateur detective Norma Haines.

In *Only Skin Deep*, Haines is helping put together the state's largest hair design show when she gets a call from a friend at the local police station. The body of famed designer Lynette LaSalle has been found in an Indianapolis motel room. She's been strangled and her legendary blonde mane has been shaved off. Later, when the bodies of two other designers are discovered also with shaven heads, it's clear their shared occupation is more than a coincidence.

Your successful series by Ann Smythe and the bestseller *The Gas Pump Murders*, by Marc Crawford, point to the continued popularity of amateur detectives. *Only Skin Deep* would make a strong addition to your line.

Sincerely,

Bonnie Booth
(513)555-5555

Encl.: three sample chapters
       synopsis
       SASE

number by five to find an average. Then count the number of lines and multiply to find the total words. For long pieces, you may want to count the words in the first three pages, divide by three and multiply by the number of pages you have.

• **Always keep a copy.** Manuscripts do get lost. To avoid expensive mailing costs, send only what is required. If you are including artwork or photos, but you are not positive they will be used, send photocopies. Artwork is hard to replace.

• **Suggest art where applicable.** Most publishers do not expect you to provide artwork and some insist on selecting their own illustrators, but if you have suggestions, please let them know. Magazine publishers work in a very visual field and are usually open to ideas.

• **Enclose a self-addressed, stamped envelope (SASE)** if you want a reply or if you want your manuscript returned. For most letters, a business-size (#10) envelope will do. Avoid using any envelope too small for an 8½ × 11 sheet of paper. For manuscripts, be sure to include enough postage and an envelope large enough to contain it.

• **Consider sending a disposable manuscript** that saves editors time and saves you money. If you are requesting a sample copy of a magazine or a book publisher's catalog, send an envelope big enough to fit.

• **When sending electronic (disk or modem) submissions,** *contact the publisher first for specific information and follow the directions carefully.* Always include a printed copy with any disk submission. *Fax or e-mail your submissions only with prior approval of the publisher.*

• **Keep accurate records.** This can be done in a number of ways, but be sure to keep track of where your stories are and how long they have been "out." Write down submission dates. If you do not hear about your submission for a long time—about three weeks to one month longer than the reporting time stated in the listing—you may want to contact the publisher. When you do, you will need an accurate record for reference.

MAILING TIPS

When mailing short correspondence or short manuscripts:

• Fold manuscripts under five pages into thirds and send in a business-size (#10) envelope.

• Mail manuscripts five pages or more unfolded in a 9 × 12 or 10 × 13 envelope.

• Mark envelopes in all caps, FIRST CLASS MAIL or SPECIAL FOURTH CLASS MANU-SCRIPT RATE.

• For return envelope, fold it in half, address it to yourself and add a stamp or, if going to a foreign country, International Reply Coupons (available at the main branch of your local post office).

• Don't send by certified mail. This is a sign of an amateur and publishers do not appreciate receiving unsolicited manuscripts this way.

• For the most current postage rates, visit the United States Postal Service online at www.usps.com.

When mailing book-length manuscripts:

FIRST CLASS MAIL over 11 ounces (@ 65 8½ × 11 20 lb.-weight pages) automatically becomes **PRIORITY MAIL.**

METERED MAIL may be dropped in any post office box, but meter strips on SASEs should not be dated.

The Postal Service provides, free of charge, tape, boxes and envelopes to hold up to two pounds for those using PRIORITY and EXPRESS MAIL.

Requirements for mailing FOURTH CLASS and PARCEL POST have not changed.

Main branches of local banks will cash foreign checks, but keep in mind payment quoted in our listings by publishers in other countries is usually payment in their currency. Also note reporting time is longer in most overseas markets. To save time and money, you may want to include a return postcard (and IRC) with your submission and forgo asking for a manuscript to be returned. If you live in Canada, see "Canadian Writers Take Note" on page 589.

RIGHTS

Know what rights you are selling. The Copyright Law states that writers are selling one-time rights (in almost all cases) unless they and the publisher have agreed otherwise. A list of various rights follows. Be sure you know exactly what rights you are selling before you agree to the sale.

• **Copyright** is the legal right to exclusive publication, sale or distribution of a literary work. As the writer or creator of a written work, you need simply to include your name, date and the copyright symbol © on your piece in order to copyright it. Be aware, however, that most editors today consider placing the copyright symbol on your work the sign of an amateur and many are even offended by it.

To get specific answers to questions about copyright (but not legal advice), you can call the Copyright Public Information Office at (202)707-3000 weekdays between 8:30 a.m. and 5 p.m. EST. Publications listed in *Novel & Short Story Writer's Market* are copyrighted *unless* otherwise stated. In the case of magazines that are not copyrighted, be sure to keep a copy of your manuscript with your notice printed on it. For more information on copyrighting your work see *The Copyright Handbook: How to Protect and Use Written Works* by Stephen Fishman (Nolo Press, 1992).

Some people are under the mistaken impression that copyright is something they have to send away for, and that their writing is not properly protected until they have "received" their copyright from the government. The fact is, you don't have to register your work with the Copyright Office in order for your work to be copyrighted; any piece of writing is copyrighted the moment it is put to paper. Registration of your work does, however, offer some additional protection (specifically, the possibility of recovering punitive damages in an infringement suit) as well as legal proof of the date of copyright.

Registration is a matter of filling out an application form (for writers, that's generally Form TX) and sending the completed form, a nonreturnable copy of the work in question and a check for $30 to the Library of Congress, Copyright Office, Register of Copyrights, 101 Independence Ave. SE, Washington DC 20559-6000. If the thought of paying $30 each to register every piece you write does not appeal to you, you can cut costs by registering a group of your works with one form, under one title for one $30 fee.

Most magazines are registered with the Copyright Office as single collective entities themselves; that is, the individual works that make up the magazine are *not* copyrighted individually in the names of the authors. You'll need to register your article yourself if you wish to have the additional protection of copyright registration.

For more information, visit the United States Copyright Office, Library of Congress, online at www.copyright.gov.

• **First Serial Rights**—This means the writer offers a newspaper or magazine the right to publish the article, story or poem for the first time in a particular periodical. All other rights to the material remain with the writer. The qualifier "North American" is often added to this phrase to specify a geographical limit to the license.

When material is excerpted from a book scheduled to be published and it appears in a magazine or newspaper prior to book publication, this is also called first serial rights.

• **One-time Rights**—A periodical that licenses one-time rights to a work (also known as simultaneous rights) buys the *nonexclusive* right to publish the work once. That is, there is nothing to stop the author from selling the work to other publications at the same time. Simultaneous sales would typically be to periodicals without overlapping audiences.

• **Second Serial (Reprint) Rights**—This gives a newspaper or magazine the opportunity to print an article, poem or story after it has already appeared in another newspaper or magazine. Second serial rights are nonexclusive—that is, they can be licensed to more than one market.

• **All Rights**—This is just what it sounds like. All Rights means a publisher may use the manuscript anywhere and in any form, including movie and book club sales, without further payment to the writer (although such a transfer, or *assignment*, of rights will terminate after 35 years). If you think you'll want to use the material later, you must avoid submitting to such markets or refuse payment and withdraw your material. Ask the editor whether he is willing to buy first rights instead of all rights before you agree to an assignment or sale. Some editors will reassign rights to a writer after a given period, such as one year. It's worth an inquiry in writing.

• **Subsidiary Rights**—These are the rights, other than book publication rights, that should be covered in a book contract. These may include various serial rights; movie, television, audiotape and other electronic rights; translation rights, etc. The book contract should specify who controls these rights (author or publisher) and what percentage of sales from the licensing of these sub rights goes to the author.

• **Dramatic, Television and Motion Picture Rights**—This means the writer is selling his material for use on the stage, in television or in the movies. Often a one-year option to buy such rights is offered (generally for 10% of the total price). The interested party then tries to sell the idea to other people—actors, directors, studios or television networks, etc. Some properties are optioned over and over again, but most fail to become dramatic productions. In such cases, the writer can sell his rights again and again—as long as there is interest in the material. Though dramatic, TV and motion picture rights are more important to the fiction writer than the nonfiction writer, producers today are increasingly interested in nonfiction material; many biographies, topical books and true stories are being dramatized.

• **Electronic Rights**—These rights cover usage in a broad range of electronic media, from online magazines and databases to CD-ROM magazine anthologies and interactive games. The editor should specify in writing if—and which—electronic rights are being requested. The presumption is that unspecified rights are kept by the writer.

Compensation for electronic rights is a major source of conflict between writers and publishers, as many book publishers seek control of them and many magazines routinely include electronic rights in the purchase of print rights, often with no additional payment. Alternative ways of handling this issue include an additional 15% added to the amount to purchase first rights to a royalty system based on the number of times an article is accessed from an electronic database.

PROMOTION TIPS

Everyone agrees writing is hard work whether you are published or not. Yet, once you arrive at the published side of the equation the work changes. Most published authors will tell you the work is still hard but it is different. Now, not only do you continue working on your next project, you must also concern yourself with getting your book into the hands of readers. It becomes time to switch hats from artist to salesperson.

While even bestselling authors whose publishers have committed big bucks to promotion are asked to help in promoting their books, new authors may have to take it upon themselves to plan and initiate some of their own promotion, sometimes dipping into their own pockets. While this does not mean that every author is expected to go on tour, sometimes at their own expense, it does mean authors should be prepared to offer suggestions for promoting their books.

Depending on the time, money and the personal preferences of the author and publisher, a promotional campaign could mean anything from mailing out press releases to setting up book signings to hitting the talk-show circuit. Most writers can contribute to their own promotion by providing contact names—reviewers, home-town newspapers, civic groups, organizations—that might have a special interest in the book or the writer.

Above all, when it comes to promotion, be creative. What is your book about? Try to capitalize on it. For example, if you've written a mystery whose protagonist is a wine connoisseur, you might give a reading at a local wine-tasting or try to set something up at one of the national wine events. For more suggestions on promoting your work see *The Writer's Guide to Promotion & Publicity*, by Elane Feldman (Writer's Digest Books).

About Our Policies

We occasionally receive letters asking why a certain magazine, publisher or contest is not in the book. Sometimes when we contact a listing, the editor does not want to be listed because they: do not use very much fiction; are overwhelmed with submissions; are having financial difficulty or have been recently sold; use only solicited material; accept work from a select group of writers only; do not have the staff or time for the many unsolicited submissions a listing may bring.

Some of the listings do not appear because we have chosen not to list them. We investigate complaints of unprofessional conduct in editors' dealings with writers and misrepresentation of information provided to us by editors and publishers. If we find these reports to be true, after a thorough investigation, we will delete the listing from future editions. See Important Listing Information on page 106 for more about our listing policies.

If a listing appeared in our book last year but is no longer listed, we list it in the General Index, beginning on page 660, with a code explaining why it is not listed. The key to those codes is given in the introduction to the General Index. Sometimes the listing does not appear because the editor did not respond in time for our press deadline, or it may not appear for any of the reasons previously mentioned above.

There is no charge to the companies that list in this book. Listings appearing in *Novel & Short Story Writer's Market* are compiled from detailed questionnaires, phone interviews and information provided by editors, publishers and awards directors. The publishing industry is volatile and changes of address, editor, policies and needs happen frequently. To keep up with the changes between editors of the book, we suggest you check the monthly Markets columns in *Writer's Digest*. Also check the market information on the *Writer's Market* website at www.writersmarket.com, or on the *Writer's Digest* website at www.writersdigest.com.

Club newsletters and small magazines devoted to helping writers also list market information. For those writers with access to online services, several offer writers' bulletin boards, message centers and chat lines with up-to-the-minute changes and happenings in the writing community. Many magazine and book publishers offer updated information for writers on their websites. Check individual listings for those website addresses.

We rely on our readers, as well, for new markets and information about market conditions. Write us if you have any new information or if you have suggestions on how to improve our listings to better suit your writing needs.

Specialized
Markets

For Mystery Writers.................................. 68

For Romance Writers.................................. 80

**For Science Fiction/Fantasy
& Horror Writers**....................................... 90

Ayelet Waldman: Writing Carpool to Carpool

BY W.E. REINKA

When Ayelet Waldman started her Mommy-Track mystery series, she went beyond 'write what you know' to "write what you are."

"I was on the mommy track," she recalls. "I wanted to write about that dilemma a woman faces when she gives up a demanding and interesting career and finds herself, much to her shock and confusion, staying home with her children like her grandmother and mother might have done."

In focusing on such a common but serious dilemma, Waldman has become a role model for writers who bemoan that there's nothing in their lives to write about. Her fan mail, 85 percent of which comes from women, indicates that Waldman's readers respond to her take on the choice between stay-at-home motherhood and a demanding career.

Ironically, Waldman did not set out to write mysteries. "The fact that I chose the mystery genre is more of an accident than what I chose to write about. I wrote my first book, *Nursery Crimes* (Prime Crime), as a mystery because I was too cowardly to write straight fiction right off the bat."

Ayelet Waldman

Photo © 2003 by Patty Williams

The series' wise-cracking, self-deprecating narrator, Juliet Applebaum, is as likely to tangle with nursing bra flaps as murder suspects. She adores her kids while conceding that playing Duplos with a toddler gets, well, boring. Humor works best when it contains germs of truth and, as Juliet stares at a closet of outgrown clothes, the reader laughs with her, not at her. "Juliet mysteries are fun to write," Waldman says. "I crack myself up. I don't know if I make anybody else laugh but I sure make myself laugh."

A Harvard-trained lawyer, Waldman gave up her job as a public defender in the federal court system after her first child, Sophie, was born,. She sometimes jokes that, while she wasn't technically writing fiction back then, her defenses of drug dealers did sometimes get creative.

W.E. REINKA, *who writes frequently about books and authors, contributes to magazines and newspapers nationwide.*

Even after she quit her job, it appeared that her husband, Pulitzer Prize-winning novelist Michael Chabon, would be the writer in the family.

Then Waldman started sneaking writing time during Sophie's naps. With some trepidation, she showed her first 50 pages to her husband. He encouraged her to "keep with it" and she has, through five Mommy Track mysteries: *Nursery Crimes*, *The Big Nap*, *A Playdate with Death*, *Death Gets a Time Out* and the forthcoming *Murder Plays House* (all Prime Crime titles).

Last year Waldman also published *Daughter's Keeper* (Sourcebooks), a more literary novel that taps her experience as a public defender in federal court. About a young woman swept away by zealous federal drug enforcement, *Daughter's Keeper* examines how she and her mother use personal tragedy to rebuild their relationship. Although the book feels light-years away from the Mommy Track mysteries, Waldman still draws on what she knows—the most gripping parts of the book come once the daughter enters the federal criminal justice system.

In the early installments of the Mommy Track series, it's hard to distinguish between Waldman and her fictional heroine, Juliet Applebaum. But, after several books, changes in Waldman's life and further development of Juliet's character mean they're no longer mirror images. "Juliet is definitely developing her own personality," Waldman says. "One thing is that I'm a lot more committed to my work than Juliet is. Writing started as a way for me to stay home with my children and it's become work that I'm really committed to. Even in later books, after Juliet opens her own private detective agency, she spends most of her time with her kids. I've learned to make time for my work. For instance, I have a babysitter now who comes in the morning to give me a few hours to work. That's not something Juliet would ever do."

"To me, discipline is the difference between a wannabe writer and a published one. It's about sitting down. If I waited for the muse, I'd be having pedicures every week. I presume that if you want to be a writer you have a certain love of language and a certain love of literature. It's all about taking yourself seriously, even if it's 350 words a day. Write a page a day and at the end of a year you'll have a novel."

Babysitter aside, Waldman still rides the Mommy Track. Daughter Sophie has been joined by three other siblings. With the family grown to six, "I write carpool to carpool," Waldman says. "I get the kids out the door in the morning, then I write until lunch time when my husband Michael and I talk about what we're both writing. After lunch, one of us picks up the kids and then my writing day is through. We're home in the afternoon with the kids."

Success allows Waldman to think like a writer, as well as a mother. She recalls that her fourth child, Abraham, was due about the same time as a Mommy Track installment. "People kept asking me 'When are you due?' And I'd answer, 'It's actually due June first but I want to get it in before I have the baby . . . Oh, you mean when is the baby due?'"

Though Waldman concedes that being married to a famous writer helped her find an agent, she earned her literary stripes through discipline. "To me, discipline is the difference between a wannabe writer and a published one. It's about sitting down. If I waited for the muse, I'd be having pedicures every week. I presume that if you want to be a writer you have a certain love of language and a certain love of literature. It's all about taking yourself seriously, even if it's 350 words a day. Write a page a day and at the end of a year you'll have a novel."

Waldman writes 1,500 words a day, not 350. While her schedule allows for about three hours writing time, when she reaches 1,500 words, she quits. "There are days when those 1,500 words come quickly and there are days when I have to eke out a little longer."

Just as her character Juliet Applebaum is refreshingly honest, Waldman doesn't dress the writing emperor in fancy clothes: "I love writing and I hate it," she says. "There are times when I'm sitting in constipated misery, hacking out my 1,500 words and I feel like Lucy in that Charlie Brown musical where's she's got an essay assignment with a word count and she's going 'very, very, very, very, very.' Those times are miserable."

She is similarly disciplined when it's time to re-write, assigning herself specific daily tasks. "The first thing I do is a fast re-write. I read the whole book in a week so I divide the total number of pages by five—for my five working days—then do that many pages each day." The second re-write takes a concentrated month. Again, Waldman divides the number of pages by her working days in a month for her daily assignments.

Once one becomes an established writer, the job includes publicity and promotions which Waldman enjoys. "I love doing the public appearances. I love reading to an audience and talking to an audience. I was a trial lawyer so you don't do that unless you're a little bit of a showboat. I even enjoy talking to reporters."

But life isn't always bliss, not even after several books. Waldman jokes about neurotically checking her Amazon sales ranking: "I fantasize about selling a gazillion copies of my books so that I never have to worry about selling a gazillion copies of my books."

Likewise, success doesn't mean that rejection stays in the rearview mirror. As usual, Waldman doesn't paint any rosy pictures. "Besides those days when it's not coming, the hardest part of writing is dealing with rejection. No matter how many people like your stuff, there are always people who don't and those people can post their views on the Internet. Somebody once called me 'moderately talented.' So days when it's not coming and I hate what I'm writing and I feel like a failure, I have this mantra as I type: 'Mod-er-ate-ly-tal-en-ted. Mod-er-ate-ly-tal-en-ted.'

The combination of internalized self-loathing and external validation of one's own self-loathing is the hardest part of being a writer."

Waldman concedes that, with success, she has become more self-confident but then quickly adds that confidence leads to more self-loathing because now she demands more of herself. All the same, she advises that feeling "insecure and miserable" after one has written six novels is different from sitting down to work feeling "insecure and miserable" as a new writer. "You need a certain amount of fear when you write but too much can be paralyzing. At least there's the knowledge, 'I have done this before. Worse comes to worst, I can write something as awful as everything else I've written. I don't know if I can be any better but I can be that bad.' "

At least until the next carpool, when the process starts all over again.

Hitchcock and Queen: Detecting Strong Fiction for Half a Century

BY I.J. SCHECTER

Alfred Hitchcock Mystery Magazine and *Ellery Queen Mystery Magazine* are two mainstays in a constantly-evolving industry. Launched in 1956 and 1941, respectively, these two venerable journals are well respected for putting out quality fiction year after year. And they remain two of the most prized markets for mystery and suspense writers, boasting circulations of 600,000 and 300,000, and paying competitive rates to both new and established writers.

Janet Hutchings

Photo © Roger Lemoine/Ace Photographic

At *Ellery Queen Mystery Magazine* (*EQMM*), more than 700 aspiring writers have seen their debut in the monthly Department of First Stories feature. Intended to set new literary standards for the mystery genre, *EQMM* has published more than 40 Nobel and Pulitzer prize winners since its inception—among them Norman Mailer, Alice Walker, Ernest Hemingway and Rudyard Kipling.

Each issue of *Alfred Hitchcock Mystery Magazine* (*AHMM*), features at least seven new mystery short stories, ranging from short-shorts to novellas. And writers published there have won Edgars, Shamuses, and Robert L. Fish awards for best first mystery short story of the year.

Linda Landrigan was promoted to editor-in-chief of *AHMM* in January of 2002, having ascended the ranks from her first position as editorial assistant, when she was first hired in 1996. Janet Hutchings has served as editor-in-chief of *EQMM* since 1991, after serving as an editor of mystery fiction for Walker & Co. Here, Landrigan and Hutchings share their thoughts on how best to submit your manuscript, what makes a mystery short story stand out for them, and how the genre has evolved.

What's your typical day like?

LL: My *ideal* day—though I know you didn't ask—is one in which I have long uninterrupted hours for concentrated reading and editing. But my typical day involves a lot of varied tasks and problem solving: getting the right computer equipment for my staff, scheduling upcoming issues, calling publishers for cover art to use in our book review column, and so forth.

JH: Indeed. The typical day is nowhere near as glamorous as an editor's job is often depicted to be. We have a lot of routine paperwork to attend to, just as in any other office—the kind of stuff that keeps a business running. Since we produce the magazines through desktop publishing, we also have a lot of work to do that formerly would have belonged to a typesetter. Then, of course, there's manuscript reading, letters to write, art to choose, and layouts to be determined. At certain times it

---

I.J. SCHECTER *is a freelance writer of fiction and essays. His latest book, a collection of short stories, is titled* The Bottom of the Mug. *His nonfiction frequently appears in* Novel & Short Story Writer's Market, *and in publications throughout the U.S. and Canada.*

gets a little more exciting—when authors are in town for awards banquets, for instance.

Do stories stay with you after the workday is over?

LL: Sure—great stories stay with me for years sometimes.

JH: I agree completely. In fact, I rarely buy a story immediately upon reading it. The stories will usually sit for a while after a day of reading and then I'll be clearer, a few days later, on what has stuck with me, which stories I liked best. When you read as much as we do, and can buy only a very few stories, it's necessary to discriminate in this way.

What, for you, makes a manuscript really sing?

LL: I look for writing that is tight, yet has a musicality and rhythm. I like to see a fully imagined world of the story, with strong characters and logical plotting that is evenly paced. I like to be surprised by a story, but I don't like surprise endings; like most mystery readers I enjoy the process of arriving at a solution as much as the final unveiling of the truth.

JH: It really is so many different things. There are different kinds of appealing stories: those I buy because of a clever plot, those that have an unforgettable voice, those with characters I can't shake, those with special atmosphere . . . it goes on.

What proportion of manuscripts reach your desk?

LL: About five percent.

JH: I look at everything, but about 75% of the manuscripts, those from unpublished authors, get read first by my associate editor. I pay special attention to those she recommends, but everything gets at least a brief look from an editor.

What are your thoughts as you read a new submission?

LL: I always anticipate loving the story.

JH: I don't think about it; I just start reading the manuscript. Unless I like the manuscript, I don't read the cover letter at all. I don't want to be influenced by what the author has to say about his story or his credits, for one thing. I just try to let the story speak for itself.

How much of a manuscript do you have to read before you know whether it's a winner?

LL: I know how difficult it is for writers—so to be as fair as possible, I try to read the entire story, unless it's obviously wrong for us.

JH: You can usually tell within the first sentence or two whether the author has control. Then you'll either be taken in by the actual story or not. Of course, even if the author has the knack for storytelling, there may still be problems. And as Linda said, some stories—no matter how good they are—simply aren't appropriate for the magazine.

You receive two publishable manuscripts but have room for only one. How do you decide?

LL: I think about what I may already have in inventory (manuscripts that I have already bought but haven't scheduled yet). Is one of the stories similar in type or tone to what I have or to what I have already published?

JH: We keep an inventory as well, so it's more a matter of which dozen of several dozen stories we'll buy. And there are so many possible factors, one being, as Linda noted, how many of each type of story we already have on hand.

What do you want to see in a cover letter?

LL: I like to see a little personal information about the author, especially publishing history, but also special areas of expertise that may bear upon the story.

JH: I like to know whether the author has been published before, because this tells us whether he or she is eligible for our Department of First Stories. We don't care about much else. If we buy the story, we'll ask for a bio then.

Photo © Roger Lemoine/Ace Photographic

Linda Landrigan

What are the top three submission don'ts?

LL: Don't strain to be trendy. Don't submit without knowing the magazine well. At least read a few issues first. And don't send a messy, typo-ridden, poorly edited manuscript.

JH: Don't fail to date your submission. If the stack gets mixed up and there's no date, you could wait a long time to hear from us. Don't use fancy type or fancy paper or all caps or italics or small type. Don't phone the editorial offices. Use reference books to get information and make all queries by regular mail.

Do you react the same way to a great story now as when you first started?

LL: I think I have a deeper appreciation and love for the art of the short story now.

JH: I'm still thrilled by a great story when I come across it, and that will never change.

What do you find harder for most writers, plot or characterization?

LL: Characterization. Characters must be fully—encyclopedically—imagined. Even minor characters. Plots happen because of the characters. I see too many stereotypes.

JH: I don't think one is inherently harder than the other, but it can be difficult to master both. It depends on the particular writer's talents.

Are there particular themes you see too much or too little of? Have certain types of stories been done to death, or are there always new ways to write even the oldest premises?

LL: A fresh approach to any situation in a story is necessary, I think. In general, spousal murders have been overdone. I am usually bored by stories about serial killers or by psychological explorations of a murderer's mind.

JH: Yes, certain themes can become tiresome quickly if not handled in an original way. I agree that the number of spouse-murder stories we see ought to make anyone afraid to get married. However, there are always new ways to write even the oldest ideas if the writer is talented and committed enough.

How can a writer determine whether he should submit to Alfred Hitchcock or Ellery Queen?

LL: Every editor has a unique sensibility. Here the standard answer is the right one: read a number of issues of each magazine, decide which you love more, then submit to that one.

JH: That's exactly right—the only way is to read each magazine. You'll definitely get a sense of the difference.

Is there a better or worse time of year to submit?

LL: No. Around September we usually get a number of Christmas-themed stories, but by that time the holiday issue (our January issue, which comes out in December) has already been sent to print. But at that time I'll eagerly read a Christmas or Hanukkah story for the next holiday issue.

JH: There is no best time to submit. We buy year-round.

Are stories appearing in your magazine often nominated for prizes? What's the nomination process?

LL: We submit all of our stories for the Edgar Allan Poe Award for best mystery short story, the private eye stories for the Shamus Award for best PI story, and the first published mystery stories for the Robert L. Fish Award. AHMM stories have won numerous awards.

JH: EQMM has had approximately 90 award nominations and around 25 winners over the past dozen years, and hundreds over the magazine's 62-year history. The nomination process is different for each award. The Edgar, the Shamus and the Arthur Ellis are by committee. The Anthony and the Agatha involve votes of convention attendees.

How has short fiction evolved during your career?

LL: I see a difference in style and tone in the early issues from the 50's and 60's. Those stories are tighter and plot-focused, less concerned with issues. Stories now have a different world to answer to.

JH: There's also come to be more diversity in the types of stories being written. When I began at EQMM most of our submissions were twist-in-the-tail suspense pieces. Now we also see a lot of PI stories, whodunits, crime stories, and so forth.

Who are your all-time favorite writers?

LL: Angela Carter, Eudora Welty, Margaret Atwood, Margaret Miller. I could go on and on.

JH: There are a number, but one of my all-time favorite mystery short-story writers who comes immediately to mind is Stanley Ellin.

What is your vision for the future?

LL: My aim is to continue a highly distinguished publishing history, to celebrate the mystery genre, and to call attention to undiscovered writers worthy of recognition.

JH: We've just started a new feature called Passport to Crime, in which we publish a story per month in translation, each month from a different country. We may continue with that, though we're giving it a one-year test first. Beyond that, my goals are the same ones Linda has articulated: to continue the high quality and diversity of fiction for which we've been known for so long and to help talented writers find a place for their work.

To find out more about Alfred Hitchcock Mystery Magazine *or* Ellery Queen Mystery Magazine, *visit www.themysteryplace.com.*

David Schanker: "Scratch a lawyer, find a writer"

BY WILL ALLISON

Like a lot of the other lawyers he meets, David Schanker always wanted to be a novelist. "There is an expression—'Scratch a lawyer, find a writer'—and it is absolutely true," he says.

David Schanker

What separates Schanker from most attorneys is that he's actually gone out and done it, publishing two acclaimed legal thrillers, *A Criminal Appeal* (1998)—nominated for the 1999 Edgar Award for Best First Novel-and *Natural Law* (2001), both from St. Martin's Press.

Though Schanker has no particular affinity for legal thrillers, he's chosen to work in the genre because the law is such an incredibly fertile source of stories.

"The law is all about human conflict and its resolution, and, in criminal cases particularly, it's about extremes of human behavior," he says. "Every case, whether civil or criminal, is a story of a problem and of human beings struggling against others or against their own nature. Studying the law has enriched my writing tremendously; I'd go so far as to say that it's given me a subject for my career."

Here, Schanker discusses how he came to be a novelist and how he balances his legal life with his literary life.

Which came first for you, writing or the law?

After graduating NYU in 1979 with a degree in film, I expected that I would make my career in some aspect of the film industry, but after a couple of years of working as a film editor (most notably as post-production supervisor on the notorious *I Spit on Your Grave*), I knew I wanted to write. I started by writing plays, and secured myself a position as an artist-in-residence at a small experimental off-off-Broadway theatre company called ReCherChez. A friend who was a writer suggested that one of my short plays, a monologue entitled "Watertower," would be suitable for publication as a short story. I submitted it to several journals, and it was published in *TriQuarterly* in 1982. That experience encouraged me to write more short fiction, and after several more acceptances, I decided to dive into fiction writing wholeheartedly. I applied to the MFA program at Columbia University and began there in the fall of 1984.

I expected that my writing degree from Columbia would enable me to get a job teaching creative writing at a college or university, a position I expected would enable me to write my

WILL ALLISON *is former editor-at-large for* Zoetrope: All-Story, *former executive editor of* Story, *and former editor of* Novel & Short Story Writer's Market. *He is also a staff member at the Squaw Valley Community of Writers and the recipient of a 2000 Ohio Arts Council Grant for fiction.*

novels while bringing home an income that would at least sustain me and my family. I was wrong about that. I had not realized the degree to which creative writing teachers were undervalued by academia. The salaries were very low, and there were, at that time, no tenure-track positions for creative writers. So I continued to work a variety of clerical jobs while writing, and eventually I decided that law school was my best bet for finding an intellectually stimulating, well-paying job.

I should say, though, that while my Columbia degree did not prove a practical success, I learned a great deal about the craft of writing as a student there. Among my teachers were John Irving, Judith Rossner, William Wilson, and Robert Towers, and my classmates included the now-famous Peter Farrelly (of the Farrelly Brothers), Tama Janowitz, Rick Moody, Jill Eisenstadt, Helen Schulman, and others lesser known. It was a wonderful experience to be part of that community of writers.

I did stop writing fiction while I was a law student, and at one point I felt certain that my writing days were over. Law school, particularly in the first year, is like boot camp—there is an overwhelming amount of work to be done, and the psychological pressure is tremendous. But in my third year of law school, when I had time to read fiction again, I started to jot some short fictional sketches about my law school experiences—sketches that eventually made their way into my second novel, *Natural Law*—and the joy of it was like coming home after a long absence.

How do you find time to work and write novels?

I am an early morning writer. I awaken at 4:30 each morning to write, and I try to get a good hour to an hour-and-a-half of writing done before it's time to wake up the family and get the day started. I consider that time to be made up of stolen moments. It's like the driving one does before the sun comes up when embarking on a long trip by car. It's not the most efficient way to work, and I'm perpetually sleep-deprived, but it makes for a good separation between my writing life and my legal life.

You publish under the name D.R. Schanker. Did you choose D.R. instead of David as a way of separating your legal and literary lives?

I chose to go with initials because of my infatuation with a few of those writers who went the same route: D.H. Lawrence, E.L. Doctorow, E.B.White, P.D. James, A.S. Byatt. It really didn't have anything to do with maintaining a separation between my careers.

At this point, I am managing to maintain a very comfortable balance between writing and the law. In my current position, I don't practice law; I work as chief of staff to the clerk of the Indiana Supreme Court. It's a job that has legal and administrative responsibilities, but I don't have cases to win or clients to please, and that makes it much less stressful than the practice. I'm thus able to free more of my time and mental energy for fiction and teaching.

How would you characterize the relationship between your legal career and your writing career?

I have to credit law school with enabling me to develop the discipline necessary to succeed as a writer. Law school forced me to get organized, to develop good study habits, to prioritize my time. Those are skills I carried over into my writing life; they enabled me not only to complete my first novel, but to persist in seeing it published and to maintain a teaching career alongside my legal and writing careers.

Aside from the fact that you're a lawyer and know the terrain, are there other reasons you choose to write legal thrillers?

I'm not particularly a fan of the legal thriller genre—I read only as much of Grisham, Turow, Fairstein, Rosenberg, etc. as I need to keep up with the market. But I find that the essential nature of the genre—that is, of centering upon conflicts between the individual and society—provides me with an excellent medium to explore the issues I care about: life, love, race, politics, sex, God, the universe, etc.

The heroine of your novels, Nora Lumsey, is an Indianapolis attorney. To what extent do your books draw upon your experiences as a lawyer in Indianapolis?

My first novel, *A Criminal Appeal*, drew upon my experiences as a law clerk for a judge on the court of appeals—my first job coming out of law school. It's the story of a law clerk who becomes dangerously involved in a case that the judge she works for is deciding. My second novel, *Natural Law*, drew upon my law school experience, but its plot—dealing with the relationships between a rural police detective, a public defender, a pair of trailer park prostitutes, and a psychopathic basketball coach—was based upon research. I see my legal experience and knowledge as providing the foundation of reality upon which my ideas can grow.

Can you provide an example of a real-life character or incident that ended up in your fiction? Is libel ever a concern?

My characters are often an amalgam of real people. Nora Lumsey, for example, is modeled on a particular kind of stubborn, big-boned Hoosier woman who draws strength from her rural roots. On the other hand, the basketball coach in Natural Law is a fictional character inspired by the public persona of a certain well-known Hoosier coach with anger-management problems. But I dare not speak his name. Fiction writers must be as careful as journalists when it comes to libel, defamation, or slander; even a groundless lawsuit can be ruinously expensive for a writer.

You also teach college writing courses. Does your legal background come in handy in the classroom?

Yes, in a number of ways. My courtroom experience has given me the confidence to deal with unruly undergraduates, and I am able to offer my students the disciplined, process-oriented approach to writing that I learned in law school and have applied to my fiction writing. Also, having suffered through my professors' use of the Socratic method in law school, I have no compunctions about calling upon students at random to answer my questions. The students hate it, as I did, but it works well to keep my classes focused.

Why do you write fiction instead of nonfiction?

I am a fiction writer by instinct—that is, I love to tell stories—but I have no interest in journalism. I like the freedom that fiction gives me to use my imagination to explore the emotional and psychological undercurrents of people and events that I may draw from the real world. In preparing to write *Natural Law*, for example, I read the transcripts of several court cases involving prostitutes, and I came to understand some factual aspects of that business. But in writing the novel, I had the opportunity to consider the thoughts that might occur to my prostitute character—that's the difference.

Resources for Mystery Writers

Below is a list of invaluable resources specifically for mystery writers. To order any of the Writer's Digest Books titles or to get a consumer book catalog, call 1-800-448-0915. You may also order Writer's Digest Books selections through www.writersdigest.com, Amazon.com, or www.barnesandnoble.com.

MAGAZINES:
- *Mystery Readers Journal*, Mystery Readers International, P.O. Box 8116, Berkeley CA 94707.
- *Writer's Digest*, 4700 East Galbraith Rd., Cincinnati OH 45236. Website: www.writersdigest.com

BOOKS:
Howdunit series (Writer's Digest Books):
- *Private Eyes: A Writer's Guide to Private Investigators*, by Hal Blythe, Charlie Sweet and John Landreth
- *Missing Persons: A Writer's Guide to Finding the Lost, the Abducted and the Escaped*, by Fay Faron
- *Deadly Doses: A Writer's Guide to Poisons*, by Serita Deborah Stevens
- *Cause of Death: A Writer's Guide to Death, Murder & Forensic Medicine*, by Keith D. Wilson, M.D.
- *Scene of the Crime: A Writer's Guide to Crime Scene Investigation*, by Anne Wingate, Ph.D.
- *Urge to Kill: How Police Take Homicide from Case to Court*, by Martin Edwards
- *Just the Facts, Ma'am: A Writer's Guide to Investigators and Investigation Techniques*, by Greg Fallis
- *Rip-off: A Writer's Guide to Crimes of Deception*, by Fay Faron

Other Writer's Digest books for mystery writers:
- *The Criminal Mind, A Writer's Guide to Forensic Psychology*, by Katherine Ramsland
- *Howdunit: How Crimes are Committed and Solved*, by John Boertlein
- *Writing Mysteries: A Handbook by the Mystery Writers of America*, edited by Sue Grafton
- *You Can Write a Mystery*, by Gillian Roberts

ORGANIZATIONS & ONLINE:
- The Mystery Writers' Forum. Website: www.zott.com/mysforum/.
- Mystery Writers of America, 17 E. 47th St., 6th Floor, New York NY 10017. Website: www.mysterywriters.org.
- The Private Eye Writers of America, 4342 Forest DeVille Dr., Apt. H, St. Louis MO 63129. Website: http://hometown.aol.com/rrandisi/myhomepage/writing.html.
- Sisters in Crime, P.O. Box 442124, Lawrence KS 66044-8933. Website: www.sistersincrime.org.
- www.writersmarket.com
- www.writersdigest.com

Katherine Sutcliffe: Moving to the Dark Side of Romance

BY DEBORAH BOUZIDEN

Katherine Sutcliffe had just finished editing proofs for *Dream Fever* (Severn House), her tenth book, when a commotion from the kitchen startled her. Going to investigate, she rounded the corner just as the last piece of sheet rock fell from the kitchen ceiling and landed at her feet. "A hard freeze had caused the water pipes to burst in our attic," she says, "and collapsed the entire thing."

By the time the insurance money arrived, Sutcliffe was ready to begin promoting *Dream Fever*. In 1992, finances were tight, but she knew to promote the book and get it noticed, she needed money. Sutcliffe presented a plan to her husband: she could use the insurance money for promotion. He left the decision to her. "It was easy," she says. "I covered the ceiling with plastic trash bags and used the money to promote."

The move paid off. *Dream Fever* was her first book to hit the top 10 on chain store bestseller lists, and the advance for her next book was enough to fix the kitchen ceiling.

Sutcliffe has been writing for as long as she can remember. While growing up, her best friends were books, notebooks and pencils. At age 13, she collaborated with a school mate, and the pair penned a thousand-page epic about a young girl who falls for a rock star. As a young adult, she wrote short stories on napkins while sitting in a booth at a local restaurant.

In 1982, when Sutcliffe quit her job as a headhunter for a computer personnel company to stay home with her children, she decided to get serious about writing, and wrote her first novel. Even though it was rejected, she continued to write—producing three more novels—until in 1985 Avon Books bought *Desire and Surrender*, her first historical romance. Sutcliffe's career took off and she hasn't looked back.

To date, Sutcliffe has had 18 novels and 6 novellas published, and she has 10 million books in print in this country alone. Nearly all of her books have hit chain store lists or the *USA Today* list. Sutcliffe's work continues to be recognized. Her 2000 bestseller *Notorious* was featured on iVillage.com as one of the seven best romances of the year, and her contemporary romance/suspense thriller *Darkling I Listen* (Jove) won the Francis Readers Award for best romantic suspense. Sutcliffe is a two-time winner of *Romantic Times*' Readers Choice Awards, and in 2001 she won *RT*'s Career Achievement Award for Storyteller of the Year.

DEBORAH BOUZIDEN *has been writing and publishing since 1985. She currently has six books available, which you can learn more about on her website at www.deborahbouziden.com.*

Here, Sutcliffe talks about her sources of inspiration, allowing her romance writing to grow and change, and the challenges facing new writers today.

How did you get the idea for your first published book, *Desire and Surrender?*

The idea came to me during a vacation to San Antonio. The story revolved around a Spanish family in San Antonio, Texas, during the Battle of the Alamo. My husband and I were at a restaurant when the lights went dim and a couple of Spanish dancers began to perform. They were so beautiful in their costumes, their dance so sexy. They flipped the switch on in my brain and for the remainder of the vacation, I crammed in all the research I could.

What kind of books do you read, and why?

I've always enjoyed the darker books more. Mostly all I've read for the last 13 years are suspense thrillers and horror. My favorite author is Stephen King, and my most prized possession, besides my children, is an autographed copy of *Misery* signed by King: "To Katherine, from your number one fan, Stephen King." I have it on a pedestal and bow in homage to it every night.

Speaking of darker books, you have stepped sideways a bit, moving away from historical romance to romantic suspense. What precipitated the move?

I had come to a crossroads in my writing. I found myself pushing the historical romance genre boundaries more and more. My frustration as a writer grew as I was forced to constantly check myself because the work was getting too dark or twisted for the genre. I was being torn between the obligations of conforming my writing to genre standards, and my desire to be all that I could be, and that meant going with my strengths and my love for writing the darker side of the human psyche.

This began in 1989, with my *Love's Illusion*. It was a historical suspense—really the first of its kind in the romance genre—about a magician who was suspected of being Jack the Ripper. I recall my editor Jackie Cantor calling and asking me if I'd had a tortured childhood—I took it as a compliment. She was the first editor who encouraged me to break out of the romance genre, pointing out that my voice was stronger when I wrote darker.

I knew that leaving historical romance and moving into the contemporary suspense market would mean starting over. Alas, making that kind of move wasn't easy, not when my entire career and name recognition had been built in historical romance. A publisher isn't eager to allow an established writer to make such an abrupt switch. And frankly, no one in publishing (except my agent) believed I could pull it off. They had no proof that I could even write a contemporary, much less a suspense thriller.

I thank God every day that an old friend and editor, Christine Zika from Avon Books, happened to move to Berkley Jove. She recognized and understood my strengths, and encouraged them. She stuck her neck out for me, which is really rare for editors these days, and said "go for it." I was in the hospital the day she called to offer me a contract for my first contemporary suspense, *Darkling I Listen*. I promised I wouldn't let her down. For the first three months of writing *Darkling*, I was hobbled to my computer, but I had never been happier in my writing career. At last I had the freedom to do my thing, and by God, I did it.

How have readers responded?

My readers have responded very enthusiastically to my romantic suspense books. But my readers are, and have been, my readers because they anticipate and appreciate my dark style of story telling. They're simply getting it in contemporary settings instead of historical.

You've been publishing books for more than 10 years now. What changes have you seen in readers and authors?

There is a greater diversity of books being published now. The genres have evolved so every reader can more easily find the kind of book they enjoy. For authors, such as myself, who once didn't fit perfectly into a specific genre niche, we now have subgenres where we can allow our voices and styles to flourish.

What is the most important thing an author must know or do with his characters?

Characterization is the most important element in any book. I develop my plots around a character's emotional crisis, which motivates his every thought, action and reaction.

When I begin to build a story, I might start with an inkling of an idea for a crisis (plot), as in a stalker after a movie star (*Darkling I Listen*), serial killer slaughtering women Jack-the-Ripper style (*Bad Moon Rising*), then I focus on the protagonist and antagonist, and develop that characterization in a manner that makes the crisis personal. I look at who, what, and why this is happening, and most importantly, what brought them to this sad and/or terrifying point in their lives. So I go back to the beginning—to the characters' childhoods—and begin to formulate the foundation of their lives that developed them into adults that must, in the present, face their demons. This means going deeply into the psyche of the characters, and that's what I most enjoy writing—showing exactly what makes a character tick. I do believe the reader gets more entertainment reading about characters they can in some way connect with, and you can't do that without making the characters human.

Why is self-promotion important? What must authors know about publishing before they start writing?

It's very important for writers to educate themselves about the business of publishing long before they actually sell a book. Understanding the process up front will prepare the writer for the often-brutal realities of the business.

A writer who has, at last, sold her first book must realize that rarely is a publisher going to promote or market a new author who is generally slammed into midlist. A writer must realize that they are a business—self-employed. Anyone going into their own business must promote and market the business if they hope to succeed.

Have your promotional efforts changed as your career has advanced?

My promotion hasn't changed a bit, especially now that I've moved into romantic suspense. I'm reaching out to a new readership, so promotion is an important now as it was in 1986 with the publication of my first book.

What is your best piece of advice for new writers?

Set realistic goals. R-E-A-L-I-S-T-I-C! Define success. If a writer is going into this business for fame and fortune only, forget it. For an aspiring author, success should be strictly the selling of the manuscript, and the continued selling of manuscripts. If money and bestseller lists happen along the way that is simply the icing on the cake.

Also, continue to learn the craft. Try to make each book better, stronger. Never settle for adequate. Learn that the delete button is your best friend. Know that every time you do a rewrite, the book is going to shine that much brighter.

The Romance Market: Ever-Evolving, Welcoming New Writers

BY ROBIN GEE

Your heroine and hero have surpassed seemingly insurmountable obstacles to their love and are finally together; now they can begin to live happily ever after. As the writer of their story, however, it's just the beginning for you. A well-written manuscript with exciting characters and a well-developed plot is only your first step; the next is to market your book to editors in a way that will get it more than just a quick glance.

This isn't as difficult as it may seem. Overall, the market is good for romance fiction. According to industry figures, romances account for more than a third of all popular fiction sales, and generate more than $1 billion in sales each year. And as of 2002, there were 51.1 million readers of romance in the U.S.

Nevertheless, publishers continue to be cautious, spending more time and advertising dollars on established authors rather than newer writers. Competition remains keen and it takes a combination of a good story, talented writing and marketing savvy to make it.

Finding a publisher requires as much care and effort as researching and writing your novel. With romance, it's primarily important to know exactly what type of romance you are writing. Is it historical? Is it contemporary? Does it contain a lot of humor? Do your characters travel through time? There are publishers and imprints for each of these types and more, but sending to the wrong ones will mark you as an amateur and result in unnecessary rejection.

The cardinal rule is: Read. Reading what's on the shelves is the easiest way of determining which publisher will be interested in your manuscript. If, for example, you plan to submit your book to Harlequin's Temptation line, read the current Temptation releases and then go to a used bookstore and look for as many past releases as you can find. Be aware that this is a love-it-or-leave-it genre; if the idea of reading a lot of romance novels puts you off, you shouldn't be trying to write them.

NOVEL MARKETS

Most romance novels are published by large, commercial publishers. Some, like Harlequin, are devoted entirely to romance, while others, like Kensington or Avon, have large romance imprints. There's a wide variety of romances being published, too. You'll find lines devoted to historicals, contemporaries, paranormal romance and time travel. Each line may also include several series such as Montana Mavericks or American Romance. Newer lines, such as Harlequin's Red Dress Ink and Simon & Schuster's Downtown Press, update traditional romance with plot lines and content intended to appeal to a more urban, hip chick. Some series feature one author, while others feature several authors writing about a common theme.

According to RWA statistics, almost half of all mass-market paperbacks are romance novels. This is where romance publishing got its start. Mass-market paperbacks are small, paperbound books usually priced between four and seven dollars. Writers on all career levels are published in this format, but most new writers start here.

Paperback romances have changed drastically from the early days of romance publishing. With a few exceptions, category romances used to be sold by the line, each one with a different cover logo so readers could identify the different lines. Authors' names were mostly pen names and were not displayed as prominently as the name of the line. While publishers continue to publish books in each of several different and distinct lines, books are now sold less by line and more by author and series.

Although you'll still find the popular "clinch" cover, with the hero and heroine in a steamy embrace, many publishers are moving away from this. Some romances now have subtle floral patterns or other such designs on the cover. Others use a combination called a "step-back" cover. A step-back is really two covers; a pattern, title and author's name on an outer cover with a couple embracing on the inside. The outer cover is usually shorter than the width of the book and sometimes has a window cut into it, framing the couple's faces. Red Dress Ink and Downtown Press covers often feature four-color photography and high-end design, and are nearly indistinguishable as romances.

Bestselling authors and those who write romances with wide appeal also appear in hardcover. Some are brought out in both hard and soft cover formats; buying the rights to both formats from a writer is typically called a hard/soft deal.

Right now there are few markets in the small and independent press for romances, unless it's a book that is literary or is aimed at a specific audience. Christian romances, for example, do very well with Christian publishers. Young adult romances can appeal to both large and small book publishers specializing in titles for young adults and children. Book packagers produce books for other publishers and quite often work with series books. Romances, especially those aimed at teens, do well in this area and some packagers may also be open to romance series for adults.

SHORT STORY MARKETS

Magazines devoted exclusively to romantic fiction appear from time to time, but unfortunately do not stay on the scene long. Mainstream women's magazines, however, remain open to stories with romance elements and some of these pay very well. Stories that mix genres—especially romantic suspense—are in demand by some of these publications. Christian magazines are also open to romance stories as are magazines aimed at seniors and teens.

Most of the large, commercial romance publishers also publish anthologies, another market for short fiction. These tend to be open mostly to established authors, but one or two slots are usually left open to new writers who have published at least one promising novel. Many are themed; holiday and travel-themed anthologies are very popular. The best way to find out about these is to watch your bookstore shelves for possible anthology series. If there's an anthology you think your story would fit, write the editor to find out if a new edition is being planned. Also, visit conventions and attend meetings of organizations such as the Romance Writers of America—networking can bring you leads on new anthology projects.

CHOOSING A MARKET FOR YOUR NOVEL

The first place to learn about book publishers and their various lines is at your local bookstore or library. It's easier than ever today to find romance series or all of the books of a favorite author. More and more publishers are reissuing series of bestselling authors and, with more shelf space in the big superstores, you're sure to find all the books you're after. There are a large number of independent used bookstores which stock romance and, now, many of these have added new titles as well. An avid reader can stock up on past books by favorite authors and even trade old ones for others.

A membership to Romance Writers of America can be most beneficial to the marketing efforts of both new and established romance writers. The group publishes the *Romance Writers Report*, a monthly publication full of market information and advice along with news about the organization. Magazines aimed at readers as well as authors, such as *Romantic Times*, can also keep you up-to-date with what's happening in the field. RWA also sponsors several conferences across the country and maintains a presence in many online forums.

As an important part of your research of the market, study the listings in this book. Develop a short list of publishers you think might be interested in your romance, then write to request their guidelines. Publishers once issued long, involved writers' guidelines for each of their lines. Now the guidelines are shorter and more flexible, but you can still obtain these and descriptions of the various lines from all the major publishers. Guidelines highlight the difference between lines and series, making it easier to identify the right publisher for your book.

ABOUT AGENTS

You do not need an agent to send a short story to a magazine. Most agents will handle short stories only if they already handle your novel, and then they do it mostly as a courtesy. For book submissions, however, a good agent can still give you an edge.

It is still possible to send unagented submissions to most romance publishers, and many writers do. Because of the volume of submissions, other types of publishers have turned to agents as a way to screen out some manuscripts, treating agents almost as "first readers." In the romance field, however, most publishers still rely on their editors to do this initial screening. Many offer standard contracts to new authors and it's hard for a writer or agent to negotiate a better deal.

While romance publishers say having an agent does not necessarily give you the edge, you may want to secure one anyway to look out for your interests or just for the peace of mind an agent can give you. Many writers who secure agents early on feel it is worth the money because they can let the agent be the "bad guy," handling contract negotiations calling editors about late payments and acting as a liaison for any author-editor disputes, regardless of how minor. Since they are just establishing a relationship with the editor, they feel these services are worth the agent's commission. Others simply feel it is their job to write the book, and an agent's job to sell it, acknowledging that a good agent knows much more about the market and has much better contacts.

Once you become an established name, however, an agent is a necessity. When discussing multi-book contracts and foreign rights, a good agent is a definite asset. And as your career grows, your agent will assist you in keeping it on track and can advise you of the best way to handle any non-romance projects you may wish to pursue.

Since it can be as hard to find a good agent as it is to find a publisher, some writers market their first book themselves and then look for an agent once they have a published book or at least a contract in hand. If you decide to look for an agent, look first at the listings of agents in this book. Many of these agents specialize in romance and know the different lines and their editors. The Romance Writers of America also publishes a list of romance agents.

Word of mouth is another good way to find an agent. The RWA regularly invites agents to speak at its conferences, where you can make an appointment to meet with one. Talking to other romance writers at conferences, at meetings and on computer bulletin boards is another good way to find out about various agents.

Approach an agent as you would a publisher, with a query letter and sample chapters or a complete manuscript, depending on the agent's guidelines. It is generally acceptable to query more than one agent at a time, but avoid sending complete manuscripts to more than one agent for consideration.

Take your time when looking for an agent and don't be afraid to ask questions. After all, your agent will be your business partner. You want to go into business with someone you trust, someone you feel has your best interests at heart. Don't hesitate to ask for references and be wary of agents who charge large fees up front. Agents who do not charge up front fees make their money from their commission (usually 15 percent) when the book is sold. An agent who charges a lot of money just to read your manuscript has less incentive to sell your book and paying a reading fee is not a guarantee of representation.

MANUSCRIPT MECHANICS

Professional presentation is important whether you're approaching an agent or publisher. Granted, a poorly written manuscript will not make much of an impression, no matter how dazzling its presentation. Yet, a well-written manuscript will remain in the slush pile only to be returned if it is sloppy and hard to read.

Ensure that your manuscript will be read and your talent has a fighting chance by making your manuscript as easy for the editor to read as possible. Manuscripts should be double-spaced with wide margins and free of typos and errors. Pay attention to details. Before printing, make sure your ink or toner cartridge is fresh, and choose a paper that will hold up to being passed around from editor to editor, such as a white bond.

Include your name, address and phone number with your submission; put your name and a consecutive page number at the top of each page. With all this in mind, however, don't worry too much about where your name or title should be placed. The bottom line is that your manuscript should be as accessible and easy to read as possible.

QUERIES, COVER LETTERS AND MANUSCRIPT FORMATS

If you are approaching book publishers and are asked to query first, chances are you will need to include a sample of your writing and some form of story outline. In fiction, your query letter should be as brief as possible. You are simply asking if they would be interested in seeing your manuscript. Keep the letter to one page, preferably only a few paragraphs. You may choose to start your letter with a hook—something special about your story, something to catch the editor's eye—but keep the hard sell to a minimum.

Be sure to identify what type of romance you have written. Show that you've done your research by mentioning which of the publisher's lines it would best fit. Information about yourself that lends credibility to your story should also be included, but avoid extraneous personal material. For example, if your heroine meets her hero in Spain and you have lived in Spain for two years, by all means mention it. If she's an independent bookstore owner and you work in such a store, that would be worth mentioning, too. Beyond this, avoid giving details about your job, hobbies, family or pets if they have nothing to do with your story. Other information to include in your query would be an estimated word count and a few of your publishing credits, if you have any. Occasionally, you will be asked to send a bio. This is usually a one- or two-paragraph biographical statement, including a brief description of your achievements.

When sending sample chapters, send three consecutive chapters. Most publishers prefer the first three. Editors want to know how your work flows and how you move from one chapter to the next.

Include a cover sheet with either a partial or complete manuscript. Put your name, address and phone number in the upper left hand corner of the page and the word count in the right. Agented authors often leave the right hand corner open for their agent's name and address, and some agents prefer their contact information to be the only material included on the cover sheet.

Center your title and byline about halfway down the page. Start your first chapter on the next page. If your chapter has a title, include it about one-third of the way down the page. Include your last name and page number in the upper right-hand corner of this and subsequent pages. Be sure the number the entire submission consecutively, all the way through to the end of the manuscript.

Along with a query and sample chapters, you may be asked to include a synopsis, outline or summary. Unfortunately, publishers tend to use these terms interchangeably, so when in doubt, check with the publisher first. A synopsis is a brief summation of your story, condensed into a page or a page-and-a-half, single spaced. An outline can from five to twenty pages, double-spaced. An outline usually follows the chapters throughout the book, listing chapter headings and a few lines about what happens in each chapter. A summary is the most subjective of these terms. Before submitting a summary of your manuscript, it's best to ask the publisher how long and detailed it should be.

For magazines and many book publishers, you will be asked to send a complete manuscript. With a complete story or novel, you include a cover letter rather than a query. Cover letters should be kept simple and again, short. Don't tell too much about your story. After all, it's there for the editor to read. Basically, you're saying: "Here I am. Here is my romance novel." As with a query letter, include what type of romance it is, what line you feel it best fits, the estimated length, a brief list of your previous publication experience (if you have any) and only the personal information that lends credibility to your story.

Whenever you correspond with an agent, editor or publisher, include a self-addressed, stamped envelope for their reply. Some writers send a disposable copy of the manuscript, but if you want it returned, you must include enough postage and a big enough box. Some writers cut costs by sending a self-addressed stamped post card with places for the publisher to check off a reply. Also, when sending to a magazine or book publisher in another country, include International Reply Coupons instead of stamps. These may be purchased at the main branch of your post office.

Tips on Writing for Red Dress Ink

Red Dress novels are not about women who have one bad date after another, says editor Margaret Marbury. Rather, they cover all aspects of being young and female and urban. And although dating happens in these stories, it is not necessarily the focal point.

Also, Red Dress titles are ultimately upbeat. "The upbeat ending could be that you know she's not going to throw in the towel," Marbury says. "She's got things around her that make her happy, and they don't necessarily have to be a man or a fabulous job. It could be just that she's content right now. She's navigated herself to a place where she's happy." Marbury doesn't rule out a romantic ending, however. "Some books warrant that. You just want it to happen. But they're not romances in the conventional sense, because in many of the books it's not about the guy; it's about something else that's going on in the heroine's life."

—David Borcherding

MORE ABOUT SUBMISSION

Many romance writers choose to writer their books under pseudonyms. In the past, some writers found themselves in messy contract disputes when the publisher owned the writer's pen name. The authors could not take the name (or their following) with them when they switched publishers. Today, thanks to organizations such as the RWA and to changes by publishers themselves, this is not as much of a problem. Many writers, however, select a pseudonym that is close to or another form of their own name. Whatever you decide, be sure you include your legal name on all correspondence with your publisher.

As do agents, most publishers will look at simultaneous queries, but they do not like simultaneous submissions. On the other hand, publishers understand that writers cannot wait a long time for their decision, so more are willing to look at them now than in the past. Keep in mind, however, that if more than one publisher expresses interest, you must decide. It's considered common courtesy to let other publishers know right away if your manuscript is sold.

Response time varies greatly with agents, magazines and book publishers. It's best to wait two to three weeks beyond the stated response time before sending a letter to check on the status of your submission. A follow-up letter should be courteous and brief, and you should include an SASE for reply.

Keep careful records of your submissions. In addition to the name of the magazine or publisher and nature of the submission, be sure to include the date you mailed it and the dates of any subsequent correspondence. If your work is accepted, keep track of your rewrite and any other deadlines. If rejected, record any useful comments or notes of encouragement accompanying the rejection. The information will not only help you manage your submissions, but also help you make informed decisions when making future submissions.

While waiting for a response, one of the best ways to relieve the anxiety is to dive into your next book. Not only does it take your mind off the wait, but it also prepares you for the very good possibility that the editor will want to buy your next book, too.

Resources for Romance Writers

Below is a list of invaluable resources specifically for romance writers. To order any of the Writer's Digest Books titles or to get a consumer book catalog, call 1-800-448-0915. You may also order Writer's Digest Books selections through www.writersdigest.com, Amazon.com or www.barnesandnoble.com.

MAGAZINES:
- *Romance Writers Report*, Romance Writers of America, 3707 FM 1960 West, Suite 555, Houston TX 77068. (281)440-6885. Fax: (281)440-7510. E-mail: info@rwanational. com.
- *Romantic Times Magazine*, 55 Bergen St., Brooklyn NY 11201. (718)237-1097. Website: www.romantictimes.com.
- *Writer's Digest*, 4700 East Galbraith Rd., Cincinnati OH 45236. Website: www.writersdigest.com.

BOOKS:
- *How To Write Romances (Revised and Updated)**, by Phyllis Taylor Pianka.
- *Keys to Success: The Professional Writer's Career Handbook*, handbook, Romance Writers of America.
- *Writing Romances: A Handbook by the Romance Writers of America*, edited by Rita Clay Estrada and Rita Gallagher.
- *You Can Write a Romance*, by Rita Clay Estrada and Rita Gallagher, Writer's Digest Books.

ORGANIZATIONS & ONLINE
- Romance Writers of America, Inc. (RWA), 3703 FM 1960 West, Suite 555, Houston TX 77068. (281)440-6885, ext. 21. Fax: (281)440-7510. E-mail: info@rwanational.com. Website: www.rwanational.com.
- Romance Writers of America regional chapters. Contact National Office (address above) for information on the chapter nearest you.
- Romance Central website: www.romance-central.com. Offers workshops and forum where romance writers share ideas and exchange advice about romance writing.
- www.writersmarket.com.
- www.writersdigest.com.

* Out of print. Check your local library.

Poppy Z. Brite

Poppy Z. Brite On Writing Her 'Exquisite' Horror

BY CANDI LACE

Long before she could weave story lines for complex, layered horror novels, Poppy Z. Brite relayed a tale called "The Bad Mouse" into a tape recorder. She was three years old, determined to share her imagination and storytelling skills with others. By age five, it was evident Brite preferred the darker plots in fiction when she created a series about bats, along with the lively short drama "Attack of the Mud Monster." That monster, caked in mud, was the firstborn character in a hair-raising family of hundreds Brite has brought to life in her fiction.

By age 12, Brite had submitted her first material to "wildly inappropriate markets," including *Redbook.* "I sold my first story at 18, so I did experience the six years of rejection that is said to be average for writers—I just started a lot earlier than most," she says. But she had already acquired readers in high school with her underground publication *The Glass Goblin.*

In 1991, Brite's writing came of age with publication of *Lost Souls,* which *Publishers Weekly* called "stylishly written and daringly provocative." Featuring a cast of sexy vampires who victimize each other in a world of sex, drugs and blood, *Lost Souls* set the stage for Brite's later novels *Drawing Blood, The Lazarus Heart,* and *Exquisite Corpse.* She has also published a canon of short stories, novellas, comics and biographical material. Today, there is rarely a horror anthology published without Brite's name in the table of contents.

Although she has seldom compromised her raw material, Brite has seen publication with some of New York's pre-eminent, mainstream publishers, among them Dell, Penguin Putnam, Simon & Schuster, and HarperCollins. She says her networking at writers' conventions, expensive promotions, collaborations with other novelists, and positive reviews are not the cause. Rather, Brite attributes her success to her unwavering passion for creating throat-clutching characters—no matter how disturbing they may be—and her dedication to developing the craft "anytime and all the time." Brite says she never had a back-up career plan, or a specific reason for writing, other than that "Writers do not have a choice. And they should not ask why, because it slows down the natural course of events on paper and their potential success," she says.

But like most writers, Brite didn't start at the top. Her first story was published in 1985 in the now-defunct quarterly *The Horror Show.* She sold several stories there before the editor invited her to be spotlighted in that publication's Rising Stars issue, featuring wide coverage on five new horror writers. Shortly after, Brite received a letter from Douglas E. Winter, who she recognized only as the biographer of Stephen King. According to Brite, it was a fledgling writer's dream call: Winter was working as a consultant on a horror line being launched by Walker & Company, and he wondered whether she had a novel in the works. Brite dropped out of the University of North Carolina and began working on what would become *Lost Souls.*

"While working on the novel and waiting to see if anyone would buy it, I went through an array of jobs, including candy maker, artist's model, short order cook, and stripper," says Brite. Although the Walker & Co. horror line never materialized, all was not lost—Delacorte published

CANDI LACE *is a writer and editor based in Atlanta. Lace has published profiles and art critiques in various publications, including* Alternative Cinema Magazine, Surface, Art Papers, Guide to Literary Agents, *and* MAKE: London's Art Forum. *She also reports for* The Covington News.

Lost Souls in 1991 as a paperback original. Impressed by the strength of the writing and the imaginative force in *Lost Souls*, Dell decided to make it the first hardcover in the Abyss horror line, signing her to a six-figure, three book contract. Thus, the first Poppy Z. Brite book was published as a paperback original and a hardcover within just a few months.

"Readers either loved it or hated it," Brite muses. "I read over 170 reviews back then, and I was very self-conscious about the exposure, but now I'm not all that inclined to read good or bad reviews," she says. With emphasis on predominantly writing to please herself, she says to please readers is centrally "a nice bonus."

Even without seeking to, Brite manages to please her fan base immensely. When Gauntlet Press released a Tenth Anniversary edition of Lost Souls (Gauntlet Press), which included lost chapters from earlier drafts, a new foreword and original artwork, copies were snatched up at a rate that broke the publishing house records. The book has also been translated into Spanish, and readers still request a follow-up to the infamous vamp character pair, "Steve and Ghost." While they also appear in a few short stories, Brite maintains she's more attracted to developing new characters than revisiting old ones.

As Brite continues to release new material at a radical speed and puts forth great effort to connect with readers, her fan base is flourishing. With established relationships under many publishers—including the renowned French press Au Diable Vauvert, which owns the French rights to Brite's novel *Liquor*—her ego remains unaffected by author status or royalties. "The thing I've found most helpful is simply to stay in touch with my readers," says Brite, who maintains a website with current information about her work, along with extra stories and promotions unavailable elsewhere. "I post on a bulletin board service in which many of my readers participate, and I do lots of interviews. That sort of thing creates word of mouth and seems to be more valuable than expensive advertising and promotion."

Brite's site generates thousands of hits per month, and inquiries to the Q&A section never stop. Nonetheless, the author reads all of the comments and spends hours responding to questions. According to one month's correspondence, Brite answered almost 50 questions on topics ranging from the characterization of gay cannibalistic serial killers (as in *Exquisite Corpse*) and her definition of "decadence," to what she wears, to the nature of her relationship with Courtney Love.

While Brite finished *Exquisite Corpse*, the third book that was supposed to fulfill her contract with Dell, rock star Love contacted her to write a biography. She agreed, and a year later, *Courtney Love: The Real Story* (S&S and Orion of UK) hit store shelves. Though the Love biography sold well, Brite doesn't consider the accomplished representation of a rock star a necessarily commendable piece in her body of writing. "She just seems like a person with a lot of advantages and a lot of problems, sometimes very generous, sometimes petty, and ultimately (like most people) quite interesting, but perhaps not as interesting as she thinks she is."

Fiction, with all those stories about vampires and carnivorous gay murders rampaging through the streets of New Orleans, intrigued Brite a great deal more. But her daring novel *Exquisite Corpse* did not receive the quick, enthusiastic welcome that *Lost Souls* and *Drawing Blood* had. In fact, announcing they could not publish the "extreme content," Dell and Penguin, Brite's UK publisher, turned down the manuscript. Not letting this adversity damage her career, Brite kept busy writing numerous short stories and travelling.

Eventually, *Exquisite Corpse* was published by Simon & Schuster and Orion, and as expected, drew various reactions. Hardcore fans either loved it or hated it for the explicit gore. Some readers criticized her portrayal of gays as promiscuous bloodsuckers and murderers. One critic openly insulted the book as a "shocking landslide for a gifted writer." In contrast, an avid fan and independent filmmaker, Max Kreuger, optioned Exquisite Corpse in 2002 to be dramatized.

Brite, like so many other writers, simply fastened her fingers to the keyboard and moved on, undaunted by negative feedback. "There is no way to please everyone who sits down to read your book," says Brite, who is constantly asked why the majority of her characters in conflict—

whether in horror, erotica or general fiction—are gay males. "I'm not sure we (men, women, gay, straight, transsexual, whatever) are really all that far apart when it comes to fears and confusion about our sexuality, so I'm always a little mystified when people are surprised that I can portray gay male sexuality in a realistic way. There are many aspects of fiction that are very challenging for me, but that's not one of them. It comes easy and feels like one of the most natural things in the world."

What could possibly challenge a writer who, according to her website, has only received two rejection slips since 1998? Research. In reading most of Brite's short stories, it is evident that they do not just describe characters, conflict and context. Tales such as "Mussolini and the Axeman's Jazz," "His Mouth Will Taste of Wormwood," "System Freeze" and "Oh Death, Where Is Thy Spatula?" are rich distillations of great mounds of research. Brite never skimps on detail, and she spends hours at the library or on the Internet. "I have bought a lot of material for research that I haven't yet used, and I have learned to be more discerning, but it is always better to have more preparatory items than less," she says.

Other aspects of her writing career that she is discerning about include editing projects and collaborations with other writers (or non-writers). "Love in Vein," a horror series she edited for HarperCollins at the request of editorial director Martin Greenburg, received critical acclaim in the genre and proved to be lucrative for Brite, but she has resisted subsequent projects. Directing such a project takes a lot of time, Brite says, and she is happier pouring over her own material.

This is not to say Brite can't work well with others. *Wrong Things* is a startling compilation of stories written with Caitlin Kiernan, another popular horror author and friend of Brite's. At one time, Brite also agreed to work alongside Ramsey Campbell, but says the relationship didn't materialize because he was deeply involved in writing a novel. Should she ever have the desire to collaborate with others, plenty of fans have begged for the opportunity, though Brite responds: "To me, writing is as intimate as having sex, and I am very selective. I would never write with strangers, nor sleep with them!"

Someone Else's Sandbox: Writing Media Tie-Ins

BY ROGER MacBRIDE ALLEN

Wander through the fiction shelves of any bookstore these days and you're likely to come across some good long stretches of shelf space given over to media tie-ins, or books based on characters, stories and plot premises from a movie, a television series, a comic book, a game, or even an earlier book series by another writer.

Media tie-ins don't even have to be books. A comic book could spawn a movie that inspires a game that is spun off into a kids' TV cartoon series that becomes the basis for a new series of graphic novels for the adult market. And then maybe someone will do a documentary about the making of the movie based on the graphic novels. In such a case, the original characters, story line, setting—the "universe" of the story—have become a franchise, and each of the various versions is there, at least in part, to serve as advertising for all the others. ("You've seen the movie and played the video game, now read the book!") This, in the parlance of the people who try to sell you things, is called synergy.

For the most part, fortunately, things don't get quite that involved. More typically, a popular television series will be the basis for a series of books that tell stories similar to what might happen in episodes of the series. Media tie-in books are usually linked to a fantasy or science fiction concept. They rarely seem to involve "realistic" dramas. There is a series of *Buffy the Vampire Slayer* novels. There isn't a series of *West Wing* novels.

I write science fiction novels for a living. The 18 or so novels I have published so far include two trilogies set in worlds created by others. I did a trilogy of *Star Wars* novels, and another trilogy set in the "Robot" universe invented by Isaac Asimov. Having written these media tie-ins, one of the most frequently asked questions I get from readers is: "I've written a really cool book set in the XYZ universe. How do I get it published?"

It's not much fun to give the answer to that question, because the answer is: "You can't." No one who mails in an unsolicited idea or story or novel to any of the media franchises ever gets it published. Period. End of story. While there *might* be exceedingly rare exceptions to this flat statement (sponsored writing contests, for example), it is 99.999 percent true. It would unwise in the extreme to spend time and effort pursuing that .001 percent.

The business process as imagined by the enthused fans who write their own novels and send them in—where the editor-in-chief himself reads the manuscript, falls in love with it, and instantly sends out a zillion-dollar check—simply never happens. It can't happen.

Besides all that, the business structure of such media tie-ins is very complex, and an inexperienced writer can wind up giving away far too much in the contract. Finally, playing in someone

---

ROGER MACBRIDE ALLEN *is the author of 17 science fiction novels—16 published and one forthcoming. Among his most recent works are a trilogy of* Star Wars *novels—*Ambush at Corellia, Assault at Selonia, *and* Showdown at Centerpoint, *and a trilogy of Asimovian Robot novels—*Caliban, Inferno, *and* Utopia. *Two of his most popular stand-alone novels are* The Ring of Charon *and* The Shattered Sphere. *His latest book is* The Game of Worlds, *a young adult novel for Avon's new "Out of Time" series. He has completed the first volume of a new trilogy for Bantam Books, entitled* The Depths of Time, *which will be published in March, 2000.*

else's sandbox—writing in an existing fictional universe where all the characters and situations are well established—just isn't the best way to get started as a professional writer. We'll take a look at why all this is so later in this article.

First, let's take a look at how media tie-ins are produced. We'll look at the business side of the process first, and then turn to the writing side of the question.

Typically, the franchise holder—for example, the studio that produced the movie or television show on which the books will be based, or the holder of the copyright of the original work-will sign a contract with a book publisher or a book packager. In exchange for a cut of the profits, the franchise holder will grant the right to publish books based on the property. Such contracts will generally specify how many books, of what length, when and where they are to be published, and so on.

"The business process as imagined by enthused fans who write their own novels and send them in—where the editor-in-chief himself reads the manuscript, falls in love with it, and instantly sends out a zillion-dollar check—simply never happens. It can't happen."

In the case of a book publisher, the publisher then turns around and signs up a writer or writers. Aside from the financial arrangements with the writers, which we'll discuss below, the process of publishing the book proceeds in more or less the usual way from there. The one exception is that, aside from the publisher needing to approve the manuscript, the franchise holder will reserve the right to approve the book outlines and the final manuscript as well.

The typical book packager deal is much more complicated. As for what a book packager *is*, exactly, explaining the deal structure is probably the best way to make that clear as well. A packager signs a contract with a franchise holder, for example, to pay X percent of whatever the packager earns from the eventual sale of books. In exchange, the packager gets the right to resell the right to publish books based on the franchise. The packager signs up a writer or writers, and then sells the whole "package" of rights obtained, plus writers hired and ready to go, plus perhaps basic story ideas, plus editorial services, to a publisher. In theory, at least, the publisher will then have out-sourced the entire process of preparing a book for publication. The packager might even provide typesetting and cover art to the publisher. In theory, all the publisher has to do is print the book and ship it. In practice, it is rarely that tidy a process.

For one thing, with a packager, there are suddenly three levels of approval required: packager, publisher, and franchise holder. With so many middlemen and so many levels of approval in the process, lines of communication and authority can get snarled-and it's the writer who usually gets caught in the middle. At one point in the writing of my three "Robot" novels, for example, some minor issue came up, and the packager called and told me not to talk to anyone at the publisher—and then the publisher called to tell me not to talk to anyone at the packager. It took a while to sort that one out.

The publisher or packager will also usually control foreign and subsidiary rights, and will sell multiple editions in multiple languages and countries, as well as audio book editions, e-book editions, and so on. These sub-rights and foreign rights can be extremely lucrative. In some cases, the packager might merely settle for breaking even on the domestic book deal, just to be able to rake in the proceeds from the foreign and subsidiary sales.

The writer/publisher/packager contract can take many forms. Normally, authors are paid on a royalty basis, receiving a percentage of the cover price of each book sold. However, many media tie-in deals operate on a work-for-hire basis, wherein the writer is paid a flat fee for delivering the manuscript. Alternately he or she is paid perhaps a half or a quarter of the standard royalties usually paid by the publisher to the author—with the packager or publisher pocketing the rest.

It is also important to bear in mind that, in most media tie-ins, the writer's contract specifies that the writer relinquishes all subsequent claim to the book. The money paid by the publisher or packager buys all rights for all time and the text becomes the franchise holder's or packager's intellectual property. The packager or the franchise holder owns the copyright to the work.

In a packager deal, so far as the publisher is concerned, the packager is the "author" of the book. The publisher pays the packager for delivering the book, and pays the packager whatever book royalties are due. An arrangement like this, where the actual writer does not own the work, and can be paid less for doing the work than someone else is for merely owning the work, is sometimes called sharecropping.

A sharecrop deal can be a bad arrangement for the writer, but it doesn't necessarily have to be. A flat fee is fine—if the fee is large enough. And even though I get a smaller royalty percentage on my *Star Wars* books than I receive for works that are completely my own, overall my *Star Wars* books have earned me more than any of the other books I have written, because they have sold, and still sell, so many copies. I get a smaller percentage, a smaller slice of the pie—but it is a very large pie.

It is, however, easy to wind up in a contract that pays too little money for too much work. This is especially true for beginning writers. They have an inherently weaker negotiating position than established writers, and they are often willing to be paid next to nothing, if only they get their names in print. Furthermore, the publisher or packager has a monopoly on the given franchise. The writer can't sell a book about the XYZ universe except to the publisher or packager who has signed with the owners of the XYZ universe. That can only add to the publisher or packager's leverage.

However the contracts are structured, the question is: how to get one of them? How to get to write and see published a book set in the world of the characters and situations you've fallen in love with?

What it boils down to is that the authors who write such media tie-in books are approached by the publisher or packager and hired to do the books. Typically, the writers hired to do such books have written and published books of their own, books that have nothing to do with any franchise, before they are approached to do the media tie-in.

They have, in other words, demonstrated the ability to write a complete, commercially publishable novel in the only way possible: by actually doing it. (Lots more people start writing books than finish writing them.) At the very least, a prospective franchise fiction writer will have written and published something—perhaps a short story or two-that the series editor has seen and liked.

All this makes it sound as if you can't join the club unless you're already a member, but that's not quite accurate. It's just that you have to join the club of writers who have published their own stuff before you can join the club of those who do media tie-in work.

These professional writers, once contracted to do so, submit outlines. The outlines are critiqued, modified, rewritten, and (with luck) approved. Part of the approval process in such cases concerns itself with whether the author's story is any good. Part of it is making sure the story idea matches the rest of the imaginary universe, and doesn't cause continuity problems for the series, now or later. (In my case, one plot line of my *Star Wars* trilogy was thrown out by Lucasfilm because what I wanted to do might interfere with future plot lines.) Only after contracts are signed, and the outlines are approved, do the writers actually write the books. And, of course, the final books are likewise subject to approval before anything gets published.

That's how it is done. Let's take a look at how it *isn't* done.

Hundreds and thousands of unsolicited story proposals, stories, book manuscripts, and so on descend on franchise holders and book publishers every year. None of them will ever be published. In fact, the vast majority of them will be returned, unopened, to sender. There are good, hard-nosed reasons for all this.

Leaving aside the potentially huge copyright issues with these unsolicited media tie-in submissions, the main problem is that most of them are badly written, or based on a bad idea, or are inaccurate or careless about the known facts in the universe in question, or are just incredibly sloppy.

A lot of these submissions are simply fan fiction (sometimes known as fanfic)—stories written by a fan of a show or movie for the fan's own amusement, then sent in to the publisher, perhaps on a whim, or at the urging of a well-meaning friend. To be very blunt indeed, a certain fraction of unsolicited media tie-in submissions are written by people who, judging by their writing, are deranged.

And, finally, for reasons that should become clear in a moment, these submissions are written by people who don't know how publishing works. If they did know, they wouldn't be making the submissions.

The risk is, of course, that the good stuff (if any) is mixed in with the bad. Even if an unsolicited *Star Trek* novel is an absolute gem, it is likely to be buried under a mountain of unpublishable gibberish that arrived in the same day's mail, heaped in the same pile with all the amateur jobs, fanfic screeds, and nut manuscripts.

But even if that perfect novel of an unsolicited manuscript were the only one to arrive, and even if the publisher was starved for material, it wouldn't matter, because no one at the publishing house would look at it. The publisher would almost certainly return it unread, for one simple reason: fear of lawsuits.

Here's why. Let's say that Fervent Fan F, who loves Media Franchise Z, writes a book set in that franchise, in which Character X marries Character Y. (Marrying characters up is a very popular notion among writers, and not much loved by the folks that control franchises. Marriages change too many things and complicate the continuity.) The book gets to Editor E, who reads the book, decides it's no good, and rejects it.

Now suppose that, two years later, in the movie series or TV series or book series or comic book series linked to the franchise, Character X does indeed marry Character Y. Or even suppose that Character X marries Z, or marries some new character never heard of before. Fervent Fan F decides that Franchise Z has stolen his idea of X getting married. Fan F goes to Lawyer L, and sues.

Now, even if Lawyer L knows there is no case at all, she might well decide to go for it anyway, in hopes that Franchise Z will offer a settlement, just to make Fervent Fan F go away.

Why Won't Publishers Use Untried Writers for Media Tie-In Projects?

"It has to do with reliability," says Ginjer Buchanan, senior executive editor and marketing director at Ace Books. "You're always taking a chance on a new writer, particularly if you are buying from proposal. Most editors don't want to run the risk with a licensed program."

And there's another side to the coin. "There are so many established writers out there interested in writing tie-ins that it's not really necessary for publishers to take a chance on a new writer," says Lucienne Diver of the Spectrum Literary Agency.

"Generally, we contact authors we feel would be appropriate to the property in question, and ask them if they would be interested," says Steve Saffel, Executive Editor at Del Rey Books. "We have authors with whom we've worked, and that familiarity allows us some assurance concerning the quality of the work we'll receive."

If there is enough bad publicity, and/or if Franchise Z concludes they are going to have a lot of trouble proving that they never heard word one from Editor E about Fan F's book, then Franchise Z might well decide it would be easier and cheaper just to pay up.

Never mind that the franchise holders thought up the Franchise Z universe, and invented Characters X and Y. They have just, in effect, been sued for violating their own copyright. And suddenly every unpublished writer in the world realizes that Franchise Z has caved in and settled one suit, and who knows, they might settle another, and another, and . . .

There is a very simple way for Franchise Z and Editor E to avoid this nightmare scenario: all they have to do is *never look at unsolicited manuscripts*. If they return the unsolicited manuscripts unopened, and/or return them with a letter stating they have not been read, and take other similar precautions, they will able to demonstrate they never saw Fan F's tale of romance and marriage. They can avoid this nuisance suit, and all the others that would almost certainly follow a settlement or a judgment against them.

Therefore, unsolicited media tie-in manuscripts don't get read. The franchise holder and the publishers thus avoid a very real and highly probable danger of lawsuit by turning their backs on the quite highly improbable hope that Fan F has written something that exactly fits in with all their future plans for the franchise, and is vastly better than anything they could get from their stable of professional writers.

So Fervent Fan F is not going to be able to publish his unsolicited *Star Wars*, or *Star Trek*, or *Buffy the Vampire Slayer*, or *Itchy and Scratchy* novel, story, poem, or comic book. Period. It can only happen if the publishers and packagers ask the writer.

There is one other danger: developing a name, not as a writer who can do a media tie-in, but as a writer who only does media tie-ins—and worse, a writer who only does them at the low end of the market. One editor I worked with warned me of this. "Remember Joe Zilch?" he asked, mentioning a writer who had appeared in a few prestigious magazines, but then settled down to cranking out a whole series of rigidly formulated media tie-ins. "He used to be a writer." In other words, no one was going to take Zilch that seriously if he ever pitched a novel that was totally his own.

In short, starting off writing media tie-ins is a tough way into the business of writing. It's also not that great a way to develop the skills of writing.

I'm glad I wrote the media tie-in books I've done. If I were approached to do similar projects in the future, I would certainly consider them. But I must confess that it is more satisfying to write my own stuff. *I'm* in charge. I get to change things. I am not tied down by plot ideas that someone else dreamed up, or forced to write around gaping holes that are enshrined in the plot logic. Besides which, writing in someone else's universe puts severe limits on what skills a writer can practice.

Books and stories are built out of three interlocking things: plot, setting, and character. If someone else has already dreamed up the people in the story, and worked out precisely what the world they live in is like, that's two out of three—character and setting—that are gone. The beginning writer will have no chance to practice creating the people and places in his story. All he's left with is plot, and even there, the his freedom will be severely limited by all the things that have already happened in the existing storyline.

A beginning writer wishing to develop his skills will do far better working on his own material, so as to give himself the chance to work on all the aspects of telling a story. And, ironically enough, the only way to get a chance to write in your favorite franchise universe is by first becoming a professional writer in your own right. You get to write in their worlds by writing in your own universe first.

Jacqueline Carey: At Ease in an Alternate Reality

BY VANESSA LYMAN

Photo © 2003 Robert Carey

Jacqueline Carey

Not long after the release of Jacqueline Carey's debut novel in 2001, a low but insistent hum began. On Internet message boards, in coffee shops, in bookstores and libraries, people who had asked people who hadn't, "Have you read it yet?"

The "it" in question was *Kushiel's Dart*, the first in what would become an acclaimed series. Set in a Europe whose history has been rewoven, the plot centers on political intrigue and the game of nations. Carey's language is rich and inventive (called "reminiscent of the best of Anne Rice" by *Library Journal*), and her story plays heavily on fables and myths. Magic and history, religion and vice, betrayal and loyalty set the story line to boiling. And the heroine—named Phèdre—is a masochistic courtesan with a love of the whip and a training in espionage.

Since the book's first release and cliffhanger ending, fans have waited impatiently for the next books in the series. When they read *Kushiel's Chosen* (2002) and *Kushiel's Avatar* (2003, all Tor), they read in order to see what scrapes Phèdre would get herself into and how she'd squeeze out again.

And Carey doesn't disappoint her readers. Here, she talks about how she borrows from history

VANESSA LYMAN *is assistant editor of Northlight Books (F&W Publications), and former assistant editor of* Novel & Short Story Writer's Market.

to inform her intricate plots, her creative promotional efforts, and her joy in becoming a full-time writer.

Your books must be very carefully plotted; they're rife with dark political intrigue that never falters. Did you plan these conspiracies out in advance or did they gel as you wrote? Did you have all three novels planned? Did the plot change because of things you discovered while writing?

I plan all the major plot elements thoroughly in advance; with the amount of intrigue involved, it's too complicated to play it fast and loose along the way. I'd get hopelessly entangled! *Kushiel's Dart* came first; once it was finished, I conceived the broader story arc that encompassed both *Chosen* and *Avatar*. There are always things I discover and incorporate during the writing process, but nothing that alters the basic structure of the plot.

Speaking of intrigue, why did you decide to focus on that rather than magic? Though the gods (should I call them that?) are active in the lives of the characters, magic and mysticism don't play nearly as strong a role as wit and pig-headedness.

To me, there's something very satisfying about an epic in which the hero or heroine is an ordinary person in extraordinary circumstances, prevailing by dint of wits, courage, or sheer persistence. When you look at Tolkien's *Lord of the Rings*, which has inspired so much contemporary fantasy, that's very much the case. Though in some ways, the Kushiel books are closer to historical fiction than fantasy; they're simply set in an alternate reality. The supernatural elements present derive from the premise that the governing mythologies are true in a literal sense.

You've said "all fantasy derives its roots from the oldest tales told by humankind, the myths and legends and fables." I noticed a fable-like storytelling in your work, especially with your second book. How deeply do legends inform your novels? Do you borrow elements from fables you know?

Oh, absolutely! I try to weave the borrowed and invented together seamlessly, so the end result has an archetypal resonance that's familiar, yet reads with fresh urgency. Sometimes it's done deliberately. The 'holmgang'—the duel on the stretched hide—comes from one of the Norse sagas. Phèdre's sojourn in La Dolorosa was inspired by *The Count of Monte Cristo*. The cleansing ritual of the *thetalos* was my invention, but its trappings were borrowed from the Eleusinian mysteries. Sometimes, it's entirely unconscious-I know it's an element I've encountered before, but I couldn't tell you where.

Legend is one thing and actual history another—you also use real geographical regions and the history and culture of that area in your story, but you change the names. Why do you choose to do it that way? It seems both limiting and liberating.

Again, it's that combination of the familiar and the strange, which is something I enjoy as a reader and a writer alike. Since I play freely with timelines—advancing some cultures, repressing others, resurrecting favorites—there's more liberty than limitations. One of my readers called it the 'cafeteria-style approach' to building an alternate history. At the same time, using actual history, geography and cultures means there's a lot of resource material out there, which enables me to do the sort of research that grounds the story in a visceral reality. I also come across some fantastic ready-made elements. The fire-temples in Drujan in *Avatar* are a good example; that's based on an actual natural phenomenon in Azerbaijan.

Tell me about taking *Kushiel's Dart* to publication. Were you at all concerned about sending a character like Phedre out into the marketplace? Why did you go with Tor?

Oh, I had all kinds of trepidation! As a cheerfully masochistic heroine, Phèdre is a provocative character, potentially controversial. I worked very hard to *not* sensationalize that aspect of her character, and in the end, all I could do was hope that readers would recognize that I was trying to transcend and subvert, not exploit, the erotic cliches involved. Still, I was tremendously relieved when the first reviews came out.

Tor is one of the best science fiction and fantasy publishers in the industry, so it wasn't a hard choice. Also, they're committed to building authors over the long run, and not merely looking for a quick score on a hot title. They've done a lot to support the Kushiel books, and I have no doubt that it was the right decision.

You've said, "Though I've written short fiction and enjoyed playing with it, I'm a bred-in-the-bone novelist and tend to think in novel-sized ideas." Care to elaborate?

I take great joy in telling stories with an epic scope, where intrigue sets events in motion that take hundreds of pages to unfold and the overall gestalt of the plot isn't visible until the end. Most of the ideas that really fire my imagination are of that ilk, and short fiction simply isn't a conducive medium for that sort of storytelling. Still, every now and then I do get inspired to write a smaller, more intimate piece—and it's nice to write something that doesn't take years to complete!

How many books did you have to write out of your system before you could sit down with Phedre's story? How long did it take to reach the point you're at now?

I wrote three novels over the course of about 10 years prior to beginning *Kushiel's Dart*. Although I learned a lot about the process with each one, none of them had that real spark of originality. Still, that's what I had to go through, first to discover my strengths as a writer, and then to find the courage to trust them. I think this is something all writers have to learn for themselves. For me, it meant taking a real creative risk in terms of the story, and turning loose my true literary voice, which is naturally baroque. When I did that, it really represented a quantum leap in the caliber of my work.

Tell me about writing fiction with a full-time job. How'd you manage it?

Because it was the thing I loved most in the world, as well as what I considered my real career, I made writing a priority. I worked an eight-to-five job and wrote for an hour or two almost every night after work; on weekends—I'd put in whatever I could. Maintaining the discipline isn't hard if you truly love the process. It's keeping hope alive during the struggling years that's tough. I just took every rejection as a challenge and kept pushing myself to get better and better, and eventually it paid off.

You recently made a significant move in your career as a fiction writer—quitting your day job and going full-time. What was the deciding factor? How has it been so far? Has it changed the way you write or has it strengthened your discipline?

My breaking point came when the demands on my time began to affect my writing. Prior to being published, I'd gotten good at balancing the day job with writing; but success creates a whole new set of issues. Novels in the pipeline have to go through the editing process, which can be time-consuming. Once that's done, there's the copyedit; and no sooner is *that* done, but the manuscript has to be proofread. If your book is going from hardcover to paperback, it should be proofread a second time. Along the way, there are various interviews, essays and news releases; and when the book comes out, as many publicity events—booksignings, talks, etc.— as the publisher sponsors or you can drum up. It all adds up, and ultimately, it got to be too much to handle while maintaining quality of life. For the past two years, my only 'vacation' has been a book tour!

So far, I'm *loving* being a full-time writer. I'm having to train myself to be less nocturnal in my writing habits, but overall, I'm getting more writing done, while feeling a lot more focused.

Plus, it's great to be able to do things like, oh, go grocery shopping in the middle of the day, or enjoy a leisurely lunch with friends.

You've worked with both types of promotion—the grand and the small. You've participated in the Tor's Women in Fantasy tour with two other fantasy writers, but you've also worked on a smaller scale, like printing up temporary tattoos just like Phedre's and distributing them through your website (though your more diehard fans have gone for the real thing). Do you have any advice on promotion based on your experiences?

Do whatever you can, as much as you're comfortable with. I've been very fortunate in terms of Tor's support—to wit, the national book tour with Sara Douglass and Juliet Marillier—but I also took initiative and demonstrated I was willing to work hard from the outset. Establish a website, and update it regularly. If there's a hook you can use, like the tattoos, go for it! I can't take any credit for people who chose to get the real thing (which is an awesome phenomenon), but I thought the temporary tats would be fun.

Stay in communication with your publicist, but don't rely solely on their efforts. Develop a list of regional media contacts. If something of note occurs—say your book wins an award—send out a press release; you may get a few articles out of it. It's often hard for writers, as we're used to being immersed in a very solitary practice, but the truth is, promotion is a necessary evil in this industry.

Another one that may sound obvious is, when it comes to public events: Practice. If you're doing a reading, rehearse it. If you've giving a talk, plan it, polish it, then rehearse it. You'll be far more comfortable, and your audience more entertained. Hey, my time is valuable; so's theirs! I figure anyone investing time to come hear me deserves my best effort.

I don't know if you've had the opportunity to compare your position to that of other writers, but have you found the fantasy field welcoming to female writers?

Yes and no. Within the genre itself, I've found readers and other writers to be quite welcoming, and Tor's Women in Fantasy campaign is indicative of their support. There's a lot of growth in romance, paranormal elements are gaining in popularity and more crossover is occurring. The one area that's markedly lacking is mainstream coverage. I encountered some statistics recently which noted that publications that do run fantasy and science fiction features, such as the *New York Times* or the *Washington Post*, tend to favor male writers by a margin of about four to one. There are a few exceptions, but overall, I don't think female writers are accorded the same weight as male writers in the genre.

Where do you foresee your career going in the next few years?

It's going to be interesting. My current work-in-progress, *Elegy for Darkness*, is a stand-alone that tackles a massive cultural icon. Essentially, it's a Tolkienesque epic fantasy . . . written as a tragedy sympathetic to the "minions of the Dark Lord." It's a very ambitious project, and I have no idea if it will put me firmly on the map or turn out to be a mere blip on the cultural radar. Either way, as of this writing, I'm mulling over what I think is a strong concept for a second D'Angeline series with a different protagonist. This is something that, believe it or not, I've had in mind as a possibility since 1999. The Kushiel books have found a wonderful readership, so I have every hope that my readers would be game for another adventure.

At a conference last year, I attended a panel on trilogies and series. There were some complaints about second books in a trilogy, because as bridges from the first, exciting installment to the powerful end novel, they tend to fall flat. As a trilogy writer, what's your opinion?

It is something that's potentially problematic, although I'm not sure the problem lies in the execution as much as it does in the expectation. A first installment benefits from the shock of the new, the capacity to surprise and delight. If you're continuing with the same characters in the same milieu, no matter how innovative your second book may be, it's going to lack the impact of the new, the sense of discovery upon venturing into the complete unknown. A final installment benefits from the fulfillment of profound resolution, and the bittersweet sense of coming to the end of a story. I think middle books are sometimes given short shrift by being perceived as a bridge between the two.

When it comes to your writing, what do you regret the most? And what makes you proudest?

There's not a lot I regret when it comes to the actual writing. No effort, however unsuccessful, is wasted if it brings you closer to your goal; every book I had to write out of my system made me a better writer. What I regret most are the dumb professional mistakes that came from being too impatient to do the research myself, and too stubborn to ask more experienced writers. The most glaring one I remember is the very first "three chapters and an outline" submission packet I put together. Not knowing that an outline simply meant a synopsis, I spent weeks developing a painstaking outline of my novel—every chapter headed by a roman numeral, major plot points under capital letters, etc. As Homer Simpson would say, "D'oh!"

As for what makes me proudest, I'm tempted to say it's sticking with it through the long struggling years; but in truth, it's probably Phèdre, who has got to be the least likely heroine ever in the annals of epic fiction. It really shouldn't work. To this day, I'm not entirely sure how I pulled it off.

Resources for Science Fiction/ Fantasy & Horror Writers

Below is a list of invaluable resources specifically for science fiction and fantasy writers. To order any of the Writer's Digest Books titles or to get a consumer book catalog, call 1-800-448-0915. You may also order Writer's Digest Books selections through www.writersdigest.com, Amazon.com, or www.barnesandnoble.com.

MAGAZINES:
- *Locus*, P.O. Box 13305, Oakland CA 94661. E-mail: locus@locusmag.com.
- *Science Fiction Chronicle*, P.O. Box 022730, Brooklyn NY 11202-0056. (718)643-9011. Fax: (718)522-3308. E-mail: sfchronicle@dnapublications.com.
- *Writer's Digest*, 4700 East Galbraith Rd., Cincinnati OH 45236. Website: www.writersdigest.com.

BOOKS (by Writer's Digest Books):
- *Aliens and Alien Societies: A Writer's Guide to Creating Extraterrestrial Life-forms*, by Stanley Schmidt
- *Worlds of Wonder, How to Write Science Fiction and Fantasy**, by David Gerrold
- *How to Write Science Fiction & Fantasy*, by Orson Scott Card
- *The Writer's Complete Fantasy Reference*, from the editors of Writer's Digest Books
- *Writing Horror**, edited by Mort Castle

ORGANIZATIONS & ONLINE:
- Science Fiction & Fantasy Writers of America, Inc., P.O. Box 877, Chestertown MD 21620. E-mail: execdir@sfwa.org. Website: www.sfwa.org/.
- Books and Writing Online: www.interzone.com/Books/books.html.
- www.writersmarket.com.
- www.locusmag.com.

* Out of print. Check your local library.

The Markets

Literary Agents... 107

Literary Magazines.. 166

Small Circulation Magazines.................. 275

Online Publications.................................. 306

Consumer Magazines............................... 332

Book Publishers.. 361

Contests & Awards................................... 472

Important Listing Information

- Listings are not advertisements. Although the information here is as accurate as possible, the listings are not endorsed or guaranteed by the editor of *Novel & Short Story Writer's Market*.
- *Novel & Short Story Writer's Market* reserves the right to exclude any listing that does not meet its requirements.

Key to Symbols and Abbreviations

- **N** New listing in all sections
- Canadian listing
- International listing
- Parent company, subsidiary, or division of major book publishing house
- **A** Agented material only
- Online publication
- Award-winning publication
- **$** Market pays money
- Accepts no submissions
- Actively seeking beginning writers
- Seeking new and established writers
- Prefers working with established writers, mostly referrals
- Only handles specific types of work
- ● Comment by editor of *Novel & Short Story Writer's Market*

ms—manuscript; **mss**—manuscripts
SASE—self-addressed, stamped envelope
SAE—self-addressed envelope
IRC—International Reply Coupon, for use on reply mail from other countries

(See Glossary for definitions of words and expressions used in writing and publishing.)

Complaint Procedure

If you feel you have not been treated fairly by a listing in *Novel & Short Story Writer's Market*, we advise you to take the following steps:
- First try to contact the listing. Sometimes one phone call or a letter can quickly clear up the matter.
- Document all your correspondence with the listing. When you write to us with a complaint, provide the details of your submission, the date of your first contact with the listing and the nature of your subsequent correspondence.
- We will enter your letter into our files and attempt to contact the listing.
- The number and severity of complaints will be considered in our decision whether or not to delete the listing from the next edition.

Literary Agents

Many publishers are willing to look at unsolicited submissions but most feel having an agent is to the writer's best advantage. In this section we include 200 agents who specialize in fiction, or publish a significant amount of fiction. These agents were also selected because of their openness to submissions from writers.

The commercial fiction field is intensely competitive. Many publishers have smaller staffs and less time. For that reason, more book publishers are relying on agents for new talent. Some publishers are even relying on agents as "first readers" who must wade through the deluge of submissions from writers to find the very best. For writers, a good agent can be a foot in the door—someone willing to do the necessary work to put your manuscript in the right editor's hands.

It would seem today that finding a good agent is as hard as finding a good publisher. Yet those writers who have agents say they are invaluable. Not only can a good agent help you make your work more marketable, an agent acts as your business manager and adviser, keeping your interests up front during and even after contract negotiations.

Still, finding an agent can be very difficult for a new writer. If you are already published in magazines, you have a better chance than someone with no publishing credits. (Many agents routinely read periodicals searching for new writers.) Although many agents do read queries and manuscripts from unpublished authors without introduction, referrals from their writer clients can be a big help. If you don't know any published authors with agents, you may want to attend a conference as a way of meeting agents. Some agents even set aside time at conferences to meet new writers.

All the agents listed here have said they are open to working with new, previously unpublished writers as well as published writers. Most do not charge a fee to cover the time and effort involved in reviewing a manuscript or a synopsis and chapters.

USING THE LISTINGS

It is especially important when contacting these busy agents that you read individual listings carefully before submitting anything. The first information after the company name includes the address and phone, fax and e-mail address (when available). **Member Agents** gives the names of individual agents working at that company (specific types of fiction an agent handles are indicated in parenthesis after that agent's name). The **Represents** section lists the types of fiction the agency works with. Reading the **Recent Sales** gives you the names of writers an agent is currently working with and, very importantly, publishers the agent has placed manuscripts with. **Writers' Conferences** identifies conferences an agent attends (and where you might possibly meet that agent). **Tips** presents advice directly from the agent to authors.

ACACIA HOUSE PUBLISHING SERVICES, LTD., 51 Acacia Rd., Toronto ON M4S 2K6, Canada. (416)484-8356. Fax: (416)484-8356. E-mail: fhanna.acacia@rogers.com. **Contact:** (Ms.) Frances Hanna. Estab. 1985. Represents 50 clients. Works with a small number of new/unpublished writers. Currently handles: 30% nonfiction books; 70% novels.

● Ms. Hanna has been in the publishing business for 30 years, first in London (UK) as a fiction editor with Barrie & Jenkins and Pan Books, and as a senior editor with a packager of mainly illustrated books. She was condensed books editor for 6 years for *Reader's Digest* in Montreal, senior editor and foreign rights manager for (the then) William Collins & Sons (now HarperCollins) in Toronto. Her husband, Vice President Bill Hanna, has over 40 years experience in the publishing business.

Member Agents: Bill Hanna, vice president (business, self-help, modern history).
Represents: Nonfiction books, novels. **Considers these fiction areas:** Action/adventure; detective/police/crime; literary; mainstream/contemporary; mystery/suspense; thriller.

○➤ This agency specializes in contemporary fiction: literary or commercial. Actively seeking "outstanding first novels with literary merit." Does not want to receive horror, occult, science fiction.

How to Contact: Query with outline and SASE. *No unsolicited mss.* No e-mail or fax queries. Responds in 6 weeks to queries. Returns materials only with SASE.

Recent Sales: Sold over 50 titles in the last year. Also made numerous international rights sales. This agency prefers not to share information on specific sales or clients.

Terms: Agent receives 15% commission on English language sales, 20% on dramatic sales, 25% commission on foreign sales. Charges clients for photocopying, postage and courier, as necessary.

Tips: "We prefer that writers be previously published, with at least a few short stories or articles to their credit. Strongest consideration will be given to those with, say, three or more published books. However, we *would* take on an unpublished writer of outstanding talent."

THE AHEARN AGENCY, INC., 2021 Pine St., New Orleans LA 70118-5456. (504)861-8395. Fax: (504)866-6434. E-mail: pahearn@aol.com. **Contact:** Pamela G. Ahearn. Estab. 1992. Member of RWA. Represents 25 clients. 20% of clients are new/unpublished writers. Currently handles: 10% nonfiction books; 90% novels.

● Prior to opening her agency, Ms. Ahearn was an agent for eight years and an editor with Bantam Books.

Represents: Nonfiction books, novels, short story collections (if stories previously published). **Considers these fiction areas:** Action/adventure; contemporary issues; detective/police/crime; ethnic; family saga; feminist; gay/lesbian; glitz; historical; humor/satire; literary; mainstream/contemporary; mystery/suspense; psychic/supernatural; regional; romance; thriller.

○ This agency specializes in historical romance; also very interested in mysteries and suspense fiction. Does not want to receive category romance, science fiction or fantasy.

How to Contact: Query with SASE. Accepts e-mail queries, no attachments. Considers simultaneous queries. Responds in 6 weeks to queries; 10 weeks to mss. Obtains most new clients through recommendations from others, solicitations, conferences.

Recent Sales: *The Amber Room*, by Steve Berry (Balantine); *The Dragon King's Palace*, by Laura Joh Rowland (St. Martin's); *Dance of Seduction*, by Sabrina Jeffries (Avon).

Terms: Agent receives 15% commission on domestic sales; 20% commission on foreign sales. Offers written contract, binding for 1 year; renewable by mutual consent.

Writers' Conferences: Moonlight & Magnolias; RWA National Conference (Orlando); Virginia Romance Writers (Williamsburg VA); Florida Romance Writers (Ft. Lauderdale FL); Golden Triangle Writers Conference; Bouchercon (Monterey, November); Malice Domestic (DC, May).

Tips: "Be professional! Always send in exactly what an agent/editor asks for, no more, no less. Keep query letters brief and to the point, giving your writing credentials and a very brief summary of your book. If one agent rejects you, keep trying—there are a lot of us out there!"

ALIVE COMMUNICATIONS, INC., 7680 Goddard St., Suite 200, Colorado Springs CO 80920. (719)260-7080. Fax: (719)260-8223. Website: www.alivecom.com. Estab. 1989. Member of CBA. Represents 200+ clients. 5% of clients are new/unpublished writers. Currently handles: 50% nonfiction books; 30% novels; 4% story collections; 5% novellas; 10% juvenile books; 1% syndicated material.

Member Agents: Rick Christian, president (blockbusters, bestsellers); Greg Johnson, vice president (popular/commercial nonfiction and fiction, Christian organizations); Jerry "Chip" MacGregor (popular/commercial nonfiction and fiction, new authors with breakout potential); Andrea Christian (gift, women's fiction/nonfiction, Christian living); Lee Hough (popular/commercial nonfiction and fiction, thoughtful spirituality, children's).

Represents: Nonfiction books, novels, short story collections, novellas, juvenile books. **Considers these fiction areas:** Action/adventure; contemporary issues; detective/police/crime; family saga; historical; humor/satire; juvenile; literary; mainstream/contemporary; mystery/suspense; religious/inspirational; thriller; westerns/frontier; young adult.

○ This agency specializes in fiction, Christian living, how-to, children's and commercial nonfiction. Actively seeking inspirational/literary/mainstream fiction and work from authors with established track record and platforms. Does not want poetry, young adult paperback, scripts, dark themes.

How to Contact: Works primarily with well-established, best-selling and career authors. Returns materials only with SASE. Obtains most new clients through recommendations from others, "On rare occasions accepts new clients through referrals."

Recent Sales: Sold 300 titles in the last year. *Left Behind series*, by Tim LaHaye and Jerry B. Jenkins (Tyndale); *Let's Roll*, by Lisa Beamer (Tyndale); *The Message*, by Eugene Peterson (NavPress); *Every Man Series*, by Stephen Arterburn (Waterbrook); *Cafe Refuge*, by Terri Blackstock (Zondervan).

Terms: Agent receives 15% commission on domestic sales; 10% commission on foreign sales. Offers written contract; 60-day written notice notice must be given to terminate contract.

Tips: "Rewrite and polish until the words on the page shine. Endorsements and great connections may help, provided you can write with power and passion. Network with publishing professionals by making contacts, joining citique groups, and attending writers' conferences in order to make personal connections in publishing and to get feedback. Alive Communications, Inc. has established itself as a premiere literary agency. Based in Colorado Springs, we serve an elite group of authors who are critically acclaimed and commercially successful in both Christian and general markets."

◪ **LINDA ALLEN LITERARY AGENCY**, 1949 Green St., Suite 5, San Francisco CA 94123-4829. (415)921-6437. **Contact:** Linda Allen. Estab. 1982. Member of AAR. Represents 35-40 clients.
Represents: Nonfiction books (adult), novels (adult). **Considers these fiction areas:** Historical; multicultural; narrative, current affairs, food/wine, health.
How to Contact: Query with SASE. Considers simultaneous queries. Responds in 3 weeks to queries. Returns materials only with SASE. Obtains most new clients through recommendations from others.
Recent Sales: This agency prefers not to share information on specific sales.
Terms: Agent receives 15% commission on domestic sales. Charges for photocopying.

◪ **MIRIAM ALTSHULER LITERARY AGENCY**, 53 Old Post Rd. N., Red Hook NY 12571. (845)758-9408. Fax: (845)758-3118. **Contact:** Miriam Altshuler. Estab. 1994. Member of AAR. Represents 40 clients. Currently handles: 45% nonfiction books; 45% novels; 5% story collections; 5% juvenile books.
• Ms. Altshuler has been an agent since 1982.
Represents: Nonfiction books, novels, short story collections, juvenile books. **Considers these fiction areas:** Literary; mainstream/contemporary; multicultural; thriller.
How to Contact: Query with SASE. Prefers to read materials exclusively. No e-mail or fax queries. Considers simultaneous queries. Responds in 2 weeks to queries; 3 weeks to mss. Returns materials only with SASE. Obtains most new clients through recommendations from others.
Terms: Agent receives 15% commission on domestic sales; 20% commission on foreign sales. No written contract. Charges clients for overseas mailing, photocopies, overnight mail when requested by author.
Writers' Conferences: Bread Loaf Writers' Conference (Middlebury VT, August).

◪ **BETSY AMSTER LITERARY ENTERPRISES**, P.O. Box 27788, Los Angeles CA 90027-0788. **Contact:** Betsy Amster. Estab. 1992. Member of AAR. Represents over 65 clients. 35% of clients are new/unpublished writers. Currently handles: 65% nonfiction books; 35% novels.
• Prior to opening her agency, Ms. Amster was an editor at Pantheon and Vintage for 10 years and served as editorial director for the Globe Pequot Press for 2 years. "This experience gives me a wider perspective on the business and the ability to give focused editorial feedback to my clients."
Represents: Nonfiction books, novels. **Considers these fiction areas:** Ethnic; literary.
○➥ Actively seeking "strong narrative nonfiction, particularly by journalists; outstanding literary fiction (the next Michael Chabon or Jhumpa Lahiri); and high profile self-help and psychology, preferably research-based." Does not want to receive poetry, children's books, romances, westerns, science fiction.
How to Contact: For fiction send query, first 3 pages and SASE. No e-mail or fax queries. Considers simultaneous queries. Responds in 1 month to queries; 2 months to mss. Obtains most new clients through recommendations from others, solicitations, conferences.
Recent Sales: *I Was Howard Hughes*, by Steven Carter (Bloomsbury); *AgeLess*, by Edward Schneider, M.D., and Elizabeth Miles (Rodale); *I Know I'm in There Somewhere: A Woman's Guide to Finding Her Inner Voice and Living a Life of Authenticity*, by Helene Brenner, Ph.D. (Gotham). Other clients include Dwight Allen, Elaine N. Aron, Lynette Brasfield, Robin Chotzinoff, Frank Clifford, Rob Cohen & David Wollock, Jan DeBlieu, Maria Amparo Escandon, Wendy Mogel, Sharon Montrose, Joy Nicholson, Katie Singer, Louise Steinman, Diana Wells.
Terms: Agent receives 15% commission on domestic sales; 20% commission on foreign sales. Offers written contract, binding for 1-2 years; 60-day notice must be given to terminate contract. Charges for photocopying, postage, long distance phone calls, messengers and galleys and books used in submissions to foreign and film agents and to magazines for first serial rights.
Writers' Conferences: Squaw Valley; Pacific Northwest Conference; San Diego Writers Conference; UCLA Writers Conference

◪ **MARCIA AMSTERDAM AGENCY**, 41 W. 82nd St., New York NY 10024-5613. (212)873-4945. **Contact:** Marcia Amsterdam. Estab. 1970. Signatory of WGA. Currently handles: 15% nonfiction books; 70% novels; 5% movie scripts; 10% TV scripts.
• Prior to opening her agency, Ms. Amsterdam was an editor.
Represents: Nonfiction books, novels, feature film, TV movie of the week, sitcom. **Considers these fiction areas:** Action/adventure; detective/police/crime; horror; mainstream/contemporary; mystery/suspense; romance (contemporary, historical); science fiction; thriller; westerns/frontier; young adult. **Considers these script subject areas:** Comedy; mainstream; mystery/suspense; romantic comedy; romantic drama.
How to Contact: Submit outline, 3 sample chapter(s), SASE. Responds in 1 month to queries.
Recent Sales: *Rosey in the Present Tense*, by Louise Hawes (Walker); *Flash Factor*, by William H. Lovejoy (Kensington).
Terms: Agent receives 15% commission on domestic sales; 20% commission on foreign sales; 10% commission on dramatic rights sales. Offers written contract, binding for 1 year. Charges clients for extra office expenses, foreign postage, copying, legal fees (when agreed upon).
Tips: "We are always looking for interesting literary voices."

APPLESEEDS MANAGEMENT, 200 E. 30th St., Suite 302, San Bernardino CA 92404. (909)882-1667.
Contact: S. James Foiles. Estab. 1988. 40% of clients are new/unpublished writers. Currently handles: 15% nonfiction books; 85% novels.
Represents: Nonfiction books, novels. **Considers these fiction areas:** Detective/police/crime; mystery/suspense.
How to Contact: Query with SASE. Responds in 2 weeks to queries; 2 months to mss.
Recent Sales: This agency prefers not to share information on specific sales.
Terms: Agent receives 10-15% commission on domestic sales; 20% commission on foreign sales. Offers written contract, binding for 1-7 years.
Tips: "Appleseeds specializes in mysteries with a detective who could be in a continuing series because readership of mysteries is expanding."

AUTHENTIC CREATIONS LITERARY AGENCY, 875 Lawrenceville-Suwanee Rd., Suite 310-306, Lawrenceville GA 30043. (770)339-3774. Fax: (770)339-7126. E-mail: ron@authenticcreations.com. Website: www.authenticcreations.com. **Contact:** Mary Lee Laitsch. Estab. 1993. Represents 70 clients. 30% of clients are new/unpublished writers. Currently handles: 60% nonfiction books; 40% novels.
● Prior to becoming agents, Ms. Laitsch was a librarian and elementary school teacher; Mr. Laitsch was an attorney and a writer.
Member Agents: Mary Lee Laitsch; Ronald Laitsch; Jason Laitsch.
Represents: Nonfiction books, novels, scholarly books. **Considers these fiction areas:** Action/adventure; contemporary issues; detective/police/crime; family saga; literary; mainstream/contemporary; mystery/suspense; romance; sports; thriller.
How to Contact: Query with SASE. No e-mail or fax queries. Considers simultaneous queries. Responds in 2 weeks to queries; 2 months to mss.
Recent Sales: Sold 15 titles in the last year. *Frankenstein—The Legacy*, by Christopher Schildt (Simon & Schuster); *Night of Dracula*, by Christopher Schildt (Simon & Schuster).
Terms: Agent receives 15% commission on domestic sales; 15% commission on foreign sales. Charges clients for photocopying.
Tips: "The tragic events of September 11 followed by the anthrax scare has changed the nature of the marketplace. Agents need to be aware of these changes and guide their authors into new directions that tap into this new market."

AUTHORS & ARTISTS GROUP, INC., 41 E. 11th St., 11th Floor, New York NY 10003. (212)944-9898. Fax: (212)944-6484. **Contact:** Al Lowman, president. Estab. 1984. Represents 50 clients. 25% of clients are new/unpublished writers. Currently handles: 95% nonfiction books; 5% novels.
● Prior to becoming an agent, Mr. Lowman was an advertising executive.
Member Agents: B.G. Dilworth (nonfiction); Al Lowman (president nonfiction).
Represents: Nonfiction books, novels. **Considers these fiction areas:** Action/adventure; contemporary issues; detective/police/crime; erotica; ethnic; gay/lesbian; horror; humor/satire; mainstream/contemporary; psychic/supernatural; religious/inspirational; thriller.
○ This agency specializes in celebrity-based autobiographies and self-help books; and any books that bring its readers to "higher ground." Actively seeking fresh full-length, adult nonfiction ideas and established novelists. Does not want to receive film and TV scripts, children's stories, poetry or short stories.
How to Contact: Fax 1 page query. Considers simultaneous queries. Responds in 3 weeks to queries. Obtains most new clients through recommendations from others.
Terms: Agent receives 15% commission on domestic sales; 20% commission on foreign sales. Charges clients for office expenses, postage, photocopying not to exceed $1,000 without permission of author.

THE AXELROD AGENCY, 49 Main St., P.O. Box 357, Chatham NY 12037. (518)392-2100. Fax: (518)392-2944. E-mail: steve@axelrodagency.com. **Contact:** Steven Axelrod. Estab. 1983. Member of AAR. Represents 20-30 clients. 1% of clients are new/unpublished writers. Currently handles: 5% nonfiction books; 95% novels.
● Prior to becoming an agent, Mr. Axelrod was a book club editor.
Represents: Nonfiction books, novels. **Considers these fiction areas:** Mystery/suspense; romance; women's.
How to Contact: Query with SASE. Considers simultaneous queries. Responds in 3 weeks to queries; 6 weeks to mss. Returns materials only with SASE. Obtains most new clients through recommendations from others.
Recent Sales: This agency prefers not to share information on specific sales.
Terms: Agent receives 15% commission on domestic sales; 20% commission on foreign sales. No written contract.
Writers' Conferences: Romance Writers of America (July).

LORETTA BARRETT BOOKS, INC., 101 Fifth Ave., New York NY 10003. (212)242-3420. Fax: (212)807-9579. E-mail: mail
orettabarrettbooks.com. **Contact:** Loretta A. Barrett or Nick Mullendore. Estab. 1990. Member of AAR. Represents 90 clients. Currently handles: 60% nonfiction books; 40% novels.
● Prior to opening her agency, Ms. Barrett was vice president and executive editor at Doubleday for 25 years.
Represents: Nonfiction books, novels. **Considers these fiction areas:** Action/adventure; confession; contemporary

issues; detective/police/crime; ethnic; family saga; feminist; gay/lesbian; glitz; historical; literary; mainstream/contemporary; mystery/suspense; psychic/supernatural; thriller.

○━ This agency specializes in general interest books. No children's or juvenile.

How to Contact: Query with SASE. No e-mail or fax queries. Considers simultaneous queries. Responds in 6 weeks to queries. Returns materials only with SASE.

Recent Sales: *The Singularity is Near*, by Ray Kurzweil (Viking); *Flesh Tones*, by MJ Rose (Ballantine Books); *The Lake of Dead Languages*, by Carol Goodman (Ballantine Books); *The Bad Witness*, by Laura Van Wormer (Mira Books).

Terms: Agent receives 15% commission on domestic sales; 20% commission on foreign sales. Offers written contract. Charges clients for shipping and photocopying.

Writers' Conferences: San Diego State University Writer's Conference; Maui Writer's Conference.

◢ **JENNY BENT, HARVEY KLINGER, INC.**, 301 W. 53rd St., New York NY 10019. (212)581-7068. Fax: (212)315-3823. E-mail: jenlbent@aol.com. Website: www.jennybent.com. **Contact:** Jenny Bent. Member of AAR. Represents 60 clients. 40% of clients are new/unpublished writers. Currently handles: 70% nonfiction books; 30% novels.

● Prior to joining her agency, Ms. Bent worked as an editor in book publishing and magazines.

Represents: Nonfiction books, novels. **Considers these fiction areas:** Ethnic; literary; mainstream/contemporary; romance.

○━ Actively seeking quality fiction and nonfiction from well-credentialed authors. Does not want to receive science fiction, New Age fiction, mysteries, thrillers, children's, self-help from non-credentialed writers.

How to Contact: Query with SASE, submit proposal package, outline, résumé, publishing history, author bio. Please always include a bio or résumé with submissions or queries. Accepts e-mail queries, but no attachments. Considers simultaneous queries. Responds in 1 month to queries; 2 months to mss. Returns materials only with SASE. Obtains most new clients through recommendations from others, solicitations, conferences.

Recent Sales: Sold 20 titles in the last year. *Red Ant House*, by Ann Cummins (Houghton Mifflin); *Makeover Moms Meal Club*, by Liz Weiss and Janice N. Bissey (Broadway).

Terms: Agent receives 15% commission on domestic sales; 25% commission on foreign sales. Offers written contract; 30 days notice must be given to terminate contract. Charges for overnight mail, out-of-office photocopies (deducted from advance).

◢ **MEREDITH BERNSTEIN LITERARY AGENCY**, 2112 Broadway, Suite 503A, New York NY 10023. (212)799-1007. Fax: (212)799-1145. Estab. 1981. Member of AAR. Represents 85 clients. 20% of clients are new/unpublished writers. Currently handles: 50% nonfiction books; 50% fiction.

● Prior to opening her agency, Ms. Bernstein served in another agency for 5 years.

Member Agents: Meredith Bernstein; Elizabeth Cavanaugh.

Represents: Nonfiction books, fiction of all kinds. **Considers these fiction areas:** Literary; mystery/suspense; romance; thriller; women's fiction.

○━ This agency does not specialize, "very eclectic."

How to Contact: Query with SASE. No e-mail or fax queries. Considers simultaneous queries. Obtains most new clients through recommendations from others, conferences, also develops and packages own ideas.

Recent Sales: *The Giftionary*, by Robyn Spizman (St. Martins); *Women for Hire*, by Tony Johnson and Robyn Spizman (Perigee).

Terms: Agent receives 15% commission on domestic sales; 20% commission on foreign sales. Charges clients $75 disbursement fee/year.

Writers' Conferences: Southwest Writers Conference (Albuquereque, August); Rocky Moutnain Writers' Conference (Denver, September); Golden Triangle (Beaumont TX, October); Pacific Northwest Writers Conference; Austin League Writers Conference; Willamette Writers Conference (Portland, OR); Lafayette Writers Conference (Lafayette, LA); Surrey Writers Conference (Surrey, BC.); San Diego State University Writers Conference (San Diego, CA).

◢ **DANIEL BIAL AGENCY**, 41 W. 83rd St., Suite 5-C, New York NY 10024-5246. (212)721-1786. Fax: (309)213-0230. E-mail: dbialagency@juno.com. **Contact:** Daniel Bial. Estab. 1992. Represents under 50 clients. 15% of clients are new/unpublished writers. Currently handles: 95% nonfiction books; 5% novels.

● Prior to opening his agency, Mr. Bial was an editor for 15 years.

Represents: Nonfiction books, novels. **Considers these fiction areas:** Action/adventure; contemporary issues; detective/police/crime; erotica; ethnic; feminist; gay/lesbian; humor/satire; literary.

How to Contact: Submit proposal package, outline. Responds in 2 weeks to queries. Returns materials only with SASE. Obtains most new clients through recommendations from others, solicitations, "good rolodex."

Terms: Agent receives 15% commission on domestic sales; 25% commission on foreign sales. Offers written contract, binding for 1 year with cancellation clause. Charges clients for overseas calls, overnight mailing, photocopying, messenger expenses.

Tips: "Publishers are looking for authors with platforms—that is, people who already have positioned themselves in order to get their books heard...and sold."

◐ **BIGSCORE PRODUCTIONS, INC.**, P.O. Box 4575, Lancaster PA 17604. (717)293-0247. Fax: (717)293-1945. E-mail: bigscore@bigscoreproductions.com. Website: www.bigscoreproductions.com. **Contact:** David A. Robie, agent; Sharon Hanby-Robie, agent; Deb Strubel, associate. Estab. 1995. Represents 50-75 clients. 25% of clients are new/unpublished writers.

Represents: Nonfiction and fiction (see website for categories of interest).

○━ This agency specializes in inspirational and self-help nonfiction and fiction and has over 40 years in the publishing and agenting business.

How to Contact: See website for submission guidelines. Query by e-mail or mail. No fax queries. Considers simultaneous queries. Responds in 1 month to proposals.

Terms: Agent receives 15% commission on domestic sales. Offers written contract, binding for 6 months. Charges clients for expedited shipping, ms photocopying and preparation, and books for subsidiary rights submissions.

Tips: "Very open to taking on new clients. Submit a well-prepared proposal that will take minimal fine-tuning for presentation to publishers. Nonfiction writers must be highly marketable and media savvy—the more established in speaking or in your profession, the better. Bigscore Productions works with all major general and Christian publishers"

◑ **DAVID BLACK LITERARY AGENCY**, 156 Fifth Ave., New York NY 10010. (212)242-5080. Fax: (212)924-6609. **Contact:** David Black, owner. Estab. 1990. Member of AAR. Represents 150 clients. Currently handles: 90% nonfiction books; 10% novels.

Member Agents: Susan Raihofer (general nonfiction to literary fiction); Gary Morris (commercial fiction to psychology); Joy E. Tutela (general nonfiction to literary fiction); Laureen Rowland (business, health).

Represents: Nonfiction books, novels. **Considers these fiction areas:** Literary; mainstream/contemporary; Commercial.

○━ This agency specializes in business, sports, politics, and novels.

How to Contact: Query with SASE, outline. No e-mail or fax queries. Considers simultaneous queries. Responds in 2 months to queries. Returns materials only with SASE.

Recent Sales: *Body for Life*, by Bill Phillips with Mike D'Orso (HarperCollins); *Walking with the Wind*, by John Lewis with Micke D'Orso (Simon & Schuster).

Terms: Agent receives 15% commission on domestic sales. Charges clients for photocopying and books purchased for sale of foreign rights.

◑ **BLEECKER STREET ASSOCIATES, INC.**, 532 LaGuardia Place, #617, New York NY 10012. (212)677-4492. Fax: (212)388-0001. **Contact:** Agnes Birnbaum. Estab. 1984. Member of AAR, RWA, MWA. Represents 60 clients. 20% of clients are new/unpublished writers. Currently handles: 75% nonfiction books; 25% novels.

● Prior to becoming an agent, Ms. Birnbaum was a senior editor at Simon & Schuster, Dutton/Signet and other publishing houses.

Represents: Nonfiction books, novels. **Considers these fiction areas:** Ethnic; historical; literary; mystery/suspense; romance; thriller; women's (interest).

○━ "We're very hands-on and accessible. We try to be truly creative in our submission approaches. We've had especially good luck with first-time authors." Does not want to receive science fiction, westerns, poetry, children's books, academic/scholarly/professional books, plays, scripts, short stories.

How to Contact: Query with SASE. No email, phone or fax queries. Considers simultaneous queries. Responds in 2 weeks to queries; 1 month to mss. Returns materials only with SASE. Obtains most new clients through recommendations from others, solicitations, conferences, "plus, I will approach someone with a letter if his/her work impresses me."

Recent Sales: Sold 30 titles in the last year. *The Art of War*, by Bevin Alexander (Crown); *The Dim Sum of All Things*, by Kim Wong Keltner (Morrow/Avon).

Terms: Agent receives 15% commission on domestic sales; 25% commission on foreign sales. Offers written contract; 30 days notice must be given to terminate contract. Charges for postage, long distance, fax, messengers, photocopies, not to exceed $200.

Tips: "Keep query letters short and to the point; include only information pertaining to book or background as writer. Try to avoid superlatives in description. Work needs to stand on its own, so how much editing it may have received has no place in a query letter."

◐ **BOOK DEALS, INC.**, 244 Fifth Ave., Suite 2164, New York NY 10001-7604. (212)252-2701. Fax: (212)591-6211. E-mail: submissions@bookdealsinc.com. Website: www.bookdealsinc.com. **Contact:** Caroline Francis Carney. Estab. 1996. Member of AAR. Represents 40 clients. 15% of clients are new/unpublished writers. Currently handles: 85% nonfiction books; 15% novels.

● Prior to opening her agency, Ms. Carney was editorial director for a consumer book imprint within Times Mirror and held senior editorial positions in McGraw-Hill and NYIF/Simon & Schuster.

Represents: Nonfiction books, novels (commercial and literary). **Considers these fiction areas:** Ethnic; literary; mainstream/contemporary; women's (contemporary); urban literature.

○━ This agency specializes in highly commercial nonfiction and books for African-American readers and women. Actively seeking well-crafted fiction and nonfiction from authors with engaging voices and impeccable credentials.

How to Contact: Query with SASE. Considers simultaneous queries.

Recent Sales: Sold 25 titles in the last year. *Self-Proclaimed*, by Rochelle Shapiro (Simon & Schuster); *Par for the Course*, by Alice Dye and Mark Shaw (HarperCollins).

Terms: Agent receives 15% commission on domestic sales; 20% commission on foreign sales. Offers written contract. Charges clients for photocopying and postage.

Tips: "If you have Internet access, please visit our website before submitting a query letter. It has a lot of insider tips to assist you in your search."

BOOKENDS, LLC, 136 Long Hill Rd., Gillette NJ 07933. (908)604-2652. E-mail: editor@bookends-inc.com. Website: www.bookends-inc.com. **Contact:** Jessica Faust or Jacky Sach. Estab. 1999. Represents 50 clients. 60% of clients are new/unpublished writers. Currently handles: 50% nonfiction books; 50% novels.

• Prior to opening their agency, Ms. Faust and Ms. Sach worked at such publishing houses as Berkley, Penguin Putnam, Macmillan and IDG.

Member Agents: Jessica Faust (mysteries, romance, relationships, business, finance, pets, general self-help); Jacky Sach (suspense thrillers, mysteries, literary fiction, spirituality, pets, general self-help)

Represents: Nonfiction books, novels. **Considers these fiction areas:** Contemporary issues; detective/police/crime; ethnic; family saga; feminist; glitz; historical; literary; mainstream/contemporary; mystery/suspense; romance; thriller.

○━ BookEnds specializes in genre fiction and personality driven nonfiction. Actively seeking romance, mystery, women's fiction, literary fiction and suspense thrillers. For nonfiction, relationships, business, general self-help, women's interest, parenting, pets, spirituality, health and psychology. Does not want to receive children's books, screenplays, science fiction, poetry, technical/military thrillers.

How to Contact: Submit outline, 3 sample chapter(s). Considers simultaneous queries. Responds in 4-6 weeks to queries; 8-10 to mss. Returns materials only with SASE. Obtains most new clients through recommendations from others, solicitations, conferences.

Recent Sales: Sold 55 titles in the last year. *Parrot Fish Don't Talk*, by Kathy Brandt (NAL); *Summer Wind*, by Barbara Gale (Harlequin).

Terms: Agent receives 15% commission on domestic sales; 20% commission on foreign sales. Offers written contract. Charges clients for photocopying, messenger, cables, overseas postage, long-distance phone calls, copies of the published book when purchases for subsidiary rights submissions. Expenses will not exceed $150.

Writers' Conferences: Central Florida Romance Writers Conference (Orlando FL, September); Emerald Coast Writers Conference (Seattle WA, October); Panhandle Professional Writer's Conference (Amarillo TX, June); Washington Romance Writers' (Harper's Ferry Retreat, April).

Tips: "When submitting material be sure to include any information that might be helpful to the agent. In your query letter you should include the title of the book, your name, your publishing history and a brief 1 or 2 sentence description of the book. Also be sure to let the agent know if you see this book as part of a series and if you've already begun work on other books. Once an agent has expressed interest in representing you it is crucial to let her know who has seen your book and even supply copies of any correspondence you've had with prospective editors."

✉ **BOOKS & SUCH**, 4788 Carissa Ave., Santa Rosa CA 94505. (707)538-4184. Fax: (707)538-3937. E-mail: jkgbooks@aol.com. Website: janetgrant.com. **Contact:** Janet Kobobel Grant. Estab. 1996. Member of CBA (associate). Represents 40 clients. 20% of clients are new/unpublished writers. Currently handles: 42% nonfiction books; 46% novels; 2% juvenile books; 10% children's picture books.

• Before becoming an agent, Ms. Grant was an editor for Zondervan and managing editor for Focus on the Family.

Represents: Nonfiction books, novels, juvenile books. **Considers these fiction areas:** Contemporary issues; family saga; historical; juvenile; mainstream/contemporary; picture books; religious/inspirational; romance; young adult.

○━ This agency specializes in "general and inspirational fiction, romance, and in the Christian booksellers market." Actively seeking "material appropriate to the Christian market."

How to Contact: Query with SASE. Considers simultaneous queries. Responds in 1 month to queries; 2 months to mss. Returns materials only with SASE. Obtains most new clients through recommendations from others, conferences.

Recent Sales: Sold 31 titles in the last year. *Gentle Passages*, by Robin Jones Gunn (Multnomah Publishers); *Fair Haven*, by BJ Hoff (W Publishing). Other clients include Janet McHenry, Jane Orcutt, Gayle Roper, Stephanie Grace Whitson.

Terms: Agent receives 15% commission on domestic sales; 15% commission on foreign sales. Offers written contract; 2 months notice must be given to terminate contract. Charges clients for postage, photocopying, telephone calls, fax and express mail.

Writers' Conferences: Romance Writers of America; Mt. Hermon Writers Conference (Mt. Hermon CA, March 22-26); Glorieta Writers Conference (Santa Fe NM, October).

Tips: "The heart of my motivation is to develop relationships with the authors I serve, to do what I can to shine the light of success on them, and to help be a caretaker of their gifts and time."

◐ **GEORGES BORCHARDT, INC.**, 136 E. 57th St., New York NY 10022. (212)753-5785. Fax: (212)838-6518. Estab. 1967. Member of AAR. Represents 200 clients. 10% of clients are new/unpublished writers. Currently handles: 60% nonfiction books; 37% novels; 1% novellas; 1% juvenile books; 1% poetry.
Member Agents: Anne Borchardt; Georges Borchardt; DeAnna Heindel; Valerie Borchardt.
Represents: Nonfiction books, novels. **Considers these fiction areas:** Literary.
    ⚬ This agency specializes in literary fiction and outstanding nonfiction.
How to Contact: Responds in 1 week to queries; 1 month to mss. Obtains most new clients through recommendations from others.
Recent Sales: Sold 100 titles in the last year. *Drop City*, by T. Coraghessan Boyle (Viking/Penguin); *Any Human Heart*, by William Boyd (Knopf); *Friendship*, by Joseph Epstein (Houghton Mifflin).
Terms: Agent receives 15% commission on domestic sales; 20% commission on foreign sales. Offers written contract. "We charge clients cost of outside photocopying and shipping manuscripts or books overseas."

Ⓝ ◐ ⊘ **THE BARBARA BOVA LITERARY AGENCY**, 3951 Gulfshore Blvd. N., PH1-B, Naples FL 34103. (941)649-7237. Fax: (239)649-7263. E-mail: bovabefore@aol.com. **Contact:** Barbara Bova. Estab. 1974. Represents 30 clients. Currently handles: 20% nonfiction books; 80% novels.
Represents: Nonfiction books, novels. **Considers these fiction areas:** Action/adventure; detective/police/crime; glitz; mystery/suspense; science fiction; thriller.
    ⚬ This agency specializes in fiction and nonfiction, hard and soft science.
How to Contact: Query with SASE. Obtains most new clients through recommendations from others.
Recent Sales: Sold 6 titles in the last year. *Saturn*, by Ben Bova; *Crystal City*, by Orson Scott Card; *Bone Cold*, by Rick Wilber.
Terms: Agent receives 15% commission on domestic sales; 20% commission on foreign sales.
Tips: This agency also handles foreign rights, movies, television, audio.

◐ **BRADY LITERARY MANAGEMENT**, P.O. Box 164, Hartland Four Corners VT 05049. **Contact:** Upton Brady. Estab. 1988. Represents 100 clients.
Represents: Nonfiction books, novels, short story collections, novellas. **Considers these fiction areas:** Literary; mainstream/contemporary.
How to Contact: Query with SASE, submit outline, first 50 pages. Responds in 2 months to queries.
Recent Sales: This agency prefers not to share information on specific sales.
Terms: Agent receives 15% commission on domestic sales; 20% commission on foreign sales. Charges clients for extensive international postage and photocopying.

◐ **THE JOAN BRANDT AGENCY**, 788 Wesley Dr., Atlanta GA 30305-3933. (404)351-8877. **Contact:** Joan Brandt. Estab. 1980. Represents 30 clients. 50% of clients are new/unpublished writers. Currently handles: 45% nonfiction books; 45% novels; 10% juvenile books.
Represents: Nonfiction books, novels, short story collections. **Considers these fiction areas:** Contemporary issues; detective/police/crime; family saga; literary; mainstream/contemporary; mystery/suspense; thriller.
How to Contact: Query with SASE. No e-mail or fax queries. Considers simultaneous queries. Returns materials only with SASE. Obtains most new clients through solicitations.
Recent Sales: This agency prefers not to share information on specific sales.
Terms: Agent receives 15% commission on domestic sales; 20% commission on foreign sales. No written contract.

◐ **BRANDT & HOCHMAN LITERARY AGENTS, INC.**, 1501 Broadway, New York NY 10036. (212)840-5760. Fax: (212)840-5776. **Contact:** Carl Brandt; Gail Hochman; Marianne Merola; Charles Schlessiger; Bill Contardi. Estab. 1913. Member of AAR. Represents 200 clients.
Represents: Nonfiction books, novels, short story collections, juvenile books, journalism. **Considers these fiction areas:** Contemporary issues; ethnic; family saga; historical; literary; mainstream/contemporary; mystery/suspense; romance; thriller; young adult.
How to Contact: Query with SASE. No fax queries. Considers simultaneous queries. Responds in 1 month to queries. Returns materials only with SASE. Obtains most new clients through recommendations from others.
Recent Sales: Sold 50 titles in the last year. This agency prefers not to share information on specific sales. Other clients include Scott Turow, Carlos Fuentes, Ursula Hegi, Michael Cunningham, Mary Pope Osborne.
Terms: Agent receives 15% commission on domestic sales; 20% commission on foreign sales. Charges clients for "manuscript duplication or other special expenses agreed to in advance."
Tips: "Write a letter which will give the agent a sense of you as a professional writer, your long-term interests as well as a short description of the work at hand."

M. COURTNEY BRIGGS, 100 N. Broadway Ave., 20th Floor, Oklahoma City OK 73102-8806. **Contact:** M. Courtney Briggs. Estab. 1994. 25% of clients are new/unpublished writers. Currently handles: 5% nonfiction books; 10% novels; 80% juvenile books; 5% multimedia.
    ● Prior to becoming an agent, Ms. Briggs was in subsidiary rights at Random House for 3 years; an associate agent and film rights associate with Curtis Brown, Ltd.; also an attorney for 12 years.

Represents: Nonfiction books, novels, juvenile books. **Considers these fiction areas:** Juvenile; mainstream/contemporary; picture books; young adult.

⦿ M. Courtney Briggs is an agent and an attorney. "I work primarily, but not exclusively, with children's book authors and illustrators. I will also consult or review a contract on an hourly basis." Actively seeking children's fiction, children's picture books (illustrations and text), young adult novels, fiction, nonfiction.

How to Contact: Query with SASE. No e-mail or fax queries. Responds in 2 weeks to queries; 6 weeks to mss. Returns materials only with SASE. Obtains most new clients through recommendations from others.

Recent Sales: This agency prefers not to share information on specific sales.

Terms: Agent receives 15% commission on domestic sales; 25% commission on foreign sales. Offers written contract; 60—day notice must be given to terminate contract.

Writers' Conferences: National Conference on Writing & Illustrating for Children (August).

◪ CURTIS BROWN, LTD., 10 Astor Place, New York NY 10003-6935. (212)473-5400. Also: 1750 Montgomery St., San Fancisco CA 94111. (415)954-8566. **Contact:** Perry Knowlton, chairman; Timothy Knowlton, CEO; Peter L. Ginsberg, president. Member of AAR; signatory of WGA.

Member Agents: Laura Blake Peterson; Ellen Geiger; Emilie Jacobson, vice president; Maureen Walters, vice president; Virginia Knowlton (literary, adult, children's); Timothy Knowlton (film, screenplays, plays; Marilyn Marlow, executive vice president; Ed Wintle (film, screenplays, plays); Mitchell Waters; Elizabeth Harding; Douglas Stewart; Kristen Manges; Dave Barber (translation rights).

Represents: Nonfiction books, novels, short story collections, novellas, juvenile books, poetry books, movie scripts, feature film, TV scripts, TV movie of the week, stage plays. **Considers these fiction areas:** Action/adventure; comic books/cartoon; confession; contemporary issues; detective/police/crime; erotica; ethnic; experimental; family saga; fantasy; feminist; gay/lesbian; glitz; gothic; hi-lo; historical; horror; humor/satire; juvenile; literary; mainstream/contemporary; military/war; multicultural; multimedia; mystery/suspense; New Age; occult; picture books; plays; poetry; poetry in translation; psychic/supernatural; regional; religious/inspirational; romance; science fiction; short story collections; spiritual; sports; thriller; translation; westerns/frontier; young adult; women's.

How to Contact: Query with SASE. Prefers to read materials exclusively. No unsolicited mss. No e-mail or fax queries. Responds in 3 weeks to queries; 5 weeks to mss. Obtains most new clients through recommendations from others, solicitations, conferences.

Recent Sales: This agency prefers not to share information on specific sales.

Terms: Offers written contract. Charges for photocopying, some postage.

◪ SHEREE BYKOFSKY ASSOCIATES, INC., 577 2nd Ave., PMB 109, New York NY 10016. E-mail: shereebee@aol.com. Website: www.shereebee.com. **Contact:** Sheree Bykofsky. Estab. 1984, incorporated 1991. Member of AAR, ASJA, WNBA. Currently handles: 80% nonfiction books; 20% novels.

● Prior to opening her agency, Ms. Bykofsky served as executive editor of The Stonesong Press and managing editor of Chiron Press. She is also the author or co-author of more than 17 books, including *The Complete Idiot's Guide to Getting Published.* Ms. Bykofsky teaches publishing at NYU and The 92nd St. Y.

Member Agents: Janet Rosen, associate; Megan Buckley, associate.

Represents: Nonfiction books, novels. **Considers these fiction areas:** Literary; mainstream/contemporary.

⦿ This agency specializes in popular reference nonfiction, commercial fiction with a literary quality and mysteries. "I have wide-ranging interests, but it really depends on quality of writing, originality, and how a particular project appeals to me (or not). I take on fiction when I completely love it—it doesn't matter what area or genre." Does not want to receive poetry, material for children, screenplays, westerns, horror, sci-fi or fantasy.

How to Contact: Query with SASE. No unsolicited mss or phone calls. Considers simultaneous queries. Responds in 1 week to queries; 1 month to mss. Returns materials only with SASE. Obtains most new clients through recommendations from others.

Terms: Agent receives 15% commission on domestic sales; 20% commission on foreign sales. Offers written contract, binding for 1 year. Charges for postage, photocopying and fax.

Writers' Conferences: ASJA (New York City); Asilomar (Pacific Grove CA); St. Petersburg; Whidbey Island; Jacksonville; Albuquerque; Austin; Columbus; Southwestern Writers; Willamette (Portland); Dorothy Canfield Fisher (San Diego); Writers Union (Maui); Pacific NW; IWWG; and many others.

Tips: "Read the agent listing carefully, and comply with guidelines."

CARLISLE & CO., 24 E. 64th St., New York NY 10021. (212)813-1881. Fax: (212)813-9567. E-mail: mtessler@carlisleco.com. Website: www.carlisleco.com. **Contact:** Michelle Tessler. Estab. 1998. Member of AAR. Represents 200 clients. Currently handles: 70% nonfiction books; 30% novels.

● Prior to opening his agency, Mr. Carlisle was the Vice President of William Morris for 18 years.

Member Agents: Michael Carlisle, Christy Fletcher, Emma Parry, Michelle Tessler, Joe Veltre. Affiliates: Donald S. Lamm, Robert Bernstein, Paul Bresnick, Diane Gedymin, Kathy Green.

Represents: Nonfiction books, fiction. **Considers these fiction areas:** Action/adventure; literary; mainstream/contemporary; mystery/suspense; thriller.

⦿ This agency has "expertise in nonfiction and literary fiction. We have a strong focus on editorial input before submission." Does not want to receive science fiction, fantasy, or romance.

How to Contact: Query with SASE. Responds in 10 days to queries; 3 weeks to mss. Obtains most new clients through recommendations from others.

Recent Sales: Sold 100 titles in the last year. *Our Inner Ape*, by Frans de Wall (Riverhead); *The Commissariat of Enlightenment*, by Ken Kalfus (Ecco/Scribner UK); *The Man I Should Have Married*, by Pamela Satran (Pocket Books).

Terms: Agent receives 15% commission on domestic sales; 20% commission on foreign sales. Offers written contract, binding for 1 book only.

Writers' Conferences: Squaw Valley Community Conference (California).

Tips: "Be sure to write as original a story as possible. Remember, you're asking the public to pay $25 for your book."

MARIA CARVAINIS AGENCY, INC., 1350 Avenue of the Americas, Suite 2905, New York NY 10019. (212)245-6365. Fax: (212)245-7196. E-mail: mca@mariacarvainisagency.com. **Contact:** Maria Carvainis, president; Frances Kuffel, executive vice president. Estab. 1977. Member of AAR, Authors Guild, Women's Media Group, ABA, MWA, RWA; signatory of WGA. Represents 70 clients. 10% of clients are new/unpublished writers. Currently handles: 34% nonfiction books; 65% novels; 1% poetry.

● Prior to opening her agency, Ms. Carvainis spent more than 10 years in the publishing industry as a senior editor with Macmillan Publishing, Basic Books, Avon Books (where she worked closely with Peter Mayer), and Crown Publishers. Ms. Carvainis has served as a member of the AAR Board of Directors and AAR Treasurer, as well as serving as chair of the AAR Contracts Committee. She presently serves on the AAR Royalty Committee.

Member Agents: Frances Kuffel (Executive Vice President); Anna Del Vecchio (Contracts Associate); Moira Sullivan (Editorial Associate); David Harvey (Literary Assistant).

Represents: Nonfiction books, novels. **Considers these fiction areas:** Literary; mainstream/contemporary; mystery/suspense; romance; thriller; young adult; Middle grade, women's fiction.

Oᴙ Does not want to receive science fiction or children's picture books.

How to Contact: Query with SASE. Responds in 1 week to queries; 3 months to mss. Obtains most new clients through recommendations from others, conferences, 60% from conferences/referrals; 40% from query letters.

Recent Sales: *The Bedwyn Series*, by Mary Balogh (Delacorte); *Hello, Darkness*, by Sandra Brown (Simon & Schuster). Other clients include Sue Erikson Boland, Pam Conrad, Phillip DePoy, Carlos Dews, Fred Haefle, Hugo Mager, Ellen Newmark, David Saxe, Kristine Rolofson, Janet Mansfield Soares, Peter Stark, Ernest Suarez.

Terms: Agent receives 15% commission on domestic sales; 20% commission on foreign sales. Offers written contract, binding for 2 years on a book-by-book basis. Charges clients for foreign postage, bulk copying.

Writers' Conferences: BEA.

CASTIGLIA LITERARY AGENCY, 1155 Camino Del Mar, Suite 510, Del Mar CA 92014. (858)755-8761. Fax: (858)755-7063. **Contact:** Julie Castiglia. Estab. 1993. Member of AAR, PEN. Represents 50 clients. Currently handles: 55% nonfiction books; 45% novels.

Member Agents: Winifred Golden; Julie Castiglia.

Represents: Nonfiction books, novels. **Considers these fiction areas:** Contemporary issues; ethnic; literary; mainstream/contemporary; mystery/suspense; women's (especially).

Oᴙ Does not want to receive horror, screenplays or academic nonfiction.

How to Contact: Query with SASE. No fax queries. Responds in 2 months to mss. Returns materials only with SASE. Obtains most new clients through recommendations from others, solicitations, conferences.

Recent Sales: Sold 21 titles in the last year.

Terms: Agent receives 15% commission on domestic sales; 25% commission on foreign sales. Offers written contract; 6-week notice must be given to terminate contract. Charges clients for Fed Ex or Messenger.

Writers' Conferences: Southwestern Writers Conference (Albuquerque NM, August); National Writers Conference; Willamette Writers Conference (OR); San Diego State University (CA); Writers at Work (Utah); Austin Conference (TX).

Tips: "Be professional with submissions. Attend workshops and conferences before you approach an agent."

CIRCLE OF CONFUSION, LTD., 107-23 71st Rd., Suite 30, Forest Hills NY 11375. E-mail: circlequeries@aol.com. **Contact:** Shelly Narine. Estab. 1990. Represents 30 clients. 40% of clients are new/unpublished writers. Currently handles: 95% movie scripts.

Member Agents: Lawrence Mattis; David Mattis; Trisha Smith.

Represents: Nonfiction books, novels, novellas, feature film, TV scripts. **Considers these fiction areas:** Action/adventure; comic books/cartoon; confession; contemporary issues; detective/police/crime; erotica; ethnic; experimental; family saga; fantasy; feminist; gay/lesbian; glitz; gothic; hi-lo; historical; horror; humor/satire; juvenile; literary; mainstream/contemporary; military/war; multicultural; multimedia; mystery/suspense; New Age; occult; picture books; plays; poetry; poetry in translation; psychic/supernatural; regional; religious/inspirational; romance; science fiction; short story collections; spiritual; sports; thriller; translation; westerns/frontier; young adult; women's.

Oᴙ Specializes in screenplays for film and TV.

How to Contact: Query with SASE. Responds in 1 month to queries; 2 months to mss. Obtains most new clients through recommendations from others, solicitations, writing contests and queries.
Terms: Agent receives 10% commission on domestic sales; 10% commission on foreign sales. Offers written contract, binding for 1 year.
Tips: "We look for writing that shows a unique voice, especially one which puts a fresh spin on commercial Hollywood genres."

WM CLARK ASSOCIATES, 355 W. 22nd St., New York NY 10011. (212)675-2784. Fax: (646)349-1658. E-mail: query@wmclark.com. Website: www.wmclark.com. **Contact:** William Clark. Estab. 1999. Member of AAR. 4.25% of clients are new/unpublished writers. Currently handles: 50% nonfiction books; 50% novels.
   • Prior to opening WCA, Mr. Clark was an agent at the Virginia Barber Literary Agency and William Morris Agency.
Represents: Nonfiction books, novels, short story collections. **Considers these fiction areas:** Contemporary issues; ethnic; historical; literary; mainstream/contemporary; Southern fiction.
   ○━ "As one of the new breed of media agents recognizing their expanded roles in today's ever-changing media landscape, William Clark represents a diverse range of commercial and literary fiction and quality nonfiction to the book publishing, motion picture, television, and new media fields."
How to Contact: Prefers to read materials exclusively. E-mail queries only. Responds in 1 month to queries.
Recent Sales: Sold 25 titles in the last year. *Hungry Ghost*, by Keith Kachtick (HarperCollins). Other clients include Russell Martin, Mian Mian, Jonathan Stone, Jocko Weyland, Carolin Young, Rev. Billy (aka Billy Talen).
Terms: Agent receives 15% commission on domestic sales; 20% commission on foreign sales. Offers written contract.
Tips: "E-mail queries should include a general description of the work, a synopsis/outline if available, biographical information, and publishing history, if any."

CLAUSEN, MAYS & TAHAN, LLC, 249 W. 34th St., Suite 605, New York NY 10001-2815. (212)239-4343. Fax: (212)239-5248. E-mail: cmtassist@aol.com. **Contact:** Stedman Mays, Mary M. Tahan. Estab. 1976. 10% of clients are new/unpublished writers. Currently handles: nonfiction books; novels.
Member Agents: Stedman Mays; Mary M. Tahan; Jena Anderson.
Represents: Nonfiction books, novels.
How to Contact: Query with SASE, proposal package, outline. No e-mail or fax queries. Considers simultaneous queries. Responds in 3 weeks to queries; 1 month to mss. Returns materials only with SASE.
Recent Sales: *And If I Perish*, by Evelyn Monahan and Rosemary Neidle-Greenlee (Knopf).
Terms: Agent receives 15% commission on domestic sales; 20% commission on foreign sales. Charges clients for postage, shipping, and photocopying.
Tips: "Research proposal writing and the publishing process. Always study your book's competition. Send a proposal and outline instead of complete manuscript for faster response. Always pitch books in writing, not over the phone."

CLIENT FIRST-A/K/A LEO P. HAFFEY AGENCY, P.O.Box 128049, Nashville TN 37212-8049. (615)463-2388. E-mail: c1st@nashville.net. Website: www.c-1st.com or www.nashville.net/~cl. **Contact:** Robin Swensen. Estab. 1990. Signatory of WGA. Represents 21 clients. 25% of clients are new/unpublished writers. Currently handles: 40% novels; 60% movie scripts.
Member Agents: Leo Haffey (attorney/agent in the motion picture industry).
Represents: Nonfiction books (self-help), novels, short story collections, novellas, feature film, animation.
   ○━ This agency specializes in movie scripts and novels for sale to motion picture industry.
How to Contact: Query with SASE, synopsis, treatment or summary. Do not send scripts/screenplays unless requested. Considers simultaneous queries. Responds in 1 week to queries; 2 months to mss. Returns materials only with SASE. Obtains most new clients through recommendations from others.
Recent Sales: This agency prefers not to share information on specific sales.
Terms: Offers written contract, binding for negotiable length of time.
Tips: "The motion picture business is a numbers game like any other. The more you write the better your chances are of success. Please send a SASE along with your query letter."

RUTH COHEN, INC., LITERARY AGENCY, P.O. Box 2244, La Jolla CA 92038-2244. (858)456-5805. **Contact:** Ruth Cohen. Estab. 1982. Member of AAR, Authors Guild, Sisters in Crime, RWA, SCBWI. Represents 45 clients. 15% of clients are new/unpublished writers. Currently handles: 60% novels; 40% juvenile books.
   • Prior to becoming an agent, Ms. Cohen served as directing editor at Scott Foresman & Company (now HarperCollins).
Represents: Novels (adult), juvenile books. **Considers these fiction areas:** Ethnic; historical; juvenile; literary; mainstream/contemporary; mystery/suspense; picture books; young adult.
   ○━ This agency specializes in "quality writing in contemporary fiction, women's fiction, mysteries, thrillers and juvenile fiction." Does not want to receive poetry, westerns, film scripts or how-to books.
How to Contact: Submit outline, 1 sample chapter(s). Responds in 3 weeks to queries. Returns materials only

with SASE. Obtains most new clients through recommendations from others, solicitations.

Recent Sales: This agency prefers not to share information on specific sales.

Terms: Agent receives 15% commission on domestic sales; 20% commission on foreign sales. Offers written contract, binding for 1 year. Charges for foreign postage, phone calls, photocopying submissions and overnight delivery of mss when appropriate.

Tips: "As the publishing world merges and changes, there seem to be fewer opportunities for new writers to succeed in the work that they love. We urge you to develop the patience, persistence and preseverance that have made this agency so successful. Prepare a well-written and well-crafted manuscript, and our combined best efforts can help advance both our careers."

☺ FRANCES COLLIN, LITERARY AGENT, P.O. Box 33, Wayne PA 19087-0033. **Contact:** Frances Collin. Estab. 1948. Member of AAR. Represents 90 clients. 1% of clients are new/unpublished writers. Currently handles: 50% nonfiction books; 48% novels; 1% textbooks; 1% poetry.

Represents: Nonfiction books, novels. **Considers these fiction areas:** Detective/police/crime; ethnic; family saga; fantasy; historical; literary; mainstream/contemporary; mystery/suspense; psychic/supernatural; regional; romance (historical); science fiction.

How to Contact: Query with SASE. Considers simultaneous queries. Responds in 1 week to queries; 2 months to mss. Obtains most new clients through recommendations from others.

Recent Sales: This agency prefers not to share information on specific sales.

Terms: Agent receives 15% commission on domestic sales; 20% commission on foreign sales. Offers written contract. Charges clients for overseas postage for books mailed to foreign agents; photocopying of mss, books, proposals; copyright registration fees; registered mail fees; passes along cost of any books purchased.

▓ ☺ COMMUNICATIONS MANAGEMENT ASSOCIATES, 1129 Sixth Ave., #1, Rockford IL 61104-3147. Fax: (815)964-3061. **Contact:** Thomas R. Lee. Estab. 1989. Represents 30 clients. 50% of clients are new/unpublished writers. Currently handles: 5% nonfiction books; 10% novels; 80% movie scripts; 5% TV scripts.

Member Agents: Jack Young.

Represents: Novels, short story collections, novellas, juvenile books, scholarly books, poetry books, feature film, TV movie of the week, animation, documentary, miniseries. **Considers these fiction areas:** Action/adventure (adventure); detective/police/crime; erotica; fantasy; historical; horror; juvenile; mainstream/contemporary; mystery/suspense; picture books; romance (historical, regency); science fiction; thriller; westerns/frontier; young adult.

　　O— This agency specializes in research, editing and financing.

How to Contact: Query with SASE, proposal package, outline, 3 sample chapter(s). Discards unwanted material. Considers simultaneous queries. Obtains most new clients through recommendations from others.

Recent Sales: Sold 2 scripts in the last year. This agency prefers not to share information on specific sales. Send query for list of credits.

Terms: Agent receives 10% commission on domestic sales; 15% commission on foreign sales. Offers written contract, binding for 2-4 months; 60 days notice must be given to terminate contract. Charges clients for postage, photocopying and office expenses; Writers reimbursed for office fees after the sale of ms.

Writers' Conferences: BEA.

Tips: "Don't let greed or fame-seeking, or anything but a sincere love of writing push you into this business."

☺ CONNOR LITERARY AGENCY, 2911 W. 71st St., Minneapolis MN 55423. (612)866-1426. Fax: (612)869-4074. E-mail: coolmkc@aol.com. **Contact:** Marlene Connor Lynch. Estab. 1985. Represents 50 clients. 30% of clients are new/unpublished writers. Currently handles: 50% nonfiction books; 50% novels.

　　● Prior to opening her agency, Ms. Connor served at the Literary Guild of America, Simon and Schuster and Random House. She is author of *What is Cool: Understanding Black Manhood in America* (Crown).

Member Agents: Deborah Coker (children's books)

Represents: Nonfiction books, novels, especially with a minority slant. **Considers these fiction areas:** Historical; horror; literary; mainstream/contemporary; multicultural; thriller; women's; suspense.

How to Contact: Query with SASE. Obtains most new clients through recommendations from others, conferences, grapevine.

Recent Sales: *Outrageous Commitments*, by Dr. Ronn Elmore (HarperCollins); *Seductions*, by Snow Starborn (Sourcebooks).

Terms: Agent receives 15% commission on domestic sales; 25% commission on foreign sales. Offers written contract, binding for 1 year.

Writers' Conferences: National Writers Union, Midwest Chapter; Agents, Agents, Agents; Texas Writer's Conference; Detroit Writer's Conference.

Tips: "Seeking previously published writers with good sales records and new writers with real talent."

☺ THE DOE COOVER AGENCY, P.O. Box 668, Winchester MA 01890. (781)721-6000. Fax: (781)721-6727. **Contact:** Doe Coover, president. Estab. 1985. Represents over 100 clients. Currently handles: 80% nonfiction books; 20% novels.

　　● Prior to becoming agents, Ms. Coover and Ms. Mohyde were editors for over a decade.

Member Agents: Doe Coover (cooking, general nonfiction); Colleen Mohyde (literary and commercial fiction, general nonfiction and journalism) Frances Kennedy (assistant)

Represents: Nonfiction books, novels. **Considers these fiction areas:** Literary; mainstream/contemporary (commercial).

○━ This agency specializes in cookbooks, serious nonfiction—particularly books on social issues—as well as fiction (literary and commercial), journalism and general nonfiction. Does not want children's books.

How to Contact: Query with SASE, outline. No e-mail or fax queries. Considers simultaneous queries. Returns materials only with SASE. Obtains most new clients through recommendations from others, solicitations.

Recent Sales: Sold 25-30 titles in the last year.

Terms: Agent receives 15% commission on domestic sales; 15% commission on foreign sales.

Writers' Conferences: BEA.

◪ CORNERSTONE LITERARY, INC., 4500 Wilshire Blvd., 3rd floor, Los Angeles CA 90010. (323)930-6039. Fax: (323)930-0407. Website: www.cornerstoneliterary.com. **Contact:** Helen Breitwieser. Estab. 1998. Member of AAR; Author's Guild. Represents 40 clients. 75% of clients are new/unpublished writers.

• Prior to founding her own boutique agency, Ms. Breitwieser was a literary agent at The William Morris Agency.

Represents: Novels. **Considers these fiction areas:** Detective/police/crime; erotica; ethnic; family saga; glitz; historical; literary; mainstream/contemporary; multicultural; mystery/suspense; romance; thriller.

○━ Actively seeking first fiction, literary. Does not want to receive science fiction, westerns, children's books, poetry, screenplays, fantasy, gay/lesbian, horror, self-help, psychology, business.

How to Contact: Query with SASE. Responds in 2 weeks to queries; 2 months to mss. Returns materials only with SASE. Obtains most new clients through recommendations from others.

Recent Sales: Sold 42 titles in the last year. *Last Breath*, by Rachel Lee (Warner); *Cold Silence*, by Danielle Girard (NAL); *Bare Necessity*, by Carole Matthews (HarperCollins). Other clients include Stan Diehl, Elaine Coffman, R.J. Kaiser, Kayla Perrin, Candice Proctor.

Terms: Agent receives 15% commission on domestic sales; 20% commission on foreign sales. Offers written contract, binding for 1 year; 60-day notice must be given to terminate contract.

Tips: "Don't query about more than one manuscript. Do not e-mail queries/submissions."

◪ CRAWFORD LITERARY AGENCY, 94 Evans Rd., Barnstead NH 03218. (603)269-5851. Fax: (603)269-2533. E-mail: crawfordlit@att.net. Winter Office: 3920 Bayside Rd., Fort Myers Beach FL 33931. (239)463-4651. Fax: (239)463-0125. **Contact:** Susan Crawford. Estab. 1988. Represents 45 clients. 10% of clients are new/unpublished writers. Currently handles: 50% nonfiction books; 50% novels.

Member Agents: Susan Crawford; Lorne Crawford (commercial fiction and nonfiction); Scott Neister (scientific/techno thrillers).

Represents: Nonfiction books, novels. **Considers these fiction areas:** Action/adventure; mystery/suspense; thriller (medical).

○━ This agency specializes in celebrity and/or media-based books and authors. Actively seeking action/adventure stories, medical thrillers, self-help, inspirational, how-to and women's issues. Does not want to receive short stories, poetry.

How to Contact: Query with SASE. Considers simultaneous queries. Responds in 3 weeks to queries. Returns materials only with SASE. Obtains most new clients through recommendations from others, solicitations, conferences.

Recent Sales: Sold 42 titles in the last year.

Terms: Agent receives 15% commission on domestic sales; 20% commission on foreign sales. Offers written contract, binding for 90 days; 100% of business is derived from commissions on ms sales.

Writers' Conferences: International Film & Television Workshops (Rockport ME); Maui Writers Conference.

Tips: "Keep learning to improve your craft. Attend conferences and network."

◖ RICHARD CURTIS ASSOCIATES, INC., 171 E. 74th St., New York NY 10021. (212)772-7363. Fax: (212)772-7393. Website: www.curtisagency.com. Estab. 1979. Member of RWA, MWA, WWA, SFWA; signatory of WGA. Represents 100 clients. 1% of clients are new/unpublished writers. Currently handles: 75% nonfiction books; 25% novels.

• Prior to opening his agency, Mr. Curtis was an agent with the Scott Meredith Literary Agency for 7 years and has authored over 50 published books.

Member Agents: Richard Curtis; Pamela Valvera.

Represents: Commercial nonfiction, commercial and literary fiction. **Considers these fiction areas:** Fantasy; romance; science fiction; thriller; young adult.

How to Contact: One-page query letter, plus no more than a one-page synopsis of proposed submission. No submission of mss unless specifically requested. If requested, submission must be accompanied by a SASE or we will assume you don't want your submission back. No e-mail or fax queries. Returns materials only with SASE.

Recent Sales: Sold 150 titles in the last year. *Ilium*, by Dan Simmons; *Suspicion of Vengeance*, by Barbara Parker;

Darwin's Children, by Greg Bear. Other clients include Jennifer Blake, Leonard Maltin, Earl Mindell and Barbara Parker.

Terms: Agent receives 15% commission on domestic sales; 25% commission on foreign sales. Offers written contract, binding for book-by-book basis. Charges for photocopying, express, international freight, book orders.

Writers' Conferences: Science Fiction Writers of America; Horror Writers of America; Romance Writers of America; World Fantasy Conference.

LIZA DAWSON ASSOCIATES, 240 W. 35th St., Suite 500, New York NY 10001. (212)465-9071. **Contact:** Liza Dawson, Caitlin Blasdell. Member of AAR, MWA, Women's Media Group. Represents 50 clients. 10% of clients are new/unpublished writers. Currently handles: 60% nonfiction books; 40% novels.

• Prior to becoming an agent, Ms. Dawson was an editor for 20 years, spending 11 years at William Morrow as vice president and 2 at Putnam as executive editor. Ms. Blasdell was a senior editor at HarperCollins and Avon.

Member Agents: Liza Dawson; Caitlin Blasdell.

Represents: Nonfiction books, novels, scholarly books. **Considers these fiction areas:** Ethnic; family saga; historical; literary; mystery/suspense; regional; science fiction (Blasdell only); thriller.

Oₘ This agency specializes in readable literary fiction, thrillers, mainstream historicals and women's fiction, academics, historians, business, journalists and psychology. Does not want to receive westerns, sports, computers, juvenile.

How to Contact: Query with SASE. Responds in 3 weeks to queries; 6 weeks to mss. Obtains most new clients through recommendations from others, conferences.

Recent Sales: Sold 40 titles in the last year.

Terms: Agent receives 15% commission on domestic sales; 20% commission on foreign sales. Offers written contract. Charges clients for photocopying and overseas postage.

Writers' Conferences: Pacific Northwest Book Conference (Seattle, July).

DeFIORE & CO., 72 Spring St., Suite 304, New York NY 10012. (212)925-7744. Fax: (212)925-9803. E-mail: info@defioreandco.com. Website: www.defioreandco.com. **Contact:** Brian DeFiore. Estab. 1999. Represents 35 clients. 50% of clients are new/unpublished writers. Currently handles: 70% nonfiction books; 30% novels.

• Prior to becoming an agent, Mr. DeFiore was Publisher of Villard Books 1997-1998; Editor-in-Chief of Hyperion 1992-1997; Editorial Director of Delacorte Press 1988-1992.

Member Agents: Brian DeFiore (popular nonfiction, business, pop culture, parenting, commercial fiction); Kate Garrick (literary fiction, crime, pop culture, politics, history, psychology, narrative nonfiction).

Represents: Nonfiction books, novels. **Considers these fiction areas:** Ethnic; gay/lesbian; literary; mainstream/contemporary; mystery/suspense; thriller.

How to Contact: Query with SASE. Considers simultaneous queries. Responds in 3 weeks to queries; 2 months to mss. Returns materials only with SASE. Obtains most new clients through recommendations from others.

Recent Sales: Sold 20 titles in the last year.

Terms: Agent receives 15% commission on domestic sales; 20% commission on foreign sales. Offers written contract; 10-day notice must be given to terminate contract. Charges clients for photocopying, overnight delivery (deducted only after a sale is made).

Writers' Conferences: Maui Writers Conference (Maui HI, September); Pacific Northwest Writers Association Conference; North Carolina Writer's Network Conference.

DHS LITERARY, INC., 2528 Elm St., Suite 350, Dallas TX 75226. (214)363-4422. Fax: (214)363-4423. E-mail: submissions@dhsliterary.com. Website: www.dhsliterary.com. **Contact:** David Hale Smith, president. Estab. 1994. Represents 35 clients. 15% of clients are new/unpublished writers. Currently handles: 60% nonfiction books; 40% novels.

• Prior to opening his agency, Mr. Smith was an editor at a newswire service.

Represents: Nonfiction books, novels. **Considers these nonfiction areas:** Biography/autobiography; business/economics; child guidance/parenting; cooking/foods/nutrition; current affairs; ethnic/cultural interests; popular culture; sports; true crime/investigative. **Considers these fiction areas:** Detective/police/crime; ethnic; literary; mainstream/contemporary; mystery/suspense; thriller; westerns/frontier.

Oₘ This agency specializes in commercial fiction and nonfiction for adult trade market. Actively seeking thrillers, mysteries, suspense, etc., and narrative nonfiction. Does not want to receive poetry, short fiction, children's books.

How to Contact: Considers simultaneous queries. Responds in 1 month to queries. Obtains most new clients through recommendations from others, editors and agents.

Recent Sales: Sold 35 titles in the last year. *The Curve of the World*, by Marcus Stevens (Algonquin); *City on Fire*, by Bill Minutaglio (Morrow).

Terms: Agent receives 15% commission on domestic sales; 25% commission on foreign sales. Offers written contract; 10-day notice must be given to terminate contract. Charges for client expenses, i.e., postage, photocopying. 100% of business is derived from commissions on sales.

Tips: "Remember to be courteous and professional, and to treat marketing your work and approaching an agent as you would any formal business matter. When in doubt, always query first via e-mail. Visit our website for more information."

SANDRA DIJKSTRA LITERARY AGENCY, 1155 Camino del Mar, PMB 515, Del Mar CA 92014-2605. (858)755-3115. Fax: (858) 794-2822. E-mail: sdla@dijkstraagency.com. **Contact:** Jill Marr. Estab. 1981. Member of AAR, Authors Guild, PEN West, Poets and Editors, MWA. Represents 200 clients. 30% of clients are new/unpublished writers. Currently handles: 50% nonfiction books; 45% novels; 5% juvenile books.
  • We specialize in a number of fields.
Member Agents: Sandra Dijkstra.
Represents: Nonfiction books, novels. **Considers these fiction areas:** Ethnic; literary; mainstream/contemporary; mystery/suspense; thriller.
How to Contact: Submit proposal package, outline, sample chapter(s), author bio, SASE. No e-mail or fax queries. Responds in 1 month to queries; 6 weeks to mss. Obtains most new clients through recommendations from others, solicitations, conferences.
Recent Sales: Sold over 40 titles in the last year. *The Hottentot Venus*, by Barbara Chase-Riboud (Doubleday); *The Lady, The Chef and the Lover*, by Marisol Konczal (Harper Collins); *End of Adolescence*, by Robert Epstein (Harcourt).
Terms: Agent receives 15% commission on domestic sales; 20% commission on foreign sales. Offers written contract. Charges clients for expenses "to cover domestic costs so that we can spend time selling books instead of accounting expenses. We also charge for the photocopying of the full ms or nonfiction proposal and for foreign postage."
Writers' Conferences: "Have attended Squaw Valley, Santa Barbara, Asilomar, Southern California Writers Conference, Rocky Mountain Fiction Writers, to name a few. We also speak regularly for writers groups such as PEN West and the Independent Writers Association."
Tips: "Be professional and learn the standard procedures for submitting your work. Give full biographical information on yourself, especially for a nonfiction project. Send no more than 50 pages of your manuscript, a very brief synopsis, detailed author bio (awards, publications, accomplishments) and a SASE. We will not respond to submissions without a SASE. Nine page letters telling us your life story, or your book's, are unprofessional and usually not read. Tell us about your book and write your query well. It's our first introduction to who you are and what you can do! Call if you don't hear within six weeks. Be a regular patron of bookstores and study what kind of books are being published. READ. Check out your local library and bookstores—you'll find lots of books on writing and the publishing industry that will help you! At conferences, ask published writers about their agents. Don't believe the myth that an agent has to be in New York to be successful—we've already disproved it!"

◙ JIM DONOVAN LITERARY, 4515 Prentice St., Suite 109, Dallas TX 75206. **Contact:** Jim Donovan, president; Kathryn Lindsey. Estab. 1993. Represents 35 clients. 20% of clients are new/unpublished writers. Currently handles: 75% nonfiction books; 25% novels.
Member Agents: Jim Donovan (president); Kathryn Lindsey.
Represents: Nonfiction books, novels. **Considers these fiction areas:** Action/adventure; detective/police/crime; historical; horror; literary; mainstream/contemporary; mystery/suspense; sports; thriller; westerns/frontier.
  ⚬⚊ This agency specializes in commercial fiction and nonfiction. Does not want to receive poetry, humor, short stories, juvenile, romance or religious work.
How to Contact: Query with SASE. Send 2- to 5-page outline and 3 sample chapters. No e-mail or fax queries. Considers simultaneous queries. Responds in 1 month to queries; 1 month to mss. Obtains most new clients through recommendations from others, solicitations.
Recent Sales: Sold 24 titles in the last year. *Given Up for Dead*, by Bill Sloan (Bantam); *Duel in the Sun*, by Curt Sampson (Pocket/Atria).
Terms: Agent receives 15% commission on domestic sales; 20% commission on foreign sales. Offers written contract, binding for 1 year; written notice must be given to terminate contract.
Tips: "The vast majority of material I receive, particularly fiction, is not ready for publication. Do everything you can to get your fiction work in top shape before you try to find an agent. I've been in the book business since 1981, in retail (as a chain buyer), as an editor, and as a published author. I'm open to working with new writers if they're serious about their writing and are prepared to put in the work necessary—the rewriting—to become publishable."

◙ DOYEN LITERARY SERVICES, INC., 1931 660th St., Newell IA 50568-7613. (712)272-3300. Website: www.barbaradoyen.com. **Contact:** (Ms.) B.J. Doyen, president. Estab. 1988. Represents 60 clients. 20% of clients are new/unpublished writers. Currently handles: 90% nonfiction books; 10% novels.
  • Prior to opening her agency, Ms. Doyen worked as a published author, teacher, guest speaker and wrote and appeared in her own weekly TV show airing in 7 states.
Represents: Nonfiction books, novels. **Considers these fiction areas:** Contemporary issues; family saga; historical; literary; mainstream/contemporary; occult; psychic/supernatural.
  ⚬⚊ This agency specializes in nonfiction and occasionally handles genre and mainstream fiction for adults. Actively seeking business, health, how-to, psychology; all kinds of adult nonfiction suitable for the major

trade publishers. Prefers fiction from published novelists only. Does not want to receive pornography, children's, poetry.

How to Contact: Query with SASE. No e-mail or fax queries. Considers simultaneous queries. Responds in 2 weeks to mss. Responds immediately to queries. Returns materials only with SASE.

Terms: Agent receives 15% commission on domestic sales; 20% commission on foreign sales. Offers written contract, binding for 1 year.

Tips: "Our authors receive personalized attention. We market aggressively, undeterred by rejection. We get the best possible publishing contracts. We are very interested in nonfiction book ideas at this time; will consider most topics. Many writers come to us from referrals, but we also get quite a few who initially approach us with query letters. Do not use phone queries unless you are successfully published or a celebrity. It is best if you do not collect editorial rejections prior to seeking an agent, but if you do, be up-front and honest about it. Do not submit your manuscript to more than one agent at a time—querying first can save you (and us) much time. We're open to established or beginning writers—just send us a terrific letter with SASE!"

DUNHAM LITERARY, INC., 156 Fifth Ave., Suite 625, New York NY 10010-7002. (212)929-0994. Website: www.dunhamlit.com. **Contact:** Jennie Dunham. Estab. 2000. Member of AAR. Represents 50 clients. 15% of clients are new/unpublished writers. Currently handles: 25% nonfiction books; 25% novels; 50% juvenile books.

• Prior to opening her agency, Ms. Dunham worked as a literary agent for Russell & Volkening. The Rhoda Weyr Agency is now a division of Dunham Literary, Inc.

Member Agents: Donna Lieberman (mainstream fiction and nonfiction, mysteries, suspense, thrillers).

Represents: Nonfiction books, novels, short story collections, juvenile books. **Considers these fiction areas:** Ethnic; juvenile; literary; mainstream/contemporary; mystery/suspense; picture books; thriller; young adult.

How to Contact: Query with SASE. No e-mail or fax queries. Responds in 1 week to queries; 2 months to mss. Obtains most new clients through recommendations from others, solicitations.

Recent Sales: *Black Hawk Down*, by Mark Bowden; *Look Back All the Green Valley*, by Fred Chappell; *Even Now*, by Susan S. Kelly.

Terms: Agent receives 15% commission on domestic sales; 20% commission on foreign sales. Writers reimbursed for office fees after the sale of ms.

DIANE DURRETT AGENCY, 727 22nd St., Sacramento CA 95818-4011. (916)492-9003. Fax: (916)444-5436. E-mail: diane_durrett@pacbell.net. **Contact:** Diane Durrett. Signatory of WGA. Currently handles: 10% novels; 90% movie scripts.

• Prior to becoming an agent, Ms. Durrett worked in print and online publishing for 10 years and served as president of the Northern California Writers & Artists association.

Represents: Novels, movie scripts, feature film. **Considers these fiction areas:** Action/adventure; detective/police/crime; historical; horror; humor/satire; literary; mainstream/contemporary; romance; science fiction; thriller.

How to Contact: Query with SASE. Responds in 2 months to queries; 2 months to mss. Returns materials only with SASE.

Terms: Agent receives 10% commission on domestic sales; 10% commission on foreign sales. Offers written contract. Charges for photocopies and postage.

Tips: "Please be sure you understand the craft of screenwriting and are using the proper format. Scripts and manuscripts should be free of spelling and grammatical errors."

DYSTEL & GODERICH LITERARY MANAGEMENT, 1 Union Square W., Suite 904, New York NY 10003. (212)627-9100. Fax: (212)627-9313. E-mail: miriam@dystel.com. Website: www.dystel.com. **Contact:** Miriam Goderich. Estab. 1994. Member of AAR. Represents 300 clients. 50% of clients are new/unpublished writers. Currently handles: 65% nonfiction books; 25% novels; 10% cookbooks.

• Dystel & Goderich Literary Management recently acquired the client list of Bedford Book Works.

Member Agents: Stacey Glick; Jane Dystel; Miriam Goderich; Michael Bourret; Jessica Papin; Jim McCarthy.

Represents: Nonfiction books, novels, cookbooks. **Considers these fiction areas:** Action/adventure; contemporary issues; detective/police/crime; ethnic; family saga; gay/lesbian; literary; mainstream/contemporary; mystery/suspense; thriller (especially).

O— This agency specializes in commercial and literary fiction and nonfiction plus cookbooks.

How to Contact: Query with SASE. Considers simultaneous queries. Responds in 1 month to queries; 6 weeks to mss. Obtains most new clients through recommendations from others, solicitations, conferences.

Recent Sales: *The Sparrow*, by Mary Russell; *Leaving Atlanta*, by Tayari Jones.

Terms: Agent receives 15% commission on domestic sales; 19% commission on foreign sales. Offers written contract, binding for book to book basis. Charges for photocopying. Galley charges and book charges from the publisher are passed on to the author.

Writers' Conferences: West Coast Writers Conference (Whidbey Island WA, Columbus Day weekend); University of Iowa Writer's Conference; Pacific Northwest Writer's Conference; Pike's Peak Writer's Conference; Santa Barbara Writer's Conference; Harriette Austin's Writer's Conference; Sandhills Writers Conference; ASU Writers Conference.

Tips: "Work on sending professional, well written queries that are concise and addressed to the specific agent the author is contacting. No Dear Sirs/Madam."

◙ **THE E S AGENCY**, 6612 Pacheco Way, Citrus Heights CA 95610. (916)723-2794. Fax: (916)723-2796. E-mail: edley07@cs.com. **Contact:** Ed Silver, president. Estab. 1995. Represents 50-75 clients. 70% of clients are new/unpublished writers. Currently handles: 50% nonfiction books; 25% novels; 25% movie scripts.
 • Prior to becoming an agent, Mr. Silver was an entertainment business manager.
Member Agents: Ed Silver.
Represents: Nonfiction books, novels, movie scripts, feature film, TV movie of the week. **Considers these fiction areas:** Action/adventure; detective/police/crime; erotica; experimental; historical; humor/satire; literary; mainstream/contemporary; mystery/suspense; thriller; young adult. **Considers these script subject areas:** Action/adventure; comedy; contemporary issues; detective/police/crime; erotica; ethnic; experimental; family saga; mainstream; mystery/suspense; romantic comedy; romantic drama; sports; thriller.
 ○┐ This agency specializes in theatrical screenplays, MOW and miniseries. Actively seeking "anything good and distinctive."
How to Contact: Query with SASE. Considers simultaneous queries. Responds in 1 month to queries. Returns materials only with SASE. Obtains most new clients through recommendations from others, queries from WGA agency list.
Recent Sales: *The Cannabible*, by Jason King; *How to Read Maya Hieroglyphs*, by John Montgomery; *Dictionary of Maya Hieroglyphs*, by John Montgomery.
Terms: Agent receives 15% commission on domestic sales; 20% commission on foreign sales; 10% commission on dramatic rights sales. Offers written contract; 30 days notice must be given to terminate contract.

◙ **ETHAN ELLENBERG LITERARY AGENCY**, 548 Broadway, #5-E, New York NY 10012. (212)431-4554. Fax: (212)941-4652. E-mail: agent@ethanellenberg.com. Website: www.ethanellenberg.com. **Contact:** Ethan Ellenberg, Michael Psaltis. Estab. 1983. Represents 80 clients. 10% of clients are new/unpublished writers. Currently handles: 25% nonfiction books; 75% novels.
 • Prior to opening his agency, Mr. Ellenberg was contracts manager of Berkley/Jove and associate contracts manager for Bantam.
Member Agents: Michael Psaltis (serious and commercial nonfiction, including science, health, popular culture, cooking, current events, politics, business, memoir and other unique projects; and commercial and literary fiction); Ethan Ellenberg
Represents: Nonfiction books, novels. **Considers these fiction areas:** Fantasy; romance; science fiction; thriller; women's.
 ○┐ This agency specializes in commercial fiction, especially thrillers, romance/women's fiction and specialized nonfiction. "We also do a lot of children's books." For children's books: Send introductory letter (with credits, if any), up to 3 picture book mss, outline and first 3 chapters for longer projects, SASE. Actively seeking commercial and literary fiction, children's books, break-through nonfiction. Does not want to receive poetry, short stories, westerns, autobiographies.
How to Contact: For fiction: Send introductory letter (with credits, if any), outline, first 3 chapters and SASE. No fax queries. Accepts e-mail queries, no attachments. Considers simultaneous queries. Responds in 2 weeks to queries; 4-6 weeks to mss. Returns materials only with SASE.
Recent Sales: Has sold over 100 titles in the last 3 years. *After Sundown*, by Madeline Baker (Kensington); *The Keys to the Universe*, by Richard Morris (Joseph Henry Press); *Grosbeck Creek*, by Clay Reynolds (Berkley).
Terms: Agent receives 15% commission on domestic sales; 10% commission on foreign sales. Offers written contract. Charges clients for "direct expenses only limited to photocopying, postage, by writer's consent only."
Writers' Conferences: RWA National; Novelists, Inc.; and other regional conferences.
Tips: "We do consider new material from unsolicited authors. Write a good clear letter with a succinct description of your book. We prefer the first three chapters when we consider fiction. For all submissions you must include SASE for return or the material is discarded. It's always hard to break in, but talent will find a home. Check our website for complete submission guidelines. We continue to see natural storytellers and nonfiction writers with important books."

◙ **NICHOLAS ELLISON, INC.**, affiliated with Sanford J. Greenburger Associates, 55 Fifth Ave., 15th Floor, New York NY 10003. (212)206-6050. Fax: (212)436-8718. **Contact:** Jennifer Cayea. Estab. 1983. Represents 70 clients. Currently handles: 50% nonfiction books; 50% novels.
 • Prior to becoming an agent, Mr. Ellison was an editor at Minerva Editions, Harper & Row and editor-in-chief at Delacorte.
Member Agents: Jennifer Cayea.
Represents: Nonfiction books, novels. **Considers these fiction areas:** Literary; mainstream/contemporary.
 ○┐ Does not want to receive self-help.
How to Contact: Query with SASE. Responds in 6 weeks to queries.
Recent Sales: *Up Country*, by Nelson DeMille (Warner); *The Anniversary*, by Amy Gutman (Little, Brown); *The Big Love*, by Sarah Dunn (Little, Brown). Other clients include Olivia Goldsmith, P.T. Deutermann, Nancy Geary.

Terms: Agent receives 15% commission on domestic sales; 20% commission on foreign sales.

◑ **ANN ELMO AGENCY, INC.**, 60 E. 42nd St., New York NY 10165. (212)661-2880, 2881. Fax: (212)661-2883. **Contact:** Lettie Lee. Estab. 1959. Member of AAR, MWA, Authors Guild.
Member Agents: Lettie Lee; Mari Cronin (plays); A.L. Abecassis (nonfiction).
Represents: Nonfiction books, novels. **Considers these fiction areas:** Contemporary issues; detective/police/crime; ethnic; family saga; historical; literary; mainstream/contemporary; mystery/suspense; regional; romance (contemporary, gothic, historical, regency); thriller.
How to Contact: Letter queries *only* with SASE. No fax queries. Responds in 3 months to queries. Obtains most new clients through recommendations from others.
Recent Sales: This agency prefers not to share information on specific sales.
Terms: Agent receives 15% commission on domestic sales; 20% commission on foreign sales. Offers written contract. Charges clients for "special mailings or shipping considerations or multiple international calls. No charge for usual cost of doing business."
Tips: "Query first, and when asked only please send properly prepared manuscript. A double-spaced, readable manuscript is the best recommendation. Include SASE, of course."

◐ **ELAINE P. ENGLISH**, Graybill & English, LLC, 1875 Connecticut Ave. NW, Suite 712, Washington DC 20009. (202)588-9798, ext. 143. Fax: (202)457-0662. E-mail: elaineengl@aol.com. Website: www.graybillandenglish.com. **Contact:** Elaine English. Member of AAR. Represents 12 clients. 50% of clients are new/unpublished writers. Currently handles: 100% novels.
   ● Ms. English is also an attorney specializing in media and publishing law.
Member Agents: Elaine English (women's fiction, including romance and mysteries).
Represents: Novels. **Considers these fiction areas:** Historical; mainstream/contemporary; multicultural; mystery/suspense; romance (including single titles); thriller; women's.
   ⟐ "While not as an agent, per se, I have been working in publishing for over fifteen years. Also, I'm affiliated with other agents who represent a broad spectrum of projects." Actively seeking women's fiction, including single title romances. Does not want to receive anything other than above.
How to Contact: Submit outline, 3 sample chapter(s), SASE. Responds in 6 weeks to queries; 6 months to mss. Returns materials only with SASE. Obtains most new clients through solicitations.
Terms: Agent receives 15% commission on domestic sales; 20% commission on foreign sales. Offers written contract; 30-day notice must be given to terminate contract. Charges only for expenses directly related to sales of manuscript (long distance, postage, copying).
Writers' Conferences: Washington Romance Writers (Harpers Ferry VA, April); RWA Nationals (New York NY, July); Georgia Romance Writers (Atlanta GA, November); Ohio Fiction Writers (October); SEAK Medical Fiction Writing for Physcians (Cape Cod, September).

◪ **FELICIA ETH LITERARY REPRESENTATION**, 555 Bryant St., Suite 350, Palo Alto CA 94301-1700. (650)375-1276. Fax: (650)401-8892. E-mail: feliciaeth@aol.com. **Contact:** Felicia Eth. Estab. 1988. Member of AAR. Represents 25-35 clients. Works with established and new writers. Currently handles: 85% nonfiction books; 15% adult novels.
Represents: Nonfiction books, novels. **Considers these fiction areas:** Ethnic; feminist; gay/lesbian; literary; mainstream/contemporary; thriller.
   ⟐ This agency specializes in "provocative, intelligent, thoughtful nonfiction on a wide array of subjects which are commercial and high-quality fiction; preferably mainstream and contemporary."
How to Contact: Query with SASE, outline. Considers simultaneous queries. Responds in 3 weeks to queries; 4-6 weeks to mss.
Recent Sales: Sold 7-10 titles in the last year. *Jane Austen in Boca*, by Paula Marantz Cohen (St. Martin's Press); *Beyond Pink and Blue*, by Dr. Leonard Sax (Doubleday/Random House); *Lavender Road to Success*, by Kirk Snyder (Ten Speed Press).
Terms: Agent receives 15% commission on domestic sales; 20% commission on foreign sales; 20% commission on dramatic rights sales. Charges clients for photocopying, express mail service—extraordinary expenses.
Writers' Conferences: Independent Writers of LA (Los Angeles); Conference of National Coalition of Independent Scholars (Berkley CA); Writers Guild.
Tips: "For nonfiction, established expertise is certainly a plus, as is magazine publication—though not a prerequisite. I am highly dedicated to those projects I represent, but highly selective in what I choose."

◪ **FARBER LITERARY AGENCY, INC.**, 14 E. 75th St., #2E, New York NY 10021. (212)861-7075. Fax: (212)861-7076. E-mail: farberlit@aol.com. Website: www.donaldfarber.com. **Contact:** Ann Farber; Dr. Seth Farber. Estab. 1989. Represents 40 clients. 50% of clients are new/unpublished writers. Currently handles: 40% nonfiction books; 15% scholarly books; 45% stage plays.
Member Agents: Ann Farber (novels); Seth Farber (plays, scholarly books, novels); Donald C. Farber (attourney, all entertainment media).
Represents: Nonfiction books, novels, juvenile books, textbooks, stage plays. **Considers these fiction areas:**

Action/adventure; contemporary issues; humor/satire; juvenile; literary; mainstream/contemporary; mystery/suspense; thriller; young adult.

How to Contact: Submit outline, 3 sample chapter(s), SASE. Prefers to read materials exclusively. Responds in 1 month to queries; 2 month to mss. Obtains most new clients through recommendations from others.

Recent Sales: Sold 5 titles in the last year. *The Eden Express*, by Mark Vonnegut (Seven Stories-Eden); *The Gardens of Frau Hess*, by Milton Marcus; *Hot Feat*, by Ed Bullins; *Bright Freedom Song*, by Gloria Houston (Harcourt Brace & Co.).

Terms: Agent receives 15% commission on domestic sales; 20% commission on foreign sales. Offers written contract, binding for 1 year. Client must furnish copies of ms, treatments and any other items for submission.

Tips: "Our attorney, Donald C. Farber, is the author of many books. His services are available to the agency's clients as part of the agency service at no additional charge."

B.R. FLEURY AGENCY, P.O. Box 149352, Orlando FL 32814-9352. (407)895-8494. Fax: (407)898-3923 or (888)310-8142. E-mail: brfleuryagency@juno.com. **Contact:** Blanche or Margaret. Estab. 1994. Signatory of WGA. Currently handles: 30% nonfiction books; 60% novels; 10% movie scripts.

Represents: Nonfiction books, novels, feature film, TV movie of the week. **Considers these fiction areas:** Fantasy; horror; humor/satire; literary; psychic/supernatural; thriller.

   O⇥ Only accepts scripts "if adapted from manuscripts by writers whom we represent."

How to Contact: Prefers to read materials exclusively. Query with one-page letter, SASE; or call for information. Accepts 1-page e-mail queries, no attachments and snail mail with no enclosures. Responds in 3 months to mss. Responds immediately to queries.

Recent Sales: Sold 5 manuscripts and 1 screenplay in the last year. This agency prefers not to share information on specific sales.

Terms: Agent receives 15% commission on domestic sales. Offers written contract, binding for as per contract. Receives screenplay commission according to WGA guidelines. Charges clients for business expenses directly related to work represented.

Tips: "Read your work aloud with someone who is not in love with you before you send it to us." E-mail queries should be 1 page maximum, no attachments. Queries with attachments or additional information will be returned unread.

THE FOGELMAN LITERARY AGENCY, 7515 Greenville, Suite 712, Dallas TX 75231. (214)361-9956. Fax: (214)361-9553. E-mail: foglit@aol.com. Website: www.fogelman.com. Also: 599 Lexington Ave., Suite 2300; New York NY 10022; (212)836-4803. **Contact:** Evan Fogelman. Estab. 1990. Member of AAR. Represents 100 clients. 2% of clients are new/unpublished writers. Currently handles: 40% nonfiction books; 40% novels; 10% scholarly books; 10% TV scripts.

   • Prior to opening his agency, Mr. Fogelman was an entertainment lawyer. He is still active in the field and serves as chairman of the Texas Entertainment and Sports Lawyers Association.

Member Agents: Evan Fogelman (nonfiction, women's fiction); Linda Kruger (women's fiction, nonfiction); Helen Brown (literary fiction).

Represents: Nonfiction books, novels. **Considers these fiction areas:** Historical; literary; mainstream/contemporary; romance (all sub-genres).

   O⇥ This agency specializes in women's fiction and nonfiction. "Zealous advocacy" makes this agency stand apart from others. Actively seeking "nonfiction of all types; romance fiction." Does not want to receive children's/juvenile.

How to Contact: Query with SASE. Considers simultaneous queries. Responds in 3 months to mss. Responds 'next business day' to queries. Returns materials only with SASE. Obtains most new clients through recommendations from others.

Recent Sales: Sold 60 titles in the last year. Other clients include Caroline Hunt, Katherine Sutcliffe, Crystal Stovall.

Terms: Agent receives 15% commission on domestic sales; 10% commission on foreign sales. Offers written contract, binding for project-to-project.

Writers' Conferences: Romance Writers of America; Novelists, Inc.

Tips: "Finish your manuscript, and see our website."

FORT ROSS, INC., RUSSIAN-AMERICAN PUBLISHING PROJECTS, 26 Arthur Place, Yonkers NY 10701-1703. (914)375-6448. Fax: (914)375-6439. E-mail: ftross@ix.netcom.com. Website: www.fortross.net. **Contact:** Dr. Vladimir P. Karsev. Estab. 1992. Represents about 100 clients. 2% of clients are new/unpublished writers. Currently handles: 50% nonfiction books; 40% novels; 10% juvenile books.

Member Agents: Ms. Olga Borodyanskaya, St. Petersburg, Russia, phone: 7-812-1738607 (fiction, nonfiction); Mr. Konstantin Paltchikov, Moscow, Russia, phone: 7-095-2035280 (romance, science fiction, fantasy, thriller); Kristin Olson, Prague, Czech Republic, phone: 420-2 2251-9639.

Represents: Nonfiction books, novels, juvenile books. **Considers these fiction areas:** Action/adventure; detective/police/crime; fantasy; horror; juvenile; mystery/suspense; romance (contemporary, gothic, historical, regency); science fiction; thriller; young adult.

O— This agency specializes in selling rights for Russian books and illustrations (covers) to American publishers and American books and illustrations for Europe; also Russian-English and English-Russian translations. Actively seeking adventure, fiction, mystery, romance, science fiction, thriller from established authors and illustrators for Russian and European markets.

How to Contact: Send published book or galleys. Accepts e-mail and fax queries. Considers simultaneous queries. Returns materials only with SASE.

Recent Sales: Sold 12 titles in the last year.

Terms: Agent receives 10% commission on domestic sales; 20% commission on foreign sales. Offers written contract, binding for 2 years; 2-month notice must be given to terminate contract.

Tips: "Established authors and book illustrators (especially cover art) are welcome for the following genres: romance, fantasy, science fiction, mystery and adventure."

LYNN C. FRANKLIN ASSOCIATES, LTD., 1350 Broadway, Suite 2015, New York NY 10018. (212)868-6311. Fax: (212)868-6312. **Contact:** Lynn Franklin and Claudia Nys. Estab. 1987. Member of PEN America. Represents 30-35 clients. 50% of clients are new/unpublished writers. Currently handles: 90% nonfiction books; 10% novels.

Represents: Nonfiction books, novels. **Considers these fiction areas:** Literary; mainstream/contemporary (commercial).

O— This agency specializes in general nonfiction with a special interest in health, biography, international affairs, and spirituality.

How to Contact: Query with SASE. No unsolicited mss. Considers simultaneous queries. Responds in 2 weeks to queries; 6 weeks to mss. Obtains most new clients through recommendations from others, solicitations.

Terms: Agent receives 15% commission on domestic sales; 20% commission on foreign sales. Offers written contract; 60-day notice must be given to terminate contract. 100% of business is derived from commissions on ms sales. Charges clients for postage, photocopying, long distance telephone if significant.

SARAH JANE FREYMANN LITERARY AGENCY, 59 W. 71st St., Suite 9B, New York NY 10023. (212)362-9277. Fax: (212)501-8240. E-mail: sjfs@aol.com. **Contact:** Sarah Jane Freymann. Represents 100 clients. 20% of clients are new/unpublished writers. Currently handles: 75% nonfiction books; 23% novels; 2% juvenile books.

Represents: Nonfiction books, novels, illustrated books. **Considers these fiction areas:** Contemporary issues; ethnic; literary; mainstream/contemporary; mystery/suspense; thriller.

How to Contact: Query with SASE. Responds in 2 weeks to queries; 6 weeks to mss. Obtains most new clients through recommendations from others.

Recent Sales: *Serenity in Motion*, by Nancy O'Hara.

Terms: Agent receives 15% commission on domestic sales; 20% commission on foreign sales. Offers written contract. Charges clients for long distance, overseas postage, photocopying. 100% of business is derived from commissions on ms sales.

Tips: "I love fresh new passionate works by authors who love what they are doing and have both natural talent and carefully honed skill."

MAX GARTENBERG, LITERARY AGENT, 521 Fifth Ave., Suite 1700, New York NY 10175. (212)292-4354. E-mail: gartenbook@att.net. **Contact:** Max Gartenberg. Estab. 1954. Represents 30 clients. 5% of clients are new/unpublished writers. Currently handles: 90% nonfiction books; 10% novels.

Represents: Nonfiction books, novels.

How to Contact: Query with SASE. Considers simultaneous queries. Responds in 2 weeks to queries; 6 weeks to mss. Obtains most new clients through recommendations from others, occasionally by "following up on good query letters"

Recent Sales: *Ogallala Blue*, by William Ashworth (W.W. Norton).

Terms: Agent receives 15% commission on first domestic sales; 10% subsequent commission on domestic sales; 15-20% commission on foreign sales.

Tips: "This is a small agency serving established writers; new writers whose work it is able to handle are few and far between. Nonfiction is more likely to be of interest here than fiction, and category fiction not at all."

GELFMAN, SCHNEIDER, LITERARY AGENTS, INC., 250 W. 57th St., New York NY 10107. (212)245-1993. Fax: (212)245-8678. **Contact:** Jane Gelfman, Deborah Schneider. Estab. 1981. Member of AAR. Represents 150 clients. 10% of clients are new/unpublished writers.

Represents: Nonfiction books, novels, 'We represent adult, general, hardcover fiction and nonfiction, literary and commercial, and some mysteries. **Considers these fiction areas:** Literary; mainstream/contemporary; mystery/suspense.

O— Does not want to receive romances, science fiction, westerns or children's books.

How to Contact: Query with SASE. Responds in 1 month to queries; 2 months to mss. Obtains most new clients through recommendations from others.

Terms: Agent receives 15% commission on domestic sales; 20% commission on foreign sales. Offers written contract. Charges clients for photocopying, messengers and couriers.

⬛ **THE GISLASON AGENCY**, 219 Main St. SE, Suite 506, Minneapolis MN 55414-2160. (612)331-8033. Fax: (612)331-8115. E-mail: gislasonbj@aol.com. Website: www.thegislasonagency.com. **Contact:** Barbara J. Gislason, literary agent. Estab. 1992. Member of Minnesota State Bar Association, Art & Entertainment Law Section (former chair), Internet Committee, Minnesota Intellectual Property Law Association Copyright Committee (former chair); also a member of SFWA, MWA, RWA, Sisters in Crime, Oak Street Arts Board (board member), Icelandic Association of Minnesota (president) and American Academy of Acupuncture and Oriental Medicine (advisory board member). 80% of clients are new/unpublished writers. Currently handles: 25% nonfiction books; 75% novels.
• Ms. Gislason became an attorney in 1980, and continues to practice Art & Entertainment Law. She has been nationally recognized as a Leading American Attorney and a Super Lawyer.
Member Agents: Deborah Sweeney (fantasy, science fiction); Kellie Hultgren (fantasy, science fiction); Lisa Higgs (Romance); Kris Olson (mystery).
Represents: Nonfiction books, novels. **Considers these fiction areas:** Fantasy; mainstream/contemporary; mystery/suspense; romance; science fiction; thriller (legal).
○➔ Do not send personal memoirs, poetry, short stories, screenplays or children's books.
How to Contact: Fiction: Query with synopsis, first 3 chapters and SASE. No e-mail or fax queries. Responds in 2 months to queries; 3 months to mss. Obtains most new clients through recommendations from others, conferences, *Literary Market Place* and other reference books.
Recent Sales: *Historical Romance # 4*, by Linda Cook (Kensington); *Dancing Dead*, by Deborah Woodworth (HarperCollins); *Autumn World*, by Joan Verba, et. al. (Dragon Stone Press).
Terms: Agent receives 15% commission on domestic sales; 20% commission on foreign sales. Offers written contract, binding for 1 year with option to renew. Charges clients for photocopying and postage.
Writers' Conferences: Romance Writers of America; Midwest Fiction Writers; University of Wisconsin Writer's Institute. Also attend state and regional writers conferences.
Tips: "Cover letter should be well written and include a detailed synopsis (if fiction) or proposal (if nonfiction), the first three chapters and author bio. Appropriate SASE required. We are looking for a great writer with a poetic, lyrical or quirky writing style who can create intriguing ambiguities. We expect a well-researched, imaginative and fresh plot that reflects a familiarity with the applicable genre. If submitting nonfiction work, explain how the submission differs from and adds to previously published works in the field. Scenes with sex and violence must be intrinsic to the plot. Remember to proofread, proofread, proofread. If the work was written with a specific publisher in mind, this should be communicated. In addition to owning an agency, Ms. Gislason practices law in the area of Art and Entertainment and has a broad spectrum of entertainment industry contacts."

⬛ **GOLDFARB & ASSOCIATES**, 1501 M St. NW, Washington DC 20005-2902. (202)466-3030. Fax: (202)293-3187. E-mail: rglawlit@aol.com. **Contact:** Ronald Goldfarb. Estab. 1966. Currently handles: 75% nonfiction books; 25% novels; increasing TV and movie deals.
• Ron Goldfarb's book (his ninth), *Perfect Villains, Imperfect Heroes*, was published by Random House. His tenth, *TV or not TV: Courts, Television, and Justice* (NYU Press), 1998. His *RFK* book is coming out in paper this year and is about to be optioned for dramatic development.
Member Agents: B. Farley Chase (New York office); Robbie Anna Hare; Kimberlee Damen, Esq.; Louise Wheatley.
Represents: Nonfiction books, novels. **Considers these fiction areas:** Action/adventure; contemporary issues; detective/police/crime; ethnic; literary; mainstream/contemporary; mystery/suspense; thriller.
○➔ This agency specializes primarily in nonfiction but has a growing interest in well-written fiction. "Given our D.C. location, we represent many journalists, politicians and former federal officials. We arrange collaborations. We also represent a broad range of nonfiction writers and novelists." Actively seeking "fiction with literary overtones; strong nonfiction ideas." Does very little children's fiction or poetry.
How to Contact: No fax queries. Responds in 1 month to queries; 2 months to mss. Obtains most new clients through recommendations from others.
Recent Sales: Sold 35 titles in the last year. *Imperfect Justice*, by Stuart Eizenstat.
Terms: Charges clients for photocopying, long distance phone calls, postage.
Writers' Conferences: Washington Independent Writers Conference; Medical Writers Conference; VCCA; participates in many ad hoc writers' and publishers' groups and events each year.
Tips: "We are a law firm which can help writers with related legal problems, Freedom of Information Act requests, libel, copyright, contracts, etc. As published authors ourselves, we understand the creative process."

⬛ **ASHLEY GRAYSON LITERARY AGENCY**, 1342 18th St., San Pedro CA 90732. Fax: (310)514-1148. Member of AAR. Represents 100 clients. 5% of clients are new/unpublished writers. Currently handles: 20% nonfiction books; 50% novels; 30% juvenile books.
Member Agents: Ashley Grayson (commercial and literary fiction, historical novels, mysteries, science fiction, thrillers, young adult); Carolyn Grayson (mainstream commercial fiction, mainstream women's fiction, romance, crime fiction, suspense, thrillers, fantasy, horror, true crime, children's and young adult, gardening, science, medical,

health, self-help, how-to, pop culture, travel, creative nonfiction); Dan Hooker (commercial fiction, mysteries, thrillers, suspense, hard science fiction, contemporary and dark fantasy, horror, young adult and middle-grade, popular subjects and treatment with high commercial potential).

⊶ "We prefer to work with published (traditional print publishing), established authors. We will give first consideration to authors who come recommended to us by our clients or other publishing professionals. We accept a very small number of new, previously unpublished authors."

How to Contact: Published authors: "We would prefer you send us a written letter with SASE to introduce yourself. If you need a fast response, you may call."

Recent Sales: Sold more than 100 titles in the last year. *Dreaming Pachinko*, by Isaac Adamson (HarperCollins); *The Sky So Big and Black*, by John Barnes (Tor); *Move Your Stuff, Change Your Life*, by Karen Rauch Carter (Simon & Schuster).

Terms: Agent receives 15% commission on domestic sales; 20% commission on foreign sales.

⬛ **SANFORD J. GREENBURGER ASSOCIATES, INC.**, 55 Fifth Ave., New York NY 10003. (212)206-5600. Fax: (212)463-8718. Website: www.greenburger.com. **Contact:** Heide Lange. Estab. 1945. Member of AAR. Represents 500 clients.

Member Agents: Heide Lange; Faith Hamlin; Theresa Park; Elyse Cheney; Dan Mandel; Julie Barer.

Represents: Nonfiction books, novels. **Considers these fiction areas:** Action/adventure; contemporary issues; detective/police/crime; ethnic; family saga; feminist; gay/lesbian; glitz; historical; humor/satire; literary; mainstream/contemporary; mystery/suspense; psychic/supernatural; regional; sports; thriller.

⊶ Does not want to receive romances or westerns.

How to Contact: Query with SASE. Considers simultaneous queries. Responds in 3 weeks to queries; 2 months to mss.

Recent Sales: Sold 200 titles in the last year. This agency prefers not to share information on specific sales. Other clients include Andrew Ross, Margaret Cuthbert, Nicholas Sparks, Mary Kurcinka, Linda Nichols, Edy Clarke and Peggy Claude Pierre, Brad Thor, Dan Brown, Sallie Bissell.

Terms: Agent receives 15% commission on domestic sales; 20% commission on foreign sales. Charges for photocopying, books for foreign and subsidiary rights submissions.

🌐 ⬛ **GREGORY & CO. AUTHORS' AGENTS**, 3 Barb Mews, London W6 7PA, England. 020-7610-4676. Fax: 020-7610-4686. E-mail: info@gregoryandcompany.co.uk. Website: www.gregoryandcompany.co.uk. **Contact:** Jane Gregory, sales; Broo Doherty, editorial; Jane Barlow/Claire Morris rights. Estab. 1987. Member of Association of Authors' Agents. Represents 60 clients. Currently handles: 10% nonfiction books; 90% novels.

● Prior to becoming an agent, Ms. Gregory was Rights Director for Chatto & Windus.

Member Agents: Jane Gregory (sales); Broo Doherty (editorial); Jane Barlow/Claire Morris (rights).

Represents: Nonfiction books, and fiction books. **Considers these fiction areas:** Action/adventure; detective/police/crime; historical; humor/satire; literary; mainstream/contemporary; multicultural; thriller; Contemporary women's fiction.

⊶ "Jane Gregory is successful at selling rights all over the world, including film and television rights. As a British agency we do not generally take on American authors." Actively seeking well-written, accessible modern novels. Does not want to receive horror, science fiction, fantasy, mind/body/spirit, children's books, screenplays and plays, short stories, poetry.

How to Contact: Query with SASE, or submit outline, 3 sample chapters, SASE. Considers simultaneous queries. Returns materials only with SASE. Obtains most new clients through recommendations from others, conferences.

Recent Sales: Sold 100 titles in the last year. *Tokyo*, by Mo Hayder (Bantam UK/Doubleday USA); *Distant Echo*, by Val McDermid (HarperCollins UK/St. Martin's Press NY); *Fox Evil*, by Minette Walters (McMillan UK/Putnam USA); *Hello, Bunny Alice*, by Laura Wilson (Orion UK/Bantam USA); *A Place of Safety*, by Natasha Cooper (Simon & Schuster UK/St. Martin's Press USA).

Terms: Agent receives 15% commission on domestic sales; 20% commission on foreign sales. Offers written contract; 3-month notice must be given to terminate contract. Charges clients for photocopying of whole typescripts and copies of book for submissions.

Writers' Conferences: CWA Conference (United Kingdom, Spring); Dead on Deansgate (Manchester, Autumn); Harrogate Literary Festival (United Kingdom, Summer); Bouchercon (location varies, Autumn).

◯ **JILL GROSJEAN LITERARY AGENCY**, 1390 Millstone Rd., Sag Harbor NY 11963-2214. (631)725-7419. Fax: (631)725-8632. E-mail: jill6981@aol.com. Website: www.hometown.aol.com/jill6981/myhomepage/index.html. **Contact:** Jill Grosjean. Estab. 1999. Represents 24 clients. 100% of clients are new/unpublished writers. Currently handles: 100% novels.

● Prior to becoming an agent, Ms. Grosjean was manager of an independent bookstore. She also worked in publishing and advertising.

Represents: Novels (exclusively). **Considers these fiction areas:** Contemporary issues; historical; humor/satire; literary; mainstream/contemporary; mystery/suspense; regional; romance.

⊶ This agency offers some editorial assistance (i.e., line-by-line edits). Actively seeking literary novels and mysteries. Does not want to receive any nonfiction subjects not indicated above.

How to Contact: Query with SASE. No cold calls, please. Considers simultaneous queries. Responds in 1 week to queries; 1 month to mss. Returns materials only with SASE. Obtains most new clients through recommendations from others, solicitations.

Recent Sales: *I Love You Like a Tomato*, by Marie Giordano (Forge Books); *Nectar*, by David C. Fickett (Forge Books); *Cycling*, by Greg Garrett (Kensington).

Terms: Agent receives 15% commission on domestic sales; 20% commission on foreign sales. No written contract. Charges clients for photocopying, mailing expenses; Writers reimbursed for office fees after the sale of ms.

Writers' Conferences: Book Passages Mystery Writer's Conference (Corte Madera CA, July); Writers' League of Texas Conference (Austin TX, July).

☑ THE GROSVENOR LITERARY AGENCY, 5510 Grosvenor Lane, Bethesda MD 20814. Phone/Fax: (301)564-6231. E-mail: dcgrosveno@aol.com. **Contact:** Deborah C. Grosvenor. Estab. 1995. Member of National Press Club. Represents 30 clients. 10% of clients are new/unpublished writers. Currently handles: 80% nonfiction books; 20% novels.

• Prior to opening her agency, Ms. Grosvenor was a book editor for 18 years.

Represents: Nonfiction books, novels. **Considers these fiction areas:** Contemporary issues; detective/police/crime; family saga; historical; literary; mainstream/contemporary; mystery/suspense; romance (contemporary, gothic, historical); thriller.

How to Contact: Send query and 3 sample chapters. No e-mail or fax queries. Responds in 1 month to queries; 2 months to mss. Returns materials only with SASE. Obtains most new clients through recommendations from others.

Recent Sales: *The Greatest Moment: The Year the Brooklyn Dodgers Won the World Series*, by Thomas Oliphant (Thomas Dunn Books); *Radical Innocent: Upton Sinclair, A Biography*.

Terms: Agent receives 15% commission on domestic sales; 20% commission on foreign sales. Offers written contract; 10-day notice must be given to terminate contract.

☑ REECE HALSEY AGENCY, 8733 Sunset Blvd., Suite 101, Los Angeles CA 90069. Fax: (310)652-7595. **Contact:** Kimberley Cameron (all queries) at Reece Halsey North. Estab. 1957. Member of AAR. Represents 40 clients. 30% of clients are new/unpublished writers. Currently handles: 30% nonfiction books; 60% novels; 10% movie scripts.

• The Reece Halsey Agency has an illustrious client list largely of established writers, including the estate of Aldous Huxley and has represented Upton Sinclair, William Faulkner and Henry Miller. Ms. Cameron has recently opened a Northern California office and all queries should be addressed to her at the Reece Halsey North office.

Member Agents: Dorris Halsey; Kimberley Cameron.

Represents: Nonfiction books, novels. **Considers these fiction areas:** Action/adventure; contemporary issues; detective/police/crime; ethnic; family saga; historical; literary; mainstream/contemporary; mystery/suspense; science fiction; thriller; women's.

O¬ This agency specializes mostly in books/excellent writing.

How to Contact: Query with SASE. Prefers to read materials exclusively. No e-mail or fax queries. Responds in 3 weeks to queries; 3 months to mss. Obtains most new clients through recommendations from others, solicitations.

Terms: Agent receives 15% commission on domestic sales; 10% commission on dramatic rights sales. Offers written contract, binding for 1 year. Requests 6 copies of ms if representing an author.

Writers' Conferences: Maui Writers Conference; ABA.

Tips: "Always send a well-written query and include a SASE with it!"

☑ REECE HALSEY NORTH, 98 Main St., #704, Tiburon CA 94920. (415)789-9191. E-mail: info@reecehalsey north.com. Website: www.reecehalseynorth.com or www.kimberleycameron.com. **Contact:** Kimberley Cameron. Estab. 1995. Member of AAR. Represents 40 clients. 30% of clients are new/unpublished writers. Currently handles: 30% nonfiction books; 70% fiction.

Member Agents: Kimberley Cameron (Reece Halsey North); Dorris Halsey (by referral only, LA office).

Represents: Nonfiction books, and fiction books. **Considers these fiction areas:** Action/adventure; comic books/cartoon; detective/police/crime; ethnic; family saga; historical; horror; literary; mainstream/contemporary; mystery/suspense; science fiction; thriller; women's.

O¬ This agency specializes in mystery, literary and mainstream fiction, excellent writing. The Reece Halsey Agency has an illustrious client list largely of established writers, including the estate of Aldous Huxley and has represented Upton Sinclair, William Faulkner and Henry Miller. Ms. Cameron has a Northern California office and all queries should be addressed to her at the Tiburon address.

How to Contact: Query with SASE. No e-mail or fax queries. Considers simultaneous queries. Responds in 1 month to queries; 3 months to mss. Obtains most new clients through recommendations from others, solicitations.

Recent Sales: *Jinn*, by Matthew Delaney (St. Martin's Press); *Final Epidemic*, by Earl Merkel (Dutton-NAL); *Sea Room*, by Norman Gautreau; *The Modern Gentleman*, by Phineas Mollod and Jason Tesauro.

Terms: Agent receives 15% commission on domestic sales. Offers written contract, binding for 1 year. Requests 8 copies of ms if representing an author.

Writers' Conferences: BEA; Maui Writers Conference; San Diego State University; Pacific Northwest; Cape Cod.

Tips: "Please send a polite, well-written query and include a SASE with it! You may also include the first ten pages of the manuscript."

THE JOY HARRIS LITERARY AGENCY, INC., 156 Fifth Ave., Suite 617, New York NY 10010. (212)924-6269. Fax: (212)924-6609. E-mail: gen.office@jhlitagent.com. **Contact:** Joy Harris. Member of AAR. Represents over 100 clients. Currently handles: 50% nonfiction books; 50% novels.

Member Agents: Leslie Daniels; Stéphanie Abou; Alexia Paul.

Represents: Nonfiction books, novels. **Considers these fiction areas:** Contemporary issues; ethnic; experimental; family saga; feminist; gay/lesbian; glitz; hi-lo; historical; humor/satire; literary; mainstream/contemporary; multicultural; multimedia; mystery/suspense; picture books; regional; short story collections; spiritual; translation; women's.

  0— Does not want to receive screenplays.

How to Contact: Query with sample chapter, outline/proposal, SASE. Considers simultaneous queries. Responds in 2 months to queries. Obtains most new clients through recommendations from clients and editors.

Recent Sales: Sold 15 titles in the last year. This agency prefers not to share information on specific sales.

Terms: Agent receives 15% commission on domestic sales; 20% commission on foreign sales. Charges clients for some office expenses.

HARTLINE LITERARY AGENCY, 123 Queenston Dr., Pittsburgh PA 15235-5429. (412)829-2495 or 2483. Fax: (412)829-2450. E-mail: joyce@hartlineliterary.com. Website: www.hartlineliterary.com. **Contact:** Joyce A. Hart. Estab. 1990. Represents 40 clients. 30% of clients are new/unpublished writers. Currently handles: 40% nonfiction books; 60% novels.

Member Agents: Joyce A. Hart, principal agent; Janet Benrey; Tamela Hancock Murray; Andrea Boeshaar.

Represents: Nonfiction books, novels. **Considers these fiction areas:** Action/adventure; contemporary issues; family saga; historical; literary; mystery/suspense (amateur sleuth, cozy); regional; religious/inspirational; romance (contemporary, gothic, historical, regency); thriller.

  0— This agency specializes in the Christian bookseller market. Actively seeking adult fiction, self-help, nutritional books, devotional, business. Does not want to receive science fiction, erotica, gay/lesbian, fantasy, horror, etc.

How to Contact: Submit outline, 3 sample chapter(s). Accepts e-mail and fax queries. Considers simultaneous queries. Responds in 2 months to queries; 3 months to mss. Returns materials only with SASE. Obtains most new clients through recommendations from others.

Recent Sales: *Every Fixed Star*, by Jane Kirkpatrick (Waterbrook); *Daughter of Liberty*, by H.M. Hostetter (Zondervan); *Happily Ever After*, by Susan Warren (Tyndale House).

Terms: Agent receives 15% commission on domestic sales. Offers written contract.

JOHN HAWKINS & ASSOCIATES, INC., 71 W. 23rd St., Suite 1600, New York NY 10010. (212)807-7040. Fax: (212)807-9555. E-mail: jha@jhaliterary.com. Website: jhaliterary.com. **Contact:** John Hawkins, William Reiss. Estab. 1893. Member of AAR. Represents over 100 clients. 5-10% of clients are new/unpublished writers. Currently handles: 40% nonfiction books; 40% novels; 20% juvenile books.

Member Agents: Moses Cardona; Warren Frazier; Anne Hawkins; John Hawkins; William Reiss; Elly Sidel.

Represents: Nonfiction books, novels, juvenile books. **Considers these fiction areas:** Action/adventure; comic books/cartoon; contemporary issues; detective/police/crime; ethnic; experimental; family saga; fantasy; feminist; gay/lesbian; glitz; gothic; hi-lo; historical; horror; humor/satire; juvenile; literary; mainstream/contemporary; military/war; multicultural; multimedia; mystery/suspense; New Age; occult; picture books; plays; poetry; poetry in translation; psychic/supernatural; regional; religious/inspirational; science fiction; short story collections; spiritual; sports; thriller; translation; westerns/frontier; young adult; women's.

How to Contact: Query with SASE, submit proposal package, outline. Considers simultaneous queries. Responds in 1 month to queries. Returns materials only with SASE. Obtains most new clients through recommendations from others.

Recent Sales: *Dead Halt on the Lunatic Line*, by Sarah Rose (Random House); *Empire of Light*, by David Czuchlewski (Putnam).

Terms: Agent receives 15% commission on domestic sales; 20% commission on foreign sales. Charges clients for photocopying.

RICHARD HENSHAW GROUP, 127 W. 24th St., 4th Floor, New York NY 10011. (212)414-1172. Fax: (435)417-5208. E-mail: submissions@henshaw.com. Website: www.rich.henshaw.com. **Contact:** Rich Henshaw. Estab. 1995. Member of AAR, SinC, MWA, HWA, SFWA. Represents 35 clients. 20% of clients are new/unpublished writers. Currently handles: 30% nonfiction books; 70% novels.

  ● Prior to opening his agency, Mr. Henshaw served as an agent with Richard Curtis Associates, Inc.

Represents: Nonfiction books, novels. **Considers these fiction areas:** Action/adventure; detective/police/crime; ethnic; family saga; fantasy; glitz; historical; horror; humor/satire; literary; mainstream/contemporary; mystery/suspense; psychic/supernatural; romance; science fiction; sports; thriller.

☞ This agency specializes in thrillers, mysteries, science fiction, fantasy and horror.
How to Contact: Query with SASE. Responds in 3 weeks to queries; 6 weeks to mss. Obtains most new clients through recommendations from others, solicitations, conferences.
Recent Sales: *Dead Soul*, by James D. Doss (St. Martin's). Other clients include Susan Wise Bauer, Jessie Wise.
Terms: Agent receives 15% commission on domestic sales; 20% commission on foreign sales. No written contract. 100% of business is derived from commissions on ms sales. Charges clients for photocopying mss and book orders.
Tips: "While we do not have any reason to believe that our submission guidelines will change in the near future, writers can find up-to-date submission policy information on our website. Always include SASE with correct return postage."

☑ **SUSAN HERNER RIGHTS AGENCY**, P.O. Box 303, Scarsdale NY 10583-0303. (914)725-8967. Fax: (914)725-8969. **Contact:** Susan Herner. Estab. 1987. Represents 100 clients. 30% of clients are new/unpublished writers. Currently handles: 60% nonfiction books; 40% novels.
Member Agents: Susan Herner, president (nonfiction, thriller, mystery, strong women's fiction).
Represents: Nonfiction books (adult), novels (adult). **Considers these fiction areas:** Action/adventure; contemporary issues; detective/police/crime; ethnic; family saga; feminist; glitz; historical; horror; literary; mainstream/contemporary; mystery/suspense; thriller.
☞ "I'm particularly looking for strong women's fiction and thrillers. I'm particularly interested in women's issues, popular science, and feminist spirituality."
How to Contact: Query with SASE, outline, sample chapter(s). Considers simultaneous queries. Responds in 1 month to queries. Returns materials only with SASE.
Recent Sales: *If Cooks Could Kill*, by Joanne Pence (Avon); *Our Improble Universe*, by Michael Mallary (Four Walls Eight Windows); *Everything You Need to Know About Latino History*, by Hemilce Novas (Plume).
Terms: Agent receives 15% commission on domestic sales; 20% commission on foreign sales; 20% commission on dramatic rights sales. Charges clients for extraordinary postage and photocopying. "Agency has two divisions: one represents writers on a commission-only basis; the other represents the rights for small publishers and packagers who do not have in-house subsidiary rights representation. Percentage of income derived from each division is currently 80-20."

☑ **FREDERICK HILL BONNIE NADELL, INC.**, 1842 Union St., San Francisco CA 94123. (415)921-2910. Fax: (415)921-2802. **Contact:** Irene Moore. Estab. 1979. Represents 100 clients.
Member Agents: Fred Hill (president); Bonnie Nadell (vice president); Irene Moore (associate).
Represents: Nonfiction books, novels. **Considers these fiction areas:** Literary; mainstream/contemporary.
How to Contact: Query with SASE. No e-mail or fax queries. Considers simultaneous queries. Returns materials only with SASE.
Recent Sales: *River of Shadows: Eadweard Muybridge and the Technological Wild West*, by Rebecca Solnit; *The Country Under My Skin*, by Gioconda Belli; *Fear Itself*, by Jonathan Nasaw.
Terms: Agent receives 15% commission on domestic sales; 20% commission on foreign sales; 15% commission on dramatic rights sales. Charges clients for photocopying.

☑ **BARBARA HOGENSON AGENCY**, 165 West End Ave., Suite 19-C, New York NY 10023. (212)874-8084. Fax: (212)362-3011. **Contact:** Barbara Hogenson. Estab. 1994. Member of AAR; signatory of WGA. Represents 60 clients. 5% of clients are new/unpublished writers. Currently handles: 35% nonfiction books; 15% novels; 50% stage plays.
● Prior to opening her agency, Ms. Hogenson was with the prestigious Lucy Kroll Agency for 10 years.
Represents: Nonfiction books, novels, theatrical stage play. **Considers these fiction areas:** Action/adventure; detective/police/crime; ethnic; historical; humor/satire; literary; mainstream/contemporary; mystery/suspense; romance (contemporary); thriller.
How to Contact: Query with SASE, outline. No unsolicited mss. Responds in 1 month to queries. Obtains most new clients through recommendations from others.
Recent Sales: *Letters of James Thurber*, by Harrison Kinney and Rosemary Thurber; *Ghosts of McDougal Street*, by Hesper Anderson; *Learning to Swim*, by Penelope Niven.
Terms: Agent receives 15% commission on domestic sales; 20% commission on foreign sales; 10% commission on dramatic rights sales. Offers written contract.

☑ **HOPKINS LITERARY ASSOCIATES**, 2117 Buffalo Rd., Suite 327, Rochester NY 14624-1507. (585)352-6268. Fax: (585)352-6270. **Contact:** Pam Hopkins. Estab. 1996. Member of AAR, RWA. Represents 30 clients. 5% of clients are new/unpublished writers. Currently handles: 100% novels.
Represents: Novels. **Considers these fiction areas:** Historical; mainstream/contemporary; romance; women's.
☞ This agency specializes in women's fiction, particularly historical, contemporary and category romance as well as mainstream work.
How to Contact: Submit outline, 3 sample chapter(s). No e-mail or fax queries. Considers simultaneous queries. Responds in 2 weeks to queries; 1 month to mss. Returns materials only with SASE. Obtains most new clients through recommendations from others, solicitations, conferences.

Recent Sales: Sold 50 titles in the last year. *The Napolean Gates*, by Merline Lovelace (Mira); *The Charmer*, by Madeline Hunter (Bantam); *Knock Me Off My Feet*, by Susan Donovan (St. Martin's).
Terms: Agent receives 15% commission on domestic sales; 20% commission on foreign sales. No written contract.
Writers' Conferences: Romance Writers of America.

HORNFISCHER LITERARY MANAGEMENT, INC., P.O. Box 50067, Austin TX 78763-0067. E-mail: jim@hornfischerliterarymanagement.com. Website: www.hornfischerliterarymanagement.com. **Contact:** James D. Hornfischer, president. Estab. 2001. Represents 45 clients. 20% of clients are new/unpublished writers. Currently handles: 90% nonfiction books; 10% novels.
 • Prior to opening his agency, Mr. Hornfischer was an agent with Literary Group International and held editorial positions at HarperCollins and McGraw-Hill. "I work hard to make an author's first trip to market a successful one. That means closely working with my clients prior to submission to produce the strongest possible book proposal or manuscript. My New York editorial background, at HarperCollins and McGraw-Hill, where I worked on books by a variety of bestselling authors such as Erma Bombeck, Jared Diamond and Erica Jong among others, is useful in this regard. In eight years as an agent I've handled two number 1 *New York Times* nonfiction bestsellers, and in 2001 one of my clients was a finalist for the Pulitzer Prize."
Represents: Nonfiction books, novels, feature film, TV movie of the week. **Considers these fiction areas:** Historical; literary; mainstream/contemporary; thriller.
 O— Actively seeking the best work of terrific writers. Does not want poetry, genre mysteries, romance or science fiction.
How to Contact: Submit proposal package, outline, 2 sample chapter(s). Considers simultaneous queries. Responds in 1 month to queries. Returns materials only with SASE. Obtains most new clients through referrals from clients; reading books and magazines; pursuing ideas with New York editors.
Recent Sales: *A Good Forest for Dying*, by Patrick Beach (Doubleday); *Pacific Alamo*, by John Wukovits (NAL); *Kings of Texas*, by Don Graham (Wiley).
Terms: Agent receives 15% commission on domestic sales; 20% commission on foreign sales. Offers written contract. Reasonable expenses deducted from proceeds after book is sold.
Tips: "When you query agents and send out proposals, present yourself as someone who's in command of his material and comfortable in his own skin. Too many writers have a palpable sense of anxiety and insecurity. Take a deep breath and realize that—if you're good—someone in the publishing world will want you."

J DE S ASSOCIATES, INC., 9 Shagbark Rd., Wilson Point, South Norwalk CT 06854. (203)838-7571. **Contact:** Jacques de Spoelberch. Estab. 1975. Represents 50 clients. Currently handles: 50% nonfiction books; 50% novels.
 • Prior to opening his agency, Mr. de Spoelberch was an editor with Houghton Mifflin.
Represents: Nonfiction books, novels. **Considers these fiction areas:** Detective/police/crime; historical; juvenile; literary; mainstream/contemporary; mystery/suspense; New Age; westerns/frontier; young adult.
How to Contact: Query with SASE. Responds in 2 months to queries. Obtains most new clients through recommendations from authors and other clients.
Terms: Agent receives 15% commission on domestic sales; 20% commission on foreign sales. Charges clients for foreign postage and photocopying.

JABBERWOCKY LITERARY AGENCY, P.O. Box 4558, Sunnyside NY 11104-0558. (718)392-5985. Fax: (718)392-5985. **Contact:** Joshua Bilmes. Estab. 1994. Member of SFWA. Represents 40 clients. 25% of clients are new/unpublished writers. Currently handles: 15% nonfiction books; 75% novels; 5% scholarly books; 5% other.
Represents: Nonfiction books, novels, scholarly books. **Considers these fiction areas:** Action/adventure; comic books/cartoon; contemporary issues; detective/police/crime; ethnic; family saga; fantasy; gay/lesbian; glitz; historical; horror; humor/satire; literary; mainstream/contemporary; psychic/supernatural; regional; science fiction; sports; thriller.
 O— This agency represents quite a lot of genre fiction and is actively seeking to increase amount of nonfiction projects. It does not handle juvenile or young adult. Book-length material only; no poetry, articles or short fiction.
How to Contact: Query with SASE. No mss unless requested. No e-mail or fax queries. Considers simultaneous queries. Responds in 2 weeks to queries. Returns materials only with SASE. Obtains most new clients through solicitations, recommendation by current clients.
Recent Sales: Sold 20 titles in the last year. *Club Dead*, by Charlaine Harris (ACE); *The Speed of Dark*, by Elizabeth Moon (Ballantine); *Deathstalker Return*, by Simon Green (ROC); *Follow Me and Die*, by Ceil Currey (Cooper Square). Other clients include Tanya Huff, Kristine Smith, Edo Van Belkom.
Terms: Agent receives 12.5% commission on domestic sales; 20% commission on foreign sales. Offers written contract, binding for 1 year. Charges clients for book purchases, photocopying, international book/ms mailing, international long distance.
Writers' Conferences: Malice Domestic (Washington DC, May); World SF Convention (Boston MA, August); Icon (Stony Brook NY, April).
Tips: "In approaching with a query, the most important things to me are your credits and your biographical

background to the extent it's relevant to your work. I (and most agents) will ignore the adjectives you may choose to describe your own work."

JCA LITERARY AGENCY, 27 W. 20th St., Suite 1103, New York NY 10011. (212)807-0888. Fax: (212)807-0461. Website: www.jcalit.com. **Contact:** Jeff Gerecke, Tony Outhwaite. Estab. 1978. Member of AAR. Represents 100 clients. 10% of clients are new/unpublished writers. Currently handles: 20% nonfiction books; 75% novels; 5% scholarly books.
Member Agents: Jeff Gerecke; Tony Outhwaite; Peter Steinberg.
Represents: Nonfiction books, novels. **Considers these fiction areas:** Action/adventure; contemporary issues; detective/police/crime; family saga; historical; literary; mainstream/contemporary; mystery/suspense; sports; thriller.
   O→ Does not want to receive screenplays, poetry, children's books, science fiction/fantasy, genre romance.
How to Contact: Query with SASE. No e-mail or fax queries. Considers simultaneous queries. Responds in 2 weeks to queries; 10 weeks to mss. Returns materials only with SASE. Obtains most new clients through recommendations from others, solicitations, conferences.
Recent Sales: *Life Sentence*, by David Ellis (Putnam); *The Heaven of Mercury*, by Brad Watson (Norton); *The Rope Eater*, by Ben Jones. Other clients include Ernest J. Gaines, Gwen Hunter, Cathy Dal.
Terms: Agent receives 15% commission on domestic sales; 20% commission on foreign sales. No written contract. "We work with our clients on a handshake basis." Charges for postage on overseas submissions, photocopying, mss for submission, books purchased for subrights submission, and bank charges, where applicable. "We deduct the cost from payments received from publishers."
Tips: "We do not ourselves provide legal, accounting, or public relations services for our clients, although some of the advice we give falls somewhat into these realms. In cases where it seems necessary we will recommend obtaining outside advice or assistance in these areas from professionals who are not in any way connected to the agency."

■ **JELLINEK & MURRAY LITERARY AGENCY**, 3623 Kumu St., Honolulu HI 96822. (808)988-8461. Fax: (808)988-8462. E-mail: jellinek@lava.net. **Contact:** Roger Jellinek. Estab. 1995. Represents 65 clients. 90% of clients are new/unpublished writers. Currently handles: 60% nonfiction books; 40% novels.
   ● Prior to becoming an agent, Mr. Jellinek was deputy editor, *New York Times Book Review* (1966-74); Editor-in-Chief, New York Times Book Co. (1975-1981); editor/packager book/TV projects (1981-1995).
Member Agents: Roger Jellinek (general fiction, nonfiction); Eden Lee Murray (general fiction, nonfiction).
Represents: Nonfiction books, novels, textbooks, movie scripts (from book clients), TV scripts (from book clients).
Considers these fiction areas: Action/adventure; confession; contemporary issues; detective/police/crime; erotica; ethnic; family saga; feminist; gay/lesbian; glitz; historical; horror; humor/satire; literary; mainstream/contemporary; multicultural; mystery/suspense; New Age; picture books; psychic/supernatural; regional; thriller; westerns/frontier.
   O→ This agency is the only literary agency in Hawaii. "Half our clients are based in Hawaii, half from all over the world. We accept submissions (after a query) via e-mail attachment; we only send out fully-edited proposals and manuscripts." Actively seeking first-rate writing.
How to Contact: Query with SASE, submit outline, 2 sample chapter(s), if requested. Accepts e-mail and fax queries. Considers simultaneous queries. Responds in 2 weeks to queries; 2 months to mss. Returns materials only with SASE. Obtains most new clients through recommendations from others, solicitations, conferences.
Recent Sales: Sold 10 titles and sold 1 scripts in the last year. *God's Photo Album*, by Shelly Mecum (HarperSan-Francisco); *The Cookie Never Crumbles*, by Wally Amos (St. Martin's Press).
Terms: Agent receives 15% commission on domestic sales; 25% commission on foreign sales. Offers written contract, binding for indefinite period; 30-day notice must be given to terminate contract. Charges clients for photocopies and postage. May refer to editing services occasionally, if author asks for recommendation. "We have no income deriving from our referrals. Referrals to editors do not imply representation."
Tips: "Would-be authors should be well read and knowledgeable about their field and genre."

LAWRENCE JORDAN LITERARY AGENCY, a Morning Star Communications, LLC company, 345 W. 121st St., New York NY 10027. (212)662-7871. Fax: (212)662-8138. E-mail: ljlagency@aol.com. **Contact:** President: Lawrence Jordan. Estab. 1978. Represents 50 clients. 25% of clients are new/unpublished writers. Works with a small number of new/previously unpublished authors. Currently handles: 70% nonfiction books; 30% novels.
   ● Prior to opening his agency, Mr. Jordan served as an editor with Doubleday & Co.
Represents: Nonfiction books, novels.
   O→ This agency specializes in general adult fiction and nonfiction. Actively seeking spiritual and religious books, mystery novels, action suspense, thrillers, biographies, autobiographies, celebrity books. Does not want to receive poetry, movie scripts, stage plays, juvenile books, fantasy novels, science fiction.
How to Contact: Query with SASE, outline. Responds in 3 weeks to queries; 6 weeks to mss.
Terms: Agent receives 15% commission on domestic sales; 20% commission on foreign sales; 20% commission on dramatic rights sales. 99% of business is derived from commissions on ms sales. Charges long-distance calls, photocopying, foreign submission costs, postage, cables and messengers.

NATASHA KERN LITERARY AGENCY, P.O. Box 2908, Portland OR 97208-2908. (503)297-6190. Website: www.natashakern.com. **Contact:** Natasha Kern. Estab. 1986. Member of RWA, MWA, SinC.

• Prior to opening her agency, Ms. Kern worked as an editor and publicist for New York publishers (Simon & Schuster, Bantam, Ballantine). "This agency has sold over 500 books."

Member Agents: Natasha Kern; Ruth Widener.

Represents: Adult commercial nonfiction and fiction. **Considers these fiction areas:** Ethnic; feminist; historical; mainstream/contemporary; mystery/suspense; religious/inspirational; romance (contemporary, historical); thriller (medical, scientific, historical).

O━ This agency specializes in commercial fiction and nonfiction for adults. "A full service agency." Does not represent sports, true crime, scholarly works, coffee table books, war memoirs, software, scripts, literary fiction, photography, poetry, short stories, children's, horror, fantasy, genre science fiction, stage plays or traditional Westerns.

How to Contact: Query with SASE, include submission history, writing credits, how long ms is. Send 2-3 page synopsis and 3-5 first pages. See web site before querying. No e-mail or fax queries. Considers simultaneous queries. Responds in 3 weeks to queries.

Recent Sales: Sold 53 titles in the last year. *Firstborn*, by Robin Lee Hatcher (Tyndale); *The Waiting Child*, by Cindy Champnella.

Terms: Agent receives 15% commission on domestic sales; 20% commission on foreign sales; 15% commission on dramatic rights sales.

Writers' Conferences: RWA National Conference, MWA National Conference and many regional conferences.

Tips: "Our idea of a Dream Client is someone who participates in a mutually respectful business relationship, is clear about needs and goals, and communicates about career planning. If we know what you need and want, we can help you achieve it. A dream client has a storytelling gift, a commitment to a writing career, a desire to learn and grow, and a passion for excellence. We want clients who are expressing their own unique voice and truly have something of their own to communicate. This client understands that many people have to work together for a book to succeed and that everything in publishing takes far longer than one imagines. Trust and communication are truly essential."

VIRGINIA KIDD AGENCY, INC., 538 E. Harford St., P.O. Box 278, Milford PA 18337-0278. (570)296-6205. Fax: (570)296-7266. E-mail: vkagency@ptd.net. **Contact:** Linn Prentis, Nanci McCloskey. Estab. 1965. Member of SFWA, SFRA. Represents 80 clients.

Member Agents: Nanci McCloskey; Linn Prentis; Christine Cohen; Vaughne Hansen.

Represents: Novels. **Considers these fiction areas:** Fantasy (special interest in non-traditional fantasy); glitz; historical; literary; mainstream/contemporary; mystery/suspense; science fiction; young adult; speculative fiction.

O━ This agency specializes in "science fiction but we do not limit ourselves to it."

How to Contact: Submit synopsis, cover letter, SASE. Prefers to read materials exclusively. Considers simultaneous queries. Responds in 1 month to queries. Obtains most new clients through recommendations.

Recent Sales: Sold 75 titles in the last year. *Changing Planes*, by Ursula K. Le Guin (Harcourt Brace); *Stories of Your Life and Others*, by Ted Chiang (Tor Books); *The Knight*, by Gene Wolfe (Tor Books). Other clients include Alan Dean Foster, Kage Baker, Wen Spencer, Eleanor Arnason, Katie Waitman, Margaret Ball.

Terms: Agent receives 15% commission on domestic sales; 20-25% commission on foreign sales; 20% commission on dramatic rights sales. Offers written contract; 60-day notice must be given to terminate contract. Charges clients occasionally for extraordinary expenses.

Tips: "If you have a novel of speculative fiction, romance, or mainstream that is really extraordinary, please query me, including a synopsis, publishing credits and a SASE."

JEFFREY M. KLEINMAN, ESQ., Graybill & English, LLC, 1875 Connecticut Ave. NW, Suite 712, Washington DC 20009. (202)588-9798. Fax: (202)457-0662. E-mail: jmkagent@aol.com. Website: www.graybillandenglish.com/jmk. **Contact:** Jeff Kleinman. Estab. 1998. 50% of clients are new/unpublished writers.

• Mr. Kleinman is a literary agent and attorney.

Represents: Nonfiction books (particularly narrative nonfiction), novels. **Considers these fiction areas:** Action/adventure; contemporary issues; ethnic; family saga; fantasy; feminist; gay/lesbian; glitz; historical; horror; humor/satire; literary; mainstream/contemporary; multimedia (tie-ins with literary projects); psychic/supernatural; regional; science fiction; thriller.

O━ This agency specializes in narrative nonfiction, nonfiction, fiction. Does not want to receive children's literature, romances, westerns or poetry.

How to Contact: Query with SASE, or send outline, 3 sample chapters, SASE. Accepts e-mail queries, no attachments. Considers simultaneous queries. Responds in 2 weeks to queries; 1 month to mss. Returns materials only with SASE. Obtains most new clients through recommendations from others, solicitations.

Recent Sales: Sold 12 titles in the last year. *Gentlemen's Blood*, by Barbara Holland (Bloomsbury); *Teasing Secrets from the Dead*, by Dr. Emily Craig (Crown); *The Lost Pet Chronicles*, by Kat Albrecht (Bloomsbury).

Terms: Agent receives 15% commission on domestic sales; 20% commission on foreign sales. Offers written contract; 30-day notice must be given to terminate contract. Charges clients for postage, long distance, photocopying.

Writers' Conferences: Wrangling on Writing (Tucson, January); Mid-Atlantic Creative Nonfiction Summer

Writer's Conference (Baltimore MD, August); Baltimore Writers (Baltimore MD, September).

HARVEY KLINGER, INC., 301 W. 53rd St., Suite 21-A, New York NY 10019. (212)581-7068. Fax: (212)315-3823. E-mail: queries@harveyklinger.com. Website: www.harveyklinger.com. **Contact:** Harvey Klinger. Estab. 1977. Member of AAR. Represents 100 clients. 25% of clients are new/unpublished writers. Currently handles: 50% nonfiction books; 50% novels.
Member Agents: Jenny Bent (literary fiction; commercial women's fiction; memoir; narrative nonfiction; self help/pop psychology); David Dunton (popular culture, with a speciality in music-related books; literary fiction; crime novels; thrillers); Wendy Silbert (narrative nonfiction; historical narrative nonfiction; politics; history; biographies; memoir; literary ficiton; business books; culinary narratives).
Represents: Nonfiction books, novels. **Considers these fiction areas:** Action/adventure; detective/police/crime; family saga; glitz; literary; mainstream/contemporary; mystery/suspense; thriller.
    O— This agency specializes in "big, mainstream contemporary fiction and nonfiction."
How to Contact: Query with SASE. No phone queries. Accepts e-mail queries. No fax queries. Responds in 2 months to queries; 2 months to mss. Obtains most new clients through recommendations from others.
Recent Sales: Sold 30 titles in the last year. *Swan Place*, by Augusta Trobaugh (Dutton); *Fund Your Future*, by Julie Stav (Berkley); *Auriel Rising*, by Elizabeth Redfern (Putnam); *A Love Supreme*, by Ashley Kahn (Viking); *Idiot Girls' Action Adventure Guide*, by Laurie Notaro; *Inside Medicine*, by Kevin Soden and Christine Dumas; *Where I Work and Other Stories*, by Ann Cummins (Houghton Mifflin); *Thirty Years of Shame*, by Mark Kemp (Free Press). Other clients include Barbara Wood, Terry Kay, Barbara De Angelis, Jill Conner Browne, Michael Farquhar, Greg Bottoms, Jeremy Jackson, Pamela Berkman, Jonetta Rose Barras, Paul Russell.
Terms: Agent receives 15% commission on domestic sales; 25% commission on foreign sales. Offers written contract. Charges for photocopying mss, overseas postage for mss.

THE KNIGHT AGENCY, P.O. Box 550648, Atlanta GA 30355. (404)816-9620. E-mail: knightagent@aol.com. Website: www.knightagency.net. **Contact:** Deidre Knight. Estab. 1996. Member of AAR, RWA, Authors Guild. Represents 65 clients. 40% of clients are new/unpublished writers. Currently handles: 50% nonfiction books; 50% novels.
Member Agents: Deidre Knight (president, agent); Pamela Harty (agent).
Represents: Nonfiction books, novels. **Considers these fiction areas:** Literary; mainstream/contemporary (commercial); romance (contemporary, paranormal, romantic suspense, historical, inspirational); women's.
    O— "We are looking for a wide variety of fiction and nonfiction. In the nonfiction area, we're particularly eager to find personal finance, business investment, pop culture, self-help/motivational and popular reference books. In fiction, we're always looking for romance; women's fiction; commercial fiction."
How to Contact: Query with SASE. Accepts e-mail queries; no attachments. No phone queries please. Considers simultaneous queries. Responds in 3 weeks to queries; 3 months to mss.
Recent Sales: Sold approximately 65 titles in the last year. *Dark Highlander*, by Karen Marie Moning (Bantam Dell); *The Healing Quilt*, by Lauraine Snelling (WaterBrook Press).
Terms: Agent receives 15% commission on domestic sales; 20-25% commission on foreign sales. Offers written contract, binding for 1 year; 30-day notice must be given to terminate contract. Charges clients for photocopying, postage, overnight courier expenses. "These are deducted from the sale of the work, not billed upfront."
Tips: "At the Knight Agency, a client usually ends up becoming a friend."

■ **ELAINE KOSTER LITERARY AGENCY, LLC**, 55 Central Park W., Suite 6, New York NY 10023. (212)362-9488. Fax: (212)712-0164. **Contact:** Elaine Koster. Member of AAR, MWA. Represents 50 clients. 10% of clients are new/unpublished writers. Currently handles: 30% nonfiction books; 70% novels.
    ● Prior to opening her agency, Ms. Koster was president and publisher of Dutton NAL.
Represents: Nonfiction books, novels. **Considers these fiction areas:** Contemporary issues; detective/police/crime; ethnic; family saga; feminist; historical; literary; mainstream/contemporary; mystery/suspense (amateur sleuth, cozy, culinary, malice domestic); regional; thriller; Chicklit.
    O— This agency specializes in quality fiction and nonfiction. Does not want to receive juvenile, screenplays, or science fiction.
How to Contact: Query with SASE, outline, 3 sample chapter(s). Prefers to read materials exclusively. No e-mail or fax queries. Responds in 3 weeks to queries; 1 month to mss. Returns materials only with SASE. Obtains most new clients through recommendations from others.
Recent Sales: Sold over 30 titles in the last year. *Tastes Like Chicken*, by Lolita Files (Simon & Schuster); *The Kite Runner*, by Khaled Hosseini (Riverhead); *Farewell Angelina*, by Virginia Swift (HarperCollins).
Terms: Agent receives 15% commission on domestic sales. Bills back specific expenses incurred doing business for a client.
Tips: "We prefer exclusive submissions. Don't e-mail or fax submissions. Please include biographical information and publishing history."

■ **KRAAS LITERARY AGENCY**, 256 Rancho Alegre Rd., Santa Fe NM 87508. (505)438-7715. Fax: (505)438-7783. Address Other: Ashley Kraas, Associate, 507 NW 22nd Ave., Suite 104, Portland OR 97210. (503)721-7442.

Estab. 1990. Represents 40 clients. 75% of clients are new/unpublished writers. Currently handles: 5% nonfiction books; 95% novels.

Represents: Nonfiction books, novels, young adult.

O— This agency specializes in adult fiction. Actively seeking "books that are well written with commercial potential." Does not want to receive short stories, plays or poetry.

How to Contact: Submit cover letter, first 50 pages of a completed ms, SASE; must include return postage and/or SASE. No e-mail or fax queries. Considers simultaneous queries. Returns materials only with SASE.

Recent Sales: *No Place Like the Chevy*, by Janet Lee Carey (Antheneum); *Night Terror*, by Chandler McGrew (Bantam); *Patriots in Petticoats*, by Shirley Raye Redmond (Random).

Terms: Agent receives 15% commission on domestic sales. Offers written contract. Charges clients for photocopying and postage.

Writers' Conferences: Southwest Writers Conference (Albuquerque NM); Durango Writers Conference (Durango CO); Wrangling with Writing (Tucson AZ); Surrey Writers Conference (Surrey BC); Schuwap Writers Conference (Schuwap BC); Willamette Writers Group (Portland OR).

PETER LAMPACK AGENCY, INC., 551 Fifth Ave., Suite 1613, New York NY 10176-0187. (212)687-9106. Fax: (212)687-9109. E-mail: renbopla@aol.com. **Contact:** Loren G. Soeiro. Estab. 1977. Represents 50 clients. 10% of clients are new/unpublished writers. Currently handles: 20% nonfiction books; 80% novels.

Member Agents: Peter Lampack (psychological suspense, action/adventure, literary fiction, nonfiction, contemporary relationships); Sandra Blanton (foreign rights); Loren G. Soeiro (literary and commercial fiction, mystery, suspense, nonfiction, narrative nonfiction).

Represents: Nonfiction books, novels. **Considers these fiction areas:** Action/adventure; detective/police/crime; family saga; historical; literary; mainstream/contemporary; mystery/suspense; thriller; Contemporary relationships.

O— This agency specializes in commercial fiction, nonfiction by recognized experts. Actively seeking literary and commercial fiction, thrillers, mysteries, suspense, psychological thrillers. Does not want to receive horror, romance, science fiction, western, academic material.

How to Contact: Query with SASE. No unsolicited mss. Accepts e-mail queries. No fax queries. Considers simultaneous queries. Responds in 3 weeks to queries; 2 months to mss. Obtains most new clients through referrals made by clients.

Recent Sales: *The Grave Maurice*, by Martha Grimes (Viking); *The Widow's Defense*, by Stephen Horn (HarperCollins); *The Sea Hunters 2*, by Clive Cussler (Putnam).

Terms: Agent receives 15% commission on domestic sales; 20% commission on foreign sales.

Writers' Conferences: BEA (Chicago, June).

Tips: "Submit only your best work for consideration. Have a very specific agenda of goals you wish your prospective agent to accomplish for you. Provide the agent with a comprehensive statement of your credentials: educational and professional."

MICHAEL LARSEN/ELIZABETH POMADA, LITERARY AGENTS, 1029 Jones St., San Francisco CA 94109-5023. (415)673-0939. E-mail: larsenpoma@aol.com. Website: www.larsen-pomada.com. **Contact:** Mike Larsen or Elizabeth Pomada. Estab. 1972. Member of AAR, Authors Guild, ASJA, PEN, WNBA, California Writers Club. Represents 100 clients. 40-45% of clients are new/unpublished writers. Currently handles: 70% nonfiction books; 30% novels.

● Prior to opening their agency, Mr. Larsen and Ms. Pomada were promotion executives for major publishing houses. Mr. Larsen worked for Morrow, Bantam and Pyramid (now part of Berkley), Ms. Pomada worked at Holt, David McKay, and The Dial Press.

Member Agents: Michael Larsen (nonfiction); Elizabeth Pomada (narrative nonfiction, books of interest to women).

Represents: Nonfiction books (adult), novels. **Considers these fiction areas:** Action/adventure; contemporary issues; detective/police/crime; ethnic; experimental; family saga; fantasy; feminist; gay/lesbian; glitz; historical; humor/satire; literary; mainstream/contemporary; mystery/suspense; religious/inspirational; romance (contemporary, gothic, historical).

O— "We have very diverse tastes. We look for fresh voices and new ideas. We handle literary, commercial and genre fiction, and the full range of nonfiction books." Actively seeking commercial and literary fiction. Does not want to receive children's books, plays, short stories, screenplays, pornography, poetry or stories of abuse.

How to Contact: Query with SASE, first 10 pages of completed novel and two page synopsis, SASE. (See brochure and website.). No e-mail or fax queries. Responds in 2 months to queries.

Recent Sales: Sold 15 titles in the last year. *Night Whispers*, by Pam Chun (Sourcebooks); *Snoopy's Guide to the Writing Life*, introduction by Barnaby Conrad and foreword by Monte Schulz (Writer's Digest); *Fox on the Rhine*, by Michael Dobson and Doug Niles (Tor).

Terms: Agent receives 15% commission on domestic sales; 20% (30% for Asia) commission on foreign sales. May charge for printing, postage for multiple submissions, foreign mail, foreign phone calls, galleys, books, and legal fees.

Writers' Conferences: Book Expo America; Santa Barbara Writers Conference (Santa Barbara); Maui Writers Conference (Maui); ASJA.

Tips: "If you can write books that meet the needs of the marketplace, and you can promote your books, now is the best time ever to be a writer. We must find new writers to make a living so we are very eager to hear from new writers whose work will interest large houses and nonfiction writers who can promote their books. Please send a SASE for a free 16-page brochure and a list of recent sales."

☑ LESCHER & LESCHER, LTD., 47 E. 19th St., New York NY 10003. (212)529-1790. Fax: (212)529-2716. **Contact:** Robert Lescher, Susan Lescher, Michael Choate. Estab. 1966. Member of AAR. Represents 150 clients. Currently handles: 80% nonfiction books; 20% novels.

Represents: Nonfiction books, novels. **Considers these fiction areas:** Literary; mystery/suspense; Commercial fiction.

  ⚊ Does not want to receive screenplays or science fiction.

How to Contact: Query with SASE. Obtains most new clients through recommendations from others.

Recent Sales: Sold 35 titles in the last year. This agency prefers not to share information on specific sales. Other clients include Neil Sheehan, Madeleine L'Engle, Calvin Trillin, Judith Viorst, Thomas Perry, Anne Fadiman, Frances FitzGerald, Paula Fox and Robert M. Parker, Jr.

Terms: Agent receives 15% commission on domestic sales; 20-25% commission on foreign sales.

☑ LEVINE GREENBERG LITERARY AGENCY, INC., 307 7th Ave., Suite 1906, New York NY 10001. (212)337-0934. Fax: (212)337-0948. Website: www.jameslevine.com. Estab. 1989. Member of AAR. Represents 250 clients. 33% of clients are new/unpublished writers. Currently handles: 70% nonfiction books; 30% novels.

  • Prior to opening his agency, Mr. Levine served as vice president of the Bank Street College of Education.

Member Agents: James Levine; Arielle Eckstut; Daniel Greenberg; Stephanie Kip Roston.

Represents: Nonfiction books, novels. **Considers these fiction areas:** Contemporary issues; literary; mainstream/ contemporary; mystery/suspense; thriller (psychological); women's.

  ⚊ This agency specializes in business, psychology, parenting, health/medicine, narrative nonfiction, psychology, spirituality, religion, women's issues and commercial fiction.

How to Contact: See www.jameslevine.com for full submission procedure. Prefers e-mail queries. Obtains most new clients through recommendations from others.

Recent Sales: *Chicken: A Self-Portrait*, by David Sterry (Regan Books/HarperCollins); *Raising Fences: A Black Man's Love Story*, by Michael Datcher (Riverhead/Penguin Putnam); *21 Dog Years: Doing Time*, by Mike Daisey (Free Press/Simon & Schuster).

Terms: Agent receives 15% commission on domestic sales; 20% commission on foreign sales. Offers written contract, binding for variable length of time. Charges clients for out-of-pocket expenses—telephone, fax, postage and photocopying—directly connected to the project.

Writers' Conferences: ASJA Annual Conference (New York City, May).

Tips: "We work closely with clients on editorial development and promotion. We work to place our clients as magazine columnists and have created columnists for *McCall's* (renamed *Rosie's*) and *Child*. We work with clients to develop their projects across various media—video, software, and audio."

☑ PAUL S. LEVINE LITERARY AGENCY, 1054 Superba Ave., Venice CA 90291-3940. (310)450-6711. Fax: (310)450-0181. E-mail: pslevine@ix.netcom.com. Website: www.netcom.com/~pslevine/lawliterary.html. **Contact:** Paul S. Levine. Estab. 1996. Member of the State Bar of California. Represents over 100 clients. 75% of clients are new/unpublished writers. Currently handles: 30% nonfiction books; 30% novels; 10% movie scripts; 30% TV scripts.

Represents: Nonfiction books, novels, movie scripts, feature film, TV scripts, TV movie of the week, episodic drama, sitcom, animation, documentary, miniseries, syndicated material (1). **Considers these fiction areas:** Action/ adventure; comic books/cartoon; confession; contemporary issues; detective/police/crime; erotica; ethnic; experimental; family saga; feminist; gay/lesbian; glitz; historical; humor/satire; literary; mainstream/contemporary; mystery/suspense; regional; religious/inspirational; romance; sports; thriller; westerns/frontier.

  ⚊ Actively seeking commercial fiction and nonfiction. Also handles children's and young adult fiction and nonfiction. Does not want to receive science fiction, fantasy or horror.

How to Contact: Query with SASE. Accepts e-mail and fax queries. Considers simultaneous queries. Responds in 1 day to queries; 2 months to mss. Returns materials only with SASE. Obtains most new clients through conferences, referrals, listings on various websites and through listings in directories.

Recent Sales: Sold 25 titles in the last year. This agency prefers not to share information on specific sales.

Terms: Agent receives 15% commission on domestic sales; 20% commission on foreign sales. Offers written contract. Charges clients for messengers, long distance, postage. "Only when incurred. No advance payment necessary."

Writers' Conferences: California Lawyers for the Arts (Los Angeles CA); National Writers Club (Los Angeles CA); "Selling to Hollywood" Writer's Connection (Glendale CA); "Spotlight on Craft" Willamette Writers Conference (Portland OR); Women in Animation (Los Angeles CA); and many others.

◑ **RAY LINCOLN LITERARY AGENCY**, Elkins Park House, Suite 107-B, 7900 Old York Rd., Elkins Park PA 19027. (215)782-8882. Fax: (215)782-8882. **Contact:** Mrs. Ray Lincoln. Estab. 1974. Represents 30 clients. 35% of clients are new/unpublished writers. Currently handles: 30% nonfiction books; 50% novels; 20% juvenile books.

Member Agents: Jerome A. Lincoln; Mrs. Ray Lincoln.

Represents: Nonfiction books, novels, juvenile books, scholarly books. **Considers these fiction areas:** Action/ adventure; contemporary issues; detective/police/crime; ethnic; family saga; fantasy; feminist; gay/lesbian; historical; humor/satire; juvenile; literary; mainstream/contemporary; mystery/suspense; psychic/supernatural; regional; romance (contemporary, gothic, historical); sports; thriller; young adult.

O→ This agency specializes in biography, nature, the sciences, fiction in both adult and chilren's categories.

How to Contact: Query with SASE. Prefers to read materials exclusively. If requested, send an outline, 2 sample chapters, SASE. No e-mail or fax queries. Responds in 2 weeks to queries. Obtains most new clients through recommendations from others.

Recent Sales: *Alexander Hamilton: A Life*, by Willard Sterne Randall (HarperCollins); *The Laser*, by Jerry Spinelli (HarperCollins); *Planet Walk*, by John Francis (Chelsea Green).

Terms: Agent receives 15% commission on domestic sales; 20% commission on foreign sales. Offers written contract. Charges clients for overseas telephone calls; upfront postage fee for unpublished authors only. "I request authors to do manuscript photocopying themselves."

Tips: "I always look for polished writing style, fresh points of view and professional attitudes. I send for balance of manuscript if it is a likely project."

◫ ◑ **LINDSEY'S LITERARY SERVICES**, 7502 Greenville Ave., Suite 500, Dallas TX 75231. (214)890-9262. Fax: (214)890-9265. E-mail: bonedges001@aol.com. **Contact:** Bonnie James; Emily Armenta. Estab. 2002. Represents 10 clients. 60% of clients are new/unpublished writers. Currently handles: 70% nonfiction books; 30% novels.

● Prior to becoming an agent, Bonnie James was a drama instructor and magazine editor, while Emily Armenta was an independent film editor and magazine editor.

Member Agents: Bonnie James (nonfiction: New Age/metaphysics, self-help, psychology, women's issues; fiction: mystery/suspense, thriller, horror, literary, mainstream, romance); Emily Armenta (nonfiction: New Age/metaphysics, self-help, psychology, women's issues; fiction: mystery/suspense, thriller, horror, literary, mainstream, romance).

Represents: Nonfiction books, novels. **Considers these fiction areas:** Action/adventure; detective/police/crime; ethnic; historical; horror; literary; mainstream/contemporary; multicultural; mystery/suspense; religious/inspirational; romance; science fiction; thriller.

O→ "We are a new agency with a clear vision and will aggressively represent our clients." Actively seeking nonfiction self-help, metaphysical, psychology, and women's issues; for fiction seeking exceptionally written books. Does not want poetry, children's books, text books.

How to Contact: Query with SASE, submit proposal package, synopsis, sample chapter(s), author bio. Considers simultaneous queries. Responds in 6 weeks to queries; 3 months to mss. Returns materials only with SASE. Obtains most new clients through recommendations from others, solicitations.

Terms: Agent receives 15% commission on domestic sales; 20% commission on foreign sales. Offers written contract, binding for 1 year; cancelable by either party with 30 days written notice notice must be given to terminate contract.

Tips: "Write a clear, concise query describing your project. Pay attention to the craft of writing. Provide complete package, including education, profession, writing credits and what you want to accomplish."

◑ **WENDY LIPKIND AGENCY**, 120 E. 81st St., New York NY 10028. (212)628-9653. Fax: (212)585-1306. **Contact:** Wendy Lipkind. Estab. 1977. Member of AAR. Represents 60 clients. Currently handles: 80% nonfiction books; 20% novels.

Represents: Nonfiction books, novels. **Considers these fiction areas:** Mainstream/contemporary; mystery/suspense (psychological suspense).

O→ This agency specializes in adult nonfiction. Does not want to receive mass market originals.

How to Contact: Prefers to read materials exclusively. Query with SASE only. Responds in 1 month to queries. Returns materials only with SASE. Obtains most new clients through recommendations from others.

Recent Sales: Sold 10 titles in the last year. *One Small Step*, by Robert Mauner (Workman); *In the Land of Lyme*, by Pamela Weintraub (Scribner).

Terms: Agent receives 15% commission on domestic sales; 20% commission on foreign sales. Sometimes offers written contract. Charges clients for foreign postage, messenger service, photocopying, transatlantic calls, faxes.

Tips: "Send intelligent query letter first. Let me know if you sent to other agents."

◑ **LITERARY AND CREATIVE ARTISTS, INC.**, 3543 Albemarle St. NW, Washington DC 20008-4213. (202)362-4688. Fax: (202)362-362-8875. E-mail: query cadc.com. Website: www.lcadc.com. **Contact:** Muriel Nellis, Jane Roberts. Estab. 1981. Member of AAR, Authors

Guild, associate member of American Bar Association. Represents 75 clients. Currently handles: 70% nonfiction books; 15% novels; 15% audio/video/film/tv.
Member Agents: Muriel Nellis; Jane Roberts; Stephen Ruwe.
Represents: Nonfiction books, novels, audio, film/TV rights.
How to Contact: Query with SASE, outline, author bio. No unsolicited mss. Responds in 3 weeks to queries.
Recent Sales: *Seasons of Grace*, by John O'Neil and Alan Jones (John Wiley and Sons); *The Origin of Minds*, by Peggy La Cerra and Roger Bingham (Harmony Books).
Terms: Agent receives 15% commission on domestic sales; 20% commission on foreign sales; 25% commission on dramatic rights sales. Charges clients for long-distance phone and fax, photocopying, shipping.
Tips: "While we prefer published writers, it is not required if the proposed work has great merit."

THE LITERARY GROUP, 270 Lafayette St., 1505, New York NY 10012. (212)274-1616. Fax: (212)274-9876. E-mail: fweimann@theliterarygroup.com. Website: www.theliterarygroup.com. **Contact:** Frank Weimann. Estab. 1985. Represents 200 clients. 65% of clients are new/unpublished writers. Currently handles: 50% nonfiction books; 50% fiction.
Member Agents: Frank Weimann (fiction, nonfiction); Ian Kleinert (nonfiction); Priya Ratneshwar (fiction).
Represents: Nonfiction books, and fiction books. **Considers these fiction areas:** Action/adventure; contemporary issues; detective/police/crime; ethnic; family saga; fantasy; feminist; horror; humor/satire; mystery/suspense; psychic/supernatural; romance (contemporary, gothic, historical, regency); sports; thriller; westerns/frontier.
    O— This agency specializes in nonfiction (true crime, military, history, biography, sports, how-to).
How to Contact: Query with SASE, outline, 3 sample chapter(s). Prefers to read materials exclusively. Responds in 1 week to queries; 1 month to mss. Returns materials only with SASE. Obtains most new clients through referrals, writers' conferences, query letters.
Recent Sales: Sold 100 titles in the last year. *Keep It Simple*, by Terry Bradshaw; *Cry Me a River*, by Ernest Hill; *Double Deal*, by Michael Corbitt and Sam Giancana. Other clients include Tommy Chong, Dr. Peter Salgo, Homer Hickman.
Terms: Agent receives 15% commission on domestic sales; 15% commission on foreign sales. Offers written contract; 30-day notice must be given to terminate contract.
Writers' Conferences: Detroit Women's Writers (MI); Kent State University (OH); San Diego Writers Conference (CA); Maui Writers Conference (HI); Austin Writers' Conference (TX).

LITWEST GROUP, LLC, Website: www.litwest.com. Represents 160 clients. 45% of clients are new/unpublished writers. Currently handles: 75% nonfiction books; 25% novels; TV, movie, Internet projects revolving around the book.
    ● Prior to opening the agency, Ms. Ellis was in academia, Mr. Preskill was in law and Ms. Mead and Ms. Boyle were in publishing.
Member Agents: Linda Mead (business, personal improvement, memoir, historical fiction/nonfiction steeped in research, ethnic/multicultural fiction/nonfiction, cozy mysteries); Nancy Ellis (mystery/suspense, religion/spiritual, parenting, psychology, science, women's literary/commercial, coming of age); Rob Preskill (men's, thrillers and mysteries where the writing is subtle, sports, travel, leisure, lifestyle, fitness, male health, business, design/architecture/art, politics, subculture, graphic novels, narrative nonfiction, literary); Katie Boyle (literary fiction, surreal, avant-garde, narrative nonfiction/memoir, contemporary culture/politics, art/music bios, graphic novels/subculture, psychology, women's issues, pop-culture, religion/spirituality).
Represents: Nonfiction books, novels, scholarly books. **Considers these fiction areas:** Contemporary issues; detective/police/crime; ethnic; family saga; feminist; historical; humor/satire; literary; mainstream/contemporary; multicultural; mystery/suspense; religious/inspirational; sports; thriller.
    O— "We are multi-faceted." Actively seeking all subjects. Does not want to receive science fiction, horror, western, cookbooks.
How to Contact: Query with SASE, outline, 3 sample chapter(s). Considers simultaneous queries. Responds in 1 month to queries. Response time varies. Returns materials only with SASE. Obtains most new clients through recommendations from others, solicitations, conferences.
Recent Sales: *The Elegant Gathering of White Snows*, by Kris Radish (Bantam). Other clients include Woodleigh Marx Hubbard, Jennifer Openshaw, Jed Diamond, Dr. Jay Gordon, Dr. Arthur White, Eric Harr, Brad Herzog, Martin Yan, Lyn Webster-Wilde, Larraine Segil.
Terms: Agent receives 15% commission on domestic sales; 20% commission on foreign sales. Offers written contract. Charges for postage and photocopying.
Writers' Conferences: Maui Writers Conference (Maui HI, Labor Day); San Diego State University Writers' Conference (San Diego CA, January); William Saroyan Writers Conference (Fresno CA, March); Santa Barbara (June) and many others.
Tips: "Clarity and precision about your work also helps the agent process."

LIVINGSTON COOKE, 278 Bloor St. E., Suite 305, Toronto ON M4W 3M4, Canada. (416)406-3390. Fax: (416)406-3389. E-mail: livcooke@idirect.ca. **Contact:** Elizabeth Griffen. Estab. 1992. Represents 200 clients. 30% of clients are new/unpublished writers. Currently handles: 50% nonfiction books; 50% novels.

- Prior to becoming an agent, Mr. Cooke was the publisher of Seal Bantam Books Canada.

Member Agents: David Johnston (film rights, literary fiction/nonfiction); Dean Cooke (literary fiction, nonfiction).
Represents: Nonfiction books, novels, juvenile books. **Considers these fiction areas:** Juvenile; literary.

O← Livingston Cooke represents some of the best Canadian writers in the world. "Through our contacts and sub-agents, we are building an international reputation for quality. Curtis Brown Canada is jointly owned by Dean Cooke and Curtis Brown New York. It represents Curtis Brown New York authors in Canada." Does not want to receive how-to, self-help, spirituality, genre fiction (science fiction, fantasy, mystery, thriller, horror).

How to Contact: Query with SASE. Accepts e-mail and fax queries. Considers simultaneous queries. Responds in 1 month to queries; 6 weeks to mss. Returns materials only with SASE. Obtains most new clients through recommendations from others.
Recent Sales: Sold 40 titles and sold 4 scripts in the last year. *Clara Callan*, by Richard B. Wright (Harperflamingo Canada); *Stanley Park*, by Timothy Taylor (Knopf Canada); *Your Mouth is Lovely*, by Nancy Richler (Harper Collins); *Spirit Cabinet*, by Paul Quarrinton (Grove/Atlantic); *Lazarus and the Hurricane*, by S. Charton/T. Swinton (St. Martin's Press); *Latitudes of Melt*, by Joan Clark (Knopf Canada); *Possesing Genius: The Bizarre Odyssey of Eintein's Brain*, by Caroline Abraham (Penguin Canada, St. Martin's Press); *Englishman's Boy*, by Guy Vanderhaeghe (Minds Eye); *Lazarus and the Hurricane*, by T. Swinton and S. Chaiton (Universal/Beacon). Other clients include Margaret Gibson, Richard Scrimger, Tony Hillerman, Robertson Davies, Brian Moore.
Terms: Agent receives 15% commission on domestic sales; 20% commission on foreign sales. Offers written contract. Charges clients for postage, photocopying, courier.

[N] [M] LOS BRAVOS LITERARY MANAGEMENT, 1811 N. Whitley Ave., Suite 1003, Los Angeles CA 90028. (323)461-5589. Fax: (323)417-4879. E-mail: marc@losbravosmanagement.com. **Contact:** Marc Gerald. Estab. 2002. Represents 25 clients. 50% of clients are new/unpublished writers. Currently handles: 70% nonfiction books; 20% novels; 10% movie scripts.

- Prior to becoming an agent, Mr. Gerald found and ran *The Syndicate*, an urban oriented publishing and entertainment company, co-owned with Wesley Snipes; found and edited W.W. Norton's Old School Books imprint; wrote and produced America's Most Wanted and numerous specials for Fox Television.

Represents: Nonfiction books, novels, feature film. **Considers these fiction areas:** Action/adventure; confession; detective/police/crime; erotica; ethnic; horror; literary; mystery/suspense; thriller; young adult; glitz.

O← "We represent a free-ranging roster of largely pop culture-leaning clients across platform. While we represent story-tellers of all stripes, the majority of our clients are artists and athletes looking to tell their story in book form, and pop culture brands seeking to impact in the publishing space."

How to Contact: Submit outline, 2 sample chapter(s). Considers simultaneous queries. Responds in 1 month to queries; 2 months to mss. Returns materials only with SASE. Obtains most new clients through recommendations from others.
Recent Sales: Sold 20 titles and sold 1 scripts in the last year. Other clients include Lil' Kim, *Gearhead Magazine*, SuicideGirls.com.
Terms: Agent receives 15% commission on domestic sales; 20% commission on foreign sales. Offers written contract. Charges clients for postage and photocopying.

[M] NANCY LOVE LITERARY AGENCY, 250 E. 65th St., New York NY 10021-6614. (212)980-3499. Fax: (212)308-6405. **Contact:** Nancy Love. Estab. 1984. Member of AAR. Represents 60-80 clients. Currently handles: 90% nonfiction books; 10% novels.
Member Agents: Nancy Love.
Represents: Nonfiction books, novels (mysteries and thrillers only). **Considers these fiction areas:** Mystery/suspense; thriller.

O← This agency specializes in adult nonfiction and mysteries. Actively seeking health and medicine (including alternative medicine), parenting, spiritual and inspirational. Does not want to receive novels other than mysteries and thrillers.

How to Contact: Query first. Fiction is only read on an exclusive basis. No e-mail or fax queries. Considers simultaneous queries. Responds in 3 weeks to queries. Returns materials only with SASE. Obtains most new clients through recommendations from others, solicitations.
Recent Sales: Sold 20 titles in the last year.
Terms: Agent receives 15% commission on domestic sales; 20% commission on foreign sales. Offers written contract. Charges clients for photocopying "if it runs over $20."
Tips: "Nonfiction author and/or collaborator must be an authority in subject area and have a platform. Send a SASE if you want a response."

[M] DONALD MAASS LITERARY AGENCY, 160 W. 95th St., Suite 1B, New York NY 10025. (212)866-8200. **Contact:** Donald Maass, Jennifer Jackson or Michelle Brummer. Estab. 1980. Member of AAR, SFWA, MWA, RWA. Represents over 100 clients. 5% of clients are new/unpublished writers. Currently handles: 100% novels.

● Prior to opening his agency, Mr. Maass served as an editor at Dell Publishing (NY) and as a reader at Gollancz (London). He is the current president of AAR.

Member Agents: Donald Maass (mainstream, literary, mystery/suspense, science fiction); Jennifer Jackson (commercial fiction, especially romance, science fiction, fantasy, mystery/suspense); Michelle Brummer (fiction: literary, contemporary, feminist, science fiction, fantasy, romance).

Represents: Novels. **Considers these fiction areas:** Detective/police/crime; fantasy; historical; horror; literary; mainstream/contemporary; mystery/suspense; psychic/supernatural; romance (historical, paranormal, time travel); science fiction; thriller; women's.

➝ This agency specializes in commercial fiction, especially science fiction, fantasy, mystery, romance, suspense. Actively seeking "to expand the literary portion of our list and expand in romance and women's fiction." Does not want to receive nonfiction, children's or poetry.

How to Contact: Query with SASE. Returns material only with SASE. Considers simultaneous queries. Responds in 2 weeks to queries; 3 months to mss.

Recent Sales: Sold over 100 titles in the last year. *No Graves as Yet*, by Anne Perry (Ballantine); *Griffone*, by Nalo Hopkinson (Warner Aspect).

Terms: Agent receives 15% commission on domestic sales; 20% commission on foreign sales.

Writers' Conferences: *Donald Maass*: World Science Fiction Convention; Frankfurt Book Fair; Pacific Northwest Writers Conference; Bouchercon and others; *Jennifer Jackson*: World Science Fiction and Fantasy Convention; RWA National and others; *Michelle Brummer*: ReaderCon; Luna Con; Frankfurt.

Tips: "We are fiction specialists, also noted for our innovative approach to career planning. Few new clients are accepted, but interested authors should query with SASE. Subagents in all principle foreign countries and Hollywood. No nonfiction or juvenile works considered."

⬤ **GINA MACCOBY AGENCY**, P.O. Box 60, Chappaqua NY 10514. (914)238-5630. **Contact:** Gina Maccoby. Estab. 1986. Represents 35 clients. Currently handles: 33% nonfiction books; 33% novels; 33% juvenile books; Represents illustrators of children's books.

Represents: Nonfiction books, novels, juvenile books. **Considers these fiction areas:** Juvenile; literary; mainstream/contemporary; mystery/suspense; thriller; young adult.

How to Contact: Query with SASE. Considers simultaneous queries. Responds in 2 months to queries. Returns materials only with SASE. Obtains most new clients through recommendations from own clients.

Recent Sales: Sold 26 titles in the last year. *The Lost Colony*, by Jean Fritz; *Eaglestrike*, by Anthony Horowitz.

Terms: Agent receives 15% commission on domestic sales; 25% commission on foreign sales. Charges clients for photocopying. May recover certain costs such as the cost of shipping books by air to Europe or Japan or legal fees.

⬤ **CAROL MANN AGENCY**, 55 Fifth Ave., New York NY 10003. (212)206-5635. Fax: (212)675-4809. E-mail: kim@carolmannagency.com. **Contact:** Kim Goldstein. Estab. 1977. Member of AAR. Represents 200 clients. 25% of clients are new/unpublished writers. Currently handles: 70% nonfiction books; 30% novels.

Member Agents: Jim Fitzgerald (fiction, popular culture, biography); Carol Mann (literary fiction, nonfiction); Leylha Ahuile (Spanish and Latin American fiction and nonfiction); Kim Goldstein (fiction and nonfiction).

Represents: Nonfiction books, novels. **Considers these fiction areas:** Literary.

➝ This agency specializes in current affairs; self-help; popular culture; psychology; parenting; history. Does not want to receive "genre fiction (romance, mystery, etc.)."

How to Contact: Query with outline/proposal and SASE. Responds in 3 weeks to queries.

Recent Sales: *America 24/7*, by Rick Smolen and David Cohen (DK); *White Guilt*, by Shelby Steele (HarperCollins). Other clients include novelist Marita Golden; journalists Tim Egan, Elizabeth Mehren, Pulitzer Prize winner Fox Butterfield and National Book Critic Award winner James Tobin; essayist Shelby Steele; sociologist Dr. William Julius Wilson; economist Thomas Sowell; and Tufts University's Elliot Pearson School of Education.

Terms: Agent receives 15% commission on domestic sales; 20% commission on foreign sales. Offers written contract.

MANUS & ASSOCIATES LITERARY AGENCY, INC., 375 Forest Ave., Palo Alto CA 94301. (650)470-5151. Fax: (650)470-5159. E-mail: manuslit@manuslit.com. Website: www.manuslit.com. **Contact:** Jillian Manus. Also: 445 Park Ave., New York NY 10022. (212)644-8020. Fax (212)644-3374. **Contact**: Janet Manus. Estab. 1985. Member of AAR. Represents 75 clients. 30% of clients are new/unpublished writers. Currently handles: 55% nonfiction books; 40% novels; 5% juvenile books.

● Prior to becoming agents, Jillian Manus was associate publisher of two national magazines and director of development at Warner Bros. and Universal Studios; Janet Manus has been a literary agent for 20 years.

Member Agents: Jandy Nelson (self-help, health, memoirs, narrative nonfiction, women's fiction, literary fiction, multicultural fiction, thrillers); Stephanie Lee (self-help, narrative nonfiction, commercial literary fiction, quirky/edgy fiction, pop culture, pop science); Christine Cummings (history, biography, science, literary fiction, mystery/suspense, pop philosophy).

Represents: Nonfiction books, novels. **Considers these fiction areas:** Literary; mainstream/contemporary; multicultural; mystery/suspense; thriller; women's; Quirky/edgy fiction.

➝ This agency specializes in commercial literary fiction, narrative nonfiction, thrillers, health, pop psychology, women's empowerment. "Our agency is unique in the way that we not only sell the material, but we edit, develop concepts and participate in the marketing effort. We specialize in large, conceptual fiction and nonfiction, and always value a project that can be sold in the TV/feature film market." Actively seeking high-concept thrillers, commercial literary fiction, women's fiction, celebrity biographies, memoirs, multicultural fiction, popular health, women's empowerment, mysteries. Does not want to receive horror, romance, science fiction/fantasy, westerns, young adult, children's, poetry, cookbooks, magazine articles. Usually obtains new clients through recommendations from editors, clients and others; conferences; and unsolicited materials.

How to Contact: Query with SASE. If requested, submit outline, 2-3 sample chapter(s). Accepts e-mail and fax queries. Considers simultaneous queries. Responds in 2 months to queries; 6 weeks to mss. Returns materials only with SASE. Obtains most new clients through recommendations from others, solicitations, conferences.

Terms: Agent receives 15% commission on domestic sales; 20-25% commission on foreign sales. Offers written contract, binding for 2 years; 60 days notice must be given to terminate contract. Charges for photocopying and postage.

Writers' Conferences: Maui Writers Conference (Maui HI, Labor Day); San Diego Writer's Conference (San Diego CA, January); Willamette Writers Conference (Willamette OR, July).

Tips: "Research agents using a variety of sources, including *LMP*, guides, *Publishers Weekly*, conferences and even acknowledgements in books similar in tone to yours."

MARCH TENTH, INC., 4 Myrtle St., Haworth NJ 07641-1740. (201)387-6551. Fax: (201)387-6552. E-mail: hchoron@aol.com. **Contact:** Harry Choron, vice president. Estab. 1982. Represents 40 clients. 30% of clients are new/unpublished writers. Currently handles: 75% nonfiction books; 25% novels.

Represents: Nonfiction books, novels. **Considers these fiction areas:** Confession; ethnic; family saga; historical; humor/satire; literary; mainstream/contemporary.

O— "Writers must have professional expertise in their field. Pefer to work with published/established writers."

How to Contact: Query with SASE. Considers simultaneous queries. Responds in 1 month to queries. Returns materials only with SASE.

Recent Sales: Sold 12 titles in the last year.

Terms: Agent receives 15% commission on domestic sales; 20% commission on foreign sales; 20% commission on dramatic rights sales. Charges clients for postage, photocopying, overseas phone expenses. "Does not require expense money upfront." Writers reimbursed for office fees after the sale of ms.

THE EVAN MARSHALL AGENCY, 6 Tristam Place, Pine Brook NJ 07058-9445. (973)882-1122. Fax: (973)882-3099. E-mail: evanmarshall@thenovelist.com. Website: www.thenovelist.com. **Contact:** Evan Marshall. Estab. 1987. Member of AAR, MWA. Currently handles: 100% novels.

● Prior to opening his agency, Mr. Marshall served as an editor with New American Library, Everest House, and Dodd, Mead & Co., and then worked as a literary agent at The Sterling Lord Agency.

Represents: Novels. **Considers these fiction areas:** Action/adventure; erotica; ethnic; historical; horror; humor/satire; literary; mainstream/contemporary; mystery/suspense; religious/inspirational; romance (contemporary, gothic, historical, Regency); science fiction; westerns/frontier.

How to Contact: Query first with SASE; do not enclose material. Responds in 1 week to queries; 2 months to mss. Obtains most new clients through recommendations from others.

Recent Sales: *In Silence*, by Erica Spindlev (Mira); *Dreaming of You*, by Dixie Kane (Kensington); *Hunter's Moon*, by Bobbi Smith (Dorchester).

Terms: Agent receives 15% commission on domestic sales; 20% commission on foreign sales. Offers written contract.

MARGRET McBRIDE LITERARY AGENCY, 7744 Fay Ave., Suite 201, La Jolla CA 92037. (858)454-1550. Fax: (858)454-2156. Estab. 1980. Member of AAR, Authors Guild.

● Prior to opening her agency, Ms. McBride worked at Random House, Ballantine Books and Warner Books.

Represents: Nonfiction books, novels, audio, video film rights. **Considers these fiction areas:** Action/adventure; detective/police/crime; ethnic; historical; humor/satire; literary; mainstream/contemporary; mystery/suspense; thriller; westerns/frontier.

O— This agency specializes in mainstream fiction and nonfiction. Does not want to receive screenplays. Does not represent romance, poetry or children's/young adult.

How to Contact: Query with synopsis or outline and SASE. Will not respond/read e-mail queries. Considers simultaneous queries. Responds in 2 months to queries. Returns materials only with SASE.

Recent Sales: Sold 22 titles in the last year. *Incriminating Evidence*, by Sheldon Siegel (Bantam); *Fierce Conversations*, by Susan Scott (Viking); *Dinner After Dark*, by Colin Cowie (Clarkson Potter).

Terms: Agent receives 15% commission on domestic sales; 25% commission on foreign sales. Charges for overnight delivery and photocopying.

HELEN McGRATH, 1406 Idaho Ct., Concord CA 94521. (925)672-6211. Fax: (925)672-6383. E-mail: hmcgrath_lit@yahoo.com. **Contact:** Helen McGrath. Estab. 1977. Currently handles: 50% nonfiction books; 50% novels.

Represents: Nonfiction books, novels. **Considers these fiction areas:** Contemporary issues; detective/police/crime; literary; mainstream/contemporary; mystery/suspense; psychic/supernatural; romance; science fiction; thriller.

How to Contact: Submit proposal with SASE. *No unsolicited mss.* Responds in 2 months to queries. Obtains most new clients through recommendations from others.

Terms: Agent receives 15% commission on domestic sales. Offers written contract. Charges clients for photocopying.

McHUGH LITERARY AGENCY, 1033 Lyon Rd., Moscow ID 83843-9167. (208)882-0107. Fax: (847)628-0146. E-mail: elisabetmch@turbonet.com. **Contact:** Elisabet McHugh. Estab. 1994. Represents 49 clients. 30% of clients are new/unpublished writers. Currently handles: 25% nonfiction books; 75% fiction.

Represents: Nonfiction books, novels. **Considers these fiction areas:** Historical; literary; mainstream/contemporary; mystery/suspense; romance; thriller; westerns/frontier.

☞ Does not handle children's books, poetry, science fiction, fantasy, horror.

How to Contact: Query by e-mail. Considers simultaneous queries. Returns materials only with SASE.

Recent Sales: *The Beginning of Children's Right in America* (McFarland & Co.); *Family Secrets* (Bantam); *Divided Loyalty* (Harlequin).

Terms: Agent receives 15% commission on domestic sales; 20% commission on foreign sales. Does not charge any upfront fees. Offers written contract. "Client must provide all copies of manuscripts needed for submissions."

Tips: "Be professional."

CLAUDIA MENZA LITERARY AGENCY, 1170 Broadway, Suite 807, New York NY 10001. (212)889-6850. **Contact:** Claudia Menza. Estab. 1983. Member of AAR. Represents 111 clients. 50% of clients are new/unpublished writers.

• Prior to becoming an agent, Ms. Menza was an editor/managing editor at a publishing company.

Represents: Nonfiction books, novels.

☞ This agency specializes in African-American fiction and nonfiction, and editorial assistance.

How to Contact: Submit outline, 1 sample chapter(s). Prefers to read materials exclusively. Responds in 2 weeks to queries; 2-4 months to mss. Returns materials only with SASE. Obtains most new clients through recommendations from others.

Recent Sales: This agency prefers not to share information on specific sales.

Terms: Agent receives 15% commission on domestic sales; 20% (if co-agent is used) commission on foreign sales; 20% commission on dramatic rights sales. Offers written contract.

DORIS S. MICHAELS LITERARY AGENCY, INC., 1841 Broadway, Suite #903, New York NY 10023. Website: www.dsmagency.com. **Contact:** Doris S. Michaels, president. Estab. 1994. Member of AAR, WNBA.

Member Agents: Faye Bender.

Represents: Novels. **Considers these fiction areas:** Literary (with commercial appeal and strong screen potential).

How to Contact: All unsolicited mss returned unopened. Query by e-mail; see submission guidelines on website. Returns materials only with SASE. Obtains most new clients through recommendations from others, conferences.

Recent Sales: Sold over 30 titles in the last year. *Cycles: How We'll Live, Work and Buy*, by Maddy Dychtwald (The Free Press); *In the River Sweet*, by Patricia Henley (Knopf); *Healing Conversations: What to Say When You Don't Know What to Say*, by Nance Guilmartin (Jossey-Bass); *The Mushroom Man*, by Sophie Powell (Peguin Putnam); *How to Become a Marketing Superstar*, by Jeff Fox (Hyperion).

Terms: Agent receives 15% commission on domestic sales; 20% commission on foreign sales. Offers written contract, binding for 1 year; 30-day notice must be given to terminate contract. 100% of business is derived from commissions on ms sales. Charges clients for office expenses, not to exceed $150 without written permission.

Writers' Conferences: BEA; Frankfurt Book Fair (Germany, October); London Book Fair; Maui Writers Conference.

MARTHA MILLARD LITERARY AGENCY, 145 W. 71st St. #8A, New York NY 10023. (973)593-9233. Fax: (973)593-9235. E-mail: marmillink@aol.com. **Contact:** Martha Millard. Estab. 1980. Member of AAR, SFWA. Represents 50 clients. Currently handles: 25% nonfiction books; 65% novels; 10% story collections.

• Prior to becoming an agent, Ms. Millard worked in editorial departments of several publishers and was vice president at another agency for four and a half years.

Represents: Nonfiction books, novels. **Considers these fiction areas:** Considers fiction depending on writer's credits and skills.

How to Contact: No unsolicited queries. No e-mail or fax queries. Returns materials only with SASE. Obtains most new clients through recommendations from others.

Recent Sales: *Backfire*, by Peter Burrows (Wiley); *Fallen Star*, by Nancy Herkness (Berkley Sensation); *The Rosetta Codex*, by Richard Paul Russ (Penguin).

Terms: Agent receives 15% commission on domestic sales; 20% commission on foreign sales. Offers written contract.

◙ **MULTIMEDIA PRODUCT DEVELOPMENT, INC.**, 410 S. Michigan Ave., Suite 724, Chicago IL 60605-1465. (312)922-3063. E-mail: mpd@mpdinc.net. **Contact:** Danielle Egan-Miller. Estab. 1971. Member of AAR, RWA, MWA, SCBWI. Represents 150 clients. 2% of clients are new/unpublished writers. Currently handles: 60% nonfiction books; 40% novels.
Member Agents: Nik Vargas (generalist).
Represents: Nonfiction books, novels. **Considers these fiction areas:** Contemporary issues; detective/police/crime; ethnic; family saga; glitz; historical; juvenile; literary; mainstream/contemporary; mystery/suspense; picture books; religious/inspirational; romance (contemporary, gothic, historical, regency, western); sports; thriller.

    O→ "We are generalists looking for professional writers with finely honed skill in writing. We are partial to authors with promotion savvy. We work closely with our authors through the entire publishing process, from proposal to after publication." Actively seeking highly commercial mainstream fiction and nonfiction. Does not want to receive poetry, short stories, plays, screenplays, articles.

How to Contact: Query by mail, SASE required. Accepts e-mail queries. No unsolicited mss accepted. Prefers to read material exclusively. Responds in 1 month to queries. Returns materials only with SASE. Obtains most new clients through "referrals, queries by professional, marketable authors."
Recent Sales: Sold 50 titles in the last year. *The Chili Queen*, by Sandra Dallas (St. Martin's Press); *In the Castle of the Flynns*, by Michael Raleigh (Sourcebooks); *Remembered Prisoners of a Forgotten War*, by Lewis H. Carlson(St. Martin's Press).
Terms: Agent receives 15% commission on domestic sales; 20% commission on foreign sales. Offers written contract, binding for 2 years. Charges clients for photocopying, overseas postage, faxes, phone calls.
Writers' Conferences: BEA (June); Frankfurt Book Fair (October); RWA (July); CBA (July); London International Book Fair (March); Boucheron (October).
Tips: "If interested in agency representation, be well informed."

◙ **JEAN V. NAGGAR LITERARY AGENCY**, 216 E. 75th St., Suite 1E, New York NY 10021. (212)794-1082. **Contact:** Jean Naggar. Estab. 1978. Member of AAR, Women's Media Group and Women's Forum. Represents 100 clients. 20% of clients are new/unpublished writers. Currently handles: 35% nonfiction books; 45% novels; 15% juvenile books; 5% scholarly books.

    ● Ms. Naggar served as president of AAR.

Member Agents: Alice Tasman (Senior Agent, narrative nonfiction, commercial/literary fiction, thrillers); Anne Engel (academic-based nonfiction for general readership); Jennifer Weltz (Director, Subsidiary Rights).
Represents: Nonfiction books, novels. **Considers these fiction areas:** Action/adventure; contemporary issues; detective/police/crime; ethnic; family saga; feminist; historical; literary; mainstream/contemporary; mystery/suspense; psychic/supernatural; thriller.

    O→ This agency specializes in mainstream fiction and nonfiction, literary fiction with commercial potential.

How to Contact: Query with SASE. Prefers to read materials exclusively. No e-mail or fax queries. Responds in 1 day to queries; 2 months to mss. Returns materials only with SASE. Obtains most new clients through recommendations from others, solicitations, conferences.
Recent Sales: *Leaving Ireland*, by Ann Moore (NAL); *The Associate*, by Phillip Margolin (HarperCollins); *Quantico Rules*, by Gene Riehl (St. Martin's Press). Other clients include Jean M. Auel, Robert Pollack, Mary McGarry Morris, Lily Prior, Susan Fromberg Schaeffer, David Ball, Elizabeth Crane, Maud Casey.
Terms: Agent receives 15% commission on domestic sales; 20% commission on foreign sales. Offers written contract. Charges for overseas mailing; messenger services; book purchases; long-distance telephone; photocopying. "These are deductible from royalties received."
Writers' Conferences: Willamette Writers Conference; Pacific Northwest Writers Conference; Breadloaf Writers Conference; Virginia Women's Press Conference (Richmond VA); Marymount Manhattan Writers Conference.
Tips: "Use a professional presentation. Because of the avalanche of unsolicited queries that flood the agency every week, we have had to modify our policy. We will now only guarantee to read and respond to queries from writers who come recommended by someone we know. Our areas are general fiction and nonfiction, no children's books by unpublished writers, no multimedia, no screenplays, no formula fiction, no mysteries by unpublished writers. We recommend patience and fortitude: the courage to be true to your own vision, the fortitude to finish a novel and polish and polish again before sending it out, and the patience to accept rejection gracefully and wait for the stars to align themselves appropriately for success."

◙ **NATIONAL WRITERS LITERARY AGENCY**, division of GTR, Inc., 3140 S. Peoria #295, Aurora CO 80014. (720)851-1959. Fax: (720)851-1960. E-mail: aajwiii@aol.com or nationalwriters@aol.com. **Contact:** Andrew J. Whelchel III. Estab. 1987. Represents 52 clients. 20% of clients are new/unpublished writers. Currently handles: 40% nonfiction books; 34% novels; 20% juvenile books; 6% scripts.
Member Agents: Andrew J. Whelchel III (screenplays, nonfiction, mystery, thriller); Jason S. Cangialosi (nonfiction); Shayne Sharpe (novels, screenplays, fantasy).
Represents: Nonfiction books, and fiction books. **Considers these fiction areas:** Action/adventure; juvenile; mainstream/contemporary; mystery/suspense; science fiction; sports; young adult.

    O→ Actively seeking "mystery/thrillers, music, business, cutting edge novels; pop culture, compelling true stories, science and technology." Does not want to receive "concept books, westerns, over-published self-help topics."

How to Contact: Query with outline and SASE. Accepts e-mail queries. No fax queries. Considers simultaneous queries. Responds in 6 weeks to queries; 2 months to mss. Returns materials only with SASE. Obtains most new clients through solicitations, conferences, or over the transom.

Recent Sales: Sold 22 titles in the last year.

Terms: Agent receives 15% commission on domestic sales; 20% commission on foreign sales; 10% commission on dramatic rights sales. Offers written contract; 30-day notice must be given to terminate contract.

Tips: "Query letters should include a great hook just as if you only had a few seconds to impress us. A professional package gets professional attention. Always include return postage!"

🖉 **KAREN NAZOR LITERARY AGENCY**, 100 Powdermill Rd., PMB 182, Acton MA 01720. (978) 266-3792. Fax: (978) 263-6230. E-mail: query@nazor.org. **Contact:** Karen Nazor. Estab. 1991. Represents 35 clients. 15% of clients are new/unpublished writers. Currently handles: 75% nonfiction books; 10% novels; 10% electronic multimedia.

● Prior to opening her agency, Ms. Nazor served a brief apprenticeship with Raines & Raines and was assistant to Peter Ginsberg, president of Curtis Brown, Ltd.

Member Agents: Kris Ashley (literary and commercial fiction).

Represents: Nonfiction books, novels, novellas. **Considers these fiction areas:** Feminist; literary; multicultural; regional; women's.

○➔ This agency specializes in "good writers! Mostly nonfiction—arts, culture, politics, technology, civil rights, etc."

How to Contact: Query (preferred) or send outline/proposal (accepted). No unsolicited mss. Responds in 2 weeks to queries; 2 months to mss. Returns materials only with SASE.

Recent Sales: Sold 12 titles in the last year. *The Secret Life of Dust*, by Hannah Holmes (John Wiley & Sons); *Childhood and Adolescent Obsessive Compulsive Disorder*, by Mitzi Waltz (O'Reilly).

Terms: Agent receives 15% commission on domestic sales; 20% commission on foreign sales. Offers written contract. Charges clients for express mail services, photocopying costs.

Tips: "I'm interested in good writers who want a long term, long haul relationship. Not a one-book writer, but a writer who has many ideas, is productive, professional, passionate and meets deadlines!"

🖉 **THE NORMA-LEWIS AGENCY**, 311 W. 43rd St., Suite 602, New York NY 10036. (212)664-0807. **Contact:** Norma Liebert. Estab. 1980. 50% of clients are new/unpublished writers. Currently handles: 60% juvenile books; 40% adult books.

Represents: Movie scripts, TV scripts, documentary, miniseries, stage plays, Juvenile and adult nonfiction and fiction. **Considers these fiction areas:** Action/adventure; detective/police/crime; family saga; historical; horror; humor/satire; juvenile; mainstream/contemporary; mystery/suspense; picture books; romance (contemporary, gothic, historical, regency); thriller; westerns/frontier; young adult.

○➔ This agency specializes in juvenile books (pre-school to high school).

How to Contact: Query with SASE. Prefers to read materials exclusively. Considers simultaneous queries. Responds in 6 weeks to queries. Returns materials only with SASE.

Recent Sales: *Viper Quarry*, by Dean Feldmeyer (Pocket Books); *Pitchfork Hollow*, by Dean Feldmeyer (Pocket Books).

Terms: Agent receives 15% commission on domestic sales; 20% commission on foreign sales.

🖉 **PARAVIEW, INC.**, 191 7th Ave., Suite 2F, New York NY 10011. (212)989-3616. Fax: (212)989-3662. E-mail: lhagan@paraview.com. Website: www.paraview.com. **Contact:** Lisa Hagan. Estab. Paraview, Inc. was established in 1988. Represents 75 clients. 50% of clients are new/unpublished writers. Currently handles: 80% nonfiction books; 10% novels; 10% scholarly books.

● Ms. Hagan has agented since 1995.

Member Agents: Lisa Hagan (fiction and nonfiction self-help).

Represents: Nonfiction books, novels. **Considers these fiction areas:** Action/adventure; contemporary issues; ethnic; feminist; literary; mainstream/contemporary; regional; romance; women's.

○➔ This agency specializes in spiritual, New Age and self-help.

How to Contact: Query including, synopsis, author, bio via email. Responds in 1 month to queries; 3 months to mss. Obtains most new clients through recommendations from editors and current clients.

Recent Sales: Sold 40 titles in the last year. *Poetry*, by Jewel Kilcher (Pocket Books); *King of the Cowboys*, by Ty Muarry (Pocket Books); *Angel Signs*, by Albert Haldane and Simha Seryaru (HarperCollins).

Terms: Agent receives 15% commission on domestic sales; 20% commission on foreign sales.

Writers' Conferences: BEA (Chicago, June); London Book Fair; E3—Electronic Entertainment Exposition.

Tips: "New writers should have their work edited, critiqued, and carefully reworked prior to submission. First contact should be via e-mail to lhagan@paraview.com."

⬥ **L. PERKINS ASSOCIATES**, 5800 Arlington Ave., Riverdale NY 10471. (718)543-5344. Fax: (718)543-5354. E-mail: lperkinsagency@yahoo.com. **Contact:** Lori Perkins. Estab. 1990. Member of AAR. Represents 50 clients. 10% of clients are new/unpublished writers.
  • Ms. Perkins has been an agent for 18 years. Her agency has an affiliate agency, Southern Literary Group. She is also the author of *The Insider's Guide to Getting an Agent* (Writer's Digest Books).
Represents: Nonfiction books, novels. **Considers these fiction areas:** Fantasy; horror; literary (dark); science fiction.
  ⚿ All of Ms. Perkins's clients write both fiction and nonfiction. "This combination keeps my clients publishing for years. I am also a published author so I know what it takes to write a book." Actively seeking a Latino *Gone With the Wind* and *Waiting to Exhale*, and urban ethnic horror. Does not want to receive "anything outside of the above categories, i.e., westerns, romance."
How to Contact: Query with SASE. Considers simultaneous queries. Responds in 6 weeks to queries; 3 months to mss. Returns materials only with SASE. Obtains most new clients through recommendations from others, solicitations, conferences.
Recent Sales: Sold 100 titles in the last year.
Terms: Agent receives 15% commission on domestic sales; 20% commission on foreign sales. No written contract. Charges clients for photocopying.
Writers' Conferences: San Diego Writer's Conference; NECON; BEA; World Fantasy.
Tips: "Research your field and contact professional writers' organizations to see who is looking for what. Finish your novel before querying agents. Read my book, *An Insider's Guide to Getting an Agent* to get a sense of how agents operate."

⬥ **ALISON J. PICARD, LITERARY AGENT**, P.O. Box 2000, Cotuit MA 02635. (508)477-7192. Fax: (508)477-7192 (Please contact before faxing.). E-mail: ajpicard@aol.com. **Contact:** Alison Picard. Estab. 1985. Represents 48 clients. 30% of clients are new/unpublished writers. Currently handles: 40% nonfiction books; 40% novels; 20% juvenile books.
  • Prior to becoming an agent, Ms. Picard was an assistant at an NYC literary agency.
Member Agents: Alison Picard (mysteries/suspense/thriller, romance, literary fiction, adult nonfiction, juvenile books).
Represents: Nonfiction books, novels, short story collections, novellas, juvenile books. **Considers these fiction areas:** Action/adventure; contemporary issues; detective/police/crime; erotica; ethnic; experimental; family saga; feminist; gay/lesbian; glitz; historical; horror; humor/satire; juvenile; literary; mainstream/contemporary; multicultural; mystery/suspense; New Age; picture books; psychic/supernatural; regional; religious/inspirational; romance; sports; thriller; young adult.
  ⚿ "Many of my clients have come to me from big agencies, where they felt overlooked or ignored. I communicate freely with my clients, and offer a lot of career advice, suggestions for revising manuscripts, etc. If I believe in a project, I will submit it to a dozen or more publishers, unlike some agents who give up after 4 or 5 rejections." Actively seeking commercial adult fiction and nonfiction, middle grade juvenile fiction. Does not want to receive sci-fi/fantasy, westerns, poetry, plays, articles.
How to Contact: Query with SASE. Considers simultaneous queries. Responds in 1 week to queries; 6 weeks to mss. Returns materials only with SASE. Obtains most new clients through recommendations from others, solicitations.
Recent Sales: Sold 27 titles in the last year. *The Shade of My Own Tree*, by Sheila Williams (Ballantine); *The Boldness of Boys*, by Susan Strong (Andrews McMeel).
Terms: Agent receives 15% commission on domestic sales; 20% commission on foreign sales. Offers written contract, binding for 1 year; 1 week notice must be given to terminate contract.
Tips: "Please don't send material without sending a query first via mail or e-mail. I don't accept phone or fax queries. Always enclose a SASE with a query."

⬥ **A PICTURE OF YOU**, 1176 Elizabeth Dr., Hamilton OH 45013-3507. (513)863-1108. Fax: (513)863-1108. E-mail: apoy1@aol.com. **Contact:** Lenny Minelli. Estab. 1993. Signatory of WGA. Represents 45 clients. 50% of clients are new/unpublished writers. Currently handles: 80% movie scripts; 10% TV scripts; 10% syndicated material.
  • Prior to opening his agency, Mr. Minelli was an actor/producer for 10 years. Also owned and directed a talent agency and represented actors and actresses from around the world.
Member Agents: Michelle Chang (fiction/nonfiction books).
Represents: Nonfiction books, novels, short story collections, novellas, feature film, TV movie of the week, episodic drama, sitcom, animation, documentary, miniseries, syndicated material. **Considers these fiction areas:** Action/adventure; detective/police/crime; erotica; ethnic; family saga; fantasy; gay/lesbian; glitz; historical; horror; literary; mainstream/contemporary; mystery/suspense; religious/inspirational; romance (contemporary, gothic, historical); thriller; westerns/frontier; young adult.
  ⚿ This agency specializes in screenplays and TV scripts.
How to Contact: Query with SASE. Accepts e-mail and fax queries. Considers simultaneous queries. Responds in 3 weeks to queries; 1 month to mss. Obtains most new clients through recommendations from others, solicitations.

Recent Sales: *Lost and Found*, by J.P. Brice; *So Long*, by Patrick Cappella.

Terms: Agent receives 10% commission on domestic sales; 15% commission on foreign sales. Offers written contract, binding for 1 year; 90-day notice must be given to terminate contract. Charges clients for postage/express mail and long distance calls.

Tips: "Make sure that the script is the best it can be before seeking an agent."

◖ PINDER LANE & GARON-BROOKE ASSOCIATES, LTD., 159 W. 53rd St., Suite 14E, New York NY 10019-6005. (212)489-0880. E-mail: pinderl@interport.net. **Contact:** Robert Thixton. Member of AAR; signatory of WGA. Represents 30 clients. 20% of clients are new/unpublished writers. Currently handles: 25% nonfiction books; 75% novels.

Member Agents: Nancy Coffey (contributing agent); Dick Duane; Robert Thixton.

Represents: Nonfiction books, novels. **Considers these fiction areas:** Contemporary issues; detective/police/crime; family saga; fantasy; gay/lesbian; literary; mainstream/contemporary; mystery/suspense; romance; science fiction.

   ◻▪ This agency specializes in mainstream fiction and nonfiction. Does not want to receive screenplays, TV series teleplays or dramatic plays.

How to Contact: Query with SASE. No unsolicited mss. Responds in 3 weeks to queries; 2 months to mss. Obtains most new clients through referrals, queries.

Recent Sales: Sold 20 titles in the last year. *The Sixth Fleet* (series), by David Meadows (Berkley); *Dark Fires*, by Rosemary Rogers (Mira Books).

Terms: Agent receives 15% commission on domestic sales; 30% commission on foreign sales. Offers written contract, binding for 3-5 years.

Tips: "With our literary and media experience, our agency is uniquely positioned for the current and future direction publishing is taking. Send query letter first giving the essence of the ms and a personal or career bio with SASE."

◖ ARTHUR PINE ASSOCIATES, INC., 250 W. 57th St., Suite 417, New York NY 10019. (215)265-7330. Fax: (212)265-4650. Estab. 1966. Represents 100 clients. 25% of clients are new/unpublished writers. Currently handles: 60% nonfiction books; 40% novels.

Member Agents: Richard Pine; Catherine Drayton; Lori Andiman; Matthew Guma.

Represents: Nonfiction books, novels. **Considers these fiction areas:** Detective/police/crime; family saga; historical; literary; mainstream/contemporary; thriller.

How to Contact: Query with SASE, outline/proposal. Prefers to read materials exclusively. No e-mail or fax queries. Responds in 1 month to queries. Obtains most new clients through recommendations from others.

Recent Sales: Sold 60 titles in the last year.

Terms: Agent receives 15% commission on domestic sales; 15% commission on foreign sales. Offers written contract.

Tips: "Our agency will consider exclusive submissions only. All submissions must be accompanied by postage or SASE. Will not read manuscripts before receiving a letter of inquiry."

◖ JULIE POPKIN, 15340 Albright St., #204, Pacific Palisades CA 90272-2520. (310)459-2834. **Contact:** Julie Popkin. Estab. 1989. Represents 35 clients. 30% of clients are new/unpublished writers. Currently handles: 70% nonfiction books; 30% novels.

   • Prior to opening her agency, Ms. Popkin taught at the university level and did freelance editing and writing.

Member Agents: Julie Popkin; Margaret McCord (fiction, memoirs, biography); Linda Schubert (nonfiction).

Represents: Nonfiction books, novels, translations. **Considers these fiction areas:** Literary; mainstream/contemporary; mystery/suspense.

   ◻▪ This agency specializes in selling book-length mss including fiction and nonfiction. Especially interested in social issues, ethnic and minority subjects, Latin American authors. Does not want to receive New Age, spiritual, romance, science fiction.

How to Contact: Query with SASE. No e-mail or fax queries. Responds in 1 month to queries; 2 months to mss. Obtains most new clients through "Mostly clients find me through guides and personal contacts."

Recent Sales: Sold 8 titles in the last year. *Two Worlds in One*, by Virginia Li (Prometheus); *The Red and the Blacklist*, by Norma Barzman (Nation Books); *Planet Earth*, by P.K. Page (Godine).

Terms: Agent receives 15% commission on domestic sales; 20% commission on foreign sales; 10% commission on dramatic rights sales. Sometimes asks for fee if ms requires extensive copying and mailing.

Writers' Conferences: BEA (Los Angeles, June); Santa Barbara (June).

Tips: "Keep your eyes on the current market. Publishing responds to changes very quickly and often works toward perceived and fresh subject matter. Historical fiction seems to be rising in interest after a long quiet period."

◖ ROBERT PRESKILL LITERARY AGENCY, Lit West Group, LLC, 2130 Fillmore St., #313, San Francisco CA 94115. (415)346-9449. Fax: (415)820-7745. E-mail: literaryagent.geo@yahoo.com. Website: www.litwest.com. **Contact:** Robert Preskill, Esq. Member of Illinois Bar; Authors Guild. 10% of clients are new/unpublished writers. Currently handles: 50% nonfiction books; 40% novels; 10% story collections.

   • Mr. Preskill formerly worked for McGraw-Hill Companies.

Member Agents: Agents of Lit West Group, LLC: Robert Preskill (literary fiction, relevant non-fiction by "experts"); Katherine Boyle (pop-culture, psychology, literary fiction); Linda Mead (business, self-help, general nonfiction, selected works of fiction); Nancy Ellis (general nonfiction, reference, self-help, young adult, fiction).

Represents: Nonfiction books, novels, short story collections, novellas. **Considers these fiction areas:** Comic books/cartoon; detective/police/crime; literary; thriller.

O→ RPLA spends extra time editing and reviewing a work once it is chosen. Much of the time we will help chart a course toward publication by assisting with marketing ideas, submitting to literary magazines and other appropriate publications and through pursuit of sub-rights. Regarding fiction, looks for things grounded in personal storytelling, subtle and powerful action, politics, issues that illuminate a deeper layer of imagery; things that take dialog and the negative space of good dialog somewhere beyond the simple experience. There are plenty of stories that pass us by on a daily basis, but we fail to see them. I am interested in those stories in the world as it exists. Does not want fantasy, romance.

How to Contact: Query with SASE. *After* query, send 3 sample chapters with SASE. Considers simultaneous queries. Responds in 1 week to queries; 10 weeks to mss. Returns materials only with SASE. Obtains most new clients through recommendations from others, solicitations.

Recent Sales: Sold 10 titles and sold 2 options on scripts in the last year. *Instant Karma*, by Mark Swartz (City Lights Publishers); *Westerfield's Chain*, by Jack Clark (St. Martin's Press); *On the Homefront*, by Jack Clark and Mary Jo Clark (Plume); *Murder for Christmas* (Morrow); *Esther Stories*, by Peter Orner (Houghton Mifflin). Other clients include Dan Whipple, Robley Wilson, Alvin Greenberg, Robert Goldberg, Alexai Galaviz-Budzlszewski.

Terms: Agent receives 15% commission on domestic sales; 20% commission on foreign sales. Offers written contract; 30-day notice must be given to terminate contract. Charges clients for project related expenses only (such as postage and photocopying).

Writers' Conferences: Maui Writers Conference (Maui HI); Asilomar Writers Conference (Pacific Grove CA); Saroyan Writers Conferance (Fresno CA); Willamet Writers Conference (Portland OR).

Tips: "I was trained through the wonderful program at University of Illinois and learned from the writing of Mark Costello, William Gass, William Maxwell, Joy Williams, Grace Paley, Richard Ford, Joan Didion, Alice Munro, Mary Gaitskill, Nathaniel West, Steve Erickson and Thoms McGuane."

◐ **SUSAN ANN PROTTER, LITERARY AGENT**, 110 W. 40th St., Suite 1408, New York NY 10018. (212)840-0480. **Contact:** Susan Protter. Estab. 1971. Member of AAR. Represents 40 clients. 5% of clients are new/unpublished writers. Works with a very small number of new/previously unpublished authors Currently handles: 50% nonfiction books; 50% novels; occasional magazine article or short story (for established clients only).

● Prior to opening her agency, Ms. Protter was associate director of subsidiary rights at Harper & Row Publishers.

Represents: Nonfiction books, novels. **Considers these fiction areas:** Detective/police/crime; mystery/suspense; science fiction; thriller.

O→ Writers must have book-length project or manuscript that is ready to be sold. Does not want to receive westerns, romance, fantasy, children's books, young adult novels, screenplays, plays, poetry, Star Wars or Star Trek.

How to Contact: Currently looking for limited number of new clients. Send short query with SASE. No unsolicited manuscripts. Responds in 3 weeks to queries; 2 months to mss.

Recent Sales: *As Above, So Below*, by Rudy Rucker (Forge); *The Light Ages*, by Ian R. Macleod (Ace); *The Hard SF Renaissance*, edited by David G. Hartwell and Kathryn Cramer (Tor).

Terms: Agent receives 15% commission on domestic sales; 15% commission on dramatic rights sales. "If, after seeing your query, we request to see your manuscript, there will be a small shipping and handling fee requested to cover cost of returning materials should they not be suitable." Charges clients for photocopying, messenger, express mail, airmail and overseas shipping expenses.

Tips: "Please send neat and professionally organized queries. Make sure to include a SASE or we cannot reply. We receive approximately 200 queries a week and read them in the order they arrive. We usually reply within two weeks to any query. Please, do not call or email queries. If you are sending a multiple query, make sure to note that in your letter. I am looking for something outstanding in a large, difficult market."

◐ **QUICKSILVER BOOKS—LITERARY AGENTS**, 50 Wilson St., Hartsdale NY 10530-2542. (914)946-8748. Fax: (914)946-8748. Website: www.quicksilverbooks.com. **Contact:** Bob Silverstein. Estab. 1973 as packager; 1987 as literary agency. Represents 50 clients. 50% of clients are new/unpublished writers. Currently handles: 75% nonfiction books; 25% novels.

● Prior to opening his agency, Mr. Silverstein served as senior editor at Bantam Books and Dell Books/Delacorte Press.

Represents: Nonfiction books, novels. **Considers these fiction areas:** Action/adventure; glitz; mystery/suspense; thriller.

O→ This agency specializes in literary and commercial mainstream fiction and nonfiction (especially psychology, New Age, holistic healing, consciousness, ecology, environment, spirituality, reference, cookbooks, narrative nonfiction). Actively seeking commercial mainstream fiction and nonfiction in most categories. Does not want to receive science fiction, pornography, poetry, or single-spaced manuscripts.

How to Contact: Query with SASE. Authors are expected to supply SASE for return of mss and for query letter responses. No e-mail or fax queries. Considers simultaneous queries. Responds in 2 weeks to queries; 1 month to mss. Returns materials only with SASE. Obtains most new clients through recommendations, listings in sourcebooks, solicitations, workshop participation.

Recent Sales: Sold over 20 titles in the last year. *Tarot D'Amour*, by Kooch and Victor Daniels (Red Wheel/Weiser).

Terms: Agent receives 15% commission on domestic sales; 20% commission on foreign sales. Offers written contract. Charges clients for photocopying of mss and proposals, but prefers authors provide actual copies; foreign mailings of books and mss.

Writers' Conferences: National Writers Union Conference (Dobbs Ferry NY, April).

Tips: "Write what you know. Write from the heart. Publishers print. Authors sell."

HELEN REES LITERARY AGENCY, 123 N. Washington St., Boston MA 02114-2113. (617)227-9014, ext. 233 or 222. **Contact:** Joan Mazmanian, Ann Collette, Helen Rees. Estab. 1983. Member of AAR. Represents 80 clients. 50% of clients are new/unpublished writers. Currently handles: 60% nonfiction books; 40% novels.

Member Agents: Ann Collette (literary fiction, women's studies, health, biography, history); Helen Rees (business, money/finance/economics, government/politics/law, contemporary issues, literary fiction).

Represents: Nonfiction books, novels. **Considers these fiction areas:** Contemporary issues; historical; literary; mainstream/contemporary; mystery/suspense; thriller.

How to Contact: Query with SASE, outline, 2 sample chapter(s). No e-mail or fax queries. Responds in 2-3 weeks to queries. Obtains most new clients through recommendations from others, solicitations, conferences.

Recent Sales: Sold 28 titles in the last year.

Terms: Agent receives 15% commission on domestic sales; 20% commission on foreign sales.

JODY REIN BOOKS, INC., 7741 S. Ash Court, Centennial CO 80122. (303)694-4430. Fax: (303)694-0687. Website: jodyreinbooks.com. **Contact:** Winnefred Dollar. Estab. 1994. Member of AAR, Authors Guild. Currently handles: 70% nonfiction books; 30% novels.

• Prior to opening her agency, Jody Rein worked for 13 years as an acquisitions editor for Contemporary Books, Bantam/Doubleday/Dell (executive editor) and Morrow/Avon (executive editor).

Member Agents: Jody Rein; Johnna Hietala.

Represents: Nonfiction books (primarily narrative and commercial nonfiction), novels (select literary novels, commercial mainstream and mystery). **Considers these fiction areas:** Literary; mainstream/contemporary; mystery/suspense.

○➤ This agency specializes in commercial and narrative nonfiction.

How to Contact: Query with SASE. No e-mail or fax queries. Considers simultaneous queries. Responds in 6 weeks to queries; 2 months to mss. Obtains most new clients through recommendations from others, solicitations.

Recent Sales: *The Lakota Way*, by Joseph Marshall III (Viking Penguin); *The Big Year*, by Mark Obmascik (The Free Press).

Terms: Agent receives 15% commission on domestic sales; 25% commission on foreign sales; 20% commission on dramatic rights sales. Offers written contract. Charges clients for express mail, overseas expenses, photocopying ms.

Tips: "Do your homework before submitting. Make sure you have a marketable topic and the credentials to write about it. Well-written books on fresh and original nonfiction topics that have broad appeal. Novels written by authors who have spent years developing their craft. Authors must be well established in their fields and have strong media experience."

JODIE RHODES LITERARY AGENCY, 8840 Villa La Jolla Dr., Suite 315, La Jolla CA 92037-1957. (858)625-0544. Fax: (858)625-0544. Website: www.writers.net and www.literaryagent.com. **Contact:** Jodie Rhodes, president. Estab. 1998. Member of AAR. Represents 50 clients. 60% of clients are new/unpublished writers. Currently handles: 60% nonfiction books; 35% novels; 5% middle to young adult books.

• Prior to opening her agency, Ms. Rhodes was a university level creative writing teacher, workshop director, published novelist and Vice President Media Director at the N.W. Ayer Advertising Agency.

Member Agents: Jodie Rhodes, president; Clark McCutcheon (fiction); Bob McCarter (nonfiction).

Represents: Nonfiction books, novels, juvenile books. **Considers these fiction areas:** Contemporary issues; ethnic; family saga; historical; juvenile; literary; mainstream/contemporary; mystery/suspense; thriller; young adult; women's.

○➤ Actively seeking "writers passionate about their books with a talent for richly textured narrative, an eye for details, and a nose for research." Does not want to receive erotica, horror, fantasy, romance, science fiction, children's books.

How to Contact: Query with brief synopsis, first 30 to 50 pages and SASE. No e-mail or fax queries. Considers simultaneous queries. Responds in 10 days to queries. Returns materials only with SASE. Obtains most new clients through recommendations from others, agent sourcebooks.

Recent Sales: Sold 25 titles in the last year. *For Material Purposes*, by Kavita Daswani (Putnam); *Tamina of the Chew*, by Denise Lamothe (Penguin).

Terms: Agent receives 15% commission on domestic sales; 20% commission on foreign sales. Offers written contract; 30-day notice must be given to terminate contract. Charges clients for fax, photocopying, phone calls and postage. "Charges are itemized and approved by writers upfront."

Writers' Conferences: Southern California Writers Conference (San Diego, mid-February); SDSU Writers Conference (San Diego, mid-January); Los Angeles Writers' Conference (Los Angeles, mid-October).

Tips: "Think your book out before you write it. Do your research, know your subject matter intimately, write vivid specifics, not bland generalities. Care deeply about your book. Don't imitate other writers. Find your own voice. We never take on a book we don't believe in, and we go the extra mile for our writers. We welcome talented new writers. We hold monthly weekend clinics on how to write a query letter and weekly writing workshops for area writers."

ANGELA RINALDI LITERARY AGENCY, P.O. Box 7877, Beverly Hills CA 90212-7877. (310)842-7665. Fax: (310)837-8143. E-mail: mail@rinaldiliterary.com. Estab. 1994. Member of AAR. Represents 50 clients. Currently handles: 40% nonfiction books; 60% novels.
 • Prior to opening her agency, Ms. Rinaldi was an editor at NAL/Signet, Pocket Books and Bantam, and the Manager of Book Development for *The Los Angeles Times*.

Represents: Nonfiction books, novels, TV and motion picture rights for clients only. **Considers these fiction areas:** Literary; Commercial; upmarket women's fiction; suspense.
 O→ Actively seeking commercial and literary fiction. Does not want to receive scripts, poetry, category romances, children's books, westerns, science fiction/fantasy, technothrillers and cookbooks.

How to Contact: Send the first 3 chapters, brief synopsis, SASE. Do not send metered mail as SASE. Considers simultaneous queries. Please advise if this is a multiple submission. Responds in 6 weeks to queries. Returns materials only with SASE.

Recent Sales: *Letters in the Attic*, by Bonnie Shimko (Academy).

Terms: Agent receives 15% commission on domestic sales; 20% commission on foreign sales. Offers written contract. Charges clients for photocopying if not provided by client.

◩ ANN RITTENBERG LITERARY AGENCY, INC., 1201 Broadway, Suite 708, New York NY 10001. (212)684-6936. Fax: (212)684-6929. **Contact:** Ann Rittenberg, president. Estab. 1992. Member of AAR. Represents 35 clients. 40% of clients are new/unpublished writers. Currently handles: 50% nonfiction books; 50% novels.

Member Agents: Ted Gideonse.

Represents: Nonfiction books, novels. **Considers these fiction areas:** Literary.
 O→ This agent specializes in literary fiction and literary nonfiction.

How to Contact: Submit outline, 3 sample chapter(s), SASE. Considers simultaneous queries. Responds in 6 weeks to queries; 2 months to mss. Obtains most new clients through referrals from established writers and editors.

Recent Sales: Sold 20 titles in the last year. *Seven Blessings*, by Ruchama King (St. Martin's Press); *All Hat*, by Brad Smith (Holt); *Meena, Heroine of Afghanistan* (St. Martin's Press).

Terms: Agent receives 15% commission on domestic sales; 20% commission on foreign sales. Offers written contract. Charges clients for photocopying only.

◩ RIVERSIDE LITERARY AGENCY, 1052 Weatherhead Hollow, Guilford VT 05301. (802)257-2677. Fax: (802)257-8907. E-mail: rivlit@sover.net. **Contact:** Susan Lee Cohen. Estab. 1991. Represents 40 clients. 20% of clients are new/unpublished writers.

Represents: Nonfiction books (adult), novels (adult), very selective.

How to Contact: Query with SASE, outline. Accepts e-mail queries. No fax queries. Considers simultaneous queries. Responds in 1 month to queries. Obtains most new clients through referrals.

Recent Sales: Sold 14 titles in the last year.

Terms: Agent receives 15% commission on domestic sales. Offers written contract. Charges clients for foreign postage, photocopying large manuscripts, express mail deliveries, etc.

◩ RLR ASSOCIATES, LTD., Literary Department, 7 W. 51st St., New York NY 10019. (212)541-8641. Fax: (212)541-6052. Website: www.rlrassociates.net/literary. **Contact:** Jennifer Unter, Ezra Fitz. Represents 50 clients. 25% of clients are new/unpublished writers. Currently handles: 70% nonfiction books; 25% novels; 5% story collections.

Member Agents: Jennifer Unter, Ezra Fitz.

Represents: Nonfiction books, novels, short story collections, scholarly books. **Considers these fiction areas:** Action/adventure; comic books/cartoon; contemporary issues; detective/police/crime; ethnic; experimental; family saga; feminist; gay/lesbian; historical; horror; humor/satire; literary; mainstream/contemporary; multicultural; mystery/suspense; sports; thriller.
 O→ "We provide a lot of editorial assistance to our clients and have connections." Actively seeking fiction (all types except for romance and fantasy), current affairs, history, art, popular culture, health, business. Does not want to receive romance or fantasy; screenplays.

How to Contact: Query with SASE. Considers simultaneous queries. Responds in 5 weeks to queries; 5 weeks to mss. Returns materials only with SASE. Obtains most new clients through recommendations from others.

Recent Sales: Sold 20 titles in the last year. Other clients include Shelby Foote, The Grief Recovery Institute, Don Wade, Don Zimmer, The Knot.com, David Plowder, PGA of America, Danny Peary, Jahnna Beecham & Malcolm Hillgartner.

Terms: Agent receives 15% commission on domestic sales; 20% commission on foreign sales. Offers written contract.

Tips: "Please check out our website for more details on our agency. No e-mail submissions please."

B.J. ROBBINS LITERARY AGENCY, 5130 Bellaire Ave., North Hollywood CA 91607-2908. (818)760-6602. Fax: (818)760-6616. E-mail: robbinsliterary@aol.com. **Contact:** (Ms.) B.J. Robbins. Estab. 1992. Member of Board of Directors, PEN American Center West. Represents 40 clients. 50% of clients are new/unpublished writers. Currently handles: 50% nonfiction books; 50% novels.

Member Agents: Rob McAndrews (commercial fiction).

Represents: Nonfiction books, novels. **Considers these fiction areas:** Contemporary issues; detective/police/crime; ethnic; literary; mainstream/contemporary; mystery/suspense; sports; thriller.

How to Contact: Submit 3 sample chapter(s), outline/proposal, SASE. No e-mail or fax queries. Considers simultaneous queries. Responds in 2 weeks to queries; 6 weeks to mss. Returns materials only with SASE. Obtains most new clients through conferences, referrals.

Recent Sales: Sold 15 titles in the last year. *Please, Please, Please,* by Renee Swindle (Dial Press); *Katie.com,* by Katherine Tarbox (Dutton); *Quickening,* by Laura Catherine Brown (Random House/Ballantine); *Snow Mountain Passage,* by James D. Houston (Knopf); *The Last Summer,* by John Hough, Jr. (Simon & Schuster).

Terms: Agent receives 15% commission on domestic sales; 20% commission on foreign sales. Offers written contract; 3-month notice must be given to terminate contract. 100% of business is derived from commissions on ms sales. Charges clients for postage and photocopying only. Writers charged for fees only after the sale of ms.

Writers' Conferences: Squaw Valley Fiction Writers Workshop (Squaw Valley CA, August); Maui Writers Conference (Maui HI); SDSU Writers Conference (San Diego CA, January).

MICHAEL D. ROBINS & ASSOCIATES, 23241 Ventura Blvd., #300, Woodland Hills CA 91364. (818)343-1755. Fax: (818)343-7355. E-mail: mdr2@msn.com. **Contact:** Michael D. Robins. Estab. 1991. Member of DGA; signatory of WGA. 10% of clients are new/unpublished writers. Currently handles: 5% nonfiction books; 5% novels; 20% movie scripts; 60% TV scripts; 10% syndicated material.

• Prior to opening his agency, Mr. Robins was a literary agent at a mid-sized agency.

Represents: Nonfiction books, novels, movie scripts, feature film, TV scripts, TV movie of the week, episodic drama, animation, miniseries, syndicated material, stage plays. **Considers these fiction areas:** Action/adventure; comic books/cartoon; detective/police/crime; family saga; fantasy; gay/lesbian; mainstream/contemporary; westerns/frontier (frontier); young adult.

How to Contact: Query with SASE. Accepts e-mail and fax queries. Considers simultaneous queries. Responds in 1 week to queries; 1 month to mss. Obtains most new clients through recommendations from others.

Recent Sales: This agency prefers not to share information on specific sales.

Terms: Agent receives 10% commission on domestic sales; 10% commission on foreign sales. Offers written contract, binding for 2 years; 4 months notice must be given to terminate contract.

LINDA ROGHAAR LITERARY AGENCY, INC., 133 High Point Dr., Amherst MA 01002. (413)256-1921. Fax: (413)256-2636. E-mail: contact@lindaroghaar.com. Website: www.lindaroghaar.com. **Contact:** Linda L. Roghaar. Estab. 1996. Represents 50 clients. 40% of clients are new/unpublished writers. Currently handles: 90% nonfiction books; 10% novels.

• Prior to opening her agency, Ms. Roghaar worked in retail bookselling for 5 years and as a publishers' sales rep for 15 years.

Represents: Nonfiction books, novels. **Considers these fiction areas:** Mystery/suspense (amateur sleuth, cozy, culinary, malice domestic).

How to Contact: Query with SASE. Accepts e-mail queries. No fax queries. Considers simultaneous queries. Responds in 2 months to queries; 4 months to mss.

Recent Sales: *Refrigerator Rights,* by Dr. Will Miller (Penguin Putnam/Perigee); *White China,* by Molly Wolf (Jossey-Bass); *Crooked Heart,* by Cristina Sumners (Bantam).

Terms: Agent receives 15% commission on domestic sales; negotiable commission on foreign sales. Offers written contract, binding for negotiable time.

THE ROSENBERG GROUP, 23 Lincoln Ave., Marblehead MA 01945. (781)990-1341. Fax: (781)990-1344. Website: www.rosenberggroup.com. **Contact:** Barbara Collins Rosenberg. Estab. 1998. Member of AAR, Recognized agent of the RWA. Represents 32 clients. 50% of clients are new/unpublished writers. Currently handles: 30% nonfiction books; 30% novels; 10% scholarly books; 30% textbooks.

• Prior to becoming an agent, Barbara was a senior editor for Harcourt.

Member Agents: Barbara Collins Rosenberg.

Represents: Nonfiction books, novels, textbooks. **Considers these fiction areas:** Literary; romance; women's.

○┅ "Barbara is well versed in the romance market (both category and single title). She is a frequent speaker at romance conferences. Actively seeking romance category or single title in contemporary "chick-lit," romantic suspense and the historical sub-genres. Does not want to receive time-travel, paranormal, or inspirational/spiritual romances.

How to Contact: Query with SASE. No e-mail or fax queries. Responds in 2 weeks to queries; 4-6 weeks to mss. Returns materials only with SASE. Obtains most new clients through recommendations from others, solicitations, conferences.

Recent Sales: Sold 26 titles in the last year.

Terms: Agent receives 15% commission on domestic sales; 15% commission on foreign sales. Offers written contract; 30 days notice must be given to terminate contract. Postage and photocopying limit of $350 per year.

Writers' Conferences: RWA Annual Conference (New York City, July 2003); Silicon Valley Romance Writers of America (October 2003).

THE GAIL ROSS LITERARY AGENCY, 1666 Connecticut Ave. NW, #500, Washington DC 20009. (202)328-3282. Fax: (202)328-9162. E-mail: jennifer@gailross.com. Website: www.gailross.com. **Contact:** Jennifer Manguera. Estab. 1988. Member of AAR. Represents 200 clients. 75% of clients are new/unpublished writers. Currently handles: 95% nonfiction books; 5% novels.

Member Agents: Gail Ross.

Represents: Nonfiction books, novels. **Considers these fiction areas:** Literary.

 ➤ This agency specializes in adult trade nonfiction.

How to Contact: Query with SASE. Considers simultaneous queries. Responds in 1 month to queries. Obtains most new clients through recommendations from others.

Recent Sales: Sold 50 titles in the last year. This agency prefers not to share information on specific sales.

Terms: Agent receives 15% commission on domestic sales; 25% commission on foreign sales. Charges for office expenses (i.e., postage, copying).

THE PETER RUBIE LITERARY AGENCY, 240 W. 35th St., Suite 500, New York NY 10001. (212)279-1776. Fax: (212)279-0927. E-mail: peterrubie@prlit.com. Website: www.prlit.com. **Contact:** Peter Rubie or June Clark (pralit@aol.com). Estab. 2000. Member of AAR. Represents 130 clients. 30% of clients are new/unpublished writers.

 ● Prior to opening his agency, Mr. Rubie was a founding partner of another literary agency at Perkins, Rubie & Associates and the fiction editor at Walker and Co.

Member Agents: June Clark (nonfiction consisting of celebrity biographies, commercial, traditional, alternative health, parenting pets, women's issues, teen nonfiction, how-to, self-help, offbeat business, food/wine, New Age, pop culture, gay issues); Peter Rubie (crime, science fiction, fantasy, literary fiction, thrillers, narrative nonfiction, business, self-help, how-to, popular, food/wine, history, commercial science, music).

Represents: Nonfiction books, novels. **Considers these fiction areas:** Action/adventure; detective/police/crime; ethnic; fantasy; gay/lesbian; historical; literary; science fiction; thriller.

How to Contact: Query with SASE. Responds in 2 months to queries; 3 months to mss. Returns materials only with SASE. Obtains most new clients through recommendations from others.

Recent Sales: Sold 30 titles in the last year. *The Emperor and the Wolf*, by Stuart Galbraith (Faber and Faber); *The Maquisarde*, by Louise Marley; *An Askew View: The Films of Kevin Smith*, by John Muir (Applause).

Terms: Agent receives 15% commission on domestic sales; 20% commission on foreign sales. Offers written contract. Charges clients for photocopying and some foreign mailings.

Tips: "We look for writers who are experts, have a strong platform and reputation in their field and have an outstanding prose style. Be professional. Subscribe to PublishersLunch.com. Read *Publishers Weekly* and genre-related magazines. Join writers' organizations. Go to conferences. Know your market, and learn your craft. Read Rubie's books *The Elements of Storytelling* (Wiley) and *The Writer's Market FAQs* (Writer's Digest Books). Go to our website for up-to-date information on clients and sales."

REGINA RYAN PUBLISHING ENTERPRISES, INC., 251 Central Park W., 7D, New York NY 10024. (212)787-5589. E-mail: queryreginaryanbooks@rcn.com. **Contact:** Regina Ryan. Estab. 1976. Currently handles: 90% nonfiction books; 5% novels; 5% juvenile books.

 ● Prior to becoming an agent, Ms. Ryan was an editor at Alfred A. Knopf, editor-in-chief of Macmillan Adult Trade, and a book producer.

Represents: Nonfiction books, novels, short story collections, juvenile books.

How to Contact: Query only by e-mail or mail with SASE. No telephone queries. Considers simultaneous queries. Responds in 1 month to queries. Returns materials only with SASE. Obtains most new clients through recommendations from others.

Recent Sales: *The Altruist*, by Walter Keady (Macadam/Cage); *Surviving Hitler*, by Andrea Warren (HarperCollins Books for Young Readers); *The Harlem Renaissance*, by Lionel Bascom (Sourcebooks/A Mediafusion Book).

Terms: Agent receives 15% commission on domestic sales; 15% commission on foreign sales. Offers written contract; 1 month, negotiable notice must be given to terminate contract. Charges clients for all out of pocket expenses, such as long distance, messengers, freight, copying, "if it's more than just a nominal amount."

Tips: "For nonfiction proposals, an analysis of the competition is essential; a sample chapter is helpful. For a fiction query, the first 10 pages are essential."

VICTORIA SANDERS & ASSOCIATES, 241 Ave. of the Americas, New York NY 10014-4822. (212)633-8811. Fax: (212)633-0525. E-mail: queriesvsa@hotmail.com. Website: www.victoriasanders.com. **Contact:** Victoria Sanders or Diane Dickensheid. Estab. 1993. Member of AAR; signatory of WGA. Represents 75 clients. 25% of clients are new/unpublished writers. Currently handles: 50% nonfiction books; 50% novels.
Member Agents: Imani Wilson (assistant literary agent).
Represents: Nonfiction books, novels. **Considers these fiction areas:** Action/adventure; contemporary issues; ethnic; family saga; feminist; gay/lesbian; literary; thriller.
How to Contact: Query with SASE. Considers simultaneous queries. Responds in 3 weeks to queries; 1 month to mss. Returns materials only with SASE. Obtains most new clients through recommendations from others, or "I find them through my reading and pursue."
Recent Sales: Sold 20 titles in the last year. *Incredible*, by Karin Slaughter (Morrow); *When Love Calls, You Better Answer*, by Bertice Berry (Doubleday).
Terms: Agent receives 15% commission on domestic sales; 20% commission on foreign sales. Offers written contract. Charges for photocopying, ms, messenger, express mail and extraordinary fees. If in excess of $100, client approval is required.
Tips: "Limit query to letter, no calls, and give it your best shot. A good query is going to get a good response."

SANDUM & ASSOCIATES, 144 E. 84th St., New York NY 10028-2035. (212)737-2011. Fax: (on request). **Contact:** Howard E. Sandum, managing director. Estab. 1987. Represents 35 clients. 20% of clients are new/unpublished writers. Currently handles: 80% nonfiction books; 20% novels.
Represents: Nonfiction books, novels (literary). **Considers these fiction areas:** Literary.
  ○➔ This agency specializes in general nonfiction.
How to Contact: Query with proposal, sample pages and SASE. Do not send full ms unless requested. Responds in 2 weeks to queries.
Terms: Agent receives 15% commission on domestic sales; adjustable commission on foreign sales; adjustable commission on dramatic rights sales. Charges clients for photocopying, air express, long-distance telephone/fax.

SCHIAVONE LITERARY AGENCY, INC., 236 Trails End, West Palm Beach FL 33413-2135. (561)966-9294. Fax: (561)966-9294. E-mail: profschia@aol.com. Website: www.freeyellow.com/members8/schiavone/index.html. **Contact:** James Schiavone, Ed.D. Estab. 1996. Member of National Education Association. Represents 40 clients. 2% of clients are new/unpublished writers. Currently handles: 50% nonfiction books; 49% novels; 1% textbooks.
  ● Prior to opening his agency, Dr. Schiavone was a full professor of development skills at the City University of New York and author of 5 trade books and 3 textbooks.
Represents: Nonfiction books, novels, juvenile books, scholarly books, textbooks, movie scripts, feature film, TV movie of the week. **Considers these fiction areas:** Contemporary issues; ethnic; family saga; historical; horror; humor/satire; juvenile; literary; mainstream/contemporary; science fiction; young adult.
  ○➔ This agency specializes in celebrity biography and autobiography. "We have a management division that handles motion picture and TV rights." Actively seeking serious nonfiction, literary fiction and celebrity biography. Does not want to receive poetry.
How to Contact: Query with SASE. Considers one page e-mail queries with no attachments. Does not accept phone or fax queries. Considers simultaneous queries. Responds in 2 weeks to queries; 6 weeks to mss. Returns materials only with SASE. Obtains most new clients through recommendations from others, solicitations, conferences.
Terms: Agent receives 15% commission on domestic sales; 20% commission on foreign sales. Offers written contract, binding for project period; written notice must be given to terminate contract. Charges clients for long distance, photocopying, postage, special handling. Dollar amount varies with each project depending on level of activity.
Writers' Conferences: Key West Literary Seminar (Key West FL, January); South Florida Writer's Conference (Miami FL, May).
Tips: "I prefer to work with established authors published by major houses in New York. I will consider marketable proposals from new/previously unpublished writers."

SUSAN SCHULMAN, A LITERARY AGENCY, 454 W. 44th St., New York NY 10036-5205. (212)713-1633/4/5. Fax: (212)581-8830. E-mail: schulman@aol.com. Website: www.susanschulmanagency.com. **Contact:** Susan Schulman, president. Estab. 1979. Member of AAR, Dramatists Guild, Women's Media Group; signatory of WGA. 10-15% of clients are new/unpublished writers. Currently handles: 70% nonfiction books; 20% novels; 10% stage plays.
Member Agents: Susan Schulman (self-help, health, business, spirituality); Christine Morin (children's books, ecology, natural sciences and business books); Bryan Leifert (plays and pitches for films).
Represents: Nonfiction books, novels. **Considers these fiction areas:** Contemporary issues; detective/police/crime; gay/lesbian; historical; literary; mainstream/contemporary; mystery/suspense; young adult.

O➤ This agency specializes in books for, by and about women's issues including family, careers, health and spiritual development, business and sociology, history and economics. Emphasizing contemporary women's fiction and nonfiction books of interest to women.

How to Contact: Query with SASE, outline/proposal, SASE. Accepts e-mail and fax queries. Considers simultaneous queries. Responds in 1 week to queries; 6 weeks to mss. Returns materials only with SASE.

Recent Sales: Sold 30 titles in the last year. *Prayers for a Non-Believer*, by Julia Cameron (Putnam); *The Half-Empty Heart*, by Alan Downs (St. Martin's Press); *The Walls Around Us*, by David Owen (Simon & Schuster).

Terms: Agent receives 15% commission on domestic sales; 7½-10% (plus 7½-10% to co-agent) commission on foreign sales; 10-20% commission on dramatic rights sales. Charges client for special messenger or copying services, foreign mail and any other service requested by client.

⬛ **LAURENS R. SCHWARTZ AGENCY**, 5 E. 22nd St., Suite 15D, New York NY 10010-5325. (212)228-2614. **Contact:** Laurens R. Schwartz. Estab. 1984. Represents 100 clients.

Represents: Nonfiction books, novels, general mix of nonfiction and fiction. Also handles movie and TV tie-ins, licensing and merchandising.

How to Contact: Query with SASE. No unsolicited mss. Responds in 1 month to queries. "Have had 18 best-sellers."

Terms: Agent receives 15% commission on domestic sales; 25% commission on foreign sales. "No client fees except for photocopying, and that fee is avoided by an author providing necessary copies or, in certain instances, transferring files on diskette or by e-mail attachment." Where necessary to bring a project into publishing form, editorial work and some rewriting provided as part of service. Works with authors on long-term career goals and promotion.

Tips: "I do not like receiving mass mailings sent to all agents. I am extremely selective—only take on one to three new clients a year. Do not send everything you have ever written. Choose one work and promote that. Always include an SASE. Never send your only copy. Always include a background sheet on yourself and a one-page synopsis of the work (too many summaries end up being as long as the work)."

⬛ **SEDGEBAND LITERARY ASSOCIATES**, 7312 Martha Lane, Fort Worth TX 76112. (817)496-3652. Fax: (425)952-9518. E-mail: queries@sedgeband.com. Website: www.sedgeband.com. **Contact:** David Duperre or Ginger Norton. Estab. 1997. 50% of clients are new/unpublished writers. Currently handles: 50% nonfiction books; 50% fiction novels.

Member Agents: David Duperre (literary, scripts, mystery, suspense); Ginger Norton (romance, horror, nonfiction, mainstream/contemporary).

Represents: Nonfiction books, novels, novellas. **Considers these fiction areas:** Action/adventure; experimental; horror; literary; mainstream/contemporary; mystery/suspense; romance.

O➤ This agency is looking for talented writers who have patience and are willing to work hard. Actively seeking new nonfiction writers, some fiction.

How to Contact: Query with SASE. No phone queries accepted. No full mss. Accepts e-mail queries with no attachments; repsonds in 1 week. Responds in 4 months to written queries Responds in 4 months to requested mss. Returns materials only with SASE. Obtains most new clients through queries, the Internet, referrals.

Recent Sales: Sold 28 titles in the last year. *The Torso Murders of Victorian London* (Mcfarland); *Kiss Me, Kat* (Lionhearted); *Silent Screams* (Gardenia Press).

Terms: Agent receives 15% commission on domestic sales; 20% commission on foreign sales. Offers written contract, binding for 1 year; 30-day written notice must be given to terminate contract. Charges clients for postage, photocopies, long distance calls, etc., "until we make a sale to an established publisher. We do not charge any reading or retainer fees."

Tips: "We care about writers and books, not just money, but we care about the industry as well. We will not represent anyone who might hurt our clients or our reputation. We expect our writers to work hard and to be patient. Do not send a rude query, it will get you nowhere. If we ask to see your book, send it as soon as possible. Don't wait around or ask a bunch of irrelevant questions about movie rights and so forth, *(at this point we haven't even offered to represent you!)*. If you can't write a synopsis, don't bother to query us. Don't handwrite your query or send us samples of your writing that are handwritten—we won't read any of it. Be professional."

⬛ **LYNN SELIGMAN, LITERARY AGENT**, 400 Highland Ave., Upper Montclair NJ 07043. (973)783-3631. **Contact:** Lynn Seligman. Estab. 1985. Member of Women's Media Group. Represents 32 clients. 15% of clients are new/unpublished writers. Currently handles: 85% nonfiction books; 15% novels.

● Prior to opening her agency, Ms. Seligman worked in the subsidiary rights department of Doubleday and Simon & Schuster, and served as an agent with Julian Bach Literary Agency (now IMG Literary Agency).

Represents: Nonfiction books, novels. **Considers these fiction areas:** Detective/police/crime; ethnic; fantasy; feminist; gay/lesbian; historical; horror; humor/satire; literary; mainstream/contemporary; mystery/suspense; romance (contemporary, gothic, historical, regency); science fiction.

O➤ This agency specializes in "general nonfiction and fiction. I do illustrated and photography books and represent several photographers for books." This agency does not handle children or young adult books.

How to Contact: Query with SASE, 1 sample chapter(s), outline/proposal. Prefers to read materials exclusively.

No e-mail or fax queries. Considers simultaneous queries. Responds in 2 weeks to queries; 2 months to mss. Returns materials only with SASE. Obtains most new clients through referrals from other writers or editors.

Recent Sales: Sold 10 titles in the last year. *Tempting a Lady and a Lady's Heart*, by Barbara Pierce.

Terms: Agent receives 15% commission on domestic sales; 25% commission on foreign sales. Charges clients for photocopying, unusual postage or telephone expenses (checking first with the author), express mail.

◗ SERENDIPITY LITERARY AGENCY, LLC, 732 Fulton St., Suite 3, Brooklyn NY 11238. (718)230-7689. Fax: (718)230-7689. E-mail: rbrooks@serendipitylit.com. Website: www.serendipitylit.com. **Contact:** Regina Brooks. Estab. 2000. Represents 30 clients. 20% of clients are new/unpublished writers. Currently handles: 60% nonfiction books; 40% novels.

- Prior to becoming an agent, Ms. Brooks was an acquisitions editor for John Wiley & Sons, Inc. and McGraw-Hill Companies.

Represents: Nonfiction books, novels, juvenile books, scholarly books, textbooks, children's. **Considers these fiction areas:** Action/adventure; confession; ethnic; historical; juvenile; literary; multicultural; mystery/suspense; picture books; romance; thriller.

- ☛ Serendipity provides developmental editing. "We help build marketing plans for nontraditional outlets." Actively seeking African-American nonfiction, computer books (nonfiction), juvenile books. Does not want to receive poetry.

How to Contact: Submit outline, 1 sample chapter(s), SASE. Prefers to read materials exclusively. Responds in 2 months to queries; 3 months to mss. Obtains most new clients through recommendations from others, conferences.

Recent Sales: This agency prefers not to share information on specific sales. Recent sales available upon request by prospective client.

Terms: Agent receives 15% commission on domestic sales; 20% commission on foreign sales. Offers written contract; 60-day notice must be given to terminate contract. Charges clients $200 upon signing for office fees or office fees will be taken from any advance. "If author requests editing services, I can offer a list of potential services." 0% of business is derived from referral to editing services.

Tips: "Looking for African-American children's books. We also represent illustrators."

◖ THE SEYMOUR AGENCY, 475 Miner St., Canton NY 13617. (315)386-1831. Fax: (315)386-1037. E-mail: marysue@slic.com. Website: www.theseymouragency.com. **Contact:** Mary Sue Seymour. Estab. 1992. Represents 100 clients. 20% of clients are new/unpublished writers. Currently handles: 70% nonfiction books; 30% novels.

- Ms. Seymour is a retired New York State certified teacher.

Represents: Nonfiction books, novels (romance). **Considers these fiction areas:** Religious/inspirational; romance (contemporary, gothic, historical, medieval, regency); westerns/frontier.

- ☛ Actively seeking nonfiction and well-written romance. Does not want to receive screenplays, short stories, poetry, general novels, New Age.

How to Contact: Query with SASE, synopsis, first 50 pages for romance. Accepts e-mail queries. No fax queries. Considers simultaneous queries. Responds in 1 month to queries; 3 months to mss. Returns materials only with SASE.

Recent Sales: *Heart of a Hunter*, by Betty Davidson (Berkley).

Terms: Agent receives 15% commission on domestic sales; 20% commission on foreign sales. Offers written contract, binding for 1 year. This agency charges unpublished authors $4.97 for sending out a copy of a manuscript; Writers reimbursed for office fees after the sale of ms.

Writers' Conferences: RWA conferences.

Tips: "Send query, synopsis and first 50 pages. If you don't hear from us, you didn't send SASE. We are looking for nonfiction and romance—women in jeopardy, suspense, contemporary, historical, regency and any well-written fiction and nonfiction by credentialed authors."

◕ SHAPIRO-LICHTMAN, Shapiro-Lichtman Building, 8827 Beverly Blvd., Los Angeles CA 90048. (310)859-8877. Fax: (310)859-7153. **Contact:** Martin Shapiro. Estab. 1969. Signatory of WGA.

Represents: Nonfiction books, novels, novellas, feature film, TV movie of the week, episodic drama, sitcom, animation (movie, TV), miniseries, soap opera, variety show. **Considers these fiction areas:** Action/adventure; comic books/cartoon; confession; contemporary issues; detective/police/crime; erotica; ethnic; experimental; family saga; fantasy; feminist; gay/lesbian; glitz; gothic; hi-lo; historical; horror; humor/satire; juvenile; literary; mainstream/contemporary; military/war; multicultural; multimedia; mystery/suspense; New Age; occult; picture books; plays; romance; science fiction; short story collections; spiritual; sports; thriller; translation; westerns/frontier; young adult.

How to Contact: Query with SASE. Responds in 10 days to queries. Returns materials only with SASE. Obtains most new clients through recommendations from others.

Recent Sales: This agency prefers not to share information on specific sales.

Terms: Agent receives 10% commission on domestic sales; 20% commission on foreign sales. Offers written contract, binding for 2 years.

WENDY SHERMAN ASSOCIATES, INC., 450 Seventh Ave., Suite 3004, New York NY 10123. (212)279-9027. Fax: (212)279-8863. E-mail: wendy@wsherman.com. **Contact:** Wendy Sherman. Estab. 1999. Member of AAR. Represents 30 clients. 30% of clients are new/unpublished writers. Currently handles: 50% nonfiction books; 50% novels.

● Prior to opening the agency, Ms. Sherman worked for The Aaron Priest agency and was vice president, executive director of Henry Holt, associate publisher, subsidary rights director, sales and marketing director.

Member Agents: Jessica Lichtenstein; Wendy Sherman.

Represents: Nonfiction books, novels. **Considers these fiction areas:** Literary; women's.

○─┐ "We specialize in developing new writers as well as working with more established writers. My experience as a publisher has proven to be a great asset to my clients."

How to Contact: Query with SASE, or send outline/proposal, 1 sample chapter. All unsolicited mss returned unopened. Considers simultaneous queries. Responds in 1 month to queries. Returns materials only with SASE. Obtains most new clients through recommendations from others.

Recent Sales: Sold 14 titles in the last year. *Real Love* , by Greg Baer, M.D. (Penguin Putnam); *The Cloud Atlas*, by Liam Callanan (Delacorte); *The Holy Thief*, by Rabbi Mark Borowitz and Alan Eisenstock (William Morrow). Other clients include D.W. Buffa, William Lashner, Nani Power, Sarah Stonich, American Dance Foundation, Howard Bahr, Lundy Bancroft, Tom Schweich, Suzanne Chazin.

Terms: Agent receives 15% commission on domestic sales; 20% commission on foreign sales. Offers written contract. Charges for photocopying of ms, messengers, express mail services, etc. (reasonable, standard expenses).

ROSALIE SIEGEL, INTERNATIONAL LITERARY AGENCY, INC., 1 Abey Dr., Pennington NJ 08534. (609)737-1007. Fax: (609)737-3708. **Contact:** Rosalie Siegel. Estab. 1977. Member of AAR. Represents 35 clients. 10% of clients are new/unpublished writers. Currently handles: 45% nonfiction books; 45% novels; 10% young adult books and short story collections for current clients.

Represents: Nonfiction books, novels, short story collections, young adult books.

How to Contact: Obtains most new clients through referrals from writers and friends.

Terms: Agent receives 15% commission on domestic sales; 20% commission on foreign sales. Offers written contract; 60-day notice must be given to terminate contract. Charges clients for photocopying.

Tips: "I'm not looking for new authors in an active way."

SILVER SCREEN PLACEMENTS, 602 65th St., Downers Grove IL 60516-3020. (630)963-2124. Fax: (630)963-1998. E-mail: silverscreen11@yahoo.com. **Contact:** William Levin. Estab. 1989. Signatory of WGA. Represents 14 clients. 80% of clients are new/unpublished writers.

● Prior to opening his agency, Mr. Levin did product placement for motion pictures/TV.

Member Agents: Bernadette LaHaie, Jeff Dudley.

Represents: Novels, movie and feature film scripts. **Considers these fiction areas:** All genres.

How to Contact: Brief. Accepts e-mail queries. No fax queries. Responds in 2 weeks to queries. Obtains most new clients through recommendations from others, listings with WGA.

Recent Sales: Sold 2 titles and sold 3 scripts in the last year. This agency prefers not to share information on specific sales. Other clients include C. Geier, N. Melamed, R. Melley, and N. Russell.

Terms: Agent receives 15% (manuscript) commission on domestic sales; 10% (screenplay) commission on dramatic rights sales. May make referrals to freelance editors. Use of said editors does not ensure representation.

Tips: "No 'cute' queries please."

JEFFREY SIMMONS LITERARY AGENCY, 10 Lowndes Square, London SWIX 9HA, England. (020)7235 8852. Fax: (020)7235 9733. **Contact:** Jeffrey Simmons. Estab. 1978. Represents 43 clients. 40% of clients are new/unpublished writers. Currently handles: 60% nonfiction books; 40% novels.

● Prior to becoming an agent, Mr. Simmons was a publisher and he is also an author.

Represents: Nonfiction books, novels. **Considers these fiction areas:** Action/adventure; confession; detective/police/crime; family saga; literary; mainstream/contemporary; mystery/suspense; thriller.

○─┐ This agency seeks to handle good books and promising young writers. "My long experience in publishing and as an author and ghostwriter means I can offer an excellent service all round, especially in terms of editorial experience where appropriate." Actively seeking quality fiction. Does not want to receive science fiction, horror, fantasy, juvenile, academic books, specialist subjects (i.e., cooking, gardening, religious).

How to Contact: Submit sample chapter, outline/proposal, IRCs if necessary, SASE. Prefers to read materials exclusively. Responds in 1 week to queries; 1 month to mss. Obtains most new clients through recommendations from others, solicitations.

Recent Sales: Sold 18 titles in the last year. *Friendly Fire*, by Picknett, Prince & Prior (mainstream); *Nelson: Love and Fame* (Yale); *Burmese Secrets* (Murray).

Terms: Agent receives 10-15% commission on domestic sales; 15% commission on foreign sales. Offers written contract, binding for lifetime of book in question or until it becomes out of print.

Tips: "When contacting us with an outline/proposal, include a brief biographical note (listing any previous publications, with publishers and dates). Preferably tell us if the book has already been offered elsewhere."

IRENE SKOLNICK LITERARY AGENCY, 22 W. 23rd St., 5th Floor, New York NY 10010. (212)727-3648. Fax: (212)727-1024. E-mail: sirene35@aol.com. **Contact:** Irene Skolnick. Estab. 1993. Member of AAR. Represents 45 clients. 75% of clients are new/unpublished writers.
Member Agents: Irene Skolnick; Laura Friedman Williams.
Represents: Nonfiction books (adult), novels (adult). **Considers these fiction areas:** Contemporary issues; literary; mainstream/contemporary.
How to Contact: Query with SASE, outline, sample chapter(s). Accepts e-mail and fax queries. Considers simultaneous queries. Responds in 1 month to queries. Returns materials only with SASE.
Recent Sales: *In Vivo*, by Allegra Goodman (Dial); *Don't Get Too Comfortable*, by David Rakoff (Doubleday); *The Pieces from Berlin*, by Michael Pye (Knopf).
Terms: Agent receives 15% commission on domestic sales; 20% commission on foreign sales. Sometimes offers criticism service; Charges for international postage, photocopying over 40 pages.

BEVERLEY SLOPEN LITERARY AGENCY, 131 Bloor St. W., Suite 711, Toronto ON M5S 1S3, Canada. (416)964-9598. Fax: (416)921-7726. E-mail: slopen@inforamp.net. Website: www.slopenagency.on.ca. **Contact:** Beverley Slopen. Estab. 1974. Represents 60 clients. 40% of clients are new/unpublished writers. Currently handles: 60% nonfiction books; 40% novels.
• Prior to opening her agency, Ms. Slopen worked in publishing and as a journalist.
Represents: Nonfiction books, novels, scholarly books, textbooks (college). **Considers these fiction areas:** Literary; mystery/suspense.
○— This agency has a "strong bent towards Canadian writers." Actively seeking "serious nonfiction that is accessible and appealing to the general reader." Does not want to receive fantasy, science fiction or children's.
How to Contact: Query with SAE and IRCs. Returns materials only with SASE (Canadian postage). Accepts short e-mail queries. Considers simultaneous queries. Responds in 2 months to queries.
Recent Sales: Sold 25 titles in the last year. *Baroque-a-nova*, by Kevin Chong (Penguin Putnam); *The Rescue of Jerusalem*, by Henry T. Aubin (Doubleday Canada, Soho Press US); *Midnight Cab*, by James W. Nichol (Knopf Canada); *Fatal Passage*, by Ken McGoogan (Carroll & Graf US, Bantam Press UK). Other clients include Modris Eksteins, Michael Marrus, Timothy Brook, Robert Fulford, Donna Morrissey, Howard Engel, Morley Torgov.
Terms: Agent receives 15% commission on domestic sales; 10% commission on foreign sales. Offers written contract, binding for 2 years; 90-day notice must be given to terminate contract.
Tips: "Please no unsolicited manuscripts."

SPECTRUM LITERARY AGENCY, 320 Central Park W., Suite 1-D, New York NY 10025. Website: www.spectrumliteraryagency.com. **Contact:** Eleanor Wood, president. Represents 80 clients. Currently handles: 10% nonfiction books; 90% novels.
Member Agents: Lucienne Diver.
Represents: Nonfiction books, novels. **Considers these fiction areas:** Contemporary issues; fantasy; historical; mainstream/contemporary; mystery/suspense; romance; science fiction.
How to Contact: Query with SASE. No e-mail or fax queries. Responds in 2 months to queries. Obtains most new clients through recommendations from authors and others.
Recent Sales: Sold over 100 titles in the last year. This agency prefers not to share information on specific sales.
Terms: Agent receives 15% commission on domestic sales. Deducts for photocopying and book orders.

THE SPIELER AGENCY, 154 W. 57th St., 13th Floor, Room 135, New York NY 10019. (212)757-4439. Fax: (212)333-2019. **Contact:** Katya Batter. Estab. 1981. Represents 160 clients. 2% of clients are new/unpublished writers.
• Prior to opening his agency, Mr. Spieler was a magazine editor.
Member Agents: Joe Spieler; John Thornton (nonfiction); Lisa M. Ross (fiction/nonfiction); Deirdre Mullane (nonfiction/fiction); Eric Myers. Spieler Agency West (Oakland, CA): Victoria Shoemaker.
Represents: Nonfiction books, literary fiction, children's books. **Considers these fiction areas:** Experimental; family saga; feminist; gay/lesbian; humor/satire; literary.
How to Contact: Query with SASE. Prefers to read materials exclusively. No fax queries. Considers simultaneous queries. Responds in 2 weeks to queries; 5 weeks to mss. Returns materials only with SASE. Obtains most new clients through recommendations.
Recent Sales: *The Clothes They Stood Up In*, by Alan Bennett (Random House).
Terms: Agent receives 15% commission on domestic sales. Charges clients for messenger bills, photocopying, postage.
Writers' Conferences: London Bookfair.

PHILIP G. SPITZER LITERARY AGENCY, 50 Talmage Farm Lane, East Hampton NY 11937. (631)329-3650. Fax: (631)329-3651. E-mail: spitzer516@aol.com. **Contact:** Philip Spitzer. Estab. 1969. Member of AAR. Represents 60 clients. 10% of clients are new/unpublished writers. Currently handles: 50% nonfiction books; 50% novels.

● Prior to opening his agency, Mr. Spitzer served at New York University Press, McGraw-Hill and the John Cushman Associates literary agency.

Represents: Nonfiction books, novels. **Considers these fiction areas:** Contemporary issues; detective/police/crime; literary; mainstream/contemporary; mystery/suspense; sports; thriller.

O→ This agency specializes in mystery/suspense, literary fiction, sports, general nonfiction (no how-to).

How to Contact: Query with SASE, outline, 1 sample chapter(s). Responds in 1 week to queries; 6 weeks to mss. Obtains most new clients through recommendations from others.

Recent Sales: *Chasing the Dime*, by Michael Connelly (Little, Brown); *White Doves at Morning*, by James Lee Burke (Hyperion); *Eleanora Duse*, by Helen Sheehy (Knopf); *Air Burial*, by Jean Shields (Carroll and Graff).

Terms: Agent receives 15% commission on domestic sales; 20% commission on foreign sales. Charges clients for photocopying.

Writers' Conferences: BEA (Chicago).

◖ **NANCY STAUFFER ASSOCIATES**, P.O. Box 1203, Darien CT 06820. (203)655-3717. Fax: (203)655-3704. E-mail: nanstauf@optonline.net. **Contact:** Nancy Stauffer Cahoon. Estab. 1989. Member of the Authors Guild. 5% of clients are new/unpublished writers. Currently handles: 15% nonfiction books; 85% novels.

Represents: Nonfiction books, novels (literary fiction). **Considers these fiction areas:** Contemporary issues; literary; mainstream/contemporary; regional.

How to Contact: Obtains most new clients through referrals from existing clients.

Recent Sales: *Ten Little Indians*, by Sherman Alexie (Grove/Atlantic); *No Enemy But Time*, by William C. Harris (St. Martin's Press); *An Unfinished Life*, by Mark Spragg.

Terms: Agent receives 15% commission on domestic sales; 20% commission on foreign sales; 20% commission on dramatic rights sales.

◖ **STEELE-PERKINS LITERARY AGENCY**, 26 Island Lane, Canandaigua NY 14424. (585)396-9290. Fax: (585)396-3579. E-mail: pattiesp@aol.com. **Contact:** Pattie Steele-Perkins. Member of AAR, RWA. Currently handles: 100% Romance and mainstream women's fiction.

Represents: Novels. **Considers these fiction areas:** Mainstream/contemporary; multicultural; romance; women's.

O→ Actively seeking romance, women's fiction and multicultural works.

How to Contact: Submit outline, 3 sample chapter(s), SASE. Considers simultaneous queries. Responds in 6 weeks to queries. Returns materials only with SASE. Obtains most new clients through recommendations from others, queries/solicitations.

Recent Sales: This agency prefers not to share information on specific sales.

Terms: Agent receives 15% commission on domestic sales. Offers written contract, binding for 1 year; 30-day notice must be given to terminate contract.

Writers' Conferences: National Conference of Romance Writers of America; Book Expo America Writers' Conferences.

Tips: "Be patient. E-mail rather than call. Make sure what you are sending is the best it can be."

STERLING LORD LITERISTIC, INC., 65 Bleecker St., New York NY 10012. (212)780-6050. Fax: (212)780-6095. **Contact:** Philippa Brophy. Estab. 1952. Signatory of WGA. Represents 600 clients. Currently handles: 50% nonfiction books; 50% novels.

Member Agents: Philippa Brophy; Laurie Liss; Chris Calhoun; Peter Matson; Sterling Lord; Claudia Cross; Neeti Madan; George Nicholson; Jim Rutman; Charlotte Sheedy.

Represents: Nonfiction books, novels, literary value considered first.

How to Contact: Query with SASE. Responds in 1 month to mss. Obtains most new clients through recommendations from others.

Recent Sales: This agency prefers not to share information on specific sales. Other clients include Kent Haruf, Dick Fancis, Mary Gordon, Sen. John McCain, Simon Winchester, James McBride, Billy Collins, Richard Paul Evans, Dave Pelzer.

Terms: Agent receives 15% commission on domestic sales; 20% commission on foreign sales. Offers written contract. Charges clients for photocopying.

◖ **STERNIG & BYRNE LITERARY AGENCY**, 3209 S. 55, Milwaukee WI 53219-4433. (414)328-8034. Fax: (414)328-8034. E-mail: jackbyrne@hotmail.com. Website: www.sff.net/people/jackbyrne. **Contact:** Jack Byrne. Estab. 1950s. Member of SFWA, MWA. Represents 30 clients. 10% of clients are new/unpublished writers. Accepting few new clients. Currently handles: 5% nonfiction books; 85% novels; 10% juvenile books.

Member Agents: Jack Byrne.

Represents: Nonfiction books, novels, juvenile books. **Considers these fiction areas:** Fantasy; horror; mystery/suspense; science fiction.

O→ "Our client list is comfortably full and our current needs are therefore quite limited." Actively seeking science fiction/fantasy by established writers. Does not want to receive romance, poetry, textbooks, highly specialized nonfiction.

How to Contact: Query with SASE. Accepts e-mail queries, no attachments. Responds in 3 weeks to queries; 3 months to mss. Returns materials only with SASE.

Recent Sales: Sold 16 titles in the last year. *When the Beast Ravens*, by E. Rose Sabin; *Stone of the Stars Trilogy*, by Alison Baird. Other clients include Jane Routley, Gerard Hourner, Betty Ren Wright, and Andre Norton.

Terms: Agent receives 15% commission on domestic sales; 20% commission on foreign sales. Offers written contract; 60-day notice must be given to terminate contract.

Tips: "Don't send first drafts; have a professional presentation...including cover letter; know your field. Read what's been done...good and bad."

STIMOLA LITERARY STUDIO, 210 Crescent Ave., Leonia NJ 07605. Phone/fax: (201)944-9886. E-mail: ltrystudio@aol.com. **Contact:** Rosemary B. Stimola. Member of AAR.

Member Agents: Rosemary B. Stimola.

Represents: Preschool through young adult fiction/nonfiction.

How to Contact: Query with SASE, or via e-mail. Responds in 3 weeks to queries; 2 months to mss. Obtains most new clients through recommendations from others, solicitations.

Recent Sales: *Gregor the Overlander*, by Suzanne Collins; *Beacon Hill Boys*, by Ken Mochizuki; *Johnny Mutton, He's So Him!*, by James Proimos.

Terms: Agent receives 15% commission on domestic sales; 20% commission on foreign sales. Offers written contract, binding for 1 year; Covers all children's literary work not previously published or under agreement. notice must be given to terminate contract.

Tips: "No phone inquiries."

⚫ ROBIN STRAUS AGENCY, INC., 229 E. 79th St., New York NY 10021. (212)472-3282. Fax: (212)472-3833. E-mail: springbird@aol.com. **Contact:** Ms. Robin Straus. Estab. 1983. Member of AAR. Currently handles: 65% nonfiction books; 35% novels.

- Prior to becoming an agent, Robin Straus served as a subsidary rights manager at Random House and Doubleday and worked in editorial at Little, Brown.

Represents: Nonfiction books, novels. **Considers these fiction areas:** Contemporary issues; family saga; historical; literary; mainstream/contemporary.

- ⚙ This agency specializes in high quality fiction and nonfiction for adults (no genre fiction; no screenplays; no books for children). Takes on very few new clients.

How to Contact: Query with brief synopsis and opening chapter or 2. Responds and returns materials only with SASE. We do not download **any** submissions. Responds in 1 month to queries; 1 month to mss. Obtains most new clients through recommendations from others.

Recent Sales: This agency prefers not to share information on specific sales.

Terms: Agent receives 15% commission on domestic sales; 20% commission on foreign sales. Offers written contract. Charges for "photocopying, express mail services, messenger and foreign postage, etc. as incurred."

🌐 ⚙ THE SUSIJN AGENCY, 3rd Floor, 64 Great Titchfield St., London W1W 7QH, England. 0044 (207)580-6341. Fax: 0044 (207)580-8626. E-mail: info@thesusijnagency.com. Website: www.thesusijnagency.com. **Contact:** Laura Susijn, Charles Buchau. Estab. 1998. Currently handles: 15% nonfiction books; 85% novels.

- Prior to becoming an agent, Ms. Susijn was a rights director at Sheil Land Associates and at Fourth Estate Ltd.

Member Agents: Laura Susijn.

Represents: Nonfiction books, novels. **Considers these fiction areas:** Literary.

- ⚙ This agency specializes in international works, selling world rights, representing non-English language writing as well as English. Emphasis on cross-cultural subjects. Self-help, romance, sagas, science fiction, screenplays.

How to Contact: Submit outline, 2 sample chapter(s). Accepts e-mail and fax queries. Considers simultaneous queries. Responds in 2 months to queries. Returns materials only with SASE. Obtains most new clients through recommendations from others, via publishers in Europe and beyond.

Recent Sales: Sold 120 titles in the last year. *Gone*, by Helena Echlin (Secker and Warburg, UK); *Daalder*, by Philibert Schogt (4 Walls 8 Windows); *Prisoner in a Red Rose Chain*, by Jeffrey Moore (Weidenfeld & Nicholson) *Smell*, by Radhika Jha (Quartet Books); *The Formula One Fanatic*, by Koen Vergeer (Bloomsbury); *A Mouthful of Glass*, by Henk Van Woerden (Granta); *Fragile Science*, by Robin Baker (Macmillan); *East of Acre Lane*, by Alex Wheatle (Fourth Estate). Other clients include Vassallucci, Podium, Atlas, De Arbeiderspers, Tiderne Skifter, MB Agency, Van Oorschot

Terms: Agent receives 15% commission on domestic sales; 15-20% commission on foreign sales. Offers written contract; 6 weeks notice must be given to terminate contract. Charges clients for photocopying, buying copies only if sale is made.

⚫ THE JOHN TALBOT AGENCY, INC., 540 W. Boston Post Rd., PMB 266, Mamaroneck NY 10543-3437. (914)381-9463. Fax: (914)381-0507. E-mail: talbotagency@mac.com. Website: www.johntalbotagency.com.

Contact: John Talbot. Estab. 1998. Member of Authors Guild. Represents 50 clients. 15% of clients are new/unpublished writers. Currently handles: 35% nonfiction books; 65% novels.

● Prior to becoming an agent, Mr. Talbot was a book editor at Simon & Schuster and Putnam Berkley.

Represents: Nonfiction books, novels. **Considers these fiction areas:** Literary; mystery/suspense.

○━ This agency specializes in commercial suspense and literary fiction "by writers who are beginning to publish in magazines and literary journals." Also narrative nonfiction, especially outdoor adventure and spirituality. Does not want to receive children's books, science fiction, fantasy, westerns, poetry, screenplays.

How to Contact: Query via e-mail only. See website for instructions.

Recent Sales: Sold 30 titles in the last year. *The Edge of Justice*, by Clinton McKinzie (Delacorte/Dell); *Crush Depth*, by Joe Buff (Morrow); *Burden*, by Tony Walters (St. Martin's Press); *Around Again*, by Suzanne Strempek Shea (Pocket Books). Other clients include Doris Meredith, Peter Telep, Clarence Major.

Terms: Agent receives 15% commission on domestic sales; 20% commission on foreign sales. Offers written contract; 60 days notice must be given to terminate contract. Charges clients for photocopying, overnight delivery, additional copies of books needed for use in sale of subsidiary rights, and fees incurred for submitting mss or books overseas.

⊌ PATRICIA TEAL LITERARY AGENCY, 2036 Vista Del Rosa, Fullerton CA 92831-1336. Phone/fax: (714)738-8333. **Contact:** Patricia Teal. Estab. 1978. Member of AAR. Represents 20 clients. Currently handles: 10% nonfiction books; 90% novels.

Represents: Nonfiction books, novels. **Considers these fiction areas:** Glitz; mainstream/contemporary; mystery/suspense; romance (contemporary, historical).

○━ This agency specializes in women's fiction and commercial how-to and self-help nonfiction. Does not want to receive poetry, short stories, articles, science fiction, fantasy, regency romance.

How to Contact: *Published authors only.* Query with SASE. No e-mail or fax queries. Considers simultaneous queries. Responds in 10 days to queries; 6 weeks to mss. Returns materials only with SASE. Obtains most new clients through conferences, recommendations from authors and editors.

Recent Sales: Sold 20 titles in the last year. *The Black Sheep's Baby*, by Kathleen Creighton (Silhouette); *Man with a Message*, by Muriel Jensen (Harlequin).

Terms: Agent receives 10-15% commission on domestic sales; 20% commission on foreign sales. Offers written contract, binding for 1 year. Charges clients for postage and phone calls.

Writers' Conferences: Romance Writers of America conferences; Asilomar (California Writers Club); BEA; Bouchercon; Hawaii Writers Conference (Maui).

Tips: "Include SASE with all correspondence. Taking on very few authors."

Ⓝ ◘ 3 SEAS LITERARY AGENCY, P.O. Box 8571, Madison WI 53708. (608)221-4306. E-mail: threeseaslit@aol.com. Website: www.threeseaslit.com. **Contact:** Michelle Grajkowski. Estab. 2000. Member of Romance Writers of America, Society of Children's Books Writers and Illustrators. Represents 40 clients. 50% of clients are new/unpublished writers. Currently handles: 30% nonfiction books; 60% novels; 10% juvenile books.

● Prior to becoming an agent, Ms. Grajkowski worked in both sales and in purchasing for a medical facility. She has a degree in journalism from the University of Wisconsin-Madison.

Represents: Nonfiction books, novels, juvenile books, scholarly books. **Considers these fiction areas:** Action/adventure; detective/police/crime; family saga; fantasy (only if there is romance in the story); historical; horror; humor/satire; juvenile; literary; mainstream/contemporary; mystery/suspense; picture books; religious/inspirational; romance; science fiction (only if there is romance in the story); thriller; westerns/frontier; young adult; Psychic/supernatural.

○━ 3 Seas focuses on romance and women's fiction. "We also handle a variety of nonfiction and children's stories. We believe in working with our clients to help plan their careers." Actively seeking authors who are committed to their careers and are determined to make it in this business. "We typically represent our clients as a whole, not just on a project-by-project basis." Does not want to receive science fiction and fantasy, unless the mss have a romance flair.

How to Contact: For fiction: Please query with first 3 chapters, a synopsis and your bio. Considers simultaneous queries. Responds in 2 months to queries; 3 months to mss. Returns materials only with SASE. Obtains most new clients through recommendations from others, conferences.

Recent Sales: Sold 20 titles in the last year. Other clients include Marshall Cook, Winnie Griggs, Diane Amos, Rebekah Shardy, Ellen Browning, Lisa Mondello, Natalie Damschroder, Juliet Blackett, Jessica Barkley, Chris deSmet, Donna Smith.

Terms: Agent receives 15% commission on domestic sales; 20% commission on foreign sales. Offers written contract, binding for 30 days.

Writers' Conferences: RWA National Conference (New York, July); Romantic Times Conference (Kansas City, October); Rocky Mountain Fiction Writers (Denver, April); New England RWA Conference (Boston, April).

◘ LYNDA TOLLS LITERARY AGENCY, P.O. Box 1785, Bend OR 97709. (541)388-3510. E-mail: blswarts@juno.com. **Contact:** Lynda Tolls Swarts. Estab. 1995. Represents 8 clients. 20% of clients are new/unpublished writers. Currently handles: 70% nonfiction books; 30% novels.

Represents: Nonfiction books, novels. **Considers these fiction areas:** Ethnic (multicultural); historical; literary; mystery/suspense; romance; contemporary, inspirational, women's.
How to Contact: Query with SASE, Nonfiction: send query including the concept of your book, market, competing titles, and your expertise. Fiction: query with synopsis and first 30 pages.
Writers' Conferences: Williamette Writers' Conference; Surrey Writers' Conference; Idaho Writers' Conference.

◻ **VENTURE LITERARY**, 8895 Towne Centre Dr., Suite 105, #141, San Diego CA 92122. (619)807-1887. E-mail: agents@ventureliterary.com. Website: www.ventureliterary.com. **Contact:** Frank R. Scatoni. Estab. 1999. Represents 30 clients. 50% of clients are new/unpublished writers. Currently handles: 95% nonfiction books; 5% novels.
  • Prior to becoming an agent, Mr. Scatoni worked as an editor at Simon & Schuster.
Member Agents: Frank R. Scatoni (general nonfiction, including biography, memoir, narrative nonfiction, sports and serious nonfiction); Greg Dinkin (general nonfiction/business, gambling).
Represents: Nonfiction books, novels. **Considers these fiction areas:** Action/adventure; detective/police/crime; literary; mainstream/contemporary; mystery/suspense; sports; thriller.
  ⚷ Specializes in nonfiction, sports, business, natural history, biography, gambling. Actively seeking nonfiction.
How to Contact: Submit proposal with 3 sample chapters. Considers simultaneous queries. Responds in 3 months to queries; 6 months to mss. Returns materials only with SASE. Obtains most new clients through recommendations from others.
Recent Sales: *Stocking Up on Sin*, by Caroline Waxler (Wiley); *The Last True Cowboys*, by Erich Krauss (Ken Singleton).
Terms: Agent receives 15% commission on domestic sales; 20% commission on foreign sales. Offers written contract. Charges clients for photocopying and postage only.
Writers' Conferences: San Diego State University Writers Conference (San Diego CA); Southern California Writers Conference (Los Angeles and San Diego).

◻ **THE VINES AGENCY, INC.**, 648 Broadway, Suite 901, New York NY 10012. (212)777-5522. Fax: (212)777-5978. E-mail: jv@vinesagency.com. Website: www.vinesagency.com. **Contact:** James C. Vines, Paul Surdi, Ali Ryan, Gary Neuwirth. Estab. 1995. Signatory of WGA; Author's Guild. Represents 52 clients. 20% of clients are new/unpublished writers. Currently handles: 50% nonfiction books; 50% novels.
  • Prior to opening his agency, Mr. Vines served as an agent with the Virginia Barber Literary Agency.
Member Agents: James C. Vines (quality and commercial fiction and nonfiction); Gary Neuwirth; Paul Surdi (women's fiction, ethnic fiction, quality nonfiction); Ali Ryan (women's fiction and nonfiction, mainstream).
Represents: Nonfiction books, novels, feature film, TV scripts. **Considers these fiction areas:** Action/adventure; contemporary issues; detective/police/crime; ethnic; experimental; family saga; feminist; gay/lesbian; historical; horror; humor/satire; literary; mainstream/contemporary; mystery/suspense; occult; psychic/supernatural; regional; romance (contemporary, historical); science fiction; sports; thriller; westerns/frontier; women's.
  ⚷ This agency specializes in mystery, suspense, science fiction, women's fiction, ethnic fiction, mainstream novels, screenplays, teleplays.
How to Contact: Submit outline, 3 sample chapter(s), SASE. Accepts e-mail and fax queries. Considers simultaneous queries. Responds in 2 weeks to queries; 1 month to mss. Returns materials only with SASE. Obtains most new clients through query letters, recommendations from others, reading short stories in magazines, soliciting conferences.
Recent Sales: Sold 48 titles and sold 5 scripts in the last year. *A Fine Dark Line*, by Joe R. Lansdale; *Loving Donovan*, by Bernice McFadden; *Bad Seed*, by Beth Saulnier.
Terms: Agent receives 15% commission on domestic sales; 25% commission on foreign sales. Offers written contract, binding for 1 year; 30 days notice must be given to terminate contract. 100% of business is derived from commissions on ms sales. Charges clients for foreign postage, messenger services, photocopying.
Writers' Conferences: Maui Writer's Conference.
Tips: "Do not follow up on submissions with phone calls to the agency. The agency will read and respond by mail only. Do not pack your manuscript in plastic 'peanuts' that will make us have to vacuum the office after opening the package containing your manuscript. Always enclose return postage."

◻ **WALES LITERARY AGENCY, INC.**, P.O. Box 9428, Seattle WA 98109-0428. (206)284-7114. E-mail: waleslit@aol.com. **Contact:** Elizabeth Wales, Meg Lemke. Estab. 1988. Member of AAR, Book Publishers' Northwest, Pacific Northwest Booksellers Association, PEN. Represents 65 clients. 10% of clients are new/unpublished writers. Currently handles: 60% nonfiction books; 40% fiction.
  • Prior to becoming an agent, Ms. Wales worked at Oxford University Press and Viking Penguin.
Member Agents: Elizabeth Wales.
  ⚷ This agency specializes in narrative nonfiction and quality, mainstream and literary fiction. Does not handle screenplays, children's literature, genre fiction, most category nonfiction.
How to Contact: Query with cover letter, writing sample (approx. 30 pages) and SASE. No phone or fax queries. Prefers regular mail queries, but accepts one-page e-mail queries with no attachments. Considers simultaneous queries. Responds in 3 weeks to queries; 6 weeks to mss. Returns materials only with SASE.

Recent Sales: *Windfalls*, by Jean Hegland (Atria/Simon & Schuster); *The Bathhouse*, by Farnoosh Moshiri Scigliano (Houghton-Mifflin); *Excerpts from a Family Medical Directory*, by Rebecca Brown (University of Wisconsin Press).

Terms: Agent receives 15% commission on domestic sales; 20% commission on foreign sales.

Writers' Conferences: Pacific NW Writers Conference (Seattle); Writers at Work (Salt Lake City); Writing Rendezvous (Anchorage); Willamette Writers (Portland).

Tips: "Especially interested in work that espouses a progressive cultural or political view, projects a new voice, or simply shares an important, compelling story. Encourages writers living in the Pacific Northwest, West Coast, Alaska and Pacific Rim countries, and writers from historically underrepresented groups, such as gay and lesbian writers and writers of color, to submit work (but does not discourage writers outside these areas). Most importantly, whether in fiction or nonfiction, the agency is looking for talented storytellers."

◙ JOHN A. WARE LITERARY AGENCY, 392 Central Park West, New York NY 10025-5801. (212)866-4733. Fax: (212)866-4734. **Contact:** John Ware. Estab. 1978. Represents 60 clients. 40% of clients are new/unpublished writers. Currently handles: 75% nonfiction books; 25% novels.

   ● Prior to opening his agency, Mr. Ware served as a literary agency with James Brown Associates/Curtis Brown, Ltd., and as an editor for Doubleday & Co.

Represents: Nonfiction books, novels. **Considers these fiction areas:** Detective/police/crime; mystery/suspense; thriller; Accessible literate noncategory fiction.

How to Contact: Query first by letter only, including SASE. No e-mail or fax queries. Considers simultaneous queries Responds in 2 weeks to queries.

Recent Sales: *Under the Banner of Heaven*, by Jon Krakauer (Doubleday); *The Traveller: A Biography of John Ledyard*, by Bill Gifford (St. Martin's); *Stealing Convenience: A Memoir of Simplicity*, by Eric Brende (HarperCollins).

Terms: Agent receives 15% commission on domestic sales; 20% commission on foreign sales; 15% commission on dramatic rights sales. Charges clients for messenger service, photocopying.

Tips: "Writers must have appropriate credentials for authorship of proposal (nonfiction) or manuscript (fiction); no publishing track record required. Open to good writing and interesting ideas by new or veteran writers."

◙ WATKINS LOOMIS AGENCY, INC., 133 E. 35th St., Suite 1, New York NY 10016. (212)532-0080. Fax: (212)889-0506. **Contact:** Katherine Fausset. Estab. 1908. Represents 150 clients.

Member Agents: Gloria Loomis (president); Katherine Fausset (agent).

Represents: Nonfiction books, novels, short story collections. **Considers these fiction areas:** Literary.

   ०━ This agency specializes in literary fiction, nonfiction.

How to Contact: Query with SASE, by standard mail only. Responds in 1 month to queries.

Recent Sales: This agency prefers not to share information on specific sales. Clients include Walter Mosley and Cornel West.

Terms: Agent receives 15% commission on domestic sales; 20% commission on foreign sales.

◙ WAXMAN LITERARY AGENCY, INC., 80 Fifth Ave., Suite 1101, New York NY 10011. Website: www.waxmanagency.com. Estab. 1997. Member of AAR. Represents 60 clients. 50% of clients are new/unpublished writers. Currently handles: 60% nonfiction books; 40% novels.

   ● Prior to opening his agency, Mr. Waxman was editor for five years at HarperCollins.

Member Agents: Scott Waxman (all categories of nonfiction, commercial fiction). **Considers these fiction areas:** Literary.

   ०━ "Looking for serious journalists and novelists with published works."

How to Contact: Query through website. All unsolicited mss returned unopened. Considers simultaneous queries. Responds in 2 weeks to queries; 6 weeks to mss. Returns materials only with SASE. Obtains most new clients through recommendations from others, solicitations, conferences.

Terms: Agent receives 15% commission on domestic sales; 25% commission on foreign sales. Offers written contract; 60 days notice must be given to terminate contract. Charges for photocopying, express mail, fax, international postage, book orders; Refers to editing services for clients only. 0% of business is derived from editing services.

◙ LYNN WHITTAKER, LITERARY AGENT, Graybill & English, LLC, 1875 Connecticut Ave. NW, Suite 712, Washington DC 20009. (202)588-9798, ext. 127. Fax: (202)457-0662. E-mail: lynnwhittaker@aol.com. Website: www.graybillandenglish.com. Estab. 1998. Member of AAR. Represents 24 clients. 10% of clients are new/unpublished writers. Currently handles: 85% nonfiction books; 15% novels.

   ● Prior to becoming an agent, Ms. Whittaker was an editor, owner of a small press, and taught at the college level.

Represents: Nonfiction books, novels, short story collections. **Considers these fiction areas:** Detective/police/crime; ethnic; historical; literary; multicultural; mystery/suspense; sports.

   ०━ "As a former editor, I especially enjoy working closely with writers to develop and polish their proposals and manuscripts." Actively seeking literary fiction, sports, history, creative nonfiction of all kinds, ethnic/

multicultural, women's stories & issues. Does not want to receive romance/women's commercial fiction, children's/young adult, religious, fantasy/horror.

How to Contact: Query with SASE, submit proposal package, outline, 2 sample chapter(s). Responds in 2 weeks to queries; 1 month to mss. Returns materials only with SASE. Obtains most new clients through recommendations from others.

Recent Sales: Clients include Michael Wilbon, Mariah Burton Nelson, Leonard Shapiro, John Tallmadge, Dorothy Sucher, Brooke Foster, James McGregor Burns.

Terms: Agent receives 15% commission on domestic sales; 20% commission on foreign sales. Offers written contract; 30 days notice must be given to terminate contract. Direct expenses for photocopying of proposals and mss, UPS/FedEx.

Writers' Conferences: Creative Nonfiction Conference, (Goucher College MD, August); Washington Independent Writers, (Washington DC, May); Hariette Austin Writers Conference, (Athens GA, July).

■ **WIESER & WIESER, INC.**, 25 E. 21st St., 6th Floor, New York NY 10010. (212)260-0860. **Contact:** Olga Wieser. Estab. 1975. 30% of clients are new/unpublished writers. Currently handles: 50% nonfiction books; 50% novels.

Member Agents: Jake Elwell (history, military, mysteries, romance, sports, thrillers); Olga Wieser (psychology, fiction, pop medical, literary fiction).

Represents: Nonfiction books, novels. **Considers these fiction areas:** Contemporary issues; detective/police/crime; historical; literary; mainstream/contemporary; mystery/suspense; romance; thriller.

○┅ This agency specializes in mainstream fiction and nonfiction.

How to Contact: Query with outline/proposal and SASE. Responds in 2 weeks to queries. Obtains most new clients through queries, authors' recommendations and industry professionals.

Recent Sales: *Mary: The Chosen One*, by Roberta Kells Dorr (Revell); *Eddie Rickenbacker*, by H. Paul Jeffers (Presidio); *Sea of Grey*, by Dewey Lambdin (St. Martin's Press); *The Voyage of the Hunley*, by Edwin P. Hoyt (Burford Books); *Cyclops*, by Jim DeFelice (Pocket); *Fire Flight*, by John Nance (Simon & Schuster).

Terms: Agent receives 15% commission on domestic sales; 20% commission on foreign sales. Offers written contract. Charges clients for photocopying and overseas mailing.

Writers' Conferences: BEA; Frankfurt Book Fair.

■ **WILLIAMS LITERARY AGENCY**, RI Box 109H, Kosciusko MS 39090-9706. (662)674-5703. Fax: (305)489-2329. E-mail: submissions@williamsliteraryagency.com. Website: williamsliteraryagency.com. **Contact:** Sheri Homan Williams. Estab. 1997. Represents 64 clients.

● Prior to becoming an agent, Sheri Homan Williams was a freelance writer and literary assistant.

Member Agents: Sheri Homan Williams, owner, literary agent (fiction, non-fiction, novels, scripts); Ann Rought, literary assistant, editor (fiction, non-fiction, novels, juvenile); Kathie Erwin, associate agent (non-fiction, scholarly); Shannon Edwards, associate agent (fiction, non-fiction, novels).

Represents: Nonfiction books, novels, juvenile books, movie scripts, feature film, TV scripts, animation, miniseries.

○┅ "Looks for well-written books with a strong plot and consistency throughout."

How to Contact: Query with SASE or submit cover letter, outline/proposal, and bio. Considers simultaneous queries. Reports in 3-6 months, depending on the number of submissions in-house. Returns materials only with SASE.

■ **WRITERS HOUSE**, 21 W. 26th St., New York NY 10010. (212)685-2400. Fax: (212)685-6550. Estab. 1974. Member of AAR. Represents 440 clients. 50% of clients are new/unpublished writers. Currently handles: 25% nonfiction books; 40% novels; 35% juvenile books.

Member Agents: Albert Zuckerman (major novels, thrillers, women's fiction, important nonfiction); Amy Berkower (major juvenile authors, women's fiction, art and decorating, psychology); Merrilee Heifetz (quality children's fiction, science fiction and fantasy, popular culture, literary fiction); Susan Cohen (juvenile and young adult fiction and nonfiction, Judaism, women's issues); Susan Ginsburg (serious and popular fiction, true crime, narrative nonfiction, personality books, cookbooks); Michele Rubin (serious nonfiction); Robin Rue (commercial fiction and nonfiction, YA fiction); Jennifer Lyons (literary, commercial fiction, international fiction, nonfiction and illustrated); Jodi Reamer (juvenile and young adult fiction and nonfiction, adult commercial fiction, popular culture); Simon Lipskar (literary and commercial fiction, narrative nonfiction); Nicole Pitesa (juvenile and young adult fiction, literary fiction); Steven Malk (juvenile and young adult fiction and non-fiction).

Represents: Nonfiction books, novels, juvenile books. **Considers these fiction areas:** Action/adventure; comic books/cartoon; confession; contemporary issues; detective/police/crime; erotica; ethnic; experimental; family saga; fantasy; feminist; gay/lesbian; glitz; gothic; hi-lo; historical; horror; humor/satire; juvenile; literary; mainstream/contemporary; military/war; multicultural; multimedia; mystery/suspense; New Age; occult; picture books; plays; poetry; poetry in translation; psychic/supernatural; regional; religious/inspirational; romance; science fiction; short story collections; spiritual; sports; thriller; translation; westerns/frontier; young adult; women's.

○┅ This agency specializes in all types of popular fiction and nonfiction. Does not want to receive scholarly, professional, poetry, plays or screenplays.

How to Contact: Query with SASE. No e-mail or fax queries. Responds in 1 month to queries. Obtains most new clients through recommendations from others.

Recent Sales: Sold 200-300 titles in the last year. *Next*, by Michael Lewis (Norton); *Art of Deception*, by Ridley Pearson (Hyperion); *Report from Ground Zero*, by Dennis Smith (Viking); *The Villa*, by Nora Roberts (Penguin/Putnam); *Captain Underpants*, by Dav Pilkey (Scholastic). Other clients include Francine Pascal, Ken Follett, Stephen Hawking, Linda Howard, F. Paul Wilson, Neil Gaiman and Laurel Hamilton.

Terms: Agent receives 15% commission on domestic sales; 20% commission on foreign sales. Offers written contract, binding for 1 year. Agency charges fees for copying manuscripts and proposals and overseas airmail of books.

Tips: "Do not send mss. Write a compelling letter. If you do, we'll ask to see your work."

WRITERS' REPRESENTATIVES, INC., 116 W. 14th St., 11th Floor, New York NY 10011-7305. (212)620-0023. E-mail: transom@writersreps.com. Website: www.writersreps.com. **Contact:** Glen Hartley or Lynn Chu. Estab. 1985. Represents 130 clients. 5% of clients are new/unpublished writers. Currently handles: 90% nonfiction books; 10% novels.
- Prior to becoming agents, Ms. Chu was a lawyer, and Mr. Hartley worked at Simon & Schuster, Harper & Row and Cornell University Press.

Member Agents: Lynn Chu; Glen Hartley; Catharine Sprinkel.

Represents: Nonfiction books, novels. **Considers these fiction areas:** Literary.
- This agency specializes in serious nonfiction. Actively seeking serious nonfiction and quality fiction. Does not want to receive motion picture/television screenplays.

How to Contact: Prefers to read materials exclusively. Considers simultaneous queries. Obtains most new clients through "recommendations from our clients."

Recent Sales: Sold 30 titles in the last year. *The Shield of Achilles*, by Philip Bobbitt; *Sisters of Salome*, by Toni Bentley; *World on Fire*, by Amy Chua; *Genius*, by Harold Bloom.

Terms: Agent receives 15% commission on domestic sales; 20% commission on foreign sales.

Tips: "Always include a SASE that will ensure a response from the agent and the return of material submitted."

WYLIE-MERRICK LITERARY AGENCY, 1138 S. Webster St., Kokomo IN 46902-6357. (765)459-8258 or (765)457-3783. E-mail: smartin@wylie-merrick.com; rbrown@wylie-merrick.com. Website: www.wylie-merrick.com. **Contact:** S.A. Martin, Robert Brown. Estab. 1999. Member of SCBWI. Currently handles: 25% nonfiction books; 25% novels; 50% juvenile books.
- Ms. Martin holds a Master's degree in Language Education and is a writing and technology curriculum specialist.

Member Agents: S.A. Martin (juvenile/middle grade/young adult); Robert Brown (adult fiction/nonfiction, young adult).

Represents: Nonfiction books (adult and juvenile), novels (adult and juvenile), juvenile books. **Considers these fiction areas:** Action/adventure; fantasy; historical; mystery/suspense; picture books; religious/inspirational; romance; science fiction; thriller; young adult (middle grade).
- This agency specializes in children's and young adult literary as well as mainstream adult fiction. Actively seeking middle-grade/young adult fiction and nonfiction; picture books; adult fiction and nonfiction.

How to Contact: Query with SASE, Include first 10 pages for novels, complete mss for picturebooks. No e-mail or fax queries. Considers simultaneous queries. Responds in 1 month to queries; 3 months to mss. Returns materials only with SASE. Obtains most new clients through recommendations from others, queries and conferences.

Recent Sales: *Full Court Pressure*, by Jon Ripslinger (Roaring Brook).

Terms: Agent receives 15% commission on domestic sales; 20% commission on foreign sales. Offers written contract. Charges clients for postage, photocopying, handling.

Tips: "We work with a small, select group of writers. We are highly selective when considering new clients, so your work must be the best it can possibly be for us to consider it. We only work with serious professionals who know their craft and the publishing industry. Anything less we reject."

ZACHARY SHUSTER HARMSWORTH, 1776 Broadway, Suite 1405, New York NY 10019. (212)765-6900. Fax: (212)765-6490. E-mail: eharmsworth@zshliterary.com. Website: www.zshliterary.com. Also: Boston Office: 729 Boylston St., 5th Floor. Phone: (617)262-2400, Fax: (617)262-2468. **Contact:** Esmond Harmsworth; Scott Gold (NY). Estab. 1996. Represents 125 clients. 20% of clients are new/unpublished writers. Currently handles: 45% nonfiction books; 45% novels; 5% story collections; 5% scholarly books.
- "Our principals include two former publishing and entertainment lawyers, a journalist and an editor/agent." Lane Zachary was an editor at Random House before becoming an agent.

Member Agents: Esmond Harmsworth (commercial and literary fiction, history, science, adventure); Todd Shuster (narrative and prescriptive nonfiction, biography, memoirs); Lane Zachary (biography, memoirs, literary fiction); Jennifer Gates (literary fiction, nonfiction).

Represents: Nonfiction books, novels. **Considers these fiction areas:** Contemporary issues; detective/police/crime; ethnic; feminist; gay/lesbian; historical; literary; mainstream/contemporary; mystery/suspense; thriller.
- This agency specializes in journalist-driven narrative nonfiction, literary and commercial fiction. Actively

seeking narrative nonfiction, mystery, commercial and literary fiction, memoirs, history, biographies. Does not want to receive poetry.

How to Contact: Query with SASE, submit 50 page sample of ms. No e-mail or fax queries. Considers simultaneous queries. Responds in 3 months to mss. Obtains most new clients through recommendations from others, solicitations, conferences.

Recent Sales: Sold 40-50 titles in the last year. *All Kinds of Minds*, by Mel Levine (Simon & Schuster). Other clients include Leslie Epstein, David Mixner.

Terms: Agent receives 15% commission on domestic sales; 20% commission on foreign sales. Offers written contract, binding for 1 work only; 30 days notice must be given to terminate contract. Charges clients for postage, copying, courier, telephone. "We only charge expenses if the manuscript is sold."

Tips: "We work closely with all our clients on all editorial and promotional aspects of their works."

☑ SUSAN ZECKENDORF ASSOC., INC., 171 W. 57th St., New York NY 10019. (212)245-2928. **Contact:** Susan Zeckendorf. Estab. 1979. Member of AAR. Represents 15 clients. 25% of clients are new/unpublished writers. Currently handles: 50% nonfiction books; 50% novels.

● Prior to opening her agency, Ms. Zeckendorf was a counseling psychologist.

Represents: Nonfiction books, novels. **Considers these fiction areas:** Detective/police/crime; ethnic; historical; literary; mainstream/contemporary; mystery/suspense; thriller.

o─┐ Actively seeking mysteries, literary fiction, mainstream fiction, thrillers, social history, parenting, classical music, biography. Does not want to receive science fiction, romance. "No children's books."

How to Contact: Query with SASE. No e-mail or fax queries. Considers simultaneous queries. Responds in 10 days to queries; 3 weeks to mss. Returns materials only with SASE.

Recent Sales: *Moment of Madness*, by Una-Mary Parker (Headline).

Terms: Agent receives 15% commission on domestic sales; 20% commission on foreign sales. Charges for photocopying, messenger services.

Writers' Conferences: Central Valley Writers Conference; The Tucson Publishers Association Conference; Writer's Connection; Frontiers in Writing Conference (Amarillo TX); Golden Triangle Writers Conference (Beaumont TX); Oklahoma Festival of Books (Claremont OK); SMU Writers Conference (NYC).

Tips: "We are a small agency giving lots of individual attention. We respond quickly to submissions."

Literary Magazines

This section contains markets for your literary short fiction. Although definitions of what constitutes "literary" writing vary, editors of literary journals agree they want to publish the "best" fiction they can acquire. Qualities they look for in fiction include creativity, style, flawless mechanics, and careful attention to detail in content and manuscript preparation. Most of the authors writing such fiction are well-read and well-educated, and many are students and graduates of university creative writing programs.

Please also review our Online Markets section, page 306, for electronic literary magazines. At a time when paper and publishing costs rise while funding to university presses continues to be cut or eliminated, electronic literary magazines are helping generate a publishing renaissance for experimental as well as more traditional literary fiction. These electronic outlets for literary fiction also benefit writers by eliminating copying and postage costs and providing the opportunity for much quicker responses to submissions. Also notice that some magazines with websites give specific information about what they offer on their websites, including updated writer's guidelines and sample fiction from their publications.

STEPPING STONES TO RECOGNITION

Some well-established literary journals pay several hundred or even several thousand dollars for a short story. Most, though, can only pay with contributor's copies or a subscription to their publication. However, being published in literary journals offers the important benefits of experience, exposure, and prestige. Agents and major book publishers regularly read literary magazines in search of new writers. Work from among these journals is also selected for inclusion in annual prize anthologies such as *The Best American Short Stories*, *Prize Stories: The O. Henry Awards*, *Pushcart Prize: Best of the Small Presses*, and *New Stories from the South: The Year's Best*.

You'll find most of the well-known prestigious literary journals listed here. Many, including *Carolina Quarterly* and *Ploughshares*, are associated with universities, while others such as *The Paris Review* are independently published.

SELECTING THE RIGHT LITERARY JOURNAL

Once you have browsed through this section and have a list of journals you might like to submit to, read those listings again, carefully. Remember that this is information editors present to help you in submitting work that fits their needs. The "Quick Start" Guide to Publishing Your Fiction, starting on page 2, will guide you through the process of finding markets for your fiction.

This is the only section in which you will find magazines that do not read submissions all year long. Whether limited reading periods are tied to a university schedule or meant to accommodate the capabilities of a very small staff, those periods are noted within listings. The staffs of university journals are usually made up of student editors and a managing editor who is also a faculty member. These staffs often change every year. Whenever possible, we indicate this in listings and give the name of the current editor and the length of that editor's term. Also be aware that the schedule of a university journal usually coincides with that university's academic year, meaning that the editors of most university publications are difficult or impossible to reach during the summer.

FURTHERING YOUR SEARCH

It cannot be stressed enough that reading the listings for literary journals is only the first part of developing your marketing plan. The second part, equally important, is to obtain fiction guidelines and read the actual journal you'd like to submit to with great care. Reading copies of these journals helps you determine the fine points of each magazine's publishing style and sensibility. There is no substitute for this type of hands-on research.

Unlike commercial periodicals available at most newsstands and bookstores, it requires a little more effort to obtain some of the magazines listed here. The super chain bookstores are doing a better job these days of stocking literaries and you can find some in independent and college bookstores, especially those published in your area. You may, however, need to send for a sample copy. We include sample copy prices in the listings whenever possible. In addition to reading your sample copies, pay close attention to the **Advice** section of each listing. There you'll often find a very specific description of the style of fiction editors at that publication prefer.

Another way to find out more about literary magazines is to check out the various prize anthologies and take note of journals whose fiction is being selected for publication there. Studying prize anthologies not only lets you know which magazines are publishing award-winning work, but it also provides a valuable overview of what is considered to be the best fiction published today. Those anthologies include:

* *Best American Short Stories*, published by Houghton Mifflin.
* *New Stories from the South: The Year's Best*, published by Algonquin Books of Chapel Hill.
* *Prize Stories: The O. Henry Awards*, published by Doubleday/Anchor.
* *Pushcart Prize: Best of the Small Presses*, published by Pushcart Press.

At the beginnings of listings, we include symbols to help you in narrowing your search. Keys to those symbols can be found on the inside front and back covers of this book.

$⬙ ACM (ANOTHER CHICAGO MAGAZINE), Left Field Press, 3709 N. Kenmore, Chicago IL 60613. E-mail: editors@anotherchicagomag.com. Website: www.anotherchicagomag.com. **Contact:** Sharon Solwitz, fiction editor. Magazine: 5½×8½; 200-220 pages; "art folio each issue." Biannual. Estab. 1977. Circ. 2,000.
Needs: Ethnic/multicultural, experimental, feminist, gay, lesbian, literary, translations, contemporary, prose poem. No religious, strictly genre or editorial. Receives 300 unsolicited mss/month. Publishes ms 6-12 months after acceptance. **Publishes 10 new writers/year.** Recently published work by Stuart Dybek and Steve Almond.
How to Contact: Responds in 3 months to queries; 6 months to mss. Accepts simultaneous, multiple submissions. Sample copy for $8 ppd. Writer's guidelines online.
Payment/Terms: Pays small honorarium when possible, contributor's copies and 1 year subscription. Acquires first North American serial rights.
Advice: "Support literary publishing by subscribing to at least one literary journal—if not ours another. Get used to rejection slips, and don't get discouraged. Keep introductory letters short. Make sure manuscript has name and address on every page, and that it is clean, neat and proofread. We are looking for stories with freshness and originality in subject angle and style, and work that encounters the world and is not stuck in its own navel."

Ⓝ $⬙ ADRIFT, Writing: Irish, Irish American and ..., 46 E. First St. #3D, New York NY 10003. **Contact:** Thomas McGonigle, editor. Magazine: 8×11; 32 pages; 60 lb. paper stock; 65 lb. cover stock; illustrations; photos. "Irish-Irish American as a basis—though we are interested in advanced writing from anywhere." Semiannual. Estab. 1983. Circ. 1,000.
Needs: Erotica, ethnic/multicultural, experimental, feminist, gay, lesbian, literary, translations. Receives 40 unsolicited mss/month. Accepts 3 mss/issue. **Publishes some new writers/year.** Recently published work by Francis Stuart. Also publishes literary criticism. Sometimes comments on rejected mss.
How to Contact: Send complete ms. SASE for return of ms. Responds as soon as possible. Sample copy for $5. Reviews fiction.
Payment/Terms: Pays on publication for first rights.
Advice: "The writing should argue with, among others, James Joyce, Flann O'Brien, Juan Goytisolo, Ingeborg Bachmann, E.M. Cioran, Max Stirner and Patrick Kavanagh."

⬙ ADVOCATE, PKA'S PUBLICATION, PKA Publications, 1881 Little Westkill Rd. CO2, Prattsville NY 12468. (518)299-3103. Tabloid: 9⅜×12¼; 32 pages; newsprint paper; line drawings; color and b&w photographs. "Eclectic for a general audience." Bimonthly. Estab. 1987. Circ. 12,000.
Needs: Adventure, children's/juvenile (5-9 years), ethnic/multicultural, experimental, fantasy, feminist, historical,

humor/satire, literary, mainstream, mystery/suspense, regional, romance, science fiction, western, young adult/teen (10-18 years), contemporary, prose poem, senior ctizen/retirement, sports. "Nothing religious, pornographic, violent, erotic, pro-drug or anti-enviroment. Currently looking for equine (horses) stories, poetry, art, photos and cartoons. The *Gaited Horse Newsletter* is currently published within the pages of PKA's *Advocate*." Receives 60 unsolicited mss/month. Accepts 6-8 mss/issue; 34-48 mss/year. Publishes ms 4 months to 1 year after acceptance. Also publishes poetry. Sometimes comments on rejected mss.

How to Contact: Send a complete ms with cover letter. Responds in 2 months to mss. No simultaneous submissions "no work that has appeared on the Internet." Sample copy for $4 (US currency for inside US; $5.25 US currency for Canada). Writer's guidelines with purchase of sample copy.

Payment/Terms: Pays contributor copies. Acquires first rights.

Advice: "The highest criterion in selecting a work is its entertainment value. It must first be enjoyable reading. It must, of course, be orginal. To stand out, it must be thought provoking or strongly emotive, or very cleverly plotted. Will consider only previously unpublished works by writers who do not earn their living principally through writing. We are currently very backed-up on short stories. We are mostly looking for art, photos, and poetry."

N $⬤ AFRICAN AMERICAN REVIEW, Saint Louis University, Shannon Hall 119, 220 N. Grand Blvd., St. Louis MO 63103-2007. (314)977-3703. Fax: (314)977-3649. Website: aar.slu.edu. **Contact:** Joe Weixlmann, editor. Magazine: 7×10; 176 pages; 60 lb., acid-free paper; 100 lb. skid stock cover; illustrations; photos. "Essays on African-American literature, theater, film, art and culture generally; interviews; poetry and fiction by African-American authors; book reviews." Quarterly. Estab. 1967. Circ. 2,067.
  ● *African American Review* is the official publication of the Division of Black American Literature and Culture of the Modern Language Association.

Needs: Ethnic/multicultural, experimental, feminist, literary, mainstream. "No children's/juvenile/young adult/teen." Receives 50 unsolicited mss/month. Accepts 40 mss/issue. Publishes ms 1-2 years after acceptance. Agented fiction 10%. Recently published work by Solon Timothy Woodward, Eugenia Collier, Jeffery Renard Allen, Raki Jones, Olympia Vernon. Length: 2,500-5,000 words; average length: 3,000 words. Also publishes literary essays, literary criticism, poetry. Sometimes comments on rejected mss.

How to Contact: Responds in 1 month to queries; 6 months to mss. Sample copy for $12. Writer's guidelines online. Reviews fiction.

Payment/Terms: Pays $25-100, 3 contributor's copies and 10 offprints. Pays on publication for first North American serial rights. Sends galleys to author.

$⬤ ☒ AGNI, Dept. NM Creative Writing Program, Boston University, 236 Bay State Rd., Boston MA 02215. (617)353-7135. Fax: (617)353-7134. E-mail: agni@bu.edu. Website: agni.bu.edu. **Contact:** Sven Birkerts, editor. Magazine: 5½×8½; 300 pages; 55 lb. booktext paper; recycled cover stock; art portfolios. "Eclectic literary magazine publishing first-rate poems, essays, translations, and stories." Biannual. Estab. 1972. Circ. 4,000.
  ● Founding editor Askold Melnyczuk won the 2001 Nora Magid Award for Literary Editing; work from *Agni* has been selected regularly (and in 2002) for inclusion in both *Pushcart Prize* and *Best American Short Stories* anthologies.

Needs: Translations, stories, prose poems. "No science fiction or romance." Receives 250 unsolicited mss/month. Accepts 2-3 mss/issue; 4-6 mss/year. Reading period September 1 through May 31 only. Publishes ms 6 months after acceptance. **Publishes 30 new writers/year.** Recently published work by Chitra Divakaruni, Ilan Stavans, Joyce Carol Oates, David Foster Wallace, Lisa Haiws, and Nicholas Montemarano.

How to Contact: Accepts submissions by mail. Responds in 2 weeks to queries; 4 months to mss. Accepts simultaneous submissions. Sample copy for $10 or online. Writer's guidelines for #10 SASE or email agni@bu.edu.

Payment/Terms: Pays $10/page up to $150, 2 contributor's copies, 1-year subscription, and 4 gift copies. Pays on publication for first North American serial rights. Rights to reprint in *AGNI* anthology (with author's consent). Sends galleys to author.

Advice: "Read *Agni* and other literary magazone carefully to understand the kinds of stories we do and do not publish. It's important for artists to support the arts."

☒ $⬤ ALASKA QUARTERLY REVIEW, ESB 208, University of Alaska-Anchorage, 3211 Providence Dr., Anchorage AK 99508. (907)786-6916. E-mail: ayaqr@uaa.alaska.edu. Website: www.uaa.alaska.edu/aqr. **Contact:** Ronald Spatz, fiction editor. Magazine: 6×9; 232-300 pages; 60 lb. Glatfelter paper; 12 pt. C15 black ink or 4-color; varnish cover stock; photos on cover only. *AQR* "publishes fiction, poetry, literary nonfiction and short plays in traditional and experimental styles." Semiannual. Estab. 1982. Circ. 2,500.

READ 'THE BUSINESS OF FICTION WRITING' section for information on manuscript preparation, mailing tips, rights and more.

• Two stories selected for inclusion in the 2004 *Prize Stories: The O. Henry Awards.*

Needs: Experimental, literary, translations, contemporary, prose poem. "If the works in *Alaska Quarterly Review* have certain characteristics, they are these: freshness, honesty, and a compelling subject. What makes a piece stand out from the multitude of other submissions? The voice of the piece must be strong—idiosyncratic enough to create a unique persona. We look for the demonstration of craft, making the situation palpable and putting it in a form where it becomes emotionally and intellectually complex. One could look through our pages over time and see that many of the pieces published in the *Alaska Quarterly Review* concern everyday life. We're not asking our writers to go outside themselves and their experiences to the absolute exotic to catch our interest. We look for the experiential and revelatory qualities of the work. We will, without hesitation, champion a piece that may be less polished or stylistically sophisticated, if it engages me, surprises me, and resonates for me. The joy in reading such a work is in discovering something true. Moreover, in keeping with our mission to publish new writers, we are looking for voices our readers do not know, voices that may not always be reflected in the dominant culture and that, in all instances, have something important to convey." Receives 200 unsolicited mss/month. Accepts 7-18 mss/issue; 15-30 mss/year. Does not read mss May 10-August 25. Publishes ms 6 months after acceptance. **Publishes 6 new writers/year.** Recently published work by Howard Norman, Douglas Light, Nicholas Montemarano, Edna Ziesk and Edith Pearlman. Publishes short shorts.

How to Contact: Accepts submissions by mail. Responds in 4 months to queries; 4 months to mss. Simultaneous submissions "undesirable, but will accept if indicated." Sample copy for $6. Writer's guidelines online.

Payment/Terms: Pays $50-200 subject to funding; pays in contributor's copies and subscriptions when funding is limited. Honorariums on publication when funding permits. Acquires first North American serial rights. Upon request, rights will be transferred back to author after publication.

Advice: "Professionalism, patience, and persistence are essential. One needs to do one's homework and know the market. The competition is very intense, and funding for the front-line journals is generally inadequate, so staffing is low. It takes time to get a response, and rejections are a fact of life. It is important not to take the rejections personally, and also to know that editors make decisions for better or worse, and they make mistakes too. Fortunately there are many gatekeepers. *Alaska Quarterly Review* has published many pieces that had been turned down by other journals—including pieces that then went on to win national awards. We also know of instances in which pieces *Alaska Quarterly Review* rejected later appeared in other magazines. We haven't regretted that we didn't take those pieces. Rather, we're happy that the authors have made a good match. Disappointment should *never* stop anyone. Will counts as much as talent, and new writers need to have confidence in themselves and stick to it."

THE ALLEGHENY REVIEW, A National Journal of Undergraduate Literature, Thomson-Shore, Inc., Box 32 Allegheny College, Meadville PA 16335. (814)332-6553. Fax: (800)706-4545. E-mail: review@allegheny.edu. Website: http://merlin2.allegheny.edu/group/review/. **Contact:** Beata M. Gomulak, senior editor. Magazine: 6×9; 100 pages; illustrations; photos. "*The Allegheny Review* is one of America's only nationwide literary magazines exclusively for undergraduate works fo poetry, fiction and nonfiction. Our intended audience is persons interested in quality literature." Annual. Estab. 1983.

• A $5 entry fee is required. Fee covers one year subscription and makes submission eligible for the Allegheny Review Literature Awards.

Needs: Adventure, ethnic/multicultural, experimental, family saga, fantasy, feminist, gay, historical, horror, humor/satire, lesbian, literary, mainstream, military/war, mystery/suspense, New Age, psychic/supernatural/occult, religious/inspirational (general), romance, science fiction, western. No "fiction not written by undergraduates—we accept nothing but fiction by currently enrolled undergraduate students. We consider anything catering to an intellectual audience." Receives 50 unsolicited mss/month. Accepts 3 mss/issue. Publishes ms 2 months after deadline after acceptance. **Publishes roughly 90% new writers/year.** Recently published work by Dianne Page, Monica Stahl and DJ Kinney. Length: 20 pages maximum; average length: varies. Publishes short shorts. Also publishes literary essays, literary criticism, poetry. Sometimes comments on rejected mss.

How to Contact: Send complete mss with a cover letter. Accepts submissions on disk. Responds in 2 weeks to queries 4 months. Send disposable copy of ms and #10 SASE for reply only to mss. Accepts multiple submissions. Sample copy for $4.

Payment/Terms: Pays 1 contributor's copy; additional copies $2. Acquires all rights. Sponsors awards/contests.

Advice: "We look for quality work that has been thoroughly revised. We look for unique voice, interesting topics and playfullness with the English language. Revise, revise, revise! And be careful how you send it—the cover letter says a lot. We definitely look for diversity in the pieces we publish."

AMERICAN LITERARY REVIEW, University of North Texas, P.O. Box 311307, Denton TX 76203-1307. (940)565-2755. Fax: (940)565-4355. E-mail: americanliteraryreview@yahoo.com. Website: www.engl.unt.edu/alr/. **Contact:** John Tait, fiction editor. Magazine: 6×9; 128 pages; 70 lb. Mohawk paper; 67 lb. Wausau Vellum cover. "Publishes quality, contemporary poems and stories." Semiannual. Estab. 1990. Circ. 900.

Needs: Literary, mainstream. "No genre works." Receives 150-200 unsolicited mss/month. Accepts 4-6 mss/issue; 8-16 mss/year. Reading period: September 1-May 1. Publishes ms within 2 years after acceptance after acceptance. Recently published work by Dana Johnson, Bill Roorbach, Cynthia Shearer, Mark Jacobs and Sylvia Wantanabe. Also publishes literary essays, poetry. Critiques or comments on rejected mss.

How to Contact: Accepts submissions by mail. Send complete ms with cover letter. Responds in 2-4 months to mss. Accepts simultaneous submissions. Sample copy for $6. Writer's guidelines for #10 SASE.

Payment/Terms: Pays in contributor's copies. Acquires one-time rights.

Advice: "We would like to see more short shorts and stylisically innovative and risk-taking fiction. We like to see stories that illuminate the various layers of characters and their situations with great artistry. Give us distinctive character-driven stories that explore the complexities of human existence." Looks for "the small moments that contain more than at first possible, that surprise us with more truth than we thought we had a right to expect."

$ 🖉 ◎ ANCIENT PATHS, A Journal of Christian Art and Literature, P.O. Box 7505, Fairfax Station VA 22039. Website: www.literatureclassics.com/ancientpaths/magazine/table.html. **Contact:** Skylar H. Burris, editor. Magazine: digest size; 40 pages; 20 lb. plain white paper; cardstock cover; illustrations. "*Ancient Paths* publishes quality fiction and creative nonfiction for a literate Christian audience. Religious themes are usually subtle, and the magazine has non-Christian readers as well as some content by non-Christian authors. However, writers should be comfortable appearing in a Christian magazine." Semiannual. Estab. 1998. Circ. 175-200.

Needs: Fantasy (Christian), historical, humor/satire, literary, mainstream, mystery/suspense (Christian), novel excerpts, religious/inspirational (general religious/literary, religious fantasy, religious mystery/suspense), science fiction (Christian), slice-of-life vignettes, western (Christian). No retelling of Bible stories. Literary fiction favored over genre fiction. Receives 5-10 unsolicited mss/month. Accepts 3-6 mss/issue; 6-12 mss/year. Publishes ms 2 months after acceptance. Recently published work by Larry Marshall Sams, Erin Tocknell, Maureen Stirsman and Chris Williams. Length: 250-2,500 words; average length: 2,000 words. Publishes short shorts. Often comments on rejected mss.

How to Contact: Send complete ms. Accepts submissions by mail, e-mail (skylar.burris@gte.net). Include estimated word count. Send SASE for return of ms or send a disposable copy of ms and #10 SASE for reply only. Responds in 1 week to queries; 4-5 weeks to mss. Accepts simultaneous and reprints, multiple submissions. Sample copy for $3.50; make checks payable to Skylar Burris *not* to *Ancient Paths*. Writer's guidelines online. Reviews fiction.

Payment/Terms: Pays $2, and 1 copy. Pays on publication for one-time rights. Not copyrighted.

Advice: "We look for fluid prose, intriguing characters, substantial themes in fiction manuscripts."

🖉 ANTHOLOGY MAGAZINE, Anthology Inc., P.O. Box 4411, Mesa AZ 85211-4411. (480)461-8200. E-mail: lisa@anthology.org. Website: www.anthology.org. **Contact:** Elissa Harris, prose editor. Magazine: 8½×11; 28 pages; 20lb. paper; 60-100 lb. cover stock; illustrations; photos. "Our intended audience is anyone who likes to read good fiction." Bimonthly. Estab. 1994. Circ. 1,000.

Needs: Adventure, fantasy (science fantasy, sword and sorcery), humor/satire, literary, mystery/suspense (amateur sleuth, police procedural, private eye/hardboiled), science fiction (hard science, soft/sociological). "No graphic horror or erotica." Receives 70-80 unsolicited mss/month. Accepts 2-3 mss/issue; 12-18 mss/year. Publishes ms 10-12 months after acceptance. **Publishes 8-10 new writers/year.** Recently published work by Elisha Porat, Kent Robinson, and Sarah Mlynowski. Average length: 3,000-5,000 words. Publishes short shorts. Also publishes poetry.

How to Contact: Accepts submissions by mail. Send complete ms with cover letter. Include estimated word count. Send SASE for reply, return of ms or send disposable copy of ms. Responds in 2-4 months to mss. No simultaneous submissions. Sample copy for 3.95. Writer's guidelines for #10 SASE. Reviews fiction.

Payment/Terms: Pays in contributor's copies; additional copies $2. Acquires first North American serial, one-time, electronic rights.

Advice: "Is there passion in writing? Is there forethought? Will the story make an emotional connection to the reader? Send for guidelines and a sample issue. If you see that your work would not only fit into, but add something to *Anthology*, then send it."

$ 🖉 ◎ 🖾 ANTIETAM REVIEW, Washington County Arts Council, 41 S. Potomac, Hagerstown MD 21740-5512. (301)791-3132. Fax: (240)420-1754. E-mail: winnie@washingtoncountyaas.com. Website: www.washcoartco uncil.org. **Contact:** Winnie Wagaman, managing editor. Magazine: 8½×11; 54-68 pages; glossy paper; light card cover; photos. A literary magazine of short fiction, poetry and black-and-white photographs. Annual. Estab. 1982. Circ. 1,500.

● Work published in *Antietam Review* has been included in the *Pushcart Prize* anthology and *Best American Short Stories*. The magazine also received a grant from the Maryland State Arts Council and Washington County Arts Council.

Needs: Condensed novels, ethnic/multicultural, experimental, feminist, literary, novel excerpts (if work as independent pieces), short stories of a literary quality. No religious, romance, erotica, confession, horror or condensed novels. Receives 100 unsolicited mss/month. Accepts 8-10 mss/year. Reads mss from September 1 to January 31. Publishes ms 2-3 months after acceptance. **Publishes 2-3 new writers/year.** Recently published work by Marc Bookman, Tom Glenn, Richard Plant, Dee Cameron, Ace Boggess, Luke Tennis and Jamie Holland. Length: 5,000 words max. Also publishes poetry.

How to Contact: Query with published clips or send complete ms. Accepts submissions by mail, e-mail, phone. Send SASE. Include estimated word count, 1-paragraph bio and list of publications. "If we hold a story, we let the writer know. Occasionally we critique returned ms or ask for rewrites." Responds in 4 months to queries. Sample copy for $6.30 (current issue). Writer's guidelines for #10 SASE.

Payment/Terms: Pays $100 and 2 contributor's copies. Pays on publication for first North American serial rights.
Advice: "We seek high-quality, well-crafted work with significant character development and shift. We seek no specific theme. We look for work that is interesting, involves the reader, and teaches us a new way to view the world. A manuscript stands out because of its energy and flow. Most of our submissions reflect the times (i.e., the news, current events) more than industry trends. We also seek a compelling voice, originality, magic. We now require *accepted* stories to be put on disk by the author to cut down on printing costs. We are seeing an increase in first-person narrative stories."

$⬛⬅️◻️ THE ANTIGONISH REVIEW, St. Francis Xavier University, P.O. Box 5000, Antigonish NS B2G 2W5 Canada. (902)867-3962. Fax: (902)867-5563. Website: www.antigonishreview.com. **Contact:** Allan Quigley, editor. Literary magazine for educated and creative readers. Quarterly. Estab. 1970. Circ. 850.
Needs: Literary, translations, contemporary, prose poem. No erotica. Receives 50 unsolicited mss/month. Accepts 6 mss/issue. Publishes ms 4 months after acceptance. **Publishes some new writers/year.** Recently published work by Arnold Bloch, Richard Butts and Helen Barolini. Sometimes comments on rejected mss.
How to Contact: Send complete ms. Accepts submissions by mail, fax. Accepts electronic (disk compatible with WordPerfect/IBM and Windows) submissions. Prefers hard copy with disk submission. Responds in 1 month to queries; 4 months to mss. No simultaneous submissions. Sample copy for $4 or online. Writer's guidelines for #10 SASE or online.
Payment/Terms: Pays $50 for stories. Pays on publication. Rights retained by author.
Advice: "Learn the fundamentals and do not deluge an editor."

$◻️ ANTIOCH REVIEW, P.O. Box 148, Yellow Springs OH 45387-0148. Website: www.antioch.edu/review. **Contact:** Fiction editor. Magazine: 6×9; 184 pages; 50 lb. book offset paper; coated cover stock; illustrations "seldom." "Literary and cultural review of contemporary issues, and literature for general readership." Quarterly. Estab. 1941. Circ. 5,100.
Needs: Experimental, literary, translations, contemporary. No science fiction, fantasy, or confessions. Receives 275 unsolicited mss/month. Accepts 5-6 mss/issue; 20-24 mss/year. June 1-September 1. Publishes ms 10 months after acceptance. Agented fiction 1-2%. **Publishes 1-2 new writers/year.** Recently published work by Gordon Lish, Jean Ross Justice, Patricia Lear, William Cobb, Leon Rooke, Valerie Leff, Stephanie Koven, Andrew Porter, and Liza Ward.
How to Contact: Accepts submissions by mail. Send complete ms with SASE, preferably mailed flat. Responds in 2 months to mss. Sample copy for $6. Writer's guidelines online.
Payment/Terms: Pays $10/printed page. Pays on publication for first, one-time rights. Rights revert to author upon publication.
Advice: "Our best advice always is to *read* the *Antioch Review* to see what type of material we publish. Quality fiction requires an engagement of the reader's intellectual interest supported by mature emotional relevance, written in a style that is rich and rewarding without being freaky. The great number of stories submitted to us indicates that fiction still has great appeal. We assume that if so many are writing fiction, many must be reading it."

◻️ APOSTROPHE, University of South Carolina Beaufort Journal of Arts, 801 Carteret St., Beaufort SC 29902. (843)521-4100. Fax: (843)521-4192. E-mail: pemalphr@gwm.sc.edu. **Contact:** Ellen Malphrus, fiction editor. Magazine: 8×5; 70 pages. "*Apostrophe* seeks excellence in writing for the thoughtful reader." Annual. Estab. 1996. Circ. 250-300.
Needs: Literary. "Does not want anything 'poorly written' or 'in bad taste'." Receives 12 unsolicited mss/month. Accepts 3-4 mss/issue. Does not read mss "during semester." Publishes ms 1-2 months after acceptance. **Publishes 3 new writers/year.** Recently published work by Evan Balkan, Mary Atwell and John Hughes. Publishes short shorts. Also publishes literary essays, literary criticism, poetry. Sometimes comments on rejected mss.
How to Contact: Send SASE for reply, return of ms or send a disposable copy of ms. Responds in 2 weeks to queries; 10 months to mss. Accepts simultaneous and reprints submissions. Sample copy for $3, 8×5 SAE and 2 first-class stamps. Writer's guidelines for SASE.
Payment/Terms: Pays 2 contributor's copies; additional copies $5.
Advice: Looks for "excellent prose style; nothing trite or clichéd; nothing 'crafted.' Don't be afraid to ignore your writing instructors, when appropriate. We prefer thoughtful construction; artful phrasing; maturity. Don't rely on anyone to teach you. Write to learn."

N️ ◻️ ◎ APPALACHIAN HERITAGE, CPO 2166, Berea KY 40404. (859)985-3699. Fax: (859)985-3903. E-mail: george-brosi@berea.edu. Website: www.berea.edu/apcenter/appheritage.html. **Contact:** George Berosi. Magazine: 6×9; 104 pages; 60 lb. stock; 10 pt. Warrenflo cover; drawings; b&w photos. "*Appalachian Heritage* is a Southern Appalachian literary magazine. We try to keep a balance of fiction, poetry, essays, scholarly works, etc., for a general audience and/or those interested in the Appalachian mountains." Quarterly. Estab. 1973. Circ. 750.
Needs: Historical, literary, regional. "We do not want to see fiction that has no ties to Southern Appalachia." Receives 60-80 unsolicited mss/month. Accepts 2-3 mss/issue; 12-15 mss/year. Publishes ms 3-6 months after acceptance. **Publishes 8 new writers/year.** Recently published work by Meridith Sue Willis, Lee Maynard, Bo Bay,

Silas House, Ron Rash, and Lee Smith. Length: 3,000 words max. Publishes short shorts. Occasionally comments on rejected mss.

How to Contact: Send complete ms. Send SASE for reply, return of ms or send a disposable copy of ms. Responds in 1 month to queries; 6 weeks to mss. Sample copy for $6. Writer's guidelines free.

Payment/Terms: Pays 3 contributor's copies; $6 charge for extras. Acquires first North American serial rights.

Advice: "Get acquainted with *Appalachian Heritage*, as you should with any publication before submitting your work."

N ☐ ◎ ARBA SICULA, St. John's University, Jamaica NY 11439. **Contact:** Gaetano Cipolla, editor. Magazine: 6×9; 180 pages; top-grade paper; good quality cover stock; illustrations; photos. Bilingual ethnic literary review (Sicilian-English) dedicated to the dissemination of Sicilian culture. Plans special fiction issue. Annual. Estab. 1979. Circ. 2,500.

Needs: Accepts ethnic literary material consisting of various forms of folklore, stories both contemporary and classical, regional, romance (contemporary, historical, young adult) and senior citizen. Material submitted must be in the Sicilian language, with English translations desirable or in English on Sicilian topics. Publishes ms 1-3 years after acceptance. **Publishes some new writers/year.** Sometimes comments on rejected mss.

How to Contact: Send complete ms. SASE. Responds in 2 months to mss. Accepts simultaneous and reprints submissions. Sample copy for $8 with 8½×11 SASE and 90¢ postage.

Payment/Terms: Pays 5 contributor's copies; $4 for additional copies. Acquires all rights.

Advice: "This review is a must for those who nurture a love of the Sicilian language."

☐ ARKANSAS REVIEW, A Journal of Delta Studies, Department of English and Philosophy, P.O. Box 1890, Arkansas State University, State University AR 72467-1890. (501)972-3043. Fax: (501)972-3045. E-mail: delta@astate.edu. Website: www.clt.astate.edu/arkreview. **Contact:** Tom Williams, fiction editor. Magazine: 8¼×11; 64-100 pages; coated, matte paper; matte, 4-color cover stock; illustrations; photos. Publishes articles, fiction, poetry, essays, interviews, reviews, visual art evocative of or responsive to the Mississippi River Delta. Triannual. Estab. 1996. Circ. 700.

Needs: Literary (essays and criticism), regional (short stories). "No genre fiction. Must have a Delta focus." Receives 30-50 unsolicited mss/month. Accepts 2-3 mss/issue; 5-7 mss/year. Publishes ms 6-12 months after acceptance. Agented fiction 1%. **Publishes 3-4 new writers/year.** Recently published work by Eric Miles Williams, Mark Sindecuse and Craig Black. Also publishes literary essays, poetry. Always comments on rejected mss.

How to Contact: Accepts submissions by e-mail, fax. Send SASE for reply, return of ms or send a disposable copy of ms. Responds in 1 week to queries; 4 months to mss. Sample copy for $7.50. Writer's guidelines for #10 SASE.

Payment/Terms: Pays 5 contributor's copies; additional copies for $5. Acquires first North American serial rights.

Advice: "We publish new writers in every issue. We look for distinguished, mature writing, surprises, a perfect ending and a story that means more than merely what went on in it. We don't like recognizable imitations of currently fashionable writers."

☐ THE ARMCHAIR AESTHETE, Pickle Gas Press, 31 Rolling Meadows Way, Penfield NY 14526. (716)388-6968. E-mail: bypaul@netacc.net. **Contact:** Paul Agosto, editor. Magazine: 5½×8½; 40-65 pages; 20 lb. paper; 110 lb. card stock color cover. "*The Armchair Aesthete* seeks quality writing that enlightens and entertains a thoughtful audience (ages 9-90) with a 'good read.'" Quarterly. Estab. 1996. Circ. 100.

Needs: Adventure, fantasy (science fantasy, sword and sorcery), historical (general), horror, humor/satire (satire), mainstream (contemporary), mystery/suspense (amateur sleuth, cozy, police procedural, private eye/hardboiled, romantic suspense), science fiction (soft/sociological), western (frontier, traditional). "No racist, pornographic, overt gore; no religious or material intended for or written by children. Receives 90 unsolicited mss/month. Accepts 13-18 mss/issue; 60-80 mss/year. Publishes ms 3-9 months after acceptance. Agented fiction 5%. **Publishes 10-15 new writers/year.** Recently published work by Teresa Bourgeoise, J. Robert Griffin, Alan Reynolds, Doug Holder, Hillary James Liberty and Valerie Corderman. Average length: 2,000 words. Publishes short shorts. Also publishes poetry. Sometimes comments on rejected mss.

How to Contact: Accepts submissions by e-mail. Send SASE for reply, return of ms or send a disposable copy of ms. Responds in 2-3 weeks to queries; 1-3 months to mss. Accepts simultaneous and reprints, multiple submis-

sions. Sample copy for $3 (paid to P. Agosto, editor) and 2 first-class stamps. Writer's guidelines for #10 SASE. Reviews fiction.

Payment/Terms: Pays 1 contributor's copy; additional copies for $3 (pay to P. Agosto, editor). Pays on publication for one-time rights.

Advice: "Clever, compelling storytelling has a good chance here. We look for a clever plot, thought-out characters, something that surprises or catches us off guard. Write on innovative subjects and situations. Submissions should be professionally presented and technically sound."

$ ☑ ARTFUL DODGE, Dept. of English, College of Wooster, Wooster OH 44691. (330)263-2577. Website: www.wooster.edu/artfuldodge. **Contact:** Editor. Magazine: 180 pages; illustrations; photos. "There is no theme in this magazine, except literary power. We also have an ongoing interest in translations from Central/Eastern Europe and elsewhere." Annual. Estab. 1979. Circ. 1,000.

Needs: Experimental, literary, translations, prose poem. "We judge by literary quality, not by genre. We are especially interested in fine English translations of significant prose writers. Translations should be submitted with original texts." Receives 40 unsolicited mss/month. Accepts 5 mss/year. **Publishes 1 new writers/year.** Recently published work by Dan Chaon, Lynne Sharon Schwartz, Robert Mooney, Joan Connor and Zbigniew Herbert; and interviews with Tim O'Brien, Lee Smith, Michael Dorris and Stuart Dybek. Average length: 2,500 words. Also publishes literary essays, literary criticism, poetry. Occasionally comments on rejected mss.

How to Contact: Accepts submissions by mail. Send complete ms with SASE. Do not send more than 30 pages at a time. Responds in 1 year to mss. Accepts simultaneous submissions if contacted immediately after being accepted elsewhere. Sample copy for $7. Writer's guidelines for #10 SASE.

Payment/Terms: Pays 2 contributor's copies and honorarium of $5/page, "thanks to funding from the Ohio Arts Council." Acquires first North American serial rights.

Advice: "If we take time to offer criticism, do not subsequently flood us with other stories no better than the first. If starting out, get as many *good* readers as possible. Above all, read contemporary fiction and the magazine you are trying to publish in."

☐ ARTISAN, a journal of craft, P.O. Box 157, Wilmette IL 60091. (847)673-7246. E-mail: artisanjnl@aol.com. **Contact:** Joan Daugherty. Tabloid: 8½×11; 36 pages. "The philosophy behind *artisan* is that anyone who strives to express themselves through their craft is an artist and artists of all genres can learn from each other." 3 times/ year. Estab. 1995. Circ. 200.

Needs: "We love to see 'literary' stories that can still appeal to a general audience—stories that are well-written and sophisticated without being stuffy." Receives 50 unsolicited mss/month. Accepts 6-8 mss/issue; 25 mss/year. Publishes ms 6-8 after acceptance. Recently published work by Joe Benevento, Kathie Giorgio and Patricia Schultheis. Length: 4,000 words; average length: 2,000 words. Publishes short shorts. Also publishes literary essays, literary criticism, poetry. Sometimes comments on rejected mss.

How to Contact: SASE for reply and send a disposable copy of ms. Accepts electronic submissions (e-mail or ASCII). Responds in 1 month to queries; 6-8 months to mss. Sample copy for $6. Guidelines for #10 SASE. Guidelines also posted on the Internet at www.members.aol.com/artisanjnl.

Payment/Terms: Pays 2 contributor's copies; additional copies $5. Acquires first rights.

Advice: "There are very few, if any, orginal stories left to tell. The difference is how you choose to tell them. Show us fresh use of language, character and story line. Make it personal."

☑ ◎ ASIAN PACIFIC AMERICAN JOURNAL, The Asian American Writer's Workshop, 16 W. 32nd St., 10th Floor, New York NY 10012. (212)494-0061. Fax: (212)494-0062. E-mail: apaj@aaww.org. Website: www.aaw w.org. **Contact:** Hanya Yanagihara, editor. Magazine: 5½×8½; 250 pages; illustrations. "We are interested in publishing works by writers from all segments of the Asian Pacific American community. The journal appeals to all interested in Asian-American literature and culture." Semiannual. Estab. 1992. Circ. 1,500.

Needs: Ethnic/multicultural, experimental, feminist, gay, historical (general), humor/satire, lesbian, literary, mainstream, novel excerpts, regional, serialized novels, translations, graphic novels. "We are interested in anything related to the Asian American community." Receives 120 unsolicited mss/month. Accepts 15 mss/issue; 30 mss/ year. Publishes ms 4-6 after acceptance. Agented fiction 5%. Recently published work by David Henry Hwang, Chitra Banerjee Divakarvni, Kimiko Hahn, Bino A. Realuyo and Rahna Rizzuto. Average length: 3,000 words. Publishes short shorts. Also publishes literary essays, poetry.

How to Contact: Include estimated word count, 3-5 sentence bio, and list of publications. Sample copy for $10.

Payment/Terms: Pays 2 contributor's copies; additional copies at 40% discount. Acquires one-time rights. Sponsors awards/contests.

Advice: "Send query with SASE."

Ⓝ ☐ THE AUX ARC REVIEW, A665 Arkansas Union, University of Arkansas, Fayetteville AR 72701. (479)575-5361. E-mail: auxarc@uark.edu. Website: www.aux-arc.com. **Contact:** Jake Swearingen, fiction editor. Annual. Estab. 2001.

Needs: Does not want genre fiction, unless extremely well done. Receives 10-30 unsolicited mss/month. Accepts 3-5 mss/issue. Does not read mss in the summer. **Publishes 2-4 new writers/year.** Recently published work by

Michael Hemmington, Thaddeus B. Bower. Length: 1,000-5,000 words; average length: 3,000 words. Publishes short shorts. Also publishes literary essays, literary criticism, poetry. Sometimes comments on rejected mss.
How to Contact: Send complete ms. Send SASE for return of ms. Responds in 2 weeks to queries; 2 months to mss. Accepts reprints, multiple submissions No simultaneous submissions. Sample copy for SASE , 8 × 11 envelope and $2 postage. Writer's guidelines online.
Payment/Terms: Pays contributor's copy. Pays on publication for one-time rights. Sponsors awards/contests.
Advice: "Clear, simple writing. Inventive situations, not set in a university setting. Revise, revise, and then revise again. One careless typo can ruin everything."

N $ ⬚ ⬚ B&A: NEW FICTION, 56 The Esplande, SR. 503, Toronto ON M5E 1A7 Canada. (416)822-8708. Ed Sluga, publisher. **Contact:** Siri Agrell, editor. 8½ × 11; 48 pages; bond paper; illustrations. "We publish new and emerging writers whose work is fresh and revealing, and impacts on a literary relationship." Quarterly. Estab. 1990. Circ. 2,000.
Needs: Experimental, literary, novel excerpts. No mystery, sci-fi, poetry. Publishes anthology periodically. Receives 20 unsolicited mss/month. Accepts 8 mss/issue; 24-40 mss/year. Publishes ms 6 months after acceptance. Length: 500-4,000 words; average length: 2,500 words.
How to Contact: Send complete ms. Should include estimated word count, short bio, list of publications with submission. SASE for reply to a query or return of ms. Accepts simultaneous submissions please advise. Sample copy for $6 (US). Writer's guidelines for #10 SASE with IRCs.
Payment/Terms: Pays $35/printed page. Pays on publication for first North American serial rights. Anthology and electronic rights Sponsors awards/contests.
Advice: "Read *B&A* first. Know what kind of literary magazine you are submitting to. If it is consistent with your work, send us your best."

⬚ THE BALTIMORE REVIEW, Baltimore Writers' Alliance, P.O. Box 410, Riderwood MD 21139. E-mail: hdiehl@bcpl.net. Website: www.baltimorewriters.org. **Contact:** Fiction Editor. Magazine: 6 × 9; 128 pages; 60 lb. paper; 10 pt. CS1 gloss film cover. Showcase for the best short stories and poetry by writers in the Baltimore area and beyond. Semiannual. Estab. 1996.
Needs: Ethnic/multicultural, literary, mainstream. "No science fiction, westerns, children's, romance, etc." Accepts 8-12 mss/issue; 16-24 mss/year. Publishes ms 1-9 months after acceptance. **Publishes "at least a few" new writers/ year.** Average length: 3,000 words. Publishes short shorts. Also publishes poetry.
How to Contact: Send SASE for reply, return of ms or send a disposable copy of ms. Responds in 1-3 months to mss. Accepts simultaneous submissions. No e-mail or fax submissions.
Payment/Terms: Pays 2 contributor's copies. Pays on publication for first North American serial rights.
Advice: "We look for compelling stories and a masterful use of the English language. We want to feel that we have never heard this story, or this voice, before. Read the kinds of publications you want your work to appear in. Make your reader believe, and care."

⬚ BARBARIC YAWP, Bone World Publishing, 3700 Country Rt. 24, Russell NY 13684-3198. (315)347-2609. **Contact:** Nancy Berbrich, fiction editor. Magazine: digest-size; 60 pages; 24lb. paper; matte cover stock. "We publish what we like. Fiction should include some bounce and surprise. Our publication is intended for the intelligent, open-minded reader." Quarterly. Estab. 1997. Circ. 120.
Needs: Adventure, experimental, fantasy (science, sword and sorcery), historical, horror, literary, mainstream, psychic/supernatural/occult, regional, religious/inspirational, science fiction (hard, soft/sociological). "We don't want any pornography, gratuitous violence or whining." Wants more humor, satire and adventure. Receives 30-40 unsolicited mss/month. Accepts 10-12 mss/issue; 40-48 mss/year. Publishes ms up to 6 months after acceptance. **Publishes 4-6 new writers/year.** Recently published work by Mark Spitzer, Jon Boilard and Karl Koweski. Length: 1,200 words; average length: 600 words. Publishes short shorts. Also publishes literary essays, literary criticism, poetry. Often comments on rejected mss.
How to Contact: Send SASE for reply, return of ms or send a disposable copy of ms. Responds in 2 weeks to queries; 4 months to mss. Accepts simultaneous and reprints, multiple submissions. Sample copy for $3. Writer's guidelines for #10 SASE.
Payment/Terms: Pays 1 contributor's copy; additional copies $3. Acquires one-time rights.
Advice: "We are primarily concerned with work that means something to the author, but which is able to transcend the personal into the larger world. Send whatever is important to you. Work must hold my interest and be well-crafted. Read, read, read; write, write, write—then send us your best. Don't get discouraged. Believe in yourself. Take risks. Do not fear rejection."

⬚ BATHTUB GIN, Pathwise Press, P.O. Box 2392, Bloomington IN 47402. (812)339-7298. E-mail: charter@blu emarble.net. Website: www.bluemarble.net/~charter/btgin.htm. **Contact:** Fiction Editor. Magazine: 8½ × 5½; 60 pages; recyled 20-lb. paper; 80-lb. card cover; illustrations; photos. "*Bathtub Gin* is looking for work that has some kick to it. We are very eclectic and publish a wide range of styles. Audience is anyone interested in new writing and art that is not being presented in larger magazines." Semiannual. Estab. 1997. Circ. 250.
Needs: Condensed novels, experimental, humor/satire, literary. "No horror, science fiction, historical unless they

go beyond the usual formula. We want more experimental fiction." Receives 20 unsolicited mss/month. Accepts 2-3 mss/issue. Does not read mss September 15-December 1 and March 15-July 1; "we publish in mid-October and mid-April." **Publishes 10 new writers/year.** Recently published work by Melissa Frederick and Allen Purdy. Publishes short shorts. Also publishes literary essays, literary criticism, poetry. Often comments on rejected mss.

How to Contact: Accepts submissions by e-mail. Send SASE for reply, return of ms or send a disposable copy of ms. Responds in 1-2 months to queries. Accepts simultaneous and reprints, multiple submissions. Sample copy for $5 with 6×9 SAE and 4 first class stamps. Writer's guidelines for #10 SASE. Reviews fiction.

Payment/Terms: Pays 1 contributor's copy; discount on additional copies. Rights revert to author upon publication.

Advice: "We are looking for writing that contains strong imagery, is complex, and is willing to take a chance with form and structure."

BEACON STREET REVIEW, 120 Boylston St., Emerson College, Boston MA 02116. E-mail: beaconstreetreview@hotmail.com. **Contact:** Prose Editor. Editors change each year. Magazine: 5½×8½; 100 pages; 60 lb. paper. The *Beacon Street Review*, a journal of new prose and poetry, is published twice a year by students in the graduate writing, literature and publishing department of Emerson College. Biannual. Estab. 1986. Circ. 1,000.

Needs: Literary. Receives 20-30 unsolicited mss/month. Accepts 4-6 mss/issue; 8-10 mss/year. Publishes ms 1-2 months after acceptance. Publishes short shorts. Also publishes poetry. Sometimes comments on rejected mss.

How to Contact: Send disposable copy of ms. Accepts simultaneous submissions with notification. Sample copy for $6 with a #10 SASE. Writer's guidelines for SASE.

Payment/Terms: Pays 3 contributor's copies; additional copies $2. Pays on publication for one-time rights. Sponsors awards/contests.

BEGINNINGS PUBLISHING, A Magazine for the Novice Writer, Beginnings Publishing, P.O. Box 92-N, Shirley NY 11967-1525. (631)645-3846. E-mail: jenineb@optonline.net. Website: www.scbeginnings.com. **Contact:** Jenine Boisits, fiction editor. Magazine: 8½×11; 54 pages; matte; glossy cover; illustrations; photographs. "*Beginnings* publishes only beginner/novice writers. We do accept articles by professionals pertaining to the craft of writing. We have had many new writers go on to be published elsewhere after being featured in our magazine." Triannual. Estab. 1999. Circ. 2,500.

• *Beginnings* ranked on *Writer's Digest's* "Top 30" list of best markets for fiction writers.

Needs: Adventure, family saga, literary, mainstream, mystery/suspense (amateur slueth), romance (contemporary), science fiction (soft/sociological), western. "No erotica, horror." Receives 425 unsolicited mss/month. Accepts 10 mss/issue; 20 mss/year. Does not read mss during January and April. Publishes ms 3-4 months after acceptance. **Publishes 100 percent new writers/year.** Recently published work by Harvey Stanbrough, Freada Dillon, Colleen Little, Mary Hoehmann. Average length: 2,500 words. Publishes short shorts. Also publishes poetry. Sometimes comments on rejected mss.

How to Contact: Send complete ms. Send disposable copy of ms and #10 SASE for reply only; however, will accept SASE for return of ms. Responds in 3 weeks to queries; 9-12 weeks to mss. Accepts simultaneous and reprints submissions. Sample copy for $4. Writer's guidelines for SASE, e-mail or on website.

Payment/Terms: Pays 1 contributor's copy; additional copies $4. Pays on publication for first North American serial, first rights.

Advice: "Originality, presentation, proper grammar and spelling a must. Non-predictable endings. Many new writers confuse showing vs. telling. Writers who have that mastered stand out. Study the magazine. Check and double check your work. Original storylines, well thought-out, keep up a good pace. Presentation is important, too! Rewrite, rewrite!"

BELLEVUE LITERARY REVIEW, A Journal of Humanity and Human Experience, Dept. of Medicine, NYU School of Medicine, 550 First Avenue, OBV-A612, New York NY 10016. (212)263-3973. Fax: (212)263-3206. E-mail: info@blreview.org. Website: http://blreview.org. **Contact:** Ronna Wineberg, fiction editor. Magazine: 6×9; 160 pages; photos. "The *BLR* is a literary journal that examines human existence through the prism of health and healing, illness and disease. We encourage creative interpretations of these themes." Semiannual. Estab. 2001. Member, CLMP.

Needs: Literary. No genre fiction. Receives 55 unsolicited mss/month. Accepts 9 mss/issue; 18 mss/year. Publishes ms 3-6 months after acceptance. Agented fiction 1%. **Publishes 3-6 new writers/year.** Recently published work by Sheila Kohler, Abraham Vergnese, Robert Oldshue and Clarence Smith. Length: 5,000 words; average length: 2,500 words. Publishes short shorts. Also publishes literary essays, poetry. Sometimes comments on rejected mss.

How to Contact: Send complete ms. Send SASE (or IRC) for return of ms or disposable copy of the ms and #10 SASE for reply only. Responds in 3-6 months to mss. Accepts simultaneous submissions. Sample copy for $7. Writer's guidelines for SASE, e-mail or on website.

Payment/Terms: Pays 2 contributor's copies; additional copies $5. Pays on publication for first North American serial rights. Sends galleys to author.

BELLINGHAM REVIEW, Mail Stop 9053, Western Washington University, Bellingham WA 98225. (360)650-4863. E-mail: bhreview@cc.wwu.edu. Website: www.wwu.edu/~bhreview. **Contact:** Fiction Editor. Magazine: 6×8¼; 150 pages; 60 lb. white paper; four color cover. "*Bellingham Review* seeks literature of palpable quality; stories, essays, and poems that nudge the limits of form or execute traditional forms exquisitely." Semiannual. Estab. 1977. Circ. 1,600.

● The editors are actively seeking submissions of creative nonfiction, as well as stories that push the boundaries of the form. The Tobias Wolff Award in Fiction Contest runs December 1-March 15; see website for guidelines or send SASE.

Needs: Experimental, humor/satire, literary, regional (Northwest). Does not want anything nonliterary. Accepts 3-4 mss/issue. Does not read ms February 2-September 30. Publishes ms 6 months after acceptance. Agented fiction 10%. **Publishes 3-4 new writers/year.** Recently published work by Christie Hodgen, Robert Van Wagoner and Joan Leegeant. Publishes short shorts. Also publishes poetry.

How to Contact: Send complete ms. Responds in 3 months to mss. Accepts simultaneous submissions. Sample copy for $7. Writer's guidelines online. Reviews fiction.

Payment/Terms: Pays as funds allow. Pays on publication. Acquires first North American serial rights.

Advice: "We look for work that is ambitious, vital, and challenging both to the spirit and the intellect."

BELLOWING ARK, A Literary Tabloid, P.O. Box 55564, Shoreline WA 98155. (206)440-0791. **Contact:** Fiction Editor. Tabloid: 11½×17½; 28 pages; electro-brite paper and cover stock; illustrations; photos. "We publish material which we feel addresses the human situation in an affirmative way. We do not publish academic fiction." Bimonthly. Estab. 1984. Circ. 650.

● Work from *Bellowing Ark* appeared in the *Pushcart Prize* anthology.

Needs: Literary, mainstream, serialized novels. "No science fiction or fantasy." Receives 10-20 unsolicited mss/month. Accepts 2-5 mss/issue; 700-1,000 mss/year. Publishes ms 6 months after acceptance. **Publishes 10-50 new writers/year.** Recently published work by Larsen Bowker, Nancy Corson Carter, Shelley Uva, Tanyo Ravicz, Susan Montag and E.R. Romaine. Publishes short shorts. Also publishes literary essays, literary criticism, poetry. Sometimes comments on rejected mss.

How to Contact: SASE. Responds in 6 weeks to mss. No simultaneous submissions. Sample copy for $4, 9½×12½ SAE and $1.43 postage.

Payment/Terms: Pays in contributor's copies. Acquires one-time rights.

Advice: "*Bellowing Ark* began as (and remains) an alternative to the despair and negativity of the Workshop/Academic literary scene; we believe that life has meaning and is worth living—the work we publish reflects that belief. Learn how to tell a story before submitting. Avoid 'trick' endings—they have all been done before and better. *Bellowing Ark* is interested in publishing writers who will develop with the magazine, as in an exteded community. We find *good* writers and stick with them. This is why the magazine has grown from 12 to 32 pages."

BELOIT FICTION JOURNAL, Box 11, 700 College St., Beloit College WI 53511. (608)363-2577. Editor-in-chief: Clint McCowan. **Contact:** Heather Skyler, managing editor. Literary magazine: 6×9; 250 pages; 60 lb. paper; 10 pt. C1S cover stock; illustrations; photos on cover; ad-free. "We are interested in publishing the best contemporary fiction and are open to all themes except those involving pornographic, religiously dogmatic or politically propagandistic representations. Our magazine is for general readership, though most of our readers will probably have a specific interest in literary magazines." Annual. Estab. 1985.

● Work first appearing in *Beloit Fiction Journal* has been reprinted in award-winning collections, including the *Flannery O'Connor* and the *Milkweed Fiction Prize* collections, and has won the Iowa Short Fiction award.

Needs: Literary, mainstream, contemporary. Wants more experimental and short shorts. Would like to see more "stories with a focus on both language and plot, unusual metaphors and vivid characters. No pornography, religious dogma, science fiction, horror, political propaganda or genre fiction." Receives 400 unsolicited mss/month. Accepts 20 mss/year. Reads mss August 1-December 1. Replies take longer in summer. Publishes ms 9 months after acceptance. **Publishes 3 new writers/year.** Recently published work by Rick Bass, A. Mannette Ansay, Gary Fincke, David Harris Ebenbach, Anne Panning and David Milofsky. Length: 250-10,000 words; average length: 5,000 words. Sometimes comments on rejected mss.

How to Contact: SASE for ms. No fax, e-mail or disk submissions. Responds in 2 weeks to queries; 2 months to mss. Accepts simultaneous submissions if identified as such. Sample copy for $12 for double issue; $7 for single issue. Writer's guidelines for #10 SASE.

Advice: "Many of our contributors are writers whose work we had previously rejected. Don't let one rejection slip turn you away from our—or any—magazine."

BERKELEY FICTION REVIEW, 10 Eshleman Hall, University of California, Berkeley CA 94720. (510)642-2892. E-mail: smh@uclink.berkeley.edu. Website: www.OCF.Berkeley.EDU/~bfr/. **Contact:** Sarah Haufrect and Julia Simon, editors. Magazine: 5½×8½; 180 pages; perfect-bound; glossy cover; some b&w art; photographs. "The mission of *Berkeley Fiction Review* is to provide a forum for new and emerging writers as well as writers already established. We publish a wide variety of contemporary short fiction for a literary audience." Annual. Estab. 1981. Circ. 1,000.

Needs: Experimental, literary, mainstream. "Quality, inventive short fiction. No poetry or formula fiction." Receives 60 unsolicited mss/month. Accepts 10-20 mss/issue. **Publishes 15-20 new writers/year.** Publishes short shorts. Occasionally comments on rejected mss.

How to Contact: Responds in 6-7 months to mss. Accepts simultaneous, multiple submissions. Sample copy for $9.50. Writer's guidelines for SASE.

Payment/Terms: Pays 1 contributor's copy. Acquires first rights. Sponsors awards/contests.

Advice: "Our criteria is fiction that resonates. Voices that are strong and move a reader. Clear, powerful prose (either voice or rendering of subject) with a point. Unique ways of telling stories—these capture the editors. Work hard, don't give up. Don't let your friends or family critique your work. Get someone honest to point out your writing weaknesses, and then work on them. Don't submit thinly veiled autobiographical stories; it's been done before—and better. With the proliferation of computers, everyone thinks they're a writer. Not true, unfortunately. The plus side though is ease of transmission and layout and diversity and range of new work."

$ ☑ BIBLIOPHILOS, A Journal of History, Literature, and the Liberal Arts, The Bibliophile Publishing Co., Inc., 200 Security Building, Fairmont WV 26554. (304)366-8107. **Contact:** Gerald J. Bobango, editor. Literary magazine: 5½×8; 68-72 pages; white glossy paper; illustrations; photos. "We see ourself as a forum for new and unpublished writers, historians, philosophers, literary critics and reviewers, and those who love animals. Audience is academic-oriented, college graduate, who believes in traditional Aristotelian-Thomistic thought and education, and has a fair streak of the Luddite in him/her. Our ideal reader owns no television, has never sent nor received e-mail, and avoids shopping malls at any cost. He loves books." Quarterly. Estab. 1981. Circ. 400.

Needs: Adventure, ethnic/multicultural, family saga, historical (general, US, Eastern Europe), horror (psychological, supernatural), humor/satire, literary, mainstream, military/war, mystery/suspense (police procedural, private eye/hardboiled, courtroom), novel excerpts, regional (New England, Middle Atlantic), romance (gothic, historical, regency period), slice-of-life vignettes, suspense, thriller/espionage, translations, western (frontier saga, traditional), utopian, Orwellian. "No 'I found Jesus and it turned my life around'; no 'I remember Mama, who was a saint and I miss her terribly'; no gay or lesbian topics; no drug culture material; nothing harping on political correctness; nothing to do with healthy living, HMOs, medical programs, or the welfare state, unless it is against statism in these areas." Receives 40 unsolicited mss/month. Accepts 5-6 mss/issue; 25-30 mss/year. Publishes ms 9 months after acceptance. **Publishes 2-6 new writers/year.** Recently published work by Mardelle Fortier, Clevenger Kehmeier, Gwen Williams, Manuel Sanchez-Lopez, Janet Tyson, Andrea C. Poe, Norman Nathan. Also publishes literary essays, literary criticism, poetry. Often comments on rejected mss.

How to Contact: Accepts submissions by mail. Query with clips of published work. Include bio, SASE and $5.25 for sample issue. Responds in 2 weeks to queries; 1 month to mss. Accepts simultaneous submissions. Sample copy for $5.25. Writer's guidelines for 9½×4 SAE with 2 first-class stamps.

Payment/Terms: Pays $25-40. Pays on publication for first North American serial rights.

Advice: "Write for specifications, send for a sample issue, then *read* the thing, study the formatting, and follow the instructions, which say query first, before sending anything. We shall not respond to unsolicited material. We don't want touchy-feely maudlin stuff where hugging kids solves all of life's problems, and we want no references anywhere in the story to e-mail, the internet, or computers, unless it's to berate them."

☑ ☑ BIG MUDDY: A JOURNAL OF THE MISSISSIPPI RIVER VALLEY, Southeast Missouri State University Press, MS2650 English Dept., Southeast MO State University, Cape Girardeau MO 63701. Website: www6.semo .edu/universitypress/. **Contact:** Susan Swartwout, editor. Magazine: 8½×5½ perfect-bound; 150 pages; acid-free paper; color cover stock; layflat lamination; illustrations; photos. "*Big Muddy* explores multidisciplinary, multicultural issues, people, and events mainly concerning the ten-state area that borders the Mississippi River, by people who have lived here, who have an interest in the area, or who know the River Basin. We publish fiction, poetry, historical essays, creative nonfiction, environmental essays, biography, regional events, photography, art, etc." Semiannual. Estab. 2001. Circ. 500.

• *Big Muddy* was *Small Press Review's* "Best Pick" in magazines-2001.

Needs: Adventure, ethnic/multicultural, experimental, family saga, feminist, historical, humor/satire, literary, mainstream, military/war, mystery/suspense, regional (Mississippi River Valley; Midwest), translations. "No romance, fantasy or children's." Receives 50 unsolicited mss/month. Accepts 2-4 mss/issue. Publishes ms 6 months after acceptance. Recently published work by John Mort, Colleen McElroy, Stephen Graham Jones, Ann Boaden, Lynn Casteel, Anna Leahy and Jim Elledge. Publishes short shorts. Also publishes literary essays, literary criticism, poetry.

How to Contact: Send SASE for return of ms or send a disposable copy of ms and #10 SASE for reply only. Responds in 10 weeks to mss. Accepts multiple submissions. Sample copy for $6. Writer's guidelines for SASE, e-mail, fax or on website. Reviews fiction.

Payment/Terms: Pays 2 contributor's copies; additional copies $5. Acquires first North American serial rights.

Advice: "In fiction manuscripts we look for clear language, avoidance of clichés except in necessary dialogue, a *fresh* vision of the theme or issue. Find some excellent and honest readers to comment on your work-in-progress and final draft. Consider their viewpoints carefully. Revise."

Ⓝ ☑ $ ☑ BIGnews, The Art and Literary Monthly, Grand Canyon Neighborhood, 302 E. 45th St., 4th Fl, New York NY 10017. (212)883-0680. Fax: (212)883-0672. E-mail: BIGnewsmag@aol.com. Website: www.main chance.org. **Contact:** Ron Grynberg, editor. Magazine: 11×17; 16 pages; tabloid paper; 50 lb. cover stock; illustrations; photos. Monthly. Estab. 2,000. Circ. 30,000.

● Received the 2002 North American Street Newspaper Association (NASNA) Awards for Best Editoriral or Essay, Best Art, Best Poetry.

Needs: Literary, mainstream. "Generally, no genre fiction." Receives 12 unsolicited mss/month. Accepts 5 mss/year. Publishes ms 2-3 months after acceptance. **Publishes 2 new writers/year.** Recently published work by Robert Sheckley, John Ray, JR., J.L. Navarro, and Tim Hall. Length: 200-5,000 words; average length: 2,700 words. Publishes short shorts. Also publishes literary essays. Sometimes comments on rejected mss.

How to Contact: Send complete ms. Accepts submissions by e-mail, fax. Send disposable copy of the ms and #10 SASE for reply only. Responds in 1 month to queries; 1 month to mss. Accepts simultaneous, multiple submissions. Sample copy for free. Writer's guidelines online.

Payment/Terms: Pays $50-75; 5 contributor's copies and a free subscription to the magazine. Pays on publication for one-time rights.

Advice: "A very busy editor has to want to read the whole thing through. Take risks. Don't write knowingly. Make it an effort of discovery."

THE BITTER OLEANDER, 4983 Tall Oaks Dr., Fayettville NY 13066-9776. (315)637-3047. Fax: (315)637-5056. E-mail: info@bitteroleander.com. Website: www.bitteroleander.com. **Contact:** Paul B. Roth. Zine specializing in poetry and fiction: 6×9; 128 pages; 55 lb. paper; 12 pt. CIS cover stock; photos. "We're interested in the surreal; deep image' particularization of natural experiences." Semiannual. Estab. 1974. Circ. 1,500.

Needs: Experimental, New Age (mystic, spiritual), translations. "No pornography; no confessional; no romance." Receives 100 unsolicited mss/month. Accepts 1-2 mss/issue; 2-4 mss/year. Does not read in July. Publishes ms 4-6 months after acceptance. Recently published work by Tom Stoner, John Michael Cummings, Sara Leslie. Average length: 2,500 words. Publishes short shorts. Also publishes literary essays, literary criticism, poetry. Always comments on rejected mss.

How to Contact: Send SASE for reply, return of ms. Responds in 1 week to queries; 1 month to mss. Accepts multiple submissions. Sample copy for $8, 7×10 SAE with 4 first-class stamps. Writer's guidelines for #10 SASE.

Payment/Terms: Pays 1 contributor's copy; additional copies $8. Acquires first rights.

Advice: "If within the first 100 words my mind drifts, the rest rarely makes it. Be yourself and listen to no one but yourself."

$ BLACK LACE, BLK Publishing CO., P.O. Box 83912, Los Angeles CA 90083-0912. (310)410-0808. Fax: (310)410-9250. E-mail: newsroom@blk.com. Website: www.blacklace.org. **Contact:** Fiction Editor. Magazine: 8⅛×10⅝; 48 pages; book stock; color glossy cover; illustrations; photos. "*Black Lace* is a lifestyle magazine for African-American lesbians. Its content ranges from erotic imagery to political commentary." Quarterly. Estab. 1991.

Needs: Ethnic/multicultural, lesbian. "Avoid interracial stories of idealized pornography." Accepts 4 mss/year. Recently published work by Nicole King, Wanda Thompson, Lynn K. Pannell, Sheree Ann Slaughter, Lyn Lifshin, JoJo and Drew Alise Timmens. Publishes short shorts. Also publishes literary essays, literary criticism, poetry.

How to Contact: Query with published clips or send complete ms. Send a disposable copy of ms. No simultaneous submissions. Accepts electronic submissions. Sample copy for $7. Writer's guidelines free.

Payment/Terms: Pays $50 and 2 contributor's copies. Acquires first North American serial rights. Right to anthologize.

Advice: *Black Lace* seeks erotic material of the highest quality. The most important thing is that the work be erotic and that it feature black lesbians or themes. Study the magazine to see what we do and how we do it. Some fiction is very romantic, other is highly sexual. Most articles in *Black Lace* cater to black lesbians between two extremes."

THE BLACK MOUNTAIN REVIEW, Black Mountain Press, P.O. Box 9, Ballyclare Co Antrim BT390JW, N. Ireland. E-mail: editors@blackmountainreview.com. Website: www.blackmountainreview.com. **Contact:** Editor. Magazine: A5; approximately 100 pages. "We publish short fiction with a contemporary flavour for an international audience." Semiannual. Estab. 1999.

Needs: Ethnic/multicultural (general), experimental, historical (literary), literary, regional (Irish), religious/inspirational (general religious, inspirational), romance (literary), science fiction (literary), translations. Publishes ms 5 months after acceptance. **Publishes many new writers/year.** Recently published work by Cathal O Searcaigh, Michael Longley and Brian Keenan. Average length: 1,500-3,000 words. Publishes short shorts. Also publishes literary essays, literary criticism, poetry. Sometimes comments on rejected mss.

How to Contact: Send SASE (or IRC) for return of ms or send a disposable copy of ms and #10 SASE for reply. Material should be supplied on 3½ inch floppy disk or by e-mail (word.txt format, preferably not attachments) with paper typescript by snail mail. Submissions *must* be accompanied with an e-mail or disk version. Responds in 2 months to queries; 4 months to mss. Accepts simultaneous submissions. Sample copy for $4.50. Writer's guidelines for SASE or by e-mail. Reviews fiction.

Payment/Terms: Pays 1 contributor's copy; additional copies $4.50. Pays on publication for one-time rights.

Advice: "We look for literary quality. Write well."

$ BLACK WARRIOR REVIEW, P.O. Box 862936, Tuscaloosa AL 35486-0027. (205)348-4518. Website: www.webdelsol.com/bwr. **Contact:** Jennifer Gravley, fiction editor. Magazine: 6×9; 200 pages; color artwork.

"We publish contemporary fiction, poetry, reviews, essays, and art for a literary audience. We publish the freshest work we can find." Semiannual. Estab. 1974. Circ. 2,000.

● Work that appeared in the *Black Warrior Review* has been included in the *Pushcart Prize* anthology, *Harper's Magazine*, *Best American Short Stories*, *Best American Poetry* and *New Short Stories from the South*.

Needs: Literary, contemporary, short and short-short fiction. Wants "work that is conscious of form and well-crafted. We are open to good experimental writing and short-short fiction. No genre fiction please." Receives 300 unsolicited mss/month. Accepts 5 mss/issue; 10 mss/year. Unsolicited novel excerpts are not considered unless the novel is already contracted for publication. Publishes ms 6 months after acceptance. **Publishes 5 new writers/year.** Recently published work by Gary Fincke, Anthony Varallo, Bret Anthony Johnston, Rick Bass, and Sherri Flick. Length: 7,500 words; average length: 2,000-5,000 words. Occasionally comments on rejected mss.

How to Contact: Send complete ms with SASE (1 story per submission). Responds in 4 months to mss. Accepts simultaneous submissions if noted. Sample copy for $8. Writer's guidelines online.

Payment/Terms: Pays up to $150, copies, and a 1-year subscription. Pays on publication for first rights.

Advice: "We look for attention to language, freshness, honesty, a convincing and sharp voice. Send us a clean, well-printed, proofread manuscript. Become familiar with the magazine prior to submission."

◯ ◎ **BLUE MESA REVIEW,** University of New Mexico, Dept. of English, Humanities Bldg., Room 217, Alburquerque NM 87131. (505)277-6155. Fax: (505)277-5573. E-mail: bluemesa@unm.edu. Website: www.unm.edu/~bluemesa. **Contact:** Julie Shigekuni. Magazine: 6×9; 300 pages; 55 lb. paper; 10 pt CS1 photos. "*Blue Mesa Review* publishes the best/most current creative writing on the market." Annual. Estab. 1989. Circ. 1,200.

Needs: Adventure, ethnic/multicultural, experimental, feminist, gay, historical, humor/satire, lesbian, literary, mainstream, regional, western. Receives 25 unsolicited mss/month. Accepts 100 mss/year. Accepts mss July 1-October 1; all submissions must be post marked by October 1; reads mss November-December; responds in January. Publishes ms 5-6 months after acceptance. Recently published work by Kathleen Spivack, Roberta Swann and Tony Mares. Publishes short shorts. Also publishes literary essays, poetry.

How to Contact: Send SASE for reply. Sample copy for $12. Writer's guidelines online. Reviews fiction.

Payment/Terms: Pays 1 contributor's copy. Acquires first North American serial rights.

Advice: "Contact us for complete guidelines. All submissions must follow our guidelines."

◙ **THE blue REVIEW,** Corba Press,. E-mail: editors@corbapress.com. Website: www.corbapress.com. **Contact:** Paul Hina and A. Scott Rinehart, editors. Magazine: 5½×8½; 30 pages; 24 lb. paper; colored cover stock. "*The blue Review* has been created for those of us who have grown tired of the modern literary conventions. Our *Review* has been invented to perpetuate subversive and mindful literary works that would otherwise fall through the cracks of an increasingly less tolerant publishing community. The current celebrated literature has its focus on writer-as-entertainer, which belittles the once highly regarded art form of writing. *The blue Review* is here to supply the writer-as-artist with the voice that has, for far too long, been absent from bookstores and many prominent small press publications." Quarterly. Estab. 2002. Circ. 100.

Needs: Experimental, historical, humor/satire, literary. "No mainstream or genre fiction. No pornography." Receives 30 unsolicited mss/month. Accepts 3 mss/issue; 12 mss/year. Publishes ms 6 months after acceptance. **Publishes 10 new writers/year.** Average length: 4,000 words. Publishes short shorts. Also publishes literary essays, poetry. Sometimes comments on rejected mss.

How to Contact: "No cover letters. No queries. E-mail submissions only." Responds in 4-6 weeks to mss. Accepts simultaneous and reprints, multiple submissions. Sample copy for $3 plus $1 s&h. Writer's guidelines online.

Payment/Terms: Pays 1 contributor's copy; additional copies $2. Acquires first rights. Not copyrighted.

Advice: "We look for stories that feel like they are being told for the first time. It is important to display fresh ideas and eccentric characters in interesting, absurd, or surreal situations. Don't be ashamed to express your unspeakable thoughts on paper. Don't be afraid of ideas just because they seem unpopular or unfashionable."

◙ ◎ **BLUELINE,** English Dept., SUNY, Postdam NY 13676. (315)267-2043. E-mail: blueline@postdam.edu. Website: www.potsdam.edu/engl/bluelinedefault.html. **Contact:** Fiction Editor. Magazine: 6×9; 200 pages; 70 lb. white stock paper; 65 lb. smooth cover stock; illustrations; photos. "*Blueline* is interested in quality writing about the Adirondacks or other places similar in geography and spirit. We publish fiction, poetry, personal essays, book reviews and oral history for those interested in Adirondacks, nature in general, and well-crafted writing." Annual. Estab. 1979. Circ. 400.

SENDING TO A COUNTRY other than your own? Be sure to send International Reply Coupons (IRC) instead of stamps for replies or return of your manuscript.

Needs: Adventure, humor/satire, literary, regional, contemporary, prose poem, reminiscences, oral history, nature/outdoors. No urban stories or erotica. Receives 8-10 unsolicited mss/month. Accepts 6-8 mss/issue. Does not read January-August. Publishes ms 3-6 after acceptance. **Publishes 2 new writers/year.** Recently published work by Joan Connor, Laura Rodley and Ann Mohin. Length: 500-3,000 words; average length: 2,500 words. Also publishes literary essays, poetry. Occasionally comments on rejected mss.
How to Contact: Accepts simultaneous submissions. Sample copy for $6.
Payment/Terms: Pays 1 contributor's copy; charges $7 each for 3 or more copies. Acquires first rights.
Advice: "We look for concise, clear, concrete prose that tells a story and touches upon a universal theme or situation. We prefer realism to romanticism but will consider nostalgia if well done. Pay attention to grammar and syntax. Avoid murky language, sentimentality, cuteness or folkiness. We would like to see more good fiction related to the Adirondacks and more literary fiction and prose poems. If manuscript has potential, we work with author to improve and reconsider for publication. Our readers prefer fiction to poetry (in general) or reviews. Write from your own experience, be specific and factual (within the bounds of you story) and if you write about universal features such as love, death, change, etc., write about them in a fresh way. Triteness and mediocrity are the hallmarks of the majority of stories seen today."

◯ BOGG, Journal of Contemporary Writing, Bogg Publications, 422 N. Cleveland St., Arlington VA 22201-1424. (703)243-6019. **Contact:** John Elsberg, US editor. Magazine: 6×9; 68-72 pages; 70 lb. white paper; 70 lb. cover stock; line illustrations. "American and British poetry, prose poems, experimental short 'fictions,' reviews, and essays on small press." Published 2 or 3 times a year. Estab. 1968. Circ. 850.
Needs: Very short experimental fiction and prose poems. "We are always looking for work with British/Commonwealth themes and/or references." Receives 25 unsolicited mss/month. Accepts 1-2 mss/issue; 3-6 mss/year. Publishes ms 3-18 after acceptance. **Publishes 25-50 new writers/year.** Recently published work by Karen Rosenberg, J. Wesley Clark, Christopher Chambers and T. Gilgore Splake. Also publishes literary essays, literary criticism. Occasionally comments on rejected mss.
How to Contact: Responds in 1 week to queries; 2 weeks to mss. Sample copy for $4 or $5 (current issue). Reviews fiction.
Payment/Terms: Pays 2 contributor's copies; reduced charge for extras. Acquires one-time rights.
Advice: "We look for voice and originality. Read magazine first. We are most interested in prose work of experimental or wry nature to supplement poetry, and are always looking for innovative/imaginative uses of British themes and references."

◼ ◯ ◉ BOOK WORLD MAGAZINE, Christ Church Publishers Ltd., 2 Caversham Street, London SW3 4AH, UK. 0207 351 4995. Fax: 0207 3514995. E-mail: leonard.holdsworth@btopenworld.com. **Contact:** James Hughes. Magazine: 64 pages; illustrations; photos. "Subscription magazine for serious book lovers, book collectors, librarians and academics." Monthly. Estab. 1971. Circ. 6,000.
Needs: Erotica, historical, humor/satire, literary, mainstream, military/war. Receives 20 unsolicited mss/month. Accepts 12 mss/issue. Publishes ms several months after acceptance. **Publishes 2 new writers/year.** Publishes short shorts. Also publishes literary essays, literary criticism.
How to Contact: Query. Send SASE for return of ms or send disposable copy of ms and #10 SASE for reply only. Responds in 3 months to queries; 3 months to mss. Accepts simultaneous submissions. Sample copy for $7.50. Writer's guidelines for SASE.
Payment/Terms: Pays on publication for one-time rights.
Advice: "Always write to us before sending any mss."

◯ BOOKPRESS, The Newspaper of the Literary Arts, The Bookery, 215 Cayuga St., Ithaca NY 14850. (607)277-2254. Fax: (607)275-9221. E-mail: bookpress@thebookery.com. Website: www.thebookery.com/bookpress. **Contact:** Jack Goldman, editor-in-chief. Newspaper: 12-16 pages; newsprint; illustrations and photos. Contains book reviews, analysis, fiction and excerpts from published work. Monthly. Estab. 1991. Circ. 6,000.
Needs: Historical, literary, regional, political science. No new age. Receives 10-12 unsolicited mss/month. Accepts 0-2 mss/issue. Does not read during the summer. Publishes ms 1-3 months after acceptance. **Publishes 5-10 new writers/year.** Recently published work by Robert Lennon, Brian Hall and Thomas Eisner. Average length: 2,000 words. Also publishes literary essays, literary criticism, poetry.
How to Contact: Send SASE for return of ms. No unsolicited e-mail submissions. Responds in 1 month to mss. Accepts simultaneous submissions. Sample copy for free. Writer's guidelines free. Reviews fiction.
Payment/Terms: Pays free subscription to newspaper.
Advice: "Send a brief, concise cover letter. No overwriting or overly cerebral academic work. The author's genuine interest and passion for the topic makes for good work."

$ ◯ BOULEVARD, Opojaz, Inc., 6614 Clayton Rd., PMB 325, Richmond Heights MO 63117. (314)862-2643. Fax: (314)781-7250. Website: www.richardburgin.com. **Contact:** Richard Burgin, editor. Magazine: 5½×8½; 150-250 pages; excellent paper; high-quality cover stock; illustrations; photos. "*Boulevard* is a diverse literary magazine presenting original creative work by well-known authors, as well as by writers of exciting promise." Triannual. Estab. 1985. Circ. 11,000.

Needs: Confessions, experimental, literary, mainstream, novel excerpts. "We do not want erotica, science fiction, romance, western, or children's stories." Receives over 600 unsolicited mss/month. Accepts about 10 mss/issue. Does not accept manuscripts between May 1 and October 1. Publishes ms 9 months after acceptance. Agented fiction 25%. **Publishes 10 new writers/year.** Recently published work by Joyce Carol Oates, Elizabeth Tallent, Josip Novakovich and Jonathan Baumbach. Length: 8,000 words maximum; average length: 5,000 words. Publishes short shorts. Also publishes literary essays, literary criticism, poetry. Sometimes comments on rejected mss.

How to Contact: Send complete ms. Accepts submissions by mail, phone. Accepts mss on disk. SASE for reply. Responds in 2 weeks to queries; 3 months to mss. Accepts multiple submissions. No simultaneous submissions. Sample copy for $8. Writer's guidelines online.

Payment/Terms: Pays $50-300. Pays on publication for first North American serial rights.

Advice: "We pick the stories that move us the most emotionally, stimulate us the most intellectually, are the best written and thought out. Don't write to get published—write to express your experience and vision of the world."

$ 🗎 ◎ 📺 BRAIN, CHILD, The Magazine for Thinking Mothers, March Press, P.O. Box 1161, Harrisonburg VA 22803. Website: www.brainchildmag.com. **Contact:** Jennifer Niesslein and Stephanie Wilkinson, co-editors. Magazine: 7¼×10; 60-100 pages; 80lb. matte cover; illustrations; photos. "*Brain, Child* reflects modern motherhood—the way it really is. We like to think of *Brain, Child* as a community, for and by mothers who like to think about what raising kids does for (and to) the mind and soul. *Brain, Child* isn't your typical parenting magazine. We couldn't cupcake-decorate our way out of a paper bag. We are more 'literary' than 'how-to,' more *New Yorker* than *Parents.* We shy away from expert advice on childrearing in favor of first-hand reflections by great writers (Jane Smiley, Barbara Ehrenreich, Anne Tyler) on life as a mother. Each quarterly issue is full of essays, features, humor, reviews, fiction, art, cartoons, and our readers' own stories. Our philosophy is pretty simple: Motherhood is worthy of literature. And there are a lot of ways to mother, all of them interesting. We're proud to be publishing articles and essays that are smart, down to earth, sometimes funny, and sometimes poignant." Quarterly. Estab. 2000. Circ. 20,000. Member, IPA, ASME.

• *Brain, Child* was winner of *Utne Reader*'s 2001 Best of the Alternative Press Award in Personal Life category, and nominated for general excellence.

Needs: Literary, mainstream. No genre fiction. Receives about 50 unsolicited mss/month. Accepts 1 mss/issue; 4 mss/year. Publishes ms 6 months after acceptance. Recently published work by Anne Tyler, Barbara Lucy Stevens and Jane Smiley. Length: 800-5,000 words; average length: 2,500 words. Also publishes literary essays. Sometimes comments on rejected mss.

How to Contact: Send complete ms. Accepts submissions by mail, e-mail (editor@brainchildmag.com). Accepts submissions by e-mail (be sure to copy and paste the ms into the body of the e-mail). Include estimated word count, brief bio and list of publications. Send SASE (or IRC) for return of ms or send a disposable copy of ms and #10 SASE for reply only. Responds in 1 month to queries; 1-3 months to mss. Accepts simultaneous and reprints, multiple submissions. Sample copy online. Writer's guidelines online. Reviews fiction.

Payment/Terms: Payment varies. Pays on publication for first North American serial, electronic rights, *Brain, Child* anthology rights. Sends galleys to author.

Advice: "We only publish fiction with a strong motherhood theme. But, like every other publisher of literary fiction, we look for well-developed characters, a compelling story, and an ending that is as strong as the rest of the piece."

🗎 ◎ THE BRIAR CLIFF REVIEW, Briar Cliff University, 3303 Rebecca St., Sioux City IA 51104-0100. (712)279-5477. E-mail: currans@briarcliff.edu. Website: www.briarcliff.edu/bcreview. **Contact:** Phil Hey or Tricia Currans-Sheehan, fiction editors. Magazine: 8½×11; 80 pages; 70 lb. Finch Opaque cover stock; illustrations; photos. "*The Briar Cliff Review* is an eclectic literary and cultural magazine focusing on (but not limited to) Siouxland writers and subjects. We are happy to proclaim ourselves a regional publication. It doesn't diminish us; it enhances us." Annual. Estab. 1989. Circ. 750.

Needs: Ethnic/multicultural, feminist, historical, humor/satire, literary, mainstream, regional. "No romance, horror or alien stories. Accepts 5 mss/year. Reads mss only between August 1 and November 1. Publishes ms 3-4 months after acceptance. **Publishes 10-14 new writers/year.** Recently published work by J. Annie MacLeod, Christine Phillips, Jenna Blum, Ken Wheaton, Jacob Appel, Laura Wilson, Cynthia Gregory and Josip Novakovich. Length: 2,500-4,000 words; average length: 3,000 words. Also publishes literary essays, literary criticism, poetry. Sometimes comments on rejected mss.

How to Contact: Send SASE for return of ms. Accepts electronic submissions (disk). Responds in 4-5 months to mss. Accepts simultaneous submissions. Sample copy for $12 and 9×12 SAE. Writer's guidelines for #10 SASE. Reviews fiction.

Payment/Terms: Pays 2 contributor's copies; additional copies available for $5. Acquires first rights.

Advice: "So many stories are just telling. We want some action. It has to move. We prefer stories in which there is no gimmick, no mechanical turn of events, no moral except the one we would draw privately."

🗎 ◎ BRILLANT CORNERS, A Journal of Jazz & Literature, Lycoming College, Williamsport PA 17701. (570)321-4279. Fax: (570)321-4090. E-mail: feinstein@lycoming.edu. **Contact:** Sascha Feinstein, editor. Journal:

6×9; 100 pages; 70 lb. Cougar opaque, vellum, natural paper; photographs. "We publish jazz-related literature—fiction, poetry and nonfiction." Semiannual. Estab. 1996. Circ. 1,200.

Needs: Condensed novels, ethnic/multicultural, experimental, literary, mainstream, romance (contemporary). Receives 10-15 unsolicited mss/month. Accepts 1-2 mss/issue; 2-3 mss/year. Does not read mss May 15-September 1. Publishes ms 4-12 after acceptance. Publishes short shorts. Also publishes literary essays, literary criticism, poetry. Rarely comments on rejected mss.

How to Contact: SASE for return of ms or send a disposable copy of ms. Accepts unpublished work only. Responds in 2 weeks to queries; 1-2 months to mss. Sample copy for $7. Reviews fiction.

Payment/Terms: Acquires first North American serial rights, sends galleys to author when possible.

Advice: "We look for clear, moving prose that demostrates a love of both writing and jazz. We primarily publish established writers, but we read all submissions carefully and welcome work by outstanding young writers."

BRYANT LITERARY REVIEW, Bryant College, 1150 Douglas Pike, Faculty Suite F, Smithfield RI 02917. (401)232-6740. Fax: (401)232-6270. E-mail: rpitt@bryant.edu. Website: http://web.bryant.edu/~blr. **Contact:** Tom Chandler. Magazine: 6×9; 125 pages; photos. Annual. Estab. 2000. Circ. 2,400. Member, CLMP.

Needs: Adventure, ethnic/multicultural, experimental, family saga, fantasy, feminist, historical, humor/satire, literary, mainstream, military/war, mystery/suspense, New Age, psychic/supernatural/occult, regional, science fiction, thriller/espionage, translations, western. "No novellas or serialized novels; only short stories." Receives 70 unsolicited mss/month. Accepts 7 mss/issue. Does not read January through August. Publishes ms 4-5 after acceptance. **Publishes 1-2 new writers/year.** Recently published work by Lyzette Wanzer, K.S. Phillips and Richard N. Bentley. Publishes short shorts. Also publishes poetry.

How to Contact: Send a disposable copy of ms and #10 SASE for reply only. Responds in 1 week to queries; 6 weeks to mss. Accepts simultaneous submissions. Sample copy for $8. Writer's guidelines by email or on website.

Payment/Terms: Pays 2 contributor's copies; additional copies $8. Pays on publication.

$ BUTTON, New England's Tiniest Magazine of Poetry, Fiction and Gracious Living, Box 26, Lunenburg MA 01462. Website: www.moonsigns.net. **Contact:** W.M. Davies, fiction editor. Magazine: 4×5; 34 pages; bond paper; color cardstock cover; illustrations; photos. "*Button* is New England's tiniest magazine of poetry, fiction, and gracious living, published once a year. As 'gracious living' is on the cover, we like wit, brevity, cleverly-conceived essay/recipe, poetry that isn't sentimental or song lyrics. I started *Button* so that a century from now, when people read it in landfills or, preferably, libraries, they'll say, 'Gee, what a great time to have lived. I wish I lived back then.'" Annual. Estab. 1993. Circ. 1,500.

Needs: Literary. "No genre fiction, science fiction, techno-thriller." Wants more of "anything Herman Melville, Henry James or Betty MacDonald would like to read." Receives 20-40 unsolicited mss/month. Accepts 1-2 mss/issue; 3-5 mss/year. Publishes ms 3-9 months after acceptance. Recently published work by Ralph Lombreglia, John Hanson Mitchell, They Might Be Giants and Lawrence Millman. Also publishes literary essays, poetry. Sometimes comments on rejected mss.

How to Contact: Send complete ms. Request guidelines. Send ms with bio, list of publications and advise how you found magazine. SASE. Responds in 1 month to queries; 2 months to mss. Sample copy for $2 and 1 34¢ stamp. Writer's guidelines for #10 SASE. Reviews fiction.

Payment/Terms: Pays $25. Pays on publication for first North American serial rights. Sends galleys to author.

Advice: "What makes a manuscript stand out? Flannery O'Connor once said, 'Don't get subtle till the fourth page,' and I agree. We look for interesting, sympathetic, believable characters and careful setting. I'm really tired of stories that start strong then devolve into dialogue uninterrupted by further exposition. Also, no stories from a mad person's POV unless it's really tricky and skillful. Please don't submit more than once a year—it's more important that you work on your craft rather than machine-gunning publications with samples, and don't submit more than 3 poems in a batch (this advice goes for other places, you'll find . . .)."

$ BYLINE, Box 5240, Edmund OK 73083-5240. (405)348-5591. E-mail: mpreston@bylinemag.com. Website: www.bylinemag.com. **Contact:** Carolyn Wall, fiction editor. Magazine "aimed at encouraging and motivating all writers toward success, with special information to help new writers. Articles center on how to write better, market smarter, sell your work." Monthly. Estab. 1981.

Needs: Literary, genre, general fiction. "Do not want to see erotica or explicit graphic content. No science fiction or fantasy." Receives 100-200 unsolicited mss/month. Accepts 1 mss/issue; 11 mss/year. Publishes ms 3 months after acceptance. **Publishes many new writers/year.** Recently published work by Joan Halperin and Greg Phillian. Also publishes literary essays, literary criticism, poetry.

How to Contact: No cover letter needed. Responds in 6-12 weeks to mss. Accepts simultaneous submissions, "if notified." Sample copy for $4. Writer's guidelines for #10 SASE.

Payment/Terms: Pays $100 and 3 contributor's copies. Pays on acceptance for first North American serial rights.

Advice: "We look for good writing that draws the reader in; conflict and character movement by story's end. We're very open to new writers. Submit a well-written, professionally prepared ms with SASE. No erotica or senseless violence; otherwise, we'll consider most any theme. We also sponsor short story and poetry contests. Read what's being published. Find a good story, not just a narrative reflection. Keep submitting."

CAIRN, St. Andrews College Press, 1700 Dogwood Mile, Laurinburg NC 28352. (910)277-5310. Fax: (910)277-5020. E-mail: press@sapc.edu. Website: www.sapc.edu/sapress.html. **Contact:** Fiction Editor. Magazine: 50-60 lb. paper. "*Cairn* is a nonprofit, student run literary magazine which seeks to publish established writers and talented students together. We occasionally publish collections by authors published in *Cairn*." Estab. 1969. Member, CLMP and AWP.

Needs: Literary, short stories and short-short fiction. "We're looking for original, quirky, imaginative short fiction with a real human insight." **Publishes 15-20 new writers/year.**

How to Contact: Send disposable copy of ms with SASE for reply only. Responds in 3-4 months to mss. Accepts simultaneous submissions with notice.

Payment/Terms: Pays 2 contributor's copies.

Advice: "Read a copy of *Cairn* to get a feel for what we publish, and follow guidelines closely."

CALLALOO, A Journal of African-American and African Diaspora Arts and Letters, Dept. of English, TAMU 4227, Texan A&M University, College Station TX 77843-4227. (979)458-3108. Fax: (979)458-3275. E-mail: callaloo@tamu.edu. Website: http://callaloo.tamu.edu. **Contact:** Charles H. Rowell, editor. Magazine: 7×10; 250 pages. "Devoted to publishing fiction, poetry, drama of the African diaspora, including North, Central and South America, the Caribbean, Europe and Africa. Visually beautiful and well-edited, the journal publishes 3-5 short stories in all forms and styles in each issue." Quarterly. Estab. 1976. Circ. 2,000.

• One of the leading voices in African-American literature, *Callaloo* has recieved NEA literature grants. Several pieces every year are chosen for collections of the year's best stories, such as *Beacon's Best*. John Edgar Wideman's "Weight" from *Callaloo* won the 2000 O. Henry Award.

Needs: Ethnic/multicultural (black culture), feminist, historical, humor/satire, literary, regional, science fiction, serialized novels, translations, contemporary, prose poem. "No romance, confessional. Would like to see more experimental fiction, science fiction and well-crafted literary fiction particularly dealing with the black middle class, immigrant communities and/or the black South." Accepts 3-5 mss/issue; 10-20 mss/year. **Publishes 5-10 new writers/year.** Recently published work by Charles Johnson, Edwidge Danticat, Thomas Glave, Nallo Hopkinson, John Edgar Wideman, Jamaica Kincaid, Percival Everett and Patricia Powell. Also publishes poetry.

How to Contact: Accepts submissions by mail. Generally accepts unpublished work, rarely accepts reprints. Responds in 2 weeks to queries; 6 months to mss. Accepts multiple submissions. Sample copy for $10. Writer's guidelines online.

Payment/Terms: Pays in contributor's copies. Aquires some rights. Sends galleys to author.

Advice: "We look for freshness of both writing and plot, strength of characterization, plausibilty of plot. Read what's being written and published, especially in journals such as *Callaloo*."

CALYX, A Journal of Art & Literature by Women, Calyc, Inc., P.O. Box B, Corvallis OR 97339. (541)753-9384. Fax: (541)753-0515. E-mail: calyx@proaxis.com. **Contact:** Editor. Magazine: 6×8; 128 pages per single issue; 60 lb. coated matte stock paper; 10 pt. chrome coat cover; original art. Publishes prose, poetry, art, essays, interviews and critical and review articles. "*Calyx* exists to publish fine literature and art by women and is committed to publishing the work of all women, including women of color, older women, working class women and other voices that need to be heard. We are committed to discovering and nurturing beginning writers." Biannual. Estab. 1976. Circ. 6,000.

Needs: Recieves approximately 1,000 unsolicited prose and poetry mss when open. Accepts 4-8 mss/issue; 9-15 mss/year. Reads mss October 1-December 31; submit only during this period. Mss received when not reading will be returned. Publishes ms 4-12 months after acceptance. **Publishes 10-20 new writers/year.** Recently published work by M. Evelina Galang, Chitrita Banerji, Diana Ma and Catherine Brady. Also publishes literary essays, literary criticism, poetry.

How to Contact: Responds in 4-12 months to mss. Accepts simultaneous submissions. Sample copy for $9.50 plus $2 postage. SASE. Reviews fiction.

Payment/Terms: "Combination of payment, free issues and 1 volume subscription.

Advice: Most mss are rejected because "the writers are not familiar with *Calyx*—writers should read *Calyx* and be familar with the publication. We look for good writing, imagination and important/interesting subject matter."

CAPERS AWEIGH, Cape Brenton Poetry & Fiction, Capers Aweigh Press, 36 Duncan Street, Glace Bay NS B1A 2L6 Canada. (902)849-0822. E-mail: capersaweigh@hotmail.com. **Contact:** Fiction Editor. Magazine: 5×8; 80 pages; bond paper; Cornwall-coated cover. "*Capers Aweigh* publishes poetry and fiction of, by and for Cape Bretoners." varies. Estab. 1992. Circ. 500.

Needs: Adventure, ethnic/multicultural, fantasy, feminist, historical, humor/satire, literary, mainstream, mystery/suspense, psychic/supernatural/occult, regional, science fiction, contemporary. List of upcoming themes available for SASE. Receives 2 unsolicited mss/month. Accepts 30 mss/issue. Publishes ms 9 months after acceptance. Recently published work by C. Fairn Kennedy and Shirley Kiju Kawi. Publishes short shorts. Also publishes literary criticism, poetry.

How to Contact: Query. Send SASE for reply or send a disposable copy of ms. Accepts electronic submissions (IBM). Sample copy for $4.95 and 6×10 SASE.

Payment/Terms: Pays free subscription to the magazine and 1 contributor's copy; additional copies for $4.95. Acquires first North American serial rights. Sponsors awards/contests.

$ ⬛ ◻ THE CAPILANO REVIEW, 2055 Purcell Way, North Vancouver BC V7J 3H5 Canada. Website: www.capcollege.bc.ca/dept/TCR/. Magazine: 6×9; 90-120 pages; book paper; glossy cover; perfect-bound; visual art. "Triannual visual and literary arts magazine that publishes only what the editors consider to be the very best fiction, poetry, drama, or visual art being produced. *TCR* editors are interested in *fresh, original work that stimulates and challenges readers.* Over the years, the magazine has developed a reputation for *pushing beyond the boundaries* of traditional art and writing. We are interested in work that is *new in concept and in execution.*" Estab. 1972. Circ. 900.
Needs: Experimental, literary, novel excerpts (previously unpublished only). "No traditional, conventional fiction. Want to see more innovative, genre-blurring work." Receives 80 unsolicited mss/month. Accepts 1 mss/issue; 3-5 mss/year. Publishes ms 2-4 months after acceptance. **Publishes some new writers/year.** Recently published work by Michael Turner, Lewis Buzbee and George Bowering. Length: 6,000 words; average length: 4,000 words. Also publishes literary essays, poetry.
How to Contact: Accepts submissions by mail. Include 2- 3-sentence bio and brief list of publications. Send Canadian SASE or IRCs for reply of ms. Responds in 1 month to queries; 4 months to mss. Accepts multiple submissions. No simultaneous submissions. Sample copy for $9. Writer's guidelines for #10 SASE with IRC or Canadian stamps or online.
Payment/Terms: Pays $50-200. Pays on publication for first North American serial rights.
Advice: "Do not send conventional realist fiction. Read the magazine before submitting and ensure your work is technically perfect."

◎ ◻ THE CARIBBEAN WRITER, The University of the Virgin Islands, RR 02, Box 10,000-Kinghill, St. Croix Virgin Islands 00850. (340)692-4152. Fax: (340)692-4026. E-mail: qmars@uvi.edu. Website: www.Caribbean Writer.com. **Contact:** Quilin B. Mars, managing editor. Magazine: 6×9; 304 pages; 60 lb. paper; glossy cover stock; illustrations; photos. "*The Caribbean Writer* is an international magazine with a Caribbean focus. The Caribbean should be central to the work, or the work should reflect a Caribbean heritage, experience or perspective." Annual. Estab. 1987. Circ. 1,500.
  ● Work published in *The Caribbean Writer* has received a Pushcart Prize and Quenepon Award.
Needs: Historical (general), humor/satire, literary, mainstream, translations, contemporary and prose poem. Receives 65 unsolicited mss/month. Accepts 60 mss/issue. **Publishes approximately 20% new writers/year.** Recently published work by Cecil Gray, Virgil Suarez and Opal Palmer Adisa. Also publishes literary essays, poetry.
How to Contact: Accepts submissions by e-mail. "Blind submissions only. Send name, address and title of manuscript on separate sheet. Title only on manuscript. Manuscripts will not be returned unless this procedure is followed." SASE (or IRC). Accepts simultaneous, multiple submissions. Sample copy for $7 and $4 postage.
Payment/Terms: Pays 2 contributor's copies. Annual prizes for best story ($400); for best poem ($300); $200 for first time publication; best work by Caribbean Author ($500); best work by Virgin Islands author ($200). Acquires one-time rights.
Advice: Looks for "work which reflects a Caribbean heritage, experience or perspective."

◻ ◻ CAROLINA QUARTERLY, Greenlaw Hall CB #3520, University of North Carolina, Chapel Hill NC 27599-3520. (919)962-0244. Fax: (919)962-3520. E-mail: cquarter@unc.edu. Website: www.unc.edu/depts/cqonli ne. **Contact:** Amy Weldon, editor-in-chief. Literary journal: 80-100 pages; illustrations. Publishes fiction for a "general literary audience." Triannual. Estab. 1948. Circ. 900-1,000.
  ● Work published in *Carolina Quarterly* has been selected for in inclusion in *Best American Short Stories*, in *New Stories for the South: The Year's Best*, and *Best of the South*.
Needs: Literary. "We would like to see more short/micro-fiction and more stories by minority/ethnic writers." Receives 150-200 unsolicited mss/month. Accepts 4-5 mss/issue; 14-16 mss/year. Does not read mss May-July. Publishes ms 4 months after acceptance. **Publishes 1-2 new writers/year.** Recently published work by Pam Durban, Elizabeth Spencer, Brad Vice, Wendy Brenner, and Nanci Kincaid. Publishes short shorts. Also publishes literary essays, poetry. Occasionally comments on rejected mss.
How to Contact: Accepts submissions by phone. Responds in 3 months to queries; 6 months to mss. No simultaneous submissions. Sample copy for $5. Writer's guidelines for SASE.
Payment/Terms: Pays in contributor's copies. Acquires first rights.

◻ ◻ CENTER, A Journal of the Literary Arts, University of Missouri, 202 Tate Hall, Columbia MO 65211. (573)884-7775. E-mail: bsw88f@mizzou.edu. Website: www.web.missouri.edu/~cwp. **Contact:** Jean Braithwaite. Magazine: 5X9; 125-200 pages; 60 lb. paper; 80 lb. dull cover; illustrations. *Center's* goal is to publish the best in literary fiction, poetry and creative nonfiction by previously unpublished and emerging writers, as well as more established writers. Semiannual. Estab. 2000. Circ. 500.
Needs: Ethnic/multicultural, experimental, humor/satire, literary, genre-crossing multimedia. Receives 30-50 unsolicited mss/month. Accepts 3-5 mss/year. Publishes ms 6 months after acceptance. **Publishes 25% new writers/year.** Recently published work by Lisa Glatt and Robert Root. Length: 10,000 words maximum; average length:

1,000 words. Publishes short shorts. Also publishes literary essays, poetry. Sometimes comments on rejected mss.
How to Contact: Send SASE (or IRC) for return of ms or send a disposable copy of ms and #10 SASE for reply only. Responds in 2 months to queries; 6 months to mss. Accepts simultaneous, multiple submissions. Sample copy for $3. Writer's guidelines for SASE. Reviews fiction.
Payment/Terms: Pays 1 contributor's copy; additional copies $3. Pays on publication for one-time rights.

CHAFFIN JOURNAL, English Department, Eastern Kentucky University, Case Annex 467, Richmond KY 40475-3102. (859)622-3080. E-mail: robert.witt@eku.edu. **Contact:** Robert Witt, editor. Magazine: 8 × 5 1/2; 120-130 pages; 70 lb. paper; 80 lb. cover. "We publish fiction on any subject; our only consideration is the quality." Annual. Estab. 1998. Circ. 150.
Needs: Ethnic/multicultural, experimental, family saga, feminist, gay, historical, humor/satire, lesbian, literary, mainstream, regional (Appalachia). "No erotica, fantasy." Receives 3-4 unsolicited mss/month. Accepts 6-8 mss/year. Does not read mss November 1 through May 31. Publishes ms 6 months after acceptance. **Publishes 2-3 new writers/year.** Recently published by Meridith Sue Willis, Raymond Abbott, Marjorie Bixler and Chris Helvey. Length: 10,000 words; average length: 5,000 words.
How to Contact: Send SASE for return of ms. Responds in 1 week to queries; 3 months to mss. Accepts simultaneous, multiple submissions. Sample copy for $5. Writer's guidelines for SASE or by e-mail.
Payment/Terms: Pays 1 contributor's copy; additional copies $5. Pays on publication for one-time rights.
Advice: "All manuscripts submitted are considered."

$ CHAPMAN, 4 Broughton Place, Edinburgh Scotland EH1 3RX. (+44)131 557 2207. Fax: (+44)131 556 9565. E-mail: chapman-pub@blueyounder.co.uk. Website: www.chapman-pub.co.uk. **Contact:** Joy Hendry, fiction editor. "*Chapman*, Scotland's quality literary magazine, is a dynamic force in Scotland, publishing poetry, fiction, criticism, reviews; articles on theatre, politics, language and the arts. Our philosophy is to publish new work, from known and unknown writers, mainly Scottish, but also worldwide." 3 times per annum. Estab. 1970. Circ. 2,000.
Needs: Literary, Scottish/ international. "No horror, science fiction." Accepts 4-6 mss/issue. **Publishes 50 new writers/year.** Recently published work by Quim Monzo, Dilys Rose and Leslie Schenck.
How to Contact: Sample copy for £6 (includes postage).
Payment/Terms: Pays by negotiation.
Advice: "Keep your stories for six months and edit carefully. We seek challenging work which attempts to explore difficult/new territory in content and form, but lighter work, if original enough, is welcome."

$ THE CHARITON REVIEW, Truman State University, Kirksville MO 63501-9915. (660)785-4499. Fax: (660)785-7486. **Contact:** Fiction editor. Magazine: 6 × 9; approximately 100 pages; 60 lb. paper; 65 lb. cover stock; photographs on cover. "We demand only excellence in fiction and fiction translation for a general and college readership." Estab. 1975. Circ. 600.
Needs: Ethnic/multicultural, experimental, literary, mainstream, novel excerpts (if they can stand alone.), translations, traditional. "We are not interested in slick or sick material." Accepts 3-5 mss/issue; 6-10 mss/year. Publishes ms 6 months after acceptance. **Publishes some new writers/year.** Recently published work by Ann Townsend, Glenn DelGrosso, Paul Ruffin and X.J. Kennedy. Also publishes literary essays, poetry. Sometimes comments on rejected mss.
How to Contact: Send complete ms. Accepts submissions by mail. No book-length mss. Responds in 1 week to queries; 1 month to mss. No simultaneous submissions. Sample copy for $5 and 7x10 SAE with 4 first-class stamps. Reviews fiction.
Payment/Terms: Pays $5/page (up to $50). Pays on publication for first North American serial rights.
Advice: "Do not ask us for guidelines: the only guidelines are excellence in all matters. Write well and study the publication you are submitting to. We are interested only in the very best fiction and fiction translation. We are not interested in slick material. We do not read photocopies, dot-matrix, or carbon copies. Know the simple mechanics of submission—SASE, no paper clips, no odd-sized SASE, etc. Know the genre (short story, novella, etc.). Know the unwritten laws. There is too much manufactured fiction; assembly-lined, ego-centered personal essays offered as fiction."

$ THE CHATTAHOOCHEE REVIEW, Georgia Perimeter College, 2101 Womack Rd., Dunwoody GA 30338-4497. (770)551-3019. Website: www.chattahoochee-review.org. **Contact:** Lawrence Hetrick, editor. Magazine: 6 × 9; 150 pages; 70 lb. paper; 80 lb. cover stock; illustrations; photos. "We publish a number of Southern writers, but *Chattahoochee Review* is not by design a regional magazine. All themes, forms, and styles are considered as long as they impact the whole person: heart, mind, intuition, and imagination." Quarterly. Estab. 1980. Circ. 1,350.
● Fiction from *The Chattahoochee Review* has been included in *Best New Stories of the South*.
Needs: "No juvenile, romance, science fiction." Accepts 5 mss/issue. Does not read ms June 1-August 31. Publishes ms 3 months after acceptance. **Publishes some new writers/year.** Recently published work by Merrill Joan Gerber, Mary Ann Taylor-Hall, Anthony Grooms and Greg Johnson. Length: 6,000 words maximum; average length: 2,500 words. Sometimes comments on rejected mss.
How to Contact: Send complete ms. Accepts submissions by mail. SASE. Responds in 2 weeks to queries; 4

months to mss. Accepts simultaneous submissions. Sample copy for $6. Writer's guidelines online. Reviews fiction.
Payment/Terms: Pays $20/page, $250 max and 2 contributor's copies. Pays on publication for first rights.
Advice: "Arrange to read magazine before you submit to it."

CHICAGO QUARTERLY REVIEW, Monadnock Group Publishers, 517 Sherman Ave., Evanston IL 60202-2815. (719)633-9794. E-mail: lawlaw58@aol.com. **Contact:** Syed Haider, Jane Lawrence and Lisa McKenaie, editors. Magazine: 6×9; 125 pages; illustrations; photos. "*CQR* was begun by a group of writers who felt there were too few venues for quality work that did not conform to preordained criteria. We continue to publish examples of solid writing not in thrall to any particular school of thought or aeshetics." Quarterly. Estab. 1994. Circ. 300.
Needs: Literary. Does not want "any work that is easily categorized, academic, obtuse or self-impressed." Receives 20-30 unsolicited mss/month. Accepts 6-8 mss/issue; 8-16 mss/year. Reading period September 1-February 29. Publishes ms 1 year after acceptance. Agented fiction 10%. **Publishes 3 new writers/year.** Recently published work by Jim Mezzanote, Kenneth Allen, Jim Henry, Jim Zervanos, D.E. Laczi and Charles Rose. Length: 5,000 words; average length: 2,500 words. Publishes short shorts. Also publishes literary essays, poetry. Sometimes comments on rejected mss.
How to Contact: Send a disposable copy of ms and #10 SASE for reply only. Responds in 2 months to queries; 6 months to mss. Accepts simultaneous, multiple submissions. Sample copy for $9.
Payment/Terms: Pays 1 contributor's copy; additional copies $6. Pays on publication for one-time rights.
Advice: "The writer's voice ought to be clear and unique, and should explain something of what it means to be human. We want well-written stories that reflect an appreciation for the rhythm and music of language; work that shows passion and commitment to the art of writing."

CHICAGO REVIEW, 5801 S. Kenwood Ave., Chicago IL 60637. (773)702-0887. E-mail: chicago-review @uchicago.edu. Website: humanities.uchicago.edu. **Contact:** William Martin, fiction editor. Magazine for a highly literate general audience: 6×9; 128 pages; offset white 60 lb. paper; illustrations; photos. Quarterly. Estab. 1946. Circ. 3,500.
● The *Chicago Review* has won two *Pushcart* prizes and an Illinois Arts Council Award.
Needs: Experimental, literary, contemporary. Receives 500 unsolicited mss/month. Accepts 5 mss/issue; 20 mss/year. **Publishes 2 new writers/year.** Recently published work by Hollis Seamon, Tome House, Rachel Klein and Doris Dörrie. Also publishes literary essays, literary criticism, poetry.
How to Contact: SASE. Responds in 3-9 months to mss. No simultaneous submissions. Sample copy for $6. Guidelines via website or SASE. Reviews fiction.
Payment/Terms: Pays 3 contributor's copies and subscription.
Advice: "We look with interest at fiction that addresses subjects inventively, work that steers clear of clichéd treatments of themes. We're always eager to read writing that experiments with language, whether it be with characters' viewpoints, tone or style. We like a strong voice capable of rejecting gimmicks in favor of subtleties. We are most impressed by writers who have read both deeply and broadly, but display their own inventiveness. However, we have been reciving more submissions and are becoming more selective."

CHIRON REVIEW, 702 N. Prairie, St. John KS 67576-1516. (620)786-4955. E-mail: chironreview@hotmail.com. Website: www.geocities.com/SoHo/Nook/1748. **Contact:** Ray Zepeda, fiction editor. Tabloid: 10×13; minimum 24 pages; newsprint; illustrations; photos. Publishes "all types of material, no particular theme; traditional and off-beat, no taboos." Quarterly. Estab. 1982. Circ. 1,200.
Needs: Experimental, humor/satire, literary, contemporary. No didactic, religious or overtly political writing. Receives 100 unsolicited mss/month. Accepts 1-6 mss/issue; 6-24 mss/year. Publishes ms 6-18 months after acceptance. **Publishes 10 new writers/year.** Recently published work by Janice Eidus, David Newman, Craig Curtis, Jay Marvin and Ad Hudler. Publishes short shorts.
How to Contact: SASE. Deadlines: November 1 (Winter), February 1 (Spring), May 1 (Summer), August 1 (Autumn). Responds in 2 months to mss. No simultaneous submissions. Sample copy for $5 ($10 overseas). Writer's guidelines for #10 SASE.
Payment/Terms: Pays 1 contributor's copies; extra copies at 50% discount. Acquires first rights.
Advice: "Research markets thoroughly."

$ CHRYSALIS READER, R.R. 1, Box 4510, Dillwyn VA 23936. (434)983-3021. Website: www.swedenborg.com. **Contact:** Robert Tucker, fiction editor. Book series: 7½×10; 192 pages; archival paper; coated cover stock; illustrations; photos. "It is very important to send for writer's guidelines and sample copies before submitting. Content of fiction, articles, reviews, poetry, etc., should be directly focused on that issue's theme and directed to the educated, intellectually curious reader." Estab. 1985. Circ. 3,000.
Needs: Adventure, experimental, historical, literary, mainstream, mystery/suspense, science fiction, fiction (leading to insight), contemporary, spiritual, sports. No religious works. Upcoming theme: "Letting Go" (Fall 2004). Receives 50 unsolicited mss/month. Accepts 15-20 mss/issue; 20-40 mss/year. Publishes ms 9 months after acceptance. **Publishes 10 new writers/year.** Recently published work by Robert Bly, Larry Dossey, Dr. Bernie Siegel, Wesley McNair, William Kloefkorn and John Hitchcock. Also publishes literary essays, literary criticism, poetry. Sometimes comments on rejected mss.

How to Contact: Query. Accepts submissions by mail, e-mail. SASE. Responds in 1 month to queries; 4 months to mss. No simultaneous submissions. Sample copy for $10 and 8½×11 SAE. Writer's guidelines online.
Payment/Terms: Pays $50-150. Pays at page-proof stage. Acquires first rights, makes work-for-hire assignments. Sends galleys to author.
Advice: Looking for "1: *Quality*; 2. appeal for our audience; 3. relevance to/illumination of an issue's theme."

$☑ CIMARRON REVIEW, Oklahoma State University, 205 Morrill Hall, OSU, Stillwater OK 74078-0135. (405)744-9476. Website: cimarronreview.okstate.edu. **Contact:** Toni Graham, Andrea Koenig, fiction editors. Magazine: 6×9; 110 pages. "Poetry and fiction on contemporary themes; personal essay on contemporary issues that cope with life in the 20th century, for educated literary readers. We work hard to reflect quality. We are eager to receive manuscripts from both established and less experienced writers that intrigue us by their unusual perspective, language, imagery and character." Quarterly. Estab. 1967. Circ. 600.
Needs: Literary-quality short stories and novel excerpts. No juvenile or genre fiction. Accepts 3-5 mss/issue; 12-15 mss/year. Publishes ms 2-6 months after acceptance. **Publishes 2-4 new writers/year.** Recently published work by Adam Braver, Gary Fincke, Catherine Brady, Nona Caspers and David Ryan. Also publishes literary essays, literary criticism, poetry.
How to Contact: Send complete ms. SASE. Responds in 2-6 months to mss. No simultaneous submissions. Sample copy for $7. Reviews fiction.
Payment/Terms: Pays 2 contributor's copies plus a year's subscription. Pays on publication for first North American serial rights.
Advice: "In order to get a feel for the kind of work we publish, please read an issue or two before submitting."

☒ ☐ ◎ THE CLAREMONT REVIEW, The Contemporary Magazine of Young Adult Writers, The Claremont Review Publishers, 4980 Wesley Rd., Victoria BC V8Y 1Y9. (250)658-5221. Fax: (250)658-5387. E-mail: editor@theClaremontReview.com. Website: www.theClaremontReview.com. **Contact:** Susan Field (business manager), Janice McCachen, Kim LeMieux and Susan Field, editors. Magazine: 6×9; 110-120 pages; book paper; soft gloss cover; b&w illustrations. "We are dedicated to publishing emerging young writers aged 13-19 from anywhere in the English-speaking world, but primarily Canada and the U.S." Biannual. Estab. 1992. Circ. 700.
Needs: Young adult/teen. "No science fiction, fantasy." Receives 20-30 unsolicited mss/month. Accepts 10-12 mss/issue; 20-24 mss/year. Publishes ms 3 months after acceptance. **Publishes 100 new writers/year.** Recently published work by Alissan Chan, Laura Ishiguro and Jason Tsai. Length: 5,000 words; average length: 1,500-3,000 words preferred. Publishes short shorts. Also publishes poetry. Always comments on rejected mss.
How to Contact: Responds in 3 months to mss. Accepts multiple submissions. Sample copy for $8.
Payment/Terms: Pays 1 contributor's copy. Additional copies for $6. Acquires first North American serial, one-time rights. Sponsors awards/contests.
Advice: Looking for "good concrete narratives with credible dialogue and solid use of original detail. It must be unique, honest and a glimpse of some truth. Send and error-free final draft with a short covering letter and bio, read us first to see what we publish."

$☑ COLORADO REVIEW, Center for Literary Publishing, Department of English, Colorado State University, Fort Collins CO 80523. (970)491-5449. Website: www.coloradoreview.com. **Contact:** Stephanie G'Schwind, editor. Literary journal: 224 pages; 60 lb. book weight paper. Estab. 1972. Circ. 1,300.
Needs: Ethnic/multicultural, experimental, literary, mainstream, contemporary. "No genre fiction." Receives 600 unsolicited mss/month. Accepts 4-5 mss/issue. Does not read mss May-August. Publishes ms within 1 year after acceptance. Recently published work by T. Alan Broughton, Erin Flanagan, Ann Hood and Robert Boswell. Also publishes poetry.
How to Contact: Send complete ms. Responds in 2 months to mss. Sample copy for $10. Writer's guidelines online. Reviews fiction.
Payment/Terms: Pays $5/page. Pays on publication for first North American serial rights. Rights revert to author upon publication. Sends galleys to author.
Advice: "We are interested in manuscripts that show craft, imagination, and a convincing voice. If a story has reached a level of technical competence, we are receptive to the fiction working on its own terms. The oldest advice is still the best: persistence. Approach every aspect of the writing process with pride, conscientiousness—from word choice to manuscript appearance. Be familiar with the *Colorado Review*; read a couple of issues before submitting your manuscript."

Ⓝ COLUMBIA: A JOURNAL OF LITERATURE AND ART, Columbia Journal, 415 Dodge Hall, New York NY 10027. (212)854-4216. Fax: (212)854-7704. E-mail: columbiajournal@columbia.edu. Website: www.columbia. edu/~tnf12. **Contact:** Christopher Hacker and Molly Johnson, editors. Magazine: 6×9; 200-250 pages; glossy cover; illustrations; photos. "We publish the very best contemporary poetry, fiction and creative nonfiction from emerging and established writers." Annual. Estab. 1977. Circ. 1,000.
Needs: Comics/graphic novels, ethnic/multicultural, experimental, historical, humor/satire, literary, translations. "We are not interested in children's literature or genre pieces, unless they can be considered to transcend the genre and be of interest to the general reader." Receives 50 unsolicited mss/month. Publishes ms 1-12 months after

acceptance. Agented fiction 70%. **Publishes 2-4 new writers/year.** Recently published work by Gary Lutz, Mary Gordon, Jonathan Lethem and Jonathan Safran Foer. Length: 5,000 words; average length: 3,000 words. Publishes short shorts. Rarely comments on rejected mss.
How to Contact: Send complete ms. Responds in 3 months to queries. Accepts simultaneous, multiple submissions. Sample copy for $8. Writer's guidelines online.
Payment/Terms: Acquires first North American serial rights. Sponsors awards/contests.

CONCHO RIVER REVIEW, Angelo State University, English Dept., Box 10894 ASU Station, San Angelo TX 76904. (325)942-2273, ext. 230. Fax: (325)942-2208. E-mail: me.hartje@angelo.edu. **Contact:** T.A. Dalrymple, fiction editor. Magazine: 6½×9; 100-125 pages; 60 lb. Ardor offset paper; Classic Laid Color cover stock; b&w drawings. "We publish any fiction of high quality—no thematic specialties." Semiannual. Estab. 1987. Circ. 300.
Needs: Ethnic/multicultural, historical, humor/satire, literary, regional, western. "No erotica; no science fiction." Receives 10-15 unsolicited mss/month. Accepts 3-6 mss/issue; 8-10 mss/year. Publishes ms 4 months after acceptance. **Publishes 4 new writers/year.** Recently published work by Gordon Alexander, Riley Froh, Gretchen Geralds and Kimberly Willis Holt. Length: 1,500-5,000 words; average length: 3,500 words. Also publishes literary essays, literary criticism, poetry.
How to Contact: Send disk copy upon acceptance. Responds in 3 weeks to queries. Accepts simultaneous submissions (if noted). Sample copy for $4. Writer's guidelines for #10 SASE. Reviews fiction.
Payment/Terms: Pays in contributor's copies; $5 charge for extras. Acquires first rights.
Advice: "We prefer a clear sense of conflict, strong characterization and effective dialogue."

⬛ CONFLUENCE, Ohio Valley Literary Group Inc., P.O. Box 336, Belpre OH 45714-0336. (304)295-6599. E-mail: confluence1989@yahoo.com. Website: www.marietta.edu/~eng/confluence.html. **Contact:** Dr. Beverly Hogue or Sandra Tritt. Magazine: 5½×8½; 100 pages; 60 lb. paper; card stock cover; illustrations. "We publish quality short stories, essays and poetry in collaboration with Marietta College." Annual. Estab. 1989. Circ. 1,000.
Needs: Ethnic/multicultural, literary, mainstream, regional. "No children's/juvenile or young adult." Receives 12 unsolicited mss/month. Accepts 4 mss/year. "We'd accept more if we received more quality fiction." Does not read mss February through August. Publishes ms 9 months after acceptance. **Publishes 6 new writers/year.** Recently published work by T.M. Bemis, Deidre Woolard, and Pearl Cannick Solomon. Length: 5,000 words; average length: 3,000 words. Publishes short shorts. Also publishes literary essays, poetry. Often comments on rejected mss.
How to Contact: Send SASE for reply, return of ms or send disposable copy of ms. Responds in 3 weeks to queries; 7 months to mss. Accepts multiple submissions. Sample copy for $6.50. Writer's guidelines for SASE or by e-mail.
Payment/Terms: Pays 3 contributor's copies; additional copies $4.50. Pays on publication for one-time rights. Sponsors awards/contests.
Advice: "We consider overall quality. We look for well-rounded characters, consistent point of view, precise wording, setting integrated into plot, dialogue that moves the plot forward, and so on. Read current short stories, avoid clichés and passive voice, and join a critique group which offers honest evaluation."

✓ $⬜ ⬛ CONFRONTATION, A Literary Journal, Long Island University, Brookville NY 11548. (516)299-2720. Fax: (516)299-2735. **Contact:** Jonna Semeiks. Magazine: 6×9; 250-350 pages; 70 lb. paper; 80 lb. cover; illustrations; photos. "We are eclectic in our taste. Excellence of style is our dominant concern." Semiannual. Estab. 1968. Circ. 2,000.
• *Confrontation* has garnered a long list of awards and honors, including the Editor's Award for Distinguished Achievement from CCLP and NEA grants. Work from the magazine has appeared in numerous anthologies including the *Pushcart Prize, Best Short Stories* and *O. Henry Prize Stories.*
Needs: Experimental, literary, mainstream, novel excerpts (if they are self-contained stories), regional, slice-of-life vignettes, contemporary, prose poem. "No 'proselytizing' literature or genre fiction." Receives 400 unsolicited mss/month. Accepts 30 mss/issue; 60 mss/year. Does not read June-September. Publishes ms 1 year after acceptance. Agented fiction approximately 10-15%. **Publishes 20-30 new writers/year.** Recently published work by Susan Vreeland, Lanford Wilson, Tom Stacey, Carol Berge and Sallie Bingham. Publishes short shorts. Also publishes literary essays, poetry.
How to Contact: Send complete ms. Accepts submissions by mail, e-mail, phone. "Cover letters acceptable, not necessary. We accept simultaneous submissions but do not prefer them." Accepts diskettes if accompanied by computer printout submissions. Responds in 3 weeks to queries; 2 months to mss. Accepts simultaneous submissions. Sample copy for $3. Writer's guidelines not available. Reviews fiction.

● **A BULLET INTRODUCES COMMENTS** by the editor of *Novel & Short Story Writer's Market* indicating special information about the listing.

Payment/Terms: <u>Pays $25-250</u>. Pays on publication for all rights.
Advice: "We look for literary merit. Keep trying."

⬛ ⬛ CONNECTICUT REVIEW, Connecticut State University System, SCSU 501 Crescent St., New Haven CT 06515. (203)392-6737. Fax: (203)248-5007. E-mail: ctreview@southernct.edu. **Contact:** Dr. Vivian Shipley, editor. Magazine: 6×9; 208 pages; white/heavy paper; glossy/heavy cover; color and b&w illustrations and photos; artwork. "*Connecticut Review* presents a wide range of cultural interests that cross disciplinary lines. The editors invite the submission of academic articles of general interest, thesis-oriented essays, translations, short stories, plays, poems and interviews." Semiannual. Estab. 1968. Circ. 4,000. CELJ, CLMJ.

• Work published in *Connecticut Review* has won the Pushcart Prize and inclusion in *Best American Poetry*, *Best American Short Stories 2000*. *CR* has also recieved the Phoenix Award for Significant Editorial Achievement, and 2001 National Public Radio's Award for Literary Excellence. *The Connecticut Review* ranked on *Writer's Digest's* "Top 30" list of best markets for fiction writers.

Needs: Literary. "Content must be under 4,000 words and suitable for circulation to libraries and high schools." Receives 250 unsolicited mss/month. Accepts 6 mss/issue; 12 mss/year. Does not read mss June-August. Publishes ms 1 year after acceptance. **Publishes 6-8 new writers/year.** Recently published work by John Searles, Michael Schiavone, Norman German, Tom Williams and Paul Ruffin. Publishes short shorts. Also publishes literary essays, poetry.
How to Contact: Send two disposable copies of ms and #10 SASE for reply only. Responds in 4 months to queries. Accepts simultaneous submissions. Sample copy for $8. Writer's guidelines for SASE.
Payment/Terms: Pays 2 contributor's copies; additional copies $8. Pays on publication for first rights. Rights revert to author on publication. Sends galleys to author.

⬛ COTTONWOOD, Box J, 400 Kansas Union, University of Kansas, Lawrence KS 66045-2115. (785)864-2516. Fax: (785)864-4298. E-mail: tlorenz@ku.edu. **Contact:** Tom Lorenz, fiction editor. Magazine: 6×9; 100 pages; illustrations; photos. "*Cottonwood* publishes high quality prose, poetry and artwork and is aimed at an audience that appreciates the same. We have a national scope and reputation wile maintaining a strong regional flavor." Semiannual. Estab. 1965. Circ. 500.
Needs: "We publish literary prose and poetry." Receives 25-50 unsolicited mss/month. Accepts 5-6 mss/issue; 10-12 mss/year. Publishes ms 6-18 months after acceptance. Agented fiction 10%. **Publishes 1-3 new writers/year.** Recently published work by Connie May Fowler, Oakley Hall and Cris Mazza. Length: 1,000-8,000 words; average length: 2,000-5,000 words. Publishes short shorts. Also publishes literary essays, literary criticism, poetry.
How to Contact: SASE for return of ms. Responds in 6 months to mss. Accepts simultaneous submissions. Sample copy for $8.50, 9×12 SAE and $1.90. Reviews fiction.
Payment/Terms: Acquires one-time rights.
Advice: "We're looking for depth and/or originality of subject matter, engaging voice and style, emotional honesty, command of the material and the structure. *Cottonwood* publishes high quality literary fiction, but we are very open to the work of talented new writers. Write something honest and that you care about and write it as well as you can. Don't hesitate to keep trying us. We sometimes take a piece from a writer we've rejected a number of times. We generally don't like clever, gimmicky writing. The style should be engaging but not claim all the attention itself."

⬛ CRAB CREEK REVIEW, P.O. Box 840, Vashon WA 98070. (206)463-5668. Website: www.crabcreekreview.org. **Contact:** Eleanor Lee, Harris Levinson, Laura Sinai and Terri Stone, editors. Magazine: 6×9 paperbound; 80-112 pages; line drawings. "Magazine publishing poetry, short stories and cover art for an audience interested in literary, visual and dramatic arts and in politics." Published twice yearly. Estab. 1983. Circ. 450.
Needs: Humor/satire, literary, translations, contemporary. No confession, erotica, horror, juvenile, preschool, religious/inspirational, romance or young adult. Receives 100 unsolicited mss/month. **Publishes some new writers/year.** Recently published work by Tommy Zurhellen, Justin Courter, Nile Lanning, Rachel Pastan, and Daniel Creason Bartlett. Length: 1,200-6,000 words; average length: 3,000 words. Publishes short shorts.
How to Contact: SASE. Responds in 2-4 months to mss. No simultaneous submissions. Sample copy for $5, subscriptions for $10. *Anniversary Anthology $3.* Writer's guidelines for SASE or on website.
Payment/Terms: Pays 2 contributor's copies; $4 charge for extras. Acquires first rights. Rarely buys reprints.
Advice: "We appreciate 'sudden fictions.' Type name and address on each piece. Enclose SASE. Send no more than one story in a packet (except for short shorts—nor more than three, ten pages total). Know what you want to say and say it in an honest, clear, confident voice."

$ ⬛ ⬛ CRAB ORCHARD REVIEW, A Journal of Creative Works, Southern Illinois University at Carbondale, English Department, Faner Hall, Carbondale IL 62901-4503. (618)453-6833. Fax: (618)453-8224. Website: www.siu.edu/~crborchd. **Contact:** Jon Tribble, managing editor. Magazine: 5½×8½; 275 pages; 55 lb. recycled paper, card cover; photo on cover. "We are a general interest literary journal published twice/year. We strive to be a journal that writers admire and readers enjoy. We publish fiction, poetry, creative nonfiction, fiction translations, interviews and reviews." Estab. 1995. Circ. 1,800.

• *Crab Orchard Review* has won a Illinois Arts Council Literary Award for prose fiction by Ricardo Cortez Cruz (2001).

Needs: Ethnic/multicultural, literary, translations, excerpted novel. No science fiction, romance, western, horror, gothic or children's. Wants more novel excerpts that also stand alone as pieces. List of upcoming themes available on website. Receives 450 unsolicited mss/month. Accepts 15-20 mss/issue; 20-40 mss/year. Reads during summer only for special issues. Publishes ms 9-12 months after acceptance. Agented fiction 1%. **Publishes 2 new writers/ year.** Recently published work by Nicole Louise Reid, S. Brady Tucker, Tayari Jones and Ira Sukrungruang. Length: 1,000-6,500 words; average length: 2,500 words. Also publishes literary essays, poetry. Rarely comments on rejected mss.

How to Contact: Send SASE for reply, return of ms. Responds in 3 weeks to queries; 9 months to mss. Accepts simultaneous submissions. Sample copy for $8. Writer's guidelines for #10 SASE. Reviews fiction.

Payment/Terms: Pays $100 minimum; $15/page maximum, 2 contributor's copies and a year subscription. Acquires first North American serial rights.

Advice: "We look for well-written, provocative, fully realized fiction that seeks to engage both the reader's senses and intellect. Don't submit too often to the same market, and don't send manuscripts that you haven't read over carefully. Writers can't rely on spell checkers to catch all errors. Always include a SASE. Read and support the journals you admire so they can continue to survive."

CRAZYHORSE, College of Charleston, Dept. of English, 66 George St., Charleston SC 29424. (843)953-7740. E-mail: crazyhorse@cofc.edu. **Contact:** Editors. Literary magazine: 8¾×8¼; 150 pages; illustrations; photos. "*Crazyhorse* publishes writing of fine quality regardless of style, predilection, subject. Editors are especially interested in original writing that engages in the work of honest communication." Raymond Carver called *Crazyhorse* "an indispensable literary magazine of the first order." Semiannual. Estab. 1961. Circ. 1,500.

Needs: All fiction of fine quality. Receives 50-100 unsolicited mss/month. Accepts 8-10 mss/issue; 16-20 mss/ year. Publishes ms 6-12 months after acceptance. Recently published work by W.D. Wethereall, Paul Zimmer and Lisa Burnell. Length: 35 pages; average length: 15 pages. Publishes short shorts. Also publishes literary essays, poetry.

How to Contact: Send SASE for return of ms or disposable copy of ms and #10 SASE for reply only. Responds in 1 week to queries; 5 weeks to mss. Accepts simultaneous submissions. Sample copy for $5. Writer's guidelines for SASE or by e-mail.

Payment/Terms: Pays 2 contributor's copies; additional copies $5. Acquires first North American serial rights. Sends galleys to author. Sponsors awards/contests.

Advice: "Write to explore subjects you care about. Clarity of language; subject is one in which something is at stake."

THE CREAM CITY REVIEW, University of Wisconsin-Milwaukee, Box 413, Milwaukee WI 53201. (414)229-4708. E-mail: creamcity@csd.uwm.edu. Website: www.uwm.edu/dept/english/creamcity.html. **Contact:** Steve Nelson, fiction editor. Magazine: 5½×8½; 200-300 pages; 70 lb. offset/ perfectbound paper; 80lb. cover stock; illustrations; photos. "General literary publication—an eclectic and electric selection of the best fiction we can find." Semiannual. Estab. 1975. Circ. 2,000.

Needs: Ethnic/multicultural, experimental, literary, regional, translations, prose poem. "Would like to see more quality fiction. No horror, formulaic, racist, sexist, pornographic, homophobic, science fiction, romance." Receives 300 unsolicited mss/month. Accepts 6-10 mss/issue. Does not read fiction or poetry April-September. **Publishes 10 new writers/year.** Recently published work by Diane Glancey, Nina de Gramont, Kate Braverman, Luis Alberto Urrea, Simon Ortiz, George Makana Clark and Pete Fromm. Publishes short shorts. Also publishes literary essays, literary criticism, poetry.

How to Contact: Responds in 6 months to mss. Accepts simultaneous, multiple submissions. Sample copy for $5 (back issue), $8 (current issue). Reviews fiction.

Payment/Terms: Pays one-year subscription. Acquires first, sends galleys to author. Rights revert to author after publication. Sponsors awards/contests.

Advice: "The best stories are those in which the reader doesn't know what is going to happen or what the writer is trying to do. Avoid formulas. Surprise us with language and stunning characters."

THE CRESCENT REVIEW, The Crescent Review, Inc., P.O. Box 7959, Shallotte NC 28470-7959. E-mail: review@mindspring.com. Website: www.crescentreview.org. **Contact:** Editor. Magazine: 6×9; 160 pages. Triannual. Estab. 1982.

• Work appearing in *The Crescent Review* has been included in *O. Henry Prize Stories*, *Best American Short Stories*, *Pushcart Prize*, *Sudden Fiction* and *Black Southern Writers* anthologies and in the *New Stories from the South*.

Needs: "Well-crafted stories." Wants shorter-length pieces (though will publish stories in the 6,000-8,000 word range). Wants stories where choice has consequences. Does not read submissions May-June and November-December. Recently published work by Madison Smartt Bell, Melinda Haynes and Julia Slavin. Length: 8,500 words max.

How to Contact: SASE. Responds in 3 months to mss. Sample copy for $9.40 plus postage. Writer's guidelines online.

Payment/Terms: Pays 2 contributor's copies; discount for contributors. Acquires first North American serial rights. Sponsors awards/contests.

Advice: "We are looking for stories told in compelling voices that capture readers' attention. We especially appreciate a light touch or humor that leavens the serious."

[N] [symbol] CRUCIBLE, English Dept., Barton College, College Station, Wilson NC 27893. (252)399-6456. Editor: Terrence L. Grimes. **Contact:** Fiction Editor. Magazine of fiction and poetry for a general, literary audience. Annual. Estab. 1964. Circ. 500.

Needs: Ethnic/multicultural, experimental, feminist, literary, regional. Would like to see more short shorts. Receives 20 unsolicited mss/month. Accepts 5-6 mss/year. Does not normally read mss from April 30 to December 1. Publishes ms 4-5 months after acceptance. **Publishes 5 new writers/year.** Recently published work by Sally Buckner.

How to Contact: Send 3 complete copies of ms unsigned with cover letter which should include a brief biography, "in case we publish." Responds in 6 weeks to queries; 4 months to mss. Sample copy for $7. Writer's guidelines free.

Payment/Terms: Pays in contributor's copies. Acquires first rights.

Advice: "Write about what you know. Experimentation is fine as long as the experiences portrayed come across as authentic, that is to say, plausible."

[symbol] CUTBANK, English Dept., University of Montana, Missoula MT 59812. (406)243-6156. E-mail: cutbank@sel way.umt.edu. Website: www.umt.edu/cutbank. **Contact:** Fiction Editor. Magazine: 5½ × 8½; 115-230 pages. "Publishes serious-minded and innovative fiction and poetry from both well known and up-and-coming authors." Semiannual. Estab. 1973. Circ. 1,000.

Needs: No "science fiction, fantasy or unproofed manuscripts. Wants innovative, challenging, well-written stories." Receives 200 unsolicited mss/month. Accepts 6-12 mss/year. Does not read mss April 15-August 15. Publishes ms 6 months after acceptance. **Publishes 4 new writers/year.** Recently published work by Padgett Powell and William Kittredge. Occasionally comments on rejected mss.

How to Contact: SASE. Responds in 4 months to mss. Accepts simultaneous submissions. Sample copy for $4 (current issue $6.95). Writer's guidelines for SASE.

Payment/Terms: Pays 2 contributor's copies. Rights revert to author upon publication, with provision *Cutbank* receives publication credit.

Advice: "Strongly suggest contributors read an issue. We have published stories by Kevin Canty, Chris Offutt and Pam Houston in recent issues, and like to feature new writers alongside more well-known names. Send only your best work."

[symbols] THE DALHOUSIE REVIEW, Dalhousie University, Halifax NS B3H 4R2 Canada. (902)494-2541. Fax: (902)494-3561. E-mail: dalhousie.review@dal.ca. Website: www.dal.ca/~dalrev/. **Contact:** Dr. Ronald Huebert, editor. Magazine: 15cm × 23cm; approximately 140 pages; photographs sometimes. Publishes articles, book reviews, short stories and poetry. Published 3 times a year. Circ. 400.

Needs: Literary. Publishes essays on history, philosophy, etc., and poetry. Recently published work by Melissa Hardy, Kim Bridgford, Eugene Dubnov and Shalom Camenietzki.

How to Contact: SASE (Canadian stamps or IRCs). Sample copy for $10 (Canadian) including postage. Reviews fiction.

Payment/Terms: Pays 10 offprints and 2 complimentary copies.

$[symbol] DAN RIVER ANTHOLOGY, Conservatory of American Letters., P.O. Box 298, Thomaston ME 04861. (207)354-0998. Fax: (207)354-8953. Website: www.americanletters.org. **Contact:** R.S. Danbury III, editor. Book: 5½ × 8½; 180 pages; 60 lb. paper; gloss 10 pt. full-color cover. Deadline every year is March 31, with acceptance/rejection by April 15, proofs out by May 15, and book released December 7. Annual. Estab. 1984. Circ. 600. *Charges reading fee: $1 for poetry; $3 for prose* (cash only, no checks)

Needs: Adventure, ethnic/multicultural, experimental, fantasy, historical, horror, humor/satire, literary, mainstream, psychic/supernatural/occult, regional, romance (contemporary and historical), science fiction, suspense, western, contemporary, prose poem, senior citizen/retirement. "Virtually anything but porn, evangelical, juvenile." Would like to see more first-person adventure." Reads "mostly in April." Length: 800-2,500 words; average length: 2,000-2,400 words. Also publishes poetry.

How to Contact: Send complete ms. No simultaneous submissions. Sample copy for $13.95 paperback, $59.95 cloth, plus $3.25 shipping. Writer's guidelines available for #10 SASE or online.

Payment/Terms: Payment "depends on your experience with us, as it is a nonrefundable advance against royalties on all sales that we can attribute to your influence. For first-timers, the advance is about 1¢/word." Pays on acceptance for all rights.

Advice: "Read an issue or two, know the market. Don't submit without reading guidelines."

$[symbols] DESCANT, Descant Arts & Letters Foundation, P.O. Box 314, Station P, Toronto ON M5S 2S8 Canada. (416)593-2557. Fax: (416)593-9362. Website: www.descant.on.ca. **Contact:** Karen Mulhallen, editor. Quarterly literary journal. Quarterly. Estab. 1970. Circ. 1,200. Member, CMPA.

● *Descant* has received the Canadian National Magazine Award in various categories, including fiction.
Needs: Ethnic/multicultural, experimental, feminist, gay, historical, humor/satire, lesbian, literary. No gothic, religious, beat. Upcoming themes: Suburbia; Latvia; Love that Dare(s) (Not). Publishes ms 16 months after acceptance. **Publishes 14 new writers/year.** Recently published work by Andrew Pyper, Douglas Glover and Judith McCormack. Also publishes literary essays, poetry.
How to Contact: Send complete ms. Accepts submissions by mail, e-mail, phone. Sample copy for $8. Writer's guidelines online.
Payment/Terms: Pays $100 (Canadian); additional copies $8. Pays on publication.
Advice: "Familiarize yourself with our magazine before submitting."

N ○ DESERT VOICES, Palo Verde College, One College Drive, Blythe CA 92225. (760)921-5449. E-mail: aminyard@paloverde.edu. **Contact:** Applewhite Minyard, editor. Magazine: 6×9; 32-46 pages; illustrations; photos. "Our magazine is intended to be a showcase for our college and local/regional writers to express themselves in a creative manner, or for other writers with experiences with our area." Semiannual. Estab. 2003. Circ. 1,500.
Needs: Adventure, ethnic/multicultural, feminist, humor/satire, literary, mainstream, regional (desert Southwest), science fiction, western. "No erotica, though sexual/sensual content is acceptable if essential to the story/poem." Receives 10-15 unsolicited mss/month. Accepts 4-5 mss/issue. Does not read during Summer. Publishes ms 6 months after acceptance. **Publishes 5-10 new writers/year.** Average length: 2,000 words. Publishes short shorts. Also publishes literary essays, poetry.
How to Contact: Send complete ms. Accepts submissions by e-mail. Include estimated word count. Send SASE (or IRC) for return of ms or disposable copy of ms and #10 SASE for reply only." Responds in 4 weeks to queries; 3 months to mss. Accepts reprints, multiple submissions. Sample copy for #10 SASE. Writer's guidelines by e-mail. Reviews fiction.
Payment/Terms: Pays on publication for one-time rights. Not copyrighted.
Advice: "Write what you feel, write what you know, write what you know you feel, write clearly, write with emotion. Write and you will be heard. We are looking for good quality fiction with a regional theme. Writers should be familiar with life in the desert southwest, though we are not interested in romanticized westerns. Poetry or artwork should meet generally accepted stylistic considerations, as well as having heart."

$ DOUBLETAKE, 55 Davis Square, Somerville MA 02144. (617)591-9389. Website: www.doubletakemagazine. org. **Contact:** Albert LaFarge, deputy editor. Magazine: 9×11; 120 pages; high quality, recycled paper, and four-color, duotone, and half-tone reproductions. "We strive to present storytelling in its many guises—visual and in words."
Needs: "Realistic fiction in all of its variety; it's very unlikely we'd ever publish science fiction or gothic horror, for example. We would like to see more fiction distinguished by literary excellence and a rare voice." Accepts 12 mss/year. **Publishes more than 10 new writers/year.** Recently published work by David Leavitt, Charles Baxter, John Luther, Deedee Agee, and Tim Johnston.
How to Contact: Send complete ms. Responds in 3 months to mss. Accepts simultaneous submissions. Sample copy for $12. Writer's guidelines online.
Payment/Terms: Pays competitively. Pays on publication for first North American serial rights.
Advice: "Use a strong, developed narrative voice. Don't attempt too much."

$ ○ ◎ DOWNSTATE STORY, 1825 Maple Ridge, Peoria IL 61614. (309)688-1409. Website: www.wiu.edu/ users/mfgeh/dss. **Contact:** Elaine Hopkins, editor. Magazine: includes illustrations. "Short fiction—some connection with Illinois or the Midwest." Annual. Estab. 1992. Circ. 500.
Needs: Adventure, ethnic/multicultural, experimental, historical, horror, humor/satire, literary, mainstream, mystery/suspense, psychic/supernatural/occult, regional, romance, science fiction, suspense, western. No porn. Accepts 10 mss/issue. Publishes ms 1 year after acceptance. **Publishes 5 new writers/year.** Publishes short shorts. Also publishes literary essays.
How to Contact: Send complete ms with a cover letter. SASE for return of ms. Responds "ASAP" to mss. Accepts simultaneous submissions. Sample copy for $8. Writer's guidelines online.
Payment/Terms: Pays $50. Pays on acceptance for first rights.

$ ○ ELLIPSIS MAGAZINE, Westminster College of Salt Lake City, 1840 S. 1300 E., Salt Lake City UT 84105. (801)832-2321. Website: www.westminstercollege.edu/ellipsis. **Contact:** Martin Murphy (revolving editor; changes every year). Magazine: 6×9; 110-120 pages; 60 lb. paper; 15 pt. cover stock; illustrations; photos. *Ellipsis Magazine* needs good literary poetry, fiction, essays, plays and visual art. Annual. Estab. 1967. Circ. 2,500.
Needs: Receives 110 unsolicited mss/month. Accepts 4 mss/issue. Does not read mss November1-July 31. Publishes ms 3 months after acceptance. **Publishes 2 new writers/year.** Length: 6,000 words; average length: 4,000 words. Also publishes poetry. Rarely comments on rejected mss.
How to Contact: Send complete ms. Accepts submissions by mail. Send SASE (or IRC) for return of ms or send disposable copy of the ms and #10 SASE for reply only. Responds in 6 months to mss. Accepts simultaneous submissions. Sample copy for $7.50. Writer's guidelines online.

Payment/Terms: Pays $50 per story and one contributor's copy; additional copies $3.50. Pays on publication for first North American serial rights. Not copyrighted.

Advice: "Have friends or mentors read your story first and make suggestions to improve it."

⬛◎ **ELYSIAN FIELDS QUARTERLY, The Baseball Review**, P.O. Box 14385, St. Paul MN 55114-0385. (651)644-8558. E-mail: info@efqreview.com. Website: www.efqreview.com. **Contact:** Tom Goldstein, editor. Magazine: 6×9; 96 pages; 60 lb. paper; gloss/varnish cover; illustrations; and photos. *Elysian Fields Quarterly* is "unique because nobody covers baseball the way that we do, in such an offbeat, irreverent manner and yet with full appreciation of the game." Quarterly. Estab. 1992. Circ. 2,500.

Needs: "Any fiction piece about baseball will be considered, provided it is not simply general fiction disguised as a baseball story by making tangential connections to baseball, but in reality is not a fiction piece about baseball." Receives 4-5 unsolicited mss/month. Accepts 2-6 mss/issue; 10-12 mss/year. Publishes ms 3-12 months after acceptance. **Publishes 10-12 new writers/year.** Recently published work by Kelly Candaele, Alvin Greenberg and Mikhail Horowitz. Length: 1,000-4,000 words; average length: 2,000-3,000 words. Also publishes literary essays, literary criticism, poetry. Very rarely comments on rejected mss.

How to Contact: Accepts submissions by e-mail. Send SASE for reply, return of ms or send disposable copy of ms. Accepts e-mail submissions, however you still must send a hardcopy of the mss. Responds in 4 months to mss. Accepts simultaneous and reprints submissions. Will occasionally consider simultaneous submissions. Sample copy for $7.95. Writer's guidelines free.

Payment/Terms: Pays 4 contributor's copies; additional copies $5. Acquires one-time, rights to reprint in any anthologies rights. Sponsors awards/contests.

Advice: "Originality, creativity, believability—is it truly a baseball story? We do not pay attention to industry trends; we just try to publish good writing, irrespective of what is being published elsewhere."

[N]⬛ **EMRYS JOURNAL**, The Emrys Foundation, P.O. Box 8813, Greenville SC 29604. (864)455-4652. Fax: (864)235-0084. E-mail: jhn@ghs.org. Website: www.emrys.org. **Contact:** Jeanine Halva-Neubauer. Catalog: 9X9¾; 120 pages; 80 lb. paper. "We publish short fiction, poetry, and essays. We are particularly interested in hearing from women and other minorities. We are mindful of the southeast but not limited to it." Annual. Estab. 1984. Circ. 400.

Needs: Feminist, literary, mainstream, regional, contemporary. No religious or science fiction mss. Accepts 18 mss/issue. Reading period: August 1-December 1. Publishes mss in April. **Publishes 1 new writer/year.** Recently published work by Mindy Friddle and Ron Rash. Length: 6,000 words; average length: 3,500 words. Publishes short shorts.

How to Contact: Send complete ms. SASE. Responds in 6 weeks to mss. Accepts multiple submissions. Sample copy for $15 and 7×10 SAE with 4 first-class stamps. Writer's guidelines for #10 SASE.

Payment/Terms: Pays in contributor's copies. Acquires first rights.

Advice: Looks for "fiction by women and minorities, especially but not exclusively southeastern."

$⬛▨ **EPOCH**, Cornell University, 251 Goldwin Smith Hall, Cornell University, Ithaca NY 14853. (607)255-3385. Fax: (607)255-6661. **Contact:** Joseph Martin, senior editor. Magazine: 6×9; 128 pages; good quality paper; good cover stock. "Well-written literary fiction, poetry, personal essays. Newcomers always welcome. Open to mainstream and avant-garde writing." Estab. 1947. Circ. 1,000.

● Work originally appearing in this quality literary journal has appeared in numerous anthologies including *Best American Short Stories*, *Best American Poetry*, *Pushcart Prize*, *The O. Henry Prize Stories*, *Best of the West* and *New Stories from the South*.

Needs: Ethnic/multicultural, experimental, literary, mainstream, novel excerpts, literary short stories. "No genre fiction. Would like to see more Southern fiction (Southern US)." Receives 500 unsolicited mss/month. Accepts 15-20 mss/issue. Does not read in summer (April 15-September 15). Publishes ms an average of 6 months after acceptance. **Publishes 3-4 new writers/year.** Recently published work by Antonya Nelson, Doris Betts and Heidi Jon Schmidt. Also publishes poetry. Critiques rejected mss when there is time. Sometimes recommends other markets.

How to Contact: Send complete ms. Accepts submissions by mail. Responds in 2 weeks to queries; 6 weeks to mss. No simultaneous submissions. Sample copy for $5. Writer's guidelines for #10 SASE.

Payment/Terms: Pays $5 and up/printed page. Pays on publication for first North American serial rights.

Advice: "Read the journals you're sending work to."

[N]⬛◎ **ERASED, SIGH, SIGH., A Journal of Death Poets and Suicide Writers**, Via Dolorosa Press, 701 East Schaaf Road, Cleveland OH 44131. E-mail: viadolorosapress@aol.com. Website: www.angelfire.com/oh2/dolorosa/index.html. **Contact:** Hyacinthe L. Raven, editor. Magazine: 5½×8½; 48 pages; parchment paper; parchment cover stock; illustrations. "We only publish writing with an existential slant whose subject is death or suicide. We print mostly poetry, but that's only because the majority of our submissions have been poems. Our audience is 18-40 year-olds, college-educated, and primarily members of the punk and goth subculture." Semiannual. Estab. 1994. Circ. 500.

Needs: Experimental, literary, mainstream. "No genre fiction. Also, no humor as our theme is of a serious tone and no children/juvenile/teen fiction as our audience is college-aged." Receives 10 unsolicited mss/month. Accepts 1-2 mss/issue; 2-4 mss/year. Publishes ms 6-12 months after acceptance. **Publishes 10 new writers/year.** Recently published work by John Sweet, John Grey, David Stone, Giovanni Malito, Lyn Lifshin. Length: 1,500 words; average length: 1,000 words. Publishes short shorts. Also publishes poetry. Sometimes comments on rejected mss.

How to Contact: Send complete ms. Accepts submissions by mail. Send disposable copy of the ms and #10 SASE for reply only. Responds in 1-2 months to queries; 1-2 months to mss. Accepts simultaneous and reprints, multiple submissions. Sample copy for $4 payable to Via Dolorosa Press. Writer's guidelines for SASE and on website.

Payment/Terms: Pays 1 contributor's copy. Pays on publication for one-time rights.

Advice: "Be familiar with our theme and the style of the poets we print—we're more likely to print fiction that has the same feel as the poetry of our regulars like John Sweet and Giovanni Malito."

EUREKA LITERARY MAGAZINE, 300 E. College Ave., Eureka College, Eureka IL 61530-1500. (309)467-6336. E-mail: llogsdon@eureka.edu. **Contact:** Jane S. Groeper, fiction editor. Magazine: 6×9; 120 pages; 70 lb. white offset paper; 80 lb. gloss cover; photographs (occasionally). "We seek to be open to the best stories that are submitted to us. We do not want to be narrow in a political sense of the word. Our audience is a combination of professors/writers and general readers." Semiannual. Estab. 1992. Circ. 500.

Needs: Adventure, ethnic/multicultural, experimental, fantasy (science), feminist, historical, humor/satire, literary, mainstream, mystery/suspense (private eye/hardboiled, romantic), psychic/supernatural/occult, regional, romance (historical), science fiction (soft/sociological), translations. Would like to see more "good social science fiction stories, good ghost stories. We try to achieve a balance between the traditional and the experimental. We do favor the traditional, though. We look for the well-crafted story, but essentially any type of story that has depth and substance to it—any story that expands us as human beings and celebrates the mystery and miracle of the creation. Make sure you have a good beginning and ending, a strong voice, excellent use of language, good insight into the human condition, narrative skill, humor—if it is appropriate to the subject." Receives 30 unsolicited mss/month. Accepts 4 mss/issue; 8-9 mss/year. Does not read mss mainly in late summer (August). **Publishes 5-6 new writers/year.** Recently published work by Jane Guill, Forrest Robinson, Ray Bradbury, Earl Coleman, Virgil Suarez, Cynthia Gallaher and Wendell Mayo. Length: 7,000-8,000 words; average length: 4,500 words. words. Publishes short shorts. Also publishes poetry.

How to Contact: Send SASE for reply, return of ms or send disposable copy of ms. Responds in 1 week to queries; 4 months to mss. Accepts simultaneous, multiple submissions. Sample copy for $7.50.

Payment/Terms: Pays free subscription to the magazine and 2 contributor's copies. Acquires first, one-time rights.

Advice: "We look for expert storytelling technique; a powerful statement about the human condition; eloquent or effective use of language—metaphor, imagery, description. Find a copy of the magazine and read it before submitting your work. Order a copy if you can."

EVANSVILLE REVIEW, University of Evansville, 1800 Lincoln Ave., Evansville IN 47722. (812)488-1042. **Contact:** Carolina Cuervo, editor. Magazine: 6×9; 180 pages; 70 lb. white paper; glossy full color cover; perfect bound. Annual. Estab. 1990. Circ. 1,000.

Needs: Does not want erotica, fantasy, experimental, or children's fiction. "We're open to all creativity. No discrimination. All fiction, screenplays, nonfiction, poetry, interviews, photo essays are anything in between." List of upcoming themes available for SASE. Receives 70 unsolicited mss/month. Does not read mss February-August. Agented fiction 2%. **Publishes 20 new writers/year.** Recently published work by John Updike, Arthur Miller, X.J. Kennedy, Jim Barnes, and Rita Dove. Also publishes literary essays, poetry.

How to Contact: Send SASE for reply, return of ms or send a disposable copy of ms. Responds in 1 month to queries; 3 months to mss. Accepts simultaneous and reprints, multiple submissions. Sample copy for $5. Writer's guidelines free.

Payment/Terms: Pays 2 contributor's copies. Pays on publication for one-time rights. Not copyrighted.

Advice: "Because editorial staff rolls over every 1-2 years, the journal always has a new flavor."

$ ⬚ ⬚ ⬚ EVENT, Douglas College, P.O. Box 2503, New Westminster BC V3L 5B2 Canada. (604)527-5293. Fax: (604)527-5095. Website: http://event.douglas.bc.ca. **Contact:** Christine Dewar, fiction editor. Magazine: 6×9; 136 pages; quality paper and cover stock. "We are eclectic and always open to content that invites involvement. Generally, we like strong narrative." Estab. 1971. Circ. 1,250.

• Fiction originally published in *Event* has been included in *The Journey Anthology* and *Best Canadian Stories*, and work published in *Event* has been nominated for numerous awards over the years. *Event* ranked on *Writer's Digest's* "Top 30" list of best markets for fiction writers.

Needs: Feminist, humor/satire, literary, regional, contemporary. "No technically poor or unoriginal pieces." Receives 100 unsolicited mss/month. Accepts 6-8 mss/issue. Publishes ms 8 months after acceptance. **Publishes 2-3 new writers/year.** Recently published work by Bill Gaston, Gary Geddes and Elisabeth Harver. Also publishes poetry.

How to Contact: Send complete ms. Accepts submissions by mail, fax. Responds in 1 month to queries; 6 months to mss. Accepts simultaneous submissions. Sample copy for $5. Writer's guidelines online.

Payment/Terms: Pays $22/page to $500. Pays on publication for first North American serial rights.

Advice: "We're looking for a strong, effective point of view; well-handled and engaging characters, attention to language and strong details."

◎ **EXHIBITION, A Journal of Visual and Literary Arts**, Bainbridge Island Arts & Humanities Council, 221 Winslow Way West Suite 201, Bainbridge Island WA 98110. (206)842-7901. E-mail: exhibition@artshum.org. Website: www.artshum.org/exhibition.html. **Contact:** Jennifer Scott. Magazine: 8½×11; 32-40 pages; artwork; photographs. "*Exhibition* is published by Bainbridge Island Arts & Humanities Council, a nonprofit organization whose mission is to create an environment on Bainbridge Island in which the arts and humanities flourish." Semiannual. Estab. 1985. Circ. 500.
Needs: Historical, humor/satire, literary, mainstream, regional (Pacific Northwest focus). "No erotica, religious, children's. Would like to receive more fiction." Receives 5 unsolicited mss/month. Accepts 0-5 mss/issue. Publishes ms 3 months after acceptance. Publishes short shorts. Also publishes literary essays, poetry. Sometimes comments on rejected mss.
How to Contact: Send SASE for return of ms or disposable copy of ms with SASE for reply only. Responds in 6 months to mss. Accepts reprints, multiple submissions. Sample copy for $7. Writer's guidelines for SASE, by e-mail or on website.
Payment/Terms: Pays 1 contributor's copy; additional copies $7. Acquires first North American serial rights.
Advice: "We unconsciously absorb and reproduce forms and styles we see most. If you want to write good fiction, watch TV less, watch people more—and read the sort of work you'd like to write."

◖ **FAULTLINE, Journal of Art and Literature**, Dept. of English and Comparitive Literature, University of California, Irvine, Irvine CA 92697-2650. (949)824-1573. E-mail: faultline@uci.edu. Website: www.humanities.uci. edu/faultline. **Contact:** Editors change in September each year. Literary magazine: 6×9; 176 pages; illustrations; photos. "We publish the very best of what we recieve. Our interest is quality and literary merit." Annual. Estab. 1992.
Needs: Translations, literary fiction up to 20 pages. "Novel excerpts are fine, but they should be self-contained. No sci-fi, mystery, westerns or romance." Receives 20-30 unsolicited mss/month. Accepts 6-9 mss/year. Does not read mss April-September. Publishes ms 9 months after acceptance. Agented fiction 10-20%. **Publishes 30-40% new writers/year.** Recently published work by Maile Meloy, Susan Emerling, Ben Miller and Joan Frank. Publishes short shorts. Also publishes literary essays, poetry.
How to Contact: Send SASE for reply, return of ms or send a disposable copy of ms. Responds in 2 weeks to queries; 4 months to mss. Accepts simultaneous submissions. Sample copy for $5. Writer's guidelines for business-size envelope.
Payment/Terms: Pays 2 contributor's copies. Pays on publication for one-time rights.
Advice: "Our commitment is to publish the best work possible from well-known and emerging authors as well as those who have been affiliated with UCI's esteemed graduate studies program."

◖ ◎ **FEMINIST STUDIES**, 0103 Taliaferro, University of Maryland, College Park MD 20742. (301)405-7415. Fax: (301)405-8395. E-mail: femstud@umail.umd.edu. Website: www.feministstudies.org. **Contact:** Shirley Lim, fiction editor. Magazine: journal-sized; about 200 pages; photographs. "Scholarly manuscripts, fiction, book review essays for professors, graduate/doctoral students; scholarly interdisciplinary feminist journal." Triannual. Estab. 1974. Circ. 7,500.
Needs: Ethnic/multicultural, feminist, gay, lesbian, contemporary. Receives 20 unsolicited mss/month. Accepts 2-3 mss/issue. "We review fiction twice a year. Deadline dates are May 1 and December 1. Authors will recieve notice of the board's decision by June 15 and January 15, respectively." Recently published work by Bell Chevigny, Betsy Gould Gibson and Joan Jacobson. Sometimes comments on rejected mss.
How to Contact: No simultaneous submissions. Sample copy for $15. Writer's guidelines free.
Payment/Terms: Pays 2 contributor's copies and 10 tearsheets. Sends galleys to authors.

$ ◖ ◩ **FICTION**, c/o Department of English, City College, 138th St. & Covenant Ave., New York NY 10031. (212)650-6319. Website: www.fictioninc.com. **Contact:** Mark J. Mirsky, editor. Magazine: 6×9; 150-250 pages; illustrations; occasionally photos. "As the name implies, we publish only fiction; we are looking for the best new writing available, leaning toward the unconventional. *Fiction* has traditionally attempted to make accessible the unaccessible, to bring the experimental to a broader audience." Semiannual. Estab. 1972. Circ. 4,000.
● Stories first published in *Fiction* have been selected for inclusion in the *Pushcart Prize* and *Best of the Small Presses* anthologies.
Needs: Experimental, humor/satire (satire), literary, translations, contemporary, literary. translations. No romance,

---

CHECK THE CATEGORY INDEXES, located at the back of the book, for publishers interested in specific fiction subjects.

science fiction, etc. Receives 200 unsolicited mss/month. Accepts 12-20 mss/issue; 24-40 mss/year. Does not read mss May-October. Publishes ms 1 year after acceptance. Agented fiction 10-20%. Recently published work by Joyce Carol Oates, Robert Musil and Romulus Linney. Publishes short shorts. Sometimes critiques rejected mss and recommends other markets. Sometimes comments on rejected mss.

How to Contact: Send complete ms with cover letter. SASE. Responds in 3 months to mss. Accepts simultaneous submissions, but please advise. Sample copy for $5. Writer's guidelines online.

Payment/Terms: Pays $114. Acquires first rights.

Advice: "The guiding principle of *Fiction* has always been to go to terra incognita in the writing of the imagination and to ask that modern fiction set itself serious questions, if often in absurd and comical voices, interrogating the nature of the real and the fantastic. It represents no particular school of fiction, except the innovative. Its pages have often been a harbor for writers at odds with each other. As a result of its willingness to publish the difficult, experimental, unusual, while not excluding the well known, *Fiction* has a unique reputation in the U.S. and abroad as a journal of future directions."

$ 🔲 ☑ THE FIDDLEHEAD, University of New Brunswick, Campus House, Box 4400, Fredericton NB E3B 5A3 Canada. (506)453-3501. Website: www.lib.und.ca/texts/fiddlehead. **Contact:** Mark A. Jarman, fiction editor. Magazine: 6×9; 128-160 pages; ink illustrations; photos. "No criteria for publication except quality. For a general audience, including many poets and writers." Quarterly. Estab. 1945. Circ. 1,000.

Needs: Literary. Receives 100-150 unsolicited mss/month. Accepts 4-5 mss/issue; 20-40 mss/year. Publishes ms 1 year after acceptance. Agented fiction small percentage. **Publishes high percentage of new writers/year.** Recently published work by Eric Miller, Tony Steele, Gina Ochsner, Liam Duncan and A.F. Moritz. Average length: 3,000 words. Publishes short shorts. Occasionally comments on rejected mss.

How to Contact: Send SASE and *Canadian* stamps or IRCs for return of mss. Responds in 6 months to mss. No simultaneous submissions. Sample copy for $10 (US).

Payment/Terms: Pays $20 (Canadian)/published page and 1 contributor's copy. Pays on publication for first or one-time rights.

Advice: "Less than 5% of the material received is published."

🄽 ☑ FILLING STATION, Filling Station Publications Society, Box 22135, Bankers Hall, Calgary AB T2P 4J5 Canada. (403)228-2385. Fax: (403)228-2385. **Contact:** Adrian Kelly, fiction editor. Magazine: 8½×11; 56 pages; 70 lb. offset paper; 80 lb. cover; illustrations; photos. "We're looking for writing that challenges the preconceptions of readers and writers alike, that crosses conventional boundaries and seeks out its own territory. We're particularly interested in new voices." Triannual. Estab. 1993. Circ. 700.

Needs: Ethnic/multicultural, experimental, feminist, gay, lesbian, literary, mainstream, regional, translations. Receives 10-15 unsolicited mss/month. Accepts 3-4 mss/issue; 10 mss/year. Publishes ms 1 year after acceptance. **Publishes 5-6 new writers/year.** Recently published work by Salma Hussain, Craig Boyko, Bill Stenson, Suzette Mays. Length: 5,000 words; average length: 2,000 words. Publishes short shorts. Also publishes literary essays, literary criticism, poetry.

How to Contact: Send complete ms. E-mail submissions/general inquiries: fiction@fillingstation.ca. Send SASE for reply, return of ms or send a disposable copy of ms. Responds in 1 month to queries; 4 months to mss. Accepts simultaneous submissions. Sample copy for $8, 9×12 SAE and 2 IRCs. Writer's guidelines for #10 SASE. Reviews fiction.

Payment/Terms: One-year subscription, beginning with the issue in which the author is published. Acquires first North American serial rights.

Advice: "We don't want work by people who know how to write but have nothing to say. Style is important, but so is the narrative framework. Also, if someone tells you it's already been done, that person is partially right—the question is how has it been done? If you are writing, you need to do it differently and get away from the familiar ruts. Beyond composition and fluid use of language, you need to make connections between things that have already been thought of but have never been connected before. Don't try to impress editors with flashy cover letters, name-dropping or stacks of credentials. Publishing, especially for small-run magazines, is increasingly expensive and difficult in an era of rising production costs and shrinking funding. The demands on any publisher in any market to seek out higher-quality work are correspondingly greater."

☑ FIRST CLASS, Four-Sep Publications, P.O. Box 86, Friendship IN 47021. E-mail: christoperm@four-sep.com. Website: www.four-sep.com. **Contact:** Christopher M, editor. Magazine: 4¼×11; 60+ pages; 24 lb./60 lb. offset paper; craft cover; illustrations; photos. "*First Class* features short fiction and poetics form the cream of the small press and killer unknowns—mingling before your very hungry eyes. I publish plays, too." Biannual. Estab. 1995. Circ. 200-400.

Needs: Erotica, literary, mainstream, science fiction (soft/sociological), post-modern. "No religious or traditional poetry, or 'boomer angst'—therapy-driven self loathing." Receives 35-50 unsolicited mss/month. Accepts 4-6 mss/issue; 10-12 mss/year. Publishes ms 1 month after acceptance. **Publishes 10-15 new writers/year.** Recently published work by Gerald Locklin, John Bennnet and B.Z. Niditch. Length: 5,000-8,000; average length: 2,000-3,000 words. Publishes short shorts. Also publishes poetry. Sometimes comments on rejected mss.

How to Contact: Send SASE and #10 SASE for reply only or send a disposable copy of ms. Responds in 1 week to queries. Accepts simultaneous and reprints submissions. Sample copy for $6. Writer's guidelines for #10 SASE. Reviews fiction.

Payment/Terms: Pays 1 contributor's copy; additional copies $5. Acquires one-time rights.

Advice: "Don't bore me with puppy dogs and the morose/sappy feeling you have about death. Belt out a good, short, thought-provoking, graphic, uncommon piece."

$ ☑ ☒ FIVE POINTS, A Journal of Literature and Art, MSC 8R0318 Georgia State University, University Plaza, 33 Gilmer St. SE, Unit 8, Atlanta GA 30303-3083. (404)651-0071. Fax: (404)651-3167. E-mail: msexton@gsu.edu. Website: www.webdelsol.com/five_points. **Contact:** Megan Sexton, associate editor. Magazine: 6×9; 200 pages; cotton paper; glossy cover; and photos. *Five Points* is "committed to publishing work that compels the imagination through the use of fresh and convincing language." Triannual. Estab. 1996. Circ. 2,000.

● Fiction first appearing in *Five Points* has been anthologized in *Best American Fiction* and Pushcart anthologies.

Needs: List of upcoming themes available for SASE. Receives 250 unsolicited mss/month. Accepts 4 mss/issue; 15-20 mss/year. Does not read mss April 30-September 1. Publishes ms 6 months after acceptance. **Publishes 1 new writer/year.** Recently published work by Frederick Busch, Ursula Hegi and Melanie Rae Thon. Average length: 7,500 words. Publishes short shorts. Also publishes literary essays, poetry. Sometimes comments on rejected mss.

How to Contact: Send SASE for reply to query. No simultaneous submissions. Sample copy for $7.

Payment/Terms: Pays $15/page minimum; $250 maximum, free subscription to magazine and 2 contributor's copies; additional copies $4. Acquires first North American serial rights. Sends galleys to author. Sponsors awards/contests.

Advice: "We place no limitations on style or content. Our only criteria is excellence. If your writing has an original voice, substance, and significance, send it to us. We will publish distinctive, intelligent writing that has something to say and says it in a way that captures and maintains our attention."

☑ ◎ FLINT HILLS REVIEW, Dept. of English, Box 4019, Emporia State University, Emporia KS 66801-5087. (620)341-6916. Fax: (620)341-5547. E-mail: webbamy@emporia.edu. Website: www.emporia.edu/fhr/. **Contact:** Amy Sage Webb, co-editor. Magazine: 9×6; 115 pages; 60 lb. paper; glossy cover; illustrations; photos. "*FHR* seeks work informed by a strong sense of place or region, especially Kansas and the Great Plains region. We seek to provide a publishing venue for writers of the Great Plains and Kansas while also publishing authors whose work evidences a strong sense of place, writing of literary quality, and accomplished use of language and depth of character development." Annual. Estab. 1996. Circ. 500. CLMP.

Needs: Ethnic/multicultural, gay, historical, regional (Plains), translations. "No religious, inspirational, children's." Want to see more "writing of literary quality with a strong sense of place." List of upcoming themes online. Receives 5-15 unsolicited mss/month. Accepts 2-5 mss/issue; 2-5 mss/year. Does not read mss April-December. Publishes ms 4 months after acceptance. **Publishes 4 new writers/year.** Recently published work by Walt McDonald, Amy Kolen, Virgil Suarez and Lisa Knopp. Average length: 3,000 words. Publishes short shorts. Also publishes literary essays, literary criticism, poetry.

How to Contact: Send a disposable copy of ms and #10 SASE for reply only. Responds in 5 weeks to queries; 6 months to mss. Accepts simultaneous, multiple submissions. Sample copy for $5.50. Writer's guidelines for SASE, by e-mail, fax or on website. Reviews fiction.

Payment/Terms: Pays 2 contributor's copies; additional copies $5.50. Acquires one-time rights.

Advice: "Strong imagery and voice, writing that is informed by place or region, writing of literary quality with depth of character development. Hone the language down to the most literary depiction that is possible in the shortest space that still provides depth of development without excess length."

☑ FLYWAY, A Literary Review, Iowa State University, 206 Ross Hall, Ames IA 50011. (515)294-8273. Fax: (515)294-6814. E-mail: flyway@iastate.edu. Website: www.flyaway.org. **Contact:** Stephen Pett, editor. Literary magazine: 6×9; 64 pages; quality paper; cover stock; some illustrations; photos. "We publish quality fiction. Our stories are accompanied by brief commentaries by their authors, the sort of thing a writer might say introducing a piece at a reading." Biannual. Estab. 1995. Circ. 500.

Needs: Literary. Receives 50 unsolicited mss/month. Accepts 2-5 mss/issue; 10-12 mss/year. Publishes ms 5 months after acceptance. **Publishes 7-10 new writers/year.** Recently published work by Naomi Shihab Nye, Gina Ochsner, Ted Kooser. Length: 5,000; average length: 3,500 words. Publishes short shorts. Often comments on rejected mss.

How to Contact: Send SASE. Sample copy for $8. Writer's guidelines for SASE.

Payment/Terms: Pays 2 contributor's copies; additional copies $6. Acquires one-time rights.

Advice: "Quality, originality, voice, drama, tension. Make it as strong as you can."

🅽 ☑ FOURTEEN HILLS, The SFSU Review, Dept. of Creative Writing, San Francisco State University, 1600 Holloway Ave., San Francisco CA 94132. (415)338-3083. E-mail: hills@sfsu.edu. Website: www.14hills.com. **Contact:** Editors change each year. Magazine: 6×9; 160 pages; 60 lb. paper; 10 point C15 cover. "*Fourteen Hills* publishes the highest quality innovative fiction and poetry for a literary audience." Semiannual. Estab. 1994. Circ. 700.

Needs: Ethnic/multicultural, experimental, gay, humor/satire, lesbian, literary, mainstream, translations. "No sexist or racist work, and no stories in which the plot has been chosen for its shock value. No genre fiction please." Receives 100 unsolicited mss/month. Accepts 8-10 mss/issue; 16-20 mss/year. Does not usually read mss during the summer. Publishes ms 2-4 months after acceptance. **Publishes 6 new writers/year.** Recently published work by Terese Svoboda, Peter Rock and Stephen Dixon. Publishes short shorts. Also publishes literary essays, poetry. Sometimes comments on rejected mss.

How to Contact: SASE for return of ms. Responds in 5 months to mss. Sample copy for $7. Writer's guidelines for #10 SASE.

Payment/Terms: Pays 2 contributor's copies. Acquires one-time, sends galleys to author rights.

Advice: "Please read an isssue of *Fourteen Hills* before submitting."

N $⊞ **FRANK, An International Journal of Contemporary Writing & Art**, Association Frank, 32 rue Edouard Vaillant, Montreuil, France. (33)(1)48596658. Fax: (33)(1)48596668. E-mail: submissions@readfrank.com. Website: www.readfrank.com or www.frank.ly. **Contact:** David Applefield. "Writing that takes risks and isn't ethnocentric is looked upon favorably." Published twice/year. Estab. 1983. Circ. 4,000.

Needs: Experimental, novel excerpts, international. "At *Frank*, we publish fiction, poetry, literary and art inter-views, and translations. We like work that falls between existing genres and has social or political consciousness." Accepts 20 mss/issue. Publishes ms 1 year after acceptance.

How to Contact: Send complete ms. Send IRC or $5 cash. Must be previously unpublished in English (world). E-mail submissions as Word attachments are welcome and should be saved in RTF. Responds in 1 month to queries; 2 months to mss. Sample copy for $10. Writer's guidelines online.

Payment/Terms: Pays $10/printed page. Pays on publication for one-time rights.

Advice: "Send your most daring and original work. At *Frank*, we like work that is not too parochial or insular, however, don't try to write for a 'French' market."

$ ⊠ ⊘ **FREEFALL MAGAZINE**, The Alexandra Writers' Centre Society, 922 Ninth Ave. SE, Calgary AB T2G 0S4 Canada. (403)264-4730. E-mail: awcs@telusplanet.net. Website: www.alexandrawriters.org. **Contact:** Sharon Drummond, editor. Magazine: 8½×11; 40 pages; bond paper; bond stock; illustrations; photos. "*FreeFall* features the best of new, emerging writers and gives them the chance to get into print along with established writers. Now in its fourteenth year, *FreeFall* seeks to attract readers looking for well-crafted stories, poetry and artwork." Semiannual. Estab. 1990. Circ. Under 500. Alberta Magazine Publishers Association (AMPA).

Needs: "No science fiction, horror." Wants to see more well-crafted literary fiction. Accepts 3-5 mss/issue; 6-10 mss/year. Does not read mss January-February, June-August. Publishes ms 6 months after acceptance. **Publishes 40% new writers/year.** Recently published work by Jan Houston, Sharon LaFrenz, Vilnis Muizieks, Bill Stenson, Dianne Wey, Joan Hoekstra, David Schultz, Janet Hunter, J. Romanov. Length: 500-3,000 words; average length: 2,500 words. Publishes short shorts. Also publishes poetry. Sometimes comments on rejected mss.

How to Contact: Send SASE (or IRC) for return of ms or send a disposable copy of ms with #10 SASE for reply only, or e-mail address for reply. Responds in 3 months to mss. Accepts reprints submissions. Sample copy for $6.50 (US). Writer's guidelines for SASE, e-mail or on website.

Payment/Terms: Pays $5 (Canadian)/printed page and 1 contributor's copy; additional copies $8.50 (US). Acquires first North American serial, one-time rights.

Advice: "We look for thoughtful word usage that conveys clear images and encourages further exploration of the story's idea and neat, clean presentation of work. Carefully read *FreeFall* guidelines before submitting. Do not fold manuscript and submit 9×11 envelope. Include SASE/IRC for reply and/or return of manuscript. You may contact us by e-mail after initial hardcopy submission. For accepted pieces a request is made for disk or e-mail copy. Web presence attracts submissions from writers all over the world."

⊠ ⊘ ◎ **FRONT & CENTRE**, Black Bile Press, 573 Gainsborough Ave., Ottawa ON K2A 2Y6 Canada. (613)729-8973. E-mail: firth@istar.ca. **Contact:** Matthew Firth, editor. Magazine: half letter-size; 40-50 pages; illustrations; photos. "We look for new fiction from Canadian and international writers—bold, aggressive work that does not compromise quality." Three issues per year. Estab. 1998. Circ. 500.

Needs: Literary ("contemporary realism/gritty urban"). "No science fiction, horror, mainstream, romance or reli-gious." Receives 30-40 unsolicited mss/month. Accepts 6-7 mss/issue; 10-20 mss/year. Publishes ms 6 months after acceptance. Agented fiction 10%. **Publishes 4-5 new writers/year.** Recently published work by Kenneth J. Harvey, David Rose, Laura Hird, Jon Boillard, Nichole McGill, and John Swan. Length: 50-4,000 words; average length: 2,500 words. Publishes short shorts. Always comments on rejected mss.

How to Contact: Send SASE (or IRC) for return of ms or send a disposable copy of ms with #10 SASE for reply only. Responds in 2 weeks to queries; 4 months to mss. Accepts multiple submissions. Sample copy for $6. Writer's guidelines for SASE or by e-mail. Reviews fiction.

Payment/Terms: Acquires first rights. Not copyrighted.

Advice: "We look for attention to detail; unique voice; not overtly derivative; bold writing; not pretentious. We should like to see more realism. Read the magazine first—simple as that!"

⊘ ◎ **FRONTIERS, A Journal of Women's Studies**, Wilson 12, Washington State University, Frontiers, Women's Studies, Pullman WA 99164-4007. (509)335-7268. Fax: (509)335-4377. E-mail: frontier@wsu.edu. **Con-**

tact: Fiction Edtitor. Magazine: 6×9; 200 pages; photos. "Women studies; academic articles in all disciplines; criticism; exceptional creative work (art, short fiction, photography, poetry)."

Needs: Feminist, lesbian, multicultural. "We want to see fiction that deals with women's lives and experience from a feminist perspective." Receives 15 unsolicited mss/month. Accepts 7-12 mss/issue. Publishes ms 6-12 months after acceptance. **Publishes 2 new writers/year.** Recently published work by Elizabeth Bell, Nadine Chapman, Tricia Currans-Sheehan and Aletha Eason.

How to Contact: SASE. Responds in 1 month to queries; 6 months to mss. Sample copy for $20. Writer's guidelines for #10 SASE.

Payment/Terms: Pays 2 contributor's copies. Acquires first North American serial rights.

Advice: "We are a *feminist* journal. *Frontiers* aims to make scholarship in women's studies, and *exceptional* creative work, accesible to a cross-disciplinary audience inside and outside academia. Read short fiction in *Frontiers* before submitting.

N 🖂 $🖂 FUGUE, English Dept., 200 Brink Hall, University of Idaho, Moscow ID 83844-1102. (208)885-6156. Fax: (208)885-5944. E-mail: fugue@uidaho.edu. Website: www.class.uidaho.edu/english/fugue/. **Contact:** Ben George and Jeff P. Jones, Co-editors. Magazine: 6×9; 125 pages; 20 lb. stock paper. By allowing the voices of established writers lend their authority to new and emerging writers, *Fugue* strives to provide its readers with the most compelling stories, poems, essays, interviews, and literary criticism possible. Semiannual. Estab. 1990. Circ. 400.

● Received a Pushcart award for a essay by Melanie Rae Thon.

Needs: Ethnic/multicultural, experimental, humor/satire, literary, romance (contemporary). Receives 80 unsolicited mss/month. Accepts 6-8 mss/issue; 12-15 mss/year. Does not read mss May 1-August 31. Publishes ms 6 months after acceptance. **Publishes 5-8 new writers/year.** Recently published work by Charles Baxter, Melanie Rae Thon, Steve Almond, Ander Monson, James McCafferty, Sonia Gernes. Length: 6,000 words; average length: 4,000 words. Publishes short shorts. Also publishes literary essays, poetry. Sometimes comments on rejected mss.

How to Contact: Send complete ms. Accepts submissions by mail. Send SASE (or IRC) for return of the ms or disposable copy of the ms and #10 SASE for reply only. Responds in 3-4 months to mss. Accepts simultaneous submissions. Sample copy for $8. Writer's guidelines for SASE or on website.

Payment/Terms: Pays $10 minimum and 1 contributor copy; additional copies $4. Pays on publication for first North American serial, electronic rights.

Advice: "The best way, of course, to determine what we're looking for is to read the journal. As the name *Fugue* indicates, our goal is to present a wide range of literary characters and language so captivating that they stick with us and invite a second reading. We are also seeking creative literary criticism which illuminates a piece of literature or a specific writer by examining that writer's personal experience."

N $🖉 🖂 FUTURES MYSTERIOUS ANTHOLOGY MAGAZINE, 3039 38th Ave. South, Minneapolis MN 55406-2140. (612)724-4023. Website: www.fmam.biz. **Contact:** Earl Staggs, editor. Magazine: 8½×11; 130 pages; illustrations; cartoons. "We nourish writers and artists; attempt to throw out the net so they can fly without fear! The futures in commodities is a good analogy for writers and artists. Their work, in many cases, is greatly undervalued. Their future market value will be higher than can be imagined. In the writing community there is a tremendous amount of energy; a rolling boil. It takes the form of many people with talent and motivation anxious to unleash their creative juices." Quarterly. Estab. 1998. Circ. 5,000.

● Publisher Babs Lakey received a Derringer Award from the Short Mystery Fiction Society.

Needs: Adventure, ethnic/multicultural, experimental, fantasy, feminist, gay, glitz, historical, horror, humor/satire, lesbian, literary, mainstream, mystery/suspense (amateur sleuth, cozy, police procedural, private eye/hardboiled), psychic/supernatural/occult, romance, science fiction, suspense, thriller/espionage, western, cartoons. "We would like to see more thrillers, more mystery and suspense. No erotica or pornography." List of upcoming themes available on the website. Receives 300 unsolicited mss/month. Accepts 45-60 mss/issue; 250 mss/year. Publishes ms 8 months after acceptance. **Publishes at least 25 new writers/year.** Recently published work by Henry Slesar, David Harford, Ashok Banker and Elizabeth Serini. Length: 500-12,000 words; average length: 2,500 words. Publishes short shorts. Also publishes literary essays, literary criticism, poetry. Sometimes comments on rejected mss.

How to Contact: Send complete ms. Accepts submissions by e-mail. Refer to online guidelines; guidelines also inside every issue. Responds in 1 week to queries; 3 months to mss. Accepts simultaneous submissions Accepts simultaneous and multiple submissions, but put each in a separate e-mail. Sample copy for $8 includes shipping. Writer's guidelines online.

Payment/Terms: Pays $10-50. Pays on publication for first rights. Sponsors awards/contests.

Advice: "Read our guidelines and do what they say—this is the first rule of being a professional! Please make the effort to read a copy before you submit."

🖉 GARGOYLE, P.O. Box 6216, Arlington VA 22206-0216. (877)327-2141 (toll free). E-mail: gargoyle@atticusb ooks.com. Website: www.atticusbooks.com. **Contact:** Richard Peabody and Lucinda Ebersole, editors. Literary magazine: 6×9; 200 pages; illustrations; photos. "*Gargoyle* began in 1976 with twin goals: to discover new voices and to rediscover overlooked talent. These days we publish a lot of fictional efforts written by poets. We have always been more interested in how a writer tells a story than in plot or story per se." Annual. Estab. 1976. Circ. 2,000.

Needs: Erotica, ethnic/multicultural, experimental, gay, lesbian, literary, mainstream, translations. "No romance, horror, science fiction." Wants "good short stories with sports and music backgrounds." Wants to see more Canadian, British, Australian and third world fiction. Receives 50-200 unsolicited mss/month. Accepts 10-15 mss/issue. Accepts submissions from Memorial Day until Labor Day. Publishes ms 6-12 months after acceptance. Agented fiction 5%. **Publishes 2-3 new writers/year.** Recently published work by Rebecca Brown, Kenneth Carroll, Wanda Coleman and Doug Rice. Length: 30 pages maximum; average length: 5-10 pages. Publishes short shorts. Also publishes literary essays, literary criticism, poetry. Sometimes comments on rejected mss.

How to Contact: Send SASE for reply, return of ms or send a disposable copy of ms. Responds in 2 weeks to queries; 3 months to mss. Accepts simultaneous submissions. Sample copy for $12.95.

Payment/Terms: Pays 1 contributor's copy; additional copies for ½ price. Acquires first North American serial, first, first British rights. Sends galleys to author.

Advice: "We have to fall in love with a particular fiction."

A GATHERING OF THE TRIBES, A Gathering of the Tribes, Inc., P.O. Box 20693, Tompkins Square Station, New York NY 10009. (212)674-3778. Fax: (212)388-9813. E-mail: info@tribes.org. Website: www.tribes.org. **Contact:** Steve Cannon. Magazine: 8½ × 10; 130 pages; glossy paper and cover; illustrations; photos. A "multicultural and multigenerational publication featuring poetry, fiction, interviews, essays, visual art, musical scores. Audience is anyone interested in the arts from a diverse perspective." Estab. 1992. Circ. 2,000-3,000.

Needs: Erotica, ethnic/multicultural, experimental, fantasy (science), feminist, gay, historical, horror, humor/satire, lesbian, literary, mainstream, romance (futuristic/time travel, gothic), science fiction (soft/sociological), translations, senior citizen/retirement. "Would like to see more satire/humor. We are open to all; just no poor writing/grammar/syntax." List of upcoming themes available for SASE. Receives 20 unsolicited mss/month. Publishes ms 3-6 months after acceptance. **Publishes 40% new writers/year.** Recently published work by Carl Watson and Hanif Kureishi. Average length: 1,500-2,500. Publishes short shorts. Also publishes literary essays, literary criticism, poetry.

How to Contact: Send complete ms. Send SASE for reply, return of ms or send a disposable copy of ms. Accepts simultaneous and reprints submissions. Sample copy for $15. Reviews fiction.

Payment/Terms: Pays 1 contributor's copy; additional copies $12-50. Sponsors awards/contests.

Advice: "Make sure your work has substance."

$ THE GEORGIA REVIEW, The University of Georgia, Athens GA 30602-9009. (706)542-3481. Fax: (706)542-0047. Website: www.uga.edu/garev. **Contact:** T.R. Hummer, editor. Journal: 7 × 10; 208 pages (average); 50 lb. woven old-style paper; 80 lb. cover stock; illustrations; photos. "Our readers are educated, inquisitive people who read a lot of work in the areas we feature, so they expect only the best in our pages. All work submitted should show evidence that the writer is at least as well-educated and well-read as our readers. Essays should be authoritative but accessible to a range of readers." Quarterly. Estab. 1947. Circ. 5,000.

● Stories first published in *The Georgia Review* have been anthologized in *Best American Short Stories*, *Best American Mystery Stories*, *Best Stories from the South* and the *Pushcart Prize Collection*. *The Georgia Review* was a finalist for the National Magazine Award in Fiction in 2003. *The Georgia Review* ranked on *Writer's Digest's* "Top 30" list of best markets for fiction writers.

Needs: "Ordinarily we do not publish novel excerpts or works translated into English, and we strongly discourage authors from submitting these." Receives 300 unsolicited mss/month. Accepts 3-4 mss/issue; 12-15 mss/year. Does not read unsolicited mss May 15-August 15. Publishes ms 6 months after acceptance. **Publishes some new writers/year.** Recently published work by Brock Clarke, Joyce Carol Oates, Guy Davenport, and Carrie Brown. Also publishes literary essays, literary criticism, poetry. Occasionally comments on rejected mss.

How to Contact: Send complete ms. Accepts submissions by mail. Responds in 2 weeks to queries; 3 months to mss. No simultaneous submissions. Sample copy for $7. Writer's guidelines online. Reviews fiction.

Payment/Terms: Pays $40/published page. Pays on publication for first North American serial rights. Sends galleys to author.

GERTRUDE, A Journal of Voice & Vision, Gertrude c/o Eric Delehoy, 7937 N Wayland Ave., Portland OR 97203. E-mail: editor@gertrudejournal.com. Website: www.gertrudejournal.com. **Contact:** Eric Delehoy, editor. Magazine: 5 × 8 1/2; 64-72 pages; perfect bound; 60 lb. paper; glossy card cover; illustrations; photos. *Gertrude* is an "annual publication featuring the voices and visions of the gay, lesbian, bisexual, transgender and supportive community." Estab. 1999. Circ. 400.

Needs: Ethnic/multicultural, feminist, gay, humor/satire, lesbian, literary, mainstream. "No romance, pornography or mystery." Wants more humorous multicultural fiction. "We'd like to publish more humor and positive portrayals of gays—steer away from victim roles, pity." Receives 15-20 unsolicited mss/month. Accepts 4-8 mss/issue; 4-8 mss/year. Publishes ms 1-2 months after acceptance. **Publishes 4-5 new writers/year.** Recently published work by Carol Guess, Demrie Alonzo, Henry Alley and Scott Pomfret. Length: 200-3,000 words; average length: 1,800 words. Publishes short shorts. Also publishes poetry.

How to Contact: Send SASE for reply to query and a disposable copy of ms. Responds in 4 months to mss.

Accepts multiple submissions. No simultaneous submissions. Sample copy for $5, 6×9 SAE and 4 1st class stamps. Writer's guidelines for #10 SASE.

Payment/Terms: Pays 1-2 contributor's copies; additional copies $4. Author retains rights. Not copyrighted.

Advice: "We look for strong characterization, imagery and new, unique ways of writing about universal experiences. Follow the construction of your work until the ending. Many stories start out with zest, then flipper and die. Show us, don't tell us."

$ ☑ ☑ THE GETTYSBURG REVIEW, Gettysburg College, Gettysburg PA 17325. (717)337-6770. Fax: (717)337-6775. E-mail: mdrew@gettysburg.com. Website: www.gettysburgreview.com. **Contact:** Mark Drew, assistant editor. Magazine: 6¼×10; 170 pages; acid free paper; full color illustrations. "Our concern is quality. Manuscripts submitted here should be extremely well written." Reading period September-May. Quarterly. Estab. 1988. Circ. 4,000.

● Work appearing in *The Gettysburg Review* has also been included in *Prize Stories: The O. Henry Awards*, *Pushcart Prize* anthology, *Best American Fiction*, *New Stories from the South*, *Harper's* and elsewhere. It is also the recipient of a Lila Wallace-Reader's Digest grant and NEA grants.

Needs: Experimental, historical, humor/satire, literary, mainstream, novel excerpts, regional, serialized novels, contemporary. "We require that fiction be intelligent, and esthetically written." Receives 350 unsolicited mss/month. Accepts 15-20 mss/issue; 60-80 mss/year. Publishes ms within 1 year after acceptance. **Publishes 1-5 new writers/year.** Recently published work by Robert Olen Butler, Joyce Carol Oates, Naeem Murr, Tom Perrotta, Alison Baker and Peter Baida. Length: 2,000-7,000 words; average length: 3,000 words. Publishes short shorts. Also publishes literary essays, literary criticism, poetry. Sometimes comments on rejected mss.

How to Contact: Send complete ms. Accepts submissions by mail, fax. SASE. Responds in 1 month to queries; 3-6 months to mss. Accepts simultaneous submissions. Sample copy for $7. Writer's guidelines online.

Payment/Terms: Pays $25/page. Pays on publication for first North American serial rights.

Advice: "Reporting time can take more than three months. It is helpful to look at a sample copy of *The Gettysburg Review* to see what kinds of fiction we publish before submitting."

☑ ◎ GINOSKO, between literary vision and spiritual realities, P.O. Box 246, Fairfax CA 94978-0246. (415)785-2802. E-mail: ginoskoeditor@aol.com. **Contact:** Robert Cesaretti, editor. Magazine: 4×6; 50-60 pages; standard paper; photo glossy cover; b&w art and photos. "Looking for literature and art that has a spiritual dimension to it: the yearning in 'Kindling' by Raymond Carver, the mythic in 'Pagan Night' by Kate Braverman, the vision of 'Revelation' by Flannery O'Connor. Published "when material permits."

Needs: Experimental, literary, stylized. "We believe there is writing that is characteristic of religious seeking in its truest sense. We do not want conventional work." Receives 10-20 unsolicited mss/month. **Publishes 4 new writers/year.** Recently published work by Ritchie Swanson and D.L. Olsen.

How to Contact: SASE for return of ms. Responds in 1-3 months to mss. Accepts simultaneous and reprints submissions. Sample copy not available.

Payment/Terms: Pays one contributor's copy. Acquires one-time rights.

Advice: "I am looking for a style that conveys spiritual hunger and yearning, yet avoids religiosity and convention— *between literary vision and spiritual realities.*"

☑ GLASS TESSERACT, Glass Tesseract. E-mail: editor@glasstesseract.com. Website: www.glasstesseract.com. **Contact:** Michael Chester, editor. Magazine: 5½×8½; 24-64 pages. Comb-bound with color frontispiece and linen paper. "Addressed to literary readership, *Glass Tesseract* is versatile, publishing stories that range in style and treatment from traditional to wide-open experimental. The purpose of the magazine is to help bring works of art into the world. Rotating selections from past, present, and future issues of the magazine appear and reappear on the website in a continual fiction and poetry kaleidoscope, optimized for online viewing." Published twice/year. A current online edition is in a PDF file, available for free, and optimized for printout. Accepts e-mail submissions only. Published once or twice/year. Estab. 2001.

Needs: Experimental, literary, mainstream. "No sentimental, moralizing, devotional, cute, coy or happy-face stories." Publishes ms 3-12 months after acceptance. Recently published work by Trevor Bundy, Shelley Ettinger, Jeremy Johnson, Ann Lewinson, David J. Marx and Helen E. Wright. Publishes short shorts. Also publishes poetry. Sometimes comments on rejected mss.

How to Contact: Responds in 4 months to mss. Accepts simultaneous and reprints, multiple submissions. Guidelines by e-mail or on the website.

MARKET CONDITIONS are constantly changing! If you're still using this book and it is 2005 or later, buy the newest edition of *Novel & Short Story Writer's Market* at your favorite bookstore or order from Writer's Digest Books by calling 1-800-448-0915.

Payment/Terms: <u>Pays 1 contributor's bound copy.</u> Bound copies are priced at a flat $12 each. For orders, inquire by e-mail for availability and magazine's current payment address. Acquires one-time rights. Sends galleys to author.
Advice: "We look for a style of language that, whether lean or rich, is artfully constructed without being pretentious, strained, or laden with clichés. We want characters who have dimensionality, not fitting into standard all-good, all-bad, all-wise, or all-innocent molds. We want story lines that emerge naturally (if not inevitably) from the nature of the characters and the language. Read the stories we have published. Send e-mail to the editor with any questions."

$ ☑ ☑ GLIMMER TRAIN STORIES, Glimmer Train Press, Inc., 710 SW Madison St., Suite 504, Portland OR 97205. (503)221-0836. Fax: (503)221-0837. <u>Website: www.glimmertrain.com.</u> **Contact:** Susan Burmeister-Brown and Linda Swanson-Davies. Magazine: 6¾×9¼; 220 pages; recycled; acid-free paper; 12 photographs. "We are interested in well-written, emotionally-moving short stories published by unknown, as well as known, writers." Quarterly. Estab. 1991. Circ. 16,000.
  • *Glimmer Train* ranked on *Writer's Digest*'s "Top 30" list of best markets for fiction writers. The magazine also sponsors an annual short story contest for new writers and a very short fiction contest.
Needs: Literary. Receives 4,000 unsolicited mss/month. Accepts 10 mss/issue; 40 mss/year. <u>Reads in January, April, July, October.</u> Publishes ms up to 2 years after acceptance. Agented fiction 10%. **Publishes 12 new writers/year.** Recently published work by Judy Budnitz, Brian Champeau, Ellen Cooney, Andre Dubus III, Thomas Kennedy, Chris Offutt, Alberto Rios and Monica Wood. Sometimes comments on rejected mss.
How to Contact: <u>Submit work online at www.glimmertrain.com.</u> Accepted work published in *Glimmer Train Stories.* Responds in 3 months to mss. No simultaneous submissions. <u>Sample copy for $9.95 on website.</u> Writer's guidelines online.
Payment/Terms: <u>Pays $500.</u> Pays on acceptance for first rights.
Advice: "When a story stays with us after the first reading, it gets another reading. Those stories that simply don't let us set them aside, get published. Read good fiction. It will often improve the quality of your own writing."

$ ☑ ☑ GRAIN LITERARY MAGAZINE, Saskatchewan Writers Guild, P.O. Box 67, Saskatoon SK S7K 3K1 Canada. (306)244-2828. Fax: (306)244-0255. Website: www.grainmagazine.ca. **Contact:** Marlis Wesseler, fiction editor. Literary magazine: 6×9; 128 pages; Chinook offset printing; chrome-coated stock; some photos. "*Grain* publishes writing of the highest quality, both traditional and innovative in nature. The *Grain* editors' aim: To publish work that challenges readers; to encourage promising new writers; and to produce a well-designed, visually interesting magazine." Quarterly. Estab. 1973. Circ. 1,600.
  • *Grain* ranked on *Writer's Digest*'s "Top 30" list of best markets for fiction writers.
Needs: Experimental, literary, mainstream, contemporary, prose poem. "No romance, confession, science fiction, vignettes, mystery." Receives 80 unsolicited mss/month. Accepts 8-12 mss/issue; 32-48 mss/year. Publishes ms 11 months after acceptance. Recently published work by J. Jill Robinson, Curtis Gillespi, John Laven. Also publishes poetry. Occasionally comments on rejected mss.
How to Contact: Accepts submissions by mail. Send complete ms with SASE (or IRC) and brief letter. Accepts queries by e-mail, mail, fax, and phone. "We expect acknowledgment if the piece is republished elsewhere." Responds in 1 month to queries; 4 months to mss. No simultaneous submissions. Sample copy for $10 or online. Writer's guidelines for #10 SASE or online.
Payment/Terms: Pays $40-175. Pays on publication for first, Canadian serial rights.
Advice: "Submit a story to us that will deepen the imaginative experience of our readers. *Grain* has established itself as a first-class magazine of serious fiction. We receive submissions from around the world. If Canada is a foreign country to you, we ask that you *do not* use U.S. postage stamps on your return envelope. If you live outside Canada and neglect the International Reply Coupons, we *will not* read or reply to your submission. We look for attention to detail, credibility, lucid use of language and metaphor and a confident, convincing voice. Sweat the small stuff. Make sure you have researched your piece, that the literal and metaphorical support one another."

$ ☑ ☑ GRAND STREET, 214 Sullivan St., Suite 6C, New York NY 10012. (212)533-2944. Fax: (212)228-9260. Website: www.grandstreet.com. **Contact:** Radhika Jones, managing editor. Magazine: 7¾×9½; 240-270 pages; illustrations; art portfolios. "We publish new fiction and nonfiction of all types." Biannual. Estab. 1981. Circ. 7,000.
  • Work published in *Grand Street* has been included in the *Best American Short Stories.* At press time, *Grand Street* was not accepting unsolicited mss. Check the website for updates.
Needs: Translations, poetry and essays. Agented fiction 90%. Recently published work by Durs Grunbin, José Saramago, Ozren Kebo, Jorge Luis Borges and Mike Davis. Length: 9,000 words; average length: 4,000 words.
Payment/Terms: Pays $250-1,000 and 2 contributor's copies. Acquires first North American serial rights. Sends galleys to author.
Advice: "We recommend that you look at a sample issue of *Grand Street* to gain a sense of what we're looking for."

$ ⊕ GRANTA, The Magazine of New Writing, Granta Publications, 2-3 Hanover Yard, Noel Rd., London NI 8BE, UK. (44)(0)20 7704 9776. Website: www.granta.com. **Contact:** Ian Jack, editor. Magazine: paperback, 256 pages approx; photos. "*Granta* magazine publishes fiction, reportage, biography and autobiography, history, travel and documentary photography. It does not publish 'writing about writing.' The realistic narrative—the story—is its primary form." Quarterly. Estab. 1979. Circ. 80,000.

Needs: Literary, novel excerpts, literary. No genre fiction. Themes decided as deadline approaches. Receives 100 unsolicited mss/month. Accepts 0-1 mss/issue; 1-2 mss/year. **Publishes 1-2 new writers/year.**

How to Contact: Send SAE and IRCs for reply, return of ms or send a disposable copy of ms. Responds in 3 months to mss. Accepts simultaneous submissions. Sample copy for $12.95. Writer's guidelines online.

Payment/Terms: Payment varies. Pays on publication. Buys world English language rights, first serial rights (minimum). "We hold more rights in pieces we commission." Sends galleys to author.

Advice: "We are looking for the best in realistic stories; originality of voice; without jargon, connivance or self-conscious 'performance'—writing that endures."

GRASSLANDS REVIEW, P.O. Box 626, Berea OH 44017-0626. E-mail: grasslandsreview@aol.com. Website: hometown.aol.com/glreview/prof/index.htm. **Contact:** Laura B. Kennelly, editor. Magazine: 6×9; 80 pages. *Grasslands Review* prints creative witing of all types; poetry, fiction, essay for a general audience. "Designed as a place for new writers to publish." Semiannual. Estab. 1989. Circ. 300.

Needs: Ethnic/multicultural, experimental, fantasy, horror, humor/satire, literary, regional, science fiction, western, contemporary, prose poem. "Nothing pornographic or overtly political or religious." Accepts 1-3 mss/issue. Reads only in October and March. Publishes ms 6 months after acceptance. **Publishes 5 new writers/year.** Recently published work by J.L. Schneider, Toiya Smith and Thérése Halscheid. Length: 100-3,500 words; average length: 1,000 words. Publishes short shorts. Also publishes poetry. Sometimes comments on rejected mss.

How to Contact: SASE. Responds in 3 months to mss. No simultaneous submissions. Sample copy for $5 old copy; $6 for most recent copy.

Payment/Terms: Pays in contributor's copies. Acquires one-time rights. Not copyrighted.

Advice: "A fresh approach, imagined by a reader for other readers, pleases our audience. We are looking for fiction which leaves a strong feeling or impression—or a new perspective on life. The *Review* began as an in-class exercise to allow experienced creative writing students to learn how a little magazine is produced. It now serves as an independant publication, attracting authors from as far away as the Ivory Coast, but its primary mission is to give unknown writers a start."

THE GREEN HILLS LITERARY LANTERN, Published by Truman State University, Division of Language & Literature, Kirksville MO 63501. (660)785-4513. E-mail: jksmith@grm.net. Website: http://ll.truman.edu/ghllweb. **Contact:** Sara King, fiction editor. Magazine: 6×9; 200-300 pages; good quality paper with glossy 4-color cover. "The mission of *GHLL* is to provide a literary market for quality fiction writers, both established and beginners, and to provide quality literature for readers from diverse backgrounds. We also see ourselves as cultural resource for North Missouri. Our publication works to publish the highest quality fiction—dense, layered, subtle, and, at the same time, fiction which grabs the ordinary reader. We tend to publish traditional short stories, but we are open to experimental forms." Annual. Estab. 1990. Circ. 500.

Needs: Ethnic/multicultural, experimental, feminist, humor/satire, literary, mainstream, regional. "Fairly traditional short stories but we are open to experimental. Our main requirement is literary merit. Wants more quality fiction about rural culture. No adventure, crime, erotica, horror, inspirational, mystery/suspense, romance." Receives 40 unsolicited mss/month. Accepts 7-10 mss/issue. Publishes ms 6-12 months after acceptance. **Publishes 0-1 new writers/year.** Recently published work by Ian MacMillan, Mark Wisniewski, Karl Harshbarger and Robert Garner McBrearty. Length: 7,000 words; average length: 3,000 words. Publishes short shorts. Also publishes poetry. Sometimes comments on rejected mss.

How to Contact: SASE for return of ms. Responds in 4 months to mss. Accepts simultaneous, multiple submissions. Sample copy for $7 (includes envelope and postage).

Payment/Terms: Pays 2 contributor's copies. Acquires one-time rights. Sends galleys to author.

Advice: "We look for strong character development, substantive plot and theme, visual and forceful language within a multilayered story. Make sure your work has the flavor of life, a sense of reality. A good story, well-crafted, will eventually get published. Find the right market for it, and above all, don't give up."

GREEN MOUNTAINS REVIEW, Johnson State College, Box A-58, Johnson VT 05656. (802)635-1350. **Contact:** Tony Whedon, fiction editor. Magazine: digest-sized; 160-200 pages. Semiannual. Estab. 1975. Circ. 1,700.

• *Green Mountains Review* has received a Pushcart Prize and Editors Choice Award.

Needs: Adventure, experimental, humor/satire, literary, mainstream, serialized novels, translations. Receives 100 unsolicited mss/month. Accepts 6 mss/issue; 12 mss/year. "Manuscripts will not be read and will be returned between March 1 and September 1." Publishes ms 6-12 months after acceptance. **Publishes 0-4 new writers/year.** Recently published work by Howard Norman, Debra Spark, Valerie Miner and Peter LaSalle. Publishes short shorts. Also publishes literary criticism, poetry. Sometimes comments on rejected mss.

How to Contact: SASE. Responds in 1 month to queries; 6 months to mss. Accepts simultaneous submissions if advised. Sample copy for $7.

Payment/Terms: Pays contributor's copies, 1-year subscription and small honorarium, depending on grants. Acquires first North American serial rights. Rights revert to author upon request.

Advice: "We're looking for more rich, textured, original fiction with cross-cultural themes. The editors are open to a wide spectrum of styles and subject matter as is apparent from a look at the list of fiction writers who have published in its pages. One issue was devoted to Vermont fiction, and another issue filled with new writing from the People's Republic of China, and a recent issue devoted to literary ethnography."

GREEN'S MAGAZINE, Fiction for the Family, Green's Educational Publications, Box 3236, Regina SK S4P 3H1 Canada. **Contact:** David Green, editor. Magazine: 5¼×8½; 96 pages; 20 lb. bond paper; matte cover stock; line illustrations. Publishes "solid short fiction suitable for family reading." Quarterly. Estab. 1972.

Needs: Adventure, fantasy, humor/satire, literary, mainstream, mystery/suspense, science fiction. "No erotic or sexually explicit fiction." Receives 20-30 unsolicited mss/month. Accepts 10-12 mss/issue; 40-50 mss/year. Publishes ms 3-6 months after acceptance. Agented fiction 1%. **Publishes 6 new writers/year.** Recently published work by Adelaide Shaw, Robert Redding, and Lou Williams. Length: 1,500-4,000 words; average length: 2,500 words. Also publishes poetry. Sometimes comments on rejected mss.

How to Contact: SASE (in Canada), SAE and IRC (for US and overseas). Responds in 2 months to mss. Sample copy for $5. Writer's guidelines for #10 SASE. Reviews fiction.

Payment/Terms: Pays in 1 contributor's copy. Acquires first North American serial rights.

Advice: "No topic is taboo, but we avoid sexuality for its own sake, and dislike material that is needlessly explicit or obscene. We look for strongly written stories that explore their characters through a subtle blending of conflicts. Plots should be appropriate, rather that overly ingenious or reliant on some *deus ex machina*. It must be a compression of experience or thoughts, in a form that is both challenging and rewarding to the reader. We have no form rejection slip. If we cannot use a submission, we try to offer constructive criticism in our personal reply. Often, such effort is rewarded with reports from our writers that following our suggestions has led to placement of the story or poem elsewhere."

THE GREENSBORO REVIEW, English Dept., 134 McIver Bldg., UNC Greensboro, P.O. Box 26170, Greensboro NC 27402-6170. (336)334-5459. E-mail: jlclark@uncg.edu/eng/mfa. **Contact:** Jim Clark, editor. Fiction editor changes each year. Send mss to the editor. Magazine: 6×9; approximately 128 pages; 60 lb. paper; 65 lb. cover. Literary magazine featuring fiction and poetry for readers interested in contemporary literature. Semiannual. Circ. 800.

● Stories for *The Greensboro Review* have been included in *The Best American Short Stories, Prize Stories: The O. Henry Awards, New Stories for the South*, and *Pushcart Prize*.

Needs: Experimental, contemporary. Accepts 6-8 mss/issue; 12-16 mss/year. Uncolicited manuscripts must arrive by September 15 to be considered for the spring issue and by February 15 to be considered for the fall issue. Manuscripts arriving after those dates may be held for the next consideration. **Publishes 10 % new writers/year.** Recently published work by Robert Morgan, George Singleton, Robert Olmstead, Jean Ross Justice, Dale Ray Phillips and Kelly Cherry.

How to Contact: Responds in 4 months to mss. Accepts multiple submissions No simultaneous submissions. Sample copy for $5.

Payment/Terms: Pays in contributor's copies. Acquires first North American serial rights.

Advice: "We want to see the best being written regardless of theme, subject or style."

THE GRIFFIN, Gwynedd-Mercy College, P.O. Box 901, 1325 Sumneytown Pike, Gwynedd Valley PA 19437-0901. (215)646-7300. Fax: (215)923-3060. E-mail: z31w@aol.com or kaler.a@gmc.edu. **Contact:** Anne K. Kaler and Susan E. Wagner, editors. Literary magazine: 8½×5½; 112 pages. "*The Griffin* is a literary journal sponsored by Gwynedd-Mercy College. Its mission is to enrich society by nurturing and promoting creative writing that demonstrates a unique and intelligent voice. We seek writing which accurately reflects the human condition with all its intellectual, emotional, and ethical challenges." Annual. Estab. 1999. Circ. 500.

Needs: Adventure, ethnic/multicultural (general), family saga, fantasy, feminist, historical, horror, humor/satire, literary, mainstream, mystery/suspense, religious/inspirational (general), romance, science fiction, thriller/espionage, western. "No slasher, graphic violence or sex." Accepts mss depending on the quality of work submitted. Receives 2-3 unsolicited mss/month. Publishes ms 3-6 months after acceptance. **Publishes 10-15 new writers/year.** Recently published work by Pat Carr, Linda Wisniewski and Michael McGregor. Length: 2,500 words; average length: 2,000 words. Publishes short shorts. Also publishes literary essays, poetry.

How to Contact: Send complete ms. Send SASE for return of ms or send disposable copy of ms and #10 SASE for reply only. Responds in 1 month to queries; 6 months to mss. Accepts simultaneous submissions "if notified." Sample copy for $6.

Payment/Terms: Pays in 2 contributor's copies; additional copies for $6. Pays on publication for one-time rights.

Advice: "Looking for well-constructed works that explore universal qualities, respect for the individual and community, justice and integrity. Check our description and criteria. Rewrite until you're sure every word counts. We publish the best work we find regardless of industry needs."

THE GSU REVIEW, Georgia State University, P.O. Box 1894, Atlanta GA 30303. (404)651-4804. Fax: (404)651-1710. E-mail: kchaple@attbi.com. Website: www.gsu.edu/wwwrev/. **Contact:** Dan Marshall, fiction editor. Magazine. "*The GSU Review* us a biannual literary magazine publishing poetry, fiction, creative nonfiction and artwork. We want orginal voices searching to rise above the ordinary. No subject or form biases." Semiannual.

Needs: Literary, novel excerpts. "No pornography." Receives 200 unsolicited mss/month. Publishes short shorts.

How to Contact: Accepts submissions by mail, e-mail. SASE for notification. Responds in 1 month to queries; 1-2 months to mss. Sample copy for $5. Writer's guidelines for SASE or on website.

Payment/Terms: Pays in contributor's copy. Acquires one-time rights.

GULF COAST, A Journal of Literature & Fine Arts, D, Dept. of English, University of Houston, Houston TX 77204-3012. (713)743-3223. Fax: (713)743-3215. Website: www.gulfcoastmag.org. **Contact:** Viet Dinh, fiction editor. Magazine: 7×9; approx. 300 pages; stock paper, gloss cover; illustrations; photos. "Innovative fiction for the literary-minded." Estab. 1987. Circ. 1,000.

• Work published in *Gulf Coast* has been selected for inclusion in the *Pushcart Prize* anthology and *Best American Short Stories*.

Needs: Ethnic/multicultural, experimental, literary, regional, translations, contemporary. "No children's, genre, religious/inspirational." Wants more "cutting-edge, experimental" fiction. Receives 150 unsolicited mss/month. Accepts 6-8 mss/issue; 12-16 mss/year. Publishes ms 6 months-1 year after acceptance. Agented fiction 5%. **Publishes 2 new writers/year.** Recently published work by Josip Novakovich, Michelle Ross, Stephen Dixon, Garry Krist, Leo Hwang-Carlos, and Greg Baxter. Publishes short shorts. Sometimes comments on rejected mss.

How to Contact: Responds in 6 months to mss. Accepts simultaneous submissions. Back issue for $6, 7×10 SAE and 4 first-class stamps. Writer's guidelines for #10 SASE or on website.

Payment/Terms: Pays contributor's copies. Acquires *small* honorarium for one-time rights rights.

Advice: "Rotating editorship, so please be patient with replies. As always, please send one story at a time."

GULF STREAM MAGAZINE, Florida International University, English Dept., Biscayne Bay Campus, 3000 N.E. 151st St., N. Miami FL 33181-3000. (305)919-5599. Editor: John Dufresne. **Contact:** Fiction Editor. Magazine: 5½×8½; 96 pages; recycled paper; 80 lb. glossy cover; cover illustrations. "We publish *good quality*—fiction, nonfiction and poetry for a predominantly literary market." Semiannual. Estab. 1989. Circ. 1,000.

Needs: Literary, mainstream, contemporary. Does not want romance, historical, juvenile or religious work. Receives 250 unsolicited mss/month. Accepts 5 mss/issue; 10 mss/year. Does not read mss during the summer. Publishes ms 3-6 months after acceptance. **Publishes 2-5 new writers/year.** Recently published work by Maureen Seaton, Charles Harper Webb, Lise Saffran, Janice Eidus, Susan Neville. Length: 7,500 words; average length: 5,000 words. Publishes short shorts. Also publishes poetry.

How to Contact: Send complete ms. SASE. Responds in 3 months to mss. Accepts simultaneous submissions "if noted." Sample copy for $5. Writer's guidelines for #10 SASE.

Payment/Terms: Pays in gift subscriptions and contributor's copies. Acquires first North American serial rights.

Advice: "Looks for good concise writing—well plotted with interesting characters. Usually longer stories do not get accepted. There are exceptions, however."

$ HAPPY, 240 E. 35th St., Suite 11A, New York NY 10016. **Contact:** Bayard, fiction editor. Magazine: 5½×8; 150-200 pages; 60 lb. text paper; 150 lb. cover; perfect-bound; illustrations; photos. Quarterly. Estab. 1995. Circ. 500.

Needs: Erotica, ethnic/multicultural, experimental, fantasy, feminist, gay, horror, humor/satire, lesbian, literary, novel excerpts, psychic/supernatural/occult, science fiction, short stories. No "television rehash or religious nonsense." Want more work that is "strong, angry, empowering, intelligent, God-like, expressive." Receives 300-500 unsolicited mss/month. Accepts 30-40 mss/issue; 100-150 mss/year. Publishes ms 6-12 months after acceptance. **Publishes 30-50% new writers/year.** Length: 6,000 words maximum; average length: 1,000-3,500 words. Publishes short shorts. Often comments on rejected mss.

How to Contact: Send complete ms. Accepts submissions by mail. Include estimated word count. Send SASE for reply, return of ms or send a disposable copy of ms. Responds in 1 month to queries. Accepts simultaneous submissions. Sample copy for $20. Writer's guidelines for #10 SASE.

Payment/Terms: Pays 1-5¢/word. Pays on publication for one-time rights.

Advice: "Excite me!"

HARD ROW TO HOE, Potato Eyes Foundation, P.O. Box 541-I, Healdsburg CA 95448. (707)433-9786. **Contact:** Joe E. Armstrong, editor. Magazine: 8½×12; 12 pages; 60 lb. white paper; illustrations; photos. "We look for literature of rural life, including environmental, Native American and foreign (English only) subjects. Book reviews, short story, poetry and a regular column. So far as we know, we are the only literary newsletter that features rural subjects." Triannual. Estab. 1982. Circ. 200.

Needs: Rural, enviromental, Native American, foreign (English only). "No urban subjects. We would like to see more fiction on current rural lifestyles." Receives 5-10 unsolicited mss/month. Accepts 2-3 mss/issue; 6-8 mss/year. Publishes ms 10 months after acceptance. **Publishes 2 new writers/year.** Recently published work by Gary Every, Victoria Gorton, and Jane Bradbury. Average length: 1,200 words. Publishes short shorts. Also publishes literary essays, poetry. Often comments on rejected mss.

How to Contact: Send complete ms. Send SASE for return of ms or send a disposable copy of ms and #10 SASE for reply only. Responds in 2 weeks to queries; 6 weeks to mss. Accepts multiple submissions. Sample copy for $3. Writer's guidelines for SASE. Reviews fiction.

Payment/Terms: Pays 2 contributor's copies; additional copies $3. Pays on publication for one-time rights.

Advice: "Work must exhibit authentic setting and dialogue."

$○ ☑ HARPUR PALATE, A Literary Journal at Binghamton University, English Department, P.O. Box 6000, Binghamton University, Binghamton NY 13902-6000. Website: harpurpalate.binghamton.edu. **Contact:** Letitia Moffitt, fiction editor. Magazine: 5½×8; 80-120 pages; coated or uncoated paper; 90 lb. coated or uncoated cover; illustrations; photos. "We believe writers should explore different genres to tell their stories. *Harpur Palate* accepts pieces regardless of genre, as long as the works pay attention to craft, structure, language, and the story well told." Semiannual. Estab. 2000. Circ. 500.

• Stories published in *Harpur Palate* have been chosen for *Best American Mystery Stories 2003* and *Best of the Rest 3*.

Needs: Adventure, ethnic/multicultural, experimental, fantasy, historical, horror, humor/satire, literary, mainstream, mystery/suspense, novel excerpts, science fiction, suspense, literary, fabulism, magical realism, metafiction, slipstream (genre blending). "No solipsistic or self-centered fiction or autobiography pretending to be fiction. No pornography, excessive profanity, or shock value for shock value's sake." Receives 150 unsolicited mss/month. Accepts 5-10 mss/issue; 12-20 mss/year. Does not read mss March 16-July 31 and October 16-December 31. Publishes ms 1-2 months after acceptance. **Publishes 5 new writers/year.** Recently published work by Hugh Cook, Scott Wolven, Lydia Davis, M. Evelina Galang and Bruce Holland Rogers. Length: 250-8,000 words; average length: 2,000-4,000 words. Publishes short shorts. Also publishes poetry. Sometimes comments on rejected mss.

How to Contact: Accepts submissions by mail, e-mail. Send complete ms with a cover letter. "Include e-mail address on cover if have one. Submitters should check our guideline information on the website for e-mail submissions." Include estimated word count, brief bio, list of publications (OK if don't have any). Send SASE for return of ms or send a disposable copy of ms and #10 SASE for reply only. Responds in 1 week to queries; 3 months to mss. Accepts simultaneous submissions if stated in the cover letter. Sample copy for $7.50, plus $1.18 shipping and handling, or on website. Writer's guidelines online.

Payment/Terms: Pays $5-20. Pays on publication for first North American serial, electronic rights. Sponsors awards/contests.

Advice: "There's nothing new under the sun, but we're looking for stories that do inventive things with fiction. We don't try to define what 'art' is or put limitations on what 'art' can be, and we try to have an eclectic mix of genre, mainstream, and experimental works in every issue. We are always interested in seeing literary speculative fiction and literary mystery/suspense as well as more mainstream stories. We would like to see more literary speculative fiction in the vein of Orwell, Huxley, Borges, García Marquez and Calvino; literary mystery in the vein of Whitehead. The editorial board chooses manuscripts during final selection meetings after the reading period deadlines. Most of us are writers and know what it's like to wait for editorial responses to arrive in the mailbox. If we would like to hold your fiction manuscript for final selection, we will inform you."

☑ HARVARD REVIEW, Harvard University, Lamont Library, Level 5, Cambridge MA 02138. (617)495-9775. E-mail: harvrev@fas.harvard.edu. Website: http://hcl.harvard.edu/houghton/departments/harvardreview/hrhome.html. Magazine: 6×9; 192-240 pages; illustrations; photographs. Semiannual. Estab. 1992. Circ. 2,000.

Needs: Literary. Receives 80-100 unsolicited mss/month. Accepts 2 mss/issue; 4 mss/year. Publishes ms 3-6 months after acceptance. **Publishes 3-4 new writers/year.** Recently published work by John Updike, David Mamet, Paul Harding and Helen Vendler. Length: 1,000-7,000 words; average length: 3,000-5,000 words. Publishes short shorts. Also publishes literary essays, literary criticism, poetry. Sometimes comments on rejected mss.

How to Contact: Send SASE for return of ms or disposable copy of ms and SASE for reply only. Responds in 2 months to queries; 3-6 months to mss. Accepts simultaneous submissions. Writer's guidelines online.

Payment/Terms: Pays 2 contributor's copies; additional copies $6. Acquires Pays on publication for first North American serial rights. Sends galleys to author.

☑ HAWAI'I PACIFIC REVIEW, Hawai'i Pacific Review, 1060 Bishop St., Honolulu HI 96813. (808)544-1108. Fax: (808)544-0862. E-mail: pwilson@hpu.edu. Website: www.hpu.edu. **Contact:** Patrice M. Wilson, editor. Magazine: 6×9; 100 pages; glossy coated cover. "*Hawai'i Pacific Review* is looking for poetry, short fiction, and personal essays that speak with a powerful and unique voice. We encourage experimental narrative techniques and poetic styles, and we welcome works in translation." Annual.

Needs: Ethnic/multicultural (general), experimental, fantasy, feminist, historical (general), humor/satire, literary, mainstream, regional (Pacific), translations. "Open to all types as long as they're well done. Our audience is adults, so nothing for children/teens." Receives 25-40 unsolicited mss/month. Accepts 5-10 mss/year. Does not read mss January-August each year. Publishes ms 10 months after acceptance. **Publishes 1-2 new writers/year.** Recently published work by Rosemary Edghill, D. Prinzo and Stephen Dixon. Publishes short shorts. Also publishes literary essays, poetry. Sometimes comments on rejected mss.

How to Contact: Send SASE for return of ms or send a disposable copy of ms and #10 SASE for reply only. Responds in 2 weeks to queries; 15 weeks to mss. Accepts simultaneous submissions. Must be cited in the cover letter. Sample copy for $5.

Payment/Terms: Pays 2 contributor's copies; additional copies $5. Pays on publication for first North American serial rights rights.

Advice: "We look for the unusual or orginal plot; prose with the texture and nuance of poetry. Character development or portrayal must be unusual/orginal; humanity shown in an original insightful way (or characters); sense or humor where applicable. Be sure it's a draft that has gone through substantial changes, with supervision from a more experienced writer if you're a beginner."

$ ☑ ☒ HAYDEN'S FERRY REVIEW, Arizona State University, Box 871502, Arizona State University, Tempe AZ 85287-1502. (480)965-1243. Fax: (480)965-2229. Website: www.haydensferryreview.org. **Contact:** Fiction editor. Editors change every 1-2 years. Magazine: 6×9; 128 pages; fine paper; illustrations; photos. "*Hayden's Ferry Review* publishes best quality fiction, poetry, and creative nonfiction from new, emerging, and established writers." Semiannual. Estab. 1986. Circ. 1,300.
   • Work from *Hayden's Ferry Review* has been selected for inclusion in *Pushcart Prize* anthologies.

Needs: Ethnic/multicultural, experimental, humor/satire, literary, regional, slice-of-life vignettes, contemporary, prose poem. Possible special fiction issue. Receives 250 unsolicited mss/month. Accepts 5 mss/issue; 10 mss/year. Publishes ms 6 months after acceptance. Recently published work by T.C. Boyle, Raymond Carver, Ken Kesey, Rita Dove, Chuck Rosenthal and Rick Bass. Publishes short shorts. Also publishes literary criticism.

How to Contact: Send complete ms. Accepts submissions by mail. SASE. Responds in 2 weeks to queries; 3 months to mss. Accepts simultaneous submissions. Sample copy for $6. Writer's guidelines online.

Payment/Terms: Pays $25-100. Pays on publication for first North American serial rights. Sends galleys to author.

$ ☑ ◎ HEARTLANDS, A Magazine of Midwest Life and Art (formerly *The Heartlands Today*), The Firelands Writing Center, Firelands College of BGSU, Huron OH 44839. (419)433-5560. E-mail: lsmithdog@aol.com. Website: www.theheartlandstoday.org. **Contact:** Fiction editor. Magazine: 8½×11; perfect bound; 160 pages; b&w illustrations; 15 photos. *Material must be set in the Midwest.* "We prefer material that reveals life in the Midwest today for a general, literate audience." Biannual. Estab. 1991.

Needs: Ethnic/multicultural, humor/satire, literary, mainstream, regional (Midwest). 2003 theme is "Our Natural World." Receives 15 unsolicited mss/month. Accepts 6 mss/issue. Does not read August-December. "We edit between January 1 and June 5." Submit then. Publishes ms 6 months after acceptance. Recently published work by Wendell Mayo, Tony Tomassi, Gloria Bowman. Also publishes literary essays, poetry. Sometimes comments on rejected mss.

How to Contact: Send SASE for ms, not needed for query. Responds in 2 months to mss. Accepts simultaneous submissions if noted. Sample copy for $5.

Payment/Terms: Pays $10-20 and 2 contributor's copies. Pays on publication for first rights.

Advice: "We look for writing that connects on a human level, that moves us with its truth and opens our vision of the world. If writing is a great escape for you, don't bother with us. We're in it for the joy, beauty or truth of the art. We look for a straight, honest voice dealing with human experiences. We do not define the Midwest, we hope to be a document of the Midwest. If you feel you are writing from the Midwest, send your work to us. We look first at the quality of the writing."

☑ HIGHWAY 14, P.O. Box 1130, Fort Collins CO 80522-1130. E-mail: editors@highway14.com. Website: www.highway14.com. **Contact:** Alex Paozols, editor. Magazine: 5¼×8⅜; 160 pages; 60 lb. white paper; card cls stock cover; illustrations; photos. "*Highway 14* is a literary fiction magazine. We reveal the consequences of enviromental destruction and pollution, frivolous culture, religious bigotry and capitalist ruin. Sometimes our pages offer a solution. Our audience ranges from people who can't get enough to read to those who have forgotten what a pleasure it is to pick up a book and leave the world." Triannual. Estab. 2002. Circ. 750.

Needs: Literary. "No poetry." Receives 90 unsolicited mss/month. Accepts 15 mss/issue; 45 mss/year. **Publishes 10 new writers/year.** Recently published work by George Singleton, Brian Evenson, Kristin Prevallet, J. Robert Lennon, Jason Ockert and Christine Hume. Sometimes comments on rejected mss.

How to Contact: Send SASE for return of ms or send disposable copy of ms and #10 SASE for reply only. Responds in 2 weeks to queries; 6 weeks to mss. Accepts simultaneous, multiple submissions. Sample copy for $10. Writer's guidelines for SASE or on website.

Payment/Terms: Pays 3 contributor's copies; additional copies $7. Acquires first rights. Not copyrighted.

Advice: "Originality is the key for us. Narcissism, sensationalism and sentimentality can often ruin a story. We admire stories that deconstruct plot and predictability with the innovative use of language. We are drawn to literature that is subtle with strong narrative, that is unassuming yet intelligent. We are eager to read stories that explore racial, ethnic, religious and culture identity with regard and disregard for landscape."

🅽 ☑ ☒ HOME PLANET NEWS, Home Planet Publications, P.O. Box 415, New York NY 10009. (718)769-2854. **Contact:** Enid Dame and Donald Lev, co-editors. Tabloid: 11½×16; 24 pages; newsprint; illustrations; photos. "*Home Planet News* publishes mainly poetry along with some fiction, as well as reviews (books, theater and art), and articles of literary interest. We see *HPN* as a quality literary journal in an eminently readable format and with content that is urban, urbane and politically aware." Triannual. Estab. 1979. Circ. 1,000.
   • *HPN* has received a small grant from the Puffin Foundation for its focus on AIDS issues.

Needs: Ethnic/multicultural, experimental, feminist, gay, historical, lesbian, literary, mainstream, science fiction (soft/sociological). No "children's or genre stories (except rarely some science fiction)." Upcoming themes: "Midrash." Publishes special fiction issue or anthology. Receives 12 unsolicited mss/month. Accepts 1 mss/issue; 3 mss/year. Reads fiction mss only from February to May. Publishes ms 1 year after acceptance. Recently published work by Maureen McNeil, Eugene Stein, B.Z. Niditch, Walter Jackman and Layle Silbert. Length: 500-2,500 words; average length: 2,000 words. Publishes short shorts. Also publishes literary criticism.

How to Contact: Send complete ms. Send SASE for reply, return of ms or send a disposable copy of the ms. Responds in 6 months to mss. Sample copy for $3. Writer's guidelines for SASE.

Payment/Terms: Pays 3 contributor's copies; additional copies $1. Acquires one-time rights.

Advice: "We use very little fiction, and a story we accept just has to grab us. We need short pieces of some complexity, stories about complex people facing situations which resist simple resolutions."

$◨ THE ICONOCLAST, 1675 Amazon Rd., Mohegan Lake NY 10547-1804. **Contact:** Phil Wagner, editor. Journal: 8½ × 5½; 40-64 pages; 20 lb. white paper; 50 lb. cover stock; illustrations. "Aimed for a literate general audience with interests in fine (but accessible) fiction and poetry." Bimonthly. Estab. 1992. Circ. 600.

Needs: Adventure, ethnic/multicultural, experimental, fantasy, humor/satire, literary, mainstream, novel excerpts, science fiction, literary. No character studies, slice-of-life, pieces strong on attitude/weak on plot. Receives 150 unsolicited mss/month. Accepts 3-6 mss/issue; 25-30 mss/year. Publishes ms 9-12 months after acceptance. **Publishes 8-10 new writers/year.** Recently published work by Stephen Graham Jones, Laura Albritton and E.G. Silverman. Publishes short shorts. Also publishes literary essays, poetry. Sometimes comments on rejected mss.

How to Contact: Send complete ms. Accepts submissions by mail. Send SASE for reply, return of ms or send a disposable copy of the ms labeled as such. Responds in 2 weeks to queries; 1 month to mss. No simultaneous submissions. Sample copy for $2.50. Writer's guidelines for #10 SASE. Reviews fiction.

Payment/Terms: Pays 1¢/word. Pays on acceptance for first North American serial rights.

Advice: "We like fiction that has something to say (and not about its author). We hope for work that is observant, intense and multi-leveled. Follow Pound's advice—'make it new.' Write what you want in whatever style you want without being gross, sensational, or needlessly explicit—then pray there's someone who can appreciate your sensibility. Read good fiction. It's as fundamental as learning how to hit, throw and catch is to baseball. With the increasing American disinclination towards literature, stories must insist on being heard. Read what is being published—then write something better—and different. Do all rewrites before sending a story out. Few editors have time to work with writers on promising stories; only polished."

$◨ ▨ THE IDAHO REVIEW, Boise State University, English Dept., 1910 University Dr., Boise ID 83725. (208)426-1002. Fax: (208)426-4373. E-mail: mwieland@boisestate.edu. **Contact:** Mitch Wieland, editor. Magazine: 6×9; 180-200 pages; acid-free accent opaque paper; coated cover stock; photos. "A literary journal for anyone who enjoys good fiction." Annual. Estab. 1998. Circ. 1,000. C.L.M.P.

● Two stories chosen for 2003 prize stories: *The O. Henry Awards*, plus one story listed as "special mention" in 2003 *Puchcart Prize.*

Needs: Experimental, literary. "No genre fiction of any type." Receives 150 unsolicited mss/month. Accepts 5-7 mss/issue; 5-7 mss/year. "We do not read from December 16-August 31." Publishes ms 1 year after acceptance. Agented fiction 5%. **Publishes 1 new writer/year.** Recently published work by Rick Bass, Melanie Rae Thon, Frederick Busch, and Edith Pearlman. Length: open; average length: 7,000 words. Publishes short shorts. Also publishes literary essays, poetry. Sometimes comments on rejected mss.

How to Contact: Send SASE for return of ms or send a disposable copy of ms and #10 SASE for reply only. Responds in 3 months to mss. Accepts simultaneous, multiple submissions. Sample copy for $8.95. Writer's guidelines for SASE. Reviews fiction.

Payment/Terms: Pays $100 when funds are available plus 2 contributor's copies; additional copies $5. Pays on publication for first North American serial rights. Sends galleys to author.

Advice: "We look for strongly crafted work that tells a story that needs to be told. We demand vision and intelligence and mystery in the fiction we publish."

◨ THE IDIOT, Anarchaos Press, P.O. Box 69163, Los Angeles CA 90069. E-mail: idiotsubmission@yahoo.com. Website: theidiotmagazine.com. **Contact:** Brian Campbell and Toni Plummer, lackeys. Magazine: 5½ × 8½; 48 pages; 20 lb. white paper; cardboard glossy cover; illustrations. "For people who enjoy Dennis Miller, Woody Allen, S.J. Perelman, James Thurber and Camus. We're looking for black comedy. Death, disease, God, religion, micronauts are all subjects of comedy. Nothing is sacred, but it needs to be funny. I don't want whimsical, I don't want amusing, I don't want some fanciful anecdote about a trip you took with your uncle when you were eight. I want laugh-out-loud-fall-on-the-floor-funny. If it's cute, give it to your mom, your sweetheart, or your puppy dog. Length doesn't matter, but most comedy is like soup. It's an appetizer, not a meal. Short is often better. Bizarre, obscure, referential and literary are all appreciated. My audience is mostly comprised of bitter misanthropes who play Russian Roulette between airings of 'The Simpsons' each day. I want dark." Annual. Estab. 1993. Circ. 250-300.

Needs: Humor/satire. Wants more short, dark humor. Publishes ms 6-12 after acceptance. **Publishes 1-3 new writers/year.** Recently published work by Joe Deasy, Dan Medeiros, Mike Buckley and Mark Romyn. Length: 2,000 words; average length: 500 words. Publishes short shorts. Also publishes poetry. Sometimes comments on rejected mss.

How to Contact: Accepts submissions by e-mail. Send SASE for reply, return of ms or send a disposable copy of ms. Responds in 1 month to queries; 3 months to mss. Accepts simultaneous and reprints submissions. Sample copy for $5.

Payment/Terms: Pays 1 contributor's copy. Acquires one-time rights. Sends galleys to author.

Advice: Nothing over 2,000 words unless it's the funniest damned thing on the face of this or any other Earth. If you're too cheap to buy a copy of our magazine, then check our website—though not nearly as funny, it will give you an idea of what we're looking for. And we have our first writing contest! See website for rules and conditions."

ILLUMINATIONS, An International Magazine of Contemporary Writing, c/o Dept. of English, College of Charleston, 66 George St., Charleston SC 29424-0001. (843)953-1920. Fax: (843)953-1924. E-mail: lewiss@ cofc.edu. Website: www.cofc.edu/illuminations. **Contact:** Simon Lewis, editor. Magazine: 5×8; 80 pages; illustrations. "*Illuminations* is one of the most challengingly eclectic little literary magazines around, having featured writers from the United States, Britain and Romania as well as Southern Africa." Annual. Estab. 1982. Circ. 400.

Needs: Literary. Receives 5 unsolicited mss/month. Accepts 1 mss/year. **Publishes 1 new writer/year.** Recently published work by Klaus de Albuquerque. Also publishes poetry. Sometimes comments on rejected mss.

How to Contact: Send SASE for reply, return of ms or send a disposable copy of ms. Responds in 2 weeks to queries; 2 months to mss. No simultaneous submissions. Sample copy for $10 and 6×9 envelope. Writer's guidelines free.

Payment/Terms: Pays 2 contributor's copies of current issue; 1 of subsequent issue. Acquires one-time rights.

ILLYA'S HONEY, The Dallas Poets Community, P.O. Box 700865, Dallas TX 75370. Website: www.dallasp oets.org. **Contact:** Ann Howells, editor. Magazine: 5½×8½; 34 pages; 24 lb. paper; glossy cover; photos. "We publish poetry and flash fiction. We try to present quality work by writers who take time to learn technique—aimed at anyone who appreciates good literature." Quarterly. Estab. 1994. Circ. 125.

Needs: Ethnic/multicultural, experimental, feminist, gay, historical, humor/satire, lesbian, literary, mainstream, regional, flash fiction. "We accept only flash (also known as micro) fiction." Receives 10 unsolicited mss/month. Accepts 2-8 mss/issue. Publishes ms 3-5 months after acceptance. **Publishes 2-3 new writers/year.** Recently published work by Paul Sampson, Susanne Bowers and Denworthy. Also publishes poetry. Sometimes comments on rejected mss.

How to Contact: Send complete ms. Send SASE for return of ms or send a disposable copy of ms and #10 SASE for reply only. Responds in 6 months to mss. Sample copy for $4. Writer's guidelines for SASE.

Payment/Terms: Pays 1 contributor's copy; additional copies $6. Pays on publication for first North American serial rights.

Advice: "We would like to see more character studies, humor."

$ IMAGE, A Journal of the Arts & Religion, The Center for Religious Humanism, 3307 Third Ave. W, Seattle WA 98119. (206)281-2988. E-mail: image@imagejournal.org. Website: www.imagejournal.org. **Contact:** Greg Wolfe. Magazine: 7×10; 136 pages; glossy cover stock; illustrations; photos. "*Image* is a showcase for the encounter between religious faith and world-class contemporary art. Each issue features fiction, poetry, essays, memoirs, an in-depth interview and articles about visual artists, film, music, etc. and glossy 4-color plates of contemporary visual art." Quarterly. Estab. 1989. Circ. 4,000. CLMP.

Needs: Humor/satire, literary, regional, religious/inspirational, translations. Receives 100 unsolicited mss/month. Accepts 2 mss/issue; 8 mss/year. Publishes ms 1 year after acceptance. Agented fiction 5%. Recently published work by Annie Dillard, David James Duncan, Bret Lott and Melanie Rae Thon. Length: 2,000-8,000 words; average length: 5,000 words. Also publishes literary essays, poetry.

How to Contact: Send SASE for reply, return of ms or send disposable copy of ms. Responds in 1 month to queries; 3 months to mss. Sample copy for $12. Reviews fiction.

Payment/Terms: Pays $10/page (100 minimum) and 4 contributor's copies; additional copies for $5. Pays on acceptance. Sends galleys to author.

Advice: "Fiction must grapple with religious faith, though the settings and subjects need not be overtly religious."

$ INDIANA REVIEW, Indiana University, Ballantine Hall 465, 1020 E. Kirkwood, Bloomington IN 47405-7103. (812)855-3439. Website: www.indiana.edu/~inreview. **Contact:** Danit Brown, fiction editor. Magazine: 6×9; 160 pages; 50 lb. paper; Glatfelter cover stock. "*Indiana Review*, a nonprofit organization run by IU graduate students, is a journal of previously unpublished poetry and fiction. Literary interviews and essays also considered. We publish innovative fiction and poetry. We're interested in energy, originality, and careful attention to craft. While we publish many well-known writers, we also welcome new and emerging poets and fiction writers." Semiannual. Estab. 1976. Circ. 2,000.

● Work published in *Indiana Review* received a Pushcart Prize (2001) and was included in *Best New American Voices* (2001). *IR* also received an Indiana Arts Council Grant and a National Endowment In the Arts grant.

Needs: Ethnic/multicultural, experimental, literary, mainstream, novel excerpts, regional, translations, literary, short fictions, translations. No genre fiction. Upcoming theme: Borders (May 2004), deadline December 2003. Receives 200 unsolicited mss/month. Accepts 7-9 mss/issue. Does not read mss mid-December to mid-January. Publishes ms an average of 3-6 months after acceptance. **Publishes 6-8 new writers/year.** Recently published work by Stuart Dybek, Marilyn Chin, Ray Gonzalez and Abby Frucht. Also publishes literary essays, poetry.

How to Contact: Send complete ms. Accepts submissions by mail. Cover letters should be *brief* and demonstrate specific familiarity with the content of a recent issue of *Indiana Review*. SASE. Responds in 2 weeks to queries; 4 months to mss. Accepts simultaneous submissions if notified *immediately* of other publication. Sample copy for $8. Writer's guidelines online.

Payment/Terms: Pays $5/page, plus 2 contributor's copies. Pays on publication for first North American serial rights. Sponsors awards/contests.

Advice: "Because our editors change each year, so do our literary preferences. It's important that potential contributors are familiar with our most recent issue of *Indiana Review* via library, sample copy or subscription. Beyond that, we look for prose that is well crafted and socially relevant. Dig deep. Don't accept your first choice descriptions when you are revising. Cliché and easy images sink 90% of the stories we reject. Understand the magazines you send to—investigate!"

INKWELL MAGAZINE, Manhattanville College, 2900 Purchase St., Purchase NY 10577. (914)323-5300. Fax: (914)694-0348. Website: www.manhattanville.edu/inkwellmag/index.htm. **Contact:** Jeremy Church, editor. Literary Journal: 7×10; 120-170 pages; 60 lb. paper; 10 pt C1S, 4/c cover; illustrations; photos. "*Inkwell Magazine* is committed to presenting top quality poetry, prose and artwork in a high quality publication. *Inkwell* is dedicated to discovering new talent, and to encouraging and bringing talents of working writers and artists to a wider audience. We encourage diverse voices and have an open submission policy for both art and literature." Annual. Estab. 1995. Circ. 1,000. Member, CLMP.

Needs: Experimental, humor/satire, literary. "No erotica, children's literature, romance, religious." List of upcoming themes available for SASE. Receives 120 unsolicited mss/month. Accepts 45 mss/issue. Does not read mss February-September. Publishes ms 2 months after acceptance. **Publishes 3-5 new writers/year.** Recently published work by Maureen Howard, Denise Shekerjian, Robert Ryser, Phyllis Carito and Susan Kelly-DeWitt. Length: 5,000 words; average length: 3,000 words. Publishes short shorts. Also publishes poetry. Sometimes comments on rejected mss.

How to Contact: Send a disposable copy of ms and #10 SASE for reply only. Responds in 2 months to queries; 4-6 months to mss. Sample copy for $6. Writer's guidelines for SASE.

Payment/Terms: Pays 1 contributor's copy; additional copies $8. Acquires first rights. Sponsors awards/contests.

Advice: "We look for well-crafted original stories with a strong voice."

INTERBANG, Dedicated to perfection in the art of writing, P.O. Box 1574, Venice CA 90294. (310)450-6372. E-mail: heather@interbang.net. Website: www.interbang.net. **Contact:** Heather Hoffman, editor. Magazine: 8½×7; 30 pages; 60 lb. paper; card cover stock; illustrations; photos. Quarterly. Estab. 1995. Circ. 2,000.

Needs: Adventure, ethnic/multicultural, experimental, family saga, fantasy (space fantasy, sword and sorcery), feminist, gay, glitz, historical (general), horror (darl fantasy, futuristic, psychological, supernatural), humor/satire, lesbian, literary, mainstream, military/war, mystery/suspense (amateur slueth, cozy, police procedural, private eye/hardboiled), New Age, psychic/supernatural/occult, regional, science fiction (hard science/technological, soft/sociological), thriller/espionage, translations. "No travel or children's." Wants to see more historical fiction, science fiction/fantasy. Receives 50 unsolicited mss/month. Accepts 5 mss/issue; 25 mss/year. Publishes ms 1 month after acceptance. Agented fiction 5%. **Publishes 50 new writers/year.** Recently published work by Sharon Mesmer, Ron Bloom, L. Fitzgerald Sjöberg. Average length: 2,500 words. Publishes short shorts. Also publishes literary essays. Sometimes comments on rejected mss.

How to Contact: Send SASE for reply, return of ms or send a disposable copy of ms. No e-mail submissions. Responds in 2 weeks to queries; 3 months to mss. Accepts simultaneous submissions. Sample copy for free. Reviews fiction.

Payment/Terms: Pays free subscription to the magazine, an *Interbang* T-shirt and 5 contributor's copies. Pays on publication for one-time rights.

Advice: "We're looking for well-written stories with strong, vivid descriptions, well-developed characters and complex themes. Focus on a consistent narrative style. We do not publish stories that read like a TV show. We want stories with style and depth."

$ ☑ THE IOWA REVIEW, 308 EPB, The University of Iowa, Iowa City IA 52242. (319)335-0462. Fax: (319)335-2535. Website: www.uiowa.edu/~iareview/. **Contact:** Fiction Editor. Magazine: 5½×8½; 200 paes; first-grade offset paper; Carolina CS1 10-pt. cover stock. "Stories, essays, poems for a general readership interested in contemporary literature." Triannual magazine. Estab. 1970. Circ. 2,000.

Needs: "We are open to a range of styles and voices and always hope to be surprised by work we then feel we need." Receives 600 unsolicited mss/month. Accepts 4-6 mss/issue; 12-18 mss/year. Does not read mss April-August. Publishes ms an average of 12-18 months after acceptance. Agented fiction less than 2%. **Publishes some new writers/year.** Recently published work by Joshua Harmon, Katherine Vaz, Mary Helen Stefaniak and Steve Tomasula. Also publishes literary essays, literary criticism, poetry.

How to Contact: Send complete ms with cover letter. "Don't bother with queries." SASE for return of ms. Responds in 3 months to queries; 3 months to mss. "We discourage simultaneous submissions." Sample copy for $7 and online. Writer's guidelines online. Reviews fiction.

Payment/Terms: Pays $25 for the first page and $15 for each additional page, plus 2 contributor's copies; additional copies 30% off cover price. Pays on publication for first North American serial, nonexclusive anthology, classroom, and online serial rights.

Advice: "We have no set guidelines as to content or length; we look for what we consider to be the best writing available to us and are pleased when writers we believe we have discovered catch on with a wider range of readers. It is never a bad idea to look through an issue or two of the magazine prior to a submission."

N $⬛ ◎ IRREANTUM, Exploring Mormon Literature, The Association for Mormon Letters, P.O. Box 51364, Provo UT 84605. (801)373-9730. Website: www.aml-online.org. **Contact:** Fiction Editor. Magazine or Zine: 8½×7½; 100-120 pages; 20 lb. paper; 20 lb. color cover; illustrations; photos. "While focused on Mormonism, *Irreantum* is a cultural, humanities-oriented magazine, not a religious magazine. Our guiding principle is that Mormonism is grounded in a sufficiently unusual, cohesive, and extended historical and cultural experience that it has become like a nation, an ethnic culture. We can speak of Mormon literature at least as surely as we can of a Jewish or Southern literature. *Irreantum* publishes stories, one-act dramas, stand-alone novel and drama excerpts, and poetry by, for, or about Mormons (as well as author interviews, essays, and reviews). The magazine's audience includes readers of any or no religious faith who are interested in literary exploration of the Mormon culture, mindset, and worldview through Mormon themes and characters. *Irreantum* is currently the only magazine devoted to Mormon literature." Quarterly. Estab. 1999. Circ. 500.

Needs: Adventure, ethnic/multicultural (Mormon), experimental, family saga, fantasy, feminist, historical, horror, humor/satire, literary, mainstream, mystery/suspense, New Age, psychic/supernatural/occult, regional (Western USA/Mormon), religious/inspirational, romance, science fiction, suspense, thriller/espionage, translations, young adult/teen. Receives 5 unsolicited mss/month. Accepts 3 mss/issue; 12 mss/year. Publishes ms 3-12 months after acceptance. **Publishes 6 new writers/year.** Recently published work by Anne Perry, Brady Udall, Brian Evenson and Robert Kirby. Length: 1,000-5,000 words; average length: 5,000 words. Publishes short shorts. Also publishes literary essays, literary criticism, poetry. Sometimes comments on rejected mss.

How to Contact: Accepts submissions by e-mail. Send complete ms with cover letter. Include brief bio and list of publications. Send a disposable copy of ms and #10 SASE for reply only. Responds in 2 weeks to queries; 2 months to mss. Accepts simultaneous and reprints, multiple submissions. Sample copy for $6. Writer's guidelines by e-mail. Reviews fiction.

Payment/Terms: Pays $0-100. Pays on publication for one-time, electronic rights.

Advice: "*Irreantum* is not interested in didactic or polemical fiction that primarily attempts to prove or disprove Mormon doctrine, history or corporate policy. We encourage beginning writers to focus on human elements first, with Mormon elements introduced only as natural and organic to the story. Readers can tell if you are honestly trying to explore the human experience or if you are writing with a propagandistic agenda either for or against Mormonism. For conservative, orthodox Mormon writers, beware of sentimentalism, simplistic resolutions, and foregone conclusions."

⬛ THE JABBERWOCK REVIEW, Mississippi State University, Drawer E, Dept. of English, Mississippi State MS 39762. (662)325-3644. E-mail: jabberwock@org.msstate.edu. Website: www.msstate.edu/org/jabberwock. **Contact:** Fiction Editor (revolving editorship). Magazine: 8½×5½; 120 pages; glossy cover; illustrations; photos. "We are located in the South—love the South—but we publish good writing from anywhere and everywhere. And from anyone. We respect writers of reputation—and print their work—but we take great delight in publishing new and emerging writers as well." Semiannual. Estab. 1979. Circ. 500.

Needs: Ethnic/multicultural, experimental, feminist, gay, literary, mainstream, regional, translations. "No science fiction, romance." Receives 150 unsolicited mss/month. Accepts 7-8 mss/issue; 15 mss/year. "We do not read during the summer (May 1 to September 1). Publishes ms 4-6 months after acceptance. Agented fiction 5%. **Publishes 1-5 new writers/year.** Recently published work by James Wilcox, Clarinda Harriss, Alan Elysheritz, Margo Rabb, Chris Mazza and Richard Lyons. Length: 250-5,000 words; average length: 4,000 words. Publishes short shorts. Also publishes literary essays, poetry. Sometimes comments on rejected mss.

How to Contact: Send SASE (or IRC) for return of ms. Responds in 5 months to mss. Accepts simultaneous submissions "with notification of such." Sample copy for $6. Writer's guidelines for SASE.

Payment/Terms: Pays 2 contributor's copies. Sponsors awards/contests.

Advice: "It might take a few months to get a response from us, but your manuscript will be read with care. Our editors enjoy reading submissions (really!) and will remember writers who are persistent and commited to getting a story 'right' through revision."

$ ✓ THE JOURNAL, The Ohio State University, 164 W. 17th Ave., Columbus OH 43210. (614)292-4076. Fax: (614)292-7816. Website: www.english.ohio-state.edu/journals/the_journal/. **Contact:** Kathy Fagan (poetry); Michelle Herman (fiction). Magazine: 6×9; 150 pages. "We're open to all forms; we tend to favor work that gives evidence of a mature and sophisticated sense of the language." Semiannual. Estab. 1972. Circ. 1,500.

Needs: Novel excerpts, literary short stories. No romance, science fiction or religious/devotional. Receives 100 unsolicited mss/month. Accepts 2 mss/issue. Publishes ms 1 year after acceptance. Agented fiction 10%. **Publishes some new writers/year.** Recently published work by Stephen Dixon, Norma Rosen, Mark Jacobs and Liza Wieland. Sometimes comments on rejected mss.

How to Contact: Accepts submissions by mail. Send complete ms with cover letter. SASE. Responds in 2 weeks to queries; 2 months to mss. Accepts simultaneous submissions No electronic submissions. Sample copy for $7 or online. Writer's guidelines online.

Payment/Terms: Pays $30. Pays on publication for first North American serial rights. Sends galleys to author.

Advice: Mss are rejected because of "lack of understanding of the short story form, shallow plots, undeveloped characters. Cure: read as much well-written fiction as possible. Our readers prefer 'psychological' fiction rather than stories with intricate plots. Take care to present a clean, well-typed submission."

$ ✓ ◎ ✪ KALEIDOSCOPE, Exploring the Experience of Disability Through Literature and the Fine Arts, Kaleidoscope Press, 701 S. Main St., Akron OH 44311-1019. (330)762-9755. Fax: (330)762-0912. Website: www.udsakron.org. **Contact:** Fiction Editor. Magazine: 8½×11; 56-64 pages; non-coated paper; coated cover stock; illustrations (all media); photos. Subscribers include individuals, agencies, and organizations that assist people with disabilities and many university and public libraries. Appreciates work by established writers as well. Especially interested in work by writers with a disability, but features writers both with and without disabilities. "Writers without a disability must limit themselves to our focus, while those with a disability may explore any topic (although we prefer original perspectives about experiences with disability)." Semiannual. Estab. 1979. Circ. 1,000.

• *Kaleidoscope* has received awards from the American Heart Association, the Great Lakes Awards Competition and Ohio Public Images.

Needs: "We look for well-developed plots, engaging characters and realistic dialogue. We lean toward fiction that emphasizes character and emotions rather than action-oriented narratives." "No fiction that is stereotypical, patronizing, sentimental, erotic, or maudlin. No romance, religious or dogmatic fiction; no children's literature." Upcoming theme: "Mental Illness" (deadline March 2004). Receives 20-25 unsolicited mss/month. Accepts 10 mss/year. Agented fiction 1%. **Publishes 1 new writers/year.** Recently published work by Ruskin Bond, Gerald R. Wheeler, Michael Levy and Robert Schuler. Also publishes poetry.

How to Contact: Accepts submissions by mail, fax. Query first or send complete ms and cover letter. Include author's education and writing background and if author has a disability, how it influenced the writing. SASE. Responds in 3 weeks to queries; 6 months to mss. Accepts simultaneous and reprints, multiple submissions. Sample copy for $6 prepaid. Writer's guidelines online.

Payment/Terms: Pays $10-125, and 2 contributor's copies; additional copies $6. Pays on publication for first, reprints permitted with credit given to original publication rights. Rights return to author upon publication.

Advice: "Read the magazine and get submission guidelines. We prefer that writers with a disability offer original perspectives about their experiences; writers without disabilities should limit themselves to our focus in order to solidify a connection to our magazine's purpose. Do not use stereotypical, patronizing and sentimental attitudes about disability."

$ ✓ ◎ KALLIOPE, a journal of women's literature & art, Florida Community College at Jacksonville, 11901 Beach Blvd., Jacksonville FL 32246. (904)646-2081. Website: www.fccj.org/kalliope. **Contact:** Fiction Editor. Magazine: 7¼×8¼; 120 pages; 70 lb. coated matte paper; Bristol cover; 16-18 halftones per issue. "*Kalliope* publishes poetry, short fiction, reviews, and b&w art, usually by women artists. We look for artistic excellence." Estab. 1978. Circ. 1,600.

Needs: Ethnic/multicultural, experimental, novel excerpts, literary. "Quality short fiction by women writers. No science fiction or fantasy. Would like to see more experimental fiction." Receives approximately 100 unsolicited mss/month. Accepts up to 10 mss/issue. Does not read mss May-August. Publishes ms 3 months after acceptance. **Publishes 3 new writers/year.** Recently published work by Edith Pearlman, Bette Howland, Susan Hubbard and Mary Gardner. Publishes short shorts. Also publishes poetry. Sometimes comments on rejected mss.

How to Contact: Send complete ms. Accepts submissions by mail. Responds in 1 week to queries; 3 months to mss. No simultaneous submissions. Sample copy for $9 (recent issue) or $4 (back copy), or see sample issues on website. Writer's guidelines online. Reviews fiction.

Payment/Terms: Pays $10 honorarium if funds are available, otherwise 2 copies or subscription. Pays on publication for first rights. "We accept only unpublished work. Copyright returned to author upon request."

Advice: "Read our magazine. The work we consider for publication will be well written and the characters and dialogue will be convincing. We like a fresh approach and are interested in new or unusual forms. Make us believe your characters; give readers an insight which they might not have had if they had not read you. We would like to publish more work by minority writers." Manuscripts are rejected because "1) nothing *happens!*, 2) it is thinly disguised autobiography (richly disguised autobiography is OK), 3) ending is either too pat or else just trails off, 4) characterization is not developed, and 5) point of view falters."

KARAMU, English Dept., Eastern Illinois University, 600 Lincoln Ave., Charleston IL 61920. (217)581-6297. **Contact:** Fiction Editor. Literary magazine: 5×8; 132-136 pages; illustrations; photos. "*Karamu* is a literary magazine of ideas and artistic expression independently produced by the faculty members and associates of Eastern Illinois University. We publish writing that captures something essential about life, which goes beyond superficial, and which develops voice genuinely. Contributions of creative non-fiction, fiction, poetry and artwork of interest to a broadly eduactated audience are welcome." Annual. Estab. 1969. Circ. 500.

● *Karamu* has received two Illinois Arts Council Awards.

Needs: Adventure, ethnic/multicultural, experimental, feminist, gay, historical, humor/satire, lesbian, literary, mainstream, regional. "No pornographic, science fiction, religious, political or didactic stories—no dogma or proselytizing." List of upcoming editorial themes available for SASE. Receives 80-90 unsolicited mss/month. Accepts 10-15 mss/issue. Does not read March 1-September 1. Publishes ms 1 year after acceptance. **Publishes 3-6 new writers/year.** Recently published work by Denise Seibert, Bill Embly, Judi Goldenberg and Daniel North. Length: 3,500 words max. Publishes short shorts. Also publishes poetry. Sometimes comments on rejected mss.

How to Contact: Send SASE for reply. Responds in 1 week to queries. Accepts simultaneous, multiple submissions. Sample copy for $7.50 or $6 for back issues. Writer's guidelines for SASE.

Payment/Terms: Pays 1 contributor's copy; additional cpies at discount. Acquires one-time rights.

Advice: Looks for "convincing, well-developed characters and plots expressing aspects of human nature or relationships in a perceptive, believable and carefully considered and written way."

KELSEY REVIEW, Mercer County College, P.O. Box B, Trenton NJ 08690. (609)586-4800. Fax: (609)586-2318. E-mail: kelsey.review@mccc.edu. Website: www.mccc.edu. **Contact:** Robin Schore. Magazine: 7X14; 98 pages; glossy paper; soft cover. "Must live or work in Mercer County, NJ." Annual. Estab. 1988. Circ. 1,750.

Needs: Regional (Mercer County only), open. Receives 10 unsolicited mss/month. Accepts 24 mss/issue. Reads mss only in May. **Publishes 8 new writers/year.** Recently published work by Bruce Petronio, James Richardson and Deborah Reggie. Publishes short shorts. Also publishes literary essays, poetry. Always comments on rejected mss.

How to Contact: SASE for return of ms. Responds in June to mss. Accepts multiple submissions. Sample copy for free.

Payment/Terms: 5 contributor's copies. Rights revert to author on publication.

Advice: Look for "quality, intellect, grace and guts. Avoid sentimentality, overwriting and self-indulgence. Work on clarity, depth and originality."

$ THE KENYON REVIEW, Walton House, 104 College Dr., Gambier OH 43022. (740)427-5208. Fax: (740)427-5417. Website: www.kenyonreview.org. **Contact:** Fiction Editor. An international journal of literature, culture, and the arts dedicated to an inclusive representation of the best in new writing (fiction, poetry, essays, interviews, criticism) from established and emerging writers. Quarterly. Estab. 1939. Circ. 5,000.

● Work published in the *Kenyon Review* has been selected for inclusion in *Pushcart Prize* anthologies and *Best American Short Stories*. Because of editor's sabbatical, unsolicited mss will not be considered again until September 1, 2004.

Needs: Condensed novels, ethnic/multicultural, experimental, feminist, gay, historical, humor/satire, lesbian, literary, mainstream, translations, contemporary. Receives 400 unsolicited mss/month. Unsolicited mss typically read only from September 1 through March 31. Publishes ms 1 year after acceptance. Recently published work by Patrick White, Roger Rosenblatt, Joyce Carol Oates, Anesa Miller, Yvonne Jackson and Michael Dahlie.

How to Contact: Accepts submissions by mail. Send complete ms with cover letter. SASE. Responds in 3-4 months to queries; 4 months to mss. No simultaneous submissions. Sample copy $10 single issue, $13 double issue (Summer/Fall), includes postage and handling. Writer's guidelines online.

Payment/Terms: Pays $10-15/page. Pays on publication for first rights.

Advice: "We look for strong voice, unusual perspective, and power in the writing."

KEREM, Creative Explorations in Judaism, Jewish Study Center Press, Inc., 3035 Porter St. NW, Washington DC 20008. (202)364-3006. Website: www.kerem.org. **Contact:** Sara R. Horowitz and Gilah Langner, editors. Magazine: 6×9; 128 pages; 60 lb. offset paper; glossy cover; illustrations; photos. "*Kerem* publishes Jewish religious, creative, literary material—short stories, poetry, personal reflections, text study, prayers, rituals, etc." Estab. 1992. Circ. 2,000.

Needs: Jewish: feminist, humor/satire, literary, religious/inspirational. Receives 10-12 unsolicited mss/month. Accepts 1-2 mss/issue. Publishes ms 2-10 months after acceptance. Also publishes literary essays, poetry.

How to Contact: Accepts submissions by e-mail. Send SASE for reply, return of ms or send disposable copy of ms. Responds in 2 months to queries; 5 months to mss. Accepts simultaneous, multiple submissions. Sample copy for $8.50. Writer's guidelines online.

Payment/Terms: Pays free subscription and 2-10 contributor's copies. Acquires one-time rights.
Advice: "Should have a strong Jewish content. We want to be moved by reading the manuscript!"

KIMERA, A Journal of Fine Writing, N. 1316 Hollis, Spokane WA 99201. E-mail: kimera@js.spokane.wa.us. Website: www.js.spokane.wa.us/kimera. **Contact:** Jan Strever, editor. Electronic and print magazine. "*Kimera* attempts to meet John Locke's challenge: Where is the head with no chimeras? We seek fiction that pushes the edge in terms of language use and craft." Semiannual online; annual print version. Estab. 1995. Circ. 2,000 (online), 300 (print).
Needs: Eclectic, energetic fiction. "Nothing badly conceived; attention to the muscularity of language." No erotica. Receives 50 unsolicited mss/month. Accepts 5 mss/issue. Publishes ms 1 year after acceptance. **Publishes some new writers/year.** Recently published work by L. Lynch and G. Thomas. Publishes short shorts. Also publishes literary essays, poetry. Sometimes comments on rejected mss.
How to Contact: Send SASE for return of ms, SASE for reply only, or disposable copy of ms. Responds in 3 weeks to queries; 3 months to mss. Accepts simultaneous submissions. Sample copy for $5. Writer's guidelines free.
Payment/Terms: Pays 1 contributor's copy. Pays on publication for first rights. Sponsors awards/contests.
Advice: "We look for clarity of language. Read other writers and previous issues."

THE KING'S ENGLISH, 3114 NE 47th Ave., Portland OR 97213. (503)709-1917. E-mail: thekingsenglish @comcast.net. Website: www.thekingsenglish.org. **Contact:** Benjamin Chambers, editor. "Our focus is literary fiction, especially if it's stuffed with strong imagery and gorgeous prose. In very rare instances, we'll include detective fiction or sci-fi/fantasy, as long as there's a strong element of suspense, the setting is unusual, and the writing first-rate." Quarterly. Estab. 2003.
Needs: Experimental, historical, literary, mainstream, mystery/suspense (private eye/hardboiled), thriller/espionage, translations. No horror, religious or heartwarming tales of redemption. Accepts 3 mss/issue; 12 mss/year. Publishes short shorts. Also publishes literary essays. Sometimes comments on rejected mss.
How to Contact: Send complete ms. Accepts submissions by mail. Responds in 2 weeks to queries; 2 months to mss. Accepts simultaneous, multiple submissions. Writer's guidelines for SASE, by e-mail or on the website.
Payment/Terms: Acquires first North American serial, one-time, electronic rights. Aquires one-time, non-exclusive rights to anthologize.
Advice: "Surprise us. With language, mostly, though concept and execution can do just as well or better. If your first page makes us long for a rainy day and a cozy armchair in which to curl up with your manuscript, you'll get our attention. Make sure your story deserves to be a long one. Write what you'd like to read. And pay no attention to advice from us."

THE KIT-CAT REVIEW, 244 Halstead Ave., Harrison NY 10528. (914)835-4833. **Contact:** Claudia Fletcher, editor. Magazine: 8½×5½; 75 pages; laser paper; colored card cover stock; illustrations. "*The Kit-Cat Review* is named after the 18th Century Kit-Cat Club, whose members included Addison, Steele, Congreve, Vanbrugh, and Garth. Its purpose is to promote/discover excellence and originality. Some issues are part anthology." The Spring issue includes the winner of the annual Gavin Fletcher Memorial Prize for Poetry of $1,000. The winning poem is published shortly thereafter in a *Kit-Cat Review* ad in the *American Poetry Review*. Quarterly. Estab. 1998. Circ. 500.
Needs: Ethnic/multicultural, experimental, literary, novel excerpts, slice-of-life vignettes. No stories with "O. Henry-type formula endings. Shorter pieces stand a better chance of publication." No science fiction, fantasy, romance, horror, or new age. Receives 40 unsolicited mss/month. Accepts 6 mss/issue; 24 mss/year. Publishes ms 6-12 months after acceptance. **Publishes 14 new writers/year.** Recently published work by Chayym Zeldis, Michael Fedo, Louis Phillips. Length: 5,000 words maximum; average length: 2,000 words. Publishes short shorts. Also publishes literary essays, literary criticism, poetry.
How to Contact: Send complete ms. Accepts submissions by mail, phone. Send SASE (or IRC) for return of ms, or send disposable copy of ms and #10 SASE for reply only. Responds in 1 week to queries; 2 months to mss. Accepts simultaneous, multiple submissions. Sample copy for $7 (payable to Claudia Fletcher). Writer's guidelines for SASE.
Payment/Terms: Pays $25-200 and 2 contributor's copies; additional copies $5. Pays on publication for first rights.

LA KANCERKLINIKO, 162 rue Paradis, P.O. Box 174, 13444 Marseille Cantini Cedex, France. (33)2-48-61-81-98. Fax: (33)2-48-61-81-98. E-mail: a.lazarus-1.septier@wanadoo.fr. **Contact:** Laurent Septier. "An Esperanto magazine which appears 4 times annually. Each issue contains 32 paages. *La Kancerkliniko* is a political and cultural magazine." Quarterly. Circ. 300.
Needs: Science fiction, short stories or very short novels. "The short story (or the very short novel) must be written only in Esperanto, eitehr original or translation from any other language." Wants more science fiction. **Publishes 2-3 new writers/year.** Recently published work by Mao Zifu, Manuel de Sabrea, Peter Brown and Aldo de'Giorgi.
How to Contact: Accepts submissions by e-mail, fax. Accepts disk submissions. Accepts multiple submissions. Sample copy for 3 IRCs from Universal Postal Union.
Payment/Terms: Pays in contributor's copies.

⬤ LAKE EFFECT, A Journal of the Literary Arts, Penn State Erie, Humanities and Social Sciences, Station Rd., Erie PA 16563-1501. (814)898-6281. Fax: (814)898-6032. E-mail: goL1@psu.edu. **Contact:** George Looney, editor-in-chief. Magazine: 5½×8½; 136-150 pages; 55lb. natural paper; 12 pt. C1S cover. "In addition to seeking strong, traditional stories, *Lake Effect* is open to more experimental, language-centered fiction as well." Annual. Estab. as *Lake Effect*, 2001; as *Tempest*, 1978. Circ. 500. Member, CLMP.

Needs: Experimental, literary, mainstream. "No children's/juvenile, fantasy, science fiction, romance or young adult/teen." Receives 30 unsolicited mss/month. Accepts 5-9 mss/issue. Publishes ms 1 year after acceptance. **Publishes 6 new writers/year.** Recently published work by Joanna Howard, Holly Clark, Michael Czyzniejewski, and Douglas Smith. Length: 4,500 words; average length: 2,600 words. Publishes short shorts. Also publishes literary essays, poetry.

How to Contact: Send SASE for return of ms or send a disposable copy of ms and #10 SASE for reply only. Responds in 3 weeks to queries; 4-6 months to mss. Accepts simultaneous submissions. Sample copy for $6. Writer's guidelines for SASE.

Payment/Terms: Pays 2 contributor's copies; additional copies $2. Acquires first, one-time rights. Not copyrighted.

Advice: "We're looking for strong, well-crafted stories that emerge from character and language more than plot. The language is what makes a story stand out (and a strong sense of voice). Be sure to let us know immediately should a submitted story be accepted elsewhere."

◎ ⬤ THE LAMP-POST, of the Southern California C.S. Lewis Society, 1106 W. 16th St., Santa Ana CA 92706. (714)836-5257. E-mail: dgclark@adelphia.com. **Contact:** David G. Clark, editor. Magazine: 5½×8½; 34 pages; 7 lb. paper; 8 lb. cover; illustrations. "We are a literary review focused on C.S. Lewis and like writers." Quarterly. Estab. 1977. Circ. 200.

Needs: "Literary fantasy and science fiction for children to adults." Publishes ms 3-12 months after acceptance. **Publishes 3-5 new writers/year.** Length: 1,000-5,000 words; average length: 2,500 words. Also publishes literary essays, literary criticism, poetry. Sometimes comments on rejected mss.

How to Contact: Send via e-mail as Word file or rich text format. Send SASE for reply, return of ms or send a disposable copy of ms. Responds in 2 weeks to mss. Accepts reprints submissions No simultaneous submissions. Sample copy for $3. Writer's guidelines for #10 SASE. Reviews fiction.

Payment/Terms: Pays 2 contributor's copies; additional copies $3. Acquires first North American serial, one-time rights.

Advice: "We look for fiction with the supernatural, mythic feel or the fiction of C.S. Lewis and Charles Williams. Our slant is Christian but we want work of literary quality. No inspirational. Is it the sort of thing Lewis, Tolkien and Williams would like—subtle, crafted fiction? If so, send it. Don't be too obvious or facile. Our readers aren't stupid."

◎ ⊞ LANDFALL/UNIVERSITY OF OTAGO PRESS, University of Otago Press, P.O. Box 56, Dunedin New Zealand. Fax: (643)479-8385. E-mail: landfall@otago.ac.nz. **Contact:** Fiction Editor.

Needs: Publishes fiction, poetry, commentary and reviews of New Zealand books.

How to Contact: Sample copy not available.

Advice: "We concentrate on publishing work by New Zealand writers, but occasionally accept work from elsewhere."

⬤ THE LAUREL REVIEW, Northwest Missouri State University, Dept. of English, Maryville MO 64468. (660)562-1739. E-mail: abenson@mail.nwmissouri.edu. **Contact:** Nancy Mayer, Rebeca Aaronsen, John Gallaher. Magazine: 6×9; 124-128 pages; good quality paper. "We publish poetry and fiction of high qulity, from the traditional to the avant-garde. We are eclectic, open and flexible. Good writing is all we seek." Biannual. Estab. 1960. Circ. 900.

Needs: Literary, contemporary. "No genre or politically polemical fiction." Receives 120 unsolicited mss/month. Accepts 3-5 mss/issue; 6-10 mss/year. Reading period: September 1-May 1. Publishes ms 1-12 months after acceptance. Agented fiction 1%. **Publishes 1-2 new writers/year.** Recently published work by Christine Sneed, Judith Kitchen and Joan Connor. Also publishes literary essays, poetry.

How to Contact: Responds in 4 months to mss. No simultaneous submissions. Sample copy for $5.

Payment/Terms: Pays 2 contributor's copies and 1 year subscription. Acquires first rights. Copyright reverts to author upon request.

Advice: "Nothing really matters to us except our perception that the story presents something powerfully felt by the writer and communicated intensely to a serious reader. (We believe, incidentally, that comedy is just as serious a matter as tragedy, and we don't mind a bit if something makes us laugh out loud; we get too little that makes us laugh, in fact.) We try to reply promptly, though we don't always manage that. In short, we want good poems and good stories. We hope to be able to recognize them, and we print what we believe to the best work submitted."

$⬤ ◎ LE FORUM, Supplement Littraire, Franco-American Research Opportunity Group, University of Maine, Franco American Center, Orono ME 04469-5719. (207)581-3764. Fax: (207)581-1455. E-mail: lisa_michaud

@umit.maine.edu. Website: www.francomaine.org. **Contact:** Lisa Michaud, managing editor. Tabloid size, magazine format: 36 pages; illustrations; photos. Publication was founded to stimulate and recognize creative expression among Franco-Americans, all types of readers, including literary and working class. This publication is used in classrooms. Circulated internationally. Quarterly. Estab. 1986. Circ. 5,000.

Needs: "We will consider any type of short fiction, poetry and critical essays having to with Franco-American experience. They must be of good quality in French or English. We are also looking for Canadian writers with French-North American experiences." Receives 10 unsolicited mss/month. Accepts 2-4 mss/issue. **Publishes some new writers/year.** Length: 750-2,500 words; average length: 1,000 words. Occasionally comments on rejected mss.

How to Contact: SASE. Responds in 3 weeks to queries; 1 month to mss. Accepts simultaneous and reprints submissions. Sample copy not available.

Payment/Terms: Pays 3 copies. Acquires one-time rights.

Advice: "Write honestly. Start with a strongly felt personal Franco-American experience. If you make us feel what you have felt, we will publish it. We stress that this publication deals specifically with the Franco-American experience."

○ **LEAPINGS LITERARY MAGAZINE**, P.O. Box 2510, Mendocino CA 95403. (707)937-4535. Fax: (707)937-3146. E-mail: editserv@compuserve.com. Website: home.inreach.com/editserv/leapings.html. **Contact:** Fiction Editor. Magazine: 5×8; 40 pages; 20 lb. paper; glossy cover; illustrations; photos. "Eclectic magazine emphasizing diversity." Semiannual. Estab. 1998. Circ. 200.

Needs: Adventure, ethnic/multicultural, experimental, fantasy, feminist, humor/satire, literary, mainstream, mystery/suspense, science fiction. "No romance." Receives 30 unsolicited mss/month. Accepts 2 mss/issue; 4 mss/year. Publishes ms 6 months after acceptance. Agented fiction 10%. **Publishes 5 new writers/year.** Recently published work by Frederick Zydek. Publishes short shorts. Also publishes literary essays, literary criticism, poetry. Sometimes comments on rejected mss.

How to Contact: Send SASE for reply, return of ms or send a disposable copy of ms. Responds in 8 weeks to mss. No simultaneous submissions. Sample copy for $5. Writer's guidelines for #10 SASE. Reviews fiction.

Payment/Terms: Pays 2 contributor's copies; additional copies $5. Pays on publication for first rights.

Advice: Looks for "good presentation and sound writing showing the writer has worked at his/her craft. Write and rewrite and only submit it when you've made the work as crisp and clear as possible."

Ⓝ ⬚ ⬚ **lichen, a literary journal**, 234-701 Rossland Road East, Whitby ON L1N 9K3 Canada. E-mail: info@lichenjournal.ca. Website: www.lichenjournal.ca. **Contact:** Ruth E. Walker and Gwynn Scheltema, fiction editors. Magazine: 5 1/4×8¼; 100 pages; 60 lb. white paper; card ⅔ with press varnish; illustrations; photos. "*lichen* publishes fiction, poetry, plays, essays, reviews, interviews, black & white art and photography by local, Canadian and international writers and artists. We present a unique mix of city and country, of innovation and tradition to a broad spectrum of readers." Semiannual. Estab. 1999. Circ. 500.

Needs: Experimental, fantasy (magic realism), feminist, gay, humor/satire, lesbian, literary. "No work that is obtuse, bigotted, banal, or hate-mongering. We will consider almost any genre or style if the work shows clarity and attention to craft." Receives 12-24 unsolicited mss/month. Accepts 5-8 mss/issue; 10-16 mss/year. Publishes ms 2-12 months after acceptance. **Publishes 4-7 new writers/year.** Recently published work by Nancy Holmes, Stan Rogal, J.J. Steinfeld, Brad Smith, George Elliott Clarke. Length: 250-3,000 words; average length: 1,000-2,500 words. Publishes short shorts. Also publishes literary essays, literary criticism, poetry. Sometimes comments on rejected mss.

How to Contact: Send complete ms. Accepts submissions by e-mail. Include estimated word count, brief bio and list of publications. Send SASE for return of ms or disposable copy of ms and #10 SASE for reply only. Responds in 1-4 weeks to queries; 3-6 months to mss. Sample copy for $10 (Canadian). Writer's guidelines online.

Payment/Terms: 1 contributor's copy and a 1-year subscription. Pays on publication for first North American serial rights.

Advice: "We look for exceptional writing that engages the reader, professional presentation in standard ms format, and an indication of knowledge of the type of writing we publish, as well as knowledge of our submission guidelines. Keep your cover letter brief, not cute."

○ **THE LICKING RIVER REVIEW**, University Center, Northern Kentucky University, Highland Heights KY 41099. (859)572-5812. E-mail: lrr@nku.edu. **Contact:** Andrew Miller, faculty advisor. Magazine: 7×11; 96 pages; photos. Annual. Estab. 1991. Circ. 1,500.

Needs: Experimental, literary, mainstream. "No erotica." Wants more experimental. Receives 40 unsolicited mss/month. Accepts 7-9 mss/year. Does not read mss December-August. Publishes ms 6 months after acceptance. **Publishes 2-3 new writers/year.** Recently published work by William Rushton, Richard Bentley, Michael Schafner, Mary Winters, Ronna Wineberg and Ryan Van Cleave. Publishes short shorts. Also publishes poetry.

How to Contact: Accepts submissions by e-mail. SASE for return of ms or send disposable copy of ms. Responds in 6 months to mss. No simultaneous submissions. Sample copy for $5.

Payment/Terms: Pays 2 contributor's copies. Pays on publication

Advice: "We look for good writing and an interesting, well-told story. Read a sample copy first. Don't do what everyone else is doing. Be fresh, orginal. Write what you like—it will show. Tell a story you care about and work on it every day until you love it before sending it out."

□ LIGHT QUARTERLY, P.O. Box 7500, Chicago IL 60680. Website: www.lightquarterly.com. **Contact:** Fiction editor. Magazine: 6×9; 64 pages; Finch opaque (60 lb.) paper; 65 lb. color cover; illustrations. Quarterly. Estab. 1992. Circ. 1,000.

Needs: Humor/satire, literary. Receives 10-40 unsolicited mss/month. Accepts 2-4 mss/issue. Publishes ms 6-24 months after acceptance. Recently published work by X.J. Kennedy, J.F. Nims and John Updike. Length: 600-2,000 words; average length: 1,200 words. Publishes short shorts. Also publishes literary essays, literary criticism, poetry. Sometimes comments on rejected mss.

How to Contact: Send SASE for reply, return of ms or send a disposable copy of ms. Responds in 1 month to queries; 4 months to mss. No simultaneous submissions. Sample copy for $6 (plus $2 for 1st class). Writer's guidelines for #10 SASE. Reviews fiction.

Payment/Terms: Pays contributor's copies (2 for domestic; 1 for foreign). Acquires first North American serial rights. Sends galleys to author.

Advice: Looks for "high literary quality; wit, allusiveness, a distinct (and distinctive) style. Read guidelines or issue first."

□ THE LISTENING EYE, Kent State University Geauga Campus, 14111 Claridon-Troy Rd., Burton OH 44021. (440)286-3840. E-mail: grace_butcher@msn.com. **Contact:** Grace Butcher, editor. Magazine: 5½×8½; 60 pages; photographs. "We publish the occasional very short story, in any subject and any style, but the language must be strong, unusual, free from cliché and vagueness. We are a shoestring operation from a small campus but we publish high-quality work." Annual. Estab. 1970. Circ. 250.

Needs: Literary. "Pretty much anything will be considered except porn." Accepts 1-2 mss/issue. Does not read mss April 15 through January 1. Publishes ms 3-4 months after acceptance. Recently published work by Lyn Lifshin. Publishes short shorts. Also publishes poetry. Sometimes comments on rejected mss.

How to Contact: Send SASE for return of ms or disposable copy of ms with SASE for reply only. Responds in 4 weeks to queries; 4 months to mss. Accepts reprints submissions. Sample copy for $3 and $1 postage. Writer's guidelines for SASE.

Payment/Terms: Pays 2 contributor's copies; additional copies $3 with $1 postage. Pays on publication for one-time rights.

Advice: "We look for powerful, unusual imagery, content and plot. Short, short."

$□ LITERAL LATTÉ, Mind Stimulating Stories, Poems & Essays, Word Sci, Inc., 61 E. Eighth St. Suite 240, New York NY 10003. (212)260-5532. E-mail: litlatte@aol.com. Website: www.literal-latte.com. **Contact:** Jeff Bockman, editor. Magazine: 11×17; 24 pages; newsprint paper; 50 lb. cover; illustrations; photos. "Publishes great writing in many flavors and styles. *Literal Latté* expands the readership for literary magazines by offering free copies in New York coffeehouses and bookstores." Bimonthly. Estab. 1994. Circ. 35,000. Member, CLMP.

Needs: Experimental, fantasy, literary, science fiction. Receives 4,000 unsolicited mss/month. Accepts 5-8 mss/issue; 40 mss/year. Agented fiction 5%. **Publishes 6 new writers/year.** Length: 500-6,000 words; average length: 4,000 words. Publishes short shorts. Often comments on rejected mss.

How to Contact: Send SASE for return of mss or send a disposable copy of ms and #10 SASE for reply only or e-mail for reply only. Responds in 6 months to mss. Accepts simultaneous, multiple submissions. Sample copy for $3. Writer's guidelines for SASE, e-mail or check website. Reviews fiction.

Payment/Terms: Pays 10 contributor's copies, a free subscrition to the magazine and 2 gift certificates; additional copies $1. Pays on publication for first, one-time rights. Sponsors awards/contests.

Advice: "Keeping free thought free and challenging entertainment are not mutually exclusive. Words make a manuscript stand out, words beautifully woven together in striking and memorable patterns."

□ ▼ THE LITERARY REVIEW, An International Journal of Contemporary Writing, Fairleigh Dickinson University, 285 Madison Ave., Madison NJ 07940. (973)443-8564. Fax: (973)443-8364. E-mail: tlr@fdu.edu. Website: www.theliteraryreview.org. **Contact:** René Steinke, editor-in-chief. Magazine: 6×9; 160 pages; professionally printed on textpaper; semigloss card cover; perfect-bound. "Literary magazine specializing in fiction, poetry, and essays with an international focus. Our audience is general with a leaning toward scholars, libraries and schools." Quarterly. Estab. 1957. Circ. 2,000.

● Work published in *The Literary Review* has been included in *Editor's Choice, Best American Short Stories* and *Pushcart Prize* anthologies. *The Literary Review* ranked on *Writer's Digest's* "Top 30" list of best markets for fiction writers.

Needs: Works of high literary quality only. Does not want to see "overused subject matter or pat resolutions to conflicts." Receives 90-100 unsolicited mss/month. Accepts 20-25 mss/year. Does not read submissions during June, July and August. Publishes ms 1½-2 years after acceptance. Agented fiction 1-2%. **Publishes 80% new writers/year.** Recently published work by Irvin Faust, Todd James Pierce, Joshua Shapiro and Susan Schwartz Senstadt. Also publishes literary essays, literary criticism, poetry. Occasionally comments on rejected mss.

How to Contact: Responds in 3-4 months to mss. Accepts multiple submissions. Sample copy for $7. Writer's guidelines for SASE. Reviews fiction.
Payment/Terms: Pays 2 contributor's copies; 25% discount for extras. Acquires first rights.
Advice: "We want original dramatic situations with complex moral and intellectual resonance and vivid prose. We don't want versions of familiar plots and relationships. Too much of what we are seeing today is openly derivative in subject, plot and prose style. We pride ourselves on spotting new writers with fresh insight and approach."

THE LONG STORY, 18 Eaton St., Lawrence MA 01843. (978)686-7638. E-mail: rpburnham@mac.com. Website: www.longstorymagazine.com. **Contact:** R.P. Burnham. Magazine: 5½×8½; 150-200 pages; 60 lb. cover stock; illustrations (b&w graphics). For serious, educated, literary people. Annual. Estab. 1983. Circ. 1,200.
Needs: Ethnic/multicultural, feminist, literary, contemporary. "No science fiction, adventure, romance, etc. We publish high literary quality of any kind, but especially look for stories that have difficulty getting published elsewhere—committed fiction, working class settings, left-wing themes, etc." Receives 30-40 unsolicited mss/month. Accepts 6-7 mss/issue. Publishes ms 3 months to 1 year after acceptance. **Publishes 50 % new writers/year.** Length: 8,000-20,000 words; average length: 8,000-12,000 words.
How to Contact: SASE. Responds in 2 months to mss. Accepts simultaneous submissions "but not wild about it." Sample copy for $6.
Payment/Terms: Pays 2 contributor's copies; $5 charge for extras. Acquires first rights.
Advice: "Read us first and make sure submitted material is the kind we're interested in. Send clear, legible manuscripts. We're not interested in commercial success; rather we want to provide a place for long stories, the most difficult literary form to publish in our country."

LOST AND FOUND TIMES, Luna Bisonte Prods, 137 Leland Ave., Columbus OH 43214. **Contact:** John M. Bennett, editor. Magazine: 5½×8½; 56 pages; good quality paper; good cover stock; illustrations; photos. Theme: experimental, avant-garde and folk literature, art. Published twice yearly. Estab. 1975. Circ. 300.
Needs: Experimental, literary, contemporary, prose poem. "No 'creative writing' workshop stories." The editor would like to see more short, extremely experimental pieces. Accepts 2 mss/issue. **Publishes some new writers/year.** Recently published work by Spryszak, Steve McComas, Willie Smith, Rupert Wondolowski, Al Ackerman. Publishes short shorts. Also publishes poetry.
How to Contact: Query with published clips. SASE. Responds in 1 week to queries; 2 weeks to mss. No simultaneous submissions. Sample copy for $7.
Payment/Terms: Pays 1 contributor's copy. Acquires Rights revert to authors rights.

LOUISIANA LITERATURE, A Review of Literature and Humanities, Southeastern Louisiana University, SLU 792, Hammond LA 70402. (504)549-5783. Fax: (504)549-5021. E-mail: ngerman@selu.edu. Website: www.selu.edu. **Contact:** Norman German, fiction editor. Magazine: 6¾×9¾; 150 pages; 70 lb. paper; card cover; illustrations. "Essays should be about Louisiana material; preference is given to fiction and poetry with Louisiana and Southern themes, but creative work can be set anywhere." Semiannual. Estab. 1984. Circ. 400 paid; 500-700 printed.
Needs: Literary, mainstream, regional. "No sloppy, ungrammatical manuscripts." Receives 100 unsolicited mss/month. Does not read mss June through July. Publishes ms 6-12 after acceptance. **Publishes 4 new writers/year.** Recently published work by Anthony Bukowski, Tim Parrish, Robert Phillips and Andrew Otis Haschemeyer. Length: 1,000-6,000 words; average length: 3,500 words. Also publishes literary essays, literary criticism, poetry. Sometimes comments on rejected mss.
How to Contact: SASE. Responds in 3 months to mss. Sample copy for $8. Reviews fiction.
Payment/Terms: Pays usually in contributor's copies. Acquires one-time rights.
Advice: "Cut out everything that is not a functioning part of the story. Make sure your manuscript is professionally presented. Use relevant specific detail in every scene. We love detail, local color, voice and craft. Any professional manuscript stands out."

THE LOUISVILLE REVIEW, College of Arts and Sciences, Spalding University, 851 S. Fourth St., Louisville KY 40203. (502)585-9911, ext. 2777. E-mail: louisvillereview@spalding.edu. Website: www.louisvillereview.org.

FOR EXPLANATIONS OF THESE SYMBOLS,
SEE THE INSIDE FRONT AND BACK COVERS OF THIS BOOK.

Contact: Sena Jeter Naslund, editor. Literary magazine. "We are a literary journal seeking original stories with fresh imagery and vivid language." Semiannual. Estab. 1976.

Needs: Literary. Receives 200+ unsolicited mss/month. Accepts 4-6 mss/issue; 8-12 mss/year. Publishes ms 6 months after acceptance. **Publishes 8-10 new writers/year.** Recently published work by Maura Stanto, Ursula Hegi, Silas House, Neela Vaswani, Jane Mayhall, Robin Lippincott, Jhumpa Lahiri. Publishes short shorts. Also publishes literary essays, poetry. Sometimes comments on rejected mss.

How to Contact: Send SASE for return of ms or send a disposable copy of ms and #10 SASE for reply only. Responds in 6 months to queries; 6 months to mss. Accepts multiple submissions. Sample copy not available.

Payment/Terms: Pays 2 contributor's copies.

LULLWATER REVIEW, Emerson University, P.O. Box 22036, Atlanta GA 30322. (404)727-6184. E-mail: gdriski@learnlink.emory.edu. Editor: Gwyneth Driskill. **Contact:** Hannah Morril, fiction editor. Magazine: 6×9; 100 pages; 60 lb. paper; photos. "*Lullwater Review* seeks submissions that are strong and original. We require no specific genre or subject." Semiannual. Estab. 1990. Circ. 2,000. Member, Council of Literary Magazines and Presses.

Needs: Adventure, condensed novels, ethnic/multicultural, experimental, fantasy, historical, humor/satire, mainstream, mystery/suspense, novel excerpts, religious/inspirational, science fiction, slice-of-life vignettes, suspense, western. "No romance or science fiction, please." Receives 75-115 unsolicited mss/month. Accepts 3-7 mss/issue; 6-14 mss/year. Does not read mss in June, July, August. Publishes ms 1-2 months after acceptance. **Publishes 25% new writers/year.** Recently published work by Greg Jenkins, Thomas Juvik, Jimmy Gleacher, Carla Vissers and Judith Sudnolt. Also publishes poetry.

How to Contact: Send complete ms. Accepts submissions by mail, e-mail (lullwaterreview@yahoo.com), phone. Responds in 1-3 months to queries; 3-6 months to mss. Accepts simultaneous submissions. Sample copy for $5. Writer's guidelines for #10 SASE.

Payment/Terms: Pays 3 contributor copies. Pays on publication for first North American serial rights. Sponsors awards/contests.

Advice: "We at the *Lullwater Review* look for clear cogent writing, strong character development and an engaging approach to the story in our fiction submissions. Stories with particularly strong voices and well-developed central themes are especially encouraged. Be sure that your manuscript is ready before mailing it off to us. Revise, revise, revise!"

$ LYNX EYE, ScribbleFest Literary Group, 542 Mitchell Dr., Los Osos CA 93402. (805)528-8146. Fax: (805)528-7676. **Contact:** Pam McCully. Magazine: 5½×8½; 120 pages; 60 lb. book paper; varied cover stock. "Each issue of *Lynx Eye* offers thoughtful and thought-provoking reading." Quarterly. Estab. 1994. Circ. 500.

Needs: Adventure, condensed novels, erotica, ethnic/multicultural, experimental, fantasy (science), feminist, gay, historical, horror, humor/satire, literary, mainstream, mystery/suspense, novel excerpts, romance, science fiction, serialized novels, translations, western. "No horror with gratuitous violence or YA stories." Receives 500 unsolicited mss/month. Accepts 30 mss/issue; 120 mss/year. Publishes ms 6 months after acceptance. **Publishes 30 new writers/year.** Recently published work by Anjali Banerjee, Jean Ryan, Karen Wendy Gilbert, Jack Random and Robert R. Gass. Length: 500-5,000 words; average length: 2,500 words. Also publishes literary essays, poetry.

How to Contact: Send complete ms. Accepts submissions by mail. Include name and address on page one; name on *all* other pages. Send SASE for reply, return of ms or send a disposable copy of ms. Responds in 3 weeks to queries; 4 months to mss. Accepts simultaneous, multiple submissions. Sample copy for $7.95. Writer's guidelines for #10 SASE.

Payment/Terms: Pays $10. Pays on acceptance for first North American serial rights.

Advice: "We consider any well-written manuscript. Characters who speak naturally and who act or are acted upon are greatly appreciated. Your high school English teacher was correct. Basics matter. Imaginative, interesting ideas are sabotaged by lack of good grammer, spelling and punctuation skills. Most submissions are contemporary/mainstream. We could use some variety. Please do not confuse confessional autobiographies with fiction."

THE MACGUFFIN, Schoolcraft College, Department of English, 18600 Haggerty Rd., Livonia MI 48152-2696. (734)462-4400, ext 5327. Fax: (734)462-4679. E-mail: macguffin@schoolcraft.edu. Website: www.macguffin.org. **Contact:** Elizabeth Kircos, fiction editor. Carol Was, poetry editor. Magazine: 6×9; 164+ pages; 60 lb. paper; 110 lb. cover; b&w illustrations; photos. "*The MacGuffin* is a literary magazine which publishes a range of material including poetry, creative nonfiction and fiction. Material ranges from traditional to experimental. We hope our periodical attracts a variety of people with many different interests." Biannual. Estab. 1984. Circ. 600.

Needs: Adventure, ethnic/multicultural, experimental, historical (general), humor/satire, literary, mainstream, translations, contemporary, prose poem. "No religious, inspirational, juvenile, romance, horror, pornography." Upcoming themes: "Humor." This will be published in July, 2004. We will consider works until May 1, 2004. Receives 35-50 unsolicited mss/month. Accepts 10-15 mss/issue; 30-50 mss/year. Does not read mss between July 1-August 15. Publishes ms 6 months to 2 years after acceptance. Agented fiction 10-15%. **Publishes 30 new writers/year.** Recently published work by Ruth Cash-Smith, Jason Schossler, and Jeff Vande Zande. Length: 100-5,000 words; average length: 2,000-2,500 words. Also publishes short shorts. Also publishes literary essays. Occasionally comments on rejected mss.

How to Contact: SASE. Responds in 4 months to mss. Sample copy for $7; current issue for $8. Writer's guidelines free.

Payment/Terms: Pays 2 contributor's copies. Acquires one-time rights.

Advice: "We want to give promising new fiction writers the opportunity to publish alongside recognized writers. Be persistent. If a story is rejected, try to send it somewhere else. When we reject a story, we may accept the next one you send us. When we make suggestions for a rewrite, we may accept the revision. There seems to be a great number of good authors of fiction, but there are far too few places for publication. However, this is changing. Make your characters come to life. Even the most ordinary people become fascinating if they live for your readers."

MAELSTROM, Hey Baby! Productions, HC # 1 Box 1624, Blakeslee PA 18610. E-mail: imaelstrom@aol.com. Website: www.geocities.com/~readmaelstrom.com. **Contact:** Christine L. Reed, editor. Magazine: 8½×7; 48 pages; full color photo cover; illustrations; photos. *Maelstrom* likes short fiction with a twist that engages the reader." Quarterly. Estab. 1997. Circ. 500.

Needs: Comics/graphic novels, experimental, horror (futuristic, psychological, supernatural), humor/satire, literary, flash fiction. Receives 30 unsolicited mss/month. Accepts 1-3 mss/issue; 15 mss/year. Publishes ms 6-12 months after acceptance. **Publishes 10 new writers/year.** Recently published work by Barbara Lefcowitz, Rob Hill and Grace Cavalieri. Length: 3,000 words; average length: 2,000 words. Publishes short shorts. Also publishes literary essays, poetry.

How to Contact: Send SASE for return of ms or send a disposable copy of ms and #10 SASE for reply only. Responds in 1 months to queries; 3-6 months to mss. Accepts simultaneous, multiple submissions. Sample copy for $4. Writer's guidelines for SASE by e-mail or on website. Reviews fiction.

Payment/Terms: Pays 1 contributor's copy; additional copies $4. Acquires one-time rights.

Advice: "We are looking for skill with language, dialogue and suspense. The story has to grab the reader in the first paragraph. Use natural language in your writing. Most work from begining writers seems stilted or choppy."

$ THE MALAHAT REVIEW, The University of Victoria, P.O. Box 1700, STN CSC, Victoria BC V8W 2Y2 Canada. (250)721-8524. Website: www.malahatreview.com. **Contact:** Marlene Cookshaw, editor. "We try to achieve a balance of views and styles in each issue. We strive for a mix of the best writing by both established and new writers." Quarterly. Estab. 1967. Circ. 1,000.

● *The Malahat Review* has received the National Magazine Award for poetry and fiction.

Needs: "General ficton and poetry." Accepts 3-4 mss/issue. Publishes ms 6 months after acceptance. **Publishes 4-5 new writers/year.** Recently published work by Niki Singh, Mark Anthony Jarman, Elizabeth Moret Ross, Andrew Pyper and Chris Fink.

How to Contact: Send complete ms. Accepts submissions by mail. "Enclose proper postage on the SASE (or send IRC)." Responds in 2 weeks to queries; 3 months to mss. No e-mail, previously published, or simultaneous submissions. Sample copy for $10 (US). Writer's guidelines online.

Payment/Terms: Pays $30/magazine page. Pays on acceptance for second serial (reprint) rights. first world rights

Advice: "We do encourage new writers to submit. Read the magazines you want to be published in, ask for their guidelines and follow them. Write for information on *Malahat*'s novella competitions."

MANGROVE, University of Miami's Literary Magazine, Americonsult, Attn: Zachary Hickman, University of Miami, Dept. of English, P.O. Box 248145, Coral Gables FL 33124-4632. (305)717-3300. Fax: (305)717-3500. E-mail: aaaprinter@aol.com. **Contact:** Zachary Hickman. Magazine: 120 pages. "Our goal at *Mangrove* is to publish the best work without discriminating with regard to theme, style or form. We publish a wide range of material." Annual. Estab. 1992. Circ. 250.

Needs: Ethnic/multicultural, literary, mainstream, regional, translations. Receives 10-20 unsolicited mss/month. Accepts 3-4 mss/issue. Publishes in May. Notifies writers of acceptance in May. Reads ms August-December. Recently published work by William Jackson and Orlando Ricardo Menes. Publishes short shorts. Also publishes poetry. Sometimes comments on rejected mss.

How to Contact: SASE for reply. Accepts simultaneous and reprints, multiple submissions. Sample copy for $6, SAE. Writer's guidelines for SASE.

Payment/Terms: Pays 3 contributor's copies. Acquires one-time rights.

Advice: "We look for stories with a distinct voice that make us look at the whole world in a different way. Send only one story at a time and send us your best."

$ MANOA, A Pacific Journal of International Writing, English Dept., University of Hawaii, Honolulu HI 96822. (808)956-3070. Fax: (808)956-3083. Website: www2.hawaii.edu/mjournal. Editor: Frank Stewart. Magazine: 7×10; 240 pages. "High quality literary fiction, poetry, essays, personal narrative, reviews. About half of each issue devoted to U.S. writing, and half new work from Pacific and Asian nations. Our audience is primarily in the U.S., although expanding in Pacific countries. U.S. writing need not be confined to Pacific settings or subjects." Semiannual. Estab. 1989. Circ. 2,500.

● *Manoa* has received numerous awards, and work published in the magazine has been selected for prize anthologies.

Needs: Literary, mainstream, translations (from US and nations in or bordering on the Pacific), contemporary,

Guideposts.

Everything We Do Is Ministry
39 Seminary Hill Road
Carmel, NY 10512

www.GuidepostsMinistries.org

A Good Creed

*If any little
word of ours
can make one life
the brighter;*

*If any song of ours
can make one heart
the lighter;*

*God help us speak
that little word,
and take our
bit of singing;*

*And drop it in
some lonely vale –
to set the echoes ringing.*

– Author unknown

excerpted novel. No Pacific exotica. Accepts 1-2 mss/issue; 2-4 mss/year. Agented fiction 10%. **Publishes 1-2 new writers/year.** Recently published work by Ha Jin, Catherine Ryan Hyde, Samrat Upadhyay and Josip Novakovich. Also publishes poetry.

How to Contact: Send complete ms. SASE. Does not accept submissions by e-mail. Responds in 3 weeks to queries; 1 month to poetry mss; 6 months to fiction to mss. Accepts simultaneous submissions. Sample copy for $10 (US). Writer's guidelines online. Reviews fiction.

Payment/Terms: Pays $100-500 normally ($25/printed page). Pays on publication for first North American serial rights. Non-exclusive and one-time print rights. Sends galleys to author.

MANY MOUNTAINS MOVING, a literary journal of diverse contemporary voices, 420 22nd St., Boulder CO 80302-7909. (303)545-9942. Fax: (303)444-6510. E-mail: mmm@mmminc.org. Website: www.mm minc.org. **Contact:** Naom Horii, editor. Magazine: 6×8 3/4; 300 pages; recycled paper; color/heavy cover; illustrations; photos. "We publish fiction, poetry, general-interest essays and art. We try to seek contributors from all cultures." Semiannual. Estab. 1994. Circ. 2,500.

• Work from *Many Mountains Moving* has been reprinted in *Pushcart* anthology and *Best American Poetry*.
See the interview with *Many Mountains Moving* editor Naomi Horii on page 222.

Needs: Ethnic/multicultural, experimental, feminist, gay, historical, humor/satire, lesbian, literary, mainstream, translations. "No genre fiction. Plans special fiction issue or anthology." Receives 400 unsolicited mss/month. Accepts 4-6 mss/issue; 12-18 mss/year. Publishes ms 2-8 months after acceptance. Agented fiction 1%. **Publishes some new writers/year.** Recently published work by Stephen Dobyns, Steven Huff, Rahna Reiko Rizzuto and Matthew Chacko. Publishes short shorts. Also publishes literary essays, poetry. Sometimes comments on rejected mss.

How to Contact: Send SASE for reply, return of ms or send a disposable copy of ms. Responds in 2 weeks to queries; 3 months to mss. Accepts simultaneous submissions. Sample copy for $6.50 and enough IRCs for 1 pound of airmail/printed matter. Writer's guidelines for #10 SASE.

Payment/Terms: Pays 2 contributor's copies; additional copies $3. Acquires first North American serial rights. Sends galleys to author "if requested." Sponsors awards/contests.

Advice: "We look for top-quality fiction with fresh voices and verve. We would like to see more humorous literary stories. Read at least one issue of our journal to get a feel for what kind of fiction we generally publish."

THE MARLBORO REVIEW, The Marlboro Review Inc., P.O. Box 243, Marlboro VT 05344-0243. (802)254-4938. E-mail: marlboro@marlbororeview.com. Website: www.marlbororeview.com. **Contact:** Helen Fremont, fiction editor. Magazine: 6×9; 80-120 pages; 60 lb. paper; photos. "We are interested in cultural, philosophical, scientific and literary issues. Approached from a writer's sensibility. Our only criterion for publication is strength of work." Semiannual. Estab. 1996. Circ. 300. CLMP, AWP.

• Works published in *The Marlboro Review* have received Pushcart Prizes.

Needs: Literary, translations. Receives 150 unsolicited mss/month. Accepts 2-3 mss/issue; 4-6 mss/year. "Accepts manuscripts September through May." Publishes ms 1 year after acceptance. Recently published work by Stephen Dobyns, Jean Valentine, Brenda Hillman, Chana Bloch, William Matthews and Alberto Rios. Length: 500-12,000 words; average length: 7,000 words. Publishes short shorts. Also publishes literary essays, literary criticism, poetry.

How to Contact: Send SASE for return of ms or send a disposable copy of ms and #10 SASE for reply only. No summer or e-mail submissions. Responds in 3 months to queries; 4 months to mss. Accepts simultaneous, multiple submissions. Sample copy for $8.75. Writer's guidelines for SASE or on website. Reviews fiction.

Payment/Terms: Pays 2 contributor's copies; additional copies $5. All rights revert to author on publication. Sends galleys to author.

Advice: "We're looking for work with a strong voice and sense of control. Do your apprenticeship first. The minimalist impulse seems to be passing and for that we are grateful. We love to see great, sprawling, musical, chance-taking fiction. *The God of Small Things* is the favorite of more than one editor here."

$ THE MASSACHUSETTS REVIEW, South College, University of Massachusetts, Amherst MA 01003-9934. (413)545-2689. Fax: (413)577-0740. Website: www.massreview.org. **Contact:** Fiction Editor. Magazine: 6×9; 172 pages; 52 lb. paper; 65 lb. vellum cover; illustrations; photos. Quarterly. Estab. 1959. Circ. 1,200.

• Stories from the *Massachusetts Review* has been anthologized in the *100 Best American Short Stories of the Century* and the *Pushcart Prize* anthology.

Needs: Short stories. Wants more prose less than 30 pages. Does not read fiction mss June 1—October 1. Publishes ms 18 months after acceptance. Agented fiction Approximately 5%. **Publishes 3-5 new writers/year.** Recently published work by Ahdaf Soueif, Elizabeth Denton and Nicholas Montemarano. Also publishes poetry. Sometimes comments on rejected mss.

How to Contact: Send complete ms. Accepts submissions by mail. No returned ms without SASE. Responds in 3 months to mss. Accepts simultaneous, multiple submissions. Sample copy for $7. Writer's guidelines online.

Payment/Terms: Pays $50. Pays on publication for first North American serial rights.

Advice: "Shorter rather than longer stories preferred (up to 28-30 pages)." Looks for works that "stop us in our tracks." Manuscripts that stand out use "unexpected language, idiosyncrasy of outlook and are the opposite of ordinary."

insider report

Many Mountains Moving: Much-needed space for writers

Naomi Horii

Photo © Edge Talent Management

Writer and editor Naomi Horii created the literary journal *Many Mountains Moving* as a labor of love. In so doing, Horii combined her passion for literature with one of her life's missions—promoting appreciation and understanding of diverse cultures by providing a much-needed literary space for writers of diverse backgrounds. But *Many Mountains Moving*, which has been called "fantastic through and through" by the *Bloomsbury Review*, transcends the boundaries of a print journal. The organization has grown into a literary community, including a monthly literature salon, readings, and an annual fiction contest, in addition to the journal.

Work from *Many Mountains Moving* has been reprinted in the prestigious *Best American Short Stories* and *Pushcart Prize* anthologies. Contributors include world-renown talents such as Isabel Allende, Amiri Baraka, Lorna Dee Cervantes, Allen Ginsberg, Ursula K. Le Guin, Lawson Fusao Inada, James Tipton, and Luis Alberto Urrea, as well as many exceptional new and emerging talents.

A writer in addition to her position as editor-in-chief, Horii understands the challenges of finding validation and publication opportunities. Of her reaction to receiving the Colorado Council on the Arts Fellowship in Fiction and the Rocky Mountain Women's Institute Fellowship in Fiction, she says: "These fellowships made a world of difference to me. I remember getting the notification from the Colorado Council on the Arts about my fellowship. I kept staring at it, thinking perhaps the letter was saying that I was being given the fellowship, but perhaps not. But I couldn't believe my eyes. I thought maybe I was delusional because I wanted it so desperately. Then finally the realization sank in.

"My dog Nina was home with me and I said to her, 'Nina, I'm a *writer*.' That's the first time I really felt I really had what it took to be a writer, that I was indeed a writer."

That validation, she says, inspired her to make time for her writing—"even a little time, no matter how many other things I had to do."

Here, Horii shares her advice for writers struggling for that validation, and discusses what she looks for in fiction published in *Many Mountains Moving*.

How are stories selected for publication in *Many Mountains Moving*?
We accept submissions from May through September. Any submissions received at any other time will be returned unread. We get thousands of manuscripts coming in, and our process is the very old-fashioned one of painstakingly going through each one. Probably ninety percent of the manuscripts we send back within a couple weeks. The other ten percent is read by a couple people, sometimes agonized over, then eventually passed to the appropriate editor for the final decision.

How has your position as editor-in-chief affected your personal writing, and conversely, how do your experiences as a writer impact your editorial decisions?

Well, my position as editor-in-chief has affected my writing by taking all of my time. I work nights, weekends, holidays—and there's always more to do. That doesn't leave much time to write. But if I did have time to write, I think it would help me dissect my own work in a way that would make it stronger. My experiences as a writer shape some of our policies; for example, we accept simultaneous submissions with notification of such with the provision that the author must notify us immediately if their work is accepted elsewhere. As a writer, I think it's a bit too much to refuse simultaneous submissions—that is, unless the publication has a big enough staff that they can respond fairly quickly to each submission. Which very few publications do.

What advice can you give writers intimidated about having their work compared to stories written by well-known authors?

Think about the fact that those well-known authors became well-known by starting out, sending their work as new writers to publications with well-known authors. Everyone has to start somewhere. Also, even the best writers don't always create the best work—they usually just keep at it longer and more consistently.

In your opinion, what's the most important element of a successful short story?

Personally, I'm big on a believable voice that draws me in and makes me want to read and care about what's happening to the characters.

What is the most common mistake you see in stories submitted to *Many Mountains Moving*?

One common problem is stories that really want to be novels but aren't—where there's too much digression and branching off not relevant to the story.

Can you tell us about *Many Mountains Moving*'s annual contest?

We'd been doing a literary awards program in the past, but we are moving to a book contest. We had our first book contest deadline for poetry last year, judged by the very exceptional poet Thom Ward. We will have our first book contest for fiction this year.

What is your vision for *Many Mountain's Moving*'s future?

We're actually in the process of revamping and relaunching as more of a hybrid between a literary journal and a commercial magazine. We're still going to have the same quality of fiction, essays, and poetry, but are going to add features like a political column, a humor column, and magazine-like feature stories.

Is there any piece of advice you've always wanted to share with authors who submit to your journal?

Keep trying, if you've read the journal and feel your work may fit our editorial tastes. People have submitted numerous times and we've had to reject the manuscripts, but then something from that same person will come along that we just can't live without.

—*Denise Meyers*

⬛ ◎ **MATRIARCH'S WAY, Journal of Female Supremacy**, Artemis Creations Publishing, 100 Chatham E, West Palm Beach FL 33417. (718)648-8215. E-mail: artemispub@sysmatrix.net. Website: www.artemiscreations. com. **Contact:** Fiction editor. Magazine: e-book format; illustrations; photos. *Matriarch's Way* is a "matriarchal feminist" publication. Biannual. Estab. 1996.

Needs: Condensed novels, erotica (quality), ethnic/multicultural, experimental, fantasy (science, sword and sorcery), feminist (radical), horror, humor/satire, literary, psychic/supernatural/occult, religious/inspirational (pagan), romance (futuristic/time travel, gothic, historical), science fiction (soft/sociological), serialized novels. "No Christian anything." Want more "femme dominant erotica and sci-fi." Upcoming themes: "Science of Matriachy" and "What it Means to be a Female 'Other.'" Receives 40 unsolicited mss/month. **Publishes 50% new writers/year.** Often comments on rejected mss.

How to Contact: Accepts submissions by e-mail (and disk.). SASE for reply or send a disposable copy of ms. Responds in 1 week to queries; 6 weeks to mss. Sample copy for $10. Reviews fiction.

Payment/Terms: Acquires one-time rights.

Advice: Looks for "a knowledge of subject, originality and good writing style. If you can best Camille Paglia, you're on your way!" Looks for "professional writing—equates with our purpose/vision—brave and outspoken."

⬛ **MEDICINAL PURPOSES, Literary Review**, Poet to Poet Inc., 86-37 120 St. #2D, c/o Catterson, Richmond Hill NY 11418. (718)847-2150. Fax: (718)847-2150. **Contact:** Thomas M. Catterson, managing editor; Anthony Scarpantonio, prose editor. Magazine: 8½×11; 40 pages; illustrations. "*Medicinal Purposes* publishes quality work that will benefit the world, though not necessarily through obvious means." Semiannual. Estab. 1995. Circ. 1,000.

Needs: Adventure, erotica, ethnic/multicultural, experimental, fantasy, feminist, gay, historical, horror, humor/satire, lesbian, literary, mainstream, mystery/suspense, psychic/supernatural/occult, regional, romance, science fiction, western, young adult/teen, senior citizen/retirement, sports. "Please no pornography, or hatemongering." Receives 15 unsolicited mss/month. Accepts 2-3 mss/issue; 8 mss/year. Publishes ms 4 months after acceptance. **Publishes 24 new writers/year.** Recently published work by Charles E. Brooks and Bernadette Miller. Length: 50-3,000 words; average length: 2,000 words. Publishes short shorts. Also publishes literary essays, poetry. Sometimes comments on rejected mss.

How to Contact: SASE. Responds in 6 weeks to queries; 8 weeks to mss. Sample copy for $9, 6×9 SAE and 4 first-class stamps. Writer's guidelines for #10 SASE.

Payment/Terms: Pays 2 contributor's copies. Acquires first rights.

Advice: "Writers should know how to write. This occurs less often than you expect. Try to be entertaining, and write a story that was worth the effort in the first place. Read guidelines first!"

$ ⬛ ◎ ⬛ **MERLYN'S PEN, Fiction, Essays and Poems by America's Teens**, Merlyn's Pen Inc., 4 King St., East Greenwich RI 02818. (401)885-5175. Fax: (401)885-5199. Website: www.merlynspen.org. **Contact:** R. Jim Stahl, publisher. Magazine: 8⅜×10⅞; 100 pages; 70 lb. paper; 12 pt. glossy cover; illustrations; photos. "We publish fiction, essays and poems by America's teen writers, age 11-19 exclusively." Published each November. Estab. 1985. Circ. 5,000.

• Winner of the Paul A. Witty Short Story Award and Selection on the New York Public Library's Book List of Recommended Reading. *Merlyn's Pen* has also received a Parent's Choice Gold Award.

Needs: Adventure, experimental, fantasy, historical, horror, humor/satire, literary, mainstream, mystery/suspense, romance, science fiction, slice-of-life vignettes, suspense, western, young adult/teen, one-act plays and dramatic monologue. "Would like to see more humor." Must be written by students in grades 6-12. Receives 1,200 unsolicited mss/month. Accepts 50 mss/issue; 50 mss/year. Publishes ms 6 months after acceptance. **Publishes 50 new writers/ year.** Length: 100-5,000 words; average length: 1,500 words. Publishes short shorts. Also publishes poetry. Sometimes comments on rejected mss.

How to Contact: Send complete ms. Send for cover-sheet template. Submissions via website only. Responds in 3 months to queries; 3 months to mss. Accepts multiple submissions. Sample articles and writer's guidelines available on website.

Payment/Terms: Pays $20-250. Pays on publication for all rights.

Advice: "Write what you *know*; write where you are. We look for authentic voice and experience of young adults."

Ⓝ ⬛ **METAL SCRATCHES**, 9251 Lake Drive NE, Forest Lake MN 55025. (651)982-1512. E-mail: metalscratc hes@aol.com. **Contact:** Kim Mark, editor. Magazine: 5½×8½; 35 pages; heavy cover-stock. "*Metal Scratches* focuses on literary fiction that examines the dark side of humanity. We are not looking for anything that is 'cute' or 'sweet'." Semiannual. Estab. 2000.

Needs: Erotica, experimental, horror (psychological), literary. "No poetry or horror as in gore." Receives 5 unsolicited mss/month. Accepts 6-8 mss/issue; 20 mss/year. Publishes ms 6 months after acceptance. **Publishes 3 new writers/year.** Length: 3,500 words; average length: 2,500 words. Publishes short shorts. Sometimes comments on rejected mss.

How to Contact: Send complete ms. Accepts submissions by e-mail. Send disposable copy of the ms and #10 SASE for reply only. Responds in 2 months to mss. Accepts simultaneous, multiple submissions. Sample copy for $4. Writer's guidelines for SASE or by e-mail.

Payment/Terms: Pays 2 contributor's copies; additional copies for $2.50. Pays on publication for one-time rights. Not copyrighted.

Advice: "Clean manuscripts prepared according to guidelines are a must. Send us something new and inventive. Don't let rejections scare you. Keep writing and keep submitting."

$ ▨ **MICHIGAN QUARTERLY REVIEW**, 3574 Rackham Bldg., 915 E. Washington, University of Michigan, Ann Arbor MI 48109-1070. (734)764-9265. Website: www.umich.edu/~mqr. **Contact:** Fiction Editor. "An interdisciplinary journal which publishes mainly essays and reviews, with some high-quality fiction and poetry, for an intellectual, widely read audience." Quarterly. Estab. 1962. Circ. 1,500.

• Stories from *Michigan Quarterly Review* have been selected for inclusion in *The Best American Short Stories*, *O. Henry* and *Pushcart Prize* volumes.

Needs: Literary. "No genre fiction written for a market. Would like to see more fiction about social, political, cultural matters, not just centered on a love relationship or dysfunctional family." Receives 200 unsolicited mss/month. Accepts 2 mss/issue; 8 mss/year. Publishes ms 1 year after acceptance. **Publishes 1-2 new writers/year.** Recently published work by Nicholas Delbanco, Elizabeth Searle, Marian Thurm and Lucy Ferriss. Length: 1,500-7,000 words; average length: 5,000 words. Also publishes literary essays, poetry.

How to Contact: Send complete ms. Accepts submissions by mail. "I like to know if a writer is at the beginning, or further along, in his or her career. Don't offer plot summaries of the story, though a background comment is welcome." SASE. Responds in 2 months to queries; 2 months to mss. No simultaneous submissions. Sample copy for $4. Writer's guidelines online.

Payment/Terms: Pays $10/published page. Pays on publication. Buys first serial rights. Sponsors awards/contests.

Advice: "There's no beating a good plot and interesting characters, and a fresh use of the English language. (Most stories fail because they're written in such a bland manner, or in TV-speak.) Be ambitious, try to involve the social world in the personal one, be aware of what the best writing of today is doing, don't be satisfied with a small slice of life narrative but think how to go beyond the ordinary."

$ ▨ ▨ **MID-AMERICAN REVIEW**, Department of English, Bowling Green State University, Bowling Green OH 43403. (419)372-2725. Fax: (419)372-6805. Website: www.bgsu.edu/midamericanreview. **Contact:** Michael Czyzniejewski, fiction editor. Magazine: 6×9; 192 pages; 60 lb. bond paper; coated cover stock. "We try to put the best possible work in front of the biggest possible audience. We publish serious fiction and poetry, as well as critical studies in contemporary literature, translations and book reviews." Semiannual. Estab. 1981.

• Work published in *Mid-American Review* has received the Pushcart Prize.

Needs: Experimental, literary, translations, memoir, prose poem, traditional. "No genre fiction. Would like to see more short shorts." Receives 500 unsolicited mss/month. Accepts 6-8 mss/issue. Publishes ms 6 months after acceptance. Agented fiction Approximately 5%. **Publishes 4-8 new writers/year.** Recently published work by Dan Chaon, Anthony Doer, and Robert Olmstead. Also publishes literary essays, poetry. Occasionally comments on rejected mss.

How to Contact: Accepts submissions by mail, phone. Send complete ms with SASE. Responds in 4 months to mss. Sample copy for $7 (current issue), $5 (back issue); rare back issues $10. Writer's guidelines online. Reviews fiction.

Payment/Terms: Pays $10/page up to $50, pending funding. Pays on publication when funding is available. Acquires first North American serial, one-time rights. Sponsors awards/contests.

Advice: "We look for well-written stories that make the reader want to read on past the first line and page. Clichéd themes and sloppy writing turn us off immediately. Read literary journals to see what's being published in today's market. We tend to publish work that is more non-traditional in style and form, but are open to all literary non-genre submissions."

▢ ▨ **MINDPRINTS, A Literary Journal**, Learning Assistance Program, Allan Hancock College, 800 S. College Dr., Santa Maria CA 93454-6399. (805)922-6966, ext. 3274. Fax: (805)922-3556. E-mail: pafahey@hancock.cc .ca.us. Website: www.hancock.cc.ca.us/studentsservices/learning_assistance/mindprints. **Contact:** Paul Fahey, editor. Magazine: 6×9; 125-150 pages; 50 lb. white offset paper; glossy cover; illustrations; photos. "*Mindprints, A Literary Journal* is one of a very few college publications created as a forum for writers and artists with disabilities or for those with an interest in the field. The emphasis on flash fiction and the fact that we are a national journal as well puts us on the cutting edge of today's market." Annual. Estab. 2000. Circ. 800.

• *Mindprints* ranked on *Writer's Digest* "Top 30" list of best fiction markets.

Needs: Literary, mainstream. Receives 20-30 unsolicited mss/month. Accepts 60 mss/year. Does not read mss June-August. Publishes ms 6 months after acceptance. **Publishes 25-30 new writers/year.** Recently published work by Tom Law, Pamelyn Casto Ingrid Reti, and Roger Paris. Length: 250-750 words; average length: 500 words. Publishes short shorts. Also publishes poetry. Often comments on rejected mss.

How to Contact: Send a disposable copy of ms and #10 SASE for reply only. Responds in 1 week to queries; 4 months to mss. Accepts simultaneous and reprints, multiple submissions. Sample copy for $6 and $2 postage or IRCs. Writer's guidelines for SASE, by e-mail or fax.

Payment/Terms: Pays 1 contributor's copy; additional copies $5. Pays on publication for one-time rights. Not copyrighted.

Advice: "We look for a great hook; a story that grabs us from the beginning; fiction and memoir with a strong voice and unusual themes; stories with a narrowness of focus yet broad in their appeal. We would like to see more flash or very short fiction. Read and study the flash fiction genre. *Flash Fiction* by Thomas, Thomas and Hazuka is highly recommended. Revise, revise, revise. Do not send manuscripts that have not been proofed. Our mission is to showcase as many voices and world views as possible. We want our readers to sample creative talent from a national and international group of published and unpublished writers and artists."

THE MINNESOTA REVIEW, A Journal of Committed Writing, Dept. of English, University of Missouri, Columbia MO 65211. (573)882-3059. Fax: (573)882-5785. E-mail: WilliamsJeff@missouri.edu. Website: http://theminnesotareview.org. **Contact:** Jeffrey Williams, editor. Magazine: 5¼×7½; approximately 200 pages; some illustrations; occasional photos. "We emphasize socially and politically engaged work." Semiannual. Estab. 1960. Circ. 1,500.
Needs: Experimental, feminist, gay, historical, lesbian, literary. Receives 50-75 unsolicited mss/month. Accepts 3-4 mss/issue; 6-8 mss/year. Publishes ms 6-12 months after acceptance. **Publishes 3-5 new writers/year.** Recently published work by E. Shaskan Bumas, Carlos Fuentes, Maggie Jaffe and James Hughes. Publishes short shorts. Also publishes literary essays, literary criticism, poetry. Occasionally comments on rejected mss.
How to Contact: SASE. Responds in 3 weeks to queries; 3 months to mss. Accepts simultaneous, multiple submissions. Sample copy for $12. Reviews fiction.
Payment/Terms: Pays in contributor's copies. Charge for additional copies. Acquires first rights.
Advice: "We look for socially and politically engaged work, particularly short, striking work that stretches boundaries."

MISSISSIPPI REVIEW, University of Southern Mississippi, Box 5144, Hattiesburg MS 39406-5144. (601)266-4321. Fax: (601)266-5757. E-mail: rief@netdoor.com. Website: www.mississippireview.com. **Contact:** Rie Fortenberry, managing editor. "Literary publication for those interested in contemporary literature—writers, editors who read to be in touch with current modes." Semiannual. Estab. 1972. Circ. 1,500.
Needs: Experimental, fantasy, humor/satire, literary, translations, contemporary, avant-garde and "art" fiction. "No juvenile or genre fiction." Quality writing. Theme issues for the print edition are solicited; theme issues for the web version are listed on the site and are open to unsolicited submissions. Buys varied amount of mss/issue. Does not read mss in summer. **Publishes 10-20 new writers/year.** Recently published work by Jason Brown, Terese Svoboda and Barry Hannag.
How to Contact: Send submissions as ASCII files int the text of your e-mail message, or as Microsoft Word or WordPerfect attachments to your message. Sample copy for $8.
Payment/Terms: Acquires first North American serial rights.

$ THE MISSOURI REVIEW, 1507 Hillcrest Hall, University of Missouri, Columbia MO 65211. (573)882-4474. Fax: (573)884-4671. Website: www.missourireview.com. **Contact:** Speer Morgan, editor. Magazine: 6×9; 212 pages. "We publish contemporary fiction, poetry, interviews, personal essays, cartoons, special features—such as 'History as Literature' series and 'Found Text' series—for the literary and the general reader interested in a wide range of subjects." Estab. 1978. Circ. 5,500.
● This magazine had stories anthologized in the *Pushcart Prize Anthology*, *Best American Short Stories*, *O. Henry Awards*, *Best American Essays*, *Best American Erotica*, and *New Stories From the South*.
Needs: Condensed novels, ethnic/multicultural, humor/satire, literary, mainstream, novel excerpts, literary. No genre fiction. Receives 400 unsolicited mss/month. Accepts 5-7 mss/issue; 16-20 mss/year. **Publishes 6-10 new writers/year.** Recently published work by Judy Troy, Willa Rabinowitz, Jesse Lee Kercheval and Michael Byers. Also publishes literary essays, poetry. Often comments on rejected mss.
How to Contact: Send complete ms. Accepts submissions by mail. May include brief bio and list of publications. Send SASE for reply, return of ms or send disposable copy of ms. International submissions via web site. Responds in 2 weeks to queries; 3 months to mss. Sample copy for $8 or online. Writer's guidelines online.
Payment/Terms: Pays $30/printed page up to $750. Offers signed contract. Sponsors awards/contests.

MM REVIEW, Finishing Line Press, P.O. Box 1016, Cincinnati OH 45201-1016. E-mail: finishingl@aol.com. Website: members.aol.com/finishingl. **Contact:** Elle Larkin. Magazine: 6×9; 35 pages; cotton paper; linen or cotton cover. "We are a literay magazine interested in publishing serious verse and excellent fiction, drama and essays." Semiannual. Estab. 1998. Circ. 500.
Needs: Literary. "No children's/juvenile or young adult/teen. No erotica." Receives 50 unsolicited mss/month. Accepts 1-4 mss/issue; 2-8 mss/year. Publishes ms 6 months after acceptance. **Publishes 20% new writers/year.**

SENDING TO A COUNTRY other than your own? Be sure to send International Reply Coupons (IRC) instead of stamps for replies or return of your manuscript.

Recently published work by Alexandra Grilikhes, Rane Arroyo, Leah Maines, Tanya Preminger and Irene Sedeora. Average length: 500-700 words. Publishes short shorts. Also publishes literary essays, poetry. Often comments on rejected mss.

How to Contact: Responds in 1 month to queries; 6 months to mss. Sample copy not available. Reviews fiction.

Payment/Terms: Pays 1 contributor's copy; additional copies $4. Pays on publication for one-time rights. "Rights revert back to authors after publication." Sends galleys to author.

Advice: "Excellence is our only criteria. We enjoy 'pushing the envelope' and are interested in experimental and cutting edge writing. We do not want 'grandma stories.' Send a clean manuscript free of typos, spelling/grammar errors and/or coffee stains! Please do not send long bios listing every place you have been published since high school plus your cat's name! No 'cute' cover letters. Writing is a business."

MOBIUS, The Journal of Social Change, 505 Christianson, Madison WI 53714. (608)242-1009. E-mail: fmschep@charter.net. Website: www.mobiusmagazine.com. **Contact:** Fred Schepartz, editor. Magazine: 8½×11; 16-24 pages; 60 lb. paper; 60 lb. cover. "Looking for fiction which uses social change as either a primary or secondary theme. This is broader than most people think. Need social relevance in one way or another. For an artistically and politically aware and curious audience." Quarterly. Estab. 1989. Circ. 1,500.

Needs: Ethnic/multicultural, experimental, fantasy, feminist, gay, historical, horror, humor/satire, lesbian, literary, mainstream, science fiction, contemporary, prose poem. "No porn, no racist, sexist or any other kind of ist. No Christian or spirituality proselytizing fiction." Wants to see more science fiction, erotica "assuming it relates to social change." Receives 15 unsolicited mss/month. Accepts 3-5 mss/issue. Publishes ms 3-9 months after acceptance. **Publishes 10 new writers/year.** Recently published work by Margaret Karmazin and Ken Byrnes. Length: 500-5,000 words; average length: 3,500 words. Publishes short shorts. Always comments on rejected mss.

How to Contact: SASE. Responds in 4 months to mss. Accepts simultaneous and reprints, multiple submissions. Sample copy for $2, 9×12 SAE and 3 first class stamps. Writer's guidelines for SASE. "Please include return postage, not IRCs, in overseas submissions."

Payment/Terms: Pays contributor's copies. Acquires one-time, electronic rights for web version.

Advice: "Note that fiction and poetry may be simultaneously published in e-version of *Mobius*. Due to space constraints of print version, some works may be accepted in e-version, but not print version. We like high impact, we like plot and character-driven stories that function like theater of the mind." Looks for "first and foremost, good writing. Prose must be crisp and polished; the story must pique my interest and make me care due to a certain intellectual, emotional aspect. Second, *Mobius* is about social change. We want stories that make some statement about the society we live in, either on a macro or micro level. Not that your story neeeds to preach from a soapbox (actually, we prefer that it doesn't), but your story needs to have *something* to say."

$☑ MOTA, An Annual Anthology of Fine Fiction, Triple Tree Publishing, P.O. Box 5684, Eugene OR 97405. (541)338-3184. Fax: (541)484-5358. E-mail: submit@tripletreepub.com. Website: www.tripletreepub.com. **Contact:** Editor. Magazine: 5½×8½; 300 pages; 60 lb. paper. "It is our intention to publish an extraordinary annual anthology of fiction, devoted to the challenging issues of our times as played out in fictional scenarios." Annual. Estab. 2002.

Needs: Adventure, erotica, ethnic/multicultural, experimental, family saga, fantasy, feminist, gay, historical, horror, humor/satire, lesbian, literary, mainstream, military/war, mystery/suspense, New Age, psychic/supernatural/occult, religious/inspirational, romance, science fiction, thriller/espionage, translations, western. Upcoming themes: Integrity (2004); Honesty (2005). Receives 30 unsolicited mss/month. Accepts 20 mss/year. **Publishes 10% new writers/year.** Length: 6,000 words; average length: 3,000 words. Publishes short shorts.

How to Contact: Send disposable copy of ms and SASE for reply only. Publishes every September. Deadline November 1 each year. Responds to queries/mss in December (after deadline) to queries. Accepts simultaneous, multiple submissions. Sample copy for $16.95 and postage. Writer's guidelines for SASE and on website.

Payment/Terms: Pays $100 and 1 contributor's copy. Pays on publication for one-time rights. Sends galleys to author.

Advice: "Be original—remember, your strength is your strangeness. Submit only your absolute best. Competition is stiff."

Ⓝ ◎ THE MUSING PLACE, The Literary & Arts Magazine of Chicago's Mental Health Community, The Thresholds, 2700 N. Lakeview, Chicago IL 60614. (773)281-3800, ext. 2465. Fax: (773)281-8790. **Contact:** Tim Collins, editor. Magazine: 8½×11; 36 pages; 60 lb. paper; glossy cover; illustrations. "We are mostly a poetry magazine by and for mental health consumers. We want to give a voice to those who are often not heard. All material is composed by mental health consumers. The only requirement for consideration of publication is having a history of mental illness." Semiannual. Estab. 1986. Circ. 1,000.

Needs: Adventure, condensed novels, ethnic/multicultural, experimental, fantasy (science fantasy, sword and sorcery), feminist, gay, historical (general), horror, humor/satire, lesbian, literary, mainstream, mystery/suspense, regional, romance, science fiction, serialized novels. Publishes ms 6 months after acceptance. Recently published work by Allen McNair, Donna Willey and Mark Goniciarz. Length: 700 words; average length: 500 words. Also publishes poetry.

How to Contact: Send complete ms. Send a disposable copy of ms. Responds in 6 months to mss. Accepts simultaneous and reprints submissions. Sample copy for $3.
Payment/Terms: Pays contributor's copies. Acquires one-time rights.

NASSAU REVIEW, Nassau Community College, State University of New York, 1 Education Dr., Garden City NY 11530-6793. (516)572-7792. **Contact:** Editorial Board. Magazine: 6½×9½; 200 pages; heavy stock paper and cover; illustrations; photos. "Looking for high-level, professionally talented fiction on any subject matter except science fiction. Intended for a college and university faculty-level audience. Not geared to college students or others of that age who have not yet reached professional competency." Annual. Estab. 1964. Circ. 1,200. Member: Council of Literary Magazines & Presses.
Needs: Historical (general), humor/satire, literary, mainstream, mystery/suspense (amateur sleuth, cozy). "No science fiction." Receives 40-50 unsolicited mss/month. Accepts 7-10 mss/year. Does not read mss April-October. Publishes ms 6 months after acceptance. **Publishes 2 new writers/year.** Recently published work by Louis Phillips, Dick Wimmer, Norbert Petsch and Mike Lipstock. Length: 2,000-6,000 words; average length: 3,000-4,000 words. Publishes short shorts. Also publishes literary essays, literary criticism, poetry.
How to Contact: Send a disposable copy of ms and #10 SASE for reply only. Responds in 2 weeks to queries; 6 months to mss. No simultaneous submissions. Sample copy for free.
Payment/Terms: Pays contributor's copies. Acquires one-time rights. Sponsors awards/contests.
Advice: "We look for narrative drive, perceptive characterization and professional competence."

NATURAL BRIDGE, English Department, University of Missouri-St. Louis, 8001 Natural Bridge Rd., St. Louis MO 63121-4499. (314)516-7327. Fax: (314)516-5781. E-mail: natural@jinx.umsl.edu. Website: www.umsl. edu/~natural. **Contact:** Ryan Stone, editor. Magazine: 6×9; 250 pages; 60 lb. opaque recycled paper; 12 pt. coated matte cover. "*Natural Bridge* is published by the UM-St. Louis MFA Program. Faculty and graduate students work together in selecting manuscripts, with a strong emphasis on originality, freshness, honesty, vitality, energy, and linguistic skill. We work closely with writers when a piece merits it." Semiannual. Estab. 1999. Circ. 400. Member, CLMP.
Needs: Literary. List of upcoming themes available for SASE or online. Receives 200 unsolicited mss/month. Accepts 35 mss/issue; 70 mss/year. Submit only July 1-August 31 and November 1-December 31. Publishes ms 9 months after acceptance. **Publishes 12 new writers/year.** Recently published work by A.E. Hotchner, Steve Stern, Brian Doyle, Jennifer Haigh and Jim Ray Daniels. Also publishes literary essays, poetry. Sometimes comments on rejected mss.
How to Contact: Send SASE for return of ms or send a disposable copy of ms and #10 SASE for reply only. Responds in 5 months to mss. Accepts simultaneous submissions. Sample copy for $8. Writer's guidelines for SASE, e-mail or on website.
Payment/Terms: Pays 2 contributor's copies and a one-year subscription; additional copies $5. Acquires first North American serial rights.
Advice: "We look for fresh stories, extremely well written, on any subject. We publish maninstream literary fiction. We want stories that work on first and subsequent readings—stories, in other words, that both entertain and resonate. Study the journal. Read all of the fiction in it, especially in a fiction-heavy issue like No. 4 or 6."

THE NEBRASKA REVIEW, University of Nebraska at Omaha, Omaha NE 68182-0324. (402)554-3159. E-mail: jreed@unomaha.edu. **Contact:** James Reed, fiction editor. Magazine: 5½×8½; 108 pages; 60 lb. text paper; chrome coat cover stock. "*TNR* attempts to publish the finest available contemporary fiction, poetry and creative nonfiction for college and literary audiences." Publishes 2 issues/year. Estab. 1973. Circ. 1,000.
  • Work published in *The Nebraska Review* was reprinted in *New Stories From the South* and the *Pushcart Prize Anthology*.
Needs: Humor/satire, literary, mainstream, contemporary. "No genre fiction." Receives 40 unsolicited mss/month. Accepts 4-5 mss/issue; 8-10 mss/year. Reads for the *Nebraska Review* Awards in Fiction and Poetry and Creative Nonfiction September 1 through November 30. Open to submission January 1-April 30; does not read May 1-August 31. Publishes ms 6-12 months after acceptance. **Publishes 2-3 new writers/year.** Recently published work by Chris Mazza, Mark Wisniewski, Stewart O'Nan, Elaine Ford and Tom Franklin. Average length: 5,000-6,000 words. Also publishes poetry.
How to Contact: Responds in 6 months to mss. Sample copy for $4.50.
Payment/Terms: Pays 2 contributor's copies and 1 year subscription; additional copies $4. Acquires first North American serial rights.
Advice: "Write stories in which the lives of your characters are the primary reason for writing and techniques of craft serve to illuminate, not overshadow, the textures of those lives. Sponsors a $500 award/year—write for rules."

NERVE COWBOY, Liquid Paper Press, P.O. Box 4973, Austin TX 78765. Website: www.onr.com/user/ junagins/nervecowboy.com.html. **Contact:** Joseph Shields or Jerry Hagins, editors. Magazine: 7×8½; 64 pages; 20 lb. paper; card stock cover; illustrations. "*Nerve Cowboy* publishes adventurous, comical, disturbing, thought-provoking, accessible poetry and fiction. We like to see work sensitive enough to make the hardest hard-ass cry, funny enough to make the most helpless brooder laugh and disturbing enough to make us all glad we're not the author of the piece." Semiannual. Estab. 1996. Circ. 350.

Needs: Literary. No "racist, sexist or overly offensive" work. Wants more unusual stories with rich description and enough twists and turns that leave the reader thinking." Receives 40 unsolicited mss/month. Accepts 2-3 mss/issue; 4-6 mss/year. Publishes ms 6-12 months after acceptance. **Publishes 5-10 new writers/year.** Recently published work by Albert Huffstickler, Celeste Bowman, Dave Newman, Marie Goyette, Charlene Logan and L. Dale Van Avken. Length: 1,500 words; average length: 750-1,000 words. Publishes short shorts. Also publishes poetry.

How to Contact: Send SASE for reply, return of ms or send a disposable copy of ms. Responds in 2 weeks to queries; 2 months to mss. Accepts reprints submissions No simultaneous submissions. Sample copy for $5. Writer's guidelines for #10 SASE.

Payment/Terms: Pays 1 contributor's copy. Acquires one-time rights.

Advice: "We look for writing which is very direct and elicits a visceral reaction in the reader. Read magazines you submit to in order to get a feel for what the editors are looking for. Write simply and from the gut."

NEW DELTA REVIEW, Louisiana State University, Dept. of English, 249 Allen Hall, Baton Rouge LA 70803-5001. (225)578-4079. E-mail: new-delta@lsu.edu. Website: www.english.lsu.edu/journals/ndr. **Contact:** Editors change every year. Check website. Magazine: 6×9; 75-125 pages; high quality paper; glossy card cover; color artwork. "We seek vivid and exciting work from new and established writers. We have published fiction from writers such as Stacy Richter, Mark Poirier and George Singleton." Semiannual. Estab. 1984. Circ. 500.

• *New Delta Review* also sponsors the Matt Clark Prizes for fiction and poetry. Work from the magazine has been included in the *Pushcart Prize* anthology.

Needs: Humor/satire, literary, mainstream, translations, contemporary, prose poem. "No Elvis stories, overwrought 'Southern' fiction, or cancer stories." Receives 150 unsolicited mss/month. Accepts 3-4 mss/issue; 6-8 mss/year. Reads from August 15-April 15. **Publishes 1-3 new writers/year.** Length: 250 words; average length: 15 pages. Publishes short shorts. Also publishes poetry. Rarely comments on rejected mss.

How to Contact: SASE (or IRC). Responds in 3 weeks to queries; 3 months to mss. No simultaneous submissions. Sample copy for $6.

Payment/Terms: Pays in contributor's copies. Charge for extras. Acquires first North American serial, electronic rights. Sponsors awards/contests.

Advice: "Our staff is open-minded and youthful. We base decisions on merit, not reputation. The manuscript that's most enjoyable to read gets the nod. Be bold, take risks, surprise us."

$ NEW ENGLAND REVIEW, Middlebury College, Middlebury VT 05753. (802)443-5075. Website: www.middlebury.edu/~nereview/. **Contact:** Stephen Donadio, editor. Magazine: 7×10; 180 pages; 50 lb. paper; coated cover stock. Serious literary only. Reads September 1 to May 31 (postmarked dates). Quarterly. Estab. 1978. Circ. 2,000.

Needs: Literary. Receives 250 unsolicited mss/month. Accepts 5 mss/issue; 20 mss/year. Does not read mss June-August. Publishes ms 6 months after acceptance. Agented fiction less than 5%. **Publishes 1-2 new writers/year.** Recently published work by Steve Almond, Padgett Powell, Peter Cameron and Joann Kobin. Publishes short shorts. Sometimes comments on rejected mss.

How to Contact: Send complete ms. "Send complete mss with cover letter. We don't want hype, or hard-sell, or summaries of the author's intentions. Will consider simultaneous submissions, but must be stated as such." SASE. Responds in 2 weeks to queries; 3 months to mss. Accepts simultaneous submissions. Sample copy for $8. Writer's guidelines online.

Payment/Terms: Pays $10/page ($20 minimum), and 2 copies. Pays on publication for first North American serial, first, second serial (reprint) rights. Sends galleys to author.

Advice: "It's best to send one story at a time, and wait until you hear back from us to try again."

NEW LAUREL REVIEW, New Orleans Poetry Forum/New Laurel Review, 828 Lesseps St., New Orleans LA 70117. (504)947-6001. **Contact:** Lee Meitzen Grue, editor. Andrea Young, poetry editor. Magazine: 6½×8; 180 pages; 60 lb. white paper; illustrations; photos. Journal of poetry, fiction, critical articles and reviews. "We have published such internationally known writers as Martha McFerren, Megan Burns and Dennis Fomento." Readership: "Literate, adult audiences as well as anyone interested in writing with significance, human interest, vitality, subtelty, etc." Published irregularly. Estab. 1970. Circ. 500. Member, Council of Editors or Learned Journals.

Needs: Ethnic/multicultural, literary, novel excerpts, translations ("cutting edge"). No "dogmatic, excessively inspirational or political" material. No science fiction. Want more classic short story and experimental short story. Receives 25 unsolicited mss/month. Accepts 1-2 mss/issue. Does not read mss during summer months and December. Agented fiction 10%. **Publishes 2-3 new writers/year.** Recently published work by Frank Durham. Publishes short shorts. Also publishes literary essays, poetry. When there is time comments on rejected mss.

How to Contact: Send SASE for reply or return of ms. Responds in 3 months to mss. No simultaneous submissions. Sample copy for $10.

Payment/Terms: Pays 1 contributor's copy; additional copies $10, discounted. Acquires first rights.

Advice: "Patience: magazines have little or no money and are staffed by working writers. Authors need to look at sample copy before submitting."

$ ▣ ▣ **NEW LETTERS**, University of Missouri-Kansas City, University House, 5101 Rockhill Rd., Kansas City MO 64110-2499. (816)235-1168. Fax: (816)235-2611. Website: umkc.edu/newletters. **Contact:** Robert Stewart, editor. Magazine: 14 lb. cream paper; illustrations. *"New Letters* is intended for the general literate reader. We publish literary fiction, nonfiction, essays, poetry. We also publish art." Quarterly. Estab. 1934. Circ. 2,500.

● *New Letters Magazine* received a Pushcart prize for fiction.

Needs: Ethnic/multicultural, experimental, humor/satire, literary, mainstream, translations, Contemporary. No genre fiction. Does not read mss May 15-October 15. Publishes ms 5 months after acceptance. Agented fiction 10%. Recently published work by Thomas E. Kennedy, Sheila Kohler, Rosellen Brown and Janet Burroway. Publishes short shorts. Rarely comments on rejected mss.

How to Contact: Send complete ms. Accepts submissions by mail. Do not submit by e-mail. Responds in 1 month to queries; 3 months to mss. No simultaneous submissions. Sample copy for $7 or sample articles on website. Writer's guidelines online.

Payment/Terms: Pays $30-75 for fiction and $15 for single poem. Pays on publication for first North American serial rights. Sends galleys to author.

Advice: "Seek publication of representative chapters in high-quality magazines as a way to the book contract. Try literary magazines first."

▢ **NEW MIRAGE QUARTERLY**, Good Samaritan Press, P.O. Box 803282, Santa Clarita CA 91380. (661)799-0694. E-mail: adorxyz@aol.com. **Contact:** Jovita Ador Lee, senior editor. Magazine: 5 × 8; 16 pages; illustrations. "We are issued by the Mirage Group of Southern California, a writers association. Much of the material we publish is the work of our members." Quarterly. Estab. 1997. Circ. 100.

Needs: Fantasy, literary, mainstream, religious/inspirational, romance, science fiction. "We would like to see more Christian literature, science fiction, romance." Receives 1 unsolicited mss/month. Publishes ms 6 months after acceptance. **Publishes 40 new writers/year.** Recently published work by Eugenia Hairston. Publishes short shorts. Also publishes literary criticism, poetry. Sometimes comments on rejected mss.

How to Contact: Send SASE for return of ms. Responds in 6 weeks to queries. Accepts simultaneous and reprints, multiple submissions. Sample copy for $7. Reviews fiction.

Payment/Terms: Pays 1 contributor's copy; additional copies $26. Pays on publication. Sends galleys to author. Not copyrighted. Sponsors awards/contests.

Advice: "The basics are important—organization, clarity, spelling, plot, etc. We recommend working with a writers' association."

$ ▢ ▣ **NEW ORLEANS REVIEW**, Box 195, Loyola University, New Orleans LA 70118. (504)865-2295. Fax: (504)865-2294. E-mail: noreview@loyno.edu. Website: www.loyno.edu/~noreview/. **Contact:** Christopher Chambers, editor. Journal: 6×9; perfect bound; 200 pages; photos. "Publishes poetry, fiction, translations, photographs, nonfiction on literature, art and film. Readership: those interested in contemporary literature and culture." Biannual. Estab. 1968. Circ. 1,300.

● Work from the *New Orleans Review* has been anthologized in *Best American Short Stories* and the *Pushcart Prize Anthology.*

Needs: "Quality fiction from traditional to experimental." No romance. Want more experimental fiction. **Publishes 12 new writers/year.** Recently published work by Gordon Lish, Michael Martone, Carolyn Sanchez and Josh Russell.

How to Contact: Accepts submissions by fax. Responds in 4 months to mss. Accepts simultaneous submissions "if we are notified immediately upon acceptance elsewhere." Sample copy for $7. Reviews fiction.

Payment/Terms: Pays $25-50 and 2 copies. Pays on publication for first North American serial rights.

Advice: "We're looking for dynamic writing that demonstrates attention to the language, and a sense of the medium, writing that engages, surprises, moves us. We're not looking for genre fiction, or academic articles. We subscribe to the belief that in order to truly write well, one must first master the rudiments: grammar and syntax, punctuation, the sentence, the paragraph, the line, the stanza. We receive about 3,000 manuscripts a year, and publish about 5% of them. Check out a recent issue, send us your best, proofread your work, be patient, be persistent."

▣ ▢ **THE NEW ORPHIC REVIEW**, New Orphic Publishers, 706 Mill St., Nelson BC V1L 4S5 Canada. (250)354-0494. Fax: (250)352-0743. **Contact:** Ernest Hekkanen, editor-in-chief. Magazine; 5½×8½; 120 pages; common paper; 100 lb. color cover. "In the traditional *Orphic* fashion, our magazine accepts a wide range of styles and approaches—from naturalism to the surreal, but, please, get to the essence of the narrative, emotion, conflict, state of being, whatever." Semiannual. Estab. 1998. Circ. 300.

Needs: Ethnic/multicultural, experimental, fantasy, historical (general), literary, mainstream. "No detective or sword and sorcery stories." List of upcoming themes available for SASE. Receives 20 unsolicited mss/month. Accepts 10 mss/issue; 22 mss/year. Publishes ms 1 year after acceptance. **Publishes 6-8 new writers/year.** Recently published work by Eveline Hasler (Swiss), Leena Krohn (Finnish), Pekka Salmi and Heinrich Müller. Length: 2,000-10,000 words; average length: 3,500 words. Publishes short shorts. Also publishes literary essays, literary criticism, poetry. Sometimes comments on rejected mss.

How to Contact: Send SASE (or IRC) for return of ms or send a disposable copy of ms and #10 SASE for reply only. Responds in 1 month to queries; 4 months to mss. Accepts simultaneous, multiple submissions. Sample copy for $15. Writer's guidelines for SASE. Reviews fiction.

Payment/Terms: Pays 1 contributor's copy; additional copies $12. Pays on publication for first North American serial rights.

Advice: "I like fiction that deals with issues, accounts for every motive, has conflict, is well-written and tackles something the is substantive. Don't be mundane; try for more, not less."

$ the new renaissance, An international magazine of ideas & opinions, emphasizing literature and the arts, The Friends of "the new renaissance", 26 Heath Rd., #11, Arlington MA 02474-3645. E-mail: marccreate @aol.com. **Contact:** Michal Anne Kucharski, co-editor. Magazine: 6×9; 144-182 pages; 70 lb. matte white paper; 4-color cover; illustrations; photos; artwork: 80 lb. dull glossy. "*tnr* is dedicated to publishing a diverse magazine, with a variety of styles, statements and tones for a sophisticated general audience. We publish assorted long & short fiction, including bilingual (Italian, German, French, Danish, Russian [Cyrillic], etc.), and Indian fiction in translation." Semiannual. Estab. 1968. Circ. 1,300.

Needs: Ethnic/multicultural (general), experimental, humor/satire, literary, psychic/supernatural/occult, regional (general), translations, psychological. "We do not want to see a heavy amount of commercial or popular fiction. Within the last two years we have been receiving too much quasi-naturalistic fiction and we like to see less." Receives 40-70 mss (January-June), 20-35 mss (September 1-October 31). Accepts 3-5 mss/issue; 6-10 mss/year. Does not read mss in July-August or November-December. Publishes ms 10-18 months after acceptance. Agented fiction 4-5%. **Publishes 1-2 new writers/year.** Recently published work by B. Wongar and M.E. McMullen. Also publishes literary essays, literary criticism, poetry. Often comments on rejected mss.

How to Contact: Send SASE (or IRC) for return of ms or send a disposable copy of ms and #10 SASE for reply. Accepts two stories if the mss are 4 pages or less. Responds in 1 month to queries; 5-7 months to mss. Sample copy not available. Writer's guidelines for SASE or by e-mail. Reviews fiction.

Payment/Terms: Pays $48-80 and 1 contributor's copy (under 30 pages), 2 copies 31-36 pages. Offers discount for additional copies. Acquires all rights; after publication, rights returned to writer.

Advice: "We're looking for the individual voice, in both style and vision. We prefer density in characterization and/ or dialogue, atmosphere, etc. We're not as interested in the 'Who Cares?' fiction. We like a story to be memorable; we leave the particulars of what to do to the individual writers. We feel that the first-person narration is becoming all too commonplace. We too often hear from writers who are not familiar with the litmag but who should be aware of, at least, what some independents are doing."

NEW STONE CIRCLE, New Stone Circle, 1185 E. 1900 North Rd., White Heath IL 61884. E-mail: m-hays@monticello.net. **Contact:** Mary Hays, fiction editor. Magazine: 8½×5½; 40-58 pages; illustrations; photos. "Our intention is to create a forum for a conversation between artists of our time." Annual. Estab. 1994. Circ. 100.

• *New Stone Circle* has won Pipistrelle Award for Best Literary Magazine.

Needs: "No racist or misogynist work." Receives 30 unsolicited mss/month. Accepts 4-5 mss/issue; 4-10 mss/ year. Agented fiction 1%. **Publishes 1-2 new writers/year.** Recently published work by Christine Chiu, Cris Mazza, Elizabeth Weiser and Jessica Inclan. Publishes short shorts.

How to Contact: Send SASE for return of ms or send a disposable copy of ms and #10 SASE for reply only. Responds in 2 months to queries; 6 months to mss. Accepts simultaneous and reprints, multiple submissions. Sample copy for $4.50. Writer's guidelines for SASE.

Payment/Terms: Pays 1 contributor's copy; additional copies $3.50. Pays on publication for one-time rights. Sends galleys to author. Sponsors awards/contests.

Advice: "Show fresh imagery. As a reader, I want to be transported to the fictional world. Keep reading, keep writing, keep sending you work out."

NEW WELSH REVIEW, Chapter Arts Centre, P.O. Box 170, Aberystwyth, Ceredigion Wales SY23 1 WZ, U.K.. 02920 665529. Fax: 02920 665529. E-mail: nwr@welshnet.co.uk. Editor: Francesca Rhydderch. **Contact:** Fiction Editor. "*NWR*, a literary quarterly ranked in the top five of British Literary magazines, publishes stories, poems and critical essays. The best of Welsh writing in English, past and present, is celebrated, discussed and debated. We seek poems, short stories, reviews, special features/articles and commentary." Quarterly.

Needs: Short fiction. "No extremes, such as extreme thriller, erotica, etc. where emphasis is placed on sensationalizing." Accepts 16-20 mss/year. **Publishes 20% new writers/year.** Recently published work by Sian James, Ron Berry, and Alun Richards.

How to Contact: Accepts mss on disk. No fax or e-mail submissions. Accepts queries by e-mail. Accepts multiple submissions.

Payment/Terms: Pays "cheque on publication and one free copy."

$ THE NEW WRITER, P.O. Box 60, Cranbrook TN17 2ZR, United Kingdom. 01580 212626. Fax: 01580 212041. E-mail: editor@the newwriter.com. Website: www.thenewwriter.com. **Contact:** Suzanne Ruthven, editor. Magazine: A4; 56 pages; illustrations; photos. Contemporary writing magazine which publishes "the best in fact, fiction and poetry." Publishes 6 issues per annum. Estab. 1996. Circ. 1,500.

Needs: "We will consider most categories apart from stories written for children. No horror, erotic or cozy fiction."

Accepts 4 mss/issue; 40 mss/year. Publishes ms 1 year after acceptance. Agented fiction 5%. **Publishes 12 new writers/year.** Recently published work by Alan Dunn, Alice Jolly, Kate Long, Annabel Lamb, Laureen Vonnegut and Stephen Finucan. Length: 2,000-5,000 words; average length: 3,500 words. Publishes short shorts. Also publishes literary essays, literary criticism, poetry. Often comments on rejected mss.

How to Contact: Query with published clips. Accepts submissions by e-mail, fax. Send SASE (or IRC) for return of ms or send a disposable copy of ms and #10 SASE for reply only. "We consider short stories from subscribers only but we may also commission guest writers." Responds in 2 months to queries; 4 months to mss. Accepts simultaneous submissions. Sample copy for SASE and A4 SAE with IRCs only. Writer's guidelines for SASE. Reviews fiction.

Payment/Terms: Pays £10 per story by credit voucher; additional copies for 1.50. Pays on publication for one-time rights. Sponsors awards/contests.

Advice: "Hone it—always be prepared to improve the story. It's a competitive market."

$⌂ NEW YORK STORIES, LaGuardia/CUNY, 31-10 Thomson Ave., Long Island City NY 11101. (718)482-5673. Website: www.newyorkstories.org. **Contact:** Daniel Caplice Lynch, editor. Magazine: 9×11; 48 pages; photos. "Our purpose is to publish quality short fiction and New York-centered nonfiction. We look for fresh approaches, artistic daring, and story telling talent. We are especially interested in work that explores NYC's diversity—ethnic, social, sexual, psychological, economic, and geographical." Estab. 1998. Circ. 1,500.

Needs: Ethnic/multicultural, experimental, feminist, gay, humor/satire, lesbian, literary, mainstream, regional. Receives 300 unsolicited mss/month. Accepts 6-8 mss/issue; up to 24 mss/year. Does not read mss June-August. Publishes ms 6 months after acceptance. Agented fiction 5%. **Publishes 2 new writers/year.** Length: 300-6,000 words; average length: 2,500-3,000 words. Publishes short shorts. Also publishes literary essays. Sometimes comments on rejected mss.

How to Contact: Send complete ms. Accepts submissions by mail, e-mail. Include 1-paragraph bio and e-mail address. Send SASE for return of ms or send disposable copy of ms. Responds in 2 weeks to queries; 6 months to mss. Accepts simultaneous and reprints submissions. Sample copy for $4. Writer's guidelines online.

Payment/Terms: Pays $100-750. Pays on publication for first North American serial rights.

Advice: "Fresh angles of vision, dark humor and psychological complexity are hallmarks of our short stories. Present characters who are 'alive.' Let them breathe. To achieve this, revise, revise, revise. Lately, the industry of publishing fiction seems to be playing it safe. We want your best—no matter what."

$⌂ NIGHT TRAIN, People, Action, Consequence, Night Train Publications, Inc., P.O. Box 6250, Boston MA 02114. E-mail: submission@nighttrainmagazine.com. Website: www.nighttrainmagazine.com. **Contact:** Rusty Barnes, fiction editor. Magazine: 6×9; 200 page; 60 lb. Glatfelter Natural paper; 12 pt. glossy laminated cover; illustrations; photos. "We publish *Night Train* for anyone interested in the best available contemporary literature. We welcome all kinds of stories, but we strongly prefer those with an edge: fiction that leaves us gasping for breath, stories with people—real people—who are actors in their own lives and accept consequences for what they do. We honor the traditions of the short story, but realize that to live, those traditions need new interpretations, new vision—a thrust forward. We provide a venue for writers to show us where the art will go, and trust them to take us there." Semiannual. Estab. 2002. Circ. 1,000.

Needs: Experimental, literary, mainstream. "A first-person, present-tense story would have to be remarkable for us to consider publishing it, but we rule out nothing. We also have a bias against stories about the pained and tortured life of writers; we're writers too, but we don't find that interesting; again, it would have to be beyond excellence for us to consider." Receives 350 unsolicited mss/month. Accepts 20-25 mss/issue; 40-50 mss/year. Publishes ms 6 months after acceptance. **Publishes 5-10 new writers/year.** Recently published work by Maryanne Stahl, Thomas Cobb and Edward Falco. Length: 250-10,000 words; average length: 3,000 words. Publishes short shorts. Often comments on rejected mss.

How to Contact: Send a disposable copy of ms and #10 SASE for reply only. Responds in 2 months to queries; 3 months to mss. Accepts simultaneous, multiple submissions. Sample copy for $9.95. Writer's guidelines for SASE or on website. Reviews fiction.

Payment/Terms: Pays 2¢/word minimum to $100 maximum, 2 contributors copies, a lifetime subscription and 2 gift subscriptions; additional copies $6.95. Pays on publication for first North American serial, electronic, one-time anthology rights. Sends galleys to author. Sponsors awards/contests.

Advice: "We want to see characters who are active participants in their own lives, who recognize the impact they have on others, who think about the things they do and suffer (or not) as a result of those actions. *Night Train* is a place where blood, bone and nerve—the basic elements of stories—matter. Careless language, ethereal subject matter or lack of grounding in the 'whys' of human behavior will make us unhappy. Please read the guidelines and aesthetic statement on our website; and look at our editor's favorite pages. They're there for one reason: to help you understand what we like."

$⌂ NIMROD, International Journal of Prose and Poetry, University of Tulsa, 600 S. College Ave., Tulsa OK 74104-3189. (918)631-3080. Fax: (918)631-3033. E-mail: nimrod@utulsa.edu. Website: www.utulsa.edu/nimrod/. **Contact:** Gerry McLoud, fiction editor. Magazine: 6×9; 192 pages,; 60 lb. white paper; illustrations; photos. "We publish one thematic issue and one awards issue each year. A recent theme was "The Celtic Fringe," a compilation of poetry and prose from all over the world. We seek vigorous, imaginative, quality writing. Our mission is to discover new writers and publish experimental writers who have not yet found a 'home' for their work." Semiannual. Estab. 1956. Circ. 3,000.

Needs: "We accept contemporary poetry and/or prose. May submit adventure, ethnic, experimental, prose poem or translations. No science fiction or romance." Receives 120 unsolicited mss/month. **Publishes 5-10 new writers/ year.** Recently published work by Felicia Ward, Ellen Bass, Jeanette Turner Hospital and Kate Small. Also publishes poetry.

How to Contact: SASE for return of ms. Accepts queries by e-mail. Does not accept submissions by e-mail unless the writer is living outside the U.S. Responds in 5 months to mss. Accepts simultaneous, multiple submissions. Sample copy for "to see what *Nimrod* is all about, send $10 for a back issue."

Payment/Terms: Pays 2 contributor's copies.

Advice: "We have not changed our fiction needs: quality, vigor, distinctive voice. We have, however, increased the number of stories we print. See current issues. We look for fiction that is fresh, vigorous, distinctive, serious and humorous, seriousl-humorous, unflinchingly serious, ironic—whatever. Just so it is quality. Strongly encourage writers to send #10 SASE for brochure for annual literary contest with prizes of $1,000 and $2,000."

96 Inc., P.O. Box 15559, Boston MA 02215-0011. (617)267-0543. Fax: (617)262-3568. E-mail: mail@96inc.c om. Website: www.96inc.com. **Contact:** Vera Gold or Nancy Mehegan, editors. Magazine: 8½ × 11; 64 pages; 20 lb. paper; matte cover; illustrations; photos. "*96 Inc.* promotes the process; integrates beginning/young with established writers; reaches out to audiences of all ages and backgrounds." Annual. Estab. 1992. Circ. 3,000.

Needs: All types of styles and subjects. Receives 200 unsolicited mss/month. Accepts 12-15 mss/issue; 30 mss/ year. Agented fiction 10%. **Publishes 2-10 new writers/year.** Recently published work by Rose Moss, Alene Bricken, Harlyn Aizley, Sharon Straits and Judith Stizel. Publishes short shorts. Also publishes literary essays, literary criticism, poetry. Sometimes comments on rejected mss.

How to Contact: Query. Send SASE for reply, return of ms or send a disposable copy of ms. Responds in 3 weeks to queries; 1 year to mss. Accepts simultaneous, multiple submissions. Sample copy for $7.50. Writer's guidelines for #10 SASE. Reviews fiction.

Payment/Terms: Pays 4 contributor's copies. Pays on publication for one-time rights.

Advice: Looks for "good writing in any style. Pays attention to the process. Read at least one issue. Be patient— it takes a very long time for readers to go through the thousands of manuscripts."

$ THE NORTH AMERICAN REVIEW, University of Northern Iowa, Cedar Falls IA 50614-0516. (319)273-6455. Fax: (319)273-4326. Website: www.webdelsol.com/NorthAmReview/NAR/. **Contact:** Grant Tracey, fiction editor. "The *NAR* is the oldest literary magazine in America and one of the most respected; though we have no prejudices about the subject matter of material sent to us, our first concern is quality." Bimonthly. Estab. 1815. Circ. under 5,000.

● Works published in *The North American Review* have won the Pushcart Prize.

Needs: Open (literary). "No flat narrative stories where the inferiority of the character is the paramount concern." Wants to see more "well-crafted literary stories that emphasize family concerns. We'd also like to see more stories engaged with environmental concerns." Reads fiction mss from January 1 to April 1 only. Publishes ms 9 months after acceptance. **Publishes 2 new writers/year.** Recently published work by Gary Gildner, Maryanne O'Hara and G.W. Clift.

How to Contact: Accepts submissions by mail, e-mail, fax, phone. Send complete ms with SASE. Responds in 3 months to queries; 3 months to mss. No simultaneous submissions. Sample copy for $5. Writer's guidelines online.

Payment/Terms: $5/350 words; $20 minimum, $100 maximum. Pays on publication for first North American serial, first rights.

Advice: "Stories that do not condescend to the reader or their character are always appealing to us. We also like stories that have characters doing things (acting upon the world instead of being acted upon). We also like a strong narrative arc. Stories that are mainly about language need not apply. Your first should be your second best line. Your last sentence should be your best. Everything in the middle should approach the two."

NORTH DAKOTA QUARTERLY, University of North Dakota, Box 7209, University Station, Grand Forks ND 58202. (701)777-3322. Fax: (701)777-2373. E-mail: ndq@sage.und.nodak.edu. Website: www.und.nodak .edu/org/ndq. **Contact:** Robert W. Lewis, editor. Jay Meek, poetry editor. Magazine: 6 × 9; 200 pages; bond paper; illustrations; photos. "*North Dakota Quarterly* is a literary journal publishing essays in the humanities; some short stories, some poetry." General audience. Quarterly. Estab. 1911. Circ. 700.

● Work published in *North Dakota Quarterly* was selected for inclusion in *The O. Henry Awards* anthology, *The Pushcart Prize Series*, and *Best American Essays*. The editors are especially interested in work by and about Native American writers.

Needs: Ethnic/multicultural, experimental, feminist, historical, humor/satire, literary. Receives 100-120 unsolicited mss/month. Accepts 4 mss/issue; 16 mss/year. Publishes ms 1 year after acceptance. **Publishes 4-5 new writers/ year.** Recently published work by Debra Marquart, Derek Wolcott, Kim Chinquee, David W. Warfield, Peter Nabokov. Average length: 3,000-4,000 words. Also publishes literary essays, literary criticism, poetry. Sometimes comments on rejected mss.

How to Contact: SASE. Responds in 3 months to mss. Sample copy for $8.
Payment/Terms: Pays 2-4 contributor's copies; 30% discount for extras. Acquires one-time rights. Sends galleys to author.

NORTHEAST ARTS MAGAZINE, P.O. Box 4363, Portland ME 04101. **Contact:** Mr. Leigh Donaldson, publisher. Magazine: 6½×9½; 32-40 pages; matte finish paper; card stock cover; illustrations; photos. Bimonthly. Estab. 1990. Circ. 750.
Needs: Ethnic/multicultural, gay, historical, literary, mystery/suspense (private eye), prose poem (under 2,000 words). "No obscenity, racism, sexism, etc." Receives 50 unsolicited mss/month. Accepts 1-2 mss/issue; 5-7 mss/ year. Publishes ms 2-4 months after acceptance. Agented fiction 20%. Publishes short shorts. Sometimes comments on rejected mss.
How to Contact: SASE. Responds in 1 month to queries; 4-6 months to mss. Accepts simultaneous submissions. Sample copy for $4.50, SAE and 75 postage. Writer's guidelines free.
Payment/Terms: Pays 2 contributor's copies. Acquires first North American serial rights.
Advice: Looks for "creative/innovative use of language and style. Unusual themes and topics."

NORTHWEST REVIEW, 369 PLC, University of Oregon, Eugene OR 97403. (541)346-3957. Website: darkwing.uoregon.edu/~engl/deptinfo/NWR.html. **Contact:** Janice MacCrae, fiction editor. Magazine: 6×9; 140-160 pages; high quality cover stock; illustrations; photos. "A general literary review featuring poems, stories, essays and reviews, circulated nationally and internationally. For a literate audience in avant-garde as well as traditional literary forms; interested in the important writers who have not yet achieved their readership." Triannual. Estab. 1957. Circ. 1,200.
Needs: Experimental, feminist, literary, translations, contemporary. Receives 150 unsolicited mss/month. Accepts 4-5 mss/issue; 12-15 mss/year. **Publishes some new writers/year.** Recently published work by Diana Abu-Jaber, Madison Smartt Bell, Maria Flook and Charles Marvin. Also publishes literary essays, literary criticism, poetry. When there is time comments on rejected mss.
How to Contact: Responds in 4 months to mss. No simultaneous submissions. Sample copy for $4. Reviews fiction.
Payment/Terms: Pays 3 contributor's copies and one-year subscription; 40% discount on extras. Acquires first rights.

$ NORTHWOODS JOURNAL, A Magazine for Writers, Conservatory of American Letters, P.O. Box 298, Thomaston ME 04861. (207)354-0998. Fax: (207)354-8953. E-mail: cal@americanletters.org. Website: www.a mericanletters.org. **Contact:** M. Hall, III fiction editor (submit fiction to S.M. Hall, III, 4709 Town-N-Country Blvd., Tampa, FL 33615). Magazine: 5½×8½; 32-64 pages; white paper; 70 lb. text cover; offset printing; some illustrations; photos. "No theme, no philosophy—for writers and for people who read for entertainment." Quarterly. Estab. 1993. Circ. 200. There is a $3 fee per story ($2 for CAL members; make checks payable to S.M. Hall, III. The magazine gets none of the reading fee).
Needs: Adventure, experimental, fantasy (science fantasy, sword and sorcery), literary, mainstream, mystery/suspense (amateur sleuth, police procedural, private eye/hard-boiled, romantic suspense), psychic/supernatural/occult, regional, romance (gothic, historical), science fiction (hard science, soft/sociological), western (frontier, traditional), sports. "Would like to see more first-person adventure. No porn or evangelical." Publishes special fiction issue or anthology. Receives 20 unsolicited mss/month. Accepts 12-15 mss/year. **Publishes 15 new writers/year.** Recently published work by Phylis Warady, Fred Zachau. Also publishes literary essays, literary criticism, poetry.
How to Contact: Send SASE for reply, return of ms or send a disposable copy of ms. In 2 days, by next deadline plus 5 days to mss to queries. No simultaneous submissions. Sample copy for $6.50 next issue, $9.75 current issue, $14.25 back issue, all postage paid. Or send 6×9 SASE with first-class postage affixed and $6.50. Writer's guidelines for #10 SASE. Reviews fiction.
Payment/Terms: Varies, " but is generally 1 cent per word or more, based on experience with us." Pays on acceptance for first North American serial rights. 50/50 split of additional sales.
Advice: "Read guidelines, read the things we've published. Know your market."

NOTRE DAME REVIEW, University of Notre Dame, English Department, Creative Writing, Notre Dame IN 46556. (574)631-6952. Fax: (574)631-8209. Website: www.nd.edu/~ndr/review.htm. **Contact:** William O'Rourke, fiction editor. Literary magazine: 6×9; 200 pages; 50 lb. smooth paper; illustrations; photos. "The *Notre Dame Review* is an independent, noncommercial magazine of contemporary American and international fiction, poetry, criticism, and art. We are especially interested in work that takes on big issues by making the invisible seen,

---

READ 'THE BUSINESS OF FICTION WRITING' section for information on manuscript preparation, mailing tips, rights and more.

that gives voice to the voiceless. In addition to showcasing celebrated authors like Seamus Heaney and Czelaw Milosz, the *Notre Dame Review* introduces readers to authors they may have never encountered before, but who are doing innovative and important work. In conjunction with the *Notre Dame Review*, the online companion to the printed magazine, the *Notre Dame Re-view* engages readers as a community centered in literary rather than commercial concerns, a community we reach out to through critique and commentary as well as aesthetic experience." Semiannual. Estab. 1995. Circ. 2,000.

• *Pushcart* prizes in fiction and poetry.

Needs: No genre fiction. Upcoming theme issues planned. List of upcoming themes or editorial calendar available for SASE. Receives 75 unsolicited mss/month. Accepts 4-5 mss/issue; 10 mss/year. Does not read mss November-January or May-August. Publishes ms 6 months after acceptance. **Publishes 1 new writers/year.** Recently published work by Ed Falco, Jarda Cerverka and David Green. Publishes short shorts. Also publishes literary criticism, poetry.

How to Contact: Send complete ms with cover letter. Include 4-sentence bio. Send SASE for response, return of ms, or send a disposable copy of ms. Responds in 4 months to mss. Accepts simultaneous submissions. Sample copy for $6. Writer's guidelines online.

Payment/Terms: Pays $5-25. Pays on publication for first North American serial rights.

Advice: "We're looking for high quality work that takes on big issues in a literary way. Please read our back issues before submitting."

OASIS, A Literary Magazine, P.O. Box 626, Largo FL 33779-0626. (727)345-8505. **Contact:** Neal Storrs, editor. Magazine: 70 pages. "The only criterion is high literary quality of writing." Quarterly. Estab. 1992. Circ. 300.

Needs: High-quality writing. Also publishes translations. Receives 150 unsolicited mss/month. Accepts 6 mss/issue; 24 mss/year. Publishes ms 4 months after acceptance. **Publishes 2 new writers/year.** Recently published work by Wendell Mayo, Al Masarik and Mark Wisniewski. Also publishes literary essays, poetry. Occasionally comments on rejected mss.

How to Contact: Send complete ms. Accepts submissions by mail, e-mail, phone. Send SASE for reply, return of ms or send a disposable copy of ms. Responds in 1 day to queries; 1 day to mss. Accepts simultaneous and reprints, multiple submissions. Sample copy for $7.50. Writer's guidelines for #10 SASE.

Payment/Terms: Pays in contributor's copies.

Advice: "If you want to write good stories, read good stories. Cultivate the critical ability to recognize what makes a story original and true to itself."

OBSIDIAN III, Literature in the African Diaspora, Dept. of English, North Carolina State University, Raleigh NC 27695-8105. (919)515-4153. Fax: (919)515-1836. E-mail: obsidian@social.chass.ncsu.edu. Website: www.ncsu.edu/chass/obsidian/index.html. **Contact:** Joyce Pettis, editor. Opal Moore, fiction editor. Magazine: 6×9; 130 pages. "Creative works in English by black writers, scholarly critical studies by all writers on black literature in English." Published 2 times/year (spring/summer, (fall/winter). Estab. 1975. Circ. 500.

Needs: Ethnic/multicultural (Pan-African), feminist, literary. All writers on black topics. Accepts 7-9 mss/year. Publishes ms 4-6 months after acceptance. **Publishes 20 new writers/year.** Recently published work by Sean Henry, R. Flowers Rivera, Terrance Hayes, Eugene Kraft,Arlene McKanic, Pearl Bothe Williams, and Kwane Dawes.

How to Contact: Accepts submissions by e-mail (disk), fax. Responds in 3 months to mss. Sample copy for $6.

Payment/Terms: Pays in contributor's copies. Acquires one-time rights. Sponsors awards/contests.

Advice: "Following proper format is essential. Your title must be intriguing and text clean. Never give up. Some of the writers we publish were rejected many times before we published them."

OHIO TEACHERS WRITE, Ohio Council of Teachers of English Language Arts, 644 Overlook Dr., Columbus OH 43214. E-mail: rmcclain@bright.net. **Contact:** Mark Jamison, editor. Editors change every 3 years. Magazine: 8½×11; 50 pages; 60 lb. white offset paper; 65 lb. blue cover stock; illustrations; photos. "The purpose of the magazine is three fold: (1) to provide a collection of fine literature for the reading pleasure of teachers and other adult readers; (2) to encourage teachers to compose literary works along with their students; (3) to provide the literate citizens of Ohio a window into the world of educators not often seen by those outside the teaching profession." Annual. Estab. 1995. Circ. 1,000. Submissions are limited to Ohio Educators.

Needs: Adventure, ethnic/multicultural, experimental, fantasy (science fantasy), feminist, gay, historical, humor/satire, lesbian, literary, mainstream, regional, religious/inspirational, romance (contemporary), science fiction (hard science, soft/sociological), western (frontier, traditional), senior citizen/retirement, sports, teaching. Receives 2 unsolicited mss/month. Accepts 7 mss/issue. "We read only in May when editorial board meets." Recently published work by Lois Spencer, Harry R. Noden, Linda J. Rice and June Langford Berkley. Publishes short shorts. Also publishes poetry. Often comments on rejected mss.

How to Contact: Send SASE with postage clipped for return of ms or send a disposable copy of ms. Accepts multiple submissions. Sample copy for $6.

Payment/Terms: Pays 2 contributor's copies; additional copies $6. Acquires first rights.

$ ONE-STORY, One-Story, LLC, P.O. Box 1326, New York NY 10156. Website: www.one-story.com. **Contact:** Maribeth Batcha and Hannah Tinti, editors. "*One-Story* is a literary magazine that contains, simply, **one story.**

It is a subscription-only magazine. Every 3 weeks subscribers are sent *One-Story* in the mail. *One-Story* is artfully designed, lightweight, easy to carry, and ready to entertain on buses, in bed, in subways, in cars, in the park, in the bath, in the waiting rooms of doctor's, on the couch, or in line at the supermarket. Subscribers also have access to a website, www.one-story.com, where they can learn more about *One-Story* authors, and hear about *One-Story* readings and events. There is always time to read one story." Estab. 2002. Circ. 2,000.

Needs: Literary, Literary short stories. *One-Story* only accepts short stories. Do not send excerpts. Do not send more than 1 story at a time. Publishes ms 3-6 months after acceptance. Recently published work by John Hodgman, Stephen Dixon, Karl Iangnemma, and Darin Strauss.

How to Contact: Send complete ms. Accepts submissions by e-mail. Accepts online submissions only. Responds in 2-6 months to mss. Accepts simultaneous submissions. Sample copy for $5. Writer's guidelines online.

Payment/Terms: Pays $100. Pays on publication for first North American serial rights. Buys the rights to publish excerpts on website and in promotional materials.

$☑ OPEN SPACES, Open Spaces Publications, Inc., PMB 134, 6327-C SW Capitol Hwy., Portland OR 97239-1937. (503)227-5764. Fax: (503)227-3401. Website: www.open-spaces.com. **Contact:** Ellen Teicher, fiction editor. Magazine: 64 pages; illustrations; photos. "*Open Spaces* is a forum for informed writing and intelligent thought. Articles are written by experts in various fields. Audience is varied (CEOs and rock climbers, politicos and university presidents, etc.) but is highly educated and loves to read good writing." Quarterly. Estab. 1997.

Needs: "Excellence is the issue—not subject matter." Accepts 2 mss/issue; 8 mss/year. Publishes ms 6 months after acceptance. **Publishes 5 new writers/year.** Recently published work by William Kittredge, Terence O'Donnell, Pattiann Rogers and David James Duncan. Publishes short shorts. Also publishes literary essays, poetry. Sometimes comments on rejected mss.

How to Contact: Accepts submissions by mail, fax. Send complete ms with a cover letter. Include short bio, social security number and list of publications. SASE for return of ms or send a disposable copy of ms. Accepts simultaneous submissions. Sample copy for $10. Writer's guidelines online.

Payment/Terms: Payment varies. Pays on publication. Rights purchased vary with author and material.

Advice: "The surest way for a writer to determine whether his or her material is right for us is to read the magazine."

☑ OTHER VOICES, University of Illinois at Chicago, 601 S. Morgan St., Chicago IL 60607. Website: webdelsol. com/other_voices. **Contact:** Lois Hauselman or Gina Frangello. Magazine: 5⅞×9; 168-205 pages; 60 lb. paper; coated cover stock; occasional photos. "Original, fresh, diverse stories and novel excerpts" for literate adults. Semiannual. Estab. 1985. Circ. 1,500.

Needs: Humor/satire, literary, contemporary, excerpted novel and one act-plays. Fiction only. "No taboos, except ineptitude and murkiness. No science fiction, romance, horror, 'chick-lit or futuristic." Receives 300 unsolicited mss/month. Accepts 17-20 mss/issue. **Publishes 6 new writers/year.** Recently published work by Aimee Bender, Wanda Coleman, Cris Mazza and Dan Chaon. Length: 5,000 words; average length: 4,000 words.

How to Contact: Send ms with SASE October 1—April 1 only. Mss received during non-reading period are returned unread. Cover letters "should be brief and list previous publications. Also, list title of submission. Most beginners' letters try to 'explain' the story—a big mistake." Responds in 10-12 weeks to mss. Accepts simultaneous submissions. Sample copy for $7 (includes postage). Writer's guidelines for #10 SASE.

Payment/Terms: Pays in contributor's copies and modest cash gratuity. Acquires one-time rights.

Advice: "There are so *few* markets for *quality* fiction! By publishing up to 40 stories a year, we provide new and established writers a forum for their work. Send us your best voice, your best work, your best best."

$☑ ◎ THE OXFORD AMERICAN, The Southern Magazine of Good Writing, The Oxford American, Inc., 303 President Clinton Ave., Little Rock AR 72201. (501)907-6418. Fax: (501)907-6419. Website: www.oxforda mericanmag.com. **Contact:** Marc Smirnoff, editor. Magazine: 8½×11; 100 pages; glossy paper; glossy cover; illustrations; photos. "*The Oxford American* is a general-interest literary magazine about the South." Bimonthly. Estab. 1992. Circ. 30,000.

● At press time, *The Oxford American* had suspended publication.

☑ OXYGEN, A Literary Magazine, Oxygen Editions, 537 Jones St., PMB 999, San Francisco CA 94102. E-mail: oxygen@slip.net. Website: www.oxygeneditions.net. **Contact:** Richard Hack, editor. Magazine: 5½×8½; 130 pages; 60 lb. vellum paper; 110 lb. laminated cover; illustrations; photos. "We are one of San Francisco's leading literary magazines, as various prize-winning authors have noted. We continue a West Coast tradition of trying new things, promoting visions of beauty, truth and communal spirit. We like work both innovative and traditional, religious or secular, pleasure-seeking. We have an ususaly broad range of work and points-of-view." Annual. Estab. 1991. Circ. 500.

Needs: "We look at almost any type of subject matter. Liveliness, depth, style, originality and economy are main considerations for selection. Please, no genre or formula fiction." Receives 50 unsolicited mss/month. Accepts 3-6 mss/issue; 3-6 mss/year. Publishes ms 4 months after acceptance. **Publishes 3-4 new writers/year.** Length: 250-5,000 words; average length: 1,750 words. Publishes short shorts. Also publishes literary essays, literary criticism, poetry.

How to Contact: Send complete ms. Responds in 4 months to mss. Accepts simultaneous and reprints, multiple submissions. Sample copy for $5. Writer's guidelines for SASE.
Payment/Terms: Pays 2 contributor's copies; additional copies $4 plus postage. Pays on publication. All rights revert to authors. Sends galleys to author.

⬤ OYSTER BOY REVIEW, P.O. Box 77842, San Francisco CA 94107-0842. E-mail: fiction@oysterboyreview.c om. Website: www.oysterboyreview.com. **Contact:** C. Earl Nelson, fiction editor. "Electronic and print magazine. "We publish kick-ass, teeth-cracking stories." Publishes 4 times a year.
Needs: No genre fiction. "Fiction the revolves around characters in conflict with themselves or each other; a plot that has a beginning, a middle, and an end; a narrative with a strong moral center (not necessarily 'moralistic'); a story with a satisfying resolution to the conflict; and an ethereal something that contributes to the mystery of a question, but does not necessarily seek or contrive to answer it." Submissions accepted January-September. **Publishes 4 new writers/year.** Recently published work by Todd Goldberg, Ken Wainio, Elisha Porat and Kevin McGowan.
How to Contact: Accepts multiple submissions. Sample copy not available.
Advice: "Keep writing, keep submitting, keep revising."

⬤ PACIFIC COAST JOURNAL, French Bread Publications, P.O. Box 56, Carlsbad CA 92018. E-mail: paccoastj @frenchbreadpublications.com. Website: www.frenchbreadpublications.com/pcj. **Contact:** Stephanie Kylkis, fiction editor. Magazine: 5½ × 8½; 40 pages; 20 lb. paper; 67 lb. cover; illustrations; b&w photos. "Slight focus toward Western North America/Pacific Rim." Quarterly. Estab. 1992. Circ. 200.
Needs: Ethnic/multicultural, experimental, feminist, historical, humor/satire, literary, science fiction (soft/sociological, magical realism). "No children's." Receives 30-40 unsolicited mss/month. Accepts 3-4 mss/issue; 10-12 mss/ year. Publishes ms 6-18 months after acceptance. **Publishes 3-5 new writers/year.** Recently published work by B.D. Love, Reinette F. Jones, and Stephanie Moore. Length: 4,000 words; average length: 2,500 words. Publishes short shorts. Also publishes literary essays, poetry. Sometimes comments on rejected mss.
How to Contact: Send SASE for reply, return of ms or send a disposable copy of ms. Also accepts e-mail address for response instead of SASE. Responds in 6-9 months to mss. Accepts simultaneous and reprints submissions. Sample copy for $2.50, 6×9 SASE and 3oz. postage. Reviews fiction.
Payment/Terms: Pays 1 contributor's copy. Acquires one-time rights.
Advice: "*PCJ* is an independent magazine and we have a limited amount of space and funding. We are looking for experiments in what can be done with the short fiction form. We don't want to see a story that you thought was okay for a mainstream litmag. We want to see something that you find you can't control through the writing process. Additionally, the best stories will enertain as well as confuse."

⬤ pacific REVIEW, Dept. of English and Comparitive Lit., San Diego State University, 5500 Campanile Dr., San Diego CA 92182-8140. E-mail: pacificREVIEW_sdsu@yahoo.com. Website: http://pacificREVIEW.sdsu.edu. **Contact:** Gwendolyn Spring Kurtz, editor-in-chief. Magazine: 6×9; 200 pages; book stock paper; paper back, extra heavy cover stock; b&w illustrations, b&w photos. "*pacific REVIEW* publishes the work of emergent literati, pairing their efforts with those of established artists. It is available at West Coast independent booksellers, university and college libraries, and is taught as text in numerous University Literature and Creative Writing classes." Circ. 2,000.
Needs: "We seek high-quality fiction and give preference to pieces that interrogate identity, in particular those works that explore identity in the context of West Coast/California and border culture." For information on theme issues see website. **Publishes 15 new writers/year.** Recently published work by Ai, Alurista, Susan Daitch, Lawrence Ferlinghetti and William T. Vollmann.
How to Contact: Responds in 3 months to mss. Sample copy for $10.
Payment/Terms: Pays 2 contributor's copies. Aquires first serial rights. All other rights revert to author rights.
Advice: "We welcome all submissions, especially those created in or in the context of the West Coast/California and the space of our borders."

⬤ PALO ALTO REVIEW, A Journal of Ideas, Palo Alto College, 1400 W. Villaret, San Antonio TX 78224. (210)921-5021. Fax: (210)9215008. E-mail: eshull@accd.edu. **Contact:** Bob Richmond and Ellen Schull, editors. Magazine: 8½×11; 64 pages; 60 lb. natural white paper (50% recycled); illustrations; photos. "Not too experimental nor excessively avant-garde, just good stories (for fiction). Ideas are what we are after. We are interested in connecting the interesting angles with which to investigate the length and breadth of the teaching/learning spectrum, life itself." Semiannual. Estab. 1992. Circ. 500-600.
Needs: Adventure, ethnic/multicultural, experimental, fantasy, feminist, historical, humor/satire, literary, mainstream, mystery/suspense, regional, romance, science fiction, translations, western. Upcoming themes available for SASE. Receives 100-150 unsolicited mss/month. Accepts 2-4 mss/issue; 4-8 mss/year. Does not read mss March-April and October-November when putting out each issue. Publishes ms 2-15 months after acceptance. **Publishes 30 new writers/year.** Recently published work by Layle Silbert, Naomi Chase, Kenneth Emberly, C.J. Hannah, Tom Juvik, Kassie Fleisher and Paul Perry. Publishes short shorts. Also publishes literary essays, literary criticism, poetry. Always comments on rejected mss.
How to Contact: Accepts submissions by e-mail. Send SASE for reply, return of ms or send a disposable copy

of ms. "Request sample copy and guidelines." Accepts submissions by e-mail only if outside the US. Responds in 4 months to mss. Accepts simultaneous submissions. Sample copy for $5. Writer's guidelines for #10 SASE or e-mail to paloaltoreview@aol.com.

Payment/Terms: Pays 2 contributor's copies; additional copies for $5. Acquires first North American serial rights.

Advice: "Good short stories have interesting characters confronted by a dilemma working toward a solution. So often what we get is 'a moment in time,' not a story. Generally, characters are interesting because readers can identify with them. Edit judiciously. Cut out extraneous verbiage. Set up a choice that has to be made. Then create tension—who wants what and why they can't have it."

PANGOLIN PAPERS, Turtle Press, P.O. Box 241, Nordland WA 98358. (360)385-3626. E-mail: trtlbluf@olympus.net. Website: www.olympus.net/cmmunity/trtlbluf/trtlbluf.htm. **Contact:** Pat Britt, managing editor. Magazine: 5½×8½; 120 pages; 24 lb. paper; 80 lb. cover. "Best quality literary fiction for an informed audience." Triannual. Estab. 1994. Circ. 500.

Needs: Experimental, humor/satire, literary, translations. "We would like to see more funny but literate stories. No genre such as romance or science fiction." Plans to publish special fiction issues or anthologies in the future. Receives 60 unsolicited mss/month. Accepts 7-10 mss/issue; 20-30 mss/year. Publishes ms 4-12 after acceptance. Agented fiction 10%. **Publishes 3-4 new writers/year.** Recently published work by Jack Nisbet and Barry Giford. Length: 100-7,000 words; average length: 3,500 words. Publishes short shorts. Also publishes literary essays. Sometimes comments on rejected mss.

How to Contact: Send SASE for reply, return of ms or send a disposable copy of ms. Responds in 2 months to mss. No simultaneous submissions. Sample copy for $6 and $1.50 postage. Writer's guidelines for #10 SASE.

Payment/Terms: Pays 2 contributor's copies. Acquires first North American serial rights. Sends galleys to author. Sponsors awards/contests.

Advice: "We are looking for orginal voices; good story, tight writing. Edit your material and cut mercilessly. Follow the rules and be honest in your work."

$ THE PARIS REVIEW, 541 E. 72nd St., New York NY 10021. (212)861-0016. Fax: (212)861-4504. Website: www.theparisreview.com. **Contact:** George A. Plimpton, editor. Other Address: 541 E. 72nd St., New York NY 10021. Magazine: 5¼×8½; about 260 pages; illustrations; photos (unsolicited artwork not accepted). "Fiction and poetry of superlative quality, whatever the genre, style or mode. Our contributors include prominent, as well as less well-known and previously unpublished writers. Writers at Work interview series includes important contemporary writers discussing their own work and the craft of writing." Quarterly.

● Work published in *The Paris Review* received five Pushcart awards.

Needs: Literary. Receives 1,000 unsolicited mss/month. **Publishes 5 new writers/year.** Recently published work by Thomas Wolfe, Denis Johnson, Melissa Pritchard, Jim Shepard and Jonathan Safran Foer. Also publishes literary essays, poetry.

How to Contact: Query. Accepts submissions by mail. SASE. Responds in 4 months to mss. Accepts simultaneous, multiple submissions. Sample copy for $15 (includes postage). Writer's guidelines online.

Payment/Terms: Payment varies depending on length. Pays on publication for all rights. Sends galleys to author. Sponsors awards/contests.

PARTING GIFTS, 3413 Wilshire, Greensboro NC 27408-2923. E-mail: rbixby@aol.com. Website: users.aol.com/marchst. **Contact:** Robert Bixby, editor. Magazine: 5×7; 72 pages. "*Parting Gifts* seeks good, powerful and short fiction that stands on its own and takes no prisoners." Semiannual. Estab. 1988.

Needs: "Brevity is the second most important criterion behind literary quality." Publishes ms within one year after acceptance. Recently published work by Ray Miller, Katherine Taylor, Curtis Smith and William Snyder, Jr. Also publishes poetry. Sometimes comments on rejected mss.

How to Contact: SASE. Responds in 1 day to queries; 1 week to mss. Accepts simultaneous, multiple submissions. Sample copy for $9. For a year subscription, $18.

Payment/Terms: Pays in contributor's copies. Acquires one-time rights.

Advice: "Read the works of Amy Hempel, Jim Harrison, Kelly Cherry, C.K. Williams and Janet Kaufman, all excellent writers who epitomize the writing *Parting Gifts* strives to promote. I look for original voice, original ideas, original setting and characters, language that makes one weep without knowing why, a deep understanding or keen observation of real people in real situations. The magazine is online, along with guidelines and feedback to authors; reading any one or all three will save a lot of postage."

PASSAGES NORTH, Northern Michigan University, Department of English, 1401 Presque Isle Ave., Marquette Mi 49855-5363. (906)227-1203. Fax: (906)227-1096. E-mail: passages@nmu.edu. Kate Myers Hanson, editor. **Contact:** John Smolens, fiction editor. Austin Hummell, poetry editor. Magazine: 8×5 1/2; 80 lb. paper. "*Passages North* publishes quality fiction, poetry and creative nonfiction by emerging and established writers." Readership: General and literary. Annual. Estab. 1979. Circ. 1,000.

Needs: Ethnic/multicultural, literary, mainstream, regional. No genre fiction, science fiction, "typical commercial press work." "Seeking more multicultural work." Receives 100-200 unsolicited mss/month. Accepts 20 mss/year. Does not read May-August. **Publishes 25% new writers/year.** Recently published work by W.P. Kinsella, Jack

Gantos, Lee Martin, Bonnie Campbell, Anthony Bukowski and Peter Orner. When there is time comments on rejected mss.
How to Contact: Responds in 2 months to mss. Accepts simultaneous submissions. Sample copy for $7. Guidelines available on the website.
Payment/Terms: Pays 2 contributor's copies. Rights revert to author upon publication.
Advice: "We look for voice, energetic prose, writers who take risks. Revise, revise. Read what we publish."

THE PATERSON LITERARY REVIEW, Passaic County Community College, One College Blvd., Paterson NJ 07505. (973)684-6555. Fax: (973)523-6085. E-mail: mgillan@pccc.cc.nj.us. Website: www.pccc.cc.nj.us/poetry. **Contact:** Maria Mazziotti Gillan, editor. Magazine: 6×9; 336 pages; 60 lb. paper; 70 lb. cover; illustrations; photos. Annual.
• Work for *PLR* has been included in the *Pushcart Prize* anthology and *Best American Poetry.*
Needs: Ethnic/multicultural, literary, contemporary. "We are interested in quality short stories, with no taboos on subject matter." Receives 60 unsolicited mss/month. Publishes ms 6-12 months after acceptance. **Publishes 5% new writers/year.** Recently published work by Robert Mooney and Abigail Stone. Also publishes literary essays, literary criticism, poetry.
How to Contact: Send SASE for reply or return of ms. "Indicate whether you want story returned." Accepts simultaneous submissions. Sample copy for $13. Reviews fiction.
Payment/Terms: Pays in contributor's copies. Acquires first North American serial rights.
Advice: Looks for "clear, moving and specific work."

PEARL, A Literary Magazine, Pearl, 3030 E. Second St., Long Beach CA 90803-5163. (562)434-4523. E-mail: pearlmag@aol.com. Website: www.pearlmag.com. **Contact:** Marilyn Johnson, editor. Magazine: 5½×8½; 96 pages; 60 lb. recycled, acid-free paper; perfect bound; coated cover; b&w drawings and graphics. "We are primarily a poetry magazine, but we do publish some *very short* fiction and nonfiction. We are interested in lively, readable prose that speaks to *real* people in direct, living language; for a general literary audience." Biannual. Estab. 1974. Circ. 600.
Needs: Humor/satire, literary, mainstream, contemporary, prose poem. "We will consider short-short stories up to 1,200 words. Longer stories (up to 4,000 words) may only be submitted to our short story contest. All contest entries are considered for publication. Although we have no taboos stylistically or subject-wise, obscure, predictable, sentimental, or cliché-ridden stories are a turn-off." Publishes an all fiction issue each year. Receives 10-20 unsolicited mss/month. Accepts 1-10 mss/issue; 12-15 mss/year. Submissions accepted September-May *only.* Publishes ms 6-12 months after acceptance. **Publishes 1-5 new writers/year.** Recently published work by Quinn Dalton, Linda Barnhart, Gina Ochsner, Helena Maria Viramontes, Lisa Glatt and Gerald Locklin. Length: 500-1,200 words; average length: 1,000 words. Also publishes poetry.
How to Contact: SASE. Responds in 2 months to mss. Accepts simultaneous, multiple submissions. Sample copy for $7 (postpaid). Writer's guidelines for #10 SASE.
Payment/Terms: Pays 1 contributor's copy. Acquires first North American serial rights. Sends galleys to author. Sponsors awards/contests.
Advice: "We look for vivid, *dramatized* situations and characters, stories written in an original 'voice,' that make sense and follow a clear narrative line. What makes a manuscript stand out is more elusive, though—more to do with feeling and imagination than anything else."

$ PEEKS & VALLEYS, A New England Fiction Journal, Davis Publications, P.O. Box 708, Newport NH 03773-0708. (603)863-5896. Fax: (603)863-8198. E-mail: hotdog@nhvt.net. Website: www.peeksandvalleys.com. **Contact:** Cindy Davis, editor. "We especially would like to see submissions by children." Quarterly. Estab. 1999.
Needs: Adventure, ethnic/multicultural, fantasy, historical, horror, humor/satire, mainstream, mystery/suspense, religious/inspirational, romance, science fiction, slice-of-life vignettes, suspense, western. No talking animals, sex, or obscenity. Receives 40 unsolicited mss/month. Accepts 7-8 mss/issue; 28-32 mss/year. Publishes ms 8 months after acceptance. **Publishes 80% new writers/year.** Length: 2,600 words; average length: 2,000 words. Publishes short shorts. Also publishes poetry. Always comments on rejected mss.
How to Contact: Send complete ms. Accepts submissions by mail. Responds in 1 month to queries; 2 months to mss. Accepts simultaneous and reprints submissions. Sample copy for $5. Writer's guidelines online.
Payment/Terms: Pays $5. Pays on acceptance for one-time, second serial (reprint) rights. Not copyrighted.
Advice: "Check our guidelines. Too many submissions are excessive length. Best chance of getting accepted is to submit humor."

$ PENINSULAR, Literary Magazine, Cherrybite Publications, Linden Cottage, 45 Burton Rd., Neston Cheshire CH64 4AE, England. 0151 353 0967. Fax: 0870 165 6282. Website: www.cherrybite.co.uk. **Contact:** Shelagh Nugent, editor. Magazine: 90 pages; card cover. "We're looking for brilliant short fiction to make the reader think/laugh/cry. A lively, up-and-coming quality magazine." Quarterly. Estab. 1985. Circ. 400.
Needs: Adventure, ethnic/multicultural (general), fantasy (space fantasy), gay, historical (general), horror (futuristic, psychological, supernatural), humor/satire, lesbian, literary, New Age, psychic/supernatural/occult, science fiction (soft, sociological), gay/lesbian, literary, New Age, psychic/supernatural/occult. No animals telling stories, clichés,

pornography, children's fiction, or purple prose. Receives 50 unsolicited mss/month. Accepts 10 mss/issue; 40 mss/year. Publishes ms 3-6 months after acceptance. **Publishes 4-5 new writers/year.** Recently published work by Alex Keegan, Sarah Klerbart, PDR Lindsay and Leigh Eduardo. Length: 1,000-4,000 words; average length: 3,000 words. Publishes short shorts. Often comments on rejected mss.

How to Contact: Send for guidelines. Prefers hard copy for submissions. Include estimated word count. Responds in 1 week to queries; 2 weeks to mss. Accepts simultaneous and reprints submissions. Sample copy for $5 (cannot accept checks, only dollar bills). Writer's guidelines online.

Payment/Terms: Pays £5 sterling/1,000 words, or can pay in copies and subscriptions. Pays on publication for one-time rights. Sponsors awards/contests.

Advice: "We look for impeccable presentation and grammar, outstanding prose, original story line and the element of difference that forbids me to put the story down. A good opening paragraph usually grabs me. Read one or two copies and study the guidelines. A beginning writer should read as much as possible. The trend seems to be for stories written in first person/present tense and for stories without end leaving the reader thinking 'so what?' Stories not following this trend stand more chance of being published by me!"

PENNSYLVANIA ENGLISH, Penn State DuBois, College Place, DuBois PA 15801. (814)375-4814. Fax: (814)375-4784. E-mail: ajv2@psu.edu "Mention Pennsylvania English in the subject line or at the beginning of the message." **Contact:** Antonio Vallone, editor. Magazine: 5½×8½; up to 180 pages; perfect bound; full color cover featuring the artwork of a Pennsylvania artist. "Our philosophy is quality. We publish literary fiction (and poetry and nonfiction). Our intended audience is literate, college-educated people." Annual. Estab. 1985. Circ. 500.

Needs: Literary, mainstream, contemporary. "No genre fiction or romance." Publishes ms 12-18 months after acceptance. **Publishes 4-6 new writers/year.** Recently published work by Dave Kress, Dan Leone and Paul West. Publishes short shorts. Also publishes literary essays, literary criticism, poetry. Sometimes comments on rejected mss.

How to Contact: SASE. Does not normally accept electronic submissions. Responds in 6 months to mss. Accepts simultaneous submissions. Sample copy not available.

Payment/Terms: Pays in 3 contributor's copies. Acquires first North American serial rights.

Advice: "Quality of the writing is our only measure. We're not impressed by long-winded cover letters detailing awards and publications we've never heard of. Beginners and professionals have the same chance with us. We receive stacks of competently written but boring fiction. For a story to rise out of the rejection pile, it takes more than the basic competence."

PEREGRINE, Amherst Writers & Artists Press, P.O. Box 1076, Amherst MA 01004-1076. (413)253-3307. Fax: (413)253-7764. E-mail: awapress@aol.com. Website: www.amherstwriters.com. **Contact:** Nancy Rose, co-editor. Magazine: 6×9; 120 pages; 60 lb. white offset paper; glossy cover. "*Peregrine* has provided a forum for national and international writers for over 21 years, and is committed to finding excellent work by new writers as well as established authors. We publish what we love, knowing that all editorial decisions are subjective, and that all work has a home somewhere." Annual.

Needs: Poetry and prose—short stories, short short. "No previously published work. No children's stories. We welcome work reflecting diversity of voice." "We like to be surprised. We look for writing that is honest, unpretentious, and memorable." Short pieces have a better chance of publication. Accepts 6-12 mss/issue. Reads October-April. Publishes ms 4 months after acceptance. **Publishes 8-10 new writers/year.** Recently published work by Dennis Maulsby, Susan Howard Case, Earl Coleman, Hedy Straus, Gerald Wheeler, Eileen Dohery, and Terry Johnson. Publishes short shorts.

How to Contact: Enclose sufficiently stamped SASE for return of ms; if disposable copy, enclose #10 SASE for response. Deadline for submission: April 1. Accepts simultaneous, multiple submissions. Sample copy for $10. Writer's guidelines for #10 SASE or on website.

Payment/Terms: Pays contributor's copies. All rights return to writer upon publication.

Advice: "We look for heart and soul as well as technical expertise. Trust your own voice. Familiarize yourself with *Peregrine*." Every ms is read by several readers; all decisions are made by editors.

PERIMETER, A Journal of International Poetry and Art, 301 W. Orion, Santa Ana CA 92707. (714)979-5597. Website: www.perimeter.home.att.net. **Contact:** Jared Miller, editor. Magazine: 5½×8½; 26 pages; 24 lb. paper. "We are a 'little magazine' featuring mostly poetry but also open to great short fiction. The spirit is avant-garde but with no allegiance to any particular movement or school." Annual. Estab. 1997. Circ. 50.

Needs: Literary. "No juvenile, science fiction, genre." Receives 2 unsolicited mss/month. Accepts 1-2 mss/year. Publishes ms 6-12 months after acceptance. **Publishes 1 new writers/year.** Recently published work by Richard Kostelanetz, Alan Catlin, and B.Z. Niditch. Length: 100-2,500 words; average length: 1,500 words. Publishes short shorts. Sometimes comments on rejected mss.

How to Contact: Send SASE for return of ms or disposable copy of ms and SASE for reply only. Sample copy for $4. Writer's guidelines for SASE or by e-mail.

Payment/Terms: Pays 1 contributor's copy; additional copies $2. Pays on publication for one-time rights.

Advice: "We look for excellent writing, imagery and word play. Rewrite, edit, read!"

N **$** **⊡** **PERMUTATIONS, The Journal of Unsettling Fiction**, Permutation Press, CA. E-mail: editor@permutationspress.com (submissions only). Website: www.permutationspress.com. **Contact:** David Anaxagoras, editor. Magazine 5½×8½; 64 pages; 60# white paper; 10pt. C1S cover stock; photos. "*Permutations* is a new small press magazine dedicated to publishing literary fiction with overtones of science fiction, fantasy and horror. We celebrate storytelling in the tradition of Ray Bradbury, Harlan Ellison, Bruce Holland Rogers, Charles Baxter, James Morrow, Neil Gaiman, Dan Simmons. Sometimes edgy, sometimes dark, always weird and wonderful." Quarterly. Estab. 2004.

Needs: Experimental, fantasy (modern, urban), horror (dark fantasy, psychological, supernatural), literary, mainstream, psychic/supernatural/occult, science fiction (soft/sociological), surreal. Accepts 5-8 mss/issue; 20-27 mss/year. Publishes ms 2 years after acceptance. Length: 500-8,000 words; average length: 3,000 words. Publishes short shorts. Often comments on rejected mss.

How to Contact: Send complete ms. Accepts submissions by e-mail. Responds in 1 month to mss. Accepts simultaneous submissions. Writer's guidelines online.

Payment/Terms: Pays $10-50. Pays on acceptance for first North American serial rights.

Advice: "*Permutations* seeks to publish modern literary fiction with overtones of science fiction, fantasy and horror. We are looking for work that is thought-provoking as well as a powerful emotional experience. Stories should on some level be off-beat, surreal, supernatural, fable, or magic realism. We encourage experimental forms, vignettes and short-shorts. We appreciate subtlety. Leave the zombies, serial killers, ray-guns, and hobbits for other markets. We want to see real characters struggling to come to terms with an enigmatic world."

⊡ **PHANTASMAGORIA**, Century College English Dept., 3300 Century Ave. N, White Bear Lake MN 55110. (651)779-3410. E-mail: allenabigail@hotmail.com. **Contact:** Abigail Allen, editor. Magazine: 5½×8½; 140-200 pages. "We publish literary fiction, poetry and essays (no scholarly essays)." Semiannual. Estab. 2001. Circ. 1,000. Member, CLMP.

Needs: Experimental, literary, mainstream. "No children's stories or young adult/teen material." Receives 120 unsolicited mss/month. Accepts 20-40 mss/issue; 40-80 mss/year. Publishes ms 6 months after acceptance. **Publishes 5-10 new writers/year.** Recently published work by Greg Mulcahy, Hiram Goza, Alvin Greenberg, Thaddeus Rutkowski and Elaine Ford. Length: 4,000 words; average length: 2,500 words. Publishes short shorts. Also publishes literary essays, poetry.

How to Contact: Send SASE (or IRC) for return of ms or send a disposable copy of ms and #10 SASE for reply only. Responds in 2 weeks to queries. Sample copy for $9. Writer's guidelines for SASE. Reviews fiction.

Payment/Terms: Pays 2 contributor' s copies. Acquires first North American serial rights.

⊡ **PHOEBE, A Journal of Literature and Arts**, George Mason University, MSN 2D6, 4400 University Dr., Fairfax VA 22030. (703)993-2915. E-mail: phoebe@gmu.edu. Website: www.gmu.edu/pubs/phoebe. **Contact:** Matt Ellsworth, fiction editor. Editors change every year. Magazine: 9×6; 116 pages; 80 lb. paper; 0-5 illustrations; 0-10 photos. "We publish mainly fiction and poetry with occasional visual art." 2 times/year. Estab. 1972. Circ. 3,000.

Needs: "Looking for a broad range of fiction and poetry. We encourage writers and poets to experiment, to stretch the boundaries of genre. No romance, western, juvenile, erotica." Receives 100 unsolicited mss/month. Accepts 3-7 mss/issue. Does not read mss in summer. Publishes ms 3-6 after acceptance. **Publishes 8-10 new writers/year.** Recently published work by Gina Ochsner, Martin Ott, Kurt Rheinheimer, Chris Haven, Amanda Holmes, W.P. Osborn and Ralph Tyler.

How to Contact: SASE. Accepts simultaneous submissions. Sample copy for $6.

Payment/Terms: Pays 2 contributor's copies. All rights revert to author.

Advice: "We are interested in a variety of fiction and poetry. We encourage writers and poets to experiment and stretch boundaries of genre. We suggest potential contributors study previous issues. Each year *Phoebe* sponsors fiction and poetry contests, with $1,000 awarded to the winning short story and poem. The deadline for both the Greg Grummer Award in Poetry and the Phoebe Fiction Prize is December 1. E-mail or send SASE for complete contest guidelines."

$ **⊡** **PIG IRON PRESS**, Pig Iron Press, P.O. Box 237, Youngstown OH 44501-0237. (330)747-6932. Fax: (330)747-0599. **Contact:** Jim Villani. Annual series: 8½×11; 144 pages; 60 lb. offset paper; 85 pt. coated cover stock; b&w illustrations; b&w 120 line photos. "Contemporary literature by new and experimental writers." Annual. Estab. 1975. Circ. 1,000.

Needs: Literary, thematic. "No mainstream." Receives 75-100 unsolicited mss/month. Accepts 60-70 mss/issue. Publishes ms 18 months after acceptance. Recently published work by Judith Hemschemeyer, Andrena Zawinski, and Jim Sanderson. Also publishes poetry.

How to Contact: Send complete ms. Responds in 4 months to queries; 4 months to mss. No simultaneous submissions. Sample copy for $6. Writer's guidelines and current theme list for #10 SASE.

Payment/Terms: Pays $5 minimum. Pays on publication for first North American serial, one-time rights. Sponsors awards/contests.

Advice: "Looking for work that is polished, compelling and magical."

○ **PIKEVILLE REVIEW**, Pikeville College, Sycamor St., Pikeville KY 41501. (606)218-5002. Fax: (606)218-5225. E-mail: eward@pc.edu. Website: www.pc.edu. **Contact:** Fiction Editor. Magazine: 8½×6; 120 pages; illustrations; photos. "Literate audience interested in well-crafted poetry, fiction, essays and reviews." Annual. Estab. 1987. Circ. 500.

Needs: Ethnic/multicultural, experimental, feminist, humor/satire, literary, mainstream, regional, translations. Receives 60-80 unsolicited mss/month. Accepts 3-4 mss/issue. Does not read mss in the summer. Publishes ms 6-8 after acceptance. **Publishes 20 new writers/year.** Recently published work by Jim Wayne Miller and Robert Morgan. Length: 15,000 words; average length: 5,000 words. Publishes short shorts. Also publishes literary essays, poetry. Often comments on rejected mss.

How to Contact: Send SASE for reply, return of ms or send a disposable copy of ms. Accepts simultaneous submissions. Sample copy for $4. Reviews fiction.

Payment/Terms: Pays 5 contributor's copies; additional copies for $4. Acquires first rights. Sponsors awards/contests.

Advice: "Send a clean manuscript with well-developed characters."

$ ▦ **PLANET-THE WELSH INTERNATIONALIST**, P.O. Box 44, Aberystwyth Ceredigion SY23 3ZZ, Cymru/Wales UK. 01970-611255. Fax: 01970-611197. Website: www.planetmagazine.org.uk. **Contact:** John Barnie, fiction editor. "A literary/cultural/political journal centered on Welsh affairs but with a strong interest in minority cultures in Europe and elsewhere." Bimonthly. Circ. 1,400.

Needs: No magical realism, horror, science fiction. Recently published work by Harriet Richards, Katie O'Reilly and Guy Vanderhaeghe.

How to Contact: No submissions returned unless accompanied by an SAE. Writers submitting from abroad should send at least 3 IRCs for return of typescript; 1 IRC for reply only. No e-mail queries. Sample copy for £4. Writer's guidelines online.

Payment/Terms: Pays £40 per 1,000 words.

Advice: "We do not look for fiction which necessarily has a 'Welsh' connection, which some writers assume from our title. We try to publish a broad range of fiction and our main criterion is quality. Try to read copies of any magazine you submit to. Don't write out of the blue to a magazine which might be completely inappropriate for your work. Recognize that you are likely to have a high rejection rate, as magazines tend to favor writers from their own countries."

$ ▣ ▽ **PLEIADES**, Pleiades Press, Department of English & Philosophy, Central Missouri State University, Martin 336, Warrensburg MO 64093. (660)543-4425. Fax: (660)543-8544. Website: www.cmsu.edu/englphil/pleiades.html. **Contact:** Susan Steinberg, fiction editor. Magazine: 5½×8½; 150 pages; 60 lb. paper; perfect-bound; 8 pt. color cover. "We publish contemporary fiction, poetry, interviews, literary essays, special-interest personal essays, reviews for a general and literary audience." Semiannual. Estab. 1991. Circ. 3,000.

● Work from *Pleiades* appears in recent volumes of *The Best American Poetry*, *Pushcart Prizes*, and *Best American Fantasy and Horror.*

Needs: Ethnic/multicultural, experimental, feminist, gay, humor/satire, literary, mainstream, novel excerpts, regional, translations, magic realism. No science fiction, fantasy, confession, erotica. Receives 100 unsolicited mss/month. Accepts 8 mss/issue; 16 mss/year. "We're slower at reading manuscripts in the summer." Publishes ms 9 months after acceptance. **Publishes 4-5 new writers/year.** Recently published work by Sherman Alexie, Edith Pearlman, Joyce Carol Oates and James Tate. Length: 2,000-6,000 words; average length: 3,000-6,000 words. Also publishes literary essays, literary criticism, poetry. Sometimes comments on rejected mss.

How to Contact: Send complete ms. Accepts submissions by mail. Include 75-100 word bio and list of publications. Send SASE for reply, return of ms or send a disposable copy of ms. Responds in 2 months to queries; 2 months to mss. Accepts simultaneous submissions. Sample copy for $5 (back issue), $6 (current issue). Writer's guidelines for #10 SASE.

Payment/Terms: Pays $10. Pays on publication for first North American serial, second serial (reprint) rights. Occasionally requests rights for TV, radio reading, website.

Advice: Looks for "a blend of language and subject matter that entices from beginning to end. Send us your best work. Don't send us formula stories. While we appreciate and publish well-crafted traditional pieces, we constantly seek the story that risks, that breaks form and expectations and wins us over anyhow."

MARKET CONDITIONS are constantly changing! If you're still using this book and it is 2005 or later, buy the newest edition of *Novel & Short Story Writer's Market* at your favorite bookstore or order from Writer's Digest Books by calling 1-800-448-0915.

$☐ ☑ PLOUGHSHARES, Emerson College, Department M, 120 Boylston St., Boston MA 02116. Website: www.pshares.org. **Contact:** Fiction Editor. "Our mission is to present dynamic, contrasting views on what is valid and important in contemporary literature, and to discover and advance significant literary talent. Each issue is guest-edited by a different writer. We no longer structure issues around preconceived themes." Estab. 1971. Circ. 6,000.

• Work published in *Ploughshares* has been selected regularly for inclusion in the *Best American Short Stories* and *O. Henry Prize* anthologies. In fact the magazine has the honor of having the most stories selected from a single issue (three) to be included in *Best American Short Stories*. Guest editors have included Richard Ford, Tim O'Brien and Ann Beattie. *Ploughshares* ranked on *Writer's Digest*'s "Top 30" list of best markets for fiction writers.

Needs: Literary, mainstream. "No genre (science fiction, detective, gothic, adventure, etc.), popular formula or commerical fiction whose purpose is to entertain rather than to illuminate." Receives 1,000 unsolicited mss/month. Accepts 30 mss/year. Reading period: postmarked August 1 to March 31. Publishes ms 6 months after acceptance. **Publishes some new writers/year.** Recently published work by Rick Bass, Joy Williams and Andre Dubus.

How to Contact: Cover letter should included "previous pubs." SASE. Responds in 5 months to mss. Accepts simultaneous submissions. Sample copy for $9 (back issue). Writer's guidelines online.

Payment/Terms: Pays $25/printed page, $50-250. Pays on publication for first North American serial rights.

Advice: "Be familiar with our fiction issues, fiction by our writers and by our various editors (e.g., Sue Miller, Tobias Wolff, Rosellen Brown, Richard Ford, Jayne Anne Phillips, James Alan McPherson) and more generally acquaint yourself with the best short fiction currently appearing in the literary quarterlies, and the annual prize anthologies (*Pushcart Prize, O. Henry Awards, Best American Short Stories*). Also realistically consider whether the work you are submitting is as good as or better than—in your own opinion—the work appearing in the magazine you're sending to. What is the level of competition? And what is its volume? Never send 'blindly' to a magazine, or without carefully weighing your prospect there against those elsewhere. Always keep a log and a copy of the work you submit."

☑ POETRY & PROSE ANNUAL, Golden Mean, P.O. Box 1175, Seaside OR 97138. (503)717-0112. E-mail: poetry@poetryproseannual.com. Website: www.poetryproseannual.com. **Contact:** Sandra Foushe. Magazine: 7 × 8½; 104 pages; semi-gloss paper; glossy cover; illustrations; photos. "*Poetry & Prose Annual* is organized and edited to be read as a whole book, the prose (both fiction and nonfiction) and poetry directed to an enlightened intelligence with a positive perspective on the world." Annual. Estab. 1997. Circ. 1,000.

Needs: Adventure, ethnic/multicultural, experimental, family saga, feminist, historical, humor/satire, literary, mainstream, mystery/suspense (amateur sleuth, cozy), New Age, regional, romance. Accepts 20-30 mss/year; 20-30 mss/year. **Publishes 40% new writers/year.** Recently published work by Mark Christopher Eades, June Stromberg, Robin Reid and Kay Kinnear. Length: 2,500 words; average length: 1,200 words. Publishes short shorts. Also publishes literary essays, poetry. Sometimes comments on rejected mss.

How to Contact: Send a disposable copy of ms and #10 SASE for reply only. Accepts simultaneous and reprints, multiple submissions with notification if the piece is accepted elsewhere. Sample copy for $10. Writer's guidelines for SASE or website.

Payment/Terms: Pays 2 contributor's copies and subscription to magazine; additional copies $8. Pays on publication for one-time, electronic rights. Sponsors awards/contests.

Advice: "We look for substantive and enlightening ideas, a writing style with clarity and ingenuity, an awareness of emotional, intellectual, and physical consciousness. Follow the submission guidelines completely and enclose all the required elements. Familiarize yourself with the editorial intent of the *Annual*. The trend toward short stories fits our format well, but we are open to longer prose, both fiction and nonfiction."

☑ POETRY FORUM SHORT STORIES, Poetry Forum, 5713 Larchmont Dr., Erie PA 16509. (814)866-2543. E-mail: 75562.670@compuserve.com. Website: www.thepoetryforum.com. **Contact:** Gunvor Skogsholm, editor. Newspaper: 7 × 8½; 34 pages; card cover; illustrations. "Human interest themes (no sexually explicit or racially biased or blasphemous material) for the general public—from the grassroot to the intellectual." Quarterly. Estab. 1989. Circ. 400.

Needs: Confessions, ethnic/multicultural, experimental, fantasy, feminist, historical, literary, mainstream, mystery/suspense, religious/inspirational, romance, science fiction, young adult/teen, contemporary, prose poem, senior citizen/retirement. "No blasphemous, sexually explicit material." Publishes annual special fiction issue. Receives 50 unsolicited mss/month. Accepts 12 mss/issue; 40 mss/year. Publishes ms 6 months after acceptance. Agented fiction 1%. **Publishes 80% new writers/year.** Recently published work by Tom Shay and James Lachard. Length: 500-5,000 words; average length: 2,000 words. Also publishes literary essays, literary criticism, poetry.

How to Contact: Accepts submissions by e-mail, fax. SASE. Responds in 2 months to mss. Accepts simultaneous and reprints submissions. Sample copy for $3. Writer's guidelines for SASE. Reviews fiction.

Payment/Terms: Acquires one-time rights.

Advice: "Tell your story with no padding as if telling it to a person standing with one hand on the door read to run out to a meeting. Have a good lead. This is the 'alpha & omega' of all good story writing. Don't start with 'This is a story about a boy and a girl.' Avoid writing how life 'ought to be,' rather write how life is."

Ⓜ POINTED CIRCLE, Portland Community College-Cascade, 705 N. Killingsworth St., Portland OR 97217. (503)978-5251. E-mail: ckimball@pcc.edu. **Contact:** Cynthia Kimball, English instructor, faculty advisor. Magazine: 80 pages; b&w illustrations; photos. "Anything of interest to educationally/culturally mixed audience." Annual. Estab. 1980.

Needs: Ethnic/multicultural, literary, regional, contemporary, prose poem. "We will read whatever is sent, but encourage writers to remember we are a quality literary/arts magazine intended to promote the arts in the community. No pornography. Be mindful of deadlines and length limits." Accepts submissions only October 1-March 1, for July 1 issue. Recently published work by J.D. McLean, Arturo Diaz, Kumaridevi Sivam.

How to Contact: Accepts submissions by e-mail, fax. Submitted materials will not be returned; SASE for notification only. Accepts multiple submissions. Sample copy for $4.50 payable to PCC. Writer's guidelines for #10 SASE.

Payment/Terms: Pays 1 copy. Acquires one-time rights.

Advice: "Looks for quality—topicality—nothing trite. The author cares about language and acts responsibly toward the reader, honors the reader's investment of time and piques the reader's interest."

Ⓜ PORCUPINE LITERARY ARTS MAGAZINE, P.O. Box 259, Cedarburg WI 53012-0259. (262)375-3128. E-mail: ppine259@aol.com. Website: members.aol.com/ppine259. **Contact:** Chris Skoczynski, fiction editor. Magazine: 5×8½; 125 pages; glossy color cover stock; art work and photos. Publishes "primarily poetry and short fiction. Novel excerpts are acceptable if self-contained. No restrictions as to theme or style." Semiannual. Estab. 1996. Circ. 1,500.

Needs: Condensed novels, ethnic/multicultural, literary, mainstream. "No pornographic or religious." Receives 30 unsolicited mss/month. Accepts 3 mss/issue; 6 mss/year. Publishes ms 1 year after acceptance. **Publishes 4-6 new writers/year.** Recently published work by Judith Ford, Holly Day, Yang Huang and Jeffrey Perso. Length: 2,000-7,500 words; average length: 3,500 words. Also publishes literary essays, poetry. Sometimes comments on rejected mss.

How to Contact: Accepts submissions by e-mail. Send SASE for reply, return of ms or send a disposable copy of ms. Responds in 2 weeks to queries; 2 months to mss. Sample copy for $5. Writer's guidelines for #10 SASE.

Payment/Terms: Pays 1 contributor's copy; additional copies for $8.95. Pays on publication for one time rights.

Advice: Looks for "believable dialogue and a narrator I can see and hear and smell. Form or join a writers' group. Read aloud. Rewrite extensively."

Ⓝ Ⓜ PORTLAND REVIEW, Portland State University, Box 347, Portland OR 97207-0347. (503)7254533. Fax: (503)725-4534. E-mail: review@vanguard.vg.pdx.edu. Website: www.portlandreview.org. **Contact:** Editors rotate. Rebecca Rich Goldweber, editor 02/03. Magazine: 9×6; 100 pages; b&w art and photos. "We seek to publish fiction in which content takes precedence over style." Quarterly. Estab. 1956. Circ. 500.

Needs: Adventure, ethnic/multicultural, experimental, feminist, gay, historical, humor/satire, lesbian, literary, mainstream, mystery/suspense, regional, science fiction. Wants more humor. Receives 100 unsolicited mss/month. Accepts 10-12 mss/issue; 30-40 mss/year. Recently published work by Ian McMillan, Heather King, and Benjamin Chambers. Also publishes literary essays, poetry.

How to Contact: Send complete ms. Send SASE for return of ms. Responds in 2-4 months to mss. Accepts simultaneous submissions. Sample copy for $7 plus $1 postage.

Payment/Terms: Pays contributor's copies. Acquires first North American serial rights.

Advice: "Our editors, and thus our taste/biases change annually, so keep trying us."

Ⓜ POTOMAC REVIEW, The Journal for Arts & Humanities, Montgomery College, Paul Peck Humanities Institute, 51 Mannakee St., Rockville MD 20850. (301)251-7417. Fax: (301)738-1745. E-mail: wattrsedge@aol.com. Website: www.montgomerycollege.edu/potomacreview. **Contact:** Christa Watters. Magazine: 5½×8½; 248 pages; 50 lb. paper; 65 lb. cover; illustrations; photos. *Potomac Review* "explores the inner and outer terrain of the Mid-Atlantic and beyond via a challenging diversity of prose, poetry and b&w artwork." Biannual. Estab. 1994. Circ. 2,000.

Needs: "Stories with a vivid, individual quality that get at 'the concealed side' of life." Humor (plus essays, cogent nonfiction of all sorts) welcome. Special section opens each issue e.g., upcoming "Beyond" for Winter 2003-04, "Within/Without" for Spring/Summer 2004. Receives 100+ unsolicited mss/month. Accepts 40-50 mss/issue. Publishes ms within 1 year after acceptance. Agented fiction 5%. **Publishes 20 new writers/year.** Recently published work by Jeffrey Hammond, Wayne Karlin, Jeffrey Scheuer, Neil Isaacs, Ann Knox, Kenneth Carroll, Hilary Tham and Ori Z. Soltes. Length: 5,000 words; average length: 2,000 words. Publishes short shorts.

How to Contact: Send SASE for reply, return of ms or send a disposable copy of ms. Responds in 3 weeks to queries; 6 months to mss. Accepts simultaneous and reprints submissions. Sample copy for $10. Writer's guidelines for #10 SASE or on website. Reviews fiction.

Payment/Terms: Pays 2 or more contibutor's copies; additional copies for a 40% discount.

Advice: "Have something to say in an original voice; check the magazine first; rewriting often trumps the original."

$ Ⓜ Ⓜ THE PRAIRIE JOURNAL, Journal of Canadian Literature, Prairie Journal Trust, P.O. Box 61203, Brentwood P.O., Calgary AB T2L 2K6 Canada. Website: www.geocities.com/prairiejournal. **Contact:** A.E. Burke, editor. Journal: 7×8½; 50-60 pages; white bond paper; Cadillac cover stock; cover illustrations. "The audience is literary, university, library, scholarly, and creative readers/writers." Semiannual. Estab. 1983. Circ. 600.

Needs: Literary, regional, Literary. No genre (romance, horror, western—sagebrush or cowboys), erotic, science fiction, or mystery. Receives 50 unsolicited mss/month. Accepts 10-15 mss/issue; 20-30 mss/year. Suggested deadlines: April 1 for spring/summer issue; October 1 for fall/winter. Publishes ms 4-6 months after acceptance. **Publishes 10 new writers/year.** Recently published work by Robert Clark and Christopher Blais. Length: 100-3,000 words; average length: 2,500 words. Also publishes literary essays, literary criticism, poetry. Sometimes comments on rejected mss.

How to Contact: Send complete ms. Accepts submissions by mail, e-mail. SASE (IRC). Include cover letter of past credits, if any. Reply to queries for SAE with 55¢ for postage or IRC. No American stamps. Responds in 2 weeks to queries; 6 months to mss. No simultaneous submissions. Sample copy for $5. Writer's guidelines online. Reviews fiction.

Payment/Terms: Pays $10-75. Pays on publication for first North American serial, electronic rights; in Canada author retains copyright with acknowledgement appreciated rights.

Advice: "We like character-driven rather than plot-centered fiction." Interested in "innovative work of quality. Beginning writers welcome! There is no point in simply republishing known authors or conventional, predictable plots. Of the genres we receive fiction is most often of the highest calibre. It is a very competitive field. Be proud of what you send. You're worth it."

☑☒ PRAIRIE SCHOONER, University of Nebraska, English Department, 201 Andrews Hall, P.O. Box 880334, Lincoln NE 68588-0334. (402)472-0911. Fax: (402)472-9771. Website: www.unl.edu/schooner/psmain.h tm. **Contact:** Hilda Raz, editor. Magazine: 6×9; 200 pages; good stock paper; heavy cover stock. "A fine literary quarterly of stories, poems, essays and reviews for a general audience that reads for pleasure." Estab. 1926. Circ. 3,200.

• *Prairie Schooner*, one of the oldest publications in this book, has garnered several awards and honors over the years. Work appearing in the magazine has been selected for anthologies including *Pushcart Prizes* and *Best American Short Stories*.

Needs: Good fiction (literary). Receives 500 unsolicited mss/month. Accepts 4-5 mss/issue. Mss are read September through May only. **Publishes 5-10 new writers/year.** Recently published work by Joyce Carol Oates, Judith Ortiz Cofer, Chitra Divakaruni, Daniel Stern and Janet Burroway. Also publishes poetry.

How to Contact: Send complete ms with SASE and cover letter listing previous publications—where, when. Responds in 4 months to mss. Sample copy for $5. Writer's guidelines and excerpts online. Reviews fiction.

Payment/Terms: Pays in contributor's copies and prize money awarded. Acquires all rights. Will reassign rights upon request after publication. Sponsors awards/contests.

Advice: "*Prairie Schooner* is eager to see fiction from beginning and established writers. Be tenacious. Accept rejection as a temporary setback and send out rejected stories to other magazines. *Prairie Schooner* is not a magazine with a program. We look for good fiction in traditional narrative modes as well as experimental, meta-fiction or any other form or fashion a writer might try. Create striking detail, well-developed characters, fresh dialogue; let the images and the situations evoke the stories' themes. Too much explication kills a lot of otherwise good stories. Be persistent. Keep writing and sending out new work. Be familiar with the tastes of the magazines where you're sending. We are receiving record number of submissions. Prospective contributors must sometimes wait longer to receive our reply."

Ⓝ $☐ ⊕ PRETEXT, Pen and Inc. Press, School of EAS, University of East Anglia, Norwich Norfolk NR1-4HE, UK. (+44)(0)1603592783. Fax: (+44)(0)1603507728. E-mail: info@penandinc.co.uk. Website: www.penand inc.co.uk. **Contact:** Katri Skala, managing editor. Magazine: 210X148 mm; 170 pages; Albury 80qsm paper; 4-color 240qsm art board cover stock; illustrations; photos. Semiannual. Estab. 1999. Member of Inpress and Independent Publishers Guild.

Needs: Ethnic/multicultural, feminist, gay, humor/satire, lesbian, literary, translations. No mass-market or non-literary work. Receives 70-80 unsolicited mss/month. Accepts 10 mss/issue; 20 mss/year. Publishes ms 6 months after acceptance. Agented fiction 30%. **Publishes 4 new writers/year.** Recently published work by Bernardine Evansto, Michele Roberts, Carol Birch, Charlie Boxer, and Douglas Cowie. Length: 6,000 words; average length: 3,000-4,000 words. Publishes short shorts. Also publishes literary essays, literary criticism, poetry. Often comments on rejected mss.

How to Contact: Send complete ms. Send SASE (or IRC) for return of the ms. Responds in 2 days to queries; 3 months to mss. Accepts simultaneous, multiple submissions. Sample copy for £7.99 (Europe) £9.99 (rest of world). Writer's guidelines for SASE, fax, e-mail or online.

Payment/Terms: Pays $50 and 1 contributor's copy. Pays on publication. Sends galleys to author.

Advice: "Looking for good writing with a sense of purpose and an awareness of literary context. Never send until you are sure it's the best it can be."

Ⓝ ☒ ☑ ◎ PRIMAVERA, Box 37-7547, Chicago IL 60637-7547. (312)324-5920. **Contact:** Editorial Board. Magazine: 5½×8½; 128 pages; 60 lb. paper; glossy cover; illustrations; photos. Literature and graphics reflecting the experiences of women: poetry, short stories, photos, drawings. "We publish original fiction that reflects the

experience of women. We select works that encompass the lives of women of different ages, races, sexual orientations and social class." Annual. Estab. 1975. Circ. 1,000.
- *Primavera* has won grants from the Illinois Arts Council, the Puffin Foundation and from Chicago Women in Publishing.

Needs: Fantasy, feminist, gay, humor/satire, lesbian, literary, science fiction. "We dislike slick stories packaged for more traditional women's magazines. We publish only work reflecting the experiences of women, but also publish manuscripts by men." Receives 40 unsolicited mss/month. Accepts 6-10 mss/issue. Publishes ms 1 year after acceptance. **Publishes some new writers/year.** Recently published work by Rawn N. James, Jr., D. Troy Sherrod, Janice Leotti, Laurie Blauner, and Therese Pampellonne. Also publishes poetry. Sometimes comments on rejected mss.
How to Contact: Send complete ms. Responds in 6 months to mss. No simultaneous submissions. Sample copy for $5; $10 for recent issues. Writer's guidelines for SASE.
Payment/Terms: Pays 2 contributor's copies. Acquires first rights.
Advice: "We're looking for artistry and deftness of untrendy, unhackneyed themes; an original slant on a well-known themes, an original use of language, and the highest quality we can find."

$ ⬚ ⬚ ⬚ PRISM INTERNATIONAL, Department of Creative Writing, Buch E462-1866 Main Mall, University of British Columbia, Vancouver BC V6T 1Z1 Canada. (604)822-2514. Fax: (604)822-3616. Website: prism.arts. ubc.ca. **Contact:** Billeh Nickerson, editor. Magazine: 6×9; 72-80 pages; Zephyr book paper; Cornwall, coated one side cover; artwork on cover. "An international journal of contemporary writing—fiction, poetry, drama, creative nonfiction and translation." Readership: "public and university libraries, individual subscriptions, bookstores—a world-wide audience concerned with the contemporary in literature." Quarterly. Estab. 1959. Circ. 1,200.
- *PRISM International* has won numerous magazine awards and stories first published in *PRISM International* have been included in the *Journey Prize Anthology* every year since 1991. *PRISM International* ranked on *Writer's Digest's* "Top 30" list of best markets for fiction writers.

Needs: Experimental, novel excerpts (up to 25 double-spaced pages), traditional. New writing that is contemporary and literary. Short stories and self-contained novel excerpts. Works of translation are eagerly sought and should be accompanied by a copy of the original. Would like to see more translations. "No gothic, confession, religious, romance, pornography, or sci-fi." Also looking for creative nonfiction that is literary, not journalistic, in scope and tone. Receives over 100 unsolicited mss/month. Accepts 70 mss/year. "*PRISM* publishes both new and established writers; our contributors have included Franz Kafka, Gabriel Garcia Marquez, Michael Ondaatje, Margaret Laurence, Mark Anthony Jarman, Gail Anderson-Dargatz and Eden Robinson." Publishes ms 4 months after acceptance. **Publishes 7 new writers/year.** Publishes short shorts. Also publishes poetry.
How to Contact: Send complete ms. Accepts submissions by mail, fax, phone. "Keep it simple. U.S. contributors take note: Do not send U.S. stamps, they are not valid in Canada. Send International Reply Coupons instead." Responds in 4 months to queries; 4 months to mss. Sample copy for $7 or on website. Writer's guidelines online.
Payment/Terms: Pays $20/printed page, and 1-year subscription. Pays on publication for first North American serial rights. Selected authors are paid an additional $10/page for digital rights. Sponsors awards/contests.
Advice: "Read several issues of our magazine before submitting. We are committed to publishing outstanding literary work. We look for strong, believeable characters; real voices; attention to language; interesting ideas and plots. Send us fresh, innovative work which also shows a mastery of the basics of good prose writing."

$ ⬚ PROVINCETOWN ARTS, Provincetown Arts, Inc., 650 Commercial St., P.O. Box 35, Provincetown MA 02657. (508)487-3167. Website: www.provincetownarts.org. **Contact:** Christopher Busa, editor. Magazine: 9×12; 184 pages; 60 lb. coated paper; 12 pcs. cover; illustrations; photos. "*Provincetown Arts* focuses broadly on the artists and writers who inhabit or visit the Lower Cape, and seeks to stimulate creative activity and enhance public awareness of the cultural life of the nation's oldest continuous art colony. Drawing upon a 75-year tradition rich in visual art, literature, and theater, *Provincetown Arts* offers a unique blend of interviews, fiction, visual features, reviews, reporting, and poetry." Annual. Estab. 1985. Circ. 8,000.
Needs: Mainstream, novel excerpts. Accepts 5 mss/issue. Publishes ms 4 months after acceptance. Recently published work by Carole Maso and Hilary Masters. Length: 500-5,000 words; average length: 3,000 words. Publishes short shorts. Also publishes literary essays, literary criticism, poetry. Sometimes comments on rejected mss.
How to Contact: Send complete ms. SASE. Responds in 3 weeks to queries; 2 months to mss. Accepts simultaneous submissions. Sample copy for $10. Writer's guidelines for #10 SASE. Reviews fiction.
Payment/Terms: Pays $75-300. Pays on publication for first, one-time, second serial (reprint) rights. Sends galleys to author.

⬚ PUCKERBRUSH REVIEW, Puckerbrush Press, 76 Maine St., Orono ME 04473. (207)866-4868/581-3832. **Contact:** Constance Hunting, editor/publisher. Magazine: 9×12; 80-100 pages; illustrations. "We publish interviews, fiction, review, poetry for a literary audience." Semiannual. Estab. 1979. Circ. 500.
Needs: Experimental, gay (occasionally), literary, Belles-lettres. "Wants to see more original, quirky and well-written fiction. No genre fiction. Nothing cliché, nothing overly sensational except in its human interest." Receives 30 unsolicited mss/month. Accepts 6 mss/issue; 12 mss/year. Publishes ms 1 year after acceptance. **Publishes 6 new writers/year.** Recently published work by John Sullivan, Merle Hillman, Wayne Burke. Publishes short shorts.

Also publishes literary essays, literary criticism, poetry. Sometimes comments on rejected mss.

How to Contact: SASE. Responds in 2 months to mss. Accepts simultaneous, multiple submissions. Sample copy for $2. Writer's guidelines for SASE. Reviews fiction.

Payment/Terms: Pays in contributor's copies.

Advice: "I don't want to see tired plots or treatments. I want to see respect for language—the right words, true views of human nature. Don't follow clichés, but don't be too outré either."

○ **PUERTO DEL SOL**, New Mexico State University, Box 3E, Las Cruces NM 88003-0001. (505)646-2345. Fax: (505)646-7755. E-mail: PUERTO@nmsu.edu. Website: www.nmsu.edu/~puerto/welcome.html. **Contact:** Kevin McIlvoy, editor-in-chief and fiction editor. Kathleene West, poetry editor. Magazine: 6×9; 200 pages; 60 lb. paper; 70 lb. cover stock. "We publish quality material from anyone. Poetry, fiction, interviews, reviews, parts-of-novels, long poems." Semiannual. Estab. 1961. Circ. 1,500.

Needs: Ethnic/multicultural, experimental, literary, mainstream, novel excerpts, translations, contemporary, prose poem. Accepts 8-10 mss/issue; 12-15 mss/year. Does not read mss March-August. **Publishes 8-10 new writers/year.** Recently published work by Dagoberto Gilb, Wendell Mayo and William H. Cobb. Also publishes literary essays, poetry. Occasionally comments on rejected mss.

How to Contact: Responds in 3 months to mss. Accepts simultaneous submissions. Sample copy for $8.

Payment/Terms: Pays 2 contributor's copies. Acquires one-time, rights revert to author rights.

Advice: "We are open to all forms of fiction, from the conventional to the wildly experimental and we are pleased to work with emerging writers."

◪ ⊕ ◎ **QUALITY WOMEN'S FICTION, Extending the Boundaries of Women's Fiction**, QWF, P.O. Box 1768, Rugby CV21 4ZA, UK. E-mail: jo@qwfmagazine.co.uk. Website: www.qwfmagazine.co.uk. **Contact:** Sally Zigmond, assistant editor. Magazine: A5; 80 pages; glossy paper. "*QWF* gets under the skin of the female experience and exposes emotional truth." Bimonthly. Estab. 1994. Circ. 1,800.

Needs: Experimental, feminist, literary. Receives 30 unsolicited mss/month. Accepts 12 mss/issue; 78 mss/year. Does not read mss June-August. Publishes ms 6-12 months after acceptance. **Publishes 15 new writers/year.** Recently published work by Kathryn Kulpa, Ruth Latta, Kirsten Marek. Length: 1,500-5,000 words; average length: 2,500 words. Publishes short shorts. Also publishes literary essays, literary criticism. Always comments on rejected mss.

How to Contact: Send complete ms. Accepts submissions by e-mail. Send SASE (or IRC) for return of ms or send disposable copy of the ms and #10 SASE for reply only. Responds in 2 months to queries; 2 months to mss. Accepts reprints submissions. Sample copy for SASE. Writer's guidelines by e-mail. Reviews fiction.

Payment/Terms: Pays 3 contributor's copies; additional copies $12. Pays on publication for First British Serial rights.

Advice: "Study the stories published on the *QWF* website."

◪ ◎ **QUARTER AFTER EIGHT, A Journal of Prose and Community**, QAE, Ellis Hall, Ohio University, Atens OH 45701. (740)593-2827. E-mail: quarteraftereight@hotmail.com. Website: www.quarteraftereight.org. **Contact:** Hayley Haugen, editor-in-chief. Magazine: 6×9; 310 pages; 20 lb. glossy cover stock; photos. "We look to publish work which challenges boundaries of genre, style, idea, and voice." Annual.

Needs: Condensed novels, erotica, ethnic/multicultural, experimental, gay, humor/satire, lesbian, literary, mainstream, translations. "No traditional, conventional fiction." Send SASE for list of upcoming themes. Receives 150-200 unsolicited mss/month. Accepts 40-50 mss/issue. Does not read mss mid-March-mid-September. Publishes ms 6-12 months after acceptance. Agented fiction 15%. **Publishes 10-15 new writers/year.** Recently published work by Virgil Suarez, Maureen Sexton and Amy England. Length: 10,000 words; average length: 3,000 words. Publishes short shorts. Also publishes literary essays, literary criticism, poetry. Sometimes comments on rejected mss.

How to Contact: Send SASE for return of ms or send a disposable copy of ms. Responds in 3 months to mss. Accepts simultaneous, multiple submissions. Sample copy for $10, 8×11 SAE and $1.60 postage. Writer's guidelines for #10 SASE. Reviews fiction.

Payment/Terms: Pays 2 contributor's copies; additional copies $10. Acquires first North American serial rights. Sponsors awards/contests.

Advice: "We look for fiction that is experimental, exploratory, devoted to and driven by language—that which succeeds in achieving the *QAE* aesthetic. Please subscribe to our journal and read what is published. We do not publish traditional lined poetry or straightforward conventional stories. We encourage writers to submit after they have gotten acquainted with the *QAE* aesthetic."

$◪ ▧ **QUARTERLY WEST**, University of Utah, 200 S. Central Campus Dr., Room 317, Salt Lake City UT 84112-9109. (801)581-3938. Website: www.utah.edu/quarterlywest. **Contact:** Jeff Chapman. Magazine: 6×9; 224 pages; 60 lb. paper; 5-color cover stock; illustrations; photos rarely. "We publish fiction, poetry, and nonfiction in long and short formats, and will consider experimental as well as traditional works." Semiannual. Estab. 1976. Circ. 1,900.

• *Quarterly West* was awarded First Place for Editorial Content from the American Literary Magazine

Awards. Work published in the magazine has been selected for inclusion in the *Pushcart Prize* anthology and *The Best American Short Stories* anthology.

Needs: Ethnic/multicultural, experimental, humor/satire, literary, mainstream, novel excerpts, slice-of-life vignettes, translations, short shorts, translations. No detective, science fiction or romance. Receives 300 unsolicited mss/month. Accepts 6-10 mss/issue; 12-20 mss/year. Reads mss between September 1 and May 1 only. "Submissions received between May 2 and August 31 will be returned unread." Publishes ms 6 months after acceptance. **Publishes 3 new writers/year.** Recently published work by Catherine Ryan Hyde, David Shields, James Tate and David Roderick.

How to Contact: Send complete ms. Accepts submissions by mail. Brief cover letters welcome. Send SASE for reply or return of ms. Responds in 6 months to mss. Accepts simultaneous submissions with notification. Sample copy for $7.50 or online. Writer's guidelines online.

Payment/Terms: Pays $15-50, and 2 contributor's copies. Pays on publication for all rights.

Advice: "We publish a special section of short shorts every issue, and we also sponsor a biennial novella contest. We are open to experimental work—potential contributors should read the magazine! We solicit occasionally, but tend more toward the surprises—unsolicited. Don't send more than one story per submission, and wait until you've heard about the first before submitting another."

$ ◙ RAIN CROW, Rain Crow Publishing, P.O. Box 11013, Chicago IL 60611. Fax: (503)214-6615. Website: www.rain-crow.com/. **Contact:** Michael S. Manley, editor. Magazine/journal: 8½×5½; 144-160 pages; white bond paper; glossy cover; illustrations; photos. "We publish new and established writers in many styles and genres. We are a publication for people passionate about the short story form." Triannual. Estab. 2001. Circ. 500. Member, CLMP.

Needs: Erotica, experimental, literary, mainstream, science fiction, translations, literary. "No propaganda, pornography, juvenile, formulaic." Receives 120-150 unsolicited mss/month. Accepts 10-12 mss/issue; 30 mss/year. Publishes ms 4 months after acceptance. **Publishes several new writers/year.** Recently published work by Susan Neville, Peter Johnson, Paul Maliszewski, Peter Hynes, Carolyn Allesio and Laura Denham. Length: 250-8,000 words; average length: 3,500 words. Publishes short shorts. Sometimes comments on rejected mss.

How to Contact: Send complete ms. Accepts submissions by mail, e-mail. Include list of publications. Send SASE for reply, return of ms or send a disposable copy of ms. Responds in 3 weeks to queries; 4 months to mss. Accepts simultaneous and reprints, multiple submissions. Sample copy for $8. Writer's guidelines online.

Payment/Terms: Pays $5-150. Pays on publication for one-time, electronic rights.

Advice: "I look for attention to craft: voice, language, character and plot working together to maximum effect. I look for stories that deserve rereading and that I would gladly recommend others read. Send your best work. Present your work professionally. Unique, credible settings and situations that entertain get the most attention."

◙ RAINBOW CURVE, P.O. Box 93206, Las Vegas NV 89193-3206. E-mail: rainbowcurve@sbcglobal.net. Website: www.rainbowcurve.net. **Contact:** Daphne Young and Julianne Bonnet, editors. Magazine: 5½×8½; 100 pages; 60 lb. paper; coated cover. "*Rainbow Curve* publishes fiction and poetry that dabble at the edge; contemporary work that evokes emotion. Our audience is those interested in exploring new worlds of experience and emotion; raw, visceral work is what we look for." Semiannual. Estab. 2002. Circ. 500.

Needs: Ethnic/multicultural, experimental, feminist, gay, lesbian, literary. "No genre fiction (romance, western, fantasy, sci-fi)." Receives 30 unsolicited mss/month. Accepts 8-10 mss/issue; 16-20 mss/year. Publishes ms 6 months after acceptance. Agented fiction 1%. **Publishes 80% new writers/year.** Recently published work by Jonathan Barrett, Trent Busch, Rob Carney, Peter Foutaine, Bridget Hoida, and Karen Toloui. Length: 500-10,000 words; average length: 7,500 words. Publishes short shorts. Sometimes comments on rejected mss.

How to Contact: Send SASE for return of ms or send a disposable copy of ms and #10 SASE for reply only. Responds in 3 months to mss. Accepts simultaneous submissions. Sample copy for $6. Writer's guidelines for SASE or on website.

Payment/Terms: Pays 1 contributor's copy; additional copies $5. Acquires one-time rights. Sends galleys to author.

Advice: "Unusual rendering of usual subjects and strong narrative voice make a story stand out. Unique glimpses into the lives of others—make it new."

ℕ ◙ RAMBUNCTIOUS REVIEW, Rambunctious Press, Inc., 1221 W. Pratt Blvd., Chicago IL 60626-4329. **Contact:** Nancy Lennon, Richard Goldman and Elizabeth Hausler, editors. Magazine: 10X7; 48 pages; illustrations; photos. Annual. Estab. 1983. Circ. 300.

READ 'THE BUSINESS OF FICTION WRITING' section for information on manuscript preparation, mailing tips, rights and more.

Needs: Experimental, feminist, humor/satire, literary, mainstream. No mystery or drama. Upcoming themes: Milestones (Winter 2004), deadline "early to middle 2004." List of upcoming themes available for SASE. Receives 30 unsolicited mss/month. Accepts 4-5 mss/issue. Does not read May-August. Publishes ms 1 year after acceptance. **Publishes 4-5 new writers/year.** Recently published work by Robert Waton, Lynn Sadler, Ben Scott. Publishes short shorts. Also publishes poetry. Sometimes comments on rejected mss.

How to Contact: Send complete ms. Send SASE for reply, return of ms or send a disposable copy of ms. Responds in 1 year to mss. Accepts simultaneous submissions. Sample copy for $4.

Payment/Terms: Pays 2 contributor's copies. Acquires one-time rights. Sponsors awards/contests.

RATTAPALLAX, Rattapallax Press, 532 La Guardia Place, Suite 353, New York NJ 10012. (212)560-7459. E-mail: info@rattapallax.com. Website: www.rattapallax.com. **Contact:** Alan Cheuse, fiction editor. Literary magazine: 6×9; 128 pages; bound; some illustrations; photos. "General readership. Our stories must be character driven with strong conflict. All accepted stories are edited by our staff and the writer before publication to ensure a well-crafted and written work." Semiannual. Estab. 1999. Circ. 2,000.

Needs: Literary. Receives 15 unsolicited mss/month. Accepts 3 mss/issue; 6 mss/year. Publishes ms 3-6 months after acceptance. Agented fiction 15%. **Publishes 3 new writers/year.** Recently published work by Stuart Dybek, Howard Norman, Dana Gioia and William P.H. Root. Length: 1,000-10,000 words; average length: 5,000 words. Publishes short shorts. Also publishes poetry. Often comments on rejected mss.

How to Contact: Send SASE for return of ms. Responds in 3 months to queries; 3 months to mss. Sample copy for $7.95. Writer's guidelines for SASE or on website.

Payment/Terms: Pays 2 contributor's copies; additional copies for $7.95. Pays on publication for first North American serial rights. Sends galleys to author.

Advice: "Character driven, well-crafted, strong conflict."

$◙ THE RAVEN CHRONICLES, A Magazine of Transcultural Art, Literature and the Spoken Word, The Raven Chronicles, 1634 11th Ave., Seattle WA 98122-2419. (206)323-4316. Fax: (206)323-4316. E-mail: editors@ravenchronicles.org. Website: www.ravenchronicles.org. **Contact:** Matt Briggs, fiction editor. Jody Aliesan, poetry editor. Jeannine Hall Gailey, online editor. Magazine: 8½×11; 80 pages; 50 lb. book; glossy cover; b&w illustrations; photos. "*The Raven Chronicles* is designed to promote transcultural art, literature and the spoken word." Triannual. Estab. 1991. Circ. 2,500-5,000.

Needs: Ethnic/multicultural, literary, regional, political, cultural essays. "No romance, fantasy, mystery or detective." Receives 300-400 unsolicited mss/month. Accepts 35-50 mss/issue; 105-150 mss/year. Publishes ms 3-6 months after acceptance. **Publishes 50-100 new writers/year.** Recently published work by David Romtvedt, Sherman Alexie, D.L. Birchfield, Nancy Redwine, Diane Glancy, Greg Hischak and Sharon Hashimoto. Length: 2,500 words (but negotiable); average length: 2,000 words. Publishes short shorts. Also publishes literary essays, literary criticism, poetry. Sometimes comments on rejected mss.

How to Contact: Send SASE for return of ms. Does not accept unsolicited submissions by e-mail (except foreign submissions). Responds in 3 months to mss. Accepts simultaneous submissions. Sample copy for $5.50. Writer's guidelines for #10 SASE.

Payment/Terms: Pays $10-40 and 2 contributor's copies; additional copies at half cover cost. Pays on publication for first North American serial rights. Sends galleys to author.

Advice: Looks for "clean, direct language, written from the heart and experimental writing. Read sample copy, or look at *Before Columbus* anthologies and *Greywolf Annual* anthologies."

◙ RE:AL, The Journal of Liberal Arts, Stephen F. Austin State University, P.O. Box 13007-SFA Station, Nacogdoches TX 75962-3007. (936)468-2059. Fax: (409)468-2614. E-mail: f_real@titan.sfasu.edu. Website: http://libweb.sfasu.edu/real/default.htm. **Contact:** W. Dale Hearell, editor. Academic journal: 6×10; perfect-bound; 175-225 pages; "top" stock. Editorial content: 30% fiction, 30% poetry, 30% scholarly essays and criticism; book reviews (assigned after query) and interviews. "Work is based on the intrinsic merit of the scholarship and creative work and its appeal to a sophisticated international readership (U.S., Canada, Great Britain, Ireland, Brazil, Puerto Rico, Italy)." Semiannual. Estab. 1968. Circ. 400.

Needs: Adventure, experimental, historical, regional, science fiction, contemporary, genre. Receives 200 unsolicited mss/month. Accepts 5-10 mss/issue. Publishes ms 1-12 months after acceptance. **Publishes 20 new writers/year.** Recently published work by Holly Kulak, Cyd Adams, John Dublin and Salem Pflueger. Occasionally comments on rejected mss.

How to Contact: SASE. Responds in 2 weeks to queries; 1 month to mss. Accepts multiple submissions No simultaneous submissions. Sample copy for $10. Writer's guidelines for SASE and on website.

Payment/Terms: Pays 2 contributor's copies; charges for extras. Rights revert to author.

Advice: "Please study an issue. *RE:AL* seeks finely crafted stories that include individualistic ideas and approaches, allowing and encouraging deeper repeated readings. Have your work checked by a well-published writer-who is not a good friend. Also proofread for grammatical and typographical errors. A manuscript must show that the writer is conscious of what he or she is attempting to accomplish in plot, character and theme. A short story isn't written but constructed; the ability to manipulate certain aspects of a story is the sign of a conscious storyteller."

N ◎ ▼ ⊕ REASONING NOVEL MAGAZINE, Forward Book Co., Room 106, 1/F, New Treasure Centre, 10 NG Fong St., San Po Kong, KLN Hong Kong 852. (852)23535856. Fax: (852)23296585. E-mail: aforward@forw ard.biz.com.hk. Website: www.hkauthors.com.hk. **Contact:** Cheng Ey Shem, publisher. Magazine: 5½×8¼; 192 pages; illustrations; photos. "The only reasoning novel magazine in Hong Kong. Our intended audience is students and teenagers." Bimonthly. Estab. 1996. Circ. 10,000. Member, Hong Kong Writer Association.

● *Reasoning Novel Magazine* received the 2nd National Reasoning Novel Awards of China.

Needs: Literary. Receives 30 unsolicited mss/month. Accepts 20 mss/issue; 120 mss/year. Publishes ms 2 months after acceptance. Agented fiction 60%. **Publishes 2-3 new writers/year.** Recently published work by Mr. Cheng Pang Nam. Length: 100,000-600,000 words; average length: 20,000 words. Publishes short shorts. Also publishes literary essays, literary criticism.

How to Contact: Send complete ms. Responds in 1 month to queries; 2 months to mss. No simultaneous submissions.

Payment/Terms: Pays on publication. Sends galleys to author.

Advice: "Submissions should have good content."

⚑ RED CEDAR REVIEW, Dept. of English, 17C Morrill Hall, Michigan State University, East Lansing MI 48824. (517)655-6307. E-mail: rcreview@msu.edu. Website: www.msu.edu/~rcreview. **Contact:** Dan Roosien, fiction editor. Magazine: 5½×8½; 100 pages. Theme: "literary—poetry and short fiction." Biannual. Estab. 1963. Circ. 400.

Needs: Literary. "Good stories with character, plot and style, any genre, but with a real tilt toward literary fiction." Accepts 3-4 mss/issue; 6-10 mss/year. Publishes ms 4 months after acceptance. **Publishes 4 new writers/year.**

How to Contact: Responds in 4 months to mss. No simultaneous submissions. Sample copy for $5.

Payment/Terms: Pays 2 contributor's copies. $6 charge for extras. Acquires first rights.

⚑ RED ROCK REVIEW, Community College of Southern Nevada, 3200 E. Cheyenne Ave. N., Las Vegas NV 89030. (702)651-4094. Fax: (702)651-4639. E-mail: richard_logsdon@ccsn.nevada.edu. Website: www.ccsn.nevada .edu/english/redrockreview/index/html. **Contact:** Dr. Richard Logsdon, senior editor. Magazine: 5×8; 125 pages. "We're looking for the very best literature. Stories need to be tightly crafted, strong is character development, built around conflict. Poems need to be tightly crafted, characterised by expert use of language." Semiannual. Estab. 1995. Circ. 250.

Needs: Experimental, literary, mainstream. Receives 350 unsolicited mss/month. Accepts 40-60 mss/issue; 80-120 mss/year. Does not read mss during summer. Publishes ms 3-5 after acceptance. **Publishes 5-10 new writers/year.** Recently published work by Willis Barnstone, Dorianne Laux, Kim Addonizio and David Benia. Length: 1,500-5,000 words; average length: 3,500 words. Publishes short shorts. Also publishes literary essays, literary criticism, poetry. Sometimes comments on rejected mss.

How to Contact: Send SASE (or IRC) for return of ms. Responds in 2 weeks to queries; 3 months to mss. Accepts simultaneous, multiple submissions. Sample copy for $5.50. Writer's guidelines for SASE, by e-mail or on website.

Payment/Terms: Pays 2 contributor's copies. Pays on acceptance for first rights.

⚑ RED WHEELBARROW, De Anza College, 21250 Stevens Creek Blvd., Cupertino CA 95014-5702. (408)864-8600. E-mail: splitterrandolph@fhda.edu. Website: www.deanza.edu/redwheelbarrow. **Contact:** Randolph Splitter, editor-in-chief. Magazine: 6×9; 100-216 pages; photos. "Contemporary poetry, fiction, creative nonfiction, b&w graphics, comics and photos." Annual. Estab. 1976 as *Bottomfish*; 2000 as *Red Wheelbarrow*. Circ. 250-500.

Needs: "Thoughtful, personal writing. We welcome submissions of all kinds, and we seek to publish a diverse range of styles and voices from around the country and the world." Receives 50-100 unsolicited mss/month. Accepts 8-10 mss/issue. Reads mss September through February. Submission deadline: January 31; publication date: Spring. Publishes ms 4 months after acceptance. Agented fiction 1%. **Publishes 0-2 new writers/year.** Recently published work by George Keithly, Bill Teitelbaum and K.P. Bath. Length: 4,000 words; average length: 2,500 words. Publishes short shorts. Also publishes poetry.

How to Contact: Accepts submissions by e-mail. Responds in 3-6 months to mss. Accepts simultaneous submissions. Sample copy for $5. Writer's guidelines online.

Payment/Terms: Pays 2 contributor's copies. Acquires first North American serial rights.

Advice: "Write freely, rewrite carefully. Resist clichés and stereotypes."

⚑ REFLECTIONS LITERARY JOURNAL, Piedmont Community College, P.O. Box 1197, Roxboro NC 27573. (336)599-1181. E-mail: thrasht@piedmont.cc.nc.us. **Contact:** Tami Sloane Thrasher, editor. Magazine: 128 pages. "We publish work which addresses and transcends humanity and cultures." Annual. Estab. 1999. Circ. 500.

Needs: Literary, translations. Receives 30 unsolicited mss/month. Accepts 5 mss/issue. Publishes ms 4 months after acceptance. **Publishes 2 new writers/year.** Recently published work by Tim McLaurin, Lynn Veach Sadler and Emily A. Kern. Length: 5,000 words; average length: 2,500 words. Publishes short shorts. Also publishes poetry.

How to Contact: Send SASE (or IRC) for return of ms or send a disposable copy of ms and #10 SASE for reply only. Sample copy for $6. Writer's guidelines for SASE or by e-mail.

Payment/Terms: Pays 1 contributor's copy; additional copies $6 pre-publication; $7 post-publication. Pays on publication for first North American serial rights. Sponsors awards/contests.
Advice: "We look for good writing with a flair, which captivates an educated lay audience. Don't take rejection letters personally. We turn away a lot of work we'd like to use simply because we don't have room for everything we like. For that reason, we're more likely to accept shorter well-written stories the longer stories of the same quality. Also, stories that contain unnecessary profanity, which is profanity that doesn't contribute to the story's plot, structure, or intended tone, are rejected immediately."

$◐ THE REJECTED QUARTERLY, A Journal of Quality Literature Rejected as Least Five Times, Black Plankton Press, P.O. Box 1351, Cobb CA 95426. E-mail: bplankton@juno.com. **Contact:** Daniel Weiss, Jeff Ludecke, fiction editors. Magazine: 8½×11; 40 pages; 60 lb. paper; 10 pt. coated cover stock; illustrations. "We want the best literature possible, regardless of genre. We do, however, have a bias toward the unusual and toward speculative fiction. We aim for a literate, educated audience. *The Rejected Quarterly* believes in publishing the highest quality rejected fiction and other writing that doesn't fit anywhere else. We strive to be different, but will go for quality every time, whether conventional or not." Published at least twice/year. Estab. 1998.
Needs: Experimental, fantasy, historical, humor/satire, literary, mainstream, mystery/suspense, romance (futuristic/time travel only), science fiction (soft/sociological), sports. Accepts poetry about being rejected. Receives 30 unsolicited mss/month. Accepts 4-6 mss/issue; 8-24 mss/year. Publishes ms 1-12 months after acceptance. **Publishes 1-2 new writers/year.** Recently published work by Vera Searles, RC Cooper and Stephen Jones. Length: 8,000 words; average length: 5,000 words. Publishes short shorts. Also publishes literary essays, literary criticism, poetry. Often comments on rejected mss.
How to Contact: Accepts submissions by e-mail. Send SASE for reply, return of ms or send a disposable copy of ms. Responds in 2 weeks to queries; 9 months to mss. Accepts reprints submissions. Sample copy for $6 (IRCs for foreign requests). Reviews fiction.
Payment/Terms: Pays $5 and 1 contributor's copy; additional copies, one at cost, others $5. Pays on acceptance for first rights. Sends galleys to author.
Advice: "We are looking for high-quality writing that tells a story or expresses a coherent idea. We want unique stories, original viewpoints and unusual slants. We are getting far too many inappropriate submissions. Please be familiar with the magazine. Be sure to include your rejection slips! Send out quality rather than quantity. Work on one piece until it is as close to a masterpiece in your own eyes as you can get it. Find the right place for it. Be selective in ordering samples, but do be familiar with where you're sending your work."

◐ RIVER CITY, Dept. of English, The University of Memphis, Memphis TN 38152. (901)678-4509. **Contact:** Thomas Russell, editor. Magazine: 7×10; 150 pages. Semiannual. Estab. 1980. Circ. 1,200.
Needs: Short stories. **Publishes some new writers/year.** Recently published work by John Updike and Susan Minot.
How to Contact: Send complete ms. Responds in 2 months to mss. Sample copy for $7.
Payment/Terms: Pays 2 contributor's copies. Acquires first North American serial rights.
Advice: "We're soliciting work from writers with a national reputation. I would prefer no cover letter. *River City* Writing Awards in Fiction: $2,000 1st prize, $500 2nd prize, $300 3rd prize. See magazine for details. Send SASE for upcoming topics and contest guidelines."

$◐ ⊻ RIVER STYX, Big River Association, 634 N. Grand Blvd., 12th Floor, St. Louis MO 63103. (314)533-4541. Fax: (314)533-3345. Website: www.riverstyx.org. **Contact:** Richard Newman, editor. Magazine: 6×9; 100 pages; color card cover; perfect-bound; b&w visual art. "*River Styx* publishes the highest quality fiction, poetry, interviews, essays, and visual art. We are an internationally distributed multicultural literary magazine." Mss read May-November. Estab. 1975.
   • *River Styx* has had stories appear in *New Stories from the South* and has been included in *Pushcart* anthologies.
Needs: Ethnic/multicultural, experimental, feminist, gay, lesbian, literary, mainstream, novel excerpts, translations, short stories, literary. "No genre fiction, less thinly veiled autobiography." Receives 350 unsolicited mss/month. Accepts 2-6 mss/issue; 6-12 mss/year. Reads only May through November. Publishes ms 1 year after acceptance. **Publishes 20 new writers/year.** Recently published work by Julianna Baggott, Philip Graham, Katherine Min, Richard Burgin, Nancy Zafris, and Eric Shade. Publishes short shorts. Also publishes poetry. Sometimes comments on rejected mss.
How to Contact: Send complete ms. Accepts submissions by mail. SASE required. Responds in 4 months to mss. Accepts simultaneous submissions "if a note is enclosed with your work and if we are notified immediately upon acceptance elsewhere." Sample copy for $7. Writer's guidelines online.
Payment/Terms: Pays 2 contributor copies, plus 1-year subscription; $8/page if funds are available. Pays on publication for first North American serial, one-time rights.
Advice: "We want high-powered stories with well-developed characters. We like strong plots, usually with at least three memorable scenes, and a subplot often helps. No thin, flimsy fiction with merely serviceable language. Short stories shouldn't be any different than poetry—every single word should count. One could argue every word counts more since we're being asked to read 10 to 30 pages."

⚫ **ROANOKE REVIEW**, Roanoke College, 221 College Lane, Salem VA 24153-3794. (540)375-2380. **Contact:** Paul Hanstedt, editor. Magazine: 6×9; 200 pages; 60 lb. paper; 70 lb. cover. "We're looking for fresh, thoughtful material that will appeal to a broader as well as literary audience. Humor encouraged." Annual. Estab. 1967. Circ. 500.

Needs: Feminist, gay, humor/satire, lesbian, literary, mainstream, regional. No pornography, science fiction or horror. Receives 50 unsolicited mss/month. Accepts 5-10 mss/year. Does not read mss March 1-September 1. Publishes ms 6 months after acceptance. Agented fiction 5%. **Publishes 5-8 new writers/year.** Recently published work by Robert Morgan, June Spence, and Bill Roorbach. Length: 1,000-6,000 words; average length: 1,500 words. Publishes short shorts. Also publishes poetry. Sometimes comments on rejected mss.

How to Contact: Send SASE for return of ms or send a disposable copy of ms and #10 SASE for reply only. Responds in 1 month to queries; 6 months to mss. Sample copy for 8×11SAE with $2 postage. Writer's guidelines for SASE.

Payment/Terms: Pays 2 contributor's copies; additional copies $5. Pays on publication for one-time rights.

Advice: "Pay attention to sentence-level writing—verbs, metaphors, concrete images. Don't forget, though, that plot and character keep us reading. We're looking for stuff that breaks the MFA story style."

$⚫ **ROCKET PRESS**, P.O. Box 2352, Aquebogue NY 11931. E-mail: testd@askjfk.com. Website: www.askjfk. com. **Contact:** Darren Johnson, editor. 16-page newspaper. "A Rocket is a transcendental, celestial traveler—innovative and intelligent fiction and poetry aimed at opening minds—even into the next century." Annual. Estab. 1993. Circ. 500-2,000.

Needs: Erotica, experimental, humor/satire, literary; special Interests (poetry). No historical, romance, academic. Publishes annual special fiction issue or anthology. Receives 20 unsolicited mss/month. Accepts 2-4 mss/issue; 8-16 mss/year. **Publishes 1 new writers/year.** Recently published work by Chris Woods, Roger Lee Kenvin and Ben Ohmart. Length: 500-2,000 words; average length: 1,000 words. Publishes short shorts. Also publishes poetry. Sometimes comments on rejected mss.

How to Contact: Accepts submissions by e-mail. "We now only accept fiction manuscripts (under 2,000 words) via e-mail. Please, no attachments. Paste story in the body of your e-mail." Responds in 3 months to mss. Accepts simultaneous submissions. Sample copy for $2.

Payment/Terms: Pays 5¢/word. Acquires one-time rights.

Advice: "Your first paragraph is crucial. Editors are swamped with submissions, so a plain or clumsy lead will send your manuscript to the recycling bin. Also, too many writers come off as self-important. When writing a cover letter really try to talk to the editor—don't just rattle off a list of publications you've been in."

⚫ **THE ROCKFORD REVIEW**, The Rockford Writers Guild, 7721 Venus St., Loves Park IL 61111. Website: http://writersguild1.tripod.com. **Contact:** Max Dodson, prose editor. Magazine: 5⅜×8½; 50 pages; b&w illustrations; b&w photos. "We look for prose and poetry with a fresh approach to old themes or new insights into the human condition." Triquarterly. Estab. 1971. Circ. 750.

Needs: Ethnic/multicultural, experimental, fantasy, humor/satire, literary, regional, science fiction (hard science, soft/sociological). "No graphic sex, translations or overly academic work." Recently published work by James Bellarosa, Sean Michael Rice, John P. Kristofco and L.S. Sedishiro. Also publishes literary essays.

How to Contact: SASE. Responds in 2 months to mss. Accepts simultaneous, multiple submissions. Sample copy for $6. Writer's guidelines for SASE.

Payment/Terms: Pays contributor's copies. "Two $25 editor's choice cash prizes per issues." Acquires first North American serial rights.

Advice: "We must understand it, and when we read it we must say 'wow.' If it makes us also laugh or cry, that is good. Read what is being published lately, and try a few samples. Like shoes, it must fit."

$⚫ ◎ ⊕ **ROOM OF ONE'S OWN, A Canadian Quarterly of Women's Literature and Criticism**, West Coast Feminist Literary Magazine Society, P.O. Box 46160, Station D, Vancouver BC V6J 5G5 Canada. Website: www.roommagazine.com. **Contact:** Growing Room Collective. Magazine: 112 pages; illustrations; photos. "*Room of One's Own* is Canada's oldest feminist literary journal. Since 1975, *Room* has been a forum in which women can share their unique perspectives on the world, each other and themselves." Quarterly. Estab. 1975. Circ. 1,000.

Needs: Feminist, literary, feminist literature—short stories, creative nonfiction, essays by, for, and about women. "No humor, science fiction, romance." Receives 60-100 unsolicited mss/month. Accepts 18-20 mss/issue; 75-80 mss/year. Publishes ms 1 year after acceptance. **Publishes 15-20 new writers/year.** Also publishes poetry.

How to Contact: Send complete ms with a cover letter. Include estimated word count and brief bio. Send a disposable copy of ms and #10 SASE or IRC for reply only. Responds in 3 months to queries; 6 months to mss. Sample copy for $7 or online. Writer's guidelines online. Reviews fiction.

Payment/Terms: Pays $35 (Canadian), and a 1-year subscription. Pays on publication for first North American serial rights.

⚫ ▼ **SALMAGUNDI**, Skidmore College, Saratoga Springs NY 12866. Fax: (518)580-5188. E-mail: pboyes@sk idmore.edu. **Contact:** Peg Boyers. Magazine: 8x5; 200-300 pages; illustrations; photos. "*Salmagundi* publishes an eclectic variety of materials, ranging from short short fiction to novellas from the surreal to the realistic. Authors include Nadine Gordimer, Russell Banks, Steven Millhauser, Gordon Lish, Clark Blaise, Mary Gordon, Joyce Carol Oates and Cynthia Ozick. Our audience is a generally literate population of people who read for pleasure." Quarterly. Estab. 1965. Circ. 4,800. Member, CLMP.

- *Salmagundi* authors are regularly represented in Pushcart collections and *Best American Short Story* collections.

Needs: Ethnic/multicultural (multicultural), experimental, family saga, gay, historical (general), literary, poetry. Receives 50-70 unsolicited mss/month. Accepts 2 mss/year. Does not read mss May 1-October 15. Publishes ms up to 2 years after acceptance years after acceptance. Agented fiction 10%. Also publishes literary essays, literary criticism, poetry.

How to Contact: Send complete ms. Accepts submissions by e-mail (pboyes@skidmore.edu). Only accepts submission by e-mail. Responds in 6 months to queries; 6 months to mss. Sample copy for $5. Writer's guidelines for #10 SASE.

Payment/Terms: 6-10 contributor's copies and subscription to magazine. Pays 6-10 contributor's copies. Acquires first, electronic rights.

Advice: "I look for excellence and a very unpredictable ability to appeal to the interests and tastes of the editors. Be brave. Don't be discouraged by rejection. Keep stories in circulation. Of course, it goes without saying: Work hard on the writing. Revise tirelessly. Study magazines and send only to those whose sensibility matches yours."

N ☐ **SALT HILL**, English Dept., Syracuse University, Syracuse NY 13244-1170. (315)425-9371. Fax: (315)443-3660. E-mail: salthill@cas.syr.edu. Website: students.syr.edu/salthill. **Contact:** Ellen Litman, editor. Magazine: 5½×8½; 120 pages; 4-color cover; illustrations; photos. Publishes fiction with "fresh imagery, original language and tonal and structural experimentation." Semiannual. Estab. 1994. Circ. 1,000. Member, CLMP.

Needs: Ethnic/multicultural, experimental, gay, humor/satire, lesbian, literary, translations. No genre fiction. Receives 40-50 unsolicited mss/month. Accepts 3-5 mss/issue; 6-10 mss/year. Publishes ms 2-8 months after acceptance. **Publishes 2 new writers/year.** Recently published work by Christine Schutt, Edra Ziesk and Mark Kipniss. Length: 6,000 words. Publishes short shorts. Also publishes literary essays, literary criticism, poetry.

How to Contact: Send complete ms. Accepts submissions by e-mail. Send SASE for reply, return of ms or send disposable copy of ms. Responds in 6 months to mss. Accepts simultaneous submissions. Sample copy for $8. Writer's guidelines for #10 SASE.

Payment/Terms: Pays 2 contributor's copies; additional copies $7. Acquires first North American serial, web rights. Sponsors awards/contests.

Advice: "Read everything you can, think about what you read, understand the stuctures, characters, etc.—then write, and write, and write again."

☐ ◎ **SAMSARA, The Magazine of Suffering**, P.O. Box 467, Ashburn VA 20146-0467. E-mail: rdfgoalie@aol. com. Website: samsara.cjb.net. **Contact:** R. David Fulcher, editor. Magazine: 8½×11; 50-80 pages; Xerox paper; poster stock cover; illustrations. "*Samsara* publishes only stories or poems relating to the theme of suffering/healing." Semiannual. Estab. 1994. Circ. 250.

Needs: Condensed novels, experimental, fantasy (science fantasy, sword and sorcery), horror, literary, mainstream, science fiction (hard science, soft/sociological). "We would like to see more fantasy and science fiction relating to suffering/healing." Receives 80 unsolicited mss/month. Accepts 17-20 mss/issue; 40 mss/year. Recently published work by Milton Kerr, Dennis Sjolie, Kim Commings, and Elizabeth Carman. Average length: 2,000 words. Publishes short shorts. Also publishes poetry. comments on rejected mss.

How to Contact: Send complete ms. Accepts submissions by mail. Send SASE for reply, return of ms or send a disposable copy of ms. Responds in 6 months to queries. Accepts simultaneous and reprints, multiple submissions. Sample copy for $5.50. Writer's guidelines for #10 SASE.

Payment/Terms: Pays 1 contributor's copy. Acquires first North American serial, second serial (reprint) rights.

Advice: "We seek out writers who make use of imagery and avoid over-writing. Symbolism and myth really make a manuscript stand out. Read a sample copy. Too many writers send work which does not pertain to the guidelines. Writers should avoid sending us splatter-punk or gore stories."

☐ **SANTA MONICA REVIEW**, Santa Monica College, 1900 Pico Blvd., Santa Monica CA 90405. (310)434-4242. **Contact:** Andrew Tonkovich, editor. Magazine: 250 pages. "The editors are committed to fostering new talent as well as presenting new work by established writers. There is also a special emphasis on presenting and promoting writers who make their home in Southern California." Estab. 1989. Circ. 4,000.

Needs: Experimental, literary, memoirs. "No crime and detective, mysogyny, footnotes, TV, dog stories." "We want more self-conscious, smart, political, humorous, digressive, meta-fiction." Receives 250 unsolicited mss/month. Accepts 10 mss/issue; 20 mss/year. Agented fiction 10%. **Publishes 5 new writers/year.** Recently published work by Ed Skoog, Trini Dalton, Judith Grossman, and John Peterson. Also publishes literary essays.

How to Contact: Send complete ms. Accepts submissions by mail. Send disposable copy of ms. Responds in 3 months to mss. Accepts simultaneous, multiple submissions. Sample copy for $7.

Payment/Terms: Pays 2 contributor's copies. Pays 2 contributor's copies. Acquires first North American serial rights. Sends galleys to author.

N ☐ THE SCRIBIA, Literary Journal, Grambling State University, P.O. Box 68, Grambling LA 71245. (318)274-2272. E-mail: hoytda@gram.edu. Website: www.gram.edu. **Contact:** Student editorial committee. Magazine: 5½×8½; 40-60 pages; standard paper; 50 lb. cover stock; illustrations. *The Scribia* publishes mostly creative work by GSU students and faculty, with some outside contributions from talented artists fro around the country. Annual. Estab. 1958. Circ. 400.

Needs: Ethnic/multicultural, literary, mainstream, regional (south), ethnic success stories. Receives 3-4 unsolicited mss/month. Accepts 3-4 mss/issue. Publishes ms 6 months after acceptance. **Publishes 1-2 new writers/year.** Recently published work by Bernie Evans. Length: 1,000 words; average length: 500 words. Publishes short shorts. Also publishes literary essays, poetry.

How to Contact: Send complete ms. Send SASE (or IRC) for return of the ms or disposable copy of the ms and #10 SASE for reply only. Responds in 2-3 weeks to queries; 6-8 months to mss. Accepts simultaneous and reprints, multiple submissions. Sample copy for free with 6×9 SASE.

Payment/Terms: Pays 2 contributor's copies. Pays on publication for one-time rights.

N $☐ ☑ SENSATIONS MAGAZINE, P.O. Box 6, Ocean Grove NJ 07756. Website: www.sensationsmag.c om. **Contact:** David Messineo. Magazine: 8½×11; 200 pages; 20 lb. paper; full color cover; color photography. "We publish short stories and poetry." Quarterly. Estab. 1987.

● *Sensations Magaizne* is one of the few markets accepting longer work and is a 3-time winner in the American Literary Magazine Awards.

Needs: Publishes 4-8 new writers/year. Recently published work by Scott Singer, Ken Sieben, Sara Clayton and Ben Pastor.

How to Contact: Accepts submissions by e-mail. "Do not submit material before reading submission guidelines." Accepts simultaneous, multiple submissions. Writer's guidelines for SASE or online.

Payment/Terms: Pays $100 for the story judged #1 by each of our three fiction editors.

Advice: "Develop long-term relationships with five magazines whose editorial opinions you respect. As the last literary magazine in America to frequently publish stories up to 30 pages double-spaced, we believe we have earned the privilege of being one of those five."

$ SHORT STUFF, For Grown-ups, Bowman Publications, 712 W. 10th St., Loveland CO 80537. (970)669-9139. "We are perhaps an enigma in that we publish only clean stories in any genre. We'll tackle any subject, but don't allow obscene language or pornographic description. Our magazine is for grown-ups, *not* X-rated 'adult' fare." Bimonthly. Estab. 1989. Circ. 10,400.

Needs: Adventure, historical, humor/satire, mainstream, mystery/suspense, romance, science fiction (seldom), suspense, western. "We want to see more humor—not essay format—real stories with humor; 1,000-word mysteries, modern lifestyles. The 1,000-word pieces have the best chance of publication." No erotica; nothing morbid or pornographic. Issues are Valentine (February/March); Easter (April/May); Mom's and Dad's (June/July); Americana (August/September); Halloween (October/November); and Holiday (December/January). Receives 500 unsolicited mss/month. Accepts 9-12 mss/issue; 76 mss/year. **Publishes 90% new writers/year.** Recently published work by Bill Hallstead, Dale Hammond and Skye Gibbons.

How to Contact: Send complete ms. Responds in 6 months to mss. Sample copy for $1.50 and 9×12 SAE with 5 first-class stamps. Writer's guidelines for #10 SASE.

Payment/Terms: Payment varies. Payment and contract upon publication. Acquires first North American serial rights.

Advice: "We seek a potpourri of subjects each issue. A new slant, a different approach, fresh viewpoints—all of these excite us. We don't like gore, salacious humor or perverted tales. Prefer third person, past tense. Be sure it is a story with a beginning, middle and end. It must have dialogue. Many beginners do not know an essay from a short story. Essays frequently used if *humorous*. We'd like to see more humor; 'clean' humor is hard to come by. Length is a big factor. Writers who can tell a good story in a thousand words are true artists and their work is highly prized by our readers. Stick to the guidelines. We get manuscripts of up to 10,000 words because the story is 'unique and deserving.' We don't even read these. Too many writers fail to include SASE. These submissions are not considered."

N ☐ ◎ SINISTER WISDOM, A Journal for the Lesbian Imagination in the Arts and Politics, Sinister Wisdom, Inc., Box 3252, Berkeley CA 94703. E-mail: sw@aalexander.org. Website: www.sinisterwisdom.org. Magazine: 5½×8½; 128-144 pages; 55 lb. stock; 10 pt C1S cover; illustrations; photos. Lesbian-feminist journal, providing fiction, poetry, drama, essays, journals and artwork. Past issues included "Lesbians of Color," "Old Lesbians/Dykes" and "Lesbians and Religion." Triannual. Estab. 1976. Circ. 2,000.

Needs: Lesbian (erotica, ethnic, experimental). No heterosexual or male-oriented fiction; no 70s amazon adventures; nothing that stereotypes or degrades women. List of upcoming themes available for SASE or on website. Receives 30 unsolicited mss/month. Accepts 6 mss/issue; 24 mss/year. Publishes ms 3-12 months after acceptance. **Publishes some new writers/year.** Recently published work by Jacqueline Miranda, Amananda Esteva and Sharon Bridgeforth. Length: 500-4,000 words; average length: 2,000 words. Publishes short shorts. Also publishes literary essays, literary criticism, poetry. Sometimes comments on rejected mss.

How to Contact: Send complete ms. Accepts submissions by e-mail. SASE. Responds in 6 months to mss.

Accepts simultaneous, multiple submissions. Sample copy for $7.50. Writer's guidelines for #10 SASE. Reviews fiction.

Payment/Terms: Pays 2 contributor's copies. Acquires one-time rights.

Advice: *Sinister Wisdom* is "a multicultural lesbian journal reflecting the art, writing and politics of our communities."

SLIPSTREAM PUBLICATIONS, Box 2071, Niagara Falls NY 14301. (716)282-2616 after 5 PM E.S.T. E-mail: editors@slipstreampress.org. Website: www.slipstreampress.org. **Contact:** Dan Sicoli, editor. Estab. 1980. Small literary press which publishes 85% poetry and 15% fiction (under 15 pages) from writers whose work may go unnoticed by larger commercial presses. Use modern fiction with strong sense of place, fresh dialogue, and well-developed characters. We only publish fiction in *Slipstream Magazine*. Publishes paperback originals.

Needs: Poetry. Holds annual Poetry Chapbook Contest.

How to Contact: Accepts unsolicited mss. Accepts queries by mail. Include brief bio. Send SASE for return of ms or send a disposable ms and SASE for reply only. Responds in 2 weeks to queries; 3 months to mss. Accepts simultaneous submissions. No electronic submissions, submissions on disk. Rarely comments on rejected mss.

Payment/Terms: Pays 2-3 contributor's copies. Publishes ms 6-12 months after acceptance. Book catalog online; ms guidelines for SASE or on website.

Advice: "Read our magazine before submitting."

THE SMALL POND MAGAZINE, Box 664, Stratford CT 06615. (203)378-4066. **Contact:** Fiction Editor. Magazine: 5½×8½; 42 pages; 60 lb. offset paper; 65 lb. cover stock; illustrations. "Features contemporary poetry, the salt of the earth, peppered with short prose pieces of various kinds. The college educated and erudite read us for good poetry, prose and pleasure." Triannual. Estab. 1964. Circ. 300.

Needs: "We rarely use the kind of genre fiction you find in slick consumer magazines. Our highest criteria is originality, even if it is a bit quirky. Don't mind O. Henry endings but they must be exceptional. Our readership consists of college grads, college staff, and a third of our subscribers are college and university libraries." No science fiction, children's. Accepts 10-12 mss/year. Publishes ms 12-18 months after acceptance. **Publishes 1-2 new writers/year.** Recently published work by Judah Jacobwitz, Charles Rammelcamp, Joshua R. Pahigian and Ruth Innes.

How to Contact: Send complete ms. Accepts submissions by mail. Responds in 2-3 months to mss. Sample copy for $4.

Payment/Terms: 2 contributor copies; back issues for $3. Acquires all rights.

Advice: "Send a sample copy first. All mss must be typed. Name and address and story title on front page, name of story on succeeding pages and paginated. I look for polished, smooth progression—no clumsy paragraphs or structures where you know the author didn't edit closely. Also, no poor grammar. Beginning and even established poets read and learn from reading lots of others' verse. Not a bad idea for fiction writers, in their genre, short or long fiction."

SNAKE NATION REVIEW, Snake Nation Press, Inc., 110 West Force St., Valdosta GA 31601. E-mail: jeana@snakenationpress.org. Website: www.snakenationpress.org. **Contact:** Jean Arambula, editor. 6×9; 110 pages; acid free 70 lb. paper; 90 lb. cover; illustrations; photos. "We are interested in all types of stories for an educated, discerning, sophisticated audience." Triannual. Estab. 1989. Circ. 2,000.

• *Snake Nation Review* ranked on *Writer's Digest's* "Top 30" list of best markets for writers.

Needs: Condensed novels, erotica, ethnic/multicultural, experimental, fantasy, gay, horror, humor/satire, lesbian, literary, mainstream, mystery/suspense, psychic/supernatural/occult, regional, science fiction, contemporary, prose poem, senior citizen/retirement. Short stories of 5,000 words or less, poems (any length), art work that will be returned after use. "We want our writers to have a voice, a story to tell, not a flat rendition of a slice of life." Plans annual anthology. Receives 200 unsolicited mss/month. Accepts 8-10 mss/issue; 40 mss/year. Publishes ms 6 months after acceptance. Agented fiction 1%. Recently published work by Robert Earl Price and O. Victor Miller. Length: 300-5,500 words; average length: 3,500 words. Publishes short shorts. Also publishes literary essays, poetry. Sometimes comments on rejected mss.

How to Contact: Send complete ms with cover letter. SASE. Responds in 3 months to queries. Sample copy for $6, 8×10 SAE and 90 postage. Writer's guidelines for SASE. Reviews fiction.

Payment/Terms: Pays 2 contributor's copies. Acquires one-time rights. Sends galleys to author.

$ SNOWY EGRET, The Fair Press, P.O. Box 29, Terre Haute IN 47808. (812)829-1910. **Contact:** Fiction Editor. Magazine: 8½×11; 50 pages; text paper; heavier cover; illustrations. "We publish works which celebrate the abundance and beauty of nature, and examine the variety of ways in which human beings interact with landscapes and living things. Nature writing from literary, artistic, psychological, philosophical, and historical perspectives." Semiannual. Estab. 1922. Circ. 400.

Needs: "No genre fiction, e.g., horror, western romance, etc." Receives 25 unsolicited mss/month. Accepts up to 6 mss/issue; up to 12 mss/year. Publishes ms 6 months after acceptance. **Publishes 20 new writers/year.** Recently published work by James Hinton, Ron Gielgun, Tom Noyes, Alice Cross and Maeve Mullin Ellis. Length: 500-10,000 words; average length: 1,000-3,000 words. Publishes short shorts. Sometimes comments on rejected mss.

How to Contact: Send complete ms. Accepts submissions by mail. Cover letter optional: do not query. SASE. Responds in 1 month to queries; 2 months to mss. Accepts simultaneous submissions if noted. Sample copy for 9×12 SASE and $8. Writer's guidelines for #10 SASE.

Payment/Terms: Pays $2/page. Pays on publication for first North American serial, second serial (reprint), one-time anthology rights, or reprints rights. Sends galleys to author.

Advice: Looks for "honest, freshly detailed pieces with plenty of description and/or dialogue which will allow the reader to identify with the characters and step into the setting; fiction in which nature affects character development and the outcome of the story."

SO TO SPEAK, A Feminist Journal of Language and Art, George Mason University, 4400 University Dr., MS 2D6, Fairfax VA 22030. (703)993-3625. E-mail: sts@gmu.edu. Website: www.gmu.edu/org/sts. **Contact:** Courtney Campbell, fiction editor. Magazine: 5½×8½; approximately 140 pages. "We are a feminist journal of language and art." Semiannual. Estab. 1988. Circ. 1,000.

Needs: Ethnic/multicultural, experimental, feminist, lesbian, literary, mainstream, regional, translations. "No science fiction, mystery, genre romance, porn (lesbian or straight)." Receives 100 unsolicited mss/month. Accepts 3-5 mss/issue; 6-10 mss/year. Publishes ms 6 months after acceptance. **Publishes 2 new writers/year.** Length: fiction up to 5,000 words; for poetry 3-5 pages per submission; average length: 4,000 words. Publishes short shorts. Also publishes literary essays, literary criticism, poetry.

How to Contact: Send complete ms. Accepts submissions by mail. Include bio (50 words maximum) and SASE. SASE for return of ms or send a disposable copy of ms. Responds in 6 months to mss. Accepts simultaneous submissions. Sample copy for $6. Writer's guidelines for #10 SASE. Reviews fiction.

Payment/Terms: Pays contributor copies. Acquires first North American serial rights. Sponsors awards/contests.

Advice: "We do not read between March 15 and August 15. Every writer has something they do exceptionally well; do that and it will shine through in the work. We look for quality prose with a definite appeal to a feminist audience. We are trying to move away from strict genre lines. We want high quality fiction, non-fiction, poetry, art, innovative and risk-taking work."

SONGS OF INNOCENCE, Pendragonian Publications, PO Box 719, New York NY 10101-0719. E-mail: mmpendragon@aol.com. **Contact:** Fiction Editor. Literary magazine/journal: 9×6; 175 pages; perfect bound; illustrations. "A literary publication which celebrates the nobler aspects of humankind and the human experience. Along with sister publication *Penny Dreadful*, we seek to provide a forum for poetry and fiction in the 19th Century/Romance/Victorian tradition." Annual. Circ. 200.

Needs: Fantasy, historical (19th century or earlier), literary, New Age, psychic/supernatural/occult. "No children's, young adult, modern tales, Christian (or anything dogmatic)." Receives 100 unsolicited mss/month. Accepts 15 mss/issue; 30 mss/year. Publishes ms up to 2 years after acceptance. Publishes short shorts. Also publishes literary essays, literary criticism, poetry. Often comments on rejected mss.

How to Contact: Send complete ms. Accepts submissions by mail, e-mail. Responds in 3 weeks to queries; 6-12 months to mss. Accepts simultaneous and reprints submissions. Sample copy for $10 and 9×6 SAE. Writer's guidelines for #10 SASE.

Payment/Terms: Pays 1 contributor copy. Pays on publication for one-time rights.

Advice: "We prefer tales set in 1910 or earlier—preferably earlier. We prefer prose in the 19th Century/Victorian style. We do not like the terse, modern, post-Hemingway 'see Dick run' style. Also should transcend genres and include a spiritual/supernatural element without becoming fantasy. Avoid strong language, sex, etc. Include name and address on the title page. Include word count on the title page. We select stories that appeal to us and do not base selection on whether one has been published elsewhere."

SONORA REVIEW, University of Arizona's Creative Writing MFA Program, University of Arizona, Dept. of English, Tucson AZ 85721. E-mail: sonora@email.arizona.edu. Website: www.coh.arizona.edu/sonora/. **Contact:** Sarah Giles, fiction editor. Magazine: 6×9; approx. 100 pages; photos. "We look for the highest quality poetry, fiction, and nonfiction, with an emphasis on emerging writers. Our magazine has a long-standing tradition of publishing the best new literature and writers. Check out our website for a sample of what we publish and our submission guidelines, or write us for a sample back issue." Semiannual. Estab. 1980. Circ. 500.

Needs: Ethnic/multicultural, experimental, literary, mainstream, novel excerpts. Receives 100 unsolicited mss/month. Accepts 2-3 mss/issue; 6-8 mss/year. Does not read in the Summer (June-August). Publishes ms 3-4 months after acceptance. **Publishes 1-3 new writers/year.** Recently published work by Meg Mullins, Dina Guidubaldi,

---

CHECK THE CATEGORY INDEXES, located at the back of the book, for publishers interested in specific fiction subjects.

Russell Tomlin, David Crouse. Also publishes literary essays, literary criticism, poetry. Sometimes comments on rejected mss.

How to Contact: Send complete ms. Accepts submissions by mail. Send disposable copy of the ms and #10 SASE for reply only. Responds in 2-5 weeks to queries; 3 months to mss. Accepts simultaneous, multiple submissions. Sample copy for $4. Writer's guidelines online. Reviews fiction.

Payment/Terms: Pays 2 contributor's copies; additional copies for $4. Pays on publication for first North American serial, one-time, electronic rights.

Advice: "Send us your best stuff."

⬛ SOUTH CAROLINA REVIEW, Strode Tower, Clemson University, Clemson SC 29634-1503. (864)656-5399. Fax: (864)656-1345. E-mail: cwayne@clemson.edu. Website: www.clemson.edu/caah/cedp. **Contact:** Wayne Chapman, editor. Magazine: 6×9; 200 pages; 60 lb. cream white vellum paper; 65 lb. cream white vellum cover stock. Semiannual. Estab. 1967. Circ. 500.

Needs: Literary, mainstream, poetry, essays, reviews. Does not read mss June-August or December. Receives 50-60 unsolicited mss/month. Recently published work by Joyce Carol Oates, Rosanne Coggeshal and Stephen Dixon. Rarely comments on rejected mss.

How to Contact: Send complete ms. Accepts submissions by mail. Requires text on disk upon acceptance in WordPerfect or Microsoft Word format. Responds in 2 months to mss. Sample copy for $10. Reviews fiction.

Payment/Terms: Pays in contributor's copies.

🗓⬛ SOUTH DAKOTA REVIEW, University of South Dakota, Box 111, University Exchange, Vermillion SD 57069. (605)677-5184. Fax: (605)677-5298. E-mail: sdreview@usd.edu. Website: www.usd.edu/engl/SDR/index .html. **Contact:** Fiction Editor. Magazine: 6×9; 140-170 pages; book paper; glossy cover stock; illustrations sometimes; photos on cover. "Literary magazine for university and college audiences and their equivalent. Emphasis is often on the American West and its writers, but will accept mss from anywhere. Issues are usually personal essay, fiction and poetry with some literary essays." Quarterly. Estab. 1963. Circ. 500.

• *Pushcart* and *Best American Essays* nominees.

Needs: Ethnic/multicultural, literary, mainstream, regional. "We like very well-written, thematically ambitious, character-centered short fiction. Contemporary Western American setting appeals, but not necessary. No formula stories, horror, or adolescent 'I' narrator." Receives 40 unsolicited mss/month. Accepts 40 mss/year. Publishes ms 1-6 months after acceptance. **Publishes 3-5 new writers/year.** Recently published work by Nathan Whiting, Dan Tobin, Frederick Zydeck.

How to Contact: Send complete ms. Accepts submissions by mail. "We like cover letters that are not boastful and do not attempt to sell the stories, but rather provide some personal information about the writer which can be used for a contributor's note." Responds in 10 weeks to mss. Sample copy for $7.

Payment/Terms: Acquires first, second serial (reprint) rights.

Advice: Rejects mss because of "careless writing; often careless typing; stories too personal ('I' confessional); aimlessness of plot; unclear or unresolved conflicts; subject matter that editor finds clichéd, senstationalized, pretentious or trivial. We are trying to use more fiction and more variety."

⬛ THE SOUTHEAST REVIEW, English Department, Florida State University, Tallahassee FL 32306-1036. (850)644-2773. E-mail: southeastreview@english.fsu.edu. Website: www.english.fsu.edu/southeastreview. **Contact:** Ed Tarkington, fiction editor. Magazine: 6×9; 160 pages; 70 lb. paper; 10 pt. Krome Kote cover; photos. "*The Southeast Review* is published for a literary audience with a sophisticated, intelligent knowledge of the fiction genre." Biannual. Estab. 1979. Circ. 6,000.

Needs: "We want stories (under 3,000 words) with striking images, fresh language and a consistent voice." Would like to see more literary fiction. "No genre fiction. We receive approximately 400 submissions per month and we accept less than 1-2% of them. We will comment briefly on rejected mss when time permits." Publishes ms 2-6 months after acceptance. **Publishes 4-6 new writers/year.** Recently published work by Greg Johnson, David Rutschman, and Charles Wright.

How to Contact: Send complete ms. Accepts submissions by mail. Responds in 3-5 months to mss. Sample copy for $5.

Payment/Terms: Pays 3 contributor's copies. Acquires first North American serial rights.

Advice: "Avoid trendy experimentation for its own sake (present-tense narration, observation that isn't also revelation). Fresh stories, moving, interesting characters and a sensitivity to language are still fiction mainstays. Also publishes winner and runners-up of the World's Best Short Story Contest sponsored by the Florida Sate University English Department."

⬛ SOUTHERN CALIFORNIA ANTHOLOGY, University of Southern California, Waite Phillips Hall, Room 404, Los Angeles CA 90089-4034. (213)740-3252. Fax: (213)740-5775. E-mail: mpw@mizar.usc.edu. Website: www.usc.edu/dept/LAS/mpw. **Contact:** Editor. Magazine: 5½×8½; 142 pages; semiglosss cover stock. "*The Southern California Anthology* is a literary review that contains an eclectic collections of previously unpublished, quality contemporary fiction, poetry and interviews with established literary people, published for adults of all professions; of particular interest to those interested in serious contemporary literature." Annual. Estab. 1983. Circ. 1,500.

Needs: Ethnic/multicultural, experimental, feminist, historical, humor/satire, literary, mainstream, regional, serialized novels. "No juvenile, religious, confession, romance, science fiction or pornography." Receives 40 unsolicited mss/month. Accepts 1-2 mss/issue. Publishes ms 4 months after acceptance. **Publishes 1-2 new writers/year.** Recently published work by James Tate, Susan Hubbard, Alice Fulton, Caremia Leonte, Stephen Dunn, Ruth Stone and Philip Appleman. Publishes short shorts.
How to Contact: Send complete ms. Cover letter should include list of previous publications. Responds in 1 month to queries; 4 months to mss. Sample copy for $4. Writer's guidelines for #10 SASE.
Payment/Terms: Pays in contributor copies. Acquires first rights.
Advice: "The *Anthology* pays particular attention to craft and style in its selection of narrative writing."

SOUTHERN HUMANITIES REVIEW, Auburn University, 9088 Haley Center, Auburn University AL 36849. Website: www.auburn.edu/english/shr/home.htm. **Contact:** Fiction Editor. Magazine: 6×9; 100 pages; 60 lb neutral pH, natural paper; 65 lb. neutral pH medium coated cover stock; occasional illustration; photos. "We publish essays, poetry, fiction and reviews. Our fiction has ranged from very traditional in form and content to very experimental. Literate, college-educated audience. We hope they read our journal for both enlightenment and pleasure." Quarterly. Estab. 1967. Circ. 800.
Needs: Fantasy, feminist, humor/satire, regional. Slower reading time in summer. Receives 25 unsolicited mss/month. Accepts 1-2 mss/issue; 4-6 mss/year. Recently published work by William Cobb, Heimito von Doderer, Greg Johnson and Dieter Kuhn. Also publishes literary essays, literary criticism, poetry. Sometimes comments on rejected mss.
How to Contact: Send complete ms. Cover letter with an explanation of the topic chosen—"special, certain book, etc., a little about the author if he/she has never submitted." Responds in 3 months to mss.
Payment/Terms: Pays in contributor copies. Rights revert to author on publication.
Advice: "Send us the ms with SASE. If we like it, we'll take it or we'll recommend changes. If we don't like it, we'll send it back as promptly as possible. Read the journal. Send typewritten, clean copy, carefully proofread. We also award annual the Hoepfner Prize of $100 for the best published essay or short story of the year. Let someone whose opinion you respect read your story and give you an honest appraisal. Rewrite, if necessary, to get the most from your story."

$ ☐ ☑ THE SOUTHERN REVIEW, 43 Allen Hall, Louisiana State University, Baton Rouge LA 70803-5005. (225)578-5108. Fax: (225)578-5098. Website: www.lsu.edu/thesouthernreview. **Contact:** John Easterly, associate editor. Magazine: 6¼×10; 240 pages; 50 lb. Glatfelter paper; 65 lb. #1 grade cover stock. No queries. Reading period: September-May. Quarterly. Estab. 1935. Circ. 3,100.
 ● Several stories published in *The Southern Review* were Pushcart Prize selections. *The Southern Review* ranked on *Writer's Digest's* "Top 30" list of best markets for fiction writers.
Needs: Literary. "We emphasize style and substantial content. No mystery, fantasy or religious mss." Receives approximately 300 unsolicited mss/month. Accepts 4-5 mss/issue. Does not read mss June-August. Publishes ms 6 months after acceptance. Agented fiction 1%. **Publishes 4-6 new writers/year.** Recently published work by William Gay, Romulus Linney, Richard Bausch and Ingrid Hill. Also publishes literary essays, literary criticism, poetry.
How to Contact: Accepts submissions by mail. Send complete ms with cover letter and SASE. "Prefer brief letters giving information on author concerning where he/she has been published before, biographical info and what he/she is doing now." Responds in 2 months to mss. Sample copy for $8. Writer's guidelines online. Reviews fiction.
Payment/Terms: Pays $12/page. Pays on publication for first North American serial rights. Sends galleys to author. Sponsors awards/contests.
Advice: "Develop a careful, clear style. Although willing to publish experimental writing that appears to have a valid artistic purpose, *The Southern Review* avoids extremism and sensationalism."

☐ SOUTHWEST REVIEW, PO Box 750374, Southern Methodist University, Dallas TX 75275-0374. (214)768-1037. Fax: (214)768-1408. E-mail: swr@mail.smu.edu. Website: www.southwestreview.org. **Contact:** Elizabeth Mills, senior editor. Magazine: 6×9; 144 pages. "The majority of our readers are college-educated adults who wish to stay abreast of the latest and best in contemporary fiction, poetry, literary criticism and books in all but the most specialized disciplines." Quarterly. Estab. 1915. Circ. 1,600.
Needs: "High literary quality; no specific requirements as to subject matter, but cannot use sentimental, religious, western, poor science fiction, pornographic, true confession, mystery, juvenile or serialized or condensed novels." Receives 200 unsolicited mss/month. Publishes ms 6-12 months after acceptance. Recently published work by Tracy Daugherty, Millicent Dillon and Mark Jacobs. Also publishes literary essays, poetry. Occasionally comments on rejected mss.
How to Contact: Send complete ms. Accepts submissions by mail. Responds in 6 months to mss. Accepts multiple submissions. Sample copy for $6. Writer's guidelines for #10 SASE or on website.
Payment/Terms: Negotiable rate and 3 contributor copies. Acquires first North American serial rights. Sends galleys to author.
Advice: "We have become less regional. A lot of time would be saved for us and for the writer if he or she looked at a copy of review before submitting. We like to receive a cover letter because it is some reassurance that the

author has taken the time to check a current directory for the editor's name. When there isn't a cover letter, we wonder whether the same story is on 20 other desks around the country."

SOUTHWESTERN AMERICAN LITERATURE, Center for the Study of the Southwest, Texas State University, 601 University Drive, San Marcos TX 78666. (512)245-2232. Fax: (512)245-7462. E-mail: mb13@swt.edu. Website: www.english.swt.edu/css. **Contact:** Twister Marquiss, assistant editor; Mark Busby, co-editor; Dickie Maurice Heaberlin, co-editor. Magazine: 6×9; 125 pages; 80 lb. cover stock. "We publish fiction, nonfiction, poetry, literary criticism and book reviews. Generally speaking we want material covering the Greater Southwest, or material written by Southwest writers." Semiannual. Estab. 1971. Circ. 300.

Needs: Ethnic/multicultural, literary, mainstream, regional. "No science fiction or romance." Receives 10-15 unsolicited mss/month. Accepts 1-2 mss/issue; 4-5 mss/year. Publishes ms 6 months after acceptance. **Publishes 1-2 new writers/year.** Recently published work by Jerry Craven, Paul Ruffin, Robert Flynn and Philip Heldrich. Length: 6,250 words; average length: 4,000 words. Publishes short shorts. Also publishes literary essays, literary criticism, poetry. Sometimes comments on rejected mss.

How to Contact: Send complete ms. Accepts submissions by mail, e-mail. Include estimated word count, 2-5 line bio and list of publications. Responds in 2 months to mss. Accepts simultaneous submissions. Sample copy for $7. Writer's guidelines free.

Payment/Terms: Pays 2 contributor copies. Acquires first rights.

Advice: "We look for crisp language, an interesting approach to material; a regional approach is desired but not required. Read widely, write often, revise carefully. We are looking for stories that probe the relationship between the tradition of Southwestern American literature and the writer's own imagination in creative ways. We seek stories that move beyond stereotype and approach the larger defining elements and also ones that, as William Faulkner noted in his Nobel Prize acceptance speech, treat subjects central to good literature—the old verities of the human heart such as honor and courage and pity and suffering, fear and humor, love and sorrow."

SPEAK UP, Speak Up Press, PO Box 100506, Denver CO 80250. (303)715-0837. Fax: (303)715-0793. E-mail: SpeakUPres@aol.com. Website: www.speakuppresss.org. **Contact:** Gretchen Bryant, senior editor. Magazine: 5½×8½; 128 pages; 55 lb. Glat. Supple Opaque Recycled Natural paper; 12 CIS cover; illustrations; photos. "*Speak Up* features the original fiction, nonfiction, poetry, plays, photography and artwork of young people 13-19 years old. *Speak Up* provides a place for teens to be creative, honest and expressive in an uncensored environment." Annual. Estab. 1999. Circ. 2,900.

Needs: Teen writers. Receives 30 unsolicited mss/month. Accepts 30 mss/issue; 30 mss/year. Publishes ms 3-12 months after acceptance. **Publishes 20 new writers/year.** Length: 5,000 words; average length: 500 words. Publishes short shorts. Also publishes literary essays, poetry.

How to Contact: Send complete ms. Accepts submissions by mail, e-mail, fax. Responds in 3 months to queries; 3 months to mss. Accepts simultaneous and reprints, multiple submissions. Sample copy for free. Writer's guidelines for #10 SASE.

Payment/Terms: Pays 2 contributor copies. Acquires first North American serial, one-time rights.

SPINDRIFT, Shoreline Community College, 16101 Greenwood Ave. North, Seattle WA 98155. (206)546-5864. E-mail: spindrift@short.cfc.edu. Website: elmo.shore.cfc.edu/spindrift. **Contact:** Literary Editor. Magazine: 140 pages; quality paper; photographs; b&w artwork. "We publish a variety of fiction, most of which would be considered literary. Authors are from all over the map, but we give priority to writers from our community." Annual. Estab. 1967. Circ. 500.

● *Spindrift* has received awards for "Best Literary Magazine" from the Community College Humanities Association both locally and nationally and awards from the Pacific Printing Industries.

Needs: Ethnic/multicultural, experimental, historical, literary, mainstream, regional, serialized novels, translations, prose poem. "No detective, science fiction, romance, religious/inspirational. We look for fresh, original work that is not forced or 'straining' to be literary." Receives 300 unsolicited mss/month. Accepts 20 mss/issue. Publishes ms 3-4 months after acceptance. **Publishes 5-6 new writers/year.** Recently published work by Ed Harkness and Virgil Suarez.

How to Contact: Send complete ms. Do not place name on ms, and please indicate multiple submissions in cover letter. Submit by Feb. 1. Responds by March 15 if SASE is included. Accepts multiple submissions. Sample copy for $8, 8×10 SAE and $1 postage; sample back issues for $2.

Payment/Terms: Pays in contributor copies. Acquires first rights. Not copyrighted.

Advice: "Let the story tell itself; don't force or overdo the language. Show the reader something new about people, situations, life itself."

SPITBALL, 5560 Fox Rd., Cincinnati OH 45239. (513)385-2268. Website: www.angelfire.com/oh5/spitball. **Contact:** Mike Shannon. Magazine: 5½×8½; 96 pages; 55 lb. Glatfelter Natural, neutral pH paper; 10 pt. CS1 cover stock; illustrations; photos. Magazine publishing "fiction and poetry about baseball exclusively for an educated, literary segment of the baseball fan population." Biannual. Estab. 1981. Circ. 2,000.

Needs: Confessions, experimental, historical, literary, mainstream, suspense. "We're looking for literary fiction about baseball *exclusively*! If it ain't about baseball, don't send it." Receives 10 unsolicited mss/month. Accepts

16-20 mss/year. Publishes ms 3 months after acceptance. Recently published work by Dallas Weibe, Michael Gilmartin and W.P. Kinsella.

How to Contact: Send complete ms. Accepts submissions by mail. brief bio about author. First time submitters are required to buy a sample copy for $6. Reporting time varies to mss. Accepts multiple submissions.

Payment/Terms: Pays in contributor copies. Acquires first North American serial rights.

Advice: "Our audience is mostly college educated and knowledgeable about baseball. The stories we have published so far have been very well written and display a firm grasp of the baseball world and its people. In short, audience response has been great because the stories are simply good as stories. Thus, mere use of baseball as a subject is no guarantee of acceptance. We are always seeking submissions. Unlike many literary magazines, we have no backlog of accepted material. Also, don't forget to tell a story! Devise a plot, make something happen!"

$☑ SPRING HILL REVIEW, A Journal of Northwest Culture, PO Box 621, Brush Prairie WA 98606. (360)892-1178. E-mail: springhillreview@aol.com. **Contact:** Lucy S.R. Austen, editor. Magazine: 11½×15; 12-16 pages; newsprint; illustrations; photos. "*SHR* is a journal of contemporary Northwest politics, arts and social and spiritual issues. It is an eclectic blend of nonfiction, fiction, poetry and artwork, aimed at baby boomers and edited from a Christian worldview. This means that we rest on the fact that human beings can live lives of dignity and meaning, first because we are created in the image of God, and then because we have been invited to live in a covenant relationship with God and with each other through Jesus Christ." Monthly. Estab. 2001. Circ. 5,000.

Needs: Adventure, ethnic/multicultural, experimental, family saga, historical, humor/satire, literary, mainstream, mystery/suspense, regional (Pacific Northwest), science fiction, translations, western, novel excerpts. "No children's, religious or romance. We are a general market publication—no overtly evangelistic material, please, and no material written for a specifically Christian audience. We welcome submissions from writers from a variety of belief systems." Receives 0-5 unsolicited mss/month. Accepts 4-6 mss/year. Publishes ms 2-4 months after acceptance. **Publishes 12-20 new writers/year.** Recently published work by Eugene C. Flinn, Robyn Parnell, Orpha Thomas. Length: 600-1,500 words; average length: 800 words. Publishes short shorts. Also publishes literary essays, poetry. Sometimes comments on rejected mss.

How to Contact: Send complete ms. Accepts submissions by mail. estimated word count, brief bio and list of publications. Send SASE for return of ms or send a disposable copy of ms and #10 SASE for reply only. Responds in 2 months to queries; 3 months to mss. Accepts simultaneous and reprints, multiple submissions. Sample copy for $2. Writer's guidelines by e-mail. Reviews fiction.

Payment/Terms: Pays $10-15. Pays on publication for first North American serial, one-time, second serial (reprint) rights.

Advice: "We look for strong characterization (show, don't tell), strong plot (although action may be interior)—even if it is initially a surprise, the denouement must be inevitable; strong sense of place. No propaganda disguised as fiction. If you're a beginning writer, say so, and be open to the possibility of feedback from an editor. If at first you don't succeed, submit your work to us again."

Ⓝ ☐ ▦ STAPLE MAGAZINE, Staple New Writing, 35 Carr Road, Walkley, Sheffield England S6 2WY. E-mail: e.barrett@shu.ac.uk. **Contact:** Elizabeth Barrett, editor. Magazines: A5; 100 pages; illustrations; photos. Quarterly. Estab. 1982. Circ. 500.

Needs: Experimental, feminist, gay, lesbian, literary. Receives 1,000 unsolicited mss/month. Accepts 5 mss/issue; 15 mss/year. Publishes ms 10 weeks after acceptance. **Publishes 3 new writers/year.** Length: 5,000 words; average length: 3,000 words. Publishes short shorts. Also publishes literary essays, literary criticism, poetry. Sometimes comments on rejected mss.

How to Contact: Send complete ms. Send SASE (or IRC) for return of ms. Responds in 8 weeks to queries; 12 weeks to mss. Accepts multiple submissions. Sample copy for $12. Writer's guidelines for SASE.

Payment/Terms: Pays 2 contributor's copies; additional copies $12. Pays on publication for one-time rights.

$☐ ◎ ▮ STONE SOUP, The Magazine by Young Writers and Artists, Children's Art Foundation, P.O. Box 83, Santa Cruz CA 95063-0083. (831)426-5557. Fax: (831)426-1161. Website: www.stonesoup.com. **Contact:** Ms. Gerry Mandel, editor. Magazine: 7×10; 48 pages; high quality paper; photos. Audience is children, teachers, parents, writers, artists. "We have a preference for writing and art based on real-life experiences; no formula stories or poems." Bimonthly. Estab. 1973. Circ. 20,000.

● This is known as "the literary journal for children." *Stone Soup* has previously won the Ed Press Golden Lamp Honor Award and the Parent's Choice Award.

Needs: Adventure, ethnic/multicultural, experimental, fantasy, historical, humor/satire, mystery/suspense, science fiction, slice-of-life vignettes, suspense. "We do not like assignments or formula stories of any kind." Receives 1,000 unsolicited mss/month. Accepts 10 mss/issue. Publishes ms 4 months after acceptance. **Publishes some new writers/year.** Also publishes literary essays, poetry. Usually comments on rejected mss.

How to Contact: Send complete ms. "We like to learn a little about our young writers, why they like to write, and how they came to write the story they are submitting." Please do not include SASE. Do not send originals. Responds only to those submissions being considered for possible publication. "If you do not hear from us in 4 to 6 weeks it means we were not able to use your work. Don't be discouraged! Try again!" No simultaneous submissions. Sample copy for $5 or online. Writer's guidelines online.

Payment/Terms: Pays $40 for stories. Authors also receive 2 copies, a certificate, and discounts on additional copies and on subscriptions. Pays on publication for all rights.

Advice: Mss are rejected because they are "derivatives of movies, TV, comic books; or classroom assignments or other formulas. Go to our website, where you can see many examples of the kind of work we publish."

$ 🗹 🌐 STORIE, all write, Leconte, Via Suor Celestina Donati 13/E, Rome 00167, Italy. (+39)06 614 8777. E-mail: storie@tiscali.it. Website: www.storie.it. **Contact:** Gianluca Bassi, editor; Barbara Pezzopane, assistant editor; George Lerner, foreign editor. Magazine: 186 pages; illustrations; photographs. "*Storie* is one of Italy's leading literary magazines. Committed to a truly crossover vision of writing, the bilingual (Italian/English) review publishes high quality fiction and poetry, interspersed with the work of alternative wordsmiths such as filmmakers and musicians. Through writings bordering on narratives and interviews with important contemporary writers, it explores the culture and craft of writing." Bimonthly. Estab. 1989. Circ. 20,000.

• *Storie* ranked on *Writer's Digest's* "Top 30" list of best markets for fiction writers.

Needs: Literary. Receives 150 unsolicited mss/month. Accepts 6-10 mss/issue; 30-50 mss/year. Does not read mss in August. Publishes ms 2 months after acceptance. **Publishes 20 new writers/year.** Recently published work by Haruki Murakami, Robert Coover, André Dubus III, T.C. Boyle, Ariel Dorfman and Tess Gallagher. Length: 2,000-6,000 words; average length: 3,000 words. Publishes short shorts. Also publishes literary essays, literary criticism, poetry. Sometimes comments on rejected mss.

How to Contact: Accepts submissions by mail, e-mail (on disk). Include brief bio. Send complete ms with cover letter. "Mss may be submitted directly by regular post without querying first; however, we do not accept unsolicited mss via e-mail. Please query via e-mail first. We only contact writers if their work has been accepted. We also arrange for and oversee a high-qulity, professional translation of the piece." Responds in 1 month to queries; 6 months to mss. Accepts multiple submissions. Sample copy for $8. Writer's guidelines online.

Payment/Terms: Pays $30-600 and 2 contributor's copies. Pays on publication for first, (in English and Italian) rights.

Advice: "More than erudite references or a virtuoso performance, we're interested in the recording of human experience in a genuine, original voice. *Storie* reserves the right to include a brief review of interesting submissions not selected for publication in a special column of the magazine."

🗹 🗹 STORYQUARTERLY, 431 Sheridan Rd., Kenilworth IL 60043. (847)256-6998. Website: www.storyquart erly.com. **Contact:** Fiction Editors. Magazine: 6×9; 500 pages; good quality paper; an all-story magazine, committed to a full range of styles and forms. "*StoryQuarterly*, an annual anthology of short stories, publishes contemporary American and international literature of high quality in a full range of styles and forms—outstanding writing and unusual insights. Annual. Estab. 1975. Circ. 5,000.

• *StoryQuarterly* ranked on *Writer's Digest's* "Top 30" list of best markets for fiction writers. *StoryQuarterly* received recognitions in *O. Henry Prize Stories, Best American Stories, Best American Essays* and *Pushcart Prize Collection* in the last 3 years. The publication also won Illinois Arts Council Awards, two apiece in the last 5 years, as well as the Dan Curley Award from the Illinois Arts Council in 2000, for the best story submitted to the Arts Council that year.

Needs: "Well-written stories, serious or humorous, that get up and run from the first page. No genre fiction, light or slight stories, pornography or sentimental stories." Receives 1,500 unsolicited mss/month. Accepts 40-50 mss/issue. **Publishes 2-5 new writers/year.** Recently published work by J.M. Coetzee, Robert Olen Butler, T. Corraghesan Boyle, Stuart Dybek, Stephen Dixon, Reginald Gibbons, Gail Godwin, Alice Hoffman, Mark Winegardner, Charles Johnson, Romulus Linney, Jim McManus and Askold Melnyczuk.

How to Contact: Responds in 2-4 months to mss. Sample copy for $8. Writer's guidelines online at website.

Payment/Terms: Pays 10 contributor's copies, plus lifetime subscription. Acquires first North American serial, one-time, copyright reverts to author after publication. electronic publishing agreement available online.

Advice: "Send one manuscript at a time to online submission site only. Click on Submissions on main webpage and link directly to submission website. No mailed submissions accepted, makes a few exceptions. Fiction selected based on command and use of the language, originality of material, sense of larger world outside the hermitage of the story. A sense of humor goes a very long way, as long as it's not simply ridicule. Intriguing openings, middles that build and create tension, and well-earned and surprising endings all figure in the composition of an outstanding story."

🗹 ◎ STRUGGLE, A Magazine of Proletarian Revolutionary Literature, Box 13261, Detroit MI 48213-0261. (213)273-9039. E-mail: timhall11@yahoo.com. **Contact:** Tim Hall, editor. Magazine: 5½×8½; 36-72 pages; 20 lb. white bond paper; colored cover; illustrations; occasional photos. Publishes material related to "the struggle of the working class and all progressive people against the rule of the rich—including their war policies, racism, exploitation of the workers, oppression of women and general culture, etc." Quarterly. Estab. 1985.

Needs: Ethnic/multicultural, experimental, feminist, historical, humor/satire, literary, regional, science fiction, translations, young adult/teen (10-18), prose poem, senior citizen/retirement. "The theme can be approached in many ways, including plenty of categories not listed here. Readers would like fiction about the anti-globalization movement, the fight against racism, prison conditions. Would also like to see more fiction that depicts life, work and struggle of the working class of every background; also the struggles of the 1930s and 60s illustrated and brought to life. No romance, psychic, mystery, western, erotica, religious." Receives 10-12 unsolicited mss/month. Recently published work by Santonio Murff, Billie Louise Jones and Theresa Dwyer. Length: 4,000 words; average length: 1,000-3,000 words. Publishes short shorts. Normally comments on rejected mss.

How to Contact: Send complete ms. Accepts submissions by mail, e-mail. "Tries to" report in 3-4 months to queries. Accepts simultaneous and reprints, multiple submissions. Sample copy for $2.50; make checks payable to Tim Hall, Special Account.

Payment/Terms: Pays 2 contributor's copies. No rights acquired. Not copyrighted.

Advice: "Write about the oppression of the working people, the poor, the minorities, women, and, if possible, their rebellion against it—we are not interested in anything which accepts the status quo. We are not too worried about plot and advanced technique (fine if we get them!)—we would probably accept things others would call sketches, provided they have life and struggle. For new writers: just describe for us a situation in which some real people confront some problem of oppression, however seemingly minor. Observe and put down the real facts. Experienced writers: try your 'committed'/experimental fiction on us. We get poetry all the time. We have increased our fiction portion of our content in the last few years. The quality of fiction that we have published has continued to improve. If your work raises an interesting issue of literature and politics, it may get discussed in letters and in my editorial. I suggest ordering a sample."

◯ SULPHUR RIVER LITERARY REVIEW, PO Box 19228, Austin TX 78760-9228. (512)292-9456. **Contact:** James Michael Robbins, editor. Magazine: 5½ × 8½; 145 pages; illustrations; photos. "*SLR* publishes literature of quality—poetry and short fiction with appeal that transcends time. Audience includes a broad spectrum of readers, mostly educated, many of whom are writers, artists and educators." Semiannual. Estab. 1978. Circ. 400.

Needs: Ethnic/multicultural, experimental, feminist, humor/satire, literary, mainstream, translations. "No religious, juvenile, teen, sports, romance or mystery. Wants to see more experimental, surreal and imaginative fiction." Receives 20 unsolicited mss/month. Accepts 4-5 mss/issue; 8-10 mss/year. Publishes ms 1-2 years after acceptance. Recently published work by Russell Thorburn, William Orem, Cara Chamberlain and Ken Holland. Publishes short shorts. Also publishes literary essays, literary criticism, poetry.

How to Contact: Send complete ms. Accepts submissions by mail. short bio and list of publications. Send SASE for reply, return of ms, or send disposable copy of ms. Responds in 1 week to queries; 1 month to mss. Sample copy for $7.

Payment/Terms: Pays 2 contributor's copies. Additional copies $7. Acquires first North American serial rights.

Advice: Looks for "quality. Imagination served perfectly by masterful control of language."

◪ A SUMMER'S READING, 409 Lakeview Drive, Sherman IL 62684-9432. (217)496-3012. **Contact:** Ted Morrissey, editor. Magazine: 8½ × 5½; 75 pages; 20 lb. paper; card cover; full color cover; b&w inside; illustrations; photos. "Unlike the majority of literary magazines, our primary reading time is the summer. We want to provide one more attractive, well-edited outlet for new, emerging and established writers and artists." Annual. Estab. 1997. Circ. 200.

Needs: Experimental, literary, translations, prose poetry. "No genre." Receives 60 unsolicited mss/month. Accepts 3-6 mss/year. Publishes ms 1 year after acceptance. **Publishes 1 new writers/year.** Recently published work by William Jackson, Barbara Peck, Christine Zilius and Mark Wisniewski. Length: 500-8,000 words; average length: 3,000-5,000 words. Publishes short shorts. Also publishes poetry. Often comments on rejected mss.

How to Contact: Send complete ms. Include estimated word count, brief bio, list of publications and e-mail address. Responds in 1 year to mss. Accepts simultaneous and reprints, multiple submissions. Sample copy for $5. Writer's guidelines by e-mail.

Payment/Terms: Pays 2 contributor's copies; additional copies $4.50. Pays on publication for one-time rights.

Advice: "We look for a combination of a plot which keeps us turning the pages and a practiced writing style. We will be fair. Your work has a better chance of getting published if it's on our desk instead of yours. Not being university affiliated, it is difficult to find reliable readers—thus reporting time is slower than we prefer."

◪ SYCAMORE REVIEW, Department of English, Purdue University, West Lafayette IN 47907. (765)494-3783. Fax: (765)494-3780. E-mail: sycamore@purdue.edu. Website: www.sla.purdue.edu/sycamore. **Contact:** Fiction Editor. Magazine: 5½ × 8½; 150-200 pages; heavy, textured, uncoated paper; heavy laminated cover. "Journal devoted to contemporary literature. We publish both traditional and experimental fiction, personal essay, poetry, interviews, drama and graphic art. Novel excerpts welcome if they stand alone as a story." Semiannual. Estab. 1989. Circ. 1,000.

Needs: Experimental, humor/satire, literary, mainstream, regional, translations. "We generally avoid genre literature, but maintain no formal restrictions on style or subject matter. No science fiction, romance, children's." Would like to see more experimental fiction. Publishes ms 11 months after acceptance. Recently published work by Lucia Perillo, June Armstrong, W.P. Osborn and William Giraldi. Also publishes poetry, "this list has included Billy Collins, Thomas Lux, Kathleen Pierce and Vandana Khanna." Also publishes poetry. Sometimes comments on rejected mss.

How to Contact: Send complete ms. Accepts submissions by mail. Include previous publications and address changes. SASE. Responds in 4 months to mss. Accepts simultaneous submissions. Sample copy for $7. Writer's guidelines for #10 SASE.

Payment/Terms: Acquires one-time rights.

Advice: "We publish both new and experienced authors but we're always looking for stories with strong emotional appeal, vivid characterization and a distinctive narrative voice; fiction that breaks new ground while still telling an interesting and significant story. Avoid gimmicks and trite, predictable outcomes. Write stories that have a ring of truth, the impact of felt emotion. Don't be afraid to submit, send your best."

$ 🌐 TAKAHE, PO Box 13-335, Christchurch 8001, New Zealand. (03)359-8133. E-mail: mark.johnstone@paradise.net.nz. Website: www.nzwriters.co.nz. **Contact:** Mark Johnstone, administrator. "A literary magazine which appears three or four times a year, and publishes short stories and poetry by both established and emerging writers. The publisher is Takahe Collective Trust, a charitable trust formed by established writers to help new writers and get them into print."

Needs: "We are particularly losing interest in stories by 'victims' of various kinds. morbid stories. We would like to see more humorous and light-hearted stories." **Publishes 20 new writers/year.** Recently published work by Graeme S. Dixon, Stuart Greenhill, David Hill, Virgil Suarez, Sally Sutton, and Chrissie Ward.

How to Contact: Send complete ms. Accepts submissions by mail. brief bio and SASE (IRC for overseas submissions). Single spacing, indented paragraphs and double quotation marks for direct speech. Any use of foreign languages must be accompanied by English translation. Accepts multiple submissions.

Payment/Terms: Pays $15 ($NZ30). Copyright reverts to author on publication

Advice: "We pay a flat rate to each writer/poet appearing in a particular issue regardless of the number/length of items. Amount is subject to change according to circumstances. Editorials and literary commentaries are by invitation only and, not being covered by our grant, are not paid for. All contributors receive two copies of the issue in which their work appears."

$ ▢ TAMEME, New Writing from North America/Nueva literatura de Norteamerica, Tameme Inc., 199 First St., Los Altos CA 94022. E-mail: editor@tameme.org. Website: www.tameme.org. **Contact:** Fiction Editor. Magazine: 6×9; 220 pages; good quality paper; heavy cover stock; illustrations. "*Tameme* is an annual bilingual magazine dedicated to publishing new writing from North America in side-by-side English-Spanish format. Our goal is to play an instrumental role in introducing important new writing from Canada and the US to Mexico, and vice versa, and to provide a forum for the art of literary translation." Estab. 1996. Circ. 1,000. Member, CLMP.

Needs: Ethnic/multicultural, literary, translations. "No genre fiction—no romance, mystery or western." Plans special fiction issue or anthology. "We are not currently reading unsolicited submissions." Receives 50-150 unsolicited mss/month. Accepts 3-4 mss/issue; 6-8 mss/year. Publishes ms 1 year after acceptance. Agented fiction 5%. **Publishes 1-3 new writers/year.** Recently published work by Fabio Morabito, Margaret Atwood, Juan Villoro, Jaime Sabines, Edwidge Danticat, A. Manette Ansay, Douglas Glover and Marianne Toussaint. Publishes short shorts. Also publishes literary essays, poetry.

How to Contact: Accepts simultaneous submissions. Sample copy for $14.95. Writer's guidelines online.

Payment/Terms: $20 per double-spaced WordPerfect page to translators; 3 contributor's copies to writers. Pays on publication for one-time rights. Sends galleys to author.

Advice: "We're looking for whatever makes us want to stand up and shout YES! Read the magazine, send for guidelines (with SASE) or check guidelines on website. We are currently not reading unsolicited submissions."

$ ▢ TAMPA REVIEW, University of Tampa Press, 401 W. Kennedy Blvd., Tampa FL 33606. (813)253-6266. Fax: (813)258-7593. Website: tampareview.ut.edu. **Contact:** Lisa Birnbaum and Kathleen Ochshorn, fiction editors. Magazine: 7½×10½; hardback; approximately 100 pages; acid-free paper; visual art; photos. An international literary journal publishing art and literature from Florida and Tampa Bay as well as new work and translations from throughout the world. Semiannual. Estab. 1988. Circ. 500.

Needs: Ethnic/multicultural, experimental, fantasy, historical, literary, mainstream, translations, Literary. "We are far more interested in quality than in genre. Nothing sentimental as opposed to genuinely moving, nor self-conscious style at the expense of human truth." Accepts 4-5 mss/issue. Reads September through December; reports January through May. Publishes ms 10 months after acceptance. Agented fiction 20%. Recently published work by Elizabeth Spencer, Lee K. Abbott, Lorrie Moore, Gordon Weaver and Tim O'Brien. Publishes short shorts. Also publishes literary essays, poetry.

How to Contact: Send complete ms. Accepts submissions by mail. Include brief bio. Responds in 5 months to mss. Accepts multiple submissions. Sample copy for $7. Writer's guidelines online.

Payment/Terms: Pays $10/printed page. Pays on publication for first North American serial rights. Sends galleys to author.

Advice: "There are more good writers publishing in magazines today than there have been in many decades. Unfortunately, there are even more bad ones. In T. Gertler's *Elbowing the Seducer*, an editor advises a young writer that he wants to hear her voice completely, to tell (he means 'show') him in a story the truest thing she knows. We concur. Rather than a trendy workshop story or a minimalism that actually stems from not having much to say, we would like to see stories that make us believe they mattered to the writer and, more importantly, will matter to a reader. Trim until only the essential is left, and don't give up belief in yourself. And it might help to attend a good writers' conference, e.g. Wesleyan or Bennington."

◙ TAPROOT LITERARY REVIEW, Taproot Writer's Workshop, Inc., Box 204, Ambridge PA 15003. (724)266-8476. E-mail: taproot10@aol.com. **Contact:** Tikvah Feinstein, editor. Magazine: 5½×8½; 93 pages; #20 paper; hard cover; attractively printed; saddle-stitched. "We select on quality, not topic. Variety and quality are our appealing features." Annual. Estab. 1987. Circ. 500.

Needs: Literary. "No pornography, religious, popular, romance fiction. Want more multicultural—displaced people living among others in new places." The majority of ms published are received through their annual contest. Receives 20 unsolicited mss/month. Accepts 6 mss/issue. **Publishes 2-4 new writers/year.** Recently published work by Rita Ariyoshi, Ellaraine Lockie, Sally Levin, and Tom Dougherty. Publishes short shorts. Also publishes poetry. Sometimes comments on rejected mss.

How to Contact: Accepts submissions by e-mail. Send for guidelines first. Send complete ms with a cover letter. Include estimated word count and bio. Responds in 6 months to mss. No simultaneous submissions. Sample copy for $5, 6×12 SAE with 5 first-class stamps. Writer's guidelines for #10 SASE.

Payment/Terms: Awards $25 in prize money for first place fiction and poetry winners each issue; certificate for 2nd and 3rd place; 1 contributor's copy. Acquires first rights. Sponsors awards/contests.

Advice: "*Taproot* is getting more fiction submissions and every one is read entirely. This takes time, so response can be delayed at busy times of year. Our contest is a good way to start publishing. Send for a sample copy and read it through. Ask for a critique and follow suggestions. Don't be offended by any suggestions—just take them or leave them and keep writing. Looks for a story that speaks in its unique voice, told in a well-crafted and complete, memorable style, a style of signature to the author. Follow writer's guidelines. Research markets. Send cover letter. Don't give up."

◙ TERMINUS:, A JOURNAL OF LITERATURE AND ART, Terminus, Inc., 1034 Hill Street, Atlanta GA 30315. E-mail: terminusmag@aol.com. Website: www.terminusmagazine.com. **Contact:** Fiction Editors. Magazine/journal: 6¾×9¾; 100 pages; heavy weight paper; card stock cover; illustrations; photos. "*Terminus* is a twice-yearly journal with the primary mission of publishing the finest writing and art across a broad range of readers. Each issue features some combination of essays, stories, poetry, art, and book reviews. We seek to publish the most thought-provocative, socially and/or culturally aware writing available. While we want to push the boundaries of general aesthetics and standards, we also want to produce writing that is accessible to a wide audience. We seek to live up to the highest standards in publishing, always growing and reaching new levels of understanding and awareness both within our immediate community and within the greater community of our country and world. We produce a CD with each issue featuring authors reading their work." Semiannual. Estab. 2002. Circ. 1,000.

Needs: Literary, translations. Receives 50 unsolicited mss/month. Accepts 2-6 mss/issue; 4-12 mss/year. Publishes ms 1 year after acceptance. Recently published work by Virgil Suarez, Askold Skalsky, Miller Williams and R.S. Gwynn. Length: 250-3,500 words; average length: 2,500 words. Publishes short shorts. Also publishes literary essays, literary criticism, poetry. Sometimes comments on rejected mss.

How to Contact: Send complete ms with a cover letter. Include estimated word count, brief bio and list of publications. Send SASE for return of ms or send a disposable copy of ms and #10 SASE for reply only. Responds in 1 month to queries; 4 months to mss. Accepts simultaneous, multiple submissions. Writer's guidelines by e-mail.

Payment/Terms: Pays 2 contributor's copies; additional copies $8. Acquires first North American serial rights.

◙ THE TEXAS REVIEW, Texas Review Press at Sam Houston State University, P.O. Box 2146, Huntsville TX 77341-2146. (936)294-1992. Fax: (936)294-3070 (inquiries only). E-mail: eng_pdr@shsu.edu. Website: www.shsu.edu. **Contact:** Paul Ruffin, editor. Magazine: 6×9; 148-190 pages; best quality paper; 70 lb. cover stock; illustrations; photos. "We publish top quality poetry, fiction articles, interviews and reviews for a general audience." Semiannual. Estab. 1976. Circ. 1,200. Member, Texas A&M University Press consortium.

Needs: Humor/satire, literary, mainstream, contemporary fiction. "We are eager enough to consider fiction of quality, no matter what its theme or subject matter. No juvenile fiction." Receives 40-60 unsolicited mss/month. Accepts 4 mss/issue; 6 mss/year. Does not read mss May-September. Publishes ms 6-12 months after acceptance. **Publishes some new writers/year.** Recently published work by George Garrett, Ellen Gilchrist and Fred Chappell. Also publishes literary essays, literary criticism, poetry. Sometimes comments on rejected mss.

How to Contact: Send complete ms. No mss accepted via fax. Send disposable copy of the ms and #10 SASE for reply only. Responds in 2 weeks to queries; 3-6 months to mss. Accepts multiple submissions. Sample copy for $5. Writer's guidelines for SASE and on the website.

Payment/Terms: Pays contributor's copies and one year subscription. Pays on publication for first North American serial, one-time rights. Sends galleys to author.

Advice: "Submit often; be aware that we reject 90% of submissions due to overwhelming number of mss sent."

READ 'THE BUSINESS OF FICTION WRITING' section for information on manuscript preparation, mailing tips, rights and more.

$⬙ THEMA, Box 8747, Metairie LA 70011-8747. (504)887-1263. **Contact:** Virginia Howard, editor. Magazine: 5½×8½; 150 pages; Grandee Strathmore cover stock; b&w illustrations. *"Thema* is designed to stimulate creative thinking by challenging writers with unusual themes, such as 'safety in numbers' and 'the power of whim.' Appeals to writers, teachers of creative writing, and general reading audience." Estab. 1988. Circ. 350.
Needs: Adventure, ethnic/multicultural, experimental, fantasy, historical, humor/satire, literary, mainstream, mystery/suspense, novel excerpts, psychic/supernatural/occult, regional, religious/inspirational, science fiction, slice-of-life vignettes, suspense, western, contemporary, sports, prose poem. "No erotica." Upcoming themes (deadlines for submission in 2004): "While you Were Out." (March 1), "Hey, Watch This!" (July 1), "Bookstore Cowboy" (November 1). Publishes ms within 6 months after acceptance. **Publishes 8 new writers/year.** Recently published work by Kaye Bache-Snyder, M.L. Krueger, Beth Bahler, and Jonathan E. Sanders. Publishes short shorts. Also publishes poetry. Sometimes comments on rejected mss.
How to Contact: Accepts submissions by mail. Send complete ms with cover letter, include "name and address, brief introduction, specifying the intended target issue for the mss." SASE. Responds in 1 week to queries; 5 months to mss. Accepts simultaneous and reprints, multiple submissions. Sample copy for $8. Writer's guidelines for #10 SASE.
Payment/Terms: Pays $10-25. Pays on acceptance for one-time rights.
Advice: "Do not submit a manuscript unless you have written it for a specified theme. If you don't know the upcoming themes, send for guidelines first, before sending a story. We need more stories told in the Mark Twain/ O. Henry tradition in magazine fiction."

⬙ 🗹 THIRD COAST, Dept. of English, Western Michigan University, Kalamazoo MI 49008-5092. (269)387-2675. Fax: (269)387-2562. Website: www.wmich.edu/thirdcoast. Glenn Deutsch, managing editor. **Contact:** Andrea Bussell and Monica Friedman, fiction editors. Magazine: 6×9; 150 pages. "We will consider many different types of fiction and favor that exhibiting a freshness of vision and approach." Semiannual. Estab. 1995. Circ. 600.
 • *Third Coast* has received *Pushcart Prize* nominations. The section editors of this publication change with the university year.
Needs: Literary. "While we don't want to see formulaic genre fiction, we will consider material that plays with or challenges generic forms." Receives 100 unsolicited mss/month. Accepts 6-8 mss/issue; 15 mss/year. Recently published work by Peter Ho Davies, Moira Crone, Lee Martin, John McNally, Peter Orner, and Mark Winegardner. Length: 9,000 words. Also publishes literary essays, poetry. Sometimes comments on rejected mss.
How to Contact: Send complete ms. Send SASE for reply or return of ms. Responds in 2 months to queries; 5 months to mss. Accepts simultaneous submissions. Sample copy for $6. Writer's guidelines for #10 SASE.
Payment/Terms: Pays 2 contributor's copies as well as a 1 year subscription to the publication; additional copies for $4. Acquires first North American serial rights.
Advice: "Of course, the writing itself must be of the highest quality. We love to see work that explores non-western contexts, as well as fiction from all walks of American (and other) experiences."

🌐 THE THIRD HALF MAGAZINE, "Amikeco", 16, Fane Close, Stamford Lincolnshire PE9 1HG, England. (01780)754193. **Contact:** Kevin Troop, fiction editor. *"The Third Half* literary magazine publishes mostly poetry, but editorial policy is to publish as much *short* short story writing as possible in separate books."
Needs: Publishes some new writers/year. Recently published work by Michael Bangerter, R. Tomas, Michael Newman and Julie Ashpool.
Payment/Terms: Pay is negotiable.

[N] 🗹 ◎ 13TH MOON, A Feminist Magazine, Dept. of English, University of Albany, Albany NY 12222. (518)442-4181. Editor: Judith Johnson. **Contact:** Fiction Editors. Magazine: 6×9; 300 pages; 50 lb. paper; heavy cover stock; illustrations; photos. "Feminist literary magazine for feminist women and men." Annual. Estab. 1973. Circ. 2,000.
Needs: Ethnic/multicultural, experimental, feminist, lesbian, literary, romance, science fiction, translations. No fiction by men. List of upcoming themes available for SASE. Receives 100 unsolicited mss/month. Accepts 30 + mss/year. Does not read mss June-August. Recently published work by F.R. Lewis, Jan Ramjerdi and Wilma Kahn. Publishes short shorts. Also publishes poetry. Sometimes comments on rejected mss.
How to Contact: Query first; send complete ms with cover letter and SASE (or IRC). Responds in 2 months to queries; 1 year to mss. Sample copy for $10 plus $3 postage. Writer's guidelines for SASE.
Payment/Terms: Pays 1 contributor's copy. Acquires first North American serial rights.
Advice: Looks for *"unusual* fiction with feminist appeal."

⬙ THORNY LOCUST, TL Press, P.O. Box 32631, Kansas City MO 64171-5631. (816)501-4178. E-mail: editors@thornylocust.com. **Contact:** Silvia Kofler. Magazine: 32 pages; illustrations; photos. *"Thorny Locust* is a literary quarterly produced in a dusty corner of the publisher's hermitage. We are interested in poetry, fiction, and artwork with some 'bite'—e.g., satire, epigrams, well-structured tirades, black humor, and bleeding heart cynicism. Absolutely no natural or artificial sweeteners, unless they're the sugar-coating on a strychnine tablet. We are not interested in polemics, gratuitous grotesques, somber surrealism, weeping melancholy, or hate-mongering. To rewrite Jack Conroy, 'We prefer polished vigor to crude banality.'" Estab. 1993. Circ. 200.

Needs: Ethnic/multicultural (general), experimental, humor/satire, literary. Receives 15-20 unsolicited mss/month. Accepts 1 mss/issue; 2-3 mss/year. Publishes ms 2 months after acceptance. Length: 250-2,000 words; average length: 1,500 words. Publishes short shorts. Also publishes poetry. Rarely comments on rejected mss.

How to Contact: Send complete ms with a cover letter. Include brief bio. Send SASE (or IRC) for return of ms or send a disposable copy of ms and #10 SASE for reply only. Responds in 3 months to queries. Accepts simultaneous submissions. Sample copy for $3. Writer's guidelines for SASE or by e-mail.

Payment/Terms: Pays 1 contributor's copy. Acquires one-time rights.

Advice: "We look for work that is witty and original. Edit your work carefully."

THOUGHT MAGAZINE, P.O. Box 117098, Burlingame CA 94011-7098. E-mail: thoughtmagazine@yahoo.com. Website: www.ThoughtMagazine.org. **Contact:** Kevin Feeney, publisher. Magazine: 8½ × 11; 50 pages; 60 lb. paper; 80 lb. cover stock; illustrations. "We publish both emerging writers as well as established talent in our literary journal focused on the art of writing, rather than the business of publishing. We publish stories that have truth to them, ones that force the reader to contemplate his own life. *Thought Magazine* is interested in a personal and collaborative relationship with its authors." Semiannual. Estab. 2000. Circ. 2,000.

Needs: Literary. "No graphic sex/violence or heavy religious themes." Receives 30-50 unsolicited mss/month. Accepts 10 mss/issue; 20 mss/year. Publishes ms 1-3 months after acceptance. **Publishes 10 new writers/year.** Recently published work by Susan Parker, Gerald Nicosia, Norman Zelaya and Shawna Chandler. Length: 1,500-8,000 words; average length: 3,000 words. Publishes short shorts. Also publishes literary essays, literary criticism. Often comments on rejected mss.

How to Contact: Send complete ms with a cover letter. Include estimated word count and brief bio. Send SASE for return of ms or send a disposable copy of ms and #10 SASE for reply only. Responds in 1 week to queries; 1 month to mss. Accepts simultaneous and reprints, multiple submissions. Sample copy for $6. Writer's guidelines for SASE, e-mail or on website.

Payment/Terms: Pays 1 contributor's copy; additional copies $6. Acquires one-time rights. Sends galleys to author upon request. Sponsors awards/contests.

Advice: "We look for stories that make the reader feel strong emotions—anger, frustration, ecstasy, excitement. Be original, be yourself, be truthful."

$ THE THREEPENNY REVIEW, P.O. Box 9131, Berkeley CA 94709. (510)849-4545. Website: www.threepennyreview.com. **Contact:** Wendy Lesser, editor. Tabloid: 10 × 17; 40 pages; Electrobrite paper; white book cover; illustrations. "We are a general interest, national literary magazine with coverage of politics, the visual arts, and the performing arts as well." Quarterly. Estab. 1980. Circ. 9,000.

• *The Threepenny Review* has received GE Writers Awards, CLMP Editor's Awards, NEA grants, Lila Wallace grants and inclusion of work in the *Pushcart Prize Anthology.*

Needs: Literary. No fragmentary, sentimental fiction. Receives 300-400 unsolicited mss/month. Accepts 3 mss/issue; 12 mss/year. Does *not* read mss June through August. Publishes ms 1 year after acceptance. Agented fiction 5%. Recently published work by Sigrid Nunez, Dagoberto Gilb, Gina Berriault and Leonard Michaels. Publishes short shorts. Also publishes literary essays, literary criticism, poetry.

How to Contact: Send complete ms. Send SASE for reply, return of ms or send a disposable copy of the ms. Responds in 1 month to queries; 2 months to mss. Accepts simultaneous submissions. Sample copy for $12 or online. Writer's guidelines online. Reviews fiction.

Payment/Terms: Pays $100 per poem or Table Talk piece. Pays on acceptance for first North American serial rights. Sends galleys to author.

$ TIMBER CREEK REVIEW, 8969 UNCG Station, Greensboro NC 27413. (336)334-2952. E-mail: timber_creek_review@hoopsmail.com. **Contact:** John M. Freiermuth, editor. Newsletter: 5½ × 8½; 80-88 pages; computer generated on copy paper; saddle-stapled with 40 lb. colored paper cover; some illustrations. "Fiction, humor/satire, poetry and travel for a general audience." Quarterly. Estab. 1992. Circ. 140-160.

Needs: Adventure, ethnic/multicultural, feminist, historical, humor/satire, literary, mainstream, mystery/suspense, regional, western, literary nonfiction. "No religious, children's, gay, romance." Receives 50 unsolicited mss/month. Accepts 30-40 mss/year. Publishes ms 2-6 months after acceptance. **Publishes 0-3 new writers/year.** Recently published work by Patricia Abbott, Jim Meirose, Brian Ames and Marcia L. Herlow.

How to Contact: Cover letter required. Accepts simultaneous submissions. Sample copy for $4.75, subscription $16.

Payment/Terms: Pays $10-35, plus subscription. Acquires one-time rights. Not copyrighted.

Advice: "Stop watching TV and read that literary magazine where your last manuscript appeared. There are no automatons here, so don't treat us like machines. We may not recognize your name at the top of the manuscript. A few lines about yourself breaks the ice, the names of 3 or 4 magazines that have published you in the last year or two would show your reality, and a bio blurb of 37 words including the names of 2 or 3 of the magazines you send the occasional subscription check (where you aspire to be?) could help. If you are not sending a check to some little magazine that is supported by subscriptions and the blood, sweat and tears of the editors, why would you send your manuscript to any of them and expect to receive a warm welcome? No requirement to subscribe or buy a sample, but they're available and are encouraged. There are no phony contests and never a reading fee. We read all year long, but may take 1 to 6 months to respond."

$◎ TIN HOUSE, McCormack Communications, Box 10500, Portland OR 97296. (503)274-4393. Fax: (503)222-1154. Website: www.tinhouse.com. **Contact:** Rob Spillman and Elissa Schappell, fiction editors. 7×9; 200 pages; 50 lb. paper; glossy cover stock; illustrations and photos. "We are a general interest literary quarterly. Our watchword is quality. Our audience is people interested in literature in all its aspects, from the mundane to the exalted." Quarterly. Estab. 1998. Circ. 5,000.
   • *Tin House* ranked on *Writer's Digest's* "Top 30" list of best markets for fiction writers.
Needs: Experimental, literary, mainstream, novel excerpts, literary. Accepts 3-4 mss/issue. Publishes ms 6 months after acceptance. Length: 5,000 words maximum; average length: 3,500 words. Publishes short shorts. Also publishes literary essays, literary criticism, poetry.
How to Contact: Send complete ms. Accepts submissions by mail. Include estimated word count. Send SASE for return of ms. Responds in 6 weeks to queries; 3 months to mss. Accepts simultaneous submissions. Sample copy for $15. Writer's guidelines online.
Payment/Terms: Pays $200-800. Pays on publication for first North American serial rights and anthology rights
Advice: "Our criteria are boldness of concept, intense level of emotion and energy, precision of observation, deployment of imagination, grace of style. Any sentence read at random is impeccable and as good as any other in the work. Do not send anything that does not make you feel like laughing or crying, or both, when you read it yourself."

◢ TOUCHSTONE LITERARY JOURNAL, PO Box 130233, Spring TX 77393-0233. E-mail: panthercreek3@ hotmail.com. **Contact:** Julia Gomez-Rivas, fiction editor. Magazine: 5½×8½; 56 pages; linen paper; coated stock cover; perfect bound; b&w illustrations; occasional photos. "We publish literary and mainstream fiction, but enjoy experimental and multicultural work as well. Our audience is middle-class, heavily academic. We are eclectic and given to whims—i.e., two years ago we devoted a 104-page issue to West African women writers." Annual. Estab. 1976. Circ. 1,000.
Needs: Humor/satire, literary, translations. "No erotica, religious, juvenile, stories written in creative writing programs that all sound alike." List of upcoming themes availabble for SASE. Receives 20-30 unsolicited mss/month. Accepts 3-4 mss/issue. Publishes ms "within the year" after acceptance. Recently published work by Ann Alejandro, Lynn Bradley, Roy Fish and Julia Mercedes Castilla. Length: 250-5,000 words; average length: 2,500 words. Publishes short shorts. Also publishes literary essays, literary criticism, poetry.
How to Contact: Send complete ms. Include estimated word count and three-sentence bio. Send SASE for return of ms. Responds in 6 weeks to mss. Accepts multiple submissions. Sample copy not available. Writer's guidelines for #10 SASE.
Payment/Terms: Pays 2 contributor's copies. Acquires one-time rights. Sends galleys to author.
Advice: "We like to see fiction that doesn't read as if it had been composed in a creative writing class. If you can entertain, edify, or touch the reader, polish your story and send it in. Don't worry if it doesn't read like our other fiction."

◢ ◎ ▼ TRANSITION, An International Review, 69 Dunster St., Cambridge MA 02138. (617)496-2845. Fax: (617)496-2877. E-mail: transition@fas.harvard.edu. Website: www.transitionmagazine.com. **Contact:** Michael Vazquez, executive editor. Magazine: 9½×6½; 150-175 pages; 70 lb. Finch Opaque paper; 100 lb. White Warren Lustro dull cover; illustrations; photos. "*Transition* magazine is a quarterly international review known for compelling and controversial writing on race, ethnicity, culture, and politics. This prestigious magazine is edited at Harvard University, and editorial board members include such heavy-hitters as Toni Morrison, Jamaica Kincaid and bell hooks. The magazine also attracts famous contributors such as Spike Lee, Philip Gourevitch and Carlos Fuentes." Quarterly. Estab. 1961. Circ. 3,500.
   • Four-time winner fo the Alternative Press Award for international reporting, (2001, 2000, 1999, 1995); finalist in the 2001 National Magazine Award in General Excellence category. *Transition* ranked on *Writer's Digest's* "Top 30" list of best markets for fiction writers.
Needs: Ethnic/multicultural, historical, humor/satire, literary, regional (African diaspora, Third World, etc.). Receives 10 unsolicited mss/month. Accepts 4-6 mss/year. Publishes ms 3-4 months after acceptance. Agented fiction 30-40%. **Publishes 1 new writers/year.** Recently published work by Geroge Makana Clark, Paul Beatty and Victor D. LaValle. Length: 4,000-8,000 words; average length: 7,000 words. Also publishes literary essays, literary criticism. Sometimes comments on rejected mss.
How to Contact: Query with published clips or send complete ms. Accepts submissions by mail. brief bio and list of publications. Send disposable copy of ms and #10 SASE for reply only. Responds in 2 months to queries; 4 months to mss. Accepts simultaneous submissions. Sample copy not available. Writer's guidelines for #10 SASE.
Payment/Terms: 3 contributor's copies. Sends galleys to author.
Advice: "We look for a non-white, alternative perspective, dealing with issues of race, ethnicity in an unpredictable, provocative way, but not exclusively."

$◢ ▼ TRIQUARTERLY, 629 Noyes St., Northwestern University, Evanston IL 60208-4302. (847)491-7614. Fax: (847)467-2096. **Contact:** Susan Firestone Hahn, editor. Magazine: 6×9¼; 240-272 pages; 60 lb. paper; heavy cover stock; illustration; photos. "A general literary quarterly. We publish short stories, novellas or excerpts from novels, by American and foreign writers. Genre or style is not a primary consideration. We aim for the general but serious and sophisticated reader. Many of our readers are also writers." Triannual. Estab. 1964. Circ. 5,000.

● Stories from *TriQuarterly* have been reprinted in *The Best American Short Stories*, *Pushcart Prizes* and *O. Henry Prize* Anthologies.

Needs: Literary, translations, contemporary. "No prejudices or preconceptions against anything *except* genre fiction (romance, science fiction, etc.)." Receives 500 unsolicited mss/month. Accepts 10 mss/issue; 30 mss/year. Does not read or accept mss between April 1 and September 30. Publishes ms 1 year after acceptance. Agented fiction 10%. **Publishes 1-5 new writers/year.** Recently published work by John Barth, Chaim Potok, Joyce Carol Oates and Robert Girardi. Publishes short shorts.

How to Contact: Send complete ms with SASE. Responds in 3 months to queries; 3 months to mss. No simultaneous submissions. Sample copy for $5. Writer's guidelines for #10 SASE.

Payment/Terms: Payment varies depending on grant support. Pays on publication for first North American serial rights. Nonexclusive reprint rights Sends galleys to author.

☑ UNBOUND, Suny Potsdam Dept. of English and Communications, Morey Hall, SUNY Potsdam, Potsdam NY 13676. (315)267-2043. E-mail: unbound@potsdam.edu. Website: www2.potsdam.edu/henryrm/unbound.html. **Contact:** Rick Henry, editor. Magazine. "*Unbound* seeks fiction that exceeds the page. We are interested in collage, avante-garde, experimental, new media, multi-media fiction that maintains a strong narrative thread." Annual. Estab. 2002.

Needs: Experimental. "No genre fiction." Publishes short shorts.

How to Contact: Send complete ms. brief bio. Send SASE for return of ms or send a disposable copy of ms and #10 SASE for reply only. Responds in 2 months to queries; 10 weeks to mss. Accepts simultaneous submissions. Sample copy not available. Writer's guidelines by e-mail.

Payment/Terms: Pays 1 contributor copy. Pays on publication for first North American serial rights.

Advice: "We look for an intelligent relationship between a fiction's form and content. Fiction need not be limited by the borders of 8½×11 sheets of paper."

☑ THE UNDERWOOD REVIEW, Hanover Press, PO Box 596, Newtown CT 06470-0596. (203)426-3388. Fax: (203)426-3398. E-mail: hanoverpress@earthlink.net. **Contact:** Faith Vicinanza, editor. Magazine: 6×9; 144-288 pages; cream paper and cover; illustrations; photos. "*The Underwood Review*, a literary/art journal, publishes poetry, short stories, interviews, essays, photography (b&w), and pen and ink artwork." Annual. Estab. 1998. Member, CLMP.

Needs: Erotica, ethnic/multicultural, experimental, family saga, fantasy, feminist, gay, humor/satire, lesbian, literary, mainstream, psychic/supernatural/occult. Receives 20 unsolicited mss/month. Accepts 10 mss/year. Publishes ms 6-8 months after acceptance. Length: 500-5,000 words; average length: 3,500 words. Publishes short shorts. Also publishes literary essays, poetry.

How to Contact: Send complete ms. Accepts submissions by mail. Responds in 3-6 weeks to queries; 3-6 months to mss. Accepts simultaneous, multiple submissions. Sample copy for $10. Writer's guidelines for #10 SASE.

Payment/Terms: 2 contributor copies. Acquires first North American serial, first, one-time rights.

Advice: Looks for fiction that is "original, edgy, risky, engaging. Open to new voices."

☐ THE UNKNOWN WRITER, PO Box 698, Ramsey NJ 07446. E-mail: unknown_writer_2000@yahoo.com. Website: www.webpan.net/~amunno/temphome.html. Magazine: 6×9; 40 pages, saddle-stitched; cardstock cover; illustrations; photos. "We exist to give newer writers a place to publish their quality writing. We want authors with limited publishing credits who have strong, detailed and compelling stories to tell. We publish work that strives to make a direct connection with the reader in a fresh, intelligent way. Our goals are to entertain our audience and to provide a literary, professional product with a small-press edge that beginning writers will be proud to list as a credit. Our intended audience is readers of all ages who prefer original, smart fiction and wish to escape the mediocrity of mainstream publications and authors." Quarterly. Estab. 1995.

● *The Unknown Writer* ranked on *Writer's Digest's* "Top 30" list of best markets for fiction writers.

Needs: Adventure, ethnic/multicultural, experimental, fantasy, gay, horror, lesbian, literary, mystery/suspense, science fiction. "No erotic, religious or graphically violent fiction." Accepts 4-5 mss/issue; 16-20 mss/year. Length: 50-5,000 words; average length: 2,500 words. Publishes short shorts. Also publishes poetry. Sometimes comments on rejected mss.

How to Contact: Send complete ms. Accepts submissions by mail, e-mail. Include estimated word count. Send SASE for return of ms or send a disposable copy of ms and #10 SASE for reply only. Accepts simultaneous, multiple submissions. Sample copy not available. Writer's guidelines online.

Payment/Terms: Pays 2 contributor's copies. Pays on publication for first rights.

Advice: "We look for strong characters, rich detail, and a clear conflict with a reasonable resolution. Please use proper spelling and grammar, consistent point of view, and a good pace. We like a quirky, imaginative bent to almost any story. We encourage future submissions when we like the style."

◖ UNMUZZLED OX, Unmuzzled Ox Foundation Ltd., 105 Hudson St., New York NY 10013. (212)226-7170. E-mail: mandreox@aol.com. **Contact:** Michael Andre, editor. Magazine: 5½×8½. "Magazine about life of an intelligent audience." Irregular frequency. Estab. 1971. Circ. 7,000.
> ● Recent issues of this magazine have included art, poetry and essays only. Check before sending submissions.

Needs: Literary, mainstream, translations, prose poetry. "No commercial fiction." Receives 20-25 unsolicited mss/month. Also publishes poetry. Sometimes comments on rejected mss.
How to Contact: "Please no phone calls and no e-mail submissions. Correspondence by *mail* only. Cover letter is significant." Responds in 1 month to queries; 1 month to mss. Sample copy not available.
Payment/Terms: Pays in contributor's copies.
Advice: "You may want to check out a copy of the magazine before you submit."

◖ UNWOUND, A Journal with Delusions of Grandeur, P.O. Box 835, Laramie WY 82073. E-mail: unwoun dmagazine@juno.com. **Contact:** Lindsay Wilson, editor. Magazine: 8½×10; 44 pages; heavy cover stock; illustrations; photos. "*Unwound* is a journal about contemporary life that seeks to recreate the world through writing and the mind that comes into contact with it. No traditional forms—I want to break with tradition. I want the work in *Unwound* to be new and to challenge old ideas." Annual. Estab. 1998. Circ. 200.
Needs: Erotica, ethnic/multicultural, humor/satire, literary, mainstream, regional (all), surrealism. Especially interested in flash fiction. Receives 5 unsolicited mss/month. Accepts 1-2 mss/issue; 2-5 mss/year. Publishes ms 1-6 month after acceptance. Agented fiction 10%. Recently published work by Daniel Crocker, Mark Wisniewski, Tim Scannel and Nathan Graziano. Length: 3,000 words; average length: 2,000 words. Publishes short shorts. Also publishes literary essays, literary criticism, poetry. Sometimes comments on rejected mss.
How to Contact: Send complete ms on disk. Include estimated word count and brief bio. SASE is a must. Send SASE for return of ms. Responds in 2 months to queries; 4 months to mss. Accepts multiple submissions. Sample copy for $4. Writer's guidelines for SASE, e-mail or on website. Reviews fiction.
Payment/Terms: Pays 1 contributor's copy; additional copies $2. Acquires one-time rights. Sends galleys to author. Not copyrighted.
Advice: "I'm looking for work that is surreal and has concerns for the image, but is still able to maintain an informal and identifiable voice. I'm looking for words and works that are trying to do something new and fresh."

$◖ ▣ VESTAL REVIEW, A flash fiction magazine, 2609 Dartmouth Dr., Vestal NY 13850. E-mail: editor @stny.rr.com. Website: www.vestalreview.net. **Contact:** Mark Budman, publisher/editor. Magazine: 8½×5½; 22 pages; heavy cover stock; illustrations. "*Vestal Review* is the magazine specializing in flash fiction (stories under 500 words). In our 13 quarterly issues up to date, we had an honor of publishing many good writers, including Aimee Bender and Mike Resnick. We accept only e-mail submissions." Quarterly. Circ. 1,500.
> ● Vestal Review received a Golden Web Award in 2002-2003.

Needs: Ethnic/multicultural, horror, literary, mainstream, speculative fiction. Receives 60-100 unsolicited mss/month. Accepts 7-8 mss/issue; 28-32 mss/year. Does not read mss March, June, September and December. Publishes ms 2-3 months after acceptance. **Publishes 2-3 new writers/year.** Recently published work by Aimee Bender, Mike Resnick, Katherine Weber, and Sam Lipsyte. Publishes short shorts. Sometimes comments on rejected mss.
How to Contact: Send complete ms with a cover letter via e-mail only. Include estimated word count, brief bio and list of publications. Responds in 1 week to queries; 2 months to mss. Accepts simultaneous, multiple submissions. Sample copy for $5. Writer's guidelines online.
Payment/Terms: Pays $0.03-0.1/word and 1 contributor's copy; additional copies $5. Pays on publication for first North American serial, electronic rights. Sends galleys to author.
Advice: "We like literary fiction, with a plot, that doesn't waste words. Don't send jokes masked as stories."

$◖ THE VINCENT BROTHERS REVIEW, The Vincent Brothers Company, 4566 Northern Circle, Riverside OH 45424. (937)367-3702. Website: www.thevincentbrothersreview.org. **Contact:** Fiction editor. Magazine: 5½×8¼; 160-175 perfect-bound pages; 60 lb. white coated paper; 60 lb. Oxford (matte) cover; b&w illustrations; photos. "*The Vincent Brothers Review*'s mission is to broaden the appreciation for creative writing and contemporary graphic arts. *TVBR*'s goal is also to serve as a bridge between the academic literary journals and the commercial slicks, between the 'zines and the established small presses. Writers must send SASE for information about upcoming theme issues. Each issue of *TVBR* contains poetry, b&w art, at least six short stories and usually one nonfiction piece. For a mainstream audience looking for an alternative to the slicks." Biannual. Estab. 1988. Circ. 450.
Needs: Adventure, condensed novels, ethnic/multicultural, experimental, feminist, historical, humor/satire, literary, mainstream, mystery/suspense (amateur sleuth, cozy, private eye), regional, science fiction (soft/sociological), serialized novels, translations, western (adult, frontier, traditional), prose poem, contemporary, senior citizen/retirement. "We love to read funny stories. Humoroues fiction is quite difficult to write-it usually appears as amusing anecdotes. We look for stories we want to pass on to other readers; stories we ourselves want to read again and again." Upcoming themes: "Taking Flight/Flight and Flying," deadline February 28; "Ohio's Ethnic Neighborhoods," deadline November 30. Receives 200-250 unsolicited mss/month. Accepts 6-15 mss/issue; 30 mss/year. Publishes ms 2-4 months after acceptance. **Publishes 4-6 new writers/year.** Recently published work by Paul Headrick, Wayne Rapp, Gerald Wheeler, Stephen Graham Jones and Jerry Gabriel. Length: 250-7,000 words; average length:

3,500 words. Publishes short shorts. Also publishes literary essays, literary criticism, poetry. Often critiques rejected mss and sometimes recommends other markets.

How to Contact: Send complete ms. Accepts submissions by mail. "Send query letter *before* sending novel excerpts or condensations! *Send only one short story at a time*—unless sending short shorts." No e-mail submissions. Responds in 1 month to queries; 3 months to mss. Accepts simultaneous, multiple submissions but not preferred. Recent sample copies are $11.50. Perfect-bound back issues are $6.50; saddle-stitched (stapled) back issues are $5. Writer's guidelines for #10 SASE. Reviews fiction.

Payment/Terms: Pays $25-350. Pays on acceptance for first North American serial rights. Sponsors awards/contests.

Advice: "We look for stories that pull us into their world immediately. Most writers mistakenly believe the first sentence is what's important. For us, it's the second sentence. It's the second sentence that lets us know the writer has command of the story and is taking us on a road we'll want to follow until we've read the last word of the story. Read, read, read some more of what the magazines are publishing. Read everything from Xeroxed 'zines to *The New Yorker*. Subscribe to at least three of the magazines/journals you like reading. Read the work of your peers."

$ WESTERN HUMANITIES REVIEW, University of Utah, English Department, 255 S. Central Campus Dr., Room 3500, Salt Lake City UT 84112-0494. (801)581-6070. Fax: (801)585-5167. Website: www.hum.utah.edu/whr. **Contact:** Karen Brennan and Robin Hemley, fiction editors. Biannual. Estab. 1947. Circ. 1,000.

Needs: Experimental (any type), literary. Does not want genre (romance, sci-fi, etc.). Receives 100 unsolicited mss/month. Accepts 3-4 mss/issue; 6-8 mss/year. Does not read mss May-August. Publishes ms 1 year after acceptance. Agented fiction 10%. **Publishes 5 new writers/year.** Recently published work by Stephen-Paul Martin and Alan Singer. Publishes short shorts. Also publishes literary essays, literary criticism, poetry. Rarely comments on rejected mss.

How to Contact: Send complete ms. Accepts simultaneous submissions. Sample copy for $10. Writer's guidelines online.

Payment/Terms: Pays $5/published page (when funds available). Pays on publication for all rights.

◨ WESTVIEW, A Journal of Western Oklahoma, Southwestern Oklahoma State University, 100 Campus Drive, Weatherford OK 73096-3098. (580)774-3168. **Contact:** Fiction Editor. Magazine: 8½ × 11; 64 pages; 24 lb. paper; slick color cover; illustrations; photos. Semiannual. Estab. 1981. Circ. 400.

Needs: Ethnic/multicultural (especially Native American), humor/satire, literary, mainstream, prose poem, contemporary. "No pornography, violence or gore. No overly sentimental work. We are particularly interested in writers of the Southwest; however, we accept work of quality from elsewhere." Receives 20 unsolicited mss/month. Accepts 5 mss/issue; 10 mss/year. Publishes ms 3-12 months after acceptance. Recently published work by Diane Glancey, Wendell Mayo, W.A. Kinsella, Jack Matthews and Mark Spencer. Average length: 2,000 words. Also publishes literary essays, literary criticism, poetry. Occasionally comments on rejected mss.

How to Contact: Send complete ms. "We welcome submissions on a 3.5 disk formatted for WordPerfect 5.0, IBM or Macintosh. Please include a hard copy printout of your submission." Responds in 2 months to queries; 2 months to mss. Accepts simultaneous submissions. Sample copy for $5.

Payment/Terms: Pays contributor's copy. Acquires first rights.

◨ WHISKEY ISLAND MAGAZINE, Dept,. of English, Cleveland State University, Cleveland OH 44115-2440. (216)687-2056. Fax: (216)687-6943. E-mail: whiskeyisland@csuohio.edu. Website: www.csuohio.edu/whiskey_island. Editors change each year. Magazine of fiction and poetry, including experimental works, with no specific theme. "We provide a forum for new writers and new work, for themes and points of view that are both meaningful and experimental, accessible and extreme." Semiannual. Estab. 1978. Circ. 2,500.

Needs: "Would like to see more short shorts, flash fiction." Receives 100 unsolicited mss/month. Accepts 46 mss/issue. **Publishes 5-10 new writers/year.** Recently published work by Vickie A. Carr and John Fulmer. Also publishes poetry.

How to Contact: Send complete ms. Accepts submissions by mail, fax. Accepts queries/mss by fax. Responds in 4 months to queries; 4 months to mss. No simultaneous submissions. Sample copy for $5.

Payment/Terms: Pays 2 contributor's copies and one-year subscription. Acquires one-time rights. Sponsors awards/contests.

Advice: "We read manuscripts September through April only. We seek a different voice, controlled language and strong opening. Childhood memoirs are discouraged."

ℕ ◨ WILLARD & MAPLE, The Literary Magazine of Champlain College, 163 South Willard Street, Freeman 302, Box 34, Burlington VT 05401. (802)865-6406. E-mail: willardandmaple@champlain.edu. **Contact:** Fiction editor. Magazine: 5½ × 8½; 100 pages; illustrations; photos. "*Willard & Maple* is a student-run literary magazine from Champlain College that publishes a wide array of poems, short stories, creative essays, short plays, pen and ink drawings, black and white photos, and computer graphics." Annual. Estab. 1996.

Needs: We accept all types of mss. Receives 20 unsolicited mss/month. Accepts 5 mss/year. Does not read mss May-September. Publishes ms 1 year after acceptance. **Publishes 10 new writers/year.** Recently published work by Jesse Rosenthal, Bill Mosler, Sandy Johnson, Erin Parker, Molly McGuill, David Jacobs. Length: 5,000 words; average length: 2,500 words. Publishes short shorts. Also publishes literary essays, poetry. Sometimes comments on rejected mss.

How to Contact: Send complete ms. Send SASE for return of ms or send disposable copy of mss and #10 SASE for reply only. Responds in 2 months to queries; 2 months to mss. Accepts simultaneous, multiple submissions. Sample copy for $8.50. Writer's guidelines for SASE or send e-mail. Reviews fiction.

Payment/Terms: Pays 2 contributor's copies; additional copies $8.50. Pays on publication for one-time rights.

Advice: "Work hard; be good; never surrender!"

$⬜⬜ WILLOW SPRINGS, 705 W. First Ave., Eastern Washington University, Spokane WA 99201. (509)623-4349. Jennifer S. Davis, editor. **Contact:** Fiction Editor. Magazine: 9×6; 128 pages; 80 lb. glossy cover. "We publish quality contemporary poetry, fiction, nonfiction, and works in translation." Semiannual. Estab. 1977. Circ. 1,500.

• *Willow Springs* is a member of the Council of Literary Magazines and Presses and AWP. The magazine has received grants from the NEA and a CLMP excellence award.

Needs: Literary, translations, short stories, prose poems, poems. "No genre fiction, please." Receives 150 unsolicited mss/month. Accepts 2-4 mss/issue; 4-8 mss/year. Does not read mss May 15-September 15. Publishes ms 4 months after acceptance. **Publishes some new writers/year.** Recently published work by James Grabill, Amy Newman and Jonathan Penne. Also publishes literary essays, literary criticism, poetry. Rarely comments on rejected mss.

How to Contact: Send complete ms. Responds in 2 months to queries; 2 months to mss. No simultaneous submissions. Sample copy for $5.50. Writer's guidelines for #10 SASE.

Payment/Terms: Pays $20-50 and 2 contributor's copies. Acquires first North American serial, first rights.

Advice: "We hope to attract good fiction writers to our magazine, and we've made a commitment to publish three-four stories per issue. We like fiction that exhibits a fresh approach to language. Our most recent issues, we feel, indicate the quality and level of our conmmitment."

⬜ WINDHOVER, A Journal of Christian Literature, University of Mary Hardin-Baylor, PO Box 8008, Belton TX 76513. (254)295-4561. E-mail: windhover@umbh.edu. **Contact:** Donna Walker-Nixon, editor. Magazine: 6×9; white bond paper. "We accept poetry, short fiction, non-fiction, creative non-fiction. *The Journal* is devoted to promoting wirters and literature with a Christian perspective and with a broad definition of that perspective." Annual. Estab. 1997. Circ. 500.

Needs: Ethnic/multicultural, experimental, family saga, fantasy, historical, humor/satire, literary. "No erotica." Receives 30 unsolicited mss/month. Accepts 5 mss/issue; 5 mss/year. Publishes ms 1 year after acceptance. **Publishes 5 new writers/year.** Recently published work by Walt McDonald, Cleatus Rattan, Greg Garrett, and Barbara Crooker. Length: 1,500-4,000 words; average length: 3,000 words. Publishes short shorts. Also publishes literary essays, poetry. Sometimes comments on rejected mss.

How to Contact: Send complete ms. Accepts submissions by mail. Estimated word count, brief bio and list of publications. Responds in 4-6 weeks to queries; 4-6 months to mss. Accepts simultaneous submissions. Sample copy for $8. Writer's guidelines by e-mail.

Payment/Terms: Pays 2 contributor's copies. Pays on publication for first rights.

Advice: "Be patient. We have an editorial board and sometimes take longer than I like. We particularly look for convincing plot and character development."

Ⓝ $⬜ ⬜ WINDSOR REVIEW, A Journal of the Arts, Dept. of English, University of Windsor, Windsor ON N9B 3P4 Canada. (519)253-4232, ext. 2290. Fax: (519)973-7050. Website: venus.uwindsor.ca/english/review.htm. **Contact:** Alistair MacLeod, fiction editor. Magazine: 6×9; perfect bound; 110 pages; illustrations; photos. "We try to offer a balance of fiction and poetry distinguished by excellence." Semiannual. Estab. 1965. Circ. 250.

Needs: Literary. No genre fiction (science fiction, romance), "but would consider if writing is good enough." Accepts 1-4 mss/issue. Publishes ms 6 months after acceptance. Recently published work by Rosemary Sullivan and Tom Wayman.

How to Contact: Send complete ms. Accepts submissions by e-mail. Send SASE for reply, return of ms or send a disposable copy of ms. Responds in 1 month to queries; 6 weeks to mss. No simultaneous submissions. Sample copy for $7 (US). Writer's guidelines online.

Payment/Terms: Pays $30 and 1 contributor's copy and a free subscription. Pays on publication for one-time rights.

Advice: "Good writing, strong characters, experimental fiction is appreciated."

$ WORCESTER MAGAZINE, 172 Shrewsbury St., Worcester MA 01604-4636. (508)755-8004. Fax: (508)755-4734. Website: www.worcestermag.com. Weekly. Estab. 1976. Circ. 40,000.

Needs: Publishes ms 3 weeks after acceptance.

How to Contact: Accepts submissions by mail, e-mail, fax.

Payment/Terms: Pays on publication for all rights.

THE WORCESTER REVIEW, Worcester County Poetry Association, Inc., 6 Chatham St., Worcester MA 01609. (508)797-4770. Website: www.geocities.com/Paris/LeftBank/6433. **Contact:** Fiction Editor. Magazine: 6×9; 100 pages; 60 lb. white offset paper; 10 pt. CS1 cover stock; illustrations; photos. "We like high quality, creative poetry, artwork and fiction. Critical articles should be connected to New England." Annual. Estab. 1972. Circ. 1,000.

Needs: Literary, prose poem. "We encourage New England writers in the hopes we will publish at least 30 percent New England but want the other 70 percent to show the best of writing from across the US." Receives 20-30 unsolicited mss/month. Accepts 2-4 mss/issue. Publishes ms 11 months after acceptance. Agented fiction less than 10%. Recently published work by Robert Pinsky, Marge Piercy, Wes McNair and Ervon Boland. Length: 1,000-4,000 words; average length: 2,000 words. Publishes short shorts. Also publishes literary essays, literary criticism, poetry. Sometimes comments on rejected mss.

How to Contact: Send complete ms. Accepts submissions by mail. Responds in 9 months to mss. Accepts simultaneous submissions only if other markets are clearly identified. Sample copy for $6. Writer's guidelines free.

Payment/Terms: Pays 2 contributor's copies and honorarium if possible. Acquires one-time rights.

Advice: "Send only one short story—reading editors do not like to read two by the same author at the same time. We will use only one. We generally look for creative work with a blend of craftsmanship, insight and empathy. This does not exclude humor. We won't print work that is shoddy in any of these areas."

WORDS LITERARY JOURNAL, 14268-66 Avenue, Surrey BC V3A-2B3 Canada. (604)599-8096. E-mail: wordsjournal@telus.net. Website: www.wordsjournal.com. **Contact:** Lois Peterson, editor. Magazine: digest size; 48-64 pages. Small press journal of fiction, poetry, essays and memoir. Triannual. Estab. 1991. Circ. 150.

Needs: Ethnic/multicultural, experimental, humor/satire, literary, mainstream. No erotica. Receives 15 unsolicited mss/month. Accepts 2 mss/issue; 8 mss/year. Publishes ms 1-6 months after acceptance. **Publishes 4 new writers/year.** Recently published work by John Ravenscroft, Jack Reuich, Wendell Mayo. Length: 1,000-4,000 words; average length: 2,500 words. Publishes short shorts. Also publishes poetry. Sometimes comments on rejected mss.

How to Contact: Send complete ms. Send SASE for return of ms or send copy of ms and #10 SASE for reply only. Responds in 2-12 weeks to mss. Accepts simultaneous and reprints, multiple submissions. Sample copy for $6; $7 (Canada). Writer's guidelines for SASE, e-mail or on website.

Payment/Terms: Pays contributor's copy; additional copies $4; $5 (Canada). Pays on publication for first North American serial rights. Sends galleys to author. Sponsors awards/contests.

Advice: "We're looking for work with a strong individual voice, fresh well-crafted language and strong characterization. Write a lot to develop a strong voice."

WORDS OF WISDOM, 8969 UNCG Station, Greensboro NC 27413. (336)334-2952. E-mail: wowmail@hoopsmail.com. **Contact:** Mikhammad Abdel-Ishara, editor. Newsletter: 5½×8½; 76-88 pages; computer-generated on copy paper; saddle-stapled with 40 lb. colored paper cover; some illustrations. "Fiction, satire/humor, poetry and travel for a general audience." Estab. 1981. Circ. 150-160.

Needs: Adventure, ethnic/multicultural, feminist, historical, humor/satire, literary, mainstream, mystery/suspense (private eye, cozy), regional, western. "No religious, children, gay or romance." Receives 50 unsolicited mss/month. Accepts 65-75 mss/year. Publishes ms 2-6 months after acceptance. **Publishes 0-5 new writers/year.** Recently published work by Tim McCoy, Robert Steiner, Susan Carrithers, David Sapp and Margene Whitler Hucek. Length: 1,200-6,000 words; average length: 3,000 words.

How to Contact: Send complete ms. Accepts submissions by mail. Responds in 1-6 months to mss. Accepts simultaneous submissions. Sample copy for free.

Payment/Terms: Offers subscription to magazine for first story published. Acquires one-time rights. Not copyrighted.

Advice: "A few lines about yourself breaks the ice, the names of three or four magazines that have published your work in the last year would show your reality, and a bio blurb of about 35 words including the names of a few magazines you send your subscription money to could help. No requirements to subscribe or buy a sample, but they are available at $15 and $4.50 and are encouraged. There are no phony contests and never a reading fee. We read all year long, but it may take one to six months to respond."

WRITING FOR OUR LIVES, Running Deer Press, 647 N. Santa Cruz Ave., Annex, Los Gatos CA 95030-4350. (408)354-8604. **Contact:** Janet M. McEwan, editor. Magazine: 5¼×8¼; 80 pages; 70 lb. recycled white paper; 80 lb. recycled cover. "*Writing For Our Lives* is a periodical which serves as a vessel for poems, short fiction, stories, letters, autobiographies, and journal excerpts from the life stories, spiritual journeys and experiences of women. Audience is women and friends of women." Annual. Estab. 1992. Circ. 500.

Needs: Ethnic/multicultural, experimental, feminist, humor/satire, lesbian, literary, translations. "Autobiographical, breaking personal or historical silence on any concerns of women's lives. No genre fiction. *Women writers only, please.*" Receives 15-20 unsolicited mss/month. Accepts 10 mss/issue; 20 mss/year. Publishes ms 2-24 months after acceptance. **Publishes 3-5 new writers/year.** Recently published work by Sabah Akbar, Anjali Banerjee, Debra Kay Vest, Lisa M. Oritz and Luci Yamamoto. Publishes short shorts. Also publishes poetry. Rarely comments on rejected mss.

How to Contact: Send complete ms. Accepts submissions by mail. "Publication date is October. Closing date for mss is August 15. Initial report immediate; next report, if any, in 1-18 months." Send 2 SASEs for reply, and one of them must be sufficient for return of ms if desired." Accepts simultaneous and reprints, multiple submissions. Sample copy for $6-8. Writer's guidelines for #10 SASE.

Payment/Terms: Acquires second serial (reprint), first worldwide english language serial rights.

Advice: "It is in our own personal stories that the real herstory of our time is told. This periodical is a place for exploring the boundaries of our empowerment to break long historical and personal silences. While honoring the writing which still needs to be held close to our hearts, we can begin to send some of our heartfelt words out into a wider circle."

⬛ XAVIER REVIEW, Xavier University, 1 Drexel Dr., New Orleans LA 70125-1098. (504)485-7944. Fax: (504)485-7197. E-mail: rcollins@xula.edu (correspondence only—no mss). **Contact:** Richard Collins, editor. Mark Whitaker, associate editor. Magazine: 6×9; 75 pages; 50 lb. paper; 12 pt. CS1 cover; photographs. Magazine of "poetry/fiction/nonfiction/reviews (contemporary literature) for professional writers, libraries, colleges and universities. Semiannual. Estab. 1980. Circ. 500.

Needs: Ethnic/multicultural, experimental, historical, literary, mainstream, regional (Southern, Latin American), religious/inspirational, serialized novels, translations. Receives 100 unsolicited mss/month. Accepts 2 mss/issue; 4 mss/year. **Publishes 2-3 new writers/year.** Recently published work by Andrei Codressa, Terrance Hayes, Naton Leslie, Alvin Aubert. Also publishes literary essays, literary criticism. Occasionally comments on rejected mss.

How to Contact: Send complete ms. Include 2-3 sentence bio. Sample copy for $5.

Payment/Terms: Pays 2 contributor's copies.

⬛ XCONNECT (formerly Crossconnect), P.O. Box 2317, Philadelphia PA 19103. (215)898-5324. Fax: (215)898-9348. E-mail: xconnect@ccat.sas.upenn.edu. Website: ccat.sas.upenn.edu/xconnect. **Contact:** David Diefer. Journal: 5½×8½; trade paper; 200 pages. "*Xconnect* publishes tri-annually on the World Wide Web and annually in print, with the best of our web issues, plus nominated work from editors in the literary community. *Xconnect: writers of the information age* is a nationally distributed, full color, journal sized book."

Needs: Experimental, literary. "Our mission—like our name—is one of connection. *Xconnect* seeks to promote and document the emergent creative artists as well as established artists who have made the transition to the new technologies of the Information Age." **Publishes 25 new writers/year.** Recently published work by Bob Perelman, John Edgar Wideman and Rachel Blau Duplessis. Rarely comments on rejected mss.

How to Contact: Accepts simultaneous and reprints submissions. Sample copy not available.

Payment/Terms: Pays 1 contributor's copy for use in print version. Author retains all rights. Regularly sends prepublication galleys.

Advice: "Persistence."

⬛ THE YALOBUSHA REVIEW, The Literary Journal of the University of Mississippi, Dept. of English Bondurant Hall, P.O. Box 1848, University Mississippi 38677. (662)915-3175. Fax: (662)915-7419. E-mail: yalobuh @olemiss.edu. Magazine: 6×9; 126 pages; illustrations; photos. Annual. Estab. 1995. Circ. 500.

Needs: Experimental, family saga, historical, humor/satire, literary, mainstream, genre. Receives 70 unsolicited mss/month. Accepts 6-8 mss/issue. Publishes ms 6 months after acceptance. **Publishes 4-6 new writers/year.** Recently published work by Steve Almond, Shay Youngblood, and Dan Chase. Length: 1,000-5,000 words; average length: 5,000 words. Publishes short shorts. Also publishes poetry.

How to Contact: Send complete ms. Accepts submissions by mail. Include a brief bio. Send disposable copy of ms and #10 SASE for reply only. Responds in 6 weeks to queries; 6 months to mss. Accepts multiple submissions. Sample copy for $10. Writer's guidelines for #10 SASE.

Payment/Terms: Acquires first rights.

Advice: "We don't read manuscripts May 15 through August 15. We look for writers with a strong, distinct voice and good stories to tell. Thrill us."

⬛ 🅜 YEMASSEE, The literary journal of the University of South Carolina, Department of English, University of South Carolina, Columbia SC 29208. (803)777-2085. Fax: (803)777-9064. E-mail: yemassee@gwm.sc .edu. Website: www.cla.sc.edu/ENGL/yemassee/index.htm. **Contact:** Carl Jenkins and Jil Carroll, editors. Magazine: 5½×8½; 70-90 pages; 60 lb. natural paper; 65 lb. cover; cover illustration. "We are open to a variety of subjects and writing styles. We publish primarily fiction and poetry, but we are also interested in one-act plays, brief excerpts of novels, and interviews with literary figures. Our essential consideration for acceptance is the quality of the work." Semiannual. Estab. 1993. Circ. 500.

• Stories from *Yemassee* have been selected for publication in *Best New Stories from the South*.

Needs: Condensed novels, ethnic/multicultural, experimental, feminist, gay, historical, humor/satire, lesbian, literary, regional. "No romance, religious/inspirational, young adult/teen, children's/juvenile, erotica. Wants more experimental work." Receives 30 unsolicited mss/month. Accepts 1-3 mss/issue; 2-6 mss/year. "We read from August-May and hold ms over to the next year if they arrive in the summer." **Publishes 6 new writers/year.** Recently published work by Robert Coover, Chris Railey, Virgil Suarez, Susan Ludvigson and Kwame Dawes. Publishes short shorts. Also publishes literary essays, poetry.

How to Contact: Send complete ms. Accepts submissions by mail. Include estimated word count, brief bio, and list of publications. Send SASE for reply, return of ms, or send disposable copy of ms. Responds in 2 weeks to queries; 4 months to mss. Accepts simultaneous submissions. Sample copy for $5. Writer's guidelines for #10 SASE.

Payment/Terms: Acquires first rights.

Advice: "Our criteria are based on what we perceive as quality. Generally that is work that is literary. We are interested in subtlety and originality, interesting or beautiful language, craft and precision. Read our journal and any other journal before you submit to see if your work seems appropriate. Send for guidelines and make sure you follow them."

🌐 ◎ YORKSHIRE JOURNAL, Smith Settle Ltd., Ilkley Rd., Otley West Yorkshire LS21 3JP, England. 01943-467958. Fax: 01943-850057. E-mail: sales@smith-settle.co.uk. Website: www.smith-settle.co.uk/index.htm. **Contact:** Mark Whitley. Magazine: 120 pages; matte art paper; art board cover stock; illustrations; photos. "We publish historical/factual articles, poetry and short stories by and about the county of Yorkshire in England." Quarterly. Estab. 1993. Circ. 3,000.

Needs: Regional. "Anything about Yorkshire." Receives 2-4 unsolicited mss/month. Accepts 2-3 mss/year. Recently published work by Denis Yeadon, Neville Slack, Mary Walsh and Alex Marwood. Average length: 1,500 words. Often comments on rejected mss.

How to Contact: Query with or without published clips. Accepts submissions by mail, e-mail. Include estimated word count and 50-word bio. Send IRCs for reply, return of ms, or send disposable copy of ms. Responds in 6 weeks to queries; 10 weeks to mss. Accepts reprints submissions. Sample copy for $10. Writer's guidelines for #10 SASE.

Payment/Terms: Pays 1 contributor copy. Pays on publication for first rights.

Advice: "Fiction must be about Yorkshire in some way. Send in an outline first, not the completed manuscript."

$ ◪ 🛇 ZOETROPE: ALL-STORY, AZ X Publications, 916 Kearney St., San Francisco CA 94133. (415)788-7500. Fax: (415)989-7910. E-mail: info@all-story.com. Website: www.all-story.com. **Contact:** Tamara Straus, editor-in-chief. Magazine: 10½×14; 60 pages; illustrations; photos. Quarterly. "*Zoetrope: All-Story* presents a new generation of classic stories. Inspired by the Coppola heritage of independence and creativity, the magazine is at once innovative and deeply traditional. It explores the intersection of fiction and film and anticipates some of its stories becoming memorable films." Estab. 1997. Circ. 3,000.

● This journal won the 2002 National Magazine Award for fiction. Stories from *Zoetrope* have received the O. Henry Prize, the Pushcart Prize and have been reprinted in *New Stories from the South* and received honorable mentions in *Best American Short Stories*.

Needs: Literary, mainstream/contemporary, one-act plays. "No genre fiction or excerpts from longer works." Receives 600 unsolicited mss/month. Accepts 5-7 mss/issue; 30-40 mss/year. Publishes ms approximately 6 months after acceptance. Agented fiction 15%. **Publishes 4-6 new writers/year.** Published work by Arthur Bradford, A.M. Homes, Jane Smiley and Susan Straight.

How to Contact: Send complete ms (no more than 1) with cover letter. Accepts queries by mail. Include estimated word count and list of publications. SASE. Accepts simultaneous submissions. Sample copy for $5.95 and 9×12 SAE and $1.70 postage. Guidelines for #10 SASE.

Payment/Terms: Pays $1,500 for first seral rights and two-year option on movie rights for unsolicited submission. $6,000 for commissioned works. Sponsors contest.

Advice: "We like fiction that really tells a full story. Voices we haven't heard before and solid prose help a story stand out."

$ ZYZZYVA, The Last Word: West Coast Writers & Artists, P.O. Box 590069, San Francisco CA 94159-0069. (415)752-4393. Fax: (415)752-4391. Website: www.zyzzyva.org. "We feature work by writers currently living on the West Coast or in Alaska and Hawaii only. We are essentially a literary magazine, but of wide-ranging interests and a strong commitment to nonfiction." Estab. 1985. Circ. 3,500.

Needs: Ethnic/multicultural, experimental, humor/satire, mainstream. Receives 300 unsolicited mss/month. Accepts 10 mss/issue; 30 mss/year. Publishes ms 3 months after acceptance. Agented fiction 5%. **Publishes 15 new writers/year.** Recently published work by Catherine Brady, Saira Ramasastry, Anthony Swifford. Publishes short shorts. Also publishes literary essays, poetry.

How to Contact: Send complete ms. Accepts submissions by mail. Responds in 1 week to queries; 1 month to mss. Sample copy for $7 or online. Writer's guidelines online.

Payment/Terms: Pays $50. Pays on acceptance. First North American serial and one-time anthology rights.

Small Circulation Magazines

This section of *Novel & Short Story Writer's Market* contains general interest, special interest, regional and genre magazines with circulations of under 10,000. Although these magazines vary greatly in size, theme, format and management, the editors are all looking for short stories. Their specific fiction needs present writers of all degrees of expertise and interests with an abundance of publishing opportunities.

Although not as high-paying as the large-circulation consumer magazines, you'll find some of the publications listed here do pay writers 1-5¢/word or more. Also, unlike the big consumer magazines, these markets are very open to new writers and relatively easy to break into. Their only criteria is that your story be well written, well presented, and suitable for their particular readership.

In this section you will also find listings for zines. Zines vary greatly in appearance as well as content. Some paper zines are photocopies published whenever the editor has material and money, while others feature offset printing and regular distribution schedules. And a few have evolved into four-color, commercial-looking, very slick publications.

DIVERSITY IN OPPORTUNITY

Among the diverse publications in this section are magazines devoted to almost every topic, every level of writing and every type of writer. Some of the markets listed here publish fiction about a particular geographic area or by authors who live in that locale.

SELECTING THE RIGHT MARKET

First, zero in on those markets most likely to be interested in your work. If you write genre fiction, check out specific sections for lists of magazines publishing in that genre (mystery, page 68; romance, page 80; science fiction/fantasy & horror, page 90). For other types of fiction, begin by looking at the Category Index starting on page 618. If your work is more general—or conversely, very specialized—you may wish to browse through the listings, perhaps looking up those magazines published in your state or region. Also check the Online Markets section for other specialized and genre publications.

In addition to browsing through the listings and using the Category Index, check the ranking codes at the beginning of listings to find those most likely to be receptive to your work. This is especially true for beginning writers, who should look for magazines that say they are especially open to new writers (□) and for those giving equal weight to both new and established writers (◨). For more explanation about these codes, see the inside front and back covers of this book.

Once you have a list of magazines you might like to try, read their listings carefully. Much of the material within each listing carries clues that tell you more about the magazine. The "Quick Start" Guide to Publishing Your Fiction starting on page 2 describes in detail the listing information common to all the markets in our book.

The physical description appearing near the beginning of the listings can give you clues about the size and financial commitment to the publication. This is not always an indication of quality, but chances are a publication with expensive paper and four-color artwork on the cover has more prestige than a photocopied publication featuring a clip art self-cover. For more information on some of the paper, binding and printing terms used in these descriptions, see Printing and Production Terms Defined on page 590.

FURTHERING YOUR SEARCH

It cannot be stressed enough that reading the listing is only the first part of developing your marketing plan. The second part, equally important, is to obtain fiction guidelines and read the actual magazine. Reading copies of a magazine helps you determine the fine points of the magazine's publishing style and philosophy. There is no substitute for this type of hands-on research.

Unlike commercial magazines available at most newsstands and bookstores, it requires a little more effort to obtain some of the magazines listed here. You may need to send for a sample copy. We include sample copy prices in the listings whenever possible. See The Business of Fiction Writing on page 59 for the specific mechanics of manuscript submission. Above all, editors appreciate a professional presentation. Include a brief cover letter and send a self-addressed envelope for a reply or a self-addressed envelope in a size large enough to accommodate your manuscript, if you would like it returned. Be sure to include enough stamps or International Reply Coupons (for replies from countries other than your own) to cover your manuscript's return. Many publishers today appreciate receiving a disposable manuscript, eliminating the cost to writers of return postage and saving editors the effort of repackaging manuscripts for return.

Most of the magazines listed here are published in the U.S. You will also find some English-speaking markets from around the world. These foreign publications are denoted with a 🌐 symbol at the beginning of listings. To make it easier to find Canadian markets, we include a 🍁 symbol at the start of those listings.

🔳 🌐 ◎ **THE ABIKO ANNUAL WITH JAMES JOYCE**, Finnegans Wake Studies, ALP Ltd., 8-1-7 Namiki, Abiko, Chiba 270-1165, Japan. (011)81-471-69-7319. E-mail: hce@jcom.home.he.jp. Website: members.jc om.home.ne.jp/hce. **Contact:** Tatsuo Hamada. Magazine: A5; 350 pages; illustrations; photos. "We primarily publish James Joyce *Finnegans Wake* essays from writers here in Japan and abroad." Annual. Estab. 1989. Circ. 300. Charges fees.
Needs: Experimental (in the vein of James Joyce), literary, inspirational. Also essays on James Joyce's *Finnegans Wake* from around the world. Receives very few unsolicited mss/month. Length: 5,000 words maximum; average length: 15 pages words. Also publishes literary essays, literary criticism, poetry. Always comments on rejected mss.
How to Contact: Send a disposable copy of ms and #10 SASE for reply only. Responds in 1 week to queries; 3 months to mss. Accepts multiple submissions. Sample copy for $20. Guidelines for SASE. "Do not send American postage. It won't fly in Japan." Reviews fiction.
Payment/Terms: Pays 1 contributor's copy; additional copies $25. Copyright reverts to author upon publication.
Advice: "We require camera-ready copy. The writer is welcome to accompany it with appropriate artwork."

🔳 $🔳 **ADVENTURES OF SWORD & SORCERY**, Double Star Press, P.O. Box 807, Xenia OH 45385. E-mail: double_star@yahoo.com. **Contact:** Randy Dannenfelser, editor. Magazine: 8½×11; 80 pages; slick cover stock; illustrations. "We publish sword and sorcery, heroic and high fantasy fiction." Quarterly. Estab. 1995. Circ. 7,000.
Needs: Fantasy. Sword and sorcery, heroic and high fantasy fiction. "We want fiction with an emphasis on action and adventure, but still cognizant of the struggles within as they play against the struggles without. Include sexual content only as required by the story, but not excessive/porn." Receives 250 unsolicited mss/month. Accepts 9 mss/issue; 36 mss/year. Publishes ms 1 year after acceptance. Agented fiction 5%. **Publishes 8 new writers/year.** Recently published work by Mike Resnick, Stephen Baxter and Darrell Schweitzer. Length: 1,000-20,000 words; average length: 5,000 words. Also publishes literary essays. Always comments on rejected mss.
How to Contact: Accepts submissions by mail, e-mail. Responds in 1 month to queries; 2 months to mss. No simultaneous submissions. Sample copy for $6. Writer's guidelines for #10 SASE. Reviews fiction.
Payment/Terms: Pays 3-6¢/word and 3 contributor copies; additional copies 40% discount plus shipping. Pays on acceptance for first North American serial rights. Sends galleys to author.
Advice: "Recently we are looking for more adventuresome work with settings other than generic medieval Europe. We look for real emotion in the prose. Think about the audience we are targeted at, and send us appropriate stories."

🔳 🌐 **ALBEDO ONE**, The Irish Magazine of Science Fiction, Fantasy and Horror, Albedo One, 2 Post Rd., Lusk, Co Dublin, Ireland. (+353)1-8730177. E-mail: bobn@eircom.net. Website: www.yellowbrickroad.ie/albedo. **Contact:** Editor, *Albedo One*. Magazine: A4; 44 pages. "We hope to publish interesting and unusual fiction by new and established writers. We will consider anything, as long as it is well-written and entertaining, though our definitions of both may not be exactly mainstream. We like stories with plot and characters that live on the page. Most of our audience are probably committed genre fans, but we try to appeal to a broad spectrum of readers—the narrow focus of our readership is due to the public-at-large's unwillingness to experiment with their reading/magazine purchasing rather than any desire on our part to be exclusive." Triannual. Estab. 1993. Circ. 900.

Needs: Comics/graphic novels, experimental, fantasy, horror, literary, science fiction. Receives more than 20 unsolicited mss/month. Accepts 15-18 mss/year. Publishes ms 1 year after acceptance. **Publishes 4 new writers/year.** Length: 2,000-5,000 words; average length: 4,000 words. Also publishes literary criticism. Sometimes comments on rejected mss.

How to Contact: Responds in 4 months to mss. Sample copy for $9. Guidelines available by e-mail or on website. Reviews fiction.

Payment/Terms: Pays $6 per story and 1 contributor's copy; additional copies $5 plus p&p. Pays on publication for first rights.

Advice: "We look for good writing, good plot, good characters. Read the magazine, and don't give up."

N ☐ **ALEMBIC**, Singularity Rising Press, P.O. Box 28416, Philadelphia PA 19149. (215)743-4927. E-mail: alembic@earthlink.net. **Contact:** Larry Farrell, editor. Magazine: 8½×11; 64 pages; bond paper; illustrations. *"Alembic* is a literary endeavor magically bordering intersecting continua."* The magazine publishes poems, stories and art. Twice a year. Estab. 1999. Circ. 100.

Needs: Fantasy (space fantasy, sword and sorcery), horror (dark fantasy, futuristic, psychological, supernatural), literary, mystery/suspense (amateur sleuth, cozy, police procedural, private eye/hardboiled), science fiction (hard science/technological, soft/sociological), thriller/espionage. No children's, religious, romance. Would like to see more mystery. Receives 15 unsolicited mss/month. Accepts 6 mss/issue; 24 mss/year. Publishes ms 1-2 years after acceptance. **Publishes 15 new writers/year.** Recently published work by William S. Frankl and Bill Glose. Length: 1,000-5,000 words; average length: 3,000 words. Publishes short shorts. Also publishes poetry. Often comments on rejected mss.

How to Contact: Not copyrighted. Sponsors contest. Send for guidelines. Responds in 9 months to mss. Accepts multiple submissions. Sample copy for $7.50. Guidelines for SASE or by e-mail. Reviews fiction.

Payment/Terms: Pays 1 contributor's copy; additional copies $5. Pays on publication for first North American serial rights. Not copyrighted.

Advice: "Fiction we publish has to grab me and make me care what will or won't happen to the characters. Write, rewrite and rewrite again. After all that, keep on submitting. A rejection never killed anyone."

N **ANY DREAM WILL DO REVIEW, Short Stories and Humor from the Secret Recesses of our Minds**, Any Dream Will Do, Inc., 1830 Kirman Ave., C1, Reno NV 89502-3381. (775)786-0345. E-mail: cassjmb@i qemail.com. Website: www.willigocrazy.org/Ch08.htm. **Contact:** Dr. Jean M. Bradt, editor and publisher. Magazine: 5½×8½; 52 pages; 20# bond paper; 12 Carolina cover stock. "The 52-page *Any Dream Will Do Review* showcases a new literary genre, psych-inspirational fiction, which attempts to fight the stigma against consumers of mental-health services by touching hearts, that is, by exposing the deepest of consumers' thoughts and emotions. In the *Review*'s stories, accomplished authors honestly reveal their most intimate secrets. See www.willigocrazy.org/Ch09a.htm for detailed instructions on how to write psych-inspirational fiction." Semiannual. Estab. 2001. Circ. 200.

Needs: Ethnic/multicultural, mainstream, psychic/supernatural/occult, romance (contemporary), science fiction (soft/sociological), psych-inspirational. No pornography, true life stories, black humor, political material, testimonials, experimental fiction, or depressing accounts of hopeless or perverted people. Accepts 10 mss/issue; 20 mss/year. Publishes ms 6 months after acceptance. **Publishes 10 new writers/year.** Publishes short shorts. Often comments on rejected mss.

How to Contact: Send complete ms. Accepts submissions by mail, e-mail (cassjmb@iqemail.com). Please submit by e-mail, if possible. If you must submit by hardcopy, please send disposable copies. Responds in 4 weeks to mss. Accepts multiple submissions. Sample copy for $10. Writer's guidelines online.

Payment/Terms: Pays in contributor's copies; additional copies $10. Acquires all rights.

Advice: "Read several stories on www.willigocrazy.org/Ch08.htm before starting to write. Proof your story many times before submitting. Make the readers think. Above all, present people (preferably diagnosed with mental illness realistically rather than with prejudice."

$ ☐ ◎ ☒ **ARTEMIS MAGAZINE, Science and Fiction for a Space-Faring Age**, LRC Publications, Inc., 1380 E. 17th St., Suite 201, Brooklyn NY 11230-6011. E-mail: magazine@lrcpubs.com. Website: www.lrcpublicatio ns.com. **Contact:** Ian Randal Stock, editor. Magazine: 8½×11; 64 pages; glossy; illustrations. "As part of the Artemis Project, we present lunar and space development in a positive light. The magazine is an even mix of science and fiction. We are a proud sponsor of the Artemis Project, which is constructing a commercial, manned moon

---

● **A BULLET INTRODUCES COMMENTS** by the editor of *Novel & Short Story Writer's Market* indicating special information about the listing.

base. We publish science articles for the intelligent layman, and near-term, near-Earth hard science fiction stories." Quarterly. Estab. 1999.

● Short stories published in Artemis have been nominated for Hugo and Nebula awards, and have been named to the Year's Best Science Fiction 6.

Needs: Adventure, science fiction, thriller/espionage. No fantasy, inspirational. Receives 200 unsolicited mss/month. Accepts 4-7 mss/issue. Publishes ms 3-12 months after acceptance. **Publishes 4 new writers/year.** Recently published work by Joseph J. Lazzaro, Fred Lerner, Allen M. Steele, Jack McDevitt, Stanley Schmidt and Jack Williamson. Length: 15,000 words maximum (shorter is better); average length: 2,000-8,000 words. Publishes short shorts. Also publishes poetry. Often comments on rejected mss.

How to Contact: Send complete ms. Accepts submissions by mail. Send a disposable copy of ms with SASE for reply. *Submissions sent without SASE will not be read.* Responds in 2 months to queries. Sample copy for $5 and a 9×12 SAE with 4 first-class stamps. Writer's guidelines for SASE or on website. Reviews fiction.

Payment/Terms: Pays 3-5¢/word, and 3 contributor's copies. Pays on acceptance. Buys first world English serial rights. Sends galleys to author.

Advice: "Write the best possible story you can. Read a lot of fiction that you like, and reread it a few times. (If it doesn't hold up to rereading, it might not be so great. And don't give me any rip-offs or current television shows, video or role-playing games, or movies). Then go over your story again, make it even better. Remember that neatness counts when you prepare your manuscript (also, knowledge of the English language and grammar, and the concepts of fiction). Then send it to the magazine that publishes fiction most like the story you've written. Remember that you're up against many hundreds of manuscripts for a very few slots in the magazine. Make your story absolutely fantastic. In my case, a science fiction story must contain both science and fiction. Remember that, to be interesting to the reader, your story will probably be about the most important moment or event in the character's life."

$◎⊕ AUREALIS, Australian Fantasy and Science Fiction, P.O. Box 2164, Mt. Waverley, Victoria 3149, Australia. Website: www.sf.org.au/aurealis. **Contact:** Keith Stevenson, fiction editor. "*Aurealis* promotes the best in science fiction, fantasy and horror to an ever-widening audience in Australia and worldwide." Semiannual. Circ. 2,500.

Needs: Fantasy, horror, science fiction. Accepts 7 mss/issue. **Publishes 4 new writers/year.** Recently published work by Robert Hood, Richard Harland, Cory Daniells and Robert N. Stephenson. Sometimes comments on rejected mss.

How to Contact: Does not accept e-mail submissions. Responds in 3 months to mss. Sample copy for $10 (Aus). Guidelines for SAE with IRC or online.

Payment/Terms: Pays $20-60 per 1,000 words, minimum of $20 and contributor's copies. Acquires First Australian Serial Rights, non-exclusive electronic rights. Have rights to include story in Collector's Edition anthology.

Advice: "We want original concepts, strong/believable characters, satisfying denouements, tightly written fiction. Look for new perspectives, write economically, and show real people in fantastic situations."

$⊠⊘ CHALLENGING DESTINY, New Fantasy & Science Fiction, Crystalline Sphere Publishing, RR #6, St. Marys ON N4X 1C8 Canada. (519)885-6012. E-mail: csp@golden.net. Website: challengingdestiny.com. **Contact:** David M. Switzer, editor. Magazine: 8×5¼; 120 pages; Kallima 10 pt. cover; illustrations. "We publish all kinds of science fiction and fantasy short stories." Quarterly. Estab. 1997. Circ. 200.

Needs: Fantasy, science fiction. No horror, short short stories. Receives 40 unsolicited mss/month. Accepts 6 mss/issue; 24 mss/year. Publishes ms 5 months after acceptance. **Publishes 6 new writers/year.** Recently published work by Uncle River, A.R. Morlan, and Ken Rand. Length: 2,000-10,000 words; average length: 6,000 words. Often comments on rejected mss.

How to Contact: Send complete ms. Accepts submissions by mail. Send SAE and IRC for reply, return of ms or send disposable copy of ms. Responds in 1 week to queries; 1 month to mss. Accepts simultaneous submissions. Sample copy for $7.50 (Canadian), $6.50 (US). Writer's guidelines for #10 SASE, 1 IRC, or online. Reviews fiction.

Payment/Terms: Pays 1¢/word (Canadian), plus 2 contributors copies. Pays on publication for first North American serial rights. Sends galleys to author.

Advice: "Manuscripts with a good story and interesting characters stand out. We look for fiction that entertains and makes you think. If you're going to write short fiction, you need to read lots of it. Don't reinvent the wheel. Use your own voice."

ℕ⊘ THE CHICAGO WRITER'S SOURCE, 1212 S. Naper Blvd. Suite 119, Naperville IL 60540. (630)688-4803. Fax: (630)548-0456. E-mail: cwseditor@aol.com. **Contact:** J. Morgan, fiction editor. Magazine: 8½×11; 12 pages; 70# white paper; illustrations. *The Chicago Writer's Source* is a quarterly publication that strives to reveal all that the city of Chicago has to offer writers. Quarterly. Estab. 2003. Circ. 250.

Needs: Mainstream, military/war (amateur sleuth), religious/inspirational, romance (gothic). Does not want children's, erotica, or pieces with excessive violence. Receives 50 unsolicited mss/month. Accepts 4 mss/year. Publishes ms 3 months after acceptance.

How to Contact: Send complete ms. Send SASE (or IRC) for return of ms or disposable copy of the ms and #10 SASE for reply only. Responds in 3 months to queries; 3 months to mss. Sample copy for $4, on the website or by e-mail.

Payment/Terms: Pays 2 contributor's copies. Pays on acceptance.

Advice: "We look for distinguished, mature writers who show love for the language and a sense that there is something at stake in the story. We want a story that somehow needs to be told. A writer will always find an audience if the work is true."

$ 🖂 ⊘ ◎ CHRISTIAN COURIER, Reformed Faith Witness, 1 Hiscott St., St. Catharines ON L2R 1C7 Canada. (905)682-8311. Fax: (905)682-8313. E-mail: editor@christiancourier.ca. **Contact:** Harry DerNederlander, editor. Tabloid: 11½×14; 20 pages; newsprint; illustrations; photos. "We assume a Christian perspective which acknowledges that this world belongs to God and that human beings are invited to serve God in every area of society." Biweekly. Estab. 1945. Circ. 4,000.

Needs: Historical, religious/inspirational, senior citizen/retirement, sports. No "sentimental 'religious' stuff; superficial moralizing." Receives 5-10 unsolicited mss/month. Accepts 12 mss/year. Does not read mss from the end of July through early August. Publishes ms 2 months after acceptance. Length: 3,000 words; average length: 1,800 words. Publishes short shorts. Also publishes literary essays, literary criticism, poetry.

How to Contact: Send complete ms. Accepts simultaneous and reprints submissions. Sample copy for free. Writer's guidelines for #10 SASE.

Payment/Terms: Pays $60-120 and 1 contributor's copy (on request). Pays 30 days after publication. Acquires one-time rights. Not copyrighted.

Advice: Looks for work "geared to a Christian audience but reflecting the real world, real dilemmas, without pat resolutions—written in an engaging, clear manner."

Ⓝ $▢ CIA—CITIZEN IN AMERICA, CIA—Citizen in America, Inc., 30 Ford St., Glen Cove, Long Island NY 11542. (516)671-4047. E-mail: ciamc@webtv.net. **Contact:** John J. Maddox, magazine coordinator. Magazine: 8¼×10½; 40-80 pages; glossy cover stock; photos. "*CIA—Citizen in America* trys to strengthen democracy here and abroad by allowing the freedom of expression in all forms possible through the press. *CIA* does not shy away from controversy." Estab. 2002.

Needs: Adventure, erotica, ethnic/multicultural, experimental, historical, humor/satire, mainstream, religious/inspirational, romance, science fiction, slice-of-life vignettes, western, war stories. No screen or plays. No works that deliberately promote racism, prejudice, or gender oriented violence. Receives 50 unsolicited mss/month. Accepts 5 mss/issue. Publishes ms 3 months after acceptance. Agented fiction 2%. Length: 250-2,500 words; average length: 1,000 words. Publishes short shorts. Also publishes literary essays, literary criticism, poetry. Sometimes comments on rejected mss.

How to Contact: Send complete ms. Accepts submissions by mail, e-mail (ciamc@webtv.net), phone. Send SASE for return of the ms or send disposable copy of ms and #10 SASE for reply only. Responds in 2 weeks to queries; 1-2 months to mss. Accepts simultaneous and reprints submissions. Sample copy for $10. Writer's guidelines for #10 SASE, e-mail or on website.

Payment/Terms: Pays $40-100. Pays on publication for first North American serial, first, one-time, simultaneous rights, makes work-for-hire assignments.

Advice: "Feel free to submit all your work. State your age with all submissions."

▢ THE CIRCLE MAGAZINE, Circle Publications, 173 Grandview Road, Wernersville PA 19565. (610)670-7017. Fax: (610)670-7017. E-mail: circlemag@aol.com. Website: www.circlemagazine.com. **Contact:** Penny Talbert, editor. Magazine: 5½×8½; 48-52 pages; white offset paper; illustrations; photos. " *The Circle* is an eclectic mix of culture and subculture. Our goal is to provide the reader with thought-provoking reading that they will remember." Quarterly.

Needs: Adventure, experimental, humor/satire, literary, mainstream, mystery/suspense, New Age, psychic/supernatural/occult, romance, science fiction, thriller/espionage. No religious fiction. Receives 400 unsolicited mss/month. Accepts 3-5 mss/issue; 12-20 mss/year. Publishes ms 1-4 months after acceptance. Recently published work by David McDaniel, Bart Stewart, Ace Boggess, and Stephen Forney. Length: 2,000-6,000 words words; average length: 2,500 words words. Publishes short shorts. Also publishes literary essays, literary criticism, poetry. Sometimes comments on rejected mss.

How to Contact: Send complete ms. Accepts submissions by mail, e-mail (circlemag@aol.com). Send complete ms with a cover letter. Include estimated word count, brief bio and list of publications. Responds in 1 month to queries; 4 months to mss. Accepts simultaneous and reprints, multiple submissions. Sample copy for $4. Writer's guidelines online.

Payment/Terms: 1 contributor's copy; additional copies $4. Pays on publication for one-time, electronic rights.

Advice: "The most important thing is that submitted fiction keeps our attention and interest. The most typical reason for rejection: bad endings! Proofread your work, and send it in compliance with our guidelines."

Ⓝ ◪ CITY SLAB, Urban Tales of the Grotesque, City Slab Publications, 1705 Summit Ave. #211, Seattle WA 98122. (206)568-4343. E-mail: dave@cityslab.com. Website: www.cityslab.com. **Contact:** Dave Lindschmidt, editor. Magazine: 8½×11; 60 pages; illustrations; photos. "*City Slab* presents the best in urban horror today. *City Slab* offers an intriguing mix of familiar voices with new discoveries. Each page is a cold, wet kiss to the genre." Evan Wright, *Rolling Stone* magazine. Quarterly. Estab. 2002.

Needs: "We're looking for taunt, multi-leveled urban horror. Start the story with action. Capture the feel of your city whether it's real or imagined and have a story to tell! We love crime fiction but there has to be a horror slant to it. Steer away from first person point of view." Publishes ms 3-6 months after acceptance. **Publishes 6 new writers/year.** Recently published work by Poppy Z. Brite, Brian Hodge, Eric Pape and Patricia Russo.

How to Contact: Accepts submissions by mail, e-mail (dave@cityslab.com). estimated word count, brief bio and list of publications. Send disposable copy of ms and #10 SASE for reply only. Responds in 6 weeks to queries; 2 months to mss. Sample copy for $6. Writer's guidelines online.

Payment/Terms: Pays on publication for first North American serial rights.

COCHRAN'S CORNER, 1003 Tyler Court, Waldorf MD 20602-2964. (301)870-1664. **Contact:** John Treasure, editor/art council. Magazine: 5½×11; 52 pages. "We publish fiction, nonfiction and poetry. Our only requirement is no strong language." For a "family" audience." Quarterly. Estab. 1986. Circ. 500.

Needs: Adventure, children's/juvenile, historical, horror, humor/satire, mystery/suspense, religious/inspirational, romance, science fiction, young adult/teen. "Mss must be free from language you wouldn't want your/our children to read." Would like to see more mystery and romance fiction. Plans a special fiction issue. Receives 50 unsolicited mss/month. Accepts 4 mss/issue; 8 mss/year. Publishes ms by next issue after acceptance. **Publishes 30 new writers/year.** Recently published work by James Hughes, Ellen Sandry, James Bennet, Susan Lee and Judy Demers. Length: 300-1,000 words; average length: 500 words. Also publishes literary essays, literary criticism, poetry.

How to Contact: Send complete ms. Accepts submissions by mail. "Right now we are forced to limit acceptance to *subscribers only.*" Send complete ms with cover letter. Responds in 3 weeks to queries; 6-8 weeks to mss. Accepts simultaneous and reprints submissions. Sample copy for $5, 9×12 SAE and 90¢ postage. Writer's guidelines for #10 SASE.

Payment/Terms: Pays in contributor's copies. Acquires one-time rights.

Advice: "I feel the quality of fiction is getting better. The public is demanding a good read, instead of having sex or violence carry the story. I predict that fiction has a good future. We like to print the story as the writer submits it if possible. This way writers can compare their work with their peers and take the necessary steps to improve and go on to sell to bigger magazines. Stories from the heart desire a place to be published. We try to fill that need. Be willing to edit yourself. Polish your manuscript before submitting to editors."

CREATIVE WITH WORDS PUBLICATIONS, Creative With Words Publications, P.O. Box 223226, Carmel CA 93922. Fax: (831)655-8627. E-mail: cwwpub@usa.net. Website: members.tripod.com/CreativeWithWords. **Contact:** Brigitta Geltrich, general editor. Booklet: 5½×8½; more than 50 pages; bond paper; illustrations/computer art work. Monthly. Estab. 1975. Circ. varies.

Needs: Ethnic/multicultural, humor/satire, mystery/suspense (amateur sleuth, private eye), regional (folklore), young adult/teen (adventure, historical). "Do not submit essays." No violence or erotica, overly religious fiction or sensationalism. "Twice a year we publish an anthology of the writings of young writers, titled, "We are Writers, Too!" List of upcoming thems available for SASE. Receives 250-500 unsolicited mss/month. Accepts 12 mss/year. Publishes ms 1-2 months after acceptance. Recently published work by Najwa Salam Brax, June K. Silconas, Steven Dotterem and David Napolin. Average length: 800 words. Publishes short shorts. Also publishes poetry. Sometimes comments on rejected mss.

How to Contact: Query with or without published clips or send complete ms. Accepts submissions by mail. Send complete ms with a cover letter with SASE. Include estimated word count. Responds in 2 weeks to queries; 2 months to mss. Sample copy for $6. For #10 SASE.

Payment/Terms: 20% reduction cost on each copy ordered, 30% reduction on each copy on order of 10 or more. Acquires one-time rights.

Advice: "We offer a great variety of themes. We look for clean family-type fiction. Also, we ask the writer to look at the world from a different perspective, research topic thoroughly, be creative, apply brevity, tell the story from a character's viewpoint, tighten dialogue, be less descriptive, proofread before submitting and be patient. We will not publish every manuscript we receive. It has to be in standard English, well-written, proofread. We do not appreciate receiving manuscripts where we have to do the proofreading and the correcting of grammar."

CRIMEWAVE, TTA Press, 5 Martins Lane, Witcham, Ely Cambs CB6 2LB UK. E-mail: ttapress@aol.com. Website: www.ttapress.com. **Contact:** Andy Cox, fiction editor. Magazine: 128 pages; lithographed, color; perfect bound. Magazine publishes "modern crime fiction from across the waterfront, from the misnamed cozy to the deceptively subtle hardboiled." Biannual. Published in June and December.

Needs: Mystery/suspense (amateur sleuth, cozy, police procedural, private eye/hardboiled), thriller/espionage. Ac-

CHECK THE CATEGORY INDEXES, located at the back of the book, for publishers interested in specific fiction subjects.

cepts 15 mss/issue. Recently published work by Chaz Brenchley, Ian Rankin, James Lovegrove and Cristopher Fowler.

How to Contact: Accepts submissions by e-mail. "Send one story at a time plus adequate return postage, or disposable ms plus 2 IRC's or e-mail address—but no e-mail submissions. No reprints." No simultaneous submissions. Sample copy for $12 US or for 4 issues: $40. Writer's guidelines online.

Payment/Terms: "Relatively modest flat fee, but constantly increasing." Acquires contract on acceptance, payment on publication.

[N] ○ CTHULHU SEX MAGAZINE, Blood, Sex and Tentacles, Cthulhu Sex, P.O. Box 3678, Grand Central Station, New York NY 10163. (347)623-4197. E-mail: stcthulhu@cthulhusex.com. Website: www.cthulhusex.com. **Contact:** Michael A. Morel, editor-in-chief. Magazine: 8¼×10⅝; 52-68 pages; 24 lb. white paper; 80 lb. glossy cover stock; illustrations; photos. "We intend to corrupt the mainstream ideals of the apparent mutual exclusivity of beauty and horror. We generally publish poetry, short stories and artwork that evoke a dark and sensual atmosphere in the genre of erotic horror. We particularly look for edgy and experimental works that explore the dark side of sensuality and have a subtle yet powerful impact. We cater to mature readers and connoisseurs of erotic horror." Quarterly. Estab. 1998. Circ. 750-1,000+. Member, Horror Writers Association.

Needs: Fantasy (dark), horror (dark fantasy, futuristic, psychological, supernatural, erotic), psychic/supernatural/occult, science fiction (dark). "We do not want to see explicit pornography, rape, rehashed vampire stories, erotica without a darker edge, serials." Receives 40-50 unsolicited mss/month. Accepts 5-7 mss/issue; 25-30 mss/year. Publishes ms 4 months after acceptance. **Publishes 5 new writers/year.** Recently published work by Wrath James White, Hertzan Chimera, Alex Severin, Mark McLaughlin. Length: 800-5,000 words; average length: 2,500 words. Publishes short shorts. Also publishes poetry. Sometimes comments on rejected mss.

How to Contact: Send complete ms. Send disposable copy of ms and #10 SASE for reply only. Responds in 2 weeks to queries; 2 months to mss. Accepts simultaneous and reprints submissions. Sample copy for $3.95. Writer's guidelines for SASE, e-mail or website.

Payment/Terms: Pays 3 contributor's copies; additional copies $3. Pays on publication for one-time, promotional rigths rights.

Advice: "We look for work that explores at least one of the elements of the theme blood, sex and tentacles. Well edited pieces are always appreciated. We want authors to use good writing to evoke a response instead of cheap TADA tactics. Have a unique plotline. We recommend prospective contributors read at least one copy of the magazine to get an idea of our content style. Do not try to sell your story; let it speak for itself."

[N] $DAKOTA OUTDOORS, South Dakota, Hipple Publishing Co., P.O. Box 669 333 W. Dakota Ave., Pierre SD 57501-0669. (605)224-7301. Fax: (605)224-9210. Monthly. Estab. 1974. Circ. 7,000.

Needs: Adventure, humor/satire. Does not want stories about vacations or subjects that don't include hunting and fishing. Receives 0-2 unsolicited mss/month. Publishes ms 1-2 months after acceptance. Agented fiction 90%. **Publishes 0-4 new writers/year.** Publishes short shorts.

How to Contact: Send complete ms. Accepts submissions by mail, e-mail. Responds in 3 months to queries. Accepts simultaneous submissions. Sample copy for 9×12 SAE and 3 first-class stamps. Writer's guidelines by e-mail.

Payment/Terms: Pays on publication.

Advice: "Submit samples of manuscript or previous works for consideration; photos or illustrations with manuscript are helpful."

[globe] DARK HORIZONS, Beech House, Chapel Lane, Moulton Cheshire CW9 8PQ, England. E-mail: darkhorizon @britishfantasysociety.org.uk. Website: www.britishfantasysociety.org.uk. **Contact:** Debbie Bennett, editor. "We are a small press fantasy magazine. Our definition of fantasy knows no bounds, covering science, heroic, dark and light fantasy and horror fiction." Biannual. Circ. 500.

Needs: Fantasy. No space opera, hard SF, horror. **Publishes 20 new writers/year.** Publishes short shorts. Also publishes poetry.

How to Contact: Send complete ms. Accepts submissions by mail. Send ms with brief cover letter and IRCs or e-mail address.

Payment/Terms: Pays in contributor's copies.

Advice: "We look for a good story with a beginning, middle, end, and point to it."

[icon] [icon] DESCANT, Ft. Worth's Journal of Fiction and Poetry, Texas Christian University, TCU Box 297270, Ft. Worth TX 76129. (817)257-6537. Fax: (817)257-6239. E-mail: descant@tcu.edu. Website: eng.tcu.edu.usefulsi tes/descant.htm. **Contact:** Dave Kuhne, editor. Magazine: 6×9; 120-150 pages; acid free paper; paper cover. "*descant* seeks high quality poems and stories in both traditional and innovative form." Annual. Estab. 1956. Circ. 500-750. Member, CLMP.

● Offers four cash awards: The $500 Frank O'Connor Award for the best story in an issue; the $250 Sandra Brown Award for an outstanding story in an issue; the $500 Betsy Colquitt Award for the best poem in an issue; the $250 Baskerville Publishers Award for outstanding poem in an issue. Several stories first published by *descant* have appeared in *Best American Short Stories*.

Needs: Literary. "No horror, romance, fantasy, erotica." Receives 20-30 unsolicited mss/month. Accepts 25-35 mss/year. Publishes ms 1 year after acceptance. **Publishes 50% new writers/year.** Recently published work by William Harrison, Annette Sanford, Miller Williams, Patricia Chao, Vonesca Stroud, and Wald McDonald. Length: 1,000-5,000 words; average length: 2,500 words. Publishes short shorts. Also publishes poetry.

How to Contact: Send complete ms. Accepts submissions by mail. Send complete ms with cover letter. Include estimated word count and brief bio. Responds in 6-8 weeks to mss. Accepts simultaneous submissions. Sample copy for $10. SASE, e-mail or fax.

Payment/Terms: Pays 2 contributor's copies, additional copies $6. Pays on publication for one-time rights. Sponsors awards/contests.

Advice: "We look for character and quality of prose. Send your best short work."

DOWN IN THE DIRT, The Publication Revealing all your Dirty Little Secrets, Scars Publications and Design, 829 Brian Court, Gurnee IL 60031-3155. (847)281-9070. E-mail: alexrand@scars.tv. Website: scars.tv. **Contact:** Alexandria Rand, editor. Magazine: 5½×8½; 60# paper; illustrations; photos. Published "as material gathers." Estab. 2000.

Needs: Adventure, ethnic/multicultural, experimental, fantasy, feminist, gay, historical, horror, lesbian, literary, mystery/suspense, New Age, psychic/supernatural/occult, science fiction. No religious or family-oriented material. Publishes ms within 1 year after acceptance. Recently published work by Simon Perchik, Jim Dewitt, Jennifer Connelly, L.B. Sedlacek, Aeon Logan, Helena Wolfe. Average length: 1,000 words. Publishes short shorts. Also publishes poetry. Always, if asked, comments on rejected mss.

How to Contact: Query with published clips or send complete ms. Accepts submissions by e-mail. Send SASE (or IRC) for return of the ms or disposable copy of the ms and #10 SASE for reply only. Responds in 1 month to queries; 1 month to mss. Accepts simultaneous and reprints, multiple submissions. Sample copy for $13. Writer's guidelines for SASE, e-mail or on the website. Reviews fiction.

DREAM FANTASY INTERNATIONAL, (formerly *Dream International Quarterly*), #H-1, 411 14th Street, Ramona CA 92065-2769. **Contact:** Charles I. Jones, Editor-in-chief. Magazine: 8½×11; 143 pages; Xerox paper; parchment cover stock; some illustrations; photos. "Although we accept material from professional writers, we encourage "new" (unpublished) writers, as well. Our hope is to attract writers interested in dreams and the dream state. We hope to extend this interest to fantasy which is dream-related or inspired. We hope to attract readers (writers) with like interests." Quarterly. Estab. 1981. Circ. 65-100.

Needs: Confessions, erotica (soft), fantasy (dream), historical, horror, humor/satire, literary, psychic/supernatural/occult, science fiction, young adult/teen (10-18), prose poem. "No material that is not dream related or dream-related fantasy. Often we receive pieces with 'dream' or 'dreams' used in the title that we find are not dream-related. We would like to see submissions that deal with dreams that have an influence on the person's daily waking life. Suggestions for making dreams beneficial to the dreamer in his/her waking life. We would also like to see more submissions dealing with lucid dreaming." Receives 35-40 unsolicited mss/month. Accepts 20 mss/issue; 50-55 mss/year. Publishes ms 8 months to 3 years after acceptance. Agented fiction 1%. **Publishes 20-30 new writers/year.** Recently published work by Timothy Scott, Carmen M. Pursifull, Richard W. Sullivan and Robert Michael O'Hearn. Publishes short shorts. Also publishes literary essays, poetry.

How to Contact: Send complete ms. Responds in 6 weeks to queries; 3 months to mss. Accepts simultaneous and reprints submissions. Sample copy for $14. For $2 and SAE with 2 first-class stamps.

Payment/Terms: Pays contributor's copies (contributors must pay $4.50 for postage and handling). Acquires first North American serial rights. Sends galleys to author.

Advice: "Both poetry and prose submissions must be concise and free of ramblings and typographical errors. The material should be interesting and appealing and something that our readers can relate to. New and 'unique' material always grabs our attention. Write about what you know. Make the reader stand up and take notice. Avoid rambling and stay away from clichés in your writing unless, of course, it is of a humorous nature and is purposefully done to make a point."

DREAMS & VISIONS, New Frontiers in Christian Fiction, Skysong Press, 35 Peter St. S., Orillia ON L3V 5A8 Canada. (705)329-1770. Fax: (705)329-1770. Website: www.bconnex.net/~skysong. **Contact:** Steve Stanton, editor. Magazine: 5½×8½; 56 pages; 20 lb. bond paper; glossy cover. "Innovative literary fiction for adult Christian readers." Semiannual. Estab. 1988. Circ. 200.

Needs: Experimental, fantasy, humor/satire, literary, mainstream, mystery/suspense, novel excerpts, religious/inspirational, science fiction (soft/sociological), slice-of-life vignettes. "We do not publish stories that glorify violence or perversity. All stories should portray a Christian world view or expand upon Biblical themes or ethics in an entertaining or enlightening manner." Receives 20 unsolicited mss/month. Accepts 7 mss/issue; 14 mss/year. Publishes ms 2-6 months after acceptance. Length: 2,000-6,000 words; average length: 2,500 words.

How to Contact: Send complete ms. Accepts submissions by mail, e-mail. Responds in 6 weeks to queries; 6 months to mss. Accepts simultaneous submissions. Sample copy for $4.95. Writer's guidelines online.

Payment/Terms: Pays 1¢/word. Pays on publication for first North American serial, one-time, second serial (reprint) rights.

Advice: "In general we look for work that has some literary value, that is in some way unique and relevant to

Christian readers today. Our first priority is technical adequacy, though we will occasionally work with a beginning writer to polish a manuscript. Ultimately, we look for stories that glorify the Lord Jesus Christ, stories that build up rather than tear down, that exalt the sanctity of life, the holiness of God, and the value of the family."

THE EDGE, TALES OF SUSPENSE, Thievin' Kitty Publications, P.O. Box 341, Marion MA 02738. E-mail: theedge@capecod.net. Website: www.blindside.net/smallpress/read/absolutes/theedge. **Contact:** Greg F. Gifune, editor. Zine specializing in varied genre suspense: digest-sized; 80-88 pages; heavy stock paper; heavy card cover. "We publish a broad range of genres, subjects and styles. While not an easy magazine to break into, we offer thrilling, 'edge of your seat' fiction from both seasoned and newer writers. We focus on the writing, not illustrations or distracting bells and whistles. Our goal is to present a quality, entertaining publication." Triannual. Estab. 1998. Circ. 1,000.

Needs: Adventure, erotica, gay, horror, lesbian, mystery/suspense (police procedural, private eye/hardboiled, noir), psychic/supernatural/occult, westerns with supernatural or horror element only. "Emphasis is on horror, crime and blends." No children's, young adult, romance, humor. Receives over 100 unsolicited mss/month. Accepts 10-12 mss/issue; 30-36 mss/year. Publishes ms 1-4 months after acceptance. Agented fiction 1-2%. **Publishes 1-6 new writers/year.** Recently published work by Ken Goldman, John Roux, Scott Urban, Stefano Donati, Suzanne Donahue, Robert Dunbar and Michael Laimo. Length: 700-8,000 words; average length: 2,500-4,500 words. Also publishes poetry. Always comments on rejected mss.

How to Contact: Send complete ms with a cover letter. Include estimated word count, brief bio and list of publications. Send SASE for reply, return of ms or send a disposable copy of ms. Responds in 8 weeks to mss. Accepts simultaneous submissions but not preferred. Sample copy for $6 U.S., $7 elsewhere (includes postage). Writer's guidelines for #10 SASE.

Payment/Terms: Pays 1 contributor's copy; additional copies $5. Acquires one-time rights.

Advice: "We look for taut, tense thrillers with realistic dialogue, engaging characters, strong plots and endings that are both powerful and memorable. Graphic violence, sex and profanity all have their place but do not have to be gratuitous. We will not accept anything racist, sexist, sacrilegious, or stories that depict children or animals in violent or sexual situations!"

THE ELOQUENT UMBRELLA, Linn-Benton Community College, 6500 SW Pacific Blvd., Albany OR 97321-3779. (541)917-4555. E-mail: terrance.millet@linnbenton.edu. **Contact:** Terrance Millet. Magazine: illustrations; photos. "*The Eloquent Umbrella's* purpose is to showcase art, photography, poetry and prose of Linn and Benton Counties in Oregon." Annual. Estab. 1990. Circ. 750.

Needs: Regional. "No slander, pornography or other material unsuitable for community reading." Accepts 50-100 mss/issue. Deadline is January 15 each year. Reads mss during winter term only; publishes in spring after acceptance. Recently published work by Chris Anderson, Roger Weaver, Charles Goodrich. Publishes short shorts. Also publishes literary essays, literary criticism, poetry.

How to Contact: Send complete ms. Accepts submissions by mail. Send complete ms with cover letter. Include 1-5 line bio. Responds in spring to mss. Accepts simultaneous, multiple submissions. Sample copy for (9×12) and $2 postage SAE. Writer's guidelines online.

Payment/Terms: Not copyrighted.

Advice: "The magazine is created by a collective editorial board and production team in a literary publication class."

ENIGMA, Audacious/Bottle Press, 402 South 25 Street, Philadelphia PA 19146. (215)545-8694. E-mail: sydx@att.net. **Contact:** Syd Bradford, publisher. Magazine: 8½×11; 100 pages; 24 lb. white paper; illustrations; photos. "Everything is done—except printing—by me, the publisher. No editors, etc. Eclectic—I publish articles, fiction, poetry." Quarterly. Estab. 1989. Circ. 90.

Needs: Adventure, experimental, fantasy, historical, horror, humor/satire. "No sentimental or religious fiction." Receives 30 unsolicited mss/month. Publishes ms 3 months after acceptance. **Publishes 20 new writers/year.** Recently published work by Richard A. Robbins, Eleanor Leslie and Diana K. Rubin. Length: 1,000-3,000 words; average length: 1,500 words. Publishes short shorts. Also publishes literary essays, literary criticism, poetry.

How to Contact: Send complete ms. Accepts submissions by mail, e-mail (sydx@att.net). Send complete ms with cover letter. Sample copy for $6. Writer's guidelines for #10 SASE. Reviews fiction.

Payment/Terms: Pays 1 contributor's copy; additional copies $6, plus $1.30 shipping and handling. Sends galleys to author. Not copyrighted.

MARKET CONDITIONS are constantly changing! If you're still using this book and it is 2005 or later, buy the newest edition of *Novel & Short Story Writer's Market* at your favorite bookstore or order from Writer's Digest Books by calling 1-800-448-0915.

Advice: "I look for imaginative writing, excellent movement, fine imagery, stunning characters."

◯ **EYES**, 3610 North Doncaster Court, Apt. X7, Saginaw MI 48603-1862. (989)498-4112. E-mail: fjm3eyes@aol.c om. **Contact:** Frank J. Mueller, editor. Magazine: 8½×11; 40 + pages. "No specific theme. Speculative fiction and surrealism most welcome. For a general, educated, not necessarily literary audience." Estab. 1991.
Needs: Horror (psychological), mainstream, contemporary ghost story. No sword/sorcery, overt science fiction, pornography, preachiness or children's fiction. "Especially looking for speculative fiction and surrealism. Would like to see more ghost stories, student writing. Dark fantasy OK, but not preferred." Accepts 5-9 mss/issue. Publishes ms 1 + years after acceptance. **Publishes 15-20 new writers/year.** Sometimes comments on rejected mss.
How to Contact: Query with or without published clips or send complete ms. Accepts submissions by mail. Query first or send complete ms. A short bio is optional. Responds in 1 month to queries; 3 + months to mss. No simultaneous submissions. Sample copy for $6, extras $4. Writer's guidelines for #10 SASE.
Payment/Terms: Pays 1 contributor's copy. Acquires one-time rights.
Advice: "Pay attention to character. A strong plot, while important, may not be enough alone to get you in the *Eyes*. Atmosphere and mood are also important. Please proofread. If you have a manuscript you like enough to see in the *Eyes*, send it to me. Above all, don't let rejections discourage you. I would encourage the purchase of a sample to get an idea of what I'm looking for. Read stories by authors such as Algernon Blackwood, Nathaniel Hawthorne, Shirley Jackson, Henry James and Poe."

$FANTASTIC STORIES OF THE IMAGINATION, P.O. Box 329, Brightwaters NY 11718. (631)666-5276. Website: www.dnapublications.com/fantastic/index.htm. **Contact:** Edward J. McFadden III, editor. Magazine: 50-72 pages; glossy paper; four color glossy cover; illustrations. "We feature science fiction in all its forms. While elements in the story must be science fiction/fantasy oriented, mixing genres is permissible." Estab. 1992. Circ. 6,000.
Needs: Fantasy (space fantasy, sword and sorcery, dark), science fiction (hard science/technological, soft/sociological), dark fantasy, futuristic. Receives 400-500 unsolicited mss/month. Accepts 8-10 mss/issue; 32-40 mss/year. Publishes ms 1-2 years after acceptance. Agented fiction 20%. **Publishes 5-10 new writers/year.** Length: 2,000-15,000 words; average length: 6,000 words. Also publishes poetry. Sometimes comments on rejected mss.
How to Contact: Send complete ms. Send SASE for return of ms or disposable copy of ms and SASE for reply only. Sample copy for $6. Writer's guidelines for SASE or on website.
Payment/Terms: Pays 1-5¢/word and 1 contributor's copy. Acquires first North American serial rights.

Ⓝ $◯ **THE FIRST LINE**, Castle Builder Press LLC., P.O. Box 0382, Plano TX 75025-0382. (972)824-0646. E-mail: submissions@thefirstline.com. Website: www.thefirstline.com. **Contact:** Robin LaBounty, manuscript coordinator. Magazine: 8×5; 56-60 pages; 20 lb. bond paper; 80 lb. cover stock. "We only publish stories that start with the first line provided. We are a collection of tales—of different directions writers can take when they start from the same place. Quarterly. Estab. 1999. Circ. 250.
Needs: Adventure, ethnic/multicultural, fantasy, gay, humor/satire, lesbian, literary, mainstream, mystery/suspense, regional, romance, science fiction, western. Receives 50 unsolicited mss/month. Accepts 12 mss/issue; 36 mss/year. Publishes ms 1 month after acceptance. **Publishes 6 new writers/year.** Length: 300-1,500 words; average length: 1,000 words. Publishes short shorts. Also publishes literary essays, literary criticism. Often comments on rejected mss.
How to Contact: Send complete ms. Accepts submissions by e-mail. Send SASE for return of ms or disposable copy of the ms and #10 SASE for reply only. Responds in 1 week to queries; 3 months to mss. Accepts multiple submissions No simultaneous submissions. Sample copy for $3. Writer's guidelines for SASE, e-mail or on website. Reviews fiction.
Payment/Terms: Pays $5 maximum and contributor's copy; additional copy $1.50. Pays on publication for rights negotiable rights.
Advice: "Don't just write the first story that comes to mind after you read the sentence. If it is obvious, chances are other people are writing about the same thing. Don't try so hard. Be willing to accept criticism."

$◯ ◎ ⊻ **FLESH AND BLOOD**, Tales of Horror & Dark Fantasy, Flesh & Blood Press, 121 Joseph St., Bayville NJ 08721. Website: www.fleshandbloodpress.com. **Contact:** Jack Fisher, editor-in-chief/publisher; Robert Swartwood, senior editor; Meghan Fatras and Teri A. Jacobs, assistant editors. Magazine: full-sized; 48-60 pages; 60 lb. paper; thick/glossy, full-color cover; "fully and lavishly illustrated. We publish fiction with heavy emphasis on the supernatural, fantastic, and/or bizarre." Quarterly. Estab. 1997. Circ. 600.
• The magazine recently won the 2001 Zine Publishing Competition Award in *Writer's Digest Magazine*, and won The Best Magazine of the Year Award in the *Jobs In Hell* newsletter contest.
Needs: Horror (dark fantasy, supernatural), slice-of-life vignettes, dark fantasy. "Nothing that isn't dark, strange, odd, and/or offbeat." Receives 250-400 unsolicited mss/month. Accepts 7-10 mss/issue; 21-36 mss/year. Publishes ms 10 months after acceptance. Agented fiction 1%. **Publishes 4-6 new writers/year.** Recently published work by Wendy Rathbone, Teri Jacobs, Jay Bonansinga and Jack Ketchum. Length: 100-6,000 words; average length: 2,000 words. Publishes short shorts. Also publishes poetry. Often comments on rejected mss.
How to Contact: Accepts submissions by mail, e-mail. Send complete ms with a cover letter. Include brief bio

and list of publications. Send SASE (or IRC) for return of ms. Responds in 2 weeks to queries; 2 months to mss. No simultaneous submissions. Sample copy for $6 (check payable to Jack Fisher). Writer's guidelines online.

Payment/Terms: Pays 4-5¢/word. Pays within 3 months of acceptance.

Advice: "Stories that mix one or more of the following elements with a horrific/weird idea/plot have a good chance: the fantastical, whimsical, supernatural, bizarre; stories should have unique ideas and be strongly written; the weirder and more offbeat, the better."

N ☐ FOLIATE OAK LITERARY MAGAZINE, Foliate Oak Online, University of Arkansas-Monticello, MCB 113, Monticello AR 71656. (870)460-1247. E-mail: foliate@uamont.edu. Website: www.uamont.edu/foliateo ak. **Contact:** Diane Payne, faculty advisor. Magazine: 6×9; 80 pages. Monthly. Estab. 1980. Circ. 500.

Needs: Adventure, comics/graphic novels, ethnic/multicultural, experimental, family saga, feminist, gay, historical, humor/satire, lesbian, literary, mainstream, science fiction (soft/sociological). No religious, sexist or homophobic work. Receives 30 unsolicited mss/month. Accepts 5 mss/issue; 40 mss/year. Does not read mss May-August. Publishes ms 1 month after acceptance. **Publishes 20 new writers/year.** Recently published work by David Barringer, Thom Didato, Joe Taylor, Molly Giles, Patricia Shevlin, Tony Hoafland. Length: 50-3,500 words; average length: 1,500 words. Publishes short shorts. Also publishes literary essays, literary criticism, poetry. Rarely comments on rejected mss.

How to Contact: Send complete ms. Accepts submissions by e-mail. Only send e-mail submissions. Responds in 1 week to queries; 2 months to mss. Accepts simultaneous and reprints, multiple submissions. Sample copy for SASE and 6×8 envelope. Writer's guidelines online. Reviews fiction.

Payment/Terms: Pays contributor's copy. Acquires electronic rights. Sends galleys to author. Not copyrighted.

Advice: "We're open to honest experimental, offbeat, realistic and surprising fiction. We will *only* accept submissions via e-mail at foliateoak@uamont.edu. *Snail Mail submissions will not be returned*!!! Please use a text-only (not rich-text or html) format, and cut and paste your submission into the body of your message. No more than three submissions per person. Excessive poetry is not smiled upon! Artwork can be e-mailed as well, but please submit only gif's or jpg's. Please limit you photos to two per submission and wait until we respond before you send more."

N $☐ FREE FOCUS/OSTENTATIOUS MIND, Wagner Press, Bowbridge Press, P.O. Box 7415, JAF Station, New York NY 10116-17415. **Contact:** Patricia Denise Coscia, editor. Editors change every year. Magazine: 8×14; 10 pages; recycled paper; illustrations; photos. "*Free Focus* is a small-press magazine which focuses on the educated women of today, and *Ostentatious Mind* is designed to encourage the intense writer, the cutting reality." Bimonthly. Estab. 1985 and 1987. Circ. 100 each.

Needs: Experimental, feminist, humor/satire, mainstream, mystery/suspense (romantic), psychic/supernatural/occult, western, young adult/teen (adventure). "X-rated fiction is not accepted." List of upcoming themes available for SASE. Plans future special fiction issue or anthology. Receives 1,000 unsolicited mss/month. Does not read mss February to August. Publishes ms 3-6 months after acceptance. **Publishes 200 new writers/year.** Recently published work by Edward Janz, Carol S. Fowler, Beth Anne Wiggins. Length: 1,000 words; average length: 500 words. Publishes short shorts. Also publishes literary essays, literary criticism, poetry. Always comments on rejected mss.

How to Contact: Query with published clips or send complete ms. Send SASE for reply. Responds in 3 months to mss. Accepts simultaneous submissions. Sample copy for $3, #10 SAE and $1 postage. Writer's guidelines for #10 SAE and $1 postage.

Payment/Terms: Pays $2.50-5 and 2 contributor's copies; additional copies $2. Pays on publication. Sends galleys to author. Sponsors awards/contests.

Advice: "This publication is for beginning writers. Do not get discouraged; submit your writing. We look for imagination and creativity; no x-rated writing."

$ FUN FOR KIDZ, Bluffton News Publishing and Printing Company, P.O. Box 227, 103 N. Main Street, Bluffton OH 45817-0227. (419)358-4610. Fax: (419)358-5027. Website: www.funforkidz.com. **Contact:** Virginia Edwards, associate editor. Magazine: 7×8; 49 pages; illustrations; photographs. "*Fun for Kidz* focuses on activity. The children are encouraged to solve problems, explore and develop character. Target age: 6-13 years." Bimonthly. Estab. 2002. Circ. 1,500.

Needs: Children's/juvenile (adventure, animal, easy-to-read, historical, mystery, preschool, series, sports). Bugs; Oceans; Animals; Camping; Fun with Stars; Healthy Fun; Summer Splash; In the Mountains; Fun with Words. List of upcoming themes for SASE. Accepts 10 mss/issue; 60 mss/year. Publishes short shorts. Also publishes poetry. Sometimes comments on rejected mss.

How to Contact: Send complete ms. Accepts submissions by mail. Send complete ms with cover letter. Include estimated word count and brief bio. Responds in 6 weeks to queries; 6 months to mss. Accepts simultaneous, multiple submissions. Sample copy for $4. Writer's guidelines for #10 SASE.

Payment/Terms: Pays 5¢/word and 1 contributor's copy. Pays on publication for first rights.

Advice: "Work needs to be appropriate for a children's publication ages 6-13 years. Request a theme list so story submitted will work into an upcoming issue."

$☐ THE FUNNY PAPER, F/J Writers Service, P.O. Box 455, Lee's MO 64063. (816)347-8862. E-mail: felixkc mo@aol.com. Website: www.angelfire.com/biz/funnypaper. **Contact:** F.H. Fellhauer, editor. Zine specializing in humor, contest and poetry: 8½ × 11; 8 pages. Published 5 times/year. No summer or Christmas. Estab. 1984.

Needs: Children's/juvenile, humor/satire, literary. "No controversial fiction." Receives 10-20 unsolicited mss/month. Accepts 1 mss/issue; 4-5 mss/year. Length: 1,000 words; average length: 295 words. Publishes short shorts. Also publishes poetry. Sometimes comments on rejected mss.

How to Contact: Accepts submissions by e-mail. Send for guidelines. Include estimated word count with submission. Send disposable copy of ms and #10 SASE for reply only. Responds in 2 weeks to queries; 1-3 months to mss. Accepts simultaneous and reprints submissions. Sample copy for $3.

Payment/Terms: Prizes for stories, jokes and poems for $5-100 (humor, inspirational, fillers). No fee. Additional copies $3. Pays on publication for first, one-time rights.

Advice: "Do your best work, no trash. We try to keep abreast of online publishing and provide information."

$🖊 FUNNY TIMES, A Monthly Humor Review, Funny Times, Inc., P.O. Box 18530, Cleveland Heights OH 44118. (216)371-8600. Fax: (216)371-8696. Website: www.funnytimes.com. **Contact:** Ray Lesser and Susan Wolpert, editors. Zine specializing in humor: tabloid; 24 pages; newsprint; illustrations. "*Funny Times* is a monthly review of America's funniest cartoonists and writers. We are the *Reader's Digest* of modern American humor with a progressive/peace-oriented/environmental/politically activist slant." Monthly. Estab. 1985. Circ. 63,000.

Needs: Humor/satire. "Anything funny." Receives hundreds unsolicited mss/month. Accepts 5 mss/issue; 60 mss/year. Publishes ms 3 months after acceptance. Agented fiction 10%. **Publishes 10 new writers/year.** Publishes short shorts.

How to Contact: Query with published clips. Include list of publications. Send SASE for return of ms or disposable copy of ms. Responds in 3 months to mss. Accepts simultaneous and reprints submissions. Sample copy for $3 or 9 × 12 SAE with 4 first-class stamps (83¢ postage). Writer's guidelines online.

Payment/Terms: Pays $50-150. Pays on publication for one-time, second serial (reprint) rights.

Advice: "It must be funny."

$🖊 🟡 GATEWAY S-F MAGAZINE, Stories of Science and Faith, GateWay Publishing House, 1833 S. Westmoorland Avenue, Los Angeles CA 90006-4621. (213)749-1044. E-mail: gateway59@hotmail.com. Website: www.geocities.com/scifieditor/index.html. **Contact:** John A.M. Darnell, editor; john.darnell@walsworth.com. Christian SF Magazine: 5½ × 8½; 140 pages; white bond paper; glossy cover; illustrations. "We are a print publication with a web edition, specializing in hard science fiction plots with Christian themes." Quarterly. Estab. 2000. Circ. 250.

Needs: Science fiction (futuristic, time travel, hard science, technological, soft/sociological, Christian), young adult/teen (science fiction). No fantasy, horror, or romance. No experimental forms such as local dialects. Receives 20-30 unsolicited mss/month. Accepts 20 mss/issue; 80 mss/year. Publishes ms 6 months after acceptance. **Publishes 40 new writers/year.** Length: 500-7,500 words; average length: 2,500 words. Publishes short shorts. Sometimes comments on rejected mss.

How to Contact: Send complete ms. Accepts submissions by e-mail (gateway59@hotmail.com). "We prefer e-mail submissions with MS Word.doc files as attachments." Include estimated word count, brief bio, postal address, e-mail address and phone number. Accepts reprints submissions. Sample copy for $7.50. For SASE, by e-mail or on website.

Payment/Terms: Pays $5-10.

Advice: "We look for good, solid writing, no typos or weak grammar, hard sf plots, Christian themes, rapid advance of plot, no experimental forms. Visit us online for a sense of what we publish."

N⃞ GAY CHICAGO MAGAZINE, Gernhardt Publications, Inc., 3115 N. Broadway, Chicago IL 60657-4522. (773)327-7271. Publisher: Paul Gernhardt. General Manager: Stacy Bridges. **Contact:** Jeff Rossen, entertainment editor. Magazine: 8½ × 11; 80-144 pages; newsprint paper and cover stock; illustrations; photos. Entertainment guide, information for the gay community.

Needs: Erotica (no explicit hard core), gay, lesbian, romance. Receives "a few" unsolicited mss/month. Accepts 10-15 mss/year.

How to Contact: Send complete ms. Send all submissions Attn: Jeff Rossen. Responds in 6 weeks to mss. Sample copy for 9 × 12 SAE and $1.45 postage first-class stamps.

Payment/Terms: Pays 5-10 contributor's copies. Acquires one-time rights.

**FOR EXPLANATIONS OF THESE SYMBOLS,
SEE THE INSIDE FRONT AND BACK COVERS OF THIS BOOK.**

N **$** 🔲 **GRASSLIMB**, Grasslimb, 4640 La Cuenta Dr., San Diego CA 92124-3011. E-mail: valerie@grasslimb.c om. Website: www.grasslimb.com/journal/. **Contact:** Valerie Polichar, editor. Magazine: 14 × 20; 8 pages; 60# white paper; illustrations. "*Grasslimb* is sold in cafés as well as in bookstores. Our readers like some insight into both the pain and the strange joys of life along with their cups of coffee. Loss, alienation and grief are subjects which draw us. Conversely, we find the beauty of the natural world compelling." Semiannual. Estab. 2002. Circ. 300.

Needs: Comics/graphic novels, ethnic/multicultural, experimental, gay, literary, mystery/suspense (crime), regional, thriller/espionage, translations. Does not want romance or religious writings. Accepts 2-4 mss/issue; 4-8 mss/year. Does not read mss in November and December. Publishes mss 3 months after acceptance. **Publishes 2 new writers/ year.** Recently published work by Leonard Ariho, Josey Foo, Matt Titus. Length: 500-2,000 words; average length: 1,500 words. Publishes short shorts. Also publishes poetry. Rarely comments on rejected mss.

How to Contact: Send complete ms. Send SASE for return of ms or disposable copy of ms and #10 SASE for reply only. Responds in 2 months to mss. Accepts simultaneous and reprints, multiple submissions. Sample copy for $2. Writer's guidelines for SASE, e-mail or on website. Reviews fiction.

Payment/Terms: Writers receive $5 minimum; $50 maximum, and 2 contributor's copies; additional copies $2. Pays on acceptance for first North American serial rights. Sends galleys to author.

Advice: "We publish brief fiction work that can be read in a single sitting over a cup of coffee. Work can be serious or light, but is generally 'literary' in nature, rather than mainstream. Remember to have your work proofread and to send short work."

$ 🔲 ◎ **HADROSAUR TALES**, Hadrosaur Productions, P.O. Box 2194, Mesilla Park NM 88047-2194. Website: www.zianet.com/hadrosaur. **Contact:** David L. Summers, editor. Zine specializing in science fiction: 5½ × 8½; 100-125 pages; 50 lb. white stock; 80 lb. cover. "*Hadrosaur Tales* is a literary science fiction and fantasy magazine published 3 times a year. We publish short stories, poetry, and articles with themes related to science fiction and fantasy. Above all, we are looking for thought-provoking ideas and good writing. Speculative fiction set in the past, present, and future is welcome. Likewise, contemporary or historical fiction is welcome as long as it has a mythic or science fictional element. Our target audience includes adult fans of the science fiction and fantasy genres along with anyone else who enjoys thought-provoking and entertaining writing." Triannual. Estab. 1995. Circ. 150.

Needs: Erotica, fantasy (space fantasy, sword and sorcery), horror, science fiction (hard science/technological, soft/ sociological). "We do not want to see stories with graphic violence. Do not send 'mainstream' fiction with no science fictional or fantastic elements. Do not send stories with copyrighted characters, unless you're the copyright holder." Receives 15 unsolicited mss/month. Accepts 7-10 mss/issue; 21-30 mss/year. Reading period is May 1- June 15 and November 1-December 15. Publishes ms 9 months after acceptance. **Publishes 8 new writers/year.** Recently published work by Justin Stanchfield, Ken Goldman, Nina Muntenu, Mark Fewell, Christina Sng, and Bonnie McDaniel. Length: 1,000-6,000 words; average length: 4,000 words. Also publishes poetry. Always comments on rejected mss.

How to Contact: Send complete ms. Accepts submissions by mail, e-mail (hadrosaur@zianet.com). Include estimated word count, brief bio and list of publications. Send SASE (or IRC) for return of ms or send a disposable copy of ms and #10 SASE for reply only. Responds in 1 week to queries; 1 month to mss. Accepts reprints submissions. No simultaneous submissions. Sample copy for $6.95. Writer's guidelines online.

Payment/Terms: Pays $6-10. Pays on acceptance for one-time rights.

Advice: "First and foremost, I look for engaging drama and believable characters. With those characters and situations, I want you to take me someplace I've never been before. The story I'll buy is the one set in a new world or where the unexpected happens, but yet I cannot help but believe in the situation because it feels real. Read absolutely everything you can get your hands on, especially stories and articles outside your genre of choice. This is a great source for original ideas."

$ 🔲 **HARDBOILED**, Gryphon Publications, P.O. Box 209, Brooklyn NY 11228. Website: www.gryphonbooks.c om. **Contact:** Gary Lovisi, editor. Magazine: Digest-sized; 100 pages; offset paper; color cover; illustrations. "Hard-hitting crime fiction and private-eye stories—the newest and most cutting-edge work and classic reprints." Semiannual. Estab. 1988. Circ. 1,000.

Needs: Mystery/suspense (private eye, police procedural, noir), hardboiled crime, and private-eye stories, all on the cutting edge. No "pastiches, violence for the sake of violence." Wants to see more nonprivate eye hardboiled. Receives 40-60 unsolicited mss/month. Accepts 10-20 mss/issue. Publishes ms 18 months after acceptance. **Publishes 5-10 new writers/year.** Recently published work by Andrew Vachss, Stephen Solomita, Joe Hensley, Mike Black. Sometimes comments on rejected mss.

How to Contact: Query with or without published clips or send complete ms. Accepts submissions by mail, fax. Query with SASE only on anything over 3,000 words. All stories must be submitted in hard copy. If accepted e-mail as an attachement in a word document. Responds in 2 weeks to queries; 1 month to mss. Accepts simultaneous and reprints submissions. Sample copy for $10 or double issue for $20 (add $1.50 book postage). Writer's guidelines for #10 SASE.

Payment/Terms: Pays $5-50. Pays on publication for first North American serial, one-time rights.

Advice: "By 'hardboiled' the editor does not mean rehashing of pulp detective fiction from the 1940s and 1950s but, rather, realistic, gritty material. We look for good writing, memorable characters, intense situations. Lovisi could be called a pulp fiction 'afficionado,' however he also publishes *Paperback Parade* and holds an annual vintage paperback fiction convention each year."

$ HORIZONS, The Jewish Family Journal, Targum Press, 22700 W. Eleven Mile Rd., Southfield MI 48034. Fax: (888)298-9992. E-mail: horizons@netvision.net.il. Website: www.targum.com. **Contact:** Miriam Zakon, chief editor. "We include fiction and nonfiction, memoirs, essays, historical, and informational articles, all of interest to the Orthodox Jew." Quarterly. Estab. 1994. Circ. 5,000.
Needs: Historical, humor/satire, mainstream, slice-of-life vignettes. Nothing not suitable to Orthodox Jewish values. Receives 4-6 unsolicited mss/month. Accepts 2-3 mss/issue; 10-12 mss/year. Publishes ms 6 months after acceptance. **Publishes 20-30 new writers/year.** Length: 300-3,000 words; average length: 1,500 words. Publishes short shorts. Also publishes poetry.
How to Contact: Send complete ms. Accepts submissions by mail, e-mail, fax. Responds in 1 week to queries; 2 months to mss. Accepts simultaneous submissions. Writer's guidelines available.
Payment/Terms: Pays $20-100. Pays 4-6 weeks after publication. Acquires one-time rights.
Advice: "Study our publication to make certain your submission is appropriate to our target market."

HYBOLICS, Da Literature and Culture of Hawaii, Hybolics, Inc., P.O. Box 3016, Aiea HI 96701. (808)366-1272. E-mail: hybolics@lava.net. Website: www.hybolics.com. **Contact:** Lee Tonouchi, co-editor. Magazine: 8½×11; 80 pages; 80 lb. coated paper; cardstock cover; illustrations; photos. "We publish da kine creative and critical work dat get some kine connection to Hawaii." Annual. Estab. 1999. Circ. 1,000.
Needs: Comics/graphic novels, ethnic/multicultural, experimental, humor/satire, literary. "No genre fiction. Wants to see more sudden fiction." Receives 50 unsolicited mss/month. Accepts 10 mss/year. Publishes ms 1 year after acceptance. **Publishes 3 new writers/year.** Recently published work by Darrell Lum, Rodney Morales, Lee Cataluna and Lisa Kanae. Length: 1,000-8,000 words; average length: 4,000 words. Publishes short shorts. Also publishes literary essays, literary criticism, poetry.
How to Contact: Send complete ms. Accepts submissions by mail. Send complete ms with a cover letter. Include estimated word count, brief bio and list of publications. Responds in 5 weeks to queries; 5 months to mss. Sample copy for $13.35. Writer's guidelines for #10 SASE.
Payment/Terms: Pays 2 contributor's copies; additional copies $7.25. Pays on publication for first rights.

ITALIAN AMERICANA, URI/CCE, 80 Washington Street, Providence RI 02903-1803. (401)277-5306. Fax: (401)277-5100. E-mail: bonomoal@etal.ui.edu. Website: www.uri.edu/prov/italian/italian.html. **Contact:** C.B. Albright, editor. Magazine: 6×9; 240 pages; varnished cover; perfect bound; photos. "*Italian Americana* contains historical articles, fiction, poetry and memoirs, all concerning the Italian experience in the Americas." Semiannual. Estab. 1974. Circ. 1,200.
Needs: Literary, Italian American. No nostalgia. Wants to see more fiction featuring "individualized characters." Receives 10 unsolicited mss/month. Accepts 3 mss/issue; 6-7 mss/year. Publishes ms up to 1 year after acceptance. Agented fiction 5%. **Publishes 2-4 new writers/year.** Recently published work by Mary Caponegro and Sal LaPuma. Average length: 20 double spaced pages words. Publishes short shorts. Also publishes literary essays, literary criticism, poetry. Sometimes comments on rejected mss.
How to Contact: Send complete ms. Accepts submissions by mail. Send complete ms (in triplicate) with a cover letter. Include 3-5 line bio, list of publications. Responds in 1 month to queries; 2 months to mss. No simultaneous submissions. Sample copy for $7. Writer's guidelines for #10 SASE. Reviews fiction.
Payment/Terms: Pays 1 contributor's copy; additional copies $7. Acquires first North American serial rights.
Advice: "Please individualize characters, instead of presenting types (i.e., lovable uncle, etc.). No nostalgia."

JEWISH CURRENTS MAGAZINE, 22 E. 17th Street, New York NY 10003-1919. (845)626-2427. Fax: (212)414-2227. E-mail: babush@ulster.net. **Contact:** Lawrence Bush. Magazine: 8½×11; 40 pages. "We are a secular, progressive, independent Jewish bimonthly, printing fiction, poetry articles and reviews on Jewish politics and history. Holocaust/Resistance, mideast peace process, Black-Jewish relations, labor struggles, women's issues. Audience is secular, left/progressive, Jewish, mostly urban." Bimonthly. Estab. 1946. Circ. 2,000.
Needs: Ethnic/multicultural, feminist, historical, humor/satire, translations, contemporary; senior citizen/retirement. "No religious, sectarian; no porn or hard sex, no escapist stuff. Go easy on experimentaion, but we're interested." "Must be well written! We are interested in *authentic* experience and readable prose; humanistic orientation. Must have Jewish theme. Could use more humor; short, smart, emotional and intellectual impact. Upcoming Themes: (submit at least 6 months in advance): "Black-Jewish Relations" (January/February); "International Women's Day, Holocaust/Resistance, Passover" (March/April); "Israel" (May/June); "Jews in the USSR and Ex-USSR" (July/August); "Jewish Book Month, Hanuka" (November/December). Receives 6-10 unsolicited mss/month. Accepts 0-1 mss/issue; 8-10 mss/year. Publishes ms 2-24 months after acceptance. Recently published work by Lanny Lefkowitz, Galena Vromen, Alex B. Stone. Length: 1,000-3,000 words; average length: 1,800 words. Publishes short shorts. Also publishes literary essays, literary criticism, poetry.
How to Contact: Send complete ms. Accepts submissions by mail. Send complete ms with cover letter. "Writers should include brief biographical information, especially their publishing histories." SASE. Responds in 2 months to mss. Sample copy for $3 with SAE and 3 first class stamps. Reviews fiction.

Payment/Terms: Pays complimentary one-year subscription and 6 contributor's copies. "We readily give reprint permission at no charge." Sends galleys to author.

Advice: Noted for "stories with Jewish content and personal Jewish experience—e.g., immigrant or Holocaust memories, assimilation dilemmas, dealing with Jewish conflicts OK. Space is increasingly a problem. Be intelligent, imaginative, intuitive and absolutely honest. Have a musical ear, and an ear for people: how they sound when they talk and also hear what they don't say."

JOURNAL OF POLYMORPHOUS PERVERSITY, Wry-Bred Press Inc., 630 First Avenue, Suite 32-P, New York NY 10016. (212)689-5473. Fax: (212)689-6859. E-mail: info@psychhumor.com. Website: www.psychhumor.com. **Contact:** Glenn Ellenbogen, editor. Magazine: 6¾ × 10; 24 pages; 60 lb. paper; antique India cover stock; illustrations with some articles. "*JPP* is a humorous and satirical journal of psychology, psychiatry, and the closely allied mental health disciplines." For "psychologists, psychiatrists, social workers, psychiatric nurses, *and* the psychologically sophisticated layman." Semiannual. Estab. 1984.

Needs: Humor/satire. "We only consider materials that are funny or that relate to psychology *or* behavior." Receives 50 unsolicited mss/month. Accepts 8 mss/issue; 16 mss/year. **Publishes many new writers/year.** Length: 4,000 words; average length: 1,500 words. Sometimes comments on rejected mss.

How to Contact: Send complete ms. Accepts submissions by mail. Send complete ms *in triplicate*. Include cover letter and SASE. Responds in 3 months to mss. Accepts multiple submissions. Sample copy for $7. Writer's guidelines for #10 SASE.

Payment/Terms: Pays 2 contributor's copies; additional copies $7.

Advice: "We will *not* look at poetry. We only want to see intelligent spoofs of scholarly psychology and psychiatry articles written in scholarly scientific language. Take a look at *real* journals of psychology and try to lampoon their *style* as much as their content. There are few places to showcase satire of the social sciences, thus we provide one vehicle for injecting a dose of humor into this often too serious area. Occasionally, we will accept a piece of creative writing written in the first person, e.g. 'A Subjective Assessment of the Oral Doctoral Defense Process: I Don't Want to Talk About It, If You Want to Know the Truth' (the latter being a piece in which Holden Caulfield shares his experiences relating to obtaining a Ph.D in Psychology). Other creative pieces have involved a psychodiagnostic evaluation of *The Little Prince* (as a psychiatric patient) and God being refused tenure (after having created the world) because of insufficient publications and teaching experiences."

KRAX MAGAZINE, 63 Dixon Lane, Leeds Yorkshire LS12 4RR, Britain, U.K. **Contact:** A. Robson, co-editor. "*Krax* publishes lighthearted, humorous and whimsical writing. It is for anyone seeking light relief at a gentle pace. Our audience has grown middle-aged along with us, especially now that we're annual and not able to provide the instant fix demanded by teens and twenties." Published 1-2 times a year.

Needs: "No war stories, horror, space bandits, boy-girl soap opera. We publish mostly poetry of a lighthearted nature but use comic or spoof fiction, witty and humorous essays. Would like to see more whimsical items, trivia ramblings or anything daft." Accepts 1 mss/issue. **Publishes 1 new writers/year.** Recently published work by Rachel Kendall, Johnny Haelterman, and Jim Sullivan.

How to Contact: Accepts submissions by mail. No specific guidelines but cover letter appreciated. Sample copy for $2.

Advice: "Don't spend too long on scene-setting or character construction as this inevitably produces an anti-climax in a short piece. We look for original settings, distinctive pacing, description related to plot, i.e. only dress character in bow tie and gumboots if you're having a candlelight dinner in The Everglades. Look at what you enjoy in all forms of fiction from strip cartoons to novels, movies to music lyrics then try to put some of this into your own writing. Send IRCs or currency notes for return postal costs."

$ LADY CHURCHILL'S ROSEBUD WRISTLET, An Occasional Outburst, Small Beer Press, 176 Prospect Ave., Northampton MA 01060. E-mail: info@lcrw.net. Website: www.lcrw.net/lcrw. **Contact:** Gavin Grant, editor. Zine: half legal size; 40 pages; 60 lb. paper; cardstock cover; illustrations; photos. Semiannual. Estab. 1996. Circ. 700.

Needs: Comics/graphic novels, experimental, fantasy, feminist, literary, science fiction, translations, short story collections. Receives 25 unsolicited mss/month. Accepts 4-6 mss/issue; 8-12 mss/year. Publishes ms 6 months after acceptance. **Publishes 2-4 new writers/year.** Recently published work by Amy Beth Forbes, Jeffrey Ford, Carol Emshwiller and Theodora Goss. Length: 200-7,000 words; average length: 3,500 words. Publishes short shorts. Also publishes literary essays, poetry. Sometimes comments on rejected mss.

How to Contact: Send complete ms with a cover letter. Include estimated word count. Send SASE (or IRC) for

---

SENDING TO A COUNTRY other than your own? Be sure to send International Reply Coupons (IRC) instead of stamps for replies or return of your manuscript.

return of ms or send a disposable copy of ms and #10 SASE for reply only. Responds in 2 weeks to queries; 1-3 month to mss. Sample copy for $4. Writer's guidelines online. Reviews fiction.

Payment/Terms: Pays $10-20 and 2 contributor's copies; additional copies $4. Pays on publication for first or one-time rights.

Advice: "I like fiction that tends toward the speculative."

$© LEADING EDGE, Magazine of Science Fiction and Fantasy, TLE Press, 3-146 JKHB, Provo UT 84602. (801)378-4455. E-mail: tle@byu.edu. Website: http://tle.byu.edu. **Contact:** Fiction director. Zine specializing in science fiction: 5½×8½; 120 pages; card stock; some illustrations. "*The Leading Edge* is dedicated to helping new writers make their way into publishing. We send back critiques with every story. We don't print anything with heavy swearing, violence that is too graphic, or explicit sex." Semiannual. Estab. 1981. Circ. 500.

Needs: Fantasy (space fantasy, sword/sorcery), science fiction (hard science/technological, soft/sociological). Receives 60 unsolicited mss/month. Accepts 6 mss/issue; 12 mss/year. Publishes ms 1-6 after acceptance. **Publishes 9-10 new writers/year.** Recently published work by Orson Scott Card and Dave Wolverton. Length: 17,000; average length: 10,000 words. Publishes short shorts. Also publishes poetry. Always comments on rejected mss.

How to Contact: Send complete ms with cover letter. Include estimated word count, brief bio and list of publications. Send disposable copy of ms and #10 SASE for reply only. Responds in 5 months to mss. Sample copy for $4.95. Writer's guidelines for SASE. Reviews fiction.

Payment/Terms: Pays 1¢/word; $100 maximum and 2 contributor's copies; additional copies $4.95. Pays on publication for first North American serial rights. Sends galleys to author.

Advice: "Don't base your story on your favorite TV show, book or game. Be original, creative and current. Base science fiction on recent science, not '50s horror flicks."

© LEFT CURVE, P.O. Box 472, Oakland CA 94604-0472. (510)763-7193. E-mail: editor@leftcurve.org. Website: www.leftcurve.org. **Contact:** Csaba Polony, editor. Magazine: 8½×11; 144 pages; 60 lb. paper; 100 pt. C1S gloss layflat lamination cover; illustrations; photos. "*Left Curve* is an artist-produced journal addressing the problem(s) of cultural forms emerging from the crises of modernity that strive to be independent from the control of dominant institutions, based on the recognition of the destructiveness of commodity (capitalist) systems to all life." Published irregularly. Estab. 1974. Circ. 2,000.

Needs: Ethnic/multicultural, experimental, historical, literary, regional, science fiction, translations, contemporary, prose poem, political. "No topical satire, religion-based pieces, melodrama." "We publish critical, open, social/political-conscious writing." Receives 12 unsolicited mss/month. Accepts 1 mss/issue. Publishes ms 12 months after acceptance. Recently published work by Peter Lengyel and Michael Filas. Length: 500-2,500 words; average length: 1,200 words. Publishes short shorts. Sometimes comments on rejected mss.

How to Contact: Send complete ms. Accepts submissions by mail, e-mail (editor@leftcurve.com). Send complete ms with cover letter. Include "statement of writer's intent, brief bio and reason for submitting to *Left Curve*." Accepts electronic submissions; "prefer 3½ disk and hard copy though we do accept e-mail submissions." Responds in 6 months to mss. For $10, 9×12 SAE and $1.24 postage. Writer's guidelines for 1 first-class stamp.

Payment/Terms: Pays contributor's copies. Rights revert to author.

Advice: "We look for continuity, adequate descriptive passages, endings that are not simply abandoned (in both meanings). Dig deep; no superficial personalisms, no corny satire. Be honest, realistic and gouge out the truth you wish to say. Understand yourself and the world. Have writing be a means to achieve or realize what is real."

[N] ◖ LIQUID OHIO, Voice of the Unheard, Grab Odd Dreams Press, P.O. Box 60265, Bakersfield CA 93386-0265. E-mail: amber@liquidohio.net. Website: www.liquidohio.net. **Contact:** Christa Hart, fiction editor. Magazine: 8½×11; 32 pages; newsprint; illustrations; photos. Quarterly. Estab. 1995. Circ. 500.

Needs: Experimental, humor/satire, literary. Receives 15-20 unsolicited mss/month. Accepts 2 mss/issue; 24-30 mss/year. Publishes ms 1-3 months after acceptance. **Publishes 15 new writers/year.** Recently published work by Marvin Pinkis, Richard Robbins and Hillary Wentworth. Length: 2,000-3,000 words; average length: 1,500-1,800 words. Publishes short shorts. Also publishes literary essays, literary criticism, poetry.

How to Contact: Send complete ms with a cover letter. Should include estimated word count. Send SASE for reply, return of ms or send a disposable copy of ms. Accepts simultaneous, multiple, reprint and electronic submissions. Responds in 1 month to queries; 3 months to mss. Sample copy for $4, 11×14 SAE and 3 first-class stamps. Writer's guidelines online.

Payment/Terms: Pays 3 contributor's copies. Acquires one-time rights.

Advice: "We like things that are different, but not too abstract or 'artsy' that one goes away saying, 'huh?' Write what you feel, not necessarily what sounds deep or meaningful—it will probably be that naturally if it's real. Send in anything you've got—live on the edge. Stories that are relatable, that deal with those of us trying to find a creative train in the world. We also love stories that are extremely unique, e.g., talking pickles, etc."

[N] ◻ LITERARY POTPOURRI, an online literary journal for contemporary adult fiction, poetry and graphic arts, Lit Pot Press, Inc., 3909 Reche Road Suite 132, Fallbrook CA 92028-3818. (760)731-3111. Fax: (760)731-3111. E-mail: litpot@adelphia.net. Website: www.literarypotpourri.com. **Contact:** Beverly Jackson, editor-in-chief. Magazine: 5½×8½; 160 pages; 60# paper; paperback and OPP cover stock; illustrations; photos.

Literary Potpourri has a simple mission: to publish literary work without abusing writers. We do not believe writers should have to wait for months to get a response for a submission. We welcome simultaneous submissions. We are unique inasmuch as we respond almost immediately, occasionally suggest other venues if the piece is not for us, and sometimes give feedback if the piece has potential. We like beginning writers with talent as well as seasoned professionals, and we'll give the outsider story a chance if it's well done. Our audience is a literary audience, who appreciates the edgy, the innovative as well as the solid plotted, emotive piece. Monthly. Estab. 2001. Circ. 1,000. Member, CLMP.

Needs: Ethnic/multicultural, humor/satire, literary. Does not want Children's, hard Sci-Fi, Religious, Romance. Receives 50 unsolicited mss/month. Accepts 4 mss/issue; 50 mss/year. Publishes ms 6 months after acceptance. **Publishes 20 new writers/year.** Recently published work by Terri Brown-Davidson, Joseph Young, Jill Mountain, Tom Sheehan, Jeffrey Hartmann, Rusty Barnes. Length: 100-5,000 words; average length: 2,500 words. Publishes short shorts. Also publishes literary essays, literary criticism, poetry. Sometimes comments on rejected mss.

How to Contact: Accepts submissions by e-mail. Send disposable copy of the ms and #10 SASE for reply only. Responds in 1 week to queries; 2 weeks to mss. Accepts simultaneous submissions. Sample copy for $10. Writer's guidelines for e-mail or on the website.

Payment/Terms: Pays $5-15 and 2 contributor's copies; additional copies $10. Pays on acceptance for first North American serial, electronic rights. Sends galleys to author.

Advice: "We look for fresh fiction with a literary bent, work that uses language and imagery effectively and is not mainstream, simplistic storytelling. We like characterization and plot, but also appreciate the abstract and absurd when well conceived. Humor and satire that move us are always appreciated. We don't want diatribes, rants, preachy or pedantic academic works."

◎ LOW BUDGET SCIENCE FICTION, Cynic Press, P.O. Box 40691, Philadelphia PA 19107. **Contact:** Joseph Farley, editor. Magazine specializing in science fiction: 8½×11; 24-40 pages; 20 lb. paper; 70 lb. cover; illustrations; photographs. "Quirky science fiction, horror and fantasy have a home here." Biannual. Estab. 2002. Circ. 100.

Needs: Fantasy (space fantasy, sword and sorcery, cross-over), science fiction (erotica, experimental, hard science/technological, cross-genre). Receives 5 unsolicited mss/month. Accepts 4-10 mss/issue. "in my sleep." Recently published work by Ernest Swallow, Joseph Farley, and Brad Wells. Publishes short shorts. Sometimes comments on rejected mss.

How to Contact: Send complete ms with cover letter. Include brief bio and list of publications. Send SASE for return of ms or send disposable copy of ms with SASE for reply only. Responds in 4 months to mss. Accepts simultaneous and reprints, multiple submissions. Sample copy for $7. Reviews fiction.

Payment/Terms: Pays 1 contributor's copy; additional copies $7. Pays on publication for one-time rights.

Advice: "Finding a good manuscript is like falling in love: you may know it when you first see it, or you may need to get familiar with it for a while."

Ⓝ ◯ MIDNIGHT TIMES, Tower Web Productions, 9561 Duffer Dr., Hillsboro MO 63050. E-mail: tepes@midnighttimes.com. Website: www.midnighttimes.com. **Contact:** Jay Manning, editor. The intention is to provide a forum for new writers to get exposure. The primary theme is darkness, but this doesn't necessarily mean evil. There can be a light at the end of the tunnel. Quarterly. Estab. 2003.

Needs: Erotica, fantasy (sword and sorcery), horror (dark fantasy, futuristic, psychological, supernatural), literary, mainstream, psychic/supernatural/occult, science fiction, vampires. No pornography. Accepts 3 mss/issue; 12 mss/year. Publishes ms 2 weeks after acceptance. **Publishes 6 new writers/year.** Length: 500-10,000 words; average length: 4,000 words. Publishes short shorts. Also publishes poetry. Sometimes comments on rejected mss.

How to Contact: Send complete ms. Accepts submissions by e-mail. Send SASE (or IRC) for return of the ms or disposable copy of the ms and #10 SASE for reply only. Responds in 1 week to queries; 2 weeks to mss. Accepts simultaneous and reprints submissions. Writer's guidelines for SASE or by e-mail or on website.

Payment/Terms: No payment. Acquires one-time rights.

Advice: "A good vampire story does not have to be a 'horror' story. Eternal darkness is a universal theme that transcends all genres. Be sure to read the classics before writing on this topic."

$◎ THE MIRACULOUS MEDAL, The Central Association of the Miraculous Medal, 475 E. Chelten Ave., Philadelphia PA 19144-5785. (215)848-1010. Website: www.cammonline.org. **Contact:** Charles Kelly, general manager. Magazine. Quarterly. Estab. 1915.

Needs: Religious/inspirational. Should not be pious or sermon-like. Receives 25 unsolicited mss/month. Accepts 2 mss/issue; 8 mss/year. Publishes ms 2 years after acceptance.

How to Contact: Accepts submissions by mail. Responds in 3 months to queries. Sample copy for 6×9 SAE and 2 first-class stamps. Writer's guidelines free.

Payment/Terms: Pays 2¢/word minimum. Pays on acceptance for first North American serial rights.

◯ ◎ MOUNTAIN LUMINARY, P.O. Box 1187, Mountain View AR 72560-1187. (870)585-2260. Fax: (870)269-4110. E-mail: ecomtn@mvtel.net. **Contact:** Anne Thiel, editor. Magazine: photos. "*Mountain Luminary* is dedicated to bringing information to people about the Aquarian Age; how to grow with its new and evolutionary energies and how to work with the resultant changes in spirituality, relationships, environment and the planet. *Mountain Luminary* provides a vehicle for people to share ideas, philosophies and experiences that deepen understanding of this evolutionary process and humankind's journey on Earth." Quarterly. Estab. 1985.

Needs: Humor/satire, metaphor/inspirational/Aquarian-Age topics. Accepts 8-10 mss/year. Publishes ms 6 months after acceptance. **Publishes 2 new writers/year.** Recently published work by Christain De Quincey and Sharda Brody.

How to Contact: Query with published clips. Accepts submissions by mail, e-mail (ecomtn@mvtel.net), fax. Query with clips of published work. SASE for return of ms. Accepts simultaneous submissions. Sample copy for free. Writer's guidelines free.

Payment/Terms: Pays 1 contributor's copy. "We may offer advertising space as payment." Acquires one-time rights.

Advice: "We look for stories with a moral—those with insight to problems on the path which raise the reader's awareness. Topical interests include: New Age/Aquarian Age, astrology, crystals, cultural and ethnic concerns, dreams, ecosystems, the environment, extraterrestrials, feminism, folklore, healing and health, holistic and natural health, inspiration, juvenile and teen issues, lifestyle, meditation, men's issues, metaphysics, mysticism, nutrition, parallel dimensions, prayer, psychic phenomenon, self-help, spirituality and women's issues."

MSLEXIA, For Women Who Write, Mslexia Publications Ltd., P.O. Box 656, Newcastle Upon Tyne NE99-2RP, United Kingdom. (00)44-191-2616656. Fax: (00)44-191-2616636. E-mail: postbag@mslexia.demon.co.uk. Website: www.mslexia.co.uk. **Contact:** Debbie Taylor, marketing manager. Magazine: A4; 60 pages; some illustrations; photos. "*Mslexia* is for women who write, who want to write, who have a specialist interest in women's writing of who teach creative writing. *Mslexia* is a blend of features, articles, advice, listings, and original prose and poetry. Many parts of the magazine are open to submission from any women. Please request contributor's guidelines prior to sending in work." Quarterly. Estab. 1999. Circ. 8,000.

Needs: No work from men accepted. Each issue is to a specific theme. Themes for SAE. Some themes include erotica, death writing from a male perspective and body image. Publishes ms 3-4 months after acceptance. **Publishes 40-50 new writers/year.** Length: 2,000 words; average length: 1,000-2,000 words. Publishes short shorts. Also publishes poetry.

How to Contact: Query. Accepts submissions by mail, e-mail (postbag@mslexia.demon.co.uk). Query first. Responds in 2 weeks to queries; 3 months to mss. For SAE, e-mail, fax or on web site.

Payment/Terms: Pays contributor's copies.

Advice: "We look for an unusual slant on the theme. Well structured, short pieces. Also intelligent, humorous, or with a strong sense of voice. Consider the theme and all obvious interpretations of it. Try to think of a new angle/slant. Dare to be different. Make sure the piece is strong on craft as well as content."

N ◯ MUDROCK: STORIES & TALES, Mudrock Press, P.O. Box 31688, Dayton OH 45437. E-mail: mudrockpress@hotmail.com. Website: www.mudrockpress.com. **Contact:** Brady Allen and Scott Geisel, editors. Magazine: 7×8½; 80-100 pages; bond paper; index cover stock; illustrations. *Mudrock* is an eclectic collection of stories, odd or not so, that people can follow, stories based in North America. We both like road stories, but we accept a wide range of genres from mainstream and realism to humor, horror, and sci-fi." Triannual. Estab. 2003. Circ. 250-500.

Needs: Ethnic/multicultural (North America), feminist, horror (dark fantasy, futuristic, psychological, supernatural), humor/satire, literary, mainstream, mystery/suspense (amateur sleuth, cozy, police procedural, private eye/hard-boiled), psychic/supernatural/occult, regional (North America), science fiction (hard science/technological, soft/sociological), thriller/espionage, western, road stories. We do not want experimental or post-modern fiction. Accepts 8-10 mss/issue; 25-30 mss/year. Publishes ms 3-12 months after acceptance. **Publishes 15-20 new writers/year.** Length: 8,000 words; average length: 3,000-6,000 words. Publishes short shorts. Sometimes comments on rejected mss.

How to Contact: Send complete ms. Send SASE for return of the ms or send disposable copy of the ms and #10 SASE for reply only. Responds in 1 month to queries; 3 months to mss. Accepts simultaneous and reprints submissions. Sample copy for $4.50 (past issue), $6 current issue. Writer's guidelines for SASE or on website.

Payment/Terms: Pays 2 contributor's copies; additional copies $5. Pays on publication for one-time rights. Sends galleys to author.

Advice: "Stories first, style second. Vivid characters and settings; compelling action and storylines. Polished mechanics—no first drafts. Edit and then edit some more. Read. Read our publication. Read other publications. Read books. Write. Write a lot. Send us a story when you think it's as good as what we publish."

READ 'THE BUSINESS OF FICTION WRITING' section for information on manuscript preparation, mailing tips, rights and more.

$ ☑ NEW ENGLAND WRITERS' NETWORK, P.O. Box 483, Hudson MA 01749-0483. (978)562-2946. E-mail: NEWNmag@aol.com. **Contact:** Liz Aleshire, fiction editor. Magazine: 8½ × 11; 24 pages; coated cover. "We are devoted to helping new writers get published and to teaching through example and content. We are looking for well-written stories that grab us from the opening paragraph." Quarterly. Estab. 1994. Circ. 200.
Needs: Adventure, condensed novels, ethnic/multicultural, humor/satire, literary, mainstream, mystery/suspense, religious/inspirational, romance. "We will consider anything except pornography or extreme violence." Accepts 5 mss/issue; 20 mss/year. Publishes ms 4-12 months after acceptance. **Publishes 10-12 new writers/year.** Recently published work by Laura Pederson, Esther Holt and Pat Car. Publishes short shorts. Also publishes poetry.
How to Contact: Send complete ms. Accepts submissions by mail. Send complete ms with cover letter. Include estimated word count. Bio on acceptance. Reads mss only from June 1 to September 1. No simultaneous submissions. Sample copy for $5.50. Writer's guidelines free.
Payment/Terms: Pays $10 for fiction, $5 for personal essays, $5 per poem and 1 contributor's copy. Pays on publication for first North American serial rights. Sponsors awards/contests.
Advice: "We are devoted to helping new writers get published and to teaching through example and content. Give us a try! Please send for guidelines and a sample."

◎ NEW METHODS, The Journal of Animal Health Technology, 24700 A N Hwy. 101, Willits CA 95490. (707)459-4535. E-mail: norwal13@yahoo.com. Website: www.geocities.com/norwal13photos.yahoo.com/norwal 13. **Contact:** Ronald S. Lippert, publisher. Newsletter ("could become a magazine again"): 8½ × 11; 2-4 pages; 20 lb. paper; illustrations; "rarely photos." Network service in the animal field educating services for mostly professionals in the animal field; e.g., animal health technicians. Monthly. Estab. 1976. Circ. 5,608.
Needs: Animals: contemporary, experimental, historical, mainstream, regional. No stories unrelated to animals. Receives 12 unsolicited mss/month. Accepts 1 mss/issue; 12 mss/year. Publishes short shorts. Occasionally comments on rejected mss.
How to Contact: Query. Accepts submissions by mail. Query first with theme, length, expected time of completion, photos/illustrations, if any, biographical sketch of author, all necessary credits or send complete ms. Responds in up to 4 months to queries. Accepts simultaneous, multiple submissions. Sample copy for $2.50. Writer's guidelines for SASE.
Payment/Terms: Acquires one-time rights. Sponsors awards/contests.
Advice: "Emotion, personal experiences—make the person feel it. We are growing."

$ ☑ ▧ NIGHT TERRORS, 1202 W. Market Street, Orrville OH 44667-1710. (330)683-0338. E-mail: dedavids on@night-terrors-publications.com. Website: www.night-terrors-publications.com. **Contact:** D.E. Davidson, editor/publisher. Magazine: 8½ × 11; 52 pages; 80 lb. glossy cover; illustrations; photos. "*Night Terrors* publishes quality, thought-provoking horror fiction for literate adults." Quarterly. Estab. 1996. Circ. 1,000.
• *Night Terrors* has had 22 stories listed in the Honorable Mention section of *The Year's Best Fantasy and Horror, Annual Collections.*
Needs: Horror, psychic/supernatural/occult. "*Night Terrors* does not accept stories involving abuse, sexual mutilation or stories with children as main characters. We publish traditional supernatural/psychological horror for a mature audience. Our emphasis is on literate work with a chill." Wants to see more psychological horror. Receives 50 unsolicited mss/month. Accepts 12 mss/issue; 46 mss/year. Publishes ms 6-12 months after acceptance. **Publishes 16 new writers/year.** Recently published work by John M. Clay, Ken Goldman and Barbara Rosen. Length: 2,000-5,000 words; average length: 3,000 words. Often comments on rejected mss.
How to Contact: Accepts submissions by mail. Send complete ms with cover letter. Include estimated word count, 50-word bio and list of publications. Send a #10 SASE or larger SASE for reply or return of ms. Responds in 1 week to queries; 3 months to mss. Accepts simultaneous submissions. Sample copy for $6 (make checks payable to Night Terrors Publications). Writer's guidelines for #10 SASE.
Payment/Terms: "Pays 2 contributor's copies for nonprofessional writers; additional copies for $4.50. Pays by arrangement with professional writers." Pays on publication for first North American serial rights. Sends galleys to author.
Advice: "I publish what I like. I like stories which involve me with the viewpoint character and leave me with the feeling that his/her fate could have or might be mine. Act professionally. Check your work for typos, spelling, grammar, punctuation, format. Send your work flat in a 9 × 12 envelope. And if you must, paper clip it, don't staple."

◎ ☐ THE NOCTURNAL LYRIC, Journal of the Bizarre, The Nocturnal Lyric, P.O. Box 542, Astoria OR 97103. E-mail: nocturnallyric@melodymail.com. Website: www.angelfire.com/ca/nocturnallyric. **Contact:** Susan Moon, editor. Magazine: 8½ × 11; 40 pages; illustrations. "Fiction and poetry submitted should have a bizarre horror theme. Our audience encompasses people who stand proudly outside of the mainstream society." 3 times/year. Estab. 1987. Circ. 400.
Needs: Horror (dark fantasy, futuristic, psychological, supernatural, satirical). "No sexually graphic material—it's too over done in the horror genre lately." Receives 25-30 unsolicited mss/month. Accepts 8-9 mss/issue; 30 mss/year. Publishes ms 1 year after acceptance. **Publishes 20 new writers/year.** Recently published work by Rene Dumas, Kevin Christinat, Eleanor Lohse, Gary Kowalski, Steven Palukaitis, and Kent Robinson. Length: 2,000

words; average length: 1,500 words. Publishes short shorts. Also publishes literary essays, poetry. Rarely comments on rejected mss.

How to Contact: Send complete ms. Accepts submissions by mail. Send complete ms with cover letter. Include estimated word count. Responds in 3 month to queries; 8 months to mss. Accepts simultaneous and reprints, multiple submissions. Sample copy for $2 (back issue); $3 (current issue). Writer's guidelines online.

Payment/Terms: Pays with discounts on subscriptions and copies of issue. Pays on acceptance. Not copyrighted. Sponsors awards/contests.

Advice: "A manuscript stands out when the story has a very original theme and the ending is not predictable. Don't be afraid to be adventurous with your story. Mainstream horror can be boring. Surreal, satirical horror is what true nightmares are all about."

N $ ⊘ ◎ ☺ NOVA SCIENCE FICTION MAGAZINE, Nova Publishing Company, 17983 Paseo Del Sol, Chino Hills CA 91709-3947. (909)393-0806. **Contact:** Wesley Kawato, editor. Zine specializing in evangelical Christian science fiction: 8½×5½; 64 pages; cardstock cover. "We publish religious science fiction short stories, no fantasy or horror. One story slot per issue will be reserved for a story written from an evangelical Christian viewpoint. We also plan to carry one article per issue dealing with science fiction wargaming." Quarterly. Estab. 1999. Circ. 25.

Needs: Science fiction (hard science/technological, soft/sociological, religious). "No stories where the villain is a religious fanatic and stories that assume the truth of evolution." Accepts 3 mss/issue; 12 mss/year. Publishes ms 3 months after acceptance. **Publishes 7 new writers/year.** Recently published work by Teri Pilcher, Travis Peary, Steve Poling, Martha Bland, Ralph Sperry, Matthew Spence, and Will Morton. Length: 250-7,000 words; average length: 4,000 words. Publishes short shorts. Sometimes comments on rejected mss.

How to Contact: Query first. Include estimated word count and list of publications. Responds in 3 months to queries and mss. Send SASE (or IRC) for return of ms. Accepts reprints, multiple submissions. Sample copy for $6. Guidelines free for SASE.

Payment/Terms: Pays $1.25-35. Pays on publication for first North American serial rights. Not copyrighted.

Advice: "Make sure your plot is believable and describe your characters well enough so I can visualize them. If I like it, I buy it. I like happy endings and heroes with a strong sense of faith."

☺ NUTHOUSE, Your Place for Humor Therapy, Twin Rivers Press, P.O. Box 119, Ellenton FL 34222. E-mail: nuthouse449@aol.com. Website: hometown.aol.com/nuthous499/index2.html. **Contact:** Dr. Ludwig "Needles" Von Quirk, chief of staff. Zine: digest-sized; 12-16 pages; bond paper; illustrations; photos. "Humor of all genres for an adult readership that is not easily offended." Published every 6 weeks. Estab. 1993. Circ. 100.

Needs: Humor/satire (erotica, experimental, fantasy, feminist, historical (general), horror, literary, main-stream/contemporary, mystery/suspense, psychic/supernatural/occult, romance, science fiction and westerns.). Plans annual "Halloween Party" issue featuring humorous verse and fiction with a horror theme. Deadline: July 31. Receives 30-50 unsolicited mss/month. Accepts 5-10 mss/issue; 50-60 mss/year. Publishes ms 6-12 months after acceptance. **Publishes 10-15 new writers/year.** Recently published work by Michael Fowler, Dale Andrew White, and Jim Sullivan. Length: 100-1,000 words; average length: 500 words. Publishes short shorts. Also publishes literary essays, literary criticism, poetry. Often comments on rejected mss.

How to Contact: Send complete ms with a cover letter. Include estimated word count, bio (paragraph) and list of publications. SASE for return of ms or send disposable copy of ms. Sample copy for $1.25 (payable to Twin Rivers Press). Writer's guidelines for #10 SASE.

Payment/Terms: Pays 1 contributor's copy. Acquires one-time rights. Not copyrighted.

Advice: Looks for "laugh-out-loud prose. Strive for original ideas; read the great humorists—Saki, Woody Allen, Robert Benchley, Garrison Keillor, John Irving—and learn from them. We are turned off by sophomoric attempts at humor built on a single, tired, overworked gag or pun; give us a story with a beginning, middle and end."

☺ THE OAK, 1530 Seventh Street, Rock Island IL 61201. (309)788-3980. **Contact:** Betty Mowery, editor. Magazine: 8½×11; 8-10 pages. "To provide a showcase for new authors while showing the work of established authors as well; to publish wholesome work, something with a message." Bimonthly. Estab. 1991. Circ. 300.

Needs: Adventure, experimental, fantasy, humor/satire, mainstream, contemporary; prose poem. No erotica or love poetry. Receives 25 unsolicited mss/month. Accepts 12 mss/issue. Publishes ms 3 months after acceptance. **Publishes 25 new writers/year.**

How to Contact: Send complete ms. Accepts submissions by mail. Send complete ms. Responds in 1 week to mss. Accepts simultaneous and reprints, multiple submissions. Sample copy for $3; subscription $10. Writer's guidelines for #10 SASE.

Payment/Terms: None, but not necessary to buy a copy in order to be published. Acquires first rights.

Advice: "I do not want erotica, extreme violence or killing of humans or animals for the sake of killing. Just be yourself when you write. Also, write *tight*. Please include SASE or manuscripts will be destroyed. Be sure name and address are on the manuscript. Study the markets for length of manuscript and what type of material is wanted."

☺ OFFICE NUMBER ONE, 2111 Quarry Rd., Austin TX 78703. E-mail: onocdingus@aol.com. **Contact:** Carlos B. Dingus, editor. Zine: 8½×11; 12 pages; 60 lb. standard paper; b&w illustrations; photos. "I look for short stories, imaginary news stories or essays (under 400 words) that can put a reader on edge—avoid profanity or obscenity, be up-beat, free the reader to see several worlds." Biannual zine specializing in satire, humor and views from alternate realities. Estab. 1989. Circ. 1,000.

Needs: Experimental, fantasy, horror, humor/satire, literary, psychic/supernatural/occult, fictional news articles, fictional reviews, limericks. Receives 16 unsolicited mss/month. Accepts 1-3 mss/issue; 16 mss/year. Publishes ms 6-12 months after acceptance. **Publishes 10-15 new writers/year.** Also publishes literary essays, poetry. Sometimes comments on rejected mss.

How to Contact: Send complete ms with optional cover letter. Include estimated word count. Send SASE for reply, return of ms or send disposable copy of ms. Will consider simultaneous submissions, reprints. Responds in 6-8 weeks to mss. Sample copy for $2 with SAE and 3 first-class stamps. Writer's guidelines for SASE.

Payment/Terms: Pays 1 contributor's copy. Additional copies for $1 plus $1.50 postage and 9×12 SASE. Aquires reprint rights for all *Office Number One* publications.

Advice: "No unnecessary words. Clear presentation. *One* good idea. Write for an audience you can identify, plan to publish more *shorter* fiction, to be more up-beat and to focus on a journalistic style. The Internet is taking away from print media, however, the Internet cannot replace print media for fiction writing."

ON SPEC, P.O. Box 4727, Station South, Edmonton AB T6E 5G6 Canada. (780)413-0215. Fax: (780)413-1538. E-mail: onspec@canada.com. Website: www.onspec.ca/. **Contact:** Diane L. Walton, editor. Magazine: $5\frac{1}{4} \times 8$; 112 pages; illustrations. "We publish speculative fiction by new and established writers, with a strong preference for Canadian authored works." Quarterly. Estab. 1989. Circ. 2,000.

Needs: Fantasy, horror, science fiction, magic realism. No media tie-in or shaggy-alien stories. No condensed or excerpted novels, religious/inspirational stories, fairy tales. "We would like to see more horror, fantasy, science fiction—well developed stories with complex characters and strong plots." Receives 100 unsolicited mss/month. Accepts 10 mss/issue; 40 mss/year. "We read manuscripts during the month after each deadline: February 28/May 31/August 31/November 30." Publishes ms 6-18 months after acceptance. **Publishes 10-15 new writers/year.** Recently published work by James Van Pelt, David Kirtle, Allen Weiss and Steve Mohn. Length: 1,000-6,000 words; average length: 4,000 words. Also publishes poetry. Often comments on rejected mss.

How to Contact: Send complete ms. Accepts submissions by mail, phone. SASE for return of ms or send a disposable copy of ms plus #10 SASE for response. Include Canadian postage or IRCs. No e-mail or fax submissions. Responds in 2 weeks to queries 2 months after deadline to mss to mss. Accepts simultaneous submissions. Sample copy for $7. Writer's guidelines for #10 SASE or on website.

Payment/Terms: Pays $50-180 for fiction. Short stories (under 1,000 words): $50 plus 1 contributor's copy. Pays on acceptance for first North American serial rights.

Advice: "We're looking for original ideas with a strong SF element, excellent dialogue, and characters who are so believable, our readers will really care about them."

ONCE UPON A WORLD, 9070 Sheep Ranch Court, Las Vegas NV 89032. E-mail: ejalward@yahoo.com. **Contact:** Emily Alward, editor. Zine: $8\frac{1}{2} \times 11$; 80-100 pages; white paper; card stock cover; pen & ink illustrations. "Our goal is to publish unique science fiction and fantasy stories which may not fit the parameters of much commerical ficiton because of its emphasis on world-building and character interaction." Annual. Estab. 1988. Circ. 150.

Needs: Fantasy, science fiction. No realistic "stories in contemporary settings"; horror; stories using Star Trek or other media characters; stories with completely negative endings. Wants to see more "stories set in worlds with alternate political, economic or family arrangements." Upcoming theme: Effective Non-lethal Counters to Violence/Terrorism (in a SF setting—deadline July 2003). Receives 20 unsolicited mss/month. Accepts 8-12 mss/issue; "varies, depending on backlog." Publishes ms 2 months to 1½ years after acceptance. **Publishes 5 new writers/year.** Recently published work by Jeff Kozzi, B.J. Nold and Don Stockard. Length: 400-10,000 words; average length: 3,000 words. Publishes short shorts. Also publishes poetry. Sometimes comments on rejected mss and recommends other markets. Sometimes comments on rejected mss.

How to Contact: Send complete ms. SASE. Responds in 2-4 weeks to queries; 2-16 weeks to mss. "Reluctantly" accepts simultaneous submissions. Sample copy for $9. Make checks payable to Emily Alward. Writer's guidelines for #10 SASE. Reviews fiction.

Payment/Terms: Pays contributor's copies. Acquires first rights, "stories copyrighted in author's name; copyrights not registered."

Advice: "Create your own unique universe, and then show its texture and how it 'works' in the story. This is a good way to try out a world that you're building for a novel. But, don't forget to also give us interesting characters with believable problems. Submit widely, but pay attention to editors' needs and guidelines—don't scattershot. Take on new challenges—i.e., never say 'I only write science fiction, romance, or even fiction in general'—you never know where your 'sideline' work is going to impress an editor. We aim to fill some niches not necessarily well-covered by larger publishers currently: science fiction; cross-genre; SF love stories; and non-cyber centered futures. Also, we see too many stories with generic, medieval-type world settings and premises."

ORB, Speculative Fiction, ORB Publications, P.O. Box 1621, West Preston, Melbourne Victoria 3072, Australia. (+61) 03 94719270. E-mail: orb@vicnet.net.au. Website: http://home.vicnet.net.au/~kendacot/Orb.

Contact: Sarah Endacott, editor. Zine specializing in speculative fiction: A5; 196 pages; 90gsm white; 200gsm full color cover; internal b&w illustrations. "An Australian speculative fiction magazine that publishes Australian authors, artwork, reviews, interviews and articles." Biannual. Estab. 1999. Circ. 500.

• *Orb* was nominated for two Ditmars in 1999 and 2 Aurealis Awards in 2000.

Needs: Fantasy (space fantasy, sword and sorcery), horror, psychic/supernatural/occult, religious/inspirational (religious fantasy), romance (futuristic/time travel), science fiction (hard science/technological, soft/sociological), young adult/teen (fantasy/science fiction). "Fiction must be from Australian writers and have some speculative content." Receives 20 unsolicited mss/month. Accepts 10-12 mss/issue; 20-30 mss/year. Publishes ms 3 months after acceptance. **Publishes 4 new writers/year.** Length: 100-10,000 words; average length: 3,000 words. Publishes short shorts. Also publishes literary essays, literary criticism. Often comments on rejected mss.

How to Contact: Send complete copy of ms with cover letter. Include estimated word count and brief bio with submission. Send SASE (or IRC) for return of ms or disposable copy of ms and #10 SASE for reply only. Responds in 3 weeks to queries; 3 months to mss. Accepts simultaneous, multiple submissions. Sample copy for $16.95 (Australian). SASE and on website.

Payment/Terms: Pays $30 (Australian dollars) and 1 contributor's copy; additional copies $16.95 (Australian). Pays on publication for first rights. Sends galleys to author.

Advice: "Challenging, controversial concepts make manuscript/stories stand out. This must accompany solid plot and characterization and clear, proficient writing style. Read widely in the genre."

⬛ ◎ 📧 OUTER DARKNESS, Where Nightmares Roam Unleashed, Outer Darkness Press, 1312 N. Delaware Place, Tulsa OK 74110. **Contact:** Dennis Kirk, editor. Zine: 8½×5½; 60-80 pages; 20 lb. paper; 90 lb. matte cover; illustrations. Specializes in imaginative literature. "Variety is something I strive for in *Outer Darkness*. In each issue we present readers with great tales of science fiction and horror along with poetry, cartoons and interviews/essays. I seek to provide readers with a magazine which, overall, is fun to read. My readers range in age from 16 to 70." Quarterly. Estab. 1994. Circ. 500.

• Fiction published in *Outer Darkness* has received honorable mention in *The Year's Best Fantasy and Horror.*

Needs: Fantasy (science), horror, mystery/suspense (with horror slant), psychic/supernatural/occult, romance (gothic), science fiction (hard science, soft/sociological). No straight mystery, pure fantasy—works which do not incorporate elements of science fiction and/or horror. Also, no slasher horror with violence, gore, sex instead of plot. Wants more "character driven tales—especially in the genre of science fiction and well-developed psychological horror. I do not publish works with children in sexual situations and graphic language should be kept to a minimum." Receives 75-100 unsolicited mss/month. Accepts 7-9 mss/issue; 25-40 mss/year. **Publishes 2-5 new writers/year.** Recently published work by Terry Campbell, Lenora Rogers, Steve Burt, Kendall Evans. Length: 1,000-5,000 words; average length: 3,000 words. Also publishes poetry. Always comments on rejected mss.

How to Contact: Send complete ms with a cover letter. Include estimated word count, 50- to 75-word bio, list of publications and "any awards, honors you have received." Send SASE for reply, return of ms or send a disposable copy of ms. Responds in 2 weeks to queries; 3 months to mss. Accepts simultaneous, multiple submissions. Sample copy for $3.95. Writer's guidelines for #10 SASE.

Payment/Terms: Pays 3 contributor's copies for fiction; 2 for poetry and 3 for art. Pays on publication for one-time rights.

Advice: "I look for strong characters and well developed plot. And I definitely look for suspense. I want stories which move—and carry the reader along with them. Be patient and persistent. Often it's simply a matter of linking the right story with the right editor. I've received many stories which were good, but not what I wanted at the time. However, these stories worked well in another horror-sci-fi zine."

Ⓝ $ OVER THE BACK FENCE, Southern Ohio's Own Magazine, Panther Publishing, LLC, P.O. Box 756, Chillicothe OH 45601. (740)772-2165. Fax: (740)773-7626. Website: www.backfence.com. "We are a regional magazine serving 30 counties in Southern Ohio. *Over The Back Fence* has a wholesome, neighborly style. It appeals to readers from young adults to seniors, showcasing art and travel opportunities in the area." Quarterly. Estab. 1994. Circ. 15,000.

Needs: Humor/satire. Receives 20 unsolicited mss/month. Accepts 2-3 mss/issue; 8-12 mss/year. Publishes ms 1 year after acceptance. Agented fiction 10%. **Publishes 4 new writers/year.** Recently published work by Debbie Farmer, Carol Lucas and Marcia Shonberg. Publishes short shorts. Also publishes poetry. Sometimes comments on rejected mss.

How to Contact: Query with published clips. Accepts submissions by mail. Responds in 3 months to queries. Accepts simultaneous submissions. Sample copy for $4 or on website. Writer's guidelines online.

Payment/Terms: Pays 10¢/word minimum, negotiable depending on experience. Pays on publication for one-time North American serial rights, makes work-for-hire assignments.

Advice: "Submitted pieces should have a neighborly, friendly quality. Our publication is a positive piece on the good things in Ohio."

Ⓝ ◻ ◎ THE PEGASUS REVIEW, P.O. Box 88, Henderson MD 21640-0088. (410)482-6736. **Contact:** Art Bounds, editor. Magazine: 5½×8½; 6-8 pages; illustrations. "*The Pegasus Review* is a bimonthly, done in a calligraphic format and occasionally illustrated. Each issue is based on a specific theme." Estab. 1980. Circ. 120.

● Because *The Pegasus Review* is done is a calligraphic format, fiction submissions must be very short. Two pages, says the editor, are the ideal length.

Needs: Humor/satire, literary, religious/inspirational, prose poem. Wants more short-shorts and theme related fiction. Upcoming themes for 2004: "Courage" (January/February); "Children" (March/April); "Conservation" (May/June); "America" (July/August); "Earth" (September/October); "Faith" (November/December). Receives 35 unsolicited mss/month. Accepts 50 mss/issue. **Publishes 10 new writers/year.** Recently published work by Patrick Fiedler, Leslie Palmer, Ronald MacKinnan Thompson, and J. Lorraine Brown. Publishes short shorts. Sometimes comments on rejected mss.

How to Contact: Send complete ms. Send brief cover letter with author's background, name and prior credits, if any. Responds in 2 months to mss. Accepts simultaneous submissions. Sample copy for $2.50. Writer's guidelines for #10 SASE.

Payment/Terms: Pays 2 contributor's copies. Acquires one-time rights. Sponsors awards/contests.

Advice: "Read, read, read. Old and new. Constantly work at honing your craft. Get involved with a local writers' group and network. Above all, keep marketing you by using *Novel & Short Story Writer's Market* and *Writer's Digest* magazine. Believe in your work and it will find not only a home, but an audience."

PINDELDYBOZ, Pindeldyboz, 21-17 25th Rd., Astoria NY 11102. Website: www.pindeldyboz.com or www.pboz. net. **Contact:** Whitney Pastorek, senior editor. Literary magazine: 5½×8½; 272 pages; illustrations. "*Pineldyboz* is dedicated to publishing work that challenges what a short story can be. We don't ask for anything specific—we only ask that people take chances. We like heightened language, events, relationships—stories that paint the world a little differently, while still showing us the places we already know." Semiannual. Estab. 2001.

Needs: Comics/graphic novels, experimental, literary, translations. Publishes ms 3 months after acceptance. Recently published work by Carrie Hoffman, Matthew Derby, Amanda Eyre Ward, Dan Kennedy, Corey Mesler, Jason Wilson and Mike Magnuson. Length: 250+; average length: 2,000 words. Publishes short shorts. Also publishes literary essays, poetry. Always comments on rejected mss.

How to Contact: Send complete copy of ms with cover letter. Accepts mss by e-mail and disk. Include brief bio and phone number with submission. Send SASE (or IRC) for return of the ms and disposable copy of ms and #10 SASE for reply only. Responds in 2 weeks to queries; 3 months to mss. Accepts simultaneous, multiple submissions. Sample copy for $12. Writer's guidelines online.

Payment/Terms: Pays 2 contributor's copies; additional copies $10. Pays on publication for one-time rights.

Advice: "Good grammar, spelling, and sentence structure help, but what's more important is a willingness to take risks. Surprise us. And we will love it."

THE PIPE SMOKER'S EPHEMERIS, The Universal Coterie of Pipe Smokers, 20-37 120 Street, College Point NY 11356-2128. **Contact:** Tom Dunn, editor. Magazine: 8½×11; 84-116 pages; offset paper and cover; illustrations; photos. Pipe smoking and tobacco theme for general and professional audience. Irregular quarterly. Estab. 1964.

Needs: Pipe smoking related: historical, humor/satire, literary. Publishes ms up to 1 year after acceptance. Length:5,000 words; average length: 2,500 words. Publishes short shorts. Occasionally comments on rejected mss.

How to Contact: Send complete ms. Accepts submissions by mail. Send complete ms with cover letter. Responds in 2 weeks to mss. Accepts simultaneous and reprints submissions. Sample copy for 8½×11 SAE and 6 first-class stamps.

Payment/Terms: Acquires one-time rights.

POSKISNOLT PRESS, Yesterday's Press, JAF Station, Box 7415, New York NY 10116-4630. **Contact:** Patricia D. Coscia, editor. Magazine: 7×8½; 20 pages; regular typing paper. Estab. 1989. Circ. 100.

Needs: Erotica, ethnic/multicultural, experimental, fantasy, feminist, gay, humor/satire, lesbian, literary, mainstream, psychic/supernatural/occult, romance, western, young adult/teen (10-18 years old), contemporary, prose poem, senior citizen/retirement. "X-rated material is not accepted!" Plans to publish a special fiction issue or anthology in the future. Receives 50 unsolicited mss/month. Accepts 30 mss/issue; 100 mss/year. Publishes ms 6 months after acceptance. Recently published work by Steve Swanbeck, Jenny D. Nasson, Carol S. Fowler. Length: 100-500 words; average length: 200 words. Publishes short shorts. Sometimes comments on rejected mss.

How to Contact: Query with published clips or send complete ms. SASE. Responds in 1 week to queries; 6 months to mss. Accepts simultaneous submissions. Sample copy for $5 with #10 SAE and $2 postage. Writer's guidelines for #10 SAE and $2 postage.

INTERESTED IN A PARTICULAR GENRE? Check our sections for: **Mystery/ Suspense**, page 68; **Romance**, page 80; **Science Fiction/Fantasy & Horror**, page 90.

Payment/Terms: Pays with subscription to magazine or contributor's copies; charges for extras. Acquires first, one-time rights.

◻ ◎ **PRAYERWORKS, Encouraging God's people to do real work of ministry—intercessory prayer**, The Master's Work, P.O. Box 301363, Portland OR 97294-9363. (503)761-2072. E-mail: vannm1@aol.com. **Contact:** V. Ann Mandeville, editor. Newsletter: 5½×8; 4 pages; bond paper. "Our intended audience is 70% retired Christians and 30% families. We publish 350-500 word devotional material—fiction, nonfiction, biographical poetry, clean quips and quotes. Our philosophy is evangelical Christian serving the body of Chirst in the area of prayer." Estab. 1988. Circ. 1,000.

Needs: Religious/inspirational. "No nonevangelical Christian. Subject matter may include anything which will build relationship with the Lord—prayer, ways to pray, stories of answered prayer, teaching on a Scripture portion, articles that will build faith, or poems will all work. We even use a series occasionally." Publishes ms 2-6 months after acceptance. **Publishes 30 new writers/year.** Recently published work by Allen Audrey and Petey Prater. Length: 350-500 words; average length: 350-500 words. Publishes short shorts. Also publishes poetry. Often comments on rejected mss.

How to Contact: Send complete ms. Accepts submissions by mail. Send complete ms with cover letter. Include estimated word count and a very short bio. Responds in 1 month to mss. Accepts simultaneous and reprints, multiple submissions. Sample copy for #10 SASE. Writer's guidelines for #10 SASE.

Payment/Terms: Pays free subscription to the magazine and contributor's copies. Pays on publication. Not copyrighted.

Advice: Stories "must have a great take-away—no preaching; teach through action. Be thrifty with words—make them count."

◩ **PROSE AX, doses of prose, poetry, and visual art**, P.O. Box 22643, Honolulu HI 96823-2643. E-mail: prose_ax@att.net. Website: www.proseax.com. **Contact:** J.C. Salazar, editor. Zine and online magazine specializing in prose, poetry and art: 8½×7; 24-30 pages; 20 lb. paper; illustrations; photos. "We are a literary journal that publishes stimulating, fresh prose and poetry. We are committed to publishing new or ethnic writers or ethnic themes. The style of our website and print version is very visual, very stylish, and I think this makes our publication different. We present fresh voices in a fresh way." Quarterly. Estab. 2000. Circ. 400-500 print; 50 unique visitors average per day to website.

• *Prose Ax* ranked on *Writer's Digest*'s "Top 30" list of best markets for emerging fiction writers.

Needs: Ethnic/multicultural (general), experimental, literary, literary fantasy (fantastic realism), novel excerpts that work well alone, flash fiction. "No genre, especially romance and mystery." Receives 30-50 unsolicited mss/month. Accepts 7-15 mss/issue. Publishes ms 1-4 months after acceptance. **Publishes 20 new writers/year.** Recently published work by Eric Paul Shafer, Ken Goldman, Suzanne Frischkorn, Jasmine Orr, Jason D. Smith, K.J. Stevens and Kenneth Champeon. Length: 50-5,000 words; average length: 1,000 words. Publishes short shorts. Also publishes literary essays, poetry. Often comments on rejected mss.

How to Contact: Accepts submissions by mail, e-mail. Send complete copy of ms with cover letter. Include estimated word count with submission. Send disposable copy of ms and #10 SASE for reply only. Responds in 1-2 months to mss. Accepts simultaneous and reprints, multiple submissions. Writer' guidelines for SASE, e-mail or on website. Reviews fiction.

Payment/Terms: Pays 2 contributor's copies; additional copies send SASE. Pays on publication for one-time, electronic rights. Sends galleys to author. Sponsors awards/contests.

Advice: "A good story has good details and descriptions. Read our zine first to see if what you write will fit in with the tone and style of *Prose Ax*. Write a little hello to us instead of sending only your mss."

💲◩ **PSI**, P.O. Box 6218, Charlottesville VA 22906-6218. Fax: (434)964-0096. E-mail: asam@publisherssyndication.com. Website: www.publisherssyndication.com. **Contact:** A.P. Samuels, editor. Magazine: 8½×11; 32 pages; bond paper; self cover. "Mystery and romance." Bimonthly. Estab. 1987.

Needs: Adventure, mystery/suspense (private eye), romance (contemporary, historical, young adult), suspense, western (traditional). No ghoulish, sex, violence. Wants to see more believable stories. Accepts 1-2 mss/issue. **Publishes 1-3 new writers/year.** Average length: 30,000 (novelettes) words. Publishes short shorts. "only on a rare occasion." Sometimes comments on rejected mss.

How to Contact: Send complete ms. Accepts submissions by mail. Send complete ms with cover letter. Responds in 2 weeks to queries; 6 weeks to mss.

Payment/Terms: Pays 1-4¢/word, plus royalty. Pays on acceptance for all rights.

Advice: "Manuscripts must be for a general audience. Just good plain story telling (make it compelling). No explicit sex or ghoulish violence."

💲 **THE PSYCHIC RADIO**, 1111 Elmwood Avenue, Rochester NY 14620-3005. (585)241-1200, ext. 1288. **Contact:** Lester Billips Jr., editor. Magazine: full size; 32-64 pages; 70 lb. text gloss; 100 lb. text gloss card cover. "My magazine uses stories, poems or essays which are either religious or are slanted toward the growing psychic/occult problem in America today." Bimonthly. Estab. 2001.

Needs: Fantasy (sword and sorcery), horror (futuristic, psychological, supernatural), New Age, psychic/supernatural/occult, religious/inspirational (general, inspirational, religious fantasy), science fiction (soft/sociological). "No plain horror. Must be slanted toward psychic-occult experience. No religious material." Accepts 1-5 mss/issue; 5-10 mss/year. Publishes ms 3-4 months after acceptance. Recently published work by Jean Reed. Publishes short shorts. Also publishes literary essays, poetry. Sometimes comments on rejected mss.

How to Contact: Send complete ms. Accepts submissions by mail. Send complete ms with cover letter. Include estimated word count and brief bio. Responds in 1 month to queries; 1 month to mss. Accepts simultaneous and reprints, multiple submissions. Sample copy for $2.50. Writer's guidelines for #10 SASE.

Payment/Terms: Pays $25-$50. Pays on publication for one-time rights.

Advice: "I look for work with relevance to the growing psychic/occult problem in America today. Be honest and be urgent."

$ ⬛ ◎ QUEEN OF ALL HEARTS, Montfort Missionaries, 26 S. Saxon Ave., Bay Shore NY 11706-8993. (631)665-0726. Fax: (631)665-4349. E-mail: montfort@optonline.net. Website: www.montfortmissionaries.com. **Contact:** Roger M. Charest, S.M.M., managing editor. Magazine: 7¾×10¾; 48 pages; self cover stock; illustrations; photos. Magazine of "stories, articles and features on the Mother of God by explaining the Scriptural basis and traditional teaching of the Catholic Church concerning the Mother of Jesus, her influence in fields of history, literature, art, music, poetry, etc." Bimonthly. Estab. 1950. Circ. 2,000.

Needs: Religious/inspirational. "No mss not about Our Lady, the Mother of God, the Mother of Jesus." Publishes ms 6-12 months after acceptance. **Publishes 6 new writers/year.** Recently published work by Richard O'Donnell and Jackie Clements-Marenda. Sometimes comments on rejected mss.

How to Contact: Send complete ms. Accepts submissions by mail, e-mail, fax, phone. Accepts queries/mss by e-mail and fax (mss by permission only). Responds in 2 months to queries. Sample copy for $2.50 with 9×12 SAE.

Payment/Terms: Pays $40-60. Pays on acceptance Not copyrighted.

Advice: "We are publishing stories with a Marian theme."

$ ⬛ ▢ ◎ QUEEN'S QUARTERLY, A Canadian Review, Queen's University, Kingston ON K7L 3N6 Canada. (613)533-2667. Fax: (613)533-6822. E-mail: qquarter@post.queensu.ca. Website: info.queensu.ca/quarterly. **Contact:** Boris Castel, editor. Magazine: 6×9; 800 pages/year; illustrations. "A general interest intellectual review, featuring articles on science, politics, humanities, arts and letters. Book reviews, poetry and fiction." Quarterly. Estab. 1893. Circ. 3,000.

Needs: Historical, literary, mainstream, novel excerpts, short stories, women's. *"Special emphasis on work by Canadian writers." Accepts 2 mss/issue; 8 mss/year. Publishes ms 6-12 months after acceptance.* **Publishes 5 new writers/year.** Recently published work by Gail Anderson-Dargatz, Tim Bowling, Emma Donohue, Viktor Carr, Mark Jarman, Rick Bowers and Dennis Bock. Also publishes literary essays, literary criticism, poetry.

How to Contact: "Send complete ms with SASE and/or IRC. No reply with insufficient postage." Responds in 2-3 months to queries. Sample copy online. Writer's guidelines online. Reviews fiction.

Payment/Terms: Pays $100-300 for fiction, 2 contributor's copies and 1-year subscription; additional copies $5. Pays on publication for first North American serial rights. Sends galleys to author.

$ ⬛ ROSEBUD, The Magazine For People Who Enjoy Good Writing, Rosebud, Inc., N3310 Asje Rd., Cambridge WI 53523. (608)423-9780. Fax: (608)423-9976. E-mail: jrodclark@smallbytes.net. Website: www.rsbd.net or www.hyperionstudio.com/rosebud. **Contact:** Roderick Clark, editor. Magazine: 7×10; 136 pages; 60 lb. matte; 100 lb. cover; illustrations. Quarterly. Estab. 1993. Circ. 9,000.

Needs: Adventure, condensed novels, ethnic/multicultural, experimental, historical (general), humor/satire, literary, mainstream, novel excerpts, psychic/supernatural/occult, regional, romance (contemporary), science fiction (soft/sociological), serialized novels, slice-of-life vignettes, suspense, translations. "No formula pieces." Each submission must fit loosely into one of the following categories to qualify: City and Shadow (urban setting), Songs of Suburbia (suburban themes), These Green Hills (nature and nostalgia), En Route (any type of travel), Mothers, Daughters, Wives (relationships), Ulysses' Bow (manhood), Paper, Scissors, Rock (childhood, middle age, old age), The Jeweled Prize (concerning love), Lost and Found (loss and discovery), Voices in Other Rooms (historic or of other culture), Overtime (involving work), Anything Goes (humor), I Hear Music (music), Season to Taste (food), Word Jazz (wordplay), Apples to Oranges (miscellaneous, excerpts, profiles). Publishes annual special fiction issue or anthology. Receives 1,200 unsolicited mss/month. Accepts 16 mss/issue; 64 mss/year. Publishes ms 1-3 months after acceptance. **Publishes 70% new writers/year.** Published work by Seamus Heany, Louis Simpson, Allen Ginsberg and Phillip Levine. Publishes short shorts. Also publishes literary essays. Often comments on rejected mss.

How to Contact: Send complete ms. SASE for return of ms. $1 handling fee. to queries; 3 months to mss. Accepts simultaneous and reprints submissions. Sample copy for $6.95 or sample articles online. Writer's guidelines for SASE or on website.

Payment/Terms: Pays $15, and 3 contributor's copies; additional copies $4.40. Pays on publication for first, one-time, second serial (reprint) rights.

Advice: "Each issue will have six or seven flexible departments (selected from a total of sixteen departments that will rotate). We are seeking stories, articles, profiles, and poems of: love, alienation, travel, humor, nostalgia and unexpected revelation. Something has to 'happen' in the pieces we choose, but what happens inside characters is much more interesting to us than plot manipulation. We like good storytelling, real emotion and authentic voice."

N **$ SKYLINE MAGAZINE**, Skyline Publications, P.O. Box 295, Stormville NY 12582-5417. (845)227-5171. Fax: (845)226-8392. Website: www.skylinepublications.com. **Contact:** Victoria Valentine, publisher/editor. "*Skyline Magazine* publishes the excellent work of both established and new authors. Our readers and authors range in age from 17-100. We hope to bring the world together by presenting all forms of the arts through individual expression. We seek fiction and nonfiction stories, human-interest articles/essays, interviews about unique and/or accomplished everyday individuals, as well as celebrities. We feel everyone has something to say that would be of interest to others. Life holds many stories and we are open to all. We normally do not publish politics or religious material. In each issue we publish at least one student author and one student artist." Bimonthly. Estab. 2001. Circ. 1,650.
Needs: Adventure, ethnic/multicultural, experimental, fantasy, historical, horror (if tasteful), humor/satire, mainstream, mystery/suspense, novel excerpts, romance, science fiction, slice-of-life vignettes, suspense, thriller/espionage, western. No erotica. Nothing political or religious. Publishes ms 1-3 months after acceptance. Publishes short shorts. Also publishes literary essays, poetry.
How to Contact: Accepts submissions by mail, e-mail (SkylineEditor@aol.com). Responds in 6-8 weeks to queries; 2-3 months to mss. No simultaneous submissions. Sample copy for $2.50, plus $1.50 postage. Writer's guidelines online or by e-mail.
Payment/Terms: Pays in contributor copies. Acquires first North American serial rights.
Advice: "Send your cleanest edited work. Stories should include strong plot and characters and surprise or powerful conclusions. Much can be said in a few pages. Send interesting, compelling stories with rewarding conclusions."

SLATE AND STYLE, Magazine of the National Federation of the Blind Writers Division, NFB Writer's Division, 2704 Beach Drive, Merrick NY 11566. (516)868-8718. Fax: (516)868-9076. E-mail: loristay@aol.com. **Contact:** Lori Stayer, fiction editor. Newsletter: 8×10; 32 print/40 Braille pages; cassette and large print. "Articles of interest to writers and resources for blind writers." Quarterly. Estab. 1982. Circ. 200.
Needs: Adventure, fantasy, humor/satire, contemporary, blindness. No erotica. "Avoid theme of death." Does not read mss in June or July. **Publishes 2 new writers/year.** Recently published work by Bonnie Lannom, Jane Lansaw, Christina Oakes, and Patricia Hubschman. Publishes short shorts. Also publishes literary criticism, poetry. When requested comments on rejected mss.
How to Contact: Accepts submissions by mail, e-mail. Responds in 3-6 weeks to queries; 3-6 weeks to mss. Sample copy for $2.50.
Payment/Terms: Pays in contributor's copies. Acquires one-time rights. Not copyrighted. Sponsors awards/contests.
Advice: "The best advice I can give is to send you work out; manuscripts left in a drawer have no chance at all."

$ SPELLBOUND MAGAZINE, A fantasy magazine for young readers, Eggplant Productions, 135 Shady Lane, Bolingbrook IL 60440. (630)460-7959. Fax: (801)720-0706. E-mail: spellbound@eggplant-productions .com. Website: www.eggplant-productions.com/spellbound/. **Contact:** Raechel Henderson Moon, fiction editor. Zine: A5; 48 pages; 20 lb. paper; 80 lb. cover stock; some illustrations. "*Spellbound* is a quarterly fantasy magazine for children ages 9-13. Our goal is to introduce children to the wonderful world of fantasy in all its forms. We publish poetry and fiction that is fun, positive and doesn't talk down to our readers." Quarterly. Estab. 1999. Circ. less than 100.
Needs: Children's/juvenile (fantasy). No after school special types of fiction. Receives 15 unsolicited mss/month. Accepts 5 mss/issue; 20 mss/year. Publishes ms 6-12 months after acceptance. **Publishes 50% new writers/year.** Length: 500-2,500 words; average length: 1,800 words. Publishes short shorts. Also publishes poetry. Always comments on rejected mss.
How to Contact: Send complete ms with cover letter. We only accept e-mail submissions. Include estimated word count, brief bio and postal mailing address. Responds in 6 weeks to queries and mss. Accepts simultaneous, multiple submissions. Sample copy for $5. Free on website.
Payment/Terms: Pays $5 and 2 contributor's copies; additional copies $2. Pays on acceptance for first World English-language rights.
Advice: "Looking for fiction that makes me feel something. I am looking for stories that use bold images and memorable characters. Ultimately, I choose the types of stories I would like to read as a child. Read the guidelines carefully. Keep in mind the age of our audience and have fun with the story."

$ STARSHIP EARTH, Black Moon Publishing, P.O. Box 484, Bellaire OH 43906. (740)676-5659. **Contact:** Ms. Silver Shadowhorse, editor. Zine specializing in the sci-fi universe: 8½×11; 60 pages; glossy paper and cover; illustrations; photos. "*Starship Earth* is geared toward science fiction fans of all ages. We do mostly nonfiction, but do print short stories. Our nonfiction focus: profiles of actors and industry people, conventions, behind the scenes articles on films and TV shows. We do cover action/adventure films and TV as well. Heavy *Star Trek* focus. We cover classic science fiction, too." Estab. 1996. Circ. 30,000.
Needs: Fantasy (science fantasy), historical (with a science fiction twist), science fiction (hard science, soft/sociological, historical). No erotic content, horror, "Sword & Sorcery," explicit violence, explicit language or religious material. "Short story needs are filled for the next year." Publishes special fiction issues or anthologies.

Receives 100-200 unsolicited mss/month. Accepts 1 mss/issue; 12 mss/year. Publishes ms 18 months after acceptance. **Publishes 10 new writers/year.** Recently published work by Jackson Frazier and Sean Kennedy. Length: 500-3,000 words; average length: 2,000-3,000 words. Publishes short shorts. Sometimes comments on rejected mss.
How to Contact: Query. Accepts submissions by mail. Include estimated word count, short bio and list of publications. Send SASE for reply, return of ms or send disposable copy of ms. Responds in 1 month to queries; 4 months to mss. Writer's guidelines for #10 SASE. Reviews fiction.
Payment/Terms: Pays 3¢/word. Pays on publication for first, one-time rights.
Advice: "Get our guidelines. Submit in the correct format. Send typed or computer printed manuscripts only. Avoid bad language, explicit sex and violence. Do not include any religious content. Manuscripts stand out when they are professionally presented."

STORYTELLER, Canada's Short Story Magazine, Tyo Communications, 858 Wingate Dr., Ottawa Ontario K1G 1S5. (613)521-9570. E-mail: info@storytellermagazine.com. Website: www.storytellermagazine.com. **Contact:** Melanie Fogel, editor. Magazine: 8½×11; 44 pages; 140 lb. bond paper; 160m gloss cover stock; illustrations. *Storyteller* is Canada's only popular fiction magazine. "We focus on entertaining stories, preferably with a Canadian slant." Quarterly. Estab. 1994. Circ. 2000.
Needs: Adventure, ethnic/multicultural (general), fantasy (twilight zone), historical (general), horror (dark fantasy, futuristic, psychological, supernatural), humor/satire, mainstream, military/war, mystery/suspense (amateur slueth, cozy, police procedural, private eye/hardboiled), psychic/supernatural/occult, romance (contemporary, futuristic/time travel, gothic, historical, regency period, roamantic suspense), science fiction (soft/sociological), thriller/espionage, western (frontier saga, traditional). "No 'hardcore' genre. No 'American' stories, there are hundreds of American magazines for Canadians readers to read. No 'agenda' stories, write a letter to your newspaper instead. No novel excerpts, experimental writing or children's stories." Publishes annual Great Canadian Story Contest issue. Receives 150-200 unsolicited mss/month. Accepts 8-11 mss/issue; 40 mss/year. Publishes ms 6-10 weeks after acceptance. **Publishes 8-12 new writers/year.** Recently published work by Ken Goldman, Vicki Cameron, Leslie Carmichael, Mary Jane Maffini, Rebecca Senese, Barbara Fradkin, Rudy Kremberg, John Ballen. Length: 2,000-6,000 words; average length: 3,500 words. Sometimes comments on rejected mss.
How to Contact: Send complete ms. Send SASE with Canadian postage. Responds in 2 months to mss. Accepts reprints, multiple submissions No simultaneous submissions. Sample copy for $5 plus shipping and postage. Writer's guidelines for SASE or on website.
Payment/Terms: Pays 5¢/word; ¼¢/word for reprints; 2 contributor's copies; additional copies $5. Acquires first North American serial rights. Sponsors awards/contests.
Advice: "We look for characters so real you can smell them, in situations that keep us asking: What happens next? A manuscript stands out when I'm still on the first page and I've forgotten I'm reading a manuscript. Don't be superficial. Short stories need all the depth of a good novel. If you don't know what kind of underwear your character prefers, or which brand of toothpaste, you don't know him/her well enough."

THE STORYTELLER, A Writer's Magazine, 2441 Washington Road, Maynard AR 72444. (870)647-2137. Fax: (870)647-2454. E-mail: storyteller1@cox-internet.com. Website: http://freewebz.com/fossilcreek. **Contact:** Regina Cook Williams, editor. Tabloid: 8½×11; 64 pages; typing paper; glossy cover; illustrations. "This magazine is open to all new writers regardless of age. I will accept short stories in any genre and poetry in any type. Please keep in mind, this is a family publication." Quarterly. Estab. 1996.
  ● Received *People's Choice Awards* and a *Pushcart Prize*. Nonsubscribers must pay reading fee: $1/poem, $2/short story.
Needs: Adventure, historical, humor/satire, literary, mainstream, mystery/suspense, religious/inspirational, romance, western, young adult/teen, senior citizen/retirement, sports. "I will not accept pornography, erotica, science fiction, New Age, foul language, graphic horror or graphic violence." Wants more well-plotted mysteries. Publishes ms 3-9 months after acceptance. **Publishes 30-50 new writers/year.** Recently published work by Mellie Justad, Rick Jankowski, Rick Magers, Barbara Deming, Dusty Richards and Tony Hillerman. Publishes short shorts. Also publishes literary essays, poetry. Sometimes comments on rejected mss.
How to Contact: Accepts submissions by mail. Send complete ms with cover letter. Include estimated word count and 5-line bio. Submission by mail only. Responds in 1 month to queries; 2 months to mss. Accepts simultaneous and reprints submissions. Sample copy for $6. Writer's guidelines for #10 SASE.
Payment/Terms: Sponsors awards/contests.
Advice: "Follow the guidelines. No matter how many times this has been said, writers still ignore this basic and most important rule." Looks for "professionalism, good plots and unique characters. Purchase a sample copy so you know the kind of material we look for. Even though this is for unpublished writers, don't send us something you would not send to paying markets." Would like more "well-plotted mysteries and suspense and a few traditional westerns. Avoid sending anything that children or young adults would not (or could not) read, such as really bad language."

$ THE STRAND MAGAZINE, P.O. Box 1418, Birmingham MI 48012-1418. (248)788-5948. Fax: (248)874-1046. E-mail: strandmag@strandmag.com. Website: strandmag@strandmag.com. **Contact:** A.F. Gulli, editor. "After an absence of nearly half a century, the magazine known to millions for bringing Sir Arthur Conan Doyle's ingenious detective, Sherlock Holmes, to the world has once again appeared on the literary scene. First launched in 1891, *The Strand*, included in its pages the works of some of the greatest writers of the 20th century: Agatha Christie, Dorothy Sayers, Margery Allingham, W. Somerset Maugham, Graham Greene, P.G. Wodehouse, H.G. Wells, Aldous Huxley and many others. In 1950, economic difficulties in England caused a drop in circulation which forced the magazine to cease publication." Quarterly. Estab. 1998. Circ. 50,000.

Needs: Horror, humor/satire, mystery/suspense (detective stories), suspense, tales of the unexpected, tales of terror and the supernatural written in the classic tradition of this century's great author's. "We are NOT interested in submissions with any sexual content." "Stories can be set in any time or place, provided they are well written and the plots interesting and well thought out." Publishes ms 4 months after acceptance.

How to Contact: SASE (IRCs if outside the US). Responds in 1 month to queries; 4 months to mss. Sample copy not available. Writer's guidelines for #10 SASE.

Payment/Terms: Pays $50-175. Pays on acceptance for first North American serial rights.

STUDIO, A Journal of Christians Writing, 727 Peel Street, Albury 2640, Australia. (+61)26021-1135. E-mail: pgrover@bigpond.com. **Contact:** Paul Grover, managing editor. Quarterly. Circ. 300.

Needs: "*Studio* publishes prose and poetry of literary merit, offers a venue for new and aspiring writers, and seeks to create a sense of community among Christians writing." Accepts 30-40 mss/year. **Publishes 40 new writers/ year.** Recently published work by Andrew Lansdown and Benjamin Gilmour.

How to Contact: Accepts submissions by mail. Send SASE. "Overseas contributors must use International postal coupons in place of stamped envelope." Responds in 1 month to mss. Sample copy for $8 (Aus).

Payment/Terms: Pays in copies; additional copies are discounted. Subscription $58 (Australian) for 4 issues (1 year). International draft in Australian dollars and IRC required, or Visa and Mastercard facilities available. "Copyright of individual published pieces remains with the author, while each edition as a whole is copyright to studio."

$ TALEBONES, Fiction on the Dark Edge, Fairwood Press, 5203 Quincy Avenue SE, Auburn WA 98092-8723. (253)735-6552. E-mail: talebones@fairwoodpress.com. **Contact:** Patrick and Honna Swenson, editors. Magazine: digest size; 84 pages; standard paper; glossy cover stock; illustrations; photos. "We like stories that have punch, but still entertain. We like dark science fiction and dark fantasy, humor, psychological and experimental works." Quarterly. Estab. 1995. Circ. 1,000.

Needs: Fantasy (dark), humor/satire, science fiction (hard science, soft/sociological, dark). "No straight slash and hack horror. No cat stories or stories told by young adults." "Would like to see more science fiction." Receives 200 unsolicited mss/month. Accepts 6-7 mss/issue; 24-28 mss/year. Publishes ms 3-4 months after acceptance. **Publishes 2-3 new writers/year.** Recently published work by Leslie What, Tony Daniel, William Barton, Nina Kiriki Hoffman. Length: 1,000-6,000 words; average length: 3,000-4,000 words. Publishes short shorts. Also publishes poetry.

How to Contact: Send complete ms. Accepts submissions by mail, e-mail (talesbones@fairwoodpress.com). Send complete ms with cover letter. Include estimated word count and 1-paragraph bio. Responds in 1 week to queries; 1 month to mss. Sample copy for $6. Writer's guidelines for #10 SASE. Reviews fiction.

Payment/Terms: Pays $1-2. Pays before publication. Acquires first North American serial rights. Sends galleys to author.

Advice: "The story must be entertaining, but should blur the boundary between science fiction and horror. Most of our stories have a dark edge to them, but often are humorous or psychological. Be polite and know how to properly present a manuscript. Include a cover letter, but keep it short and to the point."

THIRTEEN STORIES, Twilight Writers, 1111 Jervis Street, Suite 102, Vancouver BC V6E 2C5. (604)844-7556. E-mail: editor@thirteenstories.com. Website: www.thirteenstories.com. **Contact:** Jennifer M. Brooks, editor. Magazine: 4.15″ × 5.35″; 160 pages; 20# paper; 100# Topkote Coated. "*Thirteen Stories* offers a genuine venue for unpublished short stories, with a focus on new writers. Our goal is to present a quality, softcover pocketbook which is accessible, attractive and available to a broad audience in order to promote those writers who contribute their stories. We choose thirteen stories each month from our database of horror, supernatural and fantasy submissions, based on the quality of the writing and the storyline, with a leaning towards Twilight Zone and H.P. Lovecraft stories. We also try to provide a variety of 'voices' for each issue." Monthly. Estab. 2003. Circ. 200+.

Needs: Fantasy (sword and sorcery, insanity-based delusions), horror (dark fantasy, futuristic, psychological, super-

FOR EXPLANATIONS OF THESE SYMBOLS,
SEE THE INSIDE FRONT AND BACK COVERS OF THIS BOOK.

natural, humorous), mystery/suspense (police procedural), psychic/supernatural/occult, science fiction (soft/socio-logical, hard science/technological). "The publication is not suited to writing for young people (under 15 years of age), and does not work well for poetry due to the size of the pages. We are also not looking for blatant morality works, though stories which have underlying subtle moral convictions are fine." Receives 20-40 unsolicited mss/month. Accepts 13 mss/issue; 156 mss/year. Publishes ms 2 weeks after acceptance. **Publishes 24-30 new writers/year.** Recently published work by Kealan Patrick Burke, David S. Irvin, Matthew McGuire, Scott Thomas, Michael Leo Donovan, David Alexander, Lewis Carlyle, Christopher Fulbright, Andrew Scott Bear. Length: 2,000-4,500 words; average length: 2,500 words. Sometimes comments on rejected mss.

How to Contact: Accepts submissions by e-mail. Responds in 6 months to mss. Accepts simultaneous, multiple submissions. Sample copy for $5. Writer's guidelines online.

Payment/Terms: Pays 2 contributor's copies; additional copies $6. Pays on publication for one-time rights.

Advice: "Pay attention to grammar and punctuation. (It matters! Our read of the story is interrupted if we have to stop and make corrections, even if it is only in our head.) Show, don't tell. Description which invites the reader into the mind of the characters while offering a visceral connection to the situation engages the reader. Take a new perspective on the classic horror concept. Explore 'evil' and the basis of its manifestation. Push the boundaries of what evil and horror are—poke at those beliefs and emotions within yourself and see what emerges. Face your fear, and use it."

🖉 TRANSCENDENT VISIONS, Toxic Evolution Press, 251 S. Olds Blvd., 84-E, Fairless Hills PA 19030-3426. (215)547-7159. **Contact:** David Kime, editor. Zine: letter size; 24 pages; xerox paper; illustrations. "*Transcendent Visions* is a literary zine by and for people who have been labeled mentally ill. Our purpose is to illustrate how creative and articulate mental patients are." Twice a year. Estab. 1992. Circ. 200.

• *Transcendent Visions* has received excellent reviews in many underground publications.

Needs: Experimental, feminist, gay, humor/satire, lesbian. Especially interested in material dealing with mental illness. "I do not like stuff one would find in a mainstream publication. No porn." Would like to see more "quirky, nonmainstream fiction." Receives 5 unsolicited mss/month. Accepts 5-7 mss/issue; 7 mss/year. Publishes ms 3-4 months after acceptance. Recently published work by Brian McCarvill, Michael Fowler, Thomas A. Long, Lisa Donnelly, Roger D. Coleman and Emil Vachas. Publishes short shorts. Also publishes poetry.

How to Contact: Send complete ms with cover letter. Include half-page bio. Send disposable copy of ms. Responds in 3 month to mss. Accepts simultaneous and reprints submissions. Sample copy for $2.

Payment/Terms: Pays 1 contributor's copy. Pays on publication for one-time rights.

Advice: "We like unusual stories that are quirky. We like shorter pieces. Please do not go on and on about what zines you have been published in or awards you have won, etc. We just want to read your material, not know your life story. Please don't swamp me with tons of submissions. Send up to five stories. Please print or type your name and address."

🖉 ◎ UP DARE?, la Pierna Tierna Press, 13304 Rachel Road SE, Albuquerque NM 87123-5631. (505)296-9919. **Contact:** Mary M. Towne, editor. Magazine: digest-sized; 48 pages; illustrations. "The only requirement is that all submitted material must pertain to folks with physical or psychological handicaps." Bimonthly. Estab. 1997.

Needs: No smut. Looks for "honesty, plain language and message." **Publishes 10 new writers/year.** Recently published work by Denyce Hering, Kenneth Austin, Jane Lonnquist, Gordon Graves and Robert Duluty. Publishes short shorts. Also publishes poetry.

How to Contact: Accepts submissions by mail. "We will take single-spaced and even double-sided submissions so long as they are legible. We prefer to optically scan all material to avoid typos. We will not insist on a SASE if you truly have financial limitations. We're trying to make it as easy as possible. We will take short (250 words or less) pieces in Braille." Accepts multiple submissions. Sample copy for $2.50. Writer's guidelines for #10 SASE.

Advice: "Perfect structure and grammar are not as important as verisimilitude. We will not use emphemisms—a chair with a leg missing is a 'three-legged chair,' not a 'challenged seat.' We would like to hear from folks who are handicapped, but we aren't closing the door to others who understand and help or just have opinions to share. We will take reprints if the original appearance is identified."

$🖉 VIRGINIA QUARTERLY REVIEW, University of Virginia, One West Range, P.O. Box 400223, Charlottesville VA 22904-4223. (434)924-3124. Fax: (434)924-1397. Website: www.virginia.edu/vqr. **Contact:** Ted Genoways, editor. "A national journal of literature and thought. A lay, intellectual audience; people who are not out-and-out scholars but who are interested in ideas and literature." Quarterly. Estab. 1925. Circ. 4,000.

• Offers Emily Clark Balch Award for best puplished short story of the year.

Needs: Adventure, ethnic/multicultural, feminist, historical, humor/satire, literary, mainstream, mystery/suspense, novel excerpts, romance, serialized novels, translations. "No pornography." Accepts 3 mss/issue; 20 mss/year. Publishes ms 1 year after acceptance.

How to Contact: Send complete ms. SASE. Responds in 2 weeks to queries; 2 months to mss. Sample copy for $5. Writer's guidelines online.

Payment/Terms: Pays $10/page maximum. Pays on publication for first, "will transfer upon request." rights.

Advice: Looks for "stories with a somewhat Southern dialect and/or setting. Humor is welcome; stories involving cancer and geriatrics are not."

$ ☑ ◎ WEBER STUDIES, Vices and Viewpoints of the Contemporary West, 1214 University Circle, Ogden UT 84408-1214. (801)626-6473. E-mail: blroghaar@weber.edu. Website: http://weberstudies.weber.edu. **Contact:** Brad L. Roghaar, editor. Magazine: 7½×10; 120-140 pages; coated paper; 4-color cover; illustrations; photos. "We seek the following themes: preservation of and access to wilderness, environmental cooperation, insight derived from living in the West, cultural diversity, changing federal involvement in the region, women and the West, implications of population growth, a sense of place, etc. We love good writing that reveals human nature as well as natural environment." Triannual. Estab. 1984. Circ. 1,000.

Needs: Adventure, comics/graphic novels, ethnic/multicultural, experimental, feminist, gay, historical, humor/satire, literary, mainstream, military/war, mystery/suspense, New Age, psychic/supernatural/occult, regional (contemporary western U.S.), science fiction, translations, western (frontier sage, tradtional, contemporary), short story collections. No children's/juvenile, erotica, religious or young adult/teen. Receives 50 unsolicited mss/month. Accepts 3-6 mss/issue; 9-18 mss/year. Publishes ms up to 18 months after acceptance. **Publishes "few" new writers/year.** Recently published work by Rex Burns, Ron McFarland and Joseph M. Ditta. Publishes short shorts. Also publishes literary essays, poetry. Sometimes comments on rejected mss.

How to Contact: Send complete ms. Accepts submissions by mail. Send complete ms with a cover letter. Include estimated word count, bio (if necessary), and list of publications (not necessary). Responds in 3 months to mss. Accepts multiple submissions. Sample copy for $10.

Payment/Terms: Pays $70-$150. Pays on publication for first, electronic rights. Requests electronic archive permission. Sends galleys to author.

Advice: "Is it true? Is it new? Is it interesting? Will the story appeal to educated readers who are concerned with the contemporary western U.S.? Declining public interest in reading generally is of concern. We publish both print media and electronic media because we believe the future will expect both options."

Ⓝ $ ☑ ◎ WEIRD TALES, 123 Crooked Lane, King of Prussia PA 19406. (610)275-4463. E-mail: owlswick@comcast.net. **Contact:** George H. Seithers and Darrell Schweitzer, editors. Magazine: 8½×11; 68 pages; white, non-glossy paper; glossy 4-color cover; illustrations. "We publish fantastic fiction, supernatural horror for an adult audience." Quarterly. Estab. 1923. Circ. 10,000.

Needs: Fantasy (sword and sorcery), horror, psychic/supernatural/occult, translations. No hard science fiction or non-fantasy. "We want to see a wide range of fantasy, from sword and sorcery to supernatural horror. We can use some unclassifiables." Receives 400 unsolicited mss/month. Accepts 8 mss/issue; 32 mss/year. Publishes ms 6-18 months after acceptance. Agented fiction 10%. **Publishes 6 new writers/year.** Recently published work by Tanith Lee, Thomas Ligotti, Ian Watson and Lord Dunsany. Length: 10,000 words; average length: 4,000 words. Publishes short shorts. Also publishes poetry. Always comments on rejected mss.

How to Contact: Send complete ms. Send SASE for reply, return of ms or send a disposable copy of ms with SASE. Responds in 2-3 weeks to mss. Accepts multiple submissions No simultaneous submissions. Sample copy for $4.95. Writer's guidelines for #10 SASE or by e-mail. Reviews fiction.

Payment/Terms: Pays 3¢/word and 2 contributor's copies. Acquires first North American serial, plus anthology option rights. Sends galleys to author.

Advice: "We look for imagination and vivid writing. Read the magazine. Get a good grounding in the contemporary horror and fantasy field through the various 'best of the year' anthologies. Avoid the obvious clichés of technicalities of the hereafter, the mechanics of vampirism, generic Tolkien-clone fantasy. In general, it is to be honest and emotionally moving rather than clever. Avoid stories which have nothing of interest for the allegedly 'surprise' ending."

Ⓝ ◎ WISCONSIN ACADEMY REVIEW, Wisconsin Academy of Sciences, Arts & Letters, 1922 University Ave., Madison WI 53726. (608)263-1692. Fax: (608)265-3039. E-mail: jfischer@wisconsinacademy.org. Website: www.wisconsinacademy.org. **Contact:** Joan Fischer, editor. Magazine: 8½×11; 56-64 pages; 75 lb. coated paper; coated cover stock; illustrations; photos. "The *Review* reflects the focus of the sponsoring institution with its editorial emphasis on Wisconsin's intellectual, cultural, social and physical environment. It features short fiction, poetry, essays, nonfiction articles and Wisconsin-related art." Quarterly. Estab. 1954. Circ. 3,000.

Needs: "Wants well-written, journalistic pieces about new or intriguing aspects of Wisconsin thought and culture. Author must have a Wisconsin connection or fiction must have strong Wisconsin theme or setting." No genre fiction. Receives 5-6 unsolicited mss/month. Accepts 1-2 mss/issue; 6-8 mss/year. **Publishes some new writers/year.** Also publishes literary essays, literary criticism, poetry.

How to Contact: Send complete ms with SAE and state author's connection to Wisconsin, the prerequisite. Accepts multiple submissions. Sample copy for $3. Writer's guidelines for #10 SASE.

Payment/Terms: Pays 2-3 contributor's copies. Acquires first rights.

Advice: "Manuscript publication is at the discretion of the editor based on space, content and balance. We accept only previously unpublished poetry and fiction. We publish emerging as well as established authors."

Ⓝ ☑ WRITERS FOR READERS, Writers Haven Ltd., P.O. Box 465, Cave Spring GA 30124-465. (706)777-1634. E-mail: bgmc1020@aol.com. **Contact:** B.G. McElwee, editor. Magazine: 11×8½; 100 pages; 20 lb. paper; 20 lb. cover stock; illustrations; photos. The magazine was created with the primary goal of publishing previously unpublished authors. "We sell only enough ads to help pay publishing cost." Quarterly. Estab. 2002. Circ. 120.

Needs: Experimental, family saga, fantasy (space fantasy), historical (general), horror (futuristic, supernatural), humor/satire, literary, mainstream, military/war, mystery/suspense (amateur sleuth), religious/inspirational (children's religious, inspirational, religious thriller), romance (contemporary, historical, romantic suspense), science fiction (soft/sociological), thriller/espionage, western, young adult/teen (adventure, fantasy/science fiction, historical, horror, mystery/suspense, sports, western). No vulgar language or explicit sex. Publishes ms 6 months after acceptance. Recently published work by Jimmy W. Hall, Bernice Anderson, Danny Lee Ingram, Cathy Lemelin, Tim Whetstone, Thad Matheny, Bill Monday. Length: 100-5,000 words; average length: 3,000 words. Publishes short shorts. Also publishes literary essays, poetry. Often comments on rejected mss.
How to Contact: Send complete ms. Accepts submissions by e-mail. Send SASE for return of mss and disposable copy of the ms and #10 SASE for reply only. Responds in 4 weeks to queries; 6 months to mss. Accepts simultaneous and reprints submissions. Sample copy for $5. Writer's guidelines for SASE or by e-mail.
Payment/Terms: Pays contributor's copy; additional copies $5. Pays on publication for one-time rights.
Advice: "It must immediately catch the interest of the reader. Do not rewrite and rewrite your story. Write it, check it for grammar and punctuation then submit it."

N: $ ☑ ◎ ZAHIR, Unforgettable Tales, Zahir Publishing, 315 South Coast Hwy. 101, Suite U8, Encinitas CA 92024. E-mail: stempchin@zahirtales.com. Website: www.zahirtales.com. **Contact:** Sheryl Tempchin, editor. Magazine: Digest-size; 60 pages; heavy stock paper; glossy, full color cover stock; illustrations. "We publish quality speculative fiction for intelligent adult readers. Our goal is to bridge the gap between literary and genre fiction, and present a publication that is both entertaining and aesthetically pleasing." Triannual. Estab. 2003.
Needs: Fantasy (surrealism, magical realism), literary, psychic/supernatural/occult, science fiction, surrealism, magical realism. No children's stories or stories that deal with excessive violence or anything pornographic. Accepts 6-8 mss/issue; 18-24 mss/year. Publishes ms 2-12 months after acceptance. **Publishes 6 new writers/year.** Sometimes comments on rejected mss.
How to Contact: Send complete ms. Accepts submissions by e-mail (stempchin@zahirtales.com). Send SASE (or IRC) for return of ms or disposable copy of the ms and #10 SASE for reply only. Responds in 1-2 weeks to queries; 1-3 months to mss. Accepts reprints submissions No simultaneous submissions. Sample copy for $5 (US), $6.50 elsewhere. Writer's guidelines for #10 SASE, by e-mail, or online.
Payment/Terms: Pays $10 and 2 contributor's copies. Pays on publication for first, second serial (reprint) rights.
Advice: "The stories we are most likely to buy are well written, have interesting, well developed characters and/or ideas that fascinate, chill, thrill, or amuse us. They must have some element of the fantastic or surreal."

◎ ZOPILOTE, Oldie Publications, 824 S. Mill Avenue, Suite 219, Tempe AZ 85281. (480)557-7195. E-mail: zopilote1@mindspring.com. Website: www.zopilote.com. **Contact:** Marco Albarran, publisher. Magazine: 8½ × 11; 34 pages; illustrations; photos. "*Zopilote* magazine is one of the few cultural magazines that promotes indigenous and Latino cultures in the U.S. We publish material pertinent to the history, ways of life, philosophies, traditions and changes taking place right now. Bimonthly. Estab. 1993. Circ. 5,000.
Needs: Comics/graphic novels, ethnic/multicultural (indigenous Latino), historical (indigenous Latino), literary, science fiction (ancient science of the Americas), western (indigenous Latino). "No religious, romance, erotica." Receives 5-10 unsolicited mss/month. Accepts 3 mss/issue; 18-20 mss/year. Publishes ms 3-5 months after acceptance. **Publishes 60-70% new writers/year.** Recently published work by Roberto Rodriquez, Cristina Gonzalez and Carmen Vaxones Martinez. Length: 150-500 words; average length: 300 words. Publishes short shorts. Also publishes literary essays, literary criticism, poetry. Sometimes comments on rejected mss.
How to Contact: Send complete ms. Accepts submissions by mail, e-mail (zopilote1@mindspring.com). Send complete ms with cover letter. Include estimated word count, brief bio and list of publications. Responds in 6 weeks to queries; 6 weeks to mss. Accepts simultaneous and reprints, multiple submissions. Sample copy for 8½ × 11 SAE and $3 postage first-class stamps. Writer's guidelines by e-mail. Reviews fiction.
Payment/Terms: Pays 5 contributor's copies; additional copies $3.50.

Online Markets

As production and distribution costs go up and subscribers numbers fall, more and more magazines are giving up print publication and moving online. Relatively inexpensive to maintain and quicker to accept and post submissions, online fiction sites are growing fast in numbers and legitimacy. Says the editor of *EWGPresents*: "We have the means to reach a universal audience by the click of a mouse. Writers are gifted with a new medium of exposure and the future demands taking advantage of this format."

Writers exploring online opportunities for publication will find a rich and diverse community of voices. Genre sites are strong, in particular those for science fiction/fantasy and horror (see the award-winning *Scifi.com* and *Far Sector* SFFH). Mainstream short fiction markets are also growing exponentially (see *American Feed Magazine* and *Cenotaph*, among many others). Online literary journals range from the traditional (*The Barcelona Review, Paumonok Review*) to those with a decidedly more quirky, regional bent (*The Dead Mule School of Southern Literature, Big Country Peacock Chronicle*). Writers will also find here more highly experimental work that could exist no where else than in cyberspace, such as the hypertext fiction found on *Drunken Boat*.

Online journals are gaining respect for the writers who appear on their sites. As Jill Adams, publisher and editor of *The Barcelona Review*, says: "We see our Internet review, like the small independent publishing houses, as a means of counterbalancing the big-business mentality of the multi-national publishing houses. At the same time, we want to see our writers 'make it big.' Last year we heard from more and more big houses asking about some of our new writers, wanting contact information, etc. So I see a healthy trend in that big houses are, finally—after being skeptical and confused—looking at it seriously and scouting online."

While the medium of online publication is different, the traditional rules of publishing apply to submissions. Writers should research the site and archives carefully, looking for a match in sensibility for their work among the varied sites publishing. They should then follow submission guidelines exactly, and submit courteously. True, these sites aren't bound by traditional print schedules, so your work theoretically may be published more quickly. But that doesn't mean a larger staff, so do exercise patience with editors considering your manuscript.

Also, while reviewing the listings in this market section, notice they are grouped differently from other market listings. In our literary magazines section, for example, you'll find primarily only publications searching for literary short fiction. But Online Markets are grouped by medium, so you'll find publishers of mystery short stories listed next to those looking for horror next to those specializing in flash fiction, so review with care. In addition, those online markets with print counterparts, such as *North American Review*, you will find listed in the print markets sections.

A final note about online publication: like literary journals, the majority of these markets are either nonpaying or very low paying. In addition, writers will not receive print copies of the publications because of the medium. So in most cases, do not expect to be paid for your exposure.

$ ◨ THE ABSINTHE LITERARY REVIEW, P.O. Box 328, Spring Green WI 53588. E-mail: staff@absinthe-literary-review.com. Website: www.absinthe-literary-review.com. **Contact:** Charles Allen Wyman. Electronic literary magazine; print issue coming 2004-2005. "*ALR* publishes short stories, novel excerpts, poems and literary essays. Our target audience is the literate individual who enjoys creative language use, character-driven fiction and the clashing of worlds—real and surreal, poetic and prosaic, sacred and transgressive."

Needs: "Transgressive works dealing with sex, death, disease, madness, and the like; the clash of archaic with modern-day; archetype, symbolism; surrealism, philosophy, physics; existential, and post-modern flavoring; experimental or flagrantly textured (but not sloppy or casual) fiction; intense crafting of language from the writer's writer.

See website for information on our annual Eros and Thanatos issue and the Absinthe Editors' Prize. Anathemas: mainstream storytellers, "Oprah" fiction, high school or beginner fiction, poetry or fiction that contains no capital letters or punctuation, "hot" trends, genre and utterly normal prose or poetry, first, second or third drafts, pieces that exceed our stated word count (5,000 max.) by thousands of words, writers who do not read and follow our onsite guidelines." **Publishes 3-6 new writers/year.** Recently published work by Bruce Holland, Arlene Ang, Virgil Suarez, James Reidel and Dan Pope.

How to Contact: Accepts submissions by mail, e-mail. Read online guidelines, then send a single fiction submission per reading period to fiction@absinthe-literary-review.com; 3-7 poems to poetry@absinthe-literary-review.com; and single essays to essays@absinthe-literary-review.com. Sample copy not available.

Advice: "Be erudite and daring in your writing. Draw from the past to drag meaning from the present. Kill ego and cliche. Invest your work with layers of meaning that subtly reveal multiple realities. Do not submit pieces that are riddled with spelling errors and grammatical snafus. Above all, be professional. For those of you who don't understand exactly what this means, please send your manuscripts elsewhere until you have experienced the necessary epiphany."

📰 ⬭ ☑ ALIENSKIN MAGAZINE, An Online Science Fiction, Fantasy & Horror Magazine, Froggy Bottom Press, PO Box 495, Beaver PA 15009. E-mail: alienskin@alienskinmag.com. Website: www.alienskinmag.com. **Contact:** Feature fiction: K. A. Patterson; Flash fiction: Phil Adams. Online magazine. "Our magazine was created for, and strives to help, aspiring writers of SFFH. We endeavor to promote and educate genre writers, helping them learn and develop the skills they need to produce marketable short stories." Monthly. Estab. 2002. Circ. 385+ internet.

Needs: Fantasy (dark fantasy, sword and sorcery), horror (dark fantasy, futuristic, psychological, psychic/supernatural/occult), science fiction (hard science/technological, soft/sociological). "No excessive blood, gore, erotica or vulgarity. No experimental or speculative fiction that does not use basic story elements of character, conflict, action and resolution. No esoteric ruminations." Receives 50-100 unsolicited mss/month. Accepts 9-21 mss/issue; 228-252 mss/year. Publishes ms 30-60 days after acceptance. **Publishes 91-100 new writers/year.** Recently published work by Chaz Siu, Stephen D. Rogers, Wade Chabassol, Bonnie J. Rowan and Anne Skalitza. Length: 1,000-3,500 words; average length: 2,200 words. Publishes short shorts. Also publishes poetry. Always comments on rejected mss.

How to Contact: Send complete ms. Accepts submissions by e-mail. estimated word count, brief bio, name, address, and e-mail address. Send disposable copy of ms and #10 SASE for reply only. Responds in 1-2 weeks to queries; 1-2 months to mss. Accepts multiple submissions. Sample copy online. Writer's guidelines online.

Payment/Terms: ½¢/word. Pays on acceptance for first, electronic rights. Sponsors awards/contests.

Advice: "We look for interesting stories that offer something unique; stories that use basic story elements of character, conflict, action and resolution. We like the dark, twisted side of SFFH genres. Read our guidelines and follow the rules, treating the submission process as a serious business transaction. Only send stories that have been spell-checked, and proof-read at least twice. Try to remember that editors who offer a critique on manuscripts do so to help you as a writer, not to make you a writer."

☑ ☻ THE ALSOP REVIEW. E-mail: alsop@alsopreview.com. Website: www.alsopreview.com. **Contact:** Jaime Wasserman, editor. Web zine. "*The Alsop Review* publishes only the best poetry and fiction. We are not a zine since we do not publish regular issues. Rather we are a permanent showcase."

Needs: Experimental, literary. "No genre work or humor for its own sake. No pornography. We would like to see more experiemental and unconventional works. Surprise me." Recently published work by Kyle Jarrard, Dennis Must, Kristy Nielsen, Bob Riche and Linda Sue Park.

How to Contact: Accepts submissions by e-mail (jw@alsopreview.com). Accepts reprints submissions. Sample copy not available.

Payment/Terms: "None. We offer a permanent 'home' on the web for writers and will pull and add material to their pages upon request."

Advice: "Read, read, read. Treat submissions to web zines as carefully as you would a print magazine. Research the market first. For every great web zine, there are a hundred mediocre ones. Remember that once your work is on the web, chances are it will be there for a very long time. Put your best stuff out there and take advantage of the opportunities to re-publish work from print magazines."

☑ AMERICAN FEED MAGAZINE, American Feed Magazine, 35 Hinsdale Ave., Winsted CT 06098. (860)738-4897. E-mail: editor@americanfeedmagazine.com. Website: www.americanfeedmagazine.com. **Contact:** Shaw Izikson, editor. Online magazine. "We like to give a place for new voices to be heard, as well as established voices a place to get a wider audience for their work." Estab. 1994.

Needs: Adventure, ethnic/multicultural, experimental, family saga, fantasy, feminist, glitz, historical, horror, humor/satire, literary, mainstream, mystery/suspense, New Age, psychic/supernatural/occult, science fiction, thriller/espionage. Receives 100 unsolicited mss/month. Accepts 15 mss/issue. **Publishes 20 new writers/year.** Recently published work by Richard Lind, Bill Glose, Angela Conrad, Ryan Miller, Joshua Farber and Daniel LaFavbre. Average length: 1,500 words. words. Publishes short shorts. Also publishes literary essays, literary criticism, poetry. Comments on rejected mss.

How to Contact: Send complete ms. Accepts submissions by mail. Include estimated word count and brief bio. Responds in 2 months to queries; 2 months to mss. Accepts simultaneous and reprints, multiple submissions. Sample copy online. Writer's guidelines by e-mail. Reviews fiction.

Payment/Terms: Acquires one-time rights.

Advice: "Make sure the story flows naturally, not in a forced way. You don't need a vivid imagination to write fiction, poetry or anything. Just look around you, because life is usually the best inspiration."

$ART OF HORROR, 708 S. 15th, Manitowoc WI 54220. E-mail: raven13@discover-net.net. Website: www.horrorseek.com/horror/ravenbroom. **Contact:** Danielle Naibert. "We want original stories/poems that makes readers cring-gasp or double check their doors before they go to sleep at night." Quarterly. Estab. 2000. HWA Association.

• Bram Stoker recommended 2 years running.

Needs: Horror (dark fantasy, futuristic, psychological, supernatural, pulp). Receives 100+ unsolicited mss/month. Accepts 4-5 mss/issue; 18-20 mss/year. Does not read mss October, December, April. Publishes ms 1-12 months after acceptance. **Publishes 2 new writers/year.** Recently published work by Kenny Crist, Kenneth Goldman. Length: 1,200-5,000 words; average length: 2,500 words. Publishes short shorts. Also publishes poetry. Sometimes comments on rejected mss.

How to Contact: Send complete ms. Responds in 2-6 weeks to mss. No simultaneous submissions. Writer's guidelines online. Reviews fiction.

Payment/Terms: Pays $100-$500. 3 months. Acquires one-time, electronic rights. Sponsors awards/contests.

Advice: "Make a story stand out with great characters, fantastic atmosphere. Don't bore me with re-hashed plots. Skip the 10 dollar words; if I have to dig out the dictionary I know my readers won't bother reading. Be entertaining! Check your work for any errors."

ASCENT, Aspirations for Artists, Ascent, 1560 Arbutus Dr., Nanoose Bay BC C9P 9C8 Canada. E-mail: ascent@bcsupernet.com. Website: www.bcsupernet.com/users/ascent. **Contact:** David Fraser, editor. E-zine specializing in short fiction (all genres) and poetry, essays, visual art: 40 electronic pages; illustrations; photos. "*Ascent* is a quality electronic publication dedicated to promotions and encouraging aspiring writers of any genre. The focus however is toward interesting experimental writing in dark mainstream, literary, science fiction, fantasy and horror. Poetry can be on any theme. Essays need to be unique, current and have social, philosophical commentary." Quarterly. Estab. 1997.

Needs: Erotica, experimental, fantasy (space fantasy), feminist, horror (dark fantasy, futuristic, psychological, supernatural), literary, mainstream, mystery/suspense, New Age, psychic/supernatural/occult, science fiction (hard science/technological, soft/sociological). Receives 20-30 unsolicited mss/month. Accepts 5 mss/issue; 20 mss/year. Publishes ms 3 months after acceptance. **Publishes 5-10 new writers/year.** Recently published work by Taylor Graham, Janet Buck, Jim Manton, Steve Cartwright, Don Stockard, Margaret Karmazin, Bill Hughes. Length: 500-4,000 words; average length: 2,000 words. Publishes short shorts. Also publishes literary essays, literary criticism, poetry. Sometimes comments on rejected mss.

How to Contact: "Query by e-mail with word attachment." Include estimated word count, brief bio and list of publications. Responds in 1 week to queries; 3 months to mss. Accepts simultaneous and reprints, multiple submissions. Guidelines by e-mail or on website. Reviews fiction.

Payment/Terms: "No payment at this time. Rights remain with author."

Advice: "Short fiction should first of all tell a good story, take the reader to new and interesting imaginary or real places. Short fiction should use language lyrically and effectively, be experimental in either form or content and take the reader into realms where they can analyze and think about the human condition. Write with passion for your material, be concise and economical and let the reader work to unravel your story. In terms of editing, always proofread to the point where what you submit is the best it possibly can be. Never be discouraged if your work is not accepted; it may just not be the right fit for a current publication."

THE BARCELONA REVIEW, Correu Vell 12 -2, 08002, Barcelona, Spain. (00) 34 93 319 15 96. E-mail: editor@barcelonareview.com. Website: www.barcelonareview.com. **Contact:** Jill Adams, editor. "*TBR* is an international review of contemporary, cutting-edge fiction published in English, Spanish and Catalan. Our aim is to bring both new and established writers to the attention of a larger audience. Well-known writers such as Alicia Erian in the U.S., Michel Faber in the U.K., Carlos Gardini in Argentina, and Nuria Amat in Spain, for example, were not known outside their countries until appearing in *TBR*. Our multilingual format increases the audience all the more. Internationally-known writers, such as Irvine Welsh and Douglas Coupland, have contributed stories that

 A BULLET INTRODUCES COMMENTS by the editor of *Novel & Short Story Writer's Market* indicating special information about the listing.

ran in small press anthologies available only in one country. We try to keep abreast of what's happening internationally and to present the best finds every two months. Our intended audience is anyone interested in high-quality contemporary, fiction that often (but not always) veers from the mainstream; we assume that our readers are well read and familiar with contemporary fiction in general."

- *The Barcelona Review* ranked on *Writer's Digest*'s "Top 30" list of best markets for fiction writers and in the top 5 of *WD*'s best online fiction publications.

Needs: Short fiction. "Our bias is towards potent and powerful cutting-edge material; given that general criteria we are open to all styles and techniques and all genres. No slice-of-life stories, vignettes or sentimental writing, and nothing that does not measure up, in your opinion, to the quality of work in our review, which we expect submitters to be familiar with." **Publishes 20 new writers/year.** Recently published work by Louise Erdich, Adam Haslett, Mark Winegardner, Adam Johnson, Thomas Glave, Kate Atkinson, Patricia Duncker, Julie Orringer.

How to Contact: Send submissions by e-mail as an attached file. Hard copies accepted but cannot be returned. No simultaneous submissions.

Payment/Terms: "In lieu of pay we offer a highly professional Spanish translation to English language writers and vice versa to Spanish writers."

Advice: "Send top drawer material that has been drafted two, three, four times—whatever it takes. Then sit on it for a while and look at it afresh. Keep the text tight (rewrite until every unnecessary word is eliminated). Grab the reader in the first paragraph and don't let go. Keep in mind that a perfectly crafted story that lacks a punch of some sort won't cut it. Make it new, make it different. Surprise the reader in some way. Read the best of the short fiction available in your area of writing to see how yours measures up. Don't send anything off until you feel it's ready and then familiarize yourself with the content of the review/magazine to which you are submitting."

☐ ☑ BIG COUNTRY PEACOCK CHRONICLE, Online Magazine, RR1, Box 89K-112, Aspermont TX 79502. (806)254-2322. E-mail: publisher@peacockchronicle.com. Website: www.peacockchronicle.com. **Contact:** Audrey Yoeckel, owner/publisher. Online magazine. "We publish articles, commentaries, reviews, interviews, short stories, serialized novels and novellas, poetry, essays, humor, and anecdotes. Due to the nature of Internet publication, guidelines for length of written works are flexible and acceptance is based more on content. Content must be family friendly. Writings that promote hatred or violence will not be accepted. *The Big Country Peacock Chronicle* is dedicated to the preservation of community values and traditional folk cultures. In today's society, we are too often deprived of a solid feeling of community which is so vital to our security and well-being. It is our attempt to keep the best parts of our culture intact. Our goal is to build a place for individuals, no matter the skill level, to test their talents and get feedback from others in a non-threatening, friendly environment. The original concept for the magazine was to open the door to talented writers by providing not only a publishing medium for their work but support and feedback as well. It was created along the lines of a smalltown publication in order to remove some of the anxiety about submitting works for first-time publication." Quarterly. Estab. 2000.

- *Big Country Peacock Chronicle* ranked on *Writer's Digest* "Top 30" list of best markets for fiction writers.

Needs: Adventure, children's/juvenile (adventure, easy-to-read, fantasy, historical, mystery, preschool, series, sports), ethnic/multicultural (general), family saga, fantasy (space fantasy, sword and sorcery), gay, historical (general), horror (futuristic, supernatural, psychological), humor/satire, literary, military/war, mystery/suspense (amateur sleuth, police procedural, private eye/hardboiled), psychic/supernatural/occult, regional, religious/inspirational (children's religious), romance (gothic, historical, romantic suspense), science fiction (soft/sociological), thriller/espionage, translations (frontier saga, traditional), western. 'While the genre of the writing or the style does not matter, excessive or gratuitous violence, foul language and sexually explicit material is not acceptable." Accepts 2-3 (depending on length) mss/issue. Publishes ms 3 months after acceptance. Average length: 2,500 words. Publishes short shorts. Also publishes literary essays, literary criticism, poetry. Always comments on rejected mss.

How to Contact: Include estimated word count, brief bio, list of publications and Internet contact information; i.e. e-mail, website address. Responds in 3 weeks to queries; 6 weeks to mss. Accepts simultaneous and reprints, multiple submissions. Writer's guidelines online. Reviews fiction.

Payment/Terms: Acquires electronic rights. Sends galleys to author.

Advice: "We look for continuity and coherence. The work must be clean with a minimum of typographical errors. The advantage to submitting works to us is the feedback and support. We work closely with our writers, offering promotion, resource information, moral support and general help to achieve success as writers. While we recommend doing businesss with us via the Internet, we have also published writers who do not have access. For those new to the Internet, we also provide assistance with the best ways to use it as a medium for achieving success in the field."

$ ☑ BLACKBIRD, an online journal of literature and the arts, Virginia Commonwealth University Department of Fiction, PO Box 843083, Richmond VA 23284. (804)225-4729. E-mail: blackbird@vcu.edu. Website: www.blackbird.vcu.edu. **Contact:** William Tester, Mary Flinn, Gregory Donovan, editors. Online journal: 80+ pages if printed; illustrations; photos. "We strive to maintain the highest quality of writing and design, bringing the best things about a print magazine to the outside world. We publish fiction that is carefully crafted, thoughtful and suprising." Semiannual. Estab. 1978. Circ. 2,000.

Needs: Adventure, comics/graphic novels, condensed novels, confessions, erotica, ethnic/multicultural, experimental, family saga, fantasy, feminist, gay, glitz, historical, horror, humor/satire, lesbian, literary, mainstream, military/war, mystery/suspense, New Age, novel excerpts, psychic/supernatural/occult, regional, religious/inspirational, serialized novels, slice-of-life vignettes, suspense, thriller/espionage, translations, western, young adult/teen. Does not want science fiction, romance, children's Receives 50-100 unsolicited mss/month. Accepts 15 mss/issue; 8-10 mss/year. Does not read from May 15-August 15. Publishes ms 3-6 months after acceptance. **Publishes 1-2 new writers/year.** Average length: 5,000-6,500 words. Also publishes literary essays, literary criticism, poetry. Sometimes comments on rejected mss.

How to Contact: Send complete ms. Inlude cover letter, name, address, telephone number, brief biographical comment. Responds in 6 months to mss. Accepts simultaneous submissions. Sample copy not available. Writer's guidelines online.

Payment/Terms: Pays $200 for fiction, $40 for poetry. Pays on publication for first North American serial rights.

Advice: "We like a story that invites us into its world, that engages our senses, soul and mind."

THE BLUE MOON REVIEW, 14313 Winter Ridge Lane, Midlothian VA 23113. E-mail: fiction@thebluemoon.com. Website: www.thebluemoon.com. **Contact:** Theron Montgomery, fiction editor. Electronic magazine: illustrations and photos. Quarterly. Estab. 1994. Circ. 25,000.

● *The Blue Moon Review* ranked on *Writer's Digest*'s "Top 30" list of best markets for fiction writers.

Needs: Experimental, feminist, gay, lesbian, literary, mainstream, regional, translations. "No genre fiction or condensed novels." Receives 40-70 unsolicited mss/month. Accepts 7-10 mss/issue; 51-60 mss/year. Publishes ms 9 months after acceptance. Recently published work by Edward Falco, Deborah Eisenberg, Robert Sward and Aldo Alvarez. Publishes short shorts. Also publishes literary essays, literary criticism, poetry. Sometimes comments on rejected mss.

How to Contact: Send complete ms. Accepts submissions by e-mail (only.). Include a brief bio, list of publications and e-mail address if available. Does not accept submissions via regular mail. Responds in 2 months to mss. Accepts simultaneous submissions. Sample copy online. Writer's guidelines online.

Payment/Terms: Acquires first North American serial rights.

Advice: "We look for strong use of language or strong characterization. Manuscripts stand out by their ability to engage a reader on an intellectual or emotional level. Present characters with depth regardless of age and introduce intelligent concepts that have resonance and relevance."

$ N ⬚ BRADY MAGAZINE, **Where Writers Meet Writers**. E-mail: submissions@bradymagazine.com. Website: www.bradymagazine.com. **Contact:** Krissy Brady, editor. "*Brady Magazine* is not only a publication, but an online resource for writers. We offer online workshops, a directory of freelance publications, and we also give writers the opportunity to join our 'swap team' to make it easier for struggling writers to find jobs." Bimonthly. Estab. 2003.

Needs: Adventure, erotica, ethnic/multicultural, experimental, family saga, fantasy, feminist, gay, glitz, historical, horror, humor/satire, lesbian, literary, mainstream, military/war, mystery/suspense, New Age, psychic/supernatural/occult, regional, religious/inspirational, romance, science fiction, western. "Nothing that would come with artwork, as we want to concentrate on the literary end of publishing. We are very flexible when it comes to fictional genres that writers would like to submit, as we do not want *Brady Magazine* to become predictable." Receives 100-150 unsolicited mss/month. Accepts 3 mss/issue; 18 mss/year. Publishes ms 2-4 months after acceptance. **Publishes 10 new writers/year.** Length: 500-3,000 words; average length: 2,500 words. Publishes short shorts. Also publishes poetry. Always comments on rejected mss.

How to Contact: Send complete ms. Accepts submissions by e-mail. Please send submissions in the body of the e-mail; no attachments. Responds in 3 weeks to queries; 2 months to mss. Accepts simultaneous and reprints, multiple submissions. Sample copy online. Writer's guidelines by e-mail.

Payment/Terms: Pays $10 per short story. Pays on publication Not copyrighted.

Advice: "We don't really have specific criteria when selecting fiction; all we want is the writer to be comfortable and confident with the work they are sending us."

$ ⬚ THE CAFE IRREAL, **International Imagination**. E-mail: editors@cafeirreal.com. Website: www.cafeirreal.com. **Contact:** Alice Whittenburg, G.S. Evans, editors. E-zine: illustrations. "*The Cafe Irreal* is a webzine focusing on short stories and short shorts of an irreal nature." Semiannual. Member, Council of Literary Magazine and Presses.

● *The Cafe Irreal* ranked as one ot the top five online fiction markets for writers by *Writer's Digest*.

FOR EXPLANATIONS OF THESE SYMBOLS,
SEE THE INSIDE FRONT AND BACK COVERS OF THIS BOOK.

Needs: Experimental, fantasy (literary), science fiction (literary), translations. "No horror or 'slice-of-life' stories; no genre or mainstream fiction or fantasy." Accepts 10-15 mss/issue; 20-30 mss/year. Recently published work by (translations) Istvan Orkeny, Marco Denevi, and Ana Maria Shua. Publishes short shorts. Also publishes literary essays, literary criticism, poetry. Often comments on rejected mss.

How to Contact: Accepts submissions by e-mail. "No attachments, include submission in body of e-mail. Include estimated word count." Responds in 2 months to mss. Accepts reprints submissions. Sample copy online. Writer's guidelines online.

Payment/Terms: Pays on publication for electronic rights. Sends galleys to author.

Advice: "Forget formulas. Write about what you don't know, take me places I couldn't possibly go, don't try to make me care about the characters. Read short fiction by writers such as Franz Kafka, Kobo Abe, Julio Cortazar, Leonora Carrington and Stanislaw Lem. Also read our website and guidelines."

CARVE MAGAZINE, Mild Horse Press, P.O. Box 72231, Davis CA 95617. E-mail: editor@carvezine.com. Website: www.carvezine.com. **Contact:** Melvin Sterne, editor. Bimonthly online journal with annual printed "best of" anthology. *Carve Magazine* nominates for the Pushcart, O. Henry, Best American and Ezinik Anthology Series. Bimonthly. Estab. 2000. Circ. 8,500. Member, CLMP.

• Fiction appearing in *Carve Magazine* has been nominated for the Pushcart, O. Henry, Best American and e2ink Anthology Series for best online fiction.

Needs: Literary (fiction). No genre, poetry or nonfiction. Accepts Publishes 70+ stories/year. mss./year. **Publishes 10-20 new writers/year.** Recently published work by Gina Ochsner, Krista McGruder, Sefi Atta, Angela Tung, A.C Koch. Occasionally comments on rejected mss.

How to Contact: Send complete ms. Accepts submissions by e-mail. Responds in 2-3 months to mss. Accepts simultaneous submissions "if identified, except for contest." Writer's guidelines online.

Payment/Terms: Sponsors awards/contests.

Advice: "We look for stories with strong characterization, conflict, and tightly written prose. Do you know what a fictive moment is?"

CENOTAPH, Fiction for the New Millennium, Cayuse Press, PO Box 66003, Burien WA 98166-0003. E-mail: editor@cenotaph.net. Website: www.cenotaph.net. **Contact:** Paul Tylor, editor. Electronic literary journal ("electronic submissions only, please."). "Published quarterly, *Cenotaph* is fiction for the new millennium, and seeks innovative fiction, shimmering with vision and originality for a literate audience." Quarterly. Estab. 1999.

Needs: Adventure, ethnic/multicultural, fantasy, historical, literary, mainstream, mystery/suspense, science fiction, thriller/espionage, translations. "Also considers cross-genre, surrrealism, magic realism and speculative fiction." Receives 30 unsolicited mss/month. Accepts 10-12 mss/issue; 40-48 mss/year. Recently published work by Paul Tylor, Mary Chandler, Teresa White. Length: 800-2,500 words; average length: 1,500 words. Sometimes comments on rejected mss.

How to Contact: Send complete ms. Include estimated word count, 100- to 200-word bio and list of publications. Responds in 2 months to mss. Accepts reprints submissions. Sample copy not available. Writer's guidelines online.

Payment/Terms: Acquires one-time rights.

Advice: "We no longer accept postal submissions, and no postal mss will be returned. Read and study the guidelines, then follow them when submitting. We are always looking for new voices and original stories. Short works best on the Internet—we are interested in good writing, period. Your work won't make the short list if it exhibits sloppy mechanics. We're more attracted to stories under 1,000 words. We look forward to working with you."

collectedstories.com, spin a yarn, weave a story, collectedstories.com, Columbia U. Station, P.O.Box 250626, New York NY 10025. (718)609-9454. E-mail: info@collectedstories.com. Website: www.collectedstories.com. **Contact:** Dara Albanese or Wendy Ball, co-publishers. Online magazine: photos. "An online magazine devoted exclusively to literary short fiction, *collectedstories.com* publishes original short stories but also reports on various aspects related to the short form, featuring upcoming releases, author interviews, news on short story book deals, etc. The founders strive to provide short fiction with a quality venue of its own." Quarterly. Estab. 2000.

Needs: Literary. "No young adult or children's fiction." Receives 50-75 unsolicited mss/month. Accepts 4 mss/issue; 12 mss/year. Publishes ms 1 month after acceptance. **Publishes 7 new writers/year.** Recently published work by Susan Chiavell, David Fickett, Ashley Shelby. Average length: 1,800 words. Publishes short shorts.

How to Contact: Query with or without published clips or send complete ms. Include information from contact form. Accepts submission via online form or by e-mail with prior arrangement. Responds in 1 week to queries; 3 months to mss. Accepts reprints, multiple submissions. Sample copy online. Writer's guidelines online. Reviews fiction.

Payment/Terms: Writers retain copyright.

Advice: "Since stories are accepted on a revolving basis, criteria may vary in that a story is up against the best of only that particular batch under consideration for the next issue. We select the most readable stories, that is, stories that are original, compelling, or with a sense of character, and evidence of talent with prose. Writers should become familiar with a publication before submission, develop a strong hold on grammar, and thereby submit only clean, finished works for consideration."

$ ◎ CONVERSELY, Conversely, Inc., PMB #121, 3053 Fillmore St., San Francisco CA 94123-4009. E-mail: writers@conversely.com. Website: www.conversely.com. **Contact:** Alejandro Gutierrez, editor. Online magazine specializing in relationships between men and women. Illustrations; photos. "*Conversely* is dedicated to exploring relationships between women and men, every stage, every aspect, through different forms of writing, essays, memoirs, and fiction. Our audience is both female and male, mostly between 18-35 age range. We look for writing that is intelligent, provocative, and witty; we look for topics that are original and appealing to our readers." Quarterly, some sections are published biweekly. Estab. 2000.

Needs: Literary, "must be about romantic relationships between women and men." No erotica, gothic, science fiction. Receives 300 unsolicited mss/month. Accepts 1-3 mss/issue; 8-12 mss/year. Publishes ms 3 months after acceptance. **Publishes 2-4 new writers/year.** Recently published work by Tod Goldberg, Stephanie Aulenback and Jim Nichols. Length: 500-3,000 words; average length: 2,500 words.

How to Contact: "We only accept manuscript submissions through our online submissions system (no mail, no e-mail)." Go to http://conversely.com/Masth/submi.shtml to submit online. Queries by e-mail only. Responds in 2 weeks to queries; 2 months to mss. Accepts simultaneous submissions. Complete guidelines on website.

Payment/Terms: Pays $50-200. Pays on publication for electronic rights (90 days exclusive, non-exclusive thereafter) rights. Sends galleys to author.

Advice: "We look for stories that hold attention from start to finish, that cover original topics or use a fresh approach, that have a compelling narrative voice. We prefer stories that deal with relationships in an insightful, honest way, and that surprise by revealing more about a character than was expected. Keep in mind our target audience. Know when to start and know where to end, what to leave out and what it keep in."

◢ ◎ THE COPPERFIELD REVIEW, A Journal for Readers and Writers of Historical Fiction, Meredith Allard, publisher,. E-mail: info@copperfieldreview.com. Website: www.copperfieldreview.com. **Contact:** Meredith Allard, editor-in-chief. "We are an online literary journal that publishes historical fiction and articles, reviews and interviews related to historical fiction and articles, reviews and interviews related to historical fiction. We believe that by understanding the lessons of the past through historical fiction we can gain better insight into the nature of our society today, as well as a better understanding of ourselves." Quarterly. Estab. 2000.

Needs: Historical (general), romance (historical), western (frontier saga, traditional). "We will consider submissions in most fiction categories, but the setting must be historical in nature. We don't want to see anything not related to historical fiction." Receives 30 unsolicited mss/month. Accepts 7-10 mss/issue; 28-40 mss/year. Responds to mss during the months of January, April, July and October. **Publishes "between 30 and 40 percent" new writers/year.** Recently published work by RD Larson, Aidan Baker, Anthony Arthur, Lad Moore and Anu Kumar. Average length: 1,500 words. Publishes short shorts. Also publishes literary essays, literary criticism, poetry. Seldom comments on rejected mss.

How to Contact: Send complete ms. Accepts submissions by e-mail. Responds in 6 weeks to queries. Accepts simultaneous and reprints, multiple submissions. Sample copy online. Writer's guidelines online. Reviews fiction.

Payment/Terms: Acquires one-time rights.

Advice: "We wish to showcase the very best in literary historical fiction. Stories that use historical periods and details to illuminate universal truths will immediately stand out. We are thrilled to receive thoughtful work that is polished, poised and written from the heart. Be professional, and only submit your very best work. Be certain to adhere to a publication's submission guidelines, and always treat your e-mail submissions with the same care you would use with a traditional publisher. Above all, be strong and true to your calling as a writer. It is a difficult, frustrating but wonderful journey. It is important for writers to review our online submission guidelines prior to submitting."

◎ CRIMSON, Night Terrors Publications, 1202 W. Market St., Orrville OH 44667-1710. (330)683-0338. E-mail: dedavidson@night-terrors-publications.com. Website: www.night-terrors-publications.com. **Contact:** D.E. Davidson, editor/publisher. E-zine specializing in dark works: equivalent to 8½ × 5½; equivalent to 35-60 pages. "*Crimson* publishes stories submitted to *Night Terrors* magazine which the editor finds to have merit but which do not fit the concept for *Night Terrors*." Estab. 1999. Circ. 700.

Needs: "We publish any story of sufficient quality which was submitted to *Night Terrors* but for various reasons was not appropriate for that publication. This could include science fiction, horror, religious, literary, erotica, fantasy or most other adult categories of fiction. No graphic sex or violence toward children and women. No stories written specifically for *Crimson*. Please read the *Night Terrors* guidelines and write with the goal of publication there." Receives 150 unsolicited mss/month. Accepts 4 mss/issue; 24 mss/year. Publishes ms 4 months after acceptance. **Publishes 10 new writers/year.** Recently published work by A.R. Morlan, Ezra Claverie, Vera Searles and Craig

READ 'THE BUSINESS OF FICTION WRITING' section for information on manuscript preparation, mailing tips, rights and more.

Maull. Length: 2,000-5,000 words; average length: 2,500 words. Sometimes comments on rejected mss.

How to Contact: Send complete ms. Accepts submissions by mail. Include estimated word count, brief bio and list of publications. Responds in 3 weeks to queries; 10 weeks to mss. Accepts simultaneous submissions. Sample copy online. Writer's guidelines online.

Payment/Terms: 1 (printed) contributor's copy or all back issues on CD. Pays on publication for one-time rights. Sends galleys to author.

Advice: "Please read our guidelines before submitting. These are available on our website. Be professional. Do not submit stories which are less than 2,000 words or more than 5,000 words. Do not submit stories folded. Send stories only in a 9×12 envelope. Do not use small type. Please use 12 pt. New Roman or Courier or equivalent. Proof your work. Use appropriate ms format and always include SASE. Send only one story at a time."

$ ◨ DANA LITERARY SOCIETY ONLINE JOURNAL, Dana Literary Society, P.O. Box 3362, Dana Point CA 92629-8362. E-mail: ward@danaliterary.org. Website: www.danaliterary.org. **Contact:** Robert L. Ward, director. Online journal. "Fiction we publish must be thought-provoking and well-crafted. We prefer works that have a message or moral." Monthly. Estab. 2000. Circ. 8,000.

Needs: Humor/satire, "Also stories with a message or moral." "Most categories are acceptable if work is mindful of a thinking audience. No romance, children's/juvenile, religious/inspirational, pornographic, excessively violent or profane work. Would like to see more humor/satire." Receives 60 unsolicited mss/month. Accepts 3 mss/issue; 36 mss/year. Publishes ms 3 months after acceptance. **Publishes 8 new writers/year.** Recently published work by John A. Broussard, A.B. Jacobs and Beverly Newton. Length: 800-2,500 words; average length: 2,000 words. Also publishes literary essays, poetry. Often comments on rejected mss.

How to Contact: Send complete ms. Accepts submissions by mail. Responds in 2 weeks to mss. Accepts simultaneous and reprints submissions. Sample copy online. Writer's guidelines online.

Payment/Terms: Pays $50. Pays on publication for one-time rights. Not copyrighted.

Advice: "Success requires two qualities: ability and tenacity. Perfect your technique through educational resources, expansion of your scope of interests and regular reevaluation and, as required, revision of your works. Profit by a wide exposure to the writings of others. Submit works systematically and persistently, keeping accurate records so you know what went where and when. Take to heart responses and suggestions and plan your follow-up accordingly."

◉ DARGONZINE. E-mail: dargon@dargonzine.org. Website: dargonzine.org. **Contact:** Ornoth D.A. Liscomb, editor. Electronic zine specializing in fantasy. "*DargonZine* is an electronic magazine that prints original fantasy fiction by aspiring Internet writers. The Dargon Project is a collaborative anthology whose goal is to provide a way for aspiring fantasy writers on the Internet to meet and become better writers through mutual contact and collaboration as well as contact with a live readership via the Internet."

Needs: Fantasy. "Our goal is to write fantasy fiction that is mature, emotionally compelling, and professional. Membership in the Dargon Project is a requirement for publication." **Publishes 4-12 new writers/year.**

How to Contact: Guidlines available on website. Sample copy online. Writer's guidelines online.

Payment/Terms: "As a strictly noncommercial magazine, our writers' only compensation is their growth and membership in a lively writing community. Authors retain all rights to their stories." "Authors retain all rights to their stories."

Advice: "The Readers and Writers FAQs on our website provide much more detailed information about our mission, writing philosophy and value of writing for *DargonZine*."

◪ ◉ DARK MOON RISING, c/o Angela Silliman,. E-mail: fiction@darkmoonrising.com or poetry@darkmoon rising.com. Website: www.darkmoonrising.com. **Contact:** Angela Silliman, senior editor. "*Dark Moon Rising* is an intelligent and creative venue for science fiction, fantasy, horror and related genres. We publish well-crafted stories, imaginative poetry and vivid artwork. We are deeply committed to showcasing the work of both new and established writers." 6 times/year.

Needs: "We publish short (less than 7,500 words) science fiction, fantasy, horror and related genre fiction, as well as poetry and artwork fitting these genres. Our readership ranges in age and both genders, and comes from around the world. The attitude of the e-zine is to maintain something around the level of PG-13 for all published materials. We are not interested in anything with excessive strong language, intensive gore or pornography. We are also not looking for anything in the mystery or romance genres." Accepts 5-10 mss/issue. **Publishes 8-10. new writers/ year.** Recently published work by Donna Marie Robb, Angeline Hawkes-Craig, E.K. Rivera, L. Joseph Shosty, Mark Allen, T.G. Browning and J. Alan Erwin.

How to Contact: Accepts submissions by e-mail. Sample copy online. Writer's guidelines online.

Payment/Terms: "We currently offer no compensation, but we do ask for 90 day publication rights. After that, the author may request that the story be removed if it has been sold elsewhere." Acquires one-time rights.

Advice: "Read what we have online to get a feel for what we generally publish. If we like a story we'll work with you to get it just right. Have someone else read over your story for typos and missing words. As a writer, I know that when you've worked on a piece for awhile, and you know what it's supposed to say, you may overlook errors. Reading out loud also helps. Don't be afraid to submit your work! Electronic publishing is a great place for new and beginning authors to get their work published. Also, it's a great place to see what works and what doesn't. The online world is a booming market for short fiction and most magazines, zines and other short story markets will be moving into the arena in the future."

◎ **THE DEAD MULE**, P.O. Box 835, Winterville NC 28590. E-mail: contact@deadmule.com. Website: www.dea dmule.com. **Contact:** Valerie MacEwan, editor, or Phoebe Kate Foster, associate editor. Online literary journal. "*The Dead Mule* is an online literary magazine featuring Southern fiction, articles, poetry, essays, and is proud to claim a long heritage of Southern literary excellence. We consider any writing with a Southern slant. By that we mean the author needs either Southern roots or the writing must be Southern in subject matter. As the first online Southern literary journal, we've published almost 200 writers and are damn proud of it." Estab. 1996.
Needs: Literary. "Also nonfiction articles about the South including festival critiques, Nascar worshipping diatribes, and championship wrestling tributes. Always, always, stories about mules." Special poetry issue in September; special fiction issue published in the December/January *Dead Mule*. Does not read fiction from June-August.
How to Contact: Send complete ms. Accepts submissions by e-mail (deadmulesubmissions@hotmail.com). Sample copy online. Writer's guidelines online.
Advice: "What we want are writers. Pure and simple. Folks who write about the South. While long lists of previously published works are impressive, they don't matter much around here. That's why we don't include that type of information. We don't think anyone is less of a writer because their list is short. You're a writer because you say you are. Also, you've worked hard on whatever it is you wrote. Don't blow it all by not submitting correctly. If you're thinking about submitting, remember to tell us why, if it's not obvious from the content, you should be admitted to The Dead Mule School of Southern Literature. Before we read the submission, we need to know why you think you're 'Southern.' Remember, no good Southern fiction is complete without a dead mule."

$ N ◪ DREXEL ONLINE JOURNAL. Website: www.drexel.edu/doj. **Contact:** Albert DiBartolomeo, editor-in-chief. Monthly. Estab. 2001.
Needs: Adventure, ethnic/multicultural, fantasy, feminist, gay, horror, literary, mainstream, science fiction. Does not want erotica, religious or psychic work. Receives 100+ unsolicited mss/month. Accepts 2 mss/issue; 24 mss/ year. Publishes ms 2 days-2 weeks after acceptance. Agented fiction 1%. **Publishes 50% new writers/year.** Recently published work by Helen Mallon, Paula Marantz Cohen, Gary Presley, Robert Strauss. Length: 1-3,000 words; average length: 2,000 words. Publishes short shorts. Also publishes literary essays, literary criticism, poetry. Always comments on rejected mss.
How to Contact: Send complete ms. Accepts submissions by e-mail. Send SASE (or IRC) for return of ms and disposable copy of the ms and #10 SASE for reply only. Accepts simultaneous, multiple submissions. Sample copy online. Reviews fiction.
Payment/Terms: Pays $100-300. Pays on publication Sends galleys to author. Sponsors awards/contests.
Advice: "Wants work that is creative, fluid, polished and original."

$ ◎ DRUNKEN BOAT, An Online Journal of Arts & Literature, Drunken Boat, 233 Park Place #27, Brooklyn NY 11238. E-mail: editors@drunkenboat.com. Website: www.drunkenboat.com. **Contact:** Ravi Shankar, editor. Online journal. *Drunkenboat.com* is dedicated to creating an arena where works of art endemic to the medium of the web (hypertext, digital animation, music) can coexist with works of more traditional print forms of representation (poetry, critical and fictive prose, photography). It is our conviction that while digital technology will not, in the near future, supplant the print publishing industry, opportunities exist on the web to create new communities of artists and readers that are more egalitarian in terms of accessibility and less narrow in the scope of potential genre than those offered by the conventional print journal. We believe in the kind of creative cross-pollination that includes on the same site, for example, a poem and the oral reading of a thespian's monologue or a collection of short films and a collaboratively evolving work of fiction." Semiannual. Estab. 1999. Circ. 10,000.
Needs: "We don't want to see inarticulate stories with poorly developed plots and/or characters." Accepts 5 mss/ year.
How to Contact: Please direct submissions to submissions@drunkenboat.com.
Advice: "At *Drunken Boat* we are especially interested in work that utilizes the web in a dynamic way. Think of the medium of representation as an integral part of aesthetic expression. We are also looking for the highest quality work: thoughtful, provocative, musical work that evinces a knowledge of literary tradition alongside a recognition of the modern moment."

◎ **ANTONIN DVORAK'S NOCTURNE HORIZONS**, ADVORAK.COM, P.O. Box 251, Painted Post NY 14870. E-mail: visitingwriters@advorak.com. Website: www.advorak.com/horizons.
Contact: Mrs. Rebecca Dvorak. E-zine specializing in fantasy, science fiction and horror. "Our publication is hosted by a writer for his audience If you want to share Dvorak's readership, and you write similar work, submit!" Quarterly. Estab. 2001. Circ. 1,000.
Needs: Adventure, fantasy (supernatural), horror (dark fantasy, futuristic, psychological, supernatural), psychic/ supernatural/occult, romance (supernatural), science fiction (hard science/technological, soft/sociological), thriller/ espionage. "No religious, erotica, children's/juvenile, gay or feminist." Receives 20 unsolicited mss/month. Accepts 3-5 mss/issue; 12-20 mss/year. Publishes ms 2 months after acceptance. **Publishes 7 new writers/year.** Length:

1,000-10,000 words; average length: 6,000 words. Publishes short shorts. Also publishes poetry. Sometimes comments on rejected mss.

How to Contact: Send complete ms. Accepts submissions by e-mail. Send SASE (or IRC) for return of ms or send a disposable copy of ms and #10 SASE for reply only. Responds in 4-6 weeks to queries; 4-6 weeks to mss. Accepts simultaneous and reprints, multiple submissions. Sample copy online. Writer's guidelines by e-mail.

Payment/Terms: Acquires first electronic rights rights. Sends galleys to author. Not copyrighted. Sponsors awards/contests.

Advice: "We love to read a good story. Grammar and writing style can always be polished. Without a compelling story, there is nothing to polish. Write, write and write some more. Writing is a talent, but also a skill. E-zines are popping up all over the Internet. We pride ourselves on standing out. We provide a cutting-edge design and fill it with cutting-edge work."

N ◗ **ENTERZONE, hyper web text media zine art**, Borderless Publishing, 1017 Bay View Ave., Oakland CA 94610-4032. (415)672-5759. E-mail: query@ezone.org. Website: www.ezone.org. **Contact:** Briggs Nisbet, editor. E-zine. "Live on the web since 1994, *Enterzone* tries to subvert the byways of commerce and predigested 'experience' by sneaking poetry, stories, art, genre-bending and 'what is it?' to those who happen by. We are easily findable, well-linked, adequately exposd (recognized by *The New Yorker* in 1995) and committed to breaking new ground." Quarterly. Estab. 1994. Circ. 30,000.

Needs: Comics/graphic novels, ethnic/multicultural, experimental, family saga, feminist, gay, historical, humor/satire, lesbian, literary, regional, translations. "We are averse to genre fiction, with rare exceptions." Receives 10 unsolicited mss/month. Accepts 2 mss/issue; 8 mss/year. Publishes ms 1 week after acceptance. Agented fiction 5%. **Publishes 2 new writers/year.** Average length: 5,000 words. Publishes short shorts. Also publishes literary essays, literary criticism, poetry. often comments on rejected mss.

How to Contact: Query. Accepts submissions by e-mail. Send SASE (or IRC) for return of ms or send disposable copy of ms with #10 SASE for reply only. Responds in 1 month to queries; 6 months to mss. Accepts simultaneous and reprints submissions. Sample copy online. Writer's guidelines by e-mail. Reviews fiction.

Payment/Terms: Acquires first North American serial, first, one-time, electronic rights.

Advice: "We are looking for originality, voice, tone, confidence. Fiction should 'swing.' Use your best stuff right away, but boil it down."

N $◻ **EOTU, Ezine of Fiction, Art & Poetry**, Clam City Publications, 2102 Hartman, Boise ID 83704. (208)322-2408. E-mail: editor@clamcity.com. Website: www.clamcity.com/eotu.html. **Contact:** Larry Dennis. "All fiction, art and poetry needs to be published to have meaning. We do what we can to make that happen. Types of material: We are open to fiction, art and poetry of all genres, though we tend toward literary and speculative work, science fiction, fantasy and horror because that's where the editor's tastes lie." Bimonthly. Estab. 2000.

Needs: Comics/graphic novels, erotica, experimental, fantasy (space fantasy, sword and sorcery.), horror (dark fantasy, futuristic, psychological, supernatural), humor/satire, literary, psychic/supernatural/occult, romance (futuristic/time travel, gothic, love stories), science fiction (hard science/technological, soft/sociological), thriller/espionage. Receives 150 unsolicited mss/month. Accepts 12-15 mss/issue; 75-90 mss/year. **Publishes 5-10 new writers/year.** Recently published work by Bruce Boston, Marge Simon, Randy Chandler, James Dorr, s.c virtes, Nancy Bennett, Chanya Weisman, Linda Broadhurst. Length: 1-3,000 words; average length: 1,500 words. Publishes short shorts. Also publishes poetry. Rarely comments on rejected mss.

How to Contact: Send complete ms. Accepts submissions by e-mail. Send SASE for return of ms or a disposable copy of ms and #10 SASE for reply only. Responds in 2 weeks to queries; 2 months to mss. Accepts simultaneous and reprints, multiple submissions. Writer's guidelines online.

Payment/Terms: Pays $5-$30. Pays on acceptance for electronic rights.

Advice: "We go mostly on the editor's taste in fiction, art and poetry, which is for character driven stories in speculative, literary, science fiction, fantasy, and horror genres. Stories with a unique style and structure have an advantage."

◗ **EWGPRESENTS**, 406 Shady Lane, Cayce SC 29033. (803)794-8869. E-mail: ewgbet@aol.com. Website: www.ewgpresents.com. **Contact:** Betty Almond. Electronic zine. "A contemporary journal of literary quality by new and established writers. *EWGPresents* continues to provide an online forum for writers to present their works internationally, and to usher literature into the digital age."

Needs: Literary. "No pornography or excessive violence and gore beyond the legitimate needs of a story. When in doubt, leave it out." **Publishes 50-60 new writers/year.** Recently published work by Tessa Nardi, L.C. Mohr, Mary Gordon and Jeffrey L. Jackson.

How to Contact: Query. Accepts submissions by e-mail. Submissions should be directed to specific departments with work in the body of the e-mail. Sample copy online. Writer's guidelines online.

Advice: "Read and adhere to guidelines provided at the zine. We seek well-written, professionally executed fiction, with attention to basics—grammar, punctuation, usage. Be professional. Be creative. Above all, be yourself. We have the means to reach a universal audience by the click of a mouse. Writers are gifted with a new medium of exposure and the future demands taking advantage of this format."

FAILBETTER.COM, Failbetter, 63 Eighth Ave. #3A, Brooklyn NY 11217. E-mail: editor@failbetter.com. Website: www.failbetter.com. **Contact:** Thom Didato, editors. Online journal specializing in original works of fiction, poetry and art. "We are a quarterly online magazine published in the spirit of a traditional literary journal—dedicated to publishing quality fiction, poetry, and artwork. While the web plays host to hundreds, if not thousands, of genre-related sites (many of which have merit), we are not one of them.:" Quarterly. Estab. 2000. Circ. 30,000. Member, Council of Literary Magazines and Presses.

• Only online literary journal to receive Honorable Mention in 2003 *Pushcart Prize Collection*. Published works included in annual "Best of Net" Print Anthology—e2ink.

Needs: Literary, novel excerpts. "No genre fiction—romance, fantasy or science fiction." Always would like to see more "character-driven literary fiction where something happens!" Receives 25-50 unsolicited mss/month. Accepts 3-5 mss/issue; 12-20 mss/year. Publishes ms 4 months after acceptance. **Publishes 4-6 at least 1/issue. new writers/year.** Recently published work by Antonya Nelson, Tom Paine, Victor LaValle, Matthew Derby and Nathan Long. Publishes short shorts. Often comments on rejected mss.

How to Contact: Accepts submissions by e-mail. Responds in 2 weeks to queries; 2-3 month to mss. Accepts simultaneous submissions. Sample copy online. Writer's guidelines online.

Payment/Terms: Acquires one-time rights.

Advice: "Read an issue. Read our guidelines! We place a high degree of importance on originality, believing that even in this age of trends it is still possible. We are not looking for what is current or momenary. We are not concerned with length: one good sentence may find a home here, as the bulk of mediocrity will not. Most importantly, know that what you are saying could only come from you. When you are sure of this, please feel free to submit."

THE FAIRFIELD REVIEW, 544 Silver Spring Rd., Fairfield CT 06880. (203)256-1970. Fax: (203)256-1970. E-mail: fairfieldreview@hpmd.com. Website: www.fairfieldreview.org. **Contact:** Edward and Janet Granger-Happ, Pamela Pollak, editors. Electronic magazine. "Our mission is to provide an outlet for poetry, short stories and essays, from both new and established writers and students. We are accessible to the general public."

Needs: Literary. "Would like to see more stories "rich in lyrical imagery and those that are more humorous." **Publishes 20 new writers/year.** Recently published work by Nan Leslie (Pushcart nominee) and Wes Prussing.

How to Contact: Accepts submissions by e-mail. Sample copy online.

Advice: "We encourage students and first-time writers to submit their work. In addition to the submission guidelines found in each issue on our website, we recommend reading the essay 'Writing Qualities to Keep in Mind' from our Editors and Authors page on the website. Keep to small, directly experienced themes; write crisply using creative, poetic images, avoid the trite expression."

FAR SECTOR SFFH, (formerly *Deep Outside SFFH*), C&C Clocktower Books, PMB 260, 6549 Mission Gorge Rd., San Diego CA 92120. (619)501-4196. Website: www.farsector.com. **Contact:** John Cullen, editor. Web-only magazine. "*Far Sector SFFH* is a paying professional magazine for science fiction and dark imaginative fiction, aimed at people who love to read well-plotted character-driven genre fiction." Monthly. Estab. 1998. Circ. 5,000+.

Needs: Horror (dark fantasy, futuristic, psychological), science fiction (hard science/technological, soft/sociological). No pornography, excessive gore, "or vulgarity unless it directly furthers the story (sparingly, at that)." No sword and sorcery, elves, high fantasy, cookie-cutter space opera. Receives 100-150 unsolicited mss/month. Accepts 1 mss/issue; 12 mss/year. Publishes ms 3 months after acceptance. **Publishes 1-3 new writers/year.** Recently published work by Recently published Pat York, Melanie Tem, Paul Martens and Joel Best. Sometimes comments on rejected mss.

How to Contact: Send complete ms. Accepts submissions by mail. Accepts submissions by postal mail only. Send disposable copy of ms and SASE for reply. Responds in 3 months to mss. Sample copy online. Writer's guidelines online.

Payment/Terms: Pays 3¢/word. Pays within 90 days of acceptance. Acquires first, electronic rights. Sends galleys to author.

Advice: "We look for the best quality story. Genre comes second. We look for published, first-rate, professional fiction. It is most important to grab us from the first three paragraphs—not only as a common standard but because that's how we lead with both the monthly newsletter and the main page of the magazine. Please read the tips and guidelines at the magazine's website for up-to-the-moment details. Do not send envelopes asking for guidelines, please—all the info is online at our website."

FICTION INFERNO, The Literary Magazine That Burns You Up, S.O.L. Enterprises,. E-mail: editor@fictioninferno.com. Website: www.fictioninferno.com. **Contact:** Max E. Keele, publisher. E-zine specializing in literary speculative fiction. "We are a free literary journal publishing the most exciting short speculative, fantasy and strange fiction available. *Fiction Inferno* prefers to publish literate, high-quality speculative and imaginative fiction that doesn't fit elsewhere. Dangerous fiction. Experimental fiction. Subversive fiction. Outrageous fiction. We hope to reinvigorate the field of speculative fiction with an evolved iteration of the New Wave speculative vision of Phillip K. Dick, Harlan Ellison, Norman Spinrad, et. al." Quarterly. Estab. 2001. Circ. 5,000/issue.

Needs: Erotica, experimental, fantasy, horror, literary, psychic/supernatural/occult, science fiction. "No psycho-killer, religious, TV or movie inspired, dull." Receives 50 unsolicited mss/month. Accepts 3-4 mss/issue; 12 mss/

year. Publishes ms 3-6 months after acceptance. **Publishes 5 new writers/year.** Recently published work by Christopher Daly and Woody O. Carsky-Wilson. Length: 1-50,000 words; average length: 7,000 words. Publishes short shorts. Sometimes comments on rejected mss.

How to Contact: Send complete ms. Accepts submissions by e-mail. estimated word count and brief bio. Responds in 3 weeks to queries; 4 months to mss. Sample copy online. Reviews fiction.

Payment/Terms: Pays on publication for one-time, electronic rights.

Advice: "We are an Internet magazine devoted to publishing speculative fiction of literary quality, including but not limited to the genres more commonly referred to as science fiction, fantasy, horror and experimental. Our goal is to find and publish the best fiction available from authors of any and all backgrounds, whether well-established in their writing careers or just starting out. The only objective criteria for making the pages of *FI* is well-crafted, innovative fiction. Of course, the subjective criteria is we have to like it. What do we like? Inventiveness, daring, uniqueness of voice, unusual subject matter, fiction that does something."

5-TROPE. E-mail: ander@thediagram.com. Website: www.webdelsol.com/5_trope. **Contact:** Ander Monson, managing editor. Online literary journal. "We aim to publish the new and original in fiction, poetry and new media. We hope to appeal to writers and readers with a seriousness about playing with language and form." Quarterly. Estab. 1999. Circ. 5,000.

Needs: Comics/graphic novels, experimental, literary. "No religious, horror, fantasy, espionage." Receives 50 unsolicited mss/month. Accepts 6 mss/issue; 30 mss/year. Publishes ms 1-6 months after acceptance. **Publishes 5 new writers/year.** Recently published work by Gary Lutz, Maile Chapman and Sarah Levine. Length: 250-5,000 words; average length: 1,000 words. Publishes short shorts. Also publishes poetry. Sometimes comments on rejected mss.

How to Contact: Accepts submissions by e-mail. Send complete mss electronically. Sample copy online.

Payment/Terms: Acquires first rights. Sends galleys to author.

Advice: "We look for originality in language and form, coupled with a strong authorial presence. The first thing a writer should do before submitting is to read issues of the publication to get a feel for what we're looking for."

$ ◢ flashquake, An Online Journal of Flash Literature, River Road Studios, P.O. Box 2154, Albany NY 12220-0154. E-mail: dorton@flashquake.org. Website: www.flashquake.org. **Contact:** Debi Orton, publisher. E-zine specializing in flash literature. "*flashquake* is a quarterly online literary journal specifically centered around flash literature—flash fiction, flash memoir, flash plays and poetry. Our goal is to create a literary venue for all things flash. Send us your best flash, works that leave your readers thinking. We define flash as works less than 1,000 words. Shorter pieces will impress us; poetry can be up to 35 lines. We want the best story you can tell us in the fewest words you need to do it! Move us, engage us, give us a complete story that only you could have written."

Needs: Ethnic/multicultural (general), experimental, literary, flash literature of all types: fiction, memoir, plays, poetry and artwork. "Not interested in romance, graphic sex, graphic violence, gore, vampires, or work of a religious nature." Receives 25-30 unsolicited mss/month. Accepts 100-120 mss/issue. Publishes ms 1-3 months after acceptance. Publishes short shorts. Sometimes comments on rejected mss.

How to Contact: Accepts submissions by postal mail and e-mail (but prefers e-mail submissions). Submit to flashquake.org. Include estimated word count, brief bio, list of publications, mailing address and e-mail address. Guidelines and submission instructions on web site.

Payment/Terms: Pays $5-25. Pays on publication for electronic rights. Sponsors awards/contests.

Advice: "*Read our submission guidelines before submitting.* Proofread your work thoroughly! We will instantly reject your work for spelling and grammar errors. Save your document as plain text and paste it into an e-mail message. We will not open attachments. We want work that the reader will think about long after reading it, stories that compel the reader to continue reading them. We do like experimental work, but that should not be construed as a license to forget narrative clarity, plot, character development or reader satisfaction."

◼ ◢ FLUENT ASCENSION, Fierce Concepts, PO Box 6407, Glendale AZ 85312. (602)435-7523. Fax: (815)364-3780. E-mail: submissions@fluentascension.com. Website: www.fluentascension.com. **Contact:** Warren Norgaard, editor. Online magazine. Quarterly. Estab. 2003.

Needs: Comics/graphic novels, erotica, ethnic/multicultural, experimental, gay, humor/satire, lesbian, literary, translations. Receives 3-5 unsolicited mss/month. Accepts 1-3 mss/issue. Publishes short shorts. Also publishes literary essays, literary criticism, poetry. Sometimes comments on rejected mss.

How to Contact: Send complete ms. Accepts submissions by mail, e-mail. Include estimated word count, brief bio and list of publications. Send SASE (or IRC) for return of ms or send disposable copy of ms and #10 SASE for reply only. Responds in 4-8 weeks to queries; 4-8 weeks to mss. Accepts simultaneous and reprints, multiple submissions. Sample copy online. Writer's guidelines online.

Payment/Terms: Acquires electronic rights. Sponsors awards/contests.

◼ ◢ GIN BENDER POETRY REVIEW, PO Box 406, Huntington TX 75949. E-mail: ginbender@yahoo.com. Website: www.ginbender.com. **Contact:** T.A. Thompson, founder/chief editor. Online magazine. "We publish a diverse group of writers including award-winning and debut authors." Triannual. Estab. 2002.

Needs: Historical, literary, mainstream, regional. "No science fiction, horror." Receives 20 unsolicited mss/month. Accepts 2-4 mss/issue; 6-12 mss/year. Publishes ms 4 months after acceptance. **Publishes 2-4 new writers/year.** Recently published work by Christopher Woods, Elizabeth Routen and Peggy Duffy. Length: 500-1,500 words; average length: 1,000 words. Publishes short shorts. Also publishes literary essays, poetry. Sometimes comments on rejected mss.

How to Contact: Send complete ms. Accepts submissions by e-mail. Include estimated word count, brief bio and list of publications. Send disposable copy of ms and #10 SASE for reply only. Responds in 2 weeks to queries; 6 weeks to mss. Accepts reprints submissions. Sample copy online. Writer's guidelines online.

Payment/Terms: Acquires first, electronic rights.

Advice: "We look for fiction that grasps the soul momentarily. Read all the literary work you can. Study the masters and the new."

■ THE GREEN TRICYCLE, "The fun-to-read lit mag!", Cayuse Press, PO Box 66003, Burien WA 98166-0003. E-mail: editor@greentricycle.com. Website: greentricycle.com. **Contact:** B. Benepe, publisher. "*The Green Tricycle* is an online thematic literary journal, with three themes per issue. Each piece is limited to 200 words. We accept poetry, micro-fiction, mini-essays, letters and drama, as long as it addresses the theme in an original manner." Quarterly. Estab. 1999.

Needs: Literary. Wants more mystery, literary and cross-genre. "No erotica, horror, or occult—too much of that is on the Internet already." Receives 100-300 unsolicited mss/month. Accepts 30 mss/issue; 120 mss/year. Publishes ms 1-3 months after acceptance. Agented fiction 10%. **Publishes 25 new writers/year.** Recently published work by Paul Tylor and Diane Schuller. Average length: 175 words. Also publishes literary essays, poetry. Sometimes comments on rejected mss.

How to Contact: Include estimated word count, 25-30 word bio and list of publications. Responds in 2 months to mss. Sample copy online. Writer's guidelines online. Reviews fiction.

Payment/Terms: Acquires one-time rights.

Advice: "I look for originality. A creative approach to the theme catches my attention. Be original. Read the magazine. Sloppy mechanics are sickening. Write the best you can without using four-letter words."

■ THE HORSETHIEF'S JOURNAL, Celebrating the Literature of the New West, Cayuse Press, PO Box 66003, Burien WA 98166-0003. E-mail: cayuse-press@usa.com. Website: www.cayuse-press.com. **Contact:** Tiffany A. Christian, editor. Electronic literary magazine. "*The Horsethief's Journal* is a triannual online literary journal showcasing the best in contermporary poetry, short fiction and memoir for the general reader. We prefer fiction that illuminates the human condition and complements the memoir and poetry we publish. Our audience spans all ages." Triannual. Estab. 1998.

Needs: Adventure, ethnic/multicultural, historical, literary, mainstream, mystery/suspense, regional, thriller/espionage, translations. "No erotica, horror, children's, young adult, sappy romance." Receives 30 unsolicited mss/month. Accepts 2-5 mss/issue; 6-15 mss/year. Publishes ms 1-3 months after acceptance. **Publishes 3 new writers/year.** Recently published work by Paul Tylor and Mary Chandler. Average length: 1,500 words. Publishes short shorts. Also publishes literary essays, poetry. Sometimes comments on rejected mss.

How to Contact: Include estimated word count, 100-200 word bio and list of publications. Responds in 3 months to mss. Sample copy online. Writer's guidelines online. Reviews fiction.

Payment/Terms: Acquires one-time rights.

Advice: "We're looking for stories with an original slant. No cliched plots, characters or themes. Polish, polish, polish. Poor diction, grammar errors—bad mechanics in general—will get you a rejection. Read the magazine. Be original."

■ IN POSSE REVIEW ON WEB DEL SOL. E-mail: submissions@webdelsol.com. Website: www.webdelsol.com/inposse. **Contact:** Rachel Callaghan, editor. E-zine specializing in literary fiction, poetry, and creative nonfiction. "The best of literary fiction, creative nonfiction and poetry from, well, whoever writes it—we welcome all serious writers; especially those who can demonstrate fresh new style and a slightly skewed point of view. We are looking for non-PC work concerning ethnic issues. See website for details." Triannual. Estab. 1998.

Needs: Adventure, erotica, ethnic/multicultural, experimental, family saga, fantasy, feminist, gay, historical, horror, humor/satire, lesbian, literary, mystery/suspense, science fiction, western. Accepts 10 mss/issue; 90 mss/year. Publishes ms 1-3 months after acceptance. **Publishes 10 new writers/year.** Length: 3,500 words; average length: 1,500 words. Also publishes literary essays, poetry. sometimes comments on rejected mss.

How to Contact: Send complete ms. Accepts submissions by e-mail. Include estimated word count, brief bio and

---

CHECK THE CATEGORY INDEXES, located at the back of the book, for publishers interested in specific fiction subjects.

list of publications. Responds in 3 months to mss. Accepts multiple submissions No simultaneous submissions. Sample copy online. Writer's guidelines online.
Payment/Terms: Acquires one-time, electronic rights.
Advice: "We have very eclectic tastes. Whatever turns us on at the moment. Different, suprising, cutting-edge, intriguing but well-written is best. A manuscript that stands out is one we would consider printing out. Make sure you have a complete story, not a slice of life or good start. Wait after writing and re-read. Use spelling and grammar checkers."

THE JOLLY ROGER, PO Box 1087, Chapel Hill NC 27514. (919)960-0933. E-mail: drakeraft@jollyroger.com. Website: www.jollyroger.com. **Contact:** Drake Raft, editor. Electronic magazine. "Literature composed in the context of the Western Canon."
Needs: "Conservative and traditional fiction, epic poetry, prose and short stories. Looking for rhyme, meter, words that mean things, plot and character. Publishes an occasional novel or collection of short stories." **Publishes 10-20 new writers/year.** Recently published work by Drake Raft, Becket Knottingham, Elliot McGucken and Bootsy McClusky.
How to Contact: Accepts submissions by mail, e-mail, fax, phone. Sample copy online. Writer's guidelines online.

KENNESAW REVIEW, Kennesaw State University, Dept. of English, Building 27, 1000 Chastain Rd., Kennesaw GA 30144-5591. (770)423-6346. Website: www.kennesaw.edu/kr. **Contact:** Robert W. Hill, editor. Online literary journal. "Just good litrary fiction, all themes, for a eclectic audience." Triannual. Estab. 1987.
Needs: Flash fiction. "No formulaic genre fiction." Receives 25 unsolicited mss/month. Accepts 2-4 mss/issue. Publishes ms 12-18 months after acceptance. Recently published work by Jon Hansen, Donna Vitucci, Joan Frank, Luke Whisnant.
How to Contact: Send complete ms. Include previous publications. Responds in 2 months to mss. Accepts simultaneous, multiple submissions. Writer's guidelines online.
Payment/Terms: Acquires first rights. Includes Annual edition in CD or print format, or both.
Advice: "Use the language well and tell an interesting story."

LITERARY WITCHES, 2610 Broadway St., Ft. Wayne IN 46807. (260)744-9197. E-mail: novaqueer@aol.com. Website: members.aol.com/MeierAvila/index.html. **Contact:** Sabrina Counts, editor. Electronic zine. "A post-modern journal exploring diverse literary art, rooted in feminist and literary theory. We publish work which reflects and explores post-modernism, reconstruction, hypertext, transgendered experimentation, multiculturalism, queer theory, feminism, post-feminism. We are a journal of the mind and body, a cyber-gathering of academic theory and experimental fiction."
Needs: Ethnic/multicultural, experimental, feminist, gay, lesbian, literary. "Please do not send fantasy, vampire stories." Wants postmodern fiction and literature. We are especially interested in work exploring queer discourse, the body and postmodern piracy. Recently published work by Kathy Acker, Doug Rice, Michael Bode, Cheryl Meier and Marita Avila.
How to Contact: Accepts submissions by mail, e-mail. "Please submit your work in the body of e-mail along with your address and phone number, or send in hard copy." Sample copy online.
Advice: "We feature literary art by the best American authors as well as diverse or new writers. Read the publication before sending your work for consideration. Electronic publishing is very important right now. For example, *Literary Witches* is becoming involved with an electronic journal that was just awarded the first Guggenheim grant for a cyber publication. And because of continuing accessibility to cyberspace, electronic journals can be reached by diverse groups of people."

$LITEROTICAFFEINE, Digital Enterprises, P.O. Box 1074, Laguna Beach CA 92652-1074. E-mail: litcaffeine@yahoo.com. Website: www.literoticaffeine.com. **Contact:** Kevin Canelloni. "We look for well-written, literary erotica which emphasizes character development, plot, and tone. The stories must be in short story format (a beginning, middle, end). We are not looking for cheesy beginnings that shortly plunge into one long sex scene. Sex is one of the themes in our stories but we prefer it to be a subplot to otherwise engaging story." Biweekly. Estab. 1999.
Needs: Erotica. Does not want to see anything without erotic content. Publishes ms 2 weeks to 2 months after acceptance. Rarely comments on rejected mss.
How to Contact: Send complete ms. Accepts submissions by e-mail. Accepts simultaneous and reprints submissions. Writer's guidelines online.
Payment/Terms: Pays $10-$25. Pays on publication for first North American serial, electronic rights.

MARGIN: Exploring Modern Magical Realism, 321 High School Road, N.E., PMB #204, Bainbridge Island WA 98110. E-mail: smike10@qwest.net. Website: www.magical-realism.com. **Contact:** Tamara Kaye Sellman, editor. Electronic anthology specializing in magical realism. "*Margin* seeks, in a variety of ways, to answer the question 'what is magical realism?'" Estab. 2000. Circ. 30,000.

● *Margin* has received the Arete "Wave of a Site" award. The editor of *Margin* is on hiatus at publication time. Nominated for *Pushcart* and *e2ink*.

Needs: Ethnic/multicultural, fantasy, feminist, gay, historical, horror, lesbian, mainstream, psychic/supernatural/occult, science fiction, translations. "No magical realist knockoffs, no stock fantasy with elves or angels. Nothing gratuitous. If you are unsure what magical realism is, visit the website and look at our discussion of criteria before sending. Interested in academic writing; query first." Look for announcement of new contests for writers, as well. Receives 100 unsolicited mss/month. Publishes ms 6 months after acceptance. Recently published work by Gayle Brandeis, Virgil Suarez, and Brian Evenson. Also publishes literary essays, literary criticism. Sometimes comments on rejected mss.

How to Contact: Send complete ms. Accepts submissions by e-mail. We accept electronic submissions only—no attachments. See website for guidelines. Sample copy online. Writer's guidelines for SASE or online. Reviews fiction.

Payment/Terms: Negotiable.

Advice: "Technical strength, unique, engaging style, well-developed and inventive story. Surprise us by avoiding what has already been done. Manuscript must be magical realism. Do not send more than one submission at a time. You will not get a fair reading if you do. Always enclose SASE. Do not inquire before 3 months. Send us your A-list, no works in progress."

TIMOTHY MCSWEENEY'S INTERNET TENDENCY, 826 Valencia Street, San Francisco CA 94110. E-mail: websubmissions@mcsweeneys.net. Website: www.mcsweeneys.net. **Contact:** Dave Eggers, Eli Horowitz, Lee Epstein, editors. Online literary journal. "*Timothy McSweeney's Internet Tendency* is an offshoot of *Timothy McSweeney's Quarterly Concern*, a journal created by nervous people in relative obscurity, and published four times a year." Daily.

Needs: Literary. Sometimes comments on rejected mss.

How to Contact: Accepts submissions by mail, e-mail. "Submit the first 300 words of ms via e-mail to the 'print submissions' or 'web submissions' address. If the piece is under 1,000 words, paste the entire submission in the e-mail. Include a 'brief and sober' bio and cover letter. Attach the entire ms to the e-mail submission, if possible as a Microsoft Word file. Attachments in BinHex cannot be read. Stories without the author's phone number cannot be considered." Sample copy online. Writer's guidelines online.

Advice: "Do not submit your work to both the print submissions address and the web submissions address, as seemingly hundreds of writers have been doing lately. If you submit a piece of writing intended for the magazine to the web submissions address, you will confuse us, and if you confuse us, we will accidentally delete your work without reading it, and then we will laugh and never give it another moment's thought, and sleep the carefree sleep of young children. This is very, very serious."

MERCURY BOOKS, Where Words Have Wings!, Cayuse Press, PO Box 66003, Burien WA 98166-0003. E-mail: mercurybooks@email.com. Website: www.mercurybooks.com/. **Contact:** Barbara Benepe, publisher. Online magazine. "Each issue is devoted entirely to the works of one author." Biannual. Estab. 2001.

● *At presstime,* Mercury Books *was temporarily closed to submissions. See website for updates.*

Needs: Literary. "We seek to publish an author's collection of short fiction or poetry, or a mix of fiction and poetry. We will consider new or unpublished authors. The work must be outstanding and the author must be willing to work with our editorial staff."

How to Contact: "Please visit the whe website for our detailed checklist for submissions and follow them carefully. Collections chosen for publication will be announced in January and will be published later in the year. You must include your address, phone number and e-mail address so we can contact you. We will consider previously published material if you own the copyright and provide complete publication documents. Ideally we prefer a mix of new material with previously published work. We seek to become the first publisher of a writer's collected works and provide an attractive format for presentation." Accepts simultaneous and reprints, multiple submissions. Writer's guidelines online.

Payment/Terms: Acquires first, one-time electronic rights.

Advice: "Be original. Read and follow the guidelines. Please include complete documentation with any previously published work."

$ METROPOLE, P.O. Box 281, Warrensburg NY 12885. (518)623-3220. E-mail: editorial@metropolemag.com. Website: www.metropolemag.com. **Contact:** Dan Quinn. "We're looking for fiction that's literate, sophisticated, and out of the ordinary. Slice-of-life sketches are out, character sketches are out. Strange is in (but we're no looking for outright science fiction or fantasies set on one of the moons of Jupiter)." Monthly. Estab. 2001.

Needs: "Favorite recent movies will give you a clue to our taste: *Moulin Rouge*, *Run Lola Run*, *Memento*."

How to Contact: Send complete ms. Accepts submissions by e-mail. Electronic submissions are welcome, but send them in the body of hte e-mail to danquinn@metropolemag.com, not as attachments. Send SASE for reply. Responds in 4 weeks to mss. Accepts simultaneous, multiple submissions.

Payment/Terms: Pays $20 per printed page, payable on publication. Acquires first North American serial, foreign rights. All other rights are retained by the author.

Advice: "*Metropole* is a daring and rambunctious magazine, literary but very far from stuffy, somber, or traditional.

It's loaded with personality, largely that of its publisher, Anthony Sapienza. Fiction that gets selected fits with that personality; it's going to be strange and sharp-edged, sometimes funny, sometimes horrific (but not in any traditional way—no vampires or alien monsters, please). Ordinary naturalistic narratives about ordinary naturalistic problems are not going to make it here. Offbeat is too mild a term for much of our fiction, but we're not interested in self-conscious 'experimental: writing.'"

THE MID-SOUTH REVIEW, A Journey into the Heart of the South. E-mail: midsouth@yahoo.com. Website: www.geocities.com/midsouthreview. **Contact:** Jeff Martindale, editor. Online magazine. "We are an online literary journal featuring fiction, essays, and poetry with general interest in Southern culture and history. Our mission is to publish the best stories written by and about Mid-Southerners." Monthly. Estab. 2002.
Needs: Humor/satire, literary, mainstream, "anything about the South." "No gore, violence, hate, erotica, or science fiction." List of upcoming themes available online. Accepts 3-5 mss/issue. Publishes ms 2-4 months after acceptance. Recently published work by Jeff Martindale and Scottie H. Freeman. Length: 2,500 words; average length: 1,500 words. Publishes short shorts. Also publishes literary essays, poetry. Sometimes comments on rejected mss.
How to Contact: Send complete ms. Accepts submissions by e-mail. Include estimated word count and brief bio. No attachments. Place submission in the body of the e-mail. Responds in 3-4 months to queries; 3-4 months to mss. Sample copy online. Writer's guidelines online.
Payment/Terms: free subscription to magazine.
Advice: "Rewrite! Rewrite! Rewrite! Spend as much or more time rewriting your work than on your first draft. Follow submission guidelines to the letter. Incorrect submissions reduce your chance of getting published. Don't take rejection personally."

$MILLENNIUM SCIENCE FICTION & FANTASY, Jo Pop Publications, P.O. Box 8118, Roswell NM 88202-8118. E-mail: jopoppub@jopoppub.com. Website: www.jopoppub.com. **Contact:** Diana R. Moreland. E-zine with print "Best Of" quarterly. Monthly e-zine publishes science fiction, fantasy and psychological horror, "offering the best of short speculative fiction we can find." Monthly. Estab. 1993. Circ. 1,000. Member of the Horror Zine Association.
● *Millennium Science Fiction & Fantasy* ranked on *Writer's Digest's* "Top 30" list of best markets for fiction writers.
Needs: Fantasy (space fantasy), horror (dark fantasy, futuristic, psychological, supernatural), humor/satire, science fiction (hard science/technological, soft/sociological), young adult/teen (fantasy/science fiction, horror). "No explicit language, sex or violence. No graphic blood, guts or exploitation pieces." List of upcoming themes available for SASE. Receives 100 unsolicited mss/month. Accepts 4-5 mss/issue; 48-60 mss/year. Does not read mss October 31-January 1. Publishes ms 4 months after acceptance. **Publishes 1-3 new writers/year.** Recently published work by Greg F. Giyune and Patricia L. White. Length: 50-2,500 words; average length: 2,000 words. Publishes short shorts. Also publishes literary criticism, poetry. Often comments on rejected mss.
How to Contact: Send complete ms. Accepts submissions by mail, e-mail. Write "story submission" in your subject line. Include estimated word count, 50-100 word bio and list of publications. Send SASE for reply, return of ms or send a disposable copy of ms. Responds in 2 months to queries; 2 weeks to 3 months no answer to mss. Accepts reprints submissions. Sample copy for $6.50 (print issue) or online at website. Writer's guidelines for #10 SASE, online at webstie or by email. Reviews fiction.
Payment/Terms: Pays $5-10. Pays on acceptance for one-time rights. Other rights (with option to print in yearly anthology). Sponsors awards/contests.
Advice: "We have a standard rule-three grammar errors in the first paragraph is an automatic reject. We are leaning more towards e-mail submissions and welcome electronic copies of accepted manuscripts."

NUVEIN ONLINE. (626)401-3466. Fax: (626)401-3460. E-mail: editor@nuvein.com. Website: www.nuvein.com. **Contact:** Enrique Diaz, editor. Electronic Zine. "We are open to short works of fiction which explore topics divergent from the mainstream. Especially welcome are stories with a point of view opposite to traditional and stereotypical views of minorities, including women and gays. Of course we are not averse to stories dealing with such changes. Our philosophy is to provide a forum for voices rarely heard in other publications."
● Nuvein Online has received the Visionary Media Award.
Needs: Serialized novels, short fiction and graphic e-novels. Wants more "experimental cyberfiction, serialized fiction, ethnic, as well as pieces dealing with the exploration of sexuality." **Publishes 20 new writers/year.** Recently published work by J. Knight, Paul A. Toth, Rick Austin, Robert Levin, and Scott Essman.
How to Contact: Query. Accepts submissions by mail, e-mail, fax. Sample copy online.
Advice: "Read over each submission before sending it, and if you, as the writer, find the piece irresistable, e-mail it to us immediately!"

THE ORACULAR TREE, A Transformational E-Zine, The Oracular Tree, 208-167 Morgan Ave., Kitchener ON Canada N2A 2M4. E-mail: editor@oraculartree.com. Website: www.oraculartree.com. **Contact:** Teresa Hawkes, publisher. E-zine specializing in transformation. "We believe the stories we tell ourselves and each other predict the outcome of our lives. We can affect gradual social change by transforming our deeply rooted cultural stories. The genre is not as important as the message and the high quality of the writing. We accept stories, poems, articles and essays which will reach well-educated, open-minded readers around the world. We offer a forum for those who see a need for change, who want to add their voices to a growing search for alternatives." Weekly. Estab. 1977. Circ. 40,000 hits/month.

Needs: Fantasy, literary, New Age. "We'll look at any genre that is well-written and can examine a new cultural paradigm. No tired dogma, no greeting card poetry, please." Receives 20-30 unsolicited mss/month. Accepts 80-100 mss/year. Publishes mss 3 months after acceptance. **Publishes 20-30 new writers/year.** Recently published work by Dr. Richard Taylor, Dr. David Peat, Margaret Karmazin and Dr. Elaine Hatfield. Publishes short shorts. Also publishes literary essays, poetry. Often comments on rejected mss.

How to Contact: Send complete ms. Accepts submissions by e-mail. Responds in 2 weeks to queries; 2 months to mss. Accepts simultaneous and reprints, multiple submissions. Sample copy online. Writer's guidelines online.

Payment/Terms: Author retains copyright; one-time archived posting Not copyrighted.

Advice: "The underlying idea must be clearly expressed. The language should be appropriate to the tale, using creative license and an awareness of rhythm. We look for a juxtaposition of ideas that creates resonance in the mind and heart of the reader. Write from your honest voice. Trust your writing to unfold."

OUTSIDER INK, Outsider Media, 201 W. 11th St., New York NY 10014. (212)691-4345. E-mail: editor@outsidermedia.com. Website: www.outsiderink.com. **Contact:** Sean Meriwether, editor. E-zine specializing in alternative fiction, poetry and artwork. "We are an online quarterly only. Each issue contains five fiction pieces, two poetry sections, and one visual artist. A monthly feature spotlights an individual, normally an underpublished writer or poet. We have established an international readership by publishing new material with a diverse range of adult themes. We are all outsiders, artist and non-artist alike, but there are those brave enough to share their experiences with the world. Rattle my cage and demand my attention, tell me your story the way you want it to be told. I am looking for the harsh and sometimes ugly truths. Dark humor is especially appealing. Quarterly. Estab. 1999. Circ. 30,000 hits/month.

• *Outsider Ink* ranked on *Writer's Digest's* "Top 30" list of best markets for fiction writers.

Needs: Literary. "No mainstream, genre fiction, children's or religious." Receives 200 unsolicited mss/month. Accepts 5 mss/issue; 20 mss/year. Publishes ms 3 months after acceptance. **Publishes 15 new writers/year.** Recently published work by Daniel A. Olivas, Greg Wharton, Maryanne Stahl and Ray Van Horn, Jr. Average length: 2,000 words. Publishes short shorts. Also publishes poetry. Often comments on rejected mss.

How to Contact: Send complete ms. Accepts submissions by e-mail. Responds in 1 week to queries; 3 months to mss. Accepts simultaneous and reprints, multiple submissions. Sample copy online. Writer's guidelines online.

Payment/Terms: Acquires electronic rights. Sends galleys to author. Not copyrighted.

Advice: "*Outsider Ink* publishes work that isn't afraid to cover unexplored territory, both emotionally and physically. Though we want work that pushes the envelope, it should maintain a literary foundation. We aren't looking for fiction or poetry that is weird for the sake of being weird, we want prose with a point of view and a mind of its own. Take the time to familiarize yourself with the e-zine before submitting. The bulk of submissions are not accepted because they are innappropriate to the venue. We encourage new writers, and act as a launching pad to other venues. Trust your own voice when editing your own material. If you think it isn't ready yet, don't submit it—finish it first."

PAINTED BRIDE QUARTERLY, Rutgers University, 311 N. Fifth St., Camden NJ 08102-1519. (856)225-6129. Fax: (856)225-6117. E-mail: pbq@camden.rutgers.edu. Website: www.pbq.rutgers.edu. **Contact:** Kathleen Volk-Miller, managing editor. "*PBQ* seeks literary fiction, experimental and traditional." Publishes online each quarter and a print annual each spring. Estab. 1973.

Needs: Ethnic/multicultural, experimental, feminist, gay, lesbian, literary, translations. "No genre fiction." "Publishes theme-related work, check website; holds annual fiction contests. **Publishes 24 new writers/year.** Length: 5,000 words; average length: 3,000 words. Publishes short shorts. Also publishes literary essays, literary criticism, poetry. Occasionally comments on rejected mss.

How to Contact: Send complete ms. Responds in 6 months to mss. Sample copy online. Reviews fiction.

Payment/Terms: Acquires first North American serial rights.

Advice: We look for "freshness of idea incorporated with high-quality writing. We receive an awful lot of nicely written work with worn-out plots. We want quality in whatever—we hold experimental work to as strict standards as anything else. Many of our readers write fiction; most of them enjoy a good reading. We hope to be an outlet for quality. A good story gives, first, enjoyment to the reader. We've seen a good many of them lately, and we've published the best of them."

PAPERPLATES, a magazine for fifty readers, Perkolator Kommunikation, 19 Kenwood Ave., Toronto ON M6C 2R8 Canada. (416)651-2551. Fax: (416)651-2910. E-mail: magazine@paperplates.org. Website: www.paperplates.org. **Contact:** Bethany Gibson, fiction editor. Electronic magazine. Semiannual. Estab. 1990.

Needs: Condensed novels, ethnic/multicultural, feminist, gay, lesbian, literary, mainstream, translations. "No science fiction, fantasy or horror." Receives 12 unsolicited mss/month. Accepts 2-3 mss/issue; 6-9 mss/year. Publishes ms 6-8 months after acceptance. Recently published work by Celia Lottridge, C.J. Lockett, Deirdre Kessler and

Marvyne Jenoff. Length: 1,500-3,500 words; average length: 3,000 words. Publishes short shorts. Also publishes literary essays, literary criticism, poetry.

How to Contact: Accepts submissions by e-mail. Responds in 6 weeks to queries; 3 months to mss. Accepts simultaneous submissions. Sample copy online. Writer's guidelines for #10 SASE.

Payment/Terms: 1 contributor's copy. Acquires first North American serial rights.

THE PAUMANOK REVIEW. E-mail: submissions@paumanokreview.com. Website: www.paumanokreview.com. **Contact:** Katherine Arline, editor. Online literary magazine. "*TPR* is dedicated to publishing and promoting the best in world art and literature." Quarterly. Estab. 2000.

• J.P. Maney's *Western Exposures* was selected for inclusion in the *e2ink Best of the Web Anthology*.

Needs: Experimental, literary, mainstream. Receives 100 unsolicited mss/month. Accepts 6-8 mss/issue; 24-32 mss/year. Publishes ms 6 weeks after acceptance. **Publishes 4 new writers/year.** Recently published work by Patty Friedman, Elisha Porat, Barry Spacks and Walter McDonald. Length: 1,500-6,000 words; average length: 3,000 words. Publishes short shorts. Also publishes literary essays, poetry. Usually comments on rejected mss.

How to Contact: Send complete ms. Accepts submissions by e-mail. estimated word count, brief bio, list of publications and where you discovered the publication. Responds in 1 week to queries; 1 month to mss. Accepts simultaneous and reprints submissions. Sample copy online. Writer's guidelines online.

Payment/Terms: Free classified ads for the life of the magazine. Acquires one-time, anthology rights. Sends galleys to author.

Advice: "Though this is an English-language publication, it is not US or UK-centric. Please submit accordingly. *TPR* is a publication of Wind River Press, which also publishes *Critique* magazine and select print and electronic books."

PBW, 513 N. Central Ave., Fairborn OH 45324. (937)878-5184. E-mail: rianca@aol.com. Electronic disk zine; 700 pages, specializing in avant-garde fiction and poetry. "*PBW* is an experimental floppy disk that prints strange and 'unpublishable' in an above-ground-sense writing." Twice per year. Estab. 1988.

How to Contact: "Manuscripts are only taken if they are submitted on disk or by e-mail." Send SASE for reply, return of ms, or send. Sample copy not available.

Payment/Terms: All rights revert back to author Not copyrighted.

$ ◯ ◎ ▦ PERIDOT BOOKS, Tri-Annual Online Magazine of SF, Fantasy & Horror, 1225 Liberty Bell Dr., Cherry Hill NJ 08003. (856)354-0786. E-mail: submissions@peridotbooks.com. Website: www.peridotbooks.com. **Contact:** Ty Drago, editor. Online magazine specializing in science fiction fantasy and horror. "We are an e-zine by writers for writers. Our articles focus on the art, craft and business of writing. Our links and editorial policy all focus on the needs of fiction authors." Triannual. Estab. 1998.

• Peridot Books won the Page One Award for Literary Contribution.

Needs: Fantasy (space fantasy, sword and sorcery, sociological), horror (dark fantasy, futuristic, supernatural), science fiction (hard science/technological, soft/sociological). "No media tie-ins (Star Trek, Star Wars, etc., or space opera, vampires)." Receives 150 unsolicited mss/month. Accepts 8 mss/issue; 24 mss/year. Publishes ms 1-2 months after acceptance. Agented fiction 5%. **Publishes 10 new writers/year.** Length: 1,500-7,500 words; average length: 4,500 words. Also publishes literary essays, literary criticism. Often comments on rejected mss.

How to Contact: Send complete ms with a cover letter, electronic only. Include estimated word count, brief bio, list of publications and name and e-mail address in the body of the story. Responds in 6 weeks to mss. Accepts simultaneous and reprints, multiple submissions. Writer's guidelines online.

Payment/Terms: .5¢/word. Pays on publication for one-time, electronic rights.

Advice: "Give us something original, preferably with a twist. Avoid gratuitous sex or violence. Funny always scores points. Be clever, imaginative, but be able to tell a story with proper mood and characterization. Put your name and e-mail address in the body of the story. Read the site and get a feel for it before submitting."

$ ◯ ▦ PIF, 1426 Harvard Ave. #451, Seattle WA 98122-3813. (360)493-0596. E-mail: editor@pifmagazine.com. Website: pifmagazine.com. **Contact:** Rachel Sage, editor. Electronic magazine. Monthly. Estab. 1995. Circ. 10,000.

• *Pif* ranked on *Writer's Digest*'s "Top 30" list of markets for fiction writers.

Needs: Experimental, literary, very short, "micro" fiction. "No genre fiction." Receives 200-300 unsolicited mss/month. Accepts 1-2 mss/issue; 12-24 mss/year. Publishes ms 1-4 months after acceptance. **Publishes several new writers/year.** Recently published work by Julia Slavin, Brad Bryant, Richard Madelin. Publishes short shorts. Also publishes literary essays, poetry. Sometimes comments on rejected mss.

How to Contact: Accepts submissions by e-mail. Accepts simultaneous submissions. Sample copy online. Writer's guidelines online.

Payment/Terms: Pays $50-200 on publication.

THE PINK CHAMELEON, The Pink Chameleon,. E-mail: dpfreda@juno.com. Website: www.geocities.com/thepinkchameleon/index/html. **Contact:** Mrs. Dorothy Paul Freda, editor/publisher. Family-oriented electronic magazine. Annual. Estab. 2000.

Needs: Adventure, experimental, family saga, fantasy, humor/satire, literary, mainstream, mystery/suspense, religious/inspirational, romance, science fiction, thriller/espionage, western, young adult/teen, psychic/supernatural. "No violence for the sake of violence." Receives 50 unsolicited mss/month. Publishes ms within 1 year after acceptance. **Publishes 50% new writers/year.** Recently published work by Deanne F. Purcell, James W. Collins and C.T. VanHoose. Length: 500-2,500 words; average length: 2,000 words. Publishes short shorts. Also publishes literary essays, poetry. Sometimes comments on rejected mss.

How to Contact: Send complete ms. Responds in 1 month to mss. Accepts reprints, multiple submissions. No simultaneous submissions. Sample copy online. Writer's guidelines online.

Payment/Terms: "Non-Profit. Acquires one-time rights for one year but will return rights earlier on request."

Advice: "Simple, honest, evocative emotion, upbeat submissions that give hope for the future; well-paced plots; stories, poetry, articles, essays that speak from the heart. Read guidelines carefully. Use a good, but not ostentatious opening hook. Stories should have a beginning, middle and end that make the reader feel the story was worth his or her time. This also applies to articles and essays. In the latter two, wrap your comments and conclusions in a neatly packaged paragraph. Turnoffs include violence, bad language used as padding and to sensationalize. Simple, genuine and sensitive work does not need to shock with vulgarity to be interesting and enjoyable."

THE PLAZA, A Space for Global Human Relations, U-Kan, Inc., Yoyogi 2-32-1, Shibuya-ku, Tokyo 151-0053, Japan. E-mail: plaza@u-kan.co.jp. Website: www.u-kan.co.jp. **Contact:** Leo Shunji Nishida, publisher/ fiction editor. Online literary magazine. "*The Plaza* is an intercultural and bilingual magazine (English and Japanese). Our focus is 'the essence of being human.' Some works are published in both Japanese and English (translations by our staff if necessary). The most important criteria is artistic level. We look for works that reflect simply 'being human.' Stories on intercultural (not international) relations are desired. *The Plaza* is devoted to offering a spiritual place where people around the world can share their creative work. We introduce contemporary writers and artists as our generation's contribution to the continuing human heritage." Quarterly.

Needs: Wants to see more fiction "of not human beings, but of being human. Of not international, but intercultural. Of not social, but human relationships." No political themes; religious evangalism; social commentary. Accepts 2 mss/issue. **Publishes 3 new writers/year.** Recently published work by Joe Kernac, Eleanor Lohse and Kikuzou Hidari.

How to Contact: Send complete ms. Accepts submissions by e-mail, fax. Accepts multiple submissions. Sample copy online. Writer's guidelines online.

Advice: "The most important consideration is that the writer is motivated to write. If it is not moral but human, or if it is neither a wide knowledge nor a large computer-like memory, but rather a deep thinking like the quietness in the forest, it is acceptable. While the traditional culture of reading of some thousands of years may be destined to be extinct under the marvelous progress of civilization, we intend to present contemporary works as our global human heritage to readers of forthcoming generations."

PREMONITIONS, Pigasus Press, 13 Hazely Combe, Isle of Wight PO30 3AJ, England. Website: www.piga suspress.co.uk. **Contact:** Tony Lee, editor. "A magazine of quality science fiction plus articles and reviews." Biannual.

Needs: Science fiction (hard, contemporary science fiction/fantasy). "No sword and sorcery, supernatural horror." Accepts 6 mss/issue.

How to Contact: Accepts submissions by mail. "Unsolicited submissions are always welcome, but writers must enclose SAE/IRC for reply, plus adequate postage to return ms if unsuitable." Sample copy online.

Advice: "Potential contributors are advised to study recent issues of the magazine."

REALPOETIK, A Little Magazine of the Internet, 840 W. Nickerson #11, Seattle WA 98119. (206)282-3776. E-mail: salasin@scn.org. Website: www.scn.org/realpoetik. **Contact:** Fiction Editor. "We publish the new, lively, exciting and unexpected in vernacular English. Any vernacular will do." Weekly. Estab. 1993.

Needs: "We do not want to see anything that fits neatly into categories. We subvert categories." Publishes ms 2-4 months after acceptance. **Publishes 20-30 new writers/year.** Average length: 250-500 words. Publishes short shorts. Also publishes literary essays, literary criticism, poetry. Sometimes comments on rejected mss.

How to Contact: Query with or without published clips or send complete ms. Accepts submissions by e-mail. Responds in 1 month to queries. Sample copy online.

Payment/Terms: Acquires one-time rights. Sponsors awards/contests.

Advice: "Be different, but interesting. Humor and consciousness are always helpful. Write short. We're a post-modern e-zine."

THE ROSE & THORN LITERARY E-ZINE, Showcasing Emerging and Established Writers and A Writer's Resource. E-mail: BAQuinn@aol.com. Website: www.theroseandthornezine.com. **Contact:** Barbara Quinn, fiction editor. E-zine specializing in literary works of fiction, nonfiction, poetry and essays. "We created this publication for readers and writers alike. We offer inspiration from eclectic works of distinction and provide a forum for emerging and established voices. We blend contemporary writing with traditional prose and poetry in an effort to promote the literary arts and expand the venue of standard publishing." Quarterly. Circ. 12,000.

Needs: Adventure, ethnic/multicultural, experimental, fantasy, historical, horror (dark fantasy, futuristic, psychological, supernatural), humor/satire, literary, mainstream, mystery/suspense, New Age, regional, religious/inspirational

(inspirational, religious fantasy), romance (contemporary, futuristic/time travel, gothic, historical, regency, romantic suspense), science fiction, thriller/espionage, western. Receives "several hundred" unsolicited mss/month. Accepts 8-10 mss/issue; 40-50 mss/year. **"About 50% of accepted ms are from unpublished writers."** Publishes short shorts. Also publishes literary essays, poetry. Sometimes comments on rejected mss.

How to Contact: Query with or without published clips or send complete ms. Accepts submissions by e-mail. Include estimated word count, 150-word bio, list of publications and author's byline. Responds in 1 week to queries; 1 month to mss. Accepts simultaneous and reprints submissions. Sample copy for free. Writer's guidelines online.

Payment/Terms: Writer retains all rights. Sends galleys to author.

Advice: "Clarity, control of the language, evocative stories that tug at the heart and make their mark on the reader long after it's been read. We look for uniqueness in voice, style and characterization. New twists on old themes are always welcome. Use all aspects of good writing in your stories, including dynamic characters, strong narrative voice and a riveting original plot. We have eclectic tastes, so go ahead and give us a shot. Read the publication and other quality literary journals so you'll see what we look for. Always check your spelling and grammar before submitting. Reread your submission with a critical eye and ask yourself, 'does it evoke an emotional response? Have I completely captured my reader?' Check your submission for 'it' and 'was' and see if you can come up with a better way to express yourself. Be unique."

RPPS/FULLOSIA PRESS, Rockaway Park Philosophical Society, PO Box 280, Ronkonkoma NY 11779. E-mail: deanofrpps@aol.com. Website: rpps_fullosia_press.tripod.com. **Contact:** J.D. Collins, editor. E-zine. "One-person, part-time. Publishes fiction and non-fiction. Our publication is right wing and conservative but amendable to the opposition's point of view. We promote an independent American. We are anti-globabl, anti-UN. Collects unusual news from former British or American provinces. Fiction interests include military, police, private detective, courthouse stories." Monthly. Estab. 1999. Circ. 150.

Needs: Historical (American), military/war, mystery/suspense, thriller/espionage. Christmas, St. Patrick's Day, Fourth of July. Publishes ms 1 week after acceptance. **Publishes 10 new writers/year.** Recently published work by Glen Cunningham, PEter Layton, Dr. Kelly White, James Davies, Dave Waters, Andy Martin, and Peter Vetrand's class. Length: 500-2,000 words; average length: 750 words. Publishes short shorts. Also publishes literary essays. Always comments on rejected mss.

How to Contact: Query with or without published clips. Accepts submissions by e-mail. Include brief bio and list of publications. Responds in 1 month to mss. Accepts simultaneous and reprints, multiple submissions. Sample copy online. Reviews fiction.

Payment/Terms: Acquires electronic rights.

Advice: "Make your point quickly. If you haven't done so, after five pages, everybody hates you and your characters."

$ SCIFI.COM, PMB 391, 511 Avenue of the Americas, New York NY 10011-8436. (212)989-3742. E-mail: datlow@www.scifi.com. Website: www.scifi.com/scifiction/. **Contact:** Ellen Datlow, fiction editor. E-zine specializing in science fiction. "Largest and widest-ranging science fiction site on the web. Affiliated with the Sci Fi Channel, *Science Fiction Weekly*, news, reviews, comics, movies, and interviews." Weekly. Estab. 2000. Circ. 50,000/day.

● *Scifi.com* ranked on *Writer's Digest's* "Top 30" list of best markets for fiction writers. Linda Nagata's novella *Goddess*, first published on Scifi.com, was the first exclusively net-published piece of fiction to ever win the Nebula Award from Science Fiction adn Fantasy Writers of America. Andy Duncan's story "Pottawatamic Giant" won the World Fantasy Award.

Needs: Fantasy (urban fantasy), science fiction (hard science/technological, soft/sociological). "No space opera, sword and sorcery, poetry or high fantasy." Receives 100 unsolicited mss/month. Accepts 1 mss/issue; 35 mss/year. Publishes ms within 6 months after acceptance. Agented fiction 2%. Recently published work by Carol Emshwiller, Robert Reed, Nancy Kress and James P. Blaylock. Length: 1,500-20,000 words; average length: 7,500 words. Sometimes comments on rejected mss.

How to Contact: Send complete ms. Send SASE for return of ms or send a disposable copy of the ms adn #10 SASE for reply only. Responds in 2 months to mss. Writer's guidelines for SASE or on website.

Payment/Terms: Pays 20¢/word up to $3,500. Pays on acceptance for first, electronic, anthology rights.

Advice: "We look for crisp, evocative writing, interesting characters, good storytelling. Check out the kinds of fiction we publish if you can. If you read one, then you know what I want."

SHADOW VOICES. E-mail: phantomlady@geocities.com. Website: www.geocities.com/Athens/Styx/1713index. **Contact:** Vida Janulaitis, editor. Electronic zine. "If you speak of the unknown and reach into the darkness of your soul, share your deepest thoughts. Send me your poetry and short stories."

Needs: "We want well-written fiction or poetry that reveals your inner thoughts. No pornography, or racist material that may inspire someone to do harm to any form of life or property." Wants more fiction that "allows the writer to reveal a different side of life and put those feelings into words. The best writing grabs your attention from beginning and surprises you in the end." Recently published work by Taylor Graham, Rich Logsdon and Vida Janulaitis.

How to Contact: Query with or without published clips or send complete ms. Accepts submissions by e-mail. Sample copy online.

Advice: "Please edit your work carefully. I will assume poetic license. Most of all, write what's inside of you and be sincere about it. Everyone has a unique style. Make yours stand out."

N ☐ ◎ ☑ THE SITE OF BIG SHOULDERS, Chicago Writing, Art and Photography, The Site of Big Shoulders, Chicago IL. E-mail: info@sobs.org. Website: sobs.org. **Contact:** Brian Nemtusak, literary editor. Online magazine. "*The Site of Big Shoulders* features original content with a connection to the greater Chicago area by virtue of authorship or subject matter. Founded on the idea that profit corrupts media, SOBS is a non-commercial community publishing effort that focuses on high editorial quality, aesthetics and production value without regard to commercial need or mass appeal." varies. Estab. 1996. Circ. 20,000.

• This site has won the Bronze Trophy for Exceptional Creativity from the Chicago Internet Review (1998); the Artis Hot Site Award (1998) and the Juno Silver Award (1998).

Needs: Regional (greater Chicago). "We do not publish fiction that does not have a connection to the greater Chicagoland region (northeast Illinois, northwest Indiana, souteast Wisconsin)." Receives 1-5 unsolicited mss/ month. Accepts 4-8 mss/year. Publishes ms 2-12 months after acceptance. **Publishes 4-8 new writers/year.** Recently published work by Mike Beyer, Bob Nemtusak, Paul Barile and Jason Anthony Stavropoulos. Length: 200-3,000 words; average length: 1,000 words. Publishes short shorts. Also publishes literary essays, literary criticism, poetry.

How to Contact: Send complete ms. Accepts submissions by e-mail. brief bio. Responds in 3 months to queries. Accepts simultaneous and reprints, multiple submissions. Sample copy online. Writer's guidelines online.

Payment/Terms: Non-exclusive right to feature the submitted content within the Internet domain.

Advice: "We are very open to the idea of publishing hypertext or other experimental fiction. Please submit clean, edited copy."

☐ SNREVIEW, Starry Night Review—A Literary E-Zine, 197 Fairchild Ave., Fairfield CT 06825-4856. (203)366-5991. E-mail: SNReviewezine@aol.com. Website: members.aol.com/jconln1221/snreview.htm. **Contact:** Joseph Conlin, editor. E-zine specializing in literary short stories, essays and poetry. "We search for material that not only has strong characters and plot but also a devotion to imagery." Semiannual. Estab. 1999.

Needs: Literary, mainstream. Receives 10 unsolicited mss/month. Accepts 5 mss/issue; 20 mss/year. Publishes ms 6 months after acceptance. **Publishes 20 new writers/year.** Recently published work by E. Lindsey Balkan, Marie Griffin and Jonathan Lerner. Length: 1,000-7,000 words; average length: 4,000 words. Also publishes literary essays, literary criticism, poetry.

How to Contact: Accepts submissions by e-mail (only). 100 word bio and list of publications. Responds in 1 month to mss. Accepts simultaneous and reprints submissions. Sample copy online. Writer's guidelines online.

Payment/Terms: Acquires first rights.

N $☐ SONG OF THE SIREN, Mythopoeic Creative Works, Song of the Siren Publishing, P.O. Box 172, Lebanon NH 03766. E-mail: editor@song-of-the-siren.net. Website: www.song-of-the-siren.net. **Contact:** Linda Jeanne, ediotr. *Song of the Siren* is dedicated to creative works of all types inspired by mythology, folklore, and dream. "Within this category we look to publish a wide variety of styles and approaches in each issue." Monthly. Estab. 2003.

Needs: Fiction that has little if anything to do with the magazines theme. Does not want ideas that have been overdone before. Upcoming themes available on website. Accepts 3-4 mss/issue. Publishes ms 1-3 months after acceptance. Publishes short shorts. Also publishes literary essays, literary criticism, poetry. Sometimes comments on rejected mss.

How to Contact: Send complete ms. Send SASE for return of ms or disposable copy of ms and #10 SASE for reply only. Include estimated word count and brief bio in cover letter. Responds in 2-8 weeks to queries; 2-10 weeks to mss. Accepts simultaneous and reprints, multiple submissions. Sample copy online. Writer's guidelines online.

Payment/Terms: $2 minimum; $5 maximum. Or $5 per printed page and free subscription to the magazine. Pays on acceptance for electronic rights.

Advice: "Looking for a unique point of view and a different way of seeing things. Especially looking for work that taps into the raw power of mythology and dream."

N $☐ ⊕ SPOILEDINK MAGAZINE, Spoiledink.com, Dybboisgade 54 3.tv, Copenhagen 1721, Denmark. (0045) 35 81 81 02. E-mail: newsletter@spoiledink.com. Website: www.spoiledink.com. **Contact:** Scott Dille, editor. Online magazine. "We publish quality fiction, especially off-the-wall humour. Our goal is to act as a portal for great unpublished writers. We believe there are thousands of amazing writers that go unpublished. We want to fill the gap for those writers." Monthly. Estab. 2003. Circ. 3,000.

Needs: Adventure, children's/juvenile (adventure, animal), erotica, experimental, feminist, gay, horror, humor/satire, lesbian, mainstream, science fiction, thriller/espionage. Receives 30-40 unsolicited mss/month. Accepts 5-7 mss/issue. Publishes ms 1 month after acceptance. Recently published work by Scotte Dille, Jim Muri, Rebekah Chen and Alan Emmins. Length: 1,000-25,000 words; average length: 6,000 words. Publishes short shorts. Also publishes literary essays, poetry. Rarely comments on rejected mss.

How to Contact: Send complete ms. Accepts submissions by e-mail. Responds in 1 week to queries; 1 month to mss. Accepts simultaneous and reprints, multiple submissions. Sample copy online. Writer's guidelines online.

Payment/Terms: Pays $50-200. Acquires electronic rights. Sponsors awards/contests.

Advice: "Follow instructions on the site. Original well-written stories always stand out. Write in your own true voice."

STARK RAVING SANITY. E-mail: info@starkravingsanity.com. Website: www.starkravingsanity.com. **Contact:** Mike S. Dubose and H. Roger Baker II, editors. Electronic zine. "We have published short stories, poems, novel excerpts, prose poems, micro-fiction, and everything in between. Our intended audience is anyone looking for an entertaining work of substance."

Needs: "Anything goes, as long as it fits our eclectic, ever-changing tastes. We want works that illustrate a variant view of reality—but then all works do just that. So anything of quality is what we like. No hate prose or porn." **Publishes 2-3 new writers/year.** Recently published work by Joe Flowers, R.N. Friedland, Jonathan Lowe and Len Kruger.

How to Contact: Accepts submissions by e-mail. Sample copy online. Writer's guidelines online.

Advice: "In taking fiction, I like (and look for) characters who act as if they are real, situations that are interesting, and writing that sings. I will accept first-time writers if the writing does not look like it came from a first-timer. In other words, I want quality. Please be professional. Read the journal. Read and follow guidelines. And keep in mind also that we too are real people on schedules. Mutual respect, please."

STORY BYTES, Very Short Stories. E-mail: editor@storybytes.com. Website: www.storybytes.com. **Contact:** M. Stanley Bubien, editor. Electronic zine. "We are strictly an electronic publication, appearing on the Internet in three forms. First, the stories are sent to an electronic mailing list of readers. They also get placed on our website, both in PDF and HTML format."

Needs: "Stories must be very short—having a length that is the power of 2, specifically: 2, 4, 8, 16, 32, etc." No sexually explicit material. "Would like to see more material dealing with religion—not necessarily 'inspirational' stories, but those that show the struggles of living a life of faith in a realistic manner." **Publishes 33 percent new writers/year.** Recently published work by Richard K. Weems, Joseph Lerner, Lisa Cote, and Thomas Sennet.

How to Contact: Query with or without published clips or send complete ms. Accepts submissions by e-mail. "I prefer plain text with story title, authorship and word count. Only accepts electronic submissions. See website for complete guidelines." Sample copy online. Writer's guidelines online.

Advice: "In *Story Bytes* the very short stories themselves range in topic. Many explore a brief event—a vignette of something unusual, unique and at times something even commonplace. Some stories can be bizarre, while others quiet lucid. Some are based on actual events, while others are entirely fictional. Try to develop conflict early on (in the first sentence if possible!), and illustrate or resolve this conflict through action rather than description. I believe we'll find an audience for electronic published works primarily in the short story realm."

$STORY FRIENDS, Mennonite Publishing Network, 616 Walnut Ave., Scottdale PA 15683. (724)887-8500. Fax: (724)887-3111. Website: www.mph.org. **Contact:** Susan Reith, editor. "*Story Friends* is planned to nurture faith development in 4-9 year olds." Monthly. Estab. 1905. Circ. 7,000.

Needs: Children's/juvenile. Stories of everyday experiences at home, in church, in school or at a play, which provide models of Christian values. "Wants to see more fiction set in African-American, Latino or Hispanic settings. No stories about children and their grandparents or children and their elderly neighbors. I have more than enough." Publishes ms 1 year after acceptance. **Publishes 10-12 new writers/year.** Recently published work by Virginia Kroll and Lisa Harkrader.

How to Contact: Send complete ms. Responds in 2 months to queries. Accepts simultaneous submissions. Sample copy for 9×12 SAE and 2 first-class stamps. Writer's guidelines for #10 SASE.

Payment/Terms: Pays 3-5¢/word. Pays on acceptance for one-time, second serial (reprint) rights.

Advice: "I am buying more 500-word stories since we switched to a new format. It is important to include relationships, patterns of forgiveness, respect, honesty, trust and caring. Prefer exciting yet plausible short stories which offer varied settings, introduce children to wide ranges of friends and demonstrate joys, fears, temptations and successes of the readers. Read good children's literature, the classics, the Newbery winner and the Caldecott winners. Respect children you know and allow their resourcefulness and character to have a voice in your writing."

THE SUMMERSET REVIEW, 25 Summerset Dr., Smithtown NY 11787. E-mail: editor@summersetrevie w.org. Website: www.summersetreview.org. **Contact:** Joseph Levens, editor. Magazine: illustrations and photographs. "Our goal is simply to publish the highest quality fiction and essays we can find satisfying our guidelines, intended for a general audience. We love lighter pieces. We love romance and fantasy, as long isn't pure genre writing but rather something that might indeed teach us a thing or two. This a simple online literary journal of high quality material, so simple you can call it unique." Quarterly. Estab. 2002.

● Several editors-in-chief of very prominent literary publications are doing interviews for *The Summerset Review*. One has already been published in our Spring 2003 Issue: M.M.M. Hayes of StoryQuarterly.

Needs: Fantasy, humor/satire, literary, romance. No sci-fi, horror, or graphic erotica. Receives 30 unsolicited mss/month. Accepts 4 mss/issue; 18 mss/year. Publishes ms 2-3 months after acceptance. **Publishes 5-10 new writers/year.** Recently published work by Kit Chase, Eric Bosse, Pia Wilson, Michael Marisi, Sarah Maria Gonzales. Length: 8,000 words; average length: 3,000 words. Publishes short shorts. Also publishes literary essays. Often comments on rejected mss.

How to Contact: Send complete ms. Accepts submissions by e-mail. Responds in 1-2 weeks to queries; 4-6 weeks to mss. Accepts simultaneous and reprints submissions. Writer's guidelines online.

Payment/Terms: Acquires no rights, although we request credit if first published in *The Summerset Review*. Sends galleys to author.

Advice: "Style counts. We prefer innovative or at least very smooth, convincing voices. Even the dullest of premises or the complete lack of conflict make for an interesting story if it is told in the right voice and style. We like to find little, interesting facts and/or connections subtly sprinkled throughout the piece. Harsh lanaguge should be used only if/when necessary. If we are choosing between light and dark subjects, the light will usually win."

Ⓝ ◯ $TALES OF THE HOOKMAN ONLINE MAGAZINE, www.russellconnorwriting.com, 6801 Paces Trail, Apt. 338, Arlington TX 76017. (817)561-2483. E-mail: sithlords1@hotmail.com. Website: www.russellconnor writing.com. **Contact:** Russell Connor, editor-in-chief.

Needs: Fantasy (dark fantasy), horror (futuristic, psychological, supernatural, dark humor), science fiction. Publishes ms 6-12 months after acceptance. Often comments on rejected mss.

How to Contact: Send complete ms. Accepts submissions by e-mail. Responds in 2 weeks to queries; 2 months to mss. Accepts simultaneous submissions. Sample copy not available. Writer's guidelines online.

Payment/Terms: Pays honorarium.

Advice: "The best thing you can do is *submit*! Give us a shot! There are only two things we are picky about, and that's polished manuscripts and good plots. Tell me a story you might hear around a campfire. If it takes us an hour to figure out your story, you have overcomplicated it."

Ⓝ ◎ TATTOO HIGHWAY, a Journal of Prose, Poetry & Art, Tinamou Two, 4217 Fruitvale Ave, Oakland CA 94602-2519. (510)531-3604. E-mail: smcaulay@csuhayward.edu. Website: www.tattoohighway.org. **Contact:** Sara McAulay, editor. *Tattoo Highway* publishes high quality literary prose, both experimental and mainstream, including hypertext and Flash media. Each issue has a theme, and subject matter generally spins off from that. The journal is visually handsome, with unusual graphics. "We have no taboos except weak, hackneyed writing. Intended audience: grown-ups who appreciate well-crafted fiction and don't mind an occasional touch of the absurd." Semiannual. Estab. 1998.

Needs: Erotica (ethnic, general), experimental, gay, lesbian, literary, mainstream. "Please no predictable 'formula' stories. No lectures, no tracts, no sermons, on the Mount or otherwise. Graphic sex and/or violence had better be absolutely necessary to the story, and had better be exceptionally well written!" "Mass Transit"-reading period March 15-June 15 '03 (apporx; see website); "Body/Language"-reading period Sept. 15-Dec. 1 '03 (approx; see website). Accepts 5-8 mss/issue; 10-16 mss/year. Publishes ms 1 month after acceptance. Recently published work by D.S Richardson, Susan Moon, Elizabeth Wray, Adam Tavernier, Angela Costi, Stephen Newton, Yvonne Chism-Peace, Gwynne Gilson, John Gilgun, Richard Holeton. Length: 1,500 words; average length: 1,000 words. Publishes short shorts. Also publishes literary essays, poetry. Sometimes comments on rejected mss.

How to Contact: Send complete ms. Accepts submissions by e-mail. Send complete ms with cover letter. Responds in 1 week to queries; 1-2 weeks to mss. Accepts simultaneous, multiple submissions. Sample copy online.

Payment/Terms: Acquires electronic rights. Sponsors awards/contests.

Advice: "Three things: great writing, great writing, and great writing. Look at past issues online, then bring us your best stuff."

◎ THE 13TH WARRIOR REVIEW, Asterius Press, PO Box 5122, Seabrook NJ 08302-3511. E-mail: theeditor @asteriuspress.com. Website: www.asteriuspress.com. **Contact:** John C. Erianne, publisher/editor. Online magazine. Estab. 2000.

Needs: Erotica, experimental, humor/satire, literary, mainstream. Receives 200 unsolicited mss/month. Accepts 4-5 mss/issue; 10-15 mss/year. Publishes ms 6 months after acceptance. **Publishes 1-2 new writers/year.** Recently published work by George Lynn, Ehren Bivins and D. Olsen. Length: 300-3,000 words; average length: 1,500 words. Publishes short shorts. Also publishes literary essays, literary criticism, poetry. Sometimes comments on rejected mss.

How to Contact: Send complete ms. Include estimated word count, brief bio and address/e-mail. Send SASE or IRC for return of ms or send a disposable copy of ms and #10 SASE for reply only. Accepts submissions by e-mail

(test in in message body only, no file attachements). Responds in 1 week to queries; 3 weeks to mss. Accepts simultaneous submissions. Sample copy online. Reviews fiction.
Payment/Terms: Acquires first, electronic rights.

▣ ◎ **THRESHOLDS QUARTERLY, School of Metaphysics Associates Journal**, SOM Publishing, School of Metaphysics World Headquarters, 163 Moon Valley Road, Windyville MO 65783. (417)345-8411. Fax: (417)345-6668. E-mail: som@som.org. Website: www.som.org. **Contact:** Dr. Barbara Condron, editor. Electronic magazine. "The School of Metaphysics is a nonprofit educational and service organization invested in education and research in the expansion of human consciousness and spiritual evolution of humanity. For all ages and backgrounds. Themes: dreaming, healing, science fiction, personal insight, morality tales, fables, humor, spiritual insight, mystic experiences, religious articles, creative writing with universal themes." Quarterly. Estab. 1975.
Needs: Adventure, fantasy, humor/satire, psychic/supernatural/occult, religious/inspirational, science fiction. "No dark, sexual, drug-oriented fiction." Wants to see more "innovative, inspiring, uplifting work." "Dreams, Visions and Creative Imagination"; "Health and Wholeness"; "Intuitive Arts"; "Man's Spiritual Consciousness" Receives 5 unsolicited mss/month. Publishes short shorts. Also publishes literary essays, poetry. Often comments on rejected mss.
How to Contact: Include bio (1-2 paragraphs). Send SASE for reply, return of ms or send a disposable copy of ms. Sample copy not available., Writer's guidelines for 9 × 12 SAE with $1.50 first-class Stamps.
Advice: "We encourage works that have one or more of the following attributes: uplifting, educational, inspirational, entertaining, informative and innovative."

◖ **TOASTED CHEESE**, Toasted Cheese. E-mail: submit@toasted-cheese.com. Website: www.toasted-cheese.com. **Contact:** submit@toasted-cheese.com. E-zine specializing in fiction, creative non-fiction, poetry and flash fiction. "*Toasted Cheese* accepts submissions of previously unpublished fiction, flash fiction, creative non-fiction, and poetry. Our focus is on quality of work, not quantity. Some issues will therefore contain fewer/more pieces than previous issues. We don't restrict publication based on subject matter. We encourage submissions from innovative writers in all genres." Bimonthly. Estab. 2001. Circ. 2,000.
Needs: Adventure, children's/juvenile, ethnic/multicultural, experimental, fantasy, feminist, gay, historical, horror, humor/satire, lesbian, literary, mainstream, mystery/suspense, New Age, psychic/supernatural/occult, romance, science fiction, thriller/espionage, western, young adult/teen. "No fan fiction. No chapters or excerpts unless they read as a stand-alone story. No first drafts." Receives 12 unsolicited mss/month. Accepts 3-5 mss/issue; 18-30 mss/year. **Publishes 9 new writers/year.** Recently published work by Mona Wanlass, Janet Mullaney, Lori F. Dehn, Trina L. Talma and Linda Easley. Length: 500-5,000 words; average length: 1,500 words. Publishes short shorts. Also publishes poetry. Often comments on rejected mss.
How to Contact: Send complete ms. Accepts submissions by e-mail. Responds in 2 months to mss. Accepts simultaneous print submissions only; no simultaneous electronic submissions. Sample copy online. Writer's guidelines online.
Payment/Terms: Acquires electronic rights. Sponsors awards/contests.
Advice: "We are looking for clean, professional writing from writers of any level. Accepted stories will be concise and compelling. We are looking for writers who are serious about the craft: tomorrow's literary stars before they're famous. Take your submission seriously, yet remember that humor and levity are appreciated. You are submitting not to traditional 'editors' but to fellow writers who appreciate the efforts of those in the trenches."

Ⓝ **12-GAUGE.COM**, In Gauge Media LLC, 192 Washington Park, 3rd Floor, Brooklyn NY 11205. (718)852-4816. Fax: (718)222-3737. E-mail: gowan@12gauge.com or lisa@12gauge.com. Website: www.12gauge.com. **Contact:** Gowan Campbell, managing editor. Online magazine. Monthly. Estab. 1995.
Needs: Comics/graphic novels, erotica, ethnic/multicultural, experimental, gay, glitz, humor/satire, lesbian, literary, mainstream, military/war, regional, science fiction. Receives 100 unsolicited mss/month. Accepts 2 mss/issue; 24 mss/year. Publishes ms 3-4 weeks after acceptance. Length: Maximum 5,000 words (fiction); no more than 5 poems per submission; average length: 3,000 words. Publishes short shorts. Also publishes literary essays, literary criticism, poetry. Sometimes comments on rejected mss.
How to Contact: Send complete ms. Accepts submissions by e-mail. estimated word count, brief bio, list of publications and contact information. Accepts simultaneous and reprints, multiple submissions. Sample copy online. Writer's guidelines online.
Payment/Terms: Negotiable. Acquires one-time rights.
Advice: "Work must be original and shouldn't try too hard."

▣ ◎ **VQ ONLINE**, 8009 18th Lane SE, Lacey WA 98503. (360)455-4607. E-mail: jmtanaka@webtv.net. Website: community.webtv.net/JMTanaka/VQ. **Contact:** Janet Tanaka, editor. "Our readers are professional and amateur volcanologists and other volcanophiles. It is not a journal, but an interesting e-zine that features fiction, poetry, nonfiction articles, book and movie reviews, and announcements of interest to volcano scientists." Quarterly.
Needs: Serialized novels, short stories. Nothing pornographic. "Must have volcanoes as a central subject, not just window dressing." **Publishes 4-6 new writers/year.** Recently published work by Susan Mauer, Nolan Keating, Bill West and Wendall Duffield.

How to Contact: Accepts submissions by e-mail. Sample copy online.
Payment/Terms: Pays in contributor copies.
Advice: "Material must be scientifically accurate."

WAXING & WANING, A Magazine of Creative Pagan Fiction, Purple Pentacle, 1116 Wilson Ave., P.O. Box 06056, Toronto ON M3M 1G7 Canada. Fax: (416)242-7115. E-mail: editor@waxingandwaning.com. Website: www.waxingandwaning.com. **Contact:** Terri Paajanen, editor. Online magazine specializing in Pagan fiction. "There need to be Pagan characters or a Pagan element to the story line." Bimonthly. Estab. 1998. Circ. 100.
Needs: Ethnic/multicultural, fantasy, feminist, historical, horror, humor/satire, literary, mainstream, military/war, mystery/suspense, psychic/supernatural/occult, religious/inspirational, romance, science fiction. "Anything as long as there is Pagan content. No erotica, overly dark gothic." Receives 50 unsolicited mss/month. Accepts 10 mss/issue; 60 mss/year. Publishes ms 4 months after acceptance. **Publishes 80 prercent new writers/year.** Length: 1,000-6,000 words; average length: 2,500 words. Publishes short shorts. Also publishes poetry. Sometimes comments on rejected mss.
How to Contact: Send complete ms. Accepts submissions by e-mail (only). Responds in 3 weeks to queries; 2 months to mss. Accepts simultaneous and reprints, multiple submissions. Sample copy for $2. Writer's guidelines online. Reviews fiction.
Payment/Terms: Pays 1-3 contributor copies. Acquires one-time rights. Not copyrighted.
Advice: "Creativity! I want to see unique stories, not tired old witch stories. Make sure you understand what Pagan means. Read our guidelines."

WEB DEL SOL. Website: www.webdelsol.com. **Contact:** Michael Neff, editor-in-chief. Electronic magazine. "The goal of *Web Del Sol* is to use the medium of the Internet to bring the finest in contemporary literary arts to a larger audience. To that end, *WDS* not only webpublishes collections of work by accomplished writers and poets, but hosts over 25 literary arts publications on the WWW such as *Del Sol Review*, *North American Review*, *Zyzzyva*, *Global City Review*, *The Literary Review* and *The Prose Poem*." Estab. 1994.
Needs: "*WDS* publishes work considered to be literary in nature, i.e. non-genre fiction. *WDS* also publishes poetry, prose poetry, essays and experimental types of writing." **Publishes 30-40 new writers/year.** Recently published work by Robert Olen Butler, Forrest Gander, Xue Di, Michael Buceja, Martine Billen and Robley Wilson. Publishes short shorts.
How to Contact: "Submissions by e-mail from September through November and from January through March only. Submissions must contain some brief bio, list of prior publications (if any), and a short work or portion of that work, neither to exceed 1,000 words. Editors will contact if the balance of work is required." Sample copy online.
Advice: "WDS wants fiction that is absolutely cutting edge, unique and/or at a minimum, accomplished with a crisp style and concerning subjects not usually considered the objects of literary scrutiny. Read works in such publications as *Conjunctions* (www.conjunctions.com) and *North American Review* (webdelsol.com/NorthAmReview/NAR) to get an idea of what we are looking for."

WILD VIOLET, Wild Violet, PO Box 39706, Philadelphia PA 19106-9706. E-mail: wildvioletmagazine@yahoo.com. Website: www.wildviolet.net. **Contact:** Alyce Wilson, editor. Online magazine: illustrations, photos. "Our goal is to democratize the arts: to make the arts more accessible and to serve as a creative forum for writers and artists. Our audience includes English-speaking readers from all over the world, who are interested in both 'high art' and pop culture." Quarterly. Estab. 2001.
Needs: Comics/graphic novels, ethnic/multicultural, experimental, fantasy (space fantasy, sword and sorcery), feminist, gay, horror (dark fantasy, futuristic, psychological, supernatural), humor/satire, lesbian, literary, New Age, psychic/supernatural/occult, science fiction. "No stories where sexual or violent content is just used to shock the reader. No racist writings." Receives 15 unsolicited mss/month. Accepts 5 mss/issue; 20 mss/year. **Publishes 7 new writers/year.** Recently published work by Jessica DiMaio, Wayne Scheer, Jane McDonald and Eric Brown. Length: 500-6,000 words; average length: 3,000 words. Also publishes literary essays, literary criticism, poetry. Sometimes comments on rejected mss.
How to Contact: Send complete ms. Accepts submissions by e-mail. Include estimated word count and brief bio.

FOR EXPLANATIONS OF THESE SYMBOLS,
SEE THE INSIDE FRONT AND BACK COVERS OF THIS BOOK.

Send SASE for return of ms or send a disposable copy of ms and #10 SASE for reply only. Responds in 1 week to queries; 3-6 months to mss. Accepts simultaneous, multiple submissions. Sample copy online. Writer's guidelines by e-mail.

Payment/Terms: Writers receive bio and links on contributor's page. All rights retained by author. Sponsors awards/contests.

Advice: "We look for stories that are well-paced and show character and plot development. Even short shorts should do more than simply paint a picture. Manuscripts stand out when the author's voice is fresh and engaging. Avoid muddying your story with too many characters and don't attempt to shock the reader with an ending you have not earned. Experiment with styles and structures, but don't resort to experimentation for its own sake."

◘ **WILMINGTON BLUES.** E-mail: editor@wilmingtonblues.com. Website: www.wilmingtonblues.com. **Contact:** Trace Ramsey. Electronic zine.

Needs: Literary. Receives 60-80 unsolicited mss/month. Publishes ms 1 month after acceptance. Recently published work by Alex Stolis and Steve Gibbs. Length: 250-7,000 words; average length: 2,500 words. Also publishes literary essays, poetry. Often comments on rejected mss.

How to Contact: Accepts submissions by e-mail. Include estimated word count, bio and e-mail address. Responds in 2 weeks to queries; 1 month to mss. Accepts simultaneous submissions. Sample copy online. Writer's guidelines online.

Payment/Terms: Acquires one-time, electronic online archive rights.

Advice: "If your work has something to offer, it will be published. We offer comments on work that isn't accepted, and we encourage resubmission."

N ◘ **WORD RIOT, A Communication-Breakdown Production**, Word Riot Press, P.O. Box 414, Middletown NJ 07748-3143. (732)706-1272. Fax: (732)706-5856. E-mail: submissions@wordriot.org. Website: www.word riot.org. **Contact:** Jordan Rosenfeld and David Barringer, fiction editors. Online magazine. Monthly. Estab. 2002. Member, CLMP.

Needs: Humor/satire, literary, mainstream. "No fantasy, science fiction, romance." Accepts 10-12 mss/issue; 120-144 mss/year. Publishes ms 3 weeks after acceptance. Agented fiction 5%. **Publishes 8-10 new writers/year.** Length: 300-6,000 words; average length: 2,700 words. Publishes short shorts. Also publishes literary essays, poetry. Often comments on rejected mss.

How to Contact: Accepts submissions by e-mail. estimated word count and brief bio. Responds in 4-6 weeks to mss. Accepts multiple submissions. Sample copy online. Writer's guidelines online.

Payment/Terms: Acquires electronic rights. Not copyrighted. Sponsors awards/contests.

Advice: "We're always looking for something edgy or quirky. We like writers who take risks."

◘ **ZUZU'S PETALS QUARTERLY**, P.O. Box 4853, Ithaca NY 14852. (607)539-1141. Website: www.zuzu.com. **Contact:** T. Dunn, editor. Electronic magazine. "Arouse the senses; stimulate the mind." Estab. 1992.

Needs: Ethnic/multicultural, fantasy, gay, humor/satire, lesbian, literary, regional. No "romance, sci-fi, the banal, TV style plotting." Receives 300 unsolicited mss/month. Accepts 1-5 mss/issue; 4-15 mss/year. Publishes ms 4-6 months after acceptance. Agented fiction 10%. Recently published work by Norah Labiner, Jason DeBoer, Rekha Ambardak, Evan Peter, Vincent Zandri and LuAnn Jacobs. Publishes short shorts. Also publishes literary essays, literary criticism, poetry. Sometimes comments on rejected mss.

How to Contact: Send complete ms with a cover letter. Include estimated word count and list of publications. Send SASE (or IRC) for reply, return of ms or send a disposable copy of ms. Responds in 2 weeks to queries 2 weeks to 2 months to mss. Accepts simultaneous submissions. Back issue for $5. Reviews fiction.

Advice: Looks for "strong plotting and a sense of vision. Original situations and true to life reactions."

Consumer Magazines

In this section of *Novel & Short Story Writer's Market* are consumer magazines with circulations of more than 10,000. Many have circulations in the hundreds of thousands or millions. While much has been made over the shrinking consumer magazine market for fiction, new markets are opening. *Seventeen* magazine, for example, has placed new emphasis on publishing fiction. And among the oldest magazines listed here are ones not only familiar to us, but also to our parents, grandparents and even great-grandparents: *The Atlantic Monthly* (1857); *The New Yorker* (1925); *Esquire* (1933); and *Ellery Queen's Mystery Magazine* (1941).

Consumer periodicals make excellent markets for fiction in terms of exposure, prestige and payment. Because these magazines are well-known, however, competition is great. Even the largest consumer publications buy only one or two stories an issue, yet thousands of writers submit to these popular magazines.

Despite the odds, it is possible for talented new writers to break into print in the magazines listed here. Your keys to breaking into these markets are careful research, professional presentation and, of course, top-quality fiction.

TYPES OF CONSUMER MAGAZINES

In this section you will find a number of popular publications, some for a broad-based, general-interest readership and others for large but select groups of readers—children, teenagers, women, men and seniors. There are also religious and church-affiliated magazines, publications devoted to the interests of particular cultures and outlooks, and top markets for genre fiction.

SELECTING THE RIGHT MARKET

Unlike smaller journals and publications, most of the magazines listed here are available at newsstands and bookstores. Many can also be found in the library, and guidelines and sample copies are almost always available by mail or online. Start your search by reviewing the listings, then familiarize yourself with the fiction included in the magazines that interest you.

Don't make the mistake of thinking that just because you are familiar with a magazine, their fiction is the same today as when you first saw it. Nothing could be further from the truth—consumer magazines, no matter how well established, are constantly revising their fiction needs as they strive to expand their audience base.

In a magazine that uses only one or two stories an issue, take a look at the nonfiction articles and features as well. These can give you a better idea of the audience for the publication and clues to the type of fiction that might appeal to them.

If you write genre fiction, check out the specific sections for lists of magazines publishing in that genre (mystery, page 68; romance, page 80; science fiction/fantasy & horror, page 90). For other types of fiction look in the Category Index beginning on page 618. There you will find a list of markets that say they are looking for a particular subject.

FURTHERING YOUR SEARCH

See The "Quick Start" Guide to Publishing Your Fiction (page 2) for information about the material common to all listings in this book. In this section in particular, pay close attention to the number of submissions a magazine receives in a given period and how many they publish in the same period. This will give you a clear picture of how stiff your competition can be.

While many of the magazines listed here publish one or two pieces of fiction in each issue, some also publish special fiction issues once or twice a year. When possible, we have indicated this in the listing information. We also note if the magazine is open to novel excerpts as well as short fiction, and we advise novelists to query first before submitting long work.

The Business of Fiction Writing, beginning on page 59, covers the basics of submitting your work. Professional presentation is a must for all markets listed. Editors at consumer magazines are especially busy, and anything you can do to make your manuscript easy to read and accessible will help your chances of being published. Most magazines want to see complete manuscripts, but watch for publications in this section that require a query first.

As in the previous section, we've included our own comments in many of the listings, set off by a bullet (●). Whenever possible, we list the publication's recent awards and honors. We've also included any special information we feel will help you in determining whether a particular publication interests you.

The maple leaf symbol (✄) identifies our Canadian listings. You will also find some English-speaking markets from around the world. These foreign magazines are denoted with ⊕ at the beginning of the listings. Remember to use International Reply Coupons rather than stamps when you want a reply from a country other than your own.

For More Information

For more on consumer magazines, see issues of *Writer's Digest* (by F&W Publications) and other industry trade publications available in larger libraries.

For news about some of the genre publications listed here and information about a particular field, there are a number of magazines devoted to genre topics, including *The Mystery Review*, *Locus* (for science fiction); *Science Fiction Chronicle*; and *Romance Writers' Report* (available to members of Romance Writers of America).

A&U, AMERICA'S AIDS MAGAZINE, Art & Understanding, Inc., 25 Monroe St., Suite 205, Albany NY 12210-2729. (518)426-9010. Fax: (518)436-5354. Website: www.aumag.org. **Contact:** Chael Needle, managing editor. Magazine: 8⅛×10⅛; 48-72 pages; coated paper; coating u/v cover; illustrations; photos. Monthly. Estab. 1991. Circ. 205,000.

Needs: Receives 5-10 unsolicited mss/month. Accepts 0-1 mss/issue; 9 mss/year. Publishes ms 3 months after acceptance. **Publishes 1-2 new writers/year.** Recently published work by Rachel S. Thomas-Medwid, Joe Rudy, Barbara Deming, Sarah Schulman, Lee Varon, Paul Lisicki, Felice Picano. Length: less than 1,500 words; average length: 1,200 words. Also publishes literary essays, literary criticism, poetry.

How to Contact: Send complete ms. Accepts submissions by mail, fax, phone. Include estimated word count, brief bio and list of publications. Send SASE for return of ms or disposable copy of ms and #10 SASE for reply only. Prefers e-mail submissions. Responds in 1 month to queries; 2 months to mss. Accepts simultaneous, multiple submissions. Sample copy for $5. Writer's guidelines online. Reviews fiction.

Payment/Terms: Pays $50-200. Pays 2 months after publication. Acquires first North American serial rights. Sends galleys to author.

Advice: "Fiction addressing the HIV/AIDS pandemic in a honest, non-sensationalist, original way. Characters who have HIV/AIDS, going through day-to-day experiences. We are looking for shorter pieces to match space requirements."

AFRICAN VOICES, African Voices Communications, Inc., 270 W. 96th St., New York NY 10025. (212)865-2982. Fax: (212)316-3335. Website: www.africanvoices.com. **Contact:** Kim Horne, fiction editor. Magazine: 52 pages; illustrations; photos. "*African Voices* is dedicated to highlighting the art, literature, and history of people of color." Quarterly. Estab. 1992. Circ. 20,000.

Needs: Adventure, children's/juvenile, condensed novels, erotica, ethnic/multicultural, experimental, fantasy, gay, historical (general), horror, humor/satire, literary, mainstream, mystery/suspense, novel excerpts, psychic/supernatural/occult, religious/inspirational, romance, science fiction, serialized novels, slice-of-life vignettes, suspense, young adult/teen (adventure, romance), African-American. List of upcoming themes available for SASE. Publishes special fiction issue. Receives 20-50 unsolicited mss/month. Accepts 20 mss/issue. Publishes ms 3-6 months after acceptance. Agented fiction 5%. **Publishes 30 new writers/year.** Recently published work by Junot Diaz, Michel Marriott and Carol Dixon. Length: 500-2,500 words; average length: 2,000 words. Publishes short shorts. Also publishes literary essays, poetry.

How to Contact: Send complete ms. Accepts submissions by mail. Include short bio. Send SASE for return of ms. Responds in 3 months to queries. Accepts simultaneous and reprints submissions. Sample copy for $5 or online. Writer's guidelines online. Reviews fiction.
Payment/Terms: Pays $25-50. Pays on publication for first North American serial rights.
Advice: "A manuscript stands out if it is neatly typed with a well-written and interesting story line or plot. Originality encouraged. We are interested in more horror, erotic and drama pieces. *AV* wants to highlight the diversity in our culture. Stories must touch the humanity in us all."

$ ☑ AIM MAGAZINE, Aim Publishing Co., P.O. Box 1174, Maywood IL 60153. (708)344-4414. Fax: (206)543-2746. Website: aimmagazine.org. **Contact:** Ruth Apilado, associate editor. Magazine: 8½×11; 48 pages; slick paper; photos and illustrations. Publishes material "to purge racism from the human bloodstream through the written word—that is the purpose of *Aim Magazine*." Quarterly. Estab. 1975. Circ. 10,000.
Needs: Ethnic/multicultural, historical, mainstream, suspense. Open. No "religious" mss. Published special fiction issue last year; plans another. Receives 25 unsolicited mss/month. Accepts 15 mss/issue; 60 mss/year. Publishes ms 3 months after acceptance. **Publishes 40 new writers/year.** Recently published work by Christina Touregny, Thomas Lee Harris, Michael Williams and Jake Halpern. Publishes short shorts. Sometimes comments on rejected mss.
How to Contact: Send complete ms. Accepts submissions by mail, e-mail. Include SASE with cover letter and author's photograph. Responds in 2 months to queries; 1 month to mss. Accepts simultaneous submissions. Sample copy and writer's guidelines for $4 and 9×12 SAE with $1.70 postage or online.
Payment/Terms: Pays $25-35. Pays on publication for first, one-time rights.
Advice: "Search for those who are making unselfish contributions to their community and write about them. Write about your own experiences. Be familar with the background of your characters. Known for stories with social significance, proving that people from different ethnic, racial backgrounds are more alike than they are different."

$ ☑ ◎ AMERICAN GIRL, Pleasant Co. Publications, 8400 Fairway Place, Middleton WI 53562. (608)836-4848. Website: www.americangirl.com. **Contact:** Magazine Department Assistant. Magazine: 8½×11; 52 pages; illustrations; photos. "Four-color bimonthly magazine for girls age 8-12. We want thoughtfully developed children's literature with good characters and plots." Bimonthly. Estab. 1992. Circ. 700,000.
Needs: Adventure, children's/juvenile (girls 8-12 years), condensed novels, ethnic/multicultural, historical, humor/satire, slice-of-life vignettes. No romance, science fiction, fantasy. Receives 100 unsolicited mss/month. Accepts 6 mss/year. **Publishes 2-3 new writers/year.** Recently published work by Kay Thompson, Mavis Jukes and Susan Shreve. Publishes short shorts. Also publishes literary essays, poetry.
How to Contact: Query with published clips. Accepts submissions by mail. Include bio (1 paragraph). Send SASE for reply, return of ms or send a disposable copy of ms. Send SASE for guidelines. Responds in 3 months to queries. Accepts simultaneous and reprints submissions. Sample copy for $3.95 (check made out to *American Girl*) and 9×12 SAE with $1.98 postage. Writer's guidelines online.
Payment/Terms: Pays $500 minimum. Pays on acceptance for all rights. Sends galleys to author.
Advice: "We're looking for excellent character development with an interesting plot."

$ ☑ ⚇ ANALOG SCIENCE FICTION & FACT, Dell Magazine Fiction Group, 475 Park Ave. S., 11th Floor, New York NY 10016. (212)686-7188. Fax: (212)686-7414. Website: www.analogsf.com. **Contact:** Stanley Schmidt, editor. Magazine: 144 pages; illustrations; photos. Monthly. Estab. 1930. Circ. 50,000.
• Fiction published in *Analog* has won numerous Nebula and Hugo Awards. *Analog* ranked on *Writer's Digest's* "Top 30" list of best markets for fiction writers.
Needs: Science fiction (hard science/technological, soft/sociological). "No fantasy or stories in which the scientific background is implausible or plays no essential role." Receives 500 unsolicited mss/month. Accepts 6 mss/issue; 70 mss/year. Publishes ms 10 months after acceptance. Agented fiction 5%. **Publishes 3-4 new writers/year.** Recently published work by Ben Bova, Stephen Baxter, Larry Niven, Michael Swanwick, Timothy Zahn, Robert J. Sawyer, and Joan Slonczewski. Length: 2,000-80,000 words; average length: 10,000 words. Publishes short shorts. Sometimes comments on rejected mss.
How to Contact: Send complete ms with a cover letter. Include estimated word count. Send SASE for return of ms or send a disposable copy of ms and #10 SASE for reply only. Accepts multiple submissions. Sample copy for $5. Writer's guidelines online. Reviews fiction.
Payment/Terms: Pays 4¢/word for novels; 5-6¢/word for novelettes; 6-8¢/word for shorts under 7,500 words;

$450-600 for intermediate lengths. Pays on acceptance for first North American serial, nonexclusive foreign serial rights. Sends galleys to author. Not copyrighted.

Advice: "I'm looking for irresistibly entertaining stories that make me think about things in ways I've never done before. Read several issues to get a broad feel for our tastes, but don't try to imitate what you read."

$ ☒ ☑ ◎ **THE ANNALS OF SAINT ANNE DE BEAUPRÉ**, Redemptorist Fathers, P.O. Box 1000, St. Anne De Beaupré QC G0A 3C0 Canada. (418)827-4538. Fax: (418)827-4530. **Contact:** Father Roch Achard, C.S.R., editor. Magazine: 8×11; 32 pages; glossy paper; photos. "Our mission statement includes dedication to Christian family values and devotion to St. Anne." Releases 11 issues/year; July and August are one issue. Estab. 1885. Circ. 32,000.

Needs: Religious/inspirational. "No senseless mockery." Receives 50-60 unsolicited mss/month. Recently published work by Beverly Sheresh and Eugene Miller. Always comments on rejected mss.

How to Contact: Send complete ms. Include estimated word count. Send SASE for reply or return of ms. Responds in 1 month to queries. No simultaneous submissions. Sample copy and writer's guidelines for 8½×11 SAE and IRCs.

Payment/Terms: Pays 3-4¢/word. Pays on acceptance for first North American serial, first rights. "Please state rights for sale."

$ ☒ **ART TIMES, A Literary Journal and Resource for All the Arts**, P.O. Box 730, Mount Marion NY 12456-0730. (914)246-6944. Fax: (914)246-6944. Website: www.ulster.net/~arttimes. **Contact:** Raymond J. Steiner, fiction editor. Magazine: 12×15; 24 pages; Jet paper and cover; illustrations; photos. "*Art Times* covers the art fields and is distributed in locations most frequented by those enjoying the arts. Our copies are distributed throughout upstate New York counties as well as in most of the galleries of Soho, 57th Street and Madison Avenue in the metropolitan area; locations include theaters, galleries, museums, cultural centers and the like. Our readers are mostly over 40, affluent, art-conscious and sophisticated. Subscribers are located across U.S. and abroad (Italy, France, Germany, Greece, Russia, etc.)." Monthly. Estab. 1984. Circ. 24,000.

Needs: Adventure, ethnic/multicultural, fantasy, feminist, gay, historical, humor/satire, lesbian, literary, mainstream, science fiction, contemporary. "We seek quality literary pieces. Nothing violent, sexist, erotic, juvenile, racist, romantic, political, etc." Receives 30-50 unsolicited mss/month. Accepts 1 mss/issue; 11 mss/year. Publishes ms 4 years after acceptance. **Publishes 6 new writers/year.** Publishes short shorts.

How to Contact: Send complete ms. SASE. Responds in 3 months to queries; 6 months to mss. Accepts simultaneous, multiple submissions. Sample copy for 9×12 SAE and 6 first-class stamps. Writer's guidelines for #10 SASE or on website.

Payment/Terms: Pays $25 maximum (honorarium) and 1 year's free subscription. Pays on publication for first North American serial, first rights.

Advice: "Competition is greater (more submissions received), but keep trying. We print new as well as published writers."

$ ☒ ◎ ☯ **ASIMOV'S SCIENCE FICTION**, Dell Magazine Fiction Group, 475 Park Ave. S., 11th Floor, New York NY 10016. (212)686-7188. Fax: (212)686-7414. Website: www.asimovs.com. **Contact:** Gardner Dozois, editor. Magazine: 5¼×8¼ (trim size); 144 pages; 30 lb. newspaper; 70 lb. to 8 pt. C1S cover stock; illustrations; rarely prints photos. Magazine consists of science fiction and fantasy stories for adults and young adults. Publishes "the best short science fiction available." Estab. 1977. Circ. 50,000.

● Named for a science fiction "legend," *Asimov's* regularly receives Hugo and Nebula Awards. Editor Gardner Dozois has received several awards for editing including Hugos and those from *Locus* and *Science Fiction Chronicle* magazines. *Asimov* ranked on *Writer's Digest's* "Top 30" list of best markets for fiction writers.

Needs: Fantasy, science fiction (hard science, soft sociological). No horror or psychic/supernatural. Would like to see more hard science fiction. Receives approximately 800 unsolicited mss/month. Accepts 10 mss/issue. Publishes ms 6-12 months after acceptance. Agented fiction 10%. **Publishes 6 new writers/year.** Recently published work by Ursula LeGuin and Larry Niven. Publishes short shorts. Comments on rejected mss "when there is time."

How to Contact: Accepts submissions by mail. Send complete ms with SASE. Responds in 2 months to queries; 3 months to mss. Accepts reprints submissions. No simultaneous submissions. Sample copy for $5. Writer's guidelines for #10 SASE or online. Reviews fiction.

Payment/Terms: Pays 5-8¢/word. Pays on acceptance. Buys first North American serial, nonexclusive foreign serial rights; reprint rights occasionally. Sends galleys to author.

Advice: "We are looking for character stories rather than those emphasizing technology or science. New writers will do best with a story under 10,000 words. Every new science fiction or fantasy film seems to 'inspire' writers—and this is not a desirable trend. Be sure to be familiar with our magazine and the type of story we like; workshops and lots of practice help. Try to stay away from trite, clichéd themes. Start in the middle of the action, starting as close to the end of the story as you possibly can. We like stories that extrapolate from up-to-date scientific research, but don't forget that we've been publishing clone stories for decades. Ideas must be fresh.'

Ⓝ ◎ $**ATLANTA**, 1330 W. Peachtree St. NE, Suite 450, Atlanta GA 30309. (404)872-3100. Fax: (404)870-6219. Website: www.atlantamagazine.com. **Contact:** Rebecca Burns, editor. "*Atlanta* magazine articulates the special nature of Atlanta and appeals to an audience that wants to understand and celebrate the uniqueness of the region. The magazine's mission is to serve as a tastemaker by virtue of in-depth information and authoritative, provocative explorations of issues, personalities, and lifestyles." Monthly. Circ. 69,000.

Needs: Novel excerpts. Needs short stories for 2 annual reading issues—Winter & Summer. "We prefer all fiction to be by Georgia writers and/or have a Georgia/Southern theme. Receives 5 unsolicited mss/month. Accepts 7 mss/ year. Reads for Winter edition January 2004. Reads for Summer edition June 2004. Agented fiction 10%. **Publishes 2 new writers/year.** Recently published work by George Singleton, Jim Grimsley, and Pearl Cleage. Length: 1,500-5,000 words; average length: 3,000 words. Publishes short shorts. Rarely comments on rejected mss.

How to Contact: Accepts submissions by mail, e-mail. Responds in 3 months to queries. Sample copy online.

Payment/Terms: Pays on acceptance for first North American serial rights.

Advice: "Remember we want Georgia writers and Southern themes—not stories set in China, avoid bad southern gothic clichés!"

$ ⬛ THE ATLANTIC MONTHLY, 77 N. Washington St., Boston MA 02114. (617)854-7749. Fax: (617)854-7877. Website: www.theatlantic.com. **Contact:** C. Michael Curtis, senior editor. General magazine for an educated readership with broad cultural interests. Monthly. Estab. 1857. Circ. 500,000.

● *The Atlantic Monthly* won a 2003 National Magazine Award for general excellence.

Needs: Literary and contemporary fiction. "Seeks fiction that is clear, tightly written with strong sense of 'story' and well-defined characters." Receives 1,000 unsolicited mss/month. Accepts 10 mss/year. **Publishes 3-4 new writers/year.** Recently published work by Mary Gordon, Donald Hall and Roxana Robinson.

How to Contact: Send complete ms. Accepts submissions by mail. Responds in 2 months to mss. Accepts multiple submissions. No simultaneous submissions. Writer's guidelines online.

Payment/Terms: Pays $3,000. Pays on acceptance for first North American serial rights.

Advice: When making first contact, "cover letters are sometimes helpful, particularly if they cite prior publications or involvement in writing programs. Common mistakes: melodrama, inconclusiveness, lack of development, unpersuasive characters and/or dialogue."

$ ⬛ ◎ BALLOON LIFE, Balloon Life Magazine, Inc., 2336 47th Ave. SW, Seattle WA 98116-2331. (206)935-3649. Fax: (206)935-3326. E-mail: tom@balloonlife.com. Website: www.balloonlife.com. **Contact:** Tom Hamilton, editor. Magazine: 8½ × 11; 48 pages; color, b&w photos. Publishes material "about the sport of hot air ballooning. Readers participate as pilots, crew, official observers at events and spectators." Monthly. Estab. 1986. Circ. 4,000.

Needs: Humor/satire, related to hot air ballooning. "Manuscripts should involve the sport of hot air ballooning in any aspect. Prefer humor based on actual events; fiction seldom published." Accepts 4-6 mss/year. Publishes ms 3-4 months after acceptance. Length: 800-1,500 words; average length: 1,200 words. Publishes short shorts. Sometimes comments on rejected mss.

How to Contact: Send complete ms. Accepts submissions by e-mail, fax. SASE. Responds in 3 weeks to queries; 1 month to mss. Accepts simultaneous and reprints submissions. Sample copy for 9 × 12 SAE with $2 postage. Writer's guidelines for #10 SASE.

Payment/Terms: Pays $25-75 and contributor's copies. Pays on publication for all rights.

Advice: "Generally the magazine looks for humor pieces that can provide a light-hearted change of pace from the technical and current event articles. An example of a work we used was titled 'Balloon Astrology' and dealt with the character of a hot air balloon based on what sign it was born (made) under."

⬛ $ ⬛ THE BEAR DELUXE MAGAZINE, Orlo, P.O. Box 10342, Portland OR 97296. (503)242-1047. E-mail: bear@orlo.org. Website: www.orlo.org. **Contact:** Tom Webb, editor. Magazine: 11 × 14; 68 pages; newsprint paper; Kraft paper cover illustrations; photos. "*The Bear Deluxe Magazine* provides a fresh voice amid often strident and polarized environmental discourse. Street level, solution-oriented, and nondogmatic, *The Bear Deluxe* presents lively creative discussion to a diverse readership." Semiannual. Estab. 1993. Circ. 19,000.

● *The Bear Deluxe* has received a publishing grant from the Oregon Council for the Humanities, Literary Arts, Regional Arts and Culture Council.

Needs: Adventure, condensed novels, historical, horror, humor/satire, mystery/suspense, novel excerpts, western. "No detective, children's or horror." Enviromentally focused: humor/satire, literary, science fiction. "We would like to see more nontraditional forms." List of upcoming themes available for SASE. Receives 20-30 unsolicited mss/month. Accepts 2-3 mss/issue; 8-12 mss/year. Publishes ms 2 months after acceptance. **Publishes 5-6 new writers/year.** Recently published work by Peter Houlahan, John Reed and Karen Hueler. Length: 750-4,500 words; average length: 2,500 words. Publishes short shorts. Also publishes literary essays, literary criticism, poetry. Sometimes comments on rejected mss.

How to Contact: Query with or without published clips or send complete ms. Accepts submissions by mail, e-mail. Send disposable copy of mss. Responds in 3 months to queries; 6 months to mss. Accepts simultaneous and reprints submissions. Sample copy for $3. Writer's guidelines for #10 SASE or on website. Reviews fiction.

Payment/Terms: Pays free subscription to the magazine, contributor's copies and 5¢/word; additional copies for postage. Pays on publication for first, one-time rights.

Advice: "Keep sending work. Write actively and focus on the connections of man, nature, etc., not just flowery descriptions. Urban and suburban enviroments are grist for the mill as well. Have not seen enough quality humorous

insider report

Curtis: Happy to find beginners

Attention, short story writers who want to see their work published in *The Atlantic Monthly*. If you address your story directly to fiction editor C. Michael Curtis, your work will be read by the man himself.

Photo © Julia Livshin

That's right. About half the 12,000 or so short stories the magazine receives each year go to Curtis, and about half to interns. "The ones that are addressed to me, I read. I may send them to someone else for a second reading, but I read them."

Not to worry if you've already sent a story to the magazine without addressing it to Curtis. Of the interns, he says: "We've chosen young people who have impressed us with their ability to read stories swiftly and to be coherent in expressing an opinion about them, and whose views seem to roughly coincide with ours."

C. Michael Curtis

Once the interns read the stories, they pass along those with merit to Curtis for a second read. "We all respond to intelligent writing, well-shaped sentences and distinctive language, for the first few sentences, or paragraphs," he says. "By the time we've gotten to page two or three, we're interested in the story or we're not."

With all those submissions, the competition is stiff for the magazine's single short story slot per monthly issue. What makes a manuscript stand out? "I first look for language . . . and I've said, only half-seriously, that the best way to get our attention here is to write a sentence in which you use a semi-colon correctly," he says. "To find a compound-complex sentence in which the elements are under control is often enough to keep us reading, and if we are introduced to language that is inventive and off-beat, or magical in some way, we're far more likely to stay with the story."

Beyond the proper use of language, Curtis looks for the development of characters, interesting situations and a sense of resolution. "In the meantime, you just want to feel pulled into the story, often because of a kind of directness and plain language. Plain in the sense of getting to the point and not making the reader wonder what's going on."

Curtis' advice especially applies to first-time writers, since clarity and directness are frequently lacking in that group. "I read an awful lot of beginning work that involves wheel spinning, throat clearing and flights of fancy that seem on the surface to be artful, but in fact are an impediment to careful reading."

Still, he has encouragement for people who are just starting to write. "The fact that they're beginning doesn't put them at a disadvantage, unless of course they don't yet know how to write very well. We don't distinguish between veterans and beginners."

In fact, Curtis says *The Atlantic* is happier to find work by beginning writers than by more established, well-known writers. "We derive more satisfaction from having a hand in the beginning of careers and in placing our judgment against the future than in printing the work of people whose skills are well-known and widely acknowledged," he says. "You don't need a lot of imagination to discover the wonderfulness of an Oates story or an Updike story. To find work by someone no one has ever heard of is exciting."

For Curtis, the thrill of discovering a writer remains, even though he's been at it for decades. He joined *The Atlantic* in 1963, seven years after receiving a bachelor's degree in English from Cornell University. He has taught creative writing, ethics and grammar at Harvard University, Cornell and the Massachusetts Institute of Technology. His own work has appeared in *The Atlantic*, *The New Republic*, *National Review*, and *Sport*.

While finding new talent is exciting, Curtis has seen the opportunity for sharing that excitement with magazine readers reduced significantly. "In the case of *The Atlantic*, *Harper's*, and *The New Yorker*, the absolute volume of the stories has shrunk," he says. "Our magazines are a little smaller. Printing is much more expensive and instead of publishing three or four stories an issue—as we did in the '30s and '40s—we're now publishing only one."

That's unfortunate, he says: "Writers would be better served if *The Atlantic* was able to publish 30 or 40 or 50 stories a year . . . that would mean more exposure to a certain kind of enlightened audience that responds to and respects literary work."

At the same time, Curtis notes some publications have increased opportunities for short story writers. He points to new literary quarterlies, new specialized magazines and the addition of fiction in some unexpected places, such as Sunday newspaper magazines.

Curtis also has seen trends in fiction, some lasting and some short-lived. One of the trends today is stories focused on older parents and grandparents. "I suspect a lot of writers are of an age where they have parents who have survived in ways they wouldn't have 30 or 40 years ago." The magazine has published a number of stories in this vein, but has also had to turn many away.

Another trend: "An event like the World Trade Center attacks "generates a lot of stories on themes fairly directly related to the event." That trend, he expects, "will tend to end in a year or so."

—*Katie Brogan*

and ironic writing. Juxtaposition of place welcome. Action and hands-on great. Not all that interested in enviromental ranting and simple 'walks through the park.' Make it powerful, yet accessible to a wide audience."

$⦿ BOMB MAGAZINE, New Arts Publications, 594 Broadway, Suite 905, New York NY 10012-3289. (212)4313943. Fax: (212)4315880. E-mail: info@bombsite.com. Website: www.bombsite.com. Magazine: 11X14; 104 pages; 70 lb. glossy cover; illustrations; photos. Written, edited and produced by industry professionals and funded by those interested in the arts. Publishes "work which is unconventional and contains an edge, whether it be in style or subject matter." Quarterly. Estab. 1981. Circ. 36,000.

Needs: Experimental, novel excerpts, contemporary. No genre: romance, science fiction, horror, western. Upcoming theme: "The Americas," featuring work by artists and writers from Central and South America (no unsolicited mss for theme issue, please). Receives 200 unsolicited mss/month. Accepts 6 mss/issue; 24 mss/year. Publishes ms 3-6 months after acceptance. Agented fiction 70%. **Publishes 2-3 new writers/year.** Recently published work by Melanie Rae Thon, Carole Maso, Molly McQuade and Mary Jo Bang.

How to Contact: Accepts submissions by mail. SASE. Responds in 3-5 months to mss. Accepts multiple submissions. Sample copy for $7, plus $1.42 postage and handling. Writer's guidelines by e-mail.

Payment/Terms: Pays $100, and contributor's copies. Pays on publication for first, one-time rights. Sends galleys to author.

Advice: "We are committed to publishing new work that commercial publishers often deem too dangerous or difficult. The problem is, a lot of young writers confuse difficult with dreadful. Read the magazine before you even think of submitting something."

$⦿ ▣ BOSTON REVIEW, E53-407, M.I.T., Cambridge MA 02139. (617)258-0805. Fax: (617)252-1549. E-mail: bostonreview@mit.edu. Website: www.bostonreview.net. **Contact:** Junot Diaz, fiction editor. Magazine: 10¾ × 14¾; 60 pages; newsprint. "The editors are committed to a society and culture that foster human diversity and a democracy in which we seek common grounds of principle amidst our many differences. In the hope of advancing these ideals, the *Review* acts as a forum that seeks to enrich the language of public debate." Bimonthly. Estab. 1975. Circ. 20,000.

• *Boston Review* is the recipient of a Pushcart Prize in poetry.
Needs: Ethnic/multicultural, experimental, literary, regional, translations, contemporary, prose poem. "No romance, erotica, genre fiction." Receives 150 unsolicited mss/month. Accepts 4-6 mss/year. Publishes ms 4 months after acceptance. Recently published work by David Mamet, Rhonda Stamell, Jacob Appel, Elisha Porat and Diane Williams. Length: 1,200-5,000 words; average length: 2,000 words. Occasionally comments on rejected mss.
How to Contact: Send complete ms. Responds in 4 months to queries. Accepts simultaneous submissions if noted. Sample copy for $5 or online. Writer's guidelines online. Reviews fiction.
Payment/Terms: Pays $50-100, and 5 contributor's copies. Acquires first North American serial, first rights.

$◎ BOWHUNTER, The Number One Bowhunting Magazine, Primedia Consumer Media & Magazine Group, 6405 Flank Dr., Harrisburg PA 17112. (717)657-9555. Fax: (717)657-9552. E-mail: bowhunter_magazine@p rimediamags.com. Website: www.bowhunter.com. **Contact:** Dwight Schuh, editor. Magazine: 7¾ × 10½: 150 pages; 75 lb. glossy paper; 150 lb. glossy cover stock; illustrations; photos. "We are a special-interest publication, produced by bowhunters for bowhunters, covering all aspects of the sport. Material included in each issue is designed to entertain and inform readers, making them better bowhunters." Bimonthly. Estab. 1971. Circ. 1,714,666.
Needs: Bowhunting, outdoor adventure. "Writers must expect a very limited market. We buy only one or two fiction pieces a year. Writers must know the market—bowhunting—and let that be the theme of their work. No 'me and my dog' types of stories; no stories by people who have obviously nver held a bow in their hands." Receives 25 unsolicited mss/month. Accepts 1-2 mss/year. Publishes ms 3 months to 2 years after acceptance. Length: 500-2,000 words; average length: 1,500 words. Publishes short shorts. Sometimes comments on rejected mss.
How to Contact: Send complete ms. Accepts submissions by mail, e-mail, fax. Responds in 2 weeks to queries; 1 month to mss. Sample copy for $2 and 8½ × 11 SAE with appropriate postage. Writer's guidelines for #10 SASE or on website.
Payment/Terms: Pays $100-350. Pays on acceptance. Buys exclusive first, worldwide publication rights.
Advice: "We have a resident humorist who supplies us with most of the 'fiction' we need. But if a story comes through the door which captures the essence of bowhunting and we feel it will reach out to our readers, we will buy it. Despite our macho outdoor magazine status, we are a bunch of English majors who love to read. You can't bull your way around real outdoor people—they can spot a phony at 20 paces. If you've never camped out under the stars and listened to an elk bugle and try to relate that experience without really experiencing it, someone's going to know. We are very specialized; we don't want stories about shooting apples off people's heads or of Cupid's arrow finding its mark. James Dickey's *Deliverance* used bowhunting metaphorically, very effectively . . . while we don't expect that type of writing from everyone, that's the kind of feeling that characterizes a good piece of outdoor fiction."

$◎ ▣ BOYS' LIFE, Boy Scouts of America, P.O. Box 152079, Irving TX 75015-2079. (972)580-2355. Fax: (972)580-2079. Website: www.boyslife.org. **Contact:** Rich Haddaway, associate editor. Magazine: 8 × 11; 68 pages; slick cover stock; illustrations; photos. "*Boys' Life* covers Boy Scout activities and general interest subjects for ages 8 to 18, Boy Scouts, Cub Scouts and others of that age group." Monthly. Estab. 1911. Circ. 1,300,000.
Needs: Adventure, humor/satire, mystery/suspense (young adult), science fiction, western (young adult), young adult/teen, sports. "We publish short stories aimed at a young adult audience and frequently written from the viewpoint of a 10-to 16-year old boy protagonist." Receives 150 unsolicited mss/month. Accepts 12-18 mss/year. Publishes ms 1 year after acceptance. **Publishes 1 new writer/year.** Recently published work by Gary Paulsen, G. Clifton Wisler, Iain Lawrence and Ben Bova. Length: 1,000-1,500 words; average length: 1,200 words. Rarely comments on rejected mss.
How to Contact: Send complete ms. Accepts submissions by mail, fax. Responds in 2 months to queries. Sample copy for $3 and 9 × 12 SAE. Writer's guidelines for #10 SASE or online.
Payment/Terms: Pays $750 minimum. Pays on acceptance for one-time rights.
Advice: "*Boys' Life* writers understand the readers. They treat them as intelligent human beings with a thirst for knowledge and entertainment. We tend to use some of the same authors repeatedly because their characters, themes, etc., develop a following among our readers. Read at least a year's worth of the magazine. You will get a feeling for what our readers are interested in and what kind of fiction we buy."

Ⓝ $ BREAKAWAY MAGAZINE, Focus on the Family, 8605 Explorer Dr., Colorado Springs CO 80920. (719)531-3400. Website: www.breakawaymag.com. "This fast-paced, 4-color publication is designed to creatively teach, entertain, inspire, and challenge the emerging teenager. It also seeks to strengthen a boy's self-esteem, provide role models, guide a healthy awakening to girls, make the Bible relevant, and deepen their love for family, friends, church, and Jesus Christ." Monthly. Estab. 1990. Circ. 96,000.
Needs: Adventure, humor/satire, religious/inspirational, suspense. "Avoid Christian jargon, clichés, preaching, and other dialogue that isn't realistic or that interrupts the flow of the story." Receives 25 unsolicited mss/month. Accepts 4-5 mss/year. Publishes ms 5-12 months after acceptance. Agented fiction 20%. **Publishes 1-2 new writers/ year.** Recently published work by Manfred Koehler, John Jenkins, and Greg Asimakoupoulos. Length: 600-2,000 words; average length: 500 words. Publishes short shorts. Often comments on rejected mss.
How to Contact: Send complete ms. Accepts submissions by mail. Responds in 2-3 months to queries; 2-3 months to mss. Sample copy for $1.50 and 9 × 12 SASE with 3 first-class stamps. Writer's guidelines for #10 SASE.

Payment/Terms: Pays 12-15¢/word. Pays on acceptance for first North American serial, first, one-time, electronic rights.

Advice: "Be familiar with our publication and our audience. We do not want predictable stories."

$ ☑ ◎ BUGLE, Rocky Mountain Elk Foundation, P.O. Box 8249, 2291 W. Broadway, Missoula MT 59808. (406)523-4570. Fax: (406)543-7710. Website: www.elkfoundation.org. **Contact:** Don Burgess, hunting/human interest editor dburgess@rmef.org. Lee Cromrich, conservation editor lcromrich@rmef.org. Magazine: 8½×11; 114-172 pages; 55 lb. Escanaba paper; 80 lb. sterling cover, b&w, 4-color illustrations; photos. *Bugle* is the membership publication of the Rocky Mountain Elk Foundation, a nonprofit wildlife conservation group. "Our readers are predominantly hunters, many of them conservationists who care deeply about protecting wildlife habitat." Bimonthly. Estab. 1984. Circ. 132,000.

Needs: Adventure, children's/juvenile, historical, humor/satire, novel excerpts, slice-of-life vignettes, western, human interest, natural history, conservation. "We accept fiction and nonfiction stories pertaining in some way to elk, other wildlife, hunting, habitat conservation, and related issues. We would like to see more humor." Upcoming themes: "Bowhunting"; "Odd Elk Behavior"; "Hunts from Hell", stories of elk hunting adventures gone bad; "The Long Haul", vignettes revealing essential experiences of nonresident hunters journeying to the Rockies each fall to hunt elk; "Bravehearts"; stories of hunters overcoming severe physical handicaps to continue hunting. Receives 20-30 unsolicited mss/month. Accepts 3-4 mss/issue; 18-24 mss/year. Publishes ms 1-36 months after acceptance. **Publishes 12 new writers/year.** Recently published work by Rick Bass and Susan Ewing. Length: 1,500-4,500 words; average length: 2,500 words. Publishes short shorts. Also publishes literary essays, poetry.

How to Contact: Query with or without published clips or send complete ms. Accepts submissions by mail, e-mail, fax. Send SASE for reply, return of ms or send a disposable copy of ms. Responds in 1 month to queries; 3 months to mss. Accepts reprints, multiple submissions. Sample copy for $5. Writer's guidelines online.

Payment/Terms: Pays 20¢/word. Pays on acceptance for one-time rights.

Advice: "Hunting stories and essays should celebrate the hunting experience, demonstrating respect for wildlife, the land, and the hunt. Straight action-adventure hunting stories are in short supply, as are "Situation Ethics" manuscripts."

$ ☑ ◎ CALLIOPE, Exploring World History, Cobblestone Publishing Co., 30 Grove St., Suite C, Peterborough NH 03458-1454. (603)924-7209. Fax: (603)924-7380. Website: www.cobblestonepub.com. **Contact:** Rosalie Baker, editor. Magazine. "*Calliope* covers world history (east/west) and lively, original approaches to the subject are the primary concerns of the editors in choosing material. For 8-14 year olds." Estab. 1990. Circ. 11,000.

• Cobblestone Publishing also publishes the children's magazines *Appleseeds, Dig, Footsteps, Odyssey, Cobblestone* and *Faces*, some listed in this section. *Calliope* has received the Ed Press Golden Lamp and One-Theme Issue awards.

Needs: Material must fit upcoming theme; write for themes and deadlines. Childrens/juvenile (8-14 years). "Authentic historical and biographical fiction, adventure, retold legends, folktales, etc. relating to the theme." Send SASE for guidelines and theme list. Published after theme deadline. **Publishes 5-10 new writers/year.** Recently published work by Duane Damon and Amita V. Sarin. Publishes short shorts.

How to Contact: Query with or without published clips. Send SASE (or IRC) for reply. Responds in several months (if interested, responds 5 months before publication date) to mss. No simultaneous submissions. Sample copy for $4.50 and 7½×10½ SASE with 4 first-class stamps or online. Writer's guidelines for #10 SAE and 1 first-class stamp or on website.

Payment/Terms: Pays 20-25¢/word. Pays on publication for all rights.

Advice: "We primarily publish historical nonfiction. Fiction should be retold legends or folktales related to appropriate themes."

$ ☑ ◎ ☑ CAMPUS LIFE, Christianity Today, Inc., 465 Gundersen Dr., Carol Stream IL 60188. (630)260-6200. Fax: (630)260-0114. E-mail: clmag@campuslife.net. Website: www.campuslife.net. **Contact:** Chris Lutes, editor. Magazine: 8¼×11¼; 72 pages; 4-color and b&w illustrations; 4-color and b&w photos. "*Campus Life* is a magazine for high-school and early college-age teenagers. Our editorial slant is not overtly religious. The indirect style is intended to create a safety zone with our readers and to reflect our philosophy that God is interested in all of life. Therefore, we publish 'message stories' side by side with general interest, humor, etc. We are also looking for stories that help high school students consider a Christian college education." Bimonthly. Estab. 1942. Circ. 100,000.

• *Campus Life* regularly receives awards from the Evangelical Press Association.

CHECK THE CATEGORY INDEXES, located at the back of the book, for publishers interested in specific fiction subjects.

Needs: "All fiction submissions must be contemporary, reflecting the teen experience in the new milllennium. We are a Christian magazine but are *not* interested in sappy, formulaic, sentimentally religious stories. We *are* interested in well-crafted stories that portray life realistically, stories high school and college youth relate to. Writing must reflect a Christian world view. If you don't understand our market and style, don't submit." Accepts 5 mss/year. Reading and response time slower in summer. Publishes ms 5 months after acceptance. **Publishes 3-4 new writers/ year.**

How to Contact: Query. Responds in 6 weeks to queries. Sample copy for $3 and 9½ × 11 SAE with 3 first-class stamps. Writer's guidelines online.

Payment/Terms: Pays 15-20¢/word, and 2 contributor's copies. Pays on acceptance for first, one-time rights.

Advice: "We print finely-crafted fiction that carries a contemporary teen (older teen) theme. First person fiction often works best. Ask us for sample copy with fiction story. We want experienced fiction writers who have something to say to young people without getting propagandistic."

CANADIAN WRITER'S JOURNAL, P.O. Box 5180, New Liskeard ON P0J 1P0 Canada. (705)647-5424. Fax: (705)647-8366. Website: www.cwj.ca. Accepts well-written articles by all writers. Bimonthly. Estab. 1984. Circ. 350.

Needs: Requirements being met by annual contest. Send SASE for rules, or see guidelines on website. "Does not want gratuitous violence, sex subject matter." Publishes ms 9 months after acceptance. **Publishes 40 new writers/ year.** Also publishes poetry. Rarely comments on rejected mss.

How to Contact: Accepts submissions by mail, e-mail, fax, phone. Responds in 2 months to queries. Sample copy for $8, including postage. Writer's guidelines online.

Payment/Terms: Pays on publication for one-time rights.

$CAPPER'S, Ogden Publications, Inc., 1503 S.W. 42nd St., Topeka KS 66609-1265. (785)274-4300. E-mail: cappers@ogdenpubs.com. Website: www.cappers.com (includes sample items from publication, subscription information and guidelines). **Contact:** Editor. Magazine: 36-56 pages; newsprint paper and cover stock; photos. A "clean, uplifting and nonsensational newspaper for families, from children to grandparents." Biweekly. Estab. 1879. Circ. 240,000.

Needs: Serialized novels suitable for family reading. "We accept novel-length stories for serialization. No fiction containing violence, sexual references or obscenity. We would like to see more Western romance, pioneer stories." Receives 2-3 unsolicited mss/month. Accepts 4-6 stories/year. Published work by C.J. Sargent and Mona Exinger. **Published new writers within the last year.** Length: 7,000-50,000 words.

How to Contact: Send complete ms with SASE. Cover letter and/or synopsis helpful. Responds in 8 months to ms. Sample copy for $2.

Payment/Terms: Pays $75-300 for one-time serialization rights and contributor's copies. Pays on acceptance for first and second serial (reprint rights) and one-time rights.

Advice: "Since we publish in serialization, be sure your manuscript is suitable for that format. Each segment needs to be compelling enough so the reader remembers it and is anxious to read the next installment. Please proofread and edit carefully. We've seen major characters change names partway through the manuscript."

$◎ CICADA MAGAZINE, Cricket Magazine Group, P.O. Box 300, Peru IL 61354. (815)224-5803 ext. 656. Fax: (815)224-6615. E-mail: mmiklavic@caruspub.com. Website: www.cricketmag.com. **Contact:** Deborah Vetter, executive editor. Literary magazine: 128 pages; some illustrations. "*Cicada*, for ages 14 and up, publishes original short stories, poems, and first-person essays written for teens and young adults." Bimonthly. Estab. 1998. Circ. 16,000.

Needs: Adventure, fantasy, historical, humor/satire, mainstream, mystery/suspense, romance, science fiction, western, young adult/teen, sports. "Our readership is age 14-21. Submissions should be tailored for high school and college-age audience, not junior high or younger. We especially need humor and fantasy. We are also intersted in first-person, coming-of-age nonfiction (life in the Peace Corps, significant first jobs, etc.). We are currently receiving too many stories that deal with cancer." Accepts 10 mss/issue; 60 mss/year. Publishes ms 1 year after acceptance. Length: 3,000-15,000 words; average length: 5,000 words. Also publishes poetry. Sometimes comments on rejected mss.

How to Contact: Send complete ms. Accepts submissions by mail. Send SASE for return of ms or send a disposable copy of ms and #10 SASE for reply only. Responds in 3 months to mss. Accepts simultaneous and reprints submissions. Sample copy for $8.50. Writer's guidelines for SASE and on website. Reviews fiction.

Payment/Terms: Pays 25¢/word, plus 6 contributor's copies. Pays on publication for all rights.

Advice: "Quality writing, good literary style, genuine teen sensibility, depth, humor, good character development, avoidance of stereotypes. Read several issues to familiarize yourself with our style."

$◎ CLUBHOUSE MAGAZINE, Focus on the Family, 8605 Explorer Dr., Colorado Springs CO 80920. (719)531-3400. Website: www.clubhousemagazine.org. **Contact:** Jesse Florea, editor. Magazine: 8×11; 24 pages; illustrations; photos. "*Clubhouse* readers are 8-12 year old boys and girls who desire to know more about God and the Bible. Their parents (who typically pay for the membership) want wholesome, educational material with Scriptural or moral insight. The kids want excitement, adventure, action, humor, or mystery. Your job as a writer is to please both the parent and child with each article." Monthly. Estab. 1987. Circ. 114,000.

Needs: Adventure, children's/juvenile (8-12 years), humor/satire, mystery/suspense, religious/inspirational, suspense, western, holiday. Avoid contemporary, middle-class family settings (existing authors meet this need), poems (rarely printed), stories dealing with boy-girl relationships. "No science fiction." Receives 150 unsolicited mss/month. Accepts 1 mss/issue. Publishes ms 6-12 months after acceptance. Agented fiction 15%. **Publishes 8 new writers/year.** Recently published work by Sigmund Brower and Nancy Rue.

How to Contact: Send complete ms. Send SASE for reply, return of ms or send a disposable copy of ms. Responds in 2 months to mss. Sample copy for $1.50 with 9 × 12 SASE. Writer's guidelines for #10 SASE.

Payment/Terms: Pays $200 and up for first time contributor and 5 contributor's copies; additional copies available. Pays on acceptance for first North American serial, first, one-time, electronic rights.

Advice: Looks for "humor with a point, historical fiction featuring great Christians or Christians who lived during great times; contemporary, exotic settings; holiday material (Christmas, Thanksgiving, Easter, President's Day); parables; fantasy (avoid graphic descriptions of evil creatures and sorcery); mystery stories; choose-your-own adventure stories and westerns. No contemporary, middle-class family settings (we already have authors who can meet these needs) or stories dealing with boy-girl relationships."

$⃞ ◎ ▮ COBBLESTONE, Discover American History, Cobblestone Publishing, 30 Grove St., Suite C, Peterborough NH 03458-1457. (603)924-7209. Fax: (603)924-7380. Website: www.cobblestonepub.com. **Contact:** Meg Chorlian, editor. Magazine. Prefers to work with published/established writers "Each issue presents a particular theme, making it exciting as well as informative. Half of all subscriptions are for schools." All material must relate to monthly theme. Monthly. Estab. 1979. Circ. 30,000.

 • Cobblestone Press also publishes *Calliope* and *Faces* as well as *Odyssey* (science magazine), *Footsteps* (African American magazine) and *Appleseeds* (for 7-9 year olds). *Cobblestone* has received Ed Press and Parent's Choice awards.

Needs: Adventure, children's/juvenile (8-14 years old), ethnic/multicultural, historical, biographical fiction relating to theme. Has to be very strong and accurate. "American history is our primary need." Material must fit upcoming theme. Authentic historical and biographical fiction, adventure, retold legends, etc., relating to the theme." Upcoming theme available for SASE. Published after theme deadline. Publishes ms 4 months after acceptance. Publishes short shorts. Also publishes poetry.

How to Contact: Query with published clips. Accepts submissions by mail, fax. Send SASE (or IRC) for reply or send self-addressed postcard to find out if query was received. Responds in 4 months to queries. No simultaneous submissions. Sample copy for $4.95 and 7½ × 10½ SAE with 4 first-class stamps. Writer's guidelines for #10 SASE and 1 first-class stamp or on website.

Payment/Terms: Pays 20-25¢/word. Pays on publication for all rights.

Advice: Writers may send for *Cobblestone's* free catalog for a listing of subjects covered in back issues.

$◎ COUNTRY WOMAN, Reiman Publications, 5400 South 60th Street, Greendale WI 53129. (414)423-0100. Website: www.countrywomanmagazine.com. **Contact:** Kathleen Anderson, managing editor. Magazine: 8½ × 11; 68 pages; excellent quality paper; excellent cover stock; illustrations and photographs. "*Country Woman* is for contemporary rural women of all ages and backgrounds and from all over the U.S. and Canada. It includes a sampling of the diversity that makes up rural women's lives—love of home, family, farm, ranch, community, hobbies, enduring values, humor, attaining new skills and appreciating present, past and future all within the context of the lifestyle that surrounds country living." Bimonthly. Estab. 1970.

Needs: "No contemporary, urban pieces that deal with divorce, drugs, etc." Fiction must be upbeat, heartwarming and focus on a country woman as central character. "Many of our stories and articles are written by our readers!" Accepts 1 mss/issue. **Publishes 4-6 new writers/year.** Recently published work by Patricia Frederick, Monique Haen and Lorrie Ann Jackson.

How to Contact: Send complete ms. Accepts submissions by mail. All manuscripts should be sent to Kathleen Anderson, managing editor. Responds in 2 months to queries; 3 months to mss. Accepts simultaneous and reprints submissions. Sample copy for $2 and SASE. Writer's guidelines for #10 SASE.

Payment/Terms: Pays $90-125. Pays on acceptance for first North American serial, one-time, second serial (reprint) rights.

Advice: "Read the magazine to get to know our audience. Send us country-to-the-core fiction, not yuppie-country stories—our readers know the difference! Very traditional fiction—with a definite beginning, middle and end, some kind of conflict/resolution, etc. We do not want to see contemporary avant-garde fiction—nothing dealing with divorce, drugs, etc., or general societal malaise."

$⃞ ◎ ▮ CRICKET, Carus Publishing Co., P.O. Box 300, Peru IL 61354-0300. (815)224-5803. **Contact:** Marianne Carus, editor-in-chief. Magazine: 8 × 10; 64 pages; illustrations; photos. Magazine for children, ages 9-14. Monthly. Estab. 1973. Circ. 73,000.

 • *Cricket* has received a Parents Choice Award, and awards from Ed Press. Carus Corporation also publishes *Spider, the Magazine for Children, Ladybug, The Magazine for Young Children, Babybug,* and *Cicada.*

Needs: Adventure, children's/juvenile, ethnic/multicultural, fantasy, historical, humor/satire, mystery/suspense, novel excerpts, science fiction, suspense, thriller/espionage, western, folk and fairy tales. No didactic, sex, religious, or horror stories. All issues have different "mini-themes." Receives 1,100 unsolicited mss/month. Accepts 180 mss/year. Publishes ms 6-24 months after acceptance. Agented fiction 1-2%. **Publishes some new writers/year.** Recently published work by Aaron Shepard, X.J. Kennedy, and Nancy Willard.

How to Contact: Send complete ms. Responds in 3 months to mss. Accepts reprints submissions. Sample copy for $5 and 9×12 SAE. Writer's guidelines for SASE and on website.

Payment/Terms: Pays 25¢/word maximum, and 6 contributor's copies; $2.50 charge for extras. Pays on publication. Rights vary. Sends galleys to author. Sponsors awards/contests.

Advice: "Do not write *down* to children. Write about well-researched subjects you are familiar with and interested in, or about something that concerns you deeply. Children *need* fiction and fantasy. Carefully study several issues of *Cricket* before you submit your manuscript."

$ ☑ ◎ CRUSADER MAGAZINE, P.O. Box 7259, Grand Rapids MI 49510-7259. (616)241-5616. Fax: (616)241-5558. Website: www.calvinistcadets.org. **Contact:** G. Richard Broene, editor. Magazine: 8½×11; 24 pages; illustrations; photos. "*Crusader Magazine* shows boys 9-14 how God is at work in their lives and in the world around them." Estab. 1958. Circ. 10,000.

Needs: Adventure, children's/juvenile, religious/inspirational, spiritual, sports, comics. "Avoid preachiness. Avoid simplistic answers to complicated problems. Avoid long dialogue and little action." No fantasy, science fiction, fashion, horror or erotica. List of upcoming themes available for SASE or on website. Receives 60 unsolicited mss/month. Accepts 3 mss/issue; 18 mss/year. Publishes ms 4-11 months after acceptance. **Publishes 0-3 new writers/year.** Recently published work by Douglas DeVries and Betty Lou Mell. Length: 900-1,500 words; average length: 1,200 words. Publishes short shorts.

How to Contact: Send complete ms. Responds in 2 months to queries. Accepts simultaneous and reprints, multiple submissions. Sample copy for 9×12 SASE. Writer's guidelines for #10 SASE.

Payment/Terms: Pays 4-6¢/word, and 1 contributor's copy. Pays on acceptance for first North American serial, one-time, second serial (reprint), simultaneous rights. Rights purchased vary with author and material.

Advice: "On a cover sheet, list the point your story is trying to make. Our magazine has a theme for each issue, and we try to fit the fiction to the theme. All fiction should be about a young boy's interests—sports, outdoor activities, problems—with an emphasis on a Christian perspective. No simple moralisms. Avoid simplistic answers to complicated problems."

🄽 ☐ DIGRESS MAGAZINE, Promoting Independent Art, Music, and Literature, Digress Magazine, 4372 4th Street, Riverside CA 92501. (909)218-8152. E-mail: mable@digressonline.com. Website: www.digressonline.com. **Contact:** Annie Knight, editor. Magazine: 11X7; newsprint paper; illustrations. *Digress* is an art, music, and literary magazine that promotes and celebrates independent artists and the creative process, which is felt by the editor to be just as important as the creative work produced. Past issues of *Digress* has featured beginning to up and coming authors—fiction, non-fiction, and poetry, along with reviews of art shows, band performances, CD's, books, spoken word events. Quarterly. Estab. 2001. Circ. 10,000.

Needs: Erotica, ethnic/multicultural, experimental, fantasy, feminist, gay, historical, humor/satire, lesbian, literary, science fiction, translations. Receives 10-20 unsolicited mss/month. Accepts 3 mss/issue; 12 mss/year. Publishes ms 3 months after acceptance. **Publishes 25 new writers/year.** Length: 250-1,000 words; average length: 750-1,000 words. Publishes short shorts. Also publishes literary essays, literary criticism, poetry. Always comments on rejected mss.

How to Contact: Query with published clips. Accepts submissions by e-mail. Responds in 2 weeks to queries. Accepts simultaneous and reprints, multiple submissions. Sample copy for SASE. Writer's guidelines by e-mail.

Payment/Terms: Pays 3 contributor's copies; additional copies $3. Pays on publication Sends galleys to author. Not copyrighted.

Advice: "Just send it! I'm a struggling writer myself, so I understand the pain of rejection that is, unfortunately, essential to becoming a published writer."

$ ☑ ◎ DISCOVERY TRAILS, Gospel Publishing House, 1445 N. Boonville Ave., Springfield MO 65802-1894. (417)831-8000. Fax: (417)862-6059. E-mail: discoverytrails@gph.org. Website: www.radiantlife.org. **Contact:** Sinda S. Zinn, editor. Magazine: 8×10; 4 pages; coated offset paper; art illustrations; photos. *Discovery Trails* is written for boys and girls 10-12 (slanted toward older group). Fiction, adventure stories showing children applying Christian principles in everyday living are used in the paper. Weekly. Estab. 1954. Circ. 20,000.

Needs: Adventure, children's/juvenile, historical, humor/satire, mystery/suspense, religious/inspirational, spiritual, sports. No Bible fiction, "Halloween," "Easter Bunny", "Santa Claus" or science fiction stories. Accepts 2 mss/issue. Publishes ms 18 months after acceptance. **Publishes some new writers/year.** Recently published work by Ellen Javernick, Carolyn Short and Theresa Bubulka. Publishes short shorts.

How to Contact: Send complete ms. Accepts simultaneous submissions. Sample copy for #10 SASE. Writer's guidelines online.

Payment/Terms: Pays 7-10¢/word and 3 contributor's copies. Pays on acceptance for one-time, second serial (reprint), simultaneous rights.

Advice: "Know the age level and direct stories or articles relevant to that age group. Since junior-age children (grades 5 and 6) enjoy action, fiction provides a vehicle for communicating moral/spirtual principles in a dramatic framework. Fiction, if well done, can be powerful tool for relating Christian principles. It must, however, be realistic and believable in its development. Make your children be children, not overly mature for their age. We would like more serial stories. Write for contemporary children, using setting and background that includes various ethnic groups."

$ ◍ ⚑ ESQUIRE, 1790 Broadway, New York NY 10019. (212)649-4020. Website: www.esquire.com. **Contact:** Adrienne Miller, literary editor. Magazine. Monthly magazine for smart, well-off men. General readership is college educated and sophisticated, between ages 30 and 45. Written mostly by contributing editors on contract. Rarely accepts unsolicited manuscripts. Monthly. Estab. 1933. Circ. 750,000.
- *Esquire* is well-respected for its fiction and has received several National Magazine Awards. Work published in *Esquire* has been selected for inclusion in the *Best American Short Stories* and *O. Henry* anthologies.

Needs: Novel excerpts, short stories, some poetry, memoirs, and plays. No "pornography, science fiction or 'true romance' stories." Publishes special fiction issue in July. Receives 800 unsolicited mss/month. Rarely accepts unsolicited fiction. Publishes ms 2-6 months after acceptance. Recently published work by Russell Banks, Tim O'Brien, Richard Russo and David Means.
How to Contact: Send complete ms. Accepts simultaneous, multiple submissions. Writer's guidelines for SASE.
Payment/Terms: Pays in cash on acceptance, amount undisclosed. Retains first worldwide periodical publication rights for 90 days from cover date.
Advice: "Submit one story at a time. We receive over 10,000 stories a year, so worry a little less about publication, a little more about the work itself."

$ ◍ ◎ EVANGEL, Free Methodist Publishing House, P.O. Box 535002, Indianapolis IN 46253-5002. (317)244-3660. Magazine: 5½×8½; 8 pages; 2 and 4-color illustrations; color and b&w photos. Sunday school take-home paper for distribution to adults who attend church. Fiction involves people coping with everday crises, making decisions that show spiritual growth. Weekly distribution. Printed quarterly. Estab. 1897. Circ. 20,000.
Needs: Religious/inspirational. "No fiction without any semblance of Christian message or where the message clobbers the reader. Looking for more short pieces of devotional nature of 5,000 words or less than long pieces." Receives 300 unsolicited mss/month. Accepts 3-4 mss/issue; 156-200 mss/year. Publishes ms 18-36 months after acceptance. **Publishes 10 new writers/year.** Recently published work by Karen Leet and Dennis Hensley.
How to Contact: Send complete ms. Accepts submissions by mail. Responds in 4-6 weeks to queries. Accepts multiple submissions. Sample copy and writer's guidelines for #10 SASE.
Payment/Terms: Pays 4¢/word and 2 contributor's copies. Pays on publication.
Advice: "Choose a contemporary situation or conflict and create a good mix for the characters (not all-good or all-bad heroes and villians). Don't spell out everything in detail; let the reader fill in some blanks in the story. Keep him guessing." Rejects mss because of "unbelievable characters and predictable events in the story."

$ ◎ FACES, People, Places and Cultures, Cobblestone Publishing, 30 Grove St., Peterborough NH 03458. (603)924-7209. Fax: (603)924-7380. E-mail: faces@cobblestonepub.com. Website: www.cobblestonepub.com. **Contact:** Lou Waryncia, managing editor. Magazine. "*Faces* covers world culture for ages 9-14. It stands apart from other children's magazines by offering a solid look at one subject and stressing strong editorial content, color photographs throughout and original illustrations. *Faces* offers an equal balance of feature articles and activities, as well as folktales and legends." Monthly. Estab. 1984. Circ. 15,000.
- Cobblestone also publishes *Cobblestone* and *Calliope*, listed in this section.

Needs: Children's/juvenile (8-14 year-olds), ethnic/multicultural, historical, retold legends or folktales. Depends on theme. All material must relate to theme; send for theme list. Themes posted on website. Send query 6-9 months prior to theme issue publication date. Publishes ms 4 months after acceptance. Publishes short shorts.
How to Contact: Query with published clips. Accepts submissions by mail, e-mail. Send SASE for reply. Accepts simultaneous submissions. Sample copy for $4.95 and 7½×10½ (or larger) SAE with $2 postage or online. Writer's guidelines for SASE or on website.
Payment/Terms: Pays 20-25¢/word. Pays on publication for all rights.
Advice: "Study past issues of the magazine to become familiar with our style and content. Writers with anthropological and/or travel experience are particularly encouraged; *Faces* is about world culture."

FOR EXPLANATIONS OF THESE SYMBOLS,
SEE THE INSIDE FRONT AND BACK COVERS OF THIS BOOK.

$ N ◎ FIFTY SOMETHING MAGAZINE, Jet Media, 7533-C Tyler Blvd., Mentor OH 44060. (440)953-2200. Fax: (440)953-2202. "We are focusing on the 50-and-better reader." Quarterly. Estab. 1990. Circ. 10,000.
Needs: Adventure, confessions, ethnic/multicultural, experimental, fantasy, historical, humor/satire, mainstream, mystery/suspense, novel excerpts, romance, slice-of-life vignettes, suspense, western. No erotica or horror. Receives 150 unsolicited mss/month. Accepts 5 mss/issue. Publishes ms 6 months after acceptance. **Publishes 20 new writers/year.** Length: 500-1,000 words; average length: 1,000 words. Publishes short shorts.
How to Contact: Send complete ms. Responds in 3 months to queries; 3 months to mss. Accepts simultaneous and reprints submissions. Sample copy for 9 × 12 SAE and 4 first-class stamps. Writer's guidelines for #10 SASE.
Payment/Terms: Pays $10-100. Pays on publication for one-time, second serial (reprint), simultaneous rights.

$ N ◎ FIRST HAND, Experiences For Loving Men, Firsthand, Ltd., 310 Cedar Lane, Teaneck NJ 07666. (201)836-9177. Fax: (201)836-5055. **Contact:** Don Dooley, editor. Magazine: digest-size; 130 pages; illustrations. "Half of the magazine is made up of our readers' own gay sexual experience. Rest is fiction and columns devoted to health, travel, books, etc." Monthly. Estab. 1980. Circ. 70,000.
Needs: Erotica, gay. "Should be written in first person." No science fiction or fantasy. Erotica should detail experiences based in reality. Receives 75-100 unsolicited mss/month. Accepts 6 mss/issue; 72 mss/year. Publishes ms 9-18 months after acceptance. Length: 2,000-3,750 words; average length: 3,000 words. Sometimes comments on rejected mss.
How to Contact: Send complete ms. Include name, address, telephone and Social Security number and "advise on use of a pseudonym if any. Also whether selling all rights or first North American rights." Responds in 2 months to queries; 4 months to mss. No simultaneous submissions. Sample copy for $5.99. Writer's guidelines for #10 SASE.
Payment/Terms: Pays $100-150. Pays on publication. Buys all rights (exceptions made) and second serial (reprint) rights
Advice: "Avoid the hackneyed situations. Be original. We like strong plots."

◎ N A $FRICTION ZONE, Your Motorcycle Lifestyle Magazine, P.O. Box 530, Idyllwild CA 92549-0530. (909)659-9500. Fax: (909)659-8182. E-mail: editor@friction-zone.com. Website: www.friction-zone.com. **Contact:** Amy Holland. Monthly. Estab. 1999. Circ. 21,000.
Needs: "Want stories concerning motorcycling or motorcyclists. No 'first-person' fiction." Accepts 1 mss/issue; 12 mss/year. Publishes ms 1 month after acceptance. Agented fiction 100%. **Publishes 20 new writers/year.** Length: 1,000-2,000 words; average length: 1,500 words. Publishes short shorts. Often comments on rejected mss.
How to Contact: Sample copy for $4.50 or on website. Writer's guidelines for SASE.
Payment/Terms: Pays 20¢/word. Pays on publication for first North American serial rights.
Advice: "If you are not familar with the lifestyle of a motorcyclist, i.e. if your not a motorcycle rider, your work will likely not be accepted."

$ ◎ ⃞ THE GEM, Churches of God, General Conference, Box 926, Findlay OH 45839. (419)424-1961. E-mail: communications@cggc.org. Website: www.cggc.org. **Contact:** Rachel Foreman, editor. Magazine: 6 × 9; 8 pages; 50 lb. uncoated paper; illustrations (clip art). "True-to-life stories of healed relationships and growing maturity in the Christian faith for senior high students through senior citizens who attend Churches of God, General Conference Sunday Schools." Weekly. Estab. 1865. Circ. 7,000. Charge for extras (postage for mailing more than one).
Needs: Adventure, humor/satire, mainstream, religious/inspirational, senior citizen/retirement. Nothing that denies or ridicules standard Christian values. "No science fiction." Prefers personal testimony or nonfiction short stories. Receives 45 unsolicited mss/month. Accepts 20-25 mss/year. Publishes ms 4-12 months after acceptance. Length: 500-1,700 words; average length: 1,500 words.
How to Contact: Send complete ms with cover letter ("letter not essential, unless there is information about author's background which enhances story's credibility or verifies details as being authentic"). Responds in 6 months to mss. Accepts simultaneous and reprints submissions. Sample copy for #10 SASE. Writer's guidelines for #10 SASE.
Payment/Terms: Pays on publication for one-time rights.
Advice: "There is no shortcut. The key to writing well is to read everything you can and then to write and write and write."

$ ⃞ GRIT, American Life and Traditions, Ogden Publications, 1503 SW 42nd St., Topeka KS 66609-1265. (785)274-4300. Fax: (785)274-4305. E-mail: grit@grit.com. Website: www.grit.com. **Contact:** Fiction Department. Magazine: 64 pages; 30 lb. newsprint; illustrations; photos. "*Grit* is good news. As a wholesome, family-oriented magazine published for more than a century and distributed nationally, *Grit* features articles about family lifestyles, traditions, values, and pastimes. *Grit* accents the best of American life and traditions—past and present. Our readers are ordinary people doing extraordinary things, with courage, heart, determination, and imagination. Many of them live in small towns and rural areas across the country; others live in cities but share many of the values typical of small-town America." Monthly. Estab. 1882. Circ. 90,000.

● *Grit* is considered one of the leading family-oriented publications.
Needs: Adventure, condensed novels, mainstream, mystery/suspense, religious/inspirational, romance (contemporary, historical), western (frontier, traditional), nostalgia. "No sex, violence, drugs, obscene words, abuse, alcohol, or negative diatribes." "Special Storytellers issue; 5-6 manuscripts needed; submit in June." Accepts 1-2 mss/issue; 30 mss/year. **Publishes 20-25 new writers/year.** Recently published work by John Floyd, Dede Hammond, Genevieve White and Don White. Length: 1,200-6,000 words; average length: 1,500-3,000 words. Also publishes poetry.
How to Contact: Send complete ms. Accepts submissions by mail. Send SASE for return of ms. No simultaneous submissions. Sample copy and writer's guidelines for $4 and 11 × 14 SASE with 4 first-class stamps. Sample articles on website.
Payment/Terms: Pays on acceptance for first North American serial, first, one-time rights.
Advice: "Keep trying and be patient."

$ⓒ ☑ HADASSAH MAGAZINE, 50 W. 58th St., New York NY 10019. (212)688-0227. Fax: (212)446-9521. Website: www.hadassah.org. **Contact:** Zelda Shluker, maaging editor. Jewish general interest magazine: 7⅛ × 10½; 64-80 pages; coated and uncoated paper; slick, medium weight coated cover; drawings and cartoons; photos. "*Hadassah* is a general interest Jewish feature and literary magazine. We speak to our readers on a vast array of subjects ranging from politics to parenting, to midlife crisis to Mideast crisis. Our readers want coverage on social and economic issues, Jewish women's (feminist) issues, the arts, travel and health." Monthly. Circ. 300,000.
● *Hadassah* has been nominated for a National Magazine Award and has received numerous Rockower Awards for Excellence in Jewish Journalism.
Needs: Ethnic/multicultural (Jewish). No personal memoirs, "schmaltzy" or shelter magazine fiction. Receives 20-25 unsolicited mss/month. **Publishes some new writers/year.** Recently published work by Joanne Greenberg.
How to Contact: Must submit appropriate sized SASE. Responds in 4 months to mss. Sample copy and writer's guidelines for 9 × 12 SASE.
Payment/Terms: Pays $500 minimum. Pays on acceptance for first North American serial, first rights.
Advice: "Stories on a Jewish theme should be neither self-hating nor schmaltzy."

$☑ HARPER'S MAGAZINE, 666 Broadway, 11th Floor, New York NY 10012. (212)420-5720. Fax: (212)228-5889. Website: www.harpers.org. **Contact:** Lewis H. Lapham, editor. Magazine: 8 × 10¾; 80 pages; illustrations. "*Harper's Magazine* encourages national discussion on current and significant issues in a format that offers arresting facts and intelligent opinions. By means of its several shorter journalistic forms—Harper's Index, Readings, Forum, and Annotation—as well as with its acclaimed essays, fiction, and reporting, *Harper's* continues the tradition begun with its first issue in 1850: to inform readers across the whole spectrum of political, literary, cultural, and scientific affairs." Monthly. Estab. 1850. Circ. 230,000.
Needs: Humor/satire. Stories on contemporary life and its problems. Receives 50 unsolicited mss/month. Accepts 12 mss/year. Publishes ms 3 months after acceptance. **Publishes some new writers/year.** Recently published work by David Guterson, David Foster Wallace, Jonathan Franzen, Steven Millhauser, Lisa Rooney, Rick Moody and Steven Dixon.
How to Contact: Query. Responds in 6 weeks to queries. Accepts reprints submissions. Sample copy for $3.95.
Payment/Terms: Generally pays 50¢-$1/word. Pays on acceptance. Vary with author and material. Sends galleys to author.

$ HEMISPHERES, Pace Communications for United Airlines, 1301 Carolina St., Greensboro NC 27401. (336)383-5800. Website: www.hemispheresmagazine.com. **Contact:** Lisa Fann, fiction editor and Selby Bateman, senior editor. Magazine: 8 × 10; 190 pages; 45 lb. paper; 120 lb. West Vaco cover; illustrations; photos. "*Hemispheres* is an inflight magazine that interprets 'inflight' to be a mode of delivery rather than an editorial genre. As such, Hemispheres' task is to engage, intrigue and entertain its primary readers—an international, culturally diverse group of affluent, educated professionals and executives who frequently travel for business and pleasure on United Airlines. The magazine offers a global perspective and a focus on topics that cross borders as often as the people reading the magazine. That places our emphasis on ideas, concepts, and culture rather than products. We present that perspective in a fresh, artful and sophisticated graphic enviroment." Monthly. Estab. 1992. Circ. 500,000.
Needs: Adventure, ethnic/multicultural, historical, humor/satire, literary, mainstream, mystery/suspense, regional, explorations of those issues common to all people but within the context of a particular culture. Receives 30-40 unsolicited mss/month. Accepts 4 mss/year. Publishes ms 4-6 months after acceptance. **Publishes 1 new writers/year.** Recently published work by Ray Bradbury, Caroline Koeppel, Robert Olen Butler, Frederick Waterman.

INTERESTED IN A PARTICULAR GENRE? Check our sections for: **Mystery/Suspense**, page 68; **Romance**, page 80; **Science Fiction/Fantasy & Horror**, page 90.

How to Contact: Send complete ms. Accepts submissions by mail. Send a disposable copy of ms and SASE for reply. Responds in 2 months to queries; 4 months to mss. Accepts multiple submissions. Sample copy for $7.50. Writer's guidelines for #10 SASE.

Payment/Terms: Pays 50¢/word and up. Pays on acceptance for first worldwide rights. Sends galleys to author. Sponsors awards/contests.

Advice: "In our information-saturated, hyperlinked age, fiction is often viewed as a bit superfluous. It doesn't solve whatever problem we have this second, and so is often relegated to a position of entertainment—something enjoyable to be fit in around the more important aspects of life. But good fiction has much longer lasting value—it should entertain, certainly, but it should also cause us to reconsider, to look at things from another perspective, to mull over what's really important. It should encourage us to explore with new eyes the mysteries of life."

$ 回 ☑ HIGH ADVENTURE, General Council of the Assemblies of God/Royal Rangers, 1445 N. Boonville Ave., Springfield MO 65802-1894. (417)862-2781, ext. 4177. Fax: (417)831-8230. E-mail: royalrangers@ag.org. Website: www.royalrangers.ag.org. **Contact:** Rev. Jerry Parks, editor. Magazine: 8 × 10¾; 16-32 pages; 50 lb. gloss paper; illustrations; photos. "*High Adventure* is a quarterly Royal Rangers magazine for boys. This 16-page, 4-color periodical is designed to provide boys with worthwhile leisure reading to challenge them to higher ideals and greater spiritual dedication; and to perpetuate the spirit of Royal Rangers ministry through stories, crafts, ideas, and illustrations." Quarterly. Estab. 1971. Circ. 87,000.

Needs: Adventure, children's/juvenile (adventure, historical, sports, ages 5-17), historical (general), humor/satire, religious/inspirational (children's religious), young adult/teen (adventure, historical, sports), camping. No objectionable language, innuendo, immoral, or non-Christian materials. Receives 50-60 unsolicited mss/month. Accepts 8-10 mss/issue; 32-40 mss/year. Publishes ms 6-12 months after acceptance. **Publishes 10-20 new writers/year.** Publishes short shorts. Sometimes comments on rejected mss.

How to Contact: Send complete ms. Accepts submissions by mail, e-mail (royalrangers@ag.org), fax. Send a disposable copy of ms and #10 SASE for reply only. Responds in 4-6 weeks to queries; 3-6 months to mss. Accepts simultaneous and reprints, multiple submissions. Sample copy and writer's guidelines for 9 × 12 SAE and 2 first-class stamps. Writer's guidelines for SASE, by e-mail or fax.

Payment/Terms: Pays 6¢/word, plus 3 contributor's copies. Pays on publication for one-time, electronic rights. Buys first or all rights.

Advice: "Stories must capture the interest of boys age 5-17 with a positive and encouraging message."

$ ☑ 回 ☑ HIGHLIGHTS FOR CHILDREN, 803 Church St., Honesdale PA 18431-1824. (570)253-1080. Fax: (570)251-7847. Website: www.highlights.com. **Contact:** Marileta Robinson, senior editor. Magazine: 8½ × 11; 42 pages; uncoated paper; coated cover stock; illustrations; photos. "This book of wholesome fun is dedicated to helping children grow in basic skills and knowledge, in creativeness, in ability to think and reason, in sensitivity to others, in high ideals, and worthy ways of living—for children are the world's most important people. We publish stories for beginning and advanced readers. Up to 500 words for beginners (ages 3-7), up to 800 words for advanced (ages 8-12)." Monthly. Estab. 1946. Circ. 2,500,000.

 • *Highlights* has won the Paul A. Witty Short Story Award from the International Reading Association, Parent's Choice Award, Parent's Guide to Children's Media Awards, and Editorial Excellence Awards from the Association of Educational Publishers.

Needs: Adventure, children's/juvenile (ages 2-12), fantasy, historical, humor/satire, animal, contemporary, folktales, multi-cultural, problem-solving, sports. "No war, crime or violence." Unusual stories appealing to both girls and boys; stories with good characterization, strong emotional appeal, vivid, full of action. "Needs stories that begin with action rather than description, have strong plot, believable setting, suspense from start to finish." Receives 600-800 unsolicited mss/month. **Publishes 30 new writers/year.** Recently published work by Eileen Spinelli, James M. Janik, Phillis Gershator, Maryilyn Kratz and Ruskin Bond. Occasionally comments on rejected mss.

How to Contact: Send complete ms. Accepts submissions by mail. Responds in 2 months to queries. Accepts multiple submissions. Sample copy for free. Writer's guidelines for SASE or on website.

Payment/Terms: Pays $100 minimum. Pays on acceptance for all rights. Sends galleys to author.

Advice: "We accept a story on its merit whether written by an unpublished or an experienced writer. Mss are rejected because of poor writing, lack of plot, trite or worn-out plot, or poor characterization. Children *like* stories and learn about life from stories. Children learn to become lifelong fiction readers by enjoying stories. Feel passion for your subject. Create vivid images. Write a child-centered story; leave adults in the background."

$ ☑ 回 ☑ ALFRED HITCHCOCK'S MYSTERY MAGAZINE, Dell Magazines, 475 Park Ave. S., 11th Floor, New York NY 10016. (212)686-7188. Website: www.themysteryplace.com. **Contact:** Linda Landrigan, editor. Mystery fiction magazine: 5½ × 8⅜; 144 pages; 28 lb. newsprint paper; 70 lb. machine-/coated cover stock; illustrations; photos. Monthly. Estab. 1956. Circ. 184,000.

 • Stories published in *Alfred Hitchcock's Mystery Magazine* have won Edgar Awards for "Best Mystery Story of the Year," Shamus Awards for "Best Private Eye Story of the Year" and Robert L. Fish Awards for "Best First Mystery Short Story of the Year."

Needs: Mystery/suspense (amateur slueth, private eye, police procedural, suspense, etc.). No sensationalism. Number of mss/issue varies with length of mss. Recently published work by Joyce Carol Oates, Jeremiah Healy, Kathy Lynn Emerson and Jan Burke.

How to Contact: Send complete ms. Responds in 3 months to mss. Sample copy for $5. Writer's guidelines for SASE or on website.

Payment/Terms: Payment varies. Pays on publication for first, foreign rights.

$ ⬜ ◎ **HORIZONS, The Magazine of Presbyterian Women**, 100 Witherspoon St., Louisville KY 40202-1396. (502)569-5668. Fax: (502)569-8085. E-mail: sdunne@ctr.pcusa.org. Website: www.pcusa.org/horizons/. **Contact:** Sharon Dunne, assistant editor. Magazine: 8×11; 40 pages; illustrations; photos. Magazine owned and operated by Presbyterian women offering "information and inspiration for Presbyterian women by addressing current issues facing the church and the world." Bimonthly. Estab. 1988. Circ. 21,000.

Needs: Ethnic/multicultural, feminist, historical, humor/satire, literary, mainstream, religious/inspirational, translations, senior citizen/retirement. "No sex/violence or romance." List of upcoming themes available for SASE. Receives 50 unsolicited mss/month. Accepts 1 mss/issue. Publishes ms 4 months after acceptance. **Publishes 10 new writers/year.** Recently published work by Charlotte Johnson. Publishes short shorts. Also publishes literary essays, poetry. Sometimes comments on rejected mss.

How to Contact: Send complete ms. Accepts submissions by e-mail, fax. SASE or disposable copy of ms. Responds in 2 weeks to queries; 3 weeks to mss. Accepts simultaneous, multiple submissions. Sample copy for 9×12 SAE. Writer's guidelines for #10 SASE. Reviews fiction.

Payment/Terms: Pays $50/page and 2 contributor's copies; additional copies for $2.50. Pays on publication

Advice: "We are most interested in stories or articles that focus on current issues—family life, the mission of the church, and the challenges of culture and society—from the perspective of women committed to Christ."

$ ⬜ **HUMPTY DUMPTY'S MAGAZINE**, Children's Better Health Institute, P.O. Box 567, Indianapolis IN 46206-0567. (317)636-8881. Fax: (317)684-8094. Website: www.humptydumptymag.org. **Contact:** Phyllis Lybarger, editor. Magazine: 7⅝×10⅛; 36 pages; 35 lb. paper; coated cover; illustrations; some photos. "Our publication is designed to entertain and to educate young readers in healthy lifestyle habits. Fiction, poetry, pencil activities should have an element of good nutrition or fitness." Estab. 1948. Circ. 350,000.

　● *Humpty Dumpty's Magazine* is not currently considering new fiction. The Chidren's Better Health Institute also publishes *Children's Digest*, *Children's Playmate*, *Jack and Jill* and *Turtle*, some of which are listed in this section.

Needs: Juvenile health-related material. "No inanimate talking objects, animal stories and science fiction." Wants more "health and fitness stories with a positive slant." Rhyming stories should flow easily with no contrived rhymes. Receives 100-200 unsolicited mss/month. Accepts 2-3 mss/issue. Publishes ms 8 months after acceptance. **Publishes 1-2 new writers/year.**

How to Contact: Send complete ms. No queries. Accepts simultaneous, multiple submissions. Sample copy for $1.75. Writer's guidelines for SASE or on website.

Payment/Terms: Pays 22¢/word for stories, plus 10 contributor's copies. Pays on publication for all rights.

Advice: "In contemporary stories, characters should be up-to-date, with realistic dialogue. We're looking for health-related stories with unusual twists or surprise endings. We want to avoid stories and poems that 'preach.' We try to present the health material in a positive way, utilizing a light humorous approach wherever possible." Most rejected mss "are too wordy or not age appropriate."

Ⓝ $JACK AND JILL, Children's Better Health Institute, P.O. Box 567, Indianapolis IN 46206-0567. (317)636-8881. Fax: (317)684-8094. Website: www.jackandjillmag.org. "Material will not be returned unless accompanied by SASE with sufficient postage." No queries. May hold material being seriously considered for up to 1 year. Bimonthly. Estab. 1938. Circ. 200,000.

Needs: Adventure, historical, humor/satire, mystery/suspense, science fiction, sports. Wants health-related stories with a subtle lesson. Accepts 30-35 mss/year. Publishes ms 8 months after acceptance.

How to Contact: Send complete ms. Responds in 10 weeks to mss. Sample copy for $1.75. Writer's guidelines online.

Payment/Terms: Pays 15¢/word minimum. Pays on publication for all rights.

Advice: "Try to present health material in a postitive—not a negative—light. Use humor and a light approach wherever possible without minimizing the seriousness of the subject. We need more humor and adventure stories."

Ⓝ ◎ $KENTUCKY MONTHLY, Vested Interest Publications, 213 St. Clair St., Frankfort KY 40601. (502)227-0053. Fax: (502)227-5009. Website: www.kentuckymonthly.com. "We publish stories about Kentucky and by Kentuckians, including those who live elsewhere." Monthly. Estab. 1998. Circ. 40,000.

Needs: Adventure, historical, mainstream, novel excerpts. Publishes ms 3 months after acceptance.

How to Contact: Query with published clips. Accepts submissions by mail, e-mail, fax. Responds in 3 weeks to queries; 1 month to mss. Accepts simultaneous submissions. Sample copy online. Writer's guidelines online.

Payment/Terms: Pays $50-100. Pays within 3 months of publication. Acquires all rights.

$ ◨ Ⓐ 🅈 **LADIES' HOME JOURNAL**, Meredith Corporation, 125 Park Ave., 20th Floor, New York NY 10017-5516. (212)557-6600. Fax: (212)455-1313. Website: www.lhj.com. **Contact:** Editor. Magazine: 190 pages; 34-38 lb. coated paper; 65 lb. coated cover; illustrations; photos. *"Ladies' Home Journal* is for active, empowered women who are evolving in new directions. It addresses informational needs with highly focused features and articles on a variety of topics including beauty and fashion, food and nutrition, health and medicine, home decorating and design, parenting and self-help, personalities and current events." Monthly. Circ. 13,371,000.
- *Ladies' Home Journal* has won several awards for journalism.

Needs: No poetry of any kind. Book mss and short stories, *accepted only through an agent.* Return of unsolicited material can not be guranteed. Publishes ms 4-12 months after acceptance. Published work by Fay Weldon, Anita Shreve, Jane Shapiro and Anne Rivers Siddons.
How to Contact: Send complete ms. Accepts submissions by mail. Responds in 3 months to queries. Accepts simultaneous submissions. Sample copy not available. Writer's guidelines online.
Payment/Terms: Pays on acceptance for first North American serial rights. Rights bought vary with submission.
Advice: "Our readers like stories, especially those that have emotional impact. Stories about relationships between people—husband/wife, mother/son—seem to be subjects that can be explored effectively in short stories. Our readers' mail surveys attest to this fact: Readers enjoy our fiction and are most keenly tuned to stories dealing with children. Fiction today is stronger than ever. Beginners can be optimistic; if they have talent, I do believe that talent will be discovered. It is best to read the magazine before submitting."

$ ◨ ◎ 🅈 **LADYBUG, The Magazine for Young Children**, Carus Publishing Co., P.O. Box 300, Peru IL 61354-0300. (815)224-5803 ext. 656. **Contact:** Marianne Carus, editor-in-chief; Paula Morrow, editor. Magazine: 8×10; 36 pages plus 4-page pullout section; illustrations. "We look for quality writing—quality literature, no matter the subject. For young children, ages 2-6." Monthly. Estab. 1990. Circ. 134,000.
- *Ladybug* has received the Parents Choice Award; the Golden Lamp Honor Award and the Golden Lamp Award from Ed Press, and Magazine Merit awards from the Society of Children's Book Writers and Illustrators.

Needs: "Looking for age-appropriate read-aloud stories for preschoolers."
How to Contact: Send complete ms. SASE. Responds in 3 months to mss. Accepts reprints submissions. Sample copy for $5 and 9×12 SAE. Guidelines only for #10 SASE.
Payment/Terms: Pays 25¢/word (less for reprints). Pays on publication for second serial (reprint) rights. Rights purchased vary. For recurring features, pays flat fee and copyright becomes property of Cricket Magazine Group.
Advice: Looks for "well-written stories for preschoolers: age-appropriate, not condescending. We look for rich, evocative language and sense of joy or wonder."

Ⓝ $LAKE SUPERIOR MAGAZINE, Lake Superior Port Cities, Inc., P.O. Box 16417, Duluth MN 55816-0417. (218)722-5002. Fax: (218)722-4096. Website: www.lakesuperior.com. Bimonthly. Estab. 1979. Circ. 20,000.
Needs: "Wants stories that are Lake Superior related." Receives 5 unsolicited mss/month. Accepts 1-3 mss/year. Publishes ms 10 months after acceptance. **Publishes 1-6 new writers/year.** Length: 300-2,500 words; average length: 1,000 words. Publishes short shorts. Also publishes literary essays, poetry. Often comments on rejected mss.
How to Contact: Query with published clips. Accepts submissions by mail, e-mail. Responds in 3 months to queries. Sample copy for $3.95 and 5 first-class stamps. Writer's guidelines for #10 SASE.
Payment/Terms: Pays $1-125. Pays on publication for first North American serial, second serial (reprint) rights.

$☐ ◎ 🅈 **LIGUORIAN**, One Liguori Dr., Liguori MO 63057-9999. (636)464-2500. Fax: (636)464-8449. E-mail: liguorianeditor@liguori.org. Website: www.liguorian.org. **Contact:** Fr. Allan Weinert, C.S.R., editor-in-chief. Magazine: 10⅝×8; 40 pages; 4-color illustrations; photos. "Our purpose is to lead our readers to a fuller Christian life by helping them better understand the teachings of the gospel and the church and by illustrating how these teachings apply to life and the problems confronting them as members of families, the church, and society." Estab. 1913. Circ. 220,000.
- *Liguorian* received Catholic Press Association awards for 2002 including First Place for Best Short Story ("An August Night at St. Agnes," by David Nypaver).

Needs: Religious/inspirational, young adult/teen, senior citizen/retirement. "Stories submitted to *Liguorian* must have as their goal the lifting up of the reader to a higher Christian view of values and goals. We are not interested in contemporary works that lack purpose or are of questionable moral value." Receives 25 unsolicited mss/month. Accepts 12 mss/year. **Publishes 8-10 new writers/year.** Recently published work by Darlene Takarsh, Mary Beth Teymaster and Maeve Mullen Ellis. Publishes short shorts. Occasionaly comments on rejected mss.
How to Contact: Send complete ms. Accepts submissions by mail, e-mail, fax, phone. Responds in 3 months to mss. Sample copy for 9×12 SAE with 3 first-class stamps or online. Writer's guidelines for #10 SASE and on website.
Payment/Terms: Pays 10-12¢/word and 5 contributor's copies. Pays on acceptance for all rights.
Advice: "First read several issues containing short stories. We look for originality and creative input in each story we read. Since most editors must wade through mounds of manuscripts each month, consideration for the editor requires that the market be studied, the manuscript be carefully presented and polished before submitting. Our publication uses only one story a month. Compare this with the 25 or more we receive over the transom each month."

Also, many fiction mss are written without a specific goal or thrust, i.e., an interesting incident that goes nowhere is *not a story*. We believe fiction is a highly effective mode for transmitting the Christian message and also provides a good balance in an unusually heavy issue."

LILITH, The Independent Jewish Women's Magazine, 250 W. 57th Street, Suite 2432, New York NY 10107. (212)757-0818. E-mail: lilithmag@aol.com. **Contact:** Yona Zeldis McDonough, fiction editor. Magazine: 48 pages; 80 ib. cover; b&w illustrations; b&w and color photos. Publishes work relating to Jewish feminism, for Jewish feminists, feminists and Jewish households. Quarterly. Estab. 1976. Circ. 11,000; readership 25,000.
Needs: Ethnic/multicultural, feminist, lesbian, literary, religious/inspirational, translations, young adult/teen, prose poem, spiritual. "Nothing that does not in any way relate to Jews, women or Jewish women." Receives 15 unsolicited mss/month. Accepts 1 mss/issue; 4 mss/year. Publishes ms up to 1 year after acceptance. Recently published work by Leslea Newman, Marge Piercy and Gloria Goldreich. Publishes short shorts.
How to Contact: Send complete ms with cover letter, which should include a 2-line bio. Responds in 2 months to queries; 6 months to mss. Accepts simultaneous and reprints submissions Accepts simultaneous and reprint submissions but must be indicated in cover letter. Sample copy for $6. Writer's guidelines for #10 SASE. Reviews fiction.
Payment/Terms: Varies. Acquires first rights.
Advice: "Read the magazine to be familiar with the kinds of material we publish."

$ **LISTEN MAGAZINE, Celebrating Positive Choices**, The Health Connection, 55 W. Oak Ridge Dr., Hagerstown MD 21740. (301)393-3294. Fax: (301)393-2294. E-mail: listen@healthconnection.org. Website: www.listenmagazine.org. **Contact:** Anita Jacobs, editor. Magazine: 32 pages; glossy paper; illustrations; photos. "*Listen* is used in many high school classes and by professionals: medical personnel, counselors, law enforcement officers, educators, youth workers, etc. *Listen* publishes true-to-lifestories about giving teens choices about real-life situations and moral issues in a secular way." Monthly. Circ. 40,000.
Needs: Young adult/teen (easy-to-read, sports), anti-drug, alcohol, tobacco, positive role models. Upcoming themes: Tobacco (May), deadline December 2003. Publishes ms 6 months after acceptance. Length: 1,000-1,200; average length: 1,200 words.
How to Contact: Query with published clips or send complete ms. Accepts submissions by mail, e-mail, fax. Prefers submissions by e-mail. Responds in 2 months to queries. Accepts simultaneous and reprints, multiple submissions. Sample copy for $2 and 9 × 12 SASE. Writer's guidelines for SASE, by e-mail, fax or on website.
Payment/Terms: Pays $50-150, and 3 contributor's copies; additional copies $2. Pays on acceptance for first rights for use in *Listen*, reprints, and associated material.

$ **LIVE, A Weekly Journal of Practical Christian Living**, Gospel Publishing House, 1445 N. Boonville Ave., Springfield MO 65802-1894. (417)862-2781. Fax: (417)862-6059. E-mail: rl-live@gph.org. Website: www.radiantlife.org. **Contact:** Paul W. Smith, editor. "*LIVE* is a take-home paper distributed weekly in young adult and adult Sunday school classes. We seek to encourage Christians in living for God through fiction and true stories which apply Biblical principles to everyday problems." Weekly. Estab. 1928. Circ. 115,000.
Needs: Religious/inspirational, inspirational, prose poem. No preachy fiction, fiction about Bible characters, or stories that refer to religious myths (e.g., Santa Claus, Easter Bunny, etc.). No science or Bible fiction. No controversial stories about such subjects as feminism, war or capital punishment. "Inner city, ethnic, racial settings." Accepts 2 mss/issue. Publishes ms 18 months after acceptance. **Publishes 75-100 new writers/year.** Recently published work by Judy Stoner, Ginger White, Lorie Ann Johnson an Amanda Jones.
How to Contact: Send complete ms. Accepts submissions by mail, e-mail, fax. Responds in 2 weeks to queries; 2 weeks to mss. Accepts simultaneous submissions. Sample copy for #10 SASE. Writer's guidelines for #10 SASE.
Payment/Terms: Pays 7-10¢/word. Pays on acceptance for first, second serial (reprint) rights.
Advice: "Study our publication and write good, inspirational stories that will encourage people to become all they can be as Christians. Stories should go somewhere! Action, not just thought—life; interaction, not just insights. Heroes and heroines, suspense and conflict. Avoid simplistic, pietistic conclusions, preachy, critical or moralizing. We don't accept science for Bible fiction. Stories should be encouraging, challenging, humorous. Even problem-centered stories should be upbeat." Reserves the right to change the titles, abbreviate length and clarify flashbacks for publication.

$ **LIVING LIGHT NEWS**, Living Light Ministries, 5306 89th St., #200, Edmonton Alberta T6E 5P9. (780)468-6872. Fax: (780)468-6872. Website: www.lininglightnews.org. **Contact:** Jeff Caporale. Newspaper: 11 × 17; 40 pages; newsprint; electrobrite cover; illustrations; photos. "Our publication is a seeker-sensitive evangelical outreach oriented newspaper focusing on glorifying God and promoting a personal relationship with Him." Bimonthly. Estab. 1985. Circ. 24,000. Member, Evangelical Press Association.
Needs: Religious/inspirational. No Victorian-era or strongly American fiction. "We are a Northern Canadian publication interested in Christmas-related fiction foucusing on the true meaning of Christmas, humorous Christmas pieces." Christmas deadline is November 1st. Receives 3-4 unsolicited mss/month. Accepts 5 mss/year. Publishes ms 2-6 months after acceptance. **Publishes 2-6 new writers/year.** Length: 300-1,250 words; average length: 700 words. Publishes short shorts. Always comments on rejected mss.

How to Contact: Query with or without published clips or send complete ms. Accepts submissions by mail, e-mail, phone. Send SASE (or IRC) in Canadian postage for return of ms or disposable copy of ms and #10 SASE for reply only. Responds in 1 month to queries; 2 months to mss. Accepts simultaneous and reprints, multiple submissions. Sample copy for 9×13 SAE with $2.50 in IRCs or Canadian postage. Writer's guidelines for SASE, e-mail or on website.

Payment/Terms: Pays $10-100. Pays on publication

Advice: "We are looking for lively, humorous, inviting heart-warming Christmas-related fiction that focuses on the non-materialistic side of Christmas or shares God's love and grace with others. Try to write with pizzazz. We get many bland submissions. Do not be afraid to use humor and have fune."

$ THE LUTHERAN JOURNAL, Apostolic Publishing Co., Inc., 7010 6th St. N., Oakdale MN 55128. (651)702-0086. Fax: (651)702-0074. **Contact:** Vance E. Lichty. "A family magazine providing wholesome and inspirational reading material for the enjoyment and enrichment of Lutherans." Semiannual. Estab. 1938. Circ. 200,000.

Needs: Literary, religious/inspirational, romance (historical), young adult/teen, senior citizen/retirement. Must be appropriate for distribution in the churches. Accepts 3-6 mss/issue.

How to Contact: Send complete ms. Responds in 4 months to queries. Accepts simultaneous submissions. Sample copy for 9×12 SAE with 60 postage.

Payment/Terms: Pays $10-25 and one contributor's copy. Pays on publication for first rights.

$ THE MAGAZINE OF FANTASY & SCIENCE FICTION, Spilogale, Inc., P.O. Box 3447, Hoboken NJ 07030. E-mail: fandsf@aol.com. Website: www.fsfmag.com. **Contact:** Gordon Van Gelder, editor. Magazine: 5×8; 160 pages; groundwood paper; card stock cover; illustrations on cover only. "*The Magazine of Fantasy and Science Fiction* publishes various types of science fiction and fantasy short stories and novellas, making up about 80% of each issue. The balance of each issue is devoted to articles about science fiction, a science column, book and film reviews, cartoons, and competitions." Monthly. Estab. 1949. Circ. 50,000.

● The *Magazine of Fantasy and Science Fiction* won a Nebula Award for Best Novella for "Bronte's Egg" by Richard Chwedyk and a Nebula Award for Best Short Story for "Creature" by Carol Emshwiller. Also won the 2002 World Fantasy Award for Best Short Story for "Queen for a Day" by Albert E. Cowdry. The *Magazine of Fantasy & Science Fiction* ranked on *Writer's Digest's* "Top 30" list of best markets for fiction writers.

Needs: Adventure, fantasy (space fantasy, sword and sorcery), horror (dark fantasy, futuristic, psychological, supernatural), psychic/supernatural/occult, science fiction (hard science/technological, soft/sociological), young adult/teen (fantasy/science fiction, horror). No electronic submissions. "We're always looking for more science fiction." Receives 500-700 unsolicited mss/month. Accepts 5-8 mss/issue; 75-100 mss/year. Publishes ms 9-12 months after acceptance. **Publishes 1-5 new writers/year.** Recently published work by Ray Bradbury, Ursula K. Le Guin, Alex Irvine, Pat Murphy, Joyce Carol Oates and Robert Sheckley. Length: Up to 25,000 words; average length: 7,000 words. Publishes short shorts. Sometimes comments on rejected mss.

How to Contact: Send complete ms. SASE (or IRC). Responds in 2 months to queries. Accepts reprints submissions. Sample copy for $5. Writer's guidelines for SASE, by e-mail or on website.

Payment/Terms: Pays 5-8¢/word; additional copies $2.10. Pays on acceptance for first North American serial, foreign serial rights.

Advice: "A well-prepared manuscript stands out better that one with fancy doo-dads. Fiction that stands out tends to have well-developed characters and thinks through the implications of its fantasy elements. It has been said 100 times before, but read an issue of the magazine before submitting. In the wake of the recent films, we are seeing more fantasy stories about sorcerers than we can possibly publish."

$ MATURE LIVING, A Magazine for Christian Senior Adults, Lifeway Christian Resources, 1 Lifeway Plaza, Nashville TN 37234. (615)251-2000. Fax: (615)277-8272. Website: www.lifeway.com. **Contact:** David Seay, editor-in-chief. Magazine: 8½×11; 52 pages; non-glare paper; slick cover stock; full color illustrations; photos. "Our magazine is Christian in content and the material required is what would appeal to 55 and over age group: inspirational, informational, nostalgic, humorous. Our magazine is distributed mainly through churches (especially Southern Baptist churches) that buy the magazine in bulk distribute it to members in this age group." Monthly. Estab. 1977. Circ. 330,000.

Needs: Humor/satire, religious/inspirational, senior citizen/retirement. No reference to liquor, dancing, drugs, gambling; no pornography, profanity or occult. Receives 10 unsolicited mss/month. Accepts 8-10 mss/issue. Publishes ms 1 year after acceptance. Length: 600-1,200 words preferred; average length: 1,000 words.

How to Contact: Send complete ms. "No queries please." Responds in 3 months to mss. Sample copy for 9×12 SAE with 4 first-class stamps. Writer's guidelines for #10 SASE.

Payment/Terms: Pays $75-105; 3 contributor's copies. Pays on acceptance. Purchases all rights if writer agrees.

Advice: Mss are rejected because they are too long or subject matter unsuitable. "Our readers seem to enjoy an occasional short piece of fiction. It must be believable, however, and present senior adults in a favorable light."

$ MATURE YEARS, The United Methodist Publishing House, 201 Eighth Ave. S., Nashville TN 37202-0801. (615)749-6292. Fax: (615)749-6512. E-mail: matureyears@umpublishing.org. **Contact:** Marvin Cropsey, editor. Magazine: 8½×11; 112 pages; illustrations; photos. Magazine "helps persons in and nearing retirement to appropriate the resources of the Christian faith as they seek to face the problems and opportunities related to aging." Quarterly. Estab. 1954. Circ. 55,000.

Needs: Humor/satire, religious/inspirational, slice-of-life vignettes, retirement years nostalgia, intergenerational relationships. "We don't want anything poking fun at old age, saccharine stories or anything not for older adults. Must show older adults (age 55 plus) in a positive manner." Accepts 1 mss/issue; 4 mss/year. Publishes ms 1 year after acceptance. **Publishes some new writers/year.** Recently published work by Ann S. Gray, Betty Z. Walker and Vickie Elaine Legg.

How to Contact: Send complete ms. Responds in 2 weeks to queries; 2 months to mss. No simultaneous submissions. Sample copy for $5 and 9×12 SAE. Writer's guidelines for #10 SASE or by e-mail.

Payment/Terms: Pays $60-125. Pays on acceptance for first North American serial rights.

Advice: "Practice writing dialogue! Listen to people talk; take notes; master dialogue writing! Not easy, but well worth it! Most inquiry letters are far too long. If you can't sell me an idea in a brief paragraph, you're not going to sell the reader on reading your finished article or story."

$ ▥ ▣ ◎ THE MESSENGER OF THE SACRED HEART, Apostleship of Prayer, 661 Greenwood Ave., Toronto ON M4J 4B3 Canada. (416)466-1195. **Contact:** Rev. F.J. Power, S.J. and Alfred DeManche, editors. Magazine: 7×10; 32 pages; coated paper; self-cover; illustrations; photos. Monthly magazine for "Canadian and U.S. Catholics interested in developing a life of prayer and spirituality; stresses the great value of our ordinary actions and lives." Estab. 1891. Circ. 11,000.

Needs: Religious/inspirational, stories about people, adventure, heroism, humor, drama. No poetry. Stories about people, adventure, heroism, humor, drama. Accepts 1 mss/issue. comments on rejected mss.

How to Contact: Send complete ms. Responds in 1 month to queries. Sample copy for $1 and 7½×10½ SAE. Writer's guidelines for #10 SASE.

Payment/Terms: Pays 6¢/word, and 3 contributor's copies. Pays on acceptance for first North American serial, first rights.

Advice: "Develop a story that sustains interest to the end. Do not preach, but use plot and characters to convey the message or theme. Aim to move the heart as well as the mind. If you can, add a light touch or a sense of humor to the story. Your ending should have impact, leaving a moral or faith message for the reader."

$ ▣ ◎ MY FRIEND, The Catholic Magazine for Kids, Pauline Books & Media/Daughters of St. Paul, 50 St. Pauls Ave., Jamaica Plain, Boston MA 02130-3495. (617)522-8911. Fax: (617)541-9805. Website: www.myfrien dmagazine.org. **Contact:** Sister Maria Grace Dateno, editor. Magazine: 8½×11; 32 pages; smooth, glossy paper and cover stock; illustrations; photos. "*My Friend* is a 32-page monthly Catholic magazine for boys and girls. Its goal is to communicate religious truths and positive values in an enjoyable and attractive way." Theme list available. Send a SASE to the above address. Estab. 1979. Circ. 8,000.

Needs: Children's/juvenile, religious/inspirational, sports. Receives 100 unsolicited mss/month. Accepts 3-4 mss/issue; 30-40 mss/year. Publishes ms 6 months after acceptance. **Publishes some new writers/year.** Published work by Diana Jenkins and Sandra Humphrey. Length: 600-1,200 words; average length: 850 words.

How to Contact: Send complete ms. Responds in 2 months to mss. Sample copy for $2 and 9×12 SASE ($1.29). Writer's guidelines and theme list for #10 SASE.

Payment/Terms: Pays $75-150. Pays on acceptance. Buys worldwide publication rights.

Advice: "We are particularly interested in fun and amusing stories with backbone. Good dialogue, realistic character development, current lingo are necessary. We have a need for each of these types at different times. We prefer child-centered stories in a real-world setting."

$ $ ◎ NA'AMAT WOMAN, Magazine of NA'AMAT USA, the Women's Labor Zionist Organization of America, NA'AMAT USA, 350 Fifth Ave., Suite 4700, New York NY 10118. (212)563-5222. Fax: (212)563-5710. **Contact:** Judith A. Sokoloff, editor. "Magazine covering a wide variety of subjects of interest to the Jewish community—including political and social issues, arts, profiles; many articles about Israel; and women's issues. Fiction must have a Jewish theme. Readers are the American Jewish community." Estab. 1926. Circ. 20,000.

Needs: Ethnic/multicultural, historical, humor/satire, literary, novel excerpts, women-oriented. Receives 10 unsolicited mss/month. Accepts 3-5 mss/year.

How to Contact: Query with published clips or send complete ms. Accepts submissions by mail, fax. Responds in 3 months to queries; 3 months to mss. Sample copy for 9×11½ SAE and $1.20 postage. Writer's guidelines for #10 SASE.

Payment/Terms: Pays 10¢/word and 2 contributor's copies. Pays on publication for all rights.

Advice: "No maudlin nostalgia or romance; no hackneyed Jewish humor and no poetry."

$ NEW MYSTERY, The Best New Mystery Stories, 101 W. 23rd St., PH-1, New York NY 10011-7703. (212)353-3495. E-mail: editorial@newmystery.tv. Website: www.newmystery.tv. **Contact:** Editor. Magazine: 8½×11; 54 pages; illustrations; photos. "Mystery, suspense and crime." Quarterly. Estab. 1990. Circ. 90,000.

Needs: Mystery/suspense (cozy to hardboiled). "No horror or romance." Wants more suspense and espionage. Plans special annual anthology. Receives 350 unsolicited mss/month. Buys 6-10 mss/issue. Agented fiction 50%.

Publishes 1 new writer/issue. Published work by Stuart Kaminsky and Andrew Greeley. Length: 3,000-5,000 words preferred. Also buys short book reviews 500-3,000 words. Sometimes comments on rejected mss.

How to Contact: *New Mystery charges a $7 fee for purchase of a contributor's packet, which includes 2 sample copies and guidelines.* Send complete ms with cover letter. "We cannot be responsible for unsolicited manuscripts." Responds in 1 month to ms. SASE. Sample copy for $5, 9×12 SAE and 4 first-class stamps.

Payment/Terms: Pays $100-1,000. Pays on publication for negotiated rights.

Advice: Stories should have believable characters in trouble; sympathetic lead; visual language." Sponsors Annual Blaggard Award.

$⬛✉ THE NEW YORKER, The New Yorker, Inc., 4 Times Square, New York NY 10036. (212) 286-5900. E-mail: fiction@newyorker.com or poetry@newyorker.com. Website: www.newyorker.com. **Contact:** Deborah Treisman, fiction editor. A quality magazine of interesting, well-written stories, articles, essays and poems for a literate audience. Weekly. Estab. 1925. Circ. 750,000.

Needs: Accepts 1 mss/issue.

How to Contact: Send complete ms. Accepts submissions by e-mail. No more than 1 story or 6 poems should be submitted. Responds in 3 months to mss. No simultaneous submissions. Writer's guidelines online.

Payment/Terms: Payment varies. Pays on acceptance.

Advice: "Be lively, original, not overly literary. Write what you want to write, not what you think the editor would like. Send poetry to Poetry Department."

$⬛ ◎ ON THE LINE, Mennonite Publishing House, 616 Walnut Ave., Scottdale PA 15683-1999. (724)887-8500. Fax: (724)887-3111. Website: www.mph.org. **Contact:** Mary Clemens Meyer. Magazine: 7×10; 28 pages; illustrations; some photos. "*On the Line* helps upper elementary and junior high children understand and appreciate God, the created world, themselves, and others." Monthly. Estab. 1908. Circ. 5,500.

Needs: Adventure, humor/satire, religious/inspirational, everyday problems. No fantasy or fictionalized Bible stories. Wants more mystery and humorous. Problem-solving stories with Christian values for older children and young teens (9-14 years). Receives 50-100 unsolicited mss/month. Accepts 52 mss/year. Publishes ms 1 year after acceptance. **Publishes 10-20 new writers/year.** Recently published work by Judy Stoner, Karen L. Rempel-Arthur, Sandra Smith and Danielle Hammelef.

How to Contact: Send complete ms. SASE. Responds in 1 month to mss. Accepts simultaneous and reprints submissions. Sample copy for 9×12 SAE and 2 first-class stamps. Writer's guidelines for 9×12 SAE and 2 first-class stamps.

Payment/Terms: Pays 3-5¢/word. Pays on acceptance for one-time rights.

Advice: "We believe in the power of story to entertain, inspire and challenge the reader to new growth. Know children and their thoughts, feelings and interests. Be realistic with characters and events in the fiction. Stories do not need to be true, but need to *feel* true. We look for easy readibility, realistic kids and grownups, humor, fun characters and plot movement with out excessive description. Watch kids, interact with kids, listen to kids. It will show up in your writing."

$⬛ ◎ OPTIONS, The *Bi-Monthly*, AJA Publishing, P.O. Box 392, White Plains NY 10602. (914)949-0250. E-mail: info@publishinggroup.com. Website: www.youngandtight.com/men. **Contact:** Diana Sheridan, associate editor. Magazine: digest-sized; 114 pages; newsprint paper; glossy cover stock; illustrations; photos. "Stories and letters about bisexuality. Positive approach. Safe-sex encounters unless the story clearly pre-dates the AIDS situation." Estab. 1977. Circ. 25,000.

Needs: Erotica, gay, lesbian, bisexual. "First person as-if-true experiences." Accepts 8 mss/issue. "Very little" of fiction is agented. Publishes ms 10 months after acceptance. **Publishes some new writers/year.** Sometimes comments on rejected mss.

How to Contact: Send complete ms. Accepts submissions by mail, e-mail. Sample copy for $2.95 and 6×9 SAE with 5 first-class stamps. Writer's guidelines for #10 SASE or by e-mail.

Payment/Terms: Pays $100. Pays on publication for all rights.

Advice: "Read a copy of *Options* carefully and look at our spec sheet before writing anything for us. That's not new advice, but to judge from some of what we get in the mail, it's necessary to repeat. We only buy two bi/lesbian pieces per issue; need is greater for bi/gay male mss. Though we're a bi rather than a gay magazine, the emphasis is on same-sex relationships. If the readers want to read about a male/female couple, they'll buy another magazine. Gay male stories sent to *Options* will also be considered for publication in *Beau*, or one of our other gay male magazines. Must get into the hot action by 1,000 words into the story. (Sooner is fine too!) *Most important*: We *only* publish male/male stories that feature 'safe sex' practices unless the story is clearly something that took place pre-AIDS."

$⬛✉ 🏆 PLAYBOY MAGAZINE, 680 N. Lake Shore Dr., Chicago IL 60611. (312)751-8000. Website: www.playboy.com. **Contact:** Fiction Department. "As the world's largest general interest lifestyle magazine for men, *Playboy* spans the spectrum of contemporary men's passions. From hard-hitting investigative journalism to light-hearted humor, the latest in fashion and personal technology to the cutting edge of the popular culture, *Playboy* is and always has been guidebook and dream book for generations of American men.the definitive source of information and ideas for over 10 million readers each month. In addition, *Playboy*'s 'Interview' and '20 Questions' present profiles of politicians, athletes and today's hottest personalities." Monthly. Estab. 1953. Circ. 3,283,000.

Needs: Humor/satire, mainstream, mystery/suspense, science fiction, suspense. Does not consider poetry, plays, story outlines or novel-length mss. Writers should remember that the magazine's appeal is chiefly to a well-informed, young male audience. Fairy tales, extremely experimental fiction and out-right pornography all have their place, but it is not in *Playboy*. Handwritten submissions will be returned unread. Writers who submit mss without including a SASE will receive neither the ms nor a printed rejection. "We will not consider stories submitted electronically or by fax."

How to Contact: Query. Accepts submissions by mail. Responds in 1 month to queries. No simultaneous submissions. Writer's guidelines for #10 SASE or online at website.

Payment/Terms: Pays $2,000-5,000. Acquires first North American serial rights.

Advice: "*Playboy* does not consider poetry, plays, story outlines or novel-lenght manuscripts."

$ 🖂 ◎ **POCKETS**, The Upper Room, 1908 Grand Ave., P.O. Box 340004, Nashville TN 37203-0004. (615)340-7333. Fax: (615)340-7267. E-mail: pockets@upperroom.org. Website: www.pockets.org or www.upperroom.org/pockets. **Contact:** Lynn W. Gilliam, associate editor. Magazine: 7×11; 48 pages; color and 2-color illustrations; some photos. "We are a Christian, inter-denominational publication for children 6-11 years of age. Each issue reflects a specific theme." Estab. 1981. Circ. 94,000.

• *Pockets* has received honors from the Educational Press Association of America.

Needs: Adventure, ethnic/multicultural, historical (general), religious/inspirational, slice-of-life vignettes. No fantasy, science fiction, talking animals. "All submissions should address the broad theme of the magazine. Each issue is built around one theme with material which can be used by children in a variety of ways. Scripture stories, fiction, poetry, prayers, art, graphics, puzzles and activities are included. Submissions do not need to be overtly religious. They should help children experience a Christian lifestyle that is not always a neatly-wrapped moral package, but is open to the continuing revelation of God's will. Seasonal material, both secular and liturgical, is desired. No violence, horror, sexual and racial stereotyping or fiction containing heavy moralizing." Themes available by SASE. Receives 200 unsolicited mss/month. Accepts 4-5 mss/issue; 44-60 mss/year. Publishes ms 1 year to 18 months after acceptance. **Publishes 15 new writers/year.** Length: 600-1,400 words; average length: 1,200 words.

How to Contact: Send complete ms. Responds in 6 weeks to mss. Accepts reprints, multiple submissions. Sample copy for 9×12 SAE and 4 first-class stamps. Writer's guidelines, themes, and due dates available online.

Payment/Terms: Pays 14¢/word, plus 2-5 contributor's copies. Pays on acceptance for first North American serial rights. Sponsors awards/contests.

Advice: "Listen to children as they talk with each other. Send for a sample copy, guidelines and list of themes before submitting. Many manuscripts we receive are simply inappropriate. New themes published in December of each year." Include SASE.

◎ ▢ **PORTLAND MAGAZINE, Maine's City Magazine**, 722 Congress St., Portland ME 041012. (207)775-4339. Fax: (207)775-2334. E-mail: editor@portlandmonthly.com. Website: www.portlandmagazine.com. **Contact:** Colin Sargent, editor. Magazine: 200 pages; 60 lb. paper; 100 lb. cover stock; illustrations; photos. "City lifestyle magazine—fiction, style, business, real estate, controversy, fashion, cuisine, interviews and art relating to the Maine area." Monthly. Estab. 1986. Circ. 100,000.

Needs: Historical, literary (Maine connection). Query first. Receives 20 unsolicited mss/month. Accepts 1 mss/issue; 10 mss/year. **Publishes 50 new writers/year.** Recently published work by C.D.B Bryan, Joan Connor, Jason Brown, and Sebastian Junger.

How to Contact: Send complete ms. SASE.

Payment/Terms: Pays on publication for first North American serial rights.

Advice: "We publish ambitious short fiction featuring everyone from Frederick Barthelme to newly discovered fiction by Edna St. Vincent Millay."

$ ▢ **PURPOSE**, 616 Walnut Ave., Scottdale PA 15683-1999. (724)887-8500. Fax: (724)887-3111. E-mail: horsch @mph.org. Website: www.mph.org. **Contact:** James E. Horsch, editor. Magazine: 5⅜×8⅜; 8 pages; illustrations; photos. Weekly. Estab. 1968. Circ. 110,000.

Needs: Historical (related to discipleship theme), humor/satire, religious/inspirational. No militaristic/narrow patriotism or racism. Receives 100 unsolicited mss/month. Accepts 3 mss/issue; 140 mss/year. Publishes ms 8 months after acceptance. **Publishes 15-25 new writers/year.** Length: 750 words; average length: 500 words. Occasionally comments on rejected mss.

How to Contact: Send complete ms. Responds in 3 months to queries. Accepts simultaneous and reprints, multiple submissions. Sample copy and writer's guidelines for 6×9 SAE and 2 first-class stamps. Writer's guidelines free.

Payment/Terms: Pays up to 5 for stories, and 2 contributor's copies. Pays on acceptance for one-time rights.

Advice: Many stories are "situational—how to respond to dilemmas. Looking for first-person storylines. Write crisp, action moving, personal style, focused upon an individual, a group of people, or an organization. The story form is an excellent literary device to use in exploring discipleship issues. There are many issues to explore. Each writer brings a unique solution. The first two paragraphs are crucial in establishing the mood/issue to be resolved in the story. Work hard on developing these."

$ ◎ ☑ ELLERY QUEEN'S MYSTERY MAGAZINE, Dell Magazines Fiction Group, 475 Park Ave. S., 11th Floor, New York NY 10016. (212)686-7188. Fax: (212)686-7414. E-mail: elleryqueen@dellmagazines.com. Website: www.themysteryplace.com. **Contact:** Janet Hutchings, editor. Magazine: 5⅜ × 8½; 144 pages with special 240-page combined September/October issue. "*Ellery Queen's Mystery Magazine* welcomes submissions from both new and established writers. We publish every kind of mystery short story: the psychological suspense tale, the deductive puzzle, the private eye case—the gamut of crime and detection from the realistic (including the policeman's lot and stories of police procedure) to the more imaginative (including "locked rooms" and "impossible crimes"). *EQMM* has been in continuous publication since 1941. From the beginning three general criteria have been employed in evaluating submissions: We look for strong writing, an original and exciting plot, and professional craftsmanship. We encourage writers whose work meets these general criteria to read an issue of *EQMM* before making a submission." Magazine for lovers of mystery fiction. Estab. 1941. Circ. 300,000 readers.

• *EQMM* has won numerous awards and sponsors its own award for the best stories of the year, nominated by its readership.

Needs: No explicit sex or violence, no gore or horror. Seldom publishes parodies or pastiches. "We accept only mystery, crime, suspense and detective fiction." 2,500-8,00 words is the preferred range. Also publishes minute mysteries of 250 words; novellas up 20,000 words from established authors. Publishes ms 6-12 months after acceptance. Agented fiction 50%. **Publishes 10 new writers/year.** Recently published work by Jeffery Deaver, Joyce Carol Oates and Ruth Rendell. Sometimes comments on rejected mss.

How to Contact: Send complete ms. Responds in 3 months to mss. Accepts simultaneous, multiple submissions. Sample copy for $5. Writer's guidelines for SASE or online.

Payment/Terms: Pays 5-8¢/word, occasionally higher for established authors. Pays on acceptance for first North American serial rights.

Advice: "We have a Department of First Stories and usually publish at least one first story an issue, i.e., the author's first published fiction. We select stories that are fresh and of the kind our readers have expressed a liking for. In writing a detective story, you must play fair with the reader, providing clues and necessary information. Otherwise you have a better chance of publishing if you avoid writing to formula."

$ ☑ REDBOOK MAGAZINE, 224 W. 57th St., New York NY 10019. (212)649-2000. Website: www.redbookmag.com. Magazine: 8 × 10¾; 150-250 pages; 34 lb. paper; 70 lb. cover; illustrations; photos. "*Redbook* addresses young married women between the ages of 28 and 44. Most of our readers are married with children 10 and under; over 60 percent work outside the home. The articles entertain, educate and inspire our readers to confront challenging issues. Each article must be timely and relevant to *Redbook* readers' lives." Monthly. Estab. 1903. Circ. 3,200,000.

Needs: Publishes ms 6 months after acceptance.

How to Contact: *Redbook* was not accepting unsolicited mss at the time of publication. Responds in 3 months to queries; 3 months to mss. Sample copy not available. Writer's guidelines online.

Payment/Terms: Pays on acceptance. Rights purchased vary with author and material.

Advice: "Read at least the last 6 issues of the magazine to get a better understanding of appropriate subject matter and treatment."

Ⓝ ☑ ◎ $ REFORM JUDAISM, Union of American Hebrew Congregations, 633 Third Ave. 7th Floor, New York NY 10017-6778. (212)650-4240. Website: www.uahc.org/rjmag/. Magazine: 8 × 10⅞; 80-112 pages; illustrations; photos. "*Reform Judaism* is the official voice of the Union of American Hebrew Congregations, linking the institutions and affiliates of Reform Judaism with every Reform Jew. *RJ* covers developments within the Movement while interpreting events and Jewish tradition from a Reform perspective." Quarterly. Estab. 1972. Circ. 310,000.

• Recipient of The Simon Rockower Award for Excellence in Jewish Journalism for feature writing, graphic design and photography. The editor says they would publish more stories if they could find excellent, sophiticated, contemporary Jewish fiction.

Needs: Humor/satire, religious/inspirational, sophisticated, cutting-edge, superb writing. Receives 75 unsolicited mss/month. Accepts 3 mss/year. Publishes ms 3 months after acceptance. Published work by Frederick Fastow and Bob Sloan. Length: 600-2,500 words; average length: 1,500 words.

How to Contact: Send complete ms. SASE. Responds in 2 months to queries; 2 months to mss. Accepts simultaneous and reprints submissions. Sample copy for $3.50. Writer's guidelines online.

Payment/Terms: Pays 30¢/word. Pays on publication for first North American serial rights.

$ ☑ ◎ SEEK, Standard Publishing, 8121 Hamilton Ave., Cincinnati OH 45231. (513)931-4050, ext. 351. Fax: (513)931-0950. E-mail: dmedill@standardpub.com. Website: www.standardpub.com. **Contact:** Dawn A. Medill,

---

SENDING TO A COUNTRY other than your own? Be sure to send International Reply Coupons (IRC) instead of stamps for replies or return of your manuscript.

senior editor. Magazine: 5½×8½; 8 pages; newsprint paper; art and photo in each issue. "Inspirational stories of faith-in-action for Christian adults; a Sunday School take-home paper." Quarterly. Estab. 1970. Circ. 27,000.

Needs: Religious/inspirational, and religiously slanted historical and humorous fiction. No poetry. List of upcoming themes available online. Accepts 150 mss/year. Publishes ms 1 year after acceptance.

How to Contact: Send complete ms. Accepts submissions by mail, e-mail, fax. Prefers submissions by e-mail. Responds in 3 months to queries. Sample copy for 6×9 SAE with 2 first-class stamps. Writer's guidelines online.

Payment/Terms: Pays 5¢/word. Pays on acceptance for first North American serial, second serial (reprint) rights.

Advice: "Write a credible story with Christian slant—no preachments; avoid overworked themes such as joy in suffering, generation gaps, etc. Most manuscripts are rejected by us because of irrelevant topic or message, unrealistic story, or poor charater and/or plot development. We use fiction stories that are believable."

$⬛ SEVENTEEN, 1440 Broadway, 13th Floor, New York NY 10018. (212)204-4300. Fax: (212)204-3977. Website: www.seventeen.com. **Contact:** Jennifer Braunschweiger, senior editor. Magazine: 8½×11; 125-400 pages; 40 lb. coated paper; 80 lb. coated cover stock; illustrations; photos/. "*Seventeen* is a young woman's first fashion and beauty magazine. Tailored for young women in their teens and early twenties, *Seventeen* covers fashion, beauty, health, fitness, food, college, entertainment, fiction, plus crucial personal and global issues." Monthly. Estab. 1944. Circ. 2,400,000.

Needs: No science fiction, action/adventure or pornography. High quality literary fiction. Receives 200 unsolicited mss/month. Accepts 6-9 mss/year. Publishes ms 6 months after acceptance. Agented fiction 50%. **Publishes 3 new writers/year.** Recently published work by Thisbe Nissen, Meg Cabot, David Schickler and Alice Sebold.

How to Contact: Query with published clips or send complete ms. Accepts submissions by mail. Responds in 3 months to queries. Sample copy not available. Writer's guidelines available online.

Payment/Terms: Pays $500-2,000. Pays on acceptance for one-time rights.

Advice: "Respect the intelligence and sophistication of teenagers. *Seventeen* remains open to the surprise of new voices. Our commitment to publishing the work of new writers remains strong; we continue to read every submission we receive. We believe that good fiction can move the reader toward throughtful examination of her own life as well as the lives of others—providing her ultimately with a fuller appreciation of what it means to be human. While stories that focus on female teenage experience continue to be of interest, the less obvious possibilities are equally welcome. We encourage writers to submit literary short stories concerning subjects that may not be immediately identifiable as 'teenage,' with narrative styles that are experimental and challenging. Too often, unsolicited submissions possess voices and themes condescending and unsophisticated. Also, writers hesitate to send stories to *Seventeen* that they think too risqué or sophisticated. Good writing holds the imaginable and then some, and if it doesn't find its home here, we're always grateful for the introduction to a writer's work. We're more inclined to publish cutting edge fiction than simple, young adult fiction."

$⬛◎⬛ SHINE BRIGHTLY, (formerly *Touch Shine*), GEMS Girls' Clubs, P.O. Box 7259, Grand Rapids MI 49510. (616)241-5616. Fax: (616)241-5558. E-mail: sara@gemsgc.org. Website: www.gospelcom.net/gems. **Contact:** Sara Lynne Hilton, managing editor. Magazine: 8½×11; 24 pages; 50 lb. paper; 50 lb. cover stock; illustrations; photos. "Our purpose is to lead girls into a living relationship with Jesus Christ and to help them see how God is at work in their lives and the world around them. Puzzles, crafts, stories, articles and club input for girls ages 9-14." Monthly. Estab. 1971. Circ. 13,000.

• *Shine Brightly* has received awards for fiction and illustrations from the Evangelical Press Association.

Needs: Adventure (that girls could experience in their hometowns or places they might realistically visit), children's/juvenile, ethnic/multicultural, historical, humor/satire, mystery/suspense (believable only), religious/inspirational (nothing too preachy), romance (stories that deal with awakening awareness of boys are appreciated), slice-of-life vignettes, suspense (can be serialized). Write for upcoming themes. Each year has an overall theme and each month has a theme to fit with yearly themes. Receives 50 unsolicited mss/month. Accepts 3 mss/issue; 30 mss/year. Publishes ms 1 year after acceptance. **Publishes some new writers/year.** Recently published work by A.J. Schut. Length: 400-1,000 words; average length: 800 words.

How to Contact: Send complete ms. Responds in 2 months to queries. Accepts simultaneous and reprints submissions. Sample copy for 9×12 SAE with 3 first class stamps and $1. Writer's guidelines online.

Payment/Terms: Pays $20-50. Pays on publication for first North American serial, second serial (reprint), simultaneous rights.

Advice: "Try new and refreshing approaches. No fluffy fiction with Polyanna endings. We want stories dealing with real issues facing girls today. The one-parent, new girl at school is a bit overdone in our market. We have been dealing with issues like AIDS, abuse, drugs, and family relationships in our stories—more awareness-type articles."

$⬛◎ SPIDER, The Magazine for Children, Cricket Magazine Group, P.O. Box 300, Peru IL 61354. (815)224-5803. Fax: (815)224-6615. Website: www.cricketmag.com. **Contact:** Marianne Carus, editor-in-chief; Heather Delabre, editor. Magazine: 8×10; 33 pages; illustrations; photos. "*Spider* introduces 6- to 9-year-old children to the highest quality stories, poems, illustrations, articles, and activities. It was created to foster in beginning readers a love of reading and discovery that will last a lifetime. We're looking for writers who respect children's intelligence." Monthly. Estab. 1994. Circ. 87,000.

• Carus Publishing also publishes *Cricket*, *Ladybug*, *Babybug* and *Cicada*.

Needs: Adventure, children's/juvenile (6-9 years), ethnic/multicultural, fantasy (children's fantasy), historical, humor/satire, mystery/suspense, science fiction, suspense, realistic fiction, folk tales, fairy tales. No romance, horror, religious. Accepts 4 mss/issue. Publishes ms 2-3 years after acceptance. Agented fiction 2%. Recently published work by Polly Horvath, Katie Walker, and Aaron Shepard. Length: 300-1,000 words; average length: 775 words. Also publishes poetry. Often comments on rejected mss.

How to Contact: Send complete ms. Send SASE for return of ms. Responds in 4 months to mss. Accepts simultaneous and reprints submissions. Sample copy for $5. Writer's guidelines for #10 SASE or on website.

Payment/Terms: Pays 25¢/word and 2 contributor's copies; additional copies $2. Pays on publication. Rights vary.

Advice: "Read back issues of *Spider*." Look for "quality writing, good characterization, lively style, humor."

⬛ **SPINNING JENNY**, Black Dress Press, PO Box 1373, New York NY 10276. E-mail: submissions@blackdress press.com. Website: www.blackdresspress.com. **Contact:** C.E. Harrison. Magazine: 112 pages; 60 lb. paper; offset printed; perfect bound; illustrations. Literary magazine publishing short stories and novel excerpts Estab. 1994. Member, CLMP.

Needs: Experimental, literary. Publishes ms 11 months after acceptance. **Publishes 3 new writers/year.**

How to Contact: Send complete ms. Accepts submissions by mail, e-mail. Send SASE for return of ms or send a disposable copy of ms and #10 SASE for reply only. Responds in 2 months to mss.

Payment/Terms: Pays 5 contributor copies.

$⬛ ♈ ◎ **ST. ANTHONY MESSENGER**, 28 W. Liberty St., Cincinnati OH 45202-6498. (513)241-5615. Fax: (513)241-0399. E-mail: stanthony@americancatholic.org. Website: www.americancatholic.org. **Contact:** Father Pat McCloskey, O.F.M., editor. Magazine: 8 × 10¾; 60 pages; illustrations; photos. "*St. Anthony Messenger* is a Catholic family magazine which aims to help its readers lead more fully human and Christian lives. We publish articles which report on a changing church and world, opinion pieces written from the perspective of Christian faith and values, personality profiles, and fiction that entertains and informs." Estab. 1893. Circ. 324,000.

- This is a leading Catholic magazine, and has won awards for both religious and secular journalism and writing from the Catholic Press Association, the International Association of Business Communicators, the Society of Professional Journalists and the Cincinnati Editors Association.

Needs: Mainstream, religious/inspirational, senior citizen/retirement. "We do not want mawkishly sentimental or preachy fiction. Stories are most often rejected for poor plotting and characterization; bad dialogue—listen to how people talk; inadequate motivation. Many stories say nothing, are 'happenings' rather than stories." No fetal journals, no rewritten Bible stories. Receives 60-70 unsolicited mss/month. Accepts 1 mss/issue; 12 mss/year. Publishes ms 1 year after acceptance. **Publishes 3 new writers/year.** Recently published work by Geraldine Marshall Gutfreund, John Salustri, Beth Dotson, Miriam Pollikatsikis and Joseph Pici. Sometimes comments on rejected mss.

How to Contact: Send complete ms. Accepts submissions by mail, e-mail, fax. SASE for ms. "For quickest response send self-addressed stamped postcard with choices: "Yes, we're interested in publishing; Maybe, we'd like to hold for future consideration; No, we've decided to pass on the publication." Responds in 3 weeks to queries; 2 months to mss. No simultaneous submissions. Sample copy for 9 × 12 SAE with 4 first-class stamps. Writer's guidelines online. Reviews fiction.

Payment/Terms: Pays 16¢/word maximum and 2 contributor's copies; $1 charge for extras. Pays on acceptance for first North American serial, electronic, first worldwide serial rights.

Advice: "We publish one story a month and we get up to 1,000 a year. Too many offer simplistic 'solutions' or answers. Pay attention to endings. Easy, simplistic, deus ex machina endings don't work. People have to feel characters in the stories are real and have a reason to care about them and what happens to them. Fiction entertains but can also convey a point and sound values."

$⬛ ◎ **STANDARD**, Nazarene International Headquarters, 6401 The Paseo, Kansas City MO 64131. (816)333-7000. Fax: (816)333-4439. E-mail: ssm@nazarene.org. Website: www.nazarene.org. **Contact:** Everett Leadingham, editor. Magazine: 8½ × 11; 8 pages; illustrations; photos. Inspirational reading for adults. "In *Standard* we want to show Christianity in action, and we prefer to do that through stories that hold the reader's attention." Weekly. Estab. 1936. Circ. 130,000.

Needs: "Looking for stories that show Christianity in action." Accepts 200 mss/year. Publishes ms 14-18 months after acceptance. **Publishes some new writers/year.**

How to Contact: Send complete ms. SASE. Accepts simultaneous submissions. Writer's guidelines and sample copy for SAE with 2 first-class stamps.

Payment/Terms: Pays 3½¢/word for first rights; 2¢/word for reprint rights, and contributor's copies. Pays on acceptance for first or reprint rights.

Advice: "Be conscientious in your use of Scripture; don't overload your story with quotations. When you quote the Bible, quote it exactly and cite chapter, verse, and version used. (We prefer NIV). *Standard* will handle copyright matters for Scripture. Except for quotations from the Bible, written permission for the use of any other copyrighted material (especially song lyrics) is the responsibility of the writer. Keep in mind the international audience of *Standard* with regard to geographic refrences and holidays. We cannot use stories about cultural, national, or secular holidays. Do not mention specific church affiliations. *Standard* is read in a variety of denominations. Do not submit any manuscript which has been submitted to or published in any of the following: *Vista*, *Wesleyan Advocate*, *Holiness Today*, *Preacher's Magazine*, *World Mission*, *Women Alive*, or various teen and children's publications produced by WordAction Publishing Company. These are overlapping markets."

$ ◪ **STORY FRIENDS**, Mennonite Publishing Network, 616 Walnut Ave., Scottdale PA 15683. (724)887-8500. Fax: (724)887-3111. Website: www.mph.org. **Contact:** Susan Reith, editor. A magazine which portrays Jesus as a friend and helper. Nonfiction and fiction for children 4-9 years of age. Monthly.
  • The Mennonite Publishing Network also publishes *On the Line*, *Purpose* and *With* magazines.
Needs: Juvenile. Stories of everyday experiences at home, in church, in school or at play, which provide models of Christian values. "Wants to see more fiction set in African-American, Latino or Hispanic settings. No stories about children and their grandparents or children and their elderly neighbors. I have more than enough." **Publishes 10-12 new writers/year.** Published work by Virginia Kroll and Lisa Harkrader. Length: 300-800 words.
How to Contact: Send complete ms with SASE. Seasonal or holiday material should be submitted 6 months in advance. Buys reprints. Free sample copy with SASE (9 × 12).
Payment/Terms: Pays 3-5¢/word. Pays on acceptance for one-time rights. Not copyrighted.
Advice: "I am buying more 500-word stories since we switched to a new format. It is important to include relationships, patterns of forgiveness, respect, honesty, trust and caring. Prefer exciting yet plausible short stories which offer varied settings, introduce children to wide ranges of friends and demonstrate joys, fears, temptations and successes of the readers. Read good children's literature, the classics, the Newberry winner and the Caldecott winners. Respect children you know and allow their resourcefulness and character to have a voice in your writing."

$ ◪ **THE SUN**, The Sun Publishing Co., 107 N. Roberson St., Chapel Hill NC 27516. (919)942-5282. Fax: (919)932-3101. Website: www.thesunmagazine.org. **Contact:** Sy Safransky, editor. Magazine: 8½ × 11; 48 pages; offset paper; glossy cover stock; photos. "We are open to all kinds of writing, though we favor work of a personal nature." Monthly. Estab. 1974. Circ. 55,000.
Needs: Literary. Open to all fiction. Receives 500 unsolicited mss/month. Accepts 2 mss/issue. Publishes ms 6-12 months after acceptance. Recently published work by Katherine Vaz, Stephen Vaz, Alicia Erian and Steve Almond. Also publishes poetry.
How to Contact: Send complete ms. Accepts reprints submissions. Sample copy for $5. Writer's guidelines online.
Payment/Terms: Pays $300-750. Pays on publication for first, one-time rights.
Advice: "We favor honest, personal writing with an intimate point of view."

$ ◪ **TRUE CONFESSIONS**, Macfadden Women's Group, 333 Seventh Ave., New York NY 10001. (212)979-4898. Fax: (212)979-4825. E-mail: trueconfessionstales@yahoo.com. **Contact:** Pat Byrdsong, editorial director. Magazine: 8 × 10½; 112 pages; photos. "*True Confessions* is a women's magazine featuring true-to-life stories about working class women and their families." Monthly. Circ. 200,000.
Needs: "Family problems, crime, modern social problems, ie., abuse, sexual discrimination, addiction, etc. Also stories about multicultural experience—Latino, African, Asian, Native American stories encouraged. Must be written in first-person. No science fiction or third person stories. Wants to see more first-person inspirationals, thrillers, mysteries, romances with an edge." Publishes ms 4 months after acceptance. **Publishes 25 new writers/year.**
How to Contact: Query. Accepts submissions by e-mail. Responds in 3 months to queries; 15 months to mss. Sample copy for $2.99.
Payment/Terms: Pays 3¢/word or a flat $100 rate for mini-stories, and 1 contributor's copy. Pays 1 month after publication. Acquires all rights.
Advice: "Emotionally charged stories with a strong emphasis on characterization and well-defined plots are preferred. Stories should be intriguing, suspenseful, humorous, romantic, or tragic. The plots and characters should reflect American life. I want stories that cover the wide spectrum of America. I want to feel as though I intimately know the narrator and her/his motivation. If your story is dramatically gripping and/or humorous, features three-dimensional characters, and a realistic conflict, you have an excellent chance of making a sale at *True Confessions*. I suggest writers read three to four issues of *True Confessions* before sending submissions. Do not talk down to our readers. Contemporary problems should be handled with insight and a fresh angle. Timely, first-person stories told by a sympathetic narrator are always needed as well as good romantic stories."

$ ◪ ◎ **U.S. CATHOLIC**, Claretian Publications, 205 W. Monroe St., Chicago IL 60606. (312)236-7782. Fax: (312)236-8207. Website: www.uscatholic.org. **Contact:** Maureen Abood, literary editor. Magazine: 8½ × 11; 52 pages; photos. "*U.S. Catholic* is dedicated to the belief that it makes a difference whether you're Catholic. We invite and help our readers explore the wisdom of their faith tradition and apply their faith to the challenges of the 21st century." Monthly. Estab. 1935. Circ. 40,000. Member, Associated Church Press, Religious Communicators Council, Catholic Press Association.
Needs: Ethnic/multicultural, family saga, mainstream, religious/inspirational, slice-of-life vignettes. Receives 100 unsolicited mss/month. Accepts 12 mss/year. Publishes ms 2-3 months after acceptance. **Publishes 20% new writers/year.** Publishes short shorts. Also publishes poetry.
How to Contact: Send complete ms. Accepts submissions by mail, e-mail, fax, phone. Send a disposable copy

of ms and #10 SASE for reply only. Responds in 1 month to queries; 2 months to mss. Sample copy for large SASE. Guidelines by e-mail or on website. Reviews fiction.

Payment/Terms: Pays $300. Pays on acceptance for first North American serial rights.

$ ☑ THE WAR CRY, The Salvation Army, 615 Slaters Lane, Alexandria VA 22313. (703)684-5500. Fax: (703)684-5539. E-mail: war_cry@usn.salvationarmy.org. Website: www.thewarcry.com. **Contact:** Lt. Colonel Marlene Chase, editor-in-chief. Magazine: 8½×11; 24 pages; glossy; illustrations; photos. Biweekly. Estab. 1881. Circ. 400,000. Member, Evangelical Press Association.

Needs: Family saga, religious/inspirational. "No fantasy, science fiction or New Age." Upcoming themes available for #10 SASE. Receives 30 unsolicited mss/month. Accepts 5 mss/issue; 120 mss/year. Publishes ms 2 months-1 year after acceptance. **Publishes 5 new writers/year.** Recently published work by Philip Yancey and Bob Robeson. Publishes short shorts. Also publishes poetry. Sometimes comments on rejected mss.

How to Contact: Send complete ms. Send SASE for return of ms or disposable copy of ms. Maximum 5 poems/submission. Responds in 2 months to mss. Accepts simultaneous and reprints, multiple submissions. Sample copy, theme list, and writer's guidelines free for #10 SASE or online.

Payment/Terms: Pays up to 10-20¢/word; 12 for reprints, and 2 contributor's copies. Pays on acceptance for first, one-time rights.

Advice: "We publish limited amounts of fiction, so it must be outstanding. No 'flights of fancy.' Make sure fiction is realistic and involving with good characterization. Get a sample copy."

$ ☑ ◎ WINNER, Saying No To Drugs and Yes To Life, The Health Connection, 55 W. Oak Ridge Dr., Hagerstown MD 21740. (301)393-3294. Fax: (301)393-3294. E-mail: winner@healthconnection.org. Website: www .winnermagazine.org. **Contact:** Anita Jacobs, editor. Magazine: 8⅛×10⅝; 16 pages; illustrations; photos. "*Winner* is a teaching tool to help students learn the dangers in abusive substances, such as tobacco, alcohol, and other drugs, as well as at-risk behaviors. It also focuses on everyday problems such as dealing with divorce, sibling rivalry, coping with grief, and healthy diet, to mention just a few." Monthly. Estab. 1956. Circ. 12,000.

Needs: Children's/juvenile (adventure, easy-to-read, sports, ages 8-12), true-to-life stories dealing with problems preteens face. No suspense or mystery. Upcoming themes: Addictions (May), deadline September 2003. List of upcoming themes available by SASE or online. Publishes ms 6-9 months after acceptance. Also publishes poetry.

How to Contact: Send complete ms. Accepts submissions by mail, e-mail (winner@healthconnection.org), fax, phone. Send SASE for return of ms. Responds in 4-6 weeks to queries; 2-3 months to mss. Accepts simultaneous submissions. Sample copy for $2 and 9×12 SAE with 2 first-class stamps. Writer's guidelines for SASE, by e-mail, fax or on website.

Payment/Terms: Pays $50-80. Pays on acceptance for first North American serial, first rights.

Ⓝ $ ◎ WOMAN'S WEEKLY, IPC Magazines, King's Reach, Stamford St., London England 9LS. **Contact:** Gaynor Davies. Publishes 1 serial and at least 2 short stories/week.

Needs: "Short stories can be on any theme, but must have warmth. No explicit sex or violence. Serials need not be written in installments. They are submitted as complete manuscripts and we split them up, or send first installment of serial (4,500 words) and synopsis of the rest."

How to Contact: Writer's guidelines free.

Payment/Terms: Short story payment starts at £100 and rises as writer becomes a more regular contributor. Serial payments start at around £600/installment. Writer's also receive contributor's copies.

Advice: "Read the magazine and try to understand who the publication is aimed at."

$ ◻ ◎ WOMAN'S WORLD, Bauer Publishing Co., 270 Sylvan Ave., Englewood Cliffs NJ 07632. (201)569-6699. Fax: (201)569-3584. E-mail: dearww@aol.com. **Contact:** Johnene Granger, fiction editor. Magazine: 9½×11; 54 pages. "We publish short romances and mini-mysteries for all woman, ages 18-68." Weekly. Estab. 1980. Circ. 1,600,000.

Needs: Mystery/suspense, romance (contemporary). Not interested in science fiction, fantasy, historical romance, or foreign locales. No explicit sex, graphic language, or seamy settings. "We buy contemporary romances of 1,400 words. Stories must revolve around a compelling, true-to-life relationship dilemma; may feature a male or female protagonist, and may be written in either first or third person. We are *not* interested in storries of life-or-death, or fluffy, fly-away style romances. When we say romance, what we really mean is relationship, whether it's just beginning or is about to celebrate its 50th anniversary." Receives 2,500 unsolicited mss/month. Accepts 2 mss/issue; 104 mss/year. Publishes ms 4 months after acceptance. Recently published work by Linda S. Reilly, Linda Yellin and Tim Myers. Publishes short shorts.

READ 'THE BUSINESS OF FICTION WRITING' section for information on manuscript preparation, mailing tips, rights and more.

How to Contact: Send complete ms. Accepts submissions by mail. SASE. *No queries.* Responds in 2 months to mss. Sample copy not available. Writer's guidelines for #10 SASE.

Payment/Terms: Pays $500-1,000. Pays on acceptance for first North American Serial rights for 6 months.

Advice: "Familiarize yourself totally with our format and style. Read at least a year's worth of *Woman's World* fiction. Analyze and dissect it. Regarding romances, scrutinize them not only for content but tone, mood and sensibility."

N ® $□ WRITERS' FORUM, Britain's Best Magazine for Writers, Writers International Ltd., P.O. Box 3229, Bournemouth Dorset BH1 1ZS, UK. (44)1202 589828. Fax: (44)1202 589828. E-mail: editorial@writers-forum.com. Website: www.writers-forum.com. **Contact:** John Jenkins, editor. Monthly: A4; 64 pages; illustrations; photos. "In each issue *Writers' Forum* covers the *who, why, what, where, when* and *how* of writing. You will find the latest on markets, how-to articles, courses/holidays for writers and much more. There is also a short story competition in every issue—that means you have ten chances to get published and win some cash. Prizes range from 150 to £250 and there's £1,000 for the best story of the year. Monthly. Estab. 1999. Circ. 25,000.

Needs: Erotica, historical, horror (psychological), literary, mainstream, mystery/suspense (cozy, private eye/hard-boiled), romance (contemporary, futuristic/time travel, historical, romantic suspense), science fiction (soft/sociological), thriller/espionage, western (frontier saga, traditional), young adult/teen (adventure, easy-to-read, historical, problem novels, romance). Receives hundreds unsolicited mss/month. Accepts 3-4 mss/issue; 20 mss/year. Publishes ms 2-3 months after acceptance. Length: 1,000-3,000 words; average length: 1,500 words. Also publishes literary essays, literary criticism, poetry. Always comments on rejected mss.

How to Contact: Query. Accepts submissions by e-mail, fax. Send SASE (or IRC) for return of ms or send disposable copy of the ms and #10 SASE for reply only. Responds in 2-3 weeks to queries; 2-3 weeks to mss. Accepts simultaneous submissions. Sample copy for SASE (A4 envelope; $2 postage or IRCs). Writer's guidelines for SASE, e-mail or on website. Reviews fiction.

Payment/Terms: Pays $120 maximum and 1 contributor's copy; additional copies $5. Pays on publication for first rights. Sponsors awards/contests.

Advice: "A good introduction and an original slant on a common theme. Always read the competition rules and our guidelines."

N $ WRITERS' JOURNAL, The Complete Writer's Magazine, Val-Tech Media, P.O. Box 394, Perham MN 56573-0394. (218)346-7921. Fax: (218)346-7924. Website: www.writersjournal.com. "*Writers' Journal* is read by thousands of aspiring writers whose love of writing has taken them to the next step: Writing for money. We are an instructional manual giving writers the tools and information necessary to get their work published. We also print works by authors who have won our writing contests." Bimonthly. Estab. 1980. Circ. 26,000.

Needs: "We only publish winners of our fiction contests—16 contests/year." Receives 200 contest entries unsolicited mss/month. Accepts 5-7 mss/issue; 30-40 mss/year. Publishes ms 10 months after acceptance. Agented fiction 3%. **Publishes 100 new writers/year.** Also publishes poetry.

How to Contact: Accepts submissions by mail, e-mail (not as attachment). Responds in 6 weeks to queries; 6 months to mss. Accepts simultaneous submissions. Sample copy for $5.

Payment/Terms: Pays on publication for one-time rights.

Book Publishers

In this section, you will find many of the "big-name" book publishers. Many of these publishers remain tough markets for new writers or for those whose work might be considered literary or experimental. Indeed, some only accept work from established authors, and then often only through an author's agent. Although having your novel published by one of the big commercial publishers listed in this section is difficult, it is not impossible. The trade magazine *Publishers Weekly* regularly features interviews with writers whose first novels are being released by top publishers. Many editors at large publishing houses find great satisfaction in publishing a writer's first novel.

On page 585, you'll find the publishing industry's "family tree", which maps out each of the large book publishing conglomerates' divisions, subsidiaries, and imprints. Each parent company and most subsidiaries and divisions should also have listings in this section—distinguished by the ◪ icon—detailing its imprints and the address of its headquarters. Remember, most manuscripts are acquired by imprints, not their parent company, so avoid submitting to any listing with the ◪ icon.

Also listed here are "small presses" publishing four or more titles annually. Included among them are small and mid-size independent presses, university presses, and other nonprofit publishers. Introducing new writers to the reading public has become an increasingly more important role of these smaller presses at a time when the large conglomerates are taking less chances on unknown writers. Many of the successful small presses listed in this section have built their reputations and their businesses in this way and have become known for publishing prize-winning fiction.

These smaller presses also tend to keep books in print longer than larger houses. And, since small presses publish a smaller number of books, each title is equally important to the publisher, and each is promoted in much the same way and with the same commitment. Editors also stay at small presses longer because they have more of a stake in the business—often they own the business. Many smaller book publishers are writers themselves and know first-hand the importance of a close editor-author or publisher-author relationship.

TYPES OF BOOK PUBLISHERS

Large or small, the publishers in this section publish books "for the trade." That is, unlike textbook, technical or scholarly publishers, trade publishers publish books to be sold to the general consumer through bookstores, chain stores or other retail outlets. Within the trade book field, however, there are a number of different types of books.

The easiest way to categorize books is by their physical appearance and the way they are marketed. Hardcover books are the more expensive editions of a book, sold through bookstores and carrying a price tag of around $20 and up. Trade paperbacks are soft-bound books, also sold mostly in bookstores, but they carry a more modest price tag of usually around $10 to $20. Today a lot of fiction is published in this form because it means a lower financial risk than hardcover.

Mass market paperbacks are another animal altogether. These are the smaller "pocket-size" books available at bookstores, grocery stores, drug stores, chain retail outlets, etc. Much genre or category fiction is published in this format. This area of the publishing industry is very open to the work of talented new writers who write in specific genres such as science fiction, romance, and mystery.

At one time publishers could be easily identified and grouped by the type of books they do.

Today, however, the lines between hardcover and paperback books are blurred. Many publishers known for publishing hardcover books also publish trade paperbacks and have paperback imprints. This enables them to offer established authors (and a very few lucky newcomers) hard-soft deals in which their book comes out in both versions. Thanks to the mergers of the past decade, too, the same company may own several hardcover and paperback subsidiaries and imprints, even though their editorial focuses may remain separate.

CHOOSING A BOOK PUBLISHER

In addition to checking the bookstores and libraries for books by publishers that interest you, you may want to refer to the Category Index at the back of this book to find publishers divided by specific subject categories. If you write genre fiction, check our new genre sections for lists of book publishers: (mystery, page 68; romance, page 80; science fiction/fantasy & horror, page 90). The subjects listed in the Indexes are general. Read individual listings to find which subcategories interest a publisher. For example, you will find several romance publishers listed in the For Romance Writers Section, but read the listings to find which type of romance is considered—gothic, contemporary, Regency or futuristic. See The "Quick Start" Guide to Publishing Your Fiction on page 2 for more on how to refine your list of potential markets.

The icons appearing before the names of the publishers will also help you in selecting a publisher. These codes are especially important in this section, because many of the publishing houses listed here require writers to submit through an agent. A ◙ icon identifies those that mostly publish established and agented authors, while a ◯ points to publishers most open to new writers. See the inside front and back covers of this book for a complete list and explanations of symbols used in this book.

IN THE LISTINGS

As with other sections in this book, we identify new listings with a ▨ symbol. In this section, most with this symbol are not new publishers, but instead are established publishers who were unable or decided not to list last year and are therefore new to this edition.

In addition to the ▨ symbol indicating new listings, we include other symbols to help you in narrowing your search. English-speaking foreign markets are denoted by a ▦ . The maple leaf symbol ▨ identifies Canadian presses. If you are not a Canadian writer, but are interested in a Canadian press, check the listing carefully. Many small presses in Canada receive grants and other funds from their provincial or national government and are, therefore, restricted to publishing Canadian authors.

We also include editorial comments set off by a bullet (●) within listings. This is where we include information about any special requirements or circumstances that will help you know even more about the publisher's needs and policies. The ▨ symbol identifies publishers who have recently received honors or awards for their books. And the ▲ symbol indicates that a publisher accepts agented submissions only.

Each listing includes a summary of the editorial mission of the house, an overarching principle that ties together what they publish. Under the heading **Contact** we list one or more editors, often with their specific area of expertise.

Book editors asked us again this year to emphasize the importance of paying close attention to the **Needs** and **How to Contact** subheads of listings for book publishers. Unlike magazine editors who want to see complete manuscripts of short stories, most of the book publishers listed here ask that writers send a query letter with an outline and/or synopsis and several chapters of their novel. The Business of Fiction Writing, beginning on page 59 of this book, outlines how to prepare work to submit directly to a publisher.

There are no subsidy book publishers listed in *Novel & Short Story Writer's Market*. By subsidy, we mean any arrangement in which the writer is expected to pay all or part of the cost of producing, distributing, and marketing his book. We feel a writer should not be asked to share in any cost of turning his manuscript into a book. All the book publishers listed here told us that they *do not charge writers* for publishing their work. *If any of the publishers listed here ask you to pay any part of publishing or marketing your manuscript, please let us know.* See our Complaint Procedure on page 106, and on the copyright page of this book.

A NOTE ABOUT AGENTS

Some publishers are willing to look at unsolicited submissions, but most feel having an agent is to the writer's best advantage. In this section more than any other, you'll find a number of publishers who prefer submissions from agents. That's why we've included a section of agents open to submissions from fiction writers (page 107).

Be wary of those who charge large sums of money for reading a manuscript. Reading fees do not guarantee representation. Think of an agent as a potential business partner and feel free to ask tough questions about his or her credentials, experience and business practices.

For More Information

Check out issues of *Publishers Weekly* for publishing industry trade news in the U.S. and around the world or *Quill & Quire* for book publishing news in the Canadian book industry.

For more small presses see the *International Directory of Little Magazines and Small Presses* published by Dustbooks. To keep up with changes in the industry throughout the year, check issues of two small press trade publications: *Small Press Review* (also published by Dustbooks) and *Independent Publisher* (Jenkins Group, Inc.).

A&B PUBLISHERS GROUP, 1000 Atlantic Ave., Brooklyn NY 11238. (718)783-7808. Fax: (718)783-7267. E-mail: maxtay@webspan.net. **Contact:** Maxwell Taylor, production manager (children's, adult nonfiction); Wendy Gift, editor (fiction). Estab. 1992. Publishes hardcover originals, trade paperback originals and reprints. **Published 30% debut authors within the last year.** Averages 12 total titles, 12 fiction titles/year. Distributes titles through Ingram and A&B Distributors.
Needs: Published *Let That be the Reason*, by Vickie Struger.
How to Contact: Query with SASE. Agented fiction 30%. Responds in 2 months. Accepts simultaneous submissions.
Payment/Terms: Pays 5-12% royalty on net receipts. Average advance: $500-2,500. Publishes ms 18 months after acceptance. Book catalog free.
Advice: "Read, read, read. The best writers are developed from good reading. There is not enough attention to quality. Read, write and revise until you get it almost right."

HARRY N. ABRAMS, INC., La Martiniere Groupe, 100 Fifth Ave., New York NY 10011. (212)206-7715. Fax: (212)645-8437. Website: www.abramsbooks.com. **Contact:** Eric Himmel, editor-in-chief. Estab. 1949. Publishes hardcover and "a few" paperback originals. Averages 150 total titles/year.
How to Contact: Responds in 6-8 weeks to queries. No simultaneous submissions.
Payment/Terms: Pays royalty. Average advance: variable. Publishes ms 2 years after acceptance. Book catalog for $5.

ABSEY & CO., 23011 Northcrest Dr., Spring TX 77389. (281)257-2340. Fax: (281)251-4676. E-mail: abseyand co@aol.com. Website: www.absey.com. **Contact:** Edward E. Wilson, publisher. "We are interested in book-length fiction of literary merit with a firm intended audience." Publishes hardcover, trade paperback and mass market paperback originals. **Published 3-5 debut authors within the last year.** Averages 6-10 total titles, 6-10 fiction titles/year.
Needs: Juvenile, mainstream/contemporary, short story collections. "Since we are a small, new press, we are looking for book-length manuscripts with a firm intended audience." Published *Where I'm From*, by George Ella Lyon; and *Dragonfly*, by Alice McLerran.
How to Contact: Accepts unsolicited mss. Query with SASE. Responds in 3 months to queries; 9 months to mss. No simultaneous submissions, electronic submissions.

Payment/Terms: Royalty and advance vary. Publishes ms 1 year after acceptance. Ms guidelines online.
Advice: "Since we are a small, new press looking for good manuscripts, we tend to work closely and attentively with our authors. Many established authors who have been with the large New York houses have come to us to publish their work because we work closely with them."

ACADEMY CHICAGO PUBLISHERS, 363 W. Erie St., Suite 7E., Chicago IL 60610-3125. (312)751-7300. Fax: (312)751-7306. E-mail: info@academychicago.com. Website: www.academychicago.com. **Contact:** Anita Miller, senior editor. Estab. 1975. Midsize independent publisher. Publishes hardcover originals and trade paperback reprints. Averages 15 total titles/year.
• *Cutter's Island*, by Vincent Panella placed in both the *Foreword Magazine* Book of the Year contest and the 2000 Independent Publishers Awards.
Needs: Historical, mainstream/contemporary, military/war, mystery. "We look for quality work, but we do not publish experimental, avant garde novels." Biography, history, academic and anthologies. Only the most unusual mysteries, no private-eyes or thrillers. No explicit sex or violence. Serious fiction, no romance/adventure. "We will consider historical fiction that is well researched. No science fiction/fantasy, no religious/inspirational, no how-to, no cookbooks. In general, we are very conscious of women's roles. We publish very few children's books." Published *Clean Start*, by Patricia Margaret Page (first fiction); *Cutter's Island: Caesar in Captivity*, by Vincent Panella (first fiction, historical); and *Murder at the Paniomic Games*, by Michael B. Edward.
How to Contact: Does not accept unsolicited mss. Submit proposal package including 3 sample chapter(s), synopsis. Include cover letter briefly describing the content of your work. "Manuscripts without envelopes will be discarded. *Mailers* are a *must*, even from agents." Send SASE or IRC. Responds in 3 months to queries.
Payment/Terms: Pays 7-10% royalty on wholesale price. Average advance: modest. Publishes ms 18 months after acceptance. Book catalog online; ms guidelines online.
Advice: "At the moment we are swamped with manuscripts and anything under consideration can be under consideration for months."

ACE SCIENCE FICTION AND FANTASY, The Berkley Publishing Group, Penguin Group (USA), Inc., 375 Hudson St., New York NY 10014. (212)366-2000. Website: www.penguin.com. **Contact:** Susan Allison, editor-in-chief; Anne Sowards, associate editor. Estab. 1953. Publishes hardcover, paperback and trade paperback originals and reprints. Averages 75 total titles, 72 fiction titles/year.
Needs: Fantasy, science fiction. No other genre accepted. No short stories. Published *Forever Peace*, by Joe Haldeman; *Neuromancer*, by William Gibson; *King Kelson's Bride*, by Katherine Kurtz.
How to Contact: Accepts unsolicited mss. Query first with SASE or IRC. Agented fiction 85-95%. Responds in 2 months to queries; 6 months to mss. No simultaneous submissions.
Payment/Terms: Pays royalty. Offers advance. Publishes ms 1-2 years after acceptance. Ms guidelines for #10 SASE.
Advice: "Good science fiction and fantasy are almost always written by people who have read and loved a lot of it. We are looking for knowledgeable science or magic, as well as sympathetic characters with recognizable motivation. We are looking for solid, well-plotted science fiction: good action adventure, well-researched hard science with good characterization and books that emphasize characterization without sacrificing plot. In fantasy we are looking for all types of work, from high fantasy to sword and sorcery." Submit fantasy and science fiction to Anne Sowards.

ACEN PRESS, DNA Press, P.O. Box 572, Eagleville PA 19408. (610)489-8404. Fax: (208)692-2855. **Contact:** Alexander Kuklin, Ph.D., managing editor (children scientific books); Xela Schenk, operations manager (New Age). Estab. 1998. Publishes trade paperback originals. **Published 90% debut authors within the last year.** Averages 10 total titles/year.
Needs: Juvenile, science fiction, young adult. "All books should be oriented to explaining science even if they do not fall 100% under the category of science fiction."
How to Contact: Submit complete ms. Responds in 6 weeks. Accepts simultaneous submissions.
Payment/Terms: Pays 10-20% royalty. Publishes ms 4 months after acceptance. Book catalog free; ms guidelines free.
Advice: "Quick response, great relationships, high commission/royalty."

ACME PRESS, P.O. Box 1702, Westminster MD 21158-1702. (410)848-7577. **Contact:** (Ms.) E.G. Johnston, managing editor. Estab. 1991. "We operate on a part-time basis and publish 1-2 novels/year." Publishes hardcover and trade paperback originals. **Published some debut authors within the last year.** Averages 1-2 total titles/year.
Needs: Humor. "We accept submissions on any subject as long as the material is humorous; prefer full-length novels. No cartoons or art (text only). No pornography, poetry, short stories or children's material." Published *She-Crab Soup* by Dawn Langley Simmons (fictional memoir/humor); *Biting the Wall*, by J.M. Johnston (humor/mystery); and *Super Fan*, by Lyn A. Sherwood (comic/sports).
How to Contact: Accepts unsolicited mss. Submit first 3-5 chapters, synopsis, and SASE. Include query with outline/synopsis and first 50 pages. Agented fiction 25%. Responds in 2 weeks to queries; 2 months to mss. Accepts simultaneous submissions. Always comments on rejected mss.

Payment/Terms: Pays 25 author's copies and 50% of profits. Average advance: small. Publishes ms 1 year after acceptance. Book catalog for #10 SASE; ms guidelines for #10 SASE.

■ ADVENTURE BOOK PUBLISHERS, Durksen Enterprises Ltd., #712-3545-32 Ave. NE, Calgary AB T1Y 6M6 Canada. (403)285-6844. E-mail: adventure@puzzlesbyshar.com. Website: www.puzzlesbyshar.com/adventure books/. **Contact:** S. Durksen, editor. Publishes electronic and print books. **Published 20 debut authors within the last year.** Plans 40 first novels this year. Averages 30-50 total titles, 45 fiction titles/year.
Needs: Adventure, fantasy (space fantasy, sword and sorcery), historical (general), humor, military/war, mystery (amateur sleuth, cozy, police procedural, private eye/hardboiled), romance (contemporary, historical, romantic suspense), science fiction (hard science/technological, soft/sociological), thriller/espionage, western (frontier saga, traditional), young adult (adventure, fantasy/science fiction, mystery/suspense, problem novels, romance, series, sports, western). Published *Wolfe's Pack*, by Robert M. Blacketer (adventure, military); *Dangerous Game*, by Jack Petree (fiction/adventure); *Volante*, by Lisa Cortney (juvenile); and *Blood Drops Through Time*, by Christine Westendorp (historical fiction/fantasy).
How to Contact: Does not accept unsolicited mss. Query with 1-2 page synopsis via e-mail only. Accepts ms submissions "only by invitation and in accordance with guidelines given to those invited." Accepts queries by e-mail. Include estimated word count, brief bio. Responds in 1 month to queries; 5 months to mss. Accepts simultaneous submissions. Always comments on rejected mss.
Payment/Terms: Pays 20% royalty. Publishes ms approximately 7 months after acceptance. Book catalog online; ms guidelines online.
Advice: "Good stories can be told without excessive sex and violence graphically detailed for shock value only. We do not consider works of a pornographic, illegal or harmful nature. Preference is given to mainstream manuscripts as opposed to topics with time or issue limitations. Please take the time to proofread with a critical eye before submitting."

■ AGELESS PRESS, P.O. Box 5915, Sarasota FL 34277-5915. E-mail: irishope@comcast.net. **Contact:** Iris Forrest, editor. Estab. 1992. Independent publisher. Publishes paperback originals. Books: acid-free paper; notched perfect binding; no illustrations. Averages 1 total title/year.
Needs: Experimental, fantasy, humor, literary, mainstream/contemporary, mystery, new age/mystic, science fiction, short story collections, thriller/espionage. Looking for material "based on personal computer experiences." Stories selected by editor. Published *Computer Legends, Lies & Lore*, by various (anthology); and *Computer Tales of Fact and Fantasy*, by various (anthology).
How to Contact: Does not accept unsolicited mss. Query with SASE. Accepts queries by e-mail, fax, mail. Responds in 1 week. Accepts simultaneous submissions, electronic submissions, submissions on disk. Sometimes comments on rejected mss.
Payment/Terms: Average advance: negotiable. Publishes ms 6-12 months after acceptance.
Advice: "Query! Don't send work without a query!"

ALEF DESIGN GROUP, 4423 Fruitland Ave., Los Angeles CA 90058. (800)238-6724. Website: www.alefdesign. com. Estab. 1990. Publishes hardcover and trade paperback originals. **Published 40% debut authors within the last year.** Averages 25 total titles/year.
Needs: Juvenile, religious, young adult. "We publish books of Judaic interest only." Published *The Road to Exile*, by Didier Nebot (fiction).
How to Contact: Query with SASE. Responds in 6 months to mss. Accepts simultaneous submissions.
Payment/Terms: Pays 10% royalty. Offers advance. Publishes ms 3 years after acceptance. Ms guidelines for 9×12 SAE with 10 first-class stamps.

■ ALEXANDER BOOKS, Creativity, Inc., 65 Macedonia Rd., Alexander NC 28701. (828)252-9515. Fax: (828)255-8719. Website: www.abooks.com. Publishes hardcover originals and trade paperback originals and reprints. Averages 15-20 total titles, 1-2 fiction titles/year.
Needs: Mainstream/contemporary, mystery, regional (Western North Carolina), science fiction, western. "We prefer local or well-known authors or local interest settings."
How to Contact: Query with SASE or submit 3 sample chapter(s), synopsis.
Payment/Terms: Pays royalty on net receipts. Average advance: rare. Publishes ms 18 months after acceptance. Book catalog online; ms guidelines online.

ALGONQUIN BOOKS OF CHAPEL HILL, Workman Publishing, P.O. Box 2225, Chapel Hill NC 27515-2225. (919)967-0108. Website: www.algonquin.com. **Contact:** Editorial Department. Publishes hardcover originals. Averages 24 total titles/year.
How to Contact: Send query by mail before submitting work. No phone, e-mail or fax queries or submissions. Visit our website for full submission policy to queries. Sometimes comments on rejected mss.
Payment/Terms: Ms guidelines online.

■ ALTERNATIVE COMICS, 503 NW 37th Ave., Gainsville FL 32609-2204. Website: www.indyworld.com/ altcomics. **Contact:** Jeff Mason, publisher.

Needs: Comic books and graphic novels. No superhero comics, mainstream science fiction, fantasy or horror. No submissions for anthologies.
How to Contact: E-mail jmason@indyworld.com for guidelines and additional submission information.
Advice: "Pitch full proposals. Please familiarize yourself with the comics and types of books I regularly publish before sending a submission."

■ **ALYSON PUBLICATIONS, INC.**, 6922 Hollywood Blvd., Suite 1000, Los Angeles CA 90028. (323)860-6065. Fax: (323)467-0152. Website: www.alyson.com. Estab. 1980. Medium-sized publisher specializing in lesbian-and gay-related material. Publishes hardcover and trade paperback originals and reprints. Books: paper and printing varies; trade paper, perfect-bound. **Published some debut authors within the last year.** Averages 60 total titles, 25 fiction titles/year.
Imprint(s): Alyson Wonderland, Advocate Books.
Needs: "We are interested in all categories; *all* materials must be geared toward lesbian and/or gay readers." Publishes anthologies. Authors may submit to them directly. Published *Best Lesbian Love Stories of 2003* by Angela Brown; *With You in Spirit* by Steven Cooper; *Screening Party*, by Dennis Hensley.
How to Contact: Query with SASE. Accepts queries by mail. Responds in 4 months. Accepts simultaneous submissions.
Payment/Terms: Pays 8-15% royalty on net receipts. Average advance: $1,500-15,000. Book catalog and ms guidelines for 6×9 SAE with 3 first-class stamps; ms guidelines online.

AMBASSADOR BOOKS, INC., 91 Prescott St. 01605, Worcester MA 01609. (508)756-2893. Fax: (508)757-7055. Website: www.ambassadorbooks.com. **Contact:** Kathryn Conlan, acquisitions editor. Publishes hardcover and trade paperback originals. **Published 50% debut authors within the last year.** Averages 7 total titles/year.
Needs: Juvenile, literary, picture books, religious, spiritual, sports, young adult, women's. Published *Stitches*, by Kevin Morrison (children's); *What Think You of Christ?*, by John Marshall (religion); *The Man Who Met the King*, by Gerard Goggins (fiction).
How to Contact: Query with SASE or submit complete ms. Responds in 3-4 months to queries. Accepts simultaneous submissions.
Payment/Terms: Pays 8-10% royalty on retail price. Publishes ms 1 year after acceptance. Book catalog free or online at website.

◎ **AMERICAN ATHEIST PRESS**, P.O. Box 5733, Parsippany NJ 07054-6733. (908)276-7300. Fax: (908)276-7402. Website: www.atheists.org. **Contact:** Frank Zindler, editor. Estab. 1963. Publishes trade paperback originals and reprints. Publishes quarterly journal, *American Atheist*, for which are needed articles of interest to atheists. **Published 40-50% debut authors within the last year.** Averages 12 total titles/year.
Imprint(s): Gustav Broukal Press.
Needs: Humor (satire of religion or of current religious leaders), anything of particular interest to atheists. "We rarely publish any fiction. But we have occasionally released a humorous book. No mainstream. For our press to consider fiction, it would have to tie in with the general focus of our press, which is the promotion of atheism and free thought."
How to Contact: Submit outline, sample chapter(s). Responds in 4 months to queries. Accepts simultaneous submissions.
Payment/Terms: Pays 5-10% royalty on retail price. Offers advance. Publishes ms within 2 years after acceptance. Book catalog for 6½×9½ SAE; ms guidelines for 9×12 SAE.
Advice: "We will need more how-to types of material—how to argue with creationists, how to fight for state/church separation. etc. We have an urgent need for literature for young atheists."

N ◎ ◆ **ANNICK PRESS, LTD.**, 15 Patricia Ave., Willowdale ON M2M 1H9 Canada. (416)221-4802. Fax: (416)221-8400. E-mail: annick@annickpress.com. Website: www.annickpress.com. Publisher of children's books. Publishes hardcover and trade paperback originals and mass market paperback reprints. Books: offset paper; full-color offset printing; perfect library bound; full-color illustrations. Average print order: 9,000. First novel print order: 7,000. Plans 18 first novels this year. Averages 25 total titles/year. Distributes titles through Firefly Books Ltd.
 ● "Annick Press publishes *only* work by Canadian citizens or residents."
Needs: Juvenile, young adult, children's books only.
How to Contact: Does not accept unsolicited mss. Query with SASE. "Annick Press publishes only work by Canadian citizens or residents." Responds in 1 month. No simultaneous submissions. Sometimes comments on rejected mss.
Payment/Terms: Pays 8% royalty. Average advance: $2,000-4,000. Publishes ms 2 years after acceptance. Book catalog free; ms guidelines online.

N **ANTARCTIC PRESS**, 7272 Wurzbach, Suite 204, San Antonio TX 78240. (210)614-0396. Website: www.antarctic-press.com. "Antarctic Press is a Texas-based company that was started in 1984. Since then, we have grown to become one of the largest publisher of comics in the United States. Over the years we have produced over 850 titles with a total circulation of over 5 million. Among our titles are some of the most respected and longest-running independent series in comics today. Since our inception, our main goal has been to establish a series of titles that are unique, entertaining, and high in both quality and profitability. The titles we currently publish exhibit all these traits, and appeal to a wide audience." comic books, graphic novels.

Payment/Terms: Pays royalty on gross. Book catalog online; ms guidelines online.

ANVIL PRESS, 6 W. 17th Ave., Vancouver BC V5Y 1Z4 Canada. (604)876-8710. Fax: (604)879-2667. Website: www.anvilpress.com. **Contact:** Brian Kaufman, publisher. Estab. 1988. "3-person operation with volunteer editorial board." Publishes trade paperback originals. Canadian authors *only*. Books: offset or web printing; perfect bound. **Published some debut authors within the last year.** Averages 8-10 total titles/year.

Needs: Experimental, literary, short story collections. Contemporary, modern literature—no formulaic or genre. Published *The Beautiful Dead End*, by Clint Hutzulack; *Bogman's Music*, by Tammy Armstrong (poetry); *Shylock*, by Mark Leiren-Young (drama); and *Socket*, by David Zimmerman (winner of the 3-day Novel-Writing Contest).

How to Contact: Accepts unsolicited mss. Query with SASE. Include estimated word count, brief bio. Send SASE for return of ms or send a disposable ms and SASE for reply only. Responds in 2 months to queries; 6 months to mss. Accepts simultaneous submissions.

Payment/Terms: Pays 15% royalty on net receipts. Average advance: $500. Publishes ms 8 months after acceptance. Book catalog for 9×12 SAE with 2 first-class stamps; ms guidelines online.

Advice: "We are only interested in writing that is progressive in some way—form, content. We want contemporary fiction from serious writers who intend to be around for awhile and be a name people will know in years to come. Read back titles, look through our catalog before submitting."

ARCADE PUBLISHING, 141 Fifth Ave., New York NY 10010. (212)475-2633. **Contact:** Richard Seaver, Jeannette Seaver, Cal Barksdale, Greg Coamer, Darcy Falkenhagen, and Casey Ebro. Estab. 1988. Independent publisher. Publishes hardcover originals, trade paperback reprints. Books: 50-55 lb. paper; notch, perfect bound; illustrations. **Published some debut authors within the last year.** Averages 45-50 total titles, 12-15 fiction titles/ year. Distributes titles through AOL Time Warner Book.

Needs: Ethnic, historical, humor, literary, mainstream/contemporary, mystery, short story collections, suspense. Published *Trying to Save Piggy Sneed*, by John Irving; *Judge Savage*, by Tim Parks; *Music for a Life*, by Andrei Makine; *Babel*, by Barry Maitland; and *Spikes*, by Michael Griffith.

How to Contact: Does not accept unsolicited mss. *Agented submissions only.* Responds in 2 weeks.

Payment/Terms: Pays royalty on retail price, 10 author's copies. Offers advance. Publishes ms within 18 months after acceptance. Book catalog for #10 SASE; ms guidelines for #10 SASE.

ARTE PUBLICO PRESS, University of Houston, 452 Cullen Performance Hall, Houston TX 77204-2004. Fax: (713)743-3080. Website: www.artepublicopress.com. **Contact:** Dr. Nicolas Kanellos, editor. Estab. 1979. "Small press devoted to the publication of contemporary U.S.-Hispanic literature." Publishes hardcover originals, trade paperback originals and reprints. Averages 36 total titles/year.

● Arte Publico Press is the oldest and largest publisher of Hispanic literature for children and adults in the United States.

Imprint(s): Pinata Books featuring children's and young adult literature by U.S.-Hispanic literature.

Needs: Ethnic, literary, mainstream/contemporary, written by U.S.-Hispanic authors. Published *Project Death*, by Richard Bertematti (novel, mystery); *A Perfect Silence*, by Alba Ambert; *Song of the Hummingbird*, by Graciela Limon; and *Little Havana Blues: A Cuban-American Literature Anthology*, edited by Delia Poey and Virgil Suarez.

How to Contact: Accepts unsolicited mss. Query with SASE or submit outline/proposal, 2 sample chapter(s), synopsis or submit complete ms. Agented fiction 1%. Responds in 1 month to queries; 1 month to proposals; 4 months to mss. Accepts simultaneous submissions. Sometimes comments on rejected mss.

Payment/Terms: Pays 10% royalty on wholesale price. Provides 20 author's copies; 40% discount on subsequent copies. Average advance: $1,000-3,000. Publishes ms 2 years after acceptance. Book catalog free; ms guidelines online.

Advice: "Include cover letter in which you 'sell' your book—why should we publish the book, who will want to read it, why does it matter, etc."

ARTEMIS PRESS, SRS Internet Publishing, 236 W. Portal Avenue #525, San Francisco CA 94127. (866)216-7333. E-mail: info@artemispress.com. Website: www.artemispress.com. **Contact:** Susan R. Skolnick, publisher and editor-in-chief; Hedda James, editor. Estab. 2000. "Small electronic publisher of fiction and nonfiction titles of interest to the worldwide women's community. We specialize in lesbian-related works. We are open to working with new authors and provide extremely personalized services." Publishes electronic originals and electronic editions of out-of-print and previously published titles. **Published 3 debut authors within the last year.** Plans 6 first novels this year. Titles distributed and promoted online.

Needs: Adventure, ethnic, experimental, family saga, fantasy, feminist, historical, humor, lesbian, literary, mainstream/contemporary, mystery, new age/mystic, psychic/supernatural, romance, science fiction, short story collections, thriller/espionage. Published *Moon Madness and Other Stories*, by Liann Snow (short story collection); *Faith in Love*, by Liann Snow (humor/satire); *Luna Ascendings: Stories of Love*, by Renee Brown (short story collection);

Window Garden, by Janet McClellan (romance); *Never Letting Go*, by Suzanne Hollo (humor/satire); *Delicate Fears*, by E.L. Kingsley (mystery/suspense). Publishes two mystery series, the Delicate Fears series and Samantha Skellar mysteries.

How to Contact: Accepts unsolicited mss. Query with SASE. Accepts queries by e-mail. Include estimated word count, brief bio, social security number. Send copy of ms and SASE. Agented fiction 10%. Responds in 1 month to queries; 3 months to mss. Accepts simultaneous submissions, electronic submissions, submissions on disk. Often comments on rejected mss.

Payment/Terms: Pays 40% royalty. Publishes ms 6 months after acceptance. Book catalog online; ms guidelines online.

Advice: "We like to see clean manuscripts and an indication that the author has proofed and self-edited before submitting. We work collaboratively with our authors in all phrases of publication and expect the same efforts of our authors in return."

ARX PUBLISHING, 10 Canal Street, Suite 231, Bristol PA 19007. Website: www.arxpub.com. **Contact:** Claudio Salvucci, editor. Estab. 2001. Small independent publisher committed to publishing high-quality literature in the classical style. Publishes hardcover and paperback originals and hardcover reprints. Books: library, paperback binding; b&w illustrations. **Published 1 debut authors within the last year.** Plans 1 first novel this year. Averages 10 total titles, 1 fiction title/year.

Needs: Fantasy (sword and sorcery), historical (pre-modern), humor, literary, religious (religious fantasy), science fiction, young adult (adventure, fantasy/science fiction). Published *Mask of Ollock*, Robert F. Kauffman (fantasy/epic poetry); *Niamh and the Hermit*, by Emily C.A. Snyder (fantasy/fairy tale).

How to Contact: Does not accept or return unsolicited mss. Query with SASE. Accepts queries by e-mail, mail. Include estimated word count. Responds in 1 week. Accepts simultaneous submissions, electronic submissions. Rarely comments on rejected mss.

Payment/Terms: Pays 5-10% royalty. Publishes ms 1 year after acceptance. Book catalog for SASE or on website; ms guidelines online.

Advice: "Authors we publish are well-grounded in the literary classics: Vergil, Shakespeare, Tolkien, Hawthorne, etc, and are able to write 'high prose' with a good mastery of language. The story's morals must be unimpeachable and consonant with Judaeo-Christian philosopy. We will NOT publish anything New Age, Wicca, or atheistic."

ATHENEUM BOOKS FOR YOUNG READERS, Simon & Schuster, 1230 Avenue of the Americas, New York NY 10020. (212)698-2715. Fax: (212)698-2796. Website: www.simonsayskids.com. **Contact:** Caitlyn Dlouhy, executive editor (picture book, middle grade, YA fiction); Richard Jackson, editorial director, Anne Schwartz Books (picture book, YA fiction). Estab. 1960. Second largest imprint of large publisher/corporation. Publishes hardcover originals. Books: illustrations for picture books, some illustrated short novels. Plans 5 first novels this year. Averages 85 total titles/year.

Needs: Adventure, ethnic, experimental, fantasy, gothic, historical, horror, humor, mainstream/contemporary, mystery, science fiction, sports, suspense, western, animal. "We have few specific needs except for books that are fresh, interesting and well written. Fad topics are dangerous, as are works you haven't polished to the best of your ability. (The competition is fierce.) Other things we don't need at this time are safety pamphlets, ABC books, coloring books and board books. In writing picture book texts, avoid the coy and 'cutesy,' such as stories about characters with alliterative names. *Query letter only is best*. We do not accept unsolicited mss." Published *Ben Franklin's Almanac*, by Candace Fleming (non-fiction); *If I were a Lion*, by Sarah Weeks and Heather Soloman; *America*, by E.R. Frank (YA novel); and *Audrey and Barbara*, by Janet Lawson (picture book fiction; debut author).

How to Contact: Does not accept unsolicited mss. Query with SASE or IRC. Send art samples under separate cover to Ann Bobco at the above address. Accepts queries by mail. Agented fiction 70%. Responds in 3 months. Accepts simultaneous submissions.

Payment/Terms: Pays 10% royalty on retail price. Average advance: $5,000-6,500. Publishes ms 18 months after acceptance. Ms guidelines for #10 SASE.

Advice: "Write about what you know best. We look for original stories, unique and flavor-filled voices, and strong, evocative characters with whom a reader will readily embark on a literary journey."

AUNT LUTE BOOKS, P.O. Box 410687, San Francisco CA 94141. (415)826-1300. Fax: (415)826-8300. E-mail: books@auntlute.com. Website: www.auntlute.com. **Contact:** Shahara Godfrey, first reader. Small feminist and women-of-color press. Publishes hardcover and paperback originals. Averages 4 total titles/year.

Needs: Ethnic, feminist, lesbian.

How to Contact: Accepts unsolicited mss. Query with SASE or submit outline, sample chapter(s), synopsis. Responds in 4 months to mss.

Payment/Terms: Pays royalty. Book catalog free; ms guidelines free.

Advice: "We seek manuscripts, both fiction and nonfiction, by women from a variety of cultures, ethnic backgrounds and subcultures; women who are self-aware and who, in the face of all contradictory evidence, are still hopeful that the world can reserve a place of respect for each woman in it. We seek work that explores the specificities of the worlds from which we come, and which examines the intersections between the borders which we all inhabit."

AUTHORLINK PRESS, 3720 Millswood Drive, Irving TX 75062. Website: www.authorlink.com. **Contact:** Doris Booth, editor-in-chief (mainstream, women's fiction); Elaine Lanmon, associate editor (mainstream, science fiction, fantasy, horror). "Small or midsize independent publisher. Our press is best noted for true crime and criminal profiling, though our focus is broadening." Publishes paperback originals and reprints. Books: text, 60 lb. cream paper; traditionally printed; perfect-bound. Distributes titles through Ingram, Baker & Taylor. Promotes titles through direct mailings to media, booksellers and libraries, also online promotion.

Needs: Main interest true crime, women's fiction, nonfiction. Published *Harps on the Willow*, by P.T. Sherman (mainstream, debut author); *New American Review.*

How to Contact: Submit outline, synopsis. Accepts queries by e-mail. Include estimated word count, brief bio, list of publishing credits. Agented fiction 10%. Responds in 1 month to queries; 2-3 months to mss. Accepts simultaneous submissions. No electronic submissions. Sometimes comments on rejected mss.

Payment/Terms: Pays royalty on retail price or 40% of net. Publishes ms 8-12 months after acceptance.

Advice: "We are publishing fewer titles through June 2003 due to the sluggish economy, but should increase our releases in late 2003 and into 2004."

AVALON BOOKS, Thomas Bouregy & Co., Inc., 160 Madison Ave., 5th Floor, New York NY 10016. (212)598-0222. Fax: (212)979-1862. Website: www.avalonbooks.com. **Contact:** Erin Cartwright, editorial director; Mira Son, assistant editor. Estab. 1950. Publishes hardcover originals. **Published new writers within the last year.** Averages 60 total titles/year. Distributes titles through Baker & Taylor, libraries, Barnes&Noble.com and Amazon.com. Promotes titles through *Library Journal, Booklist* and local papers.

Needs: Historical (romance), mystery, romance, western. "We publish wholesome contemporary romances, mysteries, historical romances and westerns. Our books are read by adults as well as teenagers, and the characters are all adults. All mysteries are contemporary. We publish contemporary romances (four every two months), historical romances (two every two months), mysteries (two every two months) and westerns (two every two months). The manuscripts should be between 40,000 to 70,000 words. Manuscripts that are too long will not be considered. Time period and setting are the author's preference. The historical romances will maintain the high level of reading expected by our readers. The books shall be wholesome fiction, without graphic sex, violence or strong language." Published *A Golden Trail of Murder*, by John Paxson (mystery); *Renovating Love*, by Mary Leask (romance); *Shannon US Marshall*, by Charles Friend (western); *A Wanted Man*, by Nancy J. Parra (historical romance).

How to Contact: Submit first 3 sample chapters, a 2-3 page synopsis and SASE. Query with SASE or IRC. Responds in 1 month to queries; 6 months to mss.

Payment/Terms: Pays 5-15% royalty. Average advance: $1,000+. Publishes ms 8-12 months after acceptance. Book catalog online; ms guidelines online.

AVON BOOKS, HarperCollins Publishers, 10 E. 53 Street, New York NY 10022. Website: www.harpercollins.com. **Contact:** Michael Morrison, publisher. Estab. 1941. Publishes hardcover and paperback originals and reprints. Averages 400 total titles/year.

Imprint(s): Avon, EOS.

Needs: Historical, literary, mystery, romance, science fiction, young adult, health, pop culture.

How to Contact: Does not accept unsolicited mss. Query with SASE or IRC.

Payment/Terms: Varies.

BAEN PUBLISHING ENTERPRISES, P.O. Box 1403, Riverdale NY 10471-0671. (718)548-3100. Website: www.baen.com. **Contact:** Jim Baen, publisher and editor; Toni Weisskopf, executive editor. Estab. 1983. "We publish books at the heart of science fiction and fantasy." Publishes hardcover, trade paperback and mass market paperback originals and reprints. **Published new writers within the last year.** Plans 2-3 first novels this year. Averages 120 total titles, 120 fiction titles/year. Distributes titles through Simon & Schuster.

Imprint(s): Baen Science Fiction and Baen Fantasy.

Needs: Fantasy, science fiction. Interested in science fiction novels (based on real science) and fantasy novels "that at least strive for originality. Published *A Civil Campaign*, by Lois McMaster Bujold; *Ashes of Victory*, by David Weber; *Sentry Peak*, by Harry Turtledove.

How to Contact: Accepts unsolicited mss. Submit outline, 3 consecutive sample chapter(s), synopsis or submit

**FOR EXPLANATIONS OF THESE SYMBOLS,
SEE THE INSIDE FRONT AND BACK COVERS OF THIS BOOK.**

complete ms. Send SASE or IRC. Responds in 8 months to queries; 1 year to mss. No simultaneous submissions. Sometimes comments on rejected mss.

Payment/Terms: Pays royalty on retail price. Offers advance. Book catalog free; ms guidelines online.

Advice: "Keep an eye and a firm hand on the overall story you are telling. Style is important but less important than plot. Good style, like good breeding, never calls attention to itself. Read *Writing to the Point*, by Algis Budrys. We like to maintain long-term relationships with authors."

BAKER BOOKS, Baker Book House Company, P.O. Box 6287, Grand Rapids MI 49516-6287. (616)676-9185. Fax: (616)676-2315. Website: www.bakerbooks.com. **Contact:** Jeanette Thomason, special projects editor (mystery, literary, women's fiction); Lonnie Hall DuPont, editoral director (all genres); Vicki Crumpton, aquisitions editor (all genres). Estab. 1939. "Midsize publisher of work that interests Christians." Publishes hardcover and trade paperback originals and trade paperback reprints. Books: web offset print. Averages 80 total titles/year. Distributes titles through Ingram and Spring Arbor into both CBA and ABA markets worldwide.

Needs: Literary, mainstream/contemporary, mystery, picture books, religious. "We are mainly seeking fiction of two genres: contemporary women's fiction and mystery. Published *Praise Jerusalem!* and *Resting in the Bosom of the Lamb*, by Augusta Trobaugh (contemporary women's fiction); *Touches the Sky*, by James Schaap (western, literary); and *Face to Face*, by Linda Dorrell (mystery); *Flabbergasted*, by Ray Blackston; *The Fisherman*, by Larry Huntsberger.

How to Contact: Does not accept unsolicited mss. Sometimes comments on rejected mss.

Payment/Terms: Pays 14% royalty on net receipts. Offers advance. Publishes ms within 1 year after acceptance. Book catalog for 9½×12½ SAE with 3 first-class stamps; ms guidelines for #10 SASE.

Advice: "We are not interested in historical fiction, romances, science fiction, biblical narratives or spiritual warfare novels. Do not call to 'pass by' your idea."

BALLANTINE BOOKS, Random House, Inc., 1745 Broadway, New York NY 10019. (212)782-9000. Website: www.randomhouse.com/BB. Estab. 1952. "Ballantine's list encompasses a large, diverse offering in a variety of formats." Publishes hardcover, trade paperback, mass market paperback originals.

Imprint(s): Ballantine Books; Del Ray; Fawcett (mystery line); Ivy (romance); Library of Contemporary Thought; Lucas Books; One World; Wellspring.

Needs: Confession, ethnic, fantasy, feminist, gay/lesbian, historical, humor, literary, mainstream/contemporary (women's), military/war, multicultural, mystery/suspense, romance, short story collections, spiritual, general fiction.

How to Contact: *Agented submissions only.*

Terms: Pays 8-15% royalty. Average advance: variable. Ms. guidelines online.

BANCROFT PRESS, P.O. Box 65360, Baltimore MD 21209-9945. (410)358-0658. Fax: (410)764-1967. Website: www.bancroftpress.com. "Small independent press publishing literary and commercial fiction, often by journalists." Publishes hardcover and trade paperback originals. Also packages books for other publishers (no fee to authors). **Published 2 debut authors within the last year.** Plans several first novels this year. Averages 4 total titles, 2-4 fiction titles/year.

• *The Re-Appearance of Sam Webber*, by Scott Fugua, is an ALEX Award winner.

Needs: Ethnic (general), family saga, feminist, gay/lesbian, glitz, historical, humor, lesbian, literary, mainstream/contemporary, military/war, mystery (amateur sleuth, cozy, police procedural, private eye/hardboiled), New Age/mystic, regional, science fiction (hard science/technological, soft/sociological), thriller/espionage, young adult (historical, problem novels, series), thrillers. Published *Those Who Trespass*, by Bill O'Reilly (thriller); *The Re-Appearance of Sam Webber*, by Scott Fugua (literary); and *Malicious Intent*, by Mike Walker (Hollywood).

How to Contact: Accepts unsolicited mss. Query with SASE or submit outline, 2 sample chapter(s), synopsis, by mail or e-mail or submit complete ms. Accepts queries by e-mail, fax. Include brief bio, list of publishing credits. Send SASE for return of ms or send a disposable ms and SASE for reply only. Responds in 6 months to queries; 4-8 months to proposals; 6 months to mss. Accepts simultaneous submissions. Sometimes comments on rejected mss.

Payment/Terms: Pays 6-8% royalty. Pays various royalties on retail price. Average advance: $750. Publishes ms up to 3 years after acceptance. Ms guidelines online.

Advice: "Be patient, send a sample, know your book's audience."

BANTAM DELL PUBLISHING GROUP, Random House, Inc., 1745 Broadway, New York NY 10019. (212)782-9000. Fax: (212)782-8890. Website: www.bantamdell.com. Estab. 1945. "In addition to being the nation's largest mass market paperback publisher, Bantam publishes a select yet diverse hardcover list." Publishes hardcover, trade paperback and mass market paperback originals; mass market paperback reprints. Averages 350 total titles/year.

Imprint(s): Bantam Hardcover; Bantam Trade Paperback; Bantam Mass-Market; Crimeline; Domain; Fanfare; Spectra; Delacorte Press; The Dial Press; Delta; Dell.

BANTAM DOUBLEDAY DELL BOOKS FOR YOUNG READERS, Random House Children's Publishing, Random House, Inc., 1745 Broadway, New York NY 10019. (212)782-9000. Fax: (212)782-8234.

Website: www.randomhouse.com/kids. **Contact:** Michelle Poplof, editorial director. Publishes hardcover, trade paperback and mass market paperback series originals, trade paperback reprints. Averages 300 total titles/year.
• *Bud, Not Buddy*, by Christopher Paul Curtis won the Newberry Medal and the Coretta Scott King Award.
Imprint(s): Delecorte Books for Young Readers, Doubleday Books for Young Readers, Laurel Leaf; Skylark; Starfire; Yearling Books.
Needs: Adventure, fantasy, historical, humor, juvenile, mainstream/contemporary, mystery, picture books, suspense, chapter books, middle-grade. Published *Bud, Not Buddy*, by Christopher Paul Curtis; *The Sisterhood of the Traveling Pants*, by Ann Brashares.
How to Contact: Does not accept unsolicited mss. *Agented submissions only. No unsolicited mss. Accepts unsolicited queries only.* Responds in 2 months. No simultaneous submissions.
Payment/Terms: Pays royalty. Average advance: varied. Publishes ms 2 years after acceptance. Book catalog for 9×12 SASE.

BARBOUR PUBLISHING, INC., P.O. Box 719, Uhrichsville OH 44683. (740)922-6045. Fax: (740)922-5948. Website: www.barbourpublishing.com. **Contact:** Paul Muckley, senior editor (all areas); Rebecca Germany, managing editor (fiction). Estab. 1981. Publishes hardcover, trade paperback and mass market paperback originals and reprints. **Published 40% debut authors within the last year.** Averages 200 total titles/year.
Imprint(s): Heartsong Presents (contact Rebecca Germany, managing editor), Barbour Books and Promise Press (contact Paul Muckley, senior editor).
Needs: Historical, mainstream/contemporary, religious, romance, western. All submissions must be Christian mss. "All of our fiction is 'sweet' romance. No sex, no bad language, etc. Audience is evangelical/Christian, and we're looking for wholesome material. Common writer's mistakes are a sketchy proposal, an unbelievable story and a story that doesn't fit our guidelines for inspirational romances. Published *Betrayed*, by Rosey Dow and Andew Snaden (fiction).
How to Contact: Submit 3 sample chapter(s), synopsis, SASE. Responds in 1 month. Accepts simultaneous submissions.
Payment/Terms: Pays 0-12% royalty on net price or makes outright purchase of $500-5,000. Average advance: $500-2,500. Publishes ms 2 years after acceptance. Book catalog online or for 9×12 SAE with 2 first-class stamps; ms guidelines for #10 SASE or online; ms guidelines online.
Advice: "Audience is evangelical/Christian conservative, non-denominational, young and old. We're looking for *great concepts*, not necessarily a big name author or agent. We want to publish books that will sell millions, not just 'flash in the pan' releases. Send us your ideas!"

BARDSONG PRESS, P.O. Box 775396, Steamboat Springs CO 80477-5396. (970)870-1401. Fax: (970)879-2657. Website: www.bardsongpress.com. **Contact:** Ann Gilpin, editor (Celtic history/historical fiction). Estab. 1997. "Small independent press which specializes in historical novels, short stories and poetry with Celtic themes." Publishes hardcover originals and trade paperback reprints. Averages 1-2 total titles/year. Member, PMA, SPAN, CIPA.
Needs: Historical (Celtic), poetry, short stories up to 5,000 words. "We are looking for work that reflects the ageless culture, history, symbolism, mythology and spirituality that belongs to Celtic heritage. Settings can range from ancient times to early twentieth century and include the earliest European territories, the current nations of Wales, Scotland, Ireland, Cornwall, Isle of Man, Brittany and Galacia, as well as lands involved in the Celtic Diaspora. Published *In the Shadow of Dragons*, by Kathleen Cunningham Guler (historical fiction). Publishes the Macsen's Treasure Series.
How to Contact: Does not accept unsolicited mss. Query with SASE. Accepts queries by e-mail. Include brief bio, list of publishing credits. Currently not accepting novel mss. For short stories and poetry, send mss with SASE. Agented fiction 50%. Responds in 2 months to queries; 4 months to mss. Accepts simultaneous submissions, submissions on disk. No electronic submissions. Sometimes comments on rejected mss.
Payment/Terms: Payment method varies. Publishes ms 18 months after acceptance. Book catalog online; ms guidelines online.
Advice: "Please send work with Celtic theme only."

BAREFOOT BOOKS, PO Box 382207, Cambridge MA 02238-2207. (617)576-0660. Fax: (617)576-0049. Website: www.barefootbooks.com. **Contact:** Alison Keehn, associate editor (picture books and anthologies of folktales). Publishes hardcover and trade paperback originals. **Published 35% debut authors within the last year.** Averages 30 total titles/year.
Needs: Juvenile. Barefoot Books only publishes children's picture books and anthologies of folktales. "We do not publish novels. We are no longer accepting unsolicited manuscripts. We do accept query letters, and we encourage authors to send the first page of their manuscript with the query letter. Published *Daddy Island*, by Philip Wells (picture book); *Fiesta Femenina: Celebrating Women in Mexican Folktale*, by Mary-Joan Gerson (illustrated anthology).
How to Contact: Query with SASE or submit first page of ms. Responds in 2 months. Accepts simultaneous submissions.

Payment/Terms: Pays 2½-5% royalty on retail price or makes outright purchase. Offers advance. Publishes ms 2 years after acceptance. Book catalog for #10 SASE; ms guidelines online.

Advice: "Our audience is made up of children and parents, teachers and students of many different ages and cultures. Since we are a small publisher and we definitely publish for a 'niche' market, it is helpful to look at our books and our website before submitting, to see if you book would fit into our list."

BARRON'S EDUCATIONAL SERIES, INC., 250 Wireless Blvd., Hauppauge NY 11788. (631)434-3311. Fax: (631)434-3394. Website: barronseduc.com. **Contact:** Wayne Barr, managing editor/director of acquisitions. Estab. 1941. Publishes hardcover, paperback and mass market originals and software. **Published 40% debut authors within the last year.** Averages 400 total titles/year.

Needs: Juvenile.

How to Contact: Submit sample chapter(s), synopsis. Responds in 3 months. Accepts simultaneous submissions.

Payment/Terms: Pays 12-14% royalty on net receipts. Average advance: $3-4,000. Publishes ms 18 months after acceptance. Book catalog free; ms guidelines online.

Advice: "Audience is mostly educated self-learners and hobbyists. The writer has the best chance of selling us a book that will fit into one of our series. Children's books have less chance for acceptance because of the glut of submissions. SASE must be included for the return of all materials. Please be patient for replies."

BEACH HOLME PUBLISHERS, LTD., 226-2040 W. 12th Ave., Vancouver BC V6J 2G2 Canada. (604)733-4868. Fax: (604)733-4860. Website: www.beachholme.bc.ca. **Contact:** Michael Carroll, publisher; Sarah Warren, publicity and marketing coordinator. Estab. 1971. Publishes trade paperback originals. **Published 6 debut authors within the last year.** Averages 10-14 total titles/year. Titles distributed through LPG Distribution (Canada and U.S.).

Imprint(s): Sandcastle Books (YA novels), Porcepic Books (literary fiction/poetry), Prospect Books (literary nonfiction).

Needs: Experimental, literary, poetry, young adult (Canada historical/regional), adult literary fiction from authors published in Canadian literary magazines. Interested in excellent quality, imaginative writing from writers published in Canadian literary magazines. Published *North of the Equator*, by Cyril Dabydeen (short fiction); *The Moor is Dark Beneath the Moon*, by David Watmough (novel). Published *The View from Tamisheira*, by Richard Cumyn (novella).

How to Contact: Query with SASE or submit outline, 2 sample chapter(s). Responds in 4-6 months to queries. No simultaneous submissions.

Payment/Terms: Pays 10% royalty on retail price. Average advance: $500. Publishes ms 1 year after acceptance. Ms guidelines online.

Advice: "Make sure the manuscript is well written. We see so many that only the unique and excellent can't be put down. Prior publication is a must. This doesn't necessarily mean book-length manuscripts, but a writer should try to publish his or her short fiction."

FREDERIC C. BEIL, PUBLISHER, INC., 609 Whitaker St., Savannah GA 31401. (912)233-2446. Fax: (912)233-6456. Website: www.beil.com. **Contact:** Frederic C. Beil III, president; Mary Ann Bowman, editor. Estab. 1982. "Our objectives are (1) to offer to the reading public carefully selected texts of lasting value; (2) to adhere to high standards in the choice of materials and bookmarking craftsmanship; (3) to produce books that exemplify good taste in format and design; and (4) to maintain the lowest cost consistent with quality." Publishes hardcover originals and reprints. Books: acid-free paper; letterpress and offset printing; Smyth-sewn, hardcover binding; illustrations. Plans 10 first novels this year. Averages 13 total titles, 4 fiction titles/year.

Imprint(s): The Sandstone Press, Hypermedia, Inc.

Needs: Historical, literary, regional, short story collections, biography. Published *The Dry Well*, by Marlin Barton; *Joseph Jefferson*, by Arthur Bloom (biography); and *Goya, Are You With Me Now?*, by H.E. Francis (fiction).

How to Contact: Does not accept unsolicited mss. Query with SASE. Responds in 2 weeks. Accepts simultaneous submissions.

Payment/Terms: Pays 7½% royalty on retail price. Publishes ms 20 months after acceptance. Book catalog free.

Advice: "Write about what you love."

THE BERKLEY PUBLISHING GROUP, Penguin Putnam, Inc., 375 Hudson St., New York NY 10014. (212)366-2000. E-mail: online@penguinputnam.com. Website: www.penguinputnam.com. Estab. 1954. "Berkley is proud to publish in paperback some of the country's most significant best-selling authors." Publishes paperback and mass market originals and reprints. Averages approximately 800 total titles/year.

Imprint(s): Ace Books, Berkley Books, Boulevard, Diamond Books, HP Books, Jam, Jove, Perigee, Prime Crime, Riverhead Books (paperback), Berkley Sensation.

Needs: Adventure, historical, literary, mystery, romance, spiritual, suspense, western, young adult.

How to Contact: Query with SASE. *Prefers agented submissions.* Responds in 6 weeks to queries. No simultaneous submissions.

Payment/Terms: Pays 4-15% royalty on retail price. Offers advance. Publishes ms 2 years after acceptance.

◪ **BETHANY HOUSE PUBLISHERS**, 11400 Hampshire Ave. S., Minneapolis MN 55438. (952)829-2500. Fax: (952)829-2768. Website: www.bethanyhouse.com. Estab. 1956. "The purpose of Bethany House Publisher's publishing program is to relate biblical truth to all areas of life—whether in the framework of a well-told story, of a challenging book for spiritual growth or of a Bible reference work." Publishes hardcover and trade paperback originals, mass market paperback reprints. Averages 120-150 total titles/year.

Needs: Adventure, children's/juvenile, historical, juvenile, young adult. New interest in contemporary fiction. Published *The Covenant*, by Beverly Lewis (fiction).

How to Contact: Does not accept unsolicited mss. Send SASE for guidelines. Accepts queries by fax. Responds in 3 months to queries. Accepts simultaneous submissions.

Payment/Terms: Pays negotiable royalty on net price. Average advance: negotiable. Publishes ms 1 year after acceptance. Book catalog for 9×12 SAE with 5 first-class stamps; ms guidelines online.

N ◯ ◎ **BEYOND WORDS PUBLISHING, INC.**, 20827 NW Cornell Rd., Suite 500, Hillsboro OR 97124. (503)531-8700. Fax: (503)531-8773. E-mail: barbara@beyondword.com. Website: www.beyondword.com. **Contact:** Barbara Leese, editor (children's books). Estab. 1983. Mid-size independent publisher. Publishes hardcover and trade paperback originals and paperback reprints. **Published 5 debut authors within the last year.** Averages 20-25 total titles, 2 fiction titles/year. Distributed by PGW.

Needs: Children's/juvenile (historical, preschool/picture book), ethnic (picture book), religious (children's). Does not accept adult fiction. Only wants children's/young adult fiction. Published *Elizabeth's Song*, by Michael Wanberg (historical fiction).

How to Contact: Accepts unsolicited mss. Query with SASE or submit complete ms. Accepts queries by mail. Include list of publishing credits, marketing ideas. Send SASE for return of ms or send a disposable ms and SASE for reply only. Agented fiction 5%. Responds in 6 months to queries; 6 months to mss. Accepts simultaneous submissions.

Payment/Terms: Pays 10-15% royalty on publishers proceeds. Offers advance. Publishes ms 12-18 months after acceptance. Book catalog and ms guidelines for #10 SASE or online.

Advice: "Please research our press before sending you book ideas to us."

◪ ◎ **BILINGUAL PRESS**, Hispanic Research Center, Arizona State University, P.O. Box 872702, Tempe AZ 85287-2702. (480)965-3867. Fax: (480)965-8309. E-mail: brp@asu.edu. Website: www.asu.edu/brp. **Contact:** Gary Keller, editor. Estab. 1973. "University affiliated." Publishes hardcover and paperback originals and reprints. Books: 60 lb. acid-free paper; single sheet or web press printing; perfect-bound. **Published several debut authors within the last year.**

Needs: Ethnic, literary, short story collections. Always seeking Chicano, Puerto Rican, Cuban-American or other U.S. Hispanic themes with strong and serious literary qualities and distinctive and intellectually important themes. Does *not* publish children's literature or trade genres such as travelogues and adventure fiction. Also novels set in a pre-Columbian past are not likely to be published. Published *Moving Target: A Memoir of Pursuit*, by Ron Arias; *Contemporary Chicano and Chicana Art: Artists, Works, Culture, and Education*, Gary Keller, et al.; *Sofia's Saints*, by Diana López; *Luna's California Poppies*, by Alma Luz Villanueva; and *Concierto para sordos*, by Marté Montes-Huidobro.

How to Contact: Accepts unsolicited mss. Query with SASE or submit 2-3 sample chapter(s). Accepts queries by e-mail, mail. Include brief bio, list of publishing credits. Responds in 6 weeks to queries; 2-6 months to mss.

Payment/Terms: Pays 10% royalty. Average advance: $500. Publishes ms 2 years after acceptance. Book catalog free; ms guidelines by e-mail.

Advice: "Writers should take the utmost care in assuring that their manuscripts are clean, grammatically impeccable, and have perfect spelling. This is true not only of the English but the Spanish as well. All accent marks need to be in place as well as other diacritical marks. When these are missing it's an immediate first indication that the author does not really know Hispanic culture and is not equipped to write about it. We are interested in publishing creative literature that treats the U.S Hispanic experience in a distinctive, creative, revealing way. The kind of books that we publish we keep in print for a very long time irrespective of sales. We are busy establishing and preserving a U.S. Hispanic canon of creative literature."

◎ **BIRCH BROOK PRESS**, P.O. Box 81, Delhi NY 13753. Fax: (607)746-7453. Website: www.birchbrookpress.info. **Contact:** Tom Tolnay, publisher. Estab. 1982. Small publisher of popular culture and literary titles in handcrafted letterpress editions. Specializes in fiction anthologies with specific theme, and an occasional novella. "Not a good market for full-length novels." Publishes hardcover and trade paperback originals. Books: 80 lb. vellum paper; letterpress printing; wood engraving illustrations. Averages 4-6 total titles, 2-3 fiction titles/year. Member, Small Press Center, Academy of American Poets. Distributes titles through Ingram, Baker & Taylor, Barnes&Noble.com, Amazon.com. Promotes titles through website, catalogs, direct mail and group ads.

Imprint(s): Birch Brook Press, Persephone Press and Birch Brook Impressions.

Needs: Literary, regional (Adirondacks), popular culture, special interest (fly-fishing, baseball, books about books, outdoors). "Mostly we do anthologies around a particular theme generated inhouse. We make specific calls for fiction when we are doing an anthology." Plans to publish literary-quality anthology of short fiction relating to fly-fishing. Published *Magic and Madness in the Library*, edited by Eric Graeber (fiction collection); *Life & Death of* *a Book*, by William MacAdams; *Fateful Choices*, edited by Marshall Brooks and Stephanie Greene; *A Punk in Gallows, America*, by P.W. Fox; *White Buffalo*, by Peter Skinner; *Cooperstown Chronicles*, by Peter Rutkoff; *The Suspense of Loneliness*, (anthology).

How to Contact: Query with SASE or submit sample chapter(s), synopsis. Responds in 1-2 months to queries. Accepts simultaneous submissions. Sometimes comments on rejected mss.

Payment/Terms: Royalty varies. Average advance: modest. Publishes ms 1-2 years after acceptance. Book catalog for #10 SASE; ms guidelines for #10 SASE.

Advice: "Write well on subjects of interest to BBP such as outdoors, fly fishing, baseball, music, literary novellas, books about books, cultural history."

BLACK HERON PRESS, P.O. Box 95676, Seattle WA 98145. Website: www.blackheronpress.com. **Contact:** Jerry Gold, publisher. Estab. 1984. Two-person operation; no immediate plans to expand. "We're known for literary fiction. We've done several Vietnam titles and several surrealistic fictions." Publishes hardcover and trade paperback originals. **Published 1-2 debut authors within the last year.** Averages 4 total titles, 4 fiction titles/year.

● Five books published by Black Heron Press have won awards from King County Arts Commission.

Needs: Adventure, experimental, humor, literary, mainstream/contemporary, science fiction (surrealism), Vietnam war novel—literary. Published *Somebody*, by Laurie Blauner (literary fiction, debut author); *Rikers*, by Paul Volponi (adult/YA fiction, debut author); and *Moses in Sinai*, by Simone Zelitch (historical fiction).

How to Contact: Query with SASE. Responds in 3 months. Accepts simultaneous submissions.

Payment/Terms: Pays 8-9% royalty on retail price.

Advice: "A query letter should tell me: 1) number of words; 2) number of pages; 3) if ms is available on disk; 4) if parts of novel have been published; 5) if so, where? And at least scan some of our books in a bookstore or library. Most submissions we get have come to the wrong press."

BLACK LACE BOOKS, Virgin Publishing, Thames Wharf Studio, Rainville Road, London W6 9HA United Kingdom. +44 (0207) 386 3300. Fax: +44 (0207) 386 3360. E-mail: ksharp@virgin-books.co.uk. Website: www.blacklace-books.co.uk. **Contact:** Kerri Sharp, senior commissioning editor. Estab. 1993. Publishes paper originals.

Imprint(s): Nexus Fetish Erotic Fiction for Men; Paul Copperwaite, editor; Black Lace Erotic Fiction for Women; Kerri Sharp, editor. "Nexus and Black Lace are the leading imprints of erotic fiction in the UK."

Needs: Erotica. "Female writers only for the Black Lace Series." Especially needs erotic fiction in contemporary settings. Publishes 2 erotic short story anthologies by women per year.

How to Contact: Accepts unsolicited mss. Query with SASE. Include estimated word count. Agented fiction 25%. Responds in 1 month to queries; 6 months to mss. No simultaneous submissions. Always comments on rejected mss.

Payment/Terms: Pays 7½% royalty. Average advance: $1,000. Publishes ms 7 months after acceptance. Book catalog free; ms guidelines online.

Advice: "Contemporary settings are strongly preferred. Open to female authors only. Read the guidelines first."

JOHN F. BLAIR, PUBLISHER, 1406 Plaza Dr., Winston-Salem NC 27103-1470. (336)768-1374. Fax: (336)768-9194. Website: www.blairpub.com. **Contact:** Carolyn Sakowski, president. Estab. 1954. Small, independent publisher. Publishes hardcover originals and trade paperbacks. Books: Acid-free paper; offset printing; illustrations. Averages 20 total titles/year.

Needs: Prefers regional material dealing with southeastern U.S. "We publish one work of fiction per season relating to the Southeastern U.S. Our editorial focus concentrates mostly on nonfiction." Published *The Minotaur Takes a Cigarette Break*, by Steven Sherrill; *Lord Baltimore*, by Stephen Doster.

How to Contact: Accepts unsolicited mss. Query with SASE or submit complete ms. Responds in 3 months to queries. Accepts simultaneous submissions.

Payment/Terms: Royalty negotiable. Offers advance. Publishes ms 18 months after acceptance. Book catalog for 9×12 SAE with 5 first-class stamps; ms guidelines online.

Advice: "We are primarily interested in nonfiction titles. Most of our titles have a tie-in with North Carolina or the southeastern U.S. Please enclose a cover letter and outline with the manuscript. We prefer to review queries before we are sent complete manuscripts. Queries should include an approximate word count."

BLEAK HOUSE BOOKS, (formerly Diversity Incorporated), a division of Diversity Inc., 953 E. Johnson Street, Madison WI 53703. (608)259-8370. Fax: (608)259-8371. E-mail: submissions@bleakhousebooks.com. Website: www.bleakhousebooks.com. **Contact:** Benjamin LeRoy, editor-in-chief **Contact:** Alex Carr, editor. Estab. 1995. "We are a small press run by people in their 20s. We'll look at a longshot project." Publishes hardcover and paperback originals. Books: 60 lb. offset paper; offset or digitally printed; perfect-bound. Average print order: 1,000. **Published 2-3 debut authors within the last year.** Averages 3-5 total titles, 6 fiction titles/year. Member, PMA. Distributes titles through Baker & Taylor, Partners, Alpine Book.

Needs: Literary, mystery (amateur sleuth, cozy, police procedural, private eye/hardboiled), thriller/espionage, psychological. Needs "good psychological or suspense. Not formulaic, but well thought out plots and characters that get inside the reader's head." Editors select stories. Published *Red Sky, Red Dragonfly*, by John Galligan (literary/mystery, debut author); and *Murder Over Easy*, by Marshall Cook (mystery).

How to Contact: Does not accept unsolicited mss. Query with SASE. Include estimated word count, brief bio, list of publishing credits. Agented fiction 35%. Responds in 2 weeks. Accepts simultaneous submissions. No electronic submissions, submissions on disk.

Payment/Terms: Pays 6-15% royalty. Average advance: negotiable. Publishes ms 1 year after acceptance. Book catalog free; ms guidelines online.

Advice: "We are growing and often very busy. Please have patience with publishers and agents. We will accept simultaneous submissions, but please note as such. We no longer accept unsolicited manuscripts. Our mission is to publish a wide range of dark fiction that goes from cozies to psychologically disturbing thrillers. Please, if you value your work, make sure it is well edited before sending it out."

THE BLUE SKY PRESS, An imprint of Scholastic Inc., 557 Broadway, New York NY 10012. (212)343-6100. Website: www.scholastic.com. **Contact:** The editors. Estab. 1993. Blue Sky Press publishes primarily juvenile picture books. Publishes hardcover originals. Averages 12-15 total titles/year.

Needs: Adventure, fantasy, historical, humor, juvenile, mainstream/contemporary, multicultural, picture books, folktales. Published *Bluish*, by Virginia Hamilton (novel); *No, David!*, by David Shannon (picture book); and *To Every Thing There is a Season*, by Leo and Diane Dillon (multicultural/historical).

How to Contact: Does not accept unsolicited mss. *Accepting queries (with SASE) from previously published authors only.* Agented fiction 25%. Responds in 6 months to queries. No simultaneous submissions.

Payment/Terms: Pays 10% royalty on wholesale price, between authors and illustrators. Offers advance. Publishes ms 2½ years after acceptance.

THE BOOKS COLLECTIVE, 214-21, 10405 Jasper Ave., Edmonton AB T5J 3S2 Canada. (780)448-0590. Fax: (780)448-0640. E-mail: admin@bookscollective.com. Website: www.bookscollective.com. **Contact:** Candas J. Dorsey or Timothy J. Anderson. Estab. 1992. "Small independent publisher of Canadian literary fiction, poetry, contemporary memoir and speculative." Publishes hardcover and trade paperback originals. Averages 6-10 total titles/year.

Needs: Experimental, fantasy, feminist, gay/lesbian, horror, literary, mainstream/contemporary, multicultural, multimedia, plays, poetry, regional, science fiction, short story collections. Tesseract Books publishes an annual anthology of Canadian speculative short fiction and poetry. River/Slipstream publishes a variety of work. Dinosaur Soup Books publishes books by Gerri Cook and Partners in Design Books has a focus on sustainable architecture. Published *Green Music*, by Ursula Pflug (speculative fiction); *Gypsy Messenger*, by Marijan Megla (poetry); and *Running Through the Devil's Club*, by Deborah Huford (non-fiction, debut author).

How to Contact: Accepts unsolicited mss. Query with SASE or submit proposal package including 1-3 sample chapter(s), résumé, synopsis or submit complete ms. Responds in 1 month to queries; 1 month to proposals; 6 months to mss. No simultaneous submissions, electronic submissions. Sometimes comments on rejected mss.

Payment/Terms: Pays 6-12% royalty on retail price. Average advance: $250-500 (Canadian). Publishes ms 1 year after acceptance. Book catalog for 9×12 SAE with 4 first-class Canadian stamps or on website; ms guidelines online.

Advice: "Only Canadian writers have their manuscripts read. All non-Canadian writers' manuscripts returned unread. Canadian writers living abroad must use Canadian stamps on SASEs. Most of our books are solicited by the press. Timelines for manuscript consideration are long."

BOOKS FOR ALL TIMES, INC., Box 202, Warranton VA 20188. Website: www.bfat.com. **Contact:** Joe David, publisher/editor. Estab. 1981. One-man operation. Publishes paperback originals.

Needs: Literary, mainstream/contemporary, short story collections. "No novels at the moment; hopeful, though, of publishing a collection of quality short stories. No popular fiction or material easily published by the major or minor houses specializing in mindless entertainment. Only interested in stories of the Victor Hugo or Sinclair Lewis quality."

How to Contact: Query with SASE. Responds in 1 month to queries. Sometimes comments on rejected mss.

Payment/Terms: Pays negotiable advance. "Publishing/payment arrangement will depend on plans for the book."

Advice: Interested in "controversial, honest stories which satisfy the reader's curiosity to know. Read Victor Hugo, Fyodor Dostoyevsky and Sinclair Lewis for example."

BOOKS IN MOTION, 9922 E. Montgomery, Suite 31, Spokane WA 99206. (509)922-1646. Website: www.booksinmotion.com. **Contact:** Cameron Beierle, editor. Estab. 1980. "Audiobook company, national marketer." Publishes unabridged audiobook originals. **Published new writers within the last year.** Averages 100-120 total titles, 90 fiction titles/year. Distributes titles through Internet, direct mail and various retailers as well as through its own nationwide rental program. Promotes titles through nationwide rental program, catalog, Internet website features and by client newsletters.

Needs: Adventure, fantasy, historical, mainstream/contemporary, mystery, religious, romance, science fiction (non-technical), suspense, western. "Minimal profanity and no gratuitous sex. We like series using the same charismatic character. Published *Magic Kingdom for Sale*, by Terry Brooks; and *Partners in Crime*, by J.A. Jance.

How to Contact: Does not accept unsolicited mss. Query with synopsis and first chapter. Agented fiction 10%. Response time varies to queries. Accepts simultaneous submissions.

Payment/Terms: Pays 10% royalty on wholesale or retail price. Offers advance. Publishes ms 6-12 months after acceptance. Book catalog on request; manuscript guidelines on request.

Advice: "Our audience is 20% women, 80% men. Many of our audience are truck drivers, who want something interesting to listen to. We prefer a minimum of profanity and no gratuitous sex. We want novels with a strong plot. The fewer the characters, the better it will work on tape. Six-tape audiobooks sell and rent better than any other size in the unabridged format. One hour of tape is equal to 40 pages of double-spaced, 12 pitch, normal margin, typed pages."

N ◎ BORDIGHERA INC., P.O. Box 1374, Lafayette IN 47902-1374. (561)297-0207. Fax: (561)297-2657. E-mail: atamburri@fau.edu.. **Contact:** Anthony J. Tamburri and Fred Gardaphe, editors. Estab. 1990. Small, not-for-profit, press that is devoted to the dissemination of information concerning the contributions of and about Italian Americans to the cultural and art worlds of North America. Publishes hardcover and paperback originals. Books: 20-24 lb. paper; docutech printing; perfect bound; illustrations. Average print order: 350. Average first novel print order: 350. Averages 3-5 total titles, 3 fiction titles/year.

Imprint(s): Crossings (translations); Via Folios (short story); Poetry Prize (poetry).

Needs: Ethnic (Italian/American), family saga, feminist, historical, lesbian, literary, short story collections. Published *Infinite Present*, by Maura Del Serra (poetry translation); *More Italian Hours & Other Stories*, by Helen Barolini (fiction). Publishes *Voices in Italian Americana* and *Italiana* series.

How to Contact: Accepts unsolicited mss. Submit complete ms. Reading period open from October 1 to May 31. Accepts queries by e-mail, mail. Include estimated word count, brief bio. Send SASE or IRC. Responds in 4-6 weeks to queries; 4-6 months to mss. No simultaneous submissions, electronic submissions, submissions on disk. Sometimes comments on rejected mss.

Payment/Terms: Pays royalty. Publishes ms 1-2 years after acceptance.

∅ ⋈ ○ BOREALIS PRESS, LTD., 110 Bloomingdale St., Ottawa ON K2C 4A4 Canada. (613)798-9299. Fax: (613)798-9747. Website: www.borealispress.com. **Contact:** Frank Tierney, editor; Glenn Clever, editor. Estab. 1972. "Publishes Canadiana, especially early works that have gone out of print, but also novels of today and shorter fiction for young readers." Publishes hardcover and paperback originals and reprints. Books: standard book-quality paper; offset printing; perfect bound. **Published new writers within the last year.** Averages 10-20 total titles/year. Promotes titles through website, catalog distribution, fliers for titles, ads in media.

- Borealis Press has a "New Canadian Drama," with 7 books in print. The series won Ontario Arts Council and Canada Council grants.

Imprint(s): *Journal of Canadian Poetry*, Tecumseh Press Ltd., Canadian Critical Editions Series.

Needs: Adventure, ethnic, historical, juvenile, literary, mainstream/contemporary, romance, short story collections, young adult. "Only material Canadian in content and dealing with significant aspects of the human situation. Published *Blue: Little Cat Come Home to Stay*, by Donna Richards (young adult); *Biography of a Beagle*, by Gail MacMillan (novel); *The Love of Women*, by Jennifer McVaugh (comic novel).

How to Contact: Query with SASE or submit 1-2 sample chapter(s), synopsis. *No unsolicited mss.* Accepts queries by e-mail, fax. Responds in 2 months to queries. No simultaneous submissions.

Payment/Terms: Pays 10% royalty on net receipts. 3 free author's copies. Publishes ms 18 months after acceptance. Book catalog online; ms guidelines online.

Advice: "Have your work professionally edited. Our greatest challenge is finding good authors, i.e., those who submit innovative and original material."

◉ BOSON BOOKS, C & M Online Media, Inc., 3905 Meadow Field Lane, Raleigh NC 27606. (919)233-8164. Fax: (919)233-8578. E-mail: cm@cmonline.com. Website: www.cmonline.com. **Contact:** Aquisitions Editor. Estab. 1994. "We are an online book company with distribution at our website and through 10 separate distributors such as CyberRead.com, powells.com, ebooks.com, mobipocket.com and barnesandnoble.com." Publishes online originals and reprints. **Published 6 debut authors within the last year.** Member, Association of Online Publishers.

Needs: "The quality of writing is our only consideration." Publishes ongoing series of Holocaust narratives by eyewitnesses.

How to Contact: Does not accept or return unsolicited mss. Query with SASE. Electronic submissions only. Accepts queries by e-mail.

Payment/Terms: Pays 25% royalty. Book catalog online; ms guidelines online.

Advice: "We want to see only excellence in writing."

∅ ◎ BOYDS MILLS PRESS, *Highlights for Children*, 815 Church St., Honesdale PA 18431-1895. (570)253-1164. Website: www.boydsmillspress.com. **Contact:** Larry Rosler, editorial director. Estab. 1990. "Independent publisher of quality books for children of all ages." Publishes hardcover originals and trade paperback reprints. Books: Coated paper; offset printing; case binding; 4-color illustrations. **Published 2 debut authors within the last year.** Averages 50 total titles, 4 fiction titles/year. Distributes titles through independent sales reps and via order line directly from Boyds Mills Press. Promotes titles through sales and professional conferences, sales reps, reviews.

Needs: Adventure, ethnic, historical, humor, juvenile, mystery, picture books, young adult (adventure, animal, contemporary, ethnic, historical, humor, mystery, sports). "We look for imaginative stories or concepts with simple, lively language that employs a variety of literary devices, including rhythm, repetition, and when composed properly, rhyme. The stories may entertain or challenge, but the content must be age appropriate for children. For middle and young adult fiction we look for stories told in strong, considered prose driven by well-imagined characters. Published *Sharks! Strange and Wonderful*, by Laurence Pringle; *Groover's Heart*, by Carole Crowe; and *Storm's Coming!*, by Audrey B. Baird.

How to Contact: Accepts unsolicited mss. Query with SASE. Submit outline/synopsis and 3 sample chapters for novel or complete ms. Agented fiction 80%. Responds in 1 month to mss. Accepts simultaneous submissions.

Payment/Terms: Pays royalty on retail price. Average advance: variable. Time between acceptance and publication depends on "what season it is scheduled for." Book catalog online.

Advice: "Read through our recently-published titles and review our catalog. If your book is too different from what we publish, then it may not fit our list. Feel free to query us if you're not sure."

BRANDEN PUBLISHING CO., INC., P.O. Box 812094, Wellesley MA 02482. (781)235-3634. Fax: (781)790-1056. Website: www.branden.com. **Contact:** Adolph Caso, editor. Estab. 1965. Publishes hardcover and trade paperback originals, reprints and software. Books: 55-60 lb. acid-free paper; case—or perfect-bound; illustrations. Averages 15 total titles, 5 fiction titles/year.

Imprint(s): I.P.L., Dante University Press, Four Seas, Branden Publishing Co.

Needs: Ethnic (histories, integration), historical, literary, military/war, religious (historical-reconstructive), short story collections. Looking for "contemporary, fast pace, modern society. Published *I, Morgain*, by Harry Robin; *The Bell Keeper*, by Marilyn Seguin; and *The Straw Obelisk*, by Adolph Caso.

How to Contact: Does not accept unsolicited mss. Query with SASE. Paragraph query only, with author's vita and SASE. No telephone inquiries, e-mail or fax inquiries. Responds in 1 month.

Payment/Terms: Pays 5-10% royalty on net receipts and 10 author's copies. Average advance: $1,000 maximum. Publishes ms 10 months after acceptance.

Advice: "Publishing more fiction because of demand. *Do not make phone, fax or e-mail inquiries.* Do not oversubmit; single submissions only; do not procrastinate if contract is offered. Our audience is well-read general public, professionals, college students and some high school students. We like books by or about women."

GEORGE BRAZILLER, INC., 171 Madison Avenue, Suite 1105, New York NY 10016. (212)889-0909. **Contact:** Mary Taveros, production editor. Publishes hardcover and trade paperback originals and reprints.

Needs: Ethnic, gay/lesbian, literary. "We rarely do fiction but when we have published novels, they have mostly been literary novels. Published *Blindsight*, by Herve Guibert and *Papa's Suitcase*, by Gerhard Kopf (literary fiction).

How to Contact: Submit 4-6 sample chapter(s), SASE. Agented fiction 20%. Responds in 3 months to proposals.

Payment/Terms: Publishes ms 10 months after acceptance. Book catalog free; ms guidelines free.

BREAKAWAY BOOKS, P.O. Box 24, Halcottsville NY 12438. (212)898-0408. Website: www.breakaway books.com. **Contact:** Garth Battista, publisher. Estab. 1994. "Small press specializing in fine literary books on sports. We have a new line of children's illustrated books (ages 3-7)—dealing with sports, especially running, cycling, triathlon, swimming, and boating (canoes, kayaks, sailboats). Publishes hardcover and trade paperback originals. **Published 3 debut authors within the last year.** Averages 8-10 total titles, 5 fiction titles/year.

Needs: Short story collections (sports stories).

How to Contact: Accepts unsolicited mss. Query with SASE or submit complete ms. Accepts queries by e-mail. Include brief bio, list of publishing credits. Send SASE for return of ms or send a disposable ms and SASE for reply only. Agented fiction 50%. Responds in 1 month to queries; 2 months to mss. Accepts simultaneous submissions, electronic submissions.

Payment/Terms: Pays 6-15% royalty on retail price. Average advance: $2,000-3,000. Publishes ms 9 months after acceptance. Book catalog and ms guidelines free; ms guidelines online.

BROADMAN & HOLMAN, LifeWay Christian Resources, 127 Ninth Ave. N., Nashville TN 37234. (615)251-2392. Fax: (615)251-3752. **Contact:** Leonard G. Goss, editorial director (historical, romance, contemporary, suspense, western, thrillers, etc.). Estab. 1934. "Large, commericial, evangelical Christian publishing firm. We publish Christian fiction in all genres." Publishes hardcover and paperback originals. **Published 10 debut authors within the last year.** Averages 90 total titles, 25 fiction titles/year. Member, ECPA. Distributes and promotes titles "on a national and international scale through a large sales organization."

Needs: Adventure, mystery, religious (general religious, inspirational, religious fantasy, religious mystery/suspense, religious thriller, religious romance), western. "We publish fiction in all the main genres. We want not only a very good story, but also one that sets forth Christian values. Nothing that lacks a positive Christian emphasis (but do NOT preach, however); nothing that fails to sustain reader interest. Published *Sea of Glory*, by Ken Wales and David Poling (historical, debut author); *The Third Dragon*, by Frank Simon (mystery/intrique); and *Friends and Enemies*, by Steve Bly (western).

How to Contact: Does not accept unsolicited mss. Query with SASE. Accepts queries by e-mail. Include estimated word count, brief bio, list of publishing credits. Send copy of ms and SASE. Agented fiction 50%. Responds in 3

months to queries. Accepts simultaneous submissions. No electronic submissions, submissions on disk. Sometimes comments on rejected mss.
Payment/Terms: Pays negotiable royalty. Publishes ms 10 months after acceptance. Book catalog free; ms guidelines for #10 SASE.

A BROADWAY BOOKS, Doubleday Broadway Publishing Group, Random House, Inc., 1745 Broadway, New York NY 10019. (212)782-9000. Fax: (212)782-8338. Website: www.broadwaybooks.com. **Contact:** William Thomas, editor-in-chief. Estab. 1995. Broadway publishes general interest nonfiction and fiction for adults. Publishes hardcover and trade paperback originals and reprints.
Needs: Publishes a limited list of commercial literary fiction. Published *Freedomland*, by Richard Price.
How to Contact: *Agented submissions only.*

A CADMUS EDITIONS, Box 126, Tiburon CA 94920-0126. (707) 762-0510. E-mail: cebiz@cadmus-editions.com. Website: www.cadmus-editions.com. **Contact:** Jeffrey Miller, editor. Estab. 1979. Emphasis on quality literature. Publishes hardcover and paperback originals. Books: approximately 25% letterpress; 75% offset printing; perfect and case binding. Distributes titles through Small Press Distribution. Plans 3 titles this year.
Needs: Literary. Published *The Wandering Fool*, by Yunus Emre, translated by Edouard Roditi and Guzin Dino; *The Hungry Girls*, by Patricia Eakins; and *Zig-Zag*, by Richard Thornley.
How to Contact: Does not accept unsolicited mss. *Agented submissions only.* No electronic submissions.
Payment/Terms: Pays royalty.

CAITLIN PRESS, INC., P.O. Box 2387 Station B, Prince George, BC V2N 2S6 Canada. (250)964-4953. Fax: (250)964-4970. Website: www.caitlin-press.com. **Contact:** Cynthia Wilson. Estab. 1977. "We publish books about the British Columbia interior or by people from the interior." Publishes trade paperback and soft cover originals. Averages 6-7 total titles/year. Distributes titles directly from publisher and through general distribution and Harbour Publishing. Promotes titles through *BC Book World, Canadian Books in Print* and website.
Needs: Adventure, historical, humor, mainstream/contemporary, short story collections, young adult.
How to Contact: Accepts unsolicited mss. Query with SASE. Responds in 6 months to queries. Accepts simultaneous submissions.
Payment/Terms: Pays 15% royalty on net sales. Publishes ms 18 months after acceptance. Ms guidelines online.
Advice: "Our area of interest is British Columbia and Northern Canada. Submitted manuscripts should reflect our interest area."

CANADIAN INSTITUTE OF UKRAINIAN STUDIES PRESS, CIUS Toronto Publications Office, University of Toronto, 1 Spadina Crescent, Room 109, Toronto ON M5S 2J5 Canada. (416)978-6934. Fax: (416)978-2672. E-mail: cius@chass.utoronto.ca. Website: www.utoronto.ca/cius. **Contact:** Roman Senkus, director of publications; Marko Stech, managing editor. Estab. 1976. "We publish scholarship about Ukraine and Ukrainians in Canada." Publishes hardcover and trade paperback originals and reprints.
Needs: Ukrainian literary works. Published *From Nationalism to Universalism*, by Israel Kleiner; *On Sunday Morning She Gathered Herbs*, by Olha Kobylianska; and *A Concordance to the Poetic Works of Taras Shevchenko*, by Oleh Ilnytzkyj and George Hawrysch.
How to Contact: Query with SASE or submit complete ms. Accepts queries by e-mail, fax. Responds in 1 month to queries; 3 months to mss. Accepts electronic submissions.
Payment/Terms: Pays 0-2% royalty on retail price. Nonauthor-subsidy publishes 20-30% of books. Publishes ms 2 years after acceptance. Book catalog free; ms guidelines free.
Advice: "We are a scholarly press and do not normally pay our authors. Our audience consists of university students and teachers and the general public interested in Ukrainian and Ukrainian-Canadian affairs."

A CANDLEWICK PRESS, 2067 Massachusetts Ave., Cambridge MA 02140. (617)661-3330. Fax: (617)661-0565. E-mail: bigbear@candlewick.com. Website: www.candlewick.com. **Contact:** Jamie Michalak, editor; Joan Powers, editor-at-large (novelty); Liz Bicknell, editorial director/associate publisher (poetry, picture books, fiction); Mary Lee Donovan, executive editor (picture books, fiction); Kara LaReau, senior editor (picture books, fiction); Cynthia Platt, editor (nonfiction); Sarah Ketchersid, editor (board, toddler). Estab. 1991. "We are a truly child-centered publisher." Publishes hardcover originals, trade paperback originals and reprints. Averages 200 total titles/year.
Needs: Juvenile, picture books, young adult. Published *Because of Winn-Dixie*, by Kate DiCamillo; *Judy Moody*, by Kate McDonald, illustrated by Peter Reynolds, *Who Knew What He Liked* by M.T. Anderson, illustrated by

● **A BULLET INTRODUCES COMMENTS** by the editor of *Novel & Short Story Writer's Market* indicating special information about the listing.

Kevin Hawkes; and *A Poke in the 'I'*, edited by Paul Janeczko, illustrated by Chris Raschka.
How to Contact: Does not accept unsolicited mss.

☑ ◎ **CAROLRHODA BOOKS, INC.**, Lerner Publishing Group, 241 First Ave. N., Minneapolis MN 55401.
Fax: (612)332-7615. Website: www.lernerbooks.com. **Contact:** Rebecca Poole, submissions editor. Estab. 1969.
Carolrhoda Books seeks creative picture books, middle-grade fiction, historical fiction and K-6 children's nonfiction.
Publishes hardcover originals. Averages 50-60 total titles/year.
Needs: Historical, juvenile, multicultural, picture books, young reader, middle grade and young adult fiction. "We
continue to add fiction for middle grades and 8-10 picture books per year. Not looking for folktales or anthropomor-
phic animal stories." Published *The War*, by Anais Vaugelade; *Little Wolf's Haunted Hill for Small Horrors*, by Ian
Whybrow.
How to Contact: Query with SASE or submit complete ms. Query with SASE, send complete ms for picture
books. Responds in 6 months to queries. Accepts simultaneous submissions.
Payment/Terms: Pays royalty on wholesale price or makes outright purchase. Negotiates payments of advance
against royalty. Average advance: varied. Book catalog for 9×12 SAE with $3.50 postage; ms guidelines online.

Ⓐ ☻ **CARROLL & GRAF PUBLISHERS, INC.**, Avalon Publishing Group, 161 William St., New York NY
10038. (646)375-2570. Fax: (646)375-2571. Website: www.avalonpub.com. **Contact:** Herman Graf, publisher;
Phillip Turner, executive editor; Tina Pohlman, senior editor. Estab. 1982. Publishes hardcover and trade paperback
originals. Averages 120 total titles, 50 fiction titles/year.
Needs: Literary, mainstream/contemporary, mystery, science fiction, suspense, thriller. Published *Ascension*, by
Steven Galloway; *Disturbance of the Inner Ear*, by Joyce Hackett, and *Places to Look for a Mother*, by Nicole
Stansbury.
How to Contact: Does not accept unsolicited mss. *Agented submissions only.* Query with SASE. Responds in a
timely fashion to queries. Sometimes comments on rejected mss.
Payment/Terms: Pays 10-15% royalty on retail price for hardcover, 6-7½% for paperback. Offers advance com-
mensurate with the work. Publishes ms 9-18 months after acceptance. Book catalog free.

◎ **CAVE BOOKS**, 277 Clamer Rd., Trenton NJ 08628-3204. (609)530-9743. E-mail: pddb@juno.com. Website:
www.cavebooks.com. **Contact:** Paul Steward, managing editor. Estab. 1980. Small press devoted to books on caves,
karst and speleology. Fiction: novels about cave exploration only. Publishes hardcover and trade paperback originals
and reprints. Books: acid-free paper; offset printing. **Published 2 debut authors within the last year.** Averages 2
total titles, 2 fiction titles/year.
Needs: Adventure, historical, literary, caves, karst, speleology. Published *Emergence*, by Marian McConnell
(novel).
How to Contact: Accepts unsolicited mss. Query with SASE or submit complete ms. Accepts queries by e-mail.
Send SASE for return of ms or send a disposable ms and SASE for reply only. Responds in 2 weeks to queries; 3
months to mss. Accepts simultaneous submissions, electronic submissions. Sometimes comments on rejected mss.
Payment/Terms: Pays 10% royalty on retail price. Publishes ms 18 months after acceptance.
Advice: "In the last three years we have received only three novels about caves, and we have published one of
them. We get dozens of inappropriate submissions."

CHARLESBRIDGE PUBLISHING, School Division, 85 Main St., Watertown MA 02472. (617)926-0329.
Fax: (617)926-5720. Website: www.charlesbridge.com/school. Estab. 1980. Publishes educational curricula and
hardcover and paperback nonfiction and fiction children's picture books. Averages 20 total titles/year.
Needs: Multicultural, nature, science, social studies, bedtime, etc. Non-rhyming stories. Published *The Wedding*,
by Eve Bunting; *Whale Snow*, by Debby Dahl Edwardson, and *Big Blue*, by Shelley Gill.
How to Contact: Submit complete ms.
Payment/Terms: Royalty and advance vary. Publishes ms 2 years after acceptance. Ms guidelines online.

🌐 **CHRISTCHURCH PUBLISHERS LTD**, 2 Caversham Street, London SW3 4AH United Kingdom. Fax:
0044 171 351 4995. **Contact:** James Hughes, fiction editor.
Needs: "Miscellaneous fiction, also poetry. More 'literary' style of fiction, but also thrillers, crime fiction, etc."
How to Contact: Query with SASE.
Payment/Terms: Pays royalty. Offers advance. "We have contacts and agents worldwide."

◎ **CHRONICLE BOOKS FOR CHILDREN**, 85 Second St., 6th Floor, San Francisco CA 94105. (415)537-
4200. Fax: (415)537-4420. E-mail: frontdesk@chroniclebooks.com. Website: www.chroniclekids.com. **Contact:**
Victoria Rock, director of children's books; Beth Weber, managing editor; Lisa McGuiness, editor; Susan Pearson,
editor-at-large. Publishes hardcover and trade paperback originals. **Published 5% debut authors within the last
year.** Averages 40-50 total titles/year.
Needs: Mainstream/contemporary, multicultural, young adult, picture books; middle grade fiction; young adult
projects. Published *Ghost Wings*; *Dream Carver*; *Star in the Darkness*.
How to Contact: Query with synopsis and SASE. Send complete ms with SASE for picture books. Responds in

2-18 weeks to queries; 6 months to mss. Accepts simultaneous submissions. No electronic submissions, submissions on disk.

Payment/Terms: Pays 8% royalty. Average advance: variable. Publishes ms 18 months after acceptance. Book catalog for 9×12 SAE with 3 first-class stamps; ms guidelines online.

Advice: "We are interested in projects that have a unique bent to them—be it in subject matter, writing style, or illustrative technique. As a small list, we are looking for books that will lend our list a distinctive flavor. Primarily, we are interested in fiction and nonfiction picture books for children ages up to eight years, and nonfiction books for children ages up to twelve years. We publish board, pop-up, and other novelty formats as well as picture books. We are also interested in early chapter books, middle grade fiction, and young adult projects."

CIRCLET PRESS, INC., 1770 Massachusetts Ave., #278, Cambridge MA 02140. (617)864-0492. E-mail: circlet-info@circlet.com. Website: www.circlet.com. **Contact:** Cecilia Tan, publisher. Estab. 1992. Small, independent specialty book publisher. "We are the only book publisher specializing in science fiction and fantasy of an erotic nature." Publishes hardcover and trade paperback originals. Books: perfect binding; illustrations sometimes. **Published 20 debut authors within the last year.** Averages 4-6 total titles/year. Distributes titles through SCB Distribution in the US/Canada, Turnaround UK in the UK and Bulldog Books in Australia. Promotes titles through reviews in book trade and general media, mentions in *Publishers Weekly, Bookselling This Week* and regional radio/TV.

● "Our titles were finalists in the Independent Publisher Awards in both science fiction and fantasy."

Imprint(s): The Ultra Violet Library (non-erotic lesbian/gay fantasy and science fiction).

Needs: Erotica, science fiction, short stories only. "Fiction must combine both the erotic and the fantastic. The erotic content needs to be an integral part of a science fiction story, and vice versa. Writers should not assume that any sex is the same as erotica." All books are anthologies of short stories. Published *Nymph*, by Francesca Lia Block; *Sextopia*, edited by Cecilia Tan (science fiction erotica).

How to Contact: Accepts unsolicited mss. Query with SASE. Submit full short stories up to 10,000 words between April 15 and August 31. Manuscripts received outside this reading period are discarded. Queries only via e-mail. Include estimated word count, brief bio, list of publishing credits. Send SASE for return of ms or send a disposable ms and SASE for reply only. Agented fiction 5%. Responds in 1 months to queries; 6-18 months to mss. Accepts simultaneous submissions, electronic submissions. Always comments on rejected mss.

Payment/Terms: Pays 4-12% royalty on retail price or makes outright purchase. Also pays in books, if author prefers. Publishes ms 18 months after acceptance. Book catalog for 10 SAE with 2 first-class stamps; ms guidelines online.

Advice: "Read what we publish, learn to use lyrical but concise language to portray sex positively. Make sex and erotic interaction integral to your plot. Stay away from genre stereotypes. Use depth of character, internal monologue and psychological introspection to draw me in."

CITY LIGHTS BOOKS, Columbus Ave., San Francisco CA 94133. (415)362-1901. Fax: (415)362-4921. **Contact:** Robert Sharrard, editor. Estab. 1955. Publishes paperback originals. Plans 1-2 first novels this year. Averages 12 total titles, 4-5 fiction titles/year.

How to Contact: Accepts unsolicited mss. Query first. Accepts unsolicited queries/correspondence by fax. Send SASE for reply, return of ms or send a disposable copy of ms.

CLARION BOOKS, Houghton Mifflin Co., 215 Park Ave. S., New York NY 10003. Website: www.hought onmifflinbooks.com. **Contact:** Dinah Stevenson, editorial director; Michele Coppola, editor (YA, middle-grade, chapter book); Jennifer B. Greene, editor (YA, middle-grade, chapter book); Lynne Polvino, associate editor (YA, middle-grade, chapter book). Estab. 1965. "Clarion is a strong presence in the fiction market for young readers. We are highly selective in the areas of historical and contemporary fiction. We publish chapter books for children ages 7-10 and middle grade novels for ages 9-12, as well as picture books and nonfiction." Publishes hardcover originals for children. Averages 50 total titles/year.

● Clarion author Linda Sue Park received the 2002 Newbery Award for her book, *A Single Shard*. David Wiesner received the 2002 Caldecott Award for *The Three Pigs*.

Needs: Adventure, historical, humor, mystery, suspense, strong character studies. Clarion is highly selective in the areas of historical fiction, fantasy, and science fiction. A novel must be superlatively written in order to find a place on the list. Mss that arrive without an SASE of adequate size will *not* be responded to or returned. Accepts fiction translations. Published *The Green Blue Yonder*, by Alex Shearer (contemporary, middle-grade); *When My Name Was Keoko*, by Linda Sue Park (historical fiction); and *Dunk*, by David Cubar (contemporary YA).

How to Contact: Submit complete ms. No queries, please. Send to only *one* Clarion editor. Responds in 2 months. Prefers no multiple submissions.

Payment/Terms: Pays 5-10% royalty on retail price. Average advance: minimum of $4,000. Publishes ms 2 years after acceptance. Ms guidelines for #10 SASE.

CLEIS PRESS, P.O. Box 14684, San Francisco CA 94114-0684. (415)575-4700. Fax: (415)575-4705. Website: www.cleispress.com. **Contact:** Frederique Delacoste, editor. Estab. 1980. Midsize independent publisher.

Publishes trade paperback originals and reprints. **Published new writers within the last year.** Averages 20 total titles, 5 fiction titles/year.

- Cleis Press has received the Best Fiction Firecracker for *The Leather Daddy and the Femme*, by Carol Queen, the Fab Award, and the Firecracker for Outstanding Press for 1999.

Needs: Feminist, gay/lesbian, literary. "We are looking for high quality fiction by women and men." *Black Like Us* (fiction); *Sexually Speaking: Collected Sex Writings*, by Gore Vidal (essays); and *A Fragile Union*, by Joan Nestle (essays), which won a Lambda Literary Award.

How to Contact: Accepts unsolicited mss. Submit complete ms. Accepts queries by e-mail. Include brief bio, list of publishing credits. Send SASE for return of ms or send a disposable ms and SASE for reply only. Agented fiction 10%. Responds in 1 month to queries.

Payment/Terms: Pays variable royalty on retail price. Publishes ms 2 years after acceptance. Book catalog for #10 SAE with 2 first-class stamps.

COASTAL CAROLINA PRESS, 2231 Wrightsville Ave., Wilmington NC 28403. Website: www.coastalcarolina press.org. Hardcover, trade paperback and mass market paperback originals and trade paperback reprints. **Published 70% debut authors within the last year.** Averages 4 total titles/year.

Needs: Adventure, ethnic, historical, humor, juvenile, literary, mainstream/contemporary, military/war, multicultural, mystery, regional, short story collections, suspense, young adult. Publishes books with regional niche. Published *Island Murders*, by Wanda Canada (fiction).

How to Contact: Query with SASE.

Payment/Terms: Pays royalty. Publishes ms 1 year after acceptance. Book catalog online; ms guidelines online.

COFFEE HOUSE PRESS, 27 N. Fourth St., Suite 400, Minneapolis MN 55401. Fax: (612)338-4004. **Contact:** Chris Fischbach, senior editor. Estab. 1984. "Nonprofit publisher with a small staff. We publish literary titles: fiction and poetry." Publishes hardcover and trade paperback originals. Books: acid-free paper; cover illustrations. **Published some debut authors within the last year.** Plans 3,000-4,000 first novels this year. Averages 14 total titles, 6 fiction titles/year.

- This successful nonprofit small press has received numerous grants from various organizations including the NEA, the Mellon Foundation and Lila Wallace/Readers Digest Foundation.

Needs: Ethnic, experimental, literary, mainstream/contemporary, short story collections, novels. Publishes anthologies, but they are closed to unsolicited submissions. Published *Ex Utero*, by Laurie Foos (first novel); *Gunga Din Highway*, by Frank Chin (novel); and *A 38 Special & a Broken Heart*, by Jonis Agee (short stories).

How to Contact: Accepts unsolicited mss. Query with SASE. Query first with samples and SASE. Agented fiction 10%. Responds in 1 month to queries; up to 6 months to mss.

Payment/Terms: Pays 8% royalty on retail price. Provides 15 author's copies. Publishes ms 18 months after acceptance. Book catalog and ms guidelines for #10 SASE with 2 first-class stamps; ms guidelines for #10 SAE with first-class stamps.

COMMUTERS LIBRARY, Sound Room Publishers, P.O. Box 3168, Falls Church VA 22043. (703)790-8250. Fax: (703)790-8234. E-mail: glangenfeld@commuterlibrary.com. Website: www.commuterslibrary.com. **Contact:** Joe Langenfeld, editor. Estab. 1991. "Small publisher of audiobooks (many classics) with plans to publish new works of fiction and nonfiction, primarily novellas." Publishes audiobooks. Averages 80 total titles, 70 fiction titles/year.

- Audio Best of the Year for six years.

Imprint(s): Commuters Library, Joe Langenfeld (fiction and nonfiction).

Needs: Adventure, children's/juvenile, family saga, fantasy, historical, horror, humor, literary, mainstream/contemporary, military/war, mystery, new age/mystic, suspense, western, young adult.

How to Contact: Accepts unsolicited mss. Query with SASE or submit outline, 1 sample chapter(s), synopsis. Accepts queries by e-mail, fax. Include estimated word count. Accepts simultaneous submissions, submissions on disk. No electronic submissions.

Payment/Terms: Pays 5-10% royalty. Average advance: $200-1,000. Publishes ms 1 year after acceptance. Ms guidelines online.

Advice: "Audio Books are growing in popularity. Authors should consider going directly to audio for special works. Give us good writing 10,000 to 20,000 words in length."

CONSTABLE & ROBINSON, LTD., (formerly Constable Publishers), Constable & Robinson, 3 The Lanchesters, 162 Fulham Palace Rd., London WG 9ER United Kingdom. 0208-741-3663. Fax: 0208-748-7562. **Contact:** Krystyna Green, editorial director (crime fiction). Publishes hardcover and trade paperback originals. Averages 160 total titles/year.

Needs: Crime/whodunnit. Publishes "crime fiction (mysteries)." Lenth 80,000 words minimum; 130,000 words maximum. Published *A Mist of Prophecies*, by Steven Saylor; *The Yeane's Midnight*, by Ed O'Connor; *Hollow Crown*, by David Roberts.

How to Contact: *Agented submissions only.* Submit 3 sample chapter(s), synopsis, SASE. Responds in 1 month to queries; 1 month to proposals; 3 months to mss. Accepts simultaneous submissions.

Payment/Terms: Pays royalty. Offers advance. Publishes ms 1 year after acceptance. Book catalog free.
Advice: Constable & Robinson Ltd. is looking for "crime novels with good, strong identities. Think about what it is that makes your book(s) stand out from the others."

CONTEXT BOOKS, 368 Broadway, Suite 314, New York NY 10013. (212)233-4880. E-mail: info@conte xtbooks.com. Website: www.contextbooks.com. **Contact:** Beau Friedlander. Estab. 1999. Books: offset printing; cloth/paper binding; illustrations. Plans 1 first novel this year. Member, ABA. Titles distributed through Publisher's Group West. Promotes titles on a "book by book basis."
• Context Books has received an Independent Publishers Prize, NBCC nomination, QPBC News Vision and *L.A. Times* Book Prize.
Needs: Experimental, feminist, historical, literary, mainstream/contemporary, military/war, multicultural, short story collections, political. Published *After Dachau*, by Daniel Quinn (fiction); *Assorted Fire Events*, by David Means (short stories); *Mind the Doors*, by Zinovy Zinik (Russian literature).
How to Contact: Accepts unsolicited mss. Submit complete ms. Agented fiction 99.9%. Responds in 4 months to queries; 4 months to mss. Accepts simultaneous submissions. No electronic submissions, submissions on disk.
Payment/Terms: Pays 7½-15% royalty. Author's copies. Offers advance. Publishes ms 1 year after acceptance. Book catalog for 9×12 SAE; ms guidelines for #10 SASE.
Advice: "Tell me who you are in three sentences; tell me what the work accomplishes in the same."

COPPER CANYON PRESS, P.O. Box 271, Port Townsend WA 98368. (360)385-4925. Fax: (360)385-4985. Website: www.coppercanyonpress.org. **Contact:** Michael Wiegers. Estab. 1972. Publishes trade paperback originals and occasional clothbound editions. Averages 18 total titles/year.
How to Contact: Responds in 4 months to queries. Sometimes comments on rejected mss.
Payment/Terms: Pays royalty. Publishes ms 2 years after acceptance. Book catalog free; ms guidelines online.

COTEAU BOOKS, Thunder Creek Publishing Co-operative Ltd., 401-2206 Dewdney Ave., Suite 401, Regina SK S4R 1H3 Canada. (306)777-0170. Fax: (306)522-5152. E-mail: coteau@coteaubooks.com. Website: www.coteaubooks.com. **Contact:** Nik L. Burton, managing editor. Estab. 1975. "Coteau Books publishes the finest Canadian fiction, poetry, drama, and children's literature, with an emphasis on western writers." Publishes trade paperback originals and reprints. Books: #2 offset or 60 lb. hi-bulk paper; offset printing; perfect bound; 4-color illustrations. Averages 20 total titles, 6-8 fiction titles/year. Distributes titles through Fitzhenry & Whiteside.
Needs: Ethnic, fantasy, feminist, gay/lesbian, historical, humor, juvenile, literary, mainstream/contemporary, multicultural, multimedia, mystery, plays, poetry, regional, short story collections, spiritual, sports, young adult, novels, short fiction, middle years. Published *Canadian authors only*. Published *A Song for Nettie Johnson*, by Gloria Sewai; received the 2002 Governor General's Award for Fiction.
How to Contact: Accepts unsolicited mss. Submit 3-4 sample chapter(s), author bio, SASE. Accepts queries by e-mail. Responds in 2 months to queries; 6 months to mss. No simultaneous submissions. Sometimes comments on rejected mss.
Payment/Terms: Pays 10% royalty on retail price. "We're a co-operative and receive subsidies from the Canadian, provincial and local governments. We do not accept payments from authors to publish their works." Publishes ms 1 year after acceptance. Book catalog free; ms guidelines online.
Advice: "We publish short-story collections, novels, drama, nonfiction and poetry collections, as well as literary interviews and children's books. This is part of our mandate. The work speaks for itself! Be bold. Be creative. Be persistent!"

COUNTERPOINT, The Perseus Books Group, 387 Park Avenue South, 12th Fl, New York NY 10016. Website: www.counterpointpress.com. Estab. 1995. Publishes papback and hardcover originals.
Needs: Literary, short story collections. Published *Appetites*, by Caroline Knapp (literary/non-fiction); *Why Did I Ever*, by Mary Robinson (novel).
How to Contact: *Agented submissions only.*
Payment/Terms: Pays royalty. Average advance: Negotiable. Publishes ms 24 months after acceptance. Book catalog free.

COVENANT COMMUNICATIONS, INC., Box 416, American Fork UT 84003-0416. (801)756-1041. Website: www.covenant-lds.com. Averages 50+ total titles/year.
Needs: Adventure, historical, humor, juvenile, literary, mainstream/contemporary, mystery, picture books, regional, religious, romance, spiritual, suspense, young adult.
How to Contact: Submit completed manuscript with synopsis and one-page cover letter. Responds in 4 months to mss.
Payment/Terms: Pays 6½-15% royalty on retail price. Publishes ms 6-12 months after acceptance. Ms guidelines online.
Advice: Our audience is exclusively LDS (Latter-Day Saints, "Mormon").

CRICKET BOOKS, Carus Publishing, 332 S. Michigan Ave., #1100, Chicago IL 60604. (312)939-1500. Fax: (312)939-8150. Website: www.cricketbooks.net. **Contact:** Submissions editor. Estab. 1999. "Small, independent publisher able to integrate publishing with related *Cricket* and *Cobblestone* magazine groups. We publish children's fiction and nonfiction, from picture books to high young adult." Publishes hardcover and paperback originals. **Published 2 debut authors within the last year.** Plans 2 first novels this year. Averages 20 total titles, 10 fiction titles/year. Distributes titles through PGW. Promotes titles through in-house marketing.

• Received the 2002 Batchelder Award, the 2000 Bram Stoker and the 2000 Scott O'Dell.

Imprint(s): Cricket Books, picture books to young adults; Marcato Books, fiction and nonfiction for teens.

Needs: Children's/juvenile (adventure, animal, easy-to-read, fantasy, historical, mystery, preschool/picture book, sports), juvenile, young adult (adventure, easy-to-read, fantasy/science fiction, historical, horror, mystery/suspense, problem novels, romance, sports, western), early chapter books and middle-grade fiction. Plans anthologies for Christmas, dragons, poetry, and *Cricket Magazine*'s anniversary edition. Editors select stories. Published *Seek*, by Paul Fleischman (YA fiction); *Robert and the Weird and Wacky Facts*, by Barbara Seuling (chapter book); and *Scorpio's Child*, by Kezi Matthews (fiction, ages 11-14).

How to Contact: Does not accept unsolicited mss. See our website, www.cricketbooks.net, for updates on our submission policy.

Payment/Terms: Pays 10% royalty on net receipts. Open to first-time and unagented authors. Pays up to 10% royalty on retail price. Average advance: $1,500 and up. Publishes ms 18 months after acceptance. Ms guidelines online.

N: © CROSSGEN ENTERTAINMENT, INC., 4023 Tampa Rd., Suite 2400, Oldsmar FL 34677. Website: www.crossgen.com.

Needs: Comic books, graphic novels.

How to Contact: Mail sample pages, Attn: Laura Mittler. "All submission correspondence will be conducted via postal mail. No phone calls, e-mails, or website-based portfolios will be accepted at this time. When submitting work for consideration, please complete the Employment Submission Release form (found on website) and attach to your submission. No material is considered without this form. Also include a brief résumé and SASE. No submissions will be returned." Ms guidelines on website.

Advice: "Submissions for writers should take the form of 2-3 story synopses and one 5-page full script sample."

© CROSSQUARTER PUBLISHING GROUP, P.O. Box 8756, Santa Fe NM 87504. (505)438-9846. Website: www.crossquarter.com. **Contact:** Anthony Ravenscroft. Publishes case and trade paperback originals and reprints. **Published 90% debut authors within the last year.** Averages 5-10 total titles/year.

Needs: Science fiction, visionary fiction.

How to Contact: Query with SASE. Responds in 3 months to queries. Accepts simultaneous submissions.

Payment/Terms: Pays 8-10% royalty on wholesale or retail price. Publishes ms 1 year after acceptance. Book catalog for $1.75; ms guidelines online.

Advice: "Audience is earth-conscious people looking to grow into balance of body, mind, heart and spirit."

© CROSSTIME, Crossquarter Publishing Group, P.O. Box 8756, Santa Fe NM 87504. (505)438-9846. Fax: (505)438-9846. E-mail: info@crossquarter.com. Website: www.crossquarter.com. **Contact:** Anthony Ravenscroft (visionary, speculative science). Estab. 1985. Small publisher. Publishes paperback originals. Books: recycled paper; docutech or offset printing; perfect-bound. **Published 2 debut authors within the last year.** Plans 2 first novels this year. Member, SPAN, PMA.

Needs: Mystery (occult), New Age/mystic, psychic/supernatural, romance (occult), science fiction, young adult (fantasy/science fiction). Plans an anthology of Paul B. Duquette Memorial Short Science Fiction contest winners. Guidelines on website. Published *The Shamrock and the Feather*, by Dori Dalton (debut author); *Shyla's Initiative*, by Barbara Casey (occult romance); and *CrossTIME SF Anthology* (science fiction).

How to Contact: Does not accept unsolicited mss. Query with SASE. Accepts queries by e-mail. Include estimated word count, brief bio, list of publishing credits. Responds in 3 months. Accepts simultaneous submissions, electronic submissions, submissions on disk.

Payment/Terms: Pays 6-10% royalty. Publishes ms 6-9 months after acceptance. Book catalog online; ms guidelines online.

© © CROSSWAY BOOKS, Division of Good News Publishers, 1300 Crescent St., Wheaton IL 60187-5800. (630)682-4300. Fax: (630)682-4785. Website: www.crosswaybooks.org. **Contact:** Jill Carter. Estab. 1938. " 'Making a difference in people's lives for Christ' as its maxim, Crossway Books lists titles written from an evangelical Christian perspective." Midsize evangelical Christian publisher. Publishes hardcover and trade paperback originals. Averages 85 total titles, 5 fiction titles/year. Member, ECPA. Distributes titles through Christian bookstores and catalogs. Promotes titles through magazine ads, catalogs.

Needs: Historical, literary, western, Christian. "We publish fiction that falls into these categories: (1) Christian realism, or novels set in modern, true-to-life settings as a means of telling stories about Christians today in an increasingly post-Christian era; (2) supernatural fiction, or stories typically set in the 'real world' but that bring supernatural reality into it in a way that heightens our spiritual dimension; (3) historical fiction, using historical characters, times and places of interest as a mirror for our own times; (4) some genre-technique fiction (mystery, western); and (5) children's fiction. We are not interested in romance novels, horror novels, biblical novels (i.e., stories set in Bible times that fictionalize events in the lives of prominent biblical characters), issues novels (i.e., fictionalized treatments of contemporary issues), and end times/prophecy novels. We do not accept full manuscripts or electronic submissions." Published *Freedom's Shadow*, by Marlo Schalesky (historical); *The Outlaw's Twin Sister*, by Stephen Bly (western/historical); *Picture Rock*, by Stephen Bly (western/historical). Publishes The Belles of Lordsburg series (western) and The Winds of Freedom series (historical).

How to Contact: Accepts unsolicited mss. Query with SASE. Submit book summary, chapter by chapter synopsis with 2 sample chapters and SASE. Include estimated word count. Send SASE for return of ms or send a disposable ms and SASE for reply only. Agented fiction 5%. Responds in up to 3 months to queries; 3 months to mss. Accepts simultaneous submissions. No electronic submissions, submissions on disk.

Payment/Terms: Pays negotiable royalty. Average advance: negotiable. Publishes ms 18 months after acceptance. Book catalog for 9 × 12 SAE with 7 first-class stamps; ms guidelines online.

Advice: "With so much Christian fiction on the market, we are carefully looking at our program to see the direction we wish to proceed. Be sure your project fits into our guidelines and is written from an evangelical Christian worldview. 'Religious' or 'Spiritual' viewpoints will not fit."

⊠ CROWN PUBLISHING GROUP, Random House, Inc., 1745 Broadway, New York NY 10019. (212)572-2600. Fax: (212)940-7408. E-mail: crownbiz@randomhouse.com. Website: www.randomhouse.com/crown. Estab. 1933. "The group publishes a selection of popular fiction and nonfiction by both established and rising authors."
Imprint(s): Bell Tower; Clarkson Potter; Crown Business; Crown Publishers, Inc; Harmony Books; Shaye Areheart Books; Three Rivers Press.

⊘ CUMBERLAND HOUSE PUBLISHING, 431 Harding Industrial Dr., Nashville TN 37211. (615)832-1171. Fax: (615)832-0633. Website: www.cumberlandhouse.com. **Contact:** Ron Pitkin, president. Estab. 1996. "We look for unique titles with clearly defined audiences." Publishes hardcover, trade paperback and mass market originals and reprints. Averages 60 total titles/year.
Imprint(s): Cumberland House Hearthside; Julia M. Pitkin, editor-in-chief.
Needs: Historical, mystery. Writers should know "the odds are really stacked against them. Published *Roseflower Creek*, by H.L. Miles; and *Chickamauga*, by James Reasoner.
How to Contact: Does not accept unsolicited mss. Query with SASE. Agented fiction 20%. Responds in 6 months to queries. Accepts simultaneous submissions.
Payment/Terms: Pays 10-15% royalty on net receipts. Average advance: $500-5,000. Publishes ms an average of 12 months after acceptance. Book catalog for 8 × 10 SAE with 4 first-class stamps; ms guidelines online.
Advice: Audience is "adventuresome people who like a fresh approach to things. Writers should tell what their idea is, why it's unique and why somebody would want to buy it."

N ◎ DAEDAL PRESS, Daedal Fine Arts, 2315 Bel Air Road, Fallston MD 21047. (410)879-4421. Website: www.webspawner.com/users/dkdael/. **Contact:** Dorothy Keesecker (fiction), Ernest Walters (art), editors. Estab. 1968. Small press. Publishes 2-4 books per year. Original art prints folios (no reproduction lithos), lithographs, etchings, etc. hand-pulled by the artists. Publishes hardcover and paperback originals. Books: Acid-free paper; offset printing; perfect bound. Average print order: 2,000. **Published 1 debut author within the last year.** Plans 2-4 first novels this year. Distributes titles through direct mail and creative marketing.
Imprint(s): DP; Erewhon; Daedal Fine Arts.
Needs: Wants literary fiction, especially art related.
How to Contact: Accepts unsolicited mss. Query with SASE. Submit 20-25 sample pages. Accepts queries by mail. Include estimated word count, brief bio. Responds in 2-4 weeks to queries; 2-6 weeks to mss. Accepts simultaneous submissions. No submissions on disk. Sometimes comments on rejected mss.
Payment/Terms: Pays 10-20% royalty on net receipts. Pay depends on grants/awards. Publishes ms 3-6 months after acceptance. Book catalog free; ms guidelines for SASE.
Advice: "Refrain from using words like 'it,' 'little,' etc. Make the manuscript the best work it can be before sending it to editors and publishers."

N DAN RIVER PRESS, Conservatory of American Letters, P.O. Box 298, Thomaston ME 04861-0298. (207)354-0998. Fax: (207)354-0998. E-mail: cal@americanletters.org. Website: www.americanletters.org. **Contact:** Richard S. Danbury, fiction editor. Estab. 1977. "Small press publisher of fiction and biographies owned by a non-profit foundation." Publishes hardcover and paperback originals. Books: paperback; offset printing; perfect and cloth binding; illustrations. Averages 8-10 total titles, 2-3 fiction titles/year. Promotes titles through the author's sphere of influence. Distributes titles by mail order to libraries and bookstores.
Needs: Accepts anything but porn, sedition, evangelical, and children's literature. Publishes poetry and fiction anthology (submission guidelines to *Dan River Anthology* on the web). Published *Dan River Anthology 2004*, by R.S. Danbury III, editor (poetry and short stories).
How to Contact: Accepts unsolicited mss. Submit publishing history, synopsis, author bio. Cover letter or query should include estimated word count, brief bio and brief publishing history. Query should also deal with marketing ideas. Be specific ("All Women" is not a marketing idea we can work with) and social security number, #10 SASE. Include estimated word count, brief bio, list of publishing credits. Send SASE for return of ms or send a disposable

ms and SASE for reply only. Responds in 2-3 days to queries. Accepts simultaneous submissions.
Payment/Terms: Pays 10-15% royalty and 10 author's copies. Publishes ms 3-4 months after acceptance. Book catalog for 6×9 SAE with 60 postage affixed; ms guidelines online.
Advice: "Spend some time developing a following."

JOHN DANIEL AND CO., Daniel & Daniel, Publishers, Inc., P.O. Box 2790, McKinleyville CA 95519. (707)839-3495. Fax: (707)839-3242. E-mail: dand@danielpublishing.com. Website: www.danielpublishing.com. **Contact:** John Daniel, publisher. Estab. 1980. "We publish small books, usually in small editions, but we do so with pride." Publishes hardcover originals and trade paperback originals. Publishes poetry, fiction and nonfiction. Averages 4 total titles/year. Distributes through SCB Distributors. Promotes through direct mail, reviews.
Needs: Literary, poetry, short story collections. Publishes poetry, fiction and nonfiction; specializes in belles lettres, literary memoir. Published *Unplugged*, by Paul McComas (novel); *Alpha Male*, by Sam Foster (novel); *The Romantic Road*, by Yvonne West (short stories).
How to Contact: Accepts unsolicited mss. Query with SASE or submit proposal package including synopsis, 50 pages. Responds in 1 month to queries; 1 month to proposals; 2 months to mss. Accepts simultaneous submissions.
Payment/Terms: Pays 10% royalty on wholesale price. Average advance: $0-500. Publishes ms 1 year after acceptance. Book catalog free or online; ms guidelines online.
Advice: "Write for the joy of writing. That's as good as it gets.'"

Ⓝ DARK HORSE COMICS, INC., 10956 SE Main St., Milwaukie OR. Website: www.darkhorse.com. "In addition to publishing comics from top talent like Frank Miller, Mike Mignola, Stan Sakai, and internationally-renowned humorist Sergio Aragonés, Dark Horse is recognized as the world's leading publisher of licensed comics." Graphic novels, comic books.
Needs: Comic books, graphic novels. Published *Astro Boy Volume 10 TPB*, by Osamu Tezuka and Reid Fleming; *Flaming Carrot Crossover #1*, by Bob Burden and David Boswell.
How to Contact: To submit a written proposal, send a signed submission agreement (forms available online), complete synopsis, and full script via postal mail. Additional writer's guidelines online. Submissions are not returned. "Editor will respond to submission only if interested in hiring the creator."
Payment/Terms: Book catalog online.
Advice: "If you're looking for constructive criticism, show your work to industry professionals at conventions."

◐ MAY DAVENPORT, PUBLISHERS, 26313 Purissima Rd., Los Altos Hills CA 94022. (650)947-1275. Fax: (650)947-1373. E-mail: mdbooks@earthlink.net. Website: www.maydavenportpublishers.com. **Contact:** May Davenport, editor/publisher. Estab. 1976. "We prefer books which can be *used* in high schools as supplementary readings in English or creative writing courses. Reading skills have to be taught, and novels by humorous authors can be more pleasant to read than Hawthorne's or Melville's novels, war novels, or novels about past generations. Humor has a place in literature." Publishes hardcover and paperback originals. Averages 4 total titles/year. Distributes titles through direct mail order.
Imprint(s): md Books (nonfiction and fiction).
Needs: Humor, literary. "We want to focus on novels junior and senior high school teachers can share with their reluctant readers in their classrooms." Published *A Warm Familiar Feeling*, by Colby Farley; *Senoritis*, by Tate Thompson; *The Lesser Plan*, by Irvin Gay; *Making My Escape*, by David Lee Finkle.
How to Contact: Query with SASE. Responds in 1 month to queries.
Payment/Terms: Pays 15% royalty on retail price. Publishes ms 1 year after acceptance. Book catalog for #10 SASE; ms guidelines for #10 SASE.
Advice: "Just write humorous fictional novels about today's generation with youthful, admirable, believable characters to make young readers laugh. TV-oriented youth need role models in literature, and how a writer uses descriptive adjectives and similes enlightens youngsters who are so used to music, animation, special effects with stories."

▢ ◎ DAW BOOKS, INC., Penguin Putnam, Inc., 375 Hudson St., 3rd Floor, New York NY 10014-3658. (212)366-2096. Fax: (212)366-2090. E-mail: daw@penguinputnam.com. Website: www.dawbooks.com. **Contact:** Peter Stampfel, submissions editor. Estab. 1971. Publishes hardcover and paperback originals and reprints. Averages 60-80 total titles/year.
Needs: Fantasy, science fiction. "We are interested in science fiction and fantasy novels. We need science fiction more than fantasy right now, but we're still looking for both. We like character-driven books with attractive characters. We accept both agented and unagented manuscripts. Long books are absolutely not a problem. We are not seeking collections of short stories or ideas for anthologies. We do not want any nonfiction manuscripts." Published *The War of the Flowers*, by Tad Williams (fantasy).
How to Contact: Query with SASE. Simultaneous submissions "returned unread at once unless prior arrangements are made by agent."
Payment/Terms: Pays in royalties with an advance negotiable on a book-by-book basis. Book catalog free; ms guidelines online.
Advice: "We strongly encourage new writers. Research your publishers and submit only appropriate work."

A ◎ DEL REY BOOKS, Ballantine Publishing Group, Random House, Inc., 1745 Broadway, 18th Floor, New York NY 10019. (212)782-9000. Website: www.randomhouse.com/delrey. **Contact:** Betsy Mitchell, editor-in-chief; Shelly Shapiro, editorial director; Steve Saffel, executive editor; Chris Schluep, editor. Estab. 1977. "In terms of mass market, we basically created the field of fantasy bestsellers. Not that it didn't exist before, but we put the mass into mass market." Publishes hardcover, trade paperback, and mass market originals and mass market paperback reprints. Averages 120 total titles, 80 fiction titles/year.

Needs: Fantasy (should have the practice of magic as an essential element of the plot), science fiction (well-plotted novels with good characterizations, exotic locales and detailed alien creatures), alternate history. Published *Darwin's Children*, by Greg Bear; *The Gates of Dawn*, by Robert Newcomb; *Trading in Danger*, by Elizabeth Moon; *Dragon's Kin*, by Ann McCafferey and Todd McCaffrey; and *Star Wars: Unifying Force*, by James Luceno.

How to Contact: Does not accept unsolicited mss. *Agented submissions only.* Responds in 6 months to queries. No simultaneous submissions. Sometimes comments on rejected mss.

Payment/Terms: Pays royalty on retail price. Average advance: competitive. Publishes ms 1 year after acceptance. Ms guidelines online.

Advice: Has been publishing "more fiction and hardcovers, because the market is there for them. Read a lot of science fiction and fantasy, such as works by Anne McCaffrey, David Eddings, China Mieville, Arthur C. Clarke, Terry Brooks, Richard Morgan, Barbara Hambly. When writing, pay particular attention to plotting (and a satisfactory conclusion) and characters (sympathetic and well-rounded) because those are what readers look for."

A ◎ DELACORTE PRESS, Bantam Dell Publishing Group, Random House, Inc., 1745 Broadway, New York NY 10019. (212)782-9000. Fax: (212)782-9523. Website: www.randomhouse.com/kids. **Contact:** Michelle Poploff, director of properties. Publishes hardcover and trade paperback originals. Averages 36 total titles/year.

Needs: Publishes a range of young adult and middle grade fiction.

How to Contact: *Agented submissions only.* No simultaneous submissions.

Payment/Terms: Offers advance.

C ◎ DELIRIUM BOOKS, P.O. Box 338, N. Webster IN 46555. (574)594-3200. E-mail: srstaley@deliriumbooks.com. Website: www.deliriumbooks.com. **Contact:** Shane R, Staley, editor-in-chief (horror); Bob Strauss, associate editor (horror). Estab. 1999. "Delirium is one of the upcoming independent publishers in the horror genre. Noted for publishing edgy horror fiction and not afraid to push the envelope. Publishes hardcover originals and reprints. Books: 60 lb. natural/white paper; digitally printed; stitched binding. Distributes and promotes titles through website, Amazon.com, B&N.com and specialty bookstores.

Needs: Horror (psychological, supernatural). Wants "edgy novels within the horror genre." Plans anthology titled *Corrosion*; check website for guidelines and reading times. Published *Heretics*, by Greg F. Gifune (horror); *Cobwebs and Whispers*, by Scott Thomas (horror); and *Maternal Instinct*, by J.F. Gonzalez (horror).

How to Contact: Accepts unsolicited mss. Query with SASE. Accepts queries by e-mail. Include estimated word count. Responds in 2 weeks to queries; 3-6 months to mss. No simultaneous submissions, electronic submissions, submissions on disk.

Payment/Terms: Pays royalty. Book catalog online; ms guidelines online.

Advice: "Since the horror genre has been in a recent growth period, we are increasing the number of titles we publish per year. Delirium specializes in limited edition hardcovers. Delirium has been known to publish edgy fiction, extreme and hardcore. Please don't write specifically for the mainstream horror markets and submit your manuscripts to Delirium."

N ◯ ☑ DENLINGER'S PUBLISHERS, LTD., P.O. Box 1030, Edgewater FL 32132-1030. (386)424-1737. Fax: (386)428-3534. E-mail: editor@thebookden.com. Website: www.thebookden.com. **Contact:** Patricia Red, acquisitions editor (fiction-all). Estab. 1926. Denlinger's Publishers has a small dedicated staff that is interested in new technology in the field of publishing, i.e. P.O.D and electronic publication. Publishes paperback originals. **Published 95% debut authors within the last year.** Plans 20 first novels this year. Member, PMA. Distributes titles through Baker & Taylor, B&N.com, direct mail, Amazon.com and company website.

● Denlinger's Publishers won the Grand Prize Fiction Award at the 2000 Frankfurt International E-book Awards.

Needs: Adventure, ethnic, family saga, feminist, historical, horror, military/war, mystery, new age/mystic, religious, romance, science fiction, short story collections, thriller/espionage, western, young adult. Published *The Power of The Shadow*, by Darrell Pruitt (adventure/intrigue); *The Prodigal's Return*, by Dwight Geddes (multicultural); *Three Little Kings*, by David Schaafsma (adventure). Publishes the ongoing series *Wicked Witch of the West* (fantasy-teen).

How to Contact: Accepts unsolicited mss. Submit complete manuscript with cover letter. "Electronic submissions only!" Include estimated word count, brief bio. Send SASE for return of ms or send a disposable ms and SASE for reply only. Agented fiction 5%. Accepts simultaneous submissions, electronic submissions, submissions on disk.

Payment/Terms: Pays 10% royalty plus 6 contributor's copies. Publishes ms 6-9 months after acceptance. Book catalog online; ms guidelines for SASE and on website.

Advice: "Read the material on the website carefully. Do your research on questions regarding publishing *prior* to submission. We do not have time to explain the whole industry to each prospective submitter. Make sure you are comfortable with the publishing arrangement *prior* to submission. Our contract is online at www.thebookden.com/agree.html."

DESCANT PUBLISHING, P.O. Box 12973, Mill Creek WA 98082. (206)235-3357. Fax: (646)365-7513. E-mail: bret@descantpub.com. Website: www.descantpub.com. **Contact:** Alex Royal, editor (fiction). Estab. 2001. Publishes hardcover, trade paperback, mass market paperback, and electronic originals. **Published 50% debut authors within the last year.** Averages 10-12 total titles/year.
Needs: Fantasy, horror, mainstream/contemporary, mystery, religious, science fiction, suspense. Fresh storylines are critical. Published *The Stories of Those Who Were There*, by Peter Orullian (historical fiction).
How to Contact: Query with SASE. Responds in 3 months. Accepts simultaneous submissions.
Payment/Terms: Pays 6-15% royalty. Publishes ms 18 months after acceptance. Ms guidelines for #10 SASE.

A **◎** **DIAL BOOKS FOR YOUNG READERS**, Penguin Group USA, 345 Hudson St., 14th Floor, New York NY 10014. (212)366-2000. Website: www.penguinputnam.com. **Contact:** Submissions Editor. Estab. 1961. Trade children's book publisher. Publishes hardcover originals. Averages 50 total titles/year.
Needs: Adventure, fantasy, juvenile, picture books, young adult. Especially looking for "lively and well-written novels for middle grade and young adult children involving a convincing plot and believable characters. The subject matter or theme should not already be overworked in previously published books. The approach must not be demeaning to any minority group, nor should the roles of female characters (or others) be stereotyped, though we don't think books should be didactic, or in any way message-y. No topics inappropriate for the juvenile, young adult, and middle grade audiences. No plays." Published *A Year Down Yonder*, by Richard Peck; and *The Missing Mitten Mystery*, by Steven Kellog.
How to Contact: *Agented submissions only.* Query with SASE. Accepts unsolicited queries for longer works and unsolicited mss for picture books. Responds in 3 months to queries. No simultaneous submissions. Sometimes comments on rejected mss.
Payment/Terms: Pays royalty. Average advance: varies. Book catalog for 9×12 SAE with 4 first-class stamps.

A **DIAL PRESS**, Bantam Dell Publishing Group, Random House, Inc., 1745 Broadway, New York NY 10019. (212)782-9000. Fax: (212)782-9523. Website: www.randomhouse.com/bantamdell/. **Contact:** Susan Kamil, vice president, editorial director. Estab. 1924. Averages 6-12 total titles/year.
Needs: Literary (general). Published *Mary and O'Neil* (short story collection); and *Niagara Falls Over Again* (fiction).
How to Contact: *Agented submissions only.* Accepts simultaneous submissions.
Payment/Terms: Pays royalty on retail price. Offers advance. Publishes ms 18 months after acceptance.

A **DOUBLEDAY**, Doubleday Broadway Publishing Group, Random House, Inc., 1745 Broadway, New York NY 10019. (212)782-9000. Fax: (212)782-9700. Website: www.randomhouse.com. Estab. 1897. Publishes hardcover originals. Averages 70 total titles/year.
Needs: Adventure, confession, ethnic, experimental, feminist, gay/lesbian, historical, humor, literary, mainstream/contemporary, religious, short story collections.
How to Contact: *Agented submissions only.* No simultaneous submissions.
Payment/Terms: Pays royalty on retail price. Offers advance. Publishes ms 1 year after acceptance.

A **▓** **DOUBLEDAY CANADA**, Random House of Canada, A Division of Random House, Inc., 1 Toronto Street, Suite 300, Toronto ON M5C 2V6 Canada. (416)364-4449. Website: www.randomhouse.ca. Publishes hardcover and paperback originals. Averages 50 total titles/year.
Imprint(s): Seal Books (mass market publisher); Anchor Canada (trade paperback publisher).
How to Contact: Does not accept unsolicited mss. *Agented submissions only.*

A **◎** **DOUBLEDAY RELIGIOUS PUBLISHING**, Doubleday Broadway Publishing Group, Random House, Inc., 1540 Broadway, New York NY 10036. (212)354-6500. Fax: (212)782-3735. Website: www.randomhouse.com. **Contact:** Eric Major, vice president, religious division; Trace Murphy, executive editor; Andrew Corbin, editor. Estab. 1897. Publishes hardcover and trade paperback originals and reprints. Averages 45-50 total titles/year.
Imprint(s): Image Books, Anchor Bible Commentary, Anchor Bible Reference, Galilee, New Jerusalem Bible.
Needs: Religious.
How to Contact: *Agented submissions only.* Responds in 3 months to proposals. Accepts simultaneous submissions.
Payment/Terms: Pays 7½-15% royalty. Offers advance. Publishes ms 1 year after acceptance. Book catalog for SAE with 3 first-class stamps.

◪ **◎** **DOWN THERE PRESS**, Subsidiary of Open Enterprises Cooperative, Inc., 938 Howard Street #101, San Francisco CA 94103-4100. E-mail: downtherepress@excite.com. Website: www.goodvibes.com/dtp/dtp.html. **Contact:** Leigh Davidson, managing editor. Estab. 1975. Small independent press with part-time staff; part of a large worker-owned cooperative. "Devoted exclusively to the publication of sexual health books for children and adults. We publish books that are innovative, lively and practical, providing realistic physiological information with nonjudgmental techniques for strengthing sexual communication." Publishes paperback originals. Books: Web offset printing; perfect binding; some illustrations. Average print order: 5,000. First novel print order: 3,000-5,000. **Published new writers within the last year.** Averages 1-2 total titles, 1 fiction title/year. Member, Publishers Marketing Association and Northern California Book Publicity and Marketing Association.

Imprint(s): Yes Press, Red Alder Books and Passion Press (audio division).

Needs: Erotica, feminist, sex education/sex-positive nonfiction. Published *Herotica 6*, edited by Marcy Sheiner (anthology); *Sex Spoken Here: Erotic Reading Circle Stories*, edited by Carol Queen and Jack Davis (anthology); *Any 2 People Kissing*, by Kate Dominic (short stories, erotic); and *Sex Toy Tales*, edited by A. Semans and Cathy Weeks.

How to Contact: Accepts unsolicited mss. Prefers book proposals rather than entire ms. Accepts queries by mail. Include estimated word count. Send SASE for return of ms or send a disposable ms and SASE for reply only. Responds in 9 months to mss. Accepts simultaneous submissions. No electronic submissions. Sometimes comments on rejected mss.

Payment/Terms: Pays royalty. Publishes ms 18 months after acceptance. Book catalog for #10 SASE; ms guidelines for #10 SASE.

N **▨** **◻** **◎** **DRAGON MOON PRESS**, Box 64312, 5512 Fourth St. NW, Calgary AB T2K 6J0 Canada. E-mail: publisher@dragonmoonpress.com. Website: www.dragonmoonpress.com. **Contact:** Gwen Gades, publisher; Christine Mains, submissions editor. Estab. 1994. "Dragon Moon Press is dedicated to new and exciting voices in science fiction and fantasy. At Dragon Moon Press, we continue to improve how we do business and continue to seek out quality manuscripts and authors." Publishes trade paperback and electronic originals. Books: 60 lb. offset paper; offset and POD printing perfect-bound. Average print order: 250-1,000. **Published 1 debut author within the last year.** Plans 2 first novels this year. Averages 1-2 total titles, 2 fiction titles/year. "Distributed through Ingram Distribution Services. Promoted locally, through authors, and promoted online at leading retail bookstores like Amazon.com, Barnes & Noble.com, Chapters, etc."

Imprint(s): Dragon Moon Press; Gwen Gades, Christine Mains, editors.

Needs: Fantasy, science fiction (hard science/technological, soft/sociological). "We are publishing more trade paperbacks because we can print short runs as needed and not invest so heavily in traditional offset printing. We are also receiving many high quality manuscripts that we feel deserve to be published." Published *The Dragon Reborn*, by Kathleen H. Nelson (fantasy). Publishes *MOREVI: The Chronicles of Rafe and Askana*, epic fantasy series by Lisa Lee and Tee Morris.

How to Contact: Accepts unsolicited mss. Query with SASE or submit proposal package including outline, 3 sample chapter(s), synopsis. Include estimated word count, brief bio, list of publishing credits. Responds in 4 months to queries; 4 months to proposals; 8 months to mss. Accepts simultaneous submissions. No electronic submissions, submissions on disk.

Payment/Terms: Pays 8-15% royalty on retail price. Publishes ms 2 years after acceptance. Book catalog online; ms guidelines online.

Advice: "First, be patient. Read our guidelines at dragonmoonpress.com. Not following our submission guidelines can be grounds for automatic rejection. Second, we view publishing as a family affair. Be ready to participate in the process, and show some enthusiasm and understanding for what we do. Remember also, this is a business and not about egos, so keep yours on a leash! The reward with Dragon Moon Press is not so much in money as it is in the experience and the satisfaction in the final work. Show us a great story with well-developed characters and plot lines, show us that you are interested in participating in marketing and developing as an author, and show us your desire to create a great book and you may just find yourself published by Dragon Moon Press."

N **▨** **DRAWN & QUARTERLY**, P.O. Box 48056, Montreal QC H2V 4S8 Canada. E-mail: chris@drawnandquarterly.com. Website: www.drawnandquarterly.com. **Contact:** Chris Oliveras.

Needs: Graphic novels, comic books, comic book series, anthology submissions.

How to Contact: Electronic and web submissions preferred. Guidelines on website.

▨ **◻** **DREAMCATCHER PUBLISHING INC.**, One Market Square, Suite 306 Dockside, Saint John NB E2L 4Z6 Canada. (506)632-4008. E-mail: dcpub@fundy.net. Website: www.dreamcatcher.nb.ca. **Contact:** Yvonne Wilson, editor-in-chief (trade books: novels, occasional collections of short stories); Joan Allison (children's). Estab. 1998. "Dreamcatcher Publishing Inc. is small, independent and literary. We look for, but are not limited to, the work of writers from eastern Canada." Publishes paperback originals. Books: comutell coated paper; web printing; perfect binding; illustrations by artists with BFA. Average print order: 2-3,000. First novel print order: 1,000. **Published 2 debut authors within the last year.** Plans 1-2 first novels this year. Averages 4 total titles, 3 fiction titles/year. Distributes titles through CanBook (Toronto).

Needs: Children's/juvenile, humor, literary, mainstream/contemporary, romance (contemporary), short story collections, young adult (adventure, fantasy/science, mystery/suspense, problem novels), Regional (Atlantic Canada). Wants fiction with "Green" themes, "Hope" and children's stories. Published *Strange Lights at Midnight*, by Allison Mitchem (novel); *By Invitation Only*, by Gail Higgins (poetry); *The Ragged Believers*, by Robert M. Rayner (novel).

How to Contact: Query with SASE. Accepts queries by e-mail, fax, phone. Include estimated word count, brief

bio, list of publishing credits. Responds in 2 weeks to queries. Often comments on rejected mss.
Payment/Terms: Pays 7-12% royalty. Publishes ms 1-2 years after acceptance. Book catalog online; ms guidelines online.
Advice: "Be business-like. Phone first, but not until you have a well-prepared manuscript ready to show us. Our interests in fiction are eclectic, but we may say no. Never ask if we will look at an unfinished manuscript to see if it is worth finishing. Spelling and punctuation count."

DUFOUR EDITIONS, P.O. Box 7, Chester Springs PA 19425. (610)458-5005. Fax: (610)458-5005. Website: www.dufoureditions.com. **Contact:** Thomas Lavoie, associate publisher. Estab. 1948. Small independent publisher, tending toward literary fiction. Publishes hardcover originals, trade paperback originals and reprints. Averages 3-4 total titles, 1-2 fiction titles/year. Promotes titles through catalogs, reviews, direct mail, sales reps, Book Expo and wholesalers.
Needs: Literary, short story collections. "We like books that are slightly off-beat, different and well-written." Published *Tideland*, by Mitch Cullin; *The Case of the Pederast's Wife*, by Clare Elfman; *Last Love in Constantinople*, by Milorad Pavic; *Night Sounds and Other Stories*, by Karen Shoemaker; *From the Place in the Valley Deep in the Forest*, by Mitch Cullen (short stories); and *Beyond Faith and Other Stories*, by Tom Noyes.
How to Contact: Query with SASE. Accepts queries by e-mail, fax. Include estimated word count, brief bio, list of publishing credits. Responds in 3 months. Accepts simultaneous submissions.
Payment/Terms: Pays 6-10% royalty on net receipts. Average advance: $100-500. Publishes ms 18 months after acceptance. Book catalog free.

DUNDURN PRESS, LTD., 8 Market St., Suite 200, Toronto ON M5E 1M6 Canada. (416)214-5544. Website: www.dundurn.com. **Contact:** Acquisitions Editor. Estab. 1972. Dundurn prefers work by Canadian authors. First-time authors are welcome. Publishes hardcover and trade paperback originals and reprints. Averages 15 fiction titles a year.
Needs: Literary, mystery, young adult.
How to Contact: Query with SASE or submit sample chapter(s), synopsis, author bio. Responds in 1-2 months to queries. Accepts simultaneous submissions. No electronic submissions.
Payment/Terms: Pays 10% royalty on net receipts. Publishes ms an average of 1 year after acceptance. Ms guidelines online.

THOMAS DUNNE BOOKS, St. Martin's Press, 175 Fifth Ave., New York NY 10010. (212)674-5151. Website: www.stmartins.com. **Contact:** Tom Dunne. Publishes wide range of fiction and nonfiction. Publishes hardcover originals, trade paperback originals and reprints. Averages 210 total titles/year.
Needs: Mainstream/contemporary, mystery, suspense, thrillers; women's. Published *Winter's Solstice*, by Rosamunde Pilcher; and *Marines of Autumn*, by James Brady.
How to Contact: Does not accept unsolicited mss. Agents submit query or submit synopsis and 100 sample pages. Responds in 2 months to queries. Accepts simultaneous submissions.
Payment/Terms: Pays royalty. Pays 10-15% royalty on retail price for hardcover, 7½% for paperback. Average advance: varies. Publishes ms 1 year after acceptance. Book catalog free; ms guidelines free.

DUTTON CHILDREN'S BOOKS, Penguin Group, Inc., 345 Hudson St., New York NY 10014. (212)414-3700. Fax: (212)414-3397. Website: www.penguin.com. **Contact:** Stephanie Owens Lurie, president and publisher (picture books and fiction); Donna Brooks, editorial director (books for all ages with distinctive narrative style); Lucia Monfried, senior editor (picture books, easy-to-read books, fiction); Michele Coppola, editor (picture books and fiction); Julie Strauss-Gabel, editor (picture books and fiction); Alissa Heyman, associate editor (fiction, poetry, picture books); Meredith Mundy Wasinger, editor (picture books, fiction and nonfiction). Estab. 1852. Dutton Children's Books publishes fiction and nonfiction for readers ranging from preschoolers to young adults on a variety of subjects. Publishes hardcover originals as well as novelty formats. Averages 100 total titles/year.
Needs: Dutton Children's Books has a diverse, general interest list that includes picture books; easy-to-read books; and fiction for all ages, from "first chapter" books to young adult readers. Published *Miss Bindergarter Takes a Field Trip with Kindergarten*, by Joseph Slate, illustrated by Ashley Wolff (picture book); *The Day the Chickens Went on Strike*, by Erica Silverman, illustrated by Matthew Trueman (picture book); *The Boy Who Spoke Dog*, by Clay Morgan (novel); *Horace Splatty, the Cupcaked Crusader*, by Lawrence David, illustrated by Barry Gott (chapter book); and *12 Again*, by Sue Corbett (novel).
How to Contact: Does not accept unsolicited mss. Query with SASE and letter only.
Payment/Terms: Pays royalty on retail price. Offers advance.

EAKIN PRESS/SUNBELT MEDIA, INC., P.O. Box 90159, Austin TX 78709-0159. (512)288-1771. Fax: (512)288-1813. Website: www.eakinpress.com. **Contact:** Virginia Messer, publisher. Estab. 1978. Eakin specializes in Texana and Western Americana for juveniles and adults. Publishes hardcover and paperback originals and reprints. Averages 60 total titles/year.
Imprint(s): Nortex; Sunbelt/Eakin; Eakin Press, Penpoint Press.
Needs: Historical, juvenile. Juvenile fiction for grades K-12, preferably relating to Texas and the Southwest or

contemporary. Nonfiction adult with Texas or Southwest theme. Published *Inside Russia*, by Inez Jeffry.

How to Contact: Accepts unsolicited mss. Query or submit outline/synopsis and sample chapters. Agented fiction 5%. Responds in 3 months to queries. Accepts simultaneous submissions.

Payment/Terms: Pays royalty. Pays 10-12-15% royalty on net sales. Publishes ms 18 months after acceptance. Book catalog for $1.25; ms guidelines online.

Advice: "Only fiction with strong Southwest theme. We receive around 1,200 queries or unsolicited mss a year."

THE ECCO PRESS, HarperCollins, 10 E. 53rd St., New York NY 10022. (212)207-7000. Fax: (212)702-2460. Website: www.harpercollins.com. **Contact:** Daniel Halpern, editor-in-chief. Estab. 1970. Publishes hardcover and trade paperback originals and reprints. Books: acid-free paper; offset printing; Smythe-sewn binding; occasional illustrations. First novel print order: 3,000 copies. Averages 60 total titles, 20 fiction titles/year.

Needs: Literary, short story collections. "We can publish possibly one or two original novels a year." Published *Blonde*, by Joyce Carol Oates; *Pitching Around Fidel*, by S.L. Price.

How to Contact: Does not accept unsolicited mss. Query with SASE.

Payment/Terms: Pays royalty. Average advance: negotiable. Publishes ms 1 year after acceptance. Book catalog free; ms guidelines free.

Advice: "We are always interested in first novels and feel it's important that they be brought to the attention of the reading public."

ECW PRESS, 2120 Queen St. E., Suite 200, Toronto ON M4E 1E2 Canada. (416)694-3348. Fax: (416)698-9906. E-mail: info@ecwpress.com. Website: www.ecwpress.com. **Contact:** Jack David, publisher. Estab. 1979. Publishes hardcover and trade paperback originals. Averages 60 total titles/year.

Needs: Literary, mystery, poetry, short story collections, suspense.

How to Contact: Visit company website to view submission guidelines. Accepts simultaneous submissions.

Payment/Terms: Pays 8-12% royalty on net receipts. Average advance: $300-5,000. Publishes ms 18 months after acceptance. Book catalog and ms guidelines free; ms guidelines online.

Advice: "Make sure to include return postage (SASE, IRC if outside of Canada) if you wish your material to be returned."

EDGE SCIENCE FICTION AND FANTASY PUBLISHING, Box 1714, Calgary AB T2P 2L7 Canada. (403)254-0160. Fax: (403)254-0456. E-mail: editor@edgewebsite.com. Website: www.edgewebsite.com. **Contact:** Cheyenne Grewe, editorial manager (science fiction/fantasy). Estab. 1996. "We are an independent publisher of science fiction and fantasy novels in hard cover or trade paperback format. We produce high-quality books with lots of attention to detail and lots of marketing effort. We want to encourage, produce and promote thought-provoking and fun-to-read science fiction and fantasy literature by 'Bringing the magic alive: one world at a time' (as our motto says) with each new book released." Publishes hardcover and trade paperback originals. Books: natural offset paper; offset/web printing; HC/perfect binding; b&w illustration only. Average print order: 2,000-3,000. Plans 4 first novels this year. Averages 2-4 total titles/year. Member of Book Publishers Association of Alberta (BPAA), Independent Publishers Association of Canada (IPAC), Publisher's Marketing Association (PMA), Small Press Center.

Imprint(s): Edge, Alien Vistas, Riverbend.

Needs: Fantasy (space fantasy, sword and sorcery), science fiction (hard science/technological, soft/sociological). "We are looking for all types of fantasy and science fiction, except juvenile/young adult, horror, erotica, religious fiction, short stories, dark/gruesome fantasy, or poetry." Published *Throne Price*, by Lynda Williams and Alison Sinclair (science fantasy); *Keaen*, by Till Noever (fantasy); and *Orbital Burn, by K.A. Bedford*.

How to Contact: Accepts unsolicited mss. Query with SASE or submit outline, 3 sample chapter(s), synopsis. Check website for guidelines or send SAE & IRCS for same. Include estimated word count. Responds in 1 month to queries; 1 month to proposals; 4-5 months to mss. No simultaneous submissions, electronic submissions. Rarely comments on rejected mss.

Payment/Terms: Pays 10% royalty on wholesale price. Average advance: negotiable. Publishes ms 18 months after acceptance. Ms guidelines online.

Advice: "Send us your best, polished, completed manuscript. Use proper manuscript format. Take the time before you submit to get a critique from people who can offer you useful advice. When in doubt, visit our website for helpful resources, FAQs and other tips."

EERDMANS BOOKS FOR YOUNG READERS, William B. Eerdmans Publishing Co., 255 Jefferson Ave. SE, Grand Rapids MI 49503. (616)459-4591. Fax: (616)459-6540. **Contact:** Judy Zylstra, editor. Publishes picture books and middle reader and young adult fiction and nonfiction. Averages 12-15 total titles/year.

Needs: Juvenile, picture books, young adult, middle reader. Published *The Enemy Has a Face*, by Gloria Miklowitz.

How to Contact: Submit complete mss for picture books and novels or biographies under 200 pages with SASE. For longer books, send query letter and 3 or 4 sample chapters with SASE. Responds in 6 weeks to queries. Accepts simultaneous submissions.

Payment/Terms: Pays 5-7½% royalty on retail price. Publishes middle reader and YA books in 1 year; publishes picture books in 2-3 years. Book catalog for #10 SASE.

◨ ◎ ⬛ **WILLIAM B. EERDMANS PUBLISHING CO.**, 255 Jefferson Ave. SE, Grand Rapids MI 49503. (616)459-4591. Fax: (616)459-6540. Website: www.eerdmans.com. **Contact:** Jon Pott, editor-in-chief, fiction editor (adult fiction); Judy Zylstra, fiction editor (children). Estab. 1911. "Although Eerdmans publishes some regional books and other nonreligious titles, it is essentially a religious publisher whose titles range from the academic to the semi-popular. We are a midsize independent publisher. We publish the occasional adult novel, and these tend to engage deep spiritual issues from a Christian perspective." Publishes hardcover and paperback originals and reprints. **Published some debut authors within the last year.** Averages 120-130 total titles, 6-8 (mostly for children) fiction titles/year.

● Wm. B. Eerdmans Publishing Co.'s titles have won awards from the American Library Association and The American Bookseller's Association.

Imprint(s): Eerdmans Books for Young Readers.

Needs: Religious (children's, general, fantasy). Published *I Wonder as I Wander*, by Gwenyth Swain, illustrated by Ronald Himler; *Gilgamesh the Herd*, by Geraldine McCaughrean, illustrated by David Parkins; and *The Enemy Has a Face*, by Gloria D. Miklowitz (young adult); *Down in the Piney Woods* and *Mariah's Pond*, by Ethel Footman Smothers.

How to Contact: Accepts unsolicited mss. Query with SASE. Include brief bio, list of publishing credits. Send SASE for return of ms or send a disposable ms and SASE for reply only. Agented fiction 5%. Responds in 6 weeks to queries. Accepts simultaneous submissions. Sometimes comments on rejected mss.

Payment/Terms: Pays royalty. Publishes ms usually within 1 year after acceptance. Book catalog free; ms guidelines free.

Advice: "Our readers are educated and fairly sophisticated, and we are looking for novels with literary merit."

ELECTRIC WORKS PUBLISHING, 605 Ave. C.E., Bismarck ND 58501. (701)255-0356. Website: www.electricpublishing.com. **Contact:** James R. Bohe, editor-in-chief. Publishes digital books. **Published 70% debut authors within the last year.** Averages 15 total titles/year.

Needs: Adventure, ethnic, experimental, fantasy, gothic, historical, horror, humor, juvenile, literary, mainstream/contemporary, military/war, multicultural, multimedia, mystery, occult, plays, poetry in translation, regional, religious, romance, science fiction, short story collections (of 40,000 words or more), spiritual, sports, suspense, western, young adult. Published *Felling of the Son*, by Monette Bebow-Reinhard; *Marzipan*, by George Laidlaw.

How to Contact: *Electronic submissions only.* Submit ms in digital format. Responds in 5 months to queries. Accepts simultaneous submissions, electronic submissions, submissions on disk.

Payment/Terms: Pays royalty on wholesale price. Publishes ms 3 months after acceptance. Book catalog and ms guidelines online.

◨ **EMPIRE PUBLISHING SERVICE**, P.O. Box 1344, Studio City CA 91614-0344. Estab. 1960. Midsize publisher with related imprints. Publishes hardcover reprints and trade paperback originals and reprints. Book: paper varies; offset printing; binding varies. Average print order: 5,000-10,000. First novel print order: 2,500-5,000. **Published 2 debut authors within the last year.** Averages 40 total titles, 5 fiction titles/year. Distributes and promotes titles by "Sales & Marketing Distribution offices in five countries."

Imprint(s): Paul Mould Publishing, Paul Mould, editor (historical); Gaslight Publications (Sherlock Holmes); Collectors Publications (erotica).

Needs: Historical (pre-18th century), mystery (Sherlock Holmes). Plans anthology of Sherlock Holmes short stories. Published *House Calls*, by Lawrence Brown (historical, debut author).

How to Contact: Does not accept unsolicited mss. Query with SASE. Include estimated word count, brief bio, list of publishing credits, general background. Agented fiction 5%. Responds in 1 month. No simultaneous submissions, electronic submissions, submissions on disk.

Payment/Terms: Pays 6-10% royalty on retail price. Average advance: variable. Publishes ms up to 2 years after acceptance. Book catalog for #10 SASE; ms guidelines for $1 or #10 SASE.

Advice: "Send query with SASE for only the type of material we publish, historical and Sherlock Holmes."

⬛ ◎ ◭ **EOS**, HarperCollins, 10 E. 53rd St., New York NY 10022. (212)207-7000. E-mail: eossubs@harpercollins.com. Website: www.eosbooks.com. **Contact:** Diana Gill, senior editor. Estab. 1998. Publishes hardcover originals, trade and mass market paperback originals and reprints. Averages 40-46 total titles, 40 fiction titles/year.

Needs: Fantasy, science fiction. Published *The Isle of Battle*, by Sean Russell (fantasy); *Trapped*, by James Alan Gardner.

How to Contact: Does not accept unsolicited mss. *Agented submissions only. No unsolicited submissions.* Accepts

---

INTERESTED IN A PARTICULAR GENRE? Check our sections for: **Mystery/Suspense**, page 68; **Romance**, page 80; **Science Fiction/Fantasy & Horror**, page 90.

queries by e-mail. Include list of publishing credits, brief synopsis. Agented fiction 99%. Responds in 6 months to queries.

Payment/Terms: Pays royalty on retail price. Average advance: variable. Publishes ms 18-24 months after acceptance. Ms guidelines for #10 SASE.

Advice: "Know the field and our guidelines. Getting an agent is best. No unsolicited submissions. Query via e-mail only."

◐ ⊚ FAITH KIDZ BOOKS, Cook Communications Ministries, 4050 Lee Vance View, Colorado Springs CO 80918. Fax: (719)536-3265. Website: www.cookministries.com. **Contact:** Heather Gemmen, senior editor. "Faith Kidz Books publishes works of children's inspirational titles, ages 1-12, with a clear biblical value to influence children's spiritual growth." Publishes hardcover and paperback originals. Averages 40-50 total titles/year.

Needs: Historical, juvenile, picture books, religious, toddler books. "Picture books, devotionals, Bible storybooks, for an age range of 1-12. We're particularly interested in materials for beginning readers."

How to Contact: Does not accept unsolicited mss. Query with SASE. Previously published or agented authors preferred. Responds in 6 months to queries. Accepts simultaneous submissions.

Payment/Terms: Pays one flat fee. Offers advance. Publishes ms 18 months after acceptance.

ℕ FANTAGRAPHICS BOOKS, 7563 Lake City Way NE, Seattle WA 98115. Website: www.fantagraphics.com.

Needs: Graphic novels "for thinking readers." No mainstream genres—superhero, vigilante, horror, fantasy, or science fiction. Complete packages only—both art and script.

How to Contact: Send ms via postal mail with SASE and cover letter.

Payment/Terms: Allow 2-3 months for response. Ms guidelines on website.

Ⓐ FARRAR, STRAUS & GIROUX, 19 Union Square West, New York NY 10003. (212)741-6900. Publishes hardcover and trade paperback books. Averages 180 total titles/year.

Needs: Literary.

How to Contact: Responds in 2 months to queries; 2 months to proposals.

Payment/Terms: Ms guidelines free.

◯ ⊚ ▼ FARRAR, STRAUS & GIROUX BOOKS FOR YOUNG READERS, Farrar Straus Giroux, Inc., 19 Union Square W., New York NY 10003. (212)741-6900. Fax: (212)633-2427. **Contact:** Wesley Adams, senior editor (children's); Beverly Reingold, executive editor (children's); Robert Mayes, editor (children's). Estab. 1946. "We publish original and well-written materials for all ages." Publishes hardcover originals and trade paperback reprints. **Published some debut authors within the last year.** Averages 75 total titles/year.

Imprint(s): Frances Foster Books, edited by Frances Foster (children's); Melanie Kroupa Books, edited by Melanie Kroupa (children's).

Needs: Children's/juvenile, juvenile, picture books, young adult, nonfiction. "Do not query picture books; just send manuscript. Do not fax queries or manuscripts." Published *Hole in my Life*, by Jack Gantos, *George Washington's Teeth*, by Deborah Chandra and Madeline Comora, illustrated by Brock Cole; *Holes*, by Louis Sachar; *The Trolls*, by Polly Horvath; and *Tribute to Another Dead Rock Star*, by Randy Powell.

How to Contact: Query with SASE. Include brief bio, list of publishing credits. Agented fiction 25%. Responds in 2 months. Accepts simultaneous submissions. No electronic submissions, submissions on disk.

Payment/Terms: Pays royalty. Pays 2-6% royalty on retail price for paperbacks, 3-10% for hardcovers. Average advance: $3,000-25,000. Publishes ms 18 months after acceptance. Book catalog for 9 × 12 SAE with $1.87 postage; ms guidelines for #10 SASE.

Advice: "Study our list to avoid sending something inappropriate. Send query letters for long manuscripts; don't ask for editorial advice (just not possible, unfortunately); and send SASEs!"

Ⓐ FARRAR, STRAUS & GIROUX PAPERBACKS, 19 Union Square W., New York NY 10003. (212)741-6900. FSG Paperbacks emphasizes literary nonfiction and fiction, as well as poetry. Publishes hardcover and trade paperback originals and reprints. Averages 180 total titles/year.

Needs: Literary. Published *The Corrections*, by Jonathon Franzen; and *The Haunting of L.*, by Howard Norman.

How to Contact: Does not accept unsolicited mss.

FC2, Department of English, FSU, Tallahassee FL 32306-1580. (850)644-2260. E-mail: fc2@english.fsu.edu. Website: fc2.org. **Contact:** R.M. Berry, publisher (fiction); Brenda L. Mills, managing editor. Estab. 1974. Publisher of innovative fiction. Publishes hardcover and paperback originals. Books: perfect/Smyth binding; illustrations. Average print order: 2,200. **Published new writers within the last year.** Plans 2 first novels this year. Averages 6 total titles, 6 fiction titles/year. Titles distributed through Northwestern U.P.

Needs: Experimental, feminist, gay/lesbian, innovative; modernist/postmodern; avant-garde; anarchist; minority; cyberpunk. Published *Book of Lazarus*, by Richard Grossman; *Is It Sexual Harassment Yet?*, by Cris Mazza; *Liberty's Excess*, by Lidia Yuknavitch; *Aunt Rachel's Fur*, by Raymond Federman.

How to Contact: Accepts unsolicited mss. Query with SASE or submit outline, publishing history, synopsis, author bio. Send queries to: FC2, Unit for Contemporary Literature, Illinois State University, 109 Fairchild Hall,

Normal IL 61790-4241. Include brief bio, list of publishing credits. Agented fiction 5%. Responds in 3 weeks to queries; 2-6 months to mss. Accepts simultaneous submissions. Often comments on rejected mss.
Payment/Terms: Pays 10% royalty. Publishes ms 1-3 years after acceptance. Ms guidelines online.
Advice: "Be familiar with our list."

◎ **THE FEMINIST PRESS AT THE CITY UNIVERSITY OF NEW YORK**, 365 Fifth Ave., Suite 5406, New York NY 10016. (212)817-7915. Fax: (212)817-1593. E-mail: jcasella@gc.cuny.edu. Website: www.feministpress.org. **Contact:** Jean Casella, publisher. Estab. 1970. Small, nonprofit literary and educational publisher. "The Feminist Press publishes only fiction reprints by classic American women authors and translations of distinguished international women writers." Publishes hardcover and trade paperback originals and reprints. Publishes no original fiction; exceptions are anthologies and international works. "We use an acid-free paper, perfect-bind our books, four color covers; and some cloth for library sales if the book has been out of print for some time; we shoot from the original text when possible. We always include a scholarly and literary afterword, since we are introducing a text to a new audience. Average print run: 2,500." Averages 15-20 total titles, 4-8 fiction titles/year. Member, CLMP, Small Press Association. Distributes titles through Consortium Book Sales and Distribution. Promotes titles through author tours, advertising, exhibits and conferences. Charges "permission fees (reimbursement)."
Needs: Ethnic, feminist, gay/lesbian, literary, short story collections, women's. "The Feminist Press publishes only fiction reprints by classic American women authors and imports and translations of distinguished international women writers. Absolutely no original fiction is considered." Needs fiction by "U.S. women of color writers from 1920-1970 who have fallen out of print." Published *Apples From the Desert*, by Savyon Liebrecht (short stories, translation); *The Parish and the Hill*, by Mary Doyle Curran (fiction reprint); *Allegra Maud Goldman*, by Edith Konecky (fiction, reprint); and *Still Alive*, by Ruth Kluger (memoir).
How to Contact: Does not accept unsolicited mss. Query by e-mail only to jcasella@gc.cuny.edu; limit 200 words with 'submission' as subject line. Include estimated word count, brief bio, list of publishing credits. Responds in 1 month to queries; 6 months to proposals. Accepts simultaneous submissions, electronic submissions.
Payment/Terms: Pays 10% royalty on net receipts. Pays 5-10 author's copies. Average advance: $250-500. Publishes ms 18-24 months after acceptance. Book catalog online; ms guidelines online.

Ⓝ ◨ **FENN PUBLISHING COMPANY LTD.**, H.B. Fenn and Company Ltd., 34 Nixon Rd., Bolton ON L7E 1W2 Canada. (905)951-6600. Fax: (905)951-6601. Website: www.hbfenn.com. **Contact:** C. Jordan Fenn, publisher. Estab. 1982.
How to Contact: Accepts unsolicited mss. Submit complete ms. Include brief bio, list of publishing credits. Responds in 3 months. Accepts simultaneous submissions.
Payment/Terms: Pays royalty. Publishes ms 1 year after acceptance.

Ⓝ ◔ **FIRST BOOKS**, 6750 SW Franklin St. Suite A, Portland OR 97223. (503)968-6777. Website: www.firstbooks.com; www.franklinstreetbooks.com. **Contact:** Jeremy Solomon and Virginia Linman, editors. Estab. 1988. Publishes hardcover originals, paperback originals and paperback reprints. **Published 30+ debut authors within the last year.** Averages 30-60 total titles, 15 fiction titles/year. Distributes through Ingram, Butler & Taylor, Koen.
Imprint(s): Franklin Street Books
Needs: Published *Widow of Que-Moy*, by Jeff Chen (historical romance); *The Pink Eyed Detective*, by Greg Moderich (mystery); *All is Safely Gathered In*, by Peter Gray (English novel).
How to Contact: Does not accept or return unsolicited mss. Query with SASE. Accepts queries by e-mail, mail.

Ⓝ ◎ **FIVE STAR PUBLISHING**, Gale, 295 Kennedy Memorial Drive, Waterville ME 04901. (207)859-1000. Fax: (207)859-1006. E-mail: fivestar@gale.com. **Contact:** Russell Davis, editor. Estab. 1996. Publishes hardcover originals, reissues select titles as trade paperbacks. **Published 50% debut authors within the last year.**
Needs: Romance (including all sub-genres, chick lit and tart noir), literary women's fiction. "We highly recommend you read at least one of our more recent titles prior to submitting your work. Innovative new directions in storytelling and a fresh approach are a must. We want a sophisticated, compelling plot with fully developed characters that create an emotionally genuine story." Published *Chickpea Lover (Not a Cookbook)*, by D-L Nelson (romance); *The Eternal Trust*, by Melinda Rucker Haynes (paranormal romance); *The Education of Ruby Loonfoot*, by Paxton Riddle (historical women's fiction); *The Bluebird House*, by Rae Ellen Lee (contemporary women's fiction).
How to Contact: Agented fiction 40%. Responds in 6 months to queries; 1 year to mss.
Payment/Terms: Pays royalty on wholesale price. Average advance: $1,500-3,000. Publishes ms 1 year after acceptance. Book catalog free; ms guidelines for SASE or by e-mail.
Advice: "Submit your best material—surprise us with a story we haven't heard before. Portray the relationships honestly and directly. We're looking for material that has broad appeal, a distinct voice, and a believable plot with characters the reader will relate to."

◔ ◨ **FORGE AND TOR BOOKS**, Tom Doherty Associates, LLC, 175 Fifth Ave. 14th Floor, New York NY 10010. (212)388-0100. Fax: (212)388-0191. Website: www.tor.com. **Contact:** Melissa Ann Singer, senior editor (general fiction, mysteries, thriller); Patrick Nielsen Hayden, senior editor (science fiction, fantasy). Estab. 1980. "Tor Books are science fiction, fantasy, and horror, and occasionally, related nonfiction. Forge books are everything else—general fiction, historical fiction, mysteries and suspense, women's fiction, and nonfiction. Orb titles are trade paperback reprint editions of science fiction, fantasy and horror books. Publishes hardcover, trade paperback and mass market paperback originals, trade and mass market paperback reprints. **Published some debut authors within the last year.**

- *Kushiel's Dart*, by Jacqueline Carey won the John W. Campbell Memorial Award for Best Novel. See the interview with Jacqueline Carey on page 99 of this edition. Tor was named Best Publisher at the Locus Awards for the 15th consecutive year.

Imprint(s): Orb.

Needs: Historical, horror, mainstream/contemporary, mystery (amateur sleuth, police procedural, private eye/hard-boiled); science fiction, suspense, thriller/espionage, western (frontier saga, traditional), thriller; general fiction and fantasy.

How to Contact: Accepts unsolicited mss. Query with SASE. Include estimated word count, brief bio, list of publishing credits. Agented fiction 95%. Responds in 4 months to proposals. Sometimes comments on rejected mss.

Payment/Terms: Paperback: Pays 6-8% royalty for first-time authors, 8-10% royalty for established authors; Hardcover: Pays 10% first 5,000, 12½% second 5,000, 15% thereafter. Offers advance. Publishes ms 12-18 months after acceptance. Book catalog for 9×12 SAE with 2 first-class stamps.

Advice: "The writing mechanics must be outstanding for a new author to break into today's market."

FORT ROSS INC. RUSSIAN-AMERICAN PUBLISHING PROJECTS, 26 Arthur Place, Yonkers NY 10701. (914)375-6448. Fax: (914)375-6439. E-mail: fort.ross@verizon.net. Website: www.fortross.net. **Contact:** Dr. Vladimir P. Kartsev. Estab. 1992. "We welcome Russian-related manuscripts and books from well-established fantasy and romance novel writers who would like to have their novels translated in Russia and Eastern Europe by our publishing house in cooperation with the local publishers." Publishes paperback originals. **Published 3 debut authors within the last year.** Averages 10 total titles/year.

Needs: Adventure, fantasy (space fantasy, sword and sorcery), horror, mainstream/contemporary, mystery (amateur sleuth, police procedural, private eye/hardboiled), romance (contemporary, futuristic/time travel), science fiction (hard science/technological, soft/sociological), suspense, thriller/espionage.

How to Contact: Does not accept unsolicited mss. Query with SASE. Include estimated word count, brief bio, list of publishing credits. Responds in 1 month. Accepts simultaneous submissions.

Payment/Terms: Pays 4-7% royalty on wholesale price or makes outright purchase of $500-1,500. Average advance: $500-$1,000; negotiable. Publishes ms 1 year after acceptance.

FOUR WALLS EIGHT WINDOWS, 39 W. 14th St., Room 503, New York NY 10011. (212)206-8965. Fax: (212)206-8799. E-mail: edit@4w8w.com. Website: www.4w8w.com. **Contact:** Jofie Ferrari-Adler, editor. Estab. 1987. "We are a small independent publisher." Publishes hardcover originals, trade paperback originals and reprints. Books: quality paper; paper or cloth binding; illustrations sometimes. Average print order: 3,000-7,000. First novel print order: 3,000-5,000. **Published some debut authors within the last year.** Averages 35 total titles, 9 fiction titles/year. Distributes titles through Publisher's Group West, the largest independent distributor in the country. Promotes titles through author tours, bound galleys, select advertising, postcard mailing, etc.

- Four Walls Eight Windows' books have received mention from the *New York Times* as "Notable Books of the Year," and have been nominated for *L.A. Times* fiction and nonfiction prizes.

Needs: Feminist, gay/lesbian, nonfiction.

How to Contact: Does not accept unsolicited mss. Query with SASE. "Query letter accompanied by sample chapter, outline and SASE is best. Useful to know if writer has published elsewhere, and if so, where." Agented fiction 50%. Responds in 2 months to queries. Accepts simultaneous submissions, electronic submissions.

Payment/Terms: Pays royalty on retail or net price, depending on contract. Average advance: variable. Publishes ms 1-2 years after acceptance. Book catalog for 6×9 SAE with 3 first-class stamps.

Advice: "Please read our catalog and/or our website to be sure your work would be compatible with our list."

FRONT STREET, 20 Battery Park Ave., #403, Asheville NC 28801. (828)236-3097. Fax: (828)236-3098. E-mail: contactus@frontstreetbooks.com. Website: www.frontstreetbooks.com. **Contact:** Stephen Roxburgh, president and publisher; Joy Neaves, editor. Estab. 1994. "Small independent publisher of high-quality picture books and literature for children and young adults." Publishes hardcover originals. Averages 10-15 total titles/year. Distributes titles through PGW. Titles promoted on the Internet, in catalog, by sales representatives, at library and education conferences.

- *A Step from Heaven*, by An Na won the Michael L. Printz Award for 2002. Published *Carver: A Life in Poems*, by Marilyn Nelson won a Newbery Honor 2002 and a Coretta Scott King Honor.

Needs: Adventure, children's/juvenile (adventure, animal, fantasy, historical, mystery, sports), fantasy, feminist, historical, humor, juvenile, literary, picture books, science fiction, young adult (adventure, fantasy/science fiction, historical, mystery/suspense, problem novels, sports). Published *Marika*, by Andrea Cheng (YA); *Stray Voltage*, by Eugenie Doyle (YA); *My Mommy*, by Susan Paradis; (children's).

How to Contact: Accepts unsolicited mss. No longer accepting unsolicited picture books mss. Query with SASE or submit complete ms. Accepts queries by e-mail, fax. Include brief bio, list of publishing credits. Send SASE for return of ms or send a disposable ms and SASE for reply only. Agented fiction 10%. Responds in 1 month to

queries; 3 months to mss. Accepts simultaneous submissions. No electronic submissions.
Payment/Terms: Pays royalty on retail price. Offers advance. Publishes ms 1 year after acceptance. Book catalog online; ms guidelines online.

FYOS ENTERTAINMENT, LLC, P.O. Box 2021, Philadelphia PA 19103. (215)972-8067. Fax: (215)972-8076. Website: www.fyos.com. **Contact:** Tonya Marie Evans, editor-in-chief (poetry, African-America fiction); Susan Borden Evans, general manager (African-American fiction). Publishes hardcover originals and trade paperback originals. Averages 2-3 total titles/year.

Needs: Multicultural, poetry, short story collections. "We concentrate acquisition efforts on poetry and fiction of interest primarily to the African-American reader. We are looking for thought-provoking, well-written work that offers a 'quick and entertaining' read. Published *Seasons of Her*, by T. Evans; *SHINE!*, by T. Evans.

How to Contact: Query with SASE. Responds in 1-3 months to queries; 3-6 months to mss. Accepts simultaneous submissions.

Payment/Terms: Pays 10-15% royalty on retail price or a 60 (publisher)/40 (author) split of net receipts. Will also consider outright purchase opportunities. Publishes ms 1 year after acceptance. Book catalog for #10 SASE; ms guidelines online.

Advice: "Neatness counts! Present yourself and your work in a highly professional manner."

GASLIGHT PUBLICATIONS, Empire Publishing Services, P.O. Box 1344, Studio City CA 91614. (818)784-8918. **Contact:** Simon Waters, fiction editor (Sherlock Holmes only). Estab. 1960. Publishes hardcover and paperback originals and reprints. Books: paper varies; offset printing; binding varies; illustrations. Average print order: 5,000. **Published 1 debut author within the last year.** Averages 4-12 total titles, 2-4 fiction titles/year. Promotes titles through sales reps, trade, library, etc.

Needs: Sherlock Holmes only. Published *On the Scent with Sherlock Holmes*, by Walter Shepherd; *Sherlock Holmes, The Complete Bagel Street Saga*, by Robert L. Fish; and *Subcutaneously: My Dear Watson*, by Jack Tracy (all Sherlock Holmes). Publishes the Sherlock Holmes Mystery series.

How to Contact: Accepts unsolicited mss. Query with SASE. Include estimated word count, brief bio, list of publishing credits. Send SASE for return of ms or send a disposable ms and SASE for reply only. Agented fiction 10%. Responds in 2 weeks to queries; 1 year to mss.

Payment/Terms: Pays 8-10% royalty. Royalty and advance dependent on the material. Publishes ms 1-6 months after acceptance. Book catalog for 9×12 SAE with $2 first-class stamps.

Advice: "Please send only Sherlock Holmes material. Other stuff just wastes time and money."

GAY SUNSHINE PRESS and LEYLAND PUBLICATIONS, P.O. Box 410690, San Francisco CA 94141-0690. Fax: (415)626-1802. Website: www.gaysunshine.com. **Contact:** Winston Leyland, editor. Estab. 1970. Midsize independent press. Publishes hardcover originals, trade paperback originals and reprints. Books: natural paper; perfect-bound; illustrations. Average print order: 5,000-10,000. Averages 3-4 total titles/year.

- Gay Sunshine Press has received a Lambda Book Award for *Gay Roots* (volume I), named "Best Book by a Gay or Lesbian Press," and received grants from the National Endowment for the Arts.

Needs: Erotica, experimental, historical, literary, mystery, science fiction, all gay male material only. "We have a high literary standard for fiction. We desire fiction on gay themes of *high* literary quality and prefer writers who have already had work published in literary magazines. We also publish erotica, short stories and novels." Published *Out in the Castro: Promise, Desire, Activism*, large anthology with 35+ writers, artists (2002).

How to Contact: Does not accept unsolicited mss. Query with SASE. Responds in 6 weeks.

Payment/Terms: Pays royalty or makes outright purchase. Book catalog for $1.

Advice: "We continue to be interested in receiving queries from authors who have book-length manuscripts of high literary quality. We feel it is important that an author know exactly what to expect from our press (promotion, distribution, etc.) before a contract is signed. Before submitting a query or manuscript to a particular press, obtain critical feedback on your manuscript from knowledgeable people. If you alienate a publisher by submitting a manuscript shoddily prepared/typed, or one needing very extensive rewriting, or one which is not in the area of the publisher's specialty, you will surely not get a second chance with that press."

GENESIS PRESS, INC., 315 Third Ave. N, Columbus MS 39701. (662)329-9927. Fax: (662)329-9399. E-mail: books@genesis-press.com. Website: www.genesis-press.com. Publishes hardcover and trade paperback originals and reprints. **Published 50% debut authors within the last year.** Averages 30 total titles/year.

- *Tomorrow's Promise*, by Leslie Esdale won a Gold Pen Award.

Needs: Erotica, ethnic, literary, multicultural, romance, women's. Published *Cherish the Flame*, by Beverly Clark; *No Apologies*, by Seressia Glass.

How to Contact: Query with SASE or submit 3 sample chapter(s), synopsis. Responds in 2 months.

Payment/Terms: Pays 6-12% royalty on invoice price. Average advance: $750-5,000. Publishes ms 1 year after acceptance. Ms guidelines online.

Advice: "Be professional. Always include a cover letter and SASE. Follow the submission guidelines posted on our website or send a SASE for a copy."

LAURA GERINGER BOOKS, HarperCollins Children's Books, 1350 Avenue of the Americas, New York NY 10019. (212)261-6500. Website: www.harperchildrens.com. **Contact:** Laura Geringer, senior vice president/ publisher. "We look for books that are out of the ordinary, authors who have their own definite take, and artists who add a sense of humor to the text." Publishes hardcover originals. **Published some debut authors within the last year.** Averages 15-20 total titles/year.

Needs: Adventure, fantasy, historical, humor, juvenile, literary, picture books, young adult. Published *Regular Guy*, by Sarah Weeks; and *Throwing Smoke*, by Bruce Brooks.

How to Contact: Does not accept unsolicited mss. Query with SASE. Agented fiction 90%. Responds in 3 months.

Payment/Terms: Pays 10-12½% on retail price. Average advance: variable.

Advice: "A mistake writers often make is failing to research the type of books an imprint publishes, therefore sending inappropriate material."

GIVAL PRESS, P.O. Box 3812, Arlington VA 22203. (703)351-0079. Fax: (703)351-0079. E-mail: givalpress@yahoo.com. Website: www.givalpress.com. **Contact:** Robert L. Giron, publisher. Estab. 1998. A small, independent publisher that publishes quality works by a variety of authors from array walks of life. Works are in English, Spanish, and French which have a philosophical or social message. Publishes paperback originals and reprints and e-books. Books: perfect-bound. Average print order: 500. **Published 4 debut authors within the last year.** Plans 2 first novels this year. Member, PMA, Literary Council of Small Presses and Magazines. Distributes books through Ingram and BookSurge.com.

● Received a Bronze Award, 2001 *ForeWord Magazine* for fiction—translation.

Needs: Children's/juvenile (animal), ethnic, gay/lesbian, historical, lesbian, literary, short story collections. "Looking for French books with English translation." Published *Barnyard Buddies I*, by Pamela Brown (children's); *The Gay Herman Melville Reader*, by Ken Schellenberg (fiction); *The Smoke Week: Sept. 9-22, 2001*, by Ellis Avery (memoir).

How to Contact: Does not accept unsolicited mss. Query with SASE or submit outline, 2 sample chapter(s). Reading period open from May to August. Accepts queries by e-mail, mail. Include estimated word count, brief bio, list of publishing credits. Send SASE for return of ms or send a disposable ms and SASE for reply only. Agented fiction 5%. Responds in 4 months to queries.

Payment/Terms: 20 contributor's copies. Offers advance. Publishes ms 1 year after acceptance. Book catalog for SASE and on website; ms guidelines for SASE or on website.

Advice: "Study the types of books we have published—literary works with a message of high quality."

THE GLENCANNON PRESS, P.O. Box 633, Benicia CA 94510. (707)745-3933. Fax: (707)747-0311. E-mail: captjaff@pacbell.net. Website: www.glencannon.com. **Contact:** Bill Harris (maritime, maritime children's). Estab. 1993. "We publish quality books about ships and the sea." Publishes hardcover and paperback originals and hardcover reprints. Books: Smyth: perfect binding; illustrations. Average print order: 1,000. First novel print order: 750. **Published 1 debut author within the last year.** Averages 4-5 total titles, 1 fiction titles/year. Member, PMA, BAIPA. Distributes titles through Quality Books, Ingram and Baker & Taylor. Promotes titles through direct mail, magazine advertising and word of mouth.

Imprint(s): Palo Alto Books (any except maritime); Glencannon Press (merchant marine and Navy); Bill Harris, editor.

Needs: Adventure, children's/juvenile (adventure, fantasy, historical, mystery, preschool/picture book), ethnic (general), historical (maritime), humor, mainstream/contemporary, military/war, mystery, thriller/espionage, western (frontier saga, traditional maritime), young adult (adventure, historical, mystery/suspense, western). Currently emphasizing children's maritime, any age. Published *White Hats*, by Floyd Beaver (navy short stories); and *The Crafty Glencannon*, by Guy Gilpatric (merchant marine short stories).

How to Contact: Accepts unsolicited mss. Submit complete ms. Include brief bio, list of publishing credits. Send SASE for return of ms or send a disposable ms and SASE for reply only. Responds in 2 months. Accepts simultaneous submissions. Often comments on rejected mss.

Payment/Terms: Pays 10-20% royalty. Publishes ms 6-24 months after acceptance. Book catalog online.

Advice: "Write a good story in a compelling style."

DAVID R. GODINE, PUBLISHER, INC., 9 Hamilton Place, Boston MA 02108. (617)451-9600. Fax: (617)350-0250. E-mail: info@godine.com. Website: www.godine.com. **Contact:** President: David R. Godine. Estab. 1970. Small independent publisher (5-person staff). Publishes hardcover and trade paperback originals and reprints. Averages 35 total titles/year.

Imprint(s): Nonpareil Books (trade paperbacks), Verba Mundi (translations), Imago Mundi (photography).

Needs: Children's/juvenile, historical, literary. *No unsolicited mss*

How to Contact: Does not accept unsolicited mss. Query with SASE.

Payment/Terms: Pays royalty on retail price. Publishes ms 3 years after acceptance. Book catalog for 5×8 SAE with 3 first-class stamps.

Advice: "Have your agent contact us. Please no phone queries."

GOOSE LANE EDITIONS, 469 King St., Fredericton, NB E3B 1E5 Canada. (506)450-4251. Fax: (506)459-4991. Website: www.gooselane.com. **Contact:** Laurel Boone, editorial director. Estab. 1954. Publishes hardcover and paperback originals and occasional reprints. Books: some illustrations. Average print order: 3,000. First novel print order: 1,500. Averages 12-14 total titles, 4-5 fiction titles/year. Distributes titles through University of Toronto Press (UTP).

Needs: Literary (novels), mainstream/contemporary, short story collections. "Our needs in fiction never change: Substantial, character-centered literary fiction." Published *Elle*, by Douglas Glover; *A Sharp Tooth in a the Fur*, by Darryl Whitter.

How to Contact: Accepts unsolicited mss. Query with SASE "with Canadian stamps, International Reply Coupons, cash, check, or money order. No U.S. stamps please." Responds in 6 months to queries. No simultaneous submissions.

Payment/Terms: Pays 8-10% royalty on retail price. Average advance: $200-1,000, negotiable.

Advice: "We do not consider submissions from outside Canada."

GRAYWOLF PRESS, 2402 University Ave., Suite 203, St. Paul MN 55114. (651)641-0077. Fax: (651)641-0036. E-mail: wolves@graywolfpress.com. Website: www.graywolfpress.org. **Contact:** Anne Czarniecki, executive editor; Katie Dublinski, editor. Estab. 1974. Growing small literary press, nonprofit corporation. Publishes trade cloth and paperback originals. Books: acid-free quality paper; offset printing; hardcover and soft binding; illustrations occasionally. Average print order: 3,000-10,000. First novel print order: 3,000-7,500. Averages 16 total titles, 4-6 fiction titles/year. Distributes titles nationally through Farrar, Straus, & Giroux. "We have an in-house marketing staff and an advertising budget for all books we publish."

Needs: Literary, short story collections. "Familiarize yourself with our list first." Published *One Vacant Chair*, by Joe Coomer; *The House on Eccles Road*, by Judith Ktchen; *Avoidance*, by Michael Lowenthal; *Operation Monsoon*, by Shona Ramaya.

How to Contact: Query with SASE. "Please do not fax or e-mail queries or submissions." Agented fiction 90%. Responds in 3 months to queries.

Payment/Terms: Pays royalty on retail price. Average advance: $1,000-6,000. Publishes ms 18 months after acceptance. Book catalog free; ms guidelines online.

Advice: "Please review the catalog and submission guidelines being submitting your work. We rarely publish collections or novels by authors who have not published work previously in literary journals or magazines."

GREEN BEAN PRESS, P.O. Box 237, New York NY 10013. (718)965-2076. Fax: (718)965-2076. E-mail: gbpress@earthlink.net. Website: www.greenbeanpress.com. **Contact:** Ian Griffin, editor. Estab. 1993. Publishes paperback originals. Books: acid-free paper; perfect-bound. Average print order: 1,000. **Published 3 debut authors within the last year.** Averages 6 total titles, 5 fiction titles/year. Titles distributed through Ingram, Baker & Taylor. Promotion through print ads, author signings and readings, direct mail and e-mail.

Needs: Humor, literary, mystery (private eye/hardboiled), short story collections. Prefers "shorter works, averaging between 80 and 175 pages. Published *Frostbite*, by Nathan Graziano (short story); *One Last Chance*, by Brent McKnight (short story); *Do Not Look Directly Into Me*, by Daniel Crocker (short story); *Wing-Ding at Uncle Tug's*, by Jeff Grimshaw (humor/short story).

How to Contact: Does not accept unsolicited mss. Query with SASE or submit outline, 2-4 sample chapter(s), synopsis, author bio. Accepts queries by e-mail. Include brief bio. Agented fiction 10%. Responds in 2 weeks. No simultaneous submissions, electronic submissions, submissions on disk.

Payment/Terms: Pays 10-15% royalty. Publishes ms 6-12 months after acceptance. Book catalog online; ms guidelines online.

Advice: "As a result of corporate publishers' 'bestseller only' mentality, there are more and more high-quality authors out there looking for presses they can have closer, more personal relationships with. This is a great opportunity for small independent presses. Let your work speak for itself. If you feel the need to send a letter explaining every little thing about your manuscript, then the manuscript's not doing its job."

GREENE BARK PRESS, P.O. Box 1108, Bridgeport CT 06601. (203)372-4861. Fax: (203)371-5856. Website: www.greenebarkpress.com. **Contact:** Michele Hofbauer, associate publisher. Estab. 1991. "We only publish children's fiction—all subjects, but in reading picture book format appealing to ages 3-9 or all ages." Publishes hardcover originals. **Published new writers within the last year. debut authors within the last year.** Averages 5 total titles/year. Distributes titles through Baker & Taylor and Quality Books. Promotes titles through ads, trade shows (national and regional), direct mail campaigns.

Needs: Juvenile. Published *A Pumpkin Story*, by Mariko Shinju and *The Magical Trunk*, by GiGi Tegge.

How to Contact: Submit complete ms. No queries or ms by e-mail. Responds in 6 months. Accepts simultaneous submissions. No electronic submissions.

Payment/Terms: Pays 10-15% royalty on wholesale price. Publishes ms 1 year after acceptance. Book catalog for $2; ms guidelines for SASE.

Advice: Audience is "children who read to themselves and others. Mothers, fathers, grandparents, godparents who read to their respective children, grandchildren. Include SASE, be prepared to wait, do NOT inquire by telephone, fax or e-mail."

⊘ **GREENWILLOW BOOKS**, HarperCollins Publishers, 1350 Avenue of the Americas, New York NY 10019. (212)261-6500. Website: www.harperchildrens.com. **Contact:** Fiction Editor. Estab. 1974. Publishes hardcover originals and reprints. Averages 50-60 total titles/year.
Needs: Fantasy, humor, literary, mystery, picture books. Published *The Queen of Attolia*, by Megan Whalen Turner; *Bo & Mzzz Mad*, by Sid Fleishman; *Whale Talk*, by Chris Crutcher; *Year of the Griffen*, by Diana Wynne Jones.
How to Contact: Does not accept unsolicited mss.
Payment/Terms: Pays 10% royalty on wholesale price for first-time authors. Average advance: variable. Publishes ms 2 years after acceptance.

⊘ **GREYCORE PRESS**, 2646 New Prospect Road, Pine Bush NY 12566. (845)744-5081. Fax: (845)744-8081. E-mail: joan123@frontiernet.net. Website: www.greycore.com. **Contact:** Joan Schweighandt, publisher. Estab. 1999. Small independent publisher of quality fiction and nonfiction titles. Established GreyCore Kids this year. Publishes hardcover originals. Books: cloth binding. Average print order: 7,000. **Published 2 debut authors within the last year.** Averages 3 total titles, 2 fiction titles/year. Member, Dustbooks. Distributes titles through Client Distribution Services.
Needs: Children's/juvenile, literary, mainstream/contemporary. Published *One Man's Leg*, by Paul Martin; *The Water Thief*, by Robert Baldwin; *Buddha Wept*, by Rocco Lo Bosco; *When I Wished I Was Alone*, by Dave Cutler.
How to Contact: Does not accept unsolicited mss. Query with SASE. Accepts queries by e-mail, fax. Include estimated word count, list of publishing credits. Accepts simultaneous submissions. Sometimes comments on rejected mss.
Payment/Terms: Publishes ms 18 months after acceptance.
Advice: "We prefer to get cover letters that include author credentials and the ways in which writers are willing to help publicize their work. We are very small and can't keep up with the number of manuscripts we receive. Our preference is to receive a cover letter, synopsis and the author's credentials via snail mail. We will read e-mail queries too, of course, but as e-mails tend to get lost in the shuffle, our preference is snail mail, with SASE."

GROLIER PUBLISHING CO., INC, Scholastic Inc., 90 Old Sherman Turnpike, Danbury CT 06816-0001. (203)797-3500. Fax: (203)797-3197. Website: www.publishing.grolier.com. Estab. 1895. Publishes hardcover and trade paperback originals.
Imprint(s): Children's Press, Franklin Watts, Orchard Books.
How to Contact: No simultaneous submissions. Sometimes comments on rejected mss.

Ⓐ **GROVE/ATLANTIC, INC.**, 841 Broadway 4th Floor, New York NY 10003. (212)614-7850. Fax: (212)614-7886. Estab. 1952. Publishes hardcover originals, trade paperback originals and reprints. Averages 60-70 total titles/year.
Imprint(s): Grove Press (estab. 1952), Atlantic Monthly Press (estab. 1917).
Needs: Experimental, literary. Published *Four Blondes*, by Candace Bushnell (Atlantic Monthly); and *How the Dead Live*, by Will Self (Grove Press). *Agented submissions only.* Query with SASE. Accepts simultaneous submissions.
How to Contact: Does not accept unsolicited mss. *Agented submissions only.* Query with SASE. Accepts simultaneous submissions.
Payment/Terms: Pays 7½-15% royalty on retail price. Average advance: varies. Publishes ms 1 year after acceptance. Book catalog free.

⊘ **GRYPHON BOOKS**, P.O. Box 209, Brooklyn NY 11228. (718)646-6126 (after 6 p.m. EST). Website: www.gryphonbooks.com. **Contact:** Gary Lovisi, owner/editor. Estab. 1983. Publishes paperback originals and trade paperback reprints. Books: bond paper; offset printing; perfect binding. Average print order: 500-1,000. **Published some debut authors within the last year.** Averages 10-15 total titles, 12 fiction titles/year.
Imprint(s): Gryphon Books, Gryphon Doubles, Gryphon SF Rediscovery Series.
Needs: Mystery (private eye/hardboiled, crime), science fiction (hard science/technological, soft/sociological). Published *The Dreaming Detective*, by Ralph Vaughn (mystery-fantasy-horror); *The Woman in the Dugout*, by Gary Lovisi and T. Arnone (baseball novel); and *A Mate for Murder*, by Bruno Fischer (hardboiled pulp). Publishes Gryphon Double novel series.
How to Contact: "I am not looking for novels right now; *will only see a 1-page synopsis with SASE.*" Include estimated word count, brief bio, list of publishing credits, "how you heard about us." Agented fiction 5-10%. Responds in 1 month to queries; 2 months to mss. Accepts simultaneous submissions, submissions on disk. Often comments on rejected mss.
Payment/Terms: Payment varies. Publishes ms 1-3 years after acceptance. Book catalog for #10 SASE; ms guidelines for #10 SASE.
Advice: "I am looking for better and better writing, more cutting-edge material with *impact*! Keep it lean and focused."

🔯 ⊘ 🔻 **GUERNICA EDITIONS**, Box 117, Station P, Toronto, ON M5S 2S6 Canada. (416)658-9888. Fax: (416)657-8885. E-mail: guernicaeditions@cs.com. Website: www.guernicaeditions.com. **Contact:** Antonio D'Alfonso, fiction editor (novel and short story). Estab. 1978. "Guernica Editions is a small press that produces works

insider report

Lynn Pruett: Have faith in your craft

What do you get when you cross Jane Austen's *Pride and Predjudice* with David Allen Coe's "The Perfect Country and Western Song"? The answer—Lynn Pruett's debut novel *Ruby River* (Grove/Atlantic 2002). Over a decade in the making, *Ruby River* tells the story of Hattie Bohannon, a spitfire widow, and her three equally feisty daughters, all of whom work together to run a truck stop in northeastern Alabama.

"As for the novel as a whole, the idea came about one day when I was sitting in a truck stop near Ider, Alabama, reading *Pride And Prejudice*, which I was going to teach. I thought, what if you put *Pride and Prejudice* in an Alabama truck stop?" Pruett explains of her inspiration. "That semester I drafted two or three chapters. In *Pride and Prejudice*, there are five Bennett sisters; originally I had five Bohannon sisters, but as I wrote and discovered that this would be a multiple POV novel, I had to eliminate characters and story lines. So there are three Bohannon daughters and one granddaughter. I did not follow the plot or anything else from *Pride and Prejudice*. I figured the notion of having a mother with several marriage-eligible daughters working in a truck stop would create many possibilities."

Pruett's high-brow style mixed with her working class characters has proved to be a powerful and entertaining combination. Since the novel's publication the author has had both robust sales and reviews, and she has received fellowships to prestigious writers' conferences including Yaddo, The Squaw Valley Writers' Conference, and the Sewanee Writers' Conference. Now a resident of Kentucky, Pruett has also been nominated for that states' Best Literary Book Award of 2002.

But the fruits of this literary success were a long time in the making for Pruett, too long to put the minds of most aspiring writers at ease. As much as its *Pride and Prejudice* predecessor, *Ruby River* is a heartbreaking book about strong women endeavoring to persevere through adversity. Maybe this book has become such a success because of Pruett's own strength and determination. In fact, one might even say, as strong women go, Lynn Pruett is every bit as inspiring as her famous literary hero Jane Austen.

Here, Pruett talks about the importance of persistence, faith in your craft, and the support of a writing community.

So you worked on *Ruby River* all the way through your MFA at the University of Alabama?

A version of *Ruby River* was my masters thesis; it was bought by a publishing house; my editor was fired; consequently that novel was not published. I was pretty disillusioned about writing and publishing at that point. I abandoned it for about five years—had children, taught creative writing, kept writing other things, drafted a second novel. But I went back to it three years ago and lifted out pieces here and there and put it through a couple of major revisions: new characters added, old ones ditched; structural shifts, POV changes, new events, etc.

So this book does not have a chronological age; though I'd say I worked on it for eight years from its beginning as a chapter in a creative writing class to the time it was in print. Chronologically there were five years in between when I didn't work on it at all.

I bet there are lots of writers out there who are disillusioned with the publishing industry for one reason or another. How would you compare the published version of *Ruby River* **to the version that almost made it into print? Looking back on it, can you find anything positive to say about having your heart broken by a publisher?**
The published version of *Ruby River* is a much better book. It was publishable in its earlier form—I reread it last year and was surprised to feel that way about it. It had become a source of embarrassment for me, the early version, because it had "failed." Although, of course, it had not failed. The publisher had failed. It was rough going from such a joyful high to a shameful low. If I wasn't so invested in the book, I would have recognized that its failure to be published was not my fault. However, it took a long time to try again. To have faith in an industry that had acted that way. Finally, some of us absolutely have to write. And so I kept on writing. I drafted a very angry second novel which I did not send out—fortunately.

I moved away from the town where I wrote the first version of *Ruby River* and had a fresh start, a fresh look at the book, a new set of writing friends. That freed me because its old history was not known unless I shared it.

Being dropped by the publisher eventually made me more committed to *my* writing. An odd outgrowth was that I isolated this work from other readers. I showed no one the manu-script before I sent it to my agent. I had people read bits and pieces of it but I wanted to protect it this time around. I was more sure about myself as a writer. And hey, I wanted to kick ass. I have that 'Bama kick-ass' thing going. I am a writer whether or not any publisher says I am.

The old version was told in third person omniscient POV. Structurally, it was a chapter book. The published version—and this was very important to my development as a writer—is told in first and third with a variety of distances. In grad school I was told I had to write in third person and in past tense. However that was not working for my characters or for the closeness I wanted to get from some of them. To me that was risky; I'm glad Grove is flexible. They believed readers would be sophisticated enough to follow the POV shifts—it's interesting that the people who comment most on this with curiosity are writers or reviewers. In general, readers simply go with the flow, which is what I hoped.

Of course I don't like knowing I lost five years. I might be on book number three or four by now—and all the good things that can come from publishing several books might be mine right now. I don't get those years back. Honestly I am not happy to have lived through the experience; there was a lot of pain and self-doubt and anger in those years.

But I am pleased with *Ruby River* as it is now. I think it's better crafted and better written.

You've said before that the competition in grad school prevented you from showing your work to other people. But that's changed for you. What is the Kentucky Book Mafia? Who are they and why is a sense of community important to you?
I've written with several people since I came to Lexington. There was one person I did writing practices with—fast writing that honed narrative drive to a necessity; it was like doing wind

sprints once a week. Then there is KaBoom, the Kentucky Book Mafia.

It's a writing group that meets weekly. We exchange stories or essays or poems; we read another member's entire novel more than once. I occasionally showed them parts of *Ruby River*. When we chose our name we decided that the promotion of Kentucky writers was part of our mission. Then everybody else joined the MFA program at Spalding University so the focus the past two years has been mainly on writing.

Anyway, I was more experienced than anyone in the group but I joined because I wanted camaraderie. A writer is an odd person in the world. What we do makes little sense to anyone else but other writers or artists. When I was at Yaddo in February, we artists and writers would report our progress at the end of a full working day: one photographic print, one paragraph, eight notes by the composer. In KaBoom, there is the understanding of what it means to write, to give everything you have regardless of any other probable reward. It is nice to meet with people who understand and who cheer you on. Very different from the competitive atmosphere of graduate school. I needed a positive environment after my experience with the novel's initial rejection.

One thing KaBoom has done recently is start a reading series at a historic horse country inn; people pay to eat hors d'oeuvres and listen to us do a round-robin reading. We have given workshops on writing groups at conferences and written query letters for folks in search of agents. We also make books by hand.

After so many years working on *Ruby River*, have you been able to start a new project?

I am writing another novel at this point, which is pretty daunting. A good thing about having a book that's such a long time in coming is that you're mainly revising. Starting from scratch, with awkward sentences and an unknown plot . . .

—*Brad Vice*

---

of fiction and nonfiction on the viability of pluriculturalism." Publishes trade paperback originals, reprints and software. Books: various paper; offset printing; perfect binding. Average print order: 1,000. **Published 6 debut authors within the last year.** Averages 25 total titles, 18-20 fiction titles/year. Distributes titles through professional distributors.

• Two titles by Guernica Editions have won American Book Awards.

Imprint(s): Prose Series, Antonio D'Alfonso, editor, all; Picas Series, Antonio D'Alfonso, editor, reprints.

Needs: Erotica, feminist, gay/lesbian, literary, multicultural, plays, poetry, poetry in translation. "We wish to open up into the fiction world and focus less on poetry. We specialize in European, especially Italian, translations." Publishes anthology of Arab women/Italian women writers. Published *A Demon in My View*, by Len Grasparin; *A Destroyer of Compasses*, by Wade Bell; *Voices in the Desert: An Anthology of Arab-Canadian Women Writers*, edited by Elizabeth Dahab.

How to Contact: Accepts unsolicited mss. Query with SASE. Include estimated word count, brief bio, list of publishing credits. Responds in 1 month to queries; 1 year to mss. No simultaneous submissions.

Payment/Terms: Pays 8-10% royalty on retail price or makes outright purchase of $200-5,000. Average advance: $200-2,000. Publishes ms 15 months after acceptance. Book catalog online.

Advice: "Know what publishers do, and send your works only to publishers whose writers you've read and enjoyed."

ROBERT HALE LIMITED, Clerkenwell House, 45/47 Clerkenwell Green, London EC1R 0HT England. Fax: 020-7490-4958. **Contact:** Fiction editor. Publishes hardcover and trade paperback originals and hardcover reprints. **Published 30 debut authors within the last year.**

Needs: Historical (not U.S. history), mainstream/contemporary, western. Length: 40,000-150,000 words. Published *Sin City*, by Harold Robbins; *Dog Island*, by Mike Stewart; *Savage Run*, by C.J. Box.

How to Contact: Query with SASE. Accepts queries by fax.

Advice: "Write well and have a strong plot."

🖰 **HAMPTON ROADS PUBLISHING CO., INC.**, 1125 Stoney Ridge Rd., Charlottesville VA 22902. (434)296-2772. Fax: (434)296-5096. Website: www.hrpub.com. **Contact:** Frank Demarco, chief editor. Estab. 1989. "We work as a team to produce the best books we are capable of producing which will impact, uplift and contribute to positive change in the world. We publish what defies or doesn't quite fit the usual genres. We are noted for visionary fiction." Publishes hardcover and trade paperback originals. Publishes and distributes hardcover and paperback originals on subjects including metaphysics, health, complementary medicine, visionary fiction and other related topics. Average print order: 3,000-5,000. **Published 6 debut authors within the last year.** Averages 35-40 total titles, 4 fiction titles/year. Distributes titles through distributors. Promotes titles through advertising, representatives, author signings and radio-TV interviews with authors.

Needs: Literary, new age/mystic, psychic/supernatural, spiritual, visionary fiction, past-life fiction, based on actual memories. "Fiction should have one or more of the following themes: spiritual, inspirational, metaphysical, i.e., past life recall, out-of-body experiences, near death experience, paranormal. Published *Rogue Messiahs*, by Colin Wilson; *Spirit Matters*, by Michael Lerner; and *The Authenticator*, by William M. Valtos.

How to Contact: Does not accept unsolicited mss. Query with SASE or submit outline, 2 sample chapter(s), synopsis or submit complete ms. Accepts queries by e-mail, fax. Send SASE for return of ms or send a disposable ms and SASE for reply only. Agented fiction 5%. Responds in 2 months to queries; 2 months to proposals; 6 months to mss. Accepts simultaneous submissions.

Payment/Terms: Pays royalty. Average advance: $1,000-50,000. Publishes ms 1 year after acceptance. Ms guidelines online.

Advice: "Send us something new and different. Be patient. We take the time to give each submission the attention it deserves."

🅽 🖰 🌄 **HARBOR HOUSE**, 629 Stevens Crossing, Martinez CA 30907. (706)738-0354. Fax: (706)738-0354. E-mail: harborbook@knology.net. Website: harborhousebooks.com. **Contact:** E. Randall Floyd, editor. Estab. 1997. Harbor House seeks to publish the best in original fiction (mainstream, historical, horror). Publishes hardcover originals and paperback originals. Average print order: 5,000. **Published 3 debut authors within the last year.** Member, PMA. Distributes titles through the National Book Network; Ingram; Baker & Taylor.

● Received a Golden Eye Literary Award.

Imprint(s): Batwing Press.

Needs: Historical (biography), horror (psychological, supernatural), mainstream/contemporary, military/war, new age/mystic, psychic/supernatural, romance (historical), young adult (horror, mystery/suspense), civil war. Published *The Dark Side of Liberalism*, by Phil Kent (political); *Two Rivers*, by Naomi Williams (fiction).

How to Contact: Accepts unsolicited mss. Submit outline, 3 sample chapter(s). Query. Accepts queries by mail. Include estimated word count, brief bio, list of publishing credits, marketing plans. Agented fiction 10%. Responds in 4 weeks to queries; 2 months to mss. Accepts simultaneous submissions. Sometimes comments on rejected mss.

Payment/Terms: Pays 10% royalty. Average advance: $5,000. Publishes ms 6-18 months after acceptance. Book catalog online; ms guidelines online.

Advice: "We strongly encourage authors to consult our website before submitting material. We are particularly interested in developing unpublished authors."

HARCOURT, INC, Children's Books Division, 525 B St., Suite 1900, San Diego CA 92101. (619)281-6616. Fax: (619)699-6777. Website: www.harcourtbooks.com/htm/childrens_index.asp. Estab. 1919. "Harcourt Inc. owns some of the world's most prestigious publishing imprints—quality products for the juvenile, educational, scientific, technical, medical, professional and trade markets worldwide." Publishes hardcover originals and trade paperback reprints.

Imprint(s): Harcourt Children's Books, Gulliver Books, Silver Whistle, Red Wagon, Odyssey Paperbacks, Magic Carpet, Voyager Books/Libros Viajeros and Green Light Readers.

Needs: Children's/juvenile, young adult.

How to Contact: Does not accept unsolicited mss.

🅰 🌄 **HARCOURT, INC.**, Trade Division, 525 B St., Suite 1900, San Diego CA 92101. (619)699-6560. Fax: (619)699-5555. Website: www.harcourtbooks.com. **Contact:** Jeannette Larson, senior editor (general fiction); Allyn Johnston, editorial director of Harcourt Brace Children's Books. Publishes hardcover and trade paperback originals and trade paperback reprints. **Published very few debut authors within the last year.** Averages 120 total titles/year.

● Books published by Harcourt Trade Publishers have received numerous awards including the Caldecott and Newbery medals and selections as the American Library Association's "Best Books for Young Adults."

Imprint(s): Harcourt Trade Children's Books, Gulliver Books, Red Wagon Books and Silver Whistle.

Needs: Historical, mystery, picture books, Nonfiction.

How to Contact: Does not accept unsolicited mss. *Agented submissions only.* Accepts simultaneous submissions.

Payment/Terms: Pays 6-15% royalty on retail price. Average advance: $2,000 minimum. Book catalog for 9 × 12 SAE; ms guidelines online.

Advice: "Read as much current fiction as you can; familiarize yourself with the type of fiction published by a particular house; interact with young people to obtain a realistic picture of their concerns, interests and speech patterns."

☐ ◎ **HARLEQUIN AMERICAN ROMANCE**, a Harlequin book line, 300 E. 42nd Street, 6th floor, New York NY 10017. (212)682-6080. Fax: (212)682-4539. Website: www.eharlequin.com. **Contact:** Melissa Jeglinski, associate senior editor. "Upbeat and lively, fast-paced and well-plotted, American Romance celebrates the pursuit of love in the backyards, big cities and wide-open spaces of America." Publishes paperback originals and reprints. Books: newspaper print paper; web printing; perfect-bound. **Regularly publishes new writers.**
Needs: Romance (contemporary, American). Needs "all-American stories with a range of emotional and sensual content and are supported by a sense of community within the plot's framework. In the confident and caring heroine, the tough but tender hero, and their dynamic relationship that is at the center of this series, real-life love is showcased as the best fantasy of all!"
How to Contact: Accepts unsolicited mss. Query with SASE or submit complete ms. Manuscripts must be 70,000-75,000 words. Send SASE for return of ms or send a disposable ms and SASE for reply only. No simultaneous submissions, electronic submissions, submissions on disk.
Payment/Terms: Pays royalty. Offers advance. Ms guidelines online.

🔶 ☐ ◎ **HARLEQUIN BLAZE**, a Harlequin book line, 225 Duncan Mill Road, Don Mills ON M3B 3K9 Canada. (416)445-5860. Website: www.eharlequin.com. **Contact:** Birgit Davis-Todd, executive editor. "Harlequin Blaze is a hot new series that has evolved out of the very successful Temptation line. It is a vehicle to build and promote new authors who have a strong sexual edge to their stories. It is also *the* place to be for seasoned authors who want to create a sexy, sizzling, longer contemporary story." Publishes paperback originals and reprints. Books: newspaper print; web printing; perfect-bound. **Published some debut authors within the last year.**
Needs: Romance (contemporary). "Sensuous, highly romantic, innovative plots that are sexy in premise and execution. The tone of the books can run from fun and flirtatious to dark and sensual. Submissions should have a very contemporary feel—what it's like to be young and single today. We are looking for heroes and heroines in their early 20s and up. There should be a strong emphasis on the physical relationship between the couples. Fully described loves scenes along with a high level of fantasy and playfulness."
How to Contact: Accepts unsolicited mss. New authors should send a query letter outlining their story in a couple of pages. Published authors may query and/or submit chapters and a synopsis. Manuscripts must be 70,000-75,000 words. No simultaneous submissions, electronic submissions, submissions on disk.
Payment/Terms: Pays royalty. Offers advance. Ms guidelines online.
Advice: "Are you a *Cosmo* girl at heart? A fan of *Sex and the City*? Or maybe you have a sexually adventurous spirit. If so, then Blaze is the series for you!"

🔶 ☐ ◐ ◎ **HARLEQUIN DUETS**, a Harlequin book line, 225 Duncan Mill Road, Don Mills ON M3B 3K9 Canada. (416)445-5860. Website: www.eharlequin.com. **Contact:** Birgit Davis-Todd, senior editor. "Harlequin Duets are a delightful combination of romance and comedy. Fast-paced and plot driven, these novels depend upon the comedy building from the relationship between hero and heroine." Publishes paperback originals and reprints. Books: newspaper print; web printing; perfect-bound. **Regularly publishes new authors.**
Needs: Romance (Romantic comedy). "We are looking for a comic premise, a strong humourous voice, and a great romance. A high degree of sexual tension is a must, and while we encourage love scenes, they are not a requirement. So whether your story is a screwball comedy of errors or simply the lighter side of love, we are looking for entertaining romance that will bring a smile to the face of every reader."
How to Contact: Accepts unsolicited mss. Query with SASE or submit complete ms. Manuscripts must be 50,000-55,000 words. Send SASE for return of ms or send a disposable ms and SASE for reply only. No simultaneous submissions, electronic submissions, submissions on disk.
Payment/Terms: Pays royalty. Offers advance. Ms guidelines online.

🔶 🔶 ◎ **HARLEQUIN ENTERPRISES, LTD.**, 225 Duncan Mill Rd., Don Mills ON M3B 3K9 Canada. (416)445-5860. Website: www.eharlequin.com; www.mirabooks.com. **Contact:** Randall Toye, editorial director (Gold Eagle, Worldwide Library); Tara Gavin, editorial director (Silhouette, Harlequin, Steeple Hill, Red Dress Ink); Diane Moggy, editorial director (MIRA Red Dress Ink, HQN Books), Malle Vallik, editorial director (eHarlequin, New Product Development). Estab. 1949. Publishes mass market paperback originals and reprints. Books: newsprint paper; web printing; perfect-bound. **Published some debut authors within the last year.** Averages 1,500 total titles/year. Distributes titles through retail market, direct mail market and overseas through operating companies. Promotes titles through trade and consumer advertising: print, radio, TV.
Imprint(s): Harlequin Books, Silhouette, MIRA, Gold Eagle, Luna, HQN Books, World Wide Library, Mills & Boon, Steeple Hill, Red Dress Ink.
Needs: Adventure (heroic), mystery, romance, suspense (romantic suspense only).
How to Contact: Query with SASE. Responds in 6 weeks. No simultaneous submissions. Sometimes comments on rejected mss.
Payment/Terms: Pays royalty. Offers advance. Publishes ms 1-2 years after acceptance. Ms guidelines online.

☐ ◎ **HARLEQUIN HISTORICALS**, a Harlequin book line, 300 E. 42nd Street, 6th floor, New York NY 10017. (212)682-6080. Fax: (212)682-4539. Website: www.eharlequin.com. **Contact:** Tracy Farrell, senior editor. "The primary element of a Harlequin Historical novel is romance. The story should focus on the heroine and how her love for one man changes her life forever. For this reason, it is very important that you have an appealing hero and heroine, and that their relationship is a compelling one. The conflicts they must overcome and the situations they face can be as varied as the setting you have chosen, but there must be romantic tension, some spark between your hero and heroine that keeps your reader interested." Publishes paperback originals and reprints. Books: newsprint paper; perfect-bound. **Regularly publishes new writers.**
Needs: Romance (historical). "We will not accept books set after 1900. We're looking primarily for books set in North America, England or France between 1100 and 1900 A.D. We do not buy many novels set during the American Civil War. We are, however, flexible, and will consider most periods and settings. We are not looking for gothics or family sagas, nor are we interested in the kind of comedy of manners typified by straight Regencies. Historical romances set during the Regency period, however, will definitely be considered."
How to Contact: Accepts unsolicited mss. Query with SASE or submit complete ms. Manuscripts must be 99,000-105,000 words. Send SASE for return of ms or send a disposable ms and SASE for reply only. No simultaneous submissions, electronic submissions, submissions on disk.
Payment/Terms: Pays royalty. Offers advance. Ms guidelines online.

☐ ◎ **HARLEQUIN INTRIGUE**, a Harlequin Book line, 300 E. 42nd Street, 6th floor, New York NY 10017. (212)682-6080. Website: www.eharlequin.com. **Contact:** Denise O'Sullivan, associate senior editor. "These novels are taut, edge-of-the-seat, contemporary romantic suspense tales of intrigue and desire. Kidnappings, stalkings and women in jeopardy coupled with best selling romantic themes are the examples of story lines we love most." Publishes paperback originals and reprints. Books: newspaper print; perfect-bound. **Regularly publishes new writers.**
Needs: Romance (romantic suspense). "Murder mystery, psychological suspense, or thriller; the love story must be inextricably bound to the resolution where all loose ends are tied up neatly and shared dangers lead right to shared passions. As long as they're in jeopardy and falling in love, our heroes and heroines may traverse a landscape as wide as the world itself. Their lives are on the line and so are their hearts!"
How to Contact: Accepts unsolicited mss. Query with SASE or submit complete ms. Manuscripts must be 70,000-75,000 words. Send SASE for return of ms or send a disposable ms and SASE for reply only. No simultaneous submissions, electronic submissions, submissions on disk.
Payment/Terms: Pays royalty. Offers advance. Ms guidelines online.

🅽 🌐 ◎ **HARLEQUIN MILLS & BOON, LTD.**, Harlequin Enterprises, Ltd., Eton House, 18-24 Paradise Rd., Richmond Surrey TW9 1SR United Kingdom. (44)0208-288-2800. Website: www.millsandboon.co.uk. **Contact:** K. Stoecker, editorial director; Tessa Shapcott, senior editor (Harlequin Presents); Samantha Bell, senior editor (Harlequin Romance); Linda Fildew, senior editor (Mills and Boon Historicals); Sheila Hodgson, senior editor (Mills and Boon Medicals). Estab. 1908-1909. Publishes mass market paperback originals. **Published new writers within the last year.** Plans 3-4 first novels this year.
Imprint(s): Harlequin Presents (Mills and Boon Presents), Harlequin Romance (Mills and Boon Tender Romance), Mills and Boon Historicals, Mills and Boon Medicals.
Needs: Romance (contemporary, historical, regency period, medical).
How to Contact: Query with SASE or submit 3 sample chapter(s), synopsis. Responds in 5 months to mss. No simultaneous submissions.
Payment/Terms: Pays advance against royalty. Publishes ms 2 years after acceptance. Ms guidelines online.

🌐 ☐ ◎ **HARLEQUIN PRESENTS (MILLS & BOON PRESENTS)**, a Harlequin book line, Eton House, 18-24 Paradise Road, Richmond Surrey TW9 1SR United Kingdom. (44)0208 288 2800. Website: www.millsandboon.com. **Contact:** Tessa Shapcott, senior editor. "Pick up a Harlequin Presents novel and you'll enter a world full of spine-tingling passion and provacative, tantalizing, romantic excitement! Although grounded in reality, these stories offer compelling modern fantasies to readers all around the world, and there is scope within this line to develop relevant contemporary issues which touch the lives of today's women. Harlequin Presents novels capture the drama and intensity of a powerful, sexual love affair." Publishes paperback originals and reprints. Books: newspaper print; perfect-bound. **Regularly publishes new writers.**
Needs: Romance. Needs "novels written in the third person that feature spirited, independent heroines who aren't afraid to take the initiative, and breathtakingly attractive, larger-than-life heroes. The conflict between these characters should be lively and evenly matched, but always balanced by a developing romance that may include explicit lovemaking."
How to Contact: Accepts unsolicited mss. Query with SASE or submit complete ms. Manuscripts must be 50,000-55,000 words. Send SASE for return of ms or send a disposable ms and SASE for reply only. No simultaneous submissions, electronic submissions, submissions on disk.
Payment/Terms: Pays royalty. Offers advance. Ms guidelines online.

🌐 ☐ ◎ **HARLEQUIN ROMANCE (MILLS & BOON TENDER ROMANCE)**, a Harlequin book line, Eton House, 18-24 Paradise Road, Richmond Surrey TW9 1SR United Kingdom. (44)208 288 2800. Website:

www.millsandboon.co.uk. **Contact:** Bryony Green, associate senior editor. "Sparkling, fresh and emotionally fulfilling, these stories capture the rush of falling in love and deliver the ultimate in feel-good romantic fiction!" Publishes paperback originals and reprints. Books: newspaper print; perfect-bound. **Regularly publishes new writers.**

Needs: Romance. Needs "novels written in the third person from the heroine's point of view, with focus almost exclusively on the developing relationship between the protagonists. The emphasis should be on warm and tender emotions, with no sexual explicitness; lovemaking should only take place when the emotional commitment between the characters justifies it. Readers should be thrilled by the tenderness of their developing relationship, and gripped by romantic suspense as the couple strives to overcome the emotional barriers between them and find true happiness in the romance of a lifetime!"

How to Contact: Accepts unsolicited mss. Submit 3 sample chapter(s), synopsis. Manuscripts must be 50,000-55,000 words. SASE only accepted from UK. For outside the UK please send International Reply Coupons. Send SASE for return of ms or send a disposable ms and SASE for reply only. No simultaneous submissions, electronic submissions, submissions on disk.

Payment/Terms: Pays royalty. Offers advance. Ms guidelines online.

HARLEQUIN SUPERROMANCE, a Harlequin book line, 225 Duncan Mill Road, Don Mills ON M3B 3K9 Canada. (416)445-5860. Website: www.eharlequin.com. **Contact:** Laura Shin, senior editor. "The aim of Superromance novels is to produce a contemporary, involving read with a mainstream tone in its situations and characters, using romance as the major theme. To achieve this, emphasis should be placed on individual writing styles and unique and topical ideas." Publishes paperback originals and reprints. Books: newspaper print; perfect-bound. **Published 4 debut authors within the last year.**

Needs: Romance (contemporary). "The criteria for Superromance books are flexible. Aside from length, the determining factor for publication will always be quality. Authors should strive to break free of stereotypes, clichés and worn out plot devices to create strong, believable stories with depth and emotional intensity. Superromance novels are intended to appeal to a wide range of romance readers."

How to Contact: Accepts unsolicited mss. Query with SASE or submit 3 sample chapter(s), synopsis or submit complete ms. Manuscripts must be approximately 80,000 words. Send SASE for return of ms or send a disposable ms and SASE for reply only. No simultaneous submissions, electronic submissions, submissions on disk.

Payment/Terms: Pays royalty. Offers advance. Ms guidelines online.

Advice: "A general familiarity with current Superromance books is advisable to keep abreast of ever-changing trends and overall scope, but we don't want imitations and we are open to innovation. We look for sincere, heartfelt writing based on true-to-life experiences the reader can identify with."

HARLEQUIN TEMPTATION, a Harlequin book line, 225 Duncan Mills Road, Don Mills ON M3B 3K9 Canada. (416)445-5860. Website: www.eharlequin.com. **Contact:** Brenda Chin, senior editor. "Temptation is sexy, sassy, and seductive! This is one of Harlequin's boldest, most sensuous series, focusing on men and women living and loving today!" Publishes paperback originals and reprints. Books: newspaper print; perfect-bound. **Regularly publishes new writers.**

Needs: Romance. "Almost anything goes in Temptation: the stories may be humorous, topical, adventurous or glitzy, but at heart they are pure romantic fantasy."

How to Contact: Accepts unsolicited mss. Query with SASE or submit complete ms. Send SASE for return of ms or send a disposable ms and SASE for reply only. No simultaneous submissions, electronic submissions, submissions on disk.

Payment/Terms: Pays royalty. Offers advance. Ms guidelines online.

Advice: "Think fast-paced, use the desire and language of women today, add a high level of sexual tension along with strong conflicts, and then throw in a good dash of 'what if.' The results should sizzle."

HARPERCOLLINS CANADA LTD., 2 Bloor St. West, 20th Floor, Toronto ON M4W 1A8 Canada. (416)975-9334. Fax: (416)975-5223. Website: www.harpercanada.com. Harpercollins is not accepting unsolicited material at this time.

HARPERCOLLINS GENERAL BOOKS GROUP, Division of HarperCollins Publishers, 10 East 53 Street, New York NY 10022. (212)207-7000. Fax: (212)207-7633. Website: www.harpercollins.com. "HarperCollins, one of the largest English language publishers in the world, is a broad-based publisher with strengths in academic, business and professional, children's, educational, general interest, and religious and spiritual books, as well as multimedia titles." Publishes hardcover and paperback originals and paperback reprints.

Imprint(s): Access Press; Amistad Press; Avon; Ecco; Fourth Estate; HarperAudio; HarperBusiness; HarperCollins; HarperEntertainment; HarperLargePrint; HarperResource; HarperSanFranciso; HarperTorch; Perennial; Perfect-Bound; Quill; Rayo; ReganBooks; William Morrow.

HARPERTORCH, (formerly HarperPaperbacks), Imprint of HarperCollins Publishers, 10 E. 53rd St., New York NY 10022. (212)207-7000. Fax: (212)207-7901. **Contact:** Michael Morrison, publisher. Publishes paperback originals and reprints. **Published new writers within the last year.**

Needs: Mainstream/contemporary, mystery, romance (contemporary, historical, romantic suspense), suspense, thriller/espionage.
How to Contact: Does not accept unsolicited mss. Query through agent.
Payment/Terms: Pays royalty. Offers advance.

🄰 🄾 🄾 **HARVEST HOUSE PUBLISHERS,** 990 Owen Loop N., Eugene OR 97402. (541)343-0123. Fax: (541)302-0731. E-mail: manuscriptcoordinator@harvesthousepublishers.com. Website: www.harvesthousepublishe rs.com. **Contact:** Acquisitions. Estab. 1974. "Our mission is to glorify God by providing high-quality books and products that affirm biblical values, help people grow spiritually strong, and proclaim Jesus Christ as the answer to every human need." Publishes hardcover originals and reprints, trade paperback originals and reprints, and mass market paperback originals and reprints. Books: 40 lb. ground wood paper; offset printing; perfect binding. Average print order: 10,000. First novel print order: 10,000-15,000. **Published 5-6 debut authors within the last year.** Averages 160 total titles, 15-20 fiction titles/year.
Needs: Harvest House no longer accepts unsolicited manuscripts, proposals, or artwork.
How to Contact: Does not accept unsolicited mss. Responds in 1 month to queries.
Payment/Terms: Pays royalty. Book catalog free.
Advice: "Attend a writer's conference where you have an opportunity to pitch your book idea to an editor face to face. We also look at fiction represented by a reputable agent."

🄾 **HAWK PUBLISHING GROUP,** 7107 S. Yale Ave., #345, Tulsa OK 74136. (918)492-3677. Fax: (918)492-2120. Website: www.hawkpub.com. Estab. 1999. Independent publisher of general trade/commercial books, fiction and nonfiction. Publishes hardcover and trade paperback originals. **Published 4 debut authors within the last year.** Plans 2 first novels this year. Averages 6-8 total titles, 3 fiction titles/year. Member, PMA. Titles are distributed by NBN/Biblio Distribution.
Needs: Looking for good books of all kinds. Not interested in juvenile, poetry, or short story collections. Published *The Darkest Night*, by Jodie Larsen; *This Fair Land*, by K.D. Wentworth.
How to Contact: Accepts unsolicited mss. Submissions will not be returned, so send only copies. No SASE. No submissions by e-mail or by "certified mail or any other service that requires a signature." Replies "only if interested. If you have not heard from us within three months after the receipt of your submission, you may safely assume that we were not able to find a place for it in our list." Include brief bio, list of publishing credits. Accepts simultaneous submissions.
Payment/Terms: Pays royalty. Publishes ms 1-2 years after acceptance. Ms guidelines online.
Advice: "Prepare a professional submission and follow the guidelines. The simple things really do count; use 12 pt. pitch with 1″ margins and only send what is requested."

🄾 **HELICON NINE EDITIONS,** Subsidiary of Midwest Center for the Literary Arts, Inc., P.O. Box 22412, Kansas City MO 64113. E-mail: helicon9@aol.com. Website: www.heliconnine.com. **Contact:** Gloria Vando Hickok. Estab. 1990. Small not-for-profit press publishing poetry, fiction, creative nonfiction and anthologies. Publishes paperback originals. Also publishes one-story chapbooks called *feuillets*, which come with envelope, 250 print run. Books: 60 lb. paper; offset printing; perfect-bound; 4-color cover. Average print order: 1,000-5,000. **Published 1 debut author within the last year.** Distributes titles through Baker & Taylor, Brodart, Ingram, Follet (library acquisitions), Midwest Library Service, all major distributors and booksellers. Promotes titles through reviews, readings, radio and television interviews.
How to Contact: Does not accept unsolicited mss. See website for updates.
Payment/Terms: Pays royalty. Offers advance. Publishes ms 6-12 months after acceptance.
Advice: "We accept short story collections. We welcome new writers and first books. Submit a clean, readable copy in a folder or box—paginated with title and name on each page. Also, do not pre-design book, i.e., no illustrations. We'd like to see books that will be read 50-100 years from now."

HENDRICK-LONG PUBLISHING CO., INC., 10635 Toweroaks D., Houston TX 77070. (832)912-7323. Fax: (832)912-7353. E-mail: hendrick-long@worldnet.att.net. Website: www.hendricklongpublishing.com. **Contact:** Vilma Long. Estab. 1969. Publishes hardcover and trade paperback originals and hardcover reprints. Averages 4 total titles/year.
Needs: Juvenile, young adult. Published *Pioneer Children*, by Betsy Warren; *Maggie Houston*, by Jane Cook.
How to Contact: Query with SASE or submit outline, 2 sample chapter(s), synopsis. 1 month to queries, 2 months if more than one query is sent to queries. No simultaneous submissions.
Payment/Terms: Pays royalty. Pays royalty on selling price. Offers advance. Publishes ms 18 months after acceptance. Book catalog for 8½×11 or 9×12 SASE with 4 first-class stamps; ms guidelines online.

🄽 🄰 🄼 **HESPERUS PRESS,** 4 Ricket Street, London SW6 1RU UK. 44 20 7610 3331. Fax: 44 20 7610 3337. **Contact:** Jenny Rayner, editorial director (literary fiction). Estab. 2001. Hesperus is a small independent publisher of mainly classics and literary fiction. Publishes paperback originals. Books: traditional printing; sewn binding. Average print order: 5,000. Distributes titles through Trafalgar Square in the US, Grantham Book Services in the UK.

Needs: Literary. Published *Loveless Love*, by Luigi Pirandello (modern classic); *Portrait of Mr. W.H.*, by Oscar Wilde (modern classic); *Tragedy of the Korosko*, by Arthur Conan Doyle (modern classic).

How to Contact: Does not accept unsolicited mss. *Agented submissions only.*

Payment/Terms: Book catalog free.

Advice: "Find an agent to represent you."

N **HIGH COUNTRY PUBLISHERS LTD.**, 197 New Market Center, #135, Boone NC 28607. (828)964-0090. Fax: (828)262-1973. E-mail: editor@highcountrypublishers.com. Website: www.highcountrypublishers.com. **Contact:** Judith Geary, senior editor. Estab. 2001. "We are a small regional house focusing on popular fiction and memoir. At present, we are most interested in regional fiction, historical fiction and mystery fiction." Publishes hardcover originals, paperback originals and paperback reprints. Books: 60# paper; offset printing; b&w illustrations. Average print order: 1,500-5,000. First novel print order: 1,500-3,000. **Published 1 debut author within the last year.** Plans 3 first novels this year. Member, PMA, PAS, SEBA. Distributes titles through Biblio Distribution, 2 divisions of NBN books.

Needs: Ethnic, family saga, fantasy (historical), feminist, historical, mainstream/contemporary, mystery (amateur sleuth, cozy, police procedural, private eye/hardboiled), regional (southern Appalachian), romance (contemporary, historical, romantic suspense adventure), young adult (historical, mystery/suspense). Published *All Roads Lead to Murder*, by Albert A. Bell, Jr. (historical mystery); *Monteith's Mountain*, by Skip Brooks (historical suspense); *Weave Me A Song*, by Lila Hopkins (Christian romance). Publishes a mystery series.

How to Contact: Accepts unsolicited mss. Query with SASE or submit outline, 3 sample chapter(s). Reading period open from July to October. Accepts queries by e-mail, mail. Include estimated word count, brief bio, list of publishing credits. Send copy of ms and SASE. Agented fiction 10%. Responds in 6 months to queries; 6 months to mss. Accepts simultaneous submissions, electronic submissions. No submissions on disk. Often comments on rejected mss.

Payment/Terms: Pays 10% royalty. Publishes ms 6 months-2 years after acceptance. Book catalog free; ms guidelines online.

HILL STREET PRESS, 191 E. Broad St., Suite 209, Athens GA 30601-2848. (706)613-7200. Fax: (706)613-7204. E-mail: info@hillstreetpress.com. Website: www.hillstreetpress.com. **Contact:** Patrick Allen and Judy Long, editors. Estab. 1998. "Small independent press specializing in southern belles lettres especially nonfiction. We concentrate on high-quality first fiction." Publishes hardcover originals, trade paperback originals and reprints. Books: acid-free paper, conventional printing, photos/drawings. Average print order: 7,500. **Published 5 debut authors within the last year.** Plans 2 first novels this year. Averages 20 total titles, 5 fiction titles/year.

Needs: Gay/lesbian, historical, humor, lesbian, literary, mainstream/contemporary, military/war, regional (southern US), religious, sports, African American. "Reasonable length projects (50,000-85,000 words) stand a far better chance of review. Do not submit proposals for works in excess of 125,000 words in length. Published *Prime Leaf*, by Eugene Wall (literary, debut author); *The Worst Day of My Life So Far*, by M.A. Harper (literary); and *Truelove and Homegrown Tomatoes*, by Julie Cannon (mainstream, debut author).

How to Contact: Accepts unsolicited mss. Query with SASE or submit proposal package including 3 sample chapter(s), résumé, synopsis, press clips. "Let us know at the point of submission if you are represented by an agent." Include estimated word count, list of publishing credits, résumé. Send SASE for return of ms or send a disposable ms and SASE for reply only. Agented fiction 5%. Responds in 1 month to queries; 3 months to proposals; 6 months to mss. Accepts simultaneous submissions.

Payment/Terms: Pays 9-12½% royalty on wholesale price. Publishes ms 1 year after acceptance. Book catalog and ms guidelines online.

Advice: "Do not submit short stories. Your proposal is your advertisement—sell your work with proposal, query letter, résumé and 3 sample chapters."

HODDER & STOUGHTON/HEADLINE, Hodder Headline, 338 Euston Road, London NW1 3BH England. (020)7873-6000. **Contact:** Mrs. Betty Schwartz, submissions editor, Hodder & Stoughton (adult fiction, nonfiction); Caroline Stofer, submissions editor, Headline (adult fiction). "Big commercial, general book publishers of general fiction/nonfiction, thrillers, romance, sagas, contemporary, original, literary, crime." Publishes hardcover and paperback originals and paperback reprints.

Imprint(s): Coronet, Sceptre, Flame, Hodder & Stoughton, NEL, LIR (Headline, Review, Feature).

Needs: Family saga, historical (general), literary, mainstream/contemporary, mystery (amateur sleuth, cozy, police procedural, private eye/hardboiled), romance (contemporary, romantic suspense), thriller/espionage. Published *Everything's Eventual*, by Stephen King (general); *Dinner for Two*, by Mike Gayle (general, romantic comedy); *The Rice Mother*, by Rani Manicka (literary).

How to Contact: Accepts unsolicited mss. Query with SASE or submit outline, 1 sample chapter(s), synopsis. Accepts queries by e-mail. Include estimated word count, brief bio. Responds in 2 weeks to queries; 1 month to mss. Accepts simultaneous submissions.

Payment/Terms: Flat A4 SASE; ms guidelines for #10 SASE.

Advice: "Minimum 80,000 words. For popular fiction titles (i.e. thrillers) we require around 120,000 words. Send cover letter, short synopsis (1-2 pages) and first sample chapter, typewritten, double-spaced. Writing should be of good quality and commercial. No single short stories."

HOLIDAY HOUSE, INC., 425 Madison Ave., New York NY 10017. (212)688-0085. Fax: (212)421-6134. **Contact:** Suzanne Reinoehl, editor. Estab. 1935. "Holiday House has a commitment to publishing first-time authors and illustrators." Independent publisher of children's books, picture books, nonfiction and novels for young readers. Publishes hardcover originals and paperback reprints. **Published new writers within the last year.** Averages 60 total titles/year.
  • *The Wright Brothers: How They Invented the Airplane*, by Russell Freedman and published by Holiday House was a Newbery Honor Book.
Needs: Adventure, children's/juvenile, historical, humor, literary, mainstream/contemporary, Judaica and holiday, animal stories for young readers. Children's books only. Published *Sense Pass King*, by Katrin Tchana, illustrated by Trina Schart Hyman; *Dear Whiskers*, by Ann Whitehead Nagda, illustrated by Stephanie Roth; and *Helen Keller*, by Laurie Lawlor.
How to Contact: Query with SASE. "No phone calls, please." No simultaneous submissions.
Payment/Terms: Pays royalty on list price, range varies. Average advance: Flexible, depending on whether the book is illustrated. Publishes ms 1-2 years after acceptance. Ms guidelines for #10 SASE.
Advice: "We're not in a position to be too encouraging, as our list is tight, but we're always open to good writing. Please submit only one project at a time."

HOLLOWAY HOUSE PUBLISHING CO., 8060 Melrose Ave., Los Angeles CA 90046. (323)653-8060. Fax: (323)655-9452. **Contact:** Neal Colgrass, editor (multi-cultural). Estab. 1960. Publishes paperback originals. Book: Groundwood paper; offset printing; perfect binding; illustrations. Average print order: 10,000. Distributes through the National Distributer.
Imprint(s): Mankind Books (multicultural).
Needs: Comic books, erotica, ethnic, multicultural.
How to Contact: Accepts unsolicited mss. Query with SASE. Accepts queries by mail. Include estimated word count, list of publishing credits. Send SASE or IRC. Agented fiction 10%. No simultaneous submissions. Sometimes comments on rejected mss.
Payment/Terms: Publishes ms 6-12 months after acceptance.

HENRY HOLT & CO. BOOKS FOR YOUNG READERS, Henry Holt & Co., LLC, 115 W. 18th St., New York NY 10011. (212)886-9200. Website: www.henryholt.com. **Contact:** Submissions editor, Books for Young Readers. Estab. 1866 (Holt). Henry Holt Books for Young Readers publishes excellent books of all kinds (fiction, nonfiction, illustrated) for all ages, from the very young to the young adult. Publishes hardcover originals of picture books, chapter books, middle grade and young adult novels. Averages 70-80 total titles/year.
Needs: Adventure, fantasy, historical, mainstream/contemporary, multicultural, picture books, young adult. Juvenile: adventure, animal, contemporary, fantasy, history, multicultural. Picture books: animal, concept, history, multicultural, sports. Young adult: contemporary, fantasy, history, multicultural, nature/environment, problem novels, sports. Published *When Zachary Beaver Came to Town*, by Kimberly Willis Holt (middle grade fiction); *The Gospel According to Larry*, by Janet Tashjian (YA fiction); *Visiting Langston*, by Willis Perdomo, illustrated by Bryan Collier (picture book); *Keeper of the Night*, by Kimberly Willis Holt, and *Alphabet Under Construction*, by Denise Fleming (picture book).
How to Contact: Accepts unsolicited mss. Submit complete ms, attention: Submissions Editor. Include estimated word count, brief bio, list of publishing credits. Send SASE or IRC. Responds in 3-4 months to queries. No simultaneous submissions.
Payment/Terms: Pays royalty on retail price. Average advance: $3,000 and up. Publishes ms 18-36 months after acceptance. Book catalog for 8½×11 SAE with $1.75 postage; ms guidelines online.

HENRY HOLT & CO., INC., 115 W. 18th St., New York NY 10011. (212)886-9200. Fax: (212)633-0748. E-mail: publicity@hholt.com. Website: www.henryholt.com. Estab. 1866.
Imprint(s): Books for Young Readers; John Macrae Books; Metropolitan Books; Owl Books; Times Books.
How to Contact: No simultaneous submissions. Sometimes comments on rejected mss.

HOMA & SEKEY BOOKS, 138 Veterans Plaza, P.O. Box 103, Dumont NJ 07628. (201)384-6692. Fax: (201)384-6055. E-mail: info@homabooks.com. Website: www.homabooks.com. **Contact:** Shawn Ye, editor-in-chief. Estab. 1997. "We focus on publishing Asia-related titles. Both translations and original English manuscripts are welcome. Publishes hardcover and paperback originals. Books: natural paper; web press; perfect bound; illustrations. Average print order: 2,000. Average first novel print order: 1,500. **Published 3 debut authors within the last year.** Averages 7 total titles, 3 fiction titles/year. Member, PMA. Distributes titles through IPG, Ingram, Baker & Taylor, etc.
  • Received the Notable Book Award for *Father & Son: A Novel*.
Needs: Ethnic (Asian), literary, mystery, young adult (adventure, historical, mystery/suspense, romance). Wants China-related titles. Published *Father and Son*, by Sung-won Han (translation); *The General's Beard*, by Jyoung

Lee (translation); *Reflections on a Mask*; In-hun Choe (translation). Also publish a series of Modern fiction from Korea.

How to Contact: Accepts unsolicited mss. Query with SASE or submit outline, 2 sample chapter(s). Accepts queries by e-mail, mail. Include estimated word count, brief bio, list of publishing credits. Send SASE for return of ms or send a disposable ms and SASE for reply only. Responds in 4 weeks to queries; 10 weeks to mss. Accepts simultaneous submissions, electronic submissions. Always comments on rejected mss.

Payment/Terms: Pays 5-10% royalty. Publishes ms 1 year after acceptance. Book catalog for 9×12 SASE; ms guidelines online.

Advice: "Authors should be willing and able to actively participate in the publicity and promotion of their books."

Ⓝ ◻ HOT HOT HOUSE, 760 Cushing Hwy, Cohasset MA 02025. (781)383-8360. Fax: (781)383-8346. E-mail: publisher@hothousepress.com. Website: www.hothousepress.com. **Contact:** Sally Weltman, senior editor. Estab. 2000. Small, independent publisher with over four decades of experience. Publishes hardcover and paperback originals. Average print order: 5,000. First novel print order: 3,000. **Published 2 debut authors within the last year.** Member, Independent Publishers Association. Distributes through NBN.

Needs: Historical, literary, mystery, thriller/espionage. Published *All Are Naked*, by Wayne Barcomb (mystery/suspense); *Earth Angel*, by Tom McCann (fable); *Agents for Justice*, by Duke Southard (literary).

How to Contact: Accepts unsolicited mss. Query with SASE. Accepts queries by e-mail, mail. Include estimated word count, brief bio, list of publishing credits. Send SASE for return of ms or send a disposable ms and SASE for reply only. Agented fiction 30%. Responds in 1 month to queries; 1-2 months to mss. Accepts simultaneous submissions.

Payment/Terms: Pays 50% of revenue after published. Average advance: $100. Publishes ms within a year after acceptance. Book catalog online; ms guidelines for SASE.

Advice: "Make sure you have your manuscript in good shape and outline what you can/will do to promote and publicize the book."

☑ ◎ HOUGHTON MIFFLIN BOOKS FOR CHILDREN, Houghton Mifflin Company, 222 Berkeley St., Boston MA 02116. (617)351-5959. Fax: (617)351-1111. E-mail: children's_books@hmco.com. Website: www.houghtonmifflinbooks.com. **Contact:** Hannah Rodgers, submissions coordinator; Kate O'Sullivan, senior editor; Ann Rider, senior editor; Margaret Raymo, senior editor. "Houghton Mifflin gives shape to ideas that educate, inform, and above all, delight." Publishes hardcover originals and trade paperback originals and reprints. **Published 12 debut authors within the last year.** Averages 100 total titles/year. Promotes titles through author visits, advertising, reviews.

Imprint(s): Clarion Books, New York City, Walter Lorraine books.

Needs: Adventure, ethnic, historical, humor, juvenile (early readers), literary, mystery, picture books, suspense, young adult, board books. Published *Gathering Blue*, by Lois Lowry; *The Circuit*, by Francisco Jimenez; and *When I Was Older*, by Garret Freymann-Weyr.

How to Contact: Submit complete ms with appropriate-sized SASE. Responds in 4 months to queries; 4-6 months to mss. Accepts simultaneous submissions. No electronic submissions, submissions on disk.

Payment/Terms: Pays 5-10% royalty on retail price. Average advance: variable. Publishes ms 18-24 months after acceptance. Book catalog for 9×12 SASE with 3 first-class stamps; ms guidelines online.

Ⓐ HOUGHTON MIFFLIN CO., 222 Berkeley St., Boston MA 02116. Website: www.hmco.com. **Contact:** Submissions Editor. Estab. 1832. Publishes hardcover originals and trade paperback originals and reprints. **Published 5 debut authors within the last year.** Averages 250 total titles/year.

Needs: Literary. "We are not a mass market publisher. Study the current list." Published *Everything Is Illuminated*, by Jonathan Safran Foer; *The Book of Salt*, by Monique Truong; *In the Forest*, by Edna O'Brien; and *The American Heritage College Dictionary*, 4th Edition.

How to Contact: Does not accept unsolicited mss. *Agented submissions only.* Accepts simultaneous submissions.

Payment/Terms: Hardcover: pays 10-15% royalty on retail price, sliding scale or flat rate based on sales; paperback: 7½% flat rate, but negotiable. Average advance: variable. Publishes ms 3 years after acceptance. Book catalog online.

◎ HOWELLS HOUSE, P.O. Box 9546, Washington DC 20016-9546. (202)333-2182. **Contact:** W.D. Howells, publisher. Estab. 1988. "Our interests are institutions and institutional change." Publishes hardcover and trade paperback originals and reprints. Averages 4 total titles/year.

Imprint(s): The Compass Press, Whalesback Books.

Needs: Historical, literary, mainstream/contemporary.

How to Contact: Query. Responds in 2 months to proposals. No simultaneous submissions.

Payment/Terms: Pays 15% net royalty or makes outright purchase. May offer advance. Publishes ms 8 months after acceptance.

◻ ◎ HUNTINGTON PRESS, 3687 S. Procyon Avenue, Las Vegas NV 89103. (702)252-0655. E-mail: books@huntingtonpress.com. Website: www.huntingtonpress.com. **Contact:** Deke Castleman, senior editor. Publishes hardcover and paperback originals. Books: offset printing. First novel print order: 3,000-5,000. **Published 2 debut authors within the last year.** Member, PMA/SPAN.

Needs: "We focus on novels about gambling and Las Vegas."

How to Contact: Accepts unsolicited mss. Query with SASE. Accepts queries by e-mail. Responds in 1 month to queries; 2 weeks to mss. Accepts simultaneous submissions, electronic submissions, submissions on disk. Often comments on rejected mss.

Payment/Terms: Pays royalty. Book catalog free; ms guidelines for #10 SASE.

N A ◎ ∅ HYPERION BOOKS FOR CHILDREN, Hyperion, 114 Fifth Ave., New York NY 10011. (212)633-440. Fax: (212)633-4833. Website: http://disney.go.com/disneybooks/hyperionbooks/homepage.html. **Contact:** Editorial director. "The aim of Hyperion Books for Children is to create a dynamic children's program informed by Disney's creative vision, direct connection to children, and unparalleled marketing and distribution." Publishes hardcover and trade paperback originals. Averages 210 total titles/year.

Needs: Juvenile, picture books, young adult. Published *McDuff*, by Roesmary Wells and Susan Jeffers (picture book); *Split Just Right*, by Adele Griffin (middle grade).

How to Contact: *Agented submissions only.* Accepts simultaneous submissions.

Payment/Terms: Pays royalty. Average advance: varies. Publishes ms 1 year after acceptance. Book catalog free; ms guidelines free.

Advice: "Hyperion Books for Children are meant to appeal to an upscale children's audience. Study your audience. Look at and research current children's books. Who publishes what you like? Approach them."

N ⊕ ◯ IGNOTUS PRESS, BCM-Writer, London WC1N 3XX UK. E-mail: ignotuspress@aol.com. Website: www.ignotuspress.com. **Contact:** Suzanne Ruthuen. Estab. 1996. The aim of Ignotus Press is to provide a wide base of genuine information for all esoteric traditions. Publishes paperback originals, hardcover reprints, paperback reprints and e-books. Books: litho and digital printing; perfect binding; illustrations. Average first novel print order: 300. **Published 12 debut authors within the last year.** Averages 20 total titles/year.

Imprint(s): Moonraker.

Needs: Horror (psychological, supernatural), humor, new age/mystic, psychic/supernatural, religious (religious mystery/suspense, religious thriller). "Ignotus press hopes to fill the gap left by main-stream publishers who are moving away from traditional sources. What we don't want is New Age idealism, sword & sorcery, fantasy, 'mind, body & spirit', the white-light brand of modern Wicca, pseudo-spirituality or any form of neo-Hammer House of Horror fiction." Published *Wood Craft*, by Rupert Percy; *Velvet Vampire*, by Adam Thorne; *Hearth Fire*, by Fiona Walker-Craven.

How to Contact: Does not accept unsolicited mss. Submit 2 sample chapter(s). Accepts queries by mail. Include estimated word count, brief bio, list of publishing credits. Responds in 4 months. Sometimes comments on rejected mss.

Payment/Terms: Pays royalty. Pays 6 contributor's copies. Publishes ms 6-12 months after acceptance. Book catalog free; ms guidelines for SASE.

Advice: "Seriously study the guidelines and back list."

N IMAGE COMICS, 1071 M/ Batavia St., Suite A, Orange CA 92867. Website: www.imagecomics.com.

Needs: Comics and graphic novels, all genres.

How to Contact: "Image Comics accepts only proposals for new comics. This refers to writing, inking, pencilling, lettering, or coloring samples. Since Images publishes only creator-owned properties, we do not hire freelancers. Therefore, we do not accept submissions, we accept proposals." Send cover letter, one-page story synopsis for series, ms, cover mock-up via postal mail.

Payment/Terms: "Since Image Comics, Inc. owns no intellectual properties, you can be assured, accepted or not, your property will remain yours." Ms guidelines on website.

⚏ INSOMNIAC PRESS, 192 Spadina Ave., Suite 403, Toronto ON M5T 2C2 Canada. (416)504-6270. Fax: (416)504-9313. E-mail: mike@insomniacpress.com. Website: www.insomniacpress.com. Estab. 1992. "Midsize independent publisher with a mandate to produce edgy experimental fiction." Publishes trade paperback originals and reprints, mass market paperback originals, and electronic originals and reprints. First novel print order: 3,000. **Published 15 debut authors within the last year.** Plans 4 first novels this year. Averages 20 total titles, 5 fiction titles/year.

Needs: Comic books, ethnic, experimental, gay/lesbian, humor, literary, mainstream/contemporary, multicultural, mystery, poetry, suspense. We publish a mix of commercial (mysteries) and literary fiction. Published *Pray For Us Sinners*, by Patrick Taylor (novel).

How to Contact: Accepts unsolicited mss. Query via e-mail, submit proposal package including synopsis or submit complete ms. Accepts queries by e-mail. Include estimated word count, brief bio, list of publishing credits. Send SASE for return of ms or send a disposable ms and SASE for reply only. Agented fiction 5%. Responds in 1 week to queries; 2 months to proposals; 2 months to mss. Accepts simultaneous submissions. Sometimes comments on rejected mss.

Payment/Terms: Pays 10-15% royalty on retail price. Average advance: $500-1,000. Publishes ms 6 months after acceptance. Ms guidelines online.
Advice: "Visit our website, read our writer's guidelines."

◎ INTERCONTINENTAL PUBLISHING, 11681 Bacon Race Rd., Woodbridge VA 22192. (703)583-4800. Fax: (703)670-7825. E-mail: icpub@worldnet.att.net. **Contact:** H.G. Smittenaar, publisher. Publishes hardcover and trade paperback originals. Averages 3-4 total titles/year.
Needs: Mystery, suspense. Published *I'm Okay You're Dead*, by Spizer (mystery); *Dekok and the Begging Death*, by Baantjer (police procedural).
How to Contact: Submit proposal package, including 1-3 sample chapters, estimated word count and SASE. Responds ASAP to proposals. Accepts simultaneous submissions.
Payment/Terms: Pays 5% minimum royalty.
Advice: "Be original, write proper English, be entertaining."

◎ INTERLINK PUBLISHING GROUP, INC., 46 Crosby St., Northampton MA 01060. (413)582-7054. Fax: (413)582-7057. E-mail: editor@interlinkbooks.com. Website: www.interlinkbooks.com. **Contact:** Michel Moushabeck, publisher; Pam Thompson, fiction editor. Estab. 1987. "Midsize independent publisher specializing in world travel, world literature, world history and politics." Publishes hardcover and trade paperback originals. Books: 55 lb. Warren Sebago cream white paper; web offset printing; perfect binding. Average print order: 5,000. **Published new writers within the last year.** Averages 50 total titles, 2-4 fiction titles/year. Distributes titles through distributors such as Baker & Taylor. Promotes titles through book mailings to extensive, specialized lists of editors and reviews, authors read at bookstores and special events across the country.
Imprint(s): Interlink Books and Olive Branch Press.
Needs: Ethnic, international. "We are looking for translated works relating to the Middle East, Africa or Latin America." Published *House of the Winds*, by Mia Yun (first novel); *The Gardens of Light*, by Amin Maalouf (novel translated from French); and *War in the Land of Egypt*, by Yusef Al-Qaid (novel translated from Arabic). Publishes the International Folk Tales series.
How to Contact: Does not accept unsolicited mss. Query with SASE or submit outline, sample chapter(s). Responds in 3 months to queries. Accepts simultaneous submissions. No electronic submissions.
Payment/Terms: Pays 6-8% royalty on retail price. Average advance: small. Publishes ms 18 months after acceptance. Book catalog free; ms guidelines online.
Advice: "Our Emerging Voices Series is designed to bring to North America readers the one-unheard voices of writers who have achieved wide acclaim at home, but were not recognized beyond the borders of their native lands. We are also looking for folk tale collections (for adults) from around the world that fit in our International Folk Tale Series."

⬚ ◙ INVERTED-A, P.O. Box 267, Licking MO 65542. E-mail: amnfn@well.com. **Contact:** Aya Katz, chief editor (poetry, novels, political); Nets Katz, science editor (scientific, academic). Estab. 1985. Publishes paperback originals. Books: offset printing. Average print order: 1,000. Average first novel print order: 500. Distributes through Baker & Taylor, Amazon, Bowker.
Needs: Utopian, political. Needs poetry submission for our newsletter, *Inverted-A Horn*.
How to Contact: Does not accept unsolicited mss. Query with SASE. Reading period open from January 2 to March 15. Accepts queries by e-mail. Include estimated word count. Send SASE or IRC. Responds in 1 month. Accepts simultaneous submissions. Sometimes comments on rejected mss.
Payment/Terms: Pays in 10 author's copies. Publishes ms 1 year after acceptance. Ms guidelines for SASE.
Advice: "Read our books. Read the *Inverted-A Horn*. We are different. We do not follow industry trends."

⬚ ✦ ◎ ION IMAGINATION PUBLISHING, Ion Imagination Entertainment, Inc., P.O. Box 210943, Nashville TN 37221-0943. Fax: (615)646-6276. E-mail: ionimagin@aol.com. Website: www.flumpa.com. **Contact:** Keith Frickey, editor. Estab. 1994. Small independent publisher of children's fiction, multimedia and audio products. Publishes hardcover and paperback originals. Average first novel print order: 10,000. Member, SPAN and PMA.
• Received the Parents Choice National Parenting Centers Seal of Approval, Dr. Troy.
Needs: Children's/juvenile (adventure, animal, preschool/picture book, science).
How to Contact: Does not accept unsolicited mss. Query with SASE. Include brief bio, list of publishing credits. Responds in 1 month. Accepts simultaneous submissions. Sometimes comments on rejected mss.
Payment/Terms: Pays royalty.

◙ IRONWEED PRESS, P.O. Box 754208, Parkside Station, Forest Hills NY 11375. (718)544-1120. Fax: (718)268-2394. Estab. 1996. Small independent publisher. "Annually we publish only one original title, selected through our Ironweed Press Fiction Prize. The deadline is in June. For guidelines, please send SASE." See listing for Ironweed Press Fiction Prize in the Contests and Awards section. Publishes hardcover and paperback originals. Distributes titles through national wholesalers.

◙ ◎ ITALICA PRESS, 595 Main St., Suite 605, New York NY 10044-0047. (212)935-4230. Fax: (212)838-7812. E-mail: inquiries@italicapress.com. Website: www.italicapress.com. **Contact:** Ronald G. Musto and Eileen

Gardiner, publishers. Estab. 1985. Small independent publisher of Italian fiction in translation. "First time translators published. We would like to see translations of Italian writers well-known in Italy who are not yet translated for an American audience." Publishes trade paperback originals. Books: 50-60 lb. natural paper; offset printing; illustrations. Average print order: 1,500. Averages 6 total titles, 2 fiction titles/year. Distributes titles through website. Promotes titles through website.

Needs: Translations of 20th century Italian fiction. Published *Eruptions*, by Monica Sarsini; *The Great Bear*, by Ginevra Bompianai; and *Sparrow*, by Giovanni Verga.

How to Contact: Accepts unsolicited mss. Query with SASE. Accepts queries by e-mail, fax. Responds in 1 month to queries; 2 months to mss. Accepts simultaneous submissions, electronic submissions, submissions on disk.

Payment/Terms: Pays 7-15% royalty on wholesale price. Provides author's copies. Publishes ms 1 year after acceptance. Book catalog free; ms guidelines online.

Advice: "Remember we publish *only* fiction that has been previously published in Italian. A *brief* call saves a lot of postage. 90% of proposals we receive are completely off base but we are very interested in things that are right on target. Please send return postage if you want your manuscript back."

IVY LEAGUE PRESS, INC., P.O. Box 3326, San Ramon CA 94583-8326. (800)IVY-PRESS. Fax: (888)IVY-PRESS. E-mail: ivyleaguepress@worldnet.att.net. **Contact:** Maria Thomas, editor. Publishes hardcover, trade paperback and mass market paperback originals. Specializes in medical thrillers. Books: perfect binding. First novel print order: 5,000. Distributes titles through Baker & Taylor and Ingram. Promotes titles through TV, radio and print.

Needs: Mystery (medical). Medical suspense. Published *Allergy Shots*, by Robert B. Litman.

How to Contact: Does not accept unsolicited mss. Query with SASE. Include estimated word count, brief bio, list of publishing credits. Responds in 3 months. Accepts electronic submissions, submissions on disk. No simultaneous submissions. Always comments on rejected mss.

Payment/Terms: Pays royalty. Offers advance.

Advice: "If you tell a terrific story of medical suspense, one which is hard to put down, we may publish it."

IVY PUBLICATIONS, 72 Hyperion House, Somers Road, London SW21HZ United Kingdom. Estab. 1989. Small book publisher. Publishes paperback originals.

Needs: Adventure, children's/juvenile (adventure, historical), historical, humor, military/war, young adult (adventure, historical). "We are on the look-out for genius; a P.G. Wodehouse or Raymond Chandler would be most welcome."

How to Contact: Accepts unsolicited mss. Query with SASE. Accepts queries by mail. Include list of publishing credits. Accepts simultaneous submissions. No electronic submissions, submissions on disk. Sometimes comments on rejected mss.

Payment/Terms: "We pay all costs." Profit: 50% to author, 50% to publisher.

Advice: "Write in top-class English that is used by top American, British, Indian, South African writers. Meaning of words, style and grammar are our yardsticks."

JAMESON BOOKS, INC., 722 Columbus St., P.O. Box 738, Ottawa IL 61350. (815)434-7905. Fax: (815)434-7907. **Contact:** Jameson G. Campaigne, publisher/editor. Estab. 1986. "Jameson Books publishes conservative/libertarian politics and economics, history, biography, Chicago-area themes and pre-cowboy frontier novels (1750-1840)." Publishes hardcover originals. Books: free sheet paper; offset printing. Average print order: 10,000. First novel print order: 5,000. Averages 6 total titles, 6-8 fiction titles/year. Distributes titles through LPC Group/Chicago (book trade).

Needs: Very well researched western (frontier pre-1850). Interested in pre-cowboy "mountain men" in American west, before 1820 in east frontier fiction. Published *Yellowstone Kelly*, by Peter Bowen; *Wister Trace*, by Loren Estelman; and *One-Eyed Dream*, by Terry Johnston.

How to Contact: Does not accept unsolicited mss. Query with SASE or submit outline, 1 sample chapter(s), synopsis. Agented fiction 70%. Responds in 6 months. Accepts simultaneous submissions. Sometimes comments on rejected mss.

Payment/Terms: Pays 6-15% royalty on retail price. Average advance: $1,000-25,000. Publishes ms 1 year after acceptance.

JIREH PUBLISHING COMPANY, P.O. Box 4263, San Leandro CA 94579-0263. E-mail: jaholman@yahoo.com. Website: www.jirehpublishing.com. Estab. 1995. Small independent publisher. "We have just begun our fiction line." Publishes hardcover, trade paperback and electronic originals. Books: paper varies; POP and offset printed; binding varies. Average print order: varies. First novel print order: varies. Plans 2 first novels this year. Averages 2-5 total titles, 1-2 fiction titles/year. Distributes titles through online bookstores and booksellers (retailers).

Needs: Mystery, religious (Christian ebooks, general religious, mystery/suspense, thriller, romance), suspense. "We are looking for Christian values in the books that we publish."

How to Contact: Accepts unsolicited mss. Query with SASE. Accepts queries by e-mail. Include brief bio, list of publishing credits. Send SASE for return of ms or send a disposable ms and SASE for reply only. Responds in 1-2 months to queries; 3 months to mss. Accepts simultaneous submissions. No electronic submissions, submissions on disk. Sometimes comments on rejected mss.

Payment/Terms: Pays 10-12% royalty on wholesale price. Publishes ms 9-12 months after acceptance. Book catalog online; ms guidelines online.

☑ ◎ **JOURNEYFORTH**, BJU Press, 1700 Wade Hampton Blvd., Greenville SC 29614-0001. (864)242-5100, ext. 4350. E-mail: jb@bjup.com. Website: www.bjup.com. **Contact:** Nancy Lohr, manuscript editor (juvenile fiction). Estab. 1974. "Small independent publisher of excellent, trustworthy novels, information books, audio tapes and ancillary materials for readers pre-school through high school. We desire to develop in our children a love for and understanding of the written word, ultimately helping them love and understand God's word." Publishes paperback original and reprints. Books: 50 lb. white paper; Webb lithography printing; perfect-bound binding. Average print order: 5,000. **Published some debut authors within the last year.** Averages 10 total titles, 10 fiction titles/year. Distributes titles through Spring Arbor and Appalachian. Promotes titles through CBA Marketplace.

Needs: Adventure (children's/juvenile, young adult), historical (children's/juvenile, young adult), juvenile (animal, easy-to-read, series), mystery (children's/juvenile, young adult), sports (children's/juvenile, young adult), suspense (young adult), western (young adult), young adult (series). "Our fiction is all based on a moral and Christian word-view." Published *Susannah and the Secret Coins*, by Elaine Schulte (historical young adult fiction); *Arby Jenkins Meets His Match*, by Sharon Hambrick (contemporary children's fiction); *Over the Divide*, by Catherine Farnes (young adult fiction).

How to Contact: Accepts unsolicited mss. Query with SASE or submit outline, 5 sample chapter(s) or submit complete ms. Include estimated word count, brief bio, social security number, list of publishing credits. Send SASE for return of ms or send a disposable ms and SASE for reply only. Responds in 1 month to queries; 3 months to mss. Accepts simultaneous submissions.

Payment/Terms: Pays royalty. Publishes ms 12-18 months after acceptance. Book catalog free; ms guidelines online.

Advice: "Study the publisher's guidelines. Make sure your work is suitable or you waste time for you and the publisher."

Ⓝ ☑ ◎ **JUST US BOOKS, INC.**, 356 Glenwood Ave., 3rd Floor, East Orange NJ 07017. (973)672-7701. Fax: (973)677-7570. E-mail: justusbooks@aol.com. Website: www.justusbooks.com. Estab. 1988. Small independent publisher of children's books that focus on African-American experiences (fiction and nonfiction). Publishes hardcover originals, paperback originals, hardcover reprints and paperback reprints. Averages 4-8 total titles, 2-4 fiction titles/year. Member, Small Press Association; Children Book Council.

Needs: Children's/juvenile (historical, mystery, preschool/picture book), ethnic (African American), young adult (adventure, easy-to-read, historical, mystery/suspense, problem novels, series, sports.). "Young adult fiction targeted to male readers." Published *A Blessing in Disguise*, by Eleanora Tate.

How to Contact: Accepts unsolicited mss. Query with SASE. Accepts queries by mail. Send SASE for return of ms or send a disposable ms and SASE for reply only. Responds in 8-10 weeks to queries and mss. Accepts simultaneous submissions. Rarely comments on rejected mss.

Payment/Terms: Pays royalty. Book catalog online; ms guidelines for SASE or on website.

Advice: "We are looking for realistic, contemporary characters; stories and interesting plots that introduce both conflict and resolution. We will consider various themes and story-lines, but before an author submits a query we urge them to become familiar with our books."

Ⓝ ☑ **JUSTIN, CHARLES & CO., PUBLISHERS**, 20 Park Plaza, Suite 909, Boston MA 02116. (617)426-4406. E-mail: info@justincharlesbooks.com. Website: www.justincharles.com. **Contact:** Stephen Hall, publisher (general fiction, mystery). Carmen Mitchell, assistant editor (general fiction, mystery). Estab. 2002. Publishes hardcover originals and paperback originals. Plans 1 first novel this year. Distributes through the National Book Network.

Imprint(s): Kate's Mystery Books.

Needs: Humor, mainstream/contemporary, mystery (amateur sleuth, police procedural, private eye/hardboiled).

READ 'THE BUSINESS OF FICTION WRITING' section for information on manuscript preparation, mailing tips, rights and more.

Published *Dead Clever*, by Scarlet Thomas (mystery); *The Hired Gun*, by Matthew Bronton (noir); and *The White Trilogy*, by Ken Bruen (mystery/police procedural).

How to Contact: Accepts unsolicited mss. Query with SASE or submit 3-4 sample chapter(s), synopsis. Accepts queries by mail. Include brief bio, list of publishing credits. Send SASE for return of ms or send a disposable ms and SASE for reply only. Agented fiction 90%. Responds in 2 months to queries; 2-3 months to mss. Accepts simultaneous submissions. No electronic submissions, submissions on disk. Rarely comments on rejected mss.

Payment/Terms: Publishes ms 1-2 years after acceptance. Ms guidelines online.

Advice: "Please look at the types of books we have on our website and our writers guidelines."

N ⃞ ◎ KAEDEN BOOKS, P.O. Box 16190, Rocky River OH 44116-0190. (440)617-1400. Fax: (440)617-1403. E-mail: jhoyer@kaeden.com. Website: www.kaeden.com. **Contact:** Joan Hoyer, office manager. Estab. 1990. "We are an educational publisher of supplemental texts for use in the pre-K to 3rd grade market. Our materials are used by teachers in reading instruction in the classroom. These are fully illustrated books with kid-catching, interesting themes that are age appropriate." Publishes paperback originals. Books: offset printing; saddle binding; illustrations. Average print order: 5,000. **Published 6 debut authors within the last year.** Averages 8-16 total titles/year. Distributes titles through school sales representatives. Promotes titles in professional teacher and reading journals, also partnered with Thinkbox.com.

Needs: Adventure (children's/juvenile), ethnic, fantasy, historical (children's/juvenile; general), humor, mystery (children's/juvenile, amatuer sleuth), science fiction (soft/sociological), short story collections, sports (children's/juvenile), suspense (amateur sleuth), Children's/Juvenile; Animal; Series; Thriller/Espionage. Published *When I Go to Grandma's House*, by Brian P. Cleary (fiction); *Sammy's Hamburger Caper*, by Kathleen and Craig Urmston (fiction); and *The Fishing Contest*, by Joe Yung Yukisgi.

How to Contact: Accepts unsolicited mss. Query with SASE or submit outline, publishing history, synopsis, author bio, SASE. Send a disposable copy of ms and SASE for reply only. Responds only "if interested." Include brief bio, list of publishing credits..

Payment/Terms: Pays royalty. Negotiable, either royalties or flat fee by individual arrangement with author depending on book. Publishes ms 6-24 months after acceptance. Ms guidelines online.

Advice: "Our line is expanding with particular interest in fiction/nonfiction for grades two to three. Material must be suitable for use in the public school classroom, be multicultural and be high interest with appropriate word usage and a positive tone for the respective grade."

N ⃞ ◎ KAYA PRODUCTION, 116 Pinehurst Ave. #E51, New York NY 10033. (212)740-3519. E-mail: kaya@kaya.com. Website: www.kaya.com. **Contact:** Sunyoung Lee, editor. "Kaya is a small independent press dedicated to the publication of innovative literature from the Asian diaspora." Publishes hardcover originals and trade paperback originals and reprints.

Needs: "Kaya publishes Asian, Asian-American and Asian diasporic materials. We are looking for innovative writers with a commitment to quality literature."

How to Contact: Submit 2-4 sample chapter(s), synopsis, SASE. Responds in 6 months to mss. Accepts simultaneous submissions.

Payment/Terms: Book catalog free; ms guidelines online.

Advice: Audience is people interested in a high standard of literature and who are interested in breaking down easy approaches to multicultural literature.

A ⃞ KENSINGTON PUBLISHING CORP., 850 Third Ave., 16th Floor, New York NY 10022. (212)407-1500. Fax: (212)935-0699. Website: www.kensingtonbooks.com. **Contact:** Michaela Hamilton, editor in chief; Kate Duffy, editorial director (romance); John Scognamiglio, editorial director; Ann LaFarge, executive editor; Karen Thomas, editorial director (Arabesque romance, African-American fiction, Dafina Books); Amy Garvey, editor (romance, regency, historical romance). Estab. 1975. Full service trade commercial publisher, all formats. Publishes hardcover and trade paperback originals, mass market paperback originals and reprints. Averages over 500 total titles/year.

Imprint(s): Arabesque and Dafina (Karen Thomas, executive editor); Brava (Kate Duffy, editoral director); Citadel; Kensington; Pinnacle; Zebra.

Needs: Ethnic, gay/lesbian, historical, horror, mainstream/contemporary, multicultural, mystery, occult, romance (contemporary, historical, regency,), suspense, thriller/espionage, western (epic), thrillers; women's. Published *Celebration*, by Fern Michaels.

How to Contact: Does not accept unsolicited mss. *Agented submissions only. No unsolicited mss.* Responds in 1 month to queries. Accepts simultaneous submissions.

Payment/Terms: Pays 8-15% royalty on retail price or makes outright purchase. Average advance: $2,000 and up. Publishes ms 9-12 months after acceptance. Book catalog online.

◎ ALLEN A. KNOLL, PUBLISHERS, 200A W. Victoria Street, Suite 3, Santa Barbara CA 93101-3627. (805)564-3377. E-mail: bookinfo@knollpublishers.com. Website: www.knollpublishers.com. **Contact:** Submissions. Estab. 1990. "Small independent publisher, a few titles a year. Specializes in 'books for intelligent people who read for fun.' " Publishes hardcover originals. Books: offset printing; sewn binding. Titles distributed through Ingram, Baker & Taylor.

Needs: Published *The Unholy Ghost*, by Alistair Boyle (mystery); *She Died for Her Sins*, by David Champion (mystery); *He's Back*, by Theodore Roosevelt Gardner II (fiction/literature). Publishes the Gil Yates private investigator and Bomber Hanson Mystery series.

How to Contact: Does not accept unsolicited mss.

Payment/Terms: Varies. Book catalog online.

KNOPF PUBLISHING GROUP, Division of Random House, Inc., 1745 Broadway, New York NY 10019. (212)751-2600. Website: www.randomhouse.com/knopf. Estab. 1915. "Throughout history, Knopf has been dedicated to publishing distinguished fiction and nonfiction." Publishes hardcover and paperback originals.

Imprint(s): Everyman's Library; Alfred A. Knopf; Pantheon Books; Shocken Books; Vintage Anchor Publishing.

ALFRED A. KNOPF, Knopf Publishing Group, Random House, Inc., 1745 Broadway, 21st Floor, New York NY 10019. (212)751-2600. Website: www.aaknopf.com. **Contact:** Senior Editor. Estab. 1915. Book-length fiction of literary merit by known and unknown writers. Publishes hardcover and paperback originals. **Published debut authors within the last year.** Averages 200 total titles/year.

Needs: Publishes book-length fiction of literary merit by known or unknown writers. Length: 40,000-150,000 words. Published *Gertrude and Claudius*, by John Updike; *The Emperor of Ocean Park*, by Stephen Carter; and *Balzac and the Little Chinese Seamstress*, by Dai Sijie.

How to Contact: Does not accept unsolicited mss. Query with SASE or submit sample chapter(s). Send SASE or IRC. Responds in 3-5 months to queries. Accepts simultaneous submissions.

Payment/Terms: Pays 10-15% royalty. Royalty and advance vary. Offers advance. Must return advance if book is not completed or is unacceptable. Publishes ms 1 year after acceptance. Book catalog for 7½ × 10½ SAE with 5 first-class stamps; ms guidelines online.

KREGEL PUBLICATIONS, Kregel, Inc., P.O. Box 2607, Grand Rapids MI 49501. (616)451-4775. Fax: (616)451-9330. E-mail: kregelbooks@kregel.com. Website: www.kregel.com. **Contact:** Acquisitions Editor. Estab. 1949. Midsize independent Christian publisher. Publishes hardcover and trade paperback originals and reprints. Plans 5-10 first novels this year. Averages 90 total titles, 10-15 fiction titles/year. Member, ECPA.

Imprint(s): Kregel Academic & Professional, Jim Weaver (academic/pastoral); Kregel Kid Zone, Steve Barclift (children).

Needs: Adventure, children's/juvenile (adventure, historical, mystery, preschool/picture book, series, sports, Christian), historical, mystery, religious (children's, general, inspirational, fantasy/sci-fi, mystery/suspense, religious thriller, relationships), young adult (adventure). Fiction should be geared toward the evangelical Christian market. Wants "books with fast-paced, contemporary storylines—strong Christian message presented in engaging, entertaining style as well as books for juvenile and young adults, especially young women. Published *Divided Loyalties*, by L.K. Malone (action/thriller); *A Test of Love*, by Kathleen Scott (relationships); and *Jungle Hideout*, by Jeanette Windle (juvenile/adventure). Publishes the Parker Twins series, juvenile fiction.

How to Contact: Does not accept unsolicited mss. Query with SASE. Accepts queries by e-mail, fax. Include estimated word count, brief bio. Responds in 3 months. Accepts simultaneous submissions, electronic submissions, submissions on disk.

Payment/Terms: Pays 8-16% royalty on wholesale price. Average advance: $200-2,000. Publishes ms 14 months after acceptance. Book catalog for 9 × 12 SASE; ms guidelines online.

Advice: "Visit our website and review the titles listed under various subject categories. Does your proposed work duplicate existing titles? Does it address areas not covered by existing titles? Does it break new ground?"

LAST KNIGHT PUBLISHING COMPANY, P.O. Box 270006, Fort Collins Co 80527. (970)391-6857. Fax: (970)493-0924. E-mail: ckaine@lastknightpublishing.com. Website: www.LastKnightPublishing.com. **Contact:** Charles Kaine, publisher/owner. "Small independent publisher interested in various fictional forms. We are interested in books that have a niche market. We are interested in making high quality books, both by the words written and how it is printed." Publishes paperback originals. Books: 70 lb. Vellum opaque paper; offset-printed; perfect-bound. Average print order: 1,500-4,000. Average first novel print order: 1,500. **Published 1 debut author within the last year.** Plans 2-3 first novels this year.

Needs: Fantasy (space fantasy, sword and sorcery), historical, horror (dark fantasy, futuristic, supernatural), literary, mainstream/contemporary, mystery (amateur sleuth, cozy), psychic/supernatural, thriller/espionage. Published *The Breach*, by Brian Kaufman (historical fiction).

How to Contact: Accepts unsolicited mss. Query with SASE. Accepts queries by mail. Include estimated word count, brief bio, and an explanation of "why people will want to read the work." Send SASE for return of ms or send a disposable ms and SASE for reply only. Responds in 6 weeks to queries; 2-3 months to mss. Accepts simultaneous submissions. Often comments on rejected mss.

Payment/Terms: Pays royalty. Average advance: negotiable. Publishes ms 9 months after acceptance. Ms guidelines online.

LEAPFROG PRESS, P.O. Box 1495, 95 Commercial St., Wellfleet MA 02667-1495. (508)349-1925. Fax: (508)349-1180. E-mail: leapfrog@c4.net. Website: www.leapfrogpress.com. **Contact:** David Witkowsky, acquisitions editor. Estab. 1996. "We search for beautifully written literary titles and endeavor to market them aggresively to national trade and library accounts as well as to sell film, translation, foreign and book club rights." Publishes hardcover and paperback originals and paperback reprints. Books: acid-free paper; sewn binding. Average print order: 5,000. First novel print order: 4,000 (average). Member, Publishers Marketing Association, Bookbuilders of Boston and PEN. Distributes titles through Consortium Book Sales and Distribution, St. Paul, MN. Promotes titles through all national review media, bookstore readings, author tours, website, radio shows, chain store promotions, advertisements, book fairs.

- *The Devil and Daniel Silverman*, by Theodore Rozak, was nominated for the American Library Association Stonewall Award and it was a San Francisco Chronicle best seller.

Needs: "Genres often blur; we're interested in good writing. We'd love to see memoirs as well as fiction that comments on the world through the lends of personal, political or family experience." Published *The War at Home*, by Nora Eisenberg; *Just The Way You Want Me*, by Nora Eisenberg; *The German Money*, by Lev Raphael; *Junebug*, by Maureen McCoy; *Paradise Dance*, by Michael Lee; and *The Devil and Daniel Silverman*, by Theodore Roszak.
How to Contact: Query with SASE. Accepts queries by e-mail, but due to volume, does not respond unless interested. Accepts queries by e-mail. "Please see website for information. Do not call the office." Responds in 3-6 months. No simultaneous submissions. Sometimes comments on rejected mss.
Payment/Terms: Pays 4-8% royalty. Average advance: Negotiable. Publishes ms 1-2 years after acceptance.
Advice: "Because editors have so little time, you had best send them your very best work. Editors don't have a lot of time to line edit. They love to work with you but they do not want to rewrite your book for you. In fact, if you send good material that is poorly written, they may wonder if you actually can do the revisions necessary. So don't be impatient. Send your work only when you feel it is as good as you can make it, and that means knowing what's out there in the market; knowing how to create characters and a dynamite beginning and a plot that doesn't meander all over the place because you don't know where the story is going. Learn your craft. Although we have been open to the work of novice writers, we have found that we have had much of our success recently from writers who were formerly published by large NYC presses and then came to us. For that reason, we're especially interested in knowing where you have published before and if the book has a history."

LEAPING DOG PRESS, P.O. Box 222605, Chantilly VA 20153-2605. (703)864-6148. Fax: (703)484-3297. E-mail: editor@leapingdogpress.com. Website: www.leapingdogpress.com. **Contact:** Jordan Jones, editor and publisher.

LEE & LOW BOOKS, 95 Madison Ave., New York NY 10016. (212)779-4400. Fax: (212)532-6035. Website: www.leeandlow.com. **Contact:** Louise May, executive editor. Estab. 1991. "Our goals are to meet a growing need for books that address children of color, and to present literarture that all children can identify with. We only consider multicultural children's picture books. Of special interest are stories set in contemporary America." Publishes hardcover originals—picture books only. Averages 12-16 total titles/year.
Imprint(s): Bebop Books
Needs: Children's/juvenile (historical, multicultural, preschool/picture book for children ages 2-10), ethnic, juvenile, multicultural, illustrated. Published *The Pot that Juan Built*, by Nancy Andrews-Goebel; and *Love to Langston*, by Tony Medina.
How to Contact: Accepts unsolicited mss. Send complete ms with cover letter or through an agent. Send SASE for return of ms or send a disposable ms and SASE for reply only. Agented fiction 30%. Responds in 2-4 months to queries; 2-4 months to mss. Accepts simultaneous submissions. Sometimes comments on rejected mss.
Payment/Terms: Pays royalty. Offers advance. Book catalog for SASE with $1.75 postage; ms guidelines online.
Advice: "Writers should familarize themselves with the styles and formats of recently published children's books. Lee & Low Books is a multicultural children's book publisher. We would like to see more contemporary stories set in the U.S. Animal stories and folktales are not considered at this time."

LEISURE BOOKS, Dorchester Publishing Co., 276 Fifth Ave., Suite 1008, New York NY 10001-0112. (212)725-8811. Fax: (212)532-1054. E-mail: dorchedit@aol.com. Website: www.dorchesterpub.com. **Contact:** Ashley Kuehl or Leah Hultenschmidt, editorial assistants. Estab. 1970. Publishes mass market paperback originals and reprints. Publishes romances, westerns, horrors, young adult, and technothrillers only. Books: newsprint paper; offset printing; perfect-bound. Average print order: variable. First novel print order: variable. Plans 25 first novels this year. Averages 160 total titles, 145 fiction titles/year. Promotes titles through ads in *Romantic Times*, author readings, promotional items.
Imprint(s): Leisure Books (contact: Alicia Condon), Love Spell Books (contact: Christopher Keeslar).
Needs: Historical (romance), horror, romance, western, technothrillers. "We are strongly backing historical romance (90,000-100,000 words). All historical romance should be set pre-1900. Horrors and westerns are growing as well. No sweet romance, science fiction, erotica, contemporary women's fiction, mainstream or action/adventure. New YA line, contemporary and paranormal, 45,000 words." Published *Pure Temptation*, by Connie Mason (historical romance); and *Frankly My Dear*, by Sandra Hill (time-travel romance).
How to Contact: Accepts unsolicited mss. Query with SASE or submit outline, first 3 sample chapter(s), synopsis.

Mark Wisniewski: 'Writing fiction rooted in real life'

Mark Wisniewski's bio reads like a "Who's Who" of the best literary magazines in the country. Besides dozens of stories published in such places as *Virginia Quarterly Review*, *Mississippi Review*, and *The Gettysburg Review*, his first novel (*Confessions of a Polish Used-Car Salesman*, Indian Chief Publishing House) went into a second printing. Sandwiched between *Confessions* and his second novel, *Pariahs*—currently being handled by his New York agent—Wisniewski recently put together a decidedly offbeat short story collection, *All Weekend with the Lights On* (Leaping Dog Press), for which he has received much critical acclaim.

Mark Wisniewski

His fiction is often outrageous, satirical—sometimes downright grim. *The Los Angeles Times* said *Confessions* "maintains the 'grinning horror' of *Huckleberry Finn*," and *Publishers Weekly* found that the themes of *All Weekend* include "confronting the truth of our shared hopes and fears, and telling the secrets that guard our uncommon lives." But above all, Wisniewski's work is about ordinary people in ordinary situations; it's rooted in real life, whether drawn from his Polish-American grandparents or from his own varied experiences. Publication may be "a matter of striking some fiber inside a given editor on a given day," as Wisniewski admits, but he's scored enough to suggest that there's something in his stories that grabs readers—and keeps them reading.

Wisniewski himself is drawn to story. Years ago, when he was a student in Georgetown University's law school and writing short stories whenever he could, Wisniewski sensed the practice of law would bore him. "But law itself is all about conflict, which is what's at the heart of good fiction," he says. "So those three years weren't an absolute waste of time, just an expensive and inefficient way to pass it for someone who wants to write."

Once he got the law degree, that was it for Wisniewski in the legal profession. He then supported himself by teaching fiction workshops at colleges in California, Texas, Pennsylvania, and New York City. Now, finally, one passion occupies his time: his writing—well, not exactly, because Wisniewski is also a book doctor, and that's a rather heavy commitment.

Some of Wisniewski's clients are "amazingly skilled at making phone calls" just as he settles down to do his own work. Still, no great loss: "I remind myself that my 'day job' is all about the business of telling stories, then hope that the more I help improve my clients' fiction, the more practiced I'll be when it comes to improving my own."

Wisniewski has plenty of professional training to draw on: three years of MFA workshops under his belt—one at UMass-Amherst and two at UC-Davis. As a graduate student, he was a "peer feedback freak," he says. "In those days, this served me well. But since, I've found it best to bounce work off my own walls. I like to have my wife read early drafts out loud—there's a value to hearing someone other than you interpret intended cadences of sentences.

But when it comes to the final draft, you could say I become my own book doctor."

Revision, as Wisniewski sees it, is the key to success—a truth misunderstood by beginning writers. It's not running a piece through the spell check or giving it to a friend to read and receiving the hoped-for "It's good." True revision, Wisniewski believes, goes all the way down to the floor joists: "I'm talking about attacking every possible weakness that one's gut suggests might exist and turning each of those weaknesses into reasons people will love the story." If one thinks of Raymond Carver's labor at revision—up to 15 to 20 drafts per story—to perfect a style which seems so natural, so unadorned, Wisniewski's prose also strikes one as genuine and lacking artifice yet, like Carver's, finely polished. Wisniewski says he can't even guess how much he revises; it's "second-nature" by now. "I mean, if I want to see a story in print, I simply have to become that story's biggest enemy, so why not dig in and begin slashing?"

But what about those he book doctors for? Some of Wisniewski's clients "aren't ready to revise." He finds he has to "make changes for them and convince them to use the changes, in which case you become a sort of therapist." Still, there are rewards, especially when a writer calls and announces an acceptance. "Some of those days feel better than those on which my own work is accepted, because there's the added satisfaction of successful teamwork."

Where does it all begin—before the story's shaped up enough to revise? With plot? Character? Tone?

For Wisniewski, "That depends on the story." Sometimes he'll begin with a what-if plot-wise; other times he'll begin with a particular character and "put him or her up against someone or something who represents a competing value, and plot becomes a matter of having that protagonist and antagonist encounter each other." If Wisniewski's stories usually seem character-driven, like most literary fiction, he emphasizes that plot "better show up—or you don't have a story."

The hallmark of a Wisniewski story is that oddball character—and a tone that is playful, bizarre, humorous, and yet oftentimes with an undertow to it, a measure of venomous irony. Tone itself emerges in the process of revision; it gets noticed, says Wisniewski, "when I listen to the places in the story where the narrative voice sounds most natural, then try to replicate the sound of that voice throughout the piece. If it's wry, it's wry. If it's playful, it's playful. I try not to get in its way." Regarding humor, Wisniewski says, it's "a serious world out there, full of awfully serious writers. Readers could use a laugh or two." His fans will recognize the truth of this assertion even in his darker pieces.

An avid short story writer, Wisniewski does nonetheless prefer the novel, if "for no other reason than the novel has potential to reach that many more readers." *Pariahs*, a disturbing book, like much of his fiction, takes up a timely topic, that of sexual harassment of young men by Catholic priests. Excerpts have appeared in high profile literary magazines, including *TriQuarterly*, *Beloit Fiction Journal*, and *The Yale Review*. One editor in New York expressed doubts about the book-buying public being interested in the subject matter. Baffled by this response, Wisniewski has this to offer: "Then again, this is a controversial, ironic, yet dead-serious book that lays out truths society has been hiding for centuries."

This speaks volumes about Mark Wisniewski's work as a whole. If Hawthorne aimed at "the truth of the human heart," Wisniewski drags up a lot from below the surface in his own writing—what we humans hide in sins and sorrows, in yearning and desires—and as a book doctor, he labors to get other writers to do the same.

—*Jack Smith*

"All mss must be typed, double-spaced on one side and left unbound." Agented fiction 70%. Responds in 6 months to queries. No simultaneous submissions, electronic submissions.

Payment/Terms: Pays royalty on retail price. Average advance: negotiable. Publishes ms 18 months after acceptance. Book catalog free by calling (800)481-9191; ms guidelines online.

Advice: Encourage first novelists "if they are talented and willing to take direction, *and* write the kind of genre fiction we publish. Please include a brief synopsis if sample chapters are requested."

N ☉ LERNER PUBLICATIONS COMPANY, 241 First Ave. N., Minneapolis MN 55401. (612)332-3344. Fax: (612)332-7615. Website: www.lernerbooks.com. **Contact:** Jennifer Zimian, submission editor. Estab. 1959. "Midsize independent *children's* publisher." Publishes hardcover originals, trade paperback originals and reprints. Books: Offset printing; reinforced library binding; perfect binding. Average print order: 5,000. First novel print order: 5,000. Averages 200 total titles, 1-2 fiction titles/year.

Needs: Young adult (problem novels, sports, adventure, mystery). Looking for "well-written middle grade and young adult. No *adult fiction or single short stories.*"

How to Contact: Accepts unsolicited mss. Query with SASE or submit outline, 2 sample chapter(s), synopsis. Responds in 6 months to mss. Accepts simultaneous submissions.

Payment/Terms: Provides author's copies. Average advance: varied. Publishes ms 12-18 months after acceptance. Book catalog for 9×12 SAE with $3.50 postage; ms guidelines online.

N ✪ LES ÉDITIONS DU VERMILLON, 305 St. Patrick St., Ottawa ON K1N 5K4 Canada. (613)241-4032. Fax: (613)241-3109. Publishes trade paperback originals. **Published some debut authors within the last year.** Averages 15-20 total titles/year.

Needs: Juvenile, literary, religious, short story collections, young adult.

How to Contact: Query with SASE. Responds in 6 months.

Payment/Terms: Pays 10% royalty. Publishes ms 18 months after acceptance. Book catalog free.

✪ ARTHUR A. LEVINE BOOKS, Scholastic Inc., 557 Broadway, New York NY 10012. (212)343-4436. Website: www.scholastic.com. **Contact:** Arthur Levine, editorial director. "Arthur A. Levine is looking for distinctive literature, for children and young adults, for whatever's extraordinary." Averages 10-14 total titles/year.

Needs: Juvenile, picture books, young adult, middle grade novels. Published *Frida*, by Jonah Winter, illustrated by Ana Juan; *St. Michael's Scales*, by Neil Connelly (YA novel, debut author); *The Slightly True Story of Cedar B. Hartley*, by Martine Murray (middle-grade novel, debut author); and *At the Crossing-Places*, by Kevin Crossley-Holland (YA fantasy novel).

How to Contact: Query with SASE. "We are willing to work with first-time authors, with or without agent."

Payment/Terms: Pays variable royalty on retail price. Average advance: variable. Book catalog for 9×12 SASE.

N ✪ ☉ ⚑ LIGHTWAVE PUBLISHING INC., P.O. Box 160, Maple Ridge BC V2X 7G1 Canada. (804)462-7890. Fax: (604)462-8208. E-mail: mikal@lightwavepublishing.com. Website: www.lightwavepublishing.com. **Contact:** Mikal Marrs. Estab. 1991. "Small award-winning independent publisher fo Christian children's and parenting material." Publishes hardcover originals.

● Lightwave has received three Angel Awards.

Needs: Children's/juvenile (religious), religious. "We only hire 'work-for-hire' and look for good writers willing to work to detailed specifications."

How to Contact: Does not accept unsolicited mss. Query with SASE. Include brief bio, list of publishing credits. Responds in 1 month to queries. No simultaneous submissions.

Payment/Terms: Pays a lump sum. Finds writers on a work-for-hire basis. Publishes ms 8 months after acceptance. Book catalog online; ms guidelines free.

Advice: "Writer must be a team player, willing to work for hire (no royalties, limited accreditation), versatile, professional, work well to instructions and deadlines."

N ⬯ ☉ ⚑ LIONHEARTED PUBLISHING, INC., P.O. Box 618, Zephyr Cove NV 89448-0618. (775)588-1388. E-mail: editor@LionHearted.com. Website: www.lionhearted.com. **Contact:** Historical or Contemporary Acquistions Editor. Estab. 1994. "Multiple award-winning, independent publisher of single title, mass market paperback, trade, and ebook, romance novels." Publishes trade mass market paperback originals and e-books. Also expanded romance into e-book formats. Books: mass market paperback; perfect-binding. **Published 10-12 debut authors within the last year.** Averages 12-72 total titles, 12 fiction titles/year. Distributes through Ingram, Barnes & Noble, Baker & Taylor, Amazon and Internet website. Promotes titles through trade romance reader magazines, website and Internet.

Needs: Romance (contemporary, futuristic/time travel, historical, regency period, romantic suspense; over 65,000 words only), romantic comedies. Published *Lord Darver's Match*, by Susanne Marie Knight (Regency time travel); *The Only One*, by Karen Woods, *Heart of the Diamond*, by Carrie Brock (Regency romance); *Suddenly Love*, by Catherine Sellers (contemporary romance); *The Rebel's Bride*, by JoAnn Delazzari; *Family Portrait*, by Sharon Sobel (Regency romance); *Charades*; by Ann Logan (romantic suspense); *Lover's Never Lie*, by Gael Morrison (romantic suspense); *The Magic Token*, by Susanne Marie Knight (Regency romance).

How to Contact: Accepts unsolicited mss. Query with SASE or submit outline, 3 sample chapter(s), publishing history, synopsis, estimated word count, cover letter and 1 paragraph story summary in cover letter. Do not send ms by regular mail unless invited by editor. Send sample chapters in body of e-mail or label each attachment with the title. Accepts queries by e-mail. Include list of publishing credits. Agented fiction less than 10%. Responds in 1 month to queries; 3 months to mss. No simultaneous submissions. Always comments on rejected mss.

Payment/Terms: Royalties of 10% maximum on paperbacks; 30% on electronic books. Average advance: $100. Publishes ms 18-24 months after acceptance. Book catalog online; ms guidelines online.

Advice: "If you are not an avid reader and fan of romance novels, and you have not written a romance, then you do not understand the hidden code and language of ramance, so don't waste your time or an editor's by submitting to a publisher of romance. Read at least three of our novels (they are a bit different from the normal category romance). Reading our books is the smart way to discover what our editors like."

★ LITTLE, BROWN AND CO. ADULT TRADE BOOKS, Division of AOL Time Warner Book Group, 1271 Avenue of the Americas, New York NY 10020. (212)522-8700. Fax: (212)522-2067. Website: www.twbookmark.com. Estab. 1837. "The general editorial philosophy for all divisions continues to be broad and flexible, with high quality and the promise of commercial success as always the first considerations." Publishes hardcover originals and paperback originals and reprints.

Imprint(s): Arcade Books; Back Bay Books; Bulfinch Press.

A ★ LITTLE, BROWN AND CO., CHILDREN'S PUBLISHING, Division of AOL Time Warner Books Group, Time Life Building, 1271 Avenue of the Americas, 11th Floor, New York NY 10020. (212)522-8700. Website: www.twbookmark.com. Estab. 1837. "We are looking for strong writing and presentation, but no predetermined topics." Publishes hardcover originals, trade paperback reprints. Averages 70-100 total titles/year.

Imprint(s): Back Bay Books.

Needs: Adventure, ethnic, fantasy, feminist, gay/lesbian, historical, humor, juvenile, mystery, picture books, science fiction, suspense, young adult. "We are looking for strong fiction for children of all ages in any area, including multicultural. We always prefer full manuscripts for fiction."

How to Contact: *Agented submissions only.* Accepts simultaneous submissions.

Payment/Terms: Pays royalty on retail price. Average advance: negotiable. Publishes ms 2 years after acceptance. Ms guidelines online.

LITTLE, BROWN AND CO., INC., Time Warner Inc., 1271 Avenue of the Americas, New York NY 10020. (212)522-8700. Website: twbookmark.com. **Contact:** Editorial Department. Estab. 1837. "The general editorial philosophy for all divisions continues to be broad and flexible, with high quality and the promise of commercial success as always the first considerations." Medium-size house. Publishes adult and juvenile hardcover originals and paperback originals and reprints. Averages 100 total titles, varies fiction titles/year.

Imprint(s): Little, Brown; Back Bay; Bulfinch Press.

Needs: Literary, mainstream/contemporary. Published *When the Wind Blows*, by James Patterson; *Angels Flight*, by Michael Connelly; *Sea Glass*, by Anita Shreve; and *City of Bones*, by Michael Connelly.

How to Contact: Does not accept unsolicited mss. Query with SASE. No simultaneous submissions.

Payment/Terms: Pays royalty. Average advance: varying. Ms guidelines online.

A LITTLE, BROWN AND COMPANY CHILDREN'S BOOKS, Time Life Building, 1271 Avenue of the Americas, New York NY 10020. (212)5228700. Website: www.littlebrown.com. **Contact:** Submission editor. Estab. 1837. Publishes hardcover originals and trade paperback reprints. Books: 70 lb. paper; sheet-fed printing; illustrations. Distributes titles through sales representatives. Promotes titles through author tours, book signings, posters, press kits, magazine and newspapers and Beacon Hill Bookbay.

Imprint(s): Megan Tingley Books (Megan S. Tingley, executive editor).

Needs: Children's/juvenile (adventure, ethnic, historical, humor, mystery, picture books, science fiction, suspense, fantasy). Published *What Every Girl (Except Me) Knows*, by Nora Baskin; *Gossip Girl* series, by Cecily von Ziegesar.

How to Contact: *Agented submissions only.*

Payment/Terms: Pays royalty. Average advance: negotiable. Publishes ms 1-2 after acceptance.

Advice: "Writers should avoid looking for the 'issue' they think publishers want to see, choosing instead topics they know best and are most enthusiastic about/inspired by."

◎ LIVINGSTON PRESS, University of West Alabama, Station 22, Livingston AL 35470. E-mail: jwt@uwa.edu. Website: www.livingstonpress.uwa.edu. **Contact:** Joe Taylor, literary editor; Tina Jones, literary editor. Estab. 1984. "Small university press specializing in offbeat and/or Southern literature." Publishes hardcover and trade paperback originals. Books: acid free; offset; some illustrations. Average print order: 2,500. First novel print order: 2,500. Plans 3 first novels this year. Averages 9 total titles, 6 fiction titles/year.

Imprint(s): Swallow's Tale Press.

Needs: Experimental, literary, short story collections, off-beat or Southern. "We are interested in form and, of course style." Recently published *Widening the Road*, by Fred Bonnie (stories); *The High Traverse*, by Richard Blanchard (novel); *The Drinking of Spirits*, by Tom Abrams (stories).

How to Contact: Query with SASE. Accepts unsolicited mss only during December. Include estimated word count, brief bio, list of publishing credits. Send SASE for return of ms or send a disposable ms and SASE for reply only. Responds in 1 month to queries; 1 year to mss. Accepts simultaneous submissions.

Payment/Terms: Pays a choice of 12% of initial run or a combination of contributor's copies and 10% royalty of net. Publishes ms 18 months after acceptance. Book catalog for SASE; ms guidelines online.

LLEWELLYN PUBLICATIONS, Llewellyn Worldwide, Ltd., P.O. Box 64383, St. Paul MN 55164-0383. (651)291-1970. Fax: (651)291-1908. E-mail: lwlpc@llewellyn.com. Website: www.llewellyn.com. **Contact:** Nancy J. Mostad, acquisitions manager (New Age, metaphysical, occult); Barbara Moore, acquisitions editor (kits and decks), Alexander Negrete (spanish), Natalie Harter (magic), Megan Atwood (YA and childrens), Stephanie Clement (astrology). Estab. 1901. Publishes trade and mass market paperback originals. **Published 30% debut authors within the last year.** Averages 100 total titles/year.

Needs: Occult, spiritual (metaphysical). "Authentic and educational, yet entertaining."

How to Contact: Responds in 3 months to queries. Accepts simultaneous submissions.

Payment/Terms: Pays 10% royalty on wholesale price or retail price. Book catalog for 9×12 SAE with 4 first-class stamps; ms guidelines online.

LONGSTREET PRESS, INC., 2974 Hardman Court, Atlanta GA 30305. (404)254-0110. Fax: (404)254-0116. Website: www.longstreetpress.net. **Contact:** Scott Bard, president/editor. Estab. 1988. Publishes hardcover and trade paperback originals. **Published 10% debut authors within the last year.** Averages 20 total titles/year.

Needs: Literary, mainstream/contemporary (Southern fiction).

How to Contact: *Agented submissions only.* Responds in 3 months to queries. Accepts simultaneous submissions.

Payment/Terms: Pays royalty. Offers advance. Publishes ms 1 year after acceptance. Book catalog for 9×12 SAE with 4 first-class stamps or online; ms guidelines for #10 SASE or online.

LOST HORSE PRESS, 105 Lost Horse Lane, Sandpoint ID 83864. (208)255-4410. Fax: (208)255-1560. E-mail: losthorsepress@mindspring.com. **Contact:** Christine Holbert, editor (novels, novellas). Estab. 1998. Publishes hardcover and paperback originals. Books: 60-70 lb. natural paper; offset printing; b&w illustration. Average print order:1,000-2,500. First novel print order: 1,000. **Published 2 debut authors within the last year.** Plans 2 first novels this year. Averages 4 total titles, 2 fiction titles/year.

• *Woman on the Cross*, by Pierre Delattre, won the *ForeWord Magazine's* 2001 Book of the Year Award for literary fiction.

Needs: Ethnic, experimental, lesbian, literary, regional (Pacific NW), short story collections. Accepts queries by e-mail. Accepts submissions on disk. Published *Tales of a Dalai Lama*, by Pierre Delattre (literary fiction); *Love*, by Valerie Martin (short stories); *Sailing Away*, by Richard Morgan (short stories); and *Woman on the Cross*, by Pierre Delattre (literary).

How to Contact: Accepts unsolicited mss. Query with SASE or submit publishing history, author bio, or submit complete ms. Accepts queries by e-mail. Include brief bio, list of publishing credits. Send SASE for return of ms or send a disposable ms and SASE for reply only. Responds in 3 months to queries; 6 months to mss.

Payment/Terms: Publishes ms 1-2 years after acceptance. Book catalog free; ms guidelines for #10 SASE.

LOVE SPELL, Dorchester Publishing Co., Inc., 200 Madison Ave., 20th Floor, New York NY 10016. (212)725-8811. Fax: (212)532-1054. Website: www.dorchesterpub.com. **Contact:** Don D'Auria, executive editor (horror, western); Kate Seaver, editor (romance); Micaela Bombard, editorial assistant (horror, romance, western). Love Spell publishes the quirky sub-genres of romance: time-travel, paranormal, futuristic. "Despite the exotic settings, we are still interested in character-driven plots." Publishes mass market paperback originals. Books: newsprint paper; offset printing; perfect-bound. Average print order: varies. First novel print order: varies. Plans 15 first novels this year. Averages 48 total titles/year.

Needs: Romance (futuristic, time travel, paranormal, historical), science fiction, futuristic, time travel, whimsical contemporaries. "Books industry-wide are getting shorter; we're interested in 90,000 words." Published *Island*, by Richard Layman (horror); *Dark Legend*, by Chrisine Feehan (paranormal romance); and *The Dragon Lord*, by Connie Mason (historical romance).

How to Contact: Query with SASE or submit 3 sample chapter(s), synopsis. No material will be returned without

---

MARKET CONDITIONS are constantly changing! If you're still using this book and it is 2005 or later, buy the newest edition of *Novel & Short Story Writer's Market* at your favorite bookstore or order from Writer's Digest Books by calling 1-800-448-0915.

SASE. Query first. No queries by fax. "All mss must be typed, double-spaced on one side and left unbound." Agented fiction 70%. Responds in 6 months to mss. No simultaneous submissions.

Payment/Terms: Pays 4% royalty on retail price. Average advance: $2,000 average. Publishes ms 1 year after acceptance. Book catalog free by calling (800)481-9191; ms guidelines online.

Advice: "The best way to learn to write a Love Spell Romance is by reading several of our recent releases. The best written stories are usually ones writers feel passionate about—so write from your heart! Also, the market is very tight these days so more than ever we are looking for refreshing, standout original fiction."

LTDBOOKS, 200 N. Service Rd. West, Unit 1, Suite 301, Oakville ON L6M 2Y1 Canada. (905)847-6060. Fax: (905)847-6060. E-mail: publisher@ltdbooks.com. Website: www.ltdbooks.com. **Contact:** Dee Lloyd, editor; Terry Shiels, editor. Estab. 1999. "LTDBooks, an energetic presence in the rapidly expanding e-book market, is a multi-genre, royalty-paying fiction publisher specializing in high quality stories with strong characters and great ideas." Publishes electronic originals on disk or by download as well as selected trade paperback titles. Books: 3½ floppy disk with cover and jewel case, or as a download. **Published 14 debut authors within the last year.** Averages 15 total titles, 36 fiction titles/year. Member, Electronic Publishers Association. Distributes titles through the Internet, Baker & Taylor, Powells.com, Lightning Source, Contentreserve, and Amazon.com.

Needs: Adventure, fantasy (space fantasy, sword and sorcery), historical (general), horror (dark fantasy, futuristic, psychological, supernatural), literary, mainstream/contemporary, mystery (amateur sleuth, cozy, police procedural, private eye/hardboiled), romance (contemporary, futuristic/time travel, gothic, historical, regency period, romantic suspense), science fiction (hard science/technological, soft/sociological), suspense (amateur sleuth, cozy, police procedural, private eye/hardboiled), thriller/espionage, western, young adult (adventure, fantasy/science fiction, historical, horror, mystery/suspense, problem novels, romance, series, sports, western), Thriller/Espionage. Prefers queries by e-mail. "Our new trade paperback program started June 2001." Published *Pilikia is My Business*, by Mark Troy (2002 Shamus Award Finalist) and *Beaudry's Ghost* (2002 Independent Publisher Award winner for best romance).

How to Contact: Accepts unsolicited mss. Query with SASE. Follow guidelines on website. Queries via e-mail only. Include estimated word count, brief bio, list of publishing credits. Responds in 1-2 months to queries. Accepts simultaneous submissions, electronic submissions, submissions on disk. Always comments on rejected mss.

Payment/Terms: Pays 30% royalty on electronic titles and flat rate on trade paperbacks. Publishes ms more than 1 year after acceptance. Ms guidelines online.

Advice: "We publish only fiction. Many of our books are electronic (as download or on disk) with ongoing additions to our new trade paperback program. Keep in mind that trade paperback publication is not guaranteed upon acceptance of electronic publication."

LUATH PRESS LTD., 54½ Castlehill, The Royal Mile, Edinburgh Scotland EH1 2ND UK. 0044 (0)131 225 4326. Fax: 0044 (0)131 225 4324. E-mail: gavin.macdougall@luath.co.uk. Website: www.luath.co.uk. **Contact:** Gavin McDougall, editor. Estab. 1981. Committed to publishing well written books that are worth reading. Publishes paperback and hardcover originals. **Published 5-10 debut authors within the last year.** Plans 5-10 first novels this year. Member, Scottish Publishers Association.

Needs: Published *Milk Reading*, by Nick Smith (fiction); *The Fundementals of New Caledonia*, by John MacKay (fiction).

How to Contact: Accepts unsolicited mss. Query with SASE or submit complete ms. Accepts queries by e-mail, fax, phone, mail. Include estimated word count, brief bio, list of publishing credits. No submissions on disk. Never comments on rejected mss.

Payment/Terms: Pays royalty. Book catalog online.

Advice: "Check out our website, buy lots of our books, read them—and then get in touch with us."

THE LYONS PRESS, An imprint of The Globe Pequot Press, Inc., 246 Goose Lane, Guilford CT 06437. (203)458-4500. Fax: (203)458-4668. Website: www.lyonspress.com. **Contact:** Submissions editor. Estab. 1984 (Lyons & Burford), 1997 (The Lyons Press). Publishes hardcover and trade paperback originals and reprints. **Published 50% debut authors within the last year.** Averages 240 total titles/year.

Needs: Historical, military/war, short story collections (fishing, hunting, outdoor, nature), sports. Published *The Hunter, the Hammer, and Heaven*, by Robert Young Pelton.

How to Contact: Query with SASE or submit proposal package including outline, 3-5 sample chapter(s). Agented fiction 70%. Responds in 1 month to queries; 1 month to proposals. Accepts simultaneous submissions.

Payment/Terms: Pays 5-10% royalty on wholesale price. Average advance: $2,000-7,000. Publishes ms 1 year after acceptance. Book catalog online; ms guidelines online.

MACADAM/CAGE PUBLISHING, INC., 155 Sansome St., Suite 550, San Francisco CA 94104. (415)986-7502. Fax: (415)986-7414. E-mail: info@macadamcage.com. Website: www.macadamcage.com. **Contact:** Patrick Walsh and Anika Streitfeld, editors. Estab. 1999. Mid-size independent publisher. Publishes hardcover and trade paperback originals. Books: web offset printing; case binding. Average first novel print order: 5,000-15,000. **Published 10 debut authors within the last year.** Averages 25-30 total titles/year. Member, PMA, ABA, NCIBA.

Distributes titles through Baker & Taylor, Ingram, Brodart, Koen and American Wholesale. Promotes titles via in-house marketing/publicity department.

Needs: Historical, literary, mainstream/contemporary. Published *The God File*, by Frank Turner Hollon (fiction); *Ella Minnow Pea*, by Mark Dunn (fiction); *Sleep Toward Heaven*, by Amanda Eyre Ward (fiction); and *Snow Island*, by Katie Towler (fiction).

How to Contact: Accepts unsolicited mss. Submit proposal package including up to 3 sample chapter(s), synopsis, SASE. Include estimated word count, brief bio. Send SASE or IRC. Agented fiction 50%. Responds in 4 months to queries; 4 months to mss. Accepts simultaneous submissions. Often comments on rejected mss.

Payment/Terms: Pays negotiable royalties. Average advance: negotiable. Publishes ms up to 1 year after acceptance. Ms guidelines for SASE or on website.

N O M JOHN MACRAE BOOKS, Henry Holt & Co., Inc., 115 W. 18th St., New York NY 10011. (212)886-9200. Estab. 1991. "We publish literary fiction and nonfiction. Our primary interest is in language; strong, compelling writing." Publishes hardcover originals. Averages 20-25 total titles/year.

Needs: Literary, mainstream/contemporary. Published *Burning Their Boats*, by Angela Carter (novel).

How to Contact: Does not accept unsolicited mss.

Payment/Terms: Pays royalty. Average advance: varies. Publishes ms 9-12 months after acceptance.

MARINE TECHNIQUES PUBLISHING, INC., 126 Western Ave., Suite 266, Augusta ME 04330-7252. (207)622-7984. Fax: (207)621-0821. E-mail: marinetechniques@midmaine.com. **Contact:** James L. Pelletier, president/CEO (commercial marine or maritime international); Christopher S. Pelletier, vice president operations (national and international maritime related properties). **Published 15% debut authors within the last year.** Averages 3-5 total titles/year.

Needs: Must be commercial maritime/marine related.

How to Contact: Submit complete ms. Responds in 6 months. Accepts simultaneous submissions.

Payment/Terms: Pays 25-43% royalty on wholesale or retail price. Publishes ms 6-12 months after acceptance. Book catalog free.

Advice: "Audience consists of commercial marine/maritime firms, persons employed in all aspects of the marine/maritime commercial and recreational fields, persons interested in seeking employment in the commercial marine industry; firms seeking to sell their products and services to vessel owners, operators, and mangers in the commercial marine industry worldwide, etc."

A M V MARINER BOOKS, Houghton Mifflin, 222 Berkeley St., Boston MA 02116. (617)351-5000. Fax: (617)351-1202. Website: www.hmco.com. **Contact:** Paperback division. Estab. 1997. Publishes trade paperback originals and reprints.

● Mariner Books' *Interpreter of Maladies*, by debut author Jhumpa Lahiri, won the 2000 Pulitzer Prize for fiction and *The Caprice*, by Sabina Murray received the 2003 PEN/Faulkner Award.

Needs: Literary, mainstream/contemporary. Published Bella Bathurst, Anita Desai, Perri Klass and Samrat Upadhyay.

How to Contact: *Agented submissions only.* Responds in 4 months to mss.

Payment/Terms: Pays royalty on retail price or makes outright purchase. Average advance: variable. Book catalog free.

MARVEL COMICS, 10 E. 40th St., New York NY 10016. (917)472-2100. Fax: (917)472-2152. Website: www.marvel.com. Publishes hardcover originals and reprints, trade paperback reprints, mass market comic book originals, electronic reprints. Averages 650 total titles/year.

Needs: Adventure, comic books, fantasy, horror, humor, science fiction, young adult. "Our shared universe needs new heroes and villains; books for younger readers and teens needed."

How to Contact: Query with SASE or submit proposal package including synopsis. Responds in 2 months to queries; 2 months to proposals. No simultaneous submissions.

Payment/Terms: Pays on a per page work for hire basis or creator-owned which is then contracted. Pays negotiable advance. Publishes ms 4-12 months after acceptance. Ms guidelines online.

M O McBOOKS PRESS, 1D Booth Building, 520 N. Meadow St., Ithaca NY 14850. (607)272-2114. Fax: (607)273-6068. E-mail: mcbooks@mcbooks.com. Website: www.mcbooks.com. **Contact:** Editorial director. Estab. 1979. "Small independent publisher; specializes in historical nautical fiction, American publisher of Alexander Kent's Richard Bolitho series, Dudley Pope's Ramage novels." Publishes trade paperback and hardcover originals and reprints. Averages 20 total titles, 17 fiction titles/year. Distributes titles through National Book Network.

Needs: Historical (nautical), nautical and military historical. Published *Ramage and the Rebels*, by Dudley Pope (nautical fiction); *The Wicked Trade*, by Jan Needle (nautical fiction); and *Second to None*, by Alexander Kent (Douglas Reeman) (nautical fiction). Publishes the continuing Bolitho and Ramage series.

How to Contact: Accepts unsolicited mss. Query with SASE. Accepts queries by e-mail. Include list of publishing credits. Mostly agented fiction. Responds in 1 month to queries; 2 months to proposals. Accepts simultaneous submissions.

Payment/Terms: Pays 5-10% royalty on retail price. Average advance: $1,000-5,000. Ms guidelines online.
Advice: "We are small and do not take on many unpublished writers."

◎ ✉ **MARGARET K. McELDERRY BOOKS**, Simon & Schuster Children's Publishing Division, Simon & Schuster, 1230 Sixth Ave., New York NY 10020. (212)698-2761. Fax: (212)698-2796. Website: www.simonsayskids .com. **Contact:** Emma D. Dryden, vice president/editorial director. Estab. 1971. Publishes quality material for preschoolers to 18-year-olds. Publishes hardcover originals. Books: high quality paper; offset printing; three piece and POB bindings; illustrations. Average print order: 12,500. First novel print order: 7,500. **Published some debut authors within the last year.** Averages 30 total titles/year.
   • Books published by Margaret K. McElderry Books have received numerous awards including the Newbery and the Caldecott Awards.
Needs: Adventure, fantasy, historical, mainstream/contemporary, mystery, picture books, young adult (or middle grade), all categories (fiction and nonfiction) for juvenile and young adult. "We will consider any category. Results depend on the quality of the imagination, the artwork and the writing." Published *Bear Wants More*, by Karma Wilson and illustrated by Jane Chapman (picture book); *The Puppeteer's Apprentice*, by D. Anne Love (middle grade historical fiction); *Loose Threads*, by Lorie Ann Grover (middle grade fiction); and *Alchemy*, by Margaret Mahy (young adult fiction).
How to Contact: Send query letter with SASE only for picture books; query letter with first 3 chapters, SASE for middle grade and young adult novels.
Payment/Terms: Average print order is 5,000-10,000 for a first middle grade or young adult book; 7,500-20,000 for a first picture book. Pays royalty on hardcover retail price: 10% fiction; picture book, 5% author; 5% illustrator. Offers $5,000-8,000 advance for new authors. Publishes ms up to 3 years after acceptance. Ms guidelines for #10 SASE.
Advice: "Imaginative writing of high quality is always in demand; also picture books that are original and unusual. Keep in mind that McElderry is a very small imprint, so we are very selective about the books we will undertake for publication. We try not to publish any 'trend' books. Be familiar with our list and with what is being published this year by all publishing houses."

Ⓝ ◯ ◎ **MEISHA MERLIN PUBLISHING, INC.**, P.O. Box 7, Decatur GA 30031. E-mail: email@meishamerl in.com. Website: www.meishamerlin.com. **Contact:** Stephen Pagel, senior editor; Alan Siler, junior editor. Estab. 1996. Midsize independent publisher devoted exclusively to science fiction, fantasy and horror. Publishes hardcover and paperback originals and reprints. Also publishes e-books. **Published 2 debut authors within the last year.**
Needs: Fantasy (space fantasy, sword and sorcery), horror (dark fantasy, futuristic, psychological, supernatural), science fiction (hard science/technological, soft/sociological). Published *Metal of Night*, by Mark Tiedeman and *Tales of Pain and Wonder*, by Caitlia R. Kierna.
How to Contact: Accepts unsolicited mss. Query with SASE or submit first 75 pages. Accepts queries by e-mail, mail. Include estimated word count, brief bio, list of publishing credits. Send SASE for return of ms or send a disposable ms and SASE for reply only. Often comments on rejected mss.
Advice: "We look for quality and originality first, specific genre or style second."

◎ **MERIWETHER PUBLISHING, LTD.**, 885 Elkton Dr., Colorado Springs CO 80907-3557. (719)594-4422. Fax: (719)594-9916. Website: www.meriwetherpublishing.com; www.contemporarydrama.com. **Contact:** Rhonda Wray, associate editor (church plays); Ted Zapel, editor (school plays, comedies, books). Estab. 1969. "Mid-size, independent publisher of plays. We publish plays for teens, mostly one-act comedies, holiday plays for churches and musical comedies. Our books are on the theatrical arts." Publishes paperback originals and reprints. Books: quality paper; printing house specialist; paperback binding. Average print order: 5,000-10,000. **Published 25-35 debut authors within the last year.**
Needs: Mainstream/contemporary, plays (and musicals), religious (children's plays and religious Christmas and Easter plays), suspense, all in playscript format, comedy. Published *Murder in the Manor*, by Bill Hand (comic mystery play).
How to Contact: Accepts unsolicited mss. Query with SASE. Accepts queries by e-mail. Include list of publishing credits. Send SASE for return of ms or send a disposable ms and SASE for reply only. Responds in 3 weeks to queries; 2 months to mss. Accepts simultaneous submissions. Sometimes comments on rejected mss.
Payment/Terms: Pays 10% royalty on retail price or makes outright purchase. Publishes ms 6-12 months after acceptance. Book catalog and ms guidelines for $2 postage.
Advice: "If you're interested in writing comedy/farce plays, we're your best publisher."

MICAH PUBLICATIONS, INC, 255 Humphrey St., Marblehead MA 01945. (781)631-7601. Fax: (781)639-0772. E-mail: micah@micahbooks.com. Website: www.micahbooks.com. **Contact:** Roberta Kalechofsky, editor. Estab. 1975. "Two-person operation on part-time basis. Publishes about 3 titles a year." Publishes paperback originals and reprints. Books: print on demand; perfect-bound; some illustrations. Average print order: 800. First novel print order: 800.
Needs: Children's/juvenile (animal), family saga, literary, short story collections, animal stories, animal rights stories.

How to Contact: Accepts unsolicited mss. Query with SASE. Include estimated word count, brief bio, list of publishing credits. Send SASE for return of ms or send a disposable ms and SASE for reply only. Responds in 3 months to queries. Accepts simultaneous submissions. Sometimes comments on rejected mss.

Payment/Terms: Pays in 10 author's copies. Additional copies at 40% discount. Will divide spin-off benefits if there are any. Publishes ms 6-8 months after acceptance. Book catalog free; ms guidelines for SASE.

Advice: "Be honest. Make sure your work is of high literary quality. We don't have time and money to waste on anything but writing excellence."

MID-LIST PRESS, 4324 12th Ave S., Minneapolis MN 55407-3218. (612)822-3733. Fax: (612)823-8387. E-mail: guide@midlist.org. Website: www.midlist.org. **Contact:** Lane Stiles, publisher. Estab. 1989. "We are a non-profit literary press dedicated to the survival of the mid-list, those quality titles that are being neglected by the larger commercial houses. Our focus is on first-time writers, and we are probably best known for the Mid-List Press First Series Awards." Publishes hardcover and trade paperback originals. Books: acid-free paper; offset printing; perfect or Smyth-sewn binding. Average print order: 2,000. **Published 2 debut authors within the last year.** Averages 4 total titles, 2 fiction titles/year. Distributes titles through Small Press Distribution, Ingram, Baker & Taylor, Midwest Library Service, Brodart, Follet and Emery Pratt. Promotes titles through publicity, direct mail, catalogs, author's events and review and awards.

Needs: General fiction. Published *Plan Z, by Leslie Kove*, by Betsy Robinson (first fiction, novel); *Leaving the Neighborhood*, by Lucy Ferriss (first fiction, short fiction); and *Wonderful Tricks*, by Gregory Spatz (first fiction, short fiction).

How to Contact: Accepts unsolicited mss. Send query letter first. Previously published authors only. See guidelines. Agented fiction less than 10%. Responds in 3 weeks to queries; 3 months to mss. Accepts simultaneous submissions.

Payment/Terms: Pays 40-50% royalty on net receipts. Average advance: $1,000. Publishes ms 12-18 months after acceptance. Ms guidelines online.

Advice: "Write first for guidelines or visit our website before submitting a query, proposal or manuscript. And take the time to read some of the titles we've published."

MIGHTYBOOK, 10924 Grant Rd., #225, Houston TX 77070. (281)955-9855. Fax: (281)890-4818. E-mail: reaves@houston.rr.com. Website: www.mightybook.com. **Contact:** Richard Eaves, acquisitions editor. Estab. 1991. "Small independent publisher of electronic, read aloud picture books and books on audiocassette/CD, and print-on-demand books. Much of our marketing and sales are done on the Internet." Publishes electronic books. **Published 10 debut authors within the last year.** Averages 30-50 total titles, 25 fiction titles/year.

Needs: Very short children's picture books (100-200 words). Published *I Have No Tail*, by S.J. Arohalt; *Oliver's High Five*, by Beverly S. Brown; *How I Feel Happy*, by Marcia Leonard; *Purple Underwear* by Robin McKay Pimentel; and *Icky, Sticky, and Gooey*, by Kimberly Constant (debut fiction).

How to Contact: Accepts unsolicited mss. Submit complete ms with cover letter (include estimated word count and brief bio). Accepts queries by e-mail, fax, phone. Agented fiction 5%. Responds in 6 weeks to queries; 6 weeks to mss. Accepts simultaneous submissions, electronic submissions, submissions on disk.

Payment/Terms: Pays royalties of 20% gross. Publishes ms 6-9 months after acceptance. Book catalog online; ms guidelines online.

Advice: "Write short picture books with a good moral, but avoid references to violence and avoid controversial topics."

MILKWEED EDITIONS, 1011 Washington Ave. S., Suite 300, Minneapolis MN 55415. (612)332-3192. Fax: (612)215-2550. E-mail: editor@milkweed.org. Website: www.milkweed.org and www.worldashome.org. **Contact:** H. Emerson Blake, publisher; Elisabeth Fitz, first reader. Estab. 1980. Nonprofit publisher. Publishes hardcover originals and paperback originals and reprints. Books: book text quality—acid-free paper; offset printing; perfect or hardcover binding. Average print order: 4,000. First novel print order depends on book. **Published some debut authors within the last year.** Averages 15 total titles/year. Distributes through Publisher's Group West. Each book has its own marketing plan involving print ads, tours, conferences, etc.

Needs: Literary. Novels for adults and for readers 8-13. High literary quality. For adult readers: literary fiction, nonfiction, poetry, essays; for children (ages 8-12): literary novels. Translations welcome for both audiences. Published *Distant Music*, by Lee Langley; *Roofwalker*, by Susan Power (short stories); and *Hell's Bottom, Colorado*, by Laura Pritchett (first fiction, short stories).

How to Contact: Send for guidelines first, then submit complete ms. Responds in 2 months to queries; 6 months to mss. Accepts simultaneous submissions.

Payment/Terms: Pays 7½% royalty on retail price. Average advance: varied. Publishes ms 1-2 years after acceptance. Book catalog for $1.50 postage; ms guidelines online.

Advice: "Read good contemporary literary fiction, find your own voice, and persist. Familiarize yourself with our list before submitting."

MILKWEEDS FOR YOUNG READERS, Milkweed Editions, 1011 Washington Ave. S., Suite 300, Minneapolis MN 55415. (612)332-3192. Fax: (612)215-2550. Website: www.milkweed.org. **Contact:** Emerson

Blake, publisher; Elizabeth Fitz, children's reader. Estab. 1984. "Milkweeds for Young Readers are works that embody humane values and contribute to cultural understanding." Publishes hardcover and trade paperback originals. Averages 1-2 total titles/year. Distributes titles through Publishers Group West. Promotes titles individually through print advertising, website and author tours.

• *Parents Wanted*, by George Harrar, was named "Best Children's Book of the Year" in 2002 by Bank Street.

Needs: Adventure, fantasy, historical, humor, mainstream/contemporary, animal, environmental. For ages 8-13. Published *Parents Wanted*, by George Harrar; *Emma and the Ruby Ring*, by Yvonne MacGrory; *Tides*, by V.M. Caldwell (middle-grade novel) and *The Return of Gabriel*, by John Armistead.

How to Contact: Query with SASE. Agented fiction 30%. Responds in 2 months to queries. Accepts simultaneous submissions.

Payment/Terms: Pays 7½% royalty on retail price. Average advance: variable. Publishes ms 1 year after acceptance. Book catalog for $1.50; ms guidelines for #10 SASE or on the website.

Advice: "Familiarize yourself with our books before submitting. You need not have a long list of credentials—excellent work speaks for itself."

MILLS & BOON HISTORICAL ROMANCE, a Harlequin book line, Eton House, 18-24 Paradise Rd., Richmond Surrey TW9 1SR United Kingdom. (44)0208 288 2800. Website: www.millsandboon.co.uk. "This series covers a wide range of British and European historical periods from ancient Greece up to and including the World War II." Publishes paperback originals and reprints. Books: newspaper print; web printing; perfect-bound. **Published some debut authors within the last year.**

Needs: Romance. "The romance should take priority, with all the emotional impact of a growing love and should be developed over a relatively short span of time; the historical detail should be accurate, without sounding like a textbook, and should help to create a true sense of the chosen setting, so the reader becomes immersed in that time." Manuscripts must be 75,000-90,000 words.

How to Contact: Accepts unsolicited mss. "A query letter and brief synopsis is advised." Send SASE for return of ms or send a disposable ms and SASE for reply only. No simultaneous submissions, electronic submissions, submissions on disk.

Payment/Terms: Pays royalty. Offers advance. Ms guidelines for SASE and on website.

MILLS & BOON MEDICAL ROMANCE, a Harlequin book line, Eton House, 18-24 Paradise Rd., Richmond Surrey TW9 1SR United Kingdom. (44)0208 288 2800. Website: www.millsandboon.co.uk. **Contact:** Sheila Hodgson, senior editor. "These are present-day romances in a medical setting." Publishes paperback originals and reprints. Books: newspaper print; web printing; perfect-bound. **Published some debut authors within the last year.**

Needs: Romance (medical). Looking for writing with "a good balance between the romance, the medicine, and the underlying story. At least one of the main characters should be a medical professional, and developing the romance is easier if the hero and heroine work together. Medical detail should be accurate but preferably without using technical language. An exploration of patients and their illnesses is permitted, but not in such numbers as to overwhelm the growing love story. Settings can be anywhere in the world." Manuscripts must be 50,000-55,000 words.

How to Contact: Accepts unsolicited mss. Query with SASE or submit complete ms with cover letter. Send SASE for return of ms or send a disposable ms and SASE for reply only. No simultaneous submissions, electronic submissions, submissions on disk.

Payment/Terms: Pays royalty. Offers advance. Ms guidelines for SASE and on website.

Advice: "More detailed guidelines are available on request with a stamped, addressed envelope."

MINOTAUR, Imprint of St. Martin's Press, 175 Fifth Ave., New York NY 10010. (212)674-5151. **Contact:** Joe Veltre, editor. Publishes trade hardcover and paperback originals and reprints, commercial non-fiction, literary fiction and mass market paperback originals and reprints.

• Does not accept unsolicited mss.

Needs: Mystery.

How to Contact: Query with SASE. Agented fiction 99.9%. Accepts simultaneous submissions.

Payment/Terms: Pays variable royalty on net price. Average advance: varies.

MIRA BOOKS, an imprint of Harlequin, 225 Duncan Mill Rd., Don Mills ON M3B3K9 Canada. Website: www.mirabooks.com. "MIRA Books is proud to publish outstanding mainstream women's fiction for readers around the world." Publishes paperback originals.

Needs: Family saga, historical (romance), mainstream/contemporary, suspense (romance), thriller/espionage, relationship novels. Published work by Penny Jordan, Debbie Macomber, Diana Palmer, Nan Ryan and Susan Wiggs.

How to Contact: Does not accept unsolicited mss.

Payment/Terms: Pays royalty. Offers advance.

A ☑ ◎ **MOODY PUBLISHERS**, (formerly Moody Press), Moody Bible Institute, 820 N. LaSalle Blvd., Chicago IL 60610. (312)329-8047. Fax: (312)329-2019. E-mail: acquisitions@moody.edu. Website: www.moodypublishers.org. **Contact:** Acquistions Coordinator (all fiction). Estab. 1894. Small, evangelical Christian Publisher. "We publish only fiction that reflects and supports our evangelical worldview and mission." Publishes hardcover, trade and mass market paperback originals. Averages 60 total titles, 5-10 fiction titles/year. Member, CBA. Distributes and promotes titles through sales reps, print advertising, promotional events, Internet, etc.

Needs: Children's/juvenile (series), fantasy, historical, mystery, religious (children's religious, inspirational, religious mystery/suspense), science fiction, young adult (adventure, fantasy/science fiction, historical, mystery/suspense, series). Published *Courage to Run*, by Wendy Lawton (YA, debut author); *Vinegar Boy*, by Alberta Hause (YA); and *Purity Reigns*, by Stephanie Perry Moore (YA). Publishes ongoing YA series, Daughters of the Faith.

How to Contact: Accepts unsolicited mss. Query with SASE. Accepts queries by e-mail, fax. Include estimated word count, brief bio, list of publishing credits. Send SASE for return of ms or send a disposable ms and SASE for reply only. Agented fiction 90%. Responds in 2-3 months to queries. Accepts electronic submissions. No simultaneous submissions, submissions on disk.

Payment/Terms: Royalty varies. Average advance: $1,000-10,000. Publishes ms 9-12 months after acceptance. Book catalog for 9×12 SAE with 4 first-class stamps; ms guidelines for SASE and on website.

Advice: "Get to know Moody Publishers and understand what kinds of books we publish. We will decline all submissions that do not support our evangelical Christian beliefs and mission."

A **WILLIAM MORROW**, HarperCollins, 10 E. 53rd St., New York NY 10022. (212)207-7000. Fax: (212)207-7145. Website: www.harpercollins.com. **Contact:** Acquisitions Editor. Estab. 1926. Approximately half of the books published are fiction. Averages 200 total titles/year.

Needs: Publishes adult ficiton. "Morrow accepts only the highest quality submissions" in adult fiction.

How to Contact: *Agented submissions only.*

Payment/Terms: Pays standard royalty on retail price. Average advance: varying. Publishes ms 2 years after acceptance. Book catalog free.

◎ **MOUNTAIN STATE PRESS**, 2300 MacCorkle Ave. SE, Charleston WV 25304-1099. (304)357-4767. Fax: (304)357-4715. E-mail: msp1@newwave.net. Website: www.mountainstatepress.com. **Contact:** Sharon Underwood, fiction editor. Estab. 1978. "A small nonprofit press run by a board of 13 members who volunteer their time. We specialize in books about West Virginia or by authors from West Virginia. We strive to give a voice to Appalachia." Publishes paperback originals and reprints. **Published some debut authors within the last year.** Plans 2-3 first novels this year. Distributes titles through bookstores, distributors, gift shops and individual sales (Amazon.com and Barnes & Noble online carry our titles). Promotes titles through newspapers, radio, TV (local author series), mailings and book signings.

Needs: Family saga, historical (West Virginia), military/war, new age/mystic, religious. Currently compiling an anthology of West Virginia authors. Published *Mel Street: A Country Legend*, by Deniss Schuster Sr. and Larry J. Delp (biography); *Hears the Wind*, by Kate Dooley, *The Conversion of Big Jim Cane*, by Robert Elkins.

How to Contact: Accepts unsolicited mss. Query with SASE or submit complete ms with cover letter. Accepts queries by e-mail, fax. Include estimated word count, brief bio. Send SASE for return of ms or send a disposable ms and SASE for reply only. Responds in 6 months to mss. Accepts electronic submissions. Often comments on rejected mss.

Payment/Terms: Pays royalty.

Advice: "Topic of West Virginia is the best choice for our press. Send your manuscript in and it will be read and reviewed by the members of the Board of Mountain State Press. We give helpful suggestions and critique the writing."

A ☑ Ⓨ **MULTNOMAH PUBLISHERS, INC.**, P.O. Box 1720, Sisters OR 97759. (541)549-1144. Fax: (541)549-8048. E-mail: editoria@multnomahbooks.com. Website: www.multnomahbooks.com. **Contact:** Editorial department. Estab. 1987. Midsize independent publisher of evangelical fiction and nonfiction. Publishes hardcover and trade paperback originals. Books: perfect binding. Average print order: 15,000. Averages 75 total titles/year.

- Multnomah Books has received several Gold Medallion Books Awards from the Evangelical Christian Publishers Association.

Imprint(s): Multnomah Books ("Christian living and popular theology books"); Multnomah Fiction ("Changing lives through the power of story"); Multnomah Gift ("Substantive topics with beautiful, lyrical writing").

Needs: Adventure, historical, humor, literary, mystery, religious, romance, suspense, western. Published *The Protector*, by Dee Henderson (romance/suspense); *Who I Am*, by Melody Carlson (YA); and *The Ishbane Conspiracy*, by Randy Alcorn (contemporary).

How to Contact: Does not accept unsolicited mss. *Agented submissions only.* Accepts simultaneous submissions.

Payment/Terms: Pays royalty on wholesale price. Provides 100 author's copies. Offers advance. Publishes ms 1-2 years after acceptance. Ms guidelines online.

Advice: "Looking for clean, moral, uplifting fiction. We're particularly interested in contemporary women's fiction, historical fiction, superior romance and mystery/suspense."

🌐 **MY WEEKLY STORY COLLECTION**, D.C. Thomson and Co., Ltd., 22 Meadowside, Dundee DD19QJ Scotland. **Contact:** Mrs. D. Hunter, fiction editor. "Cheap paperback story library with full-colour cover. Material should not be violent, controversial or sexually explicit." Distributes titles through national retail outlets. Promotes titles through display cards in retail outlets and in-house magazine advertising.
Needs: Historical, mainstream/contemporary. Length: approximately 30,000 words.
How to Contact: Query with SASE or submit outline, 3 sample chapter(s), synopsis.
Payment/Terms: Writers are paid on acceptance.
Advice: "Avoid too many colloquialisms/Americanisms. Stories can be set anywhere."

🅰 Ⓜ ◎ **THE MYSTERIOUS PRESS**, Warner Books, 1271 Avenue of the Americas, New York NY 10020. (212)522-7200. Fax: (212)522-7990. Website: www.twbookmark.com. **Contact:** Sara Ann Freed, editor-in-chief. Estab. 1976. Publishes hardcover, trade paperback and mass market editions Books: hardcover (some Smythe-sewn) and paperback binding; illustrations rarely. First novel print order: 10,000 copies minimum. **Published some debut authors within the last year.** Averages 36-45 total titles/year.
Needs: Mystery, suspense, crime/detective novels. Published *Open and Shut*, by David Rosenfelt; *Cyanite Wells*, by Marcia Mulle.
How to Contact: *Agented submissions only.* Responds in 2 months to queries.
Payment/Terms: Pays standard, but negotiable, royalty on retail price. Average advance: negotiable. Publishes ms an average of 1 year after acceptance. Ms guidelines online.
Advice: "Write a strong and memorable novel, and with the help of a good literary agent, you'll find the right publishing house. Don't despair if your manuscript is rejected by several houses. All publishing houses are looking for new and exciting crime novels, but it may not be at the time your novel is submitted. Hang in there, keep the faith—and good luck."

◨ **NATURAL HERITAGE/NATURAL HISTORY, INC.**, P.O. Box 95, Station O, Toronto ON M4A 2M8 Canada. (416)694-7907. Fax: (416)690-0819. E-mail: submissions@naturalheritagebooks.com. Website: www.natur alheritagebooks.com. **Contact:** Jane Gibson, editor-in-chief. Publishes hardcover and trade paperback originals. **Published 50% debut authors within the last year.** Averages 12-15 total titles/year.
Imprint(s): Natural Heritage Books.
Needs: Historical, children's (age 8-12). Published *Just a Little Later with Eevo and Sim*, by Henry Shykoff.
How to Contact: Query with SASE. Responds in 4 months. No simultaneous submissions.
Payment/Terms: Pays 8-10% royalty on retail price. Offers advance. Publishes ms 2 years after acceptance. Book catalog free; ms guidelines online.
Advice: "We are a Canadian publisher in the natural heritage and history fields. We rarely publish fiction, the only exceptions being occasional historical fiction and children's chapter books."

◎ **THE NAUTICAL & AVIATION PUBLISHING CO.**, 1250 Fairmont Ave., Mt. Pleasant SC 29464. (843)856-0561. Fax: (843)856-3164. **Contact:** Melissa A. Pluta, editor. Estab. 1979. Small publisher interested in quality military and naval history and literature. Publishes hardcover originals and reprints. Averages 10-12 total titles, 1-4 fiction titles/year.
Needs: Historical, military/war (Revolutionary War, War of 1812, Civil War, WW I and II, Persian Gulf and Marine Corps history). Looks for "novels with a strong military history orientation." Published *The Black Flower*, by Howard Bahr; *Lieutenant Christopher and the Quasi-War with France*, by VADM William P. Mack; and *Rifleman Dodd*, by C.S. Forester (all military fiction).
How to Contact: Accepts unsolicited mss. Submit complete ms with cover letter and brief synopsis. Send SASE or IRC. Accepts simultaneous submissions. Sometimes comments on rejected mss.
Payment/Terms: Pays 10-12% royalty on net receipts. Average advance: rare. Book catalog free.
Advice: Encourages first novelists.

🖊 ◎ **NAVAL INSTITUTE PRESS**, US Naval Institute, 291 Wood Ave., Annapolis MD 21402-5035. (410)268-6110. Fax: (410)295-1084. E-mail: ssprinkle@usni.org. Website: www.usni.org; www.nip.org. **Contact:** Paul Wilderson, executive editor; Tom Cutler, senior acquisitions editor; Eric Mills, acquisitions editor. Estab. 1873. "Best known for introducing Tom Clancy's and Stephen Coonts' first novels. We've been publishing books for 125 years (but do very little fiction) to advance knowledge of the naval and maritime services." First novel print order: 2,500. Averages 80-90 total titles/year. Distributes titles through wholesalers such as Ingram and Baker & Taylor.
Needs: Historical, military/war. Limited to fiction on military and naval themes. Published *Dog Company Six*, by Edwin P. Simmons (Korean War novel); and *Punk's War*, by Ward Carroll (first novel).
How to Contact: Submit outline, sample chapter(s), synopsis, author bio. Send SASE or IRC. Accepts simultaneous submissions.
Payment/Terms: Pays 5-10% royalty on net receipts. Publishes ms 1 year after acceptance. Book catalog for 9×12 SASE; ms guidelines online.

🖊 ◎ **THOMAS NELSON, INC.**, Box 141000, Nashville TN 37214-1000. (615)889-9000. Website: www.thom asnelson.com. **Contact:** Acquisitions Editor. "Largest Christian book publishers." Publishes hardcover and paperback originals. Averages 100-150 total titles/year.

Needs: Publishes commercial fiction authors who write for adults from a Christian perspective. Published *Kingdom Come*, by Larry Burkett and T. Davis Bunn; *Dakota Moon* series, by Stephanie Grace Whitson (romance); and *Empty Coffin*, by Robert Wise (mystery/suspense).

How to Contact: Does not accept unsolicited mss. Responds in 3 months to queries. Accepts simultaneous submissions.

Payment/Terms: Pays royalty on net receipts. Rates negotiated for each project. Offers advance. Publishes ms 1-2 years after acceptance. Ms guidelines online.

Advice: "We are a conservative publishing house and want material which is conservative in morals and in nature."

⊘ ◎ **TOMMY NELSON**, Thomas Nelson, Inc., P.O. Box 141000, Nashville TN 37214-1000. (615)889-9000. Fax: (615)902-2219. Website: www.tommynelson.com. **Contact:** Publisher of children's Christian fiction and non-fiction for boys and girls up to age 14. "We honor God and serve people through books, videos, software and Bibles for children that improve the lives of our customers." Publishes hardcover and trade paperback originals. Averages 50-75 total titles/year.

Imprint(s): Word Kids.

Needs: Adventure, juvenile, mystery, picture books, religious. Published *Prayer of Jabez for Kids*, by Bruce Wilkinson.

How to Contact: Does not accept unsolicited mss. No simultaneous submissions.

Payment/Terms: Ms guidelines online.

Advice: "Know the CBA market. Check out the Christian bookstores to see what sells and what is needed."

Ⓐ ◐ **NEW AMERICAN LIBRARY**, Penguin Putnam, Inc., 375 Hudson St., New York NY 10014. (212)366-2000. Fax: (212)366-2889. Website: www.penguinputnam.com. **Contact:** Claire Zion, editorial director, NAL editorial (fiction, nonfiction); Ellen Edwards, executive editor (commercial women's fiction—mainstream novels and contemporary romances; mysteries in a series and single title suspense; nonfiction of all types for a general audience and historical); Laura Anne Gilman, executive editor (science fiction/fantasy/horror, mystery series, New Age); Audrey LaFehr, executive editor (contemporary and historical romance, women's suspense, multicultural fiction); Hilary Ross, associate executive editor (romances, Regencies); Doug Grad, senior editor (thrillers, suspense novels, international intrigue, technothrillers, military fiction and nonfiction, adventure nonfiction); Genny Ostertag, senior editor (mysteries, suspense, commerical women's fiction); Dan Slater, senior editor (historical fiction, adult westerns, thrillers, military fiction and nonfiction, true crime, media tie-ins); Tracy Bernstein, executive editor; Laura Ciselli, senior editor (contemporary romance, romantic suspense). Estab. 1948. Publishes mass market and trade paperback originals and reprints. **Published some debut authors within the last year.** Averages 500 total titles/year.

Imprint(s): Signet, Signet Classic, Onyx, ROC, NAL Accent.

Needs: Erotica, ethnic, fantasy, historical, horror, mainstream/contemporary, mystery, romance, science fiction, suspense, western, chicklit. "All kinds of commercial fiction." Published *The Hearing*, by John Lescroart; *Scarlet Feather*, by Maeve Binchy; *Orchard Blues*, by Stuart Woods; and *Always in My Heart*, by Catherine Anderson.

How to Contact: *Agented submissions only.* Query with SASE. "State type of book and past publishing projects." Responds in 6 months to queries. No simultaneous submissions.

Payment/Terms: Pays negotiable royalty. Average advance: negotiable. Publishes ms 1-2 years after acceptance. Book catalog for SASE.

Advice: "Write the complete manuscript and submit it to an agent or agents."

◎ **THE NEW ENGLAND PRESS, INC.**, P.O. Box 575, Shelburne VT 05482. (802)863-2520. Fax: (802)863-1510. E-mail: editorial@nepress.com. Website: www.nepress.com. **Contact:** Christopher A. Bray, managing editor. Estab. 1978. Publishes hardcover and trade paperback originals. **Published 50% debut authors within the last year.** Averages 6-8 total titles/year.

Needs: Historical (Vermont, New Hampshire, Maine). "We look for very specific subject matters based on Vermont history and heritage, including historical novels for young adults set in Northern New England. We do not publish contemporary adult fiction of any kind."

How to Contact: Query with SASE or submit 2 sample chapter(s), synopsis. Agented fiction 10%. Responds in 6-9 months to queries. Accepts simultaneous submissions.

Payment/Terms: Pays royalty on wholesale price. Publishes ms 15 months after acceptance. Book catalog free; ms guidelines online.

Advice: "Our readers are interested in all aspects of Vermont and northern New England, including hobbyists (railroad books) and students (young adult fiction and biography). No agent is needed, but our market is extremely specific and our volume is low, so send a query or outline and writing samples first. Sending the whole manuscript is discouraged. We will not accept projects that are still under development or give advances."

◐ **NEW HOPE BOOKS, INC.**, P.O. Box 38, New Hope PA 18938. (888)741-BOOK. Fax: (215)862-1205. E-mail: NewHopeBks@aol.com. Website: www.NewHopeBooks.net. **Contact:** Barbara Taylor, publisher; Tamara Hayes, assistant editor. Estab. 1999. "We are a small but quickly growing press that savors zippy, mainstream page turners, which readily adapt to feature film." Publishes hardcover and paperback originals and reprints. **Published 1 debut author within the last year.**

Needs: Adventure, literary, mainstream/contemporary, mystery, thriller/espionage. Looks for "plot-driven fiction only that tugs on the heartstrings." Published *The Boardwalkers* (murder mystery); and *A Run to Hell*, (crime/espionage), both by Frederick Schofield.

How to Contact: Does not accept unsolicited mss. Query with SASE. Submit first 3 chapters and final chapter. "Almost all of our fiction is agented." Accepts queries by e-mail. Include estimated word count. Responds in 3 months. Accepts simultaneous submissions.

Payment/Terms: Pays royalty. Average advance: negotiable. Publishes ms 1 year after acceptance. Book catalog online; ms guidelines for #10 SASE.

Advice: "Current industry trends heavily favor our approach. Submissions must perfectly fit our guidelines for consideration."

NEW VICTORIA PUBLISHERS, P.O. Box 27, Norwich VT 05055-0027. (802)649-5297. Fax: (802)649-5297. E-mail: newvic@aol.com. Website: www.newvictoria.com. **Contact:** Claudia Lamperti, editor; Re-Becca Beguin, editor. Estab. 1976. "Publishes mostly lesbian fiction—strong female protagonists. Most well known for Stoner McTavish mystery series." Small, three person operation. Publishes trade paperback originals. Averages 4-6 total titles/year. Distributes titles through Words Distributing (Oakland, CA), Airlift (London) and Bulldog Books (Sydney, Australia). Promotes titles "mostly through lesbian feminist media."

  • *Mommy Deadest*, by Jean Marcy, won the Lambda Literary Award for Mystery.

Needs: Adventure, erotica, fantasy, feminist, historical, humor, lesbian, mystery (amateur sleuth), romance, science fiction, western. "Looking for strong feminist characters, also strong plot and action. We will consider most anything if it is well written and appeals to lesbian/feminist audience. Hard copy only—no disks." Publishes anthologies or special editions. Published *Killing at the Cat*, by Carlene Miller (mystery); *Queer Japan*, by Barbara Summerhawk (anthology); *Skin to Skin*, by Martha Miller (erotic short fiction); *Talk Show*, by Melissa Hartman (novel); *Flight From Chador*, by Sigrid Brunel (adventure); and *Do Drums Beat There*, by Doe Tabor (novel).

How to Contact: Accepts unsolicited mss. Submit outline, sample chapter(s), synopsis. Accepts queries by e-mail, fax. Send SASE or IRC. No simultaneous submissions.

Payment/Terms: Pays 10% royalty. Publishes ms 1 year after acceptance. Book catalog free; ms guidelines for SASE.

Advice: "We are especially interested in lesbian or feminist mysteries, ideally with a character or characters who can evolve through a series of books. Mysteries should involve a complex plot, accurate legal and police procedural detail, and protagonists with full emotional lives. Pay attention to plot and character development. Read guidelines carefully."

NEWEST PUBLISHERS LTD., 201, 8540-109 St., Edmonton AB T6G 1E6 Canada. (780)432-9427. Fax: (780)433-3179. E-mail: info@newestpress.com. Website: www.newestpress.com. **Contact:** Ruth Linka, general manager. Estab. 1977. Publishes trade paperback originals. **Published some debut authors within the last year.** Averages 13-16 total titles/year. Promotes titles through book launches, media interviews, review copy mailings and touring.

Imprint(s): Prairie Play Series (drama), Writer as Critic (literary criticisim), Nunatak New Fiction.

Needs: Literary. "Our press is interested in Western Canadian writing." Published *Talon*, by Paulette Dube (fiction, debut author); *Icefields*, by Thomas Wharton (novel); *Blood Relations and Other Plays*, by Sharon Pollock (drama); *A Thirst to Die For*, by Ian Waddell (mystery, debut author). Publishes the Nunatak New Fiction Series.

How to Contact: Accepts unsolicited mss. Submit complete ms. Send SASE or IRC. Responds in 6 months to queries. Accepts simultaneous submissions.

Payment/Terms: Pays 10% royalty. Publishes ms 18 months after acceptance. Book catalog for 9 × 12 SASE; ms guidelines online.

Advice: "*We publish western Canadian writers only or books about western Canada.* We are looking for excellent quality and originality."

NORTH-SOUTH BOOKS, Nord-Sud Verlag AG, 1123 Broadway, Suite 800, New York NY 10010. (212)706-4545. Website: www.northsouth.com. **Contact:** Julie Amper. Estab. 1985. "The aim of North-South is to build bridges—bridges between authors and artists form different countries and between readers of all ages. We believe children should be exposd to as wide a range of artistic styles as possible with universal themes." **Published some debut authors within the last year.** Averages 100 total titles/year.

  • North-South Books is the publisher of the international bestseller, *The Rainbow Fish*.

Needs: Picture books, easy-to-read. "We are currently accepting only picture books; all other books are selected by our German office."

How to Contact: *Agented submissions only.* Does not respond unless interested to proposals. No simultaneous submissions.

Payment/Terms: Pays royalty on retail price. Offers advance. Publishes ms an average of 9-12 months after acceptance. Ms guidelines online.

W.W. NORTON CO., INC., 500 Fifth Ave., New York NY 10110. Fax: (212)869-0856. E-mail: manuscript@ww norton.com. Website: www.wwnorton.com. Midsize independent publisher of trade books and college textbooks.

Publishes literary fiction. Estab. 1923. Publishes hardcover and paperback originals and reprints. Averages 300 total titles/year.

Needs: Literary, poetry, poetry in translation, religious. High-quality literary fiction. Published *Ship Fever*, by Andrea Barrett; *Oyster*, by Jannette Turner Hospital; and *Power*, by Linda Hogan.

How to Contact: Does not accept unsolicited mss. No phone calls. Responds in 2 months to queries. No simultaneous submissions.

Payment/Terms: Pays royalty. Offers advance. Ms guidelines online.

NW WRITERS' CORP., NSpirit Cultural Newsmagazine, Ogun Books, P.O. Box 24873, Federal Way WA 98093. (253)839-3177. Fax: (253)839-3207. E-mail: nwwriterscorp@aol.com. Website: www.nwwriterscorp.com. **Contact:** Orisade Awodola, executive editor (fiction, inspirational, women's fiction, nonfiction, genealogy, history, spiritual, empowerment, black, cultural studies). Estab. 1998. Publishes hardcover and trade paperback originals and reprints. **Published 100% debut authors within the last year.** Averages 6-8 total titles/year.

Needs: Ethnic, historical, multicultural, multimedia, religious, spiritual. "We accept fiction mss based on marketability and review for filming potential." Published *Still My Tremblin' Soul*, by Carolyn Y. Parnell (suspense).

How to Contact: Query with SASE. Please do not send mss. Send a query letter with SASE or e-mail query letter to nwwriterscorp@aol.com. Responds in 1 month. Accepts simultaneous submissions.

Payment/Terms: Pays 20-25% royalty or makes outright purchase of $1,000-2,000. Publishes ms 1 year after acceptance. Book catalog online; ms guidelines online.

Advice: Audience consists of educators, business leaders, college students.

☐ ▨ OAK TREE PRESS, 2743 S. Veterans Pkwy., Suite 135, Springfield IL 62704-6402. (217)824-8001. Fax: (217)824-3424. E-mail: oaktreepub@aol.com. Website: www.oaktreebooks.com. **Contact:** Billie Johnson, publisher (mysteries, romance, nonfiction); Sarah Wasson, acquisitions editor (all); Barabara Hoffman, senior editor (children's, young adult, educational). Estab. 1998. "Small independent publisher with a philosophy of author advocacy. Welcomes first-time authors and sponsors annual mystery contest which publishes the winning entry." Publishes hardcover, trade paperback and mass market paperback originals and reprints. Books: acid-free paper; perfect-binding. First novel print order: 1,000 **Published 4 debut authors within the last year.** Plans 3 first novels this year. Averages 8-10 total titles, 8 fiction titles/year. Member: SPAN, SPAWN. Distributes through Ingram, Baker & Taylor, and Amazon.com. Promotes through website, conferences, PR, author tours.

● *Affinity for Murder*, by Anne White was an Agatha Award finalist. Published *Timeless Love*, by Mary Montague Sikes received a Prism Award.

Imprint(s): Oak Tree Press, Dark Oak Mysteries; Timeless Love; Acorn Books for Children (children's, YA).

Needs: Adventure, confession, ethnic, fantasy (romance), feminist, humor, mainstream/contemporary, mystery (amateur sleuth, cozy, police procedural, private eye/hardboiled), new age/mystic, picture books, romance (contemporary, futuristic/time travel, romantic suspense), suspense, thriller/espionage, young adult (adventure, mystery/suspense, romance). Small independent publisher with emphasis on mystery and romance novels. Published *Hearts Across Forever*, by Mary Montague Sikes (romance); *Deadfall*, by Lynda Douglas (mystery); *Number Please*, by Sheree Petree (mystery); *An Affinity for Murder*, by Anne White (mystery); and *Element Threat*, by Richard Opper (mystery/adventure).

How to Contact: Does not accept or return unsolicited mss. Query with SASE. Accepts queries by e-mail, fax. Include estimated word count, brief bio, list of publishing credits, brief description of ms. Agented fiction 5%. Responds in 4-6 weeks. Accepts simultaneous submissions, electronic submissions. No submissions on disk. Rarely comments on rejected mss.

Payment/Terms: Pays 10-20% royalty on wholesale price. Average advance: negotiable. Publishes ms 9-18 months after acceptance. Book catalog for SASE or on website; ms guidelines for SASE or on website.

Advice: "Understand the business and be eager and enthusiastic about participating in the marketing and promotion of the title."

ℕ ☑ ◎ OMNIDAWN PUBLISHING, Omnidawn Corporation, 1632 Elm Ave, Richmond CA 94805-1614. (510)237-5472. E-mail: submissions@omnidawn.com. Website: www.omnidawn.com. **Contact:** Rusty Morrison and Ken Keegan, editors (new wave fabulist). Estab. 1999. Omnidawn is a small independent publisher ran by two part-time editors and college interns. It specializes in new wave fabulist fiction. "New wave fabulist fiction has been defined as literary versions of science fiction, fantasy, and/or horror. We are also interested in literary New Age and psychic/supernatural." Publishes hardcover originals, paperback originals and e-books. Books: Archival quality paper; offset printing; trade paperback and hardcover binding. Average print order: 3,000. **Published 1-2 debut authors within the last year.** Plans 2 first novels this year. Distributes titles through Small Press Distribution.

Needs: Fantasy (new wave fabulist), horror, New Age/mystic, psychic/supernatural, science fiction.

How to Contact: Accepts unsolicited mss. Query with SASE. Accepts queries by e-mail, mail. Include estimated word count, brief bio, list of publishing credits. Send SASE for return of ms or send a disposable ms and SASE for reply only. Responds in 1 week to queries; 1-2 months to mss. Accepts simultaneous submissions. No electronic submissions, submissions on disk.

Payment/Terms: Pays 6-10% royalty. Average advance: negotiable. Publishes ms 6-12 months after acceptance. Book catalog online; ms guidelines online.

Advice: "Check our website for latest information or request guidelines via standard or e-mail."

🅰 ◎ ONE WORLD BOOKS, Ballantine Publishing Group, Inc., 1745 Broadway, 18th Floor, New York NY 10019. (212)782-9000. Fax: (212)572-4949. **Contact:** Anita Diggs, senior editor. Publishes hardcover, trade and mass market paperback originals and trade paperback reprints. **Published 50% debut authors within the last year.** Averages 24 total titles/year.
Needs: Adventure, comic books, confession, erotica, ethnic, historical, humor, literary, mainstream/contemporary, multicultural, mystery, regional, romance, suspense, strong need for commercial women's fiction. "All One World Books must be specifically written for either an African-American, Asian or Hispanic audience. Absolutely no exceptions!" Published *Bittersweet*, by Freddie Lee Johnson III.
How to Contact: *Agented submissions only.* Agented fiction 95%. Accepts simultaneous submissions.
Payment/Terms: Pays 7½-15% royalty on retail price. Average advance: $40,000-200,000. Publishes ms 18 months after acceptance.
Advice: Targets African-American, Asian and Hispanic readers. All books must be written in English.

🆓 ONI PRESS, 6336 SE Milwaukie Ave. PMB 30, Portland OR. Website: www.onipress.com.
Needs: Graphic novels, comic books.
How to Contact: Oni no longer accepts unsolicited submissions. Bring portfolios to conventions for review.

◀ ◻ ◎ ORCA BOOK PUBLISHERS, 1030 N. Park St., Victoria BC V8T 1C6 Canada. (250)380-1229. Fax: (250)380-1892. E-mail: orca@orcabook.com. Website: www.orcabook.com. **Contact:** Maggie deVries, children's book editor. Estab. 1984. Publishes hardcover and trade paperback originals, and mass market paperback originals and reprints. Books: quality 60 lb. book stock paper; illustrations. Average print order: 3,000-5,000. First novel print order: 3,000-5,000. Plans 3-4 first novels this year. Averages 30 total titles/year.
Needs: Hi-lo, juvenile (5-9 years), literary, mainstream/contemporary, young adult (10-18 years). "Ask for guidelines, find out what we publish." Looking for "children's fiction."
How to Contact: Query with SASE or submit proposal package including outline, 2-5 sample chapter(s), synopsis, SASE. Agented fiction 20%. Responds in 1 month to queries; 1 month to proposals. No simultaneous submissions. Sometimes comments on rejected mss.
Payment/Terms: Pays 10% royalty. Publishes ms 12-18 months after acceptance. Book catalog for 8½ × 11 SASE; ms guidelines online.
Advice: "We are looking to promote and publish Canadians."

🆓 ORCHISES PRESS, P.O. Box 20602, Alexandria VA 22320-1602. (703)683-1243. Fax: (703)993-1161. Website: mason.gmu.edu/~rlathbur. **Contact:** Roger Lathbury, editor-in-chief. Estab. 1983. Publishes hardcover and trade paperback originals and reprints. Averages 4-5 total titles/year.
How to Contact: Responds in 3 months to queries. Accepts simultaneous submissions.
Payment/Terms: Pays 36% of receipts after Orchises has recouped its costs. Publishes ms 1 year after acceptance. Book catalog for #10 SASE; ms guidelines online.

▦ ◢ ◎ ORIENT PAPERBACKS, A Division of Vision Books Pvt Ltd., 1590 Madarsa Rd., Kashmere Gate Delhi 110 006 India. +911-11-2386-2267. Fax: +911-11-2386-2935. E-mail: orientpbk@vsnl.com. Website: www.orientpaperbacks.com. **Contact:** Sudhir Malhotra, editor. "We are one of the largest paperback publishers in S.E. Asia and publish English fiction by authors from this part of the world."
Needs: Length: 40,000 words minimum.
How to Contact: Send cover letter, brief summary, 1 sample chapter and author's bio data. "We send writers' guidelines on accepting a proposal."
Payment/Terms: Pays royalty on copies sold.

🆓 ◢ OTHER PRESS, 307 Seventh Ave., Suite 1807, New York NY 1001. (212)414-0054. Fax: (212)414-0939. E-mail: editor@otherpress.com. Website: www.otherpress.com. **Contact:** Stacey Hague and Blake Radcliffe, editors (literary and translations). Estab. 1998. The Other Press is a small independent publisher. Publishes hardcover originals and paperback reprints. **Published 1 debut author within the last year.** Plans 3 first novels this year.
Needs: Literary. Published *The Artificial Silk Girl*, by Irmgard Keun (fiction); *Verses of Forgiveness*, by Myriam Ataki (fiction-middle eastern); *A Cleaning Woman*, by Christian Oster (fiction).
How to Contact: Accepts unsolicited mss. Query with SASE or submit outline, 2 sample chapter(s). Accepts queries by e-mail, mail. Include brief bio, list of publishing credits. Responds in 4 weeks to queries; 3 months to mss. Accepts simultaneous submissions, electronic submissions. No submissions on disk. Rarely comments on rejected mss.
Payment/Terms: Pays 7½-12% royalty. Average advance: negotiable.
Advice: "Please send us your absolute final draft of your completed manuscript and not a work in progress."

◎ ▼ OUR CHILD PRESS, P.O. Box 4379, Philadelphia PA 19118-8379. (610)308-8988. Fax: (610)407-0943. E-mail: ocp98@aol.com. Website: www.ourchildpress.com. **Contact:** Carol Hallenbeck, CEO. Estab. 1984. Publishes hardcover and paperback originals and reprints.

● Received the Ben Franklin Award for *Don't Call Me Marda*, by Sheila Welch.

Needs: Especially interested in books on adoption or learning disabilities. Published *Things Little Kids Need to Know*, by Susan Uhlig.

How to Contact: Does not accept unsolicited mss. Query with SASE. Responds in 2 weeks. Accepts simultaneous submissions. Sometimes comments on rejected mss.

Payment/Terms: Pays 5% royalty. Publishes ms 6 months after acceptance. Book catalog free.

OUTRIDER PRESS, INC., 937 Patricia, Crete IL 60417. (708)672-6630. Fax: (708)672-5820. E-mail: outriderpr@aol.com. Website: www.outriderpress.com. **Contact:** Whitney Scott, editor. Estab. 1988. Small literary press and hand bindery; publishes many first-time authors. Publishes paperback originals. Books: 70 lb. paper; offset printing; perfect bound. Average print order: 2,000. **Published 25-30 debut authors within the last year.** Distributes titles through Baker & Taylor.

● Was a *Small Press Review* "Pick" for 2000.

Needs: Ethnic, experimental, family saga, fantasy (space fantasy, sword and sorcery), feminist, gay/lesbian, historical, horror (psychological, supernatural), humor, lesbian, literary, mainstream/contemporary, mystery (amateur slueth, cozy, police procedural, private eye/hardboiled), new age/mystic, psychic/supernatural, romance (contemporary, futuristic/time travel, gothic, historical, regency period, romantic suspense), science fiction (soft/sociological), short story collections, thriller/espionage, western (frontier saga, traditional). Holds the 2004 Anthology/Contest—The Supernatural. Published *Telling Time*, by Cherie Caswell Dost; *If Ever I Cease to Love*, by Robert Klein Engler.

How to Contact: Accepts unsolicited mss. Query with SASE. Accepts queries by mail. Include estimated word count, brief bio, list of publishing credits. Agented fiction 10%. Responds in 3 weeks to queries; 4 months to mss. Accepts simultaneous submissions, electronic submissions, submissions on disk. Sometimes comments on rejected mss.

Payment/Terms: Pays honorarium. Publishes ms 6 months after acceptance. Book catalog free; ms guidelines for SASE.

Advice: "It's always best to familiarize yourself with our publications. We're especially fond of humor/irony."

PETER OWEN PUBLISHERS, 73 Kenway Rd., London SW5 0RE United Kingdom. 020-7373 5628. Fax: 020-7373 6760. E-mail: admin@peterowen.com. Website: www.peterowen.com. **Contact:** Antonia Owen, editorial director/fiction editor. "Independent publishing house from 1951. Publish literary fiction from around the world, from Russia to Japan. Publishers of Shusaku Endo, Paul and Jane Bowles, Hermann Hesse, Octavio Paz, Colette, etc." Publishes hardcover originals and trade paperback originals and reprints. Averages 20-30 total titles, 4 fiction titles/year. Titles distributed through Central Books, London and Dufour Editions, USA.

Needs: Literary. "No first novels and authors should be aware that we publish very little new fiction these days." Does not accept short stories, only excerpts from novels of normal length. Published *Angels on the Head of a Pin*, by Yuri Druzhnikov (translated literary fiction); *Cassandra's Disk*, by Angela Green (fiction); *At the Apple's Core*, by Denis O'Dell (non-fiction, music memoir).

How to Contact: Submit sample chapter(s), synopsis. Query with SASE or by e-mail. Submissions by agent preferred. Responds in 2 months to queries; 3 months to proposals. Accepts simultaneous submissions.

Payment/Terms: Pays 7½-10% royalty. Average advance: negotiable. Publishes ms 1 year after acceptance. Book catalog for SASE, SAE with IRC or on website.

Advice: "Be concise. It helps if author is familiar with our list. New fiction is very hard to sell in the UK; it is also hard to get it reviewed. At the moment we are publishing less fiction than non-fiction."

RICHARD C. OWEN PUBLISHERS, INC., P.O. Box 585, Katonah NY 10536. (914)232-3903. Website: www.rcowen.com. **Contact:** Janice Boland, director, children's books. Estab. 1982. "We believe children become enthusiastic, independent, life-long readers when supported and guided by skillful teachers who choose books with real and lasting value. The professional development work we do and the books we publish support these beliefs." Publishes hardcover and paperback originals. **Published 15 debut authors within the last year.** Averages 23 total titles/year. Distributes titles to schools via mail order. Promotes titles through website, database mailing, reputation, catalog, brochures and appropriate publications—magazines, etc.

Needs: Picture books. "Brief, strong story line, believable characters, natural language, exciting—child-appealing stories with a twist. No lists books, alphabet or counting books." Seeking short, snappy stories and articles for 7-

FOR EXPLANATIONS OF THESE SYMBOLS, SEE THE INSIDE FRONT AND BACK COVERS OF THIS BOOK.

8-year-old children (2nd grade). Subjects include humor, careers, mysteries, science fiction, folktales, women, fashion trends, sports, music, mysteries, myths, journalism, history, inventions, planets, architecture, plays, adventure, technology, vehicles. Published *Mama Cut My Hair*, by Lisa Wilkinson (fiction, debut author); *Cool*, by Steven Morse (fiction, debut author); and *Author on My Street*, by Lisa Brodie Cook (fiction).

How to Contact: Send for ms guidelines, then submit full ms with SASE via mail only. No e-mail submissions please. Responds in 5 months to mss. Accepts simultaneous submissions.

Payment/Terms: Pays 5% royalty on wholesale price. Books for Young Learners Anthologies: flat fee for all rights. Publishes ms 2-5 years after acceptance. Ms guidelines online.

Advice: "Send entire ms. Write clear strong stories with memorable characters and end with a big wind up finish. Write for today's children—about real things that interest them. Read books that your public library features in their children's room to acquaint yourself with the best modern children's literature."

N A ✍ OWL BOOKS, Henry Holt & Co., Inc., 115 W. 18th St., New York NY 10011. (212)886-9200. Fax: (212)633-0748. Website: www.henryholt.com. **Contact:** Jenifer Barth, senior editor; Tom Bissell, associate editor. Estab. 1996. Averages 135-140 total titles/year.

Needs: Literary, mainstream/contemporary. Published *White Boy Shuffle*, by Paul Beatty and *The Debt to Pleasure*, by John Lanchester.

How to Contact: Does not accept unsolicited mss. *Agented submissions only.* Query with synopsis, 1 sample chapter and SASE. Responds in 3 months to proposals. Accepts simultaneous submissions.

Payment/Terms: Pays 6-7½% royalty on retail price. Average advance: variable. Publishes ms 1 year after acceptance. Ms guidelines online.

N ☐ ◎ PALARI PUBLISHING, P.O. Box 9288, Richmond VA 23227-0288. (804)883-6112. Fax: (804)883-5234. E-mail: palaripub@aol.com. Website: www.palari.net. **Contact:** David Smitherman, fiction editor. Estab. 1998. Small publisher specializing in Southern mysteries and nonfiction. Publishes hardcover and trade paperback originals. **Published 2 debut authors within the last year.** Member, Publishers Marketing Association. Distributes titles through Baker & Taylor, Ingram, Amazon.com, mail order and website. Promotes titles through book signings, direct mail and the Internet.

Needs: Adventure, ethnic, gay/lesbian, historical, literary, mainstream/contemporary, multicultural, mystery, suspense. "Tell why your idea is unique or interesting. Make sure we are interested in your genre before submitting." Published *We're Still Here* (cultural); and *In and Out in Hollywood* (Hollywood, gay); *The Guessing Game* (mystery).

How to Contact: Accepts unsolicited mss. Query with SASE. Accepts queries by e-mail, fax. Include estimated word count, brief bio, social security number, list of publishing credits. Send SASE for return of ms or send a disposable ms and SASE for reply only. Responds in 1 month to queries; 2-3 months to mss. Accepts simultaneous submissions, electronic submissions. Often comments on rejected mss.

Payment/Terms: Pays royalty. Publishes ms 1 year after acceptance. Book catalog free; ms guidelines online.

Advice: "Send a good bio. I'm interested in a writer's experience and unique outlook on life."

PANTHEON BOOKS, Knopf Publishing Group, Random House, Inc., 745 Broadway 21-1, New York NY 10019. (212)751-2600. Fax: (212)572-6030. Website: www.pantheonbooks.com. **Contact:** Adult Editorial Department. Estab. 1942. "Small but well-established imprint of well-known larger house." Publishes hardcover and trade paperback originals and trade paperback reprints.

Needs: Quality fiction and nonfiction. Published *Crooked Little Heart*, by Anne Lamott.

How to Contact: Does not accept unsolicited mss. Query with cover letter and sample material. Send SASE or IRC. No simultaneous submissions.

Payment/Terms: Pays royalty. Offers advance.

PANTHER CREEK PRESS, P.O. Box 130233, Spring TX 77393-0233. E-mail: panthercreek3@hotmail.com. Website: www.panthercreekpress.com. **Contact:** Bobbi Sissel, editor (literary); Jerry Cooke, assistant editor (mystery); William Laufer, assistant editor (collections). Estab. 1999. "Mid-size publisher interested in Merchant-Ivory type fiction." Publishes paperback originals. Books: 60 lb. white paper; docutech-printed; perfect-pound. Average print order: 1,500. **Published 4 debut authors within the last year.** Distributes titles through Baker & Taylor, Amazon.com.

Imprint(s): Enigma Books, Jerry Cooke, editor (mystery).

Needs: Ethnic, experimental, humor, literary, mainstream/contemporary, multicultural, mystery (amateur sleuth), regional (Texana), short story collections. Published *The Caballeros of Ruby, Texas*, by Cynthia Leal Massey (literary); *Under a Riverbed Sky*, by Christopher Woods (literary collection); and *Killing Daddy: A Caprock Story*, by Sandra Gail Teichmann (literary experimental novel).

How to Contact: Does not accept unsolicited mss. Query with SASE. Accepts queries by e-mail. Include estimated word count, brief bio, list of publishing credits. Responds in 3 weeks to queries.

Payment/Terms: Pays 10% royalty. Publishes ms 1 year after acceptance. Guidelines and catalog available on website.

Advice: "We would enjoy seeing more experimental work, but 'shock' narrative does not interest us. We don't want to see thrillers, fantasies, horror. The small, thoughtful literary story that large publishers don't want to take a chance on is the kind that gets our attention."

PAPYRUS PUBLISHERS & LETTERBOX SERVICE, P.O. Box 27383-55, Las Vegas NV 89126-1383. (702)256-3838. Website: www.booksbyletterbox.com. **Contact:** Geoffrey Hutchinson-Cleaves, editor-in-chief; Jessie Ros, fiction editor. Estab. London 1946; USA 1982. Mid-size independent press. Publishes hardcover originals. Books: audio. Average print order 5,000. Promotes titles through mail, individual author fliers, author tours.
Imprint(s): Letterbox Service; Difficult Subjects Made Easy; Pet Patter Features.
Needs: "Not accepting right now. Full stocked." See website for submission policy updates.
Advice: "Don't send it, unless you have polished and polished and polished. Absolutely no established author sends off a piece that has just been 'written' once. That is the first draft of many!"

PARADISE CAY PUBLICATIONS, P.O. Box 29, Arcata CA 95518-0029. (707)822-7038. Fax: (707)822-9163. E-mail: matt@humboldt1.com. Website: www.paracay.com. **Contact:** Matt Morehouse, publisher. Publishes hardcover and trade paperback originals and reprints. Books: 50 lb. paper; offset printing; perfect bound; illustrations. Average print order: 10,000. Average first novel print order: 3,000. **Published 1 debut authors within the last year.** Averages 5 total titles, 1 fiction title/year.
Needs: Adventure (nautical, sailing). All fiction must have a nautical theme. Published *Easing Sheets*, by L.M. Lawson.
How to Contact: Query with SASE or submit proposal package including 2-3 sample chapter(s), synopsis. Responds in 1 month to queries; 1 month to proposals.
Payment/Terms: Pays 10-15% royalty on wholesale price or makes outright purchase of $1,000-10,000. Average advance: $0-2,000. Publishes ms 4 months after acceptance. Book catalog and ms guidelines free on request or online.
Advice: "Must present in a professional manner. *Must* have a strong nautical theme."

PASSEGGIATA PRESS, 420 West 14th St., Pueblo CO 81003-3404. (719)544-1038. Fax: (719)544-7911. E-mail: passegpress@cs.com. **Contact:** Donald Herdeck, publisher/editor-in-chief. Estab. 1973. "We search for books that will make clear the complexity and value of non-Western literature and culture." Small independent publisher with expanding list. Publishes hardcover and paperback originals. Books: library binding; illustrations. Average print order: 1,000-1,500. Averages 10-20 total titles, 6-8 fiction titles/year.
  • Passeggiata, formerly Three Continents Press, has published three authors awarded the Nobel Prize in Literature."
Needs: "We publish original fiction only by writers from Africa, the Caribbean, the Middle East, Asia and the Pacific. Published *Not Yet African*, by Kevin Gordon; and *Ghost Songs*; by Kathryn Abdul-Baki.
How to Contact: Query with SASE or submit outline, table of contents. State "origins (non-Western), education and previous publications. Send inquiry letter first and ms only if so requested by us. We are not a subsidy publisher, but do a few specialized titles a year with grants. In those cases we accept institutional subventions." Accepts queries by e-mail, fax. Responds in 1 week. Accepts simultaneous submissions. Sometimes comments on rejected mss.
Payment/Terms: Pays 5-10% royalty. Foundation or institution recieves 20-30 copies of book and at times royalty on first printing. We pay royalties once yearly (against advance) as a percentage of net paid receipts. Average advance: $300. Provides 10 author's copies. Sends galleys to authors.
Advice: "Submit professional work (within our parameters of interest) with well worked-over language and clean manuscripts prepared to exacting standards."

PEACHTREE PUBLISHERS, LTD., 1700 Chattahoochee Ave., Atlanta GA 30318-2112. (404)876-8761. Fax: (404)875-2578. Website: www.peachtree-online.com. **Contact:** Helen Harriss, submissions editor. Estab. 1978. Independent publisher specializing in children's literature, nonfiction and regional guides. Publishes hardcover and trade paperback originals. First novel print run 5,000. **Published 2 debut authors within the last year.** Averages 20-25 total titles, 1-2 fiction titles/year. Promotes titles through review copies to appropriate publications, press kits and book signings at local bookstores.
Imprint(s): Peachtree Jr. and FreeStone
Needs: Juvenile, young adult. "Absolutely no adult fiction! We are seeking YA and juvenile works including mystery and historical fiction, of high literary merit." Published *Sister Spider Knows All*; *Shadow of A Doubt*; *My Life and Death by Alexandra Ganarsie*.
How to Contact: Accepts unsolicited mss. Query with SASE. Query, submit outline/synopsis and 3 sample chapters, or submit complete ms with SASE. Inquiries/submissions by US mail only. E-mail and fax will not be answered. Responds in 6 months to queries; 6 months to mss. Accepts simultaneous submissions. No electronic submissions.
Payment/Terms: Pays royalty. Royalty varies. Offers advance. Publishes ms 1 year or more after acceptance. Book catalog for 9×12 SAE with 6 first-class stamps; ms guidelines online.
Advice: "Check out our website or catalog for the kinds of things we are interested in."

◎ ⬛ **PELICAN PUBLISHING CO.**, P.O. Box 3110, Gretna LA 70054. (504)368-1175. Website: www.pelicanp ub.com. **Contact:** Nina Kooij, editor-in-chief. Estab. 1926. "We seek writers on the cutting edge of ideas. We believe ideas have consequences. One of the consequences is that they lead to a bestselling book." Publishes hardcover, trade paperback and mass market paperback originals and reprints. Books: hardcover and paperback binding; illustrations sometimes. Buys juvenile mss with illustrations. Averages 90 total titles/year. Distributes titles internationally through distributors, bookstores, libraries. Promotes titles at reading and book conventions, in trade magazines, in radio interviews, print reviews and TV interviews.

• *The Warlord's Puzzle*, by Virginia Walton Pilegard was #2 on *Independent Bookseller's* Book Sense 76 list.

Needs: Historical, juvenile (regional or historical focus). "We publish maybe one novel a year, usually by an author we already have. Almost all proposals are returned. We are most interested in historical Southern novels." Published *Child to the Waters*, by James Everett Kibler (Southern short stories) and *Moon's Cloud Blanket*, by Rose Ann St. Romain (children's tale, debut author).

How to Contact: Does not accept unsolicited mss. Query with SASE or submit outline, 2 sample chapter(s), synopsis, SASE. "Not responsible if writer's only copy is sent." Responds in 1 month. No simultaneous submissions. Rarely comments on rejected mss.

Payment/Terms: Pays royalty on actual receipts. Publishes ms 9-18 months after acceptance. Book catalog for SASE; writer's guidelines for SASE or on website.

Advice: "Research the market carefully. Check our catalog to see if your work is consistent with our list. For ages 8 and up, story must be planned in chapters that will fill at least 90 double-spaced manuscript pages. Topic for ages 8-12 must be Louisiana related and historical. We look for stories that illuminate a particular place and time in history and that are clean entertainment. The only original adult work we might consider is historical fiction, preferably Civil War (not romance). Please don't send three or more chapters unless solicited. Follow our guidelines listed under 'How to Contact.'"

Ⓝ ⬛ ◨ ◎ **PEMMICAN PUBLICATIONS**, 150 Henry Ave., Main Floor RM 12, Winnipeg MB R3B 0J7. (204)589-6346. Fax: (204)589-2063. E-mail: pemmicanpublications@hotmail.com. Website: www.pemmican.mb. ca. **Contact:** Audreen Hourie, managing editor. Estab. 1980. Metis and Aboriginal children's books. Publishes paperback originals. Books: stapled binding and perfect-bound; 4-color illustrations. Average print order: 2,500. First novel print order: 1,000. **Published some debut authors within the last year.** Averages 9 total titles/year. Distributes titles through Pemmican Publications. Promotes titles through press releases, fax, catalogs and book displays.

Needs: Children's/juvenile (American Indian, easy-to-read, preschool/picture book), ethnic (Native American). Published *Red Parka Mary*, by Peter Eyvindson (children's); *Nanabosho & Kitchie Odjig*, by Joe McLellan (native children's legend); and *Jack Pine Fish Camp*, by Tina Umpherville (children's). Also publishes the Builders of Canada series.

How to Contact: Accepts unsolicited mss. Submit complete ms. Send SASE for return of ms or send a disposable ms and SASE for reply only. Accepts simultaneous submissions.

Payment/Terms: Pays 10% royalty. Provides 10 author's copies. Average advance: $350.

⬛ **PENGUIN GROUP USA**, 375 Hudson St., New York NY 10014. (212)366-2000. Website: www.penguin.c om. "The company possesses perhaps the world's most prestigious list of best-selling authors and a backlist of unparalleled breadth, depth, and quality." General interest publisher of both fiction and nonfiction.

Imprint(s): Viking (hardcover); Dutton (hardcover); The Penguin Press (hardcover); Daw (hardcover and paperback); G P Putnam's Sons (hardcover and children's); Riverhead Books (hardcover and paperback); Tarcher (hardcover and paperback); Grosset/Putnam (hardcover); Putnam (hardcover); Avery; Viking Compass (hardcover); Penguin (paperback); Penguin Classics (paperback); Plume (paperback); Signet (paperback); Signet Classics (paperback); Onyx (paperback); Roc (paperback); Topaz (paperback); Mentor (paperback); Meridian (paperback); Berkley Books (paperback); Jove (paperback); Ace (paperback); Prime Crime (paperback); HPBooks (paperback); Penguin Compass(paperback); Dial Books for Young Readers (children's); Dutton Children's Books (children's); Viking Children's Books (children's); Puffin (children's); Frederick Warne (children's); Philomel Books (children's); Grosset and Dunlap (children's); Wee Sing (children's); PaperStar (children's); Planet Dexter (children's); Berkely (hardcover); Gothom (hardcover and paperback); Portfolio (hard and paperback); NAL (hardcover).

⬛ **PENGUIN PUTNAM BOOKS FOR YOUNG READERS**, Division of Penguin Putnam Inc., 345 Hudson St., New York NY 10014. (212)366-2000. E-mail: online@penguinputnam.com. Website: penguinputnam.com. Estab. 1838. Publishes hardcover and paperback.

Imprint(s): Dial Books for Young Readers; Dutton Children's Books; Dutton Interactive; Grosset & Dunlap; Paperstar; Philomel; Planet Dexter; Platt & Munk; Playskool; PSS; Puffin Books; G P Putnam's Sons; Viking Children's Books; Frederick Warne.

◨ ◎ **PERFECTION LEARNING CORP.**, 10520 New York Ave., Des Moines IA 50322-3775. (515)278-0133. Fax: (515)278-2980. Website: perfectionlearning.com. **Contact:** Sue Thies, editorial director. Estab. 1926. "We are an educational publisher of hi/lo fiction and nonfiction with teacher support material." Publishes hardcover and trade paperback originals. **Publishes 50-100 fiction and informational; 25 workbooks titles/year. Published 10 debut authors within the last year.** Distributes titles through sales reps, direct mail and online catalog. Promotes titles through educational conferences, journals and catalogs.

Imprint(s): Cover-to-Cover; Sue Thies, editorial director (all genres).

Needs: "We are publishing hi-lo chapter books and novels as well as curriculum books, including workbooks, literature anthologies, teacher guides, literature tests, and niche textbooks for grades 3-12." Readability of ms should be at least two grade levels below interest level for hi-lo titles. "Please do not submit mss with fewer that 4,000 words or more than 30,000 words." Published *Tall Shadow*, by Bonnie Highsmith Taylor (Native American); *The Rattlesnack Necklace*, by Linda Baxter (historical fiction); and *Tales of Mark Twain*, by Peg Hall (retold short stories).

How to Contact: Accepts unsolicited mss. Query with SASE or submit outline, 2-3 sample chapter(s), synopsis or submit complete manuscript with a cover letter. Accepts queries by e-mail, fax. Include estimated word count, brief bio, list of publishing credits. Send SASE for return of ms or send a disposable ms and SASE for reply only. Responds in 2 months to proposals; 3 months to mss. Accepts simultaneous submissions.

Payment/Terms: Pays 5-7% royalty on net receipts. Average advance: $300-500. Publishes ms 6-8 months after acceptance. Book catalog for 9 × 12 SASE with $2.31 postage; ms guidelines online.

Advice: "We are an educational publisher. Check with educators to find out their needs, their students' needs and what's popular."

THE PERMANENT PRESS, 4170 Noyac Rd., Sag Harbor NY 11963. (631)725-1101. Fax: (631)725-8215. Website: www.thepermanentpress.com. **Contact:** Judith Shepard, publisher. Estab. 1978. Mid-size, independent publisher of literary fiction. "We keep titles in print and are active in selling subsidiary rights." Publishes hardcover originals. Average print order: 1,500. **Published 4 debut authors within the last year.** Averages 12 total titles, 12 fiction titles/year. Distributes titles through Ingram, Baker & Taylor and Brodart. Promotes titles through reviews.

Imprint(s): Second Chance Press.

Needs: Literary, mainstream/contemporary, mystery. Especially looking for high line literary fiction, "artful, original and arresting." Accepts any fiction category as long as it is a "well-written, original full-length novel." Published *Hail to the Chiefs*, by Barbara Holland; *Angels in the Morning*, by Sasha Troyan; *All Honest Men*, by Claude and Michelle Stanush.

How to Contact: Accepts unsolicited mss. Query with SASE or submit first 20 pages of ms. No queries by fax or e-mail. Send SASE for return of ms or send a disposable ms and SASE for reply only. Responds in 3 weeks to queries; 6 months to mss. Accepts simultaneous submissions.

Payment/Terms: Pays 10-15% royalty on wholesale price. Offers $1,000 advance for Permanent Press books; royalty only on Second Chance Press titles. Publishes ms 18 months after acceptance. Book catalog for 8 × 10 SAE with 7 first-class stamps; ms guidelines for #10 SASE.

Advice: "We are looking for good books, be the tenth novel or first one, it makes little difference. The fiction is more important than the track record. Send us the beginning of the story, it's impossible to judge something that begins on page 302. Also, no outlines—let the writing present itself."

PHILOMEL BOOKS, Penguin Putnam Inc., 345 Hudson St., New York NY 10014. (212)414-3610. **Contact:** Patricia Lee Gauch, editorial director; Michael Green, senior editor. Estab. 1980. "A high-quality oriented imprint focused on stimulating pictue books, middle-grade novels, and young adult novels." Publishes hardcover originals. Averages 20-25 total titles/year.

Needs: Adventure, ethnic, family saga, fantasy, historical, juvenile (5-9 years), literary, picture books, regional, short story collections, western (young adult), young adult (10-18 years). Children's picture books (ages 3-8); middle-grade fiction and illustrated chapter books (ages 7-10); young adult novels (ages 10-15). Particularly interested in picture book mss with original stories and regional fiction with a distinct voice. Looking for "story-driven novels with a strong cultural voice but which speak universally." Published *The Long Patrol*, by Brian Jacques; *I Am Morgan LeFay*, by Nancy Springer; and *Betty Doll*, by Patricia Palacco.

How to Contact: Does not accept unsolicited mss. Query with SASE or submit outline, 3 sample chapter(s), synopsis. Agented fiction 40%. Responds in 3 months. Accepts simultaneous submissions. Sometimes comments on rejected mss.

Payment/Terms: Pays royalty. Average advance: negotiable. Publishes ms 1-2 years after acceptance. Book catalog for 9 × 12 SAE with 4 first-class stamps; ms guidelines for #10 SASE.

Advice: "We are not a mass-market publisher and do not publish short stories independently. In addition, we do just a few novels a year."

PIATKUS BOOKS, 5 Windmill Street, London W1T 2JA UK. 0207 631 0710. Fax: 0207 436 7137. E-mail: info@piatkus.co.uk. Website: www.piatkus.co.uk. **Contact:** Gillian Green, senior editor (literary); Emma Callasher, assistant editor (literary). Estab. 1979. Piatkus is a medium sized independent publisher of non-fiction and fiction. The fiction list is highly commercial and includes women's fiction, crime and thriller as well as literary fiction. Publishes hardcover originals, paperback originals and paperback reprints. **Published 12 debut authors within the last year.** Plans 14 first novels this year. Member, IPG.

Imprint(s): Piatkus Books (fiction), Portrait (general/non-fiction).

Needs: Adventure, erotica, family saga, historical, literary, mainstream/contemporary, mystery (amateur sleuth, cozy, police procedural, private eye/hardboiled), regional, romance (contemporary, historical, regency period, romantic suspense), thriller/espionage. Published *Natural Selection*, by Bill Dare (general); *Dive From Clausen's Pier*, by Ann Packer (literary); *Three Kates*, Nora Roberts (romance/suspense).
How to Contact: Accepts unsolicited mss. Query with SASE or submit outline, 3 sample chapter(s), synopsis. Accepts queries by mail. Include estimated word count, brief bio, list of publishing credits. Send SASE for return of ms or send a disposable ms and SASE for reply only. Agented fiction 80%. Responds in 12 weeks to mss. Accepts simultaneous submissions. No submissions on disk. Rarely comments on rejected mss.
Payment/Terms: Pays royalty. Average advance: negotiable. Publishes ms 1 year after acceptance. Book catalog free; ms guidelines for SASE.
Advice: "Study our list before submitting your work."

N A ☑ ☑ PICADOR USA, St. Martin's Press, 175 Fifth Ave., New York NY 10010. Website: www.picadorusa.com. **Contact:** Frances Coady, publisher (literary fiction); Joshua Kendall, associate editor (literary fiction). Estab. 1994. Picador publishes high-quality literary fiction and nonfiction. "We are open to a broad range of subjects, well written by authoritative authors." Publishes hardcover and trade paperback originals and reprints. Averages 70-80 total titles/year. Titles distributed through Von Holtzbrinck Publishers. Titles promoted through national print advertising and bookstore coop.
  ● *The Amazing Adventures of Kavalier & Clay*, by Michael Chabon, won the Pulitzer Prize for fiction; *In America*, by Susan Sontag, won National Book Award. Jame Crace's *Being Dead* won the National Book Critics Circle Award.
Needs: Literary. Published *No One Thinks of Greenland*, by John Griesmer (first novel, literary); *Summerland, A Novel*, by Malcolm Knox (first novel, literary fiction); *Half a Heart*, by Rosellen Brown (literary fiction).
How to Contact: Does not accept unsolicited mss. *Agented submissions only.* Accepts queries by e-mail, fax, mail. Responds in 2 months to queries. Accepts simultaneous submissions.
Payment/Terms: Pays 7½-15% royalty on retail price. Average advance: varies. Publishes ms 18 months after acceptance. Book catalog for 9×12 SASE and $2.60 postage; ms guidelines for #10 SASE or online.

N ◎ ☑ PIÑATA BOOKS, Arte Publico Press, University of Houston, Houston TX 77204-2004. (713)743-2841. Fax: (713)743-3080. Website: www.artepublicopress.com. **Contact:** Nicolas Kanellos, director. Estab. 1994. Piñata Books is dedicated to the publication of children's and young adult literature focusing on US Hispanic culture by U.S. Hispanic authors. Publishes hardcover and trade paperback originals. **Published some debut authors within the last year.** Averages 10-15 total titles/year.
Needs: Adventure, juvenile, picture books, young adult. Published *Trino's Choice*, by Diane Gonzales Bertrand (ages 11-up); *Delicious Hullabaloo/Pachanga Deliciosa*, by Pat Mora (picture book); and *The Year of Our Revolution*, by Judith Ortiz Cofer (young adult).
How to Contact: Does not accept unsolicited mss. Query with SASE or submit 2 sample chapter(s), synopsis, SASE. Responds in 1 month. Accepts simultaneous submissions.
Payment/Terms: Pays 10% royalty on wholesale price. Average advance: $1,000-3,000. Publishes ms 2 years after acceptance. Book catalog and ms guidelines available via website or with #10 SASE.
Advice: "Include cover letter with submission explaining why your manuscript is unique and important, why we should publish it, who will buy it, relevance to the U.S. Hispanic culture, etc."

◎ PIG IRON PRESS, 26 N. Phelps, Box 237, Youngstown OH 44301-0237. (330)747-6932. Fax: (330)747-0599. E-mail: pigironpress@cboss.com. **Contact:** Jim Villani, publisher. Estab. 1975. Small independent publisher. Publishes hardcover originals, paperback originals and reprints. Books: 8½×11; 60 lb. offset paper; offset lithography; paper/casebound; illustration on cover only. Average print order: 1,000. Published *Semi-Private Rooms*, by Jim Sanderson (social realism); *The Harvest*, by Judith Hemschemeyer (social realism).
Needs: Adventure, experimental, science fiction, short story collections. Published *Semi-Private Rooms*, by Jim Sanderson (social realism); *The Harvest*, by Judith Hemschemeyer (social realism).
How to Contact: Does not accept unsolicited mss.

◎ PINEAPPLE PRESS, INC., P.O. Box 3889, Sarasota FL 34230. (941)359-0886. Fax: (941)351-9988. E-mail: info@pineapplepress.com. Website: www.pineapplepress.com. **Contact:** June Cussen, editor. Estab. 1982. Small independent trade publisher. Publishes hardcover and trade paperback originals. Books: quality paper; offset printing; Smyth-sewn or perfect-bound; illustrations occasionally. **Published some debut authors within the last year.** Averages 25 total titles/year. Distributes titles through Pineapple, Ingram and Baker & Taylor. Promotes titles through reviews, advertising in print media, direct mail, author signings and the World Wide Web.
Needs: Historical, literary, mainstream/contemporary, regional (Florida). Published *Point of Horror*, by Robert Macomber (novel).
How to Contact: Does not accept unsolicited mss. Query with SASE or submit outline, sample chapter(s), synopsis. Responds in 3 months to queries. Accepts simultaneous submissions.
Payment/Terms: Pays 6½-15% royalty on net receipts. Publishes ms 18 months after acceptance. Book catalog for 9×12 SAE with $1.25 postage.
Advice: "Quality first novels will be published, though we usually only do one or two novels per year. We regard

the author/editor relationship as a trusting relationship with communication open both ways. Learn all you can about the publishing process and about how to promote your book once it is published. A query on a novel without a brief sample seems useless."

🌐 ☐ **PIPERS' ASH, LTD.**, Pipers' Ash, Church Rd., Christian Malford, Chippenham, Wiltshire SN15 4BW UK. +44(01249)720-563. Fax: 0870 0568916. E-mail: pipersash@supamasu.com. Website: www.supamasu.com. **Contact:** Manuscript Evaluation Desk. Estab. 1976. "Small press publisher. Considers all submitted manuscritps fairly—without bias or favor." This company is run by book-lovers, not by accountants. Publishes hardcover and electronic originals. **Published 12 debut authors within the last year.** Averages 12 total titles, 12 fiction titles/year. Distributes and promotes titles through direct mail and the Internet.
Needs: Adventure, children's/juvenile (adventure), confession, feminist, historical, juvenile, literary, mainstream/contemporary, military/war, plays, poetry, poetry in translation, regional, religious, romance (contemporary, romantic suspense), science fiction (hard science/technological, soft/sociological), short story collections, sports, suspense, western (frontier saga, traditional), young adult (adventure, fantasy/science fiction). Currently emphasizing stage plays. "We publish 30,000-word novels and short story collections. Visit our website." Planning anthologies: short stories, science fiction, poetry. "Authors are invited to submit collections of short stories and poetry for consideration for our ongoing programs." Published *Tales out of Church*, by Rev. Andrew Sangster; *Cosmic Women*, by Margaret Karamazin; *Cross to Bear*, by Chris Spiller; *A Sailor's Song*, by Leslie Wilkie.
How to Contact: Accepts unsolicited mss. Query with SASE or submit sample chapter(s), 25-word synopsis (that sorts out the writers from the wafflers). Accepts queries by e-mail, fax, phone. Include estimated word count. Send SASE for return of ms or send a disposable ms and SASE for reply only. Responds in 1 month to queries; 3 months to mss. Accepts electronic submissions, submissions on disk. No simultaneous submissions. Always comments on rejected mss.
Payment/Terms: Pays 10% royalty on wholesale price and 5 author's copies. Publishes ms 6 months after acceptance. Book catalog for A5 SASE and on website; ms guidelines online.
Advice: "Study the market! Check your selected publisher's catalog."

✔ ◎ **PIPPIN PRESS**, 229 E. 85th St., P.O. Box 1347, Gracie Station, New York NY 10028. (212)288-4920. Fax: (732)225-1562. **Contact:** Barbara Francis, publisher and editor-in-chief; Joyce Segal, senior editor. Estab. 1987. "Small, independent children's book company, formed by the former editor-in-chief of Prentice Hall's juvenile book division." Publishes hardcover originals. Books: 135-150 GSM offset-semi-matte paper (for picture books); offset, sheet-fed printing; Smythe-sewn binding; full color, black and white line illustrations and half tone, b&w and full color illustrations. Averages 4-6 total titles/year. Distributes titles through commission sales force. Promotes titles through reviews, trade convention exhibits, as well as book fairs.
Needs: Children's/juvenile (ages 4-12), historical, humor, mystery, picture books. "We're especially looking for small chapter books for 7- to 11-year olds, especially by people of many cultures." Also interested in humorous fiction for ages 7-11. "At this time, we are especially interested in historical novels, 'autobiographical' novels, historical and literary biographies and humor." Published *A Visit from the Leopard: Memories of a Ugandan Childhood*, by Catherine Mudibo-Pinang (juvenile autobiography, middle readers; debut author); *Abigail's Drum*, by John A. Minahan (juvenile historical, middle readers debut author); and *The Spinner's Daughter*, by Amy Littlesugar (juvenile fiction, young readers; debut author).
How to Contact: Does not accept unsolicited mss. Query with SASE or IRC. Responds in 3 weeks to queries. No simultaneous submissions. Sometimes comments on rejected mss.
Payment/Terms: Pays royalty. Offers advance. Publishes ms 2 years after acceptance. Book catalog for 6×9 SASE; ms guidelines for #10 SASE.

✔ ◎ **PLEASANT COMPANY PUBLICATIONS**, 8400 Fairway Pl., Middleton WI 53562. Fax: (608)828-4768. Website: www.americangirl.com. **Contact:** Submissions Editor. Estab. 1986. Mid-size independent publisher. "Moving in new directions, and committed to high quality in all we do. Pleasant Company has specialized in historical fiction and contemporary nonfiction for girls 7-12 and is now actively seeking strong authors for middle-grade contemporary fiction for all ages." Publishes hardcover and trade paperback originals. Averages 50-60 total titles, 30 fiction titles/year.
Imprint(s): The American Girls Collection, American Girl Library, AG Fiction, History Mysteries, Girls of Many Lands.
Needs: Children's/juvenile (contemporary for girls 8-12), contemporary. "Contemporary fiction submissions should capture the spirit of contemporary American girls and also illuminate the ways in which their lives are personally

---

INTERESTED IN A PARTICULAR GENRE? Check our sections for: **Mystery/Suspense**, page 68; **Romance**, page 80; **Science Fiction/Fantasy & Horror**, page 90.

touched by issues and concerns affecting America today. We are seeking strong, well-written contemporary fiction, told from the perspective of a middle-school-age girl. No romance, picture books, poetry." Stories must feature an American girl, aged 10-13; reading level 4th-6th grade. Published *The Night Flyer*, by Elizabeth McDavid Jones (historical fiction); *Smoke Screen*, by Amy Goldman Koss (contemporary fiction); and *The Secret Voice of Gina Zhang*, by Dori Jones Yang (contemporary fiction).

How to Contact: Accepts unsolicited mss. Query with SASE or submit complete ms. Submit complete ms with cover letter for contemporary fiction. Accepts queries by e-mail, fax. Include list of publishing credits. "Tell us why the story is right for us." Send SASE for return of ms or send a disposable ms and SASE for reply only. Agented fiction 5%. Responds in 3 months to queries; 4 months to mss. Accepts simultaneous submissions.

Payment/Terms: Average advance: varies. Publishes ms 3-12 months after acceptance. Book catalog for #10 SASE; ms guidelines for for SASE or on the website.

Advice: "No picture book submissions, no doll proposals."

PLEXUS PUBLISHING, INC., 143 Old Marlton Pike, Medford NJ 08055-8750. (609)654-6500. Fax: (609)654-4309. E-mail: jbryans@infotoday.com. **Contact:** John B. Bryans, editor-in-chief. Estab. 1977. Publishes hardcover and paperback originals. **Published 70% debut authors within the last year.** Averages 4-5 total titles/year.

Needs: Mysteries and literary novels with a strong regional (southern NJ) angle. Published *Wrong Beach Island*, by Jane Kelly.

How to Contact: Query with SASE. Agented fiction 10%. Responds in 3 months. Accepts simultaneous submissions.

Payment/Terms: Pays 10-15% royalty on net receipts. Average advance: $500-1,000. Book catalog and ms guidelines for 10×13 SAE with 4 first-class stamps.

A M PLUME, (formerly Dutton Plume), Division of Penguin Putnam Inc., 375 Hudson St., New York NY 10014. (212)366-2000. Website: www.penguinputnam.com. **Contact:** Trena Keating, editor-in-chief (literary fiction). Estab. 1948. Publishes paperback originals and reprints. **Published some debut authors within the last year.**

Needs: "All kinds of commercial and literary fiction, including mainstream, historical, New Age, western, thriller, gay. Full length novels and collections." Published *Girl with a Pearl Earring*, by Tracy Chevalier; *Liar's Moon*, by Phillip Kimball; and *The True History of Paradise*, by Margaret Cezain-Thompson.

How to Contact: *Agented submissions only.* Query with SASE. "State type of book and past publishing projects." Responds in 3 months to queries. Accepts simultaneous submissions.

Payment/Terms: Pays in royalties and author's copies. Offers advance. Publishes ms 12-18 months after acceptance. Book catalog for SASE.

Advice: "Write the complete manuscript and submit it to an agent or agents."

N O POCOL PRESS, 6023 Pocol Drive, Clifton VA 20124. (703)830-5862. E-mail: chrisandtom@erols.com. Website: www.pocolpress.com. **Contact:** J. Thomas Hetrick, editor (baseball history and fiction). Pocol Press publishes first-time, unagented authors. Our fiction deals mainly with single author, short story anthologies from outstanding niche writers. Publishes paperback originals. Books: 50 lb. paper; offset printing; perfect binding. Average print order: 500. **Published 2 debut authors within the last year.** Plans 3 first novels this year. Member, Small Press Public Association. Distributes titles through website, authors, e-mail, word-of-mouth, and readings.

Needs: Horror (psychological, supernatural), literary, mainstream/contemporary, mystery (amateur sleuth), short story collections, baseball. Published *Smoke Follows Beauty*, by Brian Ames (hunting/adventure); *Parallel Lines and the Hockey Universe*, by Grant Tracey (family, sports); *Best Bet in Beantown*, by G.S. Rowe (baseball, mystery).

How to Contact: Does not accept or return unsolicited mss. Query with SASE or submit 1 sample chapter(s). Accepts queries by mail. Include estimated word count, brief bio, list of publishing credits. Responds in 2 weeks. No simultaneous submissions, submissions on disk. Sometimes comments on rejected mss.

Payment/Terms: Pays 10-12% royalty. Publishes ms 1 year or less after acceptance. Book catalog for SASE or on website; ms guidelines for SASE or on website.

Advice: "Pocol Press is unique; we publish good writing and great storytelling. Write the best stories you can. Read them to you friends/peers. Note their reaction."

N O @ POISONED PEN PRESS, 6962 E. 1st Ave. #103, Scottsdale AZ 85251. (480)945-3375. Fax: (480)949-1707. E-mail: info@poisonedpenpress.com. Website: www.poisonedpress.com. **Contact:** Barbara G. Peters, editor (mystery, fiction). Estab. 1997. Publishes hardcover originals and paperback originals. Books: 60# paper; offset printing; hardcover binding. Average print order: 3,500. First novel print order: 3,000. **Published 6 debut authors within the last year.** Plans 8 first novels this year. Member, Publishers Marketing Association, Arizona Book Publishers Associations, Publishers Association of West. Distributes through Ingram, BGT, Brodart.

● Was nominated in 2002 for the LA Times Book Prize. Also the recipient of several Edgar and Agatha nominations.

Needs: Mystery (amateur sleuth, cozy, police procedural, private eye/hardboiled, historical). Published *At Risk*, by Kit Ehrman (mystery/fiction); *Beat Until Stiff*, by Claire Johnson (mystery/fiction); *Beware the Solitary Drinker*, by Cornelius Lehane (mystery/fiction). Publishes the ongoing series *John The Eunuch Mysteries*, and the *Wesley Farrell Mysteries*.

How to Contact: Accepts unsolicited mss. Query with SASE. Accepts queries by e-mail. Responds in 1 week to queries; 3 months to mss. Accepts electronic submissions, submissions on disk. No simultaneous submissions. Often comments on rejected mss.
Payment/Terms: Pays 7.5-15% royalty. Average advance: 500-1,000. Publishes ms 4-6 months after acceptance. Book catalog online; ms guidelines online.

POLYCHROME PUBLISHING CORP., 4509 N. Francisco, Chicago IL 60625. (773)478-4455. Fax: (773)478-0786. E-mail: polypub@earthlink.net. Website: www.polychromebooks.com. Estab. 1990. Publishes hardcover originals and reprints. **Published 50% debut authors within the last year.** Averages 4 total titles/year.
Needs: Ethnic, juvenile, multicultural (particularly Asian-American), picture books, young adult. Published *Striking It Rich: Treasures from Gold Mountain; Char Siu Bad Boy*.
How to Contact: Submit synopsis and 3 sample chapters, for picture books submit whole ms. Responds in 8 months to mss. Accepts simultaneous submissions.
Payment/Terms: Pays royalty. Offers advance. Publishes ms 2 years after acceptance. Book catalog for #10 SASE; ms guidelines for #10 SASE or on the website.

⚏ ◻ PORT TOWN PUBLISHING, 601 Belknap Street, Superior WI 54880. (715)392-6843. E-mail: porttownpublish@aol.com. Website: www.porttownpublishing.begstep.com. **Contact:** Jean Hackensmith, senior fiction editor. Estab. 1999. Port Town Publishing is a small publisher of paperback fiction novels. Publishes 24 titles per year, including 12 adult fiction titles ranging in genre from romance, to sci-fi, to myster, to horror. "Our "Little Ones" line is geared to children 4-7 years old, features 6 titles per year that will address sometimes 'difficult' issues." Publishes paperback originals. Books: 20 lb. stock paper; laser printing; perfect bound; color and pencil-sketch illustrations. Average print order: 100-200. **Published 13 debut authors within the last year.** Distribute via the internet and promote through the author.
Imprint(s): Little Ones; Growing Years.
Needs: Adventure, children's/juvenile (adventure, animal, easy-to-read, fantasy, historical, mystery, preschool/picture book, series), fantasy (space fantasy, sword and sorcery), historical, horror (dark fantasy, futuristic, psychological, supernatural), mainstream/contemporary, mystery (amateur sleuth, cozy, police procedural, private eye/hardboiled), regional (Lake Superior area), romance (contemporary, futuristic/time travel, gothic, historical, regency period, romantic suspense), science fiction (hard science/technological, soft/sociological), thriller/espionage, young adult (adventure, easy-to-read, fantasy/science fiction, historical, horror, mystery/suspense, problem novels, romance, series, sports). Wants science fiction, thriller and mystery. Published *Keeper of the Spirit*, by Kim Matton (historical romance); *Shadow of Doubt*, by Linda Morelli (romantic suspense); *The Healer*, by A.J. Russo (soft thriller). Publishes *The Gitchee Gumee Saga* series.
How to Contact: Does not accept unsolicited mss. Query with SASE. Accepts queries by e-mail, mail. Include estimated word count, brief bio, list of publishing credits. Agented fiction 5%. Responds in 1 week. Accepts simultaneous submissions.
Payment/Terms: Publishes ms 1-2 years after acceptance. Book catalog online; ms guidelines online.
Advice: "We are looking for a sellable, well-plotted story above all else. We are not afraid to take on a manuscript that needs work, but we always hope the author will grow during the editorial process."

⊘ ◎ THE POST-APOLLO PRESS, 35 Marie St., Sausalito CA 94965. (415)332-1458. Fax: (415)332-8045. E-mail: tpapress@rcn.com. Website: http://users.rcn.com.tpapress. **Contact:** Simone Fattal, publisher. Estab. 1982. Specializes in "woman writers published in Europe or the Middle East who have been translated into English for the first time." Publishes trade paperback originals and reprints. Books: acid-free paper; lithography printing; perfect-bound. Average print order: 1,000. **Published some debut authors within the last year.** Averages 4 total titles/year. Distributes titles through Small Press Distribution, Berkley, California. Promotes titles through advertising in selected literary quarterlies, SPD catalog, ALA and ABA and SF Bay Area Book Festival participation.
Needs: Experimental, literary (plays), spiritual. "Many of our books are first translations into English." Published *Some Life*, by Joanne Kyger; *In/somnia*, by Etel Adnan; *9:45*, by Kit Robinson; *Where the Rocks Started*, by Marc Atherton (debut author, novel); and *Happily*, by Lyn Hejinian.
How to Contact: Submit 1 sample chapter(s), SASE. "The Post-Apollo Press is not accepting manuscripts or queries currently due to a full publishing schedule." See website for updates. Responds in 3 months to queries.
Payment/Terms: Pays 5-7% royalty on wholesale price. Publishes ms 1½ years after acceptance. Book catalog free; Book catalog and ms guidelines for #10 SASE.
Advice: "We want to see serious, literary quality, informed by an experimental aesthetic."

⊘ ⚏ ◎ PRISTINE PUBLISHING, P.O. Box 10816, San Bernardino CA 92346. (909)862-3398. Fax: (909)862-1991. E-mail: editor@pristinepublishing.com. Website: www.pristinepublishing.com. **Contact:** Liliana Monteil-Dovcette, senior editor (romance). Estab. 2001. Pristine Publishing is a small independent publisher, just getting established. Publishes paperback originals. Books: 60# white offset papre; offset printing. Average print order 5,000. Average first novel print order: 3,000-5,000. Member, PMA. Distributes through Baker & Taylor.
Imprint(s): Eternal.

Needs: Romance (contemporary, futuristic/time travel, romantic suspense, chick-lit). Published *A Family for Raffi*, by Lara Rios (romance).

How to Contact: Does not accept unsolicited mss. Query with SASE. Accepts queries by mail. Include estimated word count, brief bio, list of publishing credits. Agented fiction 30%. Accepts simultaneous submissions. Sometimes comments on rejected mss.

Payment/Terms: Pays 4-8% royalty. Average advance: negotiable. Publishes ms 12-16 months after acceptance. Book catalog online; ms guidelines online.

Advice: "In romance the trend is toward chick-lit and women's fiction. However, the nice thing about romance is the many sub-genres that continue to be popular. I would ignore trends and write what you love. Understand that as a small press, distribution is minimal. We can not and do not wish to compete with large publishers. But this is another avenue to getting published."

⬛ PUBLISHERS SYNDICATION, INTERNATIONAL, P.O. Box 6218, Charlottesville VA 22906-6218. Fax: (434)964-0096. Website: www.Publisherssyndication.com. **Contact:** A. Samuels. Estab. 1979.

Needs: Adventure, mystery (amateur sleuth, police procedural), thriller/espionage, western (frontier saga).

How to Contact: Accepts unsolicited mss. Submit complete ms. Include estimated word count. Send SASE or IRC. Responds in 1 month to mss.

Payment/Terms: Pays .05-2% royalty. Average advance: negotiable. Ms guidelines for SASE.

Advice: "The type of manuscript we are looking for is devoid of references which might offend. Remember you are writing for a general audience."

⬛ PUCKERBRUSH PRESS, 76 Main St., Orono ME 04473-1430. (207)581-3832. **Contact:** Constance Hunting, publisher/editor (fiction). Estab. 1971. "Small independent trade publisher, unique because of independent editorial stance." Publishes trade paperback originals and reprints of literary fiction and poetry. Books: perfect-bound, illustrations. Average print order: 500. **Published 3 debut authors within the last year.** Averages 3-4 total titles, 1-2 fiction titles/year. Titles distributed through Amazon.com, Baker & Taylor, Barnes & Noble.

Needs: Literary, short story collections. Published *Cora's Seduction*, by Mary Gray Hughes (short stories); *The Crow on the Spruce*, by C. Hall (Maine fiction); *Night-Sea Journey*, by M. Alpert (poetry).

How to Contact: Accepts unsolicited mss. Submit complete ms. Include cover letter. Accepts queries by phone. Include brief bio, list of publishing credits. Responds in 1 month to queries; 3 months to mss. No simultaneous submissions. Often comments on rejected mss.

Payment/Terms: Pays 10-15% royalty on wholesale price. Book catalog for large SASE and 34; ms guidelines for SASE.

Advice: "Be true to your vision, not to fashion."

⬛ PUDDING HOUSE PUBLICATIONS, 81 Shadymere Ln., Columbus OH 43213. (614)986-1881. Website: www.puddinghouse.com. **Contact:** Jennifer Bosveld, editor. Estab. 1979. "Small independent publisher seeking outrageously fresh short short stories." Publishes paperback originals. Books, chapbooks, broadsides: paper varies; side stapled; b&w illustrations. **Published some debut authors within the last year.** Promotes titles through direct mail, conference exhibits, readings, workshops.

Needs: Experimental, literary, the writing experience, liberal/alternative politics or spirituality, new approaches. Do not send novels. Only send short short stories, flash fiction, and brief narrative. Published *In the City of Mystery*, by Alan Ziegler (short stories); and *Karmic 4-Star Buckaroo*, by John Bennett (short stories).

How to Contact: Accepts unsolicited mss. Submit complete ms. For chapbook $10 reading fee. Include brief bio, list of publishing credits. Send SASE or IRC. No simultaneous submissions. Sometimes comments on rejected mss.

Payment/Terms: Pays in author's copies. Publishes ms 2-24 months after acceptance. Ms guidelines for SASE.

Advice: "Be new!"

⬛ ◎ PUFFIN BOOKS, Penguin Putnam Inc., 345 Hudson St., New York NY 10014-3657. (212)366-2000. Website: www.penguinputnam.com. **Contact:** Sharyn November, senior editor; Kristin Gilson, executive editor. Puffin Books publishes high-end trade paperbacks and paperback reprints for preschool children, beginning and middle readers, and young adults. Publishes trade paperback originals and reprints. Averages 175-200 total titles/year.

Needs: Picture books, young adult, Middle Grade; Easy-to-Read Grades 1-3. "We publish mostly paperback reprints. We do very few original titles. We do not publish original picture books." Published *A Gift for Mama*, by Esther Hautzig (Puffin chapter book).

How to Contact: Does not accept unsolicited mss. Send SASE or IRC. Responds in 3 months. No simultaneous submissions.

Payment/Terms: Royalty varies. Average advance: varies. Publishes ms 1 year after acceptance. Book catalog for 9×12 SAE with 7 first-class stamps; send request to Marketing Department.

Advice: "Our audience ranges from little children 'first books' to young adult (ages 14-16). An original idea has the best luck."

A G.P. PUTNAM'S SONS, (Adult Trade), Penguin Putnam, Inc., 375 Hudson, New York NY 10014. (212)366-2000. Fax: (212)366-2664. Website: www.penguinputnam.com. **Contact:** Acquisition Editor. Publishes hardcover and trade paperback originals. **Published some debut authors within the last year.**
Imprint(s): Putnam, Riverhead, Jeremy P. Tarcher, Perigee.
Needs: Adventure, literary, mainstream/contemporary, mystery, suspense, women's. Prefers agented submissions. Published *The Bear and the Dragon*, by Tom Clancy (adventure).
How to Contact: Does not accept unsolicited mss. *Agented submissions only.* Responds in 6 months to queries. Accepts simultaneous submissions.
Payment/Terms: Pays variable royalties on retail price. Average advance: varies. Request book catalog through mail order department; ms guidelines free.

N ☐ QUIET STORM PUBLISHING, P.O. Box 1666, Martinsburg WV 25402. (304)283-3838. Fax: (208)498-9259. E-mail: marketing@quietstormpublishing.com. Website: http://quietstormpublishing.com. **Contact:** Clint Gaige, acquisitions. Estab. 2002. Small independent press. Publishes hardcover and paperback originals. Books: cloth or trade paper bound. **Published 8 debut authors within the last year.** Averages 24 total titles, 23 fiction titles/year. Distributes through Ingram.
Needs: Historical, mystery (amateur sleuth, cozy, police procedural, private eye/hardboiled), science fiction, thriller/espionage. Published *Xin Loi, Vietnam*, by Al Sever (non-fiction/military); *Parental Source*, by Chris Freeburn (mystery); *Betoni's Prophecy*, by Elizabeth A. Merz (science fiction). Also publishes CCD Series (mystery).
How to Contact: Does not accept unsolicited mss. Query with SASE. Accepts queries by e-mail, mail. Include brief bio, list of publishing credits. Responds in 3 months. Accepts simultaneous submissions, electronic submissions, submissions on disk.
Payment/Terms: Pays royalty. Publishes ms 1-2 years after acceptance. Book catalog online; ms guidelines online.
Advice: "Understand the industry. A writer's job is far from over when they receive a contract. Publishing books is a partnership, with all parties working together toward success."

☐ QUIXOTE PRESS, 1854 345th Ave., Wever IA 52658. (800)571-2665. Fax: (319)372-7485. **Contact:** Bruce Carlson, president. Quixote Press specializes in humorous and/or regional folklore and special interest cookbooks. Publishes trade paperback originals and reprints. **Published many debut authors within the last year.**
Needs: Humor, short story collections. Published *Eating Ohio*, by Rus Pishnery (short stories about Ohio); *Lil' Red Book of Fishing Tips*, by Tom Whitecloud (fishing tales); *How to Talk Hoosier*, by Netha Bell (humor); *Cow Whisperer*, by Skip Holmes (humor); and *Flour Sack Bloomers*, by Lucy Fetterhoff (history).
How to Contact: Query with SASE. Accepts simultaneous submissions.
Payment/Terms: Pays 10% royalty on wholesale price. Publishes ms 1 year after acceptance. Book catalog for #10 SASE; by phone.
Advice: "Carefully consider marketing considerations. Audience is women in gift shops, on farm sites, direct retail outlets, wineries, outdoor sport shops, etc. Contact us at *idea* stage, not complete ms stage. Be receptive to design input by us."

N RAMSEY BOOKS, Nor-Cal Builders, Inc., 5050 Glide Drive, Suite B, Davis CA 95616-0155. (530)979-0155. Fax: (530)753-6689. E-mail: leon@ramseybooks.com. Website: www.ramseybooks.com. **Contact:** Leon Portalance, editor. Estab. 2002. Publishes trade paperback and electronic originals. Averages 8-10 total titles/year.
Needs: Adventure, fantasy, horror, mystery, science fiction, suspense, crime/detective. "We are looking for fast paced books, mixing the description in with the dialogue and action. No unneccesary pornography, violence or profanity. Make us laugh or cry."
How to Contact: Submit proposal package including 3 sample chapter(s), synopsis, via website in Word or pdf. Responds in 1 month. Accepts simultaneous submissions.
Payment/Terms: Pays 10-15% for trade paperback; 25-30% for electronic. Average advance: $500-2,000. Publishes ms 1 year after acceptance. Book catalog online; ms guidelines online.
Advice: Audience is either hands-on people who like to do things for themselves (nonfiction) or adventure, mystery, horror junkies (fiction). "Self-edit carefully using a spell check or have someone edit your work for you."

A ⊘ ◎ RANDOM HOUSE BOOKS FOR YOUNG READERS, Random House Children's Books, A Division of Random House, Inc., 1745 Broadway, New York NY 10019. (212)782-9000. Fax: (212)782-9698. Website: www.randomhouse.com/kids. **Contact:** Heidi Kilgras, editorial director (Step Into Reading); Jennifer Dussling, senior director (Stepping Stones); Jim Thomas, senior editor (fantasy).
Needs: "Random House publishes a select list of first chapter books and novels, with an emphasis on fantasy and historical fiction." Chapter books, middle-grade, young adult. Published *A to Z Mysteries*, by Ron Roy (chapter books); the Junie B. Jones series; the Magic Tree House series; and *Lady Knight*, by Tamora Pierce.
How to Contact: Does not accept unsolicited mss. *Agented submissions only.* No queries by fax. Responds in 4 months to queries. Accepts simultaneous submissions.
Advice: "We look for original, unique stories. Do something that hasn't been done before."

✖ **RANDOM HOUSE CHILDREN'S BOOKS**, Division of Random House, Inc., 1745 Broadway, New York NY 10019. (212)782-9000. Fax: (212)782-9452. Website: www.randomhouse.com/kids. **Contact:** Kate Klimo, editorial director of Random House Golden Books Young Readers Group; Beverly Horowitz, editorial director for Knopf Delacorte Dell Young Readers Group. Estab. 1925. "Producing books for preschool children through young adult readers, in all formats from board to activity books to picture books and novels, Random House Children's Books brings together world-famous franchise characters, multimillion-copy series, and top-flight, award-winning authors and illustrators."
Imprint(s): *For Knopf Delacorte Dell Young Readers Group*—Doubleday, Alfred A. Knopf, Crown, Delacorte Press, Wendy Lamb Books, David Fickling Books, Dell Dragonfly, Dell Yearling, Dell Laurel-Leaf, Bantam. *For Random House Golden Books Young Readers Group*—Golden Books, Picturebacks, Beginner Books, Step Into Reading, Stepping Stones Books, Landmark Books.

Ⓐ ✖ **RANDOM HOUSE TRADE PUBLISHING GROUP**, Random House, Inc., 1745 Broadway, 17th Floor, New York NY 10019. (212)782-9000. Fax: (212)572-4960. Website: www.randomhouse.com. Estab. 1925. "The flagship imprint of Random House, Inc." Publishes hardcover and paperback trade books. Averages 120 total titles/year.
Imprint(s): The Modern Library; Random House Trade Books; Random House Trade Paperbacks; Villard Books; Strivers Row, Ballintine Books.
Needs: Adventure, confession, experimental, fantasy, historical, horror, humor, mainstream/contemporary, mystery, suspense.
How to Contact: *Agented submissions only.* Responds in 2 months to queries. Accepts simultaneous submissions.
Payment/Terms: Pays royalty on retail price. Offers advance. Book catalog free; ms guidelines online.

✖ **RANDOM HOUSE, INC.**, Division of Bertelsmann Book Group, 1540 Broadway, New York NY 10036. (212)782-9000. Fax: (212)302-7985. E-mail: editor@randomhouse.com. Website: www.randomhouse.com. Estab. 1925. "Random House has long been committed to publishing the best literature by writers both in the U.S. and abroad."
Imprint(s): Alfred A. Knopf, Anchor Books; Ballantine Books; Bantam Hardcover; Bantam Mass Market; Bantam Trade Paperbacks; Clarkson Potter; Crimeline; Crown Books for Young Readers; Crown Publishers, Inc; CTW Publishing; Currency; Del Ray Delacorte Press; Dell; Dell Laurel-Leaf; Dell Yearling; Delta; Derrydale; The Dial Press; Discovery Books; Domain; Doubleday; Doubleday Bible Commentary; Doubleday/Galilee; Doubleday/Image; Dragonfly Books; DTP; Everyman's Library; Fanfare; Fawcett; First Choice Chapter Books; Fodor's; Grammercy Book; Harmony Books; House of Collectibles; Island; Ivy; Knopf Books for Young Readers; Knopf Paperbacks; Library of Contemporary Thought; Living Language; Main Street Books; The Modern Library; Nan A. Talese; The New Jerusalem Bible; One World; Pantheon Books; Picture Yearling; Princeton Review, Random House; Random House Children's Publishing; Random House Large Print Publishing; Random House Reference & Information Publishing; Shocken Books; Sierra Club Adult Books; Spectra; Strivers Row, Testament Books; Three Rivers Press; Times Books; Villard Books; Vintage Books; Wings Books.

Ⓝ ◯ ◎ ⊕ **RANSOM PUBLISHING LTD.**, Rose Cottage Howe Hill, Watlington Oxon OX49 5HB UK. +44 (0)1491 613711. Fax: +44 (0)1491 613733. E-mail: jenny@ransom.co.uk. Website: www.ransom.co.uk. **Contact:** Jenny Ertie, editor. Estab. 1995. Small family run company. Specialized in multimedia until 2003. Has a small but developing list of children books for home and school use. Specializes in phonics and general reading programs. Publishes paperback originals. **Published 3 debut authors within the last year.** Member, BESA (UK).
Needs: Children's/juvenile (animal, easy-to-read, preschool/picture book, series). Publishes Ransom Literacy Steps series.
How to Contact: Accepts unsolicited mss. Query with SASE or submit outline/proposal. Accepts queries by e-mail. Include estimated word count, brief bio, list of publishing credits. Responds in 1-2 weeks to queries. Accepts simultaneous submissions, electronic submissions, submissions on disk.
Payment/Terms: Pays 10% royalty on net receipts. Ms guidelines by e-mail.

Ⓝ ◯ **RAVENHAWK BOOKS**, The 6DOF Group, 7739 Broadway Blvd., #95, Tucson AZ 85710. Website: www.ravenhawk.biz. **Contact:** Carl Lasky, publisher (all fiction). Estab. 1998. "Small, independent, literary press most interested in provacative and innovative works." Publishes hardcover and paperback originals. Books: 50 or 60 lb. paper; traditional, POD, e-book printing. First novel print order: 1,000. **Published 1 debut author within the last year.** Plans 3 first novels this year. Member, SPAN. Distributes titles through Ingram, Baker & Taylor, Amazon, Borders, Barnes & Noble.
Needs: Children's/juvenile (adventure, animal, easy-to-read, fantasy, mystery, series), fantasy (space fantasy, sword and sorcery), horror (dark fantasy, futuristic, psychological, supernatural), humor, literary, mainstream/contemporary, mystery (amateur sleuth, cozy, police procedural, private eye/hardboiled), psychic/supernatural, religious (religious mystery/suspense, religious thriller), romance (contemporary, romantic suspense), science fiction (hard science/technological, soft/sociological), short story collections, thriller/espionage, young adult (adventure, easy-to-read, fantasy/science fiction, horror, mystery/suspense, problem novels, series). Planning anthology of Damon Shiller Mysteries. Published the Chaz Trenton Trilogy.

How to Contact: Does not accept unsolicited mss. Query by invitation only. Agented fiction 10%. No simultaneous submissions, electronic submissions, submissions on disk. Sometimes comments on rejected mss.

Payment/Terms: Pays 45-60% royalty. Publishes ms 18 months after acceptance. Ms guidelines for SASE; book catalog on website only.

Advice: "Write dynamic prose utilizing a multi-dimensional edge (conflict). Persistence. Although the majority of elitists that control the publishing industry won't admit it, it really is a crap shoot out there. Don't ever give up if you believe in yourself. Courage."

RED DEER PRESS, MacKimmie Library Tower, Room 813, 2500 University Dr., NW, Calgary AB T2N 1N4 Canada. (403)220-4334. Fax: (403)210-8191. E-mail: rdp@ucalgary.ca. Website: www.reddeerpress.com. **Contact:** Peter Carver, children's book editor. Estab. 1975. Publishes young adult and paperback originals "focusing on books by, about, or of interest to Canadian youth." Books: offset paper; offset printing; hardcover/perfect-bound. Average print order: 5,000. First novel print order: 2,500. Distributes titles in Canada, the US, the UK, Australia and New Zealand.

• Red Deer Press has received numerous honors and awards from the Book Publishers Association of Alberta, Canadian Children's Book Centre, the Governor General of Canada and the Writers Guild of Alberta.

Imprint(s): Northern Lights Books for Children, Northern Light Young Novels.

Needs: Young adult (juvenile and early reader), contemporary. No romance or horror. Published *A Fine Daughter*, by Catherine Simmons Niven (novel); *The Kappa Child*, by Hiromi Goto (novel); *The Dollinage*, by Martine Leavitt; and *The Game*, by Teresa Toten (nominated for the Governor General's Award).

How to Contact: Accepts unsolicited mss. Query with SASE or IRC. Responds in 6 months to mss. Accepts simultaneous submissions. No submissions on disk.

Payment/Terms: Pays 8-10% royalty. Advance is negotiable. Publishes ms 1 year after acceptance. Book catalog for 9×12 SASE.

Advice: "We're very interested in young adult and children's fiction from Canadian writers with a proven track record (either published books or widely published in established magazines or journals) and for manuscripts with regional themes and/or a distinctive voice. We publish Canadian authors exclusively."

RED DRAGON PRESS, 433 Old Town Court, Alexandria VA 22314-3545. Laura Qa, publisher. **Contact:** David Alan, editor. Estab. 1993. "Small independent publisher of innovative, progressive and experimental works. Short fiction only." Books: quality paper; offset printing; some illustrations. Average print order: 500. **Published 2-3 debut authors within the last year.** Member, Women's National Book Association. Distributes titles through Borders, Barnes & Noble, retail and wholesale, special order and direct mail order. Promotes titles through art reviews, journals, newsletters, special events, readings and signings.

Needs: Experimental, horror (dark fantasy, futuristic, psychological, supernatural), literary, psychic/supernatural, short story collections. Published *True Stories: Fiction by Uncommon Women*, by Grace Cavalieri, Susan Cole, Jean Russell, Laura Qa and Dee Snyder.

How to Contact: Accepts unsolicited mss. Query with SASE or submit 1-3 sample chapter(s). Reading fee: $5. Accepts queries by fax. Include brief bio, list of publishing credits. Send SASE for return of ms or send a disposable ms and SASE for reply only. Responds in 6 weeks to mss. Accepts simultaneous submissions. Often comments on rejected mss.

Payment/Terms: Publishes ms 6-12 months after acceptance. Book catalog for #10 SASE; ms guidelines for #10 SASE.

Advice: "Be familiar with the work of one or more of our previously published authors."

RED DRESS INK, Harlequin Enterprises, Ltd., 233 Broadway, New York NY 10279. Website: www.eharlequin.com; www.reddressink.com. **Contact:** Margaret O'Neill Marbury, senior editor; Farrin Jacobs, associate editor. "We launched Red Dress Ink to provide women with unique and irreverent stories that reflects the lifestyles of today's modern women." Publishes hardcover and trade paperback originals. Averages 24-36 total titles/year.

Needs: Adventure, confession, humor, literary, mainstream/contemporary, multicultural, regional, romance, short story collections, contemporary women's fiction. Red Dress Ink publishes "stories that reflect the lifestyles of today's urban, single women. They show life as it is, with a strong touch of humor, hipness and energy." Word length: 90,000-110,000 words. Point of view: first person/third person, as well as multiple viewpoints, if needed. Settings: urban locales in North America or well-known international settings, such as London or Paris. Tone: fun, up-to-the-minute, clever, appealing, realistic. Published *Fashionistas*, by Lynn Messina; *The Thin Pink Line*, by Lauren Baratz-Logsted; and *Engaging Men*, by Lynda Curnyn.

How to Contact: Accepts unsolicited mss. Submit proposal package including 3 sample chapter(s), synopsis, cover letter or submit complete ms. Send SASE or IRC. Accepts simultaneous submissions. No electronic submissions, submissions on disk.

Payment/Terms: Pays 7½% royalty. Offers advance. Book catalog online; ms guidelines online.

RED HEN PRESS, P.O. Box 3537, Granada Hills CA 91394. (818)831-0649. Fax: (818)831-6659. E-mail: editor@redhen.org. Website: www.redhen.org. **Contact:** Mark E. Cull, publisher/editor (fiction); Katherine Gale, poetry editor (poetry, literary fiction). Estab. 1993. Publishes trade paperback originals. **Published 10% of books from**

debut authors within the last year. Averages 10 total titles, 10 fiction titles/year.

Needs: Ethnic, experimental, feminist, gay/lesbian, historical, literary, mainstream/contemporary, poetry, poetry in translation, short story collections. "We prefer high-quality literary fiction." Published *Wedding In October*, by Geoffrey Clark; *Talking Heads: 77*, by John Domini; *Tisch*, by Stephen Dixon.

How to Contact: Query with SASE. Agented fiction 10%. Responds in 1 month. Accepts simultaneous submissions.

Payment/Terms: Publishes ms 1 year after acceptance. Book catalog and ms guidelines available via website or free; ms guidelines online.

Advice: "Audience reads poetry, literary fiction, intelligent nonfiction. If you have an agent, we may be too small since we don't pay advances. Write well. Send queries first. Be willing to help promote your own book."

THE RED PRESS PUBLISHING COMPANY, LLC, 850 Stephenson Highway, Suite 307, Troy MI 48083. E-mail: submissions@theredpress.com. Website: www.theredpress.com. **Contact:** Leah Evans, editor. Estab. 2002. A small, independent publisher with a strong emphasis on individual marketing efforts for every title. Very hands-on, very author-friendly. Publishes hardcover and paperback originals, paperback reprints and e-books. **Published 2 debut authors within the last year.** All titles are distributed through Ingram and Baker & Taylor and other major wholesalers and distributors, and are available through on-line sources including publisher's website.

Needs: Adventure, family saga, humor, mainstream/contemporary, mystery, romance, thriller/espionage, western, young adult. "Actively seeking Native American titles that are positive in their message and preferably with a modern-day setting, also seeking women sleuth/amateur detective series and mysteries. See website for additional comments regarding submissions." Published *Last Minute in Hell*, by C.D. Manning (drama). Also publishes *The Dana Ford Mystery Series*, authored by Linda Ellison (owner of The Red Press), about a child psychiatrist who searches for missing persons.

How to Contact: Does not accept unsolicited mss. Query with SASE or submit outline, synopsis. Accepts queries by e-mail, mail. Include estimated word count. Responds in 2 weeks. Accepts simultaneous submissions. Often comments on rejected mss.

Payment/Terms: Pays 10-15% royalty. Publishes ms within one year after acceptance. Book catalog online; ms guidelines online.

Advice: "Take the time to write the best piece of work you can, and be prepared to support its marketing efforts."

RED SAGE PUBLISHING, INC., P.O. Box 4844, Seminole FL 33775-4844. (727)391-3847. Fax: (727)391-3847. Website: www.redsagepub.com. **Contact:** Alexandria Kendall, editor (romance, erotica); Claire Richards, editor (romance, erotica). Estab. 1995. Publishes "romance erotica or ultra-sensual romance novellas written by romance writers. Red Sage is the leader in the publishing industry for erotic romance." Publishes trade paperback originals. Books: perfect binding. **Published 4 debut authors within the last year.** Averages 2 total titles, 1 fiction title/year. Baker & Taylor, Amazon, Walden Books, Barnes & Noble, Borders and independent bookstores as well as mail order. Promotes titles through national trade publication advertising (*Romantic Times*, *Writerspace*), author interviews and book signings.

• Red Sage Publishing recieved the Fallot Literary Award for Fiction.

Imprint(s): The *Secrets* Collection (romance, ultra-sensual), edited by Alexandria Kendall.

Needs: Romance (ultra-sensual). "Read a Secrets volume so you understand what we publish." Length : 20,000-30,000 words. Writers may submit to anthology editor.

How to Contact: Accepts unsolicited mss. Submit synopsis, first 10 pages of story, SASE. Include estimated word count, list of publishing credits. Responds in 4 months to queries; 4 months to proposals; 4 months to mss. No simultaneous submissions. Sometimes comments on rejected mss.

Payment/Terms: Pays 6% royalty on book with 4 authors. Average advance: $50. Publishes ms 1 year after acceptance. Book catalog for #10 SASE; ms guidelines for SASE or at website.

Advice: "Know what we publish and send what you think is better!"

REGAN BOOKS, HarperCollins, 10 E. 53rd St., New York NY 10022. (212)207-7400. Fax: (212)207-6951. Website: www.reganbooks.com. **Contact:** Judith Regan, president/publisher; Cal Morgan, editorial director. Estab. 1994. Publishes hardcover and trade paperback originals. Averages 75 total titles/year.

Needs: Adventure, comic books, confession, erotica, ethnic, experimental, fantasy, feminist, gay/lesbian, gothic, hi-lo, historical, horror, humor, juvenile, literary, mainstream/contemporary, military/war, multicultural, multimedia, mystery, occult, picture books, plays, poetry, poetry in translation, regional, religious, romance, science fiction, short story collections, spiritual, sports, suspense, western, young adult.

How to Contact: Does not accept unsolicited mss. *Agented submissions only.* Responds in 3 months to proposals. Accepts simultaneous submissions.

Payment/Terms: Pays royalty on retail price. Average advance: variable. Publishes ms 1 year after acceptance.

RENAISSANCE HOUSE, 9400 Lloydcrest Drive, Beverly Hills CA 90210. (310)358-5288. Fax: (310)358-5282. Website: www.renaissancehouse.net. **Contact:** Sam Laredo, publisher; Raquel Benatar, editor. Publishes hardcover and trade paperback originals. **Published 25-30% debut authors within the last year.** Averages 30 total titles/year.

Needs: Fantasy, juvenile, multicultural, picture books, legends, fables. Published *The Spirits of the Mountain*, by Raquel Benatar.

How to Contact: Query with SASE. Agented fiction 25%. Responds in 2 months. Accepts simultaneous submissions.

Payment/Terms: Pays 5-10% royalty on net receipts. Book catalog free; ms guidelines online.

RESOURCE PUBLICATIONS, INC., 160 E. Virginia St., Suite #290, San Jose CA 95112-5876. (408)286-8505. Fax: (408)287-8748. E-mail: info@rpinet.com. Website: www.rpinet.com/ml/. **Contact:** Acquisition Director. Estab. 1973. Publishes paperback originals. **Published 30% debut authors within the last year.** Averages 10 total titles/year.

Needs: Anecdotes; faith sharing stories; stories useful in preaching or teaching.

How to Contact: Query with SASE. Agented fiction 1%. Responds in 10 weeks to queries.

Payment/Terms: Pays 8% royalty (for a first project). Average advance: $250-1,000. Book catalog online; ms guidelines online.

Advice: "We are publishers and secondarily we are book packagers. Pitch your project to us for publication first. If we can't take it on that basis, we may be able to take it on as a packaging and production project."

REVELL PUBLISHING, Subsidiary of Baker Book House, P.O. Box 6287, Grand Rapids MI 49516-6287. (616)676-9185. Fax: (616)676-9573. E-mail: lhdupont@bakerbooks.com or petersen@bakerbooks.com. Website: www.bakerbooks.com. **Contact:** Sheila Ingram, assistant to the editorial director; Jane Campbell, editorial director (Chosen Books). Estab. 1870. Midsize publisher. "Revell publishes to the heart (rather than to the head). For 125 years, Revell has been publishing evangelical books for personal enrichment and spiritual growth of general Christian readers." Publishes hardcover, trade paperback and mass market originals and reprints. Average print order: 7,500. **Published some debut authors within the last year.**

Imprint(s): Spire Books.

Needs: Religious (general). Published *Triumph of the Soul*, by Michael R. Joens (contemporary); *Daughter of Joy*, by Kathleen Morgan (historical); and *Blue Mist on the Danube*, by Doris Eliane Fell (contemporary).

How to Contact: Does not accept unsolicited mss. Recommends submitting mss to The Writer's Edge (www.writersedgeservice.com) or the Evangelical Christian Publishers Association's online service, First Edition (www.ecpa.org/FE). Both services charge writers a fee to post proposals/mss. "We subscibe to both these services and regularly review the proposals which appear there, as do many other Christian publishers." Accepts queries by e-mail. Agented fiction 20%. Responds in 3 weeks to queries. Accepts simultaneous submissions. Sometimes comments on rejected mss.

Payment/Terms: Pays royalty. Publishes ms 1 year after acceptance. Ms guidelines for SASE.

RISING MOON, Northland Publishing, LLC, P.O. Box 1389, Flagstaff AZ 86002-1389. (928)774-5251. Fax: (928)774-0592. Website: www.northlandpub.com. **Contact:** Theresa Howell, kids editor. Estab. 1988. Rising Moon's objective is to provide children with entertaining and informative books that follow the heart and tickle the funny bone. Rising Moon is no longer publishing middle-grade children's fiction. Publishes hardcover and trade paperback originals. Averages 8-10 total titles/year.

Needs: Picture books (broad subjects with wide appeal and universal themes). "We are also looking for exceptional bilingual stories (Spanish/English), activity books, fractured fairy tales, and original stories with a Southwest flavor." Published *Kissing Coyotes*, by Monica Vaughan and Ken Spengler.

How to Contact: Submit complete ms with SASE of adequate size and postage. No e-mail submissions. Responds in 3 months. Accepts simultaneous submissions.

Payment/Terms: Pays royalty. Sometimes pays flat fee. Offers advance. Publishes ms 1-2 years after acceptance. Call for book catalog; ms guidelines online.

Advice: "Our audience is composed of regional southwest interest readers."

RISING TIDE PRESS, NEW MEXICO, American-Canadian Publishers, Inc., P.O. Box 136, Santa Fe NM 87502-6136. (505)983-8484. Estab. 1981. Rising Tide Press, New Mexico is a midsize publisher. Books: 8½×11; vellum bound; 140-150 pages; white trove paper.

Needs: Wants innovative fiction. Published *Empire Sweets*, by Stanley Berne (fiction).

How to Contact: Does not accept unsolicited mss.

Payment/Terms: Pays royalty. Average advance: $10,000.

RIVER CITY PUBLISHING, River City Publishing, LLC, 1719 Mulberry St., Montgomery AL 36106. (334)265-6753. Fax: (334)265-8880. E-mail: agordon@rivercitypublishing.com. Website: www.rivercitypublishing.com. **Contact:** Ashley Gordon, editor. Estab. 1989. Midsize independent publisher (10-20 books per year). Our emphasis is on Southern literary fiction and nonfiction of national appeal. Publishes hardcover and trade paperback originals and reprints. **Published 3 debut authors within the last year.** Averages 12 total titles, 4 fiction titles/year.

● Had three nominees to *ForeWord* fiction book of the year awards (2002).

Needs: Children's/juvenile (preschool/picture book), ethnic, historical, literary, multicultural, poetry, regional (southern), short story collections. Published *Speaks the Nightbird*, by Robert McCammon (historical fiction); *Baby, Let's Make a Baby*, by Kurt Curnutt (short story collection); *Lowcountry Boil*, by Carl T. Smith (suspense novel). Pubblishes the River City Poetry Series.

How to Contact: Accepts unsolicited mss. Submit proposal package including 3 sample chapter(s), synopsis. Accepts queries by e-mail. Include brief bio, list of publishing credits. Agented fiction 25%. Responds in 3 months to queries; 4 months to proposals; 1 year to mss. Accepts simultaneous submissions. Rarely comments on rejected mss.

Payment/Terms: Pays 10-15% royalty on retail price. Average advance: $500-5,000. Publishes ms 1 year after acceptance. Ms guidelines free.

Advice: "Only send your best work about which you have received outside opinions from qualified readers you trust. From approximately 1,000 submissions each year we publish 20 books; competition is fierce."

RIVER OAK PUBLISHING, Cook Communications Ministries, 4050 Lee Vance View, Colorado Springs CO 80918. (800)708-5550. E-mail: info@riveroakpublishing.com. Website: www.cookministries.com. **Contact:** Dan Benson, editorial director. Publishes hardcover, trade paperback and mass market paperback originals and reprints.

Needs: Adventure, fantasy, historical, humor, mystery, religious, romance, spiritual, sports, western.

How to Contact: Query with SASE. Agented fiction 20%. Responds in 1 month. Accepts simultaneous submissions.

Payment/Terms: Pays royalty on wholesale price. Average advance: negotiable. Publishes ms 18 months after acceptance. Ms guidelines for #10 SASE and on at the website.

A M © ROC BOOKS, New American Library, A Division of Penguin Putnam, Inc., 375 Hudson St., New York NY 10014. (212)366-2000. Website: www.penguinputnam.com. **Contact:** Laura Anne Gilman, executive editor; Jennifer Heddle, editor. "We're looking for books that are a good read, that people will want to pick up time and time again." Publishes mass market, trade and hardcover originals. Averages 48 total titles, 48 fiction titles/ year.

Needs: Fantasy, horror, science fiction. "Roc tries to strike a balance between fantasy and science fiction. We strongly discourage unsolicited submissions." Published *Shadows and Light*, by Anne Bishop; *Conquistador*, by S.M. Stirlig.

How to Contact: Does not accept unsolicited mss. Query with SASE or submit 1-2 sample chapter(s), synopsis. Responds in 2-3 months to queries. Accepts simultaneous submissions.

Payment/Terms: Pays royalty. Average advance: negotiable.

N JAMES A. ROCK & CO., PUBLISHERS, 113 N. Washington St., #347, Rockville MD 20985. Fax: (301)294-1683. Website: www.rockpublishing.com. Estab. 1977. Publishes hardcover, trade paperback, and electronic originals and reprints. Averages 10-15 total titles, 5-10 fiction titles/year.

Needs: Adventure, comic books, experimental, fantasy, gothic, horror, humor, juvenile, literary, mainstream/contemporary, multicultural, multimedia, mystery, picture books, plays, poetry, poetry in translation, regional, religious, romance, science fiction, short story collections, suspense, young adult, ghost.

How to Contact: Query with SASE. Agented fiction 50%. Responds in 1 month.

Payment/Terms: Pays 5-15% royalty. Average advance: $0-2,000. Publishes ms 9 months after acceptance. Book catalog online; ms guidelines online.

N O ROCK VILLAGE PUBLISHING, 41 Walnut Street, Middleborough MA 02346. (508)946-4738. **Contact:** Edward Lodi, editor. Estab. 1999. Small, regional (New England themed). Must be set in clearly defined New England setting. Publishes paperback originals. Books: 60# bright white paper; off set printing; perfect bound; b&w illustrations. Average print order: 1,000. Average first novel print order: 500. **Published 1 debut author within the last year.** We distribute our own books.

Needs: Ethnic, fantasy (New England), historical, horror (dark fantasy, psychological, supernatural, old fashioned ghost stories), literary, mainstream/contemporary, mystery (amateur sleuth, cozy), psychic/supernatural, regional (New England), romance (contemporary, gothic, historical, romantic suspense), short story collections, New England ghost stories. Published *The Ghost in the Gazebo—An Anthology of New England Ghost Stories*.

How to Contact: Accepts unsolicited mss. Query with SASE. Accepts queries by mail. Include estimated word count, brief bio, list of publishing credits. Responds in 1 month to queries; 1 month to mss. Accepts simultaneous submissions. Often comments on rejected mss.

Payment/Terms: Pay varies. Publishes ms 6 months after acceptance. Book catalog for 9 × 12 SASE and postage; ms guidelines for SASE.

Advice: "When you think Rock Village Publishing, think New England. If you don't know which states are included in that designation, consult a dictionary or Atlas."

M O © RONSDALE PRESS, 3350 W. 21st Ave., Vancouver BC V6S 1G7 Canada. (604)738-4688. Fax: (604)731-4548. E-mail: ronhatch@pinc.com. Website: www.ronsdalepress.com. **Contact:** Ronald B. Hatch, president/editor; Veronica Hatch, editor (YA historical). Estab. 1988. Ronsdale Press is "dedicated to publishing books that give Canadians new insights into themselves and their country." Publishes trade paperback originals. Books:

60 lb. paper; photo offset printing; perfect binding. Average print order: 1,500. **Published some debut authors within the last year.** Averages 10 total titles, 3 fiction titles/year. Distributes titles through LPG Distribution. Promotes titles through ads in BC Bookworld and Globe & Mail, and interviews on radio.

● *Ronsdale Press publishes fiction by Canadian authors only.*

Needs: Literary, short story collections, novels. Published *The City in the Egg*, by Michel Trembly (novel); *Jackrabbit Moon*, by Sheila McLeod Arnepoulos; and *When Eagles Call*, by Susan Dobbie.

How to Contact: Accepts unsolicited mss. Query with at least the first 80 pages. Short story collections must have some previous magazine publication. Accepts queries by e-mail. Send SASE or IRC. Responds in 2 weeks to queries; 3 months to mss. Accepts simultaneous submissions. Sometimes comments on rejected mss.

Payment/Terms: Pays 10% royalty on retail price. Publishes ms 6 months after acceptance. Book catalog for #10 SASE; ms guidelines online.

Advice: "We publish both fiction and poetry. Authors *must* be Canadian. We look for writing that shows the author has read widely in contemporary and earlier literature. Ronsdale, like other literary presses, is not interested in mass-market or pulp materials."

ROYAL FIREWORKS PUBLISHING, 1 First Ave., P.O. Box 399, Unionville NY 10988. (845)726-4444. Fax: (845)726-3824. E-mail: rfpress@frontiernet.net. Website: www.rfpress.com. **Contact:** William Neumann, editor (young adult); Myrna Kemnitz, editor (education). Estab. 1977. Publishes library binding and trade paperback originals, reprints and textbooks. **Published 30-50% debut authors within the last year.** Averages 75-140 total titles/year.

Needs: Young adult. "We do novels for children from 8-16. We do a lot of historical fiction, science fiction, adventure, mystery, sports, etc. We are concerned about values." Published *Hitler's Willing Warrior*, by H. Gutshe (young adult fiction); *Double Vision*, by Jerry Chris; *A Few Screws Loose*, by Mary Ann Easley (young adult fiction).

How to Contact: Submit complete ms. Agented fiction 2%. Responds in 1 month to mss. No simultaneous submissions.

Payment/Terms: Pays 5-10% royalty on wholesale price. Publishes ms 9 months after acceptance. Book catalog for $3.85; ms guidelines for #10 SASE.

Advice: "Audience is composed of gifted children, their parents and teachers, and children (8-18) who read."

RUMINATOR BOOKS, 1648 Grand Ave., St. Paul MN 55105. (651)699-7038. Fax: (651)699-7190. E-mail: books@ruminator.com. Website: www.ruminator.com. **Contact:** Pearl Kilbride. Publishes hardcover originals, trade paperback originals and reprints. Averages 8-10 total titles, 4-6 fiction titles/year.

Needs: Literary, adult fiction. Published *Facing the Congo*, by Jeffrey Tayler; *The Last Summer of Reason*, by Tahar Djaout; *An Algerian Childhood* (anthology).

How to Contact: Query with SASE or submit proposal package including outline, sample chapter(s). Agented fiction 40%. Responds in 4 months. Accepts simultaneous submissions.

Payment/Terms: Royalty varies. Average advance: varies. Publishes ms 12-18 months after acceptance. Book catalog for 6×9 SAE with 2 first-class stamps; ms guidelines for #10 SASE and on website.

SALVO PRESS, P.O. Box 9095 or 97708, Bend OR 97708. (541)330-8746. Fax: (541)330-8746. Website: www.salvopress.com. **Contact:** Scott Schmidt, publisher (mystery, suspense, thriller & espionage). Estab. 1998. "We are a small press specializing in mystery, suspense, espionage and thriller fiction. Our press publishes in trade paperback and e-book format." Books: 5½×8½; or 6×9 paper; offset printing; perfect binding. **Published 3 debut authors within the last year.** Averages 3 total titles, 3 fiction titles/year.

Needs: Adventure, literary, mystery (amateur sleuth, police procedural, private/hard boiled), science fiction (hard science/technological), suspense, thriller/espionage, espionage; thriller. "Our needs change. Check our website." Published *Fatal Network*, by Trevor Scott (mystery/thriller); *High Steaks*, by Rob Loughran (first fiction, mystery); and *Spirit Flight*, by P.R. Fittante (first fiction, adventure).

How to Contact: Does not accept unsolicited mss. Query with SASE. Include estimated word count, brief bio, list of publishing credits, "and something to intrigue me so I ask for more." Agented fiction 15%. Responds in 1 month to queries. No simultaneous submissions. Sometimes comments on rejected mss.

Payment/Terms: Pays 10-15% royalty. Publishes ms 9 months after acceptance. Book catalog and ms guidelines online; ms guidelines online.

SARABANDE BOOKS, INC., 2234 Dundee Rd., Suite 200, Louisville KY 40205. (502)458-4028. Fax: (502)458-4065. E-mail: sarabandeb@aol.com. Website: www.sarabandebooks.org. **Contact:** Sarah Gorham, editor-in-chief; Kirby Gann, managing editor. Estab. 1994. "Small literary press publishing poetry, short fiction, and literary non-fiction." Publishes hardcover and trade paperback originals. **Published some debut authors within the last year.** Averages 10 total titles, 3-4 fiction titles/year. Distributes titles through Consortium Book Sales & Distribution. Promotes titles through advertising in national magazines, sales reps, brochures, newsletters, postcards, catalogs, press release mailings, sales conferences, book fairs, author tours and reviews.

● Kiki DeLancey received the Great American Novel Award for *Novel-in-Progress*.

Needs: Literary, novellas, short novels, 250 pages maximum, 150 pages minimum. Accepts queries in September only. Published *Portrait of My Mother, Who Posed Nude in Wartime*, by Marjorie Sandor (literary fiction/short stories); *Transgressions*, by Sallie Bingham (literary fiction/short stories); *Coal Miner's Holiday*, by Kiki DeLancey (literary fiction/short stories).

How to Contact: Query with 1 sample story or chapter. Include 1 page bio and listing of publishing credits. Send SASE or IRC. Responds in 3 months. Accepts simultaneous submissions.

Payment/Terms: Pays royalty. 10% on actual income received. Also pays in author's copies. Average advance: $500-1,000. Publishes ms 18 months after acceptance. Book catalog free; ms and contest guidelines for #10 SASE or on website.

Advice: "Make sure you're not writing in a vacuum, that you've read and are conscious of contemporary literature. Have someone read your manuscript, checking it for ordering, coherence. Better a lean, consistently strong manuscript than one that is long and uneven. We like a story to have good narrative, and we like to be engaged by language, to find ourselves turning the pages with real interest."

SAXON HOUSE CANADA, P.O. Box 6947, Station A, Toronto ON M5W 1X6 Canada. (416)488-7171. Fax: (416)488-2989. Publishes hardcover originals and trade paperback reprints. Averages 4 total titles/year.

Needs: Historical, literary.

How to Contact: Submit proposal package including 3 sample chapter(s), résumé. Responds in 4 months. Accepts simultaneous submissions.

Payment/Terms: Pays royalty on wholesale price or makes outright purchase. Offers advance. Publishes ms 15 months after acceptance.

SCHOLASTIC CANADA, LTD., 175 Hillmount Rd., Markham ON L6C 1Z7 Canada. (905)887-7323. Fax: (905)887-3643. Website: www.scholastic.ca. Publishes hardcover and trade paperback originals. Averages 40 total titles/year.

   ● *This publisher works with Canadian authors only.*

Imprint(s): North Winds Press; Les Éditions Scholastic (contact Syvie Andrews, French editor).

Needs: Children's/juvenile, juvenile (middle grade), young adult. Published *The Promise of the Unicorn*, by Vicki Blum (juvenile novel).

How to Contact: *Agented submissions only.* No simultaneous submissions.

Payment/Terms: Pays 5-10% royalty on retail price. Average advance: $1,000-5,000 (Canadian). Publishes ms 1 year after acceptance. Book catalog for 8½×11 SAE with 2 first-class stamps (IRC or Canadian stamps only).

SCHOLASTIC PRESS, Scholastic Inc., 557 Broadway, New York NY 10012. (212)343-6100. Fax: (212)343-4713. Website: www.scholastic.com. **Contact:** Elizabeth Szabla, editorial director (picture books, middle grade, young adult); Dianne Hess, executive editor (picture books, middle grade, young adult); Tracy Mack, executive editor (picture books, middle grade, young adult); Lauren Thompson, senior editor (picture books, middle grade). Publishes hardcover originals. **Published some debut authors within the last year.** Averages 50 total titles/year. Promotes titles through trade and library channels.

Needs: Juvenile, picture books, novels. Wants "fresh, exciting picture books and novels—inspiring, new talent." Published *The Three Questions*, by Jon J. Muth; *A Corner of the Universe*, by Ann M. Martin; *Green Angel*, by Alice Hoffman; *8 Dear Mrs. LaRue*, by Mark Teague.

How to Contact: Does not accept unsolicited mss. *Agented submissions only.* Responds in 2 months to queries; 6-8 months to mss. No simultaneous submissions.

Payment/Terms: Pays royalty on retail price. Average advance: varies. Publishes ms 18-24 months after acceptance.

Advice: "Be a big reader of juvenile literature before you write and submit!"

SCIENCE & HUMANITIES PRESS, P.O. Box 7151, Chesterfield MO 63006-7151. (636)394-4950. E-mail: pub@sciencehumanitiespress.com. Website: www.sciencehumanitiespress.com. **Contact:** Dr. Bud Banis, publisher. Publishes trade paperback originals and reprints, and electronic originals and reprints. **Published 25% of books from debut authors within the last year.** Averages 20-30 total titles/year. Sales are primarily through the Internet, special orders, reviews in specialized media, direct sales to libraries, special organizations and use as textbooks.

Imprint(s): Science & Humanities Press, BeachHouse Books, MacroPrintBooks (large print editions), Heuristic Books, Early Editions Books.

Needs: Adventure, historical, humor, literary, mainstream/contemporary, military/war, mystery, plays, poetry, regional, romance, science fiction, short story collections, spiritual, sports, suspense, western, young adult. "We prefer books with a theme that gives a market focus. Brief description by e-mail."

How to Contact: Does not accept unsolicited mss. Responds in 2 months to queries; 2 months to proposals. Accepts simultaneous submissions.

Payment/Terms: Pays 8% royalty on retail price. Publishes ms 6-12 after acceptance. Book catalog online; ms guidelines online.

Advice: "Our expertise is electronic publishing for continuous short-run, in-house production rather than mass distribution to retail outlets. This allows us to commit to books that might not be financially successful in conventional book store environments and to keep books in print and available for extended periods of time. Books should be types that would sell steadily over a long period of time, rather than those that require rapid rollout and bookstore shelf exposure for a short time. We consider the nurturing of new talent part of our mission but enjoy experienced writers as well. We are proud that many of our books are second, third and fourth books from authors who were once first-time authors. A good book is not a one-time accident."

N ☐ ◎ SEAL PRESS, 300 Queen Anne Ave. N., #375, Seattle WA 98109. (206)722-1838. Fax: (206)285-9410. E-mail: Leslie.Miller@avalonpub.com. Website: www.sealpress.com. **Contact:** Ingrid Emerick, editor/publisher; Leslie Miller, senior editor; Christina Henry, editor. Estab. 1976. "Midsize independent feminist book publisher interested in original, lively, radical, empowering and culturally diverse books by women." Publishes trade paperback originals. Books: 55 lb. natural paper; Cameron Belt, Web or offset printing; perfect binding; illustrations occasionally. Averages 25 total titles/year. Titles distributed by Publishers Group West.
Imprint(s): Adventura (womens travel/outdoors), Live Girls (Third-Wave, pop culture, young feminist).
Needs: Ethnic, feminist, gay/lesbian, literary, multicultural. Must fall within Adventura or Live Girls imprints. "We are interested in alternative voices. Published *Valencia*, by Michelle Tea (fiction); *Navigating the Darwin Straits*, by Edith Forbes (fiction); and *Bruised Hibiscus*, by Elizabeth Nunez (fiction).
How to Contact: Does not accept unsolicited mss. Query with SASE or submit outline, 2 sample chapter(s), synopsis. Does not accept queries by e-mail or phone. Responds in 2 months to queries. Accepts simultaneous submissions.
Payment/Terms: Pays 7-10% royalty on retail price. Average advance: $3,000-5,000. Publishes ms 18 months after acceptance. Book catalog and ms guidelines for SASE or online; ms guidelines online.

★ ☑ SERENDIPITY SYSTEMS, P.O. Box 140, San Simeon CA 93452. (805)927-5259. E-mail: bookware@the grid.net. Website: www.s-e-r-e-n-d-i-p-i-t-y.com. **Contact:** John Galuszka, publisher. Estab. 1986. "Electronic publishing for IBM-PC compatible systems. We publish on disks, the Internet and CD-ROMs, plus Rocket Editions for Gemstar's RCA Reb1100 eBook reader device. Free sample e-books available at www.the-curiosity-shop.com."
Published some debut authors within the last year. Averages 6-12 total titles, 15 fiction titles/year.
Imprint(s): Books-on-Disks™, Bookware™.
Needs: "We want to see *only* works which use (or have a high potential to use) hypertext, multimedia, interactivity or other computer-enhanced features. We cannot use on-paper manuscripts. We only publish book-length works, not individual stories." Published *The Blue-Eyed Muse*, by John Peter (novel).
How to Contact: Query by e-mail or submit entire ms on disk in ASCII or HTML files. Responds in 1 month to mss. Accepts simultaneous submissions. Often comments on rejected mss.
Payment/Terms: Pays 33% royalty on wholesale price or on retail price, depending on how the books goes out. Publishes ms 2 months after acceptance. Book catalog online; ms guidelines for #10 SASE or online.
Advice: "We are interested in seeing multimedia works suitable for Internet distribution. Would like to see: more works of serious literature—novels, short stories, etc. Would like to not see: right wing adventure fantasies from 'Tom Clancy' wanna-be's."

SEVEN STORIES PRESS, 140 Watts St., New York NY 10013. (212)226-8760. Fax: (212)226-1411. E-mail: info@sevenstories.com. Website: www.sevenstories.com. **Contact:** Daniel Simon and Tom McCarthy, editors. Estab. 1995. "Publishers of a distinguished list of authors in fine literature, journalism, contemporary culture and alternative health." Publishes hardcover and trade paperback originals. Average print order: 5,000. **Published some debut authors within the last year.** Averages 40-50 total titles, 10 fiction titles/year. Distributes through Consortium Book Sales and Distribution.
Needs: Literary. Plans anthologies. Ongoing series of short story collections for other cultures (e.g., *Contemporary Fiction from Central America; from Vietnam*, etc.). Published *A Place to Live and Other Selected Essays of Natalia Ginzburg; American Falls*, by Barry Gifford; and *The Incantation of Frida K.*, by Kate Braverman.
How to Contact: Query with SASE. Include list of publishing credits. Agented fiction 60%. Accepts simultaneous submissions. Sometimes comments on rejected mss.
Payment/Terms: Pays 7-15% royalty on retail price. Offers advance. Publishes ms 1-3 years after acceptance. Book catalog and ms guidelines free; ms guidelines online.
Advice: "Writers should only send us their work after they have read some of the books we publish and find our editorial vision in sync with theirs."

A ⊕ SEVERN HOUSE PUBLISHERS, 9-15 High St., Sutton, Surrey SM1 1DF United Kingdom. (0208)770-3930. Fax: (0208)770-3850. **Contact:** Amanda Stewart, editorial director. Publishes hardcover and trade paperback originals and reprints. Averages 150 total titles/year.
Needs: Adventure, fantasy, historical, horror, mainstream/contemporary, mystery, romance, short story collections, suspense. Published *Future Scrolls*, by Fern Michaels (historical romance); *Weekend Warriors*, by Fern Michaels; *The Hampton Passion*, by Julie Ellis (romance); *Looking Glass Justice*, by Jeffrey Ashford (crime and mystery); and *Cold Tactics*, by Ted Allbeury (thriller).
How to Contact: *Agented submissions only.* Responds in 3 months to proposals. Accepts simultaneous submissions.
Payment/Terms: Pays 7½-15% royalty on retail price. Average advance: $750-5,000. Book catalog free.

N ⊠ SHORELINE, 23 Ste-Anne, Ste-Anne-de-Bellevue, Quebec H9X 111 Canada. (514)457-5733. E-mail: shoreline@sympatico.ca. Website: www.shorelinepress.ca. **Contact:** Aquisition editor. Estab. 1991. Small independent publisher of short fiction collections. Publishes trade book and paperback originals. Book: perfect bound; b&w photos. Average print order: 500. **Published 5 debut authors within the last year.** Averages 3-4 total titles, 4 fiction titles/year. Member, AELAQ. Self-distribution.

Needs: Ethnic, historical, literary, regional (Canada), religious, short story collections, education, memoir, local history, poetry. Recently published *Sheila's Take*, by Sheila Kindellan-Sheehan; *Athabasca Seasons*, by Audrey Weldon Reid; *Practice Imperfect*, by Rae Tucker Rambally.

How to Contact: Accepts unsolicited mss. Query with SASE or submit 1-5 sample chapter(s). Accepts queries by e-mail, mail. Include estimated word count, brief bio, list of publishing credits. Send SASE or IRC. Responds in 1 month to queries. No simultaneous submissions. Sometimes comments on rejected mss.

Payment/Terms: Pays 10% royalty on retail price. Publishes ms 1 year after acceptance. Ms guidelines online.

◎ SILHOUETTE BOOKS, 233 Broadway, New York NY 10279. (212)553-4200. Fax: (212)227-8969. Website: www.eharlequin.com. Estab. 1979. Publishes mass market paperback originals. Averages over 350 total titles/year.

Needs: Romance (contemporary and historical romance for adults). "We are interested in seeing submissions for all our lines. No manuscripts other than the types outlined. Manuscripts should follow our general format, yet have individuality and life of their own that will make them stand out in the readers' minds."

How to Contact: Send query letter, 2 page synopsis and SASE to head of imprint. No simultaneous submissions.

Payment/Terms: Pays royalty. Offers advance. Publishes ms 1-3 years after acceptance. Ms guidelines online.

◯ ◎ SILHOUETTE DESIRE, a Harlequin book line, 300 E. 42nd St., 6th Floor, New York NY 10017. (212)682-6080. Fax: (212)682-4539. Website: www.eharlequin.com. **Contact:** Joan Marlow Golan, senior editor. "Sensual, believable and compelling, these books are written for today's woman. Innocent or experienced, the heroine is someone we identify with; the hero is irresistible." Publishes paperback originals and reprints. Books: newspaper print; web printing; perfect-bound. **Published some debut authors within the last year.**

Needs: Romance. Looking for novels in which "the conflict is an emotional one, springing naturally from the unique characters you've chosen. The focus is on the developing relationship, set in a believable plot. Sensuality is key, but lovemaking is never taken lightly. Secondary characters and subplots need to blend with the core story. Innovative new directions in storytelling and fresh approaches to classic romantic plots are welcome." Manuscripts must be 55,000-60,000 words.

How to Contact: Accepts unsolicited mss. Query with SASE or submit complete ms. Send SASE for return of ms or send a disposable ms and SASE for reply only. No simultaneous submissions, submissions on disk.

Payment/Terms: Pays royalty. Offers advance. Ms guidelines for SASE or on website.

◯ ◎ SILHOUETTE INTIMATE MOMENTS, a Harlequin book line, 300 E. 42nd St., 6th floor, New York NY 10017. (212)682-6080. Fax: (212)682-4539. Website: www.eharlequin.com. **Contact:** Leslie Wagner, executive senior editor. "Believable characters swept into a world of larger-than-life romance are the hallmark of Silhouette Intimate Moments books. These books offer you the freedom to combine the universally appealing elements of a category romance with the flash and excitement of mainstream fiction." Publishes paperback originals and reprints. Books: newspaper print; web printing; perfect-bound. **Published some debut authors within the last year.**

Needs: Romance (contemporary). Looking for "novels that explore new directions in romantic fiction or classic plots in contemporary ways, always with the goal of tempting today's demanding reader. Adventure, suspense, melodrama, glamour—let your imagination be your guide as you blend old and new to create a novel with emotional depth and tantalizing complexity." Manuscripts must be approximately 80,000 words.

How to Contact: Accepts unsolicited mss. Query with SASE or submit complete ms. Send SASE for return of ms or send a disposable ms and SASE for reply only. No simultaneous submissions, submissions on disk.

Payment/Terms: Pays royalty. Offers advance. Ms guidelines for SASE or on website.

◯ ◎ SILHOUETTE ROMANCE, a Harlequin book line, 300 E. 42nd St., 6th Floor, New York NY 10017. (212)682-6080. Fax: (212)682-4539. Website: www.eharlequin.com. **Contact:** Mary-Theresa Hussey, senior editor. "Our ultimate goal is to give readers vibrant love stories with heightened emotional impact—books that touch readers' hearts and celebrate their values, including the traditional ideals of love, marriage and family." Publishes paperback originals and reprints. Books: newspaper print; web printing; perfect-bound. **Published some debut authors within the last year.**

Needs: Romance (contemporary traditional). Looking for "talented authors able to portray modern relationships in the context of romantic love. Although the hero and heroine don't actually make love unless married, sexual tension is vitally important. Writers are encouraged to try creative new approaches to classic romantic and contemporary fairy tale plots." Manuscripts must be approximately 53,000-58,000 words.

How to Contact: Accepts unsolicited mss. Query with SASE or submit complete ms. Send SASE for return of ms or send a disposable ms and SASE for reply only. No simultaneous submissions, submissions on disk.

Payment/Terms: Pays royalty. Offers advance. Ms guidelines for SASE or on website.

◯ ◎ SILHOUETTE SPECIAL EDITION, a Harlequin book line, 300 E. 42nd St., 6th Floor, New York NY 10017. (212)682-6080. Fax: (212)682-4539. Website: www.eharlequin.com. **Contact:** Karen Taylor Richman, senior editor. "Whether the sensuality is sizzling or subtle, whether the plot is wildly innovative or satisfying traditional, the novel's emotional vividness, its depth and dimension, clearly label it a very special contemporary romance." Publishes paperback originals. Books: newspaper print; web printing; perfect-bound. **Published some debut authors within the last year.**

Needs: Romance (contemporary). "Sophisticated, substantial and packed with emotions, Special Edition demands writers eager to probe characters deeply to explore issues that heighten the drama of living, loving and creating a family, to generate compelling romantic plots. Subplots are welcome, but must further or parallel the developing romantic relationship in a meaningful way." Manuscripts must be approximately 76,000-80,000 words.

How to Contact: Does not accept unsolicited mss. Query with SASE. No simultaneous submissions, submissions on disk.

Payment/Terms: Pays royalty. Offers advance. Ms guidelines for SASE or on website.

SILVER DAGGER MYSTERIES, The Overmountain Press, P.O. Box 1261, Johnson City TN 37605. (423)926-2691. Fax: (423)232-1252. E-mail: beth@overmtn.com. Website: www.silverdaggermysteries.com. **Contact:** Alex Foster, acquisitions editor (mystery). Estab. 1999. "Small imprint of a larger company. We publish Southern mysteries. Our house is unique in that we are a consortium of authors who communicate and work together to promote each other." Publishes hardcover and trade paperback originals and reprints. Books: 60 lb. offset paper; perfect/case binding. Average print order: 2,000-5,000; first novel print order: 2,000. **Published 6 debut authors within the last year.** Averages 30 total titles, 15 fiction titles/year. Member, PAS. Distributes titles through direct mail, Ingram, Baker & Taylor, Partners, trade shows.

- Julie Wray Herman was nominated for the Agatha Award for *Three Dirty Women & the Garden of Death.*

Needs: Mystery (amateur sleuth, cozy, police procedural, private eye/hardboiled), young adult (mystery). "We look for average-length books of 60-80,000 words." Publishes *Magnolias & Mayhem,* an anthology of Southern short mysteries. Published *Killer Looks,* by Laura Young; *Haunting Refrain,* by Ellis Vidler; and *Justice Betrayed,* by Daniel Bailey.

How to Contact: Does not accept or return unsolicited mss. Query with SASE or submit proposal package including outline, 3 sample chapter(s), synopsis, author bio. Accepts queries by mail. Include estimated word count, brief bio, list of publishing credits. Agented fiction 30%. Responds in 1 month to queries; 3 months to proposals. Accepts simultaneous submissions.

Payment/Terms: Pays 15% royalty on retail price. Publishes ms 2 years after acceptance. Book catalog and ms guidelines online; ms guidelines online.

Advice: "We are very author friendly from editing to promotion. Make sure your book is 'Southern' or set in the South before taking the time to submit."

SILVER MOON PRESS, 160 Fifth Ave., New York NY 10010. (212)242-6499. Fax: (212)242-6799. **Contact:** Hope Killcoyne, managing editor. Publishes hardcover originals. **Published 60% debut authors within the last year.** Averages 5-8 total titles/year.

Needs: Historical, multicultural, biographical. Published *Night Journey to Vicksburg,* by Susan Rowan Masters and *In the Hands of the Enemy,* by Robert Sheely.

How to Contact: Query with SASE or submit proposal package including 1-3 sample chapter(s), synopsis. Responds in 6-12 months to queries; 6-12 months to proposals. Accepts simultaneous submissions.

Payment/Terms: Pays 7-10% royalty. Average advance: $500-1,000. Publishes ms 18 months after acceptance. Book catalog for 9×12 SASE; ms guidelines for #10 SASE.

SIMON & SCHUSTER BOOKS FOR YOUNG READERS, Simon & Schuster Children's Publishing Division, 1230 Avenue of the Americas, New York NY 10020. (212)698-2851. Fax: (212)698-2796. Website: www.simonandschuster.com. **Contact:** Brenda Bowen, executive vice president; Alyssa Eisner, associate editor; Paula Wiseman, editorial director. "We're looking for complex, challenging YA novels and middle-grade fiction with a fresh, unique slant." Publishes hardcover originals. Averages 80-90 total titles, 20 fiction titles/year.

- Books from Simon & Schuster Books for Young Readers have received the following awards: 2000 Michael L. Printz Honor Award for *Hard Love,* and the 1999 Coretta Scott King Author Award and ALA Best Book for Young Adults for *Heaven* by Angela Johnson.

Needs: Children's/juvenile, fantasy, historical, humor, juvenile, mystery, picture books, science fiction, young adult (adventure, historical, mystery, contemporary fiction). "Fiction needs to be fresh, unusual and compelling to stand out from the competition. We're not looking for problem novels, stories with a moral, or rhymed picture book texts." Published *The School Story,* by Andrew Clements (middle-grade fiction); *Fever 1793,* by Laurie Anderson (young adult fiction); and *Love & Sex,* by Michael Cart, editor (young adult fiction).

How to Contact: Does not accept unsolicited mss. Query with SASE only. Agented fiction 90%. Responds in 2 months to queries. Accepts simultaneous submissions.

Payment/Terms: Pays 4-12% royalty on retail price. Average advance: varies. Publishes ms 1-3 years after acceptance. Ms guidelines for #10 SASE.

Advice: "Study our catalog and read books we have published to get an idea of our list. The fiction market is crowded and writers need a strong, fresh, original voice to stand out."

⬟ ◎ SIMON & SCHUSTER CHILDREN'S PUBLISHING, (Division of Simon & Schuster Inc.), 1230 Avenue of the Americas, New York NY 10020. (212)698-7200. E-mail: ssonlie@simonsays.com. Website: www.simonsays.com. Estab. 1924.
Imprint(s): Aladdin Paperbacks; Atheneum Books for Young Readers; Little Simon; Margaret K. McElderry Books; Simon & Schuster Books for Young Readers; Simon Spotlight.

⬟ SLG PUBLISHING, 577 S. Market St., San Jose CA 95113. Website: www.slavelabor.com.
Needs: Comics, graphic novels.
How to Contact: "We only review complete projects. All members of the creative team need to be fully committed to the project before it is submitted." Send SASE, cover letter, character descriptions and sketches, and projects via postal mail.
Terms: Negotiated upon acceptance of proposal. Ms guidelines on website.

◐ ⛊ GIBBS SMITH, PUBLISHER, P.O. Box 667, Layton UT 84041. (801)544-9800. Fax: (801)546-8853. E-mail: info@gibbs-smith.com. Website: www.gibbs-smith.com. **Contact:** Suzanne Taylor, editor (children's); Madge Baird, editorial director (humor, western); Linda Nimori, editor. Estab. 1969. Small independent press. "We publish books that make a difference." Publishes hardcover and trade paperback originals. Averages 50 total titles, 1-2 fiction titles/year.
  ● Gibbs Smith is the recipient of a Western Writers Association Fiction Award. Publishes the winner of the Peregrine Smith Poetry Contest (accepts entries only in April).
Needs: Only short works oriented to gift market. Publishes *The Peregrine Reader*, a series of anthologies based upon a variety of themes. Published *A Strong Man*, by Carol Lynn Pearson.
How to Contact: Submit synopsis with sample illustration, if applicable. Send query letter or short gift book ms directly to the editorial director. Send SASE or IRC. Agented fiction 50%. Responds in 1 month to queries; 10 weeks to proposals; 10 weeks to mss. Accepts simultaneous submissions. Sometimes comments on rejected mss.
Payment/Terms: Pays 8-14% royalty on gross receipts. Average advance: $2,000-3,000. Publishes ms 1-2 years after acceptance. Book catalog for 9×12 SAE and $2.13 in postage; ms guidelines online.

◎ ⛊ ◐ SNOWAPPLE PRESS, Box 56024, Heritage Postal Outlet, Edmonton AB T6J 6T4 Canada. (780)437-0191. **Contact:** Vanna Tessier, editor. Estab. 1991. "We focus on topics that are interesting, unusual and controversial." Small independent literary press. Publishes hardcover originals, trade paperback originals and reprints, mass market paperback originals and reprints. Books: non-acid paper; offset printing; perfect binding; illustrations. Average print order: 500. Averages 3-4 total titles, 1-2 fiction titles/year. Distributes titles through bookseller and library wholesalers. Promotes titles through press releases and reviews.
Needs: Adventure, children's/juvenile (adventure, fantasy, mystery), ethnic, experimental, fantasy, feminist, historical, literary, mainstream/contemporary, mystery, short story collections, young adult (adventure, mystery/suspense). Published *Thistle Creek*, by Vanna Tessier (short stories); *The Last Waltz of Chopin*, by Gilberto Finzi, translated by Vanna Tessier (novel).
How to Contact: Does not accept unsolicited mss. Query with SASE. Send 1-page cover letter. Include estimated word count, list of publishing credits, and 300-word bio. Responds in 1 month.
Payment/Terms: Pays 10-50% royalty on retail price or makes outright purchase. Average advance: $100-200. Publishes ms 12-18 months after acceptance.
Advice: "Query first with proper SASE and IRC's to obtain guidelines."

SOFT SKULL PRESS INC., 71 Bond St., Brooklyn NY 11217. (718)643-1599. Fax: (718)643-0879. Website: www.softskull.com. Publishes hardcover and trade paperback originals. Averages 10 total titles/year.
Needs: Confession, experimental, graphic novels, historical, literary, mainstream/contemporary, multicultural, short story collections. Agented submissions encouraged.
How to Contact: Query with SASE or submit proposal package including 1 sample chapter(s), synopsis. Responds in 2 months to proposals. No simultaneous submissions.
Payment/Terms: Pays 7-10% royalty. Average advance: $100-15,000. Publishes ms 6 months after acceptance. Book catalog free or on website; ms guidelines online.

◐ SOHO PRESS, INC., 853 Broadway, New York NY 10003. (212)260-1900. Fax: (212)260-1902. E-mail: soho@sohopress.com. Website: www.sohopress.com. **Contact:** Juris Jurjevics, editor (literary, mainstream novels); Laura Hruska, editor (literary fiction, literary mysteries); Bryan Devendorf, editor (literary fiction). Estab. 1986. "Independent publisher known for sophisticated fiction, mysteries set abroad, women's interest (no genre) novels and multicultural novels." Publishes hardcover and trade paperback originals. Books: acid free paper; perfect binding; halftone illustrations. First novel print order: 5,000. **Published 5 debut authors within the last year.** Averages 40 total titles, 34 fiction titles/year. Distributes titles through Consortium Book Sales & Distribution in the US, Hushion House in Canada, Turnaround in England.
Imprint(s): Soho Crime, edited by Laura Hruska: procedurals set abroad.
Needs: Adventure, ethnic, feminist, historical, literary, mainstream/contemporary, mystery (police procedural), suspense. Published *Since the Layoffs*, by Iain Levinson; *A Loyal Character Dancer*, by Qiu Xialong; *Beemer*™,

by Glenn Gaslin; *We Can Still Be Friends*, by Kelly Cherry; *Maisie Dobbs*, by Jacqueline Winspear; and *Murder in the Bastille*, by Cara Black. Publishes various mystery series.

How to Contact: Does not accept unsolicited mss. Query with SASE. Include estimated word count, brief bio, list of publishing credits. Agented fiction 65%. Responds in 2 months to queries. Accepts simultaneous submissions. No electronic submissions, submissions on disk. Sometimes comments on rejected mss.

Payment/Terms: Pays 10-15% royalty on retail price. Offers advance. Publishes ms within 1 year after acceptance. Book catalog for 6×9 SAE with 2 first-class stamps; ms guidelines online.

SOUNDPRINTS, Division of Trudy Corporation., 353 Main Ave., Norwalk CT 06851. (203)846-2274. Fax: (203)846-1776. E-mail: soundprints@soundprints.com. Website: www.soundprints.com. **Contact:** Chelsea Shriver, assistant editor. Estab. 1988. Publishes hardcover originals. Averages 20-40 total titles/year.

Needs: Juvenile. "Most of our books are under license from the Smithsonian Institution and are closely curated fictional stories based on fact. We never do stories of anthropomorphic animals. When we publish juvenile fiction, it will be about wildlife or history and all information in the book *must* be accurate." Published *Bumblebee at Apple Tree Lane*, by Laura Gates Galvin; *Sockeye's Journey Home: The Story of a Pacific Salmon*, by Barbara Gaines Winkelman.

How to Contact: Does not accept unsolicited mss. "Send published writing samples/résumé with a query letter for us to keep on file. Contracts with authors on a 'work-for-hire' basis to write manuscripts to our specifications depending on our needs."

Payment/Terms: Makes outright purchase.

Advice: "Our books are written for children from ages 4-8. Our most succesful authors can craft a wonderful story which is derived from authentic wildlife facts."

SOUTHERN METHODIST UNIVERSITY PRESS, P.O. Box 750415, Dallas TX 75275-0415. (214)768-1433. Fax: (214)768-1428. Website: www.tamu.edu/upress. **Contact:** Kathryn Lang, senior editor. Estab. 1937. "Small university press publishing in areas of film/theater, Southwest life and letters, medical ethics, and contemporary fiction." Publishes hardcover and trade paperback originals and reprints. Books: acid-free paper; perfect bound; some illustrations. Average print order: 2,000. **Published 2 debut authors within the last year.** Averages 10-12 total titles, 3-4 fiction titles/year. Distributes titles through Texas A&M University Press Consortium. Promotes titles through writers' publications.

Needs: Literary, short story collections, novels. "We are willing to look at 'serious' or 'literary' fiction." No "mass market, science fiction, formula, thriller, romance." Published *Slim*, by Ruth Linnea Whitney (a novel) and *It Takes a Worried Man*, by Tracy Daugherty (short stories).

How to Contact: Accepts unsolicited mss. Query with SASE. Responds in 1 week to queries; 1 month to proposals; up to 1 year to mss. No simultaneous submissions. Sometimes comments on rejected mss.

Payment/Terms: Pays up to 10% royalty on wholesale price, 10 author's copies. Average advance: $500. Publishes ms 1 year after acceptance. Book catalog free; ms guidelines online.

Advice: "We view encouraging first time authors as part of the mission of a university press. Send query describing the project and your own background. Research the press before you submit—don't send us the kinds of things we don't publish." Looks for "quality fiction from new or established writers."

SPECTRA BOOKS, Subsidiary of Random House, Inc., 1745 Broadway, New York NY 10019. (212)782-8632. Fax: (212)782-9174. Website: www.bantamdell.com. **Contact:** Anne Lesley Groell, senior editor. Estab. 1985. Large science fiction, fantasy and speculative line. Publishes hardcover originals, paperback originals and trade paperbacks.

● Many Bantam Spectra Books have recieved Hugos and Nebulas.

Needs: Fantasy, literary, science fiction. Needs include novels that attempt to broaden the traditional range of science fiction and fantasy. Strong emphasis on characterization. Especially well written traditional science fiction and fantasy will be considered. No fiction that doesn't have as least some element of speculation or the fantastic. Published *Storm of Swords*, by George R. Martin (medieval fantasy); *Ship of Destiny*, by Robin Hobb (nautical fantasy); and *Antartica*, by Stanley Robinson (science fiction).

How to Contact: Query with 3 sample chapters and a short (no more that 3 double-spaced) synopsis. Send SASE or IRC. Agented fiction 90%. Responds in 6 months. Accepts simultaneous submissions.

Payment/Terms: Pays royalty. Average advance: negotiable. Ms guidelines for #10 SASE.

Advice: "Please follow our guidelines carefully and type neatly."

SPINSTERS INK, P.O. Box 22005, Denver CO 80222. (303)761-5552. E-mail: spinster@spinsters-ink.com. Website: www.spinsters-ink.com. **Contact:** Sharon Silvas, editor. Estab. 1978. Small women's publishing company growing steadily. "We are committed to publishing works by women writing from the periphery: fat women, Jewish women, lesbians, poor women, rural women, women of color, etc." Publishes trade paperback originals and reprints. Books: 60 lb. acid-free natural paper; photo offset printing; perfect-bound; illustrations when appropriate. Average print order: 3,000. **Published 3 debut authors within the last year.** Averages 6 total titles, 10 fiction titles/year. Distributes titles through Words Distributing.

Needs: Ethnic, feminist, gay/lesbian, mystery (amateur sleuth, private eye/hardboiled), science fiction (soft/sociological), short story collections, thriller/espionage, women's. "We do not publish poetry or short fiction. We are interested in fiction that challenges, women's language that is feminist, stories that treat lifestyles with the diversity and complexity they deserve. We are also interested in genre fiction, especially mysteries." Published *Soft Voices of the Soft-bellied Warrior*, by Mary Saracino (memoir); *The Elegant Gathering of White Snows*, by Kris Radish (fiction); *Hostage to Murder*, by Val McDermid; *Perfection*, by Anita Mason; *The Kanshou*, by Sally Miller Gearhart (science fiction/fantasy, the Earthkeep series). Publishes the Earthkeep series.

How to Contact: Submit outline, sample chapter(s), synopsis. No e-mail queries. Include estimated word count, brief bio, list of publishing credits. Agented fiction 10%. Responds in 3 months. No simultaneous submissions, submissions on disk. Sometimes comments on rejected mss.

Payment/Terms: Pays 7-11% royalty on retail price. Publishes ms 18 months after acceptance. Book catalog free; ms guidelines for SASE or on website; ms guidelines online.

Advice: "Send a thorough query letter; we only accept work that is top quality."

N THE SPIRIT THAT MOVES US PRESS, P.O. Box 720820-N, Jackson Heights NY 11372-0820. (718)426-8788. **Contact:** Morty Sklar, editor/publisher. Small independent literary publisher. "We do, for the most part, simultaneous clothbound and trade paperbacks for the same title." Publishes hardcover and paperback originals. Books: 60 lb. natural acid-free paper, mostly photo-offset, some letterpress; cloth and perfect binding; illustrations. Average print order: 3,000. **Published many debut authors within the last year.** Distributes titles directly and through wholesalers. Promotes titles through direct mail and review copies, as well as advertisements in trade and consumer publications.

• The Spirit That Moves Us Press is known for having been the first U.S. publisher of Jaroslav Seifert, who won the Nobel Prize a year after they published his *The Casting of Bells*.

Needs: Literary. "Our choice of 'literary' does not exclude almost any other category—as long as the writing communicates on an emotional level, and is involved with people more than things. Nothing sensational or academic." Published *Patchwork of Dreams: Voices from the Heart of the New America*, a multi-ethnic collection of fiction and other genres; *Editor's Choice III: Fiction, Poetry, & Art from the U.S. Small Press*, and *Free Parking*, all edited by Morty Sklar.

How to Contact: Query with SASE. Include estimated word count, brief bio, whether or not ms is a simultaneous submission. Responds in 1-3 months. Sometimes comments on rejected mss.

Payment/Terms: Pays 10% royalty on net receipts, author's copies, also honorarium, depending on finances. Publishes ms 1 year after acceptance. Book catalog for 6×9 SAE and 2 first-class stamps.

Advice: "We are interested in work that is not only well written, but that gets the reader involved on an emotional level. No matter how skilled the writing is, or how interesting or exciting the story, if we don't care about the people in it, we won't consider it. Also, we are open to a great variety of styles, so just be yourself and don't try to second-guess the editor. You may have our newest collection *Patchwork of Dreams* as a sample, for $10 (regularly $14.50 with postage)."

N SPOUT PRESS, P.O. Box 581067, Minneapolis MN 55458. (612)782-9629. Website: www.spoutpress.com. **Contact:** Chris Watercott, fiction editor. Estab. 1989. "Small independent publisher with a permanent staff of three—interested in experimental fiction for our magazine and books." Publishes paperback originals. Books: perfect bound; illustrations. Average print order: 1,000. **Published 1 debut author within the last year.** Distributes and promotes books through the website and bookpeople.

Needs: Ethnic, experimental, literary, short story collections.

How to Contact: Does not accept unsolicited mss. Query with SASE. Accepts queries by mail. Include estimated word count, brief bio, list of publishing credits. Agented fiction 10%. Responds in 1 month. Accepts simultaneous submissions. Rarely comments on rejected mss.

Payment/Terms: Pays by individual arrangement with author depending on the book. Publishes ms 12-15 months after acceptance. Book catalog online; ms guidelines for SASE or on website.

Advice: "We tend to publish writers after we know their work via publication in our journal, *Spout Magazine*."

ST. ANTHONY MESSENGER PRESS, 28 W. Liberty St., Cincinnati OH 45202-6498. (513)241-5615. Fax: (513)241-0399. Website: www.americancatholic.org. Estab. 1970. Publishes trade paperback originals. Averages 15-25 total titles/year.

How to Contact: Responds in 1 month to queries; 2 months to proposals; 2 months to mss.

Payment/Terms: Pays 10-12% royalty on net receipts. Average advance: $1,000 average. Publishes ms 18 months after acceptance. Book catalog for 9×12 SAE with 4 first-class stamps; ms guidelines online.

A ST. MARTIN'S PRESS, 175 Fifth Ave., New York NY 10010. (212)674-5151. Fax: (212)420-9314. Website: www.stmartins.com. Estab. 1952. General interest publisher of both fiction and nonfiction. Publishes hardcover, trade paperback and mass market originals. Averages 1,500 total titles/year.

Imprint(s): Bedford Books; Buzz Books; Thomas Dunne Books; Forge; Minotaur; Picador USA; Stonewall Inn Editions; TOR Books; Griffin.

Needs: Fantasy, historical, horror, literary, mainstream/contemporary, mystery, science fiction, suspense, western (contemporary), general fiction; thriller.

How to Contact: *Agented submissions only. No unsolicited mss.*
Payment/Terms: Pays royalty. Offers advance. Ms guidelines online.

STARBURST PUBLISHERS, P.O. Box 4123, Lancaster PA 17604. (717)293-0939. Fax: (717)293-1945. Website: www.starburstpublishers.com. **Contact:** Editorial Department. Estab. 1982. Midsize independent press specializing in inspirational and self-help books. Publishes hardcover and trade paperback originals. **Published some debut authors within the last year.** Averages 15-20 total titles/year. Distributes titles through all major distributors and sales reps. Promotes titles through print, radio, and major distributors.
Needs: Adventure, fantasy, historical, horror, military/war, psychic/supernatural, religious, romance (contemporary, historical), suspense, western, inspirational, spiritual. "We are only looking for good wholesome fiction that inspires or teaches self-help principles. We are also looking for successfully self-published fiction."
How to Contact: Accepts unsolicited mss. Query with SASE or submit outline, 3 sample chapter(s), synopsis, author bio. Accepts queries by e-mail. Include brief bio. Agented fiction less than 25%. Responds in 1 month to queries; 2 months to mss. Accepts simultaneous submissions, submissions on disk.
Payment/Terms: Pays 6-16% royalty on wholesale price. Average advance: varies. Publishes ms 1 year after acceptance. Book catalog for 9×12 SAE with 4 first-class stamps; ms guidelines online.

STARCHERONE BOOKS, P.O. Box 303, Buffalo NY 14201-0303. (716)885-2726. E-mail: publisher@starcherone.com. Website: www.starcherone.com. **Contact:** Theodore Pelton, publisher. Estab. 2000. Small operation on part-time basis. Publishes paperback originals and reprints. Books: acid-free paper; perfect-bound; occasional illustrations. Average print order: 1,000. Average first novel print order: 1,000. **Published 2 debut authors within the last year.** Member, CLMP. Titles distributed through website, Amazon.com, independent bookstores.
Needs: Comic books, erotica, experimental, gay/lesbian, literary, short story collections. Published *Black Umbrella Stories*, by Nicole de Csipkay (debut author, short stories); *The Voice in the Closet*, by Raymond Federman (experimental); *Endorsed by Jack Chapeau*, by Theodore Pelton (debut author, short stories).
How to Contact: Accepts unsolicited mss. Send query or submit complete ms with cover letter. Accepts unsolicited mss in August and September only. Accepts contest entries between October and January. Accepts no unsolicited manuscripts from February to July. Accepts queries by e-mail. Include brief bio, list of publishing credits. Send copy of ms and SASE. Responds in 2 months to queries; 6 months to mss. No simultaneous submissions.
Payment/Terms: Publishes ms 6-12 months after acceptance. Guidelines and catalog available on website.
Advice: "Become familiar with our interests in fiction. We are interested in new strategies for creating stories and fictive texts. Do not send genre fiction unless it is unconventional in approach."

STEEPLE HILL, Harlequin Enterprises, 233 Broadway, New York NY 10279. Website: www.eharlequin.com. **Contact:** Ann Leslie Tuttle, Melissa Endlich, acquisition editors; and all Silhouette/Harlequin Historicals editors. Estab. 1997. Publishes mass market paperback originals
Imprint(s): Love Inspired.
Needs: Romance (Christian, 70,000 words), Inspirational romance. Published *A Mother at Heart*, by Carolyne Aarsen.
How to Contact: Accepts unsolicited mss. Query with SASE or submit 3 sample chapter(s), synopsis. No simultaneous submissions.
Payment/Terms: Pays royalty. Offers advance. Ms guidelines online.
Advice: "Drama, humor and even a touch of mystery all have a place in this series. Subplots are welcome and should further the story's main focus or intertwine in a meaningful way. Secondary characters (children, family, friends, neighbors, fellow church members, etc.) may all contribute to a substantial and satisfying story. These wholesome tales of romance include strong family values and high moral standards. While there is no permarital sex between characters, a vivid, exciting romance that is presented with a mature perspective, is essential. Although the element of faith must clearly be present, it should be well integrated into the characterization and plot. The conflict between the main characters should be an emotional one, arising naturally from the well-developed personalities you've created. Suitable stories should also impart an important lesson about the powers of trust and faith."

STONE BRIDGE PRESS, P.O. Box 8208, Berkeley CA 94707. (510)524-8732. Fax: (510)524-8711. Website: www.stonebridge.com. **Contact:** Peter Goodman, publisher. Estab. 1989. "Independent press focusing on books about Japan in English (business, language, culture, literature, animation)." Publishes hardcover and trade paperback originals. Books: 60-70 lb. offset paper; web and sheet paper; perfect-bound; some illustrations. Averages 8 total titles/year. Distributes titles through Consortium. Promotes titles through Internet announcements, special-interest magazines and niche tie-ins to associations.
• Stone Bridge Press received a Japan-U.S. Friendship Prize for *Life in the Cul-de-Sac*, by Senji Kuroi.
Imprint(s): The Rock Spring Collection of Japanese Literature.
Needs: Experimental, fantasy, gay/lesbian, Japan-themed. "Primarily looking at material relating to Japan. Translations only."
How to Contact: Does not accept unsolicited mss. Query with SASE. Include 1-page cover letter. Accepts queries by e-mail, fax. Agented fiction 25%. Responds in 4 months. Accepts simultaneous submissions. Sometimes comments on rejected mss.

Payment/Terms: Pays royalty on wholesale price. Average advance: variable. Publishes ms 2 years after acceptance. Book catalog for 2 first-class stamps and SASE; ms guidelines online.

Advice: "Translations only for the time being. Absolutely no commercial fiction. No poetry."

STYLEWRITER, INC., 4395 N. Windsor Dr., Provo UT 84604-6301. (866)997-8953. Fax: (801)802-7888. E-mail: query@stylewriterinc.org. Website: www.stylewriterinc.org. **Contact:** Cherrie Floyd, acquisitions editor. Estab. 2001. Publishes hardcover, trade paperback, and electronic originals and reprints. Books: 55 lb. cream, 50 lb. white paper; digital and web press printing; perfect, spiral and case bound; illustrations. Average print order varies. **Published 2 debut authors within the last year.** Averages 30 total titles, 10 fiction titles/year.

Needs: Adventure, children's/juvenile, ethnic, experimental, fantasy, feminist, gothic, historical, horror, humor, juvenile, literary, mainstream/contemporary, military/war, multicultural, mystery, poetry, religious, romance, science fiction, short story collections, spiritual, suspense, western, young adult, children. Especially interested in romance, children's, and horror. Published *The Mortal Realm*; *Lady Anne of Kelredon*; *The Mystery of the Missing Teacup*.

How to Contact: Submit proposal package including 3 sample chapter(s), synopsis. Accepts queries by e-mail, mail. Responds in 3 months. Accepts simultaneous submissions.

Payment/Terms: Pays 45-65% royalty on wholesale price. Average advance: $500-10,000. Publishes ms 1 year after acceptance. Book catalog online; ms guidelines online.

Advice: "Trust your vision but do the market research before querying."

SYNERGEBOOKS, 1235 Flat Shoals Rd., King NC 27021. (888)812-2533. Fax: (336)994-8403. E-mail: inquiries@synergebooks.com. Website: www.synergebooks.com. **Contact:** Debra Staples, editor. Estab. 1999. Small press publisher, specializing in quality ebooks from talented new writers in a myriad of genres, including print-on-demand. SynergEbooks "works together" with the author to edit and market each book. Publishes paperback originals and e-books. Books: #60 paper; print-on-demand; perfect bound; illustrations. Average first novel print order: 50. **Published 6 debut authors within the last year.** Averages 30 total titles, 20 fiction titles/year.

● Authors have received EPPIES and other awards for the past 3 years.

Needs: Adventure, children's/juvenile (adventure, animal, fantasy), family saga, horror (futuristic, psychological, supernatural), humor, mainstream/contemporary, military/war, mystery (amateur slueth, private eye/hardboiled), new age/mystic, psychic/supernatural, religious (children's religious, inspirational, religious fantasy, religious mystery/suspense, religious thriller, religious romance), romance (contemporary, futuristic/time travel, historical, regency period, romantic suspense), science fiction, short story collections, western (frontier saga, traditional), young adult (adventure, fantasy/science fiction, historical, horror, mystery/suspense, romance), native american. Published *Second Class Citizenship*, by Robert D. Hunter (Native American); *A Mother's Son*, by J.E. de Sousa (family saga); *The Blue Mosaic Vase*, by Christie Shary (fiction).

How to Contact: Accepts unsolicited mss. Query with SASE or submit outline, 3 sample chapter(s), synopsis. Accepts queries by e-mail. Include estimated word count, brief bio, list of publishing credits. Agented fiction 1%. Responds in 4 weeks to queries; 3 months to mss. Accepts simultaneous submissions. Sometimes comments on rejected mss.

Payment/Terms: Pays 25-40% royalty. Publishes ms up to 2 years after acceptance. Book catalog online; ms guidelines online.

Advice: "We do not care if you've ever been published. If your work is unique in some way, and you are willing to work together to market your book, there is a good chance you will be accepted."

T N T CLASSIC BOOKS, 360 West 36 St., #2NW, New York NY 10018-6412. (212)736-6279. Fax: (212)695-3219. E-mail: tntclassics@aol.com. **Contact:** Francine L. Trevens, editor (novels, plays). Estab. 1994. T n T Classic Books is a one-person operation that keeps gay classics in print. Publishes paperback originals and reprints. Books: offset printing; perfect binding; illustrations. Average print order: 1,000. **Published 1 debut author within the last year.** Member of the Greater NY Independent Publishers Association.

Imprint(s): Happy Task (children).

Needs: Children's/juvenile (easy-to-read), feminist, gay/lesbian, lesbian, gay plays. Publishes a anthology of monologues for actors.

How to Contact: Does not accept unsolicited mss. Query with SASE. Accepts queries by e-mail, fax. Include brief bio, list of publishing credits. Agented fiction 5%. Responds in 1 week to queries; 3 months to mss. Accepts simultaneous submissions, electronic submissions. Often comments on rejected mss.

Payment/Terms: Pays 10 contributor's copies. Publishes ms 9 months after acceptance. Book catalog for 6×9 SAE with 1 first-class stamps.

Advice: "Try us as a last resort. And remember to never stop writing creatively."

NAN A. TALESE, Random House, Inc., 1745 Broadway, New York NY 10019. (212)782-8918. Fax: (212)782-8448. Website: www.nantalese.com. **Contact:** Nan A. Talese, editorial director. "Nan A. Talese publishes nonfiction with a powerful guiding narrative and relevance to larger cultural trends and interests, and literary fiction of the highest quality." Publishes hardcover originals. Averages 15 total titles/year.

Needs: Literary. Well written narratives with a compelling story line, good characterization and use of language. We like stories with an edge. Published *Agented submissions only.* Published *The Blind Assassin*, by Margaret Atwood; *Atonement*, by Ian McEwan; and *Great Shame*, Thomas Keneally.

How to Contact: Responds in 1 week to queries; 2 weeks to mss. Accepts simultaneous submissions.

Payment/Terms: Pays variable royalty on retail price. Average advance: varies. Publishes ms 1 year after acceptance. Agented submissions only.

Advice: "We're interested in literary narrative, fiction and nonfiction—we do not publish genre fiction. Our readers are highly literate people interested in good story-telling, intellectual and psychologically significant. We want well-written material."

Ø TATTERSALL PUBLISHING, P.O. Box 308194, Denton TX 76203-8194. (940)565-0804. Fax: (940)320-8604. E-mail: cwolfe@tattersall.com. Website: www.tattersallpub.com. **Contact:** Cheryl Wolfe, associate editor (fantasy, science fiction, mystery/suspense, historical, humor/satire). Estab. 1994. Books: 70 lb. paper; offset printing; perfect or Smythe-sewn binding. Average print order: 1,000.

Needs: "Temporarily suspending acquisitions; check website for notice of reopening of submissions."

How to Contact: Often comments on rejected mss.

◎ THIRD WORLD PRESS, P.O. Box 19730, Chicago IL 60619. (773)651-0700. Fax: (773)651-7286. E-mail: TWPress3@aol.com. **Contact:** Gwendolyn Mitchell, editor. Estab. 1967. Black-owned an operated independent publisher of fiction and nonfiction books about the black experience throughout the Diaspora. Publishes hardcover and trade paperback originals and reprints. Averages 20 total titles/year. Distributes titles through Partners, Baker & Taylor and bookstores. Promotes titles through direct mail, catalogs and newspapers.

Needs: Ethnic, feminist, historical, juvenile (animal, easy-to-read, fantasy, historical, contemporary), literary, mainstream/contemporary, picture books, plays, short story collections, young adult (easy-to-read/teen, folktales, historical), African-centered; African-American materials, preschool/picture books. "We primarily publish nonfiction, but will consider fiction by and about blacks." Published *In the Shadow of the Sun*, by Michael Simanga; *Special Interest*, by Chris Benson.

How to Contact: Accepts unsolicited mss. Query with SASE or submit outline, 5 sample chapter(s), synopsis. Responds in 6 weeks to queries; 5 months to mss. Accepts simultaneous submissions.

Payment/Terms: Pays royalty on retail price. Individual arrangement with author depending on the book, etc. Offers advance. Publishes ms 18 months after acceptance. Book catalog free; ms guidelines for #10 SASE.

◨ Ø ▨ THISTLEDOWN PRESS, 633 Main St., Saskatoon SK S7H 0J8 Canada. (306)244-1722. Fax: (306)244-1762. E-mail: tdpress@thistledown.sk.ca. Website: www.thistledown.sk.ca. **Contact:** Jackie Farrie, managing editor. Estab. 1975. Publishes paperback originals—literary fiction, young adult fiction, poetry. Books: quality stock paper; offset printing; perfect-bound; occasional illustrations. Average print order 1,500-2,000. First novel print order: 1,000-1,500. **Published some debut authors within the last year.** Promotes titles through intensive school promotions, online, advertising, special offers.

● Thistledown's *Prisoner in a Red-Rose Chain*, by Jeffrey Moore won the Commonwealth Writers Prize for Best New Book. Thistledown publishes *Canadian writers only.*

Needs: Experimental, literary, short story collections, novels. Publishes anthologies. "Stories are nominated." Published *Japanese Baseball & Other Stories*, by W.P. Kinsella (short fiction); *Ariadne's Dream*, by Tess Fragoulis (novel); *A Traveller Came By: Stories About Dying*, by Séan Virgo (short fiction). Also publishes Mayer Mystery Series (mystery novels for young adults) and The New Leaf Series (first books for poetry and fiction—Saskatchewan residents only).

How to Contact: Does not accept unsolicited mss. Query with SASE. Accepts queries by e-mail, fax. Responds in 2 months to queries.

Payment/Terms: Pays royalty on retail price. Publishes ms 1-2 years after acceptance. Guidelines and book catalog available for #10 SASE.

Advice: "We are primarily looking for quality writing that is original and innovative in its perspective and/or use of language. Thistledown would like to receive queries first before submissions—perhaps with novels outline, some indication of previous publications, periodicals your work has appeared in. We are continuing to publish more fiction and are looking for new writers to add to our list. New Leaf Editions line is first books of poetry or fiction by emerging Saskatchewan authors. Familarize yourself with some of our books before submitting a query or manuscript to the press."

CHECK THE CATEGORY INDEXES, located at the back of the book, for publishers interested in specific fiction subjects.

THORNDIKE PRESS, The Gale Group, 295 Kenney Memorial Dr., Waterville ME 04901. (207)859-1000. Fax: (207)859-1006. E-mail: Hazel.Rumney@gale.com. **Contact:** Hazel Rumney, editor (romance, western, women's fiction); Jamie Knobloch, editorial director. Estab. 1979. Midsize publisher. Publishes hardcover originals, reprints and large print reprints. Books: alkaline paper; offset printing; Smythe-sewn library binding. Average print order: 1,000. Averages 112 total titles/year.
Imprint(s): Five Star (contact: Hazel Rumney).
Needs: Romance, western, women's. "We want highly original material that contains believable motivation, with little repetitive introspection. Show us how a character feels, rather that tell us. Humor is good; clichés are not." Published *Friends and Enemies*, by Susan Oleksiw (mystery); *Desperate Acts*, by Jane Claudia Coleman (romance).
How to Contact: Submit proposal package including 3 sample chapter(s), synopsis. Responds in 3 months to proposals. Accepts simultaneous submissions.
Payment/Terms: Pays royalty on wholesale price. Average advance: $1,000-2,000. Publishes ms 8 months after acceptance. Book catalog free; ms guidelines for #10 SASE.

■ ◎ TIDEWATER PUBLISHERS, Cornell Maritime Press, Inc., P.O. Box 456, Centreville MD 21617-0456. (410)758-1075. Fax: (410)758-6849. E-mail: cornell@crosslink.net. **Contact:** Charlotte Kurst, managing editor. Estab. 1938. "Tidewater Publishers issues adult nonfiction works related to the Chesapeake Bay area, Delmarva or Maryland in general. The only fiction we handle is juvenile and must have a regional focus." Publishes hardcover and paperback originals. **Published some debut authors within the last year.** Averages 7-9 total titles/year.
Needs: Regional juvenile fiction only. Published *Chesapeake ABC*, by Priscilla Cummings and illustrated by David Aiken; and *Finding Birds in the Chesapeake Marsh*, by Zora Aiken and illustrated by David Aiken.
How to Contact: Query with SASE or submit outline, sample chapter(s), synopsis. Responds in 2 months to queries. No simultaneous submissions.
Payment/Terms: Pays 7½-15% royalty on retail price. Publishes ms 1 year after acceptance. Book catalog for 10×13 SAE with 5 first-class stamps.
Advice: "Our audience is made up of readers interested in works that are specific to the Chesapeake Bay and Delmarva Peninsula area."

◎ TILBURY HOUSE, PUBLISHERS, imprint of Harpswell Press, Inc., 2 Mechanic St., Gardiner ME 04345. (207)582-1899. Fax: (207)582-8227. E-mail: tilbury@tilburyhouse.com. Website: www.tilburyhouse.com. **Contact:** Audrey Maynard, children's book editor. Estab. 1990. Publishes hardcover originals, trade paperback originals. Averages 10 total titles/year.
Needs: Regional (New England adult). Published *Lucy's Family Tree*, by Karen Schreck; *Life Under Ice*, by Mary Cerullo.
Payment/Terms: Pays royalty. Book catalog free; ms guidelines online.

TIMBERWOLF PRESS, INC., 202 N. Allen Dr., Suite A, Allen TX 75013. (972)359-0911. Fax: (972)359-0525. Website: www.timberwolfpress.com. **Contact:** Carol Woods, senior editor. Publishes trade paperback originals. **Published 25% debut authors within the last year.** Averages 24-30 total titles/year.
Needs: Fantasy, military/war, mystery, science fiction, suspense. "In addition to traditional books, we present each title in next generation fully-cast, dramatized, unabridged audio theatre, available in the usual formats; and downloadable in all formats from our website. So our stories must maintain tension and pace. Think exciting. Think breathless. Think terrific story, terrific characters, terrific writing." Published *Soldier of the Legion*, by Marshall Thomas; *Book Two Bronwyn Tetralogy: Silk & Steel*.
How to Contact: Query via e-mail only. Fiction only. Responds in 1 month to queries; 3 months to mss. Accepts simultaneous submissions.
Payment/Terms: Pays royalty on wholesale price. Offers industry standard advance or better. Publishes ms 1 year after acceptance. Book catalog and ms guidelines on website; ms guidelines online.
Advice: "We accept e-queries and e-submissions only: *submissions@timberwolfpress.com*. And polish that query. Grammar, punctuation, and spelling are as important in e-queries and e-submissions as they are in paper queries. Make sure your submission is appropriate for Timberwolf. Get on our website, www.timberwolfpress.com, to see what we do. And no paper queries!"

N ○ ● TINDAL STREET PRESS, LTD., 217 The Custard Factory, Gibb Street, Birmingham B9 4AA UK. 0121 773 8157. Fax: 0121 693 5525. E-mail: info@tindalstreet.co.uk. Website: www.tindalstreet.co.uk. **Contact:** Emma Hargrave, managing editor. Estab. 1998. "Tindal Street is an independent, prize-winning publisher of strong contemporary fiction—novels and short stories—from the English regions. We are a small press—two member staff— with a commitment to author development, diversity and excellence." Publishes paperback originals. Books: perfect bound. Average print order: 1,500-2,000. **Published 5 debut authors within the last year.** Averages 6 total titles, 6 fiction titles/year. Distributes in the UK through Turnaround and in the US through Dufour.
Needs: Ethnic, feminist, literary, mainstream/contemporary, mystery (private eye/hardboiled), short story collections. Published *Birmingham Noir*, edited by Joel Land and Steve Bishop (fiction/short stories); *Astonishing Splashes of Colour*, by Clare Morrall (contemporary fiction); *What Goes Round*, by Maeve Clarke (contemporary fiction).
How to Contact: Accepts unsolicited mss. Query with SASE or submit outline/proposal, 3 sample chapter(s).

Accepts queries by e-mail. Include brief bio, list of publishing credits. Send SASE for return of ms or send a disposable ms and SASE for reply only. Agented fiction 10-30%. Responds in 1-2 weeks to queries; 3-6 months to mss. No submissions on disk. Always comments on rejected mss.
Payment/Terms: Average advance: negotiable. Publishes ms 6-18 months after acceptance. Book catalog free.
Advice: "Please check out our list of titles and judge how well your work might fit with the aims/standards/attitudes of Tindal Street Press."

TOKYOPOP, 5900 Wilshire Blvd., Suite 2000, Los Angeles CA 90036-5020. Website: www.tokyopop.com.
Needs: Manga comics and graphic novels; kid- and teen-focused books.
How to Contact: Submissions policy on website. Send submission release agreement (forms available online) with ms. Submissions are not returned.
Advice: Carefully read submissions policy before submitting work.

TORAH AURA PRODUCTIONS, 4423 Fruitland Ave., Los Angeles CA 90058. (800)238-6724. Website: www.torahaura.com. **Contact:** Jane Golub. Estab. 1982. Publishes hardcover and trade paperback originals. **Published 2% debut authors within the last year.** Averages 25 total titles/year.
Needs: Juvenile, picture books, religious, young adult. All fiction must have Jewish interest.
How to Contact: Query with SASE. Reviews artwork/photos as part of ms package. Send photocopies. Responds in 6 months to mss. Accepts simultaneous submissions.
Payment/Terms: Pays 10% royalty on wholesale price. Offers advance. Publishes ms 3 years after acceptance. Book catalog free.

TRADEWIND BOOKS, 1809 Maritime Mews, Granville Island, Vancouver BC V6H 3W7 Canada. (604)662-4405. Fax: (604)730-0153. E-mail: tradewindbooks@eudoramail.com. Website: www.tradewindbooks.com. **Contact:** Michael Katz, publisher (picture books, young adult); Carol Frank, art director (picture books); Tiffany Stone (acquisitions editor). Publishes hardcover and trade paperback originals. **Published 10% debut authors within the last year.** Averages 5 total titles/year.
Needs: Juvenile. Published *Huevos Rancheros*; *The Jade Necklace*; *Aziz: The Storyteller*.
How to Contact: Query with SASE or submit proposal package including 2 sample chapter(s), synopsis. Agented fiction 50%. Responds in 2 months to mss. Accepts simultaneous submissions.
Payment/Terms: Pays 7% royalty on retail price. Average advance: variable. Publishes ms 3 years after acceptance. Book catalog and ms guidelines online.

TREBLE HEART BOOKS, 1284 Overlook Dr., Sierra Vista AZ 85635. (520)458-5602. Fax: (520)458-5618. Website: www.trebleheartbooks.com. **Contact:** Lee Emory, publisher. Estab. 2001. Publishes trade paperback originals and reprints.(limited), and electronic originals. **Published 10-12 debut authors within the last year.** Averages 48 total titles, 40 fiction titles/year.
Needs: Adventure, fantasy, historical, horror, humor, mainstream/contemporary, mystery, occult, religious, romance, science fiction, short story collections, spiritual, suspense, western. "Follow our guidelines. Authors are encouraged to write outside of the box here, but traditional stories and plots are also accepted if handled with a fresh twist or approach." Published *Midnight Rose*, by Denise A. Agnew; *Counselor At Large*, by Lee Emory; *Jedidiah Boone*, by Dusty Rhodes.
How to Contact: Submit proposal package including 3 sample chapter(s), synopsis or submit complete ms. Query by e-mail. Hardcopy submissions are not wanted. Accepts queries by e-mail. Responds in 3 weeks to queries; 2 months to proposals; 3-4 months to mss. No simultaneous submissions.
Payment/Terms: Pays 15-35% royalty on wholesale price or retail price. Publishes ms 6-8 months after acceptance. Ms guidelines online.
Advice: "Study our guidelines before submitting."

TRICYCLE PRESS, P.O. Box 7123, Berkeley CA 94707. (510)559-1600. Website: www.tenspeed.com.
Contact: Nicole Geiger, publisher. Estab. 1993. "Tricycle Press is a children's book publisher that publishes picture books, board books, chapter books, and middle grade novels. Like its parent company Ten Speed Press, Tricycle Press has a reputation for books that are a bit outside the mainstream." Publishes hardcover and trade paperback originals. **Published 4 debut authors within the last year.** Averages 18-20 total titles, 15-17 fiction titles/year.
  ● Received a SCBWI Golden Kite Award: Best Picture Book text for *George Hagglesberry, Grade School Alien*, by Sarah Wilson, illustrated by Chad Cameron.
Needs: Children's/juvenile (adventure, historical, chapter books, mystery, preschool/picture book), preteen. Published *Oh, and Another Thing.*, by Karen Salmansohn ('tween fiction); *Edgar & Ellen: Rare Beasts*, by Charles Ogden (middle grade series); and *Truth Is a Bright Star*, by Joan Price (middle grade adventure).
How to Contact: Accepts unsolicited mss. Board books and picture books: submit complete ms. Middle grade books and other longer projects: send complete outline and 2-3 sample chapters (ages 9-14). Include brief bio, list of publishing credits, e-mail address. Send SASE for return of ms or send a disposable ms and SASE for reply only. Agented fiction 60%. Responds in 4-6 months to mss. Accepts simultaneous submissions.
Payment/Terms: Pays 15-20% royalty on net receipts. Average advance: $0-9,000. Publishes ms 1-2 years after

acceptance. Book catalog and ms guidelines for 9×12 SASE with 3 first-class stamps or visit the website; ms guidelines online.

TURNSTONE PRESS, 607-100 Arthur St., Winnipeg MB R3B 1H3 Canada. (204)947-1555. Fax: (204)942-1555. E-mail: editor@turnstonepress.mb.ca. Website: www.ravenstonebooks.com. **Contact:** Todd Besant, managing editor. Estab. 1976. "Turnstone Press is a literary press that publishes Canadian writers with an emphasis on writers from, and writing on, the Canadian west." Focuses on eclectic new writing, prairie writers, travel writing and regional mysteries. Publishes trade paperback originals, mass market for literary mystery imprint. Books: offset paper; perfect-bound. First novel print order: 1,500. **Published 5 debut authors within the last year.** Averages 10-12 total titles/year. Distributes titles through Lit DistCo (Canada and US). Promotes titles through Canadian national and local print media and select US print advertising.

● *Moon Lake* won the Margaret Laurence Award for Fiction. Published *In the Hands of the Living God*, by Lillian Bouzane was longlisted for the Dublin IMPAC Literary Prize. Published *Hoot to Kill*, by Karen Dudley was shortlisted for the Arthur Ellis Award. Turnstone Press publishes *Canadian writers only.*

Imprint(s): Ravenstone.
Needs: Literary, regional (Western Canada), short story collections, contemporary, novels. Published *Going to the Zoo*, by Laura Lush (short fiction); *Macaws of Death*, by Karen Dudley (mystery).
How to Contact: Accepts unsolicited mss. Query with SASE, literary curriculum vitae, and 50-page sample. Include list of publishing credits. Responds in 4 months to queries. No simultaneous submissions.
Payment/Terms: Pays 10% royalty on retail price. and 10 author's copies. Offers advance. Publishes ms 1 year after acceptance. Book catalog for #10 SASE; ms guidelines online.
Advice: "As a Canadian literary press, we have a mandate to publish Canadian writers only. Do some homework before submitting works to make sure your subject matter/genre/writing style falls within the publisher's area of interest."

TYRANNOSAURUS PRESS, P.O. Box 15061, New Orleans LA 70175-5061. (504)284-3313. Fax: (206)984-0448. E-mail: info@tyrannosauruspress.com. Website: www.tyrannosauruspress.com. **Contact:** Roxanne Reiken. Estab. 2002. We are an independent press specializing in speculative fiction (science fiction & fantasy). Publishes paperback originals. **Published 1 debut author within the last year.** Member, PMA. Distributes books via Baker & Taylor and other wholesalers; promotes by numerous different means.
Needs: Fantasy (space fantasy, sword and sorcery), science fiction (hard science/technological, soft/sociological).
How to Contact: Query with SASE. Accepts queries by e-mail, mail. Include estimated word count. Responds in 4-6 weeks to queries; 3-4 months to mss. Accepts simultaneous submissions. Sometimes comments on rejected mss.
Payment/Terms: Pays 10-20% royalty on net receipts. Book catalog for SASE and on website; ms guidelines online.

UCLA AMERICAN INDIAN STUDIES CENTER, 3220 Campbell Hall, Box 951548, UCLA, Los Angeles CA 90095-1548. (310)825-7315. Fax: (310)206-7060. E-mail: aiscpubs@ucla.edu. Website: www.sscnet.uc la.edu/indian/. **Contact:** Pamela Grieman. Estab. 1979. "Nonprofit publications unit at UCLA devoted to scholarship by and/or about Indian people; we produce numerous books, bibliographies, monographs, as well as the internationally recognized quarterly *American Indian Culture and Research Journal*, which contains academic articles, commentary, literature and book reviews." Publishes hardcover and trade paperback originals. Books: 60 lb. paper; perfect-bound; b&w illustrations. **Published 2 debut authors within the last year.** Averages 4 total titles, 2-3 fiction titles/year. Member, PMA, SPD, bookpeople.
Needs: Ethnic, literary, plays, poetry, religious, short story collections, American Indian. Published *Comeuppance at Kicking Horse Casino*, by Charles Brashear (short stories).
How to Contact: Accepts unsolicited mss. Submit proposal package including synopsis or submit complete ms and cover letter. Accepts queries by e-mail. Include estimated word count, brief bio. Responds in 2 months to queries; 3 months to mss. Accepts simultaneous submissions. No electronic submissions, submissions on disk.
Payment/Terms: Pays 8% royalty on retail price. Publishes ms 8-12 months after acceptance. Book catalog and ms guidelines free and on website.

UNITY HOUSE, Unity School of Christianity, 1901 NW Blue Parkway, Unity Village MO 64065-0001. (816)524-3550 ext. 3190. Fax: (816)251-3552. Website: www.unityworldhq.org. **Contact:** Michael Maday, editor. Estab. 1903. "We are a bridge between traditional Christianity and New Age spirituality. Unity School of Christianity is based on metaphysical Christian principles, spiritual values and the healing power of prayer as a resource for daily living." Publishes hardcover and trade paperback originals and reprints. **Published 4 debut authors within the last year.** Averages 16 total titles/year.
Needs: Juvenile, picture books, spiritual, young adult, visionary fiction, inspirational, metaphysical.
How to Contact: Query with SASE. Responds in 2 weeks. No simultaneous submissions.
Payment/Terms: Pays 10-15% royalty on net receipts. Offers advance. Publishes ms 13 months after acceptance. Book catalog free; ms guidelines online.

UNIVERSITY OF ALABAMA PRESS, P.O. Box 870380, Tuscaloosa AL 35487-0380. (205)348-5180. Fax: (205)348-9201. Website: www.uapress.ua.edu. **Contact:** Dan Waterman, editor. Estab. 1945. Publishes nonfiction hardcover and paperbound originals and fiction paperback reprints. Books: acid-free paper; offset printing; perfect or case bound; illustrations. Averages 55-60 total titles, 5 fiction titles/year.
Needs: Reprints of works by contemporary Southern writers.
How to Contact: Query with SASE. Agented fiction 75%. Responds in 2 weeks to queries.
Payment/Terms: Offers advance. Book catalog free; ms guidelines online.
Advice: "Please write a clear and concise letter of inquiry, describing work in a meaty paragraph."

THE UNIVERSITY OF ALBERTA PRESS, Ring House 2, Edmonton AB T6G 2E1 Canada. (780)492-3662. Fax: (780)492-0719. E-mail: u.a.p@ualberta.ca. Website: www.uap.ualberta.ca. **Contact:** Michael Luski, acquisitions editor (all). Estab. 1969. Small independent publisher. "Academic publisher with small literary program." Publishes paperback originals and reprints. Books: acid free paper; sheet fed offset printed; perfect-bound. Average print order: 1,000. **Published 1 debut author within the last year.** Averages 18-25 total titles, 2 fiction titles/year. Member, ACP, AAUP, ACUP, BPAA. Promotes titles through in-house marketing, external distributors for Canada, U.S., UK.
Needs: Ethnic, experimental, feminist, literary, short story collections. Published *Sawbones Memorial*, by Sinclair Ross, (Canadian literary novel); *Great Canadian War Stories*, by Muriel Whitaker, ed. (short stories); and *Recurring Fictions*, by Wendy McGrath, (novel).
How to Contact: Accepts unsolicited mss. Query with SASE. Include estimated word count, brief bio, list of publishing credits. Send SASE for return of ms or send a disposable ms and SASE for reply only. Agented fiction less than 5%. Responds in 3 months to queries. No simultaneous submissions, electronic submissions, submissions on disk.
Payment/Terms: Pays maximum 10% royalty on net price. Average advance: varies. Publishes ms within 2 years after acceptance. Ms guidelines online.

UNIVERSITY OF GEORGIA PRESS, 330 Research Dr., Athens GA 30602-4901. (706)369-6130. Fax: (706)369-6131. E-mail: books@ugapress.uga.edu. Website: www.ugapress.org. Estab. 1938. University of Georgia Press is a midsized press that publishes fiction *only* through the Flannery O'Connor Award for Short Fiction competition. Publishes hardcover originals, trade paperback originals and reprints. Averages 85 total titles/year.
Needs: Short story collections published in Flannery O'Connor Award Competition. Published *Break Any Woman Down*, by Dana Johnson and *The Necessary Grace to Fall*, by Gina Ochsner, both recent award winners.
How to Contact: Query #10 SASE for guidelines and submission periods. Charges $20 submission fee. "No phone calls accepted." Responds in 2 months to queries. No simultaneous submissions.
Payment/Terms: Pays 7-10% royalty on net receipts. Average advance: rare, varies. Publishes ms 1 year after acceptance. Book catalog and ms guidelines for #10 SASE; ms guidelines online.
Advice: "Do not call editors with queries or ideas. *Always* submit them in writing."

UNIVERSITY OF IOWA PRESS, 100 Kuhl House, Iowa City IA 52242-1000. (319)335-2000. Fax: (319)335-2055. Website: www.uiowapress.org. **Contact:** Holly Carver, director; Prasenjit Gupta, acquisitions editor. Estab. 1969. Publishes hardcover and paperback originals. Average print run for a first book is 1,000-1,500. Averages 35 total titles/year.
Needs: Currently publishes the Iowa Short Fiction Award selections.
How to Contact: Competition guidelines available on website. See Competition and Awards section for further information. Responds in 6 months to queries.
Payment/Terms: Pays 7-10% royalty on net receipts. Publishes ms 1 year after acceptance. Book catalog free; ms guidelines online.

UNIVERSITY OF MICHIGAN PRESS, 839 Greene St., Ann Arbor MI 48106. (734)764-4388. Fax: (734)615-1540. E-mail: ump.fiction@umich.edu. Website: www.press.umich.edu. **Contact:** Chris Hebert, editor (regional). Midsize university press. Publishes hardcover originals and paperback reprints. Member, AAUP.
Imprint(s): Sweetwater Fiction Originals (literary/regional).
Needs: Literary, short story collections.
How to Contact: Accepts unsolicited mss. Query with SASE or submit outline, 1 sample chapter(s). Accepts queries by mail. Include brief bio, list of publishing credits. Responds in 4-6 weeks to queries; 6-8 weeks to mss. Accepts simultaneous submissions. No electronic submissions, submissions on disk. Sometimes comments on rejected mss.
Payment/Terms: Ms guidelines online.
Advice: "Aside from work published through the Michigan Literary Fiction Awards, we seek only fiction set in the Great Lakes region."

UNIVERSITY OF MISSOURI PRESS, 2910 LeMone Blvd., Columbia MO 65201. (573)882-7641. Fax: (573)884-4498. Website: www.system.missouri.edu/upress. **Contact:** Clair Willcox, acquisitions editor. Estab. 1958. "Mid-size university press." Publishes hardcover and paperback originals and paperback reprints. **Published some**

debut authors within the last year. Averages 65 total titles/year. Member, AAUP. Distributes titles through direct mail, bookstores, sales reps.

Needs: Short story collections. Published *My Favorite Lies*, by Ruth Hamel (short story collection); *Boys Keep Being Born*, by Joan Frank (short story collections); *No Visible Means of Support*, by Dabney Stuart (short story collection).

How to Contact: Responds immediately to queries; 3 months to mss.

Payment/Terms: Pays up to 10% royalty on net receipts. Publishes ms within 1 year after acceptance. Book catalog free; ms guidelines online.

🅽 🖸 🔢 ◎ UNIVERSITY OF NEVADA PRESS, MS 166, Reno NV 89557. (775)784-6573. Fax: (775)784-6200. Website: www.nvbooks.nevada.edu. **Contact:** Joanne O'Hare, editor-in-chief. Estab. 1961. "Small university press. Publishes fiction that primarily focuses on the American West." Publishes hardcover and paperback originals and reprints. Averages 35 total titles, 2 fiction titles/year. Member, AAUP

• *Strange White Male*, by Gerald Haslam won the WESTAF Award for Fiction in 2000 and *ForeWord Magazine's* second place prize for Book of the Year.

Needs: "We publish in Basque Studies, Gambling Studies, Western literature and Western history."

How to Contact: Query with SASE or submit outline, 2-4 sample chapter(s), synopsis. Include estimated word count, brief bio, list of publishing credits. Send SASE or IRC. Responds in 2 months to queries. No simultaneous submissions.

Payment/Terms: Pays 10% royalty on net receipts. Publishes ms 18 months after acceptance. Book catalog and ms guidelines free; ms guidelines online.

Advice: Publishes fiction in Western American Literature series only.

🖸 ◎ UNIVERSITY OF TEXAS PRESS, P.O. Box 7819, Austin TX 78713-7819. (512)471-7233. Fax: (512)232-7178. E-mail: utpress@uts.cc.utexas.edu. Website: www.utexas.edu/utpress/. **Contact:** Theresa May, assistant director/editor-in-chief (social sciences, Latin American studies); James Burr, sponsorings editor (humanities, classics); William Bishel (sciences; Texas history). Estab. 1952. Average print order for a first book is 1,000. **Published 50% debut authors within the last year.** Averages 90 total titles/year.

Needs: Latin American and Middle Eastern fiction only in translations. Published *Whatever Happened to Dulce Veiga?*, by Caio Fernando Abreu (novel).

How to Contact: Query with SASE or submit outline, 2 sample chapter(s). Responds in 3 months to queries. No simultaneous submissions.

Payment/Terms: Pays royalty on net receipts. Publishes ms 18-24 months after acceptance. Book catalog and ms guidelines free; ms guidelines online.

Advice: "It's difficult to make a manuscript over 400 double-spaced pages into a feasible book. Authors should take special care to edit out extraneous material. Looks for sharply focused, in-depth treatments of important topics."

🅽 🖸 UNIVERSITY OF WISCONSIN PRESS, 1930 Monroe Street, 3rd Floor, Madison WI 53711. (608)263-1110. Fax: (608)263-1132. E-mail: uwiscpress@uwpress.wisc.edu. Website: www.wisc.edu/wisconsinpress. **Contact:** Raphael Kadushin, aquisition editor. Estab. 1937. Publishes hardcover originals, paperback originals and paperback reprints. **Published 5-8 debut authors within the last year.** Averages 98 total titles, 15 fiction titles/year. Member, AAUP. Distributes titles through ads, reviews, catalog, sales reps, etc.

Imprint(s): Terrace Books, Library of American Fiction, Library of World Fiction.

Needs: Gay/lesbian, historical, lesbian, mystery, regional (Wisconsin), short story collections. Published *A Friend of Kissinger*, by David Milofsky; *Beijing*, by Philip Gambone; *Latin Moon in Manhattan*, by Jaime Manrique.

How to Contact: Does not accept unsolicited mss. Query with SASE or submit outline, 1-2 sample chapter(s), synopsis. Accepts queries by e-mail, mail. Include estimated word count, brief bio. Agented fiction 40%. Responds in 2 weeks. Rarely comments on rejected mss.

Payment/Terms: Pays royalty. Publishes ms 9-18 months after acceptance. Book catalog online; ms guidelines online.

Advice: "Make sure the query letter and sample text are well written, and read guidelines carefully to make sure we accept the genre you are submitting."

🖸 ◎ UNIVERSITY PRESS OF NEW ENGLAND, 1 Court St., Suite 250, Lebanon NH 03766. (603)448-1533. Fax: (603)448-7006. E-mail: university.press@dartmouth.edu. Website: www.upne.com. **Contact:** John Landrigan, editor. Estab. 1970. Publishes hardcover originals. Averages 85 total titles, 6 fiction titles/year.

Needs: Literary. Only New England novels, literary fiction and reprints. Published *The Round Barn*, by Suzi Wizowaty; *The Private Revolution of Geoffrey Frost*, by I.E. Fender; *The Art and Practice of Explosion*, by G.F. Michelsen.

How to Contact: Query with SASE or submit sample chapter(s). Responds in 2 months to queries.

Payment/Terms: Pays standard royalty. Book catalog and ms guidelines for 9 × 12 SASE and 5 first-class stamps; ms guidelines online.

VANDAMERE PRESS, P.O. Box 17446, Clearwater FL 33762. (727)556-0950. **Contact:** Jerry Frank, senior acquistions editor. Estab. 1984. Publishes hardcover and trade paperback originals and reprints. **Published 25% debut authors within the last year.** Averages 8-15 total titles/year.
Needs: Adventure, humor, mystery, suspense. Published *Cry Me a River*, by Patricia Hagan (fiction).
How to Contact: Submit 5-10 sample chapter(s), synopsis. Responds in 6 months to queries. Accepts simultaneous submissions.
Payment/Terms: Pays on revenues generated. Offers advance. Publishes ms 1-3 years after acceptance.
Advice: "Author's who can provide endorsements from significant published writers, celebrities, etc., will *always* be given serious consideration. Clean, easy-to-read, *dark* copy is essential. Patience in waiting for replies is essential. All unsolicited work is looked at, but at certain times of the year our review schedule will stop. No response without SASE."

VÉHICULE PRESS, Box 125, Place du Parc Station, Montreal QC H2X 4A3 Canada. (514)844-6073. Fax: (514)844-7543. Website: www.vehiculepress.com. **Contact:** Simon Dardick, president/publisher. Estab. 1973. Small publisher of scholarly, literary and cultural books. Publishes trade paperback originals. Books: good quality paper; offset printing; perfect and cloth binding; illustrations. Average print order: 1,000-3,000. Averages 15 total titles/year.
   • Véhicle Press publishes *Canadian authors only.*
Imprint(s): Signal Editions (poetry) Esplanade Books (fiction).
Needs: Feminist, literary, regional, short story collections. Published *Rousseau's Garden*, by Ann Charney; and *Telling Stories: New English Stories from Quebec*, edited by Claude Lalumiere.
How to Contact: Query with SASE. Responds in 4 months to queries.
Payment/Terms: Pays 10-15% royalty on retail price. Average advance: $200-500. "Depends on press run and sales. Translators of fiction can receive Canada Council funding, which publisher applies for." Publishes ms 1 year after acceptance. Book catalog for 9×12 SAE with IRCs.
Advice: "Quality in almost any style is acceptable. We believe in the editing process."

VIA DOLOROSA PRESS, 701 E. Schaaf Rd., Cleveland OH 44131. (216)459-0896. Fax: (216)459-0896. E-mail: viadoloroaspress@aol.com. Website: www.angelfire.com/oh2/dolorosa/. **Contact:** Hyacinthe L. Raven, editor. Estab. 1994. Via Dolorosa Press is the foremost small press publisher of cathartic, existential works. Publishes mostly chapbooks, some trade paperbacks. Books: 24# paper; offset or Xerox printing: perfect or saddleback bound. Average print order 500-750. Average first novel print order: 500. Averages 2-10 total titles, 1 fiction title/year. Titles distributed by mail-order, Barnes & Noble, College Bookstores, local and independent bookstores, and via author readings. Authors must be active in promoting their work due to our small size.
Imprint(s): Nepenthe Books.
Needs: Confession, experimental, historical, literary, mainstream/contemporary, plays, poetry, poetry in translation, short story collections, philosophical. "Consider and examine our influences: Albert Camus, Par Lagerkvist, Nathanael West. If you think someone who likes those writers would like your work, then submit it." Published *The Main Squeeze*, by Jeff Johnson; *The Gorgon's Head*, by Ned Condini.
How to Contact: Accepts unsolicited mss. Query with SASE or submit outline, synopsis. Submit first and last chapter. Accepts queries by mail. Include estimated word count, brief bio, list of publishing credits. Responds in 1-2 month to queries; 1-2 month to mss. No simultaneous submissions. Sometimes comments on rejected mss.
Payment/Terms: Pays 25% royalty and 10% of first print run. Publishes ms 9 months after acceptance. Book catalog for SASE or on website; ms guidelines online.
Advice: "Our best advice is to be familiar with our work and audience: we're more *White Pony*-era Deftones than *Faith*-era Cure. Also, be sure to include a SASE for reply otherwise you won't hear back from us!"

VIKING, Penguin Putnam Inc., 375 Hudson St., New York NY 10014. (212)366-2000. **Contact:** Acquisitions Editor. Publishes a mix of literary and popular fiction and nonfiction. Publishes hardcover and originals.
Needs: Literary, mainstream/contemporary, mystery, suspense. Published *Lake Wobegon Summer 1956*, by Garrison Keillor; *A Day Late and A Dollar Short*, by Terry McMillan; *A Common Life*, by Jan Karon; *In the Heart of the Sea*, by Nathaniel Philbrick.
How to Contact: *Agented submissions only.* Responds in 6 months to queries. Accepts simultaneous submissions.
Payment/Terms: Pays 10-15% royalty on retail price. Average advance: negotiable. Publishes ms 12-18 months after acceptance.

VIKING CHILDREN'S BOOKS, A division of Penguin Young Readers Group, 345 Hudson St., New York NY 10014. (212)366-3600. Website: www.penguin.com. **Contact:** Melanie Cecka, Elizabeth Law. "Viking Children's books publishes high quality trade hardcover books for children through young adults. These include fiction, nonfiction, and novelty books." Publishes hardcover originals. **Published some debut authors within the last year.** Averages 60 total titles/year. Promotes titles through press kits, institutional ads.
Needs: Juvenile, picture books, young adult. Published *This Lullabye*, by Sarah Dessen (novel); *Joseph Had a Little Overcoat*, by Simms Taback (picture book); *Viking it and Liking it*, by Jon Scieszka (chapter book).
How to Contact: Does not accept unsolicited mss. Send SASE or IRC. Responds in 4 months to queries.

Payment/Terms: Pays 5-10% royalty on retail price. Average advance: negotiable. Publishes ms 1 year after acceptance. Does not accept unsolicited submissions.
Advice: No "cartoony" or mass-market submissions for picture books.

A **VILLARD BOOKS**, Random House, 1745 Broadway, New York NY 10019. (212)572-2600. Website: www.atr andom.com. Estab. 1983. Publishes hardcover and trade paperback originals. Averages 40-50 total titles/year.
Needs: Commercial fiction.
How to Contact: *Agented submissions only.* Agented fiction 95%. Accepts simultaneous submissions.
Payment/Terms: Pays negotiable royalty. Average advance: negotiable.

A **VINTAGE ANCHOR PUBLISHING**, The Knopf Publishing Group, A Division of Random House, Inc., 1745 Broadway, New York NY 10019. Website: www.randomhouse.com. **Contact:** Submissions editor. Publishes trade paperback originals and reprints.
Needs: Literary, mainstream/contemporary, short story collections. Published *Snow Falling on Cedars*, by David Guterson (contemporary); and *Martin Dressler*, by Steven Millhauser (literary).
How to Contact: *Agented submissions only.* Query with SASE or submit 2-3 sample chapter(s), synopsis. Responds in 6 months to queries. Accepts simultaneous submissions. No electronic submissions.
Payment/Terms: Pays 4-8% royalty on retail price. Average advance: $2,500 and up. Publishes ms 1 year after acceptance.

🌐 ☑ **VISION BOOKS PVT LTD.**, Madarsa Rd., Kashmere Gate Delhi 110006 India. (+91)11 2862267 or (+91)11 28262201. Fax: (+91)11 2862935. E-mail: orientpbk@vsnl.com. **Contact:** Sudhir Malhotra, fiction editor.
Imprint(s): Orient Paperbacks.
Needs: "We are a large multilingual publishing house publishing fiction and other trade books."
How to Contact: "A brief synopsis should be submitted initially. Subsequently, upon hearing from the editor, a typescript may be sent."
Payment/Terms: Pays royalty.

N ☻ **VIVISPHERE PUBLISHING**, Net Pub Corporation, 2 Neptune Rd., Poughkeepsie NY 12601. (845)463-1100. Fax: (845)463-0018. Website: www.vivisphere.com. **Contact:** Acquistion editor. Estab. 1995. "Small independent publisher offering historical, nature, and other nonfiction, spiritual—and a wide range of fiction including mysteries and science fiction." Publishes paperback originals and paperback reprints. Books: 60 lb. paper; soft cover binding; illustrations. **Published 10 debut authors within the last year.** Distributes titles through Baker & Taylor.
Imprint(s): Moon Dragon, Katrina Drake (fantasy/horror); Unifont, Alois Budrys (science fiction); Saddlehorn, Vivian Allison (western).
Needs: Adventure, ethnic, fantasy, feminist, gay/lesbian, historical, horror, literary, mainstream/contemporary, military/war, mystery, new age/mystic, psychic/supernatural, religious, romance, science fiction, suspense, western. Published *Infinite Darkness/Infinite Light*, by Margaret Doner (metaphysical romance); *The Condor Tales*, by Jacques Condor (Native American Horror); *Dancing Suns*; by Karen Daniels (science fiction).
How to Contact: Accepts unsolicited mss. Query with SASE. Accepts queries by e-mail. Include brief bio, list of publishing credits. Agented fiction 50%. Responds in 3 months to queries. Accepts simultaneous submissions, electronic submissions, submissions on disk. Sometimes comments on rejected mss.
Payment/Terms: Pays 10-15% royalty and 25 author's copies. Publishes ms 3-12 months after acceptance. Book catalog free; ms guidelines for free or on website.
Advice: "Read *Self-Editing for Fiction Writers*, by Renni Browne—then, if you still don't see need for a new draft, submit query and chapters."

N ☑ ◎ **VOICES FROM MY RETREAT**, P.O. Box 1077, S, Fallsburg NY 12779. (845)436-7455. E-mail: myretreat2@aol.com. Website: www.myretreat.net. **Contact:** Cora Schwartz, editor. Estab. 1999. "Small independent publisher focusing on novels and short story collections with an international slant, i.e. characters, setting, themes." Publishes paperback originals. Averages 2 total titles, 2 fiction titles/year. Voices From My Retreat is a member of Small Press (NYC) and the International Womens Writing Guild. Distributes titles through Amazon.com or direct. Promotes titles through Amazon.com, I.W.W.G. conferences and Small Press (NYC).
Needs: Ethnic (general), experimental, feminist, historical (general), humor, literary, mainstream/contemporary, short story collections, all must have an international slant. Published *American Depression Cookbook*, by Pat Carr.
How to Contact: Does not accept unsolicited mss. Submit complete ms. Include estimated word count, brief bio. Send SASE for return of ms or send a disposable ms and SASE for reply only. Responds in 2 months to mss. Accepts simultaneous submissions. Sometimes comments on rejected mss.

Payment/Terms: Pays 10% royalty. Publishes ms 6 months after acceptance.
Advice: "Be gut level honest. We are not interested in fiction in which the author uses a point of view of the opposite sex or of a race, class, or nationality which he/she is not. We are looking for both experience and authenticity."

WALKER AND CO., Walker Publishing Co., 435 Hudson St., New York NY 10014. Fax: (212)727-0984. Website: www.walkeryoungreaders.com. **Contact:** Submissions Editor-Juvenile. Estab. 1959. Midsize independent publisher. Publishes hardcover trade originals. Average first novel print order: 2,500-3,500. Averages 25 total titles/year.
Needs: Juvenile (fiction, nonfiction), picture books (juvenile). Published *All's Fair in Love, War, and High School*, by Janette Rallison; *Flying Blind*, by Anna Myers; *Fifteen Love*, by Robert Corbert.
How to Contact: Does not accept unsolicited mss. Query with SASE. Include "a concise description of the story line, including its outcome, word length of story (we prefer 50,000 words maximum), writing experience, publishing credits, particular expertise on this subject and in this genre. Common mistakes: sounding unprofessional (i.e. too chatty, too braggardly), forgetting SASE." Agented fiction 50%. Responds in 3 months to queries. No simultaneous submissions. Sometimes comments on rejected mss.
Payment/Terms: Pays 6% on paperback, 10% on hardcover. Average advance: competitive. Publishes ms 1 year after acceptance. Book catalog for 9 × 12 SAE with 3 first-class stamps.

WALTSAN PUBLISHING, LLC, 5000 Barnett St., Fort Worth TX 76103-2006. (817)429-2512. E-mail: sandra@waltsan.com. Website: www.waltsan.com. **Published 95% debut authors within the last year.** Averages 40-60 total titles/year.
Needs: "We look at all fiction." Full-length or collections equal to full-length only. 50,000 word minimum. Published *The Returning*, by John Potter.
How to Contact: Query with SASE or submit proposal package including 3 sample chapter(s), synopsis or submit complete ms. Agented fiction 5%. Responds in 2 months to queries; 2 months to proposals; 4-6 months to mss. Accepts simultaneous submissions.
Payment/Terms: Pays 20% royalty on wholesale price. Publishes ms 9-18 months after acceptance. Book catalog online; ms guidelines online.
Advice: Audience is computer literate, generally higher income and intelligent. "When possible, authors record their manuscripts to include audio on the CD. Check our website for guidelines and sample contract." Only publishes CDs and other removable media.

WARNER BOOKS, Time & Life Building, 1271 Avenue of the Americas, New York NY 10020. (212)522-7200. Fax: (212)522-7993. Website: www.twbookmark.com. **Contact:** (Ms.) Jamie Raab, senior vice president/publisher (general nonfiction and fiction); Les Pockell, associate publisher (general nonfiction); Rick Horgan, vice president/executive editor (general nonfiction and fiction, thrillers); Amy Einhorn, editorial director, trade paperback (popular culture, business, fitness, self-help); Beth de Guzman, editorial director, mass market (fiction, romance, nonfiction); Rick Wolff, vice president/executive editor (business, humor, sports); Caryn Karmatz Rudy, senior editor (fiction, general nonfiction, popular culture); Diana Baroni, executive editor (health, fitness, general nonfiction and fiction); John Aherne, editor (popular culture, men's health, New Age, movie tie-ins, general fiction); Rolf Zettersten, vice president/Warner Faith (books for the CBA market); (Ms.) Jaime Levine, editor/Aspect (science fiction); Karen Koszto Inyik, senior editor (women's fiction). Estab. 1960. Warner publishes general interest fiction. Publishes hardcover, trade paperback and mass market paperback originals and reprints and e-books. Averages 250 total titles/year.
Imprint(s): Mysterious Press, Warner Aspect, Warner Faith, Walk Worthy, iPublish.
Needs: Fantasy, horror, mainstream/contemporary, mystery, romance, science fiction, suspense, thriller/espionage. Published *Up Country*, by Nelson DeMille; and *A Bend in the Road*, by Nicholas Sparks.
How to Contact: *Agented submissions only. No unsolicited mss.*
Payment/Terms: Pays variable royalty. Average advance: varies. Publishes ms 2 years after acceptance.

WATERBROOK PRESS, Subsidiary of Random House, 2375 Telstar Dr., Suite 160, Colorado Springs CO 80920. (719)590-4999. Fax: (719)590-8977. Website: www.waterbrookpress.com. **Contact:** Dudley Delffs, editor. Estab. 1996. Publishes hardcover and trade paperback originals. Averages 70 total titles/year.
Needs: Adventure, historical, literary, mainstream/contemporary, mystery, religious (inspirational, religious mystery/suspense, religious thriller, religious romance), romance (contemporary, historical), science fiction, spiritual, suspense. Published *A Name of Her Own*, by Jane Kirkpatrick (historical); *Women's Intuition*, by Lisa Samson (contemporary); *Thorn in My Heart*, by Liz Curtis Higgs (historical).

VISIT THE WRITER'S MARKET WEBSITE at www.writersmarket.com for hot new markets, daily market updates, writers' guidelines and much more.

How to Contact: Does not accept unsolicited mss. *Agented submissions only.* Responds in 1-2 months to queries; 1-2 months to proposals. Accepts simultaneous submissions, electronic submissions.
Payment/Terms: Pays royalty. Publishes ms 11 months after acceptance. Book catalog online.

WHITE MANE BOOKS, White Mane Publishing Company Inc., 63 W. Burd St., P.O. Box 708, Shippensburg PA 17257. (717)532-2237. Fax: (717)532-6110. E-mail: editorial@whitemane.com. Website: www.whitemane.com. **Contact:** Harold Collier, vice president. Estab. 1987. Publishes hardcover, and trade paperback originals and reprints. **Published 50% debut authors within the last year.** Averages 60 total titles/year.
Imprint(s): Burd Street Press (military history, emphasis on American Civil War, adult nonfiction); Ragged Edge Press (religious, adult nonfiction); White Mane Kids (historically based children's fiction).
Needs: Historical, juvenile (middle grade), young adult. Published *Slaves Who Dared: The Stories of Ten African American Heroes*, by Mary Garrison.
How to Contact: Query with SASE. Agented fiction 25%. Responds in 1 month. Accepts simultaneous submissions.
Payment/Terms: Pays royalty on monies received. Offers advance. Publishes ms 18 months after acceptance. Book catalog and ms guidelines free for SASE.

N ☑ ◎ WHITE WOLF, 1554 Litton Drive, Stone Mountain GA 30083. (404)292-1819. Fax: (678)382-3883. E-mail: prboulle@white-wolf.com. Website: www.white-wolf.com/fiction. **Contact:** Philippe Boulle, managing editor. Estab. 1991. Midsize independent publisher of paperback originals that tie in to media properties developed by the publisher. Publishes some creator-owned material, but only based on established relationships. Publishes paperback originals. **Published 4-5 debut authors within the last year.** Distributes titles through Ingram, Borders and specialty distributors in the game market.
Imprint(s): World of Darkness; Exalted; Sword and Sorcery; Borealis.
Needs: Fantasy, horror, science fiction. Editor sends call for submissions to writers in his pool of candidates to create an anthology. Published *Demon: Ashes of Angels Wings*, by Greg Stolze (dark fantasy); *Darkest Heart*, by Nancy A. Collins (horror); *Vampire: Sacrifice*, by Bruce Bough (dark fantasy). Series based on *Vampire: The Masquerade*.
How to Contact: Does not accept unsolicited mss. Query with SASE. Accepts queries by e-mail, mail. Include estimated word count, brief bio, list of publishing credits. Agented fiction 5%. Responds in 2 months to queries. Accepts electronic submissions. Rarely comments on rejected mss.
Payment/Terms: Pays 3-7% royalty. Pay depends on grants/awards. Average advance: 3,500. Publishes ms 6-12 months after acceptance. Book catalog online; ms guidelines for SASE or on website.
Advice: "Become familiar with our properties."

◎ ALBERT WHITMAN AND CO., 6340 Oakton St., Morton Grove IL 60053-2723. (847)581-0033. Website: www.albertwhitman.com. **Contact:** Kathleen Tucker, editor-in-chief. Estab. 1919. Albert Whitman publishes good books for children on a variety of topics: holidays (i.e., Halloween), special needs (such as diabetes) and problems like divorce. Publishes hardcover originals and paperback reprints. Averages 30 total titles/year.
Needs: Adventure, children's/juvenile, ethnic, fantasy, historical, humor, mystery, holiday, concept books (to help children deal with problems), family. Currently emphasizing picture books; de-emphasizing folk tales and bedtime stories.
How to Contact: Submit complete ms for picture books; for longer works submit query with outline and sample chapters. Agented fiction 30%. Responds in 6 weeks to queries; 3-4 months to mss. Accepts simultaneous submissions.
Payment/Terms: Pays 10% royalty for novels; 5% for picture books. Offers advance. Publishes ms an average of 18 months after acceptance. Book catalog for 8×10 SAE with 3 first-class stamps; ms guidelines for #10 SASE.

◉ WILDSIDE PRESS, P.O. Box 301, Holicong PA 18928-0301. E-mail: wildsidepress@yahoo.com. **Contact:** John Betancourt, publisher (all). Estab. 1989. "Wildside Press is a small press specializing in science fiction/fantasy, horror/mystery fiction and nonfiction." Publishes hardcover and paperback originals and hardcover and paperback reprints. Books: 60 lb. paper; varied printing; hardcover and trade paperback binding. Distributes titles through Ingram, Baker & Taylor, NASCORP, catalog.
Needs: Fantasy (space fantasy, sword and sorcery), horror (dark fantasy, supernatural), mystery (amateur sleuth, cozy, police procedural, private eye/hardboiled), science fiction (hard science/technological, soft/sociological). Seeking to "reprint early novels by well-established current authors." Published *The Misenchanted Sword*, by Lawrence Watt-Evans (fantasy); *The Mark of Merlin*, by Anne McCaffrey (suspense); and *The Branch*, by Mike Resnick (science fiction).
How to Contact: Does not accept unsolicited mss. Accepts queries by e-mail. Include estimated word count, brief bio, list of publishing credits. Agented fiction 30%. Responds in 1 week to queries. Accepts electronic submissions, submissions on disk.
Payment/Terms: Pays 3-8% royalty. Publishes ms 1 year after acceptance. Ms guidelines online.
Advice: "Query via e-mail first. Don't waste our time—we really are looking for new and reprint work from well-established authors only. *No exceptions.*"

WILLOWGATE PRESS, P.O. Box 6529, Holliston MA 01746. (508)429-8774. E-mail: willowgatepress@yahoo. com. Website: www.willowgatepress.com. **Contact:** Robert Tolins, editor. Publishes trade paperback and mass market paperback originals. **Published 50% debut authors within the last year.** Averages 3-5 total titles/year.

Needs: Fantasy, gothic, historical, horror, humor, literary, mainstream/contemporary, military/war, mystery, occult, regional, science fiction, short story collections, sports. "We are not interested in children's, erotica, or experimental."

How to Contact: Query with SASE or submit outline, plus the first 10 pages and 10 pages of the author's choosing. Do not send cash or check in lieu of stamps for return postage. "Please note, we will be closed to submissions at least through the remainder of 2003. Check the website for details." Responds in 2 months. Accepts simultaneous submissions.

Payment/Terms: Pays 5-15% royalty on retail price. Average advance: $500. Publishes ms 6 months after acceptance. Book catalog and ms guidelines online; ms guidelines online.

Advice: "If a manuscript is accepted for publication, we will make every effort to avoid lengthy delays in bringing the product to market. The writer will be given a voice in all aspects of publishing, promotion, advertising and marketing, including cover art, copy, promotional forums, etc. The writer will be expected to be an active and enthusiastic participant in all stages of the publication process. We hope to attract the finest writers of contemporary fiction and to help generate similar enthusiasm in them and in their readers. Please don't send cash or a check in lieu of stamps for return postage."

◎ **WILSHIRE BOOK CO.**, 12015 Sherman Rd., North Hollywood CA 91605-3781. (818)765-8579. Fax: (818)765-2922. E-mail: mpowers@mpowers.com. Website: www.mpowers.com. **Contact:** Melvin Powers, publisher; Marcia Powers, senior editor (adult fables). Estab. 1947. "You are not only what you are today, but also what you choose to become tomorrow." Looking for adult fables that teach principles of psychological growth. Publishes trade paperback originals and reprints. **Published 7 debut authors within the last year.** Averages 25 total titles/year. Distributes titles through wholesalers, bookstores and mail order. Promotes titles through author interviews on radio and television.

Needs: Adult allegories that teach principles of psychological growth or offer guidance in living. Minimum 25,000 words. Published *The Princess Who Believed in Fairy Tales*, by Marcia Grad; *The King in Rusty Armor*, by Robert Fisher.

How to Contact: Accepts unsolicited mss. Query with SASE or submit 3 sample chapter(s), synopsis or submit complete ms. Accepts queries by e-mail. Responds in 2 months to queries. Accepts simultaneous submissions.

Payment/Terms: Pays standard royalty. Offers advance. Publishes ms 6 months after acceptance. Ms guidelines online.

Advice: "We are vitally interested in all new material we receive. Just as you hopefully submit your manuscript for publication, we hopefully read every one submitted, searching for those that we believe will be successful in the marketplace. Writing and publishing must be a team effort. We need you to write what we can sell. We suggest that you read the successful books mentioned above or others that are similar: *Greatest Salesman in the World*, *Illusions*, *Way of the Peaceful Warrior*, *Celestine Prophecy*. Analyze them to discover what elements make them winners. Duplicate those elements in your own style, using a creative new approach and fresh material, and you will have written a book we can successfully market."

◖ **WIND RIVER PRESS**, E-mail: submissions@windriverpress.com. Website: www.windriverpress.com. **Contact:** Katherine Arline, editor (mainstream, travel, literary, historical, short story collections, translations). Estab. 2002. Publishes full and chapbook length paperback originals and reprints and electronic books. Distributes and promotes titles through Ingram, Baker & Taylor, Bowkers, Amazon.com, US and international book reviews. "Wind River Press works closely with the author to develop a cost-effective production, promotion and distribution strategy."

Needs: Historical, literary, mainstream/contemporary, short story collections. Plans anthology of works selected from Wind River Press's magazines (*Critique* and *The Paumanok Review*). Published books by Elisha Parat, Gaither Stewart and Rochelle Mass.

How to Contact: Accepts unsolicited mss. Send submission by e-mail unless previously instructed otherwise. Accepts queries by e-mail. Include estimated word count, brief bio, list of publishing credits. Agented fiction 5%. Responds in 3 weeks to queries; 2 months to mss. Accepts simultaneous submissions. Always comments on rejected mss.

Payment/Terms: Publishes ms 6 months after acceptance. Guidelines and book catalog available on website.

◖ **WINDSTORM CREATIVE, LTD**, 7419 Ebbert Dr. SE, Port Orchard WA 98367. Website: www.windstormcreative.com. **Contact:** (Ms.) Cris Newport, senior editor. Estab. 1989. Publishes trade paperback originals and reprints. **Published some debut authors within the last year.** Averages 50 total titles/year.

Needs: Adventure, erotica, experimental, fantasy, gay/lesbian, gothic, historical, humor, literary, science fiction, young adult, contemporary, bisexual. Published *Bones Become Flowers*, by Jess Mowry (contemporary fiction); *Annabel and I*, by Chris Anne Wolfe (lesbian fiction); *Journey of a Thousand Miles*, by Peter Kasting (gay fiction); *Puzzle from the Past*, by Mike and Janet Golio (young adult).

How to Contact: "You must download a submission label and form from the website. If submissions arrive

without label, they will be destroyed." Responds in 6 months to mss. Accepts simultaneous submissions.
Payment/Terms: Pays 10-15% royalty on wholesale price. Publishes ms 1-2 years after acceptance. Ms guidelines online.
Advice: "Go to the website."

◎ **WIZARDS OF THE COAST**, P.O. Box 707, Renton WA 98057-0707. (425)226-6500. Website: www.wizards .com. **Contact:** Peter Archer, editorial director. "We publish share-world fiction set in the worlds of Dungeons & Dragons, Magic: The Gathering, and Legend of the Five Rings." Publishes hardcover and trade paperback originals and trade paperback reprints. Wizard of the Coast publishes games as well, including Dungeons & Dragons role-playing game. Books: standard paperbacks; offset printing; perfect binding; b&w (usually) illustrations. Averages 50-60 total titles/year. Distributes titles through Holtzbrinck Publishing.
Imprint(s): Dragonlance Books; Forgotten Realms Books; Magic: The Gathering Books; Legend of the Five Rings Novels; D & D Novels.
Needs: Fantasy, short story collections. "We currently publish only work-for-hire novels set in our trademarked worlds. No violent or gory fantasy or science fiction." Published *Dragons of a Vanished Moon*, by Margaret Weis and Tracy Hickman (fantasy); *The Thousand Orcs*, by R.A. Salvatore (fantasy); *Condemnation*, by Richard Baker; and *Apocalypse*, by J. Robert King (fantasy).
How to Contact: Request guidelines, then query with outline/synopsis and a 10-page writing sample. Agented fiction 65%. Responds in 4 months to queries. Accepts simultaneous submissions.
Payment/Terms: Pays 4-8% royalty on retail price. Average advance: $4,000-6,000. Publishes ms 1 year after acceptance. Ms guidelines for #10 SASE.

🌐 ◎ **THE WOMEN'S PRESS**, 27, Goodge St., London England W1T 2LD. Website: www.the-womens-press.c om. **Contact:** Editorial Dept.
Needs: "Women's fiction, written by women and centered on women. Theme can be anything—all themes may be women's concern—but we look for polictical/feminist awareness, originality, wit, fiction of ideas. Includes literary fiction, crime, and teenage list *Livewire*."
Payment/Terms: Writers receive royalty, including advance.
Advice: Writers should ask themselves, "Is this a manuscript that would interest a feminist/political press? What makes the work unique? What are its selling points? Who would want to read it? Is it double-spaced and on one side of the paper only? Have I enclosed return postage?"

◎ **WOODLEY MEMORIAL PRESS**, English Dept., Washburn University, Topeka KS 66621. (785)234-1032. E-mail: amy.fleury@washburn.edu. Website: www.washburn.edu/reference/woodley-press. **Contact:** Amy Fleury, corresponding editor. Estab. 1980. "Woodley Memorial Press is a small, nonprofit press which publishes book-length poetry and fiction collections by Kansas writers only; by 'Kansas writers' we mean writers who reside in Kansas or have a Kansas connection." Publishes paperback originals.
Needs: Experimental, literary, mainstream/contemporary, short story collections. Published *Gathering Reunion*, by David Tangeman (stories and poetry); *The Monday, Wednesday, Friday Girl*, by Stuart Levine (short stories); and *Rudolph, Encouraged by His Therapist*, by Eugene Bales (satiric stories).
How to Contact: Kansas authors should query before sending ms. Submit complete ms with cover letter, if requested. Accepts queries by e-mail. Responds in 2 weeks to queries; 2 months to mss. Often comments on rejected mss.
Payment/Terms: Publishes ms 1 year after acceptance. Ms guidelines online.
Advice: "We only publish one work of fiction a year, on average, and definitely want it to be by a Kansas author. We are more likely to do a collection of short stories by a single author."

📭 ◎ **WORLDWIDE LIBRARY**, Division of Harlequin Books, 225 Duncan Mill Rd., Don Mills ON M2B 3K9 Canada. (416)445-5860. **Contact:** Feroze Mohammed, senior editor/editorial coordinator. Estab. 1979. Large commercial category line. Publishes paperback originals and reprints. "Mystery program is reprint; no originals please."
Imprint(s): Worldwide Mystery; Gold Eagle Books.
Needs: "Action-adventure series and future fiction."
How to Contact: Send SASE or IRC. Responds in 10 weeks to queries. Accepts simultaneous submissions.
Payment/Terms: Advance and sometimes royalties; copyright buyout. Publishes ms 1-2 years after acceptance.
Advice: "Publishing fiction in very selective areas."

◎ **WRITERS DIRECT**, Imprint of Titlewaves Publishing, Book Division of H&S Publishing LLC, 1351 Kuhio Highway, Kapaa HI 96746. (808)822-7449. Fax: (808)822-2312. E-mail: rinfo@hshawaii.com. Website: www.bestpl acesonearth.com. **Contact:** Rob Sanford, editor. Estab. 1985. "Small independent publishing house founded and run by published authors." Publishes hardcover and paperback originals and reprints. Books: recycled paper; digital printing; perfect binding; illustrations.
Needs: Adventure, humor, literary, mainstream/contemporary, New Age/mystic, regional (Hawaii), religious (children's religious, inspirational, religious mystery/suspense, religious thriller), thriller/espionage.

How to Contact: Accepts unsolicited mss. Query with first chapter *only*. Include estimated word count, why author wrote book and marketing plan. Send SASE for return of ms or send a disposable ms and SASE for reply only. Responds in 1 month to queries; 3 months to mss. Accepts simultaneous submissions. Sometimes comments on rejected mss.
Payment/Terms: Pays 15-35% royalty. Book catalog for legal-size SASE.
Advice: "Do what you do best and enjoy most. Your writing is an outcome of the above."

N ⊕ ◘ THE XPRESS, P.O. Box 256 94, London N17 6FP UK. 020 8801 2100. Fax: 020 8885 1322. E-mail: vibes@xpress.co.uk. Website: www.xpress.co.uk. Estab. 1991. "We are a small publisher devoted to publishing largely Black-interest contemporary fiction. Additional imprints publish classic Black literature, literary fiction, cutting edge writing by all writers not limited to Black writing, and a range of young adult titles. We are Britain's largest Black-interest publisher and have provided a forum for beginning writers of all ethnicites." Publishes paperback originals. Average print order: 2,000-5,000. First novel print order: 5,000. **Published 3 debut authors within the last year.**
Imprint(s): Drummond Hill (children's/young adult fiction); Black Classics (fiction/literary classic); Nia (fiction/literary); 20/20 (general fiction).
Needs: Children's/juvenile (adventure), erotica, ethnic, experimental, mystery (police procedural), romance (contemporary), science fiction (soft/sociological), young adult (adventure, mystery, problem novels, series). "We are looking for Black-interest contemporary fiction and erotica, and cutting edge general fiction by published writers. Publishes *Westside Storeys* anthology. Published *All Women*, by Ray Anthony (contemporary fiction); *Days of Dread*, by Anton Marks (contemporary science fiction).
How to Contact: Accepts unsolicited mss. Query with SASE. Accepts queries by mail. Include brief bio, list of publishing credits. Agented fiction 50%. Responds in 4 weeks to queries; 8 weeks to mss. Accepts simultaneous submissions, electronic submissions. Sometimes comments on rejected mss.
Payment/Terms: Average advance: $500-1,000. Advance is negotiable. Publishes ms one year after acceptance. Book catalog free; ms guidelines for SASE.
Advice: "Please do not send your ms prematurely. Have it proofread and critiqued prior to sending it to us. We receive many mss that are sloppy and not yet ready for submission."

◼ ◘ YORK PRESS, LTD., 152 Boardwalk Dr., Toronto ON M4L 3X4 Canada. (416)690-3788. Fax: (416)690-3797. E-mail: yorkpress@sympatico.ca. Website: www3.sympatico.ca/yorkpress. **Contact:** Dr. S. Elkhadem, general manager/editor. Estab. 1975. "We publish scholarly books and creative writing of an experimental nature." Publishes trade paperback originals. **Published some debut authors within the last year.** Averages 10 total titles/year.
Needs: Experimental. "Fiction of an experimental nature by well-established writers." Published *The Moonhare*, by Kirk Hampton (experimental novel).
How to Contact: Query with SASE. Responds in 2 weeks to queries. No simultaneous submissions.
Payment/Terms: Pays 10-20% royalty on wholesale price. Offers advance. Publishes ms 6 months after acceptance.

◎ ZEBRA BOOKS, Kensington, 850 Third Ave., 16th Floor, New York NY 10022. (212)407-1500. Website: www.kensingtonbooks.com. **Contact:** Michaela Hamilton, editor-in-chief; Ann La Farge, executive editor; Kate Duffy, editorial director (romance); John Scognamiglio, editorial director; Karen Thomas, editorial director; Bruce Bender, managing director (Citadel); Margaret Wolf, editor; Richard Ember, editor; Bob Shuman, senior editor; Jeremie Ruby-Strauss, senior editor; Miles Lott, editor. Publishes hardcover originals, trade paperback and mass market paperback originals and reprints. Averages 600 total titles/year.
Needs: Zebra books is dedicated to women's fiction, which includes, but is not limited to romance.
How to Contact: Submit sample chapter(s), synopsis, SASE. Please no queries. Accepts simultaneous submissions.
Payment/Terms: Publishes ms 12-18 months after acceptance. Book catalog online.

◖ ◎ ZONDERVAN, HarperCollins Publishers, 5300 Patterson Ave. SE, Grand Rapids MI 49530-0002. (616)698-6900. Fax: (616)698-3454. Website: www.zondervan.com. **Contact:** Manuscript Review Editor. Estab. 1931. "Our mission is to be the leading Christian communication company meeting the needs of people with resources that glorify Jesus Christ and promote biblical principles." Large evangelical Christian publishing house. Publishes hardcover and trade paperback originals and reprints. First novel print order: 5,000. **Published some debut authors within the last year.** Averages 120 total titles, 15-20 fiction titles/year.
Needs: Some adult fiction (mainstream, biblical). "Inklings-style" fiction of high literary quality. Christian relevance in all cases. Will *not* consider collections of short stories. Published *Jacob's Way*, by Gilbert Morris; *The Prodigy*, by Alton Gansky; and *Times and Seasons*, by Terri Blackstock and Bev Lahaye.
How to Contact: Query with SASE or submit outline,21 sample chapter(s), synopsis. Responds in 2 months.
Payment/Terms: Pays 14% royalty on net amount received on sales of cloth and softcover trade editions; 12% royalty on net amount received on sales of mass market paperbacks. Average advance: varies. Ms guidelines online.
Advice: "Almost no unsolicited fiction is published. Send plot outline and one or two sample chapters. Editors will *not* read entire manuscripts. Your sample chapters will make or break you."

Contests & Awards

In addition to honors and, quite often, cash prizes, contests and awards programs offer writers the opportunity to be judged on the basis of quality alone without the outside factors that sometimes influence publishing decisions. New writers who win contests may be published for the first time, while more experienced writers may gain public recognition of an entire body of work.

Listed here are contests for almost every type of fiction writing. Some focus on form, such as short stories, novels or novellas, while others feature writing on particular themes or topics. Still others are prestigious prizes or awards for work that must be nominated, such as the Pulitzer Prize in Fiction. Chances are no matter what type of fiction you write, there is a contest or award program that may interest you.

SELECTING AND SUBMITTING TO A CONTEST

Use the same care in submitting to contests as you would sending your manuscript to a publication or book publisher. Deadlines are very important, and where possible, we've included this information. At times contest deadlines were only approximate at our press deadline, so be sure to write or call for complete information. To locate a contest based on its monthly deadline, turn to the Contest Index by Deadline at the back of this book.

Follow the rules to the letter. If, for instance, contest rules require your name on a cover sheet only, you will be disqualified if you ignore this and put your name on every page. Find out how many copies to send. If you don't send the correct amount, by the time you are contacted to send more, it may be past the submission deadline. An increasing number of contests invite writers to query by e-mail, and many post contest information on their websites. Check listings for e-mail and website addresses.

One note of caution: Beware of contests that charge entry fees that are disproportionate to the amount of the prize. Contests offering a $10 prize, but charging $7 in entry fees, are a waste of your time and money.

If you are interested in a contest or award that requires your publisher to nominate your work, it's acceptable to make your interest known. Be sure to leave the publisher plenty of time, however, to make the nomination deadline.

AIM MAGAZINE'S SHORT STORY CONTEST, AIM Magazine, P.O. Box 1174, Maywood IL 60153. (708)344-4414. Website: www.aimmagazine.org. **Contact:** Ruth Apilado, associate editor. This annual award is for short stories that embody our goals of furthering the brotherhood of man by way of the written word. Award: $100 and publication. Competition receives 20 submissions per category. Judge: Staff members. No entry fee. Guidelines available anytime. Accepts inquiries by phone. Entries should be unpublished. Contest open to everyone. Length: 4,000 word or less. Results announced in the autumn issue. Winners notified by mail on Sept 1. For contest results, send SASE.

Ⓝ AKC GAZETTE EIGHTEENTH ANNUAL FICTION CONTEST, 260 Madison Ave., New York NY 10016. (212)696-8333. Features Editor: Josh Adams. Annual contest for short stories under 2,000 words. Award: Prizes of $350, $250 and $150 for top three entries. Top entry published in magazine. Judges: Panel. Contest requirements available for SASE. "The *Gazette* sponsors an annual fiction contest for short short stories on some subject relating to purebred dogs. Fiction for our magazine needs a slant toward the serious fancier with real insight into the human/dog bond and breed-specific purebred behavior." Deadline: September 30. Results announced in May. Winners notified by phone and mail. For contest results, send SASE.

ALABAMA STATE COUNCIL ON THE ARTS INDIVIDUAL ARTIST FELLOWSHIP, 201 Monroe St., Montgomery AL 36130-1800. (205)242-4076, ext. 224. Fax: (334)240-3269. E-mail: randy@arts.state.al.us. Website: www.arts.state.al.us. **Contact:** Randy Shoults, Literature program manager. "To recognize the achievements and potential of Alabama writers." Annual. Competition receives 25 submissions annually. Judge: independent peer panel. No entry fee. Guidelines available January 2004. For guidelines, fax, e-mail, visit website. Accepts inquiries by fax, e-mail and phone. Deadline: March 1, 2004. "Two copies of the following should be submitted: a resume and a list of published works with reviews, if available. A minimum of 10 pages of poetry or prose, but no more than 20 pages. Please label each page with title, artist's name and date. If published, indicate where and the date of publication." Results announced in June. Winners notified by mail. For contest results, send SASE, fax, e-mail or visit website.

[N] NELSON ALGREN SHORT FICTION CONTEST, *Chicago Tribune*, 435 N. Michigan Ave., LL2, Chicago IL 60611. E-mail: akostovski@tribune.com. Website: www.chicagotribune.com/extras/writtenword. **Contact:** Aleksandra Kostovski, events producer. "Honors excellence in short story writing by previously unpublished authors." Annual. Competition for short stories. Award: $5,000 grand prize, $1,500 runners-up prizes (3). Judged by a group of *Chicago Tribune* editors and contributors. No entry fee. Guidelines available by SASE, e-mail, on website. Accepts inquiries by e-mail, phone. Deadline: February 28, 2004. Entries should be unpublished. Cover letter should include name, address, phone, e-mail, word count, title. "No info on manuscript besides title and page numbers." Results announced October 2004. Winners notified by mail or phone in September. For contest results, visit website or in the *Chicago Tribune*.

[N] [] [©] ALLIGATOR JUNIPER NATIONAL WRITING CONTEST, Alligator Juniper/Prescott College, 301 Grove Ave., Prescott AZ 86301. (928)350-2012. Fax: (928)776-5137. E-mail: aj@prescott.edu. Website: www.prescott.edu/highlights/aj.html. **Contact:** Miles Waggener, managing editor. Annual competition for fiction, creative nonfiction, poetry. "We aim to publish the highest quality fiction, nonfiction and poetry." Award: $500 plus publication for 1st place in each category. Non-winners chosen for publication paid in copies. Prize categories include poetry, short story, nonfiction; receives 250 entries per category. Fiction is judged by editors and staff of *Alligator Juniper*. Entry fee $10 for each story up to 30 pages. Additional entries require additional fee. All entrants receive the next issue, a $7.50 value. Guidelines available in May for SASE, by e-mail or on website. Also accepts inquiries by e-mail, phone. Cover letter should include name, address, phone, e-mail, word count and title. "Please include this information on the manuscript." Postmark deadline: October 1. Results announced in January. Winners notified by phone. List of contest results mailed to all entrants. "Editors select work that is original, graceful, skillful, authentic, moving and memorable."

[©] AMERICAN ASSOCIATION OF UNIVERSITY WOMEN AWARD IN JUVENILE LITERATURE, AAUW, North Carolina Chapter, and North Carolina Literary and Historical Association, 4610 Mail Service Center, Raleigh NC 27699-4610. (919)733-9375. Fax: (919)733-8807. E-mail: michael.hill@ncmail.net. **Contact:** Michael Hill, awards coordinator. Award's purpose is to "select the year's best work of literature for young people by a North Carolina writer." Annual award for published books. Award: cup. Competition receives 10-15 submissions per category. Judge: three-judge panel. No entry fee. Guidelines available in August. For guidelines, send SASE, fax, e-mail or call. Accepts inquiries by fax, e-mail, phone. Annual deadline: July 15. Entries should be previously published. Contest open to "recipients of North Carolina (three year minimum)." Results announced October 15. Winners notified by mail. For contest results, send SASE, fax, e-mail.

[N] AMERICAN LITERARY REVIEW SHORT FICTION AWARD, American Literary Review, Dept. of English, Univ. of North Texas, P.O. Box 311307, Denton TX 76203-1307. (940)565-2755. Fax: (940)565-4355. Website: www.engl.unt.edu/alr. **Contact:** John Tait, fiction editor. "This biannual award for short stories is meant to award excellence in short fiction." Award: $1,000 and publication. Competition receives 400 submissions per category. Finalists sent to outside judge. Past judges have included Marly Swick, Antonya Nelson and James Agee. Entry fee $10/story. Guidelines are currently available. For guidelines, send SASE or visit website. Accepts inquiries by fax and phone. Deadline: October 1, 2003. Entries should be unpublished. Contest open to anyone not affiliated with the University of North Texas. "Only solidly crafted, character-driven stories will have the best chance for success." Winners are announced February 1 and notified by mail and phone on February 1. List of winners available for SASE.

SHERWOOD ANDERSON WRITER'S GRANT, Sherwood Anderson Foundation, 216 College Rd., Richmond VA 23229. (804)282-8008. Fax: (804)287-6052. E-mail: mspear@richmond.edu. Website: www.richmond.edu/~journalm/comp.html. **Contact:** Michael M. Spear, foundation co-president. Award to "honor, preserve, and celebrate the memory and literary work of Sherwood Anderson, American realist of the first half of the twentieth century." Annual award for short stories and chapters of novels. Award: range $5,000 to $10,000. Entries are judged

MARKET CONDITIONS are constantly changing! If you're still using this book and it is 2005 or later, buy the newest edition of *Novel & Short Story Writer's Market* at your favorite bookstore or order from Writer's Digest Books by calling 1-800-448-0915.

by a committee established by the foundation. See website for entry mail address; varies from year to year. $20 fee per entry; make checks payable to The Sherwood Anderson Foundation. Guidelines available on website. Accepts inquiries by e-mail. Annual deadline: April 1. "To apply, you should have published at least one book of fiction or have had several short stories published in major literary and/or commercial publications. There is no form to complete, but send a detailed résumé that provides a bibliography of your publications. Include a cover letter that provides a history of your writing experience and your future plans for writing projects. Also, submit two or three examples of what you consider to be your best work." The contest is open to all struggling writers in the United States. No word length specifications. "Send in your best, most vivid prose that clearly shows talent." Results announced in mid-summer each year. Winners notified by phone. For contest results, visit website.

N ANISFIELD-WOLF BOOK AWARDS, The Cleveland Foundation, 1422 Euclid Ave., Suite 1300, Cleveland OH 44115-2001. (216)861-3810. Fax: (216)861-6754. E-mail: mbryant@clevefdn.org. Website: www.writecorner.c om. **Contact:** Marcia Bryant, Communications and Marketing Administrator. Award to recognize recent books which have made important contributions to our understanding of racism or our appreciation of the rich diversity of human cultures. Annual award for novels and story collections. Award: $20,000, divided equally if multiple winners. Judges: panel of jurors. No entry fee. Guidelines available for SASE. Deadline: January 31, 2004 for books published in 2003. Previously published submissions between January 1, 2003 and December 31, 2003. "Only books written in English and published in the preceding calendar year are eligible. Plays and screenplays are not eligible, nor are works in progress. No grants are made for the completion or publication of manuscripts." Winners notified by phone. Call for list of winners.

ANNUAL FICTION CONTEST, Women In The Arts, P.O. Box 2907, Decatur IL 62524. (217)872-0811. **Contact:** Vice President. Annual competition for essays, fiction, fiction for children, plays, rhymed poetry, unrhymed poetry. Award: $15-50. Competition receives 50-100 submissions. Judges: professional writers. Entry fee $2 per submission. Unlimited entries. Guidelines available for #10 SASE. No entries returned. Do not submit drawings for any category. Double-space prose. Entries must be typed on 8½×11 white paper and must be titled. Do not put your name on any page of the manuscript. Do put your name, address, telephone number, e-mail and titles of your entries on a cover sheet. Submit one cover sheet and one check, with all entries mailed flat in one envelope. Do not staple. All entries will be subject to blind judging. Entries that do not comply with the rules may be disqualified. Deadline: November 1 annually. Published or previously unpublished submissions. Open to anyone. Entries must be original work of the author. Entries must be titled. No entries published by WITA; author retains rights. Word length: essay, up to 1,500 words; fiction, up to 1,500 words; fiction for children, up to 1,500 words (do not submit drawings); play, one act only; rhymed poetry, up to 32 lines; unrhymed poetry, up to 32 lines. Results announced March 15 annually. Winners notified by mail. "Send a perfect manuscript—no typos, Liquid Paper or holes from 3-ring binders."

ANNUAL JUVENILE-FICTION CONTEST, Women In The Arts, P.O. Box 2907, Decatur IL 62524. (217)872-0811. **Contact:** Vice President. Annual competition for essays, fiction, fiction for children, plays, rhymed poetry, unrhymed poetry. Award: $15-50. Competition receives 50-100 submissions. Judges: professional writers. Entry fee $2 per submission. Unlimited entries. Guidelines available for #10 SASE. Deadline: November 1 annually. Published or previously unpublished submissions. Open to anyone. "Entries must be original work of the author." Word length: 1,500 words maximum for fiction, essay, fiction for children; one act for plays; up to 32 lines for poetry. "Entrants must send for our contest rules and follow the specific format requirements." Winners notified by March 15.

ANTIETAM REVIEW LITERARY AWARD, *Antietam Review*, 41 S. Potomac St., Hagerstown MD 21740. (301)791-3132. Fax: (240)420-1754. E-mail: winnie@washingtoncountyarts.com. Website: http://washingtoncounty arts.com/index3.html. **Contact:** Winnie Wagaman, managing editor. Annual award to encourage and give recognition to excellence in short fiction. "We consider only previously unpublished work. We read manuscripts between June 1 and September 1." Award: $100 for the story; publication in *Antietam Review* with citation as winner of Literary Contest; and 2 copies of magazine. Competition receives 100 submissions. "We consider all fiction mss sent to *Antietam Review* Literary Contest as entries for inclusion in each issue. We look for well-crafted, serious literary prose fiction under 5,000 words." $10 fee for each story submitted. Make checks payable to *Antietam Review*. Guidelines available for #10 SASE. Accepts inquiries by phone. Deadline: September 1 (entries accepted June through September only). Results announced in January. Winners notified by phone and mail.

☐ ◎ ARIZONA COMMISSION ON THE ARTS CREATIVE WRITING FELLOWSHIPS, 417 W. Roosevelt St., Phoenix AZ 85003-1326. (602)229-8226. Fax: (602)256-0282. E-mail: pmorris@ArizonaArts.org. Website: www.ArizonaArts.org. **Contact:** Paul Morris, public information and literature director. Fellowships awarded in alternate years to Arizona fiction and creative nonfiction writers and poets. Award: $5,000-7,500. Competition receives 250 submissions. Judges: Out-of-state writers/editors. Guidelines available on website. Accepts inquiries by fax and e-mail. Deadline: September 12. Arizona resident poets and writers over 18 years of age only. Results announced by March 2004. Winners notified in writing. For contest results, visit website.

"WE WANT TO PUBLISH YOUR WORK."

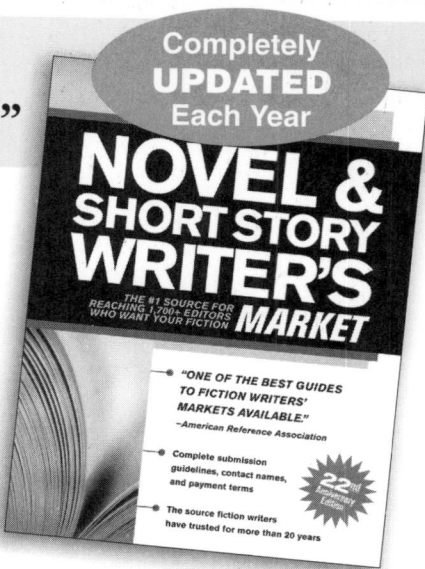

You would give anything to hear an editor speak those six magic words. So you work hard for weeks, months, even years to make that happen. You create a brilliant piece of work and a knock-out presentation, but there's still one vital step to ensure publication. You still need to submit your work to the right editors. With rapid changes in the publishing industry, it's not always easy to know who those editors are. That's why each year thousands of writers just like you turn to the most current edition of this indispensable market guide.

Keep ahead of the changes by ordering *2005 Novel & Short Story Writer's Market* today! You'll save the frustration of getting manuscripts returned in the mail stamped MOVED: ADDRESS UNKNOWN, and of NOT submitting your work to new listings because you don't know they exist. All you have to do to order next year's edition — at this year's price — is complete the attached order card and return it with your payment. Lock in the 2004 price for 2005 — order today!

2005 Novel & Short Story Writer's Market will be published and ready for shipment in November 2004.

Turn Over for More Great Books to Help Get Your Fiction Published!

OPEN HERE TO GET NEXT YEAR'S BOOK AT THIS YEAR'S PRICE!

New Writer's Digest Books!

The Complete Handbook of Novel Writing
by Meg Leder, Jack Heffron & the Editors of Writer's Digest
This compilation of the best interviews from *Writer's Digest* magazine, books and annuals will guide you through the craft, art and process of writing your novel. Includes interviews and articles from bestselling authors including Margaret Atwood, Tom Clancy, James Patterson, Nora Roberts, Kurt Vonnegut and more!
#10825-K/$17.99/400p/pb

The Writer's Digest Writing Clinic
by the Editors of Writer's Digest *magazine*
Based on one of *Writer's Digest*'s most popular columns! Top book doctors and writing instructors critique real manuscripts from beginning writers and offer practical, real-world advice for strengthening dialogue, creating believable settings and resolving plot problems. Plus, critiques of query letters, novel proposals and nonfiction book overviews.
#10870-K/$21.99/240 p/hc

Snoopy's Guide to the Writing Life
edited by Barnaby Conrad with a forward by Monte Schulz
Thirty famous writers, including Ray Bradbury, Sue Grafton and Fannie Flagg, respond to their favorite "Snoopy-at-the-typewriter" strips. Each strip inspires a reflection on some aspect of the writing life — from getting rejected to the search for new ideas. The essays are light and sometimes humorous, but they all reveal the wisdom behind the world's most literary beagle.
#10856-K/$19.99/192 p/hc

Finding Your Voice
by Les Edgerton
Les Edgerton provides tools to discover your own distinctive writing style. An ex-con-turned-published author, he offers a funny approach and down-to-earth tips on shaking off other writers' voices, silencing your inner censor, and using natural language. Plus, leading editors discuss the importance of a unique writing voice in today's competitive market.
#10836-K/$16.99/240 p/pb

2004 Children's Writer's and Illustrator's Market
edited by Alice Pope
This is the single most important resource for writers, illustrators, and photographers in the children's and young adult markets! You'll find up-to-date listings of agents and representatives, magazine and book publishers, contests and awards, toy companies, and more! And, you'll get advice on using the Internet to your best advantage, examples of great query letters, and interviews with industry experts.
#10853-K/$23.99/400 p/pb

Grammatically Correct
by Anne Stilman
Make sure your writing is smooth, clear, graceful — and correct. With this easy-to-use reference, you can quickly master the building blocks that make up good writing — including punctuation, spelling, style, usage and more. Complete with exercises and examples!
#10529-K/$19.99/352 p/hc

Pick up these helpful references today at your local bookstore, use the handy Order Card on the reverse side, or visit the Web site: www.writersdigest.com/store/books.asp.

◎ ARROWHEAD REGIONAL ARTS COUNCIL INDIVIDUAL ARTIST CAREER DEVELOPMENT GRANT, Arrowhead Regional Arts Council, 1301 Rice Lake Rd., Suite 111, Duluth MN 55811. (218)722-0952 or (800)569-8134. Fax: (218)722-4459. E-mail: aracouncil@aol.com. Website: www.aracouncil.org. **Contact:** Robert DeArmond, executive director. Award to "provide financial support to regional artists wishing to take advantage of impending, concrete opportunities that will advance their work or careers. Applicants must live in the seven-county region of Northeastern Minnesota." Award is granted 3 times a year. Competition open to short stories, novels, story collections and translations. Award: up to $1,000. Competition receives 15-20 submissions per category. Judge: ARAC Board. No entry fee. Guidelines now available. For guidelines send SASE, fax, e-mail or phone. Accepts inquiries by mail, fax, e-mail and phone. Deadline: April 30, 2004. Entries should be unpublished. Results announced June 20, 2004. Winners notified by mail. List of winners available by phone.

N: ◎ ART COOPERATIVE FICTION FELLOWSHIP, (formerly Cottonwood Fiction Fellowship), Art Cooperative, 1124 Columbia NE, Albuquerque NM 87106. E-mail: art_coop@yahoo.com. Website: www.geocities.com/art_coop. Annual competition for fiction and poetry. Judges: panel of student jurors and final judge. Entry fee $16. Include SASE for return of ms. Guidelines for SASE, e-mail or on website. Accepts inquiries by e-mail. Unpublished submissions. Limited to writers who have not published more than one novel or collection of stories. Any genre. Word length: "Interested authors should submit portfolios—suggested length between 3 and 50 pages. Portfolio may include any number of individual stories and/or a novel excerpt." Deadline: December 1.

◎ THE ART OF MUSIC ANNUAL WRITING CONTEST, Piano Press, P.O. Box 85, Del Mar CA 92014-0085. (619)884-1401. Fax: (858)755-1104. E-mail: Eaxford@aol.com. Website: www.pianopress.com. **Contact:** Elizabeth C. Axford. "Piano Press is looking for poems, short stories and essays on music-related topics only." Award: First, second, and third prizes in each of 3 age-groups. Prizes include cash and publication in the biannual anthology *The Art of Music-A Collection of Writings*. Judge: Panel of published writers. Entry fee $20/short story, essay or poem. Guidelines and entry form available on website, by SASE or by e-mail. Deadline: June 30. Contest open to all writers. Poems may be of any length and in any style, single-spaced and typed; short stories and essays should be no longer than five double-spaced, typewritten pages. "Make sure all work is fresh and original. Music related topics *only*." Results announced on October 1. Winners notified by mail. For contest results, send SASE or visit website.

☑ ◎ ARTIST TRUST ARTIST FELLOWSHIPS; GAP GRANTS, Artist Trust, 1835 12th Ave., Seattle WA 98122. (206)467-8734. Fax: (206)467-9633. E-mail: info@artisttrust.org. **Contact:** Program Director. Artist Trust has 3 grant programs for generative artists in Washington State; the GAP, Fellowship, and Twining Humber Award (THA). The GAP (Grants for Artist's Projects) is an annual award of up to $1,400 for a project proposal. The program is open to artists in all disciplines. The Fellowship grant is an award of $6,000 in unrestricted funding. Fellowships for Craft, Media, Literature and Music are awarded in odd numbered years, and Fellowships for Dance, Design, Theater and Visual Art will be awarded in even numbered years. Competition receives 700 (GAP) submissions; 500 (Fellowship); 30 (Twining Humber). Judges: Fellowship—Peer panel of 3 professional artists and arts professionals in each discipline; GAP—Interdisciplinary peer panel of 5 artists and arts professionals; THA—Selection panel of artists and arts professionals. Guidelines available in December for GAP grants; in April for Fellowship; and in November for THA; send SASE or download from website. Accepts inquiries by fax and e-mail. Deadline: late February (GAP), mid-June (Fellowship), January (Twining Humber). Results announced October (Fellowship), June (GAP), April (THA). Winners notified by mail. List of winners available by mail.

☐ ◎ THE ISAAC ASIMOV AWARD, International Association for the Fantastic in the Arts and *Asimov*'s magazine, School of Mass Communications, U. of South Florida, 4202 E. Fowler, Tampa FL 33620. (813)974-6792. Fax: (813)974-2592. E-mail: rwilber@chuma.cas.usf.edu. **Contact:** Rick Wilber, administrator. "The award honors the legacy of one of science fiction's most distinguished authors through an award aimed at undergraduate writers." Annual award for short stories. Award: $500 and consideration for publication in *Asimov's*. Winner receives all-expenses paid trip to Ft. Lauderdale, Florida, to attend conference on the Fantastic in mid-March where award is given. Competition receives 100-200 submissions. Judges: *Asimov*'s editors. Entry fee: $10 for up to 3 submissions. Guidelines available for SASE. Accepts inquiries by fax and e-mail. Deadline: December 15. Unpublished submissions. Full-time college undergraduates only. Results announced in February. Winners notified by telephone. For contest results, send SASE in March.

☼ ◐ ◎ ASTED/GRAND PRIX DE LITTERATURE JEUNESSE DU QUEBEC-ALVINE-BELISLE, Association pour l'avancement des sciences et des techniques de la documentation, 3414 Avenue du Parc, Bureau 202, Montreal QC H2X 2H5 Canada. (514)281-5012. Fax: (514)281-8219. E-mail: info@asted.org. Website: www.asted.org. **Contact:** Marie-Hélène Parent, president. "Prize granted for the best work in youth literature edited in French in the Quebec Province. Authors and editors can participate in the contest." Annual competition for fiction and nonfiction for children and young adults. Award: $1,000. Deadline: June 1. Contest entry limited to editors of books published during the preceding year. French translations of other languages are not accepted.

☑ ◎ THE ATHENAEUM LITERARY AWARD, The Athenaeum of Philadelphia, 219 S. Sixth St., Philadelphia PA 19106-3794. (215)925-2688. Fax: (215)925-3755. E-mail: erose@PhilaAthenaeum.org. Website: www.Phil

aAthenaeum.org. **Contact:** Ellen L. Rose, circulation librarian. Annual award to recognize and encourage outstanding literary achievement in Philadelphia and its vicinity. Award: A certificate bearing the name of the award, the seal of the Athenaeum, the title of the book, the name of the author and the year. Competition receives 8-10 submissions. Judged by committee appointed by Board of Directors. Guidelines available for SASE, by fax, by e-mail and on website. Accepts inquiries by fax, e-mail and phone. Deadline: December. Submissions must have been published during the preceding year. Nominations shall be made in writing to the Literary Award Committee by the author, the publisher or a member of the Athenaeum, accompanied by a copy of the book. The Athenaeum Literary Award is granted for a work of general literature, not exclusively for fiction. Juvenile fiction is not included. Results announced in Spring. Winners notified by mail. For contest results, visit website.

AWP AWARD SERIES IN POETRY, CREATIVE NONFICTION AND SHORT FICTION, AWP/ Thomas Dunne Books Novel Award, The Associated Writing Programs, Mail Stop 1E3, George Mason University, Fairfax VA 22030. (703)993-4301. Fax: (703)993-4302. E-mail: awp@gmu.edu. Website: http://awpwriter.org. **Contact:** Supriya Bhatnagar. Annual award. The AWP Award Series was established in cooperation with several university presses in order to publish and make fine fiction, nonfiction, and poetry available to a wide audience. The competition is open to all authors writing in English. Awards: $2,000 plus publication for short story collection. In addition, AWP tries to place mss of finalists with participating presses. Competition receives 400 short fiction submissions. Entry fee $20 nonmembers, $10 AWP members. Contest/award rules and guidelines available in September on website. No phone calls please. Mss must be postmarked between January 1-February 28. Only book-length mss in short story collections are eligible (150-300 pages). Cover letter should include name, address, phone, e-mail and title. "This information should appear in the cover letter only." Open to all authors writing in English regardless of nationality or residence. Manuscripts previously published in their entirety, including self-publishing, are not eligible. No mss returned. Results announced in August. Winners notified by mail or phone. For contest results, send SASE or visit website.

AWP INTRO JOURNALS PROJECT, Mail Stop 1E3, George Mason University, Fairfax VA 22030. (703)993-4308. Fax: (703)993-4302. E-mail: awp@gmu.edu. Website: www.awpwriter.org. **Contact:** Supriya Bhatnagar, publications manager. "This is a prize for students in AWP member university creative writing programs only. Authors are nominated by the head of the creative writing department. Each school may nominate no more than one work of nonfiction, one work of short fiction and three poems." Annual competition for short stories, nonfiction and poetry. Award: $50 plus publication in participating journal. 2003 journals included *Puerto del Sol*, *Quarterly West*, *Mid-American Review*, *Willow Springs*, *Bellingham Review*, *Shenandoah*, *The Journal*, *Crab Orchard Review*, *Tampa Review* and *Hayden's Ferry Review*. Judges: In 2003, Sandra Kohler (poetry), Dan Leone (short fiction), Sue William Silverman (creative nonfiction). Guidelines available in Fall 2003 for SASE or on website. Accepts inquiries by e-mail, fax and phone. Deadline: December 1. Unpublished submissions only. Results announced spring. Winners notified by mail in late spring/early summer. For contest results, send SASE or visit website.

BAKELESS LITERARY PUBLICATION PRIZES, Bread Loaf Writers' Conference Middlebury College, Middlebury College, Middlebury VT 05753. (802)443-2018. E-mail: bakeless@middlebury.edu. Website: www.middleb ury.edu/blwc/bakeless/. **Contact:** Ian Pounds, contest coordinator. "To promote new writers' careers." Annual competition for novels and story collections. Award: publication by Houghton Mifflin, some advanced money, full fellowship to attend Bread Loaf Writers' Conference. Submit as many entries as you want. Judges: Charles Baxter (fiction), Robert Pinsky (poetry). $10 fee per entry. Guidelines for SASE, e-mail and on website. Accepts inquiries by e-mail and phone. 2004 deadline: November 15. Entries should be unpublished. "Contest open to writers writing in English." Length: 200-450 pages. "Be certain the work is as close to being done as possible." Winners notified by mail with SASE. List of winners available by visiting website.

EMILY CLARK BALCH AWARDS, The Virginia Quarterly Review, One West Range, Box 400223, Charlottesville VA 22904-4223. **Contact:** Ted Genoways. Annual award "to recognize distinguished short fiction by American writers." For stories published in *The Virginia Quarterly Review* during the calendar year. Award: $500.

[N] [◎] BARD FICTION PRIZE, Bard College, Annandale-on-Hudson, New York NY 12504. (845)758-7087. Fax: (845)758-7043. E-mail: BFP@Bard.edu. Website: www.bard.edu/bfp. **Contact:** Irene Zedlacher. Purpose of award is to support young authors. Annual. Award for novels and short story collections. Award: $30,000 plus one semester as writer-in-residence. Receives hundreds of submissions per category. Judges: committee of 5 judges (authors associated with Bard College). No entry fee. Guidelines available in October by SASE, fax, phone, e-mail, or on website. Accepts inquiries by fax, e-mail, phone. Deadline: July 15, 2004. Entries should be previously published. Contest open to US citizens aged 39 and below. Cover letter should include name, address, phone, e-mail, and name of publisher where book was previously published. Results announced by October 15. Winners notified by phone. For contest results, visit website.

BEST LESBIAN EROTICA, Cleis Press, P.O. Box 4108, Grand Central Station, New York NY 10163. E-mail: tristan@puckerup.com. Website: www.puckerup.com. **Contact:** Tristan Taormino, series editor. Submit short stories, novel excerpts, other prose; poetry will be considered, but poetry is not encouraged. Accepts both unpublished and previously published material will be considered. Include cover page with author's name, title of submission(s), address, phone/fax, and e-mail. All submissions must be typed and double-spaced. Also number the pages. Length: 5,000. You may submit a maximum of 3 different pieces of work. Submit 2 hard copies of each submission. No e-mail submissions will be accepted; accepts inquiries by e-mail. All submissions must include a SASE or an e-mail address for response. No mss will be returned.

[□] [◎] "BEST OF OHIO WRITERS" CONTEST, *Ohio Writer Magazine*, P.O. Box 91801, Cleveland OH 44101. (216)421-0403. Fax: (216)791-1727. E-mail: pwlgc@msn.com. Website: www.pwlgc.com. **Contact:** Gail and Stephen Bellamy, editors. Award "to encourage and promote the work of writers in Ohio." Annual competition for short stories. Awards: $150 (1st Prize), $50 (2nd Prize). Competition receives 200 submissions. Judges: "a selected panel of prominent Ohio writers." $15 entry fee for first submission, $2 for each additional entry (includes subscription to *Ohio Writer* magazine). Guidelines available after January 1 for SASE, fax or e-mail. Accepts inquiries by e-mail and phone. Deadline: July 31. Unpublished submissions. Ohio writers only. Length: 2,500 words. "No cliché plots; we're looking for fresh, unpublished voices." Results announced November 1. Winners notified by mail. For contest results, send SASE or e-mail after November 1.

BINGHAMTON UNIVERSITY JOHN GARDNER FICTION BOOK AWARD, Binghamton University Creative Writing Program, P.O. Box 6000, Binghamton NY 13902-6000. (607)777-6134. Fax: (607)777-2408. E-mail: mgillan@binghamton.edu. Website: www.english.binghamton.edu/cwpro. **Contact:** Maria Mazzioni Gillan, director. Award's purpose is "to serve the literary community by calling attention to outstanding books of fiction." Annual award for novels, short story collections. Prize: $1,000. Competition receives approximately 500 submissions per category. Judge: "Rotating outside judges." Guidelines available for SASE and on website. Accepts inquiries by e-mail. 2004 deadline: March 1. Entries should be published in book form. Results announced in summer. For contest results, send SASE or visit website.

[◉] IRMA S. AND JAMES H. BLACK CHILDREN'S BOOK AWARD, Bank Street College, 610 W. 112th St., New York NY 10025-1898. (212)875-4450. Fax: (212)875-4558. E-mail: lindag@bnkst.edu. Website: http://streetcat.bnkst.edu/html/isb.html. **Contact:** Linda Greengrass, award director. Annual award "to honor the young children's book published in the preceding year judged the most outstanding in text as well as in art. Book must be published the year preceding the May award." Award: Press function, a scroll and seals by Maurice Sendak for attaching to award book's run. Judges: adult children's literature experts and children 6-10 years old. No entry fee. Guidelines available by SASE, fax, e-mail, or on website. Accepts inquiries by phone, fax and e-mail. Deadline: December 15. Expects to receive about 150 fiction entries for 2003 competition. "Write to address above. Usually publishers submit books they want considered, but individuals can too. No entries are returned." Winners notified by phone in April and announced in May. A list of winners will be available on website.

[◉] THE BLACK WARRIOR REVIEW LITERARY AWARD, P.O. Box 862936, Tuscaloosa AL 35486-0277. (205)348-4518. E-mail: daniel.kaplan@ua.edu. Website: www.webdelsol.com/bwr. **Contact:** Dan Kaplan. "Determined by independent judges, the award grants $500 to a fiction writer whose work has been published in the previous fall and spring issues. All works of fiction included in these issues considered." Winners listed in fall issue. Accepts inquiries by fax and e-mail.

[N] BLAGGARD AWARD FOR BEST SHORT STORY OF THE YEAR, *New Mystery Magazine*, 101 W. 23rd St., New York NY 10011. Fax: (212)353-3495. Website: www.NewMystery.com. **Contact:** Miss Linda Wong. Award to "find the best new mystery, crime or suspense writer, and promote high standards in the short story form. For writers who have never been paid for their fiction writing." Annual award for short stories. Award: publication in *New Mystery Magazine*. Competition receives approximately 3,000 submissions. Judges: editorial panel of veteran mystery writers. No entry fee. No guidelines available. Deadline: July 4. Unpublished submissions. Word length: 3,000-5,000 words. "Please mark ms 'First Mystery Award.' Study back issues of *New Mystery* for style." Sample copy: $7 plus 9×12 SAE with $1.24 postage. Results announced in May annually.

BOOK SENSE BOOK OF THE YEAR AWARD, Book Sense, 828 S. Broadway, Tarrytown NY 10591. (914)591-2665. Fax: (914)591-2720. E-mail: info@bookweb.org. Website: www.bookweb.org. **Contact:** Jill Perlstein, director marketing services. "Independent booksellers vote for the books they most enjoyed handselling in the previous year." Annual award for "fiction, nonfiction, children's illustrated, children's literature and rediscovery." Award: $2,000. Judge: "Independent bookseller members of the American Booksellers Association." No entry fee. No guidelines. Accepts inquiries by fax, e-mail, phone. All entries should be previously published. Only books first nominated for the Book Sense 76 list are eligible. Member booksellers nominate books; writers may not submit their own work. Results announced "at the Celebration of Bookselling at BookExpo America each spring." Winners notified by mail, phone or e-mail and at the Celebration of Bookselling immediately. For contest results, visit website.

BOSTON GLOBE-HORN BOOK AWARDS, Horn Book Magazine, Inc., 56 Roland St., Suite 200, Boston MA 02129. (617)628-0225. Fax: (617)628-0882. E-mail: info@hbook.com. Website: www.hbook.com. **Contact:** Anne Quirk, marketing director. Annual award. "To honor excellence in children's fiction or poetry, picture book and nonfiction published within the US." Award: $500 and engraved silver bowl first prize in each category; engraved silver plate for the 2 honor books in each category. Competition receives 1,000 submissions. No entry fee. Guidelines available after January 31 for SASE, fax, e-mail, or on website. Accepts inquiries by fax and e-mail. Entry forms or rules for SASE. Deadline: May 15. "Children's and young adult books published in the U.S. between June 1, 2002-May 31, 2003 can be submitted by publishers." Results announced in June. Winners notified by phone. For contest results, send SASE, fax, e-mail or visit website in June.

BOSTON REVIEW SHORT STORY CONTEST, Boston Review, E53-407, MIT, Cambridge MA 02139. (617)253-3642. E-mail: review@mit.edu. Website: www.bostonreview.net. **Contact:** Director. Annual award for short stories. Award: $1,000. 2003 judge was Ha Jin. Processing fee $15. Deadline: October 1. Unpublished submissions. Competition receives 500 entries. No restrictions on subject matter. Guidelines available in September for SASE, by e-mail or on website. Accepts inquiries by e-mail. Word length: 4,000 words. Winning entry published in December issue. All entrants receive a 1-year subscription to the Boston Review beginning with the December issue. Stories not returned. Results announced December 1. Winners notified by mail.

BOULEVARD SHORT FICTION CONTEST FOR EMERGING WRITERS, Boulevard, PMB 325, 6614 Clayton Rd., Richmond MO 63117. (314)862-2643. E-mail: ballymon@hotmail.com. Website: www.richardburgin.com. **Contact:** Richard Burgin, editor. Award "to recognize emerging writers who have not yet published a book of fiction, poetry or creative nonfiction with a nationally distributed press." Annual. Competition for short stories. Award: $1,500 plus publication of the winning story in Boulevard. No limit to the number of short story entries per author. Judges: staff of Boulevard magazine. $15 fee per story (includes a one-year subscription to Boulevard); make checks payable to Opajaz, Inc. Guidelines available for SASE, e-mail, on website and in publication. Accepts inquiries by e-mail, phone. Deadline: December 15. Entries should be unpublished. Length: 7,500 words. Author's name, address, phone and e-mail number, story's titled and word count and Boulevard Emerging Writers Contest should appear on page one; last name on each page is helpful. Include a 3×5 index card with your name, address and title of your submissions. Results announced in the Spring issue of Boulevard. Winners notified by mail or phone usually during February/March only through Spring issue.

THE BRIAR CLIFF REVIEW POETRY & FICTION CONTEST, The Briar Cliff Review, Briar Cliff University, 3303 Rebecca St., Sioux City IA 51104-2324. (712)279-5321. Fax: (712)279-5410. E-mail: currans@briarcliff.edu. Website: www.briarcliff.edu/bcreview. **Contact:** Tricia Currans-Sheehan, editor. Award "to reward good writers and showcase quality writing." Annual award for short stories and poetry. Award: $500 and publication in spring issue. Competition receives 100-125 submissions. No e-mail or fax submissions. Judges: editors. "All entries are read by at least 2 editors." $15 entry fee. All entrants receive a copy of the magazine with winning entries. Guidelines for SASE. Deadline: submissions between August 1 and November 1. Previously unpublished submissions. Word length: 5,000 words maximum. Results announced December or January. Winners notified by phone or by letter around December 20. For contest results, send SASE with submission. "Send us your best. We want stories with a plot."

THE BRIDPORT PRIZE, Bridport Arts Centre, South Street, Bridport, Dorset DT6 3NR United Kingdom. (01308)459444. Fax: (01308)459166. E-mail: info@bridport-arts.com. Website: www.bridportprize.co.uk. **Contact:** Frances Everitt, administrator. Awarded to "promote literary excellence, discover new talent." Annual competition for short stories. Award: £3,000 sterling (1st prize), £1,000 sterling (2nd prize), £500 sterling (3rd prize) plus various runners-up prizes and publication of approximately 10 best stories in anthology. Judge: One judge for short story (in 2003, Rose Tremain); one judge for poetry (in 2003, U.A. Fanthorpe). £6 sterling entry fee. Guidelines available January 2004; send SASE or visit website. Accepts inquiries by fax, e-mail and phone. 2004 deadline: June 30. Entries should be unpublished. Contest open to anyone. Length: 5,000 words maximum for short stories; 42 lines for poetry. Results announced in November of year of contest. Winners notified by mail or phone in September. For contest results, send SASE.

N ⊕ © **BRITISH SCIENCE FICTION ASSOCIATION AWARDS**, British Science Fiction Association, 1 Long Row Close, Everdon, Daventry, Northants NN11 3BE, United Kingdom. E-mail: bsfa@enterprise.net. Website: www.bsfa.co.uk. **Contact:** Tanya Brown, awards administrator. Award "to recognize the best novel, short story, artwork and related publication (primarily UK publication) of the previous year." Annual. Award for short stories, novels, short story collections. Award: a trophy for each category. Receives 30-35 fiction nominations. Judges: voted by BSFA membership and members of the National SF Convention (Eastercon) in the UK. No entry fee. Guidelines available in on website. Accepts inquiries by e-mail. Deadline: January 31, 2004 for nominations for 2003 award. Entries should be previously published: novel, first UK publication 2003; short story, first publication anywhere 2003. Length: depends on category; short story 40,000 word maximum. "Authors may nominate their own work. All we need for nomination is publication details, not a ms or a copy of the work. Write something popular—number of nominations gets you onto the shortlist, number of votes decides the winner!" Results announced at Eastercon, UK National SF Convention, Easter weekend. Winners notified at event/banquet or by mail, phone or e-mail. For contest results, send e-mail or visit website.

ARCH & BRUCE BROWN FOUNDATION, The Arch & Bruce Brown Foundation, PMB 503, 31855 Date Palm Dr., Suite 3, Cathedral City CA 92234. E-mail: archwrite@aol.com. Website: www.aabbfoundation.org. **Contact:** Arch Brown, president. Contest for "gay-positive works based on history." Annual contest; type of contest changes each year: short story (2004); playwriting (2005); novel (2003). Award: $1,000 (not limited to a single winner). Receives 50-100 entries. No entry fee. For guidelines, send SASE or visit website. Accepts inquiries by e-mail. 2003 deadline: November 30. Entries should be unpublished. Contest open to all writers. Cover letter and ms should include name, address, phone, e-mail and title. Results announced Spring. Winners notified by mail. For contest results, send SASE, e-mail or visit website.

🍁 ○ © **BURNABY WRITERS' SOCIETY ANNUAL COMPETITION**, 6584 Deer Lake Ave., BC V5G 3T7 Canada. (604)421-4931. E-mail: lonewolf@portal.ca. Website: www.bws.bc.ca. Annual competition to encourage creative writing in British Columbia. "Category varies from year to year." Award: $200, $100 and $50 (Canadian) prizes. Receives 400-600 entries for each award. Judge: "independent recognized professional in the field." Entry fee $5. Guidelines available for SASE or on website. Contest requirements after March for SASE. Deadline: May 31. Open to British Columbia authors only. Results announced in September. Winners notified by phone, mail or e-mail. For contest results, send SASE.

○ © **BUSH ARTIST FELLOWS PROGRAM**, Bush Foundation, E-900 First Nat'l Bank Building, 332 Minnesota St., St. Paul MN 55101-1387. Fax: (651)297-6485. E-mail: kpolley@bushfound.org. Website: www.bushfoundation.org. **Contact:** Kathi Polley, program assistant. Award to "provide artists with significant financial support that enables them to further their work and their contribution to their communities. Fellows may decide to take time for solitary work or reflection, engage in collaborative or community projects, or embark on travel or research." Annual grant. Award: $44,000 for 12-18 months. Competition receives 400-500 submissions. Literature (fiction, creative nonfiction, poetry) offered every other year. Next offered 2005. Applications available August 2004. Accepts inquiries by phone, fax and e-mail. Must meet certain publication requirements. Judges: a panel of artists and arts professionals who reside outside of Minnesota, South Dakota, North Dakota or Wisconsin. Applicants must be at least 25 years old, and Minnesota, South Dakota, North Dakota or Western Wisconsin residents. Students not eligible. Results announced in Spring 2005. Winners notified by letter. List of winners available in May and sent to all applicants.

○ © **BYLINE SHORT FICTION & POETRY AWARDS**, P.O. Box 5240, Edmond OK 73083-5240. Phone/fax: (405)348-5591. E-mail: mpreston@bylinemag.com. Website: www.bylinemag.com. **Contact:** Marcia Preston, executive editor/publisher. "To encourage our subscribers in striving for high quality writing." Annual awards for short stories and poetry. Award: $70, $35, $20 in each category. Competition receives approximately 200 submissions in each category. Judges are published writers chosen by the *ByLine* staff. Entry fee $5 for stories; $3 for poems. Guidelines available for SASE. Accepts inquiries by e-mail and phone. See website for deadline. "Judges look for quality writing, well-drawn characters, significant themes. Entries should be unpublished, not have won money in any previous contest and be suitable for publication in *ByLine*. Winners notified by mail and phone in January and announced in February issue, accompanied by photo and short bio. List of winners available for SASE, read magazine or visit website. Open to subscribers only."

N ⊕ **THE CAINE PRIZE FOR AFRICAN WRITING**, Africa GS, 2 Drayson Mews, London W8 4L4 England. +44 (0)20 73760440. Fax: +44 (0)20 79383728. E-mail: caineprize@jltaylor.com. Website: www.caineprize.com. **Contact:** Nick Elam, administrator. Award "to reward writers of African short stories." Annual. Award for short stories. Award: $15,000. Judged by a panel of 4-5 judges appointed annually. Guidelines available by fax, phone, e-mail, on website. Accepts inquiries by fax, e-mail, phone. Deadline: January 31, 2004. Entries should be previously published. "Should have been published in 5 years prior to closing date." Contest open to writers of African origin, i.e., born there or of African parentage. Length: 3,000-15,000 words. Cover letter should include name, address, phone, e-mail, title and publication where story was previously published. "Manuscripts not accepted; entries should be submitted in published form." Writer's work is submitted by publisher. Writing must reflect its

"African-ness." Results announced mid-July 2004. Winners notified at event/banquet in mid-July. For contest results, send fax, e-mail or visit website.

CALIFORNIA BOOK AWARDS, The Commonwealth Club of California, 595 Market St., San Francisco CA 94105. (415)597-4846. Fax: (415)597-6729. E-mail: bookawards@commonwealth.org. Website: www.common wealthclub.org. **Contact:** Barbara Lane, book awards manager. Annual competition for novels and story collections. Award: $2,000 (1st Prize); $300 (2nd Prize). Competition receives 400 submissions. Judges: panel of jurors. Guidelines available in July 2001 by e-mail, on website or for SASE. Accepts inquiries by phone and e-mail. Deadline: December 31. Previously published submissions that appeared in print between January 1 and December 30. "Writers must have been legal residents of California when manuscript was accepted for publication. Enter as early as possible—supply five copies of book." Winners notified in June by phone, mail or through publisher and announced in summer. List of winners available for SASE or on website.

JOHN W. CAMPBELL MEMORIAL AWARD FOR THE BEST SCIENCE FICTION NOVEL OF THE YEAR; THEODORE STURGEON MEMORIAL AWARD FOR THE BEST SCIENCE FICTION SHORT FICTION, Center for the Study of Science Fiction, English Dept., University of Kansas, Lawrence KS 66045. (785)864-3380. Fax: (785)864-1159. E-mail: jgunn@ku.edu. Website: www.ku.edu/~sfcenter. **Contact:** James Gunn, professor and director. "To honor the best novel and short science fiction of the year." Annual competition for short stories and novels. Award: Certificate. "Winners' names are engraved on a trophy." Campbell Award receives approximately 200 submissions. Judges: 2 separate juries. Accepts inquiries by e-mail and fax. Deadline: December 31. Entries must be previously published. "Ordinarily publishers should submit work, but authors have done so when publishers would not. Send for list of jurors." Entrants for the Sturgeon Award are selected by nomination only. Results announced in July. For contest results, send SASE.

CAPE FEAR CRIME FESTIVAL SHORT STORY CONTEST, Atticus, Inc., Cape Fear Crime Festival, 5828 Greenville Loop Rd., Wilmington NC 28409. (910)264-2101. Fax: (910)256-4770. E-mail: Booklady@ec.rr.c om. Website: www.galleone.com/cfcf.htm. **Contact:** Nikki Smith, contest coordinator. "The CFCF Short Story Contest was created in concert with the annual Cape Fear Crime Festival. The purpose of the story contest is to provide a forum in which to discover, publish, and promote new writers, and to introduce readers to promising authors through the publication of the contest's annual chapbook. Contest organizers are also interested in bridging the imagined gap between genre and nongenre fiction." Annual. Award for short stories. Award: "Top three stories will be awarded $100, $75, and $50, respectively, and will be published in the Story Contest chapbook, which is distributed to hundreds of Festival attendees. Winning authors will also receive free registration to the Cape Fear Crime Festival, and a free Saturday night dinner featuring a celebrated mystery author." Story should have a strong mystery or crime theme. Judges: all entries are kept anonymous and are judged by a panel of local bookstore employees, editors, and librarians to determine the semifinalists. Semifinalist stories are then passed on to a celebrity judge who determines which stories win first, second and third place. 2003 celebrity judge was author Margaret Maron. $8 fee per entry (unlimited entries); send credit card information or make checks payable to Cape Fear Crime Festival. Guidelines available in January by e-mail, and on website. Accepts inquiries by e-mail. Deadline: January 1-June 1. Entries should be unpublished. Contest open to all writers in all locations, except for those individuals who are associated with the Cape Fear Crime Festival Organization and their family members. Length: 4,000 words maximum. Cover letter should include name, address, phone, e-mail, word count and title. This information should not appear on ms. "All entries should show innovative and imaginative writing style, along with a strong mystery or crime theme. Profane or libelous language is discouraged. All winning stories are subject to editorial review and will be copyedited for grammatical errors, spelling mistakes, and libelous language." Results announced publicly at a celebratory dinner featuring a keynote speaker (usually a well-known mystery author). Winners notified by mail or e-mail no later than September 15. For contest results, send e-mail or visit website.

CAPTIVATING BEGINNINGS CONTEST, *Lynx Eye*, 542 Mitchell Dr., Los Osos CA 93402. (805)528-8146. Fax: (805)528-7876. E-mail: pamccully@aol.com. **Contact:** Pam McCully, co-editor. Annual award for stories "with engrossing beginnings, stories that will enthrall and absorb readers." Award: $100 plus publication, 1st prize; $10 each for 4 honorable mentions plus publication. Competition receives 600-700 submissions. Judges: *Lynx Eye* editors. Entry fee $5/story. Guidelines available for SASE or by e-mail. Accepts inquiries by e-mail and phone. Unpublished submissions. Length: 7,500 words or less. "The stories will be judged on the first 500 words." Guidelines available year round for SASE. Accepts inquiries by e-mail and phone. Deadline: January 31. Results announced March 15. Winners notified by mail. For contest results, send SASE after March 31.

◎ **CELTIC VOICE WRITING CONTEST**, Bardsong Press, P.O. Box 775396, Steamboat Springs CO 80477-5396. (970)870-1401. Fax: (970)879-2657. E-mail: celts@bardsongpress.com. Website: www.bardsongpress.com. **Contact:** Ann Gilpin, editor. Annual competition for short stories. Award: cash awards for category winners; publication for winners and honorable mentions. Judges: selected guest judges. $10 fee per entry. Guidelines available January 1, 2003 for SASE, e-mail or on website. Accepts inquiries by e-mail. Deadline: September 30, 2003. Entries must be unpublished. Open to all writers. "We are looking for work that reflects the ageless culture, history, symbolism, mythology and spirituality that belongs to Celtic heritage. Following the guidelines specifications closely will give the greatest chance to do well in the competition. Let your imagination soar freely." Results announced in January 2004. Winners notified by mail or e-mail. For contest results, send SASE.

◢ **THE CHELSEA AWARDS,** P.O. Box 773, Cooper Station, New York NY 10276-0773. E-mail: chelseaassoc@aol.com. **Contact:** Alfredo de Palchi. Annual competition for short stories. Award: $1,000 and publication in *Chelsea* (all entries are considered for publication), 2 free copies and discount on additional copies. Competition receives over 300 submissions. Judges: the editors. Entry fee $10 (for which entrants also receive a subscription); make checks payable to *Chelsea*. Money orders or back checks only. Guidelines available for SASE. Deadline: June 15. Unpublished submissions. Absolutely no simultaneous submissions. Manuscripts may not exceed 30 typed pages or about 7,500 words. The stories must not be under consideration elsewhere or scheduled for book publication within 8 months of the competition deadline. Include separate cover sheet with entrant's name; no name on ms. Mss will not be returned; include SASE for notification of results. Results announced August 15. Winners notified by telephone. "No submissions, notification or guidelines will be sent or responded to by e-mail. Read and follow contest guidelines. Manuscripts on which the author's name appears will be destroyed unread."

CHESTERFIELD WRITERS' FILM PROJECT, (formerly Writers' Film Project), The Chesterfield Writers Film Project, 1158 26th St., PMB 544, Santa Monica CA 90403. (213)683-3977. E-mail: info@chesterfield-co.com. Website: www.chesterfield-co.com. **Contact:** Ed Rugoff, administrator. Award "provides up to 5 yearly fellowships of $20,000 to promote and foster talented screenwriters, fiction writers and playwrights." Annual competition for short stories, novels and screenplays. Award: 5 $20,000 awards sponsored by Paramount Pictures. Judges: Mentors, panel of judges. Entry fee $39.50 U.S. dollars for each submission. Guidelines available for SASE or on website. Deadline: May 15, 2004. Published or previously unpublished submissions. "Program open to all age groups, race, religion, educational level etc. Past winners have ranged in age from early 20's to late 50's."

CHICAGO LITERARY AWARDS, *Another Chicago Magazine*, 3709 N. Kenmore, Chicago IL 60613-2901. E-mail: editors@anotherchicagomag.com. Website: www.anotherchicagomag.com. **Contact:** Editor. "To award excellence in fiction and poetry writing." Annual competition for short stories and poetry. Award: $1,000 and publication in *Another Chicago Magazine*. Competition receives 400 submissions. 2003 judges: James McManus (fiction); Albert Goldbarth (poetry). $12/story; length: 6,500; $12/set of 3 poems; length: 300 lines total. Checks payable to Left Field Press. No previously published work eligible; if work is under consideration elsewhere, *ACM* must be notified and work must be withdrawn upon acceptance elsewhere. "No names on mss; include cover page with name, address, titles, word count for fiction and line count for poetry. No mss returned." Results announced April 1. Include SASE for notification of winners; SAS postcard for acknowledgement of entry. No certified mail please.

◻◎ **CHICANO/LATINO LITERARY CONTEST,** Dept. of Spanish & Portuguese, University of California-Irvine, Irvine CA 92697-5275. (949)824-5443. Fax: (949)824-2803. E-mail: fhirsty@uci.edu. Website: www.humanities.hnet.uci.edu/spanishandportuguese/contest.html. **Contact:** Faye Hirsty, coordinator. Annual award for different genre each year; novels (2003), short stories (2004), poetry (2005) and drama (2006). Award: Usually $1,000 First Prize; $500 Second Prize; $250 Third Prize. Guidelines available in January for SASE or on website. Deadline: June 1. Entrants must be citizens or permanent residents of the U.S. Length: 225 pages, typed and double-spaced, minimum. Accepts inquiries by e-mail. Unpublished submissions only. Winners notified by letter in October. For contest results, send e-mail or visit website.

◎ **CHILDREN'S WRITERS FICTION CONTEST**, Stepping Stones, P.O. Box 8863, Springfield MO 65801-8863. (417)863-7369. E-mail: verwil@alumni.pace.edu. **Contact:** V.R. Williams, coordinator. Award to "promote writing for children by encouraging children's writers and giving them an opportunity to submit their work in competition." Annual competition for short stories and translations. Award: $260 and/or publication in *Hodge Podge*. Competition receives 160 submissions. "Judged by Goodin, Williams, Goodwin and/or associates. Entries are judged for clarity, grammar, punctuation, imagery, content and suitability for children." Entry fee $8. Guidelines available for SASE or e-mail. Accepts inquiries by phone and e-mail. Deadline: July 31. Previously unpublished submissions. Word length: 1,500 words. "Work submitted on colored paper, book format is not acceptable. Stories should have believable characters." Results announced in September. Winners notified by mail. For contest results, send SASE. "To avoid disqualification of entry, contestants must follow guidelines. If possible, the child should be the main character in the story. Stories about animals or inanimate objects should have a purpose. Children should enjoy the story, but also learn from it."

◢◎ **THE CHRISTOPHER AWARDS,** The Christophers, 12 E. 48th St., New York NY 10017-1091. (212)759-4050. Fax: (212)838-5073. E-mail: awardsinfo@christophers.org. Website: www.christophers.org. **Contact:** Judith

Trojan, program manager. Annual award "to encourage authors and illustrators to continue to produce works which affirm the highest values of the human spirit in adult and children's books." Only novels for young people are accepted. Professionally published submissions only. Award: Bronze medallion. Competition receives 500 entries of fiction/nonfiction for kids (perhaps two thirds are fiction). "Award judged by a panel of juvenile reading and subject experts. Juvenile works are 'children tested.' " No entry forms or submission fees. "Potential winners are nominated and reviewed throughout the year by juvenile book professionals, members of the Christopher staff and by specially supervised children's reading groups. Friends of The Christophers are also encouraged to nominate titles." For guidelines send 6×9 SASE, e-mail or on website. Inquiries accepted by fax, e-mail and phone. Books published in the 2003 calendar year are eligible throughout 2003. Arbitrary deadlines: June 1 through November 1 every year. Books (in multiples) may be submitted any time in between as well. Winners chosen in late January and notified by mail late February. "Awards are presented at a black-tie gala on the last Thursday in February in New York City." For contest results, send SASE, fax or visit website. Example of book award: *Love That Dog*, by Sharon Creech (children's book category 2001). "Publishers generally submit fiction/nonfiction books for young people. Authors and illustrators should familiarize themselves with our awards criteria and encourage their publishers to submit applicable titles."

𝕹 MATT CLARK PRIZE, *New Delta Review*, Louisiana State University, 249 Allen Hall, Baton Rouge LA 70803. (225)578-4079. E-mail: new-delta@lsu.edu. Website: http://english.lsu.edu/journals/ndr. **Contact:** Editors. Award in memory of Matt Clark, former teacher and coordinator of creative writing at Louisiana State University. Annual. Competition for poems and short stories. Award: $100 first place winner and publication of entry in the *New Delta Review*. Receives 75 entries. $5 fee per entry. Guidelines available in June by SASE, e-mail, on website, and in publication. Accepts inquiries by e-mail. Winners notified by mail or e-mail. For contest results, send SASE.

◘ CNW/FFWA FLORIDA STATE WRITING COMPETITION, Florida Freelance Writers Association, P.O. Box A, North Stratford NH 03590. (603)922-8338. Fax: (603)922-8339. E-mail: danakcnw@ncia.net. Website: www.writers-editors.com. **Contact:** Dana K. Cassell, executive director. Award "to recognize publishable writing." Annual competition for short stories and novels. Awards: $100 (first place), $75 (second place), $50 (third place). Competition receives 100-200 submissions in short story/novel division. Total 500+ in all divisions. Judges: published authors, teachers, editors. Entry fee ($5-20) varies with membership status and entry length. Guidelines available for SASE or on website. Deadline: March 15. Previously unpublished submissions. Winners will be notified by mail by May 31. List of winners available for SASE or visit website.

𝕹 ◘ THE CRUCIBLE POETRY AND FICTION COMPETITION, *Crucible*, Barton College, College Station, Wilson NC 27893. (252)399-6456. E-mail: tgrimes@barton.edu. **Contact:** Terrence L. Grimes, editor. Annual competition for short stories. Unpublished submissions only. Fiction should be 8,000 words or less. Award: $150 (1st prize); $100 (2nd prize) and publication in *Crucible*. Competition receives 300 entries. Judges: in-house editorial board. Guidelines available in January for SASE, e-mail or in publication. Deadline: April. "The best time to submit is December through April." Results announced in July. Winners notified by mail. For contest results, send e-mail.

◎ DANA AWARD IN SHORT FICTION, 7207 Townsend Forest Court, Browns Summit NC 27214-9634. (336)656-7009. E-mail: danaawards@pipeline.com. Website: www.danaawards.com. **Contact:** Mary Elizabeth Parker, chair. Award "to reward work that has been previously unrecognized in the area of fiction. All genres, including literary/mainstream, and speculative fiction. No work for or by persons under 16. "Let authors be aware work must meet standards of literary complexity and excellence. Character development, excellence of style are as important as the plot line." Award: $1,000. Competition receives 500 submissions annually. Entry fee $15/short story. Make checks payable to Dana Awards. Guidelines available in March by SASE, e-mail or on website. Accepts inquiries by e-mail and phone. Unpublished submissions, not under contract to any publisher. "See 'What We're Looking For' on our website for submission tips." Word length: No longer than 10,000 words, 3,000 word average preferred. Postmark deadline: October 31. Results announced March/April. Winners notified by phone, then by letter or e-mail. Send SASE with submission to receive competition results letter. For contest results, send SASE, e-mail or visit website.

DANA AWARDS: PORTFOLIO, NOVEL, SHORT FICTION, POETRY, (formerly Dana Award in the Novel), 7207 Townsend Forest Court, Browns Summit NC 27214-9634. (336)656-7009. E-mail: danaawards@pipeline.com. Website: www.danaawards.com. **Contact:** Mary Elizabeth Parker, chair. Award to "reward work that has not yet been recognized, since we know from firsthand experience how tough the literary market is." Annual competition for novels, short stories and poetry. Award: $1,000 each category. Competition receives 400 submissions for novel award, 600 for short fiction annually. Entry fees: $20 novel, $15 short story. Guidelines for SASE, e-mail or on website in March. "See website under 'What We're Looking For' for submission tips." Accepts inquiries by e-mail. Postmark deadline: October 31. Unpublished submissions and not under contract to be published. Novelists should submit first 50 pages only of a novel either completed or in progress. No novels for or by children/young adults. In-progress submissions should be as polished as possible. Short fiction: no memoirs; no stories for or by persons under 16. Multiple submissions accepted, but each must include a separate entry fee. Make checks payable to Dana Awards. Results announced March-April. Winners notified by phone, mail, or e-mail. For contest results, send SASE, e-mail, or visit website in late spring. Send SASE with submission to receive competition results letter. "We also have a fourth award, the $3,000 Portfolio Award. Content can be any mix of 3 manuscripts in novel, short fiction or poetry. See website or send SASE for guidelines (content and fees variable)."

[N] DOROTHY DANIELS ANNUAL HONORARY WRITING AWARD, Simi Valley Branch of the National League of American Pen Women, Inc., P.O. Box 1485, Simi Valley CA 93062. E-mail: cdoering@adelphia.net. **Contact:** Carol E. Doering, vice president and contest chairperson. Annual. Award for short stories. Award: $100. Receives 100-150 submissions per category. Judges: NLAPW members. $5 fee per entry; make checks payable to NLAPW-SV Branch. Guidelines available in February for SASE or e-mail. Accepts inquiries by e-mail. Deadline: July 31, 2004. Entries should be unpublished. Length: 2,000 words maximum. Cover letter should include name, address, phone, word count, title and category; name and address must not appear on ms, entry must be titled. Results announced November 5. Winners notified by mail. For contest results, send SASE.

[] [@] MARGUERITE DE ANGELI PRIZE, Delacorte Press Books for Young Readers, 1540 Broadway, New York NY 10036. (212)782-8633. Fax: (212)782-9452. Website: www.randomhouse.com. "To encourage the writing of fiction for middle grade readers (either contemporary or historical) in the same spirit as the works of Marguerite de Angeli." Open to U.S. and Canadian writers who have not previously published a novel for middle-grade readers. Annual competition for first novels for middle-grade readers (ages 7-10). Award: One BDD hardcover and paperback book contract, with $1,500 cash prize and $3,500 advance against royalties. Competition receives 350 submissions. Judges: Editors of Delacorte Press Books for Young Readers. "The judges reserve the right not to award a prize." Send SASE, fax, or visit website for guidelines; available in August. Submit between April 1 and June 30 *only*. Deadline: Submissions must be postmarked by June 30. Previously unpublished (middle-grade) fiction. Length: 80 pages minimum, 144 maximum. Manuscript: 8½×11, white paper; 12 pt font; double-spaced; consecutively numbered pages with title. Include cover letter (with title, author's name, address and phone number) and plot summary. Do not submit art. Results announced by October 31. Winners notified by phone. For contest results, send SASE or visit website.

[] [@] DELAWARE DIVISION OF THE ARTS, 820 N. French St., Wilmington DE 19801. (302)577-8278. Fax: (302)577-6561. Website: www.artsdel.org. **Contact:** Kristin Pleasanton, coordinator. "To help further careers of emerging and established professional artists." Annual awards for Delaware residents only. Awards: $10,000 for masters, $5,000 for established professionals; $2,000 for emerging professionals. Competition receives 100 submissions. Judges are out-of-state professionals in each division. Entry forms or rules available after January 1 for SASE. Deadline: August 15. Results announced in December. Winners notified by mail.

[@] DAVID DORNSTEIN MEMORIAL CREATIVE WRITING CONTEST FOR YOUNG ADULT WRITERS, Coalition for the Advancement of Jewish Education, 261 W. 35th St., Floor 12A, New York NY 10001. (212)268-4210. Fax: (212)268-4214. E-mail: cajeny@caje.org. Website: www.caje.org. **Contact:** Operations Coordinator. Purpose of award is "to perpetuate the memory of a CAJE Conference Assistant who lost his life in the explosion of PAN AM flight 103. He was a lover of short stories, which he both read and wrote, and this prize perpetuates that aspect of his life." Annual award for short stories. Award: $1,000 split between up to 3 winners. If only 1 winner, writer receives $1,000. If 2 winners, first place $750, second place $250. 3 winners, first $700, second $200, third $100. Contest receives 50 entries. Judge: "Lay committee with relevant expertise." No entry fee. For guidelines, send SASE, e-mail, visit website or call. Accepts inquiries by fax, e-mail, phone. Deadline: end of December 2003. Entries must be unpublished. "Must be on a Jewish theme or topic." Authors aged 18-35 by December 31 of competition year are eligible. Results announced by June 30. Winners notified by mail. For contest results, visit website.

[] EATON LITERARY ASSOCIATES' LITERARY AWARDS PROGRAM, Eaton Literary Associates, P.O. Box 49795, Sarasota FL 34230-6795. (941)366-6589. Fax: (941)365-4679. E-mail: eatonlit@aol.com. Website: www.eatonliterary.com. **Contact:** Richard Lawrence, vice president. Biannual award for short stories and novels. Award: $2,500 for best book-length ms, $500 for best short story. Competition receives approx. 2,000 submissions annually. Judges are 2 staff members in conjunction with an independent agency. Guidelines for SASE, fax, e-mail or on website. Accepts inquiries by fax, phone and e-mail. Deadline: March 31 for short stories; August 31 for

---

TO RECEIVE REGULAR TIPS AND UPDATES about writing and Writer's Digest publications via e-mail, send an e-mail with "SUBSCRIBE" in the subject line to writersdigest-newsletter@fwpubs.com, or sign up online at www.writersdigest.com under "E-mail newsletter signup."

book-length mss. Results announced in April and September. Winners notified by mail. For contest results, send SASE, fax, e-mail or visit website.

N EDITORS' PRIZE, *Missouri Review*, 1507 Hillcrest Hall, University of Missouri, Columbia MO 65211. (573)882-4474. Fax: (573)884-4671. E-mail: mr@missourireview.com. Website: www.missourireview.com. **Contact:** Hoa Ngo, managing editor. Award "to recognize and reward talented writers." Annual. Award for short stories, poetry and essays. Award: $2,000 fiction; $2,000 poetry; $2,000 essay. All winners will be published in *Missouri Review*. 2,000 entries total; 60% of entries for fiction. Judged by editorial staff. $15 fee per entry; send credit card information or make checks payable to *The Missouri Review*. Guidelines available in June by SASE, or on website. Deadline: October 15, 2004. Entries should be unpublished. Length: less than 25 pages. Cover letter should include name, address, phone, e-mail and title. Results announced in the spring issue. Winners notified by phone or e-mail in the Spring. For contest results, send SASE or visit website.

• See the interview with *Missouri Review* editor Speer Morgan on page 27.

THE EMILY CONTEST, West Houston Chapter Romance Writers of America, 5603 Chantilly Lane, Houston TX 77092. E-mail: ellen_watkins@juno.com. Website: http://www.poboxes.com/whrwa. **Contact:** Ellen Watkins, Emily Contest chair. Purpose is "to help people writing romance novels learn to write better books and to help them make contacts in the publishing world." Annual competition for novels. First-place entry in each category receives the Emily brooch; all finalists receive certificates. Competition receives 40-60 submissions per category. First round judges are published authors and experienced critiquers. Final round judges (for finalists) are editors at a major romance publishing house. $20 entry fee for WHRWA members, $30 for non-members. Guidelines available July 2003. For guidelines, send SASE, e-mail or visit website. Accepts inquiries by e-mail. Contest open to all unpublished romance writers. Length: first 35 pages of novel. "We look for dynamic, interesting romantic stories with a hero and heroine readers can relate to and love. Hook us from the beginning and keep the excitement level high." Results announced February 2004. Winners notified by mail or phone. For contest results, send SASE or visit website.

◙ VIRGINIA FAULKNER AWARD FOR EXCELLENCE IN WRITING, *Prairie Schooner*, P.O. Box 880334, University of Nebraska, Lincoln NE 68588-0334. (402)472-0911. Fax: (402)472-9771. E-mail: kgrey2@unl.edu. Website: www.unl.edu/schooner/psmain.htm. **Contact:** Hilda Raz, editor. "An award for writing published in *Prairie Schooner* in the previous year." Annual competition for short stories, essays, novel excerpts and translations. Award: $1,000. Judges: Editorial Board. Guidelines for SASE or on website. Accepts inquiries by fax and e-mail. "We only read mss from September 1 through May 31." Work must have been published in *Prairie Schooner* in the previous year. Results announced in Spring issue. Winners notified by mail in February or March. List of winners will be published in Spring *Prairie Schooner*.

N ◙ FAUX FAULKNER CONTEST, *Hemispheres* Magazine, *Faulkner Newsletter* of Yoknapatawpha Press and University of Mississippi, P.O. Box 248, Oxford MS 38655. (601)234-0909. E-mail: faulkner@watervalley.net. Website: www.watervalley.net/yoknapatawphapress/index.htm or www.hemispheresmagazine.com. Award "to honor William Faulkner by imitating his style, themes and subject matter in a short parody." Annual competition for a 500-word (2 pages) parody. Award: 2 round-trip tickets to Memphis, plus complimentary registration and lodging for the annual Faulkner and Yoknapatawpha Conference at the University of Mississippi. Competition receives approximately 200-300 submissions. Past judges have included George Plimpton, Tom Wicker, John Berendt and Arthur Schlesinger, Jr. (judges rotate every year or so—well-known authors). Guidelines for SASE. Deadline: March 1. Previously unpublished submissions. Results announced July 1. Winners notified May 1. Contestants grant publication rights and the right to release entries to other media and to the sponsors.

N FICTION COMPETITION AND POETRY COMPETITION, (formerly Short Fiction Competition), *Inkwell Magazine* and Manhattanville College, 2900 Purchase St., Purchase NY 10577. (914)323-7239. Fax: (914)694-3488. E-mail: inkwell@mville.edu. **Contact:** Jeremy Church, editor. "To reward excellence in fiction writing." Annual competition for short stories. Award: $1,500 and publication of the winning entry and top finalist in *Inkwell*. Competition receives roughly 800 submissions. Judge: Martha Cooley. Contests are officiated by distinguished fiction writers. $15 per entry fee. Guidelines available online at inkwelljournal.org. Deadline: October 31, 2003. Entries should be unpublished. Contest open to previously unpublished writers. Results announced Spring of 2004. Winners notified by phone in March 2004. For contest results, send SASE.

N ◙ ◙ ROBERT L. FISH MEMORIAL AWARD, Mystery Writers of America, Inc., 17 E. 47th St., 6th Floor, New York NY 10017. (212)888-8171. Fax: (212)888-8107. E-mail: mwa@mysterywriters.org. Website: www.mysterywriters.org. **Contact:** Margery Flax, office manager. Estab. 1984. Annual award "to encourage new writers in the mystery/detective/suspense short story—and, subsequently, larger work in the genre." Award: $500 and plaque. Judges: The MWA committee for best short story of the year in the mystery genre. Deadline: November 30. Submissions must be published the year prior to the award. Looking for "a story with a crime that is central to the plot that is well written and distinctive." Guidelines and application available in January by fax, e-mail or on website. Accepts inquiries by fax, e-mail and phone. Results announced in February. Winners notified by phone and e-mail. For contest results, visit website.

▦ FISH SHORT STORY PRIZE, Fish Publishing, Durrus, Bantry, Co. Cork, Ireland. Phone: (00)353(0)27 61246. E-mail: info@fishpublishing.com. Website: www.fishpublishing.com. **Contact:** Clem Cairns, editor. "Purpose is to find and publish new and exciting short fiction from all over the world: to support the short story and those that practice it." Annual. Competition for short stories. Award: Publication in Fish's anthology along with 15 other winners. $1,500 first prize, second prize is a week at Anam Cara Writers' Retreat (Ireland). Competition receives 1,800 submissions per category. Judges: stories are short-listed by a panel of readers, and the short-list is sent to independent judges who are well-known writers. $15 entry fee; make checks payable to Fish Publishing. Guidelines available in July by e-mail, on website or in publication. Accepts inquiries by e-mail and phone. Deadline: November 30 annually. Entries should be unpublished. Open to everybody except those who have won it before, or been a runner-up twice. Length: 5,000 words maximum. Cover letter should include name, address, phone, e-mail, word count and title. "Don't be afraid to write with your own voice—we value originality. Do make sure that your story is as good as you can get it. Don't try to write to please a judge or judges. Make sure it is neat and easy to read." Results announced March 17 every year. Winners notified by mail, phone or e-mail and at prize ceremony/book launch in Bantry, Co. Cork, last Saturday in June. For contest results, send SASE, e-mail or visit website.

◐ ◎ DOROTHY CANFIELD FISHER AWARD, Vermont Dept. of Libraries, 109 State St., Montpelier VT 05609-0601. (802)828-6954. Fax: (802)828-2199. E-mail: grace.greene@dol.state.vt.us. Website: www.dcfaward.org. **Contact:** Grace Greene, children's services consultant. Estab. 1957. Annual award. "To encourage Vermont schoolchildren to become enthusiastic and discriminating readers and to honor the memory of one of Vermont's most distinguished and beloved literary figures." Award: Illuminated scroll. Publishers send the committee review copies of books to consider. Only books of the current publishing year can be considered for next year's master list. Master list of titles is drawn up in March each year. Children vote each year in the spring and the award is given before the school year ends. Submissions must be "written by living American authors, be suitable for children in grades 4-8, and have literary merit. Can be nonfiction also." Accepts inquiries by e-mail. Deadline: December 1. Results announced in April. Winners notified by mail and phone. For contest results, call, write or e-mail.

Ⓝ ◎ F. SCOTT FITZGERALD SHORT STORY CONTEST, % Rockville City Hall, 111 Maryland Ave., Rockville MD 20850. (301)309-9461. Website: www.peerlessrockville.org/FSF/. **Contact:** Marilyn Mullan. Annual. Award for short stories. Award: $1,000 and receipt of award from F. Scott Fitzgerald Literary Conference Honoree Edward Albee. $25 fee per entry; make checks payable to F. Scott Fitzgerald Literary Conference Contest. Guidelines available on website. Deadline: postmarked by July 15. Entries should be unpublished. Contest open to all residents of Maryland, Virginia and Washington D.C. Length: no more than 3,000 words. Cover letter should include name, address and phone.

Ⓝ THE FLORIDA REVIEW EDITORS' AWARDS, *The Florida Review*, Department of English, UCF, Orlando FL 32817. (407)679-2038. Website: www.flreview.com. **Contact:** Jeanne Leiby, fiction editor. Annual. Competition for short stories, short nonfiction and poetry. Award: $1,000. Judged by genre editors. $15 fee per entry; make checks payable to *The Florida Review*. Guidelines available in December by SASE, phone or on website. Deadline: April 5, 2004. Entries should be unpublished. Length: 7,500 words maximum. Cover letter should include name, address, phone, e-mail, word count and title. Results announced June 1, 2004. Winners notified by mail or e-mail. For contest results, send SASE.

◻ FLORIDA STATE WRITING COMPETITION, Florida Freelance Writers Association, P.O. Box A, North Stratford NH 03590-0167. (603)922-8338. E-mail: danakcnw@ncia.net. Website: www.writers-editors.com. **Contact:** Dana K. Cassell, executive director. "To offer additional opportunities for writers to earn income and recognition from their writing efforts." Annual competition for short stories and novels. Award: varies from $50-100. Competition receives approximately 100 short stories; 60 novels; total 500+ entries in all categories. Judges: authors, editors and teachers. Entry fee from $5-20. Guidelines for SASE or on website. Deadline: March 15. Unpublished submissions. Categories include short story and novel chapter. "Guidelines are revised each year and subject to change. New guidelines are available in Summer of each year." Accepts inquiries by e-mail. Results announced May 31. Winners notified by mail. For contest results, send SASE marked "winners" or visit website.

◐ ◎ THE JOSETTE FRANK AWARD, Children's Book Committee at Bank St. College, 610 W. 112th St., New York NY 10025-1895. (212)875-4540. Fax: (212)875-4759. E-mail: bookcom@bnkst.edu. Website: www.bankstreet.edu/bookcom. **Contact:** Alice B. Belgray, committee chair. Annual award "to honor a book, or books, of outstanding literary merit in which children or young people deal in a positive and realistic way with difficulties in their world and grow emotionally and morally." Only books sent by publishers for review are considered. Books must have been published within current calendar year. Award: Certificate and cash prize. Competition receives approximately 2,000 submissions. Accepts inquiries by e-mail and fax. Deadline: November 15. Results announced in March. Winners notified through their publishers and by mail.

▦ ◻ ◎ MILES FRANKLIN LITERARY AWARD, Trust, 35 Clarence St., Sydney NSW 2000 Australia. Phone: 8295 8191. Fax: 8295 8659. E-mail: lingaldo@trust.com.au. Website: www.permanentgroup.com.au. **Contact:** Linda Ingaldo, awards administrator. Award "for the advancement, improvement and betterment of Australian literature." Annual award for novels. Award: AUS $28,000, to the author "of the novel which is of the highest literary merit for the year and which presents Australian life in any of its phases." Competition receives 60 submissions. Judges: David Marr, Dagmar Schmidmaier, Professor Elizabeth Webby, Hilary McPhee and Mark Rubbo (in 2003). $100 AU entry fee. Make checks payable to Trust Company Ltd. Guidelines available in November; send SASE, fax or e-mail. Accepts inquiries by fax, phone and e-mail. Deadline: Second Friday in December. Contest open to previously published submissions. "The novel must have been published in the year prior to competition entry and must present Australian life in any of its phases." Results announced in June. Winners notified by mail or phone.

FREEFALL MAGAZINE FICTION & POETRY CONTEST, *FreeFall* magazine, 922 Ninth Ave. SE, Calgary AB T2G 0S4 Canada. Phone/fax: (403)264-4730. E-mail: awcs@telusplanet.net. Website: www.alexandraw riters.org. **Contact:** Sherring Amsden, managing editor. Award established "to encourage the submission of quality work in fiction and poetry and give it recognition." Annual competition for short stories and poetry. Prize (fiction): 1st place, $200; 2nd place, $100. Judge: *FreeFall*'s editor and assistant editors. $10 fee per entry; make checks payable to *FreeFall* Magazine. 2004 guidelines available in January-February. For guidelines and entry form, send SASE, e-mail, phone or visit website. Accepts inquiries by e-mail and phone. Deadline: October 1, 2004. Entries should be unpublished. "Open to all writers over 18 years from any region, genre, ethnicity, etc." Length: 3,000 words maximum. Cover letter should include name, address, phone, e-mail, word count; title and word count on ms. "Carefully read and follow contest rules and guidelines for manuscript submission. Include signed contest entry form with payment." Results announced in December 2004. Winners notified by mail, phone and e-mail in December. For contest results, send SASE, e-mail or visit website.

THE FUNNY PAPER COMPETITION, F/J Writers Service, P.O. Box 455, Lee's Summit MO 64063. E-mail: felixkcmo@aol.com. Website: http://www.angelfire.com/biz/funnypaper. **Contact:** F.H. Fellhauer, editor. Award to "provide readership, help, and the opportunity to write for money to budding authors of all ages." Competition for short stories, fillers, jokes, poems, cartoons held 4 times/year. Award: $5-100. Competition receives 50-100 submissions per category. Judge: editors and selected assistants. No entry fee. Guidelines in every issue. For guidelines, send SASE or visit website. Accepts inquiries by e-mail. No deadline (unused entries are held for next contest). Entries should be unpublished, or published only if we are advised where and when. Contest open to all writers. Length: 1,000 words maximum. Results announced in each issue. Winners notified by mail on publication.

THE JOHN GARDNER MEMORIAL PRIZE FOR FICTION, (formerly The John Gardner Fiction Contest), *Harpur Palate*, English Dept., Binghamton University, Box 6000, Binghamton NY 13902-6000. E-mail: tfinley@bin ghamton.edu (for contest queries only). Website: http://harpurpalate.binghamton.edu/contests.shtml. **Contact:** John Gardner fiction contest, *Harpur Palate*. "John Gardner—novelist, poet, translator, dramatist, and teacher—helped found the creative writing program at Binghamton University. In honor of his dedication to the development of writers, *Harpur Palate* hosts the Annual John Gardner Memorial Prize for Fiction." Annual award. Prize: $500 and publication in *Harpur Palate*. Entry fee: $10/story; make checks payable to *Harpur Palate*. "You may send as many stories as you wish, but please send each story in a separate envelope along with the entry fee." Entries should be previously unpublished. "Stories may be in any genre but should not exceed 8,000 words. Don't sacrifice character for plot or plot for character. Stories that have the best chance of winning take risks with genre and style. Please include your name and contact information in the cover letter *only*. If you have an e-mail address you check regularly, please include this in your contact information. We like to make contact via e-mail first." All entrants receive a copy of the issue with the winning story and a copy of the latest back issue. Make sure your entry fee is paid by a check (drawn on U.S. bank) or money order.

GIFT OF FREEDOM AWARD, A Room Of Her Own Foundation, P.O. Box 778, Placitas NM 87043-0778. E-mail: info@aroomofherownfoundation.org. Website: www.aroomofherownfoundation.org. **Contact:** Darlene Chandler Bassett, president and founder. Award is "to provide very practical help, both materially and in professional guidance and moral support, to women who need assistance in making their creative contribution to the world." Biannual literary award for short stories, novels, short story collections, poetry, creative nonfiction and playwriting. Prize: Up to $50,000, payable over a two-year period in installments based upon the needs of the recipient. Judging: "Awarding panel will be composed of members of AROHO's Board of Directors, Advisory Council and volunteers from a wide variety of backgrounds." Each award is based upon merits of the application. $25 processing fee. For guidelines, send e-mail or visit website. 2004 deadline February 1, 2004. Entries may be either unpublished or previously published. Contest open to "U.S. female writers." Writers must submit 2 essays, each 5 double-spaced pages. "The successful applicant will have a well-articulated project concept and a clear plan for how it may be accomplished." Results announced in June 2004. Winners notified by mail, phone. List of grant winners posted on website.

GLIMMER TRAIN'S FALL SHORT-STORY AWARD FOR NEW WRITERS, Glimmer Train Press, Inc., 1211 NW Glisan St., Suite 207, Portland OR 97209. (503)221-0836. Fax: (503)221-0837. Website: www.glimm ertrain.com (includes writers' guidelines and a Q&A section for writers). **Contact:** Linda Swanson-Davies, fiction editor. Contest offered for any writer whose fiction hasn't appeared in a nationally-distributed publication with a circulation over 5,000. "We want to read your original, unpublished short (1,200-8,000 words) story." $12 reading fee. Make your submissions online (www.glimmertrain.com) by September 30. Winners will be notified and results will be posted by January 2. Winner receives $1,200, publication in *Glimmer Train Stories* and 20 copies of that issue. First/second runners-up receive $500/$300, respectively, and consideration for publication."

◻ **GLIMMER TRAIN'S FICTION OPEN,** Glimmer Train Press, Inc., 1211 NW Glisan St., Suite 207, Portland OR 97209. (503)221-0836. Fax: (503)221-0837. Website: www.glimmertrain.com (includes writers' guidelines and a Q&A section for writers). **Contact:** Linda Swanson-Davies, contest director. Contest for short story (under 20,000 words), open to all writers. Award: First place $2,000, publication in *Glimmer Train Stories* (circ. 13,000) and 20 copies of that issue. First/second runners-up receive $1,000/$600 respectively and consideration for publication. "We want to read your original, unpublished short story. No theme limitations. $15 reading fee. Make your submissions online (www.glimmertrain.com) by June 30. Winners will be notified and results will be posted by October 15."

◻ **GLIMMER TRAIN'S SPRING SHORT-STORY AWARD FOR NEW WRITERS,** Glimmer Train Press, Inc., 1211 NW Glisan St., Suite 207, Portland OR 97209. (503)221-0836. Fax: (503)221-0837. Website: www.glimmertrain.com (includes writers' guidelines and a Q&A section for writers). **Contact:** Linda Swanson-Davies, contest director. Contest offered for any writer whose fiction hasn't appeared in a nationally-distributed publication with a circulation over 5,000. "We want to read your original, unpublished short (1,200-8,000 words) story. $12 reading fee. Make your submissions online (www.glimmertrain.com) by March 31. Winners will be notified and results will be posted by July 1. Winner receives $1,200, publication in *Glimmer Train Stories* and 20 copies of that issue. First/second runners-up receive $500/$300, respectively, and consideration for publication."

◉ **GOLD MEDALLION BOOK AWARDS,** Evangelical Christian Publishers Association, 4816 S. Ash, #101, Tempe AZ 85282. (480)966-3998. Fax: (480)966-1944. E-mail: jmeegan@ecpa.org. Website: www.ecpa.org. **Contact:** Doug Ross, president. Award to "recognize quality/encourage excellence." Annual competition for 20 categories including fiction. Award: Gold Medallion plaque. Competition receives approximately 50 submissions in the fiction category. Judges: "Two rounds of judges—first round primarily Christian bookstore owners, managers and book buyers; second round primarily editors, book reviewers, industry leaders and selected Christian bookstore leaders. First round will determine five finalists in each of the 20 categories. Second round judges the finalists in each category." Entry fee of $300 for non-members. Guidelines available annually in October. Accepts inquiries by fax and e-mail. Deadline: December 1. Previously published submissions appearing during the calendar year preceding the year in which the award is to be presented. Entries must be submitted by the publisher. Results announced annually in July at the Annual Gold Medallion Book Awards Banquet. For contest results, contact the ECPA offices.

◻ **THE GREAT BLUE BEACON SHORT-SHORT STORY CONTEST,** *The Great Blue Beacon: The Newsletter for Writers of All Genres and Skill Levels,* 1425 Patriot Dr., Melbourne FL 32940-6881. (321)253-5869. E-mail: ajircc@juno.com. **Contact:** A.J. Byers, editor/publisher. Award to "recognize outstanding short-short story." Two-three contests each year for short-short stories. Awards: $50 (1st prize); $25 (2nd prize); $10 (3rd prize), plus publication of winning entry in *The Great Blue Beacon*. Receives 50-75 entries per contest. Judges: outside panel of judges. Entry fee $5 ($4 for subscribers). Guidelines available periodically when announced. For guidelines send SASE or e-mail. Accepts inquiries by e-mail and phone. Deadline: TBA. Entries should be previously unpublished. Open to all writers. Length: 1,000 words or fewer. Cover letter and first page of ms should include name, address, phone, e-mail, word count and title. Results announced two months after contest deadline. Winners notified by SASE or e-mail. For contest results, send SASE or e-mail.

Ⓝ ☑ ◎ **GREAT CANADIAN STORY CONTEST,** *Storyteller, Canada's Short Story Magazine,* 858 Wingate Dr., Ottawa ON K1G 1S5 Canada. (613)521-9570. E-mail: info@storytellermagazine.com. Website: www.storytellermagazine.com. **Contact:** Terry Tyo, publisher/managing editor. "Purpose of competition is to publish great Canadian stories." Annual. Award for short stories. Award: varies year to year. Competition receives 500-600 submissions per category. Judges: short list determined by editors; judges choose from short list. $5 Canadian (may change). Guidelines available in February by SASE or on website. Deadline: sometime in mid-April every year. Entries should be unpublished. Contest open to Canadian citizens or landed immigrants. Length: 2,000-6,000 words. "Read the magazine. The short list comprises our summer issue, so all stories must be suitable for publication in *Storyteller* to qualify." Results announced in May. Winners notified by phone or e-mail. For contest results, send SASE or visit website.

THE JUDY & A.C. GREENE LITERARY FESTIVAL CONTEST, The Living Room Theatre of Salado, P.O. Box 1023, Salado TX 76571-1023. (254)947-3104. Website: http://lrtsalado.com. **Contact:** Dr. Raymond Carver, director/producer. "The purpose of the festival is development of unpublished works by Texas writers. The Festival seeks unpublished literary works which may be adapted by staff of the Living Room Theatre for dramatic performance with two to five actors using lecture stands but no other theatrical elements." Annual competition for short stories, novels, story collections. Award: 1st prize $1,500; 3 finalists $250 each. Competition receives about 50 submissions. Judge: contest/festival staff. $20 entry fee. Guidelines available in October on website. Deadline: March 15. Entries must be unpublished. Contest open to Texas residents or former residents. Length: 30-60 minutes reading aloud time. "No poems or discursive writing." Finalists announced in May and notified by mail or e-mail. List of winners available on website. "Material will be read aloud by 2-4 performers at festival. Emphasize dialog, plot, character. Short stories and plays will be adapted to readers theatre format."

☐ **THE GREENSBORO REVIEW LITERARY AWARDS**, English Dept., 134 McIver Bldg, UNC-Greensboro, P.O. Box 26170, Greensboro NC 27402-6170. (336)334-5459. E-mail: tlkenned@uncg.edu. Website: www.uncg.edu/eng/mfa. **Contact:** Terry Kennedy, managing editor. Annual award. Award: $500. Competition receives 1,000 submissions. Judged by editors of *Greensboro Review*. Guidelines for SASE or on website. Accepts inquiries by e-mail. Deadline: September 15. Unpublished submissions. "All manuscripts meeting literary award guidelines will be considered for cash award as well as for publication in *The Greensboro Review*." Winners notified by mail, phone or e-mail. List of winners published in the Spring issue of *The Greensboro Review*.

N: GSU REVIEW ANNUAL CONTEST, *GSU Review*, GSU Review, Georgia State University, P.O. Box 1894, MSC 8R0322, Unit 8, Atlanta GA 30303. (404)651-4804. E-mail: kchaple@attbi.com. Website: www.gsu.edu/~wwwrev. **Contact:** Dan Marshall, fiction editor. Annual. Competition for short stories. Award: $1,000. Prize categories include fiction, poetry; receives over 250 entries each. $10 fee per entry; make checks payable to *GSU Review*. Guidelines available in October by SASE, on website, or in publication. Accepts inquiries by e-mail, phone. Deadline: postmarked by February 2, 2004. Entries should be unpublished. Contest open to all except faculty, staff, students of Georgia State University. Length: should not exceed 7,500 words. Cover letter should include name, address, phone, e-mail, word count and title. "Do not include this information on ms." Results announced in Spring of 2004. Winners notified by mail, phone, e-mail. For contest results, send SASE.

GULF COAST POETRY AND SHORT FICTION AWARDS, Gulf Coast: a Journal of Literature and Fine Art, University of Houston, Dept. of English, Houston TX 77204-3012. (713)743-3223. Fax: (713)743-3215. E-mail: editors@gulfcoastmag.org. Website: www.gulfcoastmag.org. **Contact:** Pablo Peschiera, managing editor. "To showcase excellent contemporary writing that pays attention to craft and language." Annual competition for short stories. Award: $1,000. Competition receives 300 submissions. $15 fee per entry. Guidelines available in Fall for SASE. Accepts inquiries by phone. Deadline: mid-February. Entries should be unpublished. Contest open to all. Length: 6,000 words or 5 poems. "Provide a short cover letter and enter what you consider to be your best work." Winners notified by mail or phone in May. List of winners available for SASE.

◎ **HAMMETT PRIZE**, International Association of Crime Writers/North American Branch, P.O. Box 8674, New York NY 10116-8674. Fax: (815)361-1477. E-mail: mfrisque@igc.org. Website: http://jmc.ou.edu/AIEP/index.htm. **Contact:** Mary A. Frisque, executive director, North American Branch. Award established "to honor a work of literary excellence in the field of crime writing by a U.S. or Canadian author." Annual award for novels, story collections by one author and also nonfiction. Award: trophy. Competition receives about 200 submissions per category. "Our reading committee seeks suggestions from publishers and they also ask the membership for recommendations. Eligible books are read by a committee of members of the organization. The committee chooses five nominated books, which are sent to three outside judges for a final decision. Judges are outside the crime writing field." No entry fee. For guidelines, send SASE or e-mail. Accepts inquiries by e-mail. Deadline: December 1, 2003. Entries should be previously published. To be eligible "the book must have been published in the U.S. or Canada during the calendar year. The author must be a U.S. or Canadian citizen or permanent resident." "Nominations announced in January; 2003 winner will be announced in Fall 2004." Winners notified by mail, phone and at awards ceremony in October 2004. For contest results, send SASE or e-mail.

◑ **DRUE HEINZ LITERATURE PRIZE**, University of Pittsburgh Press, 3400 Forbes Ave., 5th Floor, Eureka Building, Pittsburgh PA 15260. (412)383-2492. Fax: (412)383-2466. E-mail: susief@pitt.edu. Website: www.pitt.edu/press. **Contact:** Sue Borello, assistant to the director. Annual award "to support the writer of short fiction at a time when the economics of commercial publishing make it more and more difficult for the serious literary artist working in the short story and novella to find publication." Competition for story collections. Award: $15,000 and publication by the University of Pittsburgh Press. "It is imperative that entrants request complete rules of the competition by sending an SASE before submitting a manuscript." Submissions will be received only during the months of May and June. Postmark deadline: June 30. Manuscripts must be unpublished in book form. The award

MARKET CONDITIONS are constantly changing! If you're still using this book and it is 2005 or later, buy the newest edition of *Novel & Short Story Writer's Market* at your favorite bookstore or order from Writer's Digest Books by calling 1-800-448-0915.

is open to writers who have published a book-length collection of fiction or a minimum of three short stories or novellas in commercial magazines or literary journals of national distribution. Length: 150-300 typed pages. Cover letter should include name, address, phone, e-mail, title, name of publication where work was originally published. "This information should not appear on the ms." Results announced in February. Winners notified by phone. For contest results, send SASE sent with manuscript.

◪ ERNEST HEMINGWAY FOUNDATION/PEN AWARD FOR FIRST FICTION, PEN New England, P.O. Box 400725, North Cambridge MA 02140. (617)499-9550. Fax: (617)353-7134. E-mail: awards@pen-ne.org. Website: www.pen-ne.org. **Contact:** Mary Walsh, coordinator. Annual award "to give beginning writers recognition and encouragement and to stimulate interest in first books of fiction among publishers and readers." Receives 130 submissions. Award: $7,500. Novels or short story collections must have been published during calendar year under consideration. No entry fee. Entry form or rules for SASE, e-mail or on website after September. Accepts inquiries by fax, e-mail, phone. Deadline: December 13, 2003. "The Ernest Hemingway Foundation/PEN Award For First Fiction is given to an American author of the best first-published book-length work of fiction published by an established publishing house in the US each calendar year." Results announced in March. Winners notified by phone. For contest results, e-mail or visit website.

◻ LORIAN HEMINGWAY SHORT STORY COMPETITION, P.O. Box 993, Key West FL 33041-0993. (305)294-0320. E-mail: calico2419@aol.com. Website: www.shortstorycompetition.com. **Contact:** Carol Shaughnessy, co-director. Award to "encourage literary excellence and the efforts of writers who have not yet had major-market success." Annual competition for short stories. Awards: $1,000 (1st prize); $500 (2nd prize); $500 (3rd prize); honorable mentions. Competition receives approximately 850 submissions. Judges: A panel of writers, editors and literary scholars selected by author Lorian Hemingway. Entry fee $10 for each story postmarked by May 1, 2004; $15 for each story postmarked between May 1 and May 15, 2004. Guidelines available January 15 by e-mail, phone, on website or for SASE. Accepts inquiries by SASE, e-mail or visit website. Deadline: May 1-15, 2004. Unpublished submissions. "Open to all writers whose fiction has not appeared in a nationally distributed publication with a circulation of 5,000 or more." Word length: 3,000 words maximum. "We look for excellence, pure and simple—no genre restrictions, no theme restrictions—we seek a writer's voice that cannot be ignored." Results announced at the end of July during Hemingway Days Festival. Winners notified by phone prior to announcement. For contest results, send e-mail or visit website. "All entrants will receive a letter from Lorian Hemingway and a list of winners by October 1."

◻ ◎ HIGHLIGHTS FOR CHILDREN FICTION CONTEST, *Highlights for Children*, 803 Church St., Honesdale PA 18431. (570)253-1080. Fax: (570)251-7847. E-mail: eds@highlights-corp.com. Website: www.highlights.com. **Contact:** Marileta Robinson, senior editor. Award "to honor quality stories (previously unpublished) for young readers and to encourage children's writers." Annual. Contest for short stories. Awards: Three $1,000 awards plus publication in *Highlights*. "There is a different contest theme each year. We generally receive around 1,400 entries." Judges: *Highlights* editors, with input given also by outside readers. No entry fee. Guidelines available in July by SASE. Accepts inquiries by phone. Deadline: entries must be postmarked between January 1 and February 28, 2004. Entries should be unpublished. Contest open to anyone 16 years of age or older. Length: 500 words maximum for stories for beginning readers (to age 8) and 800 words for more advanced readers (ages 9 to 12). No minimum word length. Cover letter should include name, address, phone, e-mail, word count and title. "We prefer that these things appear on the manuscript as well." Results announced in June 2004. Winners notified by mail or phone. For contest results, send SASE.

THEODORE CHRISTIAN HOEPFNER AWARD, *Southern Humanities Review*, 9088 Haley Center, Auburn University AL 36849. Co-editors: Dan R. Latimer or Virginia M. Kouidis. Annual award "to award the authors of the best essay, the best short story and the best poem published in *Southern Humanities Review* each year." Award: $100 for the best short story. Judges: Editorial staff. Only published work in the current volume (4 issues) will be judged.

◪ ◻ ◎ HONOLULU MAGAZINE STARBUCKS COFFEE HAWAI'I FICTION CONTEST, *Honolulu Magazine* and Starbucks Coffee Hawai'i, 1000 Bishop St., Suite 405, Honolulu HI 96813. (808)537-9500. E-mail: akamn@pacificbasin.net. **Contact:** A. Kam Napier, managing editor. "Award to promote great writing about life in the islands. We do not accept fiction except during our annual contest, at which time we welcome it." Annual award for short stories. Award: $1,000, $500 in Starbucks merchandise and publication in the April issue of *Honolulu* Magazine. Competition receives approximately 400 submissions. Judges: editorial staff of *Honolulu* magazine. Guidelines for SASE, on website or in publication. Deadline: early December. Length: 3,000 words or less. "Stories must have a Hawai'i theme, setting and/or characters. Author should enclose name and address in separate small envelope. Do not put name on story." Winners notified by phone in February. "Remember that the judges and the magazine's readers are lifelong—or longtime—residents of Hawai'i. For us, Honolulu is a vibrant, contemporary American city—not a tourist playground."

◻ ◎ L. RON HUBBARD'S WRITERS OF THE FUTURE CONTEST, Author Services, Inc., P.O. Box 1630, Los Angeles CA 90078. (323)466-3310. Fax: (323)466-6474. E-mail: contests@authorservicesinc.com. Website: www.writersofthefuture.com. **Contact:** Rachel Deuk, contest administrator. Estab. 1983. Quarterly. Foremost competition for new and amateur writers of unpublished science fiction or fantasy short stories or novelettes. Awards $1,000, $750, $500 in quarterly prizes, $4,000 annual Grand Prize. "Contest has four quarters. There shall be three cash prizes in each quarter. In addition, at the end of the year the four first-place, quarterly winners will have their entries rejudged, and a Grand Prize winner shall be determined." Judged first by K.D. Wentworth, then by panel of 4 professional authors. No entry fee. Entrants retain all rights. Guidelines available for #10 SASE, by fax, phone, e-mail and on website. Accepts inquiries by fax, e-mail, phone. Quarterly deadlines: December 31, March 31, June 30, September 30. Year closes September 30. Entries should be unpublished. Contest open to "those who have not professionally published a novel or short novel, or more than one novelette, or more than three short stories, in any medium. Professional publication is deemed to be payment, and at least 5,000 copies or 5,000 hits." Limit 1 entry per quarter. Length: up to 17,000 words. Manuscripts: white paper, black ink; double-spaced; typed; each page appropriately numbered with title; no author name. Include cover page with author's name, address, phone number, e-mail address if available as well as estimated word count and the title of the work. Results announced quarterly. Winners notified by phone. For contest results, visit website.

INDIANA REVIEW '1/2K' PRIZE FOR SHORT-SHORTS/PROSE POEMS, *Indiana Review*, Ballantine Hall 465, 1020 E. Kirkwood Ave., Bloomington IN 47405-7103. (812)855-3439. Fax: (812)855-4253. E-mail: inreview@indiana.edu. Website: www.indiana.edu/~inreview. **Contact:** Danit Brown, fiction editor. Annual. Competition for fiction and prose poems no longer than 500 words. Award: $500 plus publication and contributor's copies. All entries considered for publication. Judges: *Indiana Review* staff and outside judges. $15 fee per entry; make checks payable to *Indiana Review*. Guidelines available in March 2004 by SASE, or on website. Accepts inquiries by e-mail, phone. Deadline: June 7. Entries should be unpublished. Length: 500 words maximum, 3 mss per entry. Cover letter should include name, address, phone, e-mail, word count and title. No identifying information on ms. "We look for command of language and form." Results announced in August. Winners notified by mail. For contest results, send SASE or visit website.

INDIANA REVIEW FICTION PRIZE, *Indiana Review*, Ballantine Hall 465, 1020 E. Kirkwood Ave., Bloomington IN 47405-7103. (812)855-3439. Fax: (812)855-4253. E-mail: inreview@indiana.edu. Website: www.indiana.edu/~inreview/. **Contact:** Danit Brown, fiction editor. Annual. Contest for fiction in any style and on any subject. Award: $1,000, publication in the *Indiana Review* and contributor's copies (1st place). Each entrant will receive the a year's subscription. Competition receives over 500 submissions. Judges: *Indiana Review* staff and outside judges. $15 entry fee. Guidelines available in June for SASE. Accepts inquiries by fax, e-mail or phone. Deadline: October 29, 2003. All entries considered for publication. Cover letter must include name, address, phone number, and title of story. Entrant's name should appear only in the cover letter, as all entries will be considered anonymously. Manuscripts will not be returned. No previously published works, or works forthcoming elsewhere, are eligible. Simultaneous submissions acceptable, but in event of entrant withdraw, contest fee will not be refunded. Length: 40 pages maximum, double spaced. Results announced by December 2003. Winners notified by mail. For contest results, send SASE. "We look for a command of language and structure, as well as a facility with compelling and unusual subject matter. It's a good idea to obtain copies of issues featuring past winners to get a more concrete idea of what we are looking for."

INDIANA UNIVERSITY WRITERS' CONFERENCE SCHOLARSHIP COMPETITION, Indiana University Writers' Conference, 464 Ballantine Hall, Bloomington IN 47401. (812)855-1877. Fax: (812)855-9535. E-mail: writecon@indiana.edu. Website: www.indiana.edu/~writecon. **Contact:** Amy Locklin, director. Competition to "provide financial assistance to conference applicants with the most promising manuscripts." Annual. Competition for short stories, poetry and creative nonfiction. Awards: between $50-150 (for use towards conference tuition/fees). "We receive approximately 60 applicants for fiction and poetry and 20 for creative nonfiction." Entries are judged anonymously by an outside judge designated by the director. The top 10 winners in fiction and poetry receive awards, and the top 2 in creative nonfiction. $25 conference application fee per entry; make checks payable to IU Writers' Conference Fund. Guidelines available in December by SASE, fax, phone, e-mail, on website, in publication. Accepts inquiries by fax, e-mail, phone. Deadline: May 3, 2004 (for receipt of ms). Entries should be unpublished. Contest open to anyone who applies to the Indiana University Writers' Conference. Length: 20 double-spaced pages of prose or 3-5 poems. Cover letter should include name, address, phone, e-mail and title. Title only on ms. Results announced mid-May. Winners notified by phone or e-mail. For contest results, send SASE, fax, e-mail or visit website.

INDIVIDUAL ARTIST FELLOWSHIP, Louisiana Division of the Arts, State of Louisiana, P.O. Box 44247, Baton Rouge LA 70804-4247. (225)342-8180. Fax: (225)342-8173. E-mail: arts@crt.state.la.us. Website: www.crt.st ate.la.us/arts. **Contact:** Dabne Liebke, literature program director. Annual cash awards in recognition of artistic excellence and to distinguish fellows of the highest artistic caliber. Competition for poetry, fiction, creative nonfiction. Award: $5,000. Fiction category receives 15 applications/year. "Peer panel reviews applications through a blind review of samples of work only. Only finalists' application packets are studied in full." Judges: panel of 5 literature experts from Louisiana and out of state. No entry fee. Guidelines and application form available in December on website, and in publication. Accepts inquiries by fax, e-mail and phone. Deadline: March 1, 2004.

Entries may be unpublished or previously published. Contest open to Louisiana residents residing in-state for part 2 years. "Students enrolled in arts-related degree or certificate granting program at grant deadline are ineligible to apply." Length: 30 pages of text (duplex 15 sheets of paper double-sided). Winners notified in June by letter or phone. For contest results, send SASE, fax, e-mail or visit the Literature page of the website.

◎ **INDIVIDUAL ARTIST FELLOWSHIP**, Nebraska Arts Council, 3838 Davenport, Omaha NE 68131-2329. (402)421-3627. Fax: (402)595-2334. E-mail: ltubach@nebraskaartscouncil.org. Website: www.nebraskaartscouncil. org. **Contact:** Lisa Tubach, program manager. Award to "recognize outstanding achievement by Nebraska writers." Competition every third year for short stories and novels. Award: $5,000 Distinguished Achievement; $1,000-2,000 Merit Awards. Competition receives 70-80 submissions per category. Judges: panel of 3. 2005 deadline for literature: November 15. Published or previously unpublished submissions. Nebraska residents only. Length: 50 pages.

◎ **INDIVIDUAL ARTIST MINI-GRANT**, Louisiana Division of the Arts, P.O. Box 44247, Baton Rouge LA 70804-4247. (225)342-8180. Fax: (225)342-8173. E-mail: arts@crt.state.la.us. Website: www.crt.state.la.us/arts. **Contact:** Dabne Liebke, literature program director. "Artist mini-grants are designed to encourage artistic development and to support the realization of specific artistic ideas, and to support specific activities related to the artist's work and career." Biannual grant competition. Award: $500. "The Artist Mini-Grant Program awards approximately 15 mini-grants each year in the Literature category." Judges: staff panel review and 3 individuals. No entry fee. Guidelines and application available by fax, phone and on website. Accepts inquiries by fax, e-mail and phone. 2003 deadlines: August 1 and December 1. Writers may apply twice/year each year but are only eligible for one grant/year. Contest open to Louisiana residents who have lived in-state for the past 2 years. "Students enrolled in arts-related degree or certificate program at grant deadline are ineligible to apply." Length: 30 pages of text (duplex 15 sheets of paper, double-sided). Sample work should always be recent material. Winners notified by phone 3 weeks after deadline and in writing. For contest results, visit website.

Ⓝ **INKWELL FICTION COMPETITION**, Inkwell-Manhattanville College, Manhattanville College, 2900 Purchase St., Box 1379, Purchase NY 10577. (914)323-7239. E-mail: inkwell@mville.edu. Website: www.inkwelljournal.org. **Contact:** Diana V. Spindler, editor. Annual. Competition for short stories. Award: $1,500. Fiction judge: Martha Cooley. $15 fee per entry (5 maximum); make checks payable to Inkwell-Manhattanville. Guidelines available by SASE. Accepts inquiries by e-mail, phone. Deadline: October 31, 2003. Entries should be unpublished. Length: 5,000 words maximum. Cover letter should include name, address, phone, e-mail, word count and title. "Do not include this information on ms." "Follow guidelines strictly and send us your best work." Results announced by January 1, 2004. Winners notified by mail or phone. For contest results, send SASE or visit website.

Ⓝ 🌐 **INTERNATIONAL IMPAC DUBLIN LITERARY AWARD**, Dublin City Council/IMPAC, Dublin City Library & Archive, 138-144 Pearse St., Dublin 2 Ireland. Phone: +353 1 674 4802. Fax: +353 1 674 4879. E-mail: dubaward@iol.ie. Website: www.impacdublinaward.ie. **Contact:** Clare Hogan, senior librarian. Award to promote high quality literary fiction. Annual. Award for novels. Award: €100,000. Competition receives 125 eligible entries. Judges: international panel. No entry fee. Guidelines available in May on website. Accepts inquiries by fax, e-mail, phone. Deadline: June. Entries should be previously published; published in 2002 for 2004 award. Novels may be published anywhere, must be in English translation if not originally published in English. Nominations from *invited* libraries only—*not* writers, publishers or agents. Results announced in March (short list); in May (winner). Winners notified by mail, phone or e-mail. For contest results, visit website.

◻ **IOWA SCHOOL OF LETTERS AWARD FOR SHORT FICTION, THE JOHN SIMMONS SHORT FICTION AWARD**, Iowa Writers' Workshop, 102 Dey House, 507 N. Clinton St., Iowa City IA 52242-1000. Annual awards for short story collections. To encourage writers of short fiction. Award: publication of winning collections by University of Iowa Press the following fall. Entries must be at least 150 pages, word processed, and submitted between August 1 and September 30. Stamped, self-addressed return packaging must accompany manuscript. Rules for SASE. Iowa Writer's Workshop does initial screening of entries; finalists (about 6) sent to outside judge for final selection. "A different well-known writer is chosen each year as judge. Any writer who has not previously published a volume of prose fiction is eligible to enter the competition for these prizes. Revised manuscripts which have been previously entered may be resubmitted."

◻ **IRONWEED PRESS FICTION PRIZE**, Ironweed Press, Inc., P.O. Box 754208, Parkside Station, Forest Hills NY 11375. (718)544-1120. Fax: (718)268-2394. E-mail: IWPress@aol.com. **Contact:** Jin Soo Kang, special projects editor. Prize established "to promote and award excellence in fiction among emerging writers." Annual award for novels and story collections. Award: $2,500 prize, publication as trade paperback. Judge: A panel of three judges (editors, agents, writers). $25 entry fee. Guidelines available November 28, 2003. Send SASE. Deadline: June 27, 2004. "The manuscript may contain published material, provided that the work as a whole has not been previously published." Contest open to all writers. Length: minimum of 20,000 words. Winner announced November 3, 2004. Winner notified by mail or phone prior to announcement. List of winners available for SASE.

◻ ◎ **JOSEPH HENRY JACKSON AWARD**, Intersection for the Arts/The San Francisco Foundation, 446 Valencia St., San Francisco CA 94103-3415. (415)626-2787. Fax: (415)626-1636. E-mail: info@theintersection.org.

Website: www.theintersection.org. **Contact:** Kevin B. Chen, program director. Award "to encourage young, unpublished writers." Annual award for short stories, novels and story collections. Award: $2,000 and certificate. Competition receives 150-200 submissions. Entry form and rules available in mid-October for SASE. Deadline: January 31. Unpublished submissions only. Applicant must be resident of northern California or Nevada for 3 consecutive years immediately prior to the deadline date. Age of applicant must be 20 through 35. Work cannot exceed 100 double-spaced, typed pages. "Submit a serious, ambitious portion of a book-length manuscript." Results announced June 15. Winners notified by mail. "Winners will be announced in letter mailed to all applicants."

🔲 **JAMES JONES FIRST NOVEL FELLOWSHIP**, Wilkes University, Wilkes-Barre PA 18766. (570)408-4530. Fax: (570)408-7829. E-mail: english@wilkes.edu. Website: www.wilkes.edu/humanities/jones.asp. **Contact:** J. Michael Lennon, English department professor. Award to "honor the spirit of unblinking honesty, determination, and insight into modern culture exemplified by the late James Jones, author of *From Here to Eternity* and other prose narrations of distinction," by encouraging the work of an American writer who has not published a book-length work of fiction. Annual award for unpublished novel, novella, or collection of related short stories in progress. Award: $6,000 for first prize; $250 honorarium for runner-up. Receives approximately 600 applications. Application fee: $20 payable to Wilkes University. Guidelines available after June 1, by e-mail or for SASE and on website. Accepts inquiries by e-mail. Deadline: Postmark March 1. Award is open to American writers who have not published a novel, novella or short story collection. Word length: 50 double-spaced pages and a two-page thematic outline. "Cover letter should include title, name, address, telephone number and e-mail address (if available)." Results announced on or near September 30. Winners notified by mail or e-mail. For contest results, send SASE, e-mail or visit website.

◎ **KATHA: INDIAN AMERICAN FICTION CONTEST**, *India Currents* Magazine, P.O. Box 21285, San Jose CA 95148. (408)274-6966. Fax: (408)274-2733. E-mail: editor@indiacurrents.com. Website: www.indiacurrents.com. **Contact:** Vandana Kumar, managing editor. Award "to encourage creative writing which has as its focus India, Indian culture, Indian-Americans and America's views of India." Annual competition for short stories. Awards: $300 (1st prize), $200 (2nd prize), $100 (3rd prize), 2 honorable mentions. Competition received 50 submissions last year. Judges: A distinguished panel of Indian-American authors. Guidelines for SASE or e-mail. Accepts inquiries by e-mail and phone. Deadline: February 20, 2004. Unpublished submissions only. Length: 3,000 words maximum. Results announced on June 1. Winners notified by mail. For contest results, send SASE. "Write about something you have experienced personally or do extensive research, so that you can write knowledgebly."

🔲 ◎ **EZRA JACK KEATS/KERLAN COLLECTION MEMORIAL FELLOWSHIP**, University of Minnesota, 113 Andersen Library, 222-21st Ave. S., Minneapolis MN 55455. (612)624-4576. Fax: (612)625-5525. E-mail: clrc@tc.umn.edu. Website: http://special.lib.umn.edu/clrc/. Award to provide "travel expenses to a talented writer and/or illustrator of children's books who wishes to use the Kerlan Collection for the furtherance of his or her artistic development." Annual competition for books of children's literature. Award: $1,500. Competition receives approximately 10 submissions. Judges: panel of non-Kerlan Collection staff; area professionals, educators, etc. Guidelines available after November for 55¢ SASE. Accepts inquiries by fax, phone and e-mail. Deadline: early May. Accepts unpublished and previously published submissions. Results announced mid June. Winners notified by phone and letter. For contest results, send SASE.

🔲 ◎ **ROBERT F. KENNEDY BOOK AWARDS**, 1367 Connecticut Ave. NW, Suite 200, Washington DC 20036. (202)463-7575. Fax: (202)463-6606. E-mail: info@rfkmemorial.org. Website: www.rfkmemorial.org. **Contact:** Book & Journalism Awards Coordinator. Endowed by Arthur Schlesinger, Jr., from proceeds of his biography, *Robert Kennedy and His Times*. Annual. "To award the author of a book which most faithfully and forcefully reflects Robert Kennedy's purposes." For books published during the calendar year. Award: $2,500 cash prize awarded in the spring. Guidelines available in the fall. Accepts inquiries by e-mail. Deadline: January 30, 2004. Looking for "a work of literary merit in fact or fiction that shows compassion for the poor or powerless or those suffering from injustice." Four copies of each book submitted should be sent, along with a $40 entry fee and entry form (available on website). Results announced Spring 2004. Winners notified by phone. For contest results, visit www.rfkmemorial.org.

🔲 ◎ **KIRIYAMA PRIZE**, (formerly Kiriyama Pacific Rim Book Prize), Kiriyama Pacific Rim Institute, 650 Delancey St., Suite 101, San Francisco CA 94107. (415)777-1628. Fax: (415)777-1646. E-mail: jeannine@kiriyamaprize.org. Website: www.kiriyamaprize.org. **Contact:** Jeannine Cuevas, prize manager. Annual competition for full-length books, fiction or non-fiction. Award: $30,000 divided equally between authors of one fiction and one nonfiction work. Competition receives 400 submissions. Judges: 2 panels of 5 judges (one panel for fiction and one for nonfiction). Guidelines available in August. Accepts inquiries by phone, mail, fax and e-mail. Deadline: October 27. All works should be published. Published entries must have appeared in print between October 1, 2002 and December 31, 2003. "The prize is open to publishers/writers world wide. Entries must concern the Pacific Rim. Writer must be nominated by publisher. Writers should prompt their publishers to do so." Results announced in Spring of 2004. Winners notified by phone.

[N] E.M. KOEPPEL SHORT FICTION AWARD, Writecorner Press, P.O. Box 16369, Jacksonville FL 32245-6369. Website: www.writecorner.com. **Contact:** Mary Sue Koeppel, editor. Annual. Award for short stories. Award: First place $1,100 and Editors Choices $100. Winning short story and several editors' choices will be published on website and will be eligible for print anthology. $15 fee per story, 2 stories for $25; make checks payable to Writecorner Press. Deadline: October 1, 2003-April 30, 2004 postmark. Entries should be unpublished. Length: 3,000 words maximum. Manuscripts must be typed with two title pages: only title may appear on the first title page. No other identification may appear on the ms. Second title page should list title of the short story, author's name, address, phone number, 3-line bio, e-mail address (optional). For contest results, visit website.

[globe] KOREAN LITERATURE TRANSLATION AWARD, Korea Literature Translation Institute, 5th Floor, Seojin Building, 149-1, Pyeong-Dong, Jongno-Gu, Seoul 110-102, Korea. Phone: 82-2-732-1442. Fax: 82-2-732-1443. E-mail: info@ltikorea.net. Website: www.ltikorea.net. **Contact:** Young-il Ko, project manager. Award in recognition of translations that have contributed to a better understanding of Korean literature overseas. Biennial. Award for translations of Korean literature published in monograph (or series) form, between January 1-December 31. Award: $20,000 grand prize; 3 work-of-merit prizes of $30,000; one special prize of $10,000 for publishers. No entry fee. Guidelines available in February on website. Accepts inquiries by fax, e-mail and phone. Entries should be published overseas in a foreign language between January 1, 1998 to December 31, 2003. Writers may not submit their own fiction. Results announced mid-September 2004. Winners notified by mail. For contest results, visit website.

[N] [globe] [target] KOREAN LITERATURE TRANSLATION CONTEST FOR NEW TRANSLATORS, Korea Literature Translation Institute (LTI Korea), 5th Floor, Seojin Building, 149-1, Pyeong-Dong, Jongno-Gu, Seoul 110-102, Korea. Phone: 82-2-732-1442. Fax: 82-2-732-1443. E-mail: info@ltikorea.net. Website: www.ltikorea.net. **Contact:** Ko Young-II, project manager. Contest "to promote the development of future translators who will eventually contribute to the promotion of Korean literature overseas." Annual. Award for short stories published between January 1, 2001 and December 31, 2003 and chosen by the translator that have not been translated previously in the target language. Award: 3 million won for winning translations in each of the four language categories (English, French, German, Spanish). No entry fee. Guidelines available on website. Accepts inquiries by fax, e-mail, phone. Submission period: August 1-30. Entries should be unpublished. Contest open to all individuals who have not had translations of Korean literature published in the target language. No word length requirement. Cover letter should include name, address, phone, e-mail and title. Writers may not submit their own fiction. Results announced in October. Winners notified by mail. For contest results, visit website.

[N] [globe] [target] LAKELAND BOOK OF THE YEAR, Cumbria Tourist Board, Ashleigh, Holly Road, Windermere, Cumbria LA23 2AO England. Phone: +44 (0)15394 44444. Fax: +44 (0)15394 44041. E-mail: info@golakes.co.uk. Website: www.golakes.co.uk. **Contact:** Paul Gardner, public relations manager. Award "to celebrate Cumbria—the Lake District and its literary talents." Annual. Award for novels and short story collections. Award: £100 each category. Prize categories vary each year depending on entries received. Chief judge: Hunter Davies. No entry fee. Guidelines available in January by fax, phone, e-mail. Accepts inquiries by fax, e-mail, phone. Deadline: March. Entries should be unpublished. Must be related to Cumbria-the Lake District. Must be published January-December of the previous year. Cover letter should include name, address, phone, e-mail and title. Results announced in June. Winners notified at event/banquet. For contest results, send fax or e-mail.

[square] THE LAWRENCE FOUNDATION AWARD, *Prairie Schooner*, 201 Andrews Hall, P.O. Box 880334, Lincoln NE 68588-0334. (402)472-0911. Fax: (402)472-9771. E-mail: kgrey2@unl.edu. Website: www.unl.edu/schooner/psmain.htm. **Contact:** Hilda Raz, editor-in-chief. Award "to honor and recognize the best short story published in *Prairie Schooner* in the past year." Annual competition for short stories. Award: $1,000. Judge: The editorial staff of *Prairie Schooner*. "Only work published in *Prairie Schooner* in the previous year is considered." Work is nominated by editorial staff. Results announced in the Spring issue. Winners notified by mail in February or March.

[square] LAWRENCE FOUNDATION PRIZE, *Michigan Quarterly Review*, 3574 Rackham Bldg., Ann Arbor MI 48109-1070. (734)764-9265. E-mail: mgr@umich.edu. Website: www.umich.edu/~mgr. **Contact:** Doris Knight, administrative assistant. "An annual cash prize awarded to the author of the best short story published in *Michigan Quarterly Review* each year." Annual competition for short stories. Award: $1,000. Competition receives approximately 500 submissions. Judges: editorial board. "Stories must already be published in *Michigan Quarterly Review*; this is not a competition in which manuscripts are read outside of the normal submission process." No entry fee. Guidelines available in December for SASE or on website. Accepts inquiries by e-mail and phone. Deadline: September. Results announced in December. Winners notified by phone or mail.

[target] LEAGUE OF UTAH WRITERS CONTEST, League of Utah Writers, 4621 W. Harman Dr., West Valley City UT 84120-3752. (801)964-0861. Fax: (801)964-0937. E-mail: crofts@numucom.com. Website: www.luwrite.com. **Contact:** Dorothy Crofts, membership chair. "The annual LUW Contest has been held since 1935 to give Utah writers an opportunity to get their works read and critiqued. It also encourages writers to keep writing in an effort to get published." Annual competition for short stories and novels. Award: 34 categories, cash award of $30/$20/ $10; children's book category, $50/$25/$15; full length book category $100/$50/$25; published writers category. Competition receives 10-100 submissions/category. Judges: professional judges who are paid for their services. Entry fee $3-6, short story; $5-12, full length book. Guidelines available after February for SASE or on website. Accepts inquiries by fax, e-mail and phone. Deadline: June 15. Both published and previously unpublished submissions. Published submissions must have appeared in print between June 2003 and June 2004. "We do have separate categories for speculative fiction, children's and teen's besides our full length book category on any subject." Word length: 1,500 words maximum, short short story; 3,000 words maximum, short story; 4,000 words maximum, speculative fiction; 90,000 word maximum, full length book; 20,000 words maximum, children's book; 50,000 words maximum, teen book; 5,000 words maximum, Agnes Burke White/Leroy Meager Short Story. "Read the contest rules and guidelines. Don't skim over them. Rules change and are revised from year to year. Don't forget to enclose your entry fee when mailing your entries." Winners will be announced at the Annual Writers Round-up in September. List of winners available at Round-up or for SASE.

LIFETIME ACHIEVEMENT AWARD, Native Writers' Circle of the Americas, English Department, University of Oklahoma, Norman OK 73019-0240. (405)325-6231. Fax: (405)325-0831. E-mail: Geary.Hobson_1@ou.edu. Website: www.worldcraftcircle.org. **Contact:** Geary Hobson, director. Award to "honor the most respected of our Native American writers. Our award is the only one given to Native American authors by Native American authors." Annual competition. Author's lifetime work as a writer. Award: $1,000. See Worldcraft Circle webpage for complete guidelines. Accepts inquiries by fax, phone, e-mail. Writers are voted on for the award by fellow American Indian writers. Writer must be nominated. Winners notified by phone initially, then by e-mail.

LILITH ANNUAL FICTION AWARD, Lilith Magazine, 250 W. 57th St., Suite 2432, New York NY 10107. (212)757-0818. Fax: (212)757-5705. E-mail: lilithmag@aol.com. Website: www.lilithmag.com. **Contact:** Yona Zeldis McDonough, fiction editor. "*Lilith*, the award-winning independent Jewish women's magazine, is offering its third annual prize in Jewish feminist fiction. We're looking for vibrant, compelling and original stories with heart, soul and chutzpah, short stories that illuminate issues central to the lives of contemporary Jewish women." Annual award for short stories. Award: $250, publication in *Lilith* and one year subscription. Receives 40 entries. $15 entry fee. Make checks payable to *Lilith Magazine* or include credit card information. For guidelines, send SASE, e-mail, visit website or call. Accepts inquiries by fax, e-mail, phone. Deadline: December 1, 2003. Entries should be unpublished. Contest open to all writers. Manuscripts should be double spaced, 2,500 words or less, with name and contact information on a separate cover sheet. "Electronic submissions, in Microsoft Word, welcome. Does not return mss. Results announced January or February 2004. Winners notified by phone.

LITERAL LATTÉ FICTION AWARD, Literal Latté, 61 E. 8th St., Suite 240, New York NY 10003. (212)260-5532. E-mail: litlatte@aol.com. Website: www.literal-latte.com. **Contact:** Edward Estlin, contributing editor. Award to "provide talented writers with three essential tools for continued success: money, publication and recognition." Annual competition for short stories. Award: $1,000 (1st prize); $300 (2nd prize); $200 (3rd prize); up to 7 honorable mentions. Competition receives 400-600 submissions. Judges: the editors. Entry fee $10 ($15 includes subscription) for each story submitted. Guidelines available for SASE, by e-mail or on website. Accepts inquiries by e-mail. Deadline: January 15. Previously unpublished submissions. Open to new and established writers worldwide. Word length: 6,000 words maximum. "The First Prize Story in the First Annual *Literal Latté* Fiction Awards has been honored with a Pushcart Prize." Winners notified by phone. List of winners available in late April for SASE or by e-mail.

LONG FICTION CONTEST INTERNATIONAL, White Eagle Coffee Store Press, P.O. Box 383, Fox River Grove IL 60021-0383. (847)639-9200. E-mail: wecspress@aol.com. Website: http://members.aol.com/wecspr ess. **Contact:** Frank E. Smith, publisher. To promote and support the long story form. Annual award for short stories. "Entries accepted from anywhere in the world; story must be written in English." Winning story receives A.E. Coppard Award—publication as chapbook plus $500, 25 contributor's copies; 40 additional copies sent to book publishers/agents and 10 press kits. Entry fee $15 U.S., ($10 for second story in same envelope). Must be in U.S. funds. Competition receives 200 entries. Guidelines available in April by SASE, e-mail or website. Accepts inquiries by e-mail. Deadline: December 15. Accepts previously unpublished submissions, but previous publication

FOR EXPLANATIONS OF THESE SYMBOLS,
SEE THE INSIDE FRONT AND BACK COVERS OF THIS BOOK.

of small parts with acknowledgements is OK. Simultaneous submissions OK. No limits on style or subject matter. Length: 8,000-14,000 words (30-50 pages double spaced) single story; may have multiparts or be a self-contained novel segment. Send cover with title, name, address, phone; second title page with title only. Submissions are not returned; they are recycled. "Previous winners include Adria Bernardi, Doug Hornig, Christy Sheffield Sanford, Eleanor Swanson, Gregory J. Wolos and Joe Hill. SASE for most current information." Results announced March 30. Winners notified by phone. For contest results, send SASE or visit website after March 30. "Write with richness and depth."

THE LONGMEADOW JOURNAL LITERARY COMPETITION, c/o Robert and Rita Morton, 6750 Longmeadow Ave, Lincolnwood IL 60710. (312)726-9789. Fax: (312)726-9772. **Contact:** Robert and Rita Morton. Award to "stimulate the young to write." Annual competition for short stories. Award: $175 (1st prize); $100 (2nd prize); 5 prizes of $50. "We publish a total of 20 stories and also Honorable Mention winners' names." Competition receives 700 submissions. Judges: Robert and Rita Morton. Guidelines for SASE or fax. Accepts inquiries by fax. Award for "short story writers between the ages of 10-19." Word length: 3,000 words or less. Winners notified by December 31, 2003.

LOS ANGELES TIMES BOOK PRIZES, *L.A. Times*, 202 W. First St., Los Angeles CA 90012. (213)237-5775. E-mail: tom.crouch@latimes.com. Website: www.latimes.com/bookprizes. **Contact:** Tom Crouch, administrative coordinator. Annual award for books published between January 1 and December 31. Award: $1,000 cash prize in each of the following categories: fiction, first fiction (the Art Seidenbaum Award), young adult fiction and mystery/thriller. In addition, the Robert Kirsch Award recognizes the body of work by a writer living in and/or writing on the American West. Entry is by nomination of juries—*no external nominations or submissions are accepted.* Juries appointed by the *L.A. Times*. No entry fee. "Works must have their first U.S. publication during the calendar year." Writers must be nominated by committee members. "The Times provides air fare and lodging in Los Angeles for the winning authors to attend the awards ceremony held in April as part of the *Los Angeles Times* Festival of Books."

THE HUGH J. LUKE AWARD, *Prairie Schooner*, 201 Andrews Hall, P.O. Box 880334, Lincoln NE 68588-0334. (402)472-0911. Fax: (402)472-9771. E-mail: kgrey2@unl.edu. Website: www.unl.edu/schooner/psmain.htm. **Contact:** Hilda Raz, editor-in-chief. Award "an annual cash prize to honor work published in the previous year in *Prairie Schooner*, including essays, fiction and poetry." Award: $250. Judge: Competition is judged by the editorial staff of *Prairie Schooner*. No entry fee. For guidelines, send SASE or visit website. "Only work published in *Prairie Schooner* in the previous year is considered." Work is nominated by the editorial staff. Results announced in the Spring issue. Winners notified by mail in February or March.

THE MAN BOOKER PRIZE FOR FICTION, Booktrust, Book House, 45 East Hill, London SW18 2QZ England. Phone: 020 8516 2973 or 020 8516 2972. Fax: 020 8516 2978. E-mail: kate@booktrust.org.uk or tarryn@booktrust.org.uk. Website: www.booktrust.org.uk or www.themanbookerprize.com. **Contact:** Kate Mervyn Jones, prizes manager; Tarryn McKay, prizes administrator. Award to the best novel of the year. Annual competition for novels. Award: £50,000. Each of the short-listed authors receive £2,500. Guidelines available for SASE, fax, e-mail or website. Judges: five judges appointed by The Booker Prize Foundation. Deadline: July. Announcement of winners October/November. Publisher will be notified. Only published submissions eligible; must be a full length novel written in English by a citizen of the Commonwealth or Republic of Ireland. List of winners available for SASE, by fax, e-mail or website.

MARSH AWARD FOR CHILDREN'S LITERATURE IN TRANSLATION, Marsh Christian Trust, University of Surrey Roehampton, Digby Stuart College, Roehampton Lane, London SW15 5PH England. E-mail: G.Lathey@roehampton.ac.uk. **Contact:** Dr. Gillian Lathey. Award to promote the publication of translated children's books in the United Kingdom. Biennial. Award for children's book translations. Award: £1,000. Judges: Patricia Crampton, Anthea Bell, Wendy Cooling, Elizabeth Hammill. No entry fee. Guidelines available by SASE. Accepts inquiries by e-mail. Deadline: June 30, 2004 for 2005 contest. Entries should be translations into English first published in the UK. Cover letter should include name, address, phone, e-mail and title. Entries must be nominated by publishers. Results announced January 2005. Winners notified by mail and at event/banquet.

WALTER RUMSEY MARVIN GRANT, Ohioana Library Association, 274 E. First Ave., Suite 300, Columbus OH 43201. (614)466-3831. Fax: (614)728-6974. E-mail: ohioana@sloma.state.oh.us. **Contact:** Linda Hengst. "To encourage young unpublished writers (30 years of age or under)." Annual competition for short stories. Award: $1,000. Guidelines for SASE. Deadline: January 31. Open to unpublished authors born in Ohio or who have lived in Ohio for a minimum of five years. Must be 30 years of age or under. Up to six pieces of prose may be submitted; maximum 60 pages, minimum 10 pages double spaced, 12 pt type.

THE MASTERS AWARD, Titan Press, P.O. Box 17897, Encino CA 91416-7897. Website: www.titanpress.info. "One yearly Grand Prize of $1,000, and four quarterly awards of 'Honorable Mention' each in either 1) fiction; 2) poetry and song lyrics; 3) nonfiction." Judges: 3 literary professionals, TBA. $15 entry fee. Awards are given on March 15, June 15, September 15 and December 15. Any submission received prior to an award date is eligible for the subsequent award. Submissions accepted throughout the year. Fiction and nonfiction must be no more than 20 pages (5,000 words); poetry no more than 150 lines. All entries must be in the English language. #10 SASE required for guidelines. "Be persistent, be consistent, be professional."

MARY McCARTHY PRIZE IN SHORT FICTION, Sarabande Books, P.O. Box 4456, Louisville KY 40204. (502)458-4028. Fax: (502)458-4065. E-mail: sarabandeb@aol.com. Website: www.sarabandebooks.org. **Contact:** Kirby Gann, managing editor. "To publish an outstanding collection of stories and/or novellas, or a short novel (less than 300 pages)." Annual competition for story collections and novella/novella collections. "The Mary McCarthy Prize in Short Fiction includes a $2,000 cash award, publication of a collection of stories, novellas, or a short novel, and a standard royalty contract." Competition receives 800-1,000 submissions per contest. Each year this contest is judged by a well-established writer. Past judges include Amy Hempel, Barry Hannah, and Rosellen Brown. Judge in 2003: Heather McHugh. $20 entry fee. Guidelines currently available. Deadline: February 15, 2003. "The collections themselves must be unpublished, but published individual stories are okay." Contest open to any writer of English (no translations) who is a citizen of the US. Length: 150-300 pages. "Read past contest winners to see the quality of writing we seek: *The Baby Can Sing*, by Judith Slater; *Head*, by William Tester; *What We Won't Do*, by Brock Clarke. Keep in mind that our final judge changes each year." Results announced July 2003. Winners notified by mail or phone in May or June. For contest results, send SASE.

N ◑ **JENNY McKEAN MOORE WRITER IN WASHINGTON**, Jenny McKean Moore Fund & The George Washington University, Dept. of English, George Washington University, Washington DC 20052. (202)994-6180. Fax: (202)994-7915. Professor of English: D. McAleavey. Annual award "of a teaching residency for a different genre each year." Award: $46,000 and an "attractive benefits package." Receives 200 submissions. Judges: George Washington University English faculty and members of the J.M. Moore Fund. Guidelines for SASE. Deadline: November 15. Previously published submissions. Results announced in February. Winners notified by phone.

◻ ◎ **McKNIGHT ARTIST FELLOWSHIPS FOR WRITERS**, Loft Literary Center, Open Book, Suite 200, 1011 Washington Ave. S., Minneapolis MN 55415. (612)215-2575. Fax: (612)215-2576. E-mail: loft@loft.org. Website: www.loft.org. **Contact:** Jerod Santek, program director. Purpose is "to give Minnesota writers of demonstrated ability the opportunity to work for a concentrated period of time on their writing." Annual award but alternates annually between creative prose and poetry. Creative Prose (fiction, essay, memoir, etc.) odd years; Poetry in even years; Children's Literature. Awards for 2005 include short stories, novels, story collections. Awards: Four $25,000 awards; a fifth $25,000 is awarded in children's literature. Judged anonymously be pre-eminent prose writers. Past judges include Dorothy Allison and Clarence Major. No entry fee. Guidelines available in September on website. Accepts inquiries by e-mail, phone. Deadline for 2005 contest: November 1, 2004. Entries should be unpublished or previously published. Competition open to legal residents of Minnesota who fulfill publication eligibility requirements as stated in guidelines. Required cover sheet should be submitted. Results announced in April. Winners notified by phone. For contest results, send SASE or visit website.

N ◎ **MELODY OF LOVE CONTEST**, Music City Romance Writers, P.O. Box 140875, Nashville TN 37214-0875. Website: http://mcrw.com. **Contact:** Trish Milburn, president. Contest to promote professionalism in romance writing. Annual. Competition for novels. Award: $50 and certificate. Categories: single title, historical, and category romance. Judges: two MCRW members (initially); final judges: editors from major publishing houses. $20 fee per entry; make checks payable to Music City Romance Writers. Guidelines available by SASE, e-mail, on website, in publication. Deadline: July 1, 2004. Entries should be unpublished. Contest open to unpublished members of the Romance Writers of America. Length: 1st chapter, 25-page limit (single spaced). "Entries must fall within current convention for romance novels." Results announced in September (finalists), in October (winners). Winners notified by phone or e-mail. For contest results, visit website.

N ◎ **MICHIGAN LITERARY FICTION AWARDS**, University of Michigan Press, 839 Greene St., Ann Arbor MI 48106. Fax: (734)615-6479. E-mail: ump.fiction@umich.edu. Website: www.press.umich.edu/fiction/index.html. **Contact:** Chris Hebert, acquisitions editor. Purpose of the award "is to provide a second chance for writers who have published at least one work of literary fiction." Annual. Award for novels and short story collections. Award: $1,000 prize money and publication. No entry fee. Guidelines available by SASE or on website. Accepts inquiries by e-mail. Deadline: July 1. Entries should be unpublished. Contest open to writers who have previously published at least one work of literary fiction. Cover letter should include name, address, phone, e-mail and title; title on every page of ms. Results announced in November. Winners notified by mail. For contest results, send SASE or visit website.

◑ **MID-LIST PRESS FIRST SERIES AWARD FOR SHORT FICTION**, Mid-List Press, 4324-12th Ave. South, Minneapolis MN 55407-3218. (612)822-3733. E-mail: guide@midlist.org. Website: www.midlist.org. **Contact:** Lane Stiles, publisher. To encourage and nurture short fiction writers who have never published a collection of fiction. Annual competition for fiction collections. Award: $1,000 advance and publication. Competition receives 300 submissions. Judges: manuscript readers and the editors of Mid-List Press. $30 entry fee. Guidelines available in February for SASE or on website. Deadline: July 1. Previously published or unpublished submissions. Word length: 50,000 words minimum. "Application forms and guidelines are available for a #10 SASE or visit our website." Results announced in January. Winners notified by phone and mail in January. Winners' list published in *Poets & Writers* and *AWP Chronicle*; also available by SASE, e-mail or on website.

◻ MID-LIST PRESS FIRST SERIES AWARD FOR THE NOVEL, Mid-List Press, 4324-12th Ave. South, Minneapolis MN 55407-3218. (612)822-3733. E-mail: guide@midlist.org. Website: www.midlist.org. **Contact:** Lane Stiles, publisher. To encourage and nurture first-time novelists. Annual competition for novels. Award: $1,000 advance and publication. Competition receives approximately 500 submissions. Judges: manuscript readers and the editors of Mid-List Press. $30 entry fee. Guidelines available in July for SASE or on website. Deadline: February 1. Unpublished submissions. Word length: minimum 50,000 words. "Application forms and guidelines are available for a #10 SASE, or visit our website." Results announced in July. Winners notified by phone and mail. Winners' list published in *Poets & Writers* and *AWP Chronicle*; also available by SASE, e-mail or on website.

◪ MILKWEED EDITIONS NATIONAL FICTION PRIZE, Milkweed Editions, 1011 Washington Ave. S., Suite 300, Minneapolis MN 55415-1246. (612)332-3192. Fax: (612)215-2550. E-mail: editor@milkweed.org. Website: www.milkweed.org. **Contact:** Elisabeth Fitz, first reader. Annual award for a novel, a short story collection, one or more novellas, or a combination of short stories and novellas. Award: $5,000 cash advance as part of any royalties agreed upon at the time of acceptance. Contest receives 3-5,000 submissions per category. Judged by Milkweed Editions. Guidelines available for SASE or check website. Accepts inquiries by e-mail and phone. Deadline: "Rolling—but 2004 winner chosen by October 2003." "Please look at previous winners: *Roofwalker*, by Susan Power; *Hell's Bottom, Colorado*, by Laura Pritchett; *Falling Dark*, by Tim Tharp; *Montana 1948*, by Larry Watson; and *Aquaboogie*, by Susan Straight—this is the caliber of fiction we are searching for. Catalog available for $1.50 postage, if people need a sense of our list." Winners are notified by phone and announced in November. See catalog for winners.

🌐◪◎ MIND BOOK OF THE YEAR, Granta House, 15-19 Broadway, London E15 4BQ England. **Contact:** Ms. A. Brackx. "To award a prize to the work of fiction or nonfiction which outstandingly furthers public understanding of the causes, experience or treatment of mental health problems." Annual competition for novels and works of nonfiction. Award: £1,000. Competition receives approximately 50-100 submissions. Judges: Michele Roberts, Blake Morrison, Fay Weldon. Deadline: December. Author's nomination is accepted. All books must be published in English in the UK.

MISSISSIPPI REVIEW PRIZE, University of Southern Mississippi/*Mississippi Review*, P.O. Box 5144 USM, Hattiesburg MS 39406-5144. (601)266-4321. Fax: (601)266-5757. E-mail: rief@netdoor.com. Website: www.missisippireview.com. **Contact:** Rie Fortenberry, managing editor. Annual award to "reward excellence in new fiction and poetry and to find new writers who are just beginning their careers." Award: $1,000 plus publication for the winning story and poem; publication for all runners-up. Competition receives 500 entries per category. Entry fee $15/story or group of 3 poems (includes copy of issue). Entries should be previously unpublished. Length: short story 50,000 words or less. Cover letter should include author's name, address, phone and e-mail numbers, word count and title of story. No manuscripts returned. Guidelines available in April for SASE, e-mail or on website. Accepts inquiries by e-mail or phone. Deadline: October 1. Winners notified in January. For contest results, send SASE or visit website.

THE MISSOURI REVIEW EDITORS' PRIZE CONTEST, 1507 Hillcrest Hall, Columbia MO 65211. (573)882-4474. Fax: (573)884-4671. Website: www.missourireview.org. **Contact:** Contest Coordinator. Annual competition for short stories, poetry and essays. Award: $2,000 for fiction and poetry, $2,000 for essay and publication in *The Missouri Review*. Competition receives more than 1,800 submissions. Judges: *The Missouri Review* editors. $15 entry fee (checks payable to *The Missouri Review*). Each fee entitles entrant to a one-year subscription to *The Missouri Review*, an extension of a current subscription, or a gift subscription. Guidelines available June for SASE. Deadline: October 15. Outside of envelope should be marked "Fiction," "Essay," or "Poetry." Enclose an index card with author's name, address, and telephone number in the left corner and, for fiction and essay entries only, the work's title in the center. Entries must be previously unpublished and will not be returned. Page length restrictions: 25 typed, double-spaced, for fiction and essays, 10 for poetry. Results announced in January. Winners notified by phone and mail. For contest results, send SASE. "Send fully realized work with a distinctive voice, style and subject."

◎ MONEY FOR WOMEN, Money for Women/Barbara Deming Memorial Fund, Inc., Box 630125, Bronx NY 10463. **Contact:** Susan Pliner, executive director. "Small grants to individual feminists in the arts." Biannual competition. Award: $500-1,500. Competition receives approximately 150 submissions. Judges: Board of Directors. Guidelines and required application available for SASE. Deadline: December 31 for fiction. Limited to U.S. and Canadian citizens. Length: 25 pages. May submit own fiction. "Only for feminists in the arts." Results announced five months after deadline. Winners notified by mail.

◎ MOONLIGHT & MAGNOLIA FICTION WRITING CONTEST: SF, F, H, Genre Writing Program, P.O. Box 180489, Richland MS 39218-0489. (601)825-7263. E-mail: hoover59@aol.com. **Contact:** K. Mark Hoover, contest administrator. This annual award is for short stories that recognizes and encourage new and unpublished writers while rewarding excellence in genre writing. Award: $250 (1st prize); $100 (2nd prize); $50 (3rd prize); top ten finalist receive certificates suitable for framing. Entries must be in competition format. Judges: David Coe; changes annually. Entry fees $7.50/story; $2.50/additional entry. Guidelines available for SASE or by e-mail. Accepts inquiries by e-mail. Deadline: December 15. Open to unpublished writers and those who have not published more than 2 stories in a nationally-distributed publication with a circulation over 5,000. Length: 10,000 words. "We are open to multiple submissions. Southern writers are encouraged to participate." Results announced January 31. Winners notified by mail, phone, or e-mail. For contest results, send SASE or e-mail.

◎ **MOTA EMERGING WRITERS CONTEST**, *Mota*, Triple Tree Publishing, P.O. Box 5684, Eugene OR 97405. (541)338-3184. Fax: (541)484-5358. E-mail: liz@tripletreepub.com. Website: www.tripletreepub.com. **Contact:** Liz Cratty, publisher. Purpose is "to seek out new, unpublished fiction writers." Annual award for short stories. Award: 1st prize, $100 and publication in *Mota*; 2nd prize, $50 and considered for publication; 3rd prize, $25 and considered for publication. Competition receives 200 submissions per category. Judge: "A panel of professional fiction authors and volume guest editor." $12 entry fee per entry. For guidelines, send SASE or visit website. Deadline: November 1. Entries should be unpublished. Contest open to "writers who are unpublished or have fewer than five short stories sold." Length: 6,000 words. "Know the volume theme: for 2004 it is Integrity; in 2005, Honesty. Write strong fiction with compelling characters and unusual problems." Results announced in December. Winners notified by phone and mail. For contest results, send SASE or visit website.

◪ ◻ ◎ **THE NATIONAL CHAPTER OF CANADA IODE VIOLET DOWNEY BOOK AWARD**, The National Chapter of Canada IODE, 254-40 Orchard View Blvd., Toronto ON M4R 1B9 Canada. (416)487-4416. Fax: (416)487-4417. Website: www.iodecanada.com. **Contact:** Sandra Connery, chair, book award committee. "The award is given to a Canadian author for an English language book suitable for children 13 years of age and under, published in Canada during the previous calendar year. Fairy tales, anthologies and books adapted from another source are not eligible." Annual competition for novels, children's literature. Award: $3,000. Competition receives 100-120 submissions. Judges: A six-member panel of judges including four National IODE officers and two non-members who are recognized specialists in the field of children's literature. Guidelines for SASE. Accepts inquiries by fax and phone. Deadline: December 31. Previously published January 1, 2003 and December 31, 2003. "The book must have been written by a Canadian citizen and must have been published in Canada during the calendar year." Word length: Must have at least 500 words of text preferably with Canadian content. Winner announced in May and notified by phone.

◼ ◻ ◎ **NATIONAL FEDERATION OF THE BLIND WRITERS' DIVISION SHORT STORY CONTEST**, National Federation of the Blind Writers' Division, 1203 S. Fairview Rd., Columbia MO 65203. (573)445-6091. **Contact:** Tom Stevens, president, Writers' Division. "To promote good writing for blind writers and Division members, blind or sighted." Annual competition for short stories. Award: $50, $40, $25, $15. Award: 2 Honorable Mentions and possible publication. Competitions receives 20 submissions. Judges: Tom Stevens and a team of associated writers judge each entry (includes Helen Stevens, Loraine Stayer). Entry fee $5/story. Guidelines available in October for SASE. Deadline: June 1, 2004. Unpublished submissions. "Entrant must be legally blind and over 18 or a member of the National Federation of the Blind Writers' Division. Story must be in English, and typed. SASE necessary." Cover letter should include name, address, phone, e-mail, word count and title; title on ms. Critique on request, $5. Word length: 3,000 maximum. Results announced July 31. Winners notified by mail. For contest results, send SASE to Lori Stayer, 2704 Beach Dr., Merrick NY 11566 or e-mail to L. Stayer at LoriStay@aol.com. Winner may be published in *Slate & Style*, the Writers' Division Magazine.

NATIONAL OUTDOOR BOOK AWARDS, Association of Outdoor Recreation and Education and Idaho State University, P.O. Box 8128, Pocatello ID 83209. (208)282-3912. Fax: (208)282-4600. E-mail: wattron@isu.edu. Website: www.isu.edu/outdoor/books. **Contact:** Ron Watters, chairman. Award "honors outstanding writing and publishing in the outdoor field." Annual competition includes awards for novels and story collections. Award: Extensive national publicity, including display of all submitted titles at the International Conference on Outdoor Recreation and Education; announcement of winning titles to the media; reviews, cover scans and publisher links of winning titles on Association website; use of award medallion and logo on book covers and promotions. Competition receives 30-50 submissions in "Literature" category. Judge: nationwide panel includes book reviewers, columnists, authors, academics and trade representatives. A $65 application fee should accompany each nominated title. Guidelines available in April for SASE, by e-mail, fax, phone or on website. Accepts inquiries by fax, e-mail, phone. Award nominations open in April and are due on or about September 1st of the award year. Entries should be previously published. "Must be bound; galleys not acceptable. Must have been released after June 1 of the previous year. Contest open to authors of any nationality, but books must be in English. Length: open. Fictional works should be entered in the "Literature" category. Results announced "early November at the International Conference on Outdoor Recreation and Education." Winners notified by mail in early November. For contest results, visit website.

◎ **NATIONAL READERS' CHOICE AWARDS**, Oklahoma Romance Writers of America, HC 68, Box 117W, Kingston OK 73439. Phone/fax: (580)564-1105. E-mail: wfergus@swbell.net. Website: www.okrwa.com. **Contact:**

Willena Ferguson, coordinator. Purpose of contest is "to provide writers of romance fiction a competition where their published novels are judged by readers." Annual award for novels. "There is no monetary award, just an annual awards banquet hosted at the Annual National Romance Writers Convention." Total annual entries between 390-425. Of the 12 categories, the least received is in novella category and the largest is the long contemporary category." Judge: "Readers in all 50 states." $25 entry fee. Checks payable to NCRA. No limit to number of entries, but each title may be entered in only one category. The 12 categories include traditional series (50-60,000 words); short contemporary series (fewer than 70,000); long contemporary series (more than 70,000); single title contemporary; short historical (100,000 or less); long historical (more than 100,000); Regency (50,000 or more); romantic suspense (50,000 or more); inspirational (50,000 or more); novella (approximately 25,000); erotic romance (50,000 or more). For guidelines, send SASE, e-mail or visit website. Entry form required; available on website. Deadline: November 20, 2003 for forms and fees (send to above address). Deadline for books receipt is January 11, 2004. Five copies of each entry must be mailed to category coordinator; contact information for coordinator will be provided by November 20. All entries must have "an original copyright date of 2003 or a first U.S. printing date of 2003 as evidenced by the copyright page or a letter from the publisher. Entry must have been available for sale in United States sometime during 2002." E-books accepted if publisher is recognized by RWA or is a member of EPIC or AED; submit a hard copy—perfect- or spiral-bound book galleys (no 3 ring binders) with ISBN—and also "e-disk and form of the book." E-books must also have evidenced 2003 copyright page. "Entries will be accepted from authors, editors, publishers, agents, readers, etc.—from whomever wishes to fill out the entry form, pay the entry fee and supply number of copies." 2003 results announced in July 2004. Winners notified by phone, if not at awards ceremony, in July 2005. List of winners will be mailed, also available by e-mail.

☐ **NATIONAL WRITERS ASSOCIATION ANNUAL NOVEL WRITING CONTEST**, National Writers Association, 3140 Peoria St., PMB 295, Aurora CO 80014. (303)841-0246. Fax: (303)841-2607. E-mail: contests@nationalwriters.com. **Contact:** Sandy Whelchel, director. Annual award to "recognize and reward outstanding ability and to increase the opportunity for publication." Award: $500 (1st prize); $300 (2nd prize); $100 (3rd prize). Award judged by editors and agents. $35 entry fee. Judges' evaluation sheets sent to each entry with SASE. Entry form and information available on Benefits section of www.nationalwriters.com. Opens December 1. Deadline: April 1. Unpublished submissions, any genre or category. Length: 20,000-100,000 words.

N ◎ ☐ **NATIONAL WRITERS ASSOCIATION ANNUAL SHORT STORY CONTEST**, National Writers Association, 3140 S. Peoria #295, Aurora CO 80014-3155. (303)841-0246. Fax: (303)841-2607. E-mail: contests@nationalwriters.com. Website: www.nationalwriters.com. **Contact:** Sandy Whelchel, executive director. Annual award to encourage and recognize writing by freelancers in the short story field. Award: $200 (1st prize); $100 (2nd prize); $50 (3rd prize). Competition receives 200 submissions for short story category. Opens April 1. Entry fee $15. Entry form and information available in January on Benefits section of www.nationalwriters.com. All entries must be postmarked by July 1. Accepts inquiries by fax, phone and e-mail. Evaluation sheets sent to each entrant if SASE provided. Unpublished submissions. Length: No more than 5,000 words. Results announced at the NWAF Summer Conference in June. Winners notified by phone or e-mail. List of winners published in *Authorship* or on website.

THE NEBRASKA REVIEW AWARD IN FICTION, The Nebraska Review, University of Nebraska at Omaha, Omaha NE 68182-0324. (402)554-3159. E-mail: jreed@unomaha.edu. **Contact:** James Reed, managing editor. Award to "recognize short fiction of the highest possible quality." Annual competition for short stories. Award: publication plus $500. Competition receives 400-500 submissions. Judges: staff. $15 entry fee for each story submitted. Guidelines for SASE. Accepts inquiries by e-mail, phone. Deadline: November 30. Previously unpublished submissions. Length: 5,000 words. Results announced March 15. Winners notified by phone, e-mail and/or mail in February. For contest results, send SASE.

◙ **NEUSTADT INTERNATIONAL PRIZE FOR LITERATURE**, *World Literature Today*, 110 Monnet Hall, University of Oklahoma, Norman OK 73019-4033. **Contact:** Robert Con Davis-Undiano, director. Biennial award to recognize distinguished and continuing achievement in fiction, poetry or drama. Awards: $50,000, an eagle feather cast in silver, an award certificate, and a special issue of *World Literature Today* devoted to the laureate. "We are looking for outstanding accomplishment in world literature. The Neustadt Prize is not open to application. Nominations are made only by members of the international jury, which changes for each award. Jury meetings are held in the fall of even-numbered years. Unsolicited manuscripts, whether published or unpublished, cannot be considered."

N ☐ ◎ **NEVADA ARTS COUNCIL ARTISTS' FELLOWSHIPS**, 716 N. Carson St., Suite A, Carson City NV 89701. (702)687-6680. Fax: (775)687-6688. Website: www.nevadaartscouncil.org. **Contact:** Fran Morrow, Artists' Services Program coordinator. Award "to honor individual artists and their artistic achievements and to support artists' efforts in advancing their careers." Annual competition for fiction, nonfiction, poetry, playwriting and writing for children and young adults. Award: $5,000 ($4,500 immediately, $500 after public service event completed). Competition receives between 150-200 submissions. Judges: Peer panels of professional artists. Guidelines available by phone, e-mail, or on website. Deadline: April. "Only available to Nevada residents." Word length: 25 pages prose and plays, 10 pages poetry. Results announced June. Winners notified by mail and phone. Entrants receive list of recipients. "Inquire about jackpot grants for Nevada residents' projects, up to $1,000."

NEW CENTURY WRITERS AWARDS, New Century Writer LLC, 32 Alfred St., Suite B, New Haven CT 06512-3927. (203)469-8824. Fax: (203)468-0333. E-mail: newcenturywriter@yahoo.com. Website: www.newcentu rywriter.org. **Contact:** Jason J. Marchi, executive director. "To discover and encourage emerging writers of fiction, screenplays and stage plays, and to provide cash awards, sponsor writing fellowships, and promote our best writers to agents, producer in the film industry, and editors in the publishing industry. Also to educate via the quarterly educational newsletter, *The Anvil*." Five annual competitions for short stories, novels/novellas, screenplays, stage plays and TV scripts. Prizes: $3,000; $1,000; $500; and four $100. Also, awards 1 or 2 Ray Bradbury Fellowships to *Zoetrope* Short Story Writer's Workshop in Belize worth $5,000 each. Publishes best 10 stories in nationally distributed anthology (lists best novels/novellas). Best stories also considered for publication in *Futures* and *Verbic- ide*. Competitions receive 2,000 submissions. Judged initially by published writers, editors, produced film makers and other film industry professionals. Past judges include editors of *Zoetrope*, Juliana Gribbins of McGraw Hill, Bari Evins of Debra Hill Entertainment, Lisa Lindo of ACMA Talent & Literary. $30 fee per entry (screenplay, stage play, novel excerpt); $15 for one short story, $20 for two short stories; $3 per poem under 100 lines. Guidelines available July 15 for 9×12 SASE, fax, e-mail or on website. Accepts inquiries by mail only. "All genres accepted. We have a diverse group of alliance companies with different tastes." Contest open to all writers. "Submit your best writing. Take the time to go over your work one more time. You do not have to be Hemingway, just tell a good, solid story." Winners notified by mail in June/July "for earlier contests and December for screenplays and stage plays." List of winners available by visiting website or send SASE.

☐ ◎ **NEW ENGLAND WRITERS SHORT, SHORT FICTION CONTEST**, New England Writers, P.O. Box 5, Windsor VT 05089-0005. (802)674-2315. E-mail: newvtpoet@aol.com. Website: http://hometown.aol.com/ newvtpoet/myhomepage/business.html or www.newenglandwriters.org. **Contact:** Frank Anthony, president. Com- petition for publication in annual *Anthology of New England Writers*. Annual competition for short stories. Marjory Bartlett Sanger Award: $300; 3-5 $30 Honorable Mentions. Competition receives 150 submissions. 2003 fiction judge: Patricia Henley; 2004 fiction judge TBA. $6 entry fee; 2 or more entries $5 each (please send 3×5 card with name, address and titles of work). Guidelines available for SASE, by e-mail, on website in November. Accepts inquiries by e-mail or phone. Deadline: June 15 postmark. Unpublished submissions. Length: 1,000 words maximum. "Strive for originality taken from your own life experience, not others. We look for creative, concise work with an unexpected ending." Results announced at annual N.E.W. conference in July. Winners notified by mail or phone right after conference. For contest results, send SASE or visit website.

☐ **NEW LETTERS LITERARY AWARDS**, *New Letters*, University House, 5101 Rockhill Rd., Kansas City MO 64110. (816)235-1168. Fax: (816)235-2611. E-mail: newletters@umkc.org. Website: www.newletters.org. **Contact:** Aleatha Ezra, assistant managing editor. Award to "find and reward good writing from writers who need the recognition and support." Annual. Award for short stories, poems and essays. Award: $1,000 cash prize and publica- tion each category. Competition receives 400-500 fiction entries. Judged anonymously. $15 fee per entry, includes a one-year subscription; send credit card information or make checks payable to New Letters. Guidelines available in January for SASE, e-mail, on website and in publication. Accepts inquiries by e-mail. Deadline: May 21,2004. Entries should be unpublished. Length: 5,000 words maximum. Cover letter should include name, address, phone, e-mail and title. Results announced in September. Winners notified by phone. For contest results, send SASE, e- mail or visit website.

NEW MILLENNIUM WRITING AWARDS, P.O. Box 2463, Knoxville TN 37901-2463. (423)428-0389. Fax: (865)428-2302. E-mail: DonWilliams7@att.net. Website: www.mach2.com/books or www.WritingAwards.com. **Contact:** Don Williams, editor. Award "to promote literary excellence in contemporary fiction." Biannual competi- tion for short stories. Award: $1,000 and publication in *New Millennium Writings*. Judges: Novelists and short story writers. Entry fee: $17. Guidelines available year round for SASE and on website. Accepts inquiries by e-mail. Deadline: mid-June and mid-November. Unpublished submissions. Length: 1,000-6,000 words. "Provide a bold, yet organic opening line, sustain the voice and mood throughout, tell an entertaining and vital story with a strong ending. *New Millennium Writings* is a forward-looking periodical for writers and lovers of good reading. It is filled with outstanding poetry, fiction, essays and other speculations on subjects both topical and timeless about life in our astonishing times. Our pages brim with prize-winning essays, humor, full-page illustrations, writing advice, poetry from writers at all stages of their careers. First-timers find their works displayed alongside well-known writers as well as profiles, interviews and tributes to famous authors such as John Updike, Sharyn McCrumb, Lee Smith, Howard Nemerov, Ken Kesey, Norman Mailer, Madison Smartt Bell, William Kennedy, David Hunter, Cormac McCarthy, Shelby Foote and more!" Results announced October and April. Winners notified by mail and phone. All entrants will receive a list of winners, plus a copy of the annual anthology. Send letter-sized SASE with entry for list.

🅽 **NEW YORK STORIES SHORT FICTION CONTEST**, *New York Stories* Magazine, Fiction Contest, NY Stories, E103, 31-10 Thomson Ave., Long Island City NY 11101. E-mail: nystories@lagcc.cuny.edu. Website: http://newyorkstories.org. **Contact:** Daniel Caplice Lynch, editor-in-chief. Competition "to recognize outstanding writing." Annual. Competition for short stories. Award: first prize, $500 and publication; second prize, $250 and consideration for publication. Judged by the editorial board. Final selection made by the editor-in-chief. $15 fee per entry; make checks payable to *New York Stories*. Guidelines available by SASE, e-mail, on website and in publication. Accepts inquiries by e-mail, phone. Deadline: September 15 every year. Entries should be unpublished. Length: less than 6,000 words. Cover letter should include name, address, phone, e-mail, word count and title. "Also include this information on the ms." Winners notified by phone or e-mail. For contest results, send SASE or visit website.

JOHN NEWBERY AWARD, American Library Association (ALA) Awards and Citations Program, Association for Library Service to Children, 50 E. Huron St., Chicago IL 60611. (312)280-2163. Fax: (312)944-7671. E-mail: alsc@ala.org. Website: www.ala.org/alsc. **Contact:** Meredith Parets, program coordinator. Annual award. Only books for children published in the US during the preceding year are eligible. Award: Medal. Entry restricted to U.S. citizens-residents. Judges: 2003 Newbery Award Selection Committee. Guidelines available on website, by fax, phone or e-mail. Accepts inquiries by fax and e-mail. Deadline: December 31. Results announced January 27. Winners notified by phone. For contest results, visit website in February.

THE NOMA AWARD FOR PUBLISHING IN AFRICA, P.O. Box 128, Witney, Oxon 0X8 5XU United Kingdom. (44)1993-775235. Fax: (44)1993-709265. E-mail: maryljay@aol.com. Website: www.nomaaward. org. **Contact:** Mary Jay. Sponsored by Kodansha Ltd. Award "to encourage publication of works by African writers and scholars in Africa, instead of abroad as is still too often the case at present." Annual competition for a new book in any of these categories: Scholarly or academic; books for children; literature and creative writing, including fiction, drama and poetry. Award: $10,000. Competition receives approximately 140 submissions. Judges: A committee of African scholars and book experts and representatives of the international book community. Chairman: Walter Bgoya. Guidelines available in November by fax, e-mail or on website. Accepts inquiries by fax, e-mail and phone. Deadline: March 31. Previously published submissions. Submissions are through publishers only. "Publishers must complete entry form and supply six copies of the published work." Maximum number of entries per publisher is 3. Results announced October. Winners notified through publishers. List of winners available from Secretariat. "The award is for an outstanding book. Content is the overriding criterion, but standards of publication are also taken into account."

NOVELLA PRIZE, *The Malahat Review*, University of Victoria, P.O. Box 1700 Stn CSC, Victoria BC V8W 2Y2 Canada. (250)721-8524. Fax: (250)472-5051. E-mail: malahat@uvic.ca. Website: www.malahatreview.com. **Contact:** Marlene Cookshaw, editor. Purpose: "To promote the writings of novellas." Biannual competition for novellas. Prizes: $500 plus payment for publication at our regular rate of $30/magazine page. Competition receives 100 submissions. Judges: "A 'blind' panel of judges/editors." editorial board and select judges. Entry fee: $30 in Canada; $40 Canadian; includes one year subscription. Guidelines available for SASE or on website. Accepts inquiries by e-mail or phone. Deadline: March 1, 2004. Entries should be unpublished. Contest open to all writers. Length: 30,000 words. Winners notified by mail 2-3 months after deadline.

O, GEORGIA! WRITING COMPETITION, O, GEORGIA TOO! WRITING COMPETITION, P.O. Box 1303, Roswell GA 30077-1303. (770)781-9705. Fax: (770)781-4676. E-mail: paulcossman@mindspring.c om. Website: www.ogeorgia.org. **Contact:** Paul Cossman, executive director. Mission: to "identify and publish new writers in order to help them launch their writing careers." Annual competition for short stories. Judges: 3 judges for fiction; all are professors or published authors. Award: publication in trade paperback book sold at Humpus Bumpus Books and other stores. Winners are also honored at a huge gala and autographing event each October. Contest receives 350 submissions. Entry fee: $15; make checks payable to O, Georgia! Writers Foundation. Guidelines available by SASE, e-mail, fax, phone and on website. Accepts inquiries by mail only. Deadline: February 15. Entries should be unpublished or previously published, but may not be anything on which another publisher holds copyright. Contest open to adults and students K-12th grades residing in the state of Georgia. Length: 4,000 words for O, Georgia! (adult competition); 2,000 words for O, Georgia Too! (kids). Cover letter should include name, address, phone, e-mail, word count, title and publications where story was previously published. Results announced June 30. Winners notified by mail. For contest results, send SASE or visit website. "Be original creative and fresh. Have good character development, good imagery and, of course good grammar and spelling."

THE FLANNERY O'CONNOR AWARD FOR SHORT FICTION, The University of Georgia Press, 330 Research Dr., Athens GA 30602-4901. (706)369-6130. Fax: (706)369-6131. E-mail: books@ugapress.uga.edu. Website: www.ugapress.org. **Contact:** Flannery O'Connor Award. Annual award "to recognize outstanding collec-

READ 'THE BUSINESS OF FICTION WRITING' section for information on manuscript preparation, mailing tips, rights and more.

tions of short fiction. Published and unpublished authors are welcome." Length: 200-275 typed double-spaced pages. Award: $1,000 and publication by the University of Georgia Press. Competition receives 330 submissions. Guidelines for SASE or on website. Accepts inquiries by mail only. Deadline: April 1-May 31. "Manuscripts cannot be accepted at any other time." Entries should be unpublished. $20 entry fee; make checks payable to UGA Press. Ms will not be returned. Results announced in November. Winners notified by mail. For contest results, send SASE or visit website.

FRANK O'CONNOR FICTION AWARD, *descant*, Dept. of English, Texas Christian University, Box 297270, Fort Worth TX 76129. (817)257-6537. Fax: (817)257-6239. E-mail: descant@tcu.edu. Website: www.eng.tcu.edu/journals/descant/index.htm. **Contact:** David Kuhne, editor. Estab. 1979 with *descant*; earlier awarded through *Quartet*. Annual award to honor the best published fiction in *descant* for its current volume. Award: $500 prize. Competition receives 500-1,000 submissions. Judge: *descant* fiction editors. No entry fee. Guidelines available for SASE or on website. Deadline: April 1. Results announced August. Winners notified by phone in July. For contest results, send SASE. "About 12 to 15 stories are published annually in *descant*. Winning story is selected from this group." Also offers the Sandra Brown Award for Short Fiction. Prize: $250. Send SASE for guidelines.

OHIO STATE UNIVERSITY PRESS, 1070 Carmack Rd., Columbus OH 43210-1002. (614)292-6930. Fax: (614)292-2065. E-mail: ohiostatepress@osu.edu. Website: www.ohiostatepress.org. **Contact:** Laurie Avery. Estab. 1957. "Small-sized university press." Publishes "scholarly and trade books." Member of Association of American University Presses (AAUP), International Association of Scholarly Publishers (IASP) and Association of American Publishers (AAP). Publishes one annual winner of poetry contest and of short fiction prize. Guidelines available on website. Accepts inquiries by e-mail and fax. Competition receives 400-500 submissions.

OHIOANA AWARD FOR CHILDREN'S LITERATURE, ALICE LOUISE WOOD MEMORIAL, Ohioana Library Association, 274 E. First Ave., Columbus OH 43201. (614)466-3831. Fax: (614)728-6974. E-mail: ohioana@sloma.state.oh.us. **Contact:** Linda Hengst, director. Competition "to honor an individual whose body of work has made, and continues to make, a significant contribution to literature for children or young adults." Annual award of $1,000. Guidelines for SASE. Accepts inquiries by fax and e-mail. Deadline: December 31 prior to year award is given. "Open to authors born in Ohio or who have lived in Ohio for a minimum of five years." Results announced in August or September. Winners notified by letter in May. For contest results, call or e-mail.

OHIOANA BOOK AWARDS, Ohioana Library Association, 274 E. First Ave., Suite 300, Columbus OH 43201. (614)466-3831. Fax: (614)728-6974. E-mail: ohioana@sloma.state.oh.us. **Contact:** Linda R. Hengst, director. Annual awards granted (only if the judges believe a book of sufficiently high quality has been submitted) to bring recognition to outstanding books by Ohioans or about Ohio. Five categories: Fiction, Nonfiction, Juvenile, Poetry and About Ohio or an Ohioan. Criteria: Books written or edited by a native Ohioan or resident of the state for at least 5 years; two copies of the book MUST be received by the Ohioana Library by December 31 prior to the year the award is given; literary quality of the book must be outstanding. Awards: Certificate and glass sculpture (up to 6 awards given annually). Each spring a jury considers all books received since the previous jury. Award judged by a jury selected from librarians, book reviewers, writers and other knowledgeable people. No entry forms are needed, but they are available July 1 of each year. "We will be glad to answer letters asking specific questions." Results announced in August or September. Winners notified by mail in May.

ORANGE BLOSSOM FICTION CONTEST, *The Oak*, 1530 Seventh St., Rock Island IL 61201. (309)788-3980. **Contact:** Betty Chezum Mowery, editor. "To build up circulation of publication and give new authors a chance for competition and publication along with seasoned writers." Annual. Competition is for short fiction. Award: Subscription to *The Oak*. Competition receives approximately 75 submissions. Judges: published authors. Entry fee six 37¢ stamps. Guidelines available in January for SASE. Word length: 500 words maximum. Prefers name, address and title on ms; no cover letter. "May be on any subject, but avoid gore and killing of humans or animals." Deadline: April 1. Results announced mid-April. Winners notified by mail. "Material is judged on content and tightness of writing as well as word lengths, since there is a 500-word limit. Guidelines for other contests available for SASE. No reply will be made without a SASE."

ORANGE PRIZE FOR FICTION, Orange pcs, %Booktrust, Book House, 45 East Hill, London SW18 2QZ England. (020)8516-2973/2. Fax: (020)8516-2978. E-mail: susy@booktrust.org.uk or tarryn@booktrust.org.uk. Website: www.orangeprize.co.uk or www.booktrust.org.uk. **Contact:** Kate Mervyn Jones, prizes manager or Tarryn McKay, prizes administrator. "This award was set up to find and reward the very best in women's fiction writing." Annual competition for novels only. Award: £30,000 and a "Bessie" statue to the winner. Number of entries varies. Judges have not been confirmed for 2003. No entry fee. Guidelines available by SASE, fax, e-mail or website. Authors should "either ask their publisher to contact Booktrust, or request a form directly themselves. However, entries must be made through publisher." Accepts inquiries by fax, e-mail, phone and post. Entries should be previously published novels by women, all nationalities. Must be published in the UK by a UK publisher. Length: full-length novel. Publishers will be notified of entry. Winner should be announced in the papers "or contact us for press release." Longlist announced in March; shortlist announced in April; winner announced in June. List of winners available by fax, e-mail or website.

◎ **OREGON BOOK AWARDS**, Literary Arts, Inc., 219 NW 12th Ave., Suite 201, Portland OR 97209. (503)227-2583. Fax: (503)243-1167. E-mail: la@literary-arts.org. Website: www.literary-arts.org. **Contact:** Kristy Athens, program coordinator. Annual award for outstanding authors of fiction, poetry, literary nonfiction, young readers and drama. Award: $500 for 8 categories. Competition receives approximately 20 submissions per genre. Judges: out-of-state experts. Guidelines available in February for SASE and on website. Accepts inquiries by phone and e-mail. Deadline: May 30. Limited to Oregon residents. Finalists announced in November; winners announced at an awards ceremony in November. List of winners available in November.

N ◎ **OREGON LITERARY FELLOWSHIPS**, Literary Arts, Inc., 219 NW 12th Ave., Suite 201, Portland OR 97209. (503)227-2583. Fax: (503)243-1167. E-mail: la@literary-arts.org. Website: www.literary-arts.org. **Contact:** Kristy Athens, program coordinator. Annual fellowships for writers of fiction, poetry, literary nonfiction, young readers and drama. Award: amount varies, $500-2,000 for approximately 18 writers. Judges: out-of-state experts. Guidelines available in February by SASE or on website. Accepts inquiries by e-mail, phone. Deadline: June 27. Limited to Oregon residents. Recipients announced in December.

◎ **DOBIE PAISANO FELLOWSHIPS**, Dobie House, 702 E. Dean Keeton St., Austin TX 78705. (512)471-8542. Fax: (512)471-9997. E-mail: aslate@mail.utexas.edu. Website: www.utexas.edu/ogs/Paisano. **Contact:** Audrey N. Slate, director. Annual fellowships for creative writing (includes short stories, novels and story collections). Award: 6 months residence at ranch; $2,000 monthly living stipend. Competition receives approximately 100 submissions. Judges: faculty of University of Texas and members of Texas Institute of Letters. $10 entry fee. Application and guidelines available after July 1, 2003 by fax, e-mail and on website. Accepts inquiries by fax, e-mail and phone. "Open to writers with a Texas connection—native Texans, people who have lived in Texas at least two years, or writers with published work on Texas and Southwest." Deadline: January 30, 2004. Results announced in May. Winners notified by telephone followed by mail. For contest results, visit website.

N ⊕ ◎ **CATHERINE PAKENHAM AWARD**, *The Sunday Telegraph*, 1 Canada Square, Canary Wharf, London E14 5DT England. Phone: 020 7538 6257. Fax: 020 7513 2512. E-mail: emma.gilbert-harris@telegraph.co.uk. **Contact:** Emma Gilbert-Harris, public relations and corporate events. Purpose of competition is "to encourage young female journalists as they begin their careers." Annual. Award for short stories, features, articles. Award: £1,000 and chance to write for a *Telegraph* publication for winner; £200 for 3 runners-up. One entry per person. No categories, candidates must choose their own topic. Judges include *Sunday Telegraph* editor Dominic Lawson and Joanna Trollope, novelist. No entry fee. Guidelines available in February 2004 by fax, phone, e-mail and in publication. Accepts inquiries by fax, e-mail, phone. Deadline: May 2004. Entries should be unpublished. Contest open to females aged 18-25 years old who are residents of UK or Ireland. Length: 700-2,000 words. Cover letter should include name, address, phone, e-mail, word count and title. Results announced in July at an awards ceremony. Winners notified by phone in July.

N ◗ **KENNETH PATCHEN COMPETITION**, Pig Iron Press, P.O. Box 237, Youngstown OH 44501. (330)747-6932. Fax: (330)747-0599. E-mail: pigironpress@cboss.com. **Contact:** Kenneth Patchen Competition. Biannual. Awards works of fiction, poetry and living in alternating years. Award: publication; $300. Judge with national visibility selected annually. Entry fee $15. Competition receives 200 submissions. Guidelines available for SASE. Reading period: January 1 to December 31. Award for fiction: 2001, 2003; fiction award for novel or short story collection, either form eligible. Previous publication of individual stories, poems or parts of novel OK. Ms should not exceed 500 typed pages. Results announced June. Winners notified by mail. For contest results, send SASE in July. "Share a voice that is spontaneous, natural and fleshy."

THE PATERSON FICTION PRIZE, The Poetry Center at Passaic County Community College, One College Boulevard, Paterson NJ 07505-1179. (973)684-6555. Fax: (973)523-6085. E-mail: mgillan@pccc.cc.nj.us. Website: www.pccc.cc.nj.us/poetry. **Contact:** Maria Mazziotti Gillan, executive director. Award to "encourage recognition of high-quality writing." Annual competition for books of short stories and novels published in the previous year. Award: $1,000. Competition expects 500 submissions this year. Judge: A different one every year. Guidelines available for SASE, e-mail or on website. Accepts inquiries by e-mail or phone. Submissions accepted after January 10, 2004. Results announced in July. Winners notified by mail. For contest results, send SASE or visit website.

◗ **PEARL SHORT STORY PRIZE**, *Pearl* Magazine, 3030 E. Second St., Long Beach CA 90803-5163. Phone/fax: (562)434-4523. E-mail: PearlMag@aol.com. Website: www.pearlmag.com. **Contact:** Marilyn Johnson, fiction editor. Award to "provide a larger forum and help widen publishing opportunities for fiction writers in the small press; and to help support the continuing publication of *Pearl*." Annual competition for short stories. Award: $250, publication in *Pearl* and 10 copies. Competition receives approximately 100 submissions. Judges: Editors of *Pearl* (Marilyn Johnson, Joan Jobe Smith, Barbara Hauk). $10 entry fee per story. Includes copy of magazine featuring winning story. Guidelines for SASE or visit website. Accepts inquiries by e-mail or fax. Deadline: May 31. Unpublished submissions. Length: 4,000 words maximum. Include a brief biographical note and SASE for reply or return of manuscript. Accepts simultaneous submissions, but asks to be notified if story is accepted elsewhere. All submissions are considered for publication in *Pearl*. "Although we are open to all types of fiction, we look most favorably upon coherent, well-crafted narratives, containing interesting, believable characters and meaningful situations." Results announced in August. Winners notified by mail. For contest results, send SASE, fax, e-mail or visit website.

◻ ◎ **WILLIAM PEDEN PRIZE IN FICTION**, *The Missouri Review*, 1507 Hillcrest Hall, University of Missouri, Columbia MO 65211. (573)882-4474. Website: www.missourireview.com. **Contact:** Speer Morgan, Evelyn Somers, Hoa Ngo, editors. Annual award "to honor the best short story published in *The Missouri Review* each year." Submissions are to be previously published in the volume year for which the prize is awarded. Award: $1,000. No application process; all fiction published in *The Missouri Review* is automatically entered.

◪ ◎ **PEN CENTER USA LITERARY AWARD IN FICTION**, (formerly PEN Center USA West Literary Award in Fiction), PEN Center USA, 672 S. LaFayette Park Place, #42, Los Angeles CA 90057. (213)365-8500. Fax: (213)365-9616. E-mail: awards@penusa.org. Website: www.penusa.org. **Contact:** Awards Coordinator. To recognize fiction writers who live in the western United States. Annual competition for published novels and story collections. Award: $1,000, plaque, and honored at a ceremony in Los Angeles. Competition receives 125 submissions. Judges: panel of writers, booksellers, editors. $25 fee for each book submitted. Guidelines available in July for SASE, fax, e-mail or on website. Accepts inquiries by fax, phone and e-mail. Deadline: December 19. Books published between January 1 and December 31 of 2003. Open only to writers living west of the Mississippi. All entries must include 4 non-returnable copies of each submission and a completed entry form. Results announced in May. Winners notified by phone and mail. For contest results, send SASE or visit website.

◎ **PEN NEW ENGLAND/L.L. WINSHIP AWARD**, P.O. Box 400725, N. Cambridge MA 02140. (617)499-9550. Fax: (617)353-7134. E-mail: awards@pen-ne.org. Website: www.pen-ne.org. **Contact:** Mary Walsh, coordinator. Award to "acknowledge and praise a work of fiction, nonfiction or poetry with a New England topic and setting and/or by an author whose main residence is New England." Annual competition for novels and poetry. Award: $2,500. Competition receives 150 submissions. Five judges. No entry fee. Guidelines available in early October for SASE, fax, e-mail or on website. Accepts inquiries by fax, e-mail and phone. Deadline: December 15 of that calendar year. Previously published submissions that appeared between January 1 and December 31 of the preceeding year. Results announced mid-March. Winners notified through publisher or PEN-NE Executive Board member. For contest results, e-mail or visit website in March.

Ⓝ ◖ ◎ **THE PEN/FAULKNER AWARD FOR FICTION**, c/o The Folger Shakespeare Library, 201 E. Capitol St. SE, Washington DC 20003. (202)675-0345. Fax: (202)608-1719. E-mail: delaney@folger.edu. Website: www.penfaulkner.org. **Contact:** Janice Delaney, PEN/Faulkner Foundation Executive Director. Annual award. "To award the most distinguished book-length work of fiction published by an American writer." Award: $15,000 for winner; $5,000 for nominees. Judges: Three writers chosen by the Trustees of the Award. Deadline: October 31. Published submissions only. Writers and publishers submit four copies of eligible titles published the current year. No juvenile. No self-published books. Authors must be American citizens.

◎ **PEW FELLOWSHIPS IN THE ARTS**, 230 S. Broad St., Suite 1003, Philadelphia PA 19102. (215)875-2285. Fax: (215)875-2276. E-mail: pewarts@mindspring.com. Website: www.pewarts.org. **Contact:** Melissa Franklin, director; Christine Miller, program associate. "The Pew Fellowships in the Arts provides financial support directly to artists so that they may have the opportunity to dedicate themselves wholly to the development of their artwork for up to two years. A goal of the Pew Fellowships in the Arts is to provide such support at a critical juncture in an artist's career, when a concentration on artistic development and exploration is most likely to contribute to personal and professional growth." Annual fellowships are awarded in three of 12 fields. Award: up to 12 $50,000 fellowships/year. Competition receives 100-200 submissions per category. Judges: a panel of artists and arts professionals. Application and guidelines available in late August for SASE and on website. Accepts inquiries by SASE, fax, e-mail, phone, website. Contest open to residents of Bucks, Chester, Delaware, Montgomery or Philadelphia counties who have lived in-county for at least 2 years. No students. Results announced annually in June. Winners notified by mail. List of winners will be mailed to entrants.

MARY ANN PFENNINGER LITERARY AWARD, GEM Literary, 340 E. Economy Rd., #305, Morristown TN 37814. (330)725-8807. E-mail: gemlit@earthlink.net. Website: www.gembooks.com. **Contact:** Darla Pfenninger, agent. Award to "honor unpublished authors in memory of the founder of the company." Annual award for novels or story collections. Award: literary representation and cash awards of $300, $100 and $50 as well as certificates for top ten. Competition receives 100 submissions. Judge: local and company readers give point values. Readers are assigned by genre; synopsis required. $20 entry fee plus return postage; send credit card information or make checks payable to Gem Literary. Guidelines available August for SASE, e-mail or visit website. Accepts inquiries by e-mail. Deadline: June 30. Entries should be unpublished but will accept self-published, or e-books. Contest open to anyone 18 years old or older. Cover letter should include name, address, phone, word count and title; title or name should be on each ms page. Results announced in August. Winners notified by mail. For contest results, send SASE or visit website. Submit "thought-provoking stories with unique characters, well written, with a sense of humor."

☐ ◎ **JAMES D. PHELAN AWARD**, Intersection for the Arts/The San Francisco Foundation, 446 Valencia St., San Francisco CA 94103-3415. (415)626-2787. Fax: (415)626-1636. E-mail: info@theintersection.org. Website: www.theintersection.org. **Contact:** Kevin B. Chen, program director. Annual award "to author of an unpublished work-in-progress of fiction (novel or short story), nonfictional prose, poetry or drama." Award: $2,000 and certificate. Competition receives more than 160 submissions. All submissions are read by three initial readers (change from year to year) who forward ten submissions each on to three judges (change from year to year). Judges are established Bay Area writers with extensive publishing and teaching histories. Rules and entry forms available after October 15 for SASE. Deadline: January 31. Unpublished submissions. Applicant must have been born in the state of California, but need not be a current resident; must be 20-35 years old. Results announced June 15. Winners notified by letter.

☐ ◎ **PLAYBOY COLLEGE FICTION CONTEST**, *Playboy* Magazine, 680 N. Lake Shore Dr., Chicago IL 60611. (312)751-8000. Website: www.playboy.com. Award "to foster young writing talent." Annual competition for short stories. Award: $3,000 plus publication in the magazine. Competition receives 2,000 submissions. Judges: Staff. Guidelines available in October *Playboy* every year. Deadline: January 1. Submissions should be unpublished. No age limit; college affiliation required. Stories should be 25 pages or fewer. "Manuscripts are not returned. Results of the contest will be sent via SASE." Results announced in February or March. Winners notified by letter. For contest results, send SASE or visit website in February.

◎ **MARY RUFFIN POOLE AWARD FOR BEST WORK OF FICTION**, North Carolina Literary and Historical Association, 4610 Mail Service Center, Raleigh NC 27699-4610. (919)733-9375. Fax: (919)733-8807. E-mail: michael.hill@ncmail.net. **Contact:** Michael Hill, awards coordinator. "Presented annually to best first published book-length work of fiction." Annual competition for novels and story collections. Award: $1,000 and an engraved plate. Competition receives 5-10 submissions per award category. Judge: three judge panel. Guidelines available July 1, 2002 for SASE, fax, e-mail or call. Deadline: July 15. Entries should be previously published (3 copies). Contest open to residents of North Carolina, minimum residency of 3 years. Winners notified by mail in October. List of winners available for SASE, fax or e-mail.

☐ **KATHERINE ANNE PORTER PRIZE FOR FICTION**, *Nimrod International Journal of Prose and Poetry*, University of Tulsa, 600 S. College, Tulsa OK 74104-3189. (918)631-3080. Fax: (918)631-3033. E-mail: nimrod@utulsa.edu. Website: www.utulsa.edu/NIMROD. **Contact:** Francine Ringold, editor-in-chief. "To award promising writers and to increase the quality of manuscripts submitted to *Nimrod*." Annual award for short stories. Award: $2,000 (1st Prize), $1,000 (2nd Prize) plus publication and two contributors copies. Competiton receives approximately 500 entries/year. Judges: editorial board and then a final judge. Past judges: Ron Carlson, Anita Shreve, Mark Doty, Gordon Lish, George Garrett, Toby Olson, John Leonard and Gladys Swan. $20 entry fee. Guidelines available after January for #10 SASE or by e-mail. Accepts inquiries by e-mail or by phone. Deadline: April 30. Previously unpublished manuscripts. Length: 7,500 words maximum. "Must be typed, double-spaced. Our contest is judged anonymously, so we ask that writers take their names off of their manuscripts. Include a cover sheet containing your name, full address, phone and the title of your work. Include a SASE for notification of the results. We encourage writers to read *Nimrod* before submission to discern whether or not their work is compatible with the style of our journal. Single issues are $10 (book rate postage included)." Results announced in July. Winners notified by mail. For contest results, send SASE with entry or visit website.

☒ **PRAIRIE SCHOONER PRIZE BOOK SERIES**, *Prairie Schooner* and the University of Nebraska Press, 201 Andrews Hall, University of Lincoln, Lincoln NE 68588-0334. (402)472-0911. Fax: (402)472-9771. E-mail: psbookseries2@unl.edu. Website: www.unl.edu/schooner/psmain.htm. **Contact:** Kelly Grey, managing editor. An annual book series competition publishing one book of short fiction by a single author each year through the University of Nebraska Press. Award: $3,000 and publication by the University of Nebraska Press. Semi-finalists chosen by a National Advisory Board; finalists and winners chosen by Hilda Raz, *Prairie Schooner*'s editor-in-chief. $25 fee per entry; make checks payable to *Prairie Schooner*. Guidelines available in late October by SASE, e-mail, or on website. Accepts inquiries by e-mail, phone. Submission period January 15 through March 15. Stories published in periodicals are eligible for inclusion, as are unpublished pieces. Contest open to all writers including non-U.S. citizens writing in English; both published and unpublished writers may enter. Length: 175-400 pages. Send one title page with title and author name; another title page with only title listed. "Send us a thoughtfully arranged collection of your best short fiction. To get an idea of what we are looking for, please read the *Prairie Schooner*."

◎ **PRAIRIE SCHOONER READERS' CHOICE AWARDS**, *Prairie Schooner*, 201 Andrews Hall, P.O. Box 880334, Lincoln NE 68588-0334. (402)472-0911. Fax: (402)472-9771. E-mail: kgrey2@unl.edu. Website: www.unl.edu/schooner/psmain.htm. **Contact:** Hilda Raz, editor-in-chief. Awards to "honor work published the previous year in *Prairie Schooner*, including poetry, essays and fiction." Award: $250 each. "We usually award 4-8 of these." Judge: the editorial staff of *Prairie Schooner*. No entry fee. For guidelines, send SASE or visit website. "Only work published in *Prairie Schooner* in the previous year is considered." Work is nominated by the editorial staff. Results announced in the Spring issue. Winners notified by mail in February or March.

THE PRESIDIO LA BAHIA AWARD, The Sons of the Republic of Texas, 1717 8th St., Bay City TX 77414. (979)245-6644. Fax: (979)244-3819. E-mail: srttexas@srttexas.org. Website: www.srttexas.org. **Contact:** Janet Hickl, administrative assistant. "To promote suitable preservation of relics, appropriate dissemination of data, and research into our Texas heritage, with particular attention to the Spanish Colonial period." Annual competition for novels. Award: "A total of $2,000 is available annually for winning participants, with a minimum first place prize of $1,200 for the best published book. At its discretion, the SRT may award a second place book prize or a prize for the best published paper, article published in a periodical or project of a nonliterary nature." Judges: recognized authorities on Texas history. No entry fee. Guidelines available in June for SASE, by fax, e-mail or on website. Accepts inquiries by mail, fax and e-mail. Entries will be accepted from June 1 to September 30. Previously published submissions and completed projects. Competition is open to any person interested in the Spanish Colonial influence on Texas culture. Cover letter should include name, address, phone and e-mail address. Results announced in November. Winners notified by mail; event/banquet in December. For contest results, send SASE, fax or e-mail.

PULITZER PRIZE IN FICTION, Columbia University, 709 Journalism Bldg., Mail Code 3865, New York NY 10027-6902. (212)854-3841. Fax: (212)854-3342. E-mail: pulitzer@www.pulitzer.org. Website: www.pulitzer.org. **Contact:** Professor Sig Gessler, administrator. Annual award for distinguished short stories, novels and story collections *first* published in U.S. in book form during the year by an American author, preferably dealing with American life. Award: $7,500 and certificate. Competition receives about 200 submissions. Guidelines and entry forms available in May 2002 for SASE, by phone, fax, e-mail and on website. Accepts inquiries by fax, phone and e-mail. Deadline: Books published between January 1 and June 30 must be submitted by July 1; books published between July 1 and October 31 must be submitted by November 1; books published between November 1 and December 31 must be submitted in galleys or page proofs by November 1. Submit 4 copies of the book, entry form, biography and photo of author and $50 handling fee. Open to American authors. Results announced April 7. Winners notified by telegram. For contest results, send SASE, fax, e-mail or visit website.

PUSHCART PRIZE, Pushcart Press, P.O. Box 380, Wainscott NY 11975. (516)324-9300. **Contact:** Bill Henderson, president. Annual award "to publish and recognize the best of small press literary work." Previously published submissions, short stories, poetry or essays on any subject. Must have been published during the current calendar year. Award: Publication in *Pushcart Prize: Best of the Small Presses*. Deadline: December 1. Nomination by small press publishers/editors only.

QSPELL BOOK AWARDS/HUGH MACLENNAN FICTION AWARD, Quebec Writers' Federation, 1200 Atwater, Montreal QC H3Z 1X4 Canada. (514)933-0878. Fax: (514)934-2485. E-mail: qspell@total.net. Website: www.Qwf.org. **Contact:** Lori Schuber, administrative director. Award "to honor excellence in writing in English in Quebec." Annual competition for fiction, poetry, nonfiction, first book and translation. Award: $2,000 (Canadian) in each category. Competition receives 15-20 submissions. Judges: panel of 3 jurors, different each year. Entry fee $10 (Canadian) per title. Guidelines for SASE. Accepts inquiries by fax and e-mail. Deadlines: May 31, 2004 (for works published October 1, 2003 to May 15, 2004); August 15, 2004 (for works published May 16, 2004 to September 30, 2004). "Writer must have resided in Quebec for three of the past five years." Books may be published anywhere. Page length: more than 48 pages. Results announced in November. Winners notified at an awards gala in November. For contest results, send SASE.

DAVID RAFFELOCK AWARD FOR PUBLISHING EXCELLENCE, National Writers Assn., 3140 S. Peoria #295, Aurora CO 80014. (303)841-0246. Fax: (303)841-2607. E-mail: contests@nationalwriters.com. Website: http://www.nationalwriters.com. **Contact:** Sandy Whelchel, executive director. Award to "assist published authors in marketing their works and promoting them." Annual award for novels, story collections. Award: $5,000 value promotional tour and services of a publicist. Judges: publishers and agents. $100 entry fee. Guidelines available for SASE, e-mail or on website. Accepts inquiries by fax, e-mail, phone. Deadline: May 1 annually. Entries should be previously published. Contest open to anyone with a published book in the English language. Winners are announced in June at the NWAF Conference and notified by mail or phone. List of winners available for SASE or visit website.

SIR WALTER RALEIGH AWARD, Historical Book Club of North Carolina and North Carolina Literary and Historical Association, 4611 Mail Service Center, Raleigh NC 27699-4610. (919)733-9375. **Contact:** Michael Hill, awards coordinator. "To promote among the people of North Carolina an interest in their own literature." Annual award for novels and short story collections. Award: Statue of Sir Walter Raleigh. Competition receives 8-12 submissions. Judges: University English and history professors. Guidelines available in August for SASE. Accepts inquiries by fax. Deadline: July 15. Book must be an original work published during the 12 months ending June 30 of the year for which the award is given. Writer must be a legal or physical resident of North Carolina for the three years preceding the close of the contest period. Authors or publishers may submit 3 copies of their book to the above address. Results announced October. Winners notified by mail. For contest results, send SASE.

THE REA AWARD FOR THE SHORT STORY, Dungannon Foundation, 53 W. Church Hill Rd., Washington CT 06794. Website: www.reaaward.org. **Contact:** Elizabeth Rea, president. Annual award "sponsored by the Dungannon Foundation, the Rea Award was established in 1986 by Michael M. Rea to honor a living U.S. or

Canadian writer who has made a significant contribution to the short story form. Award cannot be applied for. The recipient is nominated and selected by an annually appointed jury." Award: $30,000. Judges: 3 jurors. Award announced in Fall annually. Winners available on website.

🌐 **REAL WRITERS/BOOK PL@CE SHORT STORY AWARDS**, *REAL Writers* Support and Appraisal Services for Aspiring Writers, P.O. Box 170, Chesterfield, Derbyshire, S40 1FE United Kingdom. Phone/fax: (+44)01246-238492. E-mail: info@real-writers.com. Website: www.real-writers.com. **Contact:** Lynne Patrick, co-ordinator. Award to "provide a regular outlet for short fiction." Annual competition for short stories. Award: One prize of £2,500 ($3,500); ten category prizes of £100 each, including dedicated prizes for international and online entries. Winners published in an anthology, and runners-up are considered for publication in a leading magazine for writers. Competition receives 300-400 per category. Judge: Winners selected from a shortlist by a senior editor from a major publishing house. Shortlist chosen by an experienced panel. £5 or $10 entry fee; optional critique for extra fee; send credit card information or make check payable to Real Writers. Guidelines available in June for SASE, e-mail or visit website. Accepts inquiries by e-mail, phone. Deadline: November. Entries must be unpublished. Contest open to anyone. Length: 5,000 words maximum. Entry form or cover sheet should include name, address, phone, e-mail address, word count and title. Results announced in April. Winners notified by phone or mail. For contest results, visit website.

Ⓝ 🌐 ◎ **THE RED HOUSE CHILDREN'S BOOK AWARD**, Red House, The Old Malt House, Aldbourne, Marlborough Wiltshire SN8 2DW England. Phone: 01672-540629. Fax: 01672-541280. E-mail: marianneadey@aol.com. Website: www.redhousechildrensbookaward.co.uk. **Contact:** Marianne Adey, national coordinator. Purpose of award is "to find out what children choose among books of fiction published in the United Kingdom." Annual. Award for short stories, novels, short story collections. Award: silver bowl, portfolio of children's letters and pictures. Prize categories include Books for Younger Children, Books for Younger Readers, Books for Older Readers. Judged by children (60,000 reviews filled in last year). No entry fee. Guidelines available on website. Accepts inquiries by fax, e-mail, phone. Deadline: December 31, 2003. Entries should be previously published works of fiction for children, published in the UK. Either publishers or authors may submit books. Results announced in June for books published the previous year. Winners notified at event/banquet and via the publisher. For contest results, visit website.

Ⓝ ◎ **REDWRITINGHOOD.COM 100-WORD SHORT STORY CONTEST**, Bennett Enterprises, 1109 Kansas Plaza #152, Garden City KS 67846. (620)271-7932. E-mail: mui@mitone.com. Website: www.redwritinghood.com. **Contact:** Mitoné Bennett, owner/publisher. Contest to promote the art of the 100-word short story. Biannual. Competition for short stories. Award: $100, publication and contributor's copy of anthology to top prize winner; publication and contributor's copy to 25-30 other top entries. Contest receives 200 submissions per category. Judge: all entries read by Mitoné Bennett. $1 fee per entry. Guidelines available on website year round. Accepts inquiries by SASE, e-mail, phone. Deadline: July 31 and December 31 every year. Entries should be unpublished or previously published. Length: 100 words maximum. "A 100-word story is a complete story like any other. Pay attention to plot, characterization, conflict, dialogue, etc." Results announced on website usually within a month after deadline. Winners notified by e-mail.

REFLECTIONS SHORT FICTION AWARD, *Reflections Literary Journal*, Piedmont Community College, P.O. Box 1197, Roxboro NC 27573. (336)599-1181, ext. 428. E-mail: thrasht@piedmont.cc.nc.us. **Contact:** Tami Sloane Thrasher, editor. "This annual contest is designed to encourage and reward authors writing quality short fiction." Annual award for short stories. Prize: publication, $250 award and 5 contributor's copies. "We expect approximately 100 entries." Judge: each entry is evaluated and ranked by *Reflections* editorial panel, usually consisting of 6-10 readers. Judges read for appropriateness for publication in *Reflections* and for overall literary quality. $10 reading fee per story; "the fees are used exclusively for advertising and publication costs of the journal." For guidelines, send SASE or e-mail. Accepts inquiries by e-mail. Deadline: December 31 annually. Entries should be unpublished. Contest open to all writers. Length: 5,000 words maximum. "Examining a copy of the *Journal* before submitting an entry can help writers evaluate the appropriateness of their submission." Results announced in March or April. Winners notified by mail. For contest results, send SASE or e-mail.

◎ **REGIONAL BOOK AWARDS**, Mountains & Plains Booksellers Association, 19 Old Town Square, Suite 238, Ft. Collins CO 80524. (970)484-5856. Fax: (970)407-1479. E-mail: lisa@mountainsplains.org. Website: www.mountainsplains.org. **Contact:** Lisa Knudsen, director. Purpose: "to honor outstanding books set in the Mountains and Plains regions." Annual competition for one children's book and three adult books in fiction, non-fiction and poetry/art. Award: $500 and framed copy of Regional Book Awards Poster. "There are two panels of judges, one for adult books and one for children's. Each panel consists of 3-5 persons selected by the Awards Committee." Guidelines available for SASE, fax, e-mail, visit website or call. Deadline: November 1. Entries should be previously published. The book must be published for the first time within the year under consideration, November 1 through October 31. Contest open to all; "however, should relate to our region." Results announced in January. Winners notified by phone in December. For contest results, visit website.

LOUISE E. REYNOLDS MEMORIAL FICTION AWARDS, the new renaissance, 26 Heath Rd., #11, Arlington MA 02474-3645. Website: www.tnrlitmag.net. **Contact:** Louise T. Reynolds, editor-in-chief. Award established to "honor *tnr*'s founding manager, Louise E. Reynolds; to recognize and reward *tnr*'s writers; to promote interest and quality writing in independent literary magazines." Annual award is for fiction, including bilingual translations. Awards: $500, $250, $125; one $50 honorable mention. Program receives 260-275 submissions a year. Judges: Independent and new each volume. "We usually ask writers or critics who are familiar with *tnr*." Entry fee: $11.50 U.S. subscribers; $13.50 foreign; $16.50 U.S. nonsubscribers; $18.50 foreign; make checks payable to *tnr*. Guidelines available in January for SASE, e-mail or on website. Deadline: January 2-June 30 and September 1-October 31. Accepts inquiries only by e-mail. Entries should be unpublished. "All fiction submissions are tied into award program." Only fiction published in a 3-issue volume of *tnr* is considered for award. "Awards are open to all writers of literary, quality and/or serious fiction. We also publish, occasionally, light fiction, and it, too, is considered but we publish less of it." Length: 3-36 pages; double-spaced. Cover letter should include name, address, e-mail, word count and title. Include name of ms. Results announced after publication of the third issue in a volume of *tnr*. Winners notified by mail within 1 month of publication. For contest results, send SASE/IRC, e-mail or visit website.

SUMMERFIELD G. ROBERTS AWARD, The Sons of the Republic of Texas, 1717 8th St., Bay City TX 77414. (979)245-6644. Fax: (979)244-3819. E-mail: srttexas@srttexas.org. Website: www.srttexas.org. **Contact:** Janet Hickl, administrative assistant. "Given for the best book or manuscript of biography, essay, fiction, nonfiction, novel, poetry or short story that describes or represents the Republic of Texas, 1836-1846." Annual award of $2,500. Competition receives 20-35 submissions. Competition is judged by a panel comprised of winners of the last three years' competitions. No entry fee. Guidelines available in September for SASE, by fax, e-mail or on website. Accepts inquiries by fax, e-mail and phone. Deadline: January 15. "The manuscripts must be written or published during the calendar year for which the award is given. Entries are to be submitted in quintuplicate and will not be returned. Cover letter should include name, address, phone number and e-mail address." Results announced March. Winners notified by mail or phone. For contest results, send SASE, fax, e-mail.

ROMANCING THE NOVEL, Northeast Ohio RWA (Romance Writers of America), 6017 Pebble Creek Dr., Fairview PA 16415. (814)838-9972. E-mail: dkayc@aol.com. Website: http://members.aol.com/hfur/NEORWA. html. **Contact:** Debby Conrad, contest coordinator. Purpose of contest is to give writers "a chance for publication if recognized by an editor; excellent critique and advice from advanced writers." Annual. Competition for novels. Award: finalists (top 3 in each category) are read by an editor who buys in that genre. Prize categories include short contemporary romance, long contemporary romance, romantic suspense, erotic romance, inspirational romance, historical romance, paranormal romance and mainstream women's fiction. Judges: all entries are read by at least 2 experienced judges. $25 fee per entry; make checks payable to NEORWA. Guidelines available in April by SASE, e-mail, or on website. Accepts inquiries by e-mail, phone. Deadline: July 1. Entries should be unpublished. Contestants cannot be published in romantic fiction. Open to any and all members of Romance Writers of America. Cover letter should include name, address, phone, e-mail, and title; only title of ms. Results announced August 2004. Winners notified by phone or e-mail. For contest results, send e-mail or visit website.

MARJORY BARTLETT SANGER SHORT FICTION CONTEST, The Anthology of New England Writers, 151 Main St., P.O. Box 5, Windsor VT 0508-0483. (802)674-2315. E-mail: newvtpoet@aol.com. Website: www.hom etown.aol.com/newvtpoet/myhomepage/business.html. **Contact:** Dr. Frank Anthony or Susan C. Anthony, co-directors. "To discover individual writing of integrity and timelessness." Annual competition for short stories. Award: $300; three to five $30 honorable mentions. $6 one fiction entry fee; $5 each two or more entries. Guidelines for SASE, e-mail, visit website or call. Deadline: June 15. Entries should be unpublished. Contest open to all writers. Length: 1,000 words maximum. "Send your best work." Winners notified by mail or phone in July after conference. List of winners available for SASE.

THE SCARS/CC&D EDITOR'S CHOICE AWARDS, Scars Publications and Design/Children, Churches & Daddies Magazine, 829 Brian Court, Gurnee IL 60031-3155. E-mail: ccandd96@scars.tv. Website: http://scars.tv. **Contact:** Janet Kuypers, editor/publisher. Award to "showcase good writing in an annual book." Annual competition for short stories. Award: publication of story/essay and one copy of book. $13 entry fee per written piece. For guidelines, visit website. Accepts inquiries by e-mail. Deadline: "Revolves for appearing in different upcoming books as winners." Entries may be unpublished or previously published. Contest open to anyone. Length: "We appreciate shorter works. Shorter stories, more vivid and more real storylines in writing have a good chance."

VISIT THE WRITER'S MARKET WEBSITE at www.writersmarket.com for hot new markets, daily market updates, writers' guidelines and much more.

Results announced at book publication, online. Winners notified by mail when book is printed. For contest results, send SASE or e-mail.

☐ ◎ **SCIENCE FICTION WRITERS OF EARTH (SFWoE) SHORT STORY CONTEST**, Science Fiction Writers of Earth, P.O. Box 121293, Fort Worth TX 76121-1293. (817)451-8674. E-mail: sfwoe@flash.net. Website: www.flash.net/~sfwoe. **Contact:** Gilbert Gordon Reis, SFWoE administrator. Purpose "to promote the art of science fiction/fantasy short story writing." Annual award for short stories. Award: $200 (1st prize); $100 (2nd prize); $50 (3rd prize); $25 (First Honor). SFWoE will place the winning 1st prize story on their website for 180 days and pay the author $75 in addition to the $200 prize money." Competition receives approximately 250 submissions/year. Judge: Author Edward Bryant. Entry fee $5 for membership and first entry; $2 each for additional entries; make checks payable to SFWoE. Guidelines available after November for SASE, e-mail, or print from website. Accepts inquiries by e-mail and phone. Deadline: October 30. Submissions must be unpublished. The author must not have received payment for a published piece of fiction. Stories should be science fiction or fantasy, 2,000-7,500 words. Cover letter should include name, address, phone, e-mail address, word count and title. Same information should appear on ms title page. "Visit our website and read the winning story in our online newsletter to know what the judge looks for in a good story. Contestants enjoy international competition." Results announced January 31. Winners notified by mail, phone or e-mail. "Each contestant is mailed the contest results, judge's report, and a listing of the top ten contestants." Send separate SASE for complete list of the contest stories and contestants (or print from website).

◎ **SCRIPTAPALOOZA SCREENPLAY COMPETITION**, (formerly Scriptapalooza), Write Brothers, 7775 Sunset Blvd. PMB #200, Hollywood CA 90046. (323)654-5809. E-mail: info@scriptapalooza.com. Website: www.scriptapalooza.com. **Contact:** Mark Andrushko, president. Annual competition for screenwriting. Award: grand prize, $10,000. Top 3 will be considered by major production companies. Ten runners-up have loglines submitted to same production companies. Top 30 entries receive software. Competition receives 2,000-3,000 submissions. $40-50 entry fee; accepts Paypal credit card or make checks payable to Scriptapalooza. Guidelines available now. For guidelines, send SASE, e-mail or visit website. Accepts inquiries by e-mail, phone. Deadline: January 2 (earlybird deadline $40); March 1 (first deadline $45); April 15 (final deadline $50). Entries must be unpublished. Competition open to anyone 18 years or older. No pornography accepted. Length: 80-140 pages (proper screenwriting format). Results announced August 15. Winners notified by mail, phone, e-mail. For contest results, visit website.

◎ **SCRIPTAPALOOZA TELEVISION WRITING COMPETITION**, (formerly Scriptapalooza TV), *Script* Magazine, 7775 Sunset Blvd. PMB #200, Hollywood CA 90046. (323)654-5809. E-mail: info@scriptapalooza.com. Website: www.scriptapaloozatv.com. **Contact:** Mark Andrushko, president. Award to "discover talented writers who have an interest in American television writing." Semiannual competition for TV spec scripts and pilots. Award: $500 to top winner in each category (total $1,500) plus software, production company consideration and possible pitch meetings. Award: $200 second place each category; $100 third place each category. Competition receives 400-500 submissions in each category. Entry fee: $40; accepts Paypal credit card or make checks payable to Scriptapalooza. Guidelines available now. For guidelines, send SASE, visit website. Accepts inquiries by e-mail, phone. Deadline: May 15, 2004 and November 15, 2004. Entries should be unpublished. Contest open to any writer 18 years or older. Length: standard television format whether one hour, one-half hour or pilot. "Pilots should be fresh and new and easy to visualize. Spec scripts should be current with the shows, up-to-date storylines, characters, etc." Results announced February 15 and August 15. Winners notified by mail, phone or e-mail as soon as possible. For contest results, visit website.

☐ ◎ **SEVENTEEN MAGAZINE FICTION CONTEST**, *Seventeen Magazine*, 1440 Broadway, 13th Floor, New York NY 10018. (212)407-9700 or (212)204-4300. Fax: (212)204-3977. Website: www.seventeen.com. **Contact:** Attn: Fiction Contest Rules. Awarded to "honor best short fiction by a young writer." Annual competition receives 1,000-2,000 submissions. Guidelines for SASE. Rules published in late fall issue. Contest for 13-21 year olds. No entry fee. Deadline: April 30. Entries must be unpublished. Length: 3,500 words maximum. Include name, address, phone and e-mail on the upper right-hand corner of the cover page. Submissions judged by a panel of outside readers, former winners and *Seventeen*'s editors. Cash awarded to winners. First-place story published in 2004 issue. Winners notified by mail. List of winners available for SASE.

♥ ◎ **SFWA NEBULA® AWARDS**, Science-Fiction and Fantasy Writers of America, Inc., 532 La Guardia Place #632, New York NY 10012-1428. President: Michael Capobianco. Annual awards for previously published short stories, novels, novellas, novelettes. Science fiction/fantasy only. "No submissions; nominees upon recommendation of members only." Deadline: December 31. "Works are nominated throughout the year by active members of the SFWA."

ℕ **MICHAEL SHAARA AWARD FOR CIVIL WAR FICTION**, U.S. Civil War Center, LSU, Raphael Semmes Dr., Baton Rouge LA 70803. (225)578-3151. Fax: (225)578-4876. E-mail: lwood@lsu.edu. Website: www.cwc.lsu.edu. **Contact:** Leah W. Jewett, director. Competition "to encourage fresh approaches to Civil War fiction." Annual. Competition for novels. Award: $2,500. Judged for presentation of unique perspective, use of unusual approach, effective writing; contribution to existing body of Civil War literature. No entry fee. Guidelines available on website. Accepts inquiries by fax, e-mail, phone. Deadline: December 31, 2004. Entries should be previously published in 2004 for the first time. Competition open to authors of Civil War novels published for the first time in the year designated by award (i.e., for 2004 award, only novels published in 2004 are eligible). Cover letter should include name, address, phone, e-mail and title. Writers may submit their own fiction or may be nominated by publishers. Need 6 copies of novel. "Enter well before deadline." Results announced spring 2005. Winners notified by phone. For contest results, visit website.

FRANCES SHAW FELLOWSHIP FOR OLDER WOMEN WRITERS, The Ragdale Foundation, 1260 N. Green Bay Rd., Lake Forest IL 60045-1106. (847)234-1063, ext. 205. E-mail: eventsragdale@aol.com. Website: www.ragdale.org. **Contact:** Sylvia Brown, director of programming and marketing. Award to "nurture and support older women writers who are just beginning to write seriously." Annual competition for short stories, novels and poetry. Award: 6 weeks free residency at Ragdale, plus domestic travel. Competition receives 60 submissions. Judges: a panel of four anonymous women writers. Guidelines available for SASE. Accepts inquiries by fax or e-mail. Deadline: February 1. Previously unpublished submissions. Contest open to females over 55. Length: 20 pages/12 short poems. "Make your letter of application interesting, covering your desire to write and the reasons you have been thwarted to this point." Results announced in April. Winners notified by phone.

SHORT GRAIN CONTEST, *Grain* magazine, Box 67, Saskatoon SK S7K 3K1 Canada. (306)244-2828. Fax: (306)244-0255. E-mail: grainmag@sasktel.net. Website: www.grainmagazine.ca. ("E-mail entries not accepted.") **Contact:** Jennifer Still, business administrator. Annual competition for postcard stories, prose poems, dramatic monologues and creative nonfiction. Awards: 3 prizes of $500 in each category and publication in Fall issue. Competition receives 200 entries, dramatic monologue; 400 entries, prose poem; 500 entries, postcard story; 150 entries, creative nonfiction. Judges: Blind judging; J. Jill Robinson (postcard story), Zsuzsi Gartner (nonfiction), Tonja Gunvaldsen Klaassen (prose poem), Kit Brennan (dramatic monologue). Query first. $25 basic entry fee includes one-year subscription. U.S. and International entries in U.S. dollars. U.S. writers add $4 U.S. postage. International writers add $6 U.S. postage; make checks payable to Short Grain contest. Guidelines available in June by fax, e-mail, on website or for SASE or SAE and IRC. Deadline: January 31. Unpublished submissions. Contest entries must be either an original postcard story (a work of narrative fiction written in 500 words or less) or a prose poem (a lyric poem written as a prose paragraph or paragraphs in 500 words or less), a dramatic monologue (a self-contained speech given by a single character in 500 words or less) or creative nonfiction (a creative nonfiction prose piece in 5,000 words or less). Cover letter should include name, address, phone, e-mail, word count and title; title only on ms. Results announced April. Winners notified by phone, e-mail or mail. For contest results, send SASE, e-mail, fax or visit website.

SIDE SHOW SHORT STORY CONTEST, Somersault Press, 404 Vista Heights Rd., El Cerrito CA 94530. E-mail: somersaultpress@yahoo.com. **Contact:** Shelley Anderson and Jean Schiffman, editors. Award "to attract quality writers for our 300-odd page paperback fiction anthology." Awards: $100 (1st prize); $75 (2nd prize); $50 (3rd prize); $5/printed page paid to all accepted writers (on publication). Competition receives approximately 1,000 submissions. Judges: The editors of *Side Show*. Entry fee: $10 (includes sample copy of *Side Show*); make check payable to Somersault Press. No guidelines or restrictions on length or style. No genre, essays or novels. For informational leaflet, send SASE or e-mail. Accepts inquiries by e-mail. Unpublished (preferably) or previously published submissions; must have permission from previous publisher. Sample copy for $10 plus $2 postage. Multiple submissions (in same mailing envelope) encouraged (only one entry fee required for each writer). Will critique if requested. Cover letter should include name, address, e-mail, title and publications where story was previously published if applicable. "No deadline. Book published when we accept 20-30 stories." Winners notified before printing and announced upon publication.

SKIPPING STONES HONOR AWARDS, P.O. Box 3939, Eugene OR 97403-0939. (541)342-4956. Fax: (541)342-4956. E-mail: editor@skippingstones.org. Website: www.skippingstones.org. **Contact:** Arun N. Toké, executive editor. Award to "promote multicultural and/or nature awareness through creative writings for children and teens." Annual competition for short stories, novels, story collection, poetry and nonfiction. Award: honor certificates; seals; reviews; press release/publicity. Competition receives 125 submissions. Judges: "A multicultural committee of teachers, librarians, parents, students and editors." $50 entry fee ($25 for small/low income publishers/self-publishers). Guidelines for SASE or e-mail and on website. Accepts inquiries by e-mail, fax and phone. Deadline: January 15 annually. Previously published submissions that appeared in print between January 2002 and January 2004. Writer may submit own work or can be nominated by publisher, authors or illustrators. "We seek authentic, exceptional, child/youth friendly books that promote intercultural/international/intergenerational harmony and understanding through creative ways. Writings that come out of your own experiences/cultural understanding seem to have an edge." Results announced April. Winners notified through press release, personal notifications and by publishing reviews of winning titles. For contest results, send SASE, e-mail or visit website.

SKIPPING STONES YOUTH AWARDS, *Skipping Stones* Magazine, P.O. Box 3939, Eugene OR 97403-0939. (541)342-4956. E-mail: editor@skippingstones.org. Website: www.skippingstones.org. **Contact:** Arvn N.

Toké, executive editor. Award "to promote creativity and multicultural and nature awareness in youth." Annual. Award for short stories. Award: publication in Autumn issue, honor award certificate, subscription to *Skipping Stones*, 5 multicultural and/or nature books. Contest receives up to 200 submissions in four categories: fiction, nonfiction, poems and art/photos. Up to 10 winners in various categories. $3 fee per entry; make checks payable to Skipping Stones. Guidelines available in September 2003 by SASE, e-mail, or on website. Accepts inquiries by e-mail, phone. Deadline: June 20. Entries should be unpublished. Contest open to youth ages 7-17. Length: 750 words maximum. Cover letter should include name, address, phone and e-mail. "Be imaginative in your approach. Be creative. Do not use stereotypes or excessive violent language/plots. Be sensitive to cultural diversity." Results announced in September 2004. Winners notified by mail. For contest results, visit website. Everyone who enters receives the issue which features the award winners.

THE BERNICE SLOTE AWARD, *Prairie Schooner,* 201 Andrews Hall, P.O. Box 880334, Lincoln NE 68588-0334. (402)472-0911. Fax: (402)472-9771. E-mail: kgrey2@unl.edu. Website: www.unl.edu/schooner/psmain.htm. **Contact:** Hilda Raz, editor-in-chief. Award to "recognize the best work by a beginning writer published in *Prairie Schooner* in the previous year, including stories, essays and poetry." Award: $500. Judge: Competition is judged by the editorial staff of *Prairie Schooner.* No entry fee. For guidelines, send SASE, or visit website. "Only work published in *Prairie Schooner* in the previous year will be considered." Work is nominated by the editorial staff. Results announced in the Spring issue. Winners notified by mail in February or March.

🔲 ◎ **KAY SNOW CONTEST,** Willamette Writers, 9045 SW Barbur Blvd., Suite 5-A, Portland OR 97219-4027. (503)452-1592. Fax: (503)452-0372. E-mail: wilwrite@teleport.com. Website: www.willamettewriters.com. **Contact:** Marlene Moore, office manager. Award "to create a showcase for writers of all fields of literature." Annual competition for short stories; also poetry (structured and nonstructured), nonfiction, juvenile and student writers and screenwriters. Award: $300 (1st prize) in each category, second and third prizes, honorable mentions. Competition receives approximately 400 submissions. $500 Liam Callen Memorial Award for best overall entry to the contest. Judges: nationally recognized writers and teachers. $15 entry fee, nonmembers; $10, members; students free. Guidelines for #10 SASE, fax, e-mail or website. Accepts inquiries by fax, phone and e-mail. Deadline: May 15 postmark. Unpublished submissions. 2 poems with maximum 5 double-spaced pages per entry. Results announced August. Winners notified by mail and phone. For contest results, send SASE. Prize winners will be honored at the two-day August Willamette Writers Conference. Press releases will be sent to local and national media announcing the winners, and excerpts from winning entries may appear in our newsletter.

🔲 ◎ **SOCIETY OF CHILDREN'S BOOK WRITERS AND ILLUSTRATORS GOLDEN KITE AWARDS,** Society of Children's Book Writers and Illustrators, 8271 Beverly Blvd., Los Angeles CA 90048. (323)782-1010. **Contact:** Chelsea Mooser, chair. Annual award. "To recognize outstanding works of fiction, nonfiction and picture illustration for children by members of the Society of Children's Book Writers and Illustrators and published in the award year." Published submissions should be submitted from January to December of publication year. Deadline: December 15. Rules for SASE. Award: Statuette and plaque. Looking for quality material for children. Individual "must be member of the SCBWI to submit books."

🔲 ◎ **SOCIETY OF CHILDREN'S BOOK WRITERS AND ILLUSTRATORS WORK-IN-PROGRESS GRANTS,** 8271 Beverly Blvd., Los Angeles CA 90048. (323)782-1010. **Contact:** SCBWI. Annual grant for any genre or contemporary novel for young people; also nonfiction research grant and grant for work whose author has never been published. Award: $1,500 (1st prize), $500 (2nd prize). Work-in-progress. Competition receives approximately 180 submissions. Judges: Members of children's book field—editors, authors, etc. Guidelines for SASE. Deadline: February 1-May 1. Entries must be unpublished. Applicants must be SCBWI members.

◎ **SOUTH DAKOTA ARTS COUNCIL,** 800 Governors Dr., Pierre SD 57501-2294. (605)773-3131. E-mail: sdac@stlib.state.sd.us. Website: www.sdarts.org. **Contact:** Dennis Holub, executive director. "Individual Artist Grants (up to $3,000) and Artists Collaboration Grant (up to $6,000) are planned for fiscal year 2004." Guidelines and application available on website and by mail. Deadline: March 1. Grants are open only to residents of South Dakota. Students pursuing an undergraduate or graduate degree are ineligible. Applicants must submit application form with an original signature; current résumé no longer than 5 pages; appropriate examples of artistic work (see guidelines); up to 5 pages additional documentation (see guidelines); SASE with adequate postage for ms return (if desired).

🔲 **THE SOUTHERN REVIEW/LOUISIANA STATE UNIVERSITY SHORT FICTION AWARD,** *The Southern Review* and Louisiana State University English Dept., LSU, 43 Allen Hall, Baton Rouge LA 70803-5005. (225)578-5108. Fax: (225)578-5098. E-mail: bmacon@lsu.edu. Website: www.lsu.edu/thesouthernreview. **Contact:** John Easterly, associate editor. Annual award "to recognize the best first collection of short stories by an American writer published in the United States during the past year." Annual. Award for short stories. Award: $500 and possible paid reading invitation. Competition receives 40-45 submissions. Judges: committee of editors and faculty members. No entry fee. Guidelines available by SASE, fax, phone, e-mail, and on website. Accepts inquiries by fax, e-mail, phone. Deadline: January 31. Two copies to be submitted by publisher or author. Winner announced summer and notified by mail or phone.

SPUR AWARDS, Western Writers of America, Inc., 1012 Fair St., Franklin TN 37064. Phone/fax: (615)791-1444. E-mail: TNcrutch@aol.com. Website: www.westernwriters.org. **Contact:** Awards Coordinator. Purpose of award is to "reward quality in the fields of western fiction and nonfiction." Annual award for short stories and novels as well as poetry and nonfiction. Prize: trophy. Competition receives 25-30 submissions per category. No entry fee. Guidelines for 2003 competition available in August 2003. Send SASE. Deadline: December 31, 2003. Entries must be published in contest year. Contest open to all writers. Results announced annually in summer. Winners notified by mail. For contest results, send SASE.

THE STARCHERONE FICTION PRIZE, Starcherone Books, P.O. Box 303, Buffalo NY 14201-0303. Website: www.starcherone.com. Annual. Award for novels and story collections. Award: $1,500 and publication with Starcherone Books. Judges: contests will be blind-judged; author's name should appear only on title page. 2003 final judge was Cris Mazza. $25 fee per entry. Guidelines available by SASE or at www.starcherone.com/prize.htm. Deadline: January 10. Length: 400 pages maximum. "All finalists will be considered for publication." Results announced in August.

WALLACE E. STEGNER FELLOWSHIP, Creative Writing Program, Stanford University, Stanford CA 94305-2087. (650)725-1208. Fax: (650)723-3679. E-mail: gay-pierce@stanford.edu. Website: www.stanford.edu/dept/english/cw. **Contact:** Gay Pierce, program administrator. Annual award for short stories, novels, poetry and story collections. Five fellowships in fiction ($22,000 stipend plus required tuition of approximately $6,000). Competition receives 800 submissions. $50 entry fee. Guidelines available in July for SASE, by e-mail and on website. Accepts inquiries by phone and e-mail. Deadline: December 1. For unpublished or previously published fiction writers. Residency required. Word length: 9,000 words or 40 pages. Results announced April. Winners notified by telephone in mid-March. For contest results, visit website.

STONY BROOK SHORT FICTION PRIZE, Department of English, Humanities Bldg., State University of New York, Stony Brook NY 11794-5350. E-mail: Carolyn.McGrath@stonybrook.edu. Website: www.stonybrook.edu/fictionprize. **Contact:** Carolyn McGrath, director. Award "to recognize excellent undergraduate fiction." Annual competition for short stories. Award: $1,000, publication on website. Competition receives 150-200 submissions. Judges: Faculty of the Department of English & Creative Writing Program. No entry fee. Guidelines for SASE or on website. Accepts inquiries by e-mail. Deadline: March 9, 2004. Entries should be published or unpublished. "Only undergraduates enrolled full time in American or Canadian colleges and universities for the academic year 2003-2004 are eligible. Proof required. Students of all races and backgrounds are encouraged to enter." Word length: 7,500 words or less. Cover letter and ms should include name, permanent address, phone, e-mail, word count and title. Winners notified by phone; results posted on website by June 2004.

TALL GRASS WRITERS GUILD LITERARY ANTHOLOGY/CONTEST, Outrider Press, 937 Patricia, Crete IL 60417-1375. (708)672-6630 or (800)933-4680 (code 03). Fax: (708)672-5820. E-mail: outriderpr@aol.com. Website: www.OutriderPr.com. **Contact:** Whitney Scott, senior editor. 2004 competition to collect diverse writings by authors of all ages and backgrounds on the theme of the supernatural: "Things That Go Bump in the Night—From the Horrific to the Hilarious" (we love humor). Open to poetry, short stories and creative nonfiction. Annual award: publication in anthology; free copy to all published contributors. $1,000 in cash prizes. Competition receives 850 submissions. Judge: Larry Janowski. Entry fee $16.50; $12 for members; make check payable to Tallgrass Writers Guild. Guidelines and entry form available for SASE, by fax, e-mail and on website. Accepts inquiries by e-mail. Deadline: February 28, 2004. Unpublished and published submissions. Word length: 2,500 words or less. Maximum 2 prose, 8 poetry entries per person. Include SASE. Cover letter and ms should include name, address, phone, e-mail, word count and title. Results announced in May. "Must include e-mail address and SASE for response." For contest results, send e-mail.

SYDNEY TAYLOR MANUSCRIPT COMPETITION, Association of Jewish Libraries, % Rachel Glasser, 315 Maitland Ave., Teaneck NJ 07666. (201)862-0312. Fax: (201)862-0362. E-mail: rkglasser@aol.com. Website: www.jewishlibraries.org. **Contact:** Rachel Glasser, coordinator. Award to "identify and encourage writers of fiction for ages 8-11 with universal appeal of Jewish contest; story should deepen the understanding of Judaism and reveal positive aspects of Jewish life." Annual. Competition for novels. Award: $1,000. Judges: Competition committee made up of Judaic librarians. Judged for writing, originality, age appropriateness, Judaic content, and universal appeal. No entry fee. Guidelines available in July by SASE, e-mail or on website. Accepts inquiries by e-mail. Deadline: December 30. Entries should be unpublished. Length: 64 page minimum-200 page maximum, double-spaced. Cover letter should include name, address, phone, e-mail and title. Results announced April 15, 2004. Winners notified by phone or e-mail. For contest results, send e-mail or visit website.

THOUGHT MAGAZINE WRITER'S CONTEST, *Thought Magazine*, P.O. Box 117098, Burlingame CA 94011-7098. E-mail: ThoughtMagazine@yahoo.com. Website: www.ThoughtMagazine.org. **Contact:** Kevin J. Feeney, publisher. "To recognize and publish quality writing in the areas of short fiction, poetry, and short nonfiction and to identify and give exposure to writers who have not yet been published in a national magazine." Award: 1st prize-$75 plus publication in *Thought Magazine*; 2nd prize-$50 plus publication in *Thought Magazine*. "All submissions are considered for publication in *Thought Magazine*." Competition receives 100 submissions per category. "Entries are judged by the editors and a panel of judges consisting of published writers and academics." $5 entry fee/story or essay or 3 poems. Accepts inquiries by e-mail. Deadlines: April 15 and August 15. Entries should be unpublished. Contest open to all writers. Length: fiction maximum of 3,000 words. Poetry maximum of 100 lines. Include name, address, phone number and/or e-mail. "We are not interested in extreme violence or pornography. May be helpful to review a back issue available for $6." Results announced 1 month after deadlines. Winners notified by phone or e-mail. For contest results, send SASE.

JOHN TIGGES WRITING CONTEST, Loras College, 1450 Alta Vista, Dubuque IA 52004-0178. (563)588-7139. Fax: (563)588-4962. E-mail: cneuhaus@loras.edu. Website: www.loras.edu. **Contact:** Chris Neuhaus, Secretary of Continuing Education. This annual award encourages and recognizes aspiring writers as well as seasoned professionals. Prizes given for fiction, nonfiction, and poetry. Awards: $100 and publication in *Julien's Journal*, Dubuque area magazine (1st prize, fiction prize); $50 (2nd prize); and $25 (3rd prize). Poetry and nonfiction receive same monetary awards. First place in both are published in Dubuque *Telegraph Herald*. Entry fee: $5/entry. Written critiques available for contest entries, additional $15 per critique. "All requests for critiques must include SASE." Guidelines available February 2004. Accepts inquiries by fax, e-mail, or phone. Deadline: Must be "in-hand by" April 9, 2004. Entries should be unpublished. Length: fiction and nonfiction, 1,500 words—subject and style open; poetry, 40 lines maximum. Results announced at the Sinipee Writer's Workshop, April 26, 2004. Winners notified by mail, first week in May.

ROBERT TRAVER FLY-FISHING FICTION AWARD, *Fly Rod & Reel Magazine*, P.O. Box 370, Camden ME 04843-0370. (207)594-9544. Fax: (207)594-5144. E-mail: pguernsey@flyrodreel.com. Website: www.flyrodreel.com. **Contact:** Paul Guernsey, editor-in-chief. "The Traver Award is given annually for a work of short fiction that embodies an implicit love of fly-fishing, respect for the sport and the natural world in which it takes place and high literary values." Award: $2,500 and publication. Competition receives approximately 200 submissions. Judges: Members of John D. Voelker Foundation and *Fly Rod & Reel* editorial staff. Accepts inquiries by fax, e-mail, phone. Deadline: March 15. Include SASE. Winner announced in late summer/early fall publication and notified by mail upon publication.

N ⊕ ◎ THE TROLLOPE SOCIETY SHORT STORY PRIZE, The Trollope Society, 9A North St., London SW4 OHN England. Phone: +44 (0)207720 6789. Fax: +44 (0)207978 1815. E-mail: pamela@tvdox.com. Website: www.trollopestoryprize.org. **Contact:** Pamela Neville-Sington. Competition "to encourage interest in the novels of Anthony Trollope amongst young people; the emphasis is on reading and writing—for fun." Annual. Competition for short stories. Award: $1,400 to the winner; story published in the Society's quarterly journal, *Trollope*, and on website; occasionally a runner-up prize of $140. Competition receives about 30 entries, "but this is only our second year." Judges: A panel of writers and academics, including Trollope's biographer, Victoria Glendinning. No entry fee. Guidelines available in May on website. Accepts inquiries by fax, e-mail, phone. Deadline: January 15. Entries should be unpublished. Competition open to students worldwide, 21 and under. Length: 3,500 word limit. Cover letter should include name, address, phone, e-mail, word count and title. Results announced in March of each year. Winners notified by e-mail.

MARK TWAIN AWARD, Missouri Association of School Librarians, #15 Fawn Meadows Dr., Eureka MO 63025-1207. (636)938-6477. Website: www.maslonline.org. **Contact:** Kristi Berner, chair. Estab. 1970. Annual award to introduce children to the best of current literature for children and to stimulate reading. Award: A bronze bust of Mark Twain, created by Barbara Shanklin, a Missouri sculptor. A committee selects pre-list of the books nominated for the award; statewide reader/selectors review and rate the books, and then children throughout the state vote to choose a winner from the final list. Books must be published two years prior to nomination for the award list. Publishers may send books they wish to nominate for the list to the committee members. "Books should be 1) of interest to children in grades 4 through 8; 2) written by an author living in the US; 3) of literary value which may enrich children's personal lives." Results announced in May. Winners notified in April by phone. List of winners available.

THE MARK TWAIN AWARD FOR SHORT FICTION, *Red Rock Review*, NSSW English Dept., J2A, 3200 E. Cheyenne Ave., N. Las Vegas NV 89030-4296. (702)651-4094. Fax: (702)651-4639. E-mail: richard_logsdon@ccsn.nevada.edu. Website: www.ccsn.nevada.edu/english/redrockreview/index.html (includes contest guidelines and general submissions guidelines). **Contact:** Rich Logsdon, senior editor. Award to "find and publish the best available works of short fiction." Annual competition for short stories. Awards: $1,000 and publication. Competition receives 300-400 entries. Judges: Pre-judging by magazine staff and readers; winner selected by guest judge. Entry fee: $10; make checks payable to *Red Rock Review*. Guidelines available for SASE or on website. Accepts inquiries by fax, e-mail and phone. Deadline: October 31. Previously unpublished submissions. Word length: 3,500 words maximum. Author's name should not appear anywhere on manuscript. Submissions should include cover page with author's name, address, phone and e-mail address. No simultaneous submissions. "We're looking for well-crafted stories with fresh, invigorating prose." Results announced in February. Winners notified by phone. For contest results, send SASE or visit website.

VERY SHORT FICTION SUMMER AWARD, *Glimmer Train Stories*, 1211 NW Glisan St., Suite 207, Portland OR 97209. (503)221-0836. Fax: (503)221-0837. Website: www.glimmertrain.com (includes writers' guidelines and Q&A section for writers). **Contact:** Linda Swanson-Davies, editor. Annual award offered to encourage the art of the very short story. "We want to read your original, unpublished, very short story (2,000 words or less). $10 reading fee. Make your submissions online (www.glimmertrain.com) by July 31. Winners will be notified and Top 25 places will be posted by November 1." Awards: $1,200 and publication in *Glimmer Train Stories* and 20 author's copies (1st place); $500 (2nd place); $300 (3rd place).

VERY SHORT FICTION WINTER AWARD, *Glimmer Train Stories*, 1211 NW Glisan St., Suite 207, Portland OR 97209. (503)221-0836. Fax: (503)221-0837. Website: www.glimmertrain.com (includes writer's guidelines and a Q&A section for writers). **Contact:** Linda Swanson-Davies, editor. Award offered to encourage the art of the very short story. "We want to read your original, unpublished, very short story (2,000 words or less). $10 reading fee. Make your submissions online (www.glimmertrain.com) by January 31. Winners will be notified and Top 25 places will be posted by May 1." Awards: $1,200 and publication in *Glimmer Train Stories* and 20 author's copies (1st place); $500 (2nd place); $300 (3rd place).

○ ◎ **VIOLET CROWN BOOK AWARD**, Writers' League of Texas, 1501 W. Fifth St., Suite E-2, Austin TX 78703-5155. (512)499-8914. Fax: (512)499-0441. E-mail: wlt@writersleague.org. Website: www.writersleague.org. **Contact:** Stephanie Sheppard, executive director. Award "to recognize the best books published by Writers' League members over the period June 1 to May 31 in fiction, nonfiction and literary categories." Annual award: Three $1,000 cash awards and 3 trophies. Competition receives approximately 100 submissions. Judges: A panel of judges who are not affiliated with the Writers' League. Entry fee $10; send credit card information or make checks payable to Writers' League of Texas. Guidelines after January for SASE, fax, e-mail or website. Accepts inquiries by fax, e-mail or phone. Deadline: May 31. "Entrants must be Writers' League of Texas members. League members reside all over the U.S. and some foreign countries. Persons may join the League when they send in entries." Publisher may also submit entry in author's name. Results announced September. Winners notified by phone and mail. For contest results, send SASE or visit website. "Special citations are presented to finalists."

N ◎ **VOGELSTEIN FOUNDATION GRANTS**, The Ludwig Vogelstein Foundation, Inc., P.O. Box 510, Shelter Island NY 11964-0510. **Contact:** Willi Kirkham, executive director. "A small foundation awarding grants to individuals in the arts and humanities. Criteria are merit and need. No student aid given." Grants: $1,000-3,500. Foundation receives 50-100 applications. Guidelines available after September 1, before February 1 for SASE. Deadline: Last initial A-M, April 5-16, 2004; last initial N-Z, April 17-30, 2004. Results announced in November. Winners notified November-December by mail.

○ ◎ **WALDEN FELLOWSHIP**, Coordinated by: Extended Campus Programs, Southern Oregon University, 1250 Siskiyou Blvd., Ashland OR 97520-5038. (541)552-6901. Fax: (541)552-6047. E-mail: friendly@sou.edu. Website: www.sou.edu/walden. **Contact:** Brooke Friendly, arts coordinator. Award "to give Oregon writers the opportunity to pursue their work at a quiet, beautiful farm in southern Oregon." Annual competition for all types of fiction and creative nonfiction. Award: 3-6 week residencies. Competition receives approximately 30 submissions. Judges: Committee judges selected by the sponsor. Guidelines for SASE and on website. Accepts inquiries by fax and e-mail. Deadline: End of November. Oregon writers only. Word length: maximum 30 pages prose, 8-10 poems. Results announced in January. Winners notified by mail. For contest results, send SASE or visit website.

○ ◎ **EDWARD LEWIS WALLANT MEMORIAL BOOK AWARD**, The University of Hartford Department of Jewish Studies, Bloomfield Ave., West Hartford CT 06117. (860)768-4964. Sponsored by Dr. and Mrs. Irving Waltman. **Contact:** Mrs. Irving Waltman. Annual award. Memorial to Edward Lewis Wallant offering incentive and encouragement to beginning writers, for books published the year before the award is conferred in the spring. Award: $500 plus award certificate. Judges: A panel of 3 literary critics. No entry fee. Accepts inquiries by phone. Books may be submitted for consideration to Dr. Sanford Pinsker, Department of English, Franklin & Marshall College, P.O. Box 3003, Lancaster PA 17604-3003. Deadline: December 31. "Looking for creative work of fiction by an American which has significance for the American Jew. The novel (or collection of short stories) should preferably bear a kinship to the writing of Wallant. The award will seek out the writer who has not yet achieved literary prominence." Results announced January-February. Winners notified by phone.

N ◎ **WEATHERFORD AWARD**, Appalachian Center, CPO 2336, Berea College, Berea KY 40404-2336. (606)986-9341 ext. 5140. Director: Gordon McKinney. Award to "select the best work about Appalachia, monograph, fiction or poetry." Annual competition for short stories, novels and story collections. Award: $500. Competition receives 15 submissions. Judges: Committee of Appalachian writers. Deadline: December 31. Published submissions. Available only to authors who write about the Appalachian Region.

○ ◎ **WESTERN HERITAGE AWARDS**, National Cowboy and Western Heritage Museum, 1700 NE 63rd St., Oklahoma City OK 73111-7997. (405)478-6404. Fax: (405)478-4714. **Contact:** M.J. Van Deuenter, director of publications. Annual award "to honor outstanding quality in fiction, nonfiction and art literature." Submissions are to have been published during the previous calendar year. Award: The Wrangler, a replica of a C.M. Russell Bronze.

Competition receives 350 submissions. Entry fee $35. Guidelines available by SASE, fax or e-mail. Entry forms and rules available October 1 for SASE. Accepts inquiries by fax and e-mail. Deadline: November 30. Looking for "stories that best capture the spirit of the West. Submit five actual copies of the work." Results announced March 1. Winners notified by letter. For contest results, send SASE, fax or e-mail. "All work must be published by a legitimate, professional publishing company. Self published works are disqualified and the entry fee is not returned. Entries should have a broad appeal to those interested in the West, western history and the western lifestyle."

WILD VIOLET FICTION CONTEST, *Wild Violet*, P.O. Box 39706, Philadelphia PA 19106-9706. E-mail: wildvioletmagazine@yahoo.com. Website: www.wildviolet.net. **Contact:** Alyce Wilson, editor. Award's purpose is "to reward well-written fiction." Annual award for short fiction. Prize: $100 and publication in *Wild Violet* for first place; publication in *Wild Violet* for second and third place. Judge: "An independent judge to be announced on the website." Entry fee: $5. For guidelines, send e-mail or visit website. Accepts inquiries by e-mail. Deadline: March 1, 2004. Entries should be unpublished. "Contest open to any writer of any background." Length: 2,000 words. "Read previous issues of *Wild Violet* to get an idea of the type of fiction that interests this publication." Results announced in May. Winners notified by e-mail. For contest results, e-mail or visit website.

⊘ ◉ WISCONSIN INSTITUTE FOR CREATIVE WRITING FELLOWSHIP, University of Wisconsin— Creative Writing, English Department, 600 N. Park St., Madison WI 53706. Website: http://creativewritingwisc.edu. Competition "to provide time, space and an intellectual community for writers working on first books." Six annual awards for short stories, novels and story collections. Awards: $25,000/9-month appointment. Competition receives 500 submissions. Judges: English Department faculty. Guidelines available for SASE; write to Ron Kuka or check website. Deadline: February. Published or unpublished submissions. Applicants must have received an M.F.A. or comparable graduate degree in creative writing and not yet published a book. Limit 1 story up to 30 pages in length. No name on writing sample. Two letters of recommendation and vita or resume required.

ℕ ◻ TOBIAS WOLFF AWARD FOR FICTION, Mail Stop 9053, Western Washington University, Bellingham WA 98225. E-mail: bhreview@cc.wwv.edu. Website: www.wwv.edu/~bhreview. **Contact:** Fiction Editor. Annual competition for novel excerpts and short stories. Award: $1,000 and publication (1st Prize). Judge: Laura Kalpakian. Entry fee $15 for the first entry, $10/story or chapter thereafter. Guidelines available in August on website or for SASE. Deadline: December 1-March 15. Unpublished submissions. Length: 8,000 words or less per story or chapter. Winner announced in August. For contest results, send SASE.

◻ JOHN WOOD COMMUNITY COLLEGE, (formerly Quincy Writers Guild Annual Creative Writing Contest), 1301 S. 48th St., Quincy IL 62305. (217)224-6500 or (217)641-4903. Fax: (217)228-9483. E-mail: ssparks@jwcc.edu. Website: http://jwcc.edu. **Contact:** Sherry L. Sparks, director of continuing and community education. "A contest to promote new writing." Annual competition for short stories, nonfiction, poetry. Awards: Cash for 1st, 2nd, 3rd place entries; certificates for honorable mention. Competition receives approximately 150 submissions. Judges: area writing professionals. Entry fee $5 (fiction and nonfiction, each entry); $3 (poetry each entry); make checks payable to JWCC. "Guidelines are very important." Guidelines available after July for SASE, fax, e-mail, phone or on website. Accepts inquiries by e-mail or post. Deadline: April 1. Unpublished submissions. Word length: fiction and nonfiction, 2,000 words maximum; poetry, 2 pages maximum, any style. No entry form is required. No personal identification should appear on ms. A 3×5 card with author's name, address, e-mail address, title of work, and category entered must accompany each entry. Entries accepted after January 1. Winners notified by mail in late June. For contest results, send SASE, fax, e-mail or visit website after July.

WORLD FANTASY AWARDS, World Fantasy Awards Association, P.O. Box 43, Mukilteo WA 98275-0043. E-mail: sfexecsec@aol.com. Website: www.worldfantasy.org. **Contact:** Peter Dennis Pautz, president. Award to "recognize excellence in fantasy literature worldwide." Annual competition for short stories, novels, story collections, anthologies, novellas and life achievement. Award: Bust of HP Lovecraft. Competition receives approximately 600 submissions. Judge: Panel. No entry fee. Guidelines available in December for SASE or on website. Deadline: June 1. Published submissions from previous calendar year. Word length: 10,000-40,000 novella; 10,000 short story. "All fantasy is eligible, from supernatural horror to Tolkienesque to sword and sorcery to the occult, and beyond." Cover letter should include name, address, phone, e-mail, word count, title and publications where submission was previously published. Results announced November 1 at annual convention. For contest results, visit website November 1.

🌐 THE WRITERS BUREAU POETRY AND SHORT STORY COMPETITION, The Writers Bureau, Sevendale House, 7 Dale St., Manchester M1 1JB England. (+44)161 228 2362. Fax: (+44)161 228 3533. E-mail: comp@writersbureau.com. Website: www.writersbureau.com/resources.htm. **Contact:** Angela Cox, competition secretary. Annual competition for short stories and poems. Award: £1,000 (1st prize), £400 (2nd prize), £200 (3rd prize), £100 (4th prize), 6 awards of £50 (5th prize). Judges: Alison Chisolm and Iain Pattison. £4 fee per entry. Guidelines available in April. For guidelines, send SASE, fax, e-mail, visit website or call. Accepts inquiries by fax, e-mail, phone. Deadline: July 31. Entries should be unpublished. Contest open to anyone. Length: 2,000 words. Results announced September 30. Winners notified by mail. For contest results, send SASE or visit website.

WRITER'S DIGEST ANNUAL WRITING COMPETITION, (Short Story Division), *Writer's Digest*, 4700 E. Galbraith Rd., Cincinnati OH 45236. (513)531-2690, ext. 1328. E-mail: competitions@fwpubs.com. Website: www.writersdigest.com. **Contact:** Contest Director. Grand prize $1,500 cash and your choice of a trip to New York City to meet with editors and agents or a trip to the 2003 Maui Writer's Conference. Other awards include cash, reference books and certificates of recognition. Names of grand prize winner and top 10 category winners are announced in the November issue of *Writer's Digest*. Top entries published in booklet ($6). Rules and entry form available by sending SASE to *Writer's Digest* Annual Writing Competition, in January through May issues of *WD* or online. Deadline: May 31. Entry fee $10 per manuscript. All entries must be original, unpublished and not previously submitted to a *Writer's Digest* contest. Length: 4,000 words maximum genre and mainstream fiction, 2,000 for children's fiction. No acknowledgment will be made of receipt of mss nor will mss be returned. Three of the ten writing categories target short fiction: mainstream/literary, genre and children's fiction.

WRITER'S DIGEST INTERNATIONAL SELF-PUBLISHED BOOK AWARDS, *Writer's Digest*, 4700 E. Galbraith Rd., Cincinnati OH 45236. (513)531-2690, ext. 1328. E-mail: competitions@fwpubs.com. Website: www.writersdigest.com. **Contact:** Contest Director. Award to "recognize and promote excellence in self-published books." Annual competition with 9 categories: mainstream/literary fiction; genre fiction, nonfiction, inspirational (spiritual, New Age), life stories, children's and young adult books, reference books, poetry and cookbooks. Grand prize: $2,500 plus an ad in *Publishers Weekly* and promotion in *Writer's Digest* as well as a 1-year membership in Publishers Marketing Association. Category winners receive $500 and promotion in *Writer's Digest*. Both grand prize and category winners receive guaranteed distribution to bookstores and libraries through Baker & Taylor and guaranteed review in *Midwest Book Review*. Judges: Final judges are successful self-published authors and book editors. Entry fee $100 for first entry; $50 for each additional entry. Guidelines available for SASE and online. Deadline: December 16. Published submissions. Author must have paid full cost of publication and book must have been published in year of contest or two years prior.

WRITERS' FORUM SHORT STORY COMPETITION, Writers International Ltd., P.O. Box 3229, Bournemouth BH1 1ZS United Kingdom. Phone: (44) 1202 589828. Fax: (44) 1202 587758. E-mail: editorial@writers-forum.com. Website: www.writers-forum.com. **Contact:** Zena O'Toole, editorial assistant. Monthly competition for short stories. "The competition aims to promote the arts of short story writing. Prizes range from a minimum of £150 to £250 in each issue with an annual trophy and a cheque for £1,000 for the best story of the year. The competition is open to all nationalities, but entries must be in English." Judges: a panel provides a short list to the editor. Reading fee: £10 or £6 for subscribers to *Writers' Forum*; send credit card information or make checks payable to Writers International Ltd. Guidelines available for e-mail, on website and in publication. Accepts inquiries by fax, e-mail, phone. Entries should be unpublished. Length: 1,500-3,000 words. Cover letter should include name, address, phone, e-mail, word count and title. Winners notified by mail. List of winners available in the magazine.

WRITERS' JOURNAL ANNUAL FICTION CONTEST, Val-Tech Media, P.O. Box 394, Perham MN 56573-0394. (218)346-7921. Fax: (218)346-7924. E-mail: writersjournal@lakesplus.com. Website: www.writersjournal.com. **Contact:** Leon Ogroske, editor. Award: $50 (1st place); $25 (2nd place); $15 (3rd place) plus publication. Publishes prize winners and selected honorable mentions. Competition receives approximately 250 submissions/ year. Entry fee $5 each; make checks payable to Val-Tech Media. Unpublished submissions. Entry forms or rules available for SASE and on website. Accepts inquiries by fax, e-mail and phone. Deadline: January 30 annually. Maximum length is 2,000 words. "Writer's name must not appear on submission. A separate cover sheet must include: name of contest, title, word count and writer's name, address, and telephone number (e-mail address if available)." Results announced in July. Winners notified by mail. A list of winners is published in July/August issue and posted on website or available for SASE.

WRITERS' JOURNAL HORROR/GHOST CONTEST, *Writers' Journal*, P.O. Box 394, Perham MN 56573. (218)346-7921. Fax: (218)346-7924. E-mail: writersjournal@lakesplus.com. Website: http://writersjournal.com. **Contact:** Leon Ogroske, editor. Annual. Award for short stories. Award: $50 (1st place), $25 (2nd place), $15

(3rd place), plus publication. Competition receives 200 submissions per category. $5 fee per entry; make checks payable to Val-Tech Media. Guidelines available by SASE, fax, phone, e-mail, on website and in publication. Accepts inquiries by fax, e-mail, phone. Deadline: March 30 annually. Entries should be unpublished. Length: 2,000 words maximum. Cover letter should include name, address, phone, e-mail, word count and title; just title on ms. Results announced in September annually. Winners notified by mail. For contest results, send SASE, fax, e-mail or visit website.

⭕ ◎ **WRITERS' JOURNAL ROMANCE CONTEST**, Val-Tech Media, P.O. Box 394, Perham MN 56573-0394. (218)346-7921. Fax: (218)346-7924. E-mail: writersjournal@lakesplus.com. Website: www.writersjournal.com. **Contact:** Leon Ogroske, editor. Award: $50 (1st prize); $25 (2nd prize); $15 (3rd prize); publishes prize winners plus honorable mentions. Competition receives 150 submissions. Entry fee $5/entry; make checks payable to Val-Tech Media. No limit on entries per person. Guidelines available for SASE, by fax, phone, e-mail, on website and in publication. Accepts inquiries by fax, e-mail, phone. Deadline: July 30, annually. Unpublished submissions. Word length: 2,000 words maximum. Cover letter should include name, address, phone, e-mail, word count and title; just title on ms. Results announced in January/February issue. Winners notified by mail. Winners list published in *Writers' Journal Magazine* and on website. Enclose #10 SASE for winner's list or send fax or e-mail.

🌐 **WRITESPOT AUTUMN SHORT STORY COMPETITION**, WriteSpot Publishers International, P.O. Box 221, The Gap Queensland 4061 Australia. Phone: (07)3300-1948. E-mail: frontdesk@writersspot.com. Website: www.writersspot.com. **Contact:** Coordinator. "The competition is to allow writers a creative outlet. It is also used as a source for stories to be included in upcoming anthologies." Two competitions are held annually. Competition for short stories. Award: $750.; $250; $100; $50; Encouragement Award $50 value (for entrants under 18); publication also offered on up to 12 selected stories. Competition receives 100+ submissions. Judges: six members of the Publications Committee. $8 single entry fee; $12 two entries; $5 each three or more entries. Guidelines are available now and will appear on website one month prior to the opening of the competition; send SASE, e-mail, visit website or call. Accepts inquiries by e-mail and phone. Accepts inquiries by e-mail or phone. Deadline: May 28, 2004. Open to entries from February 2 to May 30. Entries should be previously unpublished. Contest open to all ages and locations. Length: 5,000 words maximum. "Work may be of any theme and should display flair and originality." Results announced June 25, 2004. Winners notified by phone and e-mail. For contest results, send SASE, e-mail or visit website.

🌐 **WRITESPOT SPRING SHORT STORY COMPETITION**, WriteSpot Publishers International, P.O. Box 221, The Gap Queensland 4061 Australia. Phone: (07)3300-1948. E-mail: frontdesk@writersspot.com. Website: www.writersspot.com. **Contact:** Coordinator. "The competition is to allow writers a creative outlet. It is also used as a source for stories to be included in upcoming anthologies." Two competitions are held annually. Competition for short stories. Award: $750.; $250; $100; $50; Encouragement Award $50 value (for entrants under 18); publication also offered on up to 12 selected stories. Competition receives 100+ submissions. Judges: members of the Publications Committee. $8 single entry fee; $12 two entries; $5 each three or more entries. Guidelines are available now and will appear on website one month prior to the opening of the competition; send SASE, e-mail, visit website or call. Accepts inquiries by e-mail and phone. Competition opens August 1, 2004. Deadline: November 14, 2004. Entries should be previously unpublished. Contest open to all ages and locations. Length: 5,000 words. "Work may be of any theme and should display flair and originality." Results announced December 6, 2004. Winners notified by phone and e-mail. For contest results, send SASE, e-mail or visit website.

📄 **ZOETROPE SHORT STORY CONTEST**, 916 Kearny St., San Francisco CA 94133. (415)788-7500. Fax: (415)989-7910. Website: www.all-story.com. Annual competition for short stories. Award: $1,000 (1st prize); $500 (2nd prize); $250 (3rd prize). 2001 judge: Robert Olen Butler. Entry fee $10. Guidelines available on website. Unpublished submissions. Word length: 5,000 words maximum. "Please mark envelope clearly 'short fiction contest.' " Winners notified in December. A list of winners will be posted on website and printed in February issue.

Resources

Conferences & Workshops 519

Writing Programs 568

Book Publishers and Their Imprints 585

Canadian Writers Take Note 589

Printing & Production Terms Defined 590

Glossary 592

Literary Agents Index 596

Contest Index by Deadline 611

Conference Index by Date 614

Category Index 618

General Index 660

Conferences & Workshops

Why are conferences so popular? Writers and conference directors alike tell us it's because writing can be such a lonely business—at conferences writers have the opportunity to meet (and commiserate) with fellow writers, as well as meet and network with publishers, editors and agents. Conferences and workshops provide some of the best opportunities for writers to make publishing contacts and pick up valuable information on the business, as well as the craft, of writing.

The bulk of the listings in this section are for conferences. Most conferences last from one day to one week and offer a combination of workshop-type writing sessions, panel discussions and a variety of guest speakers. Topics may include all aspects of writing from fiction to poetry to script-writing, or they may focus on a specific area such as those sponsored by the Romance Writers of America for writers specializing in romance, or the SCBWI conferences on writing for children's books.

Workshops, however, tend to run longer—usually one to two weeks. Designed to operate like writing classes, most require writers to be prepared to work on and discuss their work in progress while attending. An important benefit of workshops is the opportunity they provide writers for an intensive critique of their work, often by professional writing teachers and established writers.

Each of the listings here includes information on the specific focus of an event as well as planned panels, guest speakers and workshop topics. It is important to note, however, some conference directors were still in the planning stages for 2004 when we contacted them. If it was not possible to include 2004 dates, fees or topics, we have provided information from 2003 so you can get an idea of what to expect. For the most current information, it's best to send a self-addressed, stamped envelope to the director in question about three months before the date(s) listed or check the conference website.

FINDING A CONFERENCE

Many writers try to make it to at least one conference a year, but cost and location count as much as subject matter or other considerations when determining which conference to attend. There are conferences in almost every state and province and even some in Europe open to North Americans.

To make it easier for you to find a conference close to home—or to find one in an exotic locale to fit into your vacation plans—we've divided this section into geographic regions. The conferences appear in alphabetical order under the appropriate regional heading.

Note that conferences appear under the regional heading according to where they will be held, which is sometimes different from the address given as the place to register or send for information. The regions are as follows:

Northeast (page 521): Connecticut, Maine, Massachusetts, New Hampshire, New York, Rhode Island, Vermont

Midatlantic (page 527): Washington DC, Delaware, Maryland, New Jersey, Pennsylvania

Midsouth (page 530): North Carolina, South Carolina, Tennessee, Virginia, West Virginia

Southeast (page 533): Alabama, Arkansas, Florida, Georgia, Louisiana, Mississippi, Puerto Rico

Midwest (page 539): Illinois, Indiana, Kentucky, Michigan, Ohio

North Central (page 544): Iowa, Minnesota, Nebraska, North Dakota, South Dakota, Wisconsin

South Central (page 546): Colorado, Kansas, Missouri, New Mexico, Oklahoma, Texas

West (page 552): Arizona, California, Hawaii, Nevada, Utah
Northwest (page 559): Alaska, Idaho, Montana, Oregon, Washington, Wyoming
Canada (page 564)
International (page 565)

To find a conference based on the month in which it occurs, check out our new Conference Index by Date at the back of this book.

LEARNING AND NETWORKING

Besides learning from workshop leaders and panelists in formal sessions, writers at conferences also benefit from conversations with other attendees. Writers on all levels enjoy sharing insights. Often, a conversation over lunch can reveal a new market for your work or let you know which editors are most receptive to the work of new writers. You can find out about recent editor changes and about specific agents. A casual chat could lead to a new contact or resource in your area.

Many editors and agents make visiting conferences a part of their regular search for new writers. A cover letter or query that starts with "I met you at the Green Mountain Writers Conference," or "I found your talk on your company's new romance line at the Moonlight and Magnolias Writer's Conference most interesting . . ." may give you a small leg up on the competition.

While a few writers have been successful in selling their manuscripts at a conference, the availability of editors and agents does not usually mean these folks will have the time there to read your novel or six best short stories (unless, of course, you've scheduled an individual meeting with them ahead of time). While editors and agents are glad to meet writers and discuss work in general terms, usually they don't have the time (or energy) to give an extensive critique during a conference. In other words, use the conference as a way to make a first, brief contact.

SELECTING A CONFERENCE

Besides the obvious considerations of time, place and cost, choose your conference based on your writing goals. If, for example, your goal is to improve the quality of your writing, it will be more helpful to you to choose a hands-on craft workshop rather than a conference offering a series of panels on marketing and promotion. If, on the other hand, you are a science fiction novelist who would like to meet your fans, try one of the many science fiction conferences or "cons" held throughout the country and the world.

Look for panelists and workshop instructors whose work you admire and who seem to be writing in your general area. Check for specific panels or discussions of topics relevant to what you are writing now. Think about the size—would you feel more comfortable with a small workshop of eight people or a large group of 100 or more attendees?

If your funds are limited, start by looking for conferences close to home, but you may want to explore those that offer contests with cash prizes—and a chance to recoup your expenses. A few conferences and workshops also offer scholarships, but the competition is stiff and writers interested in these should find out the requirements early. Finally, students may want to look for conferences and workshops that offer college credit. You will find these options included in the listings here. Again, send a self-addressed, stamped envelope for the most current details.

For more on conferences and workshops, see "Finding the Perfect Writing Community" on page 40.

Northeast (CT, MA, ME, NH, NY, RI, VT)

THE BLUE MOUNTAIN CENTER, Blue Mountain Lake, New York NY 12812-0109. (518)352-7391. **Contact:** Harriet Barlow, director. Residencies for established writers. "Provides a peaceful environment where residents may work free from distractions and demands of normal daily life." Residencies awarded for 1 month between June 19 and November 1 (approx.). For more information, send SASE for brochure. Application deadline: February 1.

BREAD LOAF WRITERS' CONFERENCE, Middlebury College, Middlebury VT 05753. (802)443-5286. Fax: (802)443-2087. E-mail: blwc@middlebury.edu. Website: www.middlebury.edu/~blwc. **Contact:** Noreen Cargill, administrative manager. Estab. 1926. Annual. Conference held in late August. Conference duration: 11 days. Average attendance: 230. For fiction, nonfiction, poetry. Site: Held at the summer campus in Ripton, Vermont (belongs to Middlebury College).
Costs: In 2003, $1,933 (included room and board).
Accommodations: Accommodations are at Ripton. Onsite accommodations included in fee.
Additional Information: Conference information available January 2004. Accepts inquiries by fax and e-mail.

GOTHAM WRITERS' WORKSHOP, WritingClasses.com (online division), 1841 Broadway, Suite 809, New York NY 10023-7603. (212)974-8377. Fax: (212)307-6325. E-mail: dana@write.org. Website: www.writingclasses. com. **Contact:** Dana Miller, director of student affairs. Estab. 1993. "Classes held throughout the year. There are four terms, beginning in January, April, June/July, September/October." Conference duration: 10-week, 1-day, and online courses offered. Average attendance: approximately 1,300 students per term, 5,000 students per year. Offers craft-oriented creative writing courses in fiction writing, screenwriting, nonfiction writing, memoir writing, novel writing, children's book writing, playwriting, poetry, songwriting, mystery writing, science fiction writing, romance writing, television writing, sketch comedy, travel writing and business writing. Also, Gotham Writers' Workshop offers a teen program, private instruction and classes on selling your work. Site: Classes are held at various schools in New York City as well as online at www.writingclasses.com. View a sample online class on the website.
Costs: 10-week and online courses—$420 (includes $25 registration fee); 1-day courses—$150 (includes $25 registration fee). Meals and lodging not included.
Additional Information: "Participants do not need to submit workshop material prior to their first class." Sponsors a contest for a free 10-week online creative writing course (value=$420) offered each term. Students should fill out a form online at www.writingclasses.com to participate in the contest. The winner is randomly selected. For brochure send e-mail, visit website, call or fax. Accepts inquiries by SASE, e-mail, phone, fax. Agents and editors participate in some workshops.

GREAT RIVER ARTS, P.O. Box 639, Walpole NH 03608. (603)756-3638. Fax: (603)756-3302. E-mail: grai@sove r.net. Website: www.greatriverarts.org. **Contact:** Tonya Tabachnikoft, public relations. Estab. 1999. Year-round workshops. Conference duration: 3-4 days. Average attendance: 5-6 per class. "This season we are offering Art and the Children's Book and The Community of Stories, a course exploring the stories inherent through memoir writings." Site: Walpole, NH. "We use a conference center called Alyson's Orchard which is, indeed, a working apple orchard located on the shores of the Connecticut River." Past workshops included Screenwriting and Reading and Discussion with Charles Simic. Past speakers included Greg Blair (screenwriter), Charles Simic, Laurie Alberts, Douglass Whynott, Eileen Christelow, Lesle Lewis.
Costs: 2003 rates were $600-750. Does not include lodging or meals.
Accommodations: Provides list of area hotels.
Additional Information: Participants may need to submit material prior to arrival depending on course. Brochures for 2004 available in February/March 2004 by e-mail, phone, fax and on website. Accepts inquiries by e-mail, phone, fax.

GREEN MOUNTAIN WRITERS CONFERENCE, 47 Hazel St., Rutland VT 05701. (802)775-5326. E-mail: ydaley@adelphia.net. Website: www.vermontwriters.com. **Contact:** Yvonne Daley, director. Estab. 1999. Annual. Check website for 2004 conference dates. Average attendance: 40. "The conference is an opportunity for writers at all stages of their development to hone their skills in a beautiful, lakeside environment where published writers across genres share tips and give feedback." Site: Conference held at an old dance pavillion on a 5-acre site on a remote pond in Tinmouth, VT. Past features include: Place in Story—The Importance of Environment; Creating

---

CAN'T FIND A CONFERENCE? Conferences are listed by region. Check the introduction to this section for a list of regional categories. Want to attend a conference during a certain month? Check the Conferences by Date Index.

Character Through Description, Dialogue, Action, Reaction, and Thought; The Collision of Real Events and Imagination. 2003 panelists/lecturers included Yvonne Daley, Ruth Stone, David Huddle, Sydney Lea, Joan Connor, Tom Smith and Ursula Smith.

Costs: $500 (including lunch, snacks, beverages).

Accommodations: Transportation can be had at cost from area airports. Offers list of area hotels and lodging.

Additional Information: Participants mss can be read and commented on at a cost. Sponsors contests. Conference publishes a literary magazine featuring work of participants twice a year. Requirements: Free tuition, no lodging ($500); reading cost fee: $15. Essays plus 3 poems or 10 pages of fiction/nonfiction. Essays should say why the writer wants to attend conference. Length: 1,000 words. Brochures available in February, or on website before then. Brochures for SASE, e-mail, website or call. Accepts inquiries by SASE, e-mail, phone. Editors participate in conferences. "We aim to create a community of writers who support one another and serve as audience/mentors for one another. Participants often continue to correspond and share work after conferences." Further information available on website, by e-mail or by phone.

HOFSTRA UNIVERSITY SUMMER WRITERS' CONFERENCE, 250 Hofstra University, UCCE, Hempstead NY 11549. (516)463-5016. Fax: (516)463-4833. E-mail: uccelibarts@hofstra.edu. Website: www.hofstra.edu (under "Academics/Continuing Education"). **Contact:** Marion Flomenhaft, director, Liberal Arts Studies. Estab. 1972. Annual (every summer, starting week after July 4). Conference held in July 2004. Average attendance: 65. Conference offers workshops in fiction, nonfiction, poetry, juvenile fiction, stage/screenwriting and, on occasion, one other genre such as detective fiction or science fiction. Workshops in prose and poetry for high school student writers are also offered. Site: The university campus, a suburban setting. "We have had the likes of Oscar Hijuelos, Robert Olen Butler, Hilma and Meg Wolitzer, Budd Schulberg, Cynthia Ozick and Rebecca Wolf."

Costs: Check website for 2004 fees. "Continental breakfast and lunch are provided daily. Tuition also includes cost of the banquet."

Accommodations: Free bus operates between Hempstead Train Station and campus for those commuting from NYC. Dormitory rooms are available for conference.

Additional Information: "All workshops include critiquing. Each participant is given one-on-one time of ½ hour with workshop leader." Conference information available March 2004. Accepts inquiries by fax, e-mail.

◎ IWWG MEET THE AGENTS AND EDITORS: THE BIG APPLE WORKSHOPS, c/o International Women's Writing Guild, P.O. Box 810, Gracie Station, New York NY 10028-0082. (212)737-7536. Fax: (212)737-9469. E-mail: iwwg@iwwg.com. Website: www.iwwg.com. **Contact:** Hannelore Hahn, executive director. Estab. 1976. Biannual. Workshops held the second weekend in April, and the second weekend in October. Average attendance: 200. Workshops to promote creative writing and professional success. Site: Private meeting space of the New York Genealogical Society, mid-town New York City. Saturday: 1-day writing workshop. Sunday afternoon: open house/meet the agents, independent presses and editors.

Costs: $130 for the weekend.

Accommodations: Information on transportation arrangements and overnight accommodations available.

Additional Information: Accepts inquiries by fax, e-mail.

◎ IWWG SUMMER CONFERENCE, c/o International Women's Writing Guild, P.O. Box 810, Gracie Station, New York NY 10028-0082. (212)737-7536. Fax: (212)737-9469. E-mail: iwwg@iwwg.com. Website: www.iwwg.com. **Contact:** Hannelore Hahn, executive director. Estab. 1977. Annual. Conference held for one week in the summer. Average attendance: 450, including international attendees. Conference to promote writing in all genres, personal growth and professional success. Conference is held "on the tranquil campus of Skidmore College in Saratoga Springs, NY, where the serene Hudson Valley meets the North Country of the Adirondacks." 70 different workshops are offered every day. Overall theme: "Writing Towards Personal and Professional Growth."

Costs: $775 for week-long program, includes room and board.

Accommodations: Transportation by air to Albany, NY or Amtrak train available from New York City. Conference attendees stay on campus.

Additional Information: Conference information available for SASE. Accepts inquiries by fax, e-mail.

THE MACDOWELL COLONY, 100 High St., Peterborough NH 03458. (603)924-3886. Fax: (603)924-9142. E-mail: info@macdowellcolony.org. Website: www.macdowellcolony.org. **Contact:** Admissions Coordinator. Estab. 1907. Open to writers, composers, visual artists, film/video artists, interdisciplinary artists and architects. Site: Includes main building, library, 3 residence halls and 32 individual studios on over 450 mostly wooded acres, 1 mile from center of small town in southern New Hampshire. Available up to 8 weeks year-round. Provisions for the writer include meals, private sleeping room, individual secluded studio. Accommodates variable number of writers, 10 to 20 at a time

Costs: "There are no residency fees. Grants for travel to and from the Colony are available based on need. The MacDowell Colony is pleased to offer grants up to $1,000 for writers in need of financial assistance during a residency at MacDowell. At the present time, only artists reviewed and accepted by the literature panel are eligible for this grant." Application forms available. Application deadline: January 15 for summer (May-August), April 15 for fall (September-December), September 15 for winter/spring (January-April). Writing sample required. For novel, send a chapter or section. For short stories, send 2-3. Send 6 copies. Brochure/guidelines available; SASE appreciated.

MANHATTANVILLE COLLEGE SUMMER WRITERS' WEEK, School of Graduate and Professional Studies, 2900 Purchase St., Purchase NY 10577-2131. (914)694-3425. Fax: (914)694-3488. E-mail: gps@mville.edu. Website: www.manhattanville.edu. **Contact:** Ruth Dowd, R.S.C.J., dean, School of Graduate and Professional Studies. Estab. 1982. Annual. Conference held June 22-26, 2004. Average attendance: 110. Workshops include children's literature, journal writing, creative nonfiction, personal essay, poetry, screenwriting, fiction, travel writing and short fiction. The conference is designed not only for writers but for teachers of writing. Students do intensive work in the genre of their choice. Site: Manhattanville is a suburban campus 30 miles from New York City. The campus centers around Reid Castle, the administration building, the former home of Whitelaw Reid. Workshops are conducted in Reid Castle. A major author is featured as guest lecturer during the conference. Past speakers have included such authors as Toni Morrison, Andy Bienen, Gail Godwin, Richard Peck and poet Mark Doty.
Costs: Conference cost was $600 in 2003 plus $35 registration fee and $40 activity fee. For 2 credits cost is $910.
Accommodations: Students may rent rooms in the college residence halls. More luxurious accommodations are available at neighboring hotels. Check website for 2004 housing costs.
Additional Information: Conference information available March 15, 2004. For brochure send e-mail, visit website, call or fax. Accepts inquiries by SASE, e-mail, fax, phone.

[N] MARYMOUNT MANHATTAN COLLEGE WRITERS' CONFERENCE, Marymount Manhattan College, 221 E. 71st St., New York NY 10021. (212)774-4810. Fax: (212) 774-4814. E-mail: lfrumkes@mmm.edu. **Contact:** Amy Kugali and Brittany Lacour. Estab. 1993. Annual. June 2004. Conference duration: "Actual conference is one day, and there is a three-day intensive preceeding." Average attendance: 200. "We present workshops on several different writing genres and panels on publicity, editing and literary agents." Site: College/auditorium setting. 2003 conference featured 2 fiction panels, a children's book writing panel, a mystery/thriller panel and a panel focusing on how to start a book. 2003 3-day intensive included fiction writer Erica Jong, magazine writer and editor Pamela Fiori, and memoir writer Malachy McCourt. The conference itself included more than 50 authors.
Costs: $155, includes lunch and reception.
Accommodations: Provides list of area lodging.
Additional Information: 2004 conference information will be available in March by fax or phone. Also accepts inquiries by e-mail. Editors and agents sometimes attend conference.

NEW ENGLAND WRITERS CONFERENCE, P.O. Box 5, 151 Main St., Windsor VT 05089-0483. (802)674-2315. E-mail: newvtpoet@aol.com. Website: www.newenglandwriters.org. **Contact:** Dr. Frank or Susan Anthony, co-directors. Estab. 1986. Annual. Conference held third Saturday in July. Conference duration: 1 day. Average attendance: 150. The purpose is "to bring an affordable literary conference to any writers who can get there, and to expose them to emerging excellence in the craft." Site: The Old South Church on Main St. in Windsor, VT. Offers panel and seminars by prominent authors, agents, editors or publishers; open readings, contest awards and book sales/signings. Featured guest speakers have included Reeve Lindbergh (fiction, memoir), Lloyd Goodwin; Avis Smalley, April Ossman and William W. Cook.
Costs: $20 (includes refreshments). No pre-registration required.
Accommodations: Provides a list of area hotels or lodging options.
Additional Information: Sponsors poetry and fiction contests as part of conference (award announced at conference). Conference information available in May. For brochure send SASE or visit website. Accepts inquiries by SASE, e-mail, phone. "Be prepared to listen to the speakers carefully and to network among participants."

[N] NEW-CUE WRITERS' CONFERENCE AND WORKSHOP, (in honor of Rachel Carson), c/o St. Thomas Aquinas College, 125 Route 340, Sparkill NY 10976. (845)398-4247. Fax: (845)398-4224. E-mail: info@new-cue.org. Website: www.new-cue.org. **Contact:** Barbara Ward Klein, President. Estab. 1999. Biennial (on the "odd" year). Conference held June 13-16, 2004. Conference duration: Tuesday-Friday. Average attendance: 100. Participants can expect to hear award-winning authors, to enjoy guided outdoor activities, and (if selected) to read from their own work at morning sessions. Site: The 2004 New-Cue Conference and Workshop will be held once again at The Spruce Point Inn in Boothbay Harbor, Maine. The Inn is one of the finest in New England and Boothbay Harbor is the largest boating harbor north of Boston. A call for submissions will be posted with registration information in early September, 2003. In addition, there will be featured speakers each day of the Conference/Workshop. 2002 speakers were Bill McKibben, Joe Bruchac, Deborah Cramer, Andrea Cohen and Tom Horton. In addition, there were 15 concurrent sessions led by college/university faculty and published authors.
Costs: Registration costs for 2004 have not been posted. In 2002, registration was $349 and included all meals, program events, and speakers but did *not* include accommodations and travel.
Accommodations: Rooms at the Spruce Point Inn are $95-150/night (dbl. ocupancy); rooms nearby are $70-125/night (dbl. ocupancy).
Additional Information: Participants need to submit workshop material prior to arrival only if they wish to be considered for presentation during a morning session. Readings limited to 15 minutes. Deadline for submissions January 15, 2004. "The events are interdisciplinary, encouraging participants from colleges and universities, govern-

mental agencies, public and private organizations as well as amateur and published writers. This is an opportunity to participate and to enjoy the company of like-minded individuals in one of the most beautiful coastal locations on the eastern seaboard."

ODYSSEY FANTASY WRITING WORKSHOP, 20 Levesque Lane, Mont Vernon NH 03057-1420. Phone/fax: (603)673-6234. E-mail: jcavelos@sff.net. Website: www.sff.net/odyssey. **Contact:** Jeanne Cavelos, director. Estab. 1996. Annual. Workshop to be held June 14 to July 23, 2004. Conference duration: 6 weeks. Average attendance: limited to 20. "A workshop for fantasy, science fiction and horror writers that combines an intensive learning and writing experience with in-depth feedback on students' manuscripts. The only workshop to combine the overall guidance of a single instructor with the varied perspectives of guest lecturers. Also, the only such workshop run by a former New York City book editor." Site: Conference held at Southern New Hampshire University in Manchester, New Hampshire. Previous guest lecturers included: George R.R. Martin, Harlan Ellison, Ben Bova, Dan Simmons, Jane Yolen, Elizabeth Hand, Gene Wolf, Terry Brooks, Craig Shaw Gardner, Patricia McKillip and John Crowley.
Costs: In 2003: $1,400 tuition, $397.50 housing (double room), $795 (single room); $25 application fee, $500-600 food (approximate), $55 processing fee to receive college credit.
Accommodations: "Workshop students stay at Southern New Hampshire University townhouses and eat at college."
Additional Information: Students must apply and include a writing sample. Students' works are critiqued throughout the 6 weeks. Workshop information available in October. For brochure/guidelines send SASE, e-mail, visit website, call or fax. Accepts inquiries by SASE, e-mail, fax, phone.

THE PUBLISHING GAME, Peanut Butter and Jelly Press, P.O. Box 590239, Newton MA 02459. E-mail: conference@publishinggame.com. Website: www.publishinggame.com. **Contact:** Alyza Harris, manager. Estab. 1998. Monthly. Conference held monthly, in different locales across the U.S.: Boston, New York City, Philadelphia, Washington, DC, Boca Raton, San Francisco, Los Angeles, Toronto, Seattle, Chicago. Conference duration: 9 a.m. to 5 p.m. Average attendance: 20 writers. "A one-day workshop on finding a literary agent, self-publishing your book, creating a publishing house and promoting your book to bestsellerdom!" Site: "Elegant hotels across the country. Boston locations alternate between the Four Seasons Hotel in downtown Boston and The Inn at Harvard in historic Harvard Square, Cambridge." Fiction panels in 2003 include Propel Your Novel from Idea to Finished Manuscript; How to Self-Publish Your Novel; Craft the Perfect Book Package; How to Promote Your Novel; Selling Your Novel to Bookstores and Libraries. Workshop led by Fern Reiss, author and publisher of The Publishing Game series.
Costs: $195.
Accommodations: "All locations are easily accessible by public transportation." Offers discounted conference rates for participants who choose to arrive early. Offers list of area lodging.
Additional Information: Brochures available for SASE. Accepts inquiries by SASE, e-mail, phone, fax but e-mail preferred. Agents and editors attend conference. "If you're considering finding a literary agent, self-publishing your novel, or just selling more copies, this conference will teach you everything you need to know to successfully publish and promote your work."

ROBERT QUACKENBUSH'S CHILDREN'S BOOK WRITING & ILLUSTRATING WORKSHOPS, 460 E. 79th St., New York NY 10021-1443. (212)744-3822. Fax: (212)861-2761. E-mail: rqstudios@aol.com. Website: www.rquackenbush.com. **Contact:** Robert Quackenbush, director. Estab. 1982. Annual. Workshop to be held July 5-9, 2004. Conference duration: Five days. Average attendance: 10. Workshops to promote writing and illustrating books for children. "Focus is generally on picture books, easy-to-read and early chapter books." Site: Held at the Manhattan studio of Robert Quackenbush, author and illustrator of more than 170 books for children. All classes led by Robert Quackenbush.
Costs: $650 tuition covers all the costs of the workshop, but does not include housing and meals. A $100 nonrefundable deposit is required with the $550 balance due two weeks prior to attendance. 10% discount for all who enroll by June 15, or three weeks prior to conference date.
Accommodations: A list of recommended hotels and restaurants is sent upon receipt of deposit.
Additional Information: Class is for beginners and professionals. Critiques during workshop. Private consultations also available at an hourly rate. "Programs suited to your needs; individualized schedules can be designed. Write or phone to discuss your goals and you will receive a prompt reply." Conference information available 1 year prior to conference. For brochure, send SASE, e-mail, visit website, call or fax. Accepts inquiries by fax, e-mail, phone, SASE.

REMEMBER THE MAGIC IWWG ANNUAL SUMMER CONFERENCE, International Women's Writing Guild, P.O. Box 810, Gracie Station, New York NY 10028-0082. (212)737-7536. Fax: (212)737-9469. E-mail: dirhahn@aol.com. Website: www.iwwg.com. **Contact:** Hannelore Hahn. Estab. 1978. Annual. Conference held in the summer. Conference duration: 1 week. Average attendance: 500. The conference features 70 workshops held every day on every aspect of writing and the arts. Site: Saratoga Springs, 30 minutes from Albany NY and 4 hours from New York City, is blessed with every type of recreation. The town itself is a Victorian paradise, offering gingerbread houses and antique shops galore. Famous for its mineral springs; conference attendees may take baths at Spa Park. Conference attendees may also avail themselves of the famous Saratoga racing season, offering "race breakfasts" at 7:00 a.m. as well as ballet and music performances scheduled at the Saratoga Arts Festival. Workshop topics at previous conferences have included Promoting Your Book; Self-Publishing; The Art of Fiction Writing and One-Act Playwriting.

Costs: $885 for 7 days single, inclusive of meals and lodging.

Accommodations: Accommodations in modern, air-conditioned and non-air-conditioned dormitories—single and/or double occupancy. Equipped with spacious desks and window seats for gazing out onto nature. Meals served cafeteria-style with choice of dishes. Variety of fresh fruits, vegetables and salads have been found plentiful . . . even by vegetarians. Conference information is available in January. For brochure send SASE, e-mail, visit website or fax. Accepts inquiries by SASE, e-mail, phone or fax. "The conference is for women only."

◎ **SCBWI/HOFSTRA CHILDREN'S LITERATURE CONFERENCE**, University College of Continuing Education, Hofstra University, Hempstead NY 11549. (516)463-5016. Website: www.hofstra.edu/writers. **Contact:** Connie C. Epstein, Adrienne Betz and Marion Flomenhaft, co-organizers. Estab. 1985. Annual. Conference to be held April 17, 2004. Average attendance: 200. Conference to encourage good writing for children. "Purpose is to bring together various professional groups—writers, illustrators, librarians, teachers—who are interested in writing for children." Site: The conference takes place at the Student Center Building of Hofstra University, located in Hempstead, Long Island. "Each year we organize the program around a theme. Last year it was Finding Your Voice. We have two general sessions, an editorial panel and five break-out groups held in rooms in the Center or nearby classrooms." Previous agents/speakers have included: Paula Danziger and Anne M. Martin and a panel of children's book editors who critique randomly selected first-manuscript pages submitted by registrants. Special interest groups are offered in picture books, nonfiction and submission procedures with others in fiction.

Costs: $80 (previous year) for SCBWI members; $75 for nonmembers. Lunch included.

◎ **SCBWI MIDYEAR CONFERENCE, NYC**, 8271 Beverly Blvd., Los Angeles CA 90048. (323)782-1010. Fax: (323)782-1892. E-mail: conference@scbwi.org. Website: www.scbwi.org. **Contact:** Stephen Mooser. Estab. 1975. Annual. Conference held in February. Average attendance: 600. Conference is to promote writing for children: picture books; fiction; nonfiction; middle grade and young adult; meet an editor; meet an agent; financial planning for writers; marketing your book; children's multimedia; etc. Site: Manhattan.

Costs: See website for current cost.

Accommodations: Write for information; hotel names will be supplied.

Additional Information: Conference information available for SASE.

SEACOAST WRITER'S ASSOCIATION SPRING AND FALL CONFERENCES, 59 River Road, Stratham NH 03885-2358. Fax: (603)772-2720. E-mail: riverrd@tiac.net. **Contact:** Pat Parnell, conference director. Annual. Conferences held in May and October. Conference duration: 1 day. Average attendance: 60. "Our conferences offer workshops covering various aspects of fiction, nonfiction and poetry." Site: Chester College of New England in Chester, New Hampshire.

Costs: Approximately $50.

Additional Information: "We sometimes include critiques. It is up to the speaker." Spring meeting includes a contest. Categories are fiction, nonfiction (essays) and poetry. Judges vary from year to year. Conference information available for SASE April 1 and September 1. Accepts inquiries by SASE, e-mail, fax and phone.

STATE OF MAINE WRITERS' CONFERENCE, 16 Foley Avenue, Saco ME 04072. (800)330-4975. **Contact:** Jeff Belyea. Estab. 1941. Annual. Conference held in August. Conference duration: 4 days. Average attendance: 40. "We try to present a balanced as well as eclectic conference. There is quite a bit of time and attention given to poetry but we also have children's literature, travel, novels/fiction and other issues of interest to writers. Our speakers are publishers, editors, illustrators and other professionals. Our concentration is, by intention, a general view of writing to publish." Site: "We are located in Ocean Park, a small seashore village 14 miles south of Portland. Ours is a summer assembly center with many buildings from the Victorian age. The conference meets in Porter Hall, one of the assembly buildings which is listed in the National Register of Historic Places. Within recent years our guest list has included Lewis Turco, Amy MacDonald, Jeffrey Aronson, Wesley McNair, John N. Cole, Betsy Sholl, Denis Ledouz, John Tagliabue, Roy Fairfield, Oscar Greene and many others. We usually have about 10 guest presenters a year."

Costs: $90-$100 includes the conference banquet. There is a reduced fee, $50 for students ages 21 and under. The fee does not include housing.

Accommodations: An accommodations list is available. "We are in a summer resort area and motels, guest houses and restaurants abound."

Additional Information: "We have a list of about nine contests on various genres. The prizes, all modest, are awarded at the end of the conference and only to those who are registered." Send SASE for program guide and contest announcements.

Ⓝ ◎ **VERMONT COLLEGE POSTGRADUATE WRITERS' CONFERENCE**, 36 College St., Montpelier VT 05651. (802) 828-8764. E-mail: rick.zind@tui.edu. Website: http://tui.edu/vermontcollege. **Contact:** Rick Zind, conference coordinator. Estab. 1996. Annual. August 11-17, 2004. Conference duration: 6 days. Average attendance: 65-70. Conference will focus on novel and short story writing, creative nonfiction and poetry. "This is the only conference designed for the advanced writer—MFA or equivalent experience, with workshops limited to 5-7 people." Site: Held on historic Vermont College campus, overlooking Montpelier. The campus has a library, dorms, computer lab, cafeteria, and great meeting spaces. "We feature readings, lectures and master classes on a variety of topics relating to poetry, fiction and memoir writing." In 2003, speakers included Bret Lott, Ellen Lesser, Pamela Painter, Melissa Pritchard, Robin Behn and Richard Jackson.

Costs: Tuition: $800; $875 for poetry ms. Meals: $135. Lodging: $180 (private room), $120 (shared).

Accommodations: Shuttle service is available from Burlington Airport to the campus.

Additional Information: Five weeks before the conference, participants submit 20 pages for prose, 6 pages for poetry, 50 pages for poetry manuscript. Brochures available in November for SASE, by phone, by e-mail or on website. Also accepts inquiries by SASE, e-mail, phone.

VERMONT STUDIO CENTER, P.O. Box 613, Johnson VT 05656. (802)635-2727. Fax: (802)635-2730. E-mail: writing@vermontstudiocenter.org. Website: www.vermontstudiocenter.org. **Contact:** Kevin Cummins, writing program coordinator. Estab. 1984. Ongoing residencies. Conference duration: From 2-12 weeks. "Most residents stay for one month." Average attendance: 53 writers and visual artists/month. "The Vermont Studio Center is an international creative community located in Johnson, Vermont, and serving more than 500 American and international artists and writers each year (50 per month). A Studio Center Residency features secluded, uninterrupted writing time, the companionship of dedicated and talented peers, and access to a roster of two distinguished Visiting Writers each month. All VSC Residents receive three meals a day, private, comfortable housing, and the company of an international community of painters, sculptors, poets, printmakers, and writers. Writers attending residencies at the Studio Center may work on whatever they choose—no matter what month of the year they attend." Visiting writers have included Melanie Rae Thon and Larry Woiwode (December 2002); Alexander Theroux and John Keeble (January 2003); Rikki Ducornet and Charles Baxter (April 2003); Andrei Codrescu and Michelle Cliff (July 2003); John Yau and Antonya Nelson (September 2003); Jane Hamilton and Sharon Doubiago (December 2003).

Costs: "The cost of a 4-week residency is $3,300. Many applicants receive financial aid."

Accommodations: Accommodations provided.

Additional Information: Conferences may be arranged with visiting writers of the resident's genre. If conference scheduled, resident may submit up to 15 pages of ms. "We have competitions for Full Fellowships three times a year. The deadlines are February 15, June 15 and October 1. Writers should submit manuscripts of 15 pages. Application fee is $25." Writers encouraged to visit website for more information. May also e-mail, call, fax.

WESLEYAN WRITERS CONFERENCE, Wesleyan University, Middletown CT 06459. (860)685-3604. Fax: (860)685-2441. E-mail: agreene@wesleyan.edu. Website: www.wesleyan.edu/writing/conferen.html. **Contact:** Anne Greene, director. Estab. 1956. Annual. Conference held one week at the end of June. Average attendance: 100. For fiction techniques, novel, short story, poetry, screenwriting, nonfiction, literary journalism, memoir. Site: The conference is held on the campus of Wesleyan University, in the hills overlooking the Connecticut River. Meals and lodging are provided on campus. Features daily seminars, readings of new fiction, poetry and nonfiction, optional manuscript consultations and guest lectures on a range of topics including publishing. "Both new and experienced writers are welcome."

Costs: In 2003, day rate $725 (including meals); boarding students' rate of $845 (including meals and room for 5 nights).

Accommodations: "Participants can fly to Hartford or take Amtrak to Meriden, CT. We are happy to help participants make travel arrangements." Overnight participants stay on campus or in hotels.

Additional Information: Participants may attend seminars in all the genres. Scholarships and teaching fellowships are available, including the Jakobson awards for new writers of fiction, poetry and nonfiction and the Jon Davidoff Scholarships for journalists. Accepts inquiries by e-mail, phone, fax.

Ⓝ THE "WHY IT'S GREAT" WRITING WORKSHOP & RETREAT, 21 Aviation Road, Albany NY 12205. (518)453-0890; (800)720-1170. E-mail: workshop@whyitsgreat.com. Website: www.whyitsgreat.com. **Contact:** David Vigoda, director. Estab. 2003. Annual. Conference held July 2004. Conference duration: 4 days. Average attendance: 12. The fundamental activity is the appreciation and understanding of what makes great writing great. The key insight is realizing that no analysis of technique alone can be sufficient. Great writing is the melding of great technique with great heart and each must be able to get out of the way of the other even as they complete each other. Technique without heart is meaningless; heart without technique is incoherent. There are workshops about one and workshops about the other, but this is the one about cultivating and resolving the struggle between them. Fiction and nonfiction are emphasized, but poets and playwrights also benefit. Issues include thematic material, narration, and voice. Examples are drawn from all types of writing. Site: World Fellowship Center is a nonprofit organization founded in 1941 to promote peace, justice, and freedom. The vacation resort is situated on 450 undeveloped acres of beautiful woods, wetlands, and a large "forever wild" sanctuary pond in the New Hampshire Whithe Mountains. It is perfect for a writer's retreat and attracts singles, couples, and families. There are always interesting conversations to join and lots of recreational choices, including swimming, boating, and hiking. Themes are determined by particpants, according to their preferences. David Vidoda, novelist, playwright, and poet, conducts the workshop. He has published a novel *Nucleus*, a collection of stories, *Annihlating Distance*, and has had plays produced in Chicago, New York and London, as well as a radio play on National Public Radio affiliates. He is a National Endowment for the Arts Fellowship winner and a member of PEN American Center. He writes the "Why It's Great" newsletter and gave his first writing workshop 30 years ago at the University of Utah. Recently he started a publishing company, Collioure Books.

Costs: There is no charge for the 2003 workshop-retreat other than the cost of staying at World Fellowship Center. The cost ranges from $35-$77 per day per adult (less for children), including all meals, facilities, and programs. Weekly rates are available.

Accommodations: Guests arrange their own transportation. Shuttle service is available for those arriving by bus. Carpools may be available from Massachusetts and metro New York/New Jersey.

Additional Information: Brochures available August 2003 for 2004 conference. Available by phone, e-mail, or on the website. "No proof of ability is required. It doesn't matter if someone has written three novels or is still trying to get the first one started—or wrote 30 pages and froze. The workshop is non-competitive so all participants can feel safe in a group setting as they share their own work, insights, and experience."

WRITER'S VOICE OF THE WEST SIDE YMCA, 5 West 63rd Street, New York NY 10023. (212)875-4124. Fax: (212)875-4184. E-mail: wswritersvoice@ymcanyc.org. **Contact:** Fanon Howell, David Andrews. Estab. 1981. Workshop held 4 times/year (Summer, Spring, Winter and Fall). Conference duration: 1-12 weeks, 2 hours one night/week. Average attendance: 15. Workshop on "fiction, poetry, writing for performance, nonfiction, multi-genre, playwriting and writing for children." Site: Workshop held at the Westside YMCA.

Costs: $400/workshop, free for West Side Y members.

Additional Information: For workshop brochures/guidelines send SASE, e-mail, visit website, call or fax. Accepts inquiries by SASE, e-mail, fax, phone. "The Writer's Voice of the Westside Y is the largest non-academic literary arts center in the U.S."

WRITING, CREATIVITY AND RITUAL: A WOMAN'S RETREAT, 995 Chapman Road, Yorktown Heights NY 10598. (914)926-4432. E-mail: emily@emilyhanlon.com. Website: www.awritersretreat.com. **Contact:** Emily Hanlon. Estab. 1998. Annual. Retreat held September 20-October 3, 2003. Average attendance: 20 is the limit. Retreat for all kinds of creative writing. Site: Tuscany, Italy. "The retreat returns to Il Grande Prato, a restored farmhouse high in the hills near Florence. Fabulous site and the food is delicious!" Theme: "Writing from the Stillpoint—that place outside judgment, a place of creative freedom."

Costs: 2003 fees: $2,950-3,650 depending on choice of room. Includes workshop, and all meals and travel within Italy. Four days of touring, including two days in Florence with guides.

Additional Information: Conference information free and available. Accepts inquiries by e-mail, phone. "This retreat is open only to women. Enrollment is limited to 20. More than just a writing workshop or conference, the retreat is an exploration of the creative process through writing, 3-hour writing workshops daily, plus creativity workshops and time to write and explore.

YADDO, Box 395, Saratoga Springs NY 12866-0395. (518)584-0746. Fax: (518)584-1312. E-mail: yaddo@yaddo.org. Website: www.yaddo.org. **Contact:** Candace Waite, Program Director. Estab. 1900. Two seasons: large season in mid-May-August; small season is late September-May (stays from 2 weeks to 2 months; average stay is 5 weeks). Average attendance: Accommodates approximately 35 artists in large season. "Those qualified for invitations to Yaddo are highly qualified writers, visual artists, composers, choreographers, performance artists and film and video artists who are working at the professional level in their fields. Artists who wish to work collaboratively are encouraged to apply. An abiding principle at Yaddo is that applications for residencies are judged on the quality of the artists' work and professional promise." Site: Site includes four small lakes, a rose garden, woodland.

Costs: No fee is charged; residency includes room, board and studio space. Limited travel expenses are available to artists accepted for residencies at Yaddo.

Accommodations: Provisions include room, board and studio space. No stipends are offered.

Additional Information: To Apply: Filing fee is $20 (checks to Corporation of Yaddo). Two letters of recommendation are requested. Applications are considered by the Admissions Committee and invitations are issued by April (deadline: January 15) and September (deadline: August 1). Information available for SASE (55¢ postage), by e-mail, fax or phone and on website. Accepts inquiries by e-mail, fax, SASE, phone.

Midatlantic (DC, DE, MD, NJ, PA)

BALTIMORE WRITERS ALLIANCE CONFERENCE, P.O. Box 410, Riderwood MD 21139-0410. (410)377-5265. Fax: (410)377-4507. E-mail: conference@baltimorewriters.org. Website: www.baltimorewriters.org. **Contact:** Adrian King and Tracy Miller. Estab. 1993. Annual. Conference held in November. Conference duration: 1 day. Average attendance: 150-200. Conference focuses on "many areas of writing and getting published." Site: Towson University. Sessions featured in the 2002 conference included book development, poetry and freelance writers. John Gregory and Carrie Brown, Alan Cheuse, Barbara DeCesare, Marcia Talley and 20 plus others participated as speakers.

Costs: $80, includes food.

Accommodations: Provides a list of area hotels or lodging options "if asked."

Additional Information: Conference information is available August/September. For brochure e-mail, visit website or call. Accepts inquiries by e-mail and phone. Online registration available. Agents and editors participate in conference.

THE COLLEGE OF NEW JERSEY WRITERS' CONFERENCE, English Dept., The College of New Jersey, P.O. Box 7718, Ewing NJ 08628-0718. (609)771-3254. Fax: (609)637-5112. E-mail: write@tcnj.edu. Website: http://writersconference.intrasun.tcnj.edu. **Contact:** Jean Hollander, director. Estab. 1980. Annual. Conference will be held April 2004. Conference duration: 9 a.m. to 10:30 p.m. Average attendance: 600-1,000. "Conference concentrates on fiction (the largest number of participants), poetry, children's literature, play and screenwriting, magazine and newspaper journalism, overcoming writer's block, nonfiction books. Conference is held at the student center at the college in two auditoriums and workshop rooms; also Kendall Theatre on campus." The focus is on various genres: romance, detective, mystery, TV writing, etc. Topics have included "How to Get Happily Published," "How to Get an Agent," and "Earning a Living as a Writer." The conference usually presents 20 or so authors, plus 2 featured speakers, who have included Kurt Vonnegut, Salman Rushdie, Arthur Miller, Saul Bellow, Toni Morrison, Joyce Carol Oates, Spike Lee, Margaret Atwood, Joseph Heller, John Updike, Anna Quindlen, etc.

Costs: General registration $50, plus $10 for each workshop. Lower rates for students.

Additional Information: Conference information available by mail, e-mail, phone.

HIGHLIGHTS FOUNDATION FOUNDERS WORKSHOPS, 814 Court St., Honesdale PA 18437. (570)253-1172. Fax: (570)253-0179. E-mail: contact@highlightsfoundation.org. Website: www.highlightsfoundation.org. **Contact:** Kent Brown. Estab. 2000. Workshops held seasonally in March, April, May, June, September, October, November. Conference duration: 3-7 days. Average attendance: limited to 10-14. Conference focuses on children's writing: fiction, nonfiction, poetry, promotions. "Our goal is to improve, over time, the quality of literature for children by educating future generations of children's authors." Site: Highlights Founders' home in Boyds Mills, PA. Faculty/speakers in 2003 included Joy Cowley, Patricia Lee Gauch, Carolyn Yoder, Andrea Early, Stephen Swinburne, Juanita Havill, Sandy Asher, Eileen Spinelli, Rich Wallace, Neil Waldman, Kent L. Brown, Jr. and Peter Jacobi.

Costs: 2002 costs ranged from $795-995, including meals, lodging, materials.

Accommodations: Coordinates pickup at local airport. Offers overnight accommodations. "Participants stay in guest cabins on the wooded grounds surrounding Highlights Founders' home adjacent to the house/conference center."

Additional Information: "Some workshops require pre-workshop assignment." Brochure available for SASE, by e-mail, on website, by phone, by fax. Accepts inquiries by phone, fax, e-mail, SASE. Editors attend conference. "Applications will be reviewed and accepted on a first-come, first-served basis, applicants must demonstrate specific experience in writing area of workshop they are applying for—writing samples are required for many of the workshops."

HIGHLIGHTS FOUNDATION WRITING FOR CHILDREN, 814 Court St., Honesdale PA 18431. (570)253-1192. Fax: (570)253-0179. E-mail: contact@highlightsfoundation.org. Website: www.highlightsfoundation.org. **Contact:** Kent L. Brown. Estab. 1985. Annual. Conference held July 17-24, 2004; July 16-23, 2005; July 15-22, 2006. Average attendance: 100. Focuses on all genres of children's writing. Site: Chautauqua Institution. "Few cars are allowed on the grounds making for peaceful, idyllic surroundings. Architecture reflects the charm of the late 19th century." "Panels planned included Characterization, Writing Dialogue, Point of View, Developing a Plot, Think Pictures, etc. 2003 speakers included Dominic Barth, Larry Dane Brimner, Pat Broderick, Mary Lou Carney, Susan Campbell Bartoletti, Joy Cowley, Andrea Early, and more.

Costs: In 2003, $2100 with meals, gate pass, conference supplies included. Lodging and transportation extra.

Accommodations: Coordinates pickup from local airports, Jamestown, PA, Buffalo, NY, and Erie, PA. Coordinates locating lodging. "Accommodations available on the grounds—inns, hotels, guesthouses." $350-1,000 per week.

Additional Information: Participants must submit ms if participating in ms program. Brochures available December 2003 by SASE, e-mail, phone, fax or on website. Accepts inquiries by SASE, e-mail, phone, fax. Agents and editors attend conference.

JENNY McKEAN MOORE COMMUNITY WORKSHOPS, English Department, George Washington University, Washington DC 20052. (202)994-8223. Fax: (202)363-8628. **Contact:** D. McAleavey, professor. Estab. 1976. Workshop held each semester. Conference duration: One semester. Average attendance: 15. Workshop concentration varies depending on professor—usually fiction or poetry. Site: Workshop held at university.

Costs: Free.

Additional Information: Admission is competitive and by ms.

MONTROSE CHRISTIAN WRITER'S CONFERENCE, 5 Locust Street, Montrose Bible Conference, Montrose PA 18801-1112. (570)278-1001 or (800)598-5030. Fax: (570)278-3061. E-mail: mbc@montrosebible.org. Website: www.montrosebible.org. **Contact:** Donna Kosik, MBC Secretary/Registrar. Estab. 1990. Annual. Confer-

ence held in July 2004. Average attendance: 75. "We try to meet a cross-section of writing needs, for beginners and advanced, covering fiction, poetry and writing for children. It is small enough to allow personal interaction between conferences and faculty. We meet in the beautiful village of Montrose, Pennsylvania, situated in the mountains. The Bible Conference provides hotel/motel-like accommodation and good food. The main sessions are held in the chapel with rooms available for other classes. Fiction writing has been taught each year."
Costs: In 2003 registration (tuition) was $120.
Accommodations: Will meet planes in Binghamton, NY and Scranton, PA. On-site accommodations: room and board $170-255/conference; $38-57/day including food.
Additional Information: "Writers can send work ahead of time and have it critiqued for $30." The attendees are usually church related. The writing has a Christian emphasis. Conference information available April 2004. For brochure send SASE, visit website, e-mail, call or fax. Accepts inquiries by SASE, e-mail, fax, phone.

 **THE NEW JERSEY SOCIETY OF CHRISTIAN WRITERS FALL SEMINAR**, P.O. Box 405, Millville NJ 08332-0405. (856)327-1231. Fax: (856)327-0291. E-mail: daystar405@aol.com. Website: www.njscw.com. **Contact:** Dr. Mary Ann Diorio. Estab. 1992. Annual. Conference held November 6, 2004. Conference duration: 1 day. Average attendance: 30. "Our focus is Christian; we feature one speaker for the entire day; we provide a warm, nuturing environment for learing; we know how to have fun!" Conference focus varies annually; in 2003, it will be fiction. Site: Ramada Inn meeting room in Vineland, NJ. Guest speaker will be Gayle Roper, Christian novelist.
Costs: $75.
Accommodations: Provides list of area hotels for guests who choose to arrive the night before
Additional Information: Brochure available in July 2003 by e-mail, phone, fax and on website. Accepts inquiries by e-mail, phone, fax and through website.

 **OUTDOOR WRITERS ASSOCIATION OF AMERICA ANNUAL CONFERENCE**, 158 Lower Georges Valley Rd., Spring Mills PA 16875. (814)364-9557. Fax: (814)364-9558. E-mail: eking4owaa@cs.com. Website: www.owaa.org. **Contact:** Eileen King, meeting planner. Estab. 1927. Annual. Conference held June 19-23, 2004, in Spokane, WA. Average attendance: 800-950. Conference concentrates on outdoor communications (all forms of media). Featured speakers have included Don Ranley, University of Missouri, Columbia; Brig. General Chuck Yeager; Nina Leopold Bradley (daughter of Aldo Leopold); Secretary of the Interior, Bill Irwin, the only blind man to hike the Appalachian Trail.
Costs: $325 for nonmembers; "applicants must have prior approval from the Executive Director." Registration fee includes cost of most meals.
Accommodations: List of accommodations available after February. Special room rates for attendees.
Additional Information: Sponsors contests, "but all is done prior to the conference and you must be a member to enter them." Conference information available February 2004. For brochure visit website, send e-mail, call or fax. Accepts inquiries by e-mail, fax.

WILLIAM PATERSON UNIVERSITY SPRING WRITER'S CONFERENCE, English Dept., Atrium 250, 300 Pompton Rd., Wayne NJ 07470-2103. (973)720-3567. Fax: (973)720-2189. E-mail: liut@wpunj.edu. Website: http://euphrates.wpunj.edu/WritersConference. **Contact:** Timothy Liu, associate professor. Annual. Conference held in April. Conference duration: 1 day. Average attendance: 100-125. The 2004 conference will focus on the emerging writer. Several hands-on workshops are offered in many genres of creative writing, critical writing and literature. Includes reading by nationally recognized author. Site: William Paterson University campus. 2003 keynote speaker: Russell Banks. Past faculty has included Yusef Komunyakaa, Joyce Carol Oates, Susan Sontag and Jimmy Santiago Braca.
Costs: $30 (2002) includes 2 workshops, plenary readings, meals.
Additional Information: Conference information is available November/December. For brochure send e-mail, visit website, call or fax. Accepts inquiries by SASE, e-mail, phone and fax. Agents and editors participate in conference.

PENN WRITERS CONFERENCE, 3440 Market St., Suite 100, Philadelphia PA 19130. (215)898-6479. Fax: (215)573-2053. E-mail: writconf@sas.upenn.edu. Website: www.upenn.edu/writconf. **Contact:** Sue Pierce, faculty coordinator. Estab. 1995. Annual. Conference held November 8, 2004. Conference duration: 1 day. Average attendance: 200. Upcoming themes: Points of View, Fiction Addiction, Stupid Sentence Tricks, The Way You Say It. Speakers: Gregory Frost, Diane Ayres, Simone Zelitah, Elise Tuska, James Rahn, Bill Kent.

Costs: $165, includes breakfast, lunch, 2 workshops, 1 roundtable or panel lunch session, keynote speaker and reception.

Additional Information: Brochures available in September.

SANDY COVE CHRISTIAN WRITERS CONFERENCE, 60 Sandy Cove Rd., North East MD 21901-5436. (800)234-2683. Fax: (410)287-3196. E-mail: info@sandycove.org or sandycove@jameswatkins.com. Website: www.sandycove.org. **Contact:** Jim Watkins, director of conference. Estab. 1982. Annual. Conference held October 5-9, 2003. Average attendance: 150. Focus is on "all areas of writing from a Christian perspective such as: periodicals, devotionals, fiction, juvenile fiction, Sunday School curriculum, screenwriting, self-publishing, Internet writing, etc." Site: "Sandy Cove is conveniently located mid-way between Baltimore and Philadelphia, just off I-95." Located on 206 acres of woodland, near headwaters of the Chesapeake Bay. 2002 panels include historical, juvenile, women's, beginner writer. Past faculty has included Christy Allen Scannel, Bonnie Brechbill, Michael Davis, Sharon Ewell Foster, Lisa Halls Johnson, Curtis Lundgren, Doug Newton, Kristi Rector, John Riddle, Kathy Scott, Olivia Seaton, Brian Taylor, Claudia Tynes, Jim Watkins, Carol Wedeven.

Costs: In 2002, costs were full package: $624 per person, single room occupancy or $490 per person double room occupancy—includes lodging, meals, materials, seminars, sessions, private appointments and 2 ms evaluations; day guest package: $356 per person, excluding lodging.

Accommodations: No arrangements for transportation. "Hotel-style rooms, bay view available. Suites available for additional fee."

Additional Information: "For manuscript evaluations, participants may submit their manuscripts between six and two weeks prior to the conference. One copy should be sent in a 9×12 manila envelope. Include a self-addressed, stamped postcard if you want confirmation that it arrived safely." Accepts inquiries by e-mail, phone, fax. Editors and publishers participate in conference. Also offers 1 day student training for high school and college age as well as a writer's retreat—24 hours of uninterrupted writing and mentoring.

WINTER POETRY & PROSE GETAWAY IN CAPE MAY, 18 North Richards Ave., Ventnor NJ 08406-2136. (609)823-5076. E-mail: info@wintergetaway.com. Website: www.wintergetaway.com. **Contact:** Peter E. Murphy, founder/director. Estab. 1994. Annual. Workshop held January 16-19, 2004. Average attendance: 200. "Open to all writers, beginners and experienced over the age of 18. Prose workshops meet all day Saturday and Sunday and on Monday morning. Participants choose one workshop from among the following choices: short story (beginning and advanced), memoir, creative nonfiction, novel, drama, poetry, photography, storytelling and pottery. Classes are small so each person receives individual attention for the new writing or work-in-progress that they are focusing on. The workshops are held at the Grand Hotel on the oceanfront in historic Cape May, New Jersey." 2002 speakers included Barbara Hurd, Renée Ashley, Terese Svoboda, Stephen Dunn, Donna Perry, Mimi Schwartz, Robbie Clipper Sethi, and Richard Weems.

Costs: Cost for 2004 is $475 which includes breakfast and lunch for 3 days, all workshop sessions and evening activities, and a double room. Dinners are not included. Participants may choose a single room at an additional cost. Some workshops require additional material fees. Commuters who make their own arrangements are welcome. A $25 early bird discount is available if full payment is made by November 15.

Accommodations: "Participants stay in comfortable rooms, most with an ocean view, perfect for thawing out the muse. Hotel facilities include a pool, sauna and a whirlpool, as well as a lounge and disco for late evening dancing."

Additional Information: "Individual critiques may be available to prose writers at an additional cost. Work in progress should be sent ahead of time." For conference information (after September 15) send e-mail, visit website or call. Accepts inquiries by SASE, e-mail, phone. "The Winter Getaway is known for its challenging and supportive workshops that encourage imaginative risk-taking and promote freedom and transformation in the participants' writing."

Midsouth (NC, SC, TN, VA, WV)

AMERICAN CHRISTIAN WRITERS CONFERENCES, P.O. Box 110390, Nashville TN 37222. (800)21-WRITE. Fax: (615)834-7736. E-mail: ACWriters@aol.com. Website: www.ACWriters.com. **Contact:** Reg Forder, director. Estab. 1988. Annual. Conferences held throughout the year in over 2 dozen cities. Conference duration: 2 days. Average attendance: 30-80. Conference's purpose is to promote all forms of Christian writing. Site: Usually located at a major hotel chain like Holiday Inn.

Costs: $99 for one day; $189 for 2 days. Plus meals and accomodation.

Accommodations: Special rates available at host hotel.

Additional Information: Conference information available for SASE, e-mail, phone or fax. Accepts inquiries by fax, e-mail, phone, SASE.

◎ **BLUE RIDGE MOUNTAIN CHRISTIAN WRITERS CONFERENCE**, P.O. Box 128, Ridgecrest NC 28770. (828)669-3596. Fax: (828)669-3806. E-mail: Robin.Hawkins@lifeway.com. Website: www.lifeway.com/conferencecenters/ridgecrest.com. **Contact:** Robin Hawkins. Estab. 1999. Annual. Conference held April 6-11, 2003. Average attendance: 200. All areas of Christian writing, specializing in scriptwriting. Site: LifeWay Ridgecrest Conference Center, 18 miles east of Asheville NC. "Companies represented this year include Focus on the Family, Guidepost Books, LifeWay Christian Resources, Boardman & Holman, Tyndale, Walk Worth Press, Act One, Lawson Falle Publishing of Greeting Cards, Hartline Marketing and others." Faculty includes professional authors, agents and editors.
Accommodations: LifeWay Ridgecrest Conference Center.
Additional Information: Sponsors contests in published and unpublished categories for poetry and lyrics, articles and short stories, novels and novellas, and scripts. Awards include trophy and $400 scholoarship toward next year's conference. Contest entry fee: $10/entry. For brochure, send e-mail, call or fax. Accepts inquiries by e-mail, phone, fax.

CREATIVE WRITING BY THE SEA, 420 Raleigh St., Suite B, Wilmington NC 28412. (910)397-0906. Fax: (910)397-9473. E-mail: info@Retreats4Women.com. Website: www.Retreats4Women.com. **Contact:** Peg Schroeder, president. Estab. 2001. Annual. Conference held May 2004. Conference duration: 6 days. Average attendance: 11. Conference's purpose is "to nurture female fiction writers at all levels of experience." Site: Bald Head Island, NC. "We are exclusive occupants of a luxurious inn where all activities take place." Workshops led by Jill McCorkle.
Costs: In 2003, $2,375 included individual and group writing sessions, 5 nights luxurious accommodations, 1 full-body massage, daily yoga class, all gourmet meals.
Accommodations: "We provide ferry passage to the island as well as electric carts and bicycles for on-island transportation. Cars are restricted on the island. We also will make shuttle arrangements to the ferry from the airport." Lodging provided.
Additional Information: "Participants are invited, but not required, to submit manuscript in advance. Maximum 50 pages, typed, double-spaced." Brochures available in September 2002 for e-mail, by phone or on website. Accepts inquiries by e-mail, phone, fax. "Our retreat is restricted to eleven women, ages 30 or better. It is an opportunity to immerse one's self in writing while the Side Trip's staff caters to all needs. The retreat takes place on semitropical Bald Head Island, NC."

◎ **GALACTICON, KAG SPRING BREAK**, 5465 Hwy. 58, #502, Chattanooga TN 37416-1659. (423)326-0339. E-mail: galacticon@vei.net. Website: www.galacticoninc.com. **Contact:** Clara Miller, programming director. Estab. 1999. Annual. Conference held March 19-21, 2004. Average attendance: 200-250. Conference focuses on "science fiction/fantasy: novels, short stories, poetry (when we have poets for panels), music (filk and folk)." Site: Comfort Inn. 2004 schedule TBA. "In the past we have had panels on Novel vs. Short Story; Writing for Special Markets; Building Your World and/or Universe; Alternate Worlds; Choosing a Publisher; Preparing a Manuscript; Writing With Another Author; Self-Publishing; Comparative Religions." Guest speakers: "Literary GoH: P.M. Griffin, Filk GoH: Emerald Rose, KAG GoH: Lawrence Schoen of the Klingon Language Institute."
Costs: "All published authors 1 free membership; adults at the door: $35 (over 12); children at the door: $20 (6 to 12); childen under 6 free."
Accommodations: Staff will arrange pick-up at airport and/or bus station (Chattanooga, TN). Offers overnight accommodations. E-mail Galacticon for details. Hotel rooms are single and/or double: $59 plus tax/night; king: $79 plus tax/night.
Additional Information: "Con Suite with real food. 2002 featured a 'Targ' (Klingon pig) roast with trimmings. Included membership: Dealers Room, Slave Auction and Charity Auction. We have raised $345 (2001), $280 (2002) and $265 (2003) for Make-A-Wish Foundation." Brochures available for SASE, by e-mail, phone or on website. For further inquiries, contact by mail, e-mail or phone. "We have very knowledgeable and supportive attendees. We love to read, write, draw and sing. We have special programming for 6 to 12 year olds with introductions to writing (they make a book) and costuming. They have their own masquerade."

HIGHLAND SUMMER CONFERENCE, Box 7014, Radford University, Radford VA 24142-7014. (540)831-5366. Fax: (540)831-5951. E-mail: jasbury@radford.edu. Website: www.radford.edu/~arsc. **Contact:** Jo Ann Asbury, assistant to director. Estab. 1978. Annual. Conference held first 2 weeks of June 2004. Conference duration: 2 weeks. Average attendance: 25. Three hours graduate or undergraduate credits. Site: The Highland Summer Conference is held at Radford University, a school of about 9,000 students. Radford is in the Blue Ridge Mountains of southwest Virginia about 45 miles south of Roanoke, VA. "The HSC features one (two weeks) or two (one week each) guest leaders each year. As a rule, our leaders are well-known writers who have connections, either thematic or personal, or both, to the Appalachian region. The genre emphasis depends upon the workshop leader(s). In the past we have had as guest lecturers Nikki Giovanni, Sharyn McCrumb, Gurney Norman, Denise Giardinia, George Ella Lyon, Jim Wayne Miller, Wilma Dykeman and Robert Morgan."
Costs: "The cost is based on current Radford tuition for 3 credit hours plus an addidtional conference fee. On-campus meals and housing are available at additional cost. 2003 conference tuition was $505 for instate undergraduates, $625 for graduate students."
Accommodations: "We do not have special rate arrangements with local hotels. We do offer accommodations

on the Radford University Campus in a recently refurbished residence hall. (In 2003 cost was $23-32 per night.)"
Additional Information: "Conference leaders typically critique work done during the two-week conference, but do not ask to have any writing sumbitted prior to the conference beginning." Conference information available after February, 2004 for SASE. Accepts inquiries by e-mail, fax.

HILTON HEAD ISLAND WRITERS RETREAT, 40 Governors Lane, Hilton Head Island SC 29928. (843)671-5118. Fax: (843)671-5118. E-mail: bob@bobmayer.org. Website: www.bobmayer.org. **Contact:** Bob Mayer. Estab. 2002. Conference held every 2 months. Next conference held February 2004. Conference duration: 4 days. Average attendance: 10. Site: Held at the Marriott Beach & Golf Resort, ocean-side, Hilton Head Island.
Costs: $445 for 2003.
Accommodations: Special conference rates at Marriott.
Additional Information: Participants should submit cover letter, one page synopsis and first 15 pages of manuscript.

NIGHTWRITERS, 504 Duncan St., Ashland VA 23005. (800) 273-5027. Fax: (804) 798-6911. E-mail: nighwriters2000@aol.com. Website: www.nightwriters.com. **Contact:** Phyllis Theroux, founder. Estab. 1980. 2-4 times/year. May, June and October 2004. Conference duration: 5 days-2 weeks. Average attendance: 10. "The purpose of this event is to kick-start the creative process. Fiction and nonfiction exercises are used." Site: May: Henry Clay Inn, Ashland, VA; June, a private lodge in the foothills of the Sierra Mountains in California; October, a 1,300-acre Estruscan farm villa in Tuscany. Phyllis Theroux, author, editor and founder of Nightwriters.
Costs: $1,250-$2,500, includes everything but air fare. Provides transportation from nearest airport.
Additional Information: Brochures for 2004 conferences will be available late summer 2003 by phone, e-mail, on website. Also accepts inquiries by SASE or fax.

NORTH CAROLINA WRITERS' NETWORK FALL CONFERENCE, P.O. Box 954, Carrboro NC 27510-0954. (919)967-9540. Fax: (919)929-0535. E-mail: mail@ncwriters.org. Website: http://ncwriters.org. **Contact:** Carol Henderson, program coordinator. Estab. 1985. Annual. Average attendance: 450. "The conference is a weekend full of workshops, panels, readings and discussion groups. It endeavors to serve writers at all stages of development from beginning, to emerging, to established. We also encourage readers who might be considering writing. We try to have *all* genres represented. In the past we have had novelists, poets, journalists, editors, children's writers, young adult writers, storytellers, playwrights, and New York editors and agents." Site: "We hold the conference at a conference center with hotel rooms available."
Costs: "Conference registration fee for NCWN members is approximately $200 and includes two meals."
Accommodations: "Special conference hotel rates are available, but the individual makes his/her own reservations."
Additional Information: Conference information available September 1, 2003. For brochure e-mail with your mailing address, visit website, fax or phone. Accepts inquiries by SASE, phone, fax, e-mail.

SEWANEE WRITERS' CONFERENCE, 735 University Ave., Sewanee TN 37383-1000. (931)598-1141. E-mail: cpeters@sewanee.edu. Website: www.sewaneewriters.org. **Contact:** Cheri B. Peters, creative writing programs manager. Estab. 1990. Annual. 2003 conference held July 15-27. Average attendance: 110. "We offer genre-based workshops in fiction, poetry, and playwriting, and a full schedule of readings, craft lectures, panel discussions, talks, Q&A sessions and the like." Site: "The Sewanee Writers' Conference uses the facilities of the University of the South. Physically, the University is a collection of ivy-covered Gothic-style buildings, located on the Cumberland Plateau in mid-Tennessee. Invited editors, publishers, and agents structure their own presentations, but there is always opportunity for questions from the audience." 2003 faculty included Richard Bausch, Tony Earley, Barry Hannah, Robert Hass, Randall Kenan, Romulus Linney, Alison Lurie, Jill McCorkle, Alice McDermott, Dan O'Brien, Janet Peery, Mary Jo Salter, Alan Shapiro and Mark Strand.
Costs: Full conference fee (tuition, board, and basic room) is $1,325; a single room costs an additional $50.
Accommodations: Participants are housed in University dormitory rooms. Motel or B&B housing is available but not abundantly so. Dormitory shared housing costs are included in the full conference fee. Complimentary chartered bus service is available—on a limited basis—on the first and last days of the conference.
Additional Information: "We offer each participant (excepting auditors) the opportunity for a private manuscript conference with a member of the faculty. These manuscripts are due one month before the conference begins." Conference information available after February. For brochure send address and phone number, e-mail, visit website or call. "The conference has available a limited number of fellowships and scholarships; these are awarded on a competitive basis." Accepts inquiries by website, e-mail, phone, regular mail (send address and phone number.).

SHEVACON, P.O. Box 416, Verona VA 24482-0416. (540)248-4152. E-mail: themecon@juno.com. Website: www.shevacon.org. **Contact:** Crystal Ritchie, writer coordinator. Estab. 1993. Annual. 2004 conference held February 27-29. Average attendance: 400. "We are one of the smaller conventions in the SF/F genre, but we have a lot of big convention qualities." Conference focuses on Writing (science fiction and fantasy, some horror), Art (science fiction and fantasy), Gaming (science fiction and fantasy). Fiction-related panels included Stolen Stories: The Use of Historical Models; Blood on the Bulkhead: Is New Fiction Too Graphic?; Bad Guys We Want to Win: Writing

Good Villians; Scare Me, Thrill Me: Is Horror More Difficult to Write than Fiction? Writer Guest of Honor is Jim Butcher. Artist Guest of Honor is Charles Keegan.

Costs: $20 until October 31, 2003; $25 until February 1, 2004; $30 on site. "Meals are not included in the registration fee. Lodging is available at an extra fee."

Accommodations: "Shuttles from the airport are available; we do not have airline discounts." Offers overnight accommodations; "individuals must make their own reservations." Holiday Inn Roanoke Tanglewood. Conventions rate $67/night.

Additional Information: Sponsors contest. "We will be awarding our first ever scholarship at our 2003 convention, keep an eye on our website for the entry requirements for the genres of Art and Writing." For brochure send SASE or visit website. Accepts inquiries by mail, e-mail or phone.

VIRGINIA FESTIVAL OF THE BOOK, 145 Ednam Dr., Charlottesville VA 22903. (434)924-6890. Fax: (434)296-4714. E-mail: vabook@virginia.edu. Website: www.vabook.org. **Contact:** Nancy Damon, programs director. Estab. 1995. Annual. Festival held March 24-28, 2004. Average attendance: 17,100. Festival held to celebrate books and promote reading and literacy. Site: Held throughout the Charlottesville/Albemarle area.

Costs: $35 for festival luncheon and $25 fee for reception (reception free for participating authors). "All other programs free and open to the public."

Accommodations: Overnight accommodations can be found on the web at www.covingtravel.com.

Additional Information: "Authors must 'apply' to the festival to be included on a panel." Conference information is available on the website, e-mail, fax or phone. For brochure visit website. Accepts inquiries by e-mail, fax, phone. Authors, agents and editors participate in conference. "The festival is a five-day event featuring authors, illustrators and publishing professionals. The featured authors are invited to convene for discussions and readings or write and inquire to participate. All attendees welcome."

WILDACRE WRITERS WORKSHOP, 233 S. Elm St., Greensboro NC 27401-2602. (800)635-2049. Fax: (336)273-4044. E-mail: judihill@aol.com. Website: www.Wildacres.com. **Contact:** Judith Hill, director. Estab. 1985. Annual. Workshop held first week in July. Conference duration: 1 week. Average attendance: 110. Workshop focuses on novel, short story, poetry, creative nonfiction. Site: Beautiful retreat center on top of a mountain in the Blue Ridge Mountains of North Carolina. Panels planned for next workshop include 2 novel classes; 2 short story classes; 1 mystery/suspense class. Past faculty has included Gail Adam, Janice Eidus, John Dufresne and Clint McCown.

Costs: $480 (everything is included: workshop, ms critique, double room, all meals).

Accommodations: Vans available, $50 round trip

Additional Information: "New people must submit a writing sample to be accepted. Those attending send their manuscript one month prior to arrival." Workshop information is available mid-January. For brochure send e-mail or visit website. Accepts inquiries by e-mail and phone. Agents and editors participate in conference.

Southeast (AL, AR, FL, GA, LA, MS, PR [Puerto Rico])

ALABAMA WRITERS' CONCLAVE, P.O. Box 230787, Montgomery AL 36123-0787. (334)244-8920. E-mail: poettennis@aol.com. Website: www.alabamapoets.org. **Contact:** Donna Jean Tennis, editor. Estab. 1923. Annual conference held for 3 days, the first week in August. 2004 conference dates are August 5-7. Average attendance: 75-100. Conference to promote "all phases" of writing. Site: Ramsay Conference Center (University of Montevallo).

Costs: Fees for 3 days are $50 for members; $70 for nonmembers (which includes membership). Lower rates for 1- or 2-day attendance. Meals and awards banquet additional cost.

Accommodations: Accommodations available on campus. $21 for single, $42 for double.

Additional Information: "We have 'name' speakers and workshops with members helping members. We offer open mike readings every evening. We sponsor a contest each year with a published book of winners." Conference brochures and contest guidelines available for SASE, by e-mail, on website. Accepts inquiries by SASE, e-mail. Membership dues are $15 and include a quarterly newsletter. Membership information from Donna Jean Tennis at above address. Conference is "laid-back, comfortable, inexpensive and always interesting and informative!"

N ARKANSAS WRITERS' CONFERENCE, AR. Penwomen Pioneer Branch of the National League of American Penwomen, 6817 Gingerbread Lane, Little Rock AR 72204. (501)565-8889. Fax: (501)907-1055. E-mail: pvining@aristotle.net. Website: http://groups.yahoo.com/group/arpenwomen. **Contact:** Clouita Rice, registrar/treasurer. Estab. 1944. Annual. Conference held first weekend in June. Average attendance: 225. "We have a variety of subjects related to writing—we have some general sessions, some more specific, but try to vary each year's subjects."

Costs: Registration: $10; luncheon: $15; banquet: $17.50; contest entry $5.

Accommodations: "We meet at a Holiday Inn Select—rooms available at reasonable rate." Holiday Inn has a bus to bring anyone from the airport. Rooms average $69.

Additional Information: "We have 36 contest categories. Some are open only to Arkansans, most are open to all writers. Our judges are not announced before conference but are qualified, many from out of state." Conference information avaible February 15. For brochures or inquiries send SASE (include full mailing address), call or fax. "We have had 226 attending from 12 states—over 2,000 contest entries from 40 states and New Zealand, Mexico and Canada."

N HARRIETTE AUSTIN WRITERS CONFERENCE, G-9 Aderhold, University of Georgia, Athens GA 30602-7101. (706)542-3876. Fax: (706)542-0306. E-mail: hawc@coe.uga.edu. Website: www.coe.uga.edu/hawc. **Contact:** Dr. Charles Connor, program director. Estab. 1994. Annual. Conference held July 18-19, 2003, from 9 a.m. Friday morning until midnight Saturday. See website for 2004 dates. Average attendance: 400. "The purpose of the conference is to provide a supportive enviroment in which writers can meet with professionals from the publishing industry to learn about the craft of writing, becoming published and the life of a writer. Workshops focus on all aspects of writing skills and the publishing world. Attendees receive professional advice on getting published, manuscript critiques and personal consultation, and information from experts in specialized topics, such as forensic science, criminal investigation and the law. Areas of focus include a wide range of fiction (mainstream, children, young adult, women's fiction, historical, mystery, thriller, crime, etc.), and nonfiction (inspirational, historical, essays, memoirs, how-to, etc.)." Site: "The conference is held at the Georgia Center for Continuing Education on the University of Georgia campus in Athens, Georgia. The Georgia Center is a modern conference facility containing within it 400-bed hotel, restaurant, coffee shop, gift shop, theatre, auditorium, meeting rooms, banquet facilities and comprehensive support services." 2003 panels included A Day with Editor Michael Seidman; A Day with Author Terry Kay; Robert Vaughan's Observations from a 40-Year Writing Career; What Is Inspirational or Christian Fiction?; Making the Sale: What Happens After You Find an Agent; and more. Staff included Jenny Baumgartner (acquiring editor at Thomas Nelson Publishers), Doris Booth (editor-in-chief, Authorlink.com and Authorlink Press), William Clark (William Clark Assoc. Literary Agency), Lyn Deardoff (Associate Editor, Peachtree Publishers), Judy Long (editor-in-chief of Hill Street Press), Patrick Lobrutto (acquiring editor for Tor/Forge and Quill Driver Books/Word Dancer Press and a scout for the Trident Media Group), and more.
Costs: 2003 conference fees: pre-registration by July 1, $130 for Friday Intensive, $275 for entire conference; registration after July 1, $145 for Friday Intensive, $300 for entire conference; lunches included with registration and other meals optional.
Accommodations: Airport shuttle service is available every 2 hours between the conference center in Athens and Hartsfield International Airport in Atlanta. Offers overnight accommodations at the Georgia Center Hotel. 2003 rates for single occupancy range from $64-69; double occupancy from $76-83.
Additional Information: "Manuscript evaluations and a one-on-one meeting with an editor or agent are available. Submit a two-page manuscript synopsis and up to 15 double-spaced, typed sample pages. Must be received no later than four weeks prior to the conference. The number of manuscripts that can be accepted is limited, so submit early. No more than one evaluation per participant will be accepted, please. Label your manuscript as to genre or type and specify your preferred evaluator. (We cannot guarantee your first choice). A fee of $40 is charged for each evaluation. Make check payable to HAWC Manuscript Evaluations, and mail two copies of writing sample directly to Dr. Charles Connor." Sponsors contest in cooperation with Authorlink.com. Full details about the competition can be found on the Authorlink website at www.authorlink.com/. Conference information is available by May. For brochure send SASE, e-mail, visit website, call or fax. Accepts inquiries by SASE, e-mail, phone and fax. Agents and editors participate in conference. "The goal of the Harriette Austin Writers Conference is to bring writers, agents, editors and special experts together in a supportive enviroment for a productive and memorable experience. We make every effort to extend the best in professionalism and Southern hospitality. Our reputation is best expressed by those who have been here and who choose to come back again and again. Come visit us in Georgia."

FLORIDA FIRST COAST WRITERS' FESTIVAL, 9911 Old Baymeadows Rd., FCCJ Deerwood Center, Jacksonville FL 32256-8117. (904)997-2726. Fax: (904)997-2746. E-mail: kclower@fccj.edu. Website: www.fccj. edu/wf. **Contact:** Kathleen Clower, conference coordinator. Estab. 1985. Annual. Festival held May 13-15, 2004. Average attendance: 300-350. All areas; mainstream plus genre. Site: Held at Sea Turtle Inn on Atlantic Beach.
Costs: Early bird special $200 for 2 days (including lunch and banquet) or $175 for 2 days (including lunch) or $90 for each day; pre-conference workshops extra.
Accommodations: Sea Turtle Inn, (904)249-7402 or (800)874-6000, has a special festival rate.
Additional Information: Sponsors contests for short fiction, poetry and novels. Novel judges are David Poyer and Lenore Hart. Entry fees: $30, novels; $10, short fiction; $5, poetry. Deadline: December 1 for novels, short fiction, poems. Conference information available January 2004. For brochures/guidelines visit website, e-mail, fax, call. Accepts inquiries by e-mail, phone, fax. E-mail contest inquiries to hdenson@fccj.edu.

FLORIDA SUNCOAST WRITERS' CONFERENCE, University of South Florida, Division of Workforce and Professional Development, 4202 E. Fowler Ave., MHH116, Tampa FL 33620-6756. (813)974-1711. Fax: (813)974-5732. E-mail: mglakis@admin.usf.edu. Website: www.conted.usf.edu/flcenter.htm. **Contact:** Martha Lakis, conference coordinator. Estab. 1970. Annual. Held February 5-7, 2004. Conference duration: 3 days. Average attendance: 350-400. Conference covers poetry, short story, novel and nonfiction, including science fiction, detective, travel writing, drama, TV scripts, photojournalism and juvenile. "This is a working writers' conference, targeting categories and mechanics of writing and being published. Designated one of the 'Top 10 Workshops/Conferences for Writers' by *Writer's Digest*." Features panels with agents and editors. Guest speakers have included Lady P.D. James, William

Styron, David Guterson, John Updike, Joyce Carol Oates, Wally Lamb, Frank McCourt, Francine Prose, Jane Smiley and Salman Rushdie.

Costs: Call for verification.

Accommodations: Special rates available at area hotels. "All information is contained in our brochure."

Additional Information: Participants may submit work for critiquing. Extra fee charged for this service. Conference information available in November; requested by e-mail, fax, phone. Accepts inquiries by e-mail, fax, phone.

◎ FUN IN THE SUN: THE WRITE STUFF, P.O. Box 17756, Plantation FL 33318. (305)663-5779. E-mail: FRWConference@aol.com. Website: www.frwriters.org. **Contact:** Ann Schwartz, conference chair. Estab. 1986. Biannual. Conference held February 2005. Average attendance: 160. "Focus is more on fiction writing. Although the conference focuses on romance writing, the workshops are useful to writers of all genres." Site: Fort Lauderdale, FL. "Workshops include topics on art, craft and business of writing and there will be an editor/agent panel. There will also be editor/agent appointments; a live and silent auction; and an author booksigning event open to the public, in which all published authors attending the conference can participate."

Costs: $145-175; member discounts and group rates available. Includes conference meals; registration materials; attendance at all workshops and events.

Accommodations: "Driving directions from major freeway will be posted on our website." Offers overnight accommodations at conference site with special rates available."

Additional Information: "Ours is the longest-running conference of any RWA chapter." Brochures available in July for SASE, by e-mail, by phone or on website. Accepts inquiries by SASE, by e-mail, by phone. Agents and editors participate in conference. "Editors and agents will be listed on our website as they become available."

GEORGIA WRITERS SPRING FESTIVAL OF WORKSHOPS, 1071 Steeple Run, Lawrenceville GA 30043. (678)407-0703. Fax: (678)407-9917. E-mail: festival@georgiawriters.org. Website: www.georgiawriters.org. **Contact:** Geri Taran, executive director. Estab. 1995. Annual. Conference held May 22, 2004. Conference duration: 1 day. Average attendance: 200. Conference is comprehensive—all genres and business aspects of a writing career. Site: Community Center, large main area, separate rooms for sessions. Speakers have inluded Diane Martin, Terry Blackwell, Susan Graham, John Devito and many others.

Costs: 2003: $55 at the door; $50 in advance; $75 with membership ($40 annual).

HAMBIDGE CENTER, P.O. Box 339, Rabun Gap GA 30568. (706)746-5718. Fax: (706)746-9933. E-mail: center@hambidge.org. Website: www.hambidge.org. **Contact:** April Hawkins. Estab. 1934. Workshops/residencies held year round. Application deadlines: October 1 for February-August residencies; May 1 for September-December residencies. Conference duration: Residencies are from 2 weeks-2 months. "Creative artists in all disciplines use uninterrupted time to create (writers included!)." Site: Facility is located on "over 600 acres in north Georgia mountains. Rural, beautiful, private cottage/studios. Dinner served February-December. On National Register of Historic Places."

Costs: $125/week.

Accommodations: "Artists stay in one of eight residence cottage-studios. Each living area is private and equipped with kitchen and bath facilities. Accommodations vary for workshops.

Additional Information: For residencies, applicants "must submit an application ($20 application fee) and samples of work. Work is reviewed by a panel of professionals in each field." Workshop brochures/guidelines available on website or upon request with SASE. Accepts inquires by e-mail, fax, phone.

HOW TO BE PUBLISHED WORKSHOPS, P.O. Box 100031, Birmingham AL 35210-3006. (205)907-0140. E-mail: mike@writing2sell.com. Website: www.writing2sell.com. **Contact:** Michael Garrett. Estab. 1986. Workshops are offered continuously year-round at various locations. Conference duration: 1 session. Average attendance: 10-15. Workshops to "move writers of category fiction closer to publication." Site: Workshops held at college campuses and universities. Themes include "Marketing," "Idea Development" and manuscript critique.

Costs: $49-79.

Additional Information: "Special critique is offered, but advance submission is not required." Workshop information available on website. Accepts inquiries by e-mail.

KEY WEST WRITERS' WORKSHOP, 5901 College Rd., Key West FL 33040. (305)296-9081. Fax: (305)292-2392. E-mail: weinman_i@firn.edu. Website: www.firn.edu/fkcc/kwww.htm. **Contact:** Irving Weinman, director. Estab. 1996. Held 5 weekends/season (January-March). Conference duration: 5 weekends. Average attendance: 10-12. Workshop focuses on fiction and poetry. 2004 schedule includes Sharon Olds, Jan. 16-18; Lee Smith, Jan. 23-25; Robert Creeley, Jan. 30-Feb. 1; Robert Stone, Feb. 6-8; Martin Espada, Feb. 13-15.

Costs: $300 per workshop.

Accommodations: Provides a list of area hotels or lodging options.

Additional Information: "It's very competitive; many more applicants than places. Early application is essential." Workshop information is available now. For brochure send SASE, e-mail, visit website, call, fax. Accepts inquiries by SASE, e-mail, phone, fax. High standards. "Informal, intimate, intense."

◎ **MOONLIGHT AND MAGNOLIAS WRITER'S CONFERENCE**, Georgia Romance Writers, 2173 Indian Shoals Drive, Loganville GA 30052. E-mail: info@georgiaromancewriters.org. Website: www.georgiaromancewrite rs.org. **Contact:** Pam Mantovani. Estab. 1982. Annual. Conference held October 13, 2004 in the Atlanta North Hotel in Atlanta, GA. Average attendance: 175. "Conference focuses on writing of women's fiction with emphasis on romance. Includes agents and editors from major publishing houses. Previous workshops have included: beginning writer sessions, research topics, writng basics and professional issues for the published author; plus specialty sessions on writing young adult, multi-cultural, inspirational and Regency. Speakers have included experts in law enforcement, screenwriting and research. Literary raffle and advertised speaker and GRW member autographing open to the public. Published authors make up 25-30% of attendees." Brochures available for SASE in June.
Costs: $165 GRW member/$175 nonmember for conference registration. Check website for current conference fees, hotel rates and registration forms.
Additional Information: Maggie Awards for excellence are presented to unpublished writers. The Maggie Award for published writers is limited to Region 3 members of Romance Writers of America. Deadline for published Maggie is April 18. Deadline for unpublished Maggies is June 1. Entry forms and guidelines available on website. Published authors judge first round, category editors judge finals. Guidelines available for SASE in spring.

NATCHEZ LITERARY AND CINEMA CELEBRATION, P.O. Box 1307, Natchez MS 39121-1307. (601)446-1208. Fax: (601)446-1214. E-mail: carolyn.smith@colin.edu. Website: www.colin.edu/NLCC. **Contact:** Carolyn Vance Smith, co-chairman. Estab. 1990. Annual. Conference held February 25-29, 2004. Average attendance: 3,000. Conference focuses on "all literature, including film scripts." Site: 500-seat auditorium, various sizes of break-out rooms. Theme will be "Scoundrels to Statesmen: Politics in the Deep South." Scholars will speak on Huey Long, Jefferson Davis and more. Speakers include William Cooper of LSU, Gail Gilchriest, screenwriter, and others.
Costs: "About $100, includes a meal, receptions, book signings, workshops. Lectures/panel discussions are free."
Accommodations: "Groups can ask for special assistance. Usually they can be accommodated." Call (800)647-6724.
Additional Information: "Participants need to read selected materials prior to attending writing workshops. Thus, pre-enrollment is advised." Conference information is available in Fall 2003. For brochure send SASE, e-mail, visit website, call or fax. Accepts inquiries by SASE, e-mail, phone and fax. Agents and editors participate in conference.

OXFORD CONFERENCE FOR THE BOOK, Center for the Study of Southern Culture, The University of Mississippi, University MS 38677-1848. (602)915-5993. Fax: (662)915-5814. E-mail: aabadie@olemiss.edu. Website: www.olemiss.edu/depts/south. **Contact:** Ann J. Abadie, associate director. Estab. 1993. Annual. Conference held April 1-4, 2004. Average attendance: 300. "The conference celebrates books, writing and reading and deals with practical concerns on which the literary arts depend, including literacy, freedom of expression and the book trade itself. Each year's program consists of readings, lectures and discussions. Areas of focus are fiction, poetry, nonfiction and—occasionally—drama. We have, on occasion, looked at science fiction and mysteries. We always pay attention to children's literature." Site: University of Mississippi campus. Annual topics include Submitting Manuscripts/Working One's Way into Print; Finding a Voice/Reaching an Audience; The Endangered Species: Readers Today and Tomorrow. In 2003, among the more than 40 speakers were fiction writers Calvin Baker, Percival Everett, Tom Franklin, Barry Hannah, Michael Mewshaw, Scott Morris, George Singleton and Robert Stone.
Costs: "The conference is open to participants without charge."
Accommodations: Provides list of area hotels.
Additional Information: Brochures available in February 2004 by e-mail, on website, by phone, by fax. Accepts inquiries by e-mail, phone, fax. Agents and editors participate in conference.

Ⓝ **OZARK CREATIVE WRITERS, INC.**, 6817 Gingerbread Lane, Little Rock AR 72204. (501)565-8889. Fax: (501)970-1055. E-mail: pvining@aristotle.net. President: Chrissy Leister Willis. **Contact:** Peggy Vining, OCWI board. Estab. 1973. Annual. Conference always held 2nd weekend in October. Conference duration: 2½ days. Average attendance: 250. "All types of writing." Site: "Conference site is the convetion center. Very nice for a small group setting. Reserve early, prior to September 1, to insure place." Main speaker for workshop in morning sessions—usually a novelist. Satellite speakers—afternoon—various types, including a Poetry Seminar.
Costs: $60 plus approximately $40 for 2 banquets. Rooms are approximately $70/night; meals extra. Registration fee allows you to enter the writing contests.
Accommodations: Chamber of Commerce will send list; 60 rooms are blocked off for OCW prior to August 15th. Accomodations vary at hotels. Many campsites also available. "Eureka Springs is a resort town near Branson, Missouri, the foothills of the beautiful Ozark Mountains."
Additional Information: "We have approximately 20 various categories of writing contests. Selling writers are our judges. Entry fee required to enter. Brochures are available for SASE after May 1. OCWI Conference is 30 years old." Accepts inquiries by SASE, e-mail, fax, phone.

MAJORIE KINNAN RAWLINGS: WRITING THE REGION, P.O. Box 12246, Gainesville FL 32604. (888)917-7001. Fax: (352)373-8854. E-mail: shakes@ufl.edu. Website: www.writingtheregion.com. **Contact:** Norma M. Homan, executive director. Estab. 1997. Annual. Conference held July 23-27, 2003. Conference duration: 5 days. Average attendance: 100. Conference concentrates on fiction, writing for children, poetry, nonfiction, drama, screenwriting, writing with humor, setting, character, etc. Site: Conference held at historic building, formerly the Thomas Hotel

Costs: $355 for 5 days including meals; $360 "early bird" registration (breakfast and lunch); $125 single day; $75 half day.

Accommodations: Special conference rates at area hotels available.

Additional Information: Optional trip and dinner at Rawlings Home at Crosscreek offered. Evening activities and banquets also planned. Manuscript consultation on an individual basis by application only and $100 additional fee. Sponsors essay contest for registrants on a topic dealing with Marjorie Kinnan Rawlings. Call for brochures/guidelines. Accepts inquiries by fax, e-mail.

◎ **SCBWI SOUTHERN BREEZE FALL CONFERENCE, "Writing and Illustrating for Kids"**, P.O. Box 26282, Birmingham AL 35260. E-mail: jskittinger@bellsouth.net. Website: www.southern-breeze.org. **Contact:** Jo Kittinger, co-regional advisor. Estab. 1992. Annual. Conference held in October. Conference duration: One-day Saturday conference. Average attendance: 125. "All Southern Breeze SCBWI conferences are geared to the production and support of quality children's literature." Keynote speakers TBA.

Costs: About $65 for SCBWI members, $80 for nonmembers, plus lunch (about $6). Individual critiques are available for additional fees.

Accommodations: "We have a room block with a conference rate. The conference is held at a nearby school."

Additional Information: "The fall conference offers approximately 28 workshops on craft and the business of writing, including a basic workshop for those new to the children's field." Manuscript critiques are offered; manuscripts must be sent by deadline. Conference information is included in the Southern Breeze newsletter, mailed in September. Brochure is available for SASE, by e-mail or visit website for details. Accepts inquiries by SASE or e-mail. Agents and editors attend/participate in conference.

◎ **SCBWI SOUTHERN BREEZE SPRING CONFERENCE, Springmingle '04**, P.O. Box 26282, Birmingham AL 35260. E-mail: jskittinger@bellsouth.net. Website: www.southern-breeze.org. **Contact:** Jo Kittinger, regional advisor. Estab. 1992. Annual. Conference held March 5-7, 2004. Average attendance: 60. "All Southern Breeze SCBWI conferences are geared to the production and support of quality children's literature." Site: Event is held "in a hotel in one of the 3 states which compose our region: Alabama, Georgia or Mississippi." Springmingle '04 will be held in Atlanta, GA. Springmingle '04 will be an Editors' Day. Speakers will include Eileen Robinson, executive editor at Children's Press, John Rudolph, editor at Putnam, and Melanie Cecka, senior editor at Viking.

Costs: "About $165; SCBWI nonmembers pay $10-15 more. Some meals are included."

Accommodations: "We have a room block with a conference rate in the hotel conference site. Individuals make their own reservations. If we can get an airline discount, we publish this in our newsletter and on our webpage."

Additional Information: There wiil be ms critiques available this year for an additional fee. Manuscripts must be sent ahead of time. Conference information is included in the Southern Breeze newsletter, mailed in January. Brochure is available for SASE, by e-mail or visit website for details. Accepts inquiries by SASE, e-mail.

◎ **SCBWI/FLORIDA ANNUAL CONFERENCE**, 2158 Portland Ave., Wellington FL 33414. E-mail: barcafer @aol.com. Website: www.publishersupdate.com. **Contact:** Barbara Casey, Florida regional advisor. Estab. 1985. Annual. Conference duration: 2 days. Average attendance: 80. Conference to promote "all aspects of writing and illustrating for children." Site: Time and location TBA.

Costs: $200 for SCBWI members, $230 for non-SCBWI members. Ms and art evaluation, $30.

Accommodations: Special conference rates on-site.

Additional Information: Accepts inquiries by e-mail.

SOUTH FLORIDA WRITERS' CONFERENCE, P.O. Box 570415, Miami FL 33257-0415. (786)877-0136. E-mail: greenfie@hotmail.com. **Contact:** Henry Greenfield, director. Estab. 1993. Annual. Conference held mid-May. Average attendance: 125. Conference focuses on short fiction, novels, poetry, juvenile, nonfiction, freelancing, playwriting, screenwriting, self-promotion, publication, e-books. Site: Barry University main campus. "Tropical setting, university-type classrooms, theaters, cafeteria, housing." 2004 panels include stage & play reading and individual ms evaluation with agents, editors, authors. 2003 panelists included authors Edna Buchanan, John Dufresne, Joyce Sweeney, Marcia Preston and others. Agents included Jeff Herman, Elizabeth Pomada, Michael Larsen, James Schiavone, and others.

Costs: Provides overnight accommodations; double $65/night with meals, single $75/night with meals. Conference fee is $200 with 20 percent early registration discount by April 15.

Accommodations: "Individual evaluations are $35. Manuscript of 20 pages or less or three poems due April 15, 2004. Fee includes 15 minutes with agent, editor or author." Sponsors contest. "Judges are professional writers. $3,200 for plays, novels, short fiction, poetry, nonfiction, juveniles. Deadline is usually in June." Brochures/guidelines available October, 2003 by SASE or by e-mail. Accepts inquiries by SASE, by e-mail, phone, fax. Agents and editors participate in conference.

SOUTHEASTERN WRITERS ASSOCIATION, P.O. Box 774, Hinesville GA 31310-0774. (912)876-3118. E-mail: purple@southeasternwriters.com. Website: www.southeasternwriters.com. **Contact:** Hary Rubin, treasurer.

Estab. 1975. Annual. Conference held June 20-26, 2004. Average attendance: 75 (limited to 100). Conference offers classes in fiction, nonfiction, juvenile, inspirational writing, poetry, etc. Site: Epworth-by-the-Sea, St. Simons Island, GA.
Costs: 2003 costs: $260 early bird registration, $300 after April 15, $75 daily tuition.
Accommodations: Offers overnight accommodations. 2003 rates ranged from $621/single to $405/double and includes motel-style room and 3 meals/day per person.
Additional Information: Sponsors numerous contests in several genres and up to 3 ms evaluation conferences with instructors. Agents and editors participate in conference panels and/or private appointments. Complete information is available on the website, including registration forms, or send SASE for brochure.

SOUTHERN LIGHTS, P.O. Box 8604, Jacksonville FL 32239-8604. (352)687-3902. E-mail: LBarone21@comcast.net. Website: www.fcrw.net. **Contact:** Laura Barone. Estab. 1995. Annual. Conference held in May. Conference duration: 2 days. Average attendance: 100. The focus of the conference is fiction writing. Site: Holiday Inn Baymeadows, which is "close to beaches, local attractions and shopping." Past panels included plotting, character development, sexual tension, avoiding contrivances, and editor/agent appointments. Cheryl Anne Porter (St. Martins, Harlequin), Vicki Heinze (St. Martins, Silhouette, Kensington), Katherine Garbera (Silhouette, Desire), Loana Tedder (Silhouette, Kensington), Jennifer Weis (editor, St. Martins Press), and Marge Smith (Harlequin, Silhouette, Kensington) participated in the past.
Costs: $65 fee includes lunch; $55/night hotel.
Accommodations: "If request is made early we can arrange pickup at airport." Offers overnight accommodations at a special room rate at the conference site.
Additional Information: Conference information is available in March. For brochure send SASE, e-mail, visit website, or call. Accepts queries by SASE, e-mail, phone. Agents and editors participate in conference.

TOUCH OF SUCCESS WRITER'S CONFERENCE, P.O. Box 1436, Dunnellon FL 34430. (352)867-0463. Website: http://touchofsuccess.com. **Contact:** Bill Thomas, director. Estab. 1978. Annual. Conference held March 24-28, 2004. Conference duration: 5 days. Workshop focuses on journalism, nonfiction, fiction. Site: "Author's chalet in ancient storybook forest plus portions on a pontoon boat floating down a magical pristine Withlacoochee River." Workshops led by Bill Thomas, fiction and nonfiction author.
Costs: $495, includes lodging and food (we have our own chef), some local transportation, boats, kayaks, canoes as needed.
Accommodations: Provides list of area motels, lodges and condos.
Additional Information: Brochures available in November/December 2003 by SASE or on website. Accepts inquiries by SASE and phone. "Submit letter of application giving background, purpose and goals for attending this event."

WRITE IT OUT, P.O. Box 704, Sarasota FL 34230-0704. (941)359-3824. Fax: (941)359-3931. E-mail: rmillerwio@aol.com. Website: www.writeitout.com. **Contact:** Ronnie Miller, director. Estab. 1997. Workshops held 2-3 times/year in March, June, July and August. Conference duration: 5-10 days. Average attendance: 4-10. Workshops on "fiction, travel writing, poetry, memoirs. We also offer intimate, motivational, in-depth free private conferences with instructors." Site: Workshops held across the United States as well as in Italy in a Tuscan villa, in Bermuda at a hotel or in Cape Cod at an inn. Theme: "Landscape—Horizon." Past speakers include Arturo Vivante, novelist.
Costs: 2002 fees: Italy, $1,595; Bermuda, $495; Cape Cod, $610. Price includes tution, room and board in Italy, all other locations just tuition. Airfare not included.
Additional Information: "Critiques on work are given at the workshops." Conference information available year round. For brochures/guidelines e-mail, fax, phone or visit website. Accepts inquiries by fax, phone, e-mail. Workshops have "small groups, option to spend time writing and not attend classes, with personal appointments with instructors for feedback."

N WRITERS' GUILD OF ACADIANA "Getting It Write!", P.O. Box 51532, Lafayette LA 70505-1532. (337)896-2484. Fax: (337)896-2483. E-mail: dbrown1024@aol.com. **Contact:** Deborah Brown, conference director. Annual. Conference held March 21-22. Average attendance: 275. "We offer workshops in all genres of fiction writing, and poetry and screenwriting." Site: Hilton Lafayette & Towers. Speakers include Don D'Auria (editor, Dorchester Publishing), Lynn Seligman (Seligman Literary Agency), Evan Fogleman (Fogleman Literary Agency), and more.

CAN'T FIND A CONFERENCE? Conferences are listed by region. Check the introduction to this section for a list of regional categories. Want to attend a conference during a certain month? Check the Conferences by Date Index.

Costs: 2003 fees: early registration, $145 for members, $180 for nonmembers. Late registration, $155 for members, $190 for nonmembers. Fee includes meals and registration packet.

Accommodations: List of area hotels and lodging options available on request.

Additional Information: Sponsors contests for novels and short stories. Novels may be in any genre. Submit first chapter and synopsis (not to exceed 15 pages). Short stories may be in any genre. Limit 2,000 words or less. Multiple entries accepted. Fee: $10/entry. Deadline for entries: January 2004. Only open to registered participants.

◎ **WRITING STRATEGIES FOR THE CHRISTIAN MARKET**, 2712 S. Peninsula Dr., Daytona Beach FL 32118-5706. (386)322-1111. Fax: (386)322-1111*9. E-mail: rupton@cfl.rr.com. Website: www.amyfound.org. **Contact:** Rosemary Upton. Estab. 1991. Independent studies with manual. Includes Basics I, Marketing II, Business III, Building the Novel. Critique by mail with SASE. Question and answer session via e-mail or U.S. mail. Critique shop included once a month, except summer (July and August). Instructor: Rosemary Upton, novelist.

Costs: $30 for manual and ongoing support.

Additional Information: "Designed for correspondence students as well as the classroom experience, the courses are economical and include all materials, as well as the evaluation assignments." Those who have taken Writing Strategies instruction are able to attend an on-going monthly critiqueshop where their peers critique their work. Manual provided. For brochures/guidelines send SASE, e-mail, fax or call. Accepts inquiries by fax, e-mail. Independent study by mail only offered at this time.

WRITING TODAY—BIRMINGHAM-SOUTHERN COLLEGE, Box 549003, Birmingham AL 35254-9765. (205)226-4921. Fax: (205)226-3072. E-mail: dcwilson@bsc.edu. Website: www.bsc.edu. **Contact:** Annie Green, director of special events; Dee Wilson, assistant director of special events. Estab. 1978. Annual. Conference held March 12-13, 2004. Average attendance: 400. "Writing Today provides a quality event that is far more affordable than other conferences of its size and quality. The conference presents writers, editors, agents and other literary professionals from around the country to conduct workshops on a variety of literary styles and topics tailored to meet the needs of writers at every stage of development." Site: "The conference is sponsored by Birmingham-Southern College and is held on the campus in classrooms and lecture halls." Previous speakers have included Eudora Welty, Edward Albee, James Dickey, Erskine Caldwell, Ray Bradbury, Pat Conroy, John Barth, Ernest Gaines and Joyce Carol Oates.

Costs: Check website.

Accommodations: Attendees must arrange own transportation. Local hotels and motels offer special rates, but participants must make their own reservations.

Additional Information: "We usually offer a critique for interested writers. We have had poetry and short story critiques. There is an additional charge for these critiques." Conference brochures and registration forms available in March for SASE, e-mail or on website. Accepts inquiries by SASE, e-mail or fax. Sponsors the Hackney Literary Competition Awards for poetry, short story and novels. Guidelines available for SASE.

Midwest (IL, IN, KY, MI, OH)

ANTIOCH WRITERS' WORKSHOP, P.O. Box 494, Yellow Springs OH 45387. E-mail: info@antiochwritersworkshop.com. Website: www.antiochwritersworkshop.com. Estab. 1984. Annual. Conference held in early July. Conference duration: 1 week. Average attendance: 80. Workshop concentration: poetry, nonfiction and fiction. Site: Workshop located downtown in the village of Yellow Springs. Speakers have included Sue Grafton, Imogene Bolls, George Ella Lyon, Herbert Martin, John Jakes, Virginia Hamilton, William Least Heat-Moon, Sena Jeter Naslund and Natalie Goldberg.

Costs: Tuition is $500 (approximate)—lower for local and repeat—plus meals.

Accommodations: "We pick up attendees free at the airport." Accommodations made through a village host program and area hotels. Cost is $150 for week (village host program).

Additional Information: Offers mss critique sessions. Conference information available after March on website.

AWP ANNUAL CONFERENCE AND BOOKFAIR, MS 1E3, George Mason University, Fairfax VA 22030. (703)993-4303. Fax: (703)993-4302. E-mail: awpconf@gmu.edu. Website: www.awpwriter.org. **Contact:** Matt Scanlon, director of conferences. Estab. 1967. Annual. Conference held March 24-27, 2004 in Chicago IL. Conference duration: 4 days. Average attendance: 3,000. The annual conference is a gathering of 3,000+ students, teachers, writers, readers, and publishers. All genres are represented. Site: This year the conference will be held at Chicago's Palmer House Hilton. "We will offer 175 panels on everything from writing to teaching to critical analysis. In 2003 E.L. Doctorow, Lucille Clifton, Richard Busch, Alice McDermott, and Juan Felipe Herrera were special speakers.

Costs: Early registration fees: $35/student; $135/AWP member; $155/nonmember.

Accommodations: Provide airline discounts and rental-car discounts. Special rate at Palmer House Hilton: $129/night.

COLUMBUS WRITERS CONFERENCE, P.O. Box 20548, Columbus OH 43220. (614)451-3075. Fax: (614)451-0174. E-mail: AngelaPL28@aol.com. Website: www.creativevista.com. **Contact:** Angela Palazzolo, director. Estab. 1993. Annual. Conference held in August. Average attendance: 350+. "The conference covers a variety of fiction and nonfiction topics presented by writers, editors and literary agents. Writing topics have included novel, short story, children's, young adult, poetry, historical fiction, science fiction, fantasy, humor, mystery, playwriting, screenwriting, magazine writing, travel, humor, cookbook, technical, queries, book proposals and freelance writing. Other topics have included finding and working with an agent/author/editor, targeting markets, time management, obtaining grants, sparking creativity and networking." Speakers have included Lee K. Abbott, Sarah Willis, Lee Martin, Donald Maass, Rita Rosenkrantz, Sheree Bykofsky, and Patrick Lobrutto, as well as many other professionals in the writing field.

Costs: Full conference, $255 (early bird, $235); Friday only, $165 (early bird, $145); Saturday only, $185 (early bird, $165); Friday night dinner and program, $45 (early bird, $38). Conference includes Friday sessions, continental breakfast, lunch, and networking/refreshments. Also included are critiques, consultations, and a bookstore for writers.

Additional Information: Call, write, e-mail or send fax to obtain a conference brochure, available mid-summer.

DETROIT WOMEN WRITERS ANNUAL WRITER'S CONFERENCE, Detroit MI. Website: www.detwo menwriters.org. Estab. 1961. Annual. Conference held October 15-16, 2004. Conference duration: 2 days. Average attendance: 300. Holds manuscript critiques and hands-on workshops. "Themes to be determined, but typically workshops are cross-genre with an emphasis on the craft of writing and process of publication."

Additional Information: Offers Mary Kay Scholarship for cost of the conference for 6 high school and college students who submit writing samples to a judge who determines the most talented of the entries. "DWW is in negotiations with the venue for the 2004 conference. All information will be posted on our website, www.detwomen-writers.org. Queries can be made on the website."

N EASTERN KENTUCKY UNIVERSITY SUMMER CREATIVE WRITING CONFERENCE, Case Annex 467, English Dept., EKU, Richmond KY 40475. (859)622-3091. E-mail: christine.delea@eku.edu. Website: www.english.eku.edu/conferences. **Contact:** Dr. Christine Delea. Estab. 1962. Annual. June 2004. Conference duration: 5 days. Average attendance: 15. Covers poetry and fiction. Site: Eastern Kentucky University campus. 2003 conference included panel discussions on regional writing, getting published, and the writing life. 2003 faculty included Hal Blythe, Harry Brown, Christine Delea and Charlie Sweet (EKU), and guest faculty James Baker Hall and Marie Manilla.

Costs: 2003 fees were $122-335 (undergraduate/audit) and $176-487 (graduate credit).

Accommodations: Lodging on campus is $15/night. Dorms have central air, kitchen facilites are accessible. Also offers list of area hotels.

Additional Information: Participants need to submit materials by May 10. Poetry—up to 10 pages, single-spaced. Fiction—up to 20 pages, double-spaced. Brochures available in March by e-mail. Also accepts inquiries for SASE and by phone. Editors attend the conference. "Our conference is a fun, casual event geared toward beginning writers. We have a good mix of college students and those who have been out of school for awhile."

N © FESTIVAL OF FAITH AND WRITING, Calvin College/Department of English, 3201 Burton St. SE, Grand Rapids MI 49546. (616)526-6770. Fax: (616)526-8508. E-mail: ffw@calvin.edu. Website: www.calvin.edu/academic/engl/festival.htm. **Contact:** Dale Brown, director. Estab. 1990. Biennial. Conference held April 22-24, 2004. Conference duration: 3 days. Average attendance: 1,800. The Festival of Faith and Writing encourages serious, imaginative writing by all writers interested in the intersections of literature and belief. Site: The festival is held at Calvin College in the new Prince Conference Center, the Fine Arts Center, and various other venues on campus. Calvin College is located in Grand Rapids, MI, 2.5 miles north of Chicago. Focus is on fiction, nonfiction, memoir, poetry, drama, children's, young adult, academic, storytelling, critics, film, songwriting. Past speakers have included Joyce Carol Oates, Patricia Hampl, Thomas Lynch, Leif Enger, Jacqueline Woodson and Stephen G. Bloom.

Costs: Registration: $150, $75 for students with valid ID. Registration includes all sessions during the 3-day event, but does not include meals, lodging or evening concerts.

Accommodations: Shuttles are available to and from local hotels. Shuttles are also available for overflow parking lots. A list of hotels with special rates for conference attendees is available on the festival website. High school and college students can arrange on-campus lodging by e-mail.

Additional Information: The festival will sponsor a fiction writing contest in association with Paraclete Press. Leif Enger, author of *Peace Like a River*, will judge the contest. Entry requirements can be found on Paraclese Press's website. Brochures available in October for SASE. Also accepts inquiries by e-mail, phone and fax. Agents and editors attend the festival.

IMAGINATION, Cleveland State University, English Department, 2121 Euclid Ave., Cleveland OH 44115. (216)687-2532. Fax: (216)687-6943. E-mail: imagination@csuohio.edu. Website: www.csuohio.edu/poetrycenter/. **Contact:** Neal Chandler, director. Estab. 1990. Annual. Conference is held in late June/early July. Average attendance: 80. "Conference concentrates on fiction, poetry and nonfiction." Site: Held at Mather Mansion, a restored 19th century mansion on the campus of Cleveland State University. Past themes have included "Realism and Beyond" and "Business of Writing."

Additional Information: E-mail, fax or mail for brochure after January.

INDIANA UNIVERSITY WRITERS' CONFERENCE, 464 Ballantine Hall, Bloomington IN 47405-7103. (812)855-1877. Fax: (812)855-9535. E-mail: writecon@indiana.edu. Website: www.indiana.edu/~writecon. **Contact:** Amy Locklin, director. Estab. 1940. Annual. Conference/workshops held the last week of June. Average attendance: 115. "The Indiana University Writers' Conference believes in a craft-based teaching of writing. We emphasize an exploration of creativity through a variety of approaches, offering workshop-based craft discussions, classes focusing on technique, and talks about the careers and concerns of a writing life." Site: Located on the campus of Indiana University, Bloomington. Participants in the week-long conference join faculty-led workshops in fiction, poetry, and creative nonfiction, take classes on various aspects of writing, engage in one-on-one consultation with faculty members, and attend a variety of readings and social events. Previous faculty include: Raymond Carver, Gwendolyn Brooks, Andre Dubus, Kurt Vonnegut Jr., Mark Doty, Robert Olen Butler and Brenda Hillman. **Costs:** Approximately $300 for classes and $450 for classes and workshop; does not include food or housing. Scholarships and college credit options are available.
Additional Information: "In order to be accepted in a workshop, the writer must submit the work they would like critiqued. Work is evaluated before accepting applicant. Scholarship awards are based on the quality of the manuscript and are determined by an outside judge." For brochures/guidelines send SASE, visit our website, e-mail or call. Deadline for scholarship application is in early May. Apply early, as workshops fill up quickly.

KENTUCKY WOMEN WRITERS CONFERENCE, 114 Bowman Hall, University of Kentucky, Lexington KY 40506-0059. (859)257-8734. E-mail: brweber@uky.edu. Website: www.uky.edu/conferences/kywwc. **Contact:** Dr. Brenda Weber, director. Estab. 1979. Annual. March 25-27, 2004. Conference duration: 3 days. Average attendance: 300-400. Conference covers all genres: poetry, fiction, creative nonfiction, academic. The KWWC highlights a theme every year and considers both creative and academic reflections on this theme. Site: Held at the University of Kentucky and several historic downtown Lexington locations, including the Carnegie Center for Literacy and Learning. 2004 theme is History in the Making. "As it relates to fiction, this could suggest the way that fiction alters and reorganizes historical 'truths.' " 2004 speakers include Alix Strauss, Chitra Divakaroni, Sena Jeter Naslund, Mary Ann Tayler Hall, Barbara Robinette Moss and more.
Costs: $120 for 3 days. Some snacks included. Meals and accommodations are not included
Accommodations: Shuttle provided from conference hotel, downtown Lexington Radisson, conference rates $79/night.
Additional Information: Sponsors fiction writing contest. Length: 10 pages double-spaced. Prize: $100, publication on website, reading at conference. Judged by board members, authors and student interns. Brochures available in December by phone, e-mail, or on website. Inquiries also accepted by SASE. "The KWWC is always a life-changing event. Authors and participants consistently rave about the quality of programming and level of energy."

KENTUCKY WRITER'S WORKSHOP, 1050 State Park Rd., Pineville KY 40977. (606)337-3066. Fax: (606)337-7250. E-mail: Dean.Henson@mail.state.ky.us. Website: www.pinemountainpark.com. **Contact:** Dean M. Henson, special events coordinator. Estab. 1995. Annual. Workshop held each March. Average attendance: 30-60. Focuses on fiction, poetry, short stories, essays. Site: Pine Mountain State Resort Park (a Kentucky State Park). 2002 panels included Writing for 16 and Under; Grist for the Mill (transforming personal experience into fiction); The Writing Commitment; Adult Novel Writing. 2002 panelists included Martha Bennett Stiles, children's author; James Baker Hall, former poet laureate of Kentucky; Jenny Davis, novelist.
Costs: Registration fee is $30.
Accommodations: Special all-inclusive event packages available. Call for information.
Additional Information: Brochures available 2 months in advance by e-mail or phone. Accepts inquiries by SASE, e-mail, phone, fax. "Our conference features Kentucky writers of note speaking and instructing on various topics in the writing endeavor. This workshop is designed to help developing authors to improve their writing craft."

KENYON REVIEW WRITERS WORKSHOP, The Kenyon Review, Kenyon College, Gambier OH 43022. (740)427-5207. Fax: (740)427-5417. E-mail: kenyonreview@kenyon.edu. Website: www.kenyonreview.org. **Contact:** David Lynn, director. Estab. 1990. Annual. Workshop held late June. Conference duration: 8 days. Average attendance: 40-50. Participants apply in poetry, fiction or creative nonfiction, and then participate in intensive daily workshops which focus on the generation and revision of significant new work. Site: The conference takes place on the campus of Kenyon College in the rural village of Gambier, Ohio. Students have access to college computing and recreational facilities and are housed in campus housing. Fiction faculty: Margot Livesey, Erin McGraw, Claire Messud. Poetry faculty: David Baker and Janet McAdams. Nonfiction faculty: Rebecca McClanahan.
Costs: $1,700 including room and board.
Accommodations: The workshop operates a shuttle from Gambier to the airport in Columbus, Ohio. Offers overnight accommodations. Participants are housed in Kenyon College student housing. The cost is covered in the tuition.
Additional Information: Application includes a writing sample. Admission decisions are made on a rolling basis beginning February 1. Workshop information is available November 1. For brochure send e-mail, visit website, call, fax. Accepts inquiries by SASE, e-mail, phone, fax.

MAGNA CUM MURDER CRIME FICTION CONFERENCE, Ball State University, Muncie IN 47306. (765)285-8975. Fax: (765)747-9566. E-mail: kennisonk@aol.com. Website: www.magnacummurder.com. **Contact:**

Kathryn Kennison, director. Estab. 1994. Annual. Conference held in October. Average attendance: 350. "The main focus is the crime fiction novel, but attention is also paid to short stories, true crime." Site: The Radisson Hotel Roberts and the Horizon Convention Center directly across the street. Past workshops have included plotting, characterization, getting published, historical, and ethics. 2003 Guest of Honor: Jeffery Deaver. 2003 International Guest of Honor: Peter Robinson.

Costs: 2003 cost: $185 includes reception, continental breakfast and boxed lunch, banquet.

Accommodations: Offers list of area hotels or lodging options.

Additional Information: Conference information available: e-mail, visit website, call, or fax. Accepts inquiries by e-mail, phone, or fax. Agents and/or editors participate in conference.

MAUMEE VALLEY FREELANCE WRITERS' CONFERENCE, Lourdes College, Franciscan Center, 6832 Convent Blvd., Sylvania OH 43560. (419)824-3707. Fax: (419)882-3987. E-mail: gburke@lourdes.edu. Website: www.lourdes.edu. **Contact:** Gloria Buke, conference coordinator. Estab. 1997. Annual. Conference held April 3, 2004. Average attendance: 75. "The purpose is to provide a venue for freelance writers in a variety of genres. 2004 conference will include on-site agents, writing competition and bookstore." Keynote speaker for the 2003 conference was Paul Martin, author of *The Writer's Little Instruction Book*.

Costs: $89/person including continental breakfast and lunch.

Additional Information: Conference information is available in January. For brochure send SASE, e-mail, visit website, call, fax. Accepts inquiries by SASE, e-mail, phone, fax. Agents and editors participate in conference. "Evaluations show that this is a well planned, well organized conference. Every effort has been made to reach freelance writers in the Maumee Valley and Southeastern Michigan areas. We have had anywhere from 38-70 people in attendance; as the conference coordinator, it is my goal to reach for the 100+ mark—hopefully, in 2004."

MIDLAND WRITERS CONFERENCE, Grace A. Dow Memorial Library, 1710 W. St. Andrews, Midland MI 48640-2698. (989)837-3435. Fax: (989)837-3468. E-mail: ajarvis@midland-mi.org. Website: www.midland-mi.org/ gracedowlibrary. **Contact:** Ann C. Jarvis, conference coordinator. Estab. 1980. Annual. Conference held in June. Average attendance: 100. "The Conference is composed of a well-known keynote speaker and workshops on a variety of subjects including poetry, children's writing, freelancing, agents, etc. The attendees are both published and unpublished authors." Site: The Conference is held at the Grace A. Dow Memorial Library in the auditorium and conference rooms. Keynoters in the past have included Pat Conroy, Peggy Noonan, Roger Ebert and Michael Beschloss.

Costs: $60, includes lunch. Costs are approximate until plans for upcoming conferences are finalized.

Accommodations: A list of area hotels is available.

Additional Information: Conference brochures/guidelines are available in April/May. Check our website for details.

N MID-MISSISSIPPI RIVER FOLKLORE, STORYTELLING AND WRITING CONFERENCE, John Wood Community College, 1301 S. 48th St., Quincy IL 62305. (217)641-4903. Fax: (217)228-6843. E-mail: ssparks @jwcc.edu. **Contact:** Sherry Sparks. Estab. 2001. Conference duration: 1 weekend. Average attendance: 30-50. Workshop/conference covers all areas of writing, for beginners and more advanced. Site: John Wood Community College.

Costs: $35-$50; some meals included.

Accommodations: List of area hotels available.

Additional Information: Sponsors contest.

MIDWEST WRITERS WORKSHOP, Dept. of Journalism, Ball State University, Muncie IN 47306. (765)285-5587. Fax: (765)285-5997. E-mail: info@midwestwriters.org. Website: www.midwestwriters.org. **Contact:** Jama Bigger. Estab. 1974. Annual. Workshops to be in July. Average attendance: 150. Site: Conference held at New Alumni Center, Ball State University.

Costs: $275 for 3-day workshop; $90 for 1-day Intensive Session including opening reception, hospitality room and closing banquet.

Accommodations: Special hotel rates offered.

Additional Information: Manuscript evaluation for extra fee. Conference brochures/guidelines are available for SASE.

⊚ THE MINISTRY OF WRITING: AN ANNUAL COLLOQUIUM, Earlham School of Religion, 228 College Ave., Richmond IN 47374. (765)983-1423. Fax: (765)983-1688. E-mail: cummins@earlham.edu. Website: http://esr.earlham.edu/centerpage.html. **Contact:** Rita Cummins, secretary. Estab. 1990. Annual. Conference held in October, 2004. Average attendance: 42. Focuses on "the written word as important part of the ministry." 2003 keynote speaker was Pat Schneider.

Costs: In 2002, $45 until October 1; $65 after October 1. Costs included all plenary sessions, workshops, Saturday lunch, refreshments. Friday evening reception for additional $15.

Accommodations: Transportation to and from airport by arrangement only. No overnight accommodations available. Offers list of area lodging.

Additional Information: Guidelines available mid-July by e-mail, on website, by phone or by fax. Accepts inquiries by e-mail, phone, fax.

GARY PROVOST'S WRITERS RETREAT WORKSHOP, c/o Write It/Sell It, 2507 S. Boston Place, Tulsa OK 74114. (800)642-2494. E-mail: wrwwisi@cox.net. Website: www.writersretreatworkshop.com. **Contact:** Gail Provost Stockwell, co-founder and creative director. Estab. 1987. Annual. Workshop held May 23-June 1, 2003. Average attendance: 30. Focus on fiction and narrative nonfiction books in progress. All genres. "The Writers Retreat Workshop is an intensive learning experience for small groups of serious-minded writers. Founded by the late Gary Provost (one of the country's leading writing instructors) and his wife Gail, an award-winning author, the WRW is a challenging and enriching adventure. The goal of WRW core staff and visiting agents/editors/authors is for students to leave with a solid understanding of the marketplace as well as the craft of writing a novel. In the heart of a supportive and spirited community of fellow writers, students learn Gary Provost's course and make remarkable leaps in their writing, editing and marketing skills." Site: Marydale Retreat Center in Erlanger, KY (just south of Cincinnati, OH).
Costs: $1,695 for 10 days which includes all tuition, food and lodging (discount for past participants), consultations and course materials. The Marydale Retreat Center is 5 miles from the Cincinnati airport and offers shuttle services.
Additional Information: Participants are selected based upon the appropriateness of this program for the applicant's specific writing project. Participants are asked to submit a brief overview and synopsis before the workshop and are given assignments and feedback during the 10-day workshop. Workshop information available by mid-November. For brochures/guidelines call 1-800-642-2494, e-mail or visit website. Accepts inquiries by e-mail, phone, SASE.

RETREAT FROM HARSH REALITY, Mid-Michigan RWA Chapter, 6845 Forest Way, Harbor Springs MI 49740. E-mail: ptrombley@voyager.net. Website: www.midmichiganrwa.com. **Contact:** Pam Trombley, retreat chair. Estab. 1985. Annual. Conference held April 30-May 2, 2004. Average attendance: limited to 50. Conference focuses on romance and fiction writing. Site: The St. Ives Resort in Stanwood, MI. This beautiful resort is the perfect setting for a weekend of relaxation and inspiration. "We do not have panels. Emphasis is on one speaker and her or his expertise." Elizabeth Bevarly, award-winning and bestselling author, is the scheduled speaker for 2004.
Costs: Fees range from $44 (Saturday only, lunch only) to $248 (weekend package, all meals, single room).
Accommodations: On-site hotel. Choose between standard rooms or suites. Handicap-accessible rooms available.
Additional Information: Published author critique offered, 50 pages maximum, $15. Open to MMRWA members or retreat attendees. Conference information available January 2004. For brochure send SASE, e-mail, or visit website. Accepts inquiries by SASE or e-mail. "Dress is casual—sweatshirts and jeans. We have a book sale and author signing. We also have a book basket raffle and auction fundraiser for the Kalamazoo YWCA Domestic Violence Program."

ROPEWALK WRITERS' RETREAT, 8600 University Blvd., Evansville IN 47712. (812)464-1863. E-mail: ropewalk@usi.edu. Website: www.ropewalk.org. **Contact:** Linda Cleek, conference coordinator. Estab. 1989. Annual. Conference held February 27-29, 2004. Average attendance: 40. "The week-long RopeWalk Writers' Retreat gives participants an opportunity to attend workshops and to confer privately with one of four or five prominent writers. At RopeWalk you will be encouraged to write—not simply listen to others talk about writing. Each workshop will be limited to twelve participants." Site: "Historic New Harmony, Indiana, site of two nineteenth century utopian experiments, provides an ideal setting for this event with its retreat-like atmosphere and its history of creative and intellectual achievement. The New Harmony Inn and Conference Center will be headquarters for the RopeWalk Writers' Retreat. Please note that reservations at the Inn should be confirmed by May 1." 2003 faculty included Ellen Bryant Voight, Stephen Dobyns, Kevin McIlvoy, Susan Neville.
Costs: $525 (2003), includes breakfasts and lunches.
Accommodations: Information on overnight accommodations is made available. "Room-sharing assistantce; some low-cost accommodations."
Additional Information: For critiques submit mss approx. 6 weeks ahead. Brochures are available after January 15.

WALLOON WRITERS' RETREAT, P.O. Box 304, Royal Oak MI 48068-0304. (248)589-3913. Fax: (248)589-9981. E-mail: johndlamb@ameritech.net. Website: www.springfed.org. **Contact:** John D. Lamb, director. Estab. 1999. Annual. Conference held September 25-28, 2003. Average attendance: 75. Focus includes fiction, poetry, creative nonfiction. Site: Michigania is owned and operated by the University of Michigan Alumni Association. Located on Walloon Lake. Attendees stay in spruce-paneled cabins and seminars are held in a large conference lodge with fieldstone fireplaces and dining area. 2003 faculty included U.S. Poet Laureate Billy Collins, Marie Howe, Jane Hamilton, Joyce Maynard, Craig Holden, Laurel Blossom, Kathleen Ripley Leo, M.L. Liebler and Terry Wooten.
Costs: Single occupancy is $575, $500 (3 nights, 2 nights). $325 non-lodging.
Accommodations: Shuttle rides from Traverse City Airport. Offers overnight accommodations. Provides list of area lodging options.
Additional Information: Optional: Attendees may submit 3 poems or 5 pages of prose for conference with a

staff member. Brochures available Mid-June by e-mail, on website or by phone. Accepts inquiries by SASE, e-mail, phone. Editors participate in conference. "Walloon Lake in Northern Michigan is the same lake that Ernest Hemingway spent the first 19 years of his life at his family's Windemere Cottage. The area plays a role in some of his early short stories. Notably in a couple Nick Adams stories."

N WESTERN RESERVE WRITERS & FREELANCE CONFERENCE, Lakeland Community College, 7700 Clocktower Dr., Kirtland OH 44094. (440) 953-7000. E-mail: deencr@aol.com. **Contact:** Deanna Adams or Nancy Piazza, co-coordinators. Estab. 1983. Biannual. Conference held March 20, 2004. Conference duration: One day. Average attendance: 20. "The Western Reserve Writers Conferences are designed for all writers, aspiring and professional, and offer presentations in all genres—nonfiction, fiction, poetry and the business of writing." Site: Located in the main building of Lakeland Community College, the conference is easy to find and just off the I-90 freeway. The fall 2003 conference featured "some of Ohio's best writers presenting on mystery, children's and women's fiction with a focus on characterization and plotting. The fall 2003 conference featured performance poet/author Ray McNiece as keynote speaker. Also featured renowned mystery writer Les Roberts, biographer Ted Shwarz, and romance writer June Lund Shiplett. Also featured presentations on book proposals and research."
Costs: Fall conference, including lunch: $69. Spring conference, no lunch: $45.
Additional Information: Brochures for the 2004 conferences will be available in January 2004 for SASE or by fax. Also accepts inquiries by e-mail and phone, or see website. Editors and agents sometimes attend the conferences.

WRITE-TO-PUBLISH CONFERENCE, 9731 N. Fox Glen Dr., Suite 6F, Niles IL 60714-4222. (847)299-4755. Fax: (847)296-0754. E-mail: lin@writetopublish.com. Website: www.writetopublish.com. **Contact:** Lin Johnson, director. Estab. 1971. Annual. Conference held from June 2-5, 2004. Average attendance: 225. Conference on "writing all types of manuscripts for the Christian market." Site: Wheaton College, Wheaton, IL.
Costs: $375.
Accommodations: Accommodations in campus residence halls or discounted hotel rates. Cost $195-255.
Additional Information: Optional manuscript evaluation available. Conference information available in January 2004. For brochures/ guidelines visit website, e-mail, fax or call. Accepts inquiries by e-mail, fax, phone.

WRITER'S DIGEST SCHOOL, 4700 E. Galbraith Rd., Cincinnati OH 45236. (800)759-0963. Fax: (513)531-0798. E-mail: wds@fwpubs.com. Website: www.writersdigestschool.com. **Contact:** Registrar. Estab. 1920s. Correspondence course; ongoing. Conference duration: "Most courses offer a self-paced term of up to two years. We have courses in Getting Started in Writing (fiction and nonfiction), Fundamentals of Fiction, Novel Writing Workshop (beginner and advanced), Writing and Selling Short Stories, and the basics of grammar and composition." Faculty consists of up to 80 instructors, all published writers and/or editors.
Costs: Course prices range from $179-439.
Additional Information: Conference information is available by e-mail and on website. Accepts inquiries by e-mail or phone.

North Central (IA, MN, NE, ND, SD, WI)

GREEN LAKE WRITERS CONFERENCE, W2511 State Hwy 23, Green Lake WI 54941. (920)294-7364. Fax: (920)294-3848. E-mail: russanhadding@glcc.org. Website: www.glcc.org. **Contact:** Russann Hadding, program coordinator. Estab. 1948. Annual. Conference held August 14-21, 2004. Conference duration: one week. Average attendance: 75. The week is open to beginning as well as experienced writers. "We provide gifted instructors in areas of children's, nonfiction, poetry, fiction, and inspirational writing." Site: 1,000 acres, including conference lodging and meeting rooms, dining facilities, and lake frontage for recreation, 72-hole golf course. "Barbara Smith is our fiction writer instuctor. Barbara is a freelance writer, editor and medical ethicist from West Virginia." Other speakers include Ellen Kort, Patricia Lorenz, Stephen and Marlo Kirkpatrick.
Costs: Double occupancy—approximately $650—inclusive. Reduced rates for triple and quad occupancy.
Accommodations: Provides a shuttle service from airport, train station, bus station.

INTERNATIONAL MUSIC CAMP CREATIVE WRITING WORKSHOP, 1725 11th St. SW, Minot ND 58701. Phone/fax: (701)838-8472. E-mail: joe@internationalmusiccamp.com. Website: www.internationalmusiccamp.com. **Contact:** Joseph T. Alme, executive director. Estab. 1956. Annual. Conference held June 27-July 3, 2004. Average attendance: 15. "The workshop offers students the opportunity to refine their skills in thinking, composing and writing in an environment that is conducive to positive reinforcement. In addition to writing poems, essays, and stories, individuals are encouraged to work on their own area of interest with conferencing and feedback from the course instructor." Site: International Peace Garden on the border between the US and Canada. "Similar to a University Campus, several dormitories, classrooms, lecture halls and cafeteria provide the perfect site for such a workshop. The beautiful and picturesque International Peace Garden provide additional inspiration to creative thinking." Dr. Ron Fisher from Minot State University is the instructor.
Costs: The cost including meals and housing is $1,230.
Accommodations: Airline and depot shuttles are available upon request. Housing is included in the $200 fee.

Additional Information: Conference information is available in September. For brochure visit website, e-mail, call or fax. Accepts inquiries by e-mail, phone and fax. Agents and editors participate in conference.

IOWA SUMMER WRITING FESTIVAL, 100 Oakdale Campus, W310, University of Iowa, Iowa City IA 52242-1802. (319)335-4160. E-mail: iswfestival@uiowa.edu. Website: www.uiowa.edu/~iswfest. **Contact:** Amy Margolis. Estab. 1987. Annual. Festival held in June and July. Workshops are one week or a weekend. Average attendance: limited to 12/class—over 1,500 participants throughout the summer. "We offer workshops across the genres, including novel, short story, poetry, essay, memoir, humor, travel, playwriting, screenwriting, writing for children and more. All levels." Site: University of Iowa campus. Guest speakers are undetermined at this time. Readers and instructors have included Lee K. Abbott, Susan Power, Joy Harjo, Gish Jen, Abraham Verghese, Robert Olen Butler, Ethan Canin, Clark Blaise, Gerald Stern, Donald Justice, Michael Dennis Browne, Marvin Bell, Hope Edelman, Lan Samantha Chang.
Costs: $460/week; $210, weekend workshop. Discounts available for early registration. Housing and meals are separate.
Accommodations: "We offer participants a choice of accommodations: dormitory, $32/night; Iowa House, $74/night; Sharaton, $85/night (rates subject to change)."
Additional Information: Conference information available in February. Accepts inquiries by fax, e-mail, phone.

MINNEAPOLIS WRITERS' CONFERENCE, Zurah Shrine Center, 2450 Park Ave., Minneapolis MN 55404. (651)455-8039, (651)645-1345. E-mail: jamisonriverwood@aol.com. Website: www.minneapoliswriters.com. **Contact:** Merle Hanson, president. Estab. 1984. Annual. Conference held in August 2004. Conference duration: 1 day. Average attendance: 100. The conference helps writers find markets for their books by providing resources, publishing contacts, motivational support, and guidance from successful authors of fiction and nonfiction. 2003 speakers: Lorna Landvik, M.D. Lake, Joel Turnipseed, Ellen Hart and Dr. Roger McDonald.
Costs: $75; includes luncheon and continental breakfast.

UNIVERSITY OF NORTH DAKOTA WRITERS CONFERENCE, Box 7209 UND, Grand Forks ND 58202-7209. (701)777-2768. Fax: (701)777-2373. E-mail: james_mckenzie@und.nodak.edu. Website: www.undwritersconference.org. **Contact:** James McKenzie, director. Estab. 1969. Annual. Conference held March 18-22, 2002. Average attendance: 1,000/day. Covers all genres, focused around a specific theme. The conference is a regional cultural and intellectual festival that puts nationally known writers in intimate and large audience contact with other writers and the student, academic and general public. Almost all events take place in the campus memorial union which has a variety of small rooms and a 1,000 seat main hall. Fiction writers in 2003 included Julia Whitty, Ted Mooney, and Thomas Disch as writer-in-residence.
Costs: Free, open to the public.
Accommodations: Offers overnight accommodations. "Campus residence halls are available at very good prices." Invited writers stay in Hilton Garden Inn.
Additional Information: Conference information is available January 31. For brochure send SASE, e-mail, visit website, call, fax. Accepts inquiries by SASE, e-mail, phone, fax.

WISCONSIN REGIONAL WRITER'S ASSOCIATION CONFERENCES, 510 W. Sunset Ave., Appleton WI 54911-1139. (920)734-3724. Website: www.wrwa.net. **Contact:** Patricia Boverhuis, president. Estab. 1948. Annual. Conferences held in May and September "are dedicated to self-improvement through speakers, workshops, and presentations. Topics and speakers vary with each event." Average attendance: 100-150. "We honor all genres of writing. Fall conference is a two-day event featuring the Jade Ring Banquet and awards for six genre categories. Spring conference is a one-day event." Keynote speaker at the 2003 Spring conference was Dr. Zorba Paster. Agents and editors participate in each conference.
Costs: $40-75.
Accommodations: Provides a list of area hotels or lodging options. "We negotiate special rates at each facility. A block of rooms is set aside for a specific time period."
Additional Information: Award winners receive a certificate and a cash prize. First place winners of the Jade Ring contest receive a jade ring. Must be a member to enter contests. For brochure, call, write, e-mail or visit website.

WRITERS INSTITUTE, 610 Langdon St., Room 621, Madison WI 53703. (608)262-3447. Fax: (608)265-2475. Website: www.dcs.wisc.edu/lsa/writing. **Contact:** Christine DeSmet. Estab. 1989. Annual. Held July 10-11, 2003. Site: Pyle Center. Average attendance: 200. Panels planned for the 2003 conference include the craft of writing and business/marketing for writers. Marshall J. Cook, Laurel Yorke and Christine DeSmet are scheduled to participate.
Costs: $205 includes materials, breaks.
Accommodations: Provides a list of area hotels or lodging options.
Additional Information: Sponsors contest. Submit 1-page writing sample and $10 entry fee. Conference speakers are judges. Conference information is available in April. For brochure send e-mail, visit website, call, fax. Accepts inquiries by SASE, e-mail, phone, fax. Agents and editors participate in conference.

WRITING WORKSHOP, P.O. Box 65, Ellison Bay WI 54210. (920)854-4088. E-mail: clearing@theclearing.org. Website: www.theclearing.org. **Contact:** Kathy Vanderhoof, registrar. Estab. 1935. Annual. Average attendance: 16. "General writing, journal, poetry as well as fiction and nonfiction." Held in a "quiet, residential setting in deep woods on the shore of Green Bay."
Costs: $675 for double; includes lodging, meals, tuition.
Accommodations: "Two to a room with private bath in rustic log and stone buildings with meals served family-style."

South Central (CO, KS, MO, NM, OK, TX)

◎ **THE AFRICAN AMERICAN BOOK CLUB SUMMIT**, PMB 120, 2951 Marina Bay Dr., Suite 130, League City TX 77573. (866)875-1055. E-mail: pwsquare@pageturner.net. Website: www.summitatsea.com. **Contact:** Pamela Walker Williams, literary events chairman. Estab. 2000. Annual. Conference held each October on board a Carnival cruise ship; the next event is scheduled for October 19-26, 2003 on board the Carnival ship Elation. Average attendance: 200. "The purpose of the conference is to bring authors and readers together. Aspiring writers will have an opportunity to discuss and obtain information on self-publishing, marketing and writing fiction." Site: on board cruise ship. Includes pool, jacuzzi, restaurant, bar, spa, room service, wheelchair accessible, fitness center, children's facilities, air conditioning.
Costs: 2003 fees: for inside cabin, $990; for outside, $1,090. Includes cruise, conference, on-board meals, port charges and gratuities.
Accommodations: "Participants have the option to add airfare and/or shuttle service." Provides a list of area accommodations for people who choose to arrive early.
Additional Information: Brochures available on website. Accepts inquiries by e-mail, phone, fax. Agents and editors attend conference.

AGENTS! AGENTS! AGENTS! & EDITORS TOO!, The Writers' League of Texas, 1501 W. Fifth St., Austin TX 78703-5155. (512)499-8914. Fax: (512)499-0441. E-mail: wlt@writersleague.org. Website: www.writersleague. org. **Contact:** Stephanie Sheppard, executive director. Estab. 1994. Annual. Conference held Summer 2003. Conference duration: 3 days. Average attendance: 220. To help writers "learn about the business of writing and get the most up-to-date information about the writing industry." Site: Austin, Texas. In 2002 topics included Agents & Editors: The Current Market for Fiction, The Current Market for Nonfiction; Exploring Audiobooks; Realistic Dialogue; Electronic Publishing; Genre Panels; Small Press; The Author-Editor Relationship; Writing Treatments That Sell; Taking Care of Business Matters for Writers; Ways to Market Your Writing; The Agony and Ecstasy of Self-Publishing. Agents in 2002: Sheree Bykofsky, Julia Castiglia, Jim Donovan, Nancy Ellis-Bell, Lawrence Jordan, Jim Hornfischer, Marcy Posner, David Hale Smith, Andrew Stuart. Editors in 2002: George Hodgman, Stephanie Land, Julia Pastore, Darryl Wimberly. Authors in 2002: Suzy Spencer, Karen Stolz, Jim Gramon, Don Webb, Mindy Reed, Greg Garrett, Bonnie Orr, Susie Flatan, Diane Fanning, Stacey Hasbrook, Joan Hall, Paula Hamilton, David Marion Wilkinson, Vanessa Leggett.
Costs: In 2002, $195 members; $240 nonmembers; $50 optional workshops.
Accommodations: Hotel offers special conference rate.
Additional Information: "The Writers' League of Texas sponsors a manuscript contest in conjunction with the annual agents and editors conference. For guidelines please SASE or send an e-mail or check the website. Entry fees for 2003 are $20. Finalists receive a critique from and a private consultation with an agent. Winners will be announced at the agents conferences. There are no monetary prizes nor is there any offer of publication. Deadline for entry was May 1, 2003." Conference information is available in December. For brochure, send SASE, e-mail, visit website, call or fax. Accepts inquiries by SASE, e-mail, phone and fax. "As a bonus for attending the conference, participants will be offered a ten-minute consult with an agent. For those that desire a consult, early registration is encouraged."

ASPEN SUMMER WORDS WRITING RETREAT AND LITERARY FESTIVAL, 110 E. Hallam St., #116, Aspen CO 81611. (970)925-3122. Fax: (970)925-5700. E-mail: info@aspenwriters.org. Website: www.aspenwriters. org. **Contact:** Julie Comins, executive director. Estab. 1976. Annual. Conference held in late June. Conference duration: 5 days. Average attendance: Writing retreat, 72; literary festival, 200 passholders, 1,800 visitors. For fiction, creative nonfiction, poetry, magazine writing, nature writing, author readings and agent/editor meetings, and industry panels. 2003 festival featured Pam Houston, Ron Carlson, Amy Bloom (fiction), James Houston (creative nonfiction), Christopher Merrill (poetry), Laura Fraser (magazine writing), David Petersen (nature writing), Ann Patchett and Patricia Schroeder.
Costs: $375/retreat; $150/festival; $495/both; $25/private meetings with agents and editors.
Accommodations: On-campus housing $110/night single; $55/night double. Off-campus rates vary. Free shuttle.
Additional Information: New application deadlines: April 1 and May 1. Manuscripts must be submitted prior to conference for review by faculty. Brochures available for SASE, by e-mail and phone request, and on website.

N̄ BAY AREA WRITER'S LEAGUE CONFERENCE, P.O. Box 58007, Houston TX 77058. E-mail: info@bawl.org. Website: www.bawl.org. **Contact:** Conference Chair. Estab. 1989. Annual. Conference held May 7-8, 2004. Conference duration: 2 days. Average attendance: 100. For "novice writers, all genres." Site: "University classroom building in a nature preserve." Features and staff to be announced.
Costs: $85 for two days, lunch included. $50 for one day, lunch included.
Accommodations: $89 per night at first-class hotel. Cheaper accommodations, e.g. Motel 6, are available.
Additional Information: Sponsors contest for high school students, unpublished authors, published authors. Fiction categories include Novel (synopsis and 20 pages) and Short Story (5,000) words. Requires $15 entry fee. Brochures/guidelines available January 2003 for SASE, by e-mail and on website. Accepts queries by SASE, e-mail. Agents and editors participate in conference.

COLORADO MOUNTAIN WRITERS' WORKSHOP, P.O. Box 85394, Tucson AZ 85754. (520)465-1520. E-mail: mfiles@pima.edu. Website: www.sheilabender.com. **Contact:** Meg Files, director. Estab. 1999. Annual. Conference held in late June. Conference duration: 5 days. Average attendance: 30. Focuses on fiction, poetry, and personal essay. The conference is designed to lift writers, novice or experienced, to the next level. Site: Held on the campus of Colorado Mountain College, Steamboat Springs, Colorado. Features personal writing. Faculty includes Meg Files, Sheila Bender and Jack Heffron.
Costs: $300.
Accommodations: Offers overnight lodging in on-site dormitory, $365 (6 nights, also meals).
Additional Information: Brochures available in November for SASE, e-mail, website, fax or call. Accepts inquiries for SASE, e-mail, fax, phone. Editors participate in conferences. Daily activities include craft talks, small group workshops, readings and ms consultations, as well as writing time.

N̄ ◎ EAST TEXAS CHRISTIAN WRITER'S CONFERENCE, East Texas Baptist University, School of Humanities, 1209 N. Grove, Marshall TX 75670. (903)923-2269. E-mail: dbaca@etbu.edu or flower@etbu.edu. Website: www.etbu.edu. **Contact:** Delma Baca. Estab. 2002. Annual. Conference held June 5, 2004. Conference duration: 1 day (Saturday). Average attendance: 60. "Primarily we are interested in promoting quality Christian writing that would be accepted in mainstream publishing." Site: "We use the classrooms, cafeterias, etc. of East Texas Baptist University. 2003 conference themes: 10 Commandments of Powerful Writers; Editor's Perspective—Do's and Don'ts; The Writer's Life; 7 Effective Habits for Christian Writers; Writing for Youth. 2003 conference speakers: Ben Z. Grant, Albert Haley, David Jenkins, Marv Knox, Bill Wells, Bill O'Neil, and Joe Pate.
Costs: $50 for individual; $80 for a couple; $30 student. Price includes meal.
Additional Information: "Would like to expand to an opportunity to meet with agents or an editor."

◎ EMINENCE AREA ARTS COUNCIL SHORT STORY WORKSHOP, P.O. Box 551, Eminence MO 65466-0551. (573)226-5655. E-mail: hilma@socket.net. **Contact:** Hilma Hughes, administrator. Estab. 1989. Annual. Workshop held April 15-17, 2004. Conference duration: 3 days. Average attendance: 12. "The Short Story Workshop focuses on fiction of any genre." Workshop centers on the process of writing—participants leave with a finished short story. Site: "Museum and Art Gallery conference room. We have large tables with chairs for participants. There is already a large screen TV and VCR for the leaders to use. Both facilities are available and the museum is accessible to the physically challenged." Workshop led by Dr. Tam Nordgren in 2004.
Costs: $40.
Accommodations: Provides list of area lodging.
Additional Information: Participants should bring work-in-progress for critique by workshop director. Brochures available in January 2004 by e-mail or phone. Accepts inquiries by e-mail or phone. "We are a small rural community on the scenic Riverways. The workshops are an excellent opportunity to rest, relax, and get away from the rush of daily life. Many participants have valued this part of the experience as much as the learning and writing process."

◎ FLATIRONS BLUNT INSTRUMENT MYSTERY WORKSHOP, c/o FBI, P.O. Box 19486, Boulder CO 80308-2486. Website: www.trulydonovan.com/rmcsinc. **Contact:** Thora Chinnery. Estab. 1996. Annual. Conference held June 19, 2004. Average attendance: 70. Conference for "mystery writers and readers." Site: "two very large auditorium rooms at the local Elks club." 2003 speakers included Connie Willis, Ed Bryant, Christine Goff, Barbara Steinen.
Costs: 2003 fee: $65 (included continental breakfast and buffet lunch).
Additional Information: Conference information available January 2004. For brochure/guidelines send SASE, visit website. "It is the only genre-specific mystery workshop in the Rocky Mountain area. The scenery is fabulous. The conference is sponsored by the Rocky Mountain Chapter of Sisters in Crime."

FORT BEND WRITERS GUILD WORKSHOP, 12523 Folkcrest Way, Stafford TX 77477-3529. (281)498-5025. E-mail: rogerpaulding@myrealbox.com. Website: http://fortbendwritersguild.tripod.com. **Contact:** Roger Paulding. Estab. 1997. Annual. Conference held March 27, 2004. Conference duration: 1 day. Average attendance: 75. Focuses on fiction (novels) and screenwriting. Site: Held at Holiday Inn.
Costs: $50 (including buffet lunch).
Additional Information: Sponsors a contest. Submit for novel competition—first 10 pages plus one page synopsis,

entry fee $15; short story—10 pages complete, $10 each. "Judges are published novelists." First prize: $300. For brochure send SASE or e-mail.

[N] [◎] GLORIETA CHRISTIAN WRITERS' CONFERENCE, Glorieta Conference Center, P.O. Box 66810, Albuquerque NM 87193-6810. (800)433-6633. Fax: (505)899-9282. E-mail: info@classervices.com. Website: www. glorietacwc.com, or www.lifeway.com. **Contact:** Marita Littaner, director. Estab. 1997. Annual. Conference held October 13-17, 2004. Conference duration: 5 days. Average attendance: 250. For "beginners, professionals, fiction, poetry, screenwriting, writing for children, drama, magazine writing, nonfiction books." To train Christian writers in their craft, provide them with an understanding of the industry, and give opportunities to meet with publishers. Site: "Located just north of historic Santa Fe, NM, conference center with hotels and dining hall with buffet-style meals." Plans "continuing course for fiction writers and numerous one-hour workshops." 2003 speakers included James Scott Bell, Jack Cavanaugh and Liz Ezell.
Costs: 2003 rates were $275 for early registration, or $305 regular registration; meals and lodging are additional and range from $200-400 depending on housing and meal plans.
Additional Information: "The craft of writing is universal, but attendees should be aware this conference has a Christian emphasis."

NATIONAL WRITERS ASSOCIATION FOUNDATION CONFERENCE, 3140 S. Peoria, Suite 295, Aurora CO 80014. (303)841-0246. Fax: (303)841-2607. E-mail: conference@nationalwriters.com. Website: www.natio nalwriters.com. **Contact:** Sandy Whelchel, executive director. Estab. 1926. Annual. Conference held in June. Conference duration: 3 days. Average attendance: 200-300. For general writing and marketing.
Costs: $200 (approximately).
Additional Information: Awards for previous contests will be presented at the conference. Conference information available annually in December. For brochures/guidelines send SASE, visit website, e-mail, fax, or call.

THE NEW LETTERS WEEKEND WRITERS CONFERENCE, University of Missouri-Kansas City, College of Arts and Sciences Continuing Ed. Division, 4825 Troost, Room 215, Kansas City MO 64110-2499. (816)235-2736. Fax: (816)235-5279. Website: www.umkc.edu/CE/College. **Contact:** Robert Stewart. Estab. mid-70's as The Longboat Key Writers Conference. Annual. Conference held in June. Conference duration: 3 days. Average attendance: 75. For "craft and the creative process in poetry, fiction, screenwriting, playwriting and journalism; but the program also deals with matters of psychology, publications and marketing. The conference is appropriate for both advanced and beginning writers." Site: "The conference meets at the beautiful Diastole conference center of The University of Missouri-Kansas City."
Costs: Several options are available. Participants may choose to attend as a noncredit student or they may attend for 1-3 hours of college credit from the University of Missouri-Kansas City. Conference registration includes continental breakfasts, Saturday and Sunday lunch. For complete information, contact the university.
Accommodations: Information on area accomodations is made available.
Additional Information: Those registering for college credit are required to submit a ms in advance. Manuscript reading and critque are included in the credit fee. Those attending the conference for noncredit also have the option of hanving their ms critiqued for an additional fee. Accepts inquiries by phone, fax.

NIMROD ANNUAL WRITERS' WORKSHOP, *Nimrod*, University of Tulsa, 600 S. College Ave., Tulsa OK 74104. (918)631-3080. Fax: (918)631-3033. E-mail: nimrod@utulsa.edu. Website: www.utulsa.edu/nimrod. **Contact:** Francine Ringold, Ph.D., editor-in-chief. Estab. 1978. Annual. Conference held in October. Conference duration: 1 day. Average attendance: 100-150. Workshop in fiction and poetry. "Prize-winners (*Nimrod*/Hardman Prizes) conduct workshops as do contest judges. Past judges: Rosellen Brown, Stanley Kunitz, Toby Olson, Lucille Clifton, W.S. Merwin, Ron Carlson, Mark Doty, Anita Shreve and Francine Prose."
Costs: Approximately $50. Lunch provided. Scholarships available for students.
Additional Information: *Nimrod International Journal* sponsors *Nimrod*/Hardman Literary Awards: The Katherine Anne Porter Prize for fiction and The Pablo Neruda Prize for poetry. Poetry and fiction prizes: $2,000 each and publication (1st prize); $1,000 each and publication (2nd prize). Deadline: must be postmarked no later than April 30.

OKLAHOMA WRITERS FEDERATION CONFERENCE, P.O. Box 2654, Stillwater OK 74076-2654. (405)408-2141. E-mail: wileykat@cox.net. Website: www.owfi.org. **Contact:** Moira Wiley, president. Estab. 1968. Annual. Conference held the first weekend in May every year. Average attendance: 300-350. Conference covers all genres, fiction, poetry, nonfiction. Site: "Our conference is held at the Embassy Suites Hotel in Oklahoma City. It has 6 floors. Everything, all meetings are contained within the hotel."
Costs: Full conference, $100; one day only, $50; authors' banquet, $30; awards banquet, $30 (2004 fees). $125 after April 15.
Accommodations: The hotel provides a shuttle to and from airport. Embassy Suites room rates have been $89. Guests of the hotel get free buffet breakfast.
Additional Information: "The annual OWFI contest is open only to paid-up members. It features competitions for cash prizes in 28 unpublished ms categories and awards 4 trophies for the best books published during the

previous calendar year. A $20 entry fee entitles participants to enter as many categories as they want, but they may enter no single category more than once. Since the contest's purpose is to encourage writers to produce professionally acceptable manuscripts, the contest rules are very explicit and contestants must follow them closely. Novel categories include mainstream; contemporary romance; historical romance; myster/suspense; Western; science fiction/fantasy/horror. Additional categories include nonfiction book; picture book; middle reader; and young adult book; short story; short short story; column." For brochures/guidelines send SASE, e-mail, visit website, call. Agents and editors participate in conference with 10-minute one-on-one appointments available. Book room and autograph party for published authors.

ROCKY MOUNTAIN BOOK FESTIVAL, 2123 Downing St., Denver CO 80205. (303)839-8320. Fax: (303)839-8319. E-mail: ccftb@compuserve.com. Website: www.coloradocenterforthebook.org. **Contact:** Christiane Citron, executive director. Estab. 1991. Annual. Festival date TBA (possibly Fall 2004). Average attendance: 10,000. Festival promotes published work from all genres. Site: 2002 festival was held at the University of Denver's Ritchie Center. Offers a wide variety of panels.
Costs: $4 (adult); $2 (child).
Additional Information: Brochures/guidelines available. Accepts inquiries by e-mail, fax. "Please submit a copy of book, bio and publicity material for consideration."

SAN JUAN WRITERS WORKSHOP, P.O. Box 841, Ridgeway CO 81432. (970)626-4125. E-mail: lepatter@ttacs.ttu.edu. Website: http://homepage.mac.com/inkwellliterary. **Contact:** Jill Patterson, director. Estab. 2002. Annual. Workshop held May, June, July 2003. Conference duration: 3 days. Average attendance: 40. Focuses on "fiction, poetry, creative nonfiction in each session. Sessions focus on Christian writers, women writers, literature of place and advanced writers." Site: "Community Center in beautiful mountain valley town of Ouray, Colorado." 2002 panels included Christian fiction, setting in fiction, advanced fiction writing. Panelists in 2003 included Pam Houston, Kelly Cherry, Scott Cairns, Lee Martin, and Melanie Rae Thon.
Costs: $470, includes breakfast and lunch daily.
Accommodations: Offers shuttle to/from airport in Montrose, CO. Provides a list of hotels.
Additional Information: Participants must submit workshop material—10-20 pages of prose—by April 15, 2004. Brochure available January 1, 2004 by SASE, e-mail or website. Accepts inquiries by SASE, e-mail, phone. "There are social activities, including mountain cookout, champagne brunch and readings."

SOUTHWEST WRITERS CONFERENCE, 8200 Mountain Rd., NE, Suite 106, Albuquerque NM 87110-7835. (505)265-9485. Fax: (505)265-9483. E-mail: swriters@aol.com. Website: www.southwestwriters.org. **Contact:** Conference Chair. Estab. 1983. Annual. Conference held in September. Average attendance: 400. "Conference concentrates on all areas of writing and includes preconference sessions, appointments and networking." Workshops and speakers include writers and editors of all genres for all levels from beginners to advanced. 2002 keynote speaker was Debbie Macomber.
Costs: $365 and up (members); $425 and up (nonmembers); includes conference sessions and 2 luncheons
Accommodations: Usually have official airline and discount rates. Special conference rates are available at hotel. A list of other area hotels and motels is available.
Additional Information: Sponsors a contest judged by authors, editors and agents from New York, Los Angeles, etc., and from other major publishing houses. Seventeen categories. Deadline: May 1. Entry fee is $29 (members) or $39 (nonmembers). Conference information available in April. For brochures/guidelines send SASE, visit website, e-mail, fax, call. "An appointment (10 minutes, one-on-one) may be set up at the conference with the editor or agent of your choice on a first-registered/first-served basis."

STEAMBOAT SPRINGS WRITERS GROUP, Steamboat Arts Council, P.O. Box 774284, Steamboat Springs CO 80477. (970)879-8079. E-mail: MsHFreiberger@cs.com. **Contact:** Harriet Freiberger, director. Estab. 1982. Annual. Group meets Thursdays, 12:00 to 2:00 at Arts Depot; guests welcome. Conference held in July. Conference duration: 1 day. Average attendance: 30. "Our conference emphasizes instruction within the seminar format. Novices and polished professionals benefit from the individual attention and camaraderie which can be established within small groups. A pleasurable and memorable learning experience is guaranteed by the relaxed and friendly atmosphere of the old train depot. Registration is limited." Site: Restored train depot.
Costs: $35 before June 1, $45 after. Fee covers all conference activities, including lunch.
Accommodations: Lodging available at Steamboat Resorts.
Additional Information: Optional dinner and activities during evening preceding conference. Accepts inquiries by e-mail, phone, mail.

TAOS INSTITUTE OF ARTS, 108 Civic Plaza Dr., Taos NM 87571. (505)758-2793. Fax: (505)737-2466. E-mail: tia@taosnet.com. Website: www.tiataos.com. Estab. 1988. Annual. Workshops held June-October. Conference duration: 1 week. Average attendance: 12 students maximum/workshop. Covers novel and short story writing, nonfiction, poetry, travel writing, mystery writing, the business of publishing, children's book writing, free-association writing. Site: Workshops take place in a variety of locations in Taos. 2003 faculty included US poet laureate Billy Collins, Robert Westbrook, Joan Cavanaugh, Levi Romero.

Costs: $460 ($40 registration fee and $420 tuition). Meals, lodging, etc. are separate
Accommodations: Provides a list of area hotels or lodging options.

TELLURIDE WRITERS CONFERENCE, P.O. Box 2189, 100 W. Pacific St., Telluride CO 81435-2189. (970)728-4519. Fax: (970)728-3340. E-mail: jjay@telluride.lib.co.us. Website: www.telluride.lib.co.us. **Contact:** Ann Kennedy, program coordinator. Estab. 2001. Annual. Conference held May 2004. Average attendance: 50. Focuses on fiction, nonfiction, essays, short stories. Site: "Telluride is a gorgeous mountain town in Southwest Colorado. Hard to get to, hard to leave." Conference held in Public Library Program Room. In 2002, panels included How to Get Published, How to Self Promote Once Published, Do You Need an Editor?, Do You Need An Agent?, When Do You Approach a Publisher Directly?, Should You Self-Publish? 2002 faculty included Bruce Holland Rogers, fiction writing instructor and author; Michelle Curry Wright, novelist; Patricia Calhoun, magazine/newspaper editor; Sandra Bond, literary agent; P. David Smith, publisher.
Costs: $35 for Saturday presentations and panel discussion; $20 individual Sunday session with panelist (20 minute duration).
Accommodations: "Conference held during shoulder season to take advantage of inexpensive lodging." Provides attendants with list of area lodging.
Additional Information: Attendants not required to submit material prior to arrival, "though it would be nice to bring a sample of writing along if attending any of the individual sessions on Sunday." Brochures available in February/March 2003 by e-mail, phone, fax or on website. "Unpublished authors will get the most out of our conference."

TEXAS CHRISTIAN WRITERS' CONFERENCE, First Baptist Church, 6038 Greenmont, Houston TX 77092. (713)686-7209. E-mail: mlrogersll@houston.rr.com. **Contact:** Martha Rogers. Estab. 1990. Annual. Conference held August 7, 2004. Conference duration: 1 day. Average attendance: 60-65. "Focus on all genres." Site: Held at the First Baptist Church fellowship center and classrooms. 2003 faculty: Jim Stafford, Rebecca Germany, Eva Marie Everson, Jeanette Littleton. 2004: Debra White-Smith.
Costs: $60 for members of IWA, $55 for members, $75 nonmembers, discounts for seniors (60+) and couples, meal at noon, continental breakfast, and breaks.
Accommodations: Offers list of area hotels or lodging options.
Additional Information: Open conference for all interested writers. Sponsors a contest for short fiction; categories include articles, devotionals, poetry, short story, book proposals, drama. Fees: $8 member, $10 nonmember. Conference information available with SASE or e-mail. Agents participate in conference. Senior discounts available.

MARK TWAIN CREATIVE WRITING WORKSHOPS, University House, 5101 Rockhill Rd., Kansas City MO 64110-2499. (816)235-1168. Fax: (816)235-2611. E-mail: BeasleyM@umkc.edu. Website: www.newsletters.org. **Contact:** Betsy Beasley, adminstrative associate. Estab. 1990. Annual. Held first 3 weeks of June, from 9:30 to 12:30 each weekday morning. Conference duration: 3 weeks. Average attendance: 40. "Focus is on fiction, poetry and literary nonfiction." Site: University of Missouri-Kansas City Campus. Panels planned for next conference include the full range of craft essentials. Staff includes Robert Stewart, editor-in-chief of newsletters and BkMk Press.
Costs: Fees for regular and noncredit courses.
Accommodations: Offers list of area hotels or lodging options.
Additional Information: Submit for workshop 6 poems/one short story prior to arrival. Conference information is available in March by SASE, e-mail or on website. Editors participate in conference.

UNIVERSITY OF NEW MEXICO'S TAOS SUMMER WRITERS CONFERENCE, Department of English, Humanities 255, University of New Mexico, Albuquerque NM 87131-1106. (505)277-6248. Fax: (505)277-2950. E-mail: taosconf@unm.edu. Website: www.unm.edu/~taosconf. **Contact:** Sharon Oard Warner, director. Estab. 1999. Annual. Held each year in mid-July. Average attendance: 150. Workshops in novel writing, short story writing, screenwriting, poetry, creative nonfiction, travel writing and in special topics such as historical fiction, memoir and revision. For beginning and experienced writers. Site: Workshops and readings are all held at the Sagebrush Inn Conference Center, part of the Sagebrush Inn, an historic hotel and Taos landmark since 1929.
Costs: Week-long workshop tuition is $490, includes a Sunday evening Mexican buffet dinner, a Friday evening barbecue, and evening museum tour. Weekend workshop tuition is $240.
Accommodations: We offer a discounted car rental rate through the Sagebrush Inn or the adjacent Comfort Suites. Conference participants receive special discounted rates $59-99/night. Room rates at both hotels include a full, hot breakfast.
Additional Information: "Participants do not submit manuscripts in advance. Instead, they bring copies to distrubute at the first meeting of the workshop." Sponsors contest. "We offer four Merit Scholarships, the Taos Resident Writer Award, the Native Writer Award, and one D.H. Lawrence Fellowship. Scholarship awards are based on submissions of poetry and fiction." They provide tuition remission; transportation and lodging not provided. To apply, submit 10 pages of poetry or fiction along with registration and deposit. Applicants should be registered for the conference. The Fellowship is for emerging writers with one book in print, provides tuition remission and cost of lodging. Brochures available late January-early February 2003. "The conference offers a balance of special

events and free time. If participants take a morning workshiop, they'll have the afternoons free, and vice versa. We've also included several outings, including a tour of the Harwood Arts Center and a visit to historic D.H. Lawrence Ranch outside Taos."

UNIVERSITY OF THE NATIONS SCHOOL OF WRITING AND WRITERS WORKSHOPS, YWAM Woodcrest, P.O. Box 1380, Lindale TX 75771-1380. (903)882-WOOD [9663]. Fax: (903)882-1161. E-mail: writings chooltx@yahoo.com. Website: www.ywamwoodcrest.com. **Contact:** Carol Scott, School of Writing. Estab. 1983. Annual. Held September 25-December 16, 2003. Conference duration: 12 weeks, individual workshops last 1 week each. Average attendance: 6-12. Site: "We are located in East Texas about 90 miles east of Dallas. Our campus is on 107 acres of wooded area."

Costs: "Interested parties should double check fees for School of Writing as housing/food costs may vary. 2003 costs are $50 registration fee; $2,700 tuition/food/housing, plus $50 book fee." Send for information on 1-week workshop costs.

Accommodations: "We can pick up students at Tyler Airport or Mineola Amtrack train station. Otherwise, we can assist in arranging shuttle service from Dallas. Costs vary depending on number of people. Housing is dormitory-style with several students sharing a common room and shower area (one for men, one for women). Married students or family housing will vary and is arranged on an as-needed basis."

Additional Information: For brochure send e-mail, visit website or call. Editors participate in conference. "If a student desires credit for a workshop or plans to attend the full School of Writing, they must meet University of Nations prerequisite (usually just the Discipleship Training School). Although we are associated in the *Youth With A Mission* missionary organization, we welcome inquiries and attendees from all backgrounds, not just missionaries."

 **THE WRITER'S LANDSCAPE**, 304 Calle Oso, Santa Fe NM 87501. (505)471-1565. E-mail: wordharvest@yahoo.com. Website: www.sfworkshops.com. **Contact:** Jean Schaumberg. Estab. 2001. Annual. Conference held April 2004. Conference duration: 5 days. Average attendance: 30. "We use the landscape as inspiration for our writing and our inner spiritual landscape as a source of values, ideas and questions to ponder. Open to all genres and abilities." Site: Held at the Ghost Ranch Santa Fe, in downtown Santa Fe, a facility run by the Presbyterian Church. 2003 themes: Writing from Nature; The Ecology of Ideas. 2003 speakers: Tony Hillerman, Demetria Martinez and Joan Losstie.

Costs: 2003: $600 commuter; $795 resident.

Accommodations: Our host, Ghost Ranch Santa Fe, handles lodging arrangements. Simple rooms in a great location.

Additional Information: "Lots of hands-on writing in a beautiful place."

WRITERS' LEAGUE OF TEXAS SPRING AND FALL WORKSHOPS AND CLASSES, 1501 W. Fifth St., Suite E-2, Austin TX 78703-5155. (512)499-8914. Fax: (512)499-0441. E-mail: wlt@writersleague.org. Website: www.writersleague.org. **Contact:** Helen Ginger, interim executive director. Workshops held in March, April, May, September, October and November. Conference duration: Workshops held weekends; classes held one evening/week and last 2-8 weeks. Average attendance: 20 for workshops; 12 for classes. "Classes and workshops provide practical advice and guidance on various aspects of fiction, creative nonfiction and screenwriting." Site: Writers' League of Texas resource center. "There are two multipurpose classrooms, a library, three offices and a workroom." Some classes are by e-mail. "Topics for workshops and classes have included E-Publishing; Creative Nonfiction; Screenwriting Basics; Novel in Progress; Basics of Short Fiction; Technique; Writing Scenes; Journaling; Manuscript Feedback; Essays; Newspaper Columns." Instructors include Marion Winik, Emily Vander Veer, Annie Reid, Bonnie Orr, Jan Epton Seale, Susan Wade, Lila Guzman, Laurie Lynn Drummond, Darryl Wimberly, Patricia Wynn, Joan Neubauer, Graham Shelby, David Wilkinson, John Pipkin, Ann McCutchan and Dao Strom.

Costs: Workshops $50; classes $5-225.

Additional Information: Conference information is available in January and August. For brochure, send SASE, e-mail, visit website, call or fax.

WRITER'S RETREATS, 906 Chelsey Lane, Durango CO 81301-3408. (970)247-5327. E-mail: thunder@animas.net. Website: www.manuscriptdevelopment.com. **Contact:** Michael Thunder. Estab. 1998. Conference duration: 1-

2 weeks. Average attendance: 1 individual/session. Focus is on fiction and screenwriting. Site: Durango, Colorado, "beautiful mountain environment."

Costs: $1,000 coaching fee. Meals and lodging are dependant on the writer's taste and budget.

Accommodations: Provides a list of area hotels or lodging options.

Additional Information: "These writer's retreats are geared toward concepting a project, or project development. Usually writers stay one week and receive 10 hours of one-on-one coaching. The rest of their time is spent writing." For brochure send e-mail, visit website or call.

◎ **WRITERS WORKSHOP IN SCIENCE FICTION,** English Department/University of Kansas, Lawrence KS 66045-2115. (785)864-3380. Fax: (785)864-1159. E-mail: jgunn@ku.edu. Website: www.ku.edu/~sfcenter. **Contact:** James Gunn, professor. Estab. 1984. Annual. Workshop held in June. Conference duration: 2 weeks. Average attendance: 10-14. The workshop is "small, informal and aimed at writers on the edge of publication or regular publication." For writing and marketing science fiction. Site: "Housing is provided and classes meet in university housing on the University of Kansas campus. Workshop sessions operate informally in a lounge." Past guests include Frederik Pohl, SF writer and former editor and agent; John Ordover, writer and editor; and Kij Johnson and Christopher McKittrick, writers.

Costs: $400 tuition. Housing and meals are additional.

Accommodations: Several airport shuttle services offer reasonable transportation from the Kansas City International Airport to Lawrence. During past conferences, students were housed in a student dormitory at $12/day double, $22/day single.

Additional Information: "Admission to the workshop is by submission of an acceptable story. Two additional stories should be submitted by the end of May. These three stories are copied and distributed to other participants for critquing and are the basis for the first week of the workshop; one story is rewritten for the second week. The workshop offers a 3-hour session manuscript critiquing each morning. The rest of the day is free for writing, study, consultation and recreation." Information available in December. For brochures/guidelines send SASE, visit website, e-mail, fax, call. "The Writers Workshop in Science Fiction is intended for writers who have just started to sell their work or need that extra bit of understanding or skill to become a published writer."

YOUTH WITH A MISSION'S SCHOOL OF WRITING, P.O. Box 1380, Lindale TX 75771-1380. (903)882-9663. Fax: (903)882-1161. E-mail: writingschooltx@yahoo.com. Website: www.ywamwoodcrest.com. **Contact:** Carol Hatheway Scott, school leader. Estab. 1986. Annual. Held September 25-December 16, 2003. Conference duration: 7 one-week workshops or 12-week school (includes 7 week-long workshops interspersed with "project weeks"). Average attendance: 10-15. Seven one-week workshops include Nonfiction Narrative, Editing Your Writing, Fiction That Lives, Marketing Your Writing, Writing Screenplays, Writing Picture Books, Writing on a Theme (book length), Writing Magazine Articles as well as a one-day workshop in poetry. Site: "Woodcrest has 107 acres of creative possiblities. Two buildings on the site at present." Faculty members include Janice Rogers, Elaine Wright Colvin, Brian Godawa, Mona Gansberg Hodgson, Sandra Tompkins, Carol Hatheway Scott.

Costs: $20 registration (non-refundable), $175 tuition first week and $125 each additional week, $175 food/housing per week. "Book fee depends on class."

Accommodations: "We offer pick-up in Tyler, Texas (airport of bus station)." Offers overnight accommodation; dorm-style rooms.

Additional Information: Brochure available for SASE, e-mail, phone, fax. Editors attend conference.

West (AZ, CA, HI, NV, UT)

AUTHOR'S VENUE JOURNEY CONFERENCE, 600 Central Ave. SE, Suite 235, Albuquerque NM 87102. (505)244-9337. Fax: (800)853-7655. E-mail: info@authorsvenue.com. Website: www.authorsvenue.com. **Contact:** Suzanne Spletzer, executive director. Estab. 2001. Annual. Conference held April 15-18, 2004. Average attendance: 300. Conference focuses on fiction, nonfiction and screenwriting. Established "to provide education and publication opportunities for writers." Site: Hyatt Regency in Lake Tahoe, NV. Panels planned for next conference include Agents' Panel, Screenwriters Marketing Panel, Coaches Panel. 2003 faculty members include Richard Walter, Professor UCLA TV & film school; Milton Kahn, publicist; John Baker, editorial director, *Publishers Weekly*; Katherine Sands, literary agent. Sponsored by *The Writer* Magazine.

Costs: $320 for nonmembers, $250 for members until November 15, 2003. After the deadline $375 for nonmembers and $300 for members. $400 at the door.

Accommodations: Offers overnight accommodations at Hyatt Regency, $109 per night.

Additional Information: Participants must submit material for manuscript consultations prior to arrival, deadline: March 1. Manuscript consultations are $150 for 30 minutes with an editor or agent. For brochure, inquiries contact by e-mail, phone, fax, mail or visit website. "A great experience for professional writers."

◎ **AUTHOR'S VENUE SCREENWRITERS INSTITUTE,** 600 Central Avenue, SE, Suite 235, Albuquerque NM 87102. (505)244-9337. Fax: (800)853-7655. E-mail: executivedirector@authorsvenue.com. Website: www.authorsvenue.com. **Contact:** Suzanne Spletzer, executive director. Estab. 2001. Annual. Conference held April 15-18,

2004. Conference duration: 4 days. Average attendance: 50 screenwriters. Conference's purpose is to provide "education in screenwriting, connecting with professionals and producers." Offers Academy class taught by Academy Award-winning or -nominated writer. Site: Hyatt Regency in Lake Tahoe, NV. Panels include marketing and screenplay panel, scene structure, dialogue. Faculty includes Richard Walter, professor at UCLA TV and Film School. **Costs:** $320 nonmembers. $250 members. After November 15, 2003 rates are $375 non-membes, $300 members, and $400 at the door.

Accommodations: Offers overnight accommodations at Hyatt, $109 per night.

Additional Information: Academy class participants must bring screenplays to read and discuss. Accepts inquiries. Contact by mail, e-mail, phone, fax. Editors, agents, producers attend conference. Further guidelines available on website.

BIG BEAR WRITER'S RETREAT, P.O. Box 1441, Big Bear Lake CA 92315-1441. (909)585-0059. Fax: (909)266-0710. E-mail: duffen@aol.com. **Contact:** Mike Foley, director. Estab. 1995. Biannual. Conference held May, October 2004. Conference duration: 3 days. Average attendance: 15-25. Themes for 2003 included Finding New Creativity, Character and Setting, Avoiding Common Errors, Character Depth, Embracing Yourself as a Writer. Site: "A small, intimate lodge in Big Bear, San Bernardino mountains of Southern California." Retreat is hosted annually by Mike Foley, editor, *Dream Merchant Magazine*, and Tom Foley, Ph.D., artistic psychologist.

Costs: $499, includes meals and lodging.

Accommodations: Offers overnight accommodations. On-site facilites included in retreat fee.

Additional Information: Prior to arrival, submit a fiction or nonfiction sample, 10 double-spaced pages maximum. Conference information is available March 2004. For brochure send SASE, e-mail, call or fax. Accepts inquiries by SASE, e-mail, phone and fax. Editors participate in conference. "This is unlike the standard writer's conference. Participants will live as writers for a weekend. Retreat includes workshop sessions, open writing time and private counseling with retreat hosts. A weekend of focused writing, fun and friendship. This is a small group retreat, known for its individual attention to writers, intimate setting and strong bonding among participants."

BLACK RIDGE SUMMER WRITING CONFERENCE, English Dept./Southern Utah University, Cedar City UT 84720. (435)865-8088. Fax: (435)865-8169. E-mail: cook@suu.edu or english@suu.edu. **Contact:** Kay Cook, chair. Estab. 2003. Annual. Conference held July 2004. Conference duration: 5 days. Average attendance: 40. The conference provides workshop discussion in four areas: fiction, poetry, drama, and creative nonfiction. "Our purpose is two-fold: 1. to provide instruction in writing each genre; 2. to provide instruction in the teaching of the writing of each genre." Site: The facility is the Hunter Conference Center, located on the campus of Southern Utah University and built specifically for hosting various conferences. 2003 format. "Our fiction writer, Brady Udall, will discuss both the teaching and writing of short fiction and the novel. He will provide both workshop and seminar discussions." 2003 staff: Brady Udall, fiction; Aden Ross, drama; Scott Thybony, nonfiction; and Barbara Anderson, poetry. Each will also do a guest reading.

Costs: $200. Meals, etc. are not included in the fee.

Additional Information: Brochures available by phone, e-mail, or on the website.

JAMES BONNET'S STORYMAKING: THE MASTER CLASS, P.O. Box 841, Burbank CA 91503-0841. (818)567-0521. Fax: (818)567-0038. E-mail: bonnet@storymaking.com. Website: www.storymaking.com. **Contact:** James Bonnet. Estab. 1990. Conference held February, May, July 2004. Conference duration: 2 days. Average attendance: 40. Conferences focus on fiction, mystery and screenwriting. Site: 2003 seminars were held at the Hilton Resort, Palm Springs, CA (September) and Los Angeles (November). Panels for next conference include High Concept, Anatomy of a Great Idea, The Creative Process, Metaphor, The Hook, The Fundamentals of Plot, Structure, Genre, Character, Complications, Crisis, Climax, Conflict, Suspense and more. James Bonnet (author) is the scheduled speaker.

Costs: $300 per weekend.

Accommodations: Provides a list of area hotels or lodging options.

Additional Information: For brochure send SASE, e-mail, visit website, call or fax. Accepts inquiries by SASE, e-mail, phone and fax. "James Bonnet, author of *Stealing Fire From the Gods*, teaches a story structure and storymaking seminar that guides writers from inspiration to final draft."

◎ **BOUCHERON**, 507 S. 8th Street, Philadelphia PA 19147. Website: www.bconvegas2003.org. Conference held October 16-19, 2003. The Boucheron is "the world mystery and detective fiction event." Site: Riviera Hotel, Las Vegas, NV. Speakers and panelists include James Lee Burke, Ian Rankin, Ruth Rendall, S.J. Rozan.

Costs: $175 registration fee covers writing workshops, panels, reception, etc.

Accommodations: "The Riviera Hotel convention rate will be $115 per night. No reservations will be accepted until late October 2002."

Additional Information: Sponsors Anthony Award for published mystery novel; ballots due prior to conference. Information available on website.

◎ **BYU WRITING FOR YOUNG READERS WORKSHOP**, 348 HCEB, Brigham Young University, Provo UT 84602. (801)378-2568. Website: http://wfyr.byu.edu. **Contact:** Susan Overstreet. Estab. 2000. Annual. Workshop

held June 28-July 2, 2004. Average attendance: 100. Conference focuses on "all genres for children and teens." Site: Brigham Young University's Harmon Conference Center. 2002 faculty included Eve Bunting, Tony Johnston, Tim Wynne-Jones, John H. Ritter, Alane Ferguson, Lael Little, Laura Torres, Cloria Skurzynski and Cludia Mills.
Costs: $399 conference fee and closing banquet.
Accommodations: Provides list of area hotels.
Additional Information: Brochures available in March by phone and on website. Accepts inquiries by SASE, e-mail, phone. Agents and editors participate in conference.

CANYONLANDS DESERT WRITER'S WORKSHOP, P.O. Box 68, Moab UT 84532. (435)259-7750. Fax: (435)259-2335. E-mail: cfiinfo@canyonlandsfieldinst.org. Website: www.canyonlandsfieldinst.org. **Contact:** Office Manager. Estab. 1986. Annual. Conference held fall 2004. Conference duration: 5 days. Average attendance: 16-20. Conference focuses on sense of place, nature-related writing, as well as formal general writing skills and instruction. Genre emphasis each year depends on expertise of guest faculty. Site: Varies depending on guest faculty. Speakers include Ellen Maloy and Sandra Alcosser.
Costs: $440/person ($425/CFI member). A deposit of $200 is required to reserve your place.
Additional Information: Send 3-5 typed pages (double spaced) 4-5 weeks in advance, so faculty can become familiar with participants work.

CANYONLANDS WRITERS RIVER TRIP AND WORKSHOP, P.O. Box 68, Moab UT 84532. (435)259-7750. Fax: (435)259-2335. E-mail: cfiinfo@canyonlandsfieldinst.org. Website: www.canyonlandsfieldinst.org. **Contact:** Office Manager. Estab. 1998. Annual. Conference held Spring-Summer 2004. Conference duration: 5 days. Average attendance: 8-16. "Enjoy four days of instruction and critique as well as private time to do some of your own writing down Westwater Canyon of the Colorado River. You'll also learn about the fascinating geology, ecology, and history of this beautiful canyon and run both mild and exciting rapids (class I-III riverstretch)." Site: "This workshop/river trip begins with an evening motel stay and introductory seminar in Grand Junction, CO. Our five-day, four-night river trip follows." Past faculty: Scott Russell Sanders, Alison Hewthrone Deming.
Costs: See website for current information.
Additional Information: Brochures available, send SASE, e-mail, visit website, call or fax. Accepts inquiries by SASE, e-mail, phone and fax.

DESERT WRITERS WORKSHOP/CANYONLANDS FIELD INSTITUTE, P.O. Box 68, Moab UT 84532. (435)259-7750. Fax: (435)259-2335. E-mail: cfiinfo@canyonlandsfieldinst.org. Website: www.canyonlandsfieldinst.org. **Contact:** Office Manager. Estab. 1984. Annual. Held in October. Conference duration: 5 days. Average attendance: 30. Concentrations include fiction, nonfiction, poetry. Site: A ranch near Moab, Utah. "Theme is oriented toward understanding the vital connection between the national world and human communities." Faculty panel has included in past years Ann Zwinger, Pam Houston, Linda Hogan, Christopher Merrill, Terry Tempest Williams and Richard Shelton.
Costs: See website for current information.
Accommodations: At a guest ranch, included in cost.
Additional Information: Brochures are available for SASE. Accepts inquiries by phone, fax, e-mail. "Participants may submit work in advance, but it is not required. Student readings, evaluations and consultations with guest instructors/faculty are part of the workshop. Desert Writers Workshop is supported in part by grants from the Utah Arts Council and National Endowment for the Arts. A partial scholarship is available. College credit is also available for an additional fee."

◎ **IWWG EARLY SPRING IN CALIFORNIA CONFERENCE**, International Women's Writing Guild, P.O. Box 810, Gracie Station NY 10028-0082. (212)737-7536. Fax: (212)737-7536. E-mail: iwwg@iwwg.com. Website: www.IWWG.com. **Contact:** Hannelore Hahn, executive editor. Estab. 1982. Annual. Conference held second week in March. Average attendance: 80. Conference to promote "creative writing, personal growth and empowerment." Site: Bosch Bahai School, a redwood forest mountain retreat in Santa Cruz, CA.
Costs: $345 for weekend program with room and board ($325 for members); $90 per day for commuters ($80 for members); $170 for weekend program withour room and board ($150 for members).
Accommodations: Accommodations are all at conference site.
Additional Information: Conference information is available after August. For brochures/guidelines, send SASE. Accepts inquiries by e-mail, fax.

Ⓝ **KAUAI WRITERS CONFERENCE**, 4265 Marina City Dr. #301 WTN, Marina Del Rey CA 90292. (310)497-8547. E-mail: graubout@earthlink.net. Website: writer2author.com. **Contact:** Michael Levin, organizer. Estab. 2000. Annual. January 2004. Conference duration: up to 5 days. Average attendance: 30. Workshop. Purpose of conference is to teach writing and selling fiction. Site: Held at hotel. Faculty has included Donald Spato, Lew Hunter, Harry Medved.
Costs: $595.
Accommodations: Offers overnight accommodations and list of area hotels.

Additional Information: Brochures available in November on website. Accepts inquiries by SASE, e-mail, phone and fax.

LA JOLLA WRITERS CONFERENCE, P.O. Box 178122, San Diego CA 92177. (858)467-1978. Fax: (858)467-1971. E-mail: akurtz@lajollawritersconference.com. Website: www.lajollawritersconference.com. **Contact:** Antoinette Kurtz, founder. Estab. 2001. Annual. Conference held October 22-24, 2004. Conference duration: 3 days. Average attendance: 175-200. "With seminars in both fiction and nonfiction, the La Jolla Writers Conference focuses on the art, craft and business of writing. We hope to engender a sense of community, encourage self-confidence, and inspire new levels of creativity in our attendees." Site: The Hilton Resort on Mission Bay in San Diego is an extremely ambiant setting. Located in the park surrounding Mission Bay, the hotel benefits from the walking, biking and jogging paths as well as access to the Bay for boating and watersports. Speakers for 2004; Tess Gerritsen, Denise Hamilton, Michael Connelly, and many more.
Costs: $295, includes 2 meals. Double rooms approximately $150 per night with conference discount. Less expensive hotels nearby.
Additional Information: For individual read & critiques, send 10 double-spaced pages one month prior to conference.

LEAGUE OF UTAH WRITERS ROUND-UP, 4621 W. Harman Drive, W.V.C. UT 84120-3752. (801)964-0861. E-mail: crofts@numucom.com. Website: www.luwrite.com. **Contact:** Dorothy Crofts, membership chairman. Estab. 1935. Annual. Conference held every September. Conference duration: 2 days, Friday and Saturday. Average attendance: 200. "The purpose of the conference is to award the winners of our annual contest as well as offer instruction in all areas of writing. Speakers cover subjects from generating ideas to writing a novel to working with a publisher. We have something for everyone." Site: Conference held at hotel conference rooms and ballroom facilities. 2003 themes included: Essays, Mystery, Writing for Magazines. 2003 speakers included Cowboy poet Stan Tixter; poet Joel Long; publisher Duane Crowther; agent Cricket Pechsein; Lynne Finney; Shirley Kawa-Jump; editor Adam C. Olsen; Anita Stansfield (romantic/fiction); Kathleen Dalton Woodbury (fantasy/fiction); Sherry Lewis (romance/mystery); essayist Pam Williams; Carolyn Cambell (nonfiction novelist).
Costs: 2003 costs: $125 for LUW members ($90 if registered before August 31); $160 for nonmembers (fee includes 4 meals).
Accommodations: Crowne Plaza, Ogden-Hotel adjoins Conference Center at 2415 Washington Blvd. List of hotel/motel accommodations available. Special hotel rate for conference attendees $59. Register 1-800-2Crowne.
Additional Information: Opportunity for writers to meet one-on-one with literary agents from New York. Sponsors contests for 8 fiction categories, 3 open to nonmembers of League. Word limits vary from 1,500 to 90,000. Conference brochures/guidelines available for SASE, e-mail, fax, phone and on website after February 2004. Accepts inquiries by fax, e-mail, SASE.

MAUI WRITERS CONFERENCE AND RETREAT, Box 1118, Kihei HI 96753. (808)879-0061. Fax: (808)879-6233. E-mail: writers@maui.net. Website: http://mauiwriters.com. Estab. 1992. Annual. Conference held Labor Day weekend, August 28-September 1, 2003. Retreat held August 22-27, 2003. Average attendance: 1,200 conference; 200 retreat. Conference covers fiction, nonfiction, screenwriting, playwriting, children's books. Site: Wailea Marriot Resort, "Four Diamond Resort on beach in Maui, Hawaii." "Dozens of speakers, panels and workshops cover all aspects of writing and publishing fiction." Speakers from 2003 conference include Tami Hoag, Tess Gerritsen, Ben Bova, Diane Mott Davidson, John Saul, Elizabeth George, Dorothy Allison, Terry Brooks.
Costs: 2003 conference was $495-695, depending when you sign up; 2003 retreat was $975-1,075 also depending when you sign up.
Accommodations: Offers "heavily discounted rates at Wailea Marriot Resort and Maui area condos."
Additional Information: Sponsors a contest. Submit 12 pages of fiction. Judged by NY Times bestselling authors. Over $4,000 in cash prizes available. Must be attendee to participate. Guidelines/brochure available throughout the year. Send a request by letter, e-mail, fax or visit website. Accepts inquiries by phone, fax, e-mail or mail. "More than 50 agents and editors attend conference."

MENDOCINO COAST WRITERS CONFERENCE, College of the Redwoods, 1211 Del Mar Drive, Fort Bragg CA 95437. (707)961-1255. Fax: (707)961-1255. E-mail: stephengarber@earthlink.net. Website: http://mcwc. org. **Contact:** Stephen Garber, registrar. Estab. 1989. Annual. Next conference held June 3-5, 2004. Average attendance: 90. "We hope to encourage the developing writer by inviting presenters who are both fine writers and excellent teachers." Site: College of the Redwoods is a small community college located on the gorgeous northern California coast. Focuses are fiction, poetry, creative nonfiction—special areas have included children's (2003), mystery (2002), social awareness. In 2003 faculty included Carolyn See, Paula Gunn Allen, Robert McDowell, Alison Luterman, Shirley Anne Costigan, Larry Baker, Joelle Fraser, Kathy Dawson (Putnam), Nicole Geiger (Tricycle Press of Ten Speed).
Costs: Before April 20, 2004: $295 (2 days); $350 (3 days). After April 20, 2004: $350 (2 days); $400 (3 days)
Additional Information: Brochures for the the 2004 conference will be available in January by SASE, phone, e-mail, or on the website. Agents and editors participate in the conference. "The conference is small, friendly and fills up fast with many returnees."

◎ **MORMON WRITERS' CONFERENCE**, c/o AML, P.O. Box 51364, Provo UT 84605-1364. (801)579-8330. E-mail: dmichael@wwno.com. Website: www.aml-online.org. **Contact:** D. Michael Martindale, conference chair. Estab. 1999. Annual. Conference held November. Conference duration: one day, usually first Saturday of the month. Average attendance: 150. The conference will cover anything to do with writing by, for, or about Mormons, including fiction, nonfiction, theater, film, children's literature. Site: Thanksgiving Point, Lehi, UT. "Plenary speeches, panels and instructional presentations by prominent authors and artists in the LDS artistic community."
Costs: $50 including catered lunch with pre-registration. AML member and student discounts available.
Additional Information: For brochures/guidelines send SASE, e-mail, visit website. Accepts inquiries by SASE, e-mail.

◎ **MOUNT HERMON CHRISTIAN WRITERS CONFERENCE**, P.O. Box 413, Mount Hermon CA 95041-0413. (831)335-4466. Fax: (831)335-9413. E-mail: info@mhcamps.org. Website: www.mounthermon.org. **Contact:** David R. Talbott, director of adult ministries. Estab. 1970. Annual. Conferences held April 2-6, 2004 and March 18-22, 2005. Average attendance: 450. "We are a broad-ranging conference for all areas of Christian writing, including fiction, children's, poetry, nonfiction, magazines, books, educational curriculum and radio and TV script-writing. This is a working, how-to conference, with many workshops within the conference involving on-site writing assignments." Site: "The conference is sponsored by and held at the 440-acre Mount Hermon Christian Conference Center near San Jose, California, in the heart of the coastal redwoods. Registrants stay in hotel-style accommodations, and full board is provided as part of the conference fees. Meals are taken family style, with faculty joining registrants. The faculty/student ratio is about 1:6 or 7. The bulk of our faculty are editors and publisher representatives from major Christian publishing houses nationwide."
Costs: Registration fees include tution, conference sessions, resource notebook, refreshment breaks, room and board and vary from $635 (economy) to $940 (deluxe), double occupancy (2003 rates).
Accommodations: Airport shuttles are available from the San Jose International Airport. Housing is not requried of registrants, but about 95% of our registrants use Mount Hermon's own housing facilites (hotel-style double-occupancy rooms). Meals with the conference are required and are included in all fees.
Additional Information: Registrants may submit 2 works for critique in advance of the conference. No advance work is required, however. Conference brochures/guidelines are available in December by calling (888)MH-CAMPS. Accepts inquiries by e-mail, fax. "The residential nature of our conference makes this a unique setting for one-on-one interaction with faculty/staff. There is also a decided inspiration flavor to the conference, and general sessions with well-known speakers are a highlight." Brochures/registration forms available in December annually on website, by e-mail, fax or phone.

PIMA WRITERS' WORKSHOP, Pima Community College, 2202 W. Anklam Road, Tucson AZ 85709-0170. (520)206-6084. Fax: (520)206-6020. E-mail: mfiles@pimacc.pima.edu. **Contact:** Meg Files, director. Estab. 1988. Annual. Conference held in May. In 2003, May 23-25. Average attendance: 200. "For anyone interested in writing beginning or experienced writer. The workshop offers sessions on writing short stories, novels, nonfiction articles and books, children's and juvenile stories, poetry, screenplays." Site: Sessions are held in the Center for the Arts on Pima Community College's West campus. Past speakers include Michael Blake, Ron Carlson, Gregg Levoy, Nancy Mairs, Linda McCarriston, Jerome Stern, Connie Willis, Larry McMurtry, Barbara Kingsolver and Robert Morgan.
Costs: $65 (can include ms critique). Participants may attend for college credit, in which case fees are $87 for Arizona residents and $315 for out-of-state residents. Meals and accommodations not included.
Accommodations: Information on local accommodations is made available and special workshop rates are available at a specified motel close to the workshop site (about $70/night).
Additional Information: Participants may have up to 20 pages critiqued by the author of their choice. Manuscripts must be submitted 3 weeks before the workshop. Conference brochure/guidelines available for SASE. Accepts inquiries by e-mail. "The workshop atmosphere is casual, friendly, and supportive, and guest authors are very accessible. Readings, films and panel discussions are offered as well as talks and manuscript sessions."

SAN DIEGO STATE UNIVERSITY WRITERS' CONFERENCE, SDSU College of Extended Studies, 5250 Campanile Drive, San Diego CA 92182-1920. (619)594-2517. Website: www.ces.sdsu.edu. **Contact:** Kevin Carter, coordinator. Estab. 1984. Annual. Conference held on 3rd weekend in January. Conference duration: 2 days. Average attendance: 375. "This conference is held in San Diego, California, at the Doubletree Hotel, Mission Valley. Each year the SDSU Writers Conference offers a variety of workshops for the beginner and the advanced writer. This conference allows the individual writer to choose which workshop best suits his/her needs. In addition to the workshops, editor/agent appointments and office hours are provided so attendees may meet with speakers, editors and agents in small, personal groups to discuss specific questions. A reception is offered Saturday immediately following the workshops where attendees may socialize with the faculty in a relaxed atmosphere. Keynote speaker is to be determined."
Costs: Approximately $295 (2003). This includes all conference workshops and office hours, coffee and pastries in the morning, lunch and reception Saturday evening. Editor/agent appointment extra fee.
Accommodations: Doubletree, Mission Valley, (800)222-TREE. Conference rate available for SDSU Writers Conference attendees. Attendees must make their own travel arrangements.

Additional Information: Editor/Agent sessions are private, one-on-one oppurtunities to meet with editors and agents to discuss your submission. For more information fax, call or send a postcard to the above address. No SASE required.

◎ **SANTA BARBARA CHRISTIAN WRITERS CONFERENCE**, P.O. Box 42429, Santa Barbara CA 93140. (805)969-3712. **Contact:** Opal Dailey, director. Estab. 1997. Conference held October 4, 2003. Conference duration: 1 day. Average attendance: 60-70. Site: Westmont College, "liberal arts Christian College. Beautiful campus in the Montecito Foothills at Santa Barbara.
Costs: $59 for 2001. Includes continental breakfast, lunch and afternoon snack.
Additional Information: Conference information available in May. For brochure, send SASE or call. Accepts inquiries by SASE and phone. Agents and editors participate in conference.

◎ **SCBWI/INTERNATIONAL CONFERENCE ON WRITING & ILLUSTRATING FOR CHILDREN**, 8271 Beverly Blvd., Los Angeles CA 90048. (323)782-1010. Fax: (323)782-1892. E-mail: conference@scbwi.org. Website: www.scbwi.org. **Contact:** Lin Oliver, executive director. Estab. 1972. Annual. Conference held in August. Conference duration: 4 days. Average attendance: 800. Writer and illustrator workshops geared toward all levels. Covers all aspects of children's magazine and book publishing.
Costs: Approximately $400; includes all 4 days and one banquet meal. Does not include hotel room.
Accommodations: Information on overnight accommodations made available.
Additional Information: Manuscript and illustration critiques are available. Brochure/guidelines available for SASE or visit website.

Ⓝ **SOUTHERN CALIFORNIA WRITERS' CONFERENCE/L.A., OXNARD**, 1010 University Ave. #54, San Diego CA 92103. (619)233-4651. E-mail: info@writersconference.com. Website: www.writersconference.com. **Contact:** Michael Steven Gregory, executive director. Estab. 2002. Annual. Next conference October 1-3, 2004. Conference duration: 3 days. Average attendance: 250. An interactive trouble-shooting of problematic aspects of conferees' manuscripts. Emphasis on fiction and nonfiction. Lots of read-and-critique workshops in addition to panels, speakers and other sessions. Site: Held at the Radisson Hotel Oxnard, a new, business-oriented faclity where event is held and those who are lodging stay. Spacious, near the freeway, about 45 minutes from LAX. 2004 themes and panels include Fiction Read-and-Critique, First Person Narrative, Point of View, Writing Dialogue that Speaks, The Psychology of Character, Plotting the Mainstream Novel, Rewriting the Novel. 2004 speakers include Drusilla Campbell, Gary Phillips, Glen Hirschberg, Allison Burnett, Jean Jenkins, Alan Russell, Jerry Hannah and Rachel Ballon.
Costs: $275 for full conference, which includes Saturday evening banquet (lodging not included).
Accommodations: Provides a list of area hotels. Conferee discount offered by host hotel. Shuttle service discount available.
Additional Information: Advance critique followed by one-on-one consultation with reader available. Otherwise conferees bring material to read in open critique sessions. Sponsors contest. Judged by conference directors. Brochures available in June for SASE, by phone, e-mail, on website. Accepts inquiries by SASE, e-mail and phone.

SOUTHERN CALIFORNIA WRITERS' CONFERENCE/SAN DIEGO, 1010 University Ave., #54, San Diego CA 92103. (619)233-4651. E-mail: info@writersconference.com. Website: www.writersconference.com. **Contact:** Michael Steven Gregory, executive director. Estab. 1986. Annual. Conference held February 13-16, 2004. Conference duration: 4 days. Average attendance: 250. Conference focuses on facilitating mainstream fiction, nonfiction to market. Emphasis is on reading and critiquing conferees' manuscripts. "We feature interactive troubleshooting of problematic aspects of conferees' manuscripts. Emphasis on fiction and commercial nonfiction. Lots of read-and-critique workshops, panels, speakers and other sessions." Site: Shelter Pointe Hotel, located on Shelter Island near San Diego's Lindbergh Field, across the bay from downtown. 2003 themes and panels include Fiction Read-and-Critique, Mining Your Life Story For Gold, Novel Pitch: 25 Words or Less, Where Should My Novel Begin?, Creating Useful Atmosphere, Turning Your Life into Fiction, Hook 'Em and Keep 'Em Hooked, and more. Speakers will include T. Greenwood, Raymond Strait, Mark Clements, B. Abell Jurys, Glen Hirschberg, Drusilla Campbell, Anne Wilson, Penny Kramer, Bob Mayer, Mike Sirota, Carolyn Wheet.
Costs: $325 which includes all workshops and events, including Saturday evening's banquet. Day rates available.
Accommodations: Hotel lodging discount available to conferees. Shuttle service to San Diego airport. Approximately $118-130/night.
Additional Information: Sponsors contest. A 250-word "Topic" competition is announced the opening day of conference. Advance submission critiques are also available, followed by one-on-one consultation. Conference information is available in September. For brochure send e-mail, visit website, call or fax. Accepts inquiries by SASE, e-mail, phone and fax. Agents and editors participate in conference.

SQUAW VALLEY COMMUNITY OF WRITERS WORKSHOP, P.O. Box 1416, Nevada City CA 95959-1416. (530)274-8551. Fax: (530)274-0986. E-mail: sxcw@oro.net. Website: www.squawvalleywriters.org. **Contact:** Brett Hall Jones, executive director. Estab. 1969. Annual. Conference held in August. Conference duration: 7 days. Average attendance: 120. "The Fiction Workshop assists talented writers by exploring the art and craft as well as the business of writing." Offerings include daily morning workshops led by writer-teachers, editors or agents of the staff, limited to 12-13 participants; seminars; panel discussions of editing and publishing; craft colloquies; lectures; and staff readings. Past themes and panels included "Personal History in Fiction," "Narrative Structure," "Roots" and "Anatomy of a Short Story." Past faculty and speakers included Michael Chabon, Mark Childress, Janet Finch, Richard Ford, Karen Joy Fowler, Lynn Freed, Molly Giles, Sands Hall, James D. Houston, Louis B. Jones, Al Young.

Costs: Tuition is $650, which includes 6 dinners.

Accommodations: The Community of Writers rents houses and condominiums in the Valley for participants to live in during the week of the conference. Single room (one participant): $400/week. Double room (twin beds, room shared by conference participant of the same sex): $285/week. Multiple room (bunk beds, room shared with 2 or more participants of the same sex): $185/week. All room subject to availability; early requests are recommended. Can arrange airport shuttle pick-ups for a fee.

Additional Information: Admissions are based on submitted manuscript (unpublished fiction, a couple of stories or novel chapters); requiries $25 reading fee. Submit ms to Brett Hall Jones, Squaw Valley Community of Writers, P.O. Box 1416, Nevada City, CA 95959. Deadline: May 10. Notification: June 10. Brochure/guidelines available February by phone, e-mail or visit website. Accepts inquiries by SASE, e-mail, phone. Agents and editors attend/participate in conferences.

TMCC WRITERS' CONFERENCE, TMCC Community Services, 5270 Neil Road Rm 216, RTMA 1, Reno NV 89502. (775)829-9010. Fax: (775)829-9032. E-mail: kberry@tmcc.edu or mikedcroft@aol.com. Website: http://commserv.tmcc.edu or www.tmccwriters.com. Estab. 1990. Annual. 2004 conference held March 25-28 for Track A which includes critique workshops; March 27-28 for Track B. Average attendance: 125. Conference focuses on fiction (literary and mainstream), poetry, marketing to agents, publishers. Site: John Ascuaga's Nugget Hotel/Casino Resort facilites include indoor pool, spa, numerous restaurants, celebrity showrooms, casino, sportsbook. "We strive to provide a well-rounded event for fiction writers and poets." Panelists include James N. Frey (how-to writer and mystery novelist); Elizabeth Rosner (literary novelist); and Will Weaver (young adult novelist).

Costs: 4-day Track A $369; 2-day Track B $109 before February 28, $199 after. "Scholarships based on merit and financial need are awarded every December."

Accommodations: Hotel shuttle service from Reno airport available. Overnight accommodations available at site for conference rate of $90/night.

Additional Information: If participating in Track A, attendees should submit first chapter (5,000 words maximum) by January 20. Brochures available November 2003 by e-mail, phone, fax or on website. Accepts inquires by e-mail or phone. Agent will participate in conference. "This conference features an informal, friendly atmosphere where questions are encouraged. A 'Meet the Presenters' session allows for participants to mix with event speakers. No-host lunches with presenters (limited to first 9 sign-ups per lunch) will also be held. The 4-day Track A keeps each critique group small."

UCLA EXTENSION WRITERS' PROGRAM, 10995 Le Conte Avenue, #440, Los Angeles CA 90024-2883. (310)825-9415 or (800)388-UCLA. Fax: (310)206-7382. E-mail: writers@UCLAextension.org. Website: www.ucla extension.org/writers. **Contact:** Linda Venis, program director. Courses held year-round with one-day or intensive weekend workshops to 12-week courses. Writers Studio held February 5-8, 2004. A 9-month Master Class is also offered every fall. "The diverse offerings span introductory seminars to professional novel and script completion workshops. The annual Writers Studio and a number of 1-, 2- and 4-day intensive workshops are popular with out-of-town students due to their specific focus and the chance to work with industry professionals. The most comprehensive and diverse continuing education writing program in the country, offering over 500 courses a year including: screenwriting, fiction, writing for young people, poetry, nonfiction, playwriting, publishing and writing for interactive multimedia. Adult learners in the UCLA Extension Writers' Program study with professional screenwriters, fiction writers, playwrights, poets, nonfiction writers and interactive multimedia writers, who bring practical experience, theoretical knowledge, and a wide variety of teaching styles and philosophies to their classes." Site: Courses are offered in Los Angeles on the UCLA campus and in the 1010 Center in Westwood Village as well as online over the Internet.

Costs: Vary from $90 for one-day workshops to $2,850 for the 9-month master class.

Accommodations: Students make own arrangements. The program can provide assistance in locating local accommodations.

Additional Information: Writers Studio information available October. For brochures/guidelines/guide to course offerings, visit website, e-mail, fax or call. Accepts inquiries by e-mail, fax, phone. "Some advanced level classes have manuscript submittal requirements; instructions are always detailed in the quarterly UCLA Extension course catalog. An annual fiction prize, The James Kirkwood Prize in Creative Writing, has been established and is given annually to one ficion writer who has produced outstanding work in a Writers' Program course."

VOLCANO WRITERS' RETREAT, P.O. Box 163, Volcano CA 95689-0163. (209)296-7945. E-mail: khexberg@volcano.net. Website: www.volcanowritersretreat.com. **Contact:** Karin Hexberg, director. Estab. 1998. Quarterly. Weekend retreats held in January, April, and October. "Summer Camp" held in July/August. Conference duration: Weekend retreats, 3 days; Summer camp, 5 days. Average attendance: 15-20. Retreat for writing "fiction, poetry, essay, memoir." Site: Held at the St. George Hotel. Hotel is 150 years old and located in the most picturesque of all the gold country towns, Volcano.

Costs: 2003 fees: weekend, $293-318 with accomodations, $174 without; summer camp, $445-576 with accomodations, $225 without.

Accommodations: Most attendees stay at the site although individuals may make other arrangements.

Additional Information: "Absolutely no critiquing. The purpose of this retreat is to create a non-competitive, non-judgmental, safe atmosphere where we are all free to write the worst stuff in the world." Brochures/guidelines for SASE. Accepts inquiries by e-mail.

⃞N WRITERS STUDIO AT UCLA EXTENTION (formerly Los Angeles Writer's Conference), 1010 Westwood Blvd., Los Angeles CA 90024. (310)825-9415. E-mail: writers@unex.ucla.edu. Website: www.uclaextension.org. **Contact:** Rick Noguchi. Estab. 1997. Annual. Next conference February 6-8, 2004. Conference duration: 2 days. Average attendance: 150-200. Conference on creative writing, fiction, memoir. Site: Located in UCLA Extension classrooms at 1010 Westwood Village Center. Instructors include Susan Taylor Chehak, Hope Edelman, Jerrilyn Farmer, Simon Levy and Leslie Spirson.

Costs: $650 before November 30; $550 after November 30.

Accommodations: Information on overnight accommodations is available.

Additional Information: Conference brochures available in late September.

⃞N THE WRITERS WAY, P.O. Box 9191, San Rafael CA 94912. E-mail: cwcmarin@aol.com. Website: www.marinwriters.com. **Contact:** Conference Chair. Estab. 2002. Annual. Next conference October 2004. Conference duration: one day. Average attendance: 120. Site: Headlands Institute, Marin Headlands, Sausalito, CA, part of Yosemite National Institute on the Pacific Ocean, close to the Golden Gate Bridge. Beautiful setting, good food. Themes and panels include fiction, memoir, creative nonfiction. 2003 speakers included Sheldon Siegel, attorney Bob Pimm, D.P. Lyle, M.D., Jessica Barksdale Inclas and Rhys Bowen. 2004 conference will include a keynote speaker, choice of 4 workshops 3 times a day, an agents-and-editors panel.

Costs: $85 early bird, $120 at the door based on space. Non-CWC member, $140.

Accommodations: Provides list of area hotels.

Additional Information: Sponsors contest for previously unpublished work. Brochures available in June 2004 by SASE, fax, phone, e-mail, on website. Accepts inquires by SASE, e-mail, phone, fax.

◎ WRITING FOR YOUNG READERS WORKSHOP, 348 HCEB, BYU, Provo UT 84602-1532. (801)378-2568. Fax: (801)422-0745. E-mail: susan.overstreet@byu.edu. Website: http://wfyr.byu.edu. **Contact:** Susan Overstreet. Estab. 2000. Annual. Workshop held July of each year. Average attendance: limited to 125. Workshop focuses on fiction for young readers: picture books, book-length fiction, illustration and general writing. "Mornings are spent in small group workshop sessions with published author." Site: Conference Center at Brigham Young University in the foothills of the Wasatch Mountain range. Previous faculty have included Eve Bunting, Lael Littke, Claudia Mills, Tim Wynne-Jones and Alane Ferguson.

Costs: $399, includes final banquet.

Accommodations: Local lodging, airport shuttle. Lodging rates: $55-85/night.

Additional Information: Participants must bring at least one manuscript in progress to the workshop. Conference information is available April of each year. For brochure visit website, call or fax. Accepts inquiries by e-mail, phone and fax. Editors particpate in conference.

YOSEMITE WINTER LITERARY CONFERENCE, P.O. Box 230, El Portal CA 95318. (209)379-2646. Fax: (209)379-2486. E-mail: info@yosemite.org. Website: www.yosemite.org. **Contact:** Beth Pratt, vice president. Estab. 2001. Annual. Conference held annually in February. Average attendance: 100. "Through workshops, panel discussions, readings and informal sessions, participants will debate and explore the literary landscape of California, the Sierra Nevada and the American West with a distinguished group of writers, publishers, artists, photographers and scientists." Site: Ahwahnee Hotel in Yosemite National Park. 2002 panels included Workpoints, Fiction Workshops, American Indian Storytelling, Inside the Writer's Studio, Writing from Life, A Writer's Sense of Place. 2002 faculty included Francisco Alarcon, Karen Joy Fowler, Gerald Haslam, Jane Hirschfield, Pam Houston, Maxine Hong Kingston, Malcom Margolin, David Max Masumoto, Louis Owens, Al Young.

Costs: In 2002, $535 fee included opening reception, dinner banquet, park entrance fee.

Accommodations: No arrangements for transportation. Offers overnight lodging at the Ahwahnee Hotel or Yosemite Lodge.

Additional Information: Brochure available in Fall of prior year by e-mail, phone, fax or on website. Accepts inquiries by e-mail, phone, fax. Editors participate in conference.

Northwest (AK, ID, MT, OR, WA, WY)

CENTRUMS 31st PORT TOWNSEND WRITERS' CONFERENCE, Box 1158, Port Townsend WA 98368-0958. (360)385-3102. Fax: (360)385-2470. E-mail: info@centrum.org. Website: www.centrum.org. **Contact:** Sam

Hamill. Estab. 1974. Annual. Conference held mid-July. Average attendance: 180. Conference to promote poetry, fiction, creative nonfiction "featuring many of the nation's leading writers." Site: The conference is held at a seaside 700-acre state park on the Strait of Juan de Fuca. "The site is a Victorian-era military fort with miles of beaches, wooded trails and recreation facilities. The park is within the limits of Port Townsend, a historic seaport and arts community, approximately 80 miles northwest of Seattle, on the Olympic Peninsula." Guest speakers participate in addition to 10 fulltime faculty.

Costs: Approximately $395-495 tuition and $205-435 room and board.

Accommodations: "Modest room and board facilities on site." Also list of hotels/motels/inns/bed & breakfasts/private rentals available.

Additional Information: Brochures/guidelines available for SASE or on website. "The conference focus is on the craft of writing and the writing life, not on marketing."

CLARION WEST WRITERS' WORKSHOP, 340 15th Avenue E, Suite 350, Seattle WA 98112-5156. (206)322-9083. E-mail: info@clarionwest.org. Website: www.clarionwest.org. **Contact:** Leslie Howle, administrator. Estab. 1983. Annual. Workshop held June 20-July 30, 2004. Average attendance: 17. "Conference to prepare students for professional careers in science fiction and fantasy writing." Deadline for applications: April 1. Site: "Conference held in Seattle's University district, an urban site close to restaurants and cafes, but not too far from downtown." Faculty: 6 teachers (professional writers and editors established in the field). "Every week a new instructoreach a well-known writer chosen for the quality of his or her work and for professional statureteaches the class, bringing a unique perspective on speculative fiction. During the fifth week, the workshop is taught by a professional editor."

Costs: Workshop tuition: $1,400 ($100 discount if application received by March 1). Dormitory housing: $1,000, some meals included.

Accommodations: Students are strongly encouraged to stay on-site, in workshop housing at one of the University of Washington's sorority houses. Cost: $1,000, some meals included, for 6-week stay.

Additional Information: "Students write their own stories every week while preparing critiques of all the other students' work for classroom sessions. This gives participants a more focused, professional approach to their writing. The core of the workshop remains science fiction, and short stories, not novels, are the focus." Conference information available in fall 2003. For brochure/guidelines send SASE, visit website, e-mail or call. Accepts inquiries by e-mail, phone, SASE. Limited scholarships are available, based on financial need. Students must submit 20-30 pages of ms with $25 application fee by mail to qualify for admission.

FISHTRAP, P.O. Box 38, Enterprise OR 97828. (503)426-3623. E-mail: rich@fishtrap.org. Website: www.fishtrap.org. **Contact:** Rich Wardschneider, director. Estab. 1988. Winter Fishtrap Conference February 20-22, 2004; Summer workshop/conference July 5-11, 2004 (5 days workshops; 2 days conference). Average attendance: 100-120. Previous faculty has included Yusef Komunyakaa, Alfredo Vea, Andrew X. Pham, songwriter Laurie Lewis, publisher Michael Wiegers (Copper Canyon).

Costs: Winter $270-400, with meals depending on lodging. Summer, 5-day, 15-hour workshop, $290; conference $160 with meals. Food and lodging $35/day; food only, $25/day.

Accommodations: Offers overnight accommodations (see above). Also provides list of area hotels. (Nearby motels $60-100/night).

Additional Information: Five fellowships given annually. Submit 8 pages of poetry or 2,500 words of prose (no name on ms) by February 7. Entries judged by a workshop instructor. Awards announced March 15. Conference information available November 2003 (for February conference) and March 2004 (for July conference). For brochures/guidelines send SASE, e-mail, visit website or call. Accepts inquiries by SASE, e-mail, phone. Agents and editors occasionally participate in conference. "Fishtrap Gatherings are about writing and the West. They are about ideas more than mechanics and logistics of writing/publishing. Workshops are not manuscript reviews, but writing sessions."

FLATHEAD RIVER WRITERS CONFERENCE, P.O. Box 7711, Kalispell MT 59904. E-mail: hows@centurytel.net. Estab. 1990. Annual. Next conference: October 8-10, 2004. Conference duration: 3 days. Average attendance: 100. Deals with all aspects of writing, including short and long fiction and nonfiction. Site: Grouse Mountain Lodge in Whitefish, MT. 2003 speakers: Donald Maass (fiction), Kent Carrol (fiction editor).

Costs: $135 general weekend conference; includes breakfast and lunch, not lodging. $435 3-day workshop and general conference.

Accommodations: Lodging at Grouse Mountain Lodge. Approximately ½ off discount (around $100 a night).

Additional Information: "We limit attendance to 100 in order to assure friendly, easy access to presentations."

THE GLEN WORKSHOP, *Image*, 3307 Third Avenue W, Seattle WA 98119. (206)281-2988. Fax: (206)281-2335. E-mail: glenworkshop@imagejournal.org. Website: www.imagejournal.org. Estab. 1991. Annual. Workshop held in August. Conference duration: 1 week. Average attendance: 100-140. Workshop focuses on "fiction, poetry and spiritual writing, essay, memoir. Run by *Image*, a literary journal with a religious focus. The Glen welcomes writers who practice or grapple with religious faith." Site: 2003 conference held in Santa Fe, NM and featured "presentations and readings by the faculty." 2003 faculty included Robert Clark (fiction); Lauren F. Winner (spiritual writing); Julia Kasdorf; Mark Jarman.

Costs: $500-800, including room and board; $300-375 for commuters (lunch only).

Accommodations: Arrange transportation by shuttle. Accommodations included in conference cost.

Additional Information: Prior to arrival, participants may need to submit workshop material depending on the teacher. "Usually 10-25 pages." Conference information is available in February. For brochure send SASE, e-mail, visit website, call or fax. "Like *Image*, the Glen is grounded in a Christian perspective, but its tone is informal and hospitable to all spiritual wayfarers."

HAYSTACK WRITING PROGRAM, P.O. Box 1491, Portland OR 97207-1491. (503)725-4186. Fax: (503)725-4840. E-mail: snydere@pdx.edu. Website: www.haystack.pdx.edu. **Contact:** Elizabeth Snyder, director. Estab. 1968. Annual. Program runs from mid-July through first week of August. Conference duration: varies; one-week and weekend workshops are available throughout the 4-week program. Average attendance: 10-15/workshop; total program 400. Haystack's writing workshops are rich and varied, offering classes in storytelling, dangerous writing, fiction, creating characters, memoir and building narrative, among others. Site: Classes are held at the Cannon Beach Elementary School in Cannon Beach, OR, a small, coastal community. Writing courses include fiction, nonfiction, poetry, essay, and memoir. Past instructors have included David Biespiel, Annie Callan, John Daniel, Michele Glazer, Karen Karbo, Whitney Otto, Sandra Scofield, Tom Spanbauer, Eric Kimmel, Wendy Lamb, Linda Zuckerman.

Costs: Approximately $415/course (week-long); $225 (weekend). Three university credits, $485. Does not include lodging.

Accommodations: Various accommodations available including: B&B, motel, hotel, private rooms, camping, private homes. A list is provided upon registration.

Additional Information: Free brochure available after March. Accepts inquiries by e-mail and fax. University credit (graduate or undergraduate) is available. Classes are held in the local school with supplemental activities at the beach, community lecture hall, galleries and other areas of the resort town.

◎ **HEDGEBROOK**, 2197 E. Millman Road, Langley WA 98260. (360)321-4786. Fax: (360)321-2171. Website: www.hedgebrook.org. Estab. 1988. Six writers are in residence at one time. "Hedgebrook provides writing residencies to women, published or not, of all ages and from diverse backgrounds at its retreat on Whidbey Island in Washington state. Residents are chosen via a selection process and provided with residencies ranging from two weeks to two months." Site: 48-acre retreat; each writer assigned her own cottage. Meals provided.

Costs: No cost.

Additional Information: To request an application, please send a self-addressed, stamped envelope to 2197 E. Millman Road, Langley, WA 98260. Application/brochures also available from website.

IDAHO WRITERS LEAGUE CONFERENCE, 467 N. 3200 E., Lewisville ID 83431-5019. (208)754-4347. E-mail: writejoy@srv.net. Website: www.idahowritersleague.com. **Contact:** Linda Helms, conference chairman. Estab. 1940. Annual. Conference held in September. Usually last weekend in September. Site: Shilo Inn in Idaho Falls. "Chapters take turns hosting the conference and it's moved yearly around the state." Panels include poetry, characterization, selling your fiction, children's literature, writing articles. Speakers included Trudy Harris, children's authors; Robert Kirby, feature writer for *Salt Lake Tribune*; Patti Sherlock, author; Patricia Kempthorne, Idaho's first lady.

Costs: $100 includes 2 continental breakfasts, 2 luncheons, 1 banquet on Saturday night.

Accommodations: Provides list of area lodging.

Additional Information: Sponsors 2 contests; one for work written on a particular theme with various categories in fiction/nonfiction/poetry/children's fiction, and the other contest for the first 30 pages/2 chapters of a novel. Open to Idaho Writer's Leaque members only. Brochures and contest guidelines available July 15 for e-mail and on website. Accepts inquiries by SASE, e-mail, phone. Editors and agents sometimes attend conference.

LOST HORSE WRITERS' CONFERENCE, 105 Lost Horse Lane, Sandpointe ID 83864. (208)255-4410. Fax: (208)255-1560. E-mail: losthorsepress@mindspring.com. Website: www.losthorsepress.org. **Contact:** Christine Holbert, director. Estab. 2000. Annual. Conference held May 2004. Conference duration: 3 days. Average attendance: 60.

Costs: 2003 tuition, $250; lodging, $50; meals, $50. These figures may change in 2004.

Accommodations: Special conference rates at area hotels. On-site dormitory-style lodging available.

N ◎ NATURE WRITERS RETREAT WITH NORTH CASCADES INSTITUTE, North Cascades Institute, 810 Highway 20, Secro-Wooley WA 98284-9394. (360)856-5700 ext. 209. Fax: (360)859-1934. E-mail: nci@ncascades.org. Website: www.ncascades.org. **Contact:** Deb Martin, registrar. Estab. 1999. Annual. 2003 conference held October 28-31. Conference duration: 4 days. Average attendance: 32. Led by three outstanding authors and poets, the NCI Nature Writing Retreat engages amateur and professional writers alike—lectures, discussions, readings and writing exercises centered on the natural world. "Nature writing, at its simplest, strives to explore basic principles at work in nature, and to convey these in language that introduces readers to the facility and wonder of their own place in the world." Site: The 2003 conference was held at Sun Mountain Lodge, one of Washington's premier resorts. Perched atop 2,000 acres of rolling hills, the lodge is surrounded by breathtaking views of the

North Cascades and the Methow Valley. Its accommodations include elegant mountain-top rooms, world-class cuisine, outdoor pools and hot tubs. Previous faculty has included Tim McNulty and Barbara Kingsolver.

Costs: 2003 costs were $525 (triple occupancy), $595 (double), $675 (single). Included lodging and lunches.

Additional Information: Conference information is available in February. For brochure send e-mail, visit website or call. Accepts inquiries by e-mail and phone. Editors participate in conference.

NORTHWEST BOOKFEST, P.O. Box 28129, Seattle WA 98118. (206)378-1883. Fax: (206)378-1882. E-mail: info@nwbookfest.org. Website: www.nwbookfest.org. **Contact:** Eleanor Mason, executive director. Estab. 1994. Annual. Conference held October 18-19, 2003. Conference duration: 2 days, Saturday and Sunday. Average attendance: 25,000. "Northwest Bookfest is a literary festival for a region that's passionate about the written word. Over 200 local and national authors, 200 book and literacy-related exhibitors and literary activities for the entire family. All genres are represented." Site: Sand Point Magnuson Park. "We'll have over 20 fiction-related panels to be defined by volunteers and staff as authors are invited to attend."

Costs: "Bookfest is free to the public, with a $5 suggested donation, which is used to fund grants to literacy organizations throughout the region."

Accommodations: Volunteer-provided transportation is available. Provides list of area hotels/lodging options. "There are Bookfest rates offered at many area hotels."

Additional Information: "Interested authors should send books or other publicity information to Eleanor Mason, executive director, at above address." Brochures available by e-mail, phone, fax and on website in early fall, after authors are confirmed. Accepts inquiries by e-mail, phone and fax. Agents and editors attend/participate in conference.

PACIFIC NORTHWEST WRITERS CONFERENCE, P.O. Box 2016, Edmonds WA 98020-9516. (425)673-2665. Fax: (425)771-9588. E-mail: pnwa@pnwa.org. Website: www.pnwa.org. **Contact:** Sue Palmason, association executive. Annual. Conference held July 24-27, 2003. Average attendance: 300. Site: "Newly renovated, technologically advanced hotel and conference center, located near SeaTac Airport." 2002 panel included Publishing 101; Opening Lines That Grab; "And the winner is . . .": The Inside Scoop on Literary Contests; Make a Long Story Short; How to Craft an Effective Short Story; other panels on genre writing, publishing, screenwriting, creativity. Critique workshops available for additional fee. Workshops include mainstream fiction, romance, mystery, science fiction/fantasy, screenwriting. 2002 panelists included Sheree Bykofsky, agent; Kimberly Cameron, agent; Donald Maas, agent; Cynthia Black, editor at Beyond Words Publishing; Maggie Crawford, editor at Pocket Books; Jennifer Heddle, editor at Penguin Putnam's New American Library; Jill Schoolman, editor at Seven Stories Press; Jean Auel, author; Chris Vogler, author; Janice Johnson, author; Carol Orlock, author; Eric Witchey, author.

Costs: Members, $400; nonmembers $450. Some meals included. Additional fee for critique workshops.

Accommodations: Hotel shuttle to and from airport available. Offers discounted rate for overnight lodging; $124/ night in 2003.

Additional Information: Participants in critique workshops must submit 5 pages of current work-in-progress plus a 2-page synopsis, with completed registration form and workshop fee. Offers contest with 8 fiction categories: The Stella Cameron Romance Genre Contest, screenwriting, adult genre novel, adult non-genre novel, juvenile/YA novel, adult short story, juvenile short story/picture book. Entry requirements vary with category. Guidelines for contest available late fall 2003; brochure for conference available winter 2003. E-mail, call, fax or visit website for brochure/guidelines. Accepts inquiries by e-mail, phone, fax. Agents and editors participate in conference.

SAGEBRUSH WRITERS WORKSHOP, P.O. Box 1255, Big Timber MT 59011-1255. (406)932-4227. E-mail: sagebrsh@ttc-cmc.net. **Contact:** Gwen Petersen, director. Estab. 1997. Annual. Workshop held April 16-17, 2004. Conference duration: 1½ days. Average attendance: 25-30. "Each year, the workshop has a different focus. For 2002, romantic suspense." Conference features "intensive personal instruction, good food, advance critiques, well published authors/instructors, agents/editors, book sales and signings, readings." Site: Crazy Mountain Museum, Big Timber, MT. Faculty consist of one writer/instructor and 2 guest speakers.

Costs: $190, includes Saturday evening banquet dinner, Sunday lunch, all snack breaks.

Accommodations: Offers shuttle from airport by arrangement with Sagebrush. Provides a list of area hotels and/ or lodging options.

Additional Information: "Submissions optional but encouraged—up to 15 pages." Workshop information is available January. For brochure send SASE, e-mail, call or fax. Accepts inquiries by SASE, e-mail, phone and fax. Agents and editors participate in conference.

CAN'T FIND A CONFERENCE? Conferences are listed by region. Check the introduction to this section for a list of regional categories. Want to attend a conference during a certain month? Check the Conferences by Date Index.

SITKA CENTER FOR ART AND ECOLOGY, P.O. Box 65, Otis OR 97368. (541)994-5485. Fax: (541)994-8024. E-mail: info@sitkacenter.org. Website: www.sitkacenter.org. **Contact:** Dee Moore, workshop program coordinator. Estab. 1970. "Our workshop program is open to all levels and is held annually from late May until late November. We also have a residency program from September through May." Average attendance: 10-16/workshop. A variety of workshops in creative process, including book arts and other media. Site: The Center borders a Nature Conservatory Preserve, the Siuslaw National Experimental Forest and the Salmon River Estuary, located just north of Lincoln City, OR.
Costs: "Workshops are generally $50-300; they do not include meals or lodging."
Accommodations: Does not offer overnight accommodations. Provides a list of area hotels or lodging options.
Additional Information: Brochure available in February of each year by SASE, phone, e-mail, fax or visit website. Accepts inquiries by SASE, e-mail, phone, fax.

SOUTH COAST WRITERS CONFERENCE, P.O. Box 590, 29392 Ellensburg Avenue, Gold Beach OR 97444. (541)247-2741. Fax: (541)247-6247. E-mail: scwc@socc.edu. Website: www.socc.edu/scwriters. **Contact:** Janet Pretti, coordinator. Estab. 1996. Annual. Conference held February 13-14, 2004. Workshops held Friday prior to conference; conference on Saturday. Average attendance: 100. "We try to cover a broad spectrum: fiction, historical, poetry, children's, nature." Site: "Conference is held in the local high school. Pre-conference activites are held at the Event Center on the Beach." 2004 will focus on the opening chapters of the novel, and the use of outlines for novel development. 2003 sessions included Creating Plot Through Characterization, Plot Is a Verb, Original Voice, Writing Quality Fiction and Sentence Revision. 2004 keynote speaker is Kate Wilhelm; also scheduled are William Sullivan, Lori Patch, Leigh Anne Jashway, and more.
Costs: $45 for Saturday conference if registered by January 31, $55 after. $25 for 6-hour Friday workshops. No meals or lodging included.
Accommodations: Provides list of area hotels.
Additional Information: Sponsors contest. "Southwestern scholarship—open to anyone. Entry should be essay, short story, memoir or poetry between 750-1,000 words. Cost covers registration for conference and a fish-fry ticket. Deadline is Jan. 15, 2004. Judged by members of the planning committee."

WILLAMETTE WRITERS CONFERENCE, 9045 SW Barbur, Suite 5-A, Portland OR 97219-4027. (503)452-1592. Fax: (503)452-0372. E-mail: wilwrite@willamettewriters.com. Website: www.willamettewriters.com. **Contact:** Bill Johnson, office manager. Estab. 1981. Annual. Conference held in August. Conference duration: 3 days. Average attendance: 400. "Williamette Writers is open to all writers, and we plan our conference accordingly. We offer workshops on all aspects of fiction, nonfiction, marketing, the creative process, screenwriting, etc. Also we invite top notch inspirational speakers for keynote addresses. Recent theme was 'The Writers Way.' We always include at least one agent or editor panel and offer a variety of topics of interest to both fiction and nonfiction writers and screenwriters." Recent editors, agents and film producers in attendance have included: Donald Maass, Donald Maass Literary Agency; Angela Rinaldi; Bob McCoy.
Costs: Cost for 2-day conference including meals is $250 members; $285 nonmembers.
Accommodations: If necessary, these can be made on an individual basis. Some years special rates are available.
Additional Information: Conference brochure/guidelines are available in May for catalog-size SASE, e-mail, fax, phone or on website. Accepts inquiries by fax, e-mail, phone, SASE.

WRITE FROM THE HEART, 9827 Irvine Avenue, Upper Lake CA 95485. (707)275-9011. E-mail: Halbooks@HalZinaBennet.com. Website: www.HalZinaBennet.com. **Contact:** Hal. Offered 4 to 6 times a year. Conference duration: 3-5 days. Average attendance: 15-30. "Open to all genres, focusing on accessing the author's most personal and individualized sources of imagery, characterization, tensions, content, style and voice." Site: Varies; California's Mt. Shasta, Mendocino California coast, Chicago, Kansas, Colorado. Panels include Creativity and Life Experiences: Sourcing Story and Character from What You Have Lived, Getting Happily Published, and more. Instructor: Hal Zina Bennett.
Costs: $170-200 for 3 days (not including meals).
Accommodations: No arrangements for transportation. Provides list of area hotels.
Additional Information: Brochures available. Request by SASE, e-mail, phone, fax or on website. Editors participate in conference. "Hal is a personal writing coach with over 200 successfully published clients, including several bestsellers. His own books include fiction, nonfiction, poetry, published by mainstream as well as smaller independent publishers."

WRITE ON THE SOUND WRITERS' CONFERENCE, Edmonds Arts Commission, 700 Main Street, Edmonds WA 98020. (425)771-0228. Fax: (425)771-0253. E-mail: wots@ci.edmonds.wa.us. **Contact:** Kris Gillespie, conference coordinator. Estab. 1986. Annual. Conference held October 4-5, 2003. Conference duration: 2 days. Average attendance: 175. "Conference is small—good for networking—and focuses on the craft of writing rather than publishers and editors." Site: "Edmonds is a beautiful community on the shores of Puget Sound, just north of Seattle."
Costs: $99 by 9/20, $120 after 9/20 for 2 days, $65 for 1 day (2003); includes registration, morning refreshments and 1 ticket to keynote lecture

Additional Information: Brochures available August 1, 2003. Accepts inquiries by e-mail, fax.

WRITERS STUDIO, 42 N.E. Graham Street, Portland OR 97212. (503)287-2150. Fax: (503)287-2150. E-mail: jesswrites@juno.com. Website: www.writing-life.com. **Contact:** Jessica Morrell. Estab. 1998. "Every year I teach a variety of one-day and weekend workshops in Portland, Oregon, and at the Oregon Coast. Subjects range from Creative Nonfiction to Fine-tuning Fiction. At this time my schedule for 2004 is not finalized because I will be a guest speaker at a number of writing conferences, though I will be teaching workshops with Marian Pierce the first weekends in March, June and October." *Writing Out the Storm* author Jessica Morrell and short story writer Marian Pierce are scheduled to participate as faculty.
Costs: Price ranges from $60-225.
Accommodations: Provides a list of area hotels or lodging options.
Additional Information: For brochure send e-mail, call. Accepts inquiries by SASE, e-mail, phone, fax.

WRITERS WEEKEND AT THE BEACH, Ocean Park Retreat Center, Ocean Park WA 98640. (360)665-6576. E-mail: etchinson@pacifier.com. Website: www.patriciarushford.com. **Contact:** Birdie Etchison or Patricia Rushford. Estab. 1992. Annual. Conference held February 27-29, 2003. Conference duration: "Two nights, one full day and one morning." Average attendance: 50-60. "Ours is a retreat for writers with an emphasis on poetry, fiction, nonfiction." Site: "Everything is on one main lodge. Wooded setting, view of the Pacific Ocean." Mystery, romance and short story writing will be covered. 2004 Keynote speaker will be Lauraine Snelling; also presenting are Jim and Tracie Peterson, acquisitions editors for Heartsong Presents (Barbour Publishing).
Costs: $165 includes food, lodging and seminars.
Accommodations: Offers overnight lodging on-site.
Additional Information: Brochures available in November 2003 on website. Accepts inquiries by SASE, e-mail, phone. Editors and agents sometimes participate in conference.

Canada

MARITIME WRITERS' WORKSHOP, Extension & Summer Session, UNB College of Extended Learning P.O. Box 4400, Fredericton NB E3B 5A3 Canada. Phone/fax: (506)474-1144. E-mail: k4jc@unb.ca. Website: www.unb.ca/extend/writers/. **Contact:** Rhona Sawlor, coordinator. Estab. 1976. Annual. Workshop held July 2004. Average attendance: 50. "We offer small groups of ten, practical manuscript focus. Novice writers welcome. Workshops in four areas: fiction, poetry, screenwriting, writing for children. The annual Marites Writers' Workshop is practical, wide-ranging program designed to help writers develop and refine their creative writing skills. This week-long program will involve you in small group workshops, lectures and discussions, public readings and special events, all in a supportive community of writers who share a commitment to excellence. Workshop groups consist of a maximum of ten writers each. Instructors are established Canadian authors and experienced teachers with a genuine interest in facilitating the writing process of others. For over a quarter century, Maritmes Writers' Workshop has provided counsel, encouragement and direction for hundreds of developing writers." Site: University of New Brunswick, Fredericton campus. 2003: Instructors included fiction writers Joan Clark and Fred Stenson, poet Anne Simpson, children's writer Marsha Skrypuck and nonfiction writer Philip Lee.
Costs: 2004: $395, tuition.
Accommodations: On-campus accommodations and meals.
Additional Information: "Participants must submit 10-20 manuscript pages which form a focus for workshop discussions." Brochures available after March. No SASE necessary. Accepts inquiries by e-mail and fax.

SAGE HILL WRITING EXPERIENCE, Box 1731, Saskatoon SK S7K 3S1 Canada. Phone/fax: (306)652-7395. E-mail: sage.hill@sasktel.net. Website: www.lights.com/sagehill. **Contact:** Steven Ross Smith. Annual. Workshops held in August and October. Conference duration: 10-21 days. Average attendance: limited to 36-40. "Sage Hill Writing Experience offers a special working and learning opportunity to writers at different stages of development. Top quality instruction, low instructor-student ratio and the beautiful Sage Hill setting offer conditions ideal for the pursuit of excellence in the arts of fiction, poetry and playwriting." Site: The Sage Hill location features "individual accommodation, in-room writing area, lounges, meeting rooms, healthy meals, walking woods and vistas in several directions." Seven classes are held: Introduction to Writing Fiction & Poetry; Fiction Workshop; Nonfiction Workshop; Writing Young Adult Fiction Workshop; Poetry Workshop; Poetry Colloquium; Fiction Colloquium; Playwriting Lab.
Costs: Summer program, $795 (Canadian) includes instruction, accommodation, meals and all facilities. Fall Poerty Colloquium: $995.
Accommodations: On-site individual accommodations for summer programs located at Lumsden, 45 kilometers outside Regina. Fall Colloquium is at Muenster, Saskatchewan, 150 kilometers east of Saskatoon.
Additional Information: For Introduction to Creative Writing: A 5-page sample of your writing or a statement of your interest in creative writing; list of courses taken required. For workshop and colloquium program: A résumé of your writing career and a 12-page sample of your work plus 5 pages of published work required. Application deadline is April 25. Guidelines are available after January for SASE, e-mail, fax, phone or on website. Accepts

inquiries by SASE, phone, e-mail and fax. Scholarships and bursaries are available.

SUNSHINE COAST FESTIVAL OF THE WRITTEN ARTS, Box 2299, Sechelt BC V0N 3A0 Canada. (604)885-9631 or (800)565-9631. Fax: (604)885-3967. E-mail: info@writersfestival.ca. Website: www.writersfestival.ca. **Contact:** Gail Bull. Estab. 1982. Annual. Festival held August 12-15, 2004. Average attendance: 9,500. One of the longest-running Canadian writers festivals, the Sunshine Coast Festival "tries to represent all genres." Site: Held in a "500-seat pavilion set in the beautiful Rockwood Gardens in the seaside town of Sechelt, BC." Past speakers included Margaret Atwood, Arthur Black, Andreas Schroeder, Bill Richardson, Anne Petrie and Margo Button.
Costs: Individual events, $12; Festival pass, $225; student discounts. Meals and lodging are not included.
Accommodations: Information on overnight accommodations is available.
Additional Information: Conference brochures/guidelines available in May on website, by e-mail, fax or phone. Accepts inquiries by fax, e-mail, SASE, phone.

THE VANCOUVER INTERNATIONAL WRITERS FESTIVAL, 1398 Cartwright St., Vancouver BC V6H 3R8 Canada. (604)681-6330. Fax: (604)681-8400. E-mail: viwf@writersfest.bc.ca. Website: www.writersfest.bc.ca. Estab. 1988. Annual. Held in October. Average attendance: 11,000. "This is a festival for readers and writers. The program of events is diverse and includes readings, panel discussions, seminars. Lots of opportunities to interact with the writers who attend." Site: Held on Granville Island—in the heart of Vancouver. Two professional theaters are used as well as Performance Works (an open space). "We try to avoid specific themes. Programming takes place between February and June each year and is by invitation."
Costs: Tickets are $10-20 (Canadian).
Accommodations: Local tourist info can be provided when necessary and requested.
Additional Information: Festival information available on website. Accepts inquiries by e-mail, fax. "A reminder—this is a festival, a celebration, not a conference or workshop."

THE WRITERS RETREAT, 15 Canusa St., Stanstead, Quebec J0B 3E5 Canada. (819) 876-2065. Fax: (819) 876-2079. E-mail: info@writersretreat.com. Website: www.writersretreat.com. **Contact:** Anthony Lanza, program director, and Micheline Cote, executive director. Estab. 1998. Year-round. Conference duration: 5 days for "in residence" workshops. Any length of stay for residency and private mentoring. The Writers Retreat workshops feature instruction in fiction writing, nonfiction writing and screenwriting. "Our sole purpose is to provide an ambiance conducive to creativity for career and emerging writers. Residency includes a private studio and breakfast, a library with reference tools, Internet access, complimentary critique. The Writers Retreat is a full literary service retreat including residency, private mentoring, workshops, editing and submission services. It is open year-round." Site: Headquarters are located on the Vermont/Quebec border and 2 satellite facilities in Colorado and Zihuatanejo, Mexico. Workshops include The Business of Writing, Self-Editing for Publication, Story Realization, Dynamics of Dramatic Structure, and more. Faculty includes Hanna Fox, editor and publisher of Red Hummingbird Press; Laurie Horowitz, literary agent at Creative Artists Agency; Dennis Lanson, screenwriter/director/producer, and Dr. Linda Seger, script consultant.
Costs: Residency starts at $455/week. Private mentoring starts at $950/week. Workshops are $950 each. All above include lodging and breakfast.
Accommodations: Provides airport transfers by arrangement, bus transfers by arrangement.
Additional Information: Submit 20-25 pages of work 30 days prior to program start. Accepts inquiries by SASE, e-mail and phone.

International

BOOKTOWNS OF EUROPE WRITERS WORKSHOPS, P.O. Box 1626, West Chester PA 19380. (610)486-6687. Fax: (610)486-0204. E-mail: info@booktownwriters.com. Website: booktownwriters.com. **Contact:** Lenore M. Scallan, workshops coordinator. Estab. 1995. 3-4 per year. 2004 conferences due to be held in Ireland, France, Norway, and Germany. See website for 2004 dates. Average attendance: under 12 per site. "Booktowns of Europe focuses on the book-length project. We remove writers from daily distractions, provide a learning vacation atmosphere in the small villages and towns of western Europe, offer intensive support for all fiction and nonfiction topics: autobiography, biography, business, history, romance, sci-fi, self help, sports, etc. (no poetry, erotica or script-writing)." Site: Offer 3-4 sites/year throughout Europe. Panels planned for next conference include 2 daily sessions—a morning writing assignment related to the location, and an afternoon session reviewing the morning's results. Lenore M. Scallan and Bruce Mowday participate as faculty members.
Costs: $1,590 for entire package, including transportation between transfer city and workshop site; full tuition; all course materials; one half-hour private conference with workshop leader; 6 nights accomodation with daily breakfast and dinner; one afternoon/evening excursion and a welcome reception.
Accommodations: All accomodations are comfortable, 2-star European, double occupancy, first-come, first-served. 10% discount for full-time students (with university ID) and seniors, plus group discounts for groups of 6 or more. Accomodations are limited.

Additional Information: A 10-page sample chapter, excerpt and/or full treatment for the book project with a $25 fee may be submitted 60 days prior to workshop for a technical and potential marketing evaluation. The submission will be returned with a marked copy and one-page evaluation sheet at the start of the workshop program. Conference information for SASE. "The workshop environment, while intense, offers plenty of private time opportunity for participants to write. They also have free time to explore the unique distinctions of each site. One additional option: a free-ranging post-dinnertime evening discussion in which town 'locals' often take part. Attendance is not required, but these open discussions often become the most memorable parts of the workshop experience."

🌐 **INTERNATIONAL READERS THEATRE WORKSHOPS**, P.O. Box 17193, San Diego CA 92177. (619)276-1948. Fax: (858)576-7369. E-mail: wadams@san.rr.com. Website: www.readerstheatre.net. **Contact:** Bill Adams, director. Estab. 1974. Workshop held July 11-20, 2004. Average attendance: 70. Workshop on "all aspects of Readers Theatre with emphasis on scriptmaking." Site: Workshop held at Brittania Hotel in London.
Costs: "$1,595 includes housing for two weeks (twin accommodations), traditional English breakfast, complimentary mid-morning coffee break and all Institute fees."
Additional Information: "One-on-one critiques available between writer and faculty (if members)." Conference information available December 2003. For brochures/guidelines send SASE, visit website, e-mail, fax, call. Accepts inquiries by SASE, fax, phone, e-mail. Conference offers "up to 12 credits in Theatre (Speech) and/or Education from the University of Southern Maine at $143/unit."

🆕 🌐 **KILLALOE HEDGE-SCHOOL OF WRITING**, 4 Riverview, Killaloe, Co. Clare, Ireland. Phone: (+353)61 375 217. Fax: (+353)61 375 487. E-mail: khs@killaloe.ie. Website: www.killaloe.ie/khs. **Contact:** K.Thorne, secretary. Estab. 1999. Held every second weekend between October and March. Conference duration: 10 a.m Saturday till 4 p.m Sunday. Average attendance: 15-20. Holds workshops on 6 different topics: Get Started Writing; Start Your Novel; Writing a Nonfiction Book; Write for Magazines and Papers; Write Your Memoirs; Get Started Writing—Level Two. Speakers include David Rice, Catherine Thorne and others yet to be invited.
Costs: 150€ (Euro) per workshop. Includes midday meal each day. Does not include lodging.
Accommodations: Runs a shuttle from Shannon Airport.
Additional Information: "Please check out our website."

🌐 **THE MONTOLIEU WORKSHOP**, 10 Sequin Rd. W., Hartford CT 06117. (860)231-9897. Fax: (860)297-5258. E-mail: Lucy.Ferriss@trincoll.edu. Website: www.montolieu.net. **Contact:** Lucy Ferriss, director. Estab. 1997. Annual. Conference held August 2004. Conference duration: 1 week. Average attendance: 12. Conference focuses on fiction and prose poetry; translation; writing about place. Site: Hotel for writers, B&B with single- and double-room accommodations; other B&B's within the village of Montolieu. Visting writers include Stephen Tapscott, Sam Pickens, and Lucy Ferriss.
Costs: $1,300 includes room and board (breakfast and dinner).
Accommodations: Provides shuttles to Carcassonne, the beach, horseback riding, wineries, etc.
Additional Information: Writers should send 5-10 pages of prose or poetry by March 31. "The conference is located in a historic book village in the south of France. In addition to the writing workshop, centers for calligraphy, bookbinding and other book arts, as well as art galleries, abound in the village and contribute to its lively atmosphere."

🌐 **PARIS WRITERS WORKSHOP/WICE**, 20, Bd. du Montparnasse, Paris 75015, France. Phone: (331)45.66.75.50. Fax: (331)40.65.96.53. E-mail: pww@wice-paris.org. Website: www.wice-paris.org. **Contact:** Rose Burke and Marcia Lebre, directors. Estab. 1987. Annual. Conference held June-July. Average attendance: 40-50. "Conference concentrates on fiction, nonfiction, and poetry. Visiting lecturers speak on a variety of issues important to beginning and advanced writers. 2003 writers in residence are Alice Mattison (novel), Isabel Huggins (short fiction), Adam Zagajowski and Michael Steinberg (creative nonfiction). Located in the heart of Paris on the Bd. du Montparnasse, the stomping grounds of such famous American writers as Ernest Hemingway, Henry Miller and F. Scott Fitzgerald. The site consists of four classrooms, a resource center/library and private terrace."
Costs: 380 Euros—tuition only.
Additional Information: "Students submit 1 copy of complete ms or work-in-progress which is sent in advance to writer-in-residence. Each student has a one-on-one consultation with writer-in-residence." Conference information available late fall. For brochures/guidelines visit website, e-mail, call or fax. Accepts inquiries by SASE, phone, e-mail, fax. "Workshop attracts many expatriate Americans and other English language writers from all over Europe and North America. We can assist with finding a range of hotels, from budget to more luxurious accommodations. We are an intimate workshop with an exciting mix of more experienced, published writers and enthusiastic beginners."

🌐 **TÝ NEWYDD WRITERS' CENTRE**, Llanystumdwy, Cricieth Gwynedd LL52 0LW, United Kingdom. Phone: 01766-522811. Fax: 01766 523095. E-mail: tynewydd@dial.pipex.com. Website: www.tynewydd.org. **Contact:** Sally Baker, director. Estab. 1990. Year-round. Regular courses held throughout the year. Every course held Monday-Saturday. Average attendance: 14. "To give people the opportunity to work side-by-side with professional writers, in an informal atmosphere." Site: Tý Newydd, large manor house, last home of the prime minister, David

Lloyd George. Situated in North Wales, Great Britain—between mountains and sea. Past featured tutors include novelists Beryl Bainbridge and Bernice Rubens.
Costs: Single room, £360, shared room, £335 for Monday-Saturday (includes full board, tuition).
Accommodations: Transportation from railway stations arranged. Accommodation in Tŷ Newydd (onsite).
Additional Information: Conference information available by mail, phone, e-mail, fax or visit website. Accepts inquiries by SASE, e-mail, fax, phone. "More and more people come to us from the U.S. often combining a writing course with a tour of Wales."

VASTO WRITERS & ARTISTS RETREAT, 517 Sherman Ave., Evanston IL 60202. (847)328-3431. E-mail: dcysaider@aol.com. Website: www.luigimonteferrante.com. **Contact:** Luigi Monteferrente or Syed A. Haider, co-directors. Estab. 1999. Annual. 2003 conference held in June. Average attendance: limited to 10. "We run an intimate, yet international, center dedicated to supporting artists wishing to break free of the distractions of everyday life to pursue their own work on their own schedule in an inspiring setting, that of an ancient Roman municipality on the Adriatic coast. Focus is on fiction, but we are especially sensitive to our guests' own aspirations and ultimate goal: enhancing one's skill and deepening one's sense of writing as a vocation."

Writing Programs

Every year, thousands of writers seek out opportunities to improve their craft through classes—whether pursuing an undergraduate or graduate degree in creative writing, enrolling in continuing education classes, or signing up for online writing programs. In addition to giving writers instruction in the technical elements of craft, these programs also give writers a chance to have their work critiqued, critique the work of others, and provide a supportive structure within which to work. As Tracy Chevalier, bestselling author of *Girl With a Pearl Earring*, says of her in-class writing experience: "That year gave me deadlines, a critical audience, and most of all the expectation that I would write all day, every day. It was the line in the sand that I need to draw in my life, between the old life where writing was a hobby and my new life where writing is primary."

Statistics show that the number of creative writing programs in colleges and universities nationwide is growing exponentially. Associated Writing Programs (AWP), a nonprofit organization based at George Mason University in Fairfax, Virginia, estimates that in the last decade the number of programs has nearly doubled. Master's in fine arts (MFA) programs alone have jumped from 55 in 1992 to 99 last year. Reports say that last year at the country's oldest MFA program, at the University of Iowa, there were some 700 applicants for 20 openings. A *Chicago Tribune* article quoted that program's director as saying Iowa was "harder to get into than Harvard Law School."

Competition notwithstanding, writing programs can be an important—even critical—part of a writer's development. Here we've compiled a list of contact information for AWP graduate and undergraduate programs throughout the country. Use this list as a starting point to contact a program or programs near you to find out about the curriculum and tuition, faculty, and financial aid opportunities.

Alaska

UNIVERSITY OF ALASKA ANCHORAGE, Department of Creative Writing & Literary Arts, 3211 Providence Dr., Anchorage AK 99508-8252. (907)786-4330. Fax: (907)786-1382. E-mail: aycwla@uaa.alaska.edu. Website: www.uaa.alaska.edu/cwla. **Contact:** Ronald Spatz. Estab. 1987. Offers B.A. minor in creative writing, M.F.A. Average class size: 10 (workshops); 15 (craft class). Faculty includes Jo-Ann Mapson. Publishes *Alaska Quarterly Review.*

UNIVERSITY OF ALASKA AT FAIRBANKS, Box 755720, Fairbanks AK 99775-5720. (907)474-7193. E-mail: faengl@uaf.edu. **Contact:** Dept. Chair. Offers M.F.A. in creative writing. Faculty includes Frank Soos, Renee Manfredi, Anne Caston, John Reinhard. See www.uaf.edu/admissions for tuition and fees. Application deadline: March 31.

Alabama

AUBURN UNIVERSITY, English Department, 9030 Haley Center, Auburn AL 36849-5203. (334)844-4620. E-mail: english@auburn.edu. Website: www.auburn.edu/english. **Contact:** Frances Collins. Estab. 1856. Faculty includes Judy Troy. Publishes *Southern Humanities Review.*

UNIVERSITY OF ALABAMA AT BIRMINGHAM, Humanities Building 217, 900 13th St. South, Birmingham AL 35294. (205)934-4250. Fax: (205)975-8125. Website: www.uab.edu/english. **Contact:** Robert Collins. Faculty includes Dennis Covington, Larry Wharton.

UNIVERSITY OF ALABAMA AT TUSCALOOSA, Creative Writing Program, 103 Morgan Hall, Box 870244, Tuscaloosa AL 35487-0244. (205)348-0766. Fax: (205)348-1388. Website: http://bama.ua.edu/~writing/. **Contact:** Robin Behn. Offers M.F.A. Faculty includes Wendy Rawlins, Sandy Hass.

Arizona

ARIZONA STATE UNIVERSITY, Creative Writing Program, English Department, Box 870302, Tempe AZ 85287. Website: www.asu.edu/clas/english/. **Contact:** Karla Elling. Estab. 1985. Offers M.F.A. Faculty includes Ron Carlson, Melissa Pritchard.

ARIZONA WESTERN COLLEGE, Division of Communications, P.O. Box 929, Yuma AZ 85366. (602)726-1000. Website: www.azwestern.edu. **Contact:** David Coy.

NORTHERN ARIZONA UNIVERSITY, Creative Writing Program, English Department, Box 6032, Flagstaff AZ 86011. (928)523-4911. Website: www.nau.edu. **Contact:** Director, creative writing area. Offers M.A. in English with creative writing emphasis and B.A. in English. Faculty includes Jane Armstrong, Ann Cummins and Allen Woodman.

PHOENIX COLLEGE, English Dept., 1202 W. Thomas Rd., Phoenix AZ 85013. (602)285-7500. Website: www.pc.maricopa.edu. **Contact:** Jed Allen. Faculty includes David Pineda, Laraine Herring.

Arkansas

PULASKI TECHNICAL COLLEGE, 3000 West Scenic Dr., North Little Rock AR 72118. (501)771-1000. Website: www2.pulaskitech.edu. Estab. 1945.

UNIVERSITY OF ARKANSAS AT FAYETTEVILLE, The Programs in Creative Writing and Translation, English Department, Kimpel Hall 333, University of Arkansas, Fayetteville AR 72701. (501)575-4301. Fax: (479)575-5919. E-mail: mfa@uark.edu. Website: www.uark.edu/depts/english/pcwt.html. **Contact:** Molly Giles. Estab. 1966. "With up to seven intensive workshops, courses in poetics and fiction theory, our students prepare themselves for the life of the writer." Offers B.A., M.F.A. Student/teacher ratio is 6:1. Average class size: 15. Faculty includes Ellen Gilchrist, Molly Giles, Donald Hays.

UNIVERSITY OF CENTRAL ARKANSAS, 201 Donaghey Ave., Irby Room 105, Dept. of Writing, Conway AR 72035. (501)450-3344. Fax: (501)450-3343. E-mail: writing@mail.uca.edu. Website: www.uca.edu/divisions/academic/writing. **Contact:** Dr. David Harvey, chair. Offers B.A.

California

ANTIOCH UNIVERSITY AT LOS ANGELES, 13274 Fiji Way, Marina Del Rey CA 90292. (310)822-4824. Website: www.antioch.edu. **Contact:** Keith Rand.

CALARTS, 24700 McBean Pkwy., Valencia CA 91355. (661)255-1050. Website: www.calarts.edu. **Contact:** Jon Wagner.

CALIFORNIA COLLEGE OF ARTS AND CRAFTS, 1111 Eighth St., San Francisco CA 94107. (415)551-9237. Fax: (415)551-9289. E-mail: twalsh@ccac-art.edu. Website: www.ccarts.edu. **Contact:** John Laskey. Estab. 2000. Offers M.F.A. Student/teacher ratio: 8-1. Average class size: 8-15. Faculty includes Ann Williams, Michelle Richmond, Javanel Acosta, Gloria Frym.

CALIFORNIA STATE UNIVERSITY AT CHICO, English & Writing, West 1st and Salem Sts., Chico CA 95929. (530)898-5125. Fax: (413)538-2138. **Contact:** Carole Oles.

CALIFORNIA STATE UNIVERSITY AT FRESNO, 5245 N. Backer, PB 98, Fresno CA 93740-8004. (559)278-2359. Fax: (559)278-7143. **Contact:** Connie Hales.

CALIFORNIA STATE UNIVERSITY LOS ANGELES, 5151 State University Dr., Los Angeles CA 90032. (323)343-4174. Fax: (323)343-6470. Website: www.calstatela.edu/academic/english/edeptwp/. **Contact:** Dr. Mary Bush.

CALIFORNIA STATE UNIVERSITY NORTHRIDGE, 1811 Nordehoff St., Northridge CA 91330-8248. (818)677-3433. **Contact:** Dorothy Barresi.

CALIFORNIA STATE UNIVERSITY SACRAMENTO, 6000 J St., Department of English, Sacramento CA 95819-6075. (916)278-6925. Fax: (916)278-5410. **Contact:** Dr. Joshua McKinney.

CHAPMAN UNIVERSITY, 1 University Dr., Orange CA 92866. (714)997-6750. Fax: (714)997-6697. Website: www.chapman.edu/comm/english. **Contact:** Mark Axelrod.

HUMBOLDT STATE UNIVERSITY, Department of English, Arcata CA 95521. (707)826-5919. Fax: (707)826-5939. **Contact:** Jim Dodge.

IDYLLWILD ARTS ACADEMY, 52500 Temecula Rd., P.O. Box 38, Idyllwild CA 92549. (909)659-2171. **Contact:** Donald A. Put.

LOYOLA MARYMOUNT UNIVERSITY, Loyola Blvd. at W. 80th St., Los Angeles CA 90045. (310)338-7668. Fax: (310)338-7727. Website: www.lmu.edu. **Contact:** Gail Wronsky.

MILLS COLLEGE, English Dept., 5000 MacArthur Blvd., Oakland CA 94613. (510)430-2217. Fax: (510)430-3314. E-mail: tnemeth@mills.edu. Website: www.mills.edu. **Contact:** Tonianne Nemeth. Offers B.A. in literature with creative writing emphasis, M.F.A. Faculty includes Elmaz Abinader and Cornelia Nixon.

SADDLEBACK COLLEGE CREATIVE WRITING PROGRAM, Saddleback College, English Dept., 2800 Marguerite Pkwy., Mission Viejo CA 92692. (949)582-4788. Fax: (949)347-1663. Website: www.saddleback.cc.ca. us. **Contact:** Shelba Cole Rossback.

SAINT MARY'S COLLEGE OF CALIFORNIA, M.F.A. Program in Creative Writing, P.O. Box 4686, St. Mary's College, Moraga CA 94575. (925)631-4088. E-mail: writers@stmarys-ca.edu. Website: www.stmarys-ca.e du. **Contact:** Thomas Cooney, coordinator. Offers M.F.A. Faculty includes Anthony Swofford, Lysley Tenorio, Rosemary Graham.

SAN DIEGO STATE UNIVERSITY, Dept. of English and Comparative Literature, 5500 Campanile Dr., San Diego CA 92182-8140. (619)594-5234. Fax: (619)594-4998. Website: www.rohan.sdsu.edu/dept/writing. **Contact:** Sandra B. Alcosser.

SAN JOSE STATE UNIVERSITY, English Department, San Jose CA 95192-0090. (408)924-4432. Fax: (408)924-4580. Website: www.sjsu.edu/depts/english/creativewriting.htm. **Contact:** Alan Soldofsky.

SONOMA STATE UNIVERSITY, English Department N-362, 1801 E. Cotati Ave., Rohnert Park CA 94928. (707)664-2140. Fax: (707)664-4400. E-mail: merle.williams@sonoma.edu. Website: www.sonoma.edu/English/. **Contact:** Merle Williams. Estab. 1961. Mission "to develop creative writing within the context of an English B.A. or M.A. degree." Offers concentration in study, B.A., M.A. Student/teacher ratio: 25-1. Average class size: 25. Faculty includes Sherrill Jaffe. Publishes the literary journals *Zaum* and *Volt, A Magazine of the Arts*.

STANFORD UNIVERSITY, Creative Writing, Dept. of English, Stanford CA 94305-2087. (650)723-0504. Website: www.stanford.edu/dept/english/cw/. **Contact:** Tobias Wolff.

UCLA EXTENSION WRITERS' PROGRAM, 10995 LeConte Ave., Room #440, Los Angeles CA 90024. (310)825-9638. Fax: (310)206-7382. Website: www.uclaextension.org/writers. **Contact:** Rick Noguchi.

UNIVERSITY OF CALIFORNIA AT DAVIS, English Department Creative Writing, Davis CA 95616. (530)752-6117. **Contact:** Shirley Martin.

UNIVERSITY OF CALIFORNIA AT IRVINE, MFA Programs in Writing, Department of English & Literature, Irvine CA 92697-2650. (949)824-6718. Fax: (949)824-2916. Website: www.humanities.uci.edu/english. **Contact:** Geoffrey Wolff (fiction); James McMichael (poetry).

UNIVERSITY OF REDLANDS, 1200 E. Colton Ave., P.O. Box 3080, Redlands CA 92373-0999. (909)793-2121, ext. 2464. Fax: (909)748-6294. Website: www.redlands.edu. **Contact:** Patricia Geary.

UNIVERSITY OF SOUTHERN CALIFORNIA, Master of Professional Writing Program, Waite Phillips Hall 404, Los Angeles CA 90089-4034. (213)740-3252. Fax: (213)740-5775. E-mail: mpw@usc.edu. Website: www.usc. edu/dept/LAS/mpw/. **Contact:** Diana Lopez. Estab. 1941. "It is the first multidisciplinary Graduate Program in Creative Writing instituted in the nation, with concentrations in fiction, poetry, playwriting, screenwriting, TV writing, and nonfiction. The program prepares individuals for writing in all genres." Offers M.A. Student/teacher ratio: 5-1. Average class size: 10. Faculty includes Aram Saroya, Shelly Lowenkopf, John Rechy.

Colorado

COLORADO STATE UNIVERSITY, Creative Writing Program, 359 Eddy Building, Fort Collins CO 80523-3010. (970)491-6428. Fax: (970)491-5601. E-mail: english@lamar.colostate.edu. Website: www.colostate.edu. **Contact:** Assistant to the Director of Creative Writing. Offers B.A., M.F.A. Average class size: 10-16. Faculty includes Leslee Becker, Judy Doenges, David Milofsky and Steven Schwartz.

DISCOVER
A WORLD OF
WRITING
SUCCESS

Are you ready to be praised, published, and paid for your writing? It's time to invest in your future with *Writer's Digest*! Beginners and experienced writers alike have been enjoying *Writer's Digest*, the world's leading magazine for writers, for more than 80 years — and it keeps getting better! Each issue is brimming with:

- Inspiration from writers who have been in your shoes
- Detailed info on the latest contests, conferences, markets, and opportunities in every genre
- Tools of the trade, including reviews of the latest writing software and hardware
- Writing prompts and exercises to overcome writer's block and rekindle your creative spark
- Expert tips, techniques, and advice to help you get published
- And so much more!

That's a lot to look forward to every month. Let *Writer's Digest* put you on the road to writing success!

Get 2 FREE ISSUES of Writer's Digest!

NO RISK!
Send No Money Now!

☐ **Yes!** Please rush me my 2 FREE issues of *Writer's Digest* — the world's leading magazine for writers. If I like what I read, I'll get a full year's subscription (12 issues, including the 2 free issues) for only $19.96. That's 67% off the newsstand rate! If I'm not completely happy, I'll write "cancel" on your invoice, return it and owe nothing. The 2 FREE issues are mine to keep, no matter what!

Name_____

Address_____

City_____

State_____ZIP_____

Annual newsstand rate is $59.88. Orders outside the U.S. will be billed an additional $10 (includes GST/HST in Canada.) Please allow 4-6 weeks for first-issue delivery.

www.writersdigest.com

TFNM1

Get **2** FREE TRIAL ISSUES of *Writer's®* Digest

Packed with creative inspiration, advice, and tips to guide you on the road to success, *Writer's Digest* will offer you everything you need to take your writing to the next level! You'll discover how to:

- Create dynamic characters and page-turning plots
- Submit query letters that publishers won't be able to refuse
- Find the right agent or editor for you
- Make it out of the slush-pile and into the hands of the right publisher
- Write award-winning contest entries
- And more!

See for yourself by ordering your 2 FREE trial issues today!

LIGHTHOUSE WRITERS WORKSHOP, 817 27th St., Denver CO 80205. (303)297-1185. Fax: (303)292-9425. **Contact:** Andrea Dupree.

UNIVERSITY OF COLORADO BOULDER, 226 UCB, Boulder CO 80309-0146. (303)492-5213. Website: www.colorado.edu/english.

UNIVERSITY OF DENVER, English Department, Pioneer Hall, Denver CO 80208. (303)871-2885. Fax: (303)871-2853. **Contact:** Brian Evenson.

Connecticut

CENTRAL CONNECTICUT STATE UNIVERSITY, English Department, Willard Hall, 1615 Stanley St., New Britain CT 06050. (860)832-2762. Fax: (830)832-2784. **Contact:** Dr. J. Tom Hazuka.

CONNECTICUT COLLEGE, Creative Writing Program, 270 Mohegan Ave., New London CT 06320-4196. **Contact:** Charles Hartman.

SOUTHERN CONNECTICUT STATE UNIVERSITY, English Department, 501 Crescent St., New Haven CT 06515-1355. (203)392-6745. **Contact:** Tim Parrish.

TRINITY COLLEGE, 300 Summit St., Hartford CT 06106. (860)297-2464. Fax: (860)297-5258. **Contact:** J. Frederick Pfeil.

UNIVERSITY OF CONNECTICUT, 215 Glenbrook Rd. U-4025, Storrs CT 06269-4025. (860)486-3870. Fax: (860)486-1530. **Contact:** Penelope Pelizzoh.

Washington, D.C.

GEORGE WASHINGTON UNIVERSITY, 801 22nd St. NW, Washington DC 20052. (202)994-6180. Fax: (520)621-7397. **Contact:** David Aleavey.

GEORGETOWN UNIVERSITY, English Dept., Box 571131, Washington DC 20057-1131. (202)687-7435. Fax: (202)687-7483. **Contact:** James F. Slevin.

JOHNS HOPKINS UNIVERSITY, Arts & Sciences, Suite 104, 1717 Massachusettes Ave. NW, Washington DC 20036-2280. (202)452-0758. Fax: (202)530-9857. **Contact:** David Everett.

Florida

EMBRY-RIDDLE UNIVERSITY, 600 S. Clyde Morris Blvd., Daytona Beach FL 32114. (904)226-6668. **Contact:** Steve Glassman.

FLORIDA ATLANTIC UNIVERSITY, Department of English, 777 Glades Rd., Boca Raton FL 33431. (561)297-2973. **Contact:** Jason Schwartz.

FLORIDA INTERNATIONAL UNIVERSITY, Biscayne Bay Campus, 3000 NE 151st St., North Miami FL 33181. (305)919-5857. Fax: (305)919-5734. **Contact:** Dr. Les Standiford.

FLORIDA STATE UNIVERSITY, English Dept., Box 1580, Tallahassee FL 32306-1580. (850)644-4230. **Contact:** Debra Brock.

STETSON UNIVERSITY, English Department, 421 N. Woodland Blvd., Unit 8300, DeLand FL 32720. (904)822-7729. E-mail: twitek@stetson.edu.

UNIVERSITY OF CENTRAL FLORIDA, 4000 Central Florida Blvd., Orlando FL 32816. (407)823-2267. Fax: (407)823-3300. **Contact:** Judith Hemschemeyer.

UNIVERSITY OF FLORIDA, English Department, P.O. Box 117310, Gainesville FL 32611-7310. (352)392-6650. Fax: (352)392-0860. Website: www.english.ufl.edu/programs/grad/index.htm. **Contact:** Padgett Powell.

UNIVERSITY OF MIAMI, Creative Writing English Dept., P.O. Box 248142, Coral Gables FL 33124. (305)284-2182. Website: www.as.miami.edu/english. **Contact:** Fred D'Aquilar.

UNIVERSITY OF SOUTH FLORIDA, CPR 107, Dept. of English, 4202 E. Fowler Ave., Tampa FL 33620. (813)974-9570. Fax: (813)974-2270. Website: www.cas.usf.edu/english/index.html. **Contact:** Rita Ciresi.

UNIVERSITY OF TAMPA, 401 W. Kennedy Blvd., Tampa FL 33606-1490. (813)253-6216. **Contact:** Donald Morrill.

Georgia

ARMSTRONG ATLANTIC STATE UNIVERSITY, Creative Writing, 11935 Abercon St., Savannah GA 31419-1997. (912)921-5633. **Contact:** James Smith.

BERRY COLLEGE, Department of English, Box 350, Mount Berry GA 30149-5010. (706)802-6723. Fax: (706)802-6722. **Contact:** Sandra Meek.

EMORY UNIVERSITY, Creative Writing Program, N209 Callaway Center, Atlanta GA 30322. (404)727-7999. Fax: (404)727-4672. **Contact:** Lynaa Williams.

GAINESVILLE COLLEGE DIVISION OF HUMANITIES, P.O. Box 1358, Gainesville GA 30503. (770)718-3674. Fax: (770)718-3832. **Contact:** Tom Sauret.

GEORGIA COLLEGE & STATE UNIVERSITY, Creative Writing Program, CBX 44, Milledgeville GA 31061. (478)445-3509. Fax: (478)445-5961. Website: http://al.gcsu.edu.mfa.htm. **Contact:** Martin Lammon.

GEORGIA PERIMETER COLLEGE, 2101 Womack Rd., Dunwoody GA 30338. (770)551-3166. Fax: (770)551-7471. **Contact:** Lawrence Hetrick.

GEORGIA SOUTHERN UNIVERSITY, Writing and Linguistics, Box 8026, Stateboro GA 30460. (912)681-0156. Fax: (912)681-0783. **Contact:** Eric Nelson.

GEORGIA STATE UNIVERSITY, English Department, University Plaza, Atlanta GA 30303-3083. **Contact:** John William Holman.

KENNESAW STATE UNIVERSITY, Creative Writing Program, 1000 Chastain Rd., Kennesaw GA 30144-5591. (770)423-6297. **Contact:** Dr. Laura Dabundo.

MACON STATE COLLEGE, Creative Writing Program, 100 College Station Dr., Macon GA 31206.

Idaho

BOISE STATE UNIVERSITY, 1910 University Dr., Boise ID 83725-1525. (208)425-1002. Fax: (208)426-4373. Website: http://english.boisestate.edu/mfa. **Contact:** Mitch Wieland.

LEWIS-CLARK STATE COLLEGE, 500 Eighth Ave., Lewiston ID 83501. (208)792-2050. Fax: (208)792-2324. **Contact:** Claire Davis.

UNIVERSITY OF IDAHO, English Dept., Brink Hall, Room 200, P.O. Box 441102, Moscow ID 83844-1102. (208)885-6156. Fax: (208)885-6157. Website: www.its.uidaho.edu/english/CW. **Contact:** Robert Wrigley.

Illinois

ART INSTITUTE OF CHICAGO, MFA in Writing, 37 South Wabash, Chicago IL 60603. (312)899-5094. **Contact:** Rebecca Targ.

BRADLEY UNIVERSITY, English Department, Peoria IL 61625. (309)677-2463. **Contact:** Margaret Carter.

COLUMBIA COLLEGE OF CHICAGO, Fiction Writing Program, 600 S. Greenview Ave., Chicago IL 60605-1996. (312)663-1600, ext. 7615. **Contact:** Deborah Roberts.

ILLINOIS STATE UNIVERSITY, Creative Writing Program, English Dept., Campus Box 4240, Normal IL 61790-4240. **Contact:** Lucia Getsi.

KNOX COLLEGE, Knox College Creative Writing, English Department, Box K-50, Galesburg IL 61401. E-mail: rmetz@knox.edu. Website: www.knox.edu. **Contact:** Robin Metz.

NORTHWESTERN UNIVERSITY, English Major in Writing, UH 215, Evanston IL 60208-2240. (847)491-7294. **Contact:** Mary Kinzie.

SOUTHERN ILLINOIS, English Department, Carbondale IL 62901. (618)453-5321. **Contact:** Beth Lordan.

UNIVERSITY OF ILLINOIS, English Department, 608 S. Wright St., Urbana IL 61801. (217)333-4137. **Contact:** Michael Van Wellenghen.

UNIVERSITY OF ILLINOIS AT CHICAGO, 601 S. Morgan St., Chicago IL 60607. (312)413-2229. Fax: (312)413-1005. **Contact:** Eugene Wildman.

Indiana

BALL STATE UNIVERISTY, Department of English, Muncie IN 47306. (765)285-8409. **Contact:** Tom Koontz.

DEPAUW UNIVERSITY, 3232 Asbury Hall, Greencastle IN 46135. (765)658-4672. **Contact:** Tom Chiarella.

INDIANA UNIVERSITY, Purdue at Indianapolis, Cavanaugh Hall 5U2L, 425 University Blvd., Indianapolis IN 46201. (317)274-9831. Fax: (317)278-1287. **Contact:** Karen Kovacik.

INDIANA UNIVERSITY, English Dept., Ballantine Hall, 1020 E. Kirkwood Ave., Bloomington IN 47405. (812)855-9539. Fax: (812)855-9535. E-mail: ardizzon@indiana.edu. Website: www.indiana.edu/~mfawrite/. **Contact:** Tony Ardizzone.

PURDUE UNIVERSITY, Creative Writing English Dept., Heavilon Hall, West Lafayette IN 47906. (765)494-0344. Fax: (765)494-3780. **Contact:** Marianne Boruch.

UNIVERSITY OF EVANSVILLE, Creative Writing Program, 1800 Lincoln Ave., Evansville IN 47722-0001. (812)479-2977. Fax: (812)477-4079. **Contact:** Margaret McMullen.

UNIVERSITY OF NOTRE DAME, Creative Writing Program, 356 O'Shaughnessy Hall, Notre Dame IN 46556-0368. (219)631-7226.

WABASH COLLEGE, English Department, 301 W. Wabash Ave., P.O. Box 352, Crawfordsville IN 47933. **Contact:** Warren Rosenberg.

Iowa

IOWA STATE UNIVERSITY, 203 Ross Hall, Ames IA 50011. (515)294-3210. Fax: (515)294-6874. **Contact:** Fern Kupfer.

UNIVERSITY OF IOWA, Department of English, 308 EPB, Iowa City IA 52242. (319)335-0454. Fax: (319)335-2535. **Contact:** Paul Diehl.

UNIVERSITY OF IOWA WRITERS' WORKSHOP, 102 Dey House, 507 N. Clinton St., Iowa City IA 52242-1000. **Contact:** Frank Conroy.

UNIVERSITY OF NORTHERN IOWA, Creative Writing, English Department, 117 Baker Hall, Cedar Falls IA 50614-0502. (319)273-3782. Fax: (319)273-5807. Website: www.uni.edu/english/webfiles/cw. **Contact:** Grant Tracey.

Kansas

EMPORIA STATE UNIVERSITY, English Dept., Creative Writing, Box 4019, Emporia KS 66801-5087. (316)341-5216. Fax: (316)341-5547. **Contact:** Dr. Philip Heldrich.

KANSAS STATE UNIVERSITY, English Department, 106 Denison Hall, Manhattan KS 66506-0701. (785)532-6716. Fax: (785)532-2192. E-mail: english@ksu.edu. Website: www.ksu.edu/english/programs/cw.htm. **Contact:** Elizabeth Dodd, Director of Creative Writing. Estab. 1863. Mission is "teaching creative writing within the environment of a strong program in literary studies, at both the bachelor's and master's level." Offers B.A., M.A. Student/teacher ratio: 2-1 (at M.A. level). Average class size: 15. Publishes literary journal *Touchstone*.

UNIVERSITY OF KANSAS, Dept. of English, 3114 Wescoe Hall, Lawrence KS 66045. (785)864-4520. Fax: (504)862-8958. **Contact:** Lori Whitten.

WICHITA STATE UNIVERSITY, English Department, Box 14, WSU, Wichita KS 672600-0014. (316)978-3130. Fax: (316)978-3548. **Contact:** Phillip H. Schneider.

Kentucky

MOREHEAD STATE UNIVERSITY, Creative Writing Program, Box 645, Morehead KY 40351. **Contact:** Dr. Mark Minor.

MURRAY STATE UNIVERSITY, English Department, P.O. Box 9, Murray KY 42071-0009. (502)762-4730. Fax: (612)624-8228. **Contact:** Squire Babcock.

SPALDING UNIVERSITY, 851 S. Fourth St., Louisville KY 40203. (502)585-9911, ext. 2423. Fax: (502)585-5178. Website: www.spalding.edu. **Contact:** Sena Jeter Naslund.

UNIVERSITY OF LOUISVILLE, Creative Writing Program, English/Brigham Humanities 315, Louisville KY 40292. (502)852-6801. Fax: (502)852-4182. **Contact:** Jeffrey T. Skinner.

Louisiana

LOUISIANA STATE UNIVERSITY, English Department, Baton Rouge LA 70803-5001. (225)388-3124. **Contact:** Judy Kahn.

LOYOLA UNIVERSITY NEW ORLEANS, English Dept., CBX50, 6363 St. Charles Ave., New Orleans LA 70118. (504)865-2474. Fax: (504)865-2294. E-mail: biguenet@loyno.edu. Website: www.loyno.edu/english. **Contact:** John Biguenet. Estab. 1912. Offers college credit, concentration in study, B.A. Average class size: 15. Faculty includes John Biguenet. Publishes the literary journal *New Orleans Review.*

McNEESE STATE UNIVERSITY, Department of Languages, Lake Charles LA 70609. (337)475-5594. **Contact:** Dr. Miller Jones.

TULANE UNIVERSITY, Department of English, 6823 St. Charles Ave., New Orleans LA 70118. (504)865-5160. Fax: (504)862-8958. E-mail: english@tulane.edu. **Contact:** Peter R. Cooley. Estab. 1834. Mission "to provide undergraduates with a strong emphasis in creative writing within the English major. Offers concentration in study. Student/teacher ratio: 10-1. Average class size: 15. Faculty includes Josh Russell, Peter Cooley.

UNIVERSITY OF LOUISIANA AT LAFAYETTE, English Department, Box 44691, Lafayette LA 70504. (337)482-5478. **Contact:** Jerry McGuire.

UNIVERSITY OF LOUISIANA AT MUNROE, English Department, 700 University Ave, Munroe LA 71209. (318)342-1520. **Contact:** William Ryan.

UNIVERSITY OF NEW ORLEANS, English Department, Lakefront, New Orleans LA 70118. **Contact:** James Knudsen.

XAVIER UNIVERSITY OF LOUISIANA, English Department, Palmetto St., New Orleans LA 70125. (504)485-5161. Fax: (504)485-7944. **Contact:** Patrice Melnick.

Maine

UNIVERSITY OF MAINE AT FARMINGTON, Roberts Learning Center, 270 Main St., Farmington ME 04938-1720. (207)778-7454. Fax: (207)778-7452. **Contact:** Wesley McNair.

Maryland

GOUCHER COLLEGE, Creative Writing Program, 1021 Dulaney Valley Rd., Towson MD 21204. (410)337-6285. Website: www.goucher.edu/cwpromo. **Contact:** Madison Smartt Bell.

LOYOLA COLLEGE, Writing Media Department, 4501 N. Charles St., Baltimore MD 21210-2697. (410)617-2528.

SALISBURY STATE UNIVERSITY, 1101 Camden Ave., Salisbury MD 21801. (410)453-6445. **Contact:** Kathy Shaeffer.

TOWSON UNIVERSITY, English Department, Towson MD 21252. **Contact:** Clarinda Harriss.

UNIVERSITY OF MARYLAND, 3119 Susquehanna Hall, UMCP, English Department, College Park MD 20742. (301)405-3820. Fax: (301)314-7539. Website: www.inform.umd.edu/ARHU/Depts/English. **Contacts:** Michael Collier and Stanley Plumly.

Massachusetts

BOSTON COLLEGE, Carney Hall, Chestnut Hill MA 02467. (617)552-3716. **Contact:** Suzanne Matson.

BRIDGEWATER STATE COLLEGE, Tillinghast Hall, English Department, Bridgewater MA 02325. **Contact:** Dr. Iain Crawford.

EMERSON COLLEGE, English Department, 120 Boyleston St., Boston MA 02116. **Contact:** John Skoyles.

HARVARD UNIVERSITY, Barker Center, 12 Quincy St., Cambridge MA 02138. (617)495-2103. Fax: (617)496-6031. Website: www.fas.harvard.edu/english. **Contact:** Brad Watson.

LARCOM PRESS, P.O. Box 161, Prides Crossing MA 01915. (978)927-8707. Fax: (978)927-8904. **Contact:** Ann Perrott.

MIT, Program in Writing and Humanistic Studies, 14E-303, Cambridge MA 02139-4307. (617)253-7894. Fax: (617)253-6910. **Contact:** James Paradis.

UNIVERSITY OF MASSACHUSETTS AT AMHERST, Bartlett Hall, English Department, Amherst MA 01003-0515. (413)545-5459. **Contact:** Donna Johnson.

UNIVERSITY OF MASSACHUSETTS AT DARTMOUTH, English Department, 285 Old Westport Rd., North Dartmouth MA 02747-2300. (508)999-8274. Website: www.umassd.edu/cas/english. **Contact:** Edwin Thompson.

Michigan

ALPENA COMMUNITY COLLEGE, 666 Johnson St., Alpena MI 49707. (989)358-7559. (989)358-7250. **Contact:** Thomas Ray.

CENTRAL MICHIGAN UNIVERSITY, Dept. of English Language & Literature, Mt. Pleasant MI 48859. (989)774-3126. Fax: (989)774-1271. **Contact:** Eric Torgersen.

GRAND VALLEY STATE UNIVERSITY, Writing Department, 1 Campus Dr., Allendale MI 49401. (616)895-3209. Fax: (616)895-3545. Website: www.gvsu.edu/writing. **Contact:** Roger Gilles.

HOPE COLLEGE, English Department, 126 E. 10th St., Holland MI 49423. (616)395-7116. Fax: (616)395-7134. Website: www.hope.edu. **Contact:** Heather Sellers.

MICHIGAN STATE UNIVERSITY, Creative Writing Program/English, 201 Morrill Hall, East Lansing MI 48824-1036. (517)355-7570. Fax: (517)353-3755. **Contact:** Marcia Aldrich.

NORTHERN MICHIGAN UNIVERSITY, Department of English, 1401 Presque Isle Ave., Marquette MI 49855. (906)227-2711. Fax: (906)227-1096. Website: http://instruct.nmu.edu/english/bmathern. **Contact:** Beverly Matherne.

UNIVERSITY OF MICHIGAN AT ANN ARBOR, 3187 Angell Hall, Ann Arbor MI 48109-1003. (734)615-3710. Website: www.lsa.umich.edu/english/grad/graduate.htm. **Contact:** Nicholas Delbanco.

WESTERN MICHIGAN UNIVERSITY, English Department, 619 Sprau Tower, Kalamazoo MI 49008-5092. (616)387-2570. Fax: (616)387-2562. **Contact:** Michele C. McLaughlin.

Minnesota

AUGSBURG COLLEGE, 2211 Riverside Ave., Minneapolis MN 55454. (612)330-1646. Fax: (612)330-1646. **Contact:** Katherine Swanson.

COLLEGE OF ST. BENEDICT, 37 S. College Ave., Maine 216, St. Joseph MN 56374. (320)363-5399. Website: www.csbsju.edu/literaryarts. **Contact:** Mary Jane Berger.

HAMLINE UNIVERSITY, Graduate Liberal Studies, 1536 Hewitt Ave., St. Paul MN 55104-1284. (651)523-2047. Fax: (651)523-2490. E-mail: water-stone@gw.hamline.edu. Website: www.hamline.edu/graduate/gls. **Contact:** Sandy Beach, program assistant. Estab. 1994. "Hamline's M.F.A. program encourages students to explore a range of writing styles and genres in an ongoing pursuit of voice and form. Students study with engaged working writers and scholars in the context of an interdisciplinary curriculum. Our primary goals are artistic and intellectual development. Students our expected to complete the program with a unified, book-length manuscript of strong literary quality that shows mastery of the craft." Offers M.F.A., master's of liberal studies with concentration in creative writing. Student/teacher ratio: 10-1. Average class size: 12. Publishes the literary journal *Water-Stone*.

MACALESTER COLLEGE, 1600 Grand Ave., St. Paul MN 55105-1899. (651)696-6516. **Contact:** Diane Glancy.

MINNESOTA STATE UNIVERSITY AT MOOREHEAD, 1104 7th Ave. S., Moorhead MN 56563. (218)236-2764. **Contact:** Virginia Klenk.

MINNESOTA STATE UNIVERSITY MANKATO, English Department, 230 Armstrong Hall, Mankato MN 56001. (507)389-2117. Fax: (507)389-5362. Website: www.mankato.msus.edu/dept/english. **Contact:** Richard Robbins.

SOUTHWEST STATE UNIVERSITY, Writing Center English Department, 1501 State St., Marshall MN 56258. (507)537-7155. Fax: (607)255-6661. **Contact:** Eileen Thomas.

UNIVERSITY OF MINNESOTA AT MINNEAPOLIS, 209 Lind Hall, 207 Church St. SE, Minneapolis MN 55455. (612)625-4360. **Contact:** Jill Christman.

WINONA STATE, Winona MN 55987-5838. (507)457-5440. Fax: (507)457-5440. **Contact:** David Robinson.

Mississippi

MISSISSIPPI STATE UNIVERSITY, Drawer E. MS 39762, Mississippi State MS 39762. (601)325-2317. Fax: (516)287-8125. **Contact:** Joyce Harris.

UNIVERSITY OF MISSISSIPPI, Dept. of English Box 1848, Bondurant Hall, University MS 38677. (662)915-7439. Website: www.olemiss.edu/depts/english. **Contact:** Joseph Urgo.

Missouri

CENTRAL MISSOURI STATE UNIVERSITY, Dept. of English and Philosophy, Martin 336, Warrensburg MO 64093. **Contact:** Rose Marie Kinder.

DRURY UNIVERSITY, 900 N. Benton Ave., Springfield MO 65802. (417)873-7220. Website: www.drury.edu. **Contact:** Randall Fuller.

LINCOLN UNIVERSITY, Department of English MLK Hall, 820 Chestnut, Jefferson City MO 65102-0029. (573)681-5195. Fax: (573)681-5040. **Contact:** Ginger Jones.

SOUTHEAST MISSOURI STATE UNIVERSITY, English Department, MS 2650, Cape Girdeau MO 63701-4799. (573)651-5188. **Contact:** Dr. Susan Swatwout.

SOUTHWEST MISSOURI STATE UNIVERSITY, English Department, 901 S. National, Springfield MO 65804. (408)280-2143. **Contact:** Michael Burns.

STEPHENS COLLEGE, English & Creative Writing, Campus Box 2034, Columbia MO 65215. (573)442-2211, ext. 4668. Fax: (573)876-7248. **Contact:** Judith Clark.

UNIVERSITY OF MISSOURI, Program in Creative Writing, 202 Tate Hall, Columbia MO 65211. (573)884-7773. Fax: (573)884-3122. E-mail: creativewriting@missouri.edu. Website: www.missouri.edu/~cwp. **Contact:** Sharon Fisher. Offers M.A., Ph.D. Faculty includes Marly Swick, Trudy Lewis, Speer Morgan. Publishes the literary journals *Missouri Review* and *Center: A Journal for the Literary Arts*.

UNIVERSITY OF MISSOURI AT KANSAS CITY, Creative Writing, 5101 Rockhill Rd., Kansas City MO 64110. (816)235-2765. Fax: (816)235-1308. E-mail: pritchettmi@umkc.edu. Website: www.umkc.edu/english. **Contact:** Michael S. Pritchett, coordinator. Estab. 1963. Mission is "to train fiction writers and poets in the art of writing and how to continue growing as artists while pursuing careers and publication." Offers concentration in study. Student/teacher ratio: 15-1. Average class size: 15. Faculty includes Michael Pritchett, Thomas Russell. Publishes the literary journal *New Letters*.

UNIVERSITY OF MISSOURI AT ST. LOUIS, MFA Program Department of English, 8001 Natural Bridge, St. Louis MO 63121. (314)516-6845. E-mail: marytroy@umsl.edu. **Contact:** Mary Troy. Estab. 1997. Mission "to create good writers; to take those already good and make them better." Offers M.F.A. Student/teacher ratio: 5-1.

Average class size: 12. Faculty includes Mary Troy and Howard Schwartz. Publishes the literary journal *Natural Bridge*.

WASHINGTON UNIVERSITY, The Writing Program English Dept., One Brookings Dr., St. Louis MO 63130. (314)935-7130. Website: http://artsci.wustl.edu/~english/writing. **Contact:** Carolyn B. Smith.

WESTMINSTER COLLEGE, 501 Westminster Ave., Fulton MO 65251-1299. **Contact:** Wayne Zade.

Montana

UNIVERSITY OF MONTANA, Creative Writing Program, English Department, Missoula MT 59812. **Contact:** Susie Castle.

Nebraska

CREIGHTON UNIVERSITY, English Department, 2500 California Plaza, Omaha NE 68178. (402)280-5768. Fax: (402)280-2143. E-mail: mhs@creighton.edu. Website: http://mockingbird.creighton.edu/ncw/cw/htm. **Contact:** Mary Helen Stefaniak. Estab. 1992. Mission "to teach students the art and craft of writing." Offers college credit, certificate, B.A., M.A. Student/teacher ratio: 10-1. Average class size: 11. Faculty includes Brent Spencer, Mary Helen Stefaniak. Publishes the literary journal *Shadows*.

UNIVERSITY OF NEBRASKA AT KEARNEY, #202 Thomas Hall, Kearney NE 68849-1320. (308)865-8299. Fax: (308)865-8411. E-mail: emrysb@unk.edu. Website: www.unk.edu/acad/english/home.html. **Contact:** Barbara Emrys. Estab. 1999. Mission is "to introduce students to the craft of writing, and help them develop publishable work (undergraduate); and to develop a publishable thesis (graduate)." Offers concentration in study and M.A. Average class size: 15. Faculty includes A.B. Embrys, Sam Umland, Suzanne Bloomfield. Publishes the literary journals *The Carillon* and *The Reynolds Review*.

UNIVERSITY OF NEBRASKA AT LINCOLN, English Department, 202 Andrews Hall, Lincoln NE 68588-0333. (404)472-9771. Website: www.unl.edu/english/html/creative.html. **Contact:** Linda Rossiter.

UNIVERSITY OF NEBRASKA AT OMAHA, Writer's Workshop, 60th & Dodge, Omaha, NE 68182-0324. E-mail: ahomer@mail.unomaha.edu. Website: www.unomaha.edu/~fineart/wworkshop/wrkshop.html.

Nevada

UNIVERSITY OF NEVADA, LAS VEGAS, 4505 Maryland Pkwy., Box 455011, Las Vegas NV 89154-5011. (702)895-3533. Fax: (702)895-4801. **Contact:** Douglas Unger.

UNIVERSITY OF NEVADA, RENO, Department of English 098, Reno NV 89557. (702)784-6689. **Contact:** Geri McVeigh.

New Hampshire

UNIVERSITY OF NEW HAMPSHIRE, English Department, 95 Main St., Durham NH 03824. (603)862-0261. Fax: (603)862-3565. **Contact:** Margaret Love Denman.

New Jersey

ROWAN UNIVERSITY, College of Communication, 201 Mullica Hill Rd., Glassboro NJ 08028-1701. **Contact:** Pat Birmingham.

RUTGERS UNIVERSITY, English Department Armitage Hall, 311 N 5th St., Camden NJ 08102-1405. (856)225-6096. **Contact:** Kathy Volk Miller.

New Mexico

INSTITUTE OF AMERICAN INDIAN ARTS, 83 Avan Nu Po Rd., Sante Fe NM 87505. (505)424-2364. Fax: (505)424-3030. Website: www.iaiancad.org. **Contact:** Jon Davis.

NEW MEXICO STATE UNIVERSITY, Box 3001, Dept. 3E, Las Cruces NM 88003-0001. **Contact:** Christopher Burnham.

UNIVERSITY OF NEW MEXICO, English Department, Humanities Bldg. 255, Albuquerque NM 87131. (505)277-6347. Fax: (505)277-2950. E-mail: english@unm.edu. Website: www.unm.edu/~english. **Contact:** Sharon Oard Warner. Estab. 1980. "We offer students the opportunity to concentrate in poetry, prose fiction and creative nonfiction while taking courses in literature, language, and professional writing. The program, which consists of workshop, literature and publishing courses, grounds students in the rich tradition of writing." Offers concentration in study, M.A. Student/teacher ratio (graduate): 5-1. Average class size: 12. Faculty includes Sharon Oard Warner, Daniel Meuller, Julie Shigekuni, Gregory Martin. Publishes the literary journal *Blue Mesa Review*.

New York

BINGHAMTON UNIVERSITY, English Department, P.O. Box 6000, Binghamton NY 13902-6000. (607)777-2169. Fax: (607)777-2408. Website: http://english.binghamton.edu. **Contact:** Maria Gillan.

BROOKLYN COLLEGE, 2900 Bedford Ave., Brooklyn NY 11210. (718)951-5195. **Contact:** Nancy Black.

CANISIUS COLLEGE, 2001 Main St., Buffalo NY 14208. (716)888-2662. **Contact:** Mick Cochrane.

COLUMBIA UNIVERSITY SCHOOL OF THE ARTS, 415 Dodge Hall, 2960 Broadway, New York NY 10027. (212)854-4392. **Contact:** Anna Delmoro.

CORNELL UNIVERSITY, Department of English, 250 Goldwin Smith Hall, Ithaca NY 14853. (607)255-7989. Fax: (607)255-6661. **Contact:** Jenka T. Pfyfe.

EUGENE LANG COLLEGE, 66 West 12th St., New York NY 10011. (212)229-5617. **Contact:** Beatrice Banu.

HAMILTON COLLEGE CREATIVE WRITING, 198 College Hill Rd., Clinton NY 13323. (315)859-4369. **Contact:** Nat Strout.

ITHACA COLLEGE PARK HALL, Danby Rd., Ithaca NY 14850. (607)274-3138. Website: www.ithaca.edu. **Contact:** Marion MacCurdy.

NASSAU COMMUNITY COLLEGE, 6th Floor Tower, One Education Dr., Garden City NY 11530-6793. (516)572-7711.

NEW YORK UNIVERSITY, Creative Writing Room 310, 19 University Place, Room 19, New York NY 10003-4556. (212)998-8806. Fax: (212)995-4864. Website: www.nyu.edu/gsas/program/cwp. **Contact:** Melissa Hammerle.

SAINT LAWRENCE UNIVERSITY, Program in Creative Writing, English Department Richardson Hall, Canton NY 13617. (315)229-5125. Fax: (315)229-5628. **Contact:** Dr. Robert Cowser.

SARAH LAWRENCE COLLEGE, Office of Graduate Studies, 1 Mead Way, Bronxville NY 10594. (914)395-2371. Website: www.slc.edu. **Contact:** Thomas Lux.

SOUTHAMPTON COLLEGE OF LONG ISLAND UNIVERSITY, Humanities, 239 Montauk Highway, Southampton NY 11968. (631)287-8420. Website: www.southampton.liu.edu. **Contact:** Robert Pattison.

STATE UNIVERSITY OF NEW YORK, 35 New Campus Dr., Brockport NY 14420-2211. **Contact:** Stan Rubin.

STATE UNIVERSITY OF NEW YORK AT GENESEO, English Department, One College Circle, Geneseo NY 14454-1451. (716)245-5272. **Contact:** David Kelly.

SYRACUSE UNIVERSITY, 401 Hall of Languages, 100 University Place, Syracuse NY 13244. (315)443-9482. Fax: (315)443-3660. Website: www-hl.syr.edu/depts/english/cwp/cwindex.htm. **Contact:** Dr. Brooks Haxton.

North Carolina

EAST CAROLINA UNIVERSITY, Writing Program, Greenville NC 27858-4353. (252)328-6380. **Contact:** Jim Holt.

ELON UNIVERSITY, CB 2252, Elon University NC 27244. **Contact:** Kevin Boyle.

NORTH CAROLINA STATE UNIVERSITY AT RALEIGH, Department of English, Box 8105, Raleigh NC 27695-8105. (919)515-4102. **Contact:** Sharon Johnson.

ST. ANDREWS COLLEGE, 1700 Dogwood Mile, Laurinburg NC 28352. **Contact:** Ron Bays.

UNIVERSITY OF NORTH CAROLINA AT ASHEVILLE, 1 University Heights, Language & Literature Dept., Asheville NC 28804-3299. **Contact:** Kim Manning.

UNIVERSITY OF NORTH CAROLINA AT CHAPEL HILL, Greenlaw CB 3520, Department of English, Chapel Hill NC 27599-3520. **Contact:** Marianne Gingher.

UNIVERSITY OF NORTH CAROLINA AT GREENSBORO, MFA Writing Program Department of English, 134 MacIver Bldg., P.O. Box 26170, Greensboro NC 27402-6170. (336)334-5459. Website: www.uncg.edu/eng/mfa. **Contact:** James L. Clark.

UNIVERSITY OF NORTH CAROLINA WILMINGTON, English Department, 601 S. College Rd., Wilmington NC 28403. (910)962-3748. Fax: (910)962-7461. **Contact:** Lorrie Smith.

WARREN WILSON COLLEGE, MFA Program for Writers, P.O. Box 9000, Asheville NC 28815-9000. (704)298-3325. **Contact:** Peter Turchi.

WESTERN CAROLINA UNIVERSITY, English Dept., CO 305, Cullowhee NC 28723. (828)227-7264. Fax: (828)227-7266. Website: www.wcu.edu/as/english. **Contact:** Dr. Brian Railsback.

North Dakota

UNIVERSITY OF NORTH DAKOTA, Department of English, P.O. Box 7209, Grand Forks ND 58202-7209. (701)777-3321. Fax: (701)777-2373. **Contact:** Ursula Hovet.

Ohio

ASHLAND UNIVERSITY, 401 College Ave., Ashland OH 44805. (419)289-5110. **Contact:** Joe Mackall.

BOWLING GREEN STATE UNIVERSITY, English Department, 226 East Hall, Bowling Green OH 43403. (419)372-8370. Website: www.bgsu.edu/departments/creativewriting. **Contact:** Wendell Mayo.

CASE WESTERN RESERVE UNIVERSITY, English Department, 11112 Bellflower Rd., Cleveland OH 44106-7117. (216)368-2355. Fax: (216)368-5088. Website: www.cwru.edu. **Contact:** Mary Grimm.

CLEVELAND STATE UNIVERSITY, Creative Writing Program, Euclid Ave at East 24th St., Cleveland OH 44115. (216)687-4522. **Contact:** Neal Chandler.

DENISON UNIVERSITY, English Department, Creative Writing Program, Granville OH 43023. **Contact:** David Baker.

HIRAM COLLEGE, Department of English, P.O. Box 67, Hiram OH 44234. (330)569-5152. Fax: (330)569-5130. **Contact:** Joyce Dyer.

KENT STATE UNIVERSITY, English Department, P.O. Box 5190, 113 Satterfield Hall, Kent OH 44242-0001. (330)672-2067. Fax: (330)672-2567. Website: http://dept.kent.edu/wick/. **Contact:** Maggie Anderson.

MIAMI UNIVERSITY, 356 Bachelor Hall, Oxford OH 45056. (513)529-5221. Fax: (513)529-1392. **Contact:** Steven Bauer and Eric Goodman.

OHIO STATE UNIVERSITY, English Department, Creative Writing Program, 421 Denney Hall, 164 W. 17th Ave, Columbus OH 43210-1370. (614)292-2242. Fax: (614)292-7816. Website: www.english.ohio-state.edu/areas/creative_writing. **Contact:** Michelle Herman.

OHIO UNIVERSITY PROGRAM IN CREATIVE WRITING, Dept. of English Language & Literature, College of Arts & Sciences, Ellis Hall, Athens OH 45701-2979. (740)593-9938. Fax: (740)593-4181. Website: www.english.ohiou.edu/gradprogram/creativew.html. **Contact:** Darrell Spencer.

OTTERBEIN COLLEGE, English Department, Westerville OH 43081. (614)823-1560. Fax: (812)479-2320. **Contact:** Norman Cheney.

UNIVERSITY OF CINCINNATI WRITING PROGRAM, English Department, P.O. Box 21-069, Cincinnati OH 45221-0069. **Contact:** Jon Hughes.

UNIVERSITY OF TOLEDO, Department of English, 2801 W. Bancroft, Toledo OH 43606. (419)530-4408. Fax: (419)530-4440. **Contact:** Jane Bradley.

WRITERS ONLINE WORKSHOPS, 4700 E. Galbraith Rd., Cincinnati OH 45236. (800)759-0963. Fax: (513)531-0798. E-mail: wdwowadmin@fwpubs.com. Website: www.writersonlineworkshops.com. **Contact:** Joe Stollenwerk, educational services manager. Estab. 2000. Online workshop; ongoing. Course duration: 6-15 weeks. Average attendance: 10-15 per class. "We have workshops in fiction, nonfiction, memoir, poetry and proposal writings." Site: Internet-based, operated entirely on the website. Current fiction related courses include Fundamentals of Fiction, Focus on the Novel, Focus on the Short Story, Advanced Novel Writing, Advanced Story Writing, Creating Dynamic Characters, Writing Effective Dialogue, Writing the Novel Proposal, Creativity & Expression (fiction and nonfiction), and others. Costs: 6-8 week workshops, $179; 12-week, $299; 14-week, $349; 15-week, $579. Additional information available on website. Accepts inquiries by e-mail and phone.

Oklahoma

CAMERON UNIVERSITY, 2800 W. Gore Blvd., Lawton OK 73505.

OKLAHOMA STATE UNIVERSITY, Creative Writing Program, English Department, 205 Morrill Hall, Stillwater OK 74078. (405)744-6148. Fax: (405)744-6326. **Contact:** Lisa Lewis.

UNIVERSITY OF CENTRAL OKLAHOMA, 100 North University Dr., Edmond OK 73034. (405)974-5632. Fax: (405)974-3832. **Contact:** Dr. Stephen Garrison.

UNIVERSITY OF OKLAHOMA, English Department, 760 Van Vleet Oval #113, Norman OK 73019-0240. (405)325-6647. Fax: (405)325-0831.

Oregon

CLACKAMAS COMMUNITY COLLEGE, 19600 S. Molalla Ave., Oregon City OR 97045. (503)657-6958, ext. 2372. **Contact:** Emily Orlando.

LEWIS & CLARK COLLEGE, English Department, 0615 SW Palatine Hill Rd., #58, Portland OR 97219.

LINFIELD COLLEGE, Department of English, 900 SE Baker, McMinnville OR 97128-6894. (503)434-2288. Fax: (503)434-2215. **Contact:** Barbara Drake.

MOVEO ANGELUS LITERARY ARTS, 31450 NE Bell Rd., Sherwood OR 97140. **Contact:** Priska von Beroldingen.

OREGON STATE UNIVERSITY, Creative Writing Program, English Department, 238 Moreland Hall, Corvallis OR 97331-5302. (541)737-1635. Fax: (541)737-3589. Website: www.orst.edu/dept/english/orw. **Contact:** Marjorie Sandor.

UNIVERSITY OF OREGON, Program in Creative Writing, 5243 University of Oregeon, 144 Columbia Hall, Eugene OR 97403-1286. (541)346-4060. Fax: (541)346-0537. Website: http://darkwing.uoregon.edu/~crwrweb/. **Contact:** Ken Calhoon.

Pennsylvania

BLOOMSBURG UNIVERSITY, English Department, 400 E. Second St., Bloomsburg PA 17815. (570)389-3006.

BUCKNELL UNIVERSITY, Stadler Center for Poetry, Lewisburg PA 17837. (570)577-1853. Fax: (570)577-3760. **Contact:** Cynthia Hogue.

CARLOW COLLEGE, 3335 Fifth Avenue, Pittsburgh PA 15213. (412)578-6346. Fax: (412)578-8722. **Contact:** Patricia Dobler.

CARNEGIE MELLON UNIVERSITY, Creative Writing Program, English Department, Pittsburgh PA 15213-2890. (412)268-2850. **Contact:** Jim Daniels.

CHATHAM COLLEGE, Woodland Rd., Pittsburgh PA 15232. (412)365-1190. Fax: (412)365-1505. **Contact:** Jeffrey Thomson.

DICKINSON COLLEGE, English Department, P.O. Box 1773, Carlisle PA 17013. (717)245-1346. Fax: (717)254-1942. Website: www.dickinson.edu/departments/engl/cw_minor.html. **Contact:** Adrienne Sue.

KUTZTOWN UNIVERSITY, English Department, Creative Writing Program, Kutztown PA 19530. **Contact:** James V. Applewhite.

LYCOMING COLLEGE, Creative Writing Program, English Department, Williamsport PA 17701-5192. (570)321-4000. Fax: (570)321-4389. **Contacts:** G. W. Hawkes and Sascha Feinstein.

PENN STATE ERIE, The Behrend College School of Humanities & Social Sciences, Station Rd., Erie PA 16563. (814)898-6440. **Contact:** Dr. Diana Hume George.

PENNSYLVANIA STATE UNIVERSITY, University Park PA 16802-6200. (814)865-6382. Fax: (814)863-7285. **Contact:** Julia Kasdorf.

SUSQUEHANNA UNIVERSITY, Writer's Institute, Hassinger Hall, Selinsgrove PA 17870. (570)372-4164. Fax: (570)372-2774. **Contact:** Dr. Gary Fincke.

TEMPLE UNIVERSITY, Creative Writing Program, 1020 Anderson Hall, Philadelphia PA 19122-6090. (215)204-2662. **Contact:** Dr. Alan Singer.

UNIVERSITY OF PENNSYLVANIA, Creative Writing Program, English Department, Philadelphia PA 19104-6273. **Contact:** Gregory Djanikian.

UNIVERSITY OF PITTSBURGH, Department of English 526-CL, Pittsburgh PA 15260. (412)624-6508. Fax: (412)624-6639. **Contact:** Lynn Emanuel.

UNIVERSITY OF PITTSBURGH AT BRADFORD, 300 Campus Dr., Bradford PA 16701-2896. (814)362-7590. Fax: (814)362-5094. Website: www.upb.pitt.edu. **Contact:** Nancy McCabe.

UNIVERSITY OF PITTSBURGH AT JOHNSTOWN, 450 Schoolhouse Rd., Johnstown PA 15904-2912. (814)269-7140. Fax: (814)269-7196. **Contact:** Dr. Carroll Grimes.

UNIVERSITY OF SCRANTON, English Department, Creative Writing, Scranton PA 18510. (717)941-7619. **Contact:** John Meredith Hill.

Rhode Island

BROWN UNIVERSITY, English Department, Box 1852, Providence RI 02912-1852. (401)863-3260. **Contact:** Forrest Gander.

PROVIDENCE COLLEGE, English Department, River Avenue, Providence RI 02918-0001. (401)865-2587. Fax: (401)865-1192. **Contact:** Susan Fournier.

RHODE ISLAND COLLEGE, 600 Mt. Pleasant Ave., Providence RI 02908. (401)456-8115. **Contact:** Thomas Cobb.

South Carolina

CONVERSE COLLEGE, 580 East Main St., Spartanburg SC 29302. (864)596-9099. Website: www.converse.edu. **Contact:** Rick Mulkey.

UNIVERSITY OF SOUTH CAROLINA, MFA Program in Creative Writing, English Dept., Humanities Bldg., Columbia SC 29208. (803)777-2096. Fax: (803)777-9064. E-mail: dawsk@gwm.sc.edu. **Contact:** Dr. Kwame Dawes. Offers M.F.A. Student/teacher ratio: 12-1. Average class size: 12. Faculty includes Dr. Janette Turner Hospital. Publishes the literary journal *Yemassee.*

South Dakota

UNIVERSITY OF SOUTH DAKOTA, 212 Dakota Hall, 414 E. Clark, Vermillion SD 57069-2390. (605)677-5966. Fax: (605)677-5298. **Contact:** Brian Bedard.

Tennessee

DYERSBURG STATE COMMUNITY COLLEGE, 1510 Lake Rd., Dyersburg TN 38024. (901)286-3326. **Contact:** Larry Griffin.

RHODES COLLEGE, English Department, Palmer Hall, 3rd Floor, 2000 N. Parkway, Memphis TN 38112. (901)843-3979. Fax: (901)843-3728. Website: www.rhodes.edu. **Contact:** Tina Barr.

UNIVERSITY OF THE SOUTH AT SEWANEE, Creative Writing Program, SPO 735 University Ave., Sewanee TN 37383-1000. **Contact:** Cheri Peters.

UNIVERSITY OF MEMPHIS, Creative Writing Program, English Department, Patterson Hall Room 463, Memphis TN 38152. (309)341-7090. **Contact:** Thomas Russell.

Texas

ABILENE CHRISTIAN UNIVERSITY, Creative Writing Program, English Department, Abilene TX 79699. (915)674-2263. **Contact:** Beth Lana.

BAYLOR UNIVERSITY, Department of English, P.O. Box 97404, Waco TX 76798. (254)710-1768. Fax: (254)710-3894. **Contact:** Dr. William V. Davis.

HARDIN-SIMMONS UNIVERSITY, Box 15114, Abilene TX 79698. (915)670-1214. **Contact:** Robert Fink.

SAM HOUSTON STATE UNIVERSITY, Texas Review, English Department, Box 2146, Huntsville TX 77341-2146. (936)294-1992. Fax: (936)294-3070. Website: www.shsu.edu. **Contact:** Barbara Miles.

LAMAR UNIVERSITY AT BEAUMONT, Creative Writing, P.O. Box 10023, Beaumont TX 77710. (409)880-8558. Fax: (409)880-8591. **Contact:** Sam Gwynn.

MIDLAND COLLEGE MAIN CAMPUS, 3600 N. Garfield, Midland TX 79705-6397. **Contact:** Dr. Leslie M. Williams.

NORTH LAKE COLLEGE, 5001 N. MacArthur Blvd., Irving TX 75038-3899. (972)273-3551. **Contact:** Dr. Gary D. Swaim.

SOUTHERN METHODIST UNIVERSITY, Department of English, P.O. Box 0435, Dallas TX 75275. (214)768-4369. **Contact:** Jack Myers.

SOUTHWEST TEXAS STATE UNIVERSITY, Creative Writing Program, 601 University Dr., San Marcos TX 78666-4616. **Contact:** Tom Grimes.

TEXAS A&M UNIVERSITY, 4227 TAMU, College Station TX 77843-4227. (979)845-8316. Fax: (979)862-2292. **Contact:** Janet McCann.

TEXAS TECH UNIVERSITY, English Department, Box 43091, Lubbock TX 79409-3091. (806)742-2501. Fax: (806)742-2501. Website: http://english.ttu.edu. **Contact:** Madonne Meyer.

TRINITY UNIVERSITY, Department of English, 715 Stadium Dr., San Antonio TX 78212-7200. (512)736-7517. **Contact:** Peter Balbert.

UNIVERSITY OF HOUSTON, Creative Writing Program, 229 Roy Cullen Bldg., Houston TX 77204-3015. (713)743-3014. Fax: (713)743-3013. Website: www.uh.edu/cwp. **Contact:** Faith Venverloh.

UNIVERSITY OF NORTH TEXAS, English Department, P.O. Box 311307, Denton TX 76203-1307. (940)565-2050. Fax: (940)565-4355. E-mail: brodman@unt.edu. Website: www.engl.unt.edu. **Contact:** Dr. Barbara A. Rodman. Estab. 1990. Mission "to develop the craft of writing in a context of diverse literary traditions supported by studies in creative writing, literary criticism, literature." Offers B.A., M.A., Ph.D. Average class size: 6-15. Faculty includes Barbara Rodman, John Tait, Kevin Grauke. Publishes the *American Literary Review*.

UNIVERSITY OF ST. THOMAS, 3800 Montrose, Houston TX 77006. (713)525-3172. Fax: (940)565-4355. E-mail: englishstaff@stthom.edu. **Contact:** Janet Lowery.

UNIVERSITY OF TEXAS AT DALLAS, Box 830688 JD 3.1, Richardson TX 75083-0688. Website: www.utdallas.edu/~nelsen/creativity.html. **Contact:** Robert Nelsen.

UNIVERSITY OF TEXAS AT EL PASO, Bilingual MFA Program, % Dept. of English, El Paso TX 79968. (915)747-5529. Fax: (915)747-6214. **Contact:** Leslie Ullman.

UNIVERSITY OF TEXAS MICHENER CENTER, Department of English, Parlin Hall, 702 East Dean Keeton, Austin TX 78705. (512)471-1601. Fax: (512)471-9997. Website: www.utexas.edu/academic/mcw. **Contact:** James Magnuson.

UNIVERSITY OF TEXAS AT SAN ANTONIO, 6900 North Loop 1604 W., San Antonio TX 78249. (210)458-4374. Fax: (210)458-5366. **Contact:** Linda Woodson.

Utah

BRIGHAM YOUNG UNIVERSITY, English Department, 3146 JKHB, Provo UT 84602. (801)378-4939. Fax: (801)378-4720. Website: http://english.byu.edu. **Contact:** Sally T. Taylor.

UNIVERSITY OF UTAH, Department of English, Salt Lake City UT 84112-0494. (801)581-6168. Fax: (801)585-5167. Website: www.hum.utah.edu/english. **Contact:** Katharine Coles.

WESTMINSTER COLLEGE OF SALT LAKE CITY, 2840 S 1300 E., Salt Lake City UT 84105. (801)488-1654. **Contact:** Natasha Sajé.

Vermont

BENNINGTON COLLEGE, Writing Seminar, Route 67-A, Bennington VT 05201. (802)440-4452. Fax: (802)440-4454. E-mail: writing@bennington.edu. Website: www.bennington.edu. **Contact:** Liam Rector.

GODDARD COLLEGE, 123 Pitkin Rd., Plainfield VT 05663. (212)533-9209. Fax: (802)454-8301. Website: www.goddard.edu. **Contact:** Paul Selig.

VERMONT COLLEGE, MFA in Writing, Montpelier VT 05602. (802)828-8840. Fax: (802)828-8649. Website: www.tui.edu/vermontcollege. **Contact:** Louise Crowley, Administrative Director.

Virginia

HOLLINS UNIVERSITY, P.O. Box 9677, Roanoke VA 24020-1677. (540)362-6317. Fax: (540)362-6097. E-mail: creative.writing@hollins.edu. Website: www.hollins.edu/academics/academics.htm. **Contact:** R.H.W. Dillard.

JAMES MADISON UNIVERSITY, English Department, MSC 1801, Harrisonburg VA 22807. (540)568-6202. Fax: (540)568-2983. Website: www.jmu.edu/english. **Contact:** Annette Frederico.

GEORGE MASON UNIVERSITY, Creative Writing Program, English Department MSN 3E4, 4400 University Dr., Fairfax VA 22030-4444. (703)993-1180. Fax: (703)993-1161. Website: www.gmu.edu/departments/english. **Contact:** William Miller.

OLD DOMINION UNIVERSITY, Creative Writing Program, English Department, Hampton Blvd., Norfolk VA 23529. (757)683-4770. **Contact:** Dr. Michael Pearson.

ROANOKE COLLEGE, Salem VA 24153. (540)375-2380. **Contact:** Paul Hanstedt.

UNIVERSITY OF VIRGINIA, P.O. Box 400121, Charlottesville VA 22904. (434)924-6675. Fax: (434)924-1478. **Contact:** Lisa Russ Spaar.

VIRGINIA COMMONWEALTH UNIVERSITY, P.O. Box 842005, Richmond VA 23284-2005. (804)828-1329. Fax: (804)828-8684. Website: www.has.vcu.edu/eng/grad. **Contact:** Laura Browder.

VIRGINIA POLYTECHNIC INSTITUTE & STATE UNIVERSITY, Department of English, Shanks Hall, Blacksburg VA 24061-0112. (540)231-6146. Fax: (540)231-5692. **Contact:** Lucinda Roy.

Washington

EASTERN WASHINGTON UNIVERSITY, Creative Writing Program MS 1, Spokane Center, 705 W 1st Avenue, Spokane WA 99201. (509)623-4217. **Contact:** Anita O'Brien.

UNIVERSITY OF WASHINGTON, English Department, Box 351130, Seattle WA 98195. (206)543-2690. **Contact:** Susan Williams.

WASHINGTON STATE UNIVERSITY, Department of English, P.O. Box 645020, Pullman WA 99164-5020. (360)650-6846. **Contact:** Carol Westensee.

WESTERN WASHINGTON UNIVERSITY, Department of English, Bellingham WA 98225-9055. (360)650-6846. **Contact:** Kathryn Trueblood, Advisor, Creative Writing.

West Virginia

WEST VIRGINIA UNIVERSITY, English Department, P.O. Box 6296, 230 Stansbury Hall, Morgantown WV 26506-6296. (304)293-1307, ext. 451. **Contact:** James Harms.

WEST VIRGINIA WESLEYAN COLLEGE, Creative Writing Program, English Department, Buckhannon WV 26201-2995. (304)473-8701. Fax: (304)473-8864. **Contact:** Mark DeFoe.

Wisconsin

BELOIT COLLEGE, Creative Writing Program, English Department, Box 23, Beloit WI 53511-5596. (608)363-2308. **Contact:** Clint McCown.

CARDINAL STRITCH UNIVERSITY, 6801 North Yates Rd., Milwaukee WI 53217. (414)410-4193. (315)443-3660. **Contact:** Barbara Wuest.

LAKELAND COLLEGE, Creative Writing, English Department, Sheboygan WI 53062-0359. (920)565-1276. Fax: (920)565-1206. Website: www.lakeland.edu. **Contact:** Karl Elder.

MARQUETTE UNIVERSITY, P.O. Box 1881, Milwaukee WI 53201. (414)288-7179. Fax: (414)288-5433. Website: www.marquette.edu/english. **Contact:** C.J. Hribal.

UNIVERSITY OF WISCONSIN AT MADISON, English Department, Helen C. White Hall, 600 N Park St., Madison WI 53706. (608)263-3800. Fax: (608)263-3709. Website: http://creativewriting.wisc.edu. **Contact:** Ronald Wallace. Estab. 1978. Offers B.A., M.F.A. Student/teacher ratio (graduate): 2-1. Average class size: 15. Faculty includes Lorrie Moore, Jesse Lee Kercheval, Ronald Wallace. Publishes the literary journal *The Madison Review*.

UNIVERSITY OF WISCONSIN AT MILWAUKEE, English Department, P.O. Box 413, Milwaukee WI 53211. (414)229-6691. Fax: (414)229-2643. **Contact:** John Goulet.

UNIVERSITY OF WISCONSIN AT WHITEWATER, Department of Modern Language & Literature, 800 W. Main St., Whitewater WI 53190-2121. (262)472-1036. Fax: (262)472-1037. **Contact:** Donna Lewis.

Wyoming

UNIVERSITY OF WYOMING, P.O. Box 3353, Hoyt Hall 201, Laramie WY 82071-3353. (307)766-6452. Fax: (307)766-3189.

Canada

GRANT MACEWAN COLLEGE, 10700-104th Ave., RM 5-265N, Edmonton, Alberta T5J 452 Canada. (780)497-4712. Fax: (780)497-5308. E-mail: mcmannd@admin.gmcc.ab.ca. Website: www.artsci.gmcc.ab.ca. **Contact:** Don McMann.

Publishers and Their Imprints

The publishing world is constantly changing and evolving. With all of the buying, selling, reorganizing, consolidating, and dissolving, it's hard to keep publishers and their imprints straight. To help you make sense of these changes, we offer this breakdown of major publishers (and their divisions)—who owns whom and which imprints are under each company umbrella. Keep in mind that this information is constantly changing. We have provided the websites to each of the publishers so you can continue to keep an eye on this ever-evolving business.

SIMON & SCHUSTER
(Viacom, Inc.)
www.simonsays.com

Simon & Schuster Audio
Pimsleur
Simon & Schuster Audioworks
Simon & Schuster Sound Ideas

Simon & Schuster Adult Publishing
Atria Books
Downtown Press
Lisa Drew Books
Fireside
The Free Press
Kaplan
Pocket Books
Scribner
Simon & Schuster
Simon & Schuster Trade Paperback
Simple Abundance Press

Touchstone
Wall Street Journal Books

Simon & Schuster Children's Publishing
Aladdin Paperbacks
Atheneum Books for Young Readers
Little Simon®
Margaret K. McElderry Books
Simon & Schuster Books for Young Readers
Simon Pulse
Simon Spotlight®

Simon & Schuster Interactive

Simon & Schuster International
Simon & Schuster Australia
Simon & Schuster Canada
Simon & Schuster UK

HARPERCOLLINS
(subsidiary of News Corp.)
www.harpercollins.com

HarperCollins General Books Group
Access Press
Amistad Press
Avon
Ecco
Eos
Fourth Estate
Harper Design International
HarperAudio
HarperBusiness
HarperCollins

HarperEntertainment
HarperLargePrint
HarperResource
HarperSanFrancisco
HarperTorch
Perennial
PerfectBound
Quill
Rayo
ReganBooks
William Morrow

HarperCollins Children's Books Group
Avon
Greenwillow Books
HarperCollins Children's Books
HarperFestival
HarperTrophy
Joanna Cotler Books
Laura Geringer Books
Tempest

HarperCollins Australia
Angus & Robertson
Flamingo
4th Estate
HarperBusiness
HarperCollins
HarperReligious

HarperSports
Voyager

HarperCollins Canada
HarperFlamingoCanada
Perennial Canada

HarperCollins UK
Collins
Collins Education
4th Estate
Thorsons/Element
Voyager Books

Zondervan
Inspirio
Vida Publishers
Zonderkidz

RANDOM HOUSE, INC.
(Bertelsmann AG)
www.randomhouse.com

Ballantine Publishing Group
Ballantine Books
Ballantine Reader's Circle
Del Rey
Del Rey/Lucas Books
Fawcett
Ivy
One World
Wellspring

Bantam Dell Publishing Group
Bantam Hardcover
Bantam Mass Market
Bantam Trade Paperback
Crimeline
Delacorte Press
Dell
Delta
The Dial Press
Domain
DTP
Fanfare
Island
Spectra

Crown Publishing Group
Bell Tower
Clarkson Potter
Crown Business

Crown Publishers, Inc.
Harmony Books
Prima
Shaye Areheart Books
Three Rivers Press

Doubleday Broadway Publishing Group
Broadway Books
Currency
Doubleday
Doubleday Image
Doubleday Religious Publishing
Main Street/Backlist Books
Nan A. Talese

Knopf Publishing Group
Alfred A. Knopf
Anchor
Everyman's Library
Pantheon Books
Schocken Books
Vintage Anchor Publishing

Random House Adult Trade Publishing Group
The Modern Library
Random House Trade Group
Random House Trade Paperbacks
Strivers Row Books
Villard Books

Random House Audio Publishing Group

Listening Library
Random House Audible
Random House Audio
Random House Audio Assets
Random House Audio Dimensions
Random House Audio Price-less
Random House Audio Roads
Random House Audio Voices

Random House Children's Books

BooksReportsNow.com
GoldenBooks.com
Junie B. Jones
Kids@Random
Magic Tree House
Parents@Random
Seussville
Teachers@Random
Teens@Random

Knopf/Delacorte/Dell Young Readers Group

Alfred A. Knopf
Bantam
Crown
David Fickling Books
Delacorte Press
Dell Dragonfly
Dell Laurel-Leaf
Dell Yearling Books
Doubleday
Wendy Lamb Books

Random House Young Readers Group

Akiko
Arthur
Barbie
Beginner Books
The Berenstain Bears
Bob the Builder
Disney
Dragon Tales
First Time Books
Golden Books
Landmark Books
Little Golden Books

Lucas Books
Mercer Mayer
Nickelodeon
Nick, Jr.
pat the bunny
Picturebacks
Precious Moments
Richard Scarry
Sesame Street Books
Step into Reading
Stepping Stones
Star Wars
Thomas the Tank Engine and Friends

Random House Direct, Inc.

Bon Appétit
Gourmet Books
Pillsbury

Random House Information Group

Fodor's Travel Publications
Living Language
Prima Games
Princeton Review
Random House Español
Random House Puzzles & Games
Random House Reference Publishing

Random House Large Print Publishing

Random House Value Publishing

Random House International

Areté
McClelland & Stewart Ltd.
Plaza & Janés
Random House Australia
Random House of Canada Ltd.
Random House Mondadori
Random House South America
Random House United Kingdom
Transworld UK
Verlagsgruppe Random House

Waterbrook Press

Fisherman Bible Study Guides
Shaw Books
Waterbrook Press

PENGUIN GROUP (USA), INC.
(Pearson plc)
www.penguinputnam.com

Penguin Putnam, Inc. (Adult)

Ace Books

Avery
Berkley Books

Diamond Books
Jam
Prime Crime
Boulevard
Dutton
Gotham
G.P. Putnam's Sons
  Blue Hen Putnam
HPBooks
Jeremy P. Tarcher
Jove
NAL
  New American Library
Penguin
Perigee
Plume
Portfolio
Riverhead Books (paperback)
Viking

Penguin Putnam Books for Young Readers (Children)
AlloyBooks
Dial Books for Young Readers
Dutton Children's Books
Firebird
Frederick Warne
G.P. Putnam's Sons
Grosset & Dunlap
  Planet Dexter
  Platt & Munk
Philomel
Phyllis Fogelman Books
PaperStar
Planet Dexter
Platt & Munk
Playskool
Price Stern Sloan
PSS
Puffin Books
Viking Children's Books

AOL TIME WARNER BOOK GROUP
www.twbookmark.com

Warner Books
Aspect
Mysterious Press
Time Warner AudioBooks
Warner Business Books
Warner Faith
Warner Forever
Warner Vision

Little, Brown and Co.
Adult Trade Books
Back Bay Books
Bulfinch Press

Little, Brown and Co.
Children's Publishing
Megan Tingley Books

HOLTZBRINCK PUBLISHERS (Germany)
www.vhpsva.com/bookseller/HBGenInfo.html

St. Martin's Press
Griffin
Minotaur
St. Martin's Press Paperback & Reference
St. Martin's Press Trade Division
Priddy & Bicknell
Thomas Dunne Books
Truman Talley Books
Whitman Coin Books & Products

Tor Books
Forge Books
Orb Books

Henry Holt & Co.

Henry Holt Books for Young Readers
John Macrae Books
Metropolitan Books
Owl Books
Picador USA
Red Feather Books
Times Books

Farrar, Straus & Giroux
Faber and Faber
FSG Books for Young Readers
Hill and Wang
Mirasol/libros
North Point Press
Sunburst Paperback

◤ Canadian Writers Take Note

While much of the information contained in this section applies to all writers, here are some specifics of interest to Canadian writers:

Postage: When sending an SASE from Canada, you will need an International Reply Coupon. Also be aware, a GST tax is required on postage in Canada and for mail with postage under $5 going to destinations outside the country. Since Canadian postage rates are voted on in January of each year (after we go to press), contact a Canada Post Corporation Customer Service Division (located in most cities in Canada) or visit www.canadapost.ca for the most current rates.

Copyright: For information on copyrighting your work and to obtain forms, write Copyright and Industrial Design, Phase One, Place du Portage, 50 Victoria St., Room C-229, Gatineau, Quebec K1A 0C9 or call (819)997-1936. Website: www.cipo.gc.ca.

The public lending right: The Public Lending Right Commission has established that eligible Canadian authors are entitled to payments when a book is available through a library. Payments are determined by a sampling of the holdings of a representative number of libraries. To find out more about the program and to learn if you are eligible, write to the Public Lending Right Commission at 350 Albert St., P.O. Box 1047, Ottawa, Ontario K1P 5V8 or call (613)566-4378 or (800)521-5721 for information. Website: www.plr-dpp.ca/. The Commission, which is part of The Canada Council, produces a helpful pamphlet, *How the PLR System Works,* on the program.

Grants available to Canadian writers: Most province art councils or departments of culture provide grants to resident writers. Some of these, as well as contests for Canadian writers, are listed in our Contests and Awards section. For national programs, contact The Canada Council, Writing and Publishing Section, 350 Alberta St., P.O. Box 1047, Ottawa, Ontario K1P 5V8 or call (613)566-4414, ext. 5576 or (800)263-5588, ext. 5576 for information. Fax: (613)566-4410. Website: www.canadacouncil.ca.

For more information: See the Resources section of *Novel & Short Story Writer's Market* for listings of writers' organizations in Canada. Also contact The Writer's Union of Canada, 40 Wellington St. E, 3rd Floor, Toronto, Ontario M5E 1C7; call them at (416)703-8982 or fax them at (416)504-7656. E-mail: info@writersunion.ca. Website: www.writersunion.ca. This organization provides a wealth of information (as well as strong support) for Canadian writers, including specialized publications on publishing contracts; contract negotiations; the author/editor relationship; author awards, competitions and grants; agents; taxes for writers, libel issues and access to archives in Canada.

Printing & Production Terms Defined

In most of the magazine listings in this book you will find a brief physical description of each publication. This material usually includes the number of pages, type of paper, type of binding and whether or not the magazine uses photographs or illustrations.

Although it is important to look at a copy of the magazine to which you are submitting, these descriptions can give you a general idea of what the publication looks like. This material can provide you with a feel for the magazine's financial resources and prestige. Do not, however, rule out small, simply produced publications as these may be the most receptive to new writers. Watch for publications that have increased their page count or improved their production from year to year. This is a sign the publication is doing well and may be accepting more fiction.

You will notice a wide variety of printing terms used within these descriptions. We explain here some of the more common terms used in our listing descriptions. We do not include explanations of terms such as Mohawk and Karma which are brand names and refer to the paper manufacturer.

PAPER

acid-free: Paper that has a low or no acid content. This type of paper resists deterioration from exposure to the elements. More expensive than many other types of paper, publications done on acid-free paper can last a long time.

bond: Bond paper is often used for stationery and is more transparent than text paper. It can be made of either sulphite (wood) or cotton fiber. Some bonds have a mixture of both wood and cotton (such as "25 percent cotton" paper). This is the type of paper most often used in photocopying or as standard typing paper.

coated/uncoated stock: Coated and uncoated are terms usually used when referring to book or text paper. More opaque than bond, it is the paper most used for offset printing. As the name implies, uncoated paper has no coating. Coated paper is coated with a layer of clay, varnish or other chemicals. It comes in various sheens and surfaces depending on the type of coating, but the most common are dull, matte and gloss.

cover stock: Cover stock is heavier book or text paper used to cover a publication. It comes in a variety of colors and textures and can be coated on one or both sides.

CS1/CS2: Most often used when referring to cover stock, CS1 means paper that is coated only on one side; CS2 is paper coated on both sides.

newsprint: Inexpensive absorbent pulp wood paper often used in newspapers and tabloids.

text: Text paper is similar to book paper (a smooth paper used in offset printing), but it has been given some texture by using rollers or other methods to apply a pattern to the paper.

vellum: Vellum is a text paper that is fairly porous and soft.

Some notes about paper weight and thickness: Often you will see paper thickness described in terms of pounds such as 80 lb. or 60 lb. paper. The weight is determined by figuring how many pounds in a ream of a particular paper (a ream is 500 sheets). This can be confusing, however, because this figure is based on a standard sheet size and standard sheet sizes vary depending on the type of paper used. This information is most helpful when comparing papers of the same type. For example, 80 lb. book paper versus 60 lb. book paper. Since the size of the paper is the same it would follow that 80 lb. paper is the thicker, heavier paper.

Some paper, especially cover stock, is described by the actual thickness of the paper. This is expressed in a system of points. Typical paper thicknesses range from 8 points to 14 points thick.

PRINTING

letterpress: Letterpress printing is printing that uses a raised surface such as type. The type is inked and then pressed against the paper. Unlike offset printing, only a limited number of impressions can be made, as the surface of the type can wear down.

offset: Offset is a printing method in which ink is transferred from an image-bearing plate to a "blanket" and from the blanket to the paper.

sheet-fed offset: Offset printing in which the paper is fed one piece at a time.

web offset: Offset printing in which a roll of paper is printed and then cut apart to make individual sheets.

There are many other printing methods but these are the ones most commonly referred to in our listings.

BINDING

case binding: In case binding, signatures (groups of pages) are stitched together with thread rather than glued together. The stitched pages are then trimmed on three sides and glued into a hardcover or board "case" or cover. Most hardcover books and thicker magazines are done this way.

comb binding: A comb is a plastic spine used to hold pages together with bent tabs that are fed through punched holes in the edge of the paper.

perfect binding: Used for paperback books and heavier magazines, perfect binding involves gathering signatures (groups of pages) into a stack, trimming off the folds so the edge is flat and gluing a cover to that edge.

saddle stitched: Publications in which the pages are stitched together using metal staples. This fairly inexpensive type of binding is usually used with books or magazines that are under 80 pages.

Smythe-sewn: Binding in which the pages are sewn together with thread. Smythe is the name of the most common machine used for this purpose.

spiral binding: A wire spiral that is wound through holes punched in pages is a spiral bind. This is the binding used in spiral notebooks.

Glossary

Advance. Payment by a publisher to an author prior to the publication of a book, to be deducted from the author's future royalties.

All rights. The rights contracted to a publisher permitting a manuscript's use anywhere and in any form, including movie and book club sales, without additional payment to the writer.

Amateur sleuth. The character in a mystery, usually the protagonist, who does the detection but is not a professional private investigator or police detective.

Anthology. A collection of selected writings by various authors.

Association of Authors' Representatives (AAR). An organization for literary agents committed to maintaining excellence in literary representation.

Auction. Publishers sometimes bid against each other for the acquisition of a manuscript that has excellent sales prospects.

Backlist. A publisher's books not published during the current season but still in print.

Book producer/packager. An organization that may develop a book for a publisher based upon the publisher's idea or may plan all elements of a book, from its initial concept to writing and marketing strategies, and then sell the package to a book publisher and/or movie producer.

Cliffhanger. Fictional event in which the reader is left in suspense at the end of a chapter or episode, so that interest in the story's outcome will be sustained.

Clip. Sample, usually from a newspaper or magazine, of a writer's published work.

Cloak-and-dagger. A melodramatic, romantic type of fiction dealing with espionage and intrigue.

Commercial. Publishers whose concern is salability, profit and success with a large readership.

Contemporary. Material dealing with popular current trends, themes or topics.

Contributor's copy. Copy of an issue of a magazine or published book sent to an author whose work is included.

Copublishing. An arrangement in which the author and publisher share costs and profits.

Copyediting. Editing a manuscript for writing style, grammar, punctuation and factual accuracy.

Copyright. The legal right to exclusive publication, sale or distribution of a literary work.

Cover letter. A brief letter sent with a complete manuscript submitted to an editor.

"Cozy" (or "teacup") mystery. Mystery usually set in a small British town, in a bygone era, featuring a somewhat genteel, intellectual protagonist.

Cyberpunk. Type of science fiction, usually concerned with computer networks and human-computer combinations, involving young, sophisticated protagonists.

Electronic rights. The right to publish material electronically, either in book or short story form.

E-zine. A magazine that is published electronically.

Electronic submission. A submission of material by modem or on computer disk.

Experimental fiction. Fiction that is innovative in subject matter and style; avant-garde, non-formulaic, usually literary material.

Exposition. The portion of the storyline, usually the beginning, where background information about character and setting is related.

Fair use. A provision in the copyright law that says short passages from copyrighted material may be used without infringing on the owner's rights.

Fanzine. A noncommercial, small-circulation magazine usually dealing with fantasy, horror or science-fiction literature and art.

First North American serial rights. The right to publish material in a periodical before it appears in book form, for the first time, in the United States or Canada.

Flash fiction. See short short stories.

Galleys. The first typeset version of a manuscript that has not yet been divided into pages.

Genre. A formulaic type of fiction such as romance, western or horror.

Gothic. A genre in which the central character is usually a beautiful young woman and the setting an old mansion or castle, involving a handsome hero and real danger, either natural or supernatural.

Graphic novel. An adaptation of a novel into a long comic strip or heavily illustrated story of 40 pages or more, produced in paperback.

Hard science fiction. Science fiction with an emphasis on science and technology.

Hard-boiled detective novel. Mystery novel featuring a private eye or police detective as the protagonist; usually involves a murder. The emphasis is on the details of the crime.

High fantasy. Fantasy with a medieval setting and a heavy emphasis on chivalry and the quest.

Horror. A genre stressing fear, death and other aspects of the macabre.

Hypertext fiction. A fictional form, read electronically, which incorporates traditional elements of storytelling with a nonlinear plot line, in which the reader determines the direction of the story by opting for one of many author-supplied links.

Imprint. Name applied to a publisher's specific line (e.g. Owl, an imprint of Henry Holt).

Interactive fiction. Fiction in book or computer-software format where the reader determines the path the story will take by choosing from several alternatives at the end of each chapter or episode.

International Reply Coupon (IRC). A form purchased at a post office and enclosed with a letter or manuscript to a international publisher, to cover return postage costs.

Juvenile. Fiction intended for children 2-12.

Libel. Written or printed words that defame, malign or damagingly misrepresent a living person.

Literary fiction. The general category of fiction which employs more sophisticated technique, driven as much or more by character evolution than action in the plot.

Literary agent. A person who acts for an author in finding a publisher or arranging contract terms on a literary project.

Mainstream fiction. Fiction which appeals to a more general reading audience, versus literary or genre fiction. Mainstream is more plot-driven than literary fiction, and less formulaic than genre fiction.

Malice domestic novel. A mystery featuring a murder among family members, such as the murder of a spouse or a parent.

Manuscript. The author's unpublished copy of a work, usually typewritten, used as the basis for typesetting.

Mass market paperback. Softcover book on a popular subject, usually around 4 × 7, directed to a general audience and sold in drugstores and groceries as well as in bookstores.

Middle reader. Juvenile fiction for readers aged 8-13, featuring heavier text than picture books and some light illustration.

Ms(s). Abbreviation for manuscript(s).

Multiple submission. Submission of more than one short story at a time to the same editor. Do not make a multiple submission unless requested.

Narration. The account of events in a story's plot as related by the speaker or the voice of the author.

Narrator. The person who tells the story, either someone involved in the action or the voice of the writer.

New Age. A term including categories such as astrology, psychic phenomena, spiritual healing, UFOs, mysticism and other aspects of the occult.

Noir. A style of mystery involving hard-boiled detectives and bleak settings.

Nom de plume. French for "pen name"; a pseudonym.

Novella (also novelette). A short novel or long story, approximately 7,000-15,000 words.

#10 envelope. 4 × 9½ envelope, used for queries and other business letters.

Offprint. Copy of a story taken from a magazine before it is bound.

One-time rights. Permission to publish a story in periodical or book form one time only.

Outline. A summary of a book's contents, often in the form of chapter headings with a few sentences outlining the action of the story under each one; sometimes part of a book proposal.

Over the transom. A phrase referring to unsolicited manuscripts, or those that come in "over the transom."

Payment on acceptance. Payment from the magazine or publishing house as soon as the decision to print a manuscript is made.

Payment on publication. Payment from the publisher after a manuscript is printed.

Pen name. A pseudonym used to conceal a writer's real name.

Periodical. A magazine or journal published at regular intervals.

Plot. The carefully devised series of events through which the characters progress in a work of fiction.

Police procedural. A mystery featuring a police detective or officer who uses standard professional police practices to solve a crime.

Print on demand (POD). Novels produced digitally one at a time, as ordered. Self-publishing through print on demand technology typically involves some fees for the author. Some authors use POD to create a manuscript in book form to send to prospective traditional publishers.

Proofreading. Close reading and correction of a manuscript's typographical errors.

Proofs. A typeset version of a manuscript used for correcting errors and making changes, often a photocopy of the galleys.

Proposal. An offer to write a specific work, usually consisting of an outline of the work and one or two completed chapters.

Protagonist. The principal or leading character in a literary work.

Public domain. Material that either was never copyrighted or whose copyright term has expired.

Pulp magazine. A periodical printed on inexpensive paper, usually containing lurid, sensational stories or articles.

Query. A letter written to an editor to elicit interest in a story the writer wants to submit.

Reader. A person hired by a publisher to read unsolicited manuscripts.

Reading fee. An arbitrary amount of money charged by some agents and publishers to read a submitted manuscript.

Regency romance. A genre romance, usually set in England between 1811-1820.

Remainders. Leftover copies of an out-of-print book, sold by the publisher at a reduced price.

Reporting time. The number of weeks or months it takes an editor to report back on an author's query or manuscript.

Reprint rights. Permission to print an already published work whose rights have been sold to another magazine or book publisher.

Roman à clef. French "novel with a key." A novel that represents actual living or historical characters and events in fictionalized form.

Romance. The genre relating accounts of passionate love and fictional heroic achievements.

Royalties. A percentage of the retail price paid to an author for each copy of the book that is sold.

SAE. Self-addressed envelope.

SASE. Self-addressed stamped envelope.

Science fiction. Genre in which scientific facts and hypotheses form the basis of actions and events.

Second serial (reprint) rights. Permission for the reprinting of a work in another periodical after its first publication in book or magazine form.

Self-publishing. In this arrangement, the author keeps all income derived from the book, but he pays for its manufacturing, production and marketing.

Sequel. A literary work that continues the narrative of a previous, related story or novel.

Serial rights. The rights given by an author to a publisher to print a piece in one or more periodicals.

Serialized novel. A book-length work of fiction published in sequential issues of a periodical.

Setting. The environment and time period during which the action of a story takes place.

Short short story. A condensed piece of fiction, usually under 700 words.

Simultaneous submission. The practice of sending copies of the same manuscript to several editors or publishers at the same time. Some people refuse to consider such submissions.

Slant. A story's particular approach or style, designed to appeal to the readers of a specific magazine.

Slice of life. A presentation of characters in a seemingly mundane situation which offers the reader a flash of illumination about the characters or their situation.

Slush pile. A stack of unsolicited manuscripts in the editorial offices of a publisher.

Social fiction. Fiction written with the purpose of bringing about positive changes in society.

Soft/sociological science fiction. Science fiction with an emphasis on society and culture versus scientific accuracy.

Space opera. Epic science fiction with an emphasis on good guys versus bad guys.

Speculation (or Spec). An editor's agreement to look at an author's manuscript with no promise to purchase.

Speculative fiction (SpecFic). The all-inclusive term for science fiction, fantasy and horror.

Splatterpunk. Type of horror fiction known for its very violent and graphic content.

Subsidiary. An incorporated branch of a company or conglomerate (e.g. Alfred Knopf, Inc., a subsidiary of Random House, Inc.).

Subsidiary rights. All rights other than book publishing rights included in a book contract, such as paperback, book club and movie rights.

Subsidy publisher. A book publisher who charges the author for the cost of typesetting, printing and promoting a book. Also Vanity publisher.

Subterficial fiction. Innovative, challenging, nonconventional fiction in which what seems to be happening is the result of things not so easily perceived.

Suspense. A genre of fiction where the plot's primary function is to build a feeling of anticipation and fear in the reader over its possible outcome.

Synopsis. A brief summary of a story, novel or play. As part of a book proposal, it is a comprehensive summary condensed in a page or page and a half.

Tabloid. Publication printed on paper about half the size of a regular newspaper page (e.g. *The National Enquirer*).

Tearsheet. Page from a magazine containing a published story.

Theme. The dominant or central idea in a literary work; its message, moral or main thread.

Trade paperback. A softbound volume, usually around 5×8, published and designed for the general public, available mainly in bookstores.

Traditional fantasy. Fantasy with an emphasis on magic, using characters with the ability to do magic such as wizards, witches, dragons, elves, and unicorns.

Unsolicited manuscript. A story or novel manuscript that an editor did not specifically ask to see.

Urban fantasy. Fantasy that takes magical characters such as elves, fairies, vampires or wizards and places them in modern-day settings, often in the inner city.

Vanity publisher. See Subsidy publisher.

Viewpoint. The position or attitude of the first- or third-person narrator or multiple narrators, which determines how a story's action is seen and evaluated.

Western. Genre with a setting in the West, usually between 1860-1890, with a formula plot about cowboys or other aspects of frontier life.

Whodunit. Genre dealing with murder, suspense and the detection of criminals.

Work-for-hire. Work that another party commissions you to do, generally for a flat fee. The creator does not own the copyright and therefore cannot sell any rights.

Young adult. The general classification of books written for readers 12-18.

Zine. Often one- or two-person operations run from the home of the publisher/editor. Themes tend to be specialized, personal, experimental and often controversial.

Literary Agents Category Index

Agents listed in this edition of *Novel & Short Story Writer's Market* the preceeding section are indexed below according to the categories of fiction they represent. Use it to find agents who handle the specific kind of fiction you write. Then turn to those listings in the alphabetical Literary Agents section for complete contact and submission information.

Action/Adventure
Acacia House Publishing Services, Ltd. 107
Ahearn Agency, Inc., The 108
Alive Communications, Inc. 108
Amsterdam Agency, Marcia 109
Authentic Creations Literary Agency 110
Authors & Artists Group, Inc. 110
Barrett Books, Inc., Loretta 110
Bial Agency, Daniel 111
Bova Literary Agency, The Barbara 114
Brown, Ltd., Curtis 115
Carlisle & Co. 115
Circle of Confusion, Ltd. 116
Communications Management Associates 118
Crawford Literary Agency 119
Donovan Literary, Jim 121
Durrett Agency, Diane 122
Dystel & Goderich Literary Management 122
E S Agency, The 123
Farber Literary Agency, Inc. 124
Fort Ross, Inc., Russian-American Publishing Projects 125
Goldfarb & Associates 127
Greenburger Associates, Inc., Sanford J. 128
Gregory & Co. Authors' Agents 128
Halsey Agency, Reece 129
Halsey North, Reece 129
Hartline Literary Agency 130
Hawkins & Associates, Inc., John 130
Henshaw Group, Richard 130
Herner Rights Agency, Susan 131
Hogenson Agency, Barbara 131
Jabberwocky Literary Agency 132
JCA Literary Agency 133
Jellinek & Murray Literary Agency 133
Kleinman, Esq., Jeffrey M. 134
Klinger, Inc., Harvey 135
Lampack Agency, Inc., Peter 136
Larsen/Elizabeth Pomada, Literary Agents, Michael 136
Levine Literary Agency, Paul S. 137
Lincoln Literary Agency, Ray 138
Lindsey's Literary Services 138
Literary Group, The 139
Los Bravos Literary Management 140

Marshall Agency, The Evan 142
McBride Literary Agency, Margret 142
Naggar Literary Agency, Jean V. 144
National Writers Literary Agency 144
Norma-Lewis Agency, The 145
Paraview, Inc. 145
Picard, Literary Agent, Alison J. 146
Picture Of You, A 146
Quicksilver Books Literary Agents 148
RLR Associates, Ltd. 150
Robins & Associates, Michael D. 151
Rubie Literary Agency, The Peter 152
Sanders & Associates, Victoria 153
Sedgeband Literary Associates 154
Serendipity Literary Agency, LLC 155
Shapiro-Lichtman 155
Simmons Literary Agency, Jeffrey 156
3 Seas Literary Agency 160
Venture Literary 161
Vines Agency, Inc., The 161
Writers House 163
Wylie-Merrick Literary Agency 164

Cartoon/Comic
Brown, Ltd., Curtis 115
Circle of Confusion, Ltd. 116
Halsey North, Reece 129
Hawkins & Associates, Inc., John 130
Jabberwocky Literary Agency 132
Levine Literary Agency, Paul S. 137
Preskill Literary Agency, Robert 147
RLR Associates, Ltd. 150
Robins & Associates, Michael D. 151
Shapiro-Lichtman 155
Writers House 163

Confession
Barrett Books, Inc., Loretta 110
Brown, Ltd., Curtis 115
Circle of Confusion, Ltd. 116
Jellinek & Murray Literary Agency 133
Levine Literary Agency, Paul S. 137
Los Bravos Literary Management 140
March Tenth, Inc. 142
Serendipity Literary Agency, LLC 155
Shapiro-Lichtman 155

Simmons Literary Agency, Jeffrey 156
Writers House 163

Contemporary Issues
Ahearn Agency, Inc., The 108
Alive Communications, Inc. 108
Authentic Creations Literary Agency 110
Authors & Artists Group, Inc. 110
Barrett Books, Inc., Loretta 110
Bial Agency, Daniel 111
BookEnds, LLC 113
Books & Such 113
Brandt Agency, The Joan 114
Brandt & Hochman Literary Agents, Inc. 114
Brown, Ltd., Curtis 115
Castiglia Literary Agency 116
Circle of Confusion, Ltd. 116
Clark Associates, William 117
Doyen Literary Services, Inc. 121
Dystel & Goderich Literary Management 122
Elmo Agency, Inc., Ann 124
Farber Literary Agency, Inc. 124
Freymann Literary Agency, Sarah Jane 126
Goldfarb & Associates 127
Greenburger Associates, Inc., Sanford J. 128
Grosjean Literary Agency, Jill 128
Grosvenor Literary Agency, The 129
Halsey Agency, Reece 129
Harris Literary Agency, Inc., The Joy 130
Hartline Literary Agency 130
Hawkins & Associates, Inc., John 130
Herner Rights Agency, Susan 131
Jabberwocky Literary Agency 132
JCA Literary Agency 133
Jellinek & Murray Literary Agency 133
Kleinman, Esq., Jeffrey M. 134
Koster Literary Agency, LLC, Elaine 135
Larsen/Elizabeth Pomada, Literary Agents, Michael 136
Levine Greenberg Literary Agency, Inc. 137
Levine Literary Agency, Paul S. 137
Lincoln Literary Agency, Ray 138
Literary Group, The 139
Litwest Group, LLC 139
McGrath, Helen 142
Multimedia Product Development, Inc. 144
Naggar Literary Agency, Jean V. 144
Paraview, Inc. 145
Picard, Literary Agent, Alison J. 146
Pinder Lane & Garon-Brooke Associates, Ltd. 147
Rees Literary Agency, Helen 149
Rhodes Literary Agency, Jodie 149
RLR Associates, Ltd. 150
Robbins Literary Agency, B.J. 151
Sanders & Associates, Victoria 153
Schiavone Literary Agency, Inc. 153
Schulman, A Literary Agency, Susan 153

Shapiro-Lichtman 155
Skolnick Literary Agency, Irene 157
Spectrum Literary Agency 157
Spitzer Literary Agency, Philip G. 157
Stauffer Associates, Nancy 158
Straus Agency, Inc., Robin 159
Vines Agency, Inc., The 161
Wieser & Wieser, Inc. 163
Writers House 163
Zachary Shuster Harmsworth 164

Detective/Police/Crime
Acacia House Publishing Services, Ltd. 107
Ahearn Agency, Inc., The 108
Alive Communications, Inc. 108
Amsterdam Agency, Marcia 109
Appleseeds Management 110
Authentic Creations Literary Agency 110
Authors & Artists Group, Inc. 110
Barrett Books, Inc., Loretta 110
Bial Agency, Daniel 111
BookEnds, LLC 113
Bova Literary Agency, The Barbara 114
Brandt Agency, The Joan 114
Brown, Ltd., Curtis 115
Circle of Confusion, Ltd. 116
Collin, Literary Agent, Frances 118
Communications Management Associates 118
Cornerstone Literary, Inc. 119
DHS Literary, Inc. 120
Donovan Literary, Jim 121
Durrett Agency, Diane 122
Dystel & Goderich Literary Management 122
E S Agency, The 123
Elmo Agency, Inc., Ann 124
Fort Ross, Inc., Russian-American Publishing Projects 125
Goldfarb & Associates 127
Greenburger Associates, Inc., Sanford J. 128
Gregory & Co. Authors' Agents 128
Grosvenor Literary Agency, The 129
Halsey Agency, Reece 129
Halsey North, Reece 129
Hawkins & Associates, Inc., John 130
Henshaw Group, Richard 130
Herner Rights Agency, Susan 131
Hogenson Agency, Barbara 131
J de S Associates, Inc. 132
Jabberwocky Literary Agency 132
JCA Literary Agency 133
Jellinek and Murray Literary Agency 133
Klinger, Inc., Harvey 135
Koster Literary Agency, LLC, Elaine 135
Lampack Agency, Inc., Peter 136
Larsen/Elizabeth Pomada, Literary Agents, Michael 136
Levine Literary Agency, Paul S. 137

Lincoln Literary Agency, Ray 138
Lindsey's Literary Services 138
Literary Group, The 139
Litwest Group, LLC 139
Los Bravos Literary Management 140
Maass Literary Agency 140
McBride Literary Agency, Margret 142
McGrath, Helen 142
Multimedia Product Development, Inc. 144
Naggar Literary Agency, Jean V. 144
Norma-Lewis Agency, The 145
Picard, Literary Agent, Alison J. 146
Picture Of You, A 146
Pinder Lane & Garon-Brooke Associates, Ltd. 147
Pine Associates, Inc., Arthur 147
Preskill Literary Agency, Robert 147
Protter, Literary Agent, Susan Ann 148
RLR Associates, Ltd. 150
Robbins Literary Agency, B.J. 151
Robins & Associates, Michael D. 151
Rubie Literary Agency, The Peter 152
Schulman, A Literary Agency, Susan 153
Seligman, Literary Agent, Lynn 154
Shapiro-Lichtman 155
Simmons Literary Agency, Jeffrey 156
Spitzer Literary Agency, Philip G. 157
3 Seas Literary Agency 160
Venture Literary 161
Vines Agency, Inc., The 161
Ware Literary Agency, John A. 162
Whittaker, Literary Agent, Lynn 162
Wieser & Wieser, Inc. 163
Writers House 163
Zachary Shuster Harmsworth 164
Zeckendorf Assoc., Inc., Susan 165

Erotica
Authors & Artists Group, Inc. 110
Bial Agency, Daniel 111
Brown, Ltd., Curtis 115
Circle of Confusion, Ltd. 116
Communications Management Associates 118
Cornerstone Literary, Inc. 119
E S Agency, The 123
Jellinek and Murray Literary Agency 133
Levine Literary Agency, Paul S. 137
Los Bravos Literary Management 140
Marshall Agency, The Evan 142
Picard, Literary Agent, Alison J. 146
Picture Of You, A 146
Shapiro-Lichtman 155
Writers House 163

Ethnic
Ahearn Agency, Inc., The 108
Amster Literary Enterprises, Betsy 109
Authors & Artists Group, Inc. 110
Barrett Books, Inc., Loretta 110

Bent, Harvey Klinger, Inc., Jenny 111
Bial Agency, Daniel 111
Bleeker Street Associates, Inc. 112
Book Deals, Inc. 112
BookEnds, LLC 113
Brandt & Hochman Literary Agents, Inc. 114
Brown, Ltd., Curtis 115
Castiglia Literary Agency 116
Circle of Confusion, Ltd. 116
Clark Associates, William 117
Cohen, Inc., Literary Agency, Ruth 117
Collin, Literary Agent, Frances 118
Cornerstone Literary, Inc. 119
Dawson Associates, Liza 120
DeFiore and Co. 120
DHS Literary, Inc. 120
Dijkstra Literary Agency, Sandra 121
Dunham Literary, Inc. 122
Dystel & Goderich Literary Management 122
Elmo Agency, Inc., Ann 124
Eth Literary Agency, Felicia 124
Freymann Literary Agency, Sarah Jane 126
Goldfarb & Associates 127
Greenburger Associates, Inc., Sanford J. 128
Halsey Agency, Reece 129
Halsey North, Reece 129
Harris Literary Agency, Inc., The Joy 130
Hawkins & Associates, Inc., John 130
Henshaw Group, Richard 130
Herner Rights Agency, Susan 131
Hogenson Agency, Barbara 131
Jabberwocky Literary Agency 132
Jellinek and Murray Literary Agency 133
Kern Literary Agency, Natasha 134
Kleinman, Esq., Jeffrey M. 134
Koster Literary Agency, LLC, Elaine 135
Larsen/Elizabeth Pomada, Literary Agents, Michael 136
Levine Literary Agency, Paul S. 137
Lincoln Literary Agency, Ray 138
Lindsey's Literary Services 138
Literary Group, The 139
Litwest Group, LLC 139
Los Bravos Literary Management 140
March Tenth, Inc. 142
Marshall Agency, The Evan 142
McBride Literary Agency, Margret 142
Multimedia Product Development, Inc. 144
Naggar Literary Agency, Jean V. 144
Paraview, Inc. 145
Picard, Literary Agent, Alison J. 146
Picture Of You, A 146
Rhodes Literary Agency, Jodie 149
RLR Associates, Ltd. 150
Robbins Literary Agency, B.J. 151
Rubie Literary Agency, The Peter 152
Sanders & Associates, Victoria 153

Schiavone Literary Agency, Inc. 153
Seligman, Literary Agent, Lynn 154
Serendipity Literary Agency, LLC 155
Shapiro-Lichtman 155
Tolls Literary Agency, Lynda 160
Vines Agency, Inc., The 161
Whittaker, Literary Agent, Lynn 162
Writers House 163
Zachary Shuster Harmsworth 164
Zeckendorf Assoc., Inc., Susan 165

Experimental

Brown, Ltd., Curtis 115
Circle of Confusion, Ltd. 116
E S Agency, The 123
Harris Literary Agency, Inc., The Joy 130
Hawkins & Associates, Inc., John 130
Larsen/Elizabeth Pomada, Literary Agents, Michael 136
Levine Literary Agency, Paul S. 137
Picard, Literary Agent, Alison J. 146
RLR Associates, Ltd. 150
Sedgeband Literary Associates 154
Shapiro-Lichtman 155
Spieler Agency, The 157
Vines Agency, Inc., The 161
Writers House 163

Family Saga

Ahearn Agency, Inc., The 108
Alive Communications, Inc. 108
Authentic Creations Literary Agency 110
Barrett Books, Inc., Loretta 110
BookEnds, LLC 113
Books & Such 113
Brandt Agency, The Joan 114
Brandt & Hochman Literary Agents, Inc. 114
Brown, Ltd., Curtis 115
Circle of Confusion, Ltd. 116
Collin, Literary Agent, Frances 118
Cornerstone Literary, Inc. 119
Dawson Associates, Liza 120
Doyen Literary Services, Inc. 121
Dystel & Goderich Literary Management 122
Elmo Agency, Inc., Ann 124
Greenburger Associates, Inc., Sanford J. 128
Grosvenor Literary Agency, The 129
Halsey Agency, Reece 129
Halsey North, Reece 129
Harris Literary Agency, Inc., The Joy 130
Hartline Literary Agency 130
Hawkins & Associates, Inc., John 130
Henshaw Group, Richard 130
Herner Rights Agency, Susan 131
Jabberwocky Literary Agency 132
JCA Literary Agency 133
Jellinek and Murray Literary Agency 133
Kleinman, Esq., Jeffrey M. 134

Klinger, Inc., Harvey 135
Koster Literary Agency, LLC, Elaine 135
Lampack Agency, Inc., Peter 136
Larsen/Elizabeth Pomada, Literary Agents, Michael 136
Levine Literary Agency, Paul S. 137
Lincoln Literary Agency, Ray 138
Literary Group, The 139
Litwest Group, LLC 139
March Tenth, Inc. 142
Multimedia Product Development, Inc. 144
Naggar Literary Agency, Jean V. 144
Norma-Lewis Agency, The 145
Picard, Literary Agent, Alison J. 146
Picture Of You, A 146
Pinder Lane & Garon-Brooke Associates, Ltd. 147
Pine Associates, Inc., Arthur 147
Rhodes Literary Agency, Jodie 149
RLR Associates, Ltd. 150
Robins & Associates, Michael D. 151
Sanders & Associates, Victoria 153
Schiavone Literary Agency, Inc. 153
Shapiro-Lichtman 155
Simmons Literary Agency, Jeffrey 156
Spieler Agency, The 157
Straus Agency, Inc., Robin 159
3 Seas Literary Agency 160
Vines Agency, Inc., The 161
Writers House 163

Fantasy

Brown, Ltd., Curtis 115
Circle of Confusion, Ltd. 116
Collin, Literary Agent, Frances 118
Communications Management Associates 118
Curtis Associates, Inc., Richard 119
Ellenberg Literary Agency, Ethan 123
Fleury Agency, B.R. 125
Fort Ross, Inc., Russian-American Publishing Projects 125
Gislason Agency, The 127
Hawkins & Associates, Inc., John 130
Henshaw Group, Richard 130
Jabberwocky Literary Agency 132
Kidd Agency, Inc., Virginia 134
Kleinman, Esq., Jeffrey M. 134
Larsen/Elizabeth Pomada, Literary Agents, Michael 136
Lincoln Literary Agency, Ray 138
Literary Group, The 139
Maass Literary Agency 140
Perkins Associates, L. 146
Picture Of You, A 146
Pinder Lane & Garon-Brooke Associates, Ltd. 147
Robins & Associates, Michael D. 151
Rubie Literary Agency, The Peter 152
Seligman, Literary Agent, Lynn 154

Shapiro-Lichtman 155
Spectrum Literary Agency 157
Sternig & Byrne Literary Agency 158
3 Seas Literary Agency 160
Writers House 163
Wylie-Merrick Literary Agency 164

Feminist
Ahearn Agency, Inc., The 108
Barrett Books, Inc., Loretta 110
Bial Agency, Daniel 111
BookEnds, LLC 113
Brown, Ltd., Curtis 115
Circle of Confusion, Ltd. 116
Eth Literary Agency, Felicia 124
Greenburger Associates, Inc., Sanford J. 128
Harris Literary Agency, Inc., The Joy 130
Hawkins & Associates, Inc., John 130
Herner Rights Agency, Susan 131
Jellinek and Murray Literary Agency 133
Kern Literary Agency, Natasha 134
Kleinman, Esq., Jeffrey M. 134
Koster Literary Agency, LLC, Elaine 135
Larsen/Elizabeth Pomada, Literary Agents, Michael 136
Levine Literary Agency, Paul S. 137
Lincoln Literary Agency, Ray 138
Literary Group, The 139
Litwest Group, LLC 139
Naggar Literary Agency, Jean V. 144
Nazor Literary Agency 145
Paraview, Inc. 145
Picard, Literary Agent, Alison J. 146
RLR Associates, Ltd. 150
Sanders & Associates, Victoria 153
Seligman, Literary Agent, Lynn 154
Shapiro-Lichtman 155
Spieler Agency, The 157
Vines Agency, Inc., The 161
Writers House 163
Zachary Shuster Harmsworth 164

Glitz
Ahearn Agency, Inc., The 108
Authors & Artists Group, Inc. 110
Barrett Books, Inc., Loretta 110
Bial Agency, Daniel 111
BookEnds, LLC 113
Bova Literary Agency, The Barbara 114
Brown, Ltd., Curtis 115
Circle of Confusion, Ltd. 116
Cornerstone Literary, Inc. 119
DeFiore and Co. 120
Dystel & Goderich Literary Management 122
Eth Literary Agency, Felicia 124
Greenburger Associates, Inc., Sanford J. 128
Greenburger Associates, Inc., Sanford J. 128
Harris Literary Agency, Inc., The Joy 130

Hawkins & Associates, Inc., John 130
Henshaw Group, Richard 130
Herner Rights Agency, Susan 131
Jabberwocky Literary Agency 132
Jellinek and Murray Literary Agency 133
Kidd Agency, Inc., Virginia 134
Kleinman, Esq., Jeffrey M. 134
Klinger, Inc., Harvey 135
Larsen/Elizabeth Pomada, Literary Agents, Michael 136
Levine Literary Agency, Paul S. 137
Lincoln Literary Agency, Ray 138
Multimedia Product Development, Inc. 144
Picard, Literary Agent, Alison J. 146
Picture Of You, A 146
Pinder Lane & Garon-Brooke Associates, Ltd. 147
Quicksilver Books Literary Agents 148
RLR Associates, Ltd. 150
Robins & Associates, Michael D. 151
Rubie Literary Agency, The Peter 152
Sanders & Associates, Victoria 153
Schulman, A Literary Agency, Susan 153
Seligman, Literary Agent, Lynn 154
Shapiro-Lichtman 155
Spieler Agency, The 157
Teal Literary Agency, Patricia 160
Vines Agency, Inc., The 161
Writers House 163
Zachary Shuster Harmsworth 164

Hi-Lo
Brown, Ltd., Curtis 115
Circle of Confusion, Ltd. 116
Harris Literary Agency, Inc., The Joy 130
Hawkins & Associates, Inc., John 130
Shapiro-Lichtman 155
Writers House 163

Historical
Ahearn Agency, Inc., The 108
Alive Communications, Inc. 108
Allen Literary Agency, Linda 109
Barrett Books, Inc., Loretta 110
Bleeker Street Associates, Inc. 112
BookEnds, LLC 113
Books & Such 113
Brandt & Hochman Literary Agents, Inc. 114
Brown, Ltd., Curtis 115
Circle of Confusion, Ltd. 116
Clark Associates, William 117
Cohen, Inc., Literary Agency, Ruth 117
Collin, Literary Agent, Frances 118
Communications Management Associates 118
Connor Literary Agency 118
Cornerstone Literary, Inc. 119
Dawson Associates, Liza 120
Donovan Literary, Jim 121
Doyen Literary Services, Inc. 121

Durrett Agency, Diane 122
E S Agency, The 123
Elmo Agency, Inc., Ann 124
English, Elaine P. 124
Fogelman Literary Agency 125
Greenburger Associates, Inc., Sanford J. 128
Gregory & Co. Authors' Agents 128
Grosjean Literary Agency, Jill 128
Grosvenor Literary Agency, The 129
Halsey Agency, Reece 129
Halsey North, Reece 129
Harris Literary Agency, Inc., The Joy 130
Hartline Literary Agency 130
Hawkins & Associates, Inc., John 130
Henshaw Group, Richard 130
Herner Rights Agency, Susan 131
Hogenson Agency, Barbara 131
Hopkins Literary Associates 131
Hornfischer Literary Management, Inc. 132
J de S Associates, Inc. 132
Jabberwocky Literary Agency 132
JCA Literary Agency 133
Jellinek and Murray Literary Agency 133
Kern Literary Agency, Natasha 134
Kidd Agency, Inc., Virginia 134
Kleinman, Esq., Jeffrey M. 134
Koster Literary Agency, LLC, Elaine 135
Lampack Agency, Inc., Peter 136
Larsen/Elizabeth Pomada, Literary Agents, Michael 136
Levine Literary Agency, Paul S. 137
Lincoln Literary Agency, Ray 138
Lindsey's Literary Services 138
Litwest Group, LLC 139
Maass Literary Agency 140
March Tenth, Inc. 142
Marshall Agency, The Evan 142
McBride Literary Agency, Margret 142
McHugh Literary Agency 143
Multimedia Product Development, Inc. 144
Naggar Literary Agency, Jean V. 144
Norma-Lewis Agency, The 145
Picard, Literary Agent, Alison J. 146
Picture Of You, A 146
Pine Associates, Inc., Arthur 147
Rees Literary Agency, Helen 149
Rhodes Literary Agency, Jodie 149
RLR Associates, Ltd. 150
Rubie Literary Agency, The Peter 152
Schiavone Literary Agency, Inc. 153
Schulman, A Literary Agency, Susan 153
Seligman, Literary Agent, Lynn 154
Serendipity Literary Agency, LLC 155
Shapiro-Lichtman 155
Spectrum Literary Agency 157
Straus Agency, Inc., Robin 159
3 Seas Literary Agency 160

Tolls Literary Agency, Lynda 160
Vines Agency, Inc., The 161
Whittaker, Literary Agent, Lynn 162
Wieser & Wieser, Inc. 163
Writers House 163
Wylie-Merrick Literary Agency 164
Zachary Shuster Harmsworth 164
Zeckendorf Assoc., Inc., Susan 165

Horror
Amsterdam Agency, Marcia 109
Authors & Artists Group, Inc. 110
Brown, Ltd., Curtis 115
Circle of Confusion, Ltd. 116
Communications Management Associates 118
Connor Literary Agency 118
Donovan Literary, Jim 121
Durrett Agency, Diane 122
Fleury Agency, B.R. 125
Fort Ross, Inc., Russian-American Publishing Projects 125
Halsey North, Reece 129
Hawkins & Associates, Inc., John 130
Henshaw Group, Richard 130
Herner Rights Agency, Susan 131
Jabberwocky Literary Agency 132
Jellinek and Murray Literary Agency 133
Kleinman, Esq., Jeffrey M. 134
Lindsey's Literary Services 138
Literary Group, The 139
Los Bravos Literary Management 140
Maass Literary Agency 140
Marshall Agency, The Evan 142
Norma-Lewis Agency, The 145
Perkins Associates, L. 146
Picard, Literary Agent, Alison J. 146
Picture Of You, A 146
RLR Associates, Ltd. 150
Schiavone Literary Agency, Inc. 153
Sedgeband Literary Associates 154
Seligman, Literary Agent, Lynn 154
Shapiro-Lichtman 155
Sternig & Byrne Literary Agency 158
3 Seas Literary Agency 160
Vines Agency, Inc., The 161
Writers House 163

Humor/Satire
Ahearn Agency, Inc., The 108
Alive Communications, Inc. 108
Authors & Artists Group, Inc. 110
Bial Agency, Daniel 111
Brown, Ltd., Curtis 115
Circle of Confusion, Ltd. 116
Durrett Agency, Diane 122
E S Agency, The 123
Farber Literary Agency, Inc. 124
Fleury Agency, B.R. 125

Greenburger Associates, Inc., Sanford J. 128
Gregory & Co. Authors' Agents 128
Grosjean Literary Agency, Jill 128
Harris Literary Agency, Inc., The Joy 130
Hawkins & Associates, Inc., John 130
Henshaw Group, Richard 130
Hogenson Agency, Barbara 131
Jabberwocky Literary Agency 132
Jellinek and Murray Literary Agency 133
Kleinman, Esq., Jeffrey M. 134
Larsen/Elizabeth Pomada, Literary Agents, Michael 136
Levine Literary Agency, Paul S. 137
Lincoln Literary Agency, Ray 138
Literary Group, The 139
Litwest Group, LLC 139
March Tenth, Inc. 142
Marshall Agency, The Evan 142
McBride Literary Agency, Margret 142
Norma-Lewis Agency, The 145
Picard, Literary Agent, Alison J. 146
RLR Associates, Ltd. 150
Schiavone Literary Agency, Inc. 153
Seligman, Literary Agent, Lynn 154
Shapiro-Lichtman 155
Spieler Agency, The 157
3 Seas Literary Agency 160
Vines Agency, Inc., The 161
Writers House 163

Juvenile
Alive Communications, Inc. 108
Books & Such 113
Briggs, M. Courtney 114
Brown, Ltd., Curtis 115
Circle of Confusion, Ltd. 116
Cohen, Inc., Literary Agency, Ruth 117
Communications Management Associates 118
Dunham Literary, Inc. 122
Farber Literary Agency, Inc. 124
Fort Ross, Inc., Russian-American Publishing Projects 125
Hawkins & Associates, Inc., John 130
J de S Associates, Inc. 132
Lincoln Literary Agency, Ray 138
Livingston Cooke 139
Maccoby Agency, Gina 141
Multimedia Product Development, Inc. 144
National Writers Literary Agency 144
Norma-Lewis Agency, The 145
Picard, Literary Agent, Alison J. 146
Rhodes Literary Agency, Jodie 149
Schiavone Literary Agency, Inc. 153
Serendipity Literary Agency, LLC 155
Shapiro-Lichtman 155
3 Seas Literary Agency 160
Writers House 163

Literary
Acacia House Publishing Services, Ltd. 107
Ahearn Agency, Inc., The 108
Alive Communications, Inc. 108
Altshuler Literary Agency, Miriam 109
Amster Literary Enterprises, Betsy 109
Authentic Creations Literary Agency 110
Barrett Books, Inc., Loretta 110
Bent, Harvey Klinger, Inc., Jenny 111
Bernstein Literary Agency, Meredith 111
Bial Agency, Daniel 111
Black Literary Agency, David 112
Bleeker Street Associates, Inc. 112
Book Deals, Inc. 112
BookEnds, LLC 113
Borchardt, Inc., Georges 114
Brady Literary Management 114
Brandt Agency, The Joan 114
Brandt & Hochman Literary Agents, Inc. 114
Brown, Ltd., Curtis 115
Bykofsky Associates, Inc. Sheree 115
Carlisle & Co. 115
Carvainis Agency, Inc., Maria 116
Castiglia Literary Agency 116
Circle of Confusion, Ltd. 116
Clark Associates, William 117
Cohen, Inc., Literary Agency, Ruth 117
Collin, Literary Agent, Frances 118
Connor Literary Agency 118
Coover Agency, The Doe 118
Cornerstone Literary, Inc. 119
Dawson Associates, Liza 120
DeFiore and Co. 120
DHS Literary, Inc. 120
Dijkstra Literary Agency, Sandra 121
Donovan Literary, Jim 121
Doyen Literary Services, Inc. 121
Dunham Literary, Inc. 122
Durrett Agency, Diane 122
Dystel & Goderich Literary Management 122
E S Agency, The 123
Ellison, Inc., Nicholas 123
Elmo Agency, Inc., Ann 124
Eth Literary Agency, Felicia 124
Farber Literary Agency, Inc. 124
Fleury Agency, B.R. 125
Fogelman Literary Agency 125
Franklin Associates, Ltd., Lynn C. 126
Freymann Literary Agency, Sarah Jane 126
Gelfman, Schneider, Literary Agents, Inc. 126
Goldfarb & Associates 127
Greenburger Associates, Inc., Sanford J. 128
Gregory & Co. Authors' Agents 128
Grosjean Literary Agency, Jill 128
Grosvenor Literary Agency, The 129
Halsey Agency, Reece 129
Halsey North, Reece 129

Harris Literary Agency, Inc., The Joy 130
Hartline Literary Agency 130
Hawkins & Associates, Inc., John 130
Henshaw Group, Richard 130
Herner Rights Agency, Susan 131
Hill Bonnie Nadell, Inc., Frederick 131
Hogenson Agency, Barbara 131
Hornfischer Literary Management, Inc. 132
J de S Associates, Inc. 132
Jabberwocky Literary Agency 132
JCA Literary Agency 133
Jellinek and Murray Literary Agency 133
Kidd Agency, Inc., Virginia 134
Kleinman, Esq., Jeffrey M. 134
Klinger, Inc., Harvey 135
Knight Agency, The 135
Koster Literary Agency, LLC, Elaine 135
Lampack Agency, Inc., Peter 136
Larsen/Elizabeth Pomada, Literary Agents, Michael 136
Lescher & Lescher, Ltd. 137
Levine Greenberg Literary Agency, Inc. 137
Levine Literary Agency, Paul S. 137
Lincoln Literary Agency, Ray 138
Lindsey's Literary Services 138
Litwest Group, LLC 139
Livingston Cooke 139
Los Bravos Literary Management 140
Maass Literary Agency 140
Maccoby Agency, Gina 141
Mann Agency, Carol 141
Manus & Associates Literary Agency, Inc. 141
March Tenth, Inc. 142
Marshall Agency, The Evan 142
McBride Literary Agency, Margret 142
McGrath, Helen 142
McHugh Literary Agency 143
Michaels Literary Agency, Inc., Doris S. 143
Multimedia Product Development, Inc. 144
Naggar Literary Agency, Jean V. 144
Nazor Literary Agency 145
Paraview, Inc. 145
Perkins Associates, L. 146
Picard, Literary Agent, Alison J. 146
Picture Of You, A 146
Pinder Lane & Garon-Brooke Associates, Ltd. 147
Pine Associates, Inc., Arthur 147
Popkin, Julie 147
Preskill Literary Agency, Robert 147
Rees Literary Agency, Helen 149
Rein Books, Inc., Jody 149
Rhodes Literary Agency, Jodie 149
Rinaldi Literary Agency, Angela 150
Rittenberg Literary Agency, Inc., Ann 150
RLR Associates, Ltd. 150
Robbins Literary Agency, B.J. 151
Rosenberg Group, The 151

Ross Literary Agency, The Gail 152
Rubie Literary Agency, The Peter 152
Sanders & Associates, Victoria 153
Sandum and Associates 153
Schiavone Literary Agency, Inc. 153
Schulman, A Literary Agency, Susan 153
Sedgeband Literary Associates 154
Seligman, Literary Agent, Lynn 154
Serendipity Literary Agency, LLC 155
Shapiro-Lichtman 155
Sherman Associates, Inc., Wendy 156
Simmons Literary Agency, Jeffrey 156
Skolnick Literary Agency, Irene 157
Slopen Literary Agency, Beverley 157
Spieler Agency, The 157
Spitzer Literary Agency, Philip G. 157
Stauffer Associates, Nancy 158
Straus Agency, Inc., Robin 159
Susijn Agency, The 159
Talbot Agency, The John 159
3 Seas Literary Agency 160
Tolls Literary Agency, Lynda 160
Venture Literary 161
Vines Agency, Inc., The 161
Watkins Loomis Agency, Inc. 162
Waxman Literary Agency, Inc. 162
Whittaker, Literary Agent, Lynn 162
Wieser & Wieser, Inc. 163
Writers House 163
Writers' Representatives, Inc. 164
Zachary Shuster Harmsworth 164
Zeckendorf Assoc., Inc., Susan 165

Mainstream/Contemporary

Acacia House Publishing Services, Ltd. 107
Ahearn Agency, Inc., The 108
Alive Communications, Inc. 108
Altshuler Literary Agency, Miriam 109
Amsterdam Agency, Marcia 109
Authentic Creations Literary Agency 110
Authors & Artists Group, Inc. 110
Barrett Books, Inc., Loretta 110
Bent, Harvey Klinger, Inc., Jenny 111
Black Literary Agency, David 112
Book Deals, Inc. 112
BookEnds, LLC 113
Books & Such 113
Brady Literary Management 114
Brandt Agency, The Joan 114
Brandt & Hochman Literary Agents, Inc. 114
Briggs, M. Courtney 114
Brown, Ltd., Curtis 115
Bykofsky Associates, Inc. Sheree 115
Carlisle & Co. 115
Carvainis Agency, Inc., Maria 116
Castiglia Literary Agency 116
Circle of Confusion, Ltd. 116

Clark Associates, William 117
Cohen, Inc., Literary Agency, Ruth 117
Collin, Literary Agent, Frances 118
Communications Management Associates 118
Connor Literary Agency 118
Coover Agency, The Doe 118
Cornerstone Literary, Inc. 119
DeFiore and Co. 120
DHS Literary, Inc. 120
Dijkstra Literary Agency, Sandra 121
Donovan Literary, Jim 121
Doyen Literary Services, Inc. 121
Dunham Literary, Inc. 122
Durrett Agency, Diane 122
Dystel & Goderich Literary Management 122
E S Agency, The 123
Ellison, Inc., Nicholas 123
Elmo Agency, Inc., Ann 124
English, Elaine P. 124
Eth Literary Agency, Felicia 124
Farber Literary Agency, Inc. 124
Fogelman Literary Agency 125
Franklin Associates, Ltd., Lynn C. 126
Freymann Literary Agency, Sarah Jane 126
Gelfman, Schneider, Literary Agents, Inc. 126
Gislason Agency, The 127
Goldfarb & Associates 127
Greenburger Associates, Inc., Sanford J. 128
Gregory & Co. Authors' Agents 128
Grosjean Literary Agency, Jill 128
Grosvenor Literary Agency, The 129
Halsey Agency, Reece 129
Halsey North, Reece 129
Harris Literary Agency, Inc., The Joy 130
Hawkins & Associates, Inc., John 130
Henshaw Group, Richard 130
Herner Rights Agency, Susan 131
Hill Bonnie Nadell, Inc., Frederick 131
Hogenson Agency, Barbara 131
Hopkins Literary Associates 131
Hornfischer Literary Management, Inc. 132
J de S Associates, Inc. 132
Jabberwocky Literary Agency 132
JCA Literary Agency 133
Jellinek and Murray Literary Agency 133
Kern Literary Agency, Natasha 134
Kidd Agency, Inc., Virginia 134
Kleinman, Esq., Jeffrey M. 134
Klinger, Inc., Harvey 135
Knight Agency, The 135
Koster Literary Agency, LLC, Elaine 135
Lampack Agency, Inc., Peter 136
Larsen/Elizabeth Pomada, Literary Agents, Michael 136
Levine Greenberg Literary Agency, Inc. 137
Levine Literary Agency, Paul S. 137
Lincoln Literary Agency, Ray 138

Lindsey's Literary Services 138
Lipkind Agency, Wendy 138
Litwest Group, LLC 139
Maass Literary Agency 140
Maccoby Agency, Gina 141
Manus & Associates Literary Agency, Inc. 141
March Tenth, Inc. 142
Marshall Agency, The Evan 142
McBride Literary Agency, Margret 142
McGrath, Helen 142
McHugh Literary Agency 143
Multimedia Product Development, Inc. 144
Naggar Literary Agency, Jean V. 144
National Writers Literary Agency 144
Norma-Lewis Agency, The 145
Paraview, Inc. 145
Picard, Literary Agent, Alison J. 146
Picture Of You, A 146
Pinder Lane & Garon-Brooke Associates, Ltd. 147
Pine Associates, Inc., Arthur 147
Popkin, Julie 147
Rees Literary Agency, Helen 149
Rein Books, Inc., Jody 149
Rhodes Literary Agency, Jodie 149
RLR Associates, Ltd. 150
Robbins Literary Agency, B.J. 151
Robins & Associates, Michael D. 151
Schiavone Literary Agency, Inc. 153
Schulman, A Literary Agency, Susan 153
Sedgeband Literary Associates 154
Seligman, Literary Agent, Lynn 154
Shapiro-Lichtman 155
Simmons Literary Agency, Jeffrey 156
Skolnick Literary Agency, Irene 157
Spectrum Literary Agency 157
Spitzer Literary Agency, Philip G. 157
Stauffer Associates, Nancy 158
Steele-Perkins Literary Agency 158
Straus Agency, Inc., Robin 159
Teal Literary Agency, Patricia 160
3 Seas Literary Agency 160
Venture Literary 161
Vines Agency, Inc., The 161
Wieser & Wieser, Inc. 163
Writers House 163
Zachary Shuster Harmsworth 164
Zeckendorf Assoc., Inc., Susan 165

Military/War
Brown, Ltd., Curtis 115
Circle of Confusion, Ltd. 116
Hawkins & Associates, Inc., John 130
Shapiro-Lichtman 155
Writers House 163

Multimedia
Brown, Ltd., Curtis 115
Circle of Confusion, Ltd. 116

Harris Literary Agency, Inc., The Joy 130
Hawkins & Associates, Inc., John 130
Kleinman, Esq., Jeffrey M. 134
Shapiro-Lichtman 155
Writers House 163

Mystery/Suspense
Acacia House Publishing Services, Ltd. 107
Ahearn Agency, Inc., The 108
Alive Communications, Inc. 108
Amsterdam Agency, Marcia 109
Appleseeds Management 110
Authentic Creations Literary Agency 110
Axelrod Agency, The 110
Barrett Books, Inc., Loretta 110
Bernstein Literary Agency, Meredith 111
Bleeker Street Associates, Inc. 112
BookEnds, LLC 113
Bova Literary Agency, The Barbara 114
Brandt Agency, The Joan 114
Brandt & Hochman Literary Agents, Inc. 114
Brown, Ltd., Curtis 115
Carlisle & Co. 115
Carvainis Agency, Inc., Maria 116
Castiglia Literary Agency 116
Circle of Confusion, Ltd. 116
Cohen, Inc., Literary Agency, Ruth 117
Collin, Literary Agent, Frances 118
Communications Management Associates 118
Cornerstone Literary, Inc. 119
Crawford Literary Agency 119
Dawson Associates, Liza 120
DeFiore and Co. 120
DHS Literary, Inc. 120
Dijkstra Literary Agency, Sandra 121
Donovan Literary, Jim 121
Dunham Literary, Inc. 122
Dystel & Goderich Literary Management 122
E S Agency, The 123
Elmo Agency, Inc., Ann 124
English, Elaine P. 124
Farber Literary Agency, Inc. 124
Fort Ross, Inc., Russian-American Publishing Projects 125
Freymann Literary Agency, Sarah Jane 126
Gelfman, Schneider, Literary Agents, Inc. 126
Gislason Agency, The 127
Goldfarb & Associates 127
Greenburger Associates, Inc., Sanford J. 128
Grosjean Literary Agency, Jill 128
Grosvenor Literary Agency, The 129
Halsey Agency, Reece 129
Halsey North, Reece 129
Harris Literary Agency, Inc., The Joy 130
Hartline Literary Agency 130
Hawkins & Associates, Inc., John 130
Henshaw Group, Richard 130

Herner Rights Agency, Susan 131
Hogenson Agency, Barbara 131
J de S Associates, Inc. 132
JCA Literary Agency 133
Jellinek and Murray Literary Agency 133
Kern Literary Agency, Natasha 134
Kidd Agency, Inc., Virginia 134
Klinger, Inc., Harvey 135
Koster Literary Agency, LLC, Elaine 135
Lampack Agency, Inc., Peter 136
Larsen/Elizabeth Pomada, Literary Agents, Michael 136
Lescher & Lescher, Ltd. 137
Levine Greenberg Literary Agency, Inc. 137
Levine Literary Agency, Paul S. 137
Lincoln Literary Agency, Ray 138
Lindsey's Literary Services 138
Lipkind Agency, Wendy 138
Literary Group, The 139
Litwest Group, LLC 139
Los Bravos Literary Management 140
Love Literary Agency, Nancy 140
Maass Literary Agency 140
Maccoby Agency, Gina 141
Manus & Associates Literary Agency, Inc. 141
Marshall Agency, The Evan 142
McBride Literary Agency, Margret 142
McGrath, Helen 142
McHugh Literary Agency 143
Multimedia Product Development, Inc. 144
Naggar Literary Agency, Jean V. 144
National Writers Literary Agency 144
Norma-Lewis Agency, The 145
Picard, Literary Agent, Alison J. 146
Picture Of You, A 146
Pinder Lane & Garon-Brooke Associates, Ltd. 147
Popkin, Julie 147
Protter, Literary Agent, Susan Ann 148
Quicksilver Books Literary Agents 148
Rees Literary Agency, Helen 149
Rein Books, Inc., Jody 149
Rhodes Literary Agency, Jodie 149
RLR Associates, Ltd. 150
Robbins Literary Agency, B.J. 151
Roghaar Literary Agency, Inc., Linda 151
Schulman, A Literary Agency, Susan 153
Sedgeband Literary Associates 154
Seligman, Literary Agent, Lynn 154
Serendipity Literary Agency, LLC 155
Shapiro-Lichtman 155
Simmons Literary Agency, Jeffrey 156
Slopen Literary Agency, Beverley 157
Spectrum Literary Agency 157
Spitzer Literary Agency, Philip G. 157
Sternig & Byrne Literary Agency 158
Talbot Agency, The John 159
Teal Literary Agency, Patricia 160

3 Seas Literary Agency 160
Tolls Literary Agency, Lynda 160
Venture Literary 161
Vines Agency, Inc., The 161
Ware Literary Agency, John A. 162
Whittaker, Literary Agent, Lynn 162
Wieser & Wieser, Inc. 163
Writers House 163
Wylie-Merrick Literary Agency 164
Zachary Shuster Harmsworth 164
Zeckendorf Assoc., Inc., Susan 165

Occult
Brown, Ltd., Curtis 115
Circle of Confusion, Ltd. 116
Doyen Literary Services, Inc. 121
Hawkins & Associates, Inc., John 130
Shapiro-Lichtman 155
Vines Agency, Inc., The 161
Writers House 163

Picture Book
Books & Such 113
Briggs, M. Courtney 114
Brown, Ltd., Curtis 115
Circle of Confusion, Ltd. 116
Cohen, Inc., Literary Agency, Ruth 117
Communications Management Associates 118
Dunham Literary, Inc. 122
Harris Literary Agency, Inc., The Joy 130
Hawkins & Associates, Inc., John 130
Jellinek and Murray Literary Agency 133
Multimedia Product Development, Inc. 144
Norma-Lewis Agency, The 145
Picard, Literary Agent, Alison J. 146
Serendipity Literary Agency, LLC 155
Shapiro-Lichtman 155
3 Seas Literary Agency 160
Writers House 163
Wylie-Merrick Literary Agency 164

Plays
Brown, Ltd., Curtis 115
Circle of Confusion, Ltd. 116
Hawkins & Associates, Inc., John 130
Shapiro-Lichtman 155
Writers House 163

Poetry in Translation
Brown, Ltd., Curtis 115
Circle of Confusion, Ltd. 116
Hawkins & Associates, Inc., John 130
Writers House 163

Poetry
Brown, Ltd., Curtis 115
Circle of Confusion, Ltd. 116
Hawkins & Associates, Inc., John 130
Writers House 163

Psychic/Supernatural
Ahearn Agency, Inc., The 108
Authors & Artists Group, Inc. 110
Barrett Books, Inc., Loretta 110
Brown, Ltd., Curtis 115
Circle of Confusion, Ltd. 116
Collin, Literary Agent, Frances 118
Doyen Literary Services, Inc. 121
Fleury Agency, B.R. 125
Greenburger Associates, Inc., Sanford J. 128
Hawkins & Associates, Inc., John 130
Henshaw Group, Richard 130
Jabberwocky Literary Agency 132
Jellinek and Murray Literary Agency 133
Kleinman, Esq., Jeffrey M. 134
Lincoln Literary Agency, Ray 138
Literary Group, The 139
Maass Literary Agency 140
McGrath, Helen 142
Naggar Literary Agency, Jean V. 144
Picard, Literary Agent, Alison J. 146
Vines Agency, Inc., The 161
Writers House 163

Regional
Ahearn Agency, Inc., The 108
Brown, Ltd., Curtis 115
Circle of Confusion, Ltd. 116
Collin, Literary Agent, Frances 118
Dawson Associates, Liza 120
Elmo Agency, Inc., Ann 124
Greenburger Associates, Inc., Sanford J. 128
Grosjean Literary Agency, Jill 128
Harris Literary Agency, Inc., The Joy 130
Hartline Literary Agency 130
Hawkins & Associates, Inc., John 130
Jabberwocky Literary Agency 132
Jellinek and Murray Literary Agency 133
Kleinman, Esq., Jeffrey M. 134
Koster Literary Agency, LLC, Elaine 135
Levine Literary Agency, Paul S. 137
Lincoln Literary Agency, Ray 138
Nazor Literary Agency 145
Paraview, Inc. 145
Picard, Literary Agent, Alison J. 146
Stauffer Associates, Nancy 158
Vines Agency, Inc., The 161
Writers House 163

Religious/Inspirational
Alive Communications, Inc. 108
Authors & Artists Group, Inc. 110
Books & Such 113
Brown, Ltd., Curtis 115
Circle of Confusion, Ltd. 116
Hartline Literary Agency 130
Hawkins & Associates, Inc., John 130
Kern Literary Agency, Natasha 134

Larsen/Elizabeth Pomada, Literary Agents, Michael 136
Levine Literary Agency, Paul S. 137
Lindsey's Literary Services 138
Litwest Group, LLC 139
Marshall Agency, The Evan 142
Multimedia Product Development, Inc. 144
Picard, Literary Agent, Alison J. 146
Picture Of You, A 146
Seymour Agency, The 155
3 Seas Literary Agency 160
Writers House 163
Wylie-Merrick Literary Agency 164

Romance

Ahearn Agency, Inc., The 108
Amsterdam Agency, Marcia 109
Authentic Creations Literary Agency 110
Axelrod Agency, The 110
Bent, Harvey Klinger, Inc., Jenny 111
Bernstein Literary Agency, Meredith 111
Bleeker Street Associates, Inc. 112
BookEnds, LLC 113
Books & Such 113
Brandt & Hochman Literary Agents, Inc. 114
Brown, Ltd., Curtis 115
Carvainis Agency, Inc., Maria 116
Circle of Confusion, Ltd. 116
Collin, Literary Agent, Frances 118
Communications Management Associates 118
Cornerstone Literary, Inc. 119
Curtis Associates, Inc., Richard 119
Durrett Agency, Diane 122
Ellenberg Literary Agency, Ethan 123
Elmo Agency, Inc., Ann 124
English, Elaine P. 124
Fogelman Literary Agency 125
Fort Ross, Inc., Russian-American Publishing Projects 125
Gislason Agency, The 127
Grosjean Literary Agency, Jill 128
Grosvenor Literary Agency, The 129
Hartline Literary Agency 130
Henshaw Group, Richard 130
Hogenson Agency, Barbara 131
Hopkins Literary Associates 131
Kern Literary Agency, Natasha 134
Knight Agency, The 135
Larsen/Elizabeth Pomada, Literary Agents, Michael 136
Levine Literary Agency, Paul S. 137
Lincoln Literary Agency, Ray 138
Lindsey's Literary Services 138
Literary Group, The 139
Maass Literary Agency 140
Marshall Agency, The Evan 142
McGrath, Helen 142

McHugh Literary Agency 143
Multimedia Product Development, Inc. 144
Norma-Lewis Agency, The 145
Paraview, Inc. 145
Picard, Literary Agent, Alison J. 146
Picture Of You, A 146
Pinder Lane & Garon-Brooke Associates, Ltd. 147
Rosenberg Group, The 151
Sedgeband Literary Associates 154
Seligman, Literary Agent, Lynn 154
Serendipity Literary Agency, LLC 155
Seymour Agency, The 155
Shapiro-Lichtman 155
Spectrum Literary Agency 157
Steele-Perkins Literary Agency 158
Teal Literary Agency, Patricia 160
3 Seas Literary Agency 160
Tolls Literary Agency, Lynda 160
Vines Agency, Inc., The 161
Wieser & Wieser, Inc. 163
Writers House 163
Wylie-Merrick Literary Agency 164

Science Fiction

Amsterdam Agency, Marcia 109
Bova Literary Agency, The Barbara 114
Brown, Ltd., Curtis 115
Circle of Confusion, Ltd. 116
Collin, Literary Agent, Frances 118
Communications Management Associates 118
Curtis Associates, Inc., Richard 119
Dawson Associates, Liza 120
Durrett Agency, Diane 122
Ellenberg Literary Agency, Ethan 123
Fort Ross, Inc., Russian-American Publishing Projects 125
Gislason Agency, The 127
Halsey Agency, Reece 129
Halsey North, Reece 129
Hawkins & Associates, Inc., John 130
Henshaw Group, Richard 130
Jabberwocky Literary Agency 132
Kidd Agency, Inc., Virginia 134
Kleinman, Esq., Jeffrey M. 134
Lindsey's Literary Services 138
Maass Literary Agency 140
Marshall Agency, The Evan 142
McGrath, Helen 142
National Writers Literary Agency 144
Perkins Associates, L. 146
Pinder Lane & Garon-Brooke Associates, Ltd. 147
Protter, Literary Agent, Susan Ann 148
Rubie Literary Agency, The Peter 152
Schiavone Literary Agency, Inc. 153
Seligman, Literary Agent, Lynn 154
Shapiro-Lichtman 155
Spectrum Literary Agency 157

Sternig & Byrne Literary Agency 158
3 Seas Literary Agency 160
Vines Agency, Inc., The 161
Writers House 163
Wylie-Merrick Literary Agency 164

Short Story Collections
Brown, Ltd., Curtis 115
Circle of Confusion, Ltd. 116
Harris Literary Agency, Inc., The Joy 130
Hawkins & Associates, Inc., John 130
Shapiro-Lichtman 155
Writers House 163

Spiritual
Brown, Ltd., Curtis 115
Circle of Confusion, Ltd. 116
Harris Literary Agency, Inc., The Joy 130
Hawkins & Associates, Inc., John 130
Shapiro-Lichtman 155
Writers House 163

Sports
Authentic Creations Literary Agency 110
Brown, Ltd., Curtis 115
Circle of Confusion, Ltd. 116
Donovan Literary, Jim 121
Greenburger Associates, Inc., Sanford J. 128
Hawkins & Associates, Inc., John 130
Henshaw Group, Richard 130
Jabberwocky Literary Agency 132
JCA Literary Agency 133
Levine Literary Agency, Paul S. 137
Lincoln Literary Agency, Ray 138
Literary Group, The 139
Litwest Group, LLC 139
Multimedia Product Development, Inc. 144
National Writers Literary Agency 144
Picard, Literary Agent, Alison J. 146
RLR Associates, Ltd. 150
Robbins Literary Agency, B.J. 151
Shapiro-Lichtman 155
Spitzer Literary Agency, Philip G. 157
Venture Literary 161
Vines Agency, Inc., The 161
Whittaker, Literary Agent, Lynn 162
Writers House 163

Thriller/Espionage
Acacia House Publishing Services, Ltd. 107
Ahearn Agency, Inc., The 108
Alive Communications, Inc. 108
Altshuler Literary Agency, Miriam 109
Amsterdam Agency, Marcia 109
Authentic Creations Literary Agency 110
Authors & Artists Group, Inc. 110
Barrett Books, Inc., Loretta 110
Bernstein Literary Agency, Meredith 111

Bleeker Street Associates, Inc. 112
BookEnds, LLC 113
Bova Literary Agency, The Barbara 114
Brandt Agency, The Joan 114
Brandt & Hochman Literary Agents, Inc. 114
Brown, Ltd., Curtis 115
Carlisle & Co. 115
Carvainis Agency, Inc., Maria 116
Circle of Confusion, Ltd. 116
Communications Management Associates 118
Connor Literary Agency 118
Cornerstone Literary, Inc. 119
Crawford Literary Agency 119
Curtis Associates, Inc., Richard 119
Dawson Associates, Liza 120
DeFiore and Co. 120
DHS Literary, Inc. 120
Dijkstra Literary Agency, Sandra 121
Donovan Literary, Jim 121
Dunham Literary, Inc. 122
Durrett Agency, Diane 122
Dystel & Goderich Literary Management 122
E S Agency, The 123
Ellenberg Literary Agency, Ethan 123
Elmo Agency, Inc., Ann 124
English, Elaine P. 124
Eth Literary Agency, Felicia 124
Farber Literary Agency, Inc. 124
Fleury Agency, B.R. 125
Fort Ross, Inc., Russian-American Publishing Projects 125
Freymann Literary Agency, Sarah Jane 126
Gislason Agency, The 127
Goldfarb & Associates 127
Greenburger Associates, Inc., Sanford J. 128
Gregory & Co. Authors' Agents 128
Grosvenor Literary Agency, The 129
Halsey Agency, Reece 129
Halsey North, Reece 129
Hartline Literary Agency 130
Hawkins & Associates, Inc., John 130
Henshaw Group, Richard 130
Herner Rights Agency, Susan 131
Hogenson Agency, Barbara 131
Hornfischer Literary Management, Inc. 132
Jabberwocky Literary Agency 132
JCA Literary Agency 133
Jellinek and Murray Literary Agency 133
Kern Literary Agency, Natasha 134
Kleinman, Esq., Jeffrey M. 134
Klinger, Inc., Harvey 135
Koster Literary Agency, LLC, Elaine 135
Lampack Agency, Inc., Peter 136
Levine Greenberg Literary Agency, Inc. 137
Levine Literary Agency, Paul S. 137
Lincoln Literary Agency, Ray 138
Lindsey's Literary Services 138

Literary Group, The 139
Litwest Group, LLC 139
Los Bravos Literary Management 140
Love Literary Agency, Nancy 140
Maass Literary Agency 140
Maccoby Agency, Gina 141
Manus & Associates Literary Agency, Inc. 141
McBride Literary Agency, Margret 142
McGrath, Helen 142
McHugh Literary Agency 143
Multimedia Product Development, Inc. 144
Naggar Literary Agency, Jean V. 144
Norma-Lewis Agency, The 145
Picard, Literary Agent, Alison J. 146
Picture Of You, A 146
Pine Associates, Inc., Arthur 147
Preskill Literary Agency, Robert 147
Protter, Literary Agent, Susan Ann 148
Quicksilver Books Literary Agents 148
Rees Literary Agency, Helen 149
Rhodes Literary Agency, Jodie 149
RLR Associates, Ltd. 150
Robbins Literary Agency, B.J. 151
Rubie Literary Agency, The Peter 152
Sanders & Associates, Victoria 153
Serendipity Literary Agency, LLC 155
Shapiro-Lichtman 155
Simmons Literary Agency, Jeffrey 156
Spitzer Literary Agency, Philip G. 157
3 Seas Literary Agency 160
Venture Literary 161
Vines Agency, Inc., The 161
Ware Literary Agency, John A. 162
Wieser & Wieser, Inc. 163
Writers House 163
Wylie-Merrick Literary Agency 164
Zachary Shuster Harmsworth 164
Zeckendorf Assoc., Inc., Susan 165

Translation
Brown, Ltd., Curtis 115
Circle of Confusion, Ltd. 116
Harris Literary Agency, Inc., The Joy 130
Hawkins & Associates, Inc., John 130
Shapiro-Lichtman 155
Writers House 163

Westerns/Frontier
Alive Communications, Inc. 108
Amsterdam Agency, Marcia 109
Brown, Ltd., Curtis 115
Circle of Confusion, Ltd. 116
Communications Management Associates 118
DHS Literary, Inc. 120
Donovan Literary, Jim 121
Hawkins & Associates, Inc., John 130
J de S Associates, Inc. 132
Jellinek and Murray Literary Agency 133

Levine Literary Agency, Paul S. 137
Literary Group, The 139
Marshall Agency, The Evan 142
McBride Literary Agency, Margret 142
McHugh Literary Agency 143
Norma-Lewis Agency, The 145
Picture Of You, A 146
Robins & Associates, Michael D. 151
Seymour Agency, The 155
Shapiro-Lichtman 155
3 Seas Literary Agency 160
Vines Agency, Inc., The 161
Writers House 163

Womens'
Axelrod Agency, The 110
Bleeker Street Associates, Inc. 112
Book Deals, Inc. 112
Brown, Ltd., Curtis 115
Castiglia Literary Agency 116
Circle of Confusion, Ltd. 116
Connor Literary Agency 118
Ellenberg Literary Agency, Ethan 123
English, Elaine P. 124
Halsey Agency, Reece 129
Halsey North, Reece 129
Harris Literary Agency, Inc., The Joy 130
Hawkins & Associates, Inc., John 130
Hopkins Literary Associates 131
Knight Agency, The 135
Levine Greenberg Literary Agency, Inc. 137
Maass Literary Agency 140
Manus & Associates Literary Agency, Inc. 141
Nazor Literary Agency 145
Paraview, Inc. 145
Rhodes Literary Agency, Jodie 149
Rosenberg Group, The 151
Sherman Associates, Inc., Wendy 156
Steele-Perkins Literary Agency 158
Vines Agency, Inc., The 161
Writers House 163

Young Adult
Alive Communications, Inc. 108
Amsterdam Agency, Marcia 109
Books & Such 113
Brandt & Hochman Literary Agents, Inc. 114
Briggs, M. Courtney 114
Brown, Ltd., Curtis 115
Carvainis Agency, Inc., Maria 116
Circle of Confusion, Ltd. 116
Cohen, Inc., Literary Agency, Ruth 117
Communications Management Associates 118
Curtis Associates, Inc., Richard 119
Dunham Literary, Inc. 122
E S Agency, The 123
Farber Literary Agency, Inc. 124

Fort Ross, Inc., Russian-American Publishing Projects 125
Hawkins & Associates, Inc., John 130
J de S Associates, Inc. 132
Kidd Agency, Inc., Virginia 134
Lincoln Literary Agency, Ray 138
Los Bravos Literary Management 140
Maccoby Agency, Gina 141
National Writers Literary Agency 144
Norma-Lewis Agency, The 145

Picard, Literary Agent, Alison J. 146
Picture Of You, A 146
Rhodes Literary Agency, Jodie 149
Robins & Associates, Michael D. 151
Schiavone Literary Agency, Inc. 153
Schulman, A Literary Agency, Susan 153
Shapiro-Lichtman 155
3 Seas Literary Agency 160
Writers House 163
Wylie-Merrick Literary Agency 164

Contest Index by Deadline

Our deadline index organizes all the contests listed in this edition by their monthly deadline. If a contest occurs multiple times during the year (quarterly, for example), its name and page number should appear under each appropriate monthly heading. Turn to the listing's page number for specific dates and other more detailed information.

January

British Science Fiction Association Awards 479
Caine Prize for African Writing, The 479
Captivating Beginnings Contest 480
Jackson Award, Joseph Henry 491
Kennedy Book Awards, Robert F. 492
Literal Latté Fiction Award 494
Marvin Grant, Walter Rumsey 495
Paisano Fellowships, Dobie 503
Phelan Award, James D. 505
Playboy College Fiction Contest 505
Roberts Award, Summerfield G. 508
Scriptapalooza Screenplay Competition 509
Short Grain Contest 510
Skipping Stones Honor Awards 510
Southern Review/Louisiana State University Short Fiction Award, The 511
Starcherone Fiction Prize, The 512
Trollope Society Short Story Prize, The 513
Very Short Fiction Winter Award 514
Writers' Journal Annual Fiction Contest 516

February

Artist Trust Artist Fellowships; GAP Grants 475
Gift of Freedom Award 486
Gulf Coast Poetry and Short Fiction Awards 488
Highlights for Children Fiction Contest 489
Katha: Indian American Fiction Contest 492
Korean Literature Translation Award 493
McCarthy Prize in Short Fiction, Mary 496
Mid-List Press First Series Award for the Novel 497
O, Georgia! Writing Competition, O, Georgia Too! Writing Competition 501
Shaw Fellowship for Older Women Writers, Frances 510
Tall Grass Writers Guild Literary Anthology/Contest 512
Wisconsin Institute for Creative Writing Fellowship 515

March

Alabama State Council on the Arts Individual Artist Fellowship 472
Binghamton University John Gardner Fiction Book Award 477
CNW/FFWA Florida State Writing Competition 482

Eaton Literary Associates' Literary Awards Program 483
Faux Faulkner Contest, The Jack 484
Florida State Writing Competition 485
Glimmer Train's Spring Short-Story Award for New Writers 487
Greene Literary Festival Contest, The Judy & A.C. 487
Hubbard's Writers of the Future Contest, L. Ron 489
Individual Artist Fellowship 490
Jones First Novel Fellowship, James 492
Lakeland Book of the Year 493
Noma Award for Publishing in Africa, The 501
Novella Prize 501
Prairie Schooner Prize Book Series 505
Scriptapalooza Screenplay Competition 509
South Dakota Arts Council 511
Stony Brook Short Fiction Prize 512
Traver Fly-Fishing Fiction Award, Robert 513
Wild Violet Fiction Contest 515
Wolff Award for Fiction, Tobias 515
Writers' Journal Horror/Ghost Contest 516

April

Anderson Writer's Grant, Sherwood 473
Arrowhead Regional Arts Council Individual Artist Career Development Grant 475
Crucible Poetry and Fiction Competition, The 482
Florida Review Editors' Awards, The 485
Great Canadian Story Contest 487
Koeppel Short Fiction Award, E.M. 493
National Writers Association Annual Novel Writing Contest 499
Nevada Arts Council Artists' Fellowships 499
O'Connor Fiction Award, Frank 502
Orange Blossom Fiction Contest 502
Porter Prize for Fiction, Katherine Anne 505
Scriptapalooza Screenplay Competition 509
Seventeen Magazine Fiction Contest 509
Thought Magazine Writer's Contest 512
Tigges Writing Contest, John 513
Vogelstein Foundation Grants 514
Wood Community College, John 515

May

Boston Globe-Horn Book Awards 478
Burnaby Writers' Society Annual Competition 479

CONTEST INDEX BY DEADLINE

Chesterfield Writers' Film Project 481
Faulkner Award for Excellence in Writing, Virginia 484
Hemingway Short Story Competition, Lorian 489
Indiana University Writers' Conference Scholarship Competition 490
Keats/Kerlan Collection Memorial Fellowship, Ezra 492
New Letters Literary Awards 500
O'Connor Award for Short Fiction, The Flannery 501
Oregon Book Awards 503
Pakenham Award, Catherine 503
Pearl Short Story Prize 503
Qspell Book Awards/Hugh Maclennan Fiction Award 506
Raffelock Award for Publishing Excellence, David 506
Scriptapalooza Television Writing Competition 509
Snow Contest, Kay 511
Society of Children's Book Writers and Illustrators Work-In-Progress Grants 511
Violet Crown Book Award 514
Writer's Digest Annual Writing Competition (Short Story Division) 516
Writespot Autumn Short Story Competition 517

June
Art of Music Annual Writing Contest, The 475
Artist Trust Artist Fellowships; GAP Grants 475
Asted/Grand Prix de Litterature Jeunesse du Quebec-Alvine-Belisle 475
Bridport Prize, The 478
Cape Fear Crime Festival Short Story Contest 480
Chelsea Awards, The 481
Chicano/Latino Literary Contest 481
Christopher Awards, The 481
de Angeli Prize, Marguerite 483
Glimmer Train's Fiction Open 487
Heinz Literature Prize, Drue 488
Hubbard's Writers of the Future Contest, L. Ron 489
Indiana Review '1/2K' Prize for Short-Shorts/Prose Poems 490
International IMPAC Dublin Literary Award 491
Ironweed Press Fiction Prize 491
League of Utah Writers Contest 493
Marsh Award for Children's Literature in Translation 495
National Federation of the Blind Writers' Division Short Story Contest 498
New England Writers Short, Short Fiction Contest 500
New Millennium Writing Awards 500
Oregon Literary Fellowships 503
Pfenninger Literary Award, Mary Ann 504
Reynolds Memorial Fiction Awards, Louise E. 508
Sanger Short Fiction Contest, Marjory Bartlett 508
Skipping Stones Youth Awards 510
World Fantasy Awards 515

July
American Association of University Women Award in Juvenile Literature 473
Arrowhead Regional Arts Council Individual Artist Career Development Grant 475
Bard Fiction Prize 477
"Best of Ohio Writers" Contest 477
Children's Writers Fiction Contest 481
Daniels Annual Honorary Writing Award, Dorothy 483
Fitzgerald Short Story Contest, F. Scott 485
Man Booker Prize for Fiction, The 495
Melody of Love Contest 496
Michigan Literary Fiction Awards 496
Mid-List Press First Series Award for Short Fiction 496
National Writers Association Annual Short Story Contest 499
Poole Award for Best Work of Fiction, Mary Ruffin 505
Pulitzer Prize in Fiction 506
Raleigh Award, Sir Walter 506
RedWritingHood.com 100-Word Short Story Contest 507
Romancing the Novel 508
Very Short Fiction Summer Award 514
Writers Bureau Poetry and Short Story Competition, The 515
Writers' Journal Romance Contest 517

August
Delaware Division of the Arts 483
Eaton Literary Associates' Literary Awards Program 483
Individual Artist Mini-Grant 491
Korean Literature Translation Contest for New Translators 493
Qspell Book Awards/Hugh Maclennan Fiction Award 506
Thought Magazine Writer's Contest 512

September
Antietam Review Literary Award 474
Arizona Commission on the Arts Creative Writing Fellowships 474
Celtic Voice Writing Contest 481
Glimmer Train's Fall Short-Story Award for New Writers 486
Greensboro Review Literary Awards, The 488
Hubbard's Writers of the Future Contest, L. Ron 489
Iowa School of Letters Award for Short Fiction, The John Simmons Short Fiction Award 491
Lawrence Foundation Prize 493
National Outdoor Book Awards 498
New York Stories Short Fiction Contest 500
Presidio La Bahia Award, The 506

October
Boston Review Short Story Contest 478
Bush Artist Fellows Program 479

Dana Award in Short Fiction 482
Dana Awards: Portfolio, Novel, Short Fiction, Poetry 482
Editors' Prize 484
Fiction Competition and Poetry Competition 484
FreeFall Magazine Fiction & Poetry Contest 486
Indiana Review Fiction Prize 490
Inkwell Fiction Competition 491
Kiriyama Prize 492
Mississippi Review Prize 497
Missouri Review Editors' Prize Contest, The 497
PEN/Faulkner Award for Fiction, The 504
Reynolds Memorial Fiction Awards, Louise E. 508
Science Fiction Writers of Earth (SFWoE) Short Story Contest 509
Twain Award for Short Fiction, The Mark 513

November

Annual Fiction Contest 474
Annual Juvenile-Fiction Contest 474
Arrowhead Regional Arts Council Individual Artist Career Development Grant 475
Bakeless Literary Publications Prizes 476
Briar Cliff Review Poetry & Fiction Contest, The 478
Brown Foundation, Arch & Bruce 479
Christopher Awards, The 481
Fish Memorial Award, Robert L. 484
Fish Short Story Prize 485
Frank Award, The Josette 485
Individual Artist Fellowship 491
McKean Moore Writer in Washington, Jenny 496
McKnight Artist Fellowships for Writers 496
Mota Emerging Writers Contest 498
National Readers' Choice Awards 498
Nebraska Review Award in Fiction, The 499
New Millennium Writing Awards 500
Pulitzer Prize in Fiction 506
Real Writers/Book Pl@ce Short Story Awards 507
Regional Book Awards 507
Scriptapalooza Television Writing Competition 509
Walden Fellowship 514
Western Heritage Awards 514
Writespot Spring Short Story Competition 517

December

Art Cooperative Fiction Fellowship 475

Athenaeum Literary Award, The 475
AWP Intro Journals Project 476
Black Children's Book Award, Irma S. and James H. 477
Boulevard Short Fiction Contest for Emerging Writers 478
California Book Awards 480
Campbell Memorial Award, John W. 480
Dornstein Memorial Creative Writing Contest for Young Adult Writers, David 483
Fisher Award, Dorothy Canfield 485
Franklin Literary Award, Miles 485
Gold Medallion Book Awards 487
Hammett Prize 488
Hemingway Foundation/Pen Award for First Fiction, Ernest 489
Honolulu Magazine Starbucks Coffee Hawai'i Fiction Contest 489
Hubbard's Writers of the Future Contest, L. Ron 489
Individual Artist Mini-Grant 491
Lilith Annual Fiction Award 494
Long Fiction Contest International 494
Mind Book of the Year 497
Money for Women 497
Moonlight & Magnolia Fiction Writing Contest 497
National Chapter of Canada IODE Violet Downey Book Award, The 498
Newbery Award, John 501
Ohioana Award for Children's Literature, Alice Louise Wood Memorial 502
Ohioana Book Awards 502
PEN Center USA Literary Award in Fiction 504
PEN New England/L.L. Winship Award 504
Red House Children's Book Award, The 507
RedWritingHood.com 100-Word Short Story Contest 507
Reflections Short Fiction Award 507
Shaara Award for Civil War Fiction, Michael 509
Society of Children's Book Writers and Illustrators Golden Kite Awards 511
SPUR Awards 512
Stegner Fellowship, Wallace E. 512
Taylor Manuscript Competition, Sydney 512
Wallant Memorial Book Award, Edward Lewis 514
Weatherford Award 514
Writer's Digest International Self-Published Book Awards 516

Conference Index by Date

Our conference index organizes all conferences listed in this edition by the month in which they are held. If a conference bridges two months, you will find its name and page number under both monthly headings. If a conference occurs multiple times during the year (seasonally, for example), it will appear under each appropriate monthly heading. Turn to the listing's page number for exact dates and more detailed information.

January

Gotham Writers' Workshop 521
Hedgebrook 561
How to Be Published Workshops 535
Kauai Writers Conference 554
Key West Writers' Workshop 535
Killaloe Hedge-School of Writing 566
Publishing Game, The 524
San Diego State University Writers' Conference 556
Sitka Center for Art and Ecology 563
Volcano Writers' Retreat 558
Winter Poetry & Prose Getaway in Cape May 530
Writer's Digest School 544
Yaddo 527

February

Bonnet's Storymaking: The Master Class, James 553
Fishtrap 560
Florida Suncoast Writers' Conference 534
Fun in the Sun: The Write Stuff 535
Hambidge Center 535
Hedgebrook 561
Hilton Head Island Writers Retreat 532
How to Be Published Workshops 535
Key West Writers' Workshop 535
Killaloe Hedge-School of Writing 566
Natchez Literary and Cinema Celebration 536
Publishing Game, The 524
SCBWWI Midyear Conference, NYC 525
SheVaCon 532
Sitka Center for Art and Ecology 563
South Coast Writers Conference 563
Southern California Writers' Conference/San Diego 557
UCLA Extension Writers' Program 558
Writer's Digest School 544
Writers Studio at UCLA Extension 559
Writers Weekend at the Beach 564
Yaddo 527
Yosemite Winter Literary Conference 559

March

AWP Annual Conference and Bookfair 539
Fort Bend Writers Guild Workshop 547
Galacticon, Kag Spring Break 531
Hambidge Center 535
Hedgebrook 561
Highlights Foundation Founders Workshops 528
How to Be Published Workshops 535
IWWG Early Spring in California Conference 554
Kentucky Women Writers Conference 541
Kentucky Writer's Workshop 541
Key West Writers' Workshop 535
Killaloe Hedge-School of Writing 566
Publishing Game, The 524
Rocky Mountain Book Festival 549
SCBWI Southern Breeze Spring Conference 537
Sitka Center for Art and Ecology 563
TMCC Writers' Conference 558
Touch of Success Writer's Conference 538
University of North Dakota Writers Conference 545
Virginia Festival of the Book 533
Western Reserve Writer's & Freelance Conference 544
Write It Out 538
Writer's Digest School 544
Writers' Guild of Acadiana 538
Writers' League of Texas Spring and Fall Workshops and Classes 551
Writing Today--Birmingham-Southern College 539
Yaddo 527

April

Author's Venue Journey Conference 552
Author's Venue Screenwriters Institute 552
Blue Ridge Mountain Christian Writers Conference 531
Booktowns of Europe Writers Workshops 565
College of New Jersey Writers' Conference, The 528
Eminence Area Arts Council Short Story Workshop 547
Festival of Faith and Writing 540
Gotham Writers' Workshop 521
Hambidge Center 535
Hedgebrook 561
Highlights Foundation Founders Workshops 528
Hilton Head Island Writers Retreat 532
How to Be Published Workshops 535
IWWG Meet the Agents and Editors 522
Maumee Valley Freelance Writers' Conference 542

Mount Hermon Christian Writers Conference 556
Oxford Conference for the Book 536
Paterson University Spring Writer's Conference, William 529
Publishing Game, The 524
Retreat From Harsh Reality 543
Sagebrush Writers Workshop 562
SCBWI/Hofstra Children's Literature Conference 525
Sitka Center for Art and Ecology 563
Volcano Writers' Retreat 558
Writer's Digest School 544
Writer's Landscape, The 551
Writers' League of Texas Spring and Fall Workshops and Classes 551
Yaddo 527

May

Bay Area Writer's League Conference 547
Big Bear Writer's Retreat 553
Bonnet's Storymaking: The Master Class, James 553
Creative Writing by the Sea 531
Florida First Coast Writers' Festival 534
Georgia Writers Spring Festival of Workshops 535
Hambidge Center 535
Hedgebrook 561
Highlights Foundation Founders Workshops 528
How to Be Published Workshops 535
Lost Horse Writers' Conference 561
Nightwriters 532
Oklahoma Writers Federation Conference 548
Pima Writers' Workshop 556
Provost's Writers Retreat Workshop, Gary 543
Publishing Game, The 524
Retreat From Harsh Reality 543
San Juan Writers Workshop 549
Seacoast Writer's Association Spring and Fall Conferences 525
Sitka Center for Art and Ecology 563
South Florida Writers' Conference 537
Southern Lights 538
Telluride Writers Conference 550
Wisconsin Regional Writer's Association Conferences 545
Writer's Digest School 544
Writers' League of Texas Spring and Fall Workshops and Classes 551
Yaddo 527

June

Arkansas Writers'Conference 533
Aspen Summer Words Writing Retreat and Literary Festival 546
BYU Writing for Young Readers Workshop 553
Clarion West Writers' Workshop 560
Colorado Mountain Writers' Workshop 547
East Texas Writer's Conference 547
Eastern Kentucky University Summer Creative Writing Conference 540

Flatirons Blunt Instrument Mystery Workshop 547
Gotham Writers' Workshop 521
Hambidge Center 535
Hedgebrook 561
Highland Summer Conference 531
Highlights Foundation Founders Workshops 528
Hilton Head Island Writers Retreat 532
How to Be Published Workshops 535
Imagination 540
Indiana Writers' Conference 541
International Music Camp Creative Writing Workshop 544
Iowa Summer Writing Festival 545
Kenyon Review Writers Workshop 541
Manhattanville College Summer Writers' Week 523
Marymount Manhattan College Writers' Conference 523
Mendocino Coast Writers Conference 555
Midland Writers Conference 542
Mid-Mississippi River Folklore, Storytelling and Writing Conference 542
National Writers Association Foundation Conference 548
New Letters Weekend Writers Conference, The 548
New-Cue Writers' Conference and Workshop 523
Nightwriters 532
Odyssey 524
Outdoor Writers Association of America Annual Conference 529
Paris Writers Workshop/WICE 566
Provost's Writers Retreat Workshop, Gary 543
Publishing Game, The 524
Remember the MAGIC IWWG Annual Summer Conference 524
Ropewalk Writers' Retreat 543
San Juan Writers Workshop 549
Sitka Center for Art and Ecology 563
Southeastern Writers Association 537
Taos Institute of Arts 549
Twain Creative Writing Workshops, Mark 550
Vasto Writers & Artists Retreat 567
Wesleyan Writers Conference 526
Write It Out 538
Writer's Digest School 544
Writers Workshop in Science Fiction 552
Write-To-Publish Conference 544
Yaddo 527

July

Agents! Agents! Agents! & Editors Too! 546
Antioch Writers' Workshop 539
Austin Writers Conference, Harriette 534
Black Ridge Summer Writing Conference 553
Bonnet's Storymaking: The Master Class, James 553
Booktowns of Europe Writers Workshops 565
BYU Writing for Young Readers Workshop 553
Canyonlands Writers River Trip and Workshop 554

Centrums 31st Port Townsend Writers' Conference 559
Fishtrap 560
Gotham Writers' Workshop 521
Hambidge Center 535
Haystack Writing Program 561
Hedgebrook 561
Highlights Foundation Founders Workshops 528
Highlights Foundation Writing for Children 528
Hofstra University Summer Writers' Conference 522
How to Be Published Workshops 535
Imagination 540
International Readers Theatre Workshops 566
Iowa Summer Writing Festival 545
Maritime Writers' Workshop 564
Midwest Writers Workshop 542
Montrose Christian Writer's Conference 528
New England Writers Conference 523
Odyssey 524
Pacific Northwest Writers Conference 562
Paris Writers Workshop/WICE 566
Publishing Game, The 524
Quackenbush's Children's Book Writing and
    Illustrating Workshops, Robert 524
Rawlings: Writing the Region, Marjorie Kinnan 536
Remember the MAGIC IWWG Annual Summer
    Conference 524
San Juan Writers Workshop 549
Sewanee Writers' Conference 532
Sitka Center for Art and Ecology 563
Steamboat Springs Writers Group 549
Taos Institute of Arts 549
University of New Mexico's Taos Summer Writers
    Conference 550
Volcano Writers' Retreat 558
"Why It's Great" Writing Workshop & Retreat, The
    526
Wildacre Writers Workshop 533
Write It Out 538
Writer's Digest School 544
Writers Institute 545
Writing for Young Readers Workshop 559
Yaddo 527

August
Alabama Writers' Conclave 533
Booktowns of Europe Writers Workshops 565
Bread Loaf Writers' Conference 521
Clarion West Writers' Workshop 560
Columbus Writers Conference 539
Glen Workshop, The 560
Green Lake Writers Conference 544
Green Mountain Writers Conference 521
Hambidge Center 535
Haystack Writing Program 561
Hedgebrook 561
Highlights Foundation Founders Workshops 528
Hilton Head Island Writers Retreat 532

How to Be Published Workshops 535
IWWG Summer Conference 522
Maui Writers Conference and Retreat 555
Minneapolis Writers' Conference 545
Montolieu Workshop, The 566
Publishing Game, The 524
Remember the MAGIC IWWG Annual Summer
    Conference 524
Sage Hill Writing Experience 564
SCBWI/International Conference on Writing &
    Illustrating for Children 557
Sitka Center for Art and Ecology 563
Squaw Valley Community of Writers Workshops 557
State of Maine Writers' Conference 525
Sunshine Coast Festival of the Written Arts 565
Taos Institute of Arts 549
Texas Christian Writers' Conference 550
Vermont College Postgraduate Writers' Conference
    525
Volcano Writers' Retreat 558
Willamette Writers Conference 563
Write It Out 538
Writer's Digest School 544
Yaddo 527

September
Gotham Writers' Workshop 521
Hambidge Center 535
Hedgebrook 561
Highlights Foundation Founders Workshops 528
How to Be Published Workshops 535
Idaho Writers League Conference 561
League of Utah Writers Round-up 555
Maui Writers Conference and Retreat 555
Publishing Game, The 524
Sitka Center for Art and Ecology 563
Southwest Writers Conference 549
Taos Institute of Arts 549
University of the Nations School of Writing and
    Writers Workshops 551
Walloon Writers' Retreat 543
Western Reserve Writer's & Freelance Conference 544
Wisconsin Regional Writer's Association Conferences
    545
Writer's Digest School 544
Writers' League of Texas Spring and Fall Workshops
    and Classes 551
Writing, Creativity and Ritual: A Woman's Retreat 527
Yaddo 527
Youth With a Mission's School of Writing 552

October
African American Book Club Summit, The 546
Big Bear Writer's Retreat 553
Bonnet's Storymaking: The Master Class, James 553
Booktowns of Europe Writers Workshops 565
Boucheron 553

Desert Writers Workshop/Canyonlands Field Institute 554

Detroit Women Writers Annual Writer's Conference 540

Flathead River Writers Conference 560

Fort Bend Writers Guild Workshop 547

Glorieta Christian Writers' Conference 548

Gotham Writers' Workshop 521

Hambidge Center 535

Hedgebrook 561

Highlights Foundation Founders Workshops 528

Hilton Head Island Writers Retreat 532

How to Be Published Workshops 535

IWWG Meet the Agents and Editors 522

Killaloe Hedge-School of Writing 566

La Jolla Writers Conference 555

Magna Cum Murder Crime Fiction Conference 541

Ministry of Writing: An Annual Colloquium, The 542

Moonlight and Magnolias Writer's Conference 536

Nightwriters 532

Nimrod Annual Writers' Workshop 548

Northwest Bookfest 562

Ozark Creative Writers, Inc. 536

Publishing Game, The 524

Sage Hill Writing Experience 564

Sandy Cove Christian Writers Conference 530

Santa Barbara Christian Writers Conference 557

SCBWI Southern Breeze Fall Conference 537

Seacoast Writer's Association Spring and Fall Conferences 525

Sitka Center for Art and Ecology 563

Southern California Writers' Conference/L.A., Oxnard 557

Taos Institute of Arts 549

University of the Nations School of Writing and Writers Workshops 551

Vancouver International Writers Festival, The 565

Volcano Writers' Retreat 558

Write From the Heart 563

Write on the Sound Writers' Conference 563

Writer's Digest School 544

Writers' League of Texas Spring and Fall Workshops and Classes 551

Writers Way, The 559

Writing, Creativity and Ritual: A Woman's Retreat 527

Yaddo 527

Youth With a Mission's School of Writing 552

November

Baltimore Writers Alliance Conference 527

Canyonlands Desert Writer's Workshop 554

Hambidge Center 535

Hedgebrook 561

Highlights Foundation Founders Workshops 528

How to Be Published Workshops 535

Killaloe Hedge-School of Writing 566

Mormon Writers' Conference 556

New Jersey Society of Christian Writers Fall Seminar, The 529

Penn Writers Conference 529

Publishing Game, The 524

Sitka Center for Art and Ecology 563

University of the Nations School of Writing and Writers Workshops 551

Writer's Digest School 544

Writers' League of Texas Spring and Fall Workshops and Classes 551

Yaddo 527

Youth With a Mission's School of Writing 552

December

Hambidge Center 535

Hilton Head Island Writers Retreat 532

How to Be Published Workshops 535

Killaloe Hedge-School of Writing 566

Publishing Game, The 524

Sitka Center for Art and Ecology 563

University of the Nations School of Writing and Writers Workshops 551

Writer's Digest School 544

Yaddo 527

Youth With a Mission's School of Writing 552

Category Index

Our category index makes it easy for you to identify publishers who are looking for a specific type of fiction. Under each fiction category are magazines and book publishers looking for that kind of fiction. Publishers who are not listed under a fiction category either accept all types of fiction or have not indicated specific subject preferences. Also not appearing here are listings that need very specific types of fiction, e.g., "fiction about fly fishing only." To use this index to find a book publisher for your mainstream novel, for instance, go to the Mainstream/Contemporary section and look under Book Publishers. Finally, read individual listings *carefully* to determine the publishers best suited to your work.

For a listing of agents and the types of fiction they represent, see the Literary Agents Category Index beginning on page 596.

ADVENTURE

Magazines

Advocate, PKA'S Publication 167
African Voices 333
Allegheny Review, The 169
American Feed Magazine 307
American Girl 334
Anthology Magazine 170
Armchair Aesthete, The 172
Art Times 335
Artemis Magazine 277
Barbaric Yawp 174
Bear Deluxe Magazine, The 336
Beginnings Publishing 175
Bibliophilos 177
Big Country Peacock Chronicle 309
Big Muddy: A Journal of the Mississippi River Valley 177
Blackbird 309
Blue Mesa Review 179
Blueline 179
Boys' Life 339
Brady Magazine 310
Breakaway Magazine 339
Bryant Literary Review 182
Bugle 340
Capers Aweigh 183
Cenotaph 311
Chrysalis Reader 186
CIA—Citizen in America 279
Cicada Magazine 341
Circle Magazine, The 279
Clubhouse Magazine 341
Cobblestone 342
Cochran's Corner 280
Cricket 342
Crusader Magazine 343
Dakota Outdoors 281

Dan River Anthology 191
Desert Voices 192
Discovery Trails 343
Down in the Dirt 282
Downstate Story 192
Drexel Online Journal 314
Dvorak's Nocturne Horizons, Antonin 314
Edge, Tales of Suspense, The 283
Enigma 283
Eureka Literary Magazine 194
Fifty Something Magazine 345
First Line 284
Foliate Oak Literary Magazine 285
Futures Mysterious Anthology Magazine 199
Gem, The 345
Green Mountains Review 203
Green's Magazine 204
Griffin, The 204
Grit 345
Harpur Palate 206
Hemispheres 346
High Adventure 347
Highlights for Children 347
Horsethief's Journal, The 318
Iconoclast, The 208
In Posse Review on Web Del Sol 318
Interbang 210
Irreantum 211
Jack and Jill 348
Karamu 213
Kentucky Monthly 348
Leapings Literary Magazine 216
Lullwater Review 219
Lynx Eye 219
MacGuffin, The 219
Magazine of Fantasy & Science Fiction, The 351
Medicinal Purposes 224
Merlyn's Pen 224

Mota 227
Musing Place, The 227
New England Writer's Network 293
Northwoods Journal 234
Oak, The 294
Ohio Teachers Write 235
On The Line 353
Palo Alto Review 237
PEEKS & valleys 239
Peninsular 239
Pink Chameleon, The 323
Pockets 354
Poetry & Prose Annual 243
Portland Review 244
PSI 298
RE:AL 249
Rose & Thorn Literary E-Zine, The 324
Rosebud 299
Shine Brightly 356
Short Stuff 254
Skyline Magazine 300
Slate and Style 300
Spider 356
Spoiledink Magazine 326
Spring Hill Review 260
Stone Soup 260
Storyteller 301
Storyteller, The 301
Thema 265
Thresholds Quarterly 329
Timber Creek Review 266
Toasted Cheese 329
Unknown Writer, The 268
Vincent Brothers Review, The 269
Virginia Quarterly Review 303
Weber Studies 304
Words of Wisdom 272

Book Publishers

Adventure Book Publishers 365
Artemis Press 367
Atheneum Books For Young Readers 368
Bantam Dell Publishing Group 370
Bantam Doubleday Dell Books for Young Readers 370
Berkley Publishing Group, The 372
Bethany House Publishers 373
Black Heron Press 374
Books In Motion 375
Borealis Press, Ltd. 376
Boyds Mills Press 376
Broadman & Holman 377
Caitlin Press, Inc. 378
Cave Books 379
Clarion Books 380
Coastal Carolina Press 381
Commuters Library 381
Covenant Communications, Inc. 382
Denlinger's Publishers, Ltd. 386

Dial Books For Young Readers 387
Doubleday 387
Electric Works Publishing 391
Fort Ross Inc. Russian-American Publishing Projects 394
Front Street 394
Geringer Books, Laura 396
Glencannon Press, The 396
Harlequin Enterprises, Ltd. 403
Holiday House, Inc. 408
Holt & Co. Books for Young Readers, Henry 408
Houghton Mifflin Books for Children 409
IVY Publications 412
JourneyForth 413
Kaeden Books 414
Kregel Publications 415
Little, Brown and Co. Children's Publishing 420
LTDBooks 422
Marvel Comics 423
McElderry Books, Margaret K. 424
Milkweeds for Young Readers 425
Multnomah Publishers, Inc. 427
Nelson, Tommy 429
New Hope Books, Inc. 429
New Victoria Publishers 430
Oak Tree Press 431
One World Books 432
Palari Publishing 434
Paradise Cay Publications 435
Philomel Books 437
Piatkus Books 437
Pig Iron Press 438
Piñata Books 438
Pipers' Ash Ltd. 439
Port Town Publishing 441
Publishers Syndication, International 442
Putnam's Sons, G.P. 443
Ramsey Books 443
Random House Trade Publishing Group 444
Red Dress Ink 445
Red Press Publishing Company, The 446
Regan Books 446
River Oak Publishing 448
Rock & Co., Publishers, James A. 448
Salvo Press 449
Science & Humanities Press 450
Severn House Publishers 451
Snowapple Press 454
Soho Press, Inc. 454
Starburst Publishers 457
Stylewriter, Inc. 458
SynergEbooks 458
Treble Heart Books 461
Vandamere Press 465
Vivisphere Publishing 466
WaterBrook Press 467
Whitman and Co., Albert 468

Windstorm Creative, Ltd. 469
Writers Direct 470

CHILDRENS/JUVENILE
Magazines
Advocate, PKA'S Publication 167
African Voices 333
American Girl 334
Big Country Peacock Chronicle 309
Bugle 340
Clubhouse Magazine 341
Cobblestone 342
Cochran's Corner 280
Cricket 342
Crusader Magazine 343
Discovery Trails 343
Faces 344
Fun For Kidz 285
Funny Paper, The 285
High Adventure 347
Highlights for Children 347
My Friend 352
Shine Brightly 356
Spellbound Magazine 300
Spider 356
Spoiledink Magazine 326
Story Friends 327
Story Friends 358
Toasted Cheese 329
Winner 359

Book Publishers
Bethany House Publishers 373
Beyond Words Publishing, Inc. 373
Commuters Library 381
Cricket Books 382
Dreamcatcher Publishing Inc. 388
Farrar, Straus & Giroux Books for Young Readers 392
Front Street 394
Gival Press 396
Glencannon Press, The 396
Godine, Publisher, Inc., David R. 396
GreyCore Press 398
Harcourt, Inc. 402
Holiday House, Inc. 408
Ion Imagination Publishing 411
IVY Publications 412
Just Us Books, Inc. 413
Kregel Publications 415
Lee & Low Books 416
Lightwave Publishing Inc. 419
Little, Brown and Company Children's Books 420
Micah Publications, Inc 424
Moody Publishers 427
Pemmican Publications 436
Pipers' Ash Ltd. 439
Pippin Press 439
Pleasant Company Publications 439

Port Town Publishing 441
Ransom Publishing Ltd. 444
Ravenhawk™ Books 444
River City Publishing 447
Scholastic Canada, Ltd. 450
Simon & Schuster Books for Young Readers 453
Snowapple Press 454
Stylewriter, Inc. 458
SynergEbooks 458
T n T Classic Books 458
Tricycle Press 461
Whitman and Co., Albert 468
X Press, The 471

COMICS/GRAPHIC NOVELS
Magazines
Albedo One 276
Blackbird 309
Columbia: A Journal of Literature and Art 187
Enterzone 315
EOTU 315
5-Trope 317
Fluent Ascension 317
Foliate Oak Literary Magazine 285
Grasslimb 287
Hybolics 288
Lady Churchill's Rosebud Wristlet 289
Maelstrom 220
Pindeldyboz 297
12-Gauge.com 329
Weber Studies 304
Wild Violet 330
Zopilote 305

Book Publishers
Dark Horse Comics 385
Holloway House Publishing Co. 408
Insomniac Press 410
Marvel Comics 423
One World Books 432
Regan Books 446
Rock & Co., Publishers, James A. 448
Starcherone Books 457

EROTICA
Magazines
Adrift 167
African Voices 333
Ascent 308
Blackbird 309
Book World Magazine 180
Brady Magazine 310
CIA—Citizen in America 279
Digress Magazine 343
Dream Fantasy International 282
Edge, Tales of Suspense, The 283
EOTU 315
Fiction Inferno 316

First Class 196
First Hand 345
Fluent Ascension 317
Gargoyle 199
Gathering of the Tribes, A 200
Gay Chicago Magazine 286
Hadrosaur Tales 287
Happy 205
In Posse Review on Web Del Sol 318
Literoticaffeine 319
Lynx Eye 219
Matriarch's Way 224
Medicinal Purposes 224
Metal Scratches 224
Midnight Times 291
Mota 227
Options 353
Poskisnolt Press 297
Quarter After Eight 247
Rain Crow 248
Rocket Press 252
Snake Nation Review 255
Spoiledink Magazine 326
Tattoo Highway 328
Thirteenth Warrior Review, The 328
12-Gauge.com 329
Underwood Review, The 268
Unwound 269
Writers' Forum 360

Book Publishers
Black Lace Books 374
Circlet Press, Inc. 380
Down There Press 387
Gay Sunshine Press and Leyland Publications 395
Genesis Press, Inc. 395
Guernica Editions 398
Holloway House Publishing Co. 408
New American Library 429
New Victoria Publishers 430
One World Books 432
Piatkus Books 437
Regan Books 446
Starcherone Books 457
Windstorm Creative, Ltd. 469
X Press, The 471

ETHNIC/MULTICULTURAL
Magazines
ACM 167
Adrift 167
Advocate, PKA'S Publication 167
African American Review 168
African Voices 333
Aim Magazine 334
Allegheny Review, The 169
American Feed Magazine 307
American Girl 334
Antietam Review 170
Any Dream Will Do Review 277
Art Times 335
Asian Pacific American Journal 173
Baltimore Review, The 174
Bibliophilos 177
Big Country Peacock Chronicle 309
Big Muddy: A Journal of the Mississippi River Valley 177
Black Lace 178
Black Mountain Review, The 178
Blackbird 309
Blue Mesa Review 179
Boston Review 338
Brady Magazine 310
Briar Cliff Review, The 181
Brillant Corners 181
Bryant Literary Review 182
Callaloo 183
Capers Aweigh 183
Cenotaph 311
Center 184
Chaffin Journal 185
Chariton Review, The 185
CIA—Citizen in America 279
Cobblestone 342
Colorado Review 187
Columbia: A Journal of Literature and Art 187
Concho River Review 188
Confluence 188
Crab Orchard Review 189
Cream City Review, The 190
Creative With Words Publications 280
Cricket 342
Crucible 191
Dan River Anthology 191
Descant 191
Desert Voices 192
Digress Magazine 343
Down in the Dirt 282
Downstate Story 192
Drexel Online Journal 314
Enterzone 315
Epoch 193
Eureka Literary Magazine 194
Faces 344
Feminist Studies 195
Fifty Something Magazine 345
filling Station 196
First Line 284
Flint Hills Review 197
Fluent Ascension 317
Foliate Oak Literary Magazine 285
Fourteen Hills 197
Fugue 199
Futures Mysterious Anthology Magazine 199
flashquake 317

Gargoyle 199
Gathering of the Tribes, A 200
Gertrude 200
Grasslands Review 203
Grasslimb 287
Green Hills Literary Lantern, The 203
Griffin, The 204
Gulf Coast 205
Hadassah Magazine 346
Happy 205
Harpur Palate 206
Hawai'i Pacific Review 206
Hayden's Ferry Review 207
Heartlands Today, The 207
Hemispheres 346
Home Planet News 207
Horizons 348
Horsethief's Journal, The 318
Hybolics 288
Iconoclast, The 208
Illya's Honey 209
In Posse Review on Web Del Sol 318
Indiana Review 209
Interbang 210
Irreantum 211
Jabberwock Review, The 211
Jewish Currents Magazine 288
Kalliope 212
Karamu 213
Kenyon Review, The 213
Kit-Cat Review, The 214
Leapings Literary Magazine 216
Left Curve 290
Lilith Magazine 350
Literary Potpourri 290
Literary Witches 319
Long Story, The 218
Lullwater Review 219
Lynx Eye 219
MacGuffin, The 219
Mangrove 220
Many Mountains Moving 221
Margin 319
Matriarch's Way 224
Medicinal Purposes 224
Missouri Review, The 226
Mobius 227
Mota 227
Mudrock: Stories & Tales 292
Musing Place, The 227
Na'amat Woman 352
New England Writer's Network 293
New Laurel Review 229
New Letters 230
New Orphic Review, The 230
New York Stories 232
North Dakota Quarterly 233

North East Arts Magazine 234
new renaissance, the 231
Obsidian III 235
Ohio Teachers Write 235
Pacific Coast Journal 237
Painted Bride Quarterly 322
Palo Alto Review 237
Paperplates 322
Passages North 238
Paterson Literary Review 239
PEEKS & valleys 239
Peninsular 239
Pikeville Review 242
Pleiades 242
Pockets 354
Poetry & Prose Annual 243
Poetry Forum Short Stories 243
Pointed Circle 244
Porcupine Literary Arts Magazine 244
Portland Review 244
Poskisnolt Press 297
Pretext 245
Prose Ax 298
Puerto Del Sol 247
Quarter After Eight 247
Quarterly West 247
Rainbow Curve 248
Raven Chronicles, The 249
River Styx 251
Rockford Review, The 252
Rose & Thorn Literary E-Zine, The 324
Rosebud 299
Salmagundi 252
Salt Hill 253
Scribia, The 254
Shine Brightly 356
Skyline Magazine 300
Snake Nation Review 255
So to Speak 256
Sonora Review 256
South Dakota Review 257
Southern California Anthology 257
Southwestern American Literature 259
Spider 356
Spindrift 259
Spring Hill Review 260
Stone Soup 260
Storyteller 301
Struggle 261
Sulphur River Literary Review 262
Tameme 263
Tampa Review 263
Thema 265
Thirteenth Moon 265
Thorny Locust 265
Timber Creek Review 266
Toasted Cheese 329

Transition 267
12-Gauge.com 329
Underwood Review, The 268
Unknown Writer, The 268
Unwound 269
U.S. Catholic 358
Vestal Review 269
Vincent Brothers Review, The 269
Virginia Quarterly Review 303
Waxing and Waning 330
Weber Studies 304
Westview 270
Wild Violet 330
Windhover 271
Words Literary Journal 272
Words of Wisdom 272
Writing For Our Lives 272
Xavier Review 273
Yemassee 273
Zopilote 305
Zuzu's Petals Quarterly 331
Zyzzyva 274

Book Publishers

Arcade Publishing 367
Arte Publico Press 367
Artemis Press 367
Atheneum Books For Young Readers 368
Aunt Lute Books 368
Ballantine Books 370
Bancroft Press 370
Beyond Words Publishing, Inc. 373
Bilingual Press 373
Bordighera Inc. 376
Borealis Press, Ltd. 376
Boyds Mills Press 376
Branden Publishing Co., Inc. 377
Braziller, Inc., George 377
Coastal Carolina Press 381
Coffee House Press 381
Coteau Books 382
Denlinger's Publishers, Ltd. 386
Doubleday 387
Electric Works Publishing 391
Feminist Press at the City University of New York, The 393
Genesis Press, Inc. 395
Gival Press 396
Glencannon Press, The 396
High Country Publishers Ltd. 407
Holloway House Publishing Co. 408
Homa & Sekey Books 408
Houghton Mifflin Books for Children 409
Insomniac Press 410
Interlink Publishing Group, Inc. 411
Just Us Books, Inc. 413
Kaeden Books 414
Kensington Publishing Corp. 414

Lee & Low Books 416
Little, Brown and Co. Children's Publishing 420
Lost Horse Press 421
New American Library 429
NW Writers' Corp. 431
Oak Tree Press 431
One World Books 432
Outrider Press, Inc. 433
Palari Publishing 434
Panther Creek Press 434
Pemmican Publications 436
Philomel Books 437
Polychrome Publishing Corp. 441
Red Hen Press 445
Regan Books 446
River City Publishing 447
Rock Village Publishing 448
Seal Press 451
Shoreline 452
Snowapple Press 454
Soho Press, Inc. 454
Spinsters Ink 455
Spout Press 456
Stylewriter, Inc. 458
Third World Press 459
Tindal Street Press, Ltd. 460
UCLA American Indian Studies Center 462
University of Alberta Press, The 463
Vivisphere Publishing 466
Voices From My Retreat 466
Whitman and Co., Albert 468
X Press, The 471

EXPERIMENTAL
Magazines

Abiko Annual with James, The 276
ACM 167
Adrift 167
Advocate, PKA'S Publication 167
African American Review 168
African Voices 333
Alaska Quarterly Review 168
Albedo One 276
Allegheny Review, The 169
Alsop Review, The 307
American Feed Magazine 307
Antietam Review 170
Antioch Review 171
Artful Dodge 173
Ascent 308
Asian Pacific American Journal 173
B&A: New Fiction 174
Barbaric Yawp 174
Bathtub Gin 174
Bellingham Review 175
Berkeley Fiction Review 176

Big Muddy: A Journal of the Mississippi River Valley 177
Bitter Oleander, The 178
Black Mountain Review, The 178
Blackbird 309
Blue Mesa Review 179
Blue Moon Review, The 310
Bomb Magazine 338
Boston Review 338
Boulevard 180
Brady Magazine 310
Brillant Corners 181
Bryant Literary Review 182
blue Review, The 179
Cafe Irreal, The 310
Capilano Review, The 184
Center 184
Chaffin Journal 185
Chariton Review, The 185
Chicago Review 186
Chiron Review 186
Chrysalis Reader 186
CIA—Citizen in America 279
Circle Magazine, The 279
Colorado Review 187
Columbia: A Journal of Literature and Art 187
Confrontation, A Literary Journal 188
Cream City Review, The 190
Crucible 191
Dan River Anthology 191
Descant 191
Digress Magazine 343
Down in the Dirt 282
Downstate Story 192
Dreams & Visions 282
Enigma 283
Enterzone 315
EOTU 315
Epoch 193
Erased, Sigh, Sigh. 193
Eureka Literary Magazine 194
Fiction 195
Fiction Inferno 316
Fifty Something Magazine 345
filling Station 196
5-Trope 317
Fluent Ascension 317
Foliate Oak Literary Magazine 285
Fourteen Hills 197
Frank 198
Free Focus/Ostentatious Mind 285
Fugue 199
Futures Mysterious Anthology Magazine 199
flashquake 317
Gargoyle 199
Gathering of the Tribes, A 200
Gettysburg Review, The 201

Ginosko 201
Glass Tesseract 201
Grain Literary Magazine 202
Grasslands Review 203
Grasslimb 287
Green Hills Literary Lantern, The 203
Green Mountains Review 203
Greensboro Review, The 204
Gulf Coast 205
Happy 205
Harpur Palate 206
Hawai'i Pacific Review 206
Hayden's Ferry Review 207
Home Planet News 207
Hybolics 288
Iconoclast, The 208
Idaho Review, The 208
Illya's Honey 209
In Posse Review on Web Del Sol 318
Indiana Review 209
Inkwell Magazine 210
Interbang 210
Irreantum 211
Jabberwock Review, The 211
Kalliope 212
Karamu 213
Kenyon Review, The 213
King's English 214
Kit-Cat Review, The 214
Lady Churchill's Rosebud Wristlet 289
Lake Effect 215
Leapings Literary Magazine 216
Left Curve 290
Lichen 216
Licking River Review, The 216
Liquid Ohio 290
Literal Latté 217
Literary Witches 319
Lost and Found Times 218
Lullwater Review 219
Lynx Eye 219
MacGuffin, The 219
Maelstrom 220
Many Mountains Moving 221
Matriarch's Way 224
Medicinal Purposes 224
Merlyn's Pen 224
Metal Scratches 224
Mid-American Review 225
Minnesota Review, The 226
Mississippi Review 226
Mobius 227
Mota 227
Musing Place, The 227
New Letters 230
New Orphic Review, The 230
New York Stories 232

Night Train 232
North Dakota Quarterly 233
Northwest Review 234
Northwoods Journal 234
new renaissance, the 231
Oak, The 294
Office Number One 294
Ohio Teachers Write 235
Pacific Coast Journal 237
Painted Bride Quarterly 322
Palo Alto Review 237
Pangolin Papers 238
Paumanok Review, The 323
Permutations 241
Phantasmagoria 241
Pif 323
Pikeville Review 242
Pindeldyboz 297
Pink Chameleon, The 323
Pleiades 242
Poetry & Prose Annual 243
Poetry Forum Short Stories 243
Portland Review 244
Poskisnolt Press 297
Prism International 246
Prose Ax 298
Puckerbrush Review 246
Puerto Del Sol 247
Quality Women's Fiction 247
Quarter After Eight 247
Quarterly West 247
Rain Crow 248
Rainbow Curve 248
Rambunctious Review 248
RE:AL 249
Red Rock Review 250
Rejected Quarterly, The 251
River Styx 251
Rocket Press 252
Rockford Review, The 252
Rose & Thorn Literary E-Zine, The 324
Rosebud 299
Salmagundi 252
Salt Hill 253
Samsara 253
Santa Monica Review 253
Skyline Magazine 300
Snake Nation Review 255
So to Speak 256
Sonora Review 256
Southern California Anthology 257
Spindrift 259
Spinning Jenny 357
Spitball 259
Spoiledink Magazine 326
Spring Hill Review 260
Staple Magazine 260

Stone Soup 260
Struggle 261
Sulphur River Literary Review 262
Summer's Reading, A 262
Sycamore Review 262
Tampa Review 263
Tattoo Highway 328
Thema 265
Thirteenth Moon 265
Thirteenth Warrior Review, The 328
Thorny Locust 265
Tin House 267
Toasted Cheese 329
Transcendent Visions 303
12-Gauge.com 329
Unbound 268
Underwood Review, The 268
Unknown Writer, The 268
Vincent Brothers Review, The 269
Weber Studies 304
Western Humanities Review 270
Wild Violet 330
Windhover 271
Words Literary Journal 272
Writers for Readers 304
Writing For Our Lives 272
Xavier Review 273
Xconnect 273
Yalobusha Review, The 273
Yemassee 273
Zyzzyva 274

Book Publishers

Ageless Press 365
Anvil Press 367
Artemis Press 367
Atheneum Books For Young Readers 368
Beach Holme Publishers, Ltd. 372
Black Heron Press 374
Books Collective, The 375
Coffee House Press 381
Context Books 382
Doubleday 387
Electric Works Publishing 391
FC2 392
Gay Sunshine Press and Leyland Publications 395
Grove/Atlantic, Inc. 398
Insomniac Press 410
Livingston Press 420
Lost Horse Press 421
Outrider Press, Inc. 433
Panther Creek Press 434
Pig Iron Press 438
Post-Apollo Press, The 441
Pudding House Publications 442
Random House Trade Publishing Group 444
Red Dragon Press 445
Red Hen Press 445

Regan Books 446
Rock & Co., Publishers, James A. 448
Snowapple Press 454
Spout Press 456
Starcherone Books 457
Stone Bridge Press 457
Stylewriter, Inc. 458
Thistledown Press 459
University of Alberta Press, The 463
Via Dolorosa Press 465
Voices From My Retreat 466
Windstorm Creative, Ltd. 469
Woodley Memorial Press 470
X Press, The 471
York Press, Ltd. 471

FAMILY SAGA
Magazines
Allegheny Review, The 169
American Feed Magazine 307
Beginnings Publishing 175
Bibliophilos 177
Big Country Peacock Chronicle 309
Big Muddy: A Journal of the Mississippi River Valley 177
Blackbird 309
Brady Magazine 310
Bryant Literary Review 182
Chaffin Journal 185
Enterzone 315
Foliate Oak Literary Magazine 285
Griffin, The 204
In Posse Review on Web Del Sol 318
Interbang 210
Irreantum 211
Mota 227
Pink Chameleon, The 323
Poetry & Prose Annual 243
Salmagundi 252
Spring Hill Review 260
Underwood Review, The 268
U.S. Catholic 358
War Cry, The 359
Windhover 271
Writers for Readers 304
Yalobusha Review, The 273

Book Publishers
Artemis Press 367
Bancroft Press 370
Bordighera Inc. 376
Commuters Library 381
Denlinger's Publishers, Ltd. 386
High Country Publishers Ltd. 407
Hodder & Stoughton/Headline 407
Micah Publications, Inc 424
MIRA Books 426
Mountain State Press 427

Outrider Press, Inc. 433
Philomel Books 437
Piatkus Books 437
Red Press Publishing Company, The 446
SynergEbooks 458

FANTASY
Magazines
Adventures of Sword & Sorcery 276
Advocate, PKA'S Publication 167
African Voices 333
Albedo One 276
Alembic 277
AlienSkin Magazine 307
Allegheny Review, The 169
American Feed Magazine 307
Ancient Paths 170
Anthology Magazine 170
Armchair Aesthete, The 172
Art Times 335
Ascent 308
Asimov's Science Fiction 335
Aurealis 278
Barbaric Yawp 174
Big Country Peacock Chronicle 309
Blackbird 309
Brady Magazine 310
Bryant Literary Review 182
Cafe Irreal, The 310
Capers Aweigh 183
Cenotaph 311
Challenging Destiny 278
Cicada Magazine 341
Cricket 342
Cthulhu Sex Magazine 281
Dan River Anthology 191
Dargonzine 313
Dark Horizons 281
Digress Magazine 343
Down in the Dirt 282
Dream Fantasy International 282
Dreams & Visions 282
Drexel Online Journal 314
Dvorak's Nocturne Horizons, Antonin 314
Enigma 283
EOTU 315
Eureka Literary Magazine 194
Fantastic Stories of the Imagination 284
Fiction Inferno 316
Fifty Something Magazine 345
First Line 284
Futures Mysterious Anthology Magazine 199
Gathering of the Tribes, A 200
Grasslands Review 203
Green's Magazine 204
Griffin, The 204
Hadrosaur Tales 287

Happy 205
Harpur Palate 206
Hawai'i Pacific Review 206
Highlights for Children 347
Iconoclast, The 208
In Posse Review on Web Del Sol 318
Interbang 210
Irreantum 211
Lady Churchill's Rosebud Wristlet 289
Leading Edge 290
Leapings Literary Magazine 216
Lichen 216
Literal Latté 217
Low Budget Science Fiction 291
Lullwater Review 219
Lynx Eye 219
Magazine of Fantasy & Science Fiction, The 351
Margin 319
Matriarch's Way 224
Medicinal Purposes 224
Merlyn's Pen 224
Midnight Times 291
Millennium Science Fiction & Fantasy 321
Mississippi Review 226
Mobius 227
Mota 227
Musing Place, The 227
New Mirage Quarterly 230
New Orphic Review, The 230
Northwoods Journal 234
Oak, The 294
Office Number One 294
Ohio Teachers Write 235
On Spec 295
Once Upon A World 295
Oracular Tree, The 321
Orb 295
Outer Darkness 296
Palo Alto Review 237
PEEKS & valleys 239
Peninsular 239
Peridot Books 323
Permutations 241
Pink Chameleon, The 323
Poetry Forum Short Stories 243
Poskisnolt Press 297
Primavera 245
Psychic Radio, The 298
Rejected Quarterly, The 251
Rockford Review, The 252
Rose & Thorn Literary E-Zine, The 324
Samsara 253
Scifi.com 325
Skyline Magazine 300
Slate and Style 300
Snake Nation Review 255
Songs of Innocence 256

Southern Humanities Review 258
Spider 356
Starship Earth 300
Stone Soup 260
Storyteller 301
Summerset Review, The 327
Talebones 302
Tales of the Hookman Online Magazine 328
Tampa Review 263
Thema 265
Thirteen Stories 302
Thresholds Quarterly 329
Toasted Cheese 329
Underwood Review, The 268
Unknown Writer, The 268
Waxing and Waning 330
Weird Tales 304
Wild Violet 330
Windhover 271
Writers for Readers 304
Zahir 305
Zuzu's Petals Quarterly 331

Book Publishers

Ace Science Fiction and Fantasy 364
Adventure Book Publishers 365
Ageless Press 365
Artemis Press 367
Arx Publishing 368
Atheneum Books For Young Readers 368
Baen Publishing Enterprises 369
Ballantine Books 370
Bantam Dell Publishing Group 370
Bantam Doubleday Dell Books for Young Readers 370
Blue Sky Press, The 375
Books Collective, The 375
Books In Motion 375
Commuters Library 381
Coteau Books 382
DAW Books, Inc. 385
Del Rey Books 386
Descant Publishing 387
Dial Books For Young Readers 387
Dragon Moon Press 388
Edge Science Fiction and Fantasy Publishing 390
Electric Works Publishing 391
Eos 391
Fort Ross Inc. Russian-American Publishing Projects 394
Front Street 394
Geringer Books, Laura 396
Greenwillow Books 398
High Country Publishers Ltd. 407
Holt & Co. Books for Young Readers, Henry 408
Kaeden Books 414
Last Knight Publishing Company 415
Little, Brown and Co. Children's Publishing 420
LTDBooks 422

Marvel Comics 423
McElderry Books, Margaret K. 424
Meisha Merlin Publishing, Inc. 424
Milkweeds for Young Readers 425
Moody Publishers 427
New American Library 429
New Victoria Publishers 430
Oak Tree Press 431
Omnidawn Publishing 431
Outrider Press, Inc. 433
Philomel Books 437
Port Town Publishing 441
Ramsey Books 443
Random House Trade Publishing Group 444
Ravenhawk™ Books 444
Regan Books 446
Renaissance House 446
River Oak Publishing 448
ROC Books 448
Rock & Co., Publishers, James A. 448
Rock Village Publishing 448
Severn House Publishers 451
Simon & Schuster Books for Young Readers 453
Snowapple Press 454
Spectra Books 455
St. Martin's Press 456
Starburst Publishers 457
Stone Bridge Press 457
Stylewriter, Inc. 458
Timberwolf Press, Inc. 460
Treble Heart Books 461
Tyrannosaurus Press 462
Vivisphere Publishing 466
Warner Books 467
White Wolf 468
Whitman and Co., Albert 468
Wildside Press 468
Willowgate Press 469
Windstorm Creative, Ltd. 469
Wizards of the Coast 470

FEMINIST
Magazines
ACM 167
Adrift 167
Advocate, PKA'S Publication 167
African American Review 168
Allegheny Review, The 169
American Feed Magazine 307
Antietam Review 170
Art Times 335
Ascent 308
Asian Pacific American Journal 173
Big Muddy: A Journal of the Mississippi River Valley 177
Blackbird 309
Blue Mesa Review 179

Blue Moon Review, The 310
Brady Magazine 310
Briar Cliff Review, The 181
Bryant Literary Review 182
Callaloo 183
Capers Aweigh 183
Chaffin Journal 185
Crucible 191
Descant 191
Desert Voices 192
Digress Magazine 343
Down in the Dirt 282
Drexel Online Journal 314
Emrys Journal 193
Enterzone 315
Eureka Literary Magazine 194
Event 194
Feminist Studies 195
filling Station 196
Foliate Oak Literary Magazine 285
Free Focus/Ostentatious Mind 285
Frontiers 198
Futures Mysterious Anthology Magazine 199
Gathering of the Tribes, A 200
Gertrude 200
Green Hills Literary Lantern, The 203
Griffin, The 204
Happy 205
Hawai'i Pacific Review 206
Home Planet News 207
Horizons 348
Illya's Honey 209
In Posse Review on Web Del Sol 318
Interbang 210
Irreantum 211
Jabberwock Review, The 211
Jewish Currents Magazine 288
Karamu 213
Kenyon Review, The 213
Lady Churchill's Rosebud Wristlet 289
Leapings Literary Magazine 216
Lichen 216
Lilith Magazine 350
Literary Witches 319
Long Story, The 218
Lynx Eye 219
Many Mountains Moving 221
Margin 319
Matriarch's Way 224
Medicinal Purposes 224
Minnesota Review, The 226
Mobius 227
Mota 227
Mudrock: Stories & Tales 292
Musing Place, The 227
New York Stories 232
North Dakota Quarterly 233

Northwest Review 234
Obsidian III 235
Ohio Teachers Write 235
Pacific Coast Journal 237
Painted Bride Quarterly 322
Palo Alto Review 237
Paperplates 322
Pikeville Review 242
Pleiades 242
Poetry & Prose Annual 243
Poetry Forum Short Stories 243
Portland Review 244
Poskisnolt Press 297
Pretext 245
Primavera 245
Quality Women's Fiction 247
Rainbow Curve 248
Rambunctious Review 248
River Styx 251
Roanoke Review 252
Room of One's Own 252
So to Speak 256
Southern California Anthology 257
Southern Humanities Review 258
Spoiledink Magazine 326
Staple Magazine 260
Struggle 261
Sulphur River Literary Review 262
Thirteenth Moon 265
Timber Creek Review 266
Toasted Cheese 329
Transcendent Visions 303
Underwood Review, The 268
Vincent Brothers Review, The 269
Virginia Quarterly Review 303
Waxing and Waning 330
Weber Studies 304
Wild Violet 330
Words of Wisdom 272
Writing For Our Lives 272
Yemassee 273

Book Publishers

Artemis Press 367
Aunt Lute Books 368
Ballantine Books 370
Bancroft Press 370
Books Collective, The 375
Bordighera Inc. 376
Cleis Press 380
Context Books 382
Coteau Books 382
Denlinger's Publishers, Ltd. 386
Doubleday 387
Down There Press 387
FC2 392
Feminist Press at the City University of New York, The 393
Four Walls Eight Windows 394
Front Street 394
Guernica Editions 398
High Country Publishers Ltd. 407
Little, Brown and Co. Children's Publishing 420
New Victoria Publishers 430
Oak Tree Press 431
Outrider Press, Inc. 433
Pipers' Ash Ltd. 439
Red Hen Press 445
Regan Books 446
Seal Press 451
Snowapple Press 454
Soho Press, Inc. 454
Spinsters Ink 455
Stylewriter, Inc. 458
T n T Classic Books 458
Third World Press 459
Tindal Street Press, Ltd. 460
University of Alberta Press, The 463
Véhicule Press 465
Vivisphere Publishing 466
Voices From My Retreat 466

GAY

Magazines

ACM 167
Adrift 167
African Voices 333
Allegheny Review, The 169
Art Times 335
Asian Pacific American Journal 173
Big Country Peacock Chronicle 309
Blackbird 309
Blue Mesa Review 179
Blue Moon Review, The 310
Brady Magazine 310
Chaffin Journal 185
Descant 191
Digress Magazine 343
Down in the Dirt 282
Drexel Online Journal 314
Edge, Tales of Suspense, The 283
Enterzone 315
Feminist Studies 195
filling Station 196
First Hand 345
First Line 284
Flint Hills Review 197
Fluent Ascension 317
Foliate Oak Literary Magazine 285
Fourteen Hills 197
Futures Mysterious Anthology Magazine 199
Gargoyle 199
Gathering of the Tribes, A 200
Gay Chicago Magazine 286
Gertrude 200

Grasslimb 287
Happy 205
Home Planet News 207
Illya's Honey 209
In Posse Review on Web Del Sol 318
Interbang 210
Jabberwock Review, The 211
Karamu 213
Kenyon Review, The 213
Lichen 216
Literary Witches 319
Lynx Eye 219
Many Mountains Moving 221
Margin 319
Medicinal Purposes 224
Minnesota Review, The 226
Mobius 227
Mota 227
Musing Place, The 227
New York Stories 232
North East Arts Magazine 234
Ohio Teachers Write 235
Options 353
Painted Bride Quarterly 322
Paperplates 322
Peninsular 239
Pleiades 242
Portland Review 244
Poskisnolt Press 297
Pretext 245
Primavera 245
Puckerbrush Review 246
Quarter After Eight 247
Rainbow Curve 248
River Styx 251
Roanoke Review 252
Salmagundi 252
Salt Hill 253
Snake Nation Review 255
Spoiledink Magazine 326
Staple Magazine 260
Tattoo Highway 328
Toasted Cheese 329
Transcendent Visions 303
12-Gauge.com 329
Underwood Review, The 268
Unknown Writer, The 268
Weber Studies 304
Wild Violet 330
Yemassee 273
Zuzu's Petals Quarterly 331

Book Publishers
Ballantine Books 370
Bancroft Press 370
Books Collective, The 375
Braziller, Inc., George 377
Cleis Press 380

Coteau Books 382
Doubleday 387
FC2 392
Feminist Press at the City University of New York, The 393
Four Walls Eight Windows 394
Gival Press 396
Guernica Editions 398
Hill Street Press 407
Insomniac Press 410
Kensington Publishing Corp. 414
Little, Brown and Co. Children's Publishing 420
Outrider Press, Inc. 433
Palari Publishing 434
Red Hen Press 445
Regan Books 446
Seal Press 451
Spinsters Ink 455
Starcherone Books 457
Stone Bridge Press 457
T n T Classic Books 458
University of Wisconsin Press 464
Vivisphere Publishing 466
Windstorm Creative, Ltd. 469

GLITZ
Magazines
American Feed Magazine 307
Blackbird 309
Brady Magazine 310
Futures Mysterious Anthology Magazine 199
Interbang 210
12-Gauge.com 329

Book Publishers
Bancroft Press 370

HISTORICAL
Magazines
Advocate, PKA'S Publication 167
African Voices 333
Aim Magazine 334
Allegheny Review, The 169
American Feed Magazine 307
American Girl 334
Ancient Paths 170
Appalachian Heritage 171
Armchair Aesthete, The 172
Art Times 335
Asian Pacific American Journal 173
Barbaric Yawp 174
Bear Deluxe Magazine, The 336
Bibliophilos 177
Big Country Peacock Chronicle 309
Big Muddy: A Journal of the Mississippi River Valley 177
Black Mountain Review, The 178
Blackbird 309

Blue Mesa Review 179
Book World Magazine 180
Bookpress 180
Brady Magazine 310
Briar Cliff Review, The 181
Bryant Literary Review 182
Bugle 340
blue Review, The 179
Callaloo 183
Capers Aweigh 183
Caribbean Writer, The 184
Cenotaph 311
Chaffin Journal 185
Christian Courier 279
Chrysalis Reader 186
CIA—Citizen in America 279
Cicada Magazine 341
Cobblestone 342
Cochran's Corner 280
Columbia: A Journal of Literature and Art 187
Concho River Review 188
Copperfield Review, The 312
Cricket 342
Dan River Anthology 191
Descant 191
Digress Magazine 343
Discovery Trails 343
Down in the Dirt 282
Downstate Story 192
Dream Fantasy International 282
Enigma 283
Enterzone 315
Eureka Literary Magazine 194
Exhibition 195
Faces 344
Fifty Something Magazine 345
Flint Hills Review 197
Foliate Oak Literary Magazine 285
Futures Mysterious Anthology Magazine 199
Gathering of the Tribes, A 200
Gettysburg Review, The 201
Gin Bender Poetry Review 317
Griffin, The 204
Harpur Palate 206
Hawai'i Pacific Review 206
Hemispheres 346
High Adventure 347
Highlights for Children 347
Home Planet News 207
Horizons 288
Horizons 348
Horsethief's Journal, The 318
Illya's Honey 209
In Posse Review on Web Del Sol 318
Interbang 210
Irreantum 211
Jack and Jill 348

Jewish Currents Magazine 288
Karamu 213
Kentucky Monthly 348
Kenyon Review, The 213
King's English 214
Left Curve 290
Lullwater Review 219
Lynx Eye 219
MacGuffin, The 219
Many Mountains Moving 221
Margin 319
Medicinal Purposes 224
Merlyn's Pen 224
Minnesota Review, The 226
Mobius 227
Mota 227
Musing Place, The 227
Na'amat Woman 352
Nassau Review 228
New Orphic Review, The 230
North Dakota Quarterly 233
North East Arts Magazine 234
Ohio Teachers Write 235
Pacific Coast Journal 237
Palo Alto Review 237
PEEKS & valleys 239
Peninsular 239
Pockets 354
Poetry & Prose Annual 243
Poetry Forum Short Stories 243
Portland Magazine 354
Portland Review 244
Purpose 354
Queen's Quarterly 299
RE:AL 249
Rejected Quarterly, The 251
Rose & Thorn Literary E-Zine, The 324
Rosebud 299
RPPS/Fullosia Press 325
Salmagundi 252
Shine Brightly 356
Short Stuff 254
Skyline Magazine 300
Songs of Innocence 256
Southern California Anthology 257
Spider 356
Spindrift 259
Spitball 259
Spring Hill Review 260
Starship Earth 300
Stone Soup 260
Storyteller 301
Storyteller, The 301
Struggle 261
Tampa Review 263
Thema 265
Timber Creek Review 266

Toasted Cheese 329
Transition 267
Vincent Brothers Review, The 269
Virginia Quarterly Review 303
Waxing and Waning 330
Weber Studies 304
Windhover 271
Words of Wisdom 272
Writers' Forum 360
Writers for Readers 304
Xavier Review 273
Yalobusha Review, The 273
Yemassee 273
Zopilote 305

Book Publishers

Academy Chicago Publishers 364
Adventure Book Publishers 365
Arcade Publishing 367
Artemis Press 367
Arx Publishing 368
Atheneum Books For Young Readers 368
Avalon Books 369
Avon Books 369
Ballantine Books 370
Bancroft Press 370
Bantam Doubleday Dell Books for Young Readers 370
Barbour Publishing, Inc. 371
Bardsong Press 371
Beil, Publisher, Inc., Frederic C. 372
Berkley Publishing Group, The 372
Bethany House Publishers 373
Blue Sky Press, The 375
Books In Motion 375
Bordighera Inc. 376
Borealis Press, Ltd. 376
Boyds Mills Press 376
Branden Publishing Co., Inc. 377
Caitlin Press, Inc. 378
Carolrhoda Books, Inc. 379
Cave Books 379
Clarion Books 380
Coastal Carolina Press 381
Commuters Library 381
Context Books 382
Coteau Books 382
Covenant Communications, Inc. 382
Crossway Books 383
Cumberland House Publishing 384
Denlinger's Publishers, Ltd. 386
Doubleday 387
Eakin Press/Sunbelt Media, Inc. 389
Electric Works Publishing 391
Empire Publishing Service 391
Faith Kidz Books 392
Forge and Tor Books 393
Front Street 394
Gay Sunshine Press and Leyland Publications 395

Geringer Books, Laura 396
Gival Press 396
Glencannon Press, The 396
Godine, Publisher, Inc., David R. 396
Hale Limited, Robert 401
Harbor House 402
Harcourt, Inc., Trade 402
High Country Publishers Ltd. 407
Hill Street Press 407
Hodder & Stoughton/Headline 407
Holiday House, Inc. 408
Holt & Co. Books for Young Readers, Henry 408
Hot Hot House 409
Houghton Mifflin Books for Children 409
Howells House 409
IVY Publications 412
JourneyForth 413
Kaeden Books 414
Kensington Publishing Corp. 414
Kregel Publications 415
Last Knight Publishing Company 415
Leisure Books 416
Little, Brown and Co. Children's Publishing 420
LTDBooks 422
Lyons Press, The 422
MacAdam/Cage Publishing, Inc. 422
McBooks Press 423
McElderry Books, Margaret K. 424
Milkweeds for Young Readers 425
MIRA Books 426
Moody Publishers 427
Mountain State Press 427
Multnomah Publishers, Inc. 427
My Weekly Story Collection 428
Natural Heritage/Natural History, Inc. 428
Nautical & Aviation Publishing Co., The 428
Naval Institute Press 428
New American Library 429
New England Press, Inc., The 429
New Victoria Publishers 430
NW Writers' Corp. 431
One World Books 432
Outrider Press, Inc. 433
Palari Publishing 434
Pelican Publishing Co. 436
Philomel Books 437
Piatkus Books 437
Pineapple Press, Inc. 438
Pipers' Ash Ltd. 439
Pippin Press 439
Port Town Publishing 441
Quiet Storm Publishing 443
Random House Trade Publishing Group 444
Red Hen Press 445
Regan Books 446
River City Publishing 447
River Oak Publishing 448

Rock Village Publishing 448
Saxon House Canada 450
Science & Humanities Press 450
Severn House Publishers 451
Shoreline 452
Silver Moon Press 453
Simon & Schuster Books for Young Readers 453
Snowapple Press 454
Soft Skull Press Inc. 454
Soho Press, Inc. 454
St. Martin's Press 456
Starburst Publishers 457
Stylewriter, Inc. 458
Third World Press 459
Treble Heart Books 461
University of Wisconsin Press 464
Via Dolorosa Press 465
Vivisphere Publishing 466
Voices From My Retreat 466
WaterBrook Press 467
White Mane Books 468
Whitman and Co., Albert 468
Willowgate Press 469
Wind River Press 469
Windstorm Creative, Ltd. 469

HORROR
Magazines

African Voices 333
Albedo One 276
Alembic 277
AlienSkin Magazine 307
Allegheny Review, The 169
American Feed Magazine 307
Armchair Aesthete, The 172
Art of Horror 308
Ascent 308
Aurealis 278
Barbaric Yawp 174
Bear Deluxe Magazine, The 336
Bibliophilos 177
Big Country Peacock Chronicle 309
Blackbird 309
Brady Magazine 310
Cochran's Corner 280
Cthulhu Sex Magazine 281
Dan River Anthology 191
Down in the Dirt 282
Downstate Story 192
Dream Fantasy International 282
Drexel Online Journal 314
Dvorak's Nocturne Horizons, Antonin 314
Edge, Tales of Suspense, The 283
Enigma 283
EOTU 315
Eyes 284
Far Sector SFFH 316

Fiction Inferno 316
Flesh And Blood 284
Futures Mysterious Anthology Magazine 199
Gathering of the Tribes, A 200
Grasslands Review 203
Griffin, The 204
Hadrosaur Tales 287
Happy 205
Harpur Palate 206
In Posse Review on Web Del Sol 318
Interbang 210
Irreantum 211
Lynx Eye 219
Maelstrom 220
Magazine of Fantasy & Science Fiction, The 351
Margin 319
Matriarch's Way 224
Medicinal Purposes 224
Merlyn's Pen 224
Metal Scratches 224
Midnight Times 291
Millennium Science Fiction & Fantasy 321
Mobius 227
Mota 227
Mudrock: Stories & Tales 292
Musing Place, The 227
Night Terrors 293
Nocturnal Lyric, The 293
Office Number One 294
On Spec 295
Orb 295
Outer Darkness 296
PEEKS & valleys 239
Peninsular 239
Peridot Books 323
Permutations 241
Psychic Radio, The 298
Rose & Thorn Literary E-Zine, The 324
Samsara 253
Skyline Magazine 300
Snake Nation Review 255
Spoiledink Magazine 326
Storyteller 301
Strand Magazine, The 301
Tales of the Hookman Online Magazine 328
Thirteen Stories 302
Toasted Cheese 329
Unknown Writer, The 268
Vestal Review 269
Waxing and Waning 330
Weird Tales 304
Wild Violet 330
Writers' Forum 360
Writers for Readers 304

Book Publishers

Atheneum Books For Young Readers 368
Bantam Dell Publishing Group 370

Books Collective, The 375
Commuters Library 381
Delirium Books 386
Denlinger's Publishers, Ltd. 386
Descant Publishing 387
Electric Works Publishing 391
Forge and Tor Books 393
Fort Ross Inc. Russian-American Publishing Projects 394
Harbor House 402
ignotus Press 410
Kensington Publishing Corp. 414
Last Knight Publishing Company 415
Leisure Books 416
LTDBooks 422
Marvel Comics 423
Meisha Merlin Publishing, Inc. 424
New American Library 429
Omnidawn Publishing 431
Outrider Press, Inc. 433
Pocol Press 440
Port Town Publishing 441
Ramsey Books 443
Random House Trade Publishing Group 444
Ravenhawk™ Books 444
Red Dragon Press 445
Regan Books 446
ROC Books 448
Rock & Co., Publishers, James A. 448
Rock Village Publishing 448
Severn House Publishers 451
St. Martin's Press 456
Starburst Publishers 457
Stylewriter, Inc. 458
SynergEbooks 458
Treble Heart Books 461
Vivisphere Publishing 466
Warner Books 467
White Wolf 468
Wildside Press 468
Willowgate Press 469

HUMOR/SATIRE
Magazines

Advocate, PKA'S Publication 167
African Voices 333
Allegheny Review, The 169
American Feed Magazine 307
American Girl 334
Ancient Paths 170
Anthology Magazine 170
Armchair Aesthete, The 172
Art Times 335
Asian Pacific American Journal 173
Balloon Life 336
Bathtub Gin 174
Bear Deluxe Magazine, The 336

Bellingham Review 175
Bibliophilos 177
Big Country Peacock Chronicle 309
Big Muddy: A Journal of the Mississippi River Valley 177
Blackbird 309
Blue Mesa Review 179
Blueline 179
Book World Magazine 180
Boys' Life 339
Brady Magazine 310
Breakaway Magazine 339
Briar Cliff Review, The 181
Bryant Literary Review 182
Bugle 340
blue Review, The 179
Callaloo 183
Capers Aweigh 183
Caribbean Writer, The 184
Center 184
Chaffin Journal 185
Chiron Review 186
CIA—Citizen in America 279
Cicada Magazine 341
Circle Magazine, The 279
Clubhouse Magazine 341
Cochran's Corner 280
Columbia: A Journal of Literature and Art 187
Concho River Review 188
Crab Creek Review 189
Creative With Words Publications 280
Cricket 342
Dakota Outdoors 281
Dan River Anthology 191
Dana Literary Society Online Journal 313
Descant 191
Desert Voices 192
Digress Magazine 343
Discovery Trails 343
Downstate Story 192
Dream Fantasy International 282
Dreams & Visions 282
Enigma 283
Enterzone 315
EOTU 315
Eureka Literary Magazine 194
Event 194
Exhibition 195
Fiction 195
Fifty Something Magazine 345
First Line 284
Fluent Ascension 317
Foliate Oak Literary Magazine 285
Fourteen Hills 197
Free Focus/Ostentatious Mind 285
Fugue 199
Funny Paper, The 285

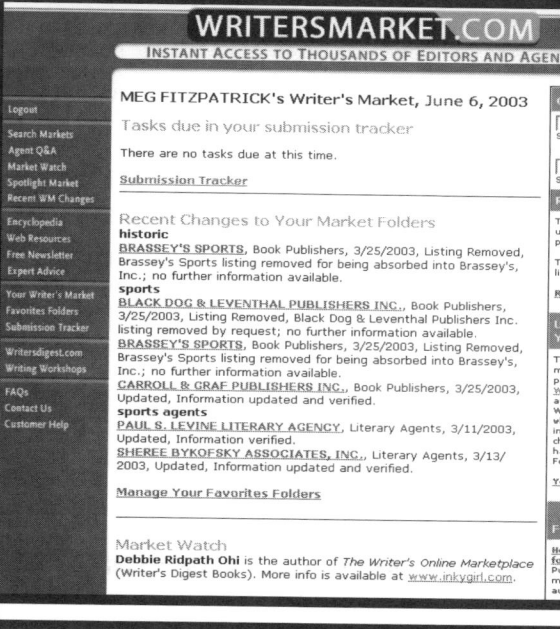

Funny Times 286
Futures Mysterious Anthology Magazine 199
Gathering of the Tribes, A 200
Gem, The 345
Gertrude 200
Gettysburg Review, The 201
Grasslands Review 203
Green Hills Literary Lantern, The 203
Green Mountains Review 203
Green's Magazine 204
Griffin, The 204
Happy 205
Harper's Magazine 346
Harpur Palate 206
Hawai'i Pacific Review 206
Hayden's Ferry Review 207
Heartlands Today, The 207
Hemispheres 346
High Adventure 347
Highlights for Children 347
Horizons 288
Horizons 348
Hybolics 288
Iconoclast, The 208
Idiot, The 208
Illya's Honey 209
Image 209
In Posse Review on Web Del Sol 318
Inkwell Magazine 210
Interbang 210
Irreantum 211
Jack and Jill 348
Jewish Currents Magazine 288
Journal of Polymorphous Perversity 289
Karamu 213
Kenyon Review, The 213
Leapings Literary Magazine 216
Lichen 216
Light Quarterly 217
Liquid Ohio 290
Literary Potpourri 290
Lullwater Review 219
Lynx Eye 219
MacGuffin, The 219
Maelstrom 220
Many Mountains Moving 221
Matriarch's Way 224
Mature Living 351
Mature Years 351
Medicinal Purposes 224
Merlyn's Pen 224
Mid-South Review, The 321
Millennium Science Fiction & Fantasy 321
Mississippi Review 226
Missouri Review, The 226
Mobius 227
Mota 227

Mountain Luminary 291
Mudrock: Stories & Tales 292
Musing Place, The 227
Na'amat Woman 352
Nassau Review 228
Nebraska Review, The 228
New Delta Review 229
New England Writer's Network 293
New Letters 230
New York Stories 232
North Dakota Quarterly 233
Nuthouse 294
new renaissance, the 231
Oak, The 294
Office Number One 294
Ohio Teachers Write 235
On The Line 353
Other Voices 236
Over The Back Fence 296
Pacific Coast Journal 237
Palo Alto Review 237
Pangolin Papers 238
Pearl 239
PEEKS & valleys 239
Pegasus Review, The 296
Peninsular 239
Pikeville Review 242
Pink Chameleon, The 323
Playboy Magazine 353
Pleiades 242
Poetry & Prose Annual 243
Portland Review 244
Poskisnolt Press 297
Pretext 245
Primavera 245
Purpose 354
Quarter After Eight 247
Quarterly West 247
Rambunctious Review 248
Reform Judaism 355
Rejected Quarterly, The 251
Roanoke Review 252
Rocket Press 252
Rockford Review, The 252
Rose & Thorn Literary E-Zine, The 324
Rosebud 299
Salt Hill 253
Shine Brightly 356
Short Stuff 254
Skyline Magazine 300
Slate and Style 300
Snake Nation Review 255
Southern California Anthology 257
Southern Humanities Review 258
Spider 356
Spoiledink Magazine 326
Spring Hill Review 260

Stone Soup 260
Storyteller 301
Storyteller, The 301
Strand Magazine, The 301
Struggle 261
Sulphur River Literary Review 262
Summerset Review, The 327
Sycamore Review 262
Talebones 302
Texas Review, The 264
Thema 265
Thirteenth Warrior Review, The 328
Thorny Locust 265
Thresholds Quarterly 329
Timber Creek Review 266
Toasted Cheese 329
Touchstone Literary Journal 267
Transcendent Visions 303
Transition 267
12-Gauge.com 329
Underwood Review, The 268
Unwound 269
Vincent Brothers Review, The 269
Virginia Quarterly Review 303
Waxing and Waning 330
Weber Studies 304
Westview 270
Wild Violet 330
Windhover 271
Word Riot 331
Words Literary Journal 272
Words of Wisdom 272
Writers for Readers 304
Writing For Our Lives 272
Yalobusha Review, The 273
Yemassee 273
Zuzu's Petals Quarterly 331
Zyzzyva 274

Book Publishers

Acme Press 364
Adventure Book Publishers 365
Ageless Press 365
American Atheist Press 366
Arcade Publishing 367
Artemis Press 367
Arx Publishing 368
Atheneum Books For Young Readers 368
Ballantine Books 370
Bancroft Press 370
Bantam Doubleday Dell Books for Young Readers 370
Black Heron Press 374
Blue Sky Press, The 375
Boyds Mills Press 376
Caitlin Press, Inc. 378
Clarion Books 380
Coastal Carolina Press 381
Commuters Library 381

Coteau Books 382
Covenant Communications, Inc. 382
Davenport, Publishers, May 385
Doubleday 387
Dreamcatcher Publishing Inc. 388
Electric Works Publishing 391
Front Street 394
Geringer Books, Laura 396
Glencannon Press, The 396
Green Bean Press 397
Greenwillow Books 398
Hill Street Press 407
Holiday House, Inc. 408
Houghton Mifflin Books for Children 409
Insomniac Press 410
IVY Publications 412
ignotus Press 410
Justin, Charles & Co., Publishers 413
Kaeden Books 414
Little, Brown and Co. Children's Publishing 420
Marvel Comics 423
Milkweeds for Young Readers 425
Multnomah Publishers, Inc. 427
New Victoria Publishers 430
Oak Tree Press 431
One World Books 432
Outrider Press, Inc. 433
Panther Creek Press 434
Pippin Press 439
Quixote Press 443
Random House Trade Publishing Group 444
Ravenhawk™ Books 444
Red Dress Ink 445
Red Press Publishing Company, The 446
Regan Books 446
River Oak Publishing 448
Rock & Co., Publishers, James A. 448
Science & Humanities Press 450
Simon & Schuster Books for Young Readers 453
Stylewriter, Inc. 458
SynergEbooks 458
Treble Heart Books 461
Vandamere Press 465
Voices From My Retreat 466
Whitman and Co., Albert 468
Willowgate Press 469
Windstorm Creative, Ltd. 469
Writers Direct 470

LESBIAN
Magazines
ACM 167
Adrift 167
Allegheny Review, The 169
Art Times 335
Asian Pacific American Journal 173
Black Lace 178

Blackbird 309
Blue Mesa Review 179
Blue Moon Review, The 310
Brady Magazine 310
Chaffin Journal 185
Descant 191
Digress Magazine 343
Down in the Dirt 282
Edge, Tales of Suspense, The 283
Enterzone 315
Feminist Studies 195
filling Station 196
First Line 284
Fluent Ascension 317
Foliate Oak Literary Magazine 285
Fourteen Hills 197
Frontiers 198
Futures Mysterious Anthology Magazine 199
Gargoyle 199
Gathering of the Tribes, A 200
Gay Chicago Magazine 286
Gertrude 200
Happy 205
Home Planet News 207
Illya's Honey 209
In Posse Review on Web Del Sol 318
Interbang 210
Karamu 213
Kenyon Review, The 213
Lichen 216
Lilith Magazine 350
Literary Witches 319
Many Mountains Moving 221
Margin 319
Medicinal Purposes 224
Minnesota Review, The 226
Mobius 227
Mota 227
Musing Place, The 227
New York Stories 232
Ohio Teachers Write 235
Options 353
Painted Bride Quarterly 322
Paperplates 322
Peninsular 239
Portland Review 244
Poskisnolt Press 297
Pretext 245
Primavera 245
Quarter After Eight 247
Rainbow Curve 248
River Styx 251
Roanoke Review 252
Salt Hill 253
Sinister Wisdom 254
Snake Nation Review 255
So to Speak 256

Spoiledink Magazine 326
Staple Magazine 260
Tattoo Highway 328
Thirteenth Moon 265
Toasted Cheese 329
Transcendent Visions 303
12-Gauge.com 329
Underwood Review, The 268
Unknown Writer, The 268
Wild Violet 330
Writing For Our Lives 272
Yemassee 273
Zuzu's Petals Quarterly 331

Book Publishers
Artemis Press 367
Aunt Lute Books 368
Bancroft Press 370
Bordighera Inc. 376
Gival Press 396
Hill Street Press 407
Lost Horse Press 421
New Victoria Publishers 430
Outrider Press, Inc. 433
T n T Classic Books 458
University of Wisconsin Press 464

LITERARY
Magazines
Abiko Annual with James, The 276
ACM 167
Adrift 167
Advocate, PKA'S Publication 167
African American Review 168
African Voices 333
Alaska Quarterly Review 168
Albedo One 276
Alembic 277
Allegheny Review, The 169
Alsop Review, The 307
American Feed Magazine 307
American Literary Review 169
Ancient Paths 170
Anthology Magazine 170
Antietam Review 170
Antigonish Review, The 171
Antioch Review 171
Apostrophe 171
Appalachian Heritage 171
Arkansas Review 172
Art Times 335
Artful Dodge 173
Ascent 308
Asian Pacific American Journal 173
Atlantic Monthly, The 336
B&A: New Fiction 174
Baltimore Review, The 174
Barbaric Yawp 174

Bathtub Gin 174
Beacon Street Review 175
Beginnings Publishing 175
Bellevue Literary Review 175
Bellingham Review 175
Bellowing Ark 176
Beloit Fiction Journal 176
Berkeley Fiction Review 176
BIGnews 177
Bibliophilos 177
Big Country Peacock Chronicle 309
Big Muddy: A Journal of the Mississippi River Valley 177
Black Mountain Review, The 178
Black Warrior Review 178
Blackbird 309
Blue Mesa Review 179
Blue Moon Review, The 310
Blueline 179
Book World Magazine 180
Bookpress 180
Boston Review 338
Boulevard 180
Brady Magazine 310
Brain, Child 181
Briar Cliff Review, The 181
Brillant Corners 181
Bryant Literary Review 182
Button 182
Byline 182
blue Review, The 179
Cairn 183
Callaloo 183
Capers Aweigh 183
Capilano Review, The 184
Caribbean Writer, The 184
Carolina Quarterly 184
Carve Magazine 311
Cenotaph 311
Center 184
Chaffin Journal 185
Chapman 185
Chariton Review, The 185
Chicago Quarterly Review 186
Chicago Review 186
Chiron Review 186
Chrysalis Reader 186
Circle Magazine, The 279
Colorado Review 187
Columbia: A Journal of Literature and Art 187
Concho River Review 188
Confluence 188
Confrontation, A Literary Journal 188
Connecticut Review 189
Crab Creek Review 189
Crab Orchard Review 189
Cream City Review, The 190

Crucible 191
collectedstories.com 311
Dalhousie Review, The 191
Dan River Anthology 191
Dead Mule, The 314
Descant 191
Desert Voices 192
Digress Magazine 343
Down in the Dirt 282
Downstate Story 192
Dream Fantasy International 282
Dreams & Visions 282
Drexel Online Journal 314
descant 281
Emrys Journal 193
Enterzone 315
EOTU 315
Epoch 193
Erased, Sigh, Sigh. 193
Eureka Literary Magazine 194
Event 194
EWGPresents 315
Exhibition 195
Failbetter.com 316
Fairfield Review, The 316
Fiction 195
Fiction Inferno 316
Fiddlehead, The 196
filling Station 196
First Class 196
First Line 284
5-Trope 317
Fluent Ascension 317
Flyway 197
Foliate Oak Literary Magazine 285
Fourteen Hills 197
Front & Centre 198
Fugue 199
Funny Paper, The 285
Futures Mysterious Anthology Magazine 199
flashquake 317
Gargoyle 199
Gathering of the Tribes, A 200
Gertrude 200
Gettysburg Review, The 201
Gin Bender Poetry Review 317
Ginosko 201
Glass Tesseract 201
Glimmer Train Stories 202
Grain Literary Magazine 202
Granta 202
Grasslands Review 203
Grasslimb 287
Green Hills Literary Lantern, The 203
Green Mountains Review 203
Green Tricycle, The 318
Green's Magazine 204

Griffin, The 204
GSU Review, The 204
Gulf Coast 205
Gulf Stream Magazine 205
Happy 205
Harpur Palate 206
Harvard Review 206
Hawai'i Pacific Review 206
Hayden's Ferry Review 207
Heartlands Today, The 207
Hemispheres 346
Highway 14 207
Home Planet News 207
Horizons 348
Horsethief's Journal, The 318
Hybolics 288
Iconoclast, The 208
Idaho Review, The 208
Illuminations 209
Illya's Honey 209
Image 209
In Posse Review on Web Del Sol 318
Indiana Review 209
Inkwell Magazine 210
Interbang 210
Irreantum 211
Italian Americana 288
Jabberwock Review, The 211
Karamu 213
Kenyon Review, The 213
King's English 214
Kit-Cat Review, The 214
Lady Churchill's Rosebud Wristlet 289
Lake Effect 215
Laurel Review, The 215
Leapings Literary Magazine 216
Left Curve 290
Lichen 216
Licking River Review, The 216
Light Quarterly 217
Lilith Magazine 350
Liquid Ohio 290
Listening Eye, The 217
Literal Latté 217
Literary Potpourri 290
Literary Witches 319
Long Story, The 218
Lost and Found Times 218
Louisiana Literature 218
Louisville Review, The 218
Lutheran Journal, The 351
Lynx Eye 219
MacGuffin, The 219
Maelstrom 220
Mangrove 220
Manoa 220
Many Mountains Moving 221

Marlboro Review, The 221
Matriarch's Way 224
McSweeney's Internet Tendency, Timothy 320
Medicinal Purposes 224
Mercury Books 320
Merlyn's Pen 224
Metal Scratches 224
Michigan Quarterly Review 225
Mid-American Review 225
Midnight Times 291
Mid-South Review, The 321
Mindprints 225
Minnesota Review, The 226
Mississippi Review 226
Missouri Review, The 226
MM Review 226
Mobius 227
Mota 227
Mudrock: Stories & Tales 292
Musing Place, The 227
Na'amat Woman 352
Nassau Review 228
Natural Bridge 228
Nebraska Review, The 228
Nerve Cowboy 228
New Delta Review 229
New England Review 229
New England Writer's Network 293
New Laurel Review 229
New Letters 230
New Mirage Quarterly 230
New Orphic Review, The 230
New York Stories 232
Night Train 232
North Dakota Quarterly 233
North East Arts Magazine 234
Northwest Review 234
Northwoods Journal 234
new renaissance, the 231
Obsidian III 235
Office Number One 294
Ohio Teachers Write 235
One-Story 235
Oracular Tree, The 321
Other Voices 236
Outsider Ink 322
Pacific Coast Journal 237
Painted Bride Quarterly 322
Palo Alto Review 237
Pangolin Papers 238
Paperplates 322
Paris Review, The 238
Passages North 238
Paterson Literary Review 239
Paumanok Review, The 323
Pearl 239
Pegasus Review, The 296

CATEGORY INDEX

Peninsular 239
Pennsylvania English 240
Perimeter 240
Permutations 241
Phantasmagoria 241
Pif 323
Pig Iron Press 241
Pikeville Review 242
Pindeldyboz 297
Pink Chameleon, The 323
Pleiades 242
Ploughshares 243
Poetry & Prose Annual 243
Poetry Forum Short Stories 243
Pointed Circle 244
Porcupine Literary Arts Magazine 244
Portland Magazine 354
Portland Review 244
Poskisnolt Press 297
Prairie Journal, The 244
Pretext 245
Primavera 245
Prose Ax 298
Puckerbrush Review 246
Puerto Del Sol 247
Quality Women's Fiction 247
Quarter After Eight 247
Quarterly West 247
Queen's Quarterly 299
Rain Crow 248
Rainbow Curve 248
Rambunctious Review 248
Rattapallax 249
Raven Chronicles, The 249
Reasoning Novel Magazine 250
Red Cedar Review 250
Red Rock Review 250
Reflections Literary Journal 250
Rejected Quarterly, The 251
River Styx 251
Roanoke Review 252
Rockford Review, The 252
Room of One's Own 252
Rose & Thorn Literary E-Zine, The 324
Rosebud 299
Salmagundi 252
Salt Hill 253
Samsara 253
Santa Monica Review 253
Scribia, The 254
Snake Nation Review 255
SNReview 326
So to Speak 256
Songs of Innocence 256
Sonora Review 256
South Carolina Review 257
South Dakota Review 257

Southern California Anthology 257
Southern Review, The 258
Southwestern American Literature 259
Spindrift 259
Spinning Jenny 357
Spitball 259
Spring Hill Review 260
Staple Magazine 260
Storie 261
Storyteller, The 301
Struggle 261
Sulphur River Literary Review 262
Summer's Reading, A 262
Summerset Review, The 327
Sycamore Review 262
Tameme 263
Tampa Review 263
Taproot Literary Review 264
Tattoo Highway 328
Terminus 264
Texas Review, The 264
Thema 265
Third Coast 265
Thirteenth Moon 265
Thirteenth Warrior Review, The 328
Thorny Locust 265
Thought Magazine 266
Threepenny Review, The 266
Timber Creek Review 266
Tin House 267
Toasted Cheese 329
Touchstone Literary Journal 267
Transition 267
Triquarterly 267
12-Gauge.com 329
Underwood Review, The 268
Unknown Writer, The 268
Unmuzzled Ox 269
Unwound 269
Vestal Review 269
Vincent Brothers Review, The 269
Virginia Quarterly Review 303
Waxing and Waning 330
Weber Studies 304
Western Humanities Review 270
Westview 270
Wild Violet 330
Willow Springs 271
Wilmington Blues 331
Windhover 271
Worcester Review, The 272
Word Riot 331
Words Literary Journal 272
Words of Wisdom 272
Writers' Forum 360
Writers for Readers 304
Writing For Our Lives 272

Xavier Review 273
Xconnect 273
Yalobusha Review, The 273
Yemassee 273
Zahir 305
Zoetrope: All-Story 274
Zopilote 305
Zuzu's Petals Quarterly 331

Book Publishers
Ageless Press 365
Ambassador Books, Inc. 366
Anvil Press 367
Arcade Publishing 367
Arte Publico Press 367
Artemis Press 367
Arx Publishing 368
Avon Books 369
Baker Books 370
Ballantine Books 370
Bancroft Press 370
Beach Holme Publishers, Ltd. 372
Beil, Publisher, Inc., Frederic C. 372
Berkley Publishing Group, The 372
Bilingual Press 373
Birch Brook Press 373
Black Heron Press 374
Bleak House Books 374
Books Collective, The 375
Books for All Times, Inc. 375
Bordighera Inc. 376
Borealis Press, Ltd. 376
Branden Publishing Co., Inc. 377
Braziller, Inc., George 377
Cadmus Editions 378
Carroll & Graf Publishers, Inc. 379
Cave Books 379
Cleis Press 380
Coastal Carolina Press 381
Coffee House Press 381
Commuters Library 381
Context Books 382
Coteau Books 382
Counterpoint 382
Covenant Communications, Inc. 382
Crossway Books 383
Daniel and Co., John 385
Davenport, Publishers, May 385
Dial Press 387
Doubleday 387
Dreamcatcher Publishing Inc. 388
Dufour Editions 389
Dundurn Press, Ltd. 389
ECW Press 390
Ecco Press, The 390
Electric Works Publishing 391
Farrar, Straus & Giroux 392
Farrar, Straus & Giroux Paperbacks 392

Feminist Press at the City University of New York, The 393
Front Street 394
Gay Sunshine Press and Leyland Publications 395
Genesis Press, Inc. 395
Geringer Books, Laura 396
Gival Press 396
Godine, Publisher, Inc., David R. 396
Goose Lane Editions 397
Graywolf Press 397
Green Bean Press 397
Greenwillow Books 398
GreyCore Press 398
Grove/Atlantic, Inc. 398
Guernica Editions 398
Hampton Roads Publishing Co., Inc. 402
Hesperus Press 406
Hill Street Press 407
Hodder & Stoughton/Headline 407
Holiday House, Inc. 408
Homa & Sekey Books 408
Hot Hot House 409
Houghton Mifflin Books for Children 409
Houghton Mifflin Co. 409
Howells House 409
Insomniac Press 410
Last Knight Publishing Company 415
Les Éditions du Vermillon 419
Little, Brown and Co., Inc. 420
Livingston Press 420
Longstreet Press, Inc. 421
Lost Horse Press 421
LTDBooks 422
MacAdam/Cage Publishing, Inc. 422
Macrae Books, John 423
Mariner Books 423
Micah Publications, Inc 424
Milkweed Editions 425
Multnomah Publishers, Inc. 427
NeWest Publishers Ltd. 430
New Hope Books, Inc. 429
Norton Co., Inc., W.W. 430
One World Books 432
Orca Book Publishers 432
Other Press 432
Outrider Press, Inc. 433
Owen Publishers, Peter 433
Owl Books 434
Palari Publishing 434
Panther Creek Press 434
Permanent Press, The 437
Philomel Books 437
Piatkus Books 437
Picador USA 438
Pineapple Press, Inc. 438
Pipers' Ash Ltd. 439
Pocol Press 440

Post-Apollo Press, The 441
Puckerbrush Press 442
Pudding House Publications 442
Putnam's Sons, G.P. 443
Ravenhawk™ Books 444
Red Dragon Press 445
Red Dress Ink 445
Red Hen Press 445
Regan Books 446
River City Publishing 447
Rock & Co., Publishers, James A. 448
Rock Village Publishing 448
Ronsdale Press 448
Ruminator Books 449
Salvo Press 449
Sarabande Books, Inc. 449
Saxon House Canada 450
Science & Humanities Press 450
Seal Press 451
Seven Stories Press 451
Shoreline 452
Snowapple Press 454
Soft Skull Press Inc. 454
Soho Press, Inc. 454
Southern Methodist University Press 455
Spectra Books 455
Spirit That Moves Us Press, The 456
Spout Press 456
St. Martin's Press 456
Starcherone Books 457
Stylewriter, Inc. 458
Talese, Nan A. 458
Third World Press 459
Thistledown Press 459
Tindal Street Press, Ltd. 460
Turnstone Press 462
UCLA American Indian Studies Center 462
University of Alberta Press, The 463
University of Michigan Press 463
University Press of New England 464
Véhicule Press 465
Via Dolorosa Press 465

MAINSTREAM/CONTEMPORARY

Magazines

Advocate, PKA'S Publication 167
African American Review 168
African Voices 333
Aim Magazine 334
Allegheny Review, The 169
American Feed Magazine 307
American Literary Review 169
Ancient Paths 170
Any Dream Will Do Review 277
Armchair Aesthete, The 172
Art Times 335
Ascent 308
Asian Pacific American Journal 173
Baltimore Review, The 174
Barbaric Yawp 174
Beginnings Publishing 175
Bellowing Ark 176
Beloit Fiction Journal 176
Berkeley Fiction Review 176
BIGnews 177
Bibliophilos 177
Big Muddy: A Journal of the Mississippi River Valley 177
Blackbird 309
Blue Mesa Review 179
Blue Moon Review, The 310
Book World Magazine 180
Brady Magazine 310
Brain, Child 181
Briar Cliff Review, The 181
Brillant Corners 181
Bryant Literary Review 182
Capers Aweigh 183
Caribbean Writer, The 184
Cenotaph 311
Chaffin Journal 185
Chariton Review, The 185
Chicago Writer's Source, The 278
Chrysalis Reader 186
CIA—Citizen in America 279
Cicada Magazine 341
Circle Magazine, The 279
Colorado Review 187
Confluence 188
Confrontation, A Literary Journal 188
Dan River Anthology 191
Desert Voices 192
Downstate Story 192
Dreams & Visions 282
Drexel Online Journal 314
Emrys Journal 193
Epoch 193
Erased, Sigh, Sigh. 193
Eureka Literary Magazine 194
Exhibition 195
Eyes 284
Fifty Something Magazine 345
filling Station 196
First Class 196
First Line 284
Foliate Oak Literary Magazine 285
Fourteen Hills 197
Free Focus/Ostentatious Mind 285
Futures Mysterious Anthology Magazine 199
Gargoyle 199
Gathering of the Tribes, A 200
Gem, The 345
Gertrude 200
Gettysburg Review, The 201

Gin Bender Poetry Review 317
Glass Tesseract 201
Grain Literary Magazine 202
Green Hills Literary Lantern, The 203
Green Mountains Review 203
Green's Magazine 204
Griffin, The 204
Grit 345
Gulf Stream Magazine 205
Harpur Palate 206
Hawai'i Pacific Review 206
Heartlands Today, The 207
Hemispheres 346
Home Planet News 207
Horizons 288
Horizons 348
Horsethief's Journal, The 318
Iconoclast, The 208
Illya's Honey 209
Indiana Review 209
Interbang 210
Irreantum 211
Jabberwock Review, The 211
Karamu 213
Kentucky Monthly 348
Kenyon Review, The 213
King's English 214
Lake Effect 215
Leapings Literary Magazine 216
Licking River Review, The 216
Louisiana Literature 218
Lullwater Review 219
Lynx Eye 219
MacGuffin, The 219
Mangrove 220
Manoa 220
Many Mountains Moving 221
Margin 319
Medicinal Purposes 224
Merlyn's Pen 224
Midnight Times 291
Mid-South Review, The 321
Mindprints 225
Missouri Review, The 226
Mobius 227
Mota 227
Mudrock: Stories & Tales 292
Musing Place, The 227
Nassau Review 228
Nebraska Review, The 228
New Delta Review 229
New England Writer's Network 293
New Letters 230
New Mirage Quarterly 230
New Orphic Review, The 230
New York Stories 232
Night Train 232

Northwoods Journal 234
Oak, The 294
Ohio Teachers Write 235
Palo Alto Review 237
Paperplates 322
Passages North 238
Paumanok Review, The 323
Pearl 239
PEEKS & valleys 239
Pennsylvania English 240
Permutations 241
Phantasmagoria 241
Pikeville Review 242
Pink Chameleon, The 323
Playboy Magazine 353
Pleiades 242
Ploughshares 243
Poetry & Prose Annual 243
Poetry Forum Short Stories 243
Porcupine Literary Arts Magazine 244
Portland Review 244
Poskisnolt Press 297
Provincetown Arts 246
Puerto Del Sol 247
Quarter After Eight 247
Quarterly West 247
Queen's Quarterly 299
Rain Crow 248
Rambunctious Review 248
Red Rock Review 250
Rejected Quarterly, The 251
River Styx 251
Roanoke Review 252
Rose & Thorn Literary E-Zine, The 324
Rosebud 299
Samsara 253
Scribia, The 254
Short Stuff 254
Skyline Magazine 300
Snake Nation Review 255
SNReview 326
So to Speak 256
Sonora Review 256
South Carolina Review 257
South Dakota Review 257
Southern California Anthology 257
Southwestern American Literature 259
Spindrift 259
Spitball 259
Spoiledink Magazine 326
Spring Hill Review 260
St. Anthony Messenger 357
Storyteller 301
Storyteller, The 301
Sulphur River Literary Review 262
Sycamore Review 262
Tampa Review 263

CATEGORY INDEX

Tattoo Highway 328
Texas Review, The 264
Thema 265
Thirteenth Warrior Review, The 328
Timber Creek Review 266
Tin House 267
Toasted Cheese 329
12-Gauge.com 329
Underwood Review, The 268
Unmuzzled Ox 269
Unwound 269
U.S. Catholic 358
Vestal Review 269
Vincent Brothers Review, The 269
Virginia Quarterly Review 303
Waxing and Waning 330
Weber Studies 304
Westview 270
Word Riot 331
Words Literary Journal 272
Words of Wisdom 272
Writers' Forum 360
Writers for Readers 304
Xavier Review 273
Yalobusha Review, The 273
Zyzzyva 274

Book Publishers

Absey & Co. 363
Academy Chicago Publishers 364
Ageless Press 365
Alexander Books 365
Arcade Publishing 367
Arte Publico Press 367
Artemis Press 367
Atheneum Books For Young Readers 368
Baker Books 370
Ballantine Books 370
Bancroft Press 370
Bantam Doubleday Dell Books for Young Readers 370
Barbour Publishing, Inc. 371
Black Heron Press 374
Blue Sky Press, The 375
Books Collective, The 375
Books for All Times, Inc. 375
Books In Motion 375
Borealis Press, Ltd. 376
Caitlin Press, Inc. 378
Carroll & Graf Publishers, Inc. 379
Chronicle Books for Children 379
Coastal Carolina Press 381
Coffee House Press 381
Commuters Library 381
Context Books 382
Coteau Books 382
Covenant Communications, Inc. 382
Descant Publishing 387
Doubleday 387

Dreamcatcher Publishing Inc. 388
Dunne Books, Thomas 389
Electric Works Publishing 391
Forge and Tor Books 393
Fort Ross Inc. Russian-American Publishing Projects 394
Glencannon Press, The 396
Goose Lane Editions 397
GreyCore Press 398
Hale Limited, Robert 401
Harbor House 402
HarperTorch 405
High Country Publishers Ltd. 407
Hill Street Press 407
Hodder & Stoughton/Headline 407
Holiday House, Inc. 408
Holt & Co. Books for Young Readers, Henry 408
Howells House 409
Insomniac Press 410
Justin, Charles & Co., Publishers 413
Kensington Publishing Corp. 414
Last Knight Publishing Company 415
Little, Brown and Co., Inc. 420
Longstreet Press, Inc. 421
LTDBooks 422
MacAdam/Cage Publishing, Inc. 422
Macrae Books, John 423
Mariner Books 423
McElderry Books, Margaret K. 424
Meriwether Publishing Ltd. 424
Milkweeds for Young Readers 425
MIRA Books 426
My Weekly Story Collection 428
New American Library 429
New Hope Books, Inc. 429
Oak Tree Press 431
One World Books 432
Orca Book Publishers 432
Outrider Press, Inc. 433
Owl Books 434
Palari Publishing 434
Panther Creek Press 434
Permanent Press, The 437
Piatkus Books 437
Pineapple Press, Inc. 438
Pipers' Ash Ltd. 439
Pocol Press 440
Port Town Publishing 441
Putnam's Sons, G.P. 443
Random House Trade Publishing Group 444
Ravenhawk™ Books 444
Red Dress Ink 445
Red Hen Press 445
Red Press Publishing Company, The 446
Regan Books 446
Rock & Co., Publishers, James A. 448
Rock Village Publishing 448

Science & Humanities Press 450
Severn House Publishers 451
Snowapple Press 454
Soft Skull Press Inc. 454
Soho Press, Inc. 454
St. Martin's Press 456
Stylewriter, Inc. 458
SynergEbooks 458
Third World Press 459
Tindal Street Press, Ltd. 460
Treble Heart Books 461
Via Dolorosa Press 465
Viking 465
Vintage Anchor Publishing 466
Vivisphere Publishing 466
Voices From My Retreat 466
Warner Books 467
WaterBrook Press 467
Willowgate Press 469
Wind River Press 469
Woodley Memorial Press 470
Writers Direct 470

MILITARY/WAR
Magazines
Allegheny Review, The 169
Bibliophilos 177
Big Country Peacock Chronicle 309
Big Muddy: A Journal of the Mississippi River Valley 177
Blackbird 309
Book World Magazine 180
Brady Magazine 310
Bryant Literary Review 182
Chicago Writer's Source, The 278
Interbang 210
Mota 227
RPPS/Fullosia Press 325
Storyteller 301
12-Gauge.com 329
Waxing and Waning 330
Weber Studies 304
Writers for Readers 304

Book Publishers
Academy Chicago Publishers 364
Adventure Book Publishers 365
Ballantine Books 370
Bancroft Press 370
Branden Publishing Co., Inc. 377
Coastal Carolina Press 381
Commuters Library 381
Context Books 382
Denlinger's Publishers, Ltd. 386
Electric Works Publishing 391
Glencannon Press, The 396
Harbor House 402
Hill Street Press 407

IVY Publications 412
Lyons Press, The 422
Mountain State Press 427
Nautical & Aviation Publishing Co., The 428
Naval Institute Press 428
Pipers' Ash Ltd. 439
Regan Books 446
Science & Humanities Press 450
Starburst Publishers 457
Stylewriter, Inc. 458
SynergEbooks 458
Timberwolf Press, Inc. 460
Vivisphere Publishing 466
Willowgate Press 469

MYSTERY/SUSPENSE
Magazines
Advocate, PKA'S Publication 167
African Voices 333
Alembic 277
Allegheny Review, The 169
American Feed Magazine 307
Ancient Paths 170
Anthology Magazine 170
Armchair Aesthete, The 172
Ascent 308
Bear Deluxe Magazine, The 336
Beginnings Publishing 175
Bibliophilos 177
Big Country Peacock Chronicle 309
Big Muddy: A Journal of the Mississippi River Valley 177
Blackbird 309
Boys' Life 339
Brady Magazine 310
Bryant Literary Review 182
Capers Aweigh 183
Cenotaph 311
Chrysalis Reader 186
Cicada Magazine 341
Circle Magazine, The 279
Clubhouse Magazine 341
Cochran's Corner 280
Creative With Words Publications 280
Cricket 342
Crimewave 280
Discovery Trails 343
Down in the Dirt 282
Downstate Story 192
Dreams & Visions 282
Edge, Tales of Suspense, The 283
Eureka Literary Magazine 194
Fifty Something Magazine 345
First Line 284
Free Focus/Ostentatious Mind 285
Futures Mysterious Anthology Magazine 199
Grasslimb 287

CATEGORY INDEX

Green's Magazine 204
Griffin, The 204
Grit 345
Hardboiled 287
Harpur Palate 206
Hemispheres 346
Hitchcock Mystery Magazine, Alfred 347
Horsethief's Journal, The 318
In Posse Review on Web Del Sol 318
Interbang 210
Irreantum 211
Jack and Jill 348
King's English 214
Leapings Literary Magazine 216
Lullwater Review 219
Lynx Eye 219
Medicinal Purposes 224
Merlyn's Pen 224
Mota 227
Mudrock: Stories & Tales 292
Musing Place, The 227
Nassau Review 228
New England Writer's Network 293
New Mystery 352
North East Arts Magazine 234
Northwoods Journal 234
Outer Darkness 296
Palo Alto Review 237
PEEKS & valleys 239
Pink Chameleon, The 323
Playboy Magazine 353
Poetry & Prose Annual 243
Poetry Forum Short Stories 243
Portland Review 244
PSI 298
Queen Mystery Magazine, Ellery 355
Rejected Quarterly, The 251
Rose & Thorn Literary E-Zine, The 324
RPPS/Fullosia Press 325
Shine Brightly 356
Short Stuff 254
Skyline Magazine 300
Snake Nation Review 255
Spider 356
Spring Hill Review 260
Stone Soup 260
Storyteller 301
Storyteller, The 301
Strand Magazine, The 301
Thema 265
Thirteen Stories 302
Timber Creek Review 266
Toasted Cheese 329
Unknown Writer, The 268
Vincent Brothers Review, The 269
Virginia Quarterly Review 303
Waxing and Waning 330

Weber Studies 304
Woman's World 359
Words of Wisdom 272
Writers' Forum 360
Writers for Readers 304

Book Publishers

Academy Chicago Publishers 364
Adventure Book Publishers 365
Ageless Press 365
Alexander Books 365
Arcade Publishing 367
Artemis Press 367
Atheneum Books For Young Readers 368
Avalon Books 369
Avon Books 369
Baker Books 370
Ballantine Books 370
Bancroft Press 370
Bantam Doubleday Dell Books for Young Readers 370
Berkley Publishing Group, The 372
Bleak House Books 374
Books In Motion 375
Boyds Mills Press 376
Broadman & Holman 377
Carroll & Graf Publishers, Inc. 379
Clarion Books 380
Coastal Carolina Press 381
Commuters Library 381
Coteau Books 382
Covenant Communications, Inc. 382
CrossTIME 383
Cumberland House Publishing 384
Denlinger's Publishers, Ltd. 386
Descant Publishing 387
Dundurn Press, Ltd. 389
Dunne Books, Thomas 389
ECW Press 390
Electric Works Publishing 391
Empire Publishing Service 391
Forge and Tor Books 393
Fort Ross Inc. Russian-American Publishing Projects 394
Gay Sunshine Press and Leyland Publications 395
Glencannon Press, The 396
Green Bean Press 397
Greenwillow Books 398
Gryphon Books 398
Harcourt, Inc., Trade 402
Harlequin Enterprises, Ltd. 403
HarperTorch 405
High Country Publishers Ltd. 407
Hodder & Stoughton/Headline 407
Homa & Sekey Books 408
Hot Hot House 409
Houghton Mifflin Books for Children 409
Insomniac Press 410
Intercontinental Publishing 411

IVY League Press, Inc. 412
Jireh Publishing Company 412
JourneyForth 413
Justin, Charles & Co., Publishers 413
Kaeden Books 414
Kensington Publishing Corp. 414
Kregel Publications 415
Last Knight Publishing Company 415
Little, Brown and Co. Children's Publishing 420
LTDBooks 422
McElderry Books, Margaret K. 424
Minotaur 426
Moody Publishers 427
Multnomah Publishers, Inc. 427
Mysterious Press, The 428
Nelson, Tommy 429
New American Library 429
New Hope Books, Inc. 429
New Victoria Publishers 430
Oak Tree Press 431
One World Books 432
Outrider Press, Inc. 433
Palari Publishing 434
Panther Creek Press 434
Permanent Press, The 437
Piatkus Books 437
Pippin Press 439
Pocol Press 440
Poisoned Pen Press 440
Port Town Publishing 441
Publishers Syndication, International 442
Putnam's Sons, G.P. 443
Quiet Storm Publishing 443
Ramsey Books 443
Random House Trade Publishing Group 444
Ravenhawk™ Books 444
Red Press Publishing Company, The 446
Regan Books 446
River Oak Publishing 448
Rock & Co., Publishers, James A. 448
Rock Village Publishing 448
Salvo Press 449
Science & Humanities Press 450
Severn House Publishers 451
Silver Dagger Mysteries 453
Simon & Schuster Books for Young Readers 453
Snowapple Press 454
Soho Press, Inc. 454
Spinsters Ink 455
St. Martin's Press 456
Stylewriter, Inc. 458
SynergEbooks 458
Timberwolf Press, Inc. 460
Tindal Street Press, Ltd. 460
Treble Heart Books 461
University of Wisconsin Press 464
Vandamere Press 465
Viking 465
Vivisphere Publishing 466
Warner Books 467
WaterBrook Press 467
Whitman and Co., Albert 468
Wildside Press 468
Willowgate Press 469
X Press, The 471

NEW AGE/MYSTIC/SPIRITUAL
Magazines

Allegheny Review, The 169
American Feed Magazine 307
Ascent 308
Bitter Oleander, The 178
Blackbird 309
Brady Magazine 310
Bryant Literary Review 182
Circle Magazine, The 279
Down in the Dirt 282
Interbang 210
Irreantum 211
Mota 227
Oracular Tree, The 321
Peninsular 239
Poetry & Prose Annual 243
Psychic Radio, The 298
Rose & Thorn Literary E-Zine, The 324
Songs of Innocence 256
Toasted Cheese 329
Weber Studies 304
Wild Violet 330

Book Publishers

Ageless Press 365
Artemis Press 367
Ballantine Books 370
Bancroft Press 370
Commuters Library 381
CrossTIME 383
Denlinger's Publishers, Ltd. 386
Hampton Roads Publishing Co., Inc. 402
Harbor House 402
ignotus Press 410
Mountain State Press 427
Oak Tree Press 431
Omnidawn Publishing 431
Outrider Press, Inc. 433
SynergEbooks 458
Vivisphere Publishing 466
Writers Direct 470

ONLINE MAGAZINES
Magazines

Absinthe Literary Review, The 306
AlienSkin Magazine 307
Alsop Review, The 307
American Feed Magazine 307

CATEGORY INDEX

Art of Horror 308
Ascent 308
Barcelona Review, The 308
Big Country Peacock Chronicle 309
Blackbird 309
Blue Moon Review, The 310
Brady Magazine 310
Cafe Irreal, The 310
Carve Magazine 311
Cenotaph 311
collectedstories.com 311
Conversely 312
Copperfield Review, The 312
Crimson 312
Dana Literary Society Online Journal 313
Dargonzine 313
Dark Moon Rising 313
Dead Mule, The 314
Drexel Online Journal 314
Drunken Boat 314
Dvorak's Nocturne Horizons, Antonin 314
Enterzone 315
EOTU 315
EWGPresents 315
Failbetter.com 316
Fairfield Review, The 316
Far Sector SFFH 316
Fiction Inferno 316
5-Trope 317
flashquake 317
Fluent Ascension 317
Gin Bender Poetry Review 317
Green Tricycle, The 318
Horsethief's Journal, The 318
In Posse Review on Web Del Sol 318
Jolly Roger, The 319
Kennesaw Review 319
Literary Witches 319
Literoticaffeine 319
Margin 319
McSweeney's Internet Tendency, Timothy 320
Mercury Books 320
Metropole 320
Mid-South Review, The 321
Millennium Science Fiction & Fantasy 321
Nuvein Online 321
Oracular Tree, The 321
Outsider Ink 322
Painted Bride Quarterly 322
Paperplates 322
Paumanok Review, The 323
PBW 323
Peridot Books 323
Pif 323
Pink Chameleon, The 323
Plaza, The 324
Premonitions 324

Realpoetik 324
Rose & Thorn Literary E-Zine, The 324
RPPS/Fullosia Press 325
Scifi.com 325
Shadow Voices 325
Site of Big Shoulders, The 326
SNReview 326
Song of the Siren 326
Spoiledink Magazine 326
Stark Raving Sanity 327
Story Bytes 327
Story Friends 327
Summerset Review, The 327
Tales of the Hookman Online Magazine 328
Tattoo Highway 328
Thirteenth Warrior Review, The 328
Thresholds Quarterly 329
Toasted Cheese 329
12-Gauge.com 329
VQ Online 329
Waxing and Waning 330
Web del Sol 330
Wild Violet 330
Wilmington Blues 331
Word Riot 331
Zuzu's Petals Quarterly 331

PSYCHIC/SUPERNATURAL/ OCCULT
Magazines

African Voices 333
Allegheny Review, The 169
American Feed Magazine 307
Any Dream Will Do Review 277
Ascent 308
Barbaric Yawp 174
Big Country Peacock Chronicle 309
Blackbird 309
Brady Magazine 310
Bryant Literary Review 182
Capers Aweigh 183
Circle Magazine, The 279
Cthulhu Sex Magazine 281
Dan River Anthology 191
Down in the Dirt 282
Downstate Story 192
Dream Fantasy International 282
Dvorak's Nocturne Horizons, Antonin 314
Edge, Tales of Suspense, The 283
EOTU 315
Eureka Literary Magazine 194
Fiction Inferno 316
Free Focus/Ostentatious Mind 285
Futures Mysterious Anthology Magazine 199
Happy 205
Interbang 210
Irreantum 211

Magazine of Fantasy & Science Fiction, The 351
Margin 319
Matriarch's Way 224
Medicinal Purposes 224
Midnight Times 291
Mota 227
Mudrock: Stories & Tales 292
Night Terrors 293
Northwoods Journal 234
new renaissance, the 231
Office Number One 294
Orb 295
Outer Darkness 296
Peninsular 239
Permutations 241
Poskisnolt Press 297
Psychic Radio, The 298
Rosebud 299
Snake Nation Review 255
Songs of Innocence 256
Storyteller 301
Thema 265
Thirteen Stories 302
Thresholds Quarterly 329
Toasted Cheese 329
Underwood Review, The 268
Waxing and Waning 330
Weber Studies 304
Weird Tales 304
Wild Violet 330
Zahir 305

Book Publishers

Artemis Press 367
CrossTIME 383
Hampton Roads Publishing Co., Inc. 402
Harbor House 402
ignotus Press 410
Last Knight Publishing Company 415
Omnidawn Publishing 431
Outrider Press, Inc. 433
Ravenhawk™ Books 444
Red Dragon Press 445
Rock Village Publishing 448
Starburst Publishers 457
SynergEbooks 458
Vivisphere Publishing 466

REGIONAL
Magazines

Advocate, PKA'S Publication 167
Appalachian Heritage 171
Arkansas Review 172
Asian Pacific American Journal 173
Barbaric Yawp 174
Bellingham Review 175
Bibliophilos 177
Big Country Peacock Chronicle 309
Big Muddy: A Journal of the Mississippi River Valley 177
Black Mountain Review, The 178
Blackbird 309
Blue Mesa Review 179
Blue Moon Review, The 310
Blueline 179
Bookpress 180
Boston Review 338
Brady Magazine 310
Briar Cliff Review, The 181
Bryant Literary Review 182
Callaloo 183
Capers Aweigh 183
Chaffin Journal 185
Concho River Review 188
Confluence 188
Confrontation, A Literary Journal 188
Cream City Review, The 190
Creative With Words Publications 280
Crucible 191
Dan River Anthology 191
Desert Voices 192
Downstate Story 192
Eloquent Umbrella, The 283
Emrys Journal 193
Enterzone 315
Eureka Literary Magazine 194
Event 194
Exhibition 195
filling Station 196
First Line 284
Flint Hills Review 197
Gettysburg Review, The 201
Gin Bender Poetry Review 317
Grasslands Review 203
Grasslimb 287
Green Hills Literary Lantern, The 203
Gulf Coast 205
Hawai'i Pacific Review 206
Hayden's Ferry Review 207
Heartlands Today, The 207
Hemispheres 346
Horsethief's Journal, The 318
Illya's Honey 209
Image 209
Indiana Review 209
Interbang 210
Irreantum 211
Jabberwock Review, The 211
Karamu 213
Kelsey Review 213
Left Curve 290
Louisiana Literature 218
Mangrove 220
Medicinal Purposes 224
Mudrock: Stories & Tales 292

Musing Place, The 227
New York Stories 232
Northwoods Journal 234
new renaissance, the 231
Ohio Teachers Write 235
Oxford American, The 236
Palo Alto Review 237
Passages North 238
Pikeville Review 242
Pleiades 242
Poetry & Prose Annual 243
Pointed Circle 244
Portland Review 244
Prairie Journal, The 244
Raven Chronicles, The 249
RE:AL 249
Roanoke Review 252
Rockford Review, The 252
Rose & Thorn Literary E-Zine, The 324
Rosebud 299
Scribia, The 254
Site of Big Shoulders, The 326
Snake Nation Review 255
So to Speak 256
South Dakota Review 257
Southern California Anthology 257
Southern Humanities Review 258
Southwestern American Literature 259
Spindrift 259
Spring Hill Review 260
Struggle 261
Sycamore Review 262
Thema 265
Timber Creek Review 266
Transition 267
12-Gauge.com 329
Unwound 269
Vincent Brothers Review, The 269
Weber Studies 304
Words of Wisdom 272
Xavier Review 273
Yemassee 273
Yorkshire Journal 274
Zuzu's Petals Quarterly 331

Book Publishers
Alexander Books 365
Bancroft Press 370
Beil, Publisher, Inc., Frederic C. 372
Birch Brook Press 373
Books Collective, The 375
Coastal Carolina Press 381
Coteau Books 382
Covenant Communications, Inc. 382
Electric Works Publishing 391
High Country Publishers Ltd. 407
Hill Street Press 407
Lost Horse Press 421

One World Books 432
Panther Creek Press 434
Philomel Books 437
Piatkus Books 437
Pineapple Press, Inc. 438
Pipers' Ash Ltd. 439
Port Town Publishing 441
Red Dress Ink 445
Regan Books 446
River City Publishing 447
Rock & Co., Publishers, James A. 448
Rock Village Publishing 448
Science & Humanities Press 450
Shoreline 452
Tilbury House, Publishers 460
Turnstone Press 462
University of Wisconsin Press 464
Véhicule Press 465
Willowgate Press 469
Writers Direct 470

RELIGIOUS/INSPIRATIONAL
Magazines
African Voices 333
Allegheny Review, The 169
Ancient Paths 170
Annals of Saint Anne de Beaupré, The 335
Barbaric Yawp 174
Big Country Peacock Chronicle 309
Black Mountain Review, The 178
Blackbird 309
Brady Magazine 310
Breakaway Magazine 339
Chicago Writer's Source, The 278
Christian Courier 279
CIA—Citizen in America 279
Clubhouse Magazine 341
Cochran's Corner 280
Crusader Magazine 343
Discovery Trails 343
Dreams & Visions 282
Evangel 344
Gem, The 345
Griffin, The 204
Grit 345
High Adventure 347
Horizons 348
Image 209
Irreantum 211
LIVE 350
Liguorian 349
Lilith Magazine 350
Living Light News 350
Lullwater Review 219
Lutheran Journal, The 351
Matriarch's Way 224
Mature Living 351

Mature Years 351
Messenger of the Sacred Heart, The 352
Miraculous Medal, The 291
Mota 227
My Friend 352
New England Writer's Network 293
New Mirage Quarterly 230
Ohio Teachers Write 235
On The Line 353
Orb 295
PEEKS & valleys 239
Pegasus Review, The 296
Pink Chameleon, The 323
Pockets 354
Poetry Forum Short Stories 243
Prayerworks 298
Psychic Radio, The 298
Purpose 354
Queen Of All Hearts 299
Reform Judaism 355
Rose & Thorn Literary E-Zine, The 324
Seek 355
Shine Brightly 356
St. Anthony Messenger 357
Story Friends 358
Storyteller, The 301
Thema 265
Thresholds Quarterly 329
U.S. Catholic 358
War Cry, The 359
Waxing and Waning 330
Writers for Readers 304
Xavier Review 273

Book Publishers
Alef Design Group 365
Ambassador Books, Inc. 366
Arx Publishing 368
Baker Books 370
Barbour Publishing, Inc. 371
Beyond Words Publishing, Inc. 373
Books In Motion 375
Branden Publishing Co., Inc. 377
Broadman & Holman 377
Covenant Communications, Inc. 382
Denlinger's Publishers, Ltd. 386
Descant Publishing 387
Doubleday 387
Doubleday Religious Publishing 387
Eerdmans Publishing Co., William 391
Electric Works Publishing 391
Faith Kidz Books 392
Hill Street Press 407
ignotus Press 410
Jireh Publishing Company 412
Kregel Publications 415
Les Éditions du Vermillon 419
Lightwave Publishing Inc. 419

Meriwether Publishing Ltd. 424
Moody Publishers 427
Mountain State Press 427
Multnomah Publishers, Inc. 427
Nelson, Tommy 429
Norton Co., Inc., W.W. 430
NW Writers' Corp. 431
Pipers' Ash Ltd. 439
Ravenhawk™ Books 444
Regan Books 446
Revell Publishing 447
River Oak Publishing 448
Rock & Co., Publishers, James A. 448
Shoreline 452
Starburst Publishers 457
Stylewriter, Inc. 458
SynergEbooks 458
Torah Aura Productions 461
Treble Heart Books 461
UCLA American Indian Studies Center 462
Vivisphere Publishing 466
WaterBrook Press 467
Writers Direct 470

ROMANCE
Magazines
Advocate, PKA'S Publication 167
African Voices 333
Allegheny Review, The 169
Any Dream Will Do Review 277
Beginnings Publishing 175
Bibliophilos 177
Big Country Peacock Chronicle 309
Black Mountain Review, The 178
Brady Magazine 310
Brillant Corners 181
Chicago Writer's Source, The 278
CIA—Citizen in America 279
Cicada Magazine 341
Circle Magazine, The 279
Cochran's Corner 280
Copperfield Review, The 312
Dan River Anthology 191
Downstate Story 192
Dvorak's Nocturne Horizons, Antonin 314
EOTU 315
Eureka Literary Magazine 194
Fifty Something Magazine 345
First Line 284
Fugue 199
Futures Mysterious Anthology Magazine 199
Gathering of the Tribes, A 200
Gay Chicago Magazine 286
Griffin, The 204
Grit 345
Irreantum 211
Lutheran Journal, The 351

Lynx Eye 219
Matriarch's Way 224
Medicinal Purposes 224
Merlyn's Pen 224
Mota 227
Musing Place, The 227
New England Writer's Network 293
New Mirage Quarterly 230
Northwoods Journal 234
Ohio Teachers Write 235
Orb 295
Outer Darkness 296
Palo Alto Review 237
PEEKS & valleys 239
Pink Chameleon, The 323
Poetry & Prose Annual 243
Poetry Forum Short Stories 243
Poskisnolt Press 297
PSI 298
Rejected Quarterly, The 251
Rose & Thorn Literary E-Zine, The 324
Rosebud 299
Shine Brightly 356
Short Stuff 254
Skyline Magazine 300
Storyteller 301
Storyteller, The 301
Summerset Review, The 327
Thirteenth Moon 265
Toasted Cheese 329
Virginia Quarterly Review 303
Waxing and Waning 330
Woman's World 359
Writers' Forum 360
Writers for Readers 304

Book Publishers
Adventure Book Publishers 365
Artemis Press 367
Avalon Books 369
Avon Books 369
Ballantine Books 370
Barbour Publishing, Inc. 371
Berkley Publishing Group, The 372
Books In Motion 375
Borealis Press, Ltd. 376
Covenant Communications, Inc. 382
CrossTIME 383
Denlinger's Publishers, Ltd. 386
Dreamcatcher Publishing Inc. 388
Electric Works Publishing 391
Five Star Publishing 393
Fort Ross Inc. Russian-American Publishing Projects 394
Genesis Press, Inc. 395
Harbor House 402
Harlequin American Romance 403
Harlequin Blaze 403

Harlequin Duets 403
Harlequin Enterprises, Ltd. 403
Harlequin Historicals 404
Harlequin Intrigue 404
Harlequin Mills & Boon, Ltd. 404
Harlequin Presents (Mills and Boon Presents) 404
Harlequin Romance (Mills & Boon Tender Romance) 404
Harlequin Superromance 405
Harlequin Temptation 405
HarperTorch 405
High Country Publishers Ltd. 407
Hodder & Stoughton/Headline 407
Kensington Publishing Corp. 414
Leisure Books 416
Lionhearted Publishing, Inc. 419
Love Spell 421
LTDBooks 422
Mills & Boon Historical Romance 426
Mills & Boon Medical Romance 426
Multnomah Publishers, Inc. 427
New American Library 429
New Victoria Publishers 430
Oak Tree Press 431
One World Books 432
Outrider Press, Inc. 433
Piatkus Books 437
Pipers' Ash Ltd. 439
Port Town Publishing 441
Pristine Publishing 441
Ravenhawk™ Books 444
Red Dress Ink 445
Red Press Publishing Company, The 446
Red Sage Publishing, Inc. 446
Regan Books 446
River Oak Publishing 448
Rock & Co., Publishers, James A. 448
Rock Village Publishing 448
Science & Humanities Press 450
Severn House Publishers 451
Silhouette Desire 452
Silhouette Intimate Moments 452
Silhouette Romance 452
Silhouette Special Edition 452
Starburst Publishers 457
Steeple Hill 457
Stylewriter, Inc. 458
SynergEbooks 458
Thorndike Press 460
Treble Heart Books 461
Vivisphere Publishing 466
Warner Books 467

CATEGORY INDEX

WaterBrook Press 467
X Press, The 471

SCIENCE FICTION
Magazines
Advocate, PKA'S Publication 167
African Voices 333
Albedo One 276
Alembic 277
AlienSkin Magazine 307
Allegheny Review, The 169
American Feed Magazine 307
Analog Science Fiction & Fact 334
Ancient Paths 170
Anthology Magazine 170
Any Dream Will Do Review 277
Armchair Aesthete, The 172
Art Times 335
Artemis Magazine 277
Ascent 308
Asimov's Science Fiction 335
Aurealis 278
Barbaric Yawp 174
Beginnings Publishing 175
Big Country Peacock Chronicle 309
Black Mountain Review, The 178
Boys' Life 339
Brady Magazine 310
Bryant Literary Review 182
Cafe Irreal, The 310
Callaloo 183
Capers Aweigh 183
Cenotaph 311
Challenging Destiny 278
Chrysalis Reader 186
CIA—Citizen in America 279
Cicada Magazine 341
Circle Magazine, The 279
Cochran's Corner 280
Cricket 342
Cthulhu Sex Magazine 281
Dan River Anthology 191
Desert Voices 192
Digress Magazine 343
Down in the Dirt 282
Downstate Story 192
Dream Fantasy International 282
Dreams & Visions 282
Drexel Online Journal 314
Dvorak's Nocturne Horizons, Antonin 314
EOTU 315
Eureka Literary Magazine 194
Fantastic Stories of the Imagination 284
Far Sector SFFH 316
Fiction Inferno 316
First Class 196
First Line 284

Foliate Oak Literary Magazine 285
Futures Mysterious Anthology Magazine 199
GateWay S-F Magazine 286
Gathering of the Tribes, A 200
Grasslands Review 203
Green's Magazine 204
Griffin, The 204
Hadrosaur Tales 287
Happy 205
Harpur Palate 206
Home Planet News 207
Iconoclast, The 208
In Posse Review on Web Del Sol 318
Interbang 210
Irreantum 211
Jack and Jill 348
La Kancerkliniko 214
Lady Churchill's Rosebud Wristlet 289
Leading Edge 290
Leapings Literary Magazine 216
Left Curve 290
Literal Latté 217
Low Budget Science Fiction 291
Lullwater Review 219
Lynx Eye 219
Magazine of Fantasy & Science Fiction, The 351
Margin 319
Matriarch's Way 224
Medicinal Purposes 224
Merlyn's Pen 224
Midnight Times 291
Millennium Science Fiction & Fantasy 321
Mobius 227
Mota 227
Mudrock: Stories & Tales 292
Musing Place, The 227
New Mirage Quarterly 230
Northwoods Journal 234
Nova Science Fiction Magazine 294
Ohio Teachers Write 235
On Spec 295
Once Upon A World 295
Orb 295
Outer Darkness 296
Pacific Coast Journal 237
Palo Alto Review 237
PEEKS & valleys 239
Peninsular 239
Peridot Books 323
Permutations 241
Pink Chameleon, The 323
Playboy Magazine 353
Poetry Forum Short Stories 243
Portland Review 244
Premonitions 324
Primavera 245
Psychic Radio, The 298

Rain Crow 248
RE:AL 249
Rejected Quarterly, The 251
Rockford Review, The 252
Rose & Thorn Literary E-Zine, The 324
Rosebud 299
Samsara 253
Scifi.com 325
Short Stuff 254
Skyline Magazine 300
Snake Nation Review 255
Spider 356
Spoiledink Magazine 326
Spring Hill Review 260
Starship Earth 300
Stone Soup 260
Storyteller 301
Struggle 261
Talebones 302
Tales of the Hookman Online Magazine 328
Thema 265
Thirteen Stories 302
Thirteenth Moon 265
Thresholds Quarterly 329
Toasted Cheese 329
12-Gauge.com 329
Unknown Writer, The 268
Vincent Brothers Review, The 269
Waxing and Waning 330
Weber Studies 304
Wild Violet 330
Writers' Forum 360
Writers for Readers 304
Zahir 305
Zopilote 305

Book Publishers
Ace Science Fiction and Fantasy 364
Acen Press 364
Adventure Book Publishers 365
Ageless Press 365
Alexander Books 365
Artemis Press 367
Arx Publishing 368
Atheneum Books For Young Readers 368
Avon Books 369
Baen Publishing Enterprises 369
Bancroft Press 370
Black Heron Press 374
Books Collective, The 375
Books In Motion 375
Carroll & Graf Publishers, Inc. 379
Circlet Press, Inc. 380
Crossquarter Publishing Group 383
CrossTIME 383
DAW Books, Inc. 385
Del Rey Books 386
Denlinger's Publishers, Ltd. 386

Descant Publishing 387
Dragon Moon Press 388
Edge Science Fiction and Fantasy Publishing 390
Electric Works Publishing 391
Eos 391
Forge and Tor Books 393
Fort Ross Inc. Russian-American Publishing Projects 394
Front Street 394
Gay Sunshine Press and Leyland Publications 395
Gryphon Books 398
Kaeden Books 414
Little, Brown and Co. Children's Publishing 420
Love Spell 421
LTDBooks 422
Marvel Comics 423
Meisha Merlin Publishing, Inc. 424
Moody Publishers 427
New American Library 429
New Victoria Publishers 430
Omnidawn Publishing 431
Outrider Press, Inc. 433
Pig Iron Press 438
Pipers' Ash Ltd. 439
Port Town Publishing 441
Quiet Storm Publishing 443
Ramsey Books 443
Ravenhawk™ Books 444
Regan Books 446
ROC Books 448
Rock & Co., Publishers, James A. 448
Salvo Press 449
Science & Humanities Press 450
Simon & Schuster Books for Young Readers 453
Spectra Books 455
Spinsters Ink 455
St. Martin's Press 456
Stylewriter, Inc. 458
SynergEbooks 458
Timberwolf Press, Inc. 460
Treble Heart Books 461
Tyrannosaurus Press 462
Vivisphere Publishing 466
Warner Books 467
WaterBrook Press 467
White Wolf 468
Wildside Press 468
Willowgate Press 469
Windstorm Creative, Ltd. 469
X Press, The 471

SERIALIZED/EXCERPTED NOVEL
Magazines
Capper's 341

SHORT STORY COLLECTIONS
Book Publishers
Absey & Co. 363
Ageless Press 365
Anvil Press 367
Arcade Publishing 367
Artemis Press 367
Ballantine Books 370
Beil, Publisher, Inc., Frederic C. 372
Bilingual Press 373
Books Collective, The 375
Books for All Times, Inc. 375
Bordighera Inc. 376
Borealis Press, Ltd. 376
Branden Publishing Co., Inc. 377
Breakaway Books 377
Caitlin Press, Inc. 378
Coastal Carolina Press 381
Coffee House Press 381
Context Books 382
Coteau Books 382
Counterpoint 382
Daniel and Co., John 385
Denlinger's Publishers, Ltd. 386
Doubleday 387
Dreamcatcher Publishing Inc. 388
Dufour Editions 389
ECW Press 390
Ecco Press, The 390
Electric Works Publishing 391
Feminist Press at the City University of New York, The 393
FYOS Entertainment, LLC 395
Gival Press 396
Goose Lane Editions 397
Graywolf Press 397
Green Bean Press 397
Kaeden Books 414
Les Éditions du Vermillon 419
Livingston Press 420
Lost Horse Press 421
Lyons Press, The 422
Micah Publications, Inc 424
Outrider Press, Inc. 433
Panther Creek Press 434
Philomel Books 437
Pig Iron Press 438
Pipers' Ash Ltd. 439
Pocol Press 440
Puckerbrush Press 442
Quixote Press 443
Ravenhawk™ Books 444
Red Dragon Press 445
Red Dress Ink 445
Red Hen Press 445
Regan Books 446

River City Publishing 447
Rock & Co., Publishers, James A. 448
Rock Village Publishing 448
Ronsdale Press 448
Science & Humanities Press 450
Severn House Publishers 451
Shoreline 452
Snowapple Press 454
Soft Skull Press Inc. 454
Southern Methodist University Press 455
Spinsters Ink 455
Spout Press 456
Starcherone Books 457
Stylewriter, Inc. 458
SynergEbooks 458
Third World Press 459
Thistledown Press 459
Tindal Street Press, Ltd. 460
Treble Heart Books 461
Turnstone Press 462
UCLA American Indian Studies Center 462
University of Alberta Press, The 463
University of Michigan Press 463
University of Missouri Press 463
University of Wisconsin Press 464
Véhicule Press 465
Via Dolorosa Press 465
Vintage Anchor Publishing 466
Voices From My Retreat 466
Willowgate Press 469
Wind River Press 469
Wizards of the Coast 470
Woodley Memorial Press 470

THRILLER/ESPIONAGE
Magazines
Alembic 277
American Feed Magazine 307
Artemis Magazine 277
Bibliophilos 177
Big Country Peacock Chronicle 309
Blackbird 309
Bryant Literary Review 182
Cenotaph 311
Circle Magazine, The 279
Cricket 342
Crimewave 280
Dvorak's Nocturne Horizons, Antonin 314
EOTU 315
Futures Mysterious Anthology Magazine 199
Grasslimb 287
Griffin, The 204
Horsethief's Journal, The 318
Interbang 210
Irreantum 211
King's English 214
Mota 227

Mudrock: Stories & Tales 292
Pink Chameleon, The 323
Rose & Thorn Literary E-Zine, The 324
RPPS/Fullosia Press 325
Skyline Magazine 300
Spoiledink Magazine 326
Storyteller 301
Toasted Cheese 329
Writers' Forum 360
Writers for Readers 304

Book Publishers
Arcade Publishing 367
Atheneum Books For Young Readers 368
Bantam Doubleday Dell Books for Young Readers 370
Berkley Publishing Group, The 372
Books In Motion 375
Carroll & Graf Publishers, Inc. 379
Clarion Books 380
Coastal Carolina Press 381
Commuters Library 381
Covenant Communications, Inc. 382
Descant Publishing 387
Dunne Books, Thomas 389
ECW Press 390
Electric Works Publishing 391
Forge and Tor Books 393
Fort Ross Inc. Russian-American Publishing Projects 394
Harlequin Enterprises, Ltd. 403
HarperTorch 405
Houghton Mifflin Books for Children 409
Insomniac Press 410
Intercontinental Publishing 411
Jireh Publishing Company 412
JourneyForth 413
Kaeden Books 414
Kensington Publishing Corp. 414
Little, Brown and Co. Children's Publishing 420
LTDBooks 422
Meriwether Publishing Ltd. 424
MIRA Books 426
Multnomah Publishers, Inc. 427
Mysterious Press, The 428
New American Library 429
Oak Tree Press 431
One World Books 432
Palari Publishing 434
Pipers' Ash Ltd. 439
Putnam's Sons, G.P. 443
Ramsey Books 443
Random House Trade Publishing Group 444
Regan Books 446
Rock & Co., Publishers, James A. 448
Salvo Press 449
Science & Humanities Press 450
Severn House Publishers 451
Soho Press, Inc. 454

St. Martin's Press 456
Starburst Publishers 457
Stylewriter, Inc. 458
Timberwolf Press, Inc. 460
Treble Heart Books 461
Vandamere Press 465
Viking 465
Vivisphere Publishing 466
Warner Books 467
WaterBrook Press 467

TRANSLATIONS
Magazines
ACM 167
Adrift 167
Agni 168
Alaska Quarterly Review 168
Antigonish Review, The 171
Antioch Review 171
Artful Dodge 173
Asian Pacific American Journal 173
Bibliophilos 177
Big Country Peacock Chronicle 309
Big Muddy: A Journal of the Mississippi River Valley 177
Bitter Oleander, The 178
Black Mountain Review, The 178
Blackbird 309
Blue Moon Review, The 310
Boston Review 338
Bryant Literary Review 182
Cafe Irreal, The 310
Callaloo 183
Caribbean Writer, The 184
Cenotaph 311
Chariton Review, The 185
Columbia: A Journal of Literature and Art 187
Crab Creek Review 189
Crab Orchard Review 189
Cream City Review, The 190
Digress Magazine 343
Enterzone 315
Eureka Literary Magazine 194
Faultline 195
Fiction 195
filling Station 196
Flint Hills Review 197
Fluent Ascension 317
Fourteen Hills 197
Gargoyle 199
Gathering of the Tribes, A 200
Grand Street 202
Grasslimb 287
Green Mountains Review 203
Gulf Coast 205
Hawai'i Pacific Review 206
Horizons 348

Horsethief's Journal, The 318
Image 209
Indiana Review 209
Interbang 210
Irreantum 211
Jabberwock Review, The 211
Jewish Currents Magazine 288
Kenyon Review, The 213
King's English 214
Lady Churchill's Rosebud Wristlet 289
Left Curve 290
Lilith Magazine 350
Lynx Eye 219
MacGuffin, The 219
Mangrove 220
Manoa 220
Many Mountains Moving 221
Margin 319
Marlboro Review, The 221
Mid-American Review 225
Mississippi Review 226
Mota 227
New Delta Review 229
New Laurel Review 229
New Letters 230
Northwest Review 234
new renaissance, the 231
Painted Bride Quarterly 322
Palo Alto Review 237
Pangolin Papers 238
Paperplates 322
Pikeville Review 242
Pindeldyboz 297
Pleiades 242
Pretext 245
Puerto Del Sol 247
Quarter After Eight 247
Quarterly West 247
Rain Crow 248
Reflections Literary Journal 250
River Styx 251
Rosebud 299
Salt Hill 253
So to Speak 256
Spindrift 259
Spring Hill Review 260
Struggle 261
Sulphur River Literary Review 262
Summer's Reading, A 262
Sycamore Review 262
Tameme 263
Tampa Review 263
Terminus 264
Thirteenth Moon 265
Touchstone Literary Journal 267
Triquarterly 267
Unmuzzled Ox 269

Vincent Brothers Review, The 269
Virginia Quarterly Review 303
Weber Studies 304
Weird Tales 304
Willow Springs 271
Writing For Our Lives 272
Xavier Review 273

WESTERN
Magazines

Advocate, PKA'S Publication 167
Allegheny Review, The 169
Ancient Paths 170
Armchair Aesthete, The 172
Bear Deluxe Magazine, The 336
Beginnings Publishing 175
Bibliophilos 177
Big Country Peacock Chronicle 309
Blackbird 309
Blue Mesa Review 179
Boys' Life 339
Brady Magazine 310
Bryant Literary Review 182
Bugle 340
CIA—Citizen in America 279
Cicada Magazine 341
Clubhouse Magazine 341
Concho River Review 188
Copperfield Review, The 312
Cricket 342
Dan River Anthology 191
Desert Voices 192
Downstate Story 192
Fifty Something Magazine 345
First Line 284
Free Focus/Ostentatious Mind 285
Futures Mysterious Anthology Magazine 199
Grasslands Review 203
Griffin, The 204
Grit 345
In Posse Review on Web Del Sol 318
Lullwater Review 219
Lynx Eye 219
Medicinal Purposes 224
Merlyn's Pen 224
Mota 227
Mudrock: Stories & Tales 292
Northwoods Journal 234
Ohio Teachers Write 235
Palo Alto Review 237
PEEKS & valleys 239
Pink Chameleon, The 323
Poskisnolt Press 297
PSI 298
Rose & Thorn Literary E-Zine, The 324
Short Stuff 254
Skyline Magazine 300

Spring Hill Review 260
Storyteller 301
Storyteller, The 301
Thema 265
Timber Creek Review 266
Toasted Cheese 329
Vincent Brothers Review, The 269
Weber Studies 304
Words of Wisdom 272
Writers' Forum 360
Writers for Readers 304
Zopilote 305

Book Publishers

Adventure Book Publishers 365
Alexander Books 365
Atheneum Books For Young Readers 368
Avalon Books 369
Barbour Publishing, Inc. 371
Berkley Publishing Group, The 372
Books In Motion 375
Broadman & Holman 377
Commuters Library 381
Crossway Books 383
Denlinger's Publishers, Ltd. 386
Electric Works Publishing 391
Forge and Tor Books 393
Glencannon Press, The 396
Hale Limited, Robert 401
JourneyForth 413
Kensington Publishing Corp. 414
Leisure Books 416
LTDBooks 422
Multnomah Publishers, Inc. 427
New American Library 429
New Victoria Publishers 430
Outrider Press, Inc. 433
Philomel Books 437
Pipers' Ash Ltd. 439
Publishers Syndication, International 442
Red Press Publishing Company, The 446
Regan Books 446
River Oak Publishing 448
Science & Humanities Press 450
St. Martin's Press 456
Starburst Publishers 457
Stylewriter, Inc. 458
SynergEbooks 458
Thorndike Press 460
Treble Heart Books 461
Vivisphere Publishing 466

YOUNG ADULT/TEEN
Magazines
Advocate, PKA'S Publication 167
African Voices 333
Blackbird 309
Boys' Life 339

Cicada Magazine 341
Cochran's Corner 280
Creative With Words Publications 280
Dream Fantasy International 282
Free Focus/Ostentatious Mind 285
GateWay S-F Magazine 286
High Adventure 347
Irreantum 211
Liguorian 349
Lilith Magazine 350
Listen Magazine 350
Lutheran Journal, The 351
Magazine of Fantasy & Science Fiction, The 351
Medicinal Purposes 224
Merlyn's Pen 224
Millennium Science Fiction & Fantasy 321
Orb 295
Pink Chameleon, The 323
Poetry Forum Short Stories 243
Poskisnolt Press 297
Storyteller, The 301
Struggle 261
Toasted Cheese 329
Writers' Forum 360
Writers for Readers 304

Book Publishers

Acen Press 364
Adventure Book Publishers 365
Alef Design Group 365
Ambassador Books, Inc. 366
Annick Press, Ltd. 366
Arx Publishing 368
Avon Books 369
Bancroft Press 370
Beach Holme Publishers, Ltd. 372
Berkley Publishing Group, The 372
Bethany House Publishers 373
Borealis Press, Ltd. 376
Boyds Mills Press 376
Caitlin Press, Inc. 378
Candlewick Press 378
Chronicle Books for Children 379
Coastal Carolina Press 381
Commuters Library 381
Coteau Books 382
Covenant Communications, Inc. 382
Cricket Books 382
CrossTIME 383
Denlinger's Publishers, Ltd. 386
Dial Books For Young Readers 387
Dreamcatcher Publishing Inc. 388
Dundurn Press, Ltd. 389
Eerdmans Books for Young Readers 390
Electric Works Publishing 391
Farrar, Straus & Giroux Books for Young Readers 392
Front Street 394
Geringer Books, Laura 396

Glencannon Press, The 396
Harcourt, Inc. 402
Harbor House 402
Hendrick-Long Publishing Co., Inc. 406
High Country Publishers Ltd. 407
Holt & Co. Books for Young Readers, Henry 408
Homa & Sekey Books 408
Houghton Mifflin Books for Children 409
Hyperion Books for Children 410
IVY Publications 412
JourneyForth 413
Just Us Books, Inc. 413
Kregel Publications 415
Lerner Publications Company 419
Les Éditions du Vermillon 419
Levine Books, Arthur A. 419
Little, Brown and Co. Children's Publishing 420
LTDBooks 422
Marvel Comics 423
McElderry Books, Margaret K. 424
Moody Publishers 427
Oak Tree Press 431
Orca Book Publishers 432
Peachtree Publishers, Ltd. 435
Philomel Books 437

Piñata Books 438
Pipers' Ash Ltd. 439
Polychrome Publishing Corp. 441
Port Town Publishing 441
Puffin Books 442
Ravenhawk™ Books 444
Red Deer Press 445
Red Press Publishing Company, The 446
Regan Books 446
Rock & Co., Publishers, James A. 448
Royal Fireworks Publishing 449
Scholastic Canada, Ltd. 450
Science & Humanities Press 450
Silver Dagger Mysteries 453
Simon & Schuster Books for Young Readers 453
Snowapple Press 454
Stylewriter, Inc. 458
SynergEbooks 458
Third World Press 459
Torah Aura Productions 461
Unity House 462
Viking Children's Books 465
White Mane Books 468
Windstorm Creative, Ltd. 469
X Press, The 471

General Index

A

A&B Publishers Group 363
A&U, America's AIDS Magazine 333
Abiko Annual with James, The 276
Abilene Christian University 582
Abrams, Inc., Harry N. 363
Absey & Co. 363
Absinthe Literary Review, The 306
Academy Chicago Publishers 364
Ace Science Fiction and Fantasy 364
Acen Press 364
ACM 167
Acme Press 364
Adrift 167
Adventure Book Publishers 365
Adventures of Sword & Sorcery 276
Advocate, PKA'S Publication 167
African American Book Club Summit, The 546
African American Review 168
African Voices 333
Ageless Press 365
Agents! Agents! Agents! & Editors Too! 546
Agni 168
Aim Magazine 334
Aim Magazine's Short Story Contest 472
AKC Gazette Eighteenth Annual Fiction Contest 472
Alabama State Council on the Arts Individual Artist Fellowship 472
Alabama Writers' Conclave 533
Alaska Quarterly Review 168
Albedo One 276
Alef Design Group 365
Alembic 277
Alexander Books 365
Algonquin Books of Chapel Hill 365
Algren Short Fiction Contest, Nelson 473
AlienSkin Magazine 307
Allegheny Review, The 169
Alligator Juniper National Writing Contest 473
Alpena Community College 575
Alsop Review, The 307
Alternative Comics 365
Alyson Publications, Inc. 366

Ambassador Books, Inc. 366
American Association of University Women Award in Juvenile Literature 473
American Atheist Press 366
American Christian Writers Conferences 530
American Feed Magazine 307
American Girl 334
American Literary Review 169
American Literary Review Short Fiction Award 473
Analog Science Fiction & Fact 334
Ancient Paths 170
Anderson Writer's Grant, Sherwood 473
Anisfield-Wolf Book Awards 474
Annals of Saint Anne de Beaupré, The 335
Annick Press, Ltd. 366
Annual Fiction Contest 474
Annual Juvenile-Fiction Contest 474
Antarctic Press 366
Anthology Magazine 170
Antietam Review 170
Antietam Review Literary Award 474
Antigonish Review, The 171
Antioch Review 171
Antioch University at Los Angeles 569
Antioch Writers' Workshop 539
Anvil Press 367
Any Dream Will Do Review 277
Apostrophe 171
Appalachian Heritage 171
Arba Sicula 172
Arcade Publishing 367
Arizona Commission on the Arts Creative Writing Fellowships 474
Arizona State University 569
Arizona Western College 569
Arkansas Review 172
Arkansas Writers'Conference 533
Armchair Aesthete, The 172
Armstrong Atlantic State University 572
Arrowhead Regional Arts Council Individual Artist Career Development Grant 475
Art Cooperative Fiction Fellowship 475
Art Institute of Chicago 572

Art of Horror 308
Art of Music Annual Writing Contest, The 475
Art Times 335
Arte Publico Press 367
Artemis Magazine 277
Artemis Press 367
Artful Dodge 173
artisan 173
Artist Trust Artist Fellowships; GAP Grants 475
Arx Publishing 368
Ascent 308
Ashland University 579
Asian Pacific American Journal 173
Asimov Award, The Isaac 475
Asimov's Science Fiction 335
Aspen Summer Words Writing Retreat and
    Literary Festival 546
Asted/Grand Prix de Litterature Jeunesse du
    Quebec-Alvine-Belisle 475
Athenaeum Literary Award, The 475
Atheneum Books For Young Readers 368
Atlanta 335
Atlantic Monthly, The 336
Auburn University 568
Augsburg College 575
Aunt Lute Books 368
Aurealis 278
Austin Writers Conference, Harriette 534
Authorlink Press 369
Author's Venue Journey Conference 552
Author's Venue Screenwriters Institute 552
Aux Arc Review, The 173
Avalon Books 369
Avon Books 369
AWP Annual Conference and Bookfair 539
AWP Award Series 476
AWP Intro Journals Project 476

B
Baen Publishing Enterprises 369
Bakeless Literary Publications Prizes 476
Baker Books 370
Balch Awards, Emily Clark 476
Ball State Univeristy 573
Ballantine Books 370
Balloon Life 336
Baltimore Review, The 174
Baltimore Writers Alliance Conference 527
Bancroft Press 370
B&A: New Fiction 174
Bantam Dell Publishing Group 370

Bantam Doubleday Dell Books for Young
    Readers 370
Barbaric Yawp 174
Barbour Publishing, Inc. 371
Barcelona Review, The 308
Bard Fiction Prize 477
Bardsong Press 371
Barefoot Books 371
Barron's Educational Series, Inc. 372
Bathtub Gin 174
Bay Area Writer's League Conference 547
Baylor University 582
Beach Holme Publishers, Ltd. 372
Beacon Street Review 175
Bear Deluxe Magazine, The 336
Beginnings Publishing 175
Beil, Publisher, Inc., Frederic C. 372
Bellevue Literary Review 175
Bellingham Review 175
Bellowing Ark 176
Beloit College 584
Beloit Fiction Journal 176
Bennington College 583
Berkeley Fiction Review 176
Berkley Publishing Group, The 372
Berry College 572
Best Lesbian Erotica 477
"Best of Ohio Writers" Contest 477
Bethany House Publishers 373
Beyond Words Publishing, Inc. 373
Bibliophilos 177
Big Bear Writer's Retreat 553
Big Country Peacock Chronicle 309
Big Muddy: A Journal of the Mississippi River
    Valley 177
BIGnews 177
Bilingual Press 373
Binghamton University 578
Binghamton University John Gardner Fiction
    Book Award 477
Birch Brook Press 373
Bitter Oleander, The 178
Black Children's Book Award, Irma S. and James
    H. 477
Black Heron Press 374
Black Lace 178
Black Lace Books 374
Black Mountain Review, The 178
Black Ridge Summer Writing Conference 553
Black Warrior Review 178
Black Warrior Review Literary Award, The 477

Blackbird 309
Blaggard Award for Best Short Story of the Year 477
Blair, Publisher, John F. 374
Bleak House Books 374
Bloomsburg University 580
Blue Mesa Review 179
Blue Moon Review, The 310
Blue Mountain Center, The 521
blue Review, The 179
Blue Ridge Mountain Christian Writers Conference 531
Blue Sky Press, The 375
Blueline 179
Bogg 180
Boise State University 572
Bomb Magazine 338
Bonnet's Storymaking: The Master Class, James 553
Book Sense Book of the Year Award 478
Book World Magazine 180
Bookpress 180
Books Collective, The 375
Books for All Times, Inc. 375
Books In Motion 375
Booktowns of Europe Writers Workshops 565
Bordighera Inc. 376
Borealis Press, Ltd. 376
Boson Books 376
Boston College 575
Boston Globe-Horn Book Awards 478
Boston Review 338
Boston Review Short Story Contest 478
Boucheron 553
Boulevard 180
Boulevard Short Fiction Contest for Emerging Writers 478
Bowhunter 339
Bowling Green State University 579
Boyds Mills Press 376
Boys' Life 339
Bradley University 572
Brady Magazine 310
Brain, Child 181
Branden Publishing Co., Inc. 377
Braziller, Inc., George 377
Bread Loaf Writers' Conference 521
Breakaway Books 377
Breakaway Magazine 339
Briar Cliff Review Poetry & Fiction Contest, The 478

Briar Cliff Review, The 181
Bridgewater State College 575
Bridport Prize, The 478
Brigham Young University 583
Brillant Corners 181
British Science Fiction Association Awards 479
Broadman & Holman 377
Broadway Books 378
Brooklyn College 578
Brown Foundation, Arch & Bruce 479
Brown University 581
Bryant Literary Review 182
Bucknell University 580
Bugle 340
Burnaby Writers' Society Annual Competition 479
Bush Artist Fellows Program 479
Button 182
Byline 182
ByLine Short Fiction & Poetry Awards 479
BYU Writing for Young Readers Workshop 553

C
Cadmus Editions 378
Cafe Irreal, The 310
Caine Prize for African Writing, The 479
Cairn 183
Caitlin Press, Inc. 378
CalArts 569
California Book Awards 480
California College of Arts and Crafts 569
California State University at Chico 569
California State University at Fresno 569
California State University Los Angeles 569
California State University Northridge 569
California State University Sacramento 569
Callaloo 183
Calliope 340
Calyx 183
Cameron University 580
Campbell Memorial Award, John W. 480
Campus Life 340
Canadian Institute of Ukrainian Studies Press 378
Canadian Writer's Journal 341
Candlewick Press 378
Canisius College 578
Canyonlands Desert Writer's Workshop 554
Canyonlands Writers River Trip and Workshop 554
Cape Fear Crime Festival Short Story Contest 480

Capers Aweigh 183
Capilano Review, The 184
Capper's 341
Captivating Beginnings Contest 480
Cardinal Stritch University 584
Caribbean Writer, The 184
Carlow College 580
Carnegie Mellon University 580
Carolina Quarterly 184
Carolrhoda Books, Inc. 379
Carroll & Graf Publishers, Inc. 379
Carve Magazine 311
Case Western Reserve University 579
Cave Books 379
Celtic Voice Writing Contest 481
Cenotaph 311
Center 184
Central Connecticut State University 571
Central Michigan University 575
Central Missouri State University 576
Centrums 31st Port Townsend Writers'
    Conference 559
Chaffin Journal 185
Challenging Destiny 278
Chapman 185
Chapman University 569
Chariton Review, The 185
Charlesbridge Publishing (School Div) 379
Chatham College 580
Chattahoochee Review, The 185
Chelsea Awards, The 481
Chesterfield Writers' Film Project 481
Chicago Literary Awards 481
Chicago Quarterly Review 186
Chicago Review 186
Chicago Writer's Source, The 278
Chicano/Latino Literary Contest 481
Children's Writers Fiction Contest 481
Chiron Review 186
Christchurch Publishers Ltd. 379
Christian Courier 279
Christopher Awards, The 481
Chronicle Books for Children 379
Chrysalis Reader 186
CIA—Citizen in America 279
Cicada Magazine 341
Cimarron Review 187
Circle Magazine, The 279
Circlet Press, Inc. 380
City Lights Books 380
City Slab 279

Clackamas Community College 580
Claremont Review, The 187
Clarion Books 380
Clarion West Writers' Workshop 560
Clark Prize, Matt 482
Cleis Press 380
Cleveland State University 579
Clubhouse Magazine 341
CNW/FFWA Florida State Writing Competition
    482
Coastal Carolina Press 381
Cobblestone 342
Cochran's Corner 280
Coffee House Press 381
collectedstories.com 311
College of New Jersey Writers' Conference,
    The 528
College of St. Benedict 575
Colorado Mountain Writers' Workshop 547
Colorado Review 187
Colorado State University 570
Columbia: A Journal of Literature and Art 187
Columbia College of Chicago 572
Columbia University School of the Arts 578
Columbus Writers Conference 539
Commuters Library 381
Concho River Review 188
Confluence 188
Confrontation, A Literary Journal 188
Connecticut College 571
Connecticut Review 189
Constable & Robinson, Ltd. 381
Context Books 382
Converse College 581
Conversely 312
Copper Canyon Press 382
Copperfield Review, The 312
Cornell University 578
Coteau Books 382
Cottonwood 189
Counterpoint 382
Country Woman 342
Covenant Communications, Inc. 382
Crab Creek Review 189
Crab Orchard Review 189
Crazyhorse 190
Cream City Review, The 190
Creative With Words Publications 280
Creative Writing by the Sea 531
Creighton University 577
Crescent Review, The 190

Cricket 342
Cricket Books 382
Crimewave 280
Crimson 312
CrossGen Enterntainmant, Inc. 383
Crossquarter Publishing Group 383
CrossTIME 383
Crossway Books 383
Crown Publishing Group 384
Crucible 191
Crucible Poetry and Fiction Competition, The 482
Crusader Magazine 343
Cthulhu Sex Magazine 281
Cumberland House Publishing 384
Cutbank 191

D

Daedal Press 384
Dakota Outdoors 281
Dalhousie Review, The 191
Dan River Anthology 191
Dan River Press 384
Dana Award in Short Fiction 482
Dana Awards: Portfolio, Novel, Short Fiction, Poetry 482
Dana Literary Society Online Journal 313
Daniel and Co., John 385
Daniels Annual Honorary Writing Award, Dorothy 483
Dargonzine 313
Dark Horizons 281
Dark Horse Comics 385
Dark Moon Rising 313
Davenport, Publishers, May 385
DAW Books, Inc. 385
de Angeli Prize, Marguerite 483
Dead Mule, The 314
Del Rey Books 386
Delacorte Press 386
Delaware Division of the Arts 483
Delirium Books 386
Denison University 579
Denlinger's Publishers, Ltd. 386
DePauw University 573
Descant 191
descant 281
Descant Publishing 387
Desert Voices 192
Desert Writers Workshop/Canyonlands Field Institute 554

Detroit Women Writers Annual Writer's Conference 540
Dial Books For Young Readers 387
Dial Press 387
Dickinson College 580
Digress Magazine 343
Discovery Trails 343
Dornstein Memorial Creative Writing Contest for Young Adult Writers, David 483
Doubleday 387
Doubleday Canada 387
Doubleday Religious Publishing 387
DoubleTake 192
Down in the Dirt 282
Down There Press 387
Downstate Story 192
Dragon Moon Press 388
Drawn & Quarterly 388
Dream Fantasy International 282
Dreamcatcher Publishing Inc. 388
Dreams & Visions 282
Drexel Online Journal 314
Drunken Boat 314
Drury University 576
Dufour Editions 389
Dundurn Press, Ltd. 389
Dunne Books, Thomas 389
Dutton Children's Books 389
Dvorak's Nocturne Horizons, Antonin 314
Dyersburg State Community College 581

E

Eakin Press/Sunbelt Media, Inc. 389
East Carolina University 578
East Texas Writer's Conference 547
Eastern Kentucky University Summer Creative Writing Conference 540
Eastern Washington University 583
Eaton Literary Associates' Literary Awards Program 483
Ecco Press, The 390
ECW Press 390
Edge Science Fiction and Fantasy Publishing 390
Edge, Tales of Suspense, The 283
Editors' Prize 484
Eerdmans Books for Young Readers 390
Eerdmans Publishing Co., William 391
Electric Works Publishing 391
Ellipsis Magazine 192
Elon University 578
Eloquent Umbrella, The 283

Elysian Fields Quarterly. 193
Embry-Riddle University 571
Emerson College 575
Emily Contest, The 484
Eminence Area Arts Council Short Story
   Workshop 547
Emory University 572
Empire Publishing Service 391
Emporia State University 573
Emrys Journal 193
Enigma 283
Enterzone 315
EOS 391
EOTU 315
Epoch 193
Erased, Sigh, Sigh. 193
Esquire 344
Eugene Lang College 578
Eureka Literary Magazine 194
Evangel 344
Evansville Review 194
Event 194
EWGPresents 315
Exhibition 195
Eyes 284

F

Faces 344
Failbetter.com 316
Fairfield Review, The 316
Faith Kidz Books 392
Fantagraphics Books 392
Fantastic Stories of the Imagination 284
Far Sector SFFH 316
Farrar, Straus & Giroux 392
Farrar, Straus & Giroux Books for Young
   Readers 392
Farrar, Straus & Giroux Paperbacks 392
Faulkner Award for Excellence in Writing,
   Virginia 484
Faultline 195
Faux Faulkner Contest, The Jack 484
FC2 392
Feminist Press at the City University of New
   York, The 393
Feminist Studies 195
Fenn Publishing Company Ltd. 393
Festival of Faith and Writing 540
Fiction 195
Fiction Competition and Poetry Competition 484
Fiction Inferno 316

Fiddlehead, The 196
Fifty Something Magazine 345
filling Station 196
First Books 393
First Class 196
First Hand 345
First Line 284
Fish Memorial Award, Robert L. 484
Fish Short Story Prize 485
Fisher Award, Dorothy Canfield 485
Fishtrap 560
Fitzgerald Short Story Contest, F. Scott 485
Five Points 197
Five Star Publishing 393
5-Trope 317
flashquake 317
Flathead River Writers Conference 560
Flatirons Blunt Instrument Mystery Workshop
   547
Flesh And Blood 284
Flint Hills Review 197
Florida Atlantic University 571
Florida First Coast Writers' Festival 534
Florida International University 571
Florida Review Editors' Awards, The 485
Florida State University 571
Florida State Writing Competition 485
Florida Suncoast Writers' Conference 534
Fluent Ascension 317
Flyway 197
Foliate Oak Literary Magazine 285
Forge and Tor Books 393
Fort Bend Writers Guild Workshop 547
Fort Ross Inc. Russian-American Publishing
   Projects 394
Four Walls Eight Windows 394
Fourteen Hills 197
Frank 198
Frank Award, The Josette 485
Franklin Literary Award, Miles 485
Free Focus/Ostentatious Mind 285
FreeFall Magazine 198
FreeFall Magazine Fiction & Poetry Contest 486
Friction Zone 345
Front & Centre 198
Front Street 394
Frontiers 198
Fugue 199
Fun For Kidz 285
Fun in the Sun: The Write Stuff 535
Funny Paper Competition, The 486

Funny Paper, The 285
Funny Times 286
Futures Mysterious Anthology Magazine 199
FYOS Entertainment, LLC 395

G
Gainesville College Division of Humanities 572
Galacticon, Kag Spring Break 531
Gardner Memorial Prize for Fiction, The John 486
Gargoyle 199
Gaslight Publications 395
GateWay S-F Magazine 286
Gathering of the Tribes, A 200
Gay Chicago Magazine 286
Gay Sunshine Press and Leyland Publications 395
Gem, The 345
Genesis Press, Inc. 395
George Mason University 583
George Washington University 571
Georgetown University 571
Georgia College & State University 572
Georgia Perimeter College 572
Georgia Review, The 200
Georgia Southern University 572
Georgia State University 572
Georgia Writers Spring Festival of Workshops 535
Geringer Books, Laura 396
Gertrude 200
Gettysburg Review, The 201
Gift of Freedom Award 486
Gin Bender Poetry Review 317
Ginosko 201
Gival Press 396
Glass Tesseract 201
Glen Workshop, The 560
Glencannon Press, The 396
Glimmer Train Stories 202
Glimmer Train's Fall Short-Story Award for New Writers 486
Glimmer Train's Fiction Open 487
Glimmer Train's Spring Short-Story Award for New Writers 487
Glorieta Christian Writers' Conference 548
Goddard College 583
Godine, Publisher, Inc., David R. 396
Gold Medallion Book Awards 487
Goose Lane Editions 397
Gotham Writers' Workshop 521

Goucher College 574
Grain Literary Magazine 202
Grand Street 202
Grand Valley State University 575
Grant MacEwan College 584
Granta 202
Grasslands Review 203
Grasslimb 287
Graywolf Press 397
Great Blue Beacon Short-Story Contest, The 487
Great Canadian Story Contest 487
Great River Arts 521
Green Bean Press 397
Green Hills Literary Lantern, The 203
Green Lake Writers Conference 544
Green Mountain Writers Conference 521
Green Mountains Review 203
Green Tricycle, The 318
Greene Bark Press 397
Greene Literary Festival Contest, The Judy & A.C. 487
Green's Magazine 204
Greensboro Review Literary Awards, The 488
Greensboro Review, The 204
Greenwillow Books 398
GreyCore Press 398
Griffin, The 204
Grit 345
Grolier Publishing Co., Inc. 398
Grove/Atlantic, Inc. 398
Gryphon Books 398
GSU Review, The 204
GSU Review Annual Contest 488
Guernica Editions 398
Gulf Coast 205
Gulf Coast Poetry and Short Fiction Awards 488
Gulf Stream Magazine 205

H
Hadassah Magazine 346
Hadrosaur Tales 287
Hale Limited, Robert 401
Hambidge Center 535
Hamilton College Creative Writing 578
Hamline University 575
Hammett Prize 488
Hampton Roads Publishing Co., Inc. 402
Happy 205
Harbor House 402
Harcourt, Inc. 402
Harcourt, Inc., Trade 402

Hard Row To Hoe 205
Hardboiled 287
Hardin-Simmons University 582
Harlequin American Romance 403
Harlequin Blaze 403
Harlequin Duets 403
Harlequin Enterprises, Ltd. 403
Harlequin Historicals 404
Harlequin Intrigue 404
Harlequin Mills & Boon, Ltd. 404
Harlequin Presents (Mills and Boon Presents) 404
Harlequin Romance (Mills & Boon Tender Romance) 404
Harlequin Superromance 405
Harlequin Temptation 405
Harpercollins Canada Ltd. 405
Harpercollins General Books Group 405
Harper's Magazine 346
HarperTorch 405
Harpur Palate 206
Harvard Review 206
Harvard University 575
Harvest House Publishers 406
Hawai'i Pacific Review 206
HAWK Publishing Group 406
Hayden's Ferry Review 207
Haystack Writing Program 561
Heartlands Today, The 207
Hedgebrook 561
Heinz Literature Prize, Drue 488
Helicon Nine Editions 406
Hemingway Foundation/Pen Award for First Fiction, Ernest 489
Hemingway Short Story Competition, Lorian 489
Hemispheres 346
Hendrick-Long Publishing Co., Inc. 406
Hesperus Press 406
High Adventure 347
High Country Publishers, Ltd. 407
Highland Summer Conference 531
Highlights for Children 347
Highlights for Children Fiction Contest 489
Highlights Foundation Founders Workshops 528
Highlights Foundation Writing for Children 528
Highway 14 207
Hill Street Press 407
Hilton Head Island Writers Retreat 532
Hiram College 579
Hitchcock Mystery Magazine, Alfred 347

Hodder & Stoughton/Headline 407
Hoepfner Award, Theodore Christian 489
Hofstra University Summer Writers' Conference 522
Holiday House, Inc. 408
Hollins University 583
Holloway House Publishing Co. 408
Holt & Co. Books for Young Readers, Henry 408
Holt And Co., Inc., Henry 408
Homa & Sekey Books 408
Home Planet News 207
Honolulu Magazine Starbucks Coffee Hawai'i Fiction Contest 489
Hope College 575
Horizons 288
Horizons 348
Horsethief's Journal, The 318
Hot Hot House 409
Houghton Mifflin Books for Children 409
Houghton Mifflin Co. 409
How to Be Published Workshops 535
Howells House 409
Hubbard's Writers of the Future Contest, L. Ron 489
Humboldt State University 570
Humpty Dumpty's Magazine 348
Huntington Press 409
Hybolics 288
Hyperion Books for Children 410

I

Iconoclast, The 208
Idaho Review, The 208
Idaho Writers League Conference 561
Idiot, The 208
Idyllwild Arts Academy 570
ignotus Press 410
Illinois State University 572
Illuminations 209
Illya's Honey 209
Image 209
Image Comics 410
Imagination 540
In Posse Review on Web Del Sol 318
Indiana Review '1/2K' Prize for Short-Shorts/ Prose Poems 490
Indiana Review 209
Indiana Review Fiction Prize 490
Indiana University 573
Indiana University 573

Indiana University Writers' Conference Scholarship Competition 490
Indiana Writers' Conference 541
Individual Artist Fellowship 490
Individual Artist Fellowship 491
Individual Artist Mini-Grant 491
Inkwell Fiction Competition 491
Inkwell Magazine 210
Insomniac Press 410
Institute of American Indian Arts 577
Interbang 210
Intercontinental Publishing 411
Interlink Publishing Group, Inc. 411
International IMPAC Dublin Literary Award 491
International Music Camp Creative Writing Workshop 544
International Readers Theatre Workshops 566
Inverted-A 411
Ion Imagination Publishing 411
Iowa Review, The 210
Iowa School of Letters Award for Short Fiction, The John Simmons Short Fiction Award 491
Iowa State University 573
Iowa Summer Writing Festival 545
Ironweed Press 411
Ironweed Press Fiction Prize 491
Irreantum 211
Italian Americana 288
Italica Press 411
Ithaca College Park Hall 578
Ivy League Press, Inc. 412
IVY Publications 412
IWWG Early Spring in California Conference 554
IWWG Meet the Agents and Editors 522
IWWG Summer Conference 522

J
Jabberwock Review, The 211
Jack and Jill 348
Jackson Award, Joseph Henry 491
James Madison University 583
Jameson Books. Inc. 412
Jewish Currents Magazine 288
Jireh Publishing Company 412
Johns Hopkins University 571
Jolly Roger, The 319
Jones First Novel Fellowship, James 492
Journal of Polymorphous Perversity 289
Journal, The 212
JourneyForth 413

Just Us Books, Inc. 413
Justin, Charles & Co., Publishers 413

K
Kaeden Books 414
Kaleidoscope 212
Kalliope 212
Kansas State University 573
Karamu 213
Katha: Indian American Fiction Contest 492
Kauai Writers Conference 554
Kaya Production 414
Keats/Kerlan Collection Memorial Fellowship, Ezra 492
Kelsey Review 213
Kennedy Book Awards, Robert F. 492
Kennesaw Review 319
Kennesaw State University 572
Kensington Publishing Corp. 414
Kent State University 579
Kentucky Monthly 348
Kentucky Women Writers Conference 541
Kentucky Writer's Workshop 541
Kenyon Review, The 213
Kenyon Review Writers Workshop 541
Kerem 213
Key West Writers' Workshop 535
Killaloe Hedge-School of Writing 566
Kimera 214
King's English 214
Kiriyama Prize 492
Kit-Cat Review, The 214
Knoll, Publishers, Allen A. 414
Knopf, Alfred A. 415
Knopf Publishing Group 415
Knox College 572
Koeppel Short Fiction Award, E.M. 493
Korean Literature Translation Award 493
Korean Literature Translation Contest for New Translators 493
Krax Magazine 289
Kregel Publications 415
Kutztown University 581

L
La Jolla Writers Conference 555
La Kancerkliniko 214
Ladies' Home Journal 349
Lady Churchill's Rosebud Wristlet 289
Ladybug 349
Lake Effect 215

Lake Superior Magazine 349
Lakeland Book of the Year 493
Lakeland College 584
Lamar University at Beaumont 582
Lamp-Post, The 215
Landfall/University of Otago Press 215
Larcom Press 575
Last Knight Publishing Company 415
Laurel Review, The 215
Lawrence Foundation Award, The 493
Lawrence Foundation Prize 493
Le Forum 215
Leading Edge 290
League of Utah Writers Contest 493
League of Utah Writers Round-up 555
Leapfrog Press 416
Leaping Dog Press 416
Leapings Literary Magazine 216
Lee & Low Books 416
Left Curve 290
Leisure Books 416
Lerner Publications Company 419
Les Éditions du Vermillon 419
Levine Books, Arthur A. 419
Lewis & Clark College 580
Lewis-Clark State College 572
Lichen 216
Licking River Review, The 216
Lifetime Achievement Award 494
Light Quarterly 217
Lighthouse Writers Workshop 571
Lightwave Publishing Inc. 419
Liguorian 349
Lilith Annual Fiction Award 494
Lilith Magazine 350
Lincoln University 576
Linfield College 580
Lionhearted Publishing, Inc. 419
Liquid Ohio 290
Listen Magazine 350
Listening Eye, The 217
Literal Latté 217
Literal Latté Fiction Award 494
Literary Potpourri 290
Literary Review, The 217
Literary Witches 319
Literoticaffeine 319
Little, Brown and Co. Adult Trade Books 420
Little, Brown and Co. Children's Publishing 420
Little, Brown and Co., Inc. 420

Little, Brown and Company Children's Books 420
LIVE 350
Living Light News 350
Livingston Press 420
Llewellyn Publications 421
Long Fiction Contest International 494
Long Story, The 218
Longmeadow Journal Literary Competition, The 495
Longstreet Press, Inc. 421
Los Angeles Times Book Prizes 495
Lost and Found Times 218
Lost Horse Press 421
Lost Horse Writers' Conference 561
Louisiana Literature 218
Louisiana State University 574
Louisville Review, The 218
Love Spell 421
Low Budget Science Fiction 291
Loyola College 574
Loyola Marymount University 570
Loyola University New Orleans 574
LTDBooks 422
Luath Press Ltd. 422
Luke Award, The Hugh J. 495
Lullwater Review 219
Lutheran Journal, The 351
Lycoming College 581
Lynx Eye 219
Lyons Press, The 422

M

MacAdam/Cage Publishing, Inc. 422
Macalester College 576
MacDowell Colony, The 522
MacGuffin, The 219
Macon State College 572
Macrae Books, John 423
Maelstrom 220
Magazine of Fantasy & Science Fiction, The 351
Magna Cum Murder Crime Fiction Conference 541
Malahat Review, The 220
Man Booker Prize for Fiction, The 495
Mangrove 220
Manhattanville College Summer Writers' Week 523
Manoa 220
Many Mountains Moving 221
Margin 319

Marine Techniques Publishing, Inc. 423
Mariner Books 423
Maritime Writers' Workshop 564
Marlboro Review, The 221
Marquette University 584
Marsh Award for Children's Literature in Translation 495
Marvel Comics 423
Marvin Grant, Walter Rumsey 495
Marymount Manhattan College Writers' Conference 523
Massachusetts Review, The 221
Masters Award, The 495
Matriarch's Way 224
Mature Living 351
Mature Years 351
Maui Writers Conference and Retreat 555
Maumee Valley Freelance Writers' Conference 542
McBooks Press 423
McCarthy Prize in Short Fiction, Mary 496
McElderry Books, Margaret K. 424
McKean Moore Writer in Washington, Jenny 496
McKnight Artist Fellowships for Writers 496
McNeese State University 574
McSweeney's Internet Tendency, Timothy 320
Medicinal Purposes 224
Meisha Merlin Publishing, Inc. 424
Melody of Love Contest 496
Mendocino Coast Writers Conference 555
Mercury Books 320
Meriwether Publishing Ltd. 424
Merlyn's Pen 224
Messenger of the Sacred Heart, The 352
Metal Scratches 224
Metropole 320
Miami University 579
Micah Publications, Inc 424
Michigan Literary Fiction Awards 496
Michigan Quarterly Review 225
Michigan State University 575
Mid-American Review 225
Midland College Main Campus 582
Midland Writers Conference 542
Mid-List Press 425
Mid-List Press First Series Award for Short Fiction 496
Mid-List Press First Series Award for the Novel 497
Mid-Mississippi River Folklore, Storytelling and Writing Conference 542

Midnight Times 291
Mid-South Review, The 321
Midwest Writers Workshop 542
Mightybook 425
Milkweed Editions 425
Milkweed Editions National Fiction Prize 497
Milkweeds for Young Readers 425
Millennium Science Fiction & Fantasy 321
Mills & Boon Historical Romance 426
Mills & Boon Medical Romance 426
Mills College 570
Mind Book of the Year 497
Mindprints 225
Ministry of Writing: An Annual Colloquium, The 542
Minneapolis Writers' Conference 545
Minnesota Review, The 226
Minnesota State University at Moorehead 576
Minnesota State University Mankato 576
Minotaur 426
MIRA Books 426
Miraculous Medal, The 291
Mississippi Review 226
Mississippi Review Prize 497
Mississippi State University 576
Missouri Review Editors' Prize Contest, The 497
Missouri Review, The 226
MIT 575
MM Review 226
Mobius 227
Money for Women 497
Montolieu Workshop, The 566
Montrose Christian Writer's Conference 528
Moody Publishers 427
Moonlight & Magnolia Fiction Writing Contest 497
Moonlight and Magnolias Writer's Conference 536
Moore Community Workshops, Jennie McKean 528
Morehead State University 574
Mormon Writers' Conference 556
Morrow, William 427
Mota 227
Mota Emerging Writers Contest 498
Mount Hermon Christian Writers Conference 556
Mountain Luminary 291
Mountain State Press 427
Moveo Angelus Literary Arts 580
Mslexia 292

Mudrock: Stories & Tales 292
Multnomah Publishers, Inc. 427
Murray State University 574
Musing Place, The 227
My Friend 352
My Weekly Story Collection 428
Mysterious Press, The 428

N

Na'amat Woman 352
Nassau Community College 578
Nassau Review 228
Natchez Literary and Cinema Celebration 536
National Chapter of Canada IODE Violet
    Downey Book Award, The 498
National Federation of the Blind Writers'
    Division Short Story Contest 498
National Outdoor Book Awards 498
National Readers' Choice Awards 498
National Writers Association Annual Novel
    Writing Contest 499
National Writers Association Annual Short Story
    Contest 499
National Writers Association Foundation
    Conference 548
Natural Bridge 228
Natural Heritage/Natural History, Inc. 428
Nature Writers Retreat With North Cascades
    Institute 561
Nautical & Aviation Publishing Co., The 428
Naval Institute Press 428
Nebraska Review Award in Fiction, The 499
Nebraska Review, The 228
Nelson Publishers, Thomas 428
Nelson, Tommy 429
Nerve Cowboy 228
Neustadt International Prize for Literature 499
Nevada Arts Council Artists' Fellowships 499
New American Library 429
New Century Writers Awards 500
New Delta Review 229
New England Press, Inc., The 429
New England Review 229
New England Writers Conference 523
New England Writer's Network 293
New England Writers Short, Short Fiction
    Contest 500
New Hope Books, Inc. 429
New Jersey Society of Christian Writers Fall
    Seminar, The 529
New Laurel Review 229

New Letters 230
New Letters Literary Awards 500
New Letters Weekend Writers Conference, The
    548
New Methods 293
New Mexico State University 577
New Millennium Writing Awards 500
New Mirage Quarterly 230
New Mystery 352
New Orleans Review 230
New Orphic Review, The 230
new renaissance, the 231
New Stone Circle 231
New Victoria Publishers 430
New Welsh Review 231
New Writer, The 231
New York Stories 232
New York Stories Short Fiction Contest 500
New York University 578
New Yorker, The 353
Newbery Award, John 501
New-Cue Writers' Conference and Workshop
    523
NeWest Publishers Ltd. 430
Night Terrors 293
Night Train 232
Nightwriters 532
Nimrod 232
Nimrod Annual Writers' Workshop 548
Ninety-six Inc. 233
Nocturnal Lyric, The 293
Noma Award for Publishing in Africa, The 501
North American Review, The 233
North Carolina State University at Raleigh 578
North Carolina Writers' Network Fall Confer-
    ence 532
North Dakota Quarterly 233
North East Arts Magazine 234
North Lake College 582
Northern Arizona University 569
Northern Michigan University 575
North-South Books 430
Northwest Bookfest 562
Northwest Review 234
Northwestern University 572
Northwoods Journal 234
Norton Co., Inc., W.W. 430
Notre Dame Review 234
Nova Science Fiction Magazine 294
Novella Prize 501
Nuthouse 294

Nuvein Online 321
NW Writers' Corp. 431

O

O, Georgia! Writing Competition, O, Georgia Too! Writing Competition 501
Oak, The 294
Oak Tree Press 431
Oasis 235
Obsidian III 235
O'Connor Award for Short Fiction, The Flannery 501
O'Connor Fiction Award, Frank 502
Odyssey 524
Office Number One 294
Ohio State University 579
Ohio State University Press 502
Ohio Teachers Write 235
Ohio University Program in Creative Writing 579
Ohioana Award for Children's Literature, Alice Louise Wood Memorial 502
Ohioana Book Awards 502
Oklahoma State University 580
Oklahoma Writers Federation Conference 548
Old Dominion University 583
Omnidawn Publishing 431
On Spec 295
On The Line 353
Once Upon A World 295
One World Books 432
One-Story 235
Oni Press 432
Open Spaces 236
Options 353
Oracular Tree, The 321
Orange Blossom Fiction Contest 502
Orange Prize for Fiction 502
Orb 295
Orca Book Publishers 432
Orchises Press 432
Oregon Book Awards 503
Oregon Literary Fellowships 503
Oregon State University 580
Orient Paperbacks 432
Other Press 432
Other Voices 236
Otterbein College 579
Our Child Press 432
Outdoor Writers Association of America Annual Conference 529
Outer Darkness 296

Outrider Press, Inc. 433
Outsider Ink 322
Over The Back Fence 296
Owen Publishers, Inc., Richard C. 433
Owen Publishers, Peter 433
Owl Books 434
Oxford American, The 236
Oxford Conference for the Book 536
Oxygen 236
Oyster Boy Review 237
Ozark Creative Writers, Inc. 536

P

Pacific Coast Journal 237
Pacific Northwest Writers Conference 562
pacific REVIEW 237
Painted Bride Quarterly 322
Paisano Fellowships, Dobie 503
Pakenham Award, Catherine 503
Palari Publishing 434
Palo Alto Review 237
Pangolin Papers 238
Pantheon Books 434
Panther Creek Press 434
Paperplates 322
Papyrus Publishers & Letterbox Service 435
Paradise Cay Publications 435
Paris Review, The 238
Paris Writers Workshop/WICE 566
Parting Gifts 238
Passages North 238
Passeggiata Press 435
Patchen Competition, Kenneth 503
Paterson Fiction Prize, The 503
Paterson Literary Review 239
Paterson University Spring Writer's Conference, William 529
Paumanok Review, The 323
PBW 323
Peachtree Publishers, Ltd. 435
Pearl 239
Pearl Short Story Prize 503
Peden Prize in Fiction, William 504
PEEKS & valleys 239
Pegasus Review, The 296
Pelican Publishing Co. 436
Pemmican Publications 436
PEN Center USA Literary Award in Fiction 504
PEN New England/L.L. Winship Award 504
PEN/Faulkner Award for Fiction, The 504
Penguin Group USA 436

Penguin Putnam Books for Young Readers 436
Peninsular 239
Penn State Erie 581
Penn Writers Conference 529
Pennsylvania English 240
Pennsylvania State University 581
Peregrine 240
Perfection Learning Corp. 436
Peridot Books 323
Perimeter 240
Permanent Press, The 437
Permutations 241
Pew Fellowships in the Arts 504
Pfenninger Literary Award, Mary Ann 504
Phantasmagoria 241
Phelan Award, James D. 505
Philomel Books 437
Phoebe 241
Phoenix College 569
Piatkus Books 437
Picador USA 438
Pif 323
Pig Iron Press 241
Pig Iron Press 438
Pikeville Review 242
Pima Writers' Workshop 556
Piñata Books 438
Pindeldyboz 297
Pineapple Press, Inc. 438
Pink Chameleon, The 323
Pipe Smoker's Ephemeris, The 297
Pipers' Ash Ltd. 439
Pippin Press 439
PLANET-The Welsh Internationalist 242
Playboy College Fiction Contest 505
Playboy Magazine 353
Plaza, The 324
Pleasant Company Publications 439
Pleiades 242
Plexus Publishing, Inc. 440
Ploughshares 243
Plume 440
Pockets 354
Pocol Press 440
Poetry & Prose Annual 243
Poetry Forum Short Stories 243
Pointed Circle 244
Poisoned Pen Press 440
Polychrome Publishing Corp. 441
Poole Award for Best Work of Fiction, Mary
    Ruffin 505

Porcupine Literary Arts Magazine 244
Port Town Publishing 441
Porter Prize for Fiction, Katherine Anne 505
Portland Magazine 354
Portland Review 244
Poskisnolt Press 297
Post-Apollo Press, The 441
Potomac Review 244
Prairie Journal, The 244
Prairie Schooner 245
Prairie Schooner Prize Book Series 505
Prairie Schooner Readers' Choice Awards 505
Prayerworks 298
Premonitions 324
Presidio La Bahia Award, The 506
Pretext 245
Primavera 245
Prism International 246
Pristine Publishing 441
Prose Ax 298
Providence College 581
Provincetown Arts 246
Provost's Writers Retreat Workshop, Gary 543
PSI 298
Psychic Radio, The 298
Publishers Syndication, International 442
Publishing Game, The 524
Puckerbrush Press 442
Puckerbrush Review 246
Pudding House Publications 442
Puerto Del Sol 247
Puffin Books 442
Pulaski Technical College 569
Pulitzer Prize in Fiction 506
Purdue University 573
Purpose 354
Pushcart Prize 506
Putnam's Sons, G.P. 443

Q

Qspell Book Awards/Hugh Maclennan Fiction
    Award 506
Quackenbush's Children's Book Writing and
    Illustrating Workshops, Robert 524
Quality Women's Fiction 247
Quarter After Eight 247
Quarterly West 247
Queen Mystery Magazine, Ellery 355
Queen Of All Hearts 299
Queen's Quarterly 299

Quiet Storm Publishing 443
Quixote Press 443

R

Raffelock Award for Publishing Excellence, David 506
Rain Crow 248
Rainbow Curve 248
Raleigh Award, Sir Walter 506
Rambunctious Review 248
Ramsey Books 443
Random House Books for Young Readers 443
Random House Children's Books 444
Random House, Inc. 444
Random House Trade Publishing Group 444
Ransom Publishing Ltd. 444
Rattapallax 249
Raven Chronicles, The 249
Ravenhawk™ Books 444
Rawlings: Writing the Region, Majorie Kinnan 536
REA Award for the Short Story, The 506
RE:AL 249
Real Writers/Book Pl@ce Short Story Awards 507
Realpoetik 324
Reasoning Novel Magazine 250
Red Cedar Review 250
Red Deer Press 445
Red Dragon Press 445
Red Dress Ink 445
Red Hen Press 445
Red House Children's Book Award, The 507
Red Press Publishing Company, The 446
Red Rock Review 250
Red Sage Publishing, Inc. 446
Red Wheelbarrow 250
Redbook Magazine 355
RedWritingHood.com 100-Word Short Story Contest 507
Reflections Literary Journal 250
Reflections Short Fiction Award 507
Reform Judaism 355
Regan Books 446
Regional Book Awards 507
Rejected Quarterly, The 251
Remember the MAGIC IWWG Annual Summer Conference 524
Renaissance House 446
Resource Publications, Inc. 447
Retreat From Harsh Reality 543

Revell Publishing 447
Reynolds Memorial Fiction Awards, Louise E. 508
Rhode Island College 581
Rhodes College 582
Rising Moon 447
Rising Tide Press, New Mexico 447
River City 251
River City Publishing 447
River Oak Publishing 448
River Styx 251
Roanoke College 583
Roanoke Review 252
Roberts Award, Summerfield G. 508
ROC Books 448
Rock & Co., Publishers, James A. 448
Rock Village Publishing 448
Rocket Press 252
Rockford Review, The 252
Rocky Mountain Book Festival 549
Romancing the Novel 508
Ronsdale Press 448
Room of One's Own 252
Ropewalk Writers' Retreat 543
Rose & Thorn Literary E-Zine, The 324
Rosebud 299
Rowan University 577
Royal Fireworks Publishing 449
RPPS/Fullosia Press 325
Ruminator Books 449
Rutgers University 577

S

Saddleback College Creative Writing Program 570
Sage Hill Writing Experience 564
Sagebrush Writers Workshop 562
St. Anthony Messenger 357
St. Anthony Messenger Press 456
Saint Lawrence University 578
St. Martin's Press 456
Saint Mary's College of California 570
Salisbury State University 574
Salmagundi 252
Salt Hill 253
Salvo Press 449
Sam Houston State University 582
Samsara 253
San Diego State University 570
San Diego State University Writers' Conference 556

San Jose State University 570
San Juan Writers Workshop 549
Sandy Cove Christian Writers Conference 530
Sanger Short Fiction Contest, Marjory Bartlett 508
Santa Barbara Christian Writers Conference 557
Santa Monica Review 253
Sarabande Books, Inc. 449
Sarah Lawrence College 578
Saxon House Canada 450
Scars/CC&D Editor's Choice Awards, The 508
SCBWI Midyear Conference, NYC 525
SCBWI Southern Breeze Fall Conference 537
SCBWI Southern Breeze Spring Conference 537
SCBWI/Florida Annual Fall Conference 537
SCBWI/Hofstra Children's Literature Conference 525
SCBWI/International Conference on Writing & Illustrating for Children 557
Scholastic Canada, Ltd. 450
Scholastic Press 450
Science & Humanities Press 450
Science Fiction Writers of Earth (SFWoE) Short Story Contest 509
Scifi.com 325
Scribia, The 254
Scriptapalooza Screenplay Competition 509
Scriptapalooza Television Writing Competition 509
Seacoast Writer's Association Spring and Fall Conferences 525
Seal Press 451
Seek 355
Sensations Magazine 254
Serendipity Systems 451
Seven Stories Press 451
Seventeen 356
Seventeen Magazine Fiction Contest 509
Severn House Publishers 451
Sewanee Writers' Conference 532
SFWA Nebula® Awards 509
Shaara Award for Civil War Fiction, Michael 509
Shadow Voices 325
Shaw Fellowship for Older Women Writers, Frances 510
SheVaCon 532
Shine Brightly 356
Shoreline 452
Short Grain Contest 510
Short Stuff 254
Side Show Short Story Contest 510

Silhouette Books 452
Silhouette Desire 452
Silhouette Intimate Moments 452
Silhouette Romance 452
Silhouette Special Edition 452
Silver Dagger Mysteries 453
Silver Moon Press 453
Simon & Schuster Books for Young Readers 453
Simon & Schuster Children's Publishing 454
Sinister Wisdom 254
Site of Big Shoulders, The 326
Sitka Center for Art and Ecology 563
Skipping Stones Honor Awards 510
Skipping Stones Youth Awards 510
Skyline Magazine 300
Slate and Style 300
SLG Publishing 454
Slipstream Publications 255
Slote Award, The Bernice 511
Small Pond Magazine, The 255
Smith, Publisher, Gibbs 454
Snake Nation Review 255
Snow Contest, Kay 511
Snowapple Press 454
Snowy Egret 255
SNReview 326
So to Speak 256
Society of Children's Book Writers and Illustrators Golden Kite Awards 511
Society of Children's Book Writers and Illustrators Work-In-Progress Grants 511
Soft Skull Press Inc. 454
Soho Press, Inc. 454
Song of the Siren 326
Songs of Innocence 256
Sonoma State University 570
Sonora Review 256
Soundprints 455
South Carolina Review 257
South Coast Writers Conference 563
South Dakota Arts Council 511
South Dakota Review 257
South Florida Writers' Conference 537
Southampton College of Long Island University 578
Southeast Missouri State University 576
Southeast Review, The 257
Southeastern Writers Association 537
Southern California Anthology 257
Southern California Writers' Conference/L.A., Oxnard 557

GENERAL INDEX

Southern California Writers' Conference/San
   Diego 557
Southern Connecticut State University 571
Southern Humanities Review 258
Southern Illinois 573
Southern Lights 538
Southern Methodist University 582
Southern Methodist University Press 455
Southern Review, The 258
Southern Review/Louisiana State University
   Short Fiction Award, The 511
Southwest Missouri State University 576
Southwest Review 258
Southwest State University 576
Southwest Texas State University 582
Southwest Writers Conference 549
Southwestern American Literature 259
Spalding University 574
Speak Up 259
Spectra Books 455
Spellbound Magazine 300
Spider 356
Spindrift 259
Spinning Jenny 357
Spinsters Ink 455
Spirit That Moves Us Press, The 456
Spitball 259
Spoiledink Magazine 326
Spout Press 456
Spring Hill Review 260
SPUR Awards 512
Squaw Valley Community of Writers Workshops
   557
St. Andrews College 579
Standard 357
Stanford University 570
Staple Magazine 260
Starburst Publishers 457
Starcherone Books 457
Starcherone Fiction Prize, The 512
Stark Raving Sanity 327
Starship Earth 300
State of Maine Writers' Conference 525
State University of New York 578
State University of New York at Geneseo 578
Steamboat Springs Writers Group 549
Steeple Hill 457
Stegner Fellowship, Wallace E. 512
Stephens College 576
Stetson University 571
Stone Bridge Press 457

Stone Soup 260
Stony Brook Short Fiction Prize 512
Storie 261
Story Bytes 327
Story Friends 327
Story Friends 358
StoryQuarterly 261
Storyteller 301
Storyteller, The 301
Strand Magazine, The 301
Struggle 261
Studio 302
Stylewriter, Inc. 458
Sulphur River Literary Review 262
Summer's Reading, A 262
Summerset Review, The 327
Sun, The 358
Sunshine Coast Festival of the Written Arts 565
Susquehanna University 581
Sycamore Review 262
SynergEbooks 458
Syracuse University 578

T

T n T Classic Books 458
Takahe 263
Talebones 302
Tales of the Hookman Online Magazine 328
Talese, Nan A. 458
Tall Grass Writers Guild Literary Anthology/
   Contest 512
Tameme 263
Tampa Review 263
Taos Institute of Arts 549
Taproot Literary Review 264
Tattersall Publishing 459
Tattoo Highway 328
Taylor Manuscript Competition, Sydney 512
Telluride Writers Conference 550
Temple University 581
Terminus 264
Texas A&M University 582
Texas Christian Writers' Conference 550
Texas Review, The 264
Texas Tech University 582
Thema 265
Third Coast 265
Third Half Magazine, The 265
Third World Press 459
Thirteen Stories 302
Thirteenth Moon 265

Thirteenth Warrior Review, The 328
Thistledown Press 459
Thorndike Press 460
Thorny Locust 265
Thought Magazine 266
Thought Magazine Writer's Contest 512
Threepenny Review, The 266
Thresholds Quarterly 329
Tidewater Publishers 460
Tigges Writing Contest, John 513
Tilbury House, Publishers 460
Timber Creek Review 266
Timberwolf Press, Inc. 460
Tin House 267
Tindal Street Press, Ltd. 460
TMCC Writers' Conference 558
Toasted Cheese 329
Tokyopop 461
Torah Aura Productions 461
Touch of Success Writer's Conference 538
Touchstone Literary Journal 267
Towson University 574
Tradewind Books 461
Transcendent Visions 303
Transition 267
Traver Fly-Fishing Fiction Award, Robert 513
Treble Heart Books 461
Tricycle Press 461
Trinity College 571
Trinity University 582
Triquarterly 267
Trollope Society Short Story Prize, The 513
True Confessions 358
Tulane University 574
Turnstone Press 462
Twain Award for Short Fiction, The Mark 513
Twain Award, Mark 513
Twain Creative Writing Workshops, Mark 550
12-Gauge.com 329
Tŷ Newydd Writers' Centre 566
Tyrannosaurus Press 462

U

U.S. Catholic 358
UCLA American Indian Studies Center 462
UCLA Extension Writers' Program 558
UCLA Extension Writers' Program 570
Unbound 268
Underwood Review, The 268
Unity House 462
University of Alabama at Birmingham 568

University of Alabama at Tuscaloosa 568
University of Alabama Press 463
University of Alaska Anchorage 568
University of Alaska at Fairbanks 568
University of Alberta Press, The 463
University of Arkansas at Fayetteville 569
University of California at Davis 570
University of California at Irvine 570
University of Central Arkansas 569
University of Central Florida 571
University of Central Oklahoma 580
University of Cincinnati Writing Program 579
University of Colorado Boulder 571
University of Connecticut 571
University of Denver 571
University of Evansville 573
University of Florida 571
University of Georgia Press 463
University of Houston 582
University of Idaho 572
University of Illinois 573
University of Illinois at Chicago 573
University of Iowa 573
University of Iowa Press 463
University of Iowa Writers' Workshop 573
University of Kansas 573
University of Louisiana at Lafayette 574
University of Louisiana at Munroe 574
University of Louisville 574
University of Maine at Farmington 574
University of Maryland 574
University of Massachusetts at Amherst 575
University of Massachusetts at Dartmouth 575
University of Memphis 582
University of Miami 571
University of Michigan at Ann Arbor 575
University of Michigan Press 463
University of Minnesota at Minneapolis 576
University of Mississippi 576
University of Missouri 576
University of Missouri at Kansas City 576
University of Missouri at St. Louis 576
University of Missouri Press 463
University of Montana 577
University of Nebraska at Kearney 577
University of Nebraska at Lincoln 577
University of Nebraska at Omaha 577
University of Nevada, Las Vegas 577
University of Nevada Press 464
University of Nevada, Reno 577
University of New Hampshire 577

University of New Mexico 578
University of New Mexico's Taos Summer
  Writers Conference 550
University of New Orleans 574
University of North Carolina at Asheville 579
University of North Carolina at Chapel Hill 579
University of North Carolina at Greensboro 579
University of North Carolina Wilmington 579
University of North Dakota 579
University of North Dakota Writers Conference
  545
University of North Texas 582
University of Northern Iowa 573
University of Notre Dame 573
University of Oklahoma 580
University of Oregon 580
University of Pennsylvania 581
University of Pittsburgh 581
University of Pittsburgh at Bradford 581
University of Pittsburgh at Johnstown 581
University of Redlands 570
University of Scranton 581
University of South Carolina 581
University of South Dakota 581
University of South Florida 571
University of Southern California 570
University of St. Thomas 582
University of Tampa 572
University of Texas at Dallas 582
University of Texas at El Paso 582
University of Texas at San Antonio 583
University of Texas Michener Center 582
University of Texas Press 464
University of Toledo 580
University of the Nations School of Writing and
  Writers Workshops 551
University of the South at Sewanee 582
University of Utah 583
University of Virginia 583
University of Washington 583
University of Wisconsin at Madison 584
University of Wisconsin at Milwaukee 584
University of Wisconsin at Whitewater 584
University of Wisconsin Press 464
University of Wyoming 584
University Press of New England 464
Unknown Writer, The 268
Unmuzzled Ox 269
Unwound 269
Up Dare 303

V

Vancouver International Writers Festival, The
  565
Vandamere Press 465
Vasto Writers & Artists Retreat 567
Véhicule Press 465
Vermont College 583
Vermont College Postgraduate Writers'
  Conference 525
Vermont Studio Center 526
Very Short Fiction Summer Award 514
Very Short Fiction Winter Award 514
Vestal Review 269
Via Dolorosa Press 465
Viking 465
Viking Children's Books 465
Villard Books 466
Vincent Brothers Review, The 269
Vintage Anchor Publishing 466
Violet Crown Book Award 514
Virginia Commonwealth University 583
Virginia Festival of the Book 533
Virginia Polytechnic Insitute & State University
  583
Virginia Quarterly Review 303
Vision Books Pvt Ltd. 466
Vivisphere Publishing 466
Vogelstein Foundation Grants 514
Voices From My Retreat 466
Volcano Writers' Retreat 558
VQ Online 329

W

Wabash College 573
Walden Fellowship 514
Walker and Company 467
Wallant Memorial Book Award, Edward Lewis
  514
Walloon Writers' Retreat 543
Waltsan Publishing, LLC 467
War Cry, The 359
Warner Books 467
Warren Wilson College 579
Washington State University 583
Washington University 577
WaterBrook Press 467
Waxing and Waning 330
Weatherford Award 514
Web del Sol 330
Weber Studies 304

Weird Tales 304
Wesleyan Writers Conference 526
West Virginia University 584
West Virginia Wesleyan College 584
Western Carolina University 579
Western Heritage Awards 514
Western Humanities Review 270
Western Michigan University 575
Western Reserve Writer's & Freelance
    Conference 544
Western Washington University 583
Westminster College 577
Westminster College of Salt Lake City 583
Westview 270
Whiskey Island Magazine 270
White Mane Books 468
White Wolf 468
Whitman and Co., Albert 468
"Why It's Great" Writing Workshop & Retreat,
    The 526
Wichita State University 573
Wild Violet 330
Wild Violet Fiction Contest 515
Wildacre Writers Workshop 533

Wildside Press 468
Willamette Writers Conference 563
Williard & Maple 270
Willow Springs 271
Willowgate Press 469
Wilmington Blues 331
Wilshire Book Company 469
Wind River Press 469
Windhover 271
Windsor Review 271
Windstorm Creative, Ltd. 469
Winner 359
Winona State 576
Winter Poetry & Prose Getaway in Cape May
    530
Wisconsin Academy Review 304
Wisconsin Institute for Creative Writing
    Fellowship 515
Wisconsin Regional Writer's Association
    Conferences 545
Wizards of the Coast 470
Wolff Award for Fiction, Tobias 515
Woman's Weekly 359
Woman's World 359
Women's Press, The 470
Wood Community College, John 515

Woodley Memorial Press 470
Worcester Magazine 271
Worcester Review, The 272
Word Riot 331
Words Literary Journal 272
Words of Wisdom 272
World Fantasy Awards 515
Worldwide Library 470
Write From the Heart 563
Write It Out 538
Write on the Sound Writers' Conference 563
Writers Bureau Poetry and Short Story
    Competition, The 515
Writer's Digest Annual Writing Competition
    (Short Story Division) 516
Writer's Digest International Self-Published
    Book Awards 516
Writer's Digest School 544
Writers Direct 470
Writers for Readers 304
Writers' Forum 360
Writers' Forum Short Story Competition 516
Writers' Guild of Acadiana 538
Writers Institute 545
Writers' Journal 360
Writers' Journal Annual Fiction Contest 516
Writers' Journal Horror/Ghost Contest 516
Writers' Journal Romance Contest 517
Writer's Landscape, The 551
Writers' League of Texas Spring and Fall
    Workshops and Classes 551
Writers Online Workshops 580
Writers Retreat, The 565
Writer's Retreats 551
Writers Studio 564
Writers Studio at UCLA Extension 559
Writer's Voice of the West Side YMCA 527
Writers Way, The 559
Writers Weekend at the Beach 564
Writers Workshop in Science Fiction 552
Writespot Autumn Short Story Competition 517
Writespot Spring Short Story Competition 517
Write-To-Publish Conference 544
Writing, Creativity and Ritual: A Woman's
    Retreat 527
Writing For Our Lives 272
Writing for Young Readers Workshop 559
Writing Strategies for the Christian Market 539
Writing Today--Birmingham-Southern College
    539
Writing Workshop 546

X

X Press, The 471
Xavier Review 273
Xavier University of Louisiana 574
Xconnect 273

Y

Yaddo 527
Yalobusha Review, The 273
Yemassee 273
York Press, Ltd. 471
Yorkshire Journal 274

Yosemite Winter Literary Conference 559
Youth With a Mission's School of Writing 552

Z

Zahir 305
Zebra Books 471
Zoetrope: All-Story 274
Zoetrope Short Story Contest 517
Zondervan 471
Zopilote 305
Zuzu's Petals Quarterly 331
Zyzzyva 274

NOTES